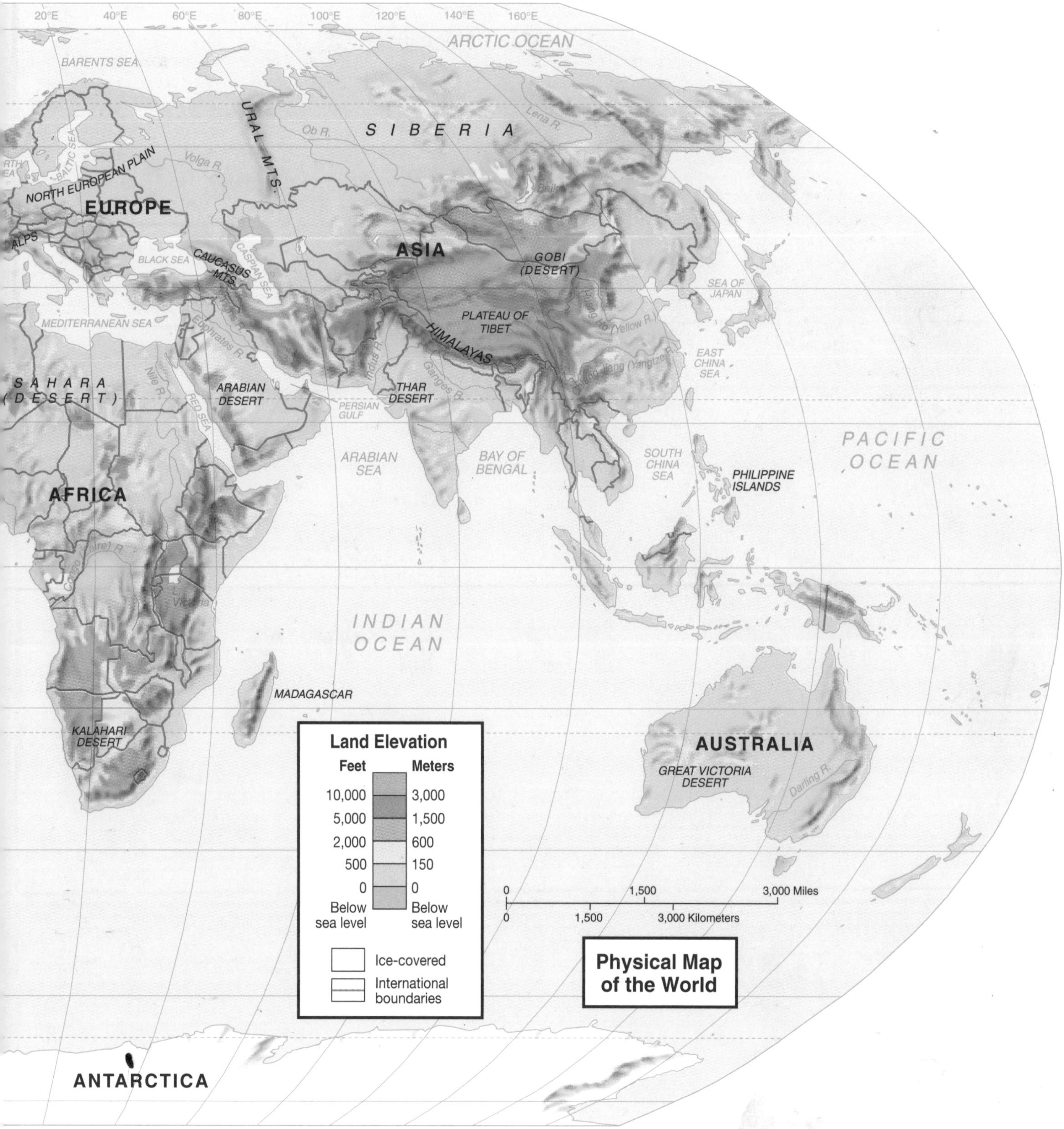

20°E
40°E
60°E
80°E
100°E
120°E
140°E
160°E
ARCTIC OCEAN
BARENTS SEA
URAL MTS.
Ob R.
S I B E R I A
Lena R.
BALTIC SEA
NORTH EUROPEAN PLAIN
Volga R.
EUROPE
ALPS
BLACK SEA
CAUCASUS MTS.
CASPIAN SEA
ASIA
GOBI (DESERT)
SEA OF JAPAN
MEDITERRANEAN SEA
Tigris R.
Euphrates R.
PLATEAU OF TIBET
Huang He (Yellow R.)
HIMALAYAS
EAST CHINA SEA
Chang Jiang (Yangtze R.)
Indus R.
Ganges R.
S A H A R A (D E S E R T)
Nile R.
RED SEA
ARABIAN DESERT
PERSIAN GULF
THAR DESERT
ARABIAN SEA
BAY OF BENGAL
SOUTH CHINA SEA
PACIFIC OCEAN
PHILIPPINE ISLANDS
AFRICA
Congo (Zaire) R.
Victoria
INDIAN OCEAN
MADAGASCAR
KALAHARI DESERT
AUSTRALIA
GREAT VICTORIA DESERT
Darling R.
Land Elevation
Feet
Meters
10,000
3,000
5,000
1,500
2,000
600
500
150
0
0
Below sea level
Below sea level
Ice-covered
International boundaries
0
1,500
3,000 Miles
0
1,500
3,000 Kilometers
Physical Map of the World
ANTARCTICA

PRIMARY SOURCE EDITION

Civilization

Past & Present

Eleventh Edition

Palmira Brummett
UNIVERSITY OF TENNESSEE

Robert R. Edgar
HOWARD UNIVERSITY

Neil J. Hackett
ST. LOUIS UNIVERSITY

George F. Jewsbury
CENTRE D'ÉTUDES DU MONDE RUSSE
ÉCOLE DES HAUTES ÉTUDES EN SCIENCES SOCIALES

Barbara Molony
SANTA CLARA UNIVERSITY

THIS BOOK HAS BENEFITED FROM THE CONTRIBUTIONS OVER MANY EDITIONS OF THE FOLLOWING AUTHORS:

T. Walter Wallbank (Late)

Alastair M. Taylor (Late)

Nels M. Bailkey

Clyde J. Lewis

PEARSON
Longman

New York Boston San Francisco
London Toronto Sydney Tokyo Singapore Madrid
Mexico City Munich Paris Cape Town Hong Kong Montréal

Executive Editor: Michael Boezi
Senior Acquisitions Editor: Janet Lanphier
Senior Development Editor: Dawn Groundwater
Development Editor: Adam Beroud
Executive Marketing Manager: Sue Westmoreland
Media and Supplements Editor: Kristi Olson
Senior Media Editor: Patrick McCarthy
Production Manager: Eric Jorgensen
Project Coordination, Text Design, and Electronic Page Makeup: Electronic Publishing Services Inc., NYC
Photo Research: Photosearch, Inc.
Cover Designer/Manager: Nancy Danahy
Cover: An ornamental mask which formed part of the regalia of the Benin King (Oba). The headdress is surmounted by representations of Portuguese merchants' heads. Ivory, early 16th century, from Benin City, Nigeria. British Museum, London, Great Britain. © Werner Forman/Art Resource, NY.
Manufacturing Buyer: Roy L. Pickering, Jr.
Printer and Binder: Courier Corporation
Cover Printer: Coral Graphic Services

Library of Congress Cataloging-in-Publication Data

Civilization past & present / Palmira Brummett ... [et al.].— 11th ed.
p. cm.
Includes bibliographical references and index.
ISBN 0-321-23613-0 — ISBN 0-321-23627-0 — ISBN 0-321-23628-9
1. Civilization. I. Brummett, Palmira Johnson

CB69.C57 2005
909—dc22 2004029985

Visit us at http://www.ablongman.com.

ISBN 0-321-42332-1 (Primary Source Edition, Complete Edition)
ISBN 0-321-42838-2 (Primary Source Edition, Volume I)
ISBN 0-321-42837-4 (Primary Source Edition, Volume II)

1 2 3 4 5 6 7 8 9 10—CRK—07 06 05

Brief Contents

Detailed Contents

*Each chapter ends with a Conclusion, Suggestions for Web Browsing, Literature and Film, and Suggestions for Reading.

Documents

Maps

Global Issues

Discovery Through Maps

Chapter Opening Image Descriptions

CHAPTER 1

Gold and lapis lazuli Goat and Tree in the form of an offering stand to the Sumerian fertility god Tammuz, from the royal burials at Ur, c. 2600–2500 B.C.E.

CHAPTER 2

The details of the lives of individual human beings in ancient times sometimes become lost in the broader discussions of economic, military, and political events. This image of a Chinese couple playing a board game shows that ordinary life with its amusements remained, and that an artisan thought it moving enough to portray it.

CHAPTER 3

The Lion capital of Sarnath, from an Ashoka column placed at the site of the Buddha's first sermon. This Lion capital is used today as a national emblem of the Republic of India.

CHAPTER 4

A view of the Acropolis of Athens, dominated by the Parthenon, the temple dedicated to the goddess Athena.

CHAPTER 5

The Forum of Rome, with the ruins of the Temple of Vesta and the Column of Phocas.

CHAPTER 6

The gold and silver domes of the Cathedral of Hagia Sophia, Novgorod, built in the mid eleventh century. Though Novgorod lies some 1000 miles to the north of Constantinople, Byzantine cultural influence penetrated deeply into the region that would one day form the heartland of Russia.

CHAPTER 7

Qur'an page with gold lettering by the fifteenth-century calligrapher Sheykh Hamdullah. For Muslims the Qur'an is eternal; craftsmen created beautiful, elaborate Qur'ans for various Muslim rulers.

CHAPTER 8

Brass statue of a queen mother, from the Court of Benin, sixteenth century.

CHAPTER 9

The Gothic-style Benedictine abbey of Mont St. Michel, constructed between the eleventh and sixtheenth centuries and built on a rocky inlet amid the sandbanks and tides between Brittany and Normandy, France.

CHAPTER 10

Refined gentlemen of the Tang and Song dynasties, seen in this detail from a scroll by tenth-century artist Gu Hongzhong, displayed their taste and culture in banquets in their own homes. Entertainment by female musicians and courtesans enhanced the opulent foods and rich decorations.

CHAPTER 11

Detail from painted Mayan vase depicting a ceremonially dressed ball player. The ball game served important social, political, and religious functions in Mayan civilization. On a very basic level, it provided the Mayan polity with entertainment. The construction of stone-paved courts, the training of players, and the holding of games also reinforced the prestige of the community. Finally, the game and its players could serve as religious offerings, with losing players sometimes being sacrificed to the gods.

CHAPTER 12

The Ottoman army under Lala Mustafa Pasha parading before the captured fortress of Tiflis. Some janissaries, carrying their gunpowder weapons, are shown in the center of the image.

CHAPTER 13

The Temple of the Golden Pavilion was commissioned by the Japanese shōgun Ashikawa Yoshimitsu in 1397. The building was intimate in scale and designed as part of a garden in which the shōgun could meditate. The building, destroyed by an arsonist in 1950, was rebuilt exactly as the original.

CHAPTER 14

Detail from *The Creation of Adam,* painted by the master Renaissance artist Michelangelo Buonarroti. Ceiling of the Sistine Chapel (1511–1512), in Rome.

CHAPTER 15

The Armada Portrait of Queen Elizabeth I was painted in 1588 to commemorate the English naval victory over the Spanish Armada. Against considerable odds, Elizabeth succeeded in mobilizing her nation to withstand Spanish diplomatic and military pressures. At the same time, she managed to maintain a certain unity in her socially and religiously diverse realm.

CHAPTER 16

This ivory saltcellar, with its carved figure of a Portuguese sailor in crow's nest, makes clear the influence of the West on the artists of Benin.

CHAPTER 17

That the small country of Holland became the richest country in Europe during the seventeenth century is a result of the hard and serious work of a diverse population, including people such as those shown in this detail from Rembrandt's *The Syndics of the Cloth Guild* (1662).

CHAPTER 18

The fury and force of the French Revolution came from people such as these Parisian women advancing on Versailles, October 5, 1789. They were about to bring the King, the Queen, and the entire National Constituent Assembly back to Paris, and the reality of the Revolution.

CHAPTER 19

Europeans usually bought slaves for the trans-Atlantic slave trade at specific locations along the west and central African coast. In *Merchant Slaves of Goree,* the French artists Grasset de St. Sauveur and Christian Labrousse depicted European and African slave traders negotiating the sale of slaves at Goree, an island off the coast of Senegal.

CHAPTER 20

Large Perspective View of the Theater District in Sakai-cho and Fukiya-cho by Okumura Masanobu (1686–1764). Japan's cities were bustling centers for the arts, culture, and mercantile activities during the Tokugawa period. Artists captured the excitement of urban life in prints depicting what they called the "floating world." This street scene by Masanobu shows theaters, teahouses, restaurants, shops, and a female street vendor selling fish.

CHAPTER 21

A man of political and military genius, Toussaint Louverture led the Haitian people in their successful struggle for independence.

CHAPTER 22

Here in the Soho Engineering Works, Birmingham, England, visitors have come to observe how the steam engines invented by James Watt are made. Note the absence of modern safety equipment and standards.

CHAPTER 23

Menelik II, the emperor of Ethiopia, stands in the middle of his generals. Crowned emperor in 1889, Menelik carried out campaigns of conquest while maintaining his kingdom's autonomy in the face of European imperialism. Ethiopia became a symbol of African independence in the black world.

CHAPTER 24

The arrival of Western gunboats and merchants in Asia in the nineteenth century usually initiated a period of economic and military domination. For the Japanese, the arrival of Commdore Perry in 1853 served as the beginning of a revolutionary change that made them competitors with the West by the end of the century.

CHAPTER 25

Diego Rivera, detail from *Dream of a Sunday Afternoon in the Alameda.* Rivera painted his 50 feet long × 15 feet high mural inside the Hotel del Prado, which is close to the Alameda Central Park in downtown Mexico City. The full mural depicts events from Mexican history from the time of the Aztecs up through the Mexican Revolution. The center panel shows the artist as a boy walking through the Alameda with his symbolic parents, the artist José Guadalupe Posada (the man in black on the far right) and one of Posada's most famous creations, "La Calavera Catrina" (the skeleton dressed as a woman). Behind the youthful Rivera stands Frida Kahlo, the artist's future wife.

CHAPTER 26

For the Germans, the proclamation of the Second Reich by William I at Versailles in the Hall of Mirrors, 1871, was a way to pay back the French for two centuries of invasions. For the French, it was an insult that would be repaid in the same place 48 years later in the dictated Treaty of Versailles that ended World War I.

CHAPTER 27

British machine gun unit at the Somme, 1916. The Battle of the Somme was one of the bloodiest engagements of World War I. In an effort to relieve pressure on the French army under siege at Verdun, the British attacked the fortified German lines at Somme. After four months of fighting which included the use of poison gas, aerial bombardment, and the first ever deployment of tanks, the British had only managed to advance eight miles. The cost in human lives: 420,000 British, 195,000 French, and 650,000 Germans. All this is a war that would not protect liberal values in Europe, but instead serve to initiate another, even deadlier war a generation later.

CHAPTER 28

Benito Mussolini and Adolf Hitler watch a Nazi parade during the Italian dictator's visit to Germany in 1937. Mussolini and his Italian compatriots invented fascism, but it was Hitler and the Nazis who would realize the totalitarian ideology's most murderous potential by initiating World War II and the Holocaust.

CHAPTER 29

In 1937, the Chinese Communist and Nationalist forces united to fight against the Japanese forces occupying China. The alliance held until the defeat of Japan, when the Communists and Nationalists resumed their struggle for control of China. The Communists would ultimately prevail by 1949. Here men from the 73rd Red Division of the 15th Army Corps offer a communist salute.

CHAPTER 30

Veiled Egyptian women demonstrate in the streets of Cairo for voting rights for women in 1922.

CHAPTER 31

In 1937, at the height of the Spanish Civil War, a woman marches toward the southern front in Madrid to join with the Republican army fighting against General Franco's nationalist forces. Supported by arms and advisors from Nazi Germany, the nationalists would prevail in a bloody conflict that would serve as a prelude to World War II.

CHAPTER 32

President Kennedy and Soviet Premier Nikita Khrushchev meet at the Vienna Summit, June 3, 1961. A series of conflicts between Washington and Moscow in the early 1960s, including the erection of the Berlin Wall and the Cuban Missile Crisis, brought the two superpowers close to nuclear war.

CHAPTER 33

On March 11, 2004, Islamic militants in a loose affiliation with al Qaeda and opposed to the United States' occupation of Iraq, which was then supported by Spain, bombed trains in multiple locations throughout Madrid. The bombings killed more than 190 commuters.

CHAPTER 34

Long lines of people wait to vote in Soweto, as South Africa holds its first election open to all its citizens in 1994.

CHAPTER 35

In the late 1980s, many Japanese women were inspired by the growth in political representation by women in local and national government. Here, women supporting feminist candidates march through Tokyo with a large banner exclaiming: "Through the power of women, we will change politics!"

To the Instructor

The eleventh edition of *Civilization Past & Present* continues to present a survey of world history, treating the development and growth of civilization as a global phenomenon in which all the world's culture systems have interacted. This new edition, like its predecessors, includes all the elements of history—social, economic, political, military, religious, aesthetic, legal, and technological—to illustrate that global interaction. One of the most significant changes in the eleventh edition is the addition of our new Asian scholar and co-author, Barbara Molony. Barbara is a professor of history at Santa Clara University and is the former director of Santa Clara's Program for the Study of Women and Gender. Well-versed in modern Asia, she significantly revised the book's Asian chapters.

With the accelerating tempo of developments in business, communication, and technology, every day each part of the world is brought into closer contact with other parts: Economic and political events that happen in even the most remote corners of the world affect each of us individually. An appreciation for and an understanding of all the civilizations of the world must be an essential aim of education. Thus, the eleventh edition of *Civilization Past & Present* emphasizes world trends and carefully avoids placing these trends within a Western conceptual basis.

CHANGES TO ORGANIZATION AND CONTENT

The eleventh edition maintains the many strengths that have made *Civilization Past & Present* a highly respected textbook. As the authors revised the text, they relied on the latest historical scholarship and profited from suggestions from adopters of the text and reviewers. Maintained throughout this compelling survey are a fluid writing style and consistent level of presentation seldom found in multi-authored texts.

While the text retains the basic organization of its predecessors, all chapters have been reviewed and revised in light of the globalization of today's changing world. The authors have carefully evaluated, revised, combined, and rewritten chapters to provide balanced coverage of all parts of the world throughout history.

One of the major changes in the eleventh edition is a new chapter, "Latin America: Independence and Dependence, 1825–1945" (Chapter 25). This new chapter provides detailed coverage of Latin America, including the political, social, and economic challenges following independence and into the twentieth century and relations between the Latin American nations and the United States.

Other chapter changes are as follows:

- **Chapter 1:** "Stone Age Societies and the Earliest Civilizations of the Near East" provides coverage of human prehistory, Egyptian civilization, and the development of smaller Near Eastern states.
- **Chapter 2:** "Ancient China—Origins to Empire: Prehistory to 220 C.E." and **Chapter 3:** "Ancient India: From Origins to 300 C.E." both include expanded coverage of gender and social history.
- **Chapter 6:** "Byzantium and the Orthodox World: Byzantium, Eastern Europe, and Russia, 325–1500" has been revised to stress the independent development of East Rome and includes enhanced information on the development of the Balkan States.
- **Chapter 9:** "The European Middle Ages, 476–1348 C.E." combines the tenth edition's Chapter 9 and Chapter 10, examining the political, religious, and social history of the entire European Middle Ages in one chapter rather than two.
- **Chapter 10:** "Culture, Power, and Trade in the Era of Asian Hegemony, 220–1350" and **Chapter 13:** "East Asian Cultural and Political Systems, 1300–1650" have been thoroughly revised and expanded, with particular attention to gender and social history.
- **Chapter 14:** "European Cultural and Religious Transformations: The Renaissance and the Reformation, 1300–1600" combines the tenth edition's Chapter 15 and Chapter 16, exploring the political, religious, and social connections between the European Renaissance and Reformation in one chapter rather than two.
- **Chapter 15:** "The Development of the European State System, 1300–1650" is a new chapter that examines the growth of the European nation-states from the late Middle Ages through the religious wars of the seventeenth century.
- **Chapter 17:** "Politics in the First Age of Capitalism, 1648–1774: Absolutism and Limited Central Power" places more emphasis on the social crises of the first phase of capitalism.
- Reorganized **Chapter 18:** "New Ideas and Their Political Consequences: The Scientific Revolution,

the Enlightenment, and the French Revolutions" combines the tenth edition's Chapter 19 and with content from Chapter 22, as the authors believe that intellectual transformations represented by the Enlightenment are directly connected to the political upheavals of French Revolutions and so should be discussed as such in one chapter.

- A recast **Chapter 19:** "Africa, 1650–1850" provides detailed coverage of Africa, including the Atlantic Slave Trade, Islamic Africa, the settlement of South Africa by Africans and Europeans, and state formation in the east and northeast of the continent.
- A recast **Chapter 20:** "Asian and Middle Eastern Empires and Nations, 1650–1815" examines political, social, and cultural developments across Asia, including the Ottoman Empire, Persia, India, China, Korea, Japan, Southeast Asia, and the Pacific.
- **Chapter 21:** "The Americas, 1650–1825: From European Dominance to Independence" offers expanded treatment of the Haitian Revolution.
- Reorganized **Chapter 22:** "Industrialization: Social, Political, and Cultural Transformations," focuses exclusively on the social, ideological, religious, and cultural effects of the Industrial Revolutions in Great Britain, Continental Europe, and the United States.
- **Chapter 23:** "Africa and the Middle East During the Age of European Imperialism" provides expanded coverage of Islam and Christianity in Africa during the colonial era.
- **Chapter 24:** "Asia, 1815–1914: India, Southeast Asia, China, and Japan" provides expanded coverage of Asian civilizations, with particular emphasis on gender and social history.
- **Chapter 26:** "Politics and Diplomacy in the West, 1815–1914" combines the tenth edition's Chapter 23 and Chapter 27, examining the political changes in Europe between the Congress of Vienna and World War I in one chapter rather than two.
- Expanded **Chapter 28:** "The USSR, Italy, Germany, and Japan: Democratic Failure and Authoritarian Government in the Interwar Period" adds coverage of Japan.
- A recast **Chapter 29:** "Forging New Nations in Asia, 1910–1950" examines political and social transformations in China, Korea, Southeast Asia, and India.
- A recast **Chapter 30:** "Emerging National Movements in the Middle East and Africa from the 1920s to 1950s" explores the rising tide of nationalism in Africa and the Middle East following World War I through the start of the Cold War.
- Expanded **Chapter 31:** "World War II: Origins and Consequences, 1919–1946" adds coverage of the postwar settlements that followed the defeat of the Axis powers in 1945.
- Reorganized **Chapter 32:** "The Bipolar World: Cold War and Decolonization, 1945–1991" prefaces its examination of the Cold War by examining the competing economic systems of the United States and the USSR. It also provides a more detailed treatment of decolonization and its relationship to the Cold War.
- Reorganized **Chapter 33:** "The United States and Europe Since 1945: Politics in an Age of Conflict and Change" now stresses the relationship between technology and social change in the United States and Europe and also provides expanded coverage of the Soviet Union and the Russian Republic.
- Reorganized **Chapter 35:** "Asia Since 1945: Political, Economic, and Social Revolutions" integrates coverage of China, Hong Kong, Taiwan, and Singapore.

The eleventh edition of *Civilization Past & Present* is a thorough revision in both its narrative and its pedagogical features. It is intended to provide the reader with an understanding of the legacies of past eras and to illuminate the way in which the study of world history gives insight into the genesis, nature, and direction of global civilization. Given the growing interdependence of the world's nations, the need for this perspective has never been greater.

NEW SPLIT

The split for the two-volume edition has changed for the eleventh edition: Volume I, To 1650, contains Chapters 1–16; Volume II, From 1300, contains Chapters 12–35. The start of Volume II at 1300 accommodates those courses that cover materials beginning earlier than 1650. The eleventh edition also includes a three-volume split edition for schools operating on the quarter system: Volume A, To 1500, contains Chapters 1–11; Volume B, From 500–1815, contains Chapters 9–20; and Volume C, From 1775, contains Chapters 18–35.

FEATURES AND PEDAGOGY

The text has been developed with the dual purpose of helping students acquire a solid knowledge of past events and, equally important, of helping them think more constructively about the significance of those events for the complex times in which we now live. A number of pedagogical features—some well tested in earlier editions and lightly revised here, and a few new ones—will assist students in achieving these goals.

GLOBAL ISSUES

MIGRATION

Why do people move from one place to another?

The history of migration is in a sense the history of humankind. All migrations involve the movement of peoples, cultures, languages, and ideas. As a result, they have shaped history around the world and played a major role in the growth of civilization. The reasons why people migrate vary. Changing environmental conditions, population pressures, economic shifts, political and religious controversies, and war and violence have all compelled people to move from one place to another. Whatever the triggering circumstance may be, the decision to migrate is ultimately driven by the human necessity or desire to find a better or more secure place to live.

Migrations have been an integral part of human experience since our early ancestors took their first tentative steps on the African savanna and began exploring and adapting to new environments. *Homo erectus* migrated from the African continent to Eurasia. Members of *Homo sapiens* followed their predecessor out of Africa and traveled further still, showing considerable ingenuity in overcoming obstacles such as the open sea to reach Australia and the cold of the northern latitudes to traverse the Bering Strait and enter the Americas.

These earliest human movements were small in scale. Extended families or clans would move into a new area and live off the land. Even with small populations, humans often placed considerable environmental strain on the land after only a short time. From 3000 B.C.E. to 500 C.E., Bantu communities migrating into central, eastern, and southern Africa could cultivate an area for only a few years before the soils were exhausted and they had to move to new land.

While environmental degradation caused by human activity has often forced people to migrate, so too have acts of nature such as droughts, floods, cold spells, and crop failures. Severe drought from around 1300 to 1100 B.C.E. likely initiated political disruptions in the eastern Mediterranean and the migrations of the Sea Peoples, Philistines, Sicilians, Sardinians, and Etruscans that followed.[1] More recently, potato blight destroyed the potato crops in Ireland between 1846 and 1850, creating widespread fam... and economic hard-...

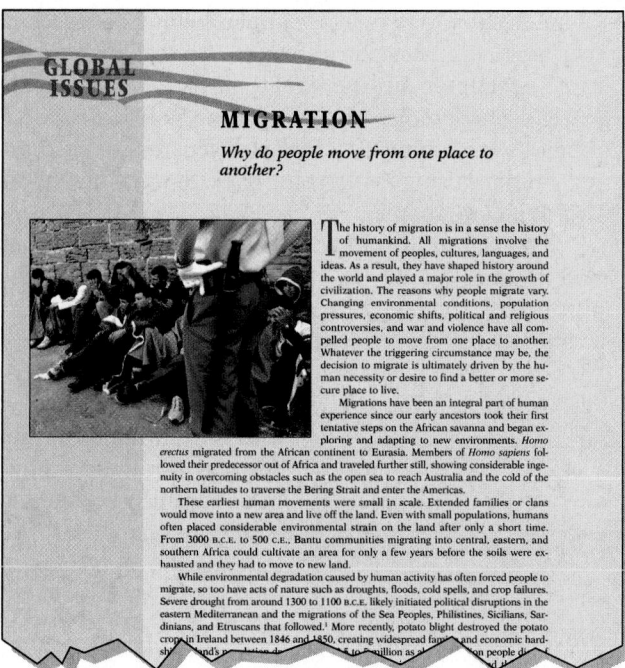

New! *Global Issues* Essays These new essays explore seven topics of unique transcultural and transhistorical significance: Migration, Religion and Government, Location and Identity, Technological Exchange, Slavery, Gender, and War and International Law. Each essay employs examples that span both history and the world's many civilizations. As pedagogical tools, the essays are intended to do more than just inform students about global topics; they also reveal challenges that have confronted and still confront civilizations the world over. The essays carefully avoid discussing their topics from a Western conceptual basis and instead strive to examine them using a global framework. Each essay uses art to illustrate its ideas and ends with critical thinking questions. Evenly distributed throughout the book, the essays appear on two-page spreads between chapters.

global economy due to transatlantic discoveries and the rise of oceanic merchant empires like those of the Dutch and the English.

The Age of the Köprülü Vizirs

Mehmed IV became sultan in 1648, facing rampant inflation, a Venetian blockade of the Dardanelles, rebellion in the provinces, and a violent struggle among palace factions, including his mother, Turhan (TOOR-hahn) Sultan, and her rival, the old Valide Sultan Kösem (KOO-sem). These senior women wielded considerable influence and controlled considerable wealth in the palace system. In 1651 Turhan ended Kösem's long-term dominance of the harem by having her strangled, but Mehmed remained enmeshed in factional politics. This internal strife was compounded by a vehement struggle between groups of conservative mullahs representing the ***ulama*** (oo-LAH-mah) and **sufis,** both of which were contending for spiritual authority and influence in the capital. By 1656 Istan-

ulama—Islamic religious authorities; men versed in Islamic sciences and law.

sufis—Islamic mystics who sought contact with Allah through prayer and ritual dance; considered a heretical movement by conservative Muslims.

New! Pronunciation Guide This new feature will help students correctly pronounce key foreign words. Pronunciations appear in parentheses immediately after the first use of a key foreign term in the text.

New! On-page Glossary This new feature provides students with concise definitions of key historical terms. Glossary definitions appear in the footer of the page in which they are discussed.

Chapter Opening Pages Chapter opening pages again feature an illustration relevant to a major chapter topic, a chapter outline, and a newly designed, easy-to-read chronology of key events—political, social, religious, and cultural—that are discussed in the chapter. Students can easily refer back to the timeline as they read the chapter.

A short text introduction previews the civilizations and themes to be discussed in the chapter. The chronology then sets the major topics within a framework easy for the student to comprehend at a glance. Chapter opening images reflect a wide range of genres, including sculpture, painting, mosaics, tapestries, and illuminated manuscripts. The images have been carefully selected to invoke a particular culture and engage the student visually.

CHAPTER
10
Culture, Power, and Trade in the Era of Asian Hegemony, 220–1350

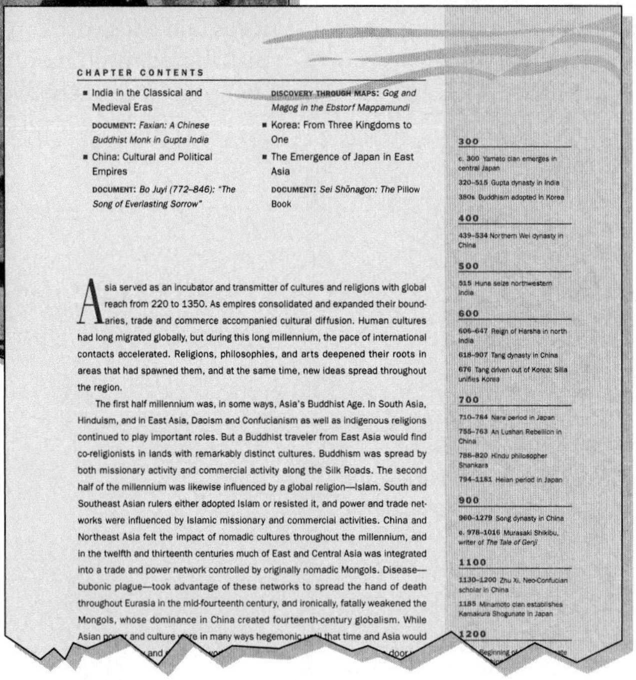
CHAPTER CONTENTS

- India in the Classical and Medieval Eras
  DOCUMENT: *Faxian: A Chinese Buddhist Monk in Gupta India*
- China: Cultural and Political Empires
  DOCUMENT: *Bo Juyi (772–846): "The Song of Everlasting Sorrow"*

DISCOVERY THROUGH MAPS: *Gog and Magog in the Ebstorf Mappamundi*

- Korea: From Three Kingdoms to One
- The Emergence of Japan in East Asia
  DOCUMENT: *Sei Shōnagon: The Pillow Book*

Asia served as an incubator and transmitter of cultures and religions with global reach from 220 to 1350. As empires consolidated and expanded their boundaries, trade and commerce accompanied cultural diffusion. Human cultures had long migrated globally, but during this long millennium, the pace of international contacts accelerated. Religions, philosophies, and arts deepened their roots in areas that had spawned them, and at the same time, new ideas spread throughout the region.

The first half millennium was, in some ways, Asia's Buddhist Age. In South Asia, Hinduism, and in East Asia, Daoism and Confucianism as well as indigenous religions continued to play important roles. But a Buddhist traveler from East Asia would find co-religionists in lands with remarkably distinct cultures. Buddhism was spread by both missionary activity and commercial activity along the Silk Roads. The second half of the millennium was likewise influenced by a global religion—Islam. South and Southeast Asian rulers either adopted Islam or resisted it, and power and trade networks were influenced by Islamic missionary and commercial activities. China and Northeast Asia felt the impact of nomadic cultures throughout the millennium, and in the twelfth and thirteenth centuries much of East and Central Asia was integrated into a trade and power network controlled by originally nomadic Mongols. Disease—bubonic plague—took advantage of these networks to spread the hand of death throughout Eurasia in the mid-fourteenth century, and ironically, fatally weakened the Mongols, whose dominance in China created fourteenth-century globalism. While Asian and culture in many ways hegemonic that time and Asia would

300
c. 300 Yamato clan emerges in central Japan
320–515 Gupta dynasty in India
380s Buddhism adopted in Korea

400
439–534 Northern Wei dynasty in China

500
515 Huns seize northwestern India

600
606–647 Reign of Harsha in north India
618–907 Tang dynasty in China
676 Tang driven out of Korea; Silla unifies Korea

700
710–784 Nara period in Japan
755–763 An Lushan Rebellion in China
788–820 Hindu philosopher Shankara
794–1181 Heian period in Japan

900
960–1279 Song dynasty in China
c. 978–1016 Murasaki Shikibu, writer of *The Tale of Genji*

1100
1130–1200 Zhu Xi, Neo-Confucian scholar in China
1185 Minamoto clan establishes Kamakura Shogunate in Japan

1200

The Great Schism of the Roman Catholic Church

In response to pressure from churchmen, rulers, scholars, and commoners throughout Europe, the papacy returned to Rome in 1377, it seemed for a time that its credibility would be regained. However, the reverse proved true. In the papal election held the following year, the **College of Cardinals** elected an Italian pope. A few months later the French cardinals declared the election invalid and elected a French pope, who returned to Avignon. During the Great **Schism** (1378–1417), as the split of the church into two allegiances was called, there were two popes, each with his college of cardinals and capital city, each claiming complete authority, each sending out papal administrators and collecting taxes, and each excommunicating the other. The nations of Europe gave allegiance as their individual political interests influenced them.

The Great Schism continued after the original rival popes died, and each group elected a replacement. Doubt and confusion caused many Europeans to question the legitimacy and holiness of the church as an institution.

The Conciliar Movement

Positive action came in the form of the Conciliar Movement. In 1395 the professors at the University of Paris proposed that a general council, representing the entire church, should meet to heal the schism. A majority of the cardinals of both factions accepted this solution, and in 1409 they met at the Council of Pisa,

College of Cardinals—Cardinals are the highest-ranking churchmen serving under the pope in the Catholic Church. Collectively, they constitute the Sacred College of Cardinals, and their duties include electing the pope, acting as his principal counselors, and aiding in governing the church.

Schism—Literally a split or division (from the Greek *schizein* = to split). The word is usually used in reference to the Great Schism (1378–1417), when there were two, and later three, rival popes, each with his own College of Cardinals.

The Conciliar Mov it represen reforming and democratizing influence in the church. But the movement was not to endure, even though the Council of Constance had decreed that general councils were superior to popes and that they should meet at regular intervals in the future. Taking steps to preserve his authority, the pope announced that to appeal to a church council without having first obtained papal consent was heretical. Together with the inability of later councils to bring about much-needed reform and with lack of support for such councils by secular

Religious Reforms and Reactions

1415	John Hus, Bohemian reformer, burned at the stake
1437–1517	Cardinal Ximenes carried out reforms of Spanish Catholic Church
c. 1450	Revival of witchcraft mania in Europe
1452–1498	Savonarola attempted religious purification of Florence
1483–1546	Martin Luther
1484–1531	Ulrich Zwingli, leader of Swiss Reformation
1491–1556	Ignatius Loyola, founder of Society of Jesus (Jesuits)
1509–1564	John Calvin, leader of Reformation in Geneva
1515–1582	St. Teresa of Avila, founder of Carmelite religious order
1517	Luther issues Ninety-Five Theses
1521	Luther declared an outcast by the Imperial Diet at Worms
1534–1549	Pontificate of Paul III
1545–1563	Council of Trent
1561–1593	Religious wars in France

Chronology Tables Throughout each chapter, brief chronology tables once again highlight the major events occurring within a text section. Whether focusing on general trends, as does European Cultural and Religious Transformations (Chapter 14), or on a single country, as does China in the Imperialist Era (Chapter 24), the chronology tables give the student an immediate summary view of a topic, at its point of discussion.

Discovery Through Maps This special feature focusing on primary maps in many chapters offers a unique historical view—be it local, city, country, world, or imagined—of the way a particular culture looked at the world at a particular time. Students tend to take the orientation of a map for granted; however, "An Islamic Map of the World" (Chapter 7) makes clear that not all peoples make the same assumptions. The world map of the famous Arab cartographer al-Idrisi is oriented, as was common at the time, with south at the top. Chapter 19's "The Myth of the Empty Land" shows how European settlers of South Africa laid claim to the South African interior by asserting that they were moving into an unpopulated area.

The discussions accompanying these maps have been expanded to emphasize their connection with the text itself; the addition of review questions help students better understand the concepts presented by the maps.

Discovery Through Maps **Map of China's Ancient Heartland, circa 1500 C.E.**

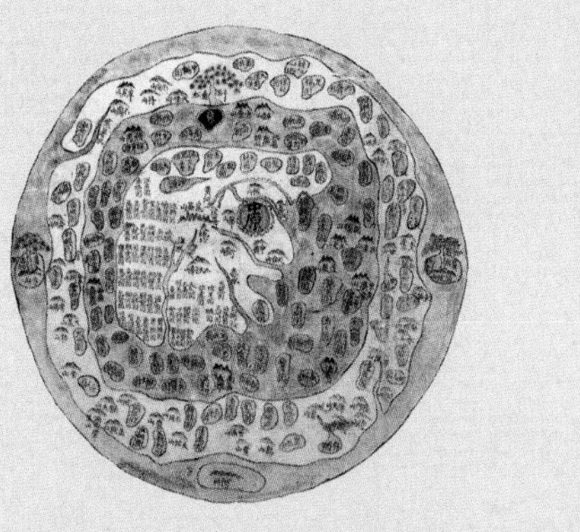

It is one of the marks of human nature that the center of the world is found in one's self-consciousness, and then in concentric circles in the family, community, and nation. This trait extends across civilizations and continents and can be seen not only in this Chinese map depicting the area known as the *Zhongyuan* (ZHONG-yoo-AHN) or heartland of ancient China, but also in maps created around the same time by Europeans as they made their voyages of discovery. The Chinese map is particularly informative because it reminds its viewers that even within China itself, the heartland was th[e] [re]pository [o]f culture and power

The map has political implications, in that it shows its viewers that the original heartland of China was the same place as the home of the Ming. This portrayal is difficult, however, for those trained to see geography in terms of a Mercator projection (see, e.g., p. 467). The Mercator projection, like the Ming map, also reflects a worldview that places the map's creators in the center–in the Mercator case, the center is in Europe. Is there any particular reason, for example, why the Greenwich Meridian (from which all longitudes on the surface of the earth are presently measured) should be the centra[l] [poi]nt of the world's geography

Excerpts from Primary Source Documents Seventeen of the more than 100 primary source documents are new. In "Muslim and Christian: Two Contemporary Perspectives" (Chapter 9), first the Christian knight, then the Muslim physician, write of the bloody fall of Jerusalem with the certainty of religious justification for his cause, and of cultural superiority. Simón Bolívar, in his powerful Proclamation to the People of Venezuela (Chapter 21), addresses his fellow-countrymen to reestablish a republican form of government in the state.

Almost every chapter now includes a document concerning the status of women in general during a particular era or details the accomplishments of a specific woman. In Chapter 35, Benazir Bhutto, Pakistan's first female prime minister, relates the dilemma of being a "foreign" student at Harvard during an era of political turmoil for both Pakistan and the United States.

Headnotes to all have been expanded to better link the documents to the text itself. Several discussion questions now follow each excerpt.

Document **Letter from Abigail Adams**

Abigail Adams, with her husband John, served as the embodiment of the American republican virtues of plain speaking, lack of ostentation, and sometimes brutal honesty. Her letter to her husband speaks to the openness and strength of their relationship. Her spelling represents the usage of the time.

31 Mar. 1776

I wish you would ever write me a Letter half as long as I write you; and tell me if you may where your Fleet are gone? What sort of Defence Virginia can make against our common Enemy? Whether it is so situated as to make an able Defence? Are not the Gentery Lords and the common people vassals, are they not like the uncivilized Natives Brittain represents us to be? I hope their Riffel Men who have shewen themselves very savage and even Blood thirsty; are not a specimen of the Generality of the people.

I am willing to allow the Colony great merrit for having produced a Washington but they have been shamefully duped by a Dunmore.

I have sometimes been ready to think that the passion for Liberty cannot be Eaquelly Strong in the Breasts of those who have been accustomed to deprive their fellow Creatures of theirs. Of this I am certain that it is not founded upon that generous and christian principal of doing to others as we would that others should do unto us. . . .

I long to hear that you have declared an independancy—and by the way in the new Code of Laws which I suppose it will be necessary for you to make I desire you would Remember the Ladies, and be more generous and favourable to them than your ancestors. Do not put such unlimited power into the hands of the Husbands. Remember all Men would be tyrants if they could. If perticuliar care and attention is not paid to the Laidies we are determined to foment a Rebelion, and will not hold ourselves bound by any Laws in which we have no voice, or Representation.

That your Sex are Naturally Tyrannical is a Truth so thoroughly established as to admit of no dispute, but such of you as wish to be happy willingly give up the harsh title of Master for the more tender and endearing one of Friend. Why then, not put it out of the power of the vicious and the Lawless to use us with cruelty and indignity with impunity. Men of Sense in all Ages abhor those customs which treat us only as the vassals of your Sex. Regard us then as Beings placed by providence under your protection and in immitation of the Supreem Being make use of that power only for our happiness.

Questions to Consider

1. Why does Abigail Adams fear that the coming political changes will not benefit women?
2. What is Adams's rationale for her critique of the way men sometimes go about doing business?
3. Would Abigail Adams think her descendants living today have fulfilled her hopes for a "proper" place for women in society?

From Abigail Smith Adams, *The Book of Abigail and John: Selected Letters of the Adams Family, 1762–1784,* eds. L. H. Butterfield, et al. (Cambridge, Mass.: Harvard University Press, 1975).

254 CIVILIZATION PAST AND PRESENT

tapping Muslim trading networks. The kingdom of Aksum became a major Red Sea power, serving as a bridge between the Mediterranean and the Indian Ocean. The Swahili city-states on the East African coast and the states of the Zimbabwe Plateau carried on extensive relations with Indian Ocean trading networks. West African savanna kingdoms created the most extensive trading network through their position overseeing trade between North Africa, the savanna, and forest regions to the south. However, within these long-distance trading networks, African states were primarily producers of raw materials.

Although most Africans remained faithful to their traditional religious beliefs and practices, many converted to Christianity and Islam in specific areas. Egypt became an early center of Christianity, while Ethiopia's rulers firmly established Christianity as their kingdom's state religion. Islam became the dominant religion of North Africa, while some rulers and traders in the West African savanna, northeastern Africa, and along the Swahili coast adopted Islam. However, until the eighteenth century, Islam remained primarily a religion of court and commerce in sub-Saharan Africa. It won few followers in small-scale societies that did not have ruling elites. This pattern is similar to other places such as Indonesia where Muslim traders established themselves but did not initially win many converts.

Suggestions for Web Browsing

You can obtain more information about topics included in this chapter at the websites listed below. See also the companion website that accompanies this text, http://www.ablongman.com/brummett, which contains an online study guide and additional resources.

Internet African History Sourcebook
http://www.fordham.edu/halsall/africa/africasbook.html

Extensive online source for links about the history of ancient Africa, including the kingdoms of Ghana, Mali, and Songhai.

Art of Benin
http://www.si.edu/ofg/Units/sorsnmafa.htm

Site of the Smithsonian Institution's National Museum of African Art displays art objects from the kingdom of Benin before Western dominance.

Great Zimbabwe
http://www.mc.maricopa.edu/~reffland/anthropology/anthro2003/legacy/africa/zimbabwe/

A 23-slide series, with commentary, that will take you through the ruins of Great Zimbabwe in southern Africa.

The Story of Africa
http://www.bbc.co.uk/worldservice/africa/features/storyofafrica/index.shtml

The radio service of the BBC presents a history of Africa from the origins of humankind to modern nation-states.

African Voices
http://www.m...si.edu/africanvo...es/

Ethiopian royal literature, see G. W. B. Huntingford, ed., *Royal Chronicles of Abyssinia: The Glorious Victories of Ama Seyon King of Ethiopia* (Clarendon Press, 1965).

Caravans of Gold (Home Vision, 1984) treats the gold trade between the Sudanic kingdoms of West Africa and the Muslim and European worlds. It is one film in an eight-part series, *Africa: The Story of a Continent*, presented by Basil Davidson, a British writer on African issues. *Lost Cities of the South* (PBS, 1999) presents a discussion of African civilizations of southern Africa, such as Mapungubwe and Great Zimbabwe. It is part of a six-part series, *Wonders of the African World*, narrated by Harvard professor Henry Louis Gates, Jr.

Suggestions for Reading

The best detailed coverage of African history can be found in two multivolume series, each containing chapters by leading scholars: *The Cambridge History of Africa*, 8 Vols. (Cambridge University Press, 1982–1984) and *The UNESCO General History of Africa*. Among other general surveys of African history are Robert July, *A History of the African People*, 4th ed. (Waveland Press, 1992); Erik Gilbert and Jonathan Reynolds, *Africa in World History from Prehistory to the Present* (Pearson Education, 2004); and Christopher Ehret, *The Civilizations of Africa: A History to 1800* (University Press of Virginia, 2002).

The best general reference work on early African history is Joseph Vogel, ed., *Encyclopedia of Precolonial Africa: Archaeology, History, Languages, Cultures, and Environments* (AltaMira Press, 1997). Another general work that examines Africa's history with a disciplinary focus is James Newman, *The Peopling of Africa: A Geographic Interpretation* (Yale University Press, 1995). A general synthesis on women in African history is Iris Berger and E. Frances White, ...

Suggestions for Reading To give the student an additional view of the various cultures and timeframes, a *Literature and Film* section at the end of each chapter offers a listing of novels, poetry, films, and videos. Readings have been updated and carefully trimmed of dated entries. Students can consult these general interpretations, monographs, and collections of traditional source materials to expand their understanding of a particular topic or to prepare reports and papers. *Suggestions for Web Browsing* have also been updated throughout.

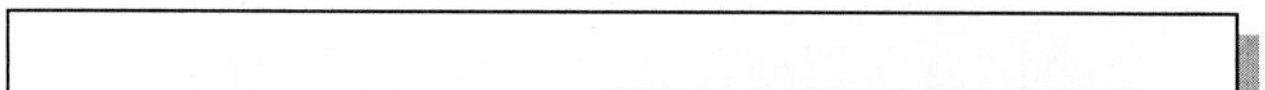

CHAPTER 6 • *Byzantium and the Orthodox World* 171

silkworms were smuggled out of China about 550 C.E., silk production flourished and became a profitable state monopoly. The state paid close attention to business: controlling the economy through a system of guilds to which all tradesmen and members of professions belonged; setting wages, profits, work hours, and prices; and even organizing bankers and doctors into compulsory corporations.

Justinian and Theodora

The dream of reclaiming the Mediterranean basin and reestablishing the Roman Empire to its former glory, however, did not die until the end of the reign of Justinian (r. 527–565). Aided by his forceful wife, Theodora, and a corps of competent assistants, he made long-lasting contributions to Byzantine and Western civilization, but gained only short-term successes in his foreign policy.

In the 520s and 530s, after earthquakes devastated much of his realm, Justinian carried out a massive project of urban renewal throughout the empire. He strengthened the walls defending Constantinople and built the monumental Hagia Sophia, which still stands. Forty windows circle the base of this great church's dome, producing a quality of light that creates the illusion that the ceiling is floating.

Justinian also reformed the government and ordered a review of all Roman law. This project led to the publication of the **Code of Justinian,** a digest of Roman and church law, texts, and other instructional materials that became the foundation of modern Western law. Following Constantine's example, Justinian saw himself ...

Emperor Justinian. Justinian bequeathed a splendid architectural and legal legacy to Europe. However, his attempt to reclaim the former glory of the Roman Empire gained only temporary success and bankrupted his treasury.

Photographs The text's more than 500 photos, most in full color, have been carefully revised to present a diverse range of images from all of the world's civilizations. Special care has again been taken to include images of the lifestyles and contributions of women for all eras and areas.

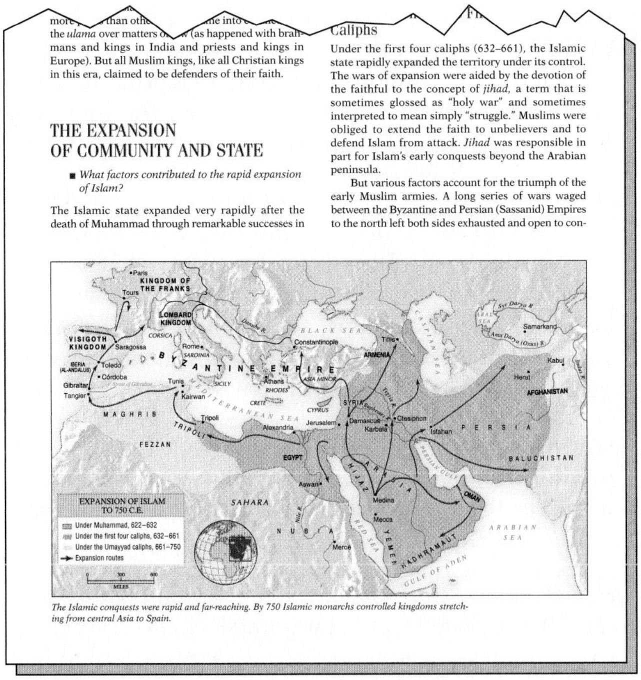

the *ulama* over matters of law (as happened with brahmans and kings in India and priests and kings in Europe). But all Muslim kings, like all Christian kings in this era, claimed to be defenders of their faith.

THE EXPANSION OF COMMUNITY AND STATE

■ *What factors contributed to the rapid expansion of Islam?*

The Islamic state expanded very rapidly after the death of Muhammad through remarkable successes in

Caliphs

Under the first four caliphs (632–661), the Islamic state rapidly expanded the territory under its control. The wars of expansion were aided by the devotion of the faithful to the concept of *jihad,* a term that is sometimes glossed as "holy war" and sometimes interpreted to mean simply "struggle." Muslims were obliged to extend the faith to unbelievers and to defend Islam from attack. *Jihad* was responsible in part for Islam's early conquests beyond the Arabian peninsula.

But various factors account for the triumph of the early Muslim armies. A long series of wars waged between the Byzantine and Persian (Sassanid) Empires to the north left both sides exhausted and open to con-

The Islamic conquests were rapid and far-reaching. By 750 Islamic monarchs controlled kingdoms stretching from central Asia to Spain.

Maps The use of full color allows students more readily to see distinctions on the more than 100 maps in the text. Some maps make clear the nature of a single distinctive event; others illustrate larger trends. For example, Trade and Cultural Interchange, c. 50 B.C.E. (Chapter 2), makes clear that an interconnected world economy existed long before the advent of modern communication and technology. The specific focus of The Persian Gulf Region, c. 1900 (Chapter 23), foretells some of today's complexities in this area of the world. A caption accompanying each map highlights the significance of the map and its relevance to a specific text topic. Many of the maps have been revised, updated, and/or increased in size. Most of the maps also include insets that show where their territory fits within a larger hemisphere or the globe.

FOR QUALIFIED COLLEGE ADOPTERS

Supplements for Instructors

MyHistoryLab With the best of Longman's multimedia solutions for history in one easy-to-use place, MyHistoryLab offers students and instructors a state-of-the-art interactive instructional solution for the World History survey course. Delivered in CourseCompass™, Blackboard™, or WebCT™, MyHistoryLab is designed to be used as a supplement to a traditional lecture course, or to administer a completely online course. MyHistoryLab provides helpful tips, review materials, and activities to make the study of history an enjoyable learning experience. Icons in the book lead students to specific assets.

MyHistoryLab includes the following features, all organized according to the text's table of contents:

- **E-Sources:** Each chapter of the book has its own collection of images, individual documents, and case studies.
- **History Bookshelf:** Read, download, or print more than 20 of the most commonly assigned works, like Plato's *The Republic,* Machiavelli's *The Prince,* or Confucius' *The Analects.*
- **History Toolkit:** Guided tutorials help students learn to analyze several types of sources.
- **Map Activities:** Each chapter contains a map activity in which students assess a map from the time period covered and take a brief geography quiz for the chapter.
- **Pre-Test and Post-Test Self-Study Quizzes with Targeted Feedback:** Two quizzes per chapter allow students to review their knowledge of the material and concepts. Chapter feedback provides links that take students directly to the relevant section of the textbook online.
- **Chapter Review Materials:** The Study Guide, PowerPoint™ presentations, flashcards, and other features will help students master the contents of the textbook and prepare for exams.
- **The Textbook Online:** Students can read the book online, or print out sections of the book to read anywhere.
- **Chapter Exam:** Each chapter has a chapter exam whose results report to the CourseCompass™, Blackboard™, or WebCT™ online gradebook.
- **Test Bank:** Create your own exams using the Test Bank from your text, and place them right in MyHistoryLab for your students to take as practice quizzes or as graded exams.
- **The Tutor Center:** On-call qualified help is available to answer student questions about MyHistoryLab when an instructor may not be available. The Tutor Center is open Sunday through Thursday from 5 PM to midnight, EST.
- **Unlimited use of Pearson's Research Navigator™:** The EBSCO ContentSelect, Academic Journal & Abstract Database, *The New York Times* Search by Subject Archive, "Best of the Web" Link

Library, and *Financial Times* Article Archive and Company Financials offer thousands of credible and reliable articles and websites to get the research process started.

- **A wealth of instructor support material:** Text-specific materials, such as instructor's manuals, test banks, and PowerPoint™ presentations simplify and enrich the teaching experience.

www.LongmanWorldHistory.com This website offers all the best of MyHistoryLab without course management features or the online e-book. As with MyHistoryLab, icons in the book lead students to specific assets on the website.

Instructor's Manual by Rick Whisonant of Winthrop University. This collection of resources includes chapter outlines, definitions, discussion suggestions, critical thinking exercises, term paper and essay topics, and audiovisual suggestions.

Companion Website (www.ablongman.com/brummett). This online course companion provides a wealth of resources for both students and instructors using *Civilization Past & Present,* Eleventh Edition. Students will find chapter summaries, test questions, and links for further research.

Test Bank and Test Generator by Susan Hellert of the University of Wisconsin at Platteville. This easy-to-customize test bank presents a wealth of multiple-choice, true-false, short-answer, and essay questions. Free to qualified college adopters.

Civilization Past & Present PowerPoint™ Presentations. Updated by Pamela Marquez of Metropolitan State College of Denver, these easy-to-customize PowerPoint™ slides outline key points of each chapter of the text and are available for download from the Companion Website (www.ablongman.com/brummett). Free to qualified college adopters.

The History Digital Media Archive CD-ROM. This CD-ROM contains hundreds of images, maps, interactive maps, and audio/video clips ready for classroom presentation, or downloading into PowerPoint™ or any other presentation software. Free to qualified college adopters.

Overhead Transparency Acetates to Accompany Civilization Past & Present. These text-specific acetates are available to all adopters. Every map is represented. Free to qualified college adopters.

Guide to Teaching World History by Palmira Brummett of the University of Tennessee at Knoxville. This guide offers explanations of major issues and themes in world history, sample syllabi and instructions on how to create a manageable syllabus, ideas for cross-cultural and cross-temporal connections, a pronunciation guide, and tips on getting through all the material. Free to qualified college adopters.

Discovering World History Through Maps and Views Overhead Transparency Acetates by Gerald Danzer of the University of Illinois at Chicago. This unique resource contains more than 100 full-color acetates of beautiful reference maps, source maps, urban plans, views, photos, art, and building diagrams. Free to qualified college adopters.

Longman World History Atlas Overhead Transparency Acetates. These acetates are available to instructors who select the *Longman World History Atlas* for their students. Free to qualified college adopters.

Historical Newsreel Video. This 90-minute video contains newsreel excerpts examining U.S. involvement in world affairs over the past 60 years. Free to qualified college adopters.

Longman-Penguin Putnam Inc. Value Bundles. Students and professors alike will love the value and quality of the Penguin books offered at a deep discount when bundled with *Civilization Past & Present,* Eleventh Edition, for qualified college adopters.

Supplements for Students

Companion Website (www.ablongman.com/brummett). This online course companion provides a wealth of resources for both students and instructors using *Civilization Past & Present,* Eleventh Edition. Students will find chapter summaries, test questions, and links for further research.

Student Study Guide in two volumes: Volume 1 (Chapters 1–17) and Volume 2 (Chapters 13–35) revised by Norman Love of El Paso Community College. Each chapter includes chapter overviews, lists of themes and concepts, map exercises, multiple-choice practice tests, and critical thinking and essay questions.

Study Card for World History. Colorful, affordable, and packed with useful information, the *Study Card for World History* makes studying easier, more efficient, and more enjoyable. Course information is distilled down to the basics, helping students quickly master the fundamentals, review a subject for understanding, or prepare for an exam. Because they are laminated for durability, Study Cards can be kept for years to come and be pulled out whenever they are needed for a quick review.

Mapping World History. This workbook was created for use in conjunction with *Discovering World History Through Maps and Views.* Designed to teach students to interpret and analyze cartographic materials as historical documents.

World History Map Workbooks, Second Edition, Volumes I and II. These workbooks, created by Glee Wilson, Kent State University, are designed to explain the correlations between historical events and geography through assignments that involve reading and interpreting maps.

Longman World History Atlas. A comprehensive collection of historical maps that reflects truly global coverage of world history. Each of the atlas's 56 maps are designed to be readable, informative, and accurate as well as beautiful.

Longman Library of World Biography Series. Each interpretive biography in the new Library of World Biography series focuses on a figure whose actions and ideas significantly influenced the course of world history. Pocket-sized and brief, each book relates the life of its subject to the broader themes and developments of the times. Series titles include:

- *Alexander the Great: Legacy of a Conqueror* by Winthrop Lindsay Adams, University of Utah
- *Benito Mussolini: The First Fascist* by Anthony L. Cardoza, Loyola University of Chicago
- *Fukuzawa Yukichi: From Samurai to Capitalist* by Helen M. Hopper, University of Pittsburg
- *Ignatius of Loyola: Founder of the Jesuits* by John Patrick Donnelly, Marquette University
- *Jacques Coeur: Entrepreneur and King's Bursar* by Kathryn L. Reyerson, University of Minnesota
- *Kato Shidzue: A Japanese Feminist* by Helen M. Hopper, University of Pittsburg
- *Simón Bolívar: Liberation and Disappointment* by David Bushnell, University of Florida
- *Vasco da Gama: Renaissance Crusader* by Glenn J. Ames, University of Toledo

Longman World History Series. These books focus on the historical significance of a particular movement, experience, or interaction. Concise and inexpensive, they bring the global connections and consequences of these events to the fore, showing students how events that happened long ago or far away can still affect them. Titles include:

- *Colonial Encounters in the Age of High Imperialism* by Scott B. Cook, Rhode Island School of Design
- *Environmentalism: A Global History* by Ramachandra Guha
- *Expansion and Global Interaction: 1200–1700* by David Ringrose, University of California at San Diego

ACKNOWLEDGMENTS

A special note of appreciation goes to the following reviewers for providing thorough and expert advice for the *Global Issues* essays. Their suggestions have been of tremendous help in the writing of this new feature:

Milan Andrejevich
Indiana University Northwest

Charles E. Bashaw
College of Charleston

Kevin W. Caldwell
Blue Ridge Community College

Peter Fraunholtz
Northeastern University

James C. Godwin II
University of Delaware

Elizabeth P. Hancock
Gainesville College

Frank Karpiel
College of Charleston

Thomas O. Kay
Wheaton College

Laurence W. Marvin
Berry College

Donald T. McGuire
SUNY Buffalo

Fannie T. Rushing
Benedictine University

Mark B. Tauger
West Virginia University

Rick Whisonant
Winthrop University

We are most grateful to the following reviewers who gave generously of their time and knowledge to provide thoughtful evaluations and many helpful suggestions for the revision of this edition.

Henry Abramson
Florida Atlantic University

Lee Annis
Montgomery College—Rockville

Daniel Ayana
Youngstown State University

James W. Brodman
University of Central Arkansas

Thomas Cary
City University

Edward R. Crowther
Adams State College

Cole P. Dawson
Warner Pacific College

Dr. Michael de Nie
State University of West Georgia

Shannon L. Duffy
Loyola University New Orleans

Charles T. Evans
Northern Virginia Community College

Ronald Fritze
University of Central Arkansas

Richard M. Golden
University of North Texas

Elizabeth P. Hancock
Gainesville College

Eric J. Hanne
Florida Atlantic University

Caroline Hoefferle
Wingate University

Roger L. Jungmeyer
Lincoln University of Missouri

Jeffrrey W. Myers
Avila University

William R. Rogers
Isothermal Community College

Daniel E. Schafer
Belmont University

Roger Schlesinger
Washington State University

William Seavey
East Carolina University

Deborah A. Symonds
Drake University

Mark B. Tauger
West Virginia University

Ted Weeks
Southern Illinois University

Rick Whisonant
Winthrop University

We also thank the many conscientious reviewers who reviewed previous editions of this book.

Henry Abramson
Florida Atlantic University

Wayne Ackerson
Salisbury State University

Jay Pascal Anglin
University of Southern Mississippi

Lee Annis
Montgomery County Community College—Maryland

Joseph Appiah
J. Sargeant Reynolds Community College

Michael Auslin
Yale University

Mark C. Bartusis
Northern State University

Charlotte Beahan
Murray State University

Martin Berger
Youngstown State University

Joel Berlatsky
Wilkes College

Jackie R. Booker
Kent State University

Mauricio Borrero
St. John's University

Darwin F. Bostwick
Old Dominion University

Robert F. Brinson Jr.
Santa Fe Community College

Robert H. Buchanan
Adams State College

Nancy Cade
Pikeville College

Michael L. Carrafiello
East Carolina University

James O. Catron Jr.
North Florida Junior College

Mark Chavalas
University of Wisconsin

William H. Cobb
East Carolina University

To the Student

We set two goals for ourselves when we wrote *Civilization Past & Present.* The first is to provide you with an understanding of the contributions of past eras in all parts of the globe to the shaping of world history. The second is to illuminate the way in which the study of world history gives us insights into the genesis, nature, and direction of our own civilization.

These are challenging tasks. However, given the globalization of all aspects of our lives, they are essential. When economies in East Asia or Latin America are in a state of crisis, the impact is felt on Wall Street. The culture of the New World—especially music and movies—has spread around the globe. When tragedies occur in the Middle East, we are all affected. Long gone are the days when an occurrence that took place far away could be isolated.

Now you are taking a course in world history to understand the development of the cultures of the world—cultures that are coming together to form a multifaceted world civilization. By understanding how and why other civilizations have chosen differing routes to their future, you can gain an understanding of why your part of civilization has succeeded or failed in attaining its potential. With an understanding of world history, you will be able to respond more knowledgeably to the changes through which you will live and to make informed choices as a world citizen.

History is the study of change over time. A historian is a person who focuses on one aspect of changes in the past, poses questions about why a particular event has taken place, proposes answers—hypotheses—and tests those hypotheses against the evidence—all of the evidence. We do not expect you to be historians at this point in your careers—to form your own hypotheses and write monographs. We have written this book, however, to enable you to study change over the entire course of human history.

We have included a number of tools to help you on your voyage through this text. The new **Global Issues essays** explore seven topics of unique transcultural and trans-historical significance: Migration, Religion and Government, Location and Identity, Technological Exchange, Slavery, Gender, and War and International Law. The essays carefully examine these topics using a global framework, employing examples that span both history and the world's many civilizations. The essays are intended to do more than just inform you about global topics; however; they also reveal challenges that have and still confront civilizations the world over.

As you begin each chapter, take five or ten minutes to look at the **chapter opening pages.** These two pages at the beginning of each chapter reveal what is to come: A photo conceptualizes a main theme of the chapter, and a chapter outline and a timeline allow you to fix beginning and end points in this part of your trip. The chapter introduction sets the stage for the content that follows and indicates the chapter's overall themes—sometimes political or economic, sometimes religious, social, or artistic. Take time to read the introduction and then thumb to the end of the chapter to read the conclusion. Next, go through the chapter reading only the main and secondary headlines. Finally, return to the beginning of the chapter and start to read—knowing in advance where you have come from and which way you are going.

Within each chapter we offer you other tools to gain an understanding of the past. Events take place in a location, and each location has particular features that affect what will happen. Thus the text includes more than 100 full-color **maps,** each with its own explanatory caption. Shaded **insets** on most of the maps help you to locate its territory on its larger hemisphere or the globe. Some maps are designed to make clear the nature of a single distinctive event; others illustrate larger trends.

Each chapter also offers new features to help you better engage with the content. The new **pronunciation guide** will help you correctly pronounce key foreign terms—after each such word within the text a pronunciation appears in parentheses. The new on-page **glossary** provides concise definitions of key historical terms and appears in the footer of the pages in which terms are discussed.

Different civilizations have different visions of themselves and their place in the world. The **Discovery Through Maps** boxes in many of the chapters will give you a notion of the way that various cultures in the world have seen themselves and their relation to the rest of the globe. For example, al-Idrisi's "An Islamic Map of the World" is oriented, as was common in Arab maps of his time, with south at the top; it is centered on the world of his own experience, the sacred city of Mecca in Arabia and the civilized realm of the Mediterranean. A late-nineteenth-century map of southern Africa perpetuated

"The Myth of the Empty Land," by which white settlers would claim that they were moving into an unpopulated land and that they had just as much right to it as Africans did.

We also include one or more excerpts from **primary source documents** in each chapter. These excerpts from original sources offer you a window into the way that the people of the time expressed themselves. The documents cover a variety of viewpoints: political, economic, legal, religious, social, artistic, and popular. For example, in "That Was No Brother," two documents—one by an African chief and the other by the English explorer Henry Morton Stanley—give two very different perceptions of the same battle.

The text's 500 **photos,** most in full color, give balanced pictorial coverage of all parts of the world and enhance the reading of each chapter by giving additional context and bringing to life the matters under discussion. For this edition, we have paid special attention in these photos to the lifestyles and contributions of women.

After you have finished each chapter you will find three features to help you prepare a paper or project or simply to learn more. The **Literature and Film** listings offer a listing of novels, poetry, films, and videos. The annotated bibliographies of **Suggestions for Reading** indicate useful general studies, monographs, and source materials. Also included is a list of **Suggestions for Web Browsing** to allow you to hook up to databases, sounds, images, or discussion groups dealing with the topics under consideration.

Robert R. Edgar
Neil J. Hackett
George F. Jewsbury
Barbara Molony

Civilization

Past & Present

CHAPTER

1

Stone Age Societies and the Earliest Civilizations of the Near East

CHAPTER CONTENTS

50,000

c. 50,000 B.C.E. *Homo sapiens*

10,000

c. 10,000 End of last ice age

c. 10,000–6000 The Aquatic Age in the Sahara

8000

c. 8000 Neolithic Revolution

6000

c. 6000 Agricultural Revolution: Occupation of Çatul Hüyük

4000

c. 3200 Emergence of civilization in Mesopotamia and Egypt

c. 2800–2300 Old Sumerian Period

c. 2700–2200 Old Kingdom of Egypt (Pyramid Age)

c. 2300–2150 Akkadian Empire

c. 2050–1800 Middle Kingdom of Egypt

2000

c. 2000–1600 Old Babylonian Empire

c. 1570–1090 New Kingdom of Egypt

c. 1450–1200 Hittite Empire

c. 745–612 Assyrian Empire

c. 586–538 Babylonian Captivity of the Jews

c. 550–332 Persian Empire

This chapter begins with an overview of the evolution of humankind on the African continent and examines the longest period of human life on the planet when our earliest ancestors invented basic tools and social structures on which all succeeding cultures would build. The skills necessary for survival were mastered over many hundred millennia as humans spread around the world, culminating in the breakthrough to farming with the domestication of plants and animals, and a settled life in villages.

Over the passage of many thousands of years, human societies located throughout Africa, Asia, and Europe continued to develop distinct cultural and technological patterns of life, but change in the patterns of everyday life was something most of the earth's early cultures avoided as frightening and disruptive. Profound change, even if extremely slow in comparison to social change in our modern world, seems to have taken place first in southwestern Asia and northeastern Africa (the Near East), where social developments were accelerated especially by the development of farming and the domestication of animals. There, along the banks of great rivers, villages evolved into towns and cities, and after the fourth millennium B.C.E. the complexity and sophistication of those cultures has led experts to label them as the world's earliest civilizations. The study of these earliest civilizations should furnish us with insights into the nature of some of humankind's most ancient institutions and oldest cultural legacies.

THE ORIGINS OF HUMANKIND

■ *What role did the African environment play in the evolution of* Homo sapiens?

Who are we? Where do we come from? Human beings have probably asked these questions ever since they have had the ability to communicate through language. For thousands of years, humans turned to religion to answer such questions. Indeed, it has only been within the last 150 years that science has put forth the theory that the human species evolved out of lower life forms. The controversy surrounding the theory of evolution continues up to today, although with decreasing intensity as more and more fossil evidence comes to light supporting the theory. Of course, the fossil record will never be complete, and paleontologists (scientists who study fossil remains in order to understand the life of past geological periods) have only skeletal remains to analyze. Nevertheless, the case for evolution appears overwhelming.

According to the theory of evolution, humans belong to the Primate order, which also includes lemurs, tarsiers, monkeys, and apes. A crucial development occurred when the ape family split into branches: tree-dwelling apes and ground-dwelling apes known as *hominids* ("prehumans" or "protohumans"). Over time and in response to environmental pressures, the hominids learned to walk upright, their legs grew longer than their arms, and their hands—no longer required for locomotion—became more dexterous. Most important, the prehuman head gradually shifted toward a more upright position, rendering superfluous much of the muscle at the back of the neck. This favored expansion of the brain, which ultimately led to modern *Homo sapiens* ("thinking man"), the only survivor of the many-branched hominid tree.

Paleontologists have discovered all of the fossil remains of the earliest ancestors of *Homo sapiens* in Africa. These include *Australopithecus africanus* (ah-STRAH-loh-pi-THEE-kuhs ah-fri-KAH-nus; "southern African ape"). First discovered in South Africa in 1924, it had an erect posture but apelike brain. In 1964 the first representative of the genus *Homo* was found at Olduvai Gorge in Tanzania at a site some 1.75 million years old. In 1973 the partial skeleton of a female named "Lucy" (for the Beatles' hit song "Lucy in the Sky with Diamonds") was found in Ethiopia and dated to about 3.8 to 3 million years ago. One of the most recent discoveries came in 1998, when South African paleontologists discovered a hominid 4 feet tall and some 3.5 million years old, whose virtually complete remains provide uniquely detailed information on the transition from ape to human.

MAP
An Introduction to the Elements of the Earth

Homo habilis ("skillful man") was the first toolmaker. Dating from about two and a half to two million years ago, *H. habilis* was less than 5 feet tall, walked

Aerial view of Olduvai Gorge in Tanzania, the site of findings by Mary Leakey and Louis S. B. Leakey, including the first representative fossils of the genus Homo.

erect, and had a well-developed opposable thumb that allowed the species to fashion tools. These fossil remains were found in association with crude tools—rocks cracked and flaked into specialized tools to cut meat and softer plants and to ward off predators. These tools expanded the nutritional options of *H. habilis*.

Later and more advanced species included *Homo ergaster,* which emerged perhaps as long as 2.3 million years ago in Africa. This species was labeled *Homo erectus* in Asia and is more widely known by that name. *H. erectus* had an upright posture, a physique very similar to modern humans, and a brain size of about 1000 cubic centimeters. *Erectus* learned to control and use fire—a major step in extending human habitation into colder latitudes—and perfected the first major standardized all-purpose tool, the Acheulean hand ax. Dubbed the Paleolithic "Swiss army knife" because it could be used for cutting, scraping, chopping, and digging, this ax remained a favorite tool long after the extinction of the species. *Erectus* was the first species to live its life primarily on the ground rather than in the trees and to demonstrate the ability to adapt to varied environments.

Around 1.6 million B.C.E. this species took the bold step of migrating out of Africa, into the Near East and Asia and eventually to the colder climate of Europe. Several theories have been advanced to explain why this movement took place out of Africa. One is that an extended dry period in the region of the present-day Sahara desert may have forced *H. erectus* to move over a wider area to collect foodstuffs. Another argument is that *H. erectus* could have moved into other regions as the species developed an ability to adapt to different environments.

From about 200,000 to 40,000 years ago, during the last ice age, a subspecies of *H. erectus*, the Neanderthals, were the principal inhabitants of Europe and spread to adjacent parts of Asia and Africa. Named for the Neander valley in western Germany where their remains were unearthed in 1856 (*thal* is the German word for "valley"), Neanderthals were slightly taller than 5 feet and had sloping foreheads, with prominent brow ridges, and thickset bodies. They were especially suited to coping with the colder climes of Europe. The inventors of many specialized tools, they were able hunters and adapted to extreme cold by using fire, wearing clothes, and living in caves. One school of thought contended that Neanderthals were the ancestors of modern Europeans until recent DNA testing of a Neanderthal skeleton showed very little overlap with the DNA of *H. sapiens*. Consequently, though sharing a common ancestor, the Neanderthals were probably not a subspecies of *sapiens.*

The culminating phase of the development of the genus *Homo* occurred around 150,000 to 100,000 years ago with the gradual emergence of *H. sapiens.* Up until a few years ago, scientists were engaged in a vigorous debate between the proponents of the "Out of Africa" school—who contend that *H. sapiens* originated exclusively in Africa and spread from there to other continents—and the multiregionalists—who argue that *H. sapiens* evolved independently in Africa, Asia, and Europe. Recent testing of mitochondrial DNA, however, strongly supports the argument for an African origin for *H. sapiens*. Mitochondrial DNA is passed on only through a mother to her offspring. By comparing DNA samples from individuals around the world and calculating the rate of mutations, geneticists have traced our human ancestors back to a hypothetical "Eve" whom they believe lived in eastern Africa some 200,000 years ago.

There is also a lively debate about the interaction between *H. sapiens* and the species of *H. erectus*. In Europe, the Cro-Magnons—*H. sapiens* named after a locality in southern France where their bones were unearthed in 1868—and Neanderthals coexisted for 50,000 years. Around 40,000 years ago, however, the Neanderthals died out, leaving the Cro-Magnons as the only hominids in Europe. Perhaps Cro-Magnons' superior brainpower and communications skills ultimately gave them a decisive advantage over Neanderthals in controlling and using food resources. We don't know for certain, but paleontologists have established that Cro-Magnon skeletons are virtually indistinguishable from those of humans today. Skillfully made flint and bone tools and polychrome paintings found on cave walls indicate that the Cro-Magnon possessed an advanced culture. By 20,000 B.C.E. Cro-Magnon and other representatives of *H. sapiens* inhabited Europe, Asia, Africa, and Australia and had moved into Americas by migrating across the Bering Strait on foot or by traveling in small boats along the coast. Today there is but one existing species of the genus *Homo.*

The Long Journey

PRELITERATE CULTURES

- *What distinguishes Paleolithic from Neolithic culture?*

In many respects we humans are eclipsed in physical endowments by numerous other creatures—in an all-species Olympic Games, we might not qualify for a medal. We cannot compete with the strength of the elephant or the speed of the antelope on land or any number of marine creatures. Our ability to defy gravity is dwarfed by insects that can jump higher and farther in terms of their size, to say nothing of birds, whose specialized structures enable them to fly and soar. Yet, a number of attributes functioning in concert allowed our species to forge ahead of all others.

They include erect posture, an opposable thumb ideal for fashioning tools, stereoscopic and color vision capable of close visual attention, and a brain whose size and multiple capabilities have enabled it to be termed the "organ of civilization."

Like other creatures, humans possess a practical intelligence for making meaningful responses to the environment. In addition, we are capable of thinking and communicating symbolically through language. The principle of symbolism gives everything a name and makes its functioning universally applicable, rather than restricting it to particular cases. By means of this capability to engage in symbolic thought and communication, humankind has created patterns of behavior and learning that can be termed *culture.* Unlike other creatures, we live also in a symbolic universe that draws on language, myth, art and religion to express aspects of human experience.

Paleolithic Culture

Making and using tools provide the first evidence of humankind's ability to employ reason to solve problems. Stone implements were the most distinctive feature of early human culture; thus, this stage is known as the **Paleolithic** or Old Stone Age. Our earliest ancestors made use of *eoliths* ("dawn stones"), bits of stone picked up to perform an immediate job. This simple utilization of what lay at hand was the first major step in toolmaking. The second consisted of *fashioning,* the haphazard preparation of a tool as need arose. The third step was *standardization,* making implements according to certain set traditions. It is with this third stage that we see the importance of symbolic thought in creating patterns of learning and behavior, transmitted in turn from one generation to the next.

In later Paleolithic cultures, toolmaking became progressively sophisticated and efficient. It was marked by a wide range of specialized tools and weapons, including implements whose primary purpose was to make other tools. The fashioning of small, specialized flints, known as *microliths,* represents a compact use of materials—indeed, the ancestor of present-day technological miniaturization. In late Paleolithic cultures, too, our ancestors applied mechanical principles to the movement of weapons. Throwers to launch spears worked on the lever principle to increase the propelling power of a hunter's arm. The bow was also invented to concentrate muscular energy to propel an arrow; it was soon also used to provide a means of twirling a stick, and this led to the invention of the rotary drill. Strictly speaking, *Paleolithic* is a cultural and not a chronological term. In fact, much of our knowledge of Paleolithic culture comes from groups surviving into modern times—for example, indigenous peoples in the rain forests

The Tool Maker

Paleolithic—An era associated with the early Stone Age and the use of simple stone implements and weapons.

As human beings faced an ever-expanding set of challenges to their existence, they invented even more sophisticated tools, as evidenced by these examples of Paleolithic toolmaking.

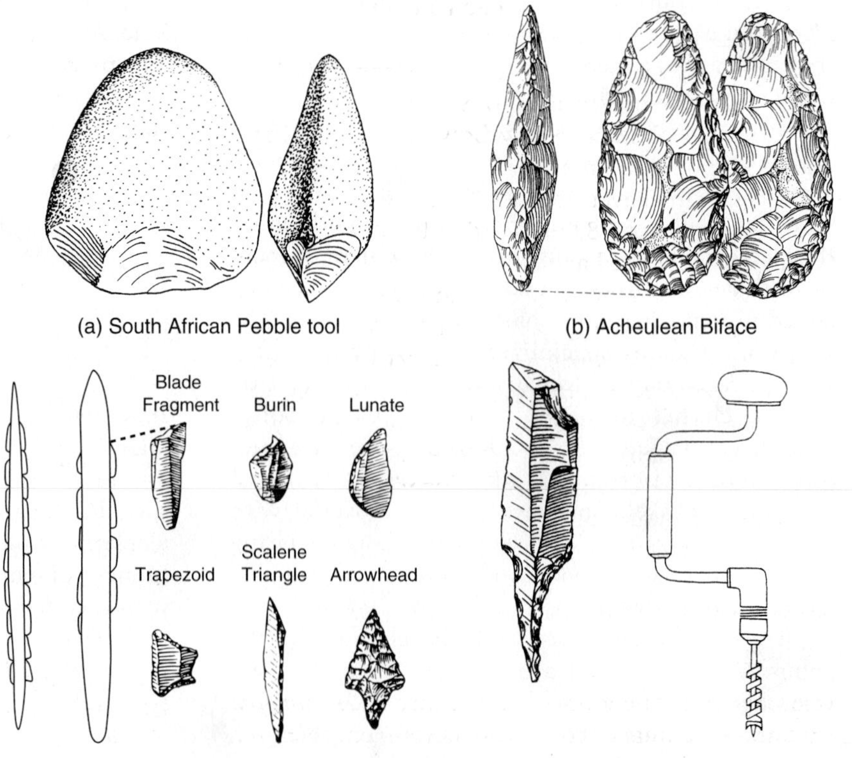

Prehistoric art in Los Toldos, Argentina, includes representations of deer and hands. Archaeologists have dated the art to around 15,000 B.C.E.

of Brazil. From an economic standpoint, the Paleolithic is also a food-gathering stage, when humans hunted, fished, and collected wild foodstuffs. Labor was divided according to sex. Men hunted, fished, and protected the group. Women picked wild plants, fruits, and nuts and prepared the food for eating; they also processed animal hides and wood into household objects and cared for the children. Men and women shared such tasks as building dwellings, making ornaments and tools, and training children for adult life.

DOCUMENT
A Need to Remember

A special achievement of late Paleolithic cultures around the world was their art. For instance, animated, realistic paintings of bison, reindeer, primitive horses, and other animals, colored in shades of black, red, yellow, and brown, have been found in more than a hundred Cro-Magnon caves in Spain and France dating from about 28,000 to 10,000 B.C.E. Cave art rivals that of civilized artists not only stylistically but also as an expression of significant human experiences. Universal in appeal, the pictures reflect the Paleolithic dependence on an abundance of game animals and success in hunting them. In addition, the artists may have believed they could wield a magical power over the spirits of animals to ensure their availability. Paleolithic artists also chiseled pictures on rock and bone and modeled figures out of clay.

The Neolithic Revolution and Advent of Agriculture

A development of enormous consequence for human societies—the shift to food-producing—took place in the ancient Near East. There, on the flanks of the mountains bordering the **Fertile Crescent,** an area of rich soil stretching northeast from the Nile River to the Tigris in what is now northern Iraq and then southeast to the Persian Gulf, was adequate rainfall to nourish wild forms of wheat and barley and provide grass for wild sheep, goats, and pigs. By 7000 B.C.E., people in that region had domesticated these grains and animals and lived in villages near their fields and herds. This momentous change ushered in the **Neolithic** or New Stone Age. The best-preserved village so far uncovered is Çatal Hüyük (chah-tahl HOO-yook; "forked mound") in southern Turkey. This 32-acre site, occupied from around 6500 to 5400 B.C.E., contains some of the most advanced features of Neolithic culture: pottery, woven textiles, mud-brick houses, shrines honoring a mother goddess, and plastered walls decorated with murals and carved reliefs. The most recent archaeological excavations at the site have raised questions about whether settled village life happened at the same time as the domestication of agriculture and whether the community had a political and religious elite.

CASE STUDY
The Neolithic Village

Neolithic artisans ground and polished stones to produce axes, adzes, and chisels with sharp cutting edges. They devised methods for drilling holes in stone, used boulders for grinding grain, and made stone bowls for storage. Skilled in their earlier role as wild food gatherers, women were responsible now for cultivating the prepared fields. They also made clay pots—decorated with geometric designs—and spun and wove textiles from cultivated flax and animal wool. The Neolithic revolution, with its "migration of skills," spread to the Balkan Peninsula by 5000 B.C.E., Egypt and Central Europe by 4000 B.C.E., and Britain and northwest India by 3000 B.C.E. The Neolithic cultures of sub-Saharan Africa, East Asia, Mesoamerica, and the Andes all developed independently from the Neolithic culture of the Fertile Crescent.

DOCUMENT
The Iceman

PRELITERATE SOCIETY AND RELIGION

- *What were the characteristics of religious beliefs among the earliest human societies?*

How can we know about those features of early cultures that are not apparent from the remains of tools and other objects? In addition to our being able to observe cultures similar to Paleolithic and Neolithic

---

Fertile Crescent—A geographic region that stretches in a semicircular arc from the eastern Mediterranean to the Persian Gulf.

Neolithic—A time period associated with the later Stone Age and the use of polished stone implements and weapons.

Discovery Through Maps

The Oldest Known Map: Çatal Hüyük

This wall painting is perhaps the oldest known map. It is also, for modern viewers, one of the most easily understood ancient maps. It is a city plan painted on two walls of a room in a Neolithic community in south-central Anatolia, near what is still the major land route in Turkey between Europe and the Near East. Radiocarbon dating has placed the image around 6200 B.C.E. It is a very large figure, nearly 9 feet wide.

By the 1960s archaeologists had uncovered 139 rooms in the complex and decided that at least 40 were used for special rites, probably of a religious nature. One of these special rooms, whose walls had often been replastered, contained this large image featuring rows of boxlike shapes. Archaeologists were amazed at the similarity between their own carefully drawn site maps and the painting on the wall. It soon became apparent that the Neolithic image was a map of the community or perhaps of the town that immediately preceded the one the dig was uncovering.

A great deal of information can be gleaned from this map:

- The town site was on a slope, with rows of houses or buildings set on graded terraces.
- The rectangular buildings and the streets set at right angles provide a gridiron look that has characterized much town planning throughout history.
- The elongated, or linear, pattern of the settlement may reflect an orientation to a major road.
- The large figure that looks like a mountain with two peaks beyond the town is, no doubt, Hasan Da-g, a volcano that was active until about 2000 B.C.E. The volcano was the source of the obsidian that was the basis of the settlement's wealth. The glassy, volcanic rock was used for making cutting tools, knives, scrapers, weapons, jewelry, ornaments, and a variety of other artifacts.

The complete map contains about 80 rooms or buildings, somewhat fewer structures than were found in the actual town that was excavated. Since the wall was replastered several times, perhaps the map was "updated." Or it may have served a ceremonial purpose for which the absolute accuracy of a civic map was unnecessary.

This map, certainly the oldest example of landscape art in addition to its function as a map, has perplexed the experts since its excavation in the 1960s. The painting certainly depicts an urban landscape, 2000 years earlier than archaeologists expected such a settlement in the area. Further excavation revealed that the town was very large by contemporary standards—perhaps home to a population exceeding 6000. A settlement of that size could not have grown enough food to support itself while accomplishing all the other tasks that Çatal Hüyük's residents did. Trade and an extensive commercial network had to be present, but there is no archaeological evidence from the site of specialized tools. Yet there is very clear proof that Çatal Hüyük possessed good pottery, well-fashioned textiles, and outstanding artwork. Some experts have speculated that the city may have served primarily as a religious center for an extensive area. In one section of the excavated town, an area of about one acre, archaeologists believe that as many as one of every three buildings may have served as a religious shrine or cult center of some sort.

Questions to Consider

1. What do you think may have been the purpose of the artist or artists who painted this map? Do you think it was intended to impart information?
2. Could the map have been constructed for a religious or ceremonial reason?
3. Why do you think that the volcano plays such a dominant part of this landscape? Could its depiction have a ceremonial or religious significance?

that still exist, the myths of Stone Age peoples throw light on their beliefs and customs. Like ourselves, our Stone Age ancestors sought to account for the origin of the universe and the meaning of existence. In often ascribing the behavior of natural phenomena to supernatural causes, Stone Age mythmakers were nonetheless seeking to make sense of what was familiar in their own lives—such as thunder and lightning and the cycle of the seasons.

Social Organization

Among all peoples, the basic social unit appeared to be the *elementary family*—parents and their offspring. In early human societies, the *extended family* was an individual family, together with a circle of related persons who usually traced their descent through their mothers and were bound together by mutual loyalty. The extended family strengthened the elementary unit in obtaining food and protecting its members against other groups. Land was communally owned but allocated to separate families. A *clan* was a group of extended families that believed that they had a common ancestor. Many peoples identified their clans by a **totem**—an animal or other natural object that was revered. Examples of totemism exist today in military insignia and the emblems of fraternal and sports organizations.

A fourth grouping, the *tribe*, comprised a number of clans. Such a community was characterized by a common speech or distinctive dialect, common cultural heritage, specific inhabited territory, and tribal chief. No community could exist or hold together unless rules governing relations among its members were recognized as binding upon all. Such rules crystallized into precedent or customary law, often attributed to a divine origin.

Correct behavior in preliterate societies consisted of not violating custom. Justice in a group acted to maintain equilibrium. Because theft disturbed economic equilibrium, justice was achieved by a settlement between the injured person and the thief. If the latter restored what had been stolen or its equivalent, the victim was satisfied, and the thief was not punished. Murder and wounding were also private matters, to be avenged by the next of kin on the principle of "an eye for an eye." Certain acts, however, such as treason, witchcraft, and incest were considered dangerous to the whole group and required punishment by the entire community—if need be, by death.

As a general rule, government in these early societies was of a democratic character. Older males—the council of elders—played a dominant role in decision-making because of their greater experience and knowledge of the group's customs and folklore. Serious decisions, such as going to war or electing a chief, required the consent of a general assembly of all adult males. The elected chief was pledged to rule in accordance with custom and in consultation with the council of elders.

Undoubtedly, the strongest single force in the life of preliterate peoples, past and present, has been religion. Religious sensibilities apparently originated in feelings of awe, as our ancestors became conscious of the universe about them. Awe and wonder led to the belief, usually called **animism**, that life exists in everything in nature—winds, stones, animals, and humans. A natural extension was belief in the existence of spirits separable from material bodies. Neanderthal people placed food and implements alongside their carefully buried dead, indicating that they believed in an afterlife and treated their forebears with affection and respect.

DOCUMENT

Early Art: Religion or Worship?

Late Paleolithic people revered the spirits of the animals they hunted as well as the spirit of fertility upon which human and animal life depended. Associated in particular with Neolithic cultures was the worship of a fertility deity, the Earth Mother (or Mother Goddess), known to us from many carved female figures with exaggerated sexual features. Fertility figurines have been excavated from Neolithic sites all over the world. At Çatal Hüyük, 33 representations of the Mother Goddess have been found, but only eight of a god who was either the goddess's son or consort. The relative scarcity of representations of male gods, together with evidence that the cult of the goddess was administered by priestesses rather than priests, supports the view that women occupied a central position in Neolithic society.

Closely associated with ancient religion was the practice of magic. In addition to revering spirits, people wanted to compel them to provide favors. For this purpose they employed magic and turned to shamans to ward off droughts, famines, floods, and plagues through what they believed to be magic powers of communication with the spirits.

Traditionally, magic has been regarded as diametrically opposed to science. Yet, as scholars are increasingly recognizing, both our ancestors and contemporary scientists believe that nature is orderly and that what is immediately perceived by the senses can be systematically classified—such as by the present-day subsistence-level Hanunóo of the Philippines. They have recorded 461 animal types and classified insect forms into 108 named categories,

totem—A symbol or emblem, usually an animal or natural object, that is associated with a family or clan.

animism—Generally, the belief that everything in the world is endowed with its own spirit.

including 13 for ants and termites.[1] Preliterate peoples must therefore be credited with a desire to acquire knowledge, both for practical purposes and for its own sake.

Further indications of this avid search for knowledge have been provided by studies of large stone monuments constructed by Neolithic peoples in at least two continents. With a computer, one astronomer found an "astonishing" number of correlations at Stonehenge in England between the alignments of stones, stone holes, and mounds and the solar and lunar positions as of 1500 B.C.E. when Stonehenge was built. These made possible a more accurate calendar and the prediction of the rising and setting of the sun and moon. But the construction of Neolithic astronomical structures had occurred long before Stonehenge. Ancient sandstone monuments in the Nile delta of Egypt indicate that their builders possessed a surprisingly complex knowledge of geometry and astronomy. Between 5000 and 7000 years old, this earliest known astronomical complex shows slabs in various configurations, including a circle that allowed the inhabitants to anticipate sunrise during the summer solstice.[2]

Before we conclude our overview of preliterate cultures, a brief summary is in order. During the first period of humankind's cultural evolution, the Paleolithic or Old Stone Age, our ancestor's toolmaking capability advanced from reliance on very simple implements—such as the standardized, all-purpose hand ax—to ever more sophisticated tools and techniques of operation. This technological evolution enabled *Homo sapiens* to move into and adapt to different environments around the world. By the time of the last glacial phase, our forebears had spread over most of the world.

Paleolithic cultures had food-gathering economies. Then, perhaps about 10,000 years ago, the Neolithic, or New Stone Age, emerged with the appearance of food-producing communities first in the Fertile Crescent of southwestern Asia and then elsewhere. Neolithic cultures are characterized by the cultivation of grains, the domestication of animals, pottery making, and the fashioning of polished stone tools. These advances occurred in different places on earth and at different times.

MESOPOTAMIA: THE FIRST CIVILIZATION

- *What factors contributed to the development of civilization in Mesopotamia?*

Historians do not agree on how best to define the term *civilization.* But most would accept the view that a civilization is a culture that has attained a degree of complexity, characterized by urban life and the interdependence of those urban residents. In other words, a civilization is a culture capable of sustaining a great number of specialists to furnish the economic, social, political, and religious needs of a large social unit. Other components of a civilization are a system of writing (originating from the need to keep records); monumental, permanent architecture in place of simple buildings; and art that is not merely decorative, like that on Neolithic pottery, but representative of people and their activities. All these characteristics of civilization first appeared together in the southern part of Mesopotamia, which came to be called Sumer.

MAP The Beginnings of Civilization in the Ancient Near East: City States and International Empires

Around 6000 B.C.E., after the agricultural revolution had begun to spread from its origins on the northern edge of the Fertile Crescent, Neolithic farmers began making their homes in the valleys of the Tigris and Euphrates Rivers themselves. Although the broad plain created by these rivers received insufficient regular rainfall to support agriculture, the eastern section was able to benefit from both rivers as sources of irrigation. Known to the Greeks as Mesopotamia (Greek for "between the rivers"), the lower sections of this plain, beginning near the point where the two rivers nearly converge, was called Babylonia. Babylonia included two geographical areas—Akkad in the north and Sumer, the delta of this river system, in the south.

Sumer had tremendous agricultural potential as long as natural environmental problems could be addressed. The rivers sometimes flooded in uncontrollable torrents. Spring and summer storms were often severe. The valley was virtually exposed on all sides to potential invaders, with no formidable natural boundaries to reduce the possibility of invasion. From the very beginning of habitation, cooperation was necessary for life to succeed. Swamps had to be drained, canals had to be dug to bring water to remote fields, and safeguards had to be constructed against flooding. These and many other related problems were solved by cooperative effort; yet the Mesopotamians continued to live in awe of their gods, whose whims might at any time bring destruction down on them.

In spite of the unpredictable nature of their gods, the Sumerians struggled to bring stability to their society. Sumerian metal workers discovered that copper, when combined with tin, produced an alloy, bronze, which was harder than copper and provided a sharper edge. The beginning of civilization in Sumer is associated with the beginning of this Bronze Age, and the new technology soon spread to Egypt, and later to Europe and Asia. Between 3500 and 3100 B.C.E. the foundations were established for a complex economy and a social order more sophisticated than any previously developed. This far more complex culture, based on large urban centers populated by interdependent and specialized workers, is what experts define as civilization.

Since the Mesopotamian plain had no stone, no metals, and no timber except its soft palm trees, these materials had to be imported, most often from the north. Water transport down the Tigris and Euphrates aided in this process. The oldest sailing boat known is represented by a model found in a Sumerian grave dating to around 3500 B.C.E. Soon after this date, wheeled vehicles appear in the form of war chariots drawn by donkeys. Another important invention was the potter's wheel, first used in Sumer soon after 3500 B.C.E.

The Emergence of Civilization in Sumer, c. 3200–2800 B.C.E.

By 3200 B.C.E. the urban centers in the region known as Sumer had developed the majority of the characteristics required to be called a civilization. Because these included the first evidence of writing, this first phase of Sumerian civilization, to about 2800 B.C.E., is called the **Protoliterate** (meaning "before literate") period.

The Sumerian language is not related to **Semitic** or **Indo-European,** the major language families that appear later in the Near East. The original home of the Semitic-speaking peoples was most likely the Arabian peninsula, and the Indo-Europeans seem to have migrated from regions around the Black and Caspian Seas. A third, much smaller language family, sometimes called Hamitic, included the Egyptians and other peoples of northeastern Africa. But the origin of the Sumerians remains a subject of speculation: Some suggest that migration from the Indus River valley might account for their arrival.

A number of the inventions and innovations of protoliterate Sumer eventually made their way to both the Nile and the Indus valleys, most likely through trade and commercial contacts. Among these inventions were wheeled vehicles and the potter's wheel. The discovery in Egypt of cylinder seals similar in shape to those used in Sumer attests to contact between the two cultures toward the end of the fourth millennium B.C.E. Certain early Egyptian art themes and architectural forms are also thought to be of Sumerian origin. And it is probable that the example of Sumerian writing stimulated the Egyptians to develop a script of their own.

The symbols on the oldest Sumerian clay tablets, the world's first writing, were pictures of concrete things such as a person's face, a sheep, a star, or a measure of grain. Some of these pictographs also represented ideas; for example, the picture of a foot was used to represent the idea of walking, and a picture of a mouth joined to that for water meant "to drink." This early pictographic writing developed into phonetic (or syllabic) writing when the scribes realized that a sign could represent a sound as well as an object or idea. Thus, the personal name Kuraka could be written by combining the pictographs for mountain *(kur),* water *(a),* and mouth *(ka).* By 2800 B.C.E. the use of syllabic writing had reduced the number of Sumerian signs from nearly 2000 to 600.

This small but beautifully crafted black diorite statue represents Gudea, the powerful king of the Sumerian city of Lagash in the late third millenium B.C.E. Contemporary poetry and inscriptions indicate that Gudea possessed great wealth and honored his gods by constructing numerous temples and shrines.

When writing, Mesopotamian scribes used a reed stylus to make wedge-shaped impressions in soft clay tablets. This cuneiform system of writing (from the Latin *cuneus,* "wedge") was adopted by many other peoples of the Near East, including the Babylonians, the Assyrians, the Hittites, and the Persians.

protoliterate—Meaning "before literacy"; the period in a society's development that precedes the development and use of a written language.

Semitic—A group of related languages that include Akkadian, Arabic, Aramaean, Canaanite, and Hebrew. The presumptive source language of these languages is thought to have originated in the Arabian Peninsula, from whence, beginning about 2500 B.C.E., Semitic-speaking tribes migrated to the Mediterranean coast, Mesopotamia, and the Nile delta. The term *Semitic* also refers to the cultures of those who speak Semitic languages.

Indo-European—A family of languages that descended from a single unrecorded language spoken in the Caucasus region more than 5000 years ago. Carried by migrating tribes to Europe and Asia, dialects of the source language eventually evolved into such varied languages as English, German, French, Spanish, Latin, Greek, Persian, and Hindi.

The Old Sumerian Period, c. 2800–2300 B.C.E

By 2800 B.C.E. the Sumerian cities had fully emerged into complex civilizations. This first historical age, called the Old Sumerian period, was characterized by constant warfare as each city attempted to protect or enlarge its land and guarantee its access to water and irrigation. Each city-state was a theocracy, a state in which the chief local god was believed to be the actual ruler. The god's earthly representative was the *ensi,* the high priest and city governor, who acted as the god's caretaker in both religious and civil functions. Though given the power to act for the god by virtue of being the human agent of the divine ruler, the *ensi* was not himself considered a divine being.

The *ensis* were powerful and sometimes autocratic rulers. Most famous is the semilegendary Gilgamesh, ruler of Uruk about 2700 B.C.E., who is known only from several epic tales. Although Gilgamesh is portrayed as an extremely powerful ruler, the epic poem also shows that Sumerian rulers could be questioned, even opposed, by some of the nobles who served as advisers in the city's council.

Early Sumerian society was highly stratified, with priests and officials of the city god and subordinate deities assuming great authority. Each temple administered extensive land holdings; that land served as the god's "estate on earth." In addition to the temple lands, a considerable part of a city's territory originally consisted of land collectively owned by clans, kinship groups comprising a number of extended families. By 2600 B.C.E. these clan lands were becoming the private property of great landowners called *lugals* (literally, "great men"). Deeds of sale record the transfer of clan lands to private owners in return for substantial payments in copper to a few clan leaders and insignificant grants of food to the remaining clan members. These private estates were worked by "clients" whose lives were regulated by the temple authorities.

In time, priests, administrators, and *ensis* began confiscating temple land and other property and asserting their authority over the common people. Their ambitions frequently led to the rise of autocratic leaders who came to power on a wave of popular discontent. Since these despots were usually *lugals,* the term *lugal* became a political title and is now generally translated as "king."

The Sumerians, like their Mesopotamian successors, made extensive use of the institution of slavery, and slaves are recorded to have worked in many capacities—as farm and urban laborers, as servants in homes and temples, and in civic positions, such as in public administration. In some cities, slaves accounted for 40 to 50 percent of the population. Slaves in Mesopotamia were not without rights, and in many cases they were treated with care. Slavery was not based on racial characteristics or cultural differences; people of the same culture became enslaved through conquest or to pay off debt. Perhaps because of the possibility that any city-state might be overtaken and its residents enslaved at the pleasure of the gods, the treatment of slaves in Mesopotamia seems generally to have been more humane than at other times and places in human history.

Sumerian women were able to attain high social prominence, usually depending on the rank of their own or their husbands' families. Men were given the greater authority than their wives in economic and legal matters, and only the husband could initiate divorce proceedings against his wife. Children were under the complete control of their parents until 20 or 21 years of age.

The Akkadian Period, c. 2300–2150 B.C.E.

To the immediate north of Sumer was the region of Akkad, inhabited by Semites who had adopted much of Sumerian culture. Appearing late in the fourth millennium B.C.E, the Akkadians were among the earliest of the Semitic peoples who migrated into Mesopotamia from the Arabian peninsula. Sargon I (2370–2315 B.C.E.), the first Akkadian ruler, conquered Sumer and went on to establish an empire that extended from the Persian Gulf almost to the Mediterranean Sea—the first true empire in history.

Very proud of his lower-class origins, Sargon boasted that his humble, unwed mother had been forced to abandon him, placing him in a reed basket and floating the basket down the river. Rescued and brought up by a gardener, Sargon rose to power through the army. As *lugal,* Sargon claimed to look after the welfare of the lower classes and to aid the rising class of private merchants. At the merchants' request, he once sent his army to far-off Asia Minor to protect a colony of them from interference by a local ruler. Sargon reputedly was a tireless worker on behalf of his people's prosperity and expanded his influence in neighboring lands through almost unending campaigns of conquest.

Early Sumer and Akkad

c. 3200–2800 B.C.E.	Protoliterate period in Sumer
c. 2800–2300 B.C.E.	Old Sumerian period
c. 2370–2315 B.C.E.	Reign of Sargon of Akkad
c. 2300–2150 B.C.E.	Akkadian dominance
c. 2150–2000 B.C.E.	Neo-Sumerian period
c. 2000–1600 B.C.E.	Old Babylonian period
c. 1792–1750 B.C.E.	Reign of Hammurabi
c. 1595 B.C.E.	Sack of Babylon by Hittites

Sargon's successors, however, were unable either to repel the attacks of hostile mountain peoples or to overcome the desire for independence of the priest-dominated Sumerian cities. As a result, the dynasty founded by Sargon collapsed about 2150 B.C.E.

The Neo-Sumerian Period, c. 2150–2000 B.C.E

Order and prosperity were restored by the *lugals* of the powerful Sumerian city of Ur. By creating a highly centralized administration in Sumer and Akkad, these rulers solved the problem of internal rebellion that had been of great concern for Sargon and his successors. The formerly temple-dominated cities became provinces administered by closely regulated governors. Religion became an arm of the state: the high priests were state appointees, and careful oversight and regulation by temple officials gave protection to a newly developing free enterprise economy that Sargon had encouraged. At the head of this bureaucratic state stood the *lugal* of Ur, now considered a living god and celebrated as a heaven-sent authority who brought order and security to the people, who were considered to be his servants.

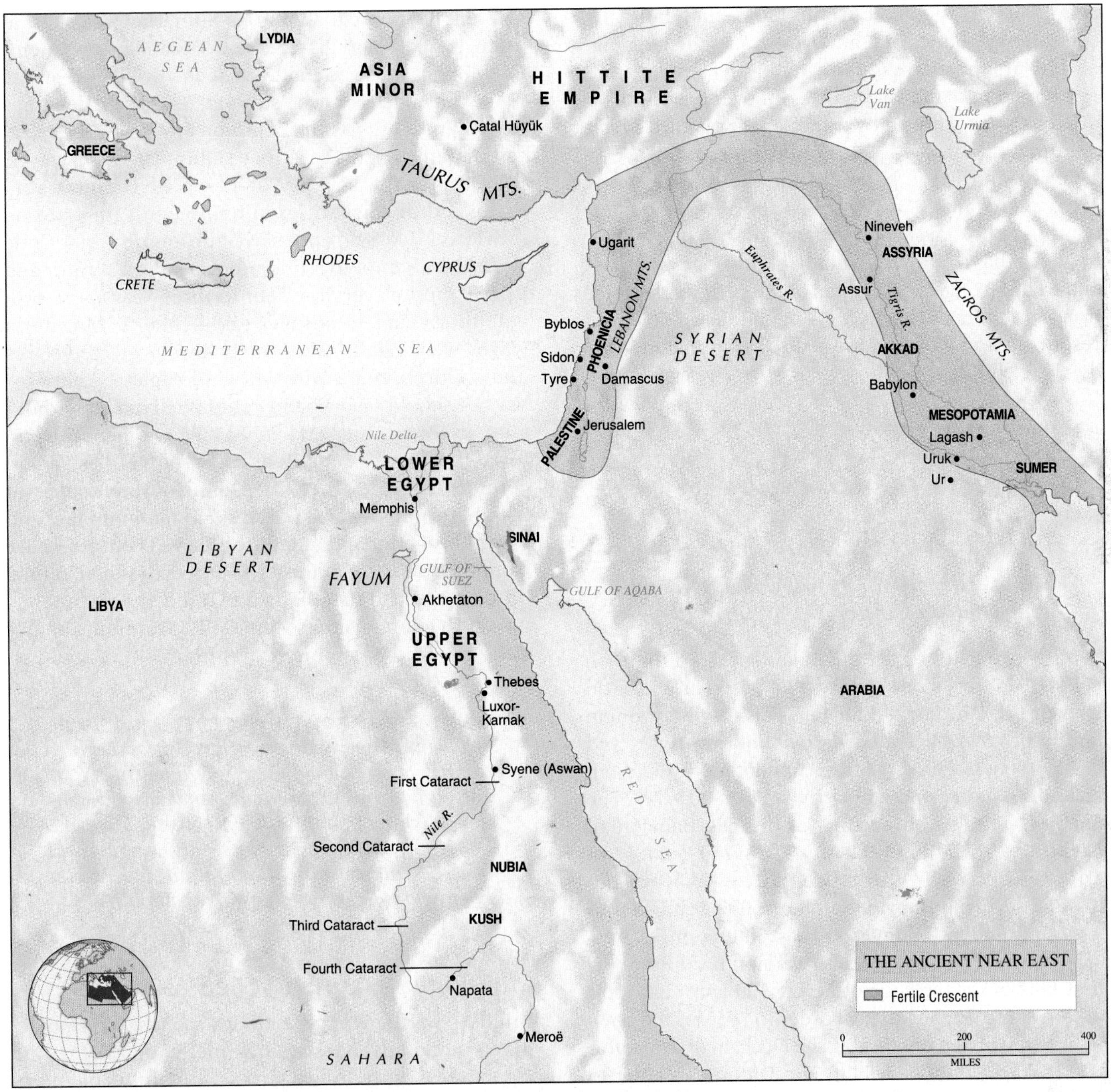

The earliest of humankind's great civilizations developed in the area that came to be called the Fertile Crescent—where rainfall was adequate to nourish wild forms of grain and grazing animals could find sufficient food.

The *lugals* of Ur, who called themselves the "vigilant shepherds" of their people, presided over a highly centralized and efficient administration. Thousands of records have been preserved from this period, detailing the meticulous regulation of commerce, agriculture, and social standards by the powerful overlords of the city. In addition, Sumerian literature and culture flourished under their direction. But the greatness of Ur lasted for little more than one hundred years.

Disaster struck Ur about 2000 B.C.E., when Elamites from what is now Iran destroyed the city. The Sumerians were never again a dominant force politically, but their cultural influence continued to be powerful throughout all subsequent civilizations in the Tigris-Euphrates valley. The Sumerians themselves disappeared as a people, but the Sumerian language continued to be written and to serve as the language of scholarship and religious ritual.

For more than two centuries following the destruction of Ur, disunity and warfare again plagued Mesopotamia, along with economic stress, a lack of security, and acute hardship for the lower classes. Many merchants, however, used the absence of state controls to become aggressive capitalists who amassed fortunes that they invested in banking operations and land. The stronger local rulers of the period attempted to assert their authority by seizing access to water resources and working toward the establishment of dynastic control.

THE BABYLONIAN EMPIRE, c. 2000–1600 B.C.E.

■ *What distinguished the Babylonians from their Sumerian predecessors?*

Semitic Amorites (from the Akkadian word *Amurru*, "West"), produced one dynasty that based its power on its control of the city of Babylon. This new Babylonian family of rulers defeated its neighboring rivals and began to build their city into a capital that would dominate most of Mesopotamia for the next 300 years. The most outstanding of the kings of this Old Babylonian Empire was Hammurabi (c. 1792–1750 B.C.E.), an extremely successful warrior who succeeded in expanding and securing Babylon's military power north into Assyria, south into Sumer, and east into Elam.

Although he was a tireless warrior, Hammurabi is best known for the code of nearly 300 laws that were given by the king "in order to prevent the powerful from oppressing the weak, in order to give justice to the orphans and widows, in order to give my land fair decisions and to give rights to the oppressed. . . ."[3] The Code of Hammurabi is a compilation of laws covering a wide variety of topics, such as property disputes, adultery, slavery, prostitution, inheritance, and public order. The collection was not exhaustive, but most likely served as guideposts for judges, as well as educated subjects, in their attempts to administer or anticipate the law. Such compilations of law date back to Sumerian codes 1400 years before Hammurabi's time, and much of the king's code echoes ancient Sumerian precedent. Hammurabi's Code made wide use of corporal punishment for offenses: based on the "eye for an eye, tooth for a tooth" principle of dispensing justice; in many cases Babylonian law was more harsh in its administration of mutilation or death as fitting punishment for crime than that by Sumerian judges, who often levied fines instead of corporal punishment. Babylonian law also made clear the privileged status of the upper classes, who suffered less severe penalties for their offenses as the common citizen, and far less severe punishments than those administered to slaves.

Hammurabi's Law Code

Hammurabi Receives His Law Code from the Gods

Despite the severity of much of Hammurabi's Code, and the disparities in treatment it imposed on the lower classes and slaves, Hammurabi's Code shows an attempt to reduce abusive interest rates and prices, limit slavery for debt to three years, and provide more care to widows and orphans. Minimum wages were established. Other laws protected wives and children; but a wife who had neglected care for her household or husband could be divorced without alimony, or the husband could take another wife and force the first to remain as a servant. Unless a son committed some grave offense, his father could not disinherit him. If the state failed to maintain law and order, the victim of that failure received compensation from the state: the value of the property stolen, or one mina of silver to the relatives of a murder victim.

In the conclusion to the Code, Hammurabi eloquently summed up his efforts to provide social justice for his people:

> *Let any oppressed man, who has a cause, come before my image as king of righteousness! Let him read the inscription on my monument! Let him give heed to my weighty words! And may my monument enlighten him as to his cause and may he understand his case! May he set his heart at ease! (and he will exclaim): Hammurabi indeed is a ruler who is like a real father to his people. . . .*[4]

Mathematics and Science

Building on the work of the Sumerians, the Babylonians made advances in arithmetic, geometry, and algebra. For ease in working with both whole numbers and fractions, they compiled tables for multiplication and division and for square and cube roots.

They knew how to solve linear and quadratic equations, and their knowledge of geometry included the theorem later formulated by the Greek philosopher Pythagoras: The square of the hypotenuse of a right-angled triangle is equal to the sum of the squares of the other two sides. They used the Sumerian system of counting based on the unit 60 (sexagesimal) rather than that based on the number 10 (decimal). The remnants of this sexagesimal system is found today in computing divisions of time—60-minute hours—and the 360-degree circle. They also adopted the Sumerian principle of place-value notation that gave numbers a value according to their position in a series. To represent zero, they employed the character for "not," which is the same as our "naught," still used colloquially for "nothing."

The Babylonians achieved little that today can be called pure science. They were most concerned with observing the natural world so that the future could be predicted. They did observe nature and collect data, the first requirement of the scientific method; but to explain natural phenomena, they were satisfied with the formulation of myths that defined things in terms of the unpredictable whims of the gods. They thought the sun, moon, and five visible planets to be gods who were able to influence human lives; accordingly, their movements were watched, recorded, and interpreted—more the study of astrology than the science of astronomy. But through their study of the world around them in an effort to predict the future, the Mesopotamians were attempting to impose an order on what they found to be a chaotic universe. Through proper reading of the signs given by the gods, some stability in the world might be achieved.

Literature and Religion

The Babylonians borrowed from the Sumerians a body of literature ranging from heroic epics that compare in scope and themes with the *Iliad* and the *Odyssey* to wisdom writings that have their counterparts in the Hebrew Old Testament. The Sumerian *Epic of Gilgamesh* records the great adventures of the heroic ruler of Uruk who supposedly lived about 2700 B.C.E. The epic poem reflects the values of a heroic age, in which great heroes seek to earn undying fame and glory. The supreme value is the eternal reputation achieved through the performance of heroic deeds. After Gilgamesh slays the fierce Bull of Heaven, he stops to proclaim his victory:

> *What man is most impressive now:*
> *Who is finest, firmest, and most fair?*
> *Isn't Gilgamesh that man above men . . . ?*
> *Who is most glorious among men?*[5]

What Gilgamesh fears most is death, which, in the Mesopotamian viewpoint replaces a glorious life on earth with a dismal existence in the House of Dust, "where dust is their fare and clay their food." The epic's central theme is Gilgamesh's search for everlasting life. He seeks out and questions Utnapishtim (oot-nah-PISH-tim), who was granted eternal life because he saved all living creatures from a great flood. (Utnapishtim's story has many similarities with the Hebrew account of Noah and the Flood). But Gilgamesh's search in not successful, and he finally concludes that he must die like all other mortals:

> *There is darkness which lets no person*
> *again see the light of day;*
> *There is a road leading away from*
> *bright and lively life. There dwell those who eat*
> *dry dust*
> *and have no cooling water to quench their*
> *awful thirst.*
> *As I stood there I saw all those who've died*
> *and even kings among those darkened souls*
> *have none of their remote and former glory.*[6]

The ancient Mesopotamians never moved far beyond this early view that immortality was reserved for the gods, and that life after death, if it existed at all, was a gloomy and terrible existence where spirits haunted the world in a continual search for food and water. Unlike the Egyptians, they did not develop an expectation of an attractive life after death as a reward for good behavior on earth. They did come to believe in divine rewards for moral conduct, but these were rewards to be enjoyed in this life—increased worldly goods, numerous offspring, long life.

The ethical content of Babylonian religion was never well developed. Numerous priesthoods—more than 30 different types of priests and priestesses are known—became preoccupied with an elaborate set of rituals, particularly those designed to ward off evil demons and predict the future through observing omens and portents. Good deeds, the priests insisted, could not protect a person from demons that have the power to make their part-human and part-animal bodies invisible. Only the proper spells, incantations, and offerings could ward off evil.

While one large class of priests provided amulets inscribed with incantations and magic formulas to expel demons, another group dealt with predicting the future. Almost anything could be viewed as an omen, but most popular were dreams, the movements of birds and animals, the internal organs of sacrificed animals, the shape taken by oil poured on the surface of water, the casting of dice, and astronomical phenomena. Such practices, called superstitions in the modern world, were in reality attempts

Worshipper statues from the square temple, Eshnunna (now Tel Asmar, Iraq).

by the Mesopotamians to obtain some semblance of control and predictability over a world ruled by chaotic and random forces.

Collapse and Disorder, c. 1600–1200 B.C.E.

The pattern of disunity and warfare, all too familiar in Mesopotamia, reasserted itself following Hammurabi's death. In 1595 B.C.E. the Hittites, an Indo-European people who had established control in Asia Minor, mounted a daring raid down the Euphrates, sacking Babylon and destroying the weakened dynasty of Hammurabi. The swift success of the Hittite raid was made possible by a new means of waging war: the use of lightweight chariots drawn by horses instead of donkeys or oxen. The next five centuries in Mesopotamia were years of disorder about which little is known; political unity dissolved, yet the cultural foundations of Mesopotamian society, and the inheritance that culture owed to the Sumerians, continued to influence the shaping of later Mesopotamian societies.

The beginnings of civilization in Egypt, and the continuous development of that great early civilization, was a development for the most part contemporary with the origins and development of civilization in Mesopotamia. Yet the circumstances under which Egyptian culture took shape, and the very nature of the Egyptian civilization, stands in contrast to the Mesopotamian achievement.

EGYPT: GIFT OF THE NILE

- *What effect did the waters of the Nile have on ancient Egyptian political and religious institutions?*

Egypt, one of Africa's earliest civilizations, is literally "the gift of the [Nile] river," as the ancient Greek historian Herodotus observed. The Nile River stretches for 4100 miles, but it is its last valley, extending 750 miles from the First **Cataract** to the Nile delta, that was the heartland of Egyptian civilization. Egyptians called the Nile valley *Kemet* ("the black land") because its soils were renewed annually by the rich black silt deposited by the floodwaters of the Blue Nile and the Apara, rivers descending from the Ethiopian highlands. Unlike the unpredictable floods of Mesopotamia, the Nile's floods rose and fell with unusual precision, reaching Aswan (ahs-WAHN) by late June and peaking in September before beginning to subside. The perennial key to successful farming was con-

cataract—Large waterfall or a series of rapids on a river such as the Nile.

trolling the Nile by diverting its floodwaters along the 10- to 20-mile-wide floodplain for irrigation. Egyptian farmers achieved this by building an elaborate network of dikes and canals.

Predynastic Egypt

The first Nile settlers were likely people who moved to the river valley as climatic changes transformed the savanna grasslands west of the Nile into desert. By 4800 B.C.E. the earliest farming communities began to appear in the western Nile delta and spread to the rest of Egypt over the next eight centuries. Recognizing the advantages of creating larger social groupings and the need to cushion themselves from the impact of droughts, floods, and plagues, farming communities started banding together to form regional chiefdoms in Lower Egypt, the area comprising the broad Nile delta north of Memphis, and Upper Egypt, which extended southward along the narrow Nile valley as far as the First Cataract at Aswan. A kingdom emerged in Upper Egypt, while Lower Egypt was divided into a number of districts (later called *nomes*) that had formerly been ruled by independent chieftains.

The Predynastic period ended soon after 3100 B.C.E. when King Menes (also known as *Narmer*) united Upper Egypt and started gradually incorporating Lower Egypt into a new kingdom with its capital at Memphis. This period has become known as the First **Dynasty,** and it marks the beginning of one of the longest-lasting civilizations in history, lasting for 3000 years.

dynasty—A series of rulers who belong to the same family or line.

Ancient Egypt

c. 3100 B.C.E.	Menes unites Upper Egypt
c. 2700 B.C.E.	Construction of Step Pyramid
c. 1720 B.C.E.	Hyksos conquer Egypt
c. 1600 B.C.E.	Oldest medical text
c. 1479–1458 B.C.E.	Regency of Queen Hatshepsut
c. 1458–1436 B.C.E.	Reign of Thutmose III
c. 1363–1347 B.C.E.	Reign of Amenhotep IV (Akhenaton)
c. 1290–1224 B.C.E.	Reign of Ramses II
c. 700s B.C.E.	Conquest of Egypt by Kush

The Old Kingdom, c. 2700–2200 B.C.E.

The kings of the Third through Sixth Dynasties—the period called the Old Kingdom or Pyramid Age—firmly established order and stability, as well as the basic elements of Egyptian civilization. The nobility lost its independence, and all power was centered in the king, or *pharaoh* (*per-ao,* "great house," originally signified the royal palace but during the New Kingdom began to refer to the king). The king had a character both divine and human. Considered a god, he also represented humans before the gods. He had the responsibility to maintain ***maat,*** that is, truth, justice, and order.

The king, along with his relatives, owned extensive tracts of land (from which he made frequent grants to temples, royal funerary cults, and private persons) and received the surplus from the crops produced on the huge royal estates. This surplus supported a large corps of specialists—administrators, priests, scribes, artists, artisans, and merchants—who labored in the pharaoh's service. The pharaoh's power and legitimacy were based on his ability to offer protection and sustain prosperity through abundant harvests. In return, his subjects gave their absolute devotion to the god-king, and Egyptians generally felt a sense of security that was rare in Mesopotamia.

The belief that the pharaoh was divine led to the construction of colossal tombs—pyramids—to preserve the pharaoh's embalmed body for eternity. The ritual of mummification was believed to restore vigor and activity to the dead pharaoh; it was his passport to eternity. The pyramid tombs, especially those of the Fourth Dynasty at Giza near Memphis, which are the most celebrated of all ancient monuments, reflect the great power and wealth of the Old Kingdom pharaohs. Although pyramid building was year-round, most construction took place during the months when the Nile overflowed its banks, and the pharaoh could expect farmers to provide their labor on construction crews. The Egyptian masses performed it primarily as an act of fidelity to their god-king, on whom the security and prosperity of Egypt depended.

The Pyramids at Giza

Security and prosperity came to an end late in the Sixth Dynasty. The burden of building and maintaining pyramid tombs for each new king exhausted the state. The Nile floods failed, and famines ensued. As the state and its god-king lost credibility, provincial rulers assumed the prerogatives of the pharaohs, including the claim to immortality, and districts became independent. Inscriptions, known as coffin texts, also began to appear in nonroyal coffins. Among other things, the

Two Accounts of an Egyptian Famine

maat—A goddess who represented the balance and harmony of the universe as well as a set of ethical concepts that encompassed "truth," "order," and "cosmic balance." One's life and personal behavior should contribute to universal order. Hence, a pharaoh maintained *maat* by ruling justly and serving the gods.

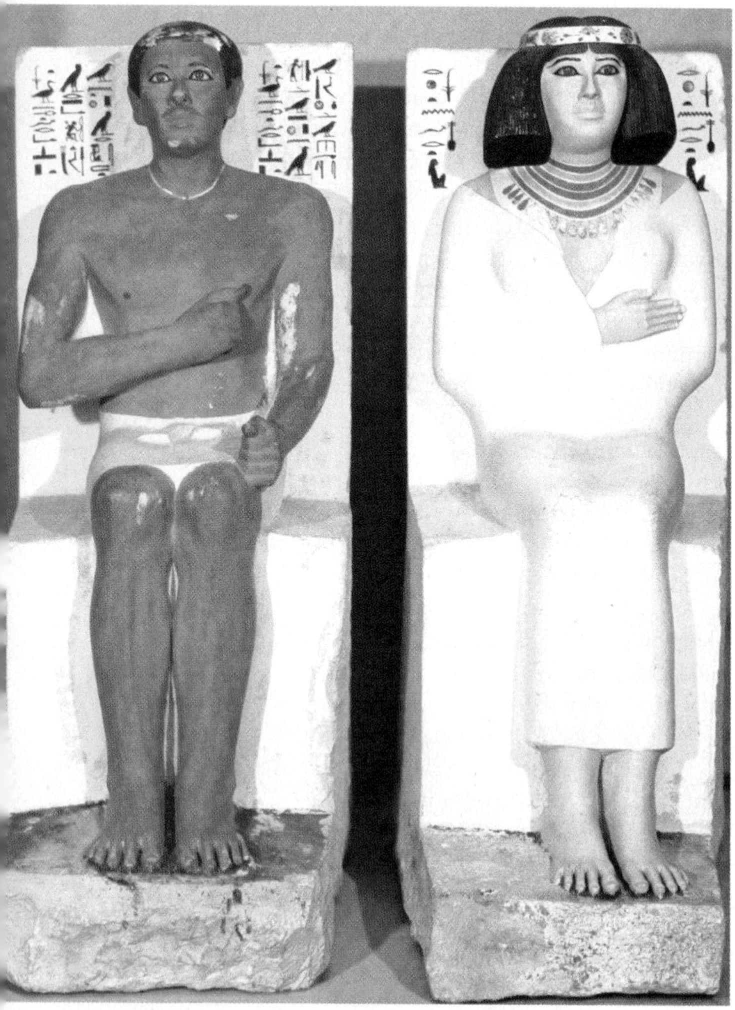

Pharoah Ra-Hotep and his wife Nofret. Ra-Hotep was a pharaoh of the Seventeenth Dynasty who ruled around 1650 B.C.E. as Egypt was under Hyksos rule. These statues raise questions of whether it is fruitful to apply modern racial classifications to ancient Egyptians.

inscriptions expressed the hope that the deceased would be reunited with their families in the afterlife. For about a century and a half, known as the First Intermediate Period (c. 2200–2050 B.C.E.), the pharaoh's central authority weakened as civil war raged among contenders for the throne and local rulers reasserted themselves. Outsiders raided and infiltrated the land. The lot of the common people became unbearable as they faced famine, robbery, and oppression. "All happiness has vanished," related a Middle Kingdom commentary on this troubled era. "I show you the land in turmoil. . . . Each man's heart is for himself. . . . A man sits with his back turned, while one slays another."[7]

The Middle Kingdom, c. 2050–1800 B.C.E

Stability was restored by the pharaohs of the Eleventh and Twelfth Dynasties, who reunited the kingdom. Stressing their role as watchful shepherds of the people, the Middle Kingdom pharaohs promoted the welfare of the downtrodden. One of them claimed, "I gave to the beggar and brought up the orphan. I gave success to the poor as to the wealthy."[8] The pharaohs of the Twelfth Dynasty revived the building of pyramids as well as the construction of public works. The largest of these, a drainage and irrigation project in the marshy Fayum (fai-YOOM) district south of Memphis, resulted in the reclamation of thousands of acres of arable land.

During the Thirteenth Dynasty, the Hyksos (HIK-sohs; "rulers of foreign lands"), a Semitic people from western Asia, assumed power over much of Egypt. The Hyksos are often portrayed as invaders who conquered Egypt around 1720 B.C.E., but now it is understood that the Hyksos migrated into Lower Egypt during the Middle Kingdom and established trading networks. During the Second Intermediate Period (c. 1800–1570 B.C.E.), they took advantage of weaknesses in the Egyptian state and gradually took control over all of Lower Egypt and many parts of Upper Egypt. The Hyksos did not sweep aside Egyptian institutions and culture. They adapted to existing Egyptian government structures, copied architectural styles and the **hieroglyphic** ("sacred carvings") system of writing, and incorporated Egyptian cults into their religious pantheon. The Hyksos army also introduced new weaponry to the Egyptians: the horse-drawn chariot and bronze weapons such as the curved sword and body armor and helmets.

The New Kingdom or Empire, c. 1570–1090 B.C.E.

Hyksos rule over Egypt lasted several centuries before a resurgent Egyptian dynasty based at Thebes challenged it. Adopting the new weapons introduced by their rulers, the Egyptians expelled the Hyksos and pursued them northwards into Phoenicia. The pharaohs of the Eighteenth Dynasty, who reunited Egypt and founded the New Kingdom, made Phoenicia the nucleus of an Egyptian empire in western Asia and conquered Nubia to the south.

The outstanding representative of this aggressive state was Thutmose III. When the union of Thutmose II and his half-sister, Hatshepsut (hat-SHEP-soot), failed to produce a male heir, Thutmose II fathered Thutmose III with a concubine. When Thutmose II died in 1479 B.C.E., Thutmose was still a child, and Hatshepsut was to act as co-regent until he came of age. Mindful of the Egyptian ideal that a son inherited the throne from the pharaoh, she legitimized her suc-

hieroglyphics—The mode of writing of ancient Egyptians that featured signs or figures to represent words.

cession by claiming that she was the designated successor of Thutmose I. She also stated that she had a divine origin as a daughter of Amon and had an oracle proclaim that Amon had chosen her to become king. She adopted all the customary royal titles; and in many of her statues and helmets, she was even depicted sporting the royal beard.

Because Hatshepsut had her own ambitions, Thutmose III had to wait for more than two decades before he assumed the throne on his own. Toward the end of his reign, he ordered Hatshepsut's name and inscriptions erased, her reliefs effaced, and her statues broken and thrown into a quarry. Historians still speculate whether he was expressing his anger at Hatshepsut or promoting his own accomplishments. Thutmose III is most noted for leading his army on 17 campaigns as far as Syria, where he set up his boundary markers on the banks of the Euphrates, called by the Egyptians "the river that runs backwards." Under his sway, Thutmose III allowed the existing rulers of conquered states to remain on their thrones, but their sons were taken as hostages to Egypt, where they were brought up, thoroughly Egyptianized, and eventually sent home to succeed their fathers as loyal vassals of Egyptian rule. Thutmose III erected *obelisks*—tall, pointed shafts of stone—to commemorate his reign and to record his wish that "his name might endure throughout the future forever and ever." The Egyptian Empire reached its peak under Amenhotep III (c. 1402–1363 B.C.E.). The restored capital at Thebes, with its temples built for the sun-god Amon east of the Nile at Luxor and Karnak, became the most magnificent city in the world. Tribute flowed in from conquered lands, and relations were expanded with Asia and the Mediterranean. To improve ties, the kings of Mitanni and Babylonia offered daughters in marriage to Amenhotep III in return for gold.

During the reign of the succeeding pharaoh, Amenhotep IV (c. 1363–1347 B.C.E.), however, the empire went into a sharp decline as the result of an internal struggle between the pharaoh and the powerful and wealthy priests of Amon, "king of the gods." The pharaoh undertook to revolutionize Egypt's religion by proclaiming the worship of the sun's disk, Aton, in place of Amon and all the other deities. Often called the first monotheist (although, as Aton's son, the pharaoh was also a god and he, not Aton, was worshipped by the Egyptians), Amenhotep changed his name to Akhenaton (akh-NAHT-in; "he who is effective for the Aton"), left Amon's city to found a new capital (Akhetaton,"horizon of Aton"), and concentrated on religious reform. By demoting Amon to a lesser status and taxing his temples, Akhenaton provoked strong opposition from Amon's priesthood. Most of Egypt's tributary princes in Asia defected when their appeals for aid against invaders went unheeded.

Akhenaton's monotheism did not survive his reign. When Akhenaton died, his 9-year-old brother, Tutankhamen (tu-tan-KAHM-in; "King Tut," c. 1347–1338 B.C.E.)—now best remembered for his small but richly furnished tomb, discovered in 1922—returned to the worship of Amon and to Memphis. Amon's priests gained revenge against Akhenaton as Tutankhamen and his successors destroyed Akhenaton's statues and tried to erase all memory of him. When Tutankhamen died in his late teens with no heir, one of his advisers, Horemheb, a general from the Nile delta region, founded the Nineteenth Dynasty (c. 1305–1200 B.C.E.).

Taking the name Ramses I, he sought to reestablish Egyptian control over Palestine and Syria. The result was a long struggle with the Hittites, who in the meantime had pushed south from Asia Minor into Syria. This struggle reached a climax in the reign of Ramses II (c. 1290–1224 B.C.E.) Ramses II regained Palestine, but when he failed to dislodge the Hittites from Syria, he agreed to a treaty. Its strikingly modern character is revealed in clauses providing for nonaggression, mutual assistance, and extradition of fugitives.

The long reign of Ramses II was one of Egypt's last periods of national grandeur. The number and size of Ramses' monuments rival those of the Pyramid Age. Outstanding among them are the great Hypostyle Hall, built for Amon at Karnak, and the temple at Abu Simbel in Nubia, with its four colossal statues of Ramses, which was raised in the 1960s to save it from inundation by the waters of the High Dam at Aswan. After Ramses II, royal authority gradually decayed as the power of the priests of Amon rose.

Third Intermediate Period, 1090–332 B.C.E.

The Third Intermediate Period was another period of transition in which the Amon priesthood at Thebes became so strong that the high priest was able to found his own dynasty and to rule over Upper Egypt. At the same time, merchant princes set up a dynasty of their own in the Nile delta. Libyans from the west moved into central Egypt, where in 940 B.C.E. they established a dynasty whose founder, Shoshenq, was a contemporary of King Solomon of Israel. Two centuries later, Egypt was conquered by the rulers of the kingdom of Kush, who established the Twenty-Fifth Dynasty. Kush's rule came to an end around 670 B.C.E. when the Assyrians of Mesopotamia made Egypt a province of their empire.

Egypt enjoyed a brief reprise of revived glory during the Twenty-Sixth Dynasty (c. 663–525 B.C.E.), which expelled the Assyrians with the aid of Greek mercenaries. The revival of ancient artistic and literary forms proved to be one of the most creative periods in Egyptian history. After attempts to expand into Syria were blocked by Nebuchadnezzar's (neh-boo-kad-NE-zahr) Babylonians, Egypt's rulers concentrated on expanding their commercial linkages throughout the region. To achieve this end, Pharaoh Necho II (c. 610–595 B.C.E.) created the first Egyptian navy. He encouraged the Greeks to establish trading colonies in the Nile delta; he put 12,000 laborers to work, digging a canal between the Nile mouth and the Red Sea (it was completed later by the Persians); and he commissioned a Phoenician expedition to search for new African trade routes.

Egypt came under Persian rule in 525 B.C.E. but was able to regain its independence in 404 B.C.E. After three brief dynasties, Egypt again fell under the Persians before coming within the domain of Alexander the Great (see Chapter 4).

Nubia and the Kingdom of Kush

Egypt's most enduring relationship was with its neighbor to the south, Nubia (NOO-bee-ah; derived from *nub*, the Egyptian word for gold), an area that stretches almost 900 miles from the town of Aswan to Khartoum, the point where the Blue and White Niles converge. The Nile gave Nubian civilization a distinctive character but in ways different from those in Egypt. As the Nile flows northward, its course is interrupted six times by cataracts that served as barriers to river traffic and Nubia's commercial contacts with Egypt. Like Egypt, many parts of Nubia east and west of the Nile are barren, so Nubian agricultural production depended on the Nile's two-mile wide floodplain.

Emerging around 4000 B.C.E., the earliest Nubian culture was made up of hunters, fishermen, farmers, and seminomadic pastoralists. This culture was distinguished for its highly skilled sculptures, ceramics, and clay figurines. Nubia also developed a healthy trade with Egypt. After a centralized state emerged in Egypt, Egyptian dynasties regarded Nubia as a source of slaves and raw materials such as gold, timber, and ivory and made several attempts to colonize Nubia. This state of hostility did not prevent Nubians from marrying into Egyptian royal families and the Egyptian state and army from recruiting Nubian administrators and archers.

Centered in a fertile area of the Nile around the Third Cataract, the Kingdom of Kush emerged around 1600 B.C.E. Its capital was at Kerma, an urban center renowned for its sophisticated temples and palaces. Kush prospered most when Egypt's fortunes declined. Although the basis of Kush's society was agriculture and animal husbandry, Kush engaged in extensive trade with Egypt to the north and African societies to the south and east.

After expelling the Hyksos, Egyptian forces reasserted their dominion over northern Nubia as far south as the Fourth Cataract, including Kerma. For the next four centuries, Egyptian administrators exploited Nubian gold to finance military campaigns in Asia and created an Egyptianized Nubian elite who spoke the Egyptian language and adopted Egyptian deities such as Amon and ritual and burial practices, including erecting pyramids.

Kush did not regain its autonomy until the eighth century B.C.E, when a new line of rulers established themselves at Napata (nah-PAH-tah) between the Third and Fourth Cataracts. The high point of Kush's power came a short time later. Taking advantage of strife in Egypt, the armies of Kush's King Piye swept through Egypt, conquering territory as far north as the Nile Delta. Although Piye proclaimed himself pharaoh

Sections of a wall painting from the tomb chapel of the treasurer Sebekhotep at Thebes show Nubians presenting gold nuggets and rings to King Thutmose IV. It dates from around 1400 B.C.E.

over Egypt and Nubia, he allowed local rulers in Egypt a measure of independence, and he cultivated the priests of the temple of Amon. His brother and successor, Shabaqo, was not so benign. He brought Egypt under the direct control of Kush and moved his capital to Thebes. He and the three pharaohs who succeeded him established the Twenty-Fifth Dynasty, which ruled Kush and Egypt for the next half century until they were forced to retreat following an Assyrian invasion. Kush's capital then moved to Meroe (MEHR-oh-wee), situated at the confluence of the Nile and APara Rivers. This site enjoyed annual rainfalls and supported a larger population. Meroe became a noted center for ironworking and weaving and exporting cotton cloth.

Kush remained in existence until 400 C.E., when it was absorbed into the Ethiopian kingdom of Aksum (ak-soom). Around the second century B.C.E. Kush's rulers started recording their royal annals in a script based on hieroglyphics and a cursive script also derived from hieroglyphics. This language, known as Meroitic, has not been translated to this day.

Egyptian Society and Economy

Egyptian society was highly stratified. Most Egyptians were poor peasants subject to forced labor for the rulers and who paid taxes to those who owned the land—the pharaoh, temples, or wealthy landowners—based on the yields of harvests.

However, class distinctions were not rigid. People could rise to a higher rank in the service of the pharaoh by joining the tiny literate elite. Pupils—usually boys—attended a scribal school for many years in which they learned to read and write hieratic script, a cursive form of hieroglyphics. Students practiced with reed pens on limestone chips or clay tablets. Scribes were in demand by the state for many tasks—writing letters, recording harvests, tracking taxes collected and owed, and keeping accounts for the Egyptian army. The most scholarly scribes assumed positions as priests, doctors, and engineers. Scribes enjoyed secure positions and were free from labor service.

Compared with the Greeks and Romans, Egyptian women enjoyed more rights, although their status at all levels of society was generally lower than that of men. Few women could qualify as scribes and thus were largely excluded from administrative positions. However, women could serve as temple priestesses, musicians, gardeners, farmers, and bakers. Some royal women, because of their positions as wives or mothers of pharaohs, had great influence in royal courts. Business and legal documents show that women shared many of the economic and legal rights of men. Women generally had rights to own, buy, sell, and inherit property without reliance on male legal

Many tomb paintings depict everyday life in Egypt. Here, two servants pick figs at the tomb of Khnumhotpes at Bani Hasan.

guardians; to negotiate legal settlements; to engage in business deals; to make wills; and to initiate litigation and testify in court. In a divorce, a woman kept any property she brought into a marriage as well as one-third of a couple's community property. When Egypt came under Greek rule, most Egyptian women preferred the option of maintaining their legal rights under Egyptian rather than Greek law.

The economy of Egypt was dominated by the divine pharaoh and his state, which owned most of the land and monopolized its commerce and industry. Because of the Nile and the proximity to the Mediterranean and Red seas, most of Egypt's trade was conducted by ships. Boats regularly plied up and down the Nile, which, unlike the Tigris and the Euphrates, is easily navigable in both directions up to the First

Document "The Great Hymn to the Aton" and Psalm 104

A notable example of New Kingdom Egyptian literature is the pharaoh Akhenaton's "Hymn to the Sun," which was found carved on the tombs of his followers. Akhenaton's Hymn reflected his dramatic break with Egyptian religious beliefs that stressed prayers to gods for health and well-being and prepared the way for "blessed" afterlife. Akhenaton conceived one omnipotent and beneficent Creator and that he was the guarantor of the afterlife. Some scholars argue that his religious reforms may have had a formative effect on the development of monotheism on the Hebrews, many of whom were perhaps enslaved in Egypt at the time of Akhenaton's reforms. The style and subject of Psalm 104 bear a striking resemblance to the king's hymn to the sun:

The Great Hymn to the Aton

Splendid you rise in heaven's lightland,
O living Aton, creator of life!
When you have dawned in eastern lightland,
You fill every land with your beauty.
You are beauteous, great, radiant,
High over every land;
Your rays embrace the lands. . . .
How many are your deeds,
Though hidden from sight;
O Sole God beside whom there is none!
You made the earth as you wished, you alone.
All peoples, herds, and flocks;
All upon earth that walk on legs,
All on high that fly on wings, . . .
You set every man in his place,
You supply their needs;
Everyone has his food,
His lifetime is counted. . .

From Miriam Lichtheim, *Ancient Egyptian Literature: A Book of Readings (Volume II: The New Kingdom)* (Berkeley: University of California Press, 1976, pp. 96–98.

Psalm 104

Bless Yahweh, my soul,
Yahweh my God, how great you are!
Clothed in majesty and glory,
wrapped in a robe of light!
You stretch the heavens out like a tent,
you build your palace on the waters above;
using the clouds as your chariot,
you advance on the wings of the wind;
you use the winds as messengers
and fiery flames as servants.
You fixed the earth on its foundations,
unshakable for ever and ever;
you wrapped it with the deep as with a robe,
the waters overtopping the mountains. . . .
The sun rises, they retire,
going back to lie down in their lairs,
and man goes to work, and to labour until dusk.
Yahweh, what variety you have created
arranging everything so wisely!
Earth is completely full of the things you have made. . . .
Glory for ever to Yahweh!
May Yahweh find joy in what he creates,
at whose glance the earth trembles,
at whose touch the mountains smoke!

From "Psalm 104," *The Jerusalem Bible*, ed. Alexander Jones (Daarton, Longman & Todd, Ltd., and Doubleday: 1966), pp. 886–888, as quoted in Perry M. Rogers, *Aspects of Western Civilization*, Vol. I (Prentice Hall: 2000), pp. 33–35.

Questions to Consider

1. How do you account for the striking similarities between Akhenaton's Hymn and Psalm 104? Do you think the Hymn might have inspired the writer of Psalm 104?
2. What are the similarities between the Aton and Yahweh? Are there any differences in the manner in which they are described?
3. Why did Akhenaton's monotheism not last beyond his reign, while the Hebrew's monotheism was sustained?

Cataract at Aswan. The current carries ships downstream, and the prevailing north wind enables them to sail upstream easily. Trade reached its height during the empire (c. 1570–1090 B.C.E.), when commerce traveled along four main routes: the Nile River to and from the south; the Red Sea, which was connected by caravan to the Nile bend near Thebes; a caravan route to Mesopotamia and southern Syria; and the Mediterranean Sea, connecting northern Syria, Cyprus, Crete, and Greece with the Nile delta. Egypt's primary imports were timber, copper, tin, and olive oil, paid for with gold from its rich mines, linens, wheat, and **papyrus** rolls made from reeds—the preferred writing materials of the ancient world (the word *paper* is derived from the Greek *papyros*).

Egyptian Religion

Religion played a central role in the everyday life of Egyptians, who attributed everything from the annual cycles of the flooding of the Nile to personal illnesses to acts of gods. The Egyptian pantheon included hundreds of gods and goddesses. Male gods usually represented rulers, creators, and insurers of fertility, while goddesses assumed roles as nurturers, magicians, and sexual temptresses. People made sacrifices and prayed to household gods to protect the well-being and health of their families. They also worshipped deities on a local and regional basis. When the Old Kingdom came into being, ruling families elevated certain local gods and religious centers such as Heliopolis (hel-YOH-POH-lis) and Thebes (in the Middle Kingdom) gained national prominence. The most important gods—such as Osiris, Horus, Re', Amun, and Hathor—had their own temples and priesthoods that conducted rituals, sacrifices, and festivals honoring the god they served. The temples owned vast properties, and the income they generated paid for the salaries and upkeep of priests.

papyrus—An early form of writing material made from the stem of the papyrus plant.

Egypt's most popular religious cult was devoted to Osiris, the fertility god of the Nile, whose death and resurrection symbolized the planting of grain and its sprouting. The Egyptian myth of fertility and life after death, according to the priests at Heliopolis, was that Osiris had been murdered by Seth, his brother, who cut the victim's body into many pieces and scattered them around Egypt. When Isis, his bereaved widow, collected all the pieces and wrapped them in linen, Osiris was resurrected so that he could father Horus, the Nile floods resumed, and vegetation revived. The Osiris cult taught that Seth was the god of violence and disorder, that Osiris was the ruler of the dead in the netherworld, and that every mummified Egyptian could become another Osiris, capable of resurrection from the dead and a blessed eternal life.

However, only a soul free of sin would be permitted to live forever. In a ceremony called "counting up character," Osiris presided over a court of 42 gods that weighed the heart of the deceased against the Feather of Truth. If the virtues of the heart were outweighed by the Feather of Truth, a horrible creature devoured it. Charms and magical prayers and spells were sold to the living as insurance policies guaranteeing them a happy outcome in the judgment before Osiris. They constitute much of what is known as the *Book of the Dead,* which was placed in tombs and coffins.

Mathematics and Science

The Egyptians were much less skilled in mathematics than the Mesopotamians. Their arithmetic was limited to addition and subtraction, which also served them when they needed to multiply and divide. They could cope with only simple algebra, but they did have considerable knowledge of practical geometry; the obliteration of field boundaries by the annual flooding of the Nile made the measurement of land a necessity. Knowledge of geometry was also essential in computing the dimensions of ramps for raising stones during the construction of pyramids. In these and other engineering projects, the Egyptians were superior to their

In this scene from the Book of the Dead, *a princess stands in the Hall of Judgment in the Underworld before a set of scales on which the jackal-headed god Anubis weighs her heart against the Feather of Truth. The baboonlike god Thoth records the result. On the left, Isis presents the princess, who has also aided her cause, with an offering to Osiris, a haunch of beef.*

Mesopotamian contemporaries. Like the Mesopotamians, the Egyptians acquired a "necessary" technology without developing a truly scientific method. Yet what has been called the oldest known scientific treatise (c. 1600 B.C.E.) was composed during the New Kingdom. Its author, possibly a military surgeon or a doctor who treated pyramid-building laborers, described cases of head and spinal injuries, dislocations, and broken bones and recommended treatments or, in the case of more serious complications, nothing at all. Other medical writings considered a range of ailments, from pregnancy complications to hippopotamus bites. To Egyptian practitioners, the causes of medical conditions had to be dealt with holistically on a spiritual as well as a physical level. Thus they prescribed a combination of medicines, rituals, magical spells, and amulets.

The Old Kingdom also produced the world's first known solar calendar, the direct ancestor of our own. In order to plan their farming operations in accordance with the annual flooding of the Nile, the Egyptians kept records and divided the calendar into three seasons—flooding, planting and growing crops, and harvesting. Each season contained four months with 30 days in each month. They observed that the Nile flood coincided with the annual appearance of the Dog Star (Sirius) on the eastern horizon at dawn, and they soon associated the two phenomena.

Monumentalism in Architecture

Because of their impressive, enduring tombs and temples, the Egyptians have been called the greatest builders in history. The earliest tomb was the mud-brick Arab *mastaba* (MAS-tuh-buh), so called because of its resemblance to a low bench. By the beginning of the Third Dynasty, stone began to replace brick, and an architectural genius named Imhotep, now honored as the "father of architecture in stone," constructed the first pyramid by piling six huge stone *mastabas* one on top of the other. Adjoining this Step Pyramid was a temple complex whose stone columns were not freestanding but attached to a wall, as though the architect were tentatively feeling his way in the use of the new medium.

The Step Pyramid of Zoser, which was built by piling six huge stone mastabas, *one of top of the other.*

The most celebrated of the true pyramids were built for the Fourth Dynasty pharaohs Khufu, Khafre, and Menkaure. Khufu's pyramid, the largest of the three, covers 13 acres and originally rose 481 feet. It is composed of 2.3 million limestone bricks, some weighing 15 tons, and all pushed and pulled into place by human muscle. This stupendous monument was built without mortar, yet some of the stones were so perfectly fitted that a knife cannot be inserted in the joints. The Old Kingdom's 80 pyramids are a striking expression of Egyptian civilization. Their dignity and massiveness reflect the religious basis of Egyptian society—the dogma that the king was a god who owned the nation and that serving him was the most important task of the people.

Just as the glory and serenity of the Old Kingdom can be seen in its pyramids, constructed as an act of loyalty by its subjects, so the power and wealth of the empire survive in the Amon temples at Thebes, made possible by the booty and tribute of conquest. On the east side of the Nile were built the magnificent temples of Karnak and Luxor. The Hypostyle Hall of the temple of Karnak, built by Ramses II, is larger than the cathedral of Notre Dame in Paris. Its forest of 134 columns is arranged in 16 rows, with the roof over a central aisle raised to allow the entry of light. This technique was later used in Roman basilicas and in Christian churches.

Sculpture and Painting

Egyptian art was essentially religious. Tomb paintings and relief sculpture depict the everyday activities that the deceased wished to continue enjoying in the afterlife, and statues glorify the god-kings in all their serenity and eternity. Since religious art is inherently conservative, Egyptian art seldom departed from the classical tradition established during the vigorous and self-assured Old Kingdom. Sculptors idealized and standardized their subjects, and the human figure is shown either looking directly ahead or in profile, with a rigidity very much in keeping with the austere architectural settings of the statues.

Yet, on two occasions an unprecedented realism appeared in Egyptian sculpture. The faces of some of the Middle Kingdom rulers appear drawn and weary, seemingly reflecting the burden of reconstructing Egypt after the collapse of the Old Kingdom. An even greater realism is seen in the portraits of Akhenaton and his queen, Nefertiti, which continued into the following reign of Tutankhamen. The portraits realistically depict the pharaoh's physical appearance such as his ungainly paunch and his happy but far from godlike family life in informal settings—the pharaoh playing with one of his young daughters on his knee or munching on a bone. The "heretic" pharaoh, who insisted on what he called "truth" in religion, seems also to have insisted on truth in art.

Painting shows the same precision and mastery of technique that are evident in sculpture. No attempt was made to show objects in perspective, and the scenes seem flat. The effect of distance was conveyed by making objects in a series or by putting one object above another. Another convention employed was to depict everything from its most characteristic angle. Often the head, arms, and legs were shown in side view while the eyes, shoulders, and chest were shown in front view.

Writing and Literary Texts

In Egypt, as in Sumer, writing began with pictures. But unlike the Mesopotamian signs, the Egyptian hieroglyphics remained primarily pictorial. At first, the hieroglyphics represented a mix of pictorial signs and one- and two-consonant signs that later came to stand for ideas and syllables. Early in the Old Kingdom the Egyptians took the further step of using alphabetical characters for 24 consonant sounds. Although they also continued to use the old pictographic and syllabic signs, the use of sound symbols had far-reaching consequences. It influenced their Semitic neighbors in Syria to produce an alphabet that, in its Phoenician form, became the forerunner of our own.

The earliest Egyptian literary works generally recorded the accomplishments of rulers or expressed religious beliefs through prayers, hymns, and funerary inscriptions. Among the latter are the *Pyramid Texts,* a collection of magic spells and ritual texts inscribed on the walls of the burial chambers of Old Kingdom pharaohs. Their recurrent theme is an affirmation that the dead pharaoh is really a god and that no obstacle can prevent him from joining his fellow gods in the heavens.

Old Kingdom literature went on to achieve a classical maturity of style and content—it stresses a "truth" that is "everlasting." Hence *The Instructions of Ptah-hotep,* addressed to the author's sons, insists that "it is the strength of truth that it endures long, and a man can say, 'I learned it from my father.'" Ptah-hotep's maxims stress the values and virtues that are important in fostering positive human relationships. To him, honesty is a good policy because it will gain one wealth and position, while affairs with other men's wives is a bad policy because it will impede one's path to success in life.[9]

DOCUMENT
Elders' Advice to Their Successors

The troubled times that followed the collapse of the Old Kingdom produced the highly personal writings of the First Intermediate Period and the Middle Kingdom. They contain protests against the ills of the day and demands for social justice. In the New Kingdom, writers composed love poems as a means of forgetting misery. The universal appeal of this literature is illustrated by the following lines.

I think I'll go home and lie very still,
feigning terminal illness,
Then the neighbors will all troop over to stare,
my love, perhaps among them
How she'll smile while the specialists snarl in
their teeth!—
She perfectly well knows what ails me.[10]

MESOPOTAMIAN SUCCESSORS TO BABYLON, c. 1600–550 B.C.E.

- *What is the legacy left by the states that succeeded the Babylonian Empire?*

The Babylonian Empire came to an end in the sixteenth century B.C.E., most probably through the raids of chariot driving invaders known as the Kassites. Primarily warriors and raiders, they ruled as a minority of conquerors over the native population. Their concern was not with the establishment of lasting political control, but rather with the accumulation of wealth for the dominant warrior class.

The Hittites

Gradually, a people known as the Hittites began to migrate into the region now known as Turkey, settle themselves as a ruling class over the native population, and establish a kingdom that by 1400 B.C.E. became the strongest power in the region and the greatest rival of the Egyptian empire. Very little was known about the Hittites until archaeologists began to unearth the remains of their civilization in Turkey at the beginning of the twentieth century. By 1920 C.E. Hittite writing had been deciphered, and it proved to be the earliest example of an Indo-European language, closely related to Greek, Latin, and Sanskrit. The Hittites began migrating into Asia Minor from the northeast as early as 2000 B.C.E. Their superior military, in particular their mastery of horse-drawn chariot warfare and mass attacks by archers using long-range bows, enabled them to conquer the native people of central Asia Minor and establish a centralized kingdom with its capital city at Hattushash (HAHT-teu-shahsh), which is near the present Turkish capital city, Ankara.

The kings of the early Hittite kingdom were aggressive monarchs who were frequently at odds with their nobles and struggled to establish an orderly succession to the throne. The early effectiveness of the Hittite monarchy was severely limited by this pattern of constant internal strife.

After 1450 B.C.E. a series of energetic Hittite kings succeeded in limiting the independence of their nobles and creating a more centralized empire that included Syria and northern Palestine, which had been left virtually undefended by the Egyptian pharaoh Akhenaton. The pharaoh Ramses II moved north from Palestine in an unsuccessful attempt to reconquer the region in the battle of Kadesh (1285 B.C.E.). Ambushed and forced back to Palestine after a bloody standoff, the pharaoh agreed to a treaty of "good peace and good brotherhood" with the Hittites in 1269 B.C.E.

The Hittite Civilization

The Hittite state under the empire differed in its organization and reflected the traditions of its Indo-European origins rather than the governmental patterns set by the older monarchies of Mesopotamia and Egypt. The king was thought to be the greatest of the nobles, but not a living god or even a god's representative on earth. Hittite nobles held large estates granted by the

The Hittites dedicated animal-shaped drinking vessels to their gods for their own private use. This vessel in the shape of a stag, made of silver with gold inlays, is 7 inches high and dates between the fifteenth to the thirteenth centuries B.C.E.

king and in return provided warriors and served on a council to advise the king and limit his arbitrary power.

The Hittites adopted the Mesopotamian cuneiform script in order to write their Indo-European language. In addition to preserving their own customs, the Hittites readily incorporated features of earlier Mesopotamian civilization that they found appealing. Sumerian and Mesopotamian literature were preserved, and Mesopotamian gods and goddesses were honored with temples and placed on equal footing with their own traditional deities. While their law codes showed great similarity to the Code of Hammurabi, they differed in prescribing more humane punishments. Instead of retaliation ("an eye for an eye"), the Hittite code made greater use of restitution and compensation.

DOCUMENT
Near Eastern Law Codes

The Hittites left their mark on later peoples of the region primarily as intermediaries. Their skills in metalworking, especially in iron, were passed eventually to their neighbors. Not especially creative in the formulation of law or literature and art, they borrowed extensively from other cultures and in turn passed their knowledge on to others, in particular to the neighboring Phrygians, Lydians, and Greeks.

The Sea Peoples

The Hittites may have been eager for the peace they concluded with Egypt in after the battle at Kadesh because of threats posed by new movements of raiding and displaced peoples—Indo-Europeans and others. A series of disruptions all over the eastern Mediterranean resulted in the overthrow of previously stable regimes now sacked and destroyed. Many survivors of these upheavals, which possibly included the fall of Troy (c. 1150 B.C.E.), fled by sea to seek new lands to plunder or settle. Collectively known as the Sea Peoples, these uprooted people included Philistines (FI-le-steens), Sicilians, Sardinians, and Etruscans. Many gave their names to the areas where they eventually settled. The collapse of the Hittite Empire, shortly after 1200 B.C.E., was partially a result of these migrations and attacks.

Scholars still hotly debate the causes behind the collapses of so many regimes for around 200 years after 1200 B.C.E. Some experts now believe that changes in warfare— especially the reliance on mobile infantry using short swords and javelins in place of the extensive use of chariots—account for the destruction of stable governments and the resulting displacement of peoples.

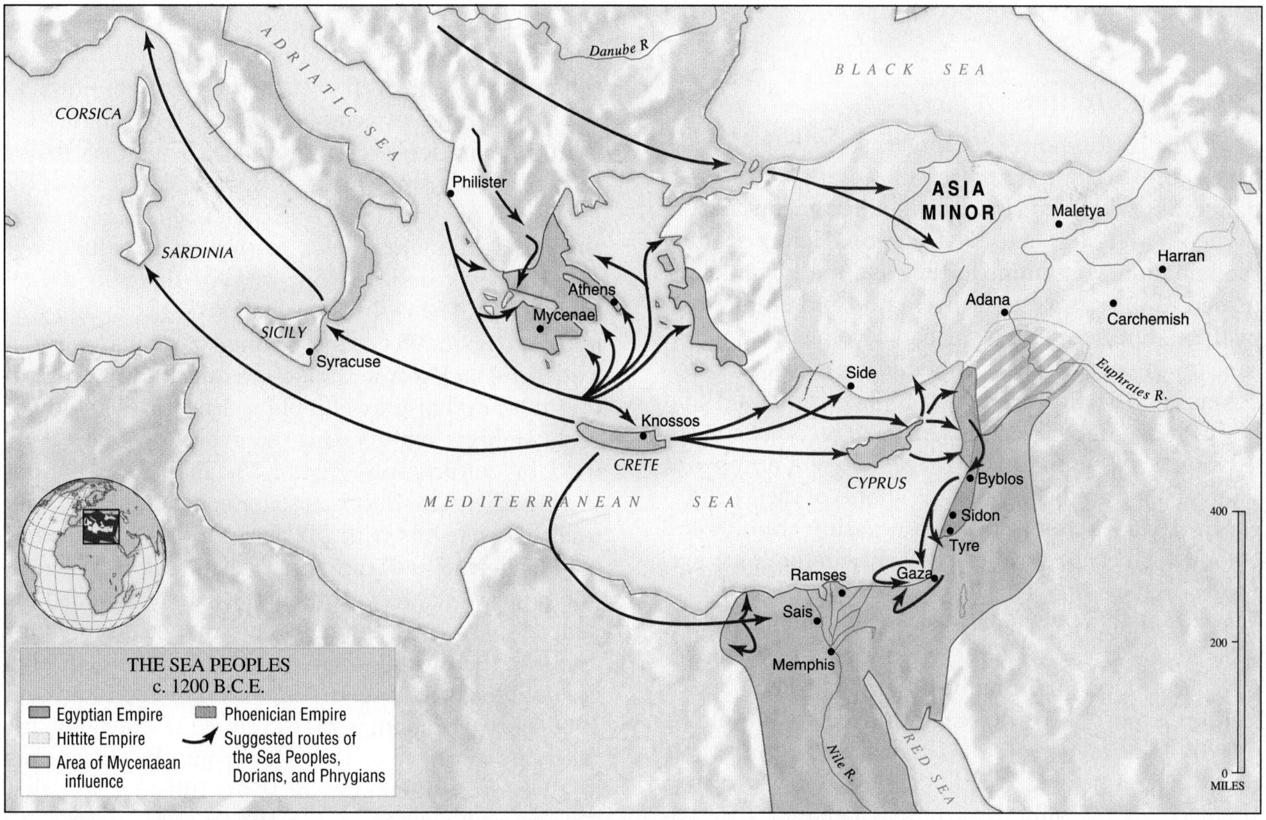

Population movements, the fall of established states, and even the introduction of new and more effective techniques of producing iron weapons may be some of the reasons for the disruption of the eastern Mediterranean around 1200 B.C.E.

The Beginnings of the Iron Age, c. 1100 B.C.E.

Shortly after the disruptions culminating with the invasion of the Sea Peoples, scholars mark the beginning of the Iron Age in the eastern Mediterranean. In fact, iron had been present in small amounts in Mesopotamia as early as one thousand years before, but the metal was seen as too precious to be employed extensively and not initially more effective than bronze. Iron weapons were used by the Hittites as early as 1400 B.C.E., and the technology used to produce iron was a fiercely guarded secret. Many scholars now suggest that, around 1100 B.C.E., partially because of the collapse of the Hittite Empire, the employment of carbonization in the production of iron tools and weapons, and a shortage in the supply of tin to aid in the manufacture of bronze, the use of iron spread from north to south in the eastern Mediterranean.

After 1200 B.C.E, with the Hittite Empire destroyed, the disorder brought by the incursions of the Sea Peoples, and Egypt in decline, the Semitic peoples of Syria and Palestine were able to assert their territorial claims in the power vacuum created by the weakness of once dominant states. For nearly 500 years, until they were conquered by the Assyrians, these peoples played a significant role in the history of the eastern Mediterranean and southwestern Asia.

The Phoenicians

Phoenicians (foh-NEE-shee-ans) is a name the Greeks gave to those Semitic peoples, called Canaanites (KAY-nah-naits), who lived along the Mediterranean coast of Syria, an area that is today Lebanon. Hemmed in by the Lebanon Mountains to the east, the Phoenicians turned to the sea for their livelihood and empire and by the eleventh century B.C.E. had become the Mediterranean's greatest traders, shipbuilders, navigators, and colonizers. To obtain silver and copper from Spain and tin from Britain, they established Gades (Cadiz) on the Atlantic coast of Spain. Carthage, one of a number of Phoenician trading posts on the shores of the Mediterranean, was a remarkably successful commercial colony and became Rome's chief rival in the third century B.C.E. (see Chapter 5).

Although the Phoenicians were essentially traders, their home cities—notably Tyre, Sidon, and Byblos—also produced manufactured goods. Their most famous export was woolen cloth dyed with the purple dye obtained from shellfish found along their coast. They were also skilled makers of furniture (made from the famous cedars of Lebanon), metalware, glassware, and jewelry. The Greeks called Egyptian papyrus rolls *biblia* ("books") because Byblos was the shipping point for this widely used writing material; later the Hebrew and Christian Scriptures were called "the Book" (Bible).

Culturally, the Phoenicians were not particularly original. They left behind no literature and little innovative art. Yet they made one of the greatest contributions to human progress, the perfection of the alphabet, which had a direct influence on the development later western European scripts. Between 1800 and 1600 B.C.E. Phoenician and neighboring Semitic peoples, influenced by Egypt's semi-alphabetical writing, started to evolve a simplified method of writing. The Phoenician alphabet of 22 consonant symbols (the Greeks later added signs for vowels) is related to the 30-character alphabet of Ugarit, a Canaanite city, which was destroyed about 1200 B.C.E. by the Sea Peoples.

The half-dozen Phoenician cities never united to form a strong state, and in the second half of the eighth century B.C.E. all but Tyre were conquered by the Assyrians. Tyre fell to the Chaldean (kahl-DEE-an) Empire in 571 B.C.E., and the one-time fiercely independent status of the Phoenicians ended with their subjugation first to the Chaldeans, and later to subsequent empires—those of the Persians, Greeks, and Romans.

The Hebrew Kingdoms

In war, diplomacy, technology, and art, the Hebrew contributions to history are of small significance; in religion and ethics, however, their contribution to world civilization was momentous. Out of the Hebrew cultural experience grew three of the world's major religions: Judaism, Christianity, and Islam.

Much of that Hebrew experience is recorded in the Old Testament, the collection of literature that the Hebrews believe was written through divine inspiration. The Old Testament's present content was approved about 90 C.E. by a council of rabbis (spiritual leaders). The Hebrew Bible is an outstanding work of literature and also a valuable source for the study of early Hebrew history and the evolution of Hebrew thought, culture, and religion. The biblical account of the history of the Hebrews (later called Israelites, and then Jews) begins with the account of a **patriarchal** clan leader named Abraham, called "the Hebrew" (a nomad or wanderer). Abraham is said to have led his people out of Ur in Sumer, where they had settled for a time in their wanderings. Most biblical scholars suggest that the date of such a migration should be around 1900 B.C.E. Abraham is then credited with leading his followers to northwestern Mesopotamia. He and his followers remained nomadic—the Bible records that Abraham moved his people to Egypt and back again to

---

patriarchal—"Father rule"; of or relating to a social system in which familial and political authority is wielded exclusively by men.

the north, and Abraham's grandson Jacob (later called Israel, and from whom the Israelites derive their name) eventually led a migration into the land of Canaan, later called Palestine.

Historians and archaeologists have raised many questions about the accuracy of biblical accounts for the early Hebrew community. No archaeological proof exists for a migration of peoples into northern Palestine around 1900 B.C.E. although no evidence exists to negate the possibility. Recently archaeologists have suggested that the culture of the age of the founders of the Hebrew community—that culture described in the early books of the Bible—best describes Hebrew culture around 1100 B.C.E., and not that probably in existence 800 years earlier.[11]

The Old Testament suggests that about 1550 B.C.E., driven by famine, some Hebrews followed Abraham's great-grandson Joseph into Egypt. Joseph's possible rise to power in Egypt and hospitable reception of his people there may be attributed to the presence of the largely Semitic Hyksos, who had conquered Egypt about 1720 B.C.E. Following the expulsion of the Hyksos by the pharaohs of the Eighteenth Dynasty, the biblical account states that the Hebrews were enslaved by the Egyptians. Shortly after 1300 B.C.E. a Hebrew leader named Moses led them out of bondage and into the wilderness of Sinai, where they entered into a pact or covenant with their God, Yahweh. The Sinai Covenant bound the people as a whole—the nation of Israel, as they now called themselves—to worship Yahweh before all other gods and to obey his Law (Torah). In return, Yahweh made the Israelites his chosen people, whom he would protect and to whom he granted Canaan, the Promised Land "flowing with milk and honey." The history of Israel from this time on is held by Jewish people to be the account of the fulfillment of this covenant.

There are no indications in Egyptian sources of a large number of Hebrews enslaved in Egypt after the Hyksos were expelled; at the same time, there are no reasons to believe that such treatment of Semitic peoples who remained in Egypt after the Hyksos did not occur. Hebrew tradition identifies Moses as the leader and eventual liberator of the Hebrews in Egypt and their leader during the Exodus (the "Road Out" in Greek), but Egyptian records give no mention of him, the demands he made of Pharaoh, or the plagues the Hebrew god supposedly visited on Egypt.

The Old Testament account of the Exodus from Egypt ends when the Israelites are led through the Sinai and arrive after 40 years of wandering in sight of Palestine. Here, they had to contend with the Canaanites, whose Semitic ancestors had migrated from Arabia early in the third millennium B.C.E. Joined by other Hebrew tribes already in Palestine, the Israelites formed a **confederacy** of 12 tribes, led by leaders called judges, and in time succeeded in subjugating the Canaanites. The biblical account of the conquest of Palestine records a bloody history of conquest and destruction of those Canaanite cities that resisted Hebrew domination—a feat mainly accomplished through the brilliant military leadership of a hero named Joshua. Recent archaeology reveals a different view: that the Hebrew occupation of Palestine was a long and slow process and that the massive destruction of Canaanite cities by Israelites as recorded in the Old Testament is not affirmed by archaeological remains. Rather, the Hebrews seemed to have absorbed, to have been absorbed, and at times to have lived in peace along with already established Canaanite communities in the region.

Leadership of the Israelites in this effort to claim their promised land seems to have been exercised by both men and women called judges—individuals among the twelve tribes of Israel who had shown uncommon degrees of courage (Judith), strength (Sampson), or divine inspiration (Samuel). The active

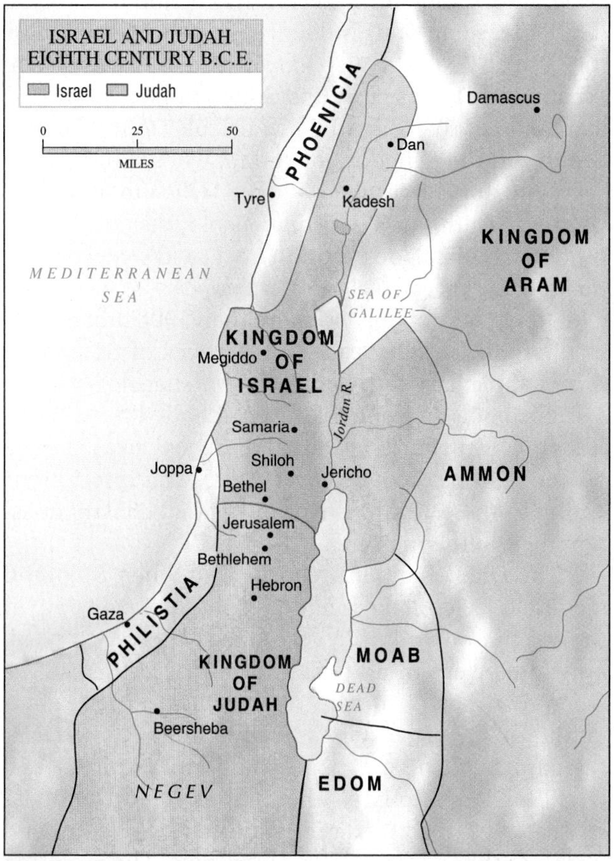

In the eighth century B.C.E., the Hebrew kingdoms of Israel and Judah often found themselves in opposition to each other, as well as being surrounded by potentially more powerful enemies.

---

confederacy—A system of government in which power is shared between existing political units with no single unit having authority over the others.

and decisive role the Old Testament attributes to Israelite women reflects the great influence they must have exercised in early Israel. Genesis describes the two sexes as being equal and necessary for human livelihood: "So God created mankind in his image, . . . male and female he created them. And God blessed them and said to them, 'Be fruitful and multiply and fill the earth and subdue it [together]'" (1:27–28). And in the Song of Songs the maiden and the youth share equally in the desire and expression of love; there is no sense of subordination of one to the other. But the continuing dangers that faced the nation led to the creation of a strong centralized monarchy, and with it came male domination and female subordination.

As the Israelites were contesting the Canaanites for dominance of the region, an even more formidable opponent appeared. The Philistines, Sea Peoples that had tried unsuccessfully to invade Egypt, and from whom the name Palestine comes, settled along the coast of Israel about 1175 B.C.E. Aided by the use of iron weapons, which were new to the region and the Hebrews, the Philistines captured the Ark of the Covenant, the sacred chest described as having mysterious powers, in which Moses had placed stone tablets inscribed with the Ten Commandments entrusted to him by Yahweh. By the middle of the eleventh century B.C.E. the Philistines appear to have been on course to dominate the entire land.

Lacking a central authority, the loose 12-tribe confederacy of Israel could not hope to ward off the Philistine danger, and a king, Saul, was chosen to unify resistance to the Philistines.

According to the Bible, Saul's reign (c. 1020–1000 B.C.E.) was not successful. Continuously undercut by tribal rivalries and overshadowed by the fame of the boy hero David, who came to prominence by slaying the Philistine giant Goliath in single combat, Saul made no attempt to transform Israel into a centralized monarchy. Saul's successor, the popular David (c. 1000–961 B.C.E.), is credited with restricting the Philistines to a narrow coastal strip to the south of Israel, and also with the consolidation of an impressively large and unified state. David also won Jerusalem from the Canaanites and made it the private domain of his royal court, separate from the existing 12 tribes. His popularity was enhanced when he placed the recovered Ark of the Covenant in his royal chapel, to which he attached a priesthood.

David was succeeded by his son Solomon (961–922 B.C.E.), under whom the Bible says Israel reached its highest degree of power and splendor as a monarchy. But the price of Solomon's vast bureaucracy, building projects (especially the palace complex and the Temple at Jerusalem), standing army (1400 chariots and 12,000 horses), and harem (700 wives and 300 concubines) was great. High taxes, forced labor, and tribal rivalries led to dissension.

Recently, archaeologists have called the Old Testament accounts of the glorious reigns of David and Solomon into question. Some scholars even suggest that a united monarchy never existed, and that even if it did, the extent of its influence is vastly overstated by the Bible. Experts also suggest that the biblical accounts of David's glory and Solomon's wealth are the work of later rulers, dating in particular to the seventh century in the Kingdom of Judah, whose rulers were searching for a glorious past upon which to base their claims of legitimacy.[12] Most archaeologists now concur that the biblical description of David's power and might is exaggerated. Jerusalem appears to have been a hill town of probably no more than 5000 inhabitants in the tenth century B.C.E., and traces of Solomon's great temple have so far evaded the archaeologists. The existence of a dynasty of kings descended from David (the so-called House of David) has been claimed to be proven by the recent discovery of several inscriptions dating to the eighth century, but other scholars question their authenticity.

The Old Testament records that when Solomon died in 922 B.C.E., the kingdom split in two—Israel in the north and Judah in the south. These two weak kingdoms were in no position to defend themselves when new, powerful empires rose again in Mesopotamia. In 722 B.C.E. the Assyrians captured Samaria, the capital of the northern kingdom, taking 27,290 Israelites into captivity (the famous "ten lost tribes" of Israel; two remained in the southern kingdom) and settling other subjects of their empire. The resulting population, called Samaritans, was ethnically, culturally, and religiously mixed, as well as deprived of any political role.

The Hebrews

c. 1800 B.C.E.	Migration of Hebrews to Palestine
c. 1550 B.C.E.	Migration to Egypt
c. 1300–1200 B.C.E.	Exodus from Egypt
c. 1020–1000 B.C.E.	Reign of Saul
c. 1000–961 B.C.E.	Reign of David
961–922 B.C.E.	Reign of Solomon
722 B.C.E.	Northern kingdom destroyed by Assyria
586 B.C.E.	Southern kingdom destroyed by Chaldeans
586–538 B.C.E.	Babylonian Captivity

The southern kingdom of Judah held out until 586 B.C.E., when Nebuchadnezzar, the Chaldean ruler of Babylon, destroyed Jerusalem and carried away a large number of its residents to his capital city. This deportation began the so-called Babylonian Captivity of the Jews (Judeans), which lasted until 538 B.C.E. While held in Babylon, the Jews were considered to be free people, allowed to engage in commerce and industry, and to practice their own religion. Some Jews abandoned their religious traditions, but most seem to have held strongly to them. It was in Babylon that the first synagogues (Greek for "gathering together") came into existence, as the Jewish communities assembled for worship and study.

DOCUMENT
Suffering Explained

In 538 B.C.E. Cyrus the Great, the king of Persia, conquered Babylon, and allowed the captives to return to Jerusalem. In 515 B.C.E. the returning exiles completed the reconstruction of the Temple destroyed by Nebuchadnezzar. But large numbers of believers never returned to Judah, which was now referred to as Judea by the Persian governors who administered it. These Jews, scattered all over the region, formed communities of worship in their cities of residence, and membership in these communities of believers became an essential component in the lives of the participants. By 500 B.C.E. the majority of Jewish believers lived outside Palestine. This "scattering" (*diaspora* in Greek) was to be a significant characteristic of Jewish existence from this time forward in their history.

The mostly peaceful Persian rule in Judea was followed by the conquest of Palestine by Alexander the Great in 332 B.C.E. After Alexander's death Judea was part of the empire ruled by the Ptolemaic dynasty of Egypt, and in 63 B.C.E. it became a Roman protectorate. Roman administration proved especially rigid and unpopular with the Jews. In 70 C.E. a revolt of the Jews against their Roman rulers was crushed, the city of Jerusalem and the temple destroyed, and the history of the Jews as a political entity ended until the twentieth century. The resulting *diaspora* from their troubled homeland sent the Jews to all the major cities of the Mediterranean, where many became influenced by the culture of the Greco-Roman world, even while others strictly adhered to their traditional beliefs and customs emphasized through instruction in the synagogues.

Hebrew Religion

The Bible states that from the time of Abraham, the Hebrews worshiped one stern, warlike tribal god whose name was not revealed to the Hebrews until the time of Moses. Yet there are traces in the Old Testament of an earlier stage of religious development that shows evidence of animism and a reverence for spirits associated with the winds, stones, and sacred springs. Gradually, beliefs became more sophisticated and developed into a worship of **anthropomorphic** gods. The god of Abraham was a god closely associated with Abraham's clan or tribe. Hebrew religion entered a more sophisticated stage of development around the thirteenth century B.C.E., when Moses is credited with directing the Hebrews toward the worship of a national god, the god of Abraham now revealed to be named Yahweh. The religion of Moses may be called monolatry—the belief that there is one god for that god's select people, but that there may exist other gods for other peoples.

Moses is credited in the Bible with being the recipient of God's law in the form of the Ten Commandments, and the leader who, with Yahweh's assistance, led the Hebrews from Egypt to the Promised Land. After their entrance into Palestine, many Hebrews adopted the **polytheism** of the Canaanites as well as the luxurious Canaanite manner of living. As a result, prophets arose who "spoke for" Yahweh (*prophetes* is Greek for "one who speaks for God"), insisting on strict adherence to the laws delivered by Moses. Between 750 and 550 B.C.E. a series of these prophets wrote down their messages and insisted that disaster would result if Yahweh's chosen people strayed from proper worship. They also developed the idea of a coming Messiah (the "anointed one" of God), a descendant of King David, who would begin a reign of peace and justice.

The destruction of Jerusalem in 586 B.C.E. and the exile in Babylon was another formative event in the evolution of Jewish thought. In accord with the prophetic warnings, Yahweh had punished his chosen people, yet the prophets also foretold that they would be allowed to return to Jerusalem and be reconfirmed as the chosen of God. Many scholars believe that the time spent in Babylon was crucial to the final achievement of true monotheism by Jewish thinkers: the destruction of Yahweh's holy city was not a sign of His weakness, but rather a sign of His power and universality, and His people's journey would serve as proof to all mankind of His glory. The Jews who returned from the Babylonian Captivity were provided a renewed faith in their destiny and a new understanding of their significance in human history.

The Aramaeans

Closely related to the Hebrews were the Aramaeans (ah-rah-MAY-ens), who occupied Syria east of the Lebanon Mountains. The most important of their little kingdoms was centered at Damascus, one of the oldest

---

anthropomorphic—Literally, "human shaped"; endowed with human characteristics.

polytheism—Belief in many gods. Though Judaism, Christianity, and Islam are monotheistic, most other religions throughout history have been polytheistic. The numerous gods may be dominated by a supreme god or a group of gods.

continuously inhabited cities in the world. The Aramaeans dominated the camel caravan trade connecting Mesopotamia, Phoenicia, and Egypt and continued to do so even after Damascus fell to the Assyrians in 732 B.C.E. The Aramaic language, which used an alphabet similar to the Phoenician, became the international language of the Mesopotamian region and the northeastern Mediterranean coast by the fifth century B.C.E. In Judea it was more commonly spoken than Hebrew among the lower classes, and was the language spoken by Jesus and his disciples.

Assyria

c. 1350 B.C.E.	Assyrian rise to power
704–681 B.C.E.	Military power at height
669–626 B.C.E.	Reign of Ashurbanipal
612 B.C.E.	Fall of Nineveh

The Assyrian Empire, c. 550–331 B.C.E.

By 700 B.C.E. the era of small states had ended with the emergence of a powerful Assyrian Empire. Two of the greatest achievements of the Assyrians were the forcible unification of weak, unstable regions of Mesopotamia and the establishment of an efficient and centralized imperial organization.

For two centuries before 700 B.C.E. the Assyrians had been attempting to transform the growing economic prosperity of northern and central Mesopotamia into a political unity. The Assyrian attempt to dominate the region began in the ninth century B.C.E; after a short period of weakness, the Assyrian monarchy regained its effectiveness in the eighth century, when the state also took over Babylon. By 671 B.C.E. the Assyrians had annexed Egypt and were the masters of the entire Fertile Crescent.

A Semitic people long residing in the hilly region of the upper Tigris, the Assyrians had experienced a thousand years of constant warfare. But their matchless army was only one of several factors that explain the success of Assyrian imperialism: a policy of calculated terrorism, an efficient system of political administration, and the support of the commercial classes that wanted political stability and unrestricted trade over large areas.

The Assyrian army, with its chariots, mounted cavalry, and sophisticated siege engines, was the most powerful ever seen in the ancient world before 700 B.C.E. Neither troops nor walls could long resist the Assyrians, whose military might seemed unstoppable. Conquered peoples were held firmly in control by systematic policies designed to terrorize. Mass deportations, like that of the Israelites, were employed as an effective means of destroying national feeling.

The well-coordinated Assyrian system of political administration was another factor in the success of the empire. Conquered lands became provinces ruled by governors who exercised extensive military, judicial, and financial powers. Their chief tasks were to ensure the regular collection of tribute (payments demanded by the conquerors) and the raising of troops for the permanent and professional army that eventually replaced the native militia of sturdy Assyrian peasants. An efficient system of communications carried the "king's word" to the governors as well as the latter's reports to the royal court—including one prophetic dispatch reading: "The king knows that all lands hate us." Nevertheless, the Assyrians should be credited with laying the foundations for some elements of the later more humane administrative systems of their successors, the Persians and Alexander the Great of Macedonia.

Assyrian Culture

The Assyrians borrowed from the cultures of other peoples and unified the elements into a new product. This is evident in Assyrian architecture and sculpture, the work of subject artisans and artists. Both arts glorified the power of the Assyrian king. The palace, serving as both residence and administrative center, replaced the temple as the characteristic architectural form. A feature of Assyrian palace architecture was the structural use of the arch and the column, both

This ancient Assyrian relief, The Dying Lion, is an example of a common theme in royal Assyrian sculpture. The prowess of the Assyrian king as hunter and leader was often emphasized through such artistic themes.

borrowed from Babylonia. Palaces were decorated with splendid relief sculptures that glorified the king as warrior and hunter. Assyrian sculptors were especially skilled in portraying realistically the ferocity and agony of charging and dying lions.

Assyrian kings were interested in preserving written as well as pictorial records of their reigns. King Ashurbanipal (ah-shoor-BAH-ni-pahl; 669–626 B.C.E.), for example, left a record of his great efforts in collecting the literary heritage of Sumer and Babylon. The 22,000 clay tablets found in the ruins of his palace at Nineveh (NI-neh-vah), in today's northern Iraq, provided modern scholars with their first direct knowledge of the bulk of this literature, which included the Sumerian *Epic of Gilgamesh.*

Downfall of the Assyrian Empire

Revolt against Assyrian terror and tribute was inevitable when Assyria's strength weakened and united opposition to Assyrian terror arose. By the middle of the seventh century B.C.E. the Assyrians had been destroyed by wars, and the Assyrian kings had to use unreliable mercenary troops and conscripted subjects. Egypt regained its independence from the Assyrians under the Twenty-Sixth Dynasty, and the Medes to the north refused to pay further tribute. The Chaldeans, tribal groups of Semites who had migrated into Babylonia, revolted in 626 B.C.E. In 612 B.C.E. they joined the Medes in destroying Nineveh, the Assyrian capital. With the fall of the capital city, Assyrian dominance was ended, much to the general satisfaction of the subjects of the Assyrian overlords.

The Lydians and the Medes

The fall of Assyria left four states to struggle over the remains of their empire: the Chaldeans and Egypt fought for control of Syria and Palestine, and Media and Lydia clashed over eastern Asia Minor.

After the collapse of the Hittite Empire about 1200 B.C.E., the Lydians succeeded in establishing a kingdom in western Asia Minor. When Assyria fell, the Lydians expanded eastward until stopped by the Medes at the Halys River, in central Turkey. Lydia profited from being in control of part of the commercial land route between Mesopotamia and the Aegean Sea, and from the possession of valuable gold-bearing streams. About 675 B.C.E. the Lydians invented coinage, which replaced the silver bars in general use up to that time. Lydia's most famous king was Croesus (KREE-sus), a monarch whose wealth was legendary. With the king's defeat by the Persians in 547 B.C.E., Lydia ceased to exist as an independent state.

The Medes were an Indo-European people who by 1000 B.C.E. had established themselves on the Iranian plateau east of Assyria. By the seventh century B.C.E. they had created in Media a strong kingdom with Ecbatana (ek-bah-TAH-nah) as its capital and with the Persians, their kinsmen to the south, as their subjects. Following the collapse of Assyria, the Medes expanded into Armenia and eastern Asia Minor, but their short-lived empire ended in 550 B.C.E. when they, too, were absorbed by the Persians.

The Chaldean (New Babylonian) Empire

While the Median kingdom controlled the northern Iranian plateau, the Chaldeans, with their capital at Babylon, became masters of the fertile crescent. Nebuchadnezzar, who had become king of the Chaldeans in 604 B.C.E., raised Babylonia to another epoch of brilliance after more than a thousand years of eclipse. By defeating the Egyptians in Syria, Nebuchadnezzar ended Egyptian hopes of recreating their empire. As we have seen, he destroyed Jerusalem in 586 B.C.E. and took thousands of captured Jews to Babylonia.

Nebuchadnezzar rebuilt the city of Babylon, making it the largest and most impressive urban center of its day. The tremendous city walls were wide enough at the top to have rows of small houses on either side. In the center of Babylon ran the famous Procession Street, which passed through the Ishtar Gate. This arch, which was adorned with brilliant tile animals, is the best remaining example of Babylonian architecture. The immense palace of Nebuchadnezzar towered terrace upon terrace, each decorated with masses of ferns, flowers, and trees. These roof gardens, the famous Hanging Gardens of Babylon, were so beautiful that they were regarded by the Greeks as one of the seven wonders of the ancient world.

Nebuchadnezzar was the last great Mesopotamian ruler, and Chaldean power quickly crumbled after his death in 562 B.C.E. Chaldean priests, whose interests included political intrigue as well as astrology, continually undermined the monarchy. Finally, in 539 B.C.E. they opened the gates of Babylon to Cyrus the Persian, allowing him to add Babylon to his impressive new empire.

THE PERSIAN EMPIRE, 550–331 B.C.E.

▪ *In what ways were the Persians innovators, and how did they also incorporate the legacies of earlier Mesopotamian societies?*

Cyrus the Persian was the greatest conqueror in the history of the ancient Near East. In 550 B.C.E. he ended Persian subjugation to the Medes by captur-

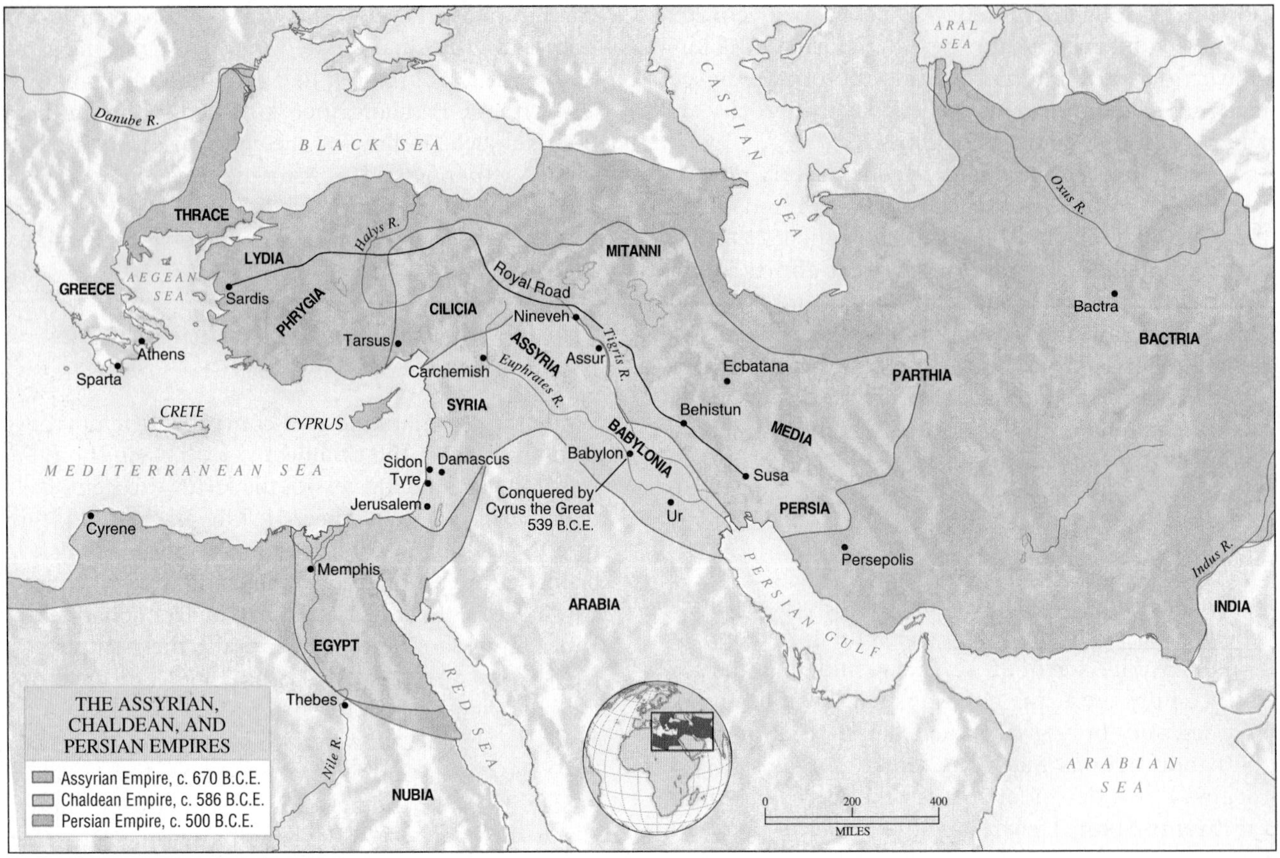

After the seventh century B.C.E. *three great empires dominated the Mesopotamian region and sought to extend their control. The Assyrian Empire extended its might into Egypt, the Chaldean into the region of the Fertile Crescent, and the Persian from Egypt in the west to the Indus River in the east.*

ing Ecbatana and ending the Median dynasty. Most of the Medes readily accepted their vigorous new ruler, who soon demonstrated that he deserved to be called "the Great." When King Croesus of Lydia moved across the Halys River in 547 B.C.E. to pick up some of the pieces of the collapsed Median Empire, Cyrus defeated him and annexed Lydia, including Greek cities on the coast of Asia Minor that were under Lydia's nominal control. Then he turned his attention eastward, establishing his power as far as the frontier of India. Babylon and its empire were also annexed to the great Persian Empire.

After Cyrus died, his son Cambyses (cam-BAI-seez; 530–522 B.C.E.) conquered Egypt. The next ruler, Darius I (522–486 B.C.E.), added the Punjab region in India and Thrace in Europe. He also began a conflict with the Greeks that continued intermittently for more than 150 years until the Persians were conquered by Alexander the Great in 331 B.C.E.

DOCUMENT
Darius the Great

Persian Government

Although built on the Assyrian model, the Persian administrative system was far more efficient and humane. The empire was divided into 20 *satrapies,* or provinces, each ruled by a governor called a *satrap.* To check the satraps, a secretary and a military official representing the "Great King, King of Kings" were installed in every province. Also, special inspectors, "the Eyes and Ears of the King," traveled throughout the realm. Imperial post roads connected the important cities. Along the Royal Road between Sardis and Susa there was a post station every 14 miles, where the king's couriers could obtain fresh horses, enabling them to cover the 1600-mile route in a week.

The Persian Empire was the first to attempt to govern many different racial groups on the principle

Persia

c. 600 B.C.E.	Union under Achaemenid kings
559–530 B.C.E.	Reign of Cyrus the Great
550 B.C.E.	Conquest of Median Empire
539 B.C.E.	Conquest of Babylon
530–522 B.C.E.	Reign of Cambyses
522–486 B.C.E.	Reign of Darius I

of equal responsibilities and rights for all peoples. So long as subjects paid their taxes and kept the peace, the king did not interfere with local religion, customs, or trade. Indeed, Darius was called "the shopkeeper" because he stimulated trade by introducing a uniform system of gold and silver coinage on the Lydian model.

Persian Religion and Art

The humaneness of the Persian rulers may have stemmed from the ethical religion founded by the prophet Zoroaster, who lived in the early sixth century B.C.E. Zoroaster attempted to replace what he called "the lie"—ritualistic, idol-worshipping cults and their Magi priests—with a religion centered on the sole god Ahura-Mazda ("Wise Lord"). This "father of Justice" demanded "good thoughts of the mind, good deeds of the hand, and good words of the tongue" from those who would attain paradise (a Persian word). This new higher religion made little progress until first Darius and then the Magi adopted it. The Magi revived many old gods as lesser deities, added much ritual, and replaced monotheism with dualism by transforming what Zoroaster had called the principle or spirit of evil into the powerful god Ahriman (the model for the Jewish Satan), the rival of Ahura-Mazda, "between which each man must choose for himself."

The complicated evolution of Zoroastrianism is revealed in its holy book, the Avesta ("The Law"), assembled in its present form between the fourth and sixth centuries C.E. Zoroastrian **eschatology**—the "doctrine

eschatology—Theological doctrine of the "last things," or the end of the world.

Document — The Majesty of Darius the Great: A Persian Royal Inscription

The Persian kings ruled their vast empire with absolute authority. But these kings were not regarded as divine beings ruling without responsibility. The power of the king had to be exercised in a reasonable and ethical manner, and in accord with the precepts of the great god of the Persians, Ahura-Mazda. The following inscription, attributed to King Darius the Great, was intended to show the Persian people that the king was an able and powerful monarch, but in addition a just and merciful administrator of his responsibilities:

A great god is Ahuramazda who created this excellent work which one sees; who created happiness for man; who bestowed wisdom and energy upon Darius the king. Says Darius the king: by the favour of Ahuramazda I am of such a kind that I am a friend to what is right, I am no friend to what is wrong. It is not my wish that to the weak is done wrong because of the mighty, it is not my wish that the weak is hurt because of the mighty, that the mighty is hurt because of the weak. What is right, that is my wish. I am no friend of the man who is a follower of the lie. I am not hot-tempered. When I feel anger rising, I keep that under control by my thinking power. I control firmly my impulses. The man who co-operates, him do I reward according to his co-operation. He who does harm, him I punish according to the damage. It is not my wish that a man does harm, it is certainly not my wish that a man if he causes damage be not punished. What a man says against a man, that does not convince me, until I have heard testimony(?) from both parties. What a man does or performs according to his powers, satisfies me, therewith I am satisfied and it gives me great pleasure and I am very satisfied and I give much to faithful men.

I am trained with both hands and feet. As a horseman I am a good horseman. As a bowman I am a good bowman, both afoot and on horseback. As a spearman I am a good spearman, both afoot and on horseback. And the skills which Ahuramazda has bestowed upon me and I have had the strength to use them, by the favour of Ahuramazda, what has been done by me, I have done with these skills which Ahuramazda has bestowed upon me.

Questions to Consider

1. What might have been the purpose of this inscription? What might have been its effect on the king's subjects who read it?
2. How does the inscription give the impression that the king's authority is unquestioned?
3. Why do you think that references to the king's skill as a hunter and a bowman are included? Are his exploits overstated or modestly listed? What purpose did these references to physical skills have?

From B. Gharib, "A Newly Found Inscription of Xerxes," *Franica Antiqua*, 1968, as quoted in Amélie Kuhrt, *The Ancient Near East: c. 3000–330 B.C.E.*, Vol. 2 (London: Routledge, 1995), p. 681.

of final things" such as the resurrection of the dead and a last judgment—also influenced later Judaism. Following the Muslim conquest of Persia in the seventh century C.E., Zoroastrianism virtually disappeared in its homeland. It exists today among the Parsees in India and in scattered communities worldwide.

In art the Persians borrowed largely from their predecessors in the fertile crescent, particularly the Assyrians. Their most important contribution was in palace architecture, the best remains of which are now found at Persepolis. Built on a high terrace in southern Iran, the royal residence was reached by a grand stairway faced with beautiful reliefs. Instead of the warfare and violence that characterized Assyrian sculpture, these reliefs depict hundreds of soldiers, courtiers, and representatives of 23 nations of the empire bringing gifts to the king for the festival of the new year.

CONCLUSION

During the Paleolithic and Neolithic periods, several technological and agricultural advances gave humans the opportunity to spread and adapt to different parts of the world. Increasingly sophisticated tools and techniques of operation allowed humans to hunt and gain control over diverse environments, while the transition from good gathering to food production made it possible for the development of the first significant civilizations along the banks of rivers.

In the second half of the fourth millennium B.C.E, the first major civilizations, Mesopotamia and Egypt, originated in river valleys: one by the Tigris and Euphrates and one by the Nile. In each instance, the complex society we call a civilization was the result of organized and cooperative efforts that were necessary to make the rivers useful to humans living along them.

Cooperation and centralized leadership resulted in interdependent urban living—the quest for order in a challenging, disorderly world. Through centralized control of religion, these early civilizations sought to understand the gods and establish harmony with them. Through creativity and inventiveness—bronze tools and weapons, the wheel, writing, and law, either in written form or revealed through the person of pharaoh—social order was established in the first cities.

Mesopotamian civilization originated in the land called Sumer. The achievements of the Sumerians served as a foundation for later Mesopotamian civilizations established by Semitic peoples migrating into the river valleys. The most significant of these later Semitic civilizations was the Babylonian Empire ruled by Hammurabi. Babylon was sacked by the Indo-European Hittites of Asia Minor, who went on to duel with Egypt over control of Syria and Palestine.

In Egypt a great civilization arose on the banks of the Nile, a civilization both monumental and timeless. The temples and tombs of the Egyptian monarchs were designed to endure forever and to preserve the satisfying and stable existence of this world into eternity. Egypt centered on the absolute rule of the pharaohs—god-kings who eventually extended their domain from Nubia to the Euphrates River.

By 1200 B.C.E. the great Near Eastern empires—Babylonian, Egyptian, and Hittite—had weakened, allowing the Semitic peoples of Syria and Palestine more opportunity to make their own cultural contributions. Although never a powerful political force in the ancient world, Israel would have a momentous impact on the future through its development of a sophisticated and influential religious tradition. Political diversity had ended by the rise of the Assyrian Empire, which unified the ancient Near East for the first time. After the fall of Assyria, the Chaldean Nebuchadnezzar constructed a new Babylonian Empire, but it was soon engulfed by the expansion of Persia. Stretching from India to Europe, the Persian Empire gave the Near East its greatest extension and power.

The achievements of these early civilizations would become the inheritance of the Greeks and eventually the Romans. Much of the social and cultural legacy of the ancient Near East remains preserved in the fabric of those Mediterranean societies, which rose to political and cultural prominence after the first civilizations declined in vitality.

Suggestions for Web Browsing

You can obtain more information about topics included in this chapter at the websites listed below. See also the companion website that accompanies this text, **http://www.ablongman.com/brummett**, which contains an online study guide and additional resources.

Fossil Hominids: Mary Leakey
http://www.talkorigins.org/faqs/homs/mleakey.html

Discussion, with images, of the life and findings of one of the twentieth century's most famous archaeologists. Links to husband Louis Leakey, son Richard Leakey, Olduvai Gorge, and fossil findings.

Human Prehistory: An Exhibition
http://users.hol.gr/~dilos/prehis.htm

Walk through six rooms of text and vivid images that discuss the works of Lyell, Huxley, and Darwin; the first humans; the first human creations; the first villages, including Çatal Hüyük, and artworks of Neolithic Greece.

Chauvet Cave
http://www.culture.gouv.fr/culture/arcnat/chauvet/en/

A French government site on a major discovery of prehistoric cave art. Contains information about the findings and many views of cave paintings at this location and others in France.

Neanderthal Museum
http://www.neanderthal.de/

Site of a German museum whose goals are to maintain and popularize the cultural heritage of the Neanderthals.

Oriental Institute Virtual Museum
http://www-oi.uchicago.edu/OI/MUS/QTVR96/QTVR96.html

An integral part of the University of Chicago's Oriental Institute, the Oriental Institute Museum offers a virtual showcase of the history, art, and archaeology of the ancient Near East.

Hammurabi
http://home.echo-on.net/~smithda/hammurabi.html

A short biography of Hammurabi, in addition to a discussion of the legal concepts he espoused in his code and a virtual recreation of the Hanging Gardens of Babylon.

Egyptian Museum
http://www.egyptianmuseum.gov.eg/

Website of the Egyptian Museum in Cairo, highlighting images of accessories and jewelry, sculptures, furniture, mummies, and written documents of ancient Egypt from the museum's enormous collection.

Museums of the Vatican: Gregorian Egyptian Museum
http://www.christusrex.org/www1/vaticano/EG-Egiziano.html

The Vatican Museum's Egyptian Museum provides images and descriptions of many of the significant objects in one of the world's best ancient Egyptian museums.

Nubia: The Land Upriver
http://ancientneareast.tripod.com/Nubia.html

The geography and early history of the Nubian peoples, from prehistoric times to the kingdom of Kush.

The Hittite Home Page
http://www.asor.org/HITTITE/HittiteHP.html

A website devoted to all things Hittite, including a useful list of links to various universities conducting excavations of Hittite sites.

Material Culture of the Ancient Canaanites, Israelites, and Related Peoples: An Information Database from Excavations
http://www.bu.edu/anep/

This site contains hundreds of images of artifacts such as weapons, tools, and jewelry, with brief histories of the cultures described.

World Cultures: Mesopotamia and Persia
http://www.wsu.edu:8080/~dee/MESO/PERSIANS.HTM

This site gives valuable information on the influence of geography on early Persian civilization, reviews Persian military history, and discusses the importance of Persian religion.

Literature and Film

Selections of Egyptian literature are presented in John Foster, *Echoes of Egyptian Voices: An Anthology of Ancient Egyptian Poetry* (University of Oklahoma Press, 1992), and R. B. Parkinson, trans. and ed., *Voices from Ancient Egypt: An Anthology of Middle Kingdom Writings* (University of Oklahoma Press, 1991).

Stephanie Dalley, ed., *Myths from Mesopotamia: Creation, the Flood, Gilgamesh, and Others* (Oxford University Press, 1998), is an excellent compilation from a variety of Mesopotamian cultures. Danny Jackson et al., eds., *The Epic of Gilgamesh* (Bolchazy Carducci, 1997), is a unique modern translation of the epic poem.

Two excellent videos are *Ancient Mesopotamia* (Schlessinger Media, 1998), and the six-video set presented by Bill Moyers on *Genesis* (PBS, 1998), in which an impressive array of experts discuss the implications and meaning of the biblical account.

Three other videos stand out: *Egypt—Beyond the Pyramids* (History Channel, 2001). This film investigates recent archaeological discoveries in Egypt, including tombs of pharaohs, temples, and cemeteries. *In Search of Human Origins* (NOVA PBS, 1994) is a three-part documentary that explores the search for human origins by scientists. *In search of History: Akhenaten: Egypt's Heretic King* (Arts and Entertainment, 1998) is a documentary portrait of Akhenaton's life and his impact on Egyptian religion and art and an exploration of his capital city, Akhetaton.

Suggestions for Reading

For comprehensive accounts of the human fossil record, the evolution of the human brain and cognitive powers, and the significance of lithic art, see Ian Tattersall, *Becoming Human: Evolution and Human Uniqueness* (Harcourt Brace, 1998), and Donald C. Johanson and Blake Edgar, *From Lucy to Language* (Simon & Schuster, 1996).

On human evolution and the spread of humankind from Africa to the rest of the world, see Noel T. Boaz, *Eco Homo: How the Human Being Emerged from the Cataclysmic History of the Earth* (HarperCollins, 1997); Ian Tattersall, *The Last Neanderthal: The Rise, Success, and Mysterious Extinction of Our Closest Relatives* (Westview Press, 1999); and Christopher Stringer and Robin McKie, *African Exodus: The Origins of Modern Humanity* (Henry Holt, 1997). Jared Diamond's *Guns, Germs and Steel: The Fates of Human Societies* (W. W. Norton, 1997) examines the impact of environment on the development of human societies in different parts of the world.

A work that deals with the origins of toolmaking in a broad cultural matrix is Kathy Schick and Nicholas Toth, *Making Silent Stones Speak: Human Evolution and the Dawn of Technology* (Simon & Schuster, 1993). On early communities, see Tim Megarry, *Society in Prehistory: The Origins of Human Culture* (New York University Press, 1996).

Fundamental forms of expression in primeval art, symbolization, the role of animals, depiction of the human figure (including fertility figurines), and the conception of space in prehistory are dealt with in Sigfried Giedion's *The Eternal Present: The Beginnings of Art* (Pantheon, 1962).

The debate between the "Out of Africa" and multiregional schools is treated in Milford Wolpoff and Rachel Caspari, *Race and Human Evolution: A Fatal Attraction* (Simon & Schuster, 1997) and Christopher Stringer and Rachel McKie, *African Exodus: The Origins of Modern Humans* (Henry Holt, 1997).

Amélie Kuhrt, *The Ancient Near East,* 2 vols. (Routledge, 1995), is an outstanding and useful overview of Mesopotamia to 330 B.C.E. William W. Hallo and William Kelly Simpson, *The Ancient Near East: A History* (Harcourt Brace, 1998), remains a good standard text. Jean Bottero et al., *Everyday Life in Ancient Mesopotamia* (Johns Hopkins University Press, 2001) gives an excellent account of the culture. Surveys of Egyptian history include Nicolas Grimal, *A History of Ancient Egypt,* trans. Ian Shaw (Blackwell, 1992), and the 14-volume *Cambridge Ancient History* (Cambridge University Press, 1970–1997). The history of Nubia and the kingdom of Kush is examined in Derek Welsby, *The Kingdom of Kush* (Wiener, 1998) and Stanley Burstein, ed., *Ancient African Civilizations: Kush and Axum* (Wiener, 1998). For the history and significance of the Hittites, see Trevor Bryce, *The Kingdom of the Hittites* (Oxford University Press, 1998). For two contrasting but well-researched interpretations of ancient Israel, see David J. Goldberg and John D. Rayner, *The Jewish People: Their History and Their Religion* (Viking, 1987), and I. Finkelstein and N. A. Silberman, *The Bible Unearthed* (The Free Press, 2001). Don Nardo, *The Persian Empire* (Lucent Books, 1998) and J. M. Cook, *The Persian Empire* (Barnes & Noble, 1998), are two of the best studies on ancient Persian history and culture.

CHAPTER

2

Ancient China—Origins to Empire

Prehistory to 220 C.E.

CHAPTER CONTENTS

6500 B.C.E.

c. 6500 Neolithic Culture in China (settled agricultural society)

1600

c. 1600–c.1027 Shang dynasty (kingship, writing system, bronze technology)

1200

c. 1027–221 Zhou dynasty

800

722–481 Spring and Autumn period

c. 551–c. 479 Life of Confucius (Kong Fuzi)

403–221 B.C.E. Period of Warring States

400

c. 372–289? Life of Mencius, Confucian advocate of good in human nature

c. 369–286 Life of Zhuangzi, Daoist celebrant of The Way

c. 310–c. 220 Life of Xunzi, Confucian advocate of need to reform human nature

221 Qin dynasty established; China united under First Emperor

213 Legalists order burning of books

206 B.C.E. Establishment of Han dynasty

100 B.C.E. Chinese silk

1 C.E.

45–116 Ban Zhao, Confucian woman scholar

66 First mention of Mahayana Buddhism

220 C.E. End of Han dynasty

The Neolithic Chinese people were a series of distinct, regional groups or cultures that have been traced back almost 10,000 years. By 200 C.E., the Chinese people belonged to an empire supported by trade routes in Asia and Africa, by a written history, and by rule by kings: they had a sense of commonality as Chinese. They also shared legendary heroes and heroines. Within both the empire and contending philosophies, there were strong attempts to maintain social differences—to keep an order that distinguished between Chinese and non-Chinese, rich and poor, and the feminine and the masculine both inside and outside the household. Such attempts at establishing and maintaining these distinctions did not always work.

Even with the maintenance of social differences during this formative period, in the face of often cataclysmic disasters, the Chinese maintained a zest for life. They reacted to human suffering by pursuing religious answers and by instituting ambitious innovations in all aspects of society from philosophy to economics. Throughout, the state retained its theoretical focus toward the amelioration of social evils and the relief of distress.

THE ORIGINS OF CHINA, 6500–221 B.C.E.

- *What developments in culture, politics, and philosophy molded prehistoric China into a civilization?*

The Neolithic Age: c. 6500–c.1600 B.C.E.

As in other parts of the world, there were tool-using humanoids *(homo erectus)* some 600,000 to 800,000 years ago on the Chinese subcontinent. Modern humans *(homo sapiens)* appeared in China around 100,000 years ago, and were hunters and gatherers during the Paleolithic period (c. 100,000–10,000 B.C.E.). They lived in a vast watershed, extending over 1000 miles from north to south and east to west and drained by two river systems that rise on the high Tibetan plateau and flow eastward to the Pacific. Three mountain ranges crisscross the river systems, diminishing in altitude as they slope eastward. The Huanghe (HWAHNG-HUH) or Yellow River crosses the highlands of the west, the deserts of the north, the hills filled with yellow silt called "loess," and the entire alluvial plain. The silt gradually builds up along the river bottom, requiring extensive dykes and river control to permit the development of agriculture. The Yangzi (YAHNG-zih) River forms the second river system. Emerging from the Tibetan highlands, it moves through gorges with cliffs 1000 or more feet high. Extensive drainage of the Yangzi valley over several centuries allowed rice agriculture to emerge in China's heartland.

Within the Chinese subcontinent, geographers have identified at least eight different ecosystems, ranging from the semitropical southeast, receiving as much as 5 feet of rain each year, to the desert-like northwest, which gets less than 4 inches of rain annu-

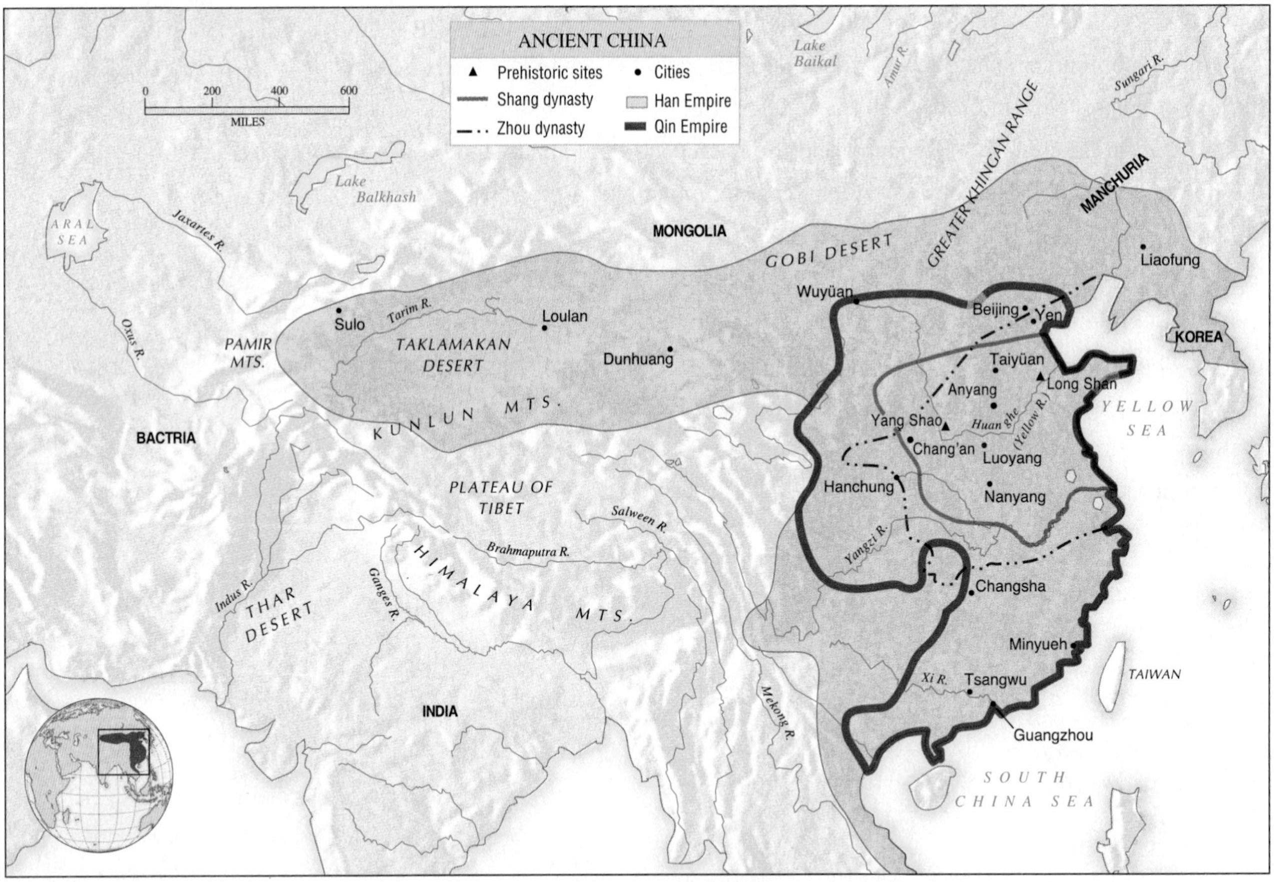

Ancient China's establishment and expansion were determined by key geographical factors. In addition to such divisions as those separating northern and southern cultures, determined by the Huanghe and Yangzi Rivers, there was geographic expansion incorporating independent peoples and states into one bureaucratic entity. By the end of the Han Empire, China had come close to achieving its natural geographic frontiers from the South China Sea to the Eurasian Steppes to the north, and the Himalayan mountains to the west. China was thus open to invasion from the north, west, and south, but conflict with "barbarians" was a stimulus to enormous cultural change.

ally. Geography, along with shifts in climate, determined the emergence of two main regional cultures by the Neolithic era.

Archaeological discoveries confirm the presence of Neolithic settlements in China before 5000 B.C.E. In each region, climate and rainfall affected the kinds of crops that were domesticated. Rice and water plants such as lotus and water chestnuts were grown in the warm, moist Yangzi valley and south of the Yangzi. Millet and wheat grew well in the drier climate of the north. In both north and south China, dogs, cattle, and pigs were raised, while buffalo were more common in the north and sheep in the south. Domestication of plants and animals in the Neolithic period may have been influenced by similar developments in West Asia, showing a sophisticated ability to adopt and develop techniques used elsewhere in Eurasia. Neolithic culture can also be divided into eastern and western geographic regions. The Yangshao (yahng-SHOW) culture of the western region (5000–3000 B.C.E.) produced geometrically painted pottery. The eastern region's culture produced beautifully crafted jade figurines and jewelry. By the late Neolithic period (3000–2000 B.C.E.), the techniques and skills were blended, as geometric designs moved westward and styles of pottery were shared. Interpreting cracks on heated bones inscribed with questions, called oracle bones, was also practiced in both areas. There is evidence that metallurgy began to be used to make weapons in this period.

Settlements surrounded by packed-earth walls appeared throughout North China. Located along the rivers, they sheltered their residents from aggressive actions of other communities. China's communities were very diverse in the Neolithic era. Some people lived in towns; some were nomadic. While the towns made institutional and technological advances, especially in the area of defense, the nomadic bands created their own effective weapons. The tension between the settled communities and the more nomadic bands had a decisive effect on the development of Chinese politics and culture.

Historians do not agree if a well-organized dynasty existed in China before the Shang dynasty in the Bronze Age. But the founding myths of China constructed a country defined by government and technology bequeathed by sage rulers. According to these myths, the earliest sages were Fu Xi (FOO SHEE), the Ox-tamer, credited with inventing the family and domesticating animals; Shen Nong, the Divine Farmer, who invented farming; and Huang Di (hoo-AHNG DEE), the Yellow King, who invented writing, silk, and pottery and was deemed the first of the **Five Sovereigns.** The last two of these five were Yao, who invented rituals, and Shun, a paragon of filial piety, who appointed wise officials. Shun's successor, Yu, is credited with developing flood control. Early historians considered Yu and his son the founders of a dynasty called Xia (shee-AH). Though such a centralized dynasty may not have existed (and is the object of debate among historians in China), the kinds of values attributed to its kings and sagely men before them created lasting Chinese institutions.

Preimperial History

before 1600 B.C.E.	"Xia"
c. 1600–1027 B.C.E.	Shang
1027–770 B.C.E.	Western Zhou
770–256 B.C.E.	Eastern Zhou
722–481 B.C.E.	Spring and Autumn period
403–221 B.C.E.	Warring States period

The sophistication of c. 4000 B.C.E. artisans can be seen in this Neolithic vessel. At the same time practical and pleasing to the eye, this bowl testifies to the aesthetic standards of everyday Chinese civilization.

Five Sovereigns—Mythical ancient kings who are believed to have ruled before hereditary dynastic succession was established.

The Bronze Age: The Shang Dynasty (c. 1600–c. 1027 B.C.E.)

The diverse cultures of northern China gave rise to a complex Bronze Age civilization sometime in the centuries after 2000 B.C.E. Several cultures remained in North China for a few centuries while one, the Shang, came to predominate by 1600 B.C.E. The Shang supposedly arose to conquer a particularly oppressive Xia overlord; the idea that sagely rule could give way, in later generations, to rule by corrupt descendents, had begun to take root. Over the 600 years of Shang rule, China developed even more complex systems of government, cities, writing, class and occupational stratification, religious ritual as the basis of the state, and sophisticated metallurgy.

Shang territorial control was not extensive, being located primarily around the Huanghe. But the spread of Shang culture stretched all the way to the Yangzi valley. In the area of Shang control, archaeological evidence of Shang capitals such as Zhengzhou (juhng-JOH) and, later, Anyang, indicates that the kings could exercise enormous power. They could demand the work of a large number of laborers and craftsmen to build their palaces and tombs. Zhengzhou, for instance, was surrounded by walls 2385 feet long, 60 feet wide, and 30 feet high. As their political and military fortunes varied, the rulers moved their capitals frequently during the six centuries of the Shang dynasty. The final Shang capital was at Anyang where the marshaling of resources and skills for the production of bronze artifacts also points to a concentration of power.

The Shang dynasty differed from its predecessors in more than simply the development of a sophisticated bronze metallurgy. Shang artisans, who lived in production centers surrounding the capital's power core with its palaces and temples, used bronze to make elaborate ceremonial and drinking vessels, weapons, pottery, and stone carvings. Not only were the bronze and other productions practical, but they were also works of art with both incised and high-relief designs. A common design was the animal mask, or *taotie* (TOW-tee-eh).

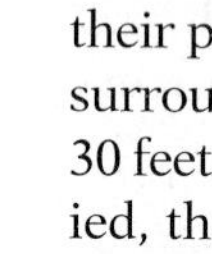

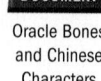

Oracle Bones and Chinese Characters

The Shang people used a system of writing that probably originated before their rule, as graphs are found on Neolithic pottery, though no documents predating Shang rule have yet been found. Shang writing can still be deciphered, because it was an early form of the same characters used in modern Chinese today. Shang writing was based on several thousand characters, some of which are **pictographs** and some of which represent sounds or meanings. Some Chinese characters consisted of two parts: one part indicating the topic of the word and the second expressing the sound. An example of the combination of two elements is the word for "family" or "home," which consists of the character for pig placed under a roof.

An Inscribed Oracle Bone

The Chinese writing system in later centuries served as the foundation for other written languages in East Asia, including Korean and Japanese. Because the writing system was not phonetic, it could be used to represent other languages as well as variations of Chinese in different locations and across the centuries. It could be imposed on conquered peoples who already spoke Chinese or a related language. Shang culture could even be extended beyond the boundaries of the king's control—including to those who spoke different languages—through transmission of ideas written in Chinese characters. Over the next three millennia, a certain degree of ideological conformity could be maintained even as diverse cultures and technological advances produced fundamental differences within China. Writing also served to advance government functions and increasingly sophisticated intellectual activities.

Most Shang writing is found on thousands of oracle bones, fragments of animal bones and tortoise shells. The religious diviners of the Shang kings dried the shells and bones and dug hollows in them to make the bones crack more easily. After the king relayed his question, the priests put a hot poker to the bones and interpreted the resulting cracks. Engravers then recorded these interpretations onto the bones. The written questions were directed at the ancestral spirits, who were believed to be closely tied to their living descendants as members of the family group. The living would ask the dead such questions as "Will the king's child be a son?" and "If we raise an army of 3000 men to drive *X* away from *Y*, will we succeed?" The practice of oracle bone divination was a form of religious ritual, accompanied by music, dancing, and animal or human sacrifices.

As the state and its activities grew more complex, the kings had to oversee not only fighting but also taxing and governing, processes facilitated by writing and record keeping. The leaders needed to record their decisions and to transmit them to their often distant subjects. These tasks were done by scribes, who became increasingly useful to the kings. Later, the scribes would grow in power to become trusted officials who would defend the monarch's power when the kings were off fighting wars or interacting with communities outside the region around the capital.

Religion played the key connective role in the maintenance of social order. The king was at the top of the Shang power structure because his ancestors were deemed best able to communicate with the supreme deity, Di, and the Shang king himself was best able to communicate with his own ancestors. The king and people worshipped other deities, including the gods controlling the Huanghe River and the mountains as well as the long-dead ancestors and recently deceased members

---

pictographs—Characters that depict an object or idea; thus, the character for "tree" originated in a drawing of a tree.

of the royal family. Ancestor worship, a key element of Shang royal power, continued in later times as veneration of ancestors and, in a particular case, as filial piety, or veneration of one's parents, the closest ancestors.

No distinction was made between the king's religious and secular powers, and his government was replicated in the structure of the patriarchal family—the state was a household that had to be managed. The Shang kings were to communicate with Di via dialogue with deceased royal kin. Such communication was accompanied by offerings to the king's ancestors in a ceremony. Offerings took various forms, including sacrifice of humans or offerings of rich foods to ancestors. Below the king on the social ladder were members of his family line or lineage who comprised the Shang aristocracy, court officials, lords who owned land, and finally what the oracle bones termed "the multitude"—common people who, unlike the kings and nobles, had no recorded ancestors and did not belong to a clan. Common people included artisans who worked in jade, bronze, wood, or leather; spun and wove silk; and devised a rich material culture, as well as peasants who lived in villages in houses partially below ground level. At the very bottom of the social order were the prisoners of war who were enslaved and forced to work on massive building projects. After their work was completed, many prisoners' heads and limbs were cut off before burial. Members of the nobility often accompanied the king to his death, and oracle bone inscriptions reveal that over 7000 captive slaves, many from the neighboring Qiang (chee-AHNG) people, were sacrificed in order to win the aid or avoid the displeasure of the spirits. As part of the ritual of human and animal sacrifice, a beerlike liquor was poured on the ground.

Unlike the common people, the kings and nobles had recorded ancestors and belonged to a clan. They were the descendants in the male line from a common ancestor whom they worshipped. The lesser levels of society each had their local gods, to whom requests to guarantee good harvests and long life were addressed. The peasants belonged to no clans, and there is no evidence that they worshipped their ancestors. Instead, their gods were the fundamental forces of nature, such as rivers, mountains, earth, wind, rain, and the stars and planets.

During the Shang period, a special group of Chinese became skilled in the use of magic, with which they attempted to manipulate the two forces of the world. They called these two opposed but complementary forces *yang* and *yin*. Yang was associated with the sun and all things male, strong, warm, and active; yin was associated with the moon and all things female, dark, cold, weak, and passive. Many centuries later, in the fourth century B.C.E., scholars speculated about these forces. In later ages Chinese thinkers would also employ these concepts to compel greater obedience and passivity from women.

The power of the kings and nobles rested on their ownership of the land, their monopoly of bronze metallurgy, their chariots, the king's religious functions and his frequent visits to subordinate domains, and a bureaucracy that was considered divine. We can see proof of the power of the Shang kings and their nobles in their imposing buildings, military superiority, and tombs. They often entered into battle across North

Chariots, whose appearance around 1200 B.C.E. attests to contact with cultures to the west of China, were a symbol of kingly power in the Shang and Zhou and were therefore sometimes buried with rulers, as in this pit in Hebei.

China and, for centuries, gained victory by using chariots, a potent technological advantage around the year 1200 B.C.E. that suggests contact with other chariot-using societies in western Asia. After death, the Shang kings' power continued when they were buried in sumptuous tombs along with those chariots and still-living servants and war captives.

Peasants might be legally free, but they had little mobility. They rarely owned land and worked plots periodically assigned to them by royal and noble landowners. They collectively cultivated the fields retained by their lords. Farming methods were primitive, not having advanced beyond the Neolithic level. Bronze was used for weapons and artwork, but not for farm tools or implements, and the peasants continued to reap wheat and millet with stone sickles and till their allotted fields with wooden plows. The inequity between the power of the king and the powerlessness of his impoverished subjects was evident by the eleventh century B.C.E. It was replaced by a new power that claimed political legitimacy due to its greater virtue.

The Zhou Dynasty (1027?–221 B.C.E.)

Around 1050 B.C.E. the Zhou frontier state, which had adopted the material advances of the Shang while preserving the cultural traditions of pre-Shang Neolithic societies, overthrew the Shang dynasty. An early Zhou history, *The Book of Documents*, later included among the classics, explained that the Shang had become corrupt and dissolute and their conquest by the virtuous Zhou was to be expected. The Zhou leader announced that Heaven *(Tian)* had given him a mandate to replace the Shang. Because the concept that Heaven indicated its will through uprisings and natural disasters was new in China, the Zhou seizure of power as *Tian*'s will was probably, in part, a rationalization for the Zhou overthrow of Shang rule. The idea of a mandate of Heaven introduced a new and very long-lasting aspect of Chinese thought: The cosmos is ruled by an impersonal and all-powerful Heaven that sits in judgment over the human ruler who links Heaven's commands and human fate. Without approval or mandate from Heaven, in other words, kingly rule was not possible. The king came to be called the "Son of Heaven."

The Zhou were a powerful western frontier tribe that took advantage of the opportunities of the wealth and increasing weakness of Shang rule. Given the Zhou's military strength, the other Chinese tribes wisely switched their loyalty to them. The Zhou went on to establish a dynasty that lasted, in one form or another, for almost 900 years (c. 1027–221 B.C.E.).

Three Zhou rulers are credited in early texts with establishing the stable Zhou state. The founder, King Wen, formed alliances with neighboring states while the Shang ruled with cruelty; Wen's son, King Wu, moved the capital eastward to Luoyang (lo-YANG) and began to fight the Shang; and the Duke of Zhou, Wu's brother, intelligently and benevolently ruled as regent for Wu's young son. After building a beautiful capital at Luoyang and conquering other states in the Yangzi valley, the Duke of Zhou stepped down to let his nephew rule.

Spread out over most of North China and the Yangzi valley, the very size of the Zhou domain made it impossible to be ruled directly from the center. States on the periphery were either ruled by Zhou relatives sent out as their representatives or allowed to stay under the jurisdiction of local chiefs. These chiefs were given hereditary titles and sent tribute to the Zhou. They also had armies that fought alongside the Zhou king's army. The king and these subordinate lords (later called vassals) were linked by kinship. Some were partrilineally related; others were related through marriage. The numbers of these subordinate rulers fluctuated greatly over the long centuries of Zhou rule. Around 800 B.C.E., there were approximately 200 domains, of which 25 or so were large enough to be important. With their hereditary

Bronze vessels, such as this one from the early tenth century B.C.E., were designed to contain water, wine, meat, or grain used during the sacrificial rites in which the Shang and Zhou prayed to the spirits of their ancestors. Animals were a major motif of ritual bronzes.

officials and various types of aristocrats, Zhou society was hierarchically arranged from the Son of Heaven on top, down through domain lords, great officials, lesser officials, and ordinary commoners.

The early Zhou kings were strong leaders who kept the allegiance of their vassals, the lords of the peripheral territories, while fighting off attacks on the frontiers. However, after two centuries, complacency set in, and a succession of weak kings led to a reduction in the central throne's power over its subordinates; taking advantage of advances in military technology, the vassals became more independent. By the eighth century B.C.E. the vassals no longer went to the Zhou capital for investiture by the Son of Heaven. As the Zhou monarchs became weaker, court officials increased their influence. Under the feudal politics of the Zhou, bureaucratic documentation became ever more complex, as the center had to define its relations with the 50 major vassal dependencies and continually changing foreign contacts. The kings' scribes, clerks, and officials wrote the documents that defined hierarchy and order and mastered the political precedents that the military men needed to exercise legitimate authority. As the state became more complex, the qualifications for state servants became more specific. Now the officials of the state, along with the nobles, could gain rank, land, wealth, and an assured future for their family, but such a bureaucracy did not ensure the strength of the reign.

The remnants of Zhou royal power disappeared completely in 771 B.C.E., when an alliance of disloyal vassals and border-area tribesmen destroyed the capital and killed the king. Part of the royal family managed to escape eastward to Luoyang, however, where the dynasty survived for another five centuries (until around 250 B.C.E.), doing little more than performing state religious rituals as the Sons of Heaven. The period before 771 is often called the "Western Zhou" to distinguish it from the era after 771 B.C.E., referred to as the "Eastern Zhou" for the location of the capital. In 335 B.C.E. some of the stronger vassals began calling themselves "kings" *(wang)*, thereby ending the sovereignty of the Zhou monarchs. Some conquered their weaker neighbors. Some pioneered new policies, based on new schools of thought developed in the East. Warfare among emerging states was incessant. During the early Eastern Zhou, also called the Spring and Autumn Period (722–481 B.C.E.), warfare often took a chivalrous form, but it turned more violent during the two and a half centuries known as the period of Warring States (403–221 B.C.E.). By 221 B.C.E. the ruler of the Qin (CHIN), the most successful of the seven largest states still existing in 300 B.C.E., had conquered all of his rivals and established a unified empire over which he was the absolute ruler.

The art of horseback riding, common among the nomads of Central Asia, greatly influenced later Zhou military strategies, supplanting the chariot-based strategy of earlier centuries. Rulers in the north developed cavalry as a defense against nomadic forces and later used their new cavalry against other Chinese states. Infantry forces drafted from the farm population were also effective against chariots. Rulers of the Warring States period began constructing increasingly complex defensive walls. The infantry adapted to new conditions by wearing tunics and trousers adopted from the nomads, an example of the interactions of non-Chinese and Chinese culture. In later centuries, the mutual influence of Chinese and "barbarian" culture would encompass military, political, intellectual and material culture. Large populations were essential to build defensive walls and raise armies. Effective rulers devised new economic and sociopolitical ways to enrich their growing populations and their resources.

Zhou Economy and Society

The contestants for power—the Jin (divided during the Warring States era into Han and Wei) in the north, the Qi (CHEE) in the east, the Chu in the Yangzi region, and the Qin in the west—recognized the connection between wealth and power. Prosperous rulers could field large armies of soldiers and laborers. New lands were claimed for agriculture from marginal fields and marshes, and the states encouraged trade in textiles, metals, woods, jade, bamboo, seafood, pearls, and animal products. During the seventh century B.C.E., the Chinese mastered the use of iron and mass-produced cast iron objects from molds, which were in wide use by the end of the third century B.C.E. The ox-drawn iron-tipped plow, together with the use of manure and the growth of large-scale irrigation and water-control projects, led to a more dependable and productive food supply and greater population growth. Zhou-era rulers also understood the necessity to build canals to improve their realm's economy and communication. The canals made it possible to move food and useful items dependably over long distances. Commerce and wealth thus grew rapidly. At the beginning of the Zhou dynasty, brightly colored shells, bolts of silk, and ingots of precious metals were used as forms of exchange; by the end of the dynasty, small round copper coins with square holes had taken their place.

Under the Zhou dynasty, merchant and artisan classes played an economically prominent, if not socially recognized, role as wealth spread beyond the nobles and court servants. Indicative of the rise in the general economic level, chopsticks and finely lacquered objects, today universally considered as symbols of Chinese and East Asian culture, were in general use by the end of the period. The continued importance of the intertwining of political power and cultural beliefs, as in the Shang era, is evident from inscriptions on bronzes. From them we know that Zhou kings, like the Shang kings, worshipped their ancestors. The Zhou kings had elaborate rituals in family temples, where they made offerings to their ancestors. The nobility, for their benefit, recorded honors they had received from the Zhou kings onto commissioned pieces of bronze. These messages were inscribed inside food containers or hidden on the backs of bells because they were meant only for the eyes of the ancestors.

Other vessels, no longer shaped in the *taotie* or animal mask form of the Shang dynasty, appear to have been used in rituals viewed by an audience. Many were inscribed with texts, suggesting their owners may have been thinking about their descendants.

The early Zhou years gave birth to the first collection of poetry, *The Book of Songs,* later canonized as one of China's great classics. The poems, composed between 1000 B.C.E. and 600 B.C.E., included love poems, poems about government officials, and poems that depict everyday lives of commoners. One poem laments the role played in the Zhou court by the powerful wives of rulers, which was a reflection of their role in the frequent disputes over succession to the throne:

Clever men build cities,
Clever women topple them . . .
Disorder does not come down from heaven;
It is produced by women.[1]

Not all royal women, however, were so poorly regarded by their contemporaries. The excavation of the tomb of Lady Hao, wife of King Wu (c. 1200 B.C.E.) contains oracle bones showing she led military expeditions, managed an estate, and carried out rituals.

It was during the time of political and social disruption of the Eastern Zhou that teachers and philosophers, longing for an idealized "good old days" of social stability of the Western Zhou, played an important role in defining and teaching values that, in continually evolving forms, would dominate Chinese society into the twentieth century. This new form of leadership found a willing audience among the people who had the most to gain from order and hierarchy, the clerks and officials who increased their influence, wealth, and legal privileges during the Zhou dynasty.

Nostalgia for the imagined past led to the conceptualizing of an entire hierarchical social order developed around an idealized monarch, with each inferior in the descending scale owing respect and obedience to his superior.

The peasant masses stood at the bottom of the hierarchy. They were controlled by government officials, landed gentry, and rural moneylenders, although, ostensibly, they were free to buy and sell land or change occupation. Most, like peasants elsewhere, were tied to their villages, where they worked as tenants or serfs and struggled to eke out an existence. Some were forced into debt slavery. To increase production and control of farmers, some rulers used their own officials rather than local intermediaries to govern the farm population. Officials gained opportunities for advancement through good performance in these jobs, and farmers were increasingly rewarded by freedom from serfdom by their own good performance. By the end of the Warring States era, rulers with more effective centralized bureaucratic control and increasingly free peasants found themselves emerging on top.

The Philosophical Schools

The rich streams of thought that appeared during the latter part of the Zhou period emerged from the very disquiet and instability of the times. During the next three centuries, some great teachers and philosophers thought deeply about the nature of humanity and the problems of society. They created a range of philosophies on how people should live. These ideas went from the extremes of living for society to living for one's own soul, and they continued to change through the centuries and shape Chinese society even today.

Confucianism: The Foundation

The first, most famous, and certainly most influential Chinese philosopher and teacher was Kong Fuzi (KONG FOO-dzih; "Master Kong, the Sage," c. 551–c. 479 B.C.E.), known in the West as Confucius after Jesuit missionaries to China in the seventeenth century Latinized his name. He was one in a line of teachers who tried to explain the universe and the place of the Chinese people within it as well as the appropriate behavior among human beings in society. Eventually viewed as the central figure in orthodox Chinese philosophy, many of his students believed the master composed or edited what were often called the Confucian classics—*The Book of Songs*, *The Book of Poetry*, *The Book of Documents*, *The Analects*, and other texts. The only work that can be accurately attributed to Confucius is *The Analects* ("Selected Sayings"), a collection of his responses to questions posed by his disciples that was passed on after his death.

Confucius belonged to the lower aristocracy of a minor state, Lu, which had been under the Duke of Zhou, idealized by Confucius and later made into a model by the master's students. Confucius was more or less a contemporary of the Buddha in India,

Document The Wisdom of Confucius

The wisdom of Confucius is celebrated across the world. Unlike some wise ancient texts that seem limited to the time in which they were written, the thoughts of the great Chinese philosopher have a relevance that transcends the moment they were expressed. In these extracts, Confucius reflects on the notions of family, power, and education.

1:1 The Master said, "To learn, and at due times to practice what one has learned, is that not also a pleasure? To have friends come from afar, is that not also a joy? To go unrecognized, yet without being embittered, is that not also to be a noble person?"

1:2 Master You [You Ruo] said, "Among those who are filial toward their parents and fraternal toward their brothers, those who are inclined to offend against their superiors are few indeed. Among those who are disinclined to offend against their superiors, there have never been any who are yet inclined to create disorder. The noble person concerns himself with the root; when the root is established, the Way is born. Being filial and fraternal—is this not the root of humaneness?"

1:3 The Master said, "Those who are clever in their words and pretentious in their appearance, yet are humane, are few indeed."

1:4 Zengzi said, "Each day I examine myself on three things: In planning on behalf of others, have I failed to be loyal? When dealing with friends, have I failed to be trustworthy? On receiving what has been transmitted, have I failed to practice it?"

1:5 The Master said, "In ruling a state of a thousand chariots, one is reverent in the handling of affairs and shows himself to be trustworthy. One is economical in expenditures, loves the people, and uses them only at the proper season."

1:7 Zixia said, "One who esteems the worthy and has little regard for sexual attraction, who in serving his parents is able to summon up his entire strength, who in serving his ruler is able to avoid himself with utmost devotion, who in interacting with friends shows himself trustworthy in his words—though it may be said of him that he has not studied. I would definitely call him learned."

1:8 The Master said, "If the noble person is not serious, he will not inspire awe, nor will his learning be sound. One should abide in loyalty and trustworthiness and should have no friends who are not his equal. If one has faults, one should not be afraid to change." . . .

1:16 The Master said. "One should not grieve that one is unrecognized by others; rather, one should grieve that one fails to recognize others." . . .

2:1 The Master said. "One who governs through virtue may be compared to the polestar, which occupies its place while the host of other stars pay homage to it." . . .

2:11 The Master said, "One who reanimates the old so as to understand the new may become a teacher."

2:12 The Master said, "The noble person is not a tool."

2:14 The Master said, "The noble person is inclusive, not exclusive: the small person is exclusive, not inclusive."

2:15 The Master said, "To learn without thinking, is unavailing; to think without learning is dangerous."

Questions to Consider

1. What do you think Confucius considers to be the traits of a "serious" person?
2. Does your professor fit the qualification expressed in 2:11? If so, why? If not, why not?
3. According to Confucius, what should be the ruler's attitude toward his people?

From the *Analects*, in William Theodore de Bary et al., eds., *Sources of Chinese Tradition*, 2nd ed., Vol. 1 (New York: Columbia University Press, 1999).

Zoroaster in Persia, and the early philosophers of Greece. To achieve his goal of improving society, Confucius did not look to the gods and spirits for assistance; he accepted the existence of Heaven *(Tian)* and spirits, but he insisted in the *Analects* that it was more important "to know the essential duties of man living in a society of men."

"We don't know yet how to serve men," he said, "How can we know about serving the spirits?" And, "We don't yet know about life, so how can we know about death?" Confucius hoped to become an adviser to a ruler, but he turned to teaching after traveling from court to court in an unsuccessful search for a ruler who would make use of his ideas.

He tried to inspire his students to be moral and prepared them to serve in government even if he himself was unable to do so. He honored the roles of learned men who served their rulers in ritual practice, record keeping, divination, and reception of guests and envoys from other rulers. He stressed that following honorable conventions and accepting hierarchy produced social harmony. Confucius advocated a fairly conservative order, though his words were reinterpreted constantly over the centuries to offer a variety of approaches to organizing the state and society.

Throughout the ages, Confucius became idealized as the authority to whom one could look for instruction on proper government and behavior.

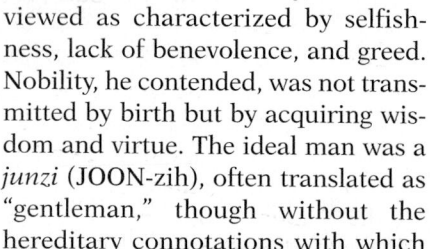

DOCUMENT Government and the Superior "Man"

Confucius was deeply disappointed with the condition of his own society, which he viewed as characterized by selfishness, lack of benevolence, and greed. Nobility, he contended, was not transmitted by birth but by acquiring wisdom and virtue. The ideal man was a *junzi* (JOON-zih), often translated as "gentleman," though without the hereditary connotations with which the word is associated in English. A *junzi* should be virtuous, righteous, humane, wise, and brave. Interactions among people should be governed by *li,* a term which covers the modern English-language connotations of propriety, manners, and ceremonial and sacred ritual. *Li* performed with a sincere heart rendered an individual human. Though *li* was manifested in each of the Five Relationships—the relationships between parent and child, ruler and subject, husband and wife, elder brother and younger brother, and friend and friend—it was most important in the family. Confucius emphasized filial piety, the respect of a child for his or her parents, above all. If the interests of one's ruler and one's parents conflicted, one's support of the parent came first. A son should never turn his father in for theft, for example.

At the same time, Confucius believed that the improvement of society was the responsibility of the ruler and that the quality of government depended on the ruler's moral character: "The way (Dao) of learning to be great consists in shining with the illustrious power of moral personality, in making a new people, in abiding in the highest goodness," he wrote.[2] Confucius's definition of the Dao as "moral personality" and the "highest goodness" was in decided contrast to the old premoral Dao, in which gods and spirits, propitiated by offerings and ritual, regulated human life for good or ill. Above all, Confucius's "new way" meant a concern for the rights of others, an adherence to a type of Golden Rule. When a disciple asked, "Is there any saying that one can act on all day, every day?" Confucius replied, "Perhaps the saying about consideration: 'Never do to others what you would not like them to do to you.'"

Confucius's view of society was hierarchical. Even though four of the Five Relationships connected a superior and an inferior (only the relationship of friend to friend was equal), all relationships were to be grounded in *ren* (often translated as benevolence, humanity, or human-relatedness), a virtue applied to all without any hierarchical dimensions.

Although Confucius called himself "a transmitter and not a creator," his redefinition of Dao and his teachings produced an ethical program for this world, by this world.[3] His desire to reemphasize the propriety and humanity of *li,* which he felt were being ignored in his day, and his redirecting of the concept of the *junzi,* or gentleman, to one whose character rather than birth defined his nobility, underscore his new ethical emphasis. As he noted, "The noble man understands what is right; the inferior man understands what is profitable."[4]

Mozi (MOH-dzih; c. 490–391 B.C.E.), born around the time of Confucius's death, took issue with Confucius's placing of priority on one's family. Mozi stressed universal love instead, though he also believed in a hierarchy headed up by those who were capable and educated. Mozi disdained wars of aggression for territorial gain and excessive mourning rituals. Though Mozi, like numerous other philosophers of the Spring and Autumn era, had a lively following in his day, his school of thought did not survive the end of the Warring States period. In the end, historians stress the contributions of Confucianists, Daoists, and Legalists because of their continuing influence on Chinese thought, but scholars like Mozi were part of a very active intellectual climate.

Mencius: The Mandate of Heaven

Mencius, or Mengzi (MUNG-dzih; c. 372–c. 289 B.C.E.) was one of two scholars whose work was largely responsible for the emergence of Confucianism as the most widely accepted philosophy in China. Born a century after the death of Confucius, Mencius was raised by a mother who, according to legend, sacrificed her own happiness to support her son's education in scholarship and righteous behavior. Mencius's mother, revered as a paragon of virtue, is supposed to have expressed the long-lasting prescription for women's position in the family: as a child, a girl is subordinate to her father; as a young adult, a woman is subordinate to her husband; and as a widow, to her son.

Mencius is best known for adding important new dimensions to Confucian thought in terms of conceptions of human nature and of the right to govern. Whereas Confucius had only implied that human nature is good, Mencius emphatically insisted that all people are innately good and tend to seek the good, just as water tends to run downhill. But goodness must be cultivated by virtuous and wise rulers. He compared human nature to a mountain, once beautiful and lush, made barren by humans and animals denuding it of vegetation. Just as the mountain's nature was not to be barren, so, too, human nature was not to be corrupt. But both needed the right conditions to flourish.

Mencius believed good kings had ruled benevolently in the past and urged rulers of his day to practice benevolence as well, by reducing taxes and making punishments less severe. In that way, he stressed, kings would gain their people's support and be invincible. Mencius went further, proposing a system of land distribution believed to have been used by ancient sage rulers. This system, called the "well-field" system, called for eight families to farm fields shaped like the Chinese character for *well* (like a modern day tic-tac-toe board), with one field in the middle farmed by all eight families for taxes. This way, Mencius argued, everyone's needs would be satisfied fairly. When the people were happy, they would support their ruler.

If the ruler was not wise and benevolent, government would be corrupt, the people hungry, and natural disasters destructive of the people's livelihood. This, Mencius averred, was Heaven's sign that the ruler was not really a true ruler. By the Confucian principle of "rectification of names," a person who was not a ruler should be removed. Such a ruler had lost the mandate of Heaven. If the Son of Heaven ruled by virtue of the permission (or mandate) of Heaven, Heaven also had the right to withdraw the mandate. Mencius's great contribution to Confucian thought was his suggestion that people's rebellion was a sign of the loss of the mandate. In fact, the phrase "removing the mandate" became the basis for the modern Chinese and Japanese terms for "revolution."

As we have seen, this concept had been used by the Zhou to justify their revolt against the Shang whom they considered corrupt. On that occasion the concept had a religious meaning. The people were to obey the Zhou ruler as the Son of Heaven, just as they worshipped Heaven through rites and rituals. Mencius, however, secularized the mandate of Heaven when he declared, "Heaven hears as the people hear; Heaven sees as the people see."[5] By redefining the concept of a heavenly mandate in this way, Mencius made the welfare of the people the ultimate standard for judging the virtue of government. Mencius advocated responsible monarchy, supporting this concept because he believed there was a need for a new, unifying leadership that could end the warring between regional states during the late Zhou period, not, however, because he believed that people had a right to express their political views. Nonetheless, the idea of the mandate of Heaven came to be associated with the idea of the people's right to rebel and to overthrow the unjust leadership of a leader who had "lost the mandate of Heaven."

Xunzi: Human Nature as Antisocial

Xunzi (SHOON-dzih; c. 310–c. 220 B.C.E.), like Mencius, interpreted and extended Confucius's ideas. Contrary to Mencius, however, Xunzi argued that human nature tended to be antisocial and needed guidance to turn toward virtue. Wise leadership, proper rituals, and even strict laws (which Mencius rejected) would make humans capable of living good lives, filled with filial piety and morality. Once a person recognizes what is good, Xunzi argued, he or she will practice goodness. Xunzi differed from some other Confucianists by arguing that an impartial Heaven did not respond to prayers or ritual: It will rain whether or not one prays for rain. But he did not reject ritual and prayer; rather he stated that ritual, like music, was an excellent way for people to express their emotions, to provide social harmony, and to order social hierarchy.

Legalism

Xunzi is appropriately considered a Confucian thinker. Two of his students, however, took some of his ideas and applied them to a different philosophical tradition that came to be called Legalism due to its emphasis on laws. Decades before Xunzi interpreted Confucianism, Lord Shang (d. 338 B.C.E.), a minister in the state of Qin, described his work as Legalist. He got rid of Qin's aristocracy; determined his subordinates' military rank by the number of heads they cut off in battle; organized territory into counties; attracted farmers to those counties by offering them houses, land, and freedom from serfdom; made people responsible for crimes committed by members of their mutual responsibility groups; and codified laws, applying them harshly without consideration for rank.

DOCUMENT Legalism: The Way of the State

Xunzi's student Han Feizi (HAN FAY-dzih; d. 233 B.C.E.) followed in Lord Shang's tradition. He advocated harsh application of laws, unmodified by family concerns. It was shocking to Confucianists that he suggested that rulers should not be expected to be moral leaders who treated their subjects with kindness. Indeed, he said, since even parents treated their newborn sons and daughters differently, thereby showing little parental love for their own daughters, how could a ruler be expected to rule subjects, with whom they had no familial bond, with morality and virtue? Equal application of the law was the only answer. Han Feizi's contemporary, Li Si (d. 208 B.C.E.), also a former student of Xunzi, put Legalist political theory into practice in Qin as its leading minister.

The Legalists argued for an elaborate system of laws defining fixed penalties for each offense, with no consideration for rank, class, or circumstances, with the important exception of the ruler, who was above the law. Judges were not to use their own consciences in estimating the gravity of a crime and arbitrarily deciding on the punishment. Their task was solely to define the crime correctly; the punishment was provided automatically by the code of law. This clashed with Confucian prioritization, in the name of human kindness, of the family, and with the notion that *ren* (benevolence) itself was a motivation for the people to support their ruler.

Daoism

A third, lasting school of thought emerged in the late Zhou era. **Daoism** contrasted greatly with Confucian ideals and practices, as it focused on natural harmony rather than social harmony. In its very earliest forms, Daoism had some political aspects, but in the third century B.C.E. its leading philosopher, Zuangzi (JWAHNG-dzih) (c. 369–c. 286 B.C.E.), embraced relativism and spiritual freedom and was adamantly apolitical. Daoists, unlike Confucianists, did not welcome rulers' intervention to improve people's livelihoods. For Confucianists, the Dao ("the way") was the ethical path for rulers' humanity in a human-centered world; for Daoists, the Dao was the way of nature with which humans should seek harmony rather than dominance.

DOCUMENT Daoism: The Way and Virtue

Two Daoist texts survive. The earliest, the *Daodejing* (DOW-deh-JING) or *Laozi* (LOW-dzih), is often attributed to Lao Dai, a sixth-century contemporary of Confucius. Most likely the book was compiled three centuries later. This poetic text is cryptic and paradoxical and open to many interpretations, because, as it suggests, the Dao itself cannot be defined. There are a few ideas that are strongly encouraged, however: that nonaction and nonbeing triumph over action and being and that silence is superior to words. Rulers should not take actions, but rather allow nature to take its course. As the *Laozi* explained, "Do not honor the worthy, and the people will not compete. Do not value rare treasures, and the people will not steal. . . A sage governs this way: He empties people's minds and fills their bellies. . . . Engage in no action and order will prevail."[6]

The other Daoist text, the *Zhuangzi*, goes much farther in rejecting politics and engagement with society. While the *Laozi* had some political uses—for instance, some rulers believed that by doing nothing their state or society could be strengthened—the *Zhuangzi* strongly rejected politics. Zhuangzi himself, believed to be the book's author, turned down government jobs and titles, preferring, he said, to drag his tail in the mud like a turtle rather than having his bones venerated after his death. Here Zhuangzi rejects both political power, which he likens to the impotence of dead bones, and social respect, suggested by his rejection of the veneration ("ancestor worship") of his bones.

Daoism was a revolt not only against society but also against the intellect's limitations. Intuition, not reason, was the source of true knowledge; and books, Daoists said, are "the dregs and refuse of the ancients." Zhuangzi even questioned the reality of the world of

---

Daoism—A philosophical school, later a religion, focusing on natural harmony and nonaction.

Document Legalism: The Theories of Han Feizi (d. 233 B.C.E.)

Throughout history, philosophers and leaders have generally differed in their notions of human nature. Some, like Confucius, counseled a due respect for the people, while others like Mencius saw the need for the people's consent in the affairs of state. The thinker Han Feizi disagreed with both Confucius and Mencius, viewing human nature as essentially evil and the average human being as incompetent.

When the sage rules the state, he does not count on people doing good of themselves, but employs such measures as will keep them from doing any evil. If he counts on people doing good of themselves, there will not be enough such people to be numbered by the tens in the whole country. But if he employs such measures as will keep them from doing evil, then the entire state can be brought up to a uniform standard. Inasmuch as the administrator has to consider the many but disregard the few, he does not busy himself with morals but with laws.

. . . Therefore, the intelligent ruler upholds solid facts and discards useless frills. He does not speak about deeds of humanity and righteousness, and he does not listen to the words of learned men.

Those who are ignorant about government insistently say: "Win the hearts of the people." If order could be procured by winning the hearts of the people, then even the wise ministers Yi Yin and Guan Zhong would be of no use. For all that the ruler would need to do would be just to listen to the people. Actually, the intelligence of the people is not to be relied upon any more than the mind of a baby. If the baby does not have his head shaved, his sores will recur; if he does not have his boil cut open, his illness will go from bad to worse. However, in order to shave his head or open the boil someone has to hold the baby while the affectionate mother is performing the work, and yet he keeps crying and yelling incessantly. The baby does not understand that suffering a small pain is the way to obtain a great benefit.

. . . The sage considers the conditions of the times . . . and governs the people accordingly. Thus though penalties are light, it is not due to charity; though punishment is heavy, it is not due to cruelty. Whatever is done is done in accordance with the circumstances of the age. Therefore circumstances go according to their time, and the course of action is planned in accordance with the circumstances.

. . . Now take a young fellow who is a bad character. His parents may get angry at him, but he never makes any change. The villagers may reprove him, but he is not moved. His teachers and elders may admonish him, but he never reforms. The love of his parents, the efforts of the villagers, and the wisdom of his teachers and elders—all the three excellent disciplines are applied to him, and yet not even a hair on his shins is altered. It is only after the district magistrate sends out his soldiers and in the name of the law searches for wicked individuals that the young man becomes afraid and changes his ways and alters his deeds. So while the love of parents is not sufficient to discipline the children, the severe penalties of the district magistrate are. This is because men become naturally spoiled by love, but are submissive to authority. . . .

That being so, rewards should be rich and certain so that the people will be attracted by them; punishments should be severe and definite so that the people will fear them; and laws should be uniform and steadfast so that the people will be familiar with them. Consequently, the sovereign should show no wavering in bestowing rewards and grant no pardon in administering punishments, and he should add honor to rewards and disgrace to punishments—when this is done, then both the worthy and the unworthy will want to exert themselves.

Questions to Consider

1. What is the function of the law, according to Legalist thinker Han Feizi?
2. What does the author believe to be the intellectual capacity of "the people?"
3. According to Han Feizi, how should a leader behave in regard to those who do good and those who do not?

the senses. He said that he once dreamed that he was a butterfly, "flying about enjoying itself." When he awakened, he was confused: "I do not know whether I was Zhuangzi dreaming that I was a butterfly, or whether now I am a butterfly dreaming that I am Zhuangzi."

Anecdotes and allegories abound in both texts, as in all mystical teachings that deal with subjects that are difficult to put into words. As the *Daodejing* put it, "The one who knows does not speak, and the one who speaks does not know." In later centuries, Daoism, which was primarily philosophical in its formative years, adopted a religious aspect. At the end of the Han dynasty, also discussed in this chapter, Daoism took on a religious coloration, and Daoists then used their beliefs in political movements and in the quest for immortality through alchemy and sexual practices. Although Confucianism and Daoism frequently sniped at each other, they never became mutually exclusive outlooks on life. Daoist intuition complemented Confucian rationalism in the search for the true way, and during the centuries to come, Chinese often attempted to follow Confucianist precepts in their social relations, while at the same time maintaining Daoist beliefs.

The diverse philosophers of the Warring States centuries reflected not only a variety of responses to the brutality of war but also the different cultural or regional environments in which they emerged. Those that left a record in the form of silk scrolls were not only attached to their time and place but also were able, through the constancy of the Chinese written language, to transcend their time. In time, these written works became part of the "Classics" considered to be the heart of Chinese philosophy.

THE QIN AND HAN EMPIRES, 221 B.C.E.–220 C.E.

- *How did Chinese leaders use Confucian and Daoist ideas to justify conflicting state policies in the name of promoting the people's welfare and the growth of the state?*

The Qin Dynasty: Unification

Two dynasties, the Qin and the Han, unified China and created a centralized empire. The Qin dynasty collapsed soon after the death of its founder, but the Han lasted for about four centuries. Together, these dynasties transformed China, but the changes were the culmination of earlier philosophical, political, and economic developments that had emerged during the turmoil of the Warring States period.

Throughout the Warring States period, there had been a widely shared hope that a king would unite China and inaugurate a great new age of peace and stability. Whereas the Confucianists believed that such a king would accomplish the task by means of his outstanding moral virtue, the Legalists substituted kingly power and rule of law as the essential elements of effective government. The rise to preeminence of the Qin state began in 361 B.C.E. when its ruler selected Lord Shang, a man imbued with Legalist principles, to be chief minister. Recognizing that the growth of Qin power depended on a more efficient and centralized bureaucratic structure, Lord Shang undermined the old hereditary nobility and created a new aristocracy based on military merit. He also undermined their privileged place in society by introducing a universal draft beginning at approximately age 15. This produced an effect of leveling social difference, as chariot and cavalry warfare, in which the nobility had played the leading role, was replaced in importance by masses of peasant infantry equipped with iron weapons. Economically, Lord Shang further weakened the old landowning nobility by granting peasants ownership of the plots they tilled. Thereafter, the peasants paid taxes directly to the local state, thus increasing its wealth and power. These reforms were essential to Qin's rise to power during the Warring States period.

Nearly a century later, King Zheng ascended the throne as a boy of nine in 247. Nine years earlier, the last Zhou king had been deposed. Aided by two ministers, former merchant Lu Buwei (LOO boo-WAY; d. 235 B.C.E.) and Li Si, King Zheng conquered the neighboring states of Han, Zhao, Wei, Chu, and Qi, thereby unifying China in 221 B.C.E. The king then declared himself *Shi Huangdi* (SHIH HWAHNG-dee) or the "First August Supreme Ruler" of the Qin, or First Emperor, as his new title is more commonly translated. Huangdi ("emperor") endured as the royal title until 1911. Shi Huangdi also enlarged China—a name derived from the word Qin—by conquests in the south as far as the coast of South China. Military expeditions

The Early Empires

221–206 B.C.E.	Qin
206 B.C.E.–9 C.E.	Former (Western) Han
9–23 C.E.	Reign of Wang Mang
23–220 C.E.	Later (Eastern) Han

entered Vietnam and Inner Mongolia as well. The emperor stated that his dynasty would endure 10,000 generations. Although it lasted just 15 years, the idea of a united China ruled by an emperor would persist into the twentieth century.

MAP China's Struggle for Cultural and Political Unity, 400 B.C.E. to 400

The First Emperor further weakened the power of the nobility by moving hundreds of thousands of leading families to the capital at Xianyang (shee-AHN-yahng), near Xi'an, where they could be closely watched. To block rebellion, he ordered the entire civilian population to surrender their weapons to the state. A single legal code replaced all local laws. Modeled on the social structure of Lord Shang, the population was organized into groups of ten families, and each person was held responsible for the actions of all the members of the group. This structure ensured that all crimes would be reported; it also increased loyalty to the state at the expense of loyalty to the family.

As part of the unifying process, the entire realm was divided into 36 commanderies which were subdivided into counties directly ruled by the emperor's centrally controlled civil and military appointees sent to replace the local families who had been moved to Xianyang. To destroy the source of the aristocracy's power and to permit the emperor's agents to tax every farmer's harvest, private ownership of land by peasants, promoted a century earlier in the state of Qin by Lord Shang, was decreed for all of China. Thus the Qin Empire reflected emerging social forces at work in China: the peasants freed from serfdom, a new military and administrative upper class, and merchants eager to increase their wealth within a larger political arena. In place of the hereditary power of the nobility, the entire population was divided into 20 ranks, each entitled to different rights, including access to a certain type of clothing and a specified amount of land, slaves, and housing. The new bureaucracy was a meritocracy in both the civil and military realms. As late as the early Zhou period, cowrie shells and cloth had been used as currency, but money had begun to circulate broadly around 500 B.C.E., and by the outset of

The tombs of the First Emperor, 210 B.C.E., have yielded most of the surviving art of that period in China. The more than 6000 figures, including these terra-cotta warriors, were not discovered until 1974 in one of the greatest archaeological finds in history.

Qin rule, the centuries of unrest had stimulated an economic boom manifested not only in support for military endeavors, but in trade routes and networks, regional specialization, and the growth of cities.

Economic growth under the First Qin Emperor's short reign was also stimulated by public works, the standardization of the written language and of currency, and the erecting of walls to keep non-Chinese nomads out. All construction was by forced labor, and under the First Emperor, 4000 miles of roads and thousands of miles of canals and waterways, one of which connected the Yangzi to the Xi River and Guangzhou (gwahng-JOH), were completed. (This surpassed the system of the Roman Empire, which was estimated to be somewhat shorter—3740 miles.) The standardization of writing entailed the introduction of new, simpler written language, and no variation was allowed. These Chinese characters, central to unification, would be used until 1949, when an even more streamlined method of writing was created.

The new, unified currency could be threaded together in strings. Moreover, weights and measures and even the length of axles (so that cart wheels would fit the grooves cut in the highways) were made uniform. Although the First Emperor, like some Warring States rulers before him, built walls to impede the incursion of nomadic tribes from central Asia, it is no longer believed that he built the 1400-mile Great Wall of China. In its present form the Great Wall was mainly the work of the sixteenth-century Ming dynasty.[7]

The Great Wall of China

The First Emperor tried to enforce intellectual conformity and to cast the Qin Legalist system as the only natural political order. He suppressed all other schools of thought, especially the Confucianists, who idealized the Zhou political order. To break the hold of the past, the emperor put into effect a Legalist proposal requiring that all privately owned books reflecting past traditions be burned and that opponents of government in the name of antiquity be beheaded. Books burned included the Confucian classics and any statements of political philosophy that countered the Qin concern for control. Legend has it that the Qin emperor had 460 Confucian scholars buried alive, but the anti-Qin hostility of later generations of Confucian scholars makes it impossible to prove whether this really happened.

Li Si and Legalist Policies of Qin Shi Huang

The First Emperor created a new cultural elite of state-appointed teachers who would give an approved reading of the traditions and lessons of history. This set in motion the precedent that "imperial governments would henceforth insist that approved texts and suitable interpretations would be used for this purpose and that teaching would be conducted along recognized lines." As recent scholarship has argued, however, much of Chinese thought was based on oral traditions handed down, and therefore the burning of books and state control of intellectual life did not eradicate late Zhou learning.[8]

The First Emperor's control of the lives of his subjects did not erase his fear of death. Three assassination attempts gave him reason to be concerned. He dispatched a group of young men and women on a fruitless quest for the mythical islands of immortality. In addition, his fear of death, along with the Qin need to demonstrate its power, led to the emperor's employment of over half a million laborers to construct a huge burial mound near the Qin capital. The location of the mound was to be kept a secret from the people, however. All artisans and laborers involved in the construction of the tomb were locked inside the tomb while alive. Nearby, over 6000 terra-cotta soldiers were presented in military formation, in three large pits. These sculptures represented figures of the Emperor's imperial guard, and no two faces of these life-size figures are alike—each head is a personal portrait.

When the First Emperor took ill and died in 210 B.C.E. while on one of his frequent tours of inspection to control his realm, he was succeeded by an inept son who was unable to control the rivalry among his father's chief aides. Qin policies had alienated not only the intellectuals and the old nobility but also the peasants, who were subjected to ruinous taxation and forced labor. Rebel armies thus rose in every province of the empire; some led by peasants, others by aristocrats. Anarchy followed, and by 206 B.C.E. the Qin dynasty had disappeared. But the idea of a unified Chinese empire, though it often failed to be created, would last until 1912, when China became a republic.

At issue in the fighting that continued for another 4 years after the end of the Qin dynasty was not only the question of succession to the throne but also the form of government. The peasant and aristocratic leaders, first allied against the Qin, became engaged in a ruthless civil war. The aristocrats, led by the brilliant general Xiang Yu (shee-AHNG YOO; 233 B.C.E.–202 B.C.E.), sought to restore the power they had possessed before the Legalist consolidation of imperial rule. Their opponents, whose main leader was Liu Bang (LEE-oo BAHNG), a peasant who became a minor government functionary, desired a centralized state. In this contest between the old order and the new, the new was the victor—China would stay united under the Han emperors and by a bureaucratic culture, based on merit, and dedicated to rule from the center.

The Han Dynasty

The Empire Consolidated

In 206 B.C.E. Liu Bang, known to history as the Emperor Gaozu (GOW-dzoo; r. 202–195 B.C.E.), defeated his aristocratic rival and established the Han

Officials conspicuously indicated their rank by the retinues of attendants that accompanied them on their travels to their posts. Officials' tombs often contained paintings, statues, or friezes depicting these retinues. This scene, carved on a tomb brick during the Later Han, shows carriages, horses, and runners.

MAP Classical China

dynasty, building a capital at Chang'an (modern Xi'an). It lasted for more than 400 years and is traditionally divided into two parts: the Former Han (206 B.C.E.–8 C.E.) and the Later Han (23–220 C.E.). The impact of these four centuries is illustrated by the fact that ethnic Chinese still call themselves "people of Han."

The empire and power sought by Gaozu and his successors were those of the Qin, but they succeeded where the Qin had failed because they attempted to balance *wu* ("military power") with *wen* ("ethical civilian rule"). To indicate his opposition to the centralized rule of the tyrannical Qin, Gaozu had initially distributed domains to supporters who would govern them as somewhat autonomous vassal states. He soon realized, however, that effective rule required centralization. He then appointed officials to carry out legal and administrative functions in the provinces. To placate the peasants, Gaozu lowered taxes and reduced forced labor. The Han tied the empire together physically as well. By100 B.C.E., the Han had established a road system that made it possible for a traveler to go from the far north to the far south in 56 days on foot or in 32 days on horseback. But the most effective tool to gain acceptance was to enlist the support of the Confucian intellectuals. The emperors recognized that an educated bureaucracy was necessary for governing their vast empire. They lifted the Qin ban on the Confucian classics and other Zhou literature. The way was open for a revival of intellectual life that had been suppressed under the Qin, and the result was yet another reformulation of Confucian thought.

In accordance with Legalist principles, now tempered by Confucian insistence on the ethical basis of government, the Han emperors established administrative organs, staffed by a salaried bureaucracy with as many as 20 levels, to rule their empire. Government officials hailed mainly from rich families who were able to educate their sons, but the door to a government career was, in principle, open to all capable men. Emperor Wudi (r. 141–87 B.C.E., "Martial Emperor"), the Han dynasty's most vigorous emperor, established a university to train future officials. The first student body numbered 50. By 8 B.C.E., there were 3000 students; the number increased to 30,000 in the Later Han. The curriculum focused on Confucianism, endearing the emperor to many scholars and legitimizing the dynasty in their skeptical eyes. The formal examination system to select officials (developed in later centuries) did not yet exist; all officials were selected after they gave evidence of their scholarly abilities. Though these officials owed their positions to political appointments, they were men of conviction. Many suffered when their convictions differed with the opinions of their rulers.

The Han dynasty devised effective ways to maintain control of power, but they were unable to address one major challenge to their control. The families of emperors' wives emerged as powerful political actors. Gaozu's widow ruled and promoted her family's interests for 15 years after Gaozu's death. At the end of the Former Han, Wang Mang, a relative of an emperor's widow, came to power briefly, attempting to establish his own dynasty, the Xin (SHIN; 9 C.E.–23 C.E.).

Wudi

After 60 years of consolidation, the Han dynasty achieved its greatest size and zenith of achievements during the long reign of Wudi. At the same time, however, Wudi raised the peasants' taxes. In addition, he increased the amount of labor and military service the peasants were forced to contribute to the state. Those taxes were lowered after his death.

Even before Wudi's reign, Han officials were concerned about the burden of taxes on the ordinary peasants. Estate holders could generally evade taxation, so peasants began to turn their land over to estate holders to whom they paid rents that were lower than official taxes. The government responded by lowering taxes on peasants and finding new revenue sources. To pay for his military expansion, Wudi increased taxes on businesses, confiscated some nobles' lands, and most controversially, started government monopolies in salt and iron production in 119 B.C.E. Salt and iron were both necessities, and the government monopolies raised a lot of money. Confucianists were horrified, however, that the Son of Heaven should be involved in something they disdained—the quest for profits. A great debate about the economic role of the state—should the state promote profit making for the people's benefit or should it stay away from enterprise for the benefit of government morality?—engaged scholars in 81 B.C.E. This classic debate is still the basis of discussions on the role and scope of government, in China and throughout the world. Should the government play an economic role, or are laissez-faire policies more effective?

Wudi may also have initiated policies concerning grain, but the timing of those policies is unclear. Certainly by 51 B.C.E. (after Wudi's death), the Ever-Normal Granary Policy had the government buy grain when it was plentiful, allowing farmers to earn a good profit, and storing it until shortfalls hit, as they always did, saving the people from famine. The price and the quantity of rice available were, thus, stabilized.

Wudi justified his expansionist policies in terms of self-defense against nomadic tribes, including the Xiongnu (SHONG-noo), known later to Europeans as the Huns. The nomads' threats had caused the Emperor Gaozu to construct a wall and to send the nomads gifts and imperial princesses as brides. In 133 B.C.E., Wudi reversed the conciliatory policy and sent huge armies to the far west, establishing military colonies there and forcing local chieftains to send their sons to China for education, in effect making them hostages. Wudi annexed a large corridor extending through the Tarim River basin of central Asia to the Pamir Mountains, close to Bactria.

Wudi sent an envoy westward to seek allies against the Xiongnu. Captured and held prisoner for ten years, this envoy eventually reached Bactria and Ferghana. His reports of the interest shown in Chinese silks by the peoples of the area is an excellent example of increasing Chinese cultural, economic, and political interaction with non-Chinese. Commercial exchanges between China and other civilizations farther west were already underway. By 101 B.C.E., Wudi conquered Ferghana, thus controlling trade routes across Central Asia. This was the beginning of centuries of what came to be called "Silk Roads," major trade routes that carried a variety of products in addition to the popular silks.

Wudi also outflanked the Xiongnu in the east by the conquest of southern Manchuria and northern Korea. In addition, he completed the conquest of South China, begun by the Qin, and added northern Vietnam to the Chinese Empire. Chinese settlers moved into all the conquered lands. In fact, just as the armies of the Roman Republic were laying the foundation of the Pax Romana in the West, the Martial Emperor was consolidating power in the East.

Han Decline

Wudi's conquests led to overextension of the empire. As costs increased and many peasants fled to the protection of the great estates, taxes on the remaining peasants increased. Advances in agricultural technology, especially new plows and irrigation systems, permitted increased output. The donkey, brought from the west by the Xiongnu, was a helpful pack animal. These improvements led to population growth—the Han Empire had more people than Rome in 2 B.C.E.—but life for farmers was precarious. The custom of multiple inheritance led to tiny farms. The central government had to rely more and more on local military commanders and great landowners for control of the population, giving them great power and prestige at its own expense. More and more peasants fell behind in their rents and were forced to sell themselves or their children into debt slavery. This decline after an initial period of increasing prosperity and power made it appear that the Han were in danger of losing the mandate of Heaven.

Wudi was followed by less powerful rulers. Two child emperors, with Wang Mang as their regent, weakened Han control. At the same time, the rise of a messianic religious movement inspired by the cult of a goddess called the Queen Mother of the West suggested that the end of the dynasty was near. Wang Mang took over the throne in 9 C.E., seeming to fulfill the cult's prophecy. Wang Mang united Confucian ethics with Legalist practice. His goal was the rejuvenation of society by employing the power of the state. Because the number of large tax-free estates had greatly increased while the number of tax-paying peasant holdings had declined in the decades before Wang Mang's rise to power, he resurrected the well-field system, cut court expenses, issued new coins, abolished slavery, and reinvigorated the Ever-Normal Granary Policy. He tried to bring back Zhou-style offices. (In 1938 a chance reading of Wang Mang's proposal inspired the "ever-normal granary" program of the American New Deal!)[9]

Wang Mang's reform program failed. The conservative bureaucracy was unequal to the difficult administrative task. The powerful landowners rebelled against the ruler who proposed to confiscate their land. To make matters worse, in 11 C.E., the Huanghe changed course dramatically, flooding enormous tracts of land. The peasants joined the wealthy in opposition to Wang Mang. Although Wang Mang rescinded his reforms, he was killed by the rebels in 23 C.E. The conflicts over landownership and tenancy, along with the concentration of power of great families, became—and remained—a major problem in Chinese history.

The Later Han dynasty never reached the heights of its predecessors. Warlords who were members of the rich landowner class seized more and more power, and widespread peasant rebellions sapped the state's resources.

Religious uprising abounded, including one led by Daoist Mother Lu. Rivalries between Confucian scholars and court **eunuchs** had always been a problem, but in the second century of the Later Han, these erupted in murderous attacks on one another. Eunuchs were in control of the throne by the 170s. The previous decades saw plagues of locusts and horrific floods. By the 180s, rebellions were occurring everywhere. The uprising of the Yellow Turbans (so named because of the yellow scarves they wore) in 184 C.E. was particularly destructive to the Later Han. This was a messianic movement joined by thousands of poverty-stricken people, who believed in what they called *Taipingdao* (tai-PING-DOW) or "The Way of Great Peace." Emerging from economic need, this movement combined folk religious Daoism with the political goal of ending the dynasty. The Yellow Turbans did not achieve their goal, but they left behind a legacy in terms of setting a precedent for other grassroots revolts.

The general who subdued the Yellow Turbans went on to slaughter over 2000 eunuchs, along with beardless men mistaken for eunuchs. Luoyang was sacked in 189.

Surviving in name only during its last 30 years, the Han dynasty ended in 220 C.E., when the throne was usurped by the son of a famous warlord. Three and a half centuries of disunity and turbulence followed—the longest period of strife in China's long history. But China eventually succeeded in reuniting. In 589 the Sui dynasty united China again. By the end of the sixth century, as a result of centuries of political and cultural transformation, China had been created.

Han Scholarship, Art, and Technology

Scholarship flourished under the Han. A major concern of scholars was the collecting and interpreting of the classics of Chinese thought produced in the Zhou period. Many of the texts destroyed under the Qin were reproduced by scholars who had memorized them earlier. When some documents assumed to be original classics were unearthed in the first century B.C.E., disputes over authenticity arose. The recovered volumes were venerated as a repository of past wisdom, while the texts written down from memory accorded more closely with scholarly currents of the Han dynasty. This encouraged studies of the past, including historical studies and the production of the world's first dictionary. This dictionary, containing 9000 characters with their meanings and pronunciations, was written by Xu Shen (SHOO SHEN; c. 54–120 C.E.). Han scholars venerated Confucius, who moved in the popular imagination from being a teacher, a man like any other, to becoming the ideal thinker and a being regarded as in some ways divine. Confucianism became the official philosophy of the state. Antiquarian interest spurred the research of Sima Qian (SIH-mah CHEN; c.145–90 B.C.E.) and Ban Gu (BAHN GOO; d. 92 C.E.). Sima Qian's work, a comprehensive history of China, the *Historical Records (Shiji)*, is a huge and highly detailed work of 130 chapters beginning with the Xia dynasty, including narratives of political events, chronological tables, and biographies. Sima Qian carefully quoted from documents, weighing evidence and bringing sophisticated historical methods to his study. He was so dedicated to his work that he chose castration over death for the crime of defending a general who had surrendered to an enemy in order to complete the *Historical Records*. Ban Gu's *History of the Former Han* was the first dynastic history written during and later approved by the following dynasty. Ban Gu, like Sima Qian, strove for historical accuracy and objectivity. Thereafter, it became customary for each dynasty to write the official history of its immediate predecessor.

DOCUMENT
Sima Qian on Qin Shi Huang

Other scholars made an important mark as well. Dong Zhongshu (DONG JONG-shoo; c. 179–104 B.C.E.), Wudi's adviser, stressed the ruler's central role in leading the people to understand the goodness in their nature. He also stressed that earthquakes, eclipses, and weather disasters were signs of a ruler's immorality and pending loss of the mandate of Heaven. The Chinese believed that the successes and failures of the past provided guidance for one's own time and for the future. As stated in the *Historical Records*, "Events of the past, if not forgotten, are teachings about the future." The state-sponsored Chinese historians wrote to affirm the intimate and unchanging and essential link—the emperor—between the heavenly order and politics, caught up in supposedly predictable cycles.[10]

Han scholars also made use of archaeological investigation as an aid to the writing of history. One scholar anticipated modern archaeologists by more than a thousand years in classifying human history by

eunuchs—Castrated men used to guard the Emperor's wives and concubines because they posed no sexual threat.

"ages": "stone" (Old Stone Age), "jade" (New Stone Age), "bronze," and "the present age" when "weapons are made of iron."[11]

Han art was clearly creative. The largely decorative art of the past, which served a religious purpose, was replaced by a realistic pictorial art (foreshadowed earlier by the individually sculpted soldiers buried near the First Emperor's tomb) portraying ordinary life. The result was the first great Chinese flowering of sculpture. Some of the finest examples of this realistic secular art are the models of the tall and spirited horses that Wudi imported from Bactria. The Han greatly admired these proud "celestial" and "blood-sweating" horses from the west, and their artists brilliantly captured the beasts' high spirit. Human figures, models, and tiles depicting everyday life are among the fine art forms. The flair for ornamentation in the visual arts and architecture are replicated in the vibrant poetry.

A masterpiece nearly 2000 years old is this lively horse of bronze, galloping and neighing with its head and tail high. To show its speed, the unknown artist, with bold imagination, placed its left hind hoof on a flying swallow, and the other three hooves in the air. The craftsmanship is extremely fine and conforms to the principles of mechanics.

Because Han buildings were made largely of wood, none remain. Ceramic models show us how houses and towers were constructed. This Han-era model of a tower, which might have been part of a single- or multistory housing compound surrounding a courtyard, indicates the use of tile, plaster, wood, and other materials.

During the Han period, China surpassed the level of technological development in the rest of the world. Notable inventions included a simple seismograph capable of indicating earthquakes several hundred miles away; the use of water power to grind grain and to operate a piston bellows for iron smelting; the horse collar, which greatly increased the pulling power of horses; paper made from cloth rags, which replaced cumbersome bamboo strips and expensive silk cloth as a writing surface; a sophisticated, labor-saving plow; and the humble but extremely useful wheelbarrow. By the end of the first century B.C.E., the Han Chinese had recognized sunspots and accurately determined the length of the calendar year, an example of the high level gained in their mathematical and observational astronomy.[12]

The Confucian Woman of the Han

Confucius had placed wives in a position subordinate to their husbands, and yin-yang theory had held that men and women were fundamentally different, but few scholars discussed women before the Han dynasty. Poetry and art had depicted women, but two writers in the Han wrote works that had the most long-lasting effects on the status of women. The first work, *Biographies of Heroic Women* by Liu Xiang (lee-OO SHANG; 79–8 B.C.E.), is a major collection of biographies of 125 exemplary women, notable for their filial piety, wise counsel to their husbands, and valor in the defense of their chastity. Such biographies were common didactic vehicles for men, and Liu Xiang's work parallels those with examples of women.

The other work was by Ban Zhao (BAN JOW; 45–116 C.E.), sister of Ban Gu, and a teacher to the girls and women in the palace. Her *Lessons for Women* were strict rules for the separation of men's and women's spheres. She elaborated on what propriety meant for women, listing four "womanly qualifications": womanly virtue, womanly words, womanly bearing, and womanly work that included sewing, weaving, and the ordering of wine and food for guests. Women were to guard their chastity and exhibit modesty and self-control, to choose their words with care, to wear clean clothing and ornaments, and to keep their bodies clean. She stated that wives should be obedient to their husbands, parents-in-law, and brothers- and sisters-in-law.

Because she knew that courtesy and righteousness could only be attained if women were educated, she stressed education. She asked: "Only to teach men and not to teach women, is that not ignoring the essential relation between them?"[13] *Lessons for Women* was passed down from Chinese men and women to girls into the twentieth century, and Ban Zhao's approach to womanhood influenced ideas in Japan and Korea as well as China.

Religious Daoism and Buddhism

The philosophical Daoism of the late Zhou era was joined by a new form of religious Daoism in the Han. While it was not until the last century of the Later Han that religious Daoism developed a written body of sacred texts and clergy able to interpret them—concepts that would have seemed alien to Zhuangzi and Laozi—other uses of Daoism emerged as early as the founding of the Qin. Both the first emperor of the Qin and Wudi of Han consulted Daoist specialists on extending their lives through elixirs, diet, and talismans in addition to sexual practices and breathing exercises. These techniques were performed by men in power and were not yet a form of popular religious expression.

By the second century of the Later Han, these Daoist-inspired practices for extending longevity were joined by an interest in alchemy to produce elixirs and combined with folk beliefs in local gods and shamanistic rituals to create a more organized religion. From these roots, religious Daoism produced several leaders able to transform peasant discontent into massive religious movements, such as the Red Eyebrows and the Yellow Turbans. Religious Daoism continued to evolve in the next several centuries.

The breakdown of the political and social order during the Later Han also produced an upsurge in philosophical Daoism. Because they had no faith in the political order or in social action that could eradicate the widespread discontent and were discouraged with Confucianism and its concern for society, educated Chinese began to turn inward. The Mahayana school of Buddhism, first mentioned in China around 66 C.E. and brought in by missionaries and traders through central Asia, provided another answer to the need for religious assurance. (For the history and beliefs of Buddhism in its country of origin, India, see the next chapter.) At first, Buddhism in China was practiced by foreigners and was not a single system of beliefs but a wide array of sects and approaches. Mahayana Buddhism came to China along with meditation, monasticism, and magic. About 148 C.E. a Buddhist missionary established a center for the translation of Buddhist writings into Chinese at the Later Han capital. Relatively few Chinese, however, were attracted to the religion during the Han dynasty. Buddhism's great attraction to converts and its influence on Chinese culture came after the fall of the Han dynasty when renewed political turmoil made its emphasis on otherworldly salvation appealing to the great majority of Chinese and its stress on compassion, transcending gender and ethnicity, particularly attractive to women. Indeed, some scholars refer to the next half millennium as China's Buddhist age, when the religion permeated culture, arts, and governance. Ten thousand temples transformed the Chinese countryside within 300 years of the fall of the Han. Religious Daoism became increasingly sophisticated and experienced great growth, too, but new Chinese developments in Buddhism particularly endeared the latter to the masses.

China and Foreign Trade

Chinese leaders had ambivalent feelings about trade with foreigners. On the one hand, they did not want to provide "the barbarians" with the means to become richer or the technology to become stronger. But to ensure stability on the northern frontier and with their

Document From *The Book of Songs:* "A Simple Rustic You Seemed"

Every Confucian gentleman was expected to memorize *The Book of Songs,* one of the five Chinese Confucian classics, along with *The Book of History, The Book of Rites,* and *The Book of Change*. The poems of *The Book of Songs* were composed between 1000 and 600 B.C.E. This particular poem is attributed to the Daoist "old master" Laozi.

A Simple Rustic You Seemed

A simple rustic you seemed,
Carrying cloth to barter for silk.
But you did not come to buy silk;
You came with a design on me.
I saw you off, wading the river Ch'i
As far as Tun-ch'iu.
"It is not that I'd put off the date,
But no good go-between you have,
Please, do not be angry;
Autumn is the time we meet again."
I climbed that ruined wall
To look towards Fu-kuan.
I did not see Fu-kuan;
My tears flowed in streams.
After I had seen Fu-kuan,
How I laughed and talked!
You'd consulted the shell and the stalks,
And there was nothing inauspicious.
You came with your carriage
And carried me away and my goods.
Before shedding from the mulberry tree,
How glossy green the leaves are!
Alas, you turtledove,
Eat not the mulberries!
Alas, you women,
Do not dally with men!
When a man dallies,
He will still be pardoned;
But when a woman dallies,
No pardon will she have.
The mulberry leaves have fallen,
All yellow and sere.
Since I came to you,
Three years I have lasted poverty.
The waters of the Ch'i are full;
They wet the curtains of my carriage.
The woman remains constant,
But the man has altered his ways;
He is lacking in faith
And changeable in his conduct.
Three years I was your wife,
I never tired of household chores.
Early I rose and late I went to bed
Not a morning was I without work.
First you found fault with me,
Then treated me with violence,
My brothers, not knowing this,
Jeered and laughed at me.
Quietly I brood over it
And myself I pity.
Together with you I was to grow old;
Old, it has made me wretched!
The Ch'i, at least, has its banks,
And the swamp, its shores.
At the feast of the "tufted hair,"
We talked and laughed gaily.
You pledged solemnly your truth,
Little reckoning that it would be broken.
No, I never thought that it could be broken,
And that this should be the end.

(Trans. Wu-chi Liu)

Questions to Consider

1. This poem gives us an indication of the role of gender in classical China. What sense do you now have regarding how expectations for women differed from expectations for men?
2. *The Book of Songs* contained folk songs, military songs, religious hymns, and love songs. The poem "A Simple Rustic" is one of the love songs. Do you think the ideas and emotions expressed here can be compared to the thoughts and sentiments in contemporary love songs? If so, why and if not, why not?
3. Do you think that this poem can be read as an expression of protest, or do you see it more as an acceptance of the composer's personal history?

From Wu-chi Liu and Irving Yuchang, eds., *Sunflower Splendor. Three Thousand Years of Chinese Poetry* (Garden City: Anchor Books, 1975), pp. 97–101.

Central Asian neighbors, the Chinese engaged in trade, especially in silk. In return they received the horses and woolen goods they needed. The Han government began to actively promote the silk business in the first century B.C.E. Some of the caravans carrying silk reached the Mediterranean basin via middlemen along trade routes stretching from Rome to China. In late nineteenth-century Europe the idea of the existence of one Silk Road was first popularized, but, in fact, there were numerous routes, most of which led to India or Persia. We have evidence of the trade from the Roman writer Pliny who criticized the decadence of those in Rome who were purchasing silk. The Latin word *serica* ("silk") came from *Seres,* the Greek word for China. Just as China was forced to form relationships beyond its borders, others were beginning to formulate images and policies for China.

In 138 B.C.E. the Han emperor Wudi sent an envoy to Bactria to seek allies against the Xiongnu. The information he brought back amounted to the Chinese discovery of western Eurasia. Intrigued above all by his envoy's report of interest in Chinese silks and his description of Central Asia's magnificent horses, Wudi resolved to open trade relations with his western neighbors. His armies pushed across the Pamir Mountains to a location close to Alexandria Eschate (Khojend), founded by Alexander the Great as the northern limit of his empire. Shortly after 100 B.C.E. silk began arriving in the Mediterranean basin, conveyed by the Parthians. Wealthy private merchants carried on this trade, which required large outlays of capital. They organized their cargoes into caravans of shaggy packhorses and two-humped Bactrian camels. When the Chinese armies moved back across the Pamirs, the Kushans of India became their middlemen, selling the silk to the Parthians and later to European merchants coming by sea to India.

It was not until about 120 C.E. that the Parthians allowed some merchants from the west to cross their land. The information they brought back about the Chinese was used by Ptolemy in constructing his map of the world. During the first and second centuries C.E.—the prosperous years of the Pax Romana—the peoples of the Roman Empire had a voracious appetite for Chinese silk, which the Romans believed was produced from the leaves of trees. In 166 C.E., according to the *History of the Later Han Dynasty,* some merchants from Da Qin ("Great Qin," the Chinese name for Rome), claiming to represent "King Antun" (Emperor Marcus Aurelius Antoninus), arrived in South China by sea across the Bay of Bengal and around the Malay peninsula.

To satisfy the Roman world's insatiable appetite for luxury goods, trade with China grew immensely in the first two centuries of the Common Era. But because such Roman exports to the East as wool, linen, glass, and metalware did not match in value Rome's imports of silk, spices, perfumes, gems, and

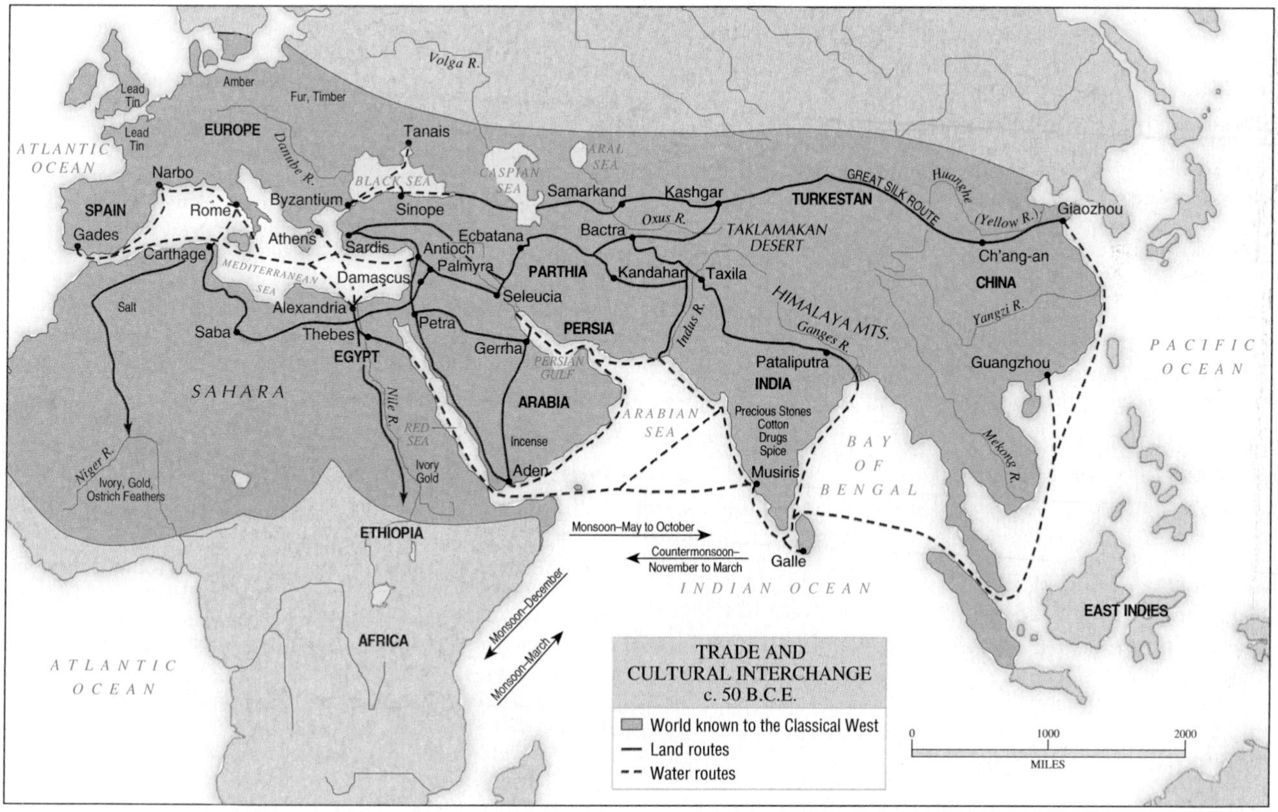

An interconnected world economy existed long before the advent of modern communications and technology. During the first century B.C.E., Africa, Asia, and Europe were drawn together in a trade cycle of raw materials and finished goods. Many items were traded across Eurasia, but the predominance of silk in the trade between the Han and Roman empires led to the routes across Central Asia being dubbed the "Silk Road."

other luxuries, the West suffered seriously from an adverse balance of trade. Gold and silver had to be continually exported to Asia. Late in the first century C.E., Pliny estimated that China and Arabia drained away annually at least 100 million sesterces (the daily wage of an unskilled Roman laborer was 4 sesterces).

For the Chinese, trade with what would come to be Europe was the least important aspect of its international commerce during the Han dynasty and continued to be so until the nineteenth century. There were, however, relations between China and the West through central Asia. Indochina, Korea, Japan, India, and the lands to the north would all come together in the next millennium to form the first global trading zone, in conjunction with the Arab markets, and would enrich and stimulate China.[14]

Early China

CONCLUSION

China was created because of, not in spite of, constant turmoil over the centuries. By the third century C.E. institutions of kingship, kinship, and empire would be in place. These would take highly different forms throughout the centuries. Nonetheless, the idea of a centralized kingdom under the mandate of Heaven was now a powerful force.

Confucian presumptions about social relationships, including the interaction between women and men in the family and between the dead and the living, had taken a strong hold. So had the Daoist philosophical and religious stream of thought that provided a counterpoint to Confucianism because of its emphasis on nonaction over social interaction and on supernatural beliefs. Buddhism was beginning to transform the entire religious landscape. The Chinese state was based primarily on Confucian concerns, however, focusing on the secular amelioration of social evils and the relief of distress.

Finally, a domestic bureaucratic model that relied on both Confucian and Legalist goals and methods was in place by the beginning of the Common Era. China was seen as a united entity inhabited by a people with shared culture and power. The imperial ambitions that had coalesced many kingdoms into one was channeled into a lively trade with the outside world, and the dynamic interaction between China and its neighbors resulted in cultural innovations and enormous social change.

Suggestions for Web Browsing

You can obtain more information about topics included in this chapter at the websites listed below. See also the companion website that accompanies this text, http://www.ablongman.com/brummett, which contains an online study guide and additional resources.

Ancient Dynasties
http://www-chaos.umd.edu/history/ancient1.html

Images and text present a view of early China, from prehistory to the era of the Warring States, 221 B.C.E.

China the Beautiful
http://www.chinapage.com/chinese.html

Extensive site exploring the art, calligraphy, poetry, literature, and music of China throughout its lengthy history.

Ancient China
http://www.wsu.edu:8080/~dee/ANCCHINA/ANCCHINA.HTM

Chinese history from 4000 to 256 B.C.E., with details about philosophy and culture.

Literature and Film

Selected Poems of Chu Yuan, ed. Dayu Sun (Universe Inc., 1999) presents a translation of representative poems by the man considered the first great Chinese poet. In the classic *Pan Chao: Foremost Woman Scholar of China* (published 1932; reprinted with an introduction by Susan Mann, Center for Chinese Studies, 2001), Nancy Lee Swann paints an insightful picture of the famous Chinese woman intellectual—a sketch of the Eastern Han period when Pan Chao (Ban Zhao) lived and wrote, of her family background, and of the literary milieu of which she was a part. In addition, Swann provides translations of writings definitively identified with Ban that survive from the years when she was active (c. 89–105 C.E.).

The Tomb of the Terra Cotta Warriors offers viewers a detailed look at one of the most surprising and important archaeological discoveries in history (The History Channel, 2001).

Suggestions for Reading

Insightful surveys and analyses of ancient China include John K. Fairbank, *China: A New History* (Belknap, 1998); Jacques Gernet, *A History of Chinese Civilization*, 2nd ed. (Cambridge University Press, 1996); Derk Bodde, Charles le Blanc, and Dorothy Borei, *Essays on Chinese Civilization* (Princeton University Press, 1981); Charles Holcombe, *The Genesis of East Asia* (University of Hawaii Press, 2002); David Keightly, ed., *The Origins of Chinese Civilization* (University of California Press, 1983); Michael Loewe, *The Pride That Was China* (St. Martin's Press, 1990); Kwang-Chih Chang, *The Archaeology of Ancient China*, 4th ed. (Yale University Press, 1987), and *Shang Civilization* (Yale University Press, 1982); Michael Loewe, John K. Fairbank, and Denis C. Twitchett, eds., *The Ch'in and Han Empires, 221 B.C.–A.D. 220* (Cambridge University Press, 1986); and Patricia Buckley Ebrey, *Cambridge Illustrated History of China* (Cambridge University Press, 1996).

The following are excellent treatments of intellectual and religious traditions: Benjamin Schwartz, *The World of Thought in Ancient China* (Harvard University Press, 1985); Frederick W. Mote, *Intellectual Foundations of China*, 2nd ed. (McGraw-Hill, 1989); A. C. Graham, *Disputers of the Tao* (Open Court Publishing, 1989); Isabelle Robinet, *Daoism: Growth of a Religion,* trans. Phyllis Brooks (Stanford University Press, 1997); and Daniel Overmyer, *Religions of China* (Harper and Row, 1986). On the fine arts, see Michael Sullivan, *The Arts of China,* 4th ed. (University of California Press, 2000), and Wen Fong, ed., *The Great Bronze Age of China* (Metropolitan Museum of Art/Knopf, 1980).

CHAPTER

3

Ancient India

From Origins to 300 C.E.

CHAPTER CONTENTS

The Indian subcontinent since ancient times has functioned as a matrix for networks of trade and culture. It has been the target of conquerors and empire builders and the origination point of philosophical and artistic trends that have radiated outward along the land-based routes linking Asia with Europe and the seaborne routes connecting South Asia to Africa, the Middle East, Southeast Asia, and East Asia. The civilizations of classical India have had a profound effect that endures to this day on the arts, literature, religion, and philosophical beliefs of the world.

The subcontinent called India was a land of sometimes dense settlement as early as the Stone Age, dating back 500,000 years. An area diverse in climate, geography, language, and ethnicity, it was, like all premodern societies, primarily a village-based agricultural society. In the ancient times discussed here, India produced an extensive civilization in the Indus valley of the northwest that ultimately declined, adopted culture and language from people who immigrated from the Iranian plateau, and later generated a second large-scale state, centered in the northeast but including large blocks of territory elsewhere throughout much of the subcontinent. Other empires rose and fell, especially in the south, throughout antiquity. Synthesizing the social ideas and the philosophical and religious beliefs and practices arising from immigration and temporary contact with those of indigenous people, India developed three major religious traditions during this time, Hinduism, Jainism, and Buddhism, the last of which spread far beyond the bounds of India to become a pan-Asian and today global religion.

2500 B.C.E.

c. 2500 Indus valley civilization develops

c. 1900–1000 Composition of the early *Rig-Veda*

c. 1900–1700 Growth of Aryan culture

1000

c. 600 Composition of the earliest *Upanishads*

500

c. 481 (perhaps as late as 400) Death of Gautama Buddha

c. 468 (perhaps as late as 447) Death of Jain Tirthamkara Mahavira

c. 400 Composition of early *Mahabharata* and *Ramayana*

321 Chandragupta Maurya establishes Mauryan kingdom

269–232 Reign of Ashoka

1

40 C.E.–200 C.E. Kushana Empire rules northern India

First century Development of Mahayana Buddhism

EARLY INDIA

- *How did indigenous culture and outside influences come together to create ancient Indian civilization?*

In this chapter we trace the important threads of Indian history to the third century C.E. This period was the formative age of Indian civilization, when its basic institutions and cultural patterns were determined.

Early Civilization in India

The term *India* is used here to refer to the entire subcontinent, an area encompassing the modern nations of Pakistan, India, Nepal, Bhutan, Bangladesh, and Sri Lanka. The term *subcontinent* is frequently used to refer to this large area. It could also be used to refer to other discrete parts of Eurasia, such as China or Europe, but such uses are not common. The Indian subcontinent is a large, irregular diamond, the lower sides of which are bounded by the warm waters of the Indian Ocean and the upper sides by the mountain walls of the Himalayas on the north and several smaller ranges on the west. The highest mountains in the world, the Himalayas, and their western counterparts divide India from the rest of Asia, making it a geographically discrete area, though never cut off from the great movements of civilization and culture. Through the Khyber Pass and other mountain passes in the northwest and across the Indian Ocean have come the armed conquerors, restless tribes, merchants, and travelers who did much to shape India's turbulent history.

In addition to the northern mountain belt, which shields India from arctic winds, the subcontinent comprises two other major geographical regions. In the north is the great plain (which came to be known as *Hindustan* after the Muslim invasions), extending from the Indus valley to the Bay of Bengal. It spans the watersheds of two great river systems, the Indus and the Ganges, which have their sources in the Himalayas. South of this great plain and separated from it in the west by the Vindhya mountain range, rises a semiarid plateau, the Deccan ("southland").

India's climate and the rhythms of Indian life are governed by the dry northeast monsoon wind of the winter and the wet southwest monsoon wind of the summer. Most parts of India receive the majority of their rainfall during the summer and autumn months of the southwest monsoon, which blows in from the Arabian Sea. The Western Ghats cause the summer monsoon to drop most of its rain on the thin Malabar Coast, making it one of the wettest areas of the globe, but the western Deccan, directly east of the Ghat range, has a semiarid climate.

India comprises an area comparable to Europe in size and internal diversity. The regions and peoples of India came to be roughly divided into two major language groups, the Indo-European in the north and the Dravidian in the south; each group embraces a number of separate languages. In the centuries between 1900 B.C.E. and 300 C.E., the emerging Hindu cultural synthesis, though modified by diverse philosophies and religions, gave the subcontinent a general cultural

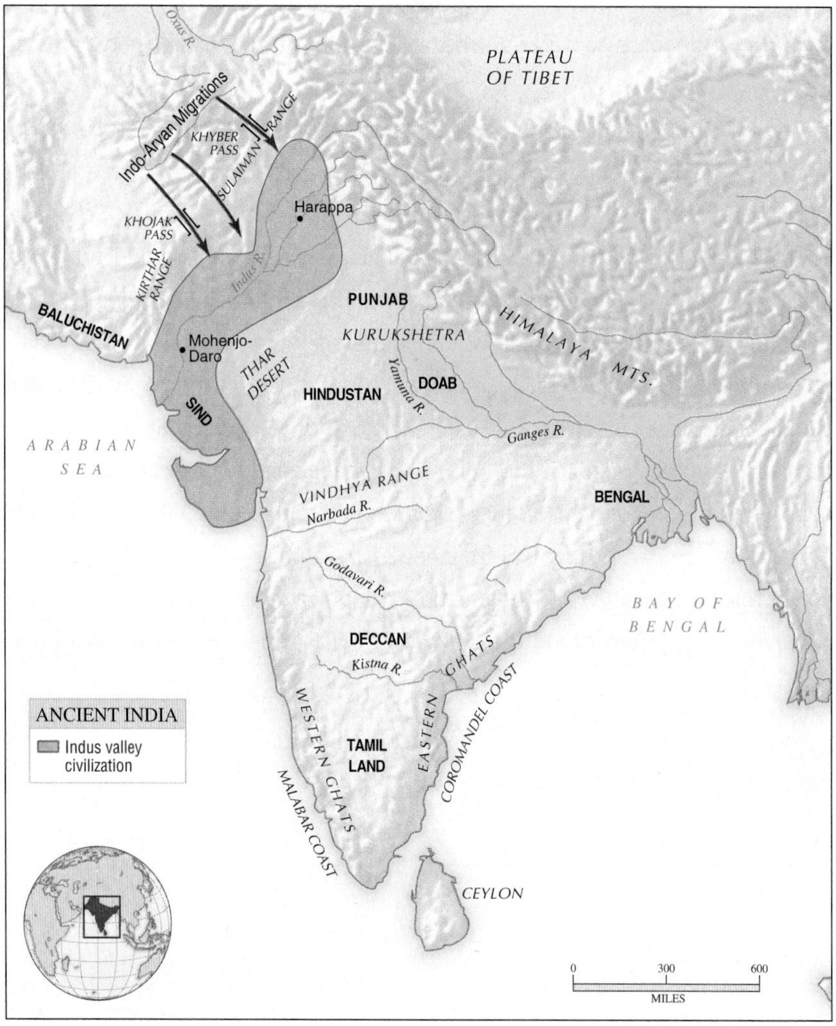

India is a peninsula protected on its northern frontiers by the Himalaya, Kirthar, and Sulaiman mountain ranges.

unity similar to the unity afforded to Europe by the spread of the Christianity in the first millennium C.E.

The Indus Civilization, c. 2500–1500 B.C.E.

Sometime before 2500 B.C.E., a counterpart of the civilizations that had emerged along the Tigris and Euphrates and the Nile appeared along the Indus River in northwestern India. This area, called the Punjab (poon-JAHB) or "land of the five rivers, is made up of an alluvial plain watered by the upper Indus and its tributaries, and the region of the lower Indus (called Sind, from *sindhu,* meaning "river," and the origin of the terms *Hindu* and *India*). This Indus valley civilization flourished until about 1700 B.C.E. Among its major cities, Mohenjo-Daro (moh-HEN-joh dah-ROH), located north of Karachi in present-day Pakistan, is believed to have been one of the largest Bronze Age cities of the world.

Archaeologists believe that the Indus valley civilization began declining sometime around 1900 B.C.E. Around that time, or perhaps a few hundred years earlier, migrants began to move into the subcontinent from the Iranian plateau. Their culture and language gradually came to dominate the north of India, as people adopted important aspects of the migrants' culture and intermixed with them. The migrants' religion, cultivated by their **Brahmans** (BRAH-muhns; seers and priests), became the foundation for much of the later cultural development of the entire subcontinent.

The rise of civilization in the Indus valley around 2500 B.C.E. resembled what had occurred in Mesopotamia nearly a thousand years earlier. In India Neolithic farmers had been living in food-producing villages situated on the hilly flanks of large river valleys since around 4000 B.C.E. These settlements spread out along the river valleys, capitalizing on their abundant water and fertile soil. Here they developed the more complex way of life we call a civilization. Some of these farming villages had grown into large cities with as many as 40,000 inhabitants by 2300 B.C.E. Excavations of two of these cities, Mohenjo-Daro in Sind and Harappa (hah-RAP-pah)

Brahmans—The priestly *varna*; highest in Hindu caste hierarchy.

The ruins at Mohenjo-Daro, a city of an estimated 30,000 to 50,000 people, are still impressive more than four millennia after the city was established. There has been much speculation concerning the function of Mohenjo-Daro's largest buildings. Were they temples, administrative centers, or perhaps granaries? Only the function of the large public bath seems at least relatively clear.

This tiny figure of a girl who may be dancing was unearthed at Mohenjo-Daro and probably dates from around 2000 B.C.E.

in the Punjab, have provided much of our knowledge of the Indus valley civilization, but other sites were widely dispersed across the whole of northwestern India. Reaching its height in the centuries around 2000 B.C.E., the Indus valley civilization produced highly organized towns and uniform weights, measures, and pottery.

Although Mohenjo-Daro and Harappa were 400 miles apart, similarities in the cities' construction and layout suggest that the Indus River made possible the maintenance of a uniform administration and economy over the entire area. The cities appear to have been carefully planned, with residential blocks arranged on a north-south grid and an elaborate drainage system with underground channels. The spacious two-storied houses of the well-to-do contained bathrooms and were constructed with the same type of baked bricks used for roads. Indeed, it was the durable bricks produced by Indus valley builders that led, in part, to the discovery of Harappa after a nineteenth-century work crew found and "recycled" its ancient bricks for a railway project.

The economy of the Indus civilization, like that of Mesopotamia and Egypt, was based on irrigation farming. Wheat and barley were the chief crops, and the state collected these grains as taxes and stored them in huge granaries. For the first known time in history, chickens were domesticated as a food source during the Indus civilization, and cotton was grown and used in making textiles. Cotton textiles would ultimately become a world trade good and an important source of wealth for South Asia. The spinning and weaving of cotton remains today one of the subcontinent's chief industries.

The nature of the society that produced Indus valley civilization is the subject of considerable controversy. Unlike Egyptian hieroglyphics, which were deciphered by modern scholars using the Rosetta Stone, the Indus valley script (400 pictographic signs) has never been deciphered. Thus, the Indus valley writings, used on engraved stamp-seals, have given rise to modern claims and counterclaims about their "true" meaning. Indus stamp seals depict bulls, rhinoceroses, and crocodiles—but they also depict horned humans, unicorns, and large figures that may or may not be gods, generating considerable speculation about the beliefs and social organization of Indus peoples.

Numerous clay mother goddess figurines have been unearthed, indicating an early version of mother-goddess worship still important in India. Such figures are also found in various forms throughout the Mediterranean world, although their exact meaning in India and elsewhere is the subject of considerable debate. Another controversial question is whether the Indus valley peoples were peaceful or warlike. Copper and bronze were used for tools and weapons, but the rarity of weapons has been used by some scholars to suggest that Indus society was peaceful. An interesting archaeological find is a set of three double graves, each with

Excavations at Mohenjo-Daro have unearthed what are often called "mother goddess figurines" such as this terra-cotta female. The figure, with her elaborate headdress, may well be a symbol of fertility but that conclusion is speculative.

a male and a female. These may be married couples buried in single graves, which may suggest an early form of a wife's duty to her husband, called *sati,* so strongly praised in later centuries.

We cannot yet solve the Indus valley controversies, but what the archaeological evidence does make clear is that the Indus valley civilization was prosperous and well organized. Trade was sufficiently well organized to obtain needed raw materials—copper, tin, silver, gold, and timber—from the mountain regions to the west; and there were active trade contacts with Mesopotamia, some 1500 miles away, as early as 2300 B.C.E. (the time of Sargon of Akkad). In addition, Indus valley seals have been found in Sumerian sites.

Excavations at Mohenjo-Daro show that decline was well underway when a series of great floods caused by earthquakes altered the course of the Indus around 1700 B.C.E and apparently severely affected the settlements along it. Other Indus valley cities, such as Harappa to the north, appear to have suffered a similar fate, although some others continued to carry on long after the decline of these two great cities. The culture of migrants entering the Indus valley through the northwest passes around 1900 B.C.E. was thus able to influence the language, religion, and culture of north India as the great Indus valley civilization was on the decline.

The Introduction of Aryan Ways in the Early Vedic Age, 1900–1000 B.C.E.

The question of the end of the Indus valley civilization and its replacement in north India by different languages and customs is a topic of heated debate among historians. While some assert that a large wave of people called Aryans invaded and conquered north India, bringing their culture with them, other historians stress that Indians already living in the north adopted the culture of a much smaller though influential group of people who immigrated from the Iranian plateau and merged with them. Thus, those who called themselves Aryans included many local people who used the term to distinguish themselves from those who did not share their culture; the distinction, these historians assert, was not between an indigenous ethnic group and immigrants from outside India, but was based more on cultural differences.

People of Aryan culture who lived in northeastern India and eastern Afghanistan inhabited tribal villages and herded cattle, sheep, goats, and horses. Their language, an early form of Sanskrit, belonged to a group of languages called Indo-European, which include Sanskrit, Persian, Celtic, English, Germanic, Italian, and Greek languages. Whether one accepts the view that a wave of semibarbaric Aryan nomads skilled at chariot warfare contributed to the weakening of the Indus valley civilization or accepts the increasingly common view that local people gradually adopted Aryan culture as they mixed with them, Aryan language and culture certainly became indigenized and dominant in northern India in the first five or six centuries after their arrival. Not all indigenous populations of the subcontinent adopted Aryan languages and cultures. Some, located in the Deccan, retained their own, which were part of the Dravidian language group. The Aryans referred to these people as *Dasas,* which had a negative connotation of "dark" enemies.

During the centuries in which Aryan culture was absorbed in north India, Aryans worshipped their gods with sacrificial rituals that were accompanied by specially composed "verses of praise and adoration," *ric* verses, which would be recited together in "hymns." The *ric* verses and the hymns they made up were regarded as the sacred compositions of inspired seers (the Brahmans), who could see the gods and understood their ways and were thus able to compose verses that could influence the gods to favor and bless Aryan men and their families. Over 1000 such hymns were gathered together in the *Rig-Veda* (reeg-VAY-dah), a collection that has been memorized and used in worship continuously for over 3500 years. (*Veda* means "knowledge," a reference to the Brahman's knowing all the hymns by memory.) The earliest part of the *Rig-Veda* was probably composed between 1900 and 1500 B.C.E., and later portions were added until about 1000 B.C.E. Both religious and secular hymns are included in the *Rig-Veda;* in the latter, the structure of society, with its occupational classifications, is revealed. Thanks to the *Rig-Veda* we know more about the Aryans than we know about the Indus civilization, for which we must still rely only on archaeological evidence because their writings have not yet been deciphered.

The early Aryan religion involved making sacrificial offerings of grain, cakes, dairy products, and animals to the gods, who embodied and controlled the forces of what we today call "nature," in return for such material gains as long life, health, many offspring, victory in war, and life in the "bright place in the sky" (heaven). The god worshipped most in the *Rig-Veda* was Indra, storm-god and patron of warriors, who is described as leading the Aryans in destroying the forts of the Dasas. Virile and boisterous, Indra personified the heroic virtues of the Aryan warrior aristocracy as he drove his chariot across the sky, wielded his thunderbolts, ate the meat of dozens of sacrificed bulls and buffaloes, and quaffed entire lakes of the stimulating ritual drink *soma,* which might have been alcoholic, narcotic, or psychedelic.

Statue of Indra, God of War

Next to Indra in popularity was Agni, the benevolent god of fire, who performed many services for the

Document *Rig-Veda:* Creation and the Kinds of Men

Like other ancient peoples, the societies of India developed a variety of creation myths. Such myths often involve stories of sacrifice and explanations for the hierarchy of beings. The Purusha Sutra of the *Rig-Veda* provides the first suggestion in ancient Vedic texts of the notion of the *varnas,* the idea that humankind is divided into four classes and their differences are based in Creation itself. The four classes are priests (Brahmans), rulers and warriors (Rajanyas or Kshatriyas), herders and merchants (Vaishyas), and the low-class workers or servants (Shudras). In this Vedic story, Purusha (the "primordial cosmic man") serves as the victim in the cosmic sacrifice from which the universe originates.

The sacrificial victim, namely Purusha, born at the very beginning, they [the gods] sprinkled with sacred water upon the sacrificial grass. With him as oblation, the gods performed the sacrifice, and also the *Sadhyas* [a class of semidivine beings] and the *rishis* [ancient seers].

From that wholly offered sacrificial oblation were born the verses and the sacred chants. . . . From it the horses were born and also those animals who have double rows of teeth; cows were born from it, from it were born goats and sheep.

When they divided Purusha, in how many different portions did they arrange him? What became of his mouth, what of his two arms? What were his two thighs and his two feet called?

His mouth became the brahman; his arms were made into the rajanya; his two thighs the vaishyas; from his two feet the shudra was born.

The moon was born from his mind, from the eye the sun was born; from the mouth Indra and Agni [Vedic gods], from the breath the wind was born.

From the navel was the atmosphere created, from the head the heaven issued forth; from the two feet was born the earth and the quarters [the four cardinal directions] from the ear. Thus did they fashion the worlds.

. . . With this sacrificial oblation did the gods offer the sacrifice. These were the first norms [dharma] of sacrifice. These greatnesses reached to the sky wherein live the ancient *Sadhyas* and gods.

Questions to Consider

1. Think about the many different ways that people can be divided. What is the system of division in this myth based on?
2. What does this myth suggest about the roles of the gods and of sacrifice in Indian society?
3. Think about other creation myths you have heard or read. How is this one similar or different?

From Ainslie T. Embree, ed., *Sources of Indian Tradition,* Vol. 1, 2nd ed. (New York: Columbia University Press, 1988), pp. 18–19.

Aryans, not least of which was conveying their ritual offerings up to the other gods. Another major Aryan god was Varuna, the sky-god. Viewed as the king of the gods, he lived in a great palace in the heavens where one of his associates was a sun-god, Mitra, known as Mithras to the Persians and, a thousand years later, widely worshipped in the Roman Empire. Varuna was the guardian of *rita,* the "right order of things." *Rita* was both the cosmic law of nature (the regularity of the seasons, for example) and the customary tribal law of the Aryans. Varuna was, thus, the divine judge.

The *Rig-Veda* is the earliest surviving work of literature in an Indo-European language, and it gives some insight into the institutions and ideas of the Early Vedic Age. Each tribe was headed by a war leader called *raja,* a word related to the Latin word for king, *rex.* Like the early kings of Sumer, Greece, and Rome, the raja was only the first among equals. Two tribal assemblies, one a small council of the great men of the tribe and the other a larger gathering of the heads of families, approved his accession to office and advised him on important matters.

The hymns in the *Rig-Veda* mention three social categories ***(varnas),*** the Brahmans or priests, the **Kshatriyas** (kuh-SHAH-tree-yas) or nobility, and the **Vaishyas** (VAI-shas) or commoners. A fourth class, the **Shudras,** the non-Aryan population of workers and serfs, was then added at the bottom of the social scale.

---

varnas—Originally occupational groups; later also four status groups connected to purity and prestige at sacred rituals.

Kshatriyas—The *varna* associated with governing and military power; second in the *varna* hierarchy.

Vaishyas—Commoner *varna;* merchants and landlords; third in the *varna* hierarchy.

Shudras—Menial workers; lowest in *varna* hierarchy.

developments, beginning around 600 B.C.E, was the composition of texts called the ***Upanishads*** (oo-PAHN-ee-shads). The second was the rise of the new non-Vedic, even anti-Vedic, monastic religions of Jainism and Buddhism sometime in the fifth century B.C.E.

In the 600s B.C.E. a radical minority of Brahmans began to embrace ascetic and mystical religious ideas and practices (early forms of yoga, meaning "spiritual discipline" and usually involving some kind of meditation) that ultimately rejected the goals and means of Vedic ritual religion and the settled village and family life that Vedic religion presumed. Some of these radical mystics recorded the *Upanishads,* which taught "secret, mystical understandings" of the human body, the breath, the mind, and the soul. The most important of these understandings was the assertion that the light of consciousness within a person was nothing less than the undiluted energy of *brahman,* the eternal, sacred creative energy that is the source and the end of all that exists (equivalent to God in monotheistic religions).

Most of the *Upanishads* taught that all things that exist—from the most sublime ideas a person could think to the crudest forms of matter—came from *brahman* energy and eventually returned to *brahman,* the only permanent reality. Beyond these ideas, the *Upanishads* taught a way for ethically pure, worthy persons (usually only Aryans, but not necessarily just Brahmans) to immerse themselves into *brahman,* which the *Upanishads* described as unsurpassably blissful. These ideas gained great power after their presentation in the *Upanishads*. A relatively tiny minority of people followed this yoga (most Aryan people continued to make use of Brahman priests and Vedic rituals). But the basic ideas, values, and meditative techniques over time greatly influenced South Asian society and came to be regarded as the supreme form of Brahman religion.

The Vedic Brahmans had thought that people live only once and that the fate of their soul is determined in that one life. (The same general idea is found in all three of the Western Abrahamic religions: Judaism, Christianity, and Islam.) Vedic Aryans hoped to live up in the heavens with the sky-gods after their death. The *Upanishads,* however, introduced the idea of the transmigration of the soul, which was entirely new in Brahman thought. (Some scholars have speculated that this idea was part of pre-Aryan culture, but there is no solid evidence of this.) Then, in texts called the *Brahmanas,* the idea was put forward that a person's deeds stayed with him or her in the form of an unseen power that would act after that person's death and condition the

Upanishads—Sacred Brahmanic scriptures collected in sixth century B.C.E. that stress *brahman* force and idea of cyclical rebirth until release through *moksha*.

Developments in Culture and Religion in India

c. 600 B.C.E.	Earliest *Upanishads*
c. 481 (perhaps as late as 400) B.C.E.	Death of Gautama Buddha
c. 468 (perhaps as late as 447) B.C.E.	Death of Mahavira
c. 300 B.C.E.	Jainism gains support in North and South India

fate of the departed soul. A deed or action was called *karman* in Sanskrit, and the unseen power of past deeds was called *karman* as well (karma in contemporary English).

The latest *Brahmana* texts sometimes express a fear that people "die again"—the accumulation of their good works, their good karma, supports them in heaven when they die, but the karma gets used up keeping the soul in heaven, and the soul then "dies" again, in heaven. This fear leads directly to the idea that when the soul dies in heaven, it descends to earth, reincarnated in another body. This new person lives and dies, and the soul goes to heaven once again, if the earthly actions of this latest lifetime have been good (that is, if they conformed with the law, or dharma [DAR-mah] as revealed in the *Vedas*). Bad deeds, bad karma, lead the soul to hell.

Eventually, the idea emerged that rebirth in sub-human forms of life was a natural consequence of violating dharma. After living a life as some kind of animal, a soul automatically moves up the ladder of life forms toward an eventual human incarnation because animals cannot violate dharma. The rebirth of the soul in a new body is called *samsara* (sam-SAH-rah), and the *Upanishads* regarded continual, unending samsara as dreary and unpleasant. The *Upanishads* taught that good deeds, including Vedic rituals, could do nothing more for a person than provide a temporary spell in heaven between incarnations. Bad deeds, of course, had far more unpleasant consequences; but worse than either hell or heaven was the prospect of living, acting, and dying over and over, forever without end. In the face of this bleak prospect, the *Upanishads* said the only truly good thing a person can do is try to escape perpetual samsara through release from desire and eventually from rebirth. That release was called *moksha* (MOHK-sha). Achieving *moksha* involves permanently escaping from karma, from

DOCUMENT
Transmigration of Souls in the *Upanishads*

samsara, and from all the pain and suffering encountered in countless lives. According to the *Upanishads*, by permanently immersing oneself in *brahman* through meditation, a person can dissolve the soul back into the holy oneness that is its ultimate source and end. The soul has "returned home"—its journey through samsara is over.

The *Upanishads* depict the first Indian gurus wandering in the forests as ascetics; there they meditated and taught their disciples. One of them summed up their quest as follows:

From the unreal lead me to the real!
From darkness lead me to light!
From death lead me to immortality!

Of course, most Indian people did not become gurus or devote their lives to meditation and asceticism; most Indians lived the life of the agriculturalist. But the powerful ideas of rebirth and *moksha* presented in the *Upanishads* and the *Brahmanas* had an enormous impact on subsequent Indian thought and social organization.

The Jains, Defenders of All Beings

Beyond the changes just noted in Vedic religious thought, two non-Vedic religions also emerged in South Asia during this time: Jainism and Buddhism. Jainism contributed to all of India (and today to the rest of the world) the unique ethical claim that the most important duty of a person is **ahimsa** (ah-

ahimsa—The practice of nonviolence toward all living things; a belief central to Jainism initially but also adopted by Buddhism and Hinduism.

Document The Jains on the Souls in All Things

The Jains, like the Buddhists, believe in conquering desire as a way of achieving Enlightenment and escaping from the cycle of rebirth. But the Jains emphasize the existence of souls in all living things. They believe all beings experience pleasure, pain, terror, and unhappiness. Hence Jain texts reveal a heightened sensitivity to the pain man can inflict by harming all things, animate and inanimate. This verse passage is taken from a Jain text depicting the speech of a prince who is trying to persuade his parents to allow him to take up a life of religion. He tries to express to them the terrible agonies suffered by beings at various levels of creation.

From clubs and knives, stakes and maces,
breaking my limbs,
An infinite number of times I have suffered
without hope.
By keen edged razors, by knives and shears,
Many times I have been drawn and quartered,
torn apart and skinned.
Helpless in snares and traps, a deer,
I have been caught and bound and fastened, and
often I have been killed.
A helpless fish, I have been caught with hooks and
nets;
An infinite number of times I have been killed and
scraped, split and gutted.
A bird, I have been caught by hawks or trapped in
nets,
Or held fast by birdlime, and I have been killed an
infinite number of times.
A tree, with axes and adzes by the carpenters
An infinite number of times I have been felled,
stripped of my bark, cut up, and sawn into
planks.
As iron, with hammer and tongs by blacksmiths
An infinite number of times I have been struck
and beaten, split and filed. . . .
Ever afraid, trembling in pain and suffering,
I have felt the utmost sorrow and agony. . . .
In every kind of existence I have suffered
Pains that have scarcely known reprieve for a
moment.

Questions to Consider

1. What problems might the Jain teachers have encountered in trying to persuade others to accept their beliefs?
2. If someone truly believed that such suffering was endured by all beings, how might it affect that person and change his or her behavior?
3. Like the Buddha, the "speaker" in this text is a prince going against the wishes of his family. What does this speech suggest about generations, change, and a family's ambitions for its sons?

From Ainslie T. Embree, ed., *Sources of Indian Tradition*, Vol. 1, 2nd ed. (New York: Columbia University Press, 1988), pp. 62–63.

HEEM-sah), which is to practice nonviolence and to cause no harm or pain to any being. Buddhism also adopted the idea of ahimsa, and, over time, many, but not all, Brahmans and their followers eventually did likewise.

Jainism places a special emphasis on the idea that all beings (including plants, insects, and minerals) have "souls" *(jiva)* and experience pain. Thus, causing pain to any other sentient beings is the biggest source of the worst possible karma. Jain texts, for example, explain in graphic detail the suffering caused to the tiny beings living in wood when it is cast upon the fire. While it is inevitable that a believer will cause pain (by drinking water and the beings that are in it, for example), a person should avoid such destructive acts as much as possible. Some Jains, who practice their faith most rigorously, gently sweep the path before them with a broom as they walk to avoid stepping on living things; they may tie cloths over their mouths to avoid inhaling any small creatures in the air.

The most significant figure in Jain belief is Mahavira (mah-hah-VEE-rah; c. 559–c. 468 B.C.E.), the faith's founder. Mahavira means "great hero." He is called the *Jina* (JEE-nah, "victor," "conqueror"), and his followers are called *Jainas* (those who "follow the Jina"), hence the Western name *Jainism* for the religion as a whole. According to Jain tradition, Mahavira was a Kshatriya prince who at the age of 30 renounced the world—his home and family and all property and status that went with them.

For over a dozen years Mahavira followed the teachings of an earlier religious teacher, Parshvanatha (parsh-vah-NAH-tah). During those years Mahavira wandered naked from place to place, lived on handouts, engaged in meditation, debated with other men who were also on holy quests, observed celibacy, and engaged in various painful ascetic practices in order to purify his soul of past karma. Nudity was a form of asceticism because it exposed the genitals and invited the painful ridicule of ordinary people. The practice of nudity was the subject of debate among later Jain ascetics and gradually died out.

Mahavira gained a great reputation as a wise and holy man, attracting many followers. Thirteen years after he resolved to starve himself to death to achieve release from the bondage of his past karma, he died after seating himself in the posture of meditation with the intention of never moving again. This deliberate form of death by inaction is seen not as an act of suicide but as the most heroic and ascetic form of nonaction humanly possible. For those whose souls were still fouled with karma, this mode of death was regarded as highly purifying, and many Jain saints have died this way throughout history.

The Jains accept the reality of samsara and karma and regard *moksha* (release from rebirth) to be the only sensible goal to pursue in life; but their way of pursuing *moksha* was very different from that of the Brahmans of the *Upanishads*. The path to *moksha* that Mahavira preached centers on the practice of asceticism, although one does not have to practice the most rigorous forms to be considered a pious Jain. To gain *moksha* a Jain must sooner or later, in this life or a future life, renounce the world and become a wandering monk or nun. But a person may be a pious lay Jaina, supporting the monks and nuns with handouts of food, clothing, and shelter and living a life that conforms to the Jain ethic (which emphasizes nonviolence but also forbids liquor, sex outside of marriage, lying, and stealing) until he or she is convinced that the time for renunciation has come.

Jains believe Mahavira died in 527 B.C.E., but modern, non-Jain historians believe he died 60 to 80 years later. Jains believe Mahavira was the twenty-fourth and last great *tirthamkara* (teer-tahm-KAH-rah; a "ford-maker," who aids his followers in crossing the swirling flood of samsara, the cycle of rebirth) in a long series of wise and powerful men in this current age. For Jains time revolves in endless cycles like a great cosmic wheel. In every age, *tirthamkaras* like Mahavira are born to teach the doctrines of Jainism to humanity. Every era consists of millions of years. The Jains also believe that when a soul gains *moksha* and escapes the cycle of rebirth forever, it ascends to the topmost point of the universe, where it exists in complete purity forever. This differs dramatically from the idea of the *Upanishads* that every individual's soul is completely submerged into *brahman*, the single "soul" of the whole universe.

DOCUMENT

Jainism: From *The Book of Sermons, The Book of Good Conduct*

Socially, Jainism was distinctive. It rejected the sacredness of the *Vedas* and thereby rejected the social stratification that assigned preeminence to the Brahmans. Interestingly, Jainism was also the first Indian religion formally to allow women to become renouncers and pursue *moksha* as nuns. The Buddha only reluctantly and belatedly allowed Buddhist laywomen to become nuns; and although some Hindu women did renounce the world from time to time, the Hindu dharma (sacred law) never formally sanctioned their doing so.

In the centuries after Mahavira the number of Jains has always been significant but never tremendously large. In spite of always being a minority religion in India, the Jains have consistently exerted greater influence than their numbers would lead anyone to expect. By 300 B.C.E. Jainism had gained significant political recognition in various kingdoms of north and south India. Also, because the ethics of their religion basically forbade farming for pious lay followers of the Jina (because tilling the soil kills so many small creatures), lay Jains were usually merchants living in cities. They often became wealthy and poured much of their wealth into the support of their religion. As a result, the Jain religion has contributed a great number of learned Jain scholars and libraries to India's cultural history.

The Middle Way of Gautama Buddha

About the same time that Mahavira lived, another ascetic and monastic religion arose in northern India. This religion, Buddhism, became popular and important in India and remained influential there for many centuries. It also spread outside India to all of Asia and today continues its expansion around the globe. Buddhism had some basic similarities to Jainism, but its root ideas were profoundly different. Both religions derive from the life and teachings of a great man; both stress the humanity of their teacher and do not rely on gods or divine rites to pursue the highest goal of life; both developed monastic institutions in which celibate men and women lived in spiritual communities, supported by a devoted laity. There is an archaic quality to many Jain doctrines, probably due to the fact that the Jain religion was never taken up by people outside of India. Buddhist doctrines, by contrast, seem very modern in certain ways, which may in part account for Buddhism's appeal to non-Indian peoples, including Europeans and Americans in the twenty-first century.

Whereas Jainism stresses purification of the soul and ascetic pain and its leader is described in military terms as a "great hero" and "victor," Buddhism's founder was a man whose leadership was the result of his "waking up," having his understanding boosted to a higher level of insight. The word *buddha* means basically "someone who has awakened from sleep." Buddhists see the Buddha's Great Awakening *(Bodhi)* as the greatest discovery of the truth of life that has ever been made. As Jains follow Mahavira's soldierly example, Buddhists seek to use the Buddha's example and his teachings so that they too may wake up and realize the benefits of Awakening (often also called Enlightenment).

The man who became the Buddha was born Siddhartha Gautama (sid-HAR-ta gow-TAH-ma), a prince of the Shakyas (SHA-kee-ahs), whose small oligarchic state was located at the foot of the Himalayas. As with many of the world's great figures, the traditional accounts of the Buddha's life contain many legends and miracles. Accordingly, Gautama was conceived when his mother dreamed one night that a white elephant entered her right side. Later the baby was born from her right side, and right after birth the baby stood up and announced that this would be his last life. Seers predicted that Gautama would become either a great king or a great sage who would see four special sights of human suffering—a sick man, an old man, a dead man, and an ascetic holy man seeking to escape suffering—after which he would renounce the world and discover a way to relieve the world's suffering.

This seated Buddha from Sarnath shows the elongated earlobes, heavy-lidded eyes, knot of hair, hand gestures, and expression of deep repose that are symbolic of the Buddha.

The traditions tell us that Gautama's father, King Shuddodana (SHOOD-doh-DAH-nah), raised him in luxury and went to great lengths to prevent the prince from ever seeing the sick, the old, or the dead.

In the prince's twenty-ninth year, however, all his father's protections proved vain in the face of fate: On three separate occasions the prince happened to see a sick man, an old man, and a dead man. These sights shocked him, and he was troubled to learn, from his chariot driver, that all people suffer sickness, old age, and death. He then happened to see a wandering ascetic who was in quest of *moksha,* and this encounter made him think very deeply about how to free himself from life's suffering. To his father's great disappointment, Gautama decided to follow that ascetic's example. He renounced his wealth and position, forsaking his wife and child.

Gautama studied meditation for a year with two different teachers, abandoning both after a while because their doctrines did not satisfy him. Then, like Mahavira, he took up the most painful and demanding forms of asceticism and practiced them with great determination and devotion. Gautama almost died from this fasting and self-torture, and after five years he concluded that these ascetic practices weakened the mind and would not lead to the end of suffering.

Gautama left his ascetic companions, who ridiculed him for his "weakness," walked down to a river and had his first bath in five years, then sat down under an expansive banyan tree (the Indian fig tree) to rest in the cool shade. (Asceticism was regarded as a kind of purifying heat by ancient Indians.) Gautama was then given a refreshing meal by a rich woman who offered a special meal once a year to the spirit of that tree. Clean, refreshed, and reinvigorated by food, Gautama was vibrantly awake as night fell. He sat up meditating all through the night; as the night progressed, his mind examined the world and its workings, and he came to understand more and more the fundamental causes for all that happens. Shortly before the dawn, he attained the key insights for understanding and then eliminating suffering, but not, according to legendary tradition, before the demon Mara (Death) and his daughters Greed, Lust, and Anger did all in their powers to prevent his grasping the truth.

Gautama summarized the truth to which he "woke up" during this Great Awakening as the Four Noble Truths, which succinctly express the entire system of Buddhist thought. The religious way of life to which the Four Noble Truths lead is often called the Middle Way. It is the way of life that is in between the normal human life of sensation, desire, and action, on the one hand, and the life of harsh asceticism, on the other. The Middle Way involves the moderate asceticism of renunciation, celibacy, and the Buddhist monastic way of life as opposed to the much more rigorous asceticism of Indian groups such as the Jains. The whole philosophy, which the Buddha taught to others, and the religious way of life to which those ideas lead is referred to in Buddhism as the *Dharma*. (The root sense of *dharma* for Hindus is "religious law" or "religious good deeds leading to a good afterlife"; Dharma, for Buddhists, has a broader meaning.)

DOCUMENT
Buddha's Sermon at Benares and The Edicts of Ashoka

Buddha's Four Noble Truths are these:

1. Suffering dominates our experience.
2. The cause of suffering is desire or craving.
3. It is possible to extinguish suffering by extinguishing its cause, thereby attaining nirvana. (*Nirvana* originally referred to a fire's going out; the Buddha's idea was to let the fire of desire go out by depriving it of its normal fuel. It resembled *moksha.*)
4. The Noble Eightfold Path leads to the extinction of desire—that is, it leads to nirvana.

The Noble Eightfold Path consists of pursuing the following eight ideals:

1. *Right views*—the intellectual conviction that the Four Noble Truths are "the Truth."
2. *Right resolve*—the decision to act according to the Four Noble Truths.
3. *Right speech*—having words be governed by the Five Moral Precepts of right conduct: do not harm any living being (ahimsa); do not take what is not given to you; do not speak falsely; do not drink intoxicating drinks; do not be sexually unchaste.
4. *Right conduct*—having deeds, like words, be governed by the Five Moral Precepts.
5. *Right livelihood*—conducting oneself ethically even in earning a living; hence such occupations as farming (which could lead to the killing of small creatures), soldiering, prostitution, and tavern keeping are disallowed.
6. *Right effort*—following the path with all one's heart and energy by renouncing the world and becoming a monk or nun.
7. *Right mindfulness*—a form of meditation that eventually produces "wisdom"; wisdom undermines desire because the wise person no longer sees his or her own self as particularly important in the world.
8. *Right concentration*—a form of meditation that uses trances to make the nonrational and unconscious layers of the person completely calm and tranquil.

Buddhism claims that desire is extinguished and nirvana attained when steps 7 and 8 of the path have been perfected—that is, when the person on the path has the wisdom to see that he or she is just one more sentient being among many and is no more valuable or important than any other (this removes the natural instinct to fight for success and even survival) and when "concentration meditation" has stilled all the powerful impulses and drives that condition every sentient being's mind. A person who has reached this nirvana of desire simply looks at his or her own condition at any given moment as "what is" and does not wish it to be otherwise, is not driven to improve it, does not envy anyone else, and does not suffer. Physical pain may be present, but the person who has reached nirvana is dissociated from it and simply sees it as one more fact of the situation of the moment. Nirvana is a happy, friendly state (in which the Buddha lived for 45 years after his Awakening), but it is not an "altered state" of consciousness and certainly not a paradise or any kind of heavenly world. Later developments in Chinese and Japanese Buddhism did create ideas about rebirth in paradise and suffering in hell, but the Buddha himself did not suggest these.

In Buddhist thought the essential element of action is the desire to get something for oneself. So, the Buddhists believe that a person who has extinguished desire no longer really performs actions, even if his or her body may be going through the motions. In other words, such a person accumulates no karma and has escaped the round of samsara. For Buddhists this nirvana amounts to gaining *moksha*.

Many peoples over time have struggled with the question of what, if anything, comes after death. The Buddha's followers were no exception. But when they asked him what happens after the devotee escapes the cycle of rebirth, the Buddha told them that the question could not be answered and was pointless anyway. Such a question, he said, "tends not to edify"; that is, it does not contribute to the one important goal. The only important thing a person can do in life is deal with suffering.

Dressed in a simple yellow robe, with begging bowl in hand, Gautama wandered through the plain of the Ganges, speaking with everyone (regardless of social class) and attracting disciples to a growing community (called the *Sangha;* SAN-gah) of monks walking the Path. He taught many sermons (the Sutras; SOO-trahs) and laid down the Rules specifying many details of the monks' daily life (the Vinaya [vee-NAH-yah] analogous to the much later Rule of St. Benedict in Medieval Europe). Resisting at first, the Buddha eventually acquiesced to demands that women be allowed to renounce the world and pursue the path and its advanced meditations on a full-time basis as nuns. Buddhist history states that while the Buddha lived, it was relatively easy to accomplish the nirvana of desire and suffering and that a great number of disciples actually did so.

At last, 80 years old and enfeebled, the Buddha was invited by a poor blacksmith to a meal. According to legend, the food included tainted mushrooms, but Gautama ate the meal rather than offend his host. Later in the day the Buddha had severe pains, and he knew death was near. Calling his disciples together, he gave them this parting message: "Be ye lamps unto yourselves. Be a refuge to yourselves. Hold fast to the truth as to a lamp. Look not for refuge to anyone beside yourselves." The Buddha had instructed that his body be burned. According to legend, his followers quarreled over possession of his ashes, which were divided into eight parts and ensconced in shrines called *stupas* (STOO-pas). Buddhist tradition credits the third century B.C.E. king Ashoka with construction of tens of thousands of stupas all over his realm, into which the ashes from the eight original stupas were subdivided. Whether or not Ashoka actually carried out this holy task, there are now stupas all over South Asia.

The Buddha stressed the fact that each person could overcome suffering only through her or his own efforts, another aspect of Buddhism that would be modified a millennium after his death by Buddhists in East Asia. Nonetheless, his followers developed a profound affection for him and were very attached to him. After his death (even to some extent during his life) many of his followers believed that mere contact with him would somehow benefit them. What the Buddha taught is a philosophy, but the movement developed by his followers, which we call Buddhism, is a religion. That religion has had a profound effect on the society, politics, and economy of South Asia and other areas, like China, Japan, and Vietnam, where Buddhism spread.

The Buddha, the Dharma he taught, and the Sangha, the community of Buddha's followers, are regarded by Buddhists as the Three Precious Jewels. Historically, as in the Jain religion, the majority of the Buddhist community are laypeople who live in the world until they sense the time is right to take the sixth step of the path, right effort, and become a monk or a nun. (In some Buddhist countries, lay Buddhists often make short retreats to a monastery for instruction from the monks and practice in meditation.) In addition to restricting their speech, conduct, and livelihood by the Five Moral Precepts, they cultivate the virtues of generosity, friendliness, and compassion. Buddhists believe that only people with great amounts of good karma ever hear the Buddhist teachings; and only those with even more good karma possess the courage and determination actually to become a monk or a nun. In the end one does not want any karma at all, good or bad, but whatever good karma a lay Buddhist accumulates will help carry that person further along the Path in this or a future life.

Buddhists who became monks or nuns donned the yellow (or orange) robe worn by all renouncers in India except the Jains (who wore white if they wore anything). Unlike their Hindu and Jain counterparts—who usually lived alone or in small assemblies without any Rule—Buddhist renouncers created the world's first monastic communities, in which people pursuing spiritual goals lived together under strict rules. Often the Buddhists lived in caves that rich lay Buddhists had cut into the sides of mountains or rock cliffs. Their only possessions were their sandals, robe, and begging bowl. They ate only one meal a day and ate only what they had received from begging. Periodically all the monks in a given area recited together all the rules of monastic life, and anyone who had violated any rule was required to make a public confession. Four sins warranted permanent expulsion from the community: fornication, stealing, murder, and making false claims of one's spiritual attainments. Large parts of the day were given over to meditation, and monks who had accomplished nirvana were known as *arhats* (AHR-hahts; "worthy ones").

Buddhist Religious Site

The Buddha was a critic of all religious and philosophical thinkers who came before him. He censured the *Vedas* and the rites of the Brahmans, considered the *Upanishads* wrong about *brahman,* and thought Mahavira's religion of ascetic purification futile. The Buddha took an agnostic stance on what really might lie beyond this world; he claimed that we, as finite, conditioned beings, had no way of knowing anything about infinite, unconditioned beings. He thought that anyone, regardless of social status, could gain nirvana, but he did not himself try to change Indian society. Though Shudras and women were admitted to Buddhist monasteries, those monasteries still tended to mirror the social structures and habits of the larger Indian society.

As with Mahavira, there is great uncertainty about exactly when the man who became the Buddha died. Buddhists have traditionally taught that he died in 526 B.C.E. Modern, non-Buddhist historians believed for many decades that 481 B.C.E. was a more accurate date. Current historical scholarship is energetically reconsidering this date and pushing it down toward 400 B.C.E. or possibly even later. Whatever the exact dates of Gautama Buddha and his contemporary Mahavira, both lived and taught in eastern India as powerful new kingdoms were in the process of turning into the Mauryan (MOW-ree-ahn) Empire (inaugurated about 320 B.C.E.). Buddhism in particular would have a significant impact on the organization of that empire.

THE MAURYAN EMPIRE AND OTHER KINGDOMS, 320 B.C.E.–300 C.E.

- *Why was Ashoka ancient India's most revered king?*

By the sixth century B.C.E., 16 major kingdoms and tribal oligarchies stretched across northern India, from modern Pakistan to Bengal. The richest and most powerful kingdom was Magadha (mah-GAH-dah), located in the eastern region that included the Ganges River. The Magadha kingdom's support of Buddhism was key to the new religion's survival and growth. The kingdom's important role in trade is seen in the presence of its coins in the far northwest of India as well. Nevertheless, it took an outside stimulus for the Magadha kingdom to attempt to build an empire. Two centuries later, a conquering general, Alexander the Great, appeared in the region. Son of a Macedonian warlord, this famous general conquered the Persian Empire (see Chapter 4), and in 326 B.C.E. brought his phalanxes into the Indus valley, defeating local Punjabi rulers. Despite his apparent ambitions to conquer India, the Punjab proved to be the easternmost territory of Alexander's empire. His weary troops refused to advance farther eastward. So, Alexander constructed a fleet and sailed to the mouth of the Indus; he then returned overland to Babylon while his fleet skirted the coast of the Arabian Sea, sailing west to the Persian Gulf.

Classical India

After Alexander's death in 323 B.C.E., the empire he had built so rapidly quickly disintegrated, and within two years his kingdom in the Punjab had completely disappeared. He had, however, helped open routes between India and countries to the West and,

The Mauryan Empire

326 B.C.E.	Alexander the Great invades India
321 B.C.E.	Chandragupta seizes Magadha
305 B.C.E.	Chandragupta defeats Seleucus
269–232 B.C.E.	Reign of Ashoka
c. 185 B.C.E.	Brahman-led revolt against last Mauryan emperor

by destroying the petty states in the Punjab, facilitated the conquests of India's own first emperor.

The Founding of the Mauryan Empire (326–184 B.C.E.)

A new era began in India in 321 B.C.E., when Chandragupta (chahn-drah-GOOP-tah) Maurya seized Pataliputra (pah-tah-li-PU-trah), capital of the state of Magadha in the Ganges valley. Chandragupta conquered northern India from this sophisticated city and founded the Mauryan dynasty, which endured until about 184 B.C.E. At its height, the empire spanned most of the subcontinent except the extreme south, although many of its territories were separated by lands ruled by other kings.

India's first empire reflected the imperial vision of its founder. Chandragupta created an administrative system of remarkable efficiency. He was also a brilliant general who extended his control westward beyond the Indus River. In 305 B.C.E. he concluded a treaty with Seleucus, the general who had inherited the major part of Alexander the Great's empire in western Asia, that ceded all territories east of Kabul to the Mauryans in return for an exchange of ambassadors and a gift of 500 war elephants to Seleucus.

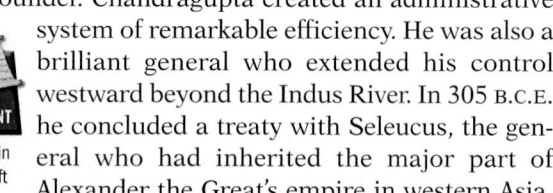

DOCUMENT
Lessons in Statecraft

Life in the Mauryan Empire

Seleucus's ambassador to the court of Chandragupta, Megasthenes, wrote a detailed account of his experiences in India in his diary, fragments of which have survived. They give a fascinating picture of life in the empire. Chandragupta's capital, Pataliputra (known today as *Patna*), covered 18 square miles and was probably the largest city in the world at the time. Outside its massive wooden walls was a deep trench used for defense and the disposal of sewage.

The remarkably advanced Mauryan Empire was divided and subdivided into provinces, districts, and villages whose headmen were appointed by the state. The old customary law, preserved and administered by the Brahman priesthood, was superseded by an extensive legal code that provided for royal interference in all matters. A series of courts, ranging from the village court presided over by the headman to the emperor's imperial court, administered the law. So busy was Chandragupta with the details of his highly organized administration that, according to Megasthenes, he had to hear court cases during his daily massage.

CASE STUDY
Hinduism and the Mauryan Empire

Two other factors struck Megasthenes as important in the administration of the empire. One was the professional army, which he reports was an enormous force of 700,000 men, 9000 elephants, and 10,000 chariots. The other was the secret police, whose numbers were so large that the Greek ambassador concluded that spies constituted a separate class in Indian society. Chandragupta, fearing conspiracies, was said to have lived in strict seclusion, attended only by women who cooked his food and in the evening bore him to his apartment, where they lulled him to sleep with music.

Of course, the historian cannot take literally the details or the numbers in Megasthenes's account. They were impressionistic and designed to create certain effects on his audience at home. Ambassadors had limited knowledge of and exposure to the daily lives of kings, and the stories of rulers and their female companions are often myths based on hearsay and conjecture. Furthermore, the counts of armies, especially of one's enemies, tended to be inflated. Nonetheless, it is clear that Megasthenes was impressed by the urban development, political organization, and military force of Chandragupta's empire.

An important indigenous source of information on Chandragupta's reign is a remarkable book, called the *Arthashastra* (ar-tah-SHAS-trah), or *Treatise on Material Gain,* written by Kautilya (kow-TIL-ya) as a guide for the king and his ministers. Said to be Chandragupta's chief adviser, Kautilya exalted royal power as the means of establishing and maintaining political and economic stability. The great evil, according to the *Arthashastra,* is anarchy, such as had existed among the small warring states in northern India. To achieve the aims of statecraft, a single authority (the king), who must employ force when necessary, was needed. Kautilya advised the king to make war on weaker kings and make peace with those who had equal or greater power. Attacking a stronger king, he said, is like "engaging . . . in a fight on foot with an elephant," while attacking an equal was like striking two unbaked jars together—both would be smashed. The king must also be wary of sons, "who are inclined to devour their begetters." Kautilya advised the king that princes should be carefully trained; but he also suggested making sacrifices in advance while the queen was pregnant and arranging for specialists to supervise her nourishment and childbirth.[1]

The *Arthashastra* is an early example of a whole genre of literature, sometimes called "mirrors for princes," that provided advice to monarchs on the best and most effective ways to rule. Later examples are found in the Middle East and Europe—for example, the medieval Persian work of Qai Qa'us and that of the Renaissance author Machiavelli. Machiavelli, like Kautilya, would advocate deception or unscrupulous means to attain desired ends. The *Arthashastra* remains in print today and has been translated into many languages. Modern leaders have been known to consult its pages.

The Mauryan state controlled and encouraged economic life. Kautilya's treatise, which is thought to reflect much actual practice, advises the ruler to "facilitate mining operations," "encourage manufacturers," "exploit forest wealth," "provide amenities" for cattle breeding and commerce, and "construct highways both on land and on water." Price controls are advocated because "all goods should be sold to the people at favorable prices," and foreign trade should be subsidized: "Shippers and traders dealing in foreign goods should be given tax exemptions to aid them in making profits."[2] Foreign trade did flourish, and the bazaars of Pataliputra displayed goods from southern India, China, Mesopotamia, and Asia Minor. Agriculture, however, remained the chief source of wealth. In theory, all land belonged to the state, which collected one-fourth of the produce as taxes. Irrigation and crop rotation were practiced, and Megasthenes states that there were no famines. The ability of the ruler to insure a regular supply of food for his kingdom was, of course, a primary measure of success.

Ashoka, India's Greatest King

Following Chandragupta's death, his son and grandson expanded the Mauryan Empire southward into the Deccan peninsula. His grandson, Ashoka (ah-SHOH-kah; r. 269–232 B.C.E.), the most renowned of all ancient Indian rulers, however, gained a reputation for being more committed to peace than to war. After eight years of expansion by military means, Ashoka attacked the kingdom of Kalinga with great brutality. The cruelty of that campaign horrified him, and he resolved never again to permit such acts of butchery. Ashoka adopted the Buddhist law of nonviolence (ahimsa) in his realm in the tenth year of his reign. The story of Ashoka's horror at the carnage of war is similar in some ways to the account of Yudhishthira (yoo-deesh-TEE-rah) in the *Mahabharata,* which also relates a king's remorse in the aftermath of battle. Scholars have pointed out that Ashoka did not renounce violence until he had completed his conquest. But for our purposes, the story of Ashoka illustrates the inherent contradictions between the idea of nonviolence and the idea that a king was by nature a warrior whose duty it was to preside over violence and death.

Throughout his empire, Ashoka had his edicts carved on rocks and stone pillars. They remain today as the oldest written documents in India yet deciphered (the Indus valley texts have not yet been deciphered) and are especially valuable for appreciating Ashoka's own construction of the spirit and purpose of his rule. For example, they contain his conception of the duty of a ruler:

> *He shall . . . personally attend the business . . . of earth, of sacred places, of minors, the aged, the afflicted, and the helpless, and of women. . . . In the happiness of his subjects lies his happiness.*[3]

Although Ashoka made Buddhism Maurya's state religion, he did not persecute the Brahmans and Hindus but proclaimed religious toleration as an official policy:

> *The king . . . honors every form of religious faith . . . whereof this is the root, to reverence one's own faith and never to revile that of others. Whoever acts differently injures his own religion while he wrongs another's.*[4]

Ashoka was a successful propagator of Buddhism. He supported the building of temples and stupas all over his empire, and the remains of many are still standing. He sent Buddhist missionaries to various lands—the Himalayan regions, Tamil Land (India's far south), Sri Lanka (Ceylon), Burma, and even as far away as Syria and Egypt, transforming Buddhism from a small Indian sect to a missionary faith. Modern Indians revere his memory, and the famous lion on the capital of one of his pillars has been adopted as the national seal of the present Indian republic.

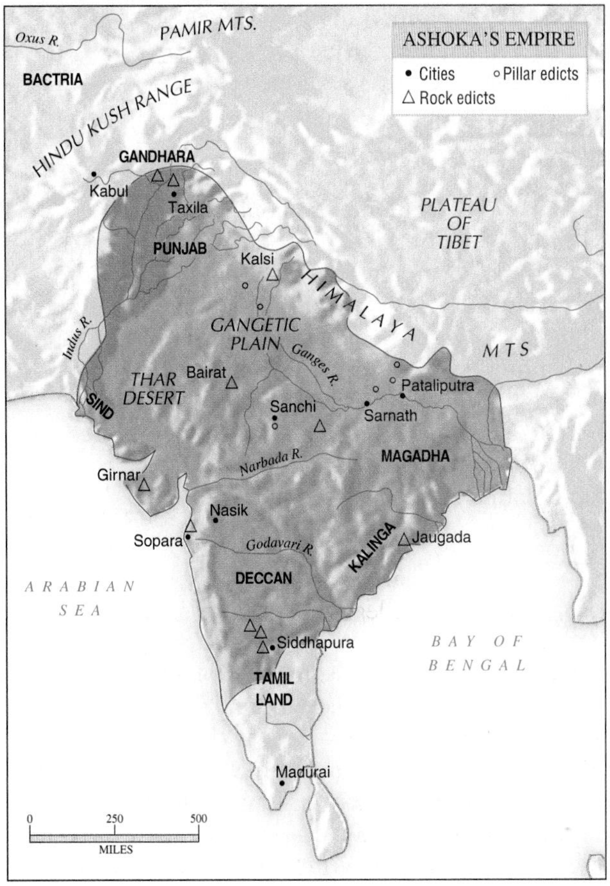

Ashoka (c. 268–233) left a written record of his reign inscribed on rocks and stone pillars all over the Mauryan Empire.

Fall of the Mauryan Empire

As so often happens, almost immediately after Ashoka's death in 233 B.C.E., the Mauryan Empire began to disintegrate. The last emperor was assassinated about 185 B.C.E. in a palace uprising led by a Brahman general. Once again, the subcontinent was politically fragmented. Northern India was overrun by a series of invaders, and the south, never controlled by the north, maintained its separate status.

The sudden collapse of the powerful Mauryan state and the grave consequences that ensued have provoked much scholarly speculation. Some historians have believed that the fall of the Mauryans can be traced to a hostile Brahman reaction against Ashoka's patronage of Buddhism. Others believe that Ashoka's inclination toward nonviolence curbed the military ardor of his people and left them vulnerable to invaders. More plausible explanations for the fall of the Mauryan state take into account the transportation and communications problems facing an empire that spanned much of the Indian subcontinent, with unsubdued areas separating territory under Mauryan control; the difficulty of financing a vast army and bureaucracy; and the intrigues of discontented regional groups within the empire.

In fact, one might argue that political division is a more natural state for large multiethnic, multilingual landmasses with diverse terrain; empires that endure and unite vast expanses of territory are the exception. No one person could directly rule all of the subcontinent; like the later Roman and Ottoman empires elsewhere, the Mauryan kingdom survived through a combination of talented leadership, economic success, flexible rule, and delegated authority.

Bactrian Greeks and Kushanas

The Mauryan Empire was the first of two attempts to unify much of north and even central India in ancient times. The second—the work of the Gupta dynasty (c. 320–550 C.E.)—was more limited in its geographical reach, but was a glorious empire nonetheless (see Chapter 10). In the five centuries between these two eras of imperial splendor, a succession of foreign invaders entered South Asia from the northwest and added new cultural elements to the Indian scene.

The first of the new invaders of India were Greeks from Bactria. They were descendants of the soldiers settled there by Alexander the Great to serve his empire in the East. After Alexander, Bactria continued as a province of the Seleucid Empire, a bastion against the attacks of nomadic tribesmen from the north and a center for trade with India to the southeast. The decline of the Seleucid Empire allowed the Bactrian Greeks to establish an independent kingdom about 245 B.C.E.

In 183 B.C.E., two years after the death of the last Mauryan emperor of India, the fourth Bactrian king, Demetrius, crossed the Hindu Kush mountains as Alexander had done 150 years earlier and occupied the northern Punjab. From his base at Taxila, Demetrius and his successors ruled Bactria and the entire Punjab (modern Afghanistan and northern Pakistan), while Taxila functioned as an important nexus of both the east-west and north-south trade.

Coins provide interesting evidence of cross-cultural artistic influences and of the self-definitions of rulers and peoples. This Bactrian coin from 170–159 B.C.E. shows the influence of Greek portraiture on South Asian money.

The Greeks in India established the farthest outpost of Hellenism in the Hellenistic Age (see Chapter 4). Their cities were not Greek enclaves in a hostile land, like Alexandria in Egypt and Antioch in Syria. The South Asian peoples were enrolled as citizens, a bilingual coinage was issued bearing Greek inscriptions on one side and Indian on the other, and at least one king, Menander, became a Buddhist. The Indo-Greek Buddhist art in the Gandhara (gahn-DAH-ra) was the greatest legacy of the era of Greek control. Some other Greeks in Bactria adopted aspects of Indian culture, including Hindu worship.

But soon after 150 B.C.E. Bactria was overrun by nomadic tribesmen. Thereafter, Greek rule in the northern subcontinent steadily declined until the last remnants disappeared late in the first century B.C.E. Hordes of nomadic peoples, migrating out of Central Asia, replaced the Greeks in Bactria and northwestern India. First to arrive were the Indo-European Scythians, who had been pushed out of Central Asia by other Indo-European nomads known in Chinese sources as the Yuezhi (yoo-EH-zhih). In their turn, the Yuezhi occupied Bactria, and about 40 C.E. they crossed the

Hindu Kush and conquered the Punjab. The Yuezhi divided into four tribes, and one, Kushana (koo-SHAH-na), took over in north India, expanding eastward to the middle Ganges valley and southward perhaps as far as the borders of the Deccan.

In contrast to the more centralized Mauryan Empire, the Kushana state was more like a loose federation—its kings were overlords rather than direct rulers—yet it gave northern India two centuries of peace and prosperity. The Kushana kingdom acted as a hub for trade routes linking India, China, and the West. Its greatest ruler, Kanishka (kah-NEESH-ka; fl. c. 120 C.E.), produced a multicultural coinage that employed Chinese, Greek, Persian, Hindu, and Buddhist devices. Kanishka gained fame as a patron of the arts and of a new form of Buddhism called **Mahayana** (MAH-hah-YAH-nah).

South India

To a large extent, India can be divided culturally into north and south. Although the south was often penetrated by northern conquerors, in general its civilizations developed in a fashion distinct from those of the north. The vast tableland of South India—the Deccan—and its fertile coastal plains remained outside the main forces of political change in the north, except, in some cases, for the 150 years of Mauryan imperial rule. The peoples of this area differed in appearance, culture, and very importantly, language—their languages were part of the Dravidian language family rather than Aryan—from the Aryan-speaking peoples of the north. Gradually, however, as Brahman priests and Buddhist monks infiltrated the south, Hinduism and Buddhism were grafted onto the existing Dravidian culture.

Politically, the south remained divided into numerous warring states. Prominent among them were three well-developed Tamil (an old Dravidian language) kingdoms in the southern third of the Deccan peninsula. These three kingdoms—Chera, Pandya, and Chola—alternated between allying to fend off northern attacks and rivalrous warfare among themselves. In the early fourth century C.E., a new dynasty, the Pallavas, took over in Chola. Under the patronage of the kings of these three states, the Tamil language developed a classically exquisite literature in the first few centuries of the Common Era. This tradition, known as the *Sangam* ("Academy") tradition, was based in the old city of Madurai in Tamil Nadu ("Tamil Land"), and it produced several anthologies of poetry, several unique epics, and a superb handbook of language and poetics. Love was an important theme in the Tamil poetry:

As a little white snake
with lovely stripes on its young body
troubles the jungle elephant
this slip of a girl
her teeth like sprouts of new rice
her wrists stacked with bangles
troubles me.[5]

Tamil society differed in several key respects from northern society. The divisions among groups of Tamils were based on their geographic origin as hill people, forest people, coastal people, and so on. Social structure was possibly matriarchal rather than patriarchal, and matrilineal inheritance was practiced until recently. Both men and women took part in the production of art, music, and dance.

By the first century B.C.E., Tamil Nadu had become an intermediary in the maritime trade extending eastward to the East Indies and westward to the Hellenistic kingdoms. Indeed, a major factor that distinguishes south India from north India is the former's orientation toward the sea. On the east and west coasts of southern India, ports developed that became important entrepots for the East-West trade and important points of cultural contact with foreign states and peoples. There, large jugs called *amphorae* have been found, evidence either of South Asian taste for Roman wine or of the Roman traders' need to bring their favored drink with them on voyages to India. The ships that brought these amphorae, as well as copper, lead, tin, and large numbers of gold coins, sailed back bearing South and Southeast Asian pepper, cotton goods, silks, cinnamon, cloves, and jewels.

EMERGENT HINDUISM AND BUDDHISM, 200 B.C.E.–300 C.E.

▪ *How did Hinduism develop as a religion based on worship of deities and Buddhism branch into two major divisions?*

Hinduism and Buddhism were not static or fixed in time; they were evolving during the classical era. In the years 200 B.C.E. to 300 C.E. the religion called Hinduism was formulating a synthesis and meeting the challenge of Buddhism. Buddhism, in turn, split into two distinct strands of interpretation. These developments were set in the context of the Indian social order that was wedded to village life, caste hierarchies, and a household based on the extended family.

Mahayana—"Greater Vehicle" branch of Buddhism; focuses on bodhisattvas who lead others to nirvana.

The Hindu Synthesis

Hinduism is not one single doctrine. It is an array of highly diverse beliefs that include the various texts of the Vedic Age, pre-Aryan Indian practices, and an evolving set of deities and rituals. Essential to Hinduism are the beliefs in the cycle of birth, death, and rebirth (samsara) and a society structured by social status and proper behavior. Beings may be born as humans in various *jatis* or as lesser creatures, depending on their actions in the previous life. A believer who accumulates good actions ascends in the hierarchy of beings in subsequent births and may ultimately escape rebirth and be absorbed into *brahman* energy.

Three Traditions of Worship and Theology: Vishnu, Shiva, and Devi

Early Aryan religion had focused on sacrifices and rituals, but later Brahmanic religion stressed personal devotion to a deity. This marked the emergence of Hinduism as a religion with increasing popular appeal. The first steps toward this were taken by Brahmans who incorporated Upanishadic thought into their teaching. In doing so, they gave the caste system additional religious support by linking it to karma and the process of reincarnation. The priests made individual salvation, now a conspicuous part of Indian religion, dependent on the uncomplaining acceptance of one's position at birth and the performance of one's dharma, which varied by caste. The belief that a person was born into a caste and died in that caste was given religious support. Marriage outside one's caste was forbidden. Of course, in practice, as in all religious systems, social reality did not always match religious ideals. In fact, some people did marry across caste lines, and some groups did apparently change caste over time. But Brahman and social sanctions against violating caste boundaries made such changes difficult.

The Upanishadic doctrine of salvation by absorption of the individual soul into *brahman* was too intellectual and remote for the average person to grasp fully. Thus, devotion to personal savior gods also emerged as an important element in Hinduism. This devotion centered on anthropomorphic deities with rich personalities and long histories.

The major Vedic gods gradually faded into the background, and three virtually monotheistic gods emerged as paramount in Hinduism: Vishnu (VISH-noo); Shiva (SHEE-va); and Devi (DAY-vee), the Goddess (sometimes called Kali (KAH-lee)). Each one of these gods became immensely popular in Hindu worship. Vishnu, Shiva, and Devi evolved from Vedic and indigenous Indian origins, and each came to be regarded by one or several different traditions as the uniquely supreme and holy God, creator of the universe. The theologies of Vishnu and Shiva were already well developed by about 200 B.C.E.; that of the Goddess was not fully developed until some time later. The theologies of these gods, as in other religious traditions, did not remain static and fixed over the ensuing centuries. In the old Vedic pantheon of the Aryans, Vishnu was a relatively minor god associated with the sun. He then developed into a pacific father-god, comforter, and savior who works continuously for the welfare of humanity. "No devotee of mine is lost," is Vishnu's

Vishnu and his consort, Lakshmi, recline upon the serpent Shesha floating on the waters of creation. Emerging out of Vishnu's navel is a lotus that serves as a throne for the god Brahma, who creates the world. This is a representation of just one of the varied Hindu creation myths. It suggests lushness, fertility, and water as the source of life. Some variants of this particular creation story note that Vishnu also created two demons who were arrogant and boastful. These demons tormented Brahma while he was trying to meditate and attacked Vishnu, thinking they were stronger than he.

promise. His followers believe that he has appeared in nine major "descents" in human form to save the world from disaster. (A predicted tenth descent has yet to happen.) Two of Vishnu's incarnations are described in the great Indian epics, as Krishna in the *Mahabharata* and as Rama (RAH-ma), the hero of the *Ramayana*. Rama saves the human race from the oppressions of a great demon, rules for many years in the city of Ayodhya, and then returns to the "City of the Gods," resuming the form of Vishnu.

Shiva, the other great popular god of classical and modern Hinduism, evolved from a minor Aryan Vedic god who was the guardian of healing herbs but whose arrows also brought disease. It is possible that another prototype of Shiva was a pre-Aryan fertility god who was worshipped in the cities of the Indus civilization. Shiva is often associated with phallic symbols. His spouse, Parvati, is the earliest expression in the Brahman texts of a powerful female goddess who was eventually recognized as a separate deity in her own right (under other names) and elevated to the status of a unique supreme and holy divinity.

Shiva's followers believe he is superior to the other gods. He personifies the cosmic force of change that destroys in order to build anew; he is often depicted with a necklace of skulls. Some representations show Shiva as the Lord of Dancers; the rhythm of his dance is that of a world continuously forming, dissolving, and reforming. He also exemplifies another major characteristic of Hinduism, the reconciliation of extremes: violence and passivity, eroticism and asceticism. Shiva is portrayed as remaining unmoved in meditation for years on end. When he emerges from his meditations, however, he is often lustful and violent.

As already noted, Shiva's wife, Parvati (followed by Vishnu's wife, Lakshmi (LAHKSH-mee)), marked the first appearance in Hinduism of a powerful female divinity. Archaeological and other evidence suggests that goddesses were worshipped in India from the time of the Indus valley civilization. But only toward the Gupta period (fourth and fifth centuries C.E.) did fully developed theologies of a supreme Goddess, Devi (the word *devi* simply means "goddess"), begin to appear. As with the development of Shiva and Vishnu, the development of Devi involved the fusion of numerous local deities into a single complex figure. The Goddess presents two faces to the world: She is a tender mother to her devotees and a ferocious warrior to those who threaten her devotees. Called "Mother" or "Bestower of Food" (Annapurna) in her benevolent moods, she can also be "the Black One" (Kali), wearing a necklace of the skulls of her victims, or Durga, a many-armed warrior riding on the back of a lion to do battle with demons. As the creative power of the universe (similar to the Vedic idea of *brahman*), she is

Lakshmi, Vishnu's consort and goddess of prosperity, beauty, and precious things, emerged from the foam of the ocean. This statuette was found half a world away from India in the ruins of ancient Pompeii in Italy, thus demonstrating the extent of trade both in Indian cultural objects and Indian ideas in the first century C.E.

referred to as Shakti ("Power," "Creative Energy"), and theologies focused on Devi as the Supreme Being of the universe are referred to as Shaktism.

As mentioned earlier, there is no centralized authority in Hinduism. The resulting "flexibility" makes Hinduism seem extremely complicated to outsiders who are used to more structured religious traditions. One aspect of this flexibility is that many versions of the theology and mythology of these deities are mixed together. For example, worshippers of Shiva often recognize Vishnu as an important and exalted creature fashioned by Shiva but who in no way rivals Shiva's divine supremacy. Worshippers of Vishnu often fit Shiva into their theology in similar ways. They also eventually included the Buddha as one of Vishnu's incarnations, and in modern times some Hindus have incorporated the Christians' Jesus into their devotions. Today many Hindus worship Jesus as a divine incarnation, but they do so as Hindus in Hindu ways; they are not Christian converts.

Most Hindus today are devotees of either Vishnu, Shiva, or Devi and their respective incarnations. But animals (especially the cow), vegetation, water, and even stones are also worshipped by some as symbols of the divine. Over time, literally thousands of deities, demigods, and lesser spirits came to form the Hindu pantheon, the world's largest.

Because the authority to teach normative ideas in Hinduism was vested in the Brahmans as a class, Hinduism is probably the world's most flexible religion. Brahmans were present in villages and towns throughout the subcontinent, and many local ideas and practices were "normalized" as "compatible with the *Vedas.*" Hinduism possesses no canon, such as the Bible or the Qur'an; no single personal founder, such as Christ or Muhammad; and no precise body of authoritative doctrine. Hindu beliefs vary dramatically among the faithful.

The serene and reclining god Vishnu is shown here in a sculpture from a sixth-century C.E. *Hindu temple. Beneath Vishnu are the five Pandavas, heroes of the* Mahabharata, *and their shared wife, Draupadi. Draupadi, along with Sita, stands as a model of Hindu womanhood: virtuous, honorable, and strong.*

The Epics

The *Mahabharata* is the great Hindu epic. Composed in verse, it contains over 75,000 stanzas, the longest work of literature in the world. It tells the tale of an all-encompassing war between rival sets of cousins, the Pandavas (pahn-DAH-vas) and the Kauravas (kow-RAH-vas). These cousins are fighting for the throne of the Bharata kingdom, in the upper Ganges plain in the region of modern Delhi. But in the epic, this great battle, lasting 18 days, is not simply a struggle for an earthly kingdom; it is ultimately a cosmic struggle between virtue and evil, a battle to set the world right.

As in the Greek *Iliad*'s account of the Trojan War, the *Mahabharata* presents a dramatic tale of heroism, vengeance, and sacrifice in which the gods directly intervene in the affairs of men. In the great Indian epic, however, it is duty that must govern the actions of kings; only through war will the proper order of the universe be restored. When the war is over and the victorious Pandavas view the horrendous slaughter of their sons, cousins, teachers, and friends, Yudhishthira, the intended king, is so shocked and horrified by the carnage that he refuses to accept the throne and wishes to retreat into the forest. Eventually, however, he is persuaded to become king. It is not his own desires or wishes that Yudhishthira must follow, but his duty.

The *Mahabharata* was shaped and embellished over time. It was incorporated into royal sacrificial ritual, and a long succession of priestly editors added many long passages on religious duties, morals, and statecraft. One of the most famous additions, incorporated into the *Mahabharata* around 200 B.C.E., was the *Bhagavad-Gita* (BAH-gah-vad GEE-tah, "The Lord's Song"), a philosophical dialogue that stressed the performance of duty (dharma) and the overcoming of passion and fear. It is still the most treasured piece in Hindu literature.

The dialogue in the *Bhagavad-Gita* takes place between Arjuna (AR-joo-na), the greatest warrior of the Pandava brothers, and Krishna, an incarnation of the god Vishnu, who takes human form and acts as Arjuna's charioteer. Arjuna is shaken by the prospect of killing his kinsmen. But Krishna, who gradually reveals himself as no ordinary charioteer, instructs Arjuna that he must give up worldly desire and personal attachment and devote himself to discipline and duty. In so doing, he will be able to attain freedom, overcome despair, and act according to his dharma, fulfilling his role in the cosmic struggle. Krishna tells Arjuna:

> *Knowledge is obscured*
> *by the wise man's eternal enemy*
> *which takes form as desire,*
> *an insatiable fire, Arjuna.*
> *The senses, mind, and understanding*
> *are said to harbor desire;*

with these desire obscures knowledge
and confounds the embodied self.
Therefore, first restrain
your senses, Arjuna,
then kill this evil
that ruins knowledge and judgment.[6]

The universal appeal of Arjuna's internal struggle and Krishna's advice has made the *Bhagavad-Gita* a world classic; it has been translated into many languages. Once Arjuna realizes that he is receiving advice from a god, he wants to know more. He wants to see the god as he really is, so he asks Krishna to reveal himself in all his majesty. Krishna obliges the unwitting Arjuna by giving him a "divine eye" with which he can see the whole universe inscribed in the god's body. But this fearful vision of world-devouring time is too much for the awestruck Arjuna. So Krishna takes mercy on him and reverts to his human form.

The other great Hindu epic, the *Ramayana,* which appears to predate the *Mahabharata,* has been likened to the Greek *Odyssey.* It recounts the tale of the exiled prince Rama and his faithful wife Sita (SEE-ta). During their banishment to the forest, Sita is kidnapped by the demon Ravana. Rama searches valiantly for his wife, whom he eventually finds, and vanquishes the

Document The *Ramayana:* The Trial of Sita

In the great Hindu epic, the *Ramayana,* King Rama rescues his wife Sita from her captor, the demon Ravana, after a lengthy struggle. Rama is overjoyed to see Sita but tormented by the shame of knowing she was touched by another male. The doubt thus cast upon her virtue forces him to repudiate her. Devastated at this rejection by her lord, Sita nevertheless proudly answers in her own defense. In a dramatic speech, she demands that a pyre be built on which she can immolate herself. The ideas of devotion, sexual purity, and masculine and feminine honor expressed here are not limited to the society of classical India. They are common in many traditional societies and continue to influence gender relations in the present day.

Rama speaks to his beloved Sita: Oh illustrious Princess, I have re-won thee and mine enemy has been defeated on the battlefield; I have accomplished all that fortitude could do; my wrath is appeased; and the insult and the one who offered it have both been obliterated by me. . . . As ordained by destiny the stain of thy separation and thine abduction by that fickle-minded titan has been expunged by me, a mortal. . . . [However] a suspicion has arisen with regard to thy conduct, and thy presence is as painful to me as a lamp to one whose eye is diseased! Henceforth go where it pleaseth thee, I give thee leave, O Daughter of Janaka. O Lovely One, the ten regions are at thy disposal; I can have nothing more to do with thee! What man of honor would give rein to his passion so far as to permit himself to take back a woman who has dwelt in the house of another? Thou hast been taken into Ravana's lap and he has cast lustful glances on thee; how can I reclaim thee, I who boast of belonging to an illustrious House [family]? . . .

Sita replies with passion: Why dost thou address such words to me, O Hero, as a common man addresses an ordinary woman? I swear to thee, O Long-Armed Warrior, that my conduct is worthy of thy respect! It is the behavior of other women that has filled thee with distrust! Relinquish thy doubts since I am known to thee! If my limbs came in contact with another's it was against my will, O Lord, and not through any inclination on my part; it was brought about by fate. That which is under my control, my heart, has ever remained faithful to thee. . . . If despite the proofs of love that I gave thee whilst I lived with thee, I am still a stranger to thee, O Proud Prince, my loss is irrevocable. . . . Raise a pyre for me, O Saumitri, this is the only remedy for my misery! These unjust reproaches have destroyed me, I cannot go on living! Publicly renounced by mine husband, who is insensible to my virtue, there is only one redress for me, to undergo the ordeal by fire!

Questions to Consider

1. Why might such an abduction be considered equivalent to a rape, even though Ravana never had sexual relations with Sita?
2. Ordeal by fire is an idea and practice found historically in a variety of regions. What does Sita's willingness to undergo such an ordeal suggest about ancient Indian society's beliefs? Why fire?
3. Why are both male and female honor so dependent upon a woman's sexual purity?
4. Why must Rama, as a king, be particularly conscious of his reputation and that of his wife?

From *The Ramayana of Valmiki,* Vol. 3, trans. Hari Prasad Shastri (London: Shanti Sadan, 1970), pp. 336–337.

enemy. Rama then gains his rightful throne. In the course of time, priestly editors transformed this simple adventure story into a book of devotion. Rama, like Krishna in the *Bhagavad-Gita,* was an incarnation of the great god Vishnu. He was viewed as the ideal ruler: a truly virtuous, mighty man who exemplifies "proper conduct and is benevolent to all creatures. Who is learned, capable, and a pleasure to behold."[7] Sita emerged as the perfect woman, devoted and faithful to her husband, yet strangely powerful. Her words were memorized by almost every Hindu bride:

> *Car and steed and gilded palace,*
> *vain are these to woman's life;*
> *Dearer is her husband's shadow*
> *to the loved and loving wife.*

Sita's abduction by the demon Ravana launches another cosmic battle between the forces of good and evil. Rama, though victorious, is dishonored because Ravana had touched his wife and taken her to his palace. He feels compelled to repudiate Sita; her abduction is viewed as a rape even though she rejected Ravana's advances. One of the most moving scenes of the *Ramayana* is that in which the loyal Sita proposes to immolate herself rather than live separated from her lord. The gods save her from the flames, thus allowing Rama honorably to take her back. But years later, wagging tongues revive the question of her "tainted" virtue, and the heroine is once again prompted to prove her purity. The figure of Sita endures as an emblem of ideal Hindu womanhood. In the Indian nationalist struggles of the twentieth century, Sita served as a symbol of femininity and of the nation itself.

Counting Time

There are many ways to understand a civilization: through its art, its buildings, its political systems, its religions, its gender relations. One interesting way to envision a people is to examine its imaginings of time. Past societies have counted time in diverse ways, and those ways then shape the people's myths. Christians and Muslims, for example, trace their histories from a creation that includes the first man, Adam. Then each faith begins counting time from the life of its particular savior or prophet, Jesus and Muhammad, respectively. Of the three great religious traditions that emerged earlier in India, Jainism and Buddhism also focus on the lives of particular holy men who taught the way of Enlightenment. But the belief in reincarnation, shared by Hindus, Buddhists, and Jains, makes Indian notions of time radically different from those of traditions in which humans have only one lifetime. In the Indian traditions, humans can and will have thousands of lifetimes. The question "What comes after death?" is intimately linked to the imagining of time.

Hindu civilization is unique among ancient world civilizations in its crafting of a particularly grand and elaborate scheme for counting time. There are many Indian creation myths, and these stories merged and shifted over time. One common Indian notion of the creation and destruction of the universe is that time is counted in eras called *mahayugas* (mah-hah-YOO-gahs). Just as individuals die and then are reborn, at the end of each era the world dissolves and then reemerges to begin a new era. Each era consists of one complete cycle of four ages: the Golden Age (1,440,000 human years), in which all beings are good and all life is comfortable; the Age of Trey (1,080,000 human years), in which some evil appears along with some suffering and difficulty in life; the Age of Deuce (720,000 human years), in which there is more evil, pain, and suffering; and the Age of Dissolution (360,000 human years), in which evil, pain, and distress predominate in human life. Before and after each age are "twilight periods" of varying length that altogether add another 720,000 years to the length of a whole cycle.

This vast expanse of human time, however, is nothing compared to the life of the god Brahma. One thousand *mahayugas* make up only one day in his existence, which lasts for 100 years of 360 days each; and as each Brahma dies, a new one is born from an egg that grows within *brahman*. In this Hindu cosmology, there have already been billions of Brahmas. According to certain ancient Hindu texts, the world is currently in an Age of Dissolution; in other words, we are approaching the end of a *mahayuga* and the halfway point in the current day of the current Brahma.

Buddhism After the Buddha

Buddhism was increasingly supported by rulers and wealthy merchants in the third century B.C.E. Its compelling message of escape from suffering and its rejection of the caste system later enhanced its popularity among other segments of society. It maintained an important position for several hundred years after that and, although other religions surpassed it in popular appeal, it survived in India until it was exterminated in the thirteenth century C.E. in the aftermath of the Muslim invasions.

The Brahmans did not sit quietly by while Buddhism challenged their power. They launched a countermovement in the second century B.C.E., reasserting their authority in the face of Buddhist successes and winning back political and economic support. This Brahman effort played a major role in giving rise to a movement of Buddhist rejuvenation, called Mahayana that began to flower about 100 B.C.E. Its followers called this movement the "Great Vehicle." Mahayana Buddhism stressed that pious Buddhists should not just seek their own personal nirvana or release from rebirth. Rather, they should imitate the Buddha directly by trying to relieve others' suffering with the message of the Dharma.

Earlier forms of Buddhism focused on the salvation of the pious individual. Mahayana Buddhism stressed the centrality of bodhisattvas (boh-dee-SAT-vas), those who postpone their own entry into the final nirvana in order to act as a compassionate and loving guide to others still suffering in the world. The Mahayana movement criticized the older forms of Buddhism calling them *Hinayana* (HEE-nah-YAH-nah) or "Lesser Vehicle" because, it said, their focus on salvation was selfish. One school of older Buddhism, Theravada (TAY-rah-VAH-dah), the so-called Doctrine of the Elders, did continue to thrive in India, but Mahayana Buddhism became more popular.

Buddhism, of course was not just a set of religious and philosophical ideas; it was a way of life. Thousands of men and women became monks and nuns, while many other lay Buddhists contributed to their support. Over time, Buddhists built monasteries, some of which became important centers of learning and way stations for traders and travelers. Monks transcribed Buddhist texts, which made their way to China and beyond, and Indian artisans carved thousands of statues of the Buddha to meet burgeoning demand. Gifts of the seven treasures (the luxury trade items gold, silver, lapis lazuli, crystal, pearl, rubies, and coral) were presented to monasteries by donors hoping to secure religious merit, good health, or nirvana for their loved ones. Some devotees venerated the Buddha along with Hindu deities, demonstrating that the lines dividing one religion from another were never as rigid in actual social practice as they often seemed. Even Roman merchants offered gifts to Buddhist monasteries; and some scholars have suggested that certain monasteries functioned as centers of trade and finance.

Buddhism (both the older Theravada and the newer Mahayana) spread outside of India and thrived in all parts of Asia. According to Sri Lankan chronicles, Buddhism was brought to Sri Lanka by missionaries sent there by the Mauryan emperor Ashoka around 250 B.C.E. After 100 B.C.E. Buddhists spread the Dharma beyond the boundaries of the subcontinent into China and central, western, and southeastern Asia. In most of those areas it took permanent root, establishing Buddhist societies, states, and monasteries that function to this day. Today the older form of Buddhism survives only in Sri Lanka and Southeast Asia, and the Mahayana is absent there; Mahayana survives in Tibet, Korea, Japan, and China. The translation of the very numerous books of the Buddhist scriptures from Sanskrit into Chinese took place during the second, third, and fourth centuries C.E., an intellectual achievement as fascinating as it is staggering. A small revival of Buddhism occurred in Maharashtra, India, in the 1950s when the Untouchable leader Dr. B. R. Ambedkar led a mass conversion of 50,000 Untouchables to Buddhism so that they might escape the oppression of Hindu "untouchability."

THE MEETING OF EAST AND WEST: NETWORKS OF EXCHANGE

▪ *What role did India play in Eurasian trade?*

In the centuries immediately preceding and following the birth of Christ, the great civilizations of the world—Indian, Chinese, and Roman—were connected by a complex network of commercial, intellectual, and diplomatic exchanges. North India and south India played different roles in these networks of exchange, one oriented primarily towards the land and the other towards the sea. Travelers and monks from China visited the holy sites in India, the monsoons carried merchants to and fro across the Indian Ocean, and the goods and ideas of the East continued to enhance and alter the societies of the Mediterranean world.

Buddhist Sculpture and Architecture

Indian thought and art would have a profound effect on the eastern and western ends of Eurasia. Conversely, the most lasting Western influence on India in the Classical Age was the influence of Greek art on Buddhist sculpture. Before the Kushana period, Indian artists were influenced by the Buddha's prohibitions against idolatry, and they refrained from portraying the Buddha in human form. His presence was indicated by symbols only, such as his footprints, his umbrella, or the tree under which he attained Enlightenment. Beginning in the first century C.E., however, the Buddha himself was portrayed in numerous statues and reliefs. Most of these early Buddha figures come from Gandhara, the center of the Kushana Empire and the earlier Greco-Bactrian kingdom.

The primary inspiration for this Gandharan Buddhist art came from Mahayana Buddhism, which viewed the Buddha as a savior. This devotional form of Buddhism used images for worship, and statues of the Buddha as well as of many bodhisattva saints were produced in large numbers. Indeed the demand for images of the Buddha and bodhisattvas was so great that it affected the economy and artistic production of South Asia. Wealthy patrons like the Kushana king Kanishka hoped to gain spiritual favor or answers to their prayers by patronizing Buddhist monks and nuns. They paid artisans to create statues, build monasteries, and carve cells in rock cliffs to accommodate the flourishing communities of monks. The overland routes which carried traders, monks, and the message of Buddhism into China are marked by these monasteries, statues of the Buddha, and rock-carved caves. A second inspiration for Gandharan art came from Greece. Apparently, Hellenistic sculptors and craftsmen migrated to Gandhara via the Central Asian trade routes. The result was an execution of Indian themes through the use of Greek artistic techniques. Thus Mahayana Buddhism and Greco-Buddhist images of the Buddha, both of which developed in the Kushana Empire, spread together throughout eastern Asia.

The Great Stupa at Sanchi, built in the first century B.C.E., contains this detailed and elegant scene from the life of the Buddha. Numerous stupas were built by King Ashoka, starting in the third century, to hold the funeral relics of the Buddha.

The magnificent buildings of the Mauryan emperors have disappeared, although archaeologists have found the ruins of a huge pillared hall at the site of the Mauryan capital which probably dates from the time of Chandragupta. Buddhist stupas, the dome-shaped monuments that were used as funeral mounds to enshrine the relics of the Buddha and Buddhist saints or to mark a holy spot, remain in great numbers. Originally made only of earth, more elaborate mounds were later fashioned out of earth faced with brick and surrounded by railings and four richly carved gateways of stone. On top of the dome was a boxlike structure surmounted by a carved umbrella, the Indian emblem that symbolizes the Buddha's princely birth. As centuries passed, the low dome was heightened in some areas into a tall, tapered structure more like a tower. Later, when Buddhism spread to other countries, the stupa type of architecture went along. Its gateway was widely copied, and the stupa itself was the prototype of the multistoried Buddhist pagodas that are common in East Asia today.

Beyond the Indian Frontiers

The Mauryan Empire had already declined by the time the Han dynasty arose in China and the Roman Empire emerged in the Mediterranean. Both empires were connected to India through trade, and the Tamil states, with their excellent ports, were well positioned to promote international commerce. While Rome experienced the prosperous years of the Pax Romana during the first and second centuries C.E., Indian merchants supplied goods to the Roman entrepots in the Middle East. South Asian ports acted as staging points for sales of Chinese silk and Indian cottons demanded in the West. Indian traders exchanged textiles for African gold and ivory and traded rice, oils, precious woods, jewels, and spices in the ports of the Arabian Sea.

Even earlier, in the years after Alexander the Great's death, India had maintained trade contacts with the Seleucid and Ptolemaic kingdoms of the Hellenistic Age over two routes, one by land and the other by sea. The most frequented route was the caravan road that extended from West Asia and Syria, crossed Mesopotamia, and then skirted the Iranian plateau to either Bactria or Kandahar before crossing the Hindu

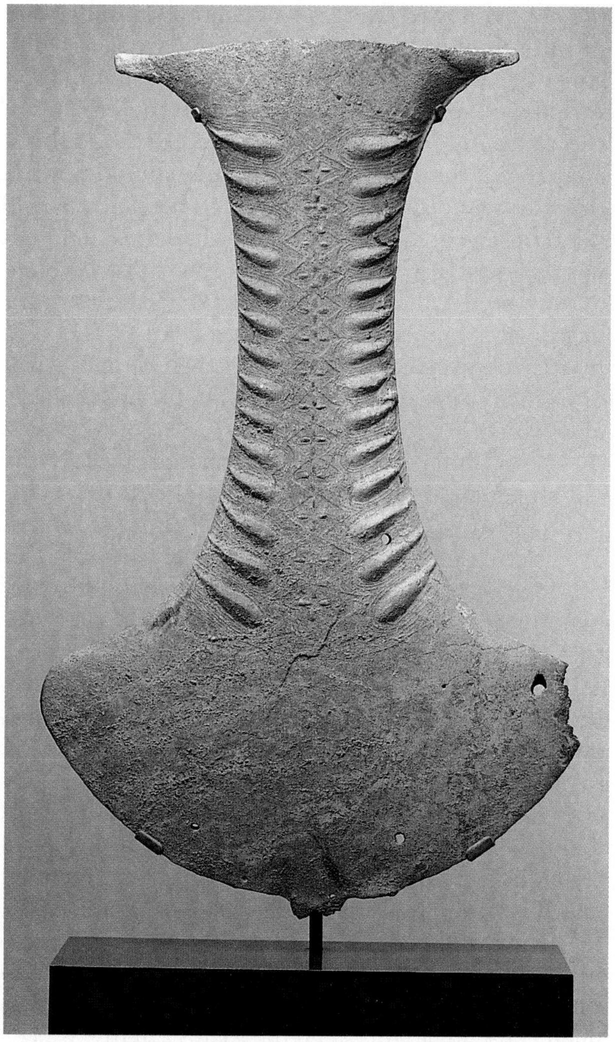

South and Southeast Asia were famous for metalworking. Bronze objects used for practical and ritual purposes (like this ceremonial blade) were highly prized and widely traded throughout the Indian Ocean region.

Vessel in the Form of an Ax. Bronze. The Metropolitan Museum of Art, Purchase, George McFadden Gift and Edit Perry Chapman Fund, 1993. (1993.525) Photograph by Bruce White © 1993 The Metropolitan Museum of Art.

Kush to reach Taxila in South Asia. The sea route that linked the eastern and western ends of Eurasia extended from China and Southeast Asia across the Bay of Bengal to India and Sri Lanka and thence across the Indian Ocean to the Red Sea ports or to the head of the Persian Gulf. From those two waterways, goods then proceeded overland and via the Mediterranean to the Middle East and into Africa and Europe.

The courts of kings and seats of power were great consumers of the goods of the East-West trade. The Mauryan and Kushana kings developed the trade passing through northern India in order to provide the foreign commodities that embellished their palace life. The Roman appetite for luxury goods from India and Southeast Asia—ivory, pearls, spices, dyes, and cotton—greatly stimulated trade in the southern kingdoms of India. Rulers vied to control and tax this lucrative commerce.

But no monarch, however great, could maintain control over the whole vast expanse of territory crossed by these trade routes. There were always middlemen. The Parthians, whose kingdom extended from the Euphrates to the borders of Bactria, levied heavy tolls on the caravan trade. The Kushanas acted as middlemen for the Chinese silk trade, selling the silk to the Parthians and later to Mediterranean merchants coming by sea to India. The Sabaean Arabs of southwestern Arabia seized the Red Sea route at Aden and were in control of much of the Mediterranean world's overseas trade with India. From Aden, the Sabaeans sent Indian goods north by caravan to Petra, which grew rich as a distribution point to Egypt via Gaza and to the north via Damascus.

So great was the demand and so lucrative the trade in Indian goods that the Roman emperor Augustus Caesar tried to break the hold of the Parthian and Arab middlemen on the Eastern trade, establishing direct commercial connections by sea with India. By 1 B.C.E. he had gained control of the Red Sea, forcing the Sabaeans out of Aden and converting the city into a Roman naval base. Ships were soon sailing from Aden directly to India across the Arabian Sea, blown by the monsoon winds.

From May to October the monsoon blows from the southwest across the Arabian Sea; between November and March the counter-monsoon blows from the northeast. Thus direct round-trip voyages, eliminating middlemen and the tedious journey along the coasts, could be made in eight months. Strabo, a Greek geographer during the time of Augustus, stated that 120 ships sailed to India every year from Egyptian ports on the Red Sea. This was an era in which early circuits of world trade developed.

When Augustus became head of the Roman world, the Tamil and Kushana rulers sent him congratulatory embassies. At least nine other embassies from India visited the Roman emperors, and Roman-Indian trade flourished. Indian birds (particularly talking parrots, costing more than human slaves) became the pets of wealthy Roman ladies, and Indian animals (lions, tigers, and buffaloes) were used in the wild beast shows of Roman emperors.

During the first century C.E., when Roman-financed ships reached the rich markets of southern India and Sri Lanka, Christianity may have accompanied them. Indian Christians today claim that their small group of about two million was founded by St. Thomas, one of Jesus' original 12 disciples, who may have sailed to India about 50 C.E. Thus, the trade routes carried more than goods. They bore travelers, envoys, pilgrims, and missionaries. Though the story of St. Thomas in India may be legendary, Buddhist philosophy was certainly spreading east and south into China and Southeast Asia.

The Balance of Trade

The balance of trade between the east and west of Eurasia from ancient times until the modern era tended to favor the countries of the East. Although Western trade with the East grew immensely in the first two centuries C.E., Roman exports such as wool, linen, glass, and metalware to the East did not match in value Rome's imports of silk, spices, perfumes, gems, and other luxuries. To make up the difference, gold and silver had continually to be exported to Asia. The discovery of large hoards of Roman coins in India seems to support claims that the Romans had to pay cash for some significant portion of their Indian goods.

Beginning in the third century, contacts between the eastern and western countries gradually declined. India entered a period of change and transition after the Mauryan Empire fell and the Kushana Empire in northeast India collapsed. In China, the Han dynasty in China broke apart. At the Western end of the trade routes, the Roman Empire's power was also circumscribed, and the hegemony of the Romans challenged. These political upheavals disrupted long-range cultural and commercial interchange but certainly did not eliminate it. The desire for diverse goods, commercial profits, and information insured the continuity of trade.

CONCLUSION

During India's formative age, three major religions were evolving on the subcontinent. Hinduism became the dominant social and religious force in India, with its notions of dharma (duty) allocated by caste. Jainism fostered the notion of ahimsa (nonviolence), which would play a powerful role in the twentieth-century Indian independence movement. Buddhism challenged the Brahman order and spread beyond the frontiers of India, ultimately to become a world religion. The great bulk of Indian thought sought not to challenge the existing social order but to explain and justify it; dharma dominated. Individual rights and desires in this world were ideally overshadowed by the requirements of eternal salvation, and freedom meant escape from the cycle of birth, death, and rebirth.

As in China, both local indigenous cultures and new languages, ideas, religions, and cultures came together to form the Indian society of antiquity. Forces of cultural and political integration at various times produced empires that spread across north India and penetrated the south. Unlike China, the written historical record can only be deciphered to the fourth century B.C.E., leaving historians more dependent on archaeological remains and engendering more heated debates about India's cultural origins.

India is today the heir of one of the longest-living civilizations in the world. By the beginning of the third century C.E., this civilization had produced a set of religious, philosophical, and literary traditions that endures to the present day. Television broadcasts of the *Ramayana* and the *Mahabharata* have been enormously successful in India in recent years. Rama and Sita remain as significant models for the virtuous male and female. Although the caste system has been challenged by the nation-state politics of modern India, it remains an essential element of Hindu identity: shaping social convention, determining political allegiance, and providing a framework for the practice of religion.

Suggestions for Web Browsing

You can obtain more information about topics included in this chapter at the websites listed below. See also the companion website that accompanies this text, **http://www.ablongman.com/brummett,** which contains an online study guide and additional resources.

Itihaas: Chronology—Ancient India
http://sify.com/itihaas/fullstory.php?id=13225643

Lengthy chronology of ancient India, 2700 B.C.E. to 1000 C.E.; most entries include subsites with text and images.

India
http://www.art-and-archaeology.com/timelines/india/india.html

Site discussing the history, sites and monuments, and classical texts of India, 600 B.C.E. to 1256 C.E.

Jainism
http://www.cs.colostate.edu/~malaiya/jainhlinks.html

Extensive site discusses the principles, traditions, and practices of Jainism and includes numerous related links.

The Buddhist Age, 500 B.C.E. to 319 C.E.
http://www.stockton.edu/~gilmorew/consorti/1cindia.htm#religdone

Text and images detail Buddha's life, the Four Truths, and the evolution of Buddhism. Related links offer analyses of Buddhist texts and a lengthy list of primary texts.

Ancient Indian History
http://www.fordham.edu/halsall/India/indiasbook.html

Comprehensive collection of documents, secondary sources on India.

The *Ramayana:* An Enduring Tradition
http://www.maxwell.syr.edu/maxpages/special/ramayana/

The Ramayana is one of the most important literary and oral texts of South Asia. This extensive site from Syracuse University offers both a short and complete story of Rama, history, images, and maps.

Literature and Film

On Indian literature, see *The Rig-Veda,* trans. Wendy Doniger (Penguin, 1986); *Upanisads,* trans. Patrick Olivelle (Oxford University Press, 1996); and *The Laws of Manu,* trans. George Bühler (Cosmo Books, 2004). For the *Mahabharata,* see J. A. van Buitenen, ed. and trans., *The Mahabharata,* 3 Vols. (University of Chicago Press, 1973–1978), and the theatrical adaptation by Jean-Claude Carrière, *The Mahabharata* (Harper & Row, 1985). The scholarly edition of the *Ramayana* is Robert P. Goldman, et al., trans., *The Ramayana of Valmiki: An Epic of Ancient India,* 7 vols. (Princeton University Press, 1984–1998). See also Nigel Frith, *The Legend of Krishna* (Schocken, 1976). Ancient Indian literature also treats intimate matters; see, e.g., Wendy Doniger and Sudhir Kakar, trans., *Kamasutra* (Oxford University Press, 2002)

Tamil literature can be sampled in A. K. Ramanujan, trans., *The Interior Landscape: Love Poems from a Classical Tamil Anthology* (Oxford University Press, 1994); and R. Parthasarathy, trans., *The Cilappatikaram of Ilanko Atikal: An Epic of South India* (Columbia University Press, 1993).

Mahabharata, directed by Peter Brooks, is based on the version by Jean-Claude Carrière. The six-hour film (1989) is highly stylized, and its interpretation of the Indian epic has been controversial. The opera *Satyagraha* by composer Philip Glass and librettist Constance De Jong premiered in 1980; a film version was made in 1983. It focuses on Gandhi but is based on the *Bhagavad-Gita. Satyagraha* was Gandhi's idea of vehemently holding to the truth against all odds and temptations.

Suggestions for Reading

Excellent surveys of ancient India may be found in Romila Thapar, ed., *Recent Perspectives of Early Indian History* (Popular Prakashan, 1995), and Stanley A. Wolpert, *A New History of India,* 7th ed. (Oxford University Press, 2004).

On pre-Aryan society see, Gregory L. Possehl, *The Indus Civilization: A Contemporary Perspective* (Altamira Press, 2003). The question of who the Aryans were is discussed in Frank Raymond Allchin, ed., *The Archaeology of Early Historic South Asia* (Cambridge University Press, 1995); Edwin Bryant, *The Quest for the Origins of Vedic Culture* (Oxford University Press, 2001); and George Erdosy, ed., *The Indo-Aryans of Ancient South Asia* (Walter de Gruyter Press, 1995). On Bactria see Frank Lee Holt, *Thundering Zeus: The Making of Hellenistic Bactria* (University California, 1999). The Mauryan civilization is analyzed by Romila Thapar, *Ashoka and the Decline of the Mauryas,* 2nd ed. (Oxford University Press, 1997).

On seafaring and India's trade, see Kenneth MacPherson, *The Indian Ocean* (Oxford University Press, 1998), and Xinru Liu, *Ancient India and Ancient China: Trade and Religious Exchanges 1–600* (Oxford University Press, 1988).

There are a number of studies of Indian religions. On Buddhism, Edward Conze, *A Short History of Buddhism* (Allen & Unwin, 1980), is a good introduction. See also Edward J. Thomas, *The Life of Buddha as Legend and History* (Routledge, 1975); Richard H. Robinson, Willard L. Johnson, and Sandra A. Wawrytko, *The Buddhist Religion: A Historical Introduction,* 4th ed. (Wadsworth, 1996); T. W. Rhys Davids, trans., *Buddhist Suttas* (Book Tree, 2000); and John S. Strong, *The Experience of Buddhism* (Wadsworth, 1995). On Hinduism, see Gavin Flood, *An Introduction to Hinduism* (Cambridge University Press, 1996); Pratima Bowes, *The Hindu Religious Tradition* (Routledge, 1978); and Sarvepalli Radhakrishnan, *The Hindu View of Life* (Allen & Unwin, 1980). For primary documents, see Ainslie Embree, ed., *Sources of Indian Tradition,* Vol. 1, 2nd ed., (Columbia University Press, 1988).

On Indian art, see Benjamin Rowland, *The Art and Architecture of India: Buddhist, Hindu, Jain,* 3rd ed. (Penguin, 1970); John Marshall, *The Buddhist Art of Gandhara* (Cambridge University Press, 1960); Heinrich Zimmer, *The Art of Indian Asia* (Princeton University Press, 1960); and Michael W. Meister, *Encyclopedia of Indian Temple Architecture,* 2 Vols. (Princeton University Press, 1983–1992).

GLOBAL ISSUES

MIGRATION

Why do people move from one place to another?

Spanish Civil Guard watching over illegal immigrants from North Africa.

The history of migration is in a sense the history of humankind. All migrations involve the movement of peoples, cultures, languages, and ideas. As a result, they have shaped history around the world and played a major role in the growth of civilization. The reasons why people migrate vary. Changing environmental conditions, population pressures, economic shifts, political and religious controversies, and war and violence have all compelled people to move from one place to another.

Migrations have been an integral part of human experience since our early ancestors took their first tentative steps on the African savanna and began exploring and adapting to new environments. *Homo erectus* migrated from the African continent to Eurasia. Members of *Homo sapiens* followed their predecessor out of Africa and traveled further still, showing considerable ingenuity in overcoming obstacles such as the open sea to reach Australia and the cold of the northern latitudes to traverse the Bering Strait and enter the Americas.

These earliest human movements were small in scale. Extended families or clans would move into a new area and live off the land. Even with small populations, humans often placed considerable environmental strain on the land after only a short time. From 3000 B.C.E. to 500 C.E., Bantu communities migrating into central, eastern, and southern Africa could cultivate an area for only a few years before the soils were exhausted and they had to move to new land.

While environmental degradation caused by human activity has often forced people to migrate, so too have acts of nature such as droughts, floods, cold spells, and crop failures. Severe drought from around 1300 to 1100 B.C.E. likely initiated political disruptions in the eastern Mediterranean and the migrations of the Sea Peoples, Philistines, Sicilians, Sardinians, and Etruscans that followed.[1] More recently, potato blight destroyed the potato crops in Ireland between 1846 and 1850, creating widespread famine and economic hardship. Ireland's population dropped from 8.5 to 5 million as about a million people died of starvation and disease and hundreds of thousands migrated to Britain and the United States. In the United States, as the Great Depression took hold in the 1930s and a 7-year drought hit the Great Plains states, tenant farmers went deeply into debt and banks called in their loans. In the hope of generating more income, farmers cultivated their fields more intensively, leading to soil erosion. Hundreds of thousands of migrants fled the "Dust Bowl" and headed west along Route 66 seeking a "promised land" in California.

From the sixteenth century onward, an important component of European conquests around the globe was the migration of its citizens to new colonies. European languages and cultures left deep imprints on the colonized societies. English settlers were especially adept at creating "Little Englands" in places such as Australia, New Zealand, Canada, and the American colonies. A common feature of these settler colonies and the states that grew out of them was the expulsion of indigenous peoples from their lands. As American settlers pushed westwards, they moved Amerindian peoples to reservations. In 1838 the U.S. government went a step further by expelling Cherokees from Georgia and sending them on the Trail of Tears to Oklahoma, a territory initially set aside for Indians. This forced migration claimed some 4000 lives.

The largest forced migration in history was the trans-Atlantic slave trade, which, over the span of 300 years, wrenched an estimated 12 million people from West and Central Africa to work as slaves on sugar plantations in Latin America, the Caribbean, and the United States. Many more millions of African slaves were taken from West Africa across the Sahara and from East Africa across the Indian Ocean to states in North Africa and the Middle East.

War and conflict have also triggered huge shifts in populations. In the fourth century C.E. the nomadic Huns of Central Asia drove westwards across the steppes into the lands occupied by Germanic tribes. The violent movement of the Huns, in turn, caused German tribes to flee further westward and eventually confront and overrun the declining western Roman Empire. The subsequent resettling of the former Roman domains by the Germanic tribes eventually led to the creation of nations such as France and England.

In the last century, wars and political conflicts have continued to be a major cause of migration. Before and during World War II, Jews in Germany and eastern Europe fled to escape persecution by the Nazis; many of those who did not manage to escape were killed. After the war millions of ethnic Germans were forcibly relocated from eastern Europe to Germany. When Communist regimes took over in Russia, China, Vietnam, and Cambodia, huge numbers of political refugees sought asylum in other countries. In the 1970s and 1980s, as civil wars erupted between guerilla groups and repressive regimes throughout Central America, hundreds of thousands of refugees fled the fighting, many of them to the United States. This trend shows no signs of abating. In 2003 the UN High Commissioner of Refugees put the total number of refugees around the world at 20.5 million.

Religion has also brought about migrations as religious minorities have sought places to practice their faiths without persecution. After the Muslim conquest of Persia in the seventh century C.E., a group of Zoroastrians migrated to India in the tenth century to escape a forced conversion to the Islamic faith. In 1685 Louis XIV of France revoked the Edict of Nantes of 1598 that guaranteed Protestant Huguenots the right to freedom of worship and made them liable to torture or jail for their beliefs. As a result, about 300,000 Huguenots left France. In 1947, the partition of British India into the new nations of India and Pakistan led to the migration of at least 10 million people who feared religious oppression. Muslims in Hindu India fled for Pakistan while Hindus and Sikhs in Muslim Pakistan fled for India. The resulting religious violence left hundreds of thousands dead.

Economic changes and population growth have also generated migrations of people from rural areas to urban centers. As European nations industrialized in the nineteenth century, rural people seeking work in factories swelled the populations of many cities and leading to problems in housing, sanitation, law enforcement, and transportation. Dramatic population growth and unemployment late in that century also led 40 million Europeans to migrate from the continent to the Americas and Australia. The ethnic makeup and national identity of countries such as Argentina were transformed as a result.

Not all economic migrations, however, have been to cities. A century ago the economic policies of European colonizers in Africa heavily favored exports from coastal areas, which forced seasonal migrants from the interior to seek work on plantations nearer the coast. With the discovery of mineral resources in southern Africa in the late nineteenth century, hundreds of thousands of male migrant workers flocked to the mines for short periods of time leaving their families behind. In both cases, the movements of these migrants between home and places of employment have continued to the present day.

In recent years, migrant workers in foreign countries have been called by many names, for example, "guest workers," "illegal aliens," and "temporary sojourners." Local people have often resented the presence of economic migrants because they are seen as threats to their jobs or way of life. Many governments have been challenged to define the status of foreign migrants and to devise policies for controlling how they enter and where and how long they stay. During the apartheid era (1948–1994) in South Africa, the white-ruled government tried to control the movements of black adults by issuing them passbooks that contained permits allowing them to work and live in areas reserved for whites.

Migration has been an integral feature of history as individuals and groups of people have moved from one place to another for a host of reasons. Some people have moved voluntarily, but over the last five centuries, many migrants have been forced to leave their homes because of war and conquest, oppressive regimes, religious intolerance, and exploitative economic systems. The result is that migration has left few countries in the modern world untouched. The United States often prides itself on being a "nation of immigrants," but as one considers the global reach of migrations, have we reached a point where it is more accurate to refer to a "world of immigrants"?

Questions

1 Why have so many people emigrated to the United States in the last 25 years?
2. How has migration been a part of your own family's history?
3. What were the causes of the world's largest migrations?

CHAPTER

4

Greece

Minoan, Mycenaean, Hellenic, and Hellenistic Civilizations, 2000–30 B.C.E.

CHAPTER CONTENTS

2000 B.C.E.

c. 2000–1200 Minoan and Mycenaean civilizations

1628? Eruption of Thera

1500 B.C.E.

1450–1150 Mycenaeans in Crete

1150–750 Greek Middle Age

1000 B.C.E.

c. 800 Homer

c. 750 Greek city-states emerge

508–502 Cleisthenes establishes democracy in Athens

500 B.C.E.

490–478 Persian Wars

470–399 Socrates

431–404 Peloponnesian War

427–347 Plato

384–322 Aristotle

359–336 Reign of Philip II of Macedonia

336–323 Reign of Alexander the Great

200 B.C.E.

200–300 Rome annexes Hellenistic states

Scarred by time, war, weather, and modern pollution, the ruins of the Athenian Acropolis stand today under a smoggy sky and overlook the trees and buildings of a vibrant city that has been modernized and beautified for the 2004 Olympic games. Because of the recent Olympics in Athens, ancient Greek civilization has received renewed attention worldwide. The renovation of the highways and subway system and new construction in preparation for the games have resulted in archaeological discoveries that add greatly to our knowledge of life in this ancient city. Celebration of contemporary Olympics in their birthplace has brought global recognition to the ancient Greeks and the significance of their cultural achievement.

In the fifth century B.C.E. the temples and statues of the Acropolis were new and gleaming, fresh from the hands of confident architects and sculptors. Today those temples, civic centers, and works of art remain ruins, yet ancient Athens and the civilization that was centered there have retained a lasting significance. The accomplishments of the ancient Greeks proved to be enduring. Their magnificent intellectual and artistic legacy helped shape much of the cultural heritage of western Europe and effect political and cultural development in Asia and Africa.

In the past historians and other scholars who specialize in western European civilization have generally tended to overemphasize the originality of Greek civilization and the positive contributions the Greeks made to their cultural heirs. Now we are able to reconstruct a more balanced picture of the ancient Greeks: one that more accurately assesses their cultural inheritance along with their original contributions. We are now much more aware of the formative influences of earlier neighboring civilizations in Africa and Asia that played an important role in influencing the shape of Greek history and culture. Our image of the ancient Greeks has become more balanced, and the recent focus of world attention on modern Athens has resulted in a renewed appreciation of the ancient Greek achievement.

MINOAN AND MYCENAEAN CIVILIZATIONS, C. 2000–1200 B.C.E.

■ *In what ways did these two early Aegean societies interact with each other?*

More than one thousand years before the emergence of the Greek civilization we call classical, two advanced cultures, one on the mainland of Greece and another centered on the island of Crete, had taken shape. Minoan (mi-NO-an) civilization with Crete as its center and the surrounding Aegean (ay-GEE-an) islands its commercial partners, was highly developed by 2000 B.C.E.; Mycenaean (mai-se-NEE-an) civilization on the mainland seems to have reached its greatest power between 1450 and 1200 B.C.E. Both civilizations appear to have collapsed shortly after 1200 B.C.E. And both of them contained elements that were to influence the development of the later so-called classical civilization of Greece.

The Minoans

The earliest of these Aegean cultures to reach a high degree of sophistication is now referred to as Minoan civilization, named after the legendary king of Crete, Minos (MEE-nos). From its center on Crete, Minoan civilization spread to the surrounding Aegean Islands, the coast of Asia Minor, and to mainland Greece itself. A narrow, 160-mile-long island, Crete served as a stepping-stone for extensive trading contacts with Europe, Asia, and Africa. Established by immigrants from Asia Minor, and made prosperous and powerful by economic and cultural contacts with Mesopotamia, Egypt, and more southern Africa, Minoan civilization achieved a high level of sophistication by 2000 B.C.E.

Minoan prosperity was based on a large-scale trading network that ranged throughout the Mediterranean: from Sicily, Greece, Asia Minor, and Syria to Africa, Sicily, and probably even Britain. The Minoans employed well-constructed ships capable of long voyages over the open sea. Chief exports were olive oil, wine, metalware, and magnificent pottery. This trading network was overseen as the monopoly of an efficient bureaucratic government under a powerful ruler whose administrative records came to be written on clay tablets, first in a form of picture writing **(hieroglyphics)**

hieroglyphics—Written characters that are pictorial in nature such as the ancient Egyptian written script. The word is Greek in origin (hieros="holy"; glyphos="writing").

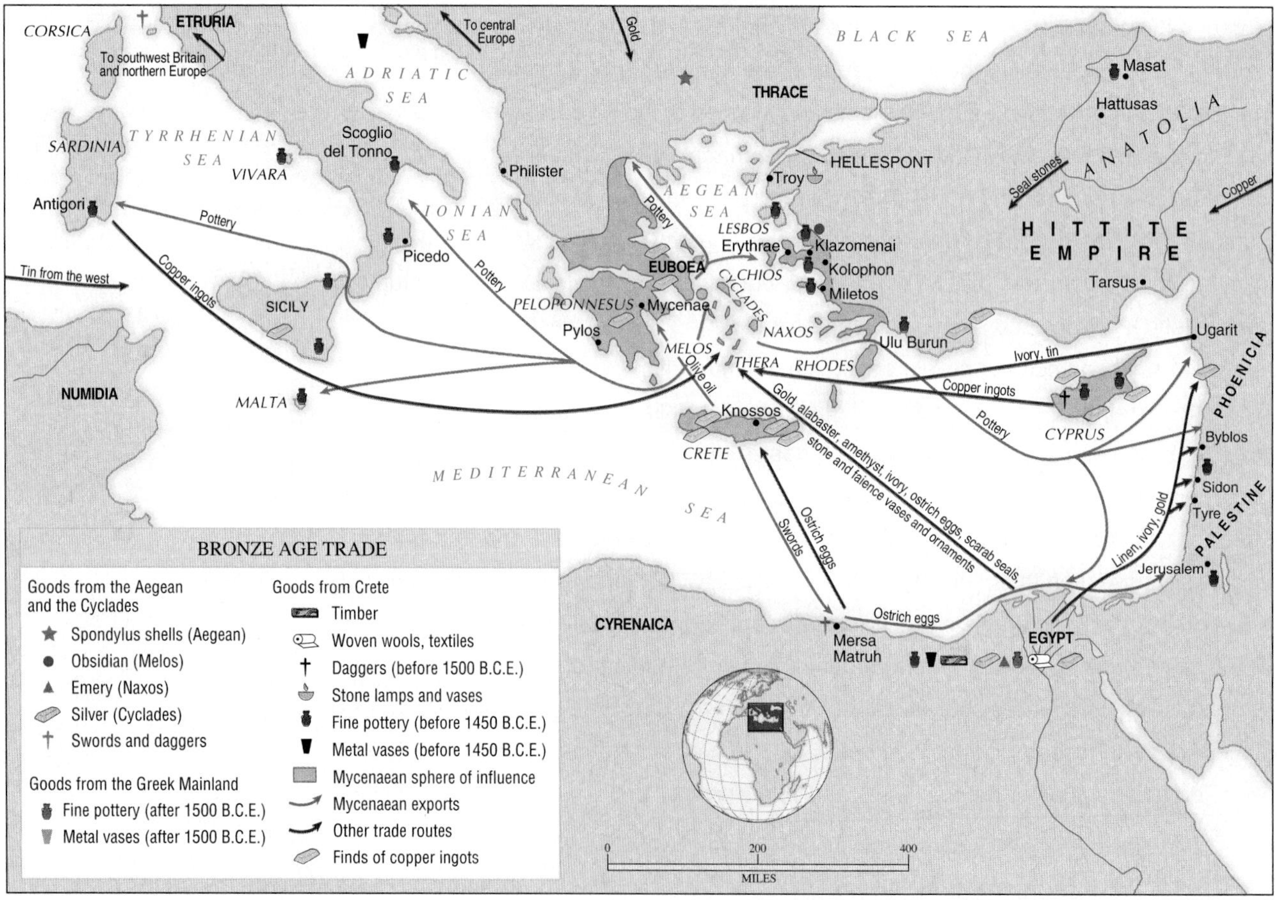

Both the Minoan and Mycenaean civilizations established wide-ranging networks throughout the Mediterranean. Evidence of trading contacts from as far away as Kush (south of Egypt) and Afghanistan has been found in Aegean Bronze Age archaeological sites.

Preclassical Greece

c. 2000–1200 B.C.E.	Minoan and Mycenaean civilizations
1628? B.C.E.	Eruption of Thera
1450–1200 B.C.E.	Mycenaeans in Crete
1150–750 B.C.E.	Greek Dark Ages

and later in a script known as Linear A, whose 87 signs represented syllables. Since neither of these early scripts has been deciphered, our knowledge of the earliest stages of Minoan civilization is incomplete and imprecise; most of what we know is derived from the material remains—walls, temples, houses, and pottery and tablet fragments—uncovered by archaeologists.

The spectacular discoveries of English archaeologist Sir Arthur Evans a century ago first brought to light this impressive civilization, whose existence had previously only been mentioned in the epics of Homer and in Greek legends such as that of the Minotaur, half bull and half man, who devoured young Greek men and women sent to it as tribute from subject Greek cities. Between 1900 and 1905 Evans excavated the ruins of a great palace at Knossos, the largest and most prosperous city in Crete after 1700 B.C.E. Rising at least three stories high and sprawling over nearly 6 acres, this "Palace of Minos," built of brick and limestone and employing unusual downward-tapering columns of wood, was a maze of royal apartments, storerooms, corridors, open courtyards, and broad stairways. Equipped with running water, the palace had a sanitation system that surpassed anything else constructed in Europe until Roman times. Walls were painted with elaborate frescoes in which the Minoans appear as a happy, peaceful people with an enthusiasm for dancing, festivals, and athletic contests. Women are shown enjoying a freedom and prominence rarely matched either in the ancient Near East or even in later classical Greece. They are not secluded in the home but are portrayed sitting with men and taking an equal part in public festivities—even as athletes and participants in religious rituals. Their dresses are very elaborate, with bright patterns and colors, pleats, and puffed sleeves. Their dresses are open in front to the waist, and their hair is carefully curled and arranged—a certain indication that Minoan women of high standing had sufficient time and wealth to devote to elaborate fashion.

One of the most notable features of Minoan culture was its art, varied in its themes, full of color, motion, and even humor. Art seems to have been an essential part of everyday life and not, as in the ancient Near East, intended to impart a religious or political message. What little is known of Minoan religion also contrasts sharply with earlier religious patterns in the Near East: There is no evidence of great temples, powerful priesthoods, or large cult statues of the gods. The principal deity was probably a Mother Goddess; her importance seems to reflect the prominence women held in Minoan society. A number of recovered statuettes show her dressed like the fashionable Minoan women who are portrayed in the murals that decorated the palace at Knossos. The Minoan Mother Goddess was perhaps an early inspiration for such later Greek goddesses as Athena, Demeter, and Aphrodite.

The Mycenaeans

Around or shortly after 2000 B.C.E., the first Indo-European Greek tribes, usually called Achaeans (ah-KEE-ahns), invaded Greece from the north, either conquered or absorbed the earlier settlers, and ruled from palaces on fortified hills at Mycenae, Pylos, Athens, and other sites in the south of Greece. By 1600 B.C.E. these Greeks—or Mycenaeans, as they are called today, after the richest of their fortresses at Mycenae—had absorbed much of the culture of the Minoans through trading contacts. But unlike

Vivid frescoes decorated the walls of many of the rooms in the Palace of Knossos. This famous Dolphin Frieze in the so-called Queen's Chamber illustrates the importance of the sea and of animals in Minoan life and art.

In contrast to some of the rigid and grandiose Mesopotamian and Egyptian statues, those of the Minoans were small and animated. This little priestess holds snakes, possibly reflecting Minoan religious rituals.

the Minoans, the Mycenaeans seemed to have been a more warlike people and sailed the seas as raiders as well as traders. Mycenaean women adopted Minoan fashions and added to Minoan styles their own cultural preferences in cosmetics, dress, and jewelry.

The Mycenaeans accumulated their wealth through agricultural production, the manufacture of superior pottery and metal tools and weapons, international trade, and probably piracy. Some of the great wealth accumulated by the kings of Mycenae—the greatest single hoard of gold, silver, and ivory objects found anywhere before the discovery of Tutankhamen's tomb—was excavated in 1876 by the amateur German archaeologist Heinrich Schliemann (1822–1890), a few years after his sensational discoveries at Troy. The royal palace on the acropolis, or citadel, of Mycenae had spacious audience rooms and apartments, fresco-lined walls, floors of painted stucco, and large storerooms. Impressive also were the royal tombs constructed by Mycenaean kings after 1500 B.C.E. These beehivelike tombs, constructed of cut stones over several tons in weight and averaging over 40 feet in height, show proof of the power and control these Mycenaean kings exercised.

The desire to expand wealth and power led the Mycenaeans to establish colonies in the eastern Mediterranean (Hittite sources refer to Achaeans in Asia Minor) and even to the conquest of Knossos about 1450 B.C.E. This Mycenaean takeover was made possible by the destruction of the mazelike palace at Knossos by fire, perhaps in the aftermath of an earthquake that weakened the palace's defenses. Minoan dominance in the Aegean and prosperity on Crete had already been reduced by the destruction caused by the spectacular eruption of the volcanic island of Thera (modern Santorini), 80 miles north of Crete, and a resultant massive tidal wave that may have struck the northern shore of the island at a height of nearly half a mile. Archaeologists and **volcanologists** now place this great eruption in 1628 B.C.E., but the resulting damage to buildings, crops, and the merchant fleet of the Minoans probably contributed to making the civilization vulnerable to Mycenaean raids. The palace at Knossos was rebuilt by the Mycenaeans only to be destroyed about 1380 B.C.E. by earthquake and fire, after which the center of civilization in the Aegean shifted to the Greek mainland.

Many of the details regarding Minoan-Mycenaean relations were unknown until after 1952, when a young English architect, Michael Ventris, startled the scholarly world by deciphering a late type of Minoan script known as Linear B, many examples of which had been found by Evans at Knossos and by later archaeologists at mainland Greek sites such as Pylos, Mycenae, and Tiryns. Before Ventris's translation, most scholars thought that Linear B had to be a written version of the Minoan language. But Ventris proved that Linear B was actually an early form of Greek written in syllabic characters. Since Linear B was Greek, the rulers of Knossos after 1450 B.C.E. must have been Mycenaean Greeks who had come to power in Crete through invasion or piracy and adopted the Minoan script to write their own language.

The Linear B texts, which are administrative documents and inventories, add greatly to our

---

volcanologists—Those who study the formation, distribution, and classification of volcanoes and their eruptions.

knowledge of Mycenaean life. The Mycenaean centers were fortified palaces and administrative offices and not, as in Crete, true cities. The bulk of the population lived in scattered villages where they worked either communal land or land held by nobles or kings. The nobles were under the close control of the kings, whose administrative records were kept daily by a large number of scribes. Prominent in these records are details of the distribution of grain and wine as wages and the collection of taxes. The most important item of income was olive oil, the major article in the wide-ranging network of Mycenaean trade, which was operated as a royal monopoly. Perhaps it was their role as merchant adventurers that led the Mycenaean kings about 1250 B.C.E. to launch an expedition against Troy to eliminate a powerful commercial rival.

Troy—Site of Homer's *Iliad*?

DOCUMENT
Homer, *The Iliad*

The city most authorities believe to have been Troy, as described to us first by the poet Homer, occupied a strategic position on the Hellespont (the strait from the Aegean to the Black Sea, now known as the Dardanelles). In such an important location, this city could command both sea traffic through the straits and land routes between Asia and Europe. For many years scholars thought that Troy existed only in the epic poems of Homer; however, Heinrich Schliemann believed otherwise. As a young man he had read Homer's *Iliad,* and he became firmly convinced that the city had truly existed. At the age of 48, having made fortunes in the California gold rush and in worldwide trade, Schliemann retired from business to prove that his dreams of ancient Troy's existence were real.

In 1870 Schliemann began excavations at the legendary site of Troy, where he unearthed nine buried cities, built one on top of the other. He discovered a treasure of golden earrings, hairpins, necklaces, and bracelets in the second city (Troy II), which led him to believe that this was the city described by Homer. Excavations in the 1930s, however, showed that Troy II had been destroyed about 2200 B.C.E., far too early to have been the scene of the Trojan War. Scholars now believe that Troy VI or VII (c. 1200–1125 B.C.E) was probably the city made famous by Homer.

Homer's account tells us that the Trojan War began because of the abduction of Helen, queen of Sparta, by the Trojan prince Paris. Under the leadership of Agamemnon, king of Mycenae, the wrathful Achaeans besieged Troy for ten long years. Homer's *Iliad* actually describes only a period of a few weeks during the tenth year of the supposed siege. There is no archaeological proof of Homer's account. But we do know that Troy VII was destroyed by fire, and there are indications that the city was besieged. Were the attackers from Greece, or perhaps did the city fall victim to the piracy and disorder associated with the coming of the Sea Peoples or the collapse of the Hittite empire around 1200 B.C.E.? Folktales of the demise of the great city passed from Mycenaean times through oral tradition and elaboration down to the eighth century, when the account attributed to the poet Homer took written form. But the facts behind the destruction of the great city on the Hellespont remain clouded in mystery.

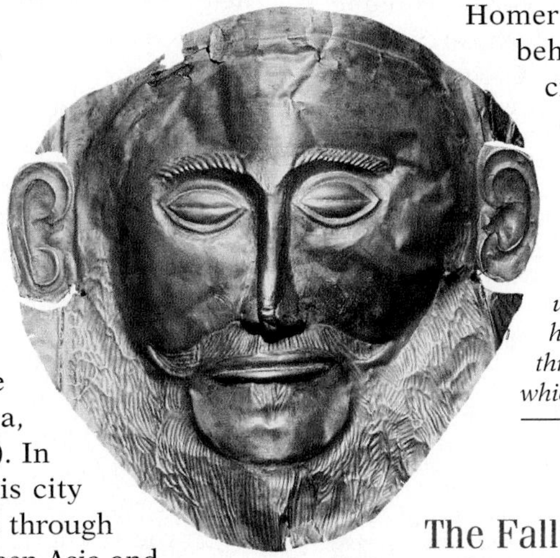

In 1876, when Heinrich Schliemann found this gold death mask at Mycenae, he excitedly telegraphed a friend: "I have looked upon the face of Agamemnon." The mask, however, dates from about 1500 B.C.E., nearly three centuries before the Trojan War, during which Agamemnon is said to have reigned.

The Fall of Mycenaean Civilization

Greek traditions recorded that around 1200 B.C.E. a new wave of Greek invaders, materially aided by weapons made of iron instead of bronze, invaded Greece from the north and conquered the Mycenaean strongholds. These newcomers may have followed in the path of the devastation caused by raiding Sea Peoples (see Chapter 1); some archaeologists suggest that invasions of new peoples caused less damage to Mycenaean sites than did the revolts of the lower classes against their powerful and autocratic overlords. First of the Mycenaean strongholds to fall was Pylos, whose Linear B archives contain numerous references to quickly undertaken preparations to meet military emergencies. We find orders directing women and children to places of safety and instructions given to makers of weapons, the navy, and food suppliers. The preparations were not in time. Pylos was sacked and burned, and all of the other major Mycenaean citadels were likewise destroyed.

THE RISE OF HELLENIC CIVILIZATION, c. 1150–500 B.C.E.

■ *How did a distinct Hellenic civilization evolve out of the Greek Dark Ages?*

The four centuries from around 1150 to 750 B.C.E., called the Greek Dark Ages, were marked by drastic depopulation and the disappearance of the major characteristics of Mycenaean civilization—centralized and bureaucratic administration, wide-ranging commerce, sophisticated art forms, monumental architecture, and writing. Although the fall of Mycenaean civilization was a catastrophic event, the end of Mycenaean dominance eventually gave rise to the emergence of a new and different civilization, called the Hellenic. Hellenic civilization receives its name from the Greek hero Hellen, a mortal who is credited with bringing humans to first inhabit Greece (Greeks ancient and modern call their country Hellas).

The Influence of Geography

MAP The Early Aegean

Geographical factors played an important part in shaping the events of Greek history. The numerous mountain ranges that crisscross the peninsula, which is about the size of the state of Maine, severely restricted internal communication and led to the development of fiercely independent city-states and the reluctance of the Greeks to unite into a single nation. The mountains cover two-thirds of the peninsula, and along the west coast, they come close to the sea, leaving few harbors or arable plains. Elsewhere the deeply indented coast provides many natural harbors. A narrow isthmus at the Gulf of Corinth made southern Greece almost an island—in fact, it was called the Peloponnesus (pe-loh-poh-NEE-sus) for "Pelop's island." The jagged coastline and the many islands offshore stimulated seagoing trade, and the rocky soil (less than a fifth of Greece is agriculturally productive) and few natural resources encouraged the Greeks to establish colonies abroad.

The Development of Hellenic Civilization

c. 1150–c. 750 B.C.E.	Greek "Dark Ages"
c. 800–750 B.C.E.	Establishment of the Greek *polis* (city-state)
c. 750–550 B.C.E.	Great age of Greek colonization
c. 650 B.C.E.	Age of Greek tyrants; *helot* revolt in Sparta
c. 600 B.C.E.	Coinage introduced in Greece
594 B.C.E.	Solon named sole *archon* in Athens
c. 560 B.C.E.	Pisistratus is tyrant in Athens
508–502 B.C.E.	Cleisthenes establishes democracy in Athens

The Homeric Age

Most of our information about the Greek Dark Ages comes from the epic poems put in written form around 750 B.C.E. and attributed to a supposedly blind Greek poet named Homer. Controversy surrounds the question of Homer's existence and whether he alone or several poets composed the *Iliad* and the *Odyssey*. The Homeric epics retain something of the material side of the Mycenaean period, handed down to Homer's time by a continuous oral tradition. But in terms of the details of political, economic, and social life, religious beliefs and practices, and the ideals that gave meaning to life, the poet could only describe what was familiar to him in his own age, probably soon after 800 B.C.E.

The values held by Homer to give meaning to life in the Homeric Age were predominantly heroic values—the strength, skill, and valor of the dominating warrior. Such was the earliest meaning of *arête* (AH-re-te), "excellence" or "virtue," a term whose meaning changed as values changed during the course of Greek culture. To obtain *arête*—defined by one Homeric hero as "to fight ever in the forefront and outdo my companions"—and the undying fame that was its reward, men would endure hardship, struggle, and even death. Honor was the just reward for one who demonstrated *arête*, and the greatest of human injustices was the denial of honor due to a great hero. Homer makes such a denial the theme of the *Iliad*, "The ruinous wrath of Achilles that brought countless ills upon the Achaeans," when Achilles, insulted by Agamemnon, withdraws from battle.

The Homeric king was essentially a war leader, hardly more than the "first among equals" among his companions—his fellow nobles who sat in his council to advise him and to check any attempt he might make to exercise arbitrary power. There was also a popular

Document Homer—*The Iliad:* Andromache and Hector

Homer's *Iliad* is mostly a story of war and carnage. Yet this great work also contains vivid and moving accounts of life and even love during the respites between battles. Homer's work served as inspiration to the Greeks of the classical period; much of the actions of heroic men and women were held up as examples of ideal conduct in times of crisis. Such inspiration can be taken from the description of an interaction between the Trojan hero Hector and his loyal wife Andromache (an-DRO-ma-kee) before Hector went out to meet certain death at the hands of the Greek Achilles:

A flash of his helmet
And off he strode and quickly reached his sturdy,
well-built house. But white-armed Andromache—
Hector could not find her in the halls.
She and the boy and a servant finely gowned
were standing on the tower, sobbing, grieving.
. . . Hector spun and rushed from his house,
back by the same way down the wide, well-paved streets
throughout the city until he reached the Scaean Gates,
the last point he would pass to gain the field of battle.
There his warm, generous wife came running up to meet him,
. . . She joined him now, and following in her steps
a servant holding the boy against her breast
in the first flush of life, only a baby
Hector's son, the darling of his eyes
and radiant as a star . . .
The great man of war breaking into a broad smile,
his gaze fixed on his son, in silence. Andromache,
pressing close beside him and weeping freely now,
clung to his hand, and urged him, called him:
"Reckless one,
my Hector—your own fiery courage will destroy you!
Have you no pity for him, our helpless son? Or me,
and the destiny that weighs me down, your widow
now so soon. Yes, soon they will kill you off,
all the Achaean forces massed for assault, and then,
bereft of you, better for me to sink beneath the earth.
What other warmth, what comfort's left for me,
once you have met your doom? Nothing but torment!
I have lost my father. Mother's gone as well.
. . . You, Hector—you are my father now, my noble mother,

a brother too, and you are my husband, young and
warm
and strong."

Questions to Consider

1. Do you think Hector and Andromache are displaying ideal conduct in this exchange?
2. Is Andromache in any way receptive to concerns *other* than her own security? What seem to be Andromache's primary goals in her conversation with Hector?
3. Is Andromache helpless to do something other than her husband's bidding? Why?

From Homer, *Iliad*, 6, 439–509, trans. Robert Fagles (New York: Penguin, 1990).

assembly of arms-bearing men, whose consent was asked whenever a crisis occurred, such as war or the recognition of a new king.

Noble women were freed from agricultural labor, but still had major responsibility for maintaining the order of the household and its accounts, supervising the upbringing of the children, and overseeing the activities of any servants attached to the estate. In most circumstances noble women had to manage the estates of their husbands when war or other duties demanded their attention. They are described by Homer as active participants in the life of their communities and even in the banquet hall conversations alongside the men. But the opportunity for leisure like that possessed by their Minoan and Mycenaean predecessors was a luxury most of these noble women probably could not enjoy.

Society was clearly aristocratic; nobles were recognized as such because of their ownership of larger estates, and their resulting influential position within

Greek civilization flourished in the mountainous lands of the eastern Mediterranean. Mainland Greece lacked arable land and navigable rivers, but its extensive coastline and fine harbors drew the Greeks to the sea for sustenance and commerce. All of the eastern Mediterranean became involved in the war between Athens and Sparta. The Spartans, surrounded by Athens's growing power, concluded that they had to go to war to prevent eventual Athenian dominance.

the tribes. Only the nobles, the *aristoi* ("best"), possessed *arête*—and the common man was reprimanded and beaten when he dared to question his superiors. Yet the commoners had certain political rights as members of the tribes; they were able to sit in the popular assembly, own land, and enjoy the protection of law as interpreted by the king.

The economy was a simple, self-sufficient agricultural system in which private ownership of land replaced the collective group ownership of Mycenaean times. Slavery was not a widely employed institution in the Greek Dark Age. Most of the estates were small, and most agricultural and domestic labor was provided by free, landless peasants. Slaves were not numerous; if slaves were to be found they were mostly employed as domestic servants on the estates of the wealthiest of the nobles.

From Oligarchy to Tyranny

The *polis* (pl. *poleis*), the term which later comes to mean the city-state—the political unit comprising the city and its people— did not carry the same meaning for the Greeks of Dark Ages. The word originally described only the physical city itself. The center of every polis was the high, fortified site, the *acropolis,* where people could take refuge from attack. In time this defensive center took on added significance as the focus of political and religious life. When commerce revived in the eighth and seventh centuries B.C.E., a trading center *(agora)* developed below the acropolis. The two areas and the surrounding territory, usually smaller than a modern county, in combination with its citizens, came to give new meaning to the word *polis*: the city and the people who share a common citizenship.

The political development of the polis was so rich and varied that it is difficult to find of a form of government not experienced—and given a lasting name—by the Greeks: monarchy, oligarchy, tyranny, and democracy. For most of the Greek Dark Ages, monarchy had been the typical form of government. But by the middle of the eighth century B.C.E., the nobles, who wished to share in the authority exercised by monarchs, had taken over the government of most city-states, ushering in an age of aristocracy ("government by the best") or **oligarchy** ("government by the few"). Exercising their superior power, the nobles in many locations abolished the popular assembly, acquired a monopoly of the best land, reduced many commoners to virtual serfdom, and forced others to seek a living on rocky, barren soil. Often the poor found relief only by emigrating overseas. In many city-states the wealthy promoted colonization as a safety valve to ward off a threatened political and economic explosion from the lower classes.

But the colonization movement was much more than just an effort to relieve the distress of the landless poor. From 750 to 550 B.C.E. the Greeks planted colonies throughout most of the Mediterranean world. Colonies were founded along the northern coast of the Aegean and around the Black Sea. So many Greeks migrated to southern Italy and eastern Sicily that the region became known as *Magna Graecia,* Great Greece. Colonies were also founded as far west as present-day France—at Massilia (modern Marseilles), for example—and Spain and on parts of the African coast. Unique was Naucratis (NAH-krah-tis) in Egypt, not a true colony but a trading post whose residents gained extraterritorial rights (their own magistrates and law courts) from the Egyptians.

VIDEO
Ephesus

Colonization not only lessened some of Greece's social problems but also stimulated rapid and significant economic development. By 600 B.C.E. economic progress and the use of coined money, probably inspired by the Lydians, had fostered the beginnings of a middle class. The Greek poleis gradually became "industrialized" as a result of concentrating on the production of specialized goods—vases, metal products, textiles, olive oil, and wine—for export in exchange for food and raw materials. But before this economic revolution was completed, the continuing land hunger of the poor contributed to a political revolution.

After 650 B.C.E. rulers known as *tyrants* seized power in many Greek states and, supported by both poorer citizens and the rising middle classes, took control of government from the nobility. Tyrants were supported also by the newly developed heavily armed infantry force: the hoplite phalanx—a formation of foot soldiers carrying overlapping shields and long spears, which replaced the aristocratic cavalry as the most important element in Greek warfare. Most tyrants were commanders of the hoplite phalanx. The hoplites, common citizens wealthy enough to furnish their own equipment, supported their commander's efforts to seize power in turn for the promise of more participation in the affairs of the polis once the tyranny was established.

A sixth-century B.C.E. amphora from the polis of Corinth. Corinthian pottery was the most popular of all such merchandise produced in Greece for two hundred years, and many examples of it are found throughout the Mediterranean region, even as far into Asia as modern Iran.

The tyrants (the word meant simply "absolute ruler" and did not at first have today's connotation of brutality) sometimes distributed land to the landless poor and, by promoting further colonization, trade, and industry, increased economic prosperity and generally made their poleis better places to live for all residents. At first exceptionally popular leaders, tyrants attempted to keep a dynastic control of their poleis by passing on their power to their sons. Within a few generations, these dynastic tyrannies tended to grow more autocratic and unpopular with the citizens, and almost all were eventually overthrown. Most Greek poleis then reverted to an aristocratic form of government with control in the hands of the nobility. The two notable exceptions to this pattern are two of the most unique of poleis: Athens and Sparta.

Athens to 500 B.C.E.

Athens and Sparta, the two city-states destined to dominate the political history of Greece during the classical period (the fifth century B.C.E. and most of the fourth), had radically different courses of development during the period prior to 500 B.C.E. The

oligarchy—Government by the few, from the Greek word oligos ("few"); political domination by a limited number of families or individuals.

political, economic, and social evolution of Athens was typical of most Greek states, but Sparta's development produced a unique way of life that inspired the admiration of other Greeks, and often their astonishment as well.

In Athens during the seventh century B.C.E., the council of nobles became most influential. The popular assembly rarely met, and the king's authority was replaced by nine magistrates, called *archons* ("rulers"), chosen annually by the aristocratic council to exercise the king's civil, military, and religious powers. While the nobles prospered on their large estates, the small farmers and sharecroppers suffered. Bad years and poor land forced them to borrow seed from the wealthy nobles, and when they were unable to repay their debts, they were sold into slavery. Small farmers called out for the cancellation of debts and the end to debt slavery, and those without any land demanded a redistribution of the land claimed by the aristocrats.

The majority of Athenian nobles finally realized that their failure to address the demand for reform might result in the rise of a tyrant, and they agreed to a policy of compromise advocated by the aristocrat Solon. In 594 B.C.E. Solon was made sole archon, with broad authority to revise the constitution of Athens in order to avoid class conflict. Solon, widely respected in Athens for his wisdom and fair dealing, instituted middle-of-the-road reforms intended to save Athens from social revolution and economic disaster.

For the lower classes, Solon agreed to canceling all debts and forbidding future debt slavery, but he rejected as too radical the demand for the redistribution of the land. His long-range solution to the economic problem was to seek full employment by stimulating trade and industry. To achieve this goal, Solon required fathers to teach their sons a trade, granted citizenship to foreign artisans and merchants who settled in Athens, and encouraged the intensive production of wine and olive oil for export.

All citizens in Athens, women included, were encouraged to work—most Athenian women citizens who did so worked at home-based small industries. Solon regulated prostitution in Athens, although such an occupation was considered unacceptable for any but foreign noncitizens.

Moderation also characterized Solon's political reforms—the common people were granted important political rights but not complete equality. Although laws continued to originate in a newly instituted Council of Four Hundred controlled by the nobles, they now had to be ratified by the popular assembly, to which Solon gave more power. And since wealth, not birth, became the qualification for membership in the new council and for the archonships, wealthy commoners could acquire full political equality. Furthermore, the assembly could now act as a court to hear appeals from the decisions of the archons and to try the archons for misdeeds in office.

Solon's reforms were very popular with the middle classes but did not completely satisfy the rich or the poor. The poor had received neither land nor full political equality, while the nobles thought Solon too radical of a reformer who had betrayed his own class. But both classes were given more political power and a sense of participation and involvement in the life of the polis. Solon's reforms moved Athens closer to the implementation of a more fully democratic constitution.

Solon advised the Athenians to accept his reforms, and then left the city and its politics for ten years, in the hope that his new constitutional reforms would take root without his interference. But rivalries between the nobles, the middle class, and the poor resulted in years of civil conflict. In 560 B.C.E., after several attempts to dominate Athens, Pisistratus (pai-SIS-tra-tus), a military hero and champion of the commoners, seized power as tyrant. He addressed the economic problems by banishing many nobles, whose lands he distributed among the poor, and by promoting commerce and industry. Together with extensive public works projects and state sponsorship of the arts—starting Athens on the road to cultural leadership in Greece—these reforms gave rise to a popular saying that "life under Pisistratus was paradise on earth." Like Solon, Pisistratus moved Athens closer to the acceptance of a more fully developed democracy by giving both the middle class and especially the commoners a real possibility to participate in governing the polis.

Pisistratus was succeeded by his son, Hippias (HIP-i-as), who proved unable to retain his father's popularity and soon became tyrannical in the modern sense of the word. The nobles, aided by a Spartan army, took the opportunity to restore aristocracy, but the majority of Athenian citizens by this time supported establishing a more democratic form of government that empowered the middle and lower classes to a greater degree than the nobles supported. The leader of the democrats, a noble named Cleisthenes (KLAIS-the-neez), established order in Athens with the cooperation of even the nobles when they were faced with the possibility of further Spartan interference.

From 508 to 502 B.C.E. Cleisthenes was given power to enact constitutional reforms that greatly reduced the remaining power of the nobility. He disbanded the old noble-dominated tribes and created ten new ones, each embracing citizens of all classes from widely scattered districts. The popular assembly acquired the right to initiate legislation and became the sovereign power in the state; there could be no appeal from its decisions. A new democratic Council of the Five Hundred, selected by lot from the ten tribes, advised the assembly and supervised the administrative actions of the archons.

Cleisthenes also has been credited with instituting the institution of *ostracism,* an annual referendum in which a quorum of citizens could vote to exile for ten years any individual thought to be a threat to the new Athenian democracy. (A quorum consisted of 6000 of the 50,000 male citizens over the age of 18. The average attendance at an Athenian assembly, whose ordinary meetings were held every ten days, was about 5000.) By 500 B.C.E. the Athenian polis had established a form of government more thoroughly democratic than in any other city in the ancient world.

The establishment of democratic government at Athens owed a great debt to the reforms of Solon and to the policies of Pisistratus, as both Athenian leaders encouraged greater participation in governance by the commoners. But the idealism of Cleisthenes was mainly responsible for establishing the democracy. Cleisthenes diminished the power and influence of the nobles in Athenian politics by reducing their ability to influence voting through their control of the tribal structure and their neighborhoods. He abolished the four Athenian tribes into which all Athenian citizens were born, and instituted in their place ten new tribes, based on neighborhood units called *demes,* which were distributed among the new tribes in such a way that no tribe could dominate a region. All citizens were enrolled on lists kept by the demes, and even if a citizen moved away from the deme in which in which he was originally enrolled, he had to return to that deme to vote and to register for military service. Cleisthenes also awarded citizenship to many resident aliens, most of whom were productive members of the middle classes. A council of 500 was established to replace the old council of 400; now 50 citizens from each of the new 10 tribes constituted this new body that was charged primarily to prepare legislation for the assembly's consideration. But final authority was given to the assembly of all citizens over the age of 18, in which any member might propose legislation, initiate debate, or argue for or against a proposal.

CASE STUDY
Comparing Athens and Sparta

By the beginning of the fifth century B.C.E., Athens was fully involved in the implementation of its new democratic institution but unsure of its security against the threat of Spartan intervention and the possibility of Persian expansion into the Aegean. Its large population and great potential for economic advantage through international trade gave the city-state great potential for growth and prosperity. But the greatest test the polis would face came from the Persian suppression of the revolt of the Greek poleis on the coast of Asia Minor and the subsequent Persian invasion of Greece.

Sparta to 500 B.C.E.

DOCUMENT
Plutarch on Life in Sparta

The early history of Sparta seems very similar to that of many Greek poleis. Sparta took steps to move from a powerful monarchy to oligarchy when the nobles installed five annually elected aristocratic magistrates, called *ephors* ("overseers"), to supervise the kings' activities. Instead of sending out colonists to satisfy the Spartans' desire for more land, the Spartans turned instead to the conquest of the neighboring region of Messenia, whose residents were forced to become state slaves *(helots).* Around 650 B.C.E., however, the Messenians revolted, and it took Sparta nearly 20 years to crush the rebellion. During this emergency that threatened the very existence of the polis, the aristocrats were forced to seek the aid of the Spartan commoners. In return, the nobles agreed to the commoners' demand for land division and more political participation. Private ownership of land was abolished, and the land allotments were divided equally among the 9000 Spartan male citizens. These land allotments were to remain with the original claimants and often came to be held by women when no male heirs to the property remained alive to claim inheritance.

In addition, the nobles established an assembly of all Spartan citizens with the right to elect the ephors and to approve or veto the proposals of the 30-member Council of Elders. While the Athenian state required only two years of military training for young men, the Spartan system—traditionally attributed to a legendary lawgiver named Lycurgus (lai-KUR-guz)—was designed to make every Spartan man a professional soldier and to keep him in a constant state of readiness for war, especially the ever-present danger of a helot revolt. To this end, Spartan society enforced an absolute subordination of the individual to the preservation of the state.

Spartan officials examined all newborn children, and any found sickly or deformed were abandoned. At the age of 7 a boy was taken from his family and placed in the charge of state educators, who taught him to bear hardship, endure discipline, and devote his life to the state. At 20 the young Spartan enrolled in the army and continued to live in barracks, where he contributed food from his allotment of land granted by the state and worked by helots. He was allowed to marry, but he continued to live in barracks, sneaking back to visit his wife only at night. After 30 he could live at home, but continued to take his meals with his company of male comrades. Finally, at 60, he was released from the army and could live at home with his family. This lifelong pattern of discipline produced some of the most formidable soldiers in human history and inspired Spartan citizens with the sense of purpose, obedience, and respect for Spartan law.

Spartan girls also received state training in order to become healthy mothers of warrior sons. Their primary service to the state was thought to be giving birth to male babies, and to that end they were instructed to strengthen their bodies for childbirth. Clad in short tunics, which other Greeks thought immodest, they engaged in running, wrestling, and throwing the discus and javelin. Their characters were to be as strong and resolute as their husbands'. As their men marched off to war, Spartan women gave them a **laconic** farewell (Laconia was another name for the Spartan homeland): "Come back *with* your shield—or *on* it."

Although many Greeks admired the Spartan way of life, few would ever desire to be a part of the Spartan regimen. The typical Spartan was an unsophisticated, uncultured fighting machine. Spartan discipline was almost universally admired, although no other Greek would wish to trade places with a Spartan who avoided the corruptions of fine food and good wine.

Although Sparta developed the finest infantry force in Greece, the state purposely remained backward culturally and economically. Trade and travel were prohibited because the city fathers feared that foreign ideas might threaten Spartan discipline. Sparta is a classic example of how intellectual stagnation accompanies rigid social conformity and military regimentation. But, through conscious design to preserve the state and the privileged status of the citizen elite, the Spartans purposely froze the natural evolution of their political and cultural institutions.

To provide additional assurance that its helots remained uncontaminated by democratic ideas, Sparta allied itself with oligarchic parties in other Peloponnesian (pe-le-pon-NEE-si-an) states and aided them in suppressing their democratic opponents. The resulting Spartan League of oligarchic states, in operation by the end of the sixth century B.C.E., was shortly to be opposed by an Athenian-led alliance of more democratic states.

laconic—Using few words, but expressing much. From Laconia, the region in which Sparta was located. Esessentially, to be laconic is to speak in a terse manner, as a Spartan did.

Persian Wars

before c. 540 B.C.E.	Persian control of Greek cities in Asia Minor
499–495 B.C.E.	Rebellion of Ionian cities in Asia Minor
490 B.C.E.	Battle of Marathon
480–479 B.C.E.	Xerxes' invasion of Greece
480 B.C.E.	Battles of Thermopylae and Salamis
479 B.C.E.	Battle of Plataea

THE GOLDEN AGE OF GREECE, 500–336 B.C.E.

- *What about this period justifies the idea of a Greek "Golden Age"?*

The leaders of a Greek economic and cultural revival after 750 B.C.E. were the Ionian Greeks, who had settled on the Aegean coast of central Asia Minor and the nearby offshore islands and the mainland region of Attica—the Athenians were also Ionian Greeks. Influenced by contacts with Phoenician traders (from whom they borrowed the alphabet in the eighth century B.C.E.) and neighboring Lydia and Egypt, the Ionians became innovators in art, science, philosophy, and literature. Ionian creativity was also evident in their commercial ventures, which spread throughout the Aegean region. It was especially because of their economic prosperity that they became the first of the Greeks to face conflict with the great powers of the Near East.

The Persian Wars

When the Persian empire and its young king Cyrus conquered Lydia in 547 B.C.E., they also took over the Ionian poleis, which had been fairly content under moderate Lydian rule. In open opposition to their Persian-appointed overlords, the Ionian cities revolted in 499 B.C.E., established democratic regimes, and appealed to the Athenians, their kinsmen, for assistance. Athens sent 20 ships—token help, and far too few to prevail over the Persians. By 494 B.C.E. the Persian king Darius I had crushed the revolt, burning the Greek polis of Miletus in revenge.

King Darius knew that Ionia was insecure as long as Athens remained free to incite the Ionian Greeks to revolt again. In 490 B.C.E. a Persian force of about 20,000 infantry and cavalry sailed across the Aegean, conquering the Greek island states along their path, and eventually encamped on the plain of Marathon, 24 miles northwest of Athens. Darius's attempt to eliminate the interference of Athens was ended when the Athenian army, half the size of the Persian force, won an overwhelming victory, slaying as many as 6400 of the invaders while losing only 192 themselves.

The battle of Marathon was one of the most decisive in ancient history. It destroyed the Greek suspicion of Persian invincibility and demonstrated, according to a contemporary Greek historian, that "free men fight better than slaves." Ten years later the Greeks were forced to prepare for a new Persian invasion under Xerxes, Darius's successor, whose objective this time was the subjection of all of Greece. Athens now had 200 warships, the largest fleet in Greece, and Sparta had agreed to head a defensive alliance of 31 states.

The Persian army was too huge to be transported by ship. Crossing the swift-flowing, mile-wide Hellespont near Troy on two pontoon bridges—a notable feat of engineering—the army marched along the Aegean coast accompanied by a great fleet carrying provisions. The Spartans wanted to abandon all of Greece except the Peloponnesus to the invaders but finally agreed to a holding action at the narrow pass of Thermopylae (ther-MO-poh-lee) in central Greece. Here 300 Spartans and a few thousand other Greeks held back the Persians for three days until the Persians discovered a mountain path to the rear of the Greek position. The Spartans fought magnificently until all were killed, along with at least 700 other Greeks. The Spartan dead were immortalized on a monument erected later at the pass, with the inscription "Go Stranger, and tell the Spartans that we lie here, obedient to their word."

The Persians then sacked Athens, whose inhabitants had been evacuated to the Peloponnesus and the islands near the bay of Salamis. Themistocles (the-MI-stoh-kleez), the leader of the democrats at Athens, had long been a strong advocate for the construction of a strong naval force, and now the Athenians were prepared to put their confidence in their ships to defeat the Persian navy in the Bay of Salamis. The battle that took place in the spring, after the Persians had spent the winter in Athens preparing for the event, was an overwhelming Greek victory. Taking full advantage of the Persians' ignorance of the tides and the inability of their ships to outmaneuver the heavier Athenian vessels designed for ramming and close combat, the Persian navy suffered near complete defeat. With 200 of his 350 ships destroyed and his lines of communication cut, Xerxes saw no alternative but to retreat to Asia, although he left a strong force in Greece. The following summer (479 B.C.E.) the Greek army, with the Spartan army in the forefront, defeated the Persian force in central Greece at Plataea. The Persian threat to the Greek mainland was ended, and the Greeks immediately began plans for campaigns to drive the Persians from the Aegean island and the Ionian coast of Asia Minor.

Athens After the Persian Wars

The prominent role the Athenians played in the Greek victory over the mighty Persian Empire exhilarated the polis and gave Athens the confidence and energy to try to assert their leadership of the Greek world during most of the remainder of the fifth century B.C.E. During this period, often described as the Golden Age of Greece, the Athenians also achieved the fullest development of their democracy, and at the same time established a formidable empire on both land and sea.

For more than 30 years (461–429 B.C.E.) during this period, the great statesman Pericles (PE-ri-kleez) guided Athenian policy. In Pericles' time actual executive power no longer resided in the archons, who were chosen by lot, but in a board of ten generals elected annually. The generals urged the popular assembly to adopt specific measures, and the success or failure of their policies determined whether they would be reelected at the end of their annual term. Pericles failed in reelection only once, and so great was his influence on the Athenians that, in the words of his contemporary, the historian Thucydides (thu-SI-di-deez), the Athenian democracy was in reality completely dominated by Pericles and his policies.

To enable even the poorest citizen to participate in government, Pericles extended payment to jurors (a panel of 6000 citizens chosen annually by lot) and to members of the assembly. Although his conservative opponents called this political bribery, Pericles insisted that it was essential to the success of democracy that all the citizens be able to participate, and so those who could not afford to miss a day's wage would be compensated at state expense.

Athenian Society

Despite the many democratic aspects of Athenian society, not all residents of Athens were given the opportunity to be fully participating citizens. Women,

slaves, and resident foreigners (with the exception of those to whom Cleisthenes had granted it) were denied citizenship and had no voice in the government. Legally, Athenian women were first the property of their fathers and then of their husbands. They could not possess property in their own name, make legal contracts, testify in the courts, or initiate divorce proceedings. The exclusion of Athenian women from public life seems significant, given the extent to which the participation in the democracy was extended to males of every social class.

An Athenian wife's function was to bear children and manage the home, where she was restricted to the women's quarters when her husband entertained his friends. Men did not marry until they were about 30, and they usually married girls half their age or less. Marriages were normally arranged through agreements between families, and prospective brides and bridegrooms seldom met before their marriage was agreed upon. Families were small, with usually no more than two children, and infanticide, usually by exposure, of unwanted infants was practiced as a means of population control. The average life expectancy in Athens was little more than 30 years, but if one were able to survive childhood, a longer life could be anticipated.

Sexual activity for men outside marriage was not a matter for negative public comment in Athens, and prostitution was common. An acceptable social institution intended to serve the needs and desires of upper-class Athenian men was spending one's leisure time with female "companions" (*hetaerae;* he-TAI-rai). These prostitutes were normally resident foreigners and therefore not subject to the social restrictions imposed on Athenian women. A few of the *hetaerae,* such as Aspasia (as-PAY-zhah), the mistress and later wife of Pericles, were cultivated women who entertained at gatherings frequented by prominent Athenian political and cultural leaders.

Although there are representations of outspoken and assertive women left for us by Athenian dramatists, actual examples of Athenian women who were publicly prominent are almost nonexistent, and the women themselves accepted their status. Athenian women enjoyed less freedom of movement and participation in the public life of the polis than most other Greek states, even Sparta. Veiled from public view, forbidden to converse with men other than their husbands, restricted to their own quarters in the home when their husbands entertained their guests—the private life of an Athenian wife was known only to her household. Yet married life seems to have been stable and peaceful. Athenian gravestones in particular attest to the love spouses felt for one another. The tie to their children was strong, and the community set high store on the honor owed by sons and daughters to their parents.

Homosexuality was an acceptable form of social conduct for Athenian men during certain periods of their lives. A sexual relationship between a mature man and a young boy just before or after the youth attained puberty was common practice. The relationship was viewed not only as sexual, but educational—a rite of initiation into adult society—and such relationships were most common among Athenian soldiers. However, male homosexuality that continued into the years when Athenians were expected to marry and produce children, as well as homosexual prostitution at any time, was not condoned. Such relationships were regarded as unnatural, and the Athenian government issued strong legal prohibitions against them.

In fifth-century Athens scholars estimate that one out of every four persons was a slave. Some were war captives and others were children of slaves, but most came from outside Greece through slave dealers. No large collections of slaves were used on agricultural estates. Small landowners might own one or more slaves, who worked in the fields alongside their masters. Those who owned many slaves—one rich Athenian owned a thousand—hired them out to private individuals or to the state, where they worked alongside Athenian citizens and received comparable wages.

Other slaves were taught a trade and set up in business. They were allowed to keep one-sixth of their wages, and many of them were able to purchase their freedom. Although a very few voices argued that slavery was contrary to nature and that all people were equal, the Greek world as a whole agreed with Aristotle that some people—non-Greeks in particular—were incapable of full human reason, and so they were by nature of inferior status and likely in need of the guidance of a master.

Athenian Imperialism

The Greek victory over Persia had been made possible by a temporary cooperation of the leading Greek city-states, but that unity quickly dissolved after the war when Sparta, envious of Athenian naval superiority and fearful of helot rebellion at home, recalled its troops and resumed its policy of isolation. Because the Persians still ruled the Ionian cities and another invasion of Greece seemed possible, Athens in 478 B.C.E. invited the city-states of the Aegean to join them in forming a defensive alliance called the Delian League. The small island of Delos, sacred to the Ionian Greeks, was chosen to be the league's headquarters and the

Document — Aristophanes on the Shortcomings of Athenian Democracy

In *The Frogs,* the comic dramatist Aristophanes (445–385 B.C.E.) exhorts the Athenians to elect better-quality leaders.

[The leader of the chorus comes forward and addresses the audience.]

We chorus folk two privileges prize:
To amuse you, citizens, and to advise.
So, mid the fun that marks this sacred day,
We'll put on serious looks, and say our say. . . .
But if we choose to strut and put on airs
While Athens founders in a sea of cares,
In days to come, when history is penned,
They'll say we must have gone clean round the bend. . . .
I'll tell you what I think about the way
This city treats her soundest men today:
By a coincidence more sad than funny,
It's very like the way we treat our money.
The noble silver drachma, that of old
We were so proud of, and the recent gold,
Coins that rang true, clean-stamped and worth their weight
Throughout the world, have ceased to circulate.
Instead, the purses of Athenian shoppers
Are full of shoddy silver-plated coppers.
Just so, when men are needed by the nation,
The best have been withdrawn from circulation.
Men of good birth and breeding, men of parts,
Well schooled in wrestling and in gentler arts,
These we abuse, and trust instead to knaves,
Newcomers, aliens, copper-pated slaves,
All rascals—honestly, what men to choose!
There was a time when you'd have scorned to use
Men so debased, so far beyond the pale,
Even as scapegoats to be dragged from jail
And flogged to death outside the city gate.
My foolish friends, change now, it's not too late!
Try the good ones again: if they succeed,
You will have proved that you have sense indeed.

Questions to Consider

1. What do you think the reaction of the Athenian theatergoers might have been to this sort of criticism?
2. What elements of Aristophanes' criticism of Athens' situation seem timeless? In what ways could a modern day satirist get by with making the same remarks?
3. Aristophanes complains that the Athens of his time is not as good as the "good old days." Are you able to understand why Aristophanes might make that remark from the section given above, and the fact that he lived and wrote during the Peloponnesian War?

From Aristophanes, *The Frogs and Other Plays,* trans. David Barrett (Baltimore: Penguin, 1964), pp. 181–183.

location of the league treasury. To maintain a 200-ship navy that would drive the Persians out and then police the seas, each state was assessed an annual payment of either ships or money, in proportion to its wealth, to the league treasury. From the beginning, Athens dominated the league. Since almost all of the 173 member states paid their assessments in money, which Athens was eager to collect, the Athenians furnished the necessary ships by building them to Athenian specifications in Athenian harbors, with cash collected from their allies.

By 468 B.C.E., after the Ionian cities had been set free and the Persian fleet had been destroyed, various league members thought it unnecessary to continue league membership. In putting down all attempts to withdraw from the league, the Athenians were motivated to some extent by the fear that a Persian danger still existed but mainly by the desire to maintain and protect the large free trade area necessary for Greek—and especially Athenian—commerce and industry. The treasury of the league was moved from Delos and incorporated into that of Athens—further indication to the league's members that Athens was in total control. The Athenians created an empire because they dared not disband the Delian League and because the league was very beneficial to a vibrant Athenian economy. By aiding in the suppression of local aristocratic factions within its subject states and at times imposing democratic governments on the allied states, Athens both eased the task of controlling its empire and emerged as the leader of a union of "democratic" states subject to Athenian control.

To many Greeks—above all to the Spartans and their allies—Athens had become an autocratic and arrogant state interested only in extending its own authority. Athens' leaders, however, justified Athenian **imperialism** on the grounds that it brought freedom, security, and prosperity to the states that recognized Athenian leadership.

The Peloponnesian War

In 431 B.C.E. the Peloponnesian War broke out between the Spartan League and the Athenian Empire. Although commercial rivalry between Athens and Sparta's major ally, Corinth, was an important factor, the conflict is a classic example of how fear of an enemy's growing power can generate a war unwanted by either side. Several incidents served to ignite the underlying tension, and Sparta finally felt it unavoidable to declare war on the Athenians, whom they considered to be the aggressors.

Sparta's hope for victory lay in its army's ability to lay siege to Athens and destroy the crops in the Athenian countryside. Pericles, for his part, relied on Athens's unrivaled navy to import sufficient food and to harass its enemies' coasts.

But Pericles' careful plans to defeat the Spartans were upset by an unexpected turn of events. In the second year of the war a plague, probably an outbreak of **typhus,** killed a third of the Athenian population, including Pericles himself. His death was a great blow to Athens, for leadership of the government passed to leaders of lesser vision and talent.

Eight more years of indecisive warfare ended in 421 B.C.E. with agreement on a compromise peace treaty. During the succeeding period Athenian imperialism was revealed in its worst form through the actions of Pericles' less able successors. In 416 B.C.E. an expedition embarked for Melos (MEE-los), a neutral Aegean island, to force it to join the Athenian Empire. When the Melians refused to join the Empire and argued that they preferred merely to be left alone, the Athenians executed all the men of military age and sold the women and children into slavery.

The war resumed in 415 B.C.E. with an Athenian expedition against Syracuse, the major Greek state in Sicily. The campaign was hastily put together and badly planned, with complete disaster as a result. Acting on the invitation of states that feared Syracusan expansion, the Athenians hoped to add Sicily to their empire and so become powerful enough to control nearly the entire Mediterranean. But bad luck and incompetent leadership resulted in the destruction of two Athenian fleets and a large Athenian army by the Syracusans, who were also supported by Sparta. The war dragged on until 404 B.C.E., when Athens surrendered after its last fleet was destroyed by a Spartan fleet, which was built with money received from Persia in exchange for possession of the Greek cities in Ionia. At home, Athens had been weakened by the plots and schemes of oligarchic politicians to whom Sparta now turned over the government. The once powerful city-state was stripped of its empire, its fleet, the defense walls that led to the port, and its army and navy.

Aftermath of the War

Anarchy and depression were the political and economic legacies of the Peloponnesian War. Having ended the threat of Athenian domination of Greece, the Spartans substituted their own form of rule that made Athenian imperialism seem mild in comparison. Everywhere, democracies were replaced by oligarchies supported by Spartan troops. The bloody regimes of these unimaginative oligarchs soon led to successful democratic revolutions at Athens and elsewhere. As one of their generals admitted, the Spartans did not know how to govern free people. Incessant warfare between city-states involved in a bewildering series of shifting alliances became typical of Greece in the fourth century B.C.E. Some alliances were even financed by Persia, which wanted to keep the Greek states disunited and weak.

Political instability in turn contributed to the economic and social problems that plagued Greece during this period. Commerce and industry lagged, and the unemployed who did not go abroad as soldiers of fortune supported authoritarian leaders and their radical schemes for redistribution of wealth. The wealthy, for their part, became increasingly reactionary and uncompromising. Many intellectuals and philosophers—including Plato and Aristotle—lost faith in democracy and joined with the wealthy in looking for an inspirational leader who would bring order and security to Greece. They found him, finally, in the person of the king of Macedonia.

The Macedonian Unification of Greece

To the north of Greece was Macedonia (ma-si-DOH-ni-ah), a region inhabited by people of the same

---

imperialism—The policy of a government to build and widen its authority by controlling other states or regions through military, political, and economic domination.

typhus—A disease characterized by exhaustion, fever, and the eruption of reddish spots on the body. Probably spread by a microorganism carried by lice and fleas.

Forensic facial reconstruction of Philip II, father of Alexander the Great, based on remains of his skull found in his tomb in Macedonia. The king had suffered an arrow wound to the eye during battle.

descent as the Greeks in the south who spoke a Greek dialect. But the Greeks considered the Macedonians backward and almost barbaric. No city-states had ever developed in Macedonia, and the land continued to be ruled by kings who were often assassinated by their own nobles if they attempted to assert too much power. But in the fourth century Macedonia emerged as a centralized, powerful state under a young and brilliant King Philip II (359–336 B.C.E.), who created the most formidable Greek army yet known by joining the well-trained Macedonian cavalry of nobles with the hoplite infantry used by the Greeks. When he was a youth, Philip had been held as a hostage at Thebes, where he acquired an appreciation of Greek culture, an understanding of Greek political weaknesses, and a desire to win for Macedonia a place of honor and power in the Greek world.

After unifying all of his home country—including a number of Greek colonies that had been established along the Macedonian coast during the earlier centuries of Macedonia's weakness—Philip turned to the Greek city-states, whose wars afforded him the opportunity first to participate through intervention and then to dominate by military superiority. Demosthenes (de-MOS-the-neez), a prominent Athenian orator and an advocate of democracy, warned constantly of the threat he believed Philip to be to Greek freedom, and urged the Athenians and other Greeks to stop the king's expansion before it was too late. Ultimately, Athens and Thebes did attempt to stop Philip's advance, but their combined forces were shattered at Chaeronea (KAY-ro-NEE-yah) in 338 B.C.E. Philip then forced the Greeks to form a league in which each state, while retaining self-government, swore to make peace and to furnish Philip with men and supplies for a campaign against Persia. Two years later, before setting out for Asia Minor, Philip was assassinated by a Macedonian noble, leaving the war against Persia as a legacy for his gifted son Alexander.

With the Macedonian victory in 338 B.C.E. and the formation of the league of Greek states firmly under the control of King Philip, the warfare between Greek states that had been almost constant for more than one hundred years came to an end. But one of the costs of this peace was the independence and self-government so prized by Greek poleis. With the Macedonian victory came changes not only in the political fabric of traditional Greek life, but cultural adaptations so significant that many scholars detect in them the beginnings of a new political and cultural order in the Mediterranean world.

THE GREEK CULTURAL ACHIEVEMENT

▪ *How did the cultural achievements of the Greeks have an impact on Western civilization and other succeeding world cultures?*

The Greeks were the first to formulate many of the Western world's fundamental concepts in politics, philosophy, science, and art. How was it that a relatively small number of people could leave such a great legacy to later civilizations? The definitive answer may always escape students, but a good part of the explanation might be found in environmental and social factors.

Unlike the older Near Eastern monarchies, the polis was not governed by a "divine" ruler, nor were the thoughts and activities of its citizens restricted by

Classical Greek Literature and Culture

c. 800 B.C.E.	Homer, *The Iliad*
c. 700–480 B.C.E.	Archaic period of Greek art
c. 700 B.C.E.	Hesiod, *Works and Days*
c. 600 B.C.E.	Thales of Miletus, "father of philosophy"
525–456 B.C.E.	Aeschylus, *Oresteia*
c. 496–406 B.C.E.	Sophocles, *Oedipus*
c. 484–c. 425 B.C.E.	Herodotus, "father of history"
c. 480–406 B.C.E.	Euripides, Athenian tragedian
c. 470–399 B.C.E.	Socrates' quest for truth
460–400 B.C.E.	Thucydides, scientific historian
c. 445–385 B.C.E.	Aristophanes, *The Frogs*
427–347 B.C.E.	Plato, *Republic*
c. 420 B.C.E.	Hippocrates' medical school
384–322 B.C.E.	Aristotle's Lyceum

powerful priesthoods. Many Greeks, and most notably the Athenians, were fond of good, wide-ranging conversation and loved debate and argument. The Greeks were religious people, but in most regards they were not overpowered by their gods and regulated by their priests. Their most creative thinkers believed that most significant questions about the world and their place within it could be answered through human resourcefulness and speculation.

The Greek Character

The Greeks felt a need to discover order and meaning both in nature and in human life. This outlook produced exceptional results in science, philosophy, and the arts. As early as the poet Hesiod (c. 700 B.C.E.), the Greeks stressed the virtue of *sophrosyne* (soh-froh-SEE-nay), moderation and self-control, as the key to happiness and fulfillment in life. Working against this virtue was *hubris,* meaning pride, arrogance, and unbridled ambition. The result of human excess and the basic cause of personal misfortune and social injustice, hubris always inspired *nemesis,* or retribution. According to the Greeks, an unavoidable law would cause the downfall or disgrace of anyone guilty of hubris. The Athenian dramatists emphasized this theme in their tragedies, and Herodotus attributed the Persian defeat by the Greeks to Xerxes' overpowering pride.

The Greeks had all the usual human frailties and failings—at times they were irrational, vindictive, and cruel. But at their best they were guided by the ideals that are described in their intellectual and artistic legacy. The philosopher Protagoras (proh-TA-goh-rahs) is credited with the statement, "Man is the measure of all things"—a statement that typifies the fundamental humanistic character of Greek thought and art.

Greek Religion

Early Greek religion, like almost all religious expressions of early civilizations, abounded in gods and goddesses who personified the forces of nature. Zeus, sky-god and wielder of thunderbolts, ruled the world from Mount Olympus with the aid of lesser deities, many of whom were his children. His power was limited only by the mysterious decrees of Fate. These gods and goddesses as described by Homer act like humans—capable of evil deeds, favoritism, and jealousy, differing from ordinary people only in their immortality. Zeus was often the unknowing victim of the plots of his wife, Hera, and other deities, and he asserted his authority through threats of violence. Hades, the place of the dead, was a subterranean land of dust and darkness, and Achilles, as Homer tells us in the *Odyssey,* would prefer to be a slave on earth than a king in Hades.

By the time of Hesiod, a more sophisticated religious interpretation had changed the vengeful and unpredictable gods of Homer into more rational dispensers of justice who rewarded the good and punished the wicked. Zeus's stature was increased when he was newly identified as the source of Fate, which was no longer considered a separate mysterious power. And from the famous **oracle** at Delphi the voice of Zeus's son Apollo urged all Greeks to follow the ideal of moderation: "Nothing in excess" and "Know yourself."

A century after Hesiod, the Orphic and Eleusinian (el-eu-SI-ni-uhn) mystery cults emerged as a type of Greek higher religion. Their initiates *(mystae)* were promised salvation in an afterlife of bliss in Elysium,

oracle—In ancient Greece, a divine message made by a god through a priest or priestess, or even through the rustling of wind through trees. Oracles were usually delivered in answer to an inquiry from an individual or polis, and the response was typically given in a form that was open to several interpretations. At Delphi, the oracle sometimes refers to the priestess who delivered the god's message.

formerly the home after death of a few heroes only. The basis of the Orphic cult was an old myth about Dionysus, a son of Zeus, who was killed and eaten by the evil Titans before Zeus arrived on the scene and burned them to ashes with his lightning bolts. Orpheus, a legendary figure, taught that Zeus then created man from the Titans' ashes. Human nature, therefore, is composed of two distinct and opposing elements: the evil Titanic element (the body) and the divine Dionysian element (the soul). Death, which frees the divine soul from the evil body, is therefore to be welcomed.

Early Greek Philosophy

What the Greeks were the first to call *philosophy* ("love of wisdom") arose from their curiosity about nature. The early Greek philosophers were called *physikoi* ("physicists") because their main interest was the investigation of the physical world. ("It is according to their wonder," wrote Aristotle, "that men begin to philosophize, pursuing science in order to know.") Later, and primarily due to the influence of Socrates, the chief concern of philosophy was not natural science but *ethics*—how people ought to act in light of moral principles.

The Mesopotamians, as noted in Chapter 1, were skilled observers of astronomical phenomena, which, like the early Greeks, they attributed to the action of the gods. But early Greek philosophers, beginning with Thales of Miletus around 600 B.C.E., changed the course of human knowledge by insisting that the phenomena of the universe could be explained by natural rather than supernatural causes. This rejection of mythological explanations led the Greeks to emphasize the use of human reason to explain the world around them.

Called the "father of philosophy," Thales speculated about the nature of the basic substance of which everything in the universe is composed. He concluded that it was water, which exists in different states and is indispensable to the maintenance and growth of organisms. Thales's successors in Ionia proposed elements other than water as this primal substance in the universe. One called it the "boundless," apparently a general concept for matter; another proposed "air," out of which all things come by a process of "rarefying and condensing"; a third asserted that fire was the "most mobile, most transformable, most active, most life-giving" element. This search for a material substance as the first principle or cause of all things culminated two centuries after Thales in the atomic theory of Democritus (de-MO-kri-tus). To Democritus (c. 460–370 B.C.E.), reality was the mechanical motion of indivisible particles, which differed in shape, size, position, and arrangement but not in quality. Moving about continuously, these particles combined to create objects.

While these and other early Greek philosophers were proposing some form of matter as the basic element in nature, Pythagoras of Samos (c. 582–500 B.C.E.) countered with the profoundly significant idea that the "nature of things" was something nonmaterial: numbers. By experimenting with a vibrating chord, Pythagoras discovered that musical harmony is based on arithmetical proportions, and he intuitively concluded that the universe was constructed of numbers and their relationships. His mystical, nonmaterial interpretation of nature, together with his belief that the human body was distinct from the soul, greatly influenced the thinking of Plato.

An important result of early Greek philosophical speculation was the further questioning of conventional beliefs and traditions. In religion, for example, Anaximander argued that thunder and lightning were caused by blasts of wind and not by Zeus's thunderbolts. Xenophanes (ze-NO-fah-neez) went on to ridicule the traditional view of the gods: "If oxen and lions had hands, . . . they would make portraits and statues of their gods in their own image."

The eroding of traditional beliefs was intensified during the last half of the fifth century B.C.E. by the activity of professional teachers, called Sophists ("intellectuals"). They taught a variety of subjects—the nucleus of our present arts and sciences—that they claimed would lead to material success. The most popular subjects they taught were methods of persuasion and successful argumentation; some even claimed to be able to teach virtue and wisdom to students who paid for their knowledge. The Sophists tried to put all conventional beliefs to the test of rational criticism and subjected human beliefs, customs, and even laws to rational analysis. Some even concluded that truth itself was relative, having no firm existence other than in the decisions and institutions of society. Such speculation questioned the existence of fixed universal standards to guide human actions.

The Contribution of Socrates

A contemporary of the early Sophists but opposed to many of their conclusions was the Athenian Socrates (SO-kra-teez). Like the Sophists, Socrates (c. 470–399 B.C.E.) turned from concern with the gods to human affairs. But unlike them, Socrates believed that by asking meaningful questions and subjecting the answers to logical analysis, agreement could be reached about ethical standards and rules of conduct in human affairs. And so he would question his fellow citizens who possessed a certain skill or particular talent in hopes of learning more about the principles that determine human behavior. He found that his fellow citizens possessed no such knowledge. Instead, he found that he was accused of undermining the institutions and values of the city-state through his constant questioning of socially accepted customs and institutions. His dislike of democracy, which he believed to be a government in which important decisions were usually made by badly informed or even totally ignorant participants, earned him the hostility of most of his fellow citizens. In spite of the growing suspicion that he was a subversive, he continued to emphasize his own individualism and his belief that the pursuit of philosophy was the best way to improve the soul and to assert that he was an ignorant man in search of knowledge, rather than a teacher of others.

In time Socrates' quest for truth led to conflict with the state. In 399 B.C.E. the Athenians, unnerved by their defeat in the Peloponnesian War and concerned about subversion from within, put Socrates on trial for introducing new gods into Athens and corrupting the youth. He was found guilty and was condemned to death. Although he was given a chance to escape that fate, he refused to do so, choosing instead to observe the polis's laws, but still retaining the right to question and analyze them.

Plato and His Theory of Ideas

After Socrates' death, philosophical leadership passed to his most famous student, Plato (427–347 B.C.E.). Like Socrates, Plato believed that truth exists, but only in the realm of thought, the spiritual world of ideas or forms. Such universal truths as beauty, good, and justice exist apart from the material world, and the beauty, good, and justice encountered in the world of the senses are only imperfect reflections of eternal and changeless ideas. The task for humans is to come to know the true reality—the eternal ideas—behind these imperfect reflections. Only the soul and the "soul's pilot," reason, can accomplish this goal, for the human soul is spiritual and immortal, and in its original state it existed beyond the "heavens" where ultimate truth also is found.

Disillusioned with the democracy that had led Athens to ruin in the Peloponnesian War and that had condemned Socrates to death, Plato put forward his concept of an ideal state in the *Republic,* the first systematic work on political science. The state's basic function, founded on the idea of justice, was the satisfaction of the common good. Plato described a kind of ideal polis in which the state regulated every aspect of life, including thought. Accordingly, poets and forms of music considered unworthy were prohibited. Private property was abolished on the grounds that it bred selfishness. Plato believed there was no essential difference between men and women; therefore, women received the same education and held the same occupations as men, including military training. Individuals belonged to one of three classes and found happiness only through their contribution to the community: workers by producing the necessities of life, warriors by guarding the state, and philosophers by ruling in the best interests of all the people.

Plato founded the Academy in Athens, the famous school that existed from about 388 B.C.E. until 529 C.E., when it was closed by the Christian emperor Justinian. Here Plato taught and encouraged his students, whom he expected to become the intellectual elite who would go on to reform society.

Aristotle, the Encyclopedic Philosopher

Plato's greatest pupil was Aristotle (384–322 B.C.E.), who set up his own school, the Lyceum (lai-SEE-um), at Athens. Reacting against the otherworldly directions of Plato's thought, Aristotle insisted that ideas have no separate existence apart from the material world—knowledge of universal ideas is the result of the painstaking collection and organization of particular facts. Aristotle's Lyceum, accordingly, became a center for the analysis of data from many branches of learning.

DOCUMENT
Aristotle on Slavery

Aristotle's works remain among the most influential contributions to Western thought. Much of his speculation deals with what he called the "philosophy of human affairs," whose object is the acquisition and maintenance of human happiness. Two kinds of virtue *(arête),* intellectual and moral, which produce two types of happiness, are described in the *Ethics.* Intellectual virtue is the product of reason, and only such people as philosophers and scientists ever attain it. Much more important for the good of society is moral virtue—virtues of character, such as justice, bravery, and temperance—which is the product less of reason than of habit and thus can be acquired by all. In this connection Aristotle introduced his "doctrine of the mean" as a guide for good conduct. He considered all moral virtues to be means between extremes; courage, for example, is the mean between cowardice and rashness. In the *Politics* Aristotle viewed the state as necessary "for the sake of the good life," because its laws and educational system provide the most effective training needed for the attainment of moral virtue and, as a result of that moral virtue—happiness. To Aristotle, the viewpoint that the state stands in opposition to the individual would not be valid.

There have probably been few geniuses whose interests were as widespread as Aristotle's. He investigated such diverse fields as biology (his minute observations include the life cycle of the gnat), mathematics, astronomy, physics, literary criticism (the concept of ***catharsis***—art as a release of emotion), rhetoric, logic (deductive and inductive), politics (he analyzed 158 Greek and foreign constitutions), ethics, and metaphysics. His knowledge was so encyclopedic that there is hardly a college course today that does not take note of what Aristotle had to say on the subject. Although his works on natural science are now mostly historical curiosities, they held a place of undisputed authority until the scientific revolution of the sixteenth and seventeenth centuries. But in no important sense are his humanistic studies, such as the *Ethics* and the *Politics,* out of date.

Medicine

Superstitions about the human body held back the development of medical science until 420 B.C.E., when Hippocrates (hip-PO-kra-teez), the "father of medicine," founded a school in which he emphasized the value of observation and the careful interpretation of symptoms. Such modern medical terms as *crisis, acute,* and *chronic* were first used by Hippocrates. He was firmly convinced that disease resulted from natural, not supernatural, causes. The Hippocratic school also gave medicine a sense of service to humanity that it has never lost. All members took the famous Hippocratic Oath, still in use today.

Despite using the empirical approach, the Hippocratic school adopted the theory that the body contained four liquids or *humors*—blood, phlegm, black bile, and yellow bile—whose proper balance was the basis of health. This popular doctrine was to impede medical progress in Europe until the seventeenth century.

The Writing of History

If history is defined as an honest attempt to find out what happened and then to explain why it happened, Herodotus (he-RO-doh-tuhs) of Halicarnassus (c. 484–c. 425 B.C.E.) deserves to be called the founder of that discipline. In his well-researched and highly entertaining history of the Persian Wars, he identified the clash of two distinct civilizations, the Greek and the Near Eastern. His portrayal of both the Greeks and the Persians was in most cases impartial, but his fondness for a good story often led him to include tall tales in his work. As he stated more than once, "My duty is to report what has been said, but I do not have to believe it."

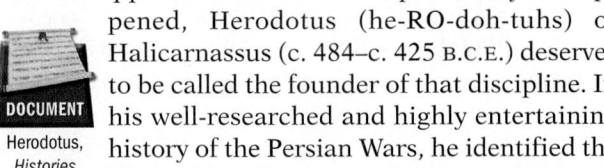

DOCUMENT
Herodotus, *Histories*

The first truly scientific historian was Thucydides (460–400 B.C.E.), who wrote a notably objective account of the Peloponnesian War. Although Thucydides was a contemporary of the events and a loyal Athenian, a reader can scarcely detect whether he favored Athens or Sparta. Thucydides believed that his history would become a useful tool for those who desire a clear picture of what has happened and, human nature being as it is, what is likely to be repeated in the future. His belief was based on his remarkable ability to analyze and explain human behavior and the nature of politics.

DOCUMENT
Thucydides on Athens

Greek Poetry and Drama

Greek literary periods can be classified according to the dominant poetic forms that reflect particular stages of the culture's development. First came the time of great epic poems, followed by periods in which lyric poetry and then drama flourished.

Sometime during the eighth century B.C.E. in Ionia, the *Iliad* and the *Odyssey,* the two great epics attributed to Homer, were set down in their present form. The *Iliad,* describing the clash of arms between the Greeks and Trojans, glorifies heroic bravery and physical strength against a background of divine intervention in human affairs. The *Odyssey,* relating the adventure-filled wanderings of Odysseus on his return to Greece after Troy's fall, places less stress on divine intervention and more on the cool resourcefulness of the hero in escaping from danger and in regaining his kingdom. These stirring epics have provided inspiration and source material for many generations of poets.

As Greek society continued to develop and seek new varieties of artistic expression, a new type of poetry, written to be sung to the accompaniment of a small stringed instrument called a lyre, became popular among the Ionian Greeks. Unlike Homer, authors of this lyric poetry sang not of legendary events but of present delights and sorrows.

DOCUMENT
Greek Poetry

Drama (also in verse) developed from the religious rites of Dionysus (son of Zeus from an affair with the daughter of the king of Tyre) in which a large chorus and its leader sang and danced. The legendary Thespis, supposedly a contemporary of Solon, added an actor called the "answerer" (*hypocrites,* the origin of our word *hypocrite*) to converse with the chorus and its leader. This innovation made dramatic dialogue possible. By

catharsis—A word which means "cleansing" in Greek, but in its application to ancient Greek tragedy, its meaning is more specifically "a purging of pity and fear"—the desired effect of the performance on the audience.

Discovery Through Maps

The World According to Herodotus, c. 450 B.C.E.

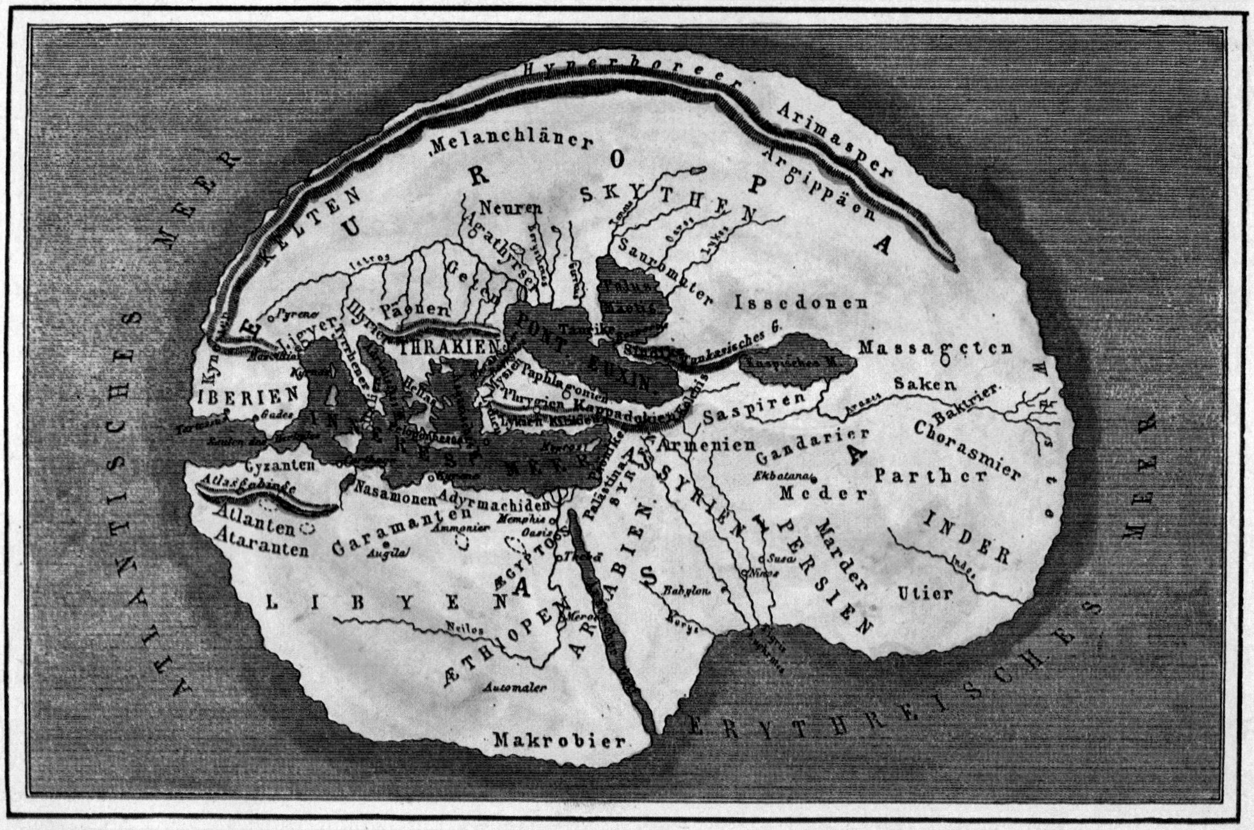

This map depicts the known world at the time of the Greek historian Herodotus, who lived and worked around 450–425 B.C.E. The map is a modern rendition of what we know Herodotus thought to be the world, as described in his writings, the *Histories*. The *Histories* was written to describe the events and circumstances that led the Greeks and the Persians to engage in war—a war that Herodotus believed changed the direction of human history. To understand why these two great powers came into conflict, the historian believed he would have to examine the origins, geographical setting, culture, and traditions of the whole empire of the Persians, as well as the background of the Greek city-states. The *Histories* became not just a listing of chronological events but an exploration of geography, sociology, and anthropology as well.

We are certain that Herodotus himself traveled extensively throughout his world in order to learn firsthand of the people he described. Most of his geographical knowledge came from his own observations or from interviews with the people he met. He seems to have believed that the earth was a flat disk, although he must have been familiar with contemporary theories that the world might be a sphere. He differed from most of his contemporaries in not picturing Europe, Africa (which he called Libya), and Asia as approximately the same size. He described Europe as being as long as both Asia and Africa put together. Yet Herodotus did not travel to the farthest reaches of the continent but relied on accounts of others; he knew nothing of the existence of Britain or Scandinavia, for example, and he did not know if Europe was surrounded by water to the west or north. His knowledge of Asia was limited to the lands of the Persian Empire. He knew that the Caspian Sea was an inland sea and not, as most of his contemporaries believed, a sea that emptied into the band of ocean that encircled the earth. He also knew that Africa was surrounded by water—a fact that the geographer Ptolemy missed 500 years later.

Questions to Consider

1. How might you account for some of the major errors in Herodotus's geographical knowledge?
2. Are there any features of the map which you find to be remarkably accurate for Herodotus's time?
3. Do you see any significance in the proportions of the map, and what region is placed in the center?

the fifth century B.C.E. in Athens, two distinct forms, tragedy and comedy, had evolved. Borrowing from the old familiar legends of gods and heroes for their plots, the tragedians reinterpreted them from the point of view of the values and problems of their own times.

In reworking the old legends of the heroic age, Aeschylus (ES-kuh-luhs; 525–456 B.C.E.) attempted to present the new values being considered regarding Greek religion, first expressed in Hesiod's work, by showing how following the old unsophisticated beliefs leads to suffering. In his trilogy, the *Oresteia,* for example, he concerned himself with hubris as applied to the murder of the hero Agamemnon by his queen following his return from the Trojan War. Aeschylus then proceeded to work out its effects—one murder after another murder until people, through suffering, learn to substitute the moral law of Zeus for the primitive law of the blood feud.

A generation later, Sophocles (c. 496–406 B.C.E.) continued to explore the themes of divine justice, morality, and ethics, while concentrating, in addition, on character development and psychological themes. Euripides (eu-RI-pi-deez; c. 480–406 B.C.E.), the last of the great Athenian tragedians, reflects the rationalism and critical spirit of the late fifth century B.C.E. His plays concentrate more on the personalities of his characters and their interesting behavior, rather than on the overriding power of fate or the gods.

Greek comedies were full of satire and scathing criticism of contemporary prominent citizens. There were no libel laws in Athens, and Aristophanes (a-ri-STO-fah-neez; c. 445–385 B.C.E.), the famous comic-dramatist and a conservative in outlook, brilliantly satirized Athenian democracy as a mob led by demagogues, the Sophists (among whom he included Socrates) as subversive, and Euripides as an opponent of civic spirit and traditional values.

Greek Architecture

During the formative, archaic period of Greek art (c. 700–480 B.C.E.), architecture flourished in Ionia, Greece, and the Greek colonies in Sicily and southern

In the Parthenon, great care was taken to design a perfect building, both structurally and visually. The topics of the Doric columns lean toward the center, and the columns are more widely spaced in the middle of each row than at the ends. All these refinements create an illusion of perfect regularity that would be lacking if the parts were actually regular. Sculpture adorned the triangular gables and part of the frieze just below the gables; another sculptured frieze ran around the walls inside the colonnade. The whole building was once painted in bright colors.

Italy. Reflecting the prosperity produced by colonization, large stone temples were constructed. Their form may have developed from wooden structures that had been influenced by the remains of Mycenaean palaces, and perhaps by Egyptian temples or the religious architecture of the Near East.

The classical phase of Greek architecture reached its zenith in Athens during the second half of the fifth century B.C.E. The Parthenon, the Erechtheum (e-rek-THEE-um), and the other temples on the Acropolis in Athens exhibit the highly developed features that make Greek structures so pleasing to the eye. All relationships, such as column spacing and height and the slight curvature of floor and roof lines, were calculated and executed with remarkable precision to achieve the illusion of a perfect balance, both structurally and visually. The three orders, or styles, usually identified by the characteristics of the columns, were the **Doric,** which was used in the Parthenon; the **Ionic,** seen in the Erechtheum; and the later and more ornate **Corinthian.**

Erectheion, Athens

Greek temples afford an interesting comparison with those of Egypt. Egyptian temples were enclosed by walls and only priests and royalty could enter the inner rooms, but the Greek temple was open, with a colonnade porch and an inside room containing a statue of the god or goddess. Animal sacrifice and ritual took place outside the temple, where the sacrificial altar was placed.

Other types of buildings, notably the theaters, stadia, and gymnasia, also express the Greek spirit and way of life. In the open-air theaters, the circular shape of the spectators' sections and the plan of the orchestra section set a style that has survived to the present day.

Greek Sculpture and Pottery

Greek sculpture is usually described as having passed through three stages of development: the archaic, the classical, and the Hellenistic periods. Greek sculpture of the archaic period, although crude in its representation of human anatomy, displays the freshness and liveliness of youth. Influenced clearly by Egyptian models, the statues of nude youths and draped maidens usually stand stiffly with clenched fists and with one foot thrust awkwardly forward. The fixed smile and formalized treatment of hair and drapery also reveal the sculptors' struggle to master the technique of their art.

The mastery of technique by 480 B.C.E. began the classical period of fifth-century Greek sculpture, whose principles of harmony and proportion shaped the development of art in the West for centuries after the Greeks. Sculpture from this period displays both the end of technical immaturity and the beginning of idealization of the human form, which reached its culmination in the dignity and poise of Phidias's (FI-dee-uhs) figures in the continuous **frieze** and **pediments** of the Parthenon. Carved with restraint and proportion, the frieze represents the citizens of Athens participating in a procession in honor of their patron goddess, Athena, which took place every four years.

The more relaxed nature of fourth-century B.C.E. Greek sculpture, while still considered classical, lacks some of the grandeur and dignity of fifth-century art. Charm, grace, and individuality characterize the work of Praxiteles (prax-IT-el-eez), the most famous sculptor of the century. These qualities can be seen in his flowing statues of the god Hermes holding the young Dionysus and of Aphrodite stepping into her bath.

The making of pottery, the oldest Greek art, started at the beginning of the Greek Middle Age (c. 1150 B.C.E.) with crude imitations of late Mycenaean forms. Soon the old Mycenaean patterns were replaced by abstract geometrical designs. With the coming of the archaic period came paintings of scenes from mythology and daily life. We are able to form an impression of what Greek painting, now lost, must have been like from surviving Greek pottery and mosaics. The buildings and sculpture we observe today as stark white marble creations were in all likelihood lavishly and brightly painted in the colors the Greeks obviously loved.

THE HELLENISTIC AGE, 336–30 B.C.E.

- *How did the Hellenistic Age differ from the Greek civilization that preceded it?*

The Hellenistic Age is the three-century period beginning with the career of Alexander the Great to the rise

---

Doric—Specific form of the capital (or crown) of a Greek column. A capital in the Doric order is squat and simple without elaborate decoration and originated in wooden temples.

Ionic—Specific form of the capital (or crown) of a Greek column. A capital of the Ionic order is usually decorated with scrolls (or volutes).

Corinthian—Specific form of the capital (or crown) of a Greek column. Corinthian capitals are the most highly decorated of the three orders of Greek columns, with carved acanthus leaves and scrolls.

frieze—In Greek architecture, a long, narrow, horizontal panel often decorated with relief sculpture and placed around the walls of a room or a temple.

pediment—The most dominant feature of the front of a Greek temple. A triangular construction that sits on top of the temple's facade.

Macedonia and Alexander

359–336 B.C.E.	Reign of Philip II
338 B.C.E.	Philip conquers Greek city-states
336–323 B.C.E.	Reign of Alexander the Great
334 B.C.E.	Alexander invades Persian Empire
331 B.C.E.	Battle at Gaugamela
327 B.C.E.	Alexander enters India
323 B.C.E.	Alexander dies

of Augustus Caesar, the first of the Roman emperors, who completed Rome's domination of the Mediterranean world by adding Greek-ruled Egypt to Rome's empire in 30 B.C.E. The Hellenistic Age, begun by the creation of Alexander the Great's vast conquests, was a period of economic expansion, cosmopolitanism, striking intellectual and artistic achievements, and the wide distribution of Greek culture.

MAP Alexander the Great and the Hellenistic Age

Alexander the Great

When Philip of Macedonia was assassinated in 336 B.C.E., his authority was claimed by his 20-year-old son, Alexander. Alexander proved himself a remarkably gifted individual from the very beginning of his reign by gaining the support of the Macedonian nobles, even though some of them suspected the young man of being involved in Philip's murder. Alexander persuaded his father's old generals and comrades to swear their loyalty to him and proceeded to demand the loyalty of the Greek League, which had been founded by his father. When the Greek city of Thebes responded to a rumor that Alexander had been killed in battle by rebelling against the Macedonians, the young king marched his army quickly to the south and ruthlessly crushed the city, selling its remaining inhabitants into slavery. The Greeks were horrified at such brutal action, but a lesson was learned, and few states dared consider rebellion in the years ahead.

Alexander is one of history's most remarkable individuals. Of average height and looks for a Macedonian, he nevertheless impressed his contemporaries as a gifted athlete, a charismatic personality, and a natural leader. Both his father, Philip, and his mother, Olympias, a princess from Illyria, were strong influ-

This small but expertly crafted ivory is thought to be a representation of King Philip, his second wife Olympias, and their young son Alexander (the Great). The three figures are probably represented as participants in a religious ritual dedicated to the god Dionysus. The object was found among the royal graves of the Macedonian monarchs in Vergina.

ences on him. Philip earned his son's respect as a king and a general, and Olympias was a forceful woman who wished great things for her son and who constantly assured the boy that his true father was not Philip, but the god Zeus.

DOCUMENT Plutarch on Alexander the Great

Having been tutored by Aristotle, Alexander was taught the superiority of Greek culture and wished to be the fulfillment of the Greek ideal. Reveling in the heroic deeds of the *Iliad,* which he always kept at his bedside, Alexander saw himself as a new Achilles waging war against barbarians when he planned to complete his father's desire to avenge the Persian attacks on Greece by conquering the Persian Empire. In 334 B.C.E. he set out with an army of 35,000 soldiers recruited from Macedonia and the Greek League. In quick succession he subdued Asia Minor, Syria, and Palestine, defeating the Persians in two great battles. He marched into Egypt, where the Egyptians welcomed him as a deliverer from their Persian masters and recognized him as pharaoh, the living god-king of Egypt.

Greatly impressed with Egypt and its traditions, Alexander wished to spend more time there. But Darius III, the Persian king, was gathering one more massive army to oppose the invader, and Alexander marched into Mesopotamia to meet the Persians for a final battle. In 331 B.C.E., at Gaugamela, near the ancient city of Nineveh, the Macedonians defeated the Persian forces. Darius III was executed by his own relatives as he fled, and Alexander became Great King of the Persian Empire. Alexander led his victorious troops to the ancient Persian capital city of Persepolis (per-SE-poh-lis), but his campaigns did not end there. He wished to command the loyalty of all Persian lands and to extend the great empire to even farther reaches. He led his troops north through Media and Bactria, then south and east into present-day Afghanistan, finally venturing as far east as the rich river valleys of India. There his weary and frightened soldiers, many of whom had been away from home for more than ten years, forced him to turn back.

DOCUMENT Descriptions of Alexandria, Egypt

In 323 B.C.E. Alexander fell ill with a mysterious fever. Perhaps he had contracted malaria in India; perhaps he fell victim to his accumulated battle wounds;

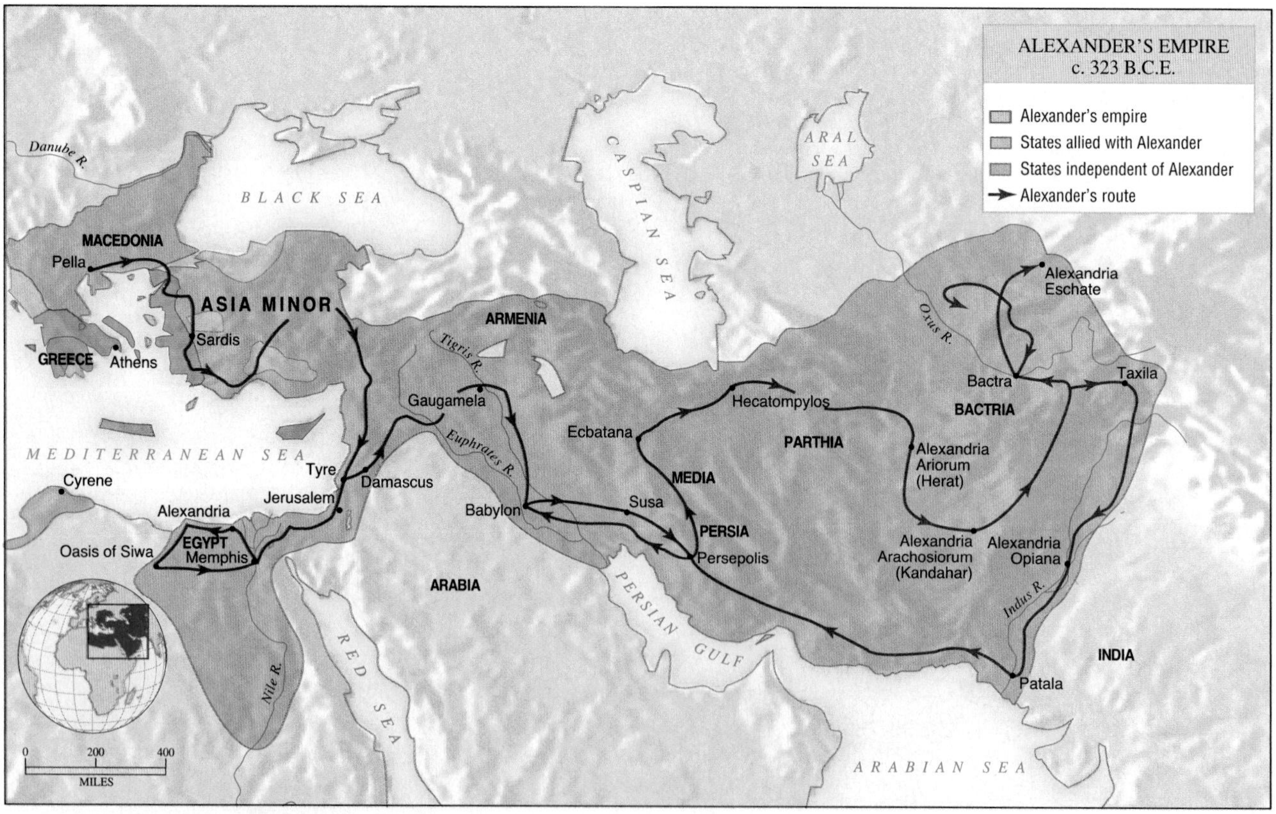

At the time of his death, Alexander had laid claim to a vast empire. One biographer claims that Alexander was planning more conquests when he recovered from his illness—perhaps north into what is now Russia or along the northern coast of Africa and eventually to Rome.

Document Arrian: Alexander the Leader

Arrian wrote his account of Alexander's campaigns in the second century C.E., almost 500 years after Alexander's death. Yet we can have great trust in most of his account, since Arrian evidently had access to accounts and diaries contemporary with Alexander. The following is a description of Alexander's inspirational leadership during an extremely difficult crossing of the southern Iranian desert in hopes of returning to Babylon:

The army was crossing a desert of sand; the sun was already blazing down upon them, but they were struggling on under the necessity of reaching water, which was still far away. Alexander, like everyone else, was tormented by thirst, but he was nonetheless marching on foot at the head of his men. It was all he could do to keep going, but he did so, and the result (as always) was that the men were better able to endure their misery when they saw that it was equally shared. As they toiled on, a party of light infantry which had gone off looking for water found some—just a wretched little trickle collected in a shallow gully. They scooped up with difficulty what they could and hurried back, with their priceless treasure, to Alexander; then, just before they reached him, they tipped the water into a helmet and gave it to him. Alexander, with a word of thanks for the gift, took the helmet and gave it full view of his troops, poured the water on the ground. So extraordinary was the effect of this action that the water wasted by Alexander was as good as a drink for every man in the army. I cannot praise this act too highly; it was a proof, if anything was, not only of his power of endurance, but also of his genius for leadership.

Questions to Consider

1. Do you think that this account could be factual, or is it most likely propaganda? Why?
2. How could such an act of wastefulness be an inspiration to an army?
3. Do you think that the myth of Alexander was, and is, perhaps more important than the historical reality of the man? Give several reasons for your answer.

From Arrian, *Anabasis*, 6.26 in A. de Selincourt, *The Campaigns of Alexander* (New York: Penguin Books, 1958).

perhaps his years of heavy drinking had taken their toll; perhaps, as rumor had it, he had been slowly poisoned by his enemies in the Macedonian camp. Whatever the case, after a short illness, and without designating an heir to his empire, Alexander died in Babylon at the age of 32.

Alexander the Great is a puzzling figure to modern historians. Some view him as a ruthless conqueror who never lost a battle and a despot who ordered even his fellow Macedonians to prostrate themselves in his presence. Others picture him as a farsighted visionary hoping to unite East and West in one world and seeking the eventual "brotherhood of man" by establishing equality for all individuals through the unity of a common Greek culture.

Mosaic of Alexander the Great

Some of Alexander's military and administrative policies sought to unify the lands he conquered and to promote what he himself called "concord and partnership in the empire" between easterners and westerners. He blended Persians with Greeks and Macedonians in his army and administration; he founded numerous cities—70, according to tradition—in the East and settled many of his followers in them; and he married two oriental princesses and encouraged his officers and men to take foreign wives. Finally, for perhaps egotistical and certainly for political reasons, he ordered the Greek city-states to accord him "divine honors."

Alexander was a remarkable blend of the romantic idealist and the practical realist, contrasting traits that he may have inherited from his parents. His mother, Olympias, who practiced the rites of the cult of Dionysus and claimed to be a descendant of the Greek hero Achilles, instilled in her son the consciousness of a divine mission that drove him onward, even to seeking the end of the earth beyond India. Much like his father, he demonstrated remarkable abilities as military commander, expert diplomat, and able political administrator. Alexander was a self-confident idealist who was excited by challenges, but meeting those challenges forced him to take actions that were practical and pragmatic. For example, he could not merely conquer the Great King of Persia; he had to act as his successor as well. Alexander ruled for only 13 years, but in many ways a large part of the world was never again the same.

The Division of Alexander's Empire

With the Greeks now masters of the ancient Near East, a new and distinctly **cosmopolitan** period in their history and culture began—the Hellenistic ("Greek-like") Age. For several decades following Alexander's sudden death, his generals competed against each other for the spoils of empire. Three major Hellenistic kingdoms emerged and maintained an uneasy balance of power until the Roman conquests of the second and first centuries B.C.E.: Egypt, ruled by Alexander's friend and general Ptolemy (TO-le-mee) and his successors; Asia, comprising most of the remaining provinces of the Persian Empire and held together with great difficulty by the dynasty founded by Seleucus (se-LEU-kus); and Macedonia and Greece, ruled by the descendants of Antigonus (an-TI-go-nuhs) the One-Eyed.

While the Antigonids in Macedonia followed the model of Alexander's father, Philip, in ruling as national kings selected by the army, the Ptolemies ruled Egypt as divine pharaohs, and some of the Seleucids attempted to have themselves recognized as "saviors" and "benefactors" of their subjects. Ptolemaic and Seleucid administrations were centralized in bureaucracies staffed mainly by Greeks, an arrangement that created a vast gulf between rulers and ruled.

Plagued by native revolts, dynastic troubles, and civil war, the Hellenistic kingdoms eventually began to crumble. Macedonia lost effective control of Greece by 250 B.C.E. when Athens asserted its independence and most of the other Greek states resisted Macedonian domination by forming two federal leagues, the Achaean and the Aetolian (a-TOH-li-an). Toward the end of the third century B.C.E. the Romans became involved in the rivalries of the city-state and Macedonian monarchy and eventually added all Greece and Macedonia into their growing empire.

The eastern reaches of Alexander's empire—Parthia, Bactria, and India—gradually broke out of Seleucid control. Pergamum, in northwestern Asia Minor, renounced its allegiance to the Seleucids and became an independent kingdom famous for its artists and scholars. By 200 B.C.E. the Romans had entered the scene, and by 30 B.C.E. Rome had annexed all but the last remaining Hellenistic state, Egypt; in that very year Cleopatra, the last reigning member of the dynasty founded by Ptolemy, was captured by the Romans and committed suicide.

HELLENISTIC SOCIETY AND CULTURE

- *What were the results of the expansion of Hellenistic civilization?*

The Hellenistic Age was a time of economic expansion and social change. In the wake of Alexander's conquests, thousands of Greeks moved eastward to begin a new era of Greek colonization, ending the long economic depression that followed the breakup of the Athenian Empire. An economic union of East and West permitted the free flow of trade, and prosperity was stimulated further when Alexander put into circulation huge amounts of Persian gold and silver and introduced a uniform coinage. The result was a much larger and more affluent middle class than had existed previously. The condition of the poor, however, was made worse by rising prices.

Greek Heritage in Turkey

By the third century B.C.E. the center of trade had shifted from Greece to the Near East. Largest of the Hellenistic cities, and much larger than any cities in Greece itself, were Antioch, in northern Syria, and Alexandria, in Egypt. The riches of India, Persia, Arabia, and the Fertile Crescent were brought by sea and land to these Mediterranean ports.

Alexandria outdistanced all other Hellenistic cities as a commercial center. Its merchants supplied the ancient world with wheat, linen, papyrus, glass, and jewelry. Boasting a population of nearly a million, the city had a double harbor in which a great lighthouse, judged one of the wonders of the ancient world, rose to a height estimated at 370 feet. Its busy streets were filled with a mixture of peoples—Greeks, Macedonians, Jews, and Egyptians. As in all other Hellenistic cities in the Near East, the privileged

---

cosmopolitan—A person or thing that belongs to all the world; free from local or national prejudices or limitations. From Greek *cosmopolites* ("citizen of the world").

Greeks and Macedonians were at the top of the social scale and the mass of native population at the bottom; the large Jewish population lived apart and was allowed a significant degree of self-government. Labor was so cheap that slavery hardly existed in Hellenistic Egypt. As a consequence, worker-organized strikes were frequent.

Hellenistic Philosophy

Developments in philosophical thought reflected the changed conditions of the Hellenistic Age. With a growing sense that individual significance was decreased in the large Hellenistic states, in which the vitality of the polis seemed to give way to a more isolated existence, philosophers concerned themselves less with the reform of society and more with the attainment of happiness for the individual. "There is no point in saving the Greeks" is the way one Hellenistic philosopher summed up the new outlook, quite in contrast to that of Socrates, Plato, and Aristotle. This emphasis on peace of mind for the individual living in an insecure world led to the rise of four principal schools of Hellenistic philosophy, all of which had their beginnings in Athens.

The Skeptics and Cynics reflected most clearly the doubts and misgivings of the times. The Skeptics hoped to achieve freedom from anxiety by denying the possibility of finding truth. The wise, they argued, will suspend judgment and not preach to others because they had learned that sensory experience, the only source of knowledge, is deceptive. They believed that real knowledge was impossible to achieve, and that it was not crucial to achieve it anyway. The Skeptics busied themselves with pointing out the errors they identified in the other opposing schools of philosophy. The Cynics believed that withdrawing from the world was the best way to deal with the miseries life held for humans. They advocated rejection of virtually all social conventions, traditions, and religious values. Cynic philosophers, most notably Diogenes of Sinope (c. 400–325 B.C.E.), wandered from city to city, dressed in rags, begging, and performing lewd acts in public to call attention to his rejection of conformity.

More socially acceptable and popular were the schools of Epicureanism and Stoicism. The Athenian Epicurus (342–270 B.C.E.) taught that happiness could be achieved simply by freeing the body from pain and the mind from fear—particularly the fear of death. To reach this dual goal, people must avoid bodily excesses, including sensual pleasures, and accept the scientific teaching of Democritus that both body and soul are composed of atoms that fall apart at death. Beyond death there is no existence and nothing to fear. Epicurus maintained that the finest pleasures are intellectual and that the gods do not concern themselves with humans, but instead spend their time pursuing true pleasure, like good Epicureans.

The Stoics, followers of Zeno (c. 336–c. 264 B.C.E.), a Semite who settled in Athens, argued in contrast to Epicureanism that the universe is controlled by some power—variously called destiny, reason, natural law, providence, or God—that determines everything that happens. Fortified by this knowledge, wise Stoics conform their will to be in harmony with natural order and "stoically" accept whatever part fortune gives to them in the drama of life. The Epicurean retreated from worldly responsibilities, but the Stoic urged participation. Stoicism's stern sense of duty and belief in the equality of all people under a single ruling force made it particularly attractive to the Roman successors to power in the Hellenistic world conquerors of the ancient world.

Science and Mathematics

The Greek concern for rational, impartial inquiry reached a high level of development in the Hellenistic period, particularly in Alexandria, where the dynasty of the Ptolemies subsidized a great research institute, the Museum, and a library of more than half a million books. Emphasizing specialization and experimentation and enriched by the inheritance of Near Eastern astronomy and mathematics, Greek science in the third century B.C.E. achieved results unmatched until the seventeenth century.

The expansion of geographical knowledge resulting from Alexander's conquests inspired scientists to make more accurate maps and to estimate the size of the earth, which had been identified as a globe through observation of its shadow in a lunar eclipse. Eratosthenes (e-rah-TOS-the-neez), the outstanding geographer of the century, drew parallels of latitude and longitude on his map of the inhabited world and calculated the circumference of the globe (within 1 percent, an error of 195 miles) by measuring the difference in the angles of the noonday sun's shadows at Aswan and Alexandria. In astronomy, Aristarchus (a-ri-STAR-kus) put forward the radical theory that the earth rotates on its axis and moves in an orbit around the sun. Most of his contemporaries, however, held to a belief in the prevailing geocentric theory, which stated that the earth was stationary and the sun revolved around it. Not only was this view supported by the powerful authority of Aristotle, but it also seemed to explain all the known facts of celestial motion. This was particularly true after Hipparchus (hi-PAR-kus) in the next century added the new idea of *epicycles*—each planet revolves in its own small orbit while moving around the earth. Aristarchus's **heliocentric theory** was forgotten until the sixteenth century C.E., when it was revived by Copernicus.

Mathematics also made great advances in the third century B.C.E. Euclid (EU-klid) systematized the theorems of plane and solid geometry, and Archimedes (ar-ke-MEE-deez) of Syracuse, who had studied at Alexandria, calculated the value of *pi,* invented a terminology for expressing numbers up to any magnitude, and established the rudiments of calculus. Archimedes also discovered specific gravity by noticing that he displaced water when submerged in his bath. And, despite his dislike for making practical use of his knowledge, he invented the compound pulley and the windlass—a lifting device consisting of a horizontal cylinder turned by a crank on which a rope or cable is wound.

The Hellenistic Greeks also contributed to the advances in medicine made earlier by Hippocrates and his school. By dissecting bodies of dead criminals, they were able to trace the outlines of the nervous system, to understand the principle of the circulation of the blood, and to ascertain that the brain, not the heart, is the true center of consciousness.

This representation of the goddess of erotic love, Aphrodite (Venus in Latin), being defended by her young son Eros (Cupid) from the advances of the god Pan, was crafted around 100 B.C.E. and is now in the Acropolis Museum in Athens. It is an excellent example of the realism, emotion, and even humor conveyed by much of Hellenistic sculpture.

Hellenistic Art and Literature

The large number of new cities that sprang up in Hellenistic times served as a tremendous impetus to new developments and experiments in architecture. These new municipalities benefited from town planning; the streets were laid out on a rectangular grid. The great public buildings were elaborate and highly ornamented; this was an age that preferred the ornate Corinthian column to the simpler Doric and Ionic styles of decoration.

Hellenistic sculptors continued and intensified the realistic, dramatic, and emotional approach that began to appear in late classical sculpture. Supported by rulers and other rich patrons in such affluent cities as Alexandria, Antioch, Rhodes, and Pergamum, they displayed their technical virtuosity by representing violent scenes, writhing forms, and dramatic poses, all with a realism that could make stone simulate flesh. Like most postclassical art, little evidence remained of the balance and restraint of classical Greek sculpture. Much of Hellenistic sculpture, with its twisted poses, contorted faces, and swollen muscles, stands in obvious contrast to the works of classical Greece seeking balance, harmony, and restraint.

Literature produced in the Hellenistic Age was generally more narrow and scholarly in its appeal than the earlier literary forms of the classical period. Scholarship flourished, and we are in debt for the

---

heliocentric theory—An astronomical theory, now proven as fact, that the sun resides at the center of the planetary system. *Heliocentric* in Greek literally means "sun centered."

Late Hellenistic sculptors avoided the stylized and perfect bodies preferred by the artists of the classical period and chose instead to portray the realistic and commonplace in their work. This famous sculpture of a drunken old woman shows not only the great skill of the artist, but also the radical shift in artistic themes now more popular and acceptable in the Hellenistic Age.

preservation of much of Greek classical literature to the subsidized scholars who worked at the Library of Alexandria. They composed epics in imitation of Homer (one new feature was romantic love, not found in Homer), long poems on fundamental subjects like the weather, and short, witty epigrams—all in a highly polished style. These sophisticated scholars also invented a new type of romantic, escapist literature: pastoral poetry extolling the unspoiled life and loves of shepherds and their rustic love interests. Some of the best of the new poetry was written at Alexandria in the third century B.C.E. by Theocritus (thee-OH-kra-tus), who also composed very realistic verses.

The Hellenistic Contribution

The greatest contribution of the Hellenistic Age was the diffusion of Greek culture throughout the ancient East and the newly rising Roman West. In the East, the cities that Alexander and his successors built were the agents for spreading Hellenistic culture from the Aegean Sea to India. Literate Asians learned Greek to facilitate trade and to read Greek literature. In Judea, upper class Jews built Greek theaters and **gymnasia** and adopted Greek speech, dress, and names.

For a time the Seleucid Empire provided the peace and economic stability necessary to ensure the partial Hellenization of a vast area. But with an insufficient number of Greeks to colonize so large an area as the Near East, the Greek cities remained only islands in an Asian ocean. As time passed, this ocean encroached more and more on the Hellenized outposts.

The gradual weakening of the loosely knit Seleucid Empire eventually resulted in the creation of independent kingdoms on the edge of the Greek world. In the middle of the third century, a nomad chieftain founded the kingdom of Parthia, situated between the Seleucid and Bactrian kingdoms. Claiming to be the heirs of the more ancient Persians, the Parthians expanded until 130 B.C.E., when they were able to take Babylonia away from Seleucid control. Although Parthia was essentially a native Iranian state, its inhabitants absorbed some Hellenistic culture. Cut off from Seleucid rule by the Parthian kingdom, Bactria also became independent. Its Greek rulers, descendants of Alexander's veterans, controlled the caravan route to India and issued some of the most beautiful of Greek coins. In 183 B.C.E. the Bactrians crossed into India and conquered the province of Gandhara. One result of the conquest was a strong Greek influence on Indian art (see Chapter 3).

In the history of western European civilization, there are few developments of greater significance than Rome's absorption of Hellenistic Greek culture and its transference of that Greek cultural heritage to later European tradition. The culture of the cosmopolitan Hellenistic Age, drawn mainly from its Greek origins, served as the vehicle through which Greece left its imprint on the Roman world. The process by which the Roman West absorbed the cultural legacy of the Greeks will be described in the next chapter.

---

gymnasia—The plural of gymnasium—an area or a room in which Greeks, usually younger men, came to exercise and converse. From Greek *gymnos* ("naked") and *gymnazein* ("to train").

CONCLUSION

The civilization developed by the ancient Greeks is certainly one of the most outstanding in the history of humanity at any time and at any place on our planet. Those cultures we usually call Western correctly look upon the ancient Greeks as one of the most significant influences in the formation of their cultures. For centuries, these Western cultures considered the Greeks to have been the sole originators of Western civilization, but more recent generations have properly recognized that the Greeks, although highly creative and original, still were influenced by the earlier civilizations of Asia and Egypt. Trade and commerce with these peoples brought knowledge of their skills and past achievements, from metalworking, war, and art to religion. The Greeks did not invent Western civilization in a vacuum.

But the ancient Greeks do deserve great admiration. They developed a culture that was quite different than any previous social achievement. Theirs was a culture that was human-centered; although observant of religion, the Greeks did not believe they were owned by the gods. The Greeks rivaled their own gods in their attempts to gain true knowledge of the secrets of philosophy and science, to produce perfection in art, architecture, and even government. Human self-confidence had never been as high, and the resulting achievements of Greek culture still remain as timeless contributions to human cultures worldwide.

Often it seems the most significant factor explaining the success of a culture contains the seeds of its greatest liability. One might propose that the independence of both individuals and city-states led to outstanding achievements. But that individuality also seems to have made it impossible for the Greeks to unify for any significant length of time or to avoid bitter rivalries and destructive war. In time, the Macedonian king Philip, and later his son Alexander, forced the Greeks to cooperate with the formation of a unified Greece, but much of the originality and creativity of that earlier vibrant Greek culture was lost in the process.

The final chapter of ancient Greek history is called the Hellenistic Age, in which Alexander and then his successors hoped to rule their new subjects in Greek fashion, imposing a superior Greek culture over their new subjects. The attempt was eventually unsuccessful. Alexander's conquest of the Persian empire has been hailed throughout the history of the West as a remarkable achievement, and largely as a noble effort to bring a superior civilization to a broader world. Even today the memory of that Western conquest of the East is remembered in Asia as one of the first of many attempts of the West to impose its brand of civilization on unwelcoming victims. Cultural exchange as well as suspicions over cultural motivations is as old as the ancient civilizations of both East and West. Yet in spite of the complexities brought about when the modern world attempts to find explanations of its difficulties in ancient rivalries, the lasting achievements of the Greeks deserve the admiration of us all. Their creativity, vitality, and humanness have left to the whole world a timeless cultural legacy.

Suggestions for Web Browsing

You can obtain more information about topics included in this chapter at the websites listed below. See also the companion website that accompanies this text, **http://www.ablongman.com/brummett,** which contains an online study guide and additional resources.

Minoan Palaces
http://dilos.com/region/crete/minoan_pictures.html

Images and text from major Minoan archaeological sites, including Knossos.

Ancient Greek World
http://www.museum.upenn.edu/Greek_World/Index.html

A presentation by the University of Pennsylvania Museum of Archaeology and Anthropology. Text and museum artifacts tell the vivid story of life in ancient Greece: land and time; daily life, economy, religion, and death.

Perseus Project
http://www.perseus.tufts.edu/

An impressive compilation of information on Greek art, architecture, and literature. One of the most useful but also scholarly sites dealing with ancient Greece.

Vatican Museum: Greek Collection
http://www.christusrex.org/www1/vaticano/GP-Profano.html

The excellent works in the Vatican's Greek collection are displayed and discussed in this outstanding site.

Daily Life in Ancient Greece
http://members.aol.com/Donnclass/Greeklife.html

A wonderfully entertaining site on ancient Greek life—gives a feel for what life would be like in a variety of Greek city-states.

Women's Life in Greece and Rome
http://www.stoa.org/diotima/anthology/wlgr/

Details about the private life and legal status of women, in addition to biographies of prominent women of ancient Greece and Rome.

Diotima: Women and Gender in the Ancient World
http://www.stoa.org/diotima/

An excellent site for information on women in ancient Greece—their political influence, occupations, dress, diet. A great range of information.

Alexander the Great
http://united-states.asinah.net/american-encyclopedia/wikipedia/a/al/alexander_the_great.html

Web page detailing the life of the king of Macedonia and conqueror of the Persian Empire.

Ancient Olympics
http://www.perseus.tufts.edu/Olympics/

Compare ancient and modern Olympic sports and read about the Olympic athletes who were famous in antiquity.

Greek Warfare
http://www.dean.usma.edu/history/web03/atlases/ancient%20warfare/ancient%20warfare%20index.htm

Informative site for ancient Greek battles, logistics, and tactics. Excellent maps and diagrams of military campaigns.

Literature and Film

Mary Renault, *The King Must Die* (Bantam, 1974), is an absorbing novel set in Mycenaean times. Several new and excellent works of historical fiction are Steven Pressfield, *Gates of Fire* (Bantam, 1999) and *The Tides of War* (Doubleday, 2000), dealing with the battle of Thermopylae and the general Alcibiades, respectively. Also outstanding are Tom Holt's *The Walled Orchard* (Warner, 1997) and *Olympiad* (Abacus, 2001). Anna Apostolou, *A Murder in Macedon* (St. Martin's, 1998), is a well-done novel dealing with the assassination of Philip, Alexander's father.

Some excellent video presentations dealing with ancient Greece are *The Mystery of the Minoans* (1999), *Atlantis—In Search of a Lost Continent* (1996; 2 tapes, Questar Edition), and *The Greeks: Crucible of Civilization* (2000; 2 tapes, PBS Home Video). Greek art and architecture are beautifully reviewed in *Art in Ancient Greece* (1994; 2 tapes, Kultur Video). *In the Footsteps of Alexander the Great* (1996; 2 tapes, PBS Home Video) is a modern trek over Alexander's ancient route through Asia.

Suggestions for Reading

John Boardman, Jasper Griffin, and Oswyn Murray, eds., *The Oxford History of the Classical World* (Oxford University Press, 1986) is one of the most comprehensive studies of ancient Greece and its culture. A shorter yet still excellent history is J. V. A. Fine, *The Ancient Greeks: A Critical History* (Belknap/Harvard University Press, 1983). John Chadwick's *The Mycenaean World* (Cambridge University Press, 1976) and Robert Drews's *The Coming of the Greeks* (Princeton University Press, 1988) are both excellent studies of the early Greek experience. For the classical period, some outstanding studies are Donald Kagan, *The Peloponnesian War* (Viking Press, 2003), and Sarah Pomeroy, *Goddesses, Whores, Wives, and Slaves: Women in Classical Antiquity* (Schocken, 1975). James Davidson's *Courtesans and Fishcakes* (St. Martin's, 1998) is a delightful study of Athenian manners and private life. Mark Munn, *The School of History: Athens in the Age of Socrates* (University of California Press, 2002) is an outstanding cultural history. For the Hellenistic period, see Peter Green's *Hellenistic History and Culture* (University of California Press, 1993) and his excellent biography of Alexander, *Alexander of Macedon: 356–323 B.C.* (Praeger, 1970).

CHAPTER

5

Roman Civilization

The Roman World, c. 900 B.C.E. to 476 C.E.

CHAPTER CONTENTS

1000 B.C.E.

c. 900 Early Iron Age in Italy; beginnings of Etruscan civilization

753 Traditional date for founding of Rome

509 Traditional date for beginning of the Republic

500 B.C.E.

390 Gauls attack and plunder Rome

264–146 Three Punic Wars: Rome ultimately defeats Carthage

133–123 Reforms of the Gracchi

c. 87–54 Catullus: poetry and epigrams

44 Julius Caesar assassinated

27 Octavian (Augustus) holds sole power

c. 25 Virgil: Epic poem *Aeneid*

4 B.C.E.–c. 30 C.E. Jesus Christ, founder of Christianity

1

c. 87–126 Plutarch: historian and biographer—*Parallel Lives*

161–180 Reign of Marcus Aurelius

313 Edict of Milan: Christians free to worship openly

325 Constantine founds new capital at Constantinople

395 Roman Empire divided into eastern and western halves

440–461 Pontificate of Leo the Great

476 Assassination of Romulus Augustulus, last Roman emperor in the West

The remains of the Roman Forum stand today in the center of a vibrant city of more than a million people—in the capital of Italy, a center of world commerce, diplomacy, and culture. That same description holds true for the Forum and the city as it was more than two thousand years ago. Originally used as a cemetery as early as the ninth century B.C.E., the Forum became a marketplace and a center of political activity two hundred years later. As Roman conquests in Italy and throughout the Mediterranean world grew, so did the importance of the Forum as the symbolic center of Rome's dominance.

Over centuries, the Romans decorated the Forum with triumphal arches and columns commemorating military conquests—constant reminders that Rome was the capital of a world state that extended from Britain to Persia, from Africa to Germany. The public buildings and temples in the Forum were Greek in style and inspiration, although more monumental and immense in appearance. And in that very design and presentation, we see two important elements of Roman culture: they readily borrowed ideas from others, especially the Greeks, if they found those ideas preferable to their own, and they very often modified and made improvements on what they borrowed. Roman ability to adapt and modify may be observed even in the empire's structure: Rome brought political stability to the Mediterranean world and in the same process perpetuated the intellectual and cultural contributions of their conquered subjects. As Rome's empire expanded, the cultural legacies of the ancient world were preserved and spread westward throughout most of Europe.

From their beginning as a simple farming community on the banks of the Tiber River to the largest and longest lasting empire of the ancient world, the Romans met one challenge after another by attempting practical solutions and efficient governmental approaches—and almost always prevailed. In the company of its formidable legions went engineers and architects, so that today, throughout the lands that were once under the rule of Rome, the remains of walls, baths, temples, amphitheaters, and aqueducts survive as reminders of the Roman contribution to shaping European civilization.

EARLY ITALY AND THE ORIGINS OF ROME: C. 900–509 B.C.E.

- *What impact did Italian geography and the various peoples of Italy have on the development of Rome?*

The history of Rome begins with small agricultural settlements in the region that eventually became the city of Rome around 900 B.C.E. The Romans themselves, however, believed that the city actually began in 753 B.C.E.—the traditional date for the founding of the city by Romulus, Rome's legendary first king. It is equally difficult to assign an end date to Rome, because long after the political dominance of Rome came to an end, the social and cultural legacies of the empire continued to influence life in lands impacted by Roman occupation. A great variety of dates might be offered to indicate the end of the empire; one such significant milestone took place in 476 C.E ., when the German chieftain Odovacer (c. 435–493 C.E.) assassinated Romulus Augustulus, the last emperor to ruler the western half of the Roman world. The first period in this remarkable span of more than a thousand years of dominance, however, ended in 509 B.C.E., according to Roman tradition, with the expulsion of the Etruscan monarch Tarquin the Proud, the seventh and last of Rome's kings, and the establishment of an aristocratic republic.

Geography and Early Settlers of Italy

Geography was crucial in shaping the course of events in Italy. The Italian peninsula is 600 miles long and about four times the size of Greece, or two-thirds that of California. A great mountainous backbone, the Apennine range, runs almost the entire length of the peninsula. But the land is not as rugged as Greece, and the mountains did not create a formidable barrier to political unification. Unlike in Greece, a network of roads could be built to link the peninsula. Furthermore, the plain of Latium (LAH-tee-um) and its major city, Rome, occupied a strategic position. The hills near what became Rome were relatively easy to defend, and once

The great variety of peoples and cultures of early Italy are portrayed on this map. Roman institutions and culture were influenced greatly by these early residents.

the Romans had begun to establish themselves as successful conquerors, they occupied a central position on the peninsula, which made it difficult for their enemies to unite successfully against them. The important central position of Rome was duplicated on a larger scale by the location of Italy itself. Italy juts into what is almost the center of the great Mediterranean sea. Once Italy was unified, its central position aided Rome in dominating the entire Mediterranean region.

Italy's most imposing valleys and useful harbors are on the western slopes of the Apennines, and the Italian peninsula extends into the western Mediterranean, not eastward. For much of its early history, therefore, cultural development in Italy was not as rapid as it might have been if the two peoples had come into close cultural contact sooner.

Both Greeks and Romans were descendants of a common Indo-European stock, and settlement of the Greek and Italian peninsulas followed broadly parallel stages. Between 2000 and 1000 B.C.E., when Indo-European peoples invaded the Aegean world, a western wing of this nomadic migration filtered into the Italian peninsula, then inhabited by indigenous Neolithic peoples. The first invaders, skilled in the use of copper and bronze, settled in the Po valley. Another wave of Indo-Europeans, equipped with iron weapons and tools, followed; in time the newer and older settlers intermingled and spread throughout the peninsula. One group, the Latins, settled in the plain of Latium, in the lower valley of the Tiber River.

As the Iron Age began in the western Mediterranean, the cultures of Italy became increasingly complex. During the ninth century B.C.E., a people known as the Etruscans established dominance throughout most of central Italy. The exact origin of the Etruscans remains uncertain. Some experts believe them to have been a non-Indo-European people who came to Italy by sea from Asia Minor. Others believe that their origin is explained through a rapid and creative growth of already resident iron-using peoples in northern Italy. Perhaps a combination of the two explanations is most likely—that native creativity fueled by contact with immigrants from the East resulted in a distinctly vibrant and creative culture. Expanding from the west

Etruscan tombs were often elaborately painted with scenes of feasting and entertainment. On these tombs youths celebrate with music and wine.

coast up to the Po valley and south to the Bay of Naples, the Etruscans organized the less-advanced and disparate Italic peoples into a loose confederation of Etruscan-dominated city-states.

In the sixth century B.C.E., Rome became one of the cities controlled by the Etruscans, at a time when that city was not highly developed politically or culturally. The Etruscans brought with them a highly effective political system under the strong direction of kings, an aristocracy of landholding nobles, and a military organization superior to any they encountered among the Italic peoples. Etruscan cultural influence was particularly strong among their Roman subjects. Much of the area around the city was made more useful through Etruscan engineering skill, marsh drainage, and agricultural technology. Their religion, which included many Eastern elements such as the worship of numerous gods and goddesses, powerful priesthoods, rituals, and sacrifices to please the gods and ward off evil, also greatly influenced the development of Roman religious belief. Their funeral customs, which helped to shape Roman practices, show the prominent role of women in Etruscan society. They are usually portrayed in Etruscan tomb paintings as appearing in public, participating in banquets along with their husbands, and in general sharing in the pleasures of life on an equal footing with men.

After 750 B.C.E. Greek colonists migrated to southern Italy and Sicily, where their colonies provided a protective buffer against powerful and prosperous Carthage, a Phoenician colony established in North Africa about 800 B.C.E. The Greeks, along with the Etruscans, had a lasting influence on Roman culture—particularly with regard to religion and their sophisticated accomplishments in art and architecture.

Rome's Origins

Legend held that Rome was founded in 753 B.C.E. by Romulus. He and his twin brother, Remus, were sons of a nearby king's daughter who had been raped by Mars, the god of war. Thrown into the Tiber River by their wicked uncle who had seized the throne, they were rescued and nurtured by a she-wolf. Other legends told the story that Romulus's ancestor was Aeneas (ay-NEE-uhs), a Trojan hero who, after the fall of Troy, founded a settlement in Latium, near what came to be Rome. The Aeneas story, perhaps invented by later mythmakers, pleased the Romans because it linked their history with that of the Greeks, whose culture they thought more sophisticated than their own.

Turning from fable to fact, modern scholars believe that in the eighth century B.C.E. the inhabitants of some small Latin settlements on hills in the Tiber valley united and established a common meeting place, the Forum, around which the city of Rome grew. Situated at a convenient place for fording the river and protected from invaders by surrounding hills and marshes, Rome was strategically located on excellent passes to both north and south. Because of their interest in gaining access to trade with the Greeks in the south, the expanding Etruscans conquered Rome about 625 B.C.E., and under their direction Rome became an important city.

MAP
Rome, Italy, and Empire

The Roman Monarchy, 753–509 B.C.E.

Rome's political growth followed a pattern of development similar to that of the Greek city-states: monarchy similar to that described by Homer, oligarchy, modified democracy, and, finally, the permanent dictatorship of the Roman emperors. In moving from oligarchy to democracy, the Romans succeeded in avoiding the intermediate Greek stage of tyranny.

The executive power, both civil and military, of Rome's seven kings (the last three were Etruscans) was called the *imperium,* (the root word for both *imperialism* and *empire*) which was symbolized by an ax bound in a bundle of rods (*fasces;* FAS-kees). Imperium was officially conferred on the king by a popular assembly made up of male citizens, and the king was expected to turn for advice to a council of nobles called the Senate. Senators held their positions for life, and they and their families belonged to the *patrician* class, the fathers of the state (*pater* means "father"). The other class of Romans, the *plebeians,* or commoners, included small farmers, artisans, and many clients, or dependents, of patrician landowners. In 509 B.C.E. the patricians, with some plebeian assistance, overthrew the Etruscan monarchy and established an aristocratic form of government, known as the Republic.

THE REPUBLIC AND THE ROMAN CONQUEST OF ITALY: 509–133 B.C.E.

- *How did the Romans conquer all of Italy and much of the Mediterranean by 130 B.C.E.?*

The history of the Roman Republic can be divided into two distinct periods. During the first, from 509 to 133 B.C.E., two themes are dominant: a change from aristocracy to a more democratic constitution, the result of the gradual extension of political and social equality to the plebeian lower class; and the expansion of Roman military and political control, first in Italy, and then throughout the Mediterranean region.

The Early Wars of Rome

509 B.C.E.	Etruscans expelled from Rome
390 B.C.E.	Gauls attack and plunder Rome
338 B.C.E.	Rome emerges victor in wars with members of the Latin League
264–241 B.C.E.	Rome wins Sicily in First Punic War
218–201 B.C.E.	Rome defeats Hannibal in Second Punic War
149–146 B.C.E.	Carthage destroyed in Third Punic War

Establishment of the Republic

In 509 B.C.E. the patricians forced out the last Etruscan king, Tarquin the Proud (Tarquinius Superbus), claiming he had acted despotically. According to the Roman historian Livy, Tarquin was the first of the Roman kings to ignore the advice of the Senate and govern in a selfish and irresponsible manner. The patricians replaced the monarchy with an aristocracy they called a *republic* (*res publica,* "commonwealth"). The imperium of the one king was shared by two new magistrates, called *consuls.* Elected annually from the patrician class, the consuls exercised power in the interest of that class. In the event of war or serious domestic emergency, an "extraordinary" magistrate called a *dictator* could be substituted for the two consuls, but the man was given absolute power for six months only. The popular assembly was retained because the patricians could control it through their plebeian clients who, in return for a livelihood, voted as their patrons directed them.

Struggle of the Orders

For more than two centuries following the establishment of the Republic, the plebeians struggled for political and social equality. Outright civil war was avoided by the willingness of the patricians to accept the demands of the plebeians, even though patrician acceptance was often reluctant and usually slow. Much of the plebeians' success in this struggle was due to their having been granted the right to organize themselves as a corporate body capable of collective action. This permission to organize, granted by the Senate early in the fifth century B.C.E., after the plebeians threatened to leave Rome and found a city elsewhere, established a sort of state within a state known as the *Concilium Plebis* (kun-SIL-I-um PLAY-bis) or "gathering of the plebians." This assembly was presided over by plebeian leaders called *tribunes* and could pass *plebiscites* ("plebeian decrees") that were binding only on the plebeian community. The tribunes were given sacred status, *sacrosanctitas* (sak-roh-SANG-ti-tahs), by the plebeian assembly in an effort to furnish them protection from any bodily harm that might come their way from patrician opponents. Tribunes also assumed the right to stop unjust or oppressive acts of the patrician consuls and Senate by uttering the word *veto* ("I forbid.").

Another major concession to plebeian interests was in the field of law. Because the consuls often interpreted Rome's unwritten customary law to suit patrician interests, the plebeians demanded that it be written down and made available for all to see. As a result, about 450 B.C.E., the law was inscribed on a dozen tablets of bronze and set up publicly in the Forum. This Code of the Twelve Tables was the first landmark development in the long history of Roman law.

In time the plebeians acquired other fundamental rights and safeguards: the rights to appeal a death sentence imposed by a consul and to be retried before the popular assembly were secured; marriage between patricians and plebeians, prohibited by the Code of the Twelve Tables, was legalized; and the enslavement of citizens for debt was abolished.

That their service in the Roman army was indispensable to the patricians greatly increased the plebeians' bargaining position in the state. Since Rome was almost constantly at war during these years, the patrician leaders of the state were more ready to accommodate plebeian demands than to face the possibility of a withdrawal of military participation by the commoners. In addition, trade and commerce in early Rome came to be dominated by the plebeian class, since the patricians avoided commercial activities in favor of concentrating their wealth on the acquisition of land and country estates.

Little by little the plebeians acquired more power in the government. In 367 B.C.E. one consulship was reserved for the plebeians, and before the end of the century, plebeians were eligible to hold other important magistracies that the patricians had created in the meantime. Among these new offices, whose powers had originally been held by the consuls, were the *praetor* (PREE-tor; in charge of the administration of justice), *quaestor* (KWEE-ster; treasurer), and *censor* (supervisor of public morals and the granting of state contracts).

The long struggle for equal status ended in 287 B.C.E. when the *Concilium Plebis* was recognized as a constitutional body, which then became known as the Tribal Assembly, and its plebiscites became laws binding on all citizens, patrician as well as plebeian.

The Roman Republic was technically a democracy, although in actual practice a senatorial aristocracy of noble patricians and rich plebeians continued to control the state. Having gained political and social equality, the plebeians were usually willing to allow the more experienced Senate to run the government from this time until 133 B.C.E., a period of almost constant warfare.

After 287 B.C.E. conflict in Roman society gradually assumed a new form. Before this time, the issue of greatest domestic importance had primarily been social and political inequality between the classes of patricians and plebeians. After equal political status was achieved, many rich plebeians were elected to the highest offices and became members of an expanded senatorial aristocracy. The new Roman "establishment" was prepared to guard its privileges even more fiercely than the old patricians had done. This fact became evident in 133 B.C.E. when a popular leader, Tiberius Gracchus (tai-BEE-ri-uhs GRAH-kuhs), arose to challenge the establishment.

This statue of a patrician with busts of his ancestors dates from either the first century B.C.E. or the first century C.E. The patricians were the aristocracy of Rome, and during the later Republic they came increasingly into conflict with senators and generals who took the part of the plebeians.

The Conquest of Italy

The growth of Rome from a small city-state to the dominant power in the Mediterranean world in less than 400 years (509–133 B.C.E.) was a remarkable achievement. Roman expansion was not deliberately planned; rather, it was the result of dealing with unsettled conditions, first in Italy and then abroad, which were thought to threaten Rome's security. Rome always claimed that its wars were defensive, waged to protect itself from potentially hostile neighbors—Etruscans in the north, land-hungry hill tribes in central Italy, and Greeks in the south. Rome subdued them all after a long, determined effort and found itself master of all Italy south of the Po valley. In the process the Romans developed the administrative skills and traits of character—both fair-mindedness and ruthlessness—that would lead to the acquisition of an empire with possessions on three continents.

Soon after driving out their Etruscan overlords in 509 B.C.E., Rome and the Latin League, composed of other Latin peoples in Latium, entered into a defensive alliance against the Etruscans. This new combination was so successful that by the beginning of the fourth century B.C.E., it had become the chief power in central Italy. But at this time (390 B.C.E.), a major disaster almost ended the history of Rome. A raiding army of Celts, called *Gauls* by the Romans, invaded Italy from central Europe, wiped out the Roman army, and almost destroyed the city by fire. The elderly members of the Senate, according to the traditional account, sat awaiting their fate with quiet dignity before they were massacred. Only a garrison on the Capitoline Hill held out under siege. After seven months and the receipt of a huge ransom in gold, the Gauls withdrew. The stubborn Romans rebuilt their city and protected it with a stone wall, part of which still stands. They also remodeled their army by replacing the solid line of fixed spears of the phalanx formation, borrowed from the Etruscans and Greeks, with much more maneuverable small units of 120 men, called *maniples,* armed with javelins instead of spears. It would be 800 years before another barbarian army would be able to conquer the city of Rome. In the years that followed Rome's recovery from the attack of the Gauls, the Latin League grew more and more alarmed at Rome's increasing strength, and war broke out between the former allies. Upon Rome's victory in 338 B.C.E. the league was dissolved, and the Latin cities were forced to sign individual treaties with Rome.

But soon after the Roman victory over the Latin League, border clashes with aggressive mountain tribes of Samnium led to three fiercely fought Samnite wars and the extension of Rome's frontiers to the Greek colonies in southern Italy by 290 B.C.E. Fearing Roman conquest, the Greeks prepared for war and called in the mercenary army of the Greek king, Pyrrhus (PEER-uhs) of Epirus, who dreamed of becoming a second Alexander the Great. Pyrrhus's war elephants, unknown in Italy, twice defeated the Romans, but at so heavy a cost that such a triumph is still called a "Pyrrhic victory." When a third battle failed to persuade the Romans to make peace, Pyrrhus returned to his homeland. By 270 B.C.E. the Roman army had subdued the Greek city-states in

Italy, and the peninsula south of the Po River was under their control.

Treatment of Conquered Peoples

Instead of killing or enslaving their defeated opponents in Italy, the Romans treated them fairly, a policy which in time created a strong loyalty to Rome throughout the peninsula. Roman citizenship was a prized possession that was not extended to all peoples in Italy until the first century B.C.E. Most defeated states were required to sign a treaty of alliance with Rome, which bound them to accept Rome's foreign policy and to supply troops for the Roman army. No tribute was required, and each allied state retained local self-government. Rome did, however, annex about one-fifth of the land its **legions** conquered in Italy, on which nearly 30 colonies were established by 250 B.C.E.

CASE STUDY
Greek and Roman Slavery

The First Punic War

After 270 B.C.E. Rome's only serious rival for dominance in the western Mediterranean was the city-state of Carthage. This prosperous state located near the modern city of Tunis began as a Phoenician colony on the northern African coast in the ninth century B.C.E. By the sixth century, Carthage had become not only independent but also the dominant commercial power in the western Mediterranean. Much more wealthy and populous than Rome, Carthage's magnificent navy controlled the northern coast of Africa, Sardinia, Corsica, western Sicily, and much of Spain. The city and its empire were governed by a commercial oligarchy of Semitic descendants of Carthage's founders. The native population was forced into service in agriculture or in the army and navy; mercenaries were also hired to secure the interests of the ruling minority.

There had been almost no conflicts of interest between Rome and Carthage before the First Punic War (from *Punicus,* Latin for "Phoenician") broke out in 264 B.C.E. In that year, Rome answered an appeal from a group of Italian mercenaries who were in control of the city of Messana, on the northern tip of Sicily next to Italy. These mercenaries were opposed by a Carthaginian force, and when the Roman Senate agreed to send an army to aid the mercenaries, a war between Carthage and Rome was the obvious result.

The First Punic War was a costly one for both combatants. Roman ground forces were quickly successful in gaining control of most of Sicily, but the Carthaginian navy was unopposed, since the Romans had no need of a navy in their conquest of Italy. Rome constructed its fleet in hurried fashion and sent it against the Carthaginians with surprising initial success. Roman engineers furnished their new vessels with an invention called the *corvus,* or "crow," a boarding bridge at the bow of a ship that, when lowered, turned a naval engagement into a land battle. After a stunning defeat of the Carthaginian navy, the Romans invaded the African coast, lost decisively, and suffered the losses of large numbers of ships through violent storms in attempting to return home. Eventually, victory for Rome came through another victory over the Carthaginian navy, but the costs of victory were high; Rome and its Italian allies lost more than 500 ships in naval engagements and storms before Carthage asked for peace in 241 B.C.E. Sicily, Sardinia, and Corsica were annexed as the first prizes in Rome's overseas empire, regulated and taxed—in contrast to Rome's allies in Italy—by Roman officials called *governors.*

The Contest with Hannibal

Stunned by its defeat in the First Punic War, Carthage concentrated on enlarging its empire in Spain. Rome's determination to prevent this led to the most famous and most difficult war in Roman history. While both powers sought a position of advantage, a young Carthaginian general, Hannibal, precipitated the Second Punic War by attacking Saguntum, a Spanish town claimed by Rome as an ally. Rome declared war, and Hannibal, seizing the initiative, in 218 B.C.E. led an army of about 40,000 men, 9000 cavalry troops, and a detachment of African elephants across the Alps into Italy. Although the crossing had cost him nearly half of his men and all but one of his elephants, Hannibal defeated the Romans in three major battles within three years, while ranging throughout Italy but not attacking Rome.

Hannibal's forces never matched those of the Romans in numbers, and the Carthaginian general was never given the reinforcements he requested from his home state. Nevertheless, Hannibal's brilliance as a commander was obvious. At the battle of Cannae (KAN-ee), in 216 B.C.E., Hannibal won his greatest victory by surrounding an army of nearly 80,000 Romans with 50,000 Carthaginians. Almost the entire Roman force was killed or captured. Even at this darkest hour of defeat, the Senate displayed the determination that was to become legendary. When the one consul who survived the battle returned to Rome to give his report, he was congratulated by the senators for "not dispairing of the Republic."

The Romans ultimately produced a general, Scipio (SI-pee-oh), who was Hannibal's match in military

---

legion—A military organizational division, originally the largest permanent unit in the Roman army. The legion was the basis of the military system by which imperial Rome conquered and ruled its empire.

strategy and who was bold enough to invade Africa. Asked to return home after 15 years spent on Italian soil, Hannibal clashed with Scipio's legions at Zama, where the Carthaginians suffered a complete defeat. The power of Carthage was broken forever by a harsh treaty imposed in 201 B.C.E. Carthage was forced to pay a huge **war indemnity,** disarm its forces, and turn Spain over to the Romans. Hannibal fled to the Seleucid Empire, where he attempted to encourage anti-Roman sentiment, and eventually committed suicide in order to avoid Roman capture.

Roman Intervention East and West

The defeat of Carthage freed Rome to turn eastward and deal with King Philip V of Macedonia. Fearful of Rome's growing power, Philip had allied himself with Hannibal during the Second Punic War. In 200 B.C.E., Rome was ready to act, following an appeal from Pergamum and Rhodes for aid in protecting the smaller Hellenistic states from Philip, who was advancing in the Aegean, and from the Seleucid emperor, who was moving into Asia Minor. The heavy Macedonian phalanxes were no match for the mobile Roman legions, and in 197 B.C.E. Philip was soundly defeated in Macedonia. His dreams of empire were ended when Rome destroyed his navy and military bases in Greece. The Romans then proclaimed the independence of Greece and were praised as liberators by the grateful Greeks.

A few years later Rome declared war on the Seleucid emperor, who had moved into Greece, urged on by Hannibal and number of Greek states that resented Rome's interference. The Romans forced the emperor to move out of Greece and Asia Minor, pay a huge indemnity, and give up his warships and war elephants. The Seleucids were checked again in 168 B.C.E. when a Roman ultimatum halted their invasion of Egypt. A Roman envoy met the advancing Seleucid army and, drawing a ring in the sand around the emperor, demanded that he decide on war or on peace with Rome before stepping out of it.

DOCUMENT
Plutarch, *The Life of Cato the Elder*

In the middle of the second century B.C.E. anti-Romanism became widespread in Greece, particularly among the poorer classes, who resented Rome's support of conservative governments and the status quo in general. In 146 B.C.E., after many Greeks had supported an attempted Macedonian revival, Rome destroyed Corinth, a hotbed of anti-Romanism, as an object lesson. The Romans also supported the oligarchic factions in all Greek states and placed Greece under the watchful eye of the governor of Macedonia, a recently established Roman province.

In the West, meanwhile, Rome's more aggressive imperialism led to suspicion of Carthage's reviving prosperity and to a demand by Roman extremists for war—*Carthago delenda est* ("Carthage must be obliterated."). Obviously provoking the Third Punic War, the Romans besieged Carthage, which resisted for three years. Rome destroyed the city in 146 B.C.E. (the same year they destroyed Corinth), killed or enslaved almost all of its surviving inhabitants, leveled the buildings, and poured salt over its borders so that nothing would ever take root on its soil again. The powerful state that had dared to defy Rome was now obliterated, and the province of Africa was created in its place.

In 133 B.C.E. Rome acquired its first province in Asia when the king of Pergamum, dying without an heir, left his kingdom to Rome. The Senate accepted the bequest and created a new province, called Asia. With provinces on three continents—Europe, Africa, and Asia—the once obscure Roman Republic was now supreme in the ancient world.

Society and Religion in Early Rome

The most important unit of early Roman society was the family. The power of the family father *(pater familias)* was absolute, and strict discipline was imposed to instill in children the virtues to which the Romans attached particular importance—loyalty, courage, self-control, and respect for laws and ancestral customs. The Romans of the early Republic were stern, hard-working, and practical. The conservative values of an agrarian society formed the values of both Roman men and women. With much of a Roman man's time taken up with military or political concerns, women had great responsibilities in supervising the upbringing of children and maintaining estates and farms.

In contrast to the frequency of divorce in the late Republic, marriage in the early Republic was viewed as a lifelong union; patrician marriages were usually arranged between families and were undertaken primarily for the creation of children, but on many occasions such marriages resulted in mutual affection between husband and wife. Nonetheless, the authority of the Roman male within his own household was usually unchallenged.

The religion of the early Romans, before their contacts with the Etruscans and Greeks, is very difficult for scholars to describe with confidence. Available evidence for their views on life after death is vague. Religious practices were concerned with appeasing and honoring the spirits *(numina)* of the family and the state by the repetition of complicated rituals and formulas. Mispronunciation of even a sin-

---

war indemnity—A payment to compensate for losses sustained or expenses incurred as a result of war. The Romans regularly imposed such war indemnities on their conquered enemies.

gle syllable was enough to cause the ritual to become ineffective. Under Etruscan influence, major gods and goddesses were personified. The sky-spirit Jupiter became the patron god of Rome; Mars, spirit of vegetation, became god of war and agriculture; and Janus, whose temple doors remained open when the army was away at war, was originally the spirit guarding the city gate.

Although early Roman religion did not have great concern with morals, it had much to do with morale. It strengthened family solidarity and enhanced a patriotic devotion to the state and its gods. But the early Romans' respect for hard work, frugality, and family and state gods was to be challenged by the effects of Rome's expansion in Italy and over much of the Mediterranean area during the early Republic.

The Late Republic

133–123 B.C.E.	Reform movement of the Gracchi
88–82 B.C.E.	First Civil War (Marius vs. Sulla)
58–49 B.C.E.	Caesar conquers Gaul
49–45 B.C.E.	Second Civil War (Pompey vs. Caesar)
44 B.C.E.	Caesar assassinated
31 B.C.E.	Third Civil War (Octavian vs. Antony)
27 B.C.E.	Octavian (Augustus) becomes ruler of Rome

THE LATE REPUBLIC: 133–30 B.C.E.

- *What were the main reasons for the failure of the Roman Republic and the consolidation of power by Augustus?*

The century following 133 B.C.E. during which Rome's frontiers reached the Euphrates and the Rhine, witnessed the failure of the Republic to solve problems generated in part by the acquisition of an empire. These years serve as a good example of the failure of a democracy and its replacement by a dictatorship. The experience of the late Republic gives support to Thucydides' judgment that a democracy is incapable of running an empire. Athens kept its democracy but lost its empire; Rome would keep its empire and loss its democracy.

Effects of Roman Expansion

The political history of Rome to 133 B.C.E. possessed two dominant themes: the gradual extension of citizenship rights in Italy and the expansion of Roman dominion over the Mediterranean world. Largely as a result of this expansion, Rome faced critical social and economic problems by the middle of the second century B.C.E.

One of the most pressing problems Rome faced was the decline in the number of small landowners, whose service and devotion had made Rome great. Burdened by frequent military service, their farms and buildings destroyed by Hannibal, and unable to compete with the cheap grain imported from the new Roman province of Sicily, small farmers sold out and moved to the great city. Here they joined the unemployed and discontented *proletariat,* so called because their only contribution was *proles,* "children." The proletariat soon were the majority of the citizens in the city.

At the same time, improved farming methods learned from the Greeks and Carthaginians encouraged rich aristocrats to buy more and more land. Abandoning the cultivation of grain, they introduced large-scale scientific production of olive oil and wine, sheep, and cattle. This change was especially profitable because an abundance of cheaply purchased slaves from conquered territory was available to work on the estates. With the increase in the availability of slave labor came worsening treatment of the labor force, as well as deteriorating conditions for the declining numbers of free laborers on these large estates. These large slave plantations, called *latifundia* (lah-ti-FUN-dee-uh), became common in many parts of Italy.

The land problem was further complicated by the government's practice of leasing part of the territory acquired in the conquest of the Italian peninsula to anyone willing to pay a percentage of the crop or animals raised on it. Only the wealthy could afford to lease large tracts of this public land, and in time, they treated it as if it were their own property. Plebeian protests led to an attempt to limit the holdings of a single individual to 320 acres of public land, but the law enacted for that purpose was never enforced.

Corruption in the government was another sign of the growing problems of the Roman Republic. Provincial officials took advantage of the opportunity to engage in graft for great profit, and aggressive Roman businessmen scrambled selfishly for the profitable state contracts to supply the armies, collect taxes and loan money in the provinces, and lease state-owned mines and forests.

Although in theory the government allowed for an unhindered participation of all male citizens, in practice it remained a senatorial oligarchy. Wars tend to strengthen the executive power in a state, and in Rome the Senate traditionally had such power. Even the tribunes, guardians of the people's rights, became, for the most part, tools of the Senate. By the middle of the second century B.C.E. the government was in the hands of a wealthy, self-serving Senate, which became increasingly incapable of coping with the problems of governing a world-state. Ordinary citizens were mostly impoverished and landless, and Rome swarmed with fortune hunters, imported slaves, unemployed farmers, and discontented war veterans. The poverty of the many, coupled with the great wealth of the few, contrasted dramatically with the old Roman traits of discipline, simplicity, and respect for authority. The next century (133–30 B.C.E.) saw Rome torn apart by internal conflict, which led to the establishment of a permanent dictatorship and the end of the Republic.

Document Columella: Roman Farm Women

Columella was a Roman citizen from Spain in the first century C.E. He served with the Roman legions and later retired to an agricultural estate, where he wrote his suggestions for how Roman farming could most efficiently be undertaken. The following excerpt from his works on agriculture describes the duties he believes should be given to the forewomen on Roman estates. Such women were usually under the supervision of a foreman; both were often slaves. Columella's listing of the forewoman's tasks gives us an insight into the wide range of duties for which such Roman farm women were held responsible:

The forewoman must not only store and guard the items which have been brought into the house and delivered to her; she should also inspect and examine them from time to time so that the furniture and clothing which have been stored do not disintegrate because of mold, and the fruits and vegetables and other necessities do not go rotten because of her neglect and slothfulness. On rainy days, or when a woman cannot do field work out of doors because of cold or frost, she should return to wool-working. Therefore, wool should be prepared and carded in advance so that she can more easily undertake and complete the required allotment of wool-working. For it will be beneficial if clothing is made at home for her and the stewards and the other valued slaves so the financial accounts of the *paterfamilias* are less strained. She ought to stay in one place as little as possible, for her job is not a sedentary one. At one moment she will have to go to the loom and teach the weavers whatever she knows better than them or, if she knows less, learn from someone who understands more. At another moment, she will have to check on those slaves who are preparing the food for the *familia*. Then she will also have to see that the kitchen, cowsheds, and even the stables are cleaned. And she will also have to open up the sickrooms occasionally, even if they are empty of patients, and keep them free of dirt, so that, when circumstance demands, a well-ordered and healthy environment is provided for the sick. She will, in addition, have to be in attendance when the stewards of the pantry and cellar are weighing something, and also be present when the shepherds are milking in the stables or bringing the lambs or calves to nurse. But she will also certainly need to be present when the sheep are sheared, and to examine the wool carefully and compare the number of fleeces with the number of sheep. Then she must turn her attention to the slaves in the house and insist that they air out the furniture and clean and polish the metal items and free them from rust, and take to the craftsmen for repair other items which require mending.

Questions to Consider

1. How do you think the responsibilities of Roman forewomen compare to modern positions of responsibility on farms?
2. Do you find it surprising that such heavy responsibilities were often given to slave women? What might be the reasons for this?
3. What duties are omitted from the list of responsibilities given by Columella, and do you see any significance in their omission?

From Columella, *On Agriculture*, 12.3.5, 6, 8, and 9, in Jo-Ann Shelton, *As the Romans Did*, 2nd ed. (New York: Oxford University Press, 1998), p. 304.

Reform Movement of the Gracchi

An awareness of Rome's serious social and economic problems led to the reform program of an idealistic and ambitious young aristocrat named Tiberius Gracchus. His reforming spirit was partly the product of newly imported philosophical arguments from Greece and an awareness that the old Roman values and customs were fast slipping away. He sought to stop Roman decline by restoring the backbone of the old Roman society, the small landowner. Supported by a **faction** of senators, Tiberius was elected tribune for the year 133 B.C.E. at the age of 29.

Tiberius proposed to the Tribal Assembly that the act limiting the holding of public land to 320 acres per male citizen, plus 160 acres for each of two grown-up sons, be reenacted. Much of the public land would continue to be held by the present occupants and their heirs as private property, but the rest was to be taken back and granted to the poor in small plots of 9 to 18 acres. The recipients were to pay a small rent and could not sell their holdings. When it became evident that the Tribal Assembly would adopt Tiberius's proposal, opposing senators persuaded one of the other tribunes to veto the measure. On the ground that a tribune who opposed the will of the people had no right to his office, Tiberius took a fateful—and, the Senate claimed, unconstitutional—step by having the assembly depose the tribune in question. The agrarian bill was then passed.

To ensure the implementation of his agrarian reform, Tiberius again violated custom by standing for reelection in the Tribal Assembly after completing his one-year term. Claiming that he sought to make himself king, partisans of the Senate murdered Tiberius and 300 of his followers.

Tiberius's work was taken up by his younger brother, Gaius Gracchus, who was elected tribune for 123 B.C.E. In addition to the allocation of public land to the poor, Gaius proposed establishing Roman colonies in southern Italy and in Africa—his enemies said near the site of Carthage. To protect the poor against speculation in the grain market (especially in times of famine), Gaius committed the government to the purchase, storage, and distribution of wheat to the urban poor at about half the actual market price. Unfortunately, what Gaius intended as a relief measure later became a dole, through which nearly free food was distributed—all too often for the advancement of astute politicians—to the entire proletariat.

Another of Gaius's proposals would have granted citizenship to Rome's Italian allies, who felt they were being mistreated by Roman officials. This proposal cost Gaius the support of the Roman proletariat, which did not wish to share the privileges of citizenship or share its control of the Tribal Assembly. In 121 B.C.E. Gaius failed to be reelected to a third term as tribune. In a further effort to guard against Gaius's leadership, the Senate again resorted to force. It decreed that the consuls could take any action deemed necessary "to protect the state and suppress the tyrants." Three thousand of Gaius's followers were killed in rioting or were arrested and executed, a fate Gaius avoided by committing suicide.

Through these actions, the Senate had shown that it had no intention of initiating needed domestic reforms or of allowing others to do so, and the deaths of Tiberius and Gaius were ominous signals of the way the Republic would decide its internal disputes in the future. In foreign affairs as well, the Senate demonstrated ineptness. Rome was forced to grant citizenship to its Italian allies after the Senate's failure to deal with their grievances pushed them into open revolt (90–88 B.C.E.). Other shortsighted actions led to the first of the three civil wars that assisted in the destruction of the Republic.

The First Civil War: Marius Against Sulla

Between 111 and 105 B.C.E. Roman armies, dispatched by the Senate and commanded by senators, failed to protect Roman business interests in Numidia, a kingdom in North Africa allied to Rome. Nor were they able to prevent Germanic tribes from overrunning southern Gaul, then a Roman province, and threatening Italy itself. Accusing the Senate of neglect and incompetence in directing Rome's foreign affairs, the Roman commercial class and common people joined together to elect Gaius Marius consul in 107 B.C.E., and the Tribal Assembly commissioned him to raise an army to put down the foreign danger. Marius first pacified North Africa and then crushed the first German threat to Rome. In the process, he created a new-style Roman army that was destined to play a major role in the turbulent history of the late Republic.

Unlike the old Roman army, which was composed of conscripts who owned their own land and thought of themselves as loyal citizens of the Republic, the new army created by Marius was recruited from landless citizens for long terms of service. These professional soldiers identified their own interests with those of their commanders, to whom they swore loyalty and looked to for bonuses of land and money, since the Senate had refused their requests for such support. Thus the character of the army changed from a militia of draftees to a "personal army" in which loyalty to the state was replaced with loyalty to the commander.

faction—A like-minded, organized group that operates within another group or government. In Rome, various factions rivaled each other for political power in the state.

Document Plutarch—The Murder of Tiberius Gracchus

In 133 B.C.E., a tribune named Tiberius Gracchus proposed a solution to a major crisis in the Roman state. Redistribution of land to the landless and unemployed residents of the city would allow these individuals to become productive citizens, strengthen the economy, and enable the Roman system of military service, which was dependent on land-owning citizens, to function more effectively. Even though such reform was thought to be necessary by many in the Roman aristocracy, Tiberius was resented for the power and prestige his land law gave him, and he was assassinated by rival aristocrats. The tradition of nonviolent domestic reform through compromise and debate was ended in Rome; many students of Roman history see in the assassination of Tiberius, and of his younger brother Gaius ten years after, the first indications of the breakdown of the Roman Republic:

. . . Flavius got to (Tiberius), and informed him that the rich men, in a sitting of the senate, seeing they could not prevail upon the consul to espouse their quarrel, had come to a final determination amongst themselves that he should be assassinated, and to that purpose had a great number of their friends and servants ready armed to accomplish it. Tiberius no sooner communicated this confederacy to those about him, but they immediately tucked up their gowns, broke the halberts which the officers used to keep the crowd off into pieces, and distributed them among themselves, resolving to resist the attack with these. Those who stood at a distance wondered, and asked what was the occasion; Tiberius, knowing they could not hear him at that distance, lifted his hand to his head wishing to intimate the great danger which he apprehended himself to be in. His Adversaries, taking notice of that action, ran off at once to the senate-house, and declared that Tiberius desired the people to bestow a crown upon him, as if this were the meaning of his touching his head. This news created general confusion in the senators, and Nasica at once called upon the consul to punish the tyrant, and defend the government. The consul mildly replied that he would not be the first to do any violence. . . . But Nasica, rising from his seat, "Since the consul," said he, "regards not the safety of the commonwealth, let every one who will defend the laws, follow me." He then, casting the skirt of his gown over his head, hastened to the capitol; those who bore him company, wrapped their gowns also about their arms, and forced their way after him. And as they were persons of the greatest authority in the city, the common people did not venture to obstruct their passing but were rather so eager to clear the way for them, that they tumbled over one another in haste. The attendants they brought with them had furnished themselves with clubs and staves from their houses, and they themselves picked up the feet and other fragments of stools and chairs, which were broken by the hasty flight of the common people. Thus armed, they made towards Tiberius, knocking down those whom they found in front of him, and those were soon wholly dispersed and many of them slain. Tiberius tried to save himself by flight. As he was running, he was stopped by one who caught hold of him by the gown; but he threw it off, and fled in his under-garment only. And stumbling over those who before had been knocked down, as he was endeavouring to get up again, Publius Satureius, a tribune, one of his colleagues was observed to give him the first fatal stroke, by hitting him upon the head with the foot of a stool. The second blow was claimed, as though it had been a deed to be proud of, by Lucius Rufus. And of the rest there fell above three hundred killed by clubs and staves only, none by an iron weapon.

This, we are told, was the first sedition amongst the Romans, since the abrogation of kingly government, that ended in the effusion of blood. . . . Tiberius himself might then have been easily induced, by mere persuasion, to give way, and certainly, if attacked at all, must have yielded without any recourse to violence and bloodshed. . . . But it is evident, that this conspiracy was fomented against him, more out of the hatred and malice which the rich men had to his person, than for the reasons which they commonly pretended against him. In testimony of which we may adduce the cruelty and unnatural insults which they used to his dead body. For they would not suffer his own brother, though he earnestly begged the favour, to bury him in the night, but threw him, together with the other corpses, into the river. Neither did their animosity stop here; for they banished some of his friends without legal process, and slew as many of the others as they could lay their hands on; amongst whom Diphanes, the orator, was slain, and one Caius Villius cruelly murdered by being shut up in a large tun with vipers and serpents.

Questions to Consider

1. Do you think that Tiberius's assassination could represent a crucial step in the decline of the Roman Republic?
2. Does Plutarch's description of the assassination give you the impression that the assassination was a well-thought-out plan, or action taken in haste? Why?
3. If Tiberius Gracchus's assassination was planned by the Senatorial opposition, what did this group have to gain by Tiberius's death? Why did they resort to violence?

From Plutarch, *Life of Tiberius Gracchus,* 16–20, in *Readings in Ancient History,* vol. 2, ed. William Davis (Boston: Allyn and Bacon, 1913) pp. 108–109.

Ambitious generals were in a position to use their military power to seize the government.

Encouraged by growing anti-Roman sentiment in the province of Asia and in Greece caused by corrupt governors, tax collectors, and moneylenders, in 88 B.C.E. the king of Pontus, in Asia Minor, declared war on Rome. The Senate ordered Cornelius Sulla, an able general and a strong supporter of the Senate's authority, to march east and restore order. As a countermove, the Tribal Assembly chose Marius for the eastern command. In effect both the Senate and the Tribal Assembly, whose power the Gracchi had revived, claimed to be the ultimate authority in the state. The result was the first of a series of civil wars between rival generals, each claiming to champion the cause of either the Senate or the Tribal Assembly. The first civil war ended in a complete victory for Sulla, who in 82 B.C.E. was appointed dictator by the Senate, not for a maximum of six months but for an unlimited term as "dictator for the revision of the constitution."

Sulla intended to restore the preeminence of the Senate. He drastically reduced the powers of the tribunes and the Tribal Assembly, giving the Senate virtually complete control of all legislation. Having massacred several thousand of the opposition, Sulla was convinced that his constitutional improvements would be permanent, and in 79 B.C.E., he voluntarily resigned his dictatorship and retired from public life.

A magnificent and idealized representation of Julius Caesar (100–44 B.C.E.), consummate politician, military strategist, and the first Roman to be awarded the title Dictator for Life. Caesar, in possession of more power than any previous Roman political leader, was assassinated in 44 B.C.E. by opponents who feared that he would destroy the Republic.

The Second Civil War: Pompey Against Caesar

The first of the civil wars and its aftermath increased both discontent and division in the state and fueled the ambitions of younger individuals eager for personal power. The first of these men to come forward was Pompey (106–48 B.C.E.), who had won fame as a military leader. In 70 B.C.E. he was elected consul. Although he was a former supporter of Sulla, he won popularity with the commoners by repealing Sulla's laws limiting the power of the tribunes and the Tribal Assembly. Pompey then put an end to disorder in the East caused by piracy (the result of the Senate's neglect of the Roman navy), the continuing threats of the king of Pontus, and the political uncertainty caused by the collapse of the Seleucid Empire. New Roman provinces and **client states** set up by Pompey brought order eastward as far as the Euphrates. These included the province of Syria—the last remnant of the once vast Seleucid Empire—and the client state of Judea, supervised by the governor of Syria.

Marcus Crassus (MAR-kuhs KRAS-suhs) was another ambitious member of the Senate who was also reputed to be the richest man in Rome resulting from his shrewd business dealings throughout the empire. Crassus was given special military command in 71 B.C.E. to crush the rebellion of nearly 70,000 slaves in southern and central Italy led by the gladiator Spartacus.

Still another ambitious and able leader beginning his public career in the 60s was Gaius Julius Caesar (100–44 B.C.E.) From a noble family, Caesar nonetheless chose to appeal to the commoners for most of his support.

Pompey, Crassus, and Caesar all found that the Senate stood in the way of their desires for more control in the state. To negate senatorial opposition, these three politicians agreed to cooperate with one another in an informal arrangement later called the First Triumvirate. All three politicians would pool their resources to help each individual member reach his personal goals in the state and subvert the opposition of the Senate. In 59 B.C.E. Julius Caesar was elected consul and worked to enact legislation favored by Pompey and Crassus. Following his consulship, Caesar spent nine years conquering Gaul, under the pretext of protecting the Gauls from the Germans across the Rhine. He accumulated a fortune in plunder and trained a loyal army of veterans. During his absence from Rome, he kept his name before the citizens by publishing an attractively written account of his military feats, *Commentaries on the Gallic War.*

client state—A kingdom or region that Rome considered to be dependent on Rome's patronage. Such states enjoyed some measure of independence but were expected to seek approval from Rome for any major undertaking. If client states failed to satisfy Roman expectations, Rome usually moved to establish permanent control.

Crassus was killed in battle against the Parthians of Persia in 53 B.C.E. Steadily becoming more fearful of Caesar's growing power, Pompey associated himself with the Senate in order to limit Caesar's authority. When the Senate demanded in 49 B.C.E. that Caesar disband his army, he crossed the Rubicon, the river in northern Italy that formed the boundary of his province, and in effect declared war on Pompey and the Senate. He marched on Rome while Pompey and most of the Senate fled to Greece, where Caesar eventually defeated them at Pharsalus (FAR-sa-luhs) in 48 B.C.E. Pompey was killed in Egypt when he sought refuge there. By 45 B.C.E. Caesar had eliminated all military threats against him, and he returned in triumph to Rome to exercise what he hoped would be unlimited power.

As he assumed the title of "dictator for the administration of public affairs," Caesar initiated far-reaching reforms. He granted citizenship to the Gauls and packed the Senate with many new non-Italian members, making it a more truly representative body as well as a rubber stamp for his policies. In the interest of the poorer citizens, he reduced debts, inaugurated a public works program, established colonies outside Italy, and decreed that one-third of the laborers on the slave-worked estates in Italy be persons of free birth. As a result, he was able to reduce from 320,000 to 150,000 the number of people in the city of Rome receiving free grain. (The population of Rome is estimated to have been 500,000 at this time.) His most enduring act was the reform of the calendar in the light of Egyptian knowledge; with minor changes, this calendar of 365 1/4 days is still in use today.

Caesar realized that the Republic was dead. In his own words, "The Republic is merely a name, without form or substance." He believed that only intelligent autocratic leadership could save Rome from continued civil war and collapse. But Caesar inspired the hatred of many, particularly those who viewed him as a high-handed egomaniac who not only had destroyed the Republic but also even aspired to having himself recognized as a god. On the Ides (fifteenth day) of March, 44 B.C.E., a group of conspirators, led by Brutus and other ex-Pompeians whom Caesar had pardoned, stabbed him to death in the Senate, and Rome was once more drawn into conflict.

The Third Civil War: Antony Versus Octavian

Following Caesar's death, his 18-year-old grandnephew and heir, Octavian (63 B.C.E.–14 C.E.), allied himself with Caesar's chief lieutenant, Mark Antony, against the conspirators and the Senate. The conspirators' armies were defeated at Philippi in Macedonia in 42 B.C.E. Then for more than a decade, Octavian and Antony exercised dictatorial power and divided the Roman world between them. But the ambitions of each man proved too great for the alliance to endure.

Antony, who took charge of the eastern half of the empire, became completely infatuated with Queen Cleopatra, the last of the Egyptian Ptolemies. He even went so far as to transfer Roman territories to her control. Octavian took advantage of Antony's blunders to propagandize Rome and Italy against Antony and his foreign lover-queen. The resulting struggle was portrayed by Octavian as a war between the Roman West and the "oriental" East. When Octavian's fleet met Antony's near Actium in Greece, first Cleopatra and then Antony deserted the battle and fled to Egypt. There Antony committed suicide, as Cleopatra did soon afterward when Alexandria was captured by Octavian in 30 B.C.E.

THE ROMAN EMPIRE AND THE *PAX ROMANA*: 30 B.C.E.–476 C.E.

- *What were the most significant achievements of the Roman Empire, and what were its greatest failures?*

At the end of a century of civil violence, Rome was at last united under one leader, Octavian, who was hailed by the grateful Romans as the "father of his country." The Republic gave way to the permanent dictatorship of the empire, and two centuries of imperial greatness, known as the *Pax Romana* ("Roman Peace"), followed. But in the third century, the empire was beset with challenges that proved disastrous: economic stagnation, Germanic invasions, and finally the loss of imperial control of the empire in the west.

Reconstruction Under Augustus

Following his triumphal return to Rome, Octavian in 27 B.C.E. announced that he would "restore the Republic." But he did so only outwardly by blending republican institutions with his own strong personal leadership. He consulted the Senate on important issues, allowed it to retain control over Italy and half of the provinces, and gave it the legislative functions of the nearly unused Tribal Assembly. The Senate in return bestowed on Octavian the title *Augustus* ("The Revered," a title previously used for gods), by which he was known thereafter.

DOCUMENT
Excerpt from Suetonius, *The Life of Augustus*

During the rest of his 45-year rule, Augustus never again held the office of dictator, and he seldom held the consulship. Throughout his career he kept the powers of a tribune, which gave him the right to initi-

The Roman Empire

14–68 C.E.	Period of the Julio-Claudian emperors
64 C.E.	Rome destroyed by fire; Emperor Nero attributes fire to Christians
69–96 C.E.	Period of the Flavian emperors
79 C.E.	Mount Vesuvius erupts, destroying Pompeii
96–180 C.E.	Period of the Antonine emperors
313 C.E.	Emperor Constantine issues Edict of Milan; Christians free to worship
378 C.E.	Battle of Adrianople; Germanic invasions into Roman Empire begin
395 C.E.	Roman Empire divided into eastern and western empires
476 C.E.	Last Roman emperor in the West assassinated

ate legislation and to veto the legislative and administrative acts of others. He also kept for himself the governorship of the frontier provinces, where the armies were stationed. Augustus's nearly total control of the army meant that his power could not be successfully challenged. From his military title, *imperator* ("victorious general"), is derived our modern term *emperor.*

Augustus constructed a constitution in which his power was in reality almost unlimited, yet disguised through his masterful use of the institutions of the old republic. He preferred the modest title of *princeps,* "first citizen" or "leader," that he felt best described his position, and his form of virtual dictatorship is therefore known as the Principate. At the beginning of the empire, then, political power was in appearances divided between the princeps and the senatorial aristocrats. This arrangement was continued by most of Augustus's successors during the next two centuries.

Seeking to heal the scars of more than a century of civil strife, Augustus concentrated on internal reform. He annexed Egypt and extended the Roman frontier to the Danube as a defense against barbarian invasions, but he failed in an attempt to conquer Germany up to the Elbe River. As a result, the Germans were never Romanized, as the Celts of Gaul and Spain were.

Through legislation and propaganda, Augustus attempted to check moral and social decline and revive the old Roman ideals and traditions. He rebuilt deteriorated temples, revived old priesthoods, and restored religious festivals. He attempted to reestablish the integrity of the family by legislating against adultery, the chief grounds for divorce, which had become quite common during the late Republic. A permanent court

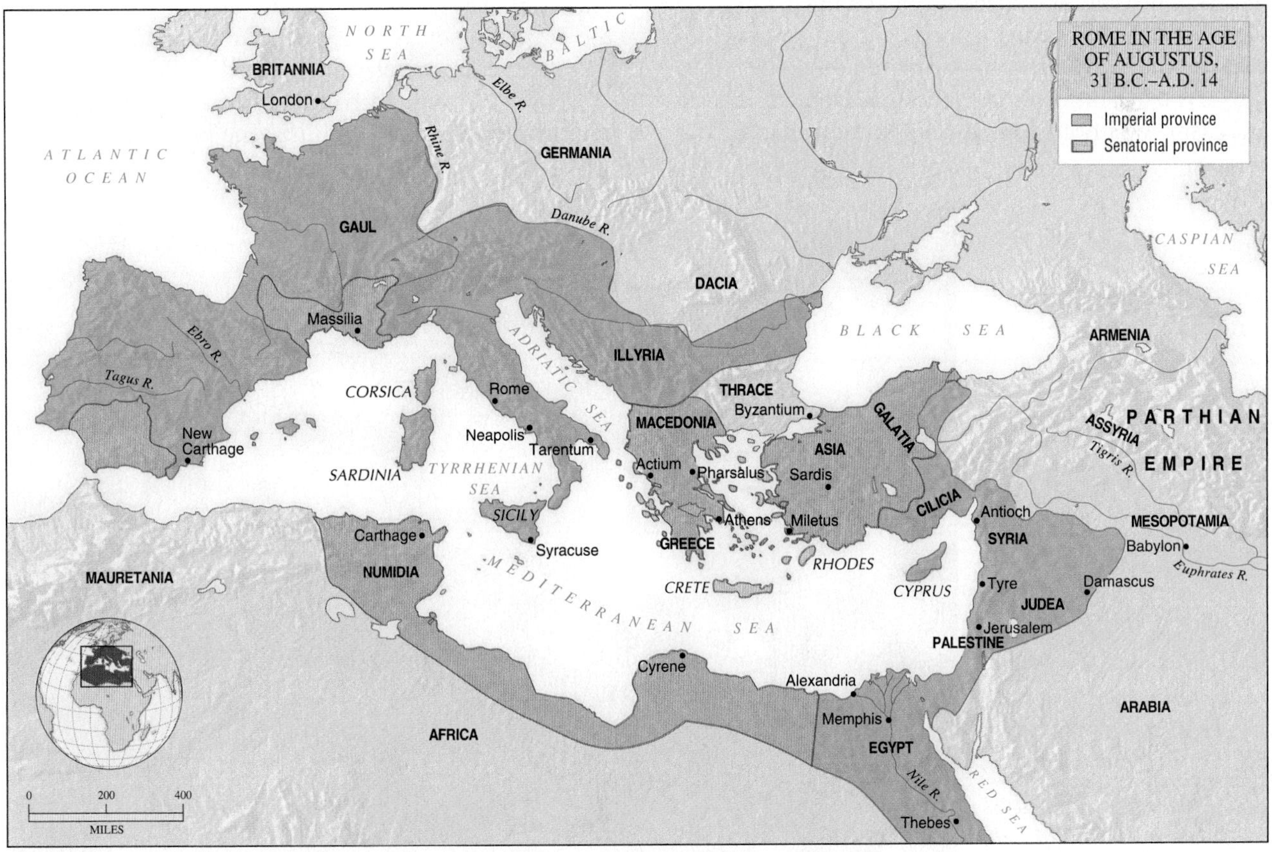

The Roman Empire at the time of Augustus.

was set up to prosecute adulterous wives and their lovers. Among those found guilty and banished from Rome were Augustus's own daughter and granddaughter. Finally, to disarm the gangs that had been terrorizing citizens, he outlawed the carrying of daggers.

Augustus greatly reduced the corruption and exploitation that had flourished in the late Republic by creating a well-paid civil service, open to all classes. He also established a permanent standing army, stationed in the frontier provinces and kept out of politics. More than 40 colonies of retired soldiers were founded throughout the empire. Augustus's reforms also gave rise to a new optimism and patriotism that were reflected in the art and literature of the Augustan Age.

DOCUMENT
Augustus on his accomplishments

The Julio-Claudian and Flavian Emperors

Augustus was followed by four descendants from among his family, the line of the Julio-Claudians, who ruled from 14 to 68 C.E. Augustus's stepson Tiberius, whom the Senate accepted as his successor, and Claudius were fairly efficient and devoted rulers; in Claudius's reign the Roman occupation of Britain began in 43 C.E. The other two rulers of this imperial line disregarded the appearance that they were only the first among all citizens: Caligula (Ka-LIG-eu-lah), Tiberius's nephew and successor, was a megalomaniac who demanded to be worshiped as a god and considered the idea of having his favorite horse elected to high office in Rome; Nero, Claudius's adopted son and successor, was notorious for his immorality, for the murders of his wife and his mother, and for beginning the persecutions of Christians in Rome. Caligula and Nero have been immortalized through history for their excesses and depravity, yet both functioned effectively as emperors for at least some duration of their reigns. Nero in particular was recognized to be intelligent and accomplished by some of his contemporaries.

The Julio-Claudian line ended in 68 C.E. when Nero, declared a public enemy by the Senate and facing army revolts, committed suicide. In the following year, four emperors were proclaimed by rival armies, with Vespasian (ves-PAY-si-an) the final victor. For nearly 30 years (69–96 C.E.) the Flavian dynasty (Vespasian followed by his two sons, Titus and Domitian) provided the empire with effective but autocratic rule. The fiction of republican institutions gave way to a scarcely veiled monarchy as the Flavians openly treated the office of emperor as theirs by right of conquest and inheritance.

The Antonines: "Five Good Emperors"

An end to autocracy and a return to the Augustan principle of an administration of equals—emperor and Senate—characterized the rule of the Antonine emperors (96–180 C.E.), under whom the empire reached the height of its prosperity and power. Selected on the basis of proven ability, these "good emperors" succeeded in establishing a spirit of confidence and optimism among the governing classes throughout the empire. Two of these emperors are especially worthy of mention.

Hadrian reigned from 117 to 138 C.E. His first important act was to stabilize the boundaries of the

The villa of the emperor Hadrian at Tivoli, a short distance away from Rome's congestion. Hadrian had the villa landscaped and decorated with replicas of famous Greek and oriental monuments.

empire. He gave up as indefensible recently conquered Armenia and Mesopotamia and erected protective walls in Germany and Britain. Hadrian traveled extensively, inspecting almost every province of the empire. New cities were founded, old ones were restored, and many public works were constructed, among them the famous Pantheon, still standing in Rome.

The last of the "five good emperors" was Marcus Aurelius (MAHR-kuhs ah-REE-lee-uhs), who ruled from 161 to 180 C.E. He preferred the study of philosophy and the quiet contemplation of his books to the blood and brutality of the battlefield. Yet he was repeatedly troubled by the invasions of the Parthians from the east and Germans from across the Danube. While engaged in his Germanic campaigns, he wrote his *Meditations,* a collection of personal thoughts notable for its Stoic idealism and love of humanity. Like a good Stoic, Marcus Aurelius died at his post at Vindobona (Vienna); at Rome his equestrian statue still stands on the Capitoline Hill.

The Pax Romana

In its finest period, the empire was a vast area stretching from Britain to the Euphrates and populated by more than 100 million people. It was welded together into an orderly and generally peaceful state, bringing stability and prosperity to the Mediterranean region and beyond. Non-Romans were equally conscious of the rich benefits derived from the Pax Romana, which began with Augustus and reached its fullest development under the Five Good Emperors. They welcomed the peace, prosperity, and administrative efficiency of the empire. Cities increased in number and were largely self-governed by their own upper-class magistrates and senates.

DOCUMENT
Excerpt from Aelius Aristides, *The Roman Oration*

Economic Prosperity

Rome's unification of the ancient Mediterranean world had far-reaching economic consequences. The

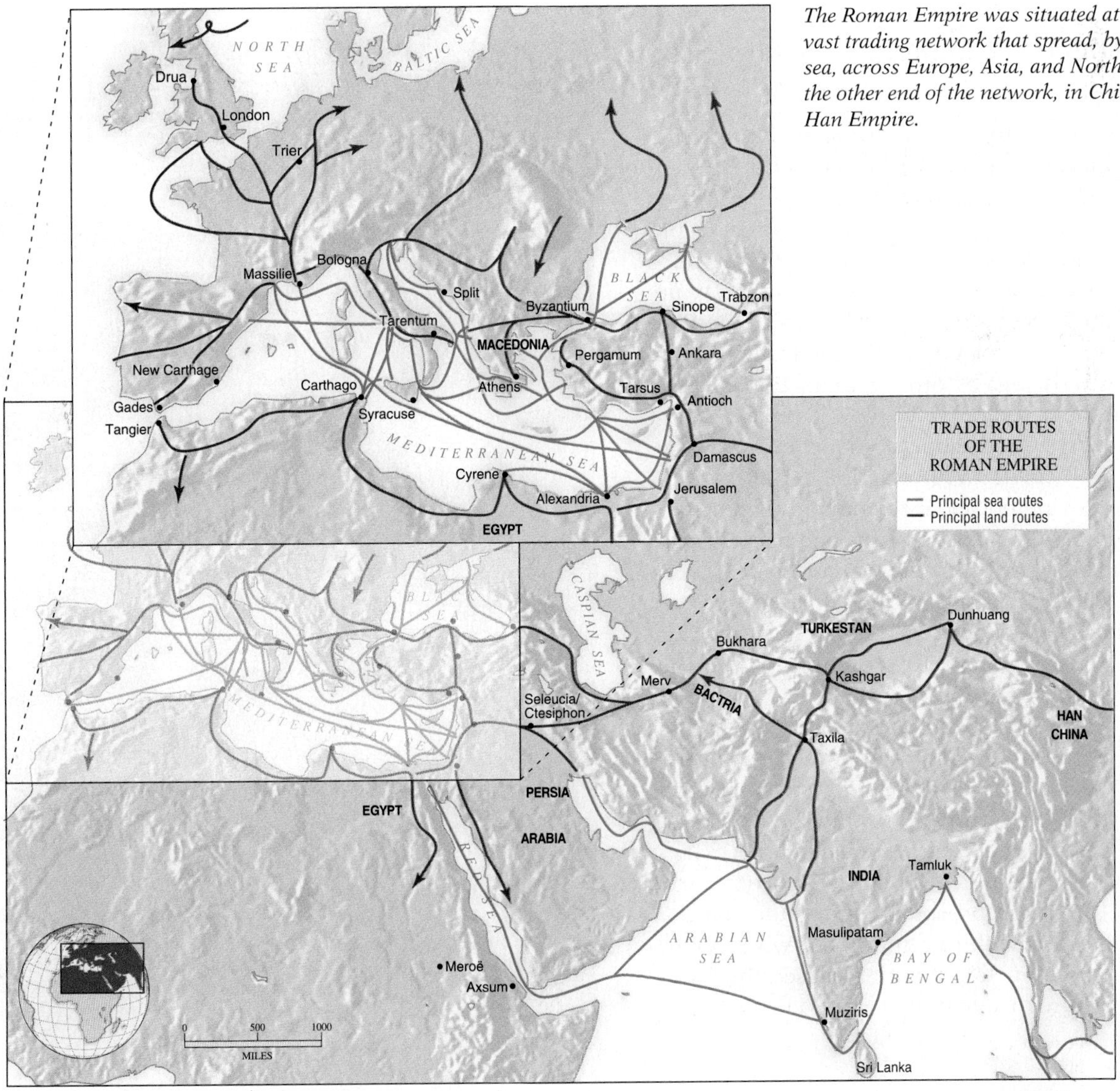

The Roman Empire was situated at one end of a vast trading network that spread, by land and sea, across Europe, Asia, and North Africa. At the other end of the network, in China, stood the Han Empire.

Pax Romana was responsible for the elimination of tolls and other artificial barriers, the suppression of piracy and lawlessness, and the establishment of a reliable coinage. Such factors, in addition to the longest period of peace the West has ever enjoyed, explain in large measure the great expansion of commerce that occurred in the first and second centuries C.E. Industry was also stimulated, but its expansion was limited since wealth remained concentrated and no mass market for industrial goods was created. Industry remained organized on a small-shop basis, with producers widely scattered, resulting in self-sufficiency.

The economy of the empire remained basically agricultural, and huge estates, the *latifundia*, prospered. On these tracts, usually belonging to absentee owners, large numbers of *coloni*, free tenants, tilled the soil as sharecroppers. The *coloni* were replacing slave labor, which was becoming increasingly hard to secure with the disappearance of the flow of war captives.

Early Evidence of Economic Stagnation

Late in the first century C.E. the first sign of economic stagnation appeared in Italy. Italian agriculture began to suffer from overproduction as a result of the loss of Italy's markets for wine and olive oil in Roman Gaul, Spain, and North Africa, which were becoming self-sufficient in those products. To aid the Italian wine producers, the Flavian emperor Domitian created an artificial scarcity by forbidding the planting of new vineyards in Italy and by ordering half the existing vineyards in the provinces to be plowed under. A century later the Five Good Emperors sought to solve the continuing problem of overproduction in Italy by subsidizing the buying power of consumers. Loans at 5 percent interest were made to ailing landowners, with the interest to be paid into the treasuries of Italian municipalities and earmarked "for girls and boys of needy parents to be supported at public expense." This system of state subsidies was soon extended to the provinces.

Also contributing to Roman economic stagnation was the continuing drain of money to the East for the purchase of such luxury goods as silks and spices and the failure of city governments within the empire to keep their finances in order, thus making it necessary for the imperial government to intervene. Such early evidence of declining prosperity foreshadowed the economic crisis of the third century C.E., when political anarchy and monetary inflation caused the economy of the empire to collapse.

Roman Society During the Empire

The social structure of Rome and of the entire empire underwent slow but significant change in the early centuries of the Common Era. At the top of the Roman social order were the old senatorial families who lived as absentee owners of huge estates and left commerce and finance to a large and wealthy middle class. In contrast to the tenements of the poor, the homes of the rich were palatial, as revealed by excavations at Pompeii, which was buried and so preserved by the eruption of the volcano Vesuvius in 79 C.E. These elaborate villas contained courts and gardens with fountains, rooms with marble walls, mosaics on the floors, and numerous frescoes and other works of art. An interesting feature of Roman furniture was the abundance of couches

Wall painting of an imaginary garden, recently excavated in the villa of Livia Drusilla, the wife of the emperor Augustus. The scene is painted on the wall of Livia's triclinium, a large living and dining area within the villa, and dates to circa 10 B.C.E. Trees, fruits, birds, and flowers of all varieties are portrayed to create a perfect natural setting.

A fresco portrait of a young woman from Pompeii. She seems to be caught in thought as she prepares to make an entry in her diary.

and the scarcity of chairs. People usually reclined, even at meals.

Roman women in the early empire were still very much the subjects of their fathers or husbands. They could not vote, they had almost no opportunity to represent their own interests in the law courts, nor could they initiate divorce proceedings unless a husband could be convicted of sorcery or murder. Women of very high social status continued to be looked upon as valuable assets in creating marriage alliances between families for eventual political or economic advantage. Wives of many emperors were regarded as representations of the ideal Roman woman, but most such highborn women were given little actual power. With the steady increase in the west of the number of noble women from the eastern empire, where women were permitted more independence of character and action, and through the growing popularity of eastern **mystery religions,** which highlighted the significance of women, the western empire began slowly to grant more rights to its female citizens.

The lower classes in the cities found recreation in social clubs, or guilds, called *collegia* (co-LEE-gee-ah), each comprising the workers of one trade. The activity of the collegia did not center on economic goals, like modern trade unions, but on the worship of a god and on feasts, celebrations, and decent burials for members. The social conditions of slaves varied greatly. Those in domestic service were often treated humanely, with their years of efficient service sometimes rewarded by emancipation or a less demanding retirement from service. Freed slaves were sometimes able to rise to positions of significance in business, letters, and the imperial service. But conditions among slaves on the large estates could be indescribably harsh. Beginning with Augustus, however, legal restrictions protected slaves from mistreatment.

Slaves in Roman Law

---

mystery religion—Secret religious cults popular in both Greece and Rome. They reached their peak of popularity in the first three centuries C.E. Their members met secretly to share meals and take part in dances and ceremonies, especially initiation rites. Observance of the proper rites and rituals were thought to provide the initiated with a blessed and blissful existence in the afterlife.

Portrait of a young Egyptian man flanked by folding doors depicting the goddess Isis (left) and the god Serapis, both of whom were associated with death and the afterlife. These paintings on wood panels date to circa 180–200 C.E. and are some of the very few remaining representations of Greco-Roman portraiture used in connection with Egyptian rites for the dead.

Recreation played a key role in Roman social life. Both rich and poor were exceedingly fond of their public baths, which in the capital alone numbered 800 during the early days of the empire. The larger baths contained enclosed gardens, promenades, gymnasia, libraries, and famous works of art as well as a sequence of cleansing rooms through which one moved—the sweat room, the warm room where sweat was scraped off by a slave (soap was unknown), the tepid room for cooling off, and the invigorating cold bath. Another popular room was the lavatory, with its long row of marble toilets equipped with comfortable arm rests.

Footraces, boxing, and wrestling were popular sports, but chariot racing and gladiatorial contests were the chief amusements. By the first century C.E. the Roman calendar had as many as 100 days set aside as holidays, the majority of which were given over to games furnished at public expense. The most spectacular sport was chariot racing. The largest of six racecourses at Rome was the Circus Maximus, a huge marble-faced structure seating about 150,000 spectators. The games, which included as many as 24 races each day, were presided over by the emperor or his representative. The crowds bet furiously on their favorite charioteers, whose fame equaled that of the sports heroes of our own day.

Of equal or greater popularity were the gladiatorial contests, organized by both emperors and private promoters as regular features on the amusement calendar. These spectacles were held in arenas, the largest and most famous of which was the Colosseum, opened in 80 C.E. The contests took various forms. Ferocious animals were pitted against armed combatants or occasionally even against unarmed men and women who had been condemned to death. Another type of contest was the fight to the death between gladiators, generally equipped with different types of weapons but matched on equal terms. It was not uncommon for the life of a defeated gladiator who had fought courageously to be spared at the request of the spectators. Although many Romans considered these bloodletting contests barbaric, they continued until the fifth century, when Christian rulers outlawed them.

IMAGE
Roman Colosseum

THE RISE OF CHRISTIANITY

- *How did Christianity grow from humble beginnings to become the sole religion of the Roman Empire?*

The growth of the Christian religion, from its modest beginnings in an obscure part of the Roman Empire to its eventual dominance as the one and only religion tolerated by that same empire that had once persecuted its followers, is a remarkable story. The rise and ultimate victory of Christianity in the Roman world has even been identified by many observers throughout Europe's history as perhaps the most significant reason for the ultimate decline and fall from dominance of the Roman Empire itself. Whether Christianity was the primary cause of Rome's demise remains a highly debated topic, but there is no controversy about the fact that the religion's growth and development in the ancient world changed not just the course of European but also of world history.

A mosaic from the third century B.C.E. depicting gladiators. Introduced to Rome by the Etruscans, gladiatorial contests grew in popularity and cruelty as Rome grew in power and population.

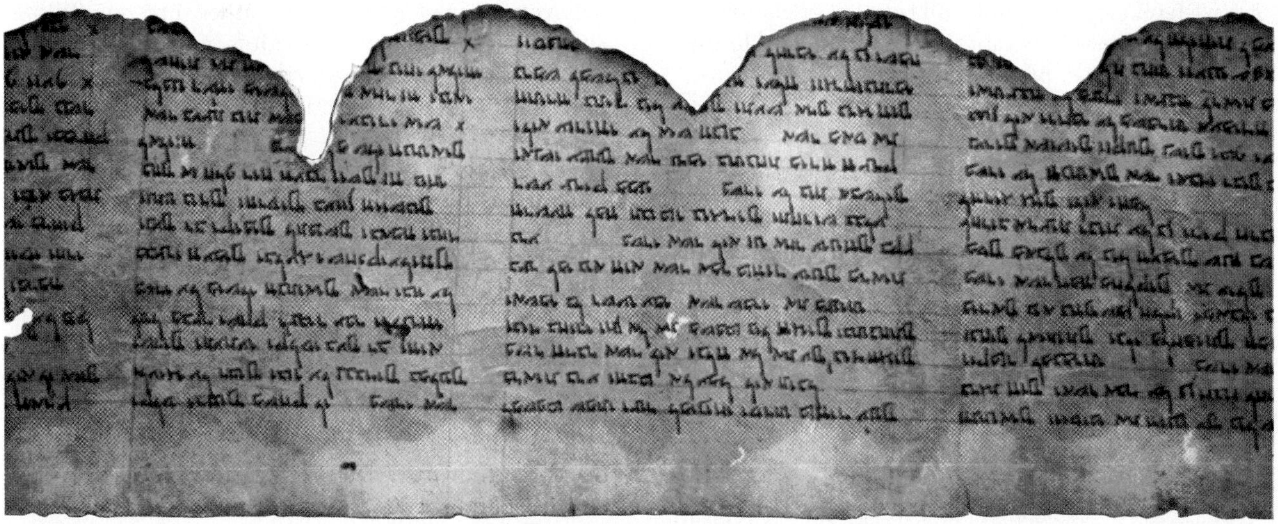

A partially unrolled section of the texts known as the Dead Sea Scrolls, now preserved and displayed at the Hebrew University in Jerusalem. The Scrolls were preserved by the Essenes, a sect of Jewish militant and religious zealots, whose nearby monastery was destroyed by the Romans in the Jewish revolt of 66–70 B.C.E.

The Jewish Background

Following the conquests of Alexander the Great in the Near East, the Ptolemies and then the Seleucids ruled Palestine. After the Jews returned from exile in Babylonia in 538 B.C.E. (see Chapter 1), they attempted to create a theocratic community based on God's law (the *Torah*) as contained in the *Pentateuch* (PEN-tah-teuk), the first five books of the Old Testament. Later they added to this record the teachings of the prophets and the writings of priests and scholars.

Jewish religious life in Jerusalem centered on the Temple at Jerusalem, and Jewish groups outside Palestine—the Jews of the Diaspora, those who did not return to Palestine after the Babylonian exile—met in local *synagogues* (from the Greek word for "assembly") for public worship and instruction in the Scriptures.

During the Hellenistic Age, Greek philosophy and culture constantly influenced the Jews outside Palestine, most of whom spoke Greek, and contributed to factionalism among the Jews in Palestine. Religious conflict often developed into open warfare.

It was in the midst of a civil war that the Roman legions first made their appearance. In 63 B.C.E. Pompey, who was then completing his pacification of Asia Minor and Syria, made Judea a Roman dependancy, subject to the Roman governor of Syria. Later, Herod the Great, a half-Jewish, half-Arab leader from Edom, was appointed king of Judea by Mark Antony and reigned from 37 to 4 B.C.E. Soon after Herod's death, Judea became a Roman administrative unit ruled by officials called *procurators*. The best-known procurator was Pontius Pilate, who ruled from 26 to 36 C.E. and under whose government Jesus was crucified. The Jews remained unhappy and divided under Roman domination. For centuries the prophets had taught that God would one day create a new Israel under a Messiah—a leader anointed by God. Many Jews lost hope in a political Messiah and an earthly kingdom and instead began to hope for a Messiah who would lead all the righteous to a spiritual kingdom.

The Life and Teaching of Jesus

The Jewish sect that became Christianity bears the unmistakable imprint of the personality of its founder, Jesus of Nazareth. According to the biblical accounts pieced together from the four Gospels, he was born in Bethlehem during Herod's reign; therefore, he must have been born by the time of Herod's death in 4 B.C.E.—probably not in the year that traditionally begins the Christian or Common Era, 1 C.E. After spending the first years of his adult life as a carpenter in the village of Nazareth, Jesus began preaching love for one's fellow human beings and urging people to turn away from sin.

Excerpt from the Gospel According to Luke

Reports of Jesus's miracles, such as casting out demons, healing the sick, raising the dead, and walking on water, spread among the Jews as he and his 12 apostles traveled from village to village. When he came to Jerusalem to observe the feast of the Passover, huge crowds greeted him enthusiastically as the promised Messiah. But his opponents, most importantly the influential sect of the **Pharisees,** accused him of distortion

Pharisees—Jewish religious party that emerged c. 160 B.C.E. in Palestine. The Pharisees believed that the Jewish oral tradition was as valid as the law presented in the Old Testament. Their belief that reason must be applied in the interpretation of the Old Testament and its application to contemporary problems has now become basic to Jewish theology.

of Jewish religious law, and with treason for claiming to be king of the Jews. He was crucified, a standard Roman penalty for treason, probably in 30 C.E.

The Spread of Christianity

Soon after Jesus's death, word spread that he had been seen alive after his crucifixion and had spoken to his disciples, giving them comfort and reassurance. Initially, there were few converts in Palestine, but the Hellenized Jews living in foreign lands, in contact with new ideas and modes of living, were less firmly committed to traditional Jewish **doctrines.** The new faith first made rapid headway among the Jewish communities in such cities as Damascus, Antioch (where its followers were first called "Christians" by the Greeks), Corinth, and Rome.

MAP
The Spread of Christianity to 300 C.E.

The first followers of Jesus had no thought of breaking away from Judaism. But because they adhered to the requirements of the Jewish law, their new message did not easily attract non-Jews. These obstacles were largely removed through more liberal and cosmopolitan teachings of an early Christian convert now known as Saint Paul. Because of his powerful influence, he has been called the second founder of Christianity.

Originally named Saul, Paul was of Jewish ancestry but a Roman citizen by birth. He was raised in the cosmopolitan city of Tarsus, in Asia Minor, and possessed a thorough knowledge of Greek culture. He was also a strict Pharisee who considered Christians to be traitors to the sacred law, and he took an active part in their persecution. One day about 33 C.E., while traveling to Damascus to prosecute the Christian community there, Saul experienced a conversion to the very beliefs he had been vigorously opposing. His conversion caused him to change his name, and also the whole course of his life—from an opponent of the new religion into the greatest of the early Christian missionaries.

Paul taught that Jesus was the Christ (from the Greek *Christos,* "Messiah"), the Son of God, and that he had died to atone for the sins of all people, and to bring salvation to Jews and Gentiles (non-Jews) alike. Adherence to the complexities of the Jewish law was unnecessary.

After covering 8000 miles teaching and preaching, Paul supposedly was put to death in Rome about 65 C.E., the same year as Peter, founder of the church at Rome, during the reign of Nero. By that time Christian communities had been established in all the major cities in the East and at Rome. Paul had performed a very important service to these infant communities of believers by instructing them, either through visits or letters, in the fundamental beliefs of the new religion. He had served as an authority by which standardization of belief could be achieved.

doctrine—A specific position that is taught or advocated. In a religious context, a doctrine is an official position that must be accepted by those who wish to consider themselves believers.

Reasons for the Spread of Christianity

The popular mystery religions that the Romans had embraced from Greece and the Near East during the troubled last century of the Republic gave spiritual satisfaction not provided by Rome's early ritualistic forms of worship. These mystery religions included the worship of the Phrygian Cybele (Si-BEH-lee), the Great Mother *(Magna Mater);* the Egyptian Isis, sister and wife of Osiris; the Greek Dionysus, called Bacchus by the Romans; and the Persian sun-god Mithras, the intermediary between humans and Ahura-Mazda, the great Lord of Light, whose sacred day of worship was called Sunday and from whose cult women were excluded. Common to all the mystery religions were the notions of a divine savior and the promise of everlasting life.

Followers of these mystery cults found Christian beliefs and practices familiar enough to convert easily to the new faith. But Christianity had far more to offer than the mystery religions did. Its founder was not a creature of myth, like the gods and goddesses of the mystery cults, but a real person whose ethical teachings were preserved by his followers and later written down. Shared with the Jews was the concept of a single omnipotent God, the God of the Hebrew Scriptures, now the God of all humanity. Moreover, Christianity was a dynamic, aggressive faith. It upheld the spiritual equality of all people—rich and poor, slave and freeborn, male and female. Women were among Jesus's audiences, and Paul's letters give much evidence of women active in the early church. One of Jesus's closest and favored followers was said to have been Mary Magdalene, a former prostitute. According to the so-called Gnostic Gospels, which the church declared heretical in the early fourth century and ordered destroyed, "Christ loved her more than all the disciples."

Christianity taught that God, the loving Father, had sent his only Son to atone for human sins and offered a vision of immortality and an opportunity to be "born again," cleansed of sin. Its converts were bound together by faith and hope, and they took seriously their obligation of caring for orphans, widows, and other unfortunates. The courage with which some of their number faced death and persecution impressed even their bitterest enemies.

Persecution of the Christians

The Roman government tolerated any religion that did not threaten the safety and stability of the empire. Christianity, however, initially was perceived as a subversive danger to society and the state. Christians, as monotheists, refused to offer sacrifice to the state cults on behalf of the emperor—not even a few grains of incense cast upon an altar. Offering sacrifice to the state cults was considered an essential patriotic rite uniting all Roman subjects in common loyalty to the imperial government. For Christians, however, there was only one God: they could sacrifice to no others. In the eyes of many Roman officials, this attitude branded them as traitors.

To the Romans, the Christians were a secret antisocial group forming a state within a state—"walling themselves off from the rest of mankind," as a pagan writer observed. Many were pacifists who refused to serve in the army, denied the legitimacy of other religious sects, and refused to associate with pagans or take part in social functions that they considered sinful or degrading.

During the first two centuries after Jesus's crucifixion, persecution of Christians was sporadic and local, such as that at Rome under Nero. But during the late third and fourth centuries, when the empire was in danger of collapse, three organized efforts were launched to suppress Christianity throughout the empire. By far the longest and most systematic campaign against the Christians, who made up perhaps one-tenth of the population in the early fourth century, was instigated by the emperor Diocletian (dai-o-KLEE-shan) from 303 to 311. He stringently imposed the death penalty on anyone who refused to sacrifice to Roman gods. But the inspired defiance of the Christian **martyrs,** who seemed to welcome death, had a persuasive effect on many observers. "The blood of the martyrs is the seed of the church" became a Christian slogan.

Church Organization

Viewing the present world as something that would end quickly with the imminent second coming of Christ and the last judgment of the living and the dead, the earliest Christians saw no need to build a formal religious bureaucracy. But after it became clear that the second coming would not be immediate, a church organization emerged to manage the day-to-day business of defining, maintaining, and spreading the faith.

At first there was little or no distinction between laity and **clergy.** Traveling teachers visited Christian communities, preaching and giving advice. But the steady growth in the number of Christians made necessary special church officials who could devote all their time to religious work, clarifying the body of Christian doctrine, conducting services, and collecting money for charitable purposes.

The earliest officials were called *presbyters* ("elders"), *deacons* ("servers"), or *bishops* ("overseers"). By the second century, the offices of bishop and presbyter had become distinct. Christian communities in villages near the main church, which was usually located in a city, were administered by priests who were responsible to a bishop. The *diocese,* a territorial administrative division under the jurisdiction of a bishop, usually corresponded to a Roman administrative district of the same name. The bishops were reputed to be the direct successors of the apostles and, like them, the guardians of Christian teaching and traditions.

A number of dioceses made up a *province.* The bishop of the most important city in each province enjoyed more prestige than his fellows and was known as an *archbishop* or *metropolitan.* The provinces were grouped into larger administrative divisions called *patriarchates.* The title of *patriarch* was applied to the bishop of such great cities as Rome, Constantinople, and Alexandria.

The bishop of Rome rose to a position of preeminence in the hierarchy of the church in the western empire. At first only one of several patriarchs, the Roman bishop gradually became recognized as the leader of the church in the West and was given the title of *pope,* from the Greek word for "father." Many factors explain the emergence of the papacy (the office and jurisdiction of the pope) at Rome. As the largest city in the West and the capital of the empire, Rome had an aura of prestige that was transferred to its bishop. After political Rome had fallen, religious Rome remained. When the empire in the West collapsed in the fifth century, the bishop of Rome emerged as a stable and dominant figure looked up to by all. The primacy of Rome was fully evident during the pontificate of Leo I, the Great (440–461), who provided both the leadership that saved Italy from invasion by the Huns (see page 158) and the major theoretical support for papal leadership of the church, the Petrine theory. This doctrine held that because Peter, whom Jesus had made leader of the apostles, was the first bishop of Rome, his authority over all Christians was handed on to his successors at Rome. The church in the East, insisting on the equality of all the apostles, never accepted the Petrine theory.

Foundations of Christian Doctrine and Worship

While the administrative structure of the church adapted to changing conditions in the West, a combination of theologians and church administrators

---

martyrs—Those who voluntarily suffer death rather than deny their religious convictions. The early Christian church saw the suffering of martyrs as a test of their faith. Many saints of the early church underwent martyrdom during the persecutions imposed by Roman authorities.

clergy—The recognized group or body of persons who are officials of a religious organization. In the early Christian church, the clergy were ordained (recognized as officials through ceremonial appointment) and considered apart from the laity, or the believers who were not officials of the church.

defined and systematized Christian beliefs, sometimes by arbitrary means. This process of fixing Christian doctrine, or *dogma,* began with Paul, who stressed Jesus's divinity and explained his death as an atonement for the sins of all humanity.

In time, differences of opinion over doctrinal matters caused many controversies. One of the most important was over a belief called *Arianism.* At issue was the relative position of the three persons of the Trinity: God the Father, God the Son, and God the Holy Spirit. The view that Father and Son were equal was vigorously denied by Arius (256–336), a priest from Alexandria. He believed that Christ logically could not fully be God because he was not of a substance identical with God and, as a created being, was not coeternal with his creator. The controversy became so serious that in 325 the emperor Constantine convened the first ecumenical church council to resolve the problem. This Council of Nicaea (ni-SEE-a) was the first of such councils in early church history. With Constantine presiding, the council found the Arian position to be a ***heresy***—an opinion or doctrine contrary to the official teaching of the church—and Christ was declared to be of the same substance as God, uncreated and coeternal with him. This mystical concept of the Trinity, essential to the central Christian doctrine of the *incarnation*—God becoming man in Christ—received official formulation in the Nicene Creed. However, Arius's views found acceptance among the Germans, and his version of the doctrine of the Trinity was adopted throughout Europe and North Africa.

The **liturgy** of the early churches was plain and simple, consisting of prayer, Scripture reading, hymns, and preaching. Early Christians worshipped God and sought salvation through individual efforts. Following the growth of church organization and proclamation of official dogma, however, the church came to be viewed as the indispensable intermediary between God and humans. Without the church, the individual could not hope for salvation.

The development of the church's dogma owed much to the church fathers of the second through fifth centuries. Since most of them were intellectuals who came to Christianity thoroughly equipped with a classical education, they maintained that Greek philosophy and Christianity were compatible. Because reason (*logos* in Greek) and truth came from God, philosophy was considered a proper tool with which one could discover God's perfection. Thus Christianity was viewed as a superior philosophy that could supersede all pagan philosophies and religions.

In the West three church fathers made highly significant contributions to the formation of Christian dogma and organization. The scholarship of Jerome (340–420) made possible the church-authorized translation of the Bible into Latin. In a revised form, it is still the official translation of the Roman Catholic Church. Jerome also justified Christian use of the literature and learning of the classical world.

Another of the church fathers, St. Ambrose (340–397), resigned his government post to become bishop of Milan, where he employed his great administrative skills to establish a model bishopric. By criticizing the actions of the strong emperor Theodosius I and forcing him to do public penance, Ambrose was the first to assert the church's superiority over the state in spiritual matters.

St. Augustine (354 – 430) was the most influential of all the church fathers in the west. At the age of 32, as he relates in his *Confessions,* one of the world's great autobiographies, he found in Christianity the answer to his long search for meaning in life. Before, he had shared the doubts of men who search for spiritual satisfaction. He blended classical logic and philosophy with Christian belief to lay the foundation of much of the church's theology.

The Regular Clergy

The secular clergy moved through the world (*saeculum;* SAI-keu-lum), administering the church's services and communicating its teachings to the laity, the common people. But another type of clergy also arose: the regular clergy, so called because they lived by a rule *(regula)* within monasteries. These monks sought seclusion from the distractions of this world in order to prepare themselves for the next. In so doing, they helped preserve and spread the heritage of the classical world along with the faith.

The monastic way of life was older than formalized Christianity, having existed among the Essenes, a militant Jewish communal group. Christian ascetics, who had abandoned worldly life to live as hermits, could be found in Egypt and the East as early as the first century C.E. They pursued spiritual perfection by denying their physical feelings, torturing themselves, and fasting. In Syria, for example, St. Simeon Stylites sat for 33 years atop a 60-foot-high pillar. A disciple then surpassed his record by three months.

---

heresy—Any belief rejected as false by religious authorities. In Christianity, the official teachings of the church were believed to be based on divine revelation, and so heretics were viewed as perversely rejecting the guidance of the church. Numerous Christian heresies appeared from the second century onwards.

liturgy—The organization of services for public worship. A standardized and formal presentation of services usually associated with public worship. In the early Christian context, the formal organization of services usually connected with the Eucharist.

In a more moderate expression of **asceticism,** Christian monks in Egypt developed a monastic life in which, seeking a common spiritual goal, they lived together under a common set of regulations. St. Basil (330–379), a Greek bishop in Asia Minor, drew up a rule based on work, charity, and a communal life that still allowed each monk to retain most of his independence. The Rule of St. Basil became the standard system in the eastern church.

In the West the work of St. Benedict (c. 480–543) paralleled St. Basil's efforts in the East. About 529 Benedict led a band of followers to a high hill between Rome and Naples, named Monte Cassino, where they erected a monastery on the site of an ancient pagan temple. For his monks Benedict composed a rule that gave order and discipline to western monasticism. Benedictine monks took three basic vows—of poverty, chastity, and obedience to the *abbot,* the head of the monastery. The daily activities of the Benedictine monks were closely regulated: They participated in eight divine services, labored in fields or workshops for six or seven hours, and spent about two hours studying and preserving the writing of Latin antiquity at a time when illiteracy was widespread throughout western Europe. Benedictine monasticism was to be one of the most dynamic civilizing forces in early medieval Europe.

Women also played an important role in monastic Christianity. In Egypt an early-fifth-century bishop declared that 20,000 women—twice the number of men—were living in desert communities as nuns. In the West several fourth-century biographies of aristocratic women describe how they turned their villas and palaces into monasteries for women of all classes and remained firmly in control of their institutions. These communities became famous for their social and educational services, in addition to providing a different way of life for women who sought alternatives to the usual pattern of marriage, motherhood, and family life.

Official Recognition and Acceptance of Christianity

In 311 the emperor Galerius (ga-LEH-ree-uhs) recognized that persecution of Christians had failed to eliminate the belief and issued an edict of toleration, making Christianity a legal religion in the East. Two years later Constantine granted Christians freedom of worship throughout the empire by issuing, in 313, the Edict of Milan, an order decreeing that Christianity would be tolerated throughout the empire.

Why Constantine did this is open to debate. His Christian biographers assert that the night before a decisive battle at the Milvian Bridge, he looked to the sky and saw a cross with the words *"Hoc vinces"* ("By this, conquer") written on it. The next day, Constantine led his troops to victory, raising the cross as his symbol. The victory also played a role in his embrace of Christianity, which allowed him to build on the support of Christians, who, at 20 percent of the empire, constituted the most organized and unified segment of the population. His actions at the Council of Nicaea (see p. 154) as a self-proclaimed "thirteenth apostle" showed that the Christian Church was to be his state church. Constantine and his mother, Helena, remained deeply committed to Christianity, but he waited until just before his death to be baptized. All of his successors but one were Christian.

This sole exception was Julian the Apostate (361–363), a military hero and scholar who had been raised a Christian but then renounced his faith and sought to revive paganism. But Julian did not persecute the Christians, and his efforts to revive paganism failed.

The emperor Theodosius I (379–395) made Christianity the official religion of the empire. Paganism was now persecuted, Christian authorities sentenced large numbers of pagan philosophers to death, pagan philosophical schools (including Plato's Academy) were closed, and non-Christian works of art and literature were destroyed. Even the Olympic games were suppressed. One famous victim of this persecution *by* Christians was the philosopher Hypatia (hi-PAY-shi-ah), who in 415 was killed by a Christian mob in Alexandria. By the age of 25, she had become famous throughout the eastern half of the empire as a lecturer on Greek philosophy. Her popularity and beauty aroused the resentment of Cyril, the archbishop of Alexandria, who had already led a mob in destroying the homes and businesses of the city's Jews. He incited the mob to abduct Hypatia, who was dragged into a nearby church and hacked to death.

The Roman Crisis of the Third Century

In the third century C.E., internal anarchy and foreign invasion drastically transformed the Roman Empire. Augustus's constitutional monarchy, in which the emperor shared power with the Senate, had changed to a despotic absolute monarchy, in which the emperors made no attempt to hide the fact that they were backed by the military and would tolerate no senatorial influence. By the late third century, the emperor was no

---

asceticism—The denial of physical or psychological desires in order to achieve a spiritual ideal or goal. The quest for spiritual purity, the need for forgiveness, and the wish to earn merit or gain access to supernatural powers all are reasons for ascetic practice. Common forms of ascetic self-denial include celibacy, abstinence, and fasting.

longer addressed as *princeps*, "first among equals," but as *dominus et deus*, "lord and god." The Principate had been replaced by the absolute rule known as the Dominate.

The transformation of the Roman Empire in the third century was foreshadowed by the reign of Commodus (KOM-moh-duhs), who in 180 C.E. began a 12-year rule characterized by incompetence, corruption, cruelty, and neglect of affairs of state. He was strangled in 192, and civil war followed for a year until the establishment of the Severan dynasty (193–235). The Severan dynasty was intimidated by the military, whose commanders the emperors attempted to placate through bribes and exorbitant favors.

After 235, when the last member of the Severan dynasty was murdered by his own troops, 50 years of bloody civil wars, Germanic invasions, and new foreign threats ensued. Of the 26 men who claimed the title of emperor during this time, only one died a natural death. Prolonged economic decline was equally deadly to the well-being of the empire as military anarchy and foreign invasions. The economy became static, inflation set in, and the concentration of land ownership in the hands of the few destroyed the small farming classes. The *latifundia*, with their fortified villas, grew as the number of *coloni*—sharecroppers—grew. As the rural tax base declined, chaotic conditions took their toll on trade, and by the end of the period, the government refused to accept its own money for taxes and required payment in goods and services.

A much needed reconstruction of the empire was accomplished by Diocletian (285–305), a rough-hewn soldier and shrewd administrator. To increase the strength of the government, he completed the trend toward autocracy, leaving the Senate in a greatly diminished role. He attempted to restructure the empire to ensure better government and an efficient succession scheme. Diocletian also tried to stop the economic decay of the empire by issuing new coins based on silver and gold and by imposing a freeze on prices and wages.

Diocletian's succession scheme collapsed when Constantine (306–337) overcame his rivals to take power. Constantine continued Diocletian's attempts to ensure the production of essential goods and services as well as the collection of taxes. He imposed decrees tying people and their children to the same occupation in the same place. Most important, he moved the capital to the site of the old Greek colony of Byzantium, renaming it Constantinople (see Chapter 6). By doing so, he, in effect, left Rome open to the attacks of the advancing Germanic peoples but ensured the continuation of Roman government in a new, safer location.

The Germanic Tribes

Waves of restless and diverse Germanic tribes were drawn into the power vacuum created during the two centuries of Rome's decline after 180. While the west-

Bust of the emperor Commodus (177–192 C.E.) portrayed as Hercules. The son of the philosopher-emperor Marcus Aurelius, Commodus was physically impressive and often dressed as Hercules and performed as a gladiator. He was one of Rome's most corrupt and despised rulers.

ernmost German tribes (Franks, Angles, and Saxons) had achieved a settled agricultural life in the third and early fourth centuries, the Goths, Vandals, and Lombards remained largely nomadic.

The economic and legal practices of the Germanic tribes set them apart from the Romans. They engaged in so little commerce that cattle, rather than money, sufficed as a measure of value. A basic factor behind Germanic restlessness seems to have been land hunger. Their numbers were increasing, much of their land was forest and swamp, and their agricultural methods were inefficient. In an effort to eliminate blood feuds, the tribal law codes of the Germans encouraged the payment of compensation as an alternative for an aggrieved kin or family seeking vengeance. For the infliction of specific injuries, a stipulated payment, termed a *bot,* was required. The amount of compensation varied according to the severity of the crime and the social position of the victim.

Lack of written laws made it necessary to hold trials to determine guilt or innocence. A person standing trial could produce oath-helpers who would swear to his innocence. If unable to obtain oath-helpers, the accused was subjected to trial by ordeal, of which there were three kinds. In the first, the defendant had to lift a small stone out of a vessel of boiling water; unless his scalded arm healed within a prescribed number of days, he was judged guilty. In the second, he had to walk blindfolded and barefoot across a floor on which lay pieces of red-hot metal; success in avoiding the metal was a sign of innocence. In the third, the bound defendant was thrown into a stream; if he sank he was innocent, but if he floated, he was guilty because water was considered a divine element that would not accept a guilty person.

According to the Roman historian Tacitus, the Germans were notorious as heavy drinkers and gamblers, but Tacitus praised their courage, respect for women, and freedom from many Roman vices. A favorite amusement was listening to the tribal bards recite old tales of heroes and gods. Each warrior leader had a retinue of followers who were linked to him by personal loyalty. The war band—*comitatus* (ko-mi-TAH-tus) in Latin—had an important bearing on the origin of medieval political patterns, which were based on similar personal bonds between vassals and their lords. The heroic values associated with the *comitatus* also continued into the Middle Ages, where they contributed to the basis of the value system of the nobility.

DOCUMENT
Tacitus, *Germania*

During the many centuries that the Romans and Germans faced each other across the Rhine-Danube frontier, there was much contact—peaceful as well as warlike—between the two peoples. Roman trade reached into German territory, and Germans entered the Roman Empire as slaves. During the troubled third century, many Germans were invited to settle on vacated lands within the empire or to serve in the Roman legions. By the fourth century, the bulk of the Roman army and its generals in the west were German.

The Germans beyond the frontiers were kept in check by force of arms, by frontier walls, by diplomacy and gifts, and by playing off one tribe against another. In the last decades of the fourth century, however, these methods proved insufficient to prevent a series of new invasions.

The Germanic Invasions

The impetus behind the increasing German activity on the frontiers in the late fourth century was the approach of the Huns. These nomads—superb horsemen and fighters from central Asia—had plundered and slain their Asian neighbors for centuries. In 372 they crossed the Volga River and soon subjugated the easternmost Germanic tribe, the Ostrogoths. Terrified at the prospect of being conquered, the Visigoths, who found themselves next in the path of the advancing Huns, petitioned the Romans to allow them to settle as allies inside the empire. Permission was granted, and in 376 the entire tribe of Visigoths crossed the Danube into Roman territory. But corrupt Roman officials soon cheated and mistreated them, and the proud Germanic tribe went on a rampage. Valens (VAH-lens), the East Roman emperor, tried to stop them, but he lost both his army and his life in the battle of Adrianople in 378.

Adrianople has been described as one of history's decisive battles since it destroyed the legend of the invincibility of the Roman legions and ushered in a century and a half of chaos. For a few years, the emperor Theodosius I held back the Visigoths, but after his death in 395, they began to migrate and pillage under their leader, Alaric. He invaded Italy, and in 410 his followers sacked Rome. The weak West Roman emperor ceded southern Gaul to the Visigoths, who soon expanded into Spain. Their Spanish kingdom lasted until the Muslim conquest of the eighth century.

To counter Alaric's threat to Italy, the Romans had withdrawn most of their troops from the Rhine frontier in 406 and from Britain the following year. A flood of Germanic tribes soon surged across the unguarded frontiers. The Vandals pushed their way through Gaul to Spain and, after pressure from the Visigoths, moved on to Africa, the granary of the empire. In 455 a Vandal raiding force sailed over from Africa, and Rome was sacked a second time. Meanwhile, the Burgundians settled in the Rhone valley, the Franks gradually spread across Gaul, and the Angles, Saxons, and Jutes invaded Britain. Although each of these tribes set up a German-ruled kingdom within the confines of the empire, only the Franks in Gaul and the Angles and Saxons in Britain managed to establish kingdoms that lasted longer than a few generations.

Meanwhile, the Huns pushed farther into Europe. Led by Attila, the "scourge of God," the mounted nomads crossed the Rhine in 451. The remaining Roman forces in Gaul, joined by the Visigoths, defeated the Huns near Troyes, France. Attila then plundered northern Italy and planned to take Rome, but disease, lack of supplies, and the dramatic appeal of Pope Leo I, whose actions brought great prestige to the papacy, caused him to return to the plains of eastern Europe. The Huns' threat disintegrated after 453, when Attila died on the night of his marriage to a Germanic princess.

The End of the West Roman Empire, 395–476 C.E.

After the death of Theodosius I in 395, the Roman Empire was divided between his two sons. The decline of Roman rule in the West was hastened as a series of weakened emperors abandoned Rome and sought safety behind the marshes at the northern Italian city of Ravenna. The leaders of the imperial army, whose ranks were now mainly German, exercised the real power.

In 475 Orestes, a German army commander, forced the Senate to elect his young son Romulus Augustulus ("Little Augustus") emperor in the West. The following year another German chieftain, Odovacar, murdered Romulus Augustulus and named himself head of the government. The murder of this boy, who ironically bore the names of the legendary founder of Rome and the founder of the empire, marks the traditional "fall" of the Roman Empire in the West, since no emperor was named to carry on the succession. Instead, the emperor in Constantinople commissioned Theodoric (thee-O-doh-rik), king of the Germanic tribe of the Ostrogoths, to lead his people into Italy and establish order. The Ostrogothic Kingdom of Italy, with its capital now at Ravenna, restored order on the peninsula, but the political unity of the western empire fell into steady decline. Because he appreciated the culture he had seen at Constantinople, Theodoric attempted to preserve much of the culture of the Roman West, but the basic fabric of society in western Europe was in gradual transition into a new construct which combined useful institutions of both older Roman and new Germanic elements. A new society was evolving.

THE ROMAN LEGACY

- *What seem to be the greatest cultural achievements of the ancient Romans, and what effects, if any, do they continue to have on the modern world?*

The Romans left a remarkable legacy to their successors. They excelled in the art of government and created a workable and enduring world-state that brought peace and order to extensive lands on three continents. For a time during the empire, probably one-third of the world's population owed allegiance to the Roman superpower. In addition to their skills in administration, the formulation and application of law, and their gifts as architects and engineers, Roman achievements in the arts, literature, philosophy, and religious thought were also greatly influential on the peoples and cultures that were the heir of their accomplishments.

Evolution of Roman Law

Of the many contributions made by the Romans in government, Roman law is one of the most significant. Roman law evolved slowly over a period of about a thousand years. At first, as in all early societies, the law was unwritten custom, handed down from the remote past, and harsh in its judgments. As noted earlier, in the fifth century B.C.E. this law was put in writing in the Code of the Twelve Tables, as the result of plebeian demand. During the remainder of the Republic, the body of Roman law (*jus civile,* "law of the citizen") was enlarged by legislation passed by the Senate and the assembly and by judicial interpretation of existing law to meet new conditions. By the second century C.E. the emperor had become the sole source of law, a responsibility he entrusted to scholars "skilled in the law" *(jurisprudentes).* These scholars were loyal to the principle of equity ("Follow the beneficial interpretation"; "The letter of the law is the height of injustice") and to Stoic philosophy with its concept of a "law of nature" *(jus naturale)* common to all people and obtainable by human reason. As a result, the absolute power of the Roman father over the family was weakened, women gained control over their property, and the principle that an accused person was innocent until proven guilty was established. Finally, in the sixth century C.E. the enormous bulk of Roman law from all sources was codified and so preserved for the future.

Roman Engineering and Architecture

Always at the hub of the sprawling empire was Rome, with close to a million inhabitants by the early days of the empire. Augustus boasted that he had found a city of brick and had left it one of marble. Nonetheless, Rome presented a great contrast of magnificence and slums, of splendid public buildings and poorly constructed tenements, which often collapsed or caught fire.

The empire's needs required a communication system of paved roads and bridges as well as huge public buildings and aqueducts. As road builders, the Romans surpassed all previous peoples. Constructed of layers of stone and gravel according to sound engineering principles, their roads were planned for the use of armies and messengers and were kept in constant repair. The earliest and best-known main Roman highway was the Appian Way. Running from Rome to the Bay of Naples, it was built about 300 B.C.E. to facilitate Rome's expansion southward. It has been said that the speed of travel possible on Roman highways was not surpassed until the early nineteenth century. In designing their bridges and aqueducts, the Romans placed a series of stone arches next to one another to provide mutual support. At times several tiers of arches were used, one above the other. Fourteen aqueducts, stretching a total of 265 miles, supplied some 50 gallons of water daily for each inhabitant of Rome.

At first the Romans copied Etruscan architectural models, but later they combined basic Greek elements with distinctly Roman innovations. By using concrete—a Roman invention—faced with brick or stone, they developed new methods for enclosing space. The Greeks' static post-and-lintel system was replaced by the more dynamic techniques of vaulting derived from the arch, also borrowed from the Etruscans.

Heavy concrete barrel vaults, cross (or groin) vaults, and domes—all so solid that they exerted no sidewise thrust—made possible the vast interiors that distinguish Roman architecture. The barrel vault was essentially a series of connected arches resembling a tunnel, and the cross vault consisted of two barrel vaults intersecting at right angles. The largest Roman domed structure is the Pantheon, the oldest massive roofed building in the world that is still intact. As its name indicates, it was dedicated to "all the gods" by the emperor Hadrian as a symbol of the union of Greeks and Romans on equal terms. The great dome rests on thick round walls of poured concrete with no window openings to weaken them. The only light enters through a great hole, 30 feet wide, at the top of the dome. The size of the dome remained unsurpassed until the twentieth century.

The Interior of the Pantheon, Rome

The typical Roman **basilica,** which served as a social and commercial center and as a law court, was not domed or vaulted. It was a rectangular structure with a light wooden ceiling held up by rows of columns that divided the interior into a central **nave** and side aisles. The roof over the nave was raised to admit light. The Roman basilica would eventually evolve into the Christian church.

Roman buildings were built to last, and their size, grandeur, and decorative richness aptly symbolized the proud imperial spirit of Rome. Whereas the Greeks designed the temple, theater, and stadium, the Romans contributed the triumphal arch, bath, basilica, amphitheater, and multistoried apartment house. Perhaps the most famous Roman building is the Colosseum, a huge amphitheater about 1/4 mile in circumference and with a seating capacity of about 45,000. On the exterior, its arches are decorated with Doric, Ionic, and Corinthian columns.

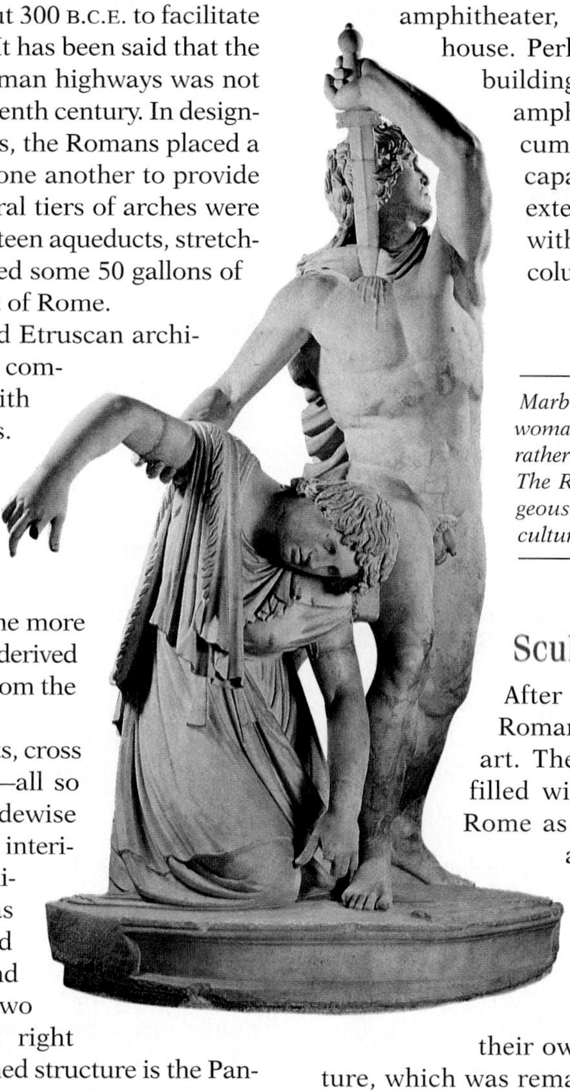

Marble representation of a dying Gallic woman and her husband committing suicide rather than be taken prisoner by the Romans. The Romans regarded the Gauls as courageous but unsophisticated in politics and culture.

Sculpture and Painting

After the conquest of Greece, many Romans acquired a passion for Greek art. The homes of the wealthy were filled with statues, either brought to Rome as plunder or copied in Greece and shipped to Rome in great number.

Although strongly influenced by Etruscan and Greek models, the Romans developed a distinctive sculpture of their own, particularly portrait sculpture, which was remarkably realistic. Their skill in

basilica—Originally a secular public building in ancient Rome, typically a large rectangular structure with an open hall and a raised platform at one or both ends. "Basilica" is also a title of honor given to a Roman Catholic or Greek Orthodox church distinguished by its antiquity or its role as an international center of worship.

nave—Main part of a Christian church, extending from the entrance (the narthex) to the transept or chancel (area around the altar). In a basilican church (see basilica), which has side aisles, nave refers only to the central section.

portraiture probably originated in the early practice of making and preserving wax images of the heads of important deceased family members. During the Principate, portraiture and relief sculpture tended to idealize the likenesses of the emperors. The Romans developed a great number of decorative motifs, such as cupids, garlands of flowers, and scrolls of various patterns, which are still used today.

What little Roman painting has been preserved clearly reflects the influence of Hellenistic Greek models. The Romans were particularly skilled in producing floor mosaics—often copies of Hellenistic paintings—and in painting frescoes. The frescoes still to be seen in Pompeii and elsewhere show that the artists drew objects in clear though idealized perspective.

Literary Rome

In literature as in art, the Romans originally turned to the Greeks for their models. Roman epic, dramatic, and lyric poetry forms were usually written in conscious imitation of the Greek masterpieces. Although first conforming to Greek examples and standards, Latin prose and poetry developed an originality and substance that ensure its value as one of the world's great literatures. Its influence was extremely strong on medieval and Renaissance literary efforts, and it continues even now on western literary themes and styles.

The Golden and Silver Ages of Latin Literature, c. 100 B.C.E.–138 C.E.

106–43 B.C.E.	Cicero: Orations and letters
c. 87–54 B.C.E.	Catullus: Poems and epigrams
c. 99–55 B.C.E.	Lucretius: Philosophical poem *On the Nature of Things*
70–19 B.C.E.	Virgil: Epic poem *Aeneid*
65–8 B.C.E.	Horace: Poems
43 B.C.E.–17 C.E.	Ovid: *The Art of Love; Metamorphoses*
59 B.C.E.–17 C.E.	Livy: *History of Rome*
c. 55 B.C.E.–117 C.E.	Tacitus: *Annals, Histories, Agricula*
c. 50 B.C.E.–127 C.E.	Juvenal: *Satires*
c. 46–c. 126 C.E.	Plutarch: *Parallel Lives*

Formal Latin literature did not begin until the mid-third century B.C.E. when a Greek slave named Livius Andronicus translated Homer's *Odyssey* and several Greek plays into Latin. By the end of that century the first of a series of Latin epics dealing with Rome's past was composed. Only a few fragments have survived.

The oldest examples of Latin literature to survive intact are the 21 comedies of Plautus (c. 254–184 B.C.E.), which were adapted from Hellenistic Greek originals but with many Roman allusions, colloquialisms, and customs added. Plautus's comedies are bawdy and vigorously humorous, and their rollicking plots of illicit love and character portraits reveal the level of culture and taste in early Rome. The works of Plautus suggest many of the types that modern comedy has assumed, including farce, burlesque, and comedy of manners.

Literature of the Late Republic and Empire

Latin literature came of age in the first century B.C.E., when an outpouring of intellectual effort coincided with the last years of the Republic. This era is often called the Ciceronian period because of the stature and lasting influence of Marcus Tullius Cicero (106–43 B.C.E.), one of the greatest masters of Latin prose and an outstanding intellectual force in Roman history.

Acclaimed as the greatest orator of his day, Cicero found time during his busy public life to write extensively on philosophy, political theory, and rhetoric. Some 900 of his letters survive. Together with 58 speeches, they give us insight into Cicero's personality as well as life in the late Republic. Cicero also made a rich contribution by passing on to the Romans and to later ages much of Greek thought—especially that of Plato and the Stoics—and at the same time interpreting philosophical concepts from the standpoint of a Roman intellectual and practical man of affairs.

Two notable poets of the Ciceronian period were Catullus (Kah-TUHL-luhs) and Lucretius (loo-KREE-shuhs). Catullus (c. 87–54 B.C.E.) was a socially active young man who wrote highly personal lyric poetry. His best-known poems are addressed to "Lesbia," an unprincipled noblewoman ten years older than he, with whom he carried on a passionate affair. Catullus's contemporary Lucretius (c. 99–55 B.C.E.) found in the philosophy of Epicurus (e-pee-KEU-ruhs) an antidote to his profound disillusionment with his fellow citizens, whom he criticized for their lack of morals and obsession for wealth and sensual pleasures.

Augustus provided the Roman world with a stability and confidence that encouraged a further outpouring of literary creativity. The literature of the Augustan Age was notable particularly for its poetry. Virgil (70–19 B.C.E.) is considered the greatest of all Roman poets. His masterpiece, the great epic poem called the *Aeneid* (ay-NEE-id), glorified the work of Augustus and emphasized Rome's destiny to conquer and rule the world. Using Homer's *Iliad* and *Odyssey* as his models, Virgil recounted the fortunes of Aeneas, the legendary founder of the Latin people, who came from Troy to Italy to fulfill his destiny.

As the most noted poet after Vergil, Horace (65–8 B.C.E.) often praised the work of Augustus and the emperor's great mission. But most of Horace's poetry is concerned with everyday human interests and moods, and succeeding generations up to the present have been attracted by his serene outlook on life.

Quite a different sort of poet was Ovid (43 B.C.E.–17 C.E.). His preference for themes of sensual love in his *Art of Love* and other poems caused Augustus to exile him from Rome. But Ovid was also a first-rate storyteller, and it is largely through his *Metamorphoses*, a witty verse collection of Greek stories about the life of the gods—not neglecting their love lives—that classical mythology was transmitted to the modern world.

The literature of the later empire, especially the period between the deaths of Augustus and Hadrian (14–138 C.E.), substituted a more critical and negative spirit for the patriotism and optimism of the Augustan Age. Despite a great emphasis on artificial stylistic devices, the period was memorable for the moral emphasis of much of its literature, seen in the historical works of Tacitus and Plutarch, the philosophical works of Seneca, and especially the poetry of Juvenal (c. 50 B.C.E.–127 C.E.), who has been called one of the greatest satiric poets, who attacked the shortcomings of Roman society and its overwhelming concern for material gain and sensual pleasures.

DOCUMENT
Juvenal, *Satires*

The Writing of History

Two Roman historians produced notable works of lasting significance during the Augustan age and the early empire. The first, Livy (59 B.C.E.–17 C.E.), was a contemporary of Vergil. His immense *History of Rome*, like the *Aeneid*, is of epic proportions and glorifies Rome's conquests and ancestral greatness. By assembling the legends and traditions of early Roman history and folding them into a continuous narrative, Livy, like Vergil, intended to advance Augustus's program of moral and social regeneration. He praised the virtues of the ancient Romans and sought to draw moral lessons from an idealized past.

Tacitus (55–117 C.E.), like his contemporary Juvenal, was concerned with the declining morality of both the Roman nobility and common citizens. In his *Germania* he contrasted the life of the idealized, simple Germanic tribes with the corrupt and immoral existence of the Roman upper classes. In the *Annals* and *Histories* he used his vivid, succinct prose to depict the shortcomings of the emperors and their courts from the death of Augustus to 96 C.E. Tacitus idealized the earlier Republic, and because he viewed the emperors as tyrants, he could not do justice to the positive contributions of imperial government.

The most famous Greek author in the empire was Plutarch (c. 46–c. 126 C.E.). He lectured on philosophy in Rome before retiring to his small hometown to pursue research on the outstanding figures in Roman and Greek history in order to discover what qualities make people great or unworthy. His *Parallel Lives*, containing 46 biographies of famous Greeks and Romans arranged in pairs for the purpose of comparison, is one of the great readable classics of world literature. Because many of the sources Plutarch used have been lost, his *Lives* is a treasure house of valuable information for the historian.

Religion and Philosophy

The turmoil of the late Republic helped erode the traditions, values, and religion of earlier Rome. For spiritual satisfaction and salvation, many Romans turned increasingly to the mystery cults of Greece (see Chapter 4) or to the Near East. Among the latter were Cybele, the Great Mother, and the Egyptian goddess Isis, who attracted the greatest number of women followers. A faithful mother herself, she extended a mother's arms to the weary of this world.

But the more intellectually sophisticated of Romans turned to Greek philosophy, particularly Epicureanism and Stoicism, for meaning. As young men, both Vergil and Horace embraced Epicureanism, but Lucretius became the most important Roman interpreter of this philosophy. In *On the Nature of Things*, Lucretius followed Epicurus in basing his explanation of the "nature of things" on materialism and atomism. He called on people to free themselves from the fear of death—which was drawing them to the emotional mystery religions of Greece and the East—since souls, like bodies, are composed of atoms that fall apart when death comes. Lucretius urged his readers to seek pleasure in the study of philosophy and not from material gain or such sensual excitements as love.

More in line with Roman taste, especially in the days of the empire, was Stoicism. The emphasis of Roman Stoicism was on living a just life, constancy to duty, courage in adversity, and service to humanity. Stoic influence had a humanizing effect on Roman law by introducing such concepts as the law of nature and the brotherhood of all, including slaves. The law of nature, as defined by Cicero, was an eternal truth that ordered all the rational thought upon which human law must be based.

One of the outstanding Roman Stoics was Seneca (4 B.C.E.–65 C.E.), Nero's tutor and a writer of moral essays and tragedies. He was regarded with high favor by the leaders of the early Christian church, for his Stoicism, like that of the ex-slave Epictetus (eh-pik-TEE-tuhs) (d. 135 C.E.) and the emperor Marcus Aurelius, had the appearance of a religious creed. He stressed an all-wise Providence, or God, and believed that each person possessed a spark of the divine.

Science in the Roman Empire

The Romans were accomplished at putting the findings of Hellenistic science to practical use, and they became extremely skilled in engineering, applied medicine, and public health. The Romans pioneered in public health service and developed the extensive practice of *hydrotherapy,* the use of mineral baths for healing. Beginning in the early empire, doctors were employed in infirmaries where soldiers, officials, and the poor could obtain free medical care. Great aqueducts and admirable drainage systems also indicate Roman concern for public health.

Characteristic of their utilitarian approach to science was their interest in amassing large encyclopedias. The most important of these was the *Natural History,* compiled by Pliny (PLI-nee) the Elder (23–79 C.E), an enthusiastic collector of all kinds of scientific odds and ends. In writing his massive work, Pliny is reputed to have read more than 2000 books. The result is an intriguing mixture of fact and fable thrown together with scarcely any method of classification. Nevertheless, it was the most widely read work on science during the empire and the early medieval period in Europe.

Two of the last great scientific minds of the ancient world were two Greeks, Claudius Ptolemy and Galen, both of whom lived in the second century C.E., an era succeeding the greatness of Hellenic civilization and the growing dominance of Rome. Ptolemy resided at Alexandria, where he became celebrated as a geographer, astronomer, and mathematician. His maps show a comparatively accurate knowledge of a broad section of the known world. But he exaggerated the size of Asia, an error that influenced Columbus to underestimate the width of the Atlantic and to set sail from Spain in search of Asia. His work on astronomy, usually called the *Almagest* ("The Great Work") from the title of the Arabic translation, presented the geocentric (earth-centered) view of the universe that prevailed until the sixteenth century. In mathematics, Ptolemy's work in improving and developing trigonometry became the basis for modern knowledge of the subject.

Galen, born in Pergamum, in Asia Minor, was a physician for a school of gladiators. His fame spread, and he was called to Rome, where he became physician to the emperor Marcus Aurelius. Galen was responsible for notable advances in physiology and anatomy; for example, he was the first to explain the mechanism of respiration. Forbidden by the Roman government to dissect human bodies, Galen experimented with animals and demonstrated that an excised heart can continue to beat outside the body and that injuries to one side of the brain produce effects in the opposite side of the body. Galen's medical encyclopedia, in which he summarized the medical knowledge of antiquity, remained the standard authority until the sixteenth century.

CONCLUSION

The story of Rome's rise from a collection of insignificant and unsophisticated villages along the banks of the Tiber to the mighty capital of an empire that included most of western Europe, the Mediterranean region, and the Near East will always remain one of the most fascinating stories in world history. Through the creation of a unified and cosmopolitan empire, the heritage of earlier near Eastern and Greek cultures was preserved, synthesized, and disseminated—and of course the Romans made significant original contributions of their own. They excelled in political theory, governmental administration, and jurisprudence. Roman military might, conquest, and pacification also enabled the growth and development of trade and commerce throughout the Mediterranean and beyond. The security of the empire, and its vast network of roads, fostered a thriving exchange of ideas as well as tangible goods. The growth and triumph of the Christian religion in the West was due in large part to the material benefits provided by the empire's infrastructure, along with the Roman capacity to adapt and refine the innovations of others.

Rome's greatest achievement was perhaps the establishment of peace and prosperity over a vast area for long periods under a stable and acceptable government. The long-enduring empire and its success in uniting a great variety of cultures and peoples under one system of government had a lasting effect on nations and peoples that came after the fall of the empire in western Europe. The cosmopolitan nature of the Roman experience and Rome's long lasting success in bringing unity and peace for centuries, and to a vast amount of territory and diverse peoples, might also serve as an example that such achievements are not impossible accomplishments.

Suggestions for Web Browsing

You can obtain more information about topics included in this chapter at the websites listed below. See also the companion website that accompanies this text, **www.ablongman.com/brummett**, which contains an online study guide and additional resources.

Museums of the Vatican: Gregorian Etruscan Museum
http://www.christusrex.org/www1/vaticano/ET1-Etrusco.html
http://www.christusrex.org/www1/vaticano/ET2-Etrusco.html

Two sites within the extensive pages of the Museums of the Vatican offer numerous images from the Etruscan period.

Timeline
http://www.exovedate.com/ancient_timeline_one.html

The history of ancient Rome, with a chronological index and links to Internet resources. Emphasis is placed on the roles of women in ancient times.

Roman Empire
http://library.advanced.org/10805/rome/html

The history of the empire is illustrated through maps and timelines. Examinations of the sources of our knowledge through Roman writers is emphasized. An extensive history of ancient Rome.

Online Encyclopedia of the Roman Empire
http://www.roman-emperors.org/

A massive site emphasizing the study of Roman history through coins and through maps of the empire.

Pompeii Forum Project
http://pompeii.virginia.edu/forummap.html

Constructed by historians and archaeologists from the University of Virginia, this site examines ancient Pompeii through a variety of photographs.

Vesuvius
http://volcano.und.nodak.edu/vwdocs/volc_images/img_vesuvius.html

A beautiful exploration of Mount Vesuvius in ancient Rome and as it appears today. Speculation on the next eruption as well.

Women's Life in Greece and Rome
http://www.stoa.org/diotima/anthology/wlgr/

Details about the private life and legal status of women, in addition to biographies of prominent women of ancient Rome.

Roman Art and Architecture
http://harpy.uccs.edu/roman/html/romarch.html

A collection of images of Roman architecture.

Literature and Film

Recommended historical novels dealing with Republican and Imperial Rome are a continuing series of mystery novels set in late Republican Rome by Steven Saylor, the most recent of which is *The Judgment of Caesar* (St. Martin's Press, 2004); Thornton Wilder, *The Ides of March* (Avon, 1975); John Williams, *Augustus* (Penguin, 1979); Robert Graves, *I Claudius* (Vintage, 1977); Marguerite Yourcenar, *Memoirs of Hadrian* (Modern Library, 1984); Lindsey Davis, *Time to Depart* (Warner, 1995); and a continuing series of novels dealing with the Roman Republic by Colleen McCullough, beginning with *The First Man in Rome* (Morrow, 1990).

A number of excellent videos available deal with Roman and early Christian themes. Outstanding Hollywood movies, spectacular for their recreations of ancient scenes, are *Ben Hur* (1959), *Spartacus* (1960), and most recently *Gladiator* (2000). More scholarly in content are *Ancient Rome: Story of an Empire* (1998; 4 tapes); *Rome: The Power and the Glory* (2001; Questar); *Catacombs of Rome* (2001; A&E Home Video); and *Rome's Lost Harbor* (2000, A&E Home Video), an excellent account of ancient Ostia. *From Jesus to Christ: The First Christians* (1998; 4 tapes, PBS Home Video) is a very good account of the beginnings of the religion. Finally, *I, Claudius* (1996; 7 tapes, BBC Production) is a classic presentation of the novel by Robert Graves.

Suggestions for Reading

H. H. Scullard, *A History of the Roman World, 753–146 B.C.*, 5th edition (Methuen, 1980); and Michael Grant, *History of Rome* (Scribner, 1979), are highly recommended general historical accounts. Also an excellent general study is Max Cary and Howard H. Scullard, *A History of Rome: Down to the Reign of Constantine*, 3rd ed. (St. Martin's Press, 1976). Ellen Macnamara, *The Etruscans* (Cambridge, 1991), is an informative study of these intriguing people. Three valuable studies of Roman society and morals are Keith Bradley, *Slavery and Society at Rome* (Cambridge University Press, 1994); Florence Dupont, *Daily Life in Ancient Rome* (Oxford University Press, 1992); and Roland Auguet, *Cruelty and Civilization: The Roman Games* (Routledge, 1994). Tom Holland, *Rubicon: The Last Years of the Roman Republic* (Doubleday, 2003) is an outstanding study of the fall of the Republic and Julius Caesar.

For the beginnings of Christianity see J. H. Hexter, *The Judeo-Christian Tradition*, 2nd ed. (Yale University Press, 1995), a brief but valuable survey; Rodney Stark, *The Rise of Christianity* (HarperCollins, 1996); and Richard E. Rubenstein, *When Jesus Became God: The Struggle to Define Christianity during the Last Days of Rome* (Harvest Books, 2000). For the later Roman Empire see Averil Cameron, *The Later Roman Empire: A.D. 284–430* (Harvard University Press, 1993), and Peter Brown, *The Making of Late Antiquity* (Harvard University Press, 1978).

CHAPTER 6

Byzantium and the Orthodox World

Byzantium, Eastern Europe, and Russia, 325–1500

CHAPTER CONTENTS

300 C.E.

325 Constantine the Great establishes his capitol in Constantinople (city dedicated May 11, 330)

361–363 Reign of Julian the Apostate

500

527–565 Reign of Justinian

c. 590 Slavic invasions begin

610–641 Heraclius saves Constantinople, defeats Persians

674–678 Arab sieges of Constantinople

700

700–1014 First Bulgarian Empire

797–802 Reign of Empress Irene

842–1071 Golden Age of Byzantium

900

900 Serbian Conversion to Christianity

988 Russian Conversion to Christianity

1071 Byzantine defeat at Manzikert

1096 First Crusade

1100

1204 Fourth Crusade; Crusaders sack Constantinople; Byzantine state disappears until 1261

1354 Turks begin to settle in Europe

1389 Battle of Kosovo

1400

1453 Fall of Constantinople, end of East Roman Empire

1462–1505 Reign of Ivan III, the Great

At its height the Roman Empire controlled the Mediterranean world, a zone that extended from the Straits of Gibraltar on the Atlantic Ocean to the Red Sea and the Black Sea. Roman bureaucrats ran a centralized administration that dictated details as small as mosaic patterns on floors in cities as distant as the present-day Constanta, Romania, and Colchester, England. Roman military leaders carried on battles in present-day Persia and along the Danube.

In the power vacuum that followed in the wake of Rome's decline, three civilizations, each sharing common Judeo-Christian roots, emerged to occupy the Mediterranean world. The civilization of western Europe, initially the weakest and most fragmented of the three civilizations, developed under the creative tension between the religious center at Rome and the political structures, such as France, north of the Alps (see Chapter 9). The Islamic world dominated the region in southwest Asia and North Africa (see Chapter 7). The Byzantine Empire, dominating the northwestern part of the Mediterranean world, carried on and modified the Roman traditions, in time transmitting a political and civilizational legacy to the peoples of the Balkans and Russia—the Orthodox world.

In this chapter we will consider the origins and development of the Orthodox world, from the founding of the Eastern Roman capitol at Constantinople—the Second Rome—to the rise of the Russian state at Moscow, the city that claimed the title of the Third Rome after the Ottoman Turks took Constantinople in 1453. When the *tsar* (the Russian word for caesar) Ivan III proclaimed Moscow to be the arena for the playing out of God's divine plan, the end of the world, and the second coming of Christ, he was embracing ideas established first in the Byzantine Empire.

BYZANTIUM: THE LATIN PHASE, 325–610

■ *Why did the East Roman—and not the West—part of the Empire survive the Germanic invasions in the two centuries after 325?*

In his wide-ranging reforms, the Roman emperor Diocletian (die-oh-KLEE-shun; r. 285–305) had wanted to bring order to the governing of the empire. To that end he imposed a new autocratic model for the emperor. He also wanted to make the transfer of power more systematic by dividing up the empire into eastern and western parts, governed by two caesars and two ***augusti.*** In theory, as each *augustus* would retire, the caesar-in-waiting would advance to take his place. Instead of resolving the problems of civil wars and regime change, Diocletian's solution led to yet another conflict, this one over control of the western half of the empire to be decided in a conflict between Maxentius and Constantine (306–337) at the battle of the Milvian Bridge in 312.

Constantine and Constantinople

Constantine's biographers assert that during the night before the battle, Constantine looked to the sky and saw a cross with the words, *"In hoc signo vinces"* ("By this, conquer") written on it. The next day, after Christ is said to have appeared in his dreams, Constantine led his troops to victory, raising the cross as his symbol. Thereafter he made an alliance with the Christians that turned a minority, though active, sect into a state religion.

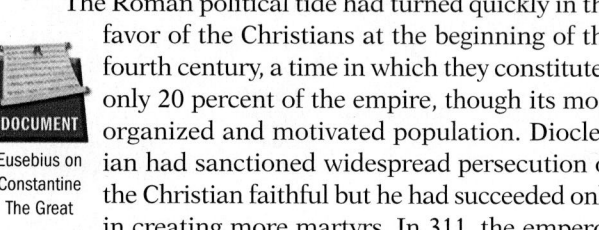

DOCUMENT
Eusebius on Constantine The Great

The Roman political tide had turned quickly in the favor of the Christians at the beginning of the fourth century, a time in which they constituted only 20 percent of the empire, though its most organized and motivated population. Diocletian had sanctioned widespread persecution of the Christian faithful but he had succeeded only in creating more martyrs. In 311, the emperor Galerius recognized that persecution had failed to stop the growth of Christianity and issued an edict of toleration, making Christianity a legal religion in the East. Two years later, Constantine and Licinius granted Christians freedom of worship throughout the empire by issuing, in 313, the **Edict of Milan.**

In 325, a number of factors convinced Constantine to move his capitol to the site of the old Greek city of Byzantium, including his new affiliation with the Christians (who were then primarily concentrated in the East), the political and defensive disadvantages of Rome, and the wealth of the eastern part of the empire. Constantine named the city after himself and dedicated it as the first Christian city on May 11, 330. He chose a site on the frontier of Europe and Asia dominating the waterway connecting the Mediterranean and Black Seas and protected on three sides by cliffs. The emperor and his successors fortified the fourth side with an impenetrable three-wall network. In the first two centuries, Visigoths, Huns, and Ostrogoths unsuccessfully threatened the city. In the seventh, eighth, and ninth centuries first Persians, then Arab forces, and finally Bulgarians besieged but failed to take Constantinople. The fortress city withstood all assaults until the Fourth Crusade in 1204. The East Roman Empire survived more 1000 years because of the security and wealth provided by Constantinople's setting.

Constantine set out enthusiastically to defend his new faith. At the Council of Nicaea, a gathering of religious leaders held to combat the **Arian heresy,** Constantine declared himself to be the "thirteenth apostle." By combining the function of head of church with that of head of state, Constantine established **caesaropapism,** a system which bestowed on the Byzantine ruler the power to impose his control over all aspects of life in his realm, both spiritual and temporal. Despite his commitment to the church, Constantine waited until just before his death to be baptized. All of his successors but one would be Christian.

Aside from his embrace and use of Christianity, Constantine continued the basic trend of Diocletian's economic and social policies. Upon his death in 337, his three sons took power as coemperors. They, in the tradition of the late Roman Empire, fell into dispute with each other until one, Constantius, emerged victorious. As they built on their father's advances, the successors faced challenges not only from the Germans, but also from the Persians. The East Romans alternately fought with and bribed the Persians, who would remain a continual threat to the East until the rise of Islam.

---

augusti—Plural of *augustus,* the title granted the first Roman emperor by the Senate in 27 B.C.E. The title passed to all of his successors. Under Diocletian's plan, the empire would be split into eastern and western parts, governed by two caesars and two *augusti.*

Edict of Milan—Constantine and Licinius in 313 granted Christians the freedom openly to worship their religion throughout the Roman Empire.

Arian heresy—The theological doctrine that affirmed that Christ demonstrably, by his suffering on the cross, was not of the same substance as God the father and therefore was less than his father.

caesaropapism—The political system in which the ruler controls all aspects of life in his realm, both secular and spiritual—he is both caesar and pope.

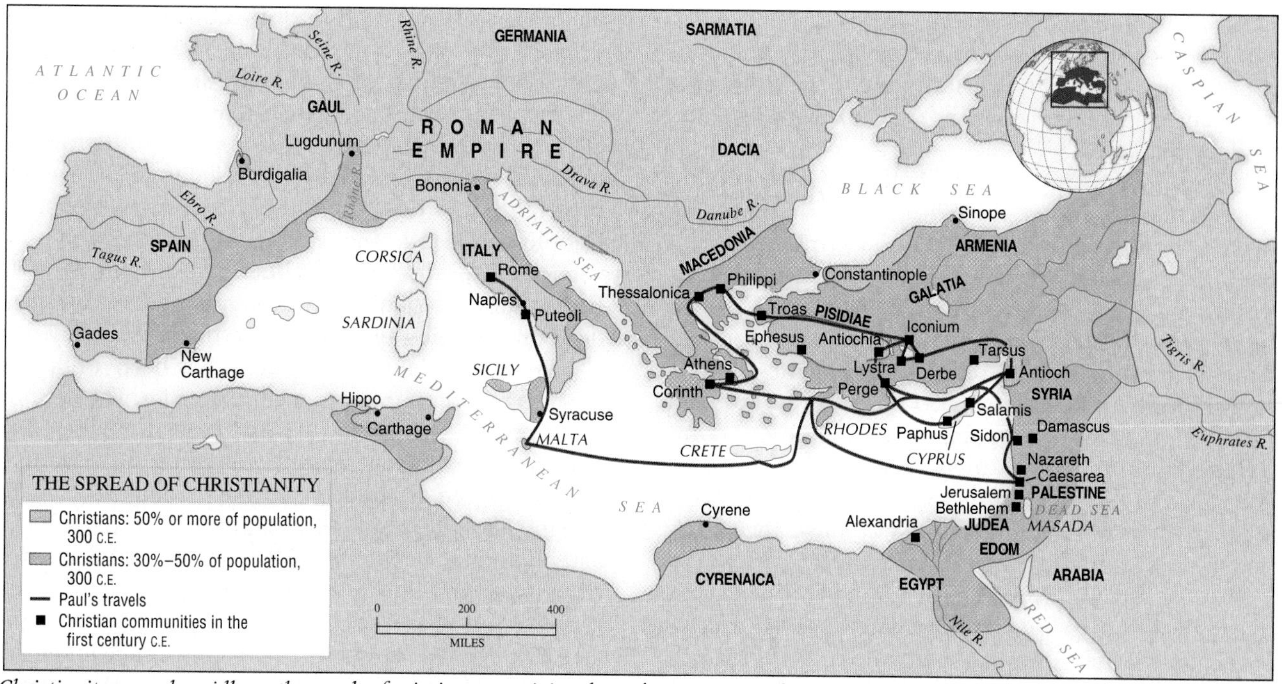

Christianity spread rapidly as the result of missionary activity along the Roman road system. The first major theological centers were Alexandria, Antioch, Ephesus, and Corinth.

This colossal head of Constantine captures the emperor's vision of himself as a strong man in control.

Julian: The Last Pagan

By aligning himself with Christianity, transferring his capitol to Constantinople, and installing a new form of government, Constantine began the Roman world's transition from a pagan to a Christian world. But, in going from Rome to the East, Constantine moved from the Latin world—centered around law, government, and public works—to the Greek, more specifically the pagan, Hellenistic world, home of the synthesis constructed by Alexander the Great that combined grandeur, polytheistic mystery cults, and Hellenic civilization. As the role of the Christian church grew between Constantine and Theodosius, the pagan world made some counterattacks.

The most prominent attempt to turn back the Christian tide was that made by Julian, called the **Apostate** (r. 361–363). Julian, a nephew of Constantine, saw three of his brothers killed by their uncles during the succession crisis after 337. Because of his age he was spared and sent into exile in the far-off city of Cappadocia. There, he received a classical Greek education, along with a thorough grounding in the study of Christianity. Even though he was baptized, he remained true to pagan Greek literature and not the Christian catechism. In 347, at the age of sixteen, he was allowed to come back to Constantinople,

Apostate—A person who abandons or renounces his religion.

where he continued his studies in Greek philosophy. In 351, he secretly renounced Christianity and continued the pursuit of **Neo-Platonism.** Four years later he went to Athens, where he was initiated into the Eleusinian cults.

In 357 Julian set out to do battle in Gaul, winning several battles along the Rhine and—at the same time—the love and loyalty of his troops, who proclaimed him to be the new Augustus. In 360 he led his forces back to Constantinople, ready to launch a revolt. Constantius, the emperor, died, however, and Julian took power peacefully. Inspired by the example of Marcus Aurelius and Octavian, he set out to be a modest and humane ruler, clearing out corrupt bureaucrats and imposing a just system of taxes. Because he served as emperor only two years, however, his style of government did not make any significant changes in the East Roman system.

Julian saw himself as a divine person, who was descended from the sun god, and carried out his rule as a religious leader. Even though he declared himself to be openly pagan, he advocated a policy of religious tolerance for all, including the anathematized Arians in Alexandria. The longer he ruled, however, the more he became opposed to the Christians, and he began to exclude them from serving in public offices. In the schools he removed Christian teachings and blocked Christians from teaching literature and philosophy. But Julian did not persecute the Christians, and his efforts to revive paganism failed. In 363, he died from wounds suffered in combat with the Persians. The two years of his reign were not enough to turn the Christian tide.

Thereafter the East Roman state resumed its attack on paganism. Theodosius the Great suppressed the Olympic Games in 393. Individual pagans faced attacks by Christian mobs. One well-known victim of this persecution was the philosopher Hypatia of Alexandria, who in 415 was killed by a Christian gang. Justinian made another attack on the 1000-year-old Greek literary and artistic traditions. He gave pagan professors an ultimatum to convert or lose the right to teach. In 528–530, when they refused to convert to Christianity, he closed Plato's Academy along with other schools in Athens. Justinian made the Christian victory complete.

Orthodoxy and Heresies

Continual theological crises occupied most of the 1128 years of the East Roman state. By establishing the precedent of the emperor as the "thirteenth apostle," Constantine gained important support from the church, and the church itself profited by becoming a state church. In a single-centered-society, heresy was not only a religious issue, but—by definition—a political crime as well. Therefore, the East Roman leaders became embroiled in the theological controversies involved in defining Orthodox Christian theology until the eighth century. Thereafter, Rome and Constantinople competed on questions of doctrine and conversions until the **Great Schism** of 1054, which split European Christianity into Roman and Greek Orthodox communities and remains to the present day.

From its origins, Christianity has been a religion that has produced important controversies. The notions of the composition of the **Trinity,** the nature of Christ, and the **Incarnation** are difficult concepts to define, let alone agree on. Added to these theological controversies was the political competition posed by the establishment of the new Christian city of Constantinople, which had no apostolic traditions such as those found at the older centers at Alexandria, Ephesus, Chalcedon, Antioch, and Rome. The head of the Orthodox church in Constantinople, the **Patriarch,** and the head of the Catholic church in Rome, the Pope, were in general accord for the first four centuries as they constructed the basis of Orthodox Christianity through their readings of the scriptures and the deliberations of the first seven ecumenical councils, which are: "assembl[ies] under the presidency of the Emperor, where every inter-communicating church was represented [and which] was the inspired body whose decisions were binding on Christendom."

In the modern, pragmatic age, the arguments over the Trinity, the nature of Christ, and the Incarnation strike secular people as being particularly abstruse and abstract. But these theological differences had important consequences, not only for the East Roman Empire but also for the development of Christianity. The Arian heresy remained strong in the West—especially in Spain—until the eighth century, and made church unity difficult. When the Muslims began their expansion in 632, people believing in **Monophysite,** Nestorian, and other heretical beliefs—especially the

Neo-Platonism—A fusing of Plato's philosophy with Aristotelian, Jewish, and Near-Eastern concepts that led logically to the belief in a universal, perfect One with which the individual soul could commune.

Great Schism—In 1054, the last in a series of breaks between the churches of Rome and Constantinople occurred. After over 950 years the two churches remain separated.

Trinity—The Christian doctrine asserting that the Father (God), the Son (Jesus Christ), and the Holy Spirit exist as a perfect unity in one godhead.

Incarnation—The putting into human form of a spirit or god. In Christianity, the appearance of the son, Jesus Christ, in human form.

Patriarch—The head of the Orthodox Church in Constantinople, or the head of the churches of Alexandria, Antioch, Moscow, and Jerusalem among others.

Monophysite—A person who believes that God the son has one single, divine nature. This is against the Orthodox view that asserts that Christ was perfect God and perfect man.

Document The Ecumenical Councils and Heresies

First Ecumenical Council:
Nicaea I, 325

Attacked the widely followed Arian heresy that asserted Christ was not of the same substance, and therefore less than the father. Instead, affirmed the full divinity of Jesus and of His being of the same substance as God the father.

Produced the creed defining Orthodox Christianity, which, with changes added in the Second Council and in the fifth century is essentially the same as that recited by Christians today. Established the date on which Easter would be celebrated.

Second Ecumenical Council:
Constantinople I, 381

Once again, Arianism condemned.

Defined the nature of the Trinity, affirmed the divinity and equality of the Holy Ghost in the Trinity.

Constantinople recognized as second in status among Christian cities, after Rome.

Third Ecumenical Council:
Ephesus, 431

Declared Mary to be Mother of God and reaffirmed the single nature of Christ, in opposition to the Nestorian view of the two natures—human and divine—and two persons of Christ, with the implied, reduced role of the Virgin Mary.

Position of Constantinople within the hierarchy of the Church strengthened.

Fourth Ecumenical Council:
Chalcedon, 451

Established the Orthodox definition of Christ as having two natures (divine and human) coexisting in one person—perfect God and perfect man, and not one single, divine nature as advanced by the Monophysites living in the east of the empire.

Fifth Ecumenical Council:
Constantinople II, 553

Another unsuccessful attempt to reconcile the Nestorian and Monophysite beliefs and bring unity to the empire.

Sixth Ecumenical Council:
Constantinople III, 680

In an attempt to heal the divisions within the empire over the Christological controversies, the doctrine of Monotheletism had emerged. In an attempt to bridge the gap between those affirming that Christ had one single, divine nature and the Orthodox position of the two natures of Christ, Monotheletism split the difference and said that Christ had one nature, but that His will was divine-human. This approach was popular in the East, but was found to be heretical at this council.

Seventh Ecumenical Council:
Nicaea II, 787

Allowed and encouraged the use of holy images in churches, thus temporarily ending the iconoclastic crisis.

Taken from Steven Runciman, *Byzantine Civilization* (Cleveland and New York: World Publishing Company, 1961), *The Cambridge Medieval History*, Vol. IV, pts. 1 and 2, (Cambridge: Cambridge University Press, 1966).

Copts in Egypt and the Syrians—accepted and even welcomed the invaders, because Islam was more tolerant to them than were the Orthodox Christians. Deeply held differences over the nature of Christ produced substantial political and diplomatic impacts.

The German Challenges

As we saw in Chapter 5, after the end of the first century, the Roman Empire faced the continual pressure of the German migrations. The Rhine-Danube frontier held for the better part of the second century C.E., but the pressure of these migrations, themselves part of a larger, 1000-year-long movement that saw people continually moving to the West from the Chinese frontier to the Atlantic, eventually caused the Rhine-Danube defensive perimeter to fall apart. During the fifth century the western part of the empire became a region dominated by the various German tribes.

The Eastern Roman capitol at Constantinople also found itself on the path of these huge and continuous population movements. Toward the end of the fourth century the Huns, a nomadic tribe of skilled horseman, left Central Asia and began moving to the West. They conquered the Ostrogoths and forced the terrified Visigoths to flee to the West. The Visigoths petitioned the Romans to allow them to settle as allies in the empire. Permission was granted in 376, and the entire tribe crossed the Danube into Roman territory. They were badly treated by corrupt Roman officials, and soon they revolted. The Emperor Valens led his forces from the safe haven of the walls of Constantinople in 378 and tried to stop them at the battle of Adrianople. Aided by the use of the stirrup and long, slashing swords, Visigoth cavalry slaughtered both the emperor and his army. This ended what was left of the Roman army's prestige. The Visigoths soon moved on to the West into Italy, and the eastern capital recovered behind its impenetrable walls. With the exception of Valens's defeat, the Germanic tribes never seriously threatened Constantinople.

Valens' successor, the Spaniard Theodosius (later called "The Great"), pacified the Visigoths and the Ostrogoths who came after them, converting a hostile invasion into a peaceful one. He agreed to make Christianity the official religion of the empire, sought to suppress other beliefs and religions, and advocated conversion of the Jews. After his death, the western portion of the Empire went into a rapid decline, until its final "fall" in 476.

East Rome, however, became stronger, maintaining its defenses against the waves of migration, codifying its laws, and becoming wealthier. Those fortunate enough to live in Constantinople enjoyed the highest standard of living in medieval Europe. The city became a world trade center by the end of the fifth century and enjoyed the continuous use of a money economy in contrast to the barter system found in western Europe. The Byzantines' wealth and taxes supported a strong military force and financed an effective government. The city built excellent sewage and water systems that permitted an increased life span. Food was abundant, with grain from Egypt and Anatolia and fish from the Aegean. Constantinople could feed as many as 1 million people when it was difficult to find a city in Europe able to sustain more than 50,000. Unlike Rome, Constantinople had several industries producing luxury goods, military supplies, hardware, and textiles. Until Justinian's reign (r. 527–565), all raw silk had been imported from China, but after

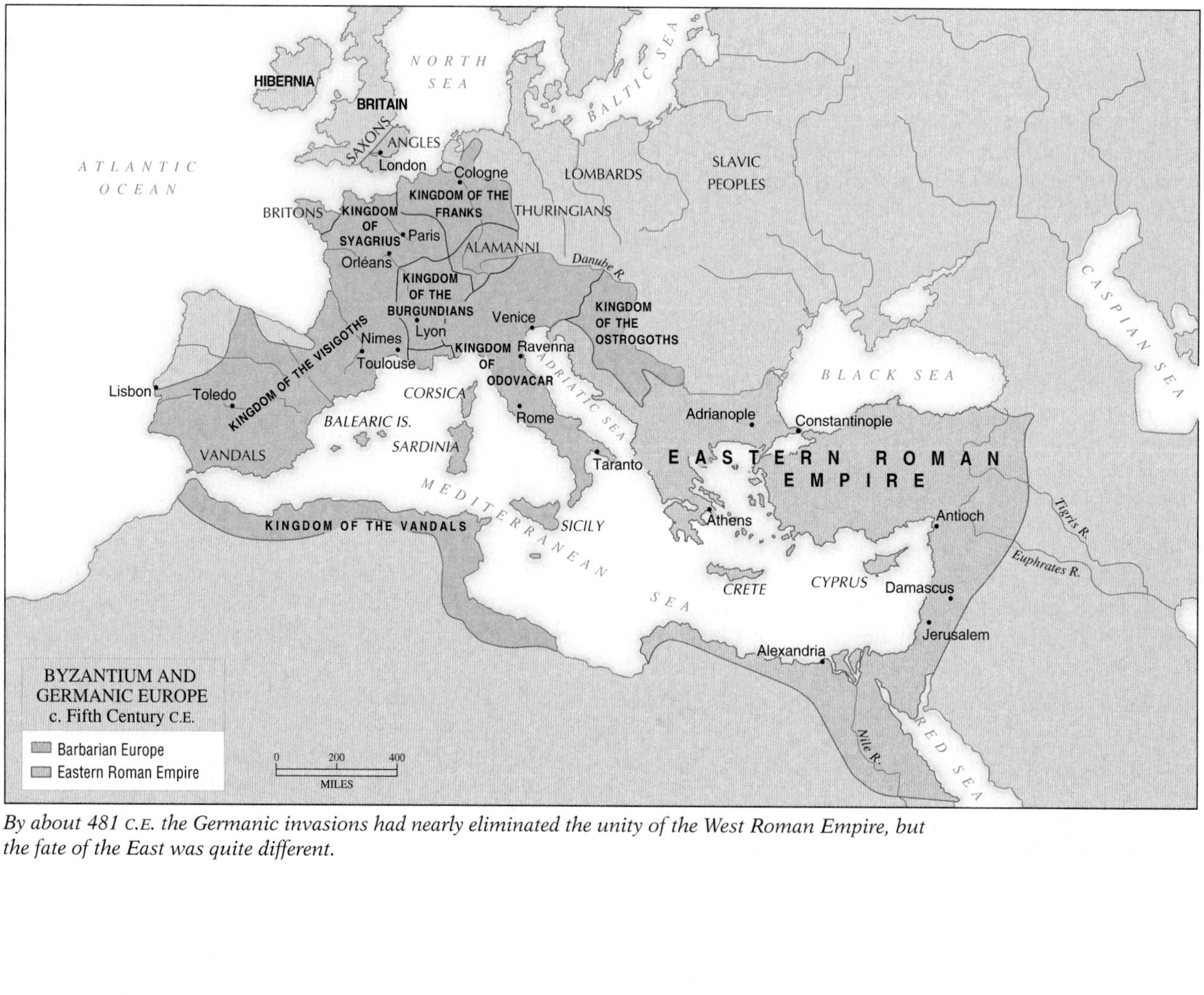

By about 481 C.E. the Germanic invasions had nearly eliminated the unity of the West Roman Empire, but the fate of the East was quite different.

silkworms were smuggled out of China about 550 C.E., silk production flourished and became a profitable state monopoly. The state paid close attention to business: controlling the economy through a system of guilds to which all tradesmen and members of professions belonged; setting wages, profits, work hours, and prices; and even organizing bankers and doctors into compulsory corporations.

Justinian and Theodora

The dream of reclaiming the Mediterranean basin and reestablishing the Roman Empire to its former glory, however, did not die until the end of the reign of Justinian (r. 527–565). Aided by his forceful wife, Theodora, and a corps of competent assistants, he made long-lasting contributions to Byzantine and Western civilization, but gained only short-term successes in his foreign policy.

In the 520s and 530s, after earthquakes devastated much of his realm, Justinian carried out a massive project of urban renewal throughout the empire. He strengthened the walls defending Constantinople and built the monumental Hagia Sophia, which still stands. Forty windows circle the base of this great church's dome, producing a quality of light that creates the illusion that the ceiling is floating.

Emperor Justinian bequeathed a splendid architectural and legal legacy to Europe. However, his attempt to reclaim the former glory of the Roman Empire gained only temporary success and bankrupted his treasury.

Hagia Sophia remains intact today, and visitors can share the awe of the Russians who visited the structure in the tenth century and said, "We knew not whether we were in heaven or on earth."

Justinian also reformed the government and ordered a review of all Roman law. This project led to the publication of the **Code of Justinian,** a digest of Roman and church law, texts, and other instructional materials that became the foundation of modern Western law. Following Constantine's example, Justinian saw himself as the thirteenth apostle and participated actively in the religious arguments of his day.

The costs of Justinian's ambitious projects triggered violence among the gangs of Constantinople. Since ancient times, groups throughout the Mediterranean

Code of Justinian—A review of all Roman laws since the beginning of the Roman Republic led to the publication of the Code, a digest of Roman and church law, texts, and other instructional materials. This became the basis of modern Western law.

pushed competitively for their own economic, social, and religious goals. Much like contemporary urban gangs, they lived in separate and well-defined neighborhoods, moved about in groups, and congregated at public events. When the factions had complaints with the emperor's policies, they chanted them in unison when Justinian was present at the circus. The most important of these were the Greens and the Blues, factions that often came to the Hippodrome—a structure that could hold 80,000 people—to support competing chariot racers in the circus.

A general dislike of Justinian's wife, Theodora, the daughter of a circus animal trainer (a background that made her almost untouchable in polite society), provided another point of contention. Her enemies believed that she behaved in an outrageous manner, espoused a heretical variant of Christianity, and had too much influence over her husband. Usually, the gangs neutralized each other's efforts. In 532, however, the Blues and the Greens joined forces to try to force Justinian from the throne. The so-called Nika rebellion, named after the victory cry of the rioters, almost succeeded. We know from Procopius's *Secret Histories* that Justinian was on the verge of fleeing until Theodora stopped him and told the emperor:

> *I do not choose to flee. Those who have worn the crown should never survive its loss. Never shall I see the day when I am not saluted as empress. If you mean to flee, Caesar, well and good. You have the money, the ships are ready, the sea is open. As for me, I shall stay.*[1]

Assisted by his generals, the emperor remained and destroyed the rebellion.

Justinian momentarily achieved his dream of reestablishing the Mediterranean rim of the Roman Empire. To carry out his plan to regain the half of the empire lost to the Germanic invaders, Justinian first had to buy the neutrality of the Persian kings who threatened not only Constantinople but also Syria and Asia Minor. After securing his eastern flank through diplomacy and bribery, he took North Africa in 533 and the islands of the western Mediterranean from the Vandals. His generals also reclaimed the southern part of Spain from the Visigoths, but no serious attempt was ever made to recover Gaul, Britain, or southern Germany.

The grandeur of the Byzantine court can be seen in this mosaic presentation of the Empress Theodora in the St. Vitale Church in Ravenna, Italy.

The old Roman tradition of the Mediterranean as Mare Nostrum *("Our Sea") died hard for Justinian. Twenty years of fighting allowed one last glimmer of the old days but exhausted his army and his treasury. A half-century after his reign, the western holdings would be lost, and the East Roman Empire would be redefined around an Anatolian, not a Mediterranean, base.*

Following Theodoric's death without a male heir in 526, civil war broke out in Italy, paving the way for Justinian's 20-year war of reconquest (535–555). Italy was ravaged from end to end by the fighting, and the classical civilization that Theodoric had carefully preserved was in large part destroyed in Rome, with Ravenna suffering extensive damage. To achieve this victory Justinian drained his treasury. Ironically, in 568, three years after his death, the last wave of Germanic invaders, the Lombards, reputed to have been the most brutal and fierce of all the Germans, poured into Italy. The emperor in the East held on to southern Italy, as well as Ravenna and Venice, but left Rome to the pope, who became the most powerful person in the city.

By a decade after Justinian's death, most of the territory he had reconquered had been lost. The Moors in Africa, Germanic peoples across Europe, and waves of nomadic tribes from Asia threatened Byzantium's boundaries. Ancient enemies such as the Persians, who had been bribed into a peaceful relationship, returned to threaten Constantinople when the money ran out, setting in motion a half-century-long battle. In addition, the full weight of the Slavic migrations came to be felt. Peaceful though they may have been, the Slavs severely strained and sometimes broke the administrative links of the state in the Balkans. Finally, the empire was split by debates regarding Christian doctrine. The stress of trying to maintain order under these burdens drove two of Justinian's successors insane.

THE AGE OF CONSOLIDATION: 610–1071

- *What were the institutional changes made by Heraclius that permitted the Byzantine Empire to maintain its dominance for the next four centuries? Why did the system finally fall?*

At the beginning of the seventh century, the East Roman Empire appeared to be on the brink of extinction. Salvation appeared from the west when Heraclius (r. 610–641), the Byzantine governor of North Africa, returned to Constantinople in 610 to overthrow the mad emperor Phocas (r. 602–610). When Heraclius arrived in the capital, conditions were so bad and the future appeared so perilous that he considered moving the government from Constantinople to Carthage in North Africa. Heraclius abandoned the hope of reunifying the old Roman Empire around its Mediterranean base and, instead, determined that Anatolia would be the foundation of the empire. During this time the use of Latin as an official language came to an end, and Greek—the language of the great majority of the population—took its place. But even with

Discovery Through Maps

A Sixth-Century Map: The Madaba Mosaic

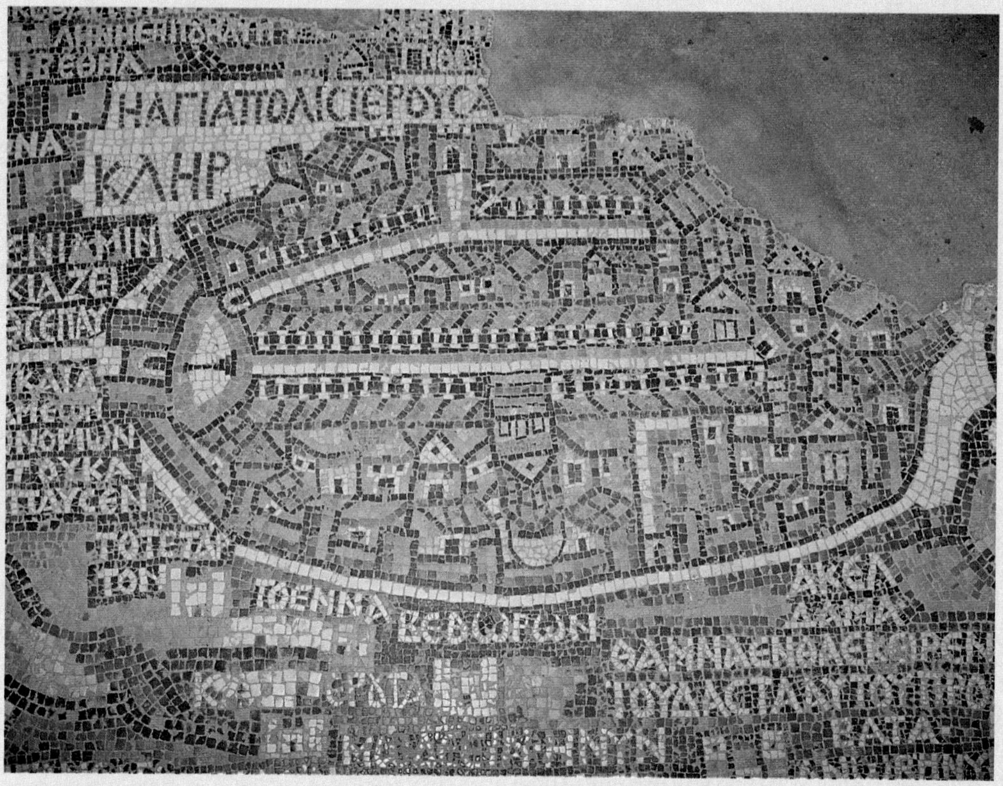

During the first part of Justinian's reign a series of earthquakes shattered buildings around the eastern Mediterranean. The emperor, who had a full treasury, embarked on a massive reconstruction program that adhered to a classical style that was copied all over the empire, even in places that had not suffered from natural disasters. One of the most impressive results of this architectural explosion was Hagia Sophia Church in Constantinople. Another, more subtle but equally revealing, was the Madaba mosaic map, found in present-day Jordan.

Although Justinian was one of the last Latin-speaking emperors of East Rome, the language used in the mosaic map is Greek, a testimony to the existence of the Greek cultural zone established by Alexander the Great in the fourth century B.C.E. that at its height extended from Gibraltar to the Indus River.

Just as Hagia Sophia spoke volumes about the wealth and power of the Christian church, this map, roughly 50 feet by 18 feet, gives remarkable detail about the eastern part of the empire. More than 150 places in present-day Israel, Jordan, Saudi Arabia, Syria, Lebanon, and part of Egypt—the area of the 12 biblical tribes, or the boundaries of Canaan promised to Abraham—are identified, along with an accurate portrayal of the roads, rivers, deserts, seas, and mountains of the region. Unlike modern maps, which are constructed with a north-south orientation, this map points to the east—toward the altar. The importance of a town can be seen by the way it is described—a small town is depicted as having a small church, whereas the unique qualities of the larger places such as Jerusalem are given more elaborate representations.

There are also other details, such as precise illustrations of places mentioned in the Bible, palm trees to indicate oases, and points at which to cross rivers on foot or by ferry boat. It is obvious that the mosaic map profited from the accounts of travelers. The care with which the unique qualities of various sites are illustrated shows that the map had more than just a decorative function: it was also to be used by Christians making pilgrimages—both those from the West and locally.

A little more than a century later, the region would be swept up in the Islamic advances, and Arabic would begin to replace Greek as the dominant language of the region. Even with that, pilgrims would continue to make their quest through the coming centuries, and the Madaba Mosaic would speak clearly to them.

To gain some notion of a modern perspective, see the map of the Spread of Christianity.

Questions to Consider

1. Locate the five patriarchates. How many are located in the eastern Mediterranean? How many in the West?
2. Why was the use of the Latin language dominant in the western half of the empire, but not the east?
3. Why do you think pious people in a number of religions make pilgrimages?

this linguistic change, the rulers referred to themselves as Romans.

Heraclius

The situation did not improve soon for the Byzantines after Heraclius's arrival. The Persians marched seemingly at will through Syria, took Jerusalem, capturing the "true cross"—the cross on which Christians believed Christ was crucified—and advanced into Egypt. The loss of Egypt to the Persians cost Constantinople a large part of its grain supply. Two fierce Asiatic invaders, the Avars and the Bulgars, pushed against Byzantium from the north. Pirates controlled the sea-lanes, and the Slavs, who had begun to move into southeast Europe in the sixth century, cut land communication across the Balkans. Facing ultimate peril, the emperor abandoned the state structure of Diocletian and Constantine.

Byzantium

325	Constantine the Great establishes capitol in Constantinople (city dedicated May 11, 330)
378	Battle of Adrianople; Visigoths defeat Roman armies, Emperor Valens killed
410	Alaric invades Italy
527–565	Reign of Justinian, construction of Hagia Sophia Cathedral
674–678	Arab sieges of Constantinople
842–1071	Golden Age of Byzantine culture and power
1054	Great schism between the Eastern Orthodox and Roman Catholic churches
1204	Fourth Crusade; Byzantium disappears until 1261
1453	Fall of Constantinople, end of East Roman Empire

Heraclius instituted a new system that strengthened his armies, tapped the support of the church and the people, and erected a more efficient, streamlined administration. He determined that the nucleus of the empire would be Anatolia (Asia Minor, the area of present-day Turkey) and that the main source of fighting men for his army would be the free peasants living there rather than mercenaries. Instead of the sprawling realm passed on by Justinian, Heraclius designed a compact state and an administration conceived to deal simultaneously with the needs of government and the challenges of defense.

This system, the **theme system,** had been tested when Heraclius ruled North Africa. Acting on the lessons of the past four centuries, he assumed that defense was a constant need and that free peasant soldiers living in the theme ("district") they were defending would be the most effective and efficient force. He installed the system in Anatolia, and his successors then spread it throughout the empire over the next two centuries. Heraclius's scheme provided sound administration and effective defense at half the former cost. As long as the theme system—with its self-supporting, landowning, free peasantry—endured, Byzantium remained strong. When the theme system and its free peasantry were abandoned in the eleventh century, the empire became weak and vulnerable.

Heraclius, buttressed by the church, fought a holy war to reclaim Jerusalem. During the 620s he applied some of the lessons of Hannibal's mobile warfare to attack Persian strength and took the enemy heartland. In 626 Heraclius stood ready to strike the final blow and refused to be drawn away by the Avar siege of Constantinople. He defeated the Persians at Nineva, marched on to Ctesiphon, and finally—symbolic of his victories—reclaimed the "true cross" and returned it to Jerusalem in 630.

The Byzantines were unable to savor their victory for long, however, because the advance of a new force, the Muslims, posed an even more dangerous threat to

theme system—Heraclius divided his realm, first in Asia Minor and then in other regions, into districts called "themes." Understanding that defense would be a continual necessity, he empowered the free peasant soldiers living in the theme to be responsible, under the leadership of a district commander, for the protection of their homelands.

The Byzantine navy coupled its prowess in battle with the secret and powerful weapon known as Greek fire, depicted here in a fourteenth-century manuscript illumination.

Byzantium than the Persians. Byzantium and Persia had previously dominated the Near East, but they were exhausted after 20 years of war. Aided by a superior cavalry, the Muslims took Syria and Palestine at the battle of Yarmuk in 636. Persia fell to them in 637, Egypt in 640. In Syria and Egypt, their advances were assisted by the anti-Constantinople sentiment provoked during the Christological controversies. Under the more tolerant Muslims, those who had a different view of the nature of Christ could freely follow their faith. A millennium of Greco-Roman rule in the eastern Mediterranean ended in a mere five years.

Constantinople's walls and the redefined Byzantine state withstood the challenge, enduring two Arab sieges in 674–678 and 717. Both times the capital faced severe land and naval attack. The Byzantines triumphed by using new techniques such as Greek fire and germ warfare. Greek fire was the medieval equivalent of napalm. It caught fire on contact with water and stuck to the hulls of the Arabs' wooden ships. The germ warfare was accomplished by sending people with small pox and other diseases into enemy camps. At the same time, the Byzantines faced the serious threats of the Bulgarians—continuing their four-century-long pressure on Constantinople—and the Slavs. Heraclius's successors built on his strong foundations by extending the theme system and protecting the free peasants—a source of taxes and soldiers.

The Heraclian dynasty saved the Byzantine state three times: in 610 and during the two Arab sieges. In the end, however, this dynasty proved the point that the political succession in East Rome was never an orderly process. Beginning with the conflicts among the sons of Constantine and continuing at least once in every century thereafter, civil war erupted around the issue of succession, usually with great violence. Notable among these episodes was that of Justinian II, Rhinometus (r. 685–695 and 705–711). His opponents removed him in 695 and, to insure that he wouldn't return, slit his nose and his tongue. He was sent off to exile across the Black Sea, in Crimea. His expulsion led to a 22-year period in which Byzantium had seven different rulers, including the exiled Justinian Rhinometus for a second tour as emperor in 705.

The Iconoclastic Period

As we have seen, from Constantine on, the Byzantine emperors played active roles in calling church councils to debate the questions concerning the nature of Christ and His relationship with the Father and the Holy Spirit. In a structure in which the emperor was both the political and spiritual leader an Orthodox Christian doctrine had to be established as a base to deal with both the secular and spiritual opponents of Constantinople. During times of war, such as the Persian invasions during Heraclius's reign, the combined force of church and state provided great strength. At other times, as in the eighth century, when arguments raged between Rome and Constantinople over the use of icons and the propagation of their particular branches of the faith, the emperor's mixing in matters of faith hurt the East Roman state.

Byzantine Emperors

306–337	Constantine the Great
361–363	Julian the Apostate
364–378	Valens
527–565	Justinian I
610–641	Heraclius I
717–741	Leo III, the Isaurian
797–802	Irene
829–842	Theophilus
867–886	Basil I, the Macedonian
886–912	Leo VI, the Wise
912–959	Constantine VII, Porphyrogenetus
963–1025	Basil II, Bulgaroctonus
1449–1453	Constantine XI

When Constantinople faced a three-sided invasion from the Arabs, Avars, and Bulgarians in 717, another powerful leader, Leo the Isaurian (r. 717–741), came forward to turn back the invaders. Over the next decade Leo rebuilt the areas ruined by war and strengthened the theme system. He reformed the law, limiting capital punishment to crimes involving treason and increasing the use of mutilation for a wide range of common crimes.

Leo took seriously his role as religious leader. He vigorously persecuted heretics and Jews, decreeing that the latter group must be baptized. In 726 he launched a theological crusade against the use of icons, pictures, and statues of religious figures such as Christ and the saints. He was concerned that icons played too prominent a role in Byzantine life and that their common use as godparents, witnesses at weddings, and objects of adoration went against the Old Testament prohibition of the worship of graven images. Accordingly, the emperor ordered the army to destroy icons. The destruction of the icons caused a violent reaction in the western part of the empire, especially in the monasteries. The government responded by mercilessly persecuting the iconophiles ("icon lovers"). The eastern part of the empire, centered in Anatolia, supported the **iconoclasm.** By trying to remove what he saw to be an abuse, Leo split his empire in two and drove a deeper wedge between the church in Rome and the church in Constantinople.

iconoclasm—The breaking of images. Under the reign of Leo the Isaurian, the empire split over the role of icons (holy images) in the life of believers. Leo wanted to destroy icons, seeming them as a worship of graven images.

In Byzantium the religious conflict over destruction of the icons had far-reaching cultural, political, and social implications. Pope Gregory II condemned iconoclasm in 731. Leo's decision to attack icons stressed the fracture lines that had existed between East and West for the past four centuries, typified by the linguistic differences between the Latin West and Greek East. As Leo's successors carried on his religious and political policies, Pope Stephen II turned to the north and struck an alliance with the Frankish king, Pepin, in 754. This was the first step in a process that a half-century later would lead to the birth of the Holy Roman Empire and the formal political split of Europe into East and West.

Empress Irene and Iconophilism

Women played a prominent role in Byzantine political life, whether openly as was the case with Justinian's wife Theodora, or more commonly as powers behind the throne. When succession led to the ascendancy of a minor, a regency council or a single regent would exercise power. Several times in Byzantine history, the Dowager Empress—the mother of the emperor in power—ruled. In 1042 the last of the Macedonian dynasty, sisters Zoe and Theodora, ruled briefly. Later on, Theodora ruled on her own in 1055. Anna Comnena (see Document), wrote of the importance of her mother and grandmother in the affairs of state.

The best-known woman who ruled in her own right was the Empress Irene. Irene was from Athens and an iconophile, a curious choice for the wife of Leo IV. She became regent for—and coemperor with—her 10-year-old son Constantine VI at Leo's death in 780, at the age of 30. She resisted attempts to overthrow her and her son and consolidated their power. In addition, she slowly worked to reverse the iconoclastic policies of her predecessors and called the Seventh Ecumenical Council to bring concord with Rome and reinstall the use of icons.

Irene extended her power during the latter part of the 780s and even after her son reached the age at which he was eligible to rule, she refused to yield any of her power. The iconoclasts rallied around Constantine VI while the iconophiles supported Irene, and finally she was forced out after the army declared its loyalty to her son in 790. Two years later, she was back after Constantine suffered defeat in several battles and proved to be incompetent and even vicious in his actions—when he sensed a potential coup from his uncles, he blinded them and cut their tongues out. His personal behavior, including openly adulterous

Document Anna Comnena

Anna Comnena, the first woman historian, was a prominent representative of the rich Byzantine intellectual life. She entered this calling after being blocked by the birth of her brother in her drive to become Byzantium's second empress and in other, later political activities. At the age of 55 she was sent off to a forced retirement and began to write a number of books, the best known of which is *The Alexiad*. She lived at the time of the first crusades, seen by the Byzantines as a western European barbarian invasion, and her descriptions of events show a marked disdain for the crusaders so revered in Western accounts. As she described herself, she was "nurtured and born in the purple, not without my full share of letters, for I carried to its highest point the art of writing Greek, nor did I neglect the study of rhetoric: I read with care the system of Aristotle and the dialogues of Plato, and fortified my mind with the quadrivium of sciences." (Quoted in Norman Baynes, *Byzantium,* Oxford: The Clarendon Press, 1961, p. 258).

On Peter the Hermit and the First Crusade

A Celt named Peter, called "Peter the Hermit," left to worship at the Holy Sepulcher. After having suffered much bad treatment at the hands of the Turks and the Saracens who were ravaging all of Asia he returned to his home only with great difficulty. Since he could not bear to have failed in his aim, he decided to begin the same voyage over again. But he understood that he should not retravel the route to the Holy Sepulcher alone for fear that a worse mishap might occur to him; and he thought up a clever scheme, which was to preach throughout all the countries of the Latins as follows: "A divine voice has ordered me to proclaim before all the nobles of France that they should all leave their homes to go worship at the Holy Sepulcher and try with all their ability and with all their passion to free Jerusalem from the domination of the [Saracens]."

Since they did [not] march in ranks or troops, they [later] fell into a Turkish ambush near Drakon and were wretchedly massacred. So many Celts and Normans were victims of the[ir] ... swords that when the bodies of the slaughtered warriors which were scattered about were [put together they formed] a high mountain of considerable dimensions, so great was the mass of bones.

From Paul Brians, trans., in *Reading About the World*, Vol. I, eds. Paul Brians et al., published by Harcourt Brace Custom Books.

Anna Comnena also wrote compellingly of the brilliance of her grandmother.

It may cause some surprise that my father the Emperor had raised his mother to such a position of honor, and that he had handed complete power over to her. Yielding up the reins of government, one might say, he ran alongside her as she drove the imperial chariot. . . .

My father reserved for himself the waging of wars against the barbarians, while he entrusted to his mother the administration of state affairs, the choosing of civil servants, and the fiscal management of the empire's revenues and expenses. One might perhaps, in reading this, blame my father's decision to entrust the imperial government to the gyneceum (the quarter of the palace reserved for women). But once you understood the ability of this woman, her excellence, her good sense, and her remarkable capacity for hard work, you would turn from criticism to admiration.

For my grandmother really had the gift of conducting the affairs of state. She knew so well how to organize and administer that she was capable of governing not only the Roman Empire but also every other kingdom under the sun. . . . She was very shrewd in seizing on whatever was called for, and clever in carrying it out with certitude. Not only did she have an outstanding intelligence, but her powers of speech matched it. She was a truly persuasive orator, in no way wordy or long-winded. . . .

She was ripe in years when she ascended the imperial throne, at the moment when her mental powers were at their most vigorous. . . .

As for her compassion toward the poor and the lavishness of her hand toward the destitute, how can words describe these things? Her house was a shelter for her needy relatives, and it was no less a haven for strangers. . . . Her expression, which revealed her true character, demanded the worship of the angels but struck terror among demons. . . .

From "The Writings of Medieval Women," Vol. 14, ed. and trans. M. Thiebaux, *Garland Library of Medieval Literature* (New York, 1987).

Questions to Consider

1. Compare and contrast the leadership qualities Anna Comnena portrays in her father and in her grandmother.
2. How would you characterize the Byzantines' attitudes toward the Crusaders? Were these caused more by civilizational or by political considerations?
3. Note Anna's description of herself in the introduction. Can you describe any other women in your study that measure up to her intellectual attainments? As you continue your study of other civilizations at this same time, cite other women you find as equals to Anna and note why.
4. Compare and contrast the frustrations faced by women in the Byzantine setting with those that continue into twenty-first century industrialized societies.

behavior—not a thing usually expected from the thirteenth apostle—led to his being increasingly isolated. Finally, in 797, Irene ordered him taken to the Purple Room, the place in which he was born, and blinded. Irene now ruled the empire in her own name—but as emperor, not empress.

Once in power she cut many taxes to gain the support of her people, gave lucrative gifts to the monasteries, and cut import duties. She gained a moment of popularity, but the state treasuries were drained. She failed to win lasting support among the eastern part of the empire for her pro-icon policies; nor could she arrange a marriage alliance with the newly proclaimed western emperor, Charlemagne, before being overthrown—a union that would have brought together the forces of East and West. As Irene spent the treasury into bankruptcy, her enemies increased. Finally, in 802 they deposed her and sent her into exile on the island of Lesbos.

The Empress Irene (r. 797–802) sought to change the anti-icon policies of her realm and make an alliance with Charlemagne, before being deposed.

The iconoclastic controversy and Irene's failed policies placed the empire in jeopardy once again. Her successor, Nicepherous (r. 802–811), after struggling to restore the bases of Byzantine power, was captured in battle with the Bulgarians in 811. Khan Krum beheaded him in July and turned his skull into a drinking cup. The iconoclasts had made a comeback, but this phase of image-breaking lacked the vigor of the first, and by 842 the policy was abandoned.

The clash over icons marked the final split between East and West. Eastern emperors were strongly impressed by Islamic culture, especially with its prohibition of images. The Emperor Theophilus (r. 829–842), for example, was a student of Muslim art and culture, and Constantinople's painting, architecture, and universities benefited from the vigor of Islamic culture. This focus on the East may have led to the final split with the West, but, by the middle of the ninth century, it also produced an East Roman state with its theological house finally in order and its borders fairly secure.

Missionary Activities

During the ninth and tenth centuries, Constantinople made its major contributions to eastern Europe and Russia. Missionaries from Constantinople set out to convert the Bulgarians and Slavic peoples in the 860s and, in the process, organized their language, laws, aesthetics, political patterns, and ethics as well as their religion. But these activities did not take place without competition. Conflict increasingly marked the relationship between the Byzantine and Roman churches. A prime example of this conflict was the competition between Patriarch Photius and Pope Nicholas I in the middle of the ninth century.

Photius excelled both as a scholar and as a religious leader. He made impressive contributions to schools in the Byzantine Empire and worked to increase Orthodoxy's influence throughout the realm. Nicholas I was Photius's equal in ambition, ego, and intellect. They collided over the attempt to convert the pagan peoples, such as the Bulgarians, caught between their spheres of influence.

Khan Boris of Bulgaria, who was as cunning and shrewd as Photius and Nicholas, saw the trend toward conversion in Europe that had been developing since the sixth century and realized the increased power he could gain with church approval of his rule. But he also wanted a separate patriarch and church for his own people and dealt with the side that gave him the better bargain. From 864 to 866 Boris changed his mind three times on the question of following Rome or Constantinople. Finally, the Byzantines gave the Bulgarians the equivalent of an autonomous (independent) church, and in return the Bulgarians entered the Byzantine cultural orbit. The resulting schism proclaimed between the churches in 867 set off a sputtering sequence of Christian warfare that continued for centuries.

The work of the Byzantine missionary brothers Cyril and Methodius was more important than Bulgarian ambitions or churchly competition. The men were natives of Thessalonica (thes-sa-LON-ee-ka), a city at the mouth of the Vardar-Morava water highway that gave access to the Slavic lands. Versed in the Slavic language, the two led a mission to Moravia, ruled by King Rastislav. He no doubt wanted to convert to Orthodoxy and enter the orbit of distant Constantinople in order to preserve as much independence for his land as he could in the face of pressure from his powerful German neighbors. Cyril and Methodius carried the faith northward in the **vernacular.** Cyril adapted Greek letters to devise an alphabet for the Slavs, and the brothers translated the liturgy and many religious books into the Slavic language. Although Germanic missionaries eventually converted the Moravians, the work of Cyril and Methodius profoundly affected all of the Slavic peoples.

Byzantium's Golden Age, 842–1071

For two centuries, a period coinciding roughly with the reign of the Macedonian dynasty (867–1056), Byzantium enjoyed political and cultural superiority over its western and eastern foes. Western Europe staggered under the blows dealt by the Saracens, Vikings, and Magyars, and the Arabs lost the momentum that had carried them forward for two centuries. Constantinople enjoyed the relative calm, wealth, and balance bequeathed by the theme system and promoted by a series of powerful rulers. The time was marked by the flowering of artists, scholars, and theologians as much as it was by the presence of great warriors. Byzantium's security and wealth encouraged an active political, cultural, and intellectual life. The widespread literacy and education among men and women of various segments of society would not be matched in Europe until eighteenth-century Paris. Unfortunately this time of well-being would come to an end at the beginning of the twelfth century.

vernacular—Using the language of the people of a local, particular region.

During the Golden Age, the population lived within the theoretical stability of the autocratic framework in which all things—political, religious, military, economic, and social—flowed from the emperor. Underneath that caesaropapistic unity, however, were the political, social, and economic struggles found in all societies. In Anatolia, the theme system based on the free soldier-peasants remained until the end of the eleventh century. The rich soil of the area combined with the dignity of self-defense to produce proud and independent families. Life was difficult, but from time to time there were religious feasts, fairs, and the occasional wandering entertainers. Still, there was always the possibility of an early frost that would wipe out a harvest and bring debt, and there were always the tax collectors. Women guaranteed the functioning of the home while also carrying on the work of the farm when their husbands were fulfilling their military obligations.

In Constantinople, a dependable supply of affordable food was guaranteed by the state and the church, again until the end of the eleventh century. Despite the wars and upheavals, the population levels remained constant in Constantinople through to 1204 and the Fourth Crusade. Among the 800,000 or so inhabitants of the city there were of, course, the homeless, numbering perhaps 30,000, and the criminal element, numbering perhaps the same. The population of the city was divided into three major groups: those who worked for the state, those who were in commerce and manufacturing, and the workers, poor people, and slaves.

The civil servants in the ninth century were the foremost proponents of Greek language and civilization, and—like the Chinese scholar gentry—their learning was as essential to their work as to the advancement of their civilization. Their pride in their position made them intolerant of foreigners, especially people from western Europe. The civil servants also carried a deep contempt for the military, who in their eyes were barbarians. For the clever and ambitious from all levels of society, the means to upward mobility was through education in the Greek classics.

Those in the second category, who made and sold things, remained subject to strict governmental controls over their work. They were frozen into a system of guilds and price controls until the theme system died at the end of the eleventh century. But with all of that, the living conditions were comparatively good—even for those who worked for the owners and merchants. The government remembered its Roman past and worked hard to keep the loyalties of the citizens of the capitol. As long as bread was cheap, the emperors had the support of the citizens of Constantinople. Free bread had ended with the loss of Egypt. The cost of food was kept low afterwards, as the supplies from Anatolia were consistent. Along with bread, a diet of dried peas and beans, green vegetables, and fish was possible even for the poorest inhabitant. If food was plentiful and cheap, clothing and shelter were less available and expensive. The homeless were the first to suffer from the bubonic plague of the eighth century and the Black Plague of the fourteenth—not to mention the always-constant small pox.

At the lower levels of society, few lived beyond the age of 60—but this was a longer life span than that found in western Europe at the same time. The life of the common laborer was difficult, jobs were aggressively sought after, and pay was low. Threatening their status from below were the large numbers of slaves kept in the Byzantine Empire. The status of slave, beyond removing one's legal identity, applied equally to some who lived very well, doing important work for their masters, as well as to those who lived an abusive life, performing the most brutal manual labor.

Except for members of the elite, such as the historian Anna Comnena, the social role of women was limited. For the most part, women of the top levels of society remained secluded and rarely went out of their houses without wearing a veil. At home it was rare for a woman to share a meal with a stranger. Within this seclusion, however, there was a lively society, an often-rich family life, and a comparatively high level of literacy and knowledge of the Greek classics. At the lower levels, women rarely were permitted by the guild structure to pursue a craft. Prostitution, which had a restricted legal standing under Constantine the Great, was practiced by a large number of women—in the thousands—in all periods of the Byzantine Empire. For women at all levels, death in childbirth was a common tragedy, and those that lived often saw their babies unable to survive the first winter, as infant mortality rates were extremely high.

DOCUMENT
Anna Comnena, *The Alexiad*

Byzantium continued its military as well as its theological dynamism. Arab armies made repeated thrusts, including one at Thessalonica in 904 that led to the loss of 22,000 people. But during the tenth century, a decline in Muslim combativeness, combined with the solidity of Byzantine defenses, brought an end to that chapter of conflict. Basil II (r. 963—1025), surnamed Bulgaroctonus (bul-ga-ROK-to-nus) or "Bulgar slayer," stopped Bulgarian challenges for more than a century at the battle of Balathista in 1014. At the same time, the Macedonian emperors dealt from a position of strength with western European powers, especially where their interests clashed in Italy. Western diplomats visiting the Byzantine court expressed outrage at the benign contempt with which the eastern emperors treated them. But the attitude merely reflected Constantinople's understanding of its role in the world.

The Byzantines continued their sometimes violent political traditions. Emperor Romanus Lecapenus I (r. 920–944) was overthrown by his sons, and in the eleventh century, succession to the throne degenerated into a power struggle between the civil and military aristocracies. Yet through all the political strife, the secular and theological schools flourished, and the emperors proved to be generous patrons of the arts. Basil I (r. 867–886) and Leo VI (r. 886–912) oversaw the collection and reform of the law codes. Leo, the most prolific lawgiver since Justinian, sponsored the greatest collection of laws of the medieval Byzantine Empire, a work that would affect jurisprudence throughout Europe. Constantine VII Porphyrogenitus (por-phi-ro-GEN-ee-tus; r. 912–959) excelled as a military leader, lover of books, promoter of an encyclopedia, and surveyor of the empire's provinces. At a time when scholarship in western Europe was almost nonexistent, Constantinople society featured a rich cultural life and widespread literacy among men and women of different classes.

The greatest contribution to European civilization from Byzantium's Golden Age was the preservation of ancient learning, especially in the areas of law, Greek science and literature, and Platonic and Aristotelian philosophy. Whereas in the West the church maintained scholarship, the men and women of Byzantium perpetuated the Greek tradition in philosophy, literature, and science. Perhaps because of this rich secular intellectual life, Byzantine monasteries—which produced many saints and mystics–showed little interest in learning or teaching about this world.

WESTERN AND TURKISH INVASIONS: 1071–1453

- *Why did the Byzantine Empire pass from being the dominant power in the region in 1015 to being so weak by 1095?*

Empires more often succumb to internal ailments than to external takeovers. This was the case with the Byzantine Empire. As long as Constantinople strengthened the foundations laid by Heraclius—the theme system and reliance on the free soldier-peasant—the empire withstood the military attacks of the strongest armies of the time. When the Byzantine leaders abandoned the pillars of their success, the state succumbed to the slightest pressure.

Byzantine Decline and the Seljuk Advance

Inflation and ambition ate away at the Heraclian structure. Too much money chased too few goods during the Golden Age. Land came to be the most profitable investment the rich could make, and the landowning magnates needed labor. Rising prices meant increased taxes. The peasant villages were collectively responsible for paying taxes, and the rising tax burden overwhelmed them. In many parts of the empire, villages sought relief by placing themselves under the control of large landowners, thus taking themselves out of the tax pool and lowering the number of peasant-soldiers. Both the state treasury and the army suffered as a result.

Until Basil II, the Macedonian emperors had tried to protect the peasantry through legislation, but the trend could not be reversed. Even though the free peasantry never entirely disappeared and each free person was still theoretically a citizen of the empire, economic and social pressures effectively destroyed the theme system. An additional factor contributing to the empire's decline was the growth of the church's holdings and the large percentage of the population taking holy orders, thus becoming exempt from taxation.

For 50 years following Basil II's death in 1025, the illusion that eternal peace had been achieved after his defeat of the Bulgarians in 1014 encouraged the opportunistic civil aristocracy, which controlled the state, to weaken the army and neglect the provinces. The next time danger arose, no strong rulers appeared to save Byzantium, perhaps because no enemies massed dramatically outside the walls of Constantinople.

New foes challenged Byzantium. The Turkish peoples, who had migrated from the region north of China to southwestern Asia around the sixth century, converted gradually to Islam. Warrior bands that formed among them fought first with and then against the Persians, Byzantines, and Arabs. The first of these Turkish bands to invade the Middle East and, eventually Anatolia, were the Seljuks (SEL-yukes). When the Seljuk Turk leader Alp Arslan (the "Victorious Lion") made a tentative probe into the empire's eastern perimeter near Lake Van in 1071, the multilingual mercenary army sent out from Constantinople fell apart even before fighting began at Manzikert. With the disintegration of the army, the only thing that could stop the Seljuk Turks' march for the next decade was the extent of their own ambition and energy.

Byzantium lost the heart of its empire when it lost Anatolia, and with it the reserves of soldiers, leaders, taxes, and food that had enabled it to survive

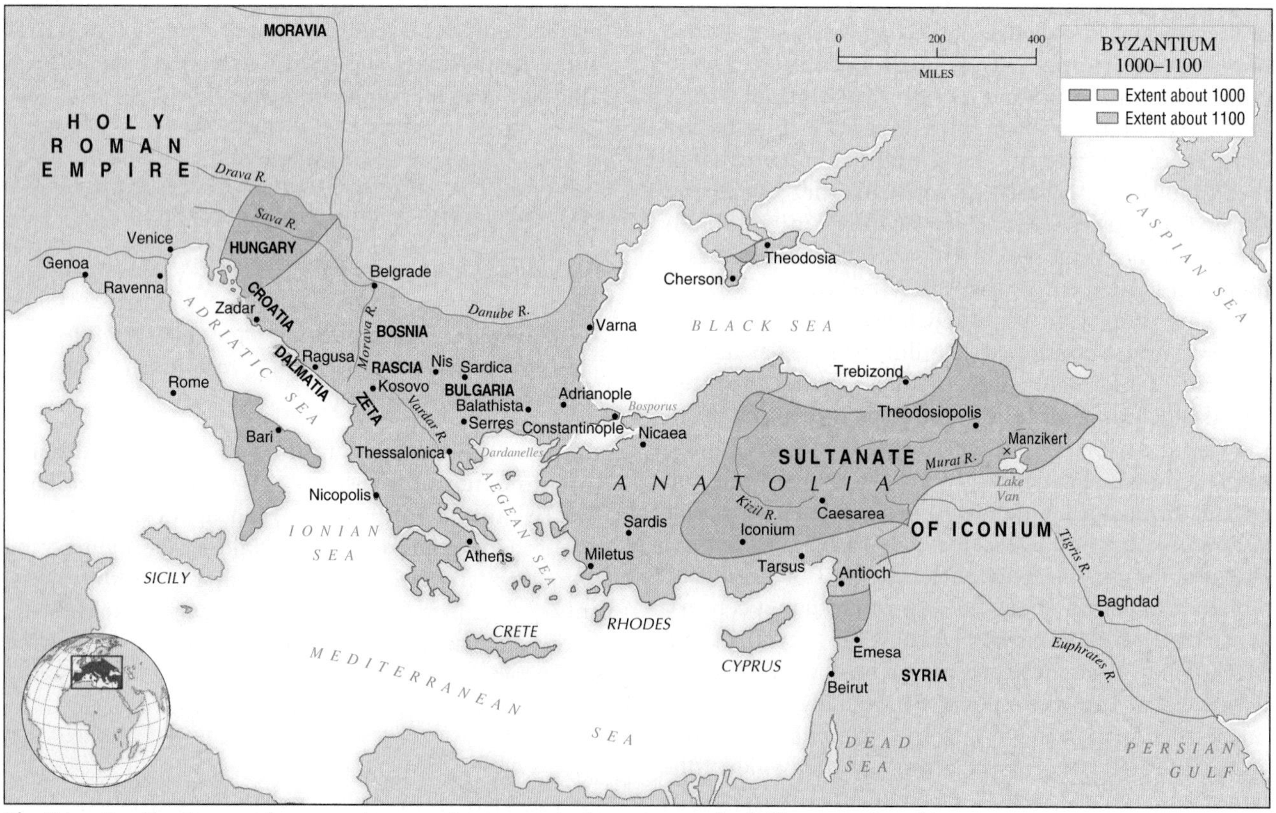

The Byzantine Empire went from a major to a minor power in the century and a half portrayed on this map. After the Turkish defeat at Manzikert in 1071, the Byzantines maintained effective control of only a small fringe of Anatolia to the east and to the north, giving in to the pressure of the Slavic migrations which had begun around the fifth century C.E. *The arrival of the Hungarians in the ninth and tenth centuries drove a wedge that prevented the Slavs from unifying.*

for four centuries. From its weakened position, the empire confronted Venice, a powerful commercial, and later political, rival. By the end of the eleventh century the Venetians had achieved undisputed trading supremacy in the Adriatic and turned their attention to the eastern Mediterranean. The Byzantines also faced the challenges of the Normans, led by Robert Guiscard, who took the last Byzantine stronghold in Italy.

The Western Crusades

The fracture in the relationship between Rome and Constantinople that had been opened during the iconoclastic controversy steadily grew into a theological gulf during the conversion competition of the ninth century. Thereafter, Rome and Constantinople developed in different ways. The Pope stood at the head of a growing community of independent states while the Emperor and his Patriarch could look to the west and north and see their allied Orthodox countries. The events leading up to the Great Schism in 1054 centered around the competition between Pope Leo IX and Patriarch Michael Cerularius. Each was ambitious for his own cause; neither cared further to maintain the fiction of Christian unity. The issues had been previously discussed: the western doctrine of the double procession of the Holy Ghost and fasting on Sunday and the eastern practices of a married clergy and the use of leavened bread in the communion service. The face-off between Pope and Patriarch led, in July of 1054, to the Roman excommunication of the eastern church's leaders and Constantinople's excommunication of the Roman church's officials. The schism between the two has never been healed.

In 1081 a politically astute and brilliant family, the Comnenians, claimed the Byzantine throne. In earlier times, with the empire at its strongest, these new rulers might have accomplished great things. But the best they could do in the eleventh and twelfth centuries after the defeat at Lake Van was to play a balance-of-power game between East and West, so well described by Anna Comnena in *The Alexiad*. In 1096 the first crusaders appeared, partly in response to the Council of Clermont, partly in response to the lure of gold and glory (see Chapter 9). Alexius Comnenus (r. 1081–1118) had appealed to Pope Urban II for help against the Seljuks, but he did not bargain on finding a host of crusaders, including the dreaded Normans and fanatic and disorganized peasants, on his doorstep. Alexius quickly got the crusaders—both peasant and noble—across the Straits of Bosporus and Dardanelles, where they won some battles that allowed the Byzantines to reclaim land lost in the previous 15 years.

Dueling Crusaders

The envy, hatred, and frustration that had been building up between the Byzantines and the Crusaders during the twelfth century finally erupted during the Fourth Crusade. The Venetians, who wanted to extend

The Crusades, viewed from the Western perspective as an epoch of bravery, were for the Byzantines and the Arabs a time of barbaric invasions. The crusaders not only failed in the long term to reclaim the Holy Land but also failed to stem the Islamic advance. By the sixteenth century, Turkish forces would be threatening Vienna.

their trade dominance in the eastern Mediterranean and the Black Sea, had control of the ships and money for this crusade. When the crusaders proved unable to pay for Venetian services rendered, they persuaded the crusaders to attack the Christian city of Zadar in Dalmatia—a commercial rival of Venice and Constantinople—before going on to the Holy Land. Constantinople itself was paralyzed by factional strife, and in 1204 for the first time an invading force captured and sacked the city. A French noble described the scene:

> *The fire . . . continued to rage for a whole week and no one could put it out. . . . What damage was done, or what riches and possessions were destroyed in the flames, was beyond the power of man to calculate. . . . The army . . . gained much booty; so much, indeed, that no one could estimate its amount or its value. It included gold and silver, table-services and precious stones, satin and silk, mantles of squirrel fur, ermine and miniver, and every choicest thing to be found on this earth. . . . So much booty had never been gained in any city since the creation of the world.*[2]

The Venetians made sure they got their share of the spoils, such as the bronze horses now found at St. Mark's Cathedral in Venice, and played a key role in placing a new emperor on the throne. The invaders ruled Constantinople until 1261. The Venetians put a stranglehold on commerce in the region and turned their hostility toward the Genoese, who threatened their trade monopoly.

The Ottoman Victory

The empire's last two centuries under the final dynasty, the Paleologus (1261–1453), saw the formerly glorious realm become a pawn in a new game. Greeks regained control of the church and the state, but there was precious little strength to carry on the ancient traditions. Byzantine coinage, which had retained its value from the fourth through the eleventh centuries, fell victim to inflation and weakness. The church, once a major pillar to help the state, became embroiled in continual doctrinal disputes. Slavic peoples such as the Bulgarians and the Serbs under Stephen Nemanja (r. 1168–1196) and Stephen Dushan (r. 1331–1355), who had posed no danger to the empire in its former strength, became threats. After Mongol invasions in the thirteenth century destroyed the exhausted Seljuk Turks, a new more formidable foe, the Ottoman or Osmanli Turks, appeared.

The Ottomans emerged from the groups of elite Turkish warriors, the *ghazis,* which came together on the northwestern frontier of Anatolia. They participated in the complex political and diplomatic relations in the Aegean area in the wake of the Fourth Crusade and were ready to take advantage of the weakened Byzantine Empire. Blessed after 1296 with a strong line of male successors and good fortune, the Ottomans rapidly expanded their power through the Balkans. They crossed the Straits into Europe in 1354 and moved up the Vardar and Morava valleys to take Serres (1383), Sofia (1385), Nis (1386), Thessalonica (1387), and finally Kosovo from the South Slavs in 1389.

The Ottoman Turks' overwhelming infantry and cavalry superiority gave them their military victories. But their administrative effectiveness, which combined strength and flexibility, solidified their rule in areas they conquered. In contrast to the Christians, both Roman and Byzantine, who were intolerant of theological differences, the Turks allowed monotheists or any believers in a "religion of the book" (the Bible, Torah, or Qur'an) to retain their faith and be ruled by a religious superior through the **millet system,** a network of religious ghettos.

In response to the Ottoman advance, the West mounted a poorly conceived and ill-fated crusade against them. The confrontation at Nicopolis on the Danube in 1396 resulted in the capture and slaughter of 10,000 knights and their attendants. Only the overwhelming force of Tamerlane (Timur the Magnificent), a Turco-Mongol ruler who defeated the Ottoman army in 1402, gave Constantinople and Europe some breathing space.

DOCUMENT
Kritovoulos on the Fall of Constantinople

The end for Constantinople came in May 1453. The last emperor, Constantine XI, and his force of 9000, half of whom were Genoese, held off 160,000 Ottomans for seven weeks. Finally, with the help of Hungarian artillerymen, the Turks breached the once impenetrable walls of the depopulated city. After 1123 years, the shining fortress fell.

DOCUMENT
Nestor-Iskander on the Fall of Constantinople

SOUTHEASTERN EUROPE TO 1500

- *What role did religion play in the formation of the various Balkan nations?*

Following in the wake of the Germanic tribes' westward march, the dominant people of eastern Europe, the Slavs, spread from the Pripet marshes west to the Elbe, east to the Urals, north to Finland, and south to the Peloponnesus. As they settled throughout eastern

---

millet system—The Ottoman Turks ruled in accord with religious law and governed their holdings as a theocratic state. Non-Turks were ruled according to their religious faith, and responsibilities for governance were handed over to the chief figures of each religious area, or millet.

East European and Russian Romes

c. 700–1014	First Bulgarian Empire
862–867	Cyril and Methodius's mission to the Moravians
865–870	Bulgarian conversion to Orthodoxy
867	First "Russian" attack on Constantinople
c. 900	Serb conversion to Orthodoxy
925	First Croat state, conversion to Catholicism
988	Russian conversion to Orthodoxy
988–1240	Kiev Rus'
1169–1389	Serbian Empire
1197–1393	Second Bulgarian Empire
1220–1243	Mongol invasions in Russia and eastern Europe
1240–1480	Mongol domination of Russia
1300s–1400s	Emergence of Wallachia and Moldavia
1389	Battle of Kosovo, Ottoman Empire begins dominance of the Balkans
1450–1468	Albanian state reaches peak under Skanderbeg
1462–1505	Reign of Tsar Ivan III, the Great

and southern Europe from the sixth through the ninth centuries, they absorbed most of the original inhabitants of the region. This mixing of peoples produced the resulting blends of nations that make up the present-day complexity of eastern Europe and Russia.

Compared to the wealth and sophistication of the Byzantines, the Slavs' economic and cultural lives were primitive, and their political and military structures were weak. Outsiders—Byzantines, Germans, Magyars, Mongols, or Turks—often ruled the various Slavic groups. Yet, before the imposition of Ottoman control, each of the Balkan peoples would have a moment of glory—the two Bulgarian empires, the Serbs under Stephen Nemanja and Stephen Dushan—in which each would create its own image of Byzantium.

Bulgaria

During the great migrations of the peoples, a warlike Finno-Tatar group arrived in the late seventh century—at a time when the Byzantine Empire was fighting for its life against the Arabs—and occupied the lands between the Balkan and the Rhodope Mountain ranges of the Balkans. Like the Huns, they were fighters and not farmers, and so after easily conquering the Slavic peoples of the region, they lived off the fruits of their subjects' labors while consolidating their positions against other invaders.

As was the case with other nomadic warrior bands, the Bulgarians within a couple of generations were absorbed by the more numerous Slavs, and became, for all intents and purposes, like other South Slavs in language and culture. They still retained their military tradition and their leadership by their Khans, however. And during the ninth and tenth centuries they posed a constant challenge to Constantinople. The great Khan Krum defeated the Emperor Nicepherous, and he led his armies far to the south of the Balkans. He even reached the walls of Constantinople, but as other leaders in the previous half-millennium, he did not possess the strength or technology to take the city.

Khan Boris cleverly set Roman and Byzantine missionaries against each other in order to gain the most advantageous terms for his conversion to Christianity. In fact he was given a national church with its own hierarchy of bishops and archbishops. Once he had joined the Byzantine side, Boris encouraged the work of missionaries from Constantinople to convert his people, and in the process accepted a Slavonic alphabet for the translations of scripture and church documents.

The First Bulgarian Empire hits its high point in the reign of Symeon (r. 893–927), a person who had been educated in Constantinople and had developed not only an appreciation for, but also a mastery of, Greek culture. Bulgaria served as the main transmission line for the spreading of Orthodoxy throughout the Balkans and into Russia. Symeon's admiration for Byzantine culture did not stop him from attempting to set up his own, independent empire however. He controlled most of the land south of present day Belgrade, up to the suburbs of Constantinople. His empire was short-lived, however, because he was in the path of yet another set of invaders coming from the east to the west: the Magyars (Hungarians), the Pechenegs, and the rising power of Russia. Finally Basil Bulgaroctonus defeated the major Bulgarian force and blinded all those who survived the battle 1014.

Bulgaria remained subdued for the next two centuries until 1185 when Peter and John Asen rebelled against Byzantine authority and successful established the Second Bulgarian Empire, and Bulgaria was a serious competitor with the weakened Byzantine Empire. Until the 1240s, Bulgaria briefly became the most important state in the Balkans, with its imitation Byzantine court and ritual. In the middle of the

In the Balkans, the new Serbian, Bulgarian, and Hungarian states grew powerful. Even though the Byzantines claimed control over the region and farther to the north and east, the Bohemian and Polish states and Russia came into existence.

thirteenth century, it fell to the Serbian Empire, and then a century later was overrun by the Ottoman Turks. Despite these reversals, the Bulgarians remained important missionaries and teachers in the spread of the Orthodox Church.

Serbia

The Serbs, a Slavic people, converted to Orthodox Christianity at roughly the same time as the Bulgarians. They too were caught in the Rome-Constantinople conversion competition, and their brothers the Croats and the Slovenes became Catholics. Despite their linguistic and ethnic similarities, the fact that the Serbs became Orthodox and the Croats and Slovenes Catholics established the foundation for centuries of tragic conflict right up to the wars in the former Yugoslavia in the 1990s.

At first the Serbs were dominated by the Bulgars, but by the 1180s, Stephen Nemanja, the Grand Zhupan, united the Serbian people. He successfully fought off both the Bulgarians and the weakened Byzantines to establish a kingdom along the Vardar and Morava river basins. His son, Stephen Nemanja II (r. 1196–1228) took advantage of the chaos created by the Fourth Crusade to consolidate his power. Like Khan Basil centuries earlier, he skillfully gained the status of king and also a Serbian national church by appealing to Rome and Constantinople for legitimacy.

Stephen Dushan (r. 1308–1355—at various times king and tsar) brought Serbia to its historic high point geographically, politically, and culturally. The Serbian ruler gained control over most of the Balkans north of Saloniki and south of the Sava River. Politically, he raised himself to the dignity of a *tsar*, or caesar—even to the point of challenging the weakened Byzantines in 1355, seeking help from both the Pope and the Turks. He died as his troops marched to Constantinople, and after that his empire fell apart. The legacy of his empire was a rich Serbian culture, based on Byzantine models, but also combining indigenous qualities and Italian influences.

As the Turks patiently advanced in the Balkans in the 1380s, the usually feuding Slavs finally united at the battle of Kosovo. After a long day of valiant fighting, which saw both the Turkish Sultan and the Serbian king die, the Ottomans emerged victorious—with control of the Balkans for the next five centuries. For the Balkan Slavs, especially the Serbs, the memory of the battle of Kosovo would be passed from generation to generation to be used by politicians in the 1990s as a tragedy to unite their people.

The collapse of Dushan's empire created such instability in the Balkans that the Ottoman Turks advanced with very little challenge. Under Sultan Murad (r. 1359–1389) they defeated the South Slavs in 1389 at the Battle of Kosovo—a date of mourning that still unites Serbian patriots today.

Romania

The Romanians, who see themselves today as "an island of Latins in a sea of Slavs," entered history as the Dacian people, settled on both sides of the Carpathian Mountain chain. They stood in the way of the Roman advance in the first century C.E. and irritated the caesars by their incursions into Roman-controlled provinces south of the Danube. The Emperor Trajan managed to defeat the Dacians and to turn the province into a productive part of the empire. These people remained under Roman rule from circa 100 to circa 275 B.C.E. and became thoroughly latinized, so much so that the Dacian culture and language died out.

The area served as a crossroads for the waves of migrating peoples coming from East to West—following the natural geographic path from the steppe frontier to the Danube valley, and from the end of Roman times to the thirteenth century, the Romanians essentially disappeared from history. After the thirteenth century the regions they inhabited became provinces: Moldavia, Wallachia, Bukovina, Bessarabia, and Transylvania. After the thirteenth century two independent, but weak, states emerged—Moldavia and Wallachia. They were threatened on all sides by the Mongols, the Russians, the Hungarians, the Bulgarians, and the Serbs. By the end of the fifteenth century they rested firmly under Ottoman control.

The Romanians were drawn into the religious orbits of whichever dominant power was the closest to where they lived. Thus, the Transylvanians became Catholic, the Wallachians became Orthodox following Serbian and Bulgarian models, and Moldavians became Orthodox with very strong influences from Russia.

Albania

The Albanians are the only indigenous Bronze Age people in the Balkans who have managed to preserve their own unique language and some of their culture. With a small population and little political and military power, they were from the first caught up in the Greek political strife of the Hellenic age, when they were subjects of the Macedonians under Philip and Alexander. In the second century B.C.E., they fell under Roman domination and their homeland became the province of Illyria (EE-lee-ree-ah). Albanians served in the Roman armies and bureaucracy—even providing several emperors, including Diocletian.

The Albanians were overwhelmed by first the Germanic and the Slavic migrations but did not assimilate with either group. They passed from being dominated by the Byzantines, to being harassed by the Bulgarians and then dominated by the Angevines during the early Crusades. Finally, after the death of Stephen Dushan, Albania entered a period of strife-filled independence, having to fight off the attentions of the Venetians and the Turks, until the arrival of their national hero Skanderbeg (r. 1443–1468). Led by Skanderbeg, Albania became a major player in Balkan affairs for one of the few times in its history. After Skanderbeg's death, however, Albania fell to the Turks. With most of the population eventually adopting Islam, Albania earned a favored position within the Ottoman Empire.

RUSSIA TO 1500

- *Of all the Slavic peoples in the Byzantine zone, why did Russia become the Third Rome and, eventually, a great power?*

Like that of eastern Europe, Russia's history is largely a product of its geography. The vast expanse of land combined with a comparatively small population has made the domination of the peasants by the landed interests, both individuals and state, one of the continuing themes in Russian history. Russia's difficulty in gaining access to the sea has had important economic and cultural consequences, stunting the growth of a merchant class and encouraging the formation of an inward-looking population.

Russia's waterways, however, have played a key role in the development of the country. The rivers, which flow north or south across the land, have served as thoroughfares for trade and cultural exchange as well as routes for invasion. Unconnected to the western European region, the rivers dictated a line of communication that led early Russian traders south to Constantinople rather than to the West. The Volkhov and Dnieper network tied together the Varangians (also known as the Vikings) and the Greeks through Russia, while the Volkhov and Volga system reached toward Central Asia.

Kiev Rus' and Vladimir

In the sixth century C.E. the eastern Slavs began moving out of the area near the Pripet marshes. The various clans went as far north as the White Sea, as far east as the Urals, and to the region south of Kiev. (Kiev Rus' describes the Kievan phase of Russian history, especially the introduction of a stronger Ukrainian historiographical tradition. The apostrophe stands for a diacritical mark in the writing of the word *Rus'* in Russian and Ukrainian.) To the north, around Lake Ilmen, the Slavs established a number of trading towns such as Novgorod, from which they founded other trading bases. By the ninth century they had accumulated sufficient wealth to attract the attention of the Varangians, who came down from the Baltic to dominate the trading routes, especially those going from the Dvina to the Dnieper to Constantinople.

Russian history is said to begin with the entry of the Varangians into eastern Slavic affairs in the 860s. One of the key controversies in Russian history revolves around the question of the Varangians' role. Did they impose themselves on the Slavs and form them into their first political units, or were the Varangians invited in by the already sophisticated, though feuding, Slavic tribes? Varying interpretations of the so-called Norman controversy can best be addressed by noting that the Slavs, like most other Europeans, fell under the wave of the northern invaders but, within two generations, assimilated them and incorporated their capabilities.

The Varangian Oleg (c. 882–913) established his seat of government at Kiev, at the transition point between the forest and steppe zones. During the tenth century Oleg and Sviatoslav (SVYAH-toe-slaf; r. 964–972) created a state that was the equal of contemporary France. Oleg took control of both Kiev and Novgorod and, with the strength gained, launched an attack on Constantinople. Sviatoslav carried Kievan power to the Danube and the lower Volga. He fell victim to the knives of Asiatic invaders, the Patzinaks. However, he left a state strong enough to endure almost a decade of internal power struggles.

The most important ruler in the Kievan phase of Russian history was Vladimir, who overcame his brothers to dominate his country from 980 to 1015. Vladimir learned his political lessons dealing with the Byzantines, and he consolidated his power in Kiev. At first, he based his rule on the pagan religion and erected statues to gods such as Perun (the god of thunder) and Volos (the god of wealth). He made peace with the Volga Bulgars to the east and worked with the Byzantines against the Bulgarians in pursuit of his diplomatic and political goals.

Constantine I, Vladimir, and the Selection of Christianity

Vladimir acknowledged the fact that the nations surrounding him were converting to one organized

Document The Acceptance of Christianity

The Christian conversion of European pagan leaders involved a complex formula of political advantage, internal rivalries, and piety. Beginning with Constantine's conversion, as described by Eusebius, the spiritual element is always emphasized as the primary cause for becoming Christian. Vladimir's conversion to Orthodoxy was a fundamental step in the division of Europe between East and West, perhaps a far more important step than any other taken in Russian history. This excerpt from the *Russian Primary Chronicle* explains in touching, if naive, detail how the decision was made.

6494 (986). Vladimir was visited by Volga Bulgars of Mohammedan [Muslim] faith. . . . Then came the Germans, asserting that they came as emissaries of the Pope. . . . The Jewish Khazars heard of these missions, and came themselves. . . . Then the Greeks sent to Vladimir a scholar. . . .

6495 (987). Vladimir summoned together his vassals and the city elders, and said to them, "Behold, the Volga Bulgars came before me urging me to accept their religion. Then came the Germans and praised their own faith; and after them came the Jews. Finally the Greeks appeared, criticizing all other faiths but commending their own, and they spoke at length, telling the history of the whole world from its beginning. . . ."

. . . The Prince and all the people chose good and wise men to the number of ten, and directed them to go first among the Volga Bulgars and inspect their faith. The emissaries went their way, and when they arrived at their destination they beheld the disgraceful actions of the Volga Bulgars and their worship in the mosque; then they returned to their own country. Vladimir then instructed them to go likewise among the Germans, and examine their faith, and finally to visit the Greeks. They thus went into Germany, and after viewing the German ceremonial, they proceeded to Tsargrad [Constantinople], where they appeared before the Emperor. . . .

Thus they returned to their own country, and the Prince called together his vassals and the elders. Vladimir then announced the return of the envoys who had been sent out, and suggested that their report be heard. He thus commanded them to speak out before his vassals. The envoys reported, "When we journeyed among the Volga Bulgars, we beheld how they worship in their temple, called a mosque, while they stand ungirt. The Volga Bulgar bows, sits down, looks hither and thither like one possessed, and there is no happiness among them, but instead only sorrow and a dreadful stench. Their religion is not good. Then we went among the Germans, and saw them performing many ceremonies in their temples; but we beheld no glory there. Then we went on to Greece, and the Greeks led us to the edifices where they worship their God, and we knew not whether we were in heaven or on earth. For on earth there is no such splendor or such beauty, and we are at a loss how to describe it. We only know that God dwells there among men, and their service is fairer than the ceremonies of other nations. . . ." Then the vassals spoke and said, "If the Greek faith were evil, it would not have been adopted by your grandmother Olga, who was wiser than all other men." Vladimir then inquired where they should all accept baptism, and they replied that the decision rested with him. . . .

By divine agency, Vladimir was suffering at that moment from a disease of the eyes, and could see nothing, being in great distress. The Princess declared to him that if he desired to be relieved of this disease, he should be baptized with all speed, otherwise it could not be cured. . . . The Bishop of Kherson, together with the Princess' priests, after announcing the tidings, baptized Vladimir, and as the Bishop laid his hand upon him, he straightway received his sight. Upon experiencing this miraculous cure, Vladimir glorified God, saying, "I have now perceived the one true God." When his followers beheld this miracle, many of them were also baptized.

Questions to Consider

1. Why do you think that Vladimir felt compelled to convert to one religion or another? Were spiritual or secular concerns more important? What did he gain by conversion?
2. Which of the possible options—Catholicism, Islam, Judaism, Orthodoxy—gave the most important advantages to Vladimir? Consider each choice and make a list of negative and positive points for the Russian ruler.
3. If you have access to a genealogy of your family, try to identify how your ancestors come to find their particular religious—or nonreligious—persuasions.

From *The Russian Primary Chronicle*, trans. Samuel H. Cross. In *Harvard Studies and Notes in Philology and Literature*, Vol. 12 (Cambridge, Mass.: Harvard University Press, 1953), pp. 183–213 passim. Reprinted by permission.

religion or another: the Poles and Hungarians to Roman Catholicism, the Khazars to Judaism, the Volga Bulgars to Islam, and the Bulgarians to Orthodox Christianity. His shrewd grandmother, Olga, had accepted Orthodox Christianity from Constantinople in 956, as had other members of his family. During the 980s Vladimir sent observers to judge the various religious alternatives. According to *The Russian Primary Chronicle,* they visited Hagia Sophia at Constantinople in 988 and were impressed with the power and wealth of the city. The observers recommended that Vladimir choose the Orthodox faith.

DOCUMENT Vladimir's Acceptance of Christianity

The story, though interesting, ignores the many concrete advantages Vladimir derived from his decision. As part of the negotiation package, Vladimir agreed to help the Byzantine emperor Basil against his enemies. In return, upon converting to Orthodoxy, he would receive the hand of the emperor's sister in marriage. After a successful campaign, Basil delayed in carrying out his part of the bargain. Vladimir moved quickly to make his point and marched into the Crimea and took the Byzantine city of Cherson. The Kiev-Byzantine arrangements were finally carried out in 990. Vladimir, now a member of the Byzantine royal family, brought his country into the Byzantine, Orthodox orbit. Even before "becoming a saint," the Chronicle tells us he destroyed the pagan statues, converted his many concubines to nuns, and forced his people to become Christians.[3] Eventually the Russians gained their own church, received their own metropolitan, and adapted Byzantine ritual, theology, and monastic practices to their own use. They also applied Byzantine governmental theories to their own social hierarchy.

After Vladimir, few great monarchs ruled during the Kievan period of Russian history. Instead, political fragmentation began to intensify. During the reign of Yaroslav the Wise (r. 1019–1054), the Kievan state reached its high point. It was the cultural and economic equal of any government in Europe, with cities larger than those found in the West. Yaroslav undertook major building projects, revised the law code, and promoted the growth of the church. He formed a dynastic alliance with Henry I of France. Unfortunately, Kiev did not long maintain its prestigious position. Yaroslav introduced a principle of succession based on the seniority system, passing the rule of Kiev from brother to brother in a given generation. This practice is in contrast with the Western one of primogeniture, under which rule is handed down to the eldest son of the ruler. Within two generations, the seniority system led to the political breakup of Kiev, although the city maintained its theoretical superiority within Russia.

Kiev also came under attack from both east and west and suffered as well from the economic decline of Constantinople. Under Vladimir Monomakh (r. 1113–1125), Kiev reemerged briefly as a center of power, but a half-century of decline soon followed. Competing centers arose at Suzdal; Galicia, where the local aristocracy dominated; Vladimir, where the prince emerged all-powerful; and Novgorod, where the assembled citizens—the *veche*—were the major force. Even before the Mongols totally destroyed the city in 1240, Kiev's era of prominence was effectively over.

For Christians of all denominations and beliefs, the Archangel Gabriel is one of the most beloved angels. He is the angel of mercy, the messenger of the incarnation and resurrection, and the bringer of consolation. It is no wonder that he figured heavily in the iconography of the Orthodox Church.

Novgorod, Moscow, and the Mongols

For more than two centuries, from 1240 to 1480, Mongols dominated Russia, and during that time, much of the land was cut off from contact with the outside world. During this period a new center of power, Moscow, emerged to serve for most of the time as collector of tribute for the Mongol court. New internal markets developed, and the Orthodox Church, unhampered by the Mongols, grew in strength and influence. The Russian city of Novgorod also managed to carry on despite the oriental overlord.

Novgorod had come under the control of the Varangians in the ninth century. However, in 997, the citizens received a charter granting them self-government, and for the next five centuries this *veche* elected its own rulers. The city boasted an aggressive and prosperous merchant class, which exploited the region from the Ural Mountains to the Baltic Sea and held its own against German merchants from the Baltic area. Novgorod was the equal of most of the cities found along the Baltic and North seas. In the middle of the thirteenth century, Alexander Nevsky, the prince of Novgorod, led his fellow citizens in struggles to repel the Teutonic Knights and the Swedes. A few years later, he showed exceptional diplomatic skill in paying homage to the Mongols, even though they had halted 60 miles outside the city and left Novgorod untouched. At a time when the rest of Russia suffered mightily under the first phase of Mongol domination, the *veche*-elected oligarchy continued to rule Novgorod.

The city's wealth and traditions permitted the *veche* to rule. These male citizens elected their princes and forced them to sign a contract setting out what they could and could not do. In the words of a typical document between ruler and city, the citizens could show their prince "the way out" if he failed to live up to the terms of his agreement. The prince could act as a leader of Novgorod only when he remained within the city's limits. The city's method of government permitted the rise of class divisions that led to more than 20 major outbreaks of violence in the thirteenth and fourteenth centuries. Changes in trade routes in the fifteenth century led to a decline in Baltic commerce, and Novgorod became dependent on Moscow for its grain supply. That dependence, in addition to the class conflict, weakened Novgorod, and in 1478 Moscow absorbed the town.

The obscure fortress town of Moscow, first mentioned in records in 1147, became the core of the new Russia. Even before the Mongol invasion, a large number of Slavs moved toward the north and east, and this migration continued for centuries as that frontier offered opportunities for the oppressed. Moscow was well-placed along a north-south river route in a protective setting of marshes and forests.

MAP
The Rise of Moscow

One of Alexander Nevsky's sons, Daniel, founded the Grand Duchy of Moscow, and he and subsequent rulers inherited Nevsky's ability to get along with the Mongols. As the Moscow princes skillfully acknowledged their inferior position to the Mongol khans, who sought tribute and recruits, the Muscovites improved their political position in relation to the other Russians by monopolizing the tax collection function for the

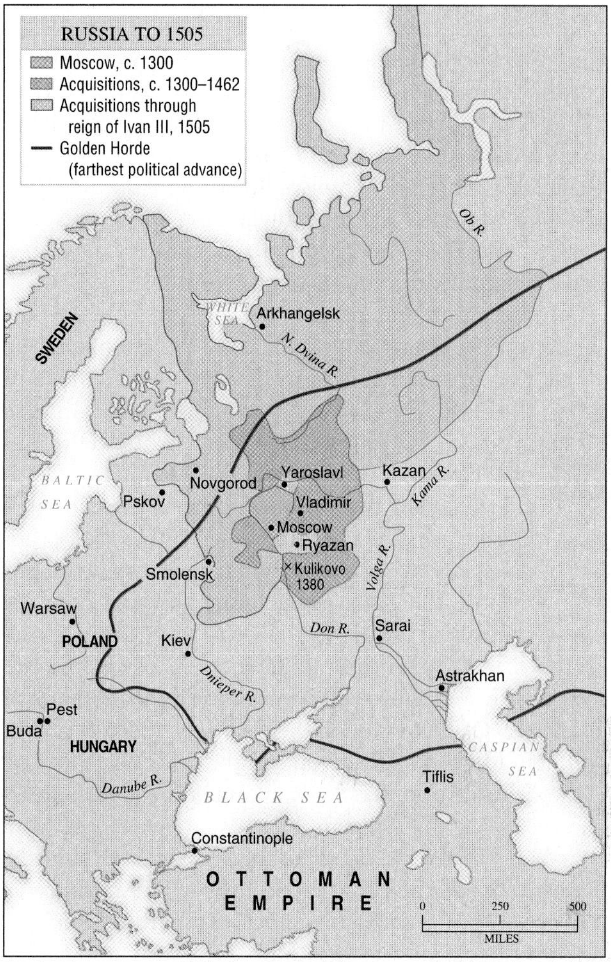

Beginning as a small fortress town, first mentioned in the chronicles in the mid-twelfth century, Moscow grew rapidly by 1500.

Mongols. In addition, at the beginning of the fourteenth century they made sure that the seat of the Russian Orthodox Church would be in Moscow, a reflection of the city's prestige.

IMAGE
St. Basil's Cathedral, Moscow

In the first century after the Mongol invasion, the Muscovite princes showed a great deal of ambition and ability, albeit in a sometimes unattractive way. For example, during his reign Ivan I Kalita (r. 1328–1341), whose surname means "moneybags," greatly increased the wealth and power of Moscow through aggressive tax collection practices.

On the surface, the fourteenth century appeared to be a time of decline, of Mongol domination and gains by the European states at Russian expense along the western boundary. The reality, however, was that Russia was laying foundations for its future with Moscow as the country's religious and political center. In 1380 Dmitri Donskoi (r. 1359–1389) defeated the Mongols at Kulikovo. Although Mongol strength was far from broken, the Russian victory had great symbolic significance.

Ivan III and the Third Rome

Civil war and invasions threatened the Moscow-based country throughout the fifteenth century. Finally, Ivan III (r. 1462–1505) made major strides to build the modern Russian state. He took Novgorod and two years later ceased acknowledging Mongol domination. He then began to advance toward the south and east against the Turks and Mongols, setting in motion a drive of expansion that lasted for centuries.

In developments of considerable symbolic importance, the Russians embraced many elements of the Roman tradition. Ivan III married the niece of the last East Roman emperor, an alliance arranged by the pope. Russians espoused the theory that Moscow was the Third Rome, the logical successor to Constantinople as the center of Christianity. In 1492 (the year 7000 in the Orthodox calendar and the beginning of a new millennium), the Muscovite metropolitan, Zosima, stated that Ivan III was "the new Emperor Constantine of the new Constantinople Moscow." Zosima for the first time called Moscow an imperial city. Philotheus of Pskov (SKOV) expounded the theory of Third Rome in full detail in the 1520s. Ivan began to use the title *tsar* ("caesar") and adopted the Roman two-headed eagle as the symbol of the Russian throne.

DOCUMENT
Filofei and the Christian Role of Moscow

Ivan opened the doors to the West ever so slightly. He established diplomatic relations with a number of European powers. He brought in Italian technicians and architects such as Aristotele Fieravanti and Pietro Antonio Solari to work on the churches, palaces, and walls of the Kremlin: the vastly expanded site of the original fortress that was the center of the town three centuries earlier. The Italian artistic tradition had no lasting cultural impact on Russia, but use of Italian artists nonetheless signified an awareness of the West. In recognition of the need to establish a standing army, Ivan began the difficult process of building up a modern state structure and increased restrictions on the Russian peasants. During the fifteenth century, Ivan was the equal of his western European colleagues Henry VII of England and Louis XI of France. After three centuries of isolation under the Mongols, the Russians were again interacting with Europe.

CONCLUSION

Byzantium made important contributions to European civilization: Greek language and learning were preserved for posterity—especially after the transmission of documents and texts to Italy, an important stage in the opening of the Renaissance; the Roman imperial system was continued and Roman law codified; and missionary activity spread Christianity throughout much of eastern Europe and Russia and fostered the development of a splendid new art dedicated to the glorification of the Christian religion. Situated at the crossroads of the East and the West, Constantinople acted as the disseminator of culture for all peoples who came in contact with the empire. This rich and turbulent city was to the early Middle Ages what Athens and Rome had been to classical times. Most importantly, by merging Roman political institutions with the Christian Church, Constantine created the form of political legitimacy that would last in Europe until the French Revolution in 1789.

From the fourth through the ninth centuries, as the Slavs moved to their new homelands, they came under the influence of dominant outside forces. In Russia and the Balkans, Byzantine patterns and traditions shaped their lives. After its initial Kievan phase, in which Vladimir made the choice to follow East Roman precedents, the Russians remained under Mongol domination even when Russia's political and religious center moved to Moscow. When the Russians regained their independence in the fifteenth century, they redefined their polity in Roman and Christian terms, claiming the legacy of the fallen city of Constantinople.

From Constantine onward, ambitious Christian leaders strengthened their control through the powerful fusion of Roman symbolism and the Christian Church. Not until the development of modern political ideologies after the French Revolution did a more potent combination of theories and symbols help governments motivate and dominate their people. In its turn, the politicians' embrace of Christ's message profoundly altered the form, if not the substance, of Christianity.

Suggestions for Web Browsing

You can obtain more information about topics included in this chapter at the websites listed below. See also the companion website that accompanies this text, **http://www.ablongman.com/brummett**, which contains an online study guide and additional resources.

Access to the Metropolitan Museum of Arts Byzantine Collection
http://www.metmuseum.org/explore/Byzantium/byzhome.html

A site providing a wide-ranging selection of Byzantine architectural and artistic triumphs.

Byzantium Studies on the Internet
http://www.fordham.edu/halsall/byzantium/

Byzantine Art
http://www.fordham.edu/halsall/byzantium/images.html

This site includes many images of icons, monasteries, Ravenna, and Hagia Sophia; it details Byzantine life in Jerusalem and offers links to related websites.

Byzantine Architecture
http://www.byzantium1200.com

See a unique experience at computer reconstructions of major Byzantine structures as they might have been in the year 1200.

Historical Tour of Jerusalem: Byzantine Period
http://gurukul.ucc.american.edu/TED/hpages/jeruselum/byzantin.htm

Short history of Jerusalem, from 324 to 638 C.E., including an image and discussion of the Madaba mosaic showing the Jerusalem Gate.

Women in Byzantium
http://www.wooster.edu/ART/wb.html

Extensive bibliography of primary and secondary sources regarding women in Byzantium.

Byzantium Through Arab Eyes
http://www.fordham.edu/halsall/source/byz-arabambas.html

An original account of a mission to Constantinople by an Arab ambassador in the late tenth century.

Literature and Film

One of the finest novels written about Byzantium is Gore Vidal's celebration of the last pagan emperor, *Julian* (Vintage, 2003). Superbly written, it is unabashedly pro-Julian and makes the fourth-century Christian hierarchy appear to be narrow and even backward in the face of the emperor's learning and sophistication. Michael Ennis gives a lively view of the tenth century in his *Byzantium* (Atlantic Monthly Press, 1989). The fortress city is seen through Viking eyes. A classic, time-travel science-fiction treatment of the reign of Justinian and his Italian campaign is provided by L. Sprague de Camp in *Lest Darkness Fall* (Prime Press, 1949), available in combined edition with David Drake's *To Bring the Light* (Baen, 1996). The author is very good at picking up the religious competition between the Arian Goth and the Orthodox Byzantines. For the most complete selection of novels, poetry, plays, movies, and music of and about Byzantium go to http://www.fordham.edu/halsall/byzantium/texts/byznov.html.

Suggestions for Reading

Two works by Arnold Hugh Martin Jones, *The Decline of the Ancient World* (Longman, 1977), and *The Later Roman Empire, 284–602: A Social, Economic, and Administrative Survey*, 2 vols. (Johns Hopkins University Press, 1986), are indispensable. Two recent and valuable studies on the impacts of the German infiltration and, later, invasions of the Roman Empire are Herwig Wolfram, *The Roman Empire and its Germanic Peoples* (University of California Press, 1998), and Leslie Webster and Michelle Brown, eds., *The Transformation of the Roman World: AD 400–900* (University of California Press, 1997).

For an exhaustive treatment of all aspects of Byzantine life, see *The Cambridge Medieval History* (Cambridge University Press, 2004, replacing Vol. 4 of the 1966–1967 edition). George Ostrogorsky, *History of the Byzantine State* (Rutgers University Press, 1957), provides a clear institutional overview. Joan M. Hussey's *The Orthodox Church in the Byzantine Empire* (Oxford University Press, 1986) is the best introduction in English to the development of the eastern variant of Christianity. Warren Treadgold provides a view of the sophistication of one period of medieval Byzantium in his *The Byzantine Revival, 780–842* (Stanford University Press, 1991). Francis Dvornik, *The Photian Schism: History and Legend* (Rutgers University Press, 1970), and *The Slavs in European History and Civilization* (Rutgers University Press, 1970), address the matters of conversion.

Charles M. Brand, *Byzantium Confronts the West, 1180–1204* (Harvard University Press, 1968), and Donald E. Queller, ed., *The Latin Conquest of Constantinople* (John Wiley & Sons, 1971), describe the tragedy of the Crusades for Byzantium and complement Steven Runciman's three-volume *History of the Crusades* (Cambridge University Press, 1987). For a view from the other side, see Amin Maalouf, *The Crusade Through Arab Eyes* (Shocken Books, 1989). Donald Nicol, *The Last Centuries of Byzantium*, 2nd ed. (Cambridge University Press, 1993), discusses the empire in its state of weakness. For an excellent discussion of the military reorganization that made the survival of the Byzantine Empire possible, see Warren Treadgold, *Byzantium and Its Army: 284–1081* (Stanford University Press, 1995). Paul Stephenson's study, *Byzantium's Balkan Frontier: A Political Study of the Northern Balkans: 900-1204* (Cambridge University Press, 2000), is a much-needed contribution to the opening chapters of the political history of the peoples of the Balkans.

John Fennell, *The Crisis of Medieval Russia, 1200–1304* (Longman, 1983), and Robert O. Crummey, *The Formation of Muscovy, 1304-1613* (Longman, 1987), are two first-rate surveys of the early phases of Russian history. Oscar Halecki, *Borderlands of Western Civilization* (Random House, 1984), gives the outlines of eastern European history, especially the northern region.

CHAPTER

7

Islam

From Its Origins to 1300

CHAPTER CONTENTS

Arabia was the birthplace of the Islamic religion; out of this desert peninsula with its commercial entrepots and oases there emerged a new vision of the world and of people's relation to the divine. That vision was based on a single, powerful god, a final prophet, and a belief in revelation. It provided a system of law, a guide for social organization, and a framework for what would become a highly diverse cultural synthesis. Human time began with the first man and woman, Adam and Eve; each believer lived in expectation of a Judgment Day, while the afterlife promised a gardenlike heaven and a fiery hell. For kingdoms and their rulers, Islam provided a universal law extending to all subjects, Muslim and non-Muslim alike. It legitimized sovereigns and promised justice to subjects. The ideal society envisioned in its sacred text, the Qur'an (or *Koran*), was one in which marriage was a preferred state, women were subordinate to men, the wealthy took care of the poor, and competing allegiances were set aside in favor of a primary allegiance to the community of believers (the *umma*). This worldview both challenged and reflected the social order of Arabia. Of course, societies and states never adhere absolutely to the ideals embedded in their sacred texts, and religious messages are interpreted in diverse ways as they extend over time and across space. Like other religious messages, the message of Islam was codified and contested. But the unity embodied in the idea of the *umma* and in the universal Sharia law has prompted some scholars to call Islamic civilization the "first world civilization." Within one century after Muhammad disseminated its message in the seventh century C.E., the power of Islam would be felt from the Indian Ocean to the Atlantic; it would transfigure age-old religious, intellectual, and political patterns.

600

622 Hijra, Muhammad's flight from Mecca to Medina

632–661 Rashidun caliphs; Islam spreads in Near East, Persia, and North Africa

661–750 Umayyad dynasty; Islam expands into Central Asia, Indus valley, Maghrib, and Spain

700

750–1258 Abbasid dynasty, high point of classical Islamic civilization

756–1031 Umayyad dynasty reestablished in Spain and North Africa

900

900–1100 Golden Age of Muslim scholarship

909–1171 Fatimid dynasty, first in North Africa, then in Egypt and Syria

1000

1095 First Crusade called

1200

1250 Mamluks seize power in Egypt

1258 Mongols conquer Baghdad

ARABIA BEFORE THE PROPHET

■ *How did the desert environment of Arabia influence Arabic culture?*

The Arabian peninsula is one-third the size of the continental United States. Most of its land is desert; rainfall is scarce, vegetation is scant, and very little of the land is suitable for agriculture. Arabia before the birth of Muhammad was a culturally isolated and economically underdeveloped region. In the relatively more fertile southwestern corner of the peninsula, however, several small Arab kingdoms once flourished in the area now known as Yemen. The most notable of these early kingdoms, Saba' (the biblical Sheba), existed as early as the eighth century B.C.E. and lasted until the third century C.E., when it was taken by the Himyarites (HEEM-yar-aits) from the south.

Aided by the domestication of the camel and the expanding trade in frankincense and spices, these kingdoms became prosperous; they formed part of a commercial network of kingdoms within and beyond the Arabian peninsula. In the north of Arabia, several kingdoms were able to establish contacts with the Byzantine and the Persian (Sassanid) empires as early as the fifth century C.E. Among the most notable of these small kingdoms were Nabataea in northwestern Arabia, which dominated Arabian trade routes until the Romans annexed the kingdom in the second century C.E., and the realm of the Lakhmids in the northeast, whose prominence was greatest around 250 to 600 C.E., until the kingdom was destroyed by the Sassanids. But in the interior of Arabia, a vast desert dotted sparsely with oases, a nomadic life based on herding was the only successful existence.

The Bedouin

The desert nomads, or *Bedouin* (BED-eu-in), lived according to ancient tribal patterns; at the head of the tribe was the male elder, or *shaykh* (SHAYK), elected and advised by the heads of the related families comprising the tribe. These men claimed authority based on family connections and personal merit. Tribes tended to be made up of three-generation families employing a gendered division of labor. The Bedouin led a precarious existence, moving their flocks from one pasture to the next, often following set patterns of migration. Aside from maintaining their herds, these nomads traded animal products for goods from the settled areas. They also relied on plunder from raids on settlements, on passing caravans, and on one another. Their nomadic existence, its hardships, and the beauty of the desert landscape are all celebrated in the poetry of pre-Islamic Arabia.

The Bedouin enjoyed a degree of personal freedom unknown in more agrarian and settled societies. They developed a code of ethics represented in the word *muru'a* (moo-ROO-ah), or "manly virtue." Far from being abrasive and rough, men proved *muru'a* through grace and restraint, loyalty to obligation and duty, a devotion to do what must be done, and respect for women. The tribe shared a corporate spirit, or *'asabiyya* (AHS-ahb-ee-yah), which reflected the shared interests and honor of the tribe.

Although Bedouin society was patriarchal (dominated by the senior males), women enjoyed a great degree of independence. They engaged in business and commerce and could sometimes wed men of their own choosing. As in all traditional agricultural societies, however, women were under the protection of men, and the honor of the tribe was vested in the sexual honor of the women. The relative freedom of the Bedouin sprang from the realities of life in the desert, as did their values and ethics. One rule of conduct was unqualified hospitality to strangers. A nomad never knew when the care of a stranger might be essential to provide the necessary water and shade to save his or her own life.

The Bedouin of the seventh century did not have a highly structured religious system. They apparently looked at life as a brief time during which to take full advantage of daily pleasure. Ideas of an afterlife were not well defined or described. The Bedouin were animists; they worshipped a large number of gods and spirits, many of whom they believed to inhabit trees, wells, and stones. Each tribe had its own gods, sometimes symbolized by sacred stones.

The Bedouin of the Arabian interior led a relatively primitive and isolated existence, but it was not in their herding camps that the message of Islam was first spoken. In the Arabian cities along the trade routes, the people came into contact with traders and travelers who brought a complex mix of artistic, religious, and philosophical influences. Among these were the monotheistic beliefs of Judaism and Christianity. Some parts of Arabia were greatly influenced by the neighboring and more highly sophisticated cultures of Byzantium, Sassanid Persia, and Ethiopia. It was out of this more urban and commercial context that the early Islamic state would emerge.

Early Mecca

On the western side of the Arabian peninsula along the Red Sea is a region known as the Hijaz, or "barrier."

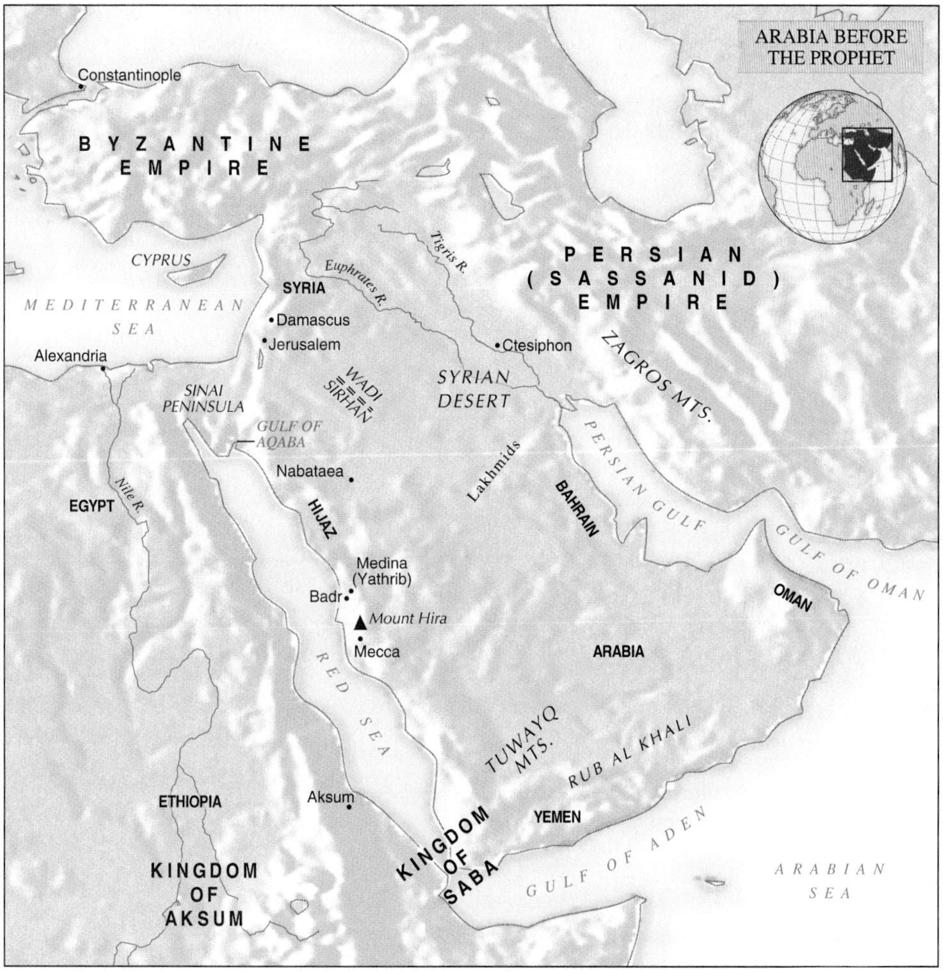

Geography played a key role in Arab history. The severity of the Arabian environment heavily influenced Bedouin social, economic, religious, and political life.

The Hijaz extends along the western coastal plain from Yemen in the south to the Sinai peninsula in the north. One of the oases in the Hijaz is Mecca, set among barren hills 50 miles inland from the sea. This site had several advantages: Mecca possessed a well (the Zamzam) of great depth, and two ancient caravan routes met there. One route ran from Africa through the peninsula to Iran and central Asia, and another, a southeast-northwest route, brought the textiles and spices of India and Southeast Asia to the Mediterranean world.

A second significant advantage for Mecca was its importance as a religious sanctuary. An ancient temple, an almost square structure built of granite blocks, stood near the well of Mecca. Known as the *Ka'ba* ("cube"), this square temple contained the sacred Black Stone. According to tradition, the stone, probably a meteorite, was originally white but had become blackened by the sins of all those who touched it. Later Muslim historians would attribute the building of the Ka'ba to the prophet Abraham or even to Adam. The Ka'ba itself was draped with the pelts of sacrificial animals and supposedly held the images and shrines of 360 gods and goddesses. For centuries, the Ka'ba had been a holy place of annual pilgrimage for the Arab tribes and a focal point of Arab culture and ritual practice. As a pilgrimage site, it also brought prestige and wealth to the tribes who controlled the city of Mecca.

By the sixth century, Mecca was controlled by the Quraysh (KOO-raysh) tribe, whose rulers organized themselves into an aristocracy of merchants and wealthy businessmen. The Quraysh engaged in lucrative trade with Byzantium and Persia, as well as with the southern Arabian tribes and the kingdom of Aksum across the Red Sea in what is now Ethiopia. In addition, a number of annual merchant fairs, such as one usually held at nearby Ukaz, were taken over by the Quraysh to extend the economic influence of Mecca. The Quraysh were also concerned with protecting the religious shrine of the Ka'ba, in addition to ensuring that the annual pilgrimage of tribes to the holy place would continue as a source of revenue for the merchants of the city.

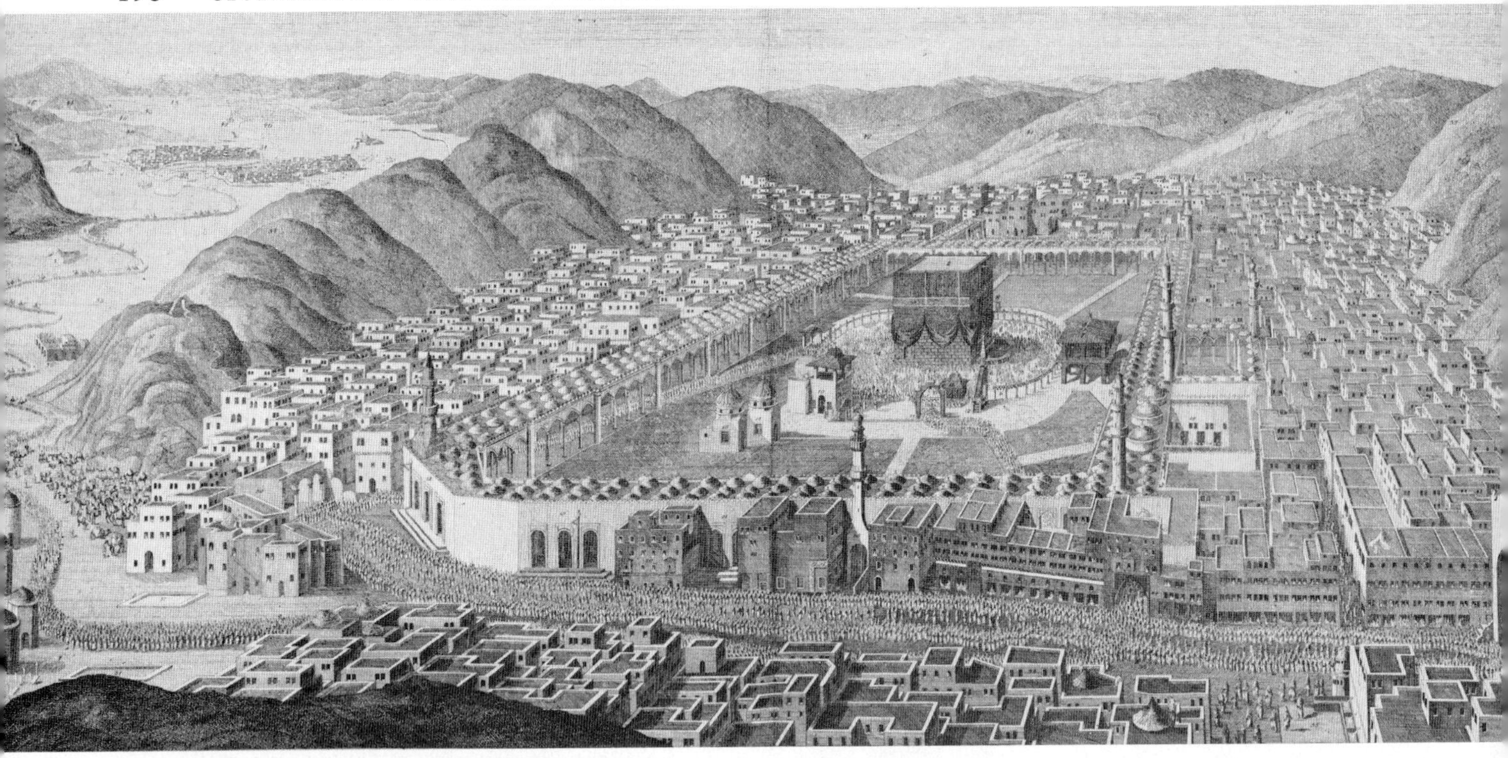

This nineteenth-century engraving depicts the city of Mecca with, at its center, the Ka'ba, a square building of stone draped with black cloth that became the focal point of Muslim worship. Each year Muslims make the pilgrimage to celebrate their unity and to worship at this most sacred shrine of Islam. The site itself and its buildings (as shown here) have been greatly expanded over the centuries since the Prophet Muhammad's time, and the number of pilgrims has dramatically increased.

MUHAMMAD, PROPHET OF ISLAM

- *What role did Muhammad play in the creation of Islam?*

Into this environment at Mecca was born a man who would revolutionize the religious, political, and social organization of his people. Muhammad (c. 570–632) came from a family belonging to the Quraysh. An orphan, he suffered the loss of both his parents and his grandfather, who cared for him after his parents' death. He was then raised by his uncle, Abu Talib, a prominent merchant of Mecca. His early years were spent helping his uncle in the caravan trade. Even as a young man, Muhammad came to be admired by his fellow Meccans as a sincere and honest person who earned the nickname al-Amin, "the trustworthy." When he was about 25 years old, he accepted employment from a wealthy widow, Khadija (cah-DEE-jah), whose caravans traded with Syria. He later married Khadija and began to take his place as a leading citizen of Mecca. Muhammad's marriage to Khadija was a long and happy one that produced two sons, who both died as infants, and two daughters. The younger, Fatima, would play an important role in the future of the fledgling Islamic state.

Biographies of the Prophet, written after his death by his followers, describe him as a handsome, large man with broad shoulders and black, shining eyes, a man who was reserved and gentle but possessed of impressive energy. Tradition relates that Muhammad was an introspective man. Often he would escape from Meccan society, which he considered too materialistic and irreligious, and spend long hours alone in a cave on nearby Mount Hira. During these hours of meditation, Muhammad searched for answers to the metaphysical questions that many thoughtful people have pondered. Muhammad's meditations sometimes produced nearly total mental and physical exhaustion. During one such solitary meditation, Muhammad heard a call that was to alter history. This initial communication from heaven came in the form of a command:

> *Recite! In the name of your Lord, who created*
> *all things, who*
> *created man from a clot [of blood].*
> *Recite! And your Lord is Most Bounteous*
> *Who teaches by the Pen,*
> *Teaches man that which he would not have*
> *otherwise known. (Qur'an 96:1–5)*

The collected revelations given to Muhammad are known as the **Qur'an** (or Koran), an Arabic word meaning "recitation" or "reading." The revelations that continued to come over the next 20 years or so were sometimes terse and short, at other times elaborate and poetic. The early revelations did not immediately persuade Muhammad that he was a messenger of God. In fact, his first reactions were fear and self-doubt. Anxious about the source and nature of his revelations, he sought the comfort and advice of Khadija.

As the revelations continued, Muhammad was persuaded that he had been called to be a messenger of divine revelation. He began to think of himself and his mission as one similar to those of prophets and messengers who had preceded him in announcing the existence of the one God, ***Allah***. Allah, "*the* God," was the same God worshipped by the Christians and Jews, but Allah had now chosen Muhammad to be his last and greatest prophet to perfect the religion revealed earlier to Abraham, Moses, the Hebrew prophets, and Jesus. The religion Muhammad preached is called ***Islam,*** which means "submission" to the will of God. The followers of Islam are called *Muslims,* "those who submit" to God's law.

Muhammad's Message and Its Early Followers

At first Muhammad had little success in attracting followers in Mecca. The early message he brought to the Arabs was strong and direct: that Allah was the one God and majestic, all-powerful, and demanding of the faith of his followers. Furthermore, Allah decreed that his followers be compassionate, ethical, and just in all their dealings:

In the name of Allah, the most Beneficent, the
Most Merciful
by the night as it enshrouds
by the day as it illuminates
by Him Who created the male and female
indeed your affairs lead to various ends.
For who gives [of himself] and acts righteously,
and conforms to goodness,
We will give him ease.
But as for him who is niggardly deeming
himself self-sufficient and rejects goodness,
We will indeed ease his path to adversity.
Nor shall his wealth save him as he perishes
for Guidance is from Us
and to Us belongs the Last and First.
(Qur'an 92:1–14)

Muhammad was able to win the early support of some of his relatives and close friends. His first converts were his wife, his cousin Ali, and Abu Bakr, a leading merchant of the Quraysh tribe, who was highly respected for his integrity. Abu Bakr remained the constant companion of the Prophet during his persecution and exile and later succeeded him as the leader of Islam. But opposition to Muhammad's message was very strong, especially from Mecca's leading citizens. Many thought Muhammad was an ambitious poet attempting to pass on his own literary creations as the word of God. Others believed him to be possessed by demons. Muhammad challenged the status quo; his strong monotheism threatened the polytheistic beliefs of Mecca and the people who obtained their income from the pilgrims to the Ka'ba. Many of Muhammad's early converts were among the poorest of the city's residents, and Mecca's leading citizens feared the possibility of social revolution.

Since Muhammad was himself a member of the Quraysh tribe, its leaders first approached his uncle Abu Talib to persuade his nephew to stop preaching. Next they tried to bribe Muhammad with the promise of a lucrative appointment as an official. When he rejected such offers, actual persecution of Muhammad's converts began, and the Quraysh attempted a commercial and social boycott of the Prophet's family. During this time of trial, Abu Talib and Khadija both died, and Muhammad's faith and resolution were greatly tested. But inspired by the spirit and example of earlier prophets such as Abraham and Moses, who were also tested and persecuted, Muhammad persevered in his faith and continued his preaching.

The Hijra

To the north of Mecca is the city of Medina, which was then called Yathrib. The residents of Medina were somewhat familiar with monotheistic beliefs, in part because of the Jewish community in residence there. While visiting Mecca, some pilgrims from Medina judged Muhammad to be a powerful and influential mediator and invited him to come to Medina to settle differences among that city's tribal chiefs. As opposition to his message increased in Mecca, Muhammad sent some of his followers to take up residence in Medina in order to escape persecution. Finally, Muhammad and Abu Bakr fled Mecca when it became known that

---

Qur'an—Literally "recitation" or "reading" in Arabic; the Islamic holy book containing the word of God (Allah) as revealed to the Prophet Muhammad through the angel Gabriel. Written in Arabic and to be read only in this language by believers.

Allah—"The God" in Arabic; the Arabic word for the same God worshipped in Christianity and Judaism.

Islam—The religion founded by the Prophet Muhammad in the seventh century A.D., a monotheistic faith drawing on elements from Judaism, Christianity, and the indigenous beliefs of the Arabian peninsula; literally "submission" in Arabic, as in "submission" to God's will.

the Quraysh intended to kill the Prophet. They were followed, but escaped, the story goes, by hiding in a narrow cave whose entrance was quickly covered by a spider's web. The Quraysh pursuers saw the web and passed on, thinking that the cave had been abandoned for a long time.

The ***Hijra*** (or *Hegira*), Muhammad's "migration" from Mecca to Medina, took place in September in the year 622. The event was such a turning point in the history of Islam that 622 is counted as year 1 of the Islamic calendar, because it marked the beginning of the Islamic state. In Medina, the Prophet met with entirely different circumstances from those in his birthplace. Muhammad's leadership turned Medina (*Madinat al-Nabi,* "City of the Prophet") into the major center of power in the Arabian peninsula.

The Community at Medina

Muhammad was received in Medina as a leader and a spiritual visionary. There, he and his followers set about the establishment of the Muslim ***umma*** or community. This new community established relations with the Medinan tribes, including the Jewish and Christian residents. Those who did not choose to accept Muhammad's faith were allowed to continue their way of life, since Christians and Jews were thought to be "people of the Book" to whom God had made himself known through earlier prophets. Ultimately, however, the Prophet's new polity came into conflict with some of the Jewish tribes of Medina and the tribes were expelled. This conflict illustrates the tension between the expansionist political policies and generally tolerant religious policies of the new state.

Hijra—The departure of the Prophet Muhammad from Mecca for Medina in 622 A.D.; considered to be the formal starting point for Islam.

umma—The community or nation of believers in Islam.

The Early Islamic State

622 The Hijra, Muhammad's migration from Mecca to Medina, year 1 of the Islamic calendar

630 The Prophet returns and takes control of Mecca, Ka'ba consecrated to Allah

632 Death of the Prophet

632–661 Rule of the first four caliphs: Abu Bakr, Umar, Uthman, Ali

638 Muslim armies take Jerusalem

651 Defeat of the Sassanids in Persia

Muhammad and his followers became steadily more aggressive in their attempts to win converts to Islam. The word ***jihad,*** meaning "struggle," was applied to the early efforts of the *umma* to win converts and conquer territory. Military encounters with the opponents of Islam began in 624, with the battle of Badr. Muhammad defeated a stronger Quraysh troop from Mecca, and the victory reinforced the resolve of the new religion's followers. Succeeding battles established the Muslims as the dominant force in Arabia, and a truce with Mecca was arranged, under which the Muslims could visit the holy city.

Return to Mecca

In 630 Muhammad returned to take control of the city of Mecca and to cleanse the Ka'ba of idols. The temple itself, together with the Black Stone, was preserved as the supreme religious center of Islam and rededicated to the One God. It is to this shrine that all devout Muslims, if able, make pilgrimage during their lifetime. Muhammad urged unbelievers and his old enemies to accept Islam and become part of the *umma.* By 632 almost all of the Arabian peninsula had (at least nominally) accepted Islam, and Muhammad had even sent ambassadors to the neighboring Byzantine and Persian Empires to announce the new religion and encourage converts. Just as Christianity began as a religion of the Jews, Islam began as a religion of the Arabs. But, over time, like Christianity, and unlike Judaism, Islam became a universal religion with a missionary spirit.

The Death of Muhammad

Muhammad died on June 8, 632, in Medina. Muslims at first refused to accept his death but were reassured by Abu Bakr, who recited this verse from the Qur'an: "Muhammad is only a messenger: many are the messengers who have died before him; if he dies, or is slain, will you turn back on your heels?" (3:144).

Muhammad had no surviving son and had not designated a successor. On the day of his death, his close companions solved the question of leadership of the faithful by agreeing on the election of Abu Bakr, who became the first successor, or **caliph** (kal-IF). Abu Bakr could not really replace Muhammad, the last prophet. However, as caliph, he was regarded as the head of the Islamic *umma;* he combined the roles

jihad—Literally "struggle" in Arabic; an Islamic term with broad meaning, ranging from the internal struggle of an individual to overcome sin to the external struggle of the faithful to address a social challenge or to fight against enemies and unbelievers in what is essentially a holy war.

caliph—The religious and political leader of the Islamic nation; successor of Muhammad.

of religious leader and head of state. Abu Bakr and his three successors in the office, Umar, Uthman, and Ali, are often referred to as the *Rashidun* (RAHSH-ee-deun), the "Rightly Guided" caliphs.

The significance of Muhammad to the birth and growth of Islam is impossible to overestimate. The Prophet and his message inspired his followers to create and work for the betterment of a society united by the Islamic faith. Ideally, tribal loyalties were replaced by loyalty to the *umma* and faith in the One God, who chose to speak to his people in their own language through a messenger who was also one of their own.

Soon after Muhammad's death, his followers began to collect and codify his teachings and actions. The result of their efforts was the **hadith,** or reports of the sayings and activities of Muhammad. The hadith have become an important source of values and ethical paths of behavior for the Islamic world. The **sunna,** the custom or practice of the Prophet, is grounded in the hadith and serves as a pattern for a model way of life to be imitated by the faithful.

hadith—A collection of the sayings, deeds, and traditions of the Prophet Muhammad, compiled by the Prophet's followers after his death to further clarify Islamic values and ethics.

This miniature depicts one of the legends of the Prophet, the Miraj or Night Journey. Muhammad, mounted on a winged part-human, part-horse steed, is believed miraculously to have ascended to heaven from Jerusalem, there enjoying a vision of God, and returning in a single night.

ISLAMIC FAITH AND LAW

▪ *What is the relationship between the Qur'an and Islamic faith and law?*

Islam places great emphasis on the necessity of obedience to God's law in addition to faith. The Qur'an is the fundamental and ultimate source of knowledge about Allah. This holy book contains both the theology of Islam and the patterns of ethical and appropriate conduct to which a Muslim must subscribe. Included in the Qur'an are some basic concepts that the Islamic community holds in common as fundamental to the faith.

The Qur'an

Muslims believe that the Qur'an contains the actual word of God as it was revealed to Muhammad through divine inspiration. These revelations to the Prophet took place over a period of more than 20 years. Before Muhammad's death, many of these messages were written down. Muhammad himself began this work of preservation, and Abu Bakr, as caliph, continued the process by compiling revelations that up to that time had been memorized by the followers and passed on by word of mouth. A complete written text of the Qur'an was produced some years after Muhammad's death, with particular care taken to eliminate discrepancies and record only one standard version. This "authorized" edition was then transmitted to various parts of the new Islamic Empire and used to guide the faithful and assist in the conversion of unbelievers. The text of the Qur'an has existed virtually unchanged for nearly 14 centuries.

The Qur'an was intended to be recited aloud; anyone who has listened to the chanting of the Qur'an can testify to its beauty, melody, and power. Much of the power of the Qur'an comes from the experience of reciting, listening, and feeling the message. The Qur'an is never to be translated from the Arabic for the purpose of worship because it is believed that translation distorts the divine message. But over time, the Qur'an was indeed translated into many languages to facilitate

DOCUMENT
The Holy Qur'an

sunna—The custom or practice of the Prophet Muhammad, grounded in the hadith; intended to serve as a model by which Muslims should conduct their lives.

Document The Qur'an

The Qur'an is one of the most significant of all religious works and one of the world's most beautiful works of literature. The following is a selection celebrating God's creation, from sura 23, titled "The Believers." It illustrates Islam's connection, through the prophets Moses and Jesus, to the sacred texts and beliefs of Judaism and Christianity. But it also points out the Islamic doctrine that God has no son. The Qur'an makes a point of rejecting the notions that God had either sons (e.g., Jesus) or daughters (goddesses in the Arabian pantheon). Note too, that the Qur'an urges men, as well as women, to "guard their modesty."

In the name of Allah, the Beneficent, the Merciful.
Successful indeed are the believers
Who are humble in their prayers,
And who shun vain conversation,
And who are payers of the poor-due;
And who guard their modesty—
Save from their wives or the [slaves] that their right hands possess, for then they are not blameworthy,
But whoso craveth beyond that, such are transgressors—
And who are shepherds of their pledge and their covenant, and who pay heed to their prayers.
These are the heirs
Who will inherit Paradise. There they will abide.
Verily We created man from a product of wet earth;
Then placed him as a drop [of seed] in a safe lodging;
Then fashioned We the drop a clot, then fashioned We the clot a little lump, then fashioned We the little lump bones, then clothed the bones with flesh, and then produced it as another creation. So blessed be Allah, the Best of Creators!
Then lo! after that ye surely die.
Then lo! on the Day of Resurrection ye are raised [again].
And We have created above you seven paths, and We are never unmindful of creation.
And We send down from the sky water in measure, and We give it lodging in the earth, and lo! We are able to withdraw it.
Then We produce for you therewith gardens of date-palms and grapes, wherein is much fruit for you and whereof ye eat;
And a tree that springeth forth from Mount Sinai that groweth oil and relish for the eaters.
And lo! in the cattle there is verily a lesson for you. We give you to drink of that which is in their bellies, and many uses have ye in them, and of them do ye eat;
And on them and on the ship ye are carried.
Then We sent Moses and his brother Aaron with Our tokens and a clear warrant
Unto Pharaoh and his chiefs, but they scorned [them] and they were despotic folk.
And they said: Shall we put faith in two mortals like ourselves, and whose folk are servile unto us?
So they denied them, and became of those who were destroyed.
And We verily gave Moses the Scripture, that haply they might go aright.
And We made the son of Mary and his mother a portent, and We gave them refuge on a height, a place of flocks and water-springs.
O ye messengers! Eat of the good things, and do right. Lo! I am Aware of what ye do.
And lo! this your religion is one religion and I am your Lord, so keep your duty unto Me.
Say: In Whose hand is the dominion over all things and He protecteth, while against Him there is no protection, if ye have knowledge?
They will say: Unto Allah [all that belongeth]. Say: How then are ye bewitched?
Nay, but We have brought them the Truth, and lo! they are liars.
Allah hath not chosen any son, nor is there any God along with Him; else would each God have assuredly championed that which he created, and some of them would assuredly have overcome others. Glorified be Allah above all that they allege.
Knower of the invisible and the visible! and exalted be He over all that they ascribe as partners [unto Him]!

Questions to Consider

1. What kind of God is suggested in these verses? Characterize him.
2. What clues do these verses give us about the society and environment of Arabia?
3. Compare this account of creation to other creation accounts you are aware of.

From Marmaduke William Pickthall, *The Meaning of the Glorious Koran: An Explanatory Translation* (London: Unwin Hyman/HarperCollins). Reprinted by permission.

scholarship and the spread of the Islamic message. As Islam spread, so too did the Arabic language. Arabic replaced many local languages as the language of administration, and gradually, some of the conquered territories adopted Arabic as the language of everyday use. The Qur'an remains the basic document for the study of Islamic theology, law, social institutions, and ethics. It forms the core of Muslim scholarship, from legal and linguistic inquiry to scientific and technical investigation.

The Holy Qur'an

The Tenets of Islamic Faith

Monotheism is the central principle of Islam. Muslims believe in the unity or oneness of God; there is no other God but Allah, and this belief is proclaimed five times daily as the believers are called to prayer with these words:

> *God is most great. I testify that there is no God but Allah. I testify that Muhammad is the Messenger of Allah. Come to prayer, come to revelation, God is most great! There is no God but Allah.*

Allah is the one and only God, unchallenged by other false divinities and unlike all others in the strength of his creative power. All life—all creation—is the responsibility of Allah alone. His nature is described in many ways and through many metaphors:

> *Allah is the light of the heaven and the earth. . . . His light is as a niche wherein is a lamp. The lamp is in a glass. The glass is as it were a shining star. [The lamp is] kindled from a blessed tree, an olive neither of the East nor of the West, whose oil would almost glow forth [of itself] though no fire touched it. Light upon light, Allah guided unto His light whom He will. And Allah speaketh to mankind in allegories, for Allah is Knower of all things.*
>
> *[This lamp is found] in houses which Allah hath allowed to be exalted and that His name shall be remembered therein. Therein do offer praise to Him at noon and evening. (Qur'an 24:35–36)*

Islam also recognizes the significance and the contributions of prophets who preceded Muhammad. From the beginnings of human history, Allah has communicated with his people either by the way of these prophets or by written scriptures:

> *Lo! We inspire thee as We inspired Noah and the Prophets after him, as We inspired Abraham and Ishmael and Isaac and Jacob and the tribes, and Jesus and Job and Jonah and Aaron and Solomon and as We imparted unto David the Psalms. (Qur'an 4:164)*

Twenty-eight such prophets are mentioned in the Qur'an as the predecessors of Muhammad, who is believed to have been Allah's final messenger. Muhammad is given no divine status by Muslims; in fact, Muhammad took great care to see that he was not worshipped as a god. He told his followers, for example, that it was not appropriate for them to bow down before him.

The creation of the universe and of all living creatures within it is the work of Allah; harmony and balance in all of creation were ensured by God. In addition to humans and other creatures on the earth, angels exist to protect humans and to pray for forgiveness for the faithful. Satan, "the Whisperer," attempts to lead people astray, and mischievous spirits called *jinn* can create havoc for believers and unbelievers alike.

Men and women are given a special status in the pattern of the universe. They can choose to obey or to reject Allah's will and deny him. Allah's message includes the belief in a Day of Resurrection when people will be held responsible for their actions and rewarded or punished accordingly for eternity. The Qur'an graphically describes heaven and hell. Those who have submitted to Allah's law—the charitable, the humble, and the forgiving—and those who have preserved his faith shall dwell in the Garden of Paradise, resting in cool shade, eating delectable foods, attended by "fair ones with wide, lovely eyes like unto hidden pearls," and hearing no vain speech or recrimination but only "Peace! Peace!" This veritable oasis is far different from the agonies of the hell that awaits sinners, the covetous, and the erring. Cast into a pit with its "scorching wind and shadow of black smoke," they will drink boiling water and suffer forever.

The Five Pillars

Over time, the Muslim community developed doctrines, laws, and institutions (like schools and courts) to put into practice its evolving religious ideals. As in other religious traditions, the spread and institutionalization of Islam was a gradual and contested process. And, as in all societies, government and social practice did not always match the religious ideals expressed in the sacred texts. But certain practices became basic to the believers.

Islam is united in the observance of the **Five Pillars,** or five essential duties that all Muslims are required to perform to the best of their abilities. These obligations are accepted by Muslims everywhere and thus serve further to unite the Islamic world. The first obligation is a basic *profession of faith,* by which a

---

Five Pillars—The five essential duties of all Muslims: (1) a profession of faith *(shahada)*; (2) prayer *(salat)* five times a day; (3) giving of alms *(zakat)*; (4) fasting *(sawm)* during the holy month of Ramadan; and (5) making a pilgrimage *(hajj)* to Mecca at least once during one's lifetime if possible.

These illustrations from a sixteenth-century Persian manuscript depict scenes from the lives of the prophets: Jesus multiplying the loaves and fishes and the staff of Moses transformed into a dragon. Artistic representation of people, events, and landscapes varies considerably from place to place, culture to culture, and over time. Moses is depicted in Jewish, Christian, and Muslim texts, but the same story can be "told" artistically in very different ways.

believer becomes a Muslim. The simple proclamation *(shahada)* is repeated in daily prayers. Belief in the One God and imitation of the exemplary life led by his Prophet are combined in the profession of faith.

Prayer (salat) is said five times a day, when Muslims are summoned to worship by the *muezzin* (myeu-EZ-in), who calls them to prayer from atop the minaret of the mosque (*masjid,* meaning "place of prostration"). During prayer, Muslims face Mecca and in so doing give recognition to the birthplace of Islam and the unity of the Islamic community. Prayer can be said alone, at work, at home, or in the mosque.

A Muslim is required to give *alms (zakat)* to the poor, orphans, and widows and to assist the spread of Islam. The payment of alms is a social and religious obligation to provide for the welfare of the *umma.* Muslims are generally expected to contribute annually in alms a percentage (usually 2.5 percent) of their total wealth and assets.

Muslims are requested to *fast (sawm)* during the holy month of Ramadan, the ninth month of the Islamic lunar calendar. From sunrise to sunset, adult Muslims in good health are to avoid food, drink, tobacco, and sexual activity. Finally, every Muslim able to do so is called to make a *pilgrimage (hajj)* to Mecca at least once in his or her lifetime, in the twelfth month of the Islamic year. The focus of the pilgrimage is the Ka'ba and a series of other sites commemorating events in the lives of the prophets Muhammad and Abraham. The *hajj* emphasizes the unity of the Islamic world community and the equality of all believers regardless of race or class.

Islamic Law

Islam is a way of life as well as a religion, and at its heart is the **Sharia,** the law provided by Allah as a guide for a proper life. The Sharia is based on the Qur'an and hadith; it gives the believers a perfect pattern of human conduct and regulates every aspect of

Sharia—Islamic law based on the word of God as manifested in the teachings of the Qu'ran and hadith.

Women associated with the Prophet are revered by the Muslim community. This manuscript image shows Fatima, Muhammad's daughter, along with Aisha and Umm Salama, two of his wives. Their fiery halos and veiled faces suggest their religious significance. Fatima is often held up as a model of Islamic womanhood and Aisha was a prominent political figure and transmitter of Islamic tradition (hadith).

a person's activities. God's decrees must be obeyed even if humans are incapable of understanding them, since the Sharia is greater than human reason. Those who study, interpret, and administer the Sharia are called *ulama,* "those who know." These men emerged, in the era after the Prophet's death, as religious scholars and leaders who administered the institutions of worship, education, and law. But there is no priesthood in Islam; all believers are equal members of the community.

Islamic law, then, permeates all aspects of human conduct and all levels of activity, from private and personal concerns to those involving the welfare of the whole state. The Sharia became the universal law of the Islamic lands. In practice, it worked in conjunction with the decrees of rulers and with customary laws that varied from region to region. Family law, set forth in the Qur'an, is based on earlier Arab tribal patterns. Islamic law emphasizes the patriarchal nature of the family and society. Marriage is expected of every Muslim man and woman unless physical infirmity or financial inability prevents it. Muslim men can marry non-Muslim women, preferably Christians or Jews, since they too are "people of the Book," but Muslim women are forbidden to marry non-Muslim men. This law reflects the notion, common in traditional societies, that the children "belong" to the father and his family. Thus, the children of a Muslim father and non-Muslim mother would be Muslims. The Qur'an had the effect of improving the status and opportunities of women, who could contract their own marriages, keep and maintain their own dowries, and manage and inherit property (unlike many Western Christian women at that time).

The Qur'an allows Muslim men to marry up to four wives, but only if each wife is treated with equal support and affection. Many modern-day Muslims interpret the Qur'an as encouraging monogamy. Polygamy, in any case, is not required; it is a practice that may have arisen to provide protection and security in early societies where women may have outnumbered men because of the toll of constant warfare.

Islamic law is considered to be God's law for all humankind, not only for the followers of Islam. Non-Muslim citizens of the Islamic state were called *dhimmis* (DHEE-mees); they received protection from the state and paid an extra head tax called the *jizya* (JIZ-yah). The Sharia courts were open to *dhimmis,* who could also appeal to juridical authorities, such as rabbis or priests, within their own communities. Disputes between Muslims and *dhimmis* were handled in the Sharia court, but a dispute between Christians might be handled within the Christian community. Islamic law sometimes designated certain dress markers for *dhimmis* to set them apart. Bearing arms, engaging in ostentatious religious displays, and corrupting Muslims (by selling them wine, for example) were also prohibited. But repeated allusions to such violations in court records suggest that these laws often were not enforced.

Thus, in addition to its theology, Islam offers to its believers a system of government, a legal foundation, and a pattern of social organization. The Islamic *umma* was, and is, an excellent example of a theocratic state, one in which power ultimately resides in God, on whose behalf political, religious, and other forms of authority are exercised. Ideally, the role of the state is to serve as the guardian of religious law. Islamic monarchs ruled in the name of Allah and called on the Sharia law to legitimize their rule. Of course, as the Islamic state evolved, some rulers were more pious than others. Some came into conflict with the *ulama* over matters of law (as happened with brahmans and kings in India and priests and kings in Europe). But all Muslim kings, like all Christian kings in this era, claimed to be defenders of their faith.

THE EXPANSION OF COMMUNITY AND STATE

- *What factors contributed to the rapid expansion of Islam?*

The Islamic state expanded very rapidly after the death of Muhammad through remarkable successes in the form of military conquest and conversion. Immediately after the Prophet's death in 632, Caliph Abu Bakr continued the effort to abolish polytheism among the Arab tribes and also to bring all of Arabia under the political control of Medina. The Muslim polity succeeded in strengthening its power throughout the Arabian peninsula and even began to launch some exploratory offensives north toward Syria.

Expansion Under the First Four Caliphs

Under the first four caliphs (632–661), the Islamic state rapidly expanded the territory under its control. The wars of expansion were aided by the devotion of the faithful to the concept of *jihad,* a term that is sometimes glossed as "holy war" and sometimes interpreted to mean simply "struggle." Muslims were obliged to extend the faith to unbelievers and to defend Islam from attack. *Jihad* was responsible in part for Islam's early conquests beyond the Arabian peninsula.

Arab Expansion and the Islamic World, 570–800 C.E.

But various factors account for the triumph of the early Muslim armies. A long series of wars waged between the Byzantine and Persian (Sassanid) Empires to the north left both sides exhausted and open to con-

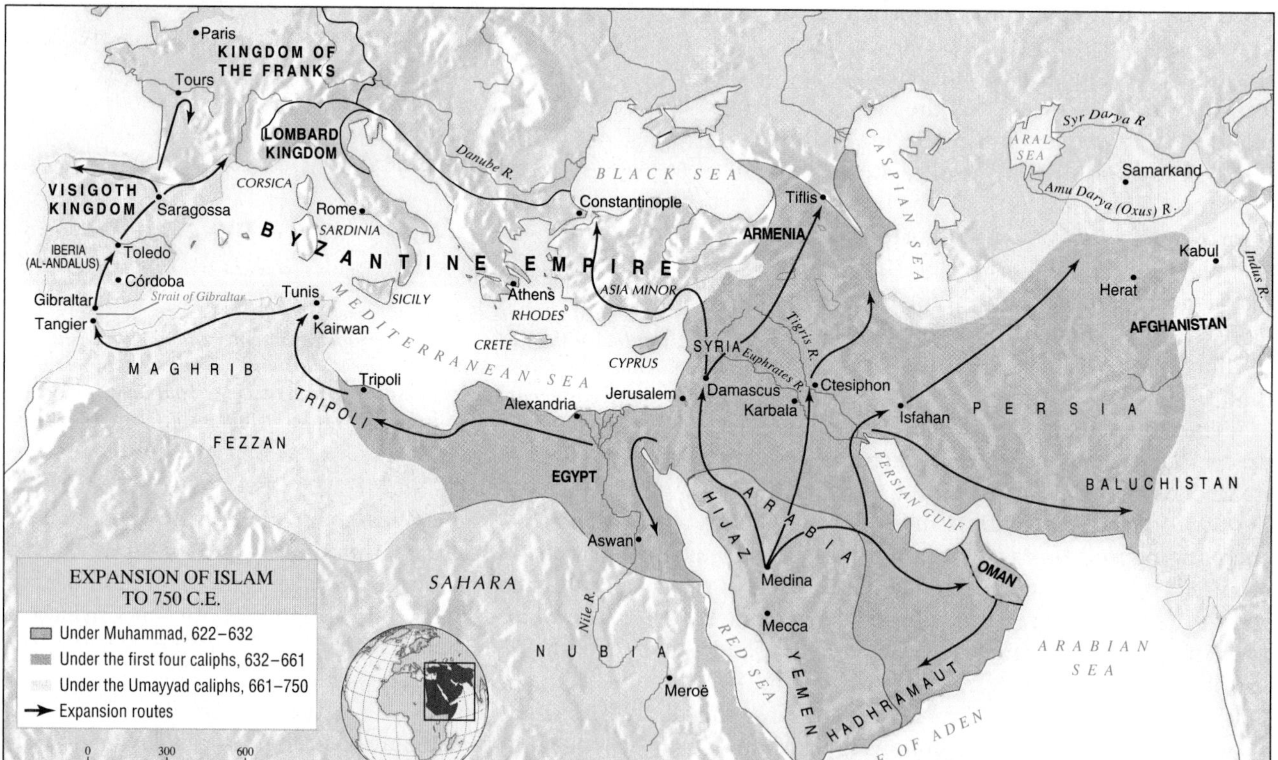

The Islamic conquests were rapid and far-reaching. By 750 Islamic monarchs controlled kingdoms stretching from central Asia to Spain.

quest. In addition, the inhabitants of Syria and Egypt, alienated by religious dissent and resenting the attempts of the Byzantine Empire to impose its brand of Christianity on the population, sought freedom from Byzantine rule. The Arabs' combined use of camels for long distance travel and swift horses for attacks was extremely effective. In 636 Arab armies conquered Syria and occupied the city of Damascus. Jerusalem was taken in 638. The Muslims then won Iraq from the Persians and in 651 defeated the last Sassanid ruler, thereby ending the 400-year-old Persian Empire. Most of Egypt had fallen with little resistance by 646, and raids had begun into the lands the Muslims called the Maghrib (MUG-reb) in North Africa west of Egypt and north of the Sahara. Within 30 years of Muhammad's death, Islam had become the dominant faith of a vast empire connecting western Asia with the Mediterranean and Africa. This area possessed a certain cultural unity under Islam, but it was politically divided.

The new Islamic territories were governed with remarkable efficiency and flexibility. The centralization of authority typical of effective military organization aided in the incorporation of new peoples. Unbelievers in the conquered territories became increasingly interested in the new religion and accepted Islam in great numbers. In addition to the power of the religious message of Islam, the imposition of a head tax on all non-Muslims and some restrictions on unbelievers' holding political office encouraged many to become converts. Accounts of the coercive imposition of Islam on conquered peoples are inexact: Jews and Christians outside Arabia generally enjoyed tolerance because they worshipped the same God as the Muslims, and many non-Muslims were active participants in the Islamic state and prospered financially and socially.

Islam was and remains one of the most effective religions in overcoming the potential barriers of race and nationality to conversion. In the early days of the spread of Islam, apart from a certain privileged position allowed Arabs and the Prophet's earliest supporters, distinctions were mostly those of economic and political rank. The new religion converted and included peoples of many ethnic origins and cultures. This egalitarian ideal of Islam undoubtedly aided its rapid and successful expansion.

Defining the Community

All Muslims shared belief in the unity of God and the practice of the Five Pillars. But Islamic civilization, like other traditions, was marked by debate and conflict over the interpretation of the law. As Islamic law was codified and as the Islamic state expanded, four main schools of legal interpretation emerged. Scholars struggled with questions of faith and reason, just as their Christian and Buddhist counterparts did. Inspired in part by the spiritual thought and practices of India, Islam also developed a set of mystical traditions that challenged the orthodoxy of the *ulama*. Meanwhile, in the political realm, not long after the death of the Prophet, the new Islamic state underwent a crisis that split the community over the question of authority.

Islam's first three caliphs—Abu Bakr (632–634), Umar (634–644), and Uthman (644–656)—were chosen in consultation with the elders and leaders of the Islamic community, setting a pattern for selecting the caliph exclusively from the Quraysh tribe of Mecca. When Uthman was assassinated by a fellow Muslim, the ensuing struggle for power ultimately split the community into two major divisions, **Sunni** and **Shia** (or Shi'ites). The Shi'ites believed that only descendents of the Prophet could command authority in the Islamic state. Because Muhammad had no surviving sons, his bloodline passed through his grandsons, the sons of his daughter Fatima and her husband Ali, the fourth caliph. Thus for the Shi'ites, the first three caliphs before Ali had been usurpers. Ali and his descendents were the only legitimate heads of the community, *imams,* who were believed to have a special knowledge of the inner meaning of the Qur'an. The Sunnis, rather than insisting on a caliph who was a direct descendant of the Prophet, accepted the first three caliphs and upheld the principle that the caliph owed his position to the consent of the Islamic community. The Sunnis argued that they followed the *sunna* of the Prophet, the patterns of behavior modeled on Muhammad's life.

The Shi'ites did not refute the validity of the sunna, but they insisted on the Qur'an as the sole and unquestioned authority on the life and teachings of the Prophet. Though originally an Arab party, the Shia in time became a more widespread Islamic movement that stood in opposition to the ruling Umayyad dynasty. That the Shia remained, in general, a minority and opposition party in part explains the evolution of its doctrine of opposition to political authorities. Notwithstanding the several major Shi'ite dynasties in Islamic history, Sunni Muslims have remained numerically dominant. Some 85 percent of the modern world's Muslims are Sunnis,

Sunni—The largest division within Islam, comprising more than 85 percent of all Muslims; the form of Islam embraced by the Umayyad state, which accepts the legitimacy of the first three caliphs and holds that the caliph's authority stems from the consent of the Islamic community.

Shia—A division in Islam representing some 10 to 15 percent of all Muslims, principally in Iran, Iraq, and Lebanon; Shi'ites deny the legitimacy of the first three caliphs and hold that the true caliphs were descended from the Prophet Muhammad through Ali, his cousin and son-in-law.

The Early Islamic Dynasties

661	Umayyad dynasty established; Damascus becomes capital
680	Muhammad's grandson Husayn killed by Umayyads at Karbala in Iraq
711	Tariq ibn Ziyad invades Spain from North Africa
750	Abbasids defeat the Umayyads and establish a new dynasty
756	Umayyads set up a new dynasty in Spain; Córdoba later becomes capital
786–809	Reign of Abbasid caliph Harun al-Rashid
909–1171	Fatimid Shi'ite dynasty in North Africa, Egypt, and Syria
1055	Seljuk Turks gain control of Baghdad but leave Abbasid caliph in place
1095	First Crusade mobilized
1250	Mamluk kingdom established in Egypt, will endure until 1517
1258	Mongols conquer Baghdad and kill Abbasid caliph, ending Abbasid dynasty

although large Shi'ite communities exist, particularly in Iran, Iraq, and Lebanon.

Umayyad Rule

Ali and his followers were opposed first by Muslims under the leadership of Muhammad's widow and favorite wife, Aisha, daughter of Abu Bakr, and later by the forces of Muawiya (MOO-AH-wee-ah), the governor of Syria and a relative of the third caliph. The power struggle for leadership in the Muslim community thus erupted into civil war. In 661, after Ali was assassinated, Muawiya proclaimed himself caliph, made Damascus his capital, and founded the Umayyad (oo-MAI-yad) dynasty, which lasted until 750. In this manner the Umayyads made the caliphate in fact, although never in law, a hereditary office rather than one chosen by election.

The Umayyads expanded the borders of Islam, but not with the spectacular successes of the years immediately after Muhammad's death. The Umayyads held Cyprus, Rhodes, and several Aegean islands, which served as bases for naval attacks on the Byzantine Empire. The Byzantines successfully defended Constantinople against persistent Umayyad attacks, and the Islamic advance toward eastern Europe was checked for the first time. The Umayyads established garrisons in central Asia to further their conquests northward across the Oxus River and southwest into India. Westward across North Africa, Umayyad armies were eventually victorious. The Berbers, a nomadic tribal people inhabiting the Maghrib, initially resisted stubbornly but eventually converted to Islam. The Berbers then aided the Umayyad armies in expanding across the Strait of Gibraltar into the weak Visigoth kingdom in Spain. General Tariq ibn Ziyad (TAHR-ik ib-in zee-YAHD) led an army across the strait into Spain in 711 (according to legend, the name *Gibraltar* is derived from *Jabal Tariq,* or "Mountain of Tariq"). After the kingdom of the Visigoths swiftly crumbled, the Muslims were able to make conquests throughout the Iberian peninsula, which they called *al-Andalus.*

The Muslims in Spain seem never to have had serious intentions of expanding their territorial holdings across the Pyrenees into what is now France, but they did engage in seasonal raids to the north. One such raiding party was defeated by Charles Martel near Tours in 732 in a battle that Europeans portrayed later as a decisive blow to Muslim expansion in Europe. But the Byzantines indeed delivered such a blow: In 717 the Byzantine emperor Leo III won a major victory over the Muslims that halted the Umayyad advance into eastern Europe.

To the east, however, the Umayyads successfully extended their rule into central Asia; by the middle of the eighth century they could claim lands as far east as Turkestan and the Indus valley. To celebrate the enduring power of Islam in the 690s the Umayyads built the Dome of the Rock in Jerusalem on the site of the old Jewish Temple. This sacred shrine is built around an enormous rock where, according to tradition, God asked Abraham to sacrifice his son Isaac. A monumental building, it reflected the power of the dynasty and its god; its interior is decorated with Qur'anic inscriptions. The Dome of the Rock has endured to the present day and has become a major site of struggle between Muslim and Jewish claims to the city they both consider holy.

The mainstay of the Umayyad dynasty's power was the ruling class, composed of an Arab military aristocracy. The Arabs formed a privileged class greatly outnumbered by non-Arab converts to Islam. Many of these converted peoples had cultures much more highly developed than that of the Arabs, and the economic and cultural life of this Islamic empire came to be dominated by these non-Arab Muslims, called ***mawali,*** or

Arabs on Horseback

Document The Early Islamic Conquests

Traditional Western historiography used the rhetorics of medieval Christian writers to portray the early Islamic conquests as sweeping and brutal. The following two excerpts from the Arabic chronicle of al-Tabari (839–923) suggest that wisdom, pragmatism, mercy, and intimidation all played a role in the early Islamic conquests. The Qur'an enjoined mercy as well as warfare, and Abu Bakr's rules of war suggest that the wise conqueror did not kill the citizens and livestock of the lands he wished to rule. In the first reading, the people who have "shaved the crown of their heads" may well be monks. But, earlier on, the passage admonishes the conquerors to leave those in hermitages alone—so the reference here is unclear. In the second passage, although the general initially calls upon God (customary in military and diplomatic messages of this era), he focuses on the power and violence of men. The Arab general Khalid ibn al-Walid's letters to the Persians offer mercy in exchange for submission, but they follow up that offer with a challenge. The *jizya* is the head tax that all non-Muslim citizens must pay to the Muslim state.

Abu Bakr (Muhammad's successor) on the Rules of War (632)

Oh People! I charge you with ten rules; learn them well!

Do not betray, or misappropriate any part of the booty; do not practice treachery or mutilation. Do not kill a young child, an old man, or a woman. Do not uproot or burn palms or cut down fruitful trees. Do not slaughter a sheep or a cow or a camel, except for food. You will meet people who have set themselves apart in hermitages; leave them to accomplish the purpose for which they have done this. You will come upon people who will bring you dishes with various kinds of food. If you partake of them, pronounce God's name over what you eat. You will meet people who have shaved the crown of their heads, leaving a band of hair around it. Strike them with the sword. Go, in God's name, and may God protect you from sword and pestilence.

Letters to the Persians (633)

In the name of God, the Merciful and the Compassionate.

From Khalid ibn al-Walid to the kings of Persia.

Praise be to God who has dissolved your order, frustrated your plans, and split your unanimity. Had he not done this to you, it would have been worse for you. Submit to our authority, and we shall leave you and your land and go by you against others. If not, you will be conquered against your will by men who love death as you love life.

In the name of God, the Merciful and the Compassionate.

From Khalid ibn al-Walid to the border chiefs of Persia.

Become Muslim and be saved. If not, accept protection from us and pay the jizya. If not, I shall come against you with men who love death as you love to drink wine.

Questions to Consider

1. Why would Abu Bakr urge his soldiers to exercise restraint and curb the destructive impulses of war?
2. Think about the idea of submission. Why does the general insist that his enemy submit and what do you think submission means for the conquered peoples?
3. What does Khalid ibn al-Walid mean when he says he shall attack "with men who love death as you love to drink wine"?

"affiliates." Because they were not Arab by birth, they were treated to a certain extent as citizens of inferior status. They were granted fewer privileges and received less from the spoils of war than did the Arabs. Resentment grew steadily among some of the non-Arab Muslims, who objected to their inferior status as a violation of the Islamic laws advocating equality. Eventually the resentment of the *mawali* and the opposition of the Shi'ites, who had been forced from power on the accession of Muawiya, helped bring about the downfall of the Umayyads.

mawali—Non-Arab Muslims; resentment against discrimination by Arab Muslims led them to oppose Umayyad rule.

The Dome of the Rock, a Muslim edifice from the seventh century, is built above the Temple Mount in Jerusalem, the site of Solomon's Temple. According to tradition, the site is also the place where Muhammad ascended into heaven on his "Night Journey." Intricate mosaic decoration covers the outer walls of the building.

Support for Umayyad rule was never universal. Hostility to the Umayyads was inflamed in 680 when an Umayyad troop massacred Husayn, the second son of Ali, and his followers at Karbala in Iraq. The killing of the grandson of the Prophet was considered a horrible affront to the Islamic community. It helped spur resentment against the ruling dynasty and made it appear illegitimate. This event introduced the theme of martyrdom into Shi'ite tradition around which opposition party unity could be mobilized. To this day, a "passion play" commemorating Husayn's death is a dramatic and important element in Shi'ite ceremonial in many communities.

THE ABBASID ERA, ZENITH OF CLASSICAL ISLAMIC CIVILIZATION

- *What roles did the cities of Baghdad, Cairo, and Córdoba play in classical Islamic civilization?*

A new dynasty, the Abbasid, was founded when a rebel army, with Shi'ite support, defeated the Umayyads. The first Abbasid caliph was Abu al-Abbas, a descendant of Muhammad's uncle, Abbas. His dynasty ruled most of the Muslim world from 750 to 1258 and built the city of Baghdad in 762 as a symbol of its wealth, power, and legitimacy. The Abbasids owed their initial support and successes in part to the discontent of the non-Arab Muslims, many of whom had become prominent leaders in Islam's cities.

The fall of the Umayyad dynasty marked the end of Arab domination within Islam. The Arab "aristocracy" had led the forces of conquest during the great period of Islamic expansion, but over time, as new dynasties established themselves, the dominant status previously held only by Arab soldiers was shared with non-Arab administrators, merchants, and scholars.

Under the Abbasids, traditional Arab patterns of tribal organization and warfare gave way to patterns of military organization and governance based on the imperial traditions of the conquered lands. The new

This sixteenth-century Persian manuscript depicts the gendered division of space in a mosque scene. Women of various ages and their children are shown in an area separated from the main mosque area by a barrier. Cultural practice has varied from region to region, but today one will often see such a separation of females and younger children from the males in rituals of worship.

Abbasid polity fostered economic prosperity, the growth of town life, and the promotion of the merchant class.

The founding of the new capital at Baghdad shifted Islam's center of gravity to the province of Iraq, whose soil, watered by the Tigris and Euphrates Rivers, had nurtured the earliest civilizations. Here the Abbasid caliphs set themselves up as potentates in the traditional style of the ancient East (particularly Persia), so that they were surrounded by a lavish court that contrasted sharply with the simplicity of the lifestyle of the Prophet and the first caliphs. One historian described the amazement of the Byzantine envoys who, on entering the Abbasid court, found a magnificent tree of silver and gold, with singing birds, also of silver and gold, perched in its leaves. The Abbasid caliph forecast that Baghdad would become the "most flourishing city in the world"; indeed, it rivaled Constantinople for that honor, situated as it was on the trade routes linking East and West. Furthermore, Abbasid patronage of scholarship and the arts produced a rich and complex culture far surpassing that in western Europe at the time. In Baghdad they founded one of the great medieval libraries, the House of Wisdom.

The Abbasid dynasty marked the high point of classical Islamic power and civilization. The empire ruled by the Abbasid caliphs was greater in size than the Roman Empire at its height; it was the product of an expansion during which the Muslim state assimilated peoples, customs, cultures, learning, and inventions on an unprecedented scale. This Islamic empire, in fact, drew from the resources of the entire known world.

Abbasid power, however, did not go unchallenged, even in the Muslim world. While the Abbasids ruled in Baghdad, rival dynasties established their sovereignty in other areas that had been incorporated into the Islamic state during the early conquests. Members of the deposed Umayyad dynasty established a new dynasty in Muslim Spain in 756 and eventually set up a glorious court in Córdoba, famous for its scholarship and patronage of the arts. In Egypt the Fatimids established a Shi'ite ruling house and developed a formidable navy that dominated the eastern Mediterranean. To bolster their legitimacy, the Fatimids claimed descent from the Prophet's daughter, Fatima; hence, the name of the dynasty. They, too, founded a new and glorious capital at Cairo, where they established al-Azhar, the famous institution of Islamic learning that has attracted scholars from throughout the Muslim world since the tenth century. Thus, the eighth to the twelfth centuries were not only the period of the classical glory of the Islamic state but also an era during which rulers in three different Muslim capitals all claimed the title "caliph." This political division stood in contrast to the Islamic world's civilizational unity, which was based on the universal Sharia law and the spread of the Arabic language.

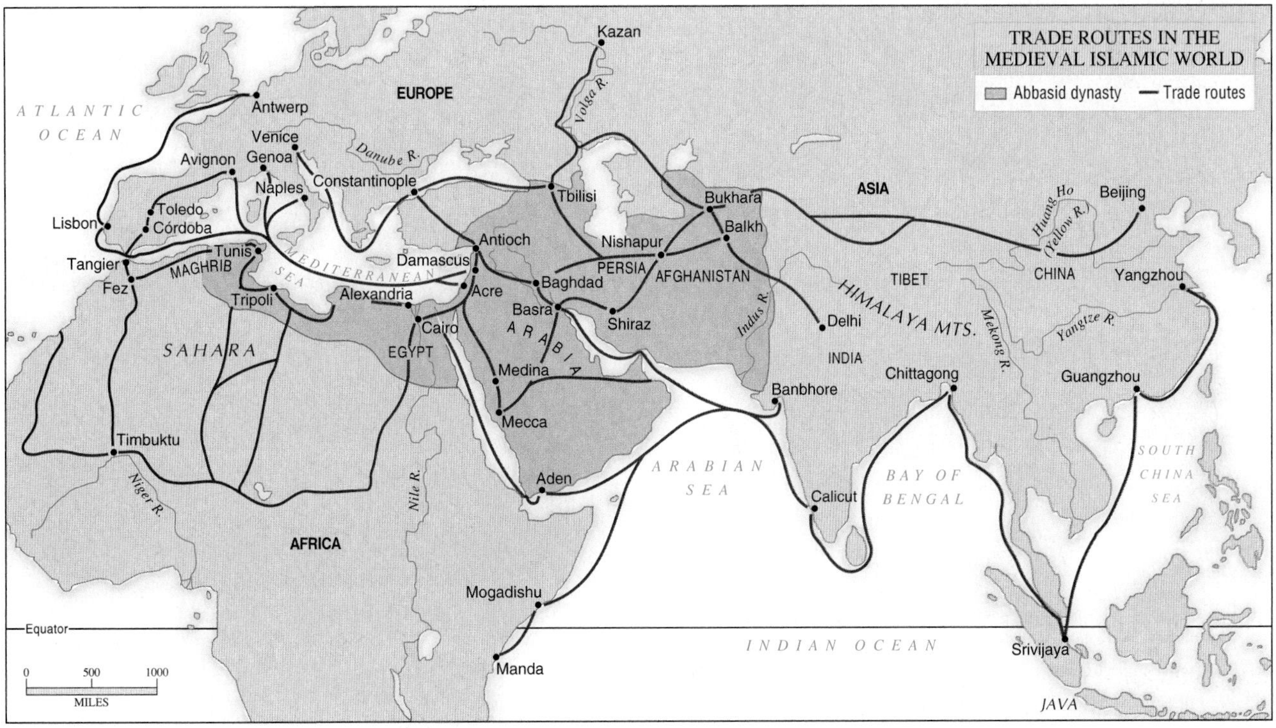

The Islamic world was embedded in a network of trading connections extending from the Atlantic to the Pacific.

Trade, Industry, and Agriculture

From the eighth century to the twelfth, the Muslim world enjoyed enormous prosperity. In close contact with three continents, merchants from the Islamic lands could move goods back and forth from China to western Europe and from Russia to central Africa. The absence of tariff barriers within the empire and the tolerance of the caliphs, who allowed non-Muslim merchants and craftsmen to reside in their territories and carry on commerce with their home countries, further facilitated trade. The presence of such important urban centers as Baghdad, Cairo, and Córdoba stimulated trade and industry throughout the Muslim world; the courts of the monarchs were great consumers of textiles, foodstuffs, arts, and crafts.

The cosmopolitan nature of Baghdad was evident in its bazaars, which contained goods from all over the known world. There were spices, minerals, and dyes from India; gems and fabrics from central Asia; honey, furs, and wax from Scandinavia and Russia; and ivory and gold from Africa. Muslim trade with Southeast Asia increased, and a large Muslim trading community established itself in the Chinese port of Guangzhou (GWANG-JOH; Canton). One bazaar in Baghdad specialized in goods from China, including silks, musk, and porcelain. In the slave markets Muslim traders bought and sold Scandinavians, Mongolians from central Asia, and Africans. Joint-stock companies flourished along with branch banking organizations, and checks (an Arabic word) drawn on one bank could be cashed with commercial agents throughout this vast network of traders. Muslim textile industries turned out excellent cottons (muslins) and silks. The steel of Damascus and Toledo, the leather of Córdoba, and the glass of Syria became internationally famous. Notable also was the art of papermaking, learned from the Chinese. Under the Abbasids, vast irrigation projects in Iraq increased cultivable land, which yielded large crops of fruits and grains. Wheat came from the Nile valley, cotton from North Africa, olives and wine from Spain, wool from eastern Asia Minor, and horses from Persia.

By the tenth century Islam was also making inroads into Africa south of the Nile and the Maghrib. Trade routes through the Sahara brought spices, leatherwork, and eventually slaves from the south to the northern coast, and, in return, caravans from the north brought luxury goods, salt, and the Islamic reli-

In the Muslim world, merchants transported goods by both land and sea. Camels carried merchants and goods on the overland routes, as shown in this manuscript illumination from the thirteenth century (above left). Sound vessels with space for both passengers and cargo, like the Indian ship depicted in this Iraqi manuscript from 1238 (above right), and reliable navigation techniques facilitated the sea trade.

gion to the early African kingdoms of Ghana and Mali. Commercial agents and missionaries carried Islam along the sea routes to central and southeastern African ports such as Mogadishu and Manda and to South and Southeast Asia.

Because the Islamic realms encompassed such a great expanse of territory, languages, and cultures, it is difficult to generalize about Islamic society. Most of the population of the Islamic world was illiterate and engaged in subsistence agriculture. In part because Muhammad was a merchant, trade was considered an honorable profession, and some merchants became quite wealthy. In general, however, the military and administrative classes possessed the greatest wealth and status. Religion, profession, gender, and class could be more important determinants of status than race (even though racism of different varieties was common here as it was in the rest of the world).

The Spectacular Reign of Harun al-Rashid

The rule of Harun al-Rashid (786–809), hero of the tales of *The Arabian Nights,* was the most spectacular of the Abbasid reigns. A contemporary of Charlemagne, who had revived the idea of a Roman Empire in the West (see Chapter 9), Harun was surely the more powerful of the two and the ruler of the more advanced culture. The two monarchs were on friendly terms, based on self-interest. Charlemagne wanted to exert pressure on the Byzantine emperor to recognize his new imperial title. Harun saw Charlemagne as an ally against the Umayyad rulers of Spain, who had broken away from Abbasid dominion. The two emperors exchanged embassies and presents. The Muslim sent the Christian rich fabrics, aromatics, and even an elephant named Abu-Lababah, meaning "the father of intelligence." Another gift, an intricate water clock from Baghdad, seems to have been regarded as miraculous in the West.

Relations between the Abbasid caliphate and the Byzantine Empire were never very cordial, and conflicts often broke out along the shifting borders that separated Christian and Muslim territories. Harun al-Rashid once responded to a communiqué from the Byzantine emperor with the following answer:

> *In the name of God, the Merciful, the Compassionate. From Harun, Commander of the Faithful, to Nicepherus, the dog of the Greeks, I have read your letter, you son of a she-infidel, and you shall see the answer before you hear it.*

This response was followed up with Abbasid raids on Byzantine possessions in Asia Minor.

In the days of Harun al-Rashid, Baghdad's wealth and splendor equaled that of Constantinople, and its chief glory was the royal palace. With its annexes for officials, the harem, and eunuchs, the caliph's residence occupied one-third of the city of Baghdad. The caliph's audience chamber was the setting for an elaborate ceremonial, which mirrored that of the Byzantines and Persians. Such court ceremonial was designed to impress the Abbasid citizens with the justice, power, and magnificence of the caliph and to intimidate foreign envoys.

Challenges to Abbasid Authority

In the tenth century a movement of migration and conquest out of central Asia began that would have a dramatic impact on the political and cultural configuration of the central Islamic lands. By the early eleventh century, Turkish peoples had moved from central Asia into the Abbasid lands, where, over time, they converted to Islam. One group, the Seljuks, after annexing most of Persia, gained control of Baghdad in 1055 and subjugated Iraq. Subsequently, they conquered Syria and Palestine at the expense of the Fatimids and proceeded to take most of Asia Minor from the Byzantines. The Seljuks permitted the Abbasids to retain nominal authority, in part to secure political legitimacy for their reign, but they themselves ruled the state. By the time of the First Crusade in 1095, which was provoked in part by the Seljuk advances, the Abbasid dynasty had lost much of its power and status in the Islamic world.

Seljuk dominance of much of the old Abbasid Empire was later challenged by the arrival of Turco-Mongol invaders from the northeastern steppes of central Asia. Early in the thirteenth century Chinggis (Genghis) Khan succeeded in uniting the animistic, tribal horsemen of Mongolia and conquering much of China and Russia; he and his successors moved on to eastern and central Asia (see Chapter 10) and ultimately conquered Persia and Iraq. In 1258 a grandson of Chinggis Khan captured Baghdad and had the caliph executed. Unlike the Seljuks, the Mongols were contemptuous of the caliph and felt no need to preserve an Abbasid successor as a figurehead to secure their legitimacy. Not only did the Abbasid dynasty come to an end, but so did most of the vast irrigation system that had supported the land. The dynasty established there by the Mongols survived for almost a century, but the Mongol invaders were eventually acculturated and absorbed into the local population.

Egypt was "saved" from the Mongol advance by the Mamluks (1250–1517). The Fatimids had been replaced by one of their own commanders, Salah al-Din, who established a new dynasty, the Ayyubids (ay-YOO-bids), who reigned from 1169–1252. Famed in the West as Saladin, it was Salah al-Din who took Jerusalem from the crusaders. The Ayyubids were in turn overthrown by their own elite "slave" guard, called *mamluks. Mamluk* literally means "slave," but these men were not slaves in the sense of people of low status who did menial tasks. Taken as captives or purchased as young men in the slave market, they were trained in the military and political arts to serve their commanders. They were converted to Islam and hence could not be held as true slaves. Indeed, they often wielded great power and wealth. After overthrowing the Ayyubids and founding their own ruling group, they formed the elite military caste of Egypt. It was the Mamluks who stopped the Mongol advance in Syria and later ejected the last of the crusaders in 1291. They ruled in Egypt and Syria until 1517, claiming the title "Protector of the Holy Places" as a result of their governance of Mecca, Medina, and also Jerusalem, the three holy cities of Islam.

ISLAMIC CULTURE

■ *What were the achievements of Islamic culture in medicine, science, mathematics, literature, art, and architecture?*

The attainments of the Muslims in the intellectual and artistic fields can be attributed not only to the Arabs but also to the peoples who embraced Islam in Persia, Iraq, Turkey, Syria, Egypt, North Africa, and Spain. Muslim learning benefited both from Islam's ability to absorb other cultures and from the native talents of the Islamic peoples. Under Abbasid rule, a great synthesis of culture and scholarship emerged, strands of which were then transmitted by traveling scholars, traders, and missionaries throughout the known world from the Mediterranean to the Indian Ocean.

MAP The Spread of Islam

The cosmopolitan spirit permeating the Abbasid dynasty supplied the tolerance necessary for a diversity of ideas, so that the science, philosophies, and literatures of ancient Greece and India alike received a cordial reception in Baghdad. Under Harun al-Rashid and his successors, the writings of Aristotle, Euclid, Ptolemy, Archimedes, Galen, and other great Greek philosophers and scientific writers were translated into Arabic. This knowledge, together with the teachings of the Qur'an, formed the basis of Muslim learning, which was in turn transmitted to scholars in Europe and Asia. In addition to being valuable transmitters of learning, Muslim scholars crafted a unique synthesis based on the genius of Arab civilization and on a continuing dialog among Muslim and non-Muslim thinkers and artists.

Advances in Medicine

The years between 900 and 1100 can be regarded as the golden age of Muslim learning. This period was particularly significant for its medical advances. Muslim students of medicine were by all measures far superior to their European contemporaries. Muslim cities had excellent pharmacies and hospitals, where physicians received instruction and training. Muslim scholars perfected surgical techniques, figured out the mode for the spread of the plague, and described the course of many diseases.

Perhaps the greatest Muslim physician was the Persian Abu Bakr Muhammad al-Razi (d. 925), better known in the West as Rhazes. Chief physician in Baghdad, he wrote more than 100 medical treatises, in which he summarized Greek medical knowledge and added his own clinical observations. His most famous work, *On Smallpox and Measles,* is the first clear description of the symptoms and treatment of these diseases.

The most influential Muslim medical treatise is the vast *Canon of Medicine,* in which the great scholar Ibn Sina, or Avicenna (d. 1037), systematically organized all Greek and Muslim medical learning. In the twelfth century, the *Canon* was translated into Latin. It was so much in demand in the West that it was issued 16 times in the last half of the fifteenth century and more than 20 times in the sixteenth, and it continued to be used until the modern era.

Progress in Other Sciences

Muslim physicists were also highly creative scientists. Al-Hasan ibn al-Haytham, or Alhazen (d. 1038), of Cairo, developed optics to a remarkable degree and challenged the theory of Ptolemy and Euclid that the eye sends visual rays to its object. The chief source of all medieval Western writers on optics, Alhazen was interested in optical reflections and illusions and examined the refraction of light rays through air and water.

Although astronomy continued to be strongly influenced by astrology, Muslim astronomers built observatories, recorded their observations over long periods, and achieved greater accuracy than the Greeks in measuring the length of the solar year and in calculating eclipses. Interest in alchemy—the attempt to change base metals into precious ones and to find the magic elixir for the preservation of human life—produced the first chemical laboratories and caused attention to be given to the value of experimentation. Muslim alchemists prepared many chemical substances (sulfuric acid, for example) and developed methods for evaporation, filtration, sublimation, crystallization, and distillation. The process of distillation, invented around 800, produced what was called *al-kuhl* ("the essence"), or alcohol, a new liquor that brought its inventors great honor in some circles.

In mathematics the Muslims were indebted to the Hindus as well as to the Greeks. From the Hindus

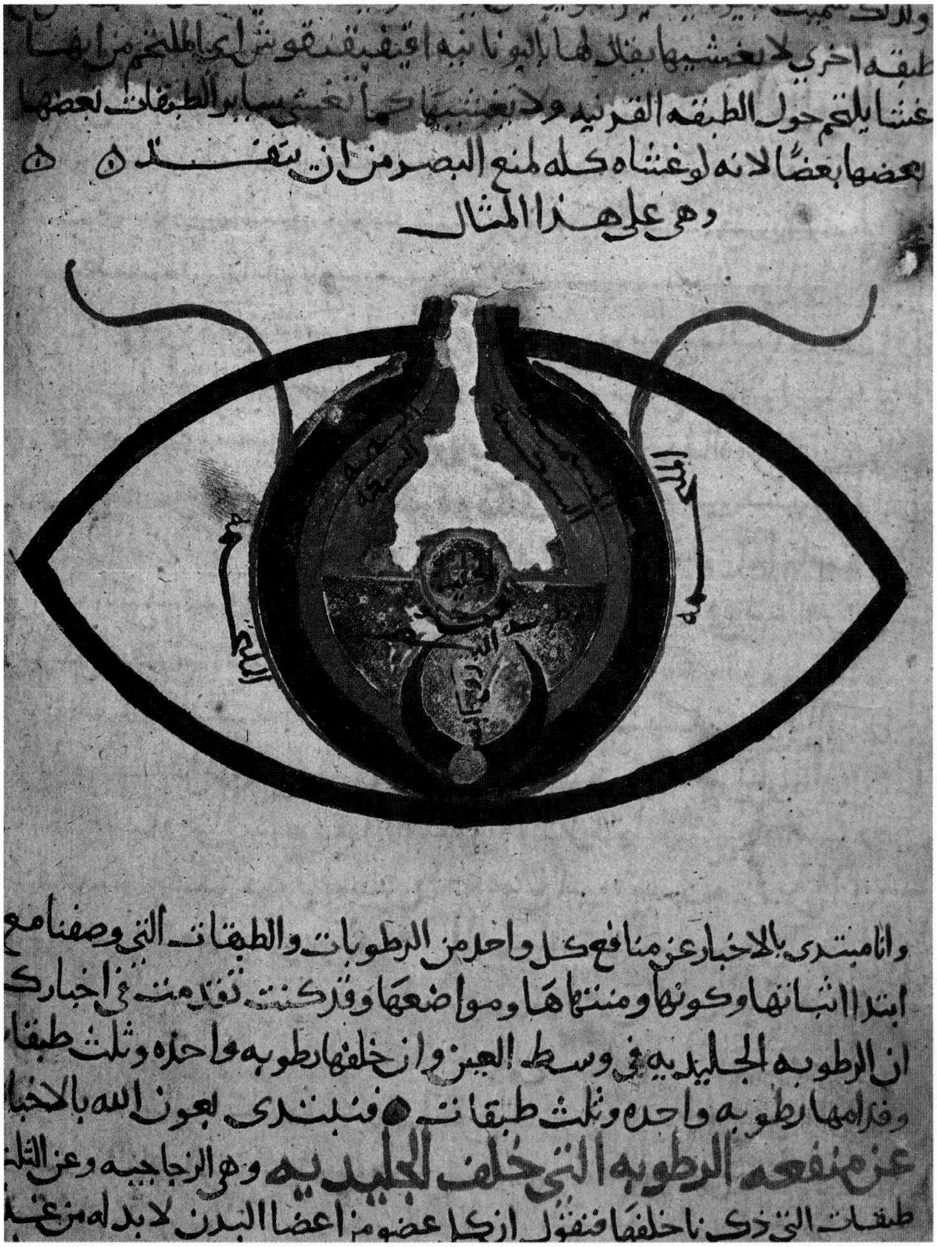

Husayn ibn Ishaq's Book of the Ten Treatises on the Eye *shows the Islamic scientist's outstandingly accurate understanding of the anatomy of the eye. Written in the tenth century, the work was still standard in the thirteenth century, when the copy shown here was made.*

came arithmetic, algebra, the zero, and the nine signs known in the West as Arabic numerals. From the Greeks came the geometry of Euclid and the fundamentals of trigonometry, which Ptolemy had established. Two Muslim mathematicians made significant contributions: al-Khwarizmi (al-KWAHR-iz-mee; d. c. 844), whose *Arithmetic* introduced Arabic numerals and whose *Algebra* first employed that mathematical term, and Omar Khayyám (d. c. 1123), the mathematician, astronomer, and poet whose work in algebra went beyond quadratics to cubic equations. Other Islamic scholars developed plane and spherical trigonometry.

In an empire that straddled continents, where trade and administration made an accurate knowledge of lands imperative, the science of geography flourished. The Muslims added to the geographical knowledge of the Greeks, whose treatises they translated, by producing detailed descriptions of the climate, manners, and customs of many parts of the known world. Developments in mapping went hand in hand with the progress of Arab seafaring, which aimed at exploiting commercial possibilities along the seaborne routes of trade.

Islamic Literature and Scholarship

To Westerners, Islamic literature may seem somewhat alien. Early Western literary styles tried to emphasize restraint and simplicity, but Muslim writers have long enjoyed literature that makes use of elegant expression, subtle combinations of words, and fanciful and even extravagant imagery.

Westerners' knowledge of Islamic literature tends to be limited to *The Arabian Nights* and the poetry of Omar Khayyám. The former is a collection of often erotic tales told with a wealth of local color that sheds light on racial and gender relations and on practices of food, dress, and cleanliness. Although *The Arabian Nights* professedly covers different facets of life at the Abbasid capital, the story is in fact often based on life in medieval Cairo. It took the literary influences of India and Persia, combined them with conventions of Arabic literature, and passed them on to the West, where they can be seen in the works of Chaucer and Boccaccio. These tales present an interesting combination of the courtly and the vulgar. The fame of Omar Khayyám's *Rubáiyát* (reu-BAI-yaht) is due at least in part to the musical (though rather free) translation of Edward Fitzgerald. The following stanzas indicate the poem's beautiful imagery and gentle resignation:

DOCUMENT *The Rubáiyát of Omar Khayyám*

A Book of Verses underneath the Bough,
A Jug of Wine, a Loaf of Bread—and Thou

Discovery Through Maps

An Islamic Map of the World

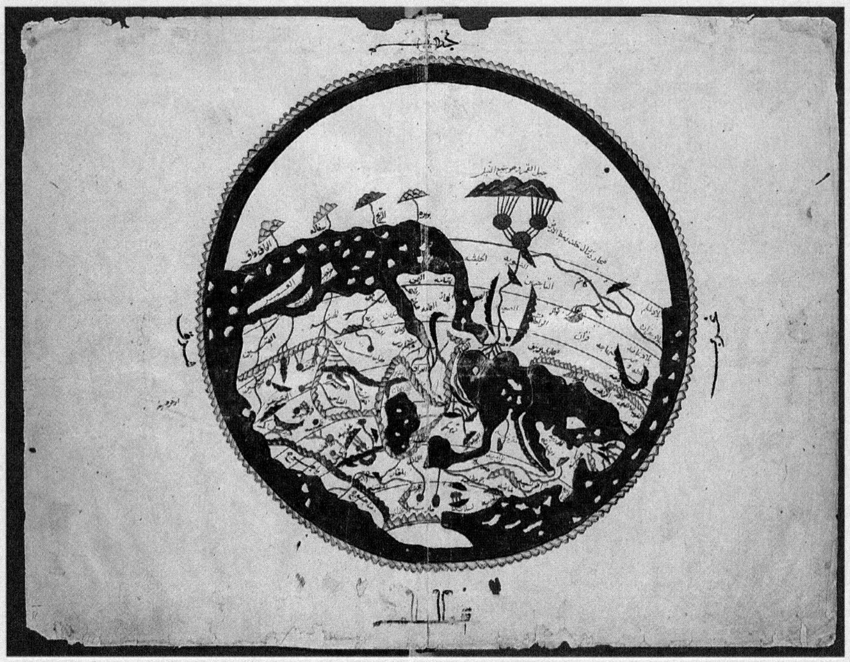

Which way is up? We tend to take the orientation of maps for granted, with north as up. For example, American world maps often depict the United States at the center and north at the top. But not all maps make those same assumptions. The world map of al-Idrisi, an Arab geographer, is a case in point. Al-Idrisi's map is oriented, as was common in Arab maps of his time, with south at the top. It is centered on the world of his own experience, the sacred city of Mecca in Arabia and the civilized realm of the Mediterranean. The map includes several distinctive features typical of this type of medieval map. The world is shown as an island encircled by a world sea. The extent of Africa is unknown; it is depicted as a giant mass occupying the upper half of the map. The Americas are not included at all.

Al-Idrisi was born in Morocco in 1100. Educated in Córdoba, he began his travels as a youth and ended up at the cosmopolitan court of King Roger of Sicily around 1138. There the king asked him to construct a world map complete with written commentary. In collaboration with other scholars, al-Idrisi crafted the map, which was engraved on silver, around the year 1154. Although the original is lost, there are various manuscript versions of al-Idrisi's world map, one of which is shown here. The Arab scholar's map was very influential and widely copied in Europe and Asia for centuries after his death in 1165. Al-Idrisi's map suggests one type of medieval worldview, and his life confirms the notion that cartographers were a valuable commodity in the Afro-Eurasian courts of the time. Rulers valued cartographers because they provided information that was practical and enlightening. They pieced together information about the world from classical sources, old maps, and the accounts of seamen, traders, and travelers. But, cartographers were also artists who made images of the ways in which peoples envisioned their own world and regions beyond their reach. Maps legitimized the power of rulers, cultures, kingdoms, and religions.

Turn the map upside down and see if you can identify the Mediterranean Sea, the Arabian Peninsula, and the Maghrib.

Questions to Consider

1. What does the world "look like" when *you* imagine it? Where and how did you learn your vision of the world?
2. The ways in which the world is represented change over time and place. Not all peoples depict land and sea in the same way. Try drawing a map of your childhood "world." What would it look like?
3. Are maps depictions of reality or do they suggest points of view?

Beside me singing in the Wilderness—
Oh, Wilderness were Paradise enow!—
Some for the Glories of This World; and some
Sigh for the Prophet's Paradise to come;
Ah, take the Cash, and let the Credit go,
Nor heed the rumble of a distant Drum! . . .
The Moving Finger writes; and, having writ,
Moves on: nor all your Piety nor Wit
Shall lure it back to cancel half a Line,
Nor all your Tears wash out a Word of it.
And that inverted Bowl they call the Sky,
Whereunder crawling coop'd we live and die,
Lift not your hands to It for help—for It
As impotently moves as you or I.[1]

The same rich imagery characterizes much Islamic prose, but *The Arabian Nights* and the *Rubáiyát* merely hint at the breadth and diversity of Islamic literature. As the first important prose work in Arab literature, the Qur'an set the stylistic pattern for all Arabic writers. With classical Arabic then "fixed" in the Qur'an, Muslim writers, spurred on by the generosity of the Islamic kings, produced a great corpus of literature. Arabic and then Persian were the languages of high culture. Poetry contests were a standard of the early Islamic courts, where the poets who contrived the most beautiful or wittiest verses received honors and rich rewards. Poetry was also used for satire. Poets used pointed verse to wound or defame their rivals, and kings used the talents of their poets to send insulting messages to their enemies. Muslim philosophy, essentially Greek in origin, was developed and modified by Islamic scholars. Like the medieval Christian philosophers, Muslim thinkers were largely concerned with reconciling the rationalism of Aristotle on the one hand and religious faith on the other. Some sought to harmonize Platonism, Aristotelianism, and Islam. The philosopher Ibn Sina (980–1037) sought to extract what was purely Aristotelian from later additions and to articulate the truths of Islam in terms of Aristotelian logic. His work had a profound effect on Islamic philosophy and was widely read in the West, where it was translated into Latin in the twelfth century.

DOCUMENT
A Mirror for Princes

Another great Islamic philosopher, Ibn Rushd, or Averroës (ah-VEHR-oh-eez; d. 1198), lived in Córdoba, where he was the caliph's personal doctor. He is famous for his marvelous commentaries on Aristotle. Ibn Rushd rejected the belief in the ultimate harmony between faith and reason along with all earlier attempts to reconcile Aristotle and Plato. He argued that parts of the Qur'an were to be taken metaphorically, not literally. But Ibn Rushd thought that most people were unable to understand either philosophy or the metaphorical meanings of the Qur'an. Those were questions for the philosophers.

DOCUMENT
The Sea of Precious Virtues

In contrast, Moses Maimonides (mai-MON-e-deez), Ibn Rushd's contemporary who was also born in Muslim Spain, sought, in his still influential *Guide to the Perplexed,* to harmonize Judaism and Aristotelian philosophy. St. Thomas Aquinas, who in the next century undertook a similar project for Christianity, was influenced by these earlier attempts to reconcile faith and reason. Although Western historiography has focused on the clash of Muslim and Christian armies in Spain, it might be better to view that territory in particular as a place where Muslim, Christian, and Jewish thinkers and writers interacted and learned from each other through a series of ongoing debates.

Islamic historiography found its finest expression in the work of Ibn Khaldun of Tunis (d. 1406), who has been called the "father of sociology." Ibn Khaldun wrote a large general history dealing particularly with human social development, focusing on the interaction of society with the physical environment. He delineated guidelines for the writing of history and ridiculed earlier historical writing, saying it was often full of stupid or thoughtless errors. Ibn Khaldun defined history in this manner:

> *It should be known that history, in matter of fact, is information about human social organization, which itself is identical with world civilization. It deals with such conditions affecting the nature of civilization as, for instance, savagery and sociability, group feelings, and the different ways by which one group of human beings achieves superiority over another. It deals with royal authority and . . . with the different kinds of gainful occupations and ways of making a living, with the sciences and crafts that human beings pursue as part of their activities and efforts, and with all the other institutions that originate in civilization through its very nature.*[2]

Ibn Khaldun conceived of history as an evolutionary process, in which societies and institutions change continually. He traveled widely in the Islamic world, serving as a judge and scholar in the courts of the Mamluks and other rulers. When he beheld the city of Cairo, he described it as a pinnacle of Islamic civilization, full of shops, gardens, scholars, and institutions of higher learning.

The Sufis

As Islamic civilization produced traditions of scholarship and philosophy, it also produced a tradition of mysticism that came to be a significant factor in the spread of Islam throughout the world. The Arabic word *tasawwuf* (tah-SAHW-woof, "mysticism") is related to the word *suf,* for the coarse woolen clothes some of the early mystics wore. The early sufis were lone ascetics who practiced physical and spiritual dis-

Document Ibn Sina's Path to Wisdom

The ways in which a person obtains an education vary considerably over time and from place to place. In the medieval Islamic world, it was customary for students to go from teacher to teacher or even from city to city seeking knowledge. Recitation and memorization were important elements of learning. Rather than working on a fixed "semester" system, a student often studied with a teacher until he mastered a particular text or body of knowledge (whether it took three months or three years). Only affluent students could afford their own books. As in many societies, formal education was reserved primarily for men; and, even among men, only an elite few were literate. Although some Muslim women became distinguished scholars and poets, girls generally received only a rudimentary education.

Ibn Sina, the famous Muslim philosopher who died in 1037, recorded the progress of his own education. His diligence, but not his pride, might in some ways serve as a model for modern students. As a young boy, Ibn Sina began his education in religion and the sciences. He remembers himself as a determined and independent student who had little patience with or respect for some of his teachers. By the time he was 16, his education was already far-reaching. Ibn Sina was raised in Bukhara, an important center of Islamic learning in Central Asia. There, he writes:

I was put under teachers of the Qur'an and of letters. By the time I was ten I had mastered the Qur'an and a great deal of literature, so that I was marvelled at for my aptitude. . . . My father sent me to a certain vegetable-seller who used the Indian arithmetic, so that I might learn it from him. Then, there came to Bukhara a man called Abu 'Abd Allah al-Natili who claimed to be a philosopher; my father invited him to stay in our house, hoping I would learn from him also. I had already occupied myself with Muslim jurisprudence, attending Isma'il the Ascetic; so I was an excellent enquirer, having become familiar with the methods of expostulation and the techniques of rebuttal according to the usages of the canon lawyers. . . . Whatever problem he [al-Natili] stated to me, I showed a better mental conception of it than he. So I continued until I had read all the straightforward parts of Logic with him; as for the subtler points, he had no acquaintance with them. From then onwards I took to reading texts by myself; I studied the commentaries, until I had completely mastered the science of Logic. Similarly with Euclid I read the first five or six figures with him, and thereafter undertook on my own account to solve the entire remainder of the book. . . . I now occupied myself with mastering the various texts and commentaries on natural science and metaphysics, until all the gates of knowledge were open to me. Next I desired to study medicine, and proceeded to read all the books that have been written on this subject. Medicine is not a difficult science, and naturally I excelled in it in a very short time, so that qualified physicians began to read medicine with me. I also undertook to treat the sick, and methods of treatment derived from practical experience revealed themselves to me such as baffle description. At the same time I continued between whiles to study and dispute on law, being now sixteen years of age.

Questions to Consider

1. Ibn Sina does not focus on the idea of learning as something that takes place in a specific building or one location. In what terms does he describe the learning process?
2. Think about writing an autobiography. When adults think back and describe their student days, is that history? What roles do memory and sense of identity play in the process?

From A. J. Arberry. *Aspects of Islamic Civilization* (Ann Arbor: University of Michigan Press, 1967), pp. 136–137.

cipline in order to transcend the material world and gain a special kind of closeness to Allah. Later, sufi orders were founded in which the devotees practiced rules of discipline, followed the path shown them by a spiritual master or *shaykh,* divorced themselves to some extent from the community, and developed rituals that ranged from the simple to the elaborate. There are many similarities between some of the sufi orders and the medieval monastic orders of Christian Europe. To be a sufi, however, one does not need to join a spiritual order; many sufis live and work in the community. What is essential to **Sufism** is the belief

Sufism—A broad term used to designate any of ascetic and mystic movements within Islam. Sufi movements have borrowed elements from Christian monasticism and Indian mysticism. The essential aim of Sufism is to achieve mystical communion with Allah.

in following a path of discipline that leads to mystical communion with Allah.

The early Muslim mystics expressed their desire for union with God in a language of love, longing, and ecstasy. This longing came to be embodied in the mystical poetry of sufis like that of the famous Jalal al-Din Rumi (1207–1273), who compared the sufi to a man "drunk with God." The *dhikr,* collective repetition of the name of God, sometimes accompanied by rhythmic movements and breathing, became part of sufi practice. It was a way of both glorifying God and transcending (like yoga) the distractions of the body and the world. In their quest for communion with God, the sufis also ran afoul of Islamic orthodoxy, because their beliefs and practices were sometimes considered extreme or blasphemous.

In the ninth century, sufis began systematically to write down the ways of the path. Communion with God meant the losing of self, however briefly. That losing or merging of self with God smacked of polytheism to many members of the *ulama.* Thus the sufis were accused of claiming to be divine and of believing they were above the law. In 922 al-Hallaj, a famous teacher and sufi in Baghdad, was executed for blasphemy after he claimed, "I am the Truth." Al-Hallaj had also alienated the authorities by claiming that the *hajj,* the pilgrimage to Mecca, was not necessary, because the sufi could pursue the pilgrimage to God from his own room. The pathos of the death of al-Hallaj is graphically described in the words of his servant, Ibrahim ibn Fatik, who wrote that al-Hallaj asked Allah to forgive those who were preparing to kill him:

> *Then he was silent. The Headsman stepped up and dealt him a smashing blow which broke his nose, and the blood ran onto his white robe. The mystic al-Shibli, who was in the crowd, cried aloud and rent his garment, and Abu Husayn al-Wasiti fell fainting, and so did other famous sufis who were there, so that a riot nearly broke out. Then the executioners did their work.*[3]

Al-Hallaj gave the sufi community in Baghdad a martyr. But in the end, the message of Sufism was too powerful and compelling for Islamic orthodoxy to ignore. Sufis were very effective in spreading the message of Islam beyond its Middle Eastern heartlands. In South and Southeast Asia, sufi asceticism and belief in mystical communion found resonances in the ascetic and mystical practices of those areas and aided the conversion of non-Muslims to Islam. By the end of the Abbasid era, Sufism had been brought into the mainstream of Islamic thought as a result of its widespread appeal and through the systematic efforts of scholars like al-Ghazali (1058–1111), who legitimized the sufi way as an acceptable path toward God. Sufism remains a powerful tool in the spread of Islam. In the United States today, Rumi's poetry remains popular, and American college students may get their first taste of Islam through the words of sufi masters.

Art and Architecture

Religious attitudes played an important part in shaping Islamic art. Because the Prophet warned against idols and their worship, there was a prohibition against pictorial representation of human and animal figures; that prohibition, however, was not always obeyed. The effect of this injunction was to encourage the development of stylized and geometrical designs. Islamic art, like other artistic traditions, borrowed extensively to forge a new and unique synthesis. Artists and craftspeople followed chiefly Byzantine and Persian models, but Central Asian, South Asian, and African motifs were also integrated into Islamic styles.

The ultimate stage of refinement of Moorish architecture, which combines Spanish and Islamic elements, is the Alhambra in Granada, the last Islamic stronghold in Spain during the Middle Ages. Slender, rhythmically spaced columns and arches covered with an intricate design of molded stucco frame the Court of the Lions, the most luxurious portion of the palace.

The Muslims excelled in the fields of architecture and the decorative arts. That Islamic architecture can boast of many large and imposing structures is not surprising; monumental building was a natural extension of the power and glory of the Islamic dynasts who wanted to celebrate their own power and glorify God. In time, original styles of building evolved; the great mosques embody such typical features as domes, arcades, and minarets, the slender towers from which the faithful are summoned to prayer. The horseshoe arch is another graceful and familiar feature of Muslim architecture.

On the walls and ceilings of their buildings, the Muslims gave full rein to their love of ornamentation and beauty of detail. The Spanish interpretation of the Islamic tradition is particularly delicate and elegant. A superb artistic example of the sophistication and wealth of the Muslim world is the Alhambra, built between 1248 and 1354 by Muslim kings in Granada, Spain. Some authorities consider it the apogee of Muslim architecture.

Restricted in their subject matter, Muslim craftspeople conceived beautiful patterns from flowers and geometrical figures. The Arabic script, one of the most graceful ever devised, was often used as a decorative motif. Muslim decorative skill also found expression in such fields as carpet and rug weaving, brass work, and the making of steel products inlaid with precious metals.

CONCLUSION

The great power of Islam's message enabled the fragmented Arab tribes to unify and expand across three continents in an astoundingly brief period. During the reigns of the first four caliphs and the century of dominance by the Umayyad dynasty, great gains were made in conquering new territories and peoples. But the Umayyad dynasty was based on a ruling hierarchy of Arabs, and the resentment of the non-Arab Islamic community helped establish the Abbasid dynasty in a new caliphate in Baghdad.

While traders, scholars, and sufis exported variants of the Islamic worldview, the Abbasid Empire provided the security, patronage, and institutional framework for a great cultural synthesis and an expanding network of international trade. As in all traditional empires of the time, agriculture provided the base for the economy of the Abbasid state, but its prosperity evolved from a combination of successful agriculture, trade, and industry.

The Islamic worldview both challenged and integrated the worldviews of the peoples it encountered in Asia, Africa, and Europe. Intellectual life was a product of that evolving synthesis. Muslim scholars participated in the rediscovery of classical (Greek) learning and the emergence of the Renaissance in Europe. They elaborated their cosmology in the course of a contentious but continuing dialog with the scholars, texts, and customs of other traditions.

Islam remains an extremely powerful force in the world. The Islamic community today is made up of leading industrialized societies as well as nations just emerging from colonialism. Present-day Muslims still derive great meaning from the teachings of Muhammad and the community he and his disciples constructed. They face the challenge of melding the world-view embedded in Islam's sacred text with the evolving conditions of the modern era, where the power of the ancient message still plays a dominant role.

Suggestions for Web Browsing

You can obtain more information about topics included in this chapter at the websites listed below. See also the companion website that accompanies this text, **http://www.ablongman.com/brummett**, which contains an online study guide and additional resources.

Internet Islamic History Sourcebook: Muhammad and Foundations—to 632 C.E.
http://www.fordham.edu/halsall/islam/islamsbook.html

Extensive online source for links about the early history of Islam, including a biography of Muhammad and the many aspects of Islam, including the role of women.

Islam and Islamic History in Arabia and the Middle East: The Message
http://www.islamic.org/Mosque/ihame/Sec1.htm

Islam and Islamic History in Arabia and the Middle East: The Golden Age.

http://www.islamic.org/Mosque/ihame/Sec7.htm

Extensive site details the origins of Islam and provides information and images about Muhammad, the Hijra, the Qur'an, Arabic writing, science and scholarship, Arabic literature, and Arabic numerals.

The Qur'an
http://islam.org/mosque/arabicscript/1/1.htm

The entire text of the Qur'an, with audio.

Islamic and Arabic Arts and Architecture
http://www.islamicart.com/

A rich and attractively designed general site, with information and images regarding architecture, calligraphy, and textiles. Includes a glossary of terms and names of important artists and architects. A subsite offers a portfolio of shrines and palaces including the Ka'ba, the Mosque of the Prophet Muhammad, the Dome of the Rock, and the Alhambra.

http://www.georgetown.edu/labyrinth

A wonderful site on medieval history which includes sections on texts and cartography.

Literature and Film

For literary sources suitable for class reading assignments and available in paperback, see the following: Robert L. Mack, ed., *Arabian Nights' Entertainments* (Oxford University Press, 1995), an annotated and historigraphically grounded edition of the Arabian Nights. Nizami, *The Story of Layla and Majnun*, trans. Rudolph Gelpke (Omega Publications, 1997), a twelfth-century classic Persian version of an Arabian folk epic of poetry, renunciation, and forbidden love. *The Legend of Seyavash* (Penguin, 1992)—one episode of the famous Persian Epic of Kings, penned in the eleventh century by Ferdowsi—is a wonderful study in notions of kingship, virtue, womanly wiles, and the mingling of Islam and animism. Usamah Ibn Munqidh, *An Arab-Syrian Gentleman and Warrior in the Period of the Crusades*, trans. P. K. Hitti (Princeton University Press, 1987), is an engaging memoir that reveals the mechanisms of cross-cultural exchange in twelfth-century Syria. Ruzbihan Baqli, *The Unveiling of Secrets: Diary of a Sufi Master*, trans. Carl Ernst (Parvardigar Press, 1997), records the personal reflections of a twelfth-century Persian Sufi. *The Adventures of Sayf Ben Dhi Yazan*, trans. Lena Jayyusi (Indiana University Press, 1999), is a folk romance composed during the medieval period of Mamluk rule in Egypt (magic, weddings, heroic feats, and day-to-day life). Ross E. Dunn, *The Adventures of Ibn Battuta: A Muslim Traveler of the 14th Century* (University of California, 1989), and Amin Maalouf, *Leo Africanus* (Dee, Ivan R., 1992), are also good student reading selections.

Films suitable for classroom presentation include *Mohammed, Messenger of God*, by Moustafa Akkad (Anchor Bay, 1976; also known as *The Message*), a popular commercial film, but one that has been acceptable in general to the Muslim community in the United States; and *Islam: Empire of Faith* (PBS, 2001), a historical assessment with commentary by various scholars of Islam.

Suggestions for Reading

Major scholarly surveys are Marshall Hodgson, *The Venture of Islam: Conscience and History of a World Civilization*, 3 vols. (University of Chicago Press, 1974), Ira Lapidus, *A History of Islamic Societies* (Cambridge University Press, 1988), and Albert Hourani, *A History of the Arab Peoples* (Warner, 1992). See also Philip K. Hitti, *The Arabs: A Short History* (Regnery, 1996), an excellent abridgment of a scholarly general history; and H. A. R. Gibb, *Mohammedanism: A Historical Survey*, 2nd ed. (Oxford University Press, 1969). See also the clear introduction to Islam by John L. Esposito, *Islam: The Straight Path*, 3rd ed. (Oxford University Press, 1998); Nehemia Levtzion and Randall Pouwels, eds., *The History of Islam in Africa* (Ohio University Press, 2000); J. Spencer Trimmingham, *The Sufi Orders in Islam* (Oxford, 1998); and Richard Fletcher, *Moorish Spain* (University of California Press, 1991).

W. Montgomery Watt, *Muhammad: Prophet and Statesman* (Oxford University Press, 1974), is a brief account of the Prophet's life and teachings. See also Karen Armstrong, *Muhammad: A Biography of the Prophet* (Harper Collins, 1992); Frederick Denny, *An Introduction to Islam*, 2nd ed. (Macmillan, 1996); and Martin Lings, *Muhammad: His Life Based on the Earliest Sources* (Inner Traditions International, 1983). For an interpretation and translation of the Qur'an, see Marmaduke William Pickthall, ed., *The Meaning of the Glorious Koran: An Explanatory Translation* (Unwin Hyman/HarperCollins). For primary source selections in translation, see James Kritzeck, ed., *Anthology of Islamic Literature* (Meridian, 1975). John Renard, *Islam and the Heroic Image* (University of South Carolina Press, 1994), is an excellent introduction to heroic Muslim personalities.

GLOBAL ISSUES

RELIGION AND GOVERNMENT

How do societies manage the relationship between their spiritual concerns and their temporal concerns?

Byzantine wall mosaic, *Christ Pantocrator Between Emperor Constantine IX Monamachus and Empress Zoe.*

Throughout history, religion and government have served as foundational institutions in the world's many societies. These two institutions (often referrred to as "church" and "state" in the West) may seem to deal with different areas of human experience, but in reality the goals of both institutions are similar. Each in its own way seeks to maintain social order, foster a sense of community, and provide hope for a more satisfying future. Nevertheless, the relationship between these two institutions has varied significantly. Some societies fused religion and government into one entity. Other societies chose to maintain mutually cooperative relationships between the two institutions. Yet in further instances, societies consciously strove to separate one institution from the other.

The origins of religion are found in humanity's spiritual concerns while the origins of government stem from humanity's temporal (worldly) concerns. Humans' spiritual concerns essentially attempt to resolve the questions of how and why the universe came into being, what humans' proper role is in the world, and what the significance is of suffering and death. Temporal concerns, on the other hand, focus at their most basic level on how best to address humans' needs for food, water, and shelter. The answers to this question involve the specialization of tasks and social organization, which inevitably form the foundation of government.

The earliest humans made little if any distinction between their spiritual concerns (religion) and their temporal concerns (government). Our earliest ancestors believed that everything in the world around them and the heavens above, both animate and inanimate, possessed a spiritual essence. Because human beings were an integral part of this holistic universe, everything they did, particularly the activity of food gathering and production, was steeped in spiritual significance.

The earliest forms of separation between religion and government probably came about as human societies grew larger, more complex, and required greater specialization from their members. Because of the increasing interdependence of individuals that naturally results from specialization, some groups or individuals within a given society showed greater ability to address the community's spiritual concerns and became their society's priests. Similarly, others showed greater ability in addressing people's temporal concerns and became their society's chiefs. These two new social groups stood at the top of their societies' social hierarchies because of the vital significance of each of their responsibilities. While the two may have often competed with one another for power, they also tended to support each other's authority. We know of only a small number of early human societies in which primary spiritual and temporal roles were likely exercised by one individual.

Many of the world's earliest civilizations, however, eventually combined religious and political authority in the person of one ruler—a priest-king. In Egypt, a truly theocratic state evolved, in which the pharaoh was seen to be a living god who governed the state. In Mesopotamia, it is likely that initially the *patesi* was both a temporal ruler and a religious authority, administering the city-state as its patron god's representative on earth. Throughout most of the history of ancient Mesopotamia, rulers were held to be mortals governing on behalf of the gods.

In ancient China, the emperor, as head of the imperial government, used a religious concept to justify his rule. "The mandate of heaven" held that the emperor ruled with the blessing of heaven, and that if the emperor ruled wisely heaven would reward the nation; if, however, he ruled unwisely, heaven would be displeased and the mandate would pass to another. In Japan, ancient tradition held that the emperor was a divine being, descended from the great sun goddess Amaterasu, the supreme deity of the Shintō religion and queen of all the *kami,* the forces inherent in nature. As civilization emerged in South Asia, the forces of religion and government became permanently intertwined in the development of the caste system, which formally enshrined priests (Brahmans) and rulers (Kshatriyas) at the top of the Hindu socioreligious hierarchy. The earliest pre-Columbian civilizations in the Americas all appear to have combined religious and governmental authority in the person of priest-kings or emperors who functioned as temporal rulers and intermediaries to the gods.

The three monotheistic religions of Judaism, Christianity, and Islam have each had different relationships with government over the course of their histories. Judaism, in its formative stages, combined many religious responsibilities of the community with the political leadership. Moses served as both a temporal leader and a prophet with religious obligations to lead his people according to God's commands. The later kings of Israel and Judah constantly sought to influence the actions of priests and prophets, who, in turn, never hesitated to involve themselves in the politics of the monarchy.

The first Christians were much more focused on spiritual matters than on temporal matters, yet they were not blind to political authority. A strong advocacy of separation of religion and government may be found in Christ's own admonition to "Leave unto Caesar that which is Caesar's, and to God the things that are God's." As Christianity became established and institutionalized in Europe, both Roman emperors and the church realized the mutual benefit of cooperation. At times that cooperation could be more accurately called dependence, especially as strong emperors such as Constantine effectively unified religious and governmental authority, giving rise to caesaropapism—the domination of the church by the emperor. As Rome fell from influence and various European monarchies were established, the church, under the direction of its popes, exerted what political influence it could. Later, as Christian Europe moved through the Renaissance, Reformation, and Enlightenment, religious influence over government weakened, ultimately giving rise to the call for separation of church and state.

Islam, from its origins, sought to unify the two institutions of religion and government. Muhammad served as both political and religious leader of the community of believers. The Prophet's successors, the caliphs, shared the same responsibility: to govern in accordance with the word of Allah as written in the Qur'an.

Religion and government, of course, continue to stand at the foundation of the world's societies today, and the appropriateness of each institution's proper or improper influence over the other is still a matter of debate. In some Islamic countries, the institutions of religion and government still overlap. The political course of Iran is currently determined by its ayatollahs (religious leaders). In Afghanistan, the mullahs, authorities on the Qur'an and Sharia (Islamic law), have strong political influence through their status as tribal spokesmen. In India, while the constitution formally separates religion and government, Hindu nationalism remains a strong force in politics. In 1998, the Hindu nationalist Bharatiya Janata party won the national elections, giving rise to new fears that non-Hindu minorities would suffer under Hindu majority rule.

In western Europe and the United States, tension continues between the two institutions on a number of levels. The French government recently banned religious dress and ostentatious display of religious symbols from its schools in an attempt to assimilate the children of Muslim immigrants into French secular culture. In the United States, religion and government run up against each other over issues such as abortion, stem cell research, public prayer, and religious symbolism in public places.

The tension between the two institutions of government and religion has been present in human society throughout history. Today, the manner in which these two institutions interact can shape a society in profound ways. In general, the separation of religion and government is thought to be more conducive to the democratic principles of equality and pluralism because such a relationship prevents religious majorities from imposing their faith on others through the power of the state. On the other hand, the unification of religion and government may promote political stability and cohesion in societies where members of one religion make up the vast majority of the population. Every society in the modern world continues to grapple with the problems related to one institution's influence over the other, with the appropriate influence of government on religion and religion on government. It is most likely that the disagreement over the proper impact each institution should have on the other will be debated into the foreseeable future.

Questions

1. Why are religion and government such powerful social institutions?
2. Should religion have some influence over government and vice versa, or should the two institutions be separated from one another?
3. What has history taught us regarding the separation of religion and government?

CHAPTER

8

African Beginnings

African Civilizations to 1500 C.E.

CHAPTER CONTENTS

"Unless you know the road you've come down, you cannot know where you are going." This proverb from the Temne people of West Africa reflects the importance that Africans place on understanding the past. And, in Africa's case, there is an extraordinarily vibrant history to consider, stretching from the emergence of our human ancestors to the development of major kingdoms and empires to the creation of modern states. Africa's geography and environment presented formidable challenges to human development, but African peoples have displayed a remarkable genius for adaptation, innovation, and ingenuity and have developed a rich tapestry of cultures, societies, and civilizations. Although there are certain cultural traits that most Africans share, Africans have created a diverse variety of social and political systems, ranging from small-scale communities in which extended families and lineages met most of their needs to large states such as Nubia, Mali, and Great Zimbabwe, with hereditary rulers, elaborate bureaucracies, and extensive trading networks.

An enduring image of Africa is that it is a collection of unchanging societies that were isolated and unaware of developments in other parts of the world. This depiction is erroneous. Africans have shared ideas and innovations with each other and been receptive to technological advances and influences from outside the continent. The trans-Saharan trade linked West African Sudanic states to the Mediterranean and Middle East; Indian Ocean trade tied the East African coastal city-states and southern Africa kingdoms to Arabia, Persia, and Asia; and the Red Sea served as a bridge connecting Aksum and Ethiopia to the Mediterranean and the Indian Ocean.

3000

c. 3000 B.C.E. Beginning of Bantu migrations

1000

700–400 B.C.E. Ironworking introduced in Nok culture, Nigeria

1 C.E.

c. 100 C.E. Establishment of kingdom of Aksum

First century Camel introduced from Asia into trans-Saharan trade

300s Rise of kingdom of Ghana, West Africa

320–350 Reign of Ezana, king of Aksum

1000

1000–1500 Peak of Swahili civilization along East African coast

1076 Almoravid attack on Ghana

1100 Building of rock churches in Ethiopia

c. 1234–1260 Reign of Malinke ruler, Sundiata Keita, founder of Mali Empire

1270 Beginning of Solomonid dynasty, Ethiopia

1290–1450 Peak of kingdom of Zimbabwe

1300s Founding of kingdom of Kongo

1307–1337 Reign of Mansa Musa in Mali

1400–1600 Rise of Edo kingdom of Benin

1434–1468 Reign of Zar'a Ya'kob, emperor of Ethiopia

THE AFRICAN ENVIRONMENT

■ *How did African farmers adapt to different environmental zones?*

Many Americans have thought of the African continent as a place of two extremes: oceans of sand dunes in the north and, to the south, an immense "jungle" teeming with wild animals. In reality, more than half of the area south of the Sahara consists of grassy plains, known as **savanna,** whereas "jungle" or tropical rain forests make up only 7 percent of the continent's land surface.

The most habitable areas have traditionally been the savannas, as their grasslands and trees favor both human settlement and long-distance trade and agriculture. The northern savanna, a region sometimes called the Sahel or Sudan (not to be confused with the modern state by the same name), stretches across the continent just south of the Sahara. Other patches of savanna are interspersed among the mountains and lakes of East Africa and another belt of grassland that runs east and west across southern Africa, north and east of the Kalahari Desert.

Between the northern and southern savannas, in the region of the equator, is dense rain forest. Although the rain forest is lush, its soils are poor because torrential rains cause soil erosion and intense heat leaches the soil of nutrients and burns off humus or organic matter that are essential for soil fertility. The rain forests also harbor insects that carry deadly diseases. Mosquitoes transmit malaria and yellow fever, and the tsetse fly is a carrier of sleeping sickness to which both humans and animals such as horses and cattle are susceptible.

Whether they sustained a living through hunting, gathering, fishing, **pastoralism,** or farming, Africans had to contend with the continent's harsh and fragile environments. Thus, African cultivators accumulated sophisticated knowledge of what food crops to grow in particular areas and how to manage their environments and sustain a living from marginal or poor soils. Permanent cultivation was a luxury that few Africans farmers were able to practice. A more prevalent approach in sparsely populated areas was "slash and burn," or **shifting cultivation.** Farmers knew that they could stay on a piece of land for a few growing seasons before soils were exhausted. Thus, every growing season, they would clear land with iron hoes and machetes and fertilize it by burning natural vegetation such as brush and tree leaves for ash. Usually after two to three years, the land lost its fertility and a family had to move on and start the cycle in another area. Shifting agriculture was especially necessary in the rain forests, where, as noted, heavy rainfall and high temperatures produced poor soils.

Cultivators learned what crops were best suited for the soils and rainfall in certain climatic zones. In rain forest areas where vegetation was dense, they favored root crops such as yams and cassava, while in the grasslands of the savanna, they grew cereal crops such as sorghum and millet.

savanna—A flat grassland dotted with trees.

pastoralism—The raising of grazing animals such as sheep and cattle.

shifting cultivation—An agricultural system in which cultivators farm land for a few growing seasons; as the soil loses its fertility, they move to another area.

AFRICAN CULTURAL PATTERNS

■ *What is the connection between kinship relations and African political systems?*

Although African societies are remarkably diverse, they often share common values, belief systems, and aesthetic styles that are reflected in their family and kinship relations and political, economic, religious, and cultural institutions.

Africans place great importance on family and kinship ties. The primary unit of social organization is the extended family, which includes not only parents and children but also a network of wives and relatives—grandparents, aunts, uncles, and cousins. Relations within families are based on descent patterns. Most African societies are patrilineal, with descent traced through the father to his sons and daughters who belong to their father's kin group. When a woman marries, she becomes part of her husband's kin group and usually no longer shares in the economic resources of her father's group. About 15 percent of African societies are matrilineal, in which descent is passed through the mother's side of the family to a mother's brother. In matrilineal societies, when a man marries, he usually goes to live at his wife's family homestead and has to work for her family for a number of years. In these societies, women live with their own kin and have at least some independent access to economic resources such as land. Many of the matrilineal societies are found in forest areas with poor soils. Because farming required large numbers of laborers, an advantage of matrilineal relationships is that they can bring together a wide network of families from both the mother's and father's side who contribute laborers to agricultural production.

Historically, families also played an important role in decisions about marriages. Marriage was not solely a private issue between a bride and a groom but was a uniting of two larger groups, such as families or clans. Strict rules stipulated whether a person could marry outside a clan or lineage. Marriage was typically accompanied by an exchange of **bridewealth,** the husband's payment of money, goods, services, or cattle to his new wife's family. Bridewealth gave a husband certain domestic rights—to establish a homestead with his wife, to use his bride's labor in his household and fields, and to attach their offspring to his kinship group. Bridewealth also cemented a social relationship between a husband and his wife's family. If a wife could not bear children or deserted her husband, her parents had to return the bridewealth. This gave the wife's family a vested interest in preserving the marriage.

Another characteristic of both matrilineal and patrilineal African societies is that they accepted **polygyny,** a man's marrying more than one wife. Although a minority of men actually took a second wife, polygyny was seen as a necessity because of high infant mortality, the need for more manpower in farming, and the desire to express status and wealth.

The family household was the foundation for building larger identities and communities—one's *lineage* contained people who could trace their descent to a common ancestor, and one's *clan* contained many lineages or people who shared kinship. Within a society, lineages and clans could be used to mobilize people for self-defense and work parties, to allocate rights to land, to raise bridewealth, and to perform religious rituals. African societies also contained groups of people who were not bound by kinship and who created larger social identities. These were secret societies that often guarded medicines, performed ritual activities, and organized defense and were cohorts of people of roughly the same age who had gone through rites-of-passage ceremonies such as circumcision.

The lineage and clan also provided the basis for political units, ranging from the most basic to the largest kingdoms. Many African societies were formed without chiefs, rulers, or centralized political institutions and operated at the village level. These are known as "stateless" societies. Authority was usually vested in a group of elders or senior members of families and lineages who conferred to work out approaches to common concerns such as deciding when to plant and to harvest, whether to move or migrate, and how to resolve disputes within a community or handle conflicts with other communities. In these egalitarian societies, reaching a consensus was an essential part of the decision-making process.

Other African societies developed slowly into chiefdoms and kingdoms that incorporated larger populations, featured elaborate hierarchies and extensive bureaucracies, and engaged in long-distance trade with other states. Even though kingdoms could be made up of many lineages or clans, they were usually dominated by one. These kingdoms were governed by hereditary rulers who wielded religious as well as political power. However, their tendencies to abuse power were often held in check by councils and courts.

There were many ways in which women shared or influenced decision-making with men. On occasion women served as officials and advisers, religious leaders, and even soldiers, and some states had women rulers. The king's wife (the queen), his sisters, and the queen mother were often powers behind the throne. In the kingdom of Abomey in West Africa, each wife of a king represented one of the kingdom's lineages and advocated its interests to the king.

The queen mother could be the actual mother of a king, or she could be an in-law, an appointee, an influential person in a society, or the wife or sister of a former ruler. She was responsible not only for looking after the king's interests, but also for serving as a unifying presence. She mediated rivalries between court factions, maintained alliances, and represented groups who were excluded in succession disputes.

Work within communities was carried out by families and kinship groups. However, specific tasks were usually determined by sex and age. Women were primarily responsible for maintaining the homestead, cultivating the fields, preparing the food, and running local markets, while men took the lead in building houses, constructing paths and roads, clearing fields, raising livestock, hunting, and conducting long-distance trade. Work parties consisting of age-mates of one or both sexes could be mobilized for communal tasks such as harvesting and planting, clearing fields, weeding, threshing, and house building. Although men usually controlled technological advances such as ironworking and blacksmithing, there were exceptions to this practice. Among the Pare of eastern Africa, women were given the responsibility for gathering and smelting iron.

An important aspect of the African heritage was its value system, which shaped all aspects of life. Paramount were a profound awareness of human interdependence and an appreciation for communal harmony and unity within the family and the larger society. The African conception of land ownership, for instance, stressed that individuals had the right to cultivate untilled land but that they could not sell or rent the land to others or pass it on to their children. Land was held in trust by the larger community.

Religion permeated the everyday experiences of Africans and was an integral part of their social and political life. Specific religious beliefs and institutions varied from society to society, but several tenets were

bridewealth—A payment a groom and his family make to the bride's family to arrange for a marriage.

polygyny—A system of marriage that allows a man to have more than one wife.

shared. African societies were polytheistic. Most had a belief in a high god or creator who was usually remote and rarely concerned with the everyday affairs of humans. Therefore, Africans were more directly engaged with other divinities, such as nature and ancestral spirits that maintained an active interest in the affairs of the living and could intercede for humans with the high god. Political leaders were often imbued with ritual authority to approach the ancestors, who provided legitimacy to the moral order and reinforced political authority.

As individuals and as communities, Africans were concerned with identifying the causes of illness and disasters such as drought, crop failures, and plagues. One way of explaining misfortune was that the high god or the ancestors were unhappy with the actions of humans. Thus, people sought the goodwill of the ancestors with prayers and ritual offerings and sacrifices at shrines. Africans also attributed misfortune to witches, who wielded evil powers and inflicted suffering on people. Those afflicted by witchcraft appealed to specialists such as diviners to diagnose the sources of evil and provide remedies for them. Women enhanced their status and prestige by serving in religious rituals as priestesses, healers, rainmakers, diviners, and spirit mediums.

Some African religious systems were extremely complex, with elaborate priesthoods and cults. The Yoruba traditionally had four levels of spiritual beings. At the top was the supreme being, Oludumare, who was served by his subordinate gods on the second level. The secondary gods had their own priests, who presided over temples and shrines. Then came the ancestors, known as *Shango*. Finally, there were the nature spirits found in the earth, mountains, rivers, and trees.

Africans were traditionally skilled and sensitive artists, particularly in sculpture, which they used to record historical events. They carved expertly in wood, ivory, and soapstone. They also fashioned statues from baked clay and cast them in bronze. An innovative technique was the *cire perdue* (SIR purdee; "lost wax") technique, which involved making a cast of the object in wax, covering it with clay, and then melting the wax and replacing it with molten bronze. The famous bronze statuary of Benin, which drew on a long tradition of metalworking in the region of present-day Nigeria, has gained international recognition for its craftsmanship and beauty. Other specific artistic traditions, producing naturalism and symbolism in a rich tapestry of styles, flourished in many early African cultures.

Many African religious ceremonies featured masked male dancers. In this photo of the Dogon people of West Africa, the masked dancers performing at a funeral ceremony are driving the spirit of the dead person from its home. The dancers also act out the Dogon myth explaining how death entered the world through the disobedience of young men.

THE PEOPLING OF AFRICA

▪ *How did the knowledge of pastoralism and agriculture spread throughout Africa?*

During the late Stone Age, human communities in Africa were small bands of foragers who based their existence on hunting wild animals and gathering wild plants. Their technology was relatively simple but effective. Small bands of hunters, armed with bows and arrows with stone barbs treated with poisons, tracked down and killed the small and large game that roamed the plains of Africa. While men conducted hunts, women were primarily responsible for gathering. With a tool kit of digging sticks, gourds, and carrying bags, they "collected a variety of wild fruits, nuts, and melons, and dug up edible roots and tubers from the ground."[1] For many foraging groups all over the world, hunting and gathering satisfied all their dietary requirements and remained a preferred way of life long after the invention of agriculture.

About 15,000 to 20,000 years ago foraging groups along the Nile River added more protein to their diets by fishing in rivers and lakes and gathering shellfish. From 10,000 B.C.E. to 6000 B.C.E, the northern half of Africa went through a wet phase known as the Aquatic Age. The region that is now the Sahara became a savanna of grassland and woodland, with an abundance of rivers and lakes. Lake Chad, for instance, formed part of a large inland sea. By fashioning bone harpoons and fishnets, people lived off the rich aquatic life. Around 3000 B.C.E. an extended dry phase set in and the vast barren area that we know now as the Sahara began to form.

Before the Sahara became a desert, the region was home to pastoralists who herded cattle, sheep, and goats. On a plateau at Tassili n-Ajjer in the central Sahara, these pastoralists left an impressive array of wall paintings depicting their lifestyles and the wild animals that roamed the region. In this painting from the Tassili frescoes, women ride oxen as their community migrates to a new settlement.

Agriculture

The dry period largely cut off sub-Saharan Africa from developments in the Mediterranean, but it was also likely a major stimulus for the development of agriculture in West Africa as communities experimented with new crops to supplement their diets. They began growing barley, wheat, and flax with simple tools such as digging sticks and wooden hoes.

In the past it was widely assumed that sub-Saharan African communities acquired agriculture by diffusion from Nile civilizations, but more recent scientific investigations have shown that plant domestication began independently in four regions: the Ethiopian highlands, the central Sudan, the West African savanna, and the West African forests. In all cases African farmers adapted crops suited to particular environments that were tested over long periods of time. For instance, around 5000 B.C.E. in the dry West African savanna, farmers developed sorghum and pearl millet, both crops requiring short growing seasons and minimal rainfall. Around 3000 B.C.E. in the grasslands of the Ethiopian highlands, farmers began cultivating *teff* (a tiny grain), finger millet, *noog* (an oil plant), sesame, and mustard. In the forests they planted *ensete* (a source of starch that looks like a banana), coffee, and qat. People chewed coffee and qat leaves as a stimulant. Around 1000 B.C.E. wheat and barley were imported from across the Red Sea. In the central Sudan agricultural communities began producing sorghum, millet, rice, cowpeas, and groundnuts as far back as 4000 B.C.E. In the West African forests, oil palms, cowpeas, and root crops such as yams were produced.

Africans also began to use domesticated animals about the same time as they adopted agriculture. The

Early African Civilizations

10,000–6000 B.C.E.	Aquatic Age
c. 4000 B.C.E.	Domestication of food crops in central Sudan
c. 3100 B.C.E.	Beginning of unification of Upper and Lower Egypt
c. 3000 B.C.E.	Sahara region begins changing into desert
c. 730 B.C.E.	Kushite conquest of Egypt
c. 700 B.C.E.	Spread of knowledge of ironworking from Egypt to Kush

earliest evidence of livestock is found in the western Egyptian desert about 8000 B.C.E. Cattle, sheep, goats, and pigs were introduced from western Asia to Egypt and North Africa and then spread much later to western, eastern, and southern Africa.

Iron Technology

Another major breakthrough for sub-Saharan African cultures was the introduction of ironworking. Although bronze and copper toolmaking had developed in western Asia, the technology had not spread to sub-Saharan Africa. This was not the case with iron technology, which reached sub-Saharan Africa by two routes. It moved first from Assyria to Egypt around 700 B.C.E. and from Egypt to Nubia in the seventh century B.C.E. Ironworking then spread southward to the Lake Victoria area around 250 B.C.E. It also appeared in West Africa around 1000 B.C.E., apparently brought south across the Sahara by Berbers, in contact with Phoenician or Carthaginian traders.

The production of several pounds of iron requires ten to 15 trees to fuel smelters. Hence, two of the earliest centers of iron smelting were in forested areas at Meroe (MEHR-oh-wee), in the Nubian kingdom of Kush, and Nok, situated on the Jos plateau in central Nigeria. Located on the Nile River in a region rich in iron ore deposits, Meroe became well-known in the fourth century B.C.E. for iron smelting and making iron tools and weapons that were key to the kingdom's success. Huge iron slag heaps still exist around the ruins of Meroe.

Archaeologists have dated ironworking sites at Nok from 1000 to 500 B.C.E. Although some contend that ironworking was an independent invention at Nok, other ironworking sites of about the same time period have recently been identified in Mauritania, southern Mali, and central Nigeria. Nevertheless, it is clear that Nok had one of the earliest ironworking sites. The Nok workers' preheating techniques and their ability to produce steel with a high carbon content were equal to those of Egypt and Rome. The Nok population included ironsmiths, craftspeople, and artists, who produced terra-cotta sculptures of remarkable realism that were strikingly similar to later art forms among the Yoruba kingdoms of Ife and Benin.

Iron production in most African societies usually took place in the dry months when rain and floods were not disruptive and agriculture was less intensive. Because their products were highly valued and could be exchanged for animals and food, ironworking specialists were persons of wealth and status who usually passed on their knowledge to close kin. Magical, ritual, and spiritual powers were often attributed to them. In some societies the ironworking craft assumed such ritualistic significance that the furnaces were hidden in secluded places.

Some scholars see the ironworking process as a metaphor that reinforced age and gender relationships. Ironworking was a preserve of the elders who

This stylized terra-cotta head, dating from about 500 B.C.E., is an outstanding example of a sculpture from the Nok culture of central Nigeria. The head, which has a human face, was probably used for religious purposes.

passed on their knowledge to young apprentices, while the smelting process was likened to a woman conceiving and giving birth. The Phoka, an ethnic group in Malawi, "described their smelting furnace as a fertile young woman while under construction, and as their 'wife' once smelting began."[2] To ensure success, male ironworkers had to observe strict abstinence while smelting, and menstruating and pregnant women were not allowed near the furnaces.

Ironworking allowed African societies to make the transition from stone to metal tools. Iron tools such as hoes, knives, sickles, spearheads, and axes made a significant difference in clearing forests and thick vegetation for agriculture, in hunting, and in waging war. When combined with the introduction of agriculture and pastoralism, the knowledge of ironworking contributed to population growth, craft specializations, trade between communities, and more complex political and economic systems. Ironworking was also a factor in the spread of Bantu groups to central, eastern, and southern Africa.

THE BANTU DISPERSION

▪ *Why did Bantu-speaking groups migrate from their original home area?*

One of the striking features of many African societies from central to eastern to southern Africa is that their languages (called Niger-Congo) and cultures have many similarities. How these societies—known as **Bantu** ("people")—came to spread over this vast area is a question that has long vexed scholars.[3]

Authorities generally agree that the original homeland for Bantu speakers was an area in present-day Cameroon near the Nigerian border. They are still not sure, however, what prompted Bantu groups to start migrating from their homeland. One explanation relates to environmental changes—as the Sahara region dried up, small groups were forced to move southward in search of new areas to farm and fish. Another explanation is that the acquisition of ironworking gave Bantu groups access to iron tools that they could use in clearing the thicker vegetation of the forest regions. However, archaeological evidence now suggests that Bantu groups did not use iron tools until after their migrations began.

Using archaeological and linguistic data, historians have had some success in reconstructing the complex movements of Bantu groups. Around 3000 B.C.E., bands of Bantu began slowly moving out of their original homeland. These Bantu groups had common lifestyles—they lived in scattered homesteads and villages and farmed root crops, foraged for food, and fished. One stream of peoples moved south into the equatorial rain forests of west Central Africa and settled in present-day Angola and Namibia. Their agriculture relied heavily on root crops and palm trees. The other stream moved east through the Congo basin and eventually settled in the area east of Lake Victoria

Around 3000 B.C.E. groups of Bantu speakers began migrating from west Central Africa and establishing farming and pastoral communities in eastern, central, and southern Africa.

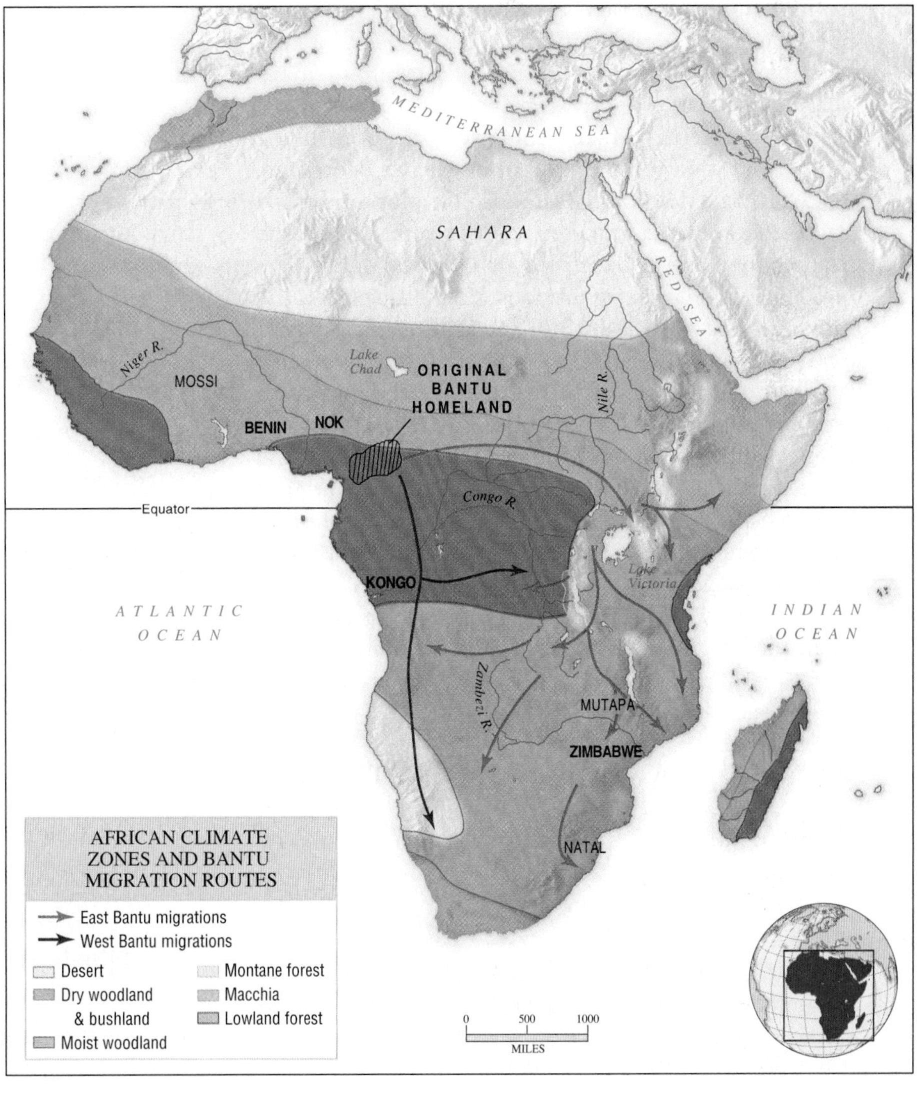

Bantu—A word meaning "people," it refers to a family of related languages spoken in central, eastern, and southern Africa.

in East Africa. There they came into contact with Cushitic-speaking peoples that had migrated from the Ethiopian highlands. The Bantu adopted their mixed farming practices—growing cereal crops such as millet and sorghum and herding cattle, sheep, and goats.

From that point, wherever Bantu groups migrated, they searched for areas that had enough summer rainfall to support cereal cultivation and their animal herds. As soils were not rich and could not support farmers for long periods, groups of people practiced shifting cultivation. The need to move on after two or three years in an area may explain why some Bantu groups, after spreading throughout East Africa, migrated southward, along tributaries of the Congo River, through the equatorial rain forest to present-day southern Congo and Zambia, where they settled in the savannas and woodland areas. Others migrated south, crossing the Zambezi and Limpopo Rivers by the fourth century of the Common Era.

As Bantu communities moved into eastern and southern Africa, they also acquired knowledge of ironworking and adopted new food crops such as the banana and the Asian yam, brought to Africa by sailors from Malaysia and Polynesia who settled on the island of Madagascar several thousand years ago. The banana had many attractive qualities. It could be grown more abundantly than root crops such as yams and without as much labor. Farmers did not have to clear out all the trees in an area for the banana to thrive. Moreover, bananas did not collect standing water and thus attracted fewer mosquitoes. In moist regions, it became a staple food and a source of mash for beer.

Throughout their migrations, Bantu societies came into contact with hunting and gathering groups. Although some scholars have portrayed the Bantu as a superior culture that overwhelmed hunting and gathering groups, recent scholarship has shown that the relationship was complex rather than one-sided. At the same time that Bantu were practicing agriculture and pastoralism, they relied on foraging for subsistence and turned to hunting and gathering bands for assistance and knowledge of local conditions. In addition, hunters and gatherers married into Bantu groups or attached themselves to Bantu groups for periods of time.

ETHIOPIA AND NORTHEASTERN AFRICA

■ *What role did the church play in strengthening the rule of Ethiopia's Solomonid dynasty?*

Situated along and inland from Africa's Red Sea coast, Ethiopia has been one of Africa's most enduring and richest civilizations. Indeed, the region between the Nile River and the Red Sea had been recognized as a major source of trade goods several thousand years before the kingdom of Ethiopia came into existence. To the Egyptians the area on the southern Red Sea coast was known as the Land of Punt, and from the Fifth Dynasty (c. 2494–2345 B.C.E.) on, Egypt's rulers regularly sent expeditions to trade for frankincense, myrrh, aromatic herbs, ebony, ivory, gold, and wild animals. The Egyptian queen Hatshepsut's funerary temple recorded a major expedition that she sent to Punt around 1470 B.C.E.

Around 800 B.C.E. traders from Saba', a kingdom on the southwestern Arabian peninsula, crossed the Red Sea, first founding trading settlements on the Eritrean coast and later a kingdom, Da'amat. The Sabaeans tapped into the ivory trade in the interior highlands, but because they were also proficient at farming in arid environments, they interacted well with farming communities of the coastal interior. The Sabaean language was similar to the Semitic languages spoken in the area, and a language called Ge'ez evolved that became the basis for oral and written communication of the elites.

By the start of the Common Era, a new state, Aksum, emerged to dominate the Red Sea trade. Taking advantage of its location between the Mediterranean and the Indian Ocean, Aksum developed extensive trading ties with Ptolemaic Egypt and the Roman Empire as well as with Asia as far east as Sri Lanka and India. In the fourth century Aksum captured elephants for Ptolemaic rulers to use in warfare against Babylon, which was

DOCUMENT
Strabo on Africa

Aksum and Ethiopia

c. 800 B.C.E.	Sabaean traders establish trading settlements on the Eritrean coast
320–350 C.E.	Reign of Ezana, king of Aksum
c. 350	Aksum conquers Kush
700–800	Aksum's control of Red Sea trade ended by Persian and Muslim forces
c. 1185–1225	Reign of Lalibela, emperor of the Ethiopian Zagwe dynasty; beginning of construction of rock churches
c. 1314–1344	Reign of Amde-Siyon, emperor of Ethiopia
1434–1468	Reign of Zar'a Ya'kob, emperor of Ethiopia

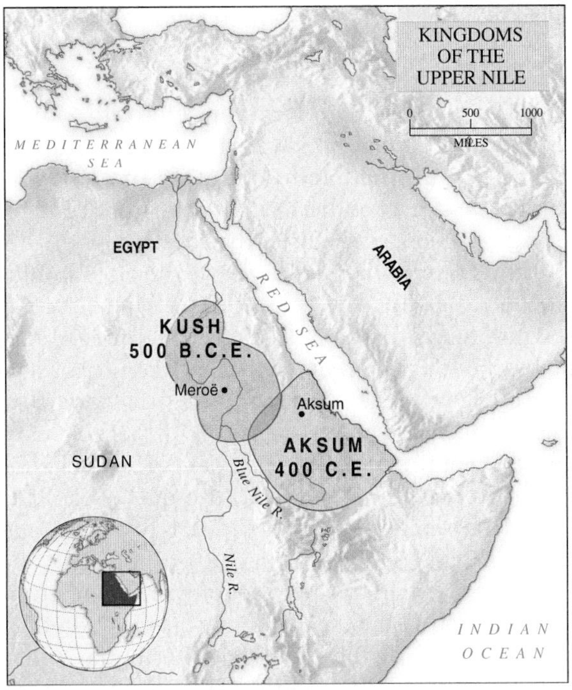

The kingdom of Kush was northeastern Africa's preeminent power until the rise of Aksum in the third and fourth centuries C.E.

importing elephants from India. The elephants were transported on specially constructed vessels.

Aksum also controlled trade with its interior, exporting slaves, gold, ivory and exotic items such as tortoise shells and rhinoceros horns in exchange for cloth, glassware and ceramic items, spices, vegetable oils, sugarcane, and wine. Aksum's capital, also called Aksum, was a major entrepot for the trade with the interior, while its bustling seaport, Adulis, prospered as the middleman for trade between the Mediterranean and the Indian Ocean. Monsoon winds dictated the rhythm of Indian Ocean trade. After July, when the summer monsoon winds were favorable, Adulis's traders set forth on their journeys. They returned in October when the prevailing winds reversed direction.

By the third and fourth centuries C.E., Aksum was at its zenith as a trading power, conquering its rival, Meroe, on the Nile, and replacing Rome as the dominant trading power on the Red Sea. Aksum minted its own bronze, silver, and gold coins with Greek inscriptions, something that only a handful of other states, such as Persia and Rome, were doing.

Aksum's best-known ruler was Ezana (320–350), who converted to Christianity toward the end of his reign, about the same time as the Roman emperor Constantine the Great. Some historians contend that Ezana conveniently converted to strengthen trading relations with the Greek-speaking world. Two Syrian brothers, Frumentius and Aedisius, have been credited with winning over Ezana to the Christian faith. Shipwrecked on the Red Sea coast, the brothers were brought to Aksum's royal court as slaves when Ezana was a child. Frumentius became an influential figure in the royal court, serving as main adviser to Ezana's mother, the queen regent. Following Ezana's conversion, Frumentius was chosen Aksum's first bishop, and Christianity was made the official state religion. Subsequently, the head of the Ethiopian church *(abuna)* was traditionally chosen by leaders of the Coptic Church in Egypt, even after Muslims gained control over Egypt.

Although Aksum's court language remained Greek, Ge'ez assumed a new prominence as the language of the Ethiopian church. The Old and New Testaments were translated into Ge'ez, which, much like Latin in the Catholic Church, became the primary language of literature and the liturgy. Several centuries after Ezana's conversion, a group of Syrian monks called the Nine Saints played a major role in spreading Christianity among rural people. The Nine Saints were known for their belief in the **Monophysite** doctrine, which held that Christ's human and divine qualities were inseparable.

The key to Aksum's continued prosperity was maintaining control over Red Sea trade. However, the Aksumites' influence in the Arabian peninsula ended in the late seventh century when a Persian expeditionary force ousted them. In 615 C.E. the Aksumite king El-Asham gave refuge to followers and family of the prophet Muhammad, who were being persecuted in Arabia. Although Muhammad directed Muslims to "leave the Abyssinians in peace,"[4] Islamic expansion late in the eighth century totally removed Aksum as a trading force in the Red Sea.

Despite Aksum's decline, some Ethiopian products such as perfume and coffee were still highly sought after. A highly prized musk was made from the glandular secretions of the civet cat. Coffee originated in Ethiopia. The coffee bean was initially chewed as a stimulant but then was made into a drink by brewing the coffee plant's leaves and berries in boiled water. Another quick-energy snack was a blend of ground coffee beans and animal fat. Finally, after someone came up with the idea of grinding roasted coffee beans, the drink rapidly spread to Arab cultures. Muslim monks drank coffee to stay awake during long periods of meditation and prayer, while coffee houses became popular gathering places throughout the Muslim world. *Qahwa* is the Arabic word from which the name *coffee* is derived.

Aksum's decline as a Red Sea power forced its rulers to migrate to the central highlands of the interior,

Monophysite—The doctrine that held that Christ has only one nature and that Christ's human and divine natures are inseparable.

where their rule continued to be plagued by conflict and warfare. There they mixed with a Cushitic-speaking people, the Agaw, who were assimilated into Aksum's political elite and also converted to Christianity. Some historians contend that the loss of commerce and revenues from the Red Sea trade led Aksum's rulers to develop a form of feudalism based on tribute from peasants that subsequent dynasties based their rule on.

The highland nobility formed the core of the Zagwe dynasty that took over in the mid-twelfth century. The Zagwes stressed their continuity with the Aksumite political order by claiming that they were descendants of Moses and encouraging the faithful to make pilgrimages to Jerusalem and Palestine. In this regard, the most enduring cultural expressions of the Zagwe dynasty were its churches, the most famous of which are the 11 awe-inspiring rock-hewn cathedrals of Roha, commissioned by the legendary Emperor Lalibela (law-lee-BAY-lah; c. 1185–1225). These impressive architectural feats, with ornate decorations and intricate workmanship, drew on Byzantine, Greek, and Roman motifs. The rock churches became the sites of pilgrimages by Christians cut off from Jerusalem by Muslim forces.

Lalibela's reign was the high point of Zagwe rule. Rivalries between feudal nobles and Muslim merchants and kingdoms were fierce, and Lalibela's successors were unable to maintain the kingdom. Yikunno-Amlak, a southern noble once imprisoned by the Zagwes, led the rebellion that overthrew them in 1270 and founded a new dynasty, the Solomonids. Like the Zagwes, the Solomonid emperors (each known as *negus*, or "king of kings") legitimized their rule by claiming a direct tie to the Aksumite past. In their royal chronicle, the *Kebre Negast* ("Glory of the Kings"), they gave an epic account of their dynasty's direct descent from the Old Testament's King Solomon. The tale related how Makeda, the queen of Sheba (Saba'), had visited Solomon to learn his techniques of rule. Instead, Solomon seduced Makeda, who bore him a son, Menelik. When Menelik later visited his father's court, he tricked Solomon and spirited the Ark of the Covenant out of Israel to Ethiopia—which church officials claim is in the Church of St. Mary of

Ethiopia's Emperor Lalibela oversaw the construction of 11 churches carved out of red volcanic rock at Roha. Shaped in the form of a Greek cross, the Church of St. George was an impressive architectural feat. Workers chipped away at the stone until they reached 40 feet down and then molded the church and hollowed out its interior.

Seyon (Zion). This story was interpreted as a sign of the covenant God was establishing with Ethiopia. Thus to the kings of the Solomonid dynasty, it was an article of faith that they were directly descended from Solomon.

To avoid the same fate as the Zagwes, the Solomonid rulers set strict rules to ensure orderly successions. To insulate royal princes from palace infighting and forming alliances with nobles in the countryside, the first Solomonid emperor crowned in 1285, Yikunno-Amlak, took the bold step of placing the princes in a remote retreat, Mount Geshen (the "mountain of the kings"). The princes lived a comfortable but monastic existence, totally isolated from the outside world. Many of them followed an ascetic life, absorbed in religious issues and gaining reputations as accomplished writers of Ge'ez poetry and composers of sacred music. When an emperor died without a designated heir, the princes provided a pool of candidates for the throne.

The first Solomonid rulers concentrated on consolidating their rule over the central highlands of Ethiopia and refrained from carrying out aggressive wars of expansion. These goals changed dramatically during the reign of Emperor Amde-Siyon ("Pillar of Zion"; c. 1314–1344), who conquered territories to the west and toward the coast and carried out aggressive campaigns against Muslim principalities to the south and east. Amde-Siyon's army had to be in a constant state of readiness because of his repeated campaigns. His soldiers were recruited from two elements: fiercely loyal regiments attached to the royal court and militias from Christian provinces that were called out for specific campaigns. The latter were based on ethnic identities and were commanded by local chiefs. Many women also followed armies, providing food for their husbands.

Amde-Siyon's campaigns against the Muslims were aimed not only at securing control over the lucrative trade in slaves and ivory but also at putting pressure on the Muslim rulers of Egypt to allow the Coptic church to send a new bishop to Ethiopia. Amde-Siyon was so successful in vanquishing his opponents that an Arab historian reported, "It is said that he has ninety-nine kings under him, and that he makes up the hundred."[5]

The Ethiopian emperor had to be constantly on guard against potential revolts against his authority by local hereditary rulers. Although he generally allowed local rulers to remain in place, he strategically placed his officials around the kingdom. Because all land within the kingdom belonged to the emperor, he maintained loyalty by granting ***gults,*** or fiefs, to nobles and to soldiers who distinguished themselves in his service, especially in newly conquered areas.

Gult-holders were bound to the emperor because he could revoke a *gult* at any time. Moreover, a *gult* owner did not own the land; he had to pay regular tribute to the emperor. In turn, the *gult* owner had the right during his lifetime to exact tribute and taxes in the form of grain, honey, cattle, and sheep from peasants who owned and worked the land. In Ethiopia tribute cattle were called "burning" because the cows were branded or "touched with fire" before they were handed over. Peasants were also expected to support any soldiers and clergy residing in their area. The major difference between the Ethiopian and European feudal systems was that the European nobility owned large estates and lived off the labor of tenants and serfs, while Ethiopian peasants kept their lands and gave up a portion of their production to the nobility.

Until Gondar was designated as the capital in the seventeenth century, Ethiopian emperors did not have a centralized bureaucracy or a fixed capital for more than a few decades at a time. Rather, they created a mobile court of family members, high officials, soldiers, priests, and retainers that moved regularly around the kingdom. This mobile court allowed the emperor to show off his power as well as encourage trade with outlying regions and to collect tribute from all his subjects. Mobile courts encamped in areas for up to four months, but they put such a strain on local resources that they were encouraged not to return for many years.

The Ethiopian monarchy assumed even greater power during the reign of Zar'a Ya'kob ("Seed of Jacob"; r. 1434–1468). Kings were usually crowned in the area where they found themselves when they took power. But Zar'a Ya'kob resurrected the tradition of kings' being crowned at the ancient capital of Aksum and stayed there an additional three years.

Within his immediate environs Zar'a Ya'kob ruled as an absolute monarch, surrounded by hundreds of courtiers and servants. To consolidate his rule, he dismissed provincial governors and replaced them with his own daughters and other female members of his family. When he held audiences at his court, he was positioned behind a curtain and communicated through a royal spokesman. When he traveled about his kingdom, his subjects had to avert their eyes on the penalty of death.

When Zar'a Ya'kob launched new campaigns of conquest to expand Ethiopia's boundaries, he was faced with the challenge of governing a diverse kingdom of many ethnic, linguistic, and religious backgrounds. He achieved his goal by exploiting the traditional feudal relationships his predecessors established with their nobles and also by reorganizing and aggressively promoting the Ethiopian church.

gult—The right to collect tribute granted to nobility and clergy by a king.

A characteristic art form of Ethiopia is wall murals. In this painting the bishop of Aksum confers a blessing on the emperor of Ethiopia at the Cathedral of St. Mary of Zion. When Zar'a Ya'kob became emperor in 1434, he chose to be crowned in Aksum because he wanted to link the monarchy with the historical prestige of that kingdom.

Under previous emperors, the state had perceived churches and monasteries as centers of Zagwe influence and struggled to win them over with gifts and land grants. Monks were especially difficult to influence because they led unpretentious lives and took their commitment to the poor seriously. Turning down a generous gift of gold and fine cloth from the Emperor Dawit, the abbot of the Dabra Halle Luya monastery in central Ethiopia provided an explanation for his decision: "We have no need for this. We have food which God ordered for us, the green of the earth and the roots of the trees. As for grain [it has] to be from the labour of our own hand." The emperor replied. "You say, 'We consume the fruit of our own labour,' but a church does not stand without land. Would it not be like a woman who has no husband?"[6] Dawit's persistence and more gifts eventually wore down the abbot's resistance.

Under Zar'a Ya'kob the Ethiopian church became a royal church, an extension of the crown that actively promoted its expansion throughout the kingdom. He granted the church extensive estates in newly conquered provinces. He appointed several bishops in these provinces. Clerics, who had previously led ascetic lives more concerned with their personal salvation, were now expected to play active roles in spreading the Christian faith. Monks recruited from monasteries were commissioned to establish churches and wage evangelical crusades to convert "pagans" and Muslims. At the same time, Zar'a Ya'kob declared war on traditional religious cults and imposed death sentences on those who practiced divination and sacrifices to gods.

The monarchy also sponsored monastic schools. The schools, mostly for boys, primarily accepted children from clerical families and the royal elite. Education typically consisted of reading and reciting religious tracts.

This was a period of the blossoming of the arts in which priests—and even Zar'a Ya'kob—played a leading role. They produced innumerable biblical translations, theological treatises, biographies of saints, historical chronicles, illuminated manuscripts, and mural paintings.

Although Zar'a Ya'kob's policies may have revived the church, they came at a cost. The church became intimately identified with imperial power and less able to develop deep roots among the common people.

Zar'a Ya'kob's reign was a high point in the Solomonid dynasty. His successors did not have the skills to hold the kingdom together, and Ethiopia went into a decline. Provincial officials and nobles seized on the weakness of the emperor to refrain from paying taxes and build up their own power. The Oromo, a pastoral people, began challenging Ethiopian control of the highland areas, and Muslims stopped sending tribute. Muslim states also grew restive. Under the military leadership of Ahmad al-Ghazi Ahmad Gran, the state of Adal launched a holy war against the Christian kingdom in 1527 that continued until 1543, when Ahmad was killed in battle.

EMPIRES OF THE WESTERN SUDAN

■ *How did trans-Saharan trade influence West African Sudanic states?*

Muslim writers called the savannas of West Africa *Bilad al-Sudan* ("Land of the Blacks"), and this region has been characterized by the longstanding trans-Saharan trade between the western savanna and the Mediterranean coast. Large camel caravans made regular trips across the dangerous desert carrying North African salt in exchange for West African gold. To the Berbers who organized these caravans,

African Empires in the Western Sudan

Document Emperor Zar'a Ya'kob's Coronation and His Concern for the Church

Beginning with the Solomonid dynasty in the twelfth century, Ethiopian monarchs commissioned courts scribes to record their accomplishments in royal chronicles. Although the chronicles were produced to glorify and lionize the ruler, they do provide valuable insights into Ethiopian political and economic life. The following passages come from the chronicles of Zar'a Ya'kob, who centralized royal administration and reshaped the church as an institution of imperial rule. They describe his coronation at Aksum and his involvement in church affairs.

When our King Zar'a [Ya'kob] went into the district of Aksum to fulfill the law and to effect the coronation ceremony according to the rites followed by his ancestors, all the inhabitants, including the priests, came to meet him and welcomed him with great rejoicing; the chiefs and all the soldiers of Tigre were on horseback carrying shield and lance, and the women, in great numbers, gave themselves up, according to the ancient custom, to endless dancing. When he entered the gates of the town the King had on his right and left the governors of Tigre and Aksum who, according to custom, both waved olive branches. . . . After arriving within the walls of Aksum the King had gold brought to him which he scattered as far as the city gate on the carpets spread along his route. This amount of gold was more than a hundred ounces. . . .

On the twenty-first of the month of Ter [January 16] the day of the death of our Holy Virgin Mary, the coronation rite was carried out, the King being seated on a stone throne. This stone, together with its supports, is only used for the coronation. There is another stone on which the King is seated when he receives the blessing, and several others to the right and left on which are seated the twelve chief judges. There is also the throne of the metropolitan bishop.

While at Aksum the Emperor made a number of regulations for the church.

During his stay at Aksum our King regulated all the institutions of the church and ordered that prayers which had up to that time been neglected should be recited each day at canonical hours. For this purpose he convened a large number of monks and founded a convent, the headship of which he entrusted to an abbot with the title of Pontiff of Aksum, who received an extensive grant of land called Nader. The King accomplished this work through devotion to the Virgin Mary and to perpetuate his own memory and that of his children and his children's children. He summoned some catechists and presented to the church a great number of ornaments and a golden ewer, revived all the old traditions, spread joy in these places, and returned thence satisfied.

Zar'a Ya'kob also founded churches and regulated religious affairs in other provinces.

Arriving in the land of Tsahay in Amhara, he went up a high and beautiful mountain, the site of which he found pleasing; at the top of this mountain and facing east he found a wall which had been raised by his father, King Dawit, with the intention of erecting a shrine. His father, however, had not had the time to complete the work, in the same way that the ancient King David, who planned to build a temple to the Lord, could not accomplish his task which was completed by his son Solomon. Our king Zar'a Ya'kob fulfilled his father's intention by building a shrine to God on the west of the mountain. Everyone, rich and poor alike and even the chiefs, were ordered to carry the stones with the result that this edifice was speedily erected. They embellished this locality, which underwent a great transformation; two churches were built there, one called Makana Gol and the other Dabra Negwadgwad. The King attached to them a certain number of priests and canons to whom he gave grants of land. He also founded a convent and placed in it monks from Dabra Libanos, whom he endowed in a similar manner.

Questions to Consider

1. Why do you think Zar'a Ya'kob selected Aksum as the site for his coronation?
2. What do these passages tell us about the relations between the Ethiopian monarchy and the church?
3. What comparisons can be made between church-state relations in Ethiopia and in European kingdoms during the same time period?

From Richard K. Pankhurst, ed., *The Ethiopian Royal Chronicles* (Oxford: Oxford University Press, 1967), pp. 34–36.

West African Sudanic Kingdoms

c. 250 B.C.E.	Jenne-jeno on Niger River settled
c. 100–40 B.C.E.	Camel introduced to trans-Saharan trade
c. 900 C.E.	State of Kanem founded
1000–1200	Hausa city-states founded
1076	Almoravid attack on Ghana
c. 1200–1235	Reign of Sumaguru, Sosso king
1300–1400	Rise of kingdom of Oyo
1307–1337	Reign of Mansa Musa in Mali
1352	Visit of Berber geographer Ibn Battuta to Mali
1464–1492	Reign of Sunni Ali, Songhai emperor
1493–1528	Reign of Askia Muhammad, Songhai emperor
1591	Morocco invades Songhai

the bend of the Niger River offered a secure watering and resting place. Here they found people who had conducted local trade for centuries before the caravans came, who knew the savanna well, and who could acquire gold from distant places. Their resulting control of the lucrative gold and salt trade brought great accumulations of wealth and was a key factor in the rise of major West African kingdoms.

Before the formation of these kingdoms, there was already a thriving interregional trade among the savanna communities. Archaeological evidence shows that in the ninth century B.C.E. some savanna communities began harnessing the floodwaters of the Niger River and started raising livestock and cultivating cereals. They formed settlements of 800 to 1000 people. The villages they lived in were unwalled and in open areas, an indication that relations between communities were mostly peaceful and cooperative. However, between 600 and 300 B.C.E., the pattern changed as villages erected walls and retreated to more remote and defensible sites—a sign that they were responding to external threats, possibly from nomadic Berbers who roamed the Sahara and occasionally raided savanna societies.

One of the earliest urban settlements, Jenne-jeno, was begun around 250 B.C.E. Situated on an inland delta of the Niger River, Jenne-jeno was ideally located because it was surrounded by water during the rainy season and was much safer for trade than other settlements. Over time, Jenne-jeno became an interregional trade center for farmers, herders, and fishermen that long predated any involvement in the trans-Saharan trade. Jenne-jeno exported food via the Niger to points to the east.

Although the Sahara was not easy to traverse, it was not impenetrable. As early as 1000 B.C.E., Carthaginians, Romans, and perhaps Greeks began establishing several routes across the Sahara for their horse- and ox-drawn chariots. One route stretched from Libya and Tunisia through the Fezzan, while the other connected Morocco to Mauritania. Trade declined with the collapse of the Roman Empire in the fourth century C.E. but was revived several centuries later, first by the Byzantine Empire and then by Arabs.

The camel, introduced from the Middle East in the first century B.C.E., became the main conveyor of goods in the trans-Saharan trade. As pack animals, camels had several advantages over horses and oxen. Carrying loads of 250 to 300 pounds, camels could travel extended distances with little water. However, they were slow and inefficient. Averaging about 20 to 30 miles a day, they generally took over two months to cross the Sahara. Moreover, attendants had to load and unload their cargo once or twice each day, and much of the provisions were used to feed attendants. Whatever the camel's liabilities, its introduction boosted the vol-

Introduced from the Middle East in the first century B.C.E., the camel was the main transporter of goods in the trans-Saharan trade between North Africa and the West African savanna.

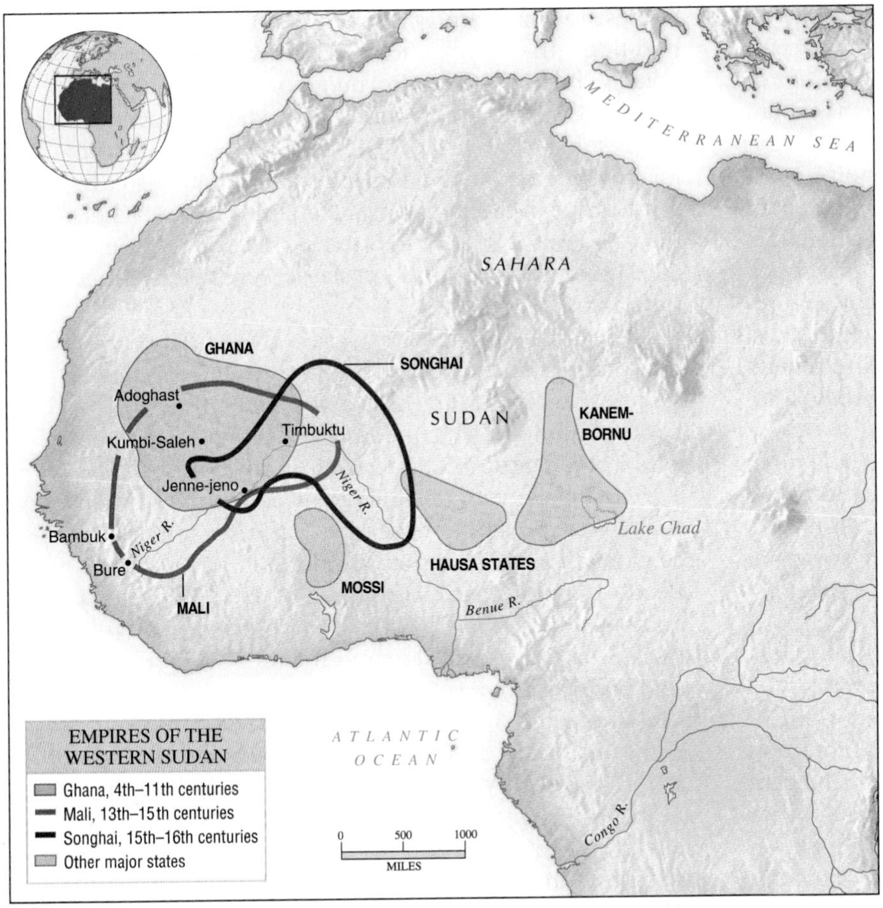

Sudanic kingdoms such as Ghana, Mali, Songhai, and Kanem-Bornu owed their power and wealth to controlling the southern part of the trans-Saharan trade.

ume of trade. The camel remained an essential part of the trans-Saharan trade until the twentieth century, when it was replaced by the automobile.

Ghana

The earliest of the Sudanic kingdoms, first known as *Aoukar* or *Wagadu*, later took the name of its war chief, Ghana (not to be confused with the modern nation of the same name). It arose on the upper Niger during the fourth century C.E. as a loose federation of village-states, inhabited by Soninke farmers. This set a pattern for future kingdoms of the savanna as a lineage or a clan asserted its authority over other groups.

The introduction of ironworking allowed the Soninke farming communities to form larger political systems. In the face of drier conditions, they applied iron tools to improving agricultural production and devised iron swords and spears to conquer neighboring groups. They also used these weapons to fend off Saharan nomads who grazed their animals in the Sahel (the southern fringe of the Sahara) and occasionally raided Soninke communities.

By about 800 C.E. Ghana had established itself as a powerful kingdom able to exact tribute from vassal states in the region. Although agricultural production contributed to Ghana's wealth, it was the expanding trans-Saharan trade with Europe and the Mediterranean world that gave Ghana even more influence. From their strategic position on the upper Niger River, the Soninke were well positioned as intermediaries to barter the salt produced from the Taghaza salt mines in the Sahara, the gold coming from Bambuk, and kola nuts and slaves captured from areas south of the savanna.

Ghana's king controlled the supply of gold within his kingdom and claimed every gold nugget coming into the country, leaving ordinary citizens the right to buy and sell only gold dust. The king was reputed to own a gold nugget so large that he bragged he could tether his horse to it. In addition, taxes were levied on every load of goods entering and leaving the country.

Ghana's gold was actually mined in Bambuk, a region eight days' journey to the west of Ghana's capital, Kumbi-Saleh, from the beds of the Senegal and Faleme Rivers. Ghana's rulers did not have direct control over Bambuk, and the persons who worked the goldfields jealously guarded information about where and how they produced the gold. They devised a strategy for negotiating with Mande traders without actually coming into direct contact with them. Al Masudi, a noted Arab traveler, described this "silent trade" around 950:

> *They have traced a boundary which no one who sets out to them ever crosses. When the merchants reach this boundary, they place their wares and cloth on the ground and then depart, and so the people of the Sudan come bearing gold which they leave beside the merchandise and then depart. The owners of the merchandise then return, and if they are satisfied with what they have found, they take it. If not, they go away again, and the people of the Sudan return and add to the price until the bargain is concluded.*[7]

Outsiders who tried to interfere in gold production soon found that less gold was offered for trade.

Traders avidly sought salt from the trans-Saharan trade because it was a crucial element in diets and a preservative for foods and skins. It was also a scarce commodity in savanna communities. A certain amount of salt could be extracted from vegetable matter or from soil, but not enough to satisfy the requirements of these savanna communities. However, in the Sahara there were large salt deposits, the best known at Taghaza, in the middle of the Sahara, about a three-week journey from both Mediterranean and Sudanese trading centers. Salt was quarried in huge 200-pound slabs, loaded on camels, and transported to trading centers like Timbuktu (tim-buk-TOO), where these slabs were distributed to other places.

Another item featured in the trade was kola nuts, which were primarily grown in the forest areas to the south of the savanna. Used to quench thirst, kola nuts were consumed mainly in the drier savanna. They did not become a major staple of the trans-Saharan exchange.

Slaves were the final component of the trans-Saharan trade. Although slavery was an established practice in some, though not all, sub-Saharan African societies, it took many shapes and forms. A common practice was that a family sent a family member—usually a child or a young adult—to serve in another household to pay off a debt or some other obligation (such as compensation for a crime) or to raise food in times of famine. In those cases, slaves were integrated into a master's family. Servile status could be of limited duration, and the slave would be sent back home as soon as the debt was repaid.

With centralized kingdoms such as Ghana and, later, Mali, slaves were bought and sold in trading transactions and were called on to perform a variety of roles—as servants, farm laborers, porters, traders, and soldiers. Most household slaves were women and children; slave women were often selected as marriage partners or concubines because a man did not have to pay bridewealth for them. Their children had all the rights of free persons.

Slave warriors had a privileged status; they could serve in high capacities as military officers, administrators, and diplomats in a king's court. Slave soldiers were the mainstays of armies and were used in raids to kidnap and capture more slaves. Most slaves were kidnapped or captured in raids on weaker communities by the stronger savanna states, especially in the forest region to the south. Muslim law enjoined Muslims from enslaving other Muslims, but this was not always observed when raiding parties were sent out.

Although savanna kingdoms created their own internal trade in slaves, the trans-Saharan slave trade was fueled primarily by demands from North African Mediterranean states. Slaves were typically taken in caravans, where they were exchanged for salt and horses. In Senegambia (si-neh-GAM-bee-ah) in the mid-fifteenth century, nine to 14 slaves could fetch one horse, while in Kanem-Bornu a horse would cost 15 to 20 slaves. In later centuries some slaves, especially those sold in Libya, were traded on to the eastern Mediterranean, the Italian peninsula, and other southern European areas. From the eighth century, when the trade was initiated, to the early twentieth century, an estimated 3.5 to 4 million slaves were taken across the Sahara.[8]

The 1200-mile journey across the desert was as perilous as the trans-Atlantic slave trade's infamous Middle Passage. Many slaves lost their lives to the harsh conditions. The majority of slaves were women who worked as domestic servants in royal households and courts or were designated as concubines. Male slaves were pressed into service in the salt mines and as caravan porters, agricultural labor, and soldiers. Because many slaves were freed or died of diseases and because so few children were born in captivity, there was a constant demand for more slaves to be sold on the market.

To reconstruct the histories of the Sudanic kingdoms, historians draw heavily on the accounts of Arab geographers, travelers, holy men, and scholars. One Arab chronicler, Al-Bakri, described Ghana at its peak in 1067. He claimed that the army was some 200,000 strong, with many contingents wearing chain mail. The king, who had not converted to Islam, was considered divine and able to intercede with the gods. He appointed all officials and served as supreme judge. His government was organized under ministers, with one responsible for his capital, Kumbi-Saleh. Princes of tributary states were held hostage at his court. When the king appeared in public, he was surrounded by highborn personal retainers holding gold swords, horses adorned with gold cloth blankets, and dogs wearing gold collars.

Ghana's capital, Kumbi-Saleh, was situated on the edge of a crop-growing area and had 15,000 to 20,000 residents. The capital was really two towns, 6 miles apart. One was a large Soninke village, where the king and his retinue lived. Close to the village was a sacred grove where traditional religious cults were practiced. The other town was occupied by Muslim merchants. The merchants' town had 12 mosques, two-story stone houses, public squares, and a market. Besides the traders, the town was also home to religious and legal scholars. Ghana's king relied on literate Muslims as treasurer, interpreters, and counselors. However influential the Muslims were, the king had to make sure that his own religious leaders were regularly consulted and that he participated in shrine and other religious activities. The first king to convert to Islam did not do so until after the Almoravid invasion in 1076.

Document Ghana, as Described by Al-Bakri

Accounts by Muslim scholars and travelers are important sources for writing the history of West Africa's Sudanic kingdoms. A Muslim geographer and theologian who lived in Spain, Al-Bakri's account of the kingdom of Ghana appeared in his *Kitab al-maslik wa-'l-mamalik ("The Book of Routes and Realms")*, published in 1040 C.E. Al-Bakri relied extensively on people who traveled to the places he describes. The following passages describe contending religious factions at Ghana's royal capital, Kumbi-Saleh.

The city of Ghana consists of two towns situated on a plain. One of these towns, which is inhabited by Muslims, is large and possesses twelve mosques, in one of which they assemble for the Friday prayer. There are salaried imams and muezzins, as well as jurists and scholars. . . . Between these two towns there are continuous habitations. The houses of the inhabitants are of stone and acacia *(sunt)* wood. The king has a palace and a number of domed dwellings all surrounded with an enclosure like a city wall *(sur)*. In the king's town, and not far from his court of justice is a mosque where the Muslims who arrive at his court *(yafid 'alayh)* pray. Around the king's town are domed buildings and groves and thickets where the sorcerers of these people, men in charge of the religious cult, live. In them too are their idols and the tombs of their kings. These woods are guarded and none may enter them and know what is there. . . . The king's interpreters, the official in charge of his treasury and the majority of his ministers are Muslims. Among the people who follow the king's religion only he and his heir apparent (who is the son of his sister) may wear sewn clothes. All other people shave their beards, and women shave their heads. The king adorns himself like a woman [wearing necklaces' round his neck] and [bracelets] on his forearms, and he puts on a high cap *(tartur)* decorated with gold and wrapped in a turban of fine cotton. He sits in audience or to hear grievances against officials *(mazalim)* in a domed pavilion around which stand ten horses covered with gold-embroidered materials. Behind the king stand ten pages holding shields and swords decorated with gold, and on his right are the sons of the [vassal] kings of his country wearing splendid garments and their hair plaited with gold. The governor of the city sits on the ground before the king and around him are ministers seated likewise. . . . The audience is announced by the beating of a drum which they call *duba,* made from a long hollow log. When the people who profess the same religion as the king approach him they fall on their knees and sprinkle dust on their heads, for this is their way of greeting him. As for the Muslims, they greet him only by clapping their hands.

Their religion is paganism and the worship of idols *(dakakyr)*. When their king dies they construct over the place where his tomb will be an enormous dome of *saj* wood. Then they bring him on a bed covered with a few carpets and cushions and place him beside the dome. At his side they place his ornaments, his weapons, and the vessels from which he used to eat and drink, filled with various kinds of food and beverages. They place there too the men who used to serve his meals. They close the door of the dome and cover it with mats and furnishings. Then the people assemble, who heap earth upon it until it becomes like a big hillock and dig a ditch around it until the mound can be reached at only one place.

They make sacrifices to their dead and make offerings of intoxicating drinks.

Question to Consider

1. What insights does Al-Bakri provide into how Sudanic kings balanced their Islamic faith with traditional religious institutions?

From N. Levtzion and J. F. P. Hopkins, *Corpus of Early Arabic Sources for West African History* (Cambridge: Cambridge University Press, 1981), pp. 79–81.

The Almoravid invasion followed Ghana's conquest of Adoghast, a Sanhaja Berber trading center, when Sanhaja Berbers rallied around an Islamic revivalist movement called the Almoravid and attacked Ghana. Although it is still a subject of debate whether the Almoravid attack was a full-scale invasion or a series of raids, Ghana had to give up Adoghast and its dominance over trade. Ghana's dominance over the gold trade was further weakened when the Bure goldfield opened up on the Niger River.

Mali

In the early thirteenth century Ghana's rule was ended by an uprising led by Sumaguru (c. 1200–1235) of the Sosso, who were related to the Soninke. Oral traditions characterize Sumaguru as a tyrant who wielded magical powers over his people. Sumaguru was overthrown in 1235 by Sundiata (SOON-dee-AH-tah), a noted hunter and magician of the Malinke Keita clan, who forged an alliance of Malinke clans and chiefdoms for that purpose. Lengthy wars followed in which Sundiata's army defeated and killed Sumaguru and routed the Sosso. Sundiata's army then embarked on campaigns of conquest throughout the territory that had been Ghana.

DOCUMENT
From Sundiata: An Epic of Old Mali

Eventually, Sundiata's Malinke created a vast empire called Mali that stretched from the Atlantic south of the Senegal River to Gao on the middle Niger River. Mali gained control of the desert gold trade and the gold-producing regions of Wangara and Bambuk. When Europeans made gold a currency in 1252, West Africa became Europe's leading supplier of gold. Several tons of gold were produced annually. Two-thirds of it was exported, while the rest was kept for conspicuous display by Mali's ruling elites.

The kingdom of Mali was at the height of its power and prosperity during the reign of Sundiata's nephew, Mansa Musa (1307–1337). Musa was perhaps the most widely known sub-Saharan African ruler throughout western Asia and Europe. He was an accomplished soldier who consolidated his kingdom's control over a vast domain. Malian and Arab merchants carried on trade with the Mediterranean coast, particularly with Algeria, Tunisia, Egypt, and the Middle East.

Mansa Musa ruled over an efficiently organized state. On the north and northeast were loosely held tributary kingdoms of diverse populations, including some Berbers. To the south were more closely controlled tributary states under resident governors appointed by the king. Elsewhere, particularly in the cities such as Timbuktu, provincial administrators governed directly in the king's name and at his pleasure. Mali's central government included ministries for finance, justice, agriculture, and foreign relations. Agricultural settlements produced food for the court, the army, and the administration, and taxes and tribute were collected from subject communities.

A devout Muslim, Musa lavishly displayed his wealth and power on a pilgrimage he took to Mecca in 1324–1325. His retinue included thousands of porters and servants and a hundred camels bearing loads of gold. In Egypt he spent so lavishly and gave away so much gold that its value in that country plummeted and did not recover for a generation:

> *This man spread upon Cairo the flood of his generosity. . . . So much gold was current in Cairo that it ruined the value of money. Let me add that gold in Egypt had enjoyed a high rate of exchange up to the moment of their arrival. But from that day onward, its value dwindled. That is how it has been for twelve years from that time, because of the great amounts of gold they brought to Egypt and spent there.*[9]

When he returned to his kingdom, Musa brought along an architect who designed mosques in Gao and Timbuktu as well as an audience chamber for Musa's palace. Musa sent students to study at Islamic schools in Morocco. They returned to found Qur'anic schools, the best known of which was at Timbuktu.

Mansa Musa's pilgrimage also caught the attention of Muslim scholars. Among them was the Moroccan geographer and traveler Ibn Battuta, who visited Mali in 1352 during the reign of Musa's brother, Mansa Sulayman (1336–1358). Battuta's account is one of the key sources for understanding the kingdom of Mali. He was favorably impressed by Mali's architecture, literature, and institutions of learning but was most laudatory about its law and justice, which guaranteed that no person "need fear brigands, thieves, or ravishers" anywhere in the vast domain. Battuta praised the king's devotion to Islam but was disappointed that so many subjects of Mali were not Muslims. He noted also that the unveiled women were attractive but lacking in humility. He was astounded that they might take lovers without arousing their husbands' jealousy and could discuss learned subjects with men.

As Mali's empire grew, Islam became an important unifying element among the political and commercial elite. Key agents for the spread of Islam were Mande traders known as Dyula (DJOO-lah), Jahanke, and Wangara, which created an extensive trading network that stretched from Senegambia on the Atlantic coast to the kingdom of Bornu to the east. Although they were largely responsible for the trade in such items as gold and kola nuts, they were Muslim teachers as well. Wherever they went, they became the lifeblood of small Muslim communities, establishing Qur'anic schools and arranging for the faithful to make pilgrimages to Mecca.

MAP
Islam and Africa: East and West

Since they operated in areas where most people were not Muslims, the Mande traders formulated religious precepts that allowed them to coexist with and accept the rule of non-Muslims. However, because there were concerns that the traders would not remain devout Muslims, they were encouraged to visit centers of Islamic learning periodically to deepen their faith.

One of the few regions where Muslims actively converted people in the countryside was in Senegambia. Despite the devoutness of kings such as

Discovery Through Maps

Mansa Musa and The Catalan Atlas of 1375

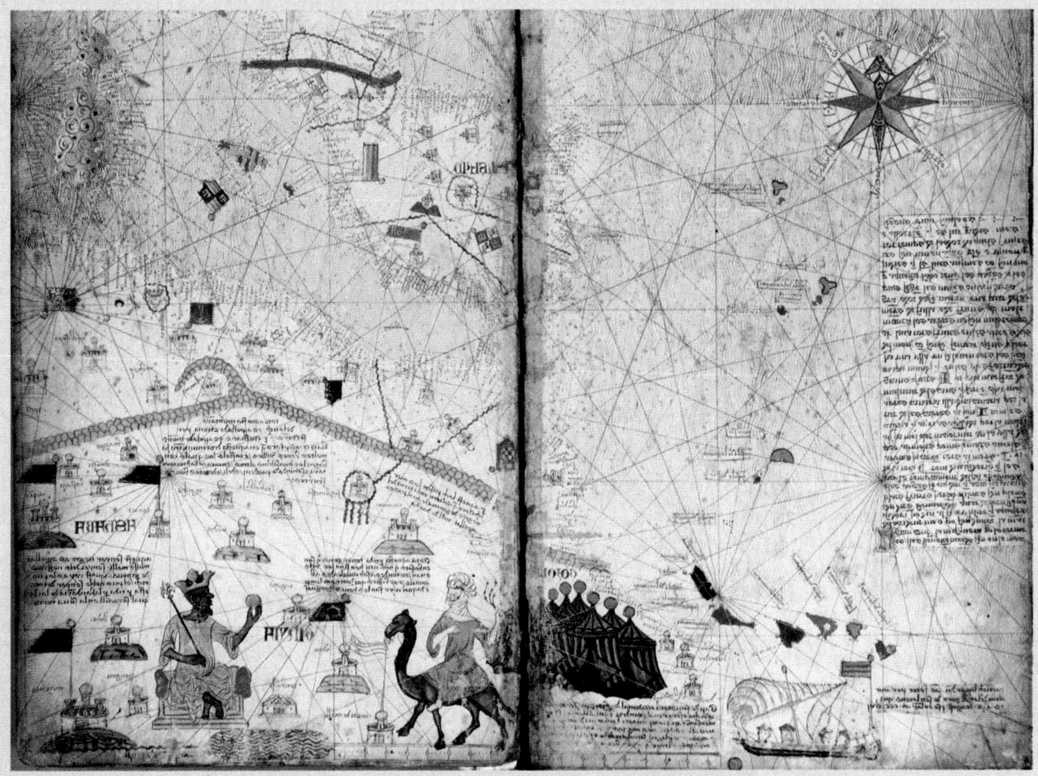

Mali's King Mansa Musa literally put himself on the map on his pilgrimage to Mecca in 1324–1325. During a lengthy stay in Cairo, he advertised his kingdom's wealth to the Mediterranean commercial world in a way that modern-day business people would appreciate. He spent extravagantly and gave away large quantities of gold. This reinforced Europe's awareness of Mali's special status—that it was a major source of gold at a time when Europe was exchanging silver for gold as its principal hard currency. Thus, when the Portuguese began exploring the African coast, one of their objectives was to establish direct contact with Mali's king.

Mansa Musa's actions left an indelible impression on outsiders' perceptions of his kingdom. Thus, it was not surprising that when Abraham Cresques, a cartographer from Majorca, was drawing the Catalan Atlas a half-century later, he made a point of highlighting Mansa Musa and his kingdom.

The Catalan Atlas was designed to promote trade between Europe and different parts of the world. For each of the atlas's 12 leaves, Cresques depended on information provided by travelers and traders, even if it was outdated. For instance, the map of Asia drew heavily from Marco Polo's travels a century earlier, while the map of West Africa relied on information passed on by Moroccan Jews who were familiar with trans-Saharan trade routes.

The map of West Africa contained several inscriptions. One was placed next to a Tuareg trader mounted on a camel. "All this region is occupied by people who veil their mouths; one only sees their eyes. They live in tents and have caravans of camels." Cresques clearly believed that Islam had a strong presence in the Sudan, as evidenced by the domes that identified Muslim centers such as Timbuktu and Gao. The map also gave an exaggerated importance to Mali's king, Mansa Musa, who is depicted holding a gold nugget in one hand and a scepter in the other as he awaits the arrival of a Muslim trader. The inscription beside him reads: "The Negro lord is called Musa Mali, lord of the Negroes of Guinea. So abundant is the gold which is found in his country that he is the richest and most noble king in all the land."

Questions to Consider

1. Why was King Mansa Musa of Mali so prominently featured in this map of the Catalan Atlas?
2. The maps in the Catalan Atlas were drawn before the European "Age of Discovery." What sources did the Catalan cartographers rely on for their knowledge of West Africa and other regions of the world?

Musa and the presence of Muslim traders in many areas, Islam was mainly a religion of court and commerce. Most people in the countryside remained faithful to their traditional religious beliefs. Muslim rulers who neglected their people's spiritual practices did so at the risk of provoking opposition. Hence, Islamic festivals were usually celebrated alongside traditional rites.

After Mansa Musa's death, his successors found the large empire increasingly difficult to govern. They were plagued by dynastic disputes, raids by desert nomads such as the Tuaregs and Sanhaja, and the restlessness of tributary states. One of the rebellious states was Songhai, centered around the bend of the Niger. Songhai had been in existence for many centuries before it was absorbed into the Malian Empire in the thirteenth century, and its principal city, Gao, was an entrepot for trade with the Maghrib and Egypt. Before the end of the fifteenth century, Songhai had won its independence, and, within another century, it had conquered Mali.

After Sunni Ali drowned in the Niger River, his son ruled for a few months before Askia Muhammad, who came from Sunni Ali's slave officer corps, deposed him and established his own dynasty. Askia Muhammad set about consolidating and reorganizing the whole empire. Although his armies seized control of the Taghaza saltworks in the Sahara, their attempts to expand control over the Hausa states to the east were not successful.

Reigning from his capital at Gao, Askia Muhammad created a centralized bureaucracy to manage finances, agriculture, and taxation, appointed administrators (usually relatives) to oversee newly created provinces, and built up a professional army featuring a cavalry of chain-mailed horsemen and an enlarged fleet of canoes, which constantly patrolled the Niger.

Unlike Sunni Ali, Askia Muhammad made peace with Muslim scholars and became their benefactor. He declared Islam the official religion. During his reign Timbuktu, Jenne-jeno, and Walata achieved recognition as centers of Islamic scholarship. Several hundred

Songhai

Songhai became the largest of the Sudanic empires, reaching its zenith during the reigns of Sunni Ali (1464–1492) and Askia Muhammad (1493–1528). Sunni Ali is remembered for his military exploits. His armies ventured out on constant campaigns of conquest, largely to the west along the Niger in what had been Mali's heartland, and captured the trading centers of Timbuktu, Walata, and Jenne-jeno.

Sunni Ali regularly feuded with Muslim scholars and clerics who accused him of not observing Muslim practices such as praying in public. They issued a condemnation of his behavior and ruled that because he was not a Muslim, he could not be recognized as a legitimate ruler. He tried to suppress his dissidents and expelled Muslim scholars from Timbuktu.

The Sankore mosque is the oldest surviving mosque in West Africa. Its pyramidlike minaret rises above the city of Timbuktu, the center of Islamic culture in the kingdom of Mali.

Muslim schools were established in Timbuktu, whose scholars developed extensive links and exchanges with scholars in the Middle East and North Africa. Its Sankore mosque became so renowned that a contemporary Arab traveler noted that more profits were being made from selling books and manuscripts there than from any other trade.

Like Mansa Musa, Askia Muhammad made a much publicized pilgrimage to Mecca. Traveling in 1497 with a large group of pilgrims, he brought thousands of gold pieces, which he freely distributed as alms to the poor and used to establish a hostel in Mecca for pilgrims from the western Sudan. Muhammad was not just expressing his faith; he was also drumming up trade with Songhai and shoring up his credentials with Muslims throughout his far-flung empire. On Muhammad's return home the Egyptian caliph recognized him as the **Caliph** of the lands of Takrur, an important distinction for any Muslim ruler.

Although a son deposed Askia Muhammad in 1528 and the kingdom was weakened by internal rivalries, Songhai remained a savanna power until 1591, when Morocco's King Ahmad al-Mansur launched an invasion of Songhai to prevent European rivals from gaining access to Sudanese gold. Taking offense at Songhai's refusal to pay a tax on salt from the Taghaza mines, al-Mansur sent a contingent of 4000 mercenaries to secure control over the Sudanic goldfields. Many died in the harsh march across the Sahara, but the survivors, armed with arquebuses (firearms mounted on a forked staff) and muskets, proved superior to the spears, swords, and bows and arrows of Songhai's soldiers. Although Morocco's impact was fleeting, Songhai was not able to recover, and the empire fragmented into many smaller kingdoms.

Kanem, Bornu, and the Hausa States

In the central Sudan, which stretches from the bend of the Niger to Lake Chad, a series of Muslim states emerged that took advantage of the fertile agricultural lands and their strategic location between the trans-Saharan trade routes to the north and the forest regions to the south. The kingdoms of Kanem and Bornu and the Hausa city-states became the most important dominant political actors.

Kanem, which lay to the northeast of Lake Chad, had been formed around 900 C.E. when groups of nomadic pastoralists unified and established the Saifawa dynasty. The ruling elite converted to Islam in the late eleventh century. As in other Sudanic states, Saifawa power and wealth were based on control of the Saharan trade. The main trade route cut through the central Sahara to the Fezzan and on to Tripoli and Egypt. Because Kanem was too far away from any sources of gold, its rulers exported ivory, ostrich feathers, and, especially, war captives from societies to the south. In return Kanem received horses that its rulers used to create a cavalry that fueled further raiding. Under Mai (king) Dunama Dibalemi (1210–1248), Kanem boasted a cavalry of 40,000 horsemen.

In the fourteenth century, one of Kanem's tributary states, Bornu, became a power in its own right, organizing its own trade and refusing to pay tribute to Kanem. During this period, Kanem's rulers were challenged by the Bulala, a non-Muslim clan, and by the deterioration of their pasturage. About 1400, the Saifawa dynasty came under attack from peoples living east of Lake Chad and moved to Bornu west of Lake Chad, where they gained access to new trading networks. At first they paid tribute to Bornu, but during the sixteenth century, Kanem's leaders gradually took over the Bornu state and began carrying out raids over an extensive area. Their rule was financed by tribute, taxes on peasants and customs levies on the trade in slaves, gold, salt and weapons between Bornu and Tripoli and Cairo.

Bornu's rulers maintained excellent relations with the Muslim world. In the early thirteenth century they established a **madrasa** in Cairo for their students studying at al-Azhar University. They developed a strong relationship with the Ottoman rulers of Tripoli and imported firearms and contracted Turkish mercenaries to train Bornu's army.

To the west of Kanem and Bornu, a group of Hausa city-states had been founded by nomadic cattle-keepers and farmers between 1000 and 1200. A common feature of Hausa villages was wooden stockades for protection. When villages grew into larger towns, they were enclosed by large walls.

Hausa city-states became important political and economic forces in the fifteenth century. All of the Hausa states were centralized, with a king and council making decisions. Islam was an important part of the trading and merchant class and the political elite.

Kano was one of the most powerful of the city-states. In the late fourteenth and fifteenth centuries, Kano's rulers made Muslim officials an integral part of their administration and invited scholars from Egypt, Tunis, and Morocco to establish centers of scholarship.

One way in which Kano's rulers thwarted lineages that were contesting for power was by appointing slaves to important state offices such as treasurer and as palace guards. They also relied on a cavalry with an officer corps to maintain their power and to raid for the slaves who labored on large royal farms. The cavalrymen wore iron helmets and coats of mail.

Caliph—The religious and political leader of the Islamic nation; successor of Muhammad.

madrasa—A theology school, usually for Sunni Muslims.

Ceremonial cavalry procession in contemporary northern Nigeria. Historically the military strength of kingdoms of the western Sudan was partly based on cavalry.

Kano produced and exported textiles, dyed cloth, and leatherwork through an extensive network in the trans-Saharan trade as well as with Yoruba and Akan states to the south.

Other significant Hausa city-states were Zazzau (ZA-zow), a supplier of slaves to Hausa states and to North Africa; Gobir, which traded with Songhai and Mali; and Katsina, an important terminus for the trans-Saharan trade. Katsina also successfully produced textiles from its cotton fields and leather goods from goat, sheep, and cattle hides. However prosperous they were, some of the Hausa states still had to pay tribute to Songhai to the west and Kanem and Bornu to the east. The Hausa states usually coexisted peacefully, although Kano and Katsina carried on a periodic war for almost a century.

A legendary Hausa ruler of the sixteenth century was Zazzau's Queen Amina. She led her armies on campaigns all the way to the banks of the Niger River and conquered Kano and Katsina. Under her rule, Zazzau controlled not only the intra-regional trade but also the region's trans-Saharan trade. Her reign is associated with the building of earthen walls around Hausa cities. She is remembered in a popular song still sung in contemporary Nigeria: "Amina, daughter of Nikatau, a woman as capable as a man."[10]

WEST AFRICAN FOREST KINGDOMS

- *How did trade in the forest kingdoms compare with those in the savannah region?*

Yams as Sources of Traditional Power in West Africa

Between the savanna grasslands and the Atlantic was forest land. Some of the forests were extensions of the savannas and were suitable for extensive human settlements; closer to the coast were rain forests that required considerable energy to clear for settlement and cultivation. The rain forests were also the home of the tsetse fly, the carrier of sleeping sickness, which limited the herding of highly susceptible livestock.

Most forest societies were built around villages and small chiefdoms sustained by agriculture and hunting. Root crops such as yams and, later, cassava were the main staples. Although they did not approach the same size as the savanna empires, some of these small chiefdoms merged and formed vibrant kingdoms.

In southwestern Nigeria, a Yoruba city-state, Ife, emerged around the eleventh century C.E. According to oral traditions, the Yoruba god of the sky, Olorun, had sent a founding ancestor, Oduduwa, to establish Ife. Anyone who subsequently made a claim to the kingship of Ife or other Yoruba states had to trace descent from Oduduwa.

To the southeast of Ife was the Edo kingdom of Benin, which rose to prominence in the fifteenth and sixteenth centuries. Benin's prosperity was based not only on commerce with the Hausa states, trading food, ivory, and kola nuts for copper and possibly salt, but also on the strength of its fishing communities on the Niger delta.

Benin was ruled by hereditary kings, known as *obas*. Advising the king was the *ozama,* a council composed of hereditary leaders who represented the main Edo lineages. They acted as a restraint on the *oba*'s powers until a thirteenth-century *oba* named Ewedo undermined the *ozama*'s powers by creating a court of men who were not members of the royal elite and who were given nonhereditary titles.

Benin remained a minor state until the rule of *Oba* Ewuare, who usurped the throne by killing his younger brother in 1440. He took over in a period of instability following the conquest of Benin by a neighboring state. Ewuare ensured that his line would succeed him by arranging that his heir be added to the *ozama* council.

Noted for his magical and healing powers, Ewuare was famous for rebuilding the capital, surrounded by a wall and featuring a broad avenue. He constructed an extensive royal palace that provided quarters for his family as well as for advisers, guilds of craftsmen, and servants. All of his freeborn subjects were expected to spend a period in the service of the palace. During Ewuare's three decades of rule, his armies expanded Benin's borders, conquering some 200 towns and extending Benin's influence far to the north and to coastal regions to the east and west. However, Ewuare did not tightly control his empire. Although he placed loyal officials in subject territories, he gave local rulers autonomy as long as they paid tribute on a regular basis. Ewuare's successors did not fare so well. The *ozama* chiefs asserted themselves and replaced, exiled, or killed a series of *obas*.

Other states developed along the forest fringe of the northern savanna. Most of them profited from the long-distance Saharan trade through the Hausa states to the north, exchanging slaves and forest products such as kola nuts for salt, leather goods, and glassware. In the Niger River region, the kingdom of Oyo emerged in the fourteenth century. The kings *(alafins)* of Oyo presided over a complex of palace councils, subkings, secret organizations, and lineage organizations at the village level. Although *alafins* claimed absolute power, they were held in check by a prime minister *(basorun)* and a council of ministers *(oyo mesi),* composed of men from the seven wards of the city of Oyo. If an *alafin* abused his authority, the prime minister could rebuke him, "The Gods reject you, the people reject you, the earth rejects you." The *alafin* then had to commit suicide.[11] This happened rarely because an *alafin*'s suicide meant that a member of the council also had to take his life. This system of checks and balances worked well until the seventeenth and eighteenth centuries.

The *alafins'* wealth was built on tolls collected from traders and their control of a slave labor force that they placed on royal farms. Oyo's rise as a regional power was due to its permanent officer corps and its cavalry, assembled with horses traded from the savanna. Because horses did not survive in the tsetse-infested forests, the cavalry was most effective in the open savannas to the southwest of Oyo.

All of these forest states are noted for their artistic achievements. Yoruba artisans created sculptures in bronze, copper, brass, and terra-cotta. Most of these artworks were used in religious contexts, as funereal pieces placed in tombs to honor ancestors and in temples. These objects showed continuity with the artistic styles of earlier civilizations such as the Nok culture of central Nigeria.

SWAHILI CITY-STATES IN EAST AFRICA

▪ *Why were small city-states established on the East African coast rather than the large states in West Africa?*

For the past 2000 years the East African, or Swahili, coast has been part of a much wider maritime trading network that linked Africa with the Near East, India, and Asia. Indeed, one scholar argues that the Indian Ocean would be better named the Afrasian Sea.[12] However, unlike the trans-Saharan trade that opened up extensive trade throughout western Africa, trade along the East African coast, with some exceptions, did not have the same impact on the East African interior until the nineteenth century.

MAP Trade Routes in Africa

The historical and cultural development of the East African coast was intimately linked to the creation of a coastal culture that dates from 100 B.C.E. to 300 C.E. with the establishment of Bantu-speaking communities along the coast north of the Tana River.

They took advantage of the fertile soils and forests along the coast to pasture their animals and to raise a great variety of food crops. They also found the creeks, rivers, lagoons, mangrove swamps, and seas ideal for fishing. Although Bantu farmers relied on subsistence agriculture and fishing, they began to expand their local and regional trading contacts and eventually linked up with merchants from the Arabian peninsula and the Persian Gulf.

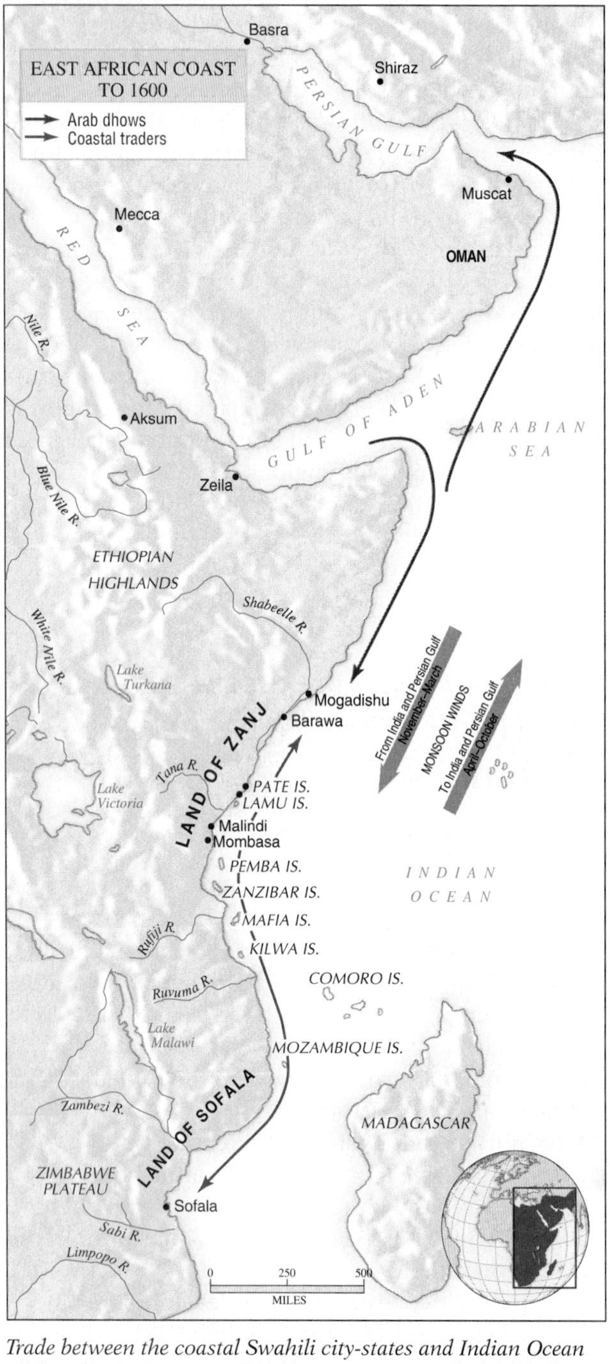

Trade between the coastal Swahili city-states and Indian Ocean trading partners was regulated by monsoon winds that blow in a southwesterly direction between November and March and in a northeasterly direction between April and October.

The language that evolved on the coast and islands was Swahili, which was based on a Bantu language spoken on the Kenyan coast. Indeed, the word *Swahili* is taken from an Arabic word *sawahil,* meaning "coast." As the language evolved, it adopted Arabic loan words, especially after the seventeenth century.

The earliest known record of the East African trade is *The Periplus of the Erythrean Sea,* a navigational guide written by a Greek trader in Alexandria, Egypt, around the first century C.E. The *Periplus* chronicles shipping ports of the Red Sea and the Indian Ocean and identifies a string of market towns on the "Azanian" (East African) coast that actively participated in the Indian Ocean trade, especially with Arabia. The most important was a port named Rhapta. Market towns exported such goods as ivory, rhinoceros horn, copra, and tortoise shells in exchange for iron tools and weapons, cloth, glass, and grain.

The Indian Ocean trade continued between 300 and 1000, but it was given a great stimulus by the spread of Islam and the settling of Muslims from Arabia and the Persian Gulf along the East African coastline from the ninth century C.E. onward. This was about the same time as Islam reached western parts of North Africa, but the spread of Islam in eastern Africa was not associated with conquest. Muslims intermixed with African communities and helped expand trading links with the Arab world. An Arab traveler described this trade on a visit to the "land of Zanj" (the East African coast) in 916:

> *The land of Zanj produces wild leopard skins. The people wear them as clothes, or export them to Muslim countries. They are the largest leopard skins and the most beautiful for making saddles. . . . They also export tortoise-shell for making combs, for which ivory is likewise used. . . . There are many wild elephants in this land but no tame ones. The Zanj do not use them for war or anything else, but only hunt and kill them for their ivory. It is from this country that come tusks weighing fifty pounds and more. They usually go to Oman, and from there are sent to China and India.*[13]

Arab boats or dhows made the Indian Ocean trade possible. They had the ability to cross the Indian Ocean three times as fast as a camel could cross the Sahara, and, with a capacity of up to 200 tons, they could carry a thousand times as much. The dhows' lateen (triangular) sails made it possible for sailors to take advantage of seasonal monsoon winds in the Indian Ocean that blow in a southwesterly direction between November and March and northeasterly between April and October. As with the Red Sea trade, the monsoon winds governed the trading calendar. It took about a month for a dhow to make the 2000-mile journey from East Africa to the Persian Gulf, and the

The Arab dhow was the primary transporter of trade goods in the Indian Ocean. The dhow's lateen sails made it possible to navigate the monsoon winds that dictated the direction of trade at different times of the year.

traders had to carry out their business according to the favorable winds, or they could not transport their goods at all. Along the East African coast itself, however, it was possible to move between the islands at most times of the year. Because the coastal trade was conducted in shallower waters, traders built small dhows with capacities of about 50 tons. These dhows typically had no deck, one mast, and palm-leaf mats for sails.

Swahili civilization flourished between 1000 and 1500, when hundreds of city-states, many of them on offshore islands, sprang up along the 1800-mile stretch from Mogadishu to Sofala on the Mozambique coast. They began as fishing villages and gradually evolved into trading centers. Most were short-lived, but those that were situated at the mouth of a river or had deep harbors and were connected to established trade routes on the African mainland—such as Malindi, Pemba, Pate, Mombasa, Mafia, and Kilwa—became regional trade centers and thrived for centuries.

Kilwa peaked as a trading center between 1250 and 1330 C.E. Kilwa had the advantage of a good supply of fresh water and several natural harbors that could handle large ships. But it became the wealthiest of the city-states because of its near monopoly over gold exported from the Zimbabwe interior. Kilwa's merchants claimed a sphere of influence over the East African coast from Kilwa southward to Sofala on the Mozambique coast, where they established an outpost to facilitate the gold trade with Africans from the interior.

The Swahili city-states were never part of an empire, nor were they dominated by any one of the city-states. Indeed, they usually competed fiercely with one another. The lack of high walls around the cities suggests that they were more concerned with protecting themselves from stray elephants than from rivals. At times, one city might exact tribute from its neighbors or a number of states might federate in time of war. Commercial competition made such cooperation difficult to maintain and curtailed political expansion on the African mainland, where kingdoms like Great Zimbabwe played one coastal city against another. Indian Ocean trade was largely free from major conflicts until the Portuguese arrived in the early sixteenth century.

Within the city-states, a Muslim commercial aristocracy exercised exclusive control over political institutions. Although they provided the capital, skills, and boats for their piece of the Indian Ocean trade, they always remained in the shadow of the Indian Ocean trading powers. The Swahili commercial elite was primarily descended from Arab and Indian settlers and indigenous Africans. A myth developed that that they were descendants of Shirazi Persians. Because the Persian Empire had once been an Indian Ocean trading power, Swahili elites probably manufactured a connection to the Persians who settled along the coast many centuries earlier. Many scholars question whether this claim has any validity.

As the Muslim Middle East became the commercial center of Eurasia, the maritime trade of the Swahili city-states figured significantly in the commercial networks of three continents. Gold, ivory, mangrove poles, amber, and slaves were the main exports. Other products commonly exported were hides and skins, cloth, rhinoceros horn, spices, and grain, in exchange for cloth, silk, beads, porcelain, gum, incense, spices (i.e., cinnamon, nutmeg, and cloves), glass, cloth, perfume, bronze, copper, and silver. Copper and silver coins were minted at Kilwa, Pate, and Mogadishu and used up and down the coast.

Kilwa, with its access to the Zimbabwean gold fields, became the major port for gold sent to Indian Ocean states and through Egypt to Europe. Gold was a mainstay of Swahili trade until gold and silver began to flow in the sixteenth century from Spanish possessions in the Americas. After that, Swahili traders turned more to exporting ivory. Iron ore, exported from Malindi and Mombasa, supplied the iron industries of India. Mangrove trees, typically found where rivers emptied into the Indian Ocean, were stripped of their branches and shipped to treeless areas throughout the southern Persian Gulf. Because mangrove poles are straight and sturdy, they made excellent materials for house construction. This trade remained healthy until the late twentieth century when oil revenues allowed Persian Gulf states to turn to steel for building materials. Slaves were shipped to the Arabian peninsula and Cambay, the capital of Gujarat, in India. There they served as domestic slaves or, as in southern Iraq, as laborers draining marshes. Their oppressive work conditions sparked off a revolt in 869 C.E. that lasted for nearly two decades. One consequence of the revolt was that few Persian Gulf households continued to rely on Africa as a source of slaves.

DOCUMENT

Excerpts from "A Description of the Coasts of East Africa and Malabar" by Duarte Barbosa

The Swahili coast attracted trading expeditions from as far away as China. In the early 1400s, a Chinese fleet under the command of Admiral Zheng He (JUHNG HUH) visited Swahili towns such as Malindi and Mogadishu, bearing porcelain, silks, lacquerware, and fine art objects and exchanging them for ivory, rhinoceros horns, incense, tortoise shell, rare woods, and exotic animals such as ostriches, zebras, and giraffes. Zheng He's ships also took back African envoys, who stayed at the Chinese court for several years.

In the early 1400s, the Chinese commissioned seven expeditions to visit all the lands of the Indian Ocean to promote trade. A Chinese fleet under the command of Admiral Zheng He visited some of the Swahili towns and took back several envoys from Malindi who brought along a giraffe as a gift to the Chinese court in 1414. The presentation of this giraffe was memorialized in a tapestry.

The governments of the city-states were usually headed by monarchs or sultans, assisted by merchant councils and advised by holy men or royal relatives. Political leadership was equated with commercial success. The king of Pate, for instance, "owned much wealth, . . . acted as an entrepreneur in ship building, trading and even mining and relied for emergency on a private army as distinct from the regular troops which he also commanded. . . ."[14] Elite families maintained their privileged status by building political and commercial alliances through intermarriage and exchanging gifts.

Although the sultans were typical Muslim rulers in most respects, the common order of succession was according to matrilineal rules. When a sultan died at Kilwa, Pate, or any of numerous other cities, the throne passed to one of the head queen's brothers. Swahili civilization was an urban culture. Most towns had a central mosque, a Qur'anic school, a marketplace, a palace, and government buildings. Some towns, such as Kilwa, Mombasa and Lamu, were densely settled; in others, settlements were dispersed. The towns were the preserves of the commercial elite, who lived in houses made of wood with coral stone foundations until the mid-fifteenth century when they replaced wood with coral rag (broken coral stone) with lime mortar. Some of the homes were two or three stories high and reflected the wealth, status, and rank of their owners. A Portuguese account of the late fifteenth century described the layout of Kilwa, a prosperous city of 12,000 people: "The streets of the city are very narrow, as the houses are very high, of three and four stories, and one can run along the tops of them upon the terraces, as the houses are very close together. . . ."[15]

With the exception of the most loyal household slaves, the Swahili traders were the only ones who lived inside the walled cities. Most slaves slept outside the city in houses made of sun-dried mud and palm-matted roofs. They came into the city to work every day. Because the towns were not self-sufficient, the traders relied on the farmers and fishermen on the mainland for foodstuffs and meat.

Swahili masons and craftsmen were celebrated for building ornate stone and coral mosques and palaces, adorned with gold, ivory, and other wealth from nearly every major port in southern Asia. Perhaps because it borrowed architectural styles from the Middle East, Kilwa impressed the famous Muslim scholar-traveler Ibn Battuta in 1331 as the most beautiful and well-constructed city he had seen anywhere. Archaeological excavations have confirmed this evaluation, revealing the ruins of enormous palaces, great mansions, elaborate mosques, arched walkways, town squares, and public fountains. The Husuni Kubwa (hoo-SOO-nee KOO-bwah) palace and trade emporium at Kilwa, built on the edge of an ocean cliff, featured domed and vaulted roofs and contained over 100 rooms, with eight to ten apartments for visiting merchants as well as their goods, and an eight-sided bathing pool in one of its many courtyards.

Constructed in the thirteenth century by the Muslim sultans of Kilwa, the Great Mosque was built from coral blocks. In the mosque's center, its arches supported a domed ceiling.

KINGDOMS OF CENTRAL AND SOUTHERN AFRICA

■ *How were southern African kingdoms tied to the Indian Ocean economy?*

By the third century C.E. central and southern Africa had been settled by migrating groups of Bantu farmers who lived in scattered homesteads or small villages and subsisted on cereal crops and animal herds. Around 1000 C.E. some of these societies began to grow in size and complexity. States were formed with ruling elites that displayed their wealth through their cattle herds. They accumulated cattle through a variety of means—raids, tribute, death dues, court fines, and bridewealth exchanges for marriages. Cattle exchanges through marriages and loans gave ruling families the opportunity to establish broader social and political networks with other powerful families. Cattle herds also financed their participation in regional trading networks and links with the Indian Ocean economy.

A common feature of the ruling elites of these new states was that they built walls, dwellings, palaces, and religious centers made of stone. Throughout the region north and south of the Limpopo River archaeologists have identified more than several hundred political centers. An early state was Mapungubwe, situated south of the Limpopo River. Mapungubwe's rulers lived in stone residences on a hilltop, while commoners lived in their traditional settlements in the surrounding valley. An estimated 3000 to 5000 people lived at Mapungubwe's political center. The elites maintained their privileged status through their control over cattle herds; the trade in such metals as tin, copper, iron, and gold; and the hunting of elephants for ivory. Tin, copper, and iron were traded regionally, but ivory and gold were designated primarily for the expanding trade with the Indian Ocean coast. Mapungubwe peaked during the thirteenth century, but its main settlement had to be abandoned soon thereafter because farmers were not able to sustain production when a climatic change produced a colder, drier environment.

Mapungubwe's successor was Great Zimbabwe ("houses of stone"), centered on a well-watered plateau north of the Limpopo. Its grandeur as a state is symbolized by its imposing granite structures, left after its rulers were forced to move northward to the Zambezi. Extending over 60 acres and supporting about 18,000 residents, the complex at Great Zimbabwe contained many structures built over several centuries. At its center was a large complex of stoneworks where the political and religious elite lived. The most impressive structure was the Great Enclosure, which likely served as the royal family's main residence. Over 800 feet in circumference, the Great Enclosure was built without mortar and featured massive freestanding walls 12 feet thick and 20 feet high. Undoubtedly, Great Zimbabwe's rulers intended their monumental architecture to enhance their power and prestige among their subjects.

Zimbabwe's king presided over an elaborate court and administration. His key advisers included the queen mother and a ritual sister, a half-sister who was appointed when a king was installed. She had to give her consent to decisions made by the royal coun-

The Great Enclosure was Great Zimbabwe's most impressive structure and likely served as the royal family's main residence. Over 800 feet in circumference, the Great Enclosure was built without mortar and featured massive, freestanding granite walls 12 feet thick and 20 feet high.

cil before they could be enacted, she kept the ritual medicines that protected the well-being of the king, and she had considerable input into the choice of a new king.

Zimbabwe's rulers combined political and sacred power. Great Zimbabwe contained a rainmaking shrine, where its rulers prayed for abundant rainfall. On a nearby hillside was a temple where they prayed and offered sacrifices to the high god Mwari and the ancestors to ensure the fertility of the land and the prosperity of the people.

Great Zimbabwe's political elite based their power on their vast cattle herds as well as the control of regional trade, particularly copper and gold. The principal sources of gold were located on the plateau west of Great Zimbabwe. Women and children were responsible for mining most gold, which they did during the dry season, when they could take time off from their farming responsibilities. They sank narrow shafts as deep as 100 feet, brought the ore to the surface, crushed it, and sifted out the gold in nearby streams. Although some of the gold was fashioned into ornamental bangles and jewelry for Zimbabwe's rulers, most of the gold was transported as a fine powder for the external trade with the coastal Swahili cities, especially Kilwa, whose prosperity depended on its ties to Zimbabwe. One historian has estimated that 7 to 10 million ounces of gold were exported from this region from the late tenth to the nineteenth centuries. Besides gold, ivory and animal skins were traded for glass beads, Indian cloth, ceramic vessels from Persia, and blue-and-white porcelain from China.

Great Zimbabwe's zenith was between 1290 and 1450. A common explanation for its sudden collapse is environmental degradation. The land no longer supported large numbers of people living in a concentrated area; trees, chopped down for firewood, had become scarce; and many wild animals had been hunted down. However, part of this interpretation is not supported by data showing that rainfall actually increased around that time. A more likely explanation for the kingdom's decline is the rise to prominence of two of its former tributary states: Torwa to the northwest and Mutapa to the north.

Oral tradition relates that Mutapa's founder was Nyatsimbe Mutota, whom Great Zimbabwe's rulers had sent north to search for an alternative source of salt. He founded the Mutapa kingdom in the well-watered Mazoe Valley south of the Zambezi River. By 1500 Mutapa's ruler, the *mwene mutapa* ("conqueror"), and his army held sway over a vast part of the upper Zimbabwe Plateau. The *mwene mutapa* did not adopt the stone building traditions of Great Zimbabwe. Instead, he lived in a palace complex within a wooden palisade. With his family, military, bureaucracy, and representatives of tributary chiefdoms, he ruled over a federation of tributary states through governors that he appointed. They paid tribute in the form of agricultural produce, iron, cattle, and especially gold, which was still the mainstay of the trade with the East African coast.

Another notable kingdom in west Central Africa was Kongo, located in a fertile agricultural area near the Atlantic coast at the mouth of the Congo River. It was formed in the fourteenth century when a petty prince named Wene led a migration, married into the local ruling family, and began developing a loose federation of states. Wene took the title of *Manikongo* ("lord of Kongo"). However, as kings of Kongo centered their political rule at their capital, Mbanza Kongo, they developed a centralized state. By the time the Portuguese arrived in the late fifteenth century, Kongo had already developed a sophisticated political system. The king, who had a professional army resident at his capital, appointed officials, usually close relatives, as his provincial administrators. The Kongo kingdom also controlled interregional trade, exchanging its cloth, woven from fibers of the raffia palm, for salt and seashells from neighboring societies.

Loango, the Capital of the Congo (Kongo)

CONCLUSION

By 1500 C.E. Africans had successfully adapted to the opportunities and constraints of Africa's challenging environments by creating a diverse range of communities and states. Critical turning points in the histories of African cultures occurred with the introduction of agriculture, herding, and ironworking. These developments spurred population growth, migrations, craft specialization, trade between communities, and more complex political and economic systems. Most Africans in 1500 still lived in scattered homesteads and small communities and earned their livelihoods from farming, herding, and hunting. However, because of trading relations with one another and with other continents, Africans began to establish kingdoms and empires in all parts of the continent and in a variety of environments. Like other early world civilizations, Egypt and Nubia evolved in the Nile River valley, but Aksum and Ethiopia emerged on a mountain plateau; Ghana, Mali, Songhay, and Great Zimbabwe in savannas; Oyo and Benin in rainforests; and the Swahili city-states on the Indian Ocean.

While Africans created their own distinct cultures and traditions, states in the West African Sudan, northeastern Africa, and the East African coast carried on vigorous commercial, technological, and intellectual exchanges with the cultures of the Indian Ocean, the Mediterranean, the Near East, and Asia, largely by tapping Muslim trading networks. The kingdom of Aksum became a major Red Sea power, serving as a bridge between the Mediterranean and the Indian Ocean. The Swahili city-states on the East African coast and the states of the Zimbabwe Plateau carried on extensive relations with Indian Ocean trading networks. West African savanna kingdoms created the most extensive trading network through their position overseeing trade between North Africa, the savanna, and forest regions to the south. However, within these long-distance trading networks, African states were primarily producers of raw materials.

Although most Africans remained faithful to their traditional religious beliefs and practices, many converted to Christianity and Islam in specific areas. Egypt became an early center of Christianity, while Ethiopia's rulers firmly established Christianity as their kingdom's state religion. Islam became the dominant religion of North Africa, while some rulers and traders in the West African savanna, northeastern Africa, and along the Swahili coast adopted Islam. However, until the eighteenth century, Islam remained primarily a religion of court and commerce in sub-Saharan Africa. It won few followers in small-scale societies that did not have ruling elites. This pattern is similar to other places such as Indonesia where Muslim traders established themselves but did not initially win many converts.

Suggestions for Web Browsing

You can obtain more information about topics included in this chapter at the websites listed below. See also the companion website that accompanies this text, **http://www.ablongman.com/brummett,** which contains an online study guide and additional resources.

Internet African History Sourcebook
http://www.fordham.edu/halsall/africa/africasbook.html

Extensive online source for links about the history of ancient Africa, including the kingdoms of Ghana, Mali, and Songhai.

Art of Benin
http://www.si.edu/ofg/Units/sorsnmafa.htm

Site of the Smithsonian Institution's National Museum of African Art displays art objects from the kingdom of Benin before Western dominance.

Great Zimbabwe
http://www.mc.maricopa.edu/~reffland/anthropology/anthro2003/legacy/africa/zimbabwe/

A 23-slide series, with commentary, that will take you through the ruins of Great Zimbabwe in southern Africa.

The Story of Africa
http://www.bbc.co.uk/worldservice/africa/features/storyofafrica/index.shtml

The radio service of the BBC presents a history of Africa from the origins of humankind to modern nation-states.

African Voices
http://www.mnh.si.edu/africanvoices/

The African Voices exhibit at the Smithsonian Institution's Museum of Natural History features discussions of history, culture and politics.

Literature and Films

The Sundiata epic of the Malian Empire is recorded in D. T. Niane, *Sundiata: An Epic of Old Mali* (Longman, 1995). For Ethiopian royal literature, see G. W. B. Huntingford, ed., *Royal Chronicles of Abyssinia: The Glorious Victories of Ama Seyon King of Ethiopia* (Clarendon Press, 1965).

Caravans of Gold (Home Vision, 1984) treats the gold trade between the Sudanic kingdoms of West Africa and the Muslim and European worlds. It is one film in an eight-part series, *Africa: The Story of a Continent,* presented by Basil Davidson, a British writer on African issues. *Lost Cities of the South* (PBS, 1999) presents a discussion of African civilizations of southern Africa, such as Mapungubwe and Great Zimbabwe. It is part of a six-part series, *Wonders of the African World,* narrated by Harvard professor Henry Louis Gates, Jr.

Suggestions for Reading

The best detailed coverage of African history can be found in two multivolume series, each containing chapters by leading scholars: *The Cambridge History of Africa,* 8 Vols. (Cambridge University Press, 1982–1984) and *The UNESCO General History of Africa.* Among other general surveys of African history are Robert July, *A History of the African People,* 4th ed. (Waveland Press, 1992); Erik Gilbert and Jonathan Reynolds, *Africa in World History from Prehistory to the Present* (Pearson Education, 2004); and Christopher Ehret, *The Civilizations of Africa: A History to 1800* (University Press of Virginia, 2002).

The best general reference work on early African history is Joseph Vogel, ed., *Encyclopedia of Precolonial Africa: Archaeology, History, Languages, Cultures, and Environments* (AltaMira Press, 1997). Another general work that examines Africa's history with a disciplinary focus is James Newman, *The Peopling of Africa: A Geographic Interpretation* (Yale University Press, 1995). A general synthesis on women in African history is Iris Berger and E. Frances White, *Women in Sub-Saharan Africa: Restoring Women to History* (Indiana University Press, 1995).

On Ethiopia, see Richard K. Pankhurst, *The Ethiopians* (Blackwell, 1998).

General works on West Africa include J. F. Ajayi and Michael Crowder, eds., *History of West Africa,* 3rd ed., Vol. 1 (Longman, 1985). A comprehensive study on Islam in Africa is Randall Pouwels and Nehemia Levtzion, eds., *The History of Islam in Africa* (Ohio University Press, 2000).

The East African coast and Swahili city-states are well covered in John Middleton, *The World of the Swahili: An African Mercantile Civilization* (Yale University Press, 1992).

The best general study on early central and southern African history is David Birmingham, ed., *History of Central Africa to 1870* (Cambridge University Press, 1981). The kingdom of Great Zimbabwe is extensively treated in Joseph Vogel, *Great Zimbabwe: The Iron Age in South Central Africa* (Garland, 1994). A detailed study of central and eastern African states is David Schoenbrun, *A Green Place, a Good Place: Agrarian Change, Gender, and Social Identity in the Great Lakes Region to the 15th Century* (Heinemann, 1998).

CHAPTER

9

The European Middle Ages, 476–1348 C.E.

CHAPTER CONTENTS

500

590–604 Pontificate of Gregory I, the Great; papacy begins to assert political influence

700

732 Charles Martel defeats Muslims at Tours

c. 790–c. 940 Viking raids and settlements throughout Europe

800

800 Charlemagne crowned emperor by the pope

843 Treaty of Verdun; division of Charlemagne's empire

900

910 Benedictine monastery at Cluny founded

962 Otto the Great crowned emperor by the Pope

987–996 Hugh Capet rules France; beginning of Capetian dynasty

1000

1066 William the Conqueror takes England at the battle of Hastings

1079–1142 Peter Abelard

1095 First Crusade

1100

1152–1190 Reign of Frederick I Barbarossa of Hohenstaufen dynasty in Germany

1154–1189 Reign of Henry II of England, founder of Plantagenet dynasty

1182–1226 St. Francis of Assisi, founder of Franciscan religious order

1198–1226 Pontificate of Innocent III, zenith of papal power

1200

1215 Magna Carta

1212–1250 Reign of Frederick II

1248 Seventh Crusade (last)

The absence of the political unity and military security once provided by the Roman Empire became an obvious fact of life in almost all of western Europe in the fourth and fifth centuries. As the unity and security of the old Roman order collapsed and Germanic chieftains claimed lands and asserted what authority they could, very slowly the civilization of Rome evolved into a culture that was a unique blending of Roman and Germanic institutions. Out of this blending of cultures emerged a distinct pattern of life in western Europe.

One of the institutions that survived the collapse of Roman order was the Christian Church, which, by the beginning of the sixth century, was still in the process of unification under the direction of the bishop of Rome, the Pope. The church increased its efficiency through the centralization of its administration, and unified its efforts to convert all of Europe and eliminate rival religions. Christian efforts to preserve knowledge and learning centered on saving art and literature of the past that was supportive exclusively of the Christian faith; for the most part the art and literature of the non-Christian past was destroyed, suppressed, or ignored—much of the intellectual heritage of the ancient world was lost forever.

The first significant state to emerge out of the fragmentation of old Roman order was that established by the Germanic tribe of the Franks, who gave northern Europe an interim of stability and progress. Military and political security was improved, and Roman Christianity was extended among the barbarian tribes of the north.

But the accomplishments of the Franks were not to be permanent. Their empire did not endure, partly because it lacked the solid economic foundation that had supported the Romans, and because of new and violent invasions. Viking, Magyar, and Muslim incursions had to be addressed through local resistance, since no effective response existed on a national or international level.

Out of the disintegration of the Frankish empire evolved an alternative political order sometimes described as feudalism. Based on formally stated agreements between individuals, this method of government was designed to provide social stability and military security in Europe. And the manorial system, the economic foundation of medieval life, provided stability to the rural economy of Europe. Both institutions attempted to insure security by resisting change and fostering self-sufficiency.

Gradually, the political and military goals of the feudal nobility became aggressive and expansionist. Monarchs once again attempted to increase their authority over the feudal nobility. The growth of trade and commerce slowly provided an economic alternative to the manorial system, and the society of the West changed in the process. In addition, the church increased its power as a political and economic force in European society, in addition to its religious leadership. The church's sponsorship of the Crusading movement of the later Middle Ages was indicative of that power and influence.

The culture of the Later European Middle Ages emerged as greatly distinct from that of the period before 500. The collective and conservative society of the earlier period gave way to a culture becoming more familiar with religious challenge, economic growth, and political centralization. The cultural conservatism and conformity that typified the earlier patterns of medieval life gave way to a society that had to adjust to a more rapid rate of change and challenge in virtually all facets of life. The roots of modern European society are easily found in the civilization of the Late Middle Ages.

THE CHURCH IN THE EARLY MIDDLE AGES

- *What role did the Church play in stabilizing western European society after the fall of the Roman Empire?*

As Europe formed a unique culture out of the remnants of Roman influence and the injection of Germanic peoples and their traditions, the church played a formative role in shaping this new social fabric. In the Early Middle Ages (500–1000), the administration of the church was centralized through the efforts of the popes and the ever more efficient bureaucracy at Rome. Missionary activity spread Christianity to the borders of the continent and provided a unified cultural and religious foundation for early European society. And, in large part, the church, its missionaries, and its copyists in monasteries should be credited with keeping at least some of the intellectual heritage of the ancient world alive in an age when learning, other than that which supported Christian belief, was considered useless and unnecessary.

The Early Medieval Papacy, 500–1000

Chapter 5 examined the growing authority of the bishops of Rome, the popes, over the Christian Church in western Europe. Not only were the bishops of Rome able to establish control over the church's hierarchy and supervise the spiritual concerns of the believers; often the early popes were looked to for political leadership and guidance in troubled times. During the pontificate of Gregory I, the Great (590–604), the papacy aggressively began to assert its political as well as its spiritual authority. After his election as pope, Gregory assumed the task of protecting Rome and its surrounding territory from the threat of invasion from the Germanic tribe of the Lombards. After successfully negotiating a peace treaty with this tribe, Gregory became the first pope to conduct himself as actual ruler of a part of what later became the Papal States.

Gregory also laid the foundation for the papal machinery of church government. He took the first step in asserting papal control of the church outside Italy by sending a mission of Benedictine monks to convert the non-Christian Anglo-Saxons. The pattern of church government that Gregory established in England—bishops supervised by archbishops, who reported to the pope—became standard.

The task of establishing papal control of the church and extending the pope's **temporal** authority was continued by Gregory's successors. In the eighth century English missionaries transferred to Germany and France the pattern of papal government they had known in England; the Donation of Pepin, a sizable grant of territory in Italy given to the pope by the Merovingian (meh-roh-VIN-gee-ahn) king (see p. 261), greatly increased the pope's temporal power by creating the Papal States.

Missionary Activities of the Church

The early Middle Ages were years of widespread and intense missionary activity. By spreading Christianity,

temporal—Having to do with time, or the present life and this world. Worldly or transitory concerns.

The bejeweled front cover of the Lindau Gospels, a work dating from the third quarter of the ninth century, is an example of Carolingian art. The Celtic-Germanic metalwork tradition has been adapted to the religious art produced during the era of Charlemagne. The main clusters of semi-precious stones adorning the gold cover have been raised so that light can penetrate beneath them to make them glow.

missionaries contributed to the confluence of Germanic and Roman cultures. Monasteries, many of which were established in remote territories far from urban centers, served not only as missionary outposts, but also as refuges for those seeking a life of contemplation and prayer, as centers of learning for scholars, and even as progressive farming centers. The dedication and enthusiasm with which many of these monks approached their faith often extended beyond the monastic walls, and resulted ultimately in the virtual elimination of paganism in Europe.

One of the most successful of early Christian missionaries was Ulfilas (OOL-fi-lahs) (c. 311–383), who spent 40 years with the Visigoths and translated most of the Bible into Gothic. Ulfilas and many other early missionaries were followers of Arius, and the heresy of Arianism (see p. 154) was adopted by all the Germanic tribes in the empire, with the exception of the Franks and the Anglo-Saxons.

Missionary activities in Ireland resulted in the founding of numerous monasteries on that island, many of them in remote and isolated locations. In the late sixth and seventh centuries, many of these Irish monks, moved by a passionate devotion to Christianity and dedicated to the elimination of heresy, traveled to Scotland, northern England, the kingdom of the Franks, and even Italy as missionaries to renew the faith and erase the effects of worldly corruption. Irish monks also eagerly pursued scholarship and the preservation of early Christian literary works, and their monasteries became storehouses for priceless manuscripts and exquisite copies of original works.

Early in the seventh century, the papacy, along with the monasteries, took a more aggressive part in directing Christian missionary efforts. Under the direction of the pope, Roman Catholicism was established throughout England, and the Irish church acknowledged the primacy of Rome.

The English church, in turn, played an important role in the expansion of Roman Catholic Christianity on the European mainland. Boniface, the greatest English missionary in the eighth century, spent 35 years among the Germanic tribes and established several important monasteries and bishoprics before he turned to the task of reforming the church in France. There, he revitalized the monasteries, organized a system of local **parishes** to bring Christianity to the countryside, and probably was instrumental in forming the alliance between the papacy and the Carolingian dynasty of kings of the Franks. Roman Catholic missionaries were also sent to work among the Scandinavian peoples and the Slavs.

The Preservation of Knowledge

One of the great contributions of the monasteries was the preservation of the learning of the early church, and some of the literature of the Greek and Roman world that early Christian leaders found compatible with the Christian faith. After the fall of Rome, learning did not entirely die out in western Europe; the knowledge of the classical world was preserved through the efforts of a small number of concerned intellectuals who recognized its lasting value. Seeing that the ability to read Greek was quickly disappearing, the sixth-century Roman scholar Boethius (boh-EE-thee-uhs) (c. 480–525) determined to preserve Greek learning by

---

parish—A local church, with its own priest, and the people under the religious care of that priest.

translating all of Plato and Aristotle into Latin. But only Aristotle's treatises on logic were translated, and these works remained the sole writings of that philosopher available in Europe until the twelfth century. Unjustly accused of treachery by the emperor, Boethius was thrown into prison, where he wrote *The Consolation of Philosophy* while awaiting execution, which eventually became a medieval textbook on philosophy.

Cassiodorus (cah-si-oh-DOH-ruhs; c. 490–c. 585), a contemporary of Boethius, devoted most of his life to the collection and preservation of classical knowledge. By encouraging the monks to copy valuable manuscripts, he was instrumental in making the monasteries centers of learning. Following his example, many monasteries established *scriptoria,* departments concerned exclusively with copying manuscripts.

During the early Middle Ages, most education took place in the monasteries. In the late sixth and seventh centuries, when political stability was not yet reestablished throughout much of the European continent, Irish monasteries provided a safe haven for learning. There, men studied Greek and Latin, copied and preserved manuscripts, and, in illuminating them, produced masterpieces of art. The *Book of Kells* is a surviving example of their skill. In the early Middle Ages, women were provided no opportunities for such pursuits; the Church limited access to reading and writing to men involved in clerical and business occupations.

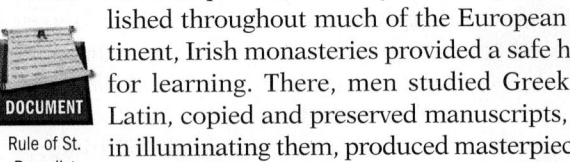

DOCUMENT
Rule of St. Benedict

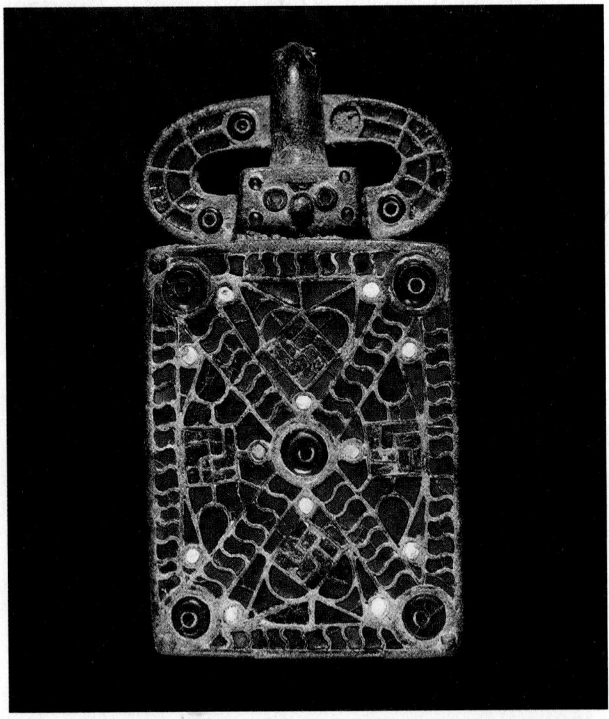

Visigothic belt buckle, circa 525–560. This elaborately crafted buckle is inlaid with finely polished red garnets and was probably worn by a prominent Spanish Visigothic woman. Most Visigothic belt buckles are of the same shape, but the patterns of decoration vary greatly, perhaps to signify the family or clan of the owner.

THE MEROVINGIANS AND CAROLINGIANS

- *How successful were the Merovingian and Carolingian monarchs in preserving Roman institutions and culture?*

In the blending of Roman and Germanic customs and institutions, the Franks played a particularly significant role. Not only was the kingdom of the Franks the most enduring of the early Germanic states, but it became, with the active support of the church, the first European kingdom that attempted to take the place of the Roman Empire in the West.

The Kingdom of the Franks Under Clovis

Before the Germanic invasions of the fourth century, the Franks lived close to the North Sea; late in the fourth century they began to migrate south and west into Roman Gaul. By 481 they occupied the northern part of Gaul as far south as the old Roman city of Paris, and in that same year, Clovis I of the Merovingian dynasty became ruler of one of the small Frankish kingdoms. By the time of his death in 511, Clovis had united the Franks into a single kingdom that stretched south to the Pyrenees.

Clovis was an intelligent manipulator of alliances and a shrewd diplomat who also used religion for political gain. He was converted to Christianity—perhaps through the influence of his Christian wife—and was baptized together with his whole army. He thus became the only Orthodox Christian ruler in the West, since the other Germanic tribes were either still pagan or followers of Arian Christianity (the heresy that maintained that Jesus was not equal to the Father and thereby not completely divine). This conversion of the Franks to Roman Christianity ultimately led to a close alliance of the Franks and the papacy.

Decline of the Merovingians—Rise of the Carolingians

Clovis's sons and grandsons extended Frankish control south to the Mediterranean and east into Germany. But after Clovis's death, the Merovingian dynasty began to decay. The Germanic tradition of treating the kingdom as personal property and dividing it among all the king's sons resulted in constant and bitter civil wars. But most importantly, the Merovingian kings proved themselves incompetent and ineffectual. Soon the Frankish state broke up into three separate kingdoms; in each, power was

The Merovingians and the Carolingians

481–511	Clovis unites Franks; beginning of Merovingian dynasty
714–741	Charles Martel mayor of the palace
732	Charles defeats Muslims at Tours
741–768	Pepin the Short mayor of the palace
751	Pepin crowned king of the Franks; beginning of Carolingian dynasty
768–814	Reign of Charlemagne
800	Charlemagne crowned emperor by the pope; beginning of Carolingian Empire
814–840	Reign of Louis the Pious
843	Treaty of Verdun divides Carolingian Empire

concentrated in the hands of the chief official of the royal household—the mayor of the palace, a powerful noble who hoped to keep the king weak and ineffectual. The Merovingian rulers became puppets—"do-nothing kings."

By the middle of the seventh century, the Frankish state had lost most of the essential characteristics of Roman civilization. The Roman system of administration and taxation had collapsed. The dukes and counts who represented the Merovinginan king received no salary and usually acted on their own initiative in commanding the fighting men and presiding over the courts in their districts. International commerce had ceased except for a small-scale trade in luxury items carried on by adventurous Greek, Syrian, and Jewish traders. The old Roman cities served mainly as centers housing the local bishops and their staffs. The virtual absence of a middle class meant that society was composed of the nobility, a union through intermarriage of aristocratic Gallo-Roman and German families who owned and exercised authority over vast estates, and, at the other end of the social scale, the peasants *(coloni)* who worked the land and were considered bound to that estate. These peasants included large numbers of formerly free German farmers. Only about 10 percent of the peasant population of Gaul maintained their status as free individuals.

Coinciding with the Merovingian decay, new waves of invaders threatened every region of Europe. A great movement of Slavic peoples from the area that is now Russia had begun around 500 C.E. From this region the Slavs pushed west, inhabiting the areas left by the Germanic tribes when they advanced into the Roman Empire. By 650 the western Slavs had reached the Elbe River, which they crossed to raid German territory. Another danger threatened western Europe from the south: in the late seventh century the Muslim Moors prepared to invade Spain from North Africa.

The kingdom of the Franks gained strength when Charles Martel became mayor of the palace (or the king's court) in 714. His military skill earned him the surname Martel, "The Hammer." Charles was responsible for introducing a major innovation in European warfare. To counteract the effectiveness of the quick-striking Muslim cavalry, Charles recruited a force of professional mounted soldiers. He rewarded his soldiers with land to enable each of them to support a family, equipment, and war horses. With such a force, Charles Martel won an important victory over the Muslim cavalry at Tours in 732.

Charles's son, Pepin the Short (741–768), legalized the power already being exercised by the mayors of the palace by requesting and receiving from the pope a decision that whoever exercised the actual power in the kingdom should be the legal ruler. In 751 Pepin was elected king by the Franks; the last Merovingian was sent off to a **monastery,** and the Carolingian dynasty came to power. In 754 the pope reaffirmed the election of Pepin by personally anointing him as king of the Franks.

Behind the pope's action was his need for a powerful protector against the Lombards, who had conquered the **Exarchate** of Ravenna (the center of Byzantine government in Italy) and were demanding tribute from the pope. Following Pepin's coronation, the pope secured his promise of armed intervention in Italy and his pledge to give the Exarchate to the papacy, once it was conquered. In 756 a Frankish army forced the Lombard king to withdraw, and Pepin gave Ravenna to the pope. The so-called Donation of Pepin made the pope a temporal ruler over the Papal States, a strip of territory that extended diagonally across northern Italy.

The alliance between the Franks and the papacy affected the course of politics and religion for centuries. It furthered the separation of the Roman from the Greek Christian Church by giving the papacy a dependable Western ally in place of the Byzantines, previously its only protector against the Lombards.

---

monastery—A house or residence of a community of religious men (monks), who live in seclusion from the world and maintain a self-sufficient communal lifestyle.

Exarchate—In the Byzantine empire, the office and/or the area ruled by an official named an exarch—a bishop ranking below the patriarch of the Eastern Orthodox Christian church.

Charlemagne and His Achievements

Under Pepin's son Charlemagne (CHAHR-leh-mayn), or Charles the Great, the Frankish state and the Carolingian dynasty reached the height of its power. Although he was certainly a successful warrior-king, leading his armies on yearly campaigns, Charlemagne, who ruled from 768 to 814, also tried to provide an effective administration for his kingdom. In addition, he had great appreciation for learning; his efforts at furthering the arts produced the revival in learning and letters known as the Carolingian Renaissance.

Charlemagne sought to extend his kingdom southward against the Muslims in Spain. He crossed the Pyrenees and eventually drove the Muslims back to the Ebro River, establishing a frontier area known as the Spanish March, centered near Barcelona. French immigrants moved into the area, later called Catalonia, giving it a character culturally distinct from the rest of Spain.

Charlemagne conquered the Bavarians and the Saxons, the last of the independent Germanic tribes, on his eastern frontier. Even farther to the east, the empire's frontier was continually threatened by the Slavs and the Avars (AY-vahrs), Asiatic nomads related to the Huns. In six campaigns, Charlemagne nearly eliminated the Avars and then set up his own military province in the Danube valley to guard against any future advances by eastern nomads. Called the East March, this territory later became Austria. Like his father Pepin, Charlemagne was deeply involved in Italian politics. The Lombards resented the attempts of the papacy to expand civil control in northern Italy. At the request of the pope, Charlemagne attacked the Lombards in 774, defeated them, and named himself their king.

This gold bust of Charlemagne was made in the fourteenth century and is housed now in the treasury of the Palace Chapel of Charlemagne in Aachen, Germany. The reliquary bust contains parts of the emperor's skull.

One of the most important events in Charlemagne's reign took place on Christmas Day, 800. In the previous year the Roman nobility had removed the pope from office, charging him with corruption. But Charlemagne came to Rome and restored the pope to his position. At the Christmas service, Charlemagne knelt before the altar and the pope placed a crown on his head while the congregation shouted: "To Charles Augustus crowned of God, great and pacific Emperor of the Romans, long life and victory!"

This ceremony demonstrated that the memory of the Roman Empire still survived as a meaningful tradition in Europe and that there was a strong desire to reestablish political unity. In fact, Charlemagne had named his capital at Aix-la-Chapelle (AX-lah-shah-PEL), "New Rome," or Aachen (AH-ken), and considered taking the title of emperor in an attempt to revive the idea of the Roman Empire in the West.

The extent of Charlemagne's empire was impressive. His territories included all of the western area of the old Roman Empire except north Africa, Britain, southern Italy, and the majority of Spain. Seven defensive provinces, or *marches,* protected the empire against hostile neighbors.

MAP The Carolingian Empire

The Carolingian territories were divided into some 300 administrative divisions, each under a count *(graf)* or, in the marches along the border, a margrave *(markgraf).* In addition, there were local military officials, the dukes. In an effort to supervise the activities of local officials, Charlemagne issued an ordinance creating the *missi dominici,* the king's envoys. Pairs of these itinerant officials, usually a bishop and a lay noble, traveled throughout the realm to check on the local administration. So that the *missi* were immune to bribes, they were chosen from men of high rank, were frequently transferred from one region to another, and no two of them were teamed for more than one year.

Charlemagne's Legacy

Charlemagne is considered one of the most significant figures of early European history. He created a state in which law and order were again enforced

Document Charlemagne: A Firsthand Look

Einhard, born in the kingdom of the Franks in circa 770 C.E., was the emperor Charlemagne's secretary and biographer. The following is an excerpt from Einhard's *Life of Charlemagne,* which he completed some years after the emperor's death. Einhard's biography of the emperor is considered one of the finest works of biography produced in the early Middle Ages. It was modeled after Roman biographies of the later emperors, and intended to give its readers an intimate glimpse of Charlemagne's character, as well as to convince them of the emperor's wisdom and majesty. The following except deals mainly with the emperor's physical appearance and private pleasures:

Charles was large and strong, and of lofty stature, though not disproportionately tall (his height is well known to have been seven times the length of his foot); the upper part of his head was round, his eyes very large and animated, nose a little long, hair fair, and face laughing and merry. Thus his appearance was always stately and dignified, whether he was standing or sitting; although his neck was thick and somewhat short, and his belly rather prominent; but the symmetry of the rest of his body concealed these defects. His gait was firm, his whole carriage manly, and his voice clear, but not so strong as his size led one to expect. His health was excellent, except during the four years preceding his death, when he was subject to frequent fevers; at the last he even limped a little with one foot. Even in those years he consulted rather his own inclinations than the advice of physicians, who were almost hateful to him, because they wanted him to give up roasts, to which he was accustomed, and to eat boiled meat instead. In accordance with the national custom, he took frequent exercise on horseback and in the chase, accomplishments in which scarcely any people in the world can equal the Franks. He enjoyed the exhalations from natural warm springs, and often practiced swimming, in which he was such an adept that none could surpass him; and hence it was that he built his palace at Aix-la-Chapelle, and lived there constantly during his latter years until his death. He used not only to invite his sons to his bath, but his nobles and friends, and now and then a troop of his retinue or bodyguard, so that a hundred or more persons sometimes bathed with him.... Charles was temperate in eating, and particularly so in drinking, for he abominated drunkenness in anybody, much more in himself and those of his household; but he could not easily abstain from food, and often complained that fasts injured his health. He very rarely gave entertainment, only on great feastdays, and then to large numbers of people. His meals ordinarily consisted of four courses, not counting the roast, which his huntsmen used to bring in on the spit; he was more fond of this than of any other dish. While at table, he listened to reading or music. . . .

Charles had the gift of ready and fluent speech, and could express whatever he had to say with the utmost clearness. He was not satisfied with command of his native language merely, but gave attention to the study of foreign ones, and in particular was such a master of Latin that he could speak it as well as his native tongue; but he could understand Greek better than he could speak it. He was so eloquent, indeed, that he might have passed for a teacher of eloquence. He most zealously cultivated the liberal arts, held those who taught them in great esteem, and conferred great honors upon them. He took lessons in grammar of the deacon Peter of Pisa, at that time an aged man. Another deacon, Albin of Britain, surnamed Alcuin, a man of Saxon extraction, who was the greatest scholar of the day, was his teacher in other branches of learning. The King spent much time and labor with him studying rhetoric, dialectics, and especially astronomy; he learned to reckon, and used to investigate the motions of the heavenly bodies most curiously, with an intelligent scrutiny. He also tried to write, and used to keep tablets and blanks in bed under his pillow, that at leisure hours he might accustom his hand to form the letters; however, as he did not begin his efforts in due season, but late in life, they met with ill success.

Questions to Consider

1. What do you suppose is Einhard's real purpose in writing this biography? Do you think it is an impartial account?
2. What could such a biography be used for, especially since it appeared after Charlemagne's death?
3. Do you think there are some exaggerations contained in this except? If so, what might they be, and why do you think they were included?

From Samuel Epes Turner, trans., *Life of Charlemagne by Einhard* (Ann Arbor: University of Michigan Press, 1960), pp. 50–57.

after three centuries of disintegration. His patronage of learning began a cultural revival that later generations would build on, producing a European civilization distinct from the Byzantine to the east and the Muslim to the south.

Charlemagne's empire was not long-lived, however, for its territories were too vast and its nobility too divisive to be held together after the dominating personality of its creator was gone. Charlemagne had no standing army; his foot soldiers were essentially the old Germanic war band summoned to fight by its war leader. The king did not have a bureaucratic administrative machine comparable to that of Roman times. The Frankish economy was agricultural and localized, and there was no system of taxation adequate to maintain an effective and permanent administration. Under Charlemagne's weak successors, the empire collapsed in the confusion of civil wars and devastating new invasions. Progress toward a centralized and effective monarchy in Europe ended with Charlemagne's death.

When he died in 814, Charlemagne was succeeded by his only surviving son, Louis the Pious, a well-meaning but ineffective ruler. Louis, in accordance with Frankish custom, divided the kingdom among his three sons, and bitter rivalry and warfare broke out among the brothers even before Louis died in 840.

In 843 the three brothers met at Verdun, where they agreed to split the Carolingian lands among themselves. Charles the Bald obtained the western part of the empire, and Louis the German the eastern; Lothair, the oldest brother, retained the title of emperor and obtained an elongated middle kingdom, which stretched 1000 miles from the North Sea to central Italy.

The Treaty of Verdun contributed to the shaping of political problems that continued into the twentieth century. Lothair's middle kingdom soon collapsed into three major parts: Lorraine in the north, Burgundy, and Italy in the south. Lorraine included Latin and German cultures, and, although it was divided in 870 between Charles and Louis, the area was disputed for centuries. Lorraine became one of the most frequent battlegrounds of Europe.

Europe Under Attack

During the ninth and tenth centuries, coinciding with the collapse of the Carolingian Empire, western Europe came under attack by Scandinavians from the

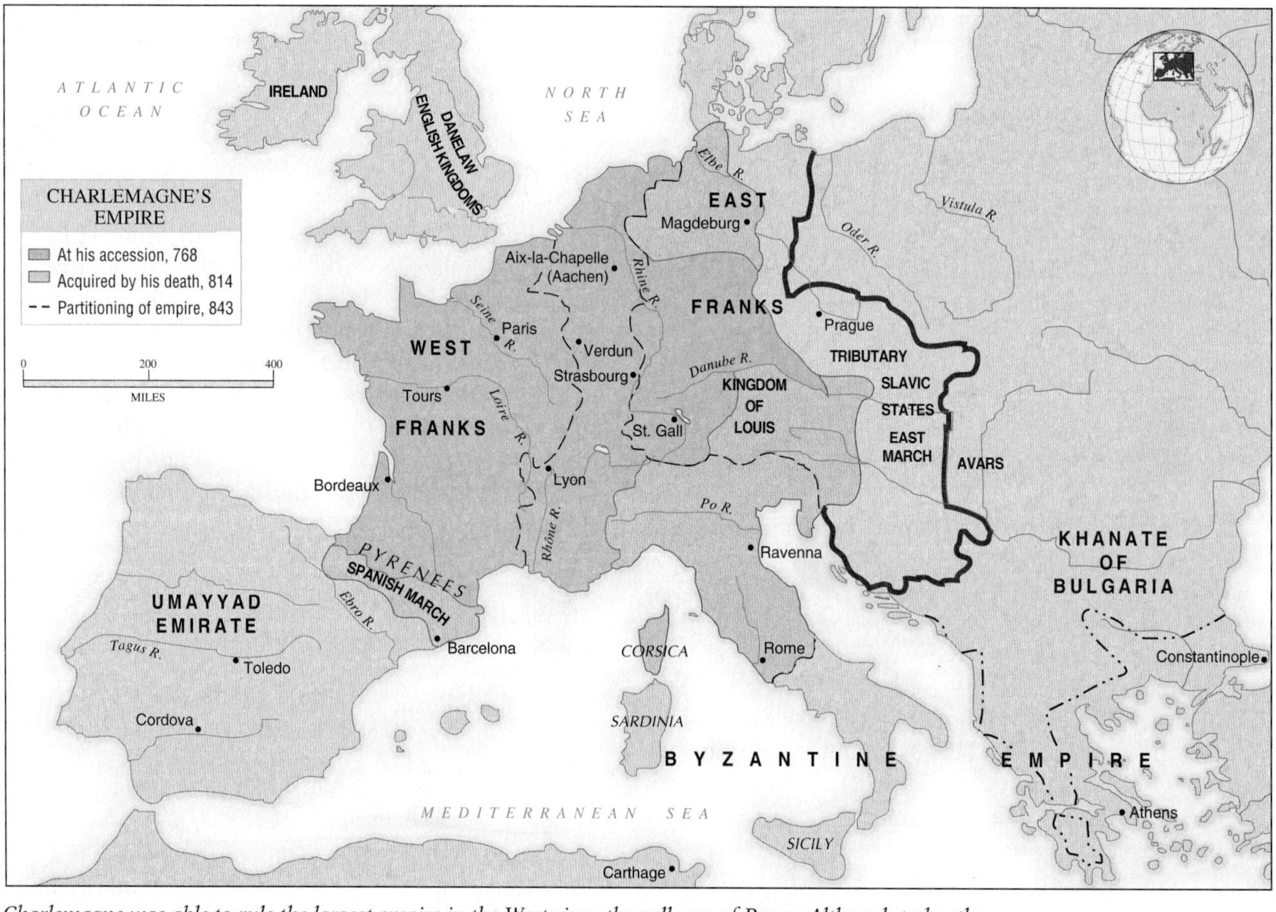

Charlemagne was able to rule the largest empire in the West since the collapse of Rome. Although today the emperor is probably remembered most for his administrative and cultural contributions, he conducted campaigns to enlarge his empire during nearly all of his reign.

north and Muslims from the south, while the Magyars, a new band of Asiatic nomads, conducted destructive raids on central Europe and northern Italy. Christian Europe was hard pressed to repel these warlike newcomers who were more threatening to life and property than the Germanic invaders of the fifth century.

From bases in North Africa, Muslim adventurers, in full command of the sea, raided the coasts of Italy and France. In 827 they began the conquest of Byzantine Sicily and southern Italy. From forts erected in southern France they penetrated far inland to attack merchant caravans even in the Alpine passes. What

New invasions in the ninth and tenth centuries threatened the stability of western Europe in much the same way the Germanic invasions had challenged the Roman Empire. Muslim, Viking, and Magyar attacks posed serious threats to Christian European political stability.

trade still existed between Byzantium and western Europe, except for that undertaken by Venice and several other Italian towns, was now almost totally cut off, and the Mediterranean Sea came under almost complete Muslim control.

The most widespread and destructive raids, however, came from Scandinavia. Swedes, Danes, and Norwegians—collectively referred to as Vikings—began to move south. Overpopulation and a surplus of young men are possible reasons for this expansion, but some scholars suggest that these raiders were defeated war bands expelled from their homeland by the emergence of strong royal power. The Vikings had developed seaworthy ships capable of carrying 100 men, powered by long oars or by sail when the wind was favorable. Viking sailors had also developed expert sailing techniques; without benefit of the compass, they were able to navigate by the stars at night and the sun by day.

The range of Viking expansion reached as far as North America to the west, the Caspian Sea to the east, and the Mediterranean to the south. Between 800 and 850, Ireland was raided repeatedly. Many monasteries, the centers of the flourishing Irish Celtic culture, were destroyed. The Icelandic Norsemen ventured on to Greenland and, later, to North America. Other raiders traveled the rivers of Russia as merchants and soldiers of fortune and founded the nucleus of a Russian state. Danes raided Britain and the shores of Germany, France, and Spain. By 840 they had occupied most of Britain north of the Thames. They devastated northwest France, destroying dozens of abbeys and towns. Unable to fend off the Viking attacks, the weak Carolingian king accepted the local Norse chieftain as duke of a Viking state, later called Normandy. Like Viking settlers elsewhere, these Northmen, or Normans, became Christian converts and eventually played an important role in shaping the future of medieval Europe.

FEUDALISM AND MANORIALISM

- *What influences did feudalism and manorialism have in shaping European society during the Middle Ages and beyond?*

Europe's response to the invasions of the ninth and tenth centuries was not uniform. By 900 the Viking occupation of England had initiated a strong national reaction, which soon led to the creation of a united British kingdom. Germany in 919 repelled the Magyar threat through the efforts of a new and able line of kings who went on to become powerful European monarchs. But Viking attacks on France accelerated a political fragmentation. Since the monarchy could not hold together its vast territory, small independent landowners surrendered both their lands and their personal freedoms to the many counts, dukes, and other local lords in return for protection and security. The decline of trade further strengthened the position of the landed nobility, whose large estates, or manors, sought to become economically self-sufficient. In addition, the nobility became increasingly dependent on military service provided by a professional force of heavily armed mounted knights, many of whom lived in the houses of their noble retainers in return for their military service.

In most parts of western Europe, where an effective centralized government was entirely absent, personal safety and security became the primary concerns of most individuals. Many historians have used the term *feudalism* to apply to the individual and unique political and social patterns resulting from political decentralization and the resulting attempts to ensure personal security.

Feudalism can be described as a system of rights and duties in which political power was exercised locally by private individuals rather than through the bureaucracy of a centralized state. In general, western European feudalism involved three basic elements: (1) a personal element, called *lordship* or *vassalage*, by which one nobleman, the *vassal*, became the follower of a stronger nobleman, the *lord;* (2) a property element, called the ***fief*** or *benefice* (usually land), which the vassal received from his lord to enable him to fulfill the obligations of being a vassal; and (3) a governmental element, the private exercise of governmental functions over vassals and fiefs.

Feudal Society

In theory, feudalism was a vast hierarchy. At the top stood the king; all the land in his kingdom in theory belonged to him. He kept large areas for his personal use (royal or crown lands) and, in return for the military service of a specified number of mounted knights, invested the highest nobles—such as dukes and counts (in Britain, earls)—with the remainder. Those nobles, in turn, in order to obtain the services of the required number of mounted warriors owed to the king, parceled out large portions of their fiefs to lesser nobles. This process, called *subinfeudation,* was continued in theory until the lowest in the scale of vassals

fief—A grant made to a vassal by a feudal lord in exchange for services. The grant usually consisted of land and the labor of the peasants who were bound to that estate. The income the land provided supported the vassal. Dignities, offices, and money rents were also given in fief.

was reached—the single knight whose fief was just sufficient to support one mounted warrior.

By maintaining the king at the head of this theoretical feudal hierarchy, the justification for monarchy was preserved, even though some feudal kings were little more than figureheads who were less powerful than their own vassals.

Relation of Lord and Vassal: The Contract

Personal bonds between lord and vassal were sometimes formally recognized. In the ceremony known as ***homage,*** the vassal knelt before his lord, or ***suzerain,*** and promised to be his "man." In the *oath of fealty* that followed, the vassal swore on the Bible or some other sacred object that he would remain true to his lord. Next, in the ritual of *investiture,* a lance, a glove, or even a clump of dirt was handed to the vassal to signify his jurisdiction over the fief. As his part of the contract, the lord was usually obliged to give his vassal protection and justice. In return, the vassal's primary duty was military service. But in addition, the vassal could be obliged to assist the lord in rendering justice in the lord's court. At certain times, as when the lord was captured and needed to be ransomed, the lord also had the right to demand special money payments, called *aids.*

The lord also had certain rights, called feudal *incidents,* regarding the administration of the fief. These included *wardship*—the right to administer the fief during the minority of a vassal's heir—and forfeiture of the fief if a vassal failed to honor his feudal obligations.

Feudal Warfare

The final authority in the early Middle Ages was force, and the general atmosphere of the era was one of potential violence. Aggressive vassals frequently made war upon their lords. But warfare was also considered the normal occupation of the nobility, for success offered glory and rich rewards. If successful, warfare might increase a noble's territory; and, if they produced nothing else, wars and raids kept nobles active. To die in battle was an appropriate end for a warrior, much preferred to death in restful circumstances.

Medieval society essentially consisted of three classes: nobles, peasants, and the clergy. Each of these groups had its tasks to perform. The nobles were primarily fighters, belonging to an honored level of society distinct from peasant workers—freemen or serfs. In an age of violence, society obviously accorded prominence to the man with the sword rather than to one with a hoe. The church drew on both the noble and peasant classes for the clergy. Although most higher churchmen were sons of nobles and held land as vassals under the feudal system, the clergy formed a class that was considered separate from the nobility and the peasantry.

homage—A pledge by a vassal to be the lord's "man" (*homo* in Latin means "man"), vowing loyalty and service to his superior. Homage created an unconditional bond between a vassal and his lord.

suzerain—A ruler, or even a state, that exercises political control over a dependent individual or state; a feudal overlord.

The Church and Feudalism

A natural development linked to the decentralization of political power in the early Middle Ages was the involvement of the church in feudalism. The unsettled conditions caused by the Viking and Magyar invasions forced church officials to enter into close relations with the only power able to offer them protection—the feudal nobles in France and Germany. Bishops and abbots often became vassals, receiving fiefs for which they were obligated to provide the usual feudal services. The papacy was also affected; during much of the tenth and early eleventh centuries, the papacy became a political prize sought by Roman nobles.

In spite of its inevitable involvement in politics, the church also sought to influence for the better the behavior of the feudal warrior nobility. In addition to attempting to add Christian virtues to the code of knightly conduct (chivalry), the church sought to impose limitations on feudal warfare. In the eleventh century bishops urged the knights to observe the "Peace of God" and the "Truce of God." The Peace of God banned from the sacraments all those who pillaged sacred places or harmed noncombatants. The Truce of God established "closed seasons" on fighting: from sunset on Wednesday to sunrise on Monday and certain longer periods, such as Lent. These attempts to impose peace, however, were generally unsuccessful.

Chivalry

One of the most interesting legacies of the Middle Ages is its concept of chivalry, a code of conduct that was to govern the behavior of all knights. Early chivalric conduct, emerging during the eleventh century, stressed the warrior virtues that were essential in medieval society: prowess in combat, courage, and loyalty to one's lord and fellow warriors. By the twelfth and thirteenth centuries, many of the rigorous aspects of earlier feudal life had given way to a more peaceful and relaxed lifestyle made possible in a more settled and secure Europe. In a sense, when feudal knights began to occupy themselves with chivalric deeds and gentlemanly pursuits of court life, feudalism itself became a dying institution.

At the height of its development, chivalry was a combination of three elements: warfare, religion, and reverence toward women. It required the knight to fight faithfully for his lord, champion the church, aid the humble, and honor women. Unfortunately, practice often differed from theory. The average knight was more superstitious than religious, and he continued to fight, plunder, and abuse women, especially those of the lower class.

From boyhood, men of the nobility underwent a rigid training for knighthood. At the age of seven, a boy was usually sent to the household of a relative, a friend, or the father's lord. There he became a page, learning the rudiments of manners, hawking, and hunting and undergoing training in the fundamentals of religion. At about 15 or 16, he became a squire and prepared himself seriously for the art of war. He learned to ride a war house with dexterity and to handle a sword, shield, and lance correctly. The squire also waited on his lord and lady at the table and learned music, poetry, and games.

If not already knighted on the battlefield for valor, the squire was usually considered eligible for knighthood at the age of 21. By the twelfth century, the church claimed a role in the ceremony, investing it with impressive symbolism. The future knight took a bath to symbolize purity and washed his weapons before the altar in an all-night vigil, confessing his sins and making a resolution to be a worthy knight. During the solemn Mass that followed, his sword was blessed on the altar by a priest. The climax of the ceremony came when the candidate, kneeling before his lord, received a light blow on the neck or shoulder (the *accolade*). The ceremony was designed to impress upon the knight that he must be virtuous and valiant, loyal to his overlord and his God.

The Lives of the Nobles

Life for the nobles centered around the castle. The earliest of these structures, mere wooden blockhouses, were built in the ninth century. Not until the twelfth and thirteenth centuries were massive castles constructed entirely of stone.

The donjon, or central tower, was the focal point of the castle; it was surrounded by an open space that contained storerooms, workshops, and a chapel. The outside walls of the castle were surrounded by turrets from which arrows, boiling oil, and various missiles might be showered upon attackers. Beyond the wall was the moat, a steep-sided ditch filled with water to deter the enemy. The only entrance to the castle lay across the drawbridge. The portcullis, a heavy iron grating that could be lowered rapidly to protect the gate, was a further barrier against intrusion.

Bodiam Castle, England

Life in the castle was anything but comfortable or ideal. The lord at first dwelt in the donjon, but by the thirteenth century, most had built more spacious quarters. Because the castle was designed for defense, it possessed no large windows, and the rooms were dark and gloomy. The stone walls were bare except for occasional tapestries hung to cut down on drafts and dampness, and a huge fireplace provided the only warmth.

The average noble derived his pleasures primarily from outdoor sports, among which warfare might be included. In peacetime the joust and tournament substituted for actual battle. The joust was a conflict between two armed knights, each equipped with a blunted lance with which one attempted to unseat the other. The tournament was a general melee in which groups of knights attacked each other. Often fierce fighting ensued, with frequent casualties.

The nobles were fond of hunting, and the constant demand for fresh meat afforded a legitimate excuse for galloping over the countryside. Most hunting was done in the nearby forests, but at times an unlucky peasant's crops might be ruined during hunts.

A similar outdoor pastime, which lords, ladies, and even high church dignitaries delighted in, was falconry: hunting with predatory birds. The hawks were reared with great care, and large groups of lords and ladies spent many afternoons eagerly wagering with one another as to whose falcon would bring down the first victim. Nobles often attended Mass with hooded falcons on their wrists.

Indoor amusements included the universally popular diversions of backgammon, dice, and chess. Nights were sometimes enlivened by the entertainment of jesters. At other times, a wandering minstrel entertained his noble hosts in exchange for a bed and a place at the table.

Noble women generally shared the lifestyles of their husbands. Even the nobility had to make the most of life in a crude and often brutal age devoid of many refinements. Like her husband, a medieval woman was expected to devote herself to days of hard work with little time for leisure. Many a noble woman was charged with the administration of the manor and the regulation of its peasants while the lord was otherwise occupied. She may also have presided over the court of the lord's vassals on occasion and generally been charged with the control of the finances for the manor.

The Early Medieval Economy: Manorialism

The economy of the early Middle Ages reflected the localism and self-sufficiency that resulted from the

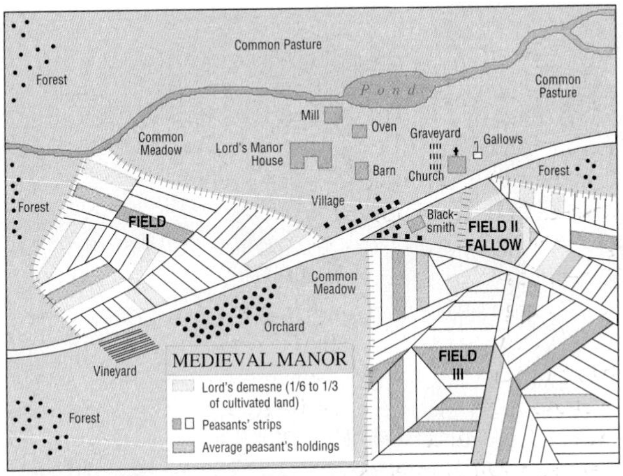

The manor, the self-contained economic unit of early medieval life, operated on a system of reciprocal rights and obligations based on custom. In return for protection, strips of arable land, and the right to use the nonarable common land, the peasant paid dues and worked on the lord's demesne. Under the three-field system, one-third of the land lay fallow so that intensive cultivation did not exhaust the soil.

lack of an effective central government in Europe. The economic and social system based on the manors, the estates held by the nobles, was referred to as *manorialism*.

The manor usually varied in size from one locality to another; a small one might contain only about a dozen households. Since the allotment of land to each family averaged about 30 acres, the smallest manors probably had about 350 acres of land suitable for farming, not counting meadows, woods, wasteland, and the lord's **demesne**—the land reserved for the lord's use alone. A large manor might contain 50 families in a total area of 5000 acres.

The center of the manor was the village, in which the thatched cottages of the peasants were grouped together along one street. Around each cottage was a space large enough for a vegetable patch, chicken yard, haystack, and stable. An important feature of the landscape was the village church, together with the priest's house and the burial ground. The lord's dwelling might be a fortified house or a more modest dwelling.

Distribution of the Land

Every manor contained arable and nonarable land. Part of the arable land was reserved for the lord and was cultivated for him by his serfs; the remainder was held by the villagers. The nonarable land, consisting of meadow, wood, and wasteland, was used in common by the villagers and the lord.

desmesne—Part of the land that is owned by the lord. The demesne is the land upon which the lord built his manor house.

From one-sixth to one-third of the arable land was given over to the lord's demesne. The arable land not held in demesne was allotted among the villagers under the open-field system, in which the fields were subdivided into strips. The strips, each containing about an acre, were separated by narrow paths of uncultivated land. The serf's holding was not all in one plot, for all soil throughout the manor was not equally fertile, and an attempt was made to give each of the villagers land of the same quality. Each tenant was really a shareholder in the village community, not only in the open fields but also in the meadow, pasture, wood, and wastelands.

Wooded land was valuable as an area to graze pigs, the most common animal on the manor. Tenants could also gather dead wood in the forest, but cutting down green wood was prohibited unless authorized by the lord.

Medieval Farming Methods

It is difficult to generalize about agricultural methods, because differences in locality, fertility of soil, crop production, and other factors resulted in a variety of farming approaches. Farming as practiced in northwestern Europe was characterized by some common factors. The implements the peasants used were extremely crude; the plow was a cumbersome instrument with heavy wheels, often requiring as many as eight oxen to pull it. (By the twelfth century the use of plow horses had become common.) Other tools included crude harrows, sickles, beetles for breaking up clods, and flails for threshing.

Inadequate methods of farming soon exhausted the soil. The average yield per acre was only 6 to 8 bushels of wheat, one-fourth the modern yield. In classical times farmers had learned that soil planted continually with one crop rapidly deteriorated. As a counteraction, they employed a two-field system: half of the arable land was planted while the other half lay fallow to recover its fertility. Medieval farmers learned that wheat or rye could be planted in the autumn as well as in the spring. As a result, by the ninth century, they were dividing the land into three fields, with one planted in the fall, another in the spring, and the third left lying fallow. This system not only kept more land in production but also required less plowing in any given year.

Both peasant men and women usually had to endure backbreaking labor. While the men usually attended to the daily manual labor of farming, peasant women cooked, cleaned, made clothing, maintained the animals, milked cows, made butter and cheese, brewed ale and beer, and nurtured the gardens. Women assisted the men during planting and

Both peasant men and women toiled in the fields. Here women reap with sickles, while behind them a man binds the sheaves.

harvesting seasons and with any seasonal or special projects endorsed by the lord. The sexes were treated fairly equally on the lower social levels in the Middle Ages—there was not much difference in the demanding lifestyle all had to endure.

Administration of the Manor

Although the lord might live on one of his manors, each manor was usually administered by such officials as the steward, the bailiff, and the reeve. The steward was the general overseer who supervised the business of all his lord's manors and presided over the manorial court. It was the bailiff's duty to supervise the cultivation of the lord's demesne; collect rents, dues, and fines; and inspect the work done by the free peasants (freemen) and the nonfree peasants (serfs). The reeve was the "foreman" of the villagers, chosen by them and representing their interests.

Freemen often lived on the manor, although they constituted only a small portion of its population. Freemen were not subject to the same demands as the serfs. The freeman did not have to work in the lord's fields himself but could send substitutes. Serfs, however, were bound to the manor and could not leave without the lord's consent. Serfdom was a hereditary status; the children of serfs were attached to the soil, just as their parents were.

The lord of the manor was bound by custom to respect certain rights of his serfs. As long as they paid their dues and services, serfs could not be evicted from their hereditary holdings. Although a serf could not appear in court against his lord or a freeman, he could appeal to the manor court against any of his fellows. To the serfs, the manor was the center of their very existence, but to the lord the manor was essentially a source of income and subsistence.

Life of the Peasants

On the manors of the Middle Ages, the margin between starvation and survival was narrow, and the life of the peasant was not easy. Famines were frequent; warfare was a constant threat; and grasshoppers, locusts, caterpillars, and rats repeatedly destroyed the crops. Men, women, and children alike had to toil long hours in the fields.

Home life offered few comforts. The typical peasant dwelling was a cottage with mud walls, clay floor, and thatched roof. The fire burned on a flat hearthstone in the middle of the floor; unless the peasant was rich enough to afford a chimney, the smoke escaped through a hole in the roof. The window openings had no glass and were stuffed with straw in the winter. Furnishings were meager, usually consisting of a table, a kneading trough for dough, a cupboard, and a bed, often either a heap of straw or a box filled with straw, which served the entire family. Pigs and chickens wandered about the cottage continually; the stable was often under the same roof, next to the family quarters.

The peasants, despite their hard, monotonous life, enjoyed a few pleasures. Wrestling was popular, as were cockfighting, a crude type of football, and fighting with quarterstaves, during which contestants stood an excellent chance of getting their heads bashed in. Dancing, singing, and drinking were popular pastimes, especially on the numerous holy days and festivals promoted by the church.

THE REVIVAL OF TRADE AND TOWNS

▪ *How did the revival of trade and towns impact the feudal and manorial systems?*

Even though manorialism attempted to secure economic self-sufficiency, an increase in trade and commercial activity in Europe was obvious after the tenth century. The opening of the Mediterranean to European trade was instrumental in increasing trade and commerce. In the eleventh century Normans and Italians broke the Muslim hold on commerce in the eastern Mediterranean, and the First Crusade (see p. 275) revived trade with the Near East. Early in the fourteenth century an all-sea route connected the Mediterranean with northern Europe via the Strait of Gibraltar. The old overland route from northern Italy through the Alpine passes to central Europe was also reopened.

Along the main European trade routes, lords set up fairs, where merchants and goods from Italy and northern Europe met. During the twelfth and thirteenth centuries the fairs of Champagne in France functioned as the major clearinghouse for this international trade.

Factors in the Revival of Towns

The resurgence of trade in Europe was a prime cause of the revival of towns; the towns arose because of trade, but they also stimulated trade by providing greater markets and by producing goods for the merchants to sell. Rivers were important in the development of medieval towns; they were natural highways on which articles of commerce could be easily transported.

Another factor contributing to the rise of towns was population growth. In Britain, for example, the population more than tripled between 1066 and 1350. The reasons for this rapid increase in population are varied. The ending of bloody foreign invasions and, in some areas, the stabilization of feudal society were contributing factors. More significant was an increase in food production brought about by the cultivation of wastelands, clearing of forests, and draining of marshes. Medieval towns were not large by modern standards. Before 1200 a European town of 20,000 was considered very large, in contrast to such cities as Baghdad, Cairo, and Constantinople—all of which were well over 50,000 in population.

Merchant and Craft Guilds

In each town the merchants and artisans organized themselves into **guilds**. There were two kinds of guilds: merchant and craft. The merchant guild, whose members were the more prosperous and influential of the town's commercial leaders, existed to ensure a monopoly of trade for its members within a given locality. All foreign merchants were supervised closely and made to pay tolls. Disputes among merchants were settled at the guild court according to its

guilds—An organization of people who practice a similar occupation and come together to protect their own professional standards and social interests.

A guild master judges the work of two craftsmen, a mason and a carpenter.

own legal code. The guilds also tried to ensure that the customers were not cheated: they checked weights and measures and insisted on a standard quality for goods. To allow only a legitimate profit, the guild fixed a "just price," which was fair to both producer and customer.

With the increase of commerce in the towns, artisans and craftspeople in each of the medieval trades—weaving, cobbling, tanning, and so on—began to organize as early as the eleventh century. The result was the craft guild, which differed from the merchant guild in that membership was limited to artisans in one particular craft.

The craft guild also differed from the merchant guild in its recognition of three distinct classes of workers: apprentices, journeymen, and master craftsmen. The apprentice was a youth who lived at the master's house and was taught the trade thoroughly. Although the apprentice received no wages, all his physical needs were supplied. Apprenticeship commonly lasted seven years. When the apprentice's schooling was finished, the youth became a journeyman. He was then eligible to receive wages and to be hired by a master. About age 23, the journeyman sought admission into the guild as a master. To be accepted he had to prove his ability. Some crafts demanded the production of a "master piece," for example, a pair of shoes that the master shoemakers would find acceptable in every way.

Very few women, usually widows of guild members, were allowed admittance into a craft guild. In Paris in 1300, for instance, there were approximately 200 craft guilds, with nearly 80 including members of both sexes. There were, however, about a dozen guilds restricted to female trades, such as the making of garments, silk, and lace.

In spite of restrictions placed on women's full participation in the guild structure, women played a vital role in the functioning of every craft guild. The home remained the center of production in every medieval town, and the wife and daughters of the master craftsman assisted him in every facet of his profession. Not only did they oversee domestic household duties, they also were relied upon to assist in the production of whatever goods the guildsman produced. They would work with the apprentices and the journeymen; if girls were placed as apprentices, they were usually supervised directly by the wife of the guildsman. The wife of the master craftsman was essential to the operation of business; in most cases, she sold merchandise, kept the financial records, and fed and paid the employees. Because of their experience and skills, such women often took over the shop after their husband's death.

The guild's functions stretched beyond business and politics into charitable and social activities. A guild member who fell into poverty received aid from the guild. The guild also provided financial assistance for the burial expense of its members and looked after their dependents. Members attended social meetings in the guildhall and periodically held processions in honor of their patron saints.

The guilds played an important role in local government. Both artisans and merchants were subject to the feudal lord or bishop in whose domain the city stood. Gradually, the citizens of the towns came to resent their overlord's collecting tolls and dues as though they were serfs. The townspeople demanded the privileges of governing themselves—of making their own laws, administering their own justice, levying their own taxes, and issuing their own coinage. The overlord resisted these demands for self-government, but the towns were able to win their independence in various ways.

THE CHURCH IN THE HIGH MIDDLE AGES: 1000–1348

■ *How did the church and its leaders hold such power and influence over European society?*

During the High Middle Ages the church became more extensively involved in the structure of society and, of necessity, more concerned with temporal affairs. Always a spiritual force in Europe, the church grew in political and economic importance through the assertive and able leadership of the papacy and the bureaucracy that served the popes in Rome. By the middle of the fourteenth century, the church had emerged as a dominant political as well as spiritual force in European life.

Monastic Reform

A religious revival, often called the "medieval reformation," began in the tenth century and grew to exercise strong influence in the twelfth and thirteenth centuries. The first manifestation of the revival was the reformed Benedictine order of monks at Cluny (KLOO-nee), in present-day France, founded in 910. The ultimate goal of these Cluniac reformers was to free the church from secular control and subject it to papal authority.

CASE STUDY
Monks and Warriors

The most aggressive advocate of church reform in the High Middle Ages was Pope Gregory VII (1073–1085), who claimed unprecedented power for the papacy. In 1075 Gregory VII formally prohibited lay investiture (bestowal of the symbols of the churchman's office by a secular official such as a king) and

Monastic Reform and the Investiture Controversy

910	Benedictine monastery at Cluny founded
1059	College of Cardinals founded
1073–1085	Pontificate of Gregory VII; struggle over lay investiture
1077	Emperor Henry IV begs forgiveness at Canossa
1091–1153	St. Bernard of Clairvaux, founder of the Cisterian religious order

threatened to excommunicate (expel from the Roman Catholic Church) any layman who performed it. The climax to the struggle occurred in Gregory's clash with the German emperor Henry IV (see p. 282).

Late in the eleventh century a second wave of monastic reform produced several new orders of monks, among which were the Cistercians. The Cistercian movement received its greatest inspiration from the efforts of St. Bernard of Clairvaux (klahr-VOH; 1091–1153). This order's abbeys were intentionally located in solitary places, and their strict discipline emphasized fasts and vigils, manual labor, and a vegetarian diet. Their churches contained neither stained glass nor statues, and Bernard denounced the beautification of churches in general as unnecessary distraction from spiritual dedication.

The Papacy's Zenith: Innocent III

Under Innocent III (1198–1216) a new type of administrator-pope emerged, and papal power reached an unprecedented height. Unlike Gregory VII and other earlier reform popes, who were monks, Innocent and other great popes of the late twelfth and thirteenth centuries were lawyers trained in the newly revived and enlarged church, or canon, law.

The unity and power of the church rested not only on a systematized, uniform religious creed but also on the most highly organized and efficient administrative system in western Europe. The church was far ahead of secular states in developing a system of courts and a body of law. Canon law was based on the Scriptures, the writings of the church fathers, and the decrees of church councils and popes. But the papacy's chief weapons to support its authority were spiritual penalties. The most powerful of these was excommunication. A person who was excommunicated was deprived of the sacraments of the church and in effect condemned to hell should a person die while excommunicated.

Interdict was also a powerful instrument of punishment and control. While excommunication was directed against individuals, interdiction suspended all public worship and withheld most sacraments in the realm of a disobedient subject. Pope Innocent III successfully applied or threatened the interdict 85 times against disobedient kings and princes.

Heresy

Heresy, the belief in doctrines officially condemned by the church, once again became a great concern in the High Middle Ages. Numerous spiritual ideas found new audiences particularly in the newly revived towns, where changing social and spiritual needs went largely ignored by churchmen more traditional in outlook.

For ten years Innocent III tried to combat the growth and popularity of new heretical groups. Unsuccessful, he instigated a crusade against the prosperous and cultured French region of Toulouse, where

Giotto, Pope Innocent III (1198–1216) Approves the Franciscan Rule. *In this predella (part of a series of paintings on the base of an altar) by the Florentine painter Giotto (1266–1337), Innocent III, accompanied by high-ranking churchmen, is shown approving the Franciscan order of monks by giving the approving document to St. Francis (center) and his humble followers. Legend says that the pope had a dream in which he was instructed by God to give approval to the Franciscans.*

the heretics were attacked in 1208 with the approval of the pope. Soon, the original religious motive was lost in a selfish rush to seize the wealth of the accused.

In 1233 a special papal court, the Inquisition, was established to cope with the rising tide of heresy and to bring about religious conformity. Those accused were tried in secret without the aid of legal counsel. Those who confessed and renounced heresy were "reconciled" with the church on performance of penance. Those who did not voluntarily confess could be tortured. If torture failed, the prisoners could be declared heretics and turned over to the secular authorities, usually to be burned at the stake.

Franciscans and Dominicans

As a more positive response to the spread of heresy and the conditions that caused it, Innocent III approved the founding of the Franciscan and Dominican orders of *friars* ("brothers"). Instead of living in remote monasteries, the friars of these orders moved among the people—especially in the quickly growing towns—ministering to their needs, preaching the Gospel, and teaching in the schools.

The Franciscans were founded by St. Francis of Assisi (c. 1182–1226), who rejected riches and emphasized a spiritual message of poverty and Christian simplicity. Love of one's fellow human beings and all God's creatures, even "brother worm," was basic in the Rule of St. Francis.

The second order of friars was founded by St. Dominic (1170–1221), a well-educated Spaniard who had fought the heretics in southern France. There, he decided that to combat the strength and zeal of its opponents, the church should have champions who could preach the Gospel with the dedication of the apostles. The friar-preachers of Dominic's order dedicated themselves to preaching as a means of maintaining the doctrines of the church and of converting heretics.

The enthusiasm and sincerity of the friars in their early years made a profound impact on an age that had grown increasingly critical of the worldliness of the church. But after they took charge of the Inquisition, became professors in the universities, and served in the papal bureaucracy in a variety of capacities, the original simplicity of the spiritual message became lost. Yet their message and zeal had done much to provide the church with moral and intellectual leadership at a time when such leadership was badly needed.

Education and the Origins of Universities

Before the twelfth century, almost all education was under the control and direction of the church. When schools run by monasteries began limiting their admissions to men preparing for church careers, students interested in educations for careers outside the church began to pressure for admittance to schools administered by cathedrals. Although the cathedral schools were still run by churchmen and taught a curriculum centered on religion, these schools steadily expanded their subject offerings to attract students who were pursuing secular careers. Cathedral schools were also more accepting of the new knowledge made available to western Europe by Byzantine and Moslem scholars. Translations of classical works of philosophy (most importantly the works of Aristotle on logic), medicine, and Roman law, accompanied by analyses and commentaries by Islamic scholars, were reintroduced to western Europe. Much of this revived interest can be attributed to an increasing interest in Islamic culture, brought about partially through contacts established during the crusades, and through the revival of international trade. The result was an intellectual revival that invigorated the interest of scholars and students in the cathedral schools.

The development of professional studies in law, medicine, and theology led to the development of universities, which soon eclipsed or expanded the cathedral schools as centers of learning. The word *university* meant a group of persons pursuing a common purpose—a guild of learners, both teachers and students, similar to a craft guild with their masters and apprentices. In the thirteenth century universities had no campuses and little or no money, and the masters taught in rented rooms or religious buildings. If the university was dissatisfied with its treatment by townspeople or the administration, it could move elsewhere. The earliest universities—at Bologna, Paris, and Oxford—were not officially founded, but in time popes or kings granted them and other universities charters of self-government.

Scholasticism

Most medieval scholars did not think of truth as something to be discovered by themselves: They saw it as already existing in the authoritative Christian and a select few non-Christian texts of antiquity. By employing reason (through the use of logic or **dialectic**), scholars of the twelfth and thirteenth centuries attempted to understand and express truth through this process of explanation. Since this task was carried out almost exclusively in the schools, these scholars are known as Scholastics, and the intellectual method they designed is called *Scholasticism*.

Scholasticism reached its highest development in the works of Thomas Aquinas (ah-KWAI-nahs;

dialectic—Logical discussion or logical argumentation.

c. 1225–1274). In his *Summa Theologica* ("summation of theology") this brilliant Dominican philosopher and theologian attempted to reconcile the works of Aristotle with church **dogma**—in other words, the truths obvious through natural reason with the truths held through faith. There can be no real contradiction between the two, he argued, since all truth comes ultimately from God. In case of an unresolved contradiction, however, faith won out because of the possibility of human error in reasoning.

Women and Learning

In the early Middle Ages, and especially after the eighth century, the convents of Europe served as centers of learned activity for a very select group of aristocratic and middle-class women who pursued an intellectual life as well as one devoted to faith. But outside the convents, a life devoted to scholarship was almost impossible for a medieval woman; the church taught that a woman should be either a housewife or a virgin in service to her God. Rarely was it possible for a woman to write, compose, or create works of scholarship or literature in such a society.

But intellectual achievement by some exceptional medieval women was possible. One such remarkable example was Hildegard of Bingen (1098–1179), the leader of a community of Benedictine nuns in Germany. Hildegard wrote a mystical work describing her visions, which she began to receive at the age of 42. She was also a skilled composer and the author of a morality play and several scientific works, which cataloged nearly 500 plants, animals, and stones, assessing their medicinal values.

THE CRUSADES

- *What was the influence of the Crusades on European and world history?*

The Crusades, a series of campaigns that began toward the end of the eleventh century, were a remarkable expression of European self-confidence and expansion in the High Middle Ages. The church was instrumental in beginning these efforts to recapture the Holy Land from Muslim control. But by the conclusion of the crusading era, the church, and the papacy in particular, had suffered a serious loss of prestige, largely because of its actions related to the crusading movement.

DOCUMENT
An Arab-Syrian Discusses the Franks

dogma—A set of beliefs that are accepted as true by a church. A doctrine put forward with authority. From a Greek word meaning "to seem (good)."

For hundreds of years peaceful pilgrims had been traveling from Europe to worship at the sites held to be significant to events described in the New Testament. But during the eleventh century, Christian pilgrims to the Holy Land became especially concerned when the Seljuk Turks, recent and fervent converts to Islam, took over Jerusalem from the more lenient Abbasid Muslims.

In 1095 Pope Urban II proclaimed the First Crusade to establish Christian control of the Holy Land. Preaching at the Council of Clermont in that year, he called on Christians to take up the cross and strive for a cause that promised not merely spiritual rewards but material gain as well. Following Urban's appeal, there was a spontaneous outpouring of religious enthusiasm. The word *crusade* itself is derived from "taking the cross," after the example of Christ.

The Crusading Expeditions

From the end of the eleventh through the thirteenth century, seven major crusades, as well as numerous small expeditions, warred against the Muslims, whom the crusaders called *Saracens*. The First Crusade, composed of feudal nobles from France, parts of Germany, and Norman Italy, marched overland through eastern Europe to Constantinople. Expecting the help of skilled European mercenaries against the Seljuk Turks, the Byzantine emperor Alexius Comnenus was shocked when confronted by a disorderly mob of crusaders and quickly ushered them out of Constantinople to fight the Turks. This First Crusade was the most successful of the seven; with not more than 5000 knights and infantry, it overcame the resistance of the Turks, who were at the time no longer united. It captured Jerusalem and a narrow strip of land stretching from there to Antioch, which became known as the Latin Kingdom of Jerusalem, and over which crusaders and Islamic armies continued to battle until the region was finally retaken by the Muslims in 1291.

IMAGE
Crusaders Besieging a Medieval Castle

The fall of Jerusalem to the Muslims, reinvigorated under the leadership of Salah-al-Din (SAH-lah-ahl-DEEN) or Saladin, the sultan of Egypt and Syria, inspired the Third Crusade in 1189. Its leaders were three of the most famous medieval kings—Frederick Barbarossa of Germany, Richard the Lion-Hearted of England, and Philip Augustus of France. Frederick drowned in Asia Minor, and, after many quarrels with Richard, Philip returned home. Saladin and Richard remained to fight but finally agreed to a three-year truce and free access to Jerusalem for Christian pilgrims.

The Fourth Crusade (1202–1204) was a disaster from both a religious and economic perspective. No kings answered the call of Pope Innocent III for the crusade, and the knights who did participate were unable to pay the Venetians

MAP
The Crusades

the agreed-on transport charges. The Venetians persuaded the crusaders to pay off their debts by capturing the Christian town of Zara on the Adriatic coast, which had long proved a successful rival to Venetian trading interests. Then, in order to eliminate Byzantine commercial competition, the Venetians pressured the crusaders to attack Constantinople itself. After conquering and sacking the great city, the crusaders set up the Latin Empire of Constantinople and forgot about their intentions of recovering the Holy Land.

The thirteenth century produced other crusading failures. The boys and girls participating in the Children's Crusade of 1212 fully expected the waters of the Mediterranean to part and make a path from southern France to the Holy Land, which they would take without fighting; instead, thousands of them were sold into slavery by the merchants of Marseilles. The Seventh Crusade was the last major attempt to regain Jerusalem; the crusading movement ended in 1291 when Acre, the last stronghold of the Christians in the Holy Land, fell to the Muslims.

The Crusader States

Four crusader states, with the kingdom of Jerusalem dominant, were established along the eastern Mediterranean coast as a result of the crusading movement. By the time Jerusalem fell to Saladin in 1187, however, only isolated pockets of Christians remained, surrounded by Muslims. The crusader states were able to cling to survival only through frequent delivery of supplies and manpower from Europe.

The crusader states were defended primarily by three semimonastic military orders: the Templars, or Knights of the Temple, so called because their first headquarters was on the site of the old Temple of Jerusalem; the Hospitalers, or Knights of St. John of Jerusalem, who were founded originally to care for the sick and wounded; and the Teutonic Knights, exclusively a German order. Combining monasticism and militarism, these orders served to protect all pilgrims and to wage perpetual war against the Muslims.

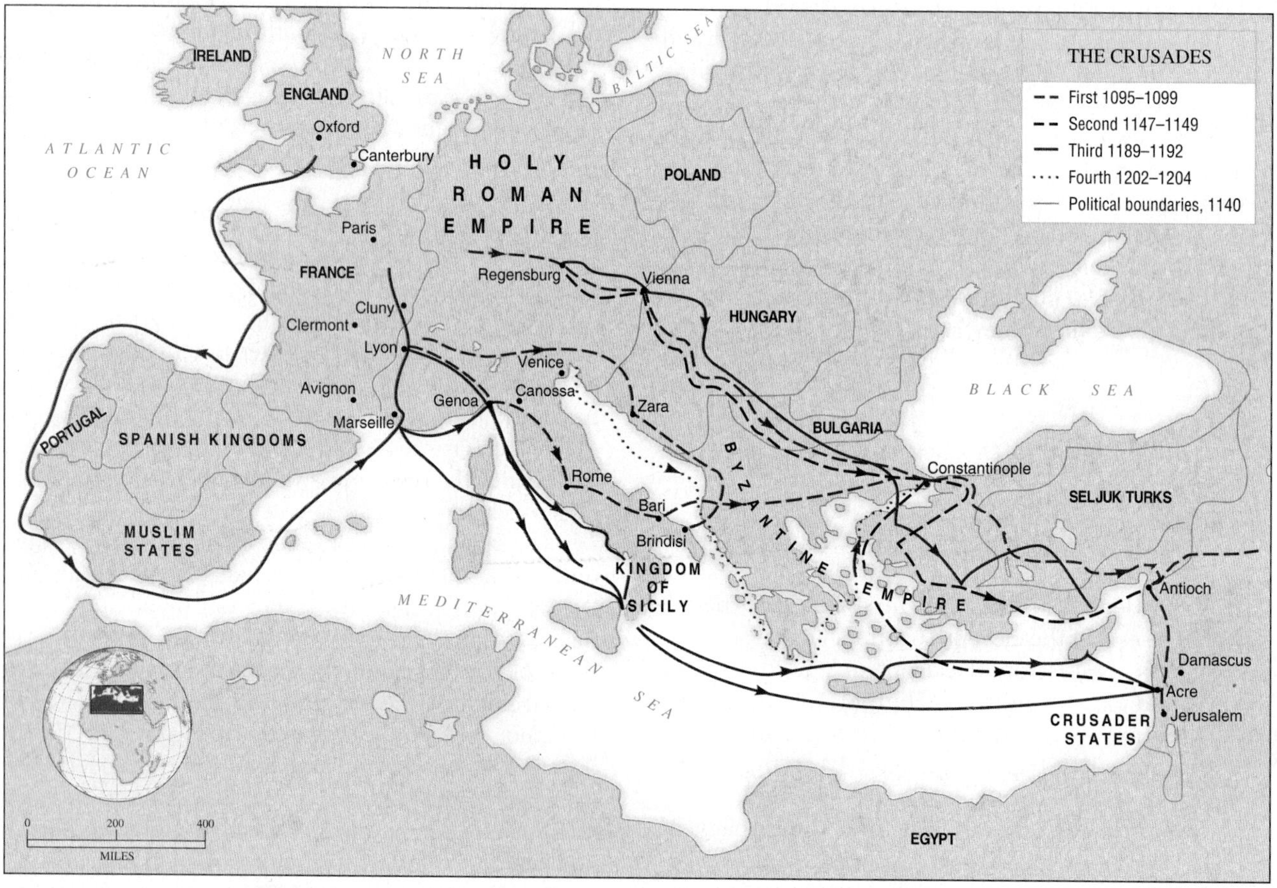

From the eleventh to the thirteenth century, seven major crusades were launched from western Europe for the purpose of taking possession of the Holy Land—portions of the eastern Mediterranean significant to Christians because of their association with the life of Jesus. Although the Crusades eventually failed to annex large amounts of territory for western states, they brought about a broadening perspective and appreciation for Byzantine and Muslim culture on the part of many western Europeans.

Document Muslim and Christian: Two Contemporary Perspectives

This first selection describes the bloody fall of Jerusalem to the Christians during the First Crusade in 1099, as witnessed by the author, a Frankish knight. He writes with the certainty of religious justification for his cause, and cultural superiority to the Muslim enemy.

In comparison to the Frankish evaluations of their Islamic rivals, the second account, from the Muslim perspective, appears in the writings of a Muslim physician who encountered the crusaders and obviously found their culture not as impressive as his own.

During this siege, we suffered so badly from thirst that we sewed up the skins of oxen and buffaloes, and we used to carry water in them for the distance of nearly six miles. We drank the water from these vessels, although it stank, and what with foul water and barley bread we suffered great distress and affliction every day, for the Saracens used to lie in wait for our men by every spring and pool, where they killed them and cut them to pieces; moreover they used to carry off the beasts into their caves and secret places in the rocks.

At last, when the pagans were defeated, our men took many prisoners, both men and women, in the Temple. They killed whom they chose, and whom they chose they saved alive. After this our men rushed round the whole city, seizing the gold and silver, horses and mules, and houses full of all sorts of goods, and they all came rejoicing and weeping from excess of gladness to worship at the Sepulchre of our Savior Jesus, and there they fulfilled their vows to him. Next morning they went cautiously up on to the Temple roof and attacked the Saracens, both men and women, cutting off their heads with drawn swords. No-one has ever seen or heard of such a slaughter of pagans, for they were burned on pyres like pyramids, and no-one save God alone knows how many there were.

From Rosalind Hill, ed., *Gesta Francorum* (London: Nelson, 1962). Reprinted by permission of Oxford University Press, Oxford.

Glory be to Allah, the creator and author of all things! Anyone who is acquainted with what concerns the Franks can only glorify and sanctify Allah the All-Powerful; for he has seen in them animals who are superior in courage and in zeal for fighting but in nothing else, just as beasts are superior in strength and aggressiveness.

I will report some Frankish characteristics and my . . . surprise as to their intelligence. . . .

Among the curiosities of medicine among the Franks, I will tell how the governor of Al-Mounaitira wrote to my uncle to ask him to send him a doctor who would look after some urgent cases. My uncle chose a Christian doctor named Thabit (?). . . . Thabit replied: "They brought before me a knight with an abscess which had formed in his leg and a woman who was wasting away with a consumptive fever. I applied a little plaster to the knight; his abscess opened and took a turn for the better; the woman I forbade certain food and improved her condition." It was at this point that a Frankish doctor came up and said: "This man is incapable of curing them." Then, turning to the knight, he asked, "Which do you prefer, to live with one leg or die with two?" "I would rather live with one leg," the knight answered. "Bring a stalwart knight," said the Frankish doctor, "and a sharp hatchet." Knight and hatchet soon appeared. I was present at the scene. The doctor stretched the patientís leg on a block of wood and then said to the knight, "Strike off his leg with the hatchet; take it off at one blow." Under my eyes the knight aimed a violent blow at it without cutting through the leg. He aimed another blow at the unfortunate man, as a result of which his marrow came from his leg and the knight died instantly. As for the woman, the doctor examined her and said, "She is a woman in whose head there is a devil who has taken possession of her. Shave off her hair!" His prescription was carried out, and like her fellows, she began once again to eat garlic and mustard. Her consumption became worse. The doctor then said, "It is because the devil has entered her head." Taking a razor, the doctor cut open her head in the shape of a cross and scraped away the skin in the centre so deeply that her very bones were showing. He then rubbed the head with salt. In her turn, the woman died instantly. After having asked them whether my services were still required and obtained an answer in the negative, I came back, having learnt to know what I had formerly been ignorant of about their medicine.

—*Usamah Ibn-Munqidh*

From G. R. Potter, trans., *The Autobiography of Ousama (1095–1188)* (London: George Routledge and Sons, 1929), pp. 172–175, 181–182, in Perry M. Rogers, *Aspects of Western Civilization*, Vol. I, 4th ed. (Prentice Hall, 2000), pp. 311–312.

Questions to Consider

1. What seem to be the most significant obstacles to cultural understanding and tolerance in these two accounts of contact between Christian and Muslim cultures?
2. How might we, as modern analysts of this medieval clash of cultures, misinterpret the sentiments expressed in these two documents? What insights might be gained from a comparison of these two viewpoints?

Significance of the Crusades

Even though the Crusades failed to achieve their permanent objective, they were much more than mere military adventures. Much of the crusading fervor spilled over into the Christian attacks against the Muslims in Spain and the Slavs in eastern Europe. The Crusades crucially weakened the Byzantine Empire and accelerated its fall. Although the early Crusades strengthened the moral leadership of the papacy in Europe, the misadventures of the later Crusades, together with the church's preaching of Crusades against Christian heretics and political opponents, weakened both the crusading ideal and respect for the papacy.

But contact with the East through the crusading movement widened the scope of many Europeans, ended their isolation, and exposed them to a civilization with much within it to be admired. The Crusades did influence the reopening of the eastern Mediterranean to Western commerce, a factor that in itself had an effect on the revival of cities and the emergence of a money economy in the West.

THE DEVELOPMENT OF EUROPEAN STATES: 1000–1348

- *How successful were European monarchs in establishing authority over their territories?*

The first three centuries of the Later Middle Ages in Europe are often described as the High Middle Ages, since many experts see in this period the full development of the earlier culture of post-Roman Europe. In this era, European monarchies struggled to emerge from the decentralized feudal organization of an earlier time. The church rose to great heights of power and authority. The revival of trade and the rebirth of towns altered the economy of Europe and offered an alternative to manorialism. And this period gave birth to developments in art, architecture, and literature that stand as some of the most significant achievements in European civilization.

The High Middle Ages witnessed the efforts of kings to assert themselves once again as forceful rulers of their lands. As we have seen, feudalism was a system founded on the decentralization of authority; the king was often no more than a figurehead in the feudal order. Now, the monarchs of most European states gradually increased their powers at the expense of their feudal nobility. Through such efforts, several of which took centuries to bear results, national monarchies began to take form on the European continent.

The Capetians and the Beginnings of France

In France, by the beginning of the tenth century, more than 30 great feudal princes were vassals of the king, but they gave him little or no support. When the last Carolingian monarch died in 987, the nobles elected one of their number, Hugh Capet (kah-PAY), count of Paris, as successor. The territory that Hugh Capet (987–996) actually controlled was a small feudal county, the Île-de-France (EEL-duh-FRAHNS), extending from Paris to Orléans. These royal lands were surrounded by many large duchies and counties, such as Flanders, Normandy, Anjou, and Champagne, which were fiercely independent.

The major accomplishment of the first four Capetian (kah-PEE-shi-ahn) kings was their success at keeping the French crown within their own family and at slowly expanding their influence, largely through marriage alliances and the efficiency of the royal courts. With the support of the church, the Capetians cleverly arranged for the election and coronation of their heirs. For 300 years the House of Capet never lacked a male heir.

Philip II Augustus

The first great expansion of the royal domain was the work of Philip II Augustus (1180–1223). Philip's great ambition was to seize from the English kings the vast territory they held in France. Philip took Normandy, Maine, Anjou, and Touraine from the English, and by doing so, he tripled the size of the monarchy's land holdings.

After the brief reign of Philip II's son Louis VIII, France came under the rule of Louis IX (1226–1270), better known as St. Louis. Louis's ideal was to rule justly, and in so doing, he became one of the most beloved kings of France. The king believed himself responsible only to God, who had put him on the throne to lead his people out of a life of sin. Just, sympathetic, and peace-loving, Louis IX convinced his subjects that the monarchy was the most important agency for ensuring their happiness and well-being.

Nation-Building in France

987–996	Reign of Hugh Capet
1108–1137	Reign of Louis VI
1180–1223	Reign of Philip II Augustus
1226–1270	Reign of Louis IX
1285–1314	Reign of Philip IV, the Fair

Height of Capetian Rule Under Philip IV

The reign of Philip IV, known as Philip the Fair (1285–1314), culminated three centuries of Capetian rule. The opposite of his saintly grandfather, Philip was a man of violence and cunning, tireless in his effort to make the monarchy supreme in France. Aware that anti-Semitism was growing in Europe in the wake of the Crusades, he expelled the Jews from France and confiscated their possessions.

Philip's need for money also brought him into conflict with the last great medieval pope. Boniface VIII refused to allow Philip to tax the French clergy and made sweeping claims to supremacy over secular powers. But Philip IV would not tolerate papal interference, and the result was the humiliation of Boniface (see Chapter 14), a blow from which the influence of the medieval papacy never recovered. In domestic affairs, the real importance of Philip's reign lay in the king's ability to increase the power and improve the organization of the royal government. Philip's astute civil servants, recruited mainly from the middle class, sought to make the power of the monarch absolute.

DOCUMENT
Summa de legibus

Philip enlarged his feudal council to include representatives of the third "estate" or class, the townspeople. This Estates-General of nobles, clergy, and burghers was used to obtain popular support for Philip's policies, including the announcement of new taxes. Philip did not ask the Estates-General's consent for his tax measures; thus, this body did not acquire a role in decisions affecting taxation. By the middle of the fourteenth century, France was well organized, unified in support of a strong monarch, and ready to assert itself as a power on the continent.

England to 1348

Most of England in 1000 was ruled by an Anglo-Saxon monarchy threatened by conquest from the Danish king Canute (ka-NOOT). In 1016 Canute conquered the island and ruled it until his death in 1035, when England returned to an Anglo-Saxon monarchy that was challenged both by the Danes and by William, the duke of Normandy, who claimed the throne on a questionable hereditary right.

William and his army of 5000 men crossed the English Channel to enforce his claim to the throne. In 1066 the duke's mounted knights defeated the English infantry at Hastings, and William became king of England (1066–1087), where he began to introduce the Norman, feudal style of administration. The new king retained some land as his royal domain and granted the remainder as fiefs to royal vassals called *tenants-in-chief*. In return for their fiefs, the tenants-in-chief provided William with a number of knights to serve in his royal army. From all the landholders in England, regardless of whether they were his immediate vassals, William exacted an oath that they would "be faithful to him against all

The Bayeux tapestry, a woolen embroidery on linen, dates from the eleventh century. Over 230 feet long, it depicts the events in the Norman conquest of England in 1066, accompanied by a commentary in Latin and surrounded by a decorative border portraying scenes from fables and everyday life.

other men." Both tenants-in-chief and lesser vassals owed their first allegiance to William.

Henry II

William was succeeded by a number of average or ineffectual rulers, but the monarchy was strengthened by Henry II (1154–1189), the founder of the Plantagenet (plahn-TAH-jehn-et), or Angevin, dynasty. As a result of his inheritance (Normandy and Anjou) and his marriage to Eleanor of Aquitaine (AH-kwi-tayn), the richest heiress in France, Henry's possessions extended from Scotland to the Pyrenees. Henry's great military skill and restless energy were important assets to his reign. He quickly began rebuilding the power of the monarchy in England.

Henry's chief contribution to the development of the English monarchy was to increase the jurisdiction of the royal courts at the expense of the feudal courts. Henry's courts also used the jury system to settle private lawsuits; circuit judges handed down quick decisions based on evidence sworn to by a jury of men selected because they were acquainted with the facts of the case. His judicial reforms stimulated the growth of the common law, one of the most important factors in unifying the English people; the decisions of the royal justices became the basis for future decisions made in the king's courts and became the law common to all English people.

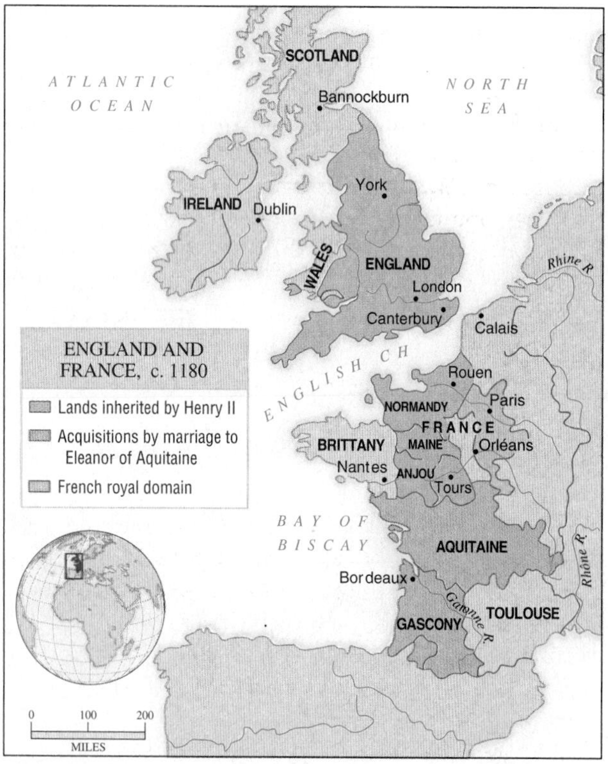

Henry II's claims to lands in France threatened to absorb the kingdom of France. Note the sizable territory claimed by the English king through his marriage to Eleanor of Aquitaine, once wife of the French king. Though it took hundreds of years, the French eventually gained control of all of the French territories claimed by England.

Thomas à Becket

Although Henry strengthened the royal courts, he was not as successful in regulating the church courts. When he appointed his trusted friend Thomas à Becket archbishop of Canterbury, the king assumed that Becket could easily be persuaded to cooperate, but the new archbishop proved stubbornly independent in upholding the authority of the church courts over the king's. After a number of disagreements in which Becket defended the independence of the English church from royal authority, Henry was reputed to have remarked that he would be relieved if someone would rid England of the troublesome Becket. Responding to this angry remark, four knights went to Canterbury and murdered Becket before the high altar of the cathedral. Popular outrage over this murder destroyed Henry's chances of reducing the power of the church courts.

The Successors of Henry II

Henry's many accomplishments were marred by the mistakes of his successors. Richard the Lion-Hearted (1189–1199) spent only five months of his ten-year reign in Britain, which he regarded as a source of money for his overseas adventures. Richard's successor, his brother John (1199–1216), was an inept and cruel ruler whose unscrupulousness cost him the support of his barons, at the time he needed them most, in his struggles with the two ablest men of the age, Philip II of France and Pope Innocent III. As feudal overlord of John's possessions in France, Philip declared John an unfaithful vassal and his claims to lands in France unwarranted. He also became involved in a struggle with Innocent III that ended in John's complete surrender.

In the meantime, the king alienated the British barons, who rebelled and in 1215 forced him to agree to the Magna Carta, a document that bound the king to observe all feudal rights and privileges. Although in later centuries people looked back on the Magna Carta as one of the most important documents in the history of political freedom, to the English nobility of John's time, the Magna Carta did not appear to break any new constitutional ground. It was essentially a feudal agreement between the barons and the king, the aristocracy and the monarchy. However, two great principles were contained in the charter: The law is above the king, and the king can be compelled by force to obey the law of the land.

A detail of the Carrow Psalter depicts the murder of Thomas à Becket by the knights of Henry II in Canterbury Cathedral. One knight has broken his sword over the archbishop's head.

The Origins of Parliament

The French-speaking Normans commonly used the word *parlement* (from *parler,* "to speak") for the great council. Anglicized as *parliament,* the term was used interchangeably with *great council* and *Curia Regis.*

Nation-Building in England

871–899	Reign of Alfred the Great of Wessex
1016–1035	Reign of Canute
1066	Battle of Hastings
1066–1087	Reign of William the Conqueror
1154–1189	Henry II begins Plantagenet dynasty
1189–1199	Reign of Richard I, the Lion-Hearted
1199–1216	Reign of John I
1215	Magna Carta
1272–1307	Reign of Edward I

Modern historians, however, generally apply the term to the great council only after 1265, when its membership was radically enlarged. Parliament first became truly influential during the reign of Edward I (1272–1307), one of England's most outstanding monarchs. Beginning with the so-called Model Parliament of 1295, Edward followed the pattern of summoning representatives of shires and towns to meetings of the great council. In calling parliaments, Edward had no intention of making any concession to popular government; rather, he hoped to build popular consensus to support his own policies.

Early in the fourteenth century the representatives of the knights and the townsmen, called the Commons, adopted the practice of meeting separately from the lords. This resulted in the division of Parliament into what came to be called the House of Commons and the House of Lords. Parliament, particularly the Commons, soon discovered its power as a major source of revenue for the king. It gradually became the custom for Parliament to exercise this power by withholding its financial grants until the king had redressed grievances, made known by petitions. Parliament also presented petitions to the king with the request that they be recognized as statutes (laws drawn up by the king and his council and confirmed in Parliament). Gradually, Parliament assumed the right to initiate legislation through petition.

Edward I was the first English king with the goal of being master of the whole island of Great Britain—Wales, Scotland, and England. In 1284, after a five-year struggle, English law and administration were imposed on Wales, and numerous attempts were made to conquer the Scots, who continued to offer Edward serious resistance up to the time of his death. By the time of Edward's death in 1307, England was efficiently organized under a strong monarchy and ready to assert itself in the quest for power on the continent.

Spain to 1348

Unification in Spain took a different course from that in either France or England. Customary rivalry between the Christian feudal nobles and royal authority was complicated by another element: religious fervor. Unification of Christian Spain was not thought possible without the expulsion of the Muslims, with their non-Christian religion and culture.

During the long struggle to drive the Muslims from Spain, patriotism blended with fierce religious devotion. This movement became known as the *Reconquista* (ree-kon-KEE-stah)—the reconquest of Spain from Muslim control. As early as the ninth century, northern Spain became committed to a religious effort to drive all Muslims out of territory Christian Spaniards considered theirs. In the early thirteenth century they captured first Cordova and Seville. The conquest of Seville effectively doubled the territory of the Spanish kingdom. From the end of the thirteenth century, when the Reconquista slowed, until the latter part of the fifteenth century, Muslim political control was confined to Granada. Until the fifteenth century, the Christian victors usually allowed their new Muslim subjects to practice their own religion and traditions. Muslim traders and artisans were protected because of their economic value, and Muslim culture—art in particular—influenced Christian designs and preferences.

Disunity in Germany and Italy

When the last Carolingian ruler of the kingdom of the East Franks died in 911, the great German dukes elected the weakest of their number to hold the title of king. But an exceptionally strong ruler inherited the throne in 936—Otto the Great (936–973), duke of Saxony and founder of the Saxon dynasty of kings. Otto attempted to control the great dukes by appointing his own relatives and favorites as their rulers. Through alliance with the church, he constructed a stronger German monarchy. Otto himself appointed German bishops and abbots, a practice known as lay investiture; since their offices were not hereditary, he expected that their first obedience was to the king.

Ivory plaque of Christ and the Emporer Otto I (962–968). This ivory carving shows Christ on a throne and in the process of blessing a model of a church presented to him by the German emporer Otto I (left) and a number of saints (right), including St. Peter, who holds his symbolic keys to the kingdom of heaven. The artist was probably influenced by both Carolingian and Byzantine artistic traditions.

Otto the Great wanted to establish a German empire, modeled after Roman and Carolingian examples. The conquest and incorporation of the Italian peninsula into that empire were Otto's primary objectives. He proclaimed himself king of Italy, and in 962 he was crowned emperor by the pope. His empire later became known as the Holy Roman Empire.

The Saxon rulers were the most powerful in Europe. They had permanently halted Magyar advances and, by utilizing the German church as an ally, reduced feudal fragmentation in their homeland. They also fostered economic progress. German eastward expansion had begun, and the Alpine passes had been freed from Muslim control and made safe for Italian merchants.

The Salian Emperors

The Saxon kings were succeeded by the Salian dynasty (1024–1125), whose members also tried to establish a centralized monarchy. Under the emperor Henry IV (1056–1106) the monarchy reached the height of its power, but it also experienced a major reverse. The revival of a powerful papacy led to a bitter conflict with Henry, centering on the king's right to appoint church officials who were also his most loyal supporters (lay investiture). This disagreement between state and church culminated in Henry's begging the pope's forgiveness at Canossa in 1077. This conflict, the Investiture Controversy, resulted in the loss of the monarchy's major sources of strength: the loyalty of the German church, now transferred to the papacy; and the support of the great nobles, now openly rebellious and insistent on their "inborn rights."

The second emperor of the new Hohenstaufen (HOH-hen-stahw-fen) dynasty, Frederick I Barbarossa ("Redbeard"), who ruled from 1152 to 1190, also sought to force the great nobles to acknowledge his overlordship. To maintain his hold over Germany, Frederick needed the resources of Italy. But encouraged by the papacy, the cities of northern Italy had joined together in the Lombard League to resist him. Frederick spent about 25 years fighting intermittently in Italy, but the final result was failure: opposition from the popes and the Lombard League was too strong. Frederick did, however, succeed in marrying his son to the heiress of the throne of the kingdom of Naples and Sicily.

The Holy Roman Empire

962	Otto the Great crowned emperor by the pope
1056–1106	Reign of Henry IV
1152–1190	Frederick I Barbarossa begins Hohenstaufen dynasty
1212–1250	Reign of Frederick II

Barbarossa's grandson, Frederick II (1212–1250), was a remarkable individual. Orphaned at an early age, Frederick was brought up as the ward of Innocent III, the most powerful medieval pope. With the pope's support, Frederick was elected emperor in 1215, one year before Innocent's death. Frederick sacrificed Germany in his efforts to unite Italy under his rule. He transferred crown lands and royal rights to the German princes in order to win their support for his Italian wars. Born in Sicily, he remained devoted to the southern part of his empire. He shaped his kingdom there into a vibrant state. Administered by paid officials who were trained at the University of Naples, which he founded for that purpose, his kingdom was the most centralized and efficiently administered in Europe.

After Frederick's death in 1250, the Holy Roman Empire never again achieved the brilliance it had once enjoyed. Later emperors usually did not try to interfere in Italian affairs, and they ceased going to Rome to receive the imperial crown from the pope. In German affairs the emperors no longer even attempted to assert their authority over the increasingly powerful nobles. By the middle of the fourteenth century Germany was hopelessly divided into more than two hundred political units, each striving for separation from the control of the other.

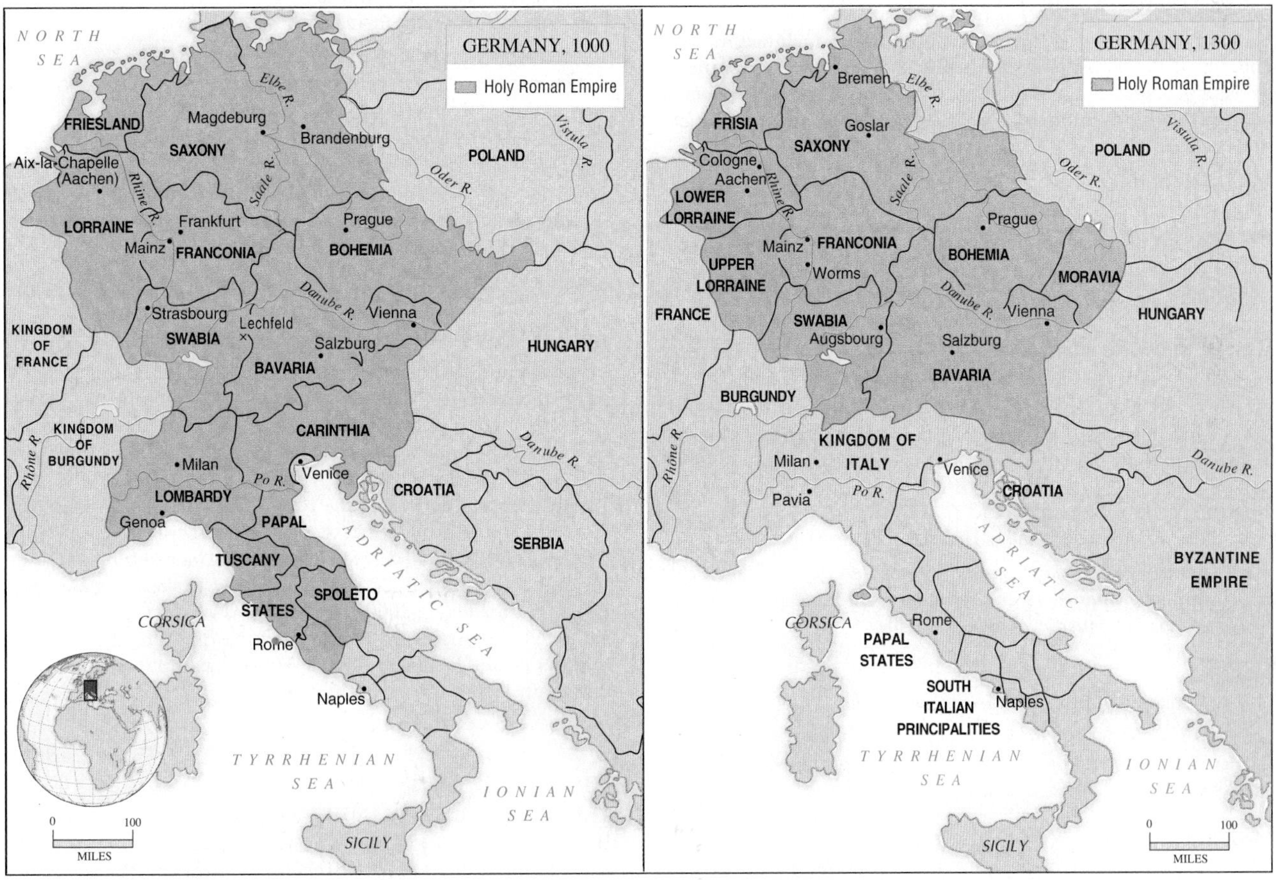

In 962, Otto the Great was crowned as Holy Roman Emperor by the pope. The dreams of recreating a Christian empire to rival the achievements of ancient Rome were never to be realized. Resistance from powerful German nobles and forceful opposition from the northern Italian communes continually frustrated the ambitions of Otto and his successors, so that the Holy Roman Empire was never able to achieve political centralization.

CONCLUSION

This chapter discusses almost one thousand years of European history: from the collapse of Roman political and economic organization, the migrations of new peoples into the old empire, and the growth in influence of a new religion and culture, to the emergence of strong European states under the leadership of ambitious monarchs. Most of the centuries that we call the European Middle Ages were times typified by conservatism and preservation. Political and economic disunity gave rise to institutions that sought to provide protection and security to all segments of society. That quest for security and stability was also evident in early European Christianity, which rejected the cultural heritage of the ancient world in return for a uniform orthodoxy of belief which sought to provide stability in troubled times. But by the eleventh century European self-imposed isolation and the quest for changelessness was challenged on several fronts. Monarchs disrupted the feudal order by setting in motion the drive toward creation of the modern nation-state. The growth of towns and revival of trade brought about new economic and social priorities. The church, once the partner of the state and the unchallenged authority in matters of spirituality and culture, came under increasing examination and challenge. The unique circumstances brought about in Europe by the collapse of Rome, the rise of Christianity, and the Germanic migrations had produced a society unlike any other in world history—one that would emerge by the fourteenth century as vibrant, creative, aggressive, and about to take a more active part in events on a world stage.

Suggestions for Web Browsing

You can obtain more information about topics included in this chapter at the websites listed below. See also the companion website that accompanies this text, **http://www.ablongman.com/brummett**, which contains an online study guide and additional resources.

Medieval Studies
http://labyrinth.georgetown.edu/

The Labyrinth project at Georgetown University offers numerous links categorized by national cultures and by artistic genre.

Women in the Middle Ages
http://info-center.ccit.arizona.edu/~ws/ws200/fall97/grp7/grp7.htm

An excellent site for examining the many activities and responsibilities of medieval women, from peasants to nobility.

Internet Medieval Sourcebook
http://www.fordham.edu/halsall/sbook.html

Extremely helpful site containing original course materials from medieval authors and secondary sources dealing with a large variety of medieval subjects.

Middle Ages
http://www.learner.org/exhibits/middleages/

This site, under the direction of the Annenberg/CBS Project, features information and exhibits illustrating what daily life was really like during the Middle Ages.

Medieval Women
http://labyrinth.georgetown.edu/display.cfm?Action=View&Category=Women

Site details the individual lives and works of medieval women, including Hildegard of Bingen; women rulers and creators; and the impact of the Crusades on women, in addition to numerous general resources.

Women Writers of the Middle Ages
http://lib.rochester.edu/camelot/womenbib.htm

Site offers bibliographies of primary and secondary sources by and about medieval women writers.

World of the Vikings
http://www.worldofthevikings.com/

This well-indexed site provides links to almost everything there is to know about these medieval seafarers—their everyday life, their travels, their influence.

Literature and Film

An excellent new edition of the Beowulf epic is Seamus Heaney, ed., *Beowulf: A New Verse Translation* (W. W. Norton, 2001). Outstanding video presentations on the Middle Ages are *Charlemagne* (2000; 5 tapes, Acorn Media); *Landmarks of Western Art: The Medieval World*, Vol. I (Kultur Video, 1999); *The Vikings* (Nova, 2000); *Just the Facts—The Middle Ages* (Goldhil Home Media, 2001); *Music of the Middle Ages* (Timeless Multimedia, 1994); *Sienna: Chronicle of a Medieval Commune* (Home Vision Entertainment, 2000); *Living in the Past: Life in Medieval Times* (Kultur Video, 2000); and *Medieval Warfare* (2000; 3 tapes, Kultur Video). An award-winning feature film set in France during this period is *The Return of Martin Guerre* (Nelson Entertainment, 1982).

Suggestions for Reading

Three excellent surveys of the early Middle Ages are Robert Bartlett, *The Making of Europe: Conquest, Colonization, and Cultural Change, 950–1350* (Princeton University Press, 1993); Rosamond McKitterick, ed., *The Early Middle Ages: Europe 400–1000* (Oxford University Press, 2001); and Richard W. Southern, *The Making of the Middle Ages* (Yale University Press, 1992). For economic and social history, see Werner Roesener, *Peasants in the Middle Ages* (Polity Press, 1996) and Frances Gies and Joseph Gies, *Women in the Middle Ages* (Perennial, 1991), *Life in a Medieval Village* (HarperPerennial, 1991), and *Marriage and Family in the Middle Ages* (HarperPerennial, 1989). For the history of the church, see Peter Brown et al., *The Rise of Western Christendom*, 2nd ed. (Blackwell, 2003), and Jaroslav Pelikan, *The Growth of Medieval Theology*, Vol. 3: The Christian Tradition (University of Chicago Press, 1978), and Michael Haren, *Medieval Thought* (Dublin University Press, 1992). On the Crusades, see Jonathan Riley-Smith, ed., *The Oxford History of the Crusades* (Oxford University Press, 1997), and Malcolm Billings, *The Cross and the Crescent* (Sterling, 1987). John Burrow, *The Ages of Man: A Study in Medieval Writing and Thought* (Oxford University Press, 1989) is an outstanding review of medieval literature.

CHAPTER

10

Culture, Power, and Trade in the Era of Asian Hegemony, 220–1350

CHAPTER CONTENTS

300

c. 300 Yamato clan emerges in central Japan

320–515 Gupta dynasty in India

380s Buddhism adopted in Korea

400

439–534 Northern Wei dynasty in China

500

515 Huna seize northwestern India

600

606–647 Reign of Harsha in north India

618–907 Tang dynasty in China

676 Tang driven out of Korea; Silla unifies Korea

700

710–784 Nara period in Japan

755–763 An Lushan Rebellion in China

788–820 Hindu philosopher Shankara

794–1181 Heian period in Japan

900

960–1279 Song dynasty in China

c. 978–1016 Murasaki Shikibu, writer of *The Tale of Genji*

1100

1130–1200 Zhu Xi, Neo-Confucian scholar in China

1185 Minamoto clan establishes Kamakura Shogunate in Japan

1200

1206 Beginning of Delhi Sultanate in India; Chinggis Khan launches invasions that create Mongol Empire

1279–1368 Yuan dynasty in China

Asia served as an incubator and transmitter of cultures and religions with global reach from 220 to 1350. As empires consolidated and expanded their boundaries, trade and commerce accompanied cultural diffusion. Human cultures had long migrated globally, but during this long millennium, the pace of international contacts accelerated. Religions, philosophies, and arts deepened their roots in areas that had spawned them, and at the same time, new ideas spread throughout the region.

The first half millennium was, in some ways, Asia's Buddhist Age. In South Asia, Hinduism, and in East Asia, Daoism and Confucianism as well as indigenous religions continued to play important roles. But a Buddhist traveler from East Asia would find co-religionists in lands with remarkably distinct cultures. Buddhism was spread by both missionary activity and commercial activity along the Silk Roads. The second half of the millennium was likewise influenced by a global religion—Islam. South and Southeast Asian rulers either adopted Islam or resisted it, and power and trade networks were influenced by Islamic missionary and commercial activities. China and Northeast Asia felt the impact of nomadic cultures throughout the millennium, and in the twelfth and thirteenth centuries much of East and Central Asia was integrated into a trade and power network controlled by originally nomadic Mongols. Disease—bubonic plague—took advantage of these networks to spread the hand of death throughout Eurasia in the mid-fourteenth century, and ironically, fatally weakened the Mongols, whose dominance in China created fourteenth-century globalism. While Asian power and culture were in many ways hegemonic until that time and Asia would continue to grow and dominate world trade until the eighteenth century, the door was open to the rise of new sites of power, particularly in Europe, during the next few hundred years.

Each Asian civilization produced significant contributions to the world's common culture. India made remarkable advances in mathematics, medicine, chemistry, textile production, and literature, and Buddhism continued its dramatic spread to East and Southeast Asia. China excelled in political organization, scholarship, and the arts, and at the same time produced such revolutionary technical inventions as printing, gunpowder, and the mariner's compass. Maritime trade flourished as Arab, Jewish, and Indian traders crisscrossed the Indian Ocean to the west of the subcontinent, while Indian and Southeast Asian traders plied the waters to the east as far as China and Japan.

Growth in the old Asian centers led naturally toward outward cultural diffusion and a varied exchange of goods, philosophies, literatures, and fashions with bordering civilizations. In Southeast Asia these arose from increasing contacts with India and China through trade, missionary efforts, colonizing, and conquest. First Korea, and then Japan, imported cultural bases from China. Similarly, nomads of Central Asia—Turks, Uighurs (WEE-ghers), Mongols, and numerous other steppe peoples—engaged in a vigorous exchange with China and India (often assimilating the cultural patterns of those civilizations) as merchants, subjects, or conquerors. The conquest of China by the Mongols during the thirteenth and fourteenth centuries facilitated the passing of those influences to the peoples of the Middle East and Europe. Nor was the diffusion of cultural influences and material culture a one-way process. The great cultural centers of Persia, India, and China adapted dress styles, military tactics, literature, and the hardy Mongol horse from the Central Asians.

INDIA IN THE CLASSICAL AND MEDIEVAL ERAS

- *What factors contributed to a diversity of religions and cultures in classical and medieval India?*

The Classical Age

The political fragmentation of India during the 500 years from 184 B.C.E. to 320 C.E. permitted the spread of new Indian religions and the introduction of ideas and technologies from east and west of India. But it was not until the reunification of India's north under the Guptas that the classical age of Hindu culture emerged. India's cultural renaissance took root in the Gupta dynasty (320–500) and attempted to recapture the territorial and cultural grandeur of the Mauryas (MOW-ree-yahs). Its monarchs gained control over northern India while fostering traditional religions, Sanskrit literature, and indigenous art. Hindu and Buddhist culture also spread widely throughout Southeast Asia in this period.

The Gupta state began its rise in 320 with the accession to power of Chandra Gupta I (not related to his earlier Mauryan namesake). His son Samudra Gupta (r. 335–375) and grandson Chandra Gupta II (r. 375–415) were successful conquerors, extending the boundaries of an original petty state in Maghada (mah-GAH-dah) until it included most of northern India, from the Himalayas to the Narmada River and east to west from sea to sea. Within this domain the Gupta monarchs developed a political structure along ancient Mauryan lines, with provincial governors, district officials, state-controlled industries, and an imperial secret service. This centralized system, however, was effective only on royal lands, which were much less extensive than in Mauryan times. With a smaller bureaucracy, the Gupta rulers depended on local authorities and communal institutions. Peasants were obligated to pay as taxes to the state one-fourth of their harvest, one-fiftieth of their cattle and gold, one-sixth of their wealth in meat, fruit, honey and trees, and a day of labor per month for road repair or irrigation maintenance. Despite such high taxes, Indian farmers appeared in reports by foreign visitors to successfully produce an abundance of food. Artisans were organized in guilds which negotiated relationships with state and religious institutions. Military forces were raised by feudal levy.

Gupta India

320	Accession of Chandra Gupta I
c. 335–375	Reign of Samudra Gupta
c. 376–414	Reign of Chandra Gupta II
515	Huna (Huns) seize northwest India; Gupta Empire collapses

Marriage alliances aided the Guptas' rise to power. Chandra Gupta I married a princess from the powerful Licchavi (leek-CHAH-vee) clan; his coins show the king and his queen, Kumaradevi (koo-MAH-rah-DEH-vee), on one side and a lion with his queen's clan name on the other. Chandra Gupta II gave his daughter, Prabhavati (prah-bah-VAH-tee) Gupta, in marriage to Rudrasena II (roo-DRAH-seh-nah), king of the powerful Vakataka dynasty in central India. Rudrasena died after a short reign, and his wife then took control of his kingdom for about 20 years as regent for her minor sons. The two kingdoms maintained close ties even after her death.

Peace and stable government under the later Guptas increased agricultural productivity and foreign trade. Commerce with Rome brought a great influx of gold and silver as well as Arabian horses into the Gupta Empire in exchange for Indian textiles, jewels, spices, perfumes, and wood. In fact, Rome's net deficit in gold exports led to the weakening of its economy. Indian traders were also active in Southeast Asia, particularly in Burma, Vietnam, and Cambodia, where they brought not only new products but also Buddhist culture. India's resulting prosperity was reflected in great public and religious buildings and in the luxuries of the elite, particularly at the Gupta court.

Although the Gupta rulers generally favored Hinduism, they practiced religious pluralism, patronizing and building temples for Hindus, Buddhists, and Jains. The Brahmans provided the Guptas with religious legitimacy, and the Guptas rewarded them with significant grants of land. Hinduism dominated the subcontinent. The Hindu revival of this period brought a great upsurge of devotion to Vishnu, Shiva, and Durga. This religious fervor was reflected in a series of religious books, the *Puranas,* which emphasized the compassion of the personal gods. The *Puranas* are a collection of myths, philosophical dialogues, ritual prescriptions, and dynastic genealogies gathered in the third and fourth centuries. The tales of the gods were popular. Among their legends, for example, is a recounting of the deeds of the goddess Durga and her fight against the buffalo demon. By promoting the devotional Hinduism reflected in these tales, the Gupta monarchs gained great favor among all classes of their subjects.

The *Bhagavad-Gita* (BAH-gah-vahd-GHEE-tah; *Song of the Blessed One*), written during this time, assured Hindus that salvation was possible, regardless of one's station in life. **Bhakti** (BAHK-tee; "devotion") was introduced as a path to salvation. Revealing himself as the Divine Savior Vishnu, the *Gita*'s protagonist Krishna explained: "Those who revere me with devotion (bhakti), they are in me and I too am in them. . . . Even those who may be of base origin, women, men of the artisan caste, and serfs, too."[1] Though inequality remained embedded in the status system that differentiated one's religious duties by caste, Hindu salvation was, in the *Bhagavad-Gita,* made accessible to all.

Much of our knowledge of Gupta society comes from the journal of a Chinese Buddhist monk, Faxian (fah-SHEN), who traveled in India for 14 years at the opening of the fifth century. Despite the Guptas' preference for Hinduism, thousands of Buddhist monks and nuns practiced their religion. Buddhist stupas (funerary mounds) dotted the landscape. In the fourth century, only Sri Lanka was more Buddhist than India. Buddhism was an important bridge linking China and India and stimulating commerce in both East and Southeast Asia.

Faxian was primarily interested in Buddhism in India, but he also commented on social customs. He reported the people to be happy, relatively free of government oppression, and inclined toward courtesy and charity. He mentions the caste system and its associations with purity and impurity, including "untouchability," the social isolation of a lowest class that is doomed to menial labor. Of course, travelers' accounts never tell the entire story and must be read with some caution. Each traveler sees bits and pieces of the society he or she is visiting and looks at the society in ways that may be very different from those of other travelers of different

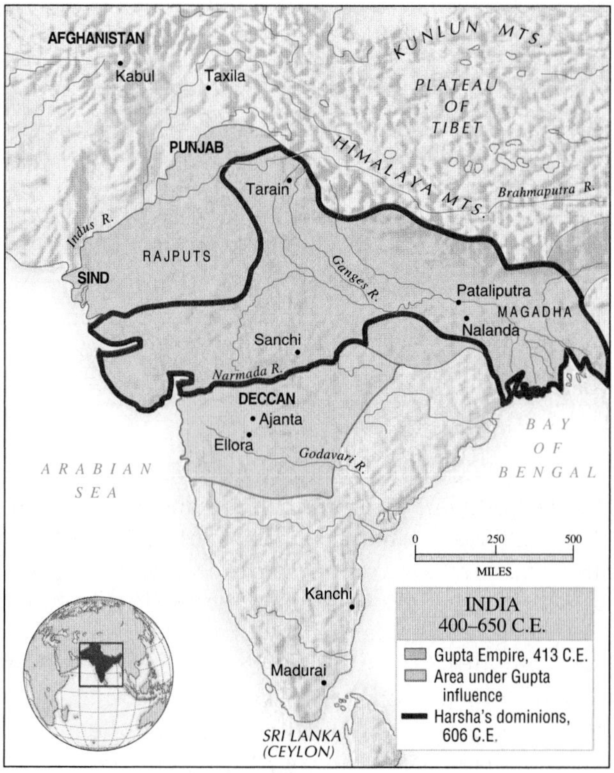

The Guptas extended their rule over northern and central India but never managed to control the southern peninsula.

bhakti—Hindu devotion.

Document Faxian: A Chinese Buddhist Monk in Gupta India

Faxian is an important source on India around 400 C.E. A Buddhist monk, he left China as a pilgrim to India in search of spiritual knowledge and Buddhist texts; he was away from home for 14 years. Faxian reached northern India on foot, via the grueling route over the mountains from China. When he returned home, he translated various Indian works and wrote the account of his travels. Faxian's story and long arduous journey illustrate both the effects of the spread of Buddhism and the draw that the Indian heartland had on Buddhists abroad. Here he describes Pataliputra (modern Patna), where Ashoka once reigned. The festival illustrates the amalgamation of Buddhist and Hindu ritual and suggests the joyous nature of some popular urban religious celebrations. Faxian's account of hospitals gives us some insight into the quality of medical care available free to the poor.

By the side of the tower of King Ashoka is built a monastery belonging to the Great Vehicle [Mahayana Buddhism], very imposing and elegant. There is also a temple belonging to the Little Vehicle [Theravada Buddhism]. Together they contain about 600 or 700 priests; their behavior is decorous and orderly. . . . Of all the kingdoms in Mid-India, the towns of this country are especially large. The people are rich and prosperous; they practice virtue and justice. Every year on the eighth day of the second month, there is a procession of images. On this occasion, they construct a four-wheeled cart, and erect upon it a tower of five stages, composed of bamboos lashed together, the whole being supported by a center post resembling a large spear with three points, in height twenty-two feet or more. So it looks like a pagoda. They then cover it with fine white linen, which they afterward paint with gaudy colors. Having made figures of the *devas* [gods], and decorated them with gold, silver, and glass, they place them under canopies of embroidered silk. Then at the four corners [of the vehicle] they construct niches in which they place figures of Buddha in a sitting posture, with a Bodhisattva [a Buddha in the making] standing in attendance. There are perhaps twenty cars thus prepared and differently decorated. During the day of the procession both priests and laymen assemble in great numbers. There are games and music, whilst they offer flowers and incense.... Then all night long they burn lamps, indulge in games and music, and make religious offerings. Such is the custom of all those who assemble on this occasion from the different countries round about. The nobles and householders of this country have founded hospitals within the city, to which the poor of all countries, the destitute, cripples, and the diseased may repair. They receive every kind of requisite help gratuitously. Physicians inspect their diseases, and according to their cases order them food and drink, medicine or decoctions, everything in fact that may contribute to their ease. When cured they depart at their convenience.

Questions to Consider

1. What does this story suggest about the institutionalization of Buddhism and its integration into city life in India?
2. Why might the people in Patna place figures of the Hindu gods and of the Buddha on the same float or cart used in a festival procession?

From Samuel Beal, ed., *Buddhist Records of the Western World,* translated from the Chinese of Hiuen Tsiang (629) (Delhi: Oriental Books, 1969), pp. lvi–lvii.

class, gender, upbringing, or motive for travel. Nonetheless, travelers like Faxian, who wrote down their observations in some detail, often provide us with the clearest glimpse we can obtain of past societies.

Gupta Art and Literature

Indian art of the Gupta period depicts a golden age of classical brilliance, combining stability and serenity with an exuberant love of life. The Gupta artistic spirit is well expressed in the 28 monasteries and temples at Ajanta, hewn out of a solid rock cliff and portraying in their wall frescoes not only the life of Buddha but also life in general: lovers embracing, beds of colorful flowers, musicians, and dancers. These sculptures reveal the beauty of the human form and provide us with a sense of Indian culture beyond that found in theological texts. The various incarnations of Vishnu and the deeds of the goddess Durga were also common subjects of Gupta sculpture. Hundreds of workers and artisans were employed in this work of building and

Classical Indian Sculpture

The Gupta era is justly renowned for its sculpture. This fifth-century terra-cotta piece shows the young Lord Krishna fighting the horse demon. According to Hindu religious tradition, Krishna, even as a baby, was formidably powerful; he battled a whole assortment of demons before reaching adolescence.

decorating temples that might, as Faxian points out, house hundreds of monks.

The Gupta era was also a golden age for literature, written in Sanskrit, the ancient language of the Brahmans. Authors supported by royal patronage poured forth a wealth of sacred, philosophical, and dramatic works in prose and poetry, including fables, fairy tales, and adventure stories featuring a wide range of characters—thieves, courtesans, hypocritical monks, and strange beasts. The *Panchatantra* is a manual of political wisdom employing animal tales to advise the king on proper rule.

The most renowned literary figure of the Gupta era was India's greatest poet and dramatist, Kalidasa, who wrote at the court of Chandra Gupta II. His best-known work in the West is *Shakuntala,* a great drama of lovers separated by adversity for many years and then by chance reunited. This universal theme of separated lovers is found in the epic stories of many Eurasian peoples in this era—the Arabian story of *Layla and Majnun,* for example.

DOCUMENT
Tales of Ten Princes

Gupta Scholarship and Science

The Gupta era brought a great stimulus to learning. Brahman traditions were revitalized, and Buddhist centers, which had spread after the Mauryan period, were given new support. The foremost Indian university, founded in the fifth century, was the Buddhist university at Nalanda in northeastern India. Accomplishments in science were no less remarkable than those in art, literature, scholarship, and philosophy. The university had a diverse population, with students from China and Southeast Asia also attending classes. The most famous Gupta scientist was the astronomer-mathematician Aryabhatta (AH-ree-ah-BAHT-tah), who lived in the fifth century. He elaborated (in verse) on quadratic equations, solstices, and equinoxes, along with the spherical shape of the earth and its rotation. Other Hindu mathematicians of this period popularized the use of a special sign for zero, passing it on later to the Arabs. Mathematical achievements were matched by those in medicine. Hindu physicians sterilized wounds, prepared for surgery by fumigation, performed cesarean operations, set bones, and were skilled in plastic surgery. They used drugs then unknown in the West, such as chaulmoogra oil for leprosy, a treatment still used during the first half of the twentieth century. With these accomplishments in pure science came many effective practical applications by Gupta craftsmen, who made soap, cement, superior dyes, and the finest tempered steel in the world.

India is famous for its rock carved temples. Kings or affluent families often financed such temples (both Hindu and Buddhist) with spectacular carvings as acts of devotion. This is the Kailasanatha Temple at Ellora, dedicated to the Hindu god Shiva and dating to approximately 765 C.E.

New Political and Religious Orders

Gupta hegemony began to collapse in the second half of the fifth century with attempted invasions by the Huna (called Xiongnu (SHONG-noo) in China and Huns in Europe) from the north. Although the Guptas held out for several decades, they ruled only in parts of northern India after 497. In 515 the Huna—who had already menaced the Roman Empire and successfully invaded Persia—seized first northwestern India and then the Ganges plain. Huna rule did not endure, but it led to several smaller kingdoms breaking free of the Gupta and prompted the migration of more Central Asian tribesmen into India. This resulted in a period in which India was generally divided into regional kingdoms rather than more expansive empires like that of the Guptas. The Central Asian tribesmen also intermarried with local populations to produce a class of fighting aristocrats known as *Rajputs* (RAHJ-poots). These fierce warriors carved out kingdoms among the Hindu states of northern India. Extensive intermarriage was common in frontier areas, blurring the boundaries between ethnolinguistic groups and even creating new identities.

In the seventh century the unity of northern India was revived for a short while by Harsha (r. 606–647), a strong leader. In 6 years he reconquered much of what had been the Gupta Empire, restoring order and partially reviving learning. However, Harsha failed in his bid to conquer the Deccan, and no ruler would do so until 1206. A tolerant leader, he was a strong supporter of Buddhism; during his reign Hinduism also grew in popularity. Harsha's support for Buddhism made possible several successful visits by Chinese ambassadors. In 643 the large delegation sent by the Tang court was received by Harsha who held a Buddhist ceremony in their honor. This diplomatic mission visited Buddhist sites and brought along an artisan to copy Buddhist architecture and sculpture. In addition to making spiritual overtures, the Chinese mission had a key commercial success—acquiring sugar-making technology from the South Asians.

When Harsha died in 647, regional kingdoms again prevailed. The period of the regional kingdoms was not a sterile one. In this era the great Hindu philosopher Shankara (c. 788–820) brilliantly argued a mystical philosophy based on the *Upanishads;* literature, especially in Tamil in the south, flourished; and Brahmans and

Buddhist monks continued to carry their religious and cultural ideas to Southeast Asia and China. Their crucial role in the "Indianization" of Southeast Asia is reflected in the great temples there. It is also reflected in Chinese sources that note 162 visits of Buddhist monks from the fifth to the eighth centuries.[2]

The Chola kingdom on India's southeastern coast played a significant role in the commercial and cultural exchange with Southeast Asia as well. The Chola had long lived in the Tamil south but were apparently a tributary lineage to the more powerful Pallavar dynasty. They began to challenge the Pallavars in the late ninth century and emerged as a ruling force in their own right within a century. Chola rulers in the eleventh century exchanged embassies with China, Sumatra, Malaya, and Cambodia; Chola fleets took Sri Lanka (Ceylon) and challenged the power of the Southeast Asian kingdom of Srivijaya (SHREE-vee-JAH-yah). When a Chola king conquered Bengal, he ordered the defeated princes to carry the holy water of the Ganges River to his new capital to celebrate his victory. Through this ceremony, he not only forced his enemies to perform a ritual act of submission but enhanced his legitimacy in Hindu terms by linking his own lands to those watered by the sacred Ganges.

Muslims in India

The prophet Muhammad founded an Arab Muslim state in Arabia in the seventh century (see Chapter 7); soon the Arab conquerors had defeated the Sassanids in Persia, and Muslim armies arrived at the boundaries of the Indian subcontinent. In 712 an Arab force seized Sind, a coastal outpost in northwestern India. During the next 300 years, Arabic-speaking Muslims established trading posts throughout the Indian Ocean region. Although the existence of the Muslim kingdom at Sind did not serve as a springboard for Arab Muslim penetration of India, Muslim traders did facilitate the integration of India into an Islamic world system. This system was a trading network that did not require participants to be Muslim but did take advantage of Muslim political expansion. The significant expansion of Muslim political control in India 300 years later, beginning in 997, had Turkish, Persian, and Afghan rather than Arabian roots.

Armies of Central Asian and Turkish slaves, originally purchased to support Muslim rulers at Baghdad, began to form independent kingdoms in Afghanistan and Persia. One of them, a kingdom ruled by Mahmud of Ghazni (MAH-mood, GAHZ-nee), launched a series of campaigns into northwestern India. He gained a reputation as a destroyer for his 17 campaigns over the course of 25 years that devastated northern India. One notable episode during these campaigns was Mahmud's destruction of Shiva's large temple complex in Gujarat and the slaughter of its defenders who, according to legend, numbered 50,000 men. These campaigns of pillage rather than conquest made Mahmud a name that to the present day evokes powerful emotions among Hindus.

DOCUMENT
Al-Biruni on India's Hindus

Mahmud is also known for the famous scholars at his court, among them Firdawsi (feer-DOW-see; 940–1020), who wrote the great epic Persian poem the *Shahnamah* (SHAH-NAH-mah), and al-Biruni (b. 973), author of a major history of India. Al-Biruni wrote that it was the caste system that prevented Muslims and Hindus from ever reaching any understanding because the Muslims considered "all men as equal, except in piety."[3] Of course, al-Biruni was minimizing the hierarchies that existed in Muslim society. But the caste system did indeed serve as a significant barrier between Hindus and Muslims (although, over time, Hindus and Muslims intermarried and some Muslim groups adapted castelike social divisions).

Firdawsi's career is an illustration of the vagaries of life at court. He spent many years writing the 60,000 verses of the *Shahnamah* but was then disappointed when the king did not reward him properly. So he penned a savage satire of Mahmud and fled to his home region of Khurasan in Persia. Legend has it that Mahmud later realized the value of Firdawsi's work and sent a large reward after him, but by the time it arrived, the poet was already dead.

The date 1206 stands out as the next significant marker of Muslim conquest in India. In the same year that the Mongol Chinggis (Genghis) Khan mobilized his campaigns of conquest and expansion in Central Asia, the general Qutb ud-Din Aibak (KOOT-buh ood-DIN ai-BAHK) seized power as sultan at Delhi. Qutb ud-Din had been a commander in the army of the Afghan ruler Muhammad of Ghur, who seized Delhi in 1193 from the Rajputs, Hindus who mounted a staunch defense in the northwest. Qutb ud-Din founded a new dynasty in 1206 that lasted for 320 years. He was followed on the throne by his son-in-law, Iltutmish (il-TOOT-mish; r. 1211–1236), and by the latter's daughter, Raziyya (ra-ZEE-yah; r. 1236–1240). According to the Muslim chronicler Minhaju-s Siraj, Sultana Raziyya was "wise, just and generous. . . . She was endowed with all the qualities befitting a king, but she was not born of the right sex, so in the estimation of men all these virtues were worthless."[4] Raziyya's father Iltutmish had himself been formally consecrated in 1229 as sultan of Delhi by a representative of the Abbasid sultan in Baghdad. Even though the Abbasid sultan wielded little power at this time, he was still a source of Islamic legitimacy for South Asian Muslim rulers. Less than 30 years later, the Abbasid caliphate would fall prey to the Mongol descendants of Chinggis Khan.

At the peak of its power in the thirteenth century, the Delhi Sultanate held not only the north but also part of the Deccan Plateau in the south. When Sultan

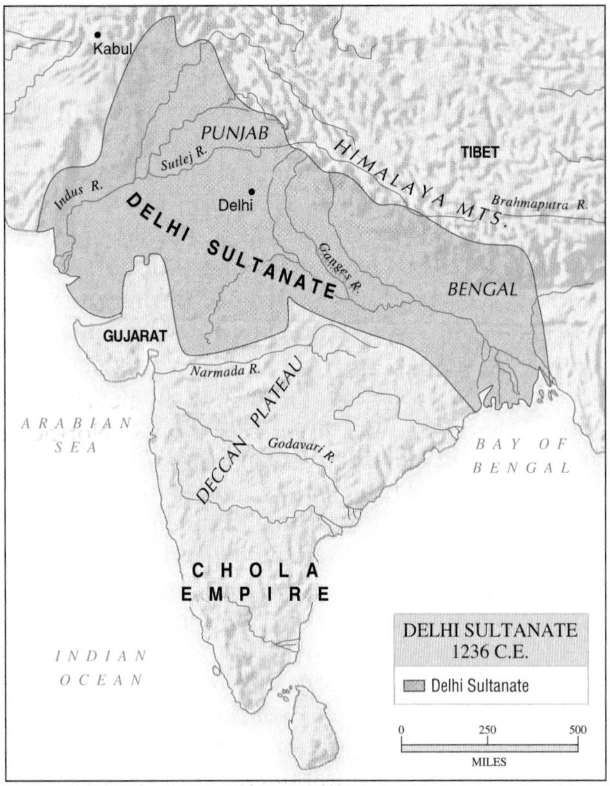

Muslim rulers established a sultanate in northern India, and Delhi flourished as its imperial capital.

Ala ud-Din (r. 1296–1316) invaded the Deccan, he called himself the "Second Alexander," a title that was emblazoned on his coins. The Delhi Sultanate also managed to ward off the Mongol invaders who seized the Punjab (poon-JAHB), thus avoiding the fate of Persia and Iraq. Delhi, under the sultanate, emerged as a great imperial capital. The Delhi sultans were patrons of the arts, builders of splendid monuments, and proponents of philosophy. The Tughluks (TOOG-looks), a Muslim dynasty who ruled Delhi for most of the fourteenth century, held an uneasy rule over the majority Hindu populace as well as over rival Muslim rulers. Ibn Battuta (IH-buhn bah-TOO-tah), the famed Muslim world traveler from north Africa, served the Tughluk court as its chief judge, observing it closely and leaving a detailed historical record. By the middle of the fourteenth century, the Tughluks had lost control of the south (upon the rise of the Hindu Vijayangar (vee-JAH-yahn-gahr) Empire in 1336) and the northeast (Sufi Muslim leaders there declared their independence of Delhi in 1338). Although experiencing brief periods of revival, the regime continued to decline internally before it was terminally fragmented by the brutal destruction of Delhi at the hands of the Turco-Mongol Timur (Tamerlane) in 1398. Timur's army wrought such destruction in Delhi that in his autobiography he denied responsibility and blamed the slaughter on his soldiers. Numerous rulers, espousing a variety of religious faiths, emerged throughout India as Delhi declined, until a century later, when Timur's great-grandson Babur would return to establish the Mughal dynasty.

DOCUMENT The Ideal Muslim King

DOCUMENT A World Traveler in India

Pre-Mughal Muslim rule in India brought some cultural integration as local lords and warriors were incorporated into the new Muslim court. Some Hindus found emotional appeal in the Muslim faith, which had no caste system, or sought to lighten their taxes and qualify for public service by converting to Islam. Others formed new religious groups synthesizing aspects of Hinduism and Islam—for example, **Sikhism.** Another typical example of cultural integration was the spread of Urdu, a spoken Indian language incorporating Persian, Arabic, and Turkish words. The Sikh religion and the Urdu language illustrate how difficult it is to maintain strict boundaries (whether ethnic, linguistic, or spiritual) between peoples who regularly interact with each other, especially in frontier areas.

DOCUMENT Indian Poetry

Cultural synthesis, however, could not eliminate Hindu-Muslim contention over polytheism, religious images, and closed castes. Many aristocratic Hindu leaders continued to resist Islam. The Muslim centuries should not be seen as a takeover of Indian society and culture by foreigners. Scholars today stress that though the rulers were Islamic, their governments ruled in ways similar to non-Islamic Indian rulers. Religion and caste remained significant barriers to assimilation, and mass conversions did not occur. The Delhi Sultanate remained a Muslim military-administrative class that ruled over a predominantly Hindu population. The impact on Buddhism was, however, far greater. The university at Nalanda and other major Buddhist centers were destroyed in 1202, driving thousands of monks and scholars to Nepal and Tibet. Buddhism was, then, effectively erased from India.

MAP The Delhi Sultanate and Mughal India

CHINA: CULTURAL AND POLITICAL EMPIRES

- *How did cross-cultural interaction with indigenous culture and ideology define China as a nation?*

The fall of the Han in 220 was followed by three and a half centuries of political disunity. Unity was regained under the Sui dynasty (589–618), consolidated under the Tang (618–907), maintained precariously under the Song (960–1279), and reasserted

---

Sikhism—Indian religion blending elements of Hinduism and Islam.

under the Yuan (1279–1368). Despite periods of internal disruption, this political system, recreated from Han precedents, survived repeated invasions and civil wars. For the 90-year Yuan dynasty, China was ruled by Central Asian invaders, the Mongols, but despite foreign control at the top, Chinese culture survived and reclaimed the emperorship in 1368. Throughout the millennium, stability resulted from a common written language, a strong family structure, an enduring Confucian tradition, an elite of scholar bureaucrats who shared power while contending for dominance, and the strength of China's economy and material culture. In the first half millennium, including the centuries of political disunity, China was part of the expanding Buddhist world. In the second half, the efforts of China's Confucian scholars promoted a flowering of Chinese culture during the expansionist Tang period, when China was the largest state in the world; during the ensuing economic prosperity of the Song; and in the Yuan period, in which China's economy dominated Eurasian trade.

Period of Division

No single dynasty was able to unite North and South China and establish a long-lasting dynasty from the fall of the Han to the rise of the Sui more than 360 years later. Yet this was a vibrant age of artistic creation, intellectual growth, and profound religious development. The divisions between north and south created dynamic differences in the two regions over time, and the reuniting of the two in the late sixth century led to a fertile synthesis of ideas and practices. Following the fall of the Han Empire various nomadic peoples, mainly Xiongnu and Yuezhi (yoo-EH-juh; "Turks"), interacted with Chinese in the border areas. At the same time, Chinese claimants to power—the ideal of a unified country persisted throughout the age of division—struggled with other Chinese as well as with sinified non-Chinese for dominance. (*Sinification* or *sinicization* meant adopting varying degrees of Chinese civilization, culture, governance, philosophy, and economic organization.) During the third century, three kingdoms vied for supremacy, and one, Jin, seemed to be on the verge of reuniting China in 280. Soon, however, succession disputes pitted Jin factions, joined by Chinese and non-Chinese allies, against one another. Unity was not to be at that time.

Xiongnu and other northern people had been invited inside the Han dynasty's borders in the second century as a way of gaining their support and decreasing the possibility of barbarian conquest. Many were used as soldiers by Chinese generals. By 304, some Xiongnu, sensing an opportunity during the fratricidal wars of the Jin, rose up, declared themselves the new kings of Han, and sacked Luoyang and Chang'an. For the next century (304–439), China was involved in constant warfare during the period known as the Sixteen Kingdoms. Many aristocrats fled southward, populating the south and bringing Chinese culture with them. This was a demographically significant move, extending the reach of Chinese civilization and developing the south's fertile agricultural economy. When, centuries later, the Grand Canal was built, food could be transported from this "rice basket" to the north, where China's defensive armies had long been dependent on either growing their own food or striking bargains with their barbarian neighbors.

In the North, a clan originally from Manchuria but sinified by the fifth century established the Northern Wei dynasty (439–534). Like other successful outsiders, the Northern Wei had adopted Chinese methods, creating an effective administration by blending their indigenous ways with Chinese ways. Throughout history, China was challenged by the question of maintaining Chinese culture and institutions—especially rule by scholars according to Confucian principles—while learning from the outsider (or barbarians, as they were ungenerously called) to create a hybrid culture, economy, and military. The question of how to maximize borrowing without compromising Chinese culture was most evident in times of strong central government. But religious, cultural, and economic blending occurred at all times. The Northern Wei instituted an **equal-field system** of land tenure that resembled the ancient "well-field" system to overcome the rise of powerful land owners whose control of land and serfs cut the tax roles. They also adopted Chinese language and dress. Their capital at Luoyang was a grand Chinese city, with palaces, 500,000 inhabitants, and 1000 Buddhist temples.

While the Northern Wei controlled the North, other rulers controlled the South. Northern aristocratic families contributed to state building through their interest in Confucianism, while leading southern families were more focused on religion and the arts. Southerners seemed somewhat effete to northerners, but when the two regions reunited in 589, the blend of both styles led to a stronger and more cultured civilization. Each region was differently influenced by foreign cultures as well, stimulating intellectual inquiry and encouraging trade.

The hallmark of the period of political disunity was its cultural growth. At the beginning of the period, the incessant military struggles led many intellectuals to abandon public service. Why bother being a serious Confucian scholar in such times, many concluded, giving themselves up to hedonism and artistic performance, often simultaneously expressing itself in

---

equal-field system—Division of land to peasants, who tilled it, rather than to wealthy landholders; adopted in China, spread to Korea and Japan.

Huge Buddhist rock carvings (these are around 50 feet tall) were commissioned by the Northern Wei at the end of the fifth century. These large figures are part of a collection of thousands of carvings at Yungang in North China. They may have been inspired by earlier Buddhist carvings, recently destroyed by the Taliban in Afghanistan.

poetry or unconventional behavior. The Seven Sages of the Bamboo Grove were the most famous of many talented poets and although one was executed for scandalous behavior, they continue to be celebrated to this day.

Buddhism and Daoism emerged as more spiritual alternatives to Confucian government service. While Daoism had indigenous roots, Buddhism came to China as part of a great expansion of a universal religion. From its origins in India, Buddhism traveled along trade routes to China, bringing international (Greek, Afghan, and Indian) arts and ideas. Missionaries aided the transmission of Buddhism as did Chinese travelers like Faxian.

Buddhism provided comfort in times of crisis. Its promise of salvation (to all, including common people), special appeal to the supposed natural compassion of women and men, offer of monastic security to men in troubled times, and long incubation within Chinese culture all ensured its popularity. China's dominant form of Buddhism, Mahayana, focused on **bodhisattvas** (BOH-dee-SAHT-vahs), individuals who had achieved salvation but chose to postpone their release from the cycle of birth and rebirth in order to save others. Bodhisattvas were technically sexless beings (though identified in popular forms of religion as female) and transcended class and culture as well as gender. The notion of salvation through faith was developed in the **Pure Land** sect of Buddhism in the fourth century; this made Buddhism increasingly appealing to those not able to enter monastic life. Developments in the Tang dynasty would broaden Buddhism's appeal further.

Daoism was encouraged to enhance its dogma and organization by the rise of Buddhism. Like Buddhists, Daoists formed monastic communities and wrote scriptures, although many of these scriptures were kept hidden from non-Daoists, unlike the widely circulated Buddhist texts. Daoists were particularly important in the study of alchemy as a route to immortality; alchemy, in turn, led to scientific discoveries. Although challenged by native Daoism, scorned by some Confucian intellectuals, and periodically persecuted by rulers jealous of its strength, Buddhism ultimately won adherents throughout China. The monarchs of the North patronized Buddhism by building splendid temples and generously endowing monasteries. From the fourth to the ninth centuries, Buddhism interacted with Chinese religious and philosophical traditions to create a complex new synthesis of ideas and art.

The Sui dynasty (589–618), descended from the Northern Wei, presented themselves as Chinese defenders of Buddhism. Emperor Wendi (r. 581–604), the first Sui ruler, and his son Yangdi (r. 604–618) established an imperial military force and a land-based militia, centralized the administration, and revived the civil service system. Between 605 and 609, Yangdi built a great waterway, the Grand Canal, to link the rice-growing Yangzi basin with northern China; this helped to overcome regional differences. This canal eventually stretched 1200 miles and permitted some later governments to locate their seats of power in the less productive but strategically important North. Building this canal, in addition to a massive conscription of soldiers (over one million) to fight in Korea, took huge amounts of labor. Disgust with this exploitation led to numerous rebellions, and in 618 Yangdi's cousin overthrew the Sui. The new Tang dynasty, like the Sui, was a hybrid of North and South, Chinese and foreign.

bodhisattvas—In Mahayana Buddhism, an enlightened being who chooses to postpone salvation to aid others in reaching enlightenment.

Pure Land—A place for those saved by faith in the Amida Buddha.

Political Developments Under the Early Tang Dynasty, 618–756

During the first half of the Tang period, China attained a new pinnacle of glory. The first three emperors, Gaozu (GOW-dzuh; r. 618–626), Taizong (TAI-dzong; r. 626–649), and Gaozong (GOW-dzong; r. 650–683), subjugated Turkish Central Asia and conquered Annam (northern Vietnam). Tang cultural influence extended north to Manchuria, east to Korea and Japan, and south to parts of Southeast Asia. It controlled Central Asia all the way to Afghanistan during the seventh century and maintained extensive trade routes. Along with territorial expansion came a deepening of state power.

The legal code of 653 combined northern and southern legal traditions, and the reemphasized **examination system** recruited officials from all regions and, in theory, all classes. This system was based on Confucian texts that were, in principle, accessible to all men (women were not allowed to take the examinations), but in reality were more likely studied in families financially able to educate their sons. This bought the elite's loyalty and focused the ideology of those who wished to be rulers, who were selected by their answers on exams based on the Confucian classics, on a unified body of scholarship. Thus, although the expansion of the empire depended on the promotion of *wu* (military), its maintenance was even more dependent on its promotion of *wen* (civil arts). Though strong supporters of Buddhism, early Tang rulers elevated the principles of Confucianism to rule the state and to define its Chinese nature.

The era of growth and grandeur was marked by the extraordinary reign of the able Empress Wu (r. 690–705), a concubine of the second and third emperors, who controlled the government for 20 years after the latter's death, eliminating her political opponents and firmly establishing the Tang dynasty. She greatly weakened the old aristocracy by favoring Buddhism and strengthening the examination system for recruiting civil servants. Moreover, she decisively defeated the Koreans, making Korea a loyal vassal state. As a woman and a widow, she was considered a usurper and was later criticized by Chinese historians and politicians who emphasized her vices, particularly her many favorites and lovers. She was overthrown in 705. Her grandson, Emperor Xuanzong (SHWAHN-dzong; r. 712–756), was also known for his long reign filled with cultural growth.

Tang rulers perfected a highly centralized government, using a complex bureaucracy organized in specialized councils, boards, and ministries, all directly responsible to the emperor. Local government functioned under 15 provincial governors, aided by subordinates down to the district level. Military commanders supervised tribute collections in semiautonomous conquered territories. Officeholders throughout the empire were, by the eighth century, usually degreeholders from government schools and universities who had qualified by passing the regularly scheduled examinations. These scholar-bureaucrats were steeped in Confucian conservatism but were more efficient than the remaining minority of aristocratic hereditary officials. The Tang retained the nationalized land register under the equal-field system, designed to check the growth of large estates, guarantee land to peasants, and relate their land tenure to both their taxes and their militia service. Until well into the eighth century, when abuses began to appear, the system worked to merge the interests of state and people.

examination system—The selection of scholar-officials through examination in Confucian texts.

Tang Economic and Social Changes

The early Tang economy was extremely prosperous, supported by thriving cities and the always busy trade routes through Central Asia, along the southeastern coast, and up and down the Grand Canal. Economic productivity, both agricultural and industrial, rose steadily during the early Tang period. The introduction of tea and wet rice from Annam turned the Yangzi area into a vast irrigated food bank and the economic base for Tang power. Tea became a staple throughout China during the Tang. More food and rising population brought increasing manufactures. Population growth was most impressive in the south, where it increased form one-quarter of the realm's population in the early seventh century to half by 742. Chinese techniques in the newly discovered craft of papermaking, along with iron casting, porcelain production, and silk processing, improved tremendously and spread west to the Middle East.

Foreign trade and influence increased significantly under the Tang emperors in a development that would continue through the Song era (960–1279). Chinese control in Central Asia facilitated trade along the old overland silk route; but as porcelain became the most profitable export and could not be easily transported by caravan, it swelled the volume of sea trade through Southeast Asia. Most of this trade left from southern ports, particularly from Guangzhou (gwahng-JOH; Canton), where more than 100,000 non-Chinese Indians, Persians, Arabs, and Malays handled the goods. Foreign merchants were equally visible at Chang'an, the Tang capital and eastern terminus of the silk route. Chang'an, a planned city of 30 square miles, not counting the imperial palace, was the largest planned city in the world, and the most populous. The imperial palace at the north of the city was flanked on either side by a market. The "West Market" dealt in foreign goods, food, and wine and exhibited foreign entertainers and magicians; the "East Market" was for domestic items. The city was vibrant, but it was also controlled, for Chang'an was planned on a grid, and every resident lived in a rectangular ward, surrounded by walls. The gate to the ward was locked at night.

Although largely state-controlled and aristocratic, Tang society was particularly responsive to new foreign stimuli, which it swiftly absorbed. A strongly pervasive Buddhism, a rising population, and steady urbanization fostered this cross-cultural exchange. Many city populations exceeded 100,000, and four cities had more than a million people. Their cosmopolitan residents enjoyed products from foreign lands, including luxury goods, musical instruments, and textiles. The foreign practice of sitting on chairs replaced sitting on floor mats. Hairstyles and games were adopted from abroad. Foreign religions, including Islam, Nestorian Christianity, Judaism, Zoroastrianism, and Manichaeism (MAN-ih-KEE-ism), were practiced freely by the thousands of international residents in Chang'an and Luoyang, though few Chinese converted to these religions as they had earlier to Buddhism. Merchants clearly benefited, but despite their wealth, they were still considered socially inferior. They often used their wealth to educate their sons for the civil service examination, thus promoting a rising class of scholar-bureaucrats. The latter, as they acquired land, gained status and power at the expense of the old aristocratic families. Conditions among artisans and the expanding mass of peasants improved somewhat, but life for them remained hard and precarious.

By the eighth century, Tang legal codes had imposed severe punishments for wifely disobedience or infidelity to husbands. New laws also limited women's rights to divorce, inheritance of property, and remarriage as widows. Women were, however, still active in the arts and literature. Although some wielded influence and power at royal courts, many were confined to harems. This subordinate position was partly balanced by the continued high status and authority of older women within families.

Class and education played an important role in women's status. Women poets were sought after by men of distinction, and one father of a poet, himself a writer of note, was promoted to a prestigious government position on the strength of his daughter's writing. Empress Wu wrote powerful poetry, some of it recalling her mother, some longing for her late husband, some expressing political ideas. Other women wrote of love and longing, military events, affairs at court, and a wide variety of topics. Not all Tang women poets were genteel. In a poem entitled "Getting It Off My Chest," Xu Yueying (SHOO yoo-eh-YING), a late Tang poet wrote: "I've broken the rules—obedience to father, husband, son. That's why I cry so much. This body? What way, what use to stick to what proper people do?"[5]

Fashions in female beauty change from place to place and over time. Figurines like this one of a mounted woman, possibly playing polo, show that physical activity and a plump physique were esteemed. This style also influenced standards of beauty in Korea and Japan at that time.

Tang Religion and Culture

Buddhism and Daoism blossomed alongside Confucian scholarship and government service. Poets, artists, architects, and painters were all inspired by religious as well as secular themes. Buddhism was particularly dynamic in the early Tang dynasty. Buddhist monasteries and temples educated children in their schools, rural temples gave lodging to travelers, and monasteries ran large-scale farms. Buddhist themes permeated folk tales. Most important, faith-based Buddhist sects, especially Pure Land, spread throughout China, offering peasants a route to salvation. Pure Land Buddhism was a vastly different form of devotion from the earlier sects that required years of good living and often many rebirths on earth before attaining salvation. **Chan** (Zen in Japanese) Buddhism developed in the Tang as well. Chan appealed more to the elite and focused on sudden enlightenment rather than scripture.

Chan—A form of Buddhism that seeks sudden enlightenment through techniques and rituals intended to quiet the mind. Known as Zen in Japan.

A fresh flowering of literature occurred during the early Tang period. It followed naturally from a dynamic society, but it was also furthered by the development of papermaking and the invention, in about 600, of block printing, which soon spread to Korea and Japan. Movable type, which would later revolutionize Europe, was little used in China during this period because it was less efficient in printing Chinese characters. Printing helped meet a growing demand for the religious and educational materials generated by Buddhism and the examination system.

Tang scholarship is best remembered for historical writing. Chinese of this period firmly believed that lessons from the past could be guides for the future. As an early Tang emperor noted, "By using a mirror of brass, you may . . . adjust your cap; by using antiquity as a mirror you may . . . foresee the rise and fall of empires."[6] In addition to universal works, the period produced many studies of particular subjects. History itself came under investigation, as illustrated by *The Understanding of History,* a work that stressed the need for analysis and evaluation in the narration of events. Writers produced works of all types, but poetry was the accepted medium, composed and repeated by emperors, scholars, singing courtesans, and common people in the marketplaces. Tang poetry was marked by ironic humor, deep sensitivity to human feeling, concern for social justice, and a near-worshipful love of nature. Two of the most famous among some 3000 recognized poets of the era were Li Bo (701–763; also known as Li Bai) and Du Fu (712–770). The former was an admitted lover of pleasure, especially of wine. A famous story about him is that during a drinking party on a lake, he leaned over the side of the boat in order to scoop out the moon and drowned. But he also had his philosophical side as seen in the following poem inspired by Daoism:

DOCUMENT
Poems by Li Bai (also known as Li Bo) and Du Fu

Zhuangzi in a dream
became a butterfly,
And the butterfly became
Zhuangzi at waking.
Which was the real, the
butterfly or the man?[7]

Du Fu, one of the great landscape poets, also wrote of suffering, especially suffering brought about by rebellions toward the end of his life.

The war-chariots rattle,
The war-horses whinny.
Each man of you has a bow and quiver at his belt. . . .
At the border where the blood of men spills like the sea—
And still the heart of Emperor Wu is beating for war. . . .
In thousands of villages, nothing grows but weeds,
And though strong women have bent to the ploughing,
East and west the furrows are all broken down . . .
It is very much better to have a daughter
Who can marry and live in the house of a neighbor,
While under the sod we bury our boys. . . .[8]

The Tang literary revival was paralleled by movements in painting and sculpture. The plastic arts, dealing with both religious and secular subjects, became a major medium for the first time in China. Small tomb statues depicted both Chinese and foreign life with realism, verve, and diversity. These figures—warriors, servants, and traders—were buried with the dead and believed to serve them in the afterlife. Religious statuary, even in Buddhist shrines, showed strong humanistic emphases, often juxtaposed with the naive sublimity of Buddhas carved in the Gandaran (Greek Hellenistic) style of northwestern India. Similar themes were developed in Tang painting, but the traditional preoccupation with nature prevailed in both the northern and southern landscape schools. The most famous Tang painter was Wu Daozi (WOO DOW-zuh), whose landscapes and religious scenes were produced at the court of the emperor Xuanzong in the early eighth century.

Tang Decline and the Transition to Premodern China

The cultural flowering of Xuanzong's reign was matched, in its early years, by vigorous and effective leadership. He fixed problems in the tax system, curbed the power of imperial relatives, and strengthened defenses against the Turks, Uighurs, and Tibetans. His method of strengthening border defenses by giving authority to commanders of military provinces backfired, however. One of these commanders, a protégé of the emperor's favorite concubine, Yang Guifei (YAHNG gwei-FAY), was doted on by the emperor to please his concubine. The commander, An Lushan, built up an army of 160,000 troops along the border, but then turned and marched on Chang'an and Luoyang in 755.

The aged emperor Xuanzong, while fleeing for his life from the capital, was forced by his troops to approve the execution of Yang Guifei, who was seen as having dominated him and his court. According to legend, he died of sorrow less than a month later. Yang

Document — Bo Juyi (772–846): "The Song of Everlasting Sorrow"

This poem by one of the late Tang dynasty's most respected poets recounts the love of Emperor Xuanzong and his beloved concubine, Yang Guifei, who was blamed by her contemporaries for the An Lushan Rebellion. Bo Juyi's poem was esteemed not only in China but also in Japan. Lady Murasaki cited it repeatedly in *The Tale of Genji.*

China's Emperor, craving beauty that might shake an empire,
Was on the throne for many years, searching, never finding,
Till a little child of the Yang clan, hardly even grown,
Bred in an inner chamber, with no one knowing her,
But with graces granted by heaven and not to be concealed,
At last one day was chosen for the imperial household.
If she but turned her head and smiled, there were cast a hundred spells,
And the powder and paint of the Six Palaces faded into nothing.
. . . There were other ladies in his court, three thousand of rare beauty,
But his favours to three thousand were concentered in one body.
. . . Her sisters and her brothers all were given titles;
And, because she so illumined and glorified her clan,
She brought to every father, every mother through the empire,
Happiness when a girl was born rather than a boy.
. . . The Emperor's eyes could never gaze on her enough—
Till war-drums, booming from Yuyang, shocked the whole earth
And broke the tunes of The Rainbow Skirt and the Feathered Coat.
The Forbidden City, the nine-tiered palace, loomed in the dust
From thousands of horses and chariots headed southwest.
The imperial flag opened the way, now moving and now pausing—
But thirty miles from the capital, beyond the western gate,
The men of the army stopped, not one of them would stir
Till under their horses' hoofs they might trample those moth-eyebrows.
Flowery hairpins fell to the ground, no one picked them up,
And a green and white jade hair-tassel and a yellow gold hair-bird.
The Emperor could not save her, he could only cover his face.
And later when he turned to look, the place of blood and tears
Was hidden in a yellow dust blown by a cold wind.
. . . And people were so moved by the Emperor's constant brooding
That they besought the Daoist priest to see if he could find her.
. . . He searched the Green Void, below, the Yellow Spring;
But he failed, in either place, to find the one he looked for.
And then he heard accounts of an enchanted isle at sea,
. . . And the lady, at news of an envoy from the Emperor of China,
Was startled out of dreams in her nine-flowered canopy.
. . . She took out, with emotion, the pledges he had given
And, through his envoy, sent him back a shell box and gold hairpin,
But kept one branch of the hairpin and one side of the box,
Breaking the gold of the hairpin, breaking the shell of the box;
Our souls belong together," she said, "like this gold and this shell—
Somewhere, sometime, on earth or in heaven, we shall surely meet."
. . . Earth endures, heaven endures; some time both shall end,
While this unending sorrow goes on and on for ever.

Questions to Consider

1. Why did the Emperor's soldiers execute Yang Guifei, and why was the Emperor unable to protect her?
2. What does this poem suggest about the role of women in the Emperor's court in the Tang?
3. Why was this poem loved not only in China but also throughout East Asia?

Excerpted from Bo Juyi (Po Chi-yi), "A Song of Unending Sorrow," in Cyril Birch, ed., *Anthology of Chinese Literature: From Early Times to the Fourteenth Century* (New York: Grove Press, 1965), pp. 266–269.

Guifei became a model of female perfidy, fueling misogynistic notions of women's control over men.

It took 8 years to put down An Lushan's rebellion, but the ensuing disruption was so extensive that the late Tang emperors never recovered their former power. In several key areas, military governors acted as independent rulers, paying no taxes to Chang'an. In the rest of China, the equal-field system was replaced with twice yearly taxation on the value of the land. This **two tax system** persisted for the next 700 years in China. Regions were allowed to fill their tax responsibilities as they wished with little government supervision. In addition, the government instituted salt, wine, and tea monopolies to raise revenues. Government receipts to merchants came to be used as a kind of currency, becoming the antecedent for paper money that was developed during the Song dynasty. Though private trade was stimulated by the government's declining economic role, government revenues declined, and taxes on peasants were raised. Falling revenues brought deterioration of the state education establishment and a corresponding drop in administrative efficiency. The government further alienated some groups by seizing Buddhist property and persecuting all "foreign" religions. Buddhism was suppressed in 841. Tens of thousands of monasteries and temples were destroyed and 250,000 monks and nuns were returned to lay life. Except for the popular sects of Pure Land and Chan, most other sects of Buddhism soon declined.

two tax system—Twice yearly tax payment based on value of land rather than on output as under the earlier equal field system.

In response to the threat posed by autonomous regional commanders, the court created armies led by eunuchs, originally personal servants to the emperor or to his women's quarters. In time, these eunuchs gained their own power, manipulating and even murdering emperors and scholar-officials. Bandits and other gangs ravaged the country after 860. Chang'an was captured in 881, and the brutal warlord who took the city killed all the foreign residents. Chang'an would never again be capital of China. In 907, the pretense of Tang rule was ended.

Political Developments During the Song Era, 960–1279

For a half-century after the fall of the Tang dynasty, China experienced political division, at times approaching anarchy. During this period of five dynasties in the north and ten kingdoms in the south, attacks by "barbarian" raiders alternated with internal con-

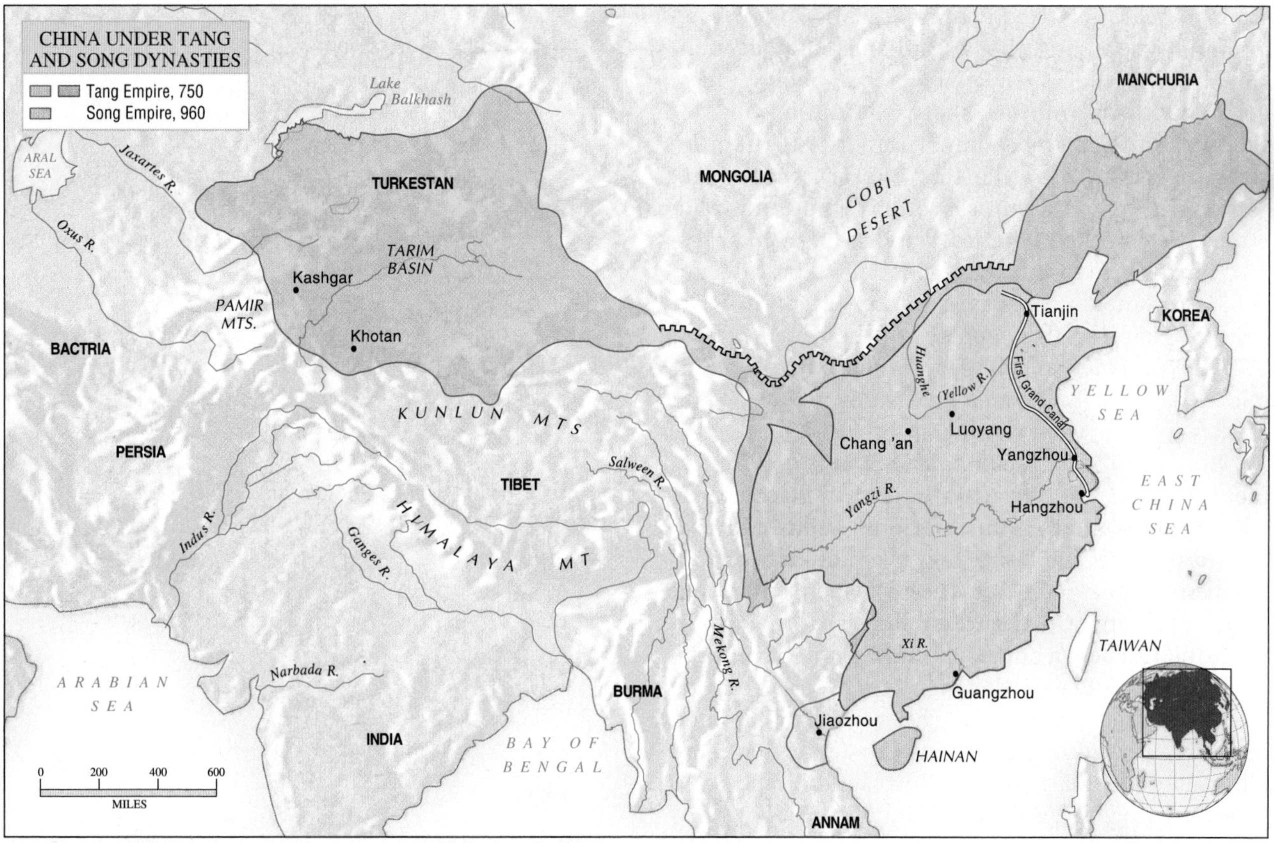

China expanded to the south, west, and north during the Tang dynasty. Northern Vietnam (Annam) and Turkish Central Asia came under Chinese control.

flicts among contending warlords. One military leader in the north—who reigned as Song Taizu (r. 960–76)—was finally able to unify all of China, founding the Song dynasty in 960. Taizu and his successors were never able to regain all the territories, however. Militarily powerful non-Chinese states bordered the Song, and the new rulers had to devise ways to keep them in check. Several were hybrid states, using Chinese methods of governance to rule over populations that included many Chinese immigrants. The Song responded by building a large military—their army had 1.25 million men by 1040—and producing large quantities of armaments. Military technology advanced as well; after using gunpowder to launch grenades, the Song invented the cannon. At the same time, scholar-officials were used to strengthen the centralizing power of the state. While this did help consolidate Song authority, in time excessive bureaucratization crept in, and rules and regulations began to impede creative governing.

Another consequence of the Song's strong focus on rule by scholar-officials was the rise of factionalism. As the state experienced mounting budgetary deficits and confronted peasant unrest, the emperor Shenzong (SHEN-dzhong; r. 1067–1085) called on an eminent statesman, Wang Anshi (WAHNG ahn-SHUH), to resolve these difficulties. Wang sponsored a thoroughgoing—and therefore threatening—reform program that granted interest-bearing agricultural loans to peasants, fixed commodity prices, provided unemployment benefits, established old-age pensions, converted labor service to monetary taxes, mobilized local militias, increased the number of schools, and reformed the examination system by stressing practical rather than literary knowledge. Although these measures brought some improvements, they evoked fanatical opposition from scholars, bureaucrats, and moneylenders. The internal debate resembled that of more than 1000 years earlier (the Salt and Iron Debates of the Han dynasty) over the propriety of the government's involvement in the economy. In the next generation most of Wang Anshi's reforms were rescinded.

Song ministers faced continuous threats along their northern and western frontiers. To placate their neighbors, the Liao (around Beijing) and the Xia (in the northwest), the Song paid them annual tribute payments in silk and silver. These payments indicated Song subordination or at least a desire for peace. In 1115, the Jurchen, a nomadic people from Manchuria, challenged the Liao. Believing the Jurchen would be good allies against their old rivals in Liao, the Song made a pact with them to divide Liao. Soon the alliance broke apart, and the Jurchen took the Song capital at Kaifeng (kai-FUHNG) in 1126. Ruling northern China, the Jurchen became increasingly sinified, ruling according to Chinese ways and intermarrying with Chinese. The Song court fled in panic to Nanjing and later set up a new capital at Hangzhou (hahng-JOH), thus bringing to an end the Song effort to govern a realm united from north to south. The period from 960 to 1127 is often called the Northern Song, and that from 1127 to 1279 the Southern Song.

After a decade of indecisive war, a treaty in 1142 stipulated that the Song had to pay tribute of silk and silver to the Jurchen whose new dynasty was called Jin (1115–1234). It also prescribed that the Jin monarch be addressed as "lord" and the Song emperor as "servant" in all official communications. The subordination of the Song was thus formalized in language and in tribute payments.

Despite these disasters, the Song rulers enjoyed somewhat better economic conditions. The country experienced unprecedented economic and cultural advances, particularly after its territory was reduced to only southern China, and it turned increasingly toward using the many canals and streams throughout the South to move products. In addition, trade with the Jin state continued as before. One and a half centuries later, a new band of Central Asian nomads, the Mongols, conquered the Jin and went on to take

Tang, Song, and Yuan China

618–907	Tang dynasty
c. 690–705	Reign of Empress Wu
701–763	Poet Li Bo
712–756	Cultural flowering under Emperor Xuanzong
712–770	Poet Du Fu
755–763	An Lushan Rebellion
960–1279	Song dynasty
1005, 1042	Song sign treaties of subordination with Liao and Xia
1019–1086	Sima Guang, historian
1067–1085	Emperor Shenzong and Wang Anshi Reforms
1126–1134	Jin dynasty established in north
1162–1227	Chinggis becomes Mongol Khan (Supreme King)
1260–1294	Khubilai becomes Khan
1279–1368	Yuan dynasty

all of the Southern Song. From 1279 to 1368, China was ruled by Mongols who established a dynasty they called Yuan.

Song Economic and Social Conditions

Economic growth was rapid. Agricultural growth sustained a population that doubled between 750 and 1100. Farmers used their surpluses to buy charcoal, tea, and wine. Many raised and sold silk, sugar, vegetables, cotton, fruit, and wood products. The government maintained some monopolies, taxed trade moderately, built great water-control projects, and aided intensive agriculture, but otherwise loosened control over individual enterprise. Rice production doubled within a century after 1050, and industry grew rapidly, pouring out, for home and foreign markets, fine silk, lacquer wares, porcelain, and paper for writing, books, money and wrapping gifts. Heavy industry, especially iron, grew rapidly, and was used for tools, suspension bridges, and nails for construction. Song economic advances were furthered by such technical innovations as water clocks, explosives for mining, hydraulic machinery, paddleboats, seagoing junks, the stern post rudder, and the mariner's compass. These commercial developments were paralleled by the development of an oceangoing navy. The resulting commercial expansion prompted banks to depend on paper currency and specialized commercial instruments. Trade with the outside world, formerly dominated by Indians and Southeast Asians, was taken over by the Chinese, who established trading colonies throughout East Asia.

The Song economic revolution exerted tremendous foreign influence abroad. Paper money, dating from the eleventh century in the south, was soon copied in the Liao state and issued by the Jin government in 1153; its use then spread steadily in all directions. Other Song economic innovations appeared quickly in coastal areas from Japan and Korea to the East Indies, where Chinese merchants were immigrant culture carriers. Song technology also spread to India, the Middle East, and even Europe. From China, Europe acquired metal horseshoes, the padded horse collar, and the wheelbarrow. Chinese mapping skills, along with the compass and the stern post ship rudder, helped prepare the way for Europe's age of expansion. Later, gunpowder and movable type, both pioneered in Song China, arrived in Europe via Asian intermediaries.

Profound and rapid change brought many tensions to Song society. Some arose from urban expansion in a population that swelled from 60 to 115 million, a growth rate of more than twice the world average. A rise in population unaccompanied by a rise in the number of officials meant that passing the exams to enter officialdom became increasingly, and frustratingly, difficult. On the other hand, life was dynamic and cosmopolitan. Cities offered residents and travelers alike access to international culture, restaurants, plays, artwork, and civic organizations. Rural life was far less exciting, but farmers could go to regularly scheduled rural markets and read printed books published on a variety of topics, including agriculture, rituals, and childbirth. The spread of books and literacy created a national culture that transcended the localism of most rural societies. Unlike Europe, cities were not islands of merchant liberation in a rural sea of aristocratic domination; rather, scholar-officials ruled everywhere. Merchants did not have power, although they could take the exams to enter the scholarly class.

Women's lives were varied though lacking in power. While lively physical activity had been encouraged in the Tang—as evidenced in art work showing women playing vigorous sports like polo—a more demure and modest demeanor was expected of women in the Song. To be sure, the extant records of the Song show women who ran inns, delivered babies as midwives, worked as entertainers, sold their sewing and weaving, wrote poetry, and served as shamans (religious mediums). As wives and mothers, women had a voice in childrearing and spouse selection for their children, despite Confucian ideas that called for women to take a back seat to men in the family. Court records in inheritance cases indicate that judges made sure that daughters received money for dowries by which they could make more successful marriages. The availability of a great number of printed materials opened doors to literature for women of educated families.

At the same time, however, the resurgence of Confucian thinking reinforced a view that demure and even physically weak women were attractive. Women were told to be modest, which limited their public role, and footbinding carried this injunction to an extreme. Begun by dancers in the tenth century, the tight binding of a little girl's feet till they were broken, bent, and ideally just three inches long came to be a symbol both of beauty and of a girl's modesty and refinement. Bound feet attracted better marriage prospects but did little to expand girls' horizons. Though it began in the Song, footbinding was still uncommon at that time and was never mentioned by the Song's greatest woman poet, Li Qingzhao (LEE ching-JOW; 1094–1152). Female infanticide, restriction on remarriage of widows, and harsh legal penalties, including death, for violating the accepted code of prescribed wifely conduct were also Song social phenomena. Women were told to put their families first, but so, too, were men. All family members were under the rule of the patriarchal (male) family head, but women were additionally burdened by their subordinate position in society as a whole.

Song Philosophy, Literature, and Art

The rapidly changing Song society was reflected in its philosophy, literature, and art. Poets wrote of people's inner lives, joys, and misfortunes. Song aesthetic expression encouraged versatility; as during the later European Renaissance, the universal man, public servant, scholar, poet, or painter was the ideal. Song's most famous woman poet, Li Qingzhao, whose work was enthusiastically promoted by her scholar husband, wrote personalized verse describing the early years of her marriage in which she and her husband engaged in lively intellectual discussions. Su Shi (1037–1101) was a northern Song poet who excelled in painting and calligraphy as well as writing. Writing his poems on his paintings, he combined the three arts of the Confucian gentleman-scholar in a single work. In another genre, Sima Guang (SUH-muh GWAHNG; 1019–1086) was an outstanding Confucian historian. Known for his bitter attacks on his contemporary Wang Anshi, he also was an astute observer of the past, looking to it for moral guidance, and a critic of those who misread historical sources. Artists depicted the beauty of nature in widely varied styles, all involving great attention to detail. Landscapes embraced all of nature in a single work, removing humans from the central position they had had in earlier works. Darker tones and sharper lines replaced the decorative lightness of Tang works. The greatest Song landscape painter was Fan Kuan (FAHN KWAHN; active 990–1020).

This Song landscape painting, Snow Mountain and Forest, *was painted by the artist Fan Kuan.*

Buddhism lost its appeal to Song's rulers as it was associated with their Liao, Xia, and Jin rivals, all of whom were ardent Buddhists. Confucianism, as a result, had a revival. The brothers Cheng Hao (1032–1085) and Cheng Yi (1033–1108) developed metaphysical approaches to Confucianism. They asserted that *li* (principle or pattern) was inherent in all things. *Qi* (CHEE; material force or energy) gives substance to things for which *li* is the blueprint. Mencius's contention that humans are fundamentally good (see Chapter 2) was always hard to explain in light of people's bad behavior. The Song **"Neo-Confucians"** could now claim that humankind's blueprint *(li)* was good but *qi* was sometimes impure and in need of cleaning. The Cheng brothers' most important follower was Zhu Xi (JOO SHEE; 1130–1200). His White Deer Grotto Academy was one of many that trained students in new approaches to Confucianism. He differed from the Chengs by ascribing greater importance to *li* over *qi* and by positing the existence of a Supreme Ultimate to which all *li* was connected. Zhu Xi contended that self-cultivation required the extension of knowledge, best achieved by the "investigation of things." In time, Neo-Confucianism was identified with Zhu Xi's philosophy, though it had many varieties and proponents.

The Song renaissance in scholarship was accompanied by significant advances in the experimental and applied sciences. Chinese doctors introduced inoculation against smallpox, and their education and hospital facilities surpassed anything in the West. In addition, there were notable achievements in astronomy, chemistry, zoology, botany, cartography, and algebra.

The Yuan Dynasty (1279–1368)

The Mongol conquest of the Song followed three-quarters of a century of Mongol growth and expansion in Central and Western Asia. The Mongol Khubilai's (1215–1294) takeover of the southern Song in 1279 furthered China's position as the center of Eurasia. Thus, although the Mongol era was a short dynasty despised by many Chinese and having a relatively minor impact on Chinese culture, it played a very significant role in world history. More than during the

Neo-Confucianism—Metaphysical form of Confucianism developed by the Cheng brothers and Zhu Xi; later became the dominant form of Confucianism throughout East Asia.

Song dynasty, with its lively international trade, and the early Ming, with its unprecedented maritime explorations, during the Yuan the five main areas of Eurasia—China, Southeast Asia, South Asia, Central Asia, and Europe—were part of a single world trading system. Europe was able to acquire Asian goods at low cost during this period; thus, when the Ming drove the Mongols out of China in 1368 and the Turks came to dominate western Asian trade routes, Europeans were inspired to seek maritime access to Asia. This, in turn, led to Europe's encounter with the Americas. Therefore, the brief Mongol period has an importance that belies both its brevity and its very limited demographic extent (the total Mongol population of about 1.5 million ruled over 100 times as many non-Mongols). Some background on earlier Central Asian tribes is helpful to understand the rise of the Mongols.

An earlier precedent for invasions out of Central Asia came from the Turkic peoples, who had figured in Eurasian history for a thousand years before the emergence of the Mongols. Between the sixth and eighth centuries, Turkic and Chinese regimes competed for control of the steppes. With Chinese support, the first Turkish Empire emerged in 552 and extended its dominion over much of Central Asia before it was conquered by the early Tang emperors. (An Lushan was of Turkish background.) During and after their imperial expansion, the Turks absorbed and transmitted much of the culture from their more advanced neighbors. Trade, religion, and warfare facilitated the process. Eastern Turks borrowed early from China, adopting Buddhism and converting their western kinsmen in far distant Ferghana. After the eighth century, when the Abbasid caliphate brought Islam to the steppes, Turkic invaders launched conquests in the Middle East and India. Through the fifteenth century, there were waves of migration and conquest out of Central Asia and into the settled territories of Eurasia. Such incursions usually brought short-term disaster to occupied regions, but effected a great synthesis of peoples and cultures and ultimately led to the establishment of Turkic regimes from India to the Middle East.

For more than five centuries before the Mongol conquests, this process had been growing in intensity. Westward and to the north of the Chinese frontiers, a series of large states, partially settled but still containing nomadic or seminomadic populations, rose and fell. Among them were the Uighur Empire of the ninth century and the Tangut state. Both of these regimes prospered by providing goods, protection, and transport for the overland trade with China, which continued to grow. For many peoples of Central Asia—Turks, Uighurs, Tanguts, Tibetans, Mongols, and a host of others—trade, especially the silk trade, was one of many stimuli that turned their attention toward the outside world in the thirteenth century.

Debate continues over what sparked Mongol expansion: climatic changes that ruined Mongol pasture lands, military capability, or the inspiration of an ambitious warlord. The Mongols, horse- and sheep-raising nomads and formidable mounted warriors, began conquering cities and trade routes in the early

Two views of Mongols as seen by their contemporaries. Left is a Persian miniature showing Mongols preparing food at their tents. Right is a Chinese painting of a mounted Mongol archer. Tents and horses were critical elements of Mongol life and status. The Mongol khans gave tents and horses as gifts to honor their subordinates and Central Asian horses were in great demand in China and Japan. In Central Asian culture a warrior was, by definition, a horseman.

thirteenth century on the way to establishing an empire that controlled most of Eurasia a century later. Beginning with Temujin, known in the West as Chinggis (1162–1227), who was selected Great Khan (Supreme King) in 1206, they claimed that they were destined by "heaven" to subdue all peoples. Chinggis was likely motivated to begin his quest for power to avenge his father's death. The Mongols were remarkably successful in launching large-scale military operations throughout Eurasia. They seized Persia, toppled the Islamic Abbasid caliphate in Baghdad, established their rule in Russia, and sacked Delhi, though they made no further inroads into India before moving on to China. From North China, they invaded Korea (1231 and 1258) and attempted unsuccessfully to invade Japan (1274 and 1281) and Java (1281 and 1292).

The Mongols have often been represented as destroyers par excellence, sacking cities, disrupting trade, and building towers of the heads of their conquered foes. The Mongols often used terror to control conquered peoples, particularly during the early conquests. Mongol commanders regularly imposed mass murder, torture, and resettlement on resisting populations. One million residents of the Chinese city of Chengdu (chuhng-DOO) were slaughtered in 1236 although that city had already been taken with little fighting. But Mongol presence also facilitated trade and diplomatic activity by providing security and postal service on Eurasian trade routes.

The Mongols Before the Conquest of the Song

Prior to their expansion in the early thirteenth century, Mongols had ranged widely in Central Asia, pitching their black felt tents, pasturing their animals, and fighting the elements much like other peoples who had raided and traded with settled Eurasian populations since the fourth century B.C.E. Mongol chiefs contended to be the "first among equals," decisions were made by councils of warriors, and women enjoyed a high degree of respect and influence. Polygamy was practiced among the warriors, but not all marriages were polygamous, and marital fidelity was enforced equally for men and women. Wives sometimes rode and fought beside their husbands; in a harsh environment where raiding and warfare were common, women as well as men had sometimes to defend the hearth and livestock.

At the opening of the thirteenth century, the Mongols began their campaign of conquests and empire building. Within less than a century, they had subdued most populations from the Pacific to the Caspian Sea,

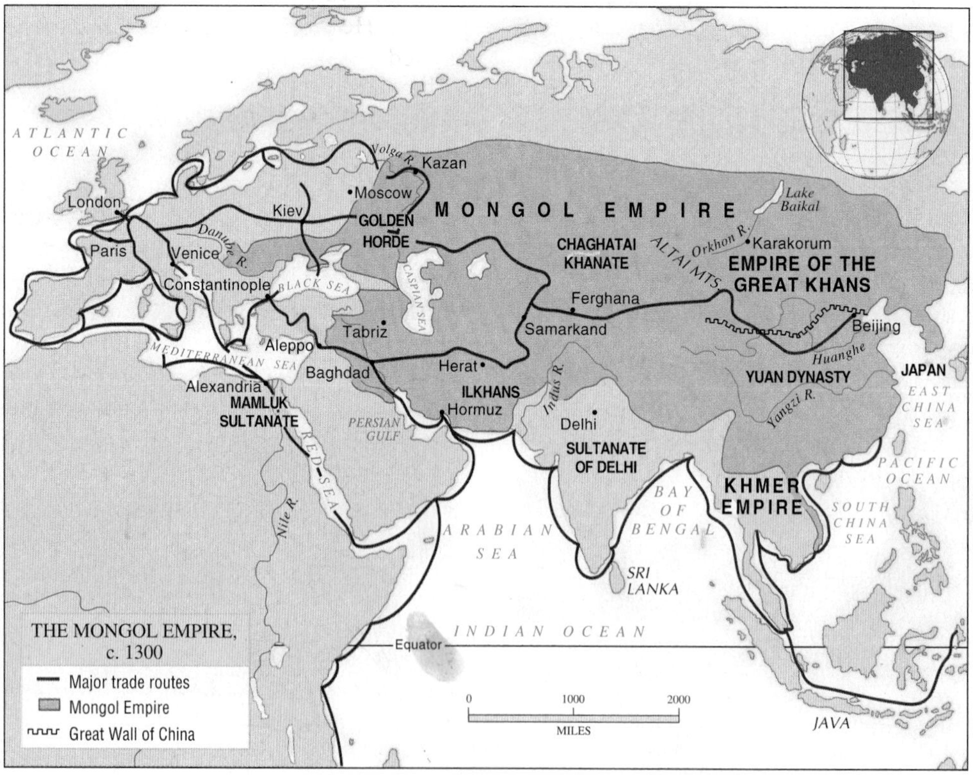

The Mongols extended their hegemony over a major part of Eurasia from the Danube to the Pacific from the mid-thirteenth to the mid-fourteenth centuries.

terrorized the rest, and gained luxuries beyond their imaginings. Trade and travel across Eurasia were facilitated. In most cases, however, they left a light cultural footprint. While the population of China did, indeed, decline from 120 million in 1207 to 60 million in 1290 (after the Mongol conquest), the cultural effects were less drastic. Chinese religion, painting, poetry, and social structure were not touched by the Mongols. Tolerance for foreign religions was promoted, but few Chinese changed their religious beliefs because of the presence of new sects.

During the first stage of their empire building, to 1241, the Mongols concentrated on the Central Asian steppe and its less developed border areas. Chinggis subordinated the Uighurs and Tanguts, seized Turkestan and Afghanistan, and invaded Persia. After his death in 1227, the campaigns halted and the Mongol forces reassembled in Mongolia to elect Chinggis's designated successor, his son Ögödei (EU-guh-dai; 1229–1241). Ögödei was granted Mongolia, from which he took the Jin Empire in northern China in 1234.

Between 1251 and 1259, during the reign of Ögödei's son, Möngke (MUHNG-kuh), Mongol armies conquered eastern Tibet (1252) and Korea (1259) while Möngke's brother, Hülegü (hoo-LEH-goo), toppled the Abbasid caliphate, absorbing every subsidiary state in Persia, Palestine, and Syria. Hülegü's campaign reflected the cosmopolitan nature of the Mongol army, with its Chinese catapult operators, and its court, with its Chinese physicians. The Mongols integrated the commanders, bureaucrats, artisans, and professionals of the conquered peoples into their armies and courts, thereby enhancing their ability to conquer and govern through borrowing the best practices of the conquered people.

Khubilai Khan (r. 1260–1294) emerged as dominant following a struggle from power among Mongol kings in 1260. After 1264 the empire broke up into four parts with only nominal central administration: Mongolia and China under Khubilai; and three other khanates in western Turkestan, Russia, and Persia and Iraq.

Mongol rulers of the mid-thirteenth century were forced to learn quickly how to organize and operate the largest imperial state that had ever existed. Although the ultimate base of authority in the sprawling Mongol territories was military power whose nucleus was a cavalry force of potentially 130,000 Mongols, civil administration and taxation were necessary. They developed a complex courier system linking the empire and created a written form of their language by using the script of the conquered Uighur people to transmit messages and records. The nomadic methods of the steppes were obviously no longer effective and had to be integrated with those of more experienced conquered bureaucrats.

Khubilai Khan hunting with his wife or a consort in a scroll painted in the late thirteenth century. Mongol women and men were expected to be vigorous and talented equestrians.

Before the conquest of the Song dynasty, Möngke revised the law code of Chinggis Khan to accommodate native cultural differences and meet practical needs. He minted coins, issued paper currency, collected taxes in money, and perfected a census system as a basis for taxes and military service. To support military operations, his state industries mined ores and produced arms. Other measures regularized trade tolls, improved roads, and provided for the safety of travelers, especially merchants. These reforms encouraged support from subject peoples, many of whom were now employed in the khan's service. Other areas were under lighter Mongol control. In these, local rulers proclaimed their submission publicly, left hostages with the khans, paid annual tribute, and provided troops for military campaigns. Such tributary rulers who served the khans loyally were guaranteed political security, honored publicly, and rewarded with lavish gifts (e.g., horses, daggers, furs, or silk garments).

China Under the Yuan Dynasty

Khubilai, who reigned as Great Khan from 1260 to 1294, turned his sights to the conquest of the Southern Song. After moving his capital to Beijing in 1264, he adopted a Chinese name for his dynasty in 1271. Like other Central Asian rulers who sought power in the east, Khubilai relied heavily on the advice of his Chinese and non-Chinese sinified advisors. One Song general offered advice on the construction of boats capable of navigating the many rivers and canals of South China. Khubilai, who had relied on cavalry and massive armies for his earlier conquests, thus became the first Central Asian conqueror of South China. Making use of a multiethnic force of Jurchen, Mongols, Persians, Uighurs, Koreans, and Chinese, Khubilai's forces laid siege to the Song. When the Yuan conquered all of China in 1279, Khubilai had gained the richest empire on earth. But even as he gained the wealth of China, the Mongol Empire had already ceased to be a unified Asian empire. Each of the four major khanates had developed its own state, and these were often at odds with one another. Though it is inaccurate to consider the Mongol realm a single political entity, the Mongol bonds of the khanates facilitated trade across the numerous Central Asian routes. Moreover, Turks and other West-Central Asians who had tried to take advantage of the commercial caravans themselves were suppressed during this period, making transport cheaper and easier.

Life under the Mongols was hard for most Chinese. While the Mongols did not prevent Chinese cultural expression, they did treat ethnic Chinese as distinctly inferior. A hierarchy dominated by foreigners was established: Mongols at the top, other peoples of Central Asia on the next rung, northern Chinese in lower positions, and southern Chinese almost completely excluded from office or public life. Taxation of Chinese was high. Many southern Chinese were subjected to serfdom or slavery. Though Khubilai retained the traditional ministries and local governmental structure, he staffed them with those in higher hierarchical positions. Generally, Mongol law prevailed, but the conquerors were often influenced by Chinese legal precedents, as in the acceptance of brutal punishments for loose or unfaithful women. Most religions were tolerated unless they violated Mongol laws.

According to Marco Polo, a Venetian traveler who arrived at Khubilai's court around 1275 and served the Khan for 17 years, the ethnic Chinese deeply resented unequal treatment. On the other hand, Polo also noted that the state insured against famine, kept order, and provided care for the sick, the aged, and the orphaned. To the awed Venetian, the Yuan state appeared fabulously wealthy, as indicated by the khan's 12,000 personal retainers, bedecked in silks, furs, fine leathers, and sparkling jewels.[9] Polo's fabulous story, dictated to a fellow prisoner of war in Genoa, reported the wondrous world of Cathay (China)—its canals, granaries, social services, technology, and such customs (strange to much of Europe) as regular bathing. Polo's account, like many travelogues of the period, is an interesting mix of fact and fantasy based on impressionistic observations and probably prompted by the desire to entertain as well as inform a specific audience. Polo was not the only observer of China, but his work at the court gave him an unusual vantage point.

DOCUMENT
Marco Polo on Chinese Society

The Yuan court's social practices, in addition to the discriminatory ethnic hierarchy, included the requirement that individuals register by occupation in order to pay labor services. In the realm of culture, the Yuan borrowed some Chinese traditions. At first, Daoism and Confucianism were subordinated to Buddhism, but both were revived during Khubilai's reign. The examination system was sporadically revived after 1315 but was weighted in favor of Mongols, so ethnic Chinese grew disillusioned. Chinese drama remained popular, influenced somewhat by the dance of Central Asia. Interest in drama encouraged the development of classical Chinese opera, a combination of singing, dancing, and acting, which reached maturity in the Yuan period. Some of the most influential Chinese painters were also producing at this time, and the novel emerged as a reflection of Chinese concerns. An example is *Romance of the Three Kingdoms*, a long and rambling tale set in late Han times but written in the fourteenth century.

During the Yuan dynasty, hosts of missionaries, traders, and adventurers continued to journey to and from Asia, Africa, and Europe. These travelers describe the opulence of China and the Mongol court. Even before the Polos, Christian missionaries had proceeded eastward, encouraged by hopes of converting the Mongols and, more important, gaining allies against the Muslims. John of Plano Carpini (PLAH-noh car-PEE-nee), dispatched by Pope Innocent IV, visited the Great Khan in 1246 but failed to convert the ruler or enlist him as a papal vassal. In fact, the khan sent him home with a letter demanding that Europe's monarchs submit to him and that the pope attend the khan's court to pay homage. Later, a Flemish Franciscan, William of Rubruck, visited Möngke's court in 1254 and 1255 and met with similar results; but another Franciscan, John of Monte Corvino, attracted thousands of converts to Christianity between his arrival in Beijing in 1289 and his death in 1322. Meanwhile, Mongol religious toleration had drawn Christians into Central Asia and Buddhists into the Middle East.

In addition to the missionaries, swarms of other people visited China and Mongolia. One was Guillaume Boucier, a Parisian architect, who trekked to Karakorum, where he constructed a palace fountain capable of dispensing four different alcoholic beverages. Other adventurers, equally distinct, moved continuously on the travel routes. Between 1325 and 1354, Ibn Battuta, the famous Muslim globetrotter from Morocco, visited Constantinople, every Middle Eastern Islamic state, India, Sri Lanka, Indonesia, and China. In Hangzhou he encountered a man from

Discovery Through Maps

Gog and Magog in the Ebstorf Mappamundi

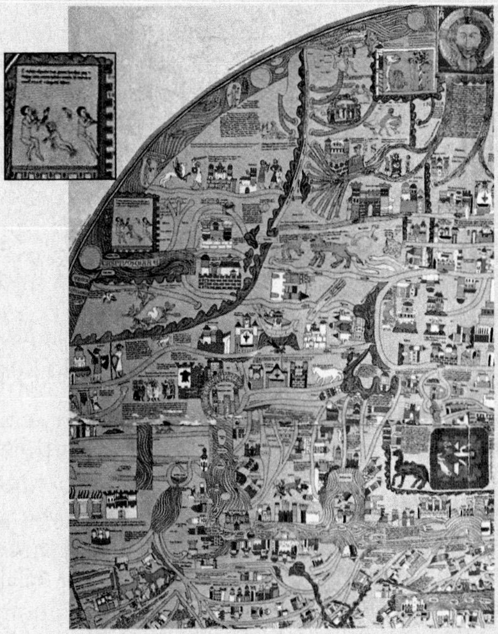

Maps depict more than geographical observations; they tell us the beliefs and imaginings of the people who produce them and reflect the point of view of the mapmaker. Historically, when people lacked a clear picture of far-off lands, they employed fantastic stories to describe what lay beyond their own known world. Like myths and folktales, maps from different eras illustrate some of the ways that societies have imagined apparently "strange" or "foreign" lands. We have seen that there was considerable commercial and intellectual exchange among Europe, India, China, and Central Asia in the years 220–1350 C.E. Nonetheless, the "Orient" remained a mysterious place in the imagination of many Westerners, a sometimes frightening place inhabited by strange creatures.

The thirteenth-century Ebstorf Mappamundi (map of the world), discovered in a Benedictine monastery in Germany, presents a geographical vision that combines Christian historiography, geographical observation, biblical mythology, the legends of Alexander the Great, and ancient tales of beastlike races inhabiting the "ends of the earth." It incorporates the idea of Gog and Magog, the homelands of apocalyptic destroyers, drawn from the New Testament (Revelation 20:7–8), into the description of the territory of northeastern Asia, the Mongol territory to the north of the Caucasus Mountains. On medieval Christian maps Gog and Magog were equated with barbarian races, with the Ten Lost Tribes of Israel, and with the armies of the Anti-Christ. According to legend, these ferocious peoples had been trapped by Alexander the Great, who built a great wall to contain them; they would break out at the end of time and overwhelm civilized societies. On the Ebsdorf map the people of Gog and Magog are tribes of savages who are shown eating human body parts and drinking blood. They are walled off in the far northeast of the world. Their identification with the Tartars suggests the fear of Turco-Mongol invaders that pervaded the mapmaker's society in the thirteenth century. Given the striking success of the Mongols' conquests in this era, it is no wonder that they came to be associated with Gog and Magog. Gog and Magog also appear on the twelfth-century Islamic world map of al-Idrīsī (see Chapter 7).

Questions to Consider

1. Why might medieval Europeans have imagined that a "hero" like Alexander the Great put a wall around such fearsome peoples?
2. Do you think the mapmakers took the idea of Gog and Magog literally? Why or why not?
3. What other examples do you know reflecting ideas about frightful peoples that live in far-off lands or about terrible events occurring at the "end of time?"

Morocco whom he had met before in Delhi. Some travelers went the opposite way. Rabban Sauma, a monk from Central Asia, traveled to Paris; and a Chinese Christian monk from Beijing, while in Europe as an envoy from the Persian khan to the pope, had audiences with the English and French kings.

Eurasian traders—Persians, Arabs, Greeks, and western Europeans—were numerous and worldly wise travelers. They were enticed by Mongol policies that lowered tolls in the commercial cities and provided special protection for merchants' goods. Land trade between Europe and China, particularly in silk and spices, increased rapidly in the fourteenth century. The main western terminals were Nizhni Novgorod, east of Moscow, where the China caravans made contact with merchants of the Hanseatic League, a coalition of German merchant companies; Tabriz, in northeastern Persia, which served as the eastern terminal for Constantinople; and the Syrian coastal cities, where the caravans met Mediterranean ships, mostly from Venice.

Expanding land trade along the old silk route did not diminish the growing volume of sea commerce. Indeed, the Mongol devastation of Middle Eastern cities provided a quick stimulus, particularly to the spice trade, which was partly redirected through the Red Sea and Egypt to Europe. Within a few decades, however, the Mamluk monopoly in Egypt drove prices up sharply, and the European demand for cheaper spices helped revive overland trade. By now, however, the southern sea route was thriving for other reasons. The Mongol conquest of China had immediately opened opportunities to Japanese and Malayan sea merchants, causing a modest commercial revolution. Later, after the government in China stabilized and became involved in the exchange, the volume of ocean trade between northeastern Asia and the Middle East surpassed that of Song times.

Although their conquests were accompanied by horrifying slaughter and wrought considerable havoc, Mongol control also spread knowledge of explosives, printing, medicine, shipbuilding, and navigation from China to the West. In the Middle East they furthered art, architecture, and historical writing. To China they brought Persian astronomy and ceramics, in addition to sorghum, a new food from India.

In the end, the Yuan dynasty was short-lived. Khubilai was its last effective leader. A powerful chancellor attempted to build a new canal to transport southern grain after the Yellow River burst its dikes in the 1340s, but his conscription of 150,000 laborers strained China's resources. In response, a messianic religion, the **White Lotus Society,** claimed numerous adherents anxious for Maitreya, the messiah Buddha, to bring about an end to suffering and injustice. Devastating epidemics hit cities already weakened by Mongol subjection; in 1232, Kaifeng lost one million people to the plague in three months. By mid-century, plague ravaged China and spread via the trade routes to the rest of Eurasia. A great rebellion, beginning in southern China and led by Zhu Yuanzhang (JOO yoo-ahn-JAHNG; 1328–1398)—known to history as Taizu, the first emperor of the Ming dynasty—ultimately ended the weakened Yuan. After the Chinese reconquered most of Mongolia and Manchuria, many northern Mongols reverted to nomadism. Others, on the western steppes, were absorbed into Turkic states.

KOREA: FROM THREE KINGDOMS TO ONE

- *How did Buddhism and Confucianism contribute to Korean culture and politics?*

In the third century C.E. the land inhabited by modern Koreans was divided in three kingdoms—one in the north and two in the south. Despite the common stereotype of Korea as an isolated "hermit kingdom," these three kingdoms were very much part of East Asian international culture. They adopted religion, arts, philosophy, and means of governance from China, transmitted culture and material goods to Japan, and fought battles against and in alliance with Chinese and Japanese rulers at various times. The fate of Koreans was closely integrated with the rise and fall of empires on the continent. By the fourteenth century, domestic and international influences led to the merger of the Korean kingdoms into one kingdom.

MAP Southeast Asia, Japan, and Korea

According to legend, Ko Chosŏn (KOH CHO-son), the earliest kingdom of Korea, was established in the third millennium B.C.E., but bronze age remnants date it from about 1500 B.C.E. Archaeological remains show that Koreans grew millet, soybeans, red beans, and rice; used ploughs and knives; developed metallurgy; and had an animistic form of religion in which all natural objects had spirits. Labor became specialized into peasant and artisan categories. In 109 B.C.E., this productive territory attracted the attention of the Han dynasty in China. Emperor Wudi conquered Ko Chosŏn and established four Chinese provincial commanderies in the north, permitting the introduction of Chinese culture. The decline of the Han allowed the newly arising Korean states to push the Chinese out and compete for dominance.

Koguryŏ (KOH-goo-ree-oh) was founded in 37 B.C.E. and by the first century C.E. had adopted a Chi-

White Lotus Society—Messianic religion that blended Manichaeism, Maitreya Buddhism, Daoism, and Confucianism. Appealed to people in times of crisis.

Korea

57 B.C.E.	Silla established
37 B.C.E.	Koguryŏ established
200s C.E.	Paekche established
383	Buddhism adopted in Korea
668	Silla defeats Paekche and Koguryŏ, unites Korea
936–1392	Koryŏ dynasty
1238	Mongol Invasion

nese style of kingship. Free peasants, living in villages under headmen, formed the bulk of society. Legal codes punished murder, theft, and bodily injury as well as female (though not male) adultery and jealousy—underscoring the importance of life and property in addition to the centrality of the polygamous, patriarchal family. The rise of the southern state of Paekche (PAIK-cheh) in the third century led Koguryŏ to strengthen its institutions: Koguryŏ's King Sosurim (r. 371–384) adopted Buddhism, set up a National Confucian Academy, and developed an administrative law code, all of which made Koguryŏ a centralized aristocratic state. In 433 Paekche formed an alliance with Silla (SHIL-lah; founded 57 B.C.E.), the other southern state. Koguryŏ fought against its Korean neighbors, sometimes in alliance with Chinese or Japanese forces. Koguryŏ was a powerful kingdom, later launching attacks on the Sui in China. (Its victories against the Sui army are part of the Korean annals of resistance.)

All three kingdoms were culturally Buddhist; Paekche adopted Buddhism in 384 and Silla in 528. Their poetry and arts followed Buddhist themes. Because most buildings were made of wood, none remain, but paintings and sculpture from this period, many with religious themes, are plentiful. A major **pagoda** (the East Asian form of the stupa) was built in Silla in 645, and lasted till it was destroyed by the Mongols in the thirteenth century.

Silla began to assert its power in the fifth century. Silla had an aristocratic society in which officials' positions were determined by "bone-rank" (that is, one's bloodline or status). Officials met in the Council of Nobles, and young men were placed in the Flower of Youth Corps, a powerful military organization. Silla allied with the Tang to defeat Koguryŏ and Paekche in the 660s, but, worried about Tang expansionism, Silla decided to push the Tang out of the Korean peninsula in 676. Lively trade between Silla and the Tang ensued, taking the place of conquest. Koreans were drawn into the international system promoted by the Tang; a Silla general in service to the Tang conquered Tashkent and Silla monks traveled to India. The eighth century, in which Pure Land Buddhism and Zen were introduced to Korea and the agricultural output was plentiful and varied, was the high point of Silla rule. By the ninth and tenth centuries, powerful landowners emerged, breaking apart the equal-field system applied in Silla.

In 936, one of many rebels succeeded in unifying the peninsula under a new dynasty he called the Koryŏ (KOH-ree-oh). This leader, King Taejo, and his immediate successors emancipated slaves (while retaining some forms of labor taxes), instituted an examination system (though preserving some aristocratic privilege), collected all arms held by private individuals, built a major university, supported Buddhism, and attempted to model the kingdom on Song Confucianism. Throughout its early years, Koryŏ faced threats from the Liao. The Jurchen's defeat of Liao and then of the northern Song left Koryŏ temporarily at peace with its neighbors. Domestically, however, the civilian leadership of Koryŏ was removed by a bloody coup by military officials in 1170, and peasant uprisings

This crown made of gold and jade is from the Kingdom of Silla and was made in the fifth or sixth century. Its opulence is a symbol for the national unification of Korea under a monarch.

pagoda—A Buddhist reliquary/monument, the East Asian equivalent of the Indian stupa.

around the same time weakened, but did not destroy, the state.

The Mongols invaded the weakened Koryŏ state in 1238. In the 1270s and 1280s, Koryŏ joined the Mongols in two unsuccessful invasions of Japan. Destructive Mongol rule led to uprisings throughout Korea in the 1340s, and soon King Kongmin (r. 1351–1374) restored Koryŏ rule. But he was doomed to failure. His bold initiatives at land reform were resisted by officials, tensions between Buddhists and Neo-Confucians of the Zhu Xi school erupted, and Japanese pirates plagued coastal trade. When he was assassinated in 1374, uprisings broke out all over Korea. The newly risen Ming dynasty in China took advantage of Koryŏ's instability, and was poised to invade in 1392. The Koryŏ general facing the Ming saw the writing on the wall, negotiated a treaty that made Korea a Ming tributary state, and marched back to the court to take over as the founder of the Yi or Chosŏ n dynasty (1392–1910).

Even in times of trouble, however, Korean culture blossomed. When the great royal library was burnt in 1126, a new collection of Buddhist works was commissioned. Movable type to print this great collection was cast and used three centuries before Gutenberg first used movable type in Europe. Buddhist works of literature, painting, and sculpture as well as a beautiful stone pagoda were also produced during the Mongol era.

THE EMERGENCE OF JAPAN IN EAST ASIA

- *Did Japan's distance from the continent allow it to retain more of its indigenous culture than the other countries of Asia in the classical and medieval eras?*

Separated from the Asian mainland by more than 100 miles of open sea since the end of the last Ice Age (around 12,000 B.C.E.), Japan was something of a curiosity to Chinese observers in the late third century C.E. These Chinese chroniclers found the Japanese law-abiding, adept at farming, fond of alcohol, expert at weaving and fishing, interested in divination, and perhaps most surprising, governed by both male and female shamanistic rulers. They described one of these rulers, Queen Himiko (also known as Pimiko), as a powerful priestess/monarch who, after her death, was interred in a remarkably large funeral mound. These tombs, some of which were twice the volume of the Great Pyramid in Egypt, tell historians that Japan was likely a hierarchical society able to mobilize labor during the tomb period, c. 300–645 C.E. The existence of religious leadership, especially female religious leadership, helps to explain the type of aristocratic society that developed in the classical age that followed the tomb period. How did Japan develop before the tomb period?

Classical Asian culture—religions, philosophies, arts, and means of governance developed on the continent—flowed into Japan first from Korea and later from China. During the Ice Age, land bridges had connected Japan with the continent. Tools dating from 30,000 B.C.E. and pottery dating from 10,000 B.C.E. (the world's oldest examples of pottery) have been found by archaeologists. Whether these were developed in Japan itself or transmitted from elsewhere is uncertain. An increasingly sophisticated Neolithic culture, called Jōmon (JOH-mon) by scholars, developed distinctive pottery and, between 5000 and 3500 B.C.E., the ancient Japanese language. But it was around 300 B.C.E. that a large migration of Koreans to Japan's westernmost large island, Kyūshū, brought about a revolution in agricultural technology (paddy-field rice) as well as bronze and iron technology. By the time the Chinese observers commented on life in Japan in the late third century, the civilization that blended the new continental ideas with indigenous culture had been established for over 600 years. The period from about 300 B.C.E. to 300 C.E. is called the Yayoi (yah-YOI) period for the district in Tokyo in which the period's pottery was first unearthed.

Clay figures like this happy dancing peasant couple were placed in the huge tombs built for Japanese uji *leaders in the third, fourth, and fifth centuries.*

The following era, the tomb period, gave birth to what might be called Japan's first organized governments, ruled by those whose remains are in the great tombs. At first, the extent of a leader's control was likely no more than a clan located in one village, but in time, successful leaders brought more and more villages under their control until they had something like a province. Political authority was intimately connected to religious authority. The original clans, called *uji,* were led by a head priest or priestess believed to be descended from the clan's own deity or *kami*. In ancient Japanese religion—later called **Shintō** ("Way of the Gods") when the introduction of Buddhism made it obvious that Japan's intrinsic belief system deserved a religious name—*kami* were believed to be everywhere in nature. The world of the living was seen as connected to the world of the gods, and governance was a part of religious ritual. Thus, women were not barred from what we would consider administrative leadership, and the Chinese observers found that fact sufficiently interesting to comment on it.

The *uji* in the Yamato region, near the area in which the cities of Nara and Kyoto were later built, possessed the most fertile agricultural land in ancient Japan. It is small wonder that the Yamato leaders, able to build on their productive wealth to support military strength, emerged as the most powerful *uji* by the fifth century. The Japanese language did not yet have its own written form, so historians rely on Chinese observers' reports from the fifth century, rich archaeological remains in tombs, and Japanese histories (*Kojiki*—Records of Ancient Matters—and *Nihongi*—Records of Japan), written in the early eighth century and based on orally transmitted tales, for evidence about people's lives at that time. Tomb artifacts throughout the period included jewels, mirrors, and, most interestingly, clay statues of human figures like warriors, musicians, courtiers, and dancing peasants, all showing expressions of joy, as well as of horses, boats and model houses. From the fifth century on, these tombs increasingly held military objects brought in by a new wave of people from the Korean peninsula. Outside the tombs, archaeological remains of peasant villages suggest farmers lived in pit dwellings.

The power of the Yamato *uji* vis-à-vis the other *uji* throughout Japan was bolstered by its alliance with Paekche. Korean artisans and scribes brought a wealth of Korean and Chinese culture with them to Japan, strengthening the prestige, authority, and administrative competence of the Yamato state. Imported weapons allowed the Yamato warriors to hold sway over their neighbors. As in Korea, Chinese characters were used to transcribe Japanese. Confucian scholarship was introduced around 513, and Buddhism made a grand entrance, possibly in 538, when the king of Paekche sent Yamato a statue of the Buddha and copies of Buddhist scriptures. Though the ties with Paekche soon ended, the coming of continental culture in general and Buddhism in particular set in motion a cultural and intellectual revolution in Japan. After Silla's unification of the Korean peninsula in the 670s, the Yamato leaders turned to the Tang dynasty for cultural models, diplomatic ties, and trade. At the same time, the Japanese retained significant indigenous customs. These included marriage practices that emphasized the central role of the bride and her family, practices that would later play an important political role. They also included the old religions of Japan. The Yamato family, while welcoming Buddhism following a sixth-century struggle between Shintō ritualists and proponents of Buddhism that was won by the latter, nevertheless retained the worship of the Shintō gods. At some earlier time, as the Yamato were rising to power, a myth of Japan's creation that blended several *uji*'s founding myths and placed the Yamato's ancestral deity Amaterasu (AH-mah-teh-RAH-soo), the sun goddess, at the top of the hierarchy, developed. The Yamato would use this to legitimize their political dominance for many centuries to come.

The victorious proponents of Buddhism, the Soga family, greatly influenced the Yamato family. During

Shintō—Indigenous Japanese religion focused on innumerable gods in nature; animistic belief system tied to government in antiquity.

Japan

c. 300 B.C.E.–300 C.E.	Yayoi period
late 200s	Queen Himiko of Yamato
c. 300	Yamato clan dominates central Japan
c. 538	Buddhism introduced to Japan
645	Taika Reform
710–784	Nara period
760s	Compilation of *Man'yōshū*
794–1181	Heian period
c. 800	Introduction of Tendai and Shingon Buddhism
995–1027	Regency of Fujiwara Michinaga
c. 1000	Lady Murasaki, *The Tale of Genji*
1185–1333	Kamakura Shogunate
1274, 1281	Mongol Invasions

his aunt's reign as the Yamato ruler, Prince Shōtoku (SHOH-toh-koo), head of the Soga, apparently undertook so many reforms that Japan was forever changed. He is credited with scholarly commentary (in flawless Chinese) on Buddhist scriptures; with building many temples, including, in 607, Hōryūji (hoh-ree-OO-jee), which contains the world's oldest extant wooden buildings; with opening diplomatic relations with the Sui and later Tang; with adopting the Chinese calendar; with reorganizing the Yamato governing structure on the model of the Confucian state to make it the central monarchy of Japan; and with writing, in 604, the "Seventeen-Article Constitution." These accomplishments were detailed in one of the eighth-century histories of Japan and undoubtedly exaggerated the Prince's personal contributions, but most of them did take place either during his service as regent to the throne or in the decades after his death. Shōtoku's death in 622 led to a struggle for power, ending with the victory of one courtly faction led by the head of the Nakatomi family (renamed Fujiwara in 645). The Yamato family retained the throne, as they do to this day, but the Fujiwara family replaced the Soga as their main advisors. In 645, the Fujiwara carried out the Taika (Great change) Reforms, which centralized economic control under the equal-field system imported from China and Korea. Two rulers, Emperor Temmu (r. 672–686) and Empress Jito (r. 686–697), implemented additional changes; they and their successors were simultaneously continental-style rulers empowered by the prestige of Confucian authority and Shintō rulers legitimized by descent from Amaterasu.

Government in the Classical Era—Nara and Heian

An important step toward Chinese-style centralization was the building of a permanent capital. In 710, the Yamato, by then considered the imperial family, built the city of Nara on the model of Chang'an. Although today's Nara is located in a different site, the eighth-century capital's grid of streets and ancient Buddhist temples are still evident in the Japanese countryside. The rise of powerful Buddhist monasteries and temples may have challenged the power of the court sufficiently to force it to abandon Nara in 784 and build a new capital, Heian (now called Kyoto), in 794. Like Nara, Heian was originally laid out on a grid pattern preserved in modern Kyoto's downtown boulevards and streets. Historians designate the years 710–784 as the Nara Period and 794–1181 (or 1185) as the Heian Period.

To make the capital the sole seat of power, the court enticed all *uji* leaders, who might be potential rivals for power, to live there by granting them titles of nobility and making the court too glamorous to avoid. Many of these *uji* families' provincial lands were con-

A fine example of architecture during the mid-Heian period in Japan is Phoenix Hall, near the modern city of Kyoto. Used by Fujiwara Michinaga as a villa, it later became a temple honoring Amida.

fiscated and redistributed under the equal-field system in the seventh and eighth centuries, but the *uji* were allowed to retain some lands, as were religious institutions and individual farmers who opened new fields to cultivation. Such private estates, unlike the lands farmed by average peasants, were exempt from taxation by the court. Though these estates, called **shōen,** were but a small percentage of Japan's cultivated fields in the eighth century, during the next several centuries peasants wishing to escape taxation commended their lands to private estate owners. This led to the gradual reduction in taxable lands, as farmers paid rents to large owners rather than the often higher taxes to the court. The replacement of tax revenues by rents did not at first appear problematic, however. The great families not only lived at or near the court but also, as we shall see, were often tied by blood to the imperial family. By the eleventh century, however, the gradual erosion of the tax base undermined the central authority of the court. In addition, the absence of a government-run military—a conscript army was one of the Chinese institutions not implemented by the Japanese court because Japan appeared not to face external enemies as did the Chinese—induced estate owners to hire guards to protect their provincial economic interests. These guards eventually became the samurai or warrior class. When they served as guards, they presented no threat to the throne, but when they banded together, as they did in the tenth century and then, most disastrously for the court, in 1181, they could become an alternate political authority to the throne.

Even during the height of the throne's power, its authority was dependent on a balance with one great family, the northern branch of the Fujiwara family. The Fujiwara had earned a special role as advisors at the time of the Taika Reform, but they preserved their dominant position through Japan's traditional marriage practices. Japanese couples married extremely young by today's standards—often as young as 12 or 13. Though girls of the elite spent most of their time indoors and spoke with men not of their immediate families from behind a screen to maintain their propriety, they were very well educated and could communicate easily by letters. Literature describes the lives of women and girls at the court as much more open, and these courtly women communicated more freely with men and with one another. In either case, women and girls played an important role in selection of their sexual and marital partners.

CASE STUDY

Women in the Imperial Courts of China and Japan

A young man interested in a woman at court might find few barriers to a liaison with her. If the young woman lived at home with her parents, courtship was a bit more complicated. The suitor would call on a potential lover by slipping, under cover of night, through the windows of her room, taking care not to wake her parents. She would speak to him, exchanging poetry and observing his character and attractiveness, from behind her screen. If his clothes, language, scholarly ability, scent, musical talent, and sensitive heart were sufficiently appealing, it was proper for her to invite him behind her screen. If not, she sent him packing, and her propriety was not compromised. If he spent the night, he would have to sneak out at the first rays of morning light. Repeated visits would trigger the parents' investigation of the young man and his career prospects, and if they approved, they would indicate the couple's marriage by leaving ritual food and drink outside their daughter's bedroom door. Thereafter, the young man could come and go during the day, as he was now part of the family as the daughter's husband. The young man would be known as the husband of his bride's house, her parents would make sure he was beautifully outfitted to present himself well at court, and in some cases, once the bride was mature enough to run her own household, the parents and other children might move to another house and leave the teenage bride in charge of her own home. Most likely, she would already have one or two children, raised in their early years by their maternal grandparents, as women usually had their first child in their teens. Grandparents thus had a particularly strong bond with their grandchildren. Property was inherited by daughters, children were their mothers' and maternal grandparents' responsibility, and respectable men and women—though not *married* women—could have more than one sexual partner. Once married, a woman should be unavailable to other men, but serial monogamy was practiced.

Fujiwara influence over the throne depended on marriage customs and family relations. When an 8-year-old boy ascended the throne as emperor in 858, his maternal grandfather, a Fujiwara who was already Grand Minister to the court, assumed even greater control as regent for his grandson. This pattern of Fujiwara patriarchs' control of child emperors, and even some adult emperors who were their grandsons or other relatives, continued for the next 200 years. The pinnacle of Fujiwara dominance was in the early eleventh century. Fujiwara Michinaga (MEE-chee-NAH-gah), who held dominion over the court from 995 to 1027, was the brother of two empresses and the father of four, the uncle of two emperors, the grandfather of two more, and the great-grandfather of another. Some non-Fujiwara protested, but until an emperor whose mother had not been a Fujiwara ascended the throne in the late eleventh century, the Fujiwara controlled the throne. Through this control, the Fujiwara were able to have the tax-free ownership status of their shōen estates confirmed, as only an official could grant that status. For the next century, retired emperors took the place of the Fujiwara as

---

shōen—A tax-free estate in Heian Japan.

regents for their youthful sons whom they placed on the throne. In the late twelfth century, disputes over succession to the throne led to the development of factions at court, and with each faction backed by a powerful samurai family, civil war raged throughout the country from 1181 to 1186. When it was over, the imperial institution survived, but it no longer had the authority to rule Japan. That power fell to the victorious samurai leader, Minamoto Yoritomo (MEE-nah-MOH-toh YOH-ree-TOH-moh; 1147–1199), his wife, Hōjō Masako (HOH-joh MAH-sah-ko; 1157–1225), and her family, who exercised their power from the medieval town of Kamakura in eastern Japan.

Classical Arts and Literature

Japanese emperors sent numerous embassies to the Tang court and brought back a continuing stream of up-to-date culture and material goods. New developments in Chinese poetry were reflected in Japanese verse; new schools of Buddhism influenced Japanese religion; and plump Tang beauties set the standard for female pulchritude at the Japanese court. Yet Japan preserved many of its own practices, including an emphasis on aristocracy, a rejection of eunuchs at court, and unique marriage customs. In 839, as the Tang dynasty was clearly declining, the court ceased to send embassies to China.

Courtly society from the Nara through the Heian periods was extraordinarily refined. The record left from those centuries includes great volumes of poetry, diaries, the world's first novel—the massive *Tale of Genji* by Lady Murasaki—as well as paintings, sculpture, temples, monasteries, and other buildings. Art works from distant lands in Eurasia, brought to Japan by travelers to China, show Japan's integration with the international culture of the Buddhist Age in the Nara and early Heian eras. And music preserved in Japan's court until the present day is the only extant record of Tang musical styles borrowed in the classical era. Impressive though this body of culture is, it was the creation of just a tiny group of people; aristocrats were no more than one tenth of one percent of the population, with urban residents influenced by those aristocrats perhaps an additional several percent.

Unlike aristocrats, farmers were not literate. Tax rates appear high, as evidenced by peasants' attempts to escape the tax roles. Pestilence devastated farmers and city-folk alike. Men, women, and children worked hard. Despite these difficulties, folk tales and written stories abound with examples of farm women's high status relative to their husbands. Women likely selected their own spouses, and many made important economic contributions to their households. Wives' infidelity was treated as a joke rather than as a capital crime in folk tales.

The poetry of the literate elite reflected the importance of sentiment. The *Man'yōshū* (mahn-YOH-shoo; *The Collection of Ten Thousand Leaves*), compiled in the 760s, contains over 4000 poems, many of which date to the fifth century, composed by emperors, empresses, courtesans, frontier guards, and commoners. These brief and direct compositions covered such themes as parting of lovers, loyalty to one's lord, love of nature, grief over the death of a child, and the Buddhist theme of the fleeting nature of human life, give us a rich sense of early Japanese society and culture. Two *Man'yōshū* poems, the first a love poem by a woman, the second a poem of grief for his wife by a man, give a sense of this collection:[10]

Court ladies and their maids in The Tale of Genji. *Heian court women were ideally plump, had hair longer than their bodies, and wore many layers of robes. The* Genji *scrolls integrated text and images.*

Oh, how steadily I love you—
You who awe me
Like the thunderous waves
That lash the seacoast of Ise!
Lady Kasa

In our chamber, where our two pillows lie,
Where we two used to sleep together,
Days I spend alone, broken-hearted:
Nights I pass, sighing till dawn.
Kakinomoto Hitomaro

Because the Japanese language did not have a written form, it was represented with Chinese characters. Aristocratic men and some women were able to read and write in Chinese and thus sought to use characters to record Japanese. The two languages are not related linguistically, so the characters were used in several different ways. One was to represent meaning—the Chinese character for "tree," for example, would be applied to the Japanese word for "tree." The other was to represent sounds without any consideration for the meaning of the character. This led to a virtually indecipherable script, so *kana,* a syllabic script, was devised in the early ninth century. Soon poetry, diaries, essays, and novels were written in this script. Aristocratic authors, especially but not exclusively women, produced an outpouring of creative works. Women's dominance in the literary arts at that time was due, in part, to the fact that men spent a lot of their time writing government documents in Chinese. But the fact that creativity, including calligraphic, artistic, and sensory abilities, was not gendered at that time, as well as the leisure time their aristocratic privilege gave them, may have had more to do with offering women opportunities to produce fine works.

The most important work of the Heian period—and some might say of the entire body of Japanese literary arts—was *The Tale of Genji*, written over the course of perhaps two decades by Lady Murasaki, who was sometimes praised, sometimes ridiculed for her exceptional knowledge of both Japanese and Chinese scholarship.[11] *The Tale of Genji* describes the life, loves, escapades, and sorrows of the sensitive and talented Prince Genji, a paragon of male virtue; his son Kaoru; Genji's steadfast male friends; and his beloved wife Murasaki. The novel is an intriguing look into courtly life around the year 1000. An excellent parallel to *Genji* is *The Pillow Book* by Sei Shōnagon (SAY SHOH-nah-gon), a contemporary and professional rival of Lady Murasaki at another empress's court. *The Pillow Book* contains often racy, amusing and satirical essays that give good insight into the life of the court.

DOCUMENT
Excerpt from Lady Murasaki Shikibu's Diary

From the sixth century through the first half of the Heian period, religious themes predominated in the arts. Statues and paintings of various manifestations of the Buddha, indicating changes in artistic style and notions of physical beauty over the centuries, were common. But decorated items for aristocratic pleasure, such as musical instruments, boxes, and tables are also among the treasury of early Japanese art. By the tenth century, paintings of highly secular themes emerged. Fans with themes from literature were made and used by court ladies, and the *Genji* scrolls of the eleventh century were a multimedia production interspersing gorgeous paintings with Murasaki's text. Comic scrolls appeared by the late Heian period. The architecture of the court and of private mansions was elegant, with raised floors of polished wood, sliding screen doors, wooden buildings connected to one another by covered corridors, windows with hinged shutters (through which suitors could climb), all surrounded by carefully landscaped gardens with streams and ponds.

The imperial treasury at Nara, built in the eighth century, contains works of art by both Japanese and continental artists, indicating Japan's increasing international contacts in the Nara period. This small silver jar depicts a hunting scene that includes a deer, still one of the symbols of Nara.

Japanese Buddhism in the Classical and Early Medieval Eras

Mahayana Buddhism reached entered Japan in the sixth century and was well established among the aristocracy by the eighth. To further the secular reach of the Nara state, the court established branch temples throughout the country, staffed by monks trained in the capital. Most commoners, especially those in the countryside, continued to carry out Shintō rituals. Except for the struggles in the sixth century, there was little conflict between Buddhism and either indigenous Shintō and the imported philosophy of Confucianism as there had been in China, and Buddhism was eventually

Document Sei Shōnagon: *The Pillow Book*

Sei Shōnagon was a contemporary and literary rival of Lady Murasaki. The two served different empresses of the reigning emperor; Sei Shōnagon 's court was considered more fashionable and Lady Murasaki's more erudite. Sei Shōnagon was a witty and talented writer. In her diary, Murasaki describes Sei Shōnagon as "a very proud person. She values herself highly and scatters her Chinese writings all about. . . . How can such a vain and reckless person end her days happily!"[11] Below is an excerpt from Sei Shōnagon 's *Pillow Book* in which she describes distressing things.

One has been expecting someone, and rather late at night there is a stealthy tapping at the door. One sends a maid to see who it is, and lies waiting, with some flutter of the breast. But the name one hears when she returns is that of someone completely different, who does not concern one at all. Of all depressing experiences, this is by far the worst.

It is very tiresome when a lover who is leaving at dawn says that he must look for a fan or a pocketbook that he left somewhere about the room last night. . . . Instead of experiencing the feelings of regret proper to such an occasion, one merely feels irritated at his clumsiness. . . . It is important that a lover should know how to make his departure. To begin with, he ought not to be too ready to get up, but should require a little coaxing. . . . He should not pull on his trousers the moment he is up, but should first of all come close to one's ear and in a whisper finish off whatever was left half-said in the course of the night. . . . If he springs to his feet with a jerk and at once begins fussing around, one begins to hate him.

I like to think of a bachelor . . . returning at dawn from some amorous excursion. . . . As soon as he is home . . . he begins to write his next-morning letter. . . . When he has washed and got into his court cloak . . . he takes the sixth chapter of the Lotus Sutra and reads it silently. Precisely at the most solemn moment of his reading, the messenger returns. . . . With an amusing if blasphemous rapidity the lover transfers his attention from the book he is reading to the business of framing an answer.

Questions to Consider

1. How important was romantic love to Heian aristocrats?
2. The ideal bachelor Sei Shōnagon describes reads Buddhist scriptures before heading off to work at the court. What other tasks take priority over his religious practice?
3. Did women have a choice in the selection of their suitors?

From "The Pillow Book of Sei Shōnagon," in Donald Keene, *Anthology of Japanese Literature* (New York: Grove Press, 1955), pp. 137–139.

indigenized as the dominant religion of Japan following new theological directions in the Heian period.

Two new sects of Buddhism were brought to Japan by student monks who had journeyed to China in 804. Tendai, introduced by Saichō in 805, and Shingon, brought back by Kūkai in 806, both made it possible to develop mass participation in Buddhist worship. Tendai doctrine stated that those who led a life of purity and contemplation could realize enlightenment and their "Buddha nature." Saichō established an important monastery at Mt. Hiei (HEE-ay), which several centuries later became a source of trouble for the court as it supported not only devotion and learning but also a large army of warrior-monks who demanded land rights and privileges. Shingon was an esoteric faith, with secret and seemingly magical rites. It was extremely popular in the Heian period, as it encouraged art, medicinal use of herbs, incantations, and pageantry. It also appealed to Shintō adherents, as its central deity was Dainichi (DAI-nee-chee), the "Great Sun" Buddha, who was identified with the Sun Goddess in the popular mind.

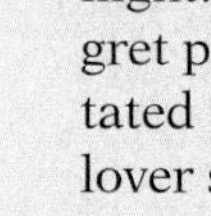

Buddhist Monks

In the mid-tenth century, itinerant monks spread a simplified version of the Tendai doctrine of enlightenment, stating that salvation was possible only for those who called on the name of Amida, the Buddha of the Pure Land. But it was not until the end of the Heian period, with its natural disasters, earthquakes, fires, and fearsome warfare that a proponent of Pure Land Buddhism succeeded in establishing a new type of Buddhism. The monk Hōnen (1133–1212) preached that faith in Amida alone, without relying on good works, was the only route to salvation. He endured persecution for his propagation of Pure Land ideas. His follower Shinran (1173–1262) took these ideas even further. He said that perfect faith was shown by uttering the name of Amida just once, and that an evil man of perfect faith was able to enter the Pure Land. Shinran broke with Buddhist tradition—eating meat,

The pagodas of Yakushi-ji at Nara. Built in the eighth century, Yakushi-ji is one of Japan's earliest wooden temple compounds. Buddhist temples of that era challenged the secular power of the government, so the emperor's court moved to Heian in 794.

marrying a nun, and advocating the equality of all occupations if performed with a pure heart. His True Pure Land sect eventually became the largest in Japan. The other important faith sect was Nichiren (NEE-chee-ren) Buddhism, founded by the monk Nichiren (1222–1282), who stated that one should place faith in the Lotus Sutra, a key Buddhist scripture, rather than Amida. Known for his Japanese nationalism, he predicted the Mongol invasions. By the twelfth century, Buddhism had spread to all classes of society.

Two major **Zen** sects were also brought back to Japan by Japanese student monks. Eisai (1141–1215) introduced the Rinzai sect and Dōgen (1200–1253) the Sōtō sect. Rinzai stressed complicated riddles to achieve enlightenment, while Sōtō emphasized long hours of meditation. Both methods were increasingly popular with samurai who were attracted to the sudden enlightenment they promised.

Early Medieval Government and Culture

Minamoto Yoritomo's victory over the other major warrior band, the Taira, in 1185 ushered in the era of warrior dominance. He never claimed the throne, as victorious generals elsewhere in Asia had, but rather had the emperor confer on him a new position, *shōgun* (great general), a title which would remain in use for most of the next 700 years. The shōgun theoretically served at the pleasure of the emperor, but (until 1868) when emperors attempted to assert their rights, the struggle was always won by the shōgun, who, of course, claimed to be serving the emperor. (An attempted imperial uprising in 1221 was suppressed.) The shōgun set up his seat of power in Kamakura, away from the capital, and the era of Kamakura dominance is called the Kamakura Period (1185–1333).

Minamoto Yoritomo's legitimacy as a ruler was based on his own institutions in addition to his symbolic subordination to the emperor. First, he made use of the loyalty of his samurai. Like feudal lords in Europe, he used a bond of loyalty to motivate his samurai warriors, whom he called "honorable house men" or vassals. These vassals were appointed constables of provinces, with the duty to raise up armies if necessary, and stewards or overseers on the shōen estates owned by the rich old Heian families. To show his authority over the estates, he allowed the stewards to collect a small amount of revenue—so small that owners did not bother to contest it as they had contested the imperial court's ability to collect taxes on private lands. By paying the small fees, however, owners acknowledged the legitimacy of Kamakura's right to collect it. During the next century, the stewards would use these locally collected resources to establish their own landed power base in the countryside, and they would eventually turn on their supposed overlords in Kamakura. Second, Minamoto Yoritomo and his successors made use of much of the provincial governing structure of the old imperial system for most of the next century. The vassal samurai were too few in number to rule on their own, so the previous system was retained in many places. Third, Minamoto established three new offices: the samurai board, which controlled the vassals; the judicial board, which settled suits over land holdings as well as criminal issues; and the administrative board, to carry out his policies. The judicial board was particularly important in gaining the support of the people, as it was known for its impartiality in settling disputes. The administrative board was headed by his Hōjō in-laws, and was used by them to increase their power after Yoritomo's death in 1199. Indeed, power passed into Hōjō hands, where it remained until the Kamakura shogunate (government by shōgun) was overthrown.

Zen—The Japanese form of Chan Buddhism. Popular with the samurai.

By the end of the thirteenth century, samurai ties to Kamakura had become attenuated. Allegiance to the dominant Hōjō was not as certain as allegiance to the Minamoto had been earlier. Far from Kamakura, samurai stewards out in the provinces developed local ties, both political and economic. When the Mongols attacked in 1274 and again in 1281, the samurai, especially those of the western island of Kyūshū, where the attack came, fought bravely, but none was rewarded, because there were no spoils of war to divide. The invasion in 1274 threw 30,000 attackers against Japan; the second invasion was mounted by 140,000. Commoners built a sea wall whose remnants are still visible today to keep the Mongols out; it helped the Japanese warriors hold the Mongols out until typhoon winds, called *kamikaze* (divine winds), blew many of the Mongol vessels out to sea, forcing them to withdraw. Japan was saved, but the invasions had some very significant outcomes. Disgruntled warriors who had fought, commoners whose labor had built the fortifications, and religious people who claimed their prayers brought about the divine winds eventually moved against Kamakura when succession disputes at court gave them an excuse to join one side or the other in the 1330s. Also, the practice of daughter inheritance and multiple inheritance gave way to unigeniture or inheritance by one son in order to keep samurai lands intact to support a mounted warrior now deemed necessary for national defense. Single inheritance weakened family ties, as younger sons sought new patrons to protect them. This strengthened the lord-vassal bond at the heart of feudalism, which became increasingly important in the next three centuries.

Kamakura was home to numerous beautiful temples, built in harmony with the verdant hills, a new style of construction. A huge outdoor Great Buddha statue that still attracts thousands of tourists every day was cast in the early Kamakura period. But much of Japan's culture in this era emanated from Heian (now increasingly called Kyoto). The court commissioned great collections of poetry as they had in earlier centuries, and court ladies wrote, for an aristocratic readership, tales of great emotional depth. Periodic markets began to bring rural people into a larger national culture, but the arts were still fairly elite. This would change in the next century, as a national culture, enhanced by new infusions of Asian styles, entered Japan.

CONCLUSION

During the centuries following the collapse of the Mauryan dynasty in India (184 B.C.E.) and, much later, the Han dynasty in China (220 C.E.), significant cultural revivals occurred in Asia. First India and then China experienced golden ages when political unity was restored and social systems were revitalized. In India, the Gupta era encouraged the development of Hindu thought, along with notable advances in painting, architecture, literature, drama, medicine, and the physical sciences. At the same time, India continued to be part of an emerging international Buddhist culture, helping to link it to other Buddhist countries along the East-West trade routes. Later, international Islam tied rising Indian dynasties, some of them Islamic, to other centers of power and trade. China experimented with blending "barbarian" and indigenous means of government in the millennium from the fall of the Han to the fall of the Mongols. Cosmopolitan blending of culture made China the East Asian center of both cultural consumption and production. Scholarship and art blossomed even in the period of disunity and flourished in the lively international Tang dynasty and the technologically sophisticated early modern Song dynasty. Korea and Japan, while retaining much of their own culture, adopted a number of aspects of Chinese governance, art, philosophy, religion, and means of communication. Rivalries at times impeded trade, but diffusion of material and other forms of culture made Eurasia a single system, often dominated by its eastern side, during much of the millennium. Over the centuries, cultural diffusion gained increasing momentum throughout Eurasia. Goods and cultural patterns spread through migrations, invasions, missionary activities, and trade to China, India, Southeast Asia, Japan, Korea, the Asian steppes, and Europe.

Suggestions for Web Browsing

You can obtain more information about topics included in this chapter at the websites listed below. See also the companion website that accompanies this text, http://www.ablongman.com/brummett, which contains an online study guide and additional resources.

Ancient and Medieval India
http://www.fordham.edu/halsall/india/indiasbook.html

Extensive collection of materials on ancient and medieval India; most entries include subsites with text and images.

Gupta Period
http://www.wsu.edu:8080/~dee/ANCINDIA/GUPTA.HTM

Indian history in the Gupta era.

Medieval India
http://www.goindiago.com/history/medieval.htm

Site discussing the history, sites and monuments, and classical texts of medieval India, 600 B.C.E.–1526 C.E.

Chinese Empire
http://www.wsu.edu/~dee/CHEMPIRE/CHEMPIRE.HTM

Chinese history from 256 B.C.E. to 1300 C.E., with details about philosophy and culture.

The Heian Era
http://www.wsu.edu:8080/~dee/ANCJAPAN/HEIAN.HTM

This site gives a valuable context to the Heian era.

Ancient Japan
http://www.wsu.edu:8080/~dee/ANCJAPAN/ANCJAPAN.HTM

Website on ancient Japan includes political, religious, and cultural history, details about women and women's communities, and a portfolio of art from the era.

Samurai Archives
http://www.samurai-archives.com/

Extensive collection of information about individuals and events in the samurai millennium.

Empires Beyond the Great Wall: The Heritage of Chinggis Khan
http://web.archive.org/web/20000815214514/http://vvv.com/khan/

A rich site (now archived) offering a biography of Chinggis Khan and information about the history and culture of the Mongol Empire.

Literature and Film

The following works give the flavor of this long millennium in India: *The Panchatantra,* trans. Arthur W. Ryder (University of Chicago, 1967); Prince Ilangô Adigal, *Shilappadikaram (The Ankle Bracelet),* trans. Alain Daniélou (New Directions, 1965); Somadeva, *Tales from the Kathäsaritsägara,* trans. Arshia Sattar (Penguin, 1994); Cornelia Dimmitt, ed., *Classical Hindu Mythology: A Reader in Sanskrit Puranas,* trans. J. A. Van Buitenen (Temple University, 1994).

For a fictional treatment about Empress Wu that offers a picture of Tang court opulence and intrigue see Evelyn McCune, *Empress* (Fawcett Columbine, 1994). For Japan, Lady Murasaki's *Tale of Genji* is available in several excellent translations. The newest is by Royall Tyler (Penguin Publishers, 2002). A 1991 animated film (subtitled) is a good introduction to the first third of the book.

Suggestions for Reading

Informative surveys of India's medieval history include Hermann A. Kulke, *A History of India,* 3rd ed. (Routledge, 1998); and Tej Ram Sharma, *The Political History of the Imperial Guptas* (Concept, 1989). On the Delhi Sultanate, see Peter Jackson, *The Delhi Sultanate: A Political and Military History* (Cambridge University Press, 2003). On women, see Tracy Pintchman, *The Rise of the Goddess in the Hindu Tradition* (State University of New York Press, 1994); and Leslie Orr, *Donors, Devotees, and Daughters of God: Temple Women in Medieval Tamilnadu* (Oxford University Press, 2000).

Two of many fine general histories of China in the post-Han, Tang, Song, and Yuan periods are Patricia Buckley Ebrey, *Cambridge Illustrated History of China* (Cambridge University Press, 1996); and Charles O. Hucker, *China's Imperial Past* (Stanford University Press, 1975). A comprehensive work on Chinese painting is *Three Thousand Years of Chinese Painting,* eds. Richard M. Barnhart, Nie Chongzheng, Lang Shaojun, James Cahill, and Wu Hung (Yale University Press, 1998). Dorothy Ko, Jahyun Kim Haboush, and Joan R. Piggott's *Women and Confucian Cultures in Premodern China, Korea, and Japan* (University of California Press, 2003) is an excellent overview of the role of women in each of the three countries. For a classic though still excellent introduction to the Song, see Jacques Gernet, *Daily Life in China on the Eve of the Mongol Invasion, 1250–76* (Stanford University Press, 1962). Valerie Hansen, *The Open Empire: A History of China to 1600* (W. W. Norton, 2000) explicates Tang and Song foreign relations and the domestic repercussions of economic expansion. On women and family relationships see Patricia Buckley Ebrey, *The Inner Quarters: Marriage and the Lives of Chinese Women in the Sung Period* (University of California Press, 1993). Katherine Bernhardt's *Women and Property in China, 960–1949* (Stanford University Press, 1999) gives us a legal history of family law in Song China with its social repercussions. On the Yuan dynasty see Elizabeth Endicott West, *Mongolian Rule in China* (Harvard University Press, 1989).

An excellent study of networks of trade and communication in the Mongol era is Janet Abu-Lughod, *Before European Hegemony: The World System,* A.D. *1250–1350* (Oxford University Press, 1989). A recent work that treats Asia as an interacting unit is Warren I. Cohen, *East Asia at the Center: Four Thousand Years of Engagement with the World* (Columbia University Press, 2000).

A solid survey of Korean history is Carter J. Eckert, et al., *Korea Old and New: A History* (Harvard University Press, 1990). Surveys of Japanese history in the classical and medieval eras include *The Cambridge History of Japan: Ancient Japan,* eds. Delmer M. Brown, John Whitney Hall, Marius B. Jansen, Madoka Kanai, and Denis Twitchett (Cambridge University Press, 1993); John W. Hall, *Government and Local Power in Japan, 500–1700* (University of Michigan Press, 1999); and Wayne Farris, *Heavenly Warriors: The Evolution of Japan's Military, 500–1300* (Harvard University Press, 1996). Karen Brazell's translation of *The Confessions of Lady Nijo* (Stanford University Press, 1976) offers a fascinating account by an itinerant woman, once a court lady, now a nun, in the early thirteenth century, and is a wonderful addition to the larger body of work on women writers in the Heian period.

CHAPTER

11

The Americas to 1492

CHAPTER CONTENTS

40,000

c. 40,000–10,000 B.C.E. Movement back and forth across the Bering Strait land bridge

10,000

10,000 B.C.E. Nomadic migrations from Asia reach tip of South America

c. 5000 B.C.E. Development of maize agriculture

2000

c. 2000 B.C.E. Divergence of Inuits and Aleuts

c. 1200 B.C.E.–150 C.E. Formative period of Mesoamerica culture (Olmec)

c. 800 B.C.E.–600 C.E. Adena and Hopewell cultures

1 C.E.

c. 150–900 Classical period in Mesoamerica culture (Maya)

c. 300 Beginning of Anasazi culture

500

c. 500–600 Beginning of Mississippian culture

c. 900–1500 Postclassical period of Mesoamerican culture (Toltec, Aztec)

1000

c. 1100–1500 Development of Inca empire

c. 1300 Height of Cahokia culture

1500

c. 1500s Inca Empire in South America reaches maturity

Early civilizations in the Americas followed a social sequence similar to that found in Africa and Eurasia. As agriculture became more diversified, food supplies increased and some cultures became more and more able to support cities, highly skilled crafts, expanding commerce, complex social structures, and the emergence of powerful states. The most noteworthy were the civilizations of the Mayas in Yucatán and Guatemala, the Aztecs in central Mexico, and the Incas in Peru. The Mayas are particularly recognized for their mathematics, solar calendar, and writing system—70 percent of which has only recently been deciphered. The Aztecs and Incas conquered large populations and governed extensive states. Each civilization produced distinctive customs, values, art, and religion, many of which have become part of the Latin American heritage. Spanish adventurers who invaded these civilizations were shocked by the religious sacrifices of human beings but astonished by the wealth, grandeur, technical efficiency, urban populations, and institutional complexity they saw in Central America and Peru. For example, Tenochtitlán (te-nohch-teet-LAHN), the Aztec capital with its 150,000 inhabitants, was larger and probably better administered than any European city of its time.

To the north of Mesoamerica, hundreds of Amerindian tribes developed diverse social patterns, languages, and economic pursuits as they adapted to the differing environments they faced. Around 4000 B.C.E. Amerindians in the southwestern part of present-day Florida founded villages along the coast in which they enjoyed a rich diet of fish, shellfish, grains, and berries and lived in accord with a sophisticated religious system that included the burial of the dead in funeral mounds. Recent archaeological finds indicate that still earlier in the present-day state of Washington, Amerindians founded villages with their own unique cultures and economic activities. The Amerindians to the north never attained the centralized power or wealth of the Mayas, Aztecs, and Incas. However, they left behind a variety of archaeological sites that attest to their sophistication and creativity.

ORIGINS OF AMERICANS AND THEIR CULTURES

■ *Does the development of Amerindian cultures support or negate the theory of parallel development?*

Many of the American cultures can be traced back to nomadic migrations from Asia to Alaska, across the Bering Strait land bridge. During the Pleistocene epoch, coinciding with the last great ice age, humans established themselves in Siberia where they built underground shelters and hunted large mammals such as mammoths. The most recent ice advance, beginning some 65,000 years ago, locked up immense amounts of global water and lowered sea levels, creating a land bridge that enabled Paleolithic people to follow the animals they hunted into North America. Later, as increasing global temperatures melted the ice and raised water levels, the bridge slowly disappeared around 10,000 years ago, after an estimated 30,000 years of sporadic human migrations. Recent discoveries indicate that there also may have been other routes of entry into the Americas, including those by sea from Iceland and Greenland and across the Pacific into Chile and Peru.

Archaeological work throughout the twentieth century continually pushed back the estimates of the time of the first permanent residents. Artifacts known as Clovis spear points, the oldest of which are about 11,200 years old, were found from Mexico to Nova Scotia. Continued discoveries across North America revised the estimates of when human beings settled in the Americas to around 20,000 years ago. Some archaeologists think humans could have lived in North America even earlier. However, the most widely accepted estimates of the first human settlement in the Americas are 14,000 years ago, with humans reaching southern Chile by circa 12,500 years ago. Recent discoveries in Peru indicate that the first city in the Americas was that at Caral, founded around 2600 B.C.E. Archaeologists believe that the pyramids built there were constructed a century before the Great Pyramid at Giza in Egypt.

Over this protracted period the Amerindians split into eight major ethnolinguistic groups and hundreds of subgroups and adapted to numerous physical environments. New research has shown the Americas to be far more densely populated in the fifteenth century than the European invaders believed—perhaps by as many as 75 million people before the massive population decline caused by climatic changes and foreign diseases such as small pox in the fifteenth and sixteenth centuries.

The development of agriculture in the Mexican highlands, along the Peruvian coastal plain, and in what is now the southwestern United States caused major changes in indigenous American culture after 7000 B.C.E. This development occurred considerably later than in the Near East, and the plants that the Amerindians domesticated were different from those in other parts of the world. They also domesticated animals such as alpacas and llamas in the Andes—there were no cattle, sheep, or horses until the Europeans arrived in 1492. The major agricultural contribution came with the cultivation of maize (corn), shortly before 5000 B.C.E., in the Tehuacán (ti-wah-CAN) valley of Mexico. From this center, maize culture spread widely. After 1000 B.C.E. it became the staple food for hundreds of societies, from the Mississippi River valley to the Argentine pampas. The Aztec Confederacy and Inca Empire, which so awed the Spanish *conquistadores* after 1500, were dependent on the raising of maize.

Beyond these mature civilizations, cultural levels varied widely among the Amerindians by the end of the fifteenth century. Some powerful cultures, like that of the Mound Builders of the Mississippi valley, borrowed heavily from Mexico. Cahokia, a major capital and trade center near contemporary St. Louis, Missouri, housed approximately 25,000 people during the thirteenth century. Other sophisticated cultures north of the Rio Grande ranged from the Pueblo of the southwest to the large Iroquois Confederacy of the eastern woodlands. In South America, complex cultures lived along the north coast and near the mouth of the Amazon. Other societies developed on Caribbean islands, in the South American pampas, and in Chile. Other Amerindians—probably a majority of them—were still hunters and gatherers. These included the Eskimo peoples of Alaska and the Inuit peoples of Arctic Canada; jungle groups such as the Jivaro (he-VAR-oh) of the upper Amazon; and the peoples of Tierra del Fuego, at the southern tip of South America.

Despite differing timeframes, Amerindian cultures differed little from cultures in Africa and Eurasia in their progression from Paleolithic hunting and food gathering to Mesolithic semifixed communities to Neolithic food production and settled communal life and then to urban centers and the emergence of political states. They also displayed common traits with other civilizations in their theocratic systems, sun cults, and human sacrifices. Like the African cultures, they were in transition from matriarchal to patriarchal institutions, although further along in the process. Finally, a common belief in monarchy among Aztecs and Incas was also typical of many other peoples in the ancient river civilizations of Eurasia.

EMERGING CIVILIZATIONS IN MESOAMERICA

▪ *What geographical and climatic factors permitted the rise of Mesoamerican civilization?*

A variety of related cultures flourished in **Mesoamerica,** a zone ranging from roughly 100 miles north of Mexico City to Costa Rica. The region varies greatly in landforms, climate, and vegetation. Two mountain ranges run through northern Mexico to join a central highland block in the region of the Valley of Mexico. The Pacific coastal region is relatively narrow while that on the Atlantic side is wide. The north and west have dry lands with sparse vegetation; the south and east are marked by tropical rain forests and savannas.

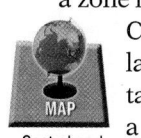

MAP Central and South American Civilizations

Despite these physical differences, the early cultures were unified by their economic interdependence, because no one region was self-sufficient. They shared a complex calendar, hieroglyphic writing, bark paper, deerskin books, team games played with balls of solid rubber, chocolate bean money, widespread upper-class polygamy, large markets, and common legends. A popular one featured a god-man symbolized by a feathered serpent. We may conveniently divide Mesoamerican history into three main periods: formative (to 150 C.E.), classical (150–900), and postclassical (900–1492).

The Formative Period

For a millennium after 1500 B.C.E., villages in the regions of Mexico and Central America grew steadily to become cities. Scattered throughout this region at the beginning of this period were some 350,000 people, living in relatively sparsely populated ceremonial trading centers and villages. Labor and stone for the massive construction projects, jade for carving, luxury goods, raw materials for the crafts, and food were brought to the centers often from distant places—without the use of horses, mules, or oxen. These goods were probably not the spoils of conquest; Olmec society left little evidence of war or violence, although some security would have been present to protect trading missions.

In these settlements artisans worked at pottery making, weaving, feather design, and masonry. Merchants ranked second only to the priesthood in social status, as they conducted trade among the temple cities. As population increased and society became more complex, priests came to dominate governments. They governed by enjoying respect and exploiting fear rather than relying on force. The general theocratic orientation is reflected most clearly in the great temple mounds; in the huge stone conical pyramid at La Venta, rising some 100 feet; and in the characteristic carved statuary that represented the dominance of the Olmec cults.

Mesoamerica—A cultural zone in Central America ranging from roughly 100 miles north of Mexico City to Costa Rica.

Mesoamerican and South American Civilizations

2500s B.C.E.–400s C.E.	Olmec
300s–900s C.E.	Mayas
900s–1200s C.E.	Toltecs
1100s–1500s C.E.	Incas
1300s–1500s C.E.	Aztecs

In time the common culture, known as the Olmec, centered in five geographical areas. One was in the Oaxaca (wah-HAHK-ah) region of western Mexico; another was in the inland Valley of Mexico; a third straddled the present Mexican-Guatemalan border; and a fourth (the later Mayan) arose in the southern highlands and lowlands of Yucatán, Honduras, and Guatemala. The fifth, and at the time most significant, area spread over some 125 miles of the eastern Mexican coast and its hinterlands, near present-day Veracruz.

Archaeological research in Olmec sites reveals exceptional wealth, technical efficiency, and artistic sensitivity. In many Olmec sites, the oldest at San Lorenzo, there were great stone buildings and pyramids dating from 1200 B.C.E. The culture is perhaps best known for its colossal heads and its fine jade carving, featuring jaguars. This cultural maturity was not matched by military advancements: San Lorenzo was destroyed by invaders about 900 B.C.E.; another ceremonial center at La Venta, in Tabasco, assumed leadership until it, too, fell, six centuries later.

Olmec influence permeated most of present-day Mexico and Central America. A few independent Olmec centers may have been established farther to the north, but it was probably more common for a number of Olmec priests and traders to live among native populations, conducting religious rites and arranging for the transport of goods to the homeland. Such enclaves were typical of regions as distant as the Pacific coast of Central America. In other places, such as the Oaxaca valley to the west, the southwestern

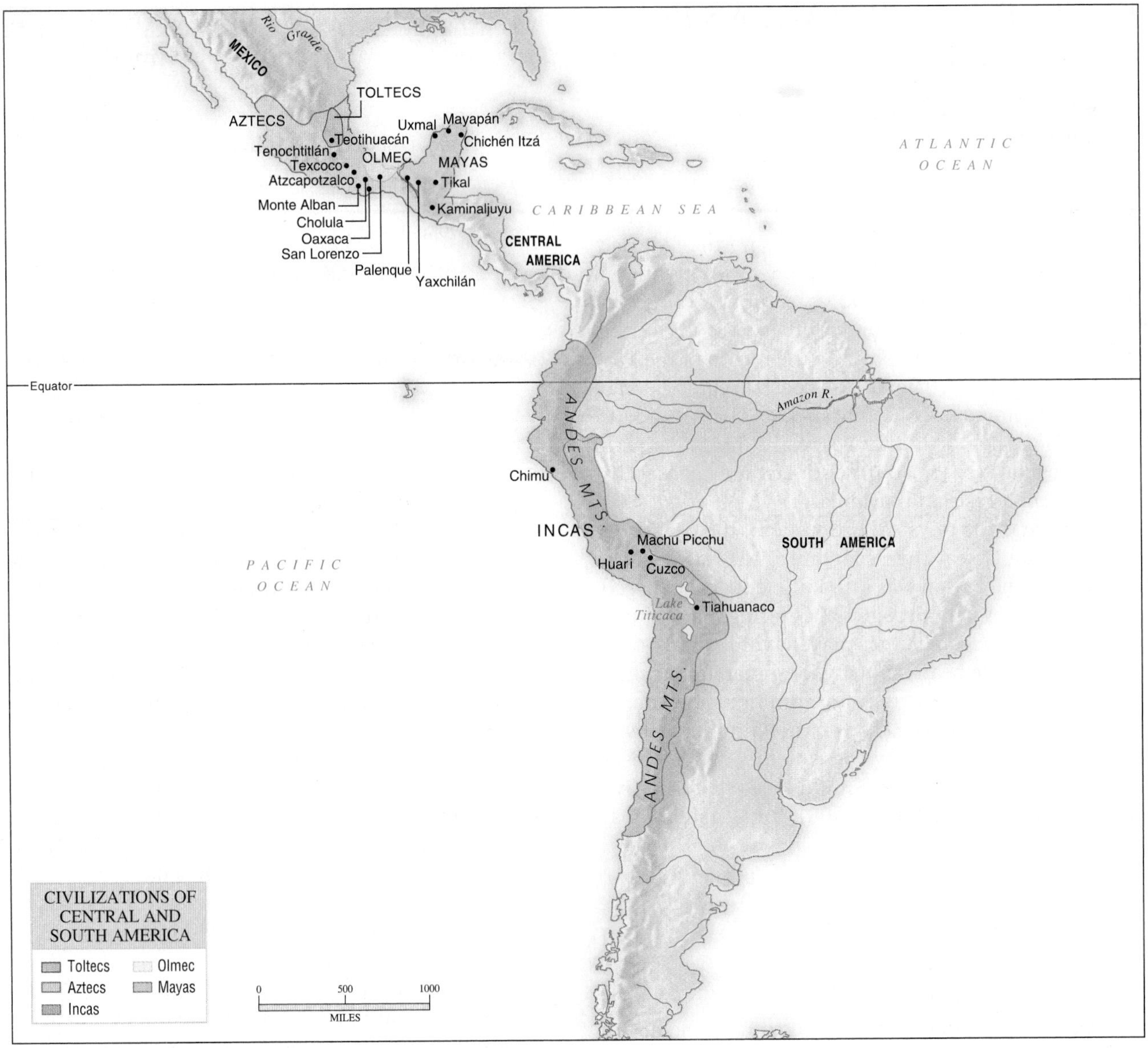

Ranging from the lowland and jungles of Central America to the arctic cold of the Andes, the civilizations of Central and South America exhibited a rich and sophisticated diversity.

Mexican highlands, or the southern Mayan regions, Olmec influence was more indirect, possibly resulting from trade or Olmec marriage into local elites. By such varied means, Olmec foundations were laid for the religion, art, architecture, and characteristic ball games—and possibly for the calendars, mathematics, and writing systems—of later civilizations, including the Mayan and the Aztec.

The Classical Period

After the fall of La Venta, Olmec prestige waned, but by the second century C.E., cultural developments progressed to a point known as the classical period, which would last until the tenth century. This was a golden age when, across the region, written communication, complex time reckoning, a pantheon of gods, interregional trade, and a 40-fold population increase over the Olmec period occurred. Hundreds of communities raised great buildings, decorated them with beautiful frescoes, produced pottery, figurines, and sculptures in large quantities. Although classical Mayan culture of the Yucatán lowlands is perhaps best known, Teotihuacán (te-oh-tee-wah-KAHN), in the northeastern valley, also generated an impressive culture.

At its peak about 500 C.E., Teotihuacán was the sixth largest city in the world, with a population of 125,000 to 200,000. Three and a half miles long and nearly two miles wide, it was laid out in a grid of sorts

The colossal Pyramid of the Sun rose above the metropolis of Teotihuacán. Measuring 650 feet at its base and 213 feet high, the structure is more than four times larger than the Great Pyramid of Khufu (Cheops) in Egypt.

and paved with a plaster floor on which clusters of imposing edifices were erected. This ceremonial center is dominated by the temple-pyramids dedicated to the moon and the sun. The first pyramid was cut off at the top to provide for a temple with a broad step ascending from a wide rectangular court. Running south is a long ceremonial axis, and adjacent to it the Pyramid of the Sun. Also truncated, it measures 650 feet at the base and rises in four terraces to 213 feet above the valley floor. The interior contains more than a million cubic yards of sun-dried bricks, and the exterior was once faced entirely with stone. As with other pyramids throughout Mesoamerica, these structures, with their ceremonial staircases, led to temples at the summit where rites and sacrifices were offered to the gods.

Teotihuacán was noted for its specialized craftspeople who came from all over Mexico and occupied designated quarters of the city. Its streets were studded with bustling markets, where all types of goods were available from foreign as well as local sources. This wealth permitted a governing elite of priests, civil officials, military leaders, and merchants to enjoy great luxury. Teotihuacán exerted a powerful influence over other states, including some among the lowland Mayas, because of its cultural reputation, social connections, and commercial advantages. When necessary, it used its formidable military power to enforce trade and tribute agreements. Above all, Teotihuacán marks the high point of priestly power over the rest of society. Thereafter, especially with the Toltecs, the cultures came to be far more military in character.

Another impressive classical center in Mexico was located at Monte Alban in the Oaxaca valley. In 200 B.C.E. it already had a population of 15,000, and its fortifications dominated the valley. In Teotihuacán's era, this concentration of temples, pyramids, and shrines was a theocratic state, still drawing tribute from adjacent hill settlements and a valley population of over 75,000 people. Although developed on a smaller scale than Teotihuacán, Monte Alban produced a similar pattern of foreign trade, class distinctions, elaborate religious architecture, artistic creativity, writing, and time reckoning. It derived most of its art styles from Teotihuacán and some from the Mayas but synthesized both in its own traditions. Politically, it remained independent through the classical era, although its elite sought the luxury goods and favor of Teotihuacán.

CLASSICAL MAYAN CIVILIZATION

- *What were the economic, political, cultural, and religious characteristics of Mayan civilization?*

While Teotihuacán and Monte Alban flourished, Mayan peoples farther south in Yucatán and Guatemala brought artistic and intellectual activity to new heights in more than 100 Mayan centers, each boasting temples, palaces, observatories, and ball courts. Although it borrowed from Teotihuacán before the latter's decay in the eighth century C.E., Mayan civilization subsequently cast a brilliant light over the whole of Mexico and Central America.

A Mayan Town

The earliest Mayas are thought to have migrated from the northwest coast of California to the Guatemalan highlands during the third millennium B.C.E. From that homeland, Yucatec- and Cholian-speaking peoples settled the northern and central lowlands, respectively, between 1500 B.C.E. and 100 C.E. Mayan villages developed steadily, many becoming ceremonial centers by the start of the Common Era. In the highlands, Kaminaljuyu (kah-MEEN-ah-leu-yeu) had by then developed architecture and primitive writing under the influence of Oaxaca and Teotihuacán. But in the early classical period, before 550 C.E., Tikal, in the central lowlands, assumed Mayan leadership as it traded with Teotihuacán and allied itself with Kaminaljuyu. The fall of Teotihuacán brought temporary confusion, soon followed by the glorious renaissance of the late classical era at Tikal, Palenque, Yaxchilán (yahks-chee-LAHN), Uxmal, and other Mayan centers.

A number of distinguished scholars such as Linda Schele and David Friedel, Jeremy Sobloff, and Michael D. Coe have given us a detailed view of the Mayas. Their communities had productive economies based not only on agriculture but also on handicrafts and long-distance trade. In often barren soil, except in some parts of the highlands, Mayan farmers used intensive agriculture, clearing, irrigating, and terracing to raise squash, chili peppers, and many other crops, including maize—which supplied 80 percent of their food. Mayan metalwork, cotton cloth, and chipped stone implements were traded widely, carried in large dugout canoes along the rivers and the Atlantic coast. Exchange was facilitated by the use of common goods as media of exchange, including cocoa beans, polished beads, salt, and lengths of cotton cloth.

Mayan society in this period was a rich mixture of old and new. An ancient kinship system prevailed among all classes, with lands assigned and controlled by the clans. Matriarchal values persisted, as indicated by some queens who retained power and influence. Women were generally respected, held some legal rights, and did some of the most important work, such as weaving. The shift toward patriarchy, however, was definite and unmistakable, as was seen in priorities accorded men in most social situations, such as being served first by women at meals. A more fundamental change involved the rise of social classes. Hereditary male nobles and priests were in most positions of authority and power, but craftspeople and merchants enjoyed privileges and status. Slaves, captured in military campaigns or kidnapped, did most of the hard work, particularly in the continuous heavy construction of ceremonial buildings. They were also subject to being used in religious sacrifice, although this was far less common than among the later Aztecs.

A hereditary priest-king, usually considered to be a descendant of a god, governed each Mayan center. He was assisted by a council of priests and nobles. His government levied taxes, supervised local government in outlying villages, and administered justice. It also was responsible for conducting foreign relations and making war. The Mayas were not very successful in large-scale military operations because their armies were drawn mainly from the nobility and were therefore limited in size. Nevertheless, armed with their obsidian-bladed weapons, they were equal to their neighbors in making war. Indeed, as time passed and cities vied for supremacy, wars became increasingly common. In the process, some centers remained independent, but most joined loosely organized leagues, based on common religious traditions, dynastic marriages, or diplomatic alignments.

Religion permeated all phases of Mayan life. Like the later Aztecs, the Mayas saw life as a burden and time as its measure, and they deified many natural phenomena, particularly the planets and stars, as powers to be appeased by human pain and suffering. Public bloodletting was part of normal ritualistic worship. Human sacrifice, usually accomplished by decapitation, was common, and wars to obtain prisoners for sacrifice were sometimes waged. The dominance of religion over everyday life is further illustrated by the general interpretation of law as religious principle and taxation as religious offerings. Economic value derived as much from the religious sanctity of a thing as from its material utility or scarcity. Moreover, education was aimed primarily at training priests; reading and writing were considered necessary religious skills, and mathematics and astronomy were valued mainly because they were required in scheduling ceremonies honoring the gods.

The two most significant achievements of the Mayas were their calendar and their writing system. Neither of these was original, but both were more efficient than those of earlier peoples. The Mayan astronomers, using only naked-eye observation, surpassed their European contemporaries. Their constant scanning of the heavens allowed them to perfect a solar calendar with 18 months of 20 days each and a five-day period for religious festivals. Using an ingenious cyclical system of notation known as the "long count," they dated events of the distant past for accurate record keeping and the scheduling of astronomical observations. Their notational mathematics, based on 20 rather than 10 as in the decimal system, employed combinations of dots and bars in vertical sequences, to indicate numbers above 20. For nonnumerical records, they combined **pictographs** and **glyphs,** which have recently been deciphered sufficiently to reveal specific historic events and their human dimensions.

DOCUMENT

Anonymous: Victory over the Underworld

These remarkable accomplishments in mathematics, astronomy, and writing were more than matched by the magnificent Mayan art and architecture. The plaza of each Mayan community was marked by at least one pyramid, topped by a temple. The one at Tikal towered to 229 feet, 16 feet higher than the Pyramid of the Sun at Teotihuacán. With their terraced sides and horizontal lines, Mayan pyramids showed a skilled sense of proportion. The highly stylized sculpture dec-

pictographs—Picture symbols.

glyphs—Symbolic characters in writing.

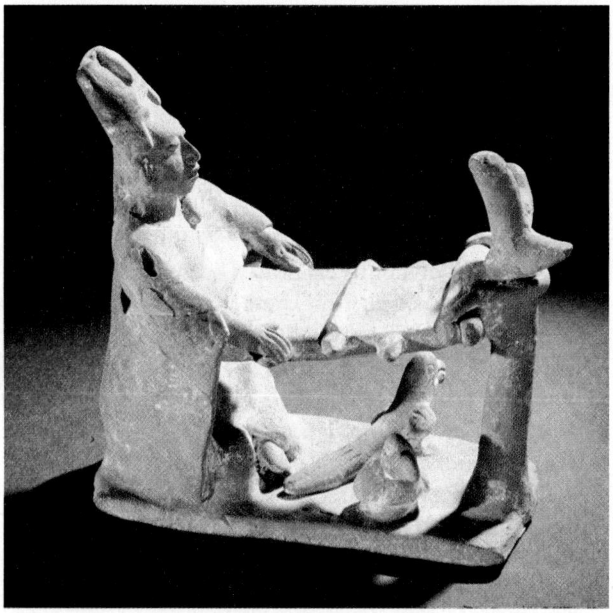

The Mesoamerican societies were at the same time sophisticated, complex, and powerful—and bloody in their human sacrifices to the gods. This seated figure, surrounded by winged messengers, seems to be looking off in the distance to anticipate what the divine powers might next demand from him.

orating their terraces is regarded by some authorities as the world's finest, even though the Mayan sculptors accomplished their intricate carving with only stone tools—there were no bronze or iron implements in the Americas at that time. The Mayas also developed mural painting to a high level of expression. Even their crafts, such as weaving, ceramics, and jewelry making, reveal a great aesthetic sense, subtlety of design, and manipulative skill.

THE POSTCLASSICAL ERA

- *Which civilizations rose to prominence after the end of the classical era of Mesoamerican civilization?*

The region's classical artistic development ended during the eighth and ninth centuries. The causes, not yet fully uncovered, have been generally attributed to factors ranging from overpopulation and internal struggles to soil exhaustion and Chichimec invasions from the north. Amid the accompanying upheavals, urban populations dwindled, and most of Teotihuacán's residents scattered in all directions, even into the Mayan lands. But there was no complete collapse; trade continued on a large scale, and the expanded use of writing indicated more social complexity and interstate competition, which contributed to intensified political conflict. Consequently, the age produced a new cultural mode, with heavier emphases on militarism, war, and gods thirsting for human blood. Among many smaller but thriving city-states, in addition to the dying Teotihuacán, were the Mayan polities of Tikal, Chichén Itzá (cheech-EN eet-SAH), and Mayapán. Farther north, the Oaxacan centers were still flourishing after the tenth century, as were Atzcapotzalco (ahts-kah-poh-TSAL-koh), Xochicalco (hoh-chee-KAL-koh), and Cholula, with its colossal pyramid.

The Toltecs

Most prominent of all these centers was Tollan, the Toltec capital. Toltec history is unclear before 980, when Topiltzin (to-PIL-tzin), a legendary king, founded the city and created a new power located in the central Valley of Mexico. His subjects were a mixture of Chichimecs and former urbanites of the area, who may have served for a while as peacekeepers in the north. Over the next two centuries, the city became a great urban complex of 120,000 people, a hub of trade, and the center of an evolving Toltec confederacy that assumed the leading role formerly played by Teotihuacán. Meanwhile, Tollan's future was shaped by a struggle for power between Topiltzin and his enemies. The king had early adopted the Teotihuacán god **Quetzalcoatl** (kets-al-koh-AHT-el), who opposed human sacrifice; but followers of the traditional Toltec war god, **Tezcatlipoca** (tez-kat-le-POH-ka), ultimately rebelled and forced Topiltzin into exile. The victorious war cult took over, steadily expanding its hegemony, by conquest and trade, into an empire stretching from the Gulf of Mexico to the Pacific, including some Mayan cities of the south.

The tumultuous political conditions of the early postclassical period finally brought disaster to the Toltecs. Failing crops and internal dissension caused great outward migrations from Tollan and abandonment of the capital at the end of the twelfth century. Shortly after, the city was burned by Chichimecs. For two centuries thereafter, the area was a land of warring states and constantly forming and dissolving federations. Some cultural continuity, however, was maintained by peoples in the Oaxaca valley, notably the Zapotecs, whose culture was as old as the Olmec. Although they struggled constantly with neighboring peoples for supremacy and survival, the Zapotecs maintained towns, temples, ball courts, and art that helped preserve Mesoamerican traditions for later times.

Quetzalcoatl—The Toltec god of the civilization, goodness, and light; literally "plumed serpent."

Tezcatlipoca—The god of the night sky and sorcery; literally "smoking mirror"; initially Toltec in origin but also adopted by subsequent peoples, including the Aztecs.

This Aztec mask is a figure within a figure, and the person wearing the mask would hope to project animal strength and unearthly terror.

Toltec militarism spread from central to southern Mexico. It left the less developed Mayan highlands relatively undisturbed but brought decline and reorientation to the old lowland centers, such as Tikal. Severe droughts also drove migrants into northern Yucatán, where a developing cistern technology provided more water. At Chichén Itzá in the tenth century, a cosmopolitan Mexican-Mayan military elite established their dominance and maintained a trading network, by land and sea, throughout the southern region. From the early thirteenth into the fifteenth century, Mayapán was a fortified center, defended by mercenaries and maintaining leverage over subkingdoms by holding hostages from dependent royal families. Trade continued to grow, along with population, among the postclassical Mayas; but art, cultural pursuits, and even architecture deteriorated. The Spaniards were later to describe the Mayan people as fiercely independent, bloodthirsty, and, like the Aztecs, inclined to sacrifice war captives' hearts on their gods' altars.

The Aztecs

Arising in the confusion of the late postclassical era, the Aztec Confederacy came to conquer and dominate central Mexico from coast to coast in less than two centuries. The Aztecs, like the Toltecs before them, retained many of their old traditions while freely borrowing from the culture, religion, and technology of their neighbors and victims. The most significant example of this borrowing was their hydraulic agriculture. It was the major factor by which they increased population in the central Mexico to more than a million people living in some 50 city-states.

The Aztecs' story really begins with the founding of the capital at Tenochtitlán; their earlier history is quite obscure. They evidently migrated from the north into central Mexico some time before 1200. For a while they were dominated by other peoples, including the Toltecs. About 1325 they settled on an island in Lake Texcoco (the site of present-day Mexico City), later connecting their new town to the mainland by causeways. In its later days Tenochtitlán was an architectural wonder. The Aztecs built a dam to control the lake level, completed a freshwater aqueduct, and created floating artificial islands where irrigated fields supplied food for the capital. Within the imperial metropolis, beautiful avenues, canals, temples, and monuments symbolized increasing Aztec power, particularly after the early fifteenth century.

Aztec Warriors

The Aztecs completed the formation of their confederacy at the same time. During the early decades at Tenochtitlán, the Aztecs had fought as tributaries of Atzcapotzalco, the dominant city-state in the valley. In 1370 they accepted a king of assumed Toltec lineage. For decades they won victories and prospered in concert with their overlords, but in 1427 they rebelled, forming a "triple alliance" with nearby Texcoco and Tlacopán, which defeated Atzcapotzalco and became the major power in the region. For the Aztecs, these events brought great change. Internally, they shifted power from the old clan leaders to a rising military aristocracy. Externally, they started a series of conquests and trading agreements. A new imperial order developed, shared at first by the other two allies but increasingly dominated by Tenochitlán, whose ruler imposed his will as head of the army, leader of the state, and chief priest. The reigns of the Aztec kings Itzcoatl (1427–1440) and his nephew Montezuma I (1440–1468), ushered in this new era of rising centralism, efficiency, and expansion. It was still in progress under the ninth monarch, Montezuma II (1502–1520), at the time of the Spanish invasion.

Xicohtencatl, the Elder: "I Say This"

As the empire expanded, so did the state-controlled economy. Its base was agricultural land, particularly floating plots installed on the lake after the 1430s. Most were built by the government. Some were allotted to the ***calpulli*** (clans)—made up of the remnants of diverse ethnic groups that came together on the island of Tenochtitlán—for distribution to families. Others were developed as estates for the monarch

calpulli—Aztec social units based on family clans.

and the nobility; the latter were worked by tenants under government supervision. Rising agricultural production supported not only the engineering, dredging, stonework, and carpentry required for heavy construction but also artisans turning out weapons, cloth, ceramics, feather work, jewelry, and hundreds of other goods. Porters from distant places backpacked over mountains to the markets of the valley. A later Spanish observer reported that the great market at Tlatelolco (tlah-tel-LOHL-koh), serving Tenochtitlán, attracted 25,000 people daily.

Conquest and the increasing wealth that accompanied it modified the ancient social structure. The old *calpulli* developed into city wards, identified largely by occupational specialties. By 1500 most *calpulli* families were headed by men. Women could inherit property and divorce their husbands but were confined mostly to household tasks, except for midwives, healers, and prostitutes. Kinship still promoted social cohesion, but class status provided major incentives. The appointed nobility *(pipiltin)*, along with the priests, held both power and social status, but they were burdened with heavy responsibilities. Moreover, they held appointed rather than hereditary posts, although they could inherit property. Commoners could be made nobles by performing superior service, particularly in war. Craftspeople and merchants paid taxes but were exempt from military service; some long-distance merchants *(pochteca)* served the government as diplomats or spies in foreign states. Peasants worked their plots and served in the army; nonmembers of *calpulli* were tenants. Their lot was hardly better than that of the numerous slaves, except for the latter's potential role as ceremonial sacrifice victims.

DOCUMENT
"Song of Tlaltecatzin"

Official documents of the period and other written accounts focus mainly on Mesoamerican social and political elites and conditions in the imperial capitals. However, recent archaeological studies throw fresh light on the lives of the Aztec common people and conditions in the provinces. Surveys of settlement patterns show that Aztec society experienced one of the most significant population explosions of premodern times. In the Valley of Mexico, the heartland of the Aztec Empire, population increased from 175,000 in the early Aztec period (1150–1350) to almost one million in the late period (1350–1519). This pattern of growth was duplicated elsewhere in the empire. To cope with this population explosion, the environment was altered: Farmers built dams and canals to irrigate cropland, constructed terraced stone walls on hillsides to form new fields, and drained swamps outside Tenochtitlán to create ***chinampas*** or floating gardens. With these changes emerged new villages and towns.

Excavations of rural sites near modern Cuernavaca (kwehr-nah-VAH-kah) disclose that provincial society was much more complex than previously thought. Commoners created a thriving marketing system whereby craft goods produced in their homes were exchanged for a variety of foreign goods. Houses at these sites were small, built of adobe brick walls supported on stone foundations. These houses were furnished with mats and baskets and had a shrine with two or three figurines and an incense burner on one of the walls. In this region the household production of cotton textiles was the major craft. All Aztec women spun and wove cloth, which provided garments, constituted the most common item of tribute demanded by the state, and served as currency in the marketplaces for obtaining other goods and services. In addition to textiles, some residents made paper out of the bark of the wild fig tree, used to produce books of pictographs and to burn in ritual offerings. According to written sources, Aztec commoners were subject to the nobles, who possessed most of the land and monopolized power in the polity. But new archaeological excavations show that the commoners were relatively prosperous people whose market system operated largely beyond state control.

The Aztec polity included subordinated allies and 38 provinces. The latter were taxed directly; most of the former paid tribute in some form; and all were denied free foreign relations. This polyglot empire was headed by a member of the royal family proclaimed to be the incarnation of the sun-god. His household was more lavish than many in Europe and swarmed with servants. A head wife supervised the concubines and scheduled their assignments, but Aztec queens rarely engaged in court intrigues or offered advice to the emperor, for he usually ruled without concern for other opinions. He was assisted in his official duties by a chief minister and subordinate bureaucracies for war, religion, justice, treasury, storehouses, and personnel. The capital and each province were administered directly by governors, most of whom were descended from former kings. They collected taxes, held court, arranged religious ceremonies, regulated economic affairs, and directed police activities. In addition, urban guilds, villages, and tribes had their own local officials. Vassal states were governed under their own laws but observed by resident Aztec emissaries. This whole system was defended by a large military organization, comprising allied forces, local militias, and an imperial guard of elite troops.

Aztec religion developed from the worship of animistic spirits, symbolizing natural forces seeking balance while in constant conflict. A pessimistic obsession with human futility also dominated the Aztec world-

Chinampas—The floating gardens the Aztecs of Tenochtitlán built and tended on Lake Texcoco.

view, perpetuating the common belief that the gods required human blood to sustain life. Thus, as they assembled their empire, the Aztecs came to envision their sun deity, **Huitzilopochtli** (wheet-tsee-loh-POHCHT-lee), as a bloodthirsty war god with an appetite for warriors captured in battle. In every city, the Aztecs built pyramids, topped by their two temples to the sun deity and Tlatelolco, god of rain. Here they honored Huitzilopochtli in great public ceremonies such as one in 1487 when bloodstained priests at the high altars tore out the living hearts of thousands of victims and held them up, quivering, to the sun. The need for sacrificial victims forced continuing conquests and later weakened the state as it faced the Spanish threat.

DOCUMENT
Admonishing Those Who Seek No Honor in War

Comparing the Aztecs and Mayas with the Romans and Greeks can be an interesting theoretical exercise. The Aztec calendar, mathematics, and writing were derived mainly from Mayan sources, somewhat the way that Roman philosophy and science were based on Greek models. Although Aztec culture spawned skilled sculptors, painters, and craftspeople who produced in great numbers, they lacked the imagination of the Mayas, whom they indirectly copied, just as Roman artists largely imitated their Greek predecessors. Similarly, both Roman and Aztec cultures were characterized by respect for discipline, practicality, directness, and force. Each was highly skilled in engineering, as attested, for example, by their aqueducts and other feats for furnishing copious amounts of water to their respective capitals. They also shared a militaristic ethos and powerful standing armies.

The Inca

The great Inca Empire in the Andean highlands of South America reached its height in the early 1500s. It extended 3500 miles between Ecuador and Chile, including almost impassable mountain ranges that separate the upper Amazon forests from the Pacific. The empire contained at least ten million people in 200 ethnolinguistic groups. It was six times the size of Texas. The capital, Cuzco, which had an estimated 200,000 inhabitants, was governed in a more centralized way than any city in Europe at the time. The Incas produced fine art and architecture and were superb engineers, but their major achievement was imperial organization. In this respect they compared favorably with the Romans and the Chinese.

MAP
Inca Expansion

A long tradition of scholarship, exemplified by researchers such as Ian Cameron, Richard W. Keating, and J. Alden Mason, gives us a detailed idea of Inca society. Although it rose very rapidly just before the Spanish conquest, Inca civilization evolved from ancient cultural foundations. Ceremonial and commercial centers had existed on the Peruvian plateau well before the Common Era. About 600 C.E. cities began rising in the highlands of the interior. During the next two centuries, tributary kingdoms drew together formerly isolated ceremonial centers of the Peruvian highlands. Some of the resulting states exercised control over the plain, along with territories in what are now Bolivia and Chile. Two kingdoms had capitals at Huari (WHA-ree) and Tiahuanaco (tee-ah-wah-NAH-koh) in south central Peru. When these states collapsed in the tenth century, they were succeeded by independent agrarian villages, which were nearly consumed by continuous warfare. A completely different situation developed along the northern coast, where the kingdom of Chimu developed a civilization, marked by extensive irrigation, rising population, centralized government, public works, high craft production, widespread trade, and an expanding tributary domain. This polity was conquered and its culture absorbed by the Incas in 1476.

The Incas created their empire while waging ruthless struggles in the highlands. According to their own legends, these "children of the sun" settled the valley of Cuzco, in the heartland of the Andes, about 1200 C.E., having migrated from the south, possibly from the region of Tiahuanaco. During the next hundred years they were a simple peasant people, organized by kinship in clans *(ayllu)*, living in villages, fulfilling mutual labor obligations, and worshipping their local demigods (*chuacas)*. To strengthen their unity and better protect themselves in constant wars for survival, they formed a monarchy, developed their military, and began taking over territory near Cuzco. In this competition they were only moderately successful during the reigns of the first seven kings, to the early fifteenth century.

Like the Aztec state at almost the same time, the Inca polity began a climactic period of rapid development with a memorable series of rulers. Viracocha (veh-rah-CO-cha) (d. 1438), the eighth emperor, turned his ragtag army into a formidable fighting machine, conquered adjoining territories, and instituted a divine monarchy, with his lineage accepted as descendants of the sun-god. His son, Pachacuti (pahch-ah-KEU-tee) (1438–1471), was a reformer, religious leader, and builder who stands among the most powerful people ever to rule in the New World, and received the admiration of the Spanish occupiers. He began arduous campaigns to the north and south, notably against Chimu. Topa Yupanqui (yeu-PAHN-kee) (1471–1493), Pachacuti's son and successor who commanded the Inca armies after 1463, completed the

Huitzilopochtli—The patron deity of the Aztecs, god of the sun and of war.

Document Father Bernabé Cobo, "Pachacuti, the Greatest Inca"

Bernabé Cobo (1582–1657) spent 61 of his 75 years in the Americas, from his first arrival in the Antilles to his death in Lima. During that time the Jesuit priest combined his duties with his qualities as a scientist and observer to write at great length about the flora and fauna of Latin and southern America. He entered into close relations with the Indians, as he spread the faith, and came to have a deep understanding of respect for them.

This selection is from Chapter 12 of his *History of the Inca Empire.* Cobo relied on Indian legends and contemporary Indian testimony, as well as earlier Spanish writings as he dealt with the civilization his countrymen had attacked. Far from viewing the Incans as barbaric and "uncivilized" as later, nineteenth-century missionaries would do, Cobo showed the capacity to understand and even admire them.

Viracocha Inca left four sons by his principal wife; they were called Pachacuti Inca Yupanqui, Inca Roca, Tupa Yupanqui, and Capac Yupanqui. The first one succeeded him in the kingdom, and concerning the rest, although they were lords and grandees, nothing is said. Pachacuti married a lady named Mama Anahuarque, native to the town of Choco, near Cuzco, and he founded a family that they call Iñaca Panaca. This king was the most valiant and warlike, wise and statesmanlike of all the Incas, because he organized the republic with the harmony, laws, and statutes that it maintained from that time until the arrival of the Spaniards. He injected order and reason into everything; eliminated and added rites and ceremonies; made the religious cult more extensive; established the sacrifices and the solemnity with which the gods were to be venerated, enlarged and embellished the temples with magnificent structures, income, and a great number of priests and ministers; reformed the calendar; divided the year into twelve months, giving each one its name; and designated the solemn fiestas and sacrifices to be held each month. He composed many elegant prayers with which the gods were to be invoked, and he ordered that these prayers be recited at the same time that the sacrifices were offered. He was no less careful and diligent in matters pertaining to the temporal welfare of the republic; he gave his vassals a method of working the fields and taking advantage of the lands that were so rough and uneven as to be useless and unfruitful; he ordered that rough hillsides be terraced and that ditches be made from the rivers to irrigate them. In short, nothing was overlooked by him in which he did not impose all good order and harmony; for this reason he was given the name of Pachacuti, which means "change of time or of the world"; this is because as a result of his excellent government things improved to such an extent that times seemed to have changed and the world seemed to have turned around; thus, his memory was very celebrated among the Indians, and he was given more honor in their songs and poems than any of the other kings that either preceded him or came after him.

After having shown himself to be so devoted to the sun and having taken the care just mentioned that all worship him in the same way that his ancestors had done, one day Pachacuti began to wonder how it was possible that a thing could be God if it was so subject to movement as the Sun, that it never stops or rests for a moment since it turns around the world every day; and he inferred from this meditation that the Sun must not be more than a messenger sent by the Creator to visit the universe; besides, if he were God, it would not be possible for a few clouds to get in front of him and obscure his splendor and rays so that he could not shine; and if he were the universal Creator and lord of all things, sometimes he would rest and from his place of rest he would illuminate all the world and command whatever he wished; and thus, there had to be another more powerful lord who ruled and governed the Sun; and no doubt this was Pachayachachic. He communicated this thought to the members of his council, and in agreement with them, he decided that Pachayachachic was to be preferred to the Sun, and within the city of Cuzco, he built the Creator his own temple which he called Quishuarcancha, and in it he put the image of the Creator of the world, Viracocha Pachayachachic.

Questions to Consider

1. What was there in Pachacuti's quest to understand the universe that would appeal to Bernabé Cobo?
2. Discuss Pachacuti's accomplishments as enumerated by Cobo. Do you think that the Spaniard's admiration came because the Incan chief possessed "European" qualities, or because he chose local solutions to local problems?
3. Would you like to be a citizen in a state led by Pachacuti? Why? Why not?

Machu Picchu, a natural fortress on a narrow ridge between two mountains, was built by the Incas probably after 1440. When the last Inca ruler died, the fortress was abandoned and lost until its rediscovery in 1911.

annexation of Chimu and extended the empire south into central Chile. The next emperor, Huayna Capac (WHAY-nah KAH-pahk) (1493–1527), completed the subjugation of Ecuador, put down rebellions, and attempted to impose order, although the empire was seething with internal discontent when the Spaniards arrived in 1532.

Despite internal problems, intensified by the steep slopes and harsh weather of the Andes, the Incas demonstrated rare technical skills in fashioning their civilization in difficult and often dangerous circumstances. They were master engineers, carrying water long distances by canals and aqueducts, using techniques borrowed from the Chimu Empire, building cities high in the Andes, and constructing networks of roads along the coast and through the mountains, along with suspension bridges and interconnecting valley roadways. All were designed to knit together a vast region that in the Inca Empire covered some 380,000 square miles.

Archaeologists have long known that the Incas gained a knowledge of canals and irrigation systems from the Chimu: Recent excavation have revealed new evidence about their sophisticated use of that technology. Canals are difficult to construct: If the slope is too narrow, the canal silts up; if it is too steep, its sides erode. Inca engineers devised different canal shapes to control the water's speed and prevent its velocity from ruining the canal. One "intervalley" canal carried water to a city from 60 miles away; it was only one of many networks, involving thousands of feeder canals, that stretched for hundreds of miles. These hydraulic techniques have been described as deserving to stand with Egypt's pyramids and China's Great Wall as among the world's greatest engineering feats. With irrigation canals constructed far removed from the water's source, the Incas farmed 40 percent more land than is achieved today. But if skills fail, land can quickly return to desert conditions. We have yet to learn what caused the destruction or abandonment of these canal systems—was it human or environmental forces, or both?

Hydraulic feats were matched by sophisticated organizational skills. To link the empire together, Inca leaders established a communication service, using state-built roads, runner-messengers, rest houses, and smoke signals. Governing by means of a divide-and-rule technique, they appealed wherever possible to traditional prejudices among conquered peoples, perpetuating feuds, courting native leaders, settling colonies of subjects among their enemies, and generally provoking disunity among potentially rebellious areas. They also relied on a common official language and the cult of divine monarchy to unify their own people, particularly the elite. Every part of their system was fitted together in a highly disciplined and integrated whole. Before the Incas, few other states had succeeded so effectively in regimenting millions of people over such great distances and against such formidable obstacles.

Like all civilized peoples, the Incas faced the problem of population expansion and a limited food supply. They solved it well enough to support large military, bureaucratic, and priestly establishments by developing what economists call a *command economy*. They used no money, no credit, and very little trade beyond local barter. The state planned all economic operations and kept all accounts. Government assigned to families the land to be worked; local family heads, under government supervision, directed workers who produced the crops and saw that harvests were brought to state warehouses. Labor taxes provided work done on public projects, the nobles' estates, and royal lands. A similar approach was used in manufacturing, with craftspeople producing in local guilds, noble households, and palace workshops. From its storehouses, the government distributed goods to individuals, to the military, and to government projects. In the process, it built roads, operated hospitals, and maintained schools. All property, even the nobles' land, was state-owned and assigned, except for distinctly personal possessions, including some luxury goods owned by the privileged classes.

This state-controlled economy functioned by way of a precisely defined class structure, built on the lingering kinship tradition. Commoners were kept loyal and disciplined by identifying the state with their ancient *ayllus*. Inca nobles maintained respect because they were all related directly or indirectly to the royal lineage and therefore shared the divine mandate to rule. They held the highest positions in government, the army, and the priesthood. A notch lower were lesser aristocrats and nobles among conquered peoples, who held local offices, up to subgovernors in the provinces. The two upper classes made up a privileged elite. Trained in special schools, they were rewarded with luxuries in food, dress, and housing. They were also exempted from taxes and cruel punishments. At the third level were common workers. They were generally confined to their villages; their work was prescribed; their dress and food were restricted; and government checked even the cleanliness of their houses. Commoners were thus little better off than the lowest class of slaves, who were often taken as prisoners of war and assigned to serve the upper classes.

The shift from kinship toward class division was accompanied by a decline of matriarchal values. Upper-class women shared some social status with their husbands, and all women could inherit property when they were widowed; but they were generally subordinated and exploited. Indeed, a fifteenth-century royal decree prohibited women from testifying in court because they were by nature “deceitful, mendacious, and fainthearted.”[1] Female commoners worked in the fields, while women of all classes were expected to keep house, mind the children, and serve the needs of men. Many were concubines or surplus wives, the number depending on the husbands’ wealth and status. The most beautiful and intelligent young girls were drafted as “chosen women.” Some would become “virgins of the sun,” serving as nuns and weavers in the temple workshops; others would become concubines of the emperor or nobles; a few would be sacrificed. All were honored as servants of the state.

All authority in the Inca state originated with the hereditary divine emperor, who exercised the power of life and death over all his subjects. He was usually aloof, even with his own immediate family, although he might, if he chose, delegate authority to the queen (his full sister after 1438) or take advice from his mother. With its thousands of servants and concubines, his court was a magnificent display of wealth and power. It was also the locus of a central government that included agencies for rituals (religion), war, treasury, accounts, and public works. The chief ministers were advisers to the Imperial Council, consisting of the emperor and four viceroys, who governed the four provinces. Each province, about the size of New York State, was divided into approximately 40 districts, under subgovernors and their assistants. Authority in the districts was further subdivided, ultimately into units of ten families. Officials at each level reported regularly to superiors and were subject to frequent inspections. This system regulated every aspect of life, including labor, justice, marriage, and even morals.

The power of the ruler depended largely on an excellent military system, which featured compulsory service. Instructors in the villages trained peasant boys for the army; the most promising were marked for advancement when they were called to active service in their twenties. They served for two years before retiring to the labor reserve and militia. The army was organized in units of 10, 50, 100, 1000, and 10,000, under officers who held complete authority over subordinates. A combat force of 200,000, with support units, was always under arms. It was supplied from military storehouses throughout the country and garrisoned in mighty stone fortresses, each with independent water sources. Troops from these centers ruthlessly suppressed any resistance to the regime.

A second base for Inca authority was religion. As the empire grew, its priests appropriated the gods of conquered peoples and included them in a vast pantheon, headed by the Inca sun-god. For example, the virgins of the sun, with their ceremonies and temples, evolved from an earlier moon goddess cult among **matrilineal** societies. War victims would on occasion be sacrificed to the sun, as would some children of “chosen women.” In later times the servants of an emperor, as well as his favorite concubines, were sent with him, at his death, to serve him in the hereafter. To emphasize the emperors’ divinity and symbolize the state’s continuity, dead emperors were mummified, seated on thrones in their sacred palaces, and attended by living servants, wives, and priests. On public occasions these figures were paraded before the people, who bowed before them in reverence. Such ceremonies were conducted by a clerical establishment of 4000 priests in the capital and many scores of thousands more throughout the country.

CASE STUDY
Death in War and Childbirth in the Americas

There was a remarkable exception to this religious mind-set in the person of the emperor Pachacuti. A highly successful military leader who largely laid the empire’s foundation by consolidating the area around Cuzco and annexing the rich Titicaca basin, this multitalented innovator established **Quechua** (KECH-wah) as the administrative language, reformed the calendar, introduced methods of terracing the hillsides and extending irrigation, and created an efficient public service. Although regarded as a direct descendant of the sun-god, Pachacuti asked himself how the sun could be the supreme deity since it never rested but

matrilineal—Tracing hereditary descent through the mother, not the father.

Quechua—A language of the Central Andes, spoken by the Incas and today the most widely spoken indigenous tongue of the Americas.

revolved endlessly around the earth. He concluded that the sun was itself a messenger sent by a more powerful being who from his place of rest could illuminate and command the world. This must be the universal Creator, Viracocha ("Lord"), who governed the sun and had brought into being all other deities. And in his honor the emperor constructed a temple in Cuzco. But, as in the case of Akhenaton, his conceptual forerunner in Egypt, Pachacuti's nascent monotheism did not prevail; later rulers continued to sacrifice victims to the sun-god—though not to the extent practiced by the Aztecs.

Order and security were dominant values in Inca cultural expression, and neither aesthetic concerns nor philosophical speculation received much attention. As we have seen, religious innovation was given short shrift, and any theorizing was subordinated to the practicalities of a state cult and the morality of power—treason and cowardice were considered the worst sins. The Incas had no written records and seem to have lacked even the pictographs of Mesoamerica. Instead they relied on oral traditions, supplemented by mnemonic devices such as the system of knotted strings called ***quipus*** (KE-peuz). These oral traditions were dealt a lethal blow by the Spanish conquest.

The Inca lunar calendar was inaccurate and provided no starting point for the identification of historical events. Although the Incas were excellent craftspeople, capable of producing fine pottery and metalwork in copper and gold, their most striking technical and cultural accomplishments were in engineering and massive architecture. Without using mortar, they fitted immense slabs of stone into temple and fortress walls. This efficiency is still exhibited in existing roads, bridges, terraced fields, and stone fortresses, such as Machu Picchu.

THE AMERINDIANS OF NORTH AMERICA

- *Why was there no unification of the North American Amerindians, such as there was in Mesoamerica?*

In the past century Hollywood and the popular media reinforced the fallacy that all Native Americans in North America constituted a single culture with a common lifestyle. The mounted, war-bonneted warrior of the plains has too often been considered the archetype of the "Red Man," presented in the "Wild West Shows" of the last century. Some Plains Indians were indeed fine mounted warriors, but they were only a fraction of the complex family of North American Indians.

European settlers found the Native Americans more diverse in their languages and appearances than the Europeans themselves. Two hundred distinct North American languages have been classified. Amerindian societies presented a wide spectrum of variation: from small bands of hunter-gatherers and farmers to well-organized states. A similar diversity was found in their arts and crafts; various regions excelled in basketry, weaving, sculpture, totem-carving, and boat making.

There is a serious debate among scholars as to the number of Native Americans at the time of the European invasions. Estimates range from as low as 2 million to as many as 18 million people in the area north of Mexico—most estimates fall between these extremes. In any case, much of North America was well populated at the end of the fifteenth century. Amerindians north of the Rio Grande did not produce the massive technological and governmental achievements found in Mesoamerica and South America. As with Paleolithic and Neolithic societies in Asia, Africa, and Europe before the Common Era, their populations were smaller, and consequently, they did not create large cities, with their complex division of labor and urban way of life. More often, they typically survived by hunting and fishing until knowledge of food raising spread north from Mesoamerica.

For North American Indians before 1492, agriculture where it could be practiced had the same effect as elsewhere in the world. A more dependable food supply made possible stable settlements in which men cleared the fields and women tended the crops. Marked population growth, with accompanying large village or town centers, and political and military power occurred in the Rio Grande, Ohio, Mississippi, and St.

North American Civilizations

c. 3000–2500 B.C.E.	Watson Brake settlements
c. 800 B.C.E.–600 C.E.	Adena and Hopewell cultures
c. 900–1300	Cahokia flourishes
c. 300 B.C.E.–1350 C.E.	Mogollon culture
c. 1100	Establishment of Navajo culture
c. 1300	Arrival of Mandans in Great Plains

quipus—A mnemonic system based on knotted strings used by the Inca to keep records and send messages.

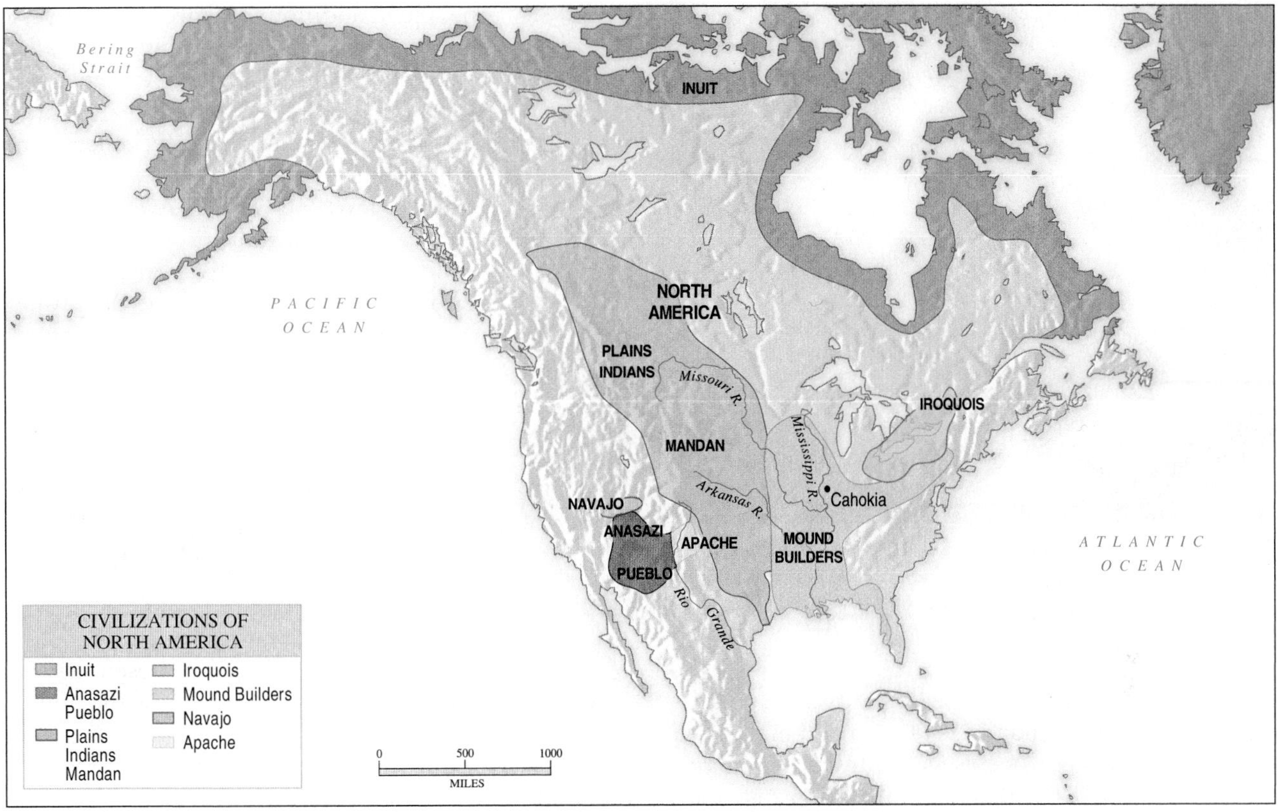

In the vastness of the North American continent, the varied environmental challenges led to the development of hundreds of different Indian tribes—more than 250 alone in the present-day state of California.

Lawrence valleys. In these places, overpopulation exhausted the soil and occasionally created environmental problems that led to the decline of the urban centers. Climate changes and European-borne pandemics in the fifteenth and sixteenth centuries devastated the Native American population, both those settled in the cities and the nomadic peoples.

The Iroquois of the Northeast Woodlands

Europeans arriving in what is now upper New York State found various groups speaking dialects of a common Iroquoian language. They had created a distinctive culture by 1000 C.E. and subsequently formed the League of the Five Nations. They used the metaphor of the longhouse, their traditional communal dwelling, to describe their political alliance: the Mohawk along the Hudson were the "keepers of the eastern door," adjoined in sequence by the Oneida, Onondaga, and Cayuga, with the Seneca, "keepers of the western door." When the Tuscarora joined in the early eighteenth century, the confederacy became known as the Six Nations. The Iroquois eventually extended their control from the Great Lakes toward the Atlantic by subjugating the nomadic, food-gathering Algonquin people.

The Iroquois had the advantage of being agriculturists with permanent villages. Some of these had several hundred residents and extensive fields where maize, beans, squash, and tobacco were grown. Fish traps were built across streams, and smokehouses preserved joints of game. Related families lived in the longhouses, long rectangular buildings protected by high wooden palisades. Women played a notable part: They owned the homes and gardens, and, since descent was matrilineal, chose the leaders. If the men chosen did not give good leadership, they could be replaced.

The Adena and Hopewell of the Ohio Valley

In the area of present-day Kentucky and Ohio, important Amerindian settlements took root between 800 B.C.E. and 600 C.E. Known generally as the Adena and Hopewell cultures, these Amerindians developed complex societies from the Missouri River to the Appalachians and from the Great Lakes to the Gulf of Mexico. Their settlements were based on the work of Indian women who, over two to three millennia,

The Great Serpent Mound in Ohio is a rich repository of the North American Indian life centered in the Adena culture. Active between 500 B.C.E. and 100 C.E. the Indians of the Adena culture had a well-developed village life and traded with other peoples from Canada to the Gulf of Mexico.

mastered the cultivation of seed plants such as sunflowers and squash and maize that arrived in the area in the fourth century B.C.E. As in Mesoamerica and South America, by 1000, maize cultivation sustained the peoples of the Ohio and Mississippi valley regions. Archaeologists think that the Hopewell and Adena cultures survived on a diet of fish, game, nuts, and other plant life.

The Adena and Hopewell cultures developed differing ways to construct their homes: the Adena chose to live in circular houses made out of poles and covered with mats and thatched roofs, while the Hopewell built round or oval houses with more protective roofs made of skins, bark from trees, and a combination of thatch and clay. They had a sophisticated view of the afterlife, as can be seen in the effort they took to bury their dead. The Native Americans near Watson Brake in northeast Louisiana (3000–2500 B.C.E.) and the peoples of the Adena culture at the beginning of the Common Era built thousands of earthen mounds for their dead. The Adena interred their deceased in vast cone-shaped mounds of earth, sometimes 500 feet around. Sometimes the dead were cremated, and the ashes were placed in the mounds along with all sorts of relics such as carved stone tablets, pipes smoked during religious ceremonies, and jewelry. The Hopewell did the same on an even larger scale for the more distinguished members of their families. Archaeologists have found evidence in these mounds of stone and clay items from both coasts, imported copper from the Great Lakes, and flaked stone items from the Tennessee valley.

Along with the impressive burial mounds, archaeologists have found indications of other projects indicating the combined efforts of hundreds of people in addition to a substantial investment of wealth. At Newark, Ohio, for example, the ceremonial site covers 4 square miles. Such enterprises indicate a long period of relative peace, generations remaining in the same place, and a substantial level of wealth. Archaeologists have also found indications of contacts with tribes across North America. Whether through trading or tribute, the Ohio valley societies had access to metals and goods found only in the Rocky Mountain area and shells from the Gulf coast. They had mastered the manufacture of tools, pottery, and copper jewelry.

The Mississippian Culture

At the end of the sixth century C.E. another major Amerindian culture made its appearance in the area just east of present-day St. Louis. Archaeologists are still investigating the origins and extent of this culture from the various burial sites, the most important of which is that at Cahokia, Illinois. Unlike the Adena and Hopewell cultures, the Mississippian culture lived in houses made out of thin pieces of wood (laths) covered with clay—so-called wattle-and-daub houses. These took various shapes in the large villages of the area. So influential was this culture that it came to dominate most of the region west of the Mississippi to the Plains, as can been seen in the Spiro Mounds in eastern Oklahoma.

The Mississippian peoples benefited from mastering the raising of maize, beans, and squash, and they tied their religion to the planting and harvesting cycles. Their burial mounds took the form of flat-topped pyramids, arranged around a central square. In the most developed regions, fortresslike palisades surrounded the site. The Cahokia complex was constructed over a period of nearly three centuries (c. 900–c. 1150). The centerpiece of the Cahokia site is a pyramid with a base of more than 18 acres, reaching a height of almost 100 feet. This is only one of more than 80 such mounds to be found at Cahokia, a city more than 6 miles long. There was no set burial practice for the Mississippian culture—remains have also been found in cemeteries, in urns, and under the floors of houses.

After the twelfth century the peoples in the Mississippian culture passed a highly complex religion along from generation to generation—an indication of their stability, continuity, and sophistication. The extent of their wealth enabled them to construct temples filled with ceremonial objects such as large stone scepters and copper plates. Their religion used symbols such as the cross, the sun, arrows surrounded by

An artist's creation of what Cahokia might have been like at its height.

semicircles, a sunburst, and—most intriguing—an outstretched hand with an eye in the palm. The art that derived from the religion featured portrayals of gods based on animals, rattlesnakes with feathers and wings, and people portrayed as birds. Vessels found at the sites indicate the presence of human sacrifice: jars with human faces painted on them and portrayals of the heads of sacrificed victims. These are indications that not only adults but also infants were given up to the higher deity the Mississippi culture believed controlled their lives.

Excavations of the Cahokia mounds give evidence of an hierarchical society that maintained order and productivity through brutality. Even though it was far distant from the Aztec and Incan Empires, there were several similarities between the political and religious systems and social repression of Cahokia and the systems in Mesoamerica and South America. For a while at the beginning of the thirteenth century, Cahokia was probably the largest city in North America, with a population larger than that of medieval London. At the end of the fourteenth century Cahokia began to decline. Archaeologists point to climate change, soil exhaustion, and the unification of those peoples Cahokia had repressed as an effective enemy force as likely causes for the end of Cahokia as a major power.

The Mogollon, the Hohokam, the Anasazi, and the Fremont Culture

The southwestern Amerindian cultures lived in the most environmentally challenging part of the continental United States, the dry and rocky regions of present-day Utah, Arizona, New Mexico, and Colorado. In response to their surroundings, they produced the most advanced levels of technology and agriculture around 300 B.C.E. The Mogollon, Hohokam, and Anasazi grew maize, beans, and squash, each group evolving its own techniques. The homes of each group were built out of adobe brick or other techniques of masonry, sometimes on extremely challenging sites. Each group also produced pottery that could rank in beauty with any in the world.

The Mogollon culture of southwestern New Mexico lasted almost 1600 years, from around 300 B.C.E. to 1350 C.E. Its people built their homes low to the ground along the tops of ridges. Villages were built around large underground buildings used for religious ceremonies and as pit houses until the eleventh century; thereafter, they built these structures at ground level. Because of the constant threat of drought, they developed a diversified economy based on hunting, gathering, and farming. Relatively isolated, they saw little need to change over the centuries.

The Hohokam culture grew along the valleys of the Salt and Gila Rivers. Its architecture was similar to that of the early Mogollon, although the Hohokam built not just ceremonial structures but also their homes inside underground pits. Perhaps learning from the Mesoamerican cultures, the Hohokam constructed an impressive network of canals, some more than 30 miles long, 6 to 10 feet deep, and 15 to 30 feet wide. The extent of these canals proves the existence not only of wealth but also of substantial social organization. The Hohokam also borrowed their religion, their burial practices, and even some of their games from the Mesoamericans.

Deriving from these two cultures was the Anasazi, which appeared around 300 C.E. Of the three cultures, the Anasazi had the most sophisticated and most impressive architecture and the largest area of influence—from the Idaho-Utah border to the Gulf of California. Early on, they built their homes in the shape of beehive-shaped domes made out of logs held together by a mudlike mortar. They grew maize and made pottery, like the Mississippian culture, and stored both in warehouse-like structures. Around 700 C.E. they took their economic development one step further by beginning the manufacture of cotton cloth. Their technological genius is apparent from their use of two forms of irrigation: runoff by building dikes and terracing hills and subsoil by constructing sand dunes at the base of hills to hold the runoff of the

The Cliff Palace of the Anasazi, Mesa Verde National Park, Colorado, is among the important Anasazi ruins to be found in the southwestern United States.

sometimes torrential rains. Their lives revolved around their religion, with ceremonies to placate the gods to hold off storms and to ensure fertility.

The Anasazi are best known today for their architectural accomplishments. Around the eleventh century they began to construct cities, with houses built in the shapes of squares and semicircles. They used all of the available materials to build these settlements; with wood, mud, and stone, they erected cliff dwellings and the equivalent of terraced apartment houses. One such structure, with some 500 living units, was the largest residential building in the North America until the completion of an apartment house in New York in 1882. At their height, these master architects constructed around a dozen towns and nearly 200 villages. The disappearance of the Anasazi around 1300 remains a mystery. It is believed that a combination of a long drought, internecine conflicts, and the arrivals of the Navajo and the Apache led to their demise.

To the north of the Anasazi there were a number of different societies spread across the Colorado Plateau and into Idaho. They were a diverse group: Some depended on farming while others were hunters and they spoke different languages. Anthropologists have labeled this group the Fremont culture. They shared traits with the Navajo in that they raised corn, used the same kinds of tools, and lived in pit houses. The culture flourished between the sixth and the fourteenth centuries. Recently one of the best-preserved settlements of the Fremont culture was revealed to have been found near Horse Canyon, Utah in the Range Creek site.

The Navajo, the Apache, and the Mandan

Three other Amerindian civilizations established their presence before the arrival of Europeans. The Navajo, the largest Native American group in the United States, came down from the north to the Southwest sometime in the eleventh century. There they borrowed extensively from the indigenous cultures.

A century or so later, the Apache, who speak a language close to that of the Navajo, arrived in the southwest and by the end of the 1500s lived in parts of the present states of Arizona, Colorado, and New Mexico. They, too, were heavily influenced by the cultures present there.

Finally, the Mandan, who based their economy on fur trading and hunting, came to the vast valley of the Missouri River from east of the Mississippi in the late 1300s. There had been Amerindians in this region since 12,000–8,000 B.C.E. who hunted on foot on the Great Plains for mammoths, mastodons, and bison using spears tipped with Clovis points. Archaeological sites in Canada indicate that Indians hunted and slaughtered buffalo for more than 7000 years. By 1000 C.E. the use of bows and arrows was common throughout the plains. When the Mandan moved west, they became yet another in a long series of Amerindians who harvested the animal wealth of the mid-continent.

The Far North: Inuit and Aleut

The appearance of the Inuit, also known as the Eskimos, is shrouded in controversy. Some observers assert that they descended from ancient seagoing peoples; others believe that they developed their culture in Alaska after the last ice age. They speak much the same language as the Aleut, whose origins are similarly unclear. It is accepted that the two groups split apart more than 4000 years ago and that they are tied more closely to Asians than the Amerindians are.

The Aleut stayed largely in the area that is now known as the Alaskan peninsula, the Aleutian Islands, and the far eastern portion of Russia. The Inuit spread along the area south of the Arctic Circle from the Bering Strait across the top of Canada to Greenland. Both peoples lived by hunting and fishing. The Aleut hunted sea lions, otters, and seals from kayaks—small boats made of a wood frame over which skins were stretched. The Inuit showed more flexibility, hunting both sea and land animals, fishing in fresh and salt water. Their diet was based primarily on the caribou, musk-ox, walruses, and whales. They used the kayak too, but supplemented it with canoes and dogsleds.

The Navajos constructed houses called hogans *to shelter themselves from the often harsh climate of the high desert in the American Southwest.*

Their greatest accomplishment in seafaring, whaling vessels was the umiak, a larger boat with a wood frame covered with caribou hide, in which several people could row.

By about 100 C.E. the Inuit had established large villages; one of the biggest, with around 400 homes, was near present-day Nome, Alaska. To counter the arctic cold, they dug as much as 20 inches into the permafrost to erect their homes, which they then covered with poles and sod. In settlements such as that near present-day Nome, archaeologists have found large structures for the performance of religious rites, led by shamans who claimed to be able to heal diseases and wounds.

CONCLUSION

Before the European invasions and colonization, the Americas produced a rich variety of highly sophisticated and complex civilizations in response to the varied environmental challenges and opportunities of the Western Hemisphere. Some of these groups made the transition from food hunting to food raising, and some did not.

In Central and South America advanced agriculture supplied the foundation to support growing populations. This in turn led to the establishment of villages, and then cities, and, finally, far-flung states. More food and more wealth made possible leisure and priestly classes who had the time and resources to consolidate their power through control of religion as well as producing an advanced art, architecture, and discoveries in mathematics and astronomy.

In North America, environmental conditions were harsher and did not permit a similar accumulation of wealth as in Central and South America. Some Indian tribes remained hunter-gatherers. Others established settled villages and complex civilizations, but without the power and sophistication of the peoples to the south.

Tragically, a combination of climate changes, pandemics—both indigenous and foreign—and European invasions diminished the population by an estimated 80 percent by 1650. Those who survived were subjugated or later forced from their lands. Although they fought bravely against overwhelming odds, the Amerindians would have to struggle to maintain their identities in the centuries to come.

Suggestions for Web Browsing

You can obtain more information about topics included in this chapter at the websites listed below. See also the companion website that accompanies this text, **http://www.ablongman.com/brummett**, which contains an online study guide and additional resources.

Mesoweb, including Illustrated Encyclopedia of Mesoamerica
http://www.mesoweb.com/

Mesoweb is devoted to ancient Mesoamerica and its cultures: the Olmec, Mayas, Aztecs, Toltecs, Mixtecs, Zapotecs, and others.

University of Pennsylvania Museum of Archaeology and Art: Mesoamerica
http://www.museum.upenn.edu/new/exhibits/galleries/mesoamericaframedoc1.html

A history of Mesoamerican culture as reflected by the many artifacts in the university's museum.

National Museum of the American Indian
http://www.nmai.si.edu/

Website of the Smithsonian Institution's National Museum of the American Indian offers a look at one of the finest and most complete collections of items from the indigenous peoples of the Western Hemisphere.

Arctic Studies Center
http://www.mnh.si.edu/arctic/

Smithsonian Institution site dedicated to the study of Arctic peoples, culture, and environments includes numerous images, as well as audio and video segments of dance and discussion.

Literature and Film

For a sensitive and moving portrayal of the Indian life before Columbus in North America see Ruth B. Hill's *Hanta Yo: An American Saga* (Doubleday, 1979). Kathleen King's *Cricket Sings: A Novel of Pre-Columbian Cahokia* (Ohio University Press, 1983) gives an imaginative presentation of life in that Mississippian metropolis. An amusing concoction is A. Tanner Smith's *Anasazi and the Viking* (Sunstock, 1992), a not-totally-inconceivable meeting of Europeans and Amerindians. Insights into the Iroquois world can be gained from Joseph Bruchac, *The Boy Who Lived with the Bears and Other Iroquois Stories* (HarperCollins, 1995). A penetrating novel first published in 1826 has been recently translated by Guillermo I. Castillo-Feliis Félix Varela, *Xicoténcatl: An anonymous historical novel about the events leading up to the conquest of the Aztec Empire* (University of Texas, 1999). Another viewpoint on the Spanish conquest from the viewpoint of Atahualpa is given in Suzanne Alles Blom, *Inca, the Scarlet Fringe* (Forge, 2000). David Drew provides a window into the rich Mayan culture in his *The Lost Chronicles of the Maya Kings* (University of California, 1999).

PBS offers presentations on the Incas and the Mayas in their *Odyssey* series. See also the PBS series: *Seeking the First Americans, Surviving Columbus, Myths and Moundbuilders,* and the *Chaco Legacy*.

Suggestions for Reading

For a useful summary of the theories of migration into the Americas, see Sasha Nemecek, "Who were the First Americans," in *Scientific American,* September 2000, pp. 80–87. A sound, in-depth introduction to indigenous cultures in the New World is Alvin M. Josephy, ed., *America in 1492* (Knopf, 1992). See also Robert Wauchope's *Indian Background of Latin American History* (Knopf, 1970).

Among the most informative works on pre-Columbian Mesoamerica are Ross Hassig, *War and Society in Ancient Mesoamerica* (University of California Press, 1992); Richard A. Dieh and Janet C. Berlo, eds., *Mesoamerica After the Decline of Teotihuacán* (Dumbarton Oaks, 1989); and Robert R. Miller, *Mexico: A History* (University of Oklahoma Press, 1989). Special insights into the Mayan experience are provided in Jeremy A. Sobloff, *A New Archeology and the Ancient Maya* (Scientific American Library, 1990). A recent study of the darker side of Aztec society is David L. Carrasco and Micah Kleist, eds., *City of Sacrifice: The Aztec Empire and the Role of Violence in Civilization* (Beacon, 1998). Michael A. Malpass presents *Daily Life in the Inca Empire* (Greenwood Press, 1996).

E. James Dixon's *Bones, Boats, and Bison* (University of New Mexico Press, 1999) guides the reader through complex archaeological questions surround the question of the first colonization in western North America. Colin G. Galloway's documentary survey of American Indian History, *First Peoples* (Bedford/St. Martin's, 1999), is the best introduction to the general discussion of Native Americans in North America.

GLOBAL ISSUES

LOCATION AND IDENTITY

Why do people use location to identify themselves?

Two foreigners on horseback with Mount Fuji and telegraph wires in the background, woodblock print, Hiroshige Utagawa, 1873.

"East is East, and West is West, and never the twain shall meet."
Ballad of East and West, Rudyard Kipling, 1889

Though Kipling's long ballad goes on to reject that assertion, most Europeans and Americans ("West") and perhaps most Asians ("East") of his day would have accepted it. Of course, it is purely arbitrary to designate one area as "West" and one as "East" on a spherical earth rotating on a north-south axis, but historians, politicians, philosophers, generals, and clerics have all done so for millennia. People have long found ways to distinguish themselves from people in other places or even from people in their own backyard, and location has been one of the ways they have done so.

When the line-drawing seems to fail—for example, Morocco, often considered part of the Middle East, is actually west of London, and Japanese maps in the nineteenth century designated the United States as the East because it lies to Japan's east—the East then gets designated as a cultural place rather than one defined by location. But whose culture? Some would say that the culture of the rulers determines the country's identity. But this can be misleading. For instance, largely Hindu (and therefore Eastern) India did not become Middle Eastern under the Muslim Mughals or Western under British rule. Maps in the twentieth century can be equally confusing. They often painted colonies in the hues of their imperialist rulers, which seems to suggest countries could be culturally relocated by a change in rulers. Is Australia Western because its settlers mostly came from Europe, even as its leaders are currently trying to join the lucrative Asian/Eastern economic zone? Are the mostly Christian Philippines Eastern or Western?

For many centuries Europeans associated continents with the cardinal directions. Asia was East, Europe was West, and Africa was South. Later, America was sometimes considered a "new" world and therefore off the directional map, and sometimes part of the West. At first glance, continents seem to be a helpful way to divide the world into areas with some internal similarities. But the continental framework also has some inconsistencies. The Panama Canal now divides North and South America and the Suez Canal divides Africa from Eurasia. Both of those canals were dug through solid ground that had been traversed by people for millennia. And what about Eurasia? If continents have been viewed, since the eighteenth century, as "large space[s] of dry land comprehending many countries all joined together, without any separation by water,"[1] Europe and Asia are no more independent continents than the world's only "subcontinent" of India.

During the Cold War, East and West took on different meanings. The Communist anthem claimed, "The East [was] Red." A line so rigid it was called "an iron curtain" supposedly divided East from West. Many countries did not fit into those categories, however, calling themselves part of the "non-aligned movement." In time, the wealthy capitalist countries, many but not all allied with the United States, came to be called the First World; the Communist countries aligned with the Soviet Union, the Second World; and all others, including Communist China, the Third World. The Second World ended with the break-up of the Soviet Union, and the First and Third Worlds are more commonly referred to as Developed Countries and Developing Countries or by the cardinal directions North and South, with most of the old Second World countries assigned to the North. But many are uncomfortable with these terms, too.

The cardinal directions do not represent the only way that location has been used to identify people and cultures. Until the late nineteenth century, for example, Chinese rulers viewed the world as centered in China, which is reflected in the name for the Chinese realm, Central Kingdom. Chinese maps paralleled this politically inspired world view. (Religiously inspired worldviews differed in China; India was placed at the center of maps by Chinese

Buddhists.) The Chinese view explained what was essentially a power relationship in terms of the ethical virtue of the emperor. Unlike Europeans, the Chinese, who divided the world into cultured and barbarian spheres, did not ascribe these qualities to the cardinal directions East and West. Instead, distance in any direction would lessen the ethical influence of the Chinese center, which was located in the emperor's court.[2] Early modern Indian geographers centered their maps on India. One Indian geographer designated Europe, at his map's margin, as "England, France, and other hat-wearing islands."[3] Medieval Islamic mapmakers centered their world on Dar al-Islam (abode of Islam). Crossing this huge stretch of territory from southern Spain to China, starting in 1325, North African adventurer Ibn Battuta found recognizable Islamic culture throughout the region.[4]

Europeans, however, were more likely to use cardinal directions to define the world's areas. These directions were conflated with cultural characteristics, most of which have been shown by historians to be inaccurate. Thus, geography became destiny—if you're in the West, you must have certain characteristics, and if you're in the East, you have a different set of cultural behaviors. This was constantly inverted as well. When those doing the defining—the "West"—decided a country had cultural characteristics that were undesirable, it could be excluded from the West or Europe by being redefined as Eastern. Even the historical insistence on calling Europe a "continent" when it met none of the usual requirements for that label was a way of setting it aside as a place with a supposedly homogenous culture, distinct from those elsewhere in Africa or the rest of Eurasia. That culture was "Western."

The ancient Greeks had divided the world they knew into three parts, which loosely corresponded to what we call Europe, Asia, and North Africa. They disagreed, however, on the boundaries between those parts. Before 500 B.C.E., the Greeks used the term "Europe" to refer to Greece and the term "Asia" for all foreign lands other than Europe. They soon expanded Europe to include the land north and west of Greece and separated "Africa" from "Asia." Later, that three-part division was given a religious underpinning when Christians asserted that God had divided the world in three parts, giving one to each son of Noah.[5] From the eleventh-century split in Christendom between a Rome-based Catholic Church and a Constantinople-based Orthodox Church, the terms *West* and *East* were increasingly used for Europe and Asia, respectively. While the East was originally a small area in the eastern Mediterranean, it grew in the popular imagination as the Europeans learned more about India and later East Asia. Seeking wealth and riches, spices and textiles, Europeans looked eastward. The East was seen as different, but not necessarily inferior.

Looking for access to the East took Columbus to a "new" world, neither Western nor Eastern but a hybrid—a "West Indies" inhabited by "Indians." In the next several centuries, European countries established relationships of imperialism over many Asians, Africans, Americans, and Australians. But it was concerning Asians that Europeans of the nineteenth century articulated theories of Western superiority. The others were viewed as barbarians, and European dominance did not seem to need explanation. Later, as categories like "Third World" and "South" replaced "East," so-called Eastern characteristics were easily transferred to Africa or South America.

The East came to be seen as the opposite of the West.[6] This was expressed in a series of stereotyped comparisons. For example, where the East contained countries whose people valued irrationality, the West esteemed rationality. Where the West promoted democracy, the East was run by autocratic rulers whose role derived from what was called, as late as the mid-twentieth century, an "Asiatic Mode of Production."[7] While the West was dynamic and thus had a history, Asia was stagnant and unchanging; and even if it had had a history in the murky past, scholars like Karl Marx and G. W. F. Hegel contended that it no longer did. While Europe enjoyed a temperate climate, permitting it to embark on industrialization, the East did not. Many outside of Europe or the United States also absorbed these stereotypes. In the late nineteenth century, Fukuzawa Yukichi, an advocate of modernizing Japan, accepted these supposed characteristics as natural and called on the Japanese to "leave Asia" and join the West. Though scholars have debunked all these notions as having no grounding in historical fact, they continue to influence the meanings of East and West.

A few additional categories were developed in the twentieth century. The Middle East (East of what? The Middle of what?) came into being as a category for military planning during World War II. Its boundaries are as shifting and political as those of Europe and Asia. Africa is also subjected to a number of different slicings—is North Africa separate from sub-Saharan Africa?

Locational designations, groupings by political allegiance, classification by assumed cultural characteristics, and organization by stages of economic development all influence each other. Assumed cultural characteristics today lead to the redrawing of geographic lines in places like the Balkans, where the break-up of Yugoslavia in the 1990s produced warfare over ethnically defined borders. But location may also lead to our ascribing cultural characteristics or history to a country that never even had that history. North-South and East-West are always relative categories and reflect power relations in addition to designations of cultural identity.

Questions

1. Why do people define their world geographically?
2. How are the ways in which people define locations related to politics or power?
3. Do nations' identities change when their rulers, ideology, or dominant religions change?

CHAPTER

12

The Islamic Gunpowder Empires, 1300–1650

CHAPTER CONTENTS

By the fourteenth century the waves of migration and conquest out of Central Asia that had established the Mongol Empire and altered the political configurations of the Islamic world had mostly ceased. Late in that century a new Turco-Mongol conqueror called Timur began a campaign that ravaged northern India, Persia, Iraq, and Anatolia, but his empire was not enduring. In the fifteenth and sixteenth centuries, however, three great Turkic empires gained preeminence in the old Mongol and Byzantine domains. The Ottoman, Safavid, and Mughal empires flourished on the bases of preexisting civilizations, Turco-Mongol military organization, and enhanced firepower; in the process they also crafted a new cultural synthesis. These empires are sometimes called the gunpowder empires because, like their European counterparts, they incorporated gunpowder weaponry into their traditional military systems. All three formed parts of a vast trading network reaching from the Pacific to the Atlantic Ocean. At the same time that the Ming Chinese were launching voyages that reached the East African coast, the Ottoman Turks were building an empire in the eastern Mediterranean that, in the sixteenth century, would dominate the region and challenge the Portuguese in the Indian Ocean.

Europeans were active in Asia during this period but exerted relatively little influence. Awed by the wealth and power of Muslim empires, they were generally held in disdain by Asian elites, who considered their own cultures superior. Akbar, the great Mughal emperor, referred to the "savage Portuguese" at his court,[1] Ottoman sultans regarded European envoys as supplicants, and the Safavid shah kept English merchants waiting for weeks while he attended to more important matters.

1300

1324 End of the reign of Osman, first Ottoman ruler

1398–1402 Timur invades India and Anatolia

1400

1453 Mehmed II conquers Constantinople

1500

1501 Ismail Safavi launches Safavid dynasty

1517 Ottomans conquer Cairo and gain control of Mecca

1517 Piri Reis world map

1520–1566 Reign of Ottoman Suleiman the Magnificent

1525 Babur, first Mughal emperor, invades India

1538–1588 Sinan Pasha, Ottoman royal architect

1556–1605 Reign of Akbar over the Mughal domains

1588–1629 Reign of Shah Abbas in Persia

1597 Shah Abbas begins building imperial Isfahan

1600

1634–1654 Taj Mahal built

1658–1707 Reign of Mughal emperor Aurangzeb in India

NEW POLITIES IN EURASIA

- *How did political conditions in Central Asia influence the rise of the Ottoman, Safavid, and Mughal empires?*

For the kingdoms of Europe, the Ottoman conquest of Constantinople in 1453 signaled a catastrophe: the end of the Eastern Roman Empire and a disruption in established commercial patterns. Preachers and writers in Europe depicted the Ottoman victories as a type of divine punishment for the sins of Christendom. Even more significant, the Ottomans symbolized a new Muslim world emerging between the eastern Mediterranean and Southeast Asia. In that expansive territory, the three new Turkic empires would hold sway for centuries. Geographically, this world was centered in Persia, under its Shi'ite Safavid (sah-FAH-weed) dynasty. Culturally, it was influenced by Persian, Arab, and Byzantine courtly traditions. To the east, the magnificent Mughal (moo-GUL) Empire emerged at a crucial crossroads of the east-west and north-south trade. Militarily, this Muslim world was dominated by the forces of the Ottoman Empire, which were far more formidable than those of any country in Europe at the time. War often raged among these contending states. Nevertheless, they shared the Islamic faith, common steppe antecedents, and Persian artistic and literary traditions.

Background: The Steppe Frontier

After the mid-fourteenth century, tumultuous conditions in Central Asia helped generate the Muslim empires to the south. The fragmented Mongol Empire left the steppe politically divided into states that dissolved and re-formed in new combinations. While the old **khanates** survived for a while, war was almost continuous along the southern steppe frontier, from the Crimea to China.

The continuing steppe influence was well illustrated by the quick rise and collapse of the Timurid (ti-MOR-id) Empire at the close of the fourteenth century. Timur the Lame, the "Tamerlane" celebrated in Western literature, who claimed descent from Ching-

khanate—A Turkic state ruled by a khan.

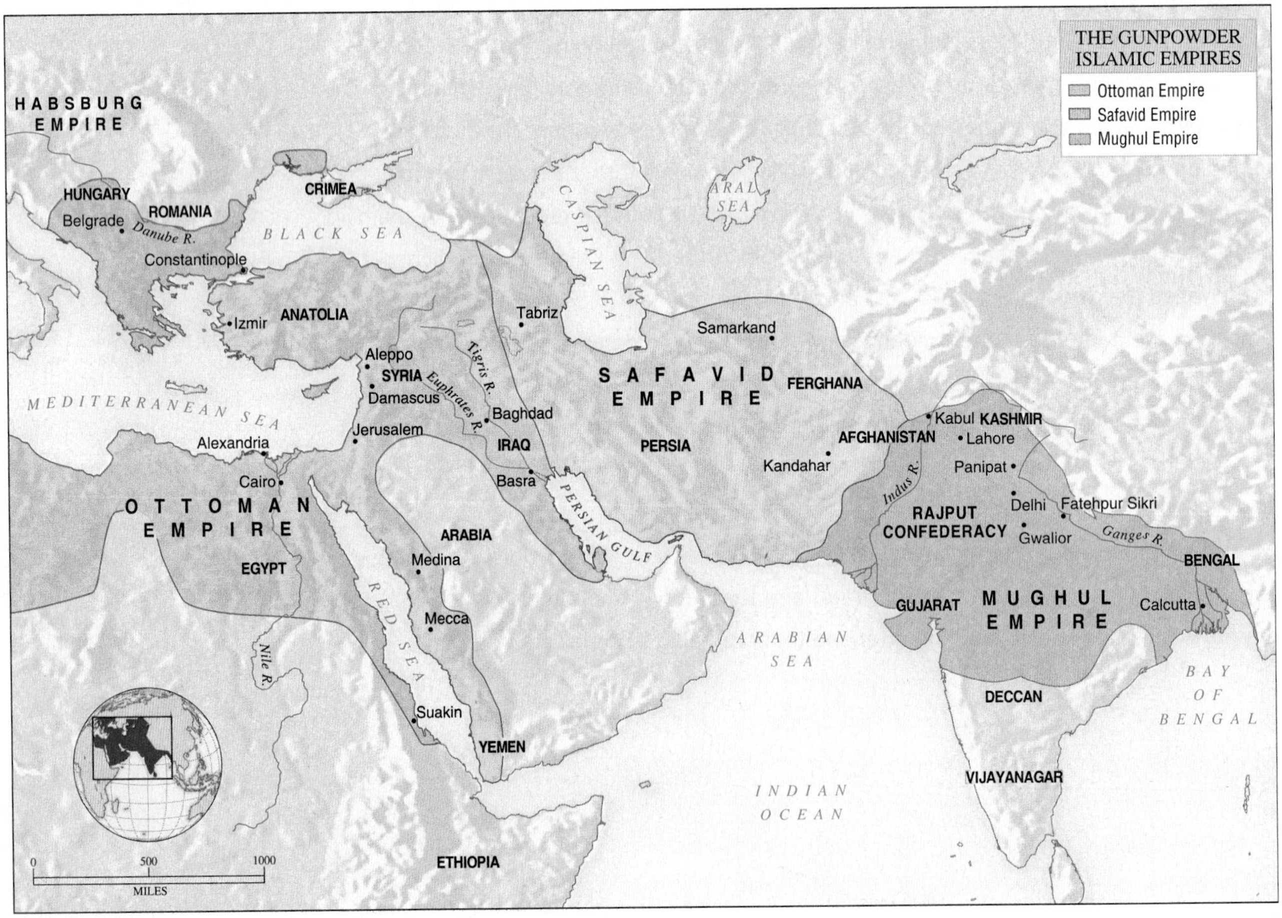

The gunpowder empires dominated south and west Asia, North Africa, and southeastern Europe in the sixteenth century.

gis (Genghis) Khan, rose to power during the 1370s as an *emir* ("commander") in the Chaghatai (chahg-HAH-tai) khanate of Central Asia. In his quest to restore the original Mongol Empire, Timur led whirlwind campaigns through the western steppe, the Crimea, Persia, and Anatolia. He crushed Ottoman resistance and carted the defeated Ottoman sultan, Bayezid I, off across Anatolia in a cage, subjecting him to ridicule. Timur terrorized northern India and was planning to invade Ming China when he died in 1405. But once Timur's army withdrew, the leaders who had submitted to him were less likely to comply with his demands. A conqueror's real domains were those from which he could effectively collect taxes and levy troops.

This miniature painting depicts the envoy of Timur at the court of the Ottoman sultan Bayezid I. The sultan is surrounded by his courtiers, with pages to his right and janissaries and officials in the foreground. Bayezid looks imposing, but he was defeated and killed by Timur. Note the fine carpets around the sultan's throne and the soldiers armed with gunpowder weapons in the foreground.

For more than a century after Timur had resurrected the spirit of Chinggis Khan, a dream of universal empire—real or imagined— lingered in the minds of his descendants, among the many Turco-Mongol rulers in northern Persia and Transoxiana (trahnz-OX-ee-ahn-ah) to its east. The Ottoman sultans, who had established their hegemony in Anatolia before Timur's time and only barely survived his onslaught, were not direct heirs of his traditions, but they too aspired to the conquests and prestige of Chinggis Khan and Alexander the Great. Russia and particularly northern India, where Muslim regimes took hold after Timur's armies devastated Delhi in 1398, were also sites of a renewed struggle for power.

Drastic change marked the steppe frontier after the late fifteenth century, as populations settled around cities and firearms moderated the advantages of tribal cavalry. Indeed, the Uzbeks, who seized most of Transoxiana in this era, were among the last steppe conquerors. Like their predecessors, they were integrated into the courtly cultures of the lands they conquered. But long after the Uzbek conquest, old nomadic traditions continued to shape the rituals and military ethos of Turco-Mongol dynasties.

THE OTTOMAN EMPIRE

▪ *How did the Ottoman Turks create and sustain their empire?*

The most powerful of the new Muslim empires was that of the Ottoman Turks. Centered in Anatolia, its military might cast long shadows over southeastern Europe, western Asia, and North Africa. By the middle of the sixteenth century the Ottoman patrimony stretched from Hungary to Ethiopia and from the borders of Morocco to Arabia and Iraq.

CASE STUDY
The Ottoman Empire in the Late Sixteenth Century

The origin myth of the Ottomans suggests the unique role that both the Central Asian warrior traditions and sufi Islam played in the legitimation of kingship. The founder of the Ottoman line was called Osman. According to legend, he was a valiant young warrior, fighting as a Seljuk subordinate on the frontiers of the Byzantine Empire in the late thirteenth century. Osman had, as a warrior must, a good horse, a strong arm, and a loyal companion. He fell in love with the daughter of a revered sufi ***shaykh*** and asked for her hand in marriage. Her father refused; but that night the *shaykh* dreamed that he saw the moon descending on his sleeping daughter, merging into her

shaykh—An Arabic term for a tribal chief or religious master.

The Ottomans

c. 1281	Osman establishes the Ottoman dynasty
1453	Ottomans capture Constantinople
1517	Sultan Selim conquers Cairo, becomes Protector of the Holy Cities
1520–1566	Reign of Suleiman the Magnificent, Ottoman Golden Age

breast. From this union grew a huge and imposing tree that spread its branches over many lands and many flowing streams. When he awoke, the *shaykh* decided to approve the marriage.

Dreams play an important role in Middle Eastern literatures, and many kings took the interpretation of dreams seriously. The legend of the *shaykh*'s dream linked the warrior tradition to the mystical religious authority of the sufis, thus legitimizing Osman's rule. His dynasty, like the tree, did endure and expand to control many and prosperous territories. As the dynasty grew more powerful, the Ottomans also falsified a genealogy linking them to the prophet Muhammad. This Ottoman claim, like Timur's claim to be a descendent of Chinggis Khan, also lent an aura of legitimacy to their rule. The Ottomans were not the first or the last family to imagine for themselves illustrious ancestors. Osman's line was spectacularly successful; it ruled for over six centuries, from the late thirteenth century until World War I.

Osman's successors won independence from their Seljuk Turk overlords and gradually conquered the surrounding principalities. They had gained control over most of Asia Minor when Timur's army invaded Anatolia, defeated the Ottomans, and forced a half-century of internal restoration. Then two remarkable sultans resumed the Ottoman conquests. The first, Mehmed II (second reign 1451–1481), took Constantinople, Romania, and the Crimea. The second, Selim I (1512–1520), annexed Kurdistan, northern Iraq, Syria,

DOCUMENT
Mehmed II

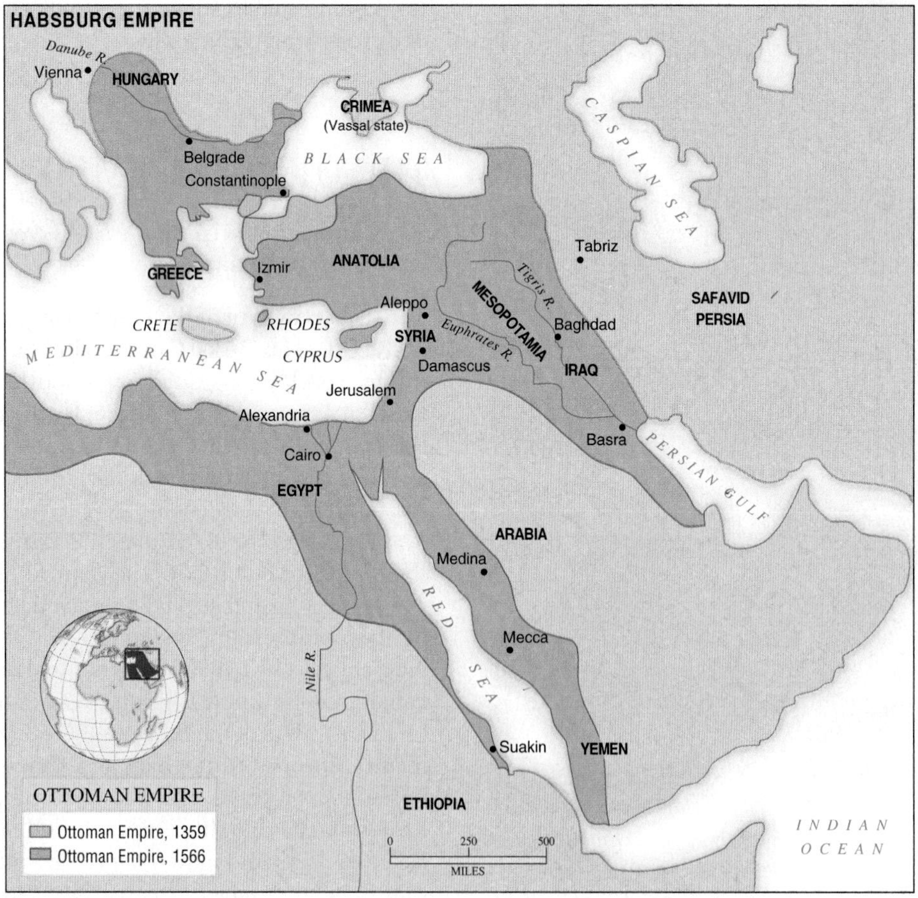

By the mid-sixteenth century the Ottoman Empire encompassed much of the Mediterranean. It included the core territories (excluding Persia) of the Middle East and extended across North Africa and into Europe.

Discovery Through Maps

The World Map of Piri Reis

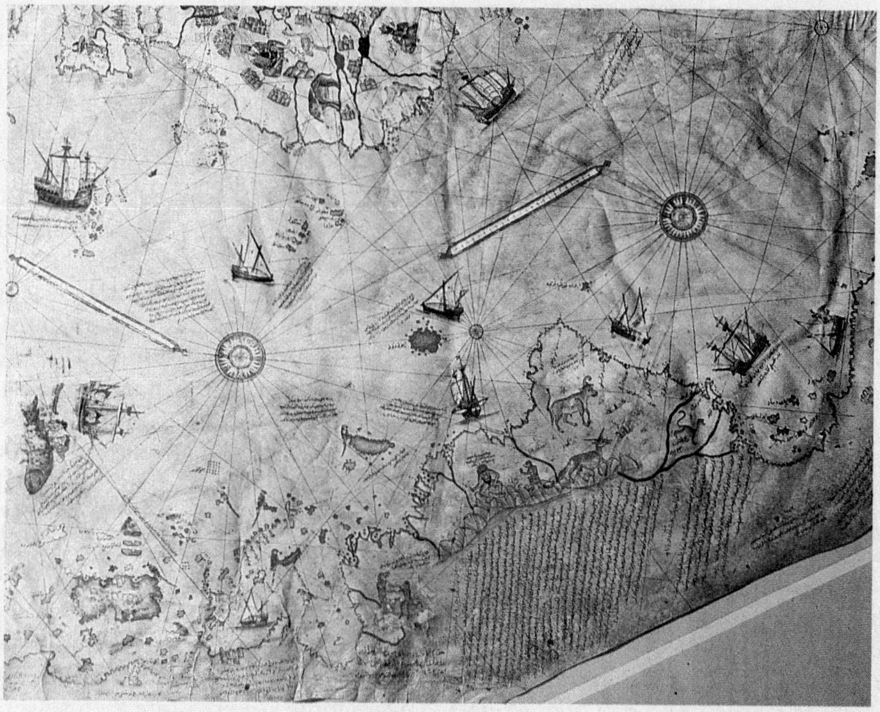

Western historiography has highlighted Europeans' "discovery" of the New World. But the Age of Discovery produced many visions of the world, only some of which were preoccupied with the Americas. Ottoman cartographers were interested in the Americas, although Ottoman ambitions for conquest were directed primarily eastward to Asia. Mapping in this era was intimately associated with the objectives of merchants and sailors, and the most famous of Ottoman cartographers was a skilled sea captain named Piri Reis. Like other members of the Ottoman military-administrative class, Piri Reis was a man of diverse talents. In 1517, when his sovereign, Sultan Selim, conquered Cairo, Piri Reis presented him with a parchment map of the world, only part of which survives. The segment reproduced here shows the Atlantic Ocean, the western shores of Africa and Europe, and the eastern shores of South and Central America. Piri Reis's map incorporates elaborate illustrations of ships, kings, wildlife, and mythical creatures. It depicts strange tales (like the sailors who landed on a whale's back, mistaking it for an island, at top left) and gives nautical distances. The cartographer provided a list of 20 Western and Islamic sources he consulted, including a map of Christopher Columbus. Piri Reis's map suggests the currents of shared knowledge that linked the scholars, merchants, and sailors of Asia, Africa, and Europe at this time. The boundaries of scholarship were fluid, and learned men eagerly sought out new information. Cartographers like Piri Reis benefited from and contributed to the knowledge assembled by peoples of many nations and religions.

For the sailor or merchant, any map that was more accurate, regardless of its provenance (Portuguese, Ottoman, Christian, Muslim), was a tool for ensuring a more successful and safer journey.

Questions to Consider

1. In the sixteenth century, why would a sea captain be a good mapmaker?
2. Think about the different kinds of maps you have seen in this text and elsewhere. How does the way a map is constructed and illustrated tell us something about the beliefs and objectives of the mapmaker and the people for whom he makes the map?
3. Why do you think there are figures of people and animals on this map?

and Egypt. Mehmed's conquests terrorized European Christendom and brought the Ottoman state considerable wealth and prestige. The sultan repopulated Constantinople, renamed Istanbul in the nineteenth century, using a combination of tax breaks and forced population transfers. The declining but intrepid old warrior was planning new campaigns when he died.

IMAGE
Mehmet II

Mehmed's son, Bayezid II, acquired further territories and built up a powerful fleet. Then, Selim's conquest of Egypt and Arabia brought added prestige: control of another great imperial capital, Cairo, and claim to the title Protector of the Holy Cities (Mecca and Medina), coveted by all Muslim monarchs. It also gave him control over the wealth and grain of Egypt and all the Mediterranean outlets of the eastern trade in spices, textiles, and jewels. Under Selim, the Ottoman navy dominated the eastern Mediterranean.

Ottoman power increased under Selim's only son, Suleiman (SOO-lay-mahn; 1520–1566). This determined campaigner soon became the most feared ruler among a generation of monarchs that included Henry VIII of England, Francis I of France, and Charles V of Spain. Suleiman's estimation of his own supremacy is illustrated in a letter to the French monarch in which Suleiman claimed glorious and elaborate titles but addressed Francis simply as "King."

Suleiman extended all his borders, particularly those touching Habsburg lands in Europe. After taking Belgrade in 1521 and the island of Rhodes from the Knights of St. John in 1522, he invaded Hungary in 1526 with 100,000 men and 300 artillery pieces. At Mohacs the Turks won an overwhelming victory. Hungary was then integrated into the Ottoman Empire. Although many Hungarian nobles were slaughtered in the war, Suleiman continued the Ottoman practice of integrating nobles and military men from his defeated foe into his own administration. If a governor submitted, he was often allowed to retain his post; this pragmatic administrative flexibility helped ensure the success of Ottoman conquests.

Suleiman aspired to the conquest of even further territory, aiming particularly at the rich agricultural lands, timber sources, and mines of eastern Europe; he also proposed to control the rich commerce of the Mediterranean. Meanwhile, his forces took Iraq from the Safavids, thus acquiring access to the Persian Gulf. This monarch, who built the great wall around Jerusalem that is still standing today, claimed to be "Lord of the two lands and two seas." His conquests provoked conflicts with the Portuguese in the Red Sea and Indian Ocean. The Portuguese imagined taking Mecca to chastise the "heathen" Ottomans, but no such attack ever materialized.

MAP
The Islamic World: The Ottoman Empire

Suleiman responded harshly to challenges to his authority. He executed his own favorite son and a grandson who rebelled against him. His palace life was marked by pomp and splendor exceeding that of Louis XIV's France. An army of servants attended him, and those men who worked in his palace inner service gained prestige and status because of their proximity to the sultan. The sultan's banquets were served on elaborate tableware of gold, silver, and an expanding collection of fine Chinese porcelain. In the hours between waking and sleeping, Suleiman met with advisers and petitioners, read, or listened to music. For amusement he watched wrestling matches and listened to court poets and jesters. He was trained in the fine art of goldsmithing, also wrote poetry, and had a keen interest in maps. Foreign ambassadors, such as those from the French king or Habsburg emperor, were forced to prostrate themselves before the sultan,

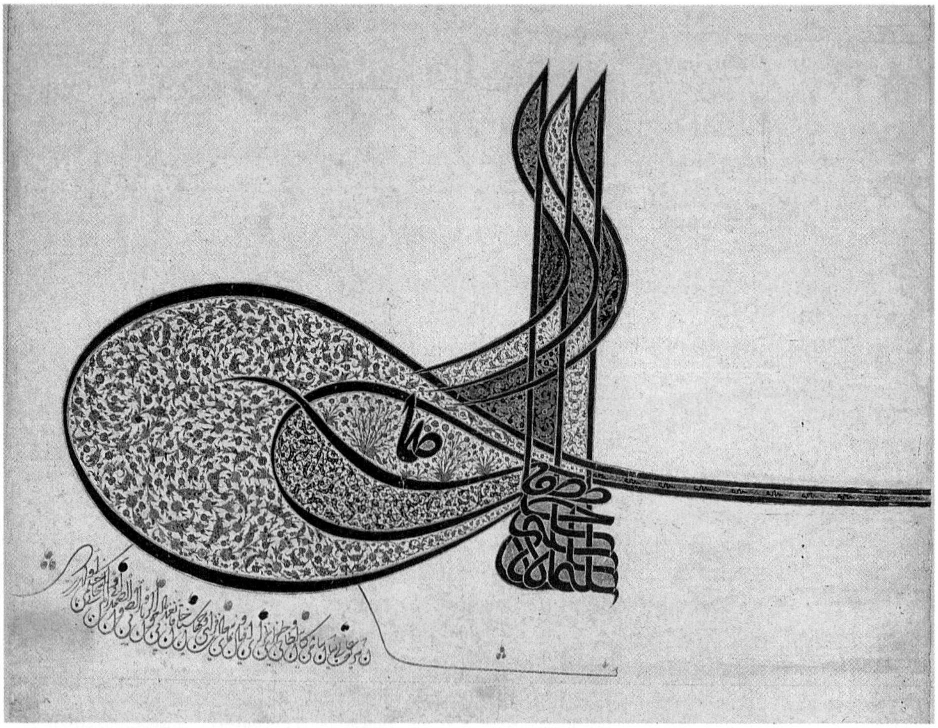

An illuminated tughra *of Sultan Suleiman. The* tughra *was the sultan's signature, used to validate imperial documents and mark coinage. It included the sultan's name and his father's name and designated the sultan as "eternally victorious." The palace employed hundreds of artists, including the designers who fashioned and illuminated such beautiful* tughras.

an indication of the perceived balance of power. European observers commented on the intimidating nature of a visit to Suleiman's court, where thousands of massed troops would stand for hours in absolute silence. In Europe he was known as Suleiman the Magnificent; in the Ottoman Empire he was called Suleiman the Lawgiver.

The sultan's rule was based on an ideal of Persian origin called the "circle of justice." This ideal stated that in order for the kingdom to be prosperous and secure, the sultan required a strong army. To provide for this army, the state needed tax revenues from its citizens, and in order for the citizens to pay their taxes they had to receive in return security and justice from the sultan. Although there were many abuses at various levels of government, the Ottoman sultans did adhere to this ideal. Any of the sultan's subjects could submit a petition to the palace asking redress of wrongs—sometimes the sultan rode out into the streets while his attendants gathered petitions from the crowd. Ottoman court records show many instances in which peasants complained to the local judge *(kadi)* that officials were extracting extra taxes or labor from them. These complaints were then forwarded to the central government, which punished or replaced the offenders.

The Empire Under Suleiman

Suleiman governed the mightiest state of his day. Extending from Poland to Yemen and from Persia to Tripoli, it included 21 provinces and many linguistic and ethnic groups, such as Magyars, Armenians, Bosnians, Albanians, Greeks, Tartars, Kurds, Arabs, Copts, and Jews. "Multiculturalism," often thought of as a twentieth-century concept, was in fact typical of many large agrarian empires of this age.

Economically, Suleiman's empire was nearly self-sufficient, with expanding production and flourishing trade. The Ottoman dominions produced annual revenues greater than those available to any contemporary European monarch and grain surpluses that gave the Ottomans considerable leverage in the Mediterranean region, where grain shortages were endemic. Merchants smuggled grain out despite government attempts to control them, and Ottoman rivals like Venice often purchased grain supplies from the sultan's **pashas.** Indeed, food has been, and still is, one of the most powerful motivating forces in history.

DOCUMENT
An Ambassador's Report on the Ottoman Empire

Power in such a far-flung empire could never be absolute. The sultan delegated authority to local governors and to pashas. Rule in distant provinces, like Egypt, was more flexible and less direct. Conquered lands closer to the capital were given to Ottoman *sipahis* (se-PAH-hee) or "fief" holders, who were expected to bring cavalry contingents for military campaigns. At other times *sipahis* lived on their lands *(timars)*, administering local affairs, collecting taxes, and keeping order. Unlike European feudal lords, they were not usually local residents and were often away in distant wars. Provincial governors *(pashas* or *beys)* were drawn from the higher-ranking Ottoman commanders. All members of this governing class were thus heavily dependent on the sultan, who might suddenly change their assignments or revoke their land holdings. By Suleiman's reign, the political power of the *sipahis* over their *timars* had been partly usurped by the sultan's central bureaucracy. It functioned under a **vizir,** or chief minister, with a host of subordinate officials. The top officials met regularly as the sultan's ***divan*** or council to advise the ruler, but his word was law (although top officials and religious authorities—the ***ulama***—might use their authority to challenge or moderate his decrees).

The Ottomans developed a unique "slave" *(kul)* system that was a major factor in their success. The system was based on the *devshirme* (dev-SHEHR-me), a levy of boys from the non-Muslim subjects of the empire, which functioned as a special type of "human tax" on the Balkan provinces. These boys were brought to the capital, converted to Islam, and taught Turkish. Most of them went to the **janissaries** (JAN-i-sehr-ees), the famed elite Ottoman infantry corps that was armed with gunpowder weapons. They formed the backbone of the formidable Ottoman armies. The smartest and most talented of the boys, however, were sent to the palace to be educated in literature, science, the arts, religion, and military skills. These boys, when they reached maturity, were given the highest military and administrative posts in the state. Ideally, the *kul* system provided the state with a group of expert administrators who, because they had been separated from their families and homes, would remain loyal to the sultan, to whom they owed everything. These "slaves," rather than occupying the lowest level of the social order, controlled much of the wealth and power in Ottoman society. Many of the buildings they endowed are still standing today. The more common type of domestic or agricultural slave did, of course, also exist in Ottoman society. Slavery and slave markets were scattered

---

pasha—Top military-administrative official (governor) in the Ottoman Empire.

vizir—A chief minister or comparable high-ranking government official in the Muslim world, but most particularly in the Ottoman Empire.

divan—A council or place of administrative assembly within the Ottoman Empire.

ulama—Islamic religious authorities; men versed in Islamic sciences and law.

janissaries—An elite Ottoman infantry corps armed with gunpowder weapons and composed mostly of converted Balkan slaves.

European writers and their audiences were fascinated by the Ottoman harem and often depicted it in exaggerated erotic terms. This engraving from a seventeenth-century French history of the Ottoman palace imagines the sultan taking his bath attended by naked harem women. In fact, this image is pure fantasy; both sexuality and reproduction in the harem were tightly controlled, and the sultan's attendants were male, not female.

throughout the Afro-Eurasian world, although Islam prohibited the enslaving of fellow Muslims.

Western literature has produced an exotic, erotic image of the Ottoman sultan's **harem** (the sacred area of the palace, or of any home, forbidden to outsiders). But much of this image is a myth produced by the overactive imaginations or hostile sentiments of European men inspired by the prospect of several hundred women in one household. In fact, sexuality in the palace was tightly controlled. Like women in other traditional patriarchal societies, most Ottoman women had to work in the fields and towns. Only the women of the elite classes could be fully veiled and secluded. In the palace, the harem women were arranged in a rigid hierarchy much like that of the men; each was paid according to her rank. Most of the women were not destined for the sultan's bed; instead they were married to the sultan's officers to create further ties of loyalty to the palace. A select few were chosen to bear the sultan's heirs.

The harem women wielded power because of their wealth, their connections, and their proximity to the sultan. The most powerful among them was the sultan's mother (the ***valide sultan***), not his wife. The *valide sultans* participated actively (although behind the scenes) in court politics. Petitioners, including pashas, applied to these high-ranking women to intercede on their behalf with the sultan. Some *valide sultans* even served a diplomatic function, corresponding with European rulers like the Venetian doge, Catherine de' Medici in France, and Queen Elizabeth in England.

In the Ottoman system, proximity to the sultan was the primary avenue to power, and membership in the royal household or military class brought with it the highest status in society. But pashas, palace women, religious officials, and members of the palace staff jockeyed for positions of power and formed alliances to advance their own interests. Harem politics, illustrated in Suleiman's reign by the contending influences of his mother and his wife, have often been blamed for weakening the Ottoman state. In fact, however, the factors that compromised Ottoman power were much more complex. Continued conquests produced serious communication and transportation problems, and long wars and failure to pay the troops on time caused rebellions in the ranks. Religious contention, provoked by the rise of the Shi'ite Safavids in Persia, also threatened the empire.

Another important factor in Ottoman politics was the fact that the eldest son had no automatic claim to the throne. The sultan's sons thus contended to succeed him, sometimes producing extended periods of interregnum. That was the case with Bayezid II, whose sons got tired of waiting for him to die and launched a civil war to determine who would sit on the throne in his stead. Once a prince established himself as sultan, he would often have his brothers exe-

---

harem—In Arabic, literally "forbidden." A sacred area of palace or home forbidden to outsiders, often but not always used to protect and sequester women.

valide sultan—The mother of the Ottoman sultan; generally the most powerful and influential woman in the empire.

Document Evliya Çelebi, "An Ottoman Official's Wedding Night"

Marriages in the Ottoman administrative system were often arranged to link powerful families, consolidate wealth, and secure loyalty. Love matches were also made, but sometimes officials were forced into marriages at the sultan's command. That was the fate of Melek Ahmed Pasha, who, after the death of his beloved first wife, was forced to marry the elderly and intransigent Fatma Sultan, daughter of Sultan Ahmed I. This passage, in which Melek Ahmed tells his tale of woe to the chronicler Evliya Çelebi, suggests that marriage to a princess, however prestigious, could be burdensome. It also illustrates the consumption of goods by royal households and the power and status of royal women, who could supersede the wishes of influential men. Note that Melek Pasha addressed his new wife as "Sultan." That title was used for royal princesses.

As soon as I entered the harem, having uttered a *besmele* [invocation of God's name], I saw her. Now I am supposed to be her husband, and this is our first night—she ought to show me just a little respect. She just sat there stock still, not moving an inch. I went up and kissed her hand.

"Pasha," she says, "welcome."

"God be praised that I have seen my sultan's smiling beauty," say I, and I shower her with all sorts of self-deprecating flatteries. Not once does she invite me to sit down. And she puts on all kinds of virginal airs, as though she weren't an ancient crone who has gone through twelve husbands!

The first pearl from her lips is this: "My dear pasha, if you want to get along with me, whether you are present at court or absent in some government post, my expenses are 15 purses each and every month. Also I owe my steward, Kermetçi Mustafa Agha, 100 purses: pay my debt in the morning. And every year I get six Marmara boatloads of firewood. And my retainers Selman Beg and Ömer Beg and Mukbil Agha and my steward get as a daily stipend 100 bushels of barley each, 10 okkas of coffee, 10 okkas of fine sugar, and nightly 10 okkas of camphor beeswax"—and on and on with suchlike nonsense, spouting these expenses like a talking inventory. Several times she pinched my cheeks. . . .

Now her stewardess and treasuress and ladies in waiting and, in short, 300 or more women came to kiss my hand and stand there in rows. "Well, my dear pasha, these are my servants of the interior. I also have as many or more manumitted [legally freed] slave girls on the exterior. Together with children and dependents, they total 700 souls. You will provide all of them with their annual stipend of silk and gauze and brocade and broadcloth. And you will pay the annual stipend of my halberdiers and cooks and gardeners and coachmen and eunuchs and *begs*, as well as those serving them, numbering 500 people. And if you don't—well, you know the consequence!"

Melek Ahmed replied: "I swear by God, my sultan," say I, "that I have just returned from the Transylvania campaign. I am a vizir who fights the holy war. In that campaign I had 7,000 men to feed. I spent 170,000 goldpieces and 600 purses. I even had to sell quite a lot of equipment and arms and armor and helmets and to borrow money from the janissary corps. . . . I am unable to bear such expenses."

After this "wedding night" Melek prayed for death and complained that he had been asked to "feed the state elephant." He vowed never to see Fatma Sultan again.

Questions to Consider

1. What does this story suggest about the lives and expenses of both males and females in the Ottoman elite class?
2. Does gender or status take precedence in the dealings of Melek and Fatma?
3. When such a story is incorporated into a history such as Evliya's, should we assume that the dialog is reported word-for-word as it occurred? What factors might affect the accuracy of this account? (Remember that Melek was Evliya's patron.)

From Robert Dankoff, trans., *The Intimate Life of an Ottoman Statesman, Melek Ahmed Pasha (1588–1662), as Portrayed in Evliya Çelebi's Book of Travels* (Albany: State University of New York Press 1991), pp. 259–261.

cuted, a grim task designed to ensure the stability of the state and avoid further struggles. A wise prince would try to gain the favor of the janissary corps, for their support might make or break him.

Religion was an integral part of government and society. But as in other Muslim lands, the religious authorities *(ulama)* did not run the government; they were subordinated to the state and the sultan. The grand **mufti,** as head of the Islamic establishment, was also the chief religious and legal adviser to the sul-

mufti—A high-ranking Islamic religious and legal adviser.

tan. The sultan approved religious appointments and might dismiss any religious officer, including the grand mufti. A corps of learned religious scholars represented the sultan as judges *(kadis),* dispensers of charities, and teachers. Non-Muslim subjects or ***dhimmis*** were regarded as inferior but were granted a significant degree of legal and religious toleration through government arrangements with their religious leaders (rabbis and priests, for example), who were responsible for their civil obedience. Non-Muslim subjects lived under their own laws and customs, pursuing their private interests within limits imposed by Islamic law and Ottoman economic needs. As in other Islamic lands, they had to pay the ***jizya,*** an additional head tax.

Ottoman society, like other societies, can be divided along different types of lines based on gender, occupation, class, religion, or race. For tax purposes, Ottoman society was divided roughly between tax-paying subjects (*reaya,* or flock) and the military-administrative class *(askeri).* This division between *askeri* and *reaya* was the primary determinant of status, crossing lines of gender, race, and sometimes religion. A woman of the *askeri* class could command authority over a man of lesser status. People of various races could be members of the *askeri* class; the chief black eunuch, for example, was one of the most powerful men in the state. Although merchants and members of the *ulama* might achieve considerable wealth and authority, they did not have access to the same type of power and status as the military administrative class.

Artistic Production

Ottoman success resulted in a vigorous cultural renaissance, most evident in monumental architecture and decorative tile work. Mehmed II rebuilt his decaying capital, from sewers to palaces. His monumental Fatih Mosque and splendid Topkapi Palace, with its fortress walls, fountains, and courtyards, were models of the new Ottoman style, which was influenced by the Byzantine artistic tradition. The palace was divided into three courts that reflected Ottoman concepts of power and space. The outer court was for public affairs, as well as stable and kitchen facilities. The second court provided a dividing line between the public and private life of the sultan. There the sultan met with diplomats and built his library. The inner court was reserved for the sultan and his intimates, a place for relaxation and privacy. Suleiman surpassed Topkapi's splendor with the beautiful and elegant Suleimaniye, his own mosque and mausoleum. These were but three architectural wonders among thousands scattered throughout the empire, many of which remain today.

In addition, the period was marked by wondrous productions in the realms of decorative arts. Calligraphy could take the form of birds or boats in official documents. Elaborate calligraphy and stunning painted tiles decorated Ottoman mosques and buildings. For example, Suleiman added luminous tiles to the Dome of the Rock in Jerusalem. Ottoman high culture also produced a great outpouring of scholarship and literature, mostly following Persian traditions but also reflecting a unique Ottoman synthesis. Poets, artists,

Portrait of a Sufi, *c. 1535, was attributed to the painter Shaykh-Zadeh who studied in Herat and then painted and instructed disciples at the Safavid Court in Tabriz. Talented painters were in great demand in the courts of the gunpowder empires. Sufi* shaykhs *often served as influential advisors to the sultans and shahs.*

dhimmis—Non-Muslim subjects of a Muslim state.

jizya—An additional head tax imposed on non-Muslims living under Muslim rule.

and historians vied for the attentions—and rewards (silver, sable furs, robes of honor, even houses)—of the sultan. Some achieved remarkable rank and success; others left the palace disheartened and poor. The great majority of artisans, however, held relatively low status. They lived and worked in the palace or in the cities, grouped often according to their occupations on "the street of the gold-thread makers" or "the street of the coppersmiths."

The Suleymaniye Mosque

Challenges to Ottoman Supremacy

Beginning in Suleiman's reign, cheap silver from the Americas and a population increase led to rising inflation, rebellions, and military mutinies, all of which weakened the government. None of the eight sultans who followed Suleiman before 1648 could duplicate his successes. Selim II was known as "the drunkard"; another sultan gained notoriety by having 19 of his brothers killed on his accession. Increasingly, the sultans did not themselves lead their troops into battle. Other problems plaguing Suleiman's successors were the rising power of the Russians and Habsburgs in Europe, stalemated wars with Persia, and the end of Ottoman naval supremacy in the Red Sea. Nonetheless, the period between 1566 and 1650 should be viewed as one of reorganization and retrenchment rather than decline. The Ottoman Empire was adjusting to newly emerging global configurations of power and commerce, and Ottoman armies still managed to gain important victories in this era, notably the reconquest of Iraq by Murad IV (1623–1640) in 1638.

With Suleiman's death the Ottoman Empire passed its zenith, but it remained a significant contender for power in the Afro-Eurasian sphere well into the eighteenth century. It continued to dominate the overland trade with Asia. Moreover, the sultans moderated Portuguese domination of the Indian Ocean, ultimately aiding the Dutch and English seaborne empires in the East while humbling their Habsburg rivals in Europe.

The Decline of the Ottomans

THE SAFAVID EMPIRE IN PERSIA

▪ *What role did Shi'ism play in the Safavid Empire?*

In the beginning of the sixteenth century a new Turkic dynasty came to power in Iran, led by a charismatic, red-headed, adolescent, sufi *shaykh*. This dynasty, emerging out of the Safavid sufi religious order, would unite Iran, challenge the Ottoman empire, and shift Iran's predominantly Sunni population to Shi'ism. The Safavid dynasty had its origins in an Islamic mystical order founded by Safi al-Din (c. 1252–1334). One of his descendants, Ismail (ruled 1501–1524), gathered an army of devoted followers and began a series of lightning campaigns that united Persia, conquered Iraq, and posed a formidable challenge to the Ottomans on their eastern frontiers. Ismail was only 14 when he seized his first territories. Although such precocity may seem unusual today, it was common enough in this era for the sons of powerful men to be trained to fight and rule while still boys.

Ismail was not only a successful military commander; he was also the head of a Shi'ite Muslim sect.

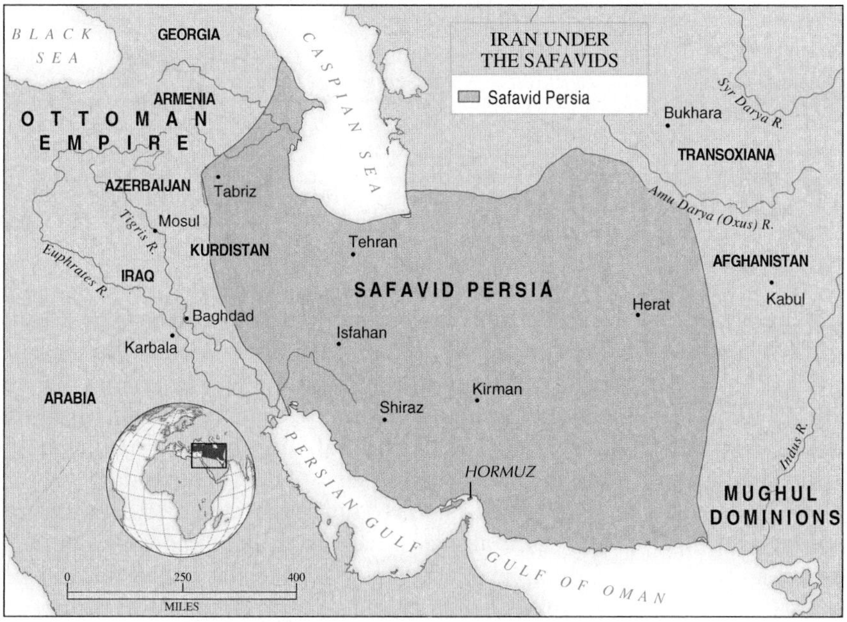

The Safavid Empire was based on the broad, semiarid Iranian plateau. The Safavids and Ottomans contended for control of Iraq and Azerbaijan.

Document The Coming of Ismail Safavi Foretold

Histories and legends of famous leaders and religious figures often recount the ways in which the coming of these men was predicted or foretold. In this selection, from an anonymous Persian manuscript, the story is told of a sufi mystic named Dede Mohammad. This sufi, or *darwish,* while returning from a pilgrimage to Mecca, becomes separated from his caravan in the desert. Dying of thirst, he is rescued by a mysterious youth who takes him to a magnificent encampment in a flowering plain. There he sees a veiled prince, whom he does not realize is the Twelfth *Imam,* a descendant of the Prophet revered by the Shi'ite Muslims who is believed to be in occultation (that is, he has disappeared but is not dead). In this vision, the Twelfth *Imam* girds and sends forth the young Ismail Safavi, thus legitimizing his reign to the Shi'ites.

After his rescue, Dede Mohammad . . . walked by the young man's side, until they came to a palace, whose cupola outrivaled the sun and moon. . . . Golden thrones were arranged side by side, and on one of the thrones a person was seated whose face was covered by a veil. Dede Mohammad, placing his hand on his breast, made a salutation, whereupon an answer to his salutation came from the veiled one, who having bidden him be seated, ordered food to be brought for him. The like of this food he had never seen in his life before. . . . As soon as he had finished his repast, he saw that a party of men had entered, bringing a boy of about fourteen years of age, with red hair, a white face, and dark grey eyes; on his head was a scarlet cap. . . . The veiled youth then said to him, "Oh! Ismail, the hour of your 'coming' has now arrived." The other replied: "It is for your Holiness to command." . . . His Holiness, taking his belt three times lifted it up and placed it on the ground again. He then, with his own blessed hands, fastened on the girdle and taking [Ismail's] cap from his head, raised it and then replaced it. . . . His Holiness then told his servants to bring his own sword which, when brought, he fastened with his own hands on the girdle of the child. Then he said, "You may now depart." [The Arab youth then guided Dede Mohammad back to his caravan, and the sufi asked his guide to reveal the identity of the veiled prince.] He replied, "Did you not know that the prince you saw was no other than the Lord of the Age?" When Dede Mohammad heard this name he stood up and said: "Oh! youth, for the love of God take me back again that I may once more kiss the feet of His Holiness [the Twelfth *Imam*], and ask a blessing of him, perchance I might be allowed to wait on him." But the youth replied: "It is impossible. You should have made your request at first. You cannot return. But you can make your request where you will, for His Holiness is everywhere present and will hear your prayers."

Questions to Consider

1. This manuscript apparently dates from the seventeenth century. Why was it important for the Safavids to relate in this way such stories of the predicted coming of Ismail?
2. The Twelfth *Imam* tied a belt or sash around Ismail's waist, placed his cap on his head, and gave him his own sword. What is the significance of this ceremony? Can you think of similar rituals that take place today?
3. What is the significance of the flowering plain in the middle of a desert and of the miraculous food?

From E. Dennison Ross, "The Early Years of Shah Ismail," *Journal of the Royal Asiatic Society* (1896), pp. 328–331.

Contemporary accounts portray him as a charismatic leader whose army thought him invincible. They followed him into battle crying *"Shaykh, Shaykh!"* The Safavid troops wore red headgear with 12 folds to commemorate the 12 Shi'ite *imams* (descendants of the prophet Muhammad); because of this headgear, they were called "redheads."

Ismail angered the Ottoman sultan by sending missionaries and agitators to stir up the sultan's subjects on the Ottoman eastern frontiers. He also launched a sometimes violent campaign to convert the Sunni Muslims of his domain to Shi'ism. Because Persia had been predominantly Sunni, he had to import Shi'ite scholars and jurists from the Arab lands, such as Syria and Iraq. Under the Safavid shahs (kings), Persia became overwhelmingly Shi'ite, as it is today.

Power is acquired not only on the field of battle but also in the arenas of reputation and diplomacy. Legends grew up around the youthful leader Ismail because of his many and rapid conquests. He was also supposed to have received the secret knowledge of the Safavi mystical order, passed down from his brother as he lay dying. Hence he had a powerful aura of both political and religious legitimacy. European rulers, including the Portuguese king and the pope, were inspired by the accounts of Ismail's victories and the rumors of his quasi-divine prowess. Hoping that the Safavids would help them defeat the Ottomans, who were Sunni Muslims, these rulers sent envoys to the young shah. Ismail had some interest in exploring possibilities with European powers, but he was apparently more interested in acquiring European artillery and defeating the Ottomans than in a Christian-Shi'ite alliance.

Because transport and communication technology was so primitive in the sixteenth century, rulers often knew little about their rivals. Diplomatic missions were thus crucially important as a means by which a ruler might establish his reputation and gain information about foreign powers. The Portuguese, for example, thought of the Safavids as barbarians, but they were interested in securing an ally against the Ottomans. Their envoy to Ismail was instructed to brag to the Safavids about the fine quality of Portuguese horses, table service, and women (all considered prize possessions). Envoys were also used to send messages of intimidation. When, in 1510, Ismail defeated Shaibani Khan, the Uzbek ruler in Central Asia, he had the Khan's skull gilded and made into a drinking cup. He sent an envoy with the grisly trophy, along with a taunting message, to the Ottoman sultan, Bayezid II. Of course, being an envoy in this era was dangerous, especially for the bearers of rude messages. The Ottoman sultans often imprisoned Safavid envoys, and messengers to the Safavid court were sometimes detained or abused. When Ismail sent another arrogant message to the Mamluk sultan in Egypt, the latter was so enraged that he sponsored a poetry contest to see which of his poets could write the most insulting reply in verse. But he did not harm Ismail's messenger because he was afraid of a Safavid invasion.

The Ottomans were intimidated by Ismail's early successes. In 1514, however, they soundly defeated Ismail's forces on the frontier between Anatolia and Persia. This victory is often attributed to the fact that the Ottomans had more and better gunpowder weaponry. Demoralized, Ismail withdrew to his palace, having lost his reputation for invincibility. After his death, the Safavids fought a series of long wars against the Ottomans to the west and the Uzbeks to the east.

None of his successors wielded the same charismatic religious power as Ismail. They were kings, not *shaykhs* (holy men), even though Ismail's son Tahmasp still claimed the headship of the Safavid sufi order. Still, the next hundred years of Safavid rule were characterized by a consolidation of state power, lavish patronage of the arts, and an exploration of diplomatic and commercial relations with Europe. European merchants visited the shah's court, trying to gain access to the coveted Iranian silk trade, but they met with little success. Tahmasp ruled for half a century (1524–1576), despite having to contend with foreign invasions, religious factionalism, and power struggles among the tribal leaders. The Safavids, with the aid of European renegades, developed their gunpowder weaponry but never to the same extent as the Ottomans. Nor did they imitate the elaborate "slave"-based hierarchy and infantry corps (janissaries) that became the basis for Ottoman success. In Persia, the tribal leaders and their cavalry-based militaries retained their position of power.

MAP The Middle East

Islam shares the story of Adam and Eve with Christianity and Judaism, with certain variations. In this Persian manuscript Adam rides a dragonlike serpent and Eve rides a peacock; these two beasts facilitated the entrance of Iblis *[Satan] into the Garden of Eden.*

The Reign of Abbas the Great

The reign of Shah Abbas (1588–1629) is considered a "golden age" of Safavid power, comparable to that of Suleiman in the Ottoman Empire. Ascending the throne at the age of 17, Abbas ultimately became a pragmatic politician, a wise statesman, a brilliant strategist, and a generous patron of the arts. During his reign, Persia acquired security, stability, and a reputation for cultural creativity, symbolized by the shah's splendid new capital at Isfahan.

Abbas directed much of his attention to the threat posed by an Ottoman-Uzbek alliance, which had almost destroyed his country. He held his holy men in political check but labored to project an image of Shi'ite piety. He reorganized his government and army, creating a personal force of "slaves" of the royal household. This force acted as a counterweight to the ambitious and often unruly tribal chiefs. Within the army, Abbas increased his artillery and musket forces, relying less on traditional cavalry. During the 1590s, he slowly recovered territory lost by his less adept predecessors.

Persia prospered under Abbas, and Isfahan was a great center of trade, production, and consumption. The government employed thousands of workers, and the shah, his family, and retainers consumed great quantities of luxury textiles, jade vessels, jeweled weapons, and exotic food items. Government monopolies, particularly in silk, promoted various crafts such as weaving and dying. Hundreds of new roads, bridges, hostels, and irrigation projects promoted agriculture, encouraged trade, and swelled urban populations. These projects also enhanced the prestige of the ruler. Contemporaries noted that a person could travel from one end of the empire to another in safety, without fear of bandits. That was a significant claim in an age when bandits roamed the countryside and merchants traveled at their own risk, often with large retinues of armed guards.

The silk trade was so lucrative that merchants on both sides conspired to get the shipments through, even when the Safavids and the Ottomans were at war. Persia was an important center in the networks of East-West trade. Its silk was in such demand in Europe that Venetian, French, and other traders would wait in the Syrian entrepots for the caravans of Persian silk to come in. They negotiated with local agents, trying to outbid each other for the rights to purchase each incoming load. One Venetian observer stated that a merchant would willingly pluck out his own eye to triumph over a competitor. The British tried for years to gain concessions from the Safavids on Persian silk. Ultimately, the shah signed a commercial agreement with the British, and the Portuguese were forcibly ejected from Hormuz in the Persian Gulf, moves allowing direct shipment of Persian silk to Europe by sea, and thus the avoidance of Ottoman tolls on the overland routes.

Persia at this time was one of the primary cultural centers of the world. It was a conduit to the West not only for the goods but also for the spiritual and literary influences of India. Meanwhile, sufi Muslim missionaries traveled to South and Southeast Asia, transmitting their own ideas and bringing a synthesis of

Nominally, this image illustrates a story about an elderly dervish who is in love with a handsome young man. But miniatures often depicted scenes of everyday life like this sixteenth-century Safavid scene of a bath house. On the roof, servants shake out towels. In the dressing room men are shown changing their clothes and an attendant brings a man who appears to be the bath keeper some food. A father carries his son into the bath while outside a servant takes care of a horse with rich saddle cloths. Inside the bath (hammam), *assisted by bath-attendants, men of various ages wash, get their hair trimmed, or enjoy a massage. The bath was a place for socializing, relaxing, and conducting business. Bathing was a same-sex activity. Women, who either attended separate baths or attended on different days, might bring their children or use the bath as an opportunity to evaluate potential brides for their sons.*

mystical ideas and practices back to the Islamic heartlands. Persia's fine arts—ceramics, tapestries, and carpets—were eagerly sought from Alexandria to Calcutta. Persian literary forms, particularly the exquisite imagery of Persian poetry, were imitated at both the Ottoman and Mughal courts, even by the rulers themselves. Persian painters explored realist styles and erotic themes. They were recruited from abroad, as were two émigrés, Khwaja Abdus Samad and Mir Sayyid Ali, who founded the famous Mughal school of painting in India.

Major Middle Eastern courts housed large workshops of artists, sometimes numbering in the hundreds. The Safavid shahs paid their painters to produce lavish manuscripts. Ismail commissioned a wondrous illustrated version of the *Epic of Kings (Shahnamah)*, a long rhyming poem by Firdawsi, that was not finished in the shah's lifetime. Five court calligraphers spent nine years transcribing a single edition of the poet Jami's *Seven Thrones*, for Prince Ibrahim Mirza; it was then turned over to a group of painters who produced its lavish illustrations. When the Ottomans conquered the Persian capital of Tabriz, they carried back many of the Safavid artists and their works as a valuable part of the booty.

Persian architecture, with its jewel-like colors, intricate geometric and floral patterns, luxurious gardens, and artificial streams, exerted considerable influence on the architecture of the Islamic world. Abbas made the capital at Isfahan a showcase for these artistic and architectural talents. One of the largest cities of its time, Isfahan had a million inhabitants. Its public life centered around a broad square (used for assemblies and polo matches), the palace compound, a huge bazaar, and the main mosque. Five hundred years later the beauty of Abbas's surviving monuments still inspires awe in visitors. As one Persian writer put it in his boyhood memoirs, "Isfahan is half the world."

THE MUGHAL EMPIRE IN SOUTH ASIA

▪ *How did the Turco-Islamic Mughals modify their rule to accommodate a Hindu majority population?*

The Safavid and Ottoman states were contemporaries of the mighty Mughal Empire in India. It too was ruled by a Turkic dynasty. But unlike the Ottoman sultans and Safavid shahs, the Mughals ruled a population that was predominantly Hindu rather than Muslim. That fact marked the Mughal Empire indelibly and helped craft its distinctive character.

The Mughals

1525	Babur invades India
1556–1605	Reign of Akbar, Mughal Golden Age
1632	Shah Jahan commissions the Taj Mahal
1658–1707	Reign of Aurangzeb, reasserts Islamic orthodoxy

Origins

The Ottoman Empire emerged out of a warrior principality in what is now Turkey, and the Safavid Empire was established by a sufi boy-king who commanded both political and religious authority in Persia. The origin of the Mughal Empire was different from each of these; one might say it was founded by a determined prince in search of a kingdom.

The establishment of the Mughal Empire was not the first instance of Muslim contact with the diverse, but predominantly Hindu, population of India. Mus-

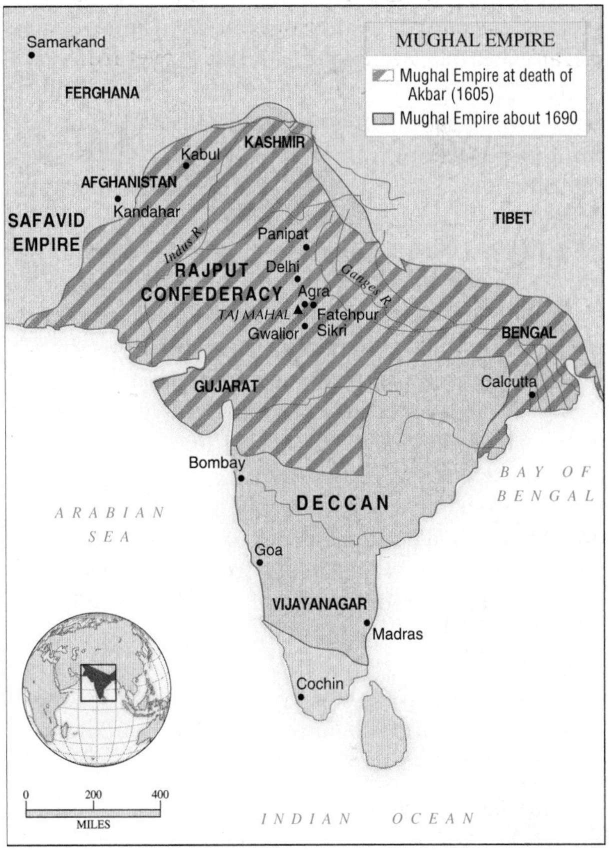

At its height the Mughal Empire comprised most of the Indian subcontinent.

lim merchants and sufi mystics had traveled to India from the Islamic heartlands for many centuries. From the seventh century onward Muslim rulers extended the frontiers of Islam eastward to the borders of South Asia. Then a Turkic warrior, Mahmud of Ghazna (c. 971–1030), gained control of Khurasan province in eastern Persia and Afghanistan and seized control of northern India. Muslim sultanates were also established on the west coast of India, and the Muslim Delhi Sultanate ruled in the thirteenth and fourteenth centuries until Timur's invasion. Thus, by the sixteenth century, much of South Asian society had had some contact with Islamic culture and political power

India is a land of many peoples, many languages, and diverse terrain. At the beginning of the sixteenth century it was politically fragmented. The Delhi Sultanate, having spawned a number of independent contending Muslim states, had been partially resurrected under the Lodi Afghan dynasty. The Rajput Confederacy held sway in the northwest, the Vijayangar Empire controlled much of southern India, and a string of commercial city-states held sway along the southwestern coast. Although many rulers had aspired to unite the entire subcontinent, that goal remained daunting.

Early in the sixteenth century, a new conqueror cast his eye on India. The adventurous Turco-Mongol ruler of Kabul, Babur ("the Tiger"; 1483–1530), was a descendant of both Timur and Chinggis Khan. Babur did not begin his career in India. He inherited the Afghan principality of Ferghana and twice conquered the Timurid capital at Samarkand before losing everything to the Uzbeks. He and his troops finally seized the throne of Kabul in 1504. Babur is a striking historical figure because, unlike many rulers of his time, he compiled his memoirs. They are a tale of triumphs and losses that reveal Babur as a straightforward narrator who built gardens wherever he went, paid careful attention to geography, was solicitous of his mother, and seemed to enjoy good wine and a good fight. He also loved to compose and recite poetry. Babur's memoirs tell of rhinoceros hunts and military relations. He notes, rather ruefully, that he had sworn to give up drink when he reached the age of 40 but now felt compelled to drink out of anxiety because he was already 39. Armed with Turkish artillery, this intrepid warrior mobilized an invasion in 1525, winning decisive battles against the Afghan Sultanate at Delhi and the Rajput Confederacy. Babur was not impressed with Indian culture. He criticized native dress, religion, and the failure of Indians to have running water in their gardens.

> *Hindustan [India] is a place of little charm. There is no beauty in its people, no graceful social intercourse, no poetic talent or understanding, no etiquette, nobility or manliness. . . . There are no good horses, meat, grapes, melons, or other fruit. There is no ice, cold water, good food or bread in the markets.*[2]

Like many travelers, Babur tended to find his own culture superior to those of other peoples. He did, however, admire the Indian systems of numbers, weights, and measures and the country's vast array of craftsmen. Speaking as a prospective ruler, he could not help but remark that "the one nice aspect of Hindustan is that it is a large country with lots of gold and money."[3] When Babur died, soon after the conquest, the hard-living and thoughtful ruler had laid the foun-

Babur, conqueror of northern India, surveying the spectacular rock-cut Hindu sculptures at Urwa fortress in Gwalior, from an illustrated manuscript of Babur's memoirs. Babur ordered these sculptures defaced, probably to fulfill the perceived Islamic prohibition against depicting the human form. Muslim rulers defaced many such Hindu and Buddhist statues, although some Muslim courts also patronized the production of images of the human form.

dations for a Mughal empire that would dominate most of the subcontinent and endure into the eighteenth century.

Babur was succeeded by his able but erratic son, Humayun (hu-MAH-yoon). After ten years of rule during which he expanded Mughal domains, Humayun was overthrown by his vassal Sher Khan. He then fled to the Safavid court of Tahmasp in Persia. The Safavid shah welcomed Humayun. It was always useful for monarchs of the time to shelter in their courts the sons or rivals of neighboring kings, as such refugees gave rulers leverage against their enemies. Rulers also demanded that vassals send their sons to reside at court; it was a practical way to ensure the loyalty of subordinates.

In 1555 Shah Tahmasp helped Humayun regain his kingdom, no doubt presuming that Humayun would prove a significant ally on the Safavids' eastern frontiers. But Humayun died shortly thereafter in a fall down his library steps—perhaps a fitting end for a learned man, but a rather ignominious one for a warrior.

The Reign of Akbar

Humayun's son Akbar (1556–1605) was 14 years old when he succeeded his father, about the same age as Shah Ismail when he commenced his reign. During a half century of rule, Akbar united northern India, advanced against the sultanates in the south of the subcontinent, and presided over a glorious courtly culture. Akbar ruled an empire more populous than those of the Ottoman sultan and the Persian shah; Mughal subjects numbered between 100 and 150 million.

Unlike Ismail, Akbar did not immediately consolidate his power. Initially, he was controlled by a regent. As often happens when a prince comes to power at an early age, powerful men in the court used the prince's youth to advance their own influence and objectives. By the age of 20, however, Akbar took charge and began a determined campaign of conquest that would continue into his old age.

This Mughal potentate was the counterpart of Suleiman in the Ottoman Empire and Shah Abbas in Safavid Persia. His reign is associated with military might, prosperity, and patronage of the arts at a spectacular level. At 13, Akbar led troops in battle; in his thirties, he challenged an enemy commander to personal combat; in late middle age, he still hunted wild animals with sword and lance. Akbar's concern for morality and social justice was indicated by his advice to a son: "Avoid religious persecution; be strong but magnanimous; accept apologies, sincerely given."[4]

A significant aspect of Akbar's reign is that he adapted the Islamic state to the conditions of ruling a non-Muslim population. In so doing, he promoted cultural synthesis, incorporated Hindus and others into the inner workings of government, and showed himself to be a pragmatic monarch. He married a number of Rajput princesses and made alliances with Hindu families, taking the men into his service. The mother of his heir, Jahangir, was a Hindu. He also abolished the *jizya,* the head tax on non-Muslims. This decision may seem like a simple matter, but the *jizya* was a standard of Islamic rule and had been institutionalized in the Sharia Islamic law. By abolishing it, Akbar gave notice to his Hindu subjects that they were granted a more equitable position vis-á-vis the Muslims, who constituted the ruling class.

Akbar also stopped taxing Hindu pilgrims, financed the construction of Hindu temples, and forbade Muslims to kill or eat the cow, which was sacred to Hindus. These measures alienated the *ulama* and the diverse Muslim elite of Turks, Afghans, Mongols, and Persians but won new support among the majority. Akbar, however, also initiated certain measures designed to force Hindu practice into compliance with Islamic law; he issued decrees outlawing Hindu child marriages and ***sati*** (the self-burning of widows), two reforms that violated Hindu traditions.

Akbar's tolerance in public administration was matched by his pursuit of knowledge and personal explorations of various religious faiths. He was devoted to certain sufi *shaykhs* and launched at his court a "house of worship," a forum for religious discussion to which he invited Muslims, Christians, Jews, Jains, Hindus, and Zoroastrians. In 1582 Akbar proclaimed a new cult, the *Din-i-Ilahi* (deen-i-eel-AH-hee), or "Divine Faith," which centered on Akbar himself and was highly influenced by **Zoroastrianism.** The new creed gained few adherents, but it further antagonized the *ulama* and demonstrated Akbar's religious eclecticism.

DOCUMENT
Akbar and the Jesuits

DOCUMENT
St. Francis Xavier, Jesuit in India

The Mughal State and Its Culture

One of the great accomplishments of the Mughal Empire was its establishment of a highly organized and intrusive central administration. In many ways like that of the Ottomans, it was designed to produce a consistent supply of taxes and troops for the government and to manage distant provinces. Akbar's military administrators, about two-thirds of whom were

---

sati—The practice by Hindu widows of self-immolation on their husbands' funeral pyres.

Zoroastrianism—A religion founded by the Persian prophet and mystic Zoroaster in the fifth century; initially monotheistic, it evolved into a dualistic faith in which the gods of light and good, led by Ahura-Mazda, opposed the gods of darkness and evil, led by Ahriman; influenced the development of Judaism and Christianity; Zoroastrians who migrated to India are known as Parsees.

foreign-born Muslims, were organized in military ranks and paid salaries according to the number of soldiers they commanded. Promotion for these military administrators, who were called ***mansabdars*** (mahn-SAHB-dahrs), was, ideally, based on merit. Their ranks were open to Hindus, and their positions were not hereditary, like those of European nobles. Like the Ottoman *kul* system, the *mansabdar* system was designed to produce loyalty to the state. Officials, in turn, were now made more dependent on the emperor. Like the Ottomans and Safavids, Akbar drew conquered foes into his service as long as they offered their submission. In this way, he took advantage of the military expertise of defeated commanders.

In the early seventeenth century the Mughal Empire was one of the wealthiest states in the world, with revenues ten times greater than those of France. Cities were numerous and large by European standards. Akbar's capital at Agra, for example, housed 200,000 people—twice the population of contemporary London. In the towns and villages, many industries flourished, particularly cotton textiles, which were exported to most of Asia and Africa. The majority of subjects were Hindu peasants. One-third to one-half of their produce, paid in land taxes, supported the army and kept the administrative elite in considerable luxury.

The early Mughal period saw a new Hindu-Muslim cultural synthesis, well illustrated in literature. Beginning with Babur, each emperor considered himself a poet, a scholar, and a collector of books. Akbar himself could not read, but he founded a great library housing over 20,000 illustrated manuscripts. The Mughals used their wealth to patronize the arts. Their literature was cosmopolitan, reflected a fresh originality, and was expressed in a variety of languages, including Turkish, Persian, Hindi, Arabic, and Urdu (an Indo-Persian fusion).

Despite the Muslim prohibition of representational figures, human or animal, painting developed rapidly as an art in the early Mughal period. Akbar had studied art as a child under Abdus Samad and Mir Sayyid Ali, two Safavid court painters whom Humayan brought to Kabul and later took to India. Akbar's royal studio employed over a hundred artists, mostly Hindus, who created works of great variety including miniatures of courtly life and large murals for Akbar's palaces.

mansabdars—Mughal military-administrative official.

In 1632 the Mughal emperor, Shah Jahan, commissioned the building of the resplendent Taj Mahal as a memorial to his late wife. Tall minarets surround a central dome, and a reflecting pool perfectly mirrors the white marble building, one of the glories of Mughal architecture. The Taj Mahal is one of the more spectacular examples of the ways in which various peoples commemorate their dead.

The royal studio produced beautifully illustrated manuscripts requiring many painters and many years to complete. Foremost among these is the spectacular *Hamzanamah* (hahm-ZAHN-ah-mah), which includes 1400 illustrations on cloth. Akbar also sponsored illustrated versions of Babur's memoirs and of the great Sanskrit epics the *Mahabharata* (MAH-he-BAH-re-te) and the *Ramayana* (rah-MAI-yah-nah). The Mughal school of painters under Jahangir, Akbar's son, produced wonderful animal and bird imagery, developed new strains of sensual and realist representation, and expertly incorporated motifs of European painting into Mughal art.

The most imposing symbols of Mughal glory are to be seen in architecture. Fusing Persian and Indic styles, it featured the lavish use of mosaics, bulbous domes, cupolas, slender spires, lofty vaulted gateways, and formal gardens, all carefully harmonized. Akbar's major building project was his palace complex at Fatehpur Sikri (fe-te-POOR SIK-ree). Akbar wanted to build his new palace on a site dedicated to a famous sufi holy man, *Shaykh* Salim Chishti. But Fatehpur Sikri became a monument to man's vanity and lack of planning. Akbar's court abandoned the complex (which took 15 years to build) after only 14 years because the water supply was inadequate. But visitors still marvel at the red sandstone blocks of the monumental fortress, which were hewn so precisely that they needed no fasteners or mortar.

Akbar's son Jahangir and his grandson Shah Jahan continued the tradition of monumental building. The latter replaced Akbar's sandstone buildings at Delhi with new ones of marble. At Agra, Shah Jahan erected the famous Taj Mahal, a tomb for his favorite wife, Mumtaz Mahal, who died while giving birth to her fifteenth child. This elaborate tomb, set in beautiful gardens, took over 20 years to build. Its luminous white marble, beautiful tracery of semiprecious stones, and elegant lines make the Taj Mahal one of the best-known buildings in the world today.

Akbar's Successors: Contesting the Hindu-Muslim Synthesis

Like most empires, the Mughal polity fared best when its administration was relatively tolerant, its treasury full, and its military successful. Jahangir (1605–1627) and Shah Jahan (1628–1658) continued Akbar's policies of relative tolerance. Jahangir was learned and artistically sensitive (as demonstrated in his memoirs), but he was also a drunkard and a drug addict, often lacking the strength to act decisively and conduct policy. He lost Kandahar to the Persians. Shah Jahan launched three costly and unsuccessful campaigns to retake Kandahar, a disastrous thrust into Central Asia, four costly invasions of the Deccan, and an extravagant expedition to oust a Portuguese enclave on the Indian coast. To compensate for these military expeditions, he had to raise land taxes, thus oppressing the peasantry.

The tension between Mughal tolerance and Muslim rule culminated in the seventeenth century with Akbar's great-grandsons, Dara Shikoh and Aurangzeb (1658–1707). Dara Shikoh took Akbar's tolerance one step further. He was a devoted sufi and wrote his own mystical works; he also studied Hindu mysticism. In the end this prince's attempt to find a middle ground between Islam and Hinduism provoked a violent response from the empire's Muslims and from his brother, Aurangzeb (OR-ang-zeb). Dara Shikoh was his father's favorite, but in the battle to succeed Shah Jahan, Aurangzeb was victorious. Charging his brother with apostasy, Aurangzeb marched him through the streets of Delhi in humiliation and had him executed.

Both sufi orders and the *ulama* opposed the ecumenicalism of Akbar and Dara Shikoh. With their support, Aurangzeb, having gained the throne, was determined to restore Sunni orthodoxy to the Mughal

Miniatures were not painted solely for artistic expression; they also suggested relationships. In this Mughal painting of Shah Jahangir and the Safavid Shah Abbas, Jahangir's artist portrayed his master as big and powerful, dominating his rather puny-looking Safavid rival. The monarchs stand on the globe, but Jahangir's lion is much more imposing than Abbas' lamb. The angels supporting the rulers' halo show the influence of European art motifs on Mughal imagery. According to the inscription on this miniature, Jahangir commissioned the painting after having a dream about Shah Abbas.

dominions. He reimposed the *jizya* and enforced the Sharia more stringently. Many Hindu temples were destroyed during his reign, and his intolerance and rigid orthodoxy weakened the Mughal hold on its diverse Hindu populations.

The Mughal Social Order

As already noted, Mughal society comprised a series of hierarchies based on a Hindu majority and a predominantly Muslim ruling class. The vast majority of

Document The Idea of Seclusion and Lady Nurjahan

The idea of seclusion (being hidden away from view) is often associated with women in Muslim societies. But historically, we find that women in all Muslim households were clearly not secluded and that "seclusion" itself is a notion that varies over time, place, class, status, and culture. Even when women were considered to be "secluded," they might have been engaged in a variety of activities that we don't ordinarily associate with seclusion. So, one question for historians, of any time, place, and group of women is: "What were those women doing?" Some examples of what elite, secluded women were doing are found in the memoirs of the Mughal emperor Jahangir. Like those of his forefather, Babur, Jahangir's memoirs are full of minute and interesting details, including discussion of the affairs of his principal wife Nurjahan (1577–1645). Nurjahan was the daughter of a Mughal vizir, and, at the end of Jahangir's reign, she, along with her brother, took over effective control of the empire. In her husband's account, we find Nurjahan portrayed as an avid hunter, an owner of estates, and a mover-and-shaker in political affairs. She engaged in all these activities while "secluded." These selections from Jahangir's memoirs (and an appendix by his historian Muhammad-Hadi) give some idea of Nurjahan's activities.

On April 16 [1617] . . . the scouts had cornered four lions. I [Jahangir] set out with the ladies of the harem to hunt them. When the lions came into view, Nurjahan Begam said, "If so commanded, I will shoot the lions." I said, "Let it be so." She hit two of them with one shot each and the other two with two shots, and in the twinkling of an eye the four lions were deprived of life with six shots. Until now such marksmanship has not been seen—from atop an elephant and from inside a howdah [covered seat] she had fired six shots, none of which missed. . . . As a reward for such marksmanship I scattered a thousand ashrafis [coins] over her head and gave her a pair of pearls and a diamond worth a lac [100,000] of rupees.

When Jahangir was suffering from chest pain and shortness of breath, his physicians could not ease his discomfort, so he committed himself to his wife's care:

> *Nurjahan Begam's remedies and experience were greater than any of the physicians', especially since she treated me with affection and sympathy. She made me drink less and applied remedies that were suitable and efficacious. Although the treatments the physicians had prescribed before were done with her approval, I now relied on her affection, gradually reduced my intake of wine, and avoided unsuitable things and disagreeable food. It is hoped that the True Physician will grant me a complete recovery from the other world.*

When Nurjahan's father died, Jahangir awarded his estate to her:

> *I awarded I'timaduddawla's jagir [a type of fief, revenue from land], household, and paraphernalia of chieftainship and amirship to Nurjahan Begam, and I ordered that her drums should be sounded after the imperial ones.*

When Mahabat Khan mounted a rebellion against Jahangir, Nurjahan escaped and mobilized for the emperor's defense:

> *[She] convened the grandees of the empire and addressed them in rebuke, saying, "It was through your negligence that things have gone so far and the unimaginable has happened. You have been disgraced before God and the people by your own actions. Now it must be made up for. Tell each other what the best thing to do is."*

Questions to Consider

1. Nurjahan was a royal woman. What do these stories suggest about class and gender as determinants of women's activities?
2. What do these excerpts suggest about the relationship between Jahangir and his wife?
3. If royal women routinely went on hunting expeditions with the emperor, how could they still be secluded?

From Wheeler Thackston, ed. and trans., *The Jahangirnama: Memoirs of Jahangir, Emperor of India* (New York: Oxford University Press, 1999), pp. xx–xxi, 219, 368, 376, 441.

the populace, as in China, the Middle East, and Europe, consisted of illiterate peasants who provided the bulk of the empire's revenue through agricultural taxes. Wealth was an important factor in determining status, but it was not the primary factor. A merchant could be very wealthy but could not achieve the same status as a member of the elite military-administrative class. Among Hindus, status was intimately linked to caste.

Mughal society, like most societies, was also patriarchal; it allocated family, religious, and political dominance to men. This system of male dominance is often attributed to Islam, but patriarchy predated Islam in India, as it did in the Middle East. In general, it would be more accurate to say that Islam both reinforced preexisting patriarchal structures and improved the position of women by forbidding female infanticide and granting women inheritance rights. In India under Islamic rule, the position of women derived from a synthesis of Hindu custom and Islamic law. Despite Akbar's reform-minded decrees, *sati* and child marriages continued. Formal education of females, as in most societies, was practically nonexistent, except in a few affluent or learned families.

The birth of a prince in the Mughal harem. This unusual scene shows the numerous female attendants of the princely court and suggests the ceremonial significance of such an event. Note the varying dress styles of the women and the rich textiles surrounding the princess.

These practices must, of course, be understood in their temporal and social contexts. In Hindu society, as in Muslim society, in which marriage is considered a preferred state (especially for women), early marriage age acted to prevent the girl's sexual purity from being compromised or questioned. By social convention, women were deemed to need male protectors, and when a woman married, she left the protection of her father or brother and became part of her husband's household. By immolating herself on her husband's funeral pyre, a widow prevented herself from becoming a social burden on her husband's family or the family she was born into.

As for female education, we should remember that the overwhelming majority of people, in all the world civilizations of this era, were illiterate. Only certain of the elites could read, and even many people of rank, like Akbar, were illiterate. Men's and women's roles were considered complementary, not equal. Because men were expected to perform the political, religious, and administrative tasks that required literacy, formal education tended to be reserved for them.

NETWORKS OF TRADE AND COMMUNICATION

- *What role do trade and communication play in the maintenance of the Ottoman, Safavid, and Mughal empires?*

The gunpowder empires emerged in a set of interconnected regions that were in turn imbedded in even more extensive networks of trade and communication. The primitive nature of transport and communications technology limited the flow of goods, knowledge, and information. But all three circulated in ways that might seem surprising, given that the only ways to get from one place to another were on foot, on animalback, or aboard oared and sailing vessels. Despite these limitations, scholars traveled from one court to another, enjoying the patronage of Ottoman, Safavid, or Mughal emperors and sharing literary, artistic, and legal traditions. The royal courts consumed prodigiously and supported the exchange of goods and culture on a grand scale. Mehmed II had his portrait painted by the famous Italian painter Bellini. Babur brought Persian artists into India, and the Safavid court imported Arab jurists. Rulers in all three empires drank from Chinese porcelain cups.

The Ottoman, Safavid, and Mughal Empires derived most of their income from agriculture. But trade was their second source of wealth. None of these empires invented the trading routes. Rather, these routes emerged and expanded across a set of well-established commercial networks linking urban centers.

They inherited these networks from their predecessors and competed with rival kingdoms to monopolize goods and collect commercial taxes. To understand how these empires worked, we must abandon the notion of modern boundaries that are marked, fixed, and defended. Rulers could not control frontiers absolutely; instead they defended and taxed key routes, fortresses, and cities. The porous nature of borders encouraged tax evaders. If officials demanded high taxes along one route, merchants might shift to another route. If taxes were collected by the camel-load, merchants stopped their beasts outside of town and repacked in order to have fewer loads.

In this context of flexible boundaries, trading communities developed that facilitated the flow of goods from one place to another. Although the Ottomans fought long wars with both Christian states in Europe and Muslim competitors in Persia and Egypt, trade among these regions was seldom squelched for long. The furs of Muscovy flowed south into the empire and the gold of Africa came north. Armenian merchants played a prominent role in the Persian silk trade, which drew European silver in large quantities into the Safavid Empire. Jewish merchants traded copper to Arab merchants, who sold it to South Asian traders in return for cotton, jewels, and spices.

Many great trading centers were scattered throughout the territories of the gunpowder empires. Babur described the emporium of Kabul, located between Persia and India, as receiving merchant caravans of 15,000 or 20,000 pack animals carrying slaves, textiles, sugar, and spices. Kabul channeled the trade of China and India westward in exchange for goods coming eastward from the Ottoman and Safavid realms.

The merchants in turn served an information function. Because communication technologies were so limited, rulers used travelers of all sorts to gain knowledge about the rest of the world. Scholars, sufis, traders, envoys, and spies all served this purpose. Monarchs used envoys as spies, and their rivals tried to control information by keeping visiting envoys sequestered and by intimidating them with military displays. Response to another ruler's challenge could never be swift because it was often months or years before a monarch received a reply or news about his envoy's fate.

Outside these channels of communication, relations between the gunpowder empires and European or East Asian states were still quite limited. Only the Ottomans had resident consuls from some of the European states in their capital. In this era, the balance of trade was tipped very much in favor of the East, with eastern goods flowing into Europe and cash flowing back. European imports, with the exception of certain kinds of textiles, were negligible by comparison.

DOCUMENT
The English in South Asia

CONCLUSION

In the three and a half centuries before 1650, Europe still lagged behind Asia in many respects. No European state, not even the polyglot empire of Charles V, could compare in manpower and resources with the realms of Suleiman or Akbar. Europeans were impressed by the resources and taxation capabilities of the Ottoman governing system. Opportunities for minorities and toleration for dissenting religions were greater in the Muslim countries than in Europe. Asian cities were usually better planned, more tastefully adorned with works of art, and even better supplied with water and with sewage disposal.

Europe's advantages, which began to be more apparent after the beginning of the seventeenth century, were most evident in the realm of technology, specifically in the production of field artillery and oceangoing ships. These technical assets helped certain of the European states gain leverage in a new age, when powerful states would depend on strategic control of sea lanes and world markets. But in the period from 1300 to 1650 it was the gunpowder empires that tended to dominate, using their resources and militaries to become the great imperial powers of that age.

Suggestions for Web Browsing

You can obtain more information about topics included in this chapter at the websites listed below. See also the companion website that accompanies this text, **http://www.ablongman.com/brummett,** which contains an online study guide and additional resources.

Islam and Islamic History in Arabia and the Middle East
http://www.islamic.org/Mosque/ihame/Sec11.htm
http://www.islamic.org/Mosque/ihame/Sec12.htm
http://www.islamic.org/Mosque/ihame/Sec13.htm

Related sites detailing the enormous legacy of the early Islamic civilization, a history of Mongol destruction and Mamluk victory, and the rise of the Ottoman Empire.

Ottoman Page
http://ottoman.home.mindspring.com/

Site dedicated to classical Ottoman history, 1300–1600, offering numerous links to other sites.

Topkapi Palace
http://www.ee.bilkent.edu.tr/~history/topkapi.html

A guide to Topkapi Palace, with numerous images of the palace rooms and grounds and its phenomenal artifacts, including portraits of the sultans, manuscripts, clothing, porcelains, and armaments.

Internet Islamic History Sourcebook: The Persians
http://www.fordham.edu/halsall/islam/islamsbook.html

Links to a variety of documents detailing the rise and spread of the Safavid Empire.

Internet Indian History Sourcebook
http://www.fordham.edu/halsall/india/indiasbook.html

Extensive indexed site of primary sources for medieval India.

Mughal Monarchs
http://rubens.anu.edu.au/student.projects/tajmahal/mughal.html

A detailed introduction to the Mughal dynasty and the city of Agra, whose images emphasize the superb architecture of the time.

Literature and Film

A short primary source on Jahangir, available in paperback, is Mutribi al-Asamm, *Conversations with Emperor Jahangir*, trans. Richard Foltz (Mazda, 1998). *The Intimate Life of an Ottoman Statesman: Melek Ahmed Pasha (1588–1662)*, trans. Robert Dankoff (SUNY Press, 1991) is a wonderful portrayal of the realities of Ottoman administration. An excellent selection of Ottoman poetry can be found in *Ottoman Lyric Poetry: An Anthology*, eds. Walter Andrews, Najaat Black, Mehmet Kalpakli (University of Texas Press, 1997).

The University of North Carolina library (Chapel Hill) has a large collection of films on the Islamic world which are cataloged by topic. These include films on the Ottoman Empire and the Modern Middle East. See listings on their website at http://www.lib.unc.edu/house/nonprint.

Suleiman the Magnificent depicts the life, accomplishments and regional significance of this Ottoman sultan.

Isfahan: A City Known as "Half the World" is a great video, in Farsi and English, about Isfahan and its historic sites. For additional information, see http://www.iranianmovies.com/reviews/isfahan.html.

Suggestions for Reading

On Inner Asia and Turkic groups, see Peter Golden, *An Introduction to the History of the Turkic Peoples* (Harassowitz, 1992). Luc Kwanten, *Imperial Nomads, a History of Central Asia, 500–1500* (University of Pennsylvania Press, 1979), is an illuminating study of a subject long neglected in standard texts.

The Ottoman Golden Age is ably depicted in Halil Inalcik, *Phoenix: The Ottoman Empire, the Classical Age 1300–1600* (Phoenix Press, 2001); Norman Itzkowitz, *The Ottoman Empire and the Islamic Tradition* (University of Oklahoma Press, 1980); and Stanford Shaw, *A History of the Ottoman Empire and Modern Turkey*, 2 vols. (Cambridge University Press, 1976–1977). On Sultan Suleiman, see Metin Kunt and Christine Woodhead, eds., *Süleyman the Magnificent and His Age* (Longman, 1995). The harem is covered in Leslie P. Peirce, *The Imperial Harem* (Oxford University Press, 1993).

On medieval Persia, see Ann Lambton, *Continuity and Change in Medieval Persia* (Persian Heritage Foundation, 1988), and David Morgan, *Medieval Persia, 1040–1797* (Longman, 1988). See also Roger Savory, *Iran Under the Safavids* (Cambridge University Press, 1980). Coverage in English of the Safavid period is still limited; an old standard is Percy M. Sykes, *A History of Persia,* (Routledge/Curzon, 2003), first published in 1938 and now in its third edition. On Safavid trade, see Rudolph Matthee, *The Politics of Trade in Safavid Iran: Silk for Silver, 1600–1730* (Cambridge University Press, 1999).

The Mughal system is ably described in John F. Richards, Gordon Johnson, and C. A. Bayly, eds., *The Mughul Empire* (Cambridge University Press, 1996); Douglas E. Streusand, *The Formation of the Mughal Empire* (Oxford University Press, 1990); and Neelam Chaudhary, *Socio-Economic History of Mughal India* (Discovery, 1987). For studies of individual emperors, see Gul Badan Begam, *The History of Humayun*, trans. A. S. Beveridge (B. R. Publishers, 1989); Bamber Gascoigne, *The Great Moghuls* (Harper & Row, 1971); and J. M. Shelat, *Akbar* (Bharatiya Bidya Bhavan, 1964).

CHAPTER 13

East Asian Cultural and Political Systems, 1300–1650

CHAPTER CONTENTS

This chapter discusses the development and mutual influences of China, Korea, Japan, and the countries of Southeast Asia from the fourteenth into the seventeenth centuries. During this time, ideologies, religions, and cultural traditions continued to be shared. Trade was maintained, though greatly modified in the middle of the period by the introduction of new players and products from Europe and the Americas and by the severe restriction of Japanese international commerce in the early seventeenth century. China was still the dominant actor in East Asia, but while its power and influence may have seemed paramount, individual nations were forming their own political and cultural traditions and identities.

Throughout its history, Chinese civilization has synthesized outside influences and its own indigenous culture. Culture rather than ethnicity generally defined what it was to be Chinese. Indeed, before the end of the seventeenth century, China was generally seen as a civilization rather than a place inhabited by a dominant ethnic group. Outsiders who adopted Chinese ways could rise to high stations, even rule China. Those who had not sufficiently assimilated Chinese culture were often not viewed as fully Chinese.

China's view of itself as a civilization was just as important as its view of itself as a political entity. Frequently called the "Central Flower," its culture and civilization were seen as having broad universal appeal. As the "Central Kingdom," a term that emphasized *political* unity, China could also justify its international relations based on the tribute system. The tribute system encompassed China's relationships with East Asian nations. It was an unequal system that required peripheral countries to indicate their loyal subordination by donating tribute to China and receiving gifts in return according to a planned schedule of visits—a form of strictly regulated trade. China acted as a protective "parent" toward neighbors who were not entirely independent of China in terms of their foreign relations. The early Ming's place in the larger Eurasian continent was perhaps even more important. It launched the world's largest maritime explorations, dominated world trade, and was deeply connected to the world's silver-based economy.

1300

1283–1317 Rama Khamheng, Thai king who established independent Thai state, created Thai alphabet

1338 Ashikaga Shogunate succeeds Kamakura Shogunate in Japan

1368–1644 Ming dynasty rules China

1392–1910 Chosŏn dynasty rules Korea

1400

15th century Islam spreads in Indonesia

15th century Nō plays flourish in Japan

15th century Vietnam and Thailand control mainland Southeast Asia

1402 Malacca founded

1403–1424 Reign of Yongle, emperor of China; Forbidden City built

1405–1433 Chinese maritime expeditions by Zheng He

1418–1450 Reign of King Sejong of Chosŏn dynasty, creator of han'gul alphabet

1467–1600 Warring States Period in Japan

1500

16th century Era of Chinese popular novels such as *The Water Margin, Journey to the West*

1557 Ming grants Portuguese traders limited operations in Macao

1592–1598 Korea repulses invasions by Japan

1600

1603 Tokugawa Shogunate in Japan begins

1627, 1636 Korea invaded by Manchus

1639 Japanese restriction of trade to Chinese, Koreans, and Dutch

In Korea, the Koryŏ dynasty, struggling with slave-owning landholders, many of whom had been allied with the Mongols who had themselves just been forced out of China, was overturned by a reformist faction in 1392. The founder of the new Chosŏn dynasty, King T'aejo (1335–1408), sent tribute missions to the Ming, cut all ties to the Mongols, and strengthened Chinese institutions in Korea. The Chosŏn dynasty was known for such cultural advances as the development of an indigenous alphabet, a lively publishing trade, an active scholarly world of competing schools of thought, and refined arts of painting and pottery that blended Korean and Chinese models. Korea retained much of its indigenous aristocratic structure during the long Chosŏn dynasty (1392–1910), but its culture was deeply imbued with neo-Confucianism, originally Chinese but now assimilated into Korean culture.

Japan was also connected with Korea and China in this era. In the first half of the three-century period, refined art collectors revered continental arts. As samurai settled in Kyoto (formerly called *Heian*) in the late fourteenth century, they outdid one another in displaying Chinese, Korean, and Japanese works readily available to wealthy collectors. Although the Ming, in theory, controlled the volume of trade within its tribute system, freebooting Japanese, Chinese, and Korean pirates imported a far greater volume of products through nongovernmental channels. Japanese ships transported products throughout northeast and Southeast Asia, purchased with various currencies, exchange of other goods, and Japanese and New World silver. In the sixteenth century, Japanese silver far surpassed New World silver as the fuel that drove the East Asian trade at the heart of the world economy.

While Confucianism was not yet established in Japan, Buddhism continued to prosper there until the end of the sixteenth century. The breakdown of peace at the end of the fifteenth century and the coming of Iberian missionaries in the sixteenth century, who brought guns along with religion, radically altered Japan's history. In 1600, Japan was once again unified, and by 1640, it would severely restrict its trade to just three partners—China, Korea, and Holland.

The lands and islands southeast of China, today called Southeast Asia, were long influenced by Indian culture and religions. Chinese culture deeply influenced Vietnam. Buddhism, Hinduism, and local religions were celebrated in the kingdoms of Southeast Asia. In Vietnam, a millennium of Chinese rule made the Chinese both despised as overlords and worthy of emulation as bearers of advanced means of governance. With the exception of a period of Mongol attack and, later, a brief occupation by Ming forces, Vietnam was politically independent of China after 939. But Vietnam's government was in many ways an ideal Confucian state, and Vietnam and China were closely bound through the tribute system.

Maritime Southeast Asia—today's Philippines, Malaysia, and Indonesia—was dependent on trade. Important maritime empires, including a succession of rulers on the island of Java, occupied most of modern Malaysia and Indonesia. In the thirteenth century, one of Java's great powers, Majapahit, held off the Mongols' attempted invasion and unified many of the islands of the Indonesian archipelago. In the fourteenth and fifteenth centuries, Islam spread to maritime Southeast Asia as merchants recognized the benefit of Muslim ties in expediting trade in the Indian Ocean. Chinese and Indian traders continued to operate throughout Southeast Asia. The coming of first Portuguese and Spanish and later British and Dutch merchants and missionaries influenced Southeast Asian life by the beginning of the seventeenth century.

CHINA: THE MING DYNASTY

▪ *In what ways can Ming China be considered an early modern state?*

Before the modern period, Chinese historians wrote the history of their country as a series of consecutive dynastic waves—as one dynasty declined after a period of growth, another would rise and receive Heaven's mandate (see Chapter 2). The struggle to overthrow the Yuan in the fourteenth century was brutal, but it contained many of the elements of dynastic change identified by contemporaries in China. That is, natural disasters and disease accompanied by religious uprisings suggested Heaven was shifting its support from the Yuan emperor to new rulers. The traditional dynastic cycle model downplays change over time. The Yuan dynasty's brevity gave it little opportunity to change China in lasting ways, and this seemed to confirm the dynastic cycle's validity. Yet, as we have seen in Chapter 10, the Yuan was at the center of a cosmopolitan Eurasian commercial world which influenced culture far beyond China's borders.

The Yuan dynasty declined after Khubilai's death in 1294. The north of China began to decline economically, and southerners suffered discriminatory treatment. Everywhere, the pre-Yuan power structure had been challenged, as the Mongols had altered civil service recruitment policies. Many peasants were brought to the brink of despair in the face of natural

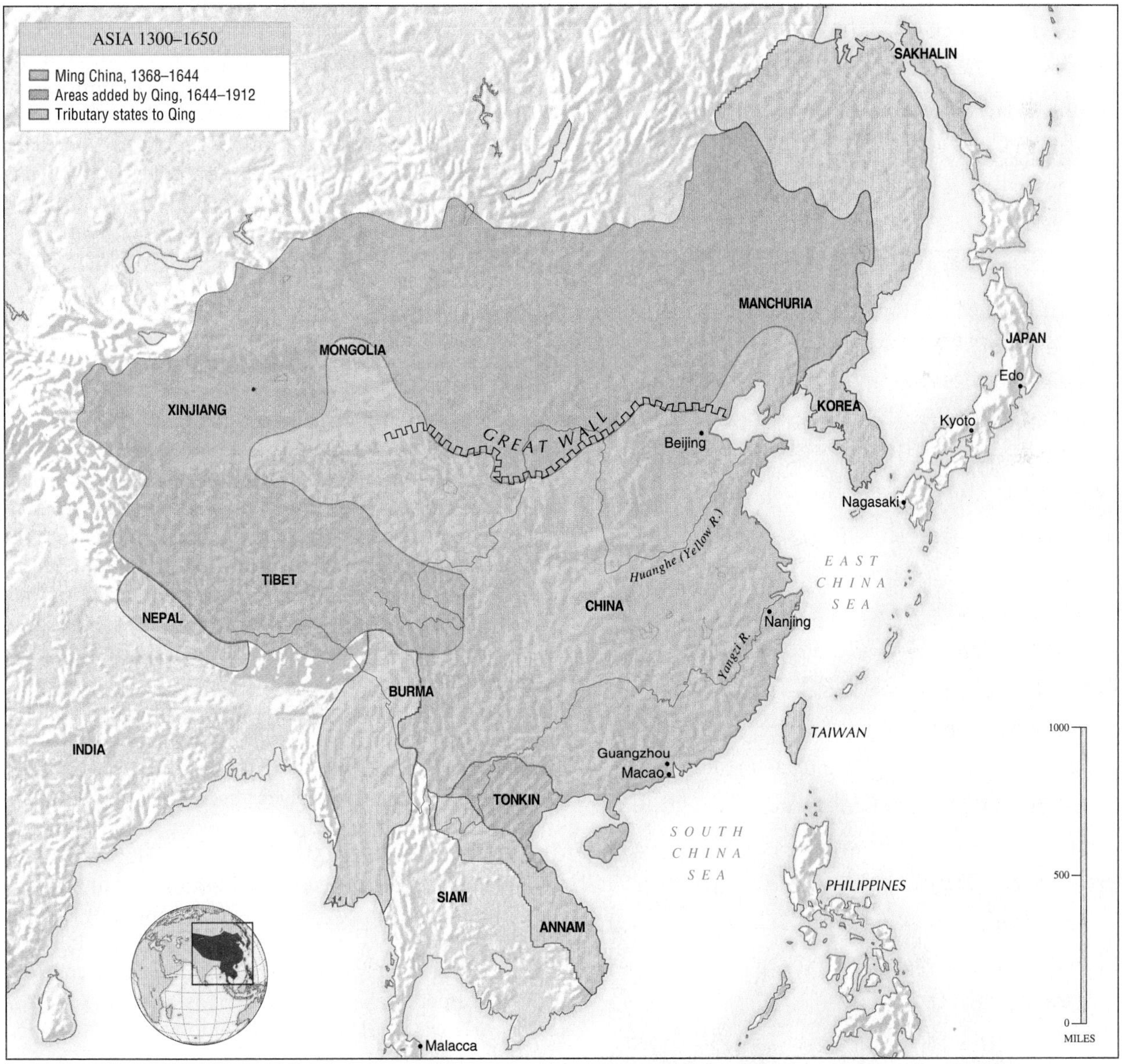

After the first two Ming emperors consolidated and expanded their rule, the rest of the dynasty remained content with the extent of their realm. The Chinese realm was greatly expanded under the Qing, who took power in the second half of the seventeenth century.

disasters in the fourteenth century, especially the Huanghe River's change in course and outbreaks of the plague. Further, the traditionally nomadic Mongol soldiers, now serving in permanent posts, lost some of their toughness and discipline. In the 39 years after Khubilai's death and the installation of the last Mongol sovereign in 1333, disorder also prevailed at the highest level of government. The Mongol royal clan had no orderly method for determining succession, and eight of the nine emperors were either overthrown or killed. Bureaucratic breakdown weakened the base of Yuan power at a time when the Mongols were severely challenged. Religious rebellions sparked by peasant discontent spread throughout southern China in the 1350s.

In 1356, a former Buddhist monk, Zhu Yuanzhang (JOO yoo-ahn-JAHNG), who had taken over the leadership of a religious-based rebel group, the **Red Turbans,** captured Nanjing. Using that city as his capital, Zhu—better known by his reign name, Ming Hongwu (hong-WOO)—conquered other warlords until he was able to march on the Yuan capital at Beijing. The Mongol emperor fled with his court to Mongolia. Hongwu thus founded a new dynasty, the Ming, without actually conquering the old. Hongwu (r. 1368–1398) attempted to assert strong imperial control, even killing thousands of scholars he believed were scheming against or ridiculing him. Neither he nor his successors were model rulers, and the last decades of Ming rule were marked by administrative failure and corruption. The strength of the Ming era lay less in its monarchs and more in the contributions of its artisans, scholars, and philosophers to a Chinese society increasingly claimed by people of all walks of life as their own.

After a period of expansion, the Ming ruled over China until factionalism, corruption, and natural disasters again led to popular uprisings, a symbol of the passage of the Mandate of Heaven, in the middle of the seventeenth century. Although modern historians often judge the Ming a failure, the three centuries were, in fact, an era of population growth, commercial expansion, and a broadening of average Chinese people's participation in the culture of the country.

Red Turbans—A branch of White Lotus Society, a millenarian Buddhist group that used Confucian and Daoist ideas as well. One of several anti-Yuan religious groups.

Portrait of Hongwu, the first emperor of the Ming dynasty.

The Early Ming Era

Hongwu was a rather brutal and paranoid emperor, although he tried to govern effectively. He believed that people should be self-sufficient and motivated to serve their community without having to be paid. He sought to lighten the tax burden of the poor and gave the families of China's 2 million soldiers plots to farm themselves to be self-supporting. More successful villagers were to look out for their less fortunate neighbors, collect village taxes, and serve their communities essentially as administrators but without formal government appointment or pay. At the level of the court, Hongwu tried to cut back the power of the **eunuchs** by forbidding them a role in politics. All these policies failed, however. Village leaders were overworked and undercompensated for their work, soldiers who were unable to support themselves absconded, and eunuchs became more powerful than ever over the next two centuries. The third Ming emperor, Hongwu's son Yongle (YAWNG-luh; r. 1403–1424), moved the capital to Beijing and transformed it into a grand city. He also undertook massive engineering projects, especially the enlarging of the Grand Canal including the construction of fifteen locks, and the expansion of the protective northern wall into the Great Wall of China we know today.

eunuchs—Castrated males who served as palace attendants and administrators for the emperor.

Discovery Through Maps

Map of China's Ancient Heartland, circa 1500 C.E.

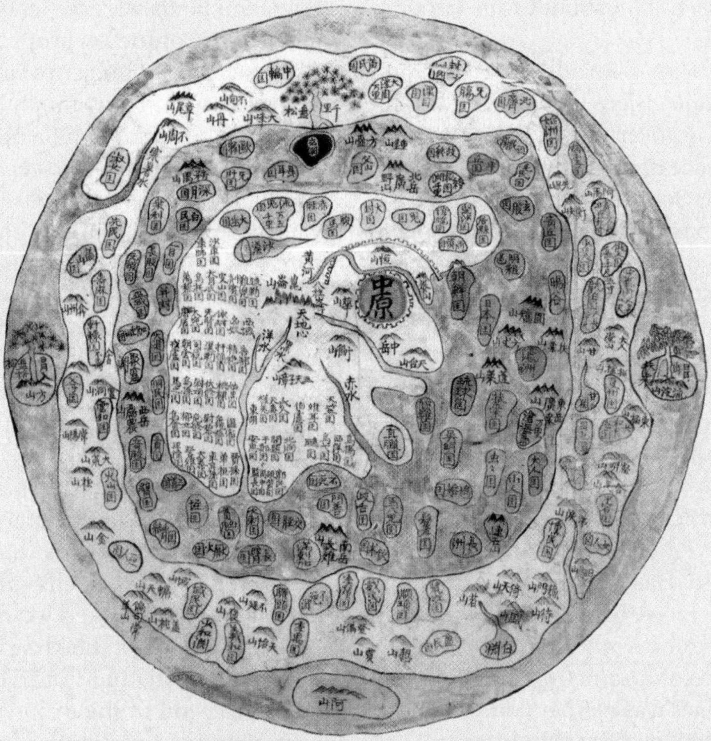

It is one of the marks of human nature that the center of the world is found in one's self-consciousness, and then in concentric circles in the family, community, and nation. This trait extends across civilizations and continents and can be seen not only in this Chinese map depicting the area known as the *Zhongyuan* (ZHONG-yoo-AHN) or heartland of ancient China, but also in maps created around the same time by Europeans as they made their voyages of discovery. The Chinese map is particularly informative because it reminds its viewers that even within China itself, the heartland was the repository of culture and power, and the farther one ventured from the center of that circle, the less likely one was to be influenced by the virtue embodied in the Son of Heaven.

By 1500, the Ming had moved their capital to Beijing, which lay in the northern region in which Chinese civilization was born; thus, the radiance of the Ming emperor was fortuitously in the same region as the birthplace of the culture he represented. In concentric circles around the Central Plain were other areas of China or countries involved in tributary relations with China. The term *central* may also be seen in a common name for China, *Zhongguo* (JONG-gwaw), meaning "Central Kingdom." The Chinese worldview placed it at the center of the world, and it was very much part of the world in terms of cultural and commercial interactions.

The map has political implications, in that it shows its viewers that the original heartland of China was the same place as the home of the Ming. This portrayal is difficult, however, for those trained to see geography in terms of a Mercator projection (see, e.g., p. 467). The Mercator projection, like the Ming map, also reflects a worldview that places the map's creators in the center–in the Mercator case, the center is in Europe. Is there any particular reason, for example, why the Greenwich Meridian (from which all longitudes on the surface of the earth are presently measured) should be the central point of the world's geography and Greenwich Mean Time should be the standard by which most clocks of the world are presently set? English dominance in the eighteenth and nineteenth centuries proved to be only a temporary moment in history, but enough to establish at least a cartographic and chronological centrality.

Questions to Consider

1. Compare and contrast this map with the view of the world on page 467. How are the maps the same? How are they different?
2. Given the particular approach of the China map, draw a simple circular map of the United States. Would Washington, D.C., or some other city be appropriately located at the center of your map? Is the Mercator Projection that is generally used today (see, for example, p. 467) necessarily better in portraying sense and relationship?

Policy in the first century of the Ming reflected a definite interest in border areas and beyond. Non-Chinese tribes, especially the Miao (mee-OW) and the Yao (YOW) in the southwest, were brought under Ming control, engendering a discussion about Chinese identity and cultural blending.

The expansive early Ming invaded Vietnam in 1407, but popular resistance there soon forced them out. The early Ming government, unlike its sixteenth-century successors, encouraged foreign trade with Japan, Southeast Asia, and India. Private trade surpassed the official trade permitted under the tribute system. Yongle regularly sent diplomatic and commercial missions to neighboring states and encouraged Chinese migration south into the Malay Archipelago and north into Mongolia. In 1405 Yongle sponsored a series of naval expeditions to potential tributary states. The greatest were led by Zheng He (JUHNG HUH), a trusted eunuch (see p. 374). The Chinese flotilla of 62 large and 225 small ships (with some ships exceeding 500 tons and carrying crews of 700) visited Sumatra, India, the Persian Gulf, Aden, and East Africa. There they exchanged porcelain for ivory, ostrich feathers, and exotic animals such as zebras and giraffes. These fancy goods were a source of fascination, but the primary purpose of the voyages was neither conquest nor trade but rather the expansion of the tribute system at the heart of Ming foreign relations. China had already penetrated the Indian Ocean while Portuguese captains were just beginning to explore the Atlantic coast of Morocco.

A Ming Naval Expedition

The voyages ended in 1433. They were considered too expensive compared to the potential gains of enrolling additional countries in the tribute system. China maintained a powerful, dominant position in that system with its closest neighbors. These neighbors received Chinese support and reciprocal gifts but were also subjected to Chinese domination—at times even invasion—and to the requirement that they humbly present gifts to the Son of Heaven, the Chinese emperor, as a sign of subordination in an almost parent-child relationship. People in distant lands were far less likely to comprehend that particular Confucian proprieties were at the heart of Chinese identity, and enrolling distant people in a tribute relationship was much less useful than demanding the subordination of a neighbor. In time, maritime exploration came to be seen as an unwise investment when costly defense against land-based border tribes was more crucial. Chinese emperors never again sponsored such path-breaking journeys.

Voyages of Zheng He

Ming China

1368–1398	Reign of Hongwu
1403–1424	Reign of Yongle, sponsor of encyclopedia
1405–1433	Naval expeditions led by Zheng He
1472–1529	Wang Yangming, philosopher
1583–1610	Matteo Ricci at Ming court
1644	Founding of Qing dynasty

Administration of the realm was seen as central to Ming power throughout the period. While foreign adventures could be curtailed, good government demanded that emperors lead by example and that the examination system bring in loyal and honest bureaucrats.

Yet despite their attempts at eliminating past problems, the Ming emperors perpetuated many of the corrupt and weak practices they wanted to reform. The excesses of court eunuchs—male children sold by their parents to be castrated for court service—continued. At the beginning of the Ming dynasty only 100 eunuchs were employed, and not in direct government posts, but by the end of the dynasty 300 years later, 100,000 were working for the throne. Eunuchs had served as court advisers and servants since the Zhou dynasty; under the Ming, they included men from Annam and Korea, some brought as tribute, and some captured in war. Under the Ming, 28 Korean-born eunuchs served as leaders of missions to Seoul. Although eunuchs served as generals, admirals, explorers, diplomats, architects, secret police, and hydraulic engineers, the majority of them were servants of low and even slave status. The increased number of eunuchs was due not only to the expansion of the imperial family under the Ming but also to the influx of men, many self-castrated, who poured into Beijing, hoping to find a secure livelihood after escaping from poverty or famine in the countryside.

The growth in the number and influence of eunuchs was paralleled by an expansion of Confucian scholarship and scholars. Preparing for a career as a bureaucrat became increasingly attractive despite the danger of repression by paranoid emperors like Hongwu. The Ming decreed that the examinations for entering the civil service be written in a strict, formal style, but at the same time they opened opportunities for students from less advanced regions of the country to pass the exams. A new lower level category was created, permitting locally successful exam candidates to become local leaders even if they were not eligible for a better government post. In time, wealthy families perpetu-

Document A Censor Accuses a Eunuch

This memorial was submitted to the emperor in 1624 by the official Yang Lien, accusing the eunuch, Wei Zhongxian (WAY jong-shee-AHN). It illustrates how the power of the eunuchs was resented by scholar-bureaucrats while giving a sense of palace politics.

A treacherous eunuch has taken advantage of his position to act as emperor. He has seized control and disrupted the government, deceived the ruler and flouted the law. He recognizes no higher authority, turns his back on the favors the emperor has conferred on him, and interferes with the inherited institutions. I beg Your Majesty to order an investigation so that the dynasty can be saved.

When Emperor Taizu [i.e., Hongwu] first established the laws and institutions, eunuchs were not allowed to interfere in any affairs outside the palace; even within it they did nothing more than clean up. Anyone who violated these rules was punished without chance of amnesty, so the eunuchs prudently were cautious and obedient. The succeeding emperors never changed these laws. Even such arrogant and lawless eunuchs as Wang Zhen (WAHNG JUHN) and Liu Jin (LEE-oh JIN) were promptly executed. Thus the dynasty lasted until today.

How would anyone have expected that, with a wise ruler like Your Majesty on the throne, there would be a chief eunuch like Wei Zhongxian, a man totally uninhibited, who destroys court precedents, ignores the ruler to pursue his selfish ends, corrupts good people, ruins the emperor's reputation as a Yao (YOW) or Xun (SHUN), and brews unimaginable disasters? The entire court has been intimidated. No one dares denounce him by name. My responsibility really is painful. But when I was supervising secretary of the office of scrutiny for war, the previous emperor personally ordered me to help Your Majesty become a ruler like Yao and Xun. I can still hear his words. If today out of fear I also do not speak out, I will be abandoning my determination to be loyal and my responsibility to serve the state. I would also be turning my back on your kindness in bringing me back to office after retirement and would not be able to face the former emperor in Heaven.

I shall list for Your Majesty Zhongxian's twenty-four most heinous crimes. Zhongxian was originally an ordinary, unreliable sort. He had himself castrated in middle age in order to enter the palace. He is illiterate, unlike those eunuchs from the directorate of ceremonial. Your Majesty was impressed by his minor acts of service and plucked him out of obscurity to confer honors on him. . . .

Our dynastic institutions require that rescripts be delegated to the grand secretaries. This not only allows for calm deliberation and protects from interference, but it assures that someone takes the responsibility seriously. Since Zhongxian usurped power, he issues the imperial edicts. If he accurately conveys your orders, it is bad enough. If he falsifies them, who can argue with him? Recently, men have been forming groups of three or five to push their ideas in the halls of government, making it as clamorous as a noisy market. Some even go directly into the inner quarters without formal permission. It is possible for a scrap of paper in the middle of the night to kill a person without Your Majesty or the grand secretaries knowing anything of it. The harm this causes is huge. The grand secretaries are so depressed that they ask to quit. Thus Wei Zhongxian destroys the political institutions that had lasted over two hundred years. This is his first great crime. . . .

One of your concubines, of virtuous and pure character, had gained your favor. Zhongxian was afraid she would expose his illegal behavior, so conspired with his cronies. They said she had a sudden illness to cover up his murdering her. Thus Your Majesty is not able to protect the concubines you favor. This is his eighth great crime. . . .

Questions to Consider

1. Discuss how this document reflects the power politics of the Ming dynasty.
2. Discuss how a similar document might have been phrased if it had been written from the perspective of a eunuch and not the palace scholar-bureaucrat.

From Patricia Buckley Ebrey, *Chinese Civilization: A Sourcebook*, 2nd ed. (New York: Free Press, 1993), pp. 263–266.

ated their status by their sons' success in the examination system. Poor boys, whose work was needed on their parents' farms, were far less likely to devote years to exam preparation. In spite of the system's theoretical openness to boys of all backgrounds, in reality only the rich had the chance to study and enter government service. By the sixteenth century, there were approximately 100,000 students preparing for exams at any given time.

As time passed, Ming rulers became resistant to innovation. Yet even this resistance had a positive aspect, in that it generated an aura of stability through most of the 1500s, when Chinese culture was a model for East Asia. Sixteenth-century European visitors were impressed by Chinese courtesy, respect for law, confidence, and stately ceremonies. They saw material prosperity in the bustling markets, stone-paved roads, and beautiful homes of Ming officials. They noted with awe the breadth of literacy and the availability of books written in vernacular language comprehensible to many readers. The elaborate Ming examination system, with its proclaimed principle of advancement on merit, often evoked favorable surprise. European commentators were lavish in their praise of Chinese justice, an attitude that would change greatly several centuries later.

Ming Society, Scholarship, and Culture

Market towns and commercial networks had been growing in China since the Song dynasty (see Chapter 10). As the population rebounded following its decline during the Yuan dynasty, market towns expanded. The distance between market towns shortened, and commercial links were improved. At the same time, other forms of social interaction developed, especially kinship (lineage) groups and community associations pledging to do good deeds and lead moral lives. Community orientation did not necessarily require that all people be treated equally, but rather humanely. During the Ming era, for instance, women became less visible to the larger society. They were to stay inside the house; widows were not supposed to remarry but rather continue to live with the family of their deceased husband; and the practice of foot binding spread throughout the country, even among commoners. The ideal of the exemplary Confucian woman was institutionalized in the form of written accounts of virtuous widows and of arches built in front of the homes of women widowed before they were 30 who reached the age of 60 without remarrying. Though Ming law, ironically, offered a financial incentive to widows' families to marry them off—if she remarried, a widow's dowry could be kept by her late husband's family, who would also earn a "bride price" from her next husband's family—widows deemed virtuous did not remarry. Morality tales written during the Ming, while likely exaggerated for didactic effect, portrayed virtuous widows as committing suicide or self-mutilation to show grief or prove their loyalty to dead husbands.

Under Ming rule, legal recognition of **concubinage** also encouraged the sale of young virgins from poor families to families of generally higher status. While women's official legal status, especially that of widows, was lowered because of stricter adherence to Confucian norms, it can also be said that women's independence was encouraged by the same ideology. New Confucian regulations and standards encouraged education for girls as well as boys. Young women, who read the more than 50 works extolling female obedience through accounts of the lives of virtuous women, were also given access to other reading material that could easily have challenged the official vision of a woman as a person confined to a household.

Even foot binding can be seen from several perspectives. The practice mutilated the foot in order to enhance a woman's desirability; mothers bound their daughters' feet to improve their marriage prospects and thus, perhaps, spare their daughters a life of hard physical labor. Farm women often did not have bound feet, as their labor was needed. On the one hand, it could be said that a life of field work liberated a woman from bound feet; on the other, bound feet usually freed a woman from backbreaking field work. Nowhere else in Asia was foot binding practiced, and yet women had subordinate status there as in most parts of the world. Thus, foot binding was a painful, mutilating practice but was itself not a cause of women's second-class status.

The Ming respect for learning and literacy was evident in officially commissioned works as well as popular works. Numerous official works were published, including vast multivolume collections, 1500 local histories, and famous medical works like *The Outline of Herb Medicine*, which took 30 years to complete. The Yongle emperor ordered the compilation of all existing literature, that is, an encyclopedia of all knowledge. It has been surmised that these works added up to more printed works than all the manuscript books throughout the world at that time. (This was also, of course, a half-century before Gutenberg

concubinage—A legal relationship of a man and a secondary wife, who usually did not have the rights and protection of a primary wife. Concubines were often obtained by rich men to produce sons.

1410. Hus was later excommunicated and called to account for himself at the Council of Constance in 1415. Even though he had been given the assurance of safe passage, he was seized and burned at the stake as a heretic, and his ashes were thrown into the Rhine. His death led to the Hussite wars (1419–1437), in which the Czechs withstood a series of crusades against them. They maintained their religious reforms until their defeat by the Habsburgs in the Thirty Years' War.

The Great Schism of the Roman Catholic Church

In response to pressure from churchmen, rulers, scholars, and commoners throughout Europe, the papacy returned to Rome in 1377, it seemed for a time that its credibility would be regained. However, the reverse proved true. In the papal election held the following year, the **College of Cardinals** elected an Italian pope. A few months later the French cardinals declared the election invalid and elected a French pope, who returned to Avignon. During the Great **Schism** (1378–1417), as the split of the church into two allegiances was called, there were two popes, each with his college of cardinals and capital city, each claiming complete authority, each sending out papal administrators and collecting taxes, and each excommunicating the other. The nations of Europe gave allegiance as their individual political interests influenced them.

The Great Schism continued after the original rival popes died, and each group elected a replacement. Doubt and confusion caused many Europeans to question the legitimacy and holiness of the church as an institution.

The Conciliar Movement

Positive action came in the form of the Conciliar Movement. In 1395 the professors at the University of Paris proposed that a general council, representing the entire church, should meet to heal the schism. A majority of the cardinals of both factions accepted this solution, and in 1409 they met at the Council of Pisa, deposed both popes, and elected a new one. But neither of the two deposed popes would give up his office, and the papal throne now had three claimants.

The intolerable situation necessitated another church council. In 1414 the Holy Roman Emperor assembled at Constance the most impressive church gathering of the period. By deposing the various papal claimants and electing Martin V as pope in 1417, the Great Schism was ended and a single papacy was restored at Rome.

The Conciliar Movement represented a reforming and democratizing influence in the church. But the movement was not to endure, even though the Council of Constance had decreed that general councils were superior to popes and that they should meet at regular intervals in the future. Taking steps to preserve his authority, the pope announced that to appeal to a church council without having first obtained papal consent was heretical. Together with the inability of later councils to bring about much-needed reform and with lack of support for such councils by secular

Religious Reforms and Reactions

1415	John Hus, Bohemian reformer, burned at the stake
1437–1517	Cardinal Ximenes carried out reforms of Spanish Catholic Church
c. 1450	Revival of witchcraft mania in Europe
1452–1498	Savonarola attempted religious purification of Florence
1483–1546	Martin Luther
1484–1531	Ulrich Zwingli, leader of Swiss Reformation
1491–1556	Ignatius Loyola, founder of Society of Jesus (Jesuits)
1509–1564	John Calvin, leader of Reformation in Geneva
1515–1582	St. Teresa of Avila, founder of Carmelite religious order
1517	Luther issues Ninety-Five Theses
1521	Luther declared an outcast by the Imperial Diet at Worms
1534–1549	Pontificate of Paul III
1545–1563	Council of Trent
1561–1593	Religious wars in France

College of Cardinals—Cardinals are the highest-ranking churchmen serving under the pope in the Catholic Church. Collectively, they constitute the Sacred College of Cardinals, and their duties include electing the pope, acting as his principal counselors, and aiding in governing the church.

Schism—Literally a split or division (from the Greek *schizein* = to split). The word is usually used in reference to the Great Schism (1378–1417), when there were two, and later three, rival popes, each with his own College of Cardinals.

rulers, the restoration of a single head of the church enabled the popes to discredit the Conciliar Movement by 1450. Not until almost a century later, when the Council of Trent convened in 1545, did a great council meet to reform the church. But by that time the church had already irreparably lost many countries to Protestantism.

While the popes refused to call councils to effect reform, they failed to bring about reform themselves. The popes busied themselves not with internal problems but with Italian politics and patronage of the arts. The issues of church reform and revitalization were largely ignored.

Political Challenges

During the fifteenth century major issues of contention between Rome and the various leaders of Europe dealt with the control of taxes and fees, the courts, the law, and trade. The Catholic Church owned vast properties and collected fortunes in tithes, fees, and religious gifts, controlling, by some estimates, between a fifth and a fourth of Europe's wealth. Impoverished secular rulers looked enviously at the church's wealth. Because the Atlantic states of England, France and Spain were more unified, they were better able to deal with Rome than states of the fragmented Holy Roman Empire.

No longer able to prevail over secular rulers by its religious authority alone after 1300, the papacy fared badly in an era of power politics in foreign relations. Free Italian cities, such as Venice and Florence, had helped build a new balance-of-power diplomacy after the 1450s. But the French invasion at the end of the fifteenth century made the peninsula an arena for desperate struggle between the Habsburg and French Valois (Val-WAH) dynasties that would last until 1559. The Papal States became a political pawn. The papacy's weaknesses were exploited by the troops of Charles V when they sacked Rome in 1527.

Spiritual and Intellectual Developments

The Roman Catholic Church faced more than just social and political challenges by 1500. At the lowest level, popular religion remained based on illiterate believers who worshipped for the magical or practical earthly benefits of the sacraments and the cults of the saints. In their short and grim lives they were far from the political intrigue and sophisticated theological disputes that would trigger the Reformations and much closer to beliefs in the existence of witches, ghosts, phantom grunting swine, and demons who might lurk around the next corner. Arguments between Augustinian and Dominican monks meant little, and dedication to the opinions of the pope in faraway Rome was weak. Of much greater concern was how to avoid going to Hell, a possibility that was constantly in evidence during this time of fragile life and early death.

At the elite levels, during the fifteenth century, humanist reformers believed that abuses in the Catholic Church resulted largely from misinterpretation of Scripture by late medieval Scholastic philosophers and theologians (see p. 274). Northern humanists like Erasmus and Sir Thomas More ridiculed later Scholastics as pedantic (see p. 412).

Intellectual conflict was not new in Europe. But the means of communicating the nature and extent of the disagreements after the 1450s was new. The printing presses, after their European introduction in the 1350s, produced 6 million publications in more than 200 European towns by 1500. There were better-educated people with a thirst to read these books, which dealt largely with religious themes, and the result was the force of mobilized public opinion.

Some of these readers responded to critics, such as the Augustinian monks, who saw the Scholastics as presumptuous and worldly. Following the teachings of St. Augustine, they believed humans to be such depraved sinners that there could be saved not through "good works," as the Church taught, but only through personal repentance and faith in God's mercy. **Augustinians** accepted only Scripture as religious truth; they believed that faith was more important than the Scholastics' manipulated power of reason. And it was to the Augustinians that Martin Luther would turn to pursue his search for understanding.

LUTHER AND THE GERMAN REFORMATION

- *Why did the most important fracture in Christendom occur in Germany?*

Martin Luther had no intention of striking the spark that launched more than a century of European conflict. Born in 1483, the son of an ambitious and tough Thuringian peasant turned miner and small businessman, he was raised by his parents under a contradictory regime of Christian love and the attendant harsh physical discipline that would affect his way of dealing with the world after 1521. Like many young boys of his time, he enjoyed the sometimes earthy and profane humor of his peasant society. Unlike many of his friends, he, as did St. Augustine 1200 years earlier, distrusted his own passionate

Martin Luther

Augustinians—Founded in 1256, a religious order dedicated to following of St. Augustine's life and teaching.

nature and became obsessed with fear of the devil and an eternity in hell. Until 1517 Luther's pursuit of his salvation was an intensely personal one, with little regard to the larger context of upheaval in which he lived.

The Search for Salvation

Martin Luther found great comfort in the teachings of the humanists and the Augustinians. After four years of studying the law, he disappointed his father by entering an Augustinian monastery at age 22, following what was to him a miraculous survival in a violent thunderstorm. As a monk, however, Luther was tormented by what he saw as his sinful nature and the fear of damnation. Then, in his mid-thirties, he read St. Paul's Epistle to the Romans and found freedom from despair in the notion of justification by faith: "Then I grasped that the justice of God is that righteousness by which through grace and sheer mercy God justifies us through faith. Thereupon, I felt myself to be reborn and to have gone through open doors into paradise."[1]

As an Augustinian, Luther entered into abstract religious debates that became more spirited because of the widespread problems of the church in central Europe. The buying and selling of church offices and charging fees to give comfort through a variety of theologically questionable ceremonies to superstitious parishioners disturbed him. But the practice that outraged Luther and brought him openly to oppose the Roman Catholic Church was the sale of indulgences. Theologically, these were shares of surplus grace, earned by Christ and the saints and available for papal dispensation to worthy souls after death. Originally, indulgences were not sold or described as tickets to heaven. By the sixteenth century, however, papal salesmen regularly peddled them as guarantees of early release from purgatory.

Luther's immediate adversary in 1517 was a **Dominican** monk named Johan Tetzel (TET-zel), commissioned by the Pope Leo X and Archbishop Albert of Mainz to sell indulgences. At the papal level, this was part of a large undertaking by which Pope Leo X hoped to finance completion of St. Peter's Basilica in Rome: The Archbishop of Mainz received 50 percent of the money for his own purposes. Tetzel used every appeal to crowds of the country people around Wittenberg (vit-en-BERG), begging them to aid their deceased loved ones and repeating the slogan "A penny in the box, a soul out of purgatory."[2] Luther and many other Germans detested Tetzel's methods and his Roman connections. He also rejected Tetzel's Dominican theology, which differed from Augustinian beliefs.

Dominicans—St. Dominic established this religious order in 1215 to go out into the world to teach and preach the word of God.

Lucas Cranach, Martin Luther and His Friends. *That Martin Luther (left) and other Protestant reformers did not suffer the same fate as John Hus a century earlier was largely due to the political support of rulers such as the Elector Frederick of Saxony (center).*

There are moments in history when the actions of a single person will link all of the prevailing and contrasting currents of an era into an explosive mixture. In Wittenberg on October 31, 1517, Martin Luther issued his Ninety-Five Theses, calling for public debate—mainly with the Dominicans—on issues involving indulgences and basic church doctrines.

This document was soon translated from Latin into German and published in all major German cities. The Theses denied the pope's power to give salvation and declared that indulgences were not necessary for a contrite and repentant Christian. Number 62, for example, stated that the "true treasure" of the Church was the "Holy Gospel of the Glory and Grace of God," and number 36 indicated that Christians truly desiring forgiveness could gain it without "letters of pardon." The resulting popular outcry forced Tetzel to leave Saxony, and Luther was almost immediately hailed as a prophet, directed by God to expose the pope and a grasping clergy.

His message was so well received because it satisfied those who wanted a return to simple faith; it also appealed to those, like the humanists, who fought church abuses and irrational authority. Luther's message provided an outlet for German resentment against Rome, and it gave encouragement to princes seeking political independence. The ensuing controversy, which soon raged far beyond Wittenberg, split all of western Christendom and focused and strengthened the social, economic, and political contradictions of the time.

Luther was soon in trouble. Although Rome was not immediately alarmed, the Dominicans levied charges of heresy against their Augustinian competitor. Having already begun his defense in a series of pamphlets, Luther continued in 1519 by debating the eminent theologian John Eck (1486–1543) at Leipzig (LEIP-zig). There Luther denied the **infallibility of the pope** and church councils, declared the Scriptures to be the sole legitimate doctrinal authority, and proclaimed that salvation could be gained only by faith. That same year a last effort at reconciliation failed completely, and in June 1520 Luther was excommunicated by the pope.

Charles V, only recently crowned emperor and aware of Luther's increased following among the princes, afforded the rebellious monk an audience before the **Imperial Diet** at Worms in 1521 to hear his defense of statements against church teachings and papal authority. If Luther recanted, he could perhaps escape his excommunication and execution. After much discussion, when the Orator of the Empire finally asked if he was prepared to recant, Luther responded:

> *Your Lordships demand a simple answer. Here it is, plain and unvarnished. Unless I am convicted of error by the testimony of Scripture or (since I put no trust in the unsupported authority of Pope or of councils, since it is plain that they have often erred and often contradicted themselves) by manifest reasoning I stand convicted by the Scriptures to which I have appealed, and my conscience is taken captive by God's word, I cannot and will not recant anything, for to act against our conscience is neither safe for us, nor open to us. On this I take my stand, I can do no other. God help me. Amen."*[3]

The Diet finally declared him an outcast. Soon afterward, as he left Worms, Luther was secretly detained for his own protection in Wartburg (VART-burg) Castle by Elector Frederick of Saxony, his secular lord. He would not burn at the stake, as did John Hus, because he enjoyed substantial political and popular support. His message had been spread by the 300,000 copies of his 30 works printed between 1517 and 1520, and he was a German hero.

The Two Kingdoms: God and the State

At Wartburg Luther set his course for the rest of his life as he began organizing an evangelical church distinct from Rome. Although he denounced much of the structure, formality, and ritual of the Catholic Church, Luther spent much of his time after the Diet of Worms building a new church for his followers. It reflected his main theological differences with Rome but kept many traditional ideas and practices. The fundamental principle of the Lutheran creed was that salvation occurred through faith that Christ's sacrifice alone could wash away sin. This departed from the Catholic doctrine of salvation by faith and good works, which required conformance to prescribed dogma and participation in rituals. The Catholic Mass became the Lutheran Communion, involving all who attended services and requiring no priestly blessing to transform the bread and wine into Christ's body and blood, which in Lutheran theory automatically "coexisted" with the wafer and the wine. Other changes included church services in German instead of Latin, an emphasis on preaching, the abolition of monasteries, and the curtailment of formal ceremonies foreign to the personal experiences of ordinary people. The Lutheran Church claimed to be a "priesthood of all believers" in which each person could receive God directly or through the Scriptures. To that end, Luther translated the Bible from Latin into German and composed the sermons that would be repeated in hundreds of Lutheran pulpits all over Germany and Scandinavia.

He took off his clerical habit in 1523 and two years later married a former nun, Katherine von Bora, who bore him six children, raised his nieces and nephews, managed his household, secured his income, entertained his colleagues, and served as his supportive companion. Luther's ideas on marriage and Christian equality promised women new opportunities, which

infallibility of the pope—The belief that popes cannot be wrong in matters of faith and doctrine.

Imperial Diet—A meeting of the political and religious leaders of the various member states of the Holy Roman Empire.

were only partly realized. He stressed the importance of wives as marriage partners for both the clergy and the **laity.** Contrary to Catholic doctrine, he even condoned divorce in cases of adultery and desertion. During the 1520s, his views drew numerous women to Wittenberg, where they found refuge from monasteries or their Catholic husbands. Some Lutheran women became wandering preachers, but they evoked protests from male ministers and legal prohibitions from many German municipal councils, including those of Nuremberg and Augsburg. Although first teaching that women were equal to men in opportunities for salvation and in their family roles, in his later writings, Luther described them as subordinate to their husbands and not meant for the pulpit.

Lutheranism recognized two main human spheres of human obligation: The first and highest was to God; the other involved a subordinate loyalty to earthly governments, which also existed in accordance with God's will. Luther's idea of "two kingdoms," one of God and one of the world, fit well with contemporary political conditions, winning him support from German and Scandinavian rulers while connecting his movement to dynastic nationalism. Luther's political orientation was clearly revealed in 1522 and 1523 during a rebellion of German knights. When Lutheran support was not forthcoming, the rebellion was quickly crushed. Luther took no part in the struggle but was embarrassed by opponents who claimed his religion threatened law and order.

DOCUMENT
Sermon at the Castle Pleissenberg

Another example of Luther's political and social conservatism was provided by a general revolt of peasants and discontented townsmen in 1524 and 1525. Encouraged by Lutheran appeals for Christian freedom, the rebels drew up petitions asking for religious autonomy. At first Luther expressed sympathy for the requests, particularly for each congregation's right to select its own pastor. Then, as violence erupted throughout central Germany in April and May 1525, imperial and princely troops crushed the rebel armies, killing an estimated 90,000 insurgents. Luther had advised rebel leaders to obey the law as God's will; when they turned to war, he penned a virulent pamphlet, *Against the Thievish and Murderous . . . Peasants.* In it he called on the princes to "knock down, strangle, . . . stab, . . . and think nothing so venomous, pernicious, or Satanic as an insurgent."[4]

There was soon a struggle for religious control in Germany between the emperor and the Lutheran princes. When Catholics sought to impose conformity in Imperial Diets during the late 1520s, Lutheran leaders drew up a formal protest (hence the appellation *protestant*). After this Augsburg Confession (1530) was rejected, the Lutheran princes organized for defense in the Schmalkaldic League. Because Charles V was preoccupied with the French and the Turks, open hostilities were minimized, but a sporadic civil war dragged on until after Luther's death in 1546. It ended with the Peace of Augsburg in 1555, when the imperial princes were permitted to choose between Lutheranism and Catholicism in their state churches, thus increasing their independence of the emperor. In addition, Catholic properties confiscated before 1552 were retained by Lutheran principalities, which provided a means for financing their policies. Although no concessions were made to other protestant groups, such as the Calvinists, this treaty shifted the European political balance against the Empire and the church.

Outside Germany, Lutheranism furnished a religious stimulus for developing national monarchies in Scandinavia. There, as in Germany, rulers welcomed not only Lutheran religious ideas but also the chance to acquire confiscated Catholic properties. They appreciated having ministers who preached obedience to constituted secular authority. In Sweden, Gustavus Vasa (goos-TA-vus VAH-sah; 1523–1560) used Lutheranism to lead a successful struggle for Swedish independence from Denmark. In turn, the Danish king, who also ruled Norway, issued an ordinance in 1537 establishing the national Lutheran Church, with its bishops as salaried officials of the state. Throughout Eastern Europe, wherever there was a German community, the Lutheran church spread—for a brief time even threatening the supremacy of the Catholic Church in Poland and Lithuania.

laity—The community of believers in the Christian Church, served by the clergy, the trained and specialized leaders of the community.

HENRY VIII AND THE ANGLICAN REFORMATION

▪ *What were the political considerations impelling Henry VIII to create the Anglican Church?*

England was affected by the same economic and social crises and changes of the fourteenth and fifteenth centuries as the rest of Europe. But unlike central Europe, England was one of the new Atlantic states characterized by national monarchies, centralized authority, and greater independence from the papacy. The Tudor dynasty adapted itself to the new conditions after the Hundred Years' War with France and the devastating War of the Roses, which destroyed much of the traditional nobility.

Legitimate Heirs and the True Church

During this time of difficult transition, it was necessary that each monarch raise a strong and healthy heir to ensure the continuity of the dynasty and the strength of England. Henry VIII (1509–1547) became the heir to the English throne when his older brother Arthur died in 1502. It had not been expected that he would be king, and his education ran to that of a true Renaissance man. He showed talent in music, literature, philosophy, jousting, hunting, and theology. Not only did he become the king of England on his father's death in 1509, but he also soon married the woman who had been his brother's wife, Catherine of Aragon (1485–1536), thus continuing the dynastic alliance with Spain. Catherine was a cultured, strong, respected woman and devoted wife: she successfully conducted a war against Scotland when Henry was campaigning in France.

Henry was a devout Roman Catholic, who gained the title "Defender of the Faith" from the pope for a pamphlet he wrote denouncing Luther and his theology. However, his immediate problem in the 1520s was the lack of a male heir. After 11 years of marriage, he had only a sickly daughter and an illegitimate son. His queen, after four earlier pregnancies, gave birth to a stillborn son in 1518, and by 1527, when she was 42, Henry had concluded that she would have no more children. His only hope for the future of his dynasty seemed to be a new marriage and a new queen. This, of course, would require an annulment of his marriage to Catherine. In 1527 he appealed to the pope, asking for the annulment.

Holbein's portrait of Henry VIII, painted in 1542, shows a man sure of himself in his royal setting. He had by this time broken with Rome, married six times in pursuit of a legitimate male heir, and turned England into a major naval power. What the portrait does not show is all of the suffering and discord he left in his wake.

Normally, the request would probably have been granted; the situation, however, was not normal. Because she had been the wife of Henry's brother, Catherine's marriage to Henry had necessitated a papal dispensation, based on her oath that the first marriage had never been consummated. Now Henry professed concern for his soul, tainted by "living in sin" with Catherine. He also claimed that he was being punished, citing a passage in the Book of Leviticus that predicted childlessness for the man who married his dead brother's wife. The pope was sympathetic and certainly aware of an obligation to the king, who had strongly supported the church. However, granting the annulment would have been admission of papal error, perhaps even corruption, in issuing the earlier dispensation. Added to the Lutheran problem, this would have doubly damaged the papacy. A more immediate concern for Henry was Catherine's nephew. As the aunt of Charles V, whose armies occupied Rome in 1527, she was able to exert considerable pressure on the pope to refuse an **annulment.**

When the pope delayed a decision, Henry began to rally his support at home. During the three years after 1531, when Catherine saw him for the last time, Henry took control of affairs. Sequestering his daughter Mary (1516–1558) and his banished wife in separate castles, he forbade them from seeing each other. The king forced the clergy into proclaiming him head of a separate, English church "as far as the law of Christ allows," extracted from Parliament the authority to appoint bishops, and designated his willing tool Thomas Cranmer (1489–1556) as archbishop of Canterbury. In 1533 Cranmer pronounced Henry's marriage to Catherine invalid; at the same time, he legalized his union with Anne Boleyn (bo-LIN), a lady of the court who was carrying his unborn child, the future Elizabeth I. Henry even forced his daughter Mary to accept him as head of the church and to admit the illegality of her mother's marriage—by implication acknowledging her own illegitimacy. Parliament also ended all payment of revenues to Rome.

Now, having little other choice, the pope excommunicated Henry, making the breach official on both sides. On his side, Henry divided up the Church's properties—some 25 percent of the wealth of the realm—to distribute to the gentry to consolidate his domestic support. In 1539 Parliament completed its

annulment—A religious or political judgment that a marriage was/is not valid, and hence no longer existed/exists.

seizure of monastery lands and the wealth of pilgrimage sites such as Canterbury Cathedral. Meanwhile, Catholics such as the former chancellor and humanist Sir Thomas More (see p. 412), who refused to swear allegiance to the new order, were executed.

There had already been a strong underground resistance movement present in England even before Henry came to power. English theologians, beginning with John Wycliffe and his followers, played an active role in the intellectual and theological debates of the High Middle Age. During the fifteenth and first part of the sixteenth centuries there was an active underground church, the Lollards, in which lay people—especially women—played an important role. William Tyndale's (1494–1536) skillful translation of the New Testament, a work marked by Lutheran influences, served as the basis for the English Bible published in 1537, which made scripture available to all literate English-speaking people. This popular Protestantism was not at all close to the new Anglican Church, which brought about little change in doctrine or ritual. The Six Articles, Parliament's declaration of the new creed and ceremonies in 1539, reaffirmed most Catholic theology except papal supremacy.

Radical Protestants and Renewed Catholics

In his later years, after the decapitation of Anne Boleyn on charges of adultery in 1536 (the year that Catherine of Aragon also died), Henry grew increasingly suspicious of popular Protestantism, which was buttressed by reformist movements spreading into England and Scotland from the Continent. Further, he refused to legalize clerical marriage, which caused great hardships among many Anglican clergymen, including some bishops, and their wives and lashed out indiscriminately at those people such as the protestant Anne Ayscough who dared to question him.

In the decade after Henry's death in 1547, religious fanaticism brought social and political upheaval. For six years, during growing political corruption, extreme protestants ruled the country and dominated the frail young king, Edward VI (1547–1553), born of Henry's third wife Jane Seymour—who died in childbirth. His government was controlled by the Regency Council, dominated first by the duke of Somerset and then, after 1549, by his rival, the duke of Northumberland. The same mix of political opportunism and religious change continued as the council members enriched themselves and pursued their ambitions. At the same time, a radical form of Protestantism swept through many parishes. The government sought political support by courting the religious radicals: it repealed the Six Articles, permitted priests to marry, replaced the Latin service with Cranmer's English version, and adopted the Forty-Two Articles, the expression of extreme Protestantism.

When Edward died in 1553, Mary Tudor came to the throne and tried to restore Catholicism through harsh persecutions, which earned her the name "Bloody Mary" from Protestant historians. The new queen possessed many of the same admirable qualities of her mother, Catherine of Aragon: dignity, intelligence, compassion, and a strong moral sense. Her religious obsession, however, eventually cost her the support of a substantial number of her subjects. Her hopeless love for her Catholic husband, Philip II of Spain—who married her in 1554—led to her being seen as a puppet of Spanish diplomacy. She restored the Catholic Church service, proclaimed papal authority in her realm, and forged an alliance with Spain. In putting down the protestants, she burned 300 of them at the stake—among whom were Cranmer, two other bishops, and 55 women. Mary died pitifully, rejected by her husband and people, but steadfast in her hope to save English Catholicism. Leaving no heir, she was compelled to name Elizabeth, her half-sister, as her successor.

PROTESTANTISM FROM SWITZERLAND TO HOLLAND: ZWINGLI AND CALVIN

- *Why were the protestants in the Rhine Valley so much more radical in their approaches than Luther or the Anglicans?*

A very different variety of church reforms took place in Switzerland and France. The leaders of these reforms were conscious of the state but not dominated by it, as the Anglicans were. Like the Lutherans, they were also concerned for the salvation of their souls, but in a much more doctrinal and often vindictive way. Calvinism was the most popular and the most conservative of the reforms, but there were many others, including multiple forms of **Anabaptism**. These movements went farther than Lutheranism and Anglicanism in rejecting Catholic dogma and ritual. Generally, they were opposed to monarchy, but their position did not become very apparent until they were deeply involved in religious wars after 1560, when they often found themselves under attack by both the Catholics and the Lutherans.

Anabaptism—A Protestant faith that holds that baptism and church membership come only when one is an adult. Anabaptists also tend to believe in a strict separation of church and state.

Document Anne Ayscough (Mrs. Thomas Kyme), English Protestant Martyr

Anne Ayscough, the daughter of Sir William Ayscough, received a good education and became remarkably independent at a time when the normal expectation was that a woman's role was to look after the house and be able to entertain guests. She read voraciously, especially Tyndale's version of the New Testament, and participated vigorously in the theological controversies of her time. She did not like the papacy, nor did she much like Henry's VIII's pet theologians and their version of English Catholicism—the Anglican Church. Duty to her family forced her to marry a Catholic husband, but soon he was not pleased when she set out to spread the Gospels by reading from the Bible to the peasants—a practice later forbidden by the law of 1543. For Anne the issues were quite clear: "[T]he papists were the agents of Antichrist and would always be opposed to the Saints of God. . . . " In standing upon her own righteousness and excluding from her heart all love of her enemies, Anne Ayscough was very much a child of her age. In 1545 she was called to London to face charges of heresy. She was then tortured—the only woman in English history put on the rack, tried, and found guilty for her refusal to believe that the wafer literally becomes the body of Christ in the communion, a process called transubstantiation.

On the eve of her execution, she wrote: "O friend most dearly beloved in God, I marvel not a little what should move you to judge in me so slender a faith as to fear death, which is the end of all misery. In the Lord I desire you not believe of me such weakness. For I doubt it not but God will perform his work in me, like as he hath begun. I understand the Council is not a little displeased, that it should be reported abroad that I was racked in the Tower. They say now that what they did there was but to frighten me; whereby I perceive they are ashamed of their uncomely doings and fear much lest the King's majesty should have information thereof. Wherefore they do not want any man to tell it abroad. Well, their cruelty God forgive them."

At the same time, she wrote Henry VIII: "I Anne Ayscough, of good memory, although God hath given me the bread of adversity and the water of trouble (yet not so much as my sins have deserved), desire this to be known unto your Grace. Forasmuch as I am by the law condemned for an evil-doer, here I take heaven and earth to record that I shall die in my innocence. And according to what I have said first and will say last, I utterly abhor and detest all heresies. And as concerning the Supper of the Lord, I believe so much as Christ hath said, therein, which he confirmed with his most blessed blood, I believe so much as he willed me to follow, and I believe so much as the Catholic church of him doth teach. For I will not forsake the commandment of his holy lips. . . ."

And as she was taken out to be executed, her final prayer was written down: "O Lord, I have more enemies now than there be hairs on my head. Yet, Lord, let them never overcome me with vain words, but fight thus, Lord, in my stead, for on thee cast I my care. With all the spite they can imagine they fall upon me, which am thy poor creature. Yet, sweet Lord, let me pay no heed to them which are against me, for in thee is my whole delight. And, Lord, I heartily desire of thee, that thou wilt of thy most merciful goodness forgive them that violence which they do and have done unto me. Open also thou their blind hearts, that they may hereafter do that thing in thy sight, which is only acceptable before thee, and to set forth thy verity aright, without all vain fantasy of sinful men. So be it, O Lord, so be it."

Anne Ayscough was burned at the stake with four companions on July 16 1546. Already viewed as a heroine by many in England, she became the best known English martyr.

Questions to Consider

1. What was there in Anne Ayscough's views that provoked such a harsh response from the leaders of the English Church, such as putting her on the rack?
2. Why were heretics burned at the stake and not, for example, hanged, or decapitated?
3. What qualities earn a person such as Anne Ayscough the accolade of being a "martyr?" What is a martyr? Whom would you consider to be martyrs during the twentieth century?

From Derek Wilson, *A Tudor Tapestry: Men, Women and Society in Reformation England* (London: Heinemann, 1972), pp. 164, 229–232.

Ulrich Zwingli

Popular Protestantism arose early in Switzerland, where many of the same difficult conditions found in the German states favored its growth. During the late medieval period, the country prospered in the growing trade between Italy and Northern Europe. Busy Swiss craftsmen and merchants in Zurich, Bern, Basel, and Geneva suffered under their Habsburg overlords and by papal policies, particularly the sale of indulgences. In 1499 the Confederation of Swiss Cantons won independence from the Holy Roman Empire and the Habsburgs. To many Swiss, this was also the first step in repudiating outside authority.

The Swiss Reformation began in Zurich, shortly after Luther published his Theses at Wittenberg. It was led by Ulrich Zwingli (OOL-rikh ZWING-lee; 1484–1531), a scholar, priest, and former military chaplain, who persuaded the city council to create a regime of clergymen and magistrates to supervise government, religion, and individual morality. Zwingli agreed with Luther in repudiating papal in favor of scriptural authority. He simplified services, preached justification by faith, attacked monasticism, and opposed clerical celibacy. More rational than Luther, he was also more interested in practical reforms, going beyond Luther in advocating additional grounds for divorce and in denying any mystical conveyance of grace by baptism or communion; both, to Zwingli, were only symbols. These differences proved irreconcilable when Luther and Zwingli met to consider merging their movements in 1529.

As Zwingli's influence spread rapidly among the northern cantons, religious controversy separated north from south, rural from urban, and feudal overlords—both lay and ecclesiastical—from towns within their dominions. When, in the 1520s, Geneva repudiated its ancient obligations and declared its independence from the local bishop and the count of Savoy, the city became a hotbed of Protestantism, with preachers streaming in from Zurich. Zwingli was killed in the religious war of 1531, after which it was decided in the Second Peace of Kappel that each Swiss canton could choose its own religion.

John Calvin

Hoping to ensure the dominance of Protestantism in Geneva after the religious wars, local reformers invited John Calvin (1509–1564) to Geneva. Calvin arrived from Basel in 1536. He was an uncompromising French reformer and a formidable foe of the ungodly, but a caring colleague and minister to humble believers. His preaching, based on his study of theology in Paris and law in Orleans, ultimately won enough followers to make his church the official religion. From Geneva, the faith spread to Scotland, Hungary, France, Italy, and other parts of Europe after the early 1540s.

In Basel he had published the first edition of his *Institutes of the Christian Religion* (1536), a theological work that transformed the general Lutheran doctrines into a rational legal system based around the concept of predestination. It also earned Calvin his invitation to Geneva. His original plan for a city government there called for domination by the clergy and banishment of all dissidents. This aroused a storm of opposition from Anabaptists—who believed in adult baptism and separation of church and state—and from the more worldly portion of the population, and Calvin was forced into exile. He moved on to Strasbourg where he associated with other reformers who helped him refine his ideas. Calvin's second regime at Geneva after 1541 involved a long struggle with the city council. His proposed ordinances for the Genevan Church gave the clergy full control over moral and religious behavior, but the council modified the docu-

Margaret of Navarre, a supporter of Protestantism, was the author of the Heptameron, *a collection of tales modeled on Boccacio's Decameron.*

ment, placing all appointments and enforcement of law under its jurisdiction.

Although recognizing the Bible as supreme law and the *Institutes* as a model for behavior, the Geneva city council did not always act on recommendations from the Consistory, Calvin's supreme church committee. For the next 14 years Calvin fought against public criticism and opposition in the council. He gradually increased his power, however, through support from the protestant refugees who poured into the city. His influence climaxed after a failed "revolt of the godless" in 1555. From that year until his death in 1564, he dominated the council, ruling Geneva with an iron hand, within the letter, but not the spirit, of the original ordinances.

Particularly in the later period, the Consistory apprehended violators of religious and moral law, sending its members into households to check every detail of private life. Offenders were reported to secular magistrates for punishment. Relatively light penalties were imposed for missing church, laughing during the service, wearing bright colors, dancing, playing cards, or swearing. Religious dissent, blasphemy, mild heresies, and adultery received heavier punishments, including banishment. Witchcraft and serious cases of heresy led to torture, and then execution—sometimes as many as a dozen or more a year. Michael Servetus (SEHR-vee-tus; 1511–1553), a Spanish theologian-philosopher and refugee from the Catholic Inquisition, was burned for heresy in Calvin's Geneva because he had denied the doctrine of the trinity.

Calvin accepted Luther's insistence on justification by faith; like Luther, he saw Christian life as a constant struggle against the devil, and he expected a coming divine retribution, an end-time, when God would redress the evils that were increasing on every side. Calvin also agreed with Luther in seeing God's power as a relief for human anxiety and a source of inner peace. Both reformers believed man to be totally depraved, but Calvin placed greater emphasis on this point, at the same time emphasizing God's immutable will and purpose. If Calvinism, to human minds, seemed contradictory in affirming man's sinful nature and his creation in God's image, this connection only proved that God's purposes were absolutely beyond human understanding. For depraved humans, God required faith and obedience, not understanding.

DOCUMENT

Calvin on Predestination

God's omnipotence was Calvin's cardinal principle. He saw all of nature as governed by a divinely ordained order, discernible to man but governed by laws that God could set aside in effecting miracles as he willed. Carried to its logical conclusion, such ideas produced Calvin's doctrine of predestination.

> *By predestination we mean the eternal decree of God, by which he determined with himself whatever he wished to happen with regard to every man. All are not created on equal terms, but some are preordained to eternal life, others to eternal damnation; and, accordingly, as each has been created for one or other of these ends, we say that he has been predestined to life or to death. . . .*[5]

In Calvin's grand scheme, as laid out precisely in the *Institutes,* his church served to aid the elect in honoring God. The human purpose was not to win salvation—for this had already been determined—but to honor God and prepare the elect for salvation. As communities of believers, congregations were committed to constant war against Satan. They also functioned to spread the Word (Scripture), educate youth, and alleviate suffering among the destitute.

Calvin was particularly ambivalent in his views on government. Ministers of the church were responsible for advising secular authorities on religious policies and resisting governments that violated God's laws. He believed that all rulers were responsible to God and subject to God's vengeance. But throughout the1540s, when he was hoping to gain the support of monarchs, he emphasized the Christian duty of obedience to secular authorities. Even then, however, he advised rulers to seek counsel from church leaders, and he ordered the faithful, among both the clergy and the laity, to disregard any government that denied them freedom in following Christ. Although willing to support any political system that furthered the true faith, Calvin always preferred representative government.

Another ambiguity in Calvin's social thought involved his attitude toward women. Unlike Catholic theologians, he did not cast women in an inferior light. In his mind, men and women were equally full of sin, but they were also equal in their chance for salvation. As he sought recruits, he stressed women's right to read the Bible and participate in church services. At the same time he saw women as naturally subordinate to their husbands in practical affairs, including the conduct of church business.

Before the Peace of Augsburg, Calvinism was strongest in France, the reformer's own homeland, where the believers were known as *Huguenots.* Calvinism made gains elsewhere but did not win political power. In Italy, the duchess of Ferrara installed the Calvinist church service in her private chapel and protected Calvinist refugees. Strasbourg in the 1530s was a free center for protestant reformers such as Matthew Zell and his wife Katherine, who befriended many Calvinist preachers, including Martin Bucer (BOOT-sur), a missionary to England during the reign of Edward VI. In the same period, John Knox spread the Calvinist message in Scotland.

More extreme than Calvinism were many divergent protestant splinter groups, each pursuing its own "inner lights." Some saw visions of the world's end, some advocated a Christian community of shared wealth, some opposed social distinctions and economic inequalities, some—these Anabaptists—repudiated infant baptism as a violation of Christian responsibility, and some denied the need for any clergy. Most of the sects emphasized biblical literalism and direct, emotional communion between the individual and God. The majority of them were indifferent or antagonistic to secular government, many favored pacifism and substitution of the church for the state.

Women were prominent among the sects, although they were usually outnumbered by men. These women were known for their biblical knowledge, faith, courage, and independence. They helped found religious communities, wrote hymns and religious tracts, debated theology, and publicly challenged the authorities. Some preached and delivered prophecies, although such activities were suppressed by male ministers by the end of the century. More women than men endured torture and suffered martyrdom. Their leadership opportunities and relative freedoms in marriage, compared to women of other religions, were bought at the high price of hardship and danger.

Persecution of the sects arose largely because of their radical ideas. But Catholics and other protestants who opposed them usually cited two revolutionary actions. The first came when some radical preachers took part in the German peasants' revolt of the 1520s and shared in the savage punishments that followed. The second came in 1534 when a Catholic army besieged Münster (MIUN-ster).

Thousands of recently arrived Anabaptist extremists had seized control and expelled dissenters from this German city near the southern Netherlands. Following their radical theology, the "regime of saints" took private property, allowed polygamy, and planned to convert the world. John of Leyden (LI-den), a former Dutch tailor who claimed divine authority, headed a terrorist regime during the final weeks before the city fell. Those who survived the fall of the city suffered horrible tortures and then execution.

Among the most damaging charges against the Münster rebels were their alleged sexual excesses and the dominant role played by women in this immorality. Such charges were mostly distortions. The initiation of **polygamy,** justified by references to the Old Testament, was a response to problems arising from a shortage of men, hundreds of whom had fled the city. Many other men were killed or injured in the fighting. Thus, the city leaders required women to marry so that they could be protected and controlled by husbands. Most Anabaptist women accepted the requirement as a religious duty. Although some paraded through the streets, shouting religious slogans, the majority prepared meals, did manual labor on the defenses, fought beside their men, and died in the fighting or at the stake. Most of the original, Catholic, Münster women, however, fiercely resisted forced marriage, choosing instead jail or execution.

Like Calvin later in Geneva, the Anabaptist regime of John of Leyden closely monitored and controlled private life and public behavior. Their theocratic state found its laws in Scripture. In looking at the laws of the city, capital punishment was applied in the following cases:

> *Whoever curses God and his holy Name or his Word shall be killed (Lev. 24).*
>
> *No one shall curse governmental authority (Ex. 22, Deut. 17), on pain of death.*
>
> *Both parties who commit adultery shall die (Ex. 20, Lev. 20, Matt. 5).*
>
> *. . . Whoever disobeys these commandments and does not truly repent, shall be rooted out of the people of God, with ban and sword, through the divinely ordained governmental authority.*[6]

For more than a century, memories of Münster plagued the protestant sects in general. Although most did not go to the extremes of "the saints," they were almost immediately driven underground throughout Europe, and their persecution continued long after they had abandoned violence. In time, they dispersed over the Continent and to North America as Mennonites, Quakers, and Baptists, to name only a few denominations. Given their suffering and oppression, voices of the radicals were among the first raised for religious liberty. Their negative experience with governments made them even more suspicious of authority than the Calvinists were. In both the Netherlands and England, they participated in political revolutions and helped frame the earliest demands for constitutional government, representative institutions, and civil liberties.

With the exception of Henry VIII's political reformation, the reformers, going back to Wycliffe and Hus and moving on through Luther and Calvin and the Anabaptists, did not believe that they were creating something new. Instead, they were trying to reclaim the purity of the early church.

---

polygamy—A type of marriage in which a husband has more than one wife.

REFORM IN THE CATHOLIC CHURCH

- *How successful was the Catholic Church in dealing with the problems that faced it?*

The era of the Protestant Reformation was also a time of rejuvenation for the Roman Catholic Church. This revival was largely caused by the same conditions that had sparked Protestantism. Throughout the fifteenth century, many sincere and devout Catholics had recognized a need for reform, and they had begun responding to the abuses in their church long before Luther acted at Wittenberg. Almost every variety of reform opinion developed within the Catholic Church. Erasmus, More, and other Christian humanists provided precedents for Luther, but none followed him out of the Catholic Church. In a category of his own was Savonarola (sa-vo-na-RO-la; 1452–1498), a Dominican friar, puritan, and mystic who ruled Florence during the last four years before his death. This "Catholic Calvin" consistently railed against the worldly living and sinful luxuries he found: His criticisms of the pope and the clergy were

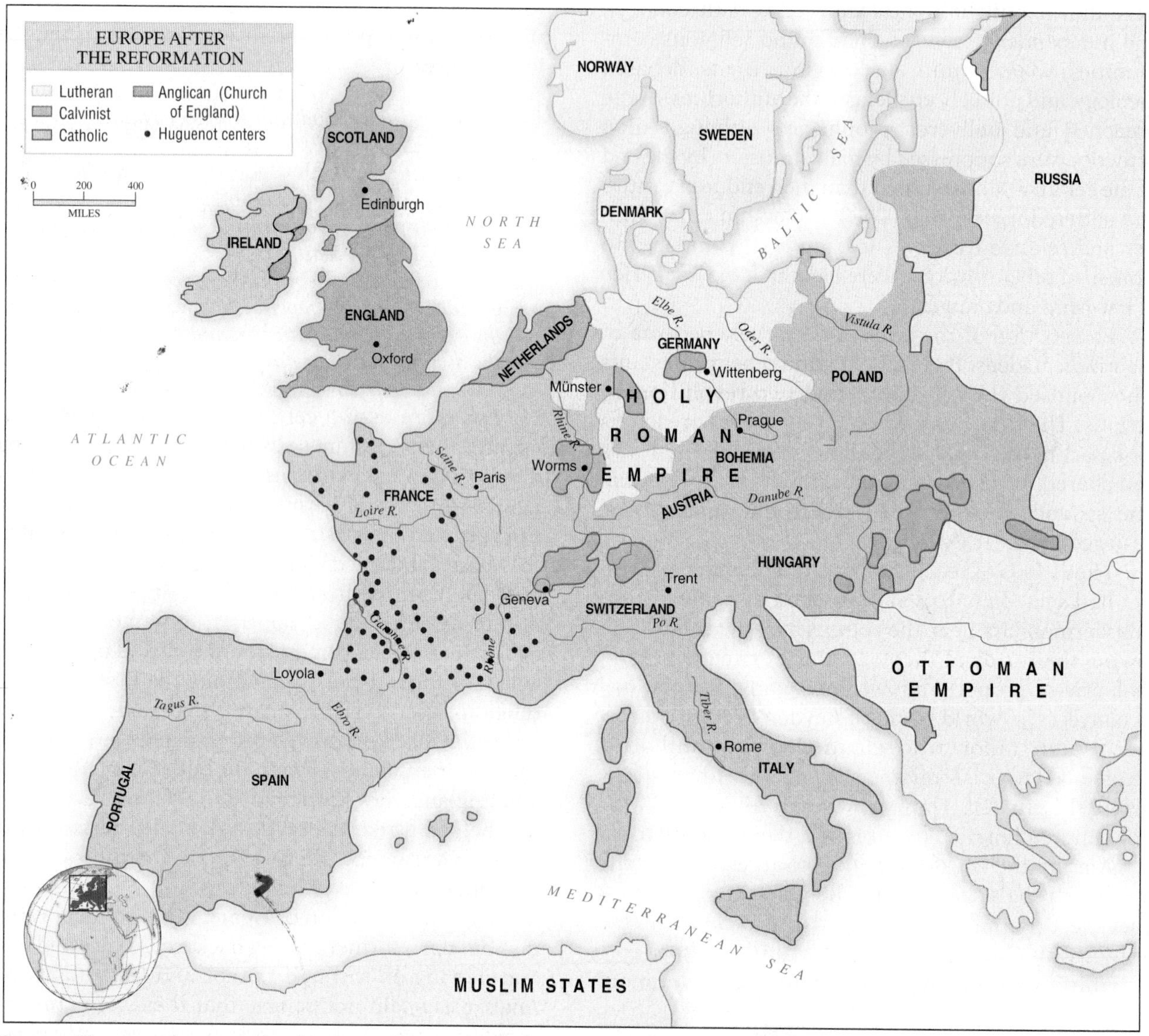

This map illustrates the geographical patterns of the Protestant Reformation. Lutheranism spread through German-speaking areas along the Baltic Sea but rarely crossed the Rhine River. The spread of Calvinism defies linguistic explanation.

much more severe than Luther's. At the other extreme of the Church was Cardinal Ximenes (1437–1517) in Spain, who carried out his own Reformation by disciplining the clergy, compiling the Complutensian Bible—eliminating many of the errors made by medieval copyists and instilling a new spirit of dedication into the monastic orders.

After the protestant revolt began, the primary Catholic reformer was Alessandro Farnese (far-NAY-se), Pope Paul III (1534–1549). Coming into office at a time when the church appeared ready to collapse, Paul struggled to overcome the troubled legacy of his Renaissance predecessors and restore integrity to the papacy. Realizing that issues raised by the protestants would have to be resolved and problems within the church corrected, he attacked the indifference, corruption, and vested interests of the clerical organization. In pursuing these reforms he appointed a commission, which reported the need for correcting such abuses as the worldliness of bishops, the traffic in benefices (church appointments with guaranteed incomes), and the transgressions of some cardinals. Their recommendations led Paul to call a church council, an idea that he continued to press against stubborn opposition for more than ten years.

When Paul died in 1549, he had already set the Roman Church on a new path, although his proposed church council, the Council of Trent, had only begun its deliberations. Perhaps his greatest contribution was his appointment of worthy members to the College of Cardinals, filling that body with eminent scholars and devout stewards of the church. As a result of his labors, the cardinals elected a succession of later popes who were prepared, intellectually and spiritually, to continue the process of regeneration.

The spirit of reform was reflected in a number of new Catholic clerical orders that sprang up in the early sixteenth century. Some of these worked with the poor, ministered to the sick, and taught. Among the better known were the Carmelites founded by St. Teresa of Avila (1515–1582) whose determination and selfless devotion became legendary. She inspired mystical faith and reforming zeal in written works such as *Interior Castle* and *The Ladder of Perfection*.

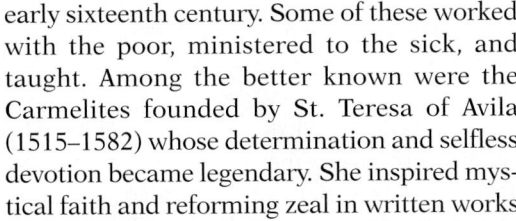

Rules for Thinking with the Church

The most significant of the new orders was the Society of Jesus, whose members are known as Jesuits. Organized along military lines, with their founder, the Spaniard Ignatius Loyola (1491–1556) as general and the pope as commander in chief, the Jesuits were an army of soldiers, sworn to follow orders and defend the faith. As preachers, teachers, confessors, organizers, diplomats, and spies, they took the field everywhere, founding schools and colleges, serving as missionaries on every continent, and working their way into government wherever possible. Their efforts were probably most responsible for the decided check that Protestantism received after the 1560s, as they zealously defended Catholicism in France, pushed the protestants out of Poland, and reclaimed southern Germany. Jesuit missions also helped Spain and Portugal develop their global empires.

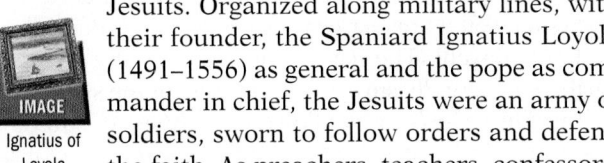

Ignatius of Loyola

Pope Paul's reform initiatives were given form by the great multinational church council, the first since 1415, which met in three sessions between 1545 and 1563 in the northern Italian city of Trent. Devoting much attention to the external struggle against Protestantism, the council also sought to eliminate internal abuses by ordering changes in church discipline and administration. It strictly forbade absenteeism, false indulgences, selling church offices, and secular pursuits by the clergy. Bishops were ordered to supervise their clergies—priests as well as monks and nuns—and to fill church positions with competent people. The Council of Trent also provided that more seminaries be established for educating priests while instructing the clergy to set examples and preach frequently to their flocks.

Rejecting all compromise, the Council of Trent retained the basic tenets of Catholic doctrine, including the necessity of good works as well as faith for salvation, the authority of church law and traditions, the sanctity of all seven sacraments, the use of only Latin in the Mass, and the spiritual value of indulgences, pilgrimages, veneration of saints, and the cult of the Virgin. The council also strengthened the power of the papacy. It defeated all attempts to place supreme church authority in any general council. When the final session voted that none of its decrees were valid without papal approval, the church became more than ever an absolute monarchy.

The full significance of Trent became evident after the 1560s when the Catholic reaction to Protestantism acquired a new vigor and militancy. Having steeled itself from within, the church and its shock troops, the Jesuits, went to war against protestants and other heretics. The new crusade was both open and secret. In Spain, Italy, and the Netherlands, the Inquisition more than ever before became the dreaded scourge of protestants and other heretics. Jesuit universities, armed with the Index of Forbidden Works, trained scholars and missionaries who would serve as priests and organizers in protestant countries such as England. Many died as martyrs, condemned by protestant tribunals, while others suffered similar fates meted out by pagans whom they sought to convert in America and Asia. But

The devotional works and personal example of St. Teresa of Avila, mystic and visionary, inspired the rebirth of Spanish Catholicism. In 1970 she was proclaimed a doctor of the church, the first woman to be so honored. The sculpture here, The Ecstasy of St. Teresa *(1645–1652), is by the Italian baroque artist Giovanni Bernini.*

Protestantism made no more significant gains in Catholic lands after Trent. Indeed, after Trent, the Catholic Church became a global church.

CONCLUSION

In could be argued that Europe's Golden Age of the Renaissance was no more than a recapitulation of that which had gone before. By resurrecting the gifts of the Greeks and Romans and learning from the science and history of the Arabs, the elites who participated in the movement were, in fact, reactionaries. But in looking back, they invented new and demanding methods of research, and the most important legacy they revived was the old Greek message that "Man Can Know." This individual liberation could be seen immediately in the artistic and architectural works as well as in the writings of Lorenzo da Valla and Machiavelli. The new humanism was not necessarily intellectually superior to the best of the scholastic thinking. However, it allowed new questions to be posed in critical ways.

Christianity had always been a religion in ferment, and the authorities in Rome and Constantinople after the Seventh Ecumenical Council had sought to stamp out those who were not in accord with orthodoxy. Luther, in many ways, echoed the thoughts of John Wycliffe and John Hus. He succeeded where they failed because of the more favorable political context he found himself in.

In many ways, the Protestant Reformation and Catholic Counter-Reformation helped create the modern world. By breaking the religious monopoly of European Catholicism, Lutheranism and Anglicanism assisted the growth of northern European national monarchies. Later, the Puritan values and "work ethic" of Calvinism helped justify the profit-seeking activities of the middle classes. Even the Catholic Church itself was transformed by the various protestant challenges. After the Council of Trent, the Catholic Counter-Reformation checked the spread of Protestantism, and the Roman Church emerged strengthened to protect and advance itself. Because the Reformation and Counter-Reformation occurred at the same time of the development of the state system (see Chapter 16), faith came to play an integral, and often dangerous, role in politics until 1648.

Because these momentous changes coincided with the beginnings of the European explorations around the world (see Chapter 15), and the construction of Portuguese, Dutch, Spanish, French, and English empires, protestant and Catholic missionaries were able to spread their messages around the globe. Political and economic imperialism were accompanied by a religious imperialism. The Christians had no doubt they were saving the heathen from hell, but this well-intentioned zealousness had mixed, and sometimes destructive, results to the peoples of Asia, Africa, and the Americas touched by European expansion.

Suggestions for Web Browsing

You can obtain more information about topics included in this chapter at the websites listed below. See also the companion website that accompanies this text, **http://www.ablongman.com/brummett**, which contains an online study guide and additional resources.

Italian Renaissance Art Project
http://www.italian-art.org

One of the very best and most comprehensive sites for reproductions of the major paintings, works of sculpture, and architecture from the Renaissance. An amazing resource of the study of Renaissance art.

Web Museum, Paris: Italian Renaissance (1420–1600)
http://www.ibiblio.org/wm/paint/tl/it-ren/

A useful site for anyone interested in the art of the Italian Renaissance, especially the work of Leonardo da Vinci, Raphael, and Michelangelo.

Florence in the Renaissance
http://www.mega.it/eng/egui/epo/secrepu.htm

A history of the Florentine Republic, with details about the city's influence on Renaissance culture.

Sistine Chapel
http://www.christusrex.org/www1/sistine/0-Tour.html

Photo collection depicting all facets of the Sistine Chapel, including images of Michelangelo's ceiling.

Michelangelo
http://www.michelangelo.com/buonarroti.html

Featuring the works of the artist beautifully illustrated and annotated. An outstanding site.

The Louvre
http://www.paris.org/Musees/Louvre

Website for one of the world's greatest museums offers many paths to some of the most beautiful Renaissance art in existence.

Medieval and Renaissance Women's History
http://womenshistory.about.com/od/medieval/

Site serves as a directory for a wide variety of discussions and references about Renaissance women painters, writers, and women of social standing.

Creative Impulse: Renaissance
http://history.evansville.net/renaissa.html

The University of Evansville's outstanding series of sites on Western civilization includes this compendium of art, history, and descriptions of daily life and culture. Includes one of the very best compilations of other sites dealing with the Renaissance.

Medieval and Renaissance Fact and Fiction
http://www.angelfire.com/mi/spanogle/medieval.html

A useful guide to Web resources for students interested in the history, culture, and literature of the Renaissance.

Northern Renaissance ArtWeb
http://www.msu.edu/~cloudsar/nrweb.htm

A collection of links for exploring the artists and literature of the Northern Renaissance.

Internet Medieval History Sourcebook: Protestant and Catholic Reformations
http://www.fordham.edu/halsall/sbook1y.html

Extensive online source for links about the Protestant and Catholic Reformations, including primary documents by or about precursors and papal critics, Luther, and Calvin and details about the Reformations themselves.

Martin Luther
http://www.wittenberg.de/e/seiten/personen/luther.html

This brief biography of Martin Luther includes links to his Ninety-Five Theses and images of related historical sites.

Tudor England
http://englishhistory.net/tudor.html/

Site detailing life in Tudor England includes biographies, maps, important dates, architecture, and music, including sound files.

Lady Jane Grey
http://www.ladyjanegrey.org/

A biography of the woman who would be queen of England for nine days, and a general history of the time.

Literature and Film

One of the best novels dealing with the Renaissance is Irving Stone, *The Agony and the Ecstasy: A Biographical Novel of Michelangelo* (New American Library, 1996). An outstanding account of the past and present of Florence is given by Mary McCarthy in *The Stones of Florence* (Harvest Books, 2002). There are also many excellent videos available on the art and architecture of the Renaissance. Some of the more notable are *The Art of the Western World: Early and High Renaissance: Realms of Light* (Kultur Video, 1994); *Leonardo Da Vinci: Renaissance Man to the World* (Madacy Entertainment, 1997); *The Art of Renaissance Science: Galileo and Perspective,* by Joseph W. Dauben for Science Television (1991); and *Florence: Cradle of the Renaissance* (Museum City Video, 1992).

The politics of the time provide a rich resource for novels. The activities of this time attracted the best attentions of Alexandre Dumas. Writing about events in France, he published *The Two Dianas,* (dealing with the time of Francis I), *The Page of the Duke of Savoy* (touching the time of the Emperor Charles V), *Ascanio* (France in the middle of the century), and *Marguerite de Valois* (touching the civil wars)—and this is only an incomplete list. Mark Twain wrote about the time of Edward VI in *The Prince and the Pauper*. More recently, Robin Maxwell sheds some light on the reign of Henry VIII in *The Secret Diary of Anne Boleyn: A Novel* (Scribner, 1998).

Filmmakers have been equally attracted to the period, especially the English scene. *A Man for All Seasons* (Columbia/Tristar, 1966), directed by Fred Zinnemann, is a fine telling of the story of Sir Thomas More. Queen Elizabeth has been the subject of films throughout the twentieth century, including *Elizabeth* (Umvd, 1998), directed by Shekhar Kapur, and indirectly in Academy Award winner *Shakespeare in Love* (Miramax, 1998), directed by John Madden. A film dealing with the period after Henry VIII is *Lady Jane* (Paramount, 1985), directed by Trevor Nunn. The 1933 film, *The Private Life of Henry VIII* (AAE Films), directed by Alexander Korda, is worth seeing. From the continent, *The Return of Martin Guerre* (Fox Lorber, 1982), directed by Daniel Vigne, does justice to Natalie Zemon Davis's fine monograph. The film of the life of *Martin Luther* (VCI Home Video, 1953) is a revealing look at the reformer.

Suggestions for Reading

Johnathan Zophy, *A Short History of Renaissance and Reformation Europe,* 2nd ed. (Prentice Hall, 1998) and John Hale, *The Civilization of Europe in the Renaissance* (Scribner, 1994) are both excellent introductions to the period. Jacob Burckhardt, *The Civilization of the Renaissance in Italy,* 2 Vols. (Torchbooks, 1958), first published in 1860, inaugurated the view that the Italian Renaissance of the fourteenth and fifteenth centuries was a momentous turning point in the history of Western civilization. The editors of this edition maintain that Burckhardt's major interpretations remain valid. Donald R. Kelley, *Renaissance Humanism* (Twayne, 1991), and Brian P. Copenhaver, *Renaissance Philosophy* (Oxford University Press, 1992) are excellent surveys. Katharina M. Wilson, ed., *Women Writers of the Renaissance and Reformation* (University of Georgia Press, 1987), is an excellent study of a neglected subject. John White, *Art and Architecture in Italy, 1250–1400,* 3rd ed. (Yale University Press, 1993) is an excellent overview. See also Charles Seymour Jr., *Sculpture in Italy, 1400–1500* (Yale University Press, 1994). Ross King, *Brunelleschi's Dome* (Walker, 2000), is an excellent account of the construction of the famous Florentine's work. Also, Silvio Bedini, *The Pope's Elephant* (Penguin, 2000), is a delightful account of Pope Leo X and his court.

A fascinating study of the attitudes of the Christian laity during the Reformation period can be found in Keith Thomas, *Religion and the Decline of Magic: Studies in Popular Beliefs in Sixteenth and Seventeenth Century England* (Oxford University Press, 1997). A useful context to the religious upheavals of the time is given by John Bossy, *Christianity in the West, 1400–1700* (Oxford University Press, 1985). On the impact of John Hus, see Thomas A. Fudge, *The Magnificent Ride: The First Reformation in Hussite Bohemia* (Ashgate Publishing, 1998). The general background of the Reformation is covered well in Steven E. Ozment, *Protestants: The Birth of a Revolution* (Doubleday, 1992). Brad S. Gregory, *Salvation at Stake: Christian Martyrdom in Early Modern Europe* (Harvard University Press, 2000), is a distinguished work of scholarship that takes the martyrs of the time at their word. Richard Marius, *Martin Luther: The Christian Between God and Death* (Belknap Press of Harvard University Press, 1999), is a superb new study of Luther to 1526. The context for the English Reformation is provided by Richard H. Britnell in *The Closing of the Middle Ages: England, 1471–1529* (Blackwell, 1997). Ulrich Gabler gives a thorough background of Ulrich Zwingli's place in history in his *Huldrych Zwingli: His Life and Work* (Clark, 1995).

William J. Bouwsma, *John Calvin* (Oxford University Press, 1988), is a scholarly portrayal of Calvin's human side, emphasizing his inner conflict against the humanistic trend of his time. On the "left wing" of Protestantism, Anthony Arthur's *The Tailor-King: The Rise and Fall of the Anabaptist Kingdom of Münster* (St. Martin's Press, 1999) is a first-rate history of the radical Reformation city-state in northern Germany. John C. Olin places the Catholic response in perspective in *The Catholic Reformation: From Savonarola to Ignatius Loyola* (Fordham University Press, 1993). R. Po-chia Hsia, *The World of Catholic Renewal 1540–1770* (Cambridge University Press, 1998), is an innovative study of the history of the Catholic Church from the run up to the Council of Trent to the suppression of the Jesuits.

CHAPTER

15

The Development of the European State System, 1300–1650

CHAPTER CONTENTS

For the greater part of the period between 1300 and 1500, Europe was militarily and economically inferior to other world civilizations. Europeans were no match for the Turkish armies, did not possess the wealth of China or India, and lacked the centralized efficiency of the Incas. From 1500 to 1650, however, the balance of military and economic power began to change, and Europe began its global expansion, a process that would continue until 1914.

Three influences contributed to this expansion. We have already discussed two of them: the changes in European thought coming out of the Renaissance and the Reformation (see Chapter 14). The third factor in the increase in European power came in the development of the nation-state system.

State structures began to be seen during the origins of modern civilizations, and the variety of state systems throughout history ranges from despotism, to empire, to religious states, to city-states, to loose federations. These states all share the same qualities: they have defined boundaries, possess the power to tax, and monopolize force. As one of the most influential analysts of the origins and dominance of the nation-state system, Charles Tilly, once noted "war made the state, and the state made war." In the thirteenth century, the most successful form of the state, the nation-state emerged, largely sparked by political opposition to the claims of papal power.

Until 1789, the typical European nation-state was inhabited in large part by people of a similar ethnic and linguistic background (the nation) and led by a king or queen who embodied the state. Tilly indicates that the nation-state succeeded because of its capacity to profit from the rise of capitalism and to mobilize the resources within its boundary to fight wars. Some scholars find the approach of linking the changes in military technology to state development to be simplistic. But it cannot be denied that as the age of gunpowder warfare arrived in the fifteenth century, a new infrastructure was demanded to support the standing army and arms factories needed to compete in the international state system. This military efficiency combined with the scientific advances coming out of the new ways of thinking and religious zeal helped propel Europe to a world force.[1]

1300

1305–1377 Babylonian Captivity of the church; papacy under French influence

1337–1453 Hundred Years' War between England and France

1350

1356 Golden Bull regulates the election of German emperors

1450

1455–1485 Wars of the Roses in England

1479 Ferdinand and Isabella begin joint rule in Spain

1492 Spain conquers Granada, unifies Spanish nation

1500

1526 Ottomans defeat Hungarians at Mohacs

1550

1556–1598 Reign of Philip II of Spain

1560s Ivan the Terrible wages war against disobedient boyars

1561–1593 Religious wars in France

1564 Start of Dutch Revolt

1571 Spanish and Venetian navy defeat Ottomans at Lepanto

1587 Dutch Republic formed

1588 English defeat Spanish Armada

1600

1618–1648 Thirty Years' War

1648 Peace of Westphalia

POLITICS IN AN AGE OF CRISIS: 1300–1500

■ *How did the crisis posed by the Black Death and its consequences change European politics?*

Europe saw many changes during the final two centuries of the late Middle Ages, some disastrous, some constructive. The suffering produced by the Black Death (bubonic plague), famine, and economic depression took a massive toll on the population (see Chapter 14) and was compounded by a number of destructive wars. Underway at the same time, however, were political changes that would have lasting effects on the growth and expansion of European power.

England and France: The Hundred Years' War

Nation-making in both England and France was greatly affected by the long conflict that colored much of both nations' history during the fourteenth and fifteenth centuries. The Hundred Years' War (1337–1453) had its origins in a fundamental conflict between the English kings, who claimed much of French territory as theirs, and the French monarchs, whose ultimate goal was a centralized France under the direct rule of the monarchy at Paris.

Another cause was the clash of French and English economic interests in Flanders. This region was falling more and more under French control, to the frustration of both the English wool-growers, who supplied the great Flemish woolen industry, and the English king, whose income came in great part from duties on wool.

A fifteenth-century portrait of Joan of Arc in battle dress. After leading the French to victory at Orléans in 1429, she was captured by the English, tried and convicted of witchcraft and heresy, and burned at the stake in 1431. The French king, Charles VII, whose kingdom she had helped save, did nothing to rescue her.

Medieval Politics, 1300–1500

1337–1453	Hundred Years' War between France and England
1356	Golden Bull regulates the election of German emperors
1386	Unification of Poland and Lithuania
1454	Treaty of Lodi brings peace to Italian city-states
1455–1485	Wars of the Roses: civil war in England
1479	Marriage of Ferdinand of Aragon and Isabella of Castile
1492	Spain conquers Granada, unifies Spanish nation
1494	France invades Italy

The first years of warfare witnessed impressive English victories. With no thought of strategy, the French knights charged the enemy and then engaged in hand-to-hand fighting. But the English had learned more effective methods. Their greatest weapon was the longbow. Six feet long and made of yew wood, the longbow shot steel-tipped arrows that were dangerous at 400 yards and deadly at 100. The usual English plan of battle called for the knights to fight dismounted. Protecting them was a forward wall of bowmen just behind a barricade of iron stakes planted in the ground to slow the enemy's cavalry charge. By the time the French cavalry reached the dismounted knights, the remaining few French were easily killed.

The revival of the French military effort and a rebirth of national spirit is associated with Joan of Arc, who inspired a series of French victories. Moved by inner voices that she believed divine, Joan persuaded the

Document The Trial of Joan of Arc

Joan of Arc (1412?–1431) is without doubt one of the most remarkable figures in European history. At the age of 13, Joan was hearing the voices of her "saints," who instructed her to come to the aid of the heir to the French throne and win for him a victory over the English at Orléans. The victory was won, Charles became king, and promptly turned his back on Joan, who was captured by the English and put on trial as a witch, a heretic, and a transvestite, since she now preferred to wear men's clothes even off the battlefield.

The following firsthand accounts were recorded by men who were witness to her trial and ultimate condemnation and execution:

Joan was dressed in men's clothes, that is, a tunic, a cape, and a short robe and other men's clothes, a costume that on our orders she had previously put aside, and had taken on women's clothes. And so we interrogated her to learn when and for what reason she had once more assumed men's clothes: "I did it on my own will," Joan declared; "I took it again because it was more lawful and convenient than to have women's clothes because I am with men; I began to wear them again because what was promised me was not observed, to wit that I should go to mass and receive the body of Christ and be freed from these irons.... I would rather die than stay in these irons; but if it is permitted for me to go to mass, and if I could be freed of these irons, and if I could be put in a decent prison and if I could have a woman to help me [her expression, *avoir femme,* is written on the minutes but not on the official transcript of the trial], I would be good and do what the church wishes."

"Since Thursday, have you heard the voices of St. Catherine and St. Margaret?" [Cauchon asked.]

"Yes."

"What have they told you?"

"God has expressed through St. Catherine and St. Margaret His great sorrow at the strong treason to which I consented in abjuring and making a revocation to save my life, and said that I was damning myself to save my life."

In the margin of the account, the author of this account wrote: "A deadly reply."

Shortly before her execution, another account of a conversation with Joan was recorded by a Dominican monk who visited her very shortly before her death:

The day that Joan was abandoned to secular judgment and delivered to be burned, I found myself in the morning in the prison with Friar Martin Ladvenu, whom the bishop of Beauvais had sent to tell her of her coming death and to induce her to true contrition and penance, and also to hear her confession, which Ladvenu did very carefully and charitably. And when he announced to the poor woman the death that she was to die that day, which her judges had ordered, and when she had understood and heard the hard and cruel death that was coming, she began to cry out sorrowfully and pitiably to tear and pull her hair. "Alas! That they treat me so horribly and cruelly that my body, clean and whole, which was never corrupted, should be today consumed and reduced to ashes! Ah! I would prefer to be beheaded seven times than to be burned like that! Alas! If I had been in an ecclesiastical prison to which I submitted myself, and if I had been guarded by men of the church, not by my enemies and adversaries, it would not have turned out for me as miserably as it has. Ah! I protest before God, the Great Judge, the great wrongs and grievances that they have done me." She then made marvelous complaint in that place of the oppression and violences that had been done to her in prison by the jailers and by the others they had made enter against her.

After these complaints, the bishop arrived, to whom she said immediately: "Bishop, I die because of you." He began to remonstrate with her, saying: "Ah, Joan, take it patiently, you will die because you have not held to what you promised us and because you return to your first witchcraft." And the poor Maid answered him: "Alas! If you had put me in the prison of a church court and handed me over to the hands of competent and agreeable ecclesiastical caretakers, this would not have happened to me. That is why I complain of you before God." That being done, I went outside and heard no more.

Questions to Consider

1. Do you feel that these accounts of Joan's actions and thoughts as she approached her execution are trustworthy? Do you think that the recorders are unbiased, or swayed toward or against her?
2. What image of Joan is created by these accounts? Does she seem to be a deluded peasant girl, a mystic visionary, or a rational martyr?
3. Are these firsthand accounts of value in illuminating Joan as a historical figure, or do they add to Joan's status as an almost mythological symbol of French resistance to the English?

From Regine Pernoud and Marie Veronique Clin, *Joan of Arc: Her Story,* trans. Jeremy duQuesnay Adams (St. Martin's Press, 1998), pp. 132–133.

Discovery Through Maps

A Pilgrim's Map of Canterbury

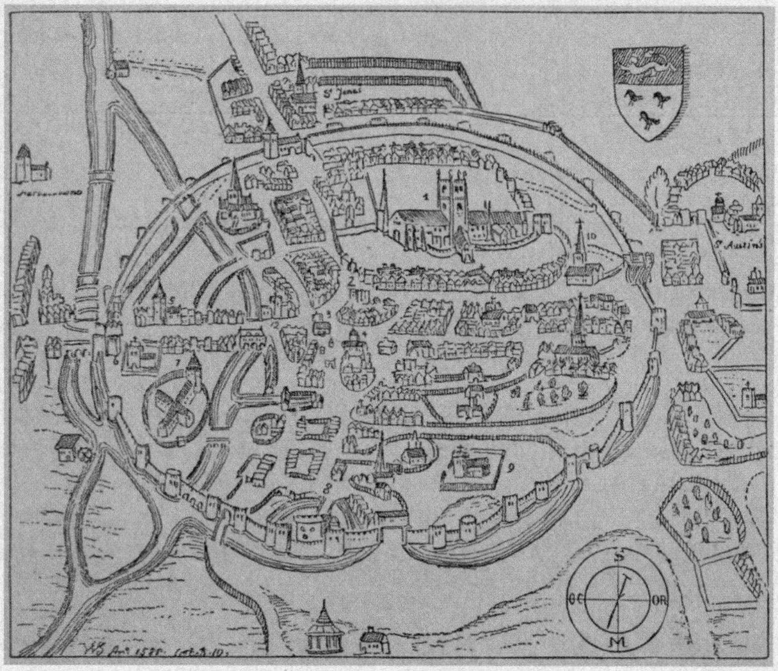

This medieval fifteenth-century map of Canterbury is in many ways a precursor of our modern tourist maps that indicate the "must see" sights of a visitor's destination. Canterbury was an English tourist attraction as early as the Roman occupation of the island—Julius Caesar and the Emperor Claudius were early visitors. But Canterbury's great fame as a pilgrimage site began when the Archbishop of Canterbury, the most influential bishop in the English Catholic Church, was killed in the cathedral by knights who claimed they were sent to conduct the assassination by the King of England, Henry II. The Archbishop, Thomas à Becket, immediately became regarded as a martyr for the cause of religious freedom. King Henry himself visited Canterbury as a pilgrim, asking forgiveness for his sins and walking barefoot to the shrine of the man he may have ordered murdered. Thomas was quickly made a saint, and the site of his murder became a destination for medieval pilgrims seeing forgiveness for their sins.

Such a pilgrimage is described by Geoffrey Chaucer in his Canterbury Tales. Chaucer prefaces this work by describing how he joined near London with a group of 29 pilgrims on their way to Canterbury to visit Thomas à Becket's shrine. To ward off the boredom of the trip, the pilgrims agree to tell tales (two on the way to Canterbury and two on the journey back), and whoever told the best tale was to be rewarded with a supper paid for by the others. Chaucer's resultant stories still remain as one of the greatest works of English literature.

Canterbury's popularity as a pilgrimage site continued throughout the Middle Ages. Although the most famous landmark remained the cathedral, the church of St. Dunstan attracted the increased attention of pilgrims in the late sixteenth century, since that church became the final resting place of the head of Sir Thomas More (1478–1535). This noted English lawyer, scholar, and humanist served as King Henry VIII's chancellor before refusing to deny the legitimacy of the king's first marriage and later failing to recognize Henry as the head of the church in England in place of the pope. More was imprisoned, refused to change his position, was put on trial, and was convicted of treason. He was beheaded in London, but his head found its final resting place in Canterbury. Henry VIII went on to confiscate much of the wealth of Canterbury, including donations of pilgrims over the centuries, in order to increase revenue. He also discouraged pilgrimage to the shrines, but Canterbury's popularity as a visitor's site has maintained its popularity to the present day.

Questions to Consider

1. How would this map serve the purposes of a visitor unfamiliar with the city of Canterbury?
2. Do you think the lack of great detail would be of concern to viewers of this map?
3. The twelve sites named and numbered on the map are almost all churches. Why do you think that is the case?

French ruler to allow her to lead an army to relieve the besieged city of Orléans. Clad in white armor and riding a white horse, she inspired confidence and a feeling of invincibility in her followers, and in 1429 Orléans was rescued from what had seemed certain conquest. Joan was captured by the enemy, found guilty of bewitching the English soldiers, and burned at the stake. But her martyrdom seemed a turning point in the long struggle.

France's development of a permanent standing army and the greater use of gunpowder also began to transform the art of war. English resistance crumbled as military superiority now turned full circle; the English longbow was outmatched by French artillery. Of the vast territories they had once controlled in France, the English retained only Calais when the war ended in 1453.

The Hundred Years' War exhausted England and fueled discontent with the monarchy in Parliament and among the common people. Baronial rivalry to control both Parliament and the crown erupted into full-scale civil war known as the Wars of the Roses (1455–1485); the white rose was the symbol of the Yorkists, and the red rose the House of Lancaster. Thirty years of bloody civil war ended in 1485 with the victory of Henry Tudor over his rivals. His victory at Bosworth Field enabled him to become Henry VII, the first of the Tudor dynasty. Henry VII (1485–1509) proved to be a popular and effective monarch, bringing national unity and security to the English people.

The Hundred Years' War left France with a new national consciousness and royal power that was stronger than ever. Shortly after the war, Louis XI (1461–1483) continued the process of consolidating royal power. Astute and tireless, yet completely lacking in scruples, Louis XI earned himself the epithet the "universal spider" because of his constant intrigues. In his pursuit of power he used any weapon—violence, bribery, treachery—to obtain his ends. The "spider king" devoted his reign to restoring prosperity to his nation and to reducing the powers of the noble families still active and ambitious after the long war. Like Henry VII in England, Louis XI was one of the "new monarchs" who worked for the creation of a subject-sovereign relationship in their kingdoms, replacing the old feudal ties of personal fidelity.

Spain: Ferdinand and Isabella and the Reconquista

Spain became strongly centralized under an assertive and aggressive monarchy in 1479, when Isabella of Castile and Ferdinand of Aragon began a joint rule that united the Iberian peninsula except for Navarre, Portugal, and Granada. The "Catholic Majesties," the title the pope conferred on Ferdinand and Isabella, set out to establish effective royal control in all of Spain.

Ferdinand and Isabella believed that the church should be subordinate to royal government. By tactful negotiations, the Spanish sovereigns induced the pope to give them the right to make church appointments in Spain and to establish a Spanish court of **Inquisition** largely free of papal control. The Spanish Inquisition confiscated the property of many *conversos* (Jews and Muslims who had converted to Christianity to avoid persecution) and terrified the Christian clergy and laity into accepting royal absolutism as well as religious orthodoxy. Although the Inquisition greatly enhanced the power of the Spanish crown, it also caused many people to flee Spain and the threat of persecution. About 150,000 Spanish Jews, mainly merchants and professional people, fled to the Netherlands, England, North Africa, and the Ottoman Empire. Calling themselves Sephardim (su-faer-DUIM), many of these exiles retained their Spanish language and culture into the twentieth century.

Inquisition—A special Roman Catholic court directed to search out and punish heretics, believers in doctrines other than those prescribed by the Church.

The uniting of Castile and Aragon, represented here by Isabella and Ferdinand, provided the foundation for the dominant Spanish state in the sixteenth century.

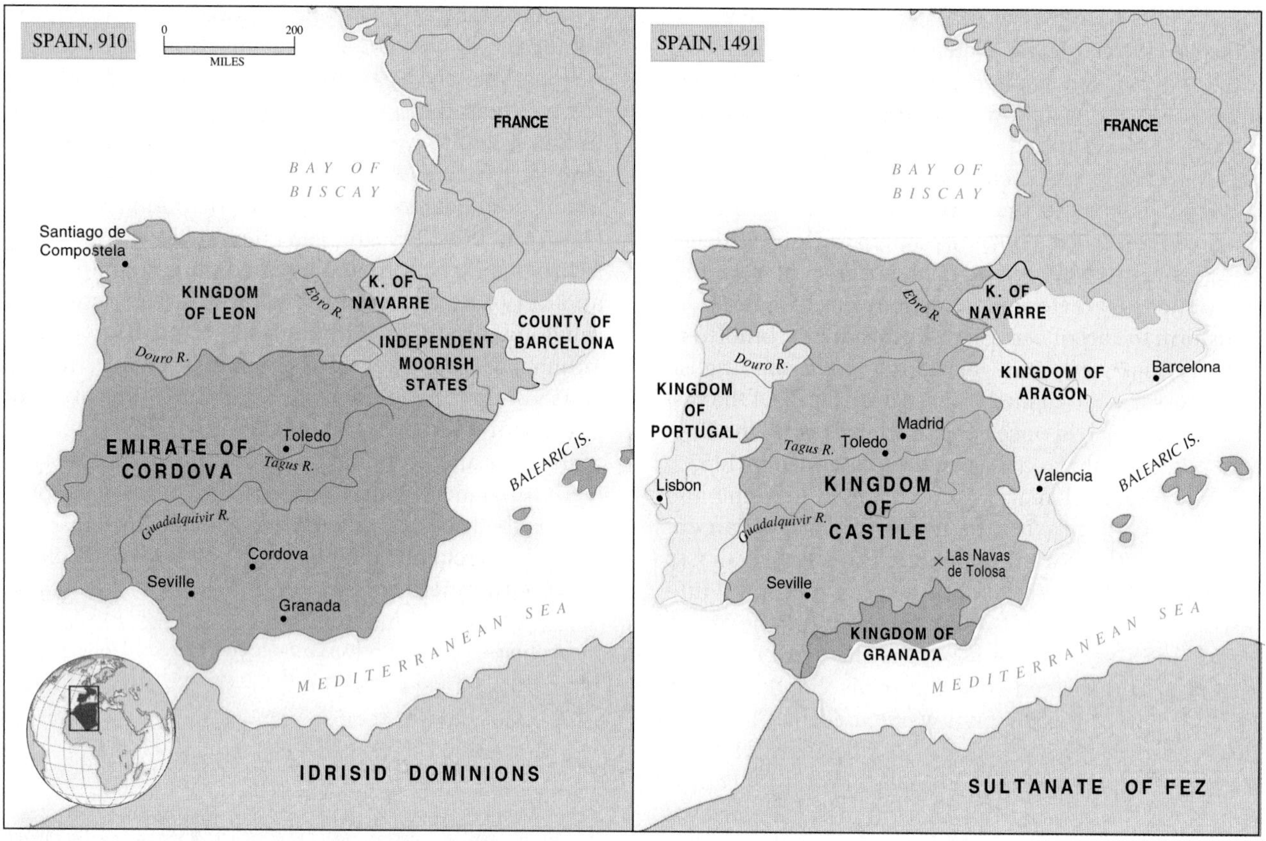

The progress of nation-building in Spain was linked to the Reconquista, the effort to expel the Muslims from the peninsula—in 1492 the kingdom of Granada, the East Muslim stronghold in Spain, fell to the Spanish.

Another manifestation of Spanish absolutism, defined by Isabella herself as "one king, one law, one faith," was the intentional neglect of the Cortes of Castile and Aragon. These representative assemblies, having emerged in the twelfth century, never were allowed by the monarchy to take an effective position as legislative bodies.

One of the most dramatic achievements of the Catholic Majesties was the completion of the *Reconquista* in 1492 with the defeat of Granada, the last Moorish state on the Iberian Peninsula. This occurred in same year that Columbus claimed the New World for Spain. Before Ferdinand died in 1516, a dozen years after Isabella, he seized the part of Navarre that lay south of the Pyrenees. This acquisition, together with the conquest of Granada, completed the unification of the Spanish nation-state.

Portugal

The western part of the Iberian Peninsula, Portugal, had a different historical evolution than did Spain. There was never a classic feudal tradition in the country, in which kings gave grants of land and positions to their vassals; rather the country was dominated by strong regional barons against whom the kings would struggle during the thirteenth century. But during the fourteenth century the centralizing power of monarchy began to impose its will over the country, and the Avis dynasty would rule Portugal from 1384 to 1580.

As will be shown in Chapter 16, the Portuguese were the first Europeans to venture out into the Atlantic in search of new business and resources. The person most known for this adventure was Prince Henry (1394–1460), the Navigator. He established an observatory where advances in navigation and ship making were made. In 1411, he crossed the Straits of Gibraltar and captured the Moroccan city of Ceuta (SIU-ta). During his life his sailors took the Azores and penetrated as far south as Senegal. In response to the economic stimulus of new markets and resources, Portugal doubled its population between 1400 and 1600 and established a global trading empire, however briefly. Then in 1580, during the reign of the Spanish Habsburg, Philip II, Spain incorporated Portugal into its realm.

Central Europe 1300–1521

Central Europe at this time included the Holy Roman Empire, Italy, and the Catholic nations of Poland, the Czech lands of Bohemia and Moravia, and Hungary. The history of this region was largely one of conflict:

political (Empire-Papacy), ethnic (German-Slav), or religious (Orthodox-Catholic). The region was, however, tied together by economics. It comprised an economic zone anchored on the west by the Rhine river, the primary route of the overland trade from the Mediterranean to the North Sea and beyond to the Baltic Sea and Russia. The cities of the **Hanseatic League** dominated the northern portions of this trade route, trading primarily in beer, wool, wood, and grain. Until the opening of the Atlantic trade routes in the sixteenth century, this zone experienced comparative economic well-being and important cultural exchange, despite the plague and wars.

The Holy Roman Empire

In the late Middle Ages, the Holy Roman Empire lapsed progressively into political disunity. In 1273 the imperial crown was given to the weak Count Rudolf of the House of Habsburg. During the remainder of the Middle Ages, the Habsburgs had amazing success in territorial acquisition; Rudolf himself acquired Austria through marriage, and, thereafter, the Habsburgs ruled their holdings from Vienna.

While the empire grew, however, its authority over its constituent states weakened. In 1356 the German nobility won significant victory in their efforts to avoid the creation of a powerful monarchy. **The Golden Bull,** a document that served as the political constitution of Germany until early in the nineteenth century, established a procedure by which seven German electors—three archbishops and four lay princes—chose the emperor. The electors and other important princes were given rights that made them virtually independent rulers, and the emperor could take no important action without the consent of the imperial feudal assembly, the Diet, which met infrequently. The empire, including 2000 independent lesser nobles, 66 autonomous cities, over 100 imperial counts, 30 secular princes, and 70 quasi-independent bishoprics was loosely governed by the Imperial Diet.

Despite the absence of political unity with the Empire, the Habsburg family managed to vastly expand its power in the fifteenth century. They achieved this primarily through successful marriage alliances and not by battle. Most marriage contracts among royal families involved a clause in which, in the case of the death of one of the participants in the marriage, all of the holdings of that person would pass to the survivor. The Habsburgs started this period of marital expansion in 1477 when Frederick III, largely ineffectual in the face of attacks by the Hungarians, arranged the marriage of his son Marximilian I to Maria of Burgundy—whose family laid claim to the lands of northeastern France and the Low Countries. Their marriage produced one son, Philip.

When Frederick died, Maximilian picked up his deceased father's Austrian lands, and then put together a marriage alliance between his son Philip and the daughter of the Spanish king, Juana. Although their marriage ended sadly, they produced a number of children, three of whom became important: Charles, Ferdinand, and Maria. Charles (1516–1556) became Holy Roman Emperor in 1519 and controlled the family's central and western holdings—including Spain and its world empire. Ferdinand headed the eastern part of the Empire, and Maria was married off to the king of Hungary, Louis II. When Louis was killed by the Turks at Mohacs in 1526, Maria Habsburg received her late husband's holdings.

The Hapsburgs' rise to power was not unnoticed at the time, and a phrase made the rounds, *Bella gerant alii, tu felix Austria nube* ("Let the others fight wars; you lucky Austrian, marry"[2]).

Because of his long reign and political skill, the Austrian monarch Frederick III (r. 1440–1493) started the successful policy of favorable marriage alliances that led to the Habsburgs ruling over a world empire in the sixteenth century.

Hanseatic League—A commercial league of mostly German cities extending from the English Channel to the eastern end of the Baltic Sea that was active between the thirteenth and seventeenth centuries.

Golden Bull—A document issued from the Holy Roman Emperor King Charles IV in 1356 that served as the political constitution of the German speaking lands until the nineteenth century.

Switzerland

In 1291, citizens in the German-speaking parts of the Alps began the drive to separate themselves from the Habsburg-dominated Empire. In 1291 the three cantons that controlled the access to Italy through the Saint Gothard Pass made an alliance to protect their independence. Fourteen years later they fought off the Habsburgs at the battle of Mortgaten, thus beginning the history of the country of Switzerland.

Because of its location on the overland route between the Mediterranean and the Rhine road to the North Sea, the region became rich. In addition, the Swiss artisans became known throughout Europe for the quality of their weapons. As we saw in Chapter 14, the region became touched by the currents of the Reformation during the career of Ulrich Zwingli.

Italy

After 1300, the middle and southern parts of the Italian peninsula gained a bit of distance from the Germans. In southern Italy, the Angevin dynasty asserted itself, while in the center the papacy worked to extend its holdings. Between Rome and the Alps, the rich and powerful city-states of Genoa, Milan, and Florence joined with Venice to construct their own diplomatic and political structures.

The years between 1300 and 1500 were not stable: As one authority notes, it was a time of threatened cities, kingdoms without kings, feudal holdings in transition to becoming principalities. Throughout the fourteenth and early fifteenth centuries the area was marked by intra-city conflicts fought using mercenary forces known as the ***condotierri*** (kon-do-TIER-ree). These mercenaries, many of them Spanish, fought for pay and would change sides in mid-battle if a better offer was made by their opponents. Economic developments shifted the political center of gravity during the 1400s to the northern cities from the Kingdom of Sicily and the Papal States.

As we saw in Chapter 14, in the northern Italian cities, new, bourgeois elites led by families such as the Medici accumulated great wealth from the wool business and banking to sponsor the great artists and thinkers of the middle classes. In 1454 they tired of their ongoing conflicts and at the Treaty of Lodi worked out a way of getting along, including exchanges of ambassadors with extraterritoriality. Unfortunately, all of the new peace was destroyed when the French invaded in 1494, and Italy became an object of and no longer a subject in European diplomacy. Incipient steps toward some sort of Italian sovereignty would have to wait nearly four centuries before being realized.

condotierri—Mercenaries employed by the Italian city-states during the conflicts of the fourteenth and fifteenth centuries.

The Catholic Frontier: Poland, Bohemia, and Hungary

East of the empire and north of the Italian peninsula, the frontiers of the Roman Catholic zone were to be found. In the tenth century, three peoples along the frontier accepted Roman Catholic Christianity: the Poles (966), the Czechs (864), and the Hungarians (1000). They joined a singular religious community that stretched from the Bug River to the Straits of Gibraltar to Iceland. Common threads uniting this community were the Latin language and a belief in papal authority. Irish and German missionaries had carried the Roman faith to this frontier area, and they were followed and sustained by a Germanic population movement, the *Drang nach Osten* ("drive to the east"). The royal families of the Poles, Czechs, and Hungarians intermarried with those of France, Luxembourg, and Austria and they participated fully in all of the major events and movements of the Western tradition. As converts to Catholicism, they proudly saw themselves, in Oscar Halecki's words, as the borderlands of civilization—facing Orthodox and even Turkish and Mongol attacks.[3]

Unlike the centralizing tendencies in western Europe where kings became stronger than their nobles, in east Central Europe—especially in Poland and Hungary—the nobles jealously guarded their authority in the fourteenth and fifteenth centuries, leading to weakened central power.

The church played a key role in both the uniting of the countries and the formation of the national identity, lending its legitimacy by converting the royal family in each country. In the course of the tenth century the Polish Piasts (895–1306), the Bohemian Přemyslids (PSHEM-ui-sleds; 895–1306), and the Hungarian Arpads (896–1310) formed the dynasties that would rule their respective countries until 1300. The Poles, Czechs, and Hungarians suffered from the Mongol invasions in the 1240s but recovered quickly within a generation. Each of their states had close commercial and cultural ties with the Germans, and—sometimes went to war with them.

The cities of Poland and Hungary tended to be dominated by Germans and Jews, the bulk of the indigenous people living as serfs. In Bohemia, however, urban life was dominated by the Czech people, still with a healthy representation of Germans and Jews. The Czechs would be the only people of eastern Europe to share fully in the urban lifestyle of Central Europe. The three countries had their individual legal traditions—the Hungarians, for example, refer to their Golden Bull of 1222 as the equivalent to the English Magna Carta in terms of its guarantees of liberties.

The region did not suffer as heavily from the Black Plague as western Europe, and as a result Poland, Bohemia, and Hungary experienced a golden age of cultural and economic development in the fourteenth century. There were universities established at Prague (1348), Krakow (1364), and Pecs (1369) and scholars from those schools participate in the humanist movement in the fifteenth century. Even with their economic and cultural progress, the three states argued over a number of issues as their respective kings sought to expand their influences and fought over regions such Silesia.

During that fourteenth century, the originating dynasties died out in Hungary and Bohemia. Foreign kings such as the Angevin Louis the Great of Hungary (1342–1382), and the Luxembourger Charles the Great of Bohemia (1333–1378) were elected by the powerful nobles and bourgeoisie of the area. The last Piast, Casimir the Great of Poland (1333–1370) led his country through its golden age, but after his death the Poles resorted to a system of elective kingship.

This well-being of the fourteenth century, however, would not last long because of the expansion of Russia to the east, Sweden to the north, and the Ottoman Empire to the south. Internal problems also would lead to a weakening of the realms. Elective kings in Poland and Hungary frittered away their central powers to satisfy the demands of the nobles who elected them. The weakening of central power hit its peak in Poland, where successive royal elections cut the powers of the monarchy until the installation of the ***Liberum* Veto**, an act that allowed one member of the nobility, the *szlachta* (SCHLOK-tah), to block a king's program by his negative vote.

In 1386 Poland united with Lithuania—the last pagan country in Europe—and became the largest state in Europe. Invasions from the east and the west, however, eroded the strength of this state. The Poles had earlier added to their own problems in 1225 when they invited the crusading order of the Teutonic knights into Poland to aid in the combat against the indigenous Baltic peoples to the north, the Prus. The Teutonic knights, out of work after failed crusades in the Eastern Mediterranean, slaughtered the Prus, established their own state based around present-day Kaliningrad (Koenigsberg), and called it Prussia. They proved a considerable threat to the Poles and were not defeated until the battle of Tannenberg in 1410. Later the Teutons would turn their territory of West Prussia over to the Poles and keep East Prussia as a fief of the Polish crown. Poland would face competition and eventual destruction by Russia, Prussia, Sweden, and Austria in the seventeenth and eighteenth centuries.

The Bohemians became the richest part of the Catholic orbit and went on to challenge the Germans politically, economically, and religiously. The Golden Bull of 1356 made the Bohemian king one of the seven electors of the Holy Roman Empire. We have already discussed the religious controversy between the Czechs and the Germans during the late fourteenth century. The creation of the Hussite Church after Jan Hus's immolation led to four crusades being preached by the Catholic Church against the forces at Prague. The Czechs successfully defended themselves under leaders such as John Žižka (ZHISH-kah) and they would continue to progress, growing economically and politically until the seventeenth century—when they were defeated in the first phase of the Thirty Years' War.

The Hungarians experienced a brilliant fifteenth century under János Hunyadi (YAWN-nosh HOON-ia-dee) and his son and successor Mathias Corvinus. As Magyar aristocrats, they ended the period of foreign kings. János Hunyadi, by his wealth and military prowess, paved the way for his son Mathias to be elected king in 1458, who came to be known as Mathias Corvinus. During his 32-year reign, Mathias established close ties with the Italian Renaissance cities, especially Florence. Scholars and artists at his court participated fully in the cultural movements of the

Matthias Corvinus was a true "renaissance man." He was a patron of the arts, supporter of artists and writers, and a collector of books and manuscripts. He was also one of the pioneers in introducing printing to Central and Eastern Europe.

***Liberum* Veto**—In order to guard against the potential power of a strong central monarchy, the Polish nobles in 1652 installed the Liberum Veto, an act that allowed one member of the nobility to block the king's program by his single negative vote in the noble assembly.

time. He founded a printing press and had one of the most important libraries in Europe. Although he was unable to increase his central power in competition with the Czechs and the Poles, he did manage to capture Vienna. After he died in 1490 from unknown causes, the Hungarian magnates went back to electing foreign kings. The Hungarians became disunited and were finally defeated by the Ottoman Turks at the battle of Mohacs (1526). Hungary was divided into three zones, the larger part controlled directly by the Ottomans.

THE RELIGIOUS-POLITICAL FUSION

- *The framers of the American Constitution demanded a total separation of church and state. What examples can you find in the wars of religion between 1517 and 1648 to support their belief in a separation of faith and politics?*

The papacy's political power had been in a continual decline since the thirteenth century. In Central Europe, local elites fought the Catholic clergy and the excluded lower classes for political control. In the Atlantic states of England, France, and Spain, the monarchs became increasingly independent of the Pope's demands. The French invasion at the end of the fifteenth century made the Italian peninsula an arena for desperate struggle between the Habsburg and French Valois dynasties that would last until 1559. The Papal States became a political pawn. The papacy's weaknesses were exploited by the troops of Charles V when they sacked Rome in 1527. Protestant leaders such as Martin Luther profited from the disarray in the Catholic world, and his followers combined religion and politics in a new and explosive way that Catholic leaders quickly learned to emulate. The result would be a series of religious-political conflicts that would last until 1648.

MAP Religious Diversity in Western Europe

Protestant Politics

The rise of the Protestants finally liberated the nation-state from any claim of authority by the church. As we saw in Chapter 14, Luther spelled out that humans have two obligations: first and most importantly, loyalty to God and second, loyalty to the earthly government. Luther's positions on church-state relations found biblical support in the words of Christ: "Therefore, render unto Caesar, that which is Caesar's and unto God, that which is God's" (Matthew 22:21).

Luther immediately gained support from German and Scandinavian rulers and in every city along the Baltic coast where there was a German-speaking majority—including in Poland and present-day Estonia. Luther supported the repression of the protesting German knights and the crushing of the Peasant's Revolt in 1524–1525. In addition, Luther said little about the Protestant princes' taking the considerable wealth of the Catholic Church

The religious split between Lutherans and Catholics soon took the form of military alliances. Lutheran princes organized for defense in the **Schmalkaldic League** and were not immediately challenged because Emperor Charles V had to deal with the French and Turkish threats. A low-intensity, sporadic civil war dragged on in the empire until after Luther's death in 1546. It ended with the Peace of Augsburg in 1555, when the imperial princes were permitted to choose between Lutheranism and Catholicism in their state churches, thus increasing their independence from the emperor. In addition, Catholic properties confiscated before 1552 were retained by Lutheran principalities, which provided a means for financing their policies.

Henry VIII's Break with Rome

In England, the conflict between the church and state had little if anything to do with differences over religious doctrine. As we saw in Chapter 14, Henry VIII (r. 1509–1547) broke from the church because he needed a legitimate male heir. When Henry's wife Catherine of Aragon failed to provide him with an heir, he sought in 1527 to have his marriage to her annulled so he could remarry. For political reasons, however, the Pope refused to grant an annulment, and Henry forced the clergy into proclaiming him head of a separate, English church.

The Anglican Church was essentially the same as the Catholic Church, with the exception that the English monarch served as the head of the church, the clergy could marry, and English replaced Latin as the official language of the church. Henry also extracted from Parliament the authority to appoint bishops, and Parliament ended all payment of revenues to Rome. In 1539 Parliament completed its seizure of monastery lands and the wealth of pilgrimage sites such as Canterbury Cathedral. While Henry's break from the church left a legacy of turmoil and strife that would last for another 150 years, his actions placed both temporal and spiritual authority in the

---

Schmalkaldic League—A defensive alliance of Lutheran princes organized in 1531 under the leadership of Philip the Magnanimous of Hesse to defend themselves against the Catholic powers of the Holy Roman Empire.

hands of the monarchy, strengthening the power of the English state.

Calvinist Variations

Calvin viewed politics as a theocratic exercise—the laws of God become the laws of the state. His plans for a city government in Geneva called for domination by the clergy—full control over moral and religious behavior—and banishment of all dissidents. Though met with grudging opposition, he gradually increased his power through support from the Protestant refugees who poured into the city. His influence climaxed after a failed "revolt of the godless" in 1555. From that year until his death in 1564, he dominated the council, ruling Geneva with an iron hand, within the letter, but not the spirit, of the original ordinances. As we saw in Chapter 15, he imposed a religious totalitarianism over Geneva, and religious police held the power to investigate every detail of private life.

DOCUMENT
Calvin on Predestination

In advising people from outside of Geneva, he said that political authorities had to consult with the church on policies. He also said, however, that it was the duty of Christians to obey the state in secular matters. When he discussed how governments should be run, he advocated the concept of representative government.

Many of the divergent Protestant splinter groups up and down the Rhine saw different lessons in scripture. The majority of them were indifferent or antagonistic to secular government; many favored pacifism and substitution of the church for the state.

The legacy of the Protestant Reformation on politics was mixed. Luther, Henry VIII, Calvin, and the Protestant radicals all advocated different combinations of the church and the state. Between 1517 and 1564, however, political life in Europe became revolutionized. The change from the concept of Christendom in 1300 to communities based on faith and allegiance imposed by the state brought with it much death, suffering, and destruction.

WARS OF RELIGIONS: THE SPANISH HABSBURGS' QUEST FOR EUROPEAN HEGEMONY, 1556–1598

- *Did Philip II of Spain use the powers of the state to spread the influence of the Catholic Church, or did he use the Church for political gain?*

After the 1560s, religious fanaticism, both Protestant and Catholic, combined with pragmatic politics to form a combustible mixture. Sometimes religious conflict caused the reshaping of the old political system to justify movements against royal authority. More often, it popularized centralized monarchies, whose rulers promised to restore order by wielding power. Despite pious declarations, kings and generals in this period conducted war with little regard for moral principles; indeed, as time passed they steadily subordinated religious concerns to dynastic ambitions or national interests. This change, however, came slowly and was completed only in 1648 after Europe was thoroughly exhausted by the human suffering and material destruction of religious wars.

Until the end of the sixteenth century, Spain, led by Philip II, attempted to impose its will over the Continent. When he took power in 1556, he looked across the Pyrenees and across the Mediterranean and saw a Europe split by religious strife and still threatened by the presence of the Ottoman Empire. In Central Europe, the Peace of Augsburg ended a short war in Germany and sought to bring an accord between the Catholics and Lutherans. Even before Calvin died in 1564, however, his movement was spreading rapidly throughout the Continent. The Council of Trent launched a formidable counteroffensive, led by the Jesuits and supported by the Spanish and Austrian Habsburgs, against all Protestants. England remained on the verge of religious civil war after the death of Queen Mary, while France plunged into three decades of conflict after the extinction of the Valois line to the throne in 1559. Religious conflict broke out in the Spanish Netherlands, and in eastern Europe, militant Catholicism reversed the gains made by Protestants in the previous half-century. Philip saw opportunity in

War and Politics in the Age of Philip II

1556–1598	Reign of Philip II of Spain
1558–1603	Reign of Elizabeth I of England
1561–1593	Religious wars in France
1566	Revolt in the Netherlands
1571	European forces defeat Turks at Lepanto
1572	Massacre of St. Bartholomew's Eve in Paris
1581	Dutch United Provinces declare independence from Spain
1587	Dutch Republic formed
1588	English defeat Spanish Armada

this tumultuous setting where the politics of religion dominated the scene in Europe.

The Era of Spanish Habsburg Dominance

Although it was a relatively underdeveloped and sparsely populated country of 8 million people, Spain, under Philip II (1556–1598), was the strongest military power in Europe. Seven centuries of resistance against the Moors (see Chapter 9) had formed a chivalric nobility that excelled in the military arts, if not also in business. This tradition, in addition to the promise of empire, saw the rigidly disciplined Spanish infantry absorb neighboring Portugal and fan out around the world as conquistadores, bringing back silver in seemingly unlimited quantities from the Americas. Working in tandem with the army was the Spanish Church, whose courts of the Inquisition, which had earlier banished the Jews, were now being used to eliminate the few remaining Moors and Spanish Protestants.

Philip willingly took on the Habsburgs' global burdens of maintaining Catholic orthodoxy, fighting the Turks, and imposing his will on his troublesome European neighbors. He considered this responsibility a part of his inheritance from his father, Charles V, whose long reign ended in 1556 when he abdicated his imperial throne and entered a monastery. At that time, Charles split his Habsburg holdings. His brother Ferdinand acquired control of Austria, Bohemia, and Hungary and became Holy Roman Emperor in 1556. Philip received Naples, Sicily, Milan, the Netherlands, Spain, and a vast overseas empire, which was much more lucrative than the traditional imperial domain in Central and eastern Europe. Indeed, the division of Habsburg lands appeared to be a blessing for Philip, allowing him to shed his father's worrisome "German problem" and concentrate more effectively on his Spanish realm.

Philip was a slightly built, somber, hardworking man. He was totally absorbed by the tasks of running a worldwide empire and rarely broke away to enjoy the luxurious life offered by his position. He seldom delegated authority, and his councilors served more as advisers than as administrators. Philip labored endlessly, reading and annotating official documents and dominating the *Cortes* (the traditional assembly of estates) of Castile. He married each of his four wives—Maria of Portugal, Mary of England, Elizabeth of France, and Anne of Austria, his niece—for political reasons; except for Mary, they bore his children but ate at his table only during official banquets. Elizabeth was his favorite, as were her daughters, who received some of his few open shows of tenderness and loving concern.

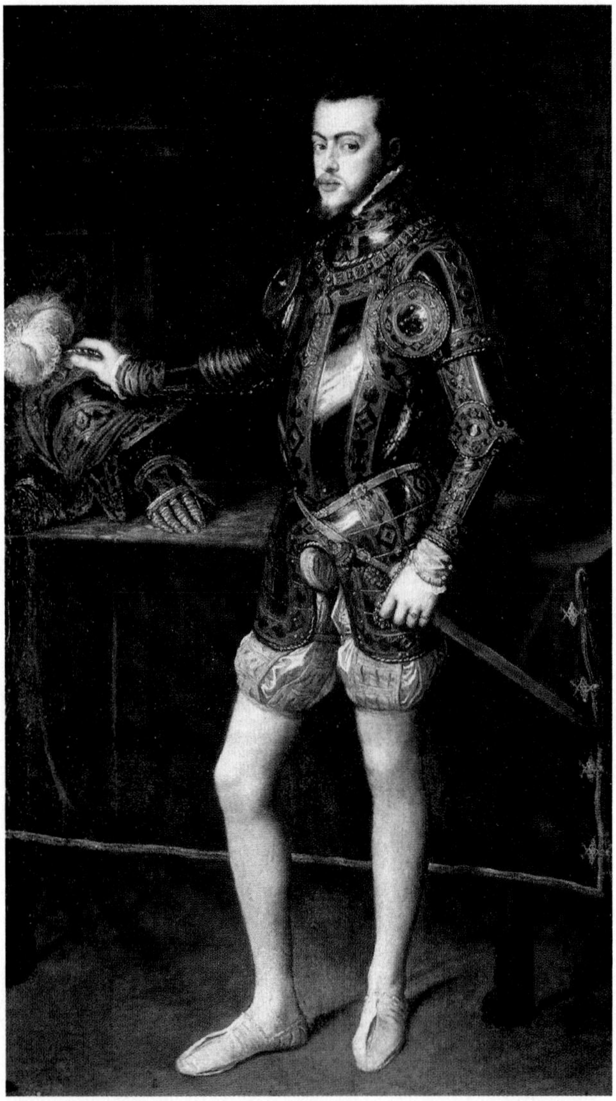

Philip II dominated the European scene during the second half of the sixteenth century. Even though he worked hard to assure Spanish Habsburg dominance, he failed to defeat the Dutch and the British and left Spain in an exhausted condition.

Philip took advantage of his role as defender of the Catholic faith. Although the church was wealthy and had unleashed the Inquisition to wipe out dissent, Philip used it to enforce Spanish traditions, arouse patriotism, and increase his popularity to strengthen the state. He was by no means a tool of the papacy: indeed, he defied more than one pope by denying jurisdiction over Spanish ecclesiastical courts, opposing the Council of Trent on clerical appointments, and fighting the Jesuits when they challenged his authority. He saw the Catholic Church as an arm of his government, and not vice versa.

Throughout his long reign, Philip continually encountered limitations to his authority. Spain had only recently been unified, and powerful nobles opposed him and his viceroys in their local councils. An overworked and overextended bureaucracy and a weak financial, communications, and industrial infrastructure placed the victories gained by the army and the state on a weak foundation. The backward Spanish sociopolitical system caused Philip many economic problems. Tax-exempt nobilities, comprising under 2 percent of the people, owned 95 percent of nonchurch land; the middle classes, overtaxed and depleted by purges of Jews and Moriscos (Spanish Muslims), were diminished; and the peasants were so exploited that production of food, particularly grains, was insufficient to feed the population. State regulation of industry and trade further limited revenues and forced primary reliance on precious metals from the Americas to fill the treasury, which ultimately produced a ruinous inflation. When his income failed to meet expenses, Philip borrowed at rising interest rates from Italian and Dutch banks. In 1557 and 1575 Philip had to suspend payments, effectively declaring national bankruptcy.

Revolt in the Netherlands

Philip's centralized rule encouraged some unity in Spain; the Netherlands, however, with its own traditions, was immediately suspicious of its foreign king who tried to enforce Catholic conformity. The Netherlands ("Low Countries") at the time also included modern Belgium, Luxembourg, and small holdings along 200 miles of marshy northern coast, an area not open to easy conquest. The geographical setting promoted strong local nobilities but also relatively independent peasants and townsmen. Even in medieval times, cities were centers of rapidly expanding commerce: of the 300 walled towns in 1560, some 19 had populations of over 10,000. (At the same time, England had only three or four of that size.) Antwerp was the commercial hub of northern Europe, serving as the crossroads of the Hanseatic League and the Italian-English trade axis. The combination of geography and wealth created a

The inherent logic of balance-of-power politics is readily evident in this map showing the extent of Habsburg—both Spanish and Austrian—holdings.

spirit of independence in religious affairs, as Lutherans, Calvinists, and Anabaptists were found in great numbers. Charles V had attempted sporadically to suppress the Protestants and had even burned a few notable heretics. But his status as a native son allowed him to maintain a tenuous stability in the region.

Anabaptist Torture in Muenster

Charles's daughter, Margaret of Parma (1522–1586) served as Philip's first regent for the Netherlands. She was sensitive to the religious complexities of her task; Philip, however, ordered a crackdown on the Protestants. Margaret introduced the Inquisition to fight heresy, a policy that forced leading nobles to leave her council and provoked vocal protests from her subjects. As the Inquisition did its work and executed prominent Protestants, the protests became loud and violent. Finally the so-called Calvinist Fury erupted in 1566, terrorizing Catholics and desecrating 400 churches. Most of the people in the Netherlands were shocked by the excesses of the radicals and voiced their support for Margaret.

Philip's response was to send the duke of Alva to the Netherlands with 10,000 Spanish troops, a great baggage train, and 2000 camp followers to establish order. Alva removed Margaret from her regency and clamped a brutal military dictatorship on the country. By decree, he centralized church administration, imposed new taxes, and established a special tribunal, soon dubbed the Council of Blood, to stamp out treason and heresy. During Alva's regime between 1567 and 1573, at least 8000 people were killed, including the powerful counts of Egmont and Horne. In addition, the Catholic terror deprived 30,000 people of their property and forced 100,000 to flee the country.

By 1568 Alva's excesses had provoked open rebellion—the first national liberation struggle, led by William of Orange (1533–1584), nicknamed William the Silent. Constant early defeats left him impoverished and nearly disgraced, but in 1572 the port of Brielle fell to his privateers, the "sea beggars," an event that triggered revolts throughout the north. Soon thereafter, William cut the dikes near Zeeland and mired down a

In his 1564 rendering of the biblical account of The Massacre of the Innocents *(1566–1567; Matthew 2:16), Pieter Brueghel the Elder anticipated well the horrors of violence that would befall the Netherlands.*

weary Spanish army. The continuing war was marked by savage ferocity, such as the sack of Antwerp by mutinous Spanish soldiers (1576). At the Spanish siege of Maestricht (MICE-treeschte) in 1579, women fought beside their men on the walls, and Spanish soldiers massacred the population, raping women first before tearing some limb from limb in the streets. That same year, in the Pacification of Ghent, Catholics and Protestants from the 17 provinces united to defy Philip, demand the recall of his army, and proclaim the authority of their traditional assembly, the States General.

Unfortunately for the rebel cause, this unity was soon destroyed by religious differences between militant northern Calvinists and Catholic southerners, particularly the many powerful nobles. The Spanish commander Alexander Farnese exploited these differences by restoring lands and privileges to the southern nobles. He was then able to win victories that induced the ten southern provinces to make peace with Spain in 1579. The Dutch, now alone, proclaimed their continued resistance to Spanish persecution and, in 1581, declared their independence from Spain. They persisted after William of Orange was assassinated in 1584, but meanwhile, the Spanish continued their war on heresy, butchering, burning, and burying alive Protestants who would not renounce their faith. The conflict lasted until a truce was negotiated in 1609.

Religious Wars in France

Although frustrated in the Netherlands, Philip did not face his father's French problem. According to the Treaty of Cateau-Cambrésis (KA-tow kam-BRAY-sees) in 1559, France gave up claims in Italy and the Netherlands. This humiliating surrender to the Habsburgs marked a definite turning point in French history. With its government bankrupt, its economy nearly prostrate, and its people disillusioned, France lost its leverage in foreign affairs as civil wars encouraged by Philip wasted the country during the next four decades.

Beneath the prevailing religious contention was another bitter struggle between the haves and have-nots. High prices, high rents, and high taxes drove the lower classes to riot and rebel against urban oligarchies, noble landlords, and government tax collectors. The social unrest continued sporadically throughout the sixteenth century. It brought no improvement of conditions for suffering peasants and town artisans, but it did frighten the wealthy nobles, merchants, and bankers whose mildly divergent interests were unified by threats from below.

By the 1560s Calvinism had become a major outlet for the frustrations of the discontented. Although outlawed and persecuted earlier, the movement grew rapidly during the decade. It converted approximately 15 percent of the population, most of whom were of the lower urban middle class; however, the leadership came mainly from the nobility, 40 to 50 percent of whom accepted Calvinism. Their motives varied—although many were sincerely religious, most pursued political ends. Even among the lesser nobles, the Calvinist side promised military employment, political prominence, and a way for taking advantage of popular discontent. The movement's potential popular support was particularly appealing to contenders for the throne among the high nobility. In 1559 the Huguenots held a secret synod in Paris that drew representatives from 72 congregations and a million members. A distinct minority, they were nevertheless well-placed and well organized with articulate spokesmen and competent military leaders.

Religious, political, and social forces combined when France suffered the loss of King Henry II in 1559, who left his crown to his sickly 15-year-old son, Francis II. His young queen was Mary Stuart (later Mary, Queen of Scots), whose uncles, the brothers Guise, took actual control of the government. They were opposed by noble families from the Huguenot camp. Francis II died in 1560, and the crown passed to his 9-year-old brother Charles. At that time, however, the real power behind the throne was Charles's mother, Catherine de Medici. Single-minded, crafty, and ready to use any means, she was determined to save the throne for one of her three sons, none of whom had produced a male heir. Exploiting the split between the Guises—the champions of the Catholic cause—and their enemies, she assumed the regency for Charles. She then attempted, through reforms of the church, to reconcile the differences between Catholics and Protestants. In this endeavor she was unsuccessful, but she kept her tenuous control, using every political strategy, including a squadron of noble women who solicited information by seducing powerful nobles.

Religious war erupted in 1561; supported by substantial Spanish financial and military interventions, it lasted through eight uneasy truces until 1593. Fanaticism evoked the most violent and inhumane acts on both sides, as destructive raids, assassinations, and torturous atrocities became commonplace. Catherine maneuvered through war and uneasy peace, first favoring the Guises and then the Bourbons. In 1572, fearing that the Huguenots were gaining supremacy, she joined a Guise plot that resulted in the murder of some 10,000 Huguenots in Paris. This Massacre of St. Bartholomew's Eve was a turning point in decisively dividing the country. The final "war of the three Henries" in the 1580s involved Catherine's third son, Henry III, who became king upon the death of Charles in 1574. The king's rivals were Henry of Guise and the

Massacre of St. Bartholomew

Protestant Henry of Navarre. When the other two Henries were assassinated, Henry of Navarre proclaimed himself king of France in 1589. Spain would have little to fear from France for the next half-century.

Elizabethan England, 1558–1603

For most of the sixteenth century, Spain built its European foreign policies on the base of an English alliance. Despite Henry's breaking his marriage with Catherine of Aragon, the Spanish ambassadors did not give up their efforts to keep England in their camp. For the better part of his reign, Philip had to deal with England's most outstanding monarch, Elizabeth I, who ruled a country that was, as the earl of Essex put it, "little in territory, not extraordinarily rich and defended only by itself."[4]

Elizabeth, a superb image maker, projected the picture of a country united behind a national church, even as her government suppressed Catholicism, put down a northern rebellion, and avoided serious troubles with Scotland and Ireland. Elizabeth dealt with potential dangers from the great Catholic powers by playing them against each other. Such successes were seen as the natural result of her brilliance and courage. This image only partly reflected reality. The "Protestant Queen" detested most of the Protestants, especially those founded on the heretical traditions of the **Lollards.** Her support for Scottish and Dutch rebels went against her fervent belief in absolute monarchy. Her celebrated coy approach in encouraging but ultimately denying prospective royal suitors, despite the diplomatic advantages of the practice, often ran counter to her emotional inclinations, throwing her into momentary rages against her advisers.

But she had learned her lesson well from Tudor politics—to compromise and discount personal feelings for the larger interests of her realm. Consequently, England became her family and her primary interest. She was especially skilled at judging people, dealing with foreign diplomats in their own languages, and projecting her charisma in public speeches. With these notable talents, she brought the English people a new sense of national pride, often expressed in Shakespeare's plays. In the second half of the sixteenth century—in contrast to France—England gave the impression of having achieved relative peace and prosperity.

Elizabeth's earliest immediate danger emerged in Scotland, where Mary of Guise was regent for her daughter Mary Stuart, queen of both France and Scotland. French troops in Scotland supported this Catholic regime. Because Mary Stuart was also a direct descendant of Henry VII of England, she was a leading claimant for the English throne and a potential rallying symbol for Catholics who hoped to reestablish their faith in England. These expectations were diminished in 1559 when a zealous Calvinist named John Knox (1505–1572), fresh from Geneva, led a revolt of Scottish nobles. Aided by English naval forces, the Scots broke religious ties with Rome, established a Presbyterian (Calvinist) state church, and, with Elizabeth's help, drove out the French soldiers.

Another serious problem loomed in Ireland, where Spanish and papal emissaries used old grievances over taxes and religion to arouse uprisings against English rule. James Maurice, an Irish leader in the southwest, began a series of revolts in 1569. Eight years later, the pope helped raise troops and money for him on the Continent. An expedition in 1579 to aid the Irish rebels was ruthlessly suppressed, but fighting dragged on for four more years. In 1601 a more serious Irish rebellion aided by 3000 Spanish troops cost Elizabeth a third of her revenues. Although never directing a successful Irish policy, as has been true of all of her successors up to the present, she managed to escape catastrophe by her stubborn persistence.

Her innate pragmatism was most beneficial in quieting English sectarian strife. She despised **Puritans** and favored rich vestments for the clergy, but she thoroughly understood the practical necessity of securing Protestant political support. Moving firmly but slowly, Elizabeth re-created a nominal Protestant national church, but one similar to her father's. The queen's policy lessened religious controversy and persecution but failed to end either completely.

Elizabeth also faced a serious danger from abroad. In 1568, after Mary Stuart was forced into exile by her Protestant subjects, she was received in England by her royal cousin. Although kept, for all intents and purposes, a prisoner, she became involved in a series of Catholic plots, which appeared even more dangerous after the pope excommunicated Elizabeth in 1570. Philip of Spain aided the plotters but still hoped to enlist Elizabeth's cooperation in creating a Catholic hegemony in Europe.

Despite all her troubles, Elizabeth's reign showed marked economic improvement. By careful—some said stingy—financial management, her government reduced debt and improved national credit. A new coinage helped make London the financial center of Europe, especially after the Spanish destruction of Antwerp. Monopolies granted to joint stock companies promoted foreign trade and brought wealth into the country. By the end of her reign in 1603, England, despite festering social and religious problems, was the most prosperous state in Europe.

Lollards—Followers of John Wycliffe who spread his doctrines both openly and secretly throughout England in the fifteenth and sixteenth centuries.

Puritans—Those English protestants in the 1500s and 1600s who found the theology and worship services of the Church of England to be not in accord with Holy Scripture.

Lepanto and the Armada

Philip's wars against Turkey—including the destruction of the Turkish fleet at Lepanto off the western coast of Greece—promoted his image as the Catholic champion, boosted Spanish morale, and revived the traditional national pride in defending the faith. When Cyprus, the last Christian stronghold in the eastern Mediterranean, fell to the Turks in 1570, Philip responded to the pope's pleas and formed a Holy League to destroy Turkish naval power. Spanish and Venetian warships, together with smaller squadrons from Genoa and the Papal States, made up a fleet of over 200 vessels that drew recruits from all over Europe. In 1571 the Holy League's fleet and the Turkish navy clashed at Lepanto, off the western coast of Greece. Christian Europe scored a major victory over the Ottoman Empire, which would never pose a naval threat again. The Spanish king could bring all of his resources to bear in northwest Europe.

Philip's diplomatic efforts, particularly his marriage to Mary Tudor in 1558, his next marriage to Elizabeth of Valois in 1560, and his clumsy efforts to court Queen Elizabeth, brought no lasting influence over English or French policies. Indeed, English captains were preying on Spanish shipping in the Atlantic, and Dutch privateers, with English and Huguenot support, were diminishing the flow of vital supplies to northern Europe. In 1580, after nine years of frustration in the Netherlands, Philip launched the first phase of his new offensive policy, using military force to validate his claim to the Portuguese throne. As king of Portugal, he gained control of the Portuguese navy and Atlantic ports, where he began assembling an oceangoing fleet, capable of operations against the Dutch and English in their home waters.

Philip's last hope for an easy solution to his problems was dashed in 1587. Pressed by the pope and the English Catholic exiles, he had tried for years to use

This detail from a painting by artists in the school of Tintoretto dealing with the Battle of Lepanto presents the decisive battle for the control of the Mediterranean in a splendid light.

Mary Stuart to overthrow Elizabeth, regain England for Catholicism, and seize control of the country. But Mary's complicity in a plot against the English queen's life was discovered, and Elizabeth finally signed a death warrant. Mary's execution confirmed Philip's earlier decision that England had to be conquered militarily. In pursuing this end, Philip planned a "great enterprise," an invasion of England blessed by the pope.

The Spanish strategy depended on a massive fleet, known as the Invincible Armada. It was ordered to meet a large Spanish army in the southern Netherlands and land this force on the English coast. But in 1588, when the Armada sailed for Flanders, Dutch ships blocked the main ports, preventing the Spanish galleons from entering the shallow waters. Philip's project was then completely ruined when the smaller and more maneuverable English ships, commanded by Charles Howard and captained by privateers such Sir Francis Drake and Sir John Hawkins, scattered the Armada in the English Channel. Retreating through the North Sea, the Spanish fleet was then battered by a severe storm, called the "Protestant wind," and forced to make a miserable return to Spain.

DOCUMENT
John Hawkins Reports on the Spanish Armada

Philip II's Failure in Europe

Contrary to English expectations, the defeat of the Armada brought no immediate shift in the international balance of power. Spain retained its military might, built new ships, and defended its sea-lanes. On the ground, the Spanish infantry would not suffer defeat until 1643 at the battle of Rocroi (ruh-KWAH). In fact, all the major combatants were exhausted, a factor that largely explains the Bourbons' acquisition of the French crown and continued Dutch independence. Lingering wars brought new opportunities for France and the Netherlands, but only more exhaustion for England and Spain.

During the last decade of Philip's life, his multiple failures foreshadowed the decline of his country. He encountered rebellion in Aragon, quarreled with Pope Clement VIII over recognizing the Bourbons (see following), and sent two more naval expeditions against England, both of which were scattered by storms. Before he died in 1598, he turned over the Netherlands to his favorite daughter Clara Isabella Eugenia and her husband, Archduke Albert, an Austrian Habsburg. He had also made peace with France. He left Spain bankrupt for the third time during his reign, having wasted the country's considerable resources and sacrificed its future to his dynastic pride. His son Philip III (r. 1598–1621), no match for his father, presided in a lazy, extravagant, and frivolous way over the beginning of the long decline of the Spanish Empire.

England experienced similar difficulties. Though sea raids on Spanish shipping continued and brought in badly needed money, all of Elizabeth's grand projects failed, such as in 1596 when the earl of Essex plundered Cadiz but missed the Spanish treasure fleet. Conflicts in France, the Netherlands, and Ireland drained her treasury, and Parliament delayed in granting her funds to continue fighting. Social and religious tensions surfaced at the turn of the seventeenth century, and the Puritans proved to be an especially irritating group for the aging queen. At her death in 1603, she left no successors, and the Stuarts took the English throne.

The Dutch declaration of independence in 1581 reflected more concern for aristocratic privilege and national survival than democratic principles, but it served as a basis for holding the northern Netherlands together. After finding no acceptable French or English person to be their king, the Dutch created a republic in 1587 and tenaciously persevered to sign a truce with Spain in 1609. As time passed, their growing maritime trade and naval power guaranteed their security.

The post-Armada stalemate most benefited the French. With the death of the last Valois claimant in 1589, the Bourbon Protestant king of Navarre was proclaimed king of France as Henry IV. This act threw the Catholic Holy League into a fanatical antiroyalist frenzy and encouraged Philip's military intervention in France to support his daughter's claim to the throne. But English aid and Henry's willingness to turn Catholic—he is said to have claimed that "Paris is worth a mass"—led to Philip's withdrawal and the Peace of Vervins in 1598. To pacify his Huguenot allies, Henry issued the Edict of Nantes, which guaranteed them some civil and religious rights and permitted them to continue holding more than a hundred fortified towns. Henry had at last gained peace for his exhausted country.

ORTHODOX EUROPE: RUSSIAN CONSOLIDATION AND OTTOMAN EXPANSION

- *In the last part of the sixteenth century, the Ottoman Empire was at its peak and Muscovite Russia was in a state of crisis. By 1700 the Turks were in a state of decline and the Russians were on the verge of becoming a major power. How do you account for the differences in the developments of the two empires?*

Russian Autocracy

As we saw in Chapter 6, Ivan III had claimed the Byzantine heritage of the Russian state and used his marriage to the niece of the last ruler of Byzantium to proclaim himself as the tsar (Russian for caesar), and he adopted the use of the two-headed eagle as the symbol for the

Russian throne. His grandson, Ivan IV (1533–1584), later surnamed "the Terrible," tried to take the next step toward the imposition of a truly imperial, autocratic rule. Ivan was three years old when his father died, and during the next decade he learned to distrust the aristocratic boyars, who showed him, his mother, and his tutors no respect as they took advantage of his youth. Once he took power in the late 1540s, he began a series of reforms to put the Russian state on a modern footing. He published a new law code, brought together representatives of the Russian population—the ***Zemski Sobor*** (ZIEM-ski so-BOR)—to reform the administration of the land, saw his forces take Kazan and Astrakhan, and opened trade with the West.

IMAGE
Ivan "the Terrible"

As would be the case with the monarchies in western and Central Europe, Ivan faced the opposition of his nobles, the boyars, to his plans to strengthen the state. After 1560 he launched a full-scale war against them. He declared most of Russia, including Moscow, to be under a martial law, enforced by a group of special forces called the *oprichniki* (oh-PREACH-nee-kee), masked men of legendary cruelty dressed in black, riding black horses, carrying broomsticks topped with dog skulls. He wanted to replace the old independent boyar class with a service nobility loyal to him. To that end he and his *oprichniki* drove 12,000 families from their lands in the dead of winter. To those who opposed him, Ivan responded with an inventive cruelty that gained him his name. As the terror increased, he lost control of himself, accidentally killing his beloved son and heir to the throne. Finally he achieved his goals, and the terror diminished. When he died in 1584, he was succeeded by another son Fedor, who was totally unequipped to face the challenge of a devastated and discontented land.

For a time Fedor ruled with the advice of his brother-in-law, Boris Godunov, a competent and ambitious boyar. For seven years the country recovered from the trauma through which it had been put by Ivan IV; however, in 1591 Ivan's last son, Dmitri, died under mysterious circumstances, and when Fedor died in 1598 without an heir, the Rurik line of rulers came to an end. Boris presented himself as the next tsar and received the acclaim of the nobles and church. However, Russia felt the effects of the same famine, economic failure, and discontent that preceded the Thirty Years' War in Central Europe. Boris's policies failed to bring the country back to even minimal prosperity. At the same time, plots against him spread throughout the country, and when he died in 1605, there was no agreed-on successor. Eight years of civil war and Polish intervention, known as the "time of troubles," devastated Russia. Finally, the Russians reunited to drive the Poles out and call a zemski sobor in 1613 to choose a new ruling family, the Romanovs.

Between 1613 and 1676, the first two Romanov tsars, Michael and Alexis, integrated most aristocrats into the state nobility and achieved some degree of stability. As in Prussia, the nobles and the government were reconciled in their common exploitation of the serfs through the Code of 1649, which established serfdom, and the primitive agricultural economy encouraged aristocratic independence. Russian ignorance and

DOCUMENT
Adan Olearius: A Foreign Traveler in Early Russia

In the second part of his reign, Ivan the Terrible lapsed into periods of insanity from time to time. In one of these periods he killed his favorite son and heir. Il'ya Repin captured this tragedy in a nineteenth century painting.

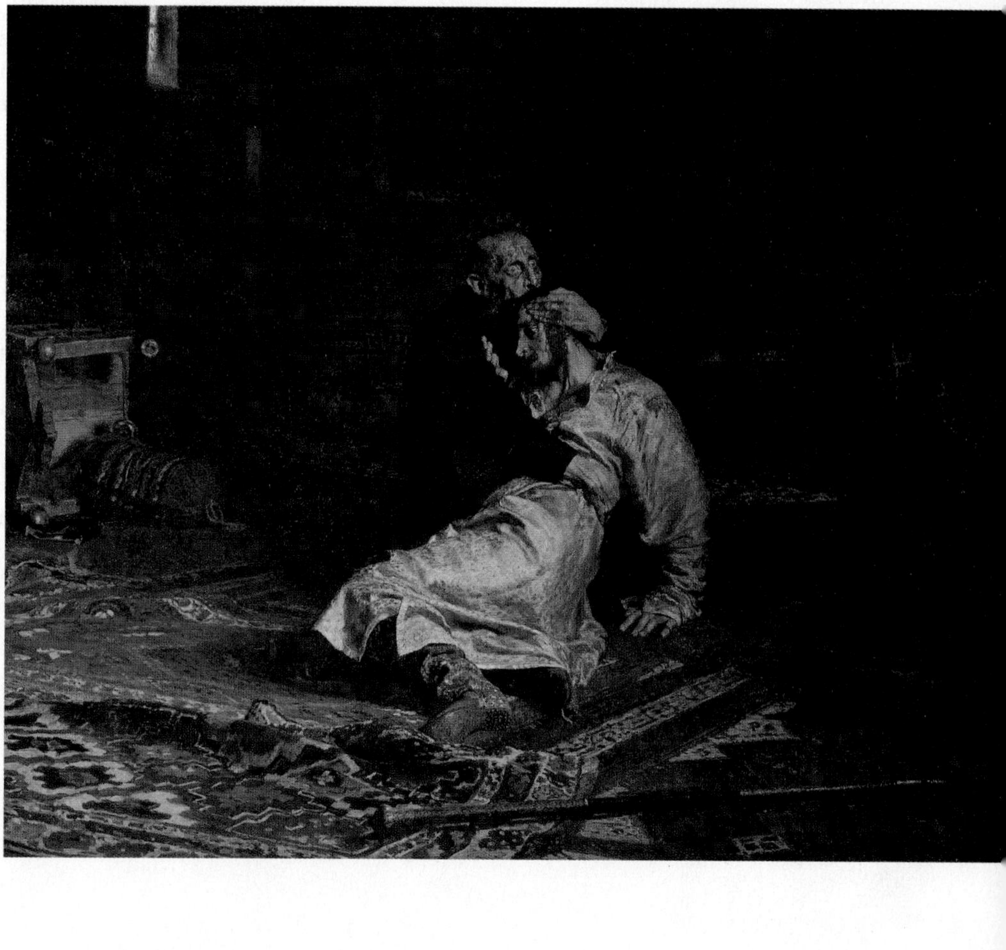

Zemski Sobor—A meeting of representatives of the Russian population—an assembly of the land—to reform the state in the 1550s and then to approve the choice of the Romanovs as the ruling family in 1613.

technical deficiencies, along with a conservative-minded nobility, made the country stagnant in comparison with Western states.

The Balkans

As we saw in Chapter 6, the nations of the Balkans took advantage of the reduced status of the Byzantine Empire and the rise of the Italian city-states to consolidate their power in the thirteenth and fourteenth centuries. The Second Bulgarian Empire, the Empire of Stephan Dushan in Serbia, and even Skanderbeg's Albania enjoyed their golden ages in the fourteenth and fifteenth century.

But after 1345, the Ottoman Turks began their biannual incursions into Europe. It was the Byzantines themselves who had invited the Turks to cross the Dardanelles during one of their periodic dynastic disputes. Three hundred years later the Ottomans would be at the gates of Vienna.

The advancing Turks found no obstacle in the weakened government at Constantinople, and as they proceeded up the rivers of the Balkans they found not much in the way of opposition from the Bulgarians, Slavs, and Romanians. In a time of economic difficulties and religious controversies, there was a considerable degree of class conflict in the area. In addition, instead of uniting against the Ottomans, the various Slavic princes squabbled with each other, mirroring the civil wars in the Byzantine world, until it was too late.

The Ottomans were nothing if not patient, and they took advantage of the conflicts within the Balkans. They understood that they did not have enough troops in the 1350s and 1360s to militarily take the area—so they advanced diplomatically, signing treaties, establishing tribute payments, and then rearming for the next advance. Then in 1362 they took Adrianople, present-day Edirne, and from there they proceeded in a measured matter through Macedonia, then to take Sofia in 1384, then Nis 1386, and southward to take Salonika in 1387. Finally on June 15, 1389, Sultan Murad I defeated the Serbian and Bosnian forces at Kosovo and effectively sealed Ottoman control over the Balkans for the next 500 years. The taking of Constantinople in 1453 completed the conquest. Only Montenegro, of all of the Balkan region, would be able to escape Ottoman rule.

DOCUMENT An Ambassador's Report on the Ottoman Empire

Thereafter the Balkans would experience a different historical development from the rest of Europe. The Ottomans ruled through a theocratic model (see Chapter 6)—all were slaves of the sultan who was, himself, the shadow of God. *Sharia* law was to be followed by Muslims, based on the Koran and other religious writings. There was no secular state.

The nations of the Balkans were ruled either as core provinces or as vassal states. In the core, the different regions were under the command of a governor—who had his miniature version of the Istanbul government. He delegated power to various regional and district authorities, while combining military and civilian authority. Then there were the vassal states—Moldavia, Wallachia, Transylvania, and Ragusa-Dubrovnik (ra-GOOZ-a dew-BROV-nik)—who were allowed to rule themselves in return for loyalty to the sultan and extensive payments in money and grain.

In the core provinces, those who were not Muslims, but followers of a religion of the book—the Bible or the Torah—were governed theocratically, also, through the *millet* system. As Peter Sugar noted, "These were parallel organizations, and each was independent within the limits of its own competence. The Ottomans had no concept corresponding to national lines of differentiation . . . but of religions. . . . The purpose of the . . . system was simply to create a secondary imperial administrative and primary legal structure for the *dhimmis* (non-Muslims in a protected position)." The chief rabbi in Istanbul had his own courts and law enforcers for Jews, as did the leaders of each Christian division—Armenian Catholics, Roman Catholics, and Orthodox Christians. The Phanariote Greeks who dominated the Orthodox structure became extremely powerful in the Balkans during Ottoman rule.

The Ottoman armies remained the most important part of the sultan's government. Before going into Europe, the military was characterized by valiant, independent volunteer horsemen, who fought when there was a war and went home when there was none. Once the empire began to expand in Europe, Sultan Orkhan began to divide the new land among his soldiers, to be given to them for their lifetime. This rewarded the forces for their work but did not create, for the moment, a hereditary service nobility. Orkhan also created a new, slave-based army, the janissaries.

As the empire grew larger, the Ottomans needed more fighters and bureaucrats. They instituted in the core area an arrangement to supply soldiers and bureaucrats, the ***devshirme*** (dev-SHIR-ma) system. Ottoman officials would go to villages throughout the Balkans and select male children whom they would take from their families and enroll in Ottoman service. The boys thus chosen would be given examinations to determine where they would serve the sultan, whether as janissaries or officials at the highest levels. This levy of Christian male children was carried on between the end of the fourteenth century and the beginning of the seventeenth system, and historians estimate that

devshirme—The Ottoman levy of Christian male children in the Balkans. More than 200,000 young boys were taken from their families to serve in the Ottoman army or bureaucracy.

around 200,000 sons were taken from their families during that time. Most of the boys taken came from the Slavic Orthodox populations.

The Balkans participated in none of the formative developments of modern European civilization. They did not experience the Renaissance or the Reformation, the Capitalist and Scientific Revolutions, nor the Enlightenment and Industrialization. The splendor of Constantinople was paid for by the exactions—human and materials—taken from the Balkans peoples. When the region reentered European affairs in the nineteenth century it lagged behind Central and western Europe.[5]

THE AUSTRIAN HABSBURGS' DRIVE FOR SUPERIORITY AND THE THIRTY YEARS' WAR

- *Why was the Thirty Years' War the most destructive military conflict in Europe until the First World War in the twentieth century?*

By 1600 the Spanish Habsburgs' golden age had ended, but the potent mixture of religious and political competition among dynasties and nations would continue with even greater intensity. Philip had taken on too much and had failed to impose his will. Now, in their turn, his cousins in Central Europe—the Austrian Habsburgs—would attempt to impose their dominance in Europe. Religious passions remained at a high pitch as increasing numbers of Calvinists and Lutherans on one side and proponents of the Catholic Counter-Reformation on the other still dreamed of the complete victory of their faith and their realms. It was a dangerous time of disruption, frustration, and fanaticism.

Europeans faced severe economic depression, along with intensified conflict in every sphere of human relations. The first few decades of the seventeenth century brought a marked decline to the European economy, even before the advent of open warfare. Prices continued to fall until about 1660, reversing the inflation of the 1500s. International trade declined, as did Spanish bullion imports from Central and South America. Heavy risks on a falling market caused failures among many foreign trading companies; only the larger houses, organized as joint-stock companies, were able to survive. A climate change, bringing on colder weather, reduced the growing season and agricultural production, and the hard times in the countryside were felt in the cities, where urban craftspeople saw their wages drop.

Tensions accompanying economic depression added to those arising from continuing religious differences. The most dangerous area for religious conflict was in Central Europe, which had directly experienced an increasingly militant Counter-Reformation since the Peace of Augsburg. Although the European power balance in 1618 resembled that of the 1500s, it was much less fixed. The power of the Habsburgs of Vienna drove even normally competitive states to come together in alliances. Underneath the facade of their sixteenth-century dominance there was a sense of vulnerability. Spain was weakening and there were other states—France, the Netherlands, and Sweden—which were growing more powerful. Under these circumstances European opposition against Austrian Habsburg dominance became almost inevitable.

War and Politics in the Age of Austrian Habsburg Dominance

1589–1610	Reign of Henry IV of France, beginning of Bourbon dynasty
1598	Edict of Nantes guarantees Protestant rights in France
1611–1632	Reign of Gustavus Adolphus in Sweden
1618–1648	Thirty Years' War
1624–1642	Cardinal Richelieu holds power in France
1643	Spanish infantry suffers first defeat at Battle of Rocroi
1648	Peace of Westphalia
1649	Independence of the United Provinces

The Bohemian and Danish Phases of the Thirty Years' War: The Habsburgs' High Tide to 1630

The Thirty Years' War, fought between 1618 and 1648, was a culmination of all these related religious and political conflicts. Almost all of western Europe except England was directly involved and suffered accordingly. Central Europe was hit particularly hard, as can be seen in an account by a soldier writing under the name Simplicissimus, suffering population declines that would take two centuries to replace.

Despite the devastation, neither Protestantism nor Catholicism won decisively. What began as a religious war in Bohemia and the German principalities turned into a complex political struggle involving the ambitions of northern German rulers, the expansionist

Document Simplicissimus on the Horrors of the Thirty Years' War

The Protestant and Catholic armies that ranged throughout Central Europe destroyed entire villages, cities, and districts. Battles were the least of the problems for the unfortunate peasants caught in the way. Accompanying the armies were thousands of camp followers who took what they wanted and destroyed the rest. In some instances it took two centuries for the devastated regions to regain their population levels and recover from the damage done by the competing forces. This account of disaster and suffering by Hans von Grimmelshausen (c. 1622–1676), the son of a German innkeeper who was left an orphan and carried away by soldiers during the Thirty Year's War, gives vivid testimony to the horrors of war. Writing under the name of Simplicissimus, he describes the arrival of an army in his home and the activities of the invaders. These ring as true for his day as they do for recent wars such as those in the Balkans, where destruction for destruction's sake and rape are common fare.

The first thing that the riders did was to stable their horses. After that, each one started to his own business which indicated nothing but ruin and destruction. While some started to slaughter, cook and fry, so that it looked as though they wished to prepare a gay feast, others stormed through the house from top to bottom as if the golden fleece of Colchis were hidden there. Others again took linen, clothing and other goods, making them into bundles as if they intended on going to market; what they did not want was broken up and destroyed. Some stabbed their swords through hay and straw as if they had not enough pigs to stab. Some shook the feathers out of the beds and filled the ticks with ham and dried meat as if they could sleep more comfortably in these. Others smashed the ovens and windows as if to announce an eternal summer. They beat copper and pewter vessels into lumps and packed the mangled pieces away. Bedsteads, tables, chairs, and benches were burned, although many stacks of dried wood stood in the yard. Earthenware pots and pans were all broken, perhaps because our guests preferred roasted meats, or perhaps they intended to eat only one meal with us. Our maid had been treated in the stable in such a way that she could not leave it any more—a shameful thing to tell! They bound the farm-hand and laid him on the earth, put a clamp of wood in his mouth and emptied a milking churn full of horrid dung water into his belly. This they called the Swedish drink, and they forced him to lead a party of soldiers to another place, where they looted men and cattle and brought them back to our yard. Among them were my dad, my mum and Ursula.

The soldiers now started to take the flints out of their pistols and in their stead screwed the thumbs of the peasants, and they tortured the poor wretches as if they were burning witches. They put one captive peasant into the bake-oven and put fire on him. Then they tied a rope around the head of another one, and twisted it with the help of a stick so tightly that blood gushed out through his mouth, nose and ears. In short everybody had his own invention to torture the peasants, and each peasant suffered his own martyrdom.... What happened to the captive women, maids and daughters I do not know as the soldiers would not let me watch how they dealt with them. I only very well remember that I heard them miserably crying in corners here and there, and I believe that my mum and Ursula had no better fate than the others.

In the midst of this misery I turned the spit and did not worry as I hardly understood what all this meant. In the afternoon I helped to water the horses and found our maid in the stable looking amazingly dishevelled. I did not recognize her but she spoke to me with pitiful voice:

"Oh, run away, boy, or the soldiers will take you with them. Look out, escape! Can't you see how evil...."

More she could not say.

Questions to Consider

1. What military roles do the physical abuse and rape mentioned by Simplicissimus play in the securing of an area? Are they just instances of bestial behavior or do they reflect military strategy?
2. In considering recent instances of conflict—for example, Yugoslavia, the Palestinian conflict, and Indonesia—do you find that the nature of warfare has changed significantly in the past four centuries?
3. Do you believe that if the local peasantry in the account you have just read had had their own weapons against the occupying army that their villages and property would have been saved?

Mark A. Kishlansky, ed., *Sources of the West: Readings in Western Civilization*, 4th edition, Longman Publishers, New York, 2001, pp. 15–18.

ambitions of Sweden, and the efforts of Catholic France to break the "Habsburg ring."

Despite the general decline of Habsburg supremacy in Spain, the early years of the war before 1629, usually cited as the Bohemian (1618–1625) and Danish (1625–1629) phases, brought a last brief revival of Habsburg prospects. The new Habsburg emperor, Ferdinand II, a fanatical Catholic, was determined to intensify the Counter-Reformation, set aside the Peace of Augsburg, and literally wipe out Protestantism in Central Europe. For a time he almost succeeded.

Ferdinand's succession came amid severe political tension. Spreading Calvinism, in addition to the aggressive crusading of the Jesuits, had earlier led to the formation of a Protestant league of German princes in 1608 and a Catholic league to counter it the next year. The two alliances had almost clashed in 1610. Meanwhile, the Bohemian Protestants had extracted a promise of toleration from their Catholic king, Rudolf II (1576–1612). In 1618 the Bohemian leaders, fearing that Ferdinand would not honor that promise, threw two of his officials out a window after heated discussions—an incident known as the **defenestration of Prague.** When Ferdinand mobilized troops, the Bohemians refused to recognize him and gave their throne to Frederick, the Protestant elector of the Palatinate, in western Germany.

defenestration of Prague—The end of negotiations between Bohemia and the Holy Roman Empire in 1618; the Bohemian representatives were so angry with the representatives of the Holy Roman Emperor that they threw them out the window.

In the short Bohemian war that followed, Frederick was quickly overwhelmed. In 1620 Ferdinand deployed two strong armies, one from Spain and the other from Catholic Bavaria, and scattered the Bohemian forces at the battle of the White Mountain, near Prague. Ferdinand gave the Bohemian lands to Maximillian of Bavaria, distributed the holdings of Bohemian Protestant nobles among Catholic aristocrats, and proceeded to stamp out Protestantism in Bohemia. Of the some 3.2 million Bohemians in 1618, mostly Protestants, all that remained 30 years later were less than 1 million people, all Catholics.

War began again in 1625 when Christian IV (r. 1588–1648), the Lutheran king of Denmark, invaded Germany. As duke of Holstein and thus a prince of the empire, he hoped to revive Protestantism and win a kingdom in Germany for his youngest son. Unlike Frederick in Bohemia, Christian had support from the English, the Dutch, and the North German princes. Their help was not enough. Ferdinand dispatched his new general, Albert von Wallenstein, to crush the Protestants in a series of overpowering campaigns. By 1629 Christian had to admit defeat and withdraw his forces, thus ending the Danish conflict with another Protestant debacle. Their successful campaigns of the 1620s gave the Habsburgs almost complete domination in Germany. In 1629 Ferdinand issued his Edict of Restitution, restoring to the Catholics all properties lost since 1552. This step seemed to be only the first step toward eliminating Protestantism

By the simplicity and starkness of his portrayal, the French artist Jacques Callot captured, in a series of 24 etchings, the senseless tragedy of the Thirty Years' War (1633). The dangling bodies in this plate dramatize the tenuousness of life in turbulent times.

completely and creating a centralized Habsburg empire in Central Europe.

The Swedish and French Phases and the Balance of Power, 1630–1648

Fearing the Counter-Reformation and the growing Habsburg, power behind it, threatened European states resumed the war in 1630. As the war rapidly spread and intensified, religious issues were steadily subordinated to power politics. This transformation could be seen in the phases of the conflict usually designated as the Swedish (1630–1635) and the French (1635–1648) because these two countries led successive and ultimately successful anti-Habsburg coalitions. By 1648 the Dutch Republic had replaced Spain as the leading maritime state and Bourbon France had become the dominant European land power.

Protestant Swedes and French Catholics challenged Ferdinand's imperial ambitions for similar political reasons. Although Gustavus Adolphus (r. 1611–1632), the Swedish king, wanted to save German Lutheranism, he was also determined to prevent a strong Habsburg state on the Baltic from restricting his own expansion and interfering with Swedish trade. A similar desire to liberate France from Habsburg encirclement motivated Cardinal Richelieu, the powerful minister of Louis XIII. Richelieu offered Gustavus French subsidies, for which the Swedish monarch promised to invade Germany and permit Catholic worship in any lands he might conquer. Thus, the Catholic cardinal and the Protestant king compromised their religious differences in the hope of achieving mutual political benefits.

Gustavus invaded Germany in 1630, while the Dutch attacked the Spanish Netherlands. With his mobile cannons and his hymn-singing Swedish veterans, Gustavus and his German allies won a series of smashing victories, climaxed in November 1632 at Lützen, near Leipzig, where Wallenstein was decisively defeated. Unfortunately for the Protestant cause, Gustavus died in the battle. A stalemate for the next three years led to the 1635 Peace of Prague and a momentary compromise between the emperor and the German Protestant states.

Sweden's warrior-king Gustavus Adolphus is portrayed here at the battle of Breitenfeld in 1631.

The situation now demanded that France act directly to further its dynastic interests. Thus, a final French phase of the war began when French troops moved into Germany and toward the Spanish borders. The French also subsidized the Dutch and Swedes and an army of German Protestant mercenaries. The Paris government continued limiting Protestantism within its borders but gladly allied with Protestant states against Spain, Austria, Bavaria, and their Catholic allies. The war that had begun in religious controversy had now become pure power politics, completing the long political transition from medieval to modern times.

For 13 more years, the seemingly endless conflict wore on. France's allies, the Swedes and northern Germans, kept Habsburg armies engaged in Germany, while French armies and the Dutch navy concentrated on Spain. In 1643 the French beat the Spaniards in the decisive battle at Rocroi, in the southern Netherlands. Next they moved into Germany, defeating the imperial forces and, with the Swedes, ravaging Bavaria.

For all practical purposes, the war was over, but years of indecisive campaigning and tortuous negotiations delayed the peace. Finally, a horde of diplomats met at Westphalia in 1644. Even then, Spain and France could reach no agreement for four years, but a settlement for the empire, the Treaty of Westphalia, was finally completed in 1648.

The Peace of Westphalia

The peace agreement at Westphalia signaled a victory for Protestantism and the German princes while almost dooming Habsburg imperial ambitions: France moved closer to the Rhine by acquiring Alsatian territory; Sweden and Brandenburg acquired lands on the Baltic; and the Netherlands and Switzerland gained recognition of their independence. The emperor was required to obtain approval from the Imperial Diet for any laws, taxes, military levies, and foreign agreements—provisions that nearly nullified imperial power and afforded the German states practical control of their foreign relations. German religious autonomy, as declared at Augsburg, was also reconfirmed, with Calvinism now permitted along with Lutheranism. In addition, Protestant states were conceded all Catholic properties taken before 1624.

In its religious terms the treaty ended the dream of reuniting Christendom. Catholics and Protestants now realized that major faiths could not be destroyed. With this admission, a spirit of toleration would gradually emerge. Although religious uniformity could be imposed within states for another century, it would not again be a serious issue in foreign affairs until the end of the twentieth century.

The Peace of Westphalia is particularly notable for confirming the new European state system. Henceforth states would customarily shape their policies in accordance with the power of their neighbors, seeking to expand at the expense of the weaker and to protect themselves—not by religion, law, or morality, but by alliances against their stronger adversaries. Based on the works of the Dutch jurist Grotius, the treaty also instituted the international conference as a means for registering power relationships among contending states, instituted the principle of the equality of all sovereign states—as seen today in the General Assembly of the United Nations—and put into practice the tools of modern diplomacy such as extraterritoriality and diplomatic immunities.

Both Spain and Austria were weakened, and the Austrian Habsburgs shifted their primary attention from Central to southeastern Europe. German disunity was perpetuated by the autonomy of so many of the microstates. France emerged from this time as the clear winner, the potential master of the Continent. The war also helped England and the Netherlands. No matter the condition of the surviving states, their future relations would be based on the pure calculus of power, both military and economic.

CONCLUSION

Despite almost constant political and religious conflict, the years between 1300 and 1650 saw the nation-state system firmly established in Europe, particularly in the Atlantic states of Spain, France, and England.

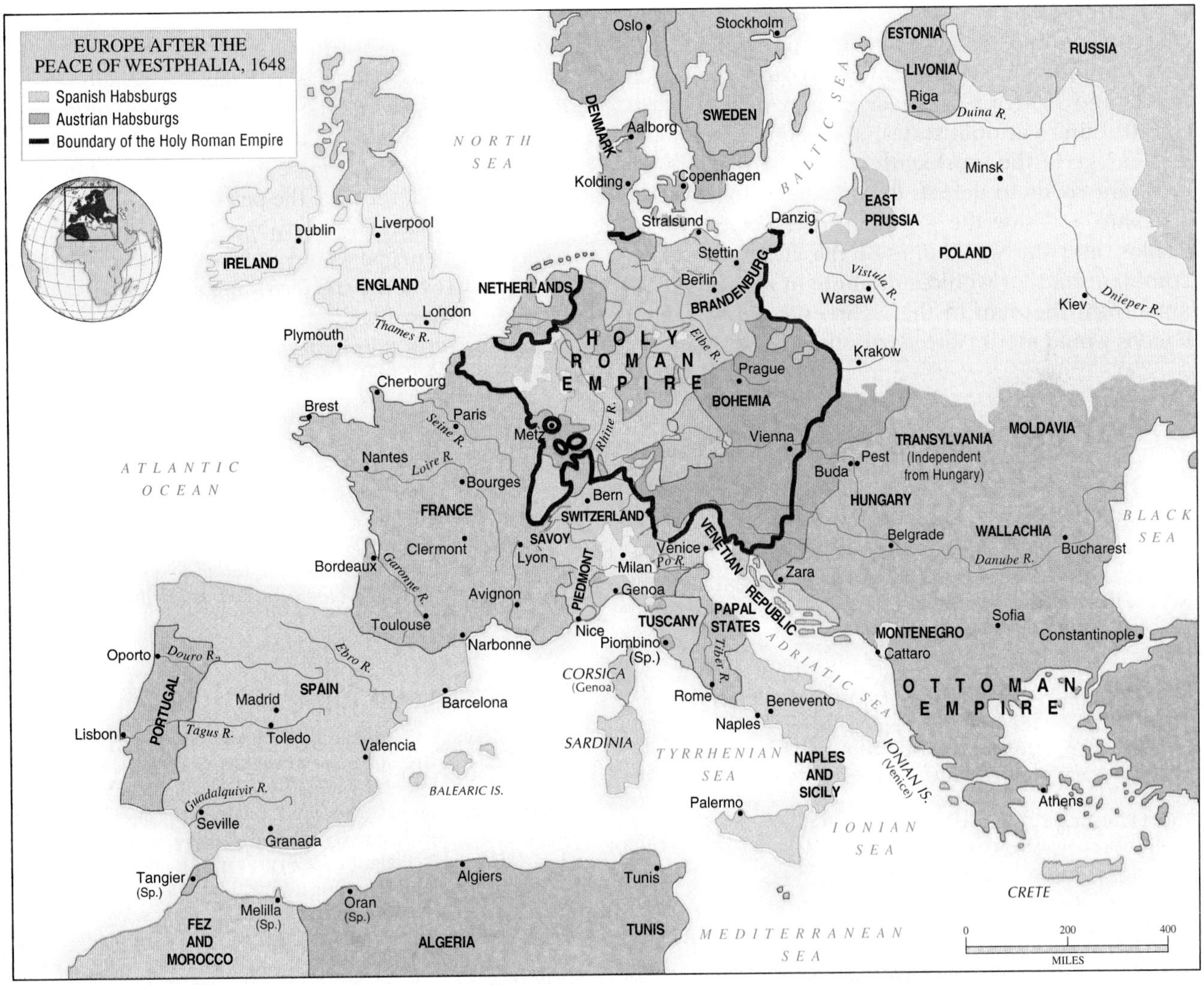

Exhausted Europeans finally agreed to put an end to the Thirty Years' War with the Treaty of Westphalia. This agreement put an end to Habsburg ambitions in Central Europe, marked the emergence of France as the major continental power, and removed religion as a factor in interstate relations. It also laid the foundations for modern international law.

Each of these three countries evolved in different ways. The political evolution of both England and France was affected by the Hundred Years' War. In England, the power of Parliament was increased, and the upsurge in the power of the nobility led to the Wars of the Roses, which ended finally with the accession of the Tudor dynasty; in France, royal power was consolidated under Louis XI, and his abilities in government made possible further progress in national unification. Nation-making in Spain was unique, since the ambitions of the monarchy were combined with the religious fervor of the Reconquista and then the Inquisition. Not until the end of the fifteenth century was the task of Spanish unification completed.

In Central and eastern Europe, state building proceeded in a haphazard and often tragic way. In the last two centuries of the Middle Ages, the Holy Roman Empire remained divided and weak; there, national unification would not be achieved until the nineteenth century. In Italy, the attempt at building a unified structure after 1454 suffered a defeat with the French invasions of a half-century later. The Italian peninsula would remain split into competing areas, also, until the nineteenth century. Poland, the Czech lands, and Hungary all made strong starts toward constructing national states, and then after a brief golden age in the fourteenth century they followed different roads to defeat. Poland opted for elective kingship and saw the growth in the powers of its nobles, and the weakening of the central state—a combination that would culminate in its disappearance from the map in the eighteenth century. The Czechs would mount a true national liberation movement against German dominance in the fifteenth century and withstand numerous attacks. However, they fell victim to Habsburg aggression in the seventeenth century. Hungary, after a shining moment under king Mathias Corvinus in the fifteenth century would be conquered by the Turks in 1526.

In eastern Europe, the Russians under Ivan III attempted to construct a strong central state, before facing chaos in the later years of his rule, and then Polish invasion during the Time of Troubles. The Romanovs slowly began to restore central power thereafter. The Balkans nations fell under the domination of the Ottoman Turks in the fourteenth and fifteenth centuries and would pursue a totally different road to state development.

The 130 years after Luther's stand at Wittenberg was an era of wrenching change for Europe. At the opening of the period, most people in their villages were still imbued with the individual, medieval concern for salvation, which gave meaning to the religious issues of the Protestant Reformation and Catholic Counter-Reformation. In the century after the Peace of Augsburg (1555), the nature of state and society changed. Initially, long and exhaustive religious wars and civil wars dominated the Continent. Later, secular political concerns became increasingly evident. But whether the wars were for faith or for state, or a combination of the two, the period until the Treaty of Westphalia ended the Thirty Years' War was the bloodiest century Europe would endure until the twentieth. Finally, in 1648, the modern state structure emerged. Europeans now lived, for better or worse, in a world of nation-states dominated by secular concerns.

Suggestions for Web Browsing

You can obtain more information about topics included in this chapter at the websites listed below. See also the companion website that accompanies this text, **http://www.ablongman.com/brummett,** which contains an online study guide and additional resources.

End of Europe's Middle Ages
http://www.ucalgary.ca/applied_history/tutor/endmiddle/

This site is developed to aid students of the late Middle Ages by providing collected links and access to primary sources.

Tudor England
http://tudor.simplenet.com/

Site detailing life in Tudor England includes biographies, maps, important dates, architecture, and music, including sound files.

The Thirty Years' War
http://www.pipeline.com/~cwa/TYWHome.htm
http://en.wikipedia.org/wiki/Thirty_Years'_War
http://www.historylearningsite.co.uk/thirty_years_war.htm

Images and explanations of Europe's bloodiest conflict, until 1914.

Peace of Westphalia
http://www.yale.edu/lawweb/avalon/westphal.htm

Complete text of the peace treaties that together made up the Treaty of Westphalia (1648), which ended the Thirty Years' War.

Literature and Film

Several recent and outstanding translations and/or editions of later medieval literature are available: Geoffrey Chaucer, *The Canterbury Tales in Modern English,* ed. Neville Coghill (Penguin, 2000); Dante Alighieri, *The Divine Comedy,* trans. Allen Mandelbaum (Knopf, 1995); and Giovanni Boccaccio, *Decameron,* trans. G. H. McWilliam (Penguin, 1996) are outstanding presentations.

This is a rich period for novels. The activities of this time attracted the best attentions of Alexandre Dumas. Writing about events in France, he produced *The Two Dianas* (dealing with the time of Francis I), *The Page of the Duke of Savoy* (touching the time of the Emperor Charles V), *Ascanio* (France in the middle of the century), and *Marguerite de Valois* (touching the civil wars), and this is only an incomplete list. Mark Twain wrote about the time of Edward VI in *The Prince and the Pauper* (1881). More recently, Robin Maxwell sheds some light on the reign of Henry VIII in *The*

Secret Diary of Anne Boleyn: A Novel (Scribner, 1998), and Reay Tannahill's *Fatal Majesty: A Novel of Mary Queen of Scots* (Griffin, 2000) offers another recent discussion of the tragic queen.

Some excellent video explorations of the late medieval period are *Siena: Chronicle of a Medieval Commune* (Metropolitan Museum of Art, 1988); *Landmarks of Western Art: The Medieval World* (Kultur Video, 1999); *Living in the Past: Life in Medieval Times* (Kultur Video, 1998); and *Medieval Warfare* (1997; Kultur Video, 3 tapes).

Filmmakers have been equally attracted to the period, especially the English scene. (All of the following are available in VHS.) Fred Zinnemann's *A Man for all Seasons* (Columbia, 1966) is a fine telling of the story of Sir Thomas More. Queen Elizabeth has been the subject of films throughout the twentieth century, including Shekhar Kapur's *Elizabeth* (Channel Four Films, 1998), and indirectly in *Shakespeare in Love* (Miramax, 1998). A film dealing with the period after Henry VIII is Trevor Nunn's *Lady Jane* (Paramount, 1986). The 1933 film, Alexander Korda's *The Private Life of Henry VIII* (London Film Productions) is worth seeing as is *Mary Queen of Scots* (Charles Jarrett, director, Universal Pictures, 1971). On the continent, *The Return of Martin Guerre* (Daniel Vigne, director, European International, 1982) does justice to Natalie Zemon Davis's fine monograph. The film of the life of Martin Luther (Louis de Rochemont Associates, 1953) is a revealing look at the reformer.

Suggestions for Reading

For the spirit of the age see David Nirenberg, *Communities of Violence: Persecution of Minorities in the Middle Ages* (Princeton University Press, 1996). See also S. Harrison Thomson, *Czechoslovakia In European History* (Frank Cass and Co. Ltd., 1965); Lonnie R. Johnson, *Central Europe: Enemies, Neighbors, Friends* (Oxford University Press, 1996); Daniel Herlihy, *The Black Death and the Transformation of the West* (Harvard University Press, 1997); and Richard Kieckhefer, *Magic in the Middle Ages* (Cambridge University Press, 2000). See also C. H. Haskins, *The Rise of Universities* (Cornell University Press, 1965).

Valuable sources of English history include Bell Henneman, ed., *The Medieval French Monarchy* (Krieger, 1973); C.B. Bouchard, *Strong of Body, Brave and Noble: Chivalry and Society in Medieval France* (Cornell, 1998); Nigel Saul, ed., *The Oxford History of Medieval England* (Oxford, 2001); and P.S.P. Goldberg, ed., *Women in Medieval English Society* (Sutton, 1997). See also Edmund King, *Medieval England, 1066–1485* (Salem House, 1989). Bernard T. Reilly, *The Medieval Spains* (Cambridge University Press, 1993), and Richard Fletcher, *Moorish Spain* (University of California Press, 1993), are excellent surveys.

On later medieval society, see Philip Ziegler, *The Black Death* (Sutton, 1998); Christopher Allmand, *The Hundred Years' War* (Cambridge University Press, 1988); Norman Cantor, *In the Wake of the Plague: The Black Death and the World It Made* (Free Press, 2001); Jonathan Sumpton, *The Hundred Years' War: Trial by Battle* (University of Pennsylvania Press, 1999); and Daniel Waley, *Later Medieval Europe: From St. Louis to Luther* (Longman, 1985).

Geoffrey Parker, *The Grand Strategy of Philip II* (Yale University Press, 1998), is the best study of the construction of the Spanish world empire. It is still important to read Fernand Braudel's *The Mediterranean and the Mediterranean World in the Age of Philip II*, 2 vols. (Harper Torchbook, 1976), translated by Siân Reynolds, for its lessons both about the age and about how to understand history in a broader context. The classic treatment of the Armada is Garrett Mattingly, *The Armada* (Houghton Mifflin, 1988).

For the Dutch rebellion see James D. Tracy's, *Holland Under Habsburg Rule* (University of California Press, 1990). Simon Schama, *The Embarrassment of Riches: An Interpretation of Dutch Culture in the Golden Age* (Knopf, 1987), and Charles R. Boxer, *The Dutch Seaborne Empire* (Penguin, 1989), depict the republic at the apex of its struggle for power and wealth. Guido Marnef, *Antwerp in the Age of Reformation* (Johns Hopkins University Press, 1996), gives the texture and detail of this extraordinary time.

French society and politics during the whole era are ably treated in Mack P. Holt, *The French Wars of Religion, 1562–1629* (Cambridge University Press, 1995), a new study of the chaotic period preceding Richelieu, with considerable emphasis on social history. Henry Heller, *Iron and Blood: Civil Wars in Sixteenth-Century France* (McGill-Queen's University Press, 1991), describes the catastrophic religious wars. For a re-creation of life just beneath the religious and political conflict see Natalie Zemon Davis's classic, *The Return of Martin Guerre* (Harvard University Press, 1984).

A revealing survey of English social history is J. A. Sharpe, *Early Modern England: A Social History, 1550–1760*, 2nd ed. (Arnold, 1997). On the growing social and political awareness of English women in the sixteenth and seventeenth centuries, see Katherine A. Henderson and Barbara McManus, *Half Humankind: Contexts and Texts of the Controversy About Women in England, 1540–1640* (University of Illinois Press, 1985), and Mary Prior, ed., *Women in English Society, 1500–1800* (Methuen, 1985). Excellent general interpretations of Elizabethan England are presented in Arthur Bryant, *The Elizabethan Deliverance* (St. Martin's Press, 1982), and David B. Quinn and A. N. Ryan, *England's Sea Empire, 1550–1642* (Allen & Unwin, 1983). Biographies worth consulting include Anne Somerset, *Elizabeth I* (Knopf, 1991), and J. Mary Wormald, *Mary, Queen of Scots* (Philip & Sons, 1988). A noteworthy special work on Elizabethan women is Susan Cahn, *The Transformation of Women's Work in England, 1500–1600* (Columbia University Press, 1987). Wallace T. MacCaffrey, *Elizabeth I, War and Politics 1588–1603* (Princeton University Press, 1992), is the best general survey of her reign.

On the less developed absolutism in eastern Europe, see Robert James Weston Evans, *The Making of the Habsburg Monarchy, 1550–1700* (Oxford University Press, 1984); see also Norman Davies, *A History of Poland*, Vol. 1 (Columbia University Press, 1981). A useful study of Prussian history in this period is Otis Mitchell, *A Concise History of Brandenburg-Prussia to 1786* (University Press of America, 1980). Development of the Romanov state is ably described in Otto Hoetzsch, *The Evolution of Russia* (Harcourt Brace, 1966), and W. Bruce Lincoln, *The Romanovs* (Dial, 1981).

Ronald G. Asch, *The Thirty Years' War, the Holy Roman Empire and Europe, 1618–1648* (St. Martin's Press, 1997), is a brief up-to-date survey with a good appreciation of the historiographical conflicts surrounding this event that adds to, but does not replace, Cicely V. Wedgewood's classic *The Thirty Years' War* (Anchor Books, 1961). Joseph Polisensky discusses the by-products of the war in *War and Society in Europe, 1618–1648* (Cambridge University Press, 1978). Michael Roberts, *Sweden's Age of Greatness* (St. Martin's Press, 1973), gives good coverage of both the political and military events in this conflict.

TECHNOLOGICAL EXCHANGE

How does technology move from one culture to another?

First trial of Maxim machine gun by English troops in Africa, 1887.

Technology has played a decisive role in human history, but its movement between cultures is often overlooked. Indeed, while American society tends to stress the creative genius of individual inventors such as Thomas Edison and the Wright brothers, technological innovations such as the light bulb and the airplane rest on a vast body of knowledge that stretches both back in time and around the world. It is, in fact, a universal tendency for individuals and societies to build on past discoveries, whatever their place of origin.

Traditionally, most world cultures have been open to beneficial new technologies originating from other cultures. Between 800 and 1300 C.E. Islamic civilization became dominant in the sciences in part because it eagerly absorbed the scientific knowledge of other civilizations such as Greece, Persia, and India. Caliphs and wealthy patrons sponsored medical centers, observatories, and libraries that translated foreign scientific treatises and undertook their own scientific investigations. Their efforts helped Muslim scientists make advances in mathematics, astronomy, medicine, and navigation. During this era, Arabic became the language of science, and both technological innovations and classical learning flowed from the Islamic world to Europe, where they helped stimulate the Renaissance.

Technology has often moved from its culture of origin to new cultures only to undergo further development there and then be transmitted on to other cultures and even back to its culture of origin, which was the case with gunpowder technology. A range of societies had experimented with explosives, but it was the Chinese who first invented gunpowder in the mid-ninth century C.E., initially only to make fireworks for religious and entertainment purposes. It would take another three centuries before they applied this technology to warfare, with the invention of rockets, bombs, and mortars. In the thirteenth century, the invading Mongols, in turn, helped to spread gunpowder technology from China across Asia to the Islamic world and Europe. Muslims and Christians alike were quick to recognize the potential of this new technology. When two English nobles in Spain witnessed the battle of Tarifa in 1340, they observed an Arab army fielding cannons against a Spanish force. They took that knowledge back with them to England, where it was immediately put to use in their wars with the French.

The Europeans, in fact, were so quick to embrace and develop gunpowder technology that it was the Portuguese and not the Chinese who first introduced muskets to East Asia in the early sixteenth century. The Japanese quickly accepted the new technology and begun manufacturing their own muskets. In a very short time, they were making guns equal to, if not better than, those made by the Europeans. This trend, however, would not last. In the seventeenth century, the samurai, the warrior class of Japan, opposed production of guns because they recognized that guns would endanger their exclusive status in Japanese society.

The Japanese only changed their view about guns out of necessity some 200 years later when a relatively small British force defeated China in the Opium War during the 1840s and Matthew Perry's warships anchored in Edo Bay in 1853. The Meiji emperor's embrace of modernization came out of the realization that Japan had to rapidly assimilate Western weapons of war if it wanted to fend off Western domination. Japanese scientists and officers studied English, French, and German military science, and the government poured money into the armament industry. Foreigners were admitted as teachers and technicians, and Japanese students were sent to American and European universities. The Imperial University, established in 1886, set up a faculty of engineering with departments specifically for explosives and shipbuilding. Japan's embrace of Western technology paid dividends when it defeated first China in the Sino-Japanese War of 1894–1895 and then Russia in the Russo-Japanese War of 1905.

Given the military and economic advantages offered by many technologies, it should not be surprising that many nations have sought to secure their own technologies and acquire or even steal the "protected" technologies of other nations. The Chinese closely guarded the secrets of silk and porcelain production for centuries until spies finally managed to carry those secrets abroad and break the Chinese monopoly. In the nineteenth century, Europeans may have eagerly sold the finished products of their technologies in the Americas, Asia, and Africa, but they generally kept the most advanced technologies for themselves, particularly weapons. Hilaire Belloc's famous couplet stated the truth bluntly: "Whatever else we have got / The Maxim gun and they have not."

The Europeans also sought to ensure that the manufacture of finished products—and thus the industry and profits—remained in their home countries. The colonized peoples of Africa and Asia, then, became the consumers of finished products and were prevented from developing their own manufacturing capabilities—a legacy that continues to challenge many countries in the developing world today.

Over the last two centuries one way some countries have sought to protect valuable technologies and encourage inventiveness in their people is through the issuing of patents, which give inventors an exclusive monopoly on the production of their invention for a number of years. Patented technologies are generally honored in the developed world, but cases of counterfeiting and piracy are rampant in the developing world. Of course, patent or no patent, if a business or individual is to have any chance of protecting a technology, it must recognize its value in the first place. This wasn't the case of the American company Western Electric and the transistor. American scientists had invented the transistor, but American electronics companies still relied on vacuum tubes in their products and were not prepared to apply the new technology in their manufacturing. Instead, a Japanese firm, Tokyo Telecommunications, recognized the importance of transistors and bought the rights from Western Electric when it sold its patent in 1954. Within a few years, the Japanese company had designed a transistor radio, and, after changing its name to Sony, it became a world leader in mass-producing electronics products.

Today, the dominant new economic technologies of our times are embodied in the Internet and information technology (IT). While these technologies have been exchanged freely around the world, their benefits have not reached all people. Because of the costs of achieving connectivity, a "digital divide" has emerged in which access to the Internet, for example, is often limited to urban elites in developing countries. On the other hand, some new technologies such as cell phones have opened up communications and business opportunities in remote areas of the world and are often even more ubiquitous in developing countries than they are in the West.

With advances to communication and transportation technology making the world smaller and smaller by the day, it seems certain the rate of technological exchange between cultures will only accelerate in the future.

Questions

1. What reasons might a culture have for rejecting a new technology coming from another culture?
2. Can you think of any situations in which counterfeiting and piracy of a technology would be morally acceptable?
3. Why is technological exchange inevitable?

CHAPTER

16

Global Encounters

Europe and the New World Economy, 1400–1650

CHAPTER CONTENTS

During the fifteenth century, European nations began a process of exploration, conquest, and trade, affecting almost all areas of the world. Their activities were mirrored in other parts of the world as Asian and Arab states took the lead in expanding their trading networks and their connections with each other. The processes were furthered by improved navigational technology and the resulting expansion of trade that encouraged long sea voyages by Arabs, Japanese, and Chinese. Likewise, sea power, rather than land-based armies, was the key to Europe's becoming a significant force in various parts of the world, especially the Americas and Africa.

European endeavors overseas were obviously related—both as cause and as effect—to trends set in motion as Europe emerged from the medieval era. The Crusades and the Renaissance stimulated European curiosity; the Reformation produced thousands of zealous missionaries seeking converts in foreign lands and refugees searching for religious freedom; and the monarchs of emerging sovereign states sought revenues, first by trading in the Indian Ocean and later by exploiting new worlds. Perhaps the most permeating influence was the rise of European capitalism, with its monetary values, profit-seeking motivations, investment institutions, and consistent impulses toward economic expansion. Some historians have labeled this whole economic transformation the Commercial Revolution. Others have used the phrase to refer to the shift in trade routes from the Mediterranean to the Atlantic. Interpreted either way, the Commercial Revolution and its accompanying European expansion helped usher in a modern era, largely at the expense of Africans and Amerindians.

Europe's Commercial Revolution developed in two quite distinct phases. The first phase involved Portugal and Spain; the second phase, after 1600, was led by the Netherlands, England, and to some extent France. The second fostered a maritime imperialism based more on trade and finance than the more directly exploitative systems of the first phase.

1300

1394–1460 Prince Henry the Navigator

1400

1400s Iberian navigators develop new naval technology; Spain and Portugal stake claims in Asia, Africa, and the Americas; Atlantic slave trade begins

1492 Christopher Columbus reaches San Salvador

1498 Vasco da Gama rounds Cape of Good Hope, reaches India

1500

1513 Vasco de Balboa reaches Pacific Ocean

1519 Hernando Cortés arrives in Mexico, defeats Aztecs

1520 Ferdinand Magellan rounds South America

1600

c. 1600 Second phase of European overseas expansion begins

1609 Henry Hudson establishes Dutch claims in North America; English East India Company chartered

1620 Pilgrims land at Plymouth

THE IBERIAN GOLDEN AGE

- *What motivated the Portuguese and Spanish to develop global commercial networks?*

Portugal and Spain, the two Iberian states, launched the new era in competition with each other, although neither was able to maintain initial advantages over the long term. Portugal lacked the manpower and resources required by an empire spread over three continents. Spain wasted its new wealth in waging continuous wars while neglecting to develop its own economy. In 1503 Portuguese pepper cost only one-fifth as much as pepper coming through Venice and the eastern Mediterranean. Within decades, gold and silver from the New World poured into Spain. Iberian bullion and exotic commodities, flowing into northern banks and markets, provided a major stimulus to European capitalism. This early European impact abroad also generated great cultural diffusion, promoting an intercontinental spread of peoples, plants, animals, and knowledge that the world had never seen before. But it also destroyed Amerindian states and weakened societies in Africa.

Conditions Favoring Iberian Expansion

A number of conditions invited Iberian maritime expansion in the fifteenth century. Muslim control over the eastern caravan routes, particularly after the Turks took Constantinople in 1453, brought rising prices in Europe. At the same time, the sprawling Islamic world lacked both unity and intimidating sea power, and China, after 1440, had abandoned its extensive naval forays into the Indian Ocean. Because Muslim and Italian rivals prevented the Iberian states from tapping into the spice trade in the eastern Mediterranean and the gold trade in West Africa, Portugal and Spain sought alternative sea routes to the East, where their centuries-old struggle with Muslims in the Mediterranean might be continued on the ocean shores of sub-Saharan Africa and Asia.

During the 1400s, Iberian navigators became proficient in new naval technology and tactics. They adopted the compass (which came from China through the Middle East), the **astrolabe,** and the triangular **lateen sail** that gave their ships the ability to take advantage of winds coming from oblique angles and cut weeks off longer voyages. They also learned to tack against the wind, thus partly freeing them from hugging the coast on long voyages. This skill was important because prevailing winds and ocean currents made it impossible for Portuguese sailors to go farther south than Cape Bojador (bo-hyah-DOR) and still return home. In 1434, a Portuguese seafarer learned that it was possible to sail west toward the Canary Islands and catch trade winds that allowed ships to proceed home. This discovery opened up a new era of exploration.

The Iberians, especially the Portuguese, were also skilled cartographers and chartmakers. But their main advantages lay with their ships and naval guns. The stormy Atlantic required broad bows, deep keels, and complex square rigging for driving and maneuvering fighting ships. Armed with brass cannons, such ships could sink enemy vessels without ramming or boarding at close range. They could also batter down coastal defenses. Even the much larger Chinese junks were no match for the European ships' maneuverability and firepower.

A strong religious motivation augmented Iberian naval efficiency. Long and bitter wars with the Muslim Moors had left the Portuguese and Spanish with an obsessive drive to convert non-Christians or destroy them in the name of Christ. Sailors with Columbus recited prayers every night, and Portuguese seamen were equally devout. Every maritime mission was regarded as a holy crusade.

For two centuries Iberians had hoped to expand their influence in Muslim lands by launching a new Christian crusade in concert with Ethiopia. The idea

Portuguese and Spanish Exploration and Expansion

1470–1541	Francisco Pizarro
1474–1566	Bartolomé de Las Casas
1479	Treaty of Alcacovas
1494	Treaty of Tordesillas
1509–1515	Alfonso de Albuquerque serves as eastern viceroy of Portugal
1510–1554	Francisco de Coronado
1510	Portuguese acquire Goa, in India
1531	Pizarro defeats Incas in Peru
c. 1550	Spanish introduce plantation system to Brazil
1565	St. Augustine founded; first European colony in North America

astrolabe—An instrument used in navigation for calculating latitude.

lateen sail—A triangular sail that is set at a 45-degree angle to the mast and takes advantage of winds coming from oblique angles.

originated with twelfth-century crusaders in the Holy Land; it gained strength later with Ethiopian migrants at Rhodes, who boasted of their king's prowess against the infidels. Thus arose the myth of "Prester John," a mighty Ethiopian monarch and potential European ally against Mongols, Turks, and Muslims. In response to a delegation from Zar'a Ya'kob, the reigning emperor, a few Europeans visited Ethiopia after 1450. These and other similar contacts greatly stimulated the determination to find a new sea route to the East that might link the Iberians with the legendary Ethiopian king and bring Islam under attack from two sides.

DOCUMENT "The Land of Prester John"

This dream of war for the cross was sincere, but it also served to rationalize more worldly concerns. Both Spain and Portugal experienced dramatic population growth between 1400 and 1600. The Spanish population increased from 5 to 8.5 million; the Portuguese population more than doubled, from 900,000 to 2 million, despite a manpower loss of 125,000 in the sixteenth century. Hard times in rural areas prompted migration to cities, where dreams of wealth in foreign lands encouraged fortune seeking overseas. Despite the obvious religious zeal of many Iberians, particularly among those in holy orders, a fervent desire for gain was the driving motivation for most migrants.

The structures of the Iberian states provided further support for overseas expansion. In both, the powers of the monarchs had been recently expanded and were oriented toward maritime adventure as a means to raise revenues, divert the Turkish menace, spread Catholic Christianity, and increase national unity. The Avis dynasty in Portugal, after usurping the throne and alienating the great nobles in 1385, made common cause with the gentry and middle classes, who prospered in commercial partnership with the government. In contrast, Spanish nobles, particularly the Castilians, were very much like Turkish aristocrats, who regarded conquest and plunder as their normal functions and sources of income. Thus, the Portuguese and Spanish political systems worked in different ways toward similar imperial ends.

Staking Claims

During the late fifteenth century, both Portugal and Spain staked claims abroad. Portugal gained a long lead over Spain in Africa and Asia. But after conquering Granada, the last Moorish state on the Iberian peninsula, and completely uniting the country, the Spanish monarchs turned their attention overseas. The resulting historic voyage of Columbus established Spanish claims to most of the Western Hemisphere.

The man most responsible for Portugal's ambitious exploits was Prince Henry (1394–1460), known as "the Navigator" because of his famous observatory at

Using ships like these broad-beamed carracks, the Portuguese controlled much of the carrying trade with the East in the fifteenth and sixteenth centuries.

Sagres (SAH-greesh), where skilled mariners planned voyages and recorded their results. As a young man in 1415, Henry directed the Portuguese conquest of Ceuta (see-YOO-tah), a Muslim port on the Moroccan coast, at the western entrance to the Mediterranean. This experience imbued him with a lifelong desire to divert the West African gold trade from Muslim caravans to Portuguese ships. He also shared the common dream of winning Ethiopian Christian allies against the Turks. Such ideas motivated him for 40 years as he sent expeditions down the West African coast, steadily charting and learning from unknown waters.

Before other European states began extensive explorations, the Portuguese had navigated the West African coast to its southern tip. Henry's captains claimed the Madeira Islands in 1418 and the Azores in 1421. A thousand miles to the west of Portugal, these uninhabited islands were settled to produce, among other things, wheat for bread-starved Lisbon.

By 1450 the Portuguese had explored the Senegal River and then traced the Guinea coast during the next decade. After Henry's death in 1460, they pushed south, reaching Benin in the decade after 1470 and Kongo, on the southwest coast, in 1482. Six years later, Bartolomeu Dias rounded southern Africa, but his disgruntled crew forced him to turn back. Nevertheless, King John II of Portugal (1481–1495) was so excited by the prospect of a direct route to India that he named Dias's discovery the "Cape of Good Hope."

Spain soon challenged Portuguese supremacy. The specific controversy was over the Canary Islands, some of which were occupied by Castilians in 1344 and others by Portuguese after the 1440s. The issue, which produced repeated incidents, was ultimately settled in 1479 by the Treaty of Alcacovas (ahl-KAHS-ko-vahsh), which recognized exclusive Spanish rights in the Canaries but banned Spain from the Madeiras, the Azores, the Cape Verdes, and West Africa. Spanish ambitions were thus temporarily frustrated until Columbus provided new hope.

Christopher Columbus (1451–1506), a Genoese sailor with an impossible dream, had been influenced by Marco Polo's journal to believe that Japan could be reached by a short sail directly westward. Although he underestimated the distance by some 7000 miles and was totally ignorant of the intervening continents, Columbus persistently urged his proposals on King John of Portugal and Queen Isabella of Spain, who was captivated by Columbus's dream and became his most steadfast supporter until her death in 1504. Having obtained her sponsorship, Columbus sailed from Palos, Spain, in three small ships on August 3, 1492. He landed on San Salvador in the West Indies on October 12, thinking he had reached his goal. In three more attempts he continued his search for an Asian passage. His voyages touched the major Caribbean islands, Honduras, the Isthmus of Panama, and Venezuela. Although he never knew it, he had claimed a new world for Spain.

Christopher Columbus and the Round World

Columbus's first voyage posed threats to Portuguese interests in the Atlantic and called for compromise if war was to be averted. At Spain's invitation, the pope issued a "bull of demarcation," establishing a north-south line about 300 miles west of the Azores. Beyond this line all lands were opened to Spanish claims. The Portuguese protested, forcing direct negotiations, which produced the Treaty of Tordesillas (tor-dhai-SEE-lyahs) in 1494. It moved the line some 500 miles farther west. Later explorations showed that the last agreement gave Spain most of the New World but left eastern Brazil to Portugal.

Motivated by a desire to find a sea route to India that bypassed the overland caravan routes controlled by Muslim states, Prince Henry the Navigator was a leading figure in promoting Portuguese explorations down the West African coast. Ironically he seldom left Portugal himself. When he died in 1460, his sailors had reached the Canary Islands, but by the end of that century, Vasco da Gama had sailed from Portugal to India.

The Developing Portuguese Empire

Through the first half of the sixteenth century, the Portuguese developed a world maritime empire while maintaining commercial supremacy. They established trading posts around both African coasts and a falter-

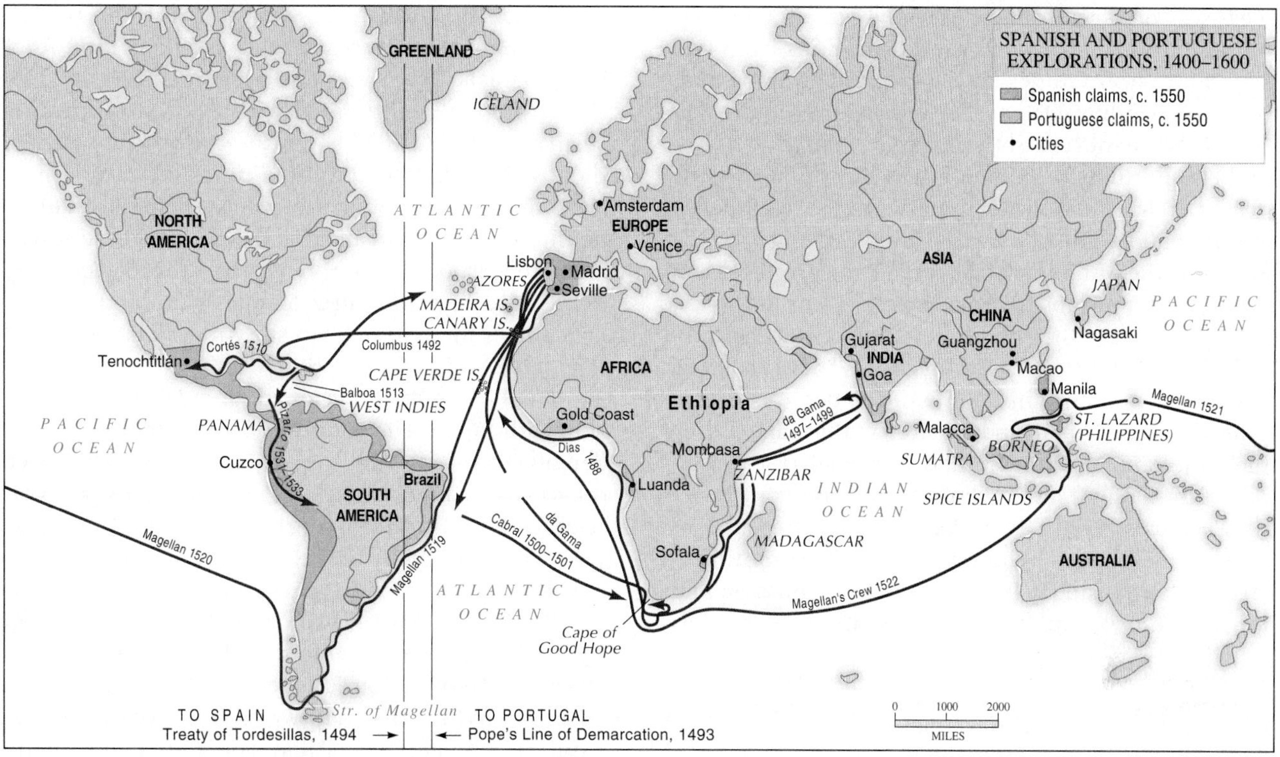

From the mid-fifteenth to the mid-sixteenth centuries, Portugal and Spain took advantage of new naval technology and tactics to become the leading seafaring nations in the world.

ing colony in Brazil, but their most extensive operations were in southern Asia, where they gained control of shipping routes and dominated the Indian Ocean spice trade.

Two voyages at the turn of the sixteenth century laid the foundations for the Portuguese interests in the Americas and the Orient. In 1497 Vasco da Gama (1469–1524) left Lisbon, Portugal, in four ships, rounding the Cape of Good Hope after 93 days on the open sea. While visiting and raiding the East African ports, da Gama picked up an Arab pilot, who brought the fleet across the Indian Ocean to Calicut (KAL-i-kut), on the western coast of India. When he returned to Lisbon in 1499, da Gama had lost two ships and a third of his men, but his cargo of pepper and cinnamon returned the cost of the expedition 60 times over. Shortly afterward, Pedro Cabral (1468–1520), commanding a large fleet on a second voyage to India, bore too far west and sighted the east coast of Brazil. The new western territory was so unpromising that it was left unoccupied until 1532, when a small settlement was established at São Vicente. In the 1540s it had attracted only some 2000 settlers, mostly men, although a few Portuguese women came after the arrival of the lord protector's wife and her retinue in 1535. The colony served mostly as a place to send convicts, and by 1600 it had only 25,000 European residents.

Brazil was neglected in favor of extensive operations in the Indian Ocean and Southeast Asia, where the Portuguese sought to gain control of the spice trade by taking over flourishing port cities, places strategically located on established trade routes. The most striking successes were achieved under Alfonso de Albuquerque, eastern viceroy from 1509 to 1515. He completed subjugation of the Swahili city-states and established fortified trading posts in Mozambique and Zanzibar. After a decisive naval victory over an Arab fleet (1509), Albuquerque's force captured Hormuz (hor-MOOZ) six years later, thus disrupting Arab passage from the Persian Gulf. In 1510 the Portuguese acquired Goa on the west coast of India; it became a base for aiding Hindus against Indian Muslims and conducting trade with Gujerat (goo-ja-RAHT), a major producer of cloth. The next year a Portuguese force took Malacca, a Muslim stronghold in Malaya, which controlled trade with China and the Spice Islands, through the narrow straits opposite Sumatra (soo-MAH-trah). Although a Portuguese goal was to spread the Christian faith at the expense of Islam, the expulsion of Muslim traders had the opposite effect. These traders moved to the Malaysian peninsula and founded new Muslim states.

The Indian Ocean had previously been open to all traders, but the Portuguese network left no room for competitors, and rival traders, especially Muslims, were squeezed out of their previous settlements. Portuguese officials financed their operations from two sources, customs duties and a tax levied on ships trading in the Indian Ocean. All ships were required to stop at Portuguese ports and take a ***cartaz.***

The Portuguese presence was largely felt on the ocean; it had very little impact on the land-based empires and trading networks of the Ottomans, the Safavids, the Mughuls, and the Chinese. On the Asian mainland, for instance, the Portuguese were mostly supplicants because they had to interact with well-established and more powerful states. They acquired temporary influence in Laos and Cambodia but were expelled from Vietnam and enslaved in Burma. In China their diplomatic blunders and breaches of etiquette offended Ming officials, who regarded the Portuguese as cannibals. In 1519 a Portuguese representative angered the Chinese by, among other things, starting to erect a fort in Canton harbor without permission and buying Chinese children as slaves. Chinese officials responded by jailing and executing a group of Portuguese emissaries who had been visiting Beijing. After being banished from Chinese ports in 1522 and 1544, the Portuguese cooperated with Chinese smuggling rings off South China before Chinese officials granted them strictly regulated trading rights in Macao (mah-KOU) in 1554. Although the Chinese generally had little interest in European goods, the Portuguese served a useful purpose by supplying the Chinese economy with Indian manufactures such as cloth and Indonesian spices and silver from the Americas reexported through Europe.

The Portuguese developed an extensive relationship with Japan. The connection was established accidentally in 1542 when three Portuguese traders landed off southern Japan after a storm blew their ship off course. At the time Japanese *daimyo* (feudal lords) were contending with each other for power, and Portuguese traders prospered by selling matchlock muskets to rival factions.

A Japanese View of European Missionaries

The Jesuit priests who followed the merchants in 1549 had great success in winning converts. While the *daimyo* Nobunaga was gaining mastery over his opponents, he

cartaz—A license issued by the Portuguese that permitted non-Portuguese traders to operate in areas of the Indian Ocean controlled by the Portuguese.

In the sixteenth century a Japanese artist depicted the Portuguese as "Southern Barbarians" in a decorative screen.

encouraged the Catholics because they were useful allies against Buddhist sects opposing him. By the 1580s, the Catholics were claiming as many as 150,000 adherents. However, as Japan became unified in the late sixteenth century, Nobunaga's successors began regarding Christians as a divisive threat. They perceived the arrival of Spanish Franciscan friars in 1592 as an additional danger because they had recently scored major successes in winning converts in the Philippines. Japanese officials issued a series of anti-Christian edicts that led to the persecution and killing of thousands of Christians. Following the suppression of a Christian peasant revolt in 1637–1638, the Japanese government expelled all Europeans except for a small contingent of Dutch traders who were confined to a small island in the Nagasaki harbor.

Long before this expulsion, the Portuguese Empire had begun to decline. It did not have the special skills or fluid capital required by a global empire and had become dependent on the bankers and spice brokers of northern Europe for financing. This deficiency was magnified by Albuquerque's failure to recruit women from home who might have produced a Portuguese governing elite in the colonies. To make matters worse, the home population dropped steadily after 1600. Thus the relatively few Portuguese men overseas mated with local women. Most were concubines, prostitutes, or slaves—regarded generally as household pets or work animals. These conditions contributed largely to a decided weakening of morale, economic efficiency, and military power. After the turn of the seventeenth century, the Portuguese lost ground to the Omani Arabs in East Africa, the Spanish in the Philippines, and the Dutch in both hemispheres. Despite a mild later revival, their empire never regained its former glory.

THE PORTUGUESE AND AFRICA

■ *How did Africans respond to the opportunities offered by trade with the Portuguese?*

The Portuguese came to Africa as traders rather than settlers. Their original goal was to find a way around Muslim middlemen who controlled the trans-Saharan caravan trade and to gain direct access to the fabled goldfields of West Africa. Muslim kingdoms of the Sudan, such as Mali, Kanem-Bornu, and the Hausa states, dominated trade in the West African interior and were reluctant to open up their trade to Europeans. Therefore, the Portuguese concentrated their efforts on establishing commercial bases along the West African coast.

MAP
Africa, Europe, and the World

The Portuguese in West Africa

Africa was not of primary importance to the Portuguese, especially after they opened up sea routes to Asia. Thus, they selectively established links with African states where they could trade for goods of value such as gold, which could be traded anywhere in the world, and slaves, which were initially taken to southern Portugal as laborers. The first bases of operation for Portuguese seafarers were at Cape Verde, Arguin (ahr-GWEEN), and Senegambia.

CASE STUDY
Portuguese Travelers in Africa

Although the Portuguese conducted hit-and-run raids for slaves and plunder, they soon learned that if they expected to sustain a profitable trade in gold, they could not afford to alienate African rulers. When the Portuguese arrived on the Gold Coast (present-day Ghana) in 1471, they found Akan states carrying on a vigorous trade to the north through Muslim Dyula traders. Still hoping to develop trade links with the kingdom of Mali, the Portuguese sent several envoys with Dyula traders to Mali in the late fifteenth century. However, Mali's king sent a clear signal about his lack of interest in ties with Portugal by informing the envoy that he recognized only three kings beside himself—the rulers of Yemen, Cairo, and Baghdad.

From that point on, the Portuguese concentrated on establishing a profitable relationship with Akan leaders, exchanging firearms (that could not be obtained through Mali), copper and brass objects, textiles, slaves, and later cowrie shells for gold. From their fort at Elmina ("the mine"), established in 1482, the Portuguese exported close to half a ton of gold annually for the next half century. Because the Akan required slave labor to clear forests for arable agricultural land, the Portuguese brought slaves from the region of Benin and Kongo. It took several more

The Portuguese and Africa

1482	Portuguese establish Fort Elmina on Gold Coast; Portuguese reach kingdom of Kongo
1506–1543	Reign of Nzinga Mbemba, king of Kongo
1506	Portuguese seize Sofala
1571	Portuguese establish colony of Angola
1607	King of Mutapa kingdom signs treaty with Portugal
1698	Portuguese driven from East African coast by Omani Arabs

centuries before Akan states actively participated in selling rather than buying slaves.

The Portuguese also initiated contacts with the kingdom of Benin, located in the forests of southwestern Nigeria. The kings of Benin, called *obas,* had governed their land since the eleventh century. When the Portuguese arrived, Benin possessed a formidable army and was at the peak of its power. Edo, the walled capital, was a bustling metropolis with wide streets, markets, and an efficient municipal government. The huge royal palace awed Europeans who chanced to see it, although the Portuguese—and later the Dutch—were generally prohibited from living in the city. The few European visitors who gained entrance were amazed by Benin's metalwork, such as copper birds on towers, copper snakes coiled around doorways, and beautifully cast bronze statues.

Benin artists cast brass plaques that adorned the oba's palace walls. The plaques depicted important events in Benin's history, including the engagement with the Portuguese. The two Portuguese soldiers in this plaque are notable for their long wavy hair and military uniforms.

The first Portuguese emissary who arrived at oba Ozuola's court in 1486 was sent back to Lisbon with gifts, including a Maltese-type cross. The cross excited the Portuguese who interpreted it as a sign that Benin was near Prester John's kingdom and that its inhabitants would be receptive to conversion to Christianity. However, when Ozuola admitted Catholic missionaries to his kingdom in the early 1500s in the hope of securing Portuguese muskets, the Portuguese made acceptance of Christianity a precondition for receiving arms. Although the missionaries converted several of Ozuola's sons and high-ranking officials, their influence ended at Ozuola's death.

Portugal believed that it could manipulate Benin's rulers to extend Portuguese trade over a much wider area, but the obas did not regard trade with the Portuguese as a vital necessity and did not allow them to establish a sizable presence in the kingdom. The obas controlled all transactions, and Portuguese traders duly paid taxes, observed official regulations, and conducted business only with the obas' representatives.

The Portuguese traded brass and copper items, textiles, and cowrie shells for pepper, cloth, beads, and slaves. Because Benin did not have access to sources of gold, the Portuguese took the slaves from Benin and traded them for gold with the Akan states, which needed laborers for clearing forests for farmland. However, in 1516, Benin decided to curtail the slave trade and offered only female slaves for purchase.

Although effectively limited in Benin, Portuguese traders openly operated among nearby coastal states, where they gained some political influence. They were particularly successful in the small kingdom of Warri, a Niger delta vassal state of Benin. Shortly after 1600, the Warri crown prince was educated in Portugal and brought home a Portuguese queen. Warri supplied large numbers of slaves, as did other nearby states, which were now competing fiercely with one another. Before long, even Benin would accept dependence on the slave trade in order to control its tributaries and hold its own against Europeans.

The Portuguese and the Kongo Kingdom

Farther south, near the mouth of the Congo River, the Portuguese experienced their most intensive involvement in Africa. There, Portuguese seafarers found the recently established Kongo kingdom of several million people, ruled by a king who was heavily influenced by the queen mother and other women on his royal council. Although the Kongo initially perceived the Europeans as water or earth spirits, Kongo's king, Nzinga Nkuwu, soon came to regard them as a potential ally against neighboring African

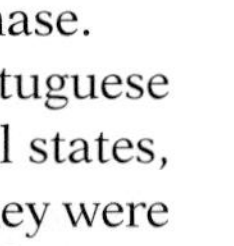

Loango, Capital of the Kingdom of the Congo

Discovery Through Maps

Savage Pictures: Sebastian Munster's Map of Africa

Voyages of exploration in the fifteenth and sixteenth centuries greatly expanded European knowledge of the rest of the world. However, mapmakers who knew very little about the geography and peoples of continents such as Africa still tended to rely on outdated information or stereotypical representations. Thus, when Sebastian Munster (1489–1552 C.E.), a professor of Hebrew and mathematics at Basel, the home of Switzerland's oldest university, developed an interest in maps, he turned to Ptolemy (90–168 C.E.), a celebrated astronomer, geographer, and mathematician of Alexandria, Egypt, whose theories about the universe influenced the European and Arab worlds for many centuries. When Ptolemy's *Guide to Geography* was published in Florence around 1400, it was the first atlas of the world.

Ptolemy's view of the world heavily influenced Munster when he began drawing his own world atlas. First published in 1544, Munster's *Cosmographia Universalis* went through 46 editions and was translated into six languages. It was the first collection to feature individual maps of Europe, Asia, the Americas, and Africa.

Munster's map of Africa relied not only on Ptolemy but also on Portuguese and Arab sources. However, it still contained many errors. The map identified the source of the Nile far to the south and, based on the assumption that the Senegal was connected to the Niger River in West Africa, showed a river flowing westward to the Atlantic.

The *Cosmographia* was also a descriptive geography, providing an accompanying narrative and drawings of prominent figures, the customs and manners of societies, and the products, animals, and plants of regions. Munster's Africa map depicted a lone human figure that bore no resemblance to Africans and a large elephant at the southern end of the continent. His rendering of Africa conformed to Jonathan Swift's satirical lines:

> *So Geographers in Africa-Maps*
> *With Savage-Pictures fill their Gaps;*
> *And o'er unhabitable Downs*
> *Place Elephants for want of Towns.*

Questions to Consider

1. Why do you think Muster chose to rely on Ptolemy's views rather than on more recent information?
2. Compare the portrayal of Africa in Munster's map with that in Abraham Cresque's Catalan map. Why does Cresque's map contain so much more detail than Munster's?

states. In the 1480s he invited the Portuguese to send teachers, technicians, missionaries, and soldiers. His son, Nzinga Mbemba (1506–1543), who converted to Catholicism in 1491, consolidated the control of the Catholic faction at his court, making Portuguese the official language and Catholicism the state religion. He encouraged his court to adopt European dress and manners while changing his own name to Don Afonso. Many friendly letters subsequently passed between him and King Manuel of Portugal.

This mutual cooperation did not last long. While the Portuguese were prepared to assist Afonso's kingdom, their desire for profits won out over their humanitarian impulses. Portuguese traders, seeking slaves for their sugar plantations at São Tomé (SAH-o TO-mai) and Principe, ranged over Kongo. By 1530 some 4000 to 5000 slaves were being taken from Kongo annually. No longer satisfied with treaty terms that gave them prisoners of war and criminals, the traders ignored the laws and bought everyone they could get, thus creating dissension and weakening the country. Driven to despair, Afonso wrote to his friend and ally Manuel: "There are many traders in all corners of the country. They bring ruin. . . . Every day, people are enslaved and kidnapped, even nobles, even members of the King's own family."[1] Such pleas brought no satisfactory responses. For a while, Afonso tried to curb the slave trade; however, he was shot by disgruntled Portuguese slavers while he was attending Mass in 1430. Afonso's successors were no more successful, and Portuguese slavers operated with impunity throughout Kongo and in neighboring areas.

The Portuguese crown also turned its attention to the Mbundu kingdom to the south of Kongo. In 1520 Manuel established contact with the Mbundu king, Ngola. However, when the Portuguese government agreed to deal with Ngola through Kongo, São Tomé slavers were given a free hand to join with Mbundu's rulers to attack neighboring states. Using African mercenaries known as pombeiros equipped with firearms and sometimes allied with feared Imbangala warriors, the slavers and their allies began a long war of conquest. In 1571 the Portuguese crown issued a royal charter to establish the colony of Angola, situated on the Atlantic coast south of the Kongo kingdom. Although Portugal had ambitious plans to create an agricultural colony for white settlement and to gain control over a silver mine and the salt trade in the interior, Angola was never a successful venture. Few settlers immigrated, and Angola remained a sleepy outpost, consisting of a handful of Portuguese men, even fewer Portuguese women, a growing population of Afro-Portuguese, and a majority of Africans. The colony functioned primarily as a haven for slavers. By the end of the sixteenth century, 10,000 slaves were flowing annually through Luanda (loo-AHN-dah), Angola's capital.

The Portuguese in East Africa

Portuguese exploits in East Africa were similar to those in Kongo and Angola. The Swahili city-states along the coast north of the Zambezi (zam-BEE-zee) River were tempting targets for Portuguese intervention because they were strategically well located for trade with Asia. However, because they rarely engaged in wars with each other or supported sizeable militaries, they could not effectively defend themselves against a ruthless Portuguese naval force that sacked and plundered city-states from Kilwa to Mombasa. At Mombasa Portuguese sailors broke into houses with axes, looted, and killed before setting the town afire. The sultan of Mombasa wrote to the sultan of Malindi: "[They] raged in our town with such might and terror that no one, neither man nor woman, neither the old or the young, nor even the children, however small, was spared to live."[2]

DOCUMENT "Of the Coasts of East Africa and Malabar"

Although a few city-states such as Malindi (mah-LEEN-dee) escaped the wrath of the Portuguese by becoming allies, the Portuguese usually relied on coercion to keep the city-states in line. They constructed fortified stations from which they attempted to collect tribute and maintain trade with the interior. An early station at Mozambique became the main port of call for vessels on the Asia route. In the 1590s the Portuguese built a fort at Mombasa, hoping to intimidate other cities and support naval operations against Turks and Arabs in the Red Sea. Although the Portuguese dominated trade in gold and ivory along the East African coast, they could not control the whole coastline and Swahili merchants continued to trade with their traditional partners. However, local industries such as ironworking and weaving virtually disappeared under Portuguese rule. When Omani Arabs expelled the Portuguese from the Swahili coast in 1698, the Swahili did not lament their departure. A Swahili proverb captured Swahili sentiment: "Go away, Manuel [the king of Portugal], you have made us hate you; go, and carry your cross with you."[3]

On the southeast coast the Portuguese were drawn to the Zimbabwean plateau by reports of huge gold mines. The Portuguese needed gold to finance their trade for spices in the Indian Ocean, while Shona kingdoms desired beads and cotton cloth from India. The Portuguese seized Sofala in 1506, diminishing the role of Muslim traders and positioning themselves as the middlemen for the gold trade with the coast. After establishing trading settlements along the Zambezi River at Sena and Tete, the Portuguese developed a close relationship with the Karanga kingdom of Mutapa, which received Portuguese traders and Catholic missionaries. This relationship soured when the king of Mutapa ordered the death of a Jesuit missionary in 1560. In the 1570s the Portuguese retaliated

Document Portuguese Encounters with Africans

The Portuguese had very specific objectives in Africa. They usually established amicable relations with stronger states, while they were more likely to coerce weaker states such as the Swahili city-states in East Africa. When Vasco da Gama dealt with the ruler of Kilwa, an island off the East African coast, he showed little patience for the subtleties of diplomacy and quickly resorted to threats to achieve his aims. This document records an exchange between da Gama and the King of Kilwa.

In the case of the Kingdom of the Kongo, the Portuguese were dealing with a state that clearly defined its interests and did not regard Portugal as a superior nation. Kongo's king, Don Afonso, who converted to Catholicism, wrote a series of letters to the king of Portugal in 1526. These letters demonstrate the complex relationship between the Kongolese leadership and the Portuguese. Afonso complains about Portuguese involvement in the slave trade but also conveys a request for doctors and apothecaries to treat illnesses.

KING IBRAHIM OF KILWA: Good friendship was to friends like brothers are and that he would shelter the Portuguese in his city and harbor . . . to pay tribute each year in money or jewelry was not a way to a good friendship, it was tributary subjugation . . . to pay tribute was dishonor . . . it would be like to be a captive . . . such friendship he did not want with subjugation . . . because even the sons did not want to have that kind of subjugation with their own parents.

VASCO DA GAMA: Take it for certain that if I so decide your city would be grounded by fire in one single hour and if your people wanted to extinguish the fire in town, they would all be burned and when you see all this happen, you will regret all you are telling me now and you will give much more than what I am asking you now, it will be too late for you. If you are still in doubt, it is up to you to see it.

KING IBRAHIM: Sir, if I had known that you wanted to enslave me, I would not have come and I would have fled into the forest, for it is better for me to be a fox but free, than a dog locked up in a golden chain.

From Chapurukha M. Kusimba, *The Rise and Fall of Swahili States* (Walnut Creek: AltaMira Press, 1999), pp. 161–162.

Moreover, Sir, in our Kingdom there is another great inconvenience which is of little service to God, and this is that many of our people [*naturaes*], keenly desirous as they are of the wares and things of your Kingdoms, which are brought here by your people, freed and exempt men; and very often it happens that they kidnap even noblemen and the sons of noblemen, and our relatives, and take them to be sold to the white men who are in our Kingdoms; and for this purpose they have concealed them, and others are brought during the night so that they might not be recognized.

And as soon as they are taken by the white men they are immediately ironed and branded with fire, and when they are carried to be embarked, if they are caught by our guards' men the whites allege that they have brought them but they cannot say from whom, so that it is our duty to do justice and to restore to the freemen their freedom, but it cannot be done if your subjects feel offended, as they claim to be.

And to avoid such a great evil we passed a law so that any white man living in our Kingdoms and wanting to purchase goods in any way should first inform three of our noblemen and officials of our court . . . who should investigate if the mentioned goods are captives or freemen, and if cleared by them there will be no further doubt nor embargo for them to be taken and embarked. But if the white men do not comply with it they will lose the aforementioned goods. . . .

[1526] Sir, Your Highness has been kind enough to write to us saying that we should ask in our letters for anything we need, and that we shall be provided with everything, and as the peace and health of our Kingdom depend on us . . . it happens that we have continuously many and different diseases which put us very often in such a weakness that we reach almost the last extreme; and the same happens to our children, relatives and natives owing to the lack in this country of physicians and surgeons who might know how to cure properly such diseases.

And to avoid such a great error and inconvenience, since it is from God in the first place and then from your Kingdoms and from Your Highness that all the good and drugs and medicines have come to save us, we beg of you to be agreeable and kind enough to send us two physicians and two apothecaries and all the necessary things to stay in our kingdoms. . . .

From Basil Davidson, *African Past* (Boston: Little, Brown and Co., 1964), pp. 192–194.

Questions to Consider

1. Why did the Portuguese treat the kings of Kongo and Kilwa in different ways?
2. What do the letters from the King of the Kongo reveal about the involvement of his people and the Portuguese in the slave trade?

by sending several expeditionary forces up the Zambezi to seize control over the gold-producing areas. The Portuguese believed the gold came from rich mines, when, in reality, African peasants recovered most of the gold from riverbeds during the winter months. In any event, these adventures ended disastrously as drought, disease (especially malaria), and African resisters decimated the Portuguese forces.

A series of internal rebellions and wars with neighboring states, however, forced Mutapa's rulers to turn to the Portuguese for assistance. In 1607 they signed a treaty that ceded control of gold production to the Portuguese. For the rest of the century the Portuguese regularly intervened in Mutapa's affairs until the forces of Mutapa and a rising power, Changamire, combined to expel the Portuguese from the Zimbabwean plateau. Along the Zambezi River the Portuguese crown granted huge land concessions ***(prazos)*** to Portuguese settlers *(prazeros)* who ruled them as feudal estates. Over time, the *prazeros* loosened their ties with Portugal's officials and became virtually independent. In the absence of Portuguese women, *prazeros* intermarried with Africans and adopted African culture.

The tale of Prester John, the mythical Ethiopian Christian monarch who held the Muslims at bay, had long captivated Portugal's monarchs. Thus, they initially responded positively when the astute Ethiopian empress Eleni made diplomatic overtures. Eleni, the daughter of a Muslim king, had married the Ethiopian emperor Baeda Maryam and converted to Christianity. After his death in 1478, she remained an influential figure as regent during the reigns of two of her sons and two grandsons. Recognizing that the interests of both Ethiopia and Portugal would be served by defeating Muslim states on the Red Sea coast, she wrote Portugal's king in 1509 proposing an alliance against the Ottoman Turks. She reasoned that the combination of Ethiopia's army and Portugal's sea forces would be very potent. However, the Portuguese, disappointed that Ethiopia did not meet their grand expectations of a kingdom ruled by Prester John, were reluctant to sign a pact.

After Eleni's death in 1522, her projected alliance was not completed for several decades. In 1541, the army of Muslim leader Ahmad Gran of the kingdom of Adal had come close to conquering Ethiopia. This time, the Portuguese responded to Ethiopian appeals by dispatching 400 Portuguese musketeers who helped to defeat the Muslims. The following year, however, Muslim forces, augmented by Turkish soldiers, rallied and defeated the Portuguese contingent, killing its commander, Christopher da Gama, Vasco's son. When the Ethiopians eventually pushed the Muslims out, they enticed some of the Portuguese soldiers to stay on by granting them large estates in the countryside. Subsequent Ethiopian rulers called on descendants of the Portuguese in their conflicts with the Turks.

The Portuguese impact on Africa was not as immediately disastrous as Spanish effects on the New World. The Portuguese did not have the manpower or arms to dictate the terms of trade with most African states. However, they did inflict severe damage in Kongo, Angola, Zimbabwe, and the Swahili city-states. Their most destructive involvement was the slave trade.

By the end of the sixteenth century the Portuguese had moved an estimated 240,000 slaves from West and Central Africa; 80 percent were transported after 1575. These trends foreshadowed much greater disasters for African societies in the seventeenth and eighteenth centuries as the Atlantic slave trade expanded (see Chapter 19).

THE GROWTH OF NEW SPAIN

- *What factors contributed to the Spanish conquest of Amerindian societies?*

While Portugal concentrated on Asian and African trade, Spain won a vast empire in America. Soon after 1492, Spanish settlements were established in the West Indies, most notably on Hispaniola (ees-pah-nee-O-lah) and Cuba. By 1500, as the American continents were recognized and the passage to Asia remained undiscovered, a host of Spanish adventurers—the ***conquistadora***—set out for the New World with dreams of acquiring riches. From the West Indies they crossed the Caribbean to eastern Mexico, fanning out from there in all directions, toward Central America, the Pacific, and the vast North American hinterlands.

In Mexico the Spaniards profited from internal problems within the Aztec Empire. By the early 1500s, the Aztecs ruled over several million people in a vast kingdom that stretched from the Gulf of Mexico to the Pacific Ocean and from present-day central Mexico to Guatemala. However, unrest ran rampant among many recently conquered peoples, who were forced to pay tribute and taxes and furnish sacrificial victims to their Aztec overlords.

In 1519 Spanish officials in Cuba, excited by reports of a wealthy Amerindian civilization from two

prazo—A land grant from the Portuguese crown to a Portuguese settler *(prazero)* in the Zambezi river valley in Mozambique that gave the settler control over tribute and labor service from local residents.

conquistadora—The Spanish soldiers who conquered Mexico and Peru.

expeditions to the Yucatán (yoo-kah-TAHN) peninsula, dispatched Hernando Cortés (1485–1574) with 11 ships, 600 fighting men, 200 servants, 16 horses, 32 crossbows, 13 muskets, and 14 mobile cannons. Before marching against the Aztec capital, he destroyed 10 of his 11 ships to prevent his men from turning back. He had the good luck to secure two interpreters. One was an Amerindian woman, Malitzin, later christened Doña Marina, who became a valuable interpreter and intelligence gatherer as well as bearing Cortés a son. As Cortés's band marched inland, he added thousands of Amerindian warriors to his small force. He easily enlisted Amerindian allies, such as the Cempoala who had suffered under Aztec rule. By contrast, the loyalty of the Tlaxcalan (tlash-KAH-lahn) was secured only after Cortez's force demonstrated the superiority of its firearms, steel swords, and armor and horses (that the Aztecs initially thought were deer).

DOCUMENT
Cortez to King Charles V of Spain

The Aztec emperor Moctezuma II's initial view of the Spaniards was shaped by an Aztec belief that the Spaniards were representatives of the white-skinned and bearded Teotihuacán (tay-o-tee-wah-KAHN) god, Quetzalcoatl (KAT-SAL-KWA-tel), who had been exiled by the Toltecs in the tenth century C.E. He forbade human sacrifice and had promised to return from across the sea to enforce his law. However, as reports of Spanish victories came to his attention, Moctezuma had second thoughts as Cortés approached the Aztec capital, Tenochtitlán (te-noch-teet-lahn), a city of more than 150,000 people. Thus, Moctezuma warily welcomed Cortés as a guest in his father's palace. Although surrounded by a host of armed Aztecs, Cortés seized the ruler and informed him that he must cooperate or die. The bold scheme worked temporarily. But when Cortés left the capital to return to the coast, his commander attacked an unarmed crowd at a religious festival, killing many Aztec notables. The massacre touched off a popular uprising. Cortés returned with reinforcements, but when he placed Moctezuma on a wall to pacify the Aztecs, they renounced their former ruler as a traitor and stoned and killed him. Neither the Aztecs nor the Spaniards showed any mercy in the fierce fighting that followed. The Aztecs ultimately drove a battered band of terrified Spaniards from the city in the narrowest of escapes. Later, having regrouped and gained new Amerindian allies, Cortés wore down the Aztecs in a bloody siege during which some Spanish prisoners were sacrificed in full view of their comrades. The outcome of the fighting was in doubt when a smallpox epidemic, accidentally introduced by a Spanish soldier, broke out, killing many thousands of Aztecs who had no immunity to the disease. Finally, in August 1521, some 60,000 exhausted and half-starved defenders surrendered.

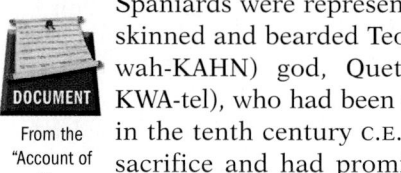

DOCUMENT
From the "Account of Alva Ixtlilxochitl"

As the inheritors of the Aztec empire, the Spaniards found the Aztec's hierarchical system suited to their needs. They replaced an urbanized Aztec elite with their own and gave privileged positions to Amerindian allies such as the Tlaxcalans. The Spanish ruled from Tenochtitlán, rebuilt as Mexico City, which became the capital of an expanding Spanish empire.

Although *conquistadora* steadily penetrated the interior, the fierce Mayas of Yucatán and Guatemala put up a determined resistance until the 1540s. By then, Spanish settlements had been established throughout Central America. The first colony in North America was founded at St. Augustine, on Florida's

An illustration from the Codex Azacatitlán of the Spanish arriving in Mexico. Standing next to Cortés is Malitzin, the Aztec woman who served as his interpreter.

east coast, in 1565. Meanwhile, numerous expeditions, including those of Hernando de Soto (1500–1542) and Francisco de Coronado (1510–1554), explored what is now California, Arizona, New Mexico, Colorado, Texas, Missouri, Louisiana, and Alabama. Spanish friars established a mission at Santa Fe in 1610, providing a base for later missions. All these new territories, known as New Spain, were administered from Mexico City after 1542.

The viceroyalty of Mexico later sponsored colonization of the Philippines, a project justified by the historic voyage of Ferdinand Magellan (1480–1521). Encouraged by the exploits of Vasco de Balboa (1479–1519), who had crossed Panama and discovered the Pacific Ocean in 1513, Magellan sailed from Spain in 1520, steered past the ice-encrusted straits at the tip of South America, and endured a 99-day voyage to the Philippines. He made an unwise choice by intervening in a conflict between two sheikdoms, and he lost his life in a battle with the inhabitants of Mactan Island. Many of Magellan's crew died after terrible suffering from **scurvy.** This illness explains why only one of Magellan's five ships completed this first circumnavigation of the world. However, the feat established a Spanish claim to the Philippines. It also prepared the way for the first tiny settlement of 400 Mexicans at Cebu in 1571. By 1580, when the Philippine capital at Manila had been secured against attacking Portuguese, Chinese, and Moro fleets, the friars were beginning conversions that would reach half a million by 1622. The colony prospered in trade with Asia but remained economically dependent on annual galleons bearing silver from Mexico. Because the Spanish were excluded from China, they relied on a community of Chinese merchants in Manila to trade the silver in the Chinese market for luxury items such as porcelain, silk, and lacquer ware.

The Development of Spanish South America

As in Mexico, the Spanish exploited unique opportunities as well as epidemics in their process of empire building in Peru. Just before they arrived, the recently formed Inca state had been torn apart by a succession crisis. When the emperor Huayna Capac and his heir apparent suddenly died of smallpox in 1526, the claim of his son Huascar (was-KAR) to the throne was contested by Atahualpa, a half-royal son who had been Huayna Capac's favorite. Their conflict, which soon destroyed nearly every semblance of imperial unity, was a major factor in the surprisingly easy triumph of a handful of Spanish freebooters over a country of more than ten million people, scattered through Peru and Ecuador in hundreds of mountain towns and coastal cities.

Francisco Pizarro (1470–1541), the son of an illiterate peasant, was the conqueror of Peru. After two earlier exploratory visits, he landed on the northern coast in January 1531 with a tiny privately financed army of 207 men and 27 horses. For more than a year he moved south, receiving some reinforcements as he plundered towns and villages. Leaving a garrison of 60 soldiers in a coastal base, he started inland in September 1532 with a Spanish force of fewer than 200. About the same time, word came that Altahualpa's forces had defeated Huascar's in battle and were poised to capture the imperial capital, Cuzco. Pizarro now posed as a potential ally to both sides. At Cajamarca he met and captured Altahualpa, slaughtering some 6000 unarmed retainers of the Inca monarch. He next forced Altahualpa to fill a room with 26,000 pounds of silver and over 13,000 pounds of gold. Then, having collected the ransom, Pizarro executed his royal prisoner and proclaimed Manco, the young son of Altahualpa's dead brother, as emperor.

Thus, upon arriving in Cuzco with their puppet ruler, the Spaniards were welcomed as deliverers and quickly secured tentative control of the country. Manco, after suffering terrible indignities from the Spaniards, organized a rebellion in 1536. Although his army of 60,000 heavily outnumbered Pizarro's 200 Spaniards, they could not score a decisive victory. Manco and his supporters retreated to the northwest to a mountain outpost at Vilacamba where an independent Inca kingdom survived until the Spanish captured and executed the last Inca emperor in 1572.

Although the *conquistadora* had triumphed over the Incas, political anarchy still reigned in Peru as the *conquistadora* split into two factions led by the Pizarro and Almagro families. When Pizarro was assassinated in his palace in 1542, it touched off a bloody civil war that raged for six years.

The period was marked by an obsessive Spanish rape of the country, along with cruel persecution of its Amerindian population, and by ruthless contention, involving every degree of greed and brutality, among the conquerors. Meanwhile, marauding expeditions moved south into Chile and north through Ecuador into Colombia. Expeditions from Chile and Peru settled in Argentina, founding Buenos Aires. Relationships between *conquistadora* and Amerindian women were common, and they

scurvy—A disease contracted on voyages of longer than a month because sailors' diets lacked sufficient quantities of vitamins B and C.

produced a new ***mestizo*** population in Paraguay. Despite this dynamic activity, there was no effective government at Lima, the capital, until the end of the sixteenth century.

Along with brutality, Spaniards in the post-conquest era also demonstrated unprecedented fortitude and courage. Pizarro's Spaniards were always outnumbered in battle. They faced nearly unendurable torments, including scorching heat, disease-carrying insects, air too thin for breathing, and cold that at times could freeze a motionless man into a lifeless statue. Amid the terrible hardships of this male-dominated era, both Amerindian and Spanish women played significant roles. As in Mexico, Amerindian women were camp-following concubines who prepared food and bore children; in addition to traditional feminine tasks, some Spanish women fought beside the men when necessary. Ines Suarez achieved distinction by donning armor and leading the defense of Santiago, Chile, shortly after its founding in 1541. Some women were present on all the pioneering ventures, and others were direct participants in the terrible sacrifices of the civil wars.

To govern Mexico and Peru the Spanish established two viceroyalties that by 1600 contained over 200 towns with a Spanish and mestizo population of 200,000. By then, the empire was in decline. Peruvian silver, the main source of Spanish wealth, was either running out or requiring very expensive mining operations; the Amerindian labor force was depleted, and African slaves were both scarce and expensive. Spain's deteriorating home economy and waning sea power presented even more serious problems.

MAP
European Empires in Latin America, 1660

IBERIAN SYSTEMS IN THE NEW WORLD

▪ *What role did Amerindian and African labor play in the Spanish and Portuguese economic systems?*

European expansion overseas after the fifteenth century brought revolutionary change to all the world's peoples, but the Iberian period before 1600 was unique in its violence and ruthless exploitation. Not only were highly organized states destroyed in the New World, but whole populations were wiped out by European diseases, shock, and inhumane treatment. This tragic catastrophe was accompanied by a decided change in the racial composition of Iberian America as an influx of African slaves, along with continued Spanish and Portuguese immigration, led to a variegated racial mixture, ranging through all shades of color between white and black. Fortunately, the Amerindian population began recovering in the mid-1600s, and their cultures, combining with Iberian and African, formed a new configuration, to be known later as Latin American.

The arrival of the Spanish and Portuguese in America led to a mixing of three cultures: European, African, and Amerindian. This painted wooden bottle, done in Inca style and dating from about 1650, shows the mix. The three figures are an African drummer, a Spanish trumpeter, and an Amerindian official.

The General Nature of Regimes

Iberian regimes in America faced serious problems. Their vast territories, far greater than the homelands, contained nearly impassable deserts, mountains, and dense rain forests. Supplies had to be moved thousands of miles, often across open seas. Communications were difficult, wars with indigenous peoples were frequent, and disease was often rampant. Such conditions help explain, if not justify, the brutality of Iberian imperialism.

DOCUMENT
New Laws for the Treatment and Preservation of the Indians

With all their unique features, Iberian overseas empires were similar to Roman or Turkish provinces: they were meant to produce revenues. In theory, all Spanish lands were the king's personal property. The Council of the Indies, which directed the viceroys in Mexico City and Lima, advised him on colonial affairs. The highborn Spanish viceroys were aided (and limited) by councils *(audiencias)*, made up of aristocratic lawyers from Spain. Local governors, responsible to the viceroys, functioned with their advisory councils ***(cabildos)*** of officials. Only the rich normally sat in such bodies; poor Spaniards and mestizos had little voice, even in their own taxation. Most taxes, however, were collected by Amerindian chiefs ***(caciques)***, still acting as rulers of Amerindian peasant villages.

mestizo—A person of Spanish and Indian descent.

cabildos—Town councils whose members were usually appointed by the governor.

cacique—An Amerindian chief who assisted the Spanish in collecting taxes from his subjects.

Portuguese Brazil was less directly controlled than the Spanish colonies. It languished for years under almost unrestricted domination of 15 aristocratic "captains" who held hereditary rights of taxing, disposing lands, making laws, and administering justice. In return, they sponsored settlement and paid stipulated sums to the king. This quasi-feudal administration was abandoned in 1548. When Philip II became king of Portugal in 1580, he established municipal councils, although these were still dominated by the hereditary captains.

Iberian Economies in America

Both the philosophies and the structures of the Iberian states limited colonial trade and industry. Most Spanish and Portuguese immigrants were disinclined toward productive labor. With few exceptions, commercial contacts were limited to the homelands; Mexican merchants fought a steadily losing battle to maintain independent trade with Peru and the Philippines. Local trade grew modestly in supplying the rising towns, some crafts developed into large-scale industrial establishments, and a national transport system, based on mule teams, became a major Mexican industry. So did smuggling, as demand for foreign goods rose higher and higher.

Agriculture, herding, and mining silver, however, were the main economic pursuits. The early gold sources soon ran out, but silver strikes in Mexico and Peru poured a stream of wealth back to Spain in the annual treasure fleets, convoyed by warships from Havana to Seville. Without gold to mine, many Spanish aristocrats acquired conquered Amerindian land, raising wheat, rice, indigo, cotton, coffee, and sugarcane. Cattle, horses, and sheep were imported and bred on ranches in the West Indies, Mexico, and Argentina. Brazil developed similar industries, particularly those related to brazilwood (for which the country was given its name), sugar, livestock, and coffee. Although Iberian economic pursuits in America were potentially productive, revealing numerous instances of initiative and originality, they were largely repressed by bureaucratic state systems.

Before 1660, plantations (large estates that used servile labor to grow crops) were not typical for agriculture in Iberian America, although they were developing in certain areas. The Spanish tried plantations in the Canaries, later establishing them in the West Indies, the Mexican lowlands, and Central America and along the northern coasts of South America. Even in such areas, which were environmentally suited for intensive single-crop cultivation, it was not easy to raise the capital, find the skilled technicians, and pay for the labor the system required.

The Spanish initially dealt with the labor problem in Mexico and Peru by forcing Amerindians on the labor market with taxation, but so many died from the devastating impact of European diseases that the Spanish turned to Africans for slave labor. Besides being separated from their families and societies, Africans slaves were mobile and could be shipped anywhere (see p. 563). By the 1550s, some 3000 African slaves were in Peru, working in gold mines and on cattle ranches and participating in a variety of unskilled and skilled occupations in the capital, Lima. At the end of the century, Africans, although replaced in the mines by Amerindians, continued to labor on coastal plantations and serve in elite households. Some 75,000 slaves were in the

Amerindian slaves work a Spanish sugar plantation on the island of Hispaniola. Spanish treatment of the Amerindians was often brutal.

Spanish colonies by 1600; more than 100,000 more arrived in the next four decades.

Portugal established sugar plantations on its Atlantic islands (Madeira, Cape Verde, and São Tomé). São Tomé was uninhabited when the Portuguese settled on it in 1485. Because the island is situated on the equator and receives abundant rainfall, it was an ideal setting to begin sugar production a half century later. São Tomé was also near Angola, a primary source of slaves. This experience created a direct link between the production of sugar and African slave labor. São Tomé also witnessed the resistance of slaves, who, much like the Maroons in Jamaica, fled the sugar plantations for the safety of the mountainous interior.

São Tomé, Cape Verde, and Madeira were the models when the Portuguese introduced the plantation system into northern Brazil around 1550. Like the Spanish, the Portuguese initially recruited Amerindian labor, but after a smallpox epidemic in the 1560s killed off many Amerindians, they began to rely on African slaves as the primary laborers on plantations. By the early 1600s, 30,000 Africans were annually being brought to Brazil. After 1650, as Dutch, British, and French possessions in the Caribbean islands were drawn into the sugar economy, they, as well as Portuguese Brazil, became the largest importers of unfree labor from Africa.

Some slaves were brutally oppressed as laborers in the mines, and others sweated on Spanish or Brazilian plantations. Slaves were also teamsters, overseers, personal servants, and skilled artisans. Particularly in the Spanish colonies, a good many earned their freedom, attaining a social status higher than that of Amerindian peasants. Free blacks, both men and women, operated shops and small businesses. Prostitution was common among black and **mulatto** women, a profession that went hand-in-hand with the sexual exploitation of female slaves as concubines and breeders.

Iberian Effects on Amerindian Life

The Spanish and Portuguese brought terrible disaster to most Amerindians. Having seen their gods mocked and their temples destroyed, many accepted Christianity as the only hope for survival, as well as salvation, while toiling for their Iberian masters. Some died from overwork, some were killed, and others simply languished as their cultures disintegrated. The most dangerous adversity was disease—European or African—to which Amerindians had no immunities.

mulatto—A person of European and African descent.

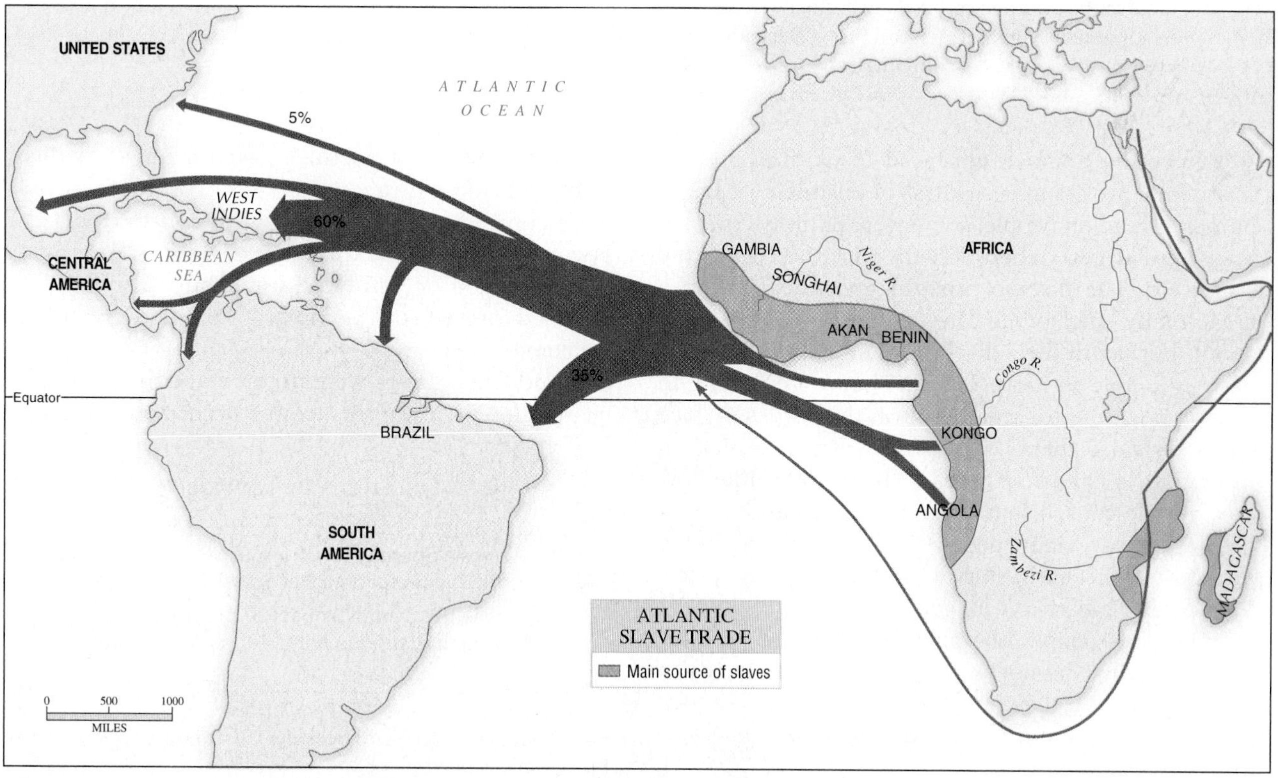

Africans were forcibly captured in raids and kidnappings in the interior of Africa and taken to the coast. After they were sold to European traders, the slaves were transported across the Atlantic to work on sugar plantations in the New World.

Epidemics arrived with Columbus and continued throughout the sixteenth century. Smallpox on Hispaniola in 1518 left only 1000 Amerindians alive there. Cortés's men carried the pox to Mexico, where it raged while he fought his way out of Tenochtitlán. From Mexico the epidemic spread through Central America, reaching Peru in 1526. It killed the reigning emperor and helped start the civil war that facilitated Pizarro's conquest. Following these smallpox disasters in the 1540s and 1570s, a wave of measles, along with other successive epidemics, continued depleting the population.

Depopulation of Amerindians was caused in part by their enslavement, despite disapproval by the Catholic Church and the Spanish government. The worst excesses came early. Original settlers on Hispaniola herded the Arawaks to work like animals; they soon became extinct. A whole indigenous population of the Bahamas—some 40,000 people—were carried away as slaves to Hispaniola, Cuba, and Puerto Rico. Cortés captured slaves before he took Tenochtitlán; other Amerindians, enslaved in Panama, were regularly sent to Peru. Before Africans arrived in appreciable numbers, the Portuguese organized "Indian hunts" in the forests to acquire slaves.

Another more common labor system in the Spanish colonies was the ***encomienda.*** This system was instituted in Mexico by Cortés as a way of using Amerindian caciques to collect revenues and provide labor. It was similar to European feudalism and manorialism, involving a royal grant that permitted the holder *(encomendero)* to take income or labor from specified lands and the people living on them. Many

---

encomienda—A system of control over land and Indian labor granted to a Spanish colonist *(encomendero).*

Document — Disease and the Spanish Conquest

Diseases introduced by Europeans had a devastating impact on indigenous societies in the New World. This account of the impact of a smallpox epidemic among the Aztecs appeared in the Florentine Codex, an invaluable history of the Aztecs published in the mid-sixteenth century. Written in Nahuátl, the Aztec language and translated into Spanish, the books were based on information gathered by Aztec scribes under the supervision of a Franciscan priest Bernadino de Sahagún. This story of the smallpox epidemic drew on eyewitness accounts of individuals who lived through the Spanish conquest.

Before the Spanish appeared to us, first an epidemic broke out, a sickness of pustules. . . . Large bumps spread on people, some were entirely covered. They spread everywhere, on the face, the head, the chest, etc. The disease brought great desolation; a great many died of it. They could no longer walk about, but lay in their dwellings and sleeping places, no longer able to move or stir. They were unable to change position, to stretch out on their sides or face down, or raise their heads. And when they made a motion, they called out loudly. The pustules that covered people caused that covered people caused great desolation. very many people died of them, and many just starved to death; starvation reigned, and no one took care of others any longer.

On some people, the pustules appeared only far apart, and they did not suffer greatly, nor did many of them die of it. But many people's faces were spoiled by it, their faces and noses were made rough. Some lost an eye or were blinded.

This disease of pustules lasted a full sixty days; after sixty days it abated and ended. When people were convalescing and reviving, the pustules disease began to move in the direction of Chalco. And many were disabled or paralyzed by it, but they were not disabled forever. . . . The Mexica warriors were greatly weakened by it.

And when things were in this state, the Spaniards came, moving toward us from Tetzcoco.

Questions to Consider

1. What was more responsible for the Spanish conquest of the Aztecs—Spanish weapons, armor, horses or the diseases that accompanied the Spanish?
2. What was the overall impact of diseases such as smallpox on the indigenous populations of the Americas?

From James Lockhart, *We People Here: Nahuatl Accounts of the Conquest of Mexico* (Berkeley: University of California Press, 1993), pp. 180–182.

encomenderos lashed and starved their Amerindian laborers, working men and women to exhaustion or renting them to other equally insensitive masters. Amerindian women on the *encomiendas* were generally used as wet nurses, cooks, or maids or as sex slaves by the owners and the caciques, who served as overseers.

The *encomienda* system was slowly but steadily abandoned after the 1550s largely because of the efforts of a former *conquistadore* and *encomendero*, Bartolomé de Las Casas (1474–1566). A Dominican friar, he protested the cruel treatment of Amerindians and persuaded Charles V that they should hold the same rights as other subjects. His efforts led to the New Law of 1542, which ended existing *encomiendas* upon the death of their holders, prohibited Amerindian slavery, and gave Amerindians full protection under Spanish law. Most of these provisions, however, were rescinded when the law evoked universal protest and open rebellion in Peru. Although later governors gradually eliminated *encomiendas,* many Amerindians were put on reservations and hired out as contract laborers under the direction of their caciques and local officials *(corrigodores)*. This practice eliminated some of the worst excesses of the *encomiendas,* but corrupt officials often exploited their wards, particularly in Peru.

DOCUMENT
From "In Defense of the Indians"

Such physical hardships were matched by others of a psychological nature, which were almost equally damaging to Amerindians. The Spaniards insisted on forcing Christian conversion even while they raped and destroyed, as Pizarro did before executing Atahualpa. Except when they used Amerindian authorities to support their regimes, the Spaniards went out of their way to insult, shame, and degrade their unfortunate subjects. In the new social milieu, Amerindians were constantly reminded of their lowly status, unworthy of human consideration. For example, Cortés, who had multiple Amerindian mistresses, passed off Malitzin to one of his captains; Pizarro forced Manco, while still an ally, to give his young Inca queen to the conqueror. Such indignities, repeated by the hundreds among both Spanish and Portuguese, left many Amerindians demoralized to the point of utter despair.

Their distress was alleviated to some extent by missions, established by the Dominican and Jesuit religious orders. These afforded Amerindians the most effective protection and aid. Las Casas led the way in founding such settlements, where Amerindians were shielded from white exploitation, instructed in Christianity, and educated or trained in special skills. The prevailing philosophy in the missions stressed patient persuasion. Large mission organizations developed in Brazil, Venezuela, Paraguay, and upper California. But even the Amerindians protected by the missions died rapidly in this alien way of life.

Moved by the simplicity and gentle nature of the Amerindians, Bartolomé de Las Casas launched a vigorous campaign to ensure their protection. His Apologetic History of the Indies *(1566) is an indictment of the Spaniards' harsh treatment of the Amerindians.*

Although most Amerindians were demoralized by their misfortunes, some resisted. In Yucatán and Guatemala, where the Mayas did not believe the Spaniards were gods, bloody fighting lasted until the 1540s. About that time, the Spanish put down a revolt on the Mexican Pacific coast with great difficulty. As the silver mines opened in northern Mexico into the 1590s, the Chichimecs, relatives of the Apaches of North America, conducted a border war, using horses and captured muskets. In Peru an Inca rebellion, led first by Manco, was subdued only in 1577. The most stubborn resistance came from the Araucanians of southern Chile, who fought the Spaniards successfully until the close of the sixteenth century.

The full Iberian impact on Amerindian culture is difficult to assess, although there can be no denying that it was disastrous. A conservative estimate of Amerindian population losses puts the proportion at 25 percent during the era to 1650, but some recent figures place losses much higher, up to 95 percent of the pre-1492 total of 100 million. Signs of mental deterioration were also evident in prevalent alcoholism, which began among Amerindians shortly after the conquest.

Spanish Colonial Society and Culture

Spanish colonial society was stratified but somewhat flexible. A small elite of officials and aristocrats contended over politics, policy toward subject peoples, and foreign trade. Merchants and petty officials were on a lower social level but above mestizos, mulattoes, and **zambos.** Amerindians were considered incompetent wards of the home government, and African slaves were legally designated as beneath the law, but there were numerous individual exceptions. Many Amerindians went from their rural homes to the towns, mines, or **haciendas;** some caciques enjoyed wealth and privilege; and a few established Amerindian families retained their nobility as early Spanish allies. Similarly, some African slaves were overseers, privileged personal servants, and involved in urban crafts such as tailoring, shoemaking, carpentry, and blacksmithing; others acquired freedom and became prosperous merchants; still others escaped slavery, organized free communities, and successfully defended their independence.

Women in Spanish American society were a numerical minority. They played ambiguous roles, reflecting the traditional ideal of male superiority. They were excluded from male contacts throughout childhood, not allowed to join in dinner conversations, educated in cloistered schools to become wives and mothers, married in their teens to further family interests, and legally subordinated to their husbands. Most could not serve in public office or qualify as lawyers. Those who did not marry, particularly women of the upper classes, usually entered convents. There was, however, another side to the story. Spanish law guaranteed a wife's dowry rights, a legal protection against the squandering of her wealth, and leverage to limit her husband's activities. The courts recognized separations and at times even granted annulments in cases of wife abuse. Women, particularly widows, operated businesses. Some were wealthy, powerful, and even cruel *encomenderas,* supervising thousands of workers. Whatever their special roles, Iberian matrons defended religion, sponsored charities, dictated manners, and taught their children family values. They civilized the empires conquered by their men.

Both the unique environment and the mix of peoples shaped Spanish colonial culture toward a new distinctive unity. From southwestern Europe came its aristocratic government, disdain for manual labor, a preference for dramatic over precise expression, and ceremonial Catholic Christianity. From Amerindian traditions came characteristic foods, art forms, architecture, legends, and practical garments like the poncho and serape, as well as substantial vocabulary. From Africa came agricultural knowledge, crafts, and animal husbandry. By 1650 this characteristic colonial culture was being preserved in its own universities, such as those at Lima and Mexico City, both founded more than a century earlier.

BEGINNINGS OF NORTHERN EUROPEAN EXPANSION

- *What were the experiences of the Dutch, French, and British with their colonies of European settlement?*

European overseas expansion after 1600 entered a second phase, comparable to developments at home. As Spain declined, so did the Spanish Empire and that of Portugal, which was unified with Spain by a Habsburg king after 1580 and plagued with its own developing imperial problems. These conditions afforded opportunities for the northern European states. The Dutch between 1630 and 1650 almost cleared the Atlantic of Spanish warships while taking over most of the Portuguese posts in Brazil, Africa, and Asia. The French and English also became involved on a smaller scale, setting up a global duel for empire in the eighteenth century.

The Shifting Commercial Revolution

Along with this second phase of expansion came a decisive shift in Europe's Commercial Revolution. Expanding foreign trade, new products, an increasing supply of bullion, and rising commercial risks created new problems, calling for energetic initiatives. Because the Spanish and Portuguese during the sixteenth century had depended on quick profits, weak home industries, and poor management, wealth flowed through their hands to northern Europe, where it was invested in productive enterprises. Later it generated a new imperial age.

European markets after the sixteenth century were swamped with a bewildering array of hitherto rare or unknown goods. New foods from America included potatoes, peanuts, maize (Indian corn), tomatoes, and fish from Newfoundland's Grand Banks. In an era without refrigeration, imported spices—such as pepper, cloves, and cinnamon—were valued for making spoiled

zambo—A person of African and Indian descent.

hacienda—An estate or plantation belonging to elite families.

Marketplace at Antwerp. In the sixteenth century, Antwerp was the leading city in international commerce. As many as 500 ships a day docked in its bustling harbor, and as many as 1000 wagons arrived each week carrying the overland trade.

foods palatable. Sugar became a common substitute for honey, and the use of cocoa, the Aztec sacred beverage, spread throughout Europe. Coffee and tea from the New World and Asia would also soon change European social habits. Similarly, North American furs, Chinese silks, and cottons from India and Mexico revolutionized clothing fashions. Furnishings of rare woods and ivory and luxurious oriental carpets appeared more frequently in the homes of the wealthy. The use of American tobacco became almost a mania among all classes, further contributing to the booming European market.

Imported gold and, even more significant, silver probably affected the European economy more than all other foreign goods. After the Spaniards had looted Aztec and Inca treasure rooms, the gold flowing from America and Africa subsided to a respectable trickle; but 7 million tons of silver poured into Europe before 1660. Spanish prices quadrupled, and because most new bullion went to pay for imports, prices more than tripled in northern Europe. Rising inflation hurt landlords who depended on fixed rents and creditors who were paid in cheap money, but the bullion bonanza ended a centuries-long gold drain to the East, with its attendant money shortage. It also increased the profits of merchants selling on a rising market, thus greatly stimulating northern European capitalism.

At the opening of the sixteenth century, Italian merchants and moneylenders, mainly Florentines, Venetians, and Genoese, dominated the rising Atlantic economy. The German Fugger banking house at Augsburg also provided substantial financing. European bankers, particularly the Fuggers and the Genoese, suffered heavily from the Spanish economic debacles under Charles V and Philip II. As the century passed, Antwerp, in the southern Netherlands, became the economic hub of Europe. It was the center for the English wool trade as well as a transfer station, drawing southbound goods from the Baltic and Portuguese goods from Asia. It was also a great financial market, dealing in commercial and investment instruments. The Spanish sack of the city in 1576 ended Antwerp's supremacy, which passed to Amsterdam and furthered Dutch imperial ventures.

Meanwhile, northern European capitalism flourished in nearly every category. Portuguese trade in Africa and Asia was matched by that of the Baltic and the North Atlantic. Northern joint-stock companies pooled capital for privateering, exploring, and commercial venturing. The Dutch and English East India companies, founded early in the seventeenth century, were but two of the better-known stock companies. In England common fields were enclosed for capitalistic sheep runs. Throughout western Europe, domestic manufacturing, in homes or workshops, was competing with the guilds. Large industrial enterprises, notably in mining, shipbuilding, and cannon casting, were becoming common. Indeed, the superiority of English and Swedish cannons caused the defeat of the Spanish Armada and Catholic armies in the Thirty Years' War.

The Dutch Empire

By 1650 the Dutch were supreme in both southern Asia and the South Atlantic. Their empire, like that of the Portuguese earlier, was primarily commercial; even their North American settlements specialized in fur trading with the Indians. They acquired territory where necessary to further their commerce but tried to act pragmatically in accordance with Asian cultures rather than by conquest. An exception was their colony in Java, where the Dutch drive for monopolizing the spice trade led them to take direct control of the island. Unlike the Spanish and the Portuguese, the Dutch made little attempt to spread Christianity.

Dutch involvement in the Indian Ocean was the direct result of the Spanish absorption of Portugal in 1580. The Spanish restricted the flow of spices, especially pepper, to Northern Europe, and Dutch seafarers set out to control the sources of the trade. Systematic Dutch naval operations commenced in 1595 when the first Dutch fleet entered the East Indies. Dutch captains soon drove the Portuguese from the Spice Islands. Malacca, the Portuguese bastion, fell after a long siege in 1641. The Dutch also occupied Sri Lanka (SHREE-lahn-KAH) and blockaded Goa, thus limiting Portuguese operations in the Indian Ocean. Although largely neglecting East Africa, they seized all Portuguese posts on the west coast north of Angola. Across the Atlantic, they conquered and held part of Brazil for a few decades, drove Spain from the Caribbean, and captured a Spanish treasure fleet. Decisive battles off the English Channel coast near Kent (1639) and off Brazil (1640) delivered final blows to the Spanish navy. What the English began in 1588, the Dutch completed 50 years later.

Dutch Exploration and Expansion

1576	Sack of Antwerp; Amsterdam becomes commercial hub of Europe
1595	First Dutch fleet enters East Indies
1609	Henry Hudson explores Hudson River
1621	Dutch form West India Company
1624	Dutch found New Amsterdam on Manhattan Island
1641	Dutch drive Portuguese out of Malacca

Five Dutch trading companies initially conducted trade with Asia, but the Dutch state decided their competition with each other cut into profits and established the Dutch East India Company. Chartered in 1602 and given a monopoly over all operations between the Cape of Good Hope in South Africa and the Strait of Magellan, it conserved resources and cut costs. In addition to its trade and diplomacy, the company sponsored explorations of Australia, Tasmania, New Guinea, and the South Pacific.

The Dutch Empire in the East was established primarily by Jan Pieterszoon Coen, governor-general of the Indies for two periods between 1619 and 1629 and founder of the company capital at Batavia in northwestern Java. At first he cooperated with local rulers in return for a monopoly over the spice trade. When this involved him in costly wars against local sultans as well as their Portuguese and English customers, Coen determined to control the trade at its sources. In the ensuing numerous conflicts and negotiations, which outlasted Coen, the Dutch acquired all of Java, most of Sumatra, the spice-growing Moluccas (mol-U-kuz), and part of Sri Lanka. They began operating their own plantations, overseen by Dutch settlers and worked by thousands of slaves brought in from such diverse areas as East Africa, Bengal, Persia, and Japan. The plantations produced cinnamon, nutmeg, cloves, sugar, tea, tobacco, and coffee, but it was pepper that reaped the highest profits. In the seventeenth century 7 million pounds of pepper were shipped to Europe annually.

Although commercially successful in Asia, the Dutch were not able to found flourishing colonial settlements. Many Dutchmen who went to the East wanted to make their fortunes and return home; those willing to stay were usually mavericks, uninterested in establishing families but instead pursuing temporary sexual liaisons with female slaves or servants. For a while after 1620 the company experimented with a policy of bringing European women to the Indies, but such efforts were abandoned when the venture failed to enlist much interest at home or in the foreign stations. Consequently, the Dutch colonies in Asia, as well as those in Africa, the Caribbean, and Brazil, remained primarily business ventures with less racial mixing than in the Iberian areas.

After resuming war with Spain in 1621, the Dutch formed the West India Company, charged with overtaking the diminishing Spanish and Portuguese holdings in West Africa and America. The company wasted no time. It soon supplanted the Portuguese in West Africa; by 1630 it had taken over the slave trade with America. After driving the Spanish from the Caribbean, the Dutch

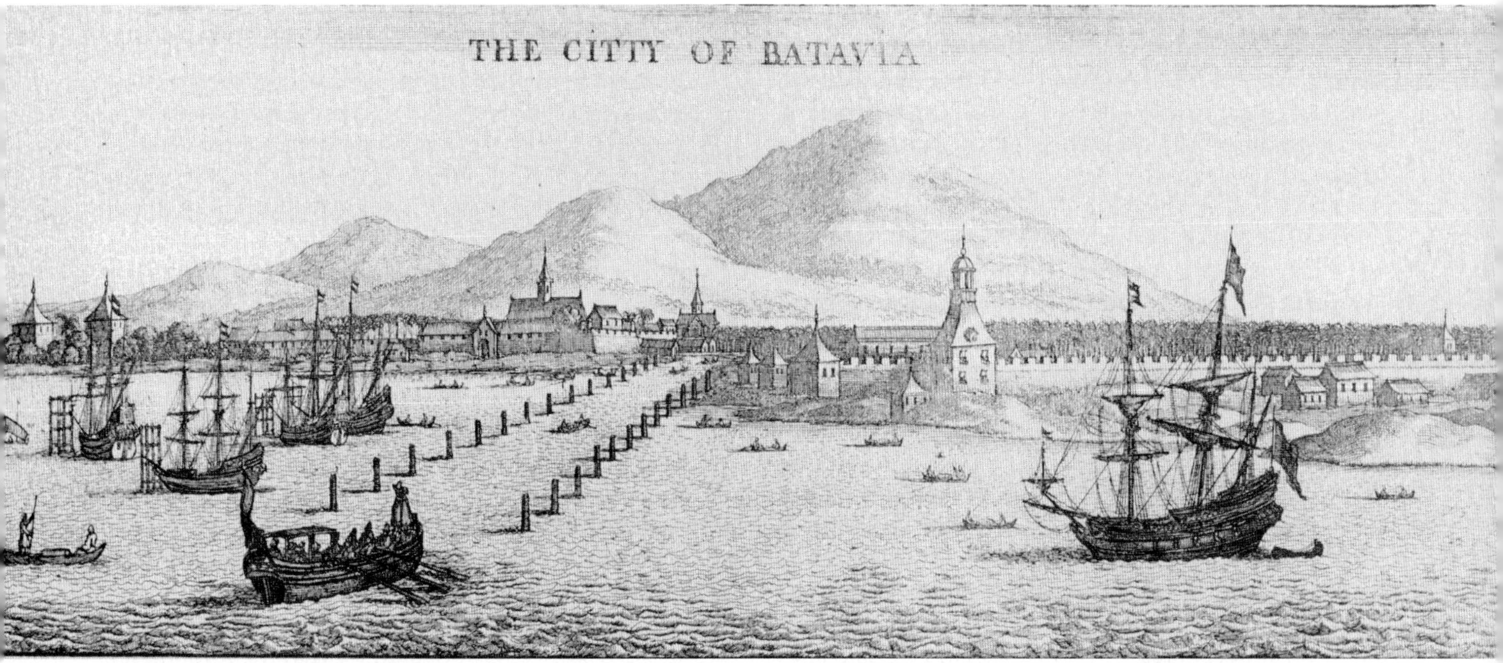

Batavia (present-day Djakarta), on the island of Java, became the headquarters of the Dutch East India Company when the Dutch ousted the Portuguese and took command of the East Indies trade in the seventeenth century.

invited other European planters to the West Indies as customers, keeping only a few bases for themselves. The company then launched a successful naval conquest of Brazil, from the mouth of the Amazon south to the San Francisco River. In Brazil the Dutch learned sugar planting, passing on their knowledge to the Caribbean and applying it directly in the East Indies.

Dutch settlements in North America never amounted to much because of the company's commercial orientation. In 1609 Henry Hudson (d. 1611), an Englishman sailing for the Dutch, explored the river (ultimately named for him) and established Dutch claims while looking for a northwest passage. Fifteen years later the company founded New Amsterdam on Manhattan Island; over the next few years it built a number of frontier trading posts in the Hudson valley and on the nearby Connecticut and Delaware Rivers. Some attempts were made to encourage planting by selling large tracts to wealthy proprietors ***(patroons).*** Agriculture, however, remained secondary to the fur trade, which the company developed in alliance with the Iroquois tribes. This arrangement hindered settlement; in 1660 only 5000 Europeans were in the colony.

The French Empire

French exploration began early, but no permanent colonies were established abroad until the start of the seventeenth century. The country was so weakened by religious wars that most of its efforts, beyond fishing, privateering, and a few failed attempts at settlement, had to be directed toward internal stability. While the Dutch were winning their empire, France was involved in the land campaigns of the Thirty Years' War. Serious French empire building thus had to be delayed until after 1650, during the reign of Louis XIV.

Early French colonization in North America was based on claims made by Giovanni da Verrazzano (1485–1528) and Jacques Cartier (1491–1557). The first, a Florentine mariner commissioned by Francis I in 1523, traced the Atlantic coast from North Carolina to Newfoundland. Eleven years later Cartier made one of two voyages exploring the St. Lawrence River. These French expeditions duplicated England's claim to eastern North America.

French colonial efforts during the sixteenth century were dismal failures. They resulted partly from French experiences in exploiting the Newfoundland fishing banks and conducting an undeclared naval war in the Atlantic against Iberian treasure ships and trading vessels after 1520. In 1543 Cartier tried unsuccessfully to establish a colony in the St. Lawrence valley. No more serious efforts were made until 1605, when a French base was established at Port Royal, on Nova Scotia. It was meant to be a fur-trading center and capital for the whole St. Lawrence region. In 1608, Samuel de Champlain (1567–1635), who had been an aide to the governor of the Nova Scotia colony, acted for a French-chartered company in founding Quebec on the St. Lawrence. The company brought in colonists, but the little community was disrupted in 1627 when

patroon—An owner of a landed estate granted by the Dutch West India Company in New York and New Jersey.

British troops took the town and forced Champlain's surrender. Although when Champlain came back as governor the fort was returned to France by a treaty in 1629, growth was slowed by the company's emphasis on fur trading, the bitterly cold winters, and skirmishes with Indians. Only a few settlers had arrived by Champlain's death in 1635, and just 2500 Europeans were in Quebec as late as 1663. Nevertheless, Montreal was established in 1642, after which French trapper-explorers began penetrating the region around the headwaters of the Mississippi.

Elsewhere, the French seized opportunities afforded by the decline of Iberian sea power. They acquired the isle of Bourbon (BOOR-bon), later known as Réunion, in the Indian Ocean (1642) for use as a commercial base. In West Africa they created a sphere of commercial interest at the mouth of the Senegal River, where they became involved in the slave trade with only slight opposition from the Dutch. Even more significant was the appearance of the French in the West Indies. They occupied part of St. Kitts in 1625 and later acquired Martinique, Guadeloupe, and Santo Domingo. Fierce attacks by Carib Indians limited economic development before 1650. However, by the late eighteenth century, Santo Domingo had become the crown jewel of France's Caribbean possessions. Possessing half of the Caribbean's slave population, the island was the largest producer of sugar in America, and—after coffee was introduced in 1723—the world's largest coffee producer until the Haitian revolution of 1791.

British and French Exploration and Colonization

1485–1528	Giovanni da Verrazzano
1491–1557	Jacques Cartier
1497–1498	John Cabot establishes English claims in North America
1567–1635	Samuel de Champlain founds Quebec
1605	French establish base at Port Royal, in Nova Scotia
1607	First English colony in North America founded at Jamestown
1627	British conquer Quebec
1629	Puritans settle near Boston
1632–1635	English Catholics found colony of Maryland
1642	Montreal established

The English Empire

In terms of power and profit, English foreign expansion before 1650 was not impressive. Like French colonialism, it was somewhat restricted by internal political conditions, particularly the poor management and restrictive policies of the early Stuart kings, which led to civil war in the 1640s. A number of circumstances, however, promoted foreign ventures. The population increased from 3 to 4 million between 1530 and 1600, providing a large reservoir of potential indentured labor; religious persecution encouraged migration of nonconformists; and holders of surplus capital were seeking opportunities for investment. Such conditions ultimately produced a unique explosion of English settlement overseas.

During the sixteenth century, English maritime operations were confined primarily to exploring, fishing, smuggling, and plundering. English claims to North America were registered in 1497 and 1498 by two voyages of John Cabot, who explored the coast of North America from Newfoundland to Virginia but found no passage to Asia. For the next century, English expeditions sought such a northern passage, both in the East and in the West. All of them failed, but they resulted in explorations of Hudson Bay and the opening of a northeastern trade route to Russia. From the 1540s, English captains, including the famous John Hawkins of Plymouth, indulged in sporadic slave trading in Africa and the West Indies, despite Spanish restrictions.

After failures in Newfoundland and on the Carolina coast, the first permanent English colony in America was founded in 1607 at Jamestown, Virginia. For a number of years the colonists suffered from lack of food and other privations, but they were saved by their leader, Captain John Smith (1580–1631), whose romantic rescue by the Indian princess Pocahontas (1595–1617) is an American legend. Jamestown set a significant precedent for all English colonies in North America. By the terms of its original charter, the London Company, which founded the settlement, was authorized to supervise government for the colonists, but they were to enjoy all the rights of native Englishmen. Consequently, in 1619 the governor called an assembly to assist in governing. This body would later become the Virginia House of Burgesses, one of the oldest representative legislatures still operating.

Shortly after the founding of Jamestown, large-scale colonization began elsewhere. In 1620 a group of English Protestants, known as Pilgrims, landed at Plymouth. Despite severe hardships, they survived, and their experiences inspired other religious dissenters against the policies of Charles I. In 1629 a number of English Puritans formed the Massachusetts Bay Company and settled near Boston, where their charter gave them the rights to virtual self-government. From this first enclave, emigrants moved out to other areas in present-day Maine, Rhode Island, and Connecticut. By 1642 more than 25,000 people had migrated to New England, laying the foundations for a number of future colonies. Around the same time (1632–1635), a group of English Catholics, fleeing Stuart persecution, founded the Maryland colony. These enterprises firmly planted English culture and political institutions in North America.

Life in the English settlements was hard during those first decades, but a pioneering spirit and native colonial pride was already evident. Food was scarce, disease was ever-present, and conflicts with Amerindians were not uncommon. Yet from the beginning, and more than in other European colonies, settlers looked to their future in the new land because they had left so little behind in Europe. Most were expecting to stay, establish homes, make their fortunes, and raise families. The first Puritans included both men and women; a shipload of "purchase brides" arrived in 1619 at Jamestown to lend stability to that colony. This was but the first of many such contingents, all eagerly welcomed by prospective husbands. In addition, many women came on their own as indentured servants.

Anglo-American colonial women faced discrimination but managed to cope with it pragmatically. They were legally dependent on their husbands, who controlled property and children; a widow acquired these rights, but it was not easy to outlive a husband. Hard work and frequent pregnancies—mothers with a dozen children were not uncommon—reduced female life expectancies. Nevertheless, many women developed a rough endurance, using their social value to gain confidence and practical equality with their husbands, although some did this more obviously than others. This independent spirit was exemplified by Anne Hutchinson (1591–1643), who was banished from Massachusetts for her heretical views and founded a dissenting religious settlement in Rhode Island. Another freethinker was Anne Bradstreet (c. 1612–1672), who, although painfully aware that men considered her presumptuous, wrote thoughtful poetry.

The English government considered the rough coasts and wild forests of North America less important in this period than footholds in the West Indies and Africa, where profits were expected in planting and slave trading. Therefore, a wave of English migrants descended on the West Indies after the Dutch opened the Caribbean. In 1613 English settlers invaded Bermuda, and by the 1620s others had planted colonies on St. Kitts, Barbados, Nevis, Montserrat (mawn-suh-RAHT), Antigua (ahn-TEE-gwah), and the Bahamas. Tobacco planting was at first the major enterprise, bringing some prosperity and the promise of more. The white population expanded dramatically, especially on Barbados, which was not subject to Carib Indian attacks. There, the English population increased from 7,000 to 37,000 in seven years. As yet, there were few African slaves on the English islands, although some were already being imported for the sugar plantations.

This is an anonymous engraving made around 1776 of the Mohawk chief and diplomat Tiyanoga. He was an ally for the British and known to them as "King Hendrick." In this portrait, one can see the influence of European trade goods in Tiyanoga's dress. His shirt is made of linen or calico, and his mantle and breechcloth of English wool duffels.

Meanwhile, English slaving posts in West Africa were beginning to flourish, and English adventurers were starting operations in Asia. Captain John Lancaster took four ships to Sumatra and Java in 1601, returning with a profitable cargo of spices. But expansion outside of the Caribbean was difficult because the Dutch were uncooperative. In the Moluccas, for example, they drove out the English in the 1620s, after repeated clashes. The English fared better in India. By 1622 the British East India Company, which had been chartered in 1600, had put the Portuguese out of business in the Persian Gulf. Subsequently, the English established trading posts on the west coast of India at Agra, Bombay, Masulipatam, Balasore, and Surat. The station at Madras, destined to become the English bastion on the east coast, was founded in 1639. The East India Company prospered from the trade in Indian cotton and silk cloth for the English and European markets.

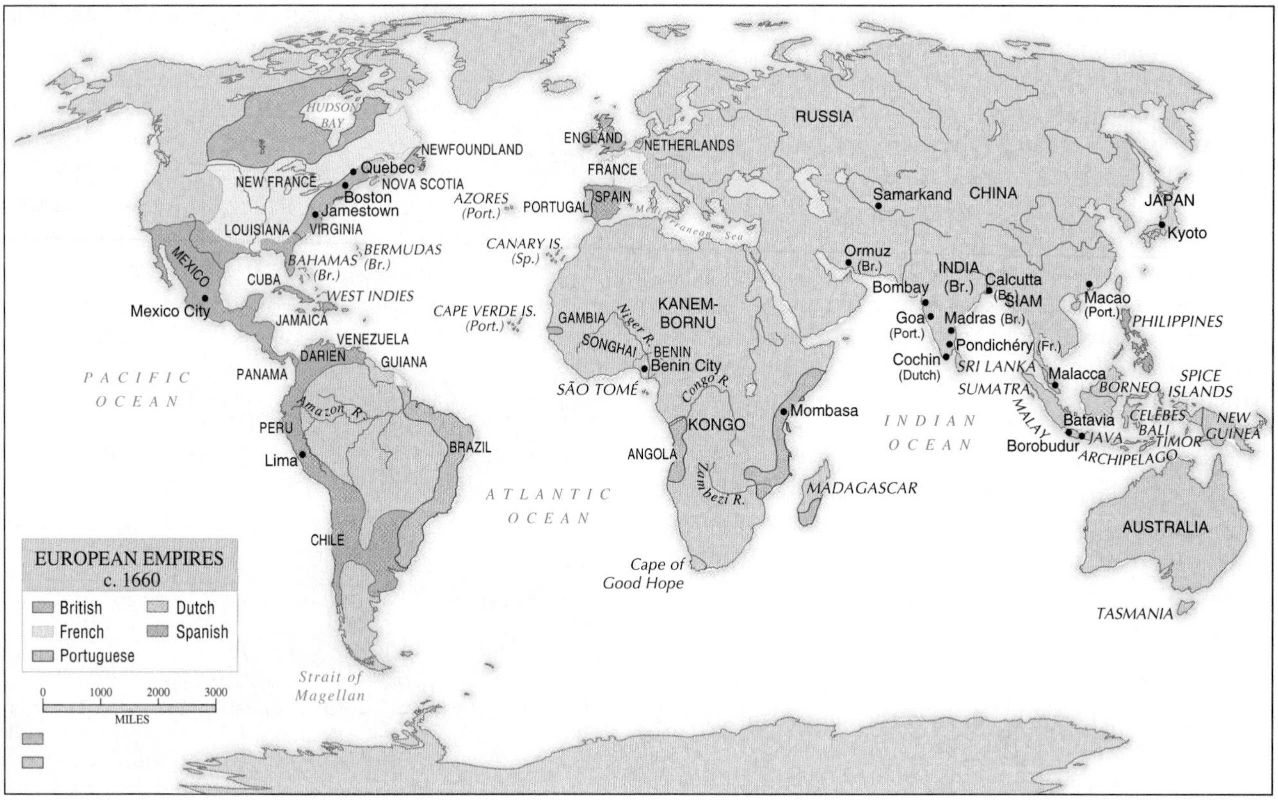

By the late 1600s the Portuguese and Spanish, the pioneers in global exploration, had been displaced in many regions by the English, French, and Dutch.

CONCLUSION

Between 1450 and 1650, the era of the early Commercial Revolution, Europeans faced outwards toward a new world and, following precedents set by earlier Eurasian empires, initiated their own age of oceanic expansion. In the process they stimulated capitalistic development, found a sea route to Asia, became more familiar with Africa, began colonizing America, and proved the world to have a spherical surface. For most of the period Spain and Portugal monopolized the new ocean trade and profited most from exploiting American gold and silver. Only after 1600, when leadership shifted toward the Dutch, French, and English, did European colonialism show signs of developing in new directions.

Overseas expansion exerted a tremendous effect on European culture and institutions. Spain's political predominance in the sixteenth century was largely bought with Amerindian treasure, and Spain's eventual decline was mainly caused by the squandering of wealth on war rather than on investment and the influx of American bullion, which inflated Spanish money and discouraged Spanish economic development. Northern European capitalism, developing in financial organization, shipbuilding, metalworking, manufacturing, and agriculture, brought a new vitality to northern economies in response to Spanish and Portuguese purchasing power. Economic advantages also contributed to Protestant victories in the Thirty Years' War.

By the late seventeenth century, the Europeans had experienced mixed results in their encounters with societies around the world. In the Indian Ocean, where they engaged well-established states, such as in China, Japan, and India, they usually had to respect their laws and authority and even do their bidding and had little impact on land-based trading networks. The Portuguese were run out of China twice before they came to respect Chinese law, and other Europeans fared worse. All were ultimately excluded from Japan. Southern India was not entirely open, as the Portuguese found by the end of the period. In the main, Turks, Arabs, Chinese, Japanese, Thais, and Vietnamese felt superior to Europeans and were usually able to defend their interests with effective action.

Where they dealt with smaller states and city-states, such as in Indonesia and East Africa, Europeans were more likely to directly intervene or dominate their affairs. Sri Lanka and the Spice Islands of the Malay archipelago, which were vulnerable to sea attack, came under domination, direct or indirect, and were exploited by the Portuguese and the Dutch.

In the New World the European impact was both dramatic and tragic. Portuguese captains and Spanish *conquistadora,* as well as diseases such as smallpox, nearly destroyed indigenous peoples and subjected most of the survivors to terrible hardships, indignities, cultural deprivations, and psychological injuries. However, the Portuguese and Spanish in America generated a new cultural synthesis, blending European, Amerindian, and African elements to produce a richness and variety not present in any of the parent cultures. This integration was largely accomplished by racial mixing, which created a new Latin American stock in the Western Hemisphere.

The European impact on Africa was less apparent at the time but perhaps more damaging in the long run than what happened to the Amerindians of Latin America. When the Portuguese began exploring the African coastline, they were more concerned with scoring quick profits through gold exports than with establishing stable, long-term relationships with African states. Moreover, with the exception of Angola or landed estates along the Zambezi River, the Portuguese did not have the manpower or resources to conquer or influence the political affairs of African states. However, as the Atlantic slave trade increased, the Portuguese and African states, especially along the Atlantic and Indian Ocean coasts, became bound up in a destructive process that would run its tragic course over the next few centuries.

Suggestions for Web Browsing

You can obtain more information about topics included in this chapter at the websites listed below. See also the companion website that accompanies this text, **http://www.ablongman.com/brummett**, which contains an online study guide and additional resources.

Age of Discovery
http://www.win.tue.nl/cs/fm/engels/discovery/#age

An excellent collection of resources that includes text, images, and maps relating to the early years of European expansion.

Internet Medieval History Sourcebook: Exploration and Expansion
http://www.fordham.edu/halsall/sbook1z.html

Extensive online source for links about Western exploration and expansion, including primary documents by or about da Gama, Columbus, Drake, and Magellan.

Columbus Navigation Home Page
http://www1.minn.net/~keithp/

Extensive information regarding the life and voyages of Christopher Columbus.

Internet African History Sourcebook
http://www.fordham.edu/halsall/africa/africasbook.html

Extensive online source for links about African history, including primary documents about the slave trade and by people who opposed it, supported it, and were its victims.

Literature and Film

Two major documentary series marked the quincentennial of Columbus's 1492 voyage in different ways. *Columbus and the Age of Discovery* (1991) is a seven-part series that primarily treats European exploration and expansion in the New World, while *500 Nations* (1995) is an eight-part series that examines Native American history before and after the arrival of Europeans. *Conquistadores* (2001) is Michael Wood's presentation of European explorers/conquerors such as Cortés and Pizarro.

Mexican writer Carlos Fuentes has written a major epic, *Terra Nostra*, trans. Margaret Peden (Farrar, Straus, and Giroux, 1976) and a collection of short stories and novellas, *The Orange Tree*, trans. Alfred MacAdam (Farrar, Straus, and Giroux, 1994), with Spanish exploration and conquest of the New World as their backdrop. James Lackhart's *We People Here: Nahuatl Accounts of the Conquest of Mexico* (University of California Press, 1993) presents indigenous Indian narratives of the Spanish conquest compiled by a Franciscan priest in the sixteenth century.

Suggestions for Reading

Several excellent works, which cover the subject of European exploration and colonization, are Geoffrey V. Scammell, *The First Imperial Age: European Overseas Expansion, 1400–1700* (Unwin Hyman, 1989); Anthony Pagden, eds., *European Encounters with the New World* (Yale University Press, 1993); and Nicholas Canny and Anthony Pagden, *Colonial Identity in the Atlantic World* (Princeton University Press, 1989). European encounters with other peoples are treated in Urs Bitterli, *Cultures in Conflict: Encounters Between European and Non-European Cultures, 1492–1800* (Stanford University Press, 1989), and Stuart Schwartz, ed., *Implicit Understandings: Observing, Reporting, and Reflecting on the Encounters between Europeans and Other Peoples in the Early Modern Era* (Cambridge University Press, 1994).

Books on the Iberian New World are Tzvetan Todorov, *The Conquest of America* (Harper&Row, 1984) and Mark A. Burkholder, *Colonial Latin America* (Oxford University Press, 1989). Works on Columbus include Felipe Fernandez-Armesto, *Columbus* (Oxford University Press, 1992), and John Yewell, Chris Dodge, and Jan De Surey, *Confronting Columbus: An Anthology* (McFarland, 1992).

For a penetrating study of Latin American social conditions, see Louisa Hoberman and Susan M. Socolow, eds., *Cities and Society in Colonial Latin America* (University of New Mexico Press, 1986).

Luis Martin, *Daughters of the Conquistadores* (Southern Methodist University Press, 1989) documents the significant role of women in the grueling process of colonization. Good coverage of the Spanish campaigns in Peru is provided in Susan Ramirez, *The World Upside Down: Cross-Cultural Contact and Conflict in Sixteenth-Century Peru* (Stanford University Press, 1996).

On political, economic, and social conditions, see Leslie B. Simpson, *The Encomienda in New Spain*, 3rd ed. (University of California Press, 1982). Edward Murguca, *Assimilation, Colonialism, and the Mexican American People* (University Press of America, 1989), depicts the racial and cultural synthesis in colonial Mexico.

A respected work on Portuguese exploration and colonization is A. J. R. Russell-Wood, *A World on the Move: The Portuguese in Africa, Asia and America, 1415–1808* (St. Martin's Press, 1992). On the Portuguese in Asia, see Michael Pearson, *The Indian Ocean* (Routledge, 2003).

A sound treatment of Dutch imperial development is Charles R. Boxer, *The Dutch Seaborne Empire* (Penguin, 1989). French colonialism in America is covered in William J. Eccles, *France in America* (Michigan State University Press, 1990), and the British Empire in William R Lewis, Nicholas Canny, P. J. Marshall, and Alaine Low, eds., *The Origins of Empire: British Overseas Enterprise to the Close of the Seventeenth Century* (Oxford University Press, 1998).

CHAPTER

17

Politics in the First Age of Capitalism, 1648–1774

Absolutism and Limited Central Power

CHAPTER CONTENTS

A century and a half of European turmoil came to an end in 1648. As we saw in Chapter 15, the new political system after the Treaty of Westphalia would be based on *raison d'état,* calculated policies to further the growth of the individual states. State structures took one of two forms thereafter: either the absolutist model perfected by Louis XIV of France or the limited central power approach found in the Netherlands and England. During this time, however, politics and diplomacy—with the numerous "Balance of Power wars"—were not the most important developments.

Capitalism—an economic system based on private ownership of property, individual risk taking, and market determination of the prices of goods—became the basis of the economy, and by implication, political power. Rich states with great resources and comparatively efficient bureaucracies grew stronger while nations such as Poland, which remained mired in its medieval political and economic structure, literally disappeared from the map.

France and England—after gaining domination over Holland—extended their influence and markets around the globe as Spain entered a period of relative stagnation. These two states probed for advantage with the powers of Africa and Asia in the late seventeenth and eighteenth centuries. The peoples of the Americas also became caught up in the Europeans' global economic and political competition.

1550

1587 Dutch Republic formed

1588–1679 Thomas Hobbes, author of *Leviathan* (1651), which provided secular, contractual justification for absolutism

1600

1603–1625 Reign of James I of England, beginning of Stuart dynasty

1619–1683 Jean Baptiste Colbert, finance minister for Louis XIV

1640–1688 Reign of Frederick William the Great Elector of Prussia

1642–1648 English Civil War

1643–1715 Reign of Louis XIV of France, the Sun King

1648 Peace of Westphalia

1649–1653 French Civil War, the Fronde, revolt of the nobility against absolutism

1650

1688 Glorious Revolution in England

1689–1725 Reign of Peter the Great of Russia

1700

1707 Act of Union between England and Scotland

1713 Peace of Utrecht

1713–1740 Reign of Frederick William I of Prussia

1715–1774 Reign of Louis XV of France

CAPITALISM AND THE FORCES OF CHANGE

■ *What role do economics and politics play in determining the success or failure of a state?*

Dynamic economic and social forces challenged all European governments, no matter what their form, in the seventeenth and eighteenth century. Every part of Europe, from Britain to Russia, to the colonies around the world, and every social class, from peasants to the most tradition-bound nobles, felt the insecurity and restlessness inherent in the economic and social transformation. Governments with sufficient flexibility survived these changes; those that could not adapt were weakened or destroyed.

Expanding Capitalism

The primary force driving change was an energetic capitalistic economy developing so rapidly that it could hardly be controlled or even predicted. **Capitalism** generated new economic pursuits that developed almost spontaneously outside established institutions. It also created unprecedented increases in the volume of trade by dealing both in precious goods and in bulk commodities. Eastern Europe and the Baltic supplied grains, timber, fish, and naval stores while western Europe supplied manufactures for its outlying regions and overseas trade. Dutch, English, and French merchant-bankers controlled shipping and credit. Plantation agriculture in the tropics, particularly the cultivation of Caribbean sugar, produced the greatest profits for overseas commerce. The African slave trade, along with its many supporting industries, also became an integral part of the intercontinental economic system. The New World economy widened European horizons while contributing to European wealth. New foods such as potatoes, yams, lima beans, tapioca, and peanuts became part of the European diet. Tropical plantation crops such as rice, coffee, tea, cocoa, and sugar ceased to be luxuries.

These new markets and resources contributed greatly to the development of modern capitalistic institutions. As the volume rose, great public banks chartered by governments replaced earlier family banks like the Fuggers of Augsburg. The Bank of Amsterdam (1609) and the Bank of England (1694) are typical examples. Such banks, holding public revenues and creating credit by issuing notes, made large amounts of capital available for favored enterprises and the state.

The Rise of Capitalism

1600	English East India companies formed
1602	Dutch East India Company
1609	Bank of Amsterdam opens
c. 1688	Lloyds of London begins operation
1694	Bank of England is chartered
1698	London Stock Exchange opens
1724	Paris Bourse is established

Building on this seventeenth-century foundation, four new conditions produced the commercial boom in the century and a half after Westphalia. First, government demand for goods reached astronomical heights as huge standing armies and navies required mountains of food, clothing, arms, and ammunition. Second, a rising European population created another expanding market, demanding bulk commodities, while the increasing average life span allowed businessmen to amass more profits for investment over the course of their lives. Developing plantation agriculture in tropical colonies provided a third stimulus to foreign trade. Finally, Brazilian gold and diamond strikes stimulated the growth of capitalistic enterprises after the 1730s by driving up prices and creating greater profits.

MAP European Population Density, c. 1600

The resulting economic changes brought promising but sometimes disturbing results. As wealth increased beyond all expectations, investment and production rose accordingly in textiles, coal, iron, and shipbuilding. With enterprises growing larger, partnerships and **joint-stock companies** began replacing individually owned companies, as had happened earlier in foreign trade. At the same time, specialization became common in new phases of wholesaling and retailing operations.

Expansion and increasing complexity were accompanied by a steady monetary inflation. Wages, for example, increased far less than food prices, thus depressing the condition of workers. Nobles on the Continent who received fixed fees from their peasants, and English landlords who had leased their fields on long-term contracts were hurt badly. Conversely, landowners who rented to short-term tenants or received payment in kind, profited, as did other capitalistic investors, who became wealthy from the general

capitalism—An economic system based on private ownership of property, individual risk taking, and market determination of the price of goods.

joint-stock companies—A business or other enterprise in which the ownership is divided among a number of stock holders who jointly share the profits and the risks.

Capitalist agriculture, shown here in the rolling and spinning of tobacco, demanded a large and dependable supply of labor. Slaves or indentured servants in the North American colonies did the hard work that returned a profit for European investors.

increase in the cost of goods. At times, their profits soared in a wildly speculative "boom and bust" market.

International trade was the most obvious indicator of European business prosperity. An even larger trade with overseas areas encouraged the formation of East India Companies in Austria and Prussia as clones of their older and better-known English, Dutch, and French counterparts. The resulting trade in sugar, silk, cotton, tobacco, and various luxury products generated whole new European industries. Perhaps more of an impact came from the African slave trade, centered in Liverpool and Bordeaux (bor-DOH), which reached its peak during the eighteenth century. Altogether, the total foreign trade of Britain and France increased by some 450 percent. The Dutch, in imperial decline, experienced a notable decrease.

The Growth of Free Enterprise

Prosperity threatened government attempts to control the economy. As opportunities for profit increased, capitalists searched for profits outside state-sponsored enterprises and even beyond the legal limits set by governments and traditions. Some of these endeavors were deliberate efforts to evade the law; others—perhaps most—were responses to opportunity. This rising free enterprise capitalism, as distinct from mercantilist state capitalism, was evident in every phase of the pre-1789 economy.

A growing demand for food encouraged the trend in capitalist agriculture: the large-scale trading of agricultural goods as commodities in national and international markets. Soaring food prices lured surplus capital into land and improvements. This trend was most typical of England, but the agricultural boom, on a slightly smaller scale, extended to France, the Dutch Republic, the Low Countries, Prussia, and even the wine producers of Italy and Spanish Catalonia. Wherever it developed, capitalistic agriculture emphasized efficiency and profits, which usually required procedures that did not fit in with the traditional cooperative methods and servile labor of rural villages.

Four Englishmen pioneered the movement. Jethro Tull (1674–1741) carefully plowed the land planted in neat rows using a drill he invented and kept the plants well cultivated as they grew to maturity. Viscount Charles Townshend (1674–1738), nicknamed "Turnip

Townshend," specialized in restoring soil fertility by such methods as applying clay-lime mixtures and planting turnips in **crop rotation.** Robert Bakewell (1725–1795) attacked the problem of scrawny cattle. Through selective breeding, he was able to increase the size of meat animals and also the milk yields from dairy cows. Another Englishman, Arthur Young (1741–1820), an ardent advocate for the new agriculture, made lecture tours throughout Europe and recorded his observations. He popularized the advantages of well-equipped farms and economical agricultural techniques and did much to free European agriculture from the less productive methods of the past.

New agricultural techniques demanded large capital investment and complete control of the land. Common fields, where villagers shared customary rights, could not be cultivated with the new methods. The land needed to be drained, irrigated, fertilized, and cultivated by scientific methods. Selective stockbreeding could not be practiced with an unregulated community herd. Landlords and investors who wanted to use the new methods brought about a devastating destruction of traditional society by trying to fence or enclose their acres. By outright purchase, foreclosure, suit, fraud, or even legislation, they tried to free their lands from old manorial restrictions, particularly from traditional rights to community use of the commons.

The gentry used their political dominance to improve their economic position, especially in the countryside. Although English manorial fees and services were abolished in the seventeenth century, many villages had retained their medieval rights to pasturage and fuel gathering on the commons. These rights were lost to enclosures. From 1750 until the end of the century, 40,000 to 50,000 small farms disappeared into large estates under the **Enclosure Acts.** Some of the peasants forced from the land went to the cities, some became agricultural laborers at pitifully poor wages, and others went into parish poorhouses, which were soon overflowing. This movement was strongest in England but also was seen on the Continent. Inflation and buyouts in France, particularly in the north, drove many peasants from the land, but they were so important as taxpayers that the government managed to restrict the movement. Consequently, French landlords were still complaining about manorial restrictions until 1789. But in England, the gentry—unlike many of their colleagues on the Continent—had already embraced capitalism and were powerful in Parliament: They were able to pass 2000 enclosure laws between 1760 and 1800.

In industry the movement toward free enterprise produced the so-called domestic system, which involved contractual arrangements between capitalistic brokers and handworkers. Brokers supplied materials to the workers in their homes and later collected the products, to be sent through another stage of finishing or sold directly on the market. The system became common in industries where demand was high, profits were large, and capital was available. Domestic manufacturing moved early to the country, away from the regulations imposed by city guilds. The advantages and disadvantages were those associated with unregulated industry. Contracts were freely negotiated and prices were usually low, but capitalists and consumers faced considerable risks. Workers, particularly women and children, were easier to exploit than the guilds were.

Domestic industry was common all over western Europe after 1500, reaching a climax of growth in the eighteenth century. Although most typical of England, it also developed rapidly in northern France, the Low

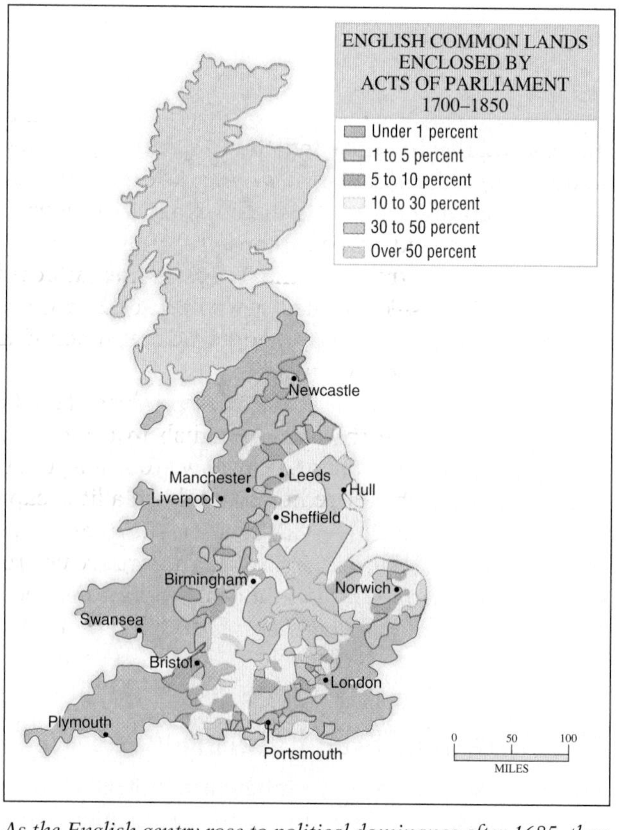

As the English gentry rose to political dominance after 1685, they used their strength in parliament to push through the Enclosure Acts, shutting the peasantry out from access to common lands.

crop rotation—The practice of planting different crops in successive seasons on the same plot of land so as to preserve the soil's fertility. Otherwise, if the same crop is planted year after year on the same plot of land the soil will become exhausted, and the land will have to lie fallow for at least a year to recover its fertility.

Enclosure Acts—A series of laws passed after 1760 that favored capitalist agriculture. Common lands were divided up, farming plots were combined, poor peasants lost the right to scavenge in the former common lands, and gates had to be installed at the boundaries around farms. The end result was to drive poor peasants off the land.

The ART of STOCKING-FRAME-WORK-KNITTING.
Engrav'd for the Universal Magazine 1750 for J. Hinton at the Kings Arms in St. Paul's Church Yard LONDON.

The individual, human skills needed to perform the art of stocking frame work knitting came to be done by machines by the beginning of the nineteenth century.

Countries, and southern Germany. It was involved in all essential processes of the woolen industries, notably spinning, weaving, fulling, and dyeing. The system also spread among other textile industries, such as linens and cottons, which provided a decided stimulus to the trend in the 1700s. Other affected industries were silk, lace, leather, paper, glass, pottery, and metals. By 1750, English domestic manufacturing employed over 4 million workers.

The career of Ambrose Crowley illustrates the domestic system in the infant English iron industry. Crowley started as a blacksmith who worked as a guildsman in Greenwich, where he accumulated a little capital. Around 1680 he moved to a small Durham village and built a domestic organization for the large-scale production of hardware. By 1700 the village had become a thriving town of 1500 workers. Crowley, who rented them their houses and supplied some of their tools as well as ore and fuel, employed most of them. The village produced nails, locks, bolts, hammers, spades, and other tools, which Crowley marketed elsewhere. A wealthy and respected citizen, he was knighted in 1706.

British industry benefited from the political system in place. Because most guild monopolies had passed with the seventeenth century, domestic industry faced few legal obstacles, but it did experience frequent functional crises. Despite widespread business prosperity, wages failed to keep up with the steady inflation. Between 1756 and 1786 wages rose by 35 percent but food prices increased by more than 60 percent. Workers also had to accept periodic unemployment, even in good times. They were thus inclined to resist the wage system and agitate for state intervention against low wages and high prices. Their bitter discontent was expressed in violent riots, most notably in 1765 and 1780.

Joint-stock companies were drastically reoriented in the late seventeenth century. Companies such as the Dutch and English East India Companies pooled the resources of many investors. In the late seventeenth century, exchanges for buying and selling stock—or **stock exchanges**—were becoming common, as were maritime insurance companies such as Lloyds of London, which began operations about 1688. Originally, joint-stock companies were exclusive monopolies, both in their areas of operation and in their limited number of stockholders. They were generally criti-

---

stock exchanges—Places where stocks—certificates representing the ownership of a part of a company or enterprise—were bought and sold.

cized, and their trading rights were regularly violated by competitors and smugglers. Under pressure, the British East India Company and similar firms steadily liberalized their policies until ultimately most stocks were sold on the open market. Sales of stock greatly increased opportunities for investment and multiplied the number of joint-stock companies. By 1715 more than 140 existed in England. This situation also encouraged a huge, speculative bull market on stock exchanges, which sprang up in taverns and coffeehouses all over western Europe. The London Stock Exchange opened in 1698 and the Paris Bourse in 1724; both were involved in the mania of speculation that collapsed the South Sea and Mississippi Companies in 1719–1720. Despite these disasters, such institutions become necessary to the private sector of Europe's economy in the early 1700s.

Banking performed a similarly necessary role. In a sense, the banks of Sweden, Amsterdam, and London were examples of state operation; their directors were often government advisers, authorized to perform semiofficial functions such as issuing notes and financing public debts. In another sense, however, these institutions became integral parts of the free market economy, providing the necessary credit for business enterprise while creating their own nonofficial commercial methods and institutions. Moreover, smaller banks developed within the private monetary and credit systems. The first English country bank was founded as a private enterprise in 1716 at Bristol; by 1780 there were 300 in the country.

Major insurance companies, banks, and stock exchanges formed an integrated institutional system, functioning in a free international market. Their standardized procedures became so complicated that ordinary people could not understand them. That strange new world of business enterprise, unlike the political world, was not controlled directly by anyone, not even by the power of concentrated capital. Goods and credit, commodity prices and wages, monetary values and stock quotations all interacted according to their own laws, which could be studied but not accurately predicted. Participants in this system learned that the number of losers could and often did outnumber the winners.

SOCIAL CRISES DURING THE CAPITALIST REVOLUTION

- *Capitalism rewards those who are the most efficient. What happened to those people—noble and peasant—who were unable to compete in the capitalist market?*

The Aristocracy and the Commoners

Ignoring the mass discontent and middle-class frustrations, the old regimes continued to depend largely on local authorities, military officers, and bureaucrats, drawn almost exclusively from nobilities and wealthy commoners. Governments therefore legalized privilege, conferring social status, political power, and fabulous wealth on a small elite while dooming the masses to grinding poverty. The system cut across class lines. Most of the clergy and nobles were as poor as some peasants, and the great majority of the urban middle classes were denied the leisured comfort of the wealthy bankers and merchants.

The aristocratic nature of the old regimes derived partly from encroachments on royal prerogatives by European nobilities after the Peace of Westphalia. Temporarily checked by such strong monarchs as Louis XIV and Peter the Great, the nobles retained or regained political power in the Habsburg domain, Germany, and Poland. Early in the eighteenth century, they did the same in Sweden, Spain, Russia (after Peter's death), and particularly in Louis XV's France.

Europe's old regimes were topped by official ruling classes of high clergy and nobles. Combined, these two privileged orders accounted for less than 2 percent of the total European population; the great magnates, who enjoyed real wealth and power, were concentrated in only 5000 families, among some 4 million titled aristocrats. Most of the true elite lived in city mansions and palaces, far away from their broad acres in the country. For their high incomes, tax immunities, and numerous honors, they contributed almost nothing beyond decoration to church and state.

France provides a good illustration of the system. There the church owned 20 percent of the land and collected returns equal to half those from royal estates. Some of the monies supported education, social work, and charities, but most went to 11,000 of the 130,000 members of the clergy, particularly to 123 bishops and 28 archbishops. Some of their annual incomes exceeded the equivalent of $1 million—the equal of what top-ranking CEOs earn today—but many of the overworked lower clergy existed on $100 a year. Among the 400,000 nobles, only 1000 families were represented at Versailles, where their members held numerous honorific appointments requiring no work. Titled nobles held 20 percent of the land, most by feudal tenures, which permitted them to collect numerous customary fees from their peasants. From all such sources, high French nobles probably averaged an annual equivalent of well over $100,000. Many, including some of the royal **intendants,** were former wealthy nonnobles who had bought their titles or offices.

intendants—Officials working for the king.

Fantastic hairstyles, like that shown in this engraving, were one of the ways in which members of the French upper class displayed their extravagance.

Conspicuous consumption was typical of the high European nobility, such as the Fitzwilliamses in Ireland, the Newcastles in England, the Schonbrüns (SHOUN-brun) in Bohemia, the Radziwills (RODZH-veel) in Poland, and the Esterhazys (ES-ter-haz-ee) in Hungary. Prince Esterhazy owned about 10,000 acres, including 29 estates, 160 market towns, and 414 villages; his annual revenues exceeded the equivalent of $400,000. With such wealth, the magnates built elaborate city dwellings and sumptuous country retreats, filling them with priceless handcrafted furniture, rich tapestries, and fine works of art. While most people scratched for food, the high nobles enjoyed meats, fruits, and rare delicacies that were literally unknown among common people. Generally, the top aristocrats lived lavishly in a fantasy world, marred only by the dull ceremonies accompanying their brilliant but busy social activities.

Beneath this aristocratic superstructure lived millions of European commoners, 80 percent of whom were peasants. Except in Sweden, where they could protest to the parliament, they were unrepresented in government. Three-fourths were landless, and many were serfs, bound to their villages, not only in Russia, Poland, and Prussia but also in Denmark. Among city-dwellers, only 11 percent were merchants, shopkeepers, artisans, and professionals. This proportion was higher in the Netherlands, England, and northern Italy, but generally lower elsewhere, particularly in eastern Europe. At the bottom of urban society was the mass of indigent poor, barely able to survive. Commoners of all economic levels paid most of the taxes. They were subject to legal discrimination in favor of the nobility, from whom they were also separated by differences in education, speech, manners, dress, and social customs.

This general pattern was evident in the French **Third Estate.** Including some 26 million people, it was more varied in its extremes than the first two estates, the clergy and nobles. At the top were about 75,000 wealthy bankers and merchants who had not bothered to buy titles. Another 3 million urban dwellers consisted largely of shopkeepers, lawyers, doctors, craftsmen, and street people, these last being most prevalent in Paris and port cities. The great mass of commoners in France, as in Europe generally, was the 23 million rural peasants. Most held some property rights to their lands, but many were tenants and about a million were still serfs in 1789. Almost all peasants, serf or free, paid fees to their local nobles. Government taxes were irregular but heavy everywhere; the *taille* (TIE-yeh), or main land tax, fell heaviest on the class that was least able to pay. French peasants lived better than serfs in eastern Europe or the starving farm laborers of England, but life in a French village was a constant struggle for survival.

The Challenge of Population Growth

Europe experienced a population explosion in the eighteenth century. The number of people there increased more than 58 percent, from about 118 million in 1700 to 185 million a century later; some 50 million of this increase came after 1750. Population growth during the era was much higher in Europe than in Asia or Africa; in fact, in percentage terms it had never been as rapid before and has never been exceeded since. In the past, historians have emphasized rising life expectancy (falling death rates) as the cause. They have attributed this lower mortality to an improved social environment, involving such conditions as cleaner clothes and dishes, made possible by the new textile and pottery industries; better water and sewage facilities, following wider use of iron piping; and better medical treatment, particularly in reducing infant mortality. However, other recent

Third Estate—Under the social system of pre-1789 France, society was divided by function: The first estate—the clergy—prayed; the second estate—the nobles—fought; and the third estate—the rest of society—worked. Established in the tenth century, the Estate System was an anachronism by the eighteenth century.

studies have suggested that a major cause for population growth was rising fertility in response to more productive agriculture and increasing food supplies, which also encouraged rural people to marry earlier and have more children to work the land. Whatever the cause, population expansion triggered major social changes, including rising economic demand, the growth of cities, an increasing labor surplus, vagabondage, and extensive migration.

Nearly every part of Europe experienced this tremendous expansion between 1650 and 1800. The English population rose from 5 million to over 9 million; that of Russia increased from 17 to 36 million; and the French population rose from 21 to 28 million. Other areas, which had earlier seen declines, posted gains: The Spanish population rose from 7.5 million to 11 million, while that of Italy expanded from 11 to 19 million. The increased number of people who could not afford to remain in their ancestral homes either migrated overseas or moved to urban areas, where 10 percent of Europe's population lived by 1800.

People moved in all directions. Some, like the Swiss and Irish, became foreign mercenaries. Others, like 300,000 French Huguenots (hyu-ge-NO), moved to escape religious persecution: 40,000 of them settled in England, and 20,000 of the most skilled went to Prussia. Both the Prussian and Russian governments regularly imported specialized craftsmen. German peasants by the thousands also went east to acquire land in Hungary or Russia. And the New World enticed many. In the eighteenth century, more than 750,000 English and 100,000 Irish settlers arrived in North America, the largest national contingents of a European migration to the Americas that numbered more than 2 million people.

Cities grew rapidly in the West, the main area of commerce—both domestic and foreign—and finance. Most affected were the English towns and cities, where populations generally increased faster than those of rural areas. The scope and significance of the trend may be quickly illustrated by a few figures. London's population rose from 400,000 to over 800,000 between the Peace of Utrecht (1713) and the French Revolution (1789). Other English cities, such as Bristol, Norwich, Liverpool, Leeds, Halifax, and Birmingham, which had been country towns in the 1600s, became medium-sized cities of between 20,000 and 65,000 inhabitants. On the Continent, the population of Paris reached 750,000 by 1789, and the number of residents in Bordeaux, Nantes, Le Havre, and Marseilles (mar-SEIL-e) all increased appreciably. Farther east were other expanding cities—Hamburg, Frankfurt, Geneva, Vienna, Berlin; the last two each had more than 100,000 inhabitants in the eighteenth century. In no city did the basic services of police, health, and employment keep pace with the increase in population.

Cities, of course, were the breeding grounds of ideas and contention. There were books and newspapers, coffeehouses, sailors from foreign lands, and varied populations, exchanging views and challenging prejudices. Violent spectacles, such as animal baiting and cockfighting, provided common amusements. Urban life was not only exciting, it was also more impersonal, dangerous, and frustrating. Using every kind of trick and deceit, a large criminal element flourished in the streets. Mobs were easily formed and more easily aroused, particularly in London and Paris, which regularly faced riots in the eighteenth century. Unlike the relatively placid inhabitants of rural villages, city-dwellers thrived on danger, diversity, and unpredictability. One person in three in the cities was unemployed in the eighteenth century. While the unemployed men sought relief in the proliferating gin

William Hogarth cast a critical and unsparing eye on the desperate conditions of the poor in London during the eighteenth century. In Gin Lane *(1751) he depicted the alcoholism that allowed the poor to escape momentarily the misery of their lives.*

mills of London, many women had no choice but to practice prostitution to feed their children.

Oppressive Conditions for Women

Post-1648 society was especially oppressive to women, whose general prospects declined despite some slight gains among those in the upper classes. Poor widows were hit hardest, as suggested by the number starving in English workhouses. Women died, on the average, five years younger than men, a fact explained largely by the high proportion that died in childbirth. A significant factor was malnutrition, because poor women lacked calcium in their diets and were therefore subject to hemorrhaging. For most women among the rural and urban poor, life was a nightmare of deprivation, suffering, and struggling to survive.

This situation was particularly true for poor country women, as noted by the British writer Arthur Young, who described a French peasant woman of 28 years who appeared to be 60 or 70. Capitalistic agriculture depressed farm wages, forcing farm laborers to leave the villages in search of work. Women had to stay and eke out support for the children by domestic spinning or weaving. Some went to work in the fields for lower pay and longer hours than men. As work opportunities diminished, thousands took to the roads, carrying their babies and begging for food. Many died with their children by the roadsides; others joined criminal gangs of robbers or smugglers. The hardiest and the most determined reached the cities, where the best hope for a displaced peasant woman was employment as a cook or maid with a well-to-do family.

In the cities a poor woman's life was not much better than in the villages. The lucky few in household service were paid much less than men, assigned cramped quarters, fed leftovers, and frequently exploited sexually by their masters. Alternate employment was extremely limited because women were denied membership in most craft guilds. A few could find work outside the guilds, spinning, weaving, sewing, or working leather in starvation-wage sweatshops. Others took dirtier and heavier jobs in the metal trades and in the coalfields, both above and below the ground. Another option, reluctantly chosen by many women, was prostitution. This ancient profession was growing rapidly in every large city, with 50,000 known female prostitutes in London and more than 40,000 in Paris by the late 1700s. Social degradation, venereal disease, and continuous harassment marked their lives as civil authorities allowed them to operate but subjected them to periodic imprisonment.

A vast social chasm separated poor women from those of the wealthy classes; yet even at the top, another broad gulf divided the sexes. Royal and noble women exercised considerable political power, but except for numerous ruling monarchs, they operated as satellites of the men they manipulated. Among both aristocratic women and those of the wealthy middle class, many were withdrawn from meaningful work as mothers and homemakers to become social ornaments for the husbands. Legally, upper-class wives remained subordinated to their husbands in the disposition of property and rights to divorce; the double standard of marital fidelity remained supreme, both socially and legally. Indeed, despite their improved education and their artistic and literary pursuits, women were still regarded as childlike, irresponsible, and passion-ruled by such eminent eighteenth-century men as Rousseau, Frederick the Great, and Lord Chesterfield.

The Prevalence of Human Misery

A significant base for popular discontent against governments after Westphalia was an ever-prevalent misery among the ever-growing numbers of the poor. The various wars destroyed crops, ruined cities, created hordes of starving refugees, and depopulated whole provinces. Armies contributed to prevailing diseases, such as smallpox, typhus, and malaria. Lack of sanitation and the presence of horse manure on roads and streets attracted swarming flies, which spread typhoid and infantile diarrhea among thousands of children. While epidemics of plague spread throughout Central Europe, rickets and tuberculosis reflected malnutrition among half the workers, who could not achieve marginal proficiency. Mortality rates were appalling: Half of the children died before they reached 6 years old, one woman in five died in childbirth, and life expectancy was only about 28 years. For a large proportion of Europeans, unemployment, homelessness, grinding poverty, and hunger were inevitable. Indeed, horrible reality could be escaped only on rare affordable occasions in alcohol.

Although sometimes exciting, life in the cities was also miserable for the urban poor, who made up 20 to 40 percent of city populations. Many had come in from the country, seeking survival. Without homes, friends, or steady work, they lived as best they could, toiling at transitory menial jobs, begging, stealing, or selling themselves as prostitutes. Only a social notch higher were the apprentices and journeymen of the decaying craft guilds, who also faced real hardships. The discipline, particularly for apprentices, was difficult; hours were long; and wages were barely enough to buy food. Crowded into filthy quarters, without adequate light, air, or bathing facilities, they lived dull lives conditioned by ignorance, squalor, disease, and crime. Bad as these conditions were, they might always get worse, for as the guilds faced competition,

Document Conditions Among Eighteenth-Century French Peasants

British writer Arthur Young made these observations just before the French Revolution. He saw better conditions elsewhere but was appalled at the backward state of French agriculture and the great gap in living standards between the nobility and the lower classes in the country.

SEPTEMBER 1ST. To Combourg. The country has a savage aspect; husbandry not much further advanced, at least in skill, than among the Hurons, which appears incredible amidst enclosures; the people almost as wild as their country, and their town of Combourg one of the most brutal filthy places that can be seen; mud houses, no windows, and a pavement so broken, as to impede all passengers, but ease none; yet here is a château, and inhabited. Who is this Mons. de Chateaubriand, the owner, that has nerves strung for a residence amidst such filth and poverty? Below this hideous heap of wretchedness is a fine lake, surrounded by well-wooded enclosures. Coming out of Hédé, there is a beautiful lake belonging to Mons. de Blossac, Intendant of Poitiers, with a fine accompaniment of wood. A very little cleaning would make here a delicious scenery. There is a [Château de Blossac], with four rows of trees, and nothing else to be seen from the windows in the true French style. Forbid it, taste, that this should be the house of the owner of that beautiful water; and yet this Mons. de Blossac has made at Poitiers the finest promenade in France!. . .

SEPT. 5TH. To Montauban. The poor people seem poor indeed; the children terribly ragged, if possible worse clad than if with no clothes at all; as to shoes and stockings they are luxuries. A beautiful girl of six or seven years playing with a stick, and smiling under such a bundle of rags as made my heart ache to see her. They did not beg, and when I gave them anything seemed more surprised than obliged. One-third of what I have seen of this province seems uncultivated, and nearly all of it in misery. . . .

JULY 11TH. Pass [Les] Islettes, a town (or rather collection of dirt and dung) of new features, that seem to mark, with the faces of the people, a country not French.

JULY 12TH. Walking up a long hill, to ease my mare, I was joined by a poor woman, who complained of the times, and that it was a sad country. Demanding her reasons, she said her husband had but a morsel of land, one cow, and a poor little horse, yet they had a *franchar* (42 lb.) of wheat, and three chickens, to pay as a quit-rent to one seigneur; and four *franchar* of oats, one chicken and 1 *sou* to pay to another, besides very heavy *tailles* and other taxes. She had seven children, and the cow's milk helped to make the soup. But why, instead of a horse, do not you keep another cow? Oh, her husband could not carry his produce so well without a horse; and asses are little used in the country. It was said, at present, that *something was to be done by some great folks for such poor ones, but she did not know who nor how,* but God send us better, *car les tailles et les droits nous écrasent* [because the *tailles* and other taxes are crushing us]. This woman, at no great distance, might have been taken for sixty or seventy, her figure was so bent, and her face so furrowed and hardened by labour; but she said she was only twenty-eight. An Englishman who had not travelled cannot imagine the figure made by infinitely the greater part of the countrywomen in France; it speaks, at the first sight, hard and severe labour. I am inclined to think, that they work harder than the men, and this, united with the more miserable labour of bringing a new race of slaves into the world, destroys absolutely all symmetry of person and every feminine appearance. . . .

Questions to Consider

1. Young writes just before the French Revolution—what do you see in the first paragraph of the selection that would provoke a violent reaction?
2. Young was an agricultural reformer in England. How did he characterize the nature of the methods used by the French peasants in preparing their land?
3. What was the effect of the rural situation in France on women?
4. It is alleged that peasants have little understanding of the economic and political system in which they find themselves. Did the woman with whom Young talked on July 12th comprehend why her life was so hard?

From Arthur Young, *Travels in France*, ed. Constantia Maxwell (Cambridge: Cambridge University Press, 1929), pp. 107 ff.

many shops were forced to close, leaving their journeymen to become wandering artisans among the vagabonds on the roads.

Most of these pitiful derelicts were products of the century's most serious social challenge, rural poverty. Despite a general prosperity lasting until about 1770, European peasants suffered severely from ravaging armies and increasing agricultural specialization. High agricultural prices turned aristocrats into aspiring capitalists, willing to gouge their peasants in seeking greater profits. Some nobles, particularly on the Continent, revived and enforced their old manorial rights to fees and services. Others moved in an opposite direction by eliminating the peasants' medieval rights and using hired labor to work their lands. Either way, the peasants lost a substantial amount of their livelihood and were likely to become criminals, vagrants, or part of an alienated subculture. They ceased to be assets to the state—as either taxpayers or soldiers—becoming instead potentially dangerous and expensive liabilities.

Although faring better than the serfs of eastern Europe, western peasants still faced terrible conditions. Some in France were reduced from tenants to laborers when merchants bought up land to profit from rising food prices. Under Louis XV, some 30,000 rural vagrants thronged French roads. About 35 percent of the peasants who had managed to acquire land were still paying manorial fees and services to local lords in accordance with feudal law. Earlier, these exactions had hurt the peasants' pride more than their chances for survival; when the practice was stepped up during the depression of the 1780s, many lost their lands.

Responses to the plight of the urban and rural poor were crude and cruel. It was felt that the way to eliminate vagrancy was through punishment. The approach was similar to the brutal beating of military delinquents, the condemning of criminals to galley slavery, or the confinement of debtors on rotting prison ships. For the poor, similar punitive solutions were sought in the British parish workhouses and the French "beggar depots." At the end of the century, the English workhouses held 100,000 inmates, compared with 230,000 in the French depots. Both systems, like others all over Europe, perpetuated abominable living conditions while denying hope for the unfortunate victims. In England, the workhouses were favored by some large landowners, who welcomed cheap labor supplied by the state. Other taxpayers opposed the cost of improving the workhouses and tried to push vagrants into other parishes. Even a pregnant woman or one with a sick child might be given a few pennies and turned away.

Ultimately, the governments built larger workhouses for fewer parishes, attempting to spread the cost of poverty relief. Such policies destroyed the initiative of the poor and conditioned them to seek public assistance. The simmering pressure of the discontent of the multitudes could be denied for a while, but in the 1770s and 1780s across Europe, mass outbreaks of violence and finally revolution would be the price to be paid. (See Chapter 18.)

Protests, Riots, and Rebellions

Injustice and misery among women and the poor were obvious sources of discontent, but even more dangerous for old regimes were changing attitudes among the higher classes. A general spirit of change and hope, coupled with the chaotic confusion and inefficiency of most monarchies, aroused general feelings of dissatisfaction, particularly among members of the lower middle class and lesser nobles, who were too numerous to be absorbed into the established system. Even some favored aristocrats showed a casual indifference to royal authority and a stubborn determination to defend their privileges. Potential middle-class rebels, particularly lawyers, were well equipped to voice grievances, which they did often by the late 1700s. Although lacking education and opportunities to register direct protests, city workers and peasants sometimes did express their despair in sporadic riots and futile local uprisings.

Because their testimony must be taken from official records, often from the statements of tortured captives, no one can accurately describe peasant attitudes on the Continent at that time. They surely varied from place to place, as did the conditions. Where life was hardest, they regularly resorted to individual acts of violence, such as killing animals or burning outbuildings. Generally, they lacked long-range political objectives but could be aroused en masse by immediate threats to their well-being. Seventy-three peasant rebellions occurred in eighteenth-century Europe, notoriously in Poland (1730s), Bohemia (1775), and in Russia, the great Pugachev (poo-gah-CHOV) revolt (1773–1775). Suffering English farm laborers rioted six times between 1710 and 1772. Although generally more docile, French peasants precipitated violent upheavals in 1709, 1725, 1740, 1749, and 1772. In his writings, Arthur Young recognized their surly attitudes and contempt for authority. In 1789, when they could express grievances to delegates headed for the **Estates-General,** they were universally bitter against feudal exactions and government taxes.

Urban workers were usually more aggressive and perhaps better informed than peasants but more

---

Estates-General—A national meeting in France of representatives of the three estates to present petitions to the king.

confused by the complexities of their problems. While their numbers increased with the size of cities, they became alienated from the upper classes by periodic unemployment and inflation. Rioting among workers and the idle poor of the cities was thus common, notably in London and Paris. Such outbreaks, however, were more violent than politically significant. Workers did recognize two potential enemies: the capitalist, who contracted for labor and influenced government to eliminate welfare, and the guild, which exploited the journeyman in favor of the master. To combat these enemies, workers occasionally organized in England and France. The organizations were weak, however, and their efforts usually failed for want of leadership.

Middle-class discontent, like that of some peasants, arose more from thwarted expectations than from terrible suffering. Upward mobility, from middle class to aristocracy, was a by-product of economic prosperity all over Europe, particularly in England and France. The movement took many forms—purchase of land and titles, marriage, even reward for personal services of lawyers, doctors, tutors, or governesses. This middle-class struggle for respectability was individually competitive, as long as opportunities were open. But in time, room at the top became limited, as old regimes stabilized and more of the middle class sought to climb the social ladder. At this point, ambitious middle-class outsiders became dangerously hostile to the system.

Most dissenting action came from men, but women were also represented among the malcontents. They were regularly involved in local uprisings against the high cost of bread, the introduction of machines to depress labor, and rising taxes. In 1770 a mob of Parisian women left their workplaces to protest the deportation of their vagrant children to the colonies. Such actions were not yet aimed directly against old regimes, but later (as we shall see in Chapter 18) other French and English women would go further to champion women's rights, along with the "rights of man."

More dangerous to monarchical establishments than outside opposition was aristocratic opposition from within. Gains by the nobles in Sweden, Spain, Austria, and even France increased their confidence and whetted their appetites for more power. As old regimes wavered, nobles at the top were frantically determined to maintain their positions; indeed, they professed to believe that they were more legitimate rulers than the kings. This was partly an effort to combat middle-class influence, for nobles were often heavily in debt and feared legal reforms that might require them to pay. At the same time, most lesser nobles resented the court cliques; a few even dreamed of helping the middle classes change the system. Noble opinions were indeed varied, promising weakening support for royal authority but refusing cooperation with kings in curtailing privileges. On this last point, nearly all nobles were in total agreement.

LOUIS XIV, THE SUN KING: THE MODEL FOR EUROPEAN ABSOLUTISM

- *Why did most European countries follow the absolutist trend of government between 1650 and 1789? What advantages and disadvantages do an absolutist government bring to a state?*

The word ***absolutism,*** which is applied to regimes such as that of Louis XIV (1638–1715, r. 1643–1715), is somewhat misleading. Despite his grandiose role-playing, Louis faced problems arising from preindustrial technology, diverse ethnic groups, local customs, traditional rights, and nobles who still commanded formidable followings, both regionally and nationally. But he was helped by the post-1648 obsession for security and by economic growth.

MAP Absolutism: France, England, and Russia, 1600-1700

Foundations of Absolutism

The prevailing respect for power was most clearly revealed in theoretical justifications for absolute monarchy. Some of these, such as the arguments advanced by Bishop Jacques Bossuet (BOS-siu-ay), employed the older idea of "divine right," claiming that rulers were agents of God's will. The most influential secular justification for absolutism came from the English philosopher Thomas Hobbes (1588–1679), whose political treatise, *Leviathan,* appeared in 1651. Unlike Bossuet, he did not see God as the source of political authority. According to Hobbes, people created governments as a protection against themselves because human life was naturally "poor, nasty, brutish, and short." Forced by human nature to surrender their freedoms to the state, people have no rights under government except obedience. Monarchs were therefore legitimately entitled to absolute authority, limited only by their own deficiencies and by the power of other states.

Neither Hobbes nor Bossuet described the workings of the monarchy of Louis XIV. Louis and his colleagues functioned within institutional systems carried over from the medieval past. Their success or failure depended on their ability to shape old feudal struc-

absolutism—The political system in which the ruler has total power, with no limitations.

tures into centralized states. In this process, none succeeded completely in eliminating aristocratic influence and local tradition as limits to royal authority. Their proclaimed absolutism reflected a trend, rather than an accomplished fact. But one goal that Louis and other monarchs across Europe shared was a desire to dominate and control their nobles, many of whom came from families with far more distinguished lineages than those of the kings. To these nobles, the king was simply *primus inter pares* (PREE-moos in-ter pa-REES) or "first among equals." Centralizing kings could not tolerate such familiarity.

The attempted absolutism of Louis XIV followed a long monarchical tradition of French kings trying to centralize power. Francis I in the early sixteenth century had increasingly subordinated the feudal nobility and created a centralized administration. Henry IV and his chief minister, the duke of Sully (suil-EE; 1560–1641) produced a balanced budget and a treasury surplus in little more than a decade. At the same time, Henry ended the nobles' control of hereditary offices and council seats. This centralization was temporarily disrupted in 1610 when Henry was assassinated, but the queen, Marie de' Medici (MEH-de-chee; 1573–1642) served as a regent for her young son Louis XIII until 1617 when he, at the age of 15, seized power to rule for himself. For the next thirteen years, after he restored her to his council, they continued their duel for power. Marie favored a pro-Spanish and Catholic policy, while Louis—following the advice of the Cardinal Richelieu (REESH-e-lieu; 1585–1642)—saw the Habsburgs and the papacy as the main threats to French interests.

Cardinal Richelieu finally came out the winner in this contest for power, and Marie de' Medici was banished from France in 1631. Richelieu worked ceaselessly to increase the king's powers over the nobles: he organized a royal civil service, restricted the traditional local courts, brought local government under central control, outlawed dueling, prohibited fortified castles, stripped the Huguenots of their military defenses, and developed strong military and naval forces loyal only to the king. His policies were carried on after his death by his colleague, Cardinal Mazarin (1602–1661), who, for all intents and purposes, ran the government until his death, when the 23-year-old Louis XIV could finally take direct control of the state. During the time of Mazarin's supervision, a civil war, the Fronde (1649–1653), was waged by some of the highest-ranking French nobles against the king. More than once, Louis barely escaped being captured by the rebel forces.

The memories of the Fronde and the impact of the lessons he received from Mazarin prepared Louis well to be an absolute monarch. His personal political convictions were clearly revealed in a characteristic statement: "All power, all authority resides in the hands of the king, and there can be no other in his kingdom than that which he establishes. The nation does not form a body in France. It resides entirely in the person of the king."[1] Louis also claimed authority over the French church and the religion of his subjects, enforcing that authority in contention with both Protestants and the papacy. The king was involved in a long struggle with the pope over revenues. In 1685 he revoked the Edict of Nantes, by which in 1598 Henry IV had granted freedom of worship to Protestant Huguenots. The new law subjected Protestants to torture or imprisonment. Luckily for them, but not for France, some 300,000 escaped to other lands, taking with them valuable skills and knowledge.

During his long reign, Louis worked at projecting an image of himself to France as a "Grand Monarch," a figure worthy of awe well as worship. But the reality of his personal life at court was marked by a casual, frivolous, morality. Louis shared his bed with numerous

Louis XIV in Robes of State *(1701), by court painter Hyacinthe Rigaud. The portrait captures the splendor of the Grand Monarch, known as the Sun King, who believed himself to be the center of France as the sun was the center of the solar system.*

Document Louis XIV to His Son

This memoir, designed to instruct a young prince who never became king, nevertheless provides revealing insights into Louis's personal rationalizations for his one-dimensional view of government.

I laid a rule on myself to work regularly twice every day, and for two or three hours each time with different persons, without counting the hours which I passed privately and alone, nor the time which I was able to give on particular occasions to any special affairs that might arise. There was no moment when I did not permit people to talk to me about them, provided that they were urgent; with the exception of foreign ministers who sometimes find too favourable moments in the familiarity allowed to them, either to obtain or to discover something, and whom one should not hear without being previously prepared.

I cannot tell you what fruit I gathered immediately I had taken this resolution. I felt myself, as it were, uplifted in thought and courage; I found myself quite another man, and with joy reproached myself for having been too long unaware of it. This first timidity, which a little self-judgment always produces and which at the beginning gave me pain, especially on occasions when I had to speak in public, disappeared in less than no time. The only thing I felt then was that I was King, and born to be one. I experienced next a delicious feeling, hard to express, and which you will not know yourself except by tasting it as I have done. . . .

All that is most necessary to this work is at the same time agreeable: for, in a word, my son, it is to have one's eyes open to the whole earth; to learn each hour the news concerning every province and every nation, the secrets of every court, the mood and the weaknesses of each Prince and of every foreign minister; to be well-informed on an infinite number of matters about which we are supposed to know nothing; to elicit from our subjects what they hide from us with the greatest care; to discover the most remote opinions of our own courtiers and the most hidden interests of those who come to us with quite contrary professions. I do not know of any other pleasure we would not renounce for that, even if curiosity alone gave us the opportunity. . . .

I gave orders to the four Secretaries of State no longer to sign anything whatsoever without speaking to me; likewise to the Controller, and that he should authorise nothing as regards finance without its being registered in a book which must remain with me, and being noted down in a very abridged abstract form in which at any moment, and at a glance, I could see the state of the funds, and past and future expenditure.

The Chancellor received a like order, that is to say, to sign nothing with the seal except by my command, with the exception only of letters of justice, so called because it would be an injustice to refuse them, a procedure required more as a matter of form than of principle. . . . I let it be understood that whatever the nature of the matter might be, direct application must be made to me when it was not a question that depended only on my favour; and to all my subjects without distinction I gave liberty to present their case to me at all hours, either verbally or by petitions. . . .

Regarding the persons whose duty it was to second my labours, I resolved at all costs to have no prime minister; and if you will believe me, my son, and all your successors after you, the name shall be banished for ever from France, for there is nothing more undignified than to see all the administration on one side, and on the other, the mere title of King. . . .

Questions to Consider

1. Given Louis' experience with the Cardinal Mazarin, who virtually kept the reins of power, why do you think he tells his son to have no prime minister? How does having a prime minister correlate with absolutist?
2. How would you characterize Louis' management style? A hands-off delegator of power or a micro-manager?
3. What do you think Louis finds most enjoyable about his job?

From *A King's Lesson in Statecraft: Louis XIV: Letters to His Heirs*, in Harry J. Carroll et al., eds., *The Development of Civilization*, Vol. 2 (Glenview, Ill.: Scott, Foresman, 1970), pp. 120–121.

women, each of whom was designated in her time as the "head mistress"—and rarely his wife, the Spanish *infanta.* He shared none of his power with them and was extremely wary of their efforts to extract political favors.

The Functioning of French Absolutism

To symbolize his life-giving presence in the council chamber, Louis had a rising sun painted on his official chair. He constantly strove to inspire awe of the monarchy, as was evidenced by his great palace at Versailles, a short distance from Paris. It was set in 17,000 beautifully landscaped acres. The parks and buildings, surrounded by a 40-mile wall, contained 1400 fountains, 2000 statues, and innumerable rooms decorated with marble columns, painted ceilings, costly draperies, mirrored walls, and handcrafted furniture.

The most striking characteristic of the government of Louis XIV was the decided contrast between central and local functions. In the provinces he had to contend with entrenched local authorities and legal structures, which remained despite his attempts at centralization. They constituted an obstacle that hindered the enforcement of royal edicts and the collection of revenues. At Versailles the situation was quite different. There, Louis was the final authority and arbiter of fashion. Theoretically, he made all major decisions. He was the supreme lawgiver, the chief judge, the commander of all military forces, and the head of all administration.

With access to Louis XIV being necessary to gain power in France, the king was surrounded by ambitious courtiers and courtesans, such as the witty and beautiful Athénaïs de Montespan.

The aristocracy through which Louis funneled his power dominated France with clear distinctions precisely defined by law. The rest of French society consisted of unprivileged taxpaying commoners, including merchants, craftsmen, and, above all, peasants. Most peasants owed dues and services to their landlords, although they were no longer bound to the soil as serfs. Commoners, including middle-class townspeople, paid most of the taxes, which were used to finance frequent wars and extravagant royal courts.

In France during the reign of Louis XIV, an alliance paired royal government with wealthy merchant-bankers in the king's attempt to gain the most money he could from the capitalists to support his ambitious plans. The result was a system of national economic regulations known as **mercantilism,** which had originated earlier but was adopted generally by European governments through the late seventeenth century. The trend was accentuated by the expansion of overseas trade, the expenses incurred in wars, and the economic depression of the middle 1600s.

Louis's comptroller of finance, Jean-Baptiste Colbert (1619–1683), installed mercantilism at the expense of Dutch overseas commerce. He created a comprehensive system of tariffs and trade prohibitions, levied against foreign imports. French luxury industries—silks, laces, fine woolens, and glass—were subsidized or developed in government shops. The state imported skilled workers and prescribed the most minute regulations for each industry. Colbert also improved internal transportation by building roads and canals. He chartered overseas trading companies, granting them monopolies on commerce with North America, the West Indies, India, Southeast Asia, and the Middle East. In all of this, he tried

---

mercantilism—Governmental regulation of all aspects of the economy.

The Reign of Louis XIV

1638	Birth of Louis XIV
1643	Louis ascends to the throne under the aegis of Cardinal Mazarin
1649–1653	Revolt of the nobles in the Fronde
1661	Death of Mazarin: Louis takes personal control
1661–1685	First phase of rule: Colbert installs mercantilism, Louvois reforms army
1670–1713	Four wars of Louis XIV
1685	Revocation of Edict of Nantes
1715	Death of Louis XIV

to harness the energies of capitalism—but ultimately failed.

"Bullionism" was one of the system's basic principles. It sought to increase precious metals within a country by achieving a "favorable balance of trade," in which the monetary value of exports exceeded the value of imports. The result was, in a sense, a national profit. This became purchasing power in the world market, an advantage shared most directly by the government and favored merchants. Louis's advisers believed state economic regulation to be absolutely necessary for gaining a favorable balance. They used subsidies, chartered monopolies, taxes, tariffs, harbor tolls, and direct legal prohibitions to encourage exports and limit imports. For the same purpose, French state enterprises received advantages over private competitors. Because Colbert viewed the world market in terms of competing states, he emphasized the importance of colonial expansion. He regarded colonies as favored markets for French products and as sources of cheap raw materials.

Louis's able minister of war, the Marquis de Louvois (lou-VWAH; 1641–1691), revolutionized the French army. In addition to infantry and cavalry, he organized special units of supply, ordnance, artillery, engineers, and inspectors. Command ranks, combat units, drills, uniforms, and weapons were standardized for the first time in Europe. Louvois also improved weaponry by such innovations as the bayonet, which permitted a musket to be fired while the blade was attached. By raising military pay, providing benefits, and improving conditions of service, the war minister increased the size of the army from 72,000 to 400,000, a force larger than all belligerents put together at any one time during the Thirty Years' War. Louvois also improved and expanded the navy. In addition to a Mediterranean galley fleet based at Toulon, the overseas forces by 1683 consisted of 217 warships, operating from Atlantic ports and served by numerous shipyards. The new navy was also part of Colbert's grand strategy for building an enormous overseas dominion. In the last decades of the seventeenth century, the French Empire extended to North America, Africa, and Asia.

Madame de Maintenon, shown here with her niece, exercised considerable influence in the court of Louis XIV.

bullionism—A theory that states that wealth is to be found only in precious metals, and trade policy should guarantee a favorable balance of trade to insure a continuous increase in the amount of precious metals held by the state.

THE GRAVITATIONAL PULL OF FRENCH ABSOLUTISM

▪ *Why did most European states admire and try to imitate French absolutism?*

The popular image of Louis XIV as the Sun King symbolized his position in France but also implied that the French system exerted an influence on other European states. Like all such symbolism, the idea was only partly true. As much as it was a response to the French example, royal authority was accepted because it promised efficiency and security, the greatest political needs of the time. Yet, French wealth and power certainly generated European admiration and imitation. Countries across the Continent imitated various aspects of the political theater created by Louis in Versailles and also copied the economic and military policies of the Sun King.

The Germanic Satellites

Among the most obvious satellites of the French sun were the numerous German principalities of the Holy Roman Empire. The 1648 Treaty of Westphalia recognized more than 300 sovereign states in the empire. Without serious responsibilities to the emperor and with treasuries filled with the proceeds of confiscated church properties, their rulers struggled to increase their prerogatives and dabble in international diplomacy. Many sought French alliances against the Habsburg emperor; those who could traveled to France and attended Louis's court. Subsequently, many a German palace became a miniature Versailles. Even the tiniest states were likely to have standing armies, state churches, court officials, and economic regulations. The elector of Brandenburg demonstrated the ultimate deference to the French model. Although sincerely loyal to his wife, he copied Louis XIV by taking an official mistress and displaying her at court without requiring her to perform the duty usually associated with the position.

Scandinavia

The era of the Sun King also witnessed an upsurge of royal authority in Scandinavia. After an earlier aristocratic reaction against both monarchies, Frederick III (r. 1648–1670) in Denmark and Charles XI (r. 1660–1697) in Sweden broke the power of the nobles and created structures similar to the French model. Frederick in 1661 forced the assembled high nobility to accept him as their hereditary king. Later royal edicts proclaimed the king's right to issue laws and impose taxes. A similar upheaval in Sweden (1680) allowed Charles to achieve financial independence by seizing the nobles' lands. Both kingdoms developed thoroughly centralized administrations. Sweden, particularly, resembled France with its professional army, navy, national church, and mercantilist economy. Although Swedish royal absolutism was limited by the nobles in 1718, the Danish system remained into the nineteenth century.

Spain and Portugal: Irregular Orbits

Unlike the Scandinavian and German states, most European governments resembled Louis's system more in their direction of development than in their specific institutions. As agricultural economies became commercialized, changing the developing interests of monarchs and commoners, rulers sought to be free of their feudal councils and exercise more authority. Some states during this period had not developed as far in this direction as France had; others were already finding absolutism at least partly outmoded. Although all felt the magnetic pull of French absolutism, their responses varied according to their traditions and local conditions.

The process is well illustrated by a time lag in the Spanish and Portuguese monarchies. United by Spanish force in 1580 and divided again by a Portuguese revolt in 1640, the two kingdoms were first weakened by economic decay and then nearly destroyed by the costs of the Thirty Years' War and their own mutual conflicts, which lasted until Spain accepted Portuguese independence in 1668. Conditions deteriorated further under the half-mad King Alfonso VI (r. 1656–1668) in Portugal and the feeble-minded Charles II (r. 1665–1700) in Spain.

The nobilities, having exploited these misfortunes to regain their dominant position in both countries, could not be easily dislodged. In Portugal not until the 1680s did Pedro II (r. 1683–1706) restore a semblance of royal authority. His successor, John V (r. 1706–1750), aided by new wealth from Brazilian gold and diamond strikes, centralized the administration, perfected mercantilism, and extended control over the church. In Spain similar developments followed the War of the Spanish Succession and the granting of the Spanish crown to Louis XIV's Bourbon grandson, Philip V (r. 1700–1746). Philip brought to Spain a corps of French advisers, including the Princesse des Ursins (pran-SESS days ur-SAN), a spy for Louis XIV. Philip then followed French precedents by imposing centralized ministries, local intendants, and economic regulations.

The Habsburgs

Aristocratic limits on absolutism, so evident in the declining kingdoms of Portugal and Spain, were even more typical of the Habsburg monarchy in eastern Europe. The Thirty Years' War had diverted Habsburg attention from the Holy Roman Empire to lands under the family's direct control. By 1700 the Habsburgs held the archduchy of Austria, a few adjacent German areas, the kingdom of Bohemia, and the kingdom of Hungary, recently conquered from the Turks. This was a very large domain, stretching from Saxony in the north to the Ottoman Empire in the southeast. It played a leading role in the continental wars against Louis XIV after the 1670s.

Leopold I (r. 1657–1705) was primarily responsible for strengthening the Austrian imperial monarchy during this period. In long wars with the French and the Turks, Leopold modernized the army, not only increasing its numbers but also instilling professionalism and loyalty in its officers. He created central administrative councils, giving each responsibility for an arm of the imperial government or a local area. He staffed these high administrative positions with court nobles, rewarded and honored like those in France. Other new nobles, given lands in the home provinces, became political tools for subordinating the local estates. Leopold suppressed Protestantism in Bohemia and Austria while keeping his own Catholic Church under firm control. In 1687 the Habsburgs were accepted as hereditary monarchs in Hungary, a status they had already achieved in Austria and Bohemia.

In the eighteenth century Maria Theresa (r. 1740–1780) confronted Leopold's problems all over again. When she inherited her throne at the age of 22, her realm, lacking both money and military forces, faced threats from Prussia. In the years after Leopold's time, the nobles had regained much of their former power and were rebuilding their dominions at the expense of the monarchy. Known as "Her Motherly Majesty," Maria was a religious and compassionate woman, but she put aside this gentle image to hasten much needed internal reforms. Count Haugwitz (HOG-vitz), her reforming minister, rigidly enforced new laws that brought provincial areas under more effective royal control.

Despite its glitter and outward trappings, the Habsburg Empire was not a good example of absolutism. Its economy was almost entirely agricultural and, therefore, dependent on serf labor. This situation perpetuated the power of the nobles and diminished revenues available to the crown. In addition, subjects of the monarchy comprised a mixture of nationalities and languages—German, Czech, Magyar, Croatian, and Italian, to name only a few. Lacking ethnic unity, the various areas persisted in their localism. Even the reforms of Leopold and Maria Theresa left royal authority existing more in name than in fact. Imposed on still functioning medieval institutions, the Habsburg regime was a strange combination of absolutist theory and feudal fact.

Poland: The Last Medieval State

While Habsburg absolutism wavered in an irregular orbit around the French sun, Poland stood completely outside of the France-centered political and economic system. Local trade and industry were even more insignificant in its economy, the peasants were more depressed, and land-controlling lesser nobles—some 10 percent of the population—grew wealthy by supplying grain for Western merchants. Nobles avoided military service and most taxes; they were lords and masters of their serfs. More than 50 local assemblies dominated their areas, admitting no outside jurisdiction. The national diet (council), which was elected by the local bodies, chose a king who had no real authority. In effect Poland was 50 small and independent feudal estates.

Absolutism in Prussia

The rise of the Hohenzollerns (HO-hen-zol-lerns) was among the most striking political developments of the era. These relatively unimportant nobles, who once occupied a castle on Mount Zollern in southern Germany, pursued their ambitious policies through marriage, intrigue, religious factionalism, and war. By the early seventeenth century, they held lands scattered across northern Germany. The Thirty Years' War was almost disastrous for the Hohenzollerns but conditioned them to austerity, perseverance, and iron discipline.

Two reigns laid permanent foundations for the later monarchy. Frederick William (r. 1640–1688), called "the Great Elector," used his small but well-trained army to win eastern Pomerania at the end of the Thirty Years' War. In the near-anarchy that prevailed in Germany immediately after Westphalia, he reformed the administration in Brandenburg, created a strong army of 30,000 soldiers, intimidated the nobles in Prussia and Cleves, and won central control over all three areas. His son Frederick I (r. 1688–1713) exploited Russia's victory over Sweden to annex western Pomerania. As a reward for fighting France, he was also recognized as "King in Prussia" by the Peace of Utrecht in 1713.

After Utrecht, Prussia became a drill yard, with the monarch Frederick William I (r. 1713–1740) as drillmaster. This crusty soldier-king demanded hard work and absolute obedience from his subjects. He once told a group of them, "We are king and master and can do what we like." On another occasion he proclaimed, "I need render account to no one as to the matter in which I conduct . . . affairs."[2] With such unabashed absolutism, he reorganized the government under the so-called **General Directory,**

General Directory—The efficient, centralized organization of the Prussian state in 1722.

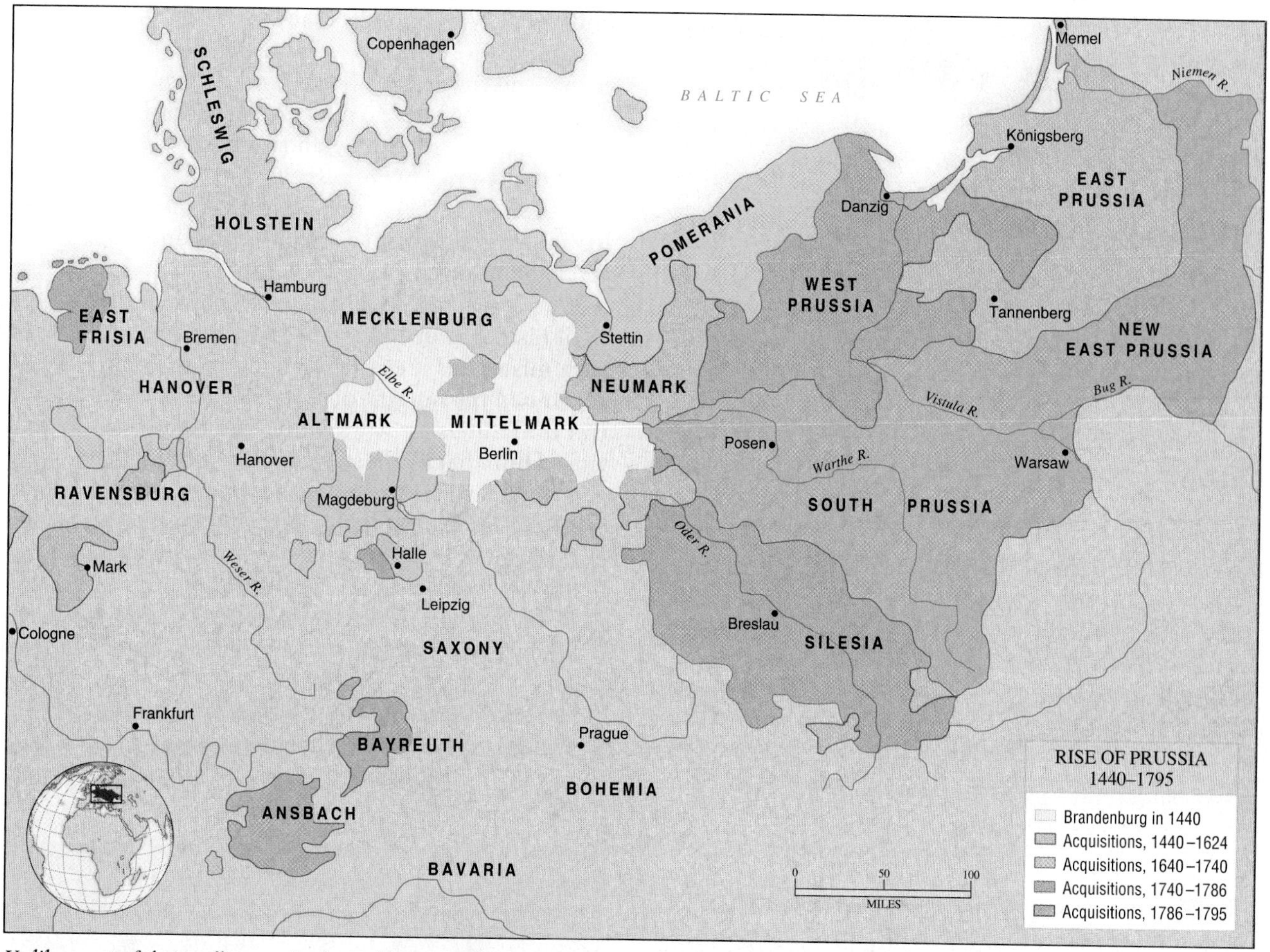

Unlike most of their colleagues in the Holy Roman Empire, the electors of Brandenburg showed a single-minded drive over the centuries to expand from their bases in Berlin and Königsberg to become a major European power at the end of the eighteenth century.

established a civil service for local administration, created a royal supreme court, taxed the nobles, required the nobles to train for professional military careers, and built an army of 80,000, considered the best trained and best equipped in Europe. At the end of his reign, the Hohenzollern monarchy was ready for military expansion.

Frederick William I held high hopes for his son Frederick II (r. 1740–1786). The young prince, however, reacted against his Spartan training, secretly seeking escape in music, art, and philosophy. When caught after attempting flight to France, he was forced to witness the beheading of his accomplice and best friend. More years of severe training and discipline brought him in line with his father's wishes but robbed the future king of the capacity for personal feeling. In later years, while retaining his cultural interests and mingling freely with writers and artists, he developed no lasting relationships, particularly not with women. He married early to escape his father's household, and then ignored his wife, Elizabeth, subjecting her to a courteous but cold formality. Neither she nor any of his frequent but temporary mistresses could influence his judgment. Neither did he confide in his family after the old king died. Wilhelmina, the sister who had shared his youthful enmity against their father, lost his confidence as they both matured. Such was the price he paid to become a superb administrator, a master of Machiavellian diplomacy, and—as we shall see—the greatest soldier of his day.

In 1780, the Prussia of Frederick II, called "the Great," was regarded as a perfectly functioning absolute monarchy. Stretching some 500 miles across northern Germany between the Elbe and Niemen Rivers, its flourishing population had grown from 750,000 in 1648 to 5 million. For 23 years, between 1740 and 1763, it had waged nearly continuous war, with 200,000 men often in the field. Consequently, the government ran as precisely as an efficient army. Like any good commander, Frederick claimed all ultimate authority. He required rigid discipline and deference to superiors from civilian officials as well as from military officers. Prussian nobles were honored over merchants or nonnoble

This portrait of Frederick II of Prussia adorns the lid of a snuffbox. A patron of the arts and sciences as well as an able military leader and administrator, Frederick devoted himself to strengthening his country's military power while he also engaged in the study of philosophy, history, and poetry.

officials and were permitted complete mastery over their serfs. Frederick's mercantilism stressed tariff protection for agriculture, encouraged industry with government subsidies, imported artisans, and sought economic self-sufficiency as a means of achieving military superiority.

Russian Autocracy

A new era in Russian history began with Peter I, "the Great" (r. 1682–1725). When he was 10 years old, Peter's half-sister Sophia staged a palace coup, in which her troops looted the palace, killing many of Peter's maternal uncles. For seven years, while Sophia ruled as regent for Peter and his handicapped half-brother, Ivan, the young co-tsar lived in fear and insecurity. Later, Peter roamed the quarter reserved for foreigners, without discipline or much formal education. He recruited and drilled his own guard regiments and learned about boats and Western ways. When he was 16, his mother arranged his marriage to a young noblewoman. From the beginning this was a mismatch; after impregnating his wife, Peter abandoned her within three months. He was now a young giant, weighing 230 pounds and standing 6 feet 8 inches tall, with a temper to match. Fortunately, he also had a sharp mind and boundless energy. Perhaps unfortunately for Russia, he despised Moscow, the traditions of the Russian court, and the culture of his country. In his efforts to westernize Russia, he would drive a wedge between the elites of the country and the masses that would last through the twentieth century.

CASE STUDY Reflections on the Accomplishments of Peter the Great

After 1689 Peter took control of the country and his life. When Sophia failed in an attempt to become sole ruler, he forced her into a convent, although his brother Ivan remained co-tsar until his death in 1696. Peter amused himself with mistresses and wild drinking parties but continued his pursuit of Western knowledge. His difficulties in wars with the Turks convinced him that he must modernize his army and build a navy. In 1697 he traveled incognito as a member of a great embassy to Poland, Germany, the Netherlands, and England. He worked as a common ship carpenter in the Netherlands, learning Dutch methods firsthand. Back in Moscow, Peter crushed a rebellion of his palace guards with savage cruelty, began extensive reforms, and conducted new wars against the Turks and Swedes in efforts to gain "a window on the sea." He achieved this goal in 1703 when he founded St. Petersburg as his

DOCUMENT Lomonosov to Peter the Great

IMAGE Winter Palace at St. Petersburg

Larger than life for the era in which he lived, the 6-foot 8-inch Tsar Peter the Great remains one of the most controversial figures in Russian history. Liberals see him as a positive force for opening his country to the West. Conservatives see him as a negative factor in Russian history for the same reason.

future capital on the Baltic. That same year Peter met Marfa Skavronska (ska-vron-SKA), a Lithuanian peasant girl who became his mistress, campaign companion, and, after the tsarina's death in a convent, his wife.

Peter's reforms enforced Russian absolutism, in fact as well as in theory. He centralized the government, replacing all representative bodies with an appointed council and appointed ministries. Royal military governors assumed local authority. The Chancery of Police maintained order and collected information from an elaborate spy network. By forcing his nobles to shave their beards and don European-style attire, he conditioned them to accept change and become living symbols of his power over them. They were now required to serve in the army, the government, or industry. Peter also officially abolished the office of patriarch as head of the state church, substituting a synod of bishops, dominated by a secular official, the procurator, who represented the tsar. In copying European mercantilism, Peter established factories, mines, and shipyards, importing technical experts along with thousands of laborers. He levied tariffs to protect native industries and taxed almost everything, including births, marriages, and caskets. As revenues increased, he improved the army and navy, both of which were expanded, professionalized, and equipped with efficient Western weapons.

DOCUMENT
On the Corruption of Morals in Russia

Before and after Peter's time, Russian absolutism reached into the forested wastes of Siberia. Russian Cossacks and fur traders explored this enormous territory between 1580 and 1651. During the seventeenth century, it remained a vast game preserve, exploited by the Russian government for its fur. Agents responsible to the Siberian Bureau in Moscow or St. Petersburg governed the relatively peaceful native peoples, collecting tribute from them in furs and a percentage from the profits of chartered companies. Given the financial succession of the tightly regulated fur trade, the government discouraged settlement in Siberia. In the eighteenth century, however, restrictions were lightened and western Siberia, between the Ob and Yenesei Rivers, began

From 1696 to 1725 Peter the Great allowed his country only one year of peace. For the rest of his time he radically changed the form and nature of his government in order to pursue war. At the end he had achieved his much desired "Window on the West" on the Baltic.

attracting colonists; convicts and political prisoners were transported there as well. Some 400,000 settlers had arrived by 1763, but Siberia was largely undeveloped until the late nineteenth century.

After his death in 1725, Peter's policies continued to affect Russian politics through the eighteenth century. In reaction, the nobles worked constantly to regain their former freedom from the state, while the "old believers," Orthodox Christians who refused to recognize seventeenth-century religious reforms, maintained an underground existence. Another striking characteristic of the period was the prominence of female rulers. Of the seven monarchs between 1725 and 1801, only three were men, and they reigned for just six and a half disastrous years. The four tsarinas were Catherine I (r. 1725–1727), Peter's camp-following second wife and the first Russian empress; Anna Ivanovna (r. 1730–1740), daughter of Peter's half-brother, Ivan; Elizabeth (r. 1741–1762), daughter of Peter and Catherine I; and Catherine II (r. 1762–1796), known as "the Great." All tried to continue Peter's policies of turning his country away from its roots toward western Europe. Anna Ivanovna allowed the Baltic Germans too much power, thus alienating their Russian subjects. Elizabeth avoided this mistake while further consolidating the central government and winning new respect in western Europe for Russian military power. She laid the foundations for the long and successful reign of Catherine the Great, whose role as an "enlightened despot" will be discussed in Chapter 18.

HOLLAND AND ENGLAND: LIMITED CENTRAL POWER

- *What social and economic factors impelled Holland and England to pursue the political model of limited central power?*

In the century between the Dutch rebellion and the British **Glorious Revolution,** constitutional government took root in the Netherlands and survived and prospered in England. The Dutch profited from the declining fortunes of the Spaniards and established global trading dominance. Protected by its island geography and strengthened by its traditions, England carried on a sometimes bloody argument about its political structure. In both countries, rapidly developing commerce and increasing social mobility encouraged a direct transition from feudalism to constitutional government, without a prolonged intermediate stage of centralized monarchy.

Glorious Revolution—This event took place in 1688 and ended the Stuart dynasty's rule in England.

The Dutch Experiment

The Dutch blazed the trail to modernity in Europe in the first half of the seventeenth century, a period described as a time of an "Embarrassment of Riches."[3] They staged the first modern national liberation struggle; conducted the first modern guerrilla war; set up the first modern republic; established the first modern banks, insurance companies, and stock markets; created the first modern capitalist agriculture; and were among the first to practice the recycling of resources. After a long and tenacious struggle against the Spaniards, they went on to establish a global trading network (see Chapter 16) that gave them the highest quality of life in Europe. Unfortunately, their lack of military power led to their being dominated by the English in the 1660s. But their precedent-setting contributions established the foundations of modern political and economic life in the West.

The internal Dutch power balance shifted during the early seventeenth century. Republicans, representing the great urban merchants, supported religious toleration, limited central authority, and peace. The monarchists, representing a majority of the urban lower classes and the nobles, especially the House of Orange, wanted a Calvinist state church, strong stadtholders (provincial governors), a large army, and an aggressive foreign policy against the Habsburgs. Until 1619 the republicans held power, but their leader, John Oldenbarnveldt (OL-den-barn-feldt; 1547–1619), was ultimately overthrown and executed after a royalist uprising. Between 1619 and the Peace of Westphalia, the country was ruled by domineering stadtholders, who conducted the war against Spain and acquired a status approaching that of European kings.

In the mid-seventeenth century the Dutch enjoyed prosperity and power far beyond their limited population base and territory. During the interval between the decline of Spain and the rise to dominance of modern France and England, the Dutch enjoyed naval, commercial, and colonial supremacy. This predominance, of course, could only be temporary. The Netherlands had not enough people nor defensible boundaries to afford long-term competition with France in Europe or with England overseas. But even as a secondary power, which it was destined to become after 1650, it remained economically progressive, culturally advanced, and a pioneer in developing constitutional government. Because of its liberal system, it became the refuge for many of Europe's finest scientists and philosophers.

Jan Steen, who graphically portrayed daily life in Holland, gave a vivid presentation of The Fish Market at Leiden *(1625–1626) in the seventeenth century. Note the variety of dress and activities Steen portrays.*

The English Debate

Between the death of Queen Elizabeth in 1603 and the Glorious Revolution in 1688, the English carried on a fundamental debate about the nature of government. At its base were the questions of the control of property, the role of law, the nature of the state, and the notion of sovereignty. The Stuart dynasty and its allies upheld the centrality of the monarch as the fundamental principle of government. Arrayed against them were individuals who saw the nation's will as expressed through Parliament as the primary principle of government. The Stuarts saw their legitimacy in birth and "the natural order of things," whereas the parliamentary forces referred to four centuries of legal traditions and practices.

Crown vs. Parliament

James, a cousin of Elizabeth and the son of Mary Stuart, had learned his lessons well in 36 years as king of Scotland. He was rational and learned and a fervent believer in monarchical divine right. He also hated parliaments and Presbyterians but recognized the need for taking what "can be" over what "should be" in political affairs. During his English reign (1603–1625), James maintained a shaky stability while tentatively pursuing unpopular policies that led to his being not very successful with Parliament. The problems here were mostly financial, involving rejection of his revenue proposals. Outside the political arena in the first part of the seventeenth century, the religious climate became more radical. English Protestants suspected first James and then his successor, Charles, of being pro-Catholics.

DOCUMENT
On the Divine Right of Kings

James's political skills were not to be found in his successor, Charles. After enduring many stormy debates with Parliament, he accepted the Petition of Right in 1628. This document affirmed ancient English rights by securing parliamentary approval of taxes, abolishing arbitrary imprisonment, ending the quartering of soldiers with citizens, and prohibiting martial law in peacetime. But Charles's cooperative attitude was only temporary. From 1629 to 1640 he ruled without Parliament, alienating much of English society, particularly the Puritan church reformers and the gentry. The king's personal rule cut him off from an understanding of what the parliamentary forces really wanted and deepened the suspicions of Charles's opponents. When his archbishop tried to force the Anglican prayer book on the Scottish kirk ("church"), the Scots rebelled and invaded England in 1640. Charles was forced to conclude a humiliating peace by paying the invaders to withdraw.

After agreeing to buy off the Scots, Charles called Parliament to raise the money and secure his future finances. When it insisted on debating other issues, this "Short Parliament" was dismissed after it sat for little more than three weeks. The government then resorted to forceful measures: It imprisoned dissidents, imposed more illegal taxes, forced loans from merchants, and impressed men for the army, measures that made the situation only worse. Desperate for funds and facing mounting public hostility, the king called what would become known as the "Long Parliament," because it sat through 20 years of constitutional debate and civil war. Finally, in January 1642, he left the capital for York, and Parliament took the unprecedented action of declaring, without royal approval, its legal authority over national military forces.

The ensuing civil war would last another seven years; the government would alternate between a republic and a monarchy, but the prospects for English absolutism were doomed forever. The parliamentary forces made alliance with the Scots, organized their forces into a national army, and enlisted popular support by appeals to radical Protestantism. In 1646, after defeating the royalists decisively at Marston Moor (1644) and Naseby (1645), they accepted Charles from the Scots, who had taken him prisoner. After four long years, the war now seemed to be over. Almost immediately, however, new conflicts arose between Parliament and its army. Conservative Presbyterians in Parliament, fearful of radical Protestantism in the ranks, were anxious to demobilize the army. Most officers, including the leading commanders Oliver Cromwell (1599–1658) and Lord Fairfax (1612–1671), supported the men and their demands for back pay.

Some rebels in the army advocated truly democratic reforms. Their most striking proposals originated with a civilian group known as **"Levellers"** because they advocated reforms to favor the common people. They were led by the former army officer "honest John Lilburne" (1614–1657). As it turned out, the radical dream was only a side issue in maneuvers for power among the Presbyterian Parliament, the conservative army officers, and the radical soldiers. When Charles escaped in November and began negotiations with the Scots, the officers suppressed the mutineers, shooting some of the Leveller leaders and imprisoning others. Although Charles managed to renew the war, he lost his last battle at Preston in August 1648. Again, the officers professed to consider the radical program while they tried unsuccessfully to extract a promise from Charles to free protestant churches from state control. Finally resorting to force, they again outlawed the Levellers while purging Parliament of 143 Presbyterian opponents. The remaining "Rump Parliament," under the dominance of Oliver Cromwell, then abolished the House of Lords, executed the king after a perfunctory trial, and declared England a republic.

For the next 11 years, Cromwell's military regime was able to perpetuate itself in different forms. At first, the Rump and a Council of State, dominated by Cromwell, governed the country while crushing all resistance in Scotland and Ireland. In 1653 more contention between Rump politicians and the council resulted in dissolution of the token Parliament and creation of a thinly veiled dictatorship. A new constitution, the Instrument of Government, written by Cromwell's henchmen, assigned him extensive powers as Lord Protector. Two years later, Cromwell finally dismissed the Instrument's impotent Parliament and instead ruled through military governors. His regimes during the **interregnum** were able to

DOCUMENT
Cromwell Abolishes the English Monarchy

England: From Stuart Ambition to Parliamentary Power

1603	James VI of Scotland becomes James I of England
1625	Charles I becomes king of England
1628	Petition of Right
1629	Charles I dissolves Parliament
1640	Short Parliament; Long Parliament convenes
1642–1648	Civil war
1649	Charles I executed
1649–1660	Various attempts at a Puritan Commonwealth
1660	Charles II restored to the English throne
1670	Secret Treaty of Dover between France and England
1685	James II becomes king of England
1688	Glorious Revolution
1689	William II and Mary II come to the throne of England
1702–1714	Queen Anne, the last of the Stuarts
1714	George I of Hanover becomes king of England

levellers—A group during the English civil war that advocated total economic, social, political, and religious equality.

interregnum—The period of time between kings.

The English Civil War led to the beheading of a monarch, seen by the parliamentary forces as guilty of exercising extra-constitutional powers. Ironically, Oliver Cromwell—shown here dissolving the Long Parliament—in his role as Lord Protector generated heated opposition to his rule from people who believed him also to be overreaching his authority.

increase trade and raise respect for England abroad, but they were never popular, a fact attested to by the continued life of the radical movements, which enlisted popular support and required government countermeasures until after the mid-1650s. Despite ultimate radical failures, the period of the civil war and the interregnum, which ended two years after Cromwell's death in 1658, brought significant changes to England.

Restoration and "Glorious" Revolution

The period from 1660 to 1688 would be marked by increasingly severe struggles between the Stuarts and Parliament. Initially, almost everyone welcomed the new ruler, Charles II (1660–1685), called back from exile in France and restored to the throne, with his lavish court and his mistresses. But Charles, the cleverest politician of the Stuart line, exploited this common desire for normality to avoid the terms of his restoration, which bound him to rule in cooperation with Parliament. Charles cleverly manipulated the English political system to get what he wanted in the first, comparatively relaxed, years of the Restoration. However, political opposition against him began to harden, precipitating a crisis by 1681. In the last part of his reign, he dismissed four Parliaments and governed without the legislative branch, taking advantage of the strong desire among the propertied classes to avoid another civil war. The Whig opposition, however, which represented the desires of the lesser landowners and their business allies in the cities, had forced a resignation from Charles II's first minister, imprisoned the second, excluded the king's Catholic supporters from public office, and provided individuals with legal security against arbitrary arrest and imprisonment.

Charles's brother James II (1685–1688) proved to be an even more determined absolutist. Like Charles, he was an admirer of Louis XIV. While Charles concealed his Catholic sympathies, his brother was openly Catholic. When James' wife gave birth to a prince who was widely regarded as a potential Catholic king, parliamentary leaders and Protestant aristocrats met and offered the crown to the former heir Mary Stuart, the Protestant daughter of James by an earlier marriage. Mary accepted the offer with the provision that her husband, William of Orange, be co-ruler. William landed at Dover with an efficient Dutch army and forced James to flee into exile. This "Glorious Revolution" ultimately pushed England far in the direction of limited monarchy.

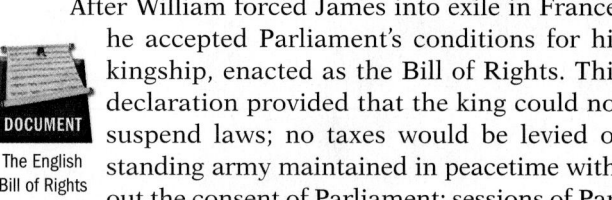

DOCUMENT
The English Bill of Rights

After William forced James into exile in France, he accepted Parliament's conditions for his kingship, enacted as the Bill of Rights. This declaration provided that the king could not suspend laws; no taxes would be levied or standing army maintained in peacetime without the consent of Parliament; sessions of Parliament would be held frequently; freedom of speech in Parliament would be assured; subjects would have the right of petition and be free of excessive fines, bail, or cruel punishments; the king would be a protestant.

Other parliamentary acts supplemented the Bill of Rights and consolidated the Revolution. In 1689 the Mutiny Act required parliamentary approval for extending martial law more than one year. In 1693, when Parliament failed to renew the customary Licensing Act, the country achieved practical freedom of the press. Finally, in the Act of Settlement in 1701, Parliament prescribed a protestant succession to the throne and barred the monarch from declaring war, removing judges, or even leaving the country without parliamentary consent. The Glorious Revolution permanently limited the English monarchy, guaranteed important legal rights, and helped popularize the ideal, if not the practice, of popular sovereignty.

Whigs and Tories

After 1688, the landed gentry—functionally a lower aristocracy of landed capitalists with a variety of economic interests—gained almost complete control of the House of Commons. From their base in the Whig alliance, they shaped state policy through a prime minister and a cabinet system that became responsible to Parliament, not the king. The gentry made government a closed system, putting members of their class into most of the public offices, lucrative positions in the Anglican Church, and commissioned ranks in the army and navy. These privileges were shared only with the few remaining nobles (220 in 1790) who sat in the House of Lords.

After the reign of William and Mary, English leaders looked to the German principality of Hanover for the next monarchs. The first two Hanoverian kings, George I (r. 1714–1727) and George II (r. 1727–1760), relied on their chief advisors (prime ministers) to work with Parliament. Sir Robert Walpole (1676–1745) first held this post, managing a Whig political machine. Walpole insisted that the entire ministry (cabinet) should act as a body; single members who could not agree were expected to resign. Later he learned the practicality of resigning with his whole cabinet when they could not command a parliamentary majority. This pragmatically developed system of cabinet government and ministerial responsibility provided the constitutional machinery needed to apply the principles of the Glorious Revolution while permitting Parliament to avoid awkward conflicts with royal authority.

English politics, so dynamic in the mid-1600s, became stagnant by the end of George II's reign in 1760. The next Hanoverian king, George III (r. 1760–1820), imposed his personality and policies more directly on British politics than did his predecessors. First, he alienated many commercial and colonial interests by opposing an aggressive policy toward France. Then, he began implementing powers never claimed by his Hanoverian predecessors, who had been virtual captives of Whig politicians. In only a few years, using lavish bribes and patronage (methods developed earlier by Walpole), George's ministers eroded Whig influence and gained control of Parliament. By 1770 they had filled the House of Commons with their supporters, known as "the King's Friends" (Tories). During George's first 12 years as the head of government, his policies made domestic enemies and produced a determined opposition party. This trouble at home was less serious, in the long run, than that provoked in the American colonies. George Grenville (1712–1770), the king's chief minister after 1763, devised a comprehensive plan to settle problems in North America left after the Seven Years' War, which sparked the movement leading to the American Revolution.

BREAKING THE BANK: DIPLOMACY AND WAR IN THE AGE OF ABSOLUTISM: 1650–1774

- *In the century and a half after 1650 there were outbursts of European war every 20 years or so. Why were the various states so ready to fight, and not negotiate?*

Because of dynastic and colonial rivalries, Europeans were constantly involved in conflicts during the age of absolutism. Fighting took place overseas in America, Africa, and Asia—not only against non-Europeans but also in global wars among European colonial powers. At the same time, wars raged on the Continent as dynastic states competed for predominance. While Spain, Sweden, and Poland were declining, Prussia, Russia, and Austria were becoming first-class powers.

Along with England and its dominance overseas, the last three exerted major influences on the European balance of power.

From Westphalia to Utrecht: The Dominance of France

France was the strongest and most threatening military power in Europe from the Peace of Westphalia (1648) to the Treaty of Utrecht (1713). Louis XIV first dreamed of expanding French frontiers to the Rhine; later, he coveted the Spanish crown. Colbert also helped him plan the conquest of a large overseas empire in America, Africa, and Asia. The diplomacy of other European states in the era centered largely on their common efforts to unite against French expansion.

Russian policy was one important exception to this general trend. In early wars with the Turks, Peter the Great took Azov, on the Black Sea. His main target in the later Great Northern War (1709–1721) was Sweden, but his preparatory diplomacy failed when his allies, Denmark and Poland, were quickly defeated by the Swedish warrior-king Charles XII (r. 1697–1712). The Swedes next invaded Russia. They were met with a "scorched earth" withdrawal before being annihilated at Poltava (1709). The war ended in 1721 with Sweden exhausted and Peter gaining a section of the Baltic coast, where he had already begun building his new capital at St. Petersburg.

The three Anglo-Dutch naval wars between 1652 and 1674 showed the balance-of-power principle in one of its more intricate applications. Conflicting commercial and colonial interests of the two maritime states were the immediate issues. At the same time, both belligerents were increasingly aware of danger from a powerful and aggressive France. The Dutch were most directly affected because French expansion toward the northern Rhine threatened the survival of the Netherlands as a nation. To deal with this problem, the Dutch tacitly accepted English maritime supremacy while preparing for an Anglo-Dutch alignment against Louis XIV. Ultimately, the French menace was more decisive than naval action in ending Anglo-Dutch hostilities.

After 1670 Louis was the prime mover in European diplomacy. He fought four major wars, each with overseas campaigns. In the first, Louis claimed the Spanish Netherlands (Belgium). Thwarted by the Dutch and their allies, he next bought off Charles II of England in the Treaty of Dover and attacked the Dutch directly. Frustrated again by a combination of enemies, he tried in the 1690s to annex certain Rhineland districts. This time, almost all of Europe allied against him and forced him to back down. The climax to these repeated French efforts came between 1701 and 1713, in the War of the Spanish Succession, when Louis sought to secure the Spanish throne for his grandson Philip. Although he finally succeeded in this project, the victory was a hollow one.

In this most destructive of Louis's wars, women played a major part behind the scenes. In England during the early years, Sarah Churchill, wife of the English supreme commander, the duke of Marlborough, consistently pressured Queen Anne (r. 1702–1714) and members of Parliament for vigorous prosecution of the war. On the other side, at the Spanish court and elsewhere on the continent, Mary of Modena, in exile with her husband, the deposed James II of England, exerted all of her influence to bolster support for France. Other women were most instrumental in bringing peace. Among them were Madame de Maintenon (men-te-NON) and Princesse des Ursins, who helped persuade Louis to drop the idea of uniting the French and Spanish Bourbon monarchies. In England after about 1709, Anne, a patient and plodding monarch, but one with at least some common sense, freed herself from Sarah Churchill's influence and guided her ministers toward the Peace of Utrecht.

Louis could not overcome all of the power balanced against him. As France became stronger, it invariably provoked more formidable counteralliances. At first, Louis faced Spain, the Netherlands, Sweden, and some German states. In the last two wars, England led an alliance that included almost all of western Europe. In this anti-French alignment, Anglo-Dutch commercial rivalry and other traditional prejudices, such as Anglo-Dutch hatred of Spain, were subordinated to the balance-of-power principle.

The Treaty of Utrecht (1713) ushered in a period of general peace, lasting some 30 years. Philip V, Louis's grandson, was confirmed as king of Spain, with the provision that the thrones of France and Spain would never be united. Since Spain had been declining for a century and France was drained financially, the Bourbon succession promised little for French ambitions in Europe. In fact, Spain had surrendered the southern Netherlands (Belgium) and its Italian holdings (Naples, Milan, and Sardinia) to the Austrian Habsburgs. In addition, Savoy was ceded to Sicily, which was subsequently traded (in 1720) to Austria for Sardinia. The duke of Savoy was also recognized as king, as was Frederick I of Prussia. The House of Savoy would unify Italy in the nineteenth century, and the Hohenzollerns would accomplish the same for Germany.

By the Treaty of Utrecht, almost all the participants except Britain lost more in the wars than they gained. The Dutch had borne the cost of most land fighting against the French; France had been demoralized by a three-front war and a Huguenot uprising, for which it received no tangible compensation except the retention of Alsace; and Spain lost heavily to the Austrian Habsburgs. Britain, by contrast, received the North American properties of Newfoundland and Nova Scotia from France in addition to French acceptance of British claims to the Hudson Bay area. Britain also retained the Mediterranean naval bases at Gibraltar and Minorca it had taken from Spain. Even more important commercially were the concessions permitting Britain to supply Spanish America with slaves and to land one shipload of goods each year at Porto Bello in Panama. These stipulations helped Britain become the leading colonial power in Europe.

From Utrecht to Paris: An Unstable Balance

The balance of European power wavered dangerously in the eighteenth century. Prussia and Russia—and even Habsburg Austria—attained great military potential, and each was tempted by power vacuums in Poland and the Ottoman Empire. The situation was complicated by the difficulty in determining which of the Eastern states was the most serious threat and therefore the logical object of counteralliances. To confuse matters further, both Britain and France were absorbed in their growing colonial rivalry, in which Britain was the obvious frontrunner. Major conflicts were on the way.

By 1730, it was apparent that France and Britain would soon clash over their conflicting colonial ambitions. Both empires were rapidly increasing their wealth and populations. In the Caribbean, French sugar production had surpassed that of the British, while French slavers were not only supplying their own islands but also challenging British trading privileges in Spanish America, as defined at Utrecht. On the other side of the world, the British and French were also scrambling to obtain influence among the petty rulers of southern India. The two powers, each with Native American allies, were fighting sporadic little wars in North America. In the preliminary diplomatic testing, French size and military force in Europe were balanced against British financial resources, naval power, and a larger American colonial population.

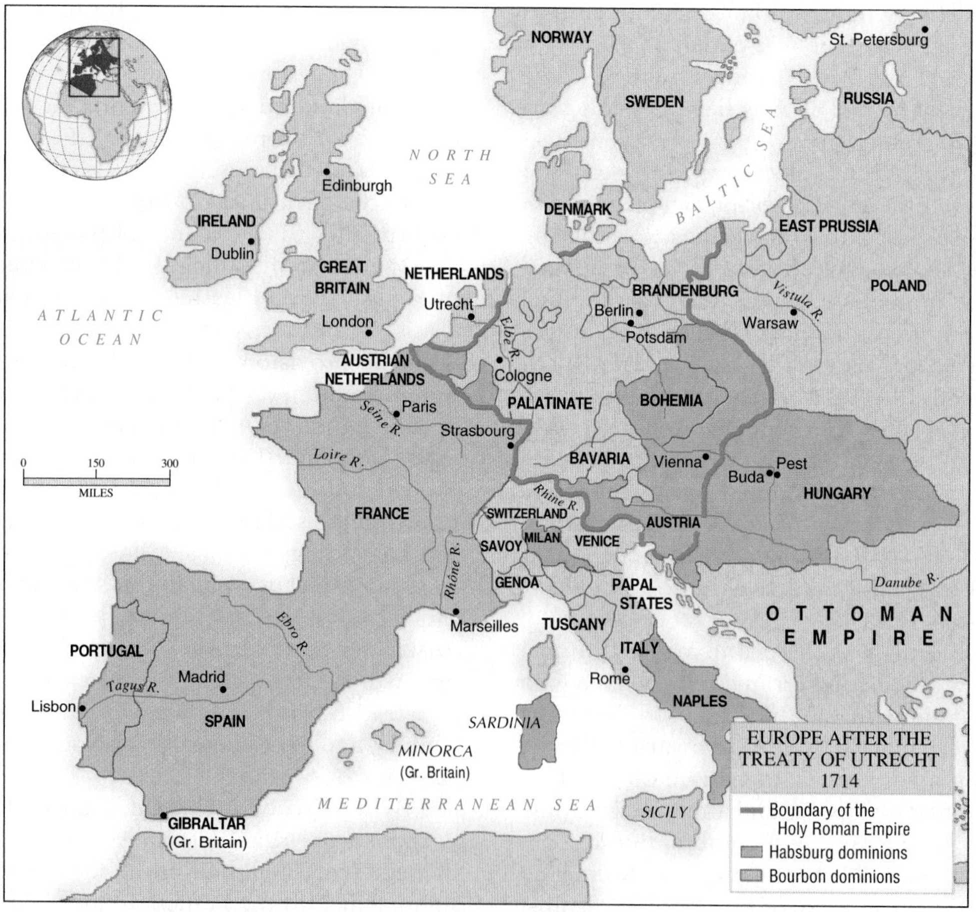

The Treaty of Utrecht confirmed the expansion of French power in Europe after the half century of wars of Louis XIV, the increased strength of Brandenburg Prussia, and the decline of the Habsburg Empire.

Discovery Through Maps

The Elegant Destruction of Poland

After the century and a half of continent-wide upheaval caused by the Reformation, Counter-Reformation, wars of religion, and Thirty Years' War, Europeans sought to impose stability through international law and absolutism. Concepts like "balance of power," *"raison d'état,"* and reason replaced the passions of the religious wars of the sixteenth and the first half of the seventeenth centuries.

This did not mean that peace came to Europe—far from it. War came to be more organized, professional, and limited as state competition took on not only a military but also an economic dimension. In the new arena of 1648 politics, state relations were conducted with almost mathematical precision. States took stock of their strength in terms of population, economic strength, and military power. They ranked themselves and their neighbors and then attacked when it seemed possible, in search of national interest, not religious truth. The wars of Louis XIV sought to gain France its "natural boundaries" of the Pyrenees and the Rhine. The Prussians sought to unify their diverse holdings in north-central Europe. Peter the Great led Russia into war against its neighbors in search of a "Window on the West."

In the last third of the eighteenth century Poland paid the price for its inability to adapt to the modern world. Since the fourteenth century the Polish nobility had tenaciously fought the attempts by their kings to assemble a strong army, preferring often to lose the first battle against invaders while waiting for the nobles to come to the country's defense. Poland after the seventeenth century fell under the influence of the Russians and the Prussians, and not until the 1770s did the Poles try to reform their institutions. It was too late. National interests led Prussia, Russia, and Austria to partition the country in 1772. After the French Revolution broke out, the Russians and Prussians partitioned the country again in 1793 and then, after a doomed national resistance, removed Poland as a state from the map of Europe. The Polish nation remained divided among the three partitioning powers until 1918.

This engraving by Le Mire is a rather caustic commentary on what was, after all, the murder of a nation-state. Here we have the monarchs of Russia, Prussia, and Austria regally carving up Poland while the Polish king, Stanislaus Poniatowski, grabs his crown to keep from losing that too. Le Mire captures the "civilized" nature of post-1648 state relations, in which *raison d'état* imposed no moral or ethical limits.

Questions to Consider

1. What had Poland done to deserve being carved up by these monarchs?
2. Do you think the artist is celebrating the occasion he portrays, or is he being sarcastic?
3. What role does the angel play in this scene? What were the religious faiths of the Prussians, Russians, and Austrians?

Conflict began in 1739 over British trade in Spanish America. An English captain testified before Parliament that Spanish authorities had boarded his vessel and cut off his ear, which he displayed wrapped in cotton. The "War of Jenkins's Ear" soon spread, with France immediately offering support to Spain. Frederick of Prussia, meanwhile, seized Silesia, part of the family holdings of the Habsburg heiress Maria Theresa, who had just succeeded to the Austrian throne. France and Spain now aligned with Frederick, along with the German states of Saxony and Bavaria. Fearful of France, Britain and the Netherlands, now allied with Hanover, joined Austria in 1742. By 1745, Prussia had almost knocked Austria out of the war, but fighting dragged on overseas in North America and India until 1748. The resulting Peace of Aix-la-Chapelle (ex la sha-PELLE) left Frederick with Silesia and the colonial positions of Britain and France about the same as they had been in 1739.

The agreements at Aix-la-Chapelle brought no peace but only a short truce of eight years. During the cessation of hostilities, France and Britain prepared to renew their global conflict. At the same time, Maria Theresa, having learned some lessons in international politics and having effected some necessary internal reforms, joined with Tsarina Elizabeth of Russia to negotiate an alliance against Frederick. The Austro-Russian alliance also included Sweden and some German states. Maria Theresa's greatest coup, however, was recruiting France, the old Habsburg enemy, possibly with help from Madame de Pompadour, Louis XV's mistress, who despised Frederick. Prussia was now effectively isolated, but so was Britain, which was more concerned about colonial issues than aggression on the Continent. Britain, therefore, formed a new alliance with Prussia against France, Russia, and Austria. This swapping of alliances, the famous diplomatic revolution of the 1750s, was another notable attempt at balance-of-power politics in both the European and world theaters.

Beginning in 1756, war raged relentlessly on three continents—Europe, North America, and Asia (India). Known in American history as the French and Indian War, the conflict in Europe is called the Seven Years' War. Attacked on all sides by three major powers, Frederick marched and wheeled his limited forces, winning battles but seeing little prospect for ultimate victory. He tried without success to buy Madame de Pompadour's influence for peace. Later he described his nearly hopeless predicament, comparing himself to a man assaulted by flies: "When one flies off my cheek, another comes and sits on my nose, and scarcely has it been brushed off then another flies up and sits on my forehead, on my eyes, and everywhere else."[4]

Frederick was saved and the war won by the narrowest of margins when a new pro-Prussian tsar, Peter III, recalled the Russian armies from the gates of Berlin and withdrew from the war. Austria then sued for peace, leaving Frederick with Silesia.

The end of the Seven Years' War in 1763 confirmed the status of Prussia and Russia as great powers and prepared for a new diplomatic order in eastern Europe. Despite its great losses, Prussia gained enormously in prestige—its internal damage would not be revealed until the nineteenth century— and Russia regained the military reputation it had achieved under Peter I without winning any striking victories. Austria lost prestige and military strength but managed to retain its respectability. The Ottoman Empire and Poland were the real losers in the postwar decades. In 1772 Poland lost half its territory to the Russians, Prussians, and Austrians in a three-way partition, despite Maria Theresa's protestations of remorse. In 1793 and 1795, Poland was eliminated entirely in two final partitions. The Ottoman Empire, meanwhile, lost the Crimea and most of the Ukraine to the aggressive expansionist policies of Catherine the Great of Russia.

Much more significant than the war's effects on eastern Europe was its impact on Anglo-French colonial rivalry. Britain gained even more than it had at Utrecht, while French colonial hopes were all but destroyed. By the Peace of Paris (1763), France lost to Britain the St. Lawrence valley and the trans-Appalachian area east of the Mississippi. Spain also ceded Florida to Britain, receiving Louisiana west of the Mississippi from France as compensation. In the West Indies, France gave up Granada, Dominica, and St. Lucia. The French kept their main trading stations in India but were not permitted to fortify them or continue their political ties with local rulers. Meanwhile, the British East India Company not only extended its political influence but also acquired Bengal. The Peace of Paris made Britain's the largest, wealthiest, and most powerful empire in the world. At the end of the last round of warfare, however, all of Europe's governments were economically exhausted. The balance-of-power warfare between kings was soon to be challenged by a new kind of ideological war in the French Revolution, a war between peoples believing in opposing ideas.

ECONOMIC CHALLENGES

- *Why were the European states—both absolutist and limited-power—unable to respond successfully to the challenges and opportunities provided by capitalism?*

Floating atop the dynamic changes of Europe, the governments, especially on the Continent, continued in the first half of the eighteenth century to act in a "business as usual" manner. Regimes did not adapt to changing conditions, and the result was increasing political weakness and misuse of power. By midcentury, the aristocratic social structure acquired the sanctity of tradition, the confidence of long experience, and the insensitivities of old age. Although no longer as typically cruel or exploitative as in the past, its governing classes had become extremely selfish and unresponsive to the larger needs of the countries that supported them in such a rich manner and incapable of understanding the potential opportunities presented by the changes of the century.

The Failure of State Controlled Economies

Eighteenth-century monarchs faced many problems in competing with traditional local authorities, but they encountered even more pressing difficulties in enforcing mercantilist regulations. In the sixteenth century, merchant-bankers had accepted the system because they shared common interests with kings in combating the Catholic Church and the feudal nobilities. As time passed, however, monarchical states became increasingly more paternalistic and ordered, while capitalism developed spontaneously toward more freedom from state control.

Bureaucrats and Smugglers

The development, as well as the success, of mercantilism varied widely from East to West. In Prussia and Russia reforms were imposed through state control and worked well, compared with previous attempts; state-imported craftsmen and tools from western Europe continued to improve the economies of both monarchies. Habsburg efforts met with less success because the empire was unable to impose regulations effectively on the aristocracy. Meanwhile, most continental states in western Europe could not easily keep their controlled manufactures competitive in the world market.

In France, government regulations favored luxury goods over bulk commodities, which limited French participation in world trade. Reliance on urban guilds created another limitation. These medieval monopolies were given the responsibility for enforcing thousands of minute regulations in every aspect of industry. Government inspectors then sought to monitor the regulatory actions of the guilds. The system, which suffered from vested interests, local politics, corruption, and bureaucratic confusion, provoked periodic confrontations, particularly when it was extended into the countryside. In 1770 the guilds and the French government attempted to stop the domestic production of printed cotton cloth (calicoes). More than 16,000 people died in the resulting violent conflicts and subsequent executions. On one day in Valence, 631 offenders were sentenced to the galleys, 58 were put to torture on the wheel, and 77 were hanged. Yet despite all such efforts, printed calicoes continued to be made and sold illegally.

Difficulties in industry were mild compared with those in foreign trade and public finance. France and England attempted the careful control of external commerce, but the increased volume and consequent promise of rich profits from such enterprise encouraged widespread smuggling. No government of a coastal state was sufficiently wealthy to police a long and irregular coastline. Moreover, the coast guards, port authorities, and customs officials charged with enforcing trade restrictions were usually so corrupt that they were ineffective. Thus, despite feeble efforts to stop it, illegal trade flowed with growing pressure through rotten and fragile mercantilist sieves, violating increasingly complicated commercial laws. To meet this problem, governments resorted to private contractors, often granting immunity from the laws as payment for enforcing the regulations. The resulting monopolies assumed and usually abused government authority.

British controls were probably more successful than the French or the Spanish, but they were extremely costly in the long run. A great body of officials—more than 1250 in London alone—cost the government more than the amounts they were supposed to save in revenues. In the second half of the eighteenth century, the government imposed stricter controls over the trade of the American colonies. As a result, smugglers took over much of the English coastline, and the colonies were pushed toward armed rebellion.

Smuggling was big business in the colonies, where it exceeded legal trade in the 1700s. West Indian planters of all nationalities conducted illicit commerce with English colonial merchants. New England timber and manufactures were regularly exchanged for French molasses, which was then made into rum and smuggled into Europe. Half the trade of Boston in 1750 violated British laws; Rhode Island and Pennsylvania merchants grew rich supplying the French during the Seven Years' War; and 80 percent of all tea used in the English colonies before 1770 came in free of duties. In addition, large quantities of tobacco were landed illegally in England with the connivance of Virginia and Carolina planters.

Smuggling was just as common in Europe, where every seacoast swarmed with illegal traders. Families grew wealthy in the business, and fathers trained their sons to maintain their enterprises. Contraband runners and government agents engaged in a continual civil war, using intelligence operations, pitched battles, and prepared sieges. Systematic enforcement was almost impossible because officials were bribed or personally involved, witnesses refused to testify, and juries often acquitted offenders caught in the act. During their classic era after the Seven Years' War, English smugglers operated openly in almost all English west coastal ports, including Bristol and Liverpool. On the other side of the country, desperate smuggling cliques roamed Kent, Sussex, and East Anglia. One of these, the notorious Hawkhurst gang of 500 armed men, forced farmers to store smuggled goods. The booty was then moved under armed convoys from depot to depot and on to waiting London merchants. When the government attempted to stop this traffic, a near civil war resulted, but smuggling was not appreciably curtailed.

The Crisis in Public Finance

Public finance was a serious problem even for Britain, the most commercially advanced state in Europe. In 1700, after war with France, the state debt reached 13 million pounds sterling and was secured by the Bank of England. The public debt continued to rise, despite the government's efforts in the 1720s to eliminate it with profits from its overseas trading monopoly, the South Sea Company. Unfortunately, following a wild speculation in South Sea stock, the venture failed. Succeeding colonial wars with France drove the debt still higher. By 1782 it had risen to 232 million pounds. Britain was very wealthy and, therefore, could easily carry this tremendous burden, but the debt nevertheless contributed to internal political unrest.

The most obvious weaknesses involved the abuse of state powers or the inability to use them for the public good. Early absolute monarchs had promised to correct abuses in state churches. Such establishments now held great wealth but continued to persecute thousands of dissenting subjects for their religious beliefs. Some kings had vowed to bring their states economic prosperity and security. Under mercantilism, their state enterprises and monopolies favored wealthy patrons and throttled trade. Even state military systems were controlled by aristocratic officers, many of whom bought their commissions and commanded local private armies. Even royal provincial agents and judges often existed beside and shared authority with thousands of lingering manorial courts and local officials, operating under the authority of local feudal lords.

The causes of the financial crisis could also be found in the political inefficiency took many other forms. Laws were a perplexing mix of variable local customs, feudal presumptions, and royal decrees. Provincial tolls were imposed on trade within states; on the Rhine River alone there were 38 toll stations between Basel and Rotterdam. Coinage, as well as weights and measures, sometimes differed in adjoining provinces. Overlapping authorities confused courts and officials about their jurisdictions. Public servants avoided responsibilities, fearing they would be blamed for error, a situation that produced bureaucratic delay and elaborate red tape. Every form of bribery, fraud, and distortion characterized governments at every level. Such evils were difficult to combat because legalized privilege was so common.

LOUIS XV AND THE DECLINE OF EUROPEAN ABSOLUTISM: 1715–1774

■ *Why did French absolutism become an ineffective and corrupt form of government?*

The absolutists and their supporters in France—perhaps 2 percent of the population—made an inadequate response to the economic and social pressures of the time. After his death in 1715, Louis XIV was succeeded by his 5-year-old great-grandson. Known as "the Well-Beloved," the new king reigned as Louis XV until 1774 but never ruled as a Sun King, partly because of his personal weaknesses, but largely because the inflexible institutions of absolutism could not contain or direct the dynamic changes of the eighteenth-century world. In middle age, with most of his royal prerogatives still intact, Louis was openly pessimistic about the future of his dynasty. He might easily have delivered the famous prophecy, stated by his mistress Madame de Pompadour (1721–1764), but usually attributed to him: *"Après moi, le déluge"* (a-pre mwa le DAY-loozh; "After me, the Flood"). France, the model of absolutist government for Europe, faced a severe crisis, as did the other governments that imitated the French example.

Such royal cynicism reflected the old regime's knowledge that it could do little to control the revolutionary developments of the time. Two centuries of war and foreign expansion had changed the basic way of life for most people and generated high expectations, particularly among the expanding urban middle classes—around 8 percent of the population—who benefited most by the worldwide explosion of foreign trade. Encouraged by the philosophies of the Enlightenment (see Chapter 18), they became more aggressive in improving their position, gaining social recognition, and demanding personal happiness outside the limits imposed by typical monarchical states and their privileged social orders.

Old Regime Monarchs

France

1715–1774	Louis XV
1774–1792	Louis XVI

Habsburgs

1711–1740	Charles VI
1740–1780	Maria Theresa
1780–1790	Joseph II

Prussia

1713–1740	Frederick William I
1740–1786	Frederick the Great
1786–1797	Frederick William II

Russia

1730–1740	Anna
1741–1762	Elizabeth
1762	Peter III
1762–1796	Catherine II

Great Britain

1714–1727	George I
1727–1760	George II
1760–1820	George III

Facing such challenges, those states could not respond effectively. They had earlier promised pragmatic compromise, whereby centralized government would maintain the interests of wealthy merchant-bankers and landed aristocrats. By the mid-eighteenth century, the system could no longer satisfy its supporters, nor could it absorb any more of the lesser nobles or the excluded middle class as each group grew more numerous. Indeed, with their expensive wars, ballooning debts, outmoded laws, passive bureaucrats, and corrupt officials, the absolute monarchies generally displayed striking political weaknesses and obvious misuses of the powers they managed to wield.

Despite all efforts at centralization, Louis XIV left a chaotic system of councils and committees, each with its own expanding network of officials and clerks, whose conflicting claims to authority were barely less perplexing than their complicated procedures. During the next reign the selling of offices became a main source of revenue and patronage. There was no body comparable to the English Parliament for registering public opinion; the French Estates-General was last called in 1614. Government was most deficient in handling revenues, which it attempted to do without budgets, precise accounting, or standard assessments. French local government was even more chaotic. Late medieval districts, with their bailiffs and seneschals, coexisted with largely ceremonial provincial governors and royal intendants who struggled to placate other officials and influence local government after the seventeenth century. Some 360 different legal codes and 200 customs schedules applied in different parts of the country. Attempts to achieve uniformity invariably provoked strong reactions from local interests.

The French government, like some others, was severely damaged by the laziness of King Louis XV, who hated the tedium of governing and was more interested in beautiful women. Well into the 1740s, he left most power in the hands of an able minister, Cardinal Fleury (fleu-REE), who had maintained peace and reasonable stability since Louis was a boy. Even in his early reign, however, "mistress power" enlisted the king's fancy; later it influenced his policies. Louis's Polish queen endured a series of rivals who were installed in the palace near the king's bedchamber, granted titles, showered with costly gifts, and paraded by Louis in public. The best known of them was Jeanne-Antoinette Poisson (PWA-sohn), of nonnoble parentage, who became Madame de Pompadour. She received 17 estates, had a personal staff of 50 attendants, enjoyed nearly unlimited access to the royal treasury, and advised Louis on public policy, particularly during the Seven Years' War. A later famous royal mistress, Madame Du Barry (1743–1793), was another woman of nonnoble origin who played the palace game better than the noble ladies at court, whom she overcame in a series of backbiting struggles for Louis's favor. Until he died in 1774, she reveled in her power, jewels, and luxurious houses. Such behavior earned France a reputation for "petticoat governance."

Other European kings squandered fortunes on mistresses, palaces, courts, and idle aristocrats, thus contributing to their common problem of rising public debt. Their financial difficulties also arose from their military expenses in attempting to protect colonial possessions and play the game of dynastic power politics in Europe. In the late 1700s, each of the great continental powers (France, Russia, and Austria) kept standing armies of 250,000 men. Rulers might have borne such heavy expenses if they could have governed by brute force, as former emperors had done, but they were prevented from doing so by their dependence on an international market, which supplied their vital material needs only in exchange for goods, bullion, or credit. Ultimately, they were forced to borrow, putting their states at the mercy of bankers and their own credit ratings. Such financial accountability, almost unknown in the ancient world, placed a serious restriction on monarchical policies in this era.

For France, where the economy was less expansive and commanded less foreign credit, the problem was more serious. Badly weakened by Louis XIV's wars, France averted financial disaster in the 1720s and 1730s only because of Fleury's peaceful foreign policy and reduced military spending. After 1742, however, deficits mounted steadily while France fought three major wars. In 1780, the French debt was so large that interest payments absorbed over half the annual income of approximately $33.8 million. Admittedly, the French debt was not excessive in comparison with Britain's. What the French lacked, however, was the Dutch capital that poured into England. Without adequate foreign credit, France was thrown back on its own resources, which caused a tripling of taxes between 1715 and 1785. The ensuing tax burden, in addition to the growing anxiety of wealthy government creditors, created the most serious threat to the Old Regime in France.

Necker Concealing the Deficit (Cartoon, 1789)

CONCLUSION

The most important occurrence of the century and a half between the Treaty of Westphalia and the outbreak of the French Revolution was the Capitalist Revolution. This revolution developed so rapidly that it could hardly be controlled or even predicted. The absolutist governments tried to ride the waves of economic growth and even control them through schemes such as mercantilism. But the economic changes came so fast that, linked with a vastly expanding population, no matter how the kings might try, they could not control the new economic pursuits that developed almost spontaneously outside of established institutions.

Even with that, the absolutist governments tried to impose central control—sanctioned by God— over the society, economy, church, culture, and military systems during this time. This system of government responded to the perceived need for stability and order after a century of religious wars. As absolutism was the system of government in France under Louis XIV—Europe's strongest power—it tended to be copied by almost all of the European states of the era. However, the structural weaknesses of a centralized control over a continent undergoing the revolutionary social and economic changes of the Capitalist Revolution became evident. The incapacity of the kings to impose their theoretical power led to massive corruption. The aristocracy could not or would not serve as transmitters of royal power, and across Europe, the nobles began a drive to reclaim the power they had lost to centralizing kings. Wars and the luxurious tastes of the monarchs drained the state treasuries and spread misery to the expanding populations. By the middle of the eighteenth century the absolutist system had come to be known as the *ancien régime*—the Old Regime—and it did not work any more.

The Dutch and the English went against the absolutist trends of the day, with differing results. The Netherlands emerged under the political, financial, military dominance of the British, while England proceeded to build a world empire. But in each case, these examples of limited government provided a different political alternative for those who had become disaffected with absolutism. When the British succeeded in ousting the Stuarts in 1688, the resulting political and theoretical doctrines established the precedent for the American Revolution a century later.

The limited central powers proved better able to ride the waves of change that swept the globe in the seventeenth and eighteenth century. Even though the political process was not marked by idealism in England, the diversity of the goals of the political elites provided a suitable framework to absorb the demographic, financial, and social changes that affected the country during the century.

Suggestions for Web Browsing

You can obtain more information about topics included in this chapter at the websites listed below. See also the companion website that accompanies this text, **http://www.ablongman.com/brummett**, which contains an online study guide and additional resources.

Internet Modern History Sourcebook: The Early Modern World
http://www.fordham.edu/halsall/mod/modsbook03.html

Online source for numerous documents about the expanding global power of the Dutch and the British.

Trade Products in Early Modern History
http://www.bell.lib.umn.edu/Products/Products.html

University of Minnesota site chronicles the development of global trade, in particular, by the Dutch and the British, as they search for a variety of products, from beaver to tulips, from coffee to tobacco.

Age of the Sun King *(L'Age d'Or)*
http://www.geocities.com/Paris/Rue/1663/index.html

Extensive site describing, with text and images, the world of France under Louis XIV.

Internet Modern History Sourcebook: The *Ancien Régime*
http://www.fordham.edu/halsall/mod/hs1000.html#ancien

Extensive online source for links about the ancien régime, *including primary documents by or about Louis XIV and Cardinal Richelieu and the enlightened despotism of Catherine the Great and Frederick II.*

Frederick the Great of Prussia
http://members.tripod.com/~Nevermore/king.html

Extensive site on the king of Prussia and his times.

The Glorious Revolution of 1688
http://www.thegloriousrevolution.com

The site includes a range of documents and images regarding the important legal and political precedents set in motion by the Glorious Revolution of 1688.

Literature and Film

Most of the novels listed here have also served as the bases of major films: Alexandre Dumas captured the drama of this period in his *The Three Musketeers* (1844), *The Man in the Iron Mask* (originally published as part of the *Vicomte de Bragelonne,* 1848–1850), and *The Count of Monte Cristo* (1844). Victor Hugo contributed *The Hunchback of Notre Dame* (1831), which takes place at the beginning of this period. Sir Walter Scott wrote *Rob Roy* (1817) and *The Pirate* (1822). A later author, Rafael Sabatini, wrote a fine swashbuckler of a book with titled *Captain Blood* (1922). Daniel Defoe captured the spirit of the English Civil War with *Memoirs of a Cavalier: Or a Military Journal of the Wars in Germany and the Wars in England from the Year 1632 to the Year 1648* (1722). He also added to the canon with *Moll Flanders* (1722). Henry Fielding's *The History of Tom Jones, a Foundling* (1749), is a rollicking view into some of the social realities in England in the eighteenth century. More recently, Nancy Mitford and Amanda Foreman have made a fine reassessment of *Madame Pompadour* and her world (New York Review of Books, 2001).

An opulent portrayal of many different aspects of eighteenth century life is Stanley Kubrick's film masterpiece *Barry Lyndon* (Hawk Films, 1975).

Suggestions for Reading

Dynamic European economic growth is strongly emphasized in Fernand Braudel, *Civilization and Capitalism, Vol. 2: The Wheels of Commerce* (Harper & Row, 1986). See also Gunnar Persson, *Pre-Industrial Economic Growth, Social Organization, and Technological Progress in Europe* (Blackwell, 1988).

For a view of the development of French absolutism to the depths of the Old Regime, see Emmanuel Le Roy Ladurie, *The Ancien Régime: A History of France, 1610–1774,* trans. Mark Greengrass (Blackwell, 1998). A general treatment of absolutism is found in John Miller, *Absolutism in Seventeenth-Century Europe* (St. Martin's Press, 1990). A revisionist views of absolutism is found in Nicholas Henshall, *The Myth of Absolutism* (Longman, 1992).

French political and social affairs are studied in Roger Mettam, *Power and Faction in Louis XIV's France* (Blackwell, 1987). Changes in the European class structure are treated in George Rude, *Europe in the Eighteenth Century: Aristocracy and the Bourgeois Challenge* (Harvard University Press, 1985) and Colin Mooers, *The Making of Bourgeois Europe* (Verso, 1991). Some obvious social threats to European monarchies are described in M. S. Anderson, *War and Society in Europe of the Old Regime, 1618–1789* (St. Martin's Press, 1988); and Frederick Krantz, *History from Below: French and English Popular Protest, 1600–1800* (Blackwell, 1988). On negative conditions affecting European women, see Marilyn Boxer and Jean H. Quatgaert, *Connecting Spheres: Women in the Western World* (Oxford University Press, 1987).

On French government and classes see Guy Chaussinand-Nogaret, *The French Nobility in the Eighteenth Century* (Cambridge University Press, 1985). On the role of eighteenth-century French women, see Joan Landes, *Women and the Public Sphere in the Age of the French Revolution* (Cornell University Press, 1988).

Jonathan I. Israel, *The Dutch Republic and the Hispanic World* (Oxford University Press, 1986), and Charles R. Boxer, *The Dutch Seaborne Empire* (Penguin, 1989), discuss the world trading empire of the Dutch. Social backgrounds are treated in Sherrin Marshall, *The Dutch Gentry, 1500–1650: Family, Faith, and Fortune* (Greenwood, 1987). On the decisive conflict with the English, see J. R. Jones, *The Anglo-Dutch Wars of the Seventeenth Century* (Addison-Wesley, 1996). Simon Schama provides a brilliant view into the seventeenth century in the Netherlands in *An Embarrassment of Riches: An Interpretation of Dutch Culture in the Golden Age* (Vintage, 1997).

On the reigns of the first two Stuart monarchs and the English civil war, see Maurice Ashley, *The English Civil War* (St. Martin's, 1990), and Derek Hirst, *Authority and Conflict in England, 1603–1658* (Harvard University Press, 1986). A recent book on the radical fringe is David Petegorsky, *Left-Wing Democracy in the English Civil War: Gerrard Winstanley and the Digger Movement* (Alan Sutton, 1997). For a broad selection of contemporary accounts of the civil war, see John Eric Adair, *By the Sword Divided: Eyewitness Accounts of the English Civil War* (Alan Sutton, 1998).

Among the best treatments of Charles II and his problems are Kenneth H. D. Haley, *Politics in the Reign of Charles II* (Blackwell, 1985). On James II and the Glorious Revolution, see John Childs, *The Army, James II, and the Glorious Revolution* (St. Martin's, 1981) and K. Merle Chacksfield, *The Glorious Revolution, 1688* (Wincanton, 1988).

CHAPTER 18

New Ideas and Their Political Consequences

The Scientific Revolution, the Enlightenment, and the French Revolutions

Originally, Quesnay and his followers opposed the comptroller of finance Jean-Baptiste Colbert's (KOL-bair) policy of subordinating agriculture to government-controlled industry. This narrow emphasis later developed into a comprehensive theory based on natural law. Quesnay, for example, compared the circulation of money to the circulation of blood. He likened mercantilist controls to tourniquets, which shut off a life-giving flow. Quesnay also denounced the mercantilist theory of bullionism, arguing that prosperity depended on production, not gold and silver in the royal treasury. According to another physiocrat, Robert Turgot (tur-GOH; 1720–1781), selfish profit-seeking in a free market would necessarily result in the best service and the most goods for society.

The most influential advocate of the new economic theory was a leader in the Scottish Enlightenment, Adam Smith, a professor of moral philosophy at Glasgow University, who had visited France and exchanged ideas with the physiocrats. In 1776 Smith published *An Inquiry into the Nature and Causes of the Wealth of Nations,* in which he set forth his ideas. The work has since become the Bible of classical economic liberalism, extolling the doctrine of free enterprise or **laissez-faire** (lay-SAY fehr) economics.

Smith was indebted to the physiocrats for his views on personal liberty, natural law, and the role of the state as a mere "passive policeman." He argued that increased production depended largely on division of labor and specialization. Because trade increased specialization, it also increased production. The growing volume of trade, in turn, depended on each person's being free to pursue individual self-interest. In seeking private gain, each individual was also guided by an "invisible hand," also known as the law of supply and demand, in meeting society's needs. As he wrote:

> *It is not from the benevolence of the butcher, the brewer, or the baker that we expect our dinner, but from their reward to their own interests. We address ourselves not to their humanity, but to their self-love.*

Smith regarded all economic controls, by the state or by guilds and trade unions, as injurious to trade. He scoffed at the mercantilist idea that the wealth of a nation depended on achieving a surplus of exports, amassing bullion, and crippling the economies of other countries. In Smith's view, trade should work to the benefit of all nations, which would follow if trade were free. In such a natural and free economic world, the prosperity of each nation would depend on the prosperity of all. He also saw colonies as potential economic drains on a colonial power.

laissez-faire—Literally "leave it alone," the economic doctrine of free enterprise and open markets advocating non-intervention by the state, more commonly, "hands off."

The Political Critique of the Old Regime

Although proponents of the moderate Enlightenment were not revolutionaries and most favored monarchy and an aristocratic social order, they were avid reformers. In this role they developed a tightly organized philosophy, purportedly based on scientific principles and contradicting every argument for absolute monarchy as it generally existed in the eighteenth century. The case against absolutism, as presented by the *philosophes* and their foreign sympathizers, condemned divine right monarchy, hereditary aristocracies by birth, state churches, and mercantilism. Each was found to be irrational, unnatural, and therefore basically unsound.

The thinkers in the Enlightenment saw the arbitrary policies of absolute monarchs as violations of innate rights, which are required by human nature. The most fundamental part of this nature was reason, the means by which people learned and realized their potential. Learning, as described by Locke in his *Essay Concerning Human Understanding* (1690), consisted entirely of knowledge gained through the senses, interpreted by reason, and stored in memory. Locke admitted no internal sources of knowledge; he insisted that the mind at birth is like a blank piece of paper (*tabula rasa*) on which experience writes.

Later thinkers took this idea further than Locke wanted to go, seeing the absence of innate ideas as an indication that moral judgments were only the mind's response to pleasure or pain. Whether this was true or whether the mind was guided by what the Scottish moderate Thomas Reid called "common sense," the individual was primarily a thinking and judging being who required maximum freedom to operate effectively. The best government, therefore, was the government that ruled least. This argument for human freedom was the heart of the anti-absolutist case.

Political freedom, like religious freedom, depended ultimately on government, the source of most restrictions or coercion. For this reason political principles in the case against absolutism were fundamental to all others. They were developed in two main categories: ideas concerning individual rights and ideas concerning the organization of government. Both categories involved efforts that were directed at securing individual freedom against unnatural abuses of authority.

According to Locke and most political theorists of the Enlightenment, government existed to maintain order, protect property, defend against foreign enemies, and protect the natural rights of its people. This idea contradicted the divine right theory, which was held by most reigning monarchs in the seventeenth and eighteenth centuries. Locke, along with many other Enlightenment thinkers including Rousseau, answered the divine right doctrine with the opposing theory of a social contract.

Locke agreed with Hobbes that the base of power was the people. But instead of seeing people as nasty and brutish, Locke saw that an existence in a free and equal society would bring out the best in human beings, as long as their property was defended and they lived in a state of reason. Locke asserted that people voluntarily came together to form governments for the protection of their basic rights, and it was the consent of the people—and that alone—that gave legitimacy to a government. He did not invent the concept of the social contract—the Huguenots in France had discussed it a century earlier. Hobbes had used the contract idea to justify royal authority; Locke turned Hobbes's argument around in his *Second Treatise on Government,* contending that political systems were originally formed by individuals for defense of their natural rights to life, freedom, and property, against local or foreign enemies. Such individuals voluntarily ceded to government the responsibility for protecting their natural rights. In this transaction, government's authority was derived from the governed. It was not absolute but was limited to performing the functions for which it was constituted. When its authority was used for other purposes, the contract was broken and the people were justified in forming another government.

As insurance against abuses of political authority, theorists of the Enlightenment generally advocated the separation of powers. Locke, for example, proposed that kings, judges, magistrates, and legislatures should share authority and thus check one another. Spinoza also stressed the need for local autonomy and a locally based militia to guard against power concentrated in a central government. Montesquieu, although somewhat skeptical about natural laws and Locke's version of the social contract, advocated the separation of powers in his *Spirit of the Laws,* as did most of the other *philosophes.*

Political freedom and guarantees for human rights were common goals, but ideas concerning the ideal form of government varied considerably. The majority of the *philosophes* were not necessarily opposed to monarchy, despite their rejection of the divine right principle. Voltaire and Montesquieu believed that rule by a "benevolent despot," aided by an aristocracy of integrity and talent, was the most likely way to attain desirable reforms. A few monarchs

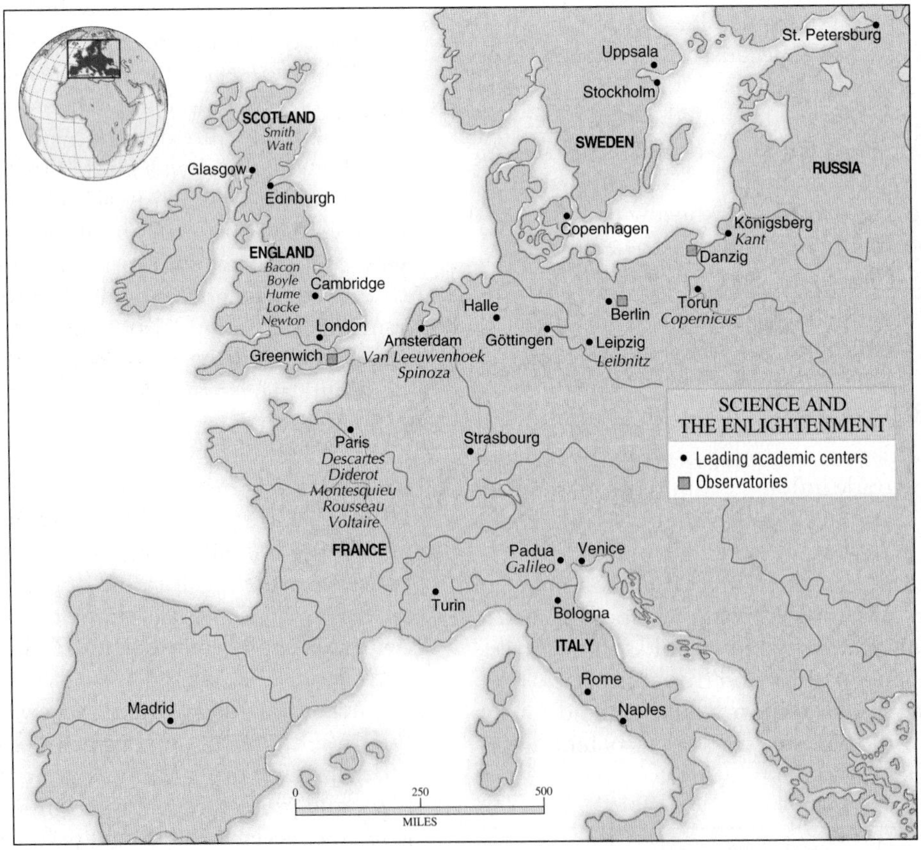

Scientific advances and Enlightenment contributions came from all parts of Europe, from Königsburg in East Prussia to Glasgow in Scotland.

were inspired by this revived Platonic ideal of the philosopher king, but the results of their policies did not always match their principles.

Perhaps the most popular form of government, particularly during the early Enlightenment, was constitutional monarchy on the English model. Locke, of course, was the recognized spokesman for the Glorious Revolution and the limited English monarchy established by Parliament. Both Voltaire and Diderot were very much impressed with the English system as they understood it. Montesquieu praised it as a practical balance of traditional forces, which secured liberty without sacrificing order.

These differences over forms of government were inconsequential compared with the points of political agreement among thinkers of the Enlightenment. All of them rejected the idea of divine right monarchy and considered monarchs to be the public servants of their peoples and to be obligated to maintain natural rights for all. These rights to life, liberty, and property, as construed by the *philosophes* and their friends abroad, seriously threatened absolutist systems.

It was Locke who made the most forceful political statement. In a state of nature, said Locke, people have two powers: to do what is necessary for the preservation of their rights and to respect the rights of others. These two powers naturally devolved into the legislative and the executive functions; of the two, the legislative function was the more important, for it was here where people maintained their dignity. The executive power was inferior to that of the legislature. It could not enslave or destroy any right or go against the foundations of the laws of nature. If it did so, the people had the right to overthrow it.

THE FAILURE OF MONARCHICAL REFORM

- *Why were the "enlightened" despots unable to implement reforms that matched their philosophical ideals?*

As old regimes faltered after the middle of the eighteenth century, an urgent need to respond to the problems of the day challenged the rulers of major European states. Neither the nobles nor the clergy, despite their high social status and political power, could provide the necessary leadership because they were committed to protecting their privileges, particularly immunity from taxation, which threatened the financial security of most countries. Responding to the literature of the Enlightenment, action by the enlightened despots did bring some curtailment of mercantilism, peasant exploitation, and government repression and seemed to offer a belated "best hope" for solving the problem. This hope, however, soon proved to be inadequate.

"Enlightened Despotism": Frederick of Prussia, Catherine of Russia, and Joseph of Austria

Some eighteenth-century kings earned recognized historical reputations—some generated by themselves—as "enlightened despots." Perhaps the major figure in this "monarch's age of repentance" was Frederick II of Prussia, known as "the Great," who became a model ruler during the second half of his reign. An avowed admirer of Voltaire, Frederick, in his writings, popularized the ideal monarch as the "first servant of the state," the "father of his people," and the "last refuge of the unfortunate."[3] "Old Fritz," as his subjects called him, was slavishly committed to his principles. He left his bed at five each morning and worked until dark, reading reports, supervising, traveling, listening to complaints, and watching every aspect of government.

Under Frederick, Prussia was considered the best-governed state in Europe. Within only a few years it recovered economically from the terrible ravages of war, largely through the state's aid in distributing seed, livestock, and tools. Frederick lessened the burdens of serfs on crown estates, imported new crops, attracted skilled immigrants, opened new lands, and tried to promote new industries, such as silk and other textiles. He codified the law and reorganized the courts, along with the civil service. Following ideas he had learned from French philosophy, he established civil equality for Catholics, abolished torture in obtaining confessions from criminals, decreed national compulsory education, and took control of the schools away from the church. Until he died in 1786, Frederick worked diligently at improving Prussia.

Frederick's contemporary, Catherine II of Russia, was also known in her time as an enlightened despot and as "the Great." Having learned the politics of survival at the Russian court, she had conspired with palace guards to kill her erratic husband, Peter, and have herself declared tsarina in 1762. She was a ruthless Machiavellian in foreign affairs, with far more lovers than many male monarchs. She also was a sensitive woman who appreciated the arts, literature, and the advantages of being considered enlightened. She corresponded with Voltaire and gave Diderot a pension. The latter even stayed at her court for a year, meeting with her daily for private discussions on intellectual subjects, including how to improve her empire.

DOCUMENT
Catherine the Great's Constitution

Catherine's reign brought considerable enlightenment and social progress to St. Petersburg society. She subsidized artists and writers, permitted publication of controversial works, established libraries, patronized galleries, and transformed the capital city with beautiful architecture. Catherine also founded hospitals and orphanages, notably those providing foundling children with improved education, one of her main interests. During the decade after 1775, she tried to start a national system of elementary and secondary schools. In that same year she began a reorganization of local government, including the cities, one of many administrative reforms that literally demilitarized civil administration in the empire by turning it over to her partners in assassination, the nobility. She secularized church land, restricted the use of torture, and won acclaim for her much publicized orders to a royal commission charged with modernizing and codifying Russian laws.

Detail of Catherine's Palace in Pushkin

Catherine's program, however, like Frederick's, was limited in scope and significance. Almost every reform had been attempted or suggested earlier and enhanced royal authority. For example, rigid state control and political indoctrination of the curriculum were fixed in the new educational system. Local government after 1775 was controlled by aristocratic landowners, while aristocrats in the commission sabotaged the much heralded legal reforms. Such deference to the aristocracy was typical of Catherine's later internal policies following the disastrous peasant revolt of the 1770s. The nobles' hysteria forced her to issue a charter giving them freedom from taxes, release from compulsory government service, and guaranteed ownership of their serfs. The reaction thus begun was continued during the French Revolution, when Catherine reversed most of her earlier stated liberal opinions and imposed severe censorship. Her political legacy was a rigid autocracy, based on support from an aristocratic elite infected by Western liberal ideals.

Even though Catherine II spoke of governing Russia in accordance with Enlightenment principles, the condition of the Russian peasant reached its lowest point during her reign.

The most radical of the would-be benevolent despots was Joseph II (1780–1790), the son of Maria Theresa and her successor as Habsburg ruler of Austria. He was intelligent and well educated; indeed, Catherine considered him to be one of the reform leaders of her generation. He was also completely converted to the principles of the new philosophers. "I have made philosophy the legislator of my empire," he wrote to a friend in 1781, shortly after his accession.[4] During his whole reign, he fancied himself a royal voice of reason, fighting for human progress against ignorance, superstition, and vice.

Joseph's reign was an explosion of reform effort that threatened to destroy much of the old aristocratic Habsburg structure. He proposed to simplify Catholic services, abolish the monasteries, take over church lands, remove religion from education, and grant civil equality to Protestants and Jews. Attacking the ancient landed establishment head on, he planned to tax the nobles, abolish entail of their lands, and free the serfs. With increasing revenues, he hoped to finance national education, balance the budget, and improve opportunities for industry and trade. The whole undertaking would be consolidated and regulated under a comprehensive code of laws.

Despite their theoretical benefits, Joseph's endeavors aroused a storm of protest, lasting through the reign and bringing him practical failure. For all of his interest in progress, Joseph was a hardheaded and narrow-minded autocrat, determined to build a state on an Enlightenment model. His administrative reforms were aimed not only at higher efficiency but also at centralized government over all the multinational Habsburg territories. His attempted unification of administration seriously alienated the Hungarians and provoked revolts in the Low Countries, Bohemia, and the Tyrol. Peasants were angry because he subjected them to compulsory military service, the clergy harangued against him, and the nobles conspired to hinder the conduct of government at every level. He died in 1790, painfully aware of his unfulfilled ideals.

The French Dilemma

The last Bourbon kings in France before the Revolution, Louis XV and his grandson Louis XVI (1774–1792), responded halfheartedly to these reforming ideas. Although he was almost indifferent to affairs of state and dozed through his council meetings, Louis XV abolished serfdom on royal lands, tried twice to tax the nobles, and attempted to curtail the special privileges of the traditional courts, particularly the most aristocratic *parlement* (par-le-MON) court of Paris. Each attempt led to years of controversy between the government and the nobles; in each instance Louis ultimately gave up the fight.

Louis XVI was well-meaning but poorly educated, lazy, and shy. Avoiding government business, he spent his happiest hours in a workshop, tinkering with locks. His child bride, the frivolous Habsburg princess Marie Antoinette, furnished him with no wisdom or practical support. Although dimly aware of problems, Louis was no more successful than his grandfather: the clamor of the nobles forced him to abandon proposals for eliminating the more undeserved pensions and levying a very modest tax on all landed property.

THE FRENCH REVOLUTION: THE DOMESTIC PHASE, 1789–1799

▪ *What group played the most important role in bringing an end to the* ancien régime *in France?*

The structural problems of France and the inequities found in that country came under the critical examination of the Enlightenment thinkers throughout the eighteenth century. Very few of the governmental, social, or religious institutions withstood the test of reason successfully. However, viewed from the outside, France in 1789 was the center of Europe, the most populous and cultured state of the time, with its thousand-year-old social, political, and economic structure. Its fragility was soon to be revealed.

France, Revolution, and Europe: 1789-1815

Versailles and the Estates-General: May–June 1789

The process of revolution, by default, proceeded quickly toward its long-delayed climax during the summer of 1789. Louis XVI, who had succeeded his grandfather in 1774, was intelligent but lacked initiative. He managed in one way or another to alienate most of his subjects through indecision and bad political judgment; his extravagant Austrian queen, Marie Antoinette (1755–1793), was unpopular in her own right. Louis's lapse of leadership led first to discord in top echelons of authority before May 1789 and then to mob action in July of that year. The outbreak of widespread violence in the cities and countryside dominated all subsequent political decisions.

Between Louis's succession in 1774 and 1789, his finance ministers faced continuously rising national deficits. The debt ultimately reached an equivalent of $6 billion (in 2004 dollars), with interest payments absorbing half of annual revenues. French financial support of the American revolutionary wars against the English brought diplomatic success, but added to the financial problems.

Because loans to cover shortfalls were becoming almost impossible to raise, the government in 1787 and 1788 sought help from Assemblies of Notables (prominent nobles and high churchmen). But these bodies refused gifts or taxes without audits of royal accounts and other fiscal reforms. Louis then forced the courts *(parlements)* to register new laws authorizing more taxes and loans. The crisis was intensified by poor harvests caused by spring floods in 1788,

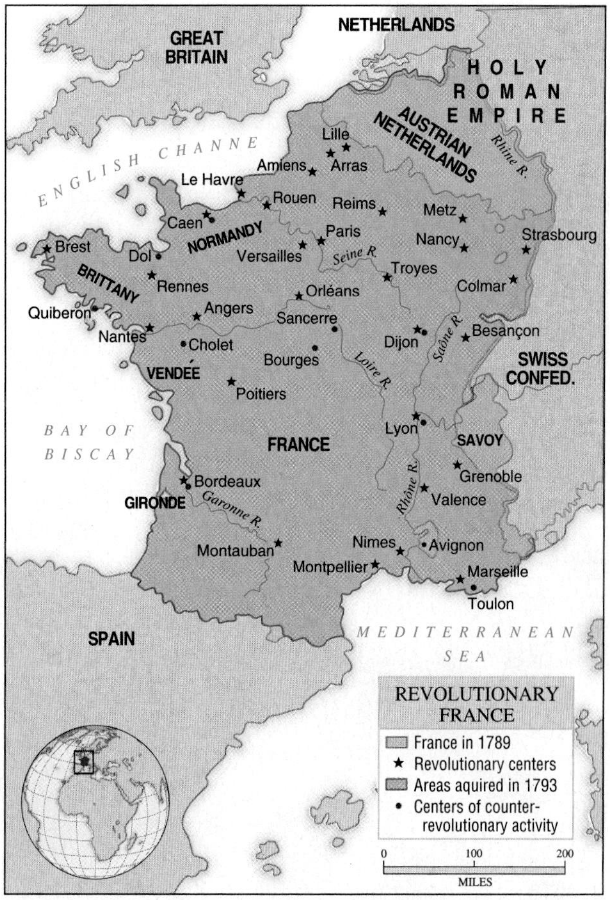

France, the model of an absolutist state and the foremost model of an "old regime," shocked and then threatened its neighbors with its thoroughgoing revolution in the five years after 1789.

followed by devastating hailstorms in July 1788 that destroyed the second planting. France endured the second coldest winter of the century in 1788–1789. Merchants holding stocks of grain drove the price of bread up to the highest level in 75 years. By the spring of 1789, the country was seething with unrest, and the government was out of money once again.

With no other recourse, Louis now bowed to the Notables and agreed to call the **Estates-General,** the nation's medieval representative assembly, which had not met since 1614. The Notables saw the Estates-General meeting as a way to leverage more advantages from the king in return for their support in ending the financial crisis. By blindly pursuing their narrow interests in the decade before 1789, they lit the fuse leading to the revolutionary explosion that destroyed their millennium-old position of superiority in French society.

During the spring of 1789, amid feverish excitement but little open hostility among the estates, electors of each order—the clergy (the First Estate); the nobles, a diverse group of which perhaps 5 percent were in the truly ancient families (the Second Estate); and the commoners (the Third Estate)—met in local assemblies across the country to select representatives. A few women participated among the clergy and nobles, but the 4.3 million electors in the Third Estate were all males, aged 25 or older, who paid the head tax. They, nevertheless, included most peasants, urban craftsmen, merchants, and professionals, comprising a much larger number of voters than those holding the parliamentary franchise in Britain.

After the delegates were elected, they compiled lists of reform proposals, the *cahiers* (kai-YEAS). The Third Estate requested a national legislature, a jury system, freedom of the press, and equitable taxes; there was no mention of overthrowing the monarchy or eliminating the aristocracy. The delegates themselves were not revolutionaries—most were moderate reformers. Of the more than 1100 delegates in the three orders, about 90 of 285 nobles were more or less sympathetic to the views of the bourgeoisie and 205 of 308 clergy were from nonnoble families. The 621 members of the Third Estate included 380 lawyers, 85 businessmen, and 64 landowners; 267 were officeholders.

Once the Estates-General convened on May 5 at Versailles, the economic question—the issue that had led the king to call the Estates-General—was instantly forgotten. The Third Estate insisted that voting should be by head rather than by chamber—which had traditionally been the case, because it had more members than the other two estates combined. Voting by head had already been adopted in some regional assemblies, and the principle had been requested in a large majority of the *cahiers.* During weeks of wrangling on this issue, some members of the clergy joined the Third Estate.

Estates-General—France's medieval representative assembly, consisting of the First Estate (the clergy), the Second Estate (the nobles), and the Third Estate (the commoners).

Locked out of their meeting hall on the king's orders, aroused delegates to the Estates-General, primarily members of the Third Estate, convened at a nearby indoor tennis court, where they swore the historic "Tennis Court Oath." The painting is by Jacques-Louis David.

On June 17, the Third Estate declared itself the national legislature and invited members of the other estates to attend its sessions. Two days later, most of the clergy voted to accept the invitation. Then, on June 20, when members found their meeting hall closed, ostensibly to prepare for the king's upcoming address, delegates of the Third Estate moved a half-mile to an indoor tennis court (*jeu de paume;* zhu de POM-e), where they solemnly swore not to disband until they had produced a French constitution. Later, after defying a royal order to reconvene separately, they declared themselves the National Constituent Assembly of France—a group legally elected to write a constitution.

At this point the delegates had declared—and won—a revolution in principle, but their full understanding of the process or even their commitment to it would develop only with time. Few members among the middle-class majority were merchants seeking free trade. Many were landowners, officeholders, or judges; many others were disappointed at not yet becoming nobles. Liberal aristocrats were willing to give up some privileges, including their manorial fees and tax immunities, in return for enlightened reforms that would improve the administration of government.

Die-hard support for the Old Regime was concentrated primarily among the relatively impoverished local "nobles of the sword" and the traditional peasants from remote communities. Sensing what was to come, however, there were many other nobles who chose to leave France, to become émigrés.

Suffering and Explosion in Paris and the Provinces: July–August 1789

Another factor, however, was already exerting its powerful influence. Economic depression in the late 1780s, particularly rising bread prices in the cities, prompted unrest and violence among more than 20 million French workers and peasants. This unfocused force of frustration and violence would, for the next five years, constantly overwhelm the plans and goals of the various governments' leaders.

Although grudgingly accepting the National Assembly on June 27, Louis tried to placate the nobles by bringing 18,000 troops to the vicinity of Versailles. Middle-class members of the Assembly, nearly panicking in fear of military intervention and a bloody response, appealed for popular support. In Paris, the forces of public order were in a confused state as many of the soldiers, especially among the *gardes-françaises* (gardz fran-SAEZ), who were supposed to protect stocks of grain and weapons, refused to follow the orders of their officers. As the contradictory rumors swirled in from Versailles on the morning of July 14, Parisians broke into military storerooms and took an estimated 30,000 rifles and cannons with little or no resistance. Later that day, an estimated 100,000 Parisian shopkeepers, workers, and women demolished the Bastille in Paris, as well as similar buildings in other cities in France. The significance of the action was not in the prisoners they liberated—a small group of obscure nobles. The Bastille—a medieval fortress—had served as the most visible symbol of the Old Regime, and its fall clearly demonstrated the rapidly growing popular defiance. Paris became an independent city with its own middle-class council and its own National Guard.

Meanwhile, other urban uprisings and peasant violence in the country consolidated the Assembly's position. As for the king, he had completely lost control and even comprehension of events, as can be seen by the entry he made in his journal for July 14, the day of the fall of the Bastille: *"Rien"* (ree-EN; "Nothing.").

The most dramatic action of the Assembly occurred on the night of August 4, 1789. By then, order had been restored in the cities, but peasants all over France were still rising against their lords—burning, pillaging, and sometimes murdering—in desperate efforts to destroy records of their manorial obligations. Faced with this violence, known as the Great Fear, the Assembly ultimately chose to grant concessions. Consequently, on that fateful night, nobles and clergy rose in the Assembly to renounce tithes, serfdom, manorial duties, feudal privileges, unequal taxes, and the sale of offices. The Old Regime, which had evolved over ten centuries, legally disappeared in a few hours. This was the real French Revolution.

Moderate Phase of the Revolution: August 1789–September 1791

To define its political principles and set its course, the Assembly issued the *Declaration of the Rights of Man and Citizen* on August 26. Intended as a preamble to a new constitution, it proclaimed human "inalienable rights" to liberty, property, security, and resistance to oppression. It also promised free speech, press, and religion, consistent with public order. Property was declared inviolate unless required for "public safety," in which case the owner was to receive "just compensation." All (male) citizens were to be equal before the law and eligible for public office on their qualifications. Taxes were to be levied only by common consent. Other accents on civil equality and property rights indicated the document's middle-class orientation.

Declaration of the Rights of Man and the Citizen

A climax to the summer upheaval came in October. Louis tried to delay taking official action to carry out the Assembly's decrees of August 4, and he was anxiously awaiting the arrival of a trusted regiment from Flanders. Meanwhile, angry Parisians marched and rioted in the streets. Two months later, on October 5, after the Flanders regiment had arrived, some 6000 women, many of them armed, marched to Versailles, accompanied by the National Guard under Lafayette. It was symbolic of the disconnection between Louis XVI and the events of his country that no preparation had been made to anticipate the arrival of this group. He had been out hunting, and, to his surprise, he was met by a deputation of six women who presented their demands. In the face of this confrontation, the king signed the decrees of August 4. Other women entered the hall where the Assembly was sitting, disrupted proceedings, and forced an adjournment. The next day, October 6, after a mob stormed the palace and killed some guards, the king and his family returned to Paris as virtual prisoners, their carriage surrounded by women carrying pikes on which were impaled the heads of the murdered bodyguards.

Shortly after the march on Versailles, the Assembly achieved some political stability by declaring martial law, to be enforced by the sometimes dependable National Guard. During the next two years, the Assembly's leaders followed the Enlightenment principles and the statements of the *Declaration* in attempting to reorganize France. Because most came from the middle class, with a preponderance of lawyers and a sprinkling of nobles, they were committed to change but also determined to keep order, protect property, and further their own special interests. Thus, as they achieved their goals, they became increasingly satisfied and conservative. Good harvests and the lowering of food prices also favored them.

One thing remained constant during the revolutionary year of 1789: France was bankrupt. And this financial distress remained one of the new government's most immediate concerns. The Assembly attempted to solve the problem by seizing church properties and using them as a base for new issues of paper currency, the *assignats* (AHS-seen-yat). Members also voted to eliminate tithes, largely in an attempt to placate Catholic peasants. Some would have gone further, but many were reluctant to abolish the state church completely, believing that it could be controlled and used to help defend property. Consequently, the Assembly decreed a "Civil Constitution of the Clergy," which made all clericals salaried public servants, abolished all archbishoprics, and reduced the number of bishoprics. Monastic orders were simply dissolved. Incumbent churchmen were required to swear loyalty to the nation, but only seven bishops and half the clergy conformed. The remainder became bitterly hostile to the government and exerted great influence, particularly among the peasants.

Understandably, the Assembly's economic policies were aimed at winning middle-class support. It therefore assured payment to holders of government bonds, secured not only by impending sales of confiscated church lands but also by lands taken from nobles who had fled the country. Most of this property was sold to middle-class speculators, who resold it to wealthy land-grabbers and social climbers; very little of it was ever acquired by peasants. The Assembly also abolished all internal tolls, industrial regulations, and guilds, thus throwing open to all the chance to work in the arts and crafts. It banned trade unions and decreed that wages be set by individual bargaining. Except for a few remaining controls on foreign trade, the Assembly applied the doctrines of Adam Smith and the physiocrats, substituting free competition for economic controls.

The Assembly dashed some of the high hopes held by French women. The early Revolution enlisted many, not only from the poor rioting Parisians of the shops and markets but also from those of the middle class, whose salons were political centers. Other women were already prominent in the political clubs of the era, forming women's patriotic societies and proposing female militias. In addition, some women were involved in a strong feminist movement, a cause taken up by the Friends of Truth, an organization that regularly lobbied the Assembly for free divorce, women's education, and women's civil rights. Its pleas, however, were largely ignored. Two women, Claire "Rose" Lacombe and Pauline Leon (po-LEEN LAY-on), who had struggled to survive the economic hardships of 1788 led the most important women's club, the Society of Republican Revolutionary Women. Lacombe was an actress; Leon was the daughter of a chocolate maker who tried to keep the family business going. Together, they often appeared before the Assembly, stating their case to improve women's place in society and, when war broke out, demanding the right to bear arms. The royalist Olympe de Gouges (OH-lamp duh GOOZHE) also fought for the cause through her manifestos and arguments before the assembly. However, it was not a promising epoch for women. The Society of Republican Revolutionary Women was shut down because of its radical leadership and programs: de Gouges, along with other women leaders, died by the guillotine in 1793.

The Assembly's Enlightenment ideology clashed with its rising conservatism on the issue of policy toward the French West Indies (see Chapter 21). News from France in 1789 brought violent altercations on Santo Domingo and Martinique, where planters, merchants, poor whites, mulattoes, and slaves evaluated the Revolution according to their diverse interests. Planters in the Assembly differed on trade policies and colonial autonomy but concurred in their fanatic defense of slavery and their opposition to civil rights for free mulattoes. Meanwhile, mulattoes in France

Document *Declaration of the Rights of Man and Citizen*

This moderate middle-class document of the French Revolution was inspired by the American Declaration of Independence. Notice, however, that it differs slightly in its precise mention of property rights.

The National Assembly recognizes and declares, in the presence and under the auspices of the Supreme Being, the following rights of man and citizen.

1. Men are born and remain free and equal in rights. Social distinctions can be based only upon the common good.
2. The aim of every political association is the preservation of the natural and imprescriptible rights of man. These rights are liberty, property, security, and resistance to oppression. . . .
3. Liberty consists in the power to do anything that does not injure others; accordingly, the exercise of the natural rights of each man has no limits except those that assure to the other members of society the enjoyment of these same rights. These limits can be determined only by law.
4. The law can forbid only such actions as are injurious to society. Nothing can be forbidden that is not forbidden by the law, and no one can be constrained to do that which it does not decree.
5. Law is the expression of the general will. All citizens have the right to take part personally, or by their representatives, in its enactment. It must be the same for all, whether it protects or punishes.
6. No man can be accused, arrested, or detained, except in the cases determined by the law and according to the forms which it has prescribed. Those who call for, expedite, execute, or cause to be executed arbitrary orders should be punished; but every citizen summoned or seized by virtue of the law ought to obey instantly. . . .
7. The law ought to establish only punishments that are strictly and obviously necessary, and no one should be punished except by virtue of a law established and promulgated prior to the offense and legally applied.
8. Every man being presumed innocent until he has been declared guilty, if it is judged indispensable to arrest him, all severity that may not be necessary to secure his person ought to be severely suppressed by law.
9. No one should be disturbed on account of his opinions, even religious, provided their manifestation does not trouble the public order as established by law.
10. The free communication of thoughts and opinions is one of the most precious of the rights of man; every citizen can then speak, write, and print freely, save for the responsibility for the abuse of this liberty in the cases determined by law.
11. The guarantee of the rights of man and citizen necessitates a public force; this force is then instituted for the advantage of all and not for the particular use of those to whom it is entrusted.
12. For the maintenance of the public force and for the expenses of administration a general tax is indispensable; it should be equally apportioned among all the citizens according to their means.
13. All citizens have the right to ascertain, by themselves or through their representatives, the necessary amount of public taxation, to consent to it freely, to follow the use of it, and to determine the quota, the assessment, the collection, and the duration of it. . . .
14. Society has the right to require of every public agent an account of his administration.
15. Any society in which the guarantee of the rights is not assured, or the separation of powers not determined, has no constitution.
16. Property being a sacred and inviolable right, no one can be deprived of it, unless a legally established public necessity evidently requires it, under the condition of a just and prior indemnity.

Questions to Consider

1. What themes of the Enlightenment do you find see reflected in this declaration?
2. Does this document strike you as a conservative, liberal, or radical statement?
3. What role does private property play in the construction of the new society?

From Mark A. Kishlansky, ed., *Sources of the West: Readings in Western Civilization*, Volume II, fourth edition, Longman Publishers, New York and London, pp. 115–117.

Document Olympe de Gouges on the Rights of Women

Olympe de Gouges's (1745–1793) father was a butcher and her mother took in washing. As a child, she had no advantage except for her beauty, which brought her marriage to a rich man close to the age of her father. She soon became a widow and had enough money to go to Paris in 1788, where she tried to enter the public debates of the time. However because of her lack of education, she wrote badly, and was not taken seriously.

Another reason she was not taken seriously by French men was because of her radical feminist views, even though she was a royalist. Nonetheless, she wrote more than 30 pamphlets and manifestos, including the *Declaration of the Rights of Woman*. She was a courageous woman who spoke her mind, especially during the time of mass executions of the Committee of Public Safety. She soon joined the ranks of the victims and was guillotined in 1793, at the age of 48.

Man, are you capable of being just? It is a woman who poses the question; you will not deprive her of that right at least. Tell me, what gives you sovereign empire to oppress my sex? Your strength? Your talents? Observe the Creator in his wisdom; survey in all her grandeur that nature with whom you seem to want to be in harmony, and give me, if you dare, an example of this tyrannical empire.

Declaration of the Rights of Woman and the Female Citizen

For the National Assembly to decree in its last sessions, or in those of the next legislature.

Preamble Mothers, daughters, sisters [and] representatives of the nation demand to be constituted into a national assembly. Believing that ignorance, omission, or scorn for the rights of woman are the only causes of public misfortunes and of the corruption of governments, [the women] have resolved to set forth in a solemn declaration the natural, inalienable, and sacred rights of woman in order that this declaration, constantly exposed before all the members of the society, will ceaselessly remind them of their rights and duties; in order that the authoritative acts of women and the authoritative acts of men may be at any moment compared with and respectful of the purpose of all political institutions; and in order that citizens' demands, henceforth based on simple and incontestable principles, will always support the constitution, good morals, and the happiness of all. Consequently, the sex that is as superior in beauty as it is in courage during the suffering of maternity recognized and declares in the presence and under the auspices of the Supreme Being, the following Rights of Woman and of Female Citizens.

Article 1 Woman is born free and lives equal to man in her rights. Social distinctions can be based only on the common utility.

Article 2 The purpose of any political association is the conservation of the natural and imprescriptible rights of woman and man; these rights are liberty, property, security, and especially resistance to oppression.

Article 3 The principle of all sovereignty rests essentially with the nation, which is nothing but the union of woman and man; no body and no individual can exercise any authority which does not come expressly from it [the nation].

Article 4 Liberty and justice consist of restoring all that belongs to others; thus, the only limits on the exercise of the natural rights of woman are perpetual male tyranny; these limits are to be reformed by the laws of nature and reason. . . .

Article 7 No woman is an exception: she is accused, arrested, and detained in cases determined by law. Women, like men, obey this rigorous law. . . .

Article 11 The free communication of thoughts and opinions is one of the most precious rights of woman, since the liberty assures the recognition of children by their fathers. Any female citizen thus may say freely, I am the mother of a child which belongs to you, without being forced by a barbarous prejudice to hide the truth; [an exception may be made] to respond to the abuse of this liberty in cases determined by the law. . . .

Article 13 For the support of the public force and the expenses of administration, the contributions of woman and man are equal; she share all the duties [*corvees*] and all the painful tasks; therefore, she must have the same share in the distribution of positions, employments, offices, honors and jobs [*industrie*]. . . .

Article 15 The collectivity of women, joined for tax purposed to the aggregate of men, has the right to demand an accounting of his administration from any public agent. . . .

Article 17 Property belongs to both sexes whether united or separate; for each it is an inviolable and sacred right; no on can be deprived of it, since it is the true patrimony of nature, unless the legally determined public need obviously dictates it, and then only with a just and prior indemnity.

Questions to Consider

1. What are the major differences between the *Declarations of the Rights of Man and Citizen* and the *Declaration of the Rights of Woman and the Female Citizen*?
2. What points made by Olympe de Gouges seem to you to be applicable to the drive for women's equal rights today?
3. In your opinion, why did male French revolutionaries pay so little attention to the efforts of their female counterparts?

Mark A. Kishlansky, ed., *Sources of the West: Readings in Western Civilization*, Volume II, fourth edition, Longman Publishers, New York and London, pp. 115–117.

spread their pamphlets and petitioned the Assembly, supported by the *Amis des Noirs* (ah-MEE day nwha; "Friends of the Blacks"), whose supporters also angrily attacked slavery in the Assembly hall. The chamber was left divided and nearly impotent. It first gave the island governments complete control over their blacks and mulattoes; then, yielding to the radicals, it granted political rights to mulattoes born of free parents. This was only a temporary solution to a difficult political and social problem.

After two years of tedious controversy, the Assembly finally produced the Constitution of 1791, which made France a limited monarchy. It assigned the law-making function to the single-chambered Legislative Assembly, which would meet automatically every two years. Louis became a figurehead, allowed to select ministers and temporarily veto laws but denied budgetary control or the right to dismiss the legislature. He had fewer powers than the new American president, George Washington, and he could also be legally deposed. In addition, the constitution created an independent and elected judiciary and completely reorganized local government on three levels—departments, districts, and communes—with elected officials relatively free of supervision from Paris. Despite implications in the *Declaration,* only male citizens who paid a specified minimum of direct taxes acquired the vote; millions could not vote. Property qualifications were even higher for deputies to the Assembly and national officials. Women were made "passive citizens," without the vote, but marriage became a civil contract, with divorce open to both parties. Other individual rights under a new law code were guaranteed to all citizens, including Jews, according to the principles of the *Declaration.*

On September 30, 1791, the Assembly dissolved itself after mandating that no present member of the Assembly was to be eligible for election to the new legislative body. It had passed more than 2000 laws that combined to end feudalism, serfdom, an irrational provincial system, conflicting courts, sale of offices, and absolute monarchy itself. It had not, however, made all citizens equal, even before the law, a point repeatedly emphasized by radical agitators and their followers among the angry street people of Paris.

The Drift Toward Radicalism: September 1791–June 1793

For more than a year before the new constitution was completed, the moderate conservative Assembly, which wanted to protect property rights and middle-class advances, had come under the increasing pressure of radicals, who wanted to carry out fundamental political and social reforms. Despite all efforts of the National Guard, unrest in the country and mob action in the cities disturbed the uneasy peace. Particularly in Paris after the spring of 1790, radical members of the Assembly played on popular fears and suspicions, encouraged by condemnations of the Revolution from émigré nobles and foreign royalists. Tensions within France were further aggravated by secret efforts by the king and queen to enlist foreign support. In June 1791, when the king—who opposed the state loyalty oath imposed on the clergy—and his family were caught trying to flee the country, the situation deteriorated. People in favor of a republic called for Louis to be removed. Angry crowds gathered, and the Guard fired on them, killing 15 people. The resulting wave of discontent would continue to intimidate national lawmakers, shaping their policies for the next three years.

In this charged atmosphere, the new and inexperienced Legislative Assembly met on October 1, 1791. Its prospects during the fall were not promising. The sullen king continued his secret plotting with foreign supporters while a 20 percent drop in the value of *assignats,* the Revolutionary government's currency, alarmed middle-class investors. Public opinion in the cities became more radical as the popular press mounted a virulent and often vulgar campaign against Louis and the Assembly, and crowds in Paris and the port cities cursed the government. On the other side, opponents of the Revolution began to act against it. Full-scale revolts threatened to erupt among Catholic peasants in Vendée (von-DAY), Avignon (ah-veen-YON), Brittany, and Mayenne. The divisions and apprehensions in the country were naturally reflected in the Assembly.

At first, the delegates formed themselves into three groups whose location in the meeting hall provided the political vocabulary for the future: conservatives to the right of the podium, moderates in the center, and liberals to the left. In Paris in 1791 the delegates on the right supported the limited monarchy; the undecided—roughly half of the delegates—were in the center; and on the left was a diverse group split by their geographical origins—for example, the **Girondins** (ZHEE-rohn-DAN) from the southwest of the country and the **Jacobins** from Paris—and political goals, and united only by their distrust for the king and his supporters. A majority could agree only on their repudiation of the Declaration of Pillnitz (August 1791), in which the Austrian and Prussian rulers threatened military intervention if Louis XVI were not properly treated.

The Girondists exploited this foreign threat in emotional appeals that rallied the center behind a war to

Girondins—Radical members of the National Assembly (seated on the left) from the southwest of France.

Jacobins—Radical members of the National Assembly (seated on the left) from Paris.

"save the Revolution." Debate gave way to action as the country slipped toward armed conflict during the spring of 1792. The stage was set in February, when Austria and Prussia formed an alliance, a move accented in March when the young and aggressive Francis II (1768–1835) succeeded his comparatively liberal father as Holy Roman Emperor. Louis and his queen, Marie Antoinette, were now hopeful for a war that might set them free. The Girondins savored their newfound dominance, which gave them control of the ministry in March. The Jacobins, under Georges-Jacques Danton (1759–1794) and Maximilien Robespierre (maks-e-MIL-i-en rob-es-PEE-er; 1758–1794), argued against entering a war, noting that, in France's economic condition, war would harm the Revolution and end government economic aid for the common people.

There was a moment of general elation when France declared war on Austria and Prussia in April. But despair soon set in when it became obvious that revolutionary enthusiasm was no match for Austrian and Prussian military discipline. There were too few trained French recruits, led by too few dependable officers, and the armies soon retreated in disorder amid mass desertions from an invasion of the Austrian Netherlands (in present day Belgium). Only the enemy's caution and concern about a Russia advance from the east prevented a complete French disaster. Despair, however, turned to mass determination in July, when the Prussian duke of Brunswick, who commanded the invading armies, issued a threat to destroy Paris if the French royal family was harmed.

In the wake of the military collapse and the Prussian threat, the Girondist rabble-rousers in the Assembly began to lose their support and came under the attack of Danton, the Jacobin deputy prosecutor for the **Paris Commune.** Danton was an enormous brute of a man with a voice of commanding power who mesmerized angry street audiences when he denounced the king as a traitor to France and those who did not share Jacobin views as fools, or worse. On August 10 an incited throng of Parisians, women as well as men, broke into the palace, terrorized the royal family, massacred the Swiss guards, and looted the premises. There followed the Jacobin-directed "September Massacres," in which, under the continual pressure of the mob, the Paris Commune seized power from the Legislative Assembly, deposed the king, and executed some 2000 suspected royalists and priests who did not support the Revolution. As there was no longer a king, it was necessary to call for a new national constitutional convention with members elected by universal male suffrage to prepare the way for a new government. The Jacobin pogrom spread throughout France, even after September 22, when the new National Convention declared France a republic.

Two days earlier, a revitalized French army defeated the Prussians at Valmy, in northern France. This victory fused radicalism with nationalism as French armies began successful advances in the Austrian Netherlands, the Rhineland, and Savoy. Confirmed by their victory in November, the Convention declared universal revolutionary war by promising "fraternity to all peoples who wish to recover their liberty" and ordered inhabitants of occupied countries to accept revolutionary principles. Led by Danton, the lawyer Robespierre—a fanatical follower of Rousseau—and Jean-Paul Marat (mah-RAH; 1743–1793)—the publisher of a violent paper that consistently denounced traitors—the radical Jacobins were now riding a rising tide. But the Girondists, despite their continued enthusiasm for the war, were now the conservatives of the Convention. They had become mainly the spokesmen for wealthy middle-class provincials, who advocated clemency for the king. On this major issue, the execution of Louis XVI, the Jacobins finally triumphed by one vote—despite foreign ambassadors' bribes—and Louis was decapitated on January 21, 1793. Marie

As revolutionary justice condemned an increasing number of people to death after 1791, the guillotine provided an efficient means to decapitate the guilty. The advocates of using the guillotine proclaimed it to be humane because the only thing the condemned would feel would be a "slight breeze at the back of the neck." Here the head of Louis XVI is being shown to the crowd.

Paris Commune—The city government of Paris in Revolutionary France.

Antoinette followed her husband to the guillotine nine months later on October 16, 1793.

Early French military advances had alarmed European capitals, but the execution of Louis XVI and his queen proved to be the decisive factor in turning all of Europe against France. Britain, Austria, Prussia, Spain, the Netherlands, and Sardinia formed the First Coalition in February and March 1793. Coalition forces soon expelled French troops from the Austrian Netherlands and Germany, after which France was invaded at a half-dozen places around its borders. In the ensuing military crisis, the Convention initiated a nationwide effort to raise a new levy of 300,000 men from quotas assigned to every unit of local government. Lazare Carnot (kar-NO; 1753–1823), the republic's minister of war, reorganized the armed forces by opening promotion to all ranks and meshing volunteers with old-line units. His efforts, along with a national patriotic response, brought a hard-won but belated stability.

As in the previous year, threats from abroad generated an internal crisis during the spring of 1793. Execution of the king spurred full-scale civil war in Brittany and the Vendée as peasant armies, led by royalist émigrés and supplied by British ships, fought regular battles against troops of the Republic. Meanwhile in Paris, worsening hunger among the poor widened the breach between Jacobins and Girondins. Again, furious mobs entered the Convention hall, protesting food prices and demanding price controls. Such a measure was pushed through the Convention in April by the *Enragés* (ahn-razh-AY), an extremist faction of the Jacobins led by the radical journalist Jacques Hébert (AY-behr; 1755–1794). When the Girondins staged uprisings in Marseilles, Lyons, Bordeaux, and Toulon, left-wing Jacobins in the Paris Commune called another armed mob into the Convention on May 31, 1793, and purged that body of any remaining Girondists. Others throughout France, wherever the Convention still retained authority, were arrested or driven into hiding.

The Jacobin Republic

The Convention was now a "rump" council of the most extreme Jacobins. Their power was secured after July 12 when Charlotte Corday (1768–1793), a young Girondist sympathizer, came to Paris from Caen and murdered Marat. He had been an adored leader of the *Enragés*, and his death infuriated the street people, including a contingent of revolutionary women who cursed Corday as they followed her to the guillotine. The general anti-Girondist mania brought the Convention under the domination of Robespierre, who remained in power until the late spring of 1794. During that time, revolutionary France, in a convulsion of

Jacques-Louis David, The Death of Marat *(1793). David's painting extols Marat as a martyr of the Revolution.*

patriotic violence, reorganized itself, suppressed internal strife, drove out foreign invaders, and catapulted the radical Jacobin party to a pinnacle of power.

The regime achieved its success largely through rigid dictatorship and terror. The 12-member **Committee of Public Safety,** headed first by Danton, and after July by Robespierre, decided security policies. Subordinate committees were established for the departments, districts, and communes. These bodies deliberately forced conformity and used neighbors to inform on neighbors and sons and daughters to testify against their parents. Suspected traitors were brought to trial before revolutionary tribunals, with most suspects receiving quick death sentences. Between September 1793 and July 1794 some 25,000 victims were dragged to public squares in carts—the famous *tumbrels* (toom-BREL)—and delivered to the

Committee of Public Safety—A 12-member group that decided security policies for the Jacobin administration.

guillotines. Ultimately, the **Reign of Terror,** or simply the Terror, as this period came to known, destroyed most of the revolutionaries, including the Girondists (September 1793), the Dantonists (April 1794), and Robespierre himself (July 1794).

While it lasted, the Jacobin dictatorship was remarkably efficient in its war efforts, as it mobilized all of France to fight and changed the nature of European warfare. The Convention made all males between 18 and 40 eligible for military service, a policy known as the *levée en masse* (le-VAY on MAHSS; "mass conscription"), which ultimately produced a force of 800,000, the largest standing army ever assembled in France. Its officers were promoted on merit and encouraged to exercise initiative. Soldiers were lionized in public festivals and provided with special entertainments, while 300 civilian commissars monitored morale and combat readiness. Between 1793 and 1795, these French citizen armies put down all internal rebellions while fighting a series of remarkably successful campaigns against foreign invaders as well. They regained all lost French territory, annexed Belgium, and occupied other areas that extended to the Rhine, the Alps, and the Pyrenees, thus gaining in two years the "natural frontiers" that Louis XIV had dreamed about. By 1794 Prussia and Spain had left the coalition and the Netherlands had become a French ally. Only Britain, Austria, and Sardinia remained at war with France.

Despite their stated beliefs in free enterprise as an ideal, the Jacobins created a war economy, which operated under extensive controls. Government agencies conscripted labor and took over industries, directing them to produce large quantities of uniforms, arms, medical supplies, and equipment. In Paris alone, 258 forges made 1000 gun barrels a day. Reacting to bread riots and the revolutionary women's condemnation of monopolists and speculators, the Convention imposed price controls, rationing, and fixed wages while issuing currency without reference to bank reserves or market demand. The government also punished profiteers, used the property of émigrés to relieve poverty, sold land directly to peasants, and freed the peasants from all compensatory payments to their old lords.

Many other changes reflected a strange combination of reason and fanaticism. The regime prohibited all symbols of status, such as knee breeches, powdered wigs, and jewelry. It abolished titles; people had to be addressed as "citizen" or "citizeness." Streets were renamed to commemorate Revolutionary events or to honor revolutionary heroes. The calendar was reformed by dividing each month into three weeks of ten days each and giving the months poetic new names; July, for example, became Thermidor (hot) to avoid referring to the tyrant Julius Caesar. The Revolution took on a semireligious character in ceremonies and fêtes, which featured attractive young women as living symbols of reason, virtue, and duty. Along with these changes came a strong reaction against Christianity: churches were closed and religious images destroyed. For a while, "Worship of the Supreme Being" was substituted for Roman Catholicism, although, in 1794, religion became a private matter.

Colonial problems, which had confounded the National and Legislative Assemblies, were met head-on by the Jacobin Convention. The grant of citizenship to free blacks and mulattoes of the islands in 1792 had drawn the mulattoes to the government side, but their armies, enlisted by the governors, faced determined insurrection from royalists and resentful escaped slaves. Sometimes, the two anti-Convention forces were united with support from Spain or the British. In the late spring of 1793, the late spring of 1793, the governor of Santo Domingo issued a decree freeing all former slaves and calling on them to join against foreign enemies. His strategy narrowly averted a British conquest. The chamber responded by freeing all slaves in French territories and giving them full citizenship rights. Later, Napoleon would reimpose slavery in the colonies, where it would last until 1848.

Unfortunately, the revolutionary women in France were not so successful. At first, they were welcomed as supporters by the radical Jacobins, until the latter gained power; then, the Jacobins regarded revolutionary women as troublemakers. In October 1793, the Convention refused to hear a group of women who wanted to protest violations of the Constitution. During the next six months, the government repressed women's societies and imprisoned their leaders. Although the Jacobin legislature denied women the vote, it did improve their education, medical care, and property rights.

Because they regulated the economy and showed concern for the lower classes, the Jacobins have often been considered as forerunners of socialism. The Constitution of 1793, which was developed by the Convention but suspended almost immediately because of the war, does not support this interpretation. It did provide public assistance for the poor and aided the unemployed in seeking work, but it also guaranteed private property, included a charter of individual liberties, confirmed the Constitution of 1791's emphasis on local autonomy, and provided for the Central Committee, appointed by the departments. The greatest difference, in comparison with the Constitution of 1791, was the right to vote, which was granted to all adult males. Although the Jacobin constitution indi-

---

Reign of Terror—The period, roughly from September 1793 to July 1794, in which the Jacobin Dictatorship executed some 25,000 people by the guillotine.

cated a concern for equality of opportunity, it also revealed its authors as eighteenth-century radical liberals who followed Rousseau rather than Locke.

Conservative Counter-Revolution and the End of the Terror

The summer of 1794 brought a conservative reaction against radical revolution. With French arms victorious everywhere, rigid discipline no longer seemed necessary, but Robespierre, still committed to Rousseau's "republic of virtue," was determined to continue the Terror. When he demanded voluntary submission to the "general will" as necessary for achieving social equality, justice, and brotherly love, many practical politicians among his colleagues doubted his sanity. Others wondered if they would be among those next eliminated to purify society. They therefore cooperated to condemn him in the Convention. In July 1794, his enemies sent him to the guillotine with 20 of his supporters, amid great celebration.

Robespierre's fall ended the Terror and initiated a revival of the pre-Jacobin past. In 1794, the Convention eliminated the Committee of Public Safety; the next year, it abolished the revolutionary tribunal and the radical political clubs and freed thousands of political prisoners. It also banned women from attendance in the Convention hall, an act that symbolized the return to a time when women's political influence was confined to the ballroom, the bedroom, and the salon. Indeed, as the exiled Girondists, émigré royalists, and nonconforming priests returned to France, Parisian politics moved from the streets to the drawing rooms of the elite, such as that of the former courtesan Madame Tallien (TAL-lee-en; 1773–1835), which became a center of high-society gossip and political intrigue. Outside Paris, by the summer of 1795, armed reactionary "white" terrorists roamed the countryside, seeking out and murdering former Jacobins. Everywhere, the earlier reforming zeal and patriotic fervor gave way to conservative cynicism.

Before it dissolved itself in 1795, the Convention proclaimed still another constitution and established a new political system known as the Directory, which governed France until 1799. The new government was headed by an executive council of five members (directors) appointed by the upper house of a bicameral (two-house) legislature. Assemblies of electors in each department selected deputies to the two chambers. These electors were chosen by adult male taxpayers, but the electors themselves had to be substantial property owners. Indeed, they numbered only some 20,000 in a total population of more than 25 million. Government was thus securely controlled by the upper middle classes, a condition also evident by the return to free trade.

The Directory was conspicuously conservative and antidemocratic, but it was also antiroyalist. A Bourbon restoration would have also restored church and royalist lands, which had been largely acquired by wealthy capitalists during the Revolution. Politicians who had participated in the Revolution or voted for the execution of Louis XVI had even greater reason to fear restoration of the monarchy. In pursuing this antiroyalist path at a time when royalist principles were regaining popularity, the government had to depend on the recently developed professional military establishment. More than once between 1795 and 1797, army action protected the government against royalists and radicals. The Directory also encouraged further military expansion, hoping to revive patriotic revolutionary fervor. Except for young military officers such as Napoleon Bonaparte, bureaucrats, members

The French Revolutions

1787–1789	Bad weather cuts down on grain harvest, drives up bread prices
August 1788	Louis XVI announces meeting of Estates-General to be held May 1789
May 5, 1789	Estates-General convenes
June 1789	Third Estate declares itself the National Assembly, Oath of the Tennis Court
July 14, 1789	Storming of the Bastille, revolution of peasantry begins
June 1791	Louis XVI and family attempt to flee Paris, are captured and returned
April 1792	France declares war on Austria
January 1793	Louis XVI executed
1793–1794	Reign of Terror
1799	Napoleon overthrows the Directory and seizes power
1804	Napoleon proclaims himself emperor of the French
September 1812	French army reaches Moscow, is trapped by Russian winter
1813	Napoleon defeated at Leipzig
June 15, 1815	Napoleon is defeated at Waterloo and exiled to island of St. Helena

of the landowning middle classes, merchants in large cities, and some professionals, the majority of people in 1796 were worse off than they had been two decades before. But the Directory paid little attention to the majority of people and protected its own.

THE FRENCH REVOLUTION: THE NAPOLEONIC PHASE, 1799–1815

- *What influence did Napoleon have on European history?*

Even as a student, Napoleon considered himself a man of destiny, and he worked hard to construct the image he wanted to project to the future. As soon as the ship carrying him to exile in St. Helena set sail in 1815, his partisans and detractors began a debate over his career that continues to the present day. Whatever the viewpoint of the participants in that debate, all agree that few people have as decisively affected their times and set in motion developments that so profoundly altered the future as did Napoleon Bonaparte.

Napoleon the Corsican

Revolutions favor the bright, the ambitious, and the lucky. Napoleon Bonaparte (1769–1821) had all three qualities in abundance. He was born on Corsica to a low-ranking Florentine noble family in 1769, the year after control of that island passed from Genoa to France. At the age of 10, he was placed by his father in the military academy at Brienne (bree-EN). Six years later, he received his officer's commission. At the beginning of the French Revolution, he was a 20-year-old officer, doomed to a mediocre future by his family's modest standing and the restrictions of the Old Regime. Ten years later, he ruled France. The Revolution gave him the opportunity to rise rapidly, the result of his intelligence, ability, charm, and daring.

Napoleon arrived at the right time—a generation earlier or later, the situation would not have allowed him to gain power. He took advantage of the gutting of the old officer class by the revolutionary wars and the destruction of what was left of the older by the Jacobins to rise quickly to a prominent position from which he could appeal to the Directory. That self-interested group of survivors asked the Corsican to break up a right-wing uprising in October 1795. The following year, the Directory gave Napoleon command of the smallest of the three armies sent to do battle with the Austrians.

The two larger forces crossed the Rhine on their way to attack the Habsburgs while, as a diversionary move, Napoleon's corps went over the Alps into Italy. Contrary to plan, the main forces accomplished little while Napoleon, intended as no more than bait, crushed the Sardinians and then the Austrians in a series of brilliant campaigns. As he marched across northern Italy he picked off Venice and was well on the road to Vienna when the Austrians approached him to make peace. Without instructions from his government, Napoleon negotiated the Treaty of Campo Formio (FORM-ee-oh; 1797) and returned home a hero.

This heroic portrait by Antoine-Jean Gros shows Napoleon at the age of 27, a time when he was leading his troops at the battle of Arcola in northern Italy in November 1796.

After considering an invasion of Britain in the first part of 1798—a cross-Channel task he deemed impossible—Napoleon set out, with the Directory's blessing, to strike at Britain's economy by attacking its colonial structure. He would invade Egypt, expose the weakness of the Ottoman Empire, and from there launch an attack on India. The politicians were as much impressed by this grand plan as they were relieved to get the increasingly popular Napoleon out of town. He successfully evaded the British fleet in the Mediterranean, landed in Egypt, and took Alexandria and

Cairo in July. The British admiral Horatio Nelson (1758–1805), however, found the French fleet and sank it at Aboukir on August 1, 1798. Even though their supply lines and access to France were cut off, Napoleon's forces fought a number of successful battles against the Turks in Syria and Egypt.

The fact remained that the French armies were stranded in Egypt and would be forced to remain there until 1801, when a truce allowed them to come home. This development would normally be regarded as a defeat, yet when Napoleon abandoned his army in August 1799, slipped by the British fleet, and returned to Paris, he was given a frenzied, triumphant homecoming. In public appearances, he adopted a modest pose and gave addresses on the scientific accomplishments of the expedition, such as the finding of the Rosetta Stone, a discovery that provided the first clue in the deciphering of Egyptian hieroglyphics.

Napoleon, his brothers, and the Abbé Sieyès (ab-AY see-YES)—the former vicar general and author of the important 1789 pamphlet "What Is the Third Estate?"—sought to take advantage of the political crisis surrounding the Directory. The Second Coalition, led by Russia and Great Britain, threatened France from the outside, while a feverish inflation ravaged the economy domestically. Various political factions courted Napoleon, whose charisma made him seem the likely savior of the country. In the meantime, he and his confederates planned their course. They launched a clumsy, though successful, coup in November 1799 and replaced the Directory with the Consulate. The plotters shared the cynical belief that "constitutions should be short and obscure" and that democracy meant that the rulers rule and the people obey.

The takeover ended the revolutionary decade. France remained, in theory, a republic, but nearly all power rested with the 31-year-old Napoleon, who ruled as First Consul. Still another constitution was written and submitted to a vote of the people. Only half of the eligible voters went to the polls, but an overwhelming majority voted in favor of the new constitution: 3,011,007 in favor versus 1,562 against.

New Foundations

Ten years of radical change made France ready for one-man rule, but of a type much different from that exercised by the Bourbon monarchy. The events of 1789 had overturned the source of legitimate political power. Now it came not from God but from the people. The social structure of the Old Regime was gone and with it the privileges of hereditary and created nobility. The church no longer had financial or overt political power. The old struggles between kings and nobles, nobles and bourgeoisie, peasants and landlords, and Catholics and Protestants were replaced by the rather more universal confrontation between rich and poor.

There had been three attempts to rebuild the French system in the ten years of revolution: the bourgeois-constitutional efforts to 1791, the radical programs to 1794, and the rule to 1799 by survivors who feared both the right and the left. Although each attempt had failed, each left valuable legacies to the new France. The first attempt established the power of the upper middle classes; the second showed the great power of the state to mobilize the population; and the third demonstrated the usefulness of employing former enemies in day-to-day politics.

Ever the pragmatic tactician, Napoleon used elements from the Old Regime and the various phases of the Revolution to reconstruct France. He built an autocracy far more powerful than Louis XVI's government. He took advantage of the absence of the old forms of competition to central power from the nobility and the feudal structure that had been destroyed in the name of liberty, equality, and brotherhood. He used the mercantile policies, military theories, and foreign policy goals of the Old Regime, the ambitions of the middle class, and the mobilization policies of the Jacobins. All he asked from those who wished to serve him was loyalty. Defrocked priests, renegade former nobles, reformed Jacobins, small businessmen, and enthusiastic soldiers all played a role. His unquestioning acceptance of the ambitious brought him popularity because ten years of constant change had compromised most politically active people in some form of unprincipled, immoral, or illegal behavior.

Napoleon built his state on the *philosophes*' conception of a system in which all French men would be equal before the law. The Revolution destroyed the sense of personal power of a sovereign and substituted what the British historian Lord Acton would later in the century call the "tyranny of the majority." The French state accordingly could intervene more effectively than ever before, limited only by distance and communication problems.

The mass democratic army created by the total mobilization of both people and resources was one of the best examples of the new state system. A revolutionary society had fought an ideological war, and the experience changed the nature of combat forever. Because advancement and success were based on valor and victory, rather than bloodlines or privilege, the army profited from the new social structure and sought to preserve and extend it. The army best symbolized the great power of the French nation unleashed by the Revolution. Many of the economic and diplomatic problems that preceded the Revolution remained, but Napoleon's new state structure provided inspired solutions.

Taking advantage of his military supremacy, Napoleon gained breathing space for his domestic reforms by making peace with the Second Coalition by March 1802. He then set about erecting the governing structure of France, which remained virtually intact into the 1980s. He developed an administration that was effective in raising money, assembling an army, and exploiting the country's resources. His centralized government ruled through prefects, powerful agents in the provinces who had almost complete control of local affairs and were supported by a large police force. He then established a stable monetary policy based on an honest tax-collecting system, backed by up-to-date accounting procedures. The Bank of France that he created remains a model of sound finance.

Napoleon knew that the country he ruled was overwhelmingly Catholic and that national interest dictated that he come to terms with the papacy. Through the Concordat of 1801 with Pope Pius VII, the pope gained the right to approve the bishops whom the First Consul appointed to the reestablished Catholic Church. The state permitted seminaries to be reopened and paid priests' salaries. Pius regained control of the Papal States and saw his church recognized as the religion of the majority in France. The church thus resumed its position of prominence, but without its former power and wealth.

Napoleon viewed education as a way to train useful citizens to become good soldiers and bureaucrats, and he pursued the development of mass education by trying to increase the number of elementary schools, secondary schools, and special institutes for technical training. The schools were to be used to propagandize the young to serve the state through "directing political and moral opinion." Overarching the entire system was the University of France, which was more an administrative body to control education than a teaching institution. Napoleon had neither the time nor the resources to put mass education in place during his lifetime, although he did gain immediate success in training the sons—but rarely the daughters—of the newly arrived middle classes to become state functionaries.

Perhaps his greatest accomplishment came in the field of law. Building on reforms begun ten years earlier, he assembled a talented team of lawyers to bring order to the chaotic state of French jurisprudence. At the time he took power, the country was caught in the transition from 366 separate local systems to a uniform code. By 1804 the staff had compiled a comprehensive civil law code (called the **Code Napoléon** after 1807) that was a model of precision and equality when compared to the old system. The code ensured the continuation of the gains made by the middle classes in the previous decade and emphasized religious toleration and abolition of the privileges held under the old order. Unfortunately, the code perpetuated the inferior status of women in the areas of civil rights, financial activities, and divorce. Nonetheless, it has served as the basis for law codes in many other countries.

The price France paid for these gains was rule by a police state that featured censorship, secret police, spies, and political trials, which sent hundreds to their deaths and thousands into exile. Order did prevail, however, and for the first time in a decade, it was safe to travel the country's roads. Napoleon also reduced the "representative assemblies" to meaningless rubber stamps. Liberty, equality, and brotherhood meant little in a land where the First Consul and his police could deny a person's freedom and right of association because of a perceived intellectual or political conflict.

To consolidate all of the changes, Napoleon proclaimed himself emperor in December 1804. Fifteen years after the outbreak of the Revolution, France had a new monarch. In a plebiscite, the nation approved the change by 3,572,329 to 2,579. As Napoleon took the crown in his hands from Pope Pius VII, who had come from Rome for the occasion, and crowned himself, the First French Republic came to an end.

Napoleon as Military Leader

War had been France's primary occupation since 1792, and, on the whole, it had been a profitable enterprise. The French had gained much land and money, as well as the opportunity to export the Revolution. Napoleon's reforms helped make his country even stronger in battle. At the end of 1804, Napoleon embarked on a series of campaigns designed to show France's invincibility. A key to French success was the emperor himself, who employed his own remarkable genius in leading his strong and wealthy country.

Napoleon brought intellectual strength, sensitivity to mood and opportunity, and bravery to the task of making war. He had been trained in the most advanced methods of his day, and he had better, more mobile artillery and more potent powder to blow holes through the enemy's lines. He worked well with a talented command staff, to which he gave much responsibility to wield their divisions as conditions dictated. Finally, he was the ultimate leader. Whether as lieutenant, general, First Consul, or

---

Code Napoléon—A civil law code instituted by Napoleon's administration in 1804. It formed the basis for many legal systems throughout Europe.

emperor, Napoleon inspired masses of soldiers in a dramatic way. At the same time, he mobilized the home front through the use of the press and skillfully written dispatches.

Beneath this image making, the supreme commander was extremely flexible in his use of resources, always changing his tactics. He was pragmatic, moved rapidly, and lived off the land. He won the loyalty of his men by incentives and rewards, not brutal discipline. He set many military precedents, among them the use of ideological and economic warfare, as well as the rapid simultaneous movement of a large number of military columns. These columns could quickly converge on a given point with devastating results, breaking the will of the enemy. Finally, he personally led his troops into battle, exposing himself to incredible dangers with little regard for his own safety.

His nemesis was Great Britain, and during 1803 and 1804, he prepared a cross-Channel invasion. But the inability of the French navy to control the Channel and the formation of the Third Coalition (Great Britain, Russia, Austria, and Sweden) forced him to march eastward. In October 1805 Admiral Nelson and the British ended Napoleon's hopes of dominating the seas by destroying the joint French-Spanish fleet at the battle of Trafalgar.

France did far better on land, gaining mastery over the Continent by the end of 1807. Napoleon totally demoralized the Third Coalition in battles at Ulm (October 1805) and Austerlitz (December 1805). He then annihilated the Prussians, who had entered the conflict in the battles at Jena and Auerstadt (October 1806). He occupied Berlin, where he established the **Continental System,** a blockade of the Continent that was an effort to defeat Britain by depriving it of trade with the rest of Europe. Finally, in June 1807, he defeated the Russians at the battle of Friedland and forced Tsar Alexander I to sign the Tilsit Treaty in July. This treaty, ratified on a raft anchored in the middle of the Nieman River, brought the two major land powers of Europe together in an alliance against Britain.

At the beginning of 1808, Napoleon stood supreme in Europe, leading France to a dominance it had never experienced before and has not experienced since. Several of his relatives occupied the thrones of neighboring countries. The rest of the continent appeared to be mere satellites revolving around, this time, a Napoleonic sun.

Napoleon's Revolution in Europe

As he achieved his military goals, Napoleon set in motion a chain reaction of mini-revolutions that had a profound impact on the rest of the century. British sea power stood in the way of France's total domination of the Continent. Even though the British economy suffered under the impact of the Continental System (exports dropped by 20 percent, with a resultant cutback in production and rise in unemployment), the damage was not permanent. The Continental System inadvertently contributed to Britain's economic development by forcing it to industrialize quickly as it sought new markets and methods. Safe behind their wall of ships, the British turned out increasing quantities of goods as they passed through the early phases of industrialization.

Napoleon's armies carried French ideological baggage and institutional reforms across the Continent. Even though the emperor consolidated the Revolution in a conservative way in France, he broke apart his opponents' fragile social and governmental structures when he marched across the Rhine. Napoleon consciously spread the messages of liberty, equality, and brotherhood with all of the antifeudal, antiprivilege, and antirepressive themes inherent in the revolutionary triad. Where the French governed directly, they used the Code Napoléon and the reformed administrative practices.

The French presence triggered a hostile wave of nationalistic resentments. Many Europeans saw Napoleon as an imperialist, and the people he had "emancipated" began to realize that they had exchanged an old form of despotism for a new one. By posing as the champion of the Revolution, Napoleon sowed the seeds of the opposition that would work against him later, especially in Prussia. With the exception of the Poles, who had labored under Russian dominance and now served Napoleon well, the rest of Europe reacted against the French yoke.

The most significant rebellion took place in Portugal and Spain. Napoleon's entry into those countries to topple the passive Bourbons and strengthen the leaky Continental System was uncharacteristically shortsighted. The emperor had a serious fight on his hands in the Peninsular War that followed. Guerrilla uprisings soon broke out, supported by a British expeditionary force and supplies. These bloody wars tied down 200,000 to 300,000 French troops over a period of five years and drained the French treasury. The invasion of Spain also prompted a series of uprisings in the New World that gave birth to modern Latin American history (see Chapter 21).

The social and political changes the French triggered in Germany were equally profound. When he redrew the map of Europe after his victories, Napoleon destroyed the remnants of the Holy Roman Empire and, in so doing, erased 112 states of that ancient league. Only six of the former 50 free cities retained their status. Further, by changing the territorial

---

Continental System—An economic system Napoleon imposed on Europe to prevent countries from trading with Great Britain.

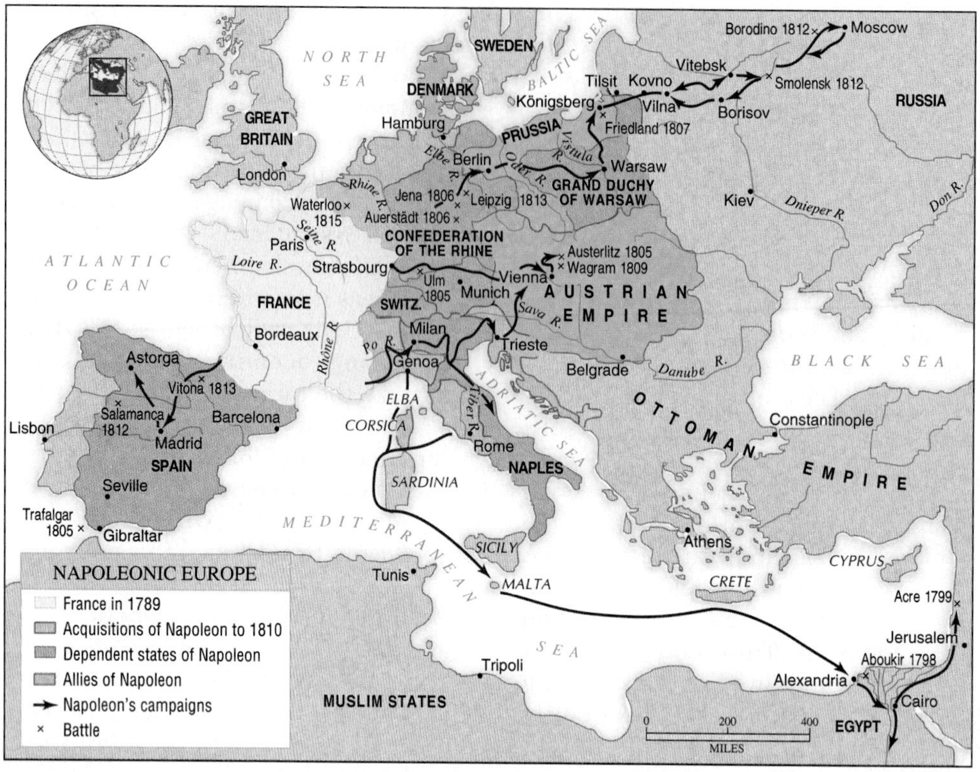

Napoleon combined the military advances of the ancien régime *and the unleashed democratic forces of the Revolution to achieve in ten years what Louis XIV had failed to accomplish in a half century: the domination of Europe.*

arrangements of other areas, he reduced the number of German political units from more than 300 to 39. All over Germany, a wave of nationalism stirred the politically conscious population and prepared the way for the liberation movement.

Napoleon's Downfall

Opposition to Napoleon grew in both Austria and Russia. After the valiant but unsuccessful campaigns against the French in 1809, culminating in the bloody battle of Wagram, Vienna became a docile, though unreliable, ally. Napoleon's marriage to Marie Louise, the daughter of Francis I of Austria, proved to be only a tenuous tie between the French emperor and the Habsburgs. In Russia the Tilsit Treaty had never been popular, and the economic hardships brought on by the Continental System made a break in the alliance virtually inevitable. By the end of 1810 France and Russia prepared to go to war against each other.

The emperor prepared carefully for his attack on Russia. Food supply would be a major problem for the 611,000 troops—half of them non-French—in the first and second lines of the invasion because his forces would be too large to live off the land. Furthermore his army took with them over 200,000 animals, which required forage and water. The invasion force delayed its march until late June to ensure that the Russian plains would furnish sufficient grass to feed the animals.

The Russian campaign was both a success and a failure for Napoleon. The French did gain their objective—the city of Moscow—but the Russians refused to surrender. Shortly after the French occupied Moscow, fires broke out, destroying three-fourths of the city. After spending 33 days in the burned shell of the former capital waiting in vain for the tsar, who was 400 miles north in St. Petersburg, to agree to peace, Napoleon gave orders to retreat. He left the city on October 19. To remain would have meant having his lines cut by winter and being trapped with no supplies. His isolation in Moscow would have encouraged his enemies in Paris. Leaving the city, as it turned out, condemned most of his men to death. As the remnants of Napoleon's forces marched west in October and November, they were forced to retrace virtually the same route they had used in the summer. They suffered starvation, attacks by partisans, and the continual pressure of Russian forces. Thousands perished daily, and by the end of November, only about 10,000 of the original force had made their escape from Russia.

Russia, which had stood alone against the French at the beginning of 1812, was soon joined by Prussia, Austria, and Britain in 1813 and 1814 in what came to be known as the War of Liberation. While British armies under the duke of Wellington (1769–1852) helped clear the French forces out of Spain, the allied troops pushed Napoleon's forces westward. A combination of Napoleon's genius and the difficulties in coordinating the allied efforts prolonged the war, but in October 1813, the French suffered a decisive defeat at Leipzig in the Battle of the Nations, one year to the day after Napoleon had fled Moscow.

The allies sent peace offers to Napoleon, but he refused them. After Leipzig the Napoleonic Empire rapidly disintegrated, and by the beginning of 1814, the allies had crossed the Rhine and invaded France. At the end of March, the Russians, Austrians, and Prussians took Paris. Two weeks later, Napoleon abdicated his throne, receiving in return sovereignty over Elba, a small island between Corsica and Italy.

Napoleon arrived in Elba in May and established rule over his 85-square-mile kingdom. He set up a mini-state, complete with an army, a navy, and a court. He soon exhausted the possibilities of Elba and in February and March 1815 he eluded the British fleet and returned to France to begin his campaign to regain power "within one hundred days." His former subjects, bored with the restored Bourbon Louis XVIII, gave him a tumultuous welcome. Napoleon entered Paris, raised an army of 300,000 men, and sent a message to the allies gathered to make peace at Vienna that he desired to rule France and only France. The allies, who were on the verge of breaking up their alliance, united, condemned Napoleon as an enemy of peace, and sent forces to France to put him down once and for all.

At the battle of Waterloo on June 18, 1815, the duke of Wellington, supported by Prussian troops under Field Marshall Gebhard von Blücher (fon BLOOK-er; 1749–1819), narrowly defeated Napoleon. The vanquished leader sought asylum with the British, hoping to live in exile in either England or the United States. But the allies, taking no chances, shipped him off to the bleak South Atlantic island of St. Helena, 5000 miles from Paris. Here he set about writing his autobiography. He died of cancer in 1821 at the age of 51.

Even with the brief flurry of the One Hundred Days, Napoleon had no hope of re-creating the grandeur of his empire as it was in 1808. The reasons for this are not hard to determine. Quite simply, Napoleon was the heart and soul of the empire, and after 1808, his physical and intellectual vigor began to weaken. Administrative and military developments reflected this deterioration as Napoleon began to appoint sycophants to positions of responsibility. Further, by 1812, the middle classes, on which he depended, began suffering the economic consequences of his policies. The Continental System and continual warfare made their effects deeply felt through decreased trade and increased taxes. Even though some war contractors profited, the costs of Napoleon's ambitions began to make Frenchmen long for peace.

MAP The Empire of Napoleon in 1812

Outside France, the growth of nationalistic resistance on the Continent worked against the dictator, who first stimulated it by exporting the call for liberty, equality, and brotherhood. Equally important, the 25 years of French military superiority disappeared as other nations adopted and improved on the new methods of fighting. Finally, the balance-of-power principle made itself felt. France could not eternally take on the whole world.

CONCLUSION

Copernicus asked the fundamental questions about whether or not the earth moved, repeating a process of inquiry that in the West went back to the Ionian Greeks: similar inquiries were to be found in India, China, and Egypt. When, after extensive mathematical calculations, he established the heliocentric theory, his findings were published, to be read and challenged. As others improved on his findings and established the natural laws that defined the motion of the planets, scientific inquiries became widely admired in some parts of Europe and widely attacked by Christian churches in others. The surprising discoveries of astronomers produced a new view of the individual's place in the universe; their perspective was apparently proved mathematically by Sir Isaac Newton in the law of gravitation. His laws, along with the other laws of science, suggested that human reason operated effectively only when it was interpreting sensory experience. Material reality was accepted by some thinkers as the only reality. Therefore, the natural laws affecting human society were also considered basically materialistic. Respect for Enlightenment philosophy, many of whose early participants contributed to the Scientific Revolution, was largely derived from the successes and popularity of science.

Within this political context, the eighteenth-century Age of Reason brought a new vision of the future to European civilization. Its proponents thought they had discovered a simple way to achieve perpetual human happiness. They sought to deliver people from irrational restraints so that they might act freely in accordance with a universal human nature. On the one hand, their writings promised that pursuit of self-interest would benefit society; on the other, it promised that a free human reason would produce sound moral judgments. In other words, individual freedom furthered the operation of natural laws. Believing they had learned these laws, eighteenth-century rationalists thought they had found the secret of never-ending progress.

Although the *philosophes* and their prototypes outside of France were not revolutionaries, their ideas promised to undermine absolutism in all of its phases. Deism questioned the necessity of state churches and clergies. The physiocrats, Adam Smith, and other early economic liberals demonstrated the futility of mercantilism. The Enlightenment's political principles substituted the social contract for divine right while emphasizing the natural human rights of political freedom and justice.

This reasonable search for natural law, and the demand that all things must stand the test of reason came at a time when colonial wars had forced France to go deeper into debt. Louis XVI's fiscal problems forced him to call the Estates-General—the representatives of the French people—in May 1789 to meet for the first time in 175 years. The subject of debate passed quickly from discussion of debt to considerations of social and political reform of the *ancien régime.* The old system collapsed under the weight of these considerations and, two months later, plunged into the maelstrom of revolution from which it emerged only ten years later, again under the control of a single leader—this time the Corsican-born Napoleon, who, thereafter, carried out his own version of the French revolution that touched all of Europe and much of the Western world.

Suggestions for Web Browsing

You can obtain more information about topics included in this chapter at the websites listed below. See also the companion website that accompanies this text, **http://www.ablongman.com/brummett,** which contains an online study guide and additional resources.

Galileo Project
http://es.rice.edu/ES/humsoc/Galileo/

A hypertext source of information about the life and work of Galileo Galilei and the science of his time.

Internet Modern History Sourcebook: The Scientific Revolution and the Enlightenment
http://www.fordham.edu/halsall/mod/modsbook09.html

Extensive online source for links about the Scientific Revolution and the Enlightenment, including primary documents by or about Copernicus, Kepler, Galileo, Descartes, Adam Smith, and John Locke.

Catherine the Great
http://members.tripod.com/~Nevermore/CGREAT.HTM

A treasure trove of materials on the Enlightened Empress.

Eighteenth-Century Fashion
http://www.marquise.de/en/1700/index.shtml

A virtual guided tour of European fashion during the rococo period.

French Revolution
http://otal.umd.edu/~fraistat/romrev/frbib.html

Lists several major websites and a selected general bibliography dedicated to the French Revolution.

Marie Antoinette
http://www2.lucidcafe.com/lucidcafe/library/95nov/antoinette.html

A short biography of the queen, with related Web sites offering portraits, genealogy, and life at Versailles.

Napoleon
http://www.napoleonseries.org/

Site provides extensive bibliographic and general historical information about Napoleon and his times.

Military History: Napoleonic Wars (1800–1815)
http://www.cfcsc.dnd.ca/links/milhist/nap.html

Canadian Forces College site lists links on the biographies of Napoleon and Nelson, campaigns and battles, museums, naval operations, and reenactments.

The Congress of Vienna
http://members.aol.com/varnix/congress/

A good collection of documents and images from the Congress that put Europe back together again.

Literature and Film

Alexander Pope captured the spirit of the age his *Essay on Man* (1733). Jonathan Swift used satire for political criticism in *Gulliver's Travels* (1726). Voltaire's *Candide* (1759) is a fine critique of contemporary society. Daniel Defoe's *Robinson Crusoe* (1719) is a pathbreaking novel. Johann Wolfgang von Goethe's *The Sorrow of Young Werther* (1774) set the stage for modern romantic novels. See Neal Stephenson's three-volume series on the Scientific Revolution, *The Baroque Cycle*, beginning with *Quicksilver* (2003–2004)

Milos Forman's film *Amadeus* (Warner, 1984) is superb. Gérard Corbiau's *Farinelli: Il Castrato* (Columbia/Tristar, 1995) gives splendid insights into the society of the time. Marvin Chomsky captures eighteenth-century Russia in his film *Catherine the Great* (A & E Entertainment, 1995).

Two panoramic novels stand head and shoulders above the rest for this period, Charles Dickens's *A Tale of Two Cities* (1859) and Leo Tolstoy's *War and Peace* (1864–1869). There are several film versions of each. Rafael Sabatini's *Scaramouche: A Romance of the French Revolution* (1921) is a good, epic, read. Two recent historical novels deserve attention, Sandra Gulland's trilogy on

CHAPTER CONTENTS

1550

c. 1581–1663 Queen Njinga, ruler of Ndongo kingdom, Angola

1650

1632–1667 Reign of Ethiopian Emperor Fasilidas

1672–1727 Reign of Moroccan Sultan Mulay Ismail

1685 Portuguese invade kingdom of Kongo

1700

1713 British obtain right to sell slaves in Spanish ports

c. 1717 Death of Asante King Osei Tutu, West Africa

1725 Fulani Muslims launch jihad in Futo Jalon, West Africa

1750

1779 First Xhosa-European war in eastern Cape, South Africa

1780s Peak decade of transatlantic slave trade

1800

1816 Shaka becomes king of Zulu people

1834 Beginning of Great Trek of Afrikaners

1840 Zanzibar becomes center for Omani Arab rule

1850

1868 Suicide of Tewodros II of Ethiopia

The mid-seventeenth to the mid-nineteenth centuries was a period of sometimes gentle and sometimes violent change in the states and societies of Africa. These states faced a set of challenges prompted by both external interventions and internal transformations. The internal upheavals took the forms of regional conflicts, the formation of new kingdoms, the expansion of Islam, migrations, and economic shifts. The external threats primarily came from the intrusion of Dutch and British settlers in southern Africa and a dramatic upswing in the Atlantic slave trade.

Arabs in North Africa and the Middle East had long maintained a slave trade with Africans in the interior of West Africa and on the East African coast. Europeans had also been involved for several centuries in a slave trade with Africans along the West and Central African coasts, but in the eighteenth century as the demand increased for slaves to work on the sugar plantations in the Americas, Portuguese, British, Dutch, and French slavers bought many more slaves from African states that rarely allowed European traders to intrude in their affairs. In the seventeenth century alone, around six million Africans were sold into the transatlantic slave trade. Although the slave trade was destructive, the transatlantic trade opened up exchanges with the Americas in crops such as cassava, peanuts, and maize that benefited African agriculture and increased African populations. In the late eighteenth century, as European nations entered the industrial age, European traders began shifting away from trading for slaves to trading for commodities such as palm oil and palm kernels.

The European presence and influence in Africa was largely limited to coastal areas. However, at the southern tip of Africa, where Europeans could survive in a temperate climate, the Dutch and British established colonies. Dutch settlers primarily engaged in subsistence pastoralism, while the British were interested in commercial farming. But both required land that they conquered from indigenous Africans.

These centuries also saw the political map of Africa being redrawn as some older states that participated in the transatlantic slave trade declined and many new ones were created throughout the continent. In northeastern Africa the long-established kingdom of Ethiopia saw its monarchy weakened and nobles assert their autonomy.

In East Africa the kingdoms of Buganda and Rwanda developed. Holy wars contributed to the spread of Islam and the emergence of Muslim kingdoms across the West African Sudan. And, in southern Africa in the early eighteenth century, the Zulu and Basotho, responding to changing trade patterns and increased conflict, established major kingdoms.

THE ATLANTIC SLAVE TRADE

- *What factors contributed to the creation and the growth of the Atlantic slave trade?*

Throughout the seventeenth century Europeans became increasingly active in the Atlantic slave trade, which combined to create a huge international complex of enterprises involving the economies of four continents. The western Saharan coast was the setting for the beginning of the Atlantic slave trade in 1441. To win the favor of Prince Henry the Navigator, a Portuguese sea captain kidnapped one man and one woman who were sold into the Mediterranean slave market. The slave trade reached its peak three centuries later as a major component in the rapidly expanding capitalism of northern Europe. Because it was conducted in partnerships between Africans and Europeans, the trade was a less obvious short-term danger to African interests than the migrating Dutch settlers in South Africa, but it posed a more serious long-term threat.

The full historical significance of the slave trade can best be understood if it is viewed in its broader setting. Europe's economy at the time derived large profits from bulk plantation commodities such as sugar, tobacco, and coffee. The most productive European plantations, which were located in the West Indies, depended primarily on slave labor from West Africa. Thus, slaving ports, such as Liverpool and Bristol in England and Bordeaux and Nantes in France, became thriving centers of a new prosperity. Related industries—such as shipbuilding, sugar refining, distilling, and textile and hardware manufacturing—also flourished. All contributed much to the development of European capitalism and ultimately to the Industrial Revolution.

Northern Europe's commercial impetus reached West Africa in the middle of the seventeenth century. The Portuguese, after losing the whole Atlantic coast to the Dutch, won back only Angola. For a while, the Dutch nearly monopolized the trade. After seizing Elmina on the Gold Coast in 1637, the Dutch West India Company was taking almost 7000 slaves a year a decade later. In the 1630s the English also established footholds on the Gold Coast at Cormantin and Cape Castle; by 1700 they had seven other posts in the area. The French, meanwhile, acquired St. Louis on the Senegal in the north, which allowed them to control most trade as far south as the Gambia River. In the resulting triangular competition, the Dutch faced constant pressure from their two rivals but maintained their dominance from a dozen strong Gold Coast forts.

CASE STUDY
Portuguese Travelers in Africa

By 1700 England was challenging Dutch predominance. Having defeated the Dutch at sea in the late 1600s, Britain next defeated France in the War of the Spanish Succession. At the ensuing Peace of Utrecht in 1713, Britain obtained the right to sell 4800 slaves each year in Spanish ports. Another advantage after 1751 was the British shift from a monopolistic chartered company to an association of merchants, which increased incentives by opening opportunities for individual traders. Finally, in the continuing Anglo-French colonial wars of the eighteenth century, the British fleet consistently hampered French operations. For these reasons, by 1785, the British were transporting thousands more slaves from West Africa than all of their competitors combined.

Despite this regional competition among Europeans, they conducted trade locally as a black-white partnership, largely on African terms. Africans leaders, who refused to grant any European nation a monopoly over the slave trade in their territories, were adept at playing one European group off another. Europeans, largely confined to their fortified settlements, recognized that they could easily be excluded from trade if they did not establish amicable working relationships with Africans. Hence, they learned to rely on African rulers who not only enforced their authority but also eagerly took profits from regular port fees, rents on the **barracoons** or slave stockades, and a contracted percentage on the sale of slaves.

MAP
African Empires in the Western Sudan

Europeans also turned to a class of Westernized blacks and Afro-Europeans who served as critical intermediaries and power brokers between Europeans and

---

barracoons—Slave stockades on the African coast. Barracoons were generally run by Europeans and supplied by African rulers, who leased the land for the buildings to the Europeans. Slaves were held in the stockades until shipped across the Atlantic to European colonies.

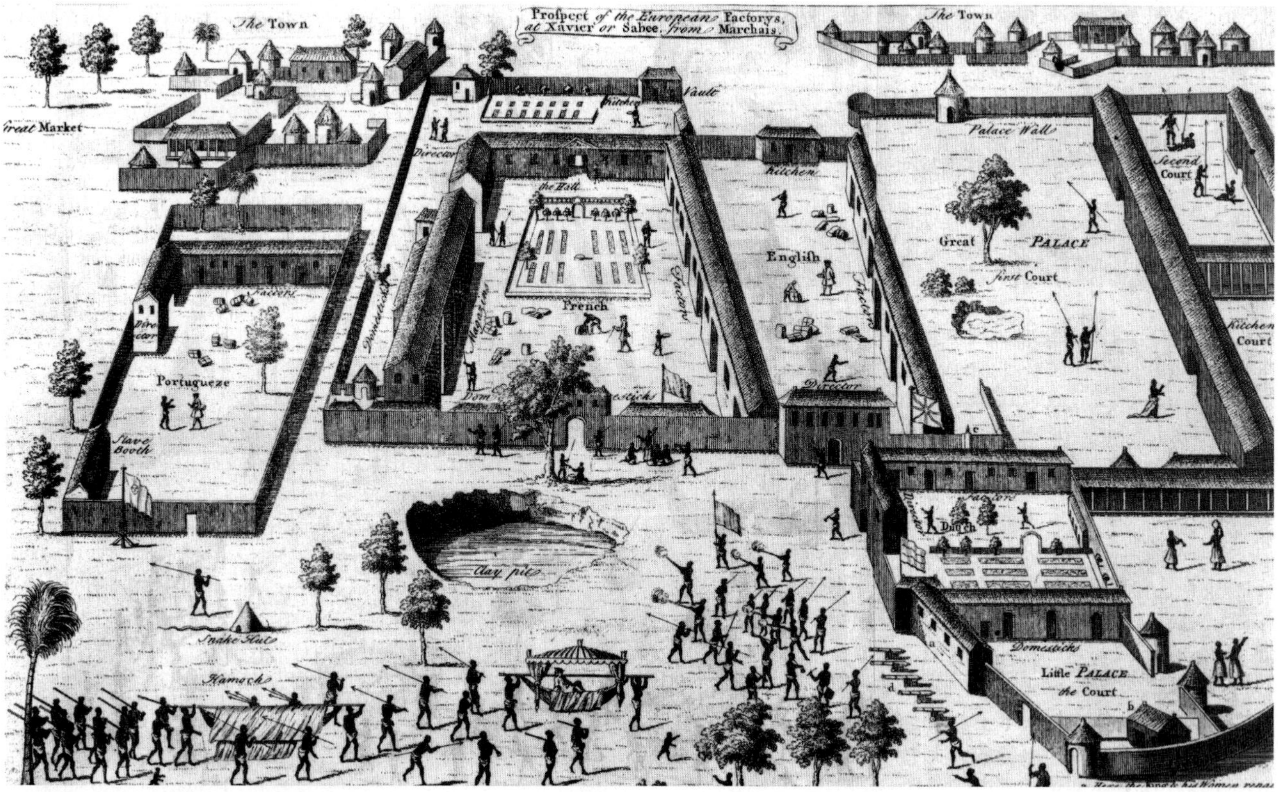

This drawing is the layout of a European slave-trading center in West Africa in the mid-eighteenth century.

Africans. Many adopted European dress, and a few were lionized in Europe or became Christian missionaries. Some found work as guides, clerks, or interpreters, while others developed trading networks or participated actively in the slave trade. For example, Mae Aurelia Correia, the African wife of a Portuguese army captain posted to Portuguese Guinea, supplemented her husband's meager wages by venturing into the slave trade as well as by establishing peanut plantations that relied on slave labor. Most European traders were not so successful. Plagued by an unhealthy climate and surrounded by suspicious inhabitants, they led short and dreary lives in their remote exiles.

Most slaves awaiting shipment in West African barracoons had been kidnapped or taken in war by other rival tribes, although some were sold by their tribe or family to pay off debts, as punishment for breaking laws, or in times of famine and hunger. Only a few were seized directly by white raiders. Slaves were usually forcibly marched to the coast in gangs, chained or roped together, and worn down by poor food, lack of water, unattended illnesses, and brutal beatings. Once in the barracoons, where they might stay for several months, they were stripped and examined for physical defects by ship doctors and then displayed before captains who were looking to buy their cargoes. The bargaining was hard and complex as slaves were exchanged for cloth (Indian textiles were preferred because they were durable and their colors did not run in hot climates), manufactured goods, bar iron, agricultural implements, alcohol, and firearms and gunpowder.

About twice as many men as women were enslaved and shipped abroad. The traditional explanation for this imbalance is that men brought the highest prices in overseas markets because they could cope with the physical demands imposed on plantation laborers. But recent research has shown that women were just as likely to be assigned the harshest field work and that they fetched roughly the same prices as men. An important reason more women slaves were kept in Africa was that they were more desired as domestic slaves in royal households, as concubines, and as agricultural laborers, and that they were less likely to resist. The British Royal African Company reinforced this imbalance by issuing a standing order to their ship captains to purchase two males for every female.

After spending time in the barracoons, slaves met a worse nightmare during the notorious **Middle Passage,** the voyage that typically took a month from

Middle Passage—The collective name applied to the shipment of African slaves across the Atlantic throughout the time of the Atlantic slave trade. The voyage at sea generally took one to two months, depending on the destination, and most slaves were confined within the ship's hold. Mortality rates for the slaves ranged as high as 20 percent.

Africa to Brazil and two months to the Caribbean and the United States. Slaves were separated according to age and gender. Women usually huddled together on a ship's open deck. To prevent rebellions, male slaves were chained together in pairs, in lower decks, each person allotted a space 16 inches wide by 30 inches high. Children, who made up about 10 percent of slaves, were placed in separate quarters.

The treatment of slaves was abominable. White crews frequently resorted to threats of violence and lashings to control slaves. Slaves who contracted diseases were frequently thrown overboard. When slaves refused to eat, a special device, the *speculum oris* or "mouth opener," was used to force-feed them. Some slaves jumped into the sea while being exercised. In 1694 the British captain of the *Hannibal* commented on the despondency of slaves in these conditions: "The negroes are so wilful and loth to leave their own country, that they have often leap'd out of the canoes, boats and ships, into the sea, and kept under water till they were drowned to avoid being taken up and saved by our boats. . . ."[1]

Through the early seventeenth century, the cramped and unsanitary conditions and poor diets of slaves on board led to mortality rates of as many as 20 percent on each voyage. Most died from the dehydration caused by gastrointestinal illnesses such as dysentery and communicable diseases such as smallpox and fevers. With improved diets and quicker crossings, the mortality rate dropped to less than 10 percent by the end of the eighteenth century. European crews on these voyages did not fare any better. Because of diseases such as malaria and yellow fever that they contracted off the African coast, their mortality rate was almost as high as the slaves.

Over 300 slave mutinies took place during the Middle Passage. Most occurred shortly after ships left the African coast. Most of them failed, and rebels were punished with savage brutality. In 1797 women slaves on the *Thomas* rebelled a few days before the ship was due to land in Barbados. As they were exercising on deck, they seized guns from an unlocked musket closet and took control of the ship. After freeing the rest of the slaves, they were no closer to freedom because none of them knew how to sail the ship. The ship drifted for more than a month until a British warship captured the slaves and resold them into slavery.

The harsh conditions of the Middle Passage did not shake the Christian faith of slave ship captains, who stood to pocket from 2 to 5 percent of the proceeds from slaves they sold. "This day," British slave trader John Newton confided to his journal in 1752, "I have reason . . . to beg a public blessing from Almighty God upon our voyage. . . ." After four voyages, however, Newton underwent a dramatic conversion and left slaving for the ministry. His legacy is his moving hymn of atonement, "Amazing Grace."

DOCUMENT
"A Defense of the Slave Trade"

The era after the Peace of Utrecht has been termed the slave century. Between 1600 and 1700, when the slave-trading companies were mostly state-chartered monopolies, some 1.5 million slaves were carried across the Atlantic. During the next century when much more trade was being conducted by individual captains outside the forts, more than 6 million slaves were taken to the Americas. With higher prices for slaves on Caribbean sugar plantations fueling demand, the trade peaked in the 1780s when 750,000 Africans were taken from West and Central Africa.

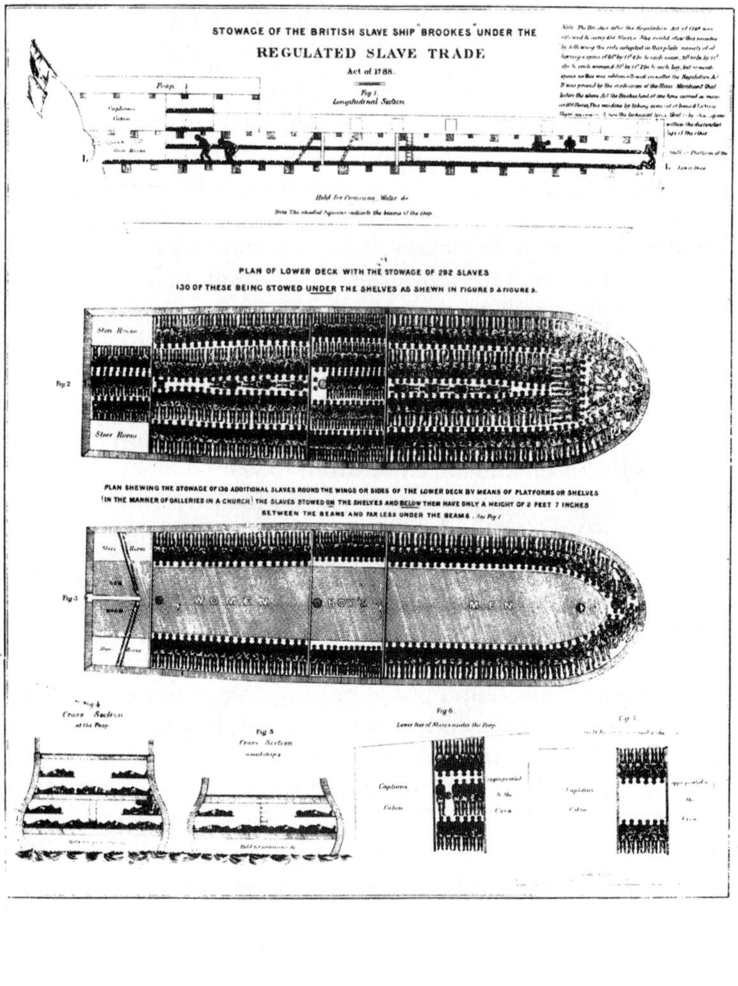

This diagram shows how slaves were packed into cargo holds for the notorious Middle Passage to the Americas. The plan was a model of efficiency as slave traders sought to maximize profits by filling their ships up to and beyond capacity.

Document A Slave's Memoir

Kidnapped into slavery when he was eleven, Olaudah Equiano was taken by British slavers first to Barbados and then to Virginia. Sold to a Quaker businessman from Philadelphia, he eventually purchased his freedom. In later life, he became an antislavery campaigner in England, and he published a best-selling autobiography in the late 1780s that dramatized the horrors of the slave trade.

The first object which saluted my eyes when I arrived on the coast was the sea, and a slave ship which was then riding at anchor and waiting for its cargo. These filled me with astonishment, which was soon converted into terror when I was carried on board. I was immediately handled and tossed up to see if I were sound by some of the crew, and I was now persuaded that I had gotten into a world of bad spirits and that they were going to kill me. Their complexions too differing so much from ours, their long hair and the language they spoke (which was very different from any I had ever heard) united to confirm me in this belief. Indeed such were the horrors of my views and fears at the moment that, if ten thousand worlds had been my own, I would have freely parted with them all to have exchanged my condition with that of the meanest slave in my own country. When I looked around the ship too and saw a large furnace or copper boiling and a multitude of black people of every description chained together, every one of their countenances expressing dejection and sorrow, I no longer doubted my fate; and quite overpowered with horror and anguish, I fell motionless on the deck and fainted. When I recovered a little I found some black people about me, who I believed were some of those who had brought me on board and had been receiving their pay; they talked to me in order to cheer me, but all in vain. I asked them if we were not to be eaten by those white men with horrible looks, red faces, and loose hair. They told me I was not, and one of the crew brought me a small portion of spirituous liquor in a wine glass, but being afraid of him I would not take it out of his hand.

The stench of the hold while we were on the coast was so intolerably loathsome that it was dangerous to remain there for any time, and some of us had been permitted to stay on the deck for the fresh air; but now that the whole ship's cargo were confined together it became absolutely pestilential. The closeness of the place and the heat of the climate, added to the number in the ship, which was so crowded that each had scarcely room to run himself, almost suffocated us. This produced copious perspirations, so that the air soon became unfit for respiration from a variety of loathsome smells, and brought on a sickness among the slaves, of which many died, thus falling victims to the improvident avarice, as I may call it, of their purchasers. This wretched situation was again aggravated by the galling of the chains, now become insupportable, and the filth of the necessary tubs, into which the children often fell and were almost suffocated. The shrieks of the women and the groans of the dying rendered the whole a scene of horror almost inconceivable. Happily perhaps for myself I was soon reduced so low here that it was thought necessary to keep me almost always on deck, and from my extreme youth I was not put in fetters.

Questions to Consider

1. What effect did the deplorable conditions on the slave ship have on the psychology of the slaves?
2. What impact do you think Equiano's description of conditions on the slave ship might have had on the campaign in England to abolish slavery?

From Paul Edwards, ed., *Equiano's Travels: His Autobiography, The Interesting Narrative of the Life of Olaudah Equiano or Gustavus Vassa the African* (London: Heinemann Educational Books, 1967).

DOCUMENT
An African Pamphleteer Attacks Slavery

Denmark was the first European state to end the slave trade in 1803, but it was Britain's decision to abolish the trade four years later that had the most far-reaching consequences. The ideals of the Enlightenment, in addition to the lobbying efforts of abolitionist movements in England, had prepared the way for this act, but even more decisive factors were the declining profitability of Britain's Caribbean plantations, a rise in the price of slaves, and pressures from British industrialists, who found it more profitable to invest in wage labor in European factories than in the sugar plantations. Although a British squadron did patrol the Atlantic after 1807, looking for slavers, the slave trade was not dramatically affected. Around that time, however, West Africans began making adjustments to their trading relations with the outside world.

There was more to the Atlantic exchange than the trafficking in human beings. Africa's population was still expanding despite the devastation of the slave trade. New foods imported from the Americas, such as manioc (cassava), which could be grown in poor soils in forested areas, and maize (corn), soon became staples because they could contribute many more calories to people's diets than other mainstays, such as sorghum and millet. Europeans also introduced oranges, lemon, limes, pineapples, groundnuts (peanuts), and guavas to the African continent. In return, yams (sweet potatoes, which were the main provision for slaves on slave ships), sorghum, plantains, bananas, and melegueta pepper ("grains of paradise") made their way from Africa to the Americas. Groundnuts, which had come from South America, had made their way to the lower Congo region, where local people gave it the name *nguba*. After slaves from this area transplanted *nguba* to the Caribbean, peanuts were then taken to North America, where it was known as the "goober pea."

Whatever its unintended consequences, the Atlantic slave trade was a degrading experience for all the Europeans, Arabs, and Africans who participated in it. An estimated 12 million people were lost to Africa through the Atlantic slave trade over three centuries, and this number does not include the hundreds of thousands of slaves who died en route from their point of capture to the slave ports, in the cramped barracoons, and in the "floating tombs" that transported slaves to the New World.

African States and the Atlantic Slave Trade

Forms of domestic slavery were practiced in most African societies. Slaves were part of households and worked with the master's family in chores and agricultural labor. The slave status did not last long, and slaves were usually freed within one to two generations. In centralized states, more demands were imposed on slaves, who lived in separate quarters and were less likely to end their bondage through **manumission.** As the demand for slaves from plantations across the Atlantic escalated, African societies were confronted with the choice of whether or not to participate. Although some refused to participate, others seized advantage of the heightened demand for slaves to amass more power by investing in firearms and horses.

DOCUMENT
Mungo Park, "Slavery in Africa"

One example was the Yoruba kingdom of Oyo, situated inland on the savanna. Drawing on revenues derived from the slave trade, the Oyo *alafin* or king traded for horses from the north and assembled a cavalry that conquered the savanna region to the southwest all the way to the coast. Oyo's royal farms were tilled by slaves captured in warfare and the Sahelian slave trade, but as Oyo's rulers tapped into the Atlantic trade, surplus slaves were sold to European traders in exchange for firearms, cloth, and **cowrie shells,** which were a widespread form of currency in West Africa.

The *alafin* was not an absolute ruler. He governed with the advice of a seven-man council of state, the *oyo mesi,* and they in turn were overseen by a secret society of religious and political notables. If the *alafin* lost the backing of his counselors, they could force him to commit suicide. A turning point in Oyo's history came in the late eighteenth century when a senior counselor in the *oyo mesi* usurped the authority of the *alafin*. This bid for power set off a period of instability and internal revolts by tributary states and the Sokoto Caliphate (SOH-ko-to) that led to Oyo's collapse by the 1830s.

Of all the West African states, Dahomey (dah-HOH-may), located west of the Oyo kingdom, was particularly affected by the slave trade. Although a tributary state to Oyo for many years, Dahomey managed to maintain its autonomy, and in the mid-seventeenth century, it became a major power in its own right when its authoritarian rulers created a highly centralized state. Power revolved around the king, who passed his throne directly to his eldest son and appointed local chiefs who did not come from an established lineage. An influential figure in the palace was the queen mother, who was usually chosen from a recently conquered territory. Her presence helped to integrate her people with the king; she played a pivotal role in selecting a new king.

The royal elite rigidly monopolized the slave trade and every aspect of the economy. Everyone was required to perform military service, even women, who provided an elite palace guard and who, in the early nineteenth century, served as a key regiment in major wars against Dahomey's rivals, including Oyo. As a way of balancing power with male officials, the king allocated offices and responsibilities to the 5000 to 6000 women known as *ahosi* who served the royal court. Some were wives captured in warfare; some were wives provided by different lineages; and some were slaves. Although the legal status of female slaves

manumission—The practice of freeing slaves from bondage. Conditions in Africa for granting freedom might include a female slave who bears a child by her master or a slave buying freedom from a master for an agreed-upon price.

cowrie shells—The cowrie, a marine gastropod, is common in the Indian Ocean, particularly around the Maldive Islands. Used as a currency in West Africa, cowrie shells were but one trade item offered by Europeans in exchange for slaves.

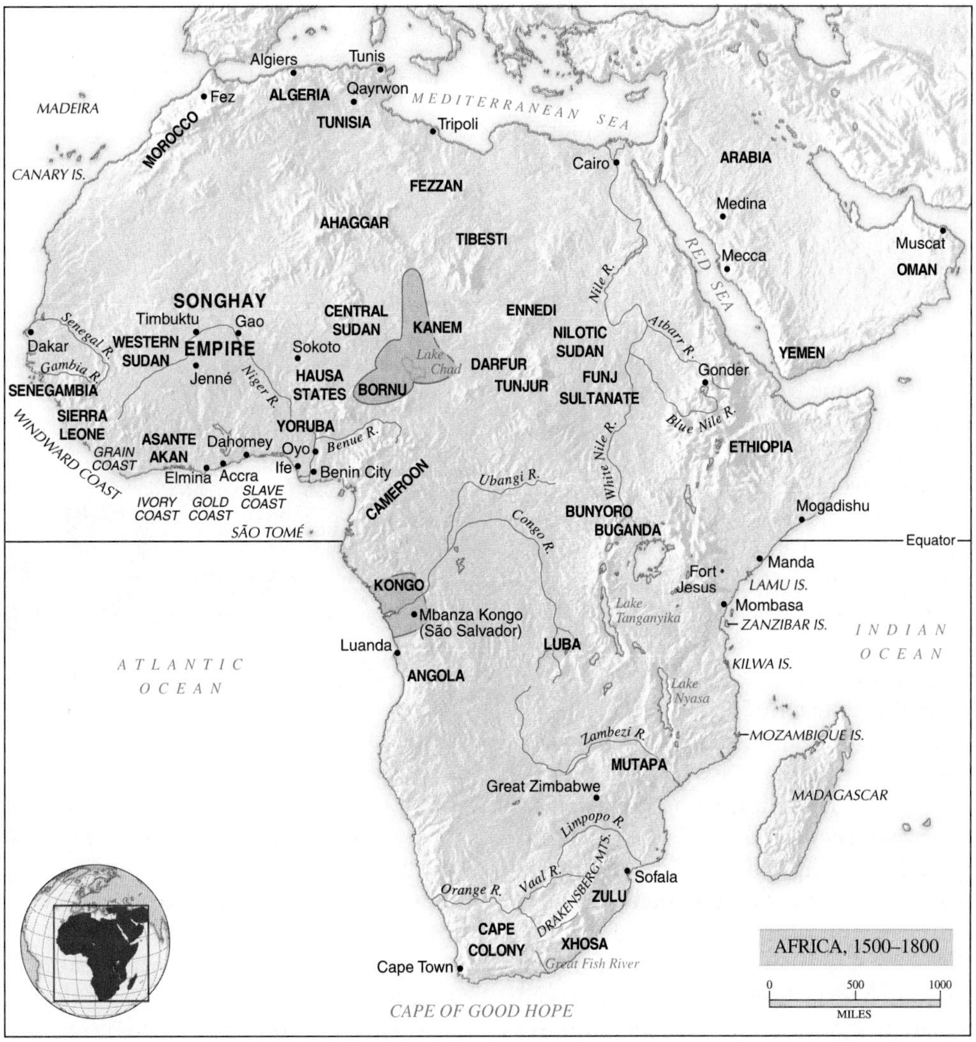

From 1500 to 1800, Africans lived under a variety of political systems, ranging from small-scale societies to expansive monarchies. Powerful kingdoms emerged in every region.

was fixed, they were allowed to accumulate wealth and to assume many roles, including managing the king's resources, trading, owning private property, and serving as soldiers and ministers of state. Because of their unquestioned loyalty to the throne, female slaves were regularly appointed to the highest offices, including that of the queen mother, who did not have to be related to the king.

Another prominent regional state was Asante, a kingdom founded by Akan peoples in the gold-producing forests of the Gold Coast interior. Akan peoples had formed states based on the trade in gold, kola nuts, and slaves to the north and gold, slaves, and ivory to the Portuguese on the coast. But in the late seventeenth century, the Akan states were absorbed into the Asante kingdom, founded by *Asantehene* (king) Osei Tutu (OH-say too-too; d. 1717). Ruling from his capital at Kumasi, Osei Tutu transformed a loose confederation into a centralized state. He boosted his authority by using a consultative body, the Kotoko Council, and the Akan judicial system. He adopted the Golden Stool as the unifying symbol of Asante kingship and identity. When Osei Tutu died in battle, his successor, Opoku Ware (c. 1720–1750), extended Asante's boundaries to the savanna regions in the north and to the fringes of the forests in the south. As many as three million people lived within its dominion. The wars of expansion from the 1680s on were major factors in Asante's involvement in the Atlantic slave trade. Slaves captured in war or sent as tribute by conquered territories were deployed in gold mines and food-producing plantations or assimilated into families. However, once the Asante kingdom began selling slaves to European traders, its revenues from slave sales eventually eclipsed the proceeds from the gold trade.

The southwest coast, from the Congo River to the Cunene River, was the largest source of slaves for

Queen Njinga of the Ndongo kingdom of Angola negotiated a treaty with the Portuguese in 1622. When an African had an audience before a Portuguese official, the African was normally expected to stand. Queen Njinga, however, ordered a female servant to kneel on all fours and sat on her back.

the transatlantic trade. Roughly 40 percent of all slaves taken during the slave trade era came from this region. Although Dutch and British slavers were active in the area, Portuguese involvement in the Kongo kingdom's affairs was particularly intrusive. The kingdom witnessed civil strife throughout much of the seventeenth century. The Portuguese took advantage of the disorder to invade Kongo in 1685, leaving the central government in shambles and fragmenting the kingdom into ministates.

A movement to restore stability and cohesion to the kingdom was inspired by Kimpa Vita (known to the Portuguese as Doña Beatrice), a woman of noble birth. As a teenager she claimed to have died and been reborn and to have been possessed by the spirit of St. Anthony in 1702. Her Antonian movement combined Kongo and Christian beliefs. She preached a personal religious experience that did not rely on Catholic priests, and her acolytes advocated the reunification of the kingdom under a king that she would choose. Although her message was very popular among peasants who longed for peace, it threatened Capuchin priests and royal factions vying for the kingship. After her opponents captured her, she was tried and convicted of treason and heresy and burned at the stake in 1706.

The Angolan hinterland suffered even more than the Kongo, and rulers had to maneuver constantly to protect their sovereignty. Queen Anna Njinga (c. 1581–1663) of the Ndongo kingdom was a survivor who was prepared to deal with most anyone. Succeeding her brother in 1618 in a kingdom that did not have a tradition of female sovereigns, she had to fend off hostile lineage groups that traditionally chose kings. To counter their opposition she signed a treaty with the Portuguese in 1622 that allowed slave traders to operate in her kingdom, and she converted to Catholicism. However, Portuguese support was short-lived, and Queen Njinga, who led her troops into battle, organized a spirited resistance. She also moved east, resuscitating the nearby Matamba kingdom and taking advantage of their recognition of queens as rulers. Proceeds from slave trading gave her the resources to build up an army. When the Dutch entered Angola in 1641, she seized an opportunity to break free from the Portuguese and allied with the Dutch. However, after the Portuguese counterattacked with troops from Brazil, she negotiated another treaty with Portuguese officials in 1656 that opened her kingdom to Catholic missionaries and to Portuguese slavers in return for Portuguese recognition of her rule.

The Portuguese eventually conquered Ndongo and other kingdoms. When Brazil's sugar plantations required massive numbers of slave laborers in the 1600s, the Portuguese, operating from their coastal ports of Luanda and Benguela, turned Angola into a vast slave-hunting preserve. Armed bands of Portuguese mercenaries regularly intervened in conflicts in African kingdoms, while the kingdoms of Kasanje, Matamba, and Ovimbundu (OH-vim-BOON-doo) assisted the Portuguese by trading or raiding for slaves in remote inland areas.

THE END OF THE SLAVE TRADE IN WEST AFRICA

- *What changes took place in African societies as the Atlantic slave trade came to an end?*

On the West African coast, African societies were adapting to the tapering off of the Atlantic slave trade. Britain, which in the late 1700s was responsible for more than half of the slaves exported from Africa, and the United States had abolished the slave trade in 1807. Other European nations followed suit in subsequent decades. A British antislavery squadron patrolled the West and East African coasts, intercepting slave ships. Although the antislavery squadron managed to free about 160,000 slaves, it was a fraction of the overall slave trade. Between 1807 and 1888, close to 3 million more Africans were enslaved and shipped overseas, largely to sugar, coffee, and cotton plantations in Cuba and Brazil (see pp. 734, 736).

Britain and France established colonies in Sierra Leone and Gabon respectively for freed slaves. Sierra Leone's capital, Freetown, became the center for assimilating Africans from West, Central, and even East Africa and created a Krio or Creole community. A significant number of Krios were Yorubas who had been sold into slavery as a result of Oyo's wars. Some were Muslims who established mosques in Freetown. Others were among the first to take advantage of mission schools and to convert to Christianity. Some became missionaries in their own right. Samuel Crowther returned to his Yoruba homeland, and rose to become Bishop of the Anglican Church. Other Krios applied their entrepreneurial skills and knowledge to establish an extensive coastal trading network and tap into the legitimate trade.

Freed African-American slaves were settled in a territory established by the **American Colonization Society** (ACS) for former slaves that wished to return voluntarily to Africa and for blacks captured on slave ships by the American antislavery squadron. The ACS selected a strip of territory in the Cape Mesurado area and pressured local Africans into ceding them the land. However, the black settlers who landed after 1821 had a difficult time adjusting. They were susceptible to diseases and looked down their noses at agriculture. When they declared themselves independent from the ACS and founded Liberia (from the Latin word liber, "free") in 1847, their population numbered only a few thousand.

The Americo-Liberians (as the settlers came to be called) patterned themselves on the United States, adopting the English language and a constitution based on the U.S. model and naming their capital Monrovia (after President James Monroe). Although their official motto was "Love of Liberty Brought Us Here," they did not extend freedom to indigenous Africans, who were regarded as uncivilized and backward. A caste system developed in which Americo-Liberians dominated politics and exploited the labor of indigenous Africans, who were not allowed to qualify for citizenship until 1904. Although Liberia's economy sputtered in the face of intense competition with European traders and the civil service was riddled with corruption, Liberia managed to survive the European scramble for Africa and to remain an independent republic through the colonial period.

DOCUMENT
The History of Mary Prince

African societies involved in the transatlantic slave trade adjusted to its winding down in various ways. Some societies were so dependent on slave exports that they found it difficult to cope. Other societies shifted from exporting slaves to trading for more domestic slaves. The Asante kingdom in the Gold Coast acquired more domestic slaves to increase gold and kola nut production for trading with Europeans and the West African interior.

For many societies, the slave trade had been a negligible part of their overall trade, and African entrepreneurs and European merchants expanded their trading links. One African export Europeans sought was gum arabic, extracted from acacia trees and used for dyes in European textile factories. Another was palm oil, a key ingredient in candles and soap and the main lubricant for Europe's industrial machinery before the discovery of petroleum oil. Peanuts (called groundnuts) and latex were also important exports.

This shift to "legitimate" commerce did not necessarily lead to improvements or opportunities in the lives of many Africans. There was an increased demand for domestic slaves to till fields for certain products as well as porters to carry goods to the coast. Along the coast east of the Niger delta, where palm oil was a major export, palm oil production was organized on gender lines: Men cut down the nuts from trees, and women extracted the oil. Although the male heads of households were the main beneficiaries of palm oil production, they gave women the proceeds from palm kernels. The demand for palm kernel oil escalated in the 1880s when William Lever began selling Sunlight, a sweet-smelling soap made from palm kernel oil and coconut oil, to a mass market in England. Some women entrepreneurs used the profits from palm kernel sales to expand their involvement in palm oil production. However, the most important beneficiaries of the trade were not the producers but the rulers and merchants. In the Niger River delta, towns vying for control of the trade fought a series of wars.

ISLAMIC AFRICA

- *What explains the rapid expansion of Islam in the West African Sudan in the eighteenth and nineteenth centuries?*

American Colonization Society—An organization founded in the United States in 1816 to promote the emigration of free African Americans to a settlement along the coast of West Africa that eventually was known as Liberia.

At the end of the eighteenth century, Islam remained a vibrant force in certain regions of Africa. Muslim West Africa was beginning to experience a cultural revival and was expanding its following beyond traders and rulers. Islam was carried by a wave of religious zeal, which arose on the Senegal River and spread east across the savanna regions to Guinea and the Hausa states and to the upper Nile. In East Africa, however, Islam remained a coastal religion with limited appeal beyond the Swahili city-states.

Meanwhile, across the continent in the west, Morocco was under the control of a dynasty that established itself in 1631 and remains in power today. Sultan Mulay Ismail (1672–1727) corresponded with Louis XIV of France and sent an ambassador to the court of Charles II in England. His uncontested power was based on a large standing army, including a force of black slaves who were recruited or captured in the Sudan as children and trained for specialized tasks. The sultan proved himself an exceptionally competent administrator, a wily military commander, and a patron of the arts. Morocco's economy was based on a combination of agriculture, trade, and privateering, although its piratic activity was minor compared to that of Algiers and Tunis. Under Mulay Ismail's successors, Morocco prospered. It was not integrated into the Islamic heartlands but remained connected to them by long-standing traditions of commercial and intellectual exchange. Each year Moroccan pilgrims and scholars made their ways by land and sea to the shrines of Mecca and to the great academic institutions of the Middle East.

In the West African savanna region, Muslim states had languished as the trans-Saharan gold trade declined after 1650. The Moroccan conquest in 1591 had broken the Songhay Empire into many rival small kingdoms, but as Moroccan administrators intermarried with local people, their ties with Morocco weakened. The Moroccans themselves were displaced by the Tuaregs, another group of desert invaders, in 1737.

The region around Lake Chad was the center of one of the region's most important states, Kanem-Bornu, which became an important center of Islamic learning. The high point of Bornu's power was during the reign of *Mai* (king) Idris Aloma (c. 1542–c. 1619). After being exposed to the wider Muslim world on a pilgrimage to Mecca, he imported firearms from North Africa and employed Turkish musketeers and advisers to command his army. To lessen the possibility of revolt, which had plagued his predecessors, he placed trusted allies, rather than close relatives, in key positions around his kingdom. For over a century, Kanem-Bornu exerted a stabilizing force in the region around Lake Chad, but its power steadily waned during the eighteenth century. By that time, the Hausa city-states, notably Kano, Katsina, and Gobir, were becoming prominent, as they profited from the expanding trade in slaves now moving across the central Sahara to the Mediterranean.

In West Africa the political map of the interior savanna dramatically changed in the eighteenth century as Fulani Muslim holy men launched a series of jihads and established new Muslim states across the region: Fulani-Tukolor kingdoms along the Senegal River in the west, the Sokoto Caliphate among the Hausa states and the sultanates of Tunjur, Darfur, and Funj in the region south of Egypt.

In the west, Islam rapidly spread through a series of successful holy wars led by Fulani holy men who criticized the lax moralities and heretical policies of West African Muslims, particularly the rulers. The Fulani were cattle-keepers who, by the fifteenth century, had spread across the West African savanna, often pasturing their herds in regions controlled by farming societies. In the highlands of Futa Jalon, the Fulani chafed at their Jalonke rulers' taxation and restrictions on pasture land. In 1725, they joined with Muslim traders and clerics to launch a *jihad* that by 1776 brought the area under Muslim and Fulani domination. Because of the war, slave raiding increased, and many captives were sold to work on local plantations or to European slavers at the Senegambian coast. In Futa Toro, in the middle valley of the Senegal River, other Fulani reformers joined with Tukolor Muslims to wage another *jihad*. They claimed that the Fulani elite had strayed from the Muslim faith, and they aimed to reestablish a kingdom based on Islamic law.

Their efforts inspired Fulani Muslims in the eastern Sudan—the most notable being Usman dan Fodio (1754–1817), son of a Muslim teacher and himself a scholar of some repute. When he began preaching in 1774, he stressed the fundamental principles of living a disciplined and devout Muslim life. Several decades later he began denouncing Muslim rulers in his home state of Gobir for ignoring Sharia law, for enslaving other Muslims, and for tolerating what he perceived to be immoral practices such as public dancing and the playing of drums and fiddles. Because his criticisms drew the ire of Gobir's ruling elite, he and his followers decided to leave for a safe haven to the west. When a Hausa ruler lifted the exemption of Muslims from taxes, Usman mobilized his students, Fulani pastoralists, and Hausa peasants and declared a holy war against Hausa rulers in 1804. Usman's movement succeeded in overthrowing most of the Hausa states and unifying them into the centralized Sokoto Caliphate. This new state, with a capital at Sokoto on the lower Niger, encompassed several hundred thousand square miles.

Usman was Caliph, while his brother Abdullahi and son Muhammad Bello (1781–1837) consolidated the caliphate. Usman retired in 1817 and Muhammad

Bello succeeded him. Sokoto's rulers introduced a government based on Muslim administrative structures and were patrons of Muslim scholarship and schools. Although a Hausa aristocracy was replaced by a Fulani nobility, the latter allowed Hausa political and religious elites in the emirates a measure of local autonomy as long as they paid an annual tribute and recognized the caliph's political and religious authority.

Usman dan Fodio's revolution brought mixed results for women. He encouraged education among elite women and supported women who disobeyed husbands who did not educate them. His wives and daughters were educated and became noted for their writings. However, women were expected to remain in seclusion and were excluded from meaningful roles in elite decision-making. The queen mother *(magajiya)* lost her power to veto decisions by male rulers and found her influence restricted to ritual matters.

The creation of the Sokoto Caliphate made little difference to the Hausa peasantry and slaves who served in households and tilled the fields of large plantations. Although elite women were freed up from agricultural production and expanded their production of indigo-dyed cloth, they were replaced in the fields by female slaves imported into the Caliphate. Hausa traders maintained their prosperous links with Tripoli to the north and the Atlantic coast. Their trade items included kola nuts, grain, salt, slaves, cattle, and cloth, which made their way to countries as far away as Egypt and Brazil.

AFRICANS AND EUROPEAN SETTLEMENT IN SOUTHERN AFRICA

▪ *What was the impact of European settlement on African societies in southern Africa?*

While tropical diseases such as malaria prevented Europeans from permanently settling in many parts of Africa, southern Africa had a temperate climate that made it possible for first the Dutch and then the English to establish colonies of trade and settlement in the Cape. Although the Dutch settlers later created a myth that the region south of the Limpopo River was unsettled and thus open to whoever could claim it (see p. 577), the area had been populated for many centuries by indigenous African societies with varied economies and political systems. They vigorously resisted the expansion of European settlers into the interior.

The earliest inhabitants of southern Africa were San (SAHN) hunters and gatherers and Khoikhoi (koi-koi), hunters and gatherers who had taken up sheep and cattle-keeping. These were followed by Bantu-speaking groups that crossed the Limpopo River around the third century of the Common Era. These groups relied on mixed agriculture and herding cattle and sheep for their livelihoods. As they migrated into different parts of the region, the Bantu-speaking societies divided into two linguistic subfamilies. The Nguni (Swazi, Zulu, and Xhosa) largely settled to the east of the Drakensberg mountain range and spread down the Indian Ocean coast as far south as the Great Fish River, the point where the summer rainfall was insufficient for their agriculture. As this strip of land was hilly and well watered by rainfall coming off the ocean, Nguni families established scattered homesteads and formed small clan-based chiefdoms. Although splits in ruling families were common, as long as land was plentiful, factions could break away and form their own chiefdoms. The other Bantu-speaking group, the Sotho/Tswana (SOO-too/TSWAH-nah), populated the drier, rolling plains west of the Drakensberg Mountains. Because the grasslands were sparse, Sotho/Tswana cattle-keepers managed their scarce resources by clustering in villages and pasturing their cattle in outlying areas. Those nearest the Kalahari Desert created extensive villages, some containing as many as 10,000 to 20,000 people.

Small groups of Khoikhoi that inhabited the southwestern Cape were the first to make contact with European seafarers. In the late sixteenth century, Portuguese and English ships on the long voyage to India and Southeast Asia began making the harbor at Table Bay a regular stopover for rest and replenishment. Because they needed a reliable source of fresh meat, Europeans depended on the Khoikhoi, who were usually willing to part with their old and sick cattle, in exchange for iron, copper, tobacco, and beads.

The English and Portuguese were followed by the Dutch East India Company, which founded a permanent settlement at Table Bay in 1652. European settlers encountered a mix of African societies that had populated the region for many centuries. Because the company's primary goal was providing meat, fruits, and vegetables for its employees, its first governor, Jan van Riebeeck, had strict instructions to avoid friction and win the cooperation of the Khoikhoi. Only a few years later, however, the company made several fateful decisions that led to clashes with Khoikhoi bands.

Because their fruit and vegetable gardens did not yield enough, in 1657, the company allowed some of its soldiers to establish their own farms a short distance from the main company settlement. Dependent on its cattle trade with the Khoikhoi, the company decided to import slaves from elsewhere to work the farms. The first batches of slaves came from western and central Africa, but, thereafter, the company turned to the Indian Ocean for most. The majority of slaves came from Mozambique and Madagascar, while the rest were brought over from India, Malaya, and Indonesia.

Over the next 150 years the Dutch colony, populated by a mix of Dutch, German, and Scandinavian settlers and Huguenot refugees fleeing persecution in France, developed a distinctive character. Company officials and personnel made up an elite at Cape Town; a second group included slaveholders whose plantations in the Cape Town vicinity produced fruit and wine; and a third group, the Boers (*boer* is the Dutch word for "farmer"; the settlers did not begin calling themselves Afrikaners until the late nineteenth century), consisted of migratory pastoralists called ***trekboers***. By 1800 there were about 21,000 Europeans in the colony, compared to a slave population of about 25,000.

The gradual expansion of company farms into the interior alarmed the Khoikhoi, who saw their grazing lands threatened by Dutch takeover. As wars broke out with Khoikhoi groups in the Cape peninsula, the trekboers steadily began conquering Khoikhoi territory farther and farther from the company settlement.

Boer families lived a pastoral lifestyle, relying largely on their own resources and preferring infrequent contact with company officials in Cape Town. Boer men believed that it was their birthright to stake out farms of around 6000 acres apiece. They expected their sons to claim other farms of the same size, usually at the expense of indigenous people. By 1800 the Boers had extended the colony's boundaries 300 miles north and 500 miles east along the Indian Ocean coast.

For most of the eighteenth century, Khoikhoi and San bands resisted Boer expansion by carrying on guerrilla skirmishing. The Khoikhoi and San groups that wanted to maintain their autonomy migrated farther into the interior; others, who lost their herds, supplemented the slave population as servants or apprentices to Boers. White settlers began to refer to Dutch-speaking Khoikhoi and San, freed slaves, and mixed-race servants as "Cape Coloureds."

The Boers' first contacts with Xhosa chiefdoms were at the Great Fish River in the early 1700s. Although they initially worked out a mutually beneficial trading relationship, as more Boers moved into Xhosa territory, conflicts erupted, largely over land and cattle. The first war between the two groups broke out in 1779. Over the next century, eight more were to take place between Xhosa chiefdoms and Europeans. Unlike the small Khoikhoi and San bands, which lacked unity, Xhosa farmers outnumbered the Boers and lived in chiefdoms prepared to defend their land vigorously. Moreover, the Boers' advantage in armaments was slight. Two wars between Xhosa and Boers ended in stalemates, broken only by the entrance of the British into the Cape in 1795.

When France invaded the Netherlands in 1795, the British responded to an appeal by the Dutch royal house and colonized the Cape. Controlling the sea route around the Cape of Good Hope also allowed the British to protect the passage to India. After handing control of the Cape back to the Dutch in 1803, the British returned several years later and established a dominant presence in the Cape and southern Africa for the next century. The British were primarily interested in increased commercial ties with the Cape by expanding wine and wool production. The British relationship with European farmers who actively participated in the market economy was more amicable than that with Boer cattlekeepers, who kept their involvement in the market economy to a minimum. Throughout the nineteenth century, British strategic and economic interests would repeatedly clash with the desires of Boer pastoralists to maintain their independent lifestyle.

African State Formation

In the first decades of the nineteenth century, African societies in southeastern Africa were swept up in a period of political transformation known as the ***Mfecane*** ("the scattering"). Its origins can be traced to increased competition by chiefdoms for grazing land following a series of severe droughts and for control of first the ivory and then the cattle trade with the Portuguese at Delagoa Bay. However, it was the Zulu clan, a minor actor when the Mfecane began, that became the region's most formidable military power.

The Zulu owed their rise in prominence to their king, Shaka (c. 1786–1828). When he was born about 1786, his father was chief of the Zulu clan, which was later part of the Mthethwa (im-TE-twah) Confederacy ruled by Dingiswayo (DEEN-gis-WAI-yoh; c. 1770s–1816). When Shaka's father rejected his mother, Shaka was forced to spend his childhood among his mother's people. As a young man, he enrolled in one of Dingiswayo's fighting regiments. Young men of about 16 to 18 traditionally went to circumcision schools for a number of months to prepare themselves for manhood. Because Dingiswayo needed soldiers who could be called into battle on short notice, he abolished the circumcision schools and enrolled his young men directly into regiments.

Shaka soon distinguished himself as a warrior, and he rose rapidly in Dingiswayo's army. On his father's death in 1815, Shaka assumed the chieftaincy of the Zulu. Shaka assumed the chieftaincy of the Zulu on his

trekboers—Migrant farmers who moved eastward from the Cape of Good Hope in the eighteenth century.

Mfecane—A term that historians use to describe a period of heightened warfare and state formation in the early nineteenth century in southern Africa.

Print of Shaka, King of the Zulus. Shaka established a major kingdom based on innovations in battle tactics and weaponry.

father's death in 1815 and became leader of the entire confederacy a few years later, after Dingiswayo was killed in a trap laid by enemies. He regrouped his followers and won over others; eventually, he vanquished his opponents. He then began constructing, primarily by cattle raiding, a major kingdom between the Phongolo and Tugela rivers that dominated southeastern Africa.

Shaka was best known for adopting new weapons and battle strategies that revolutionized warfare. He armed the Zulu army with a short stabbing spear that was not thrown but used in close fighting. He employed the buffalo horn formation, which allowed his soldiers to engage an opponent while the horns or flanks surrounded them. He drilled his soldiers so that they could march long distances on short notice. He also transformed his clan into a major kingdom of about 25,000 people by assimilating large numbers of war captives. He created a new hierarchy in which power was centered in his kingship and status was based not on descent but on achievement in the military regiments. He assigned his generals (indunas) to regimental villages around his kingdom. Groups of young women were also attached to regiments to produce food and carry out domestic chores. They eventually became the wives of the warriors who were not allowed to marry until Shaka gave his permission.

Shaka's repeated raids for cattle and captives throughout the area proved to be his downfall, as his regiments tired of constant campaigns. Several of his half-brothers and one of his generals conspired against him and assassinated him in 1828.

During the Mfecane, refugee groups escaped Shaka's domination by migrating to other parts of the region. Some headed much farther north, adopting Shaka's fighting methods and establishing kingdoms on the Shakan model in Mozambique, Zimbabwe, Malawi, and Tanzania. Still other peoples survived by creating new kingdoms that knit together clans and refugees. One kingdom forged in this way was Moshoeshoe's Basotho kingdom.

The son of a minor chief, Moshoeshoe (moh-SWESH-shwee; c. 1786–1870) gained a reputation as a cattle raider as a young man. He succeeded his father as refugee groups began streaming into his area in the foothills of the Drakensberg. To escape their raids, in 1824 Moshoeshoe moved his small following to an impregnable, flat-topped mountain called Thaba Bosiu. Over the next several decades, he creatively built a kingdom that became one of the most powerful in the region. Moshoeshoe accumulated vast cattle herds through raiding, and he used ***mafisa,*** a traditional practice of lending cattle to destitute men so they could establish their own homesteads, to win their loyalty. Moshoeshoe married many times to build up political alliances with neighboring chiefs and placed his sons and brothers as governors in different part of the expanding Basotho kingdom. He

Moshoeshoe photographed in 1860, during the visit of Prince Alfred to South Africa. Although he liked to wear European dress on formal occasions with whites, he preferred traditional dress among his own subjects. Renowned for his diplomatic skills, he was able to maintain his kingdom's independence for many decades from Afrikaner and British colonizers.

mafisa—A traditional practice among South African tribes of lending cattle to destitute men so they could establish their own homesteads.

Document "Song of the Afflicted"

This song, collected in the 1830s by a French missionary residing in the Basotho kingdom, was a lament sung by women who were mourning their menfolk lost in battle.

Song of the Afflicted

Older Widows:
We are left outside!
We are left to grief!
We are left to despair,
Which only makes our woes more bitter!
Would that I had wings to fly up to the sky!
Why does not a strong cord come down from the sky?
I would tie it to me, I would mount,
I would go there to live.

The new widow:
O fool that I am!
When evening comes, I open my window a little,
I listen in the silence, I look;
I imagine that he is coming back!

The dead man's fighting sister:
If women, too, went to war,
I would have gone, I would have thrown darts beside him;
My brother would not be dead;
Rather, my mother's son would have turned back half way,
He would have pretended he had hurt his foot against a stone.

All the women:
Alas! Are they really gone?
Are we abandoned indeed?
But where have they gone
That they cannot come back?
That they cannot come back to see us?
Are they really gone?
Is the underworld insatiable?
Is it never filled?

Question to Consider

1. Look for other songs sung by women in wartime or by men as they went off to war. How do the sentiments of this song compare with them?

From M. J. Daymond et al., eds., *Women Writing Africa The Southern Region* (Feminist Press, 2003), pp. 85–86.

armed his warriors with battle-axes and formed a cavalry using ponies bred for the rugged mountain terrain.

Moshoeshoe is best remembered for his diplomatic skills. He was prepared to fight if necessary, but he preferred to negotiate wherever possible. On many occasions he managed to salvage difficult situations by engaging in diplomacy and exploiting divisions among opponents. When a band of Ndebele warriors raided his kingdom for cattle in the late 1820s, Moshoeshoe's forces easily repulsed them. However, Moshoeshoe sent cattle to the retreating Ndebele warriors so they would not go home empty-handed and provoke another raid from their ruler.

The Great Trek and British-Afrikaner Relations

As African kingdoms in southern Africa were undergoing a period of transformation, groups of Boers were preparing to escape British control by migrating into the interior of southern Africa. Prompted by the Napoleonic wars, Britain resumed control over the Cape Colony in 1806 to protect the sea-lanes around the Cape of Good Hope. The British were intent on expanding commercial opportunities through wine and wool production; the Boers resented any interference with their pastoral way of life.

Relations between the two groups deteriorated in the next decades. At first the British won Boer approval for a law that tied Khoikhoi servants to white farmers, but after a humanitarian outcry from missionaries over abuses of servants, the British instituted an ordinance giving Khoikhoi farm laborers equal rights. Britain also abolished the slave trade in 1807, driving up the price of slaves, and in 1834, it emancipated the slaves. However, this action did not improve the conditions of former slaves as most of them, unskilled and uneducated, ended up as free but servile labor on white farms. The last straw for the Boers came in 1836 when the British handed back land to Xhosa chiefdoms whose land had been conquered in a recently completed war.

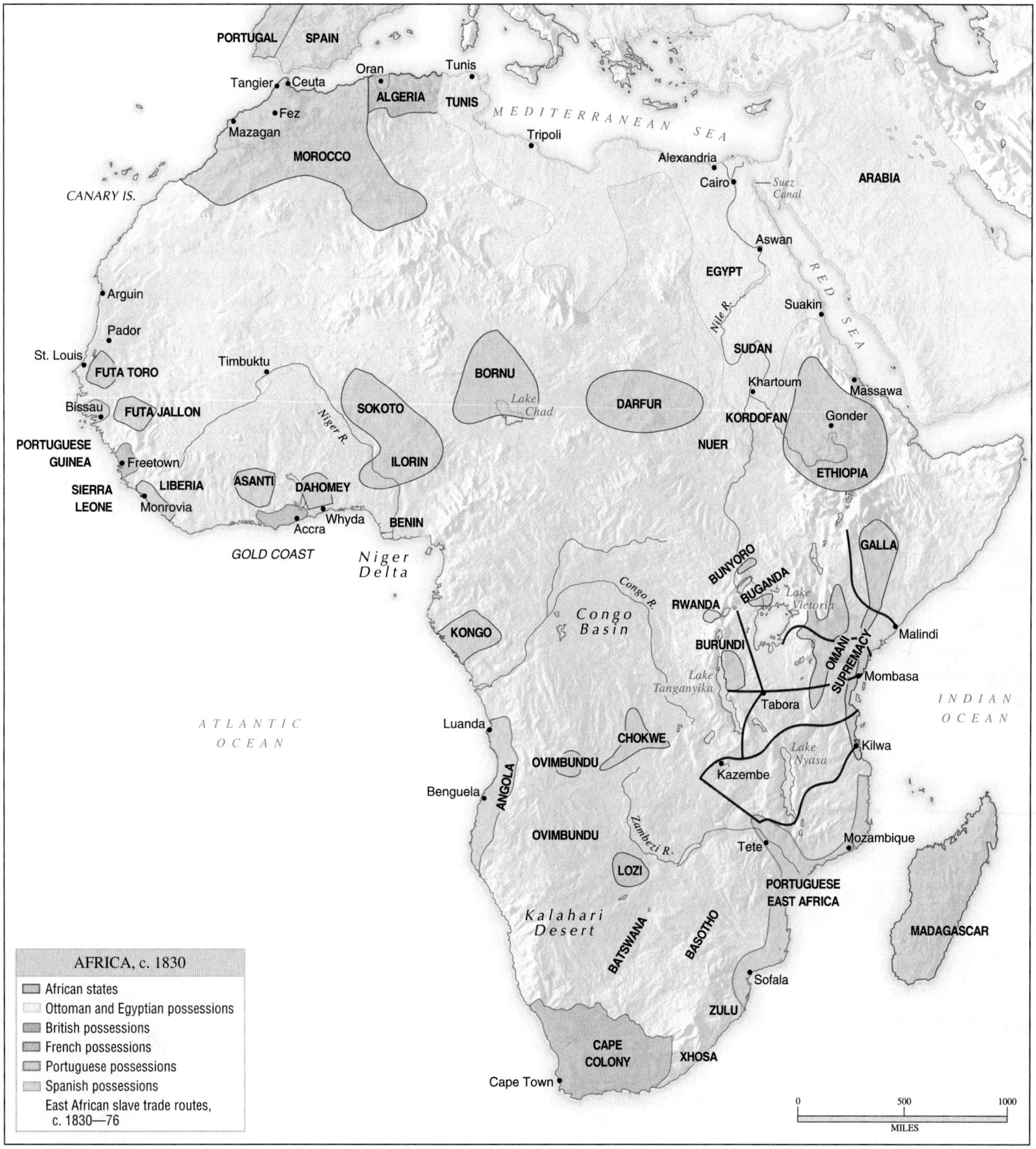

Before the European conquest of Africa in the late nineteenth century, Africans in all parts of the continent were establishing new kingdoms or expanding old ones.

To many Boers, who had very little personal capital other than their herds and found it virtually impossible to purchase land in the Cape Colony, the solution was to escape further British interference by heading northeast for the high plateau, or **veld.** In the mid-1830s bands of migrants known as ***voortrekkers*** undertook a migration called the Great Trek in their ox-drawn wagons to lands where they could restore their way of life and maintain their domination over blacks. Each band numbered several hundred people. A total of about 15,000 *voortrekkers* eventually participated in the migration.

veld—The high plateau region within the interior of South Africa.

voortrekker—An Afrikaner farmer who migrated into the interior of South Africa in the 1830s as part of the Great Trek.

The primary transportation of voortrekker *groups that migrated into the interior of southern Africa were light and strong wagons that were ideally suited to the rough terrain they were forced to cross. Despite their maneuverability, they could carry a surprising amount of household and other goods. This picture shows a wagon crossing a particularly difficult river.*

Because the Boers were pastoralists, many African rulers treated them initially as another group of cattle-keepers migrating through their lands. When *voortrekker* groups reached Moshoeshoe's kingdom, he allocated land for them to pasture their cattle temporarily. Because African societies did not have a concept of private land ownership, Moshoeshoe was not ceding the land. However, the Boers regarded the land as their own and refused to part with it. One of Moshoeshoe's sons compared the situation to a person inviting a guest to sit down in his home and the guest taking ownership of the chair.

The *voortrekkers* established two republics: the Orange Free State and the Transvaal. For the rest of the century they solidified their control by engaging in wars of land conquest against African kingdoms. In the meantime, the British prevented the Boers from having direct access to the Indian Ocean by extending their own settlement along the eastern coast north of the Cape and founding the colony of Natal.

African rulers such as Moshoeshoe became adept at dealing with both the Boers and the British and taking advantage of the rivalry between them. He invited three French Protestant missionaries to reside in his kingdom so that he could draw on their knowledge of European life and politics. He used them as scribes to send diplomatic exchanges to British officials.

Moshoeshoe's overtures to the British were initially successful. When the British drew a boundary line between the Basotho and the Boers in 1843, they favored Moshoeshoe's claims. British policy shifted a few years later to absorb the Boer states, and Moshoeshoe saw the boundary redrawn to favor Orange Free State claims. He fought a British force to a draw in 1852 and, after the British changed their policy again and withdrew from the Boer Republics in 1854, he waged two wars with the Orange Free State. The first war in 1858 ended inconclusively, but in the second, the Boers were on the verge of destroying his kingdom when Moshoeshoe successfully appealed to the British government for protection in 1868.

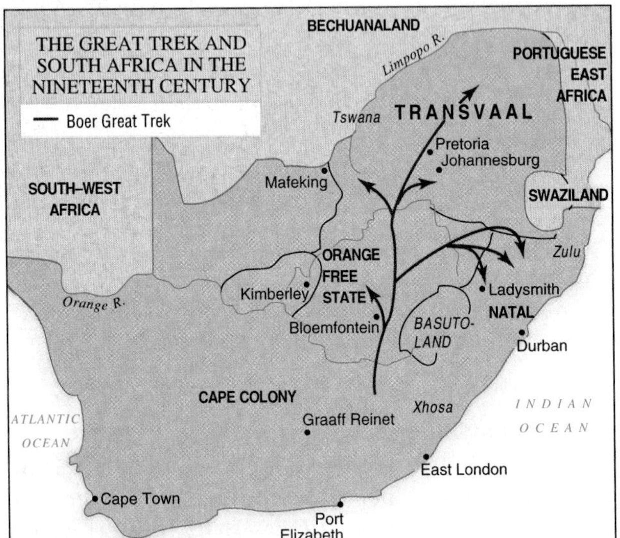

In the 1830s bands of Afrikaners migrated from the Cape into the interior of South Africa. Through the conquest of African lands, they established two republics, the Transvaal and the Orange Free State.

Discovery Through Maps

The Myth of the Empty Land

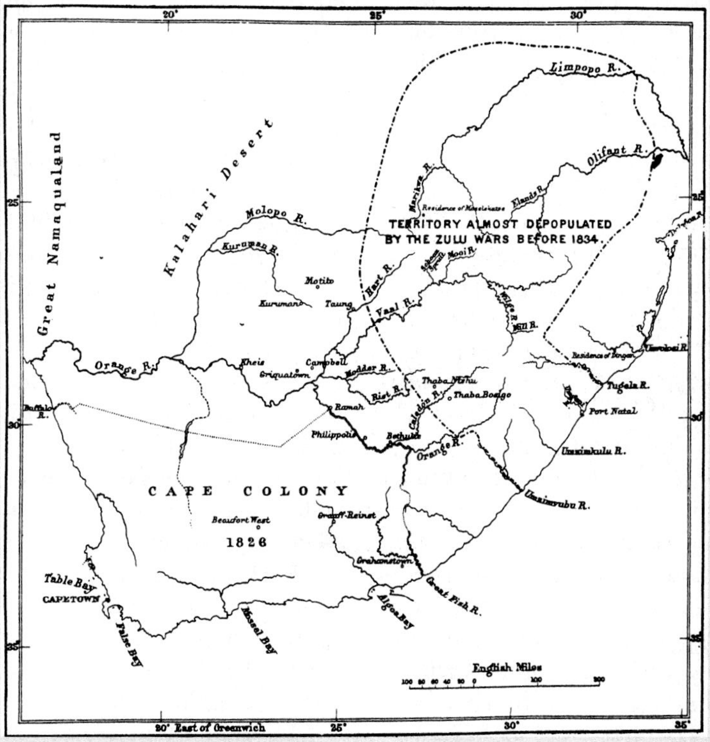

European settlement in various parts of the world was usually accompanied by the conquest of land from indigenous peoples. Because the settlers did not have a historic claim to the land, they often constructed their own versions of the past to justify their right to be there. In South Africa, one myth that white settlers created was that Dutch settlers arrived in southern Africa about the same time as Bantu-speaking peoples, the ancestors of most present-day Africans—in the mid-seventeenth century. Hence, white settlers could claim that, as they migrated from the western Cape into the interior of South Africa, they were moving into an unpopulated land that was up for grabs. Europeans could lay claim to the land, and they had just as much right to it as Africans did.

A variation of the "myth of the empty land" was based on a late-nineteenth-century map drawn by George McCall Theal, a Canadian who settled in the Cape in 1861. Theal's map shows the South African interior virtually depopulated because many Africans had been displaced by the wars of the Zulu king Shaka in the 1820s and 1830s (see p. 573). Thus, the Boers who trekked into the interior in the 1830s were settling on land no longer occupied by Africans. In a speech delivered to a Cape Town audience in 1909, Theal clearly revealed his motives for the way he drew his map. "We must . . . prove," he declared, "to these people [Africans] that we were no more intruders than they were, and that they enjoyed as much as they were entitled to." He added, "In reality this country was not the Bantu's originally any more than it was the white man's, because the Bantus were also immigrants . . . most of their ancestors migrated to South Africa in comparatively recent times."

Theal's "myth of the empty land" became an article of faith for many white South Africans until late in the twentieth century. His interpretation was a standard feature in South African history textbooks used in both white and black schools, and South African government propaganda relied on it to justify the apartheid system to the international community.

Questions to Consider

The ownership of disputed land has been a thorny issue in many countries.

1. Are there myths that settler groups have devised in other parts of the world to justify their conquests and domination of indigenous peoples and the land?
2. How accurate is the claim of Theal's map that "Zulu Wars" had depopulated the interior of South Africa before Afrikaners set out on the Great Trek?

From Christopher Saunders, *The Making of the South African Past: Major Historians on Race and Class* (Cape Town: David Philip, 1988), p. 39; Marianne Cornevin, *Apartheid Power and Historical Falsification* (Paris: UNESCO, 1980), p. 79.

In 1877 British policy shifted in response to diamond discoveries in the interior of the Cape Colony. Desiring to create a unified regional labor market, Lord Carnarvon, the Colonial Secretary, established a confederation of white-ruled states in the region and took over the Transvaal with little resistance from the Afrikaners (the name taken by the Boers about this time). The British attempted to win Afrikaner compliance by launching offensives against their main African rivals, the Pedi and Zulu kingdoms.

Although the Zulu had coexisted peacefully with British and Afrikaners for many decades, the British now perceived them as an obstacle to white control and manufactured a war against the Zulu kingdom. They launched a propaganda war, depicting the Zulu King Cetshwayo (c. 1832–1884) as an oppressive tyrant who had lost the support of his people and threatened the stability of the region. After the British issued an ultimatum demanding that Cetshwayo disband the age regiments, the basis of his power, within 30 days, a war was inevitable.

Contrary to British expectations, Cetshwayo had the full support of his army and most of his kingdom. The war started disastrously for the British when, in January 1879, the Zulu army caught a British column by surprise at Isandhlwana and overwhelmed them. A handful of British soldiers survived the battle. Cetshwayo hoped the British would end their aggression following their defeat, but they renewed their efforts and, six months later, put an end to the Zulu kingdom by carving it into 13 small pieces and exiling Cetshwayo.

This victory did not improve British relations with Transvaal Afrikaners. In 1881 they rebelled against British rule and scored a series of military successes. The British agreed to pull out of the Transvaal, although they still claimed to have a voice in its foreign affairs.

MAP South Africa

AFRICAN STATE FORMATION IN EASTERN AND NORTHEASTERN AFRICA

■ *How was eastern Africa integrated into the global economy?*

During the eighteenth century, strong new kingdoms arose in the south central and eastern sections of Africa. Portuguese intervention in these regions, like that elsewhere in Africa, proved equally calamitous. In the seventeenth century Portuguese settlers in Sena and Tete in the Zambezi River valley had intervened to support the *Mwene Mutapa* or king in a civil war within the Mutapa state; they won concessions from the king to extend trading fairs and gold-mining operations in the Zimbabwean highlands. When the *Mwene Mutapa* then attempted to curb Portuguese adventurers, they deposed him and installed a successor they could influence.

The fragmentation of the Mutapa Kingdom created a power vacuum on the Zimbabwean plateau. Young men who lacked cattle to start their own homesteads joined the armies of wealthy patrons who were contesting for power. The most successful of these warlords was Dombo (d. 1695), who took the title *Changamire*. In the late seventeenth century his *Rozvi* soldiers conquered the remnants of Mutapa and other kingdoms in the region. Then, Dombo's army turned its attention to the Portuguese, expelling them from the trading fairs. Thereafter, the Portuguese were allowed to trade in the interior only through African agents.

The Portuguese presence in the Zambezi River valley was restricted to the ***prazos,*** huge estates run by Portuguese settlers (*prazeros)* who, over time, intermarried with Africans and assimilated into local African cultures. When they failed to eke out a living from agriculture, the prazeros became warlords whose slave armies exacted tribute from clients and hunted elephants for the ivory trade.

In East Africa, most states remained small, except in the region west of Lake Victoria, where two kingdoms, Bunyoro and Buganda, vied for power. Bunyoro dominated a confederation based on village-based chiefdoms that paid tribute to Bunyoro and contributed regiments for cattle raids against neighboring societies. Bunyoro's economy was based on hunting, herding, and agriculture. In the late eighteenth century, those clans most likely to protect themselves against Bunyoro's raids, formed Buganda, a rival kingdom to the northwest of Lake Victoria. Buganda's king (*kabaka*) allocated lands to territorial chiefs and distributed land to lesser chiefs. Buganda's staple food was the banana, which had a high caloric yield and thrived in the rich, fertile soils bordering Lake Victoria. The banana could be produced on an annual basis, unlike the shifting cultivation practiced in most savanna regions of Africa. Because cattle did not thrive within Buganda's borders, Buganda's regiments regularly carried out cattle raids in neighboring chiefdoms to the west.

In East Africa, Islam was largely restricted to the coastal area, despite the fact that two centuries of Portuguese tyranny were brought to an end in 1698

prazos—Leased crown estates in the Zambezi River valley under Portuguese control.

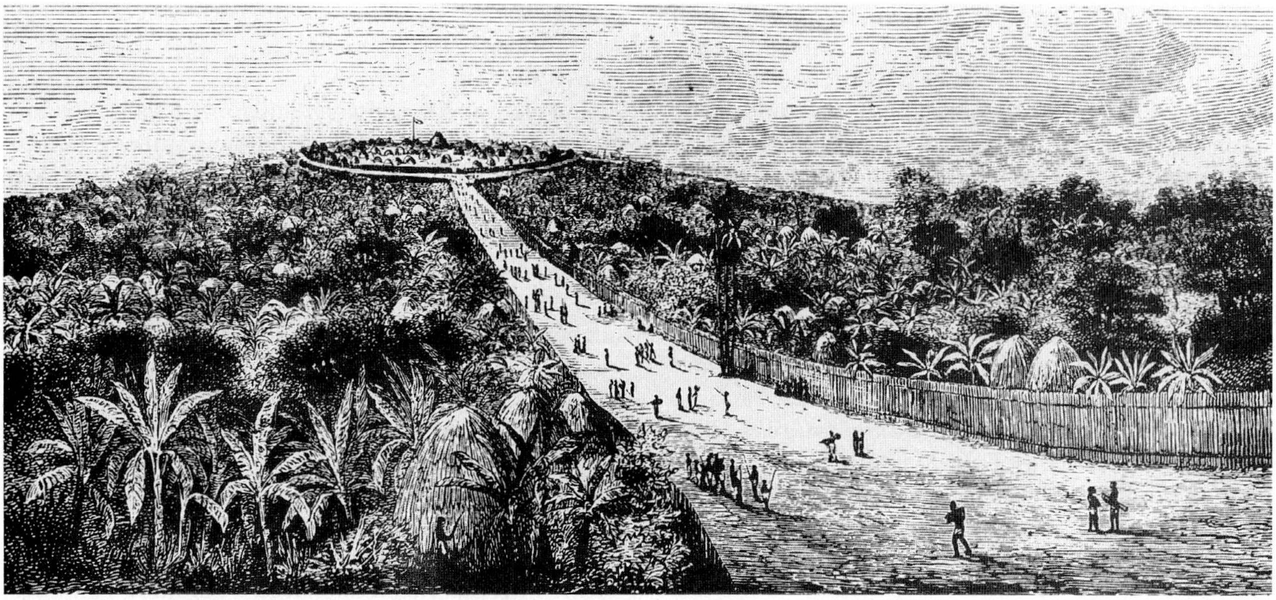

Buganda, a kingdom situated west of Lake Victoria, became a regional power in the late eighteenth century. A wide avenue led to the royal palace at its capital, Rubaga.

after a three-year siege of Fort Jesus by Omani Arabs responding to appeals of the Swahili city-states. The Portuguese retreated to their bases in southern Mozambique, but their expulsion did not bring peace and stability to the Swahili states, which fought among themselves. Pate, benefiting from immigrants from the Hadramaat that developed its trading capacity, eclipsed Kilwa as the leading Swahili state.

Oman, on the southeastern coast of the Arabian peninsula, was a major producer of dates. Oman's rulers took advantage of their new position and exported dates to East Africa in exchange for slaves for their plantations. In the late eighteenth century the Omani ruling dynasty, the Busaids, set up a headquarters on Zanzibar and established a stranglehold over commerce along the East African coast. Non-Omani traders were excluded from trading along the coast, and Zanzibar merchants had to give the Busaids a 5 percent tax on the worth of their goods.

Zanzibar became so important to the Busaids that Sultan Sayyid Said (1791–1856), who had made trips to the island for over a decade and who had built palaces for himself and his family, transferred most of his court and government there in 1840. The sultan also welcomed a British agent of the East India Company to reside in Zanzibar and to keep the lines of communication open with the British government.

The British had dispatched an anti-slavery squadron to the Indian Ocean. They first established a boundary that prohibited slave trading to India, but allowed the Omanis to sustain their slave operations on the East African coast to Oman and the western Persian Gulf region. Eventually the British began pressuring Said to give up his slave operations, and his compromise was to build up clove plantations on Zanzibar. In 1848, the British limited the slave trade to eastern Africa and its naval squadron aggressively stopped any Arab vessel thought to be transporting slaves. Zanzibar became a base for British ships and British officials dictated policy to the Omanis. Although Zanzibar did not become a British protectorate until 1890 it had long since lost its autonomy.

Throughout the nineteenth century East and Central Africa were increasingly drawn into the world economy through long-distance trade. Gold and ivory had long been exported to China and India, but now ivory was in demand by European middle classes for luxury items such as combs, billiard balls, piano keys, and cutlery handles. Elephant herds paid an enormous price; 33 elephants were slaughtered for every ton of ivory exported. The scourge of slavery also ravaged the region. During the nineteenth century, several million people were enslaved. Half of them were sent to southern Arabia, Sudan, and Ethiopia, while the rest ended up on French sugar plantations on the Indian Ocean islands of Mauritius and Réunion; on Brazilian sugar plantations, whose owners found West African slaves too highly priced; and on Arab-run clove plantations on Zanzibar and nearby islands.

The long-distance trade largely consisted of ivory and slaves brought from the interior to the coast in exchange for trade beads and cotton cloth, much of it produced by American textile mills. The trade between the coast and the interior opened up new opportunities for middlemen trading groups. The Yao, Nyamwezi (nyam-WAY-zee), Afro-Portuguese, Kamba, and Swahili Arabs controlled routes in different parts of the region and recruited thousands of porters for their caravans. As Swahili merchants established trading centers such as Tabora in the interior to facilitate and oversee their networks, the Swahili language increasingly became the lingua franca along trading routes. With imported firearms and slave armies, some of the leading warlords established conquest states based on their control over the slave trade. Mirambo (1840–1884), a Nyamwezi chief, and Tippu Tip (c. 1830–1905), who was of Arab and Nyamwezi parentage, carved out domains east and west of Lake Tanganyika, respectively.

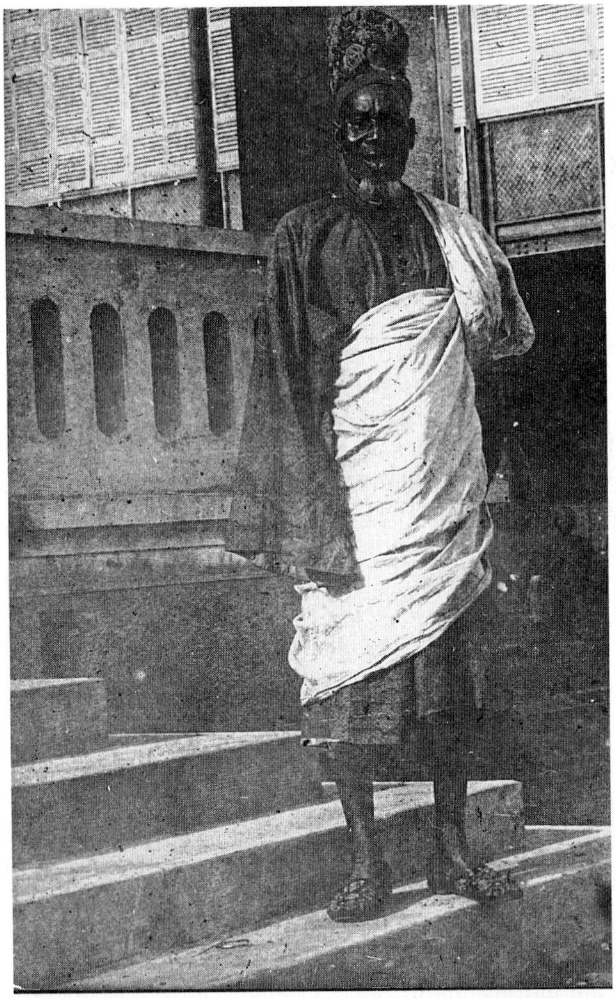

Born of Arab and Nyamwezi parents, Tippu Tip was a warlord who established a state west of Lake Tanganyika to exploit the slave trade.

This was the era when a distinct Swahili identity developed along the coast and the maturing Swahili language, assimilating Arabic words to a greater degree into its vocabulary, produced its earliest poetry. The primary language of traders was Swahili, which spread from the coast to far into the interior.

Many African kingdoms such as Rwanda were not dependent on the long-distance trade for their survival. Rwanda was composed of three main groups: the Twa, who were hunter-gatherers; the Hutu, Bantu-speaking farmers; and the Tutsi, a pastoral Nilotic people who were the last to settle in the area. Over the centuries Tutsi clans had established a patron-client relationship with Twa and Hutu clans, but the lines between the groups were not clearly drawn. Hutu and Tutsi intermarried and shared a common language, religious beliefs, and cultural institutions, and the distinctions between Tutsi patrons and Hutu clients were often blurred.

However, in the late nineteenth century the Nyiginya, a Tutsi clan led by King Rwabugiri, conquered other Tutsi and Hutu clans. Rwabugiri's state was highly centralized and favored the Tutsi minority, who served as administrators, tax collectors, and army commanders and controlled grazing land. Hutu chiefs were in charge of agricultural lands but tended Tutsi cattle and paid tribute to their Tutsi overlords.

While new states were rising in East Africa, the oldest African polity, the Kingdom of Ethiopia, was fragmenting. A source of trouble was the presence of Catholic missionaries. In 1607 Emperor Za-Dengel, hoping to attract more Portuguese arms and musketeers to counter his rivals from the nobility, invited Jesuit priest Pedro Pais to his court as a teacher, diplomat, and adviser. However, when Za-Dengel ignored Pais's advice and issued a proclamation banning the customary observance of the Saturday Sabbath, the nobles rose up and overthrew him. The Emperor Susneyos (soos-NAY-yohs; 1604–1632) consolidated the relationship with the Jesuits and secretly converted to Catholicism in 1612. He, too, subsequently forbade the observance of Saturday Sabbath as well as renouncing the monophysite belief that Christ had both human and divine qualities. Susneyos's public conversion to Catholicism in 1622 and the zealous policies of Bishop Alphonso Mendez, head of the Jesuit mission after 1625, incurred the wrath of the Ethiopian church. Mendez tried to Catholicize the Ethiopian orthodox faith by reordaining Ethiopian priests, reconsecrating the churches, and banning circumcision. Land was transferred from the Ethiopian church to the Catholics. A bloody rebellion forced Susneyos to reestablish the orthodox faith in 1632. However, he had lost so much support that he abdicated. When his son, Fasilidas (fah-SIL-e-deez; 1632–1667), expelled the Jesuits several years later, a popular song captured Ethiopian sentiment:

At length the Sheep of Ethiopia free'd
From the Bold Lyons of the West . . .
Rejoyce, rejoyce, Sing Hallelujahs all,
No More the Western Wolves
Our Ethiopia shall enthrall.[2]

During that era, Ethiopia's trading relationships with Europe and the Ottoman Empire declined, but slaves, coffee, and salt were still exported through the Nile valley and the Red Sea. Fasilidas founded his capital around 1635 at Gonder, a prosperous market town north of Lake Tana. The capital was situated close to the fertile agricultural lands of the Blue Nile and the juncture of three major caravan routes. Muslim traders, who dominated the trade between Ethiopia and Muslim states, lived in a separate part of town from the Christians.

During his reign, Fasilidas began reshaping the monarchy, continuing his father's policy of outmaneuvering his rivals by integrating the Muslim Oromo into his nobility. However, his policies eventually reduced Gonder's power, as the nobles expanded their personal fiefdoms around the kingdom and the Oromo asserted their autonomy. In effect Gonder's emperors became local potentates. One exception was Iyasu II (c. 1730–1755), who ruled with the support of his astute mother, Mentewab, who was crowned queen at his coronation and served at the same time as his queen mother. Her leadership abilities were demonstrated in 1732 when a rebel faction assaulted Gonder's castle, and she presented a plan of action to the council. "If I am a woman by the manner of my creation," she candidly told her councilors, "my gifts, which I have received from God, from below [on earth] and from above [heaven], are those of a man amongst men."[3]

An Oromo, Mentewab brought many of her ethnic group into the court and the army, and she became a master at dealing with court factions and intrigues. When her son died and was succeeded by her grandson, Iyo'as, she continued to play a pivotal role in his court. One of her strategies for extending her influence was granting *gults* (land grants) and endowments to churches, which in turn legitimized her and her ruling line through their chronicles.

However, following Iyasu's reign, civil war erupted, and provincial rulers asserted their power over Gonder. The lowest point came in 1769 when Tegray's ruler, Mika'el, conspired to strangle one emperor and poison another four months later. The years between 1769 and 1855 are known as the "era of the princes" because nobles entrenched their power at the expense of a series of powerless emperors who reigned in Gonder. A royal chronicler plaintively asked: "How is it that the kingdom has become contemptible to striplings and slaves?"[4]

This state of affairs ended in the mid-nineteenth century when Kasa Haylu, a noble from western Ethiopia, began conquering various provinces and consolidating the kingdom under one ruler. In 1855 he took the name Téwodros II (tay-WHO-drohs) and was crowned emperor. His goal was to modernize Ethiopia and build up relations with European nations. He depicted himself as a latter-day Prester John, the ruler of a Christian outpost surrounded by hostile Muslim states. He made overtures to the British government for support on that basis, but to the British, Ethiopia counted for little when compared to the Ottomans and Egypt. When Téwodros grew frustrated at the absence of a British response, he took hostage a group of Europeans, including the British consul to Ethiopia. Although he was trying to win concessions by holding the prisoners, the British grew tired of his impudence and dispatched a large Anglo-Indian expeditionary force to lay siege to Téwodros at his fortress, Maqdala, in 1868. By then, his iron-fisted rule had lost him the support of most of his nobles who refused to send soldiers. The British won a quick victory and freed the prisoners, but rather than submit to the British, Téwodros put a gun into his mouth and killed himself.

CONCLUSION

By the mid-nineteenth century many parts of Africa had been integrated into the world economy to varying degrees. In the mid-seventeenth century parts of Africa were harshly introduced to global commerce through the slave trade that wrenched millions of people from sub-Saharan Africa to service plantation economies in the Americas, North Africa, and the Middle East. Although the slave trade introduced new plants such as cassava and maize to the African continent from the Americas, the slave trade contributed little to African economic development and to the kingdoms that participated in it.

Some kingdoms such as Kongo and Oyo collapsed through their involvement in the slave trade, while many new ones were established. Islamic jihads created a series of Muslim kingdoms in the Sudanic region of West Africa. In southern Africa, new political states such as the Zulu and Basotho kingdoms were established during the Mfecane.

Once the plantation economy declined and the slave trade began to wind down in the nineteenth century and as Europe's industrial economy expanded, Europeans sought new trading relationship with Africans. A legitimate trade developed in resources such as palm oil and palm kernels that could be converted into soap, lubricants, and lamp oil for the European market. However the relationship favored Europeans as Africans sold raw resources and bought manufactured goods or finished products from non-African traders.

With the exception of southern Africa, where Dutch and British settlers seized African lands first on the coast and then in the interior, European contacts with the rest of Africa were largely limited to economic relationships in coastal areas and were controlled by Africans. However, in the last quarter of the nineteenth century, rivalries among the major powers of Europe led to a mad scramble in which European nations conquered and took direct control of almost all of Africa. The European colonizers imposed their own political boundaries and initiated economic and social changes that Africans are still coping with.

Suggestions for Web Browsing

You can obtain more information about topics included in this chapter at the websites listed below. See also the companion website that accompanies this text, **http://www.ablongman.com/brummett,** which contains an online study guide and additional resources.

Excerpts from Slave Narratives
http://www.vgskole.net/prosjekt/slavrute/primary.htm

This site contains over 40 first-person accounts of slavery in the Americas and African life written between 1682 and 1937.

Liberian Letters
http://etext.lib.virginia.edu/subjects/liberia/

This site features more than 50 original letters from freed American slaves in nineteenth century Liberia to their former masters and associates in Virginia.

Cape Slavery in South Africa
http://www.museums.org.za/iziko/slavery/slavery_world.html

A presentation of aspects of slavery (slave lives, resistance, emancipation) in the Dutch Cape Colony from 1658 to 1838.

End of the Slave Trade in Africa
http://www.fordham.edu/halsall/africa/africasbook.html

Documents regarding the termination of slave trade in Africa, from the Internet African History Sourcebook.

Literature and Film

A prominent early twentieth-century South Africa politician and journalist, Solomon Plaatje set his novel *Mhudi* (Passagiatta Press, 1986) during the wars of the Mfecane, while contemporary writer Andre Brink treated a slave uprising in the western Cape in the early nineteenth century in *A Chain of Voices* (Morrow, 1994). Beverly Mack and Jean Boyd, *The Collected Works of Nana Asma'u* (African Historical Sources, No. 9, 1998) is a collection of the poetry and other writings of the daughter of a famed West African cleric, Usman dan Fodio. Marcia Wright's *Strategies of Slaves and Women* (Lillian Barber Press, 1993) presents the life histories of nineteenth-century East and Central African women.

Suggestions for Reading

Several general studies on the transatlantic slave trade are Joseph Inikori and Stanley Engerman, eds., *The Atlantic Slave Trade* (Duke University Press, 1992), and Edward Reynolds, *Stand the Storm: A History of the Atlantic Slave Trade* (Alllison and Busby, 1989). For the effects of the slave trade on Africans, see Patrick Manning et al., eds., *Slavery and African Life* (Cambridge University Press, 1990), and John Thornton, *Africa and Africans in the Making of the Atlantic World, 1400–1680,* 2nd ed. (Cambridge University Press, 1998).

Usman dan Fodio's jihads and the creation of the Sokoto Caliphate are treated in Mervyn Hiskett, *The Sword of Truth: The Life and Times of the Shehu Usman dan Fodio* (Northwestern University Press, 1994). The decline of the Atlantic slave trade and the expansion of trade with Europe are traced in Robin Law, *From Slave Trade to "Legitimate" Commerce: The Commercial Transition in Nineteenth-Century West Africa* (Cambridge University Press, 1996).

Long-distance trade and state formation in eastern Africa are treated in Abdul Sheriff, *Spices and Ivory in Zanzibar* (Ohio University Press, 1987), and Edward Alpers, *Ivory and Slaves in East Central Africa* (Heinemann, 1975). Ethiopia's church and state are dealt with in Donald Crummey, *Land and Society in the Christian Kingdom of Ethiopia* (University of Illinois Press, 2000).

Slavery in the Cape Colony is examined in Nigel Worden, *Slavery in Dutch South Africa* (Cambridge University Press,

1985), and Robert Shell, *Children of Bondage: A Social History of the Slave Society at the Cape of Good Hope, 1652–1838* (Wesleyan University Press, 1994).

Norman Etherington's *Great Treks: The Transformation of Southern Africa, 1815–1954* (Longman, 2001) provides overviews of the Mfecane in southern Africa. John Laband has written a comprehensive treatment of nineteenth-century Zulu history, *The Rise and Fall of the Zulu Nation* (Arms & Armour, 1997). Moshoeshoe's life is treated in biographies by Leonard Thompson, *Survival in Two Worlds: Moshoeshoe of Lesotho, 1786–1870* (Oxford University Press, 1975).

Studies on nineteenth-century South Africa include Timothy Keegan, *Colonial South Africa and the Origins of the Racial Order* (University of Virginia Press, 1996), and Jeff Peires, *The Dead Will Arise: Nongqawuse and the Great Xhosa Cattle-Killing Movement of 1856–7* (Indiana University Press, 1989).

SLAVERY

Why has slavery been so widespread?

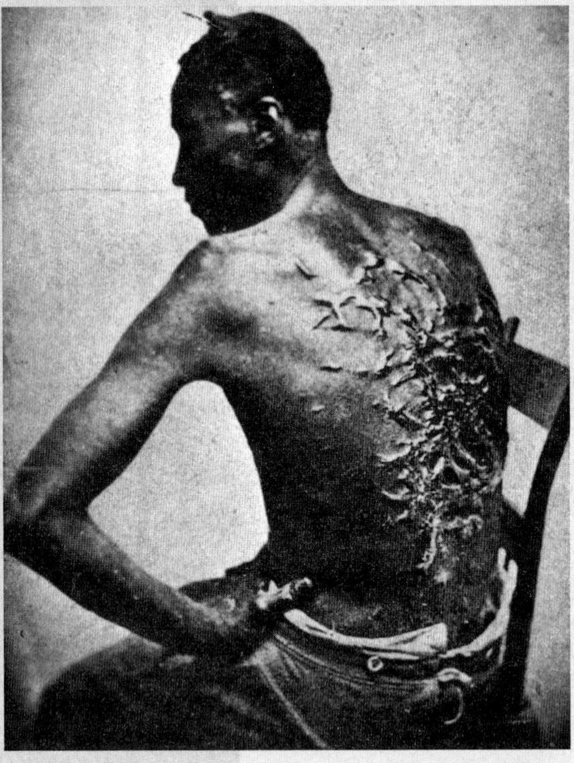

Back of plantation slave whipped by his owner, Captain John Lyon, Louisiana, 1863.

Slavery—the practice of people forcing other people into servitude and treating them as property—has existed for most of history. While the specific reasons why any one culture practiced slavery have varied, the simplest explanation for the existence of slavery is that, wherever and whenever it has occurred, certain people possessed the power to control other people absolutely, found it economically rewarding to do so, and faced little ethical or political opposition to their actions.

Traditionally, most slaves have been taken from outside the tribe, nation, or ethnic group that enslaved them, usually as war captives or kidnap victims. Most societies only extended social rights and protections to their own members, which made outsiders or "others" vulnerable to exploitation, particularly if they came from hostile communities. When slavery occurred within a group, those enslaved were generally singled out as punishment for criminal behavior, as debt repayment, or, as in the case of women and children, because of economic and physical vulnerability.

Most slaves have been used as agricultural workers. Agriculture was the primary source of wealth up until the nineteenth century, and the labor of slaves was needed to generate income for their masters. Slaves, however, have also served as artisans, soldiers, domestic servants, laborers, courtesans, prostitutes, and eunuchs. In certain cultures, notably the Ottoman and Arabic civilizations, slaves could rise to comparatively high stations when they showed great abilities as military leaders or administrators. In some cultures, slaves could buy their freedom or win it on the death of their masters. In others, slavery was a permanent condition, passed on from one generation to the next.

No one knows exactly when or where slavery originated. Some claim the institution is almost as old as the first *Homo sapiens*. The early Sumerians owned slaves who were usually captives taken in raids or wars. Early legal documents from the region between Mesopotamia and Egypt show the existence of debt slavery, a practice in which a person who could not repay his debt presented himself as payment. In fifth century B.C.E. Athens, one person in four was a slave, but their treatment varied widely, with some slaves considered members of the family while other slaves were forced to work in mines or as rowers in galleys. In ancient Rome, large numbers of slaves were taken from the various conquered peoples throughout the empire. Slave revolts were commonplace, often the result of brutal treatment in the large agricultural estates, where slaves served as both laborers and overseers. The founders of the Christian Church offered conflicting views on slavery. In the book of Colossians in the New Testament, St. Paul instructed slaves to obey their masters. Paul also urged the masters to treat their slaves as they would their brothers.

In China, war captives, criminals, and women of poor families made up the enslaved class as early as the Shang dynasty (1600–1027 B.C.E.). The archaeological record shows slaves toiling in workshops and fields, constrained by leashes and under the control of whips. Despite a long history of slavery, the Chinese showed an ethical discomfort with it. When the Emperor Wang Mang (8–23 C.E.) came to power, he forbade the buying and selling of slaves. Despite attempts to prevent slavery, the selling of indentured slaves remained a fixture of Chinese culture into the twentieth century.

Various forms of slavery have also existed in other Asian civilizations. Longstanding Hindu and Muslim legal codes justified the conditions under which bondage was lawful. Criminal activity could lead to enslavement as could being the target of a holy war. In the thirteenth and fourteenth centuries, the Mongols took so many Russian artisans as slaves that the knowledge of several crafts disappeared from Russia. Between 1400 and 1650, the Ottomans took over 200,000 mainly Orthodox Christian boys from their parents in the Balkans, converted these slaves to Islam, and trained them to be janissaries, elite infantry soldiers. Some of these slaves eventually rose to high positions within the Ottoman government.

Slavery was also practiced in the Americas. Mayan, Aztec, and Incan civilizations enslaved conquered peoples. Evidence of slavery can be found at the archaeological site at Cahokia in present-day Illinois and among the Plains Indians in the eighteenth and nineteenth centuries. When the Spanish conquistador Francisco Coronado traveled through the Pueblo towns of New Mexico in the sixteenth century, he found that people owned the slaves from present-day Kansas. Though a slave trade in the Americas predated European penetration, Europeans greatly intensified the trade after they integrated the region into their global trading networks after 1492.

Africa became the major source of slaves for both the Indian and Atlantic Ocean trades after 1300. The overseas trade grew progressively over the years as first Arabs along Africa's east coast and then later Europeans along the continent's west coast began to participate in and expand Africa's own internal slave trade. In the foreign and domestic market, slaves were paid for in cloth, tobacco, metal goods, weapons, or alcohol. Both African sellers and the European and Arab buyers found the slave trade to be profitable and continually tried to tilt the advantage of transactions in their favor.

In the Atlantic trade, Portuguese, Spanish, Dutch, French, and English merchants dealt in African slaves as part of their global commerce after the fifteenth century. Portugal started the Atlantic trade, and Spain and Holland followed suit thereafter, but by the mid-seventeenth century and throughout the eighteenth century England and France assumed leading roles in the trade. Ironically, at the same time these two nations were profiting from the slave trade, they also served as seedbeds for the Enlightenment, the intellectual and political movement that led to the principles of universal human rights. Enlightenment writers such as John Locke and Voltaire made fortunes investing in companies that participated in the slave trade, just as many of the nobles and bourgeoisie of their countries did. From the sixteenth century to the nineteenth century, some 12 million Africans were shipped across the Atlantic to the Americas and the Caribbean where most were forced to work in agriculture. Racism, specifically the belief that Africans were inherently inferior to Europeans and so deserving of enslavement, was a distinguishing characteristic of the Atlantic slave trade and slavery in the Americas.

In the Indian Ocean slave trade, Arab traders dominated from the fourteenth century through the sixteenth century. Beginning in the seventeenth century, however, the Dutch integrated the East African, South Asian, and Southeast Asian circuits of trade across the Indian Ocean, which had long been the "great highway" for eastern hemispheric migration, trade, and cultural diffusion. The Dutch transported slaves to their colonial holdings in the Netherlands East Indies (now Indonesia) and to other Indian Ocean ports. The volume of the Indian Ocean trade fluctuated between 15 and 30 percent of the Atlantic slave trade. By the end of the seventeenth century, slaves made up more than half the population of Dutch colonies and other Indian Ocean ports.

The international effort to abolish slavery is a relatively new movement that only began to take shape in Europe and its colonies in the middle of the eighteenth century. As the Enlightenment and English reform movements stressed the equality of all human beings, a growing number of people started to oppose slavery. Slaves began to resist enslavement more vigorously. Haitian independence in 1804 marked the conclusion of the world's first successful slave revolt. In the United States, many freed slaves joined the abolition movement. At the same time, the development of machines and more efficient methods of production began to reduce the demand for labor in agriculture, and other economic areas. By the middle of the nineteenth century the United States and most European nations had made slavery illegal. In other parts of the world, slavery continued into the twentieth century. Today, all governments of the world condemn slavery. Nevertheless, traditional forms of slavery still exist in remote and lawless regions of Mauritania, Sudan, Myanmar, Pakistan, and Brazil. The growing number of women and children transported across international borders and forced into prostitution or unpaid factory work also represent a new form of involuntary labor that has been likened to slavery.

Questions

1. Why have so many societies kept slaves?
2. Why did the treatment of slaves vary so much from one culture to another?
3. What conditions do you think finally led to the abolition of legal slavery? What allows various forms of illegal slavery to exist today?

CHAPTER 20

Asian and Middle Eastern Empires and Nations, 1650–1815

CHAPTER CONTENTS

The late seventeenth through the early nineteenth centuries were a period of sometimes gentle and sometimes violent transformation for the countries of Asia and the Middle East. The states in these regions faced a set of challenges prompted primarily by internal upheavals and but also by new external threats. The internal upheavals took the forms of regional conflict, economic turmoil, and population growth. The external threats coalesced around the ambitions of certain European states whose growing military and economic power enabled them to launch wars of expansion to the far corners of the globe.

For the three countries of East Asia—China, Japan, and Korea—these centuries were an era of great growth and continued domination of Eurasian trade and production. By the nineteenth century, however, these East Asian countries would face the kind of internal turmoil, fueled by external pressure, experienced earlier in Asian countries farther to the west.

In 1650 most of India and the Middle East was incorporated into traditional agrarian empires ruled by the Ottomans, the Safavids, and the Mughals. These dynasties capitalized on their military successes and durable state structures to project a sense of legitimacy and permanence to their populations. They cultivated and benefited from extensive trading networks reaching from East Asia to Europe. But no dynastic system exists free of internal struggles for power. As each empire experienced the effects of systemic changes in world economic systems in the seventeenth century, it simultaneously contended with challenges from within. For the Ottomans, the challenge came from the pasha households resisting the central authority of the sultan. In Persia, the shahs (kings) struggled to retain the loyalties of their tribal military forces. In India, the long rule of Aurangzeb was a high point in Mughal power. Soon after his death, though, sustained military struggles with the Hindu Maratha confederacy sapped the power of the empire, which had, before Aurangzeb's rule, sought to accommodate the faith of its Hindu subjects.

Southern Europeans, particularly the Portuguese, penetrated the Indian Ocean in the sixteenth century and, relying on advances in naval weaponry, rapidly militarized this important trading zone. Soon after the Portuguese and the Spanish altered the

1600

1622 Ottoman Sultan Osman II deposed

1640 Tokugawa trade limited to Chinese, Koreans, Dutch

1644–1912 Qing dynasty

1650

1658–1707 Reign of Mughal emperor Aurangzeb in India

1662–1722 Reign of Emperor Kangxi in China

1680–1720s Golden age of literature and arts in Tokugawa Japan

1700

1707–1720 Maratha and Rajput rebellions curtail Mughal power

1718–1730 Tulip Period, Ottoman Empire

1720 Müteferrika Ottoman language press founded in Istanbul

1723 Afghan invasion of Iran

1724–1776 Reign of King Yŏngjo in Korea

1736–1739 Nadir Shah becomes shah in Iran, invades India

1736–1796 Reign of Qianlong in China

1750

1750s Beginning of Dutch domination in Indonesia

1752 Burmese invasion of Thailand

1757 Battle of Plassey

1759 Chinese confine European traders to Guangzhou

1768–1779 Three voyages of Captain James Cook

1771–1801 Tay Son Uprising in Vietnam

1782 Founding of Chakri dynasty in Thailand

1789–1807 Reign of Selim III, Ottoman reformer

1794 Dutch East India Company collapses

1794 Qajar dynasty emerges in Persia

1796–1804 White Lotus Uprising in China

configuration of trade, the Dutch, French, and English moved into Asia, bringing with them their own contests and rivalries with one another. In 1600, these rivalries were mainly for a share of the Asian trade. Dutch power throughout East Asia peaked in the seventeenth century, and thereafter was confined to Indonesia. France and Britain then moved their rivalries to India (and the New World). By the middle of the eighteenth century, what had begun as the Europeans' quest for a share of Asian trade became both an effort to dominate that trade and a bold imperialist grab for territory. The Europeans' actions fundamentally changed the configuration of trade and politics in South, Southeast, and West Asia.

At the end of this period, large areas of Asia and the Middle East were still free of European political domination, but their continued independence was becoming more doubtful. The Ottoman Empire continued to rule an empire spanning three continents, and the Qajar dynasty had consolidated its rule in Iran. The major contenders for power in India were the Marathas, the Mughals, and a variety of regional warlords. Europeans, however, had begun to expand their influence in Asian economic affairs, and the British East India Company had itself become a regional force in South Asia.

East Asia continued to play the dominant role in the world economy until the early nineteenth century. Before the Industrial Revolution in England transformed the European economy, the inhabitants of China, Japan, and Korea enjoyed more access to a variety of products and lower rates of abject poverty than anywhere else in the world. China produced one-third of the world's entire economic output in 1750. Japan was the largest producer of silver until the late seventeenth century, which, together with the silver from the New World, supported the world's trade system. Many of the world's largest cities—sustained by sophisticated banking systems and complex transportation and communication networks—were located in East Asia in the eighteenth century. In the next century, the Industrial Revolution, however, gave Western imperialists operating in Asia decisive economic and military advantages, and this, together with internal wars and agricultural distress, led this dynamic region into a rapid decline.

THE OTTOMANS IN THE EARLY MODERN ERA

- *Did attempts at modernization using European models strengthen or weaken the Ottoman Empire in the eighteenth century?*

By the seventeenth century the Muslim world stretched from the Atlantic to the Pacific. In a millennium, the spread of Islam from Arabia had indeed been phenomenal. But after 1700, Muslim rulers from Anatolia to Indonesia, like their counterparts in Africa, found it increasingly difficult to keep the European imperialists at bay. As European states expanded their military power and infringed on the routes of maritime trade from East to West, they developed new world systems of interregional trade that in part supplanted older commercial systems based in and controlled by Middle Eastern and Asian states and merchants. Control of trade in the eighteenth-century world slipped out of the hands of merchants in Istanbul, Isfahan, and Cairo. For the Ottoman sultans, who for centuries had terrorized European armies and dictated the terms of trade, that ideological and economic adjustment was not easily made. Even in the great Islamic empires, economic changes, vested interests, and prolonged warfare drained state treasuries and made it difficult for traditional rulers to restructure their empires and compete with the emergent powers of Europe.

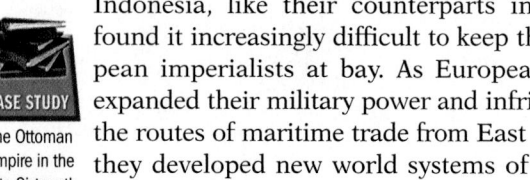

CASE STUDY
The Ottoman Empire in the Late Sixteenth Century

Ottoman Reorganization and Reform

The early seventeenth century in the Ottoman Empire was marked by a series of rebellions, one culminating in the deposition and execution of the ill-starred Sultan Osman II in 1622. Although the empire was still vast and powerful, it had lost the glory of the Golden Age associated with the reign of Suleiman (SOO-leh-mahn) the Magnificent. Many explanations have been advanced for the weaknesses of the empire in this time period: corruption, the intrigues of harem women, retention of princes in the harem rather than their being sent out to govern and fight in the provinces. Although these were factors, the more telling reasons were changes in the global economy (linked to late-sixteenth-century inflation and population growth), competition among the various pasha households for position and prestige, and the reorganization required when the empire reached the limits of its expansion. Economic factors fuelled Ottoman rebellions when **janissaries** did not receive their pay, peasants fled the plots that could no longer sustain the burgeoning population, and demobilized auxiliary soldiers (with no hope of earning a living) became bandits preying upon the countryside.

The Ottoman Empire was surprisingly large and surprisingly long-lived. No empire of any duration can remain static, and the institutions of the Ottomans had to change over time. As the ranks of the janissaries were inflated, as the *timar* ("fiefs") of the traditional cavalry became hereditary, and as a state based on expansion and conquest exhausted its resources fighting long wars on two fronts, the empire began to take a different form from the one it had in the days of Mehmed the Conqueror. All of these changes occurred in the context of a shift in the global economy due to transatlantic discoveries and the rise of oceanic merchant empires like those of the Dutch and the English.

janissaries—An elite Ottoman infantry corps armed with gunpowder weapons and comprised mostly of converted Balkan slaves.

The Age of the Köprülü Vizirs

Mehmed IV became sultan in 1648, facing rampant inflation, a Venetian blockade of the Dardanelles, rebellion in the provinces, and a violent struggle among palace factions, including his mother, Turhan (TOOR-hahn) Sultan, and her rival, the old Valide Sultan Kösem (KOO-sem). These senior women wielded considerable influence and controlled considerable wealth in the palace system. In 1651 Turhan ended Kösem's long-term dominance of the harem by having her strangled, but Mehmed remained enmeshed in factional politics. This internal strife was compounded by a vehement struggle between groups of conservative mullahs representing the ***ulama*** (oo-LAH-mah) and **sufis,** both of which were contending for spiritual authority and influence in the capital. By 1656 Istan-

ulama—Islamic religious authorities; men versed in Islamic sciences and law.

sufis—Islamic mystics who sought contact with Allah through prayer and ritual dance; considered a heretical movement by conservative Muslims.

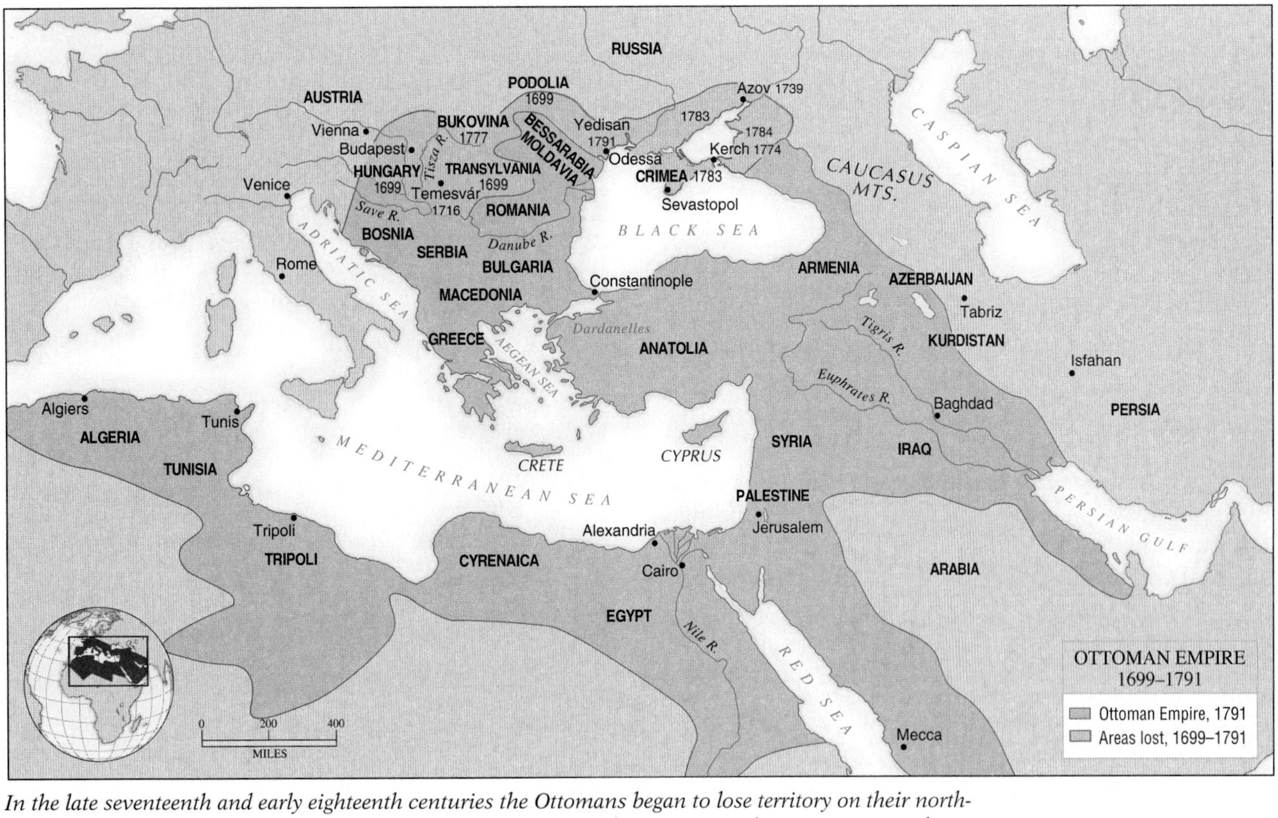

In the late seventeenth and early eighteenth centuries the Ottomans began to lose territory on their northern frontiers. As the eighteenth century progressed Russia emerged as a primary threat to Ottoman dominance in the region.

bul was in a panic as the Venetians vanquished the Ottoman fleet in the Dardanelles, provincial rebels seized much of eastern Anatolia, and food supplies became scarce. In the midst of this crisis, the empire required drastic measures; it found a man willing to take such measures in the person of a 79-year-old pasha named Mehmet Köprülü (MEH-met koo-PROO-loo; 1586–1661). Köprülü is a striking example of the power that elderly members of the military-administrative class could achieve if they managed to survive the challenges of multiple military campaigns and the competition within the palace system.

The sultan granted Mehmed Köprülü extraordinary powers. The pasha then suppressed the rebels in the provinces and broke the Venetian blockade of the Dardanelles. He used the sweeping powers granted him by the sultan to quell opposition and gain some control over the military. For two generations Köprülü and members of his family served as reformist **vizirs** (veh-ZEERS), attempting to bring some power back into the hands of the central government. They launched campaigns against Austria and Poland, took Crete, and reformed taxes. They also struck thousands of men from the rolls of the janissaries, which had become bloated with nonmilitary men who collected pay but did not fight. The problems of the empire, however, were not solved; conscription had depopulated the countryside, and Russia was emerging as a major threat to the north. **"Tax farms"** which the government sold to finance its wars, were becoming hereditary. The empire thus entered the next century in a precarious military and economic state.

The Tulip Period

The eighteenth century for the Ottomans is framed by a period of literary and artistic florescence at its beginning and a period of concerted military reform at its end. The century began inauspiciously, with a massive revolt in the capital that deposed the sultan and brought Ahmed III (1703–1730) to the throne. During his reign, the Ottomans were successful in battle against Russia but lost decisively to the Austrians. In 1718 Ibrahim Pasha became grand vizir and under his influence Ahmed launched a program of building, entertainments, and patronage of the arts that was later called the Tulip Period because of the fashion for extravagant gardens. Tulips were the rage, and rare varieties sold for fabulous sums. Ibrahim supervised the building of a pleasure palace for the sultan called the "Place of Happiness," a model for other palaces and their luxurious lifestyles.

In the Tulip Period, Ottoman elites became great consumers of European, particularly French, styles in fashion and decor, and European artists were imported to enhance life among the elite. Yirmisekiz Chelebi Mehmed (YEER-mee-SEH-keez she-LEH-bee), sent to Paris by Ibrahim, sent back reports on French zoos, gardens, women, publications, and shops as well as on arms and military schools. It was an era when the Ottomans became highly conscious of the need to emulate Western military tactics and technology and when the fashions of the French court were admired and imitated, in part, by elite Ottoman women. The luxuries of the Tulip Period were cele-

Images of women appeared more frequently in eighteenth-century Ottoman miniatures than in earlier Ottoman art. This late-eighteenth-century work depicting childbirth in the harem also illustrates the influence of European fashions in ladies' dress styles. While the midwife delivers the child, a cradle stands by to receive it.

vizir—A chief minister in the Ottoman government.

tax farms—Farms controlled by government administrators who could collect revenues from the farmers, remit most to the ruler, and use the rest to support their own interests.

brated in verse by poets, such as Nedim (d. 1730), who were experimenting with new styles: "This year, border your crimson shawl in mink, / And if the tulip cups are lacking, bring wine cups in their stead."[1] Tulips, fur-lined garments, and wine cups were all markers of elite status and wealth. Scholarship also continued to flourish under the sultan's patronage. The first Ottoman Turkish language press was founded by Ibrahim Müteferrika (EE-brah-heem MOO-teh-FEH-ree-kah) in 1720, producing maps, a dictionary, and works on science, history, and geography. The press had been opposed by some of the religious authorities but was permitted so long as it did not print books on religious subjects. The extravagance of the Tulip Period, however, did not mesh well with the conditions of economic depression and political conflict in which the empire found itself. Ahmed's reign ended as it had begun, with a violent rebellion in the capital that produced prolonged rioting and forced the sultan's abdication.

Eighteenth-Century War, Relations, and Reform

Although the empire still had its share of cultural and military successes, overall, the eighteenth century was characterized by the extension of more special commercial privileges (capitulations) to European states, loss of Ottoman territory, and a growing willingness to employ European military advisers, tactics, training methods, and technology. Travel, of Ottomans to Europe and of Europeans to the Ottoman Empire, intensified beyond the merchant activities that had for centuries connected the two regions. The Ottomans also began sending ambassadors to European courts and receiving ambassadors from more European states in return, a sign of the empire's growing weakness and need for communication. The empire had been a dominant power for centuries, and its rulers were generally persuaded of their own cultural superiority. But Ottoman military defeats prompted some Ottoman elites to consider significant military reform in order to duplicate or (they hoped) even surpass the successes of Europe. To that end, Sultan Mahmud I (r. 1730–1754) brought in the French mercenary Comte de Bonneval to help modernize the military; Mustafa III (r. 1757–1774) hired the Hungarian Baron de Tott to revamp his artillery corps and establish a military school; and Abdülhamid I (ahb-dool-HAH-mid; r. 1774–1789) imported numerous foreign military advisers. All of these attempts were vehemently opposed by the janissaries, who saw them as a threat to their own status and position.

Throughout the century, the Ottomans fought intermittently with European foes and with a series of new military leaders in Persia. The government was entangled, in alliances and competing interests, with Britain, France, Austria, and Russia, all of which had designs on certain segments of Ottoman territory. The empire had already lost Hungary and Transylvania to Austria by the Peace of Carlowitz in 1699, and it surrendered to the Austrian emperor the right to intervene in the affairs of Catholics in Ottoman territory. A series of eighteenth-century wars with Russia culminated in the 1774 Treaty of Küchük Kaynarca (koo-CHOOK kai-NAHR-kah), under which the Ottomans paid a large indemnity, gave up the Crimea, allowed Russia to interfere in the affairs of Orthodox Christians in the empire, and granted Russia commercial access to the Black Sea. By granting foreign powers like Austria and Russia rights to intervene on behalf of Ottoman Christian subjects, the empire was allowing these states to undermine its sovereignty and autonomy. These concessions suggested that Christians in the empire could appeal to outside powers and circumvent the authority of Ottoman law.

Several factors demonstrate the weakness of Ottoman central control over the provinces. The semi-independent governors *(ayan)* and their private armies challenged the dictates of the palace in the provinces. In Iraq, Egypt, Tunis, Tripoli, and Algeria, Mamluk ("slave") or janissary garrisons created their own military regimes, often intermarrying with the local elites and refusing to cooperate with Ottoman decrees. A puritanical religious revival in Arabia, the Wahhabi (wah-HAH-bee) movement, founded by Muhammad ibn Abd al-Wahhab (1703–1792), joined forces with the Sa'ud family and seized control of Mecca in 1803, an enormous blow to Ottoman prestige. The Wahhabis were a true fundamentalist movement; they argued that Islam had to be purified and all innovations (such as Sufism) eliminated. This movement had a long-term and powerful influence on the development of Arabia.

Meanwhile, European powers also aggressively intervened in Ottoman affairs; Austria and Russia stirred up revolts in the Balkans, and in 1798 Napoleon invaded Ottoman Egypt. The Ottoman regime was powerless to stop Napoleon, requiring British assistance to defeat his forces. Although the British destroyed Napoleon's fleet and forced him to flee shortly after the invasion, the French occupation both demonstrated Ottoman weakness and left a lasting legacy of scholarship on Egypt produced by Napoleon's entourage. Their studies and images of Egypt, brought back to France, helped fuel a new European interest in travel to, and interpretation of the "Orient," its goods, and its culture.

Document — Lady Montagu, Florence Nightingale, and the Myths of "Orient"

In the eighteenth and early nineteenth centuries, the Ottoman Empire stepped up its exchange of ambassadors with the states of Europe. This same time period, particularly after Napoleon's invasion of Egypt in 1798, witnessed a dramatic increase in the number of affluent European travelers who journeyed to various parts of the empire. They came not only for diplomatic and military purposes but also to seek adventure, acquire antiquities, and see the sights. Among these travelers were women of the elite classes like Lady Mary Wortley Montagu, wife of the British Ambassador to Istanbul in 1716, and Florence Nightingale, who later served as a nurse in the Crimean War. Florence Nightingale traveled to Egypt in 1849–1850, nominally for her health, but actually to seek out and explore the remains of ancient Egypt and to avoid her parents' efforts to have her marry. Lady Montagu, well educated and a member of London's literary circles, came as the young and independent-minded wife of a foreign ambassador.

Like the accounts of all travelers, the letters of these women were colored by their own knowledge and expectations and by the limitations (affected, among other things, by gender and class) on what they saw and experienced of the cultures they visited. But attitude is also an important factor in the tales of travelers, and these two women were very different from one another. Both traveled in elite circles, were interested in buying up antiquities (including Egyptian mummies), and employed ethnic stereotypes; neither had much regard for the poorer classes. But while Ms. Nightingale was seeking a religious "mission," Lady Montagu was ecumenical and irreverent. While Nightingale found the Egyptians barbaric and less than human, Montagu learned Turkish, visited harems, and characterized the Ottomans as very human (and sometimes superior to the English). Nightingale seemed to prefer the architecture of Cairo to the Cairene people, while Montagu traveled veiled as a Turkish woman so that she could explore the city. Each woman suggested in her letters that she was communicating an image of the "real" Egypt or the "real" Turkey. But, in the end, Nightingale's letters convey a romantic reverence for lost antiquity combined with a horror of the Egyptian people (especially the peasants), while Montagu, writing more than a century earlier, presented a much more complex image of Ottoman beliefs and society.

You cannot conceive of the painfulness of the impression made upon one by the population here.... One goes riding out, and one really feels inclined to believe that this is the kingdom of the devil and to shudder under this glorious sun.... I cannot describe it. In Italy one felt they were children, and their dawn was coming; here one feels as if they were demons; and their sun was set ... and out of these huts come crawling creatures, half-clothed, even in this country, where it is a shame for a woman to show her face. They do not strike one as half-formed beings, who will grow up and grow more complete, but as evil degraded creatures. I have never seen misery before but I felt, "Oh, how I should like to live here! What would I give to take this field!" But here, one turns away one's face ... thanking God that one is not here to stay.

From Florence Nightingale, *Letters From Egypt: A Journey on the Nile, 1849–1850,* ed. Anthony Sattin (New York: Wiedenfeld and Nicholson, 1987), pp. 39–40.

[Letter to a Lady friend, 17 June 1717] I heartily beg your ladyships' pardon, but I really could not forbear laughing at your letter and the commissions you are pleased to honor me with. You desire me to buy you a Greek slave who is to be mistress of a thousand good qualities. The Greeks are subjects and not slaves [of the Ottoman Empire]. Those who are to be bought in that manner are either such as are taken in war or stolen by the Tartars from Russia, Circassia, or Georgia, and are such miserable, awkward, poor wretches you would not think any of them worthy to be your housemaid. The fine slaves that wait upon the great ladies or serve the pleasures of the great men are all bought at the age of eight or nine years old and educated with great care to accomplish them in singing, dancing, embroidery, etc. They are commonly Circassians and their patron never sells them except as a punishment for some great fault. If ever they grow weary of them, they either present them to a friend or give them their freedoms.

From *The Turkish Embassy Letters of Lady Mary Wortley Montagu*, ed. Malcolm Jack (London: Virago Press, 2000), pp. 103–105.

Questions to Consider

1. Lady Montagu was not an expert on slavery in the Ottoman Empire, but she did know more than her correspondents. What does her letter suggest about certain types of slavery in the empire and about English misperceptions?
2. What kinds of difference do you think it makes whether or not a traveler learns the language of the country she or he is visiting?
3. What do these letters suggest about the differences class and gender make in the ways a traveler portrays the society he or she is visiting?

The Reforms of Selim III

Selim III (seh-LEEM; 1789–1807) is often considered the first major Ottoman reformer, but his reform program was not new. Like several of his eighteenth-century predecessors, he proposed military and tax reforms as avenues to restore the empire to its past glory. Selim opened new technical schools to train officers and modernized arms production. He drastically cut the janissary rolls to get rid of noncombatants, but he mollified the traditional military corps by increasing pay and modernizing barracks. Offending the janissaries had proved disastrous for various of his predecessors. Most of Selim's efforts and resources, however, went to modernizing the navy and training a "new model" army of 23,000 men. It was a European-style infantry corps (with European-style uniforms), composed primarily of Turkish peasants and staffed in part with French officers. Selim hoped that this new army would help restore the empire to its former position of power and be more amenable to modern techniques of warfare. But the empire was not yet ready to break the entrenched power of its traditional military forces; Selim was deposed by a janissary uprising in 1807. Eliminating the janissaries was a task that would fall to his successor, Mahmud II (1807–1839). Although Selim's new army was disbanded, his reforms opened up the empire to further European influence, especially in the realm of military training.

Selim III's efforts to reform the Ottoman state were thwarted by the janissaries, who deposed the sultan, imprisoned him, and later assassinated him.

MUSLIM POLITICS IN PERSIA

▪ *How did Persian relations with the Europeans change in the early modern era?*

The Safavid (sah-FAH-vid) Empire in Persia suffered from many of the same problems that afflicted the Ottomans, although Persia was more isolated from the conflicts of the European great powers than the Ottoman Empire was. The tribal confederations in Persia remained powerful throughout the period of Safavid rule and, after the reign of Abbas (1588–1629), increasingly challenged the central government's authority. Despite weak rulers and an Ottoman invasion of Iraq, however, the Safavid Empire remained intact and relatively secure for almost a century after Abbas died. But the eighteenth century would bring in new warlords to rule the Safavid domains and place Persia in a military squeeze between the Russians to the north, the Ottomans to the west, the Mughals to the east, and the British to the south.

The Middle East, Europe, and the World

The end of Safavid rule was initiated by an Afghan invasion in 1723 that forced Shah Husein to surrender. Although members of the Safavid family controlled parts of Persia for some years afterward, this invasion effectively ended the dynasty's rule over the region. Both the Russians and the Ottomans capitalized on Safavid distress by invading northern and western Persia. Afghan rule was not destined to last long, however. A new Turkic military commander of the Afshar tribe from eastern Persia allied himself with a Safavid prince and defeated the Afghans. By 1736, Nadir (na-DEER) Khan had defeated the Ottomans in an engagement near Tabriz and declared himself shah ("king"). This new warlord reformed the government, reorganized the army, and favored both Sunni and Shia branches of Islam, thereby alienating the Shi'ite *ulama* and gaining some favor with the Ottomans. By 1747 Nadir had regained lost territories, conquered western Afghanistan, plundered the Mughal capital at Delhi, and extended Persian hegemony over the Uzbeks to the north. But his visions of unifying and ruling a Sunni and Shi'ite empire came to nothing when he was assassinated by his own men.

Persia was once again politically fragmented, but soon—between 1750 and 1779—another tribal warlord, Karim Khan Zand, emerged and gained control

Middle East and South Asia

1622	Sultan Osman II deposed in an Ottoman rebellion
1637–1680	Shivaji Bhonsle, celebrated early leader of Marathas in India
1656–1691	Age of the Köprülü vizirs in the Ottoman Empire
1658–1707	Rule of Mughal emperor Aurangzeb in India
1690	British East India Company acquired land to develop base at Calcutta
1700	Mughal emperor grants British the right to trade and collect taxes in Bengal
1718–1730	Tulip Period
1723	Afghan invasion of Iran leads to end of Safavid Empire
1739	Invading army of Nadir Shah sacks Mughal capital at Delhi
1747	Durrani dynasty comes to power in Afghanistan
1765	Mughal emperor grants British administrative control over Bengal
1774	Treaty of Küchük Kaynarca after Russian defeat of Ottomans
1789–1807	Reign of the reformist Ottoman sultan Selim III
1794–1924	Qajar dynasty in Iran
1800	Anglo-Persian defense treaty

over most of the region. Karim Khan's reign was one of relative success and prosperity. He invaded Iraq, raided Ottoman territory, and encouraged trade relations with the British in the Persian Gulf. At his death, the country lapsed again into savage contention among tribal leaders. Zand successors ruled parts of Persia until 1794, but the Qajar (kah-JAR) dynasty, which was to rule until 1924, finally managed to replace them.

As the century drew to a close, Russia, Britain, and France were all competing for Persian trade, and Persia was drawn more directly into European power politics. An Anglo-Persian defense and commercial treaty in 1800 encouraged the Qajar shah to expect aid against the Afghans and Russia; when this was not forthcoming, he accepted a French military mission to train his troops. This entente collapsed when the French and Russians signed a temporary truce, demonstrating the precarious nature of alliances made with European states. The British then regained the advantage as advisers and commercial partners of the shah.

Thus Persia, like the Ottoman Empire, was increasingly drawn into the economic and military spheres of European powers, where once those same powers had come as petitioners seeking trade privileges in the Middle East. This shift in the balance of power in the late eighteenth and early nineteenth centuries did not radically alter life for the vast majority of citizens of these large agrarian empires. But it did begin to alter basic structures of economic and military organization and to produce a group of elite men who were more conversant with European ways.

EARLY MODERN INDIA UNDER THE MUGHALS

- *Which domestic and international factors eroded Mughal power in the seventeenth and eighteenth centuries?*

The Mughal Empire was one of the world's wealthiest and most powerful states: Its rich traditions, art, and literature affected the whole Indian subcontinent. Mughal power culminated in the long reign of Aurangzeb (ow-RAHNG-zeb; r. 1658–1707), a period marked by military and administrative success. Aurangzeb's policies, however, began to alter the imperial order, based on tolerance, established by the great Akbar (r. 1556–1605). The new emperor, who learned the entire Qur'an by heart, was a champion of Islamic orthodoxy; he saw himself as a man of great piety and patronized Islamic leaders, reversing his predecessors' balanced respect for all religions. He destroyed a number of Hindu temples and schools, although it should be noted that he did support some other Hindu temples. His attacks on some religious institutions may have had as much to do with his punishment of those temples' Hindu patrons for their presumed disloyalty as it did with anti-Hinduism. He reimposed the *jizya,* the poll tax on non-Muslims, and dismissed Hindus from government service (he cut their numbers on his staff to just 25 percent). Until about 1679, he was occupied in securing his northern frontiers, so he did not push these pro-Muslim policies vigorously at first; this changed later when he adopted a less tolerant policy.

DOCUMENT
Aurangzeb, Mughal Ruler

These abuses did not provoke mass rebellion among the Mughal subjects, who were primarily Hindu peasants, but they did make Mughal rule intolerable to many. They provoked military challenges from Hindu warlords, which, accompanied by social and economic changes, weakened Mughal rule. Several factors may have undermined the Mughals after the reign of Aurangzeb. Though some historians blame the emperor himself for failure of administration, others contend that his era was fairly successful, leading to the rise of competing forces. For instance, the Mughals rewarded the Marathas (ma-RAH-tahs), a powerful tribal confederation in the south that had ambitions to expand their territory and power, with government posts for their successes and their support. The Marathas and others soon became political and military competitors. The growth of the Mughal economy and international trade also brought in New World silver; this, together with the development of cash crops, new technologies, and new trading opportunities—all desirable developments—led to competing economic elites. The Mughals had never controlled certain areas of India, and those areas' rulers saw an opportunity to develop increasing independence from the Mughals.

MAP The Delhi Sultanate and Mughal India

One such group was the Marathas. To fight them, Aurangzeb virtually moved his capital to a battle camp in the Deccan, staying in a tent city in the field and heading an unwieldy host of 500,000 servants, 50,000 camels, and 30,000 elephants, in addition to fighting men. By 1690, after terrible losses, he had overcome most resistance, but the south could not be permanently pacified. Time and again, the aging ruler was forced to undertake new campaigns; when he died in 1707, it was in the Deccan.

Architecture and the arts during the reign of Aurangzeb were austere and religious. Wine, song, and dance were not allowed in courtly festivals. The emperor did encourage various projects in law and theology. As in the Ottoman Empire, when revenues declined, Aurangzeb employed tax farming to provide quick government income; tax farms were farms controlled by administrators who could collect revenues from the farmers, remit most to the emperor, and use the rest to support an army. The farms enriched corrupt officials at the expense of both Hindu and Muslim peasants. Peasants had little recourse against the government although they could take their complaints to the Islamic Sharia courts. After Aurangzeb died, Mughal authority was further decentralized, and South Asia was increasingly divided among rival kingdoms. A period of civil war ensued until Muhammad Shah (r. 1719–1748) succeeded to the imperial throne. Described by one contemporary as "never without a mistress in his arms and a glass in his hand," this indolent monarch made some effort to placate Hindus, with little practical result. Local Muslim dynasties ruled in the south and in Bengal; the Sikhs (SEEKS), a sect based on a Hindu-Muslim synthesis, became autonomous in the northwest; the Hindu Rajputs (RAHJ-poots), once Mughal allies, began to break away; and the fierce Hindu Marathas, whom Aurangzeb had tried to subdue over a period of 30 years, extended their sway over much of central India. The impotence of the empire was most effectively demonstrated in 1739 when the army of the Persian Nadir Shah burned and looted the Mughal capital at Delhi, killing some 30,000 and carrying away the imperial Peacock Throne, which would become a centerpiece of the Persian treasury.

Nadir Shah's invasion was but a prelude to the anarchic conditions that prevailed after Muhammad Shah's death in 1748. Mughal power met major military challenges from three directions: the Afghans in the north, the Marathas in the south, and later the British from their base in Bengal in the northeast. When Nadir Shah (1736–1747) was assassinated in 1747, his Afghan troops elevated one of their commanders, Ahmad Khan (1747–1773), to the position of shah. He took the title *Durr-i Durran* ("Pearl of Pearls"), after which his line was called the Durrani. Uniting the Afghans and conquering a vast territory—which comprised eastern Persia, present-day Afghanistan, the major part of Uzbek Turkestan, and much of northwestern India including Kashmir and the Punjab—he established a dynasty that would survive in Afghanistan into the twentieth century. During one campaign in India, Ahmad sacked Delhi (1756), decisively defeating the Marathas and helping to open the country to the British. At Panipat in 1761 his Afghans (employing their superior light artillery) crushed a huge Maratha army. But after Ahmad's death in 1772, the Afghans lost power in India, and his sprawling tribal state lapsed into almost continuous civil war.

The Afghans were a serious threat, but it was the Maratha Confederacy in the northwestern Deccan that had earlier emerged as the most powerful force to challenge Mughal supremacy. The first great Maratha leader was Shivaji Bhonsle (shee-VAH-jee BONS-le; 1630?–1680). At the age of 17, Shivaji began to build a small regional state by capturing forts and passes through the Western Ghat Mountains. He seized some territory from the kingdom of Bijapur, whose sultan sent an army under the general Afzal Khan to discipline him. Shivaji retreated to one of his hill forts, and in a famous episode, the two generals met to negotiate. Both bore arms, and in close combat Shivaji managed to disembowel Afzal Khan with a "tiger claw" (a steel weapon) concealed in the palm of his hand. Aurangzeb sent several armies to discipline Shivaji, but the Maratha chief proved illusive, raiding Mughal territory and the prosperous port of Surat on the west coast of India. When Shivaji was called to court to negotiate with the Mughal emperor, Aurangzeb publicly humiliated him. This episode set the stage for a new series of campaigns, during which Shivaji challenged the Mughal armies and extended his territory in the Deccan.

Shivaji's family had been agriculturalists, not members of the Hindu warrior or ruling caste (Kshatriya). But Shivaji was functionally a warrior nonetheless, and his rise to power illustrates the movement of a family over time from one caste group to another. To legitimize his rule, Shivaji sent to the holy Hindu city of Varanasi, where he persuaded a distinguished brahman to supply him with a Kshatriya genealogy and devise ceremonies of Hindu kingship. In these elaborate ceremonies, Shivaji offered sacrifices to the gods and received gifts from brahmans and nobles, thus reviving the notion of Hindu kingship in the subcontinent. In general, Hindu ceremonial was resurrected under the Marathas after long centuries of Muslim Mughal rule. After his death, Shivaji was immortalized in Maratha tales and ballads, and today he is celebrated as a hero figure by Hindu nationalists.

From the base established by Shivaji, various Marathas continued their wars of resistance against the Mughals, sometimes fragmented by civil war, sometimes losing territory or being co-opted by Mughal offers of position and wealth. Shortly after Aurangzeb's death, several Maratha leaders began to expand their territories into Malwa, Gujarat, and Rajasthan. In the second half of the eighteenth century, the Marathas gained control over central and north India, reducing the Mughal emperor to the status of puppet ruler. Elsewhere in India, Mughal power was challenged by the rise in power of tax farmers, princely rulers of territories, and provincial governors as well as ambitious lawbreakers. In the north and east, the Mughals also came up against the forces of a new power jockeying for position in the subcontinent, the British East India Company.

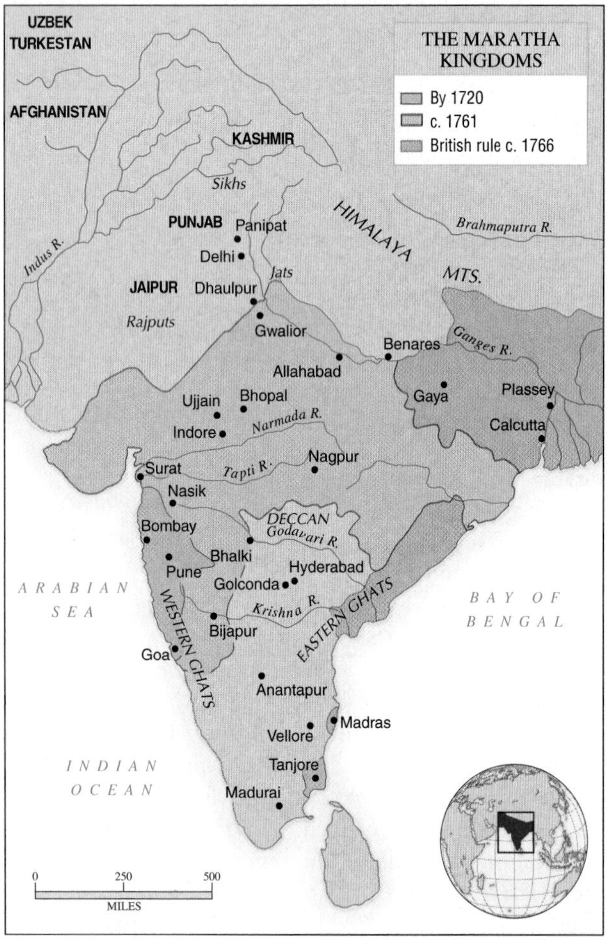

The Marathas in the Deccan rebelled against Mughal rule and won many victories against the Mughal kings. In the seventeenth and eighteenth centuries, first the Marathas and then the British posed formidable challenges to Mughal sovereignty.

The Europeans in India

As was the case in Africa, the Portuguese were the first European power to establish themselves along the coasts of South Asia and exploit the rich commerce of the subcontinent. The Dutch, French, and English followed, and by the seventeenth century, all four powers had commercial bases in India. All were attracted by the rich trade in spices and jewels and especially by the wonderful variety and volume of Indian textiles. As in Africa, the Europeans did not initially penetrate inland; their commercial ventures were dependent on the elaborate and complex networks of traders, financiers, and middlemen already conducting trade into the interior and along the routes connecting India to China, Southeast Asia, Africa, and the Middle East.

Portuguese Church in Southern India

Of the European powers, the Dutch dominated in Southeast Asia, but it was the British who managed to gain ascendancy in South Asia. They established bases in India through negotiation and commercial exchange then later extended their power and territory by force. In 1601 a group of British merchants petitioned Queen Elizabeth to grant them a monopoly over trade with "the East." Although the newly chartered East India Company (EIC) claimed a monopoly over all trade between India and Europe, what it actually acquired was a monopoly over all trade between British territory and India. The peoples of "the East," of course, had no obligation to honor such charters, but this was an era of sweeping European claims to trade and territory in various areas of the globe; the charters did give such merchant companies a legal advantage over competitors among their own countrymen.

The British presence in India exerted an increasing influence on the arts. This work of an Indian painter, inscribed in Persian and dated about 1760, depicts an official of the British East India Company smoking a water pipe and receiving an Indian visitor. Some British officials, like the one shown here, adopted South Asian furnishings; others adopted Indian styles of dress, food, and entertainment or married Indian women.

From an early "**factory**" in Surat, the British expanded to bases in Madras, Bombay (ceded to Britain by the Portuguese as a dowry for the English King Charles II's bride), and Bengal (the territory surrounding the mouth of the Ganges river). In 1690 a Company agent acquired a piece of land in the Ganges delta that the British swiftly developed into the commercial entrepot known as Calcutta. By 1700 the Company had a charter from the Mughal emperor to trade and collect taxes in the area, and by 1750 the population of Calcutta reached around 500,000. It was a major port for the Company and for Indian and independent European traders.

Calcutta provides an interesting case study for the ways (besides direct conquest) in which the British established their power in India. The Company used its bases to extend its commercial affairs inland and employed its own private army to forge alliances with local rulers. Both sides benefited (the local rulers receiving money and military assistance against their enemies from the British) although various local lords resisted British incursions. Because the balance of trade was much in favor of India, Britain sent thousands of pounds in silver to pay for its purchases. By 1800 the wealth (especially taxes) generated by the Company's activities provided a substantial portion of Britain's income.

DOCUMENT
Abu Taleb on the West and Western Influence

The British East India Company in the eighteenth century provides a clear illustration of the establishment of a new world order based on seaborne circuits of trade and the extension of European imperial power beyond the port cities of Asia and Africa. Where the Dutch, British, and French established agricultural estate colonies in Africa and Southeast Asia, in South Asia they directed their attentions, at least initially, primarily to commercial establishments. There were direct links, however, between these regions, as the Indian Ocean served not only as a medium for the transport of goods to the West but also as an arena for the circulation of slaves, workers, and mariners among the burgeoning colonies of imperial Europe.

The trade conducted by the EIC is also noteworthy for its role in **mercantilism** in the eighteenth century and for its political role in the latter part of the century. By 1750, the British market was saturated with Indian calicoes and other fabrics of high quality and low cost. Low cost was possible because Indian textile workers could maintain a decent standard of living at lower wages than could their counterparts in Europe. This was due to the higher productivity of India's agriculture, which led to lower food prices in India than in Europe; workers thus needed less income to feed themselves. The cost of fabric was kept down, and resources were freed up for other types of investment. Indian textile production grew rapidly. India accounted for 25 percent of all world manufacturing in 1750 due to enormous textile sales to Europe, Asia, and the Americas. Though the British government responded to the large volume of textile

factory—European commercial office and warehouse in India or China, headed by a factor.

mercantilism—Economic and political policy that regarded wealth as a measure of a nation's strength; mercantilist countries promoted companies that helped produce a favorable balance of trade.

imports by imposing stiff tariffs, the volume of trade remained high; the EIC carried this profitable trade.

In the second half of the century, the East India Company became increasingly involved in local politics, building its own domain in Bengal and challenging the authority of the local ruler, Siraj ud-Dawla (see-RAHJ ood-DOW-lah), who asserted his independence as Mughal power declined. In 1756, Siraj ud-Dawla retaliated by seizing Calcutta and demanding increased payments from the EIC for the privilege of trading there. The Company then sent a military force of 2000 men under Robert Clive, who crushed Siraj ud-Dawla's army in the battle of Plassey in 1757. Clive went on to defeat the French and Dutch establishments in Bengal. In 1760, the British defeated the French at Pondicherry, a decisive battle in the Seven Years' War (1756–1763). By the Treaty of Allahabad (al-LAH-ah-bahd) in 1765, the Mughal emperor granted the British administrative control of Bengal. The Company thus became one of many Indian provincial "lords." The British then extended their power inland using a combination of military force and commercial treaty. They gained hegemony over a great circuit of trade from India to China and to England, exchanging Indian opium for Chinese tea (all the rage in England) and English silver for Indian silk.

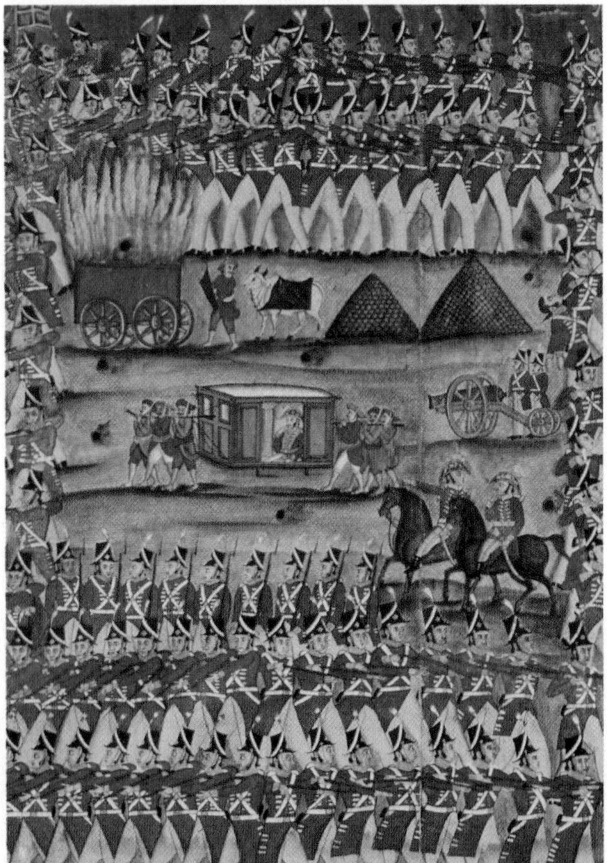

A major opponent to British incursion into India was Tipu Sultan, called the "Tiger of Mysore." This painting by an unknown Indian artist shows British soldiers unsuccessfully fighting Tipu's forces in 1780. The British defeated Tipu in 1799.

By the end of the century, the Mughal ruler Shah Alam II was collecting a British pension, and William Jones and other officials were cultivating British interest in Sanskrit classics (as the entourage of Napoleon cultivated scholarship in Egyptian and Arabic cultures). While the Ottoman and Persian empires suffered military defeats and increasing economic subordination to European powers in this era, the Mughal Empire surrendered large segments of its territory, first to the Marathas and then to the British. The Mughals could only look on as the British East India Company, employing Indian armies, extended its sway over the subcontinent.

THE QING DYNASTY BEFORE THE OPIUM WAR

- *How did the Manchu emperors make their dynasty acceptable to ethnic Chinese?*

Between 1644, when the Qing rulers took Beijing, and the early decades of the nineteenth century, China was the most populous and prosperous country on earth. In 1700, China, Europe, and India each accounted for approximately 23 percent of the world's gross domestic product. In 1820, China's share had risen to about 33 percent and Europe's to about 27 percent, while India's declined to about 16 percent. China produced one-third of the world's manufactured goods in 1750, but that percentage began to decline rapidly after 1820. What historians call the "long eighteenth century"—from the late seventeenth century to the early nineteenth—was an era of splendor and growth for China. Its economy grew steadily while its literature, art, and philosophy evoked admiration from Asian and European intellec-

Qing China

1644	Founding of the Qing (Manchu) dynasty
1662–1722	Reign of Kangxi
1736–1796	Reign of Qianlong
1759	Guangzhou (Canton) system established
1793	Macartney Mission to China
1796–1804	White Lotus uprising

tuals alike. Although impossible to predict, however, the seeds of later decline were already being sown by 1820.

The Manchus came to power after Ming loyalists called on them to help put down the rebel Li Zicheng (LEE zuh-CHUNG) in Beijing. The Manchus had developed a state north of the Great Wall in the decades before 1644. The inhabitants of Manchuria were controlled by military units called "banners"; their previously tribal government was organized as a bureaucracy with laws modeled on the Ming code; and script was created to represent the spoken language. In the 1630s, Hong Taiji (TAI-jee), the son of the Manchu Nurhachi (noor-HAH-chee; 1559–1616) who had begun the process of Manchu state-building several decades earlier, proclaimed the founding of the Qing (CHING) dynasty, thereby challenging the Ming's right to rule China. Still, the Manchus seemed preferable to the rebel Chinese, and Ming loyalists like General Wu Sangui (WOO sahn-GWEH; 1612–1678) asked for Manchu assistance.

Manchu Imperial Rule

Upon coming over the Great Wall, the Manchus showed they meant to rule. They honored the Ming by giving a proper burial to the last Ming emperor but soon moved the Chinese inhabitants of Beijing to the southern part of the city while they occupied the northern part. Land was confiscated from Chinese farmers to support the Qing military banner forces. Men were required to adopt the Qing queue hairstyle as an indication of loyalty, and women were prohibited from binding their feet. The former, of course, could be enforced, while the latter, a more private practice, could be continued by Han Chinese as a covert indicator of their non-Manchu ethnicity, as women were more often indoors and their feet remained unseen.

The Manchus' first order of business was establishing military control of the Chinese realm. Emperor Shunzhi (SHOON-jih; r. 1644–1661) and his powerful successor Kangxi (KANG-shee; r. 1662–1722) conquered Ming loyalist factions in the south with the help of General Wu Sangui. When the Ming loyalists mounted armed resistance, they were brutally suppressed. One resister, Zheng Chenggong (ZHUNG cheng-GONG; 1624–1662), known to Westerners of his day as Coxinga, fled to Taiwan where he ousted the Dutch occupiers in 1662. His son held out until Kangxi's forces defeated him in 1683. The last uprising against the Qing was staged by Wu Sangui himself, but like the others, he and his followers were defeated in 1681.

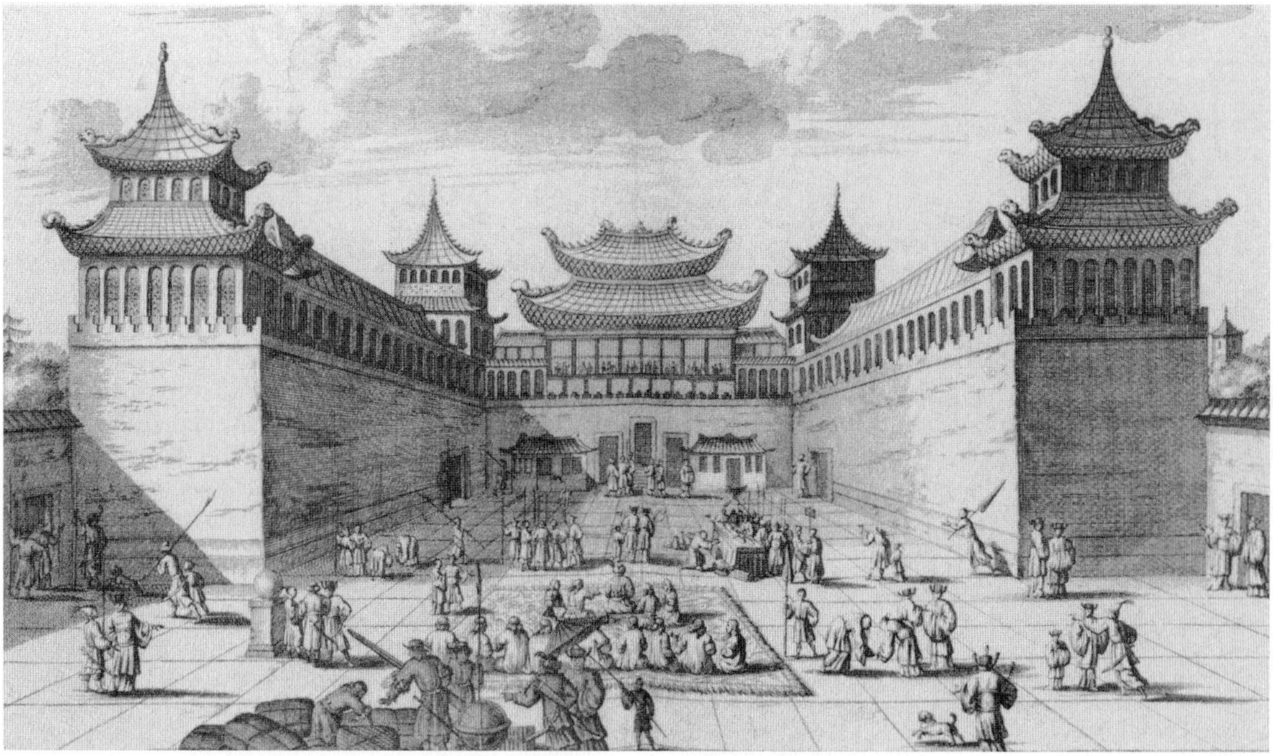

The 1689 treaty between Russia and China was the first treaty that China concluded with any Western power. In this contemporary engraving, the Russian ambassador is ceremonially greeted as he arrives for an audience with Emperor Kangxi. Note how the scale of the Chinese Imperial Palace in relationship to the Chinese figures and to the Russians suggests Chinese power over the foreign presence. Notice also how the Russians in this image have a globe of the world with them.

Kangxi extended Qing control over an enormous realm. After defeating opponents, using Chinese troops and generals, the emperor destroyed a Russian Cossack base and signed the Treaty of Nerchinsk in 1689. This treaty both eliminated the possibility of a Russian alliance with the Mongols against China and established normal relations between Russia and the Qing without imposition of a tributary relationship. In 1696 and 1697, Kangxi led troops against the Mongols and defeated them. In 1720, his armies invaded and installed a pro-Chinese Dalai Lama in Tibet. Later, during the reign of his son, the Russians recognized Chinese sovereignty over Mongolia under the Treaty of Kaikhta (1727). And, under his grandson, the Qing extended their control to Chinese Central Asia, an area with a large Muslim population permitted to retain its religion.

Jesuit missionaries were welcome at both the Ming and early Qing courts. This engraving shows a pioneering Jesuit in China, Matteo Ricci, and a Chinese convert in the late Ming dynasty.

To underscore Qing legitimacy as a Chinese dynasty, Kangxi held a special examination in 1679 to recruit scholars to write a Ming history and other works. He patronized Zhu Xi (JOO SHEE) Confucianism. At the same time, he was fascinated by Western mathematics and sciences, and supported the Jesuits at the court. He issued an edict of religious toleration in 1692, permitting conversion to Christianity, provided Chinese converts continued to practice ancestral rites of respect. The Vatican, however, rejected Kangxi's position and sent an envoy to Beijing to assert control over Chinese Catholics. Kangxi then expelled missionaries who would not accept Chinese Christians' performance of ancestor worship.

Though the Qing tried to maintain their identity and dominance, they recognized the need to bring Chinese into the government. Paralleling the Manchu military banners, the Qing created banner forces made up of Chinese troops. In civil administration, the Qing encouraged Chinese to take exams for bureaucratic posts, most of which Chinese came to occupy. At the top levels of government, a dual administrative structure was formed in which most provinces had Chinese governors while governors-general, who were usually Manchus, ruled over two provincial governors. At the level of the top government ministers, each of the six boards had a Manchu and a Chinese minister, and half the Grand Secretaries were Chinese.

The Kangxi era was a time of creative artistic work. While many scholars took part in the compilation of the Ming history, many others refused to serve the Qing. The latter included nonconformist painters like Bada Shuren (c. 1626–1705) and philosophers like Gu Yanwu (1613–1682) whose focus on practical learning influenced later Qing philosophers.

Kangxi died an old man with 56 children. His designated heir became cruel and mentally unstable, but Kangxi, disappointed, failed to appoint an alternative before his death. The next emperor, Yongzheng (YONG-jung; r. 1723–1735), staged a coup, overthrew his incompetent brother, and ascended the throne. Like his father, Yongzheng was an effective, hard-working ruler. He established a new senior bureaucracy, the Grand Council, headed by the ministers of the six boards. He simplified the tax system and reformed the payment of local administrators so they would not be dependent on informal channels of income which opened them up to corruption. He also outlawed hereditary servitude, thus freeing members of enslaved classes.

Yongzheng's death was not followed by turmoil or a coup, as he had set up a secure system to make sure his designated heir would assume the throne. Qianlong (chen-LONG; r. 1736–1796, d. 1799) ushered in the most prosperous period in China's early

The Kangxi Emperor attempted to model himself on the ideal Chinese ruler, permitting him to consolidate Manchu power over the country during his 60-year reign.

modern history. The territorial boundaries of China extended far into Central Asia, and its wealth and productivity dwarfed those of any other country in the world.

Qianlong's capital at Beijing and numerous other cities were among the world's largest in 1800, but China was primarily agricultural. Farm production grew steadily because of crop specialization, improved irrigation and fertilizers, and new plants from the Americas that could be grown where Chinese crops could not thrive. Silk production engaged many farmers, requiring the cultivation of mulberry trees (their leaves were the silkworms' food) as well as the careful tending of the worms. Farmers and urban folk alike had to buy food—especially farmers who planted tobacco, cotton, or mulberry trees—spurring the expansion of markets throughout the countryside. Chinese products were sold all over the realm and exported throughout the world. Chinese vessels shipped much of this trade until the end of the eighteenth century, when foreign shippers replaced them. The Chinese economy absorbed a great deal of silver from the mines of Japan and South America—that is, until the British discovered a product that the Chinese would consume in ever greater amounts and which would reverse the balance of trade by the early nineteenth century, opium.

IMAGE The Forbidden City, China

Economic growth in the first half of the Qianlong reign was great, but its benefits were localized. Some regions did much better than others. The coastal region and towns along the Yangzi River and Pearl River delta were much more involved in local and international trade, and grew much faster. New industries led to new social arrangements such as "sisterhoods" for unmarried women or married women who worked away from their husbands' families. Sisterhoods offered lodging and support to women in silk and other kinds of production in the southeastern region of China.

Economic growth had some serious negative effects as well. Families decided to have more children than they could have had in more difficult economic times. While individual families did not notice any ill effects of having large families—in fact, having more children to help on the farm would lead to higher family income—after several decades of population growth, China as a whole began to experience population pressure at the end of the eighteenth century, leading to migration and conflict with indigenous people living in areas to which the Chinese migrated. Population growth also led to depletion of resources, especially trees whose wood was used as fuel, and deforestation led to serious flooding.

The Qianlong emperor's reign was the pinnacle of Qing success. Qianlong ruled wisely and expanded the realm until the last 25 years of his reign, when he allowed a corrupt underling to manipulate the strings of power. As a vigorous young man, depicted here at his inauguration in 1735 with his empress, Qianlong sponsored the collection of a great encyclopedia.

Society and Culture

Eighteenth-century society was more conservative than earlier times. Laws against behaviors considered sexually deviant became much more stringent. From time to time, officials banned plays or novels for violating Confucian morality. At the same time, the government fostered education as conducive to ethical behavior, and this led to the expansion of literacy. Public governance and popular society were seen as intertwined and most efficient and ethical when locally influential families took on the responsibility for promoting the livelihoods of their nonelite neighbors. Of course, this led to meddling by puritanical officials in their neighbors' lives.

The status of women was also affected by puritanical values. Widows continued to be discouraged from remarrying, and arches commemorating "virtuous widows" (widows who did not remarry) sprang up all over China. Young girls continued to have their feet bound. On the other hand, women writers were encouraged to express their creativity in the eighteenth century. Families prided themselves on having talented daughters, and prospective bridegrooms sought out brides with poetic sensibility. Male poet Yuan Mei (yoo-AHN MAY; 1716–1797) was a particular fan of women poets, gathering a group of lively women writers around himself and declaring that they surpassed men in many ways. His detractors believed he was encouraging too much sensuality in women.

Though Confucianists disparaged novels, some of China's finest fiction writing was produced during the Qing dynasty. Wu Jingzi (WOO JING-zuh; 1701–1754) wrote *The Scholars*, a satire on the examination system. The best-loved novel was *The Dream of the Red Chamber* (also called *The Dream of Red Mansions* and *The Story of the Stone*) by Cao Xueqin (TSOW shweh-CHIN; 1715–1764). The novel has a large number of characters and is centered around three cousins, one boy and two girls. The three lead an idyllic upper-class life of culture and literature until the boy is forced to marry one of the girls and the other cousin dies. The male protagonist passes the exams but then abandons his declining family to seek truth in religion. The novel is an exquisite study of relationships between generations, the sexes, and masters and servants. Elite family politics are played out against the tale of family decline.

The eighteenth century came to an end with the death of the emperor Qianlong. Years earlier, however, Qianlong had become attached to a handsome, bright young bodyguard named Heshen (huh-SHEN), whom he appointed to high-ranking posts. Heshen developed a network of graft and corruption; however, his fall came immediately after Qianlong's death. His plundering of China's wealth was devastating. Heshen's confiscated wealth was 800 million ounces of silver, and his cronies serving in appointive posts throughout China stole millions more. When impoverished commoners joined the White Lotus religious uprising

Document

Lan Dingyuan, County Magistrate: Depraved Religious Sects Deceive People

Lan Dingyuan (1680–1733) was a magistrate in a county near Guangzhou. Magistrates served at the lowest level of the Chinese bureaucracy but had wide-ranging responsibilities, including administration, collecting taxes, and enforcing laws, at the local level. Educated as Confucian public servants, magistrates, like all government officials, found religious deviance from Confucianism particularly unethical. White Lotus beliefs were also threatening because of the role White Lotus adherents had played in dynastic change at the end of the Yuan dynasty several hundred years earlier. Lan Dingyuan kept notes of his trials, and here we see how he dealt with this heretical sect.

The people of Chaoyang believed in spirits and often talked about gods and Buddhas. . . . [L]adies of the gentry families joined together to go to the temples to worship the Buddha. In this way, heretical and depraved teachings developed and the so-called Latter Heaven sect became popular. . . . The sect also called itself the "White Lotus" or the "White Willow."

Zhan Yucan's wife, Lin, was thought to be the "Miraculous Lady." She claimed to possess the ability to summon wind and rain and to give orders to gods and spirits. She was the leader of the Latter Heaven sect and was assisted by her paramour, Hu Aqui, who called himself the "Ben Peak Divine Gentleman." These two cast spells and used magic charms and waters to cure illness and to help pray for heirs. They also claimed to be able to help widows meet their deceased husbands at night.

The people of Chaoyang adored them madly; hundreds of men and women worshipped them as their masters. . . . [M]embers of the sect had . . . already constructed a large building in the northern part of the county where they established a preaching hall and gathered several hundred followers . . . I dispatched runners (office assistants to the magistrate) to apprehend the sect leaders, but the runners were afraid to offend the gods lest the soldiers of hell punish them. Besides the local officials and many of the influential families favored the sect. So they all escaped.

I, therefore, went to the place myself, pushed my way into the front room, and arrested the Divine Lady. Then I went further into the house to search for her accomplices. . . . It was indeed an ideal place to hide criminals. . . . Finally, the local rowdies as well as certain influential families, knowing they could no longer hide him, handed over Hu Aqiu (the Divine Gentleman).

In fact, these people had no special powers whatsoever, but used incense and costumes to bewilder people. The foolish people who trembled on just hearing the names of gods and spirits were impressed when they saw the Divine Lady had no fear of gods and goddesses. Hu Aqiu, who accompanied her, wore rouge, female clothing, and a wig. People believed Hu was the genuine Empress Lady of the Moon and never suspected he was a man.

When these pious women entered his bedroom and ascended to the upper chamber, they would be led to worship the Maitreya Buddha and to recite the charms of the Precious Flower sutra. The stupefying incense was burned and the women would faint and fall asleep so the leaders of the sect could do whatever they pleased. . . . Later members would cast spells and give the women cold water the drink to revive them. The so-called "praying for heirs" and the "meeting with a deceased husband" occurred while the women were dreaming and asleep.

The members of the Latter Heaven sect were extremely evil; even hanging their heads out on the streets would have been insufficient punishment for their crimes. However, this had been a year of bad harvest, so the villagers already had lots of worries. . . . Therefore, sympathetic to the people's troubles and wanting to end the matter, I destroyed the list of those involved which the culprits had divulged during the trial.

I had Lin, the "divine Lady," and Hu Aqui beaten and put in the collar, lacing them outside the court so the people could scorn them, beat them, and finally kill them. . . . I inquired further into the matter so that the other accomplices could repent and start a new life. I confiscated the sect's building, destroyed the concealed rooms, and converted it into a literary academy dedicated to the worship of the five great [neo-Confucian] teachers. Thus the filthy was swept away and the clean restored.

. . . I went to the academy to lecture or discuss literature with the people of the county. . . . As formal study developed, heretical beliefs ceased to exist. . .

Questions to Consider

1. Was the county magistrate more concerned about the criminals' sexual exploitation of women or about the rise of heretical sects?
2. How did the punishment of the criminals and the rehabilitation of the local inhabitants validate the ethical role of Confucianism in the Qing dynasty?

From Patricia Buckley Ebrey, ed., *Chinese Civilization and Society: A Sourcebook* (New York: The Free Press, 1993), pp. 295–296.

(1796–1804), government resources were not immediately available to meet the challenge. The **White Lotus movement** promised social equality among classes and a better status for women, all to be delivered by the Buddha of the future, Maitreya (mai-TRAY-ah). Eventually the movement was suppressed. At the same time, ethnic tensions arose as Chinese migrated to border regions in search of better farmland.

The next challenge came from overseas. Concerned about the rise of trade with the English and others, in 1759 the Qing sought to regulate foreign commerce by restricting it to Guangzhou (gwahng-JOH) and placing an official merchant guild in charge of dealing with Britain's official counterpart, the East India Company. For several decades, this system worked, but as England began to sell massive quantities of opium to offset its purchases of Chinese tea, China began to suffer (see Chapter 24). The world's greatest empire in 1700 would, by 1900, succumb to imperialism, famine, and civil war. China's way of relating to the world—the **tribute system**—was fundamentally at odds with Western practices of international relations. When King George III of England attempted to set up a permanent trade representative in Beijing in 1793, Qianlong rebuffed the British attempt because it did not accord with the practices of the tribute system. China did not need foreign products, Qianlong stated; moreover, Britain's representative, Lord George Macartney, failed to perform the kowtow, a bow of submission, to the emperor.

Asia and Oceania, 1800. Most of Asia was still free of imperialism in 1800. The Philippines were under Spanish control, and Indonesia was under Dutch control, but British inroads into India had just begun. French domination of Vietnam and Europeans' encroachment on China would occur in the nineteenth century.

KOREA IN THE SEVENTEENTH AND EIGHTEENTH CENTURIES

- *Late Chosŏn history has long been seen as stagnant and rigidly old-fashioned. In what ways is this characterization incorrect?*

The struggles against the Japanese and the Manchus in the 1590s and from the 1620s to 1630s showed Koreans that they needed to strengthen their military. During the early seventeenth century, the Chosŏn dynasty refocused its attention on defense and strengthened its military. At the same time, serious factional struggles disrupted effective administration at Seoul. The factions were mainly concerned about power and influence, often framing their differences in terms of morality. Feuding factions disputed such issues as the proper length of the mourning period for the king's mother or the propriety of a concubine's son being designated an heir. Factionalism abated in the eighteenth century, when two strong kings ruled ably—King Yŏngjo (YONG-joh; r. 1724–1776) and his grandson King Chŏngjo (CHONG-joh; r. 1776–1800). Korea's economy, scholarship, and arts flourished during the eighteenth century.

King Yŏngjo was a patron of Confucian propriety. A scholar himself, he sponsored Confucian ceremonies

Korea

1627, 1636	Manchu invasions
1724–1776	Reign of King Yŏngjo
1776–1800	Reign of King Chŏngjo
late 17th–early 18th centuries	*Silhak* scholarship flourished

---

White Lotus movement—A millenarian religious movement combining elements of Confucianism and Daoism along with its predominantly Buddhist emphasis on salvation by the Buddha of the future.

tribute system—Foreign relations system placing China in a dominant position with neighboring countries who must pay tribute to China and receive protection in return.

and rituals. His behavior inspired the factions to cool their rivalries. He reduced one of the taxes paid by commoners and instituted land taxes on wealthy landowners. He ended the problem of homelessness. The economy developed rapidly, and the population increased by 50 percent. Though an effective and conscientious monarch, Yŏngjo committed a controversial and, to many, a cruel act; in 1762 he executed his son Sado, the designated heir, when the latter was clearly deranged and guilty of murder himself. This led to a renewal of factional divisions between the supporters and opponents of Yŏngjo. When Chŏngjo ascended the throne, he honored his executed father's spirit, thereby challenging his grandfather's actions and keeping the factionalism alive. Despite the disputes within the ruling class, however, the eighteenth century was a time of growth both economically and culturally.

Painters like Kim Hongdo (b. 1745) and Shin Yunbok (b. 1758) focused on Korean themes rather than simply following the previously dominant Chinese conventions. Kim, in particular, was known for his depictions of the everyday life of people at work or children in school. Other artists refined ceramic crafts. Writers, a number of them women, made **han'gul** (HAHN-gool) their medium of expression in the eighteenth century. Diaries, novels, and poetry written in han'gul were more expressive than the stiffer works written in the foreign language used for official government work, Chinese.

Yangban thinkers also were developing new approaches to learning. Observing that the farmers were not enjoying the wealth that accompanied economic growth, seventeenth-century scholar Yu Hyŏngwŏn (YOO HYONG-won) decided to undertake an extensive "investigation of things," the practice advocated by Zhu Xi, China's great Neo-Confucian scholar (see Chapter 10). Yu's massive work, which called for reform in government, the military, and the land system, inspired eighteenth-century scholars to undertake *silhak* (SHIL-hahk) or "practical learning." *Silhak* scholars, appalled by the plight of the peasants, advocated reforms that threatened the privileges of their fellow yangban. Some scholars who had international experience in China suggested that Koreans should emulate their Chinese counterparts who called for changes when circumstances demanded new policies. Some were impressed with Western studies they observed in China, including knowledge of astronomy, medicine, and Christianity. A few *silhak* scholars even formed an underground circle of Christians in 1754. In time, the number of adherents to the Western religion grew, and the government cracked down in bloody purges in 1801, 1811, 1849, and 1866.

Other social changes in the nineteenth century—new economic and power configurations—appeared following a century of growth. For example, many who had been slaves either bought their freedom or abandoned their owners, and became a new group of laborers who worked for wages. At the ruling class level, sons of concubines were entering the government as trained specialists (clerks, accountants, and other jobs), challenging the old aristocracy. These new specialists were often concerned with social reform, and many were attracted to Catholicism. Even yangban disrupted the old order, especially in areas far from Seoul. At the other end of the spectrum, farmers and miners revolted on several occasions during the nineteenth century. Thus, the stage was set for the end of the Chosŏn dynasty, as Western and, later, Japanese pressure challenged the Seoul government.

han'gul—An indigenous Korean script.

Shin Yunbok, Enjoying Lotuses While Listening to Music *(late eighteenth/early nineteenth century). Shin was one of Korea's most beloved painters. Shin's favorite themes were romantic and he often portrayed kiseang (artistic courtesans) with yangban men. The hats in this picture are the black horsehair hats that were the mark of the yangban male.*

Japan

1600–1868	Tokugawa shogunate
1640	Restriction of trade to Holland, Korea, China
1657	Death of Hayashi Razan, Neo-Confucian scholar; Great Edo fire
1688–1704	Genroku era, golden age of arts and literature
1730–1801	Motoori Norinaga, proponent of National Learning

EARLY MODERN JAPAN: THE TOKUGAWA PERIOD

- *What developments in early modern Japan helped set the stage for modernization in the late nineteenth century?*

Tokugawa Ieyasu's victory in the battle of Sekigahara in 1600, his assumption of the title of shōgun in 1603, the pacification of rowdy masterless samurai, the establishment of means of controlling the *daimyō*, and the regulation and limitation of foreign trade and contacts cemented Tokugawa rule by 1650. Japan was not yet a modern state, with its reach extending to every segment of society. But the Tokugawa shogunate did establish mechanisms to control the realm, acting as a superordinate ruler over self-regulating status groups. These statuses were the four Confucian status groups, recast for Japanese use as samurai, farmer, artisan, and merchant. In reality, the status groups were more fractured than that. Villages, cities, and towns had a variety of means of governance, depending on their relationship to their *daimyō* (for more on *daimyō*, see Chapter 13). Groups that did not fit into one of these four statuses, including those involved in the theatre or sex trades, had their own governing structure. Professional physicians and scholars could come from any status background.

The shogunate involved itself as little as possible in the day-to-day oversight of the status groups. If these groups stayed out of trouble and paid their taxes, the Tokugawa shōguns generally left them alone, sometimes issuing a warning to behave in a moral way but rarely finding reason to enforce such a decree. The one group that the Tokugawa did control was its own status group—the *daimyō*—by moving *daimyō* around for strategic placement and by the **alternate attendance system.**

The alternate attendance system required *daimyō* to spend alternate years in their domain castle and their Edo-based mansion, from which they performed attendance on the shōgun. The *daimyō*'s wives and children had to remain in Edo like hostages in fancy cages. Travel was closely controlled both to prevent clashes between the huge retinues of samurai that accompanied the *daimyō* and to make sure no firearms were being smuggled into Edo or *daimyō* wives smuggled out—signs of a possible *daimyō* plot against the shōgun. Two-thirds of the *daimyō*'s tax revenues were consumed in maintaining an elegant mansion in Edo to show off in front of their *daimyō* neighbors, in going back and forth across the countryside every year, in feeding and housing samurai both on the road and in Edo, and in having duplicate staffs in the domain and in Edo.

The *daimyō* were technically the top rulers within their domains, with their own legal and fiscal systems. The Tokugawa collected taxes from the rice crops of their own lands, which produced about one-quarter of the realm's rice output at the beginning of the period. The *daimyō* took in taxes from their own domains. Though the *daimyō* did not have to pay regular taxes to the shogunate, they did have to respond to demands to pay for projects the shogunate desired. For example, the domain of Satsuma was ordered to build 300 wooden ships to transport rocks for Tokugawa Ieyasu's castle. The costs were high, but the economic consequences were even greater. New jobs were created for lumberjacks, sailors, shipbuilders, and suppliers of food, clothing, and lodging. The transported rocks were cut from quarries with tools made of iron, which itself had to be mined, smelted, and crafted into tools. Resources were spread around when workers used their wages to buy other goods. This is but one example of thousands in which the Tokugawa's political attempts to control the *daimyō* led to unintended economic and social growth which, in the eighteenth century, came to define Japan as a nation rather than a collection of status groups.

The Tokugawa and the World

Although later Japanese considered Japan to have been a "closed country" during the Tokugawa period, Tokugawa Ieyasu had no interest in completely cutting off trade with the Chinese, Koreans, and selected Europeans. Gold, silver, and copper were plentiful in Tokugawa mines in the seventeenth century, affording the Japanese plenty of funds to buy silk from China, herbs and medicines from Korea, and

DOCUMENT Closed Country Edict of 1635

alternate attendance system—Tokugawa system of controlling *daimyō* (nobles) by requiring them to attend shogunal court every other year and to leave their wives and children at the shogunal court when they were away.

exotic plants and woods from Southeast Asia. What the shōguns did not want was Christian missionary activity, leading them to seek alternate ways of trading without bringing in missionaries.

Although Portuguese traders hauled much of the silk and other products entering Japanese ports in the early years of the Tokugawa regime, they were soon supplanted by others, especially Korean, Chinese, and, until 1640, Japanese traders. Trade with Korea went through the island of Tsu. The volume of trade with Korea and China was huge. In one decade alone (1615–1625), a conservative estimate asserts that Japan exported 130,000–160,000 kilograms (286,000–352,000 pounds) of silver for imports from China. Japan's silver exports, entering the world monetary system through the China trade, played a significant role in global commerce until the 1680s when the Tokugawa silver mines began to be depleted.

Soon, however, diplomatic and commercial relations became increasingly controlled. By the 1640s, relations with foreign countries were limited, and Japanese ships were no longer permitted to take part in international trade. Sailors blown off course were not allowed to come home—unless they were returning from Korea or the Ryūkyū Islands—under penalty of death.

Tokugawa policy changed because they became serious about controlling the introduction of Christianity to Japan. The Dutch, who had already driven the English out of the Japan trade by their more aggressive trade practices, next persuaded the Tokugawa to kick out the Spanish and Portuguese merchants, whom they considered too interested in promoting Christianity. The Dutch convinced the shōgun that Holland would not be interested in proselytizing. For the next two centuries, only the Chinese, Koreans, and Dutch could take part in the lucrative trade with Japan.

At the dawn of the Tokugawa era, the shōgun was worried about Buddhists as well as Christians. But by the middle of the century, Buddhism had been brought under government control. Confucian attacks on Buddhism deprived it of the intellectual vitality it had demonstrated in the medieval period. In addition, the requirement that every Japanese register as a member of a Buddhist temple to indicate rejection of Christianity, which may have appeared supportive of Buddhism, actually made the religion an instrument of Tokugawa policy. This deprived it of vitality as well. Christians were controlled more aggressively, with converts forced to renounce their religion. The Shimabara uprising, put down by the Tokugawa with Dutch assistance in 1638, was the last major Christian rebellion.

Both Korea and China were countries the Tokugawa could trust, but the relations with each of these differed greatly, as the Tokugawa rejected involvement with the Chinese tribute system which would have required Japan to subordinate itself to the Ming and later the Qing. The Tokugawa unease with the Manchu emperors may have also contributed to their lack of desire to become involved in the tribute system. The Manchu occupation of Seoul in 1627 raised fears that the Manchus would continue on to invade Japan as the Mongols had 350 years earlier. The Tokugawa even debated sending troops to aid the Koreans in repelling the Manchus; in the end, they did not. With Korea, the Tokugawa conducted foreign relations on the basis of equality. Unlike the case of Korea's relations with the Chinese court, Korean envoys to Edo did not prostrate themselves in a gesture of subordination.

At the end of the seventeenth century, Qing Emperor Kangxi lifted the century-long limits on official Chinese trade with Japan. This encouraged even greater trade between the two countries. Once the maximum official trade was reached, unlicensed trade was conducted at ports throughout western Japan. The Dutch, worried about increased competition from the Chinese, told the Tokugawa that Kangxi was influenced by Jesuits. The shogunate began inspecting imported Chinese books for references to Christianity and decided in 1687 to restrict Chinese merchants to the tiny island of Deshima in Nagasaki Harbor, where the Dutch had been forced to live and operate since 1640. Nagasaki grew quickly as a center of trade in the late seventeenth century. In the next century, however, the volume of trade leveled off due to use of domestically produced goods instead of imports and to growing shortages in silver and other precious metals. In addition, concern about the detrimental environmental effects of mining to promote trade began to surface in the 1680s.

Economic Growth and Social Change

The seventeenth century was an era of rapid growth. Peace permitted farmers to look forward to predictable harvests. The Tokugawa and the *daimyō* regularized weights and measures. They established policies for village self-governance: They prohibited the sale of people and possession of luxury goods; and they required more fortunate villagers to help the poor, maintain roads and bridges, and organize village families into mutual-responsibility groups.

Self-governance, a prime example of the Tokugawa policy of rule by status, was at the heart of the system. Taxes were assessed on the whole-village level by local officials. The village leadership, which varied among villages from a single individual to a council of influential families, then determined each family's annual portion of the village tax bill. Villages often hid a large part of their productivity increases from the tax assessor. Not all farmers were equally able to stash away income. Some domains experienced exploitative or corrupt government or bad weather while others prospered.

Woodblock print of Mt. Fuji by Hokusai. Landscape prints flourished during the nineteenth century in Japan. Mt. Fuji, which could be clearly seen from Edo, was a favorite theme. Here Hokusai shows a bustling rural road.

Peace was not the only reason for rapid growth. Policies like the alternate attendance system and the requirement that samurai live in castle-towns were also instrumental in both rural and urban growth. The *daimyō* converted the rice they received as taxes into cash in two major rice markets—Edo for domains in the east and Osaka for domains in the west. By 1720, these cities, as well as the castle towns and the old capital of Kyoto, accounted for 10 percent of the population. Edo was by then the world's largest city, with over a million inhabitants, and Kyoto and Osaka together had about 800,000. All those people needed to eat and be housed and clothed.

The alternate attendance system forced most *daimyō* to live beyond their means, so merchants extended them high-interest loans in advance of their next tax receipts. Determining rice futures as well as handling the transfer of cash from the merchant house to the *daimyō's* Edo mansion or castle in his domain turned some of these merchants into bankers and created a system of Japan-wide financing that transcended the official fiscal independence of the *daimyō* domains. Roads, sea-routes, transportation companies, and communications companies sprang up in the seventeenth and eighteenth centuries to meet the needs of the alternate attendance system, leading to economic growth unintended by the Tokugawa when they set that system up.

Money flowed into the guest houses and restaurants along the *daimyō's* procession routes, and from there to the villages that supplied the workers in those establishments. That cash was used to buy commercial fertilizers and to develop new irrigation devices and farm tools like threshing machines. These new technologies opened new fields and permitted farm families to work more efficiently. New technologies were spread to remote villages through printed agricultural guidebooks as literacy expanded for both, men and women. Urban demands for fruits, vegetables, and fibers (silk, hemp, and cotton) encouraged farm families to use some of the surplus available from their increased productivity for goods sold by traveling merchants. Villagers were connected to the cities in additional ways, especially as carpenters and artisans. The demand for labor drove up the cost of labor, making the large extended family of the Warring States period less efficient than the nuclear family. The old village structure, dominated by a few large families, changed to one of numerous nuclear families.

Growth of the urban economy was even more remarkable. In the medieval period, Kyoto had been the only large city. Markets had developed near Buddhist temples, but they were relatively small. Seventeenth-century castle-towns gathered purveyors of goods and services to the *daimyō* and samurai; most had a population that was half commoner and half samurai. The alternate attendance system led to post-station towns every few miles along the highways, and material and artistic culture flowed easily as the samurai rotated between Edo and the small provincial towns. Though the population of the biggest cities stopped growing around 1720, regional towns continued to grow and become integrated across the various regions of Japan.

Officials were not the only ones who moved about the country. Traveling merchants brought goods to the rural areas, and maritime companies developed freight lines to haul goods cheaply. Pilgrims and sightseers, a large number of them women over the age of 40, added to the bustle and excitement of inter-urban travel. Few Japanese remained untouched by urban culture and goods by the end of the eighteenth century. The long arm of the city reached into the rural environment as well. During the building frenzy of the first few decades of the Tokugawa period, hundreds of castles and mansions, thousands of houses for samurai and merchants, and countless ships, temples, and shops depleted the resources of wood throughout Japan. Fires also ravaged the wooden cities, making lumber even more scarce. The 1657 Edo fire dwarfed all previous fires; much of the city was destroyed and 100,000 people were killed. In the eighteenth century, planners began reforestation and other environmental programs, but it took disasters like the great Edo fire to alert them to the need for environmental policies.

Economic growth, the development of cities whose culture and wealth were increasingly dominated by people of the lowest Confucian status (merchants), and the declining wealth of samurai were unintended and ironic consequences of policies undertaken to preserve a political order with the shōgun on top, the *daimyō* and samurai under control but supported by tax revenues and the right to rule, and agriculture at the center of the economy. Economic development eroded the conservative system the Tokugawa had tried to create.

When disasters occurred, such as famines in the 1730s and 1780s caused by crop failures due to unusually bad weather, the government tried a variety of reform measures in response. Most of these were conservative, seeking to reinforce Confucian morality and cutting government expenditures. During the famines of the 1730s, the shōgun Yoshimune (YOH-shee-MOO-neh; r. 1716–1745), widely respected as moral and conscientious, attempted to cut expenses, encourage agriculture, regularize taxes, standardize the diverse legal systems throughout Japan, and relax the ban on foreign technical books. He also ordered the dismissal of nearly half the court ladies to save money. With such policies, Yoshimune hoped to restore the efficiency of the past, but his policies were only temporary remedies rather than permanent solutions for the country's problems. More innovative solutions were sought in the 1780s by the shogunal advisor Tanuma Okitsugu (TAH-noo-mah OH-kee-TSOO-goo; 1719–1788), who tried to encourage foreign trade, develop the northern island of Hokkaido, open new mines, and charter new monopolies. But his reforms, which took a completely different path from Yoshimune's policies of retrenchment, were also unsuccessful in stemming the disasters brought on by the forces of nature. A few *daimyō* were able to implement economic policies in their domains that allowed their own areas not only to pull through the hard times but also to grow, but economic policies at the highest levels of the shogunate were generally unsuccessful in the middle and end of the Tokugawa period. By the middle of the nineteenth century, when the shogunate was facing American pressure to open its ports (see Chapter 24), it was the economically successful domains that were able to challenge the Tokugawa shogunate's claim of political legitimacy.

In other important ways, the system the Tokugawa intended to create was undermined by the actual behavior of the people. Samurai men were transformed by their occupations as bureaucrats and their education at state expense from warriors willing to lay down their lives for their feudal lords to diligent organization men striving to get ahead in life.

Women also challenged stereotyped notions of their behavior. Neo-Confucian ideology placed women below men in the status hierarchy, but women's roles and status varied greatly by class. Samurai women were dependent on their husbands, who received annual stipends. To continue to receive those stipends, samurai had to have male heirs, so their wives had to be tolerant of their husbands' taking of concubines or secondary wives to guarantee the family's continuity. Samurai marriages were usually arranged with little or no input from the future bride and groom. Samurai women were expected to be submissive to their husbands and their parents-in-law.

Merchant-class women were often well educated in math and literature, helped to run their families' shops, and frequently had a voice in the selection of their husbands. In fact, business owners often adopted a talented employee as a son-in-law, who then inherited and ran the business along with his wife, the daughter of the original owner. If the marriage did not work out, the hapless son-in-law might be divorced and a better match found. Merchant-class women often enjoyed the arts and culture of the cities.

Farm women's opportunities were very much determined by their families' wealth. The poorest had rough lives, with many of them forced to work as day laborers, domestic servants, or even as prostitutes in brothels located along the highways used by the *daimyō's* processions. Middle and upper-income farm women, however, had in some ways more opportunities than their urban counterparts. Many were educated alongside their brothers in the Buddhist temple schools that sprang up all over Japan to teach the children of the commoner classes. When they reached adolescence, village girls, like the boys in boys' associations, became members of girls' associations where they learned crafts like needlework and made important friendships. During major festivals, the boys' and girls' associations mingled, and young men and women often chose their own marriage partners based on friendships and intimate relations formed at those times. Divorce for marital incompatibility was common, and multiple marriages were not looked down upon as long as the partners were monogamous during the marriage. Farm men and women were equally important to their families' economic well-being; women planted while men reaped, and both, as well as their children, threshed the rice. Sons usually inherited, but daughters, if particularly respected by their parents or in the absence of sons, could inherit and marry a man expected to become an adopted son-in-law. Women became the skilled silk workers, bringing in cash incomes to their families. And when some farmers became entrepreneurs in the late Tokugawa period, setting up silk-reeling mills and other enterprises, teenage girls were often the wage earners for their families. Women were usually not members of the village assembly, but in some cases, they did represent their families at official events.

The official ideology concerning women was grim, but in reality most played a more important role and had greater latitude in relation to their families than that suggested in official documents. No women had "rights" in the modern sense, but neither did men.

Early Modern Scholarship and Ideology

Urbanization in the seventeenth and eighteenth centuries produced new cultural and social practices in the cities and towns. At the dawn of the seventeenth century, urban culture was samurai culture. Most scholars called Kyoto their home in the seventeenth century, but in the eighteenth, many lived in Edo as well. Many scholars were outside the four-status system; some were scholars in official posts and many of those had samurai status. But other scholars came from every type of background and earned their living as teachers, advisors, or physicians. Zhu Xi Confucianism enticed a number of scholars in the seventeenth century. Hayashi Razan (HAH-yah-shee RAH-zan; 1583–1657) and Yamazaki Ansai (YAH-mah-ZAH-kee AHN-sai; 1618–1682) both started out as Buddhist clerics but later abandoned religion for the more secular Confucian learning. Hayashi's school of thought was particularly appreciated by the shogunate. Hayashi contended that the five Confucian relationships were natural and proper. The shōgun should be elevated above all others, except for the politically powerless emperor, who was to be considered, Yamazaki added, the "heaven" from which the shōgun received the Japanese Mandate of Heaven. Thus, Zhu Xi Confucianism was blended with Shintō, the ancient Japanese indigenous religion.

Hayashi's school was considered orthodox by the shogunate, but not all scholars agreed with its point of view. Some followed the Chinese thinker Wang Yangming and called for activism in the face of social injustice. These scholars often courted banishment or other forms of punishment. Another scholar created a cult of masculinity called the "Way of the Warrior" or ***bushidō*** (BOO-shee-DOH) that elevated the samurai and shōgun as upholders of military values. Yet others, such as Ogyū Sorai (OH-gyoo so-RAI; 1666–1728) rejected Neo-Confucianism and called for a study of ancient texts themselves.

Confucianism was not the only school of thought in the Tokugawa period. Early in the period, students of history began the study of Japan's past. In the eighteenth century, an eminent literary scholar, Motoori Norinaga (MOH-toh-OH-ree NOH-ree-NAH-ga, 1730-1801) undertook a massive study of *The Tale of Genji* and other classics from the Heian and pre-Heian eras (see Chapter 10). His work, which stressed the centrality of Japan and the role of Japan's ancient Shintō gods, was not intended as political, but it inspired later scholars who advocated the restoration of the power of the emperor.

Another strand of scholarship was called "Dutch Learning." While not specifically Dutch, this scholarship started with the translation of Dutch books—the only Western books allowed in Japan and only after 1720 at that—and expanded to encompass a wide variety of studies in medicine, geography, astronomy, ship building, and other technical subjects. At the end of the eighteenth century, scholars of Dutch Learning were able to comprehend the growth of Western expansionism and, alarmed, wished to discuss military and political subjects. But these were restricted by shogunate law.

Other important schools of thought supported the way of the merchant class. Merchants were at the bottom of the Confucian hierarchy, but the Kaitokudō (KAI-TOH-koo-doh) Merchant Academy in Osaka stressed the importance of commerce and the morality of merchants. In Kyoto, Ishida Baigan (EE-shee-dah BAI-gan) attracted thousands of followers with his "Heart Learning," a religion based on a synthesis of Buddhism, Confucianism, and Shintō that honored merchants who were honest and frugal and carried out their trade as if it were a "calling." Respect for merchants facilitated the transition to modern economic development in the Meiji era (see Chapter 24).

Culture and Society

Non-samurai folk, with the help of creative samurai, developed a lively urban society whose values were exemplified through its arts. Arts and culture were increasingly accessible to less elite consumers as new materials and techniques, particularly printing, brought literature and visual arts into many hands.

The art prized during the late sixteenth century, such as paintings of the Kanō school, were still valued in the seventeenth century. In addition, a new aesthetic was developing among cultivated gentlemen—the polite accomplishments of skilled amateur poetry, painting, tea ceremony, music, and calligraphy—that resembled similar movements in China and Korea at the time. Less refined culture appealed to an enormous market of commoners and samurai. Sensuality was at the heart of this great cultural outpouring. Much of this culture was produced in sections of large cities like Edo, Kyoto, and Osaka, which set aside as zones of sexuality called "pleasure quarters," initially created to marginalize and control sexuality so that the samurai could focus on their duty to their *daimyō* lords. Brothels, teahouses, artists' and writers' studios, theatres, and restaurants were crammed into these zones. Although these zones were aimed at men, many women did take part, both as workers in the brothels and as audience members at plays and other artistic performances. To be sure, life for

bushidō—Literally "the way of the warrior," this philosophy called on samurai to dedicate themselves unto death to their feudal lord and to live frugally and ethically.

those in the brothels was not all pleasurable. The quarters were surrounded by moats and gates, and women sex workers were not permitted to leave. Sold to brothels as young girls, many experienced a tough life, despite their often elegant clothing, artistic accomplishments, and genteel bearing.

The culture of the "pleasure quarters" had its own rules, which countered Confucian sensibility and morality. For example, according to conventional belief, actors were to be looked down upon, but they were the heroes of this culture, along with the finely dressed "dandies" who prided themselves on their knowledge of song lyrics, literature, and the latest gossip from the world of the theatre. Its heroines were famous courtesans and gifted geisha (GAY-shah) or female entertainers, who were trained in the arts from an early age. The restrictions on the freedom of these women, however, belied the exalted status they seemed to enjoy.

It was in these crowded areas of sexuality that urban culture flourished. Perhaps because so many there seemed to be tossed about by the uncertainties of life and fortune, the world of the arts came to be known as the **"floating world,"** a concept taken from Buddhism. Poets, playwrights, novelists, and wood-block artists created art meant for mass consumption. The consumer market was increasingly sophisticated, and printing and literacy exploded in the late seventeenth century. There were over 700 publishing companies in Kyoto alone around 1800. Texts and pictures alike were produced by woodblock prints and were cheap enough to be readily accessible.

Artists like poet Matsuo Bashō (1644–1694), novelist and storyteller Ihara Saikaku (1642–1693), playwright Chikamatsu Monzaemon (1653–1724), and woodblock artists Hishikawa Moronobu (1620?–1694), Katsushika Hokusai (1760–1849), and Andō Hiroshige (1797–1858) were esteemed during their own lifetimes and continued to be highly regarded for their artistic accomplishments.

Son of a minor samurai, poet Matsuo Bashō (MAH-tsoo-oh ba-SHOH) established himself as the major practitioner of a poetic form called haikai. But he felt constrained by the conventional haikai style, so developed a new form called haiku. His own studies of Zen, Chinese literature, and medieval Japanese poetry informed his enormous poetic output. The haiku, a 17-syllable form, evokes mood and suggests linkages between seemingly dissimilar objects.

On a withered branch
A crow has settled—
Autumn nightfall[2]

floating world—The area in which art, literature, and prostitution flourished in early modern Japan.

Bashō's most popular work was his travel writing, *Narrow Road to the North,* a volume of poetry and prose recounting his long journey throughout the island of Honshū.

Bashō's contemporary, Ihara Saikaku (EE-hah-rah SAI-kah-koo), was one of many highly successful prose writers of his day. Until the last year of his life, his tales were racy stories laced with a bit of propriety. His characters revel in pleasure—popular book titles included *The Life of an Amorous Man* (published in 1682) and *The Life of an Amorous Woman* (1686)—but despite their hedonistic lifestyle, they suffer loneliness at the end of their lives. In his 1688 novel, *The Eternal Storehouse of Japan,* Saikaku focused on practical

Woodblock prints, like this portrait of a courtesan and her attendants, depicted the life of workers and customers in the "floating world" of urban culture in the Tokugawa period. These prints made art readily available to a mass audience. They also helped to spread new fashions and culture beyond urban areas.

Document Ihara Saikaku: "The Umbrella Oracle"

Ihara Saikaku embodied the lively urban culture of Japan's "floating world" in the late seventeenth century. This short story is from his 1685 collection, *Tales from the Provinces.* Japanese loved to travel throughout the Japanese islands in the Tokugawa period—foreign travel was not permitted at that time—and for those who could not get away, tales of exotic places were an enjoyable substitute. Note the urbane city-based writer's humorous treatment of country folk.

To the famous "Hanging Temple of Kannon" in the Province of Kii, someone had once presented twenty oil-paper umbrellas which . . . were hung beside the temple for the use of any and all who might be caught in the rain or snow. . . .

One day in the spring of 1649, however, a certain villager borrowed one of the umbrellas and, while he was returning home, had it blown out of his hands by a violent "divine wind." . . . Borne aloft by the wind, the umbrella landed finally in the little hamlet of Anazato, far in the mountains of the island of Kyushu. The people of this village had from ancient times been completely cut off from the world . . . and had never even seen an umbrella! . . .

Finally, one local wise man stepped forth and proclaimed, . . . "Though I hesitate to utter that August Name, this is without a doubt the God of the Sun. . . ." All present were filled with awe. . . . The whole population of the village went up into the mountains and, gathering wood and rushes, built a shrine that the deity's spirit might be transferred hence from [the Great Shrine of] Ise. . . .

At the time of the summer rains the site upon which the shrine was situated became greatly agitated, and the commotion did not cease. When the umbrella was consulted, the following oracle was delivered: "All this summer the sacred hearth has been simply filthy. . . . [L]et there not be a single cockroach left alive! I have also one other request. I desire you to select a beautiful young maiden as a consolation offering for me. If this is not done within seven days, . . . I will rain you all to death! . . ."

The villagers were frightened out of their wits. . . [T]he young maidens, weeping and wailing, strongly protested the umbrella god's cruel demand. . . . They had come to attach a peculiar significance to the odd shape the deity had assumed.

At this juncture, a young and beautiful widow from the village stepped forward, saying, "Since it is for the god, I will offer myself in place of the young maidens."

All night long the beautiful widow waited in the shrine, but she did not get a bit of affection. Enraged, she charged into the inner sanctum, grasped the divine umbrella firmly in her hands and screaming, "Worthless deceiver!" she tore it apart, and threw the pieces as far as she could!

Questions to Consider

1. What was Ihara Saikaku's attitude toward rural people?
2. Contrast the behavior of widows advocated in Qing China with that accepted in Tokugawa Japan.
3. How does this short story show that Japanese worshipped both Buddhist and Shintō religion?

Excerpt from Ihara Saikaku, "The Umbrella Oracle," in Donald Keene, ed., *Anthology of Japanese Literature* (New York: Grove Press, 1955), pp. 354–356.

concerns of the merchant class rather than sensual pleasures, and his last book (*Worldly Mental Calculations*, 1692) was a pessimistic tale of poverty.

Theatre was most dynamic in the seventeenth and early eighteenth centuries. Nō plays from the medieval period continued to be performed but were rapidly supplanted by plays with secular themes. Many of these new plays highlighted the dilemmas of life of the merchant class, contrasting the all-too-human struggle between fulfilling one's duty and following one's heart. Two major forms predominated: kabuki (kah-BOO-kee), which used human actors, and bunraku (BOON-rah-koo), which used almost life-sized puppets and an on-stage chorus.

Kabuki was developed by a woman dancer named Okuni who brought this new form of performance to Edo in 1603. Soon female kabuki troupes were all the rage. But when these performance troupes were linked to prostitution, women actors were outlawed in 1629. Women's roles came to be performed by men and boys, just as in English theatre in Shakespeare's day. Kabuki plays used highly sophisticated staging, with revolving stages, opulent costumes and make-up, and grandiose gestures by the actors. The actors had widely enthusiastic followers who bought prints of those they idolized.

Chikamatsu Monzaemon (CHEE-kah-MAH-tsoo mon-ZAH-eh-mon), who wrote both kabuki and puppet plays, was Japan's greatest playwright of the Tokugawa period, and arguably of all time. He preferred writing puppet plays, as kabuki actors took liberties with the lines playwrights penned. Like Shakespeare, Chikamatsu wrote both historical plays and plays with deep human emotions. The latter often focused on tragic lovers whose duty to their families or employers prevented them from marrying. The lovers had no recourse but to run away and commit double suicide, deemed a pure gesture of intense romantic love. Chikamatsu's plays, in which emotion was always balanced with duty, showed that even in the floating world hedonism had its consequences. The Tokugawa government was so appalled by the rash of love suicides that followed the performance of some of Chikamatsu's plays that it banned all plays about love suicides.

Pictorial art was intimately connected with prose and poetry in the Tokugawa period. Illuminated books combined text and images, bringing affordable art to a mass readership. Woodblock prints were the breakthrough artistic form of the late seventeenth century. Earlier in the century, erotic themes in paintings called *shunga* (SHOON-ga) or pictures of spring were popular, and these themes were continued when woodblock prints first developed. Hishikawa Moronobu (HEE-shee-KAH-wa MOH-roh-NOH-boo) elevated the humble print to a major art form, depicting travel scenes, handsome actors, beautiful courtesans, gardens, and the bustle of urban street life as well as erotica. His work set the standards for the ukiyo-e (OO-kee-yoh EH), the pictures of the floating world, that characterize the Tokugawa period for many modern viewers. The form he developed continued to reign during the rest of the period. Katsushika Hokusai (kah-TSOO-shkah HOHK-sai) and Andō Hiroshige (an-DOH hee-ROH-shee-gheh) perfected the art of landscape prints that are still immensely popular in Japan and the rest of the world.

SOUTHEAST ASIA: POLITICAL AND CULTURAL INTERACTIONS

- *Was the fact that Southeast Asia had for centuries been an international crossroads a factor in its colonization by Europeans in the early modern era?*

The late seventeenth century was a time of turmoil on the Southeast Asian mainland. Only Laos had enjoyed sustained peace and a degree of good relations with its neighbors during the long reign of Souligna-Vongsa (soo-LIG-na-VONG-sa; r. 1633?–1694). In addition to struggles among the states of Southeast Asia, European pressure altered interstate relations. The Dutch and English chartered trading companies competed for commercial dominance. The Dutch pushed the English out of the Indonesian archipelago in 1623 and captured Malacca from the Portuguese in 1641. Though the Dutch were at first more interested in trade than administration, by the end of the eighteenth century the Dutch claimed administrative control of Indonesia, forcing the inhabitants to grow crops like coffee, sugar, indigo, and spices and destroying any products the Indonesians might wish to grow that could undercut Dutch profits.

The French also attempted to trade in Southeast Asia, but placed equal emphasis on missionary activity. Alexhandre de Rhodes, a Jesuit priest, spent four decades in Vietnam, converting some Vietnamese to Christianity. He is most noted for devising the Roman-alphabet-based script for the Vietnamese language. Because of Vietnamese antagonism toward Christian missionary activities in the late seventeenth century, the French turned toward Thailand, where the king was more hospitable toward missionaries. But the French pushed their luck too far, attempting to capitalize on their acceptance in Thailand by sending warships and demanding special privileges. While the Thai king was away from the capital, Thai nobles pushed the French out in 1688, thereby ending French hopes in Southeast Asia until they moved into Vietnam in the nineteenth century.

The Spanish came to Southeast Asia in 1521, when Ferdinand Magellan, on his round-the-world

Southeast Asia

1633–1694	Reign of King Souligna-Vongsa in Laos
1623	Dutch begin exclusive trade in East Indies/Indonesia
1624	Alexhandre de Rhodes arrives in Vietnam; later develops script
1752–1782	Burmese incursion into Thailand
1771–1802	Tay Son uprising ends Le dynasty in Vietnam
1782	Chakri ascends Thai throne; founds dynasty
1802–1820	Reign of Gia Long in Vietnam

journey, arrived (and was promptly killed) in the Philippines. Four decades later, the Spaniards established their colony there, focusing on establishing Christianity in the islands not already converted to Islam. Catholic priests dominated villages in the Philippines, acting as administrative as well as religious leaders. The Filipinos were generally allowed only religious education and were denied the learning necessary to assume self-government. Spain's presence in the Philippines allowed the triangular trade between South America, Japan, and the Philippines, which permitted silver to become the basis of the great East Asian trade machine.

Meanwhile, domestic and interstate turmoil rent the Southeast Asian mainland. In 1752, Burmese leader Alaungpaya (AH-lowng-PAH-yah; r. 1752–1760) drove the Mons from the Burmese capital and continued fighting southward. In 1760 Alaungpaya entered Thai territory and destroyed the beautiful Thai city of Ayuthaya (AH-yoo-TAI-yah). The Burmese assault on Thailand was halted when the Qing threatened Burma. Burma fended off the Qing, but later Burmese attacks on Thailand proved futile as the Thais gradually gained power on the Southeast Asian mainland. At first, the Thais were hampered by factionalism. But in 1782, General Chakri (CHAHK-ree) emerged on top, assumed the royal title, and united Thailand. He extended Thai influence over Laos, Cambodia, and Malaya. The Chakri dynasty continues to reign in Thailand. The first Chakri ruler, Rama I, restored culture and religion after the Burmese sack of Ayuthaya. He convened a major Buddhist council in 1788, wrote and supervised an extensive collection of royal writings, and established a climate for lively production of prose and poetry.

Vietnam also underwent turmoil in this era. The Le dynasty, founded in 1428, had suffered defeat at the hands of the Mac dynasty (1527–1592). But in 1592, the Trinh (TRIN) helped the Le to regain the throne in the northern part of Vietnam. The Le's power did not extend to the south, where the Nguyen (noo-EN) family ruled. The Nguyen continued moving southward; by 1720, they wiped out the old Cham (Cambodian) kingdom and controlled both Saigon and Phnom Penh (PNOM PEN). Southern Vietnamese culture became a blend of Cambodian and Vietnamese traditions. Chinese institutions, so influential in the north, were less important in the south. Indigenous deities were incorporated into culture under the Nguyen. As elsewhere in Southeast Asia, the status of women was relatively high.

By the middle of the eighteenth century, government mismanagement and excessive taxation, accompanied by natural disasters, led to great suffering among the peasants. Rebellions, the most significant of which exploded in the region of Tay Son in 1771, broke out throughout Vietnam. The Tay Son Uprising was led by three brothers and gained the support of hill people, farmers in the lowland river basins, and small-scale merchants. One of the brothers was declared emperor, and for the first time in centuries, the north and south were united. The Qing sent in 200,000 troops to support the Le, but they failed. The Trinh were driven out in the north, and the Nguyen were almost defeated in the south. But one Nguyen prince, Nguyen Anh (noo-EN AHN), fled to Thailand, and with the help of a French priest, Pigneau de Behaine (pee-NEEOH duh be-EN), Chinese merchants in Saigon, and other foreigners, Nguyen Anh reclaimed the throne. De Behaine got the French throne to agree to help the Nguyen, but the French monarchy fell in the Revolution of 1789, and when Nguyen Anh took the royal capital at Hue in 1801 only four Frenchmen were among his forces. Nevertheless, the French had gotten their feet in Vietnam's door, and later the whole country fell under French imperialism.

Nguyen Anh declared himself Emperor Gia Long (r. 1802–1820) in 1802. Gia Long and his successor Minh Mang (r. 1820–1841) restored the power of the throne, wrote a legal code modeled on that of the Qing, and set up a Chinese-style administration. They built roads and fortifications. They encouraged the arts. Poetry by both men and women flourished. The most revered writer was Nguyen Du (1765–1820), author of *The Tale of Kieu*, whose protagonist was a dutiful daughter who suffered great sexual adversity to rescue her father. Nguyen Du, a supporter of the Trinh, saw his work as paralleling his life under rulers he deemed illegitimate. Ho Xuan Huang (HO shoo-AHN hoo-AHNG), a woman poet who lived around the same time as Nguyen Du, wrote poems that called for sexual equality and mocked stuffy social norms.

Farther south, in Indonesia, the European presence was much more compelling and the native resistance much weaker, in part because thousands of migrating Chinese had diluted the Islamic values and loyalties of Muslim societies in the Malay Archipelago. By 1750 the Dutch had subordinated most native dynasties in Malaya, Java, Sumatra, and the other islands. In the process, imported plantation agriculture brought an economic revolution that conditioned much life and labor in the whole area. For more than a century, a Muslim Malay people, known in history as the Bugis (BOO-ghees), challenged Dutch supremacy. Originating on the island of Celebes, the Bugis first won fame as sea rovers and mercenary warriors, serving all sides in the competitive spice trade through the city of Macassar (mah-CAH-sar). When the Dutch took Macassar in 1667, the Bugis scattered from Borneo to the Malay Peninsula, where they concentrated at Selangor. Through conquest, intermarriage, and intrigue, they gained control of Jahore, Perak, and Kedah on the mainland while extending their influence to Borneo and Sumatra. The Bugis fought two wars against Dutch Malacca in 1756 and 1784 but were ultimately forced to accept Dutch overlordship.

While the Dutch were consolidating their control over the Indonesian islands, the British were also expanding their trade through the Malacca Straits and seeking a naval port to counter the French who still had a presence in India in the Bay of Bengal until 1760. In 1786 the British obtained Penang on the Malay coast. Later, when France made the Netherlands a satellite state during the Napoleonic era, Britain temporarily took Malacca and Java. Penang then became a rapidly expanding center of British influence in Malaya. By the nineteenth century, Dutch fortunes shifted, and they gained control of present day Indonesia.

EUROPEANS ON NEW PACIFIC FRONTIERS

▪ *How did the quest for trade turn Europeans into major actors in the Pacific region?*

Except for Spanish traders and colonists in the Philippines, the North Pacific area was almost unknown to Europeans before 1550, but many came during the next two centuries. Some of this contact involved Russian ships cruising southward toward Japan from Kamchatka (kahm-CHAHT-kah); at the same time, the French and British penetrated the North Pacific from Polynesia. By the late eighteenth century, when Western ships regularly arrived at Guangzhou from Hawaii or other Polynesian islands, East Asians began to feel the Western world crowding in on them.

DOCUMENT
A European View of Asia

Russians moved out toward the Pacific in 1632, when they established Yakutsk (yah-KOOTSK) in eastern Siberia. From there, adventurers drifted down the Lena, first reaching the Arctic and later sailing east to the open Pacific. Their discoveries were ignored until 1728, when Vitus Bering (VEE-toos BE-ring; 1680–1741), a Danish navigator sailing for Peter the Great, charted what was later named the Bering Strait, which links the Arctic and Pacific Oceans. This discovery opened the North Pacific to Russia during the eighteenth century. Meanwhile, the Russians founded Okhotsk (aw-KOTSK) on the Pacific coast opposite the Kamchatka peninsula. At Okhotsk, and at other timbered forts in Siberia, Russian governors and their Cossack soldiers exacted tribute in furs from a society of nomadic hunters. Relations between the conquerors and their subjects were not particularly friendly; indeed, local populations around the forts were often wiped out by direct violence or European diseases.

Europeans in the Pacific

1728	Vitus Bering charts Bering Strait
1779	Captain Cook killed in Hawaii
1788	Botany Bay established as British penal colony in Australia
1790	Unification of Hawaiian Islands by King Kamehameha

Shortly after Bering's expeditions, French and English navigators began their own extensive explorations. The most significant were those of the French noble Louis de Bougainville (loo-EE duh boo-gan-VEE; 1729–1811) and the famous English captain James Cook (1729–1779). Bougainville visited much of southern Polynesia, the Sandwich (Hawaiian) Islands, Australia, New Guinea, and New Britain. Cook's three voyages between 1768 and 1779 went beyond the known waters of the South Pacific to Antarctica and north of Alaska to the Arctic coasts, where Cook made contact with the Russians. Although he was later killed in Hawaii, Cook's journals fired European imaginations and encouraged European migration across the Pacific. Botany Bay in eastern Australia, established by the English as a penal colony in 1788, soon became a colony of settlement. Meanwhile, a swarm of Western traders, whalers, missionaries, and beachcombers descended on the South Pacific islands and the North Pacific coasts.

Perhaps the most striking feature of relations between Europeans and Pacific islanders was the contrast in gender roles. Male islanders, unlike European men, were used to female leadership; men were less possessive; and sexual indulgence was considered by both men and women as pleasurable but not overly significant. Polynesian women in Tahiti or Hawaii, when they learned that sex could be exchanged easily for European goods, met European ships when they anchored. Their preference for iron nails—no iron being found on the islands—resulted in European sailors almost dismantling their own ships.

After Cook's time, original cultures in Polynesia rapidly declined as trade goods, rum, and guns stimulated avarice, status seeking, competition for power, violence, and war. With European help, local rulers—male and female—fought to dominate their islands. Such conflict was particularly true of Hawaii in the decade after 1790, where a Hawaiian chief, Kamehameha (kah-MEH-hah-MEH-hah), used European ships and cannons to unite the three main islands. Sexual commerce with Europeans also brought syphilis to the islands, blame for which was long disputed by the French and the English. Other European imports included cattle, smallpox, and missionaries. Challenged by Christian condemnation, the old religion was largely abandoned, whole communities were harmed by alcohol consumption and alcoholism, and other evidences of psychological malaise, such as suicide, became prevalent.

European expansion in the Pacific brought significant changes for East Asia, particularly in maritime commerce. After the middle of the eighteenth century, the British began replacing the Dutch as the major European traders, a trend climaxed by the collapse of the Dutch East India Company in 1794. At Guangzhou the number of British and American ships increased dramatically after 1790. Seeking a product that might be exchanged profitably for Chinese silk and tea, the British first concentrated on cotton and then later opium from India. When the opium trade created friction with Chinese officials, British merchants began seeking furs, particularly sea otter skins, which were obtained in the North Pacific. Hawaiian ports soon became busy centers for fitting ships and recruiting sailors. By 1815, European expansion into the Pacific had radically altered the structure of commerce.

CONCLUSION

At the beginning of the nineteenth century, the Ottoman Empire continued to endure, as it would into the twentieth century with the bulk of its expansive territories, including some in Europe, intact. To the east, the Qajars consolidated their power and ruled Iran for a century, despite the territorial ambitions of Russia and Britain. The Mughals, however, had lost considerable ground to their Maratha and British rivals.

Like the recently formed Sikh state, that of the Marathas remained strong and challenged the military authority of the British in India in the first half of the nineteenth century. France had recently lost influence in Vietnam—which it would regain by the end of the nineteenth century—and was acutely aware of a revived Thailand. To Vietnam's north, China continued to be the world's largest power at the end of the eighteenth century, maintaining tributary relations with its neighbors, outproducing the rest of the world, managing great domestic growth while balancing the needs of the Manchu regime with the indigenous culture of the people, and dominating international trade. But domestic corruption, social tensions at China's boundaries due to population pressures, and creeping imperialism began to undermine Chinese strength and wealth in the early nineteenth century. Korea, long accustomed to its subordinate status vis-à-vis China, developed its own fine arts and crafts. Its eighteenth-century monarchs ruled efficiently, and its creative scholars developed an exciting form of "practical learning" which produced reforms. Japan's vibrant urban society, as well as its growing regional wealth, developed institutions of government and society that set the stage for its dynamic modernization in the late nineteenth century.

Suggestions for Web Browsing

You can obtain more information about topics included in this chapter at the websites listed below. See also the companion website that accompanies this text, **http://www.ablongman.com/brummett**, which contains an online study guide and additional resources.

Islam and Islamic History in Arabia and the Middle East:
On the coming of the West, see
http://www.islamic.org/Mosque/ihame/Sec14.htm.
On the Ottomans, see
http://www.islamic.org/Mosque/ihame/Sec13.htm.

Internet East Asia History Sourcebook:
http://www.fordham.edu/halsall/eastasia/eastasiasbook.html

Extensive online source for links about the history of East Asia, including primary documents regarding exploration, European imperialism, the legal system, and literature and arts.

Literature and Film

The following works provide an overview: Walter Andrews et al., trans., *Ottoman Lyric Poetry* (University of Texas, 1997); Kemal Silay, *Anthology of Turkish Literature* (Indiana University Press, 1998); *Evliya Çelebi in Bitlis*, ed. & trans., Robert Dankoff (Brill, 1990), the section on eastern Anatolia of the famous book of travels by the Ottoman raconteur Evilya Çelebi; and Sir John Chardin, *Travels in Persia 1673–1677* (Dover, 1988 reprint of 1927 edition).

The famous novel of Qing society *Dream of the Red Chamber* is available in various translations. See, for example, Cao Xueqin, *The Story of the Stone, The Golden Days,* trans. David Hawkes, Vol. 1 (Viking Press, 1973). For a multifaceted account of woman's place as writer during the Qing that includes representative translations of poetry, see Susan Mann, *Precious Records: Women in China's Long Eighteenth Century* (Stanford University Press, 1997). For an overview of the vibrant urban culture of Tokugawa Japan along with translations of some of the most famous short fiction of the Genroku era, see Howard

Hibbett, *The Floating World in Japanese Fiction,* 2nd ed. (Charles E. Tuttle Co., 2002).

Japanese film directors of the mid-twentieth century doted on the Tokugawa period. Numerous excellent commercial films give an insight into seventeenth-, eighteenth-, and nineteenth-century life. Kurosawa's depictions of samurai and their values may be seen in *Seven Samurai* (Toho, 1954) and *Yojimbo* ("The Bodyguard"; Kurosawa Production, 1961); a moving depiction of an early nineteenth-century physician is available in his *Red Beard* (Kurosawa Production, 1965). Filmmaker Mizoguchi Kenzo's insightful examinations of the status and roles of Tokugawa women in *The Life of Oharu: The Life of A Woman by Saikaku* (Koi Productions, 1952) are an excellent accompaniment to Ihara Saikaku's novels.

Suggestions for Reading

For background on the Ottoman Empire, see Donald Quataert, *The Ottoman Empire, 1700–1922* (Cambridge University Press, 2000); Bruce McGowan, *Economic Life in the Ottoman Empire, 1600–1800* (Cambridge University Press, 1982); Suraiya Faroqhi, *Pilgrims and Sultans: The Hajj under the Ottomans 1517–1683* (I. B. Tauris, 1994); Fatma M. Göçek, *East Encounters West* (Oxford University Press, 1987); and David Morgan, *Medieval Persia, 1040–1797* (Longman, 1988).

On the Mughal Empire, see John Richards, Gordon Johnson, and C. A. Bayly, eds., *The Mughal Empire* (Cambridge University Press, 1996); K. N. Chaudhuri, *Asia Before Europe* (Cambridge University Press, 1990); Sushil Chaudhury, Michel Morineau, Maurice Aymard, Jacques Revel, and Immanuel Wallerstein, eds., *Merchants, Companies and Trade: Europe and Asia in the Early Modern Era* (Cambridge University Press, 1999); Susan Bayly, *Caste, Society and Politics in India from the Eighteenth Century to the Modern Age* (Cambridge University Press, 1999); Matthew Edney, *Mapping an Empire: The Geographical Construction of British India, 1765–1843* (Oxford University Press, 1999); and Om Prakash, *The Dutch East India Company and the Economy of Bengal, 1630–1720* (Princeton University Press, 1985).

Among the best general surveys of Southeast Asia in this period is Anthony Reid, *Southeast Asia in the Age of Commerce, 1450–1680* (Yale University Press, 1988).

Qing China studies include Willard J. Peterson, ed., *The Cambridge History of China,* Vol. 9, part 1 (Cambridge University Press, 2001); Jonathan D. Spence, *The Search for Modern China* (W. W. Norton, 1990); and Pamela Crossley, *The Manchus* (Blackwell, 1997). R. Bin Wong, *China Transformed: Historical Change and the Limits of European Experience* (Cornell University Press, 1998), and Kenneth Pomeranz, *The Great Divergence: China, Europe, and the Making of the Modern World Economy* (Princeton University Press, 2001), place China in the world context. Jonathan Lipman, *Familiar Strangers: A History of Muslims in Northwest China* (University of Washington Press, 1998) discusses an important ethnic minority. Dorothy Ko, *Every Step a Lotus: Shoes for Bound Feet* (University of California Press, 2001) examines the meaning of foot binding in Chinese history.

Andrew C. Nahm, *Tradition and Transformation: A History of the Korean People* (Hollym International, 1988), and Carter J. Eckert et al., *Korea Old and New: A History* (Harvard University Press, 1990), offer fine treatments of major Korean developments during the period. On the roles of Korean women, see Laurel Kendall and Mark Peterson, eds., *Korean Women* (East Rock Press, 1983).

The best overview of the Tokugawa period is Conrad Totman, *Early Modern Japan* (University of California Press, 1993). Gregory M. Pflugfelder, *Cartographies of Desire* (University of California Press, 1999), offers a unique perspective on culture in the urban "pleasure quarters." On rural social change, see Anne Walthall, *Social Protest and Popular Culture in Eighteenth-Century Japan* (University of Arizona Press, 1986), and Stephen Vlastos, *Peasant Protests and Uprisings in Tokugawa Japan* (University of California Press, 1986). For Japanese intellectual developments, see Herman Ooms, *Tokugawa Ideology* (Princeton University Press, 1989). On women, see Gail Lee Bernstein, *Recreating Japanese Women, 1600–1945* (University of California Press, 1991).

CHAPTER 21

The Americas, 1650–1825

From European Dominance to Independence

CHAPTER CONTENTS

1650

1655 England seizes Jamaica

1675

1690–1760 Increased silver exports from New World to Europe

1700

1713 Treaty of Utrecht increases British influence in the Americas

1750

1750–1770 Enlightenment Administrative Reforms in Spanish Empire

1756–1773 French and Indian War

1763 Treaty of Paris sanctions British dominance in North America

1775

1775–1783 American Revolution

1787 Constitutional Convention

1791–1803 Haitian Revolution

1800

1808 Napoleon removes Spanish and Portuguese monarchs, opens generation of Latin American Revolution

1810–1821 Mexican Revolution

1823 Monroe Doctrine

As we saw in Chapter 16, for the Amerindians, the European invasion at the end of the fifteenth century through the sixteenth century brought with it war, disease, and abuse leading to a two-century loss of population that killed from an estimated 80 percent of the population in Mexico and Central America to around 30 percent in North and South America. After the terrible losses of the previous two centuries, the Amerindian population began to stabilize in 1600, but the demographic mix in the Americas was far different from that found in 1500.

For the Europeans, the entry into the New World brought with it an expanding trade in new products and an increasing supply of precious metals. Greater risks for increased wealth created new challenges. The Spanish and Portuguese, during the sixteenth century, were the first to take up these challenges. They created economic systems that depended on the imports of gold and silver from the New World. But, they did not develop new industries and they managed their business affairs poorly. The wealth they brought across the Atlantic flowed through their hands to the northern Europeans, who continued the new imperialism in the America. For the Europeans—northern and southern—the Americas posed the possibilities of profit and peril.

In Central and South America, the Spanish and Portuguese worked through the church to generate a new cultural synthesis, blending European, Amerindian, and African elements to produce a richness and variety not present in any of the parent cultures. Racial mixing, which created a new Latin American population and culture in the Western Hemisphere, ensured the continuity and development of this rich synthesis. The intermarriage of the Amerindians, Africans, and Europeans created a diverse society. However, the hierarchy of birth and race dominated life in the New World, as in the old.

In the eighteenth century, the influences of the Enlightenment thinkers gave the ambitious middle classes in North America and the Creoles, or *corillos,* in Central and South America a new vocabulary to define themselves and their futures. The English colonies moved first for independence followed by the Haitians. After Napoleon imposed his rule on the Iberian Peninsula in 1808, the much more complex wave of independence movements in the south unfolded. Although middle-class spokesmen dominated events in both the north and south, underneath their rhetoric were serious social and ethnic tensions that provided the often uncontrollable force propelling the independence movements. By 1825, with the exception of Canada and islands such as Cuba, the hemisphere was politically free. It was still, however, economically dominated by European powers.

THE IBERIAN COLONIES: 1650–1789

- *What effects did the Spanish have on their New World colonies?*

As the Europeans began the task of exploiting the riches to be found in the New World, they sponsored the immigration of their own populations and the mass importation of African slaves. In the process, the European invaders nearly destroyed the indigenous peoples' cultures and religions. They subjected most of the survivors to terrible hardships, indignities, cultural deprivations, and psychological injuries. The plight of Latin American peasants today began with Spanish and Portuguese imperial and cultural policies of the sixteenth century.

The Iberian powers carried out these policies to maintain their footholds in their massive new colonies. Spain governed an empire stretching from present-day California to Buenos Aires in the southern part of South America that was rich with economic potential. Once Portugal regained its independence from Spain in 1640, it, too, saw much the same promise in Brazil.

The Spanish Empire

Spain created an imposing administrative framework to consolidate its control of its conquests in the New World. The Spaniards faced many obstacles: distance, the lack of efficient transportation and communications links, and pockets of Amerindians, among others, who did not acknowledge Spanish authority and remained ready to fight. The Spaniards built a series of fortified administrative centers such as Santa Fe in today's New Mexico in 1573 and dispatched their missionaries to convert the Indians to Christianity.

As long as the Habsburgs ruled Spain, they pursued a rule characterized by a certain decentralization that reflected the geographical and political realities of the time. When the Bourbons took the Spanish throne during the eighteenth century, there was a marked effort toward centralization, sometimes following "enlightened despots" theories described in Chapter 18. In the 1750s and 1760s, Spanish America underwent several reforms that brought colonial administration and finance more closely under the supervision of Madrid.

Society

In Spanish America, at the top of the social hierarchy were those people born in Spain called variously *peninsulares* (pay-neen-seu-LAHR-ays) or *europeos* (eu-roh-PAY-ohs). As the eighteenth century came to a close, their numbers increased significantly—to the dismay of the Creoles—to perhaps 300,000 people at the end of the eighteenth century. They monopolized high political and church offices as well as leadership positions in business and the arts. Europeo women dominated local society.

One step down on the social scale came the group that dominated colonial society, the white population born in New World, the Creoles. Equally conscious of the social superiority of the European-born and the competition from the ambitious mixed blood population below, they fought tenaciously to maintain their position near the top of the social pyramid. At the end of the eighteenth century, they numbered around 3 million. They possessed the **haciendas** (ah-see-END-es) and mines, positions in municipal offices and universities, and dominated the middle clergy. The intellectual and political elites came from this group, and it was in their libraries that were found the works of Montesquieu, Voltaire, and Rousseau.

Poorer, and more numerous than the Creoles were the people of color. These people of mixed blood—the **mestizos** (the European and Indian population), the

---

hacienda—A plantation or large agricultural establishment in Spanish America.

mestizos—In Spanish America, people of Spanish and Indian ancestry.

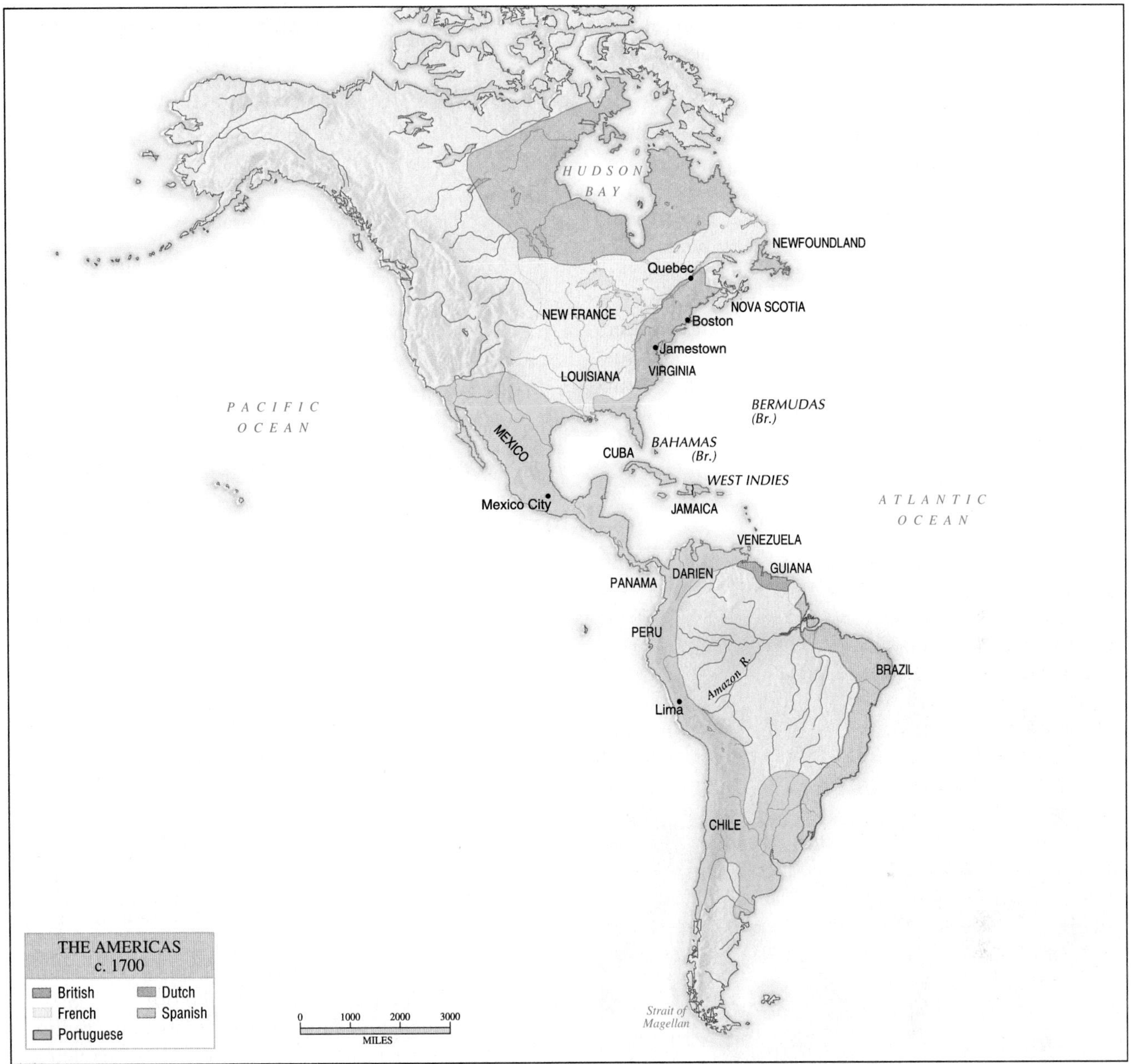

After the initial wave of European explorers and conquerors had finished their work, the peoples of North and South America found themselves in the spheres of influence of the British, French, Portuguese, Dutch, and Spanish.

mulattoes (European and African), and **zambos** (Indian and African)—were the free workers, small business people, and independent farmers. A huge social and legal gap separated them from the Creoles.

Despite European immigration, importation of slaves, and emerging mixed social groups, the indigenous Indians remained the most numerous part of the population. They had legal standing and were, in principle, free. However, given their economic and social standing, the freedom brought them little advantage.

mulattoes—People of European and African ancestry.
zambos—People of Indian and African ancestry.

At the bottom of the social scale were the slaves, regarded as property—increasingly valuable property, as the prices of slaves soared. During the seventeenth and eighteenth centuries, the number of Africans grew rapidly in the New World. Although African slaves in the Iberian empires had a less oppressive life than those found in the English colonies, they, early on, worked to improve their status in society. African slaves in the West Indies were among the most organized, and at the end of the eighteenth century fought to gain their freedom in Haiti.

Led by the Dominican and the Franciscan orders, the Spanish church labored to convert everyone in the New World to Christianity. There was an impressive amount of suppleness in their approach, as they tried to reach the Indian populations in their own languages after the failure of the initial drive to make them accept the faith through the Castilian tongue. There was a classic disdain for the local civilizations and their ways of life—but also the admission that, at least in their ignorance, the Indians were not likely to have been tainted by heresy. The Spanish and Portuguese constructed churches that took the baroque aesthetic to sometimes bizarre, but artistically impressive, extremes. Toward the frontiers where the Indians maintained their traditional customs, such as in Paraguay or California, the Jesuits were active. They instilled a discipline that was at the same time paternalistic and severe until their order was disbanded in 1767.

As can be seen from the setting of the house and the quality of the clothing, this is a portrait of an upper-class family in Latin America. This mixing of population allowed the peoples of Central and South America largely to avoid the often violent racism of North America.

Latin America: From Colonization to the Eve of Independence

1600–1660	Dutch move into former Portuguese- and Spanish-dominated areas
1655	Cromwell seizes island of Jamaica
1713	Treaty of Utrecht diminishes Spanish influence in Latin and South America
1690–1760	Vast increase in silver exports from Mexico and South America
1750–1770	High point of enlightened reforms in Spanish colonial government

Economics

Spanish America in the seventeenth and eighteenth centuries was an important part of a powerful global economic system knit together by the Spanish fleet. There was an around-the-world trading system that went from Africa to India to China to the Philippines to Mexico to the Caribbean and back to Europe. Precious metals were a significant part of the cargo between Spanish America and Spain. Imported gold and, even more significant, silver affected the European economy more than all other foreign goods. Into the middle of the seventeenth century the New World possessed the mercury mines needed to process silver.

After the Spaniards had looted Aztec and Inca treasure rooms, the gold flowing from America and Africa subsided to a comparative trickle, but 7 million tons of silver poured into Europe before 1760. Spanish prices quadrupled, and because most new bullion went to pay for imports, prices more than tripled in northern Europe. Rising inflation hurt landlords who depended on fixed rents and creditors who were paid in cheap money, but the bullion bonanza ended a centuries-long gold drain to the East, with its attendant money shortage. It also increased the profits of merchants selling on a rising market, thus greatly stimulating northern European capitalism.

Food items shipped in bulk provided the other great economic activity. After the decline of the ***encomienda*** (en-koh-MAY-AHN-dah) system (see Chapter 16), more and more of the production came from the plantations, the haciendas, that produced the agricultural products for domestic use and for

encomienda—Spanish institution, similar to feudalism and manorialism, that gave settlers authority over indigenous people to collect tribute or impose labor demands—at the same time, however, they had to provide protection to the Amerindians and Christianize them.

export. The plantation was generally constructed in the form of a square with fields of sugar cane or tobacco or coffee interspersed with fields of corn and potatoes to feed the workers. The buildings at the center were those of the master, usually in brick and wood. Around them were the houses of the overseers, and then those of the slaves with their individual gardens. In the typical plantation there would be the buildings to produce the sugar or cure the tobacco or coffee and a hospital. Typically, half of the slaves would be used to raise and the transport the cane, tobacco, or coffee beans to be processed, and the other half produced the finished product. Plantations were not known for their economic efficiency but rather for their wasteful practices and inefficient land use. As the soil became exhausted, progressive plantation owners introduced an agricultural rotation with crops that were not as financially rewarding as sugar, coffee, or tobacco. Other owners simply abandoned their land and went elsewhere.

Slaves suffered from tropical illnesses and from a wretched level of hygiene; on arrival from Africa, they were particularly prone to dysentery. Because of the nature of the work and the traumas of their conditions, it was rare for a slave to work beyond the age of 40. Infant mortality rates among the slave population were high, and women died frequently in childbirth because of lack of care, infection, and insufficient diet.

Brazil and the West Indies produced sugar, tobacco, or coffee. Mexico—with its Indian population's traditions—raised corn, beans, and peppers. Wines, potatoes, and oils came from South America. In all sectors, production was limited by often primitive planting and harvesting methods and by a lack of labor. The New World was not immune from the world depression that characterized the first half of the seventeenth century, and graft, smuggling, and piracy were natural results of economic distress. In the nature of the absolutist economics of the time, all business had to be done within either the Spanish or the Portuguese empire, through Seville and Cadiz, or through Lisbon. However, pirates and smugglers plagued the Iberian powers. In 1628 the Dutch captured 80 tons of silver from the Spaniards—as grave a setback as their defeat in the battle of Rocroi (rohk-KWAH) would be fifteen years later. By the end of the seventeenth century, even the fiction of centralized control was abandoned. The Spanish fleet was incapable of servicing the empire, and more and more trade was carried out by the merchant vessels of the Northwest—the Dutch, English, and French, who provided Spain with its markets for bulk trade, while stealing its precious metals. After the Treaty of Utrecht (1713), the Spaniards lost even more influence in the region. The British gained the right under the treaty to sell slaves in Spanish America and to make a once a year visit to important ports to sell some 500 tons of their goods. The British leveraged these openings to further penetrate the Spanish markets.

This print, taken from the trip of John Mawe to the interior of Brazil in the first part of the nineteenth century, makes clear the treatment of slaves by their Portuguese masters.

Brazil—Portugal in the New World

By the Treaty of Tordesillas (tohr-deh-SEE-yahs) (1494), the Pope issued a "bull of demarcation" to divide the lands in the New World contested between Portugal and Spain. This line was drawn in such a way that the Lisbon government received the area that would come to be known as Brazil, the largest state in present-day South America. Even when Spain absorbed Portugal in 1580, the administration of the two colonial regions remained separated for a period of 60 years.

Compared to the vast and comparatively well-organized and populated Spanish holdings, Portuguese Brazil was a loosely ruled area under the authority of a governor-general living there. After 1600

"The other side of the coin" of seventeenth-century Dutch wealth was captured by the artist Zacharius Wagner in his image of the activities of a Dutch West Indies plantation.

there were about 80,000 people—a mixture of perhaps one-third white and mixed-race, one-third Indian, and one-third African. With their lack of population and armed strength, the Portuguese in Brazil generally remained dominated by the Spaniards. Later, in the middle part of the seventeenth century, they were powerless to oppose the incursions of the French and the Dutch in Brazil. The French had already entered from the north under Henry IV in 1594. The Dutch posed a serious challenge, especially after they founded their West Indies Company in 1621. For the next 30 years, they launched a multifaceted effort toward Brazil: smuggling and piracy combined with normal commercial relations.

Sugar remained the major enterprise to the end of the seventeenth century. The raising of sugar cane spread from the island of Madeira to Brazil in the middle of the sixteenth century. Production went from 2000 tons in 1560 to more than 14,000 tons in 1600. When the Dutch took the port of Bahia and then Recife (ray-SEE-fay), they established their own sugar plantations nearby, and by 1629 there were nearly 350 sugar mills. The owners of the sugar mills typically rented the land to farmers to raise, cut, and transport the cane. Once the cane was brought to the mills, it was processed by European technicians overseeing the work of slaves—in the 1630s the Dutch brought in 23,000 African slaves to their part of Brazil to work in their sugar mills. Sugar production fell toward the end of the seventeenth century because of exhaustion of the soil. By that time, the Dutch had already transferred most of their sugar industry to the island of Curaçao (koo-rah-SAOW).

Once they regained their independence from Spain in 1640, the Portuguese increased the selling of slaves, principally to work in the production of sugar. They also took advantage of the Dutch wars with the British to reclaim their holdings to the north after 1654. For the rest of the seventeenth and into the eighteenth century, the Portuguese allied themselves with the English for help against the Dutch, the French, and the Spaniards. A close commercial connection was set up as the Portuguese sold their wines and sugars to England and had the protection of the British navy. Precious metals discoveries were made just as the sugar production died out in Brazil. There were 725 kg of gold exported in 1699, 9,000 in 1714, and 20,000 in 1725, the same year that the diamond strike occurred. The majority of the precious metals discovered at the beginning of the eighteenth century found their way to the vaults of the Bank of England. In return for these products and precious metals, British goods flooded Portugal and Brazil.

Discovery Through Maps

The Island of California

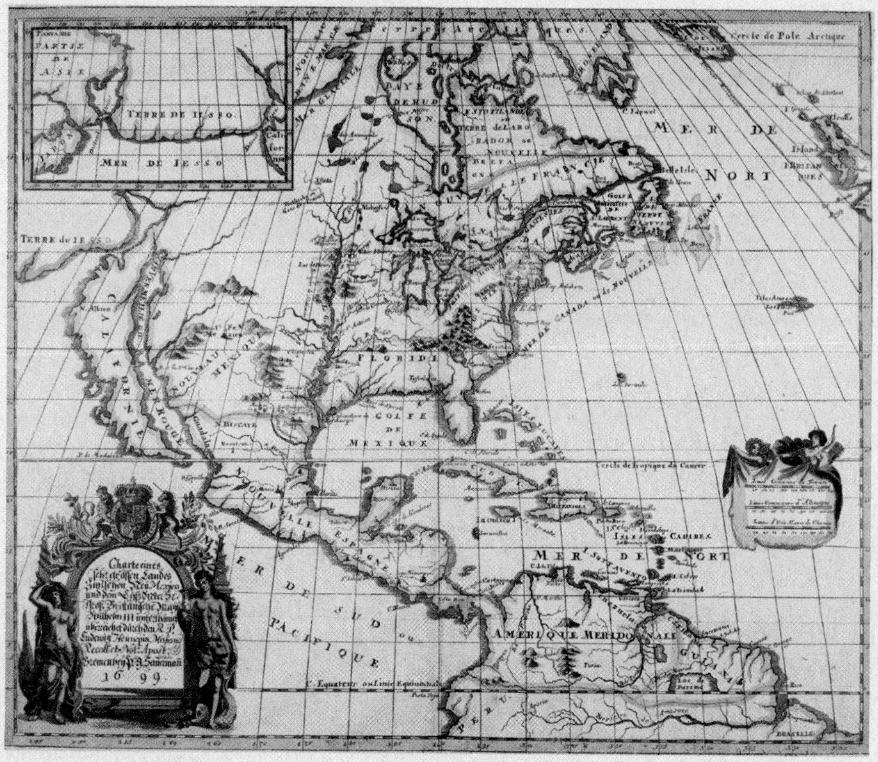

The new discovery of a very large country located in America between New Mexico and the Glacial Sea, with the necessary maps and figures and natural and moral history and the advantages to be gained there. . . . At Utrecht, the Merchant Guillaume Broedelet's Book Store, 1697.

This late seventeenth-century map of the New World, drawn by Louis Hennepin (b. 1640), shows as an island what would later become the state of California. Hennepin's map is a collection of the observations made by French explorers up and down the Mississippi and Missouri Rivers and of the charts made by seafarers in the previous century. The five Great Lakes are there, even if Lake Michigan is called Lake Illinois. Although the cartographer placed the Rio Grande in present-day Alabama, the rest of the details are quite accurate.

Hennepin seems to have consulted—either directly or indirectly—the findings of Sebastian Vizcaino's 1602 voyage in search of safe harbors for the Spanish merchant fleet crossing the Pacific from Manila. Spanish shipping drew the attentions of pirates—both quasi-officially sponsored such as Sir Francis Drake and the merely criminal—and Vizcaino searched with not much success to find a place where they might shelter after their long crossing. He must have tired of looking, for he did not find that best of harbors—San Francisco Bay. When he came back to Mexico, however, he carried with him a wealth of information about what would become California.

The person most responsible for spreading the word that California was an island was Father Antonio Ascension, who traveled with Vizcaino. As he was summarizing his notes and preparing a report for his superiors, he depicted California as an island. Unfortunately for him, the Spanish boat carrying his report was picked off by the Dutch—at that time in the process of replacing Spain as the preeminent naval power—and the priest's findings ended up in Holland. Ascension's hypothesis of California as an island came to be accepted by Dutch cartographers, the most advanced of the time.

For the next 150 years, California appeared on maps printed around the world as an island, until cartographers at last attached it to the rest of what would become the United States.

Questions to Consider

1. Find the part of the country in which you live on Hennepin's map. How accurately is it portrayed?
2. It is often said that cartographers plagiarized shamelessly—and uncritically— in the seventeenth century. Given Hennepin's presentation of California, do you think that this is true?
3. What difficulties faced a mapmaker like Hennepin in the seventeenth century?

THE WEST INDIES

■ *What made the West Indies so valuable for the European powers?*

From the tip of Florida down to South America, the West Indies served as the first stop for the Europeans on their way to the New World and remain as points of contention into the twenty-first century. Columbus claimed the region for Spain on his arrival in 1492. A century later, there remained precious few of the Indian population—save for the Caribs who, by their ferocious struggles, maintained their independence. Scattered among the islands there were several thousands Spaniards, a large number of mulattoes, mestizos, zambos, and African slaves.

As we saw in Chapter 16, the islands served as an essential element of the triangular trade routes between the Iberian powers, the West Indies, North America, and attracted all of the European maritime powers. The English staked their claims in 1620 to Saint Christopher, Barbados, Santa-Lucia, St. Kitts, Nevis, Montserrat (mon-ser-RAH), Antigua (ahn-TEE-gwa), and the Bahamas. The Dutch were more interested in the islands closer to the present day Venezuela, and took Aruba, Curaçao, and Bonaire. The French in 1625 claimed part of St. Kitts, and, ten years later, Martinique, Dominique, and Guadeloupe. Because the sugar boom was just beginning, the French islands would soon become very profitable. However, fierce attacks by the Caribs limited economic development in this era before 1650. In 1655, Cromwell seized the island of Jamaica for the English, while the French picked off Tortuga and the western part of Santo Domingo.

Until the nineteenth century, the islands were the center for continual competition, and between 1648 and 1789, they often changed hands in the wake of the European wars. From their islands, the Europeans raided their neighbors' shipping and commerce, whether as filibusters—people making unauthorized war on another state—or pirates. In addition, the French, Dutch, and English used their islands as bases to pick off Spanish shipping and to penetrate the Spanish market in the New World. Gangs of thieves in the interiors of the islands—and pirates roaming among them—took advantage of the competition among the major powers. It was a war zone, in brief, whether sparked by personal profit, national ambitions, or the desire to extend the faith as the Protestant nations fought the Catholics, and vice versa.

In the seventeenth century, the governments in Europe tried to consolidate their positions in the islands. Richelieu granted trade monopolies to merchants from La Rochelle, Nantes, and Rouen to deal in tobacco, indigo, and other goods. Colbert established the Company of the West Indies as part of his mercantilistic schemes. A significant part of his emphasis was the trade in slaves which was run out of Bordeaux, and which became the source of the wealth of many of the French bourgeoisie, including Voltaire. Curaçao became the main center for the Dutch and Jamaica for the British.

To lure people from the continent the British and French used indentures under which a person would agree to sign himself and his labor over to his sponsor for a certain number of years before he could become free. More than 6000 such contracts were signed in La Rochelle, France, alone—people seeking to escape debt, artisans wanting to become rich, and those simply seeking adventure. However, the British and French could not find enough people to go to their islands through the indentures and at the beginning of the eighteenth century, debt prisoners, galley slaves, and prostitutes were forcibly shipped across the Atlantic to populate the islands. Another important source of population for the islands was the Huguenots who fled France after the revocation of the Edict of Nantes in 1685. The majority of them went to the English and the Dutch islands. But the most important need for labor was filled by a vast increase in the

Slaveholders, even the most enlightened, suffered few moral doubts about the buying and selling of human beings. This is proven by their lack of concern for the treatment of people such as those shown here, as long as they were able to work.

amount of African slaves brought under horrible conditions to the new world.

Variations of the racial hierarchy in Spanish America were to be found in the West Indies. At the top of the pyramid were the Europeans, followed by those whites born in the islands, the people of color, and then the slaves. Not all slaves lived the same; they filled many different roles and did work ranging from management positions in the plantations down to common laborers. As in the Spanish world, it was a brutal life, marked by violence and racism, complicated by the inequities of the racial hierarchy. At the end of the eighteenth century, beginning in Haiti, a powerful resentment building among the lower classes would erupt.

As in Spanish America and Brazil, the plantation system prevailed, concentrating on the production of a single item, whether sugar, tobacco, coffee, or cotton. The sugar industry in the islands continued to prosper during the eighteenth century, especially in the French islands of Martinique, Guadeloupe, and part of Santo Domingo. Even though sugar was the dominant crop at the beginning of the century there, toward the end of the century, coffee came to dominate. The same tendencies could be found on the other islands.

Perhaps reflecting its economic growth, the West Indies underwent a population boom during the century. The French part of Santo Domingo went from 130,000 in 1730 to over a half million by the time of the French Revolution—of that number 465,000 were slaves; in Guadeloupe, in the same time, the population went from 35,000 to 106,000, of which 89,000 were slaves. The percentage of the French economy found in the Atlantic trade went from 13 percent in 1715 to 28 percent in 1785, and the Atlantic trade played a similar role in the other economies of western Europe.

BREAKING AWAY: THE CREATION OF THE UNITED STATES OF AMERICA

- *How did British policies and actions in its American colonies lead to the American Revolution?*

During the 1600s, English settlers had come to America for several reasons: to search for religious freedom, to seek political refuge, and to better their lot in life. Soon people from other European nations arrived, and the culture began to take on an identity of its own. The North American colonies got caught up in the world struggle that was the Seven Years' War; the view from London was that they should pay higher taxes to ensure their own defense. The problem was made more severe with the accession of King George III (1760–1820), who lacked the political finesse of his two Hanoverian predecessors.

A New Consciousness

From almost the beginning, the American colonies had gone in a direction different than that of England. Most Puritan (Calvinist) settlers in New England opposed the early Stuart kings; during the **Restoration,** a host of rebels fled to America. Many Catholics, favored by the later Stuarts and persecuted at home after **the Glorious Revolution,** came to the colonies, particularly to Maryland. By 1775 some 40 percent of the colonial population was of non-English stock, mostly from Ireland and southern Germany. After 1750 a popular party in Massachusetts opposed British ways, particularly British attempts to restrict colonial manufacturing, dictate terms for colonial foreign trade, and influence the actions of colonial legislatures.

Experience in self-government conditioned colonial development. Except for an unsuccessful attempt at colonial domination under James II, England had steadily relaxed controls. This trend was particularly typical of relations between the colonies and the home government under the corrupt and static Whig oligarchy, whose leaders became proponents of stability as they gained power. Preoccupied by more pressing political concerns at home, they allowed the colonists relative freedom to conduct their own affairs. In contrast, radical political opinion, driven deep underground in England after 1649, ran much nearer to the surface in America, where Locke's later emphasis on the social contract appealed to a people who had created their own governments in the wilderness and who were somewhat suspicious of a distant king. By 1763 only Maryland and New Hampshire had not attained practical autonomy, and even they were well on their way to doing so when the shooting began in 1775.

Colonial political thought was shaped as much by growth and mobility as by historical circumstances. Over 2 million Europeans seeking a better life arrived in the eighteenth century. They formed a vast lower class of indentured servants, tenants, and manual workers, sharply differentiated from wealthy New England merchants or southern planters. Many other immigrants, mainly Scotch-Irish, pushed toward the frontiers and settled on free or cheap western land. Its easy availability fostered the idea of property as an

---

Restoration—The return to the English throne in 1660 of the Stuart dynasty. The Restoration lasted during the reigns of Charles II and James II.

The Glorious Revolution—The English revolution in 1688 in which the Stuarts were driven from power in England by the forces supporting the Parliament.

individual's birthright, so that Prime Minister George Grenville's restriction on westward migration after 1763 aroused general resentment against an assumed English effort to monopolize land for a privileged aristocracy. Land speculators condemned the policy as a violation of free enterprise and, at the same time, found a common interest with craftsmen, merchants, and planters, who felt themselves dominated and exploited by British mercantilism.

Pressure from England helped bring the variety of individual complaints into a united resistance. John Adams (1735–1826), looking back on the Revolution, was well aware of this maturing American nationalism. He wrote:

> *But what do we mean by the American Revolution? Do we mean the American war? The Revolution was effected before the war commenced . . . in the minds and hearts of the people. . . . This . . . was the real American Revolution.*[1]

The Roots of Rebellion

The North American phase of the Seven Years' War saw important combat between the British and the French from the Great Lakes up to the Gulf of St. Lawrence and along the Ohio River Valley. For the most part, the Indians caught between the European competitors aligned themselves with the French, whom they saw as traders to deal with and not settlers intent on taking their lands. Owing to their superior fleet, which defeated the French navy and cut off reinforcements, the British ultimately won in the New World. The Peace of Paris of 1763 that ended the Seven Years' War gave the British control of most of North America east of the Mississippi River.

Once victory was achieved, the costs of triumph had to be paid. The Grenville program brought all the major differences between Britain and the colonies into focus. With foreign enemies out of Canada and Florida, new land beckoned colonists who no longer felt the need for British protection. They naturally abhorred new taxes and trade controls required by rising imperial costs. British troops, under the circumstances, were regarded as oppressors rather than defenders or peacekeepers. To make matters worse, a general economic depression, reflecting British postwar financial difficulties in the late 1760s, hit most colonial economies hard, particularly that of New England.

The first colonial protests came with the Grenville program, when the 1764 Sugar Act—an act to enforce British dominance over the market on imported molasses—prompted arguments against "taxation without representation" in colonial newspapers and pamphlets. These reactions were mild, however, in comparison with those following the **Stamp Act** a year later. The Stamp Act required all legal documents and other printed matter to carry a special tax stamp. Colonial assemblies in Massachusetts and New York denounced the law as "tyranny," and a "Stamp Act Congress," convening in New York, petitioned the king to repeal the law. Mob actions occurred in a number of places, but they were less effective than boycotts of English goods, imposed by a thousand colonial merchants. Soon hundreds of English tradesmen were petitioning Parliament, pleading that the taxes be rescinded. Their appeal was successful in 1766, although Parliament issued a declaration affirming its absolute right to legislate for the colonies.

Having repealed the Stamp Act, Parliament almost immediately enacted other revenue measures. Charles Townshend (1725–1767), the new chancellor of the exchequer, had Parliament levy duties on imported paint, paper, lead, wine, and tea. Other laws decreed that admiralty courts, which functioned without juries, should sit in specified ports and enforce all trade regulations. In response, some Boston merchants, mainly the habitual smugglers, generated lively protests. The big wholesalers, who saw renewed boycotts of British goods as a means for reducing their overstocked warehouses, joined them. Samuel Adams (1722–1803), the main radical leader, whipped up anti-British feeling on Boston streets. This culminated on March 5, 1770, when soldiers fired into an unruly mob, killing five people. Some lesser American merchants began to waver, but nonimportation agreements had cut British imports by 50 percent and induced Parliament to repeal most duties on the very day of the Boston Massacre.

For a while, the colonies seemed angry but pacified, until Lord North (1732–1792), the king's new chief minister, persuaded Parliament to grant a two-thirds cut in duties on East India Company tea delivered to American ports. Because the company could

The North American Evolution

1756–1763	French and Indian War
1763	Treaty of Paris increases English dominance in North America
1775–1783	American Revolution
1776	Declaration of Independence
1787	Constitutional Convention
1803	Louisiana Purchase
1823	Monroe Doctrine

Stamp Act—Revenue-raising measures passed by the English Parliament in 1765 to force the colonies in North America to pay their share of defense costs.

thus undersell smugglers and legitimate tea merchants, both of these groups again resorted to political radicalism. The tea was turned away from most American ports. In what became known as the Boston Tea Party, Sam Adams's "patriots," thinly disguised as Indians, stole onto a ship and dumped its load of tea into the harbor. Parliament retaliated with the "Intolerable Acts," which closed the port of Boston, revoked the Massachusetts Charter, and provided that political offenders be tried in England.

Contentions between the home government and the colonies deteriorated into armed conflict by 1775 and complete separation by the following year. This result was not planned, hoped for, or even foreseen by the colonists. The true rebels consisted largely of the merchants, smugglers, and large landowners who were most hurt by the new British policies, supported by doctrinaire leaders of aroused city dwellers and small farmers. Although not originally committed to independence, both groups dreamed of a future America as a center of power, prosperity, and freedom.

The resulting conflagration was also a civil war, with many colonists remaining loyal to the crown. More than 20 percent of the citizenry remained loyal to Britain, and no more than one-sixth of the male population ever took up arms. Indeed, Benjamin Franklin's son was a Loyalist leader and the last royal governor of New Jersey. Most colonists were probably apolitical, intent on their own affairs, but a vocal majority of the politically minded—whether New England merchants, Virginia planters, urban intellectuals, or simple farmers—formed an angry and determined opposition. Their outlook combined Locke's political ideas with a spirit of rough frontier independence; it was also nationalistic in its dawning awareness that many English ways were foreign to American needs and values.

The Revolutionary War

By September 1774 the Boston crisis had created a revolutionary climate. Representatives of 12 colonies, meeting in the First Continental Congress at Philadelphia, denounced British tyranny, proclaimed political representation to be a natural right, and made plans for armed resistance. In April of the next year, the explosive situation around Boston finally led to a conflict between British regulars and the Massachusetts militia at nearby Lexington and Concord in which eight Americans and 293 English soldiers were killed. Those "shots heard round the world" marked the beginning of the American Revolution.

The war begun at Lexington and Concord lasted eight years. British troops, besieged in Boston, failed to break out in June 1775 at Bunker Hill. Shortly afterward, General George Washington (1732–1799) accepted command of American forces from the recently convened Second Continental Congress. Long after the British had abandoned Boston in March 1776, his outnumbered and ill-provisioned troops fought defensive battles for survival, an ordeal climaxed at Valley Forge, in Pennsylvania, in the desolate winter of 1777–1778, when the ragged American army almost disintegrated from cold, hunger, and desertion. It was a time, in Thomas Paine's words, "to try men's souls," but it was also a time for dreams of renewed liberties and new opportunities.

The turning point of the war came in October 1777. Having occupied New York and Philadelphia, the British tried to split the country with an army moving south from Canada. Its crushing defeat at Saratoga, in upper New York, effected a diplomatic revolution. France, which had been a cautious and unofficial supplier, now entered the war on the American side and soon persuaded its Spanish ally to do the same. The Dutch followed, in a desperate effort to save their American trade. With its sea power thus countered, the British pulled their two main armies back to defensive positions in New York and Virginia. The war reached its conclusion in the southern campaigns in 1781, when French and American troops, aided by the French fleet, forced the British commander, Lord Cornwallis (1738–1805), to surrender at Yorktown, Virginia. This defeat, along with many threats abroad, caused the British to recognize the Americans' independence in the Treaty of Paris (1783).

Creating a Nation: The Logic of Locke

While the war continued, American political leaders were forming a new nation. Thomas Paine's *Common Sense,* published early in 1776 as an emotional plea for liberty, inflamed popular passions and helped convince the American Congress to break with England. In June a congressional committee drafted a formal statement of principles. The resulting Declaration of Independence, written by Thomas Jefferson, first announced the creation of the United States. In claiming for every individual "certain unalienable rights . . . to life, liberty, and the pursuit of happiness," it also used typical natural law theory in a direct appeal to radical opinion.

DOCUMENT
The Declaration of Independence

An angrier radicalism, born of army wages not paid and taxes incurred among poor civilians, marked the late war years. Economic depression and other hardships created suspicions of the highborn and wealthy leaders who were so prominent in national government.

DOCUMENT
Reflections on Revolutions

This localism was evident in the **Articles of Confederation,** a national constitution finally ratified by the states in 1781. It stipulated that

Articles of Confederation—The first national constitution for the United States, ratified in 1781.

taxation, control of trade, and issuance of money all be left to the sovereign states, each represented by one vote in Congress. Major decisions required the assent of nine states, and amendments required unanimous agreement of all 13. Although Congress could make war and peace, maintain armies, and conduct Indian affairs, it was financially dependent on the states for these functions. The system was designed to protect liberties against a distant central government dominated by an upper class.

The 1780s, under the Articles of Confederation, brought serious postwar problems. With so much power distributed among the states, the national government was severely hampered in negotiating commercial treaties with foreign states, maintaining adequate military forces, promoting internal economic development, and maintaining domestic order. While the states contended with one another, former soldiers and impoverished civilians demanded back pay, pensions, land, and cheap paper money to pay their debts. In Massachusetts a former army officer named Daniel Shays (1747–1825) even led a brief rebellion. George Washington and other national leaders, convinced that the prevailing disunity and disorder threatened not only property but also the new nation's very survival, urged a reconsideration of the Articles. Their efforts led to a convening of delegates from 12 state legislatures who met in Philadelphia from May to September 1787.

The Constitution of the United States

Because few radicals attended the convention, its delegates were concerned primarily with protecting property and strengthening the union. The arguments of the framers of the Constitution were expressed in a series of newspaper articles that came to be known collectively as the ***Federalist Papers.*** In these essays, people such as Alexander Hamilton and James Madison debated the future power of the United States government, its presidency, the legislature, civil rights, and the powers to be left to the states.

Almost immediately, the framers gave up amending the Articles of Confederation and began work on

Federalist Papers—Articles by, among others, Alexander Hamilton and James Madison, supporting the writing of a new constitution to replace the Articles of Confederation.

The effectiveness of the work done by the Constitutional Convention can be seen by the fact that the United States still follows its provisions, only slightly amended, more than two centuries later.

a new constitution. By allowing each state equal representation in the Senate, the upper house of Congress, they compromised a conflict between large and small states. Another divisive issue was resolved by allowing slaveholding states to count 60 percent of their slaves in the population on which their allocation of seats in the lower house of Congress would be based. With these two questions settled, the convention's work progressed rapidly.

A fundamental principle of the completed Constitution was Montesquieu's separation of powers. This was revealed in the carefully defined distinction between powers granted to the national and state governments and, even more specifically, in the division of functions among the branches of the central government. Congress was to make the laws, the president was to execute them, and the courts were to interpret them. The president could veto laws passed by Congress, but the latter, by a two-thirds vote, could override a presidential veto. The Supreme Court later expanded its original charge of interpreting laws to interpreting the Constitution itself, thus acquiring the right to declare any law "unconstitutional."

In recognizing the principle of popular sovereignty, the Constitution was similar to the Articles of Confederation; it differed in its centralization of government and in its securities against disorder. Proclaiming itself the supreme law of the land, the Constitution specifically prohibited the states from coining money, levying customs duties, and conducting foreign diplomacy. The president, as chief executive, commanded the national military forces, an arrangement that could protect against popular unrest and disorder. Most of the delegates to Philadelphia favored property qualifications for voting, an idea that they abandoned only because it was politically impractical. They indicated their distrust of democracy, however, by avoiding the direct popular election of senators and presidents: Senators would be chosen by the legislature of their particular states while the president would be chosen by a separate, electoral college.

The process of ratifying the Constitution precipitated a great political debate. Congress, dominated by so-called Federalist proponents, ignored the amending provisions of the Articles and appealed directly to the states. Anti-Federalists, who opposed ratification, were alarmed but were generally overwhelmed by arguments from the wealthier, more articulate, and better-educated Federalists, who supported the Constitution. By promising written guarantees of individual liberties—the later Bill of Rights, the first ten amendments to the new Constitution—the Federalists ultimately won the required nine states, and the Constitution was formally adopted on July 2, 1788. Three years later, the first ten amendments were added, guaranteeing freedom of religion, speech, and the press and protecting the people against arbitrary government. Thus the radicals left a lasting legacy, despite the Federalist triumph.

From Theory to Reality

After winning their greatest victory, the Federalists dominated American politics for more than a decade. In 1789 George Washington was elected to the first of his two four-year terms as president under the terms of the Constitution. His administration imposed a high tariff, chartered a national bank, paid public debts at face value, negotiated a commercial treaty with England, and, after 1794, opposed the French Revolution. Ironically, some French revolutionaries, such as the Marquis de Lafayette (1757–1834), who had helped win American independence, were bitterly denounced by American leaders a decade later.

When trade relations with the British began to improve in the 1790s, the French waged an undeclared war on American shipping, taking over 800 ships in the last three years of the decade. This, in addition to the undiplomatic activities of the French embassy, deeply affected the emerging party politics of the young country. Meanwhile, southern slaveholders were deeply suspicious of the French policies in their revolutionary parliaments toward slavery in their colonies in the Caribbean.

The United States benefited from one aspect of Napoleon's activities. In the seventeenth century, French explorers had laid claim to the region between the Mississippi River and the Rocky Mountains, naming it Louisiana in honor of their king. They ceded the region to the Spanish in 1763 and then took it back at the beginning of the nineteenth century. The French had never surveyed the full extent of the area and had no hope of exploiting it in the near future. As a way to block the British and the Spaniards and to make sure the port of New Orleans would remain in at least neutral hands, Napoleon sold Louisiana for $15 million to the United States in 1803. Thomas Jefferson had to take some distinctly unconstitutional steps to buy the land, but, as a result, the Louisiana Purchase doubled the land area of the new country and set a precedent for land acquisition and expansion.

Unfulfilled Dreams

The war for American rights and liberties left much unfinished business. For decades after 1783 the right to vote was restricted to propertied white male citizens. Flagrantly omitted were the common people, women, African Americans, and Native Americans, all of whom were denied full civil equality, freedom, and human justice, despite their important

Abigail Adams personified the best qualities of the new American woman at the end of the eighteenth century. She spoke plainly, openly, and affectionately as she discussed the shape of the new nation with her husband and future president, John.

contributions to the American cause. The suffering of African Americans and Native Americans was particularly severe

Many blacks who had been promised their freedom during the revolutionary wars continued to be enslaved by their owners. Even laws against slavery were not always enforced. In the northern states, emancipation was often legally delayed for decades, so that in 1810 there were still more than a total of 35,000 slaves in New York, New Jersey, and Pennsylvania. The conservative reaction of the 1790s, stimulated by debates in the Constitutional Convention, and the invention of the cotton gin, which gave a new impetus to cotton planting, confirmed the South's emotional commitments to slavery. American slaves after the 1790s were further from the rights of "all men" than they had been before the Revolution. This injustice was the ultimate cause for a subsequent bloody and tragic civil war.

Another abandonment of human rights affected Native Americans. Between 1700 and 1763, thousands of white settlers poured into Indian lands west of the Appalachian mountains. The result was bloody warfare, marked by atrocities on both sides. Looking to the British for protection, most of the tribes fought against Americans during the Revolution, only to have their territories put under control of their enemies in the peace of 1783. Protracted negotiations with the American government led to more surrenders and numerous treaties, all of which were broken as the flood of white land speculators and settlers moved westward. In desperation, the Indians attempted unification and a hopeless resistance. Subsequently, their Ohio federation was crushed in 1794 at the battle of Fallen Timbers; about the same time, the Cherokee union in the South collapsed. During the preceding 18 years, the Cherokees alone had lost 40,000 square miles of territory. In the same period, all Indian populations east of the Mississippi fell by more than 45 percent. By 1800, enforced living on land set aside for Indians was already promoting the disintegration of Native American cultures.

Among the Indian nations caught up in the changes following the American Revolution were the Miami Indians of the Ohio valley. Little Turtle, chief of the Miamis, led his people to victory over American armies twice before being forced to abandon his land.

Document — Letter from Abigail Adams

Abigail Adams, with her husband John, served as the embodiment of the American republican virtues of plain speaking, lack of ostentation, and sometimes brutal honesty. Her letter to her husband speaks to the openness and strength of their relationship. Her spelling represents the usage of the time.

31 Mar. 1776

I wish you would ever write me a Letter half as long as I write you; and tell me if you may where your Fleet are gone? What sort of Defence Virginia can make against our common Enemy? Whether it is so situated as to make an able Defence? Are not the Gentery Lords and the common people vassals, are they not like the uncivilized Natives Brittain represents us to be? I hope their Riffel Men who have shewen themselves very savage and even Blood thirsty; are not a specimen of the Generality of the people.

I am willing to allow the Colony great merrit for having produced a Washington but they have been shamefully duped by a Dunmore.

I have sometimes been ready to think that the passion for Liberty cannot be Eaquelly Strong in the Breasts of those who have been accustomed to deprive their fellow Creatures of theirs. Of this I am certain that it is not founded upon that generous and christian principal of doing to others as we would that others should do unto us. . . .

I long to hear that you have declared an independancy—and by the way in the new Code of Laws which I suppose it will be necessary for you to make I desire you would Remember the Ladies, and be more generous and favourable to them than your ancestors. Do not put such unlimited power into the hands of the Husbands. Remember all Men would be tyrants if they could. If perticuliar care and attention is not paid to the Laidies we are determined to foment a Rebelion, and will not hold ourselves bound by any Laws in which we have no voice, or Representation.

That your Sex are Naturally Tyrannical is a Truth so thoroughly established as to admit of no dispute, but such of you as wish to be happy willingly give up the harsh title of Master for the more tender and endearing one of Friend. Why then, not put it out of the power of the vicious and the Lawless to use us with cruelty and indignity with impunity. Men of Sense in all Ages abhor those customs which treat us only as the vassals of your Sex. Regard us then as Beings placed by providence under your protection and in immitation of the Supreem Being make use of that power only for our happiness.

Questions to Consider

1. Why does Abigail Adams fear that the coming political changes will not benefit women?
2. What is Adams's rationale for her critique of the way men sometimes go about doing business?
3. Would Abigail Adams think her descendants living today have fulfilled her hopes for a "proper" place for women in society?

From Abigail Smith Adams, *The Book of Abigail and John: Selected Letters of the Adams Family, 1762–1784*, eds. L. H. Butterfield, et al. (Cambridge, Mass.: Harvard University Press, 1975).

HAITI: THE FIRST SUCCESSFUL SLAVE REVOLUTION

▪ *How were the Haitians able to throw off French rule?*

The same currents of discontent and violent frustrations seen in France in the summer of 1789 (see Chapter 18) were present in the West Indies at the same time. The middle-class intellectuals and political elites were as informed of the Enlightenment writings as their French colleagues. And they were just as distant from the suffering of the people as were the delegates gathered at Versailles for the meeting of the Estates General. The shock waves generated by the outbreak of the French Revolution were especially deeply felt in Santo Domingo.

The French Revolution's Impact on Santo Domingo

Just as there was discontent in the French countryside over the abuses of the old regime, so too was there violent resentment of the slaves and mulattoes who sought justice from the Creoles or those who had come directly from France to control the colonial administration and the plantations in the West Indies. The free mulattoes in Haiti, the western part of the island of Santo Domingo, deeply resented the Creoles and the French, who treated them as slaves without rights. Their drive for respect and equality was supported by the slave population, who would later serve as their soldiers.

News from France in the summer of 1789 sparked violent uprisings on Santo Domingo and Martinique, especially among those who read or heard about *The Declaration of the Rights of Man and Citizen*. Those who sought satisfaction from the **National Constituent Assembly** shared increased frustrations in the next two years as it became evident that the Assembly's Enlightenment ideology would be set aside on the question of maintaining property, especially on the questions of slaves as property, the major issue of policy toward the French West Indies.

Slave Revolt in Saint Domingue, 1791

Planters in the Assembly differed on trade policies and colonial autonomy but concurred in their defense of slavery and their opposition to civil rights for free mulattoes. Meanwhile, mulattoes in France spread their pamphlets and petitioned the Assembly, supported by the *Amis des Noirs* (ah-MEE day nwah) ("Friends of the Blacks"), whose supporters also angrily attacked slavery in the Assembly hall. The chamber was left divided and nearly impotent. First, it gave the island governments complete control over their blacks and mulattoes; then, yielding to the radicals, it granted political rights to mulattoes born of free parents. Finally, it bowed to the planters and repealed this last measure in September 1791.

Toussaint Louverture and Haitian Independence

In response, Toussaint Louverture (TOO-san loo-ver-TURE; 1744–1803) and Jean-Jacques Dessalines (DES-sal-een; 1758–1806) began a revolutionary war that would last 12 years. There had been slave uprisings during the eighteenth century, just as there had been peasant outbreaks in Europe from the Atlantic coast to the Urals. Without a coherent program and united leadership, the slaves—like the peasants—were defeated. The situation changed by the end of the century. The American Revolution had a significant effect on the islands. The rich saw the possibility of liberation from the controls of the empire, and the poor saw the possibilities of freedom.

These visions, and the mixed messages of the French Revolution, provided the oppressed 90 percent with the unifying ideology they had lacked. In calling for support, Toussaint Louverture said, "Brothers and friends, I am Toussaint Louverture, perhaps you've heard of me. I seek vengeance. I want liberty and equality to reign in Santo Domingo. I will work to make them exist. Unite with us."[2] Combining a genius for military maneuver with a subtle understanding of the international forces at work, Louverture assembled a disciplined and victorious army.

Back in Paris, the French revolutionary assemblies continued to struggle over the policy to be adopted toward the colonies. Not only were there conflicting voices over the issue, the uprising led to a tripling of the price of sugar in Paris at the end of the summer of 1791. The authorities in the islands and in Paris began to deal in small steps with the "problem." The grant of citizenship to free blacks and mulattoes in the West Indies had drawn some mulattoes to the government side, but it was insufficient and led to insurrection uniting royalists on the island and resentful escaped slaves. This uprising complicated an already complex situation, and the Spanish and British took advantage to intervene in the French-controlled part of Santo Domingo to link up with the disaffected coalition.

Finally in the late spring of 1793, the harried governor of Santo Domingo issued a decree freeing all former slaves and calling on them to join against the foreign enemies. In February 1794, the Convention in Paris received a delegation from Santo Domingo and heard a plea for liberty from a 101-year-old former slave woman. The chamber responded by freeing all slaves in French territories and giving them full citizenship rights.

Toussaint Louverture, newly promoted by Paris to the rank of general, united all of the slave and mulatto forces into a single front and defeated the British forces. In 1797 Louverture was made commander-in-chief of the island by the French government. After noting the reactionary drift of French politics and understanding that he and his followers faced a unique opportunity, Louverture, later Governor-for-Life, began moving his country from the status of colony toward independence from France.

In 1802, Napoleon ordered slavery be reimposed in the colonies and sent a large force to Haiti to put down Louverture's government and force the African population back into servitude. Given the overwhelming power

---

National Constituent Assembly—At the meeting of the Estates General in the summer of 1789, the Third Estate, joined by elements of the other two estates, declared itself to be the National Constituent Assembly, a group legally elected to write a constitution for France.

of the French forces, Lourverture was forced to resort to guerrilla tactics. Stymied by the resistance, the French forces called for a truce and negotiations. Louverture went in good faith to the meeting, fell into a trap, and was captured. Even though he died the next year in a prison in eastern France, his forces remained united under Dessalines. After a series of bloody battles, the Haitian army forced the French to withdraw from the island. In November 1803, Dessalines and his colleagues declared the establishment of the nation of Haiti in 1804.

The declaration of Haitian independence marked the only success of a slave revolution in history and guaranteed continued liberty to more than 500,000 people of color. Internal discord—Dessalines, the first African to head a republic, would be assassinated two years later—and external pressures plagued the island until the middle of the century, when it claimed its status as the Republic of Haiti.

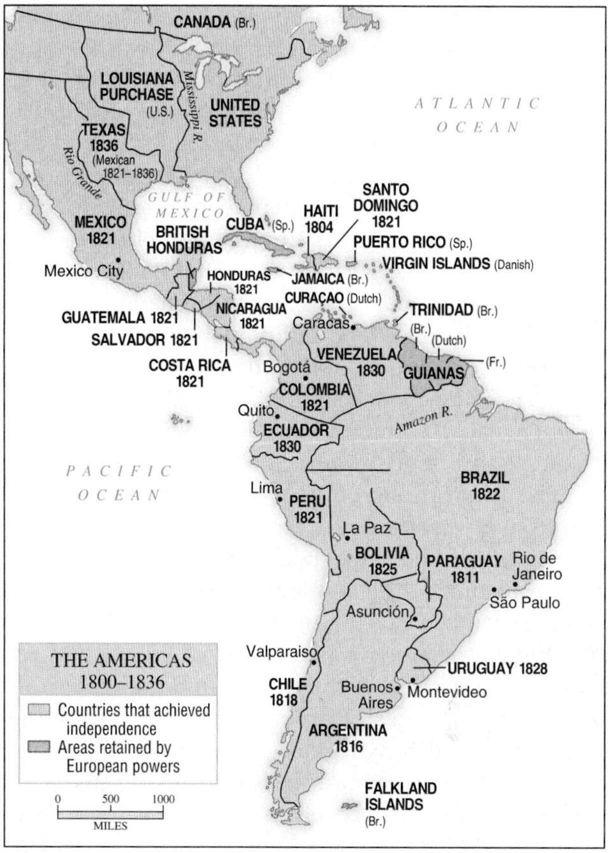

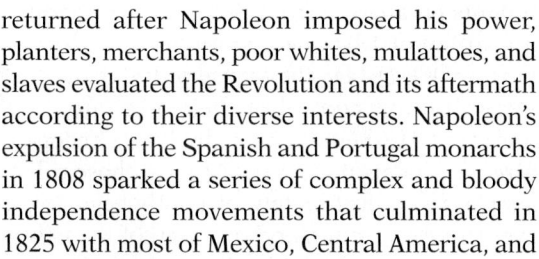

By overthrowing the Spanish king in 1808, Napoleon set in motion 20 years of independence movements in Central and South America.

THE LATIN AMERICAN REVOLUTIONS

▪ *How did Napoleon's wars in Europe influence events across the ocean in Latin America?*

Between 1789 and 1799, the French Revolution caused great excitement in Latin America. When calm returned after Napoleon imposed his power, planters, merchants, poor whites, mulattoes, and slaves evaluated the Revolution and its aftermath according to their diverse interests. Napoleon's expulsion of the Spanish and Portugal monarchs in 1808 sparked a series of complex and bloody independence movements that culminated in 1825 with most of Mexico, Central America, and South America gaining political liberty.

Latin Americans Obtain Independence

Revolutions in Mexico and Central and South America

Napoleon's eviction of the Spanish and Portuguese monarchs in 1808 unleashed the festering forces of discontent and ambition in Spanish and Portuguese America that had built up in the previous two centuries. Unlike the American Revolution, in which there was an argument for liberty made on the basis of a violated social contract, there was no concept of Spanish or Portuguese citizenship violated. Rather, each level of society read the signs coming from Europe in a different way. The Creoles initially dominated the independence movements, but when it became apparent in several countries that they had little concern for the rest of society, the mixed races, the Indians, and African slaves began to pursue their own destiny. There was not a single, unified movement toward independence in Mexico, Central America, and South America. There were several, and all were different. The only shared factor is that the fall of the three-centuries-old Spanish and Portuguese rule led to an uncertain future under American and European dominance.

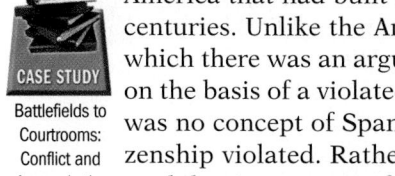

Battlefields to Courtrooms: Conflict and Agency in the Americas

Fracture Zones and Frustrations

There were three distinct struggles for independence in Latin America: Mexico between the peasant uprising in 1810 and the conservative coup d'état in 1821; Simón Bolívar's movement to liberate the northern part of South America and part of Central America; and San Martín's campaign based in the southern part of South America. Each of these movements felt the impact of three key events that took place in Europe (see Chapter 18): Napoleon's eviction of Ferdinand VII in 1808; Ferdinand's return to the throne in 1814; and the Congress System's crushing of the 1820 Spanish liberal revolution.

If the Creoles—perhaps one-fifth of the population (15 percent in Peru, 20 percent in Mexico)—borrowed ideas and examples from abroad to justify their emergence into a dominant position, the other four-fifths played an equally important role. In varying ways, depending on the location, the mixed races, the Indians, and slaves had begun their revolution for justice and equality—against the Creoles—in the eighteenth century. The periodic uprisings of these three groups and the success of the Haitians had frightened the Creoles, and the end of Spanish and Portuguese control gave them, also, the chance to pursue their goals. The independence movement from 1808 to 1825 in much of Latin America was as much a civil war as it was a classic European revolution.

The frustrations of the racial hierarchy fueled a massive resentment. The Creoles feared the *peninsulares,* who were becoming more and more numerous during the eighteenth century. They especially distrusted the Spanish Bourbon reforms of enlightened despotism that spoke of equality of all under a law code, a unitary state, and the recentralization of the Spanish Empire's economy. During the seventeenth and early eighteenth centuries, the Spanish government's mercantile control had weakened, allowing the Creoles to profit enormously—they could carry on their business with little regard for Spain. The reforms of the Spanish king Charles III (1759–1788) threatened the local businessmen and manufacturers by favoring Spanish made goods over those made in the New World and encouraging the production of raw materials for the "mother country."

The Creoles were also uncomfortably trapped between the presumptions of superiority of the *peninsulares* and the miserable masses. But they were far from wanting a revolution—aside from the few who had entered into commercial contact with the British. They were somewhat comfortable in the corrupt framework of the empires—they had no experience in self-government and had no desire to construct a new, multiracial society. The Creoles simply wanted what they saw as their just share of the wealth. Above all, they wanted nothing that would benefit those beneath them in the social hierarchy.

Once Napoleon made his move in 1808, there was a power vacuum that was not filled for the next two years. However, by 1810, in each of the regions of Mexico, Central America, and South America, the Creoles accepted the end of Spanish control and imposed their rule on the towns in which they lived. Peru remained the most faithful to the Spanish monarchy, and even though the Creoles were active in Lima, they had little impact in the countryside, where the Indians constituted a power center of their own. The Spanish did not go easily, fiercely resisting the forces of independence until 1826.

Mexico

The Mexican independence movement began earlier than any of those in Central and South America. The Mexican Creole class was smaller than that in the rest of Spanish America and far more conservative. Between 1808 and 1810, anti-Bonapartist sentiment shifted to a general rejection of the European monarchy in Creole circles throughout the viceroyalty of New Spain. But the elites were slow to mobilize their forces.

An enlightened provincial Creole priest, Miguel Hidalgo (ee-DAL-goh; 1753–1811), actually began the revolution on September 16, 1810, when he issued a call for universal freedom (the date is celebrated in Mexico today as the *Dia del Grito,* the Day of the Call). Hidalgo led his ragged army of Indians, mestizos, and idealists first to Guanajuato (gwa-ne-WAT-oh) where they carried out a great massacre, and then to the gates of Mexico City, where they stopped. Although Hidalgo was condemned by the colonial bishops and executed for treason six months after his uprising began, his cause was taken up by others, including José María Morelos (1765–1815), a radical mestizo parish priest who became an effective guerrilla leader. Unfortunately, the popular movement fell apart because of a lack of organization and shared goals.

The Creoles in Mexico City felt threatened by the threats of Hidalgo and Morelos, and by the liberal sentiments emanating from Spain in the liberal revolution of 1820. Led by Augustin de Iturbide (1783–1824), the conservative classes moved to take control of their own fate. In August 1821, the last Spanish viceroy recognized the independence of Mexico, whose ruling classes, unfortunately, promptly began to struggle over the constitution and the form of the new government. Iturbide, a Creole landowner and officer who had fought as a Spanish loyalist until 1816, became emperor of Mexico for a turbulent 10-month reign in 1822–1823. After Iturbide's death, Antonio López de Santa Anna (1794–1876) dominated politics for the next quarter century, at the end of which Mexico lost the northern half of its territory to the United States. Santa Anna, who emulated Napoleon's opportunism more successfully than he did many of the Frenchman's other qualities, became president or dictator of the Mexican republic 11 times between 1833 and 1855. His career as a military leader included several disastrous incidents, notably his humiliating defeat and capture by Texan rebels at San Jacinto in April 1836, six weeks after he had exterminated their comrades at the secularized Franciscan mission in San Antonio known as the Alamo and a month after he had mercilessly massacred Texan prisoners at Goliad.

DOCUMENT The Plan of Iguala

DOCUMENT Edward Thornton Tayloe's Journal

Augustin de Iturbide brought a conservative end to the Mexican revolution. He served as emperor of Mexico for ten months in 1822–1823.

Simón Bolívar and the Northern Revolt

The charismatic leader who stepped into the void in the northern part of South American and Central America was Simón Bolívar (1783–1830). Born in Caracas of a rich Creole family, he was educated in Europe, where he joined the Masons. After completing his rationalist education in Paris during the last years of the **Directory,** Bolívar returned to his native Venezuela to exploit colonial resistance to the Napoleonic takeover of Spain in 1808.

IMAGE The Great Liberator, Simón Bolívar

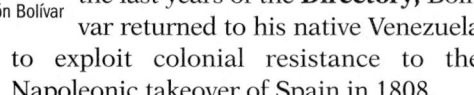

Bolívar, called "The Liberator," stepped into this situation by issuing a series of inflammatory and visionary messages calling for the liberation of Venezuela and Gran Colombia (modern-day Colombia, Panama, Ecuador, and Venezuela). From this base he hoped to expand the liberation movement to include all of Spanish South America. Instead, he found himself entrapped in a multidimensional civil war involving opportunistic Creoles, fervent royalists, and frustrated and angry people of color.

He declared an all-out war against the Spaniards in 1813, but Spanish loyalist forces frequently defeated him. He was forced to flee to Jamaica in 1815 to try to get English assistance, which was not immediately forthcoming. Then, he went to the new republic of Haiti to try to get arms and money in return for declaring an end to slavery. Despite the setbacks, he kept fighting—winning major victories in 1817—and made use of skills as an orator and as a tactician. He eventually forced the remnants of the Spanish military and administrative personnel to return to Spain.

He proposed a constitution for the newly independent regions that favored the elites of the new nations. This document was much like the one written by the French Directory, and he saw himself as something of a Caesarlike figure. He dreamed of an independent continent, the north made up of the nation-states of Venezuela, Colombia, Ecuador, Peru, and Bolivia, but he ran afoul of liberal critics and local loyalties, and the various regions went their own ways. He went into exile in 1827 and eventually died, discouraged, in 1830.

Simón Bolívar and his army battle the Spanish at Araure in Venezuela. Although the Spanish were better trained and equipped, Bolívar led his soldiers with such personal valor that he managed to liberate four countries.

Directory—The political institution that governed France from 1795–1799.

Document Simón Bolívar, Proclamation to the People of Venezuela

Simón Bolívar is considered to be one of the most charismatic and ambitious men in the history of the Americas. His Proclamation to the People of Venezuela, made on June 15, 1813, is one of his most powerful statements. It is a combination of an exhortation and an ultimatum.

SIMÓN BOLÍVAR, Liberator of Venezuela, Brigadier of the Union, General in Chief of the Northern Army

To his fellow-countrymen:

Venezuelans: An army of our brothers, sent by the Sovereign Congress of New Granada, has come to liberate you. Having expelled the oppressors from the provinces of Mérida and Trujillo, it is now among you.

We are sent to destroy the Spaniards, to protect the Americans, and to reestablish the republican governments that once formed the Confederation of Venezuela. The states defended by our arms are again governed by their former constitutions and tribunals, in full enjoyment of their liberty and independence, for our mission is designed only to break the chains of servitude which still shackle some of our towns, and not to impose laws or exercise acts of dominion to which the rules of war might entitle us.

Moved by your misfortunes, we have been unable to observe with indifference the afflictions you were forced to experience by the barbarous Spaniards, who have ravished you, plundered you, and brought you death and destruction. They have violated the sacred rights of nations. They have broken the most solemn agreements and treaties. In fact, they have committed every manner of crime, reducing the Republic of Venezuela to the most frightful desolation. Justice therefore demands vengeance, and necessity compels us to exact it. Let the monsters who infest Colombian soil, who have drenched it in blood, be cast out forever; may their punishment be equal to the enormity of their perfidy, so that we may eradicate the stain of our ignominy and demonstrate to the nations of the world that the sons of America cannot be offended with impunity.

Despite our just resentment toward the iniquitous Spaniards, our magnanimous heart still commands us to open to them for the last time a path to reconciliation and friendship; they are invited to live peacefully among us, if they will abjure their crimes, honestly change their ways, and cooperate with us in destroying the intruding Spanish government and the reestablishment of the Republic of Venezuela.

Any Spaniard who does not, by every active and effective means, work against tyranny in behalf of this just cause, will be considered and enemy and punished; as a traitor to the nation, he will inevitably by shot by a firing squad. On the other hand, a general and absolute amnesty is granted to those who come over to our army with or without their arms, as well as to those who render aid to the good citizens who are endeavoring to throw off the yoke of tyranny. Army officers and civil magistrates who proclaim the government of Venezuela and join us shall retain their posts and positions; in a word, those Spaniards who render outstanding service to the State shall be regarded and treated as Americans.

And you Americans who, by error or treachery, have been lured from the paths of justice, are informed that your brothers, deeply regretting the error of your ways, have pardoned you as we are profoundly convinced that you cannot be truly to blame, for only the blindness and ignorance in which you have been kept up to now by those responsible for your crimes could have induced you to commit them. Fear not the sword that comes to avenge you and to sever the ignoble ties with which your executioners have bound you to their own fate. You are hereby assured, with absolute impunity, of your honor, lives, and property. The single title, "Americans," shall be your safeguard and guarantee. Our arms have come to protect you, and they shall never be raised against a single one of you, our brothers.

This amnesty is extended even to the very traitors who most recently have committed felonious acts, and it shall be so religiously applied that no reason, cause, or pretext will be sufficient to oblige us to violate our offer, however extraordinary and extreme the occasion you may give to provoke our wrath.

Spaniards and Canary Islanders, you will die, though you be neutral, unless you actively espouse the cause of America's liberation. Americans, you will live, even if you have trespassed.

General Headquarters, Trujillo, June 15, 1813. The 3d [year].

SIMÓN BOLÍVAR

Questions to Consider

1. What is Bolívar's attitude toward Spain and Spaniards?
2. How does Bolívar seek to use an "amnesty" to his own advantage?
3. What form of government does Bolívar seek for the region?

From Vicente Lecuna, comp., *Selected Writings of Bolívar,* trans. Lewis Bertrand (New York, The Colonial Press, 1951), pp. 31–32.

José de San Martín and Southern Independence

Argentina, Uruguay, and Chile were liberated by the stoic, Spanish-educated officer José de San Martín (1778–1850), a man as austere and reserved as Bolívar was flashy and outgoing. San Martín, the son of Spanish aristocrats (in present-day Argentina), went to Spain to study when he was 7 years old. He served for 22 years in the Spanish army, before deciding to fight for the independence of Argentina in 1812. San Martín found a difficult political situation in the south, and determined that the key to the final defeat of Spain was to strike at the heart of their strength in Peru, the Spanish stronghold in the New World. The first step toward this goal was to prepare the way to Argentinean independence in 1816. Then, aided by his Chilean friend Bernardo O'Higgins, he liberated Chile in 1817, crossing the Andes under difficult conditions. Wherever his armies went, he liberated slaves.

DOCUMENT: Symbolism and Contested Identities in Argentina

After two years of planning, San Martín launched an attack on Peru by shipping troops around Tierra del Fuego to the Pacific coast. His army took Lima, but the Spanish armies were still in the mountains. In an attempt to gain help in evicting the Spaniards, he met with Bolívar at Guayaquil (gway-ya-KEEL). The two could never forge an alliance, partly because of personality differences and partly because of San Martín's preference for a constitutional monarchy like that of Britain or of France under the Constitution of 1791. They also disagreed on military tactics. After the meeting, San Martín abandoned the struggle and went into exile. Bolívar continued the fight and bestowed a constitution on Peru in 1825, although the last Spanish forces didn't leave until 1826. San Martín spent the rest of his life in France, frustrated by his failure to achieve constitutional monarchies in the nations he liberated. Despite the disappointment, he could take some satisfaction in being viewed as the liberator of the south of the Continent.

The Spanish colonies freed by San Martín may have rejected his desires for a constitutional monarchy, but the Portuguese in Brazil embraced that governmental form. King John VI of Portugal had fled his country in 1807 and for the next 14 years ruled the Portuguese Empire from Rio de Janeiro. Returning to Lisbon after the Portuguese revolution of 1821, the king left his son Dom Pedro as regent of Brazil. Impatient with the reactionary behavior of the Lisbon government, Pedro declared himself emperor of an independent Brazil in 1822. After a stormy interlude in which there was a struggle over the form of government and independence movements of regions wanting to break away from Brazil, Pedro stepped down in 1831 and handed the country to his son Pedro II under a regency, until he ruled in his own right as a constitutional monarch in 1840.

Independence in Latin America

1789–1803	Haitian Revolution
1804	Declaration of Haitian independence
1806–1825	Latin American Wars of Independence
1821	Spanish recognition of Mexican independence
1826	Last Spanish forces leave South America

The Social and Economic Consequences of the Latin American Revolutions

The social and economic consequences of the Latin American revolutions were far different from those in North America and Europe. The area was much poorer and more divided. The new nations of Latin America remained the economic colonies of Europe, even if they were free. The wars of independence, the establishment of new states, and the chaotic aftermath of the time dealt a heavy blow to economic development. The conditions of the indigenous Indian population declined as the new liberal regimes confiscated the large landholdings of the religious orders, which had served to insulate the surviving Indians from direct confrontations with the Europeans' economic and technological dominance. As in every country since the Reformation in which church property was bought up by the monied classes, the local population was reorganized into a new labor force more profitable to the new owners. In Latin America, the owners simply reorganized the Indian communities into a labor force and drove the unproductive and the mestizos off the land. This movement in some countries has continued in one form or another to the present day. The one great advantage gained in the independence movements was the end of slavery.

The Latin American church, led largely by *peninsulares* but staffed by the Creoles, was shattered by the national revolutions. When reconstituted with greatly reduced property and clerical personnel, the church desperately sought to win the protection of the more conservative elements in the Creole elite by opposing liberalism in any form. Since the church had been the exclusive instrument of education and social welfare before liberation, and since the ruling classes showed little interest in providing for the continuation of schools, orphanages, and relief for the lower classes, the misery of the Latin American poor grew more acute throughout the nineteenth century.

The legal and social standing of women did not benefit from political independence, controlled as it was by the often reactionary Creole class. Individual Creole women, such as Bolívar's astute mistress, Manuela Sanches, made major contributions to the revolution, but the adoption of the **Napoleonic Code** in the 1820s had the same negative impact on women's legal status in South America as it did in Europe at the same time.

It can be argued that in the wake of Napoleon's deposing the Spanish Bourbons, Latin America suffered a decline in political stability and internal economic health. The peasants and urban laborers of Indian and mixed-blood descent, the culture-shaping church, and women of all classes paid a heavy price for liberation from the Spanish and Portuguese overlords. The sole group to gain was the secular, male Creole leadership. Nevertheless, what Napoleon had destroyed was gone, and no serious attempt was made to restore the old colonial regime.

In the **Monroe Doctrine,** proclaimed in 1823, the United States let Europe know that the Western Hemisphere—including Latin America—was no longer open to colonization. For the Latin Americans, the British navy was more important for blocking the old empires from returning than was the declaration of the still young and militarily weak United States. Independence yielded the sad political results of military dictatorships that defended only the interests of the Creole class, a tendency that continued in some Latin American countries to the end of the twentieth century. Political weakness made the region the pawn of the Europeans and the North Americans.

MAP
The Americas: 1700-1900

CONCLUSION

In the opening phases of the Capitalist Revolution in the sixteenth and early seventeenth centuries, European markets were swamped with a bewildering array of hitherto rare or unknown goods from the Americas. Potatoes, peanuts, maize (Indian corn), and tomatoes were among the new foods consumed by all levels of European society. Sugar became a common substitute for honey, and the use of cocoa, the Aztec sacred beverage, spread throughout Europe. Coffee would also soon change European social habits. Similarly, North American furs and cottons from Mexico revolutionized clothing fashions. Furnishings of rare woods from Brazil appeared more frequently in the homes of the wealthy. The use of American tobacco became almost a mania among all classes, further contributing to the booming market in Europe for goods from the Americas.

The peoples of the New World paid a heavy price for this change in European tastes and habits. Those who survived the devastating impacts of European diseases and plantation labor became caught up in a social and cultural revolution that continues to the present day. In the Iberian colonies and the West Indies, not enough of the indigenous population survived, and because of the demands of the increasing commerce, there was a labor shortage. The demand for African slaves constantly grew. In North America, despite the large numbers of European immigrants, there was a similar shortage of workers, and thousands of Africans were brought against their will to work in the middle and southern sections of the English colonies.

By the end of the eighteenth century, these currents of economic exploitation and racial injustice came to be wrapped in the arguments of the Enlightenment, which were used by different social classes to defend or advance their interests in different ways. The shock waves of European events opened the doors to revolutionary change in the Americas. In the wake of the after effects of the French and English wars, the English colonists of North America carried out a war that led to the creation of the United States of America. The diverse nature of the rebels found common expression in the concept of a violated social contract to justify their rebellion. To the south, the spin-offs of the French Revolution and Napoleon triggered the independence movements in Haiti and the rest of Mexico, Central America, and South America. These movements to liberation were far more disunited and led some of the independence drives to resemble civil wars from time to time. By 1825 most of the Western Hemisphere had attained political freedom, if not stability and economic independence.

Napoleonic Code—The comprehensive French civil law code compiled in 1804.

Monroe Doctrine—U.S. declaration in 1823 that the Western Hemisphere was no longer open to European colonization and that incursions from the Old Continent would not be welcome.

Suggestions for Web Browsing

You can obtain more information about topics included in this chapter at the websites listed below. See also the companion website that accompanies this text, http://www.ablongman.com/brummett, which contains an online study guide and additional resources.

Military History: American Revolution (1775–1783)
http://militaryhistory.about.com/od/revolutionarywa1/

Site lists links on the biographies of Washington and Paine, battles, museums, reenactments, literature, and other aspects of the era.

Women in the American Revolution
http://info-center.ccit.arizona.edu/~ws/ws200/fall97/grp11/part7.htm

Bibliography providing insight into the role of women during the American Revolution.

Haitian History
http://www.webster.edu/~corbetre/haiti/history/history.htm

Images and background for the Haitian independence struggle.

Simón Bolívar
http://www.geocities.com/Athens/Acropolis/7609/eng/toc.html

A collection of studies and primary sources from the life of the liberator.

Mexican Independence
http://www.mexonline.com/grito.htm

Access to documents and studies of Mexican history.

Literature and Film

Natty Bumpo, the hero of James Fenimore Cooper's *Leatherstocking Tales*—which include *The Pioneers, The Last of the Mohicans* (1826), *The Prairie* (1827), *The Pathfinder* (1840), and *The Deerslayer* (1841)—embodies the conflict between preserving nature unspoiled and developing the land in the name of progress.

Recent films on the revolutionary events in North America are Rolland Emmerich's *The Patriot* (Columbia/Tristar, 2000) and Michael Mann's *The Last of the Mohicans* (Fox, 1992). PBS offers a rich range of videotapes on this era. Ken Burns' *Thomas Jefferson* (TSIN-DXO-FXA, 1996) and David Sutherland's *George Washington: The Man Who Wouldn't Be King* (AMEI-505-FXA, 1992) are splendid achievements. The *Africans in America* series (1998; WGBH Boston, 4 videos, AFRA-DXO-FXA) studies the Africans' fight to survive and maintain their culture from 1600 to the Civil War.

The struggle for independence brought a flood of patriotic writings, mostly poetry, although it also produced the first Spanish-American novel—*The Itching Parrot* (1816) by Mexican author JoséJoaquín Fernández de Lizardi (translated with an introduction by Katherine Anne Porter: Doubleday, 1942). In Argentina, the songs of gauchos gave inspiration to the poetry of Hilario Ascasubi and José Hernández. (Most translations of the works of these authors unfortunately are now out of print.)

Suggestions for Reading

A key work to understanding the contrasting motivations of imperial expansion is by Anthony Padgen, *Lords of All the World: Ideologies of Empire in Spain, Britain, and France, 1492–1830* (Yale University Press, 1998). See also Mark A. Burkholder, *Colonial Latin America* (Oxford University Press, 1989).

Robert Leckie, *George Washington's War* (HarperCollins, 1992), and Page Smith, *A New Age Now Begins: A People's History of the American Revolution*, 2 vols. (Penguin, 1989), are detailed and colorful narratives. Bernard Bailyn's, *The Ideological Origins of the American Revolution* (Belknap Press, 1992) remains an essential study. Ronald Hoffman and Peter J. Albert have edited *Women in the Age of the American Revolution* (University of Virginia Press, 1989), a collection of pertinent essays on the hardships and heroics of women in the Revolution. Leslie Bethell, ed., *The Cambridge History of Latin America*, Vol. 2 (Cambridge University Press, 1984), is encyclopedic in its coverage and superb in its research. To understand the Western Hemisphere south of the Rio Grande, see D. A. Brading's *The First America: The Spanish Monarchy, Creole Patriots and the Liberal State 1492–1862* (Cambridge University Press, 1994). For studies of some of the major figures of the Latin American independence movements see Robert Harvey's beautifully written *Liberators: Latin America's Struggle for Independence 1810–1830* (Overlook Press, 2002). See also C. L. R. James's study of the Haitian Revolution, *The Black Jacobins: Toussaint L'Ouverture and the San Domingo Revolution* (Vintage, 1989).

CHAPTER

22

Industrialization

Social, Political, and Cultural Transformations

CHAPTER CONTENTS

Industrialization quickened the transition from a rural to an urban way of life after 1760: it produced a revolution in the way human beings live equal to that made by the Neolithic—or Agricultural—Revolution in the fifth millennium B.C.E.

Whether for cotton cloth in the eighteenth century or for computers today, industrialization produced (and produces) more goods of a higher quality at a cheaper price. The incremental steps that led to increased textile production and to the making of other goods in all industries continue to be repeated to this day. Liberation from the productive limitations imposed by dependence on human and animal power is the great gift of industrialization. That gift, however, was (and is) paid for by the suffering of the first generations of workers in the factory system—whether in eighteenth and nineteenth century England or in the industrializing regions of Southeast Asia and Africa today.

As the workers labored in the factories, the middle classes, the foremost advocates of capitalism and industrialization, became richer and more powerful. Because of their wealth and creativity, the middle classes dominated the countries of northern and western Europe and North America during the nineteenth century. Their ascension came at the same time as the decline of the old, noble-based regimes. The middle classes recast ideology, culture, religion, and society in their own images. Through their economic power, they exported their way of life around the world.

Industrialized countries dominated the globe economically and politically by the end of the nineteenth century. The Europeans directly ruled practically all of Africa. Although China remained technically independent, it was controlled in many areas by industrialized powers. India fell directly under British rule, as did several parts of the Ottoman Empire. America expanded across the Pacific to Asia at the end of the century. Because of its reforms, only Japan was able to choose its own pace of change in the face of the European advance.

1780

1785 Invention of general purpose steam engine

1785 Invention of power loom

1800

c. 1800 Invention of cotton gin

1813–1901 Life and work of Giuseppi Verdi

1820

1825 Repeal of the Combination Acts permits the formation of labor unions

1829 Invention of steam locomotive, George Stephenson's *Rocket*

1837–1901 Queen Victoria of the United Kingdom

1840

1847 Marx and Engels issue *The Communist Manifesto*

1856 Bessemer develops new process for making steel

1859 Charles Darwin publishes *On the Origin of the Species*

1860

1864–1876 First International

1875 German Social Democratic (Marxist) party established

1880

1889–1914 Second International

1900

1903 Russian Social Democratic party splits into Menshevik and Bolshevik factions

THE INDUSTRIAL REVOLUTION: BRITISH PHASE

■ *Why did industrialization begin in Great Britain?*

During the eighteenth century, Great Britain had the advantage of not being one of the battlefields of Europe. Far away from the wars of the time, British workers and craftsmen individually developed new machines and power sources to the solve the problems of making more cotton cloth for a growing population. In so doing they made the first steps toward industrialization and set in motion a process that is still going on around the globe.

Revolution in the Making of Cotton

1733	John Kay patents flying shuttle
1764	James Hargreaves invents spinning jenny
1769	Richard Arkwright invents water frame
1779	Samuel Crompton invents water mule
1785	Edmund Cartwright invents power loom
c. 1800	Invention of cotton gin

The Revolution in the Making of Cloth

Practical people seeing the need for greater output solved the basic problems of increasing production. In the many steps from raw cotton to finished cloth, there were bottlenecks—primarily in making yarn and weaving the strands together. In 1733 John Kay (1704–1764), a spinner and mechanic, patented the first of the great machines, the flying shuttle. This device made it possible for one person to weave wide bolts of cloth by using a spring mechanism that sent the shuttle across the loom. This invention upset the balance between the weavers of cloth and the spinners of yarn: ten spinners were now required to produce the yarn needed by one weaver.

James Hargreaves (d. 1778), a weaver and carpenter, eliminated that problem of imbalance in 1764 with his spinning jenny, a mechanical spinning wheel that allowed the spinners to keep up with the weavers. Five years later, a barber named Richard Arkwright (1732–1792) built the water frame that made it possible to spin many threads into yarn at the same time. Ten years after that, Samuel Crompton (1753–1827), a spinner, combined the spinning jenny and water frame into the water mule, which, with some variations, is still used today. By this time, the makers of yarn were outpacing the weavers, but in 1785 Edmund Cartwright (1743–1823) invented the power loom, which mechanized the weaving process. In two generations, what had once been a home-based craft became an industry.

The demands of the new machines outran the supply of cotton. Since most of the material came from the United States, the demand exceeded the capability of the slave-based southern economy to create the supply. The best worker could not prepare more than 5 or 6 pounds of cotton per day because of the problems of removing the seeds. American inventor Eli Whitney (1765–1825), among others, devised the cotton gin, a machine that enabled a worker to clean more than 50 times as much cotton a day. This device, coincidentally, played a major role in the perpetuation of slavery in the United States for another half century.

Finally, the textile industry became so large that it outgrew the possibilities of its power source: falling water. Steam came to drive the machines of industrializing Britain. In the first part of the eighteenth century, mechanic Thomas Newcomen (1663–1729) made an "atmospheric engine" in which a piston was raised by injected steam. As the steam condensed, the piston returned to its original position. Newcomen's unwieldy and inefficient device was put to use pumping water out of mines. James Watt (1736–1819), a builder of scientific instruments at the University of Glasgow, perfected Newcomen's invention. Watt's steam engine was also first used to pump water out of mines. It saved the large amounts of energy lost by the Newcomen engine and led to an increase in coal productivity. After 1785 it was also used to make cloth and drive ships and locomotives. The application of steam to weaving made it possible to expand the use of cloth-making machines to new areas, and after 1815, hand looms began to disappear from commercial textile making, replaced by the undoubted superiority of the cloth-making machines.

These inventors made their contributions in response to the need to solve particular problems of production. Their machines and the new power sources expanded productivity and transformed society in ways never before imagined.

Britain's Advantages

Industrialization began in Great Britain in the eighteenth century for a number of reasons. Though neither the richest nor the most populous country in Western Europe, Britain possessed at virtually all levels of society a hardworking, inventive, risk-taking private sector that received strong support from the government. Industrialization could not begin and grow without individual business owners who took a chance on something new. The British maintained this close tie between private initiative and creative governmental support throughout the eighteenth and nineteenth centuries.

Thanks to early governmental support of road improvements and canal construction, Britain had a better transportation network than any other country in Europe. The British also had mastery of the seas, excellent ports, and a large merchant fleet. They enjoyed the advantage of living safely on their island, away from the carnage of war, even during the Napoleonic conflicts. The chance to industrialize in stable conditions gave them the opportunity to profit from war contracts between 1792 and 1815. Finally, the Bank of England served as a solid base for economic growth by providing the money and financial stability for English businessmen.

Probably the most important factor was the relative flexibility of the British social and political systems. Members of the elite, unlike their colleagues on the Continent, pursued their wealth in the new industrial framework with great energy. At the same time, the middle classes, who had no land in the countryside and were excluded from political life until reforms in the second half of the nineteenth century, poured their enthusiasm and inventiveness into developing new businesses and technologies. The rising economic tide eventually included the workers after 1850. They benefited from gradual reforms granted to stifle any chance of revolution from below.

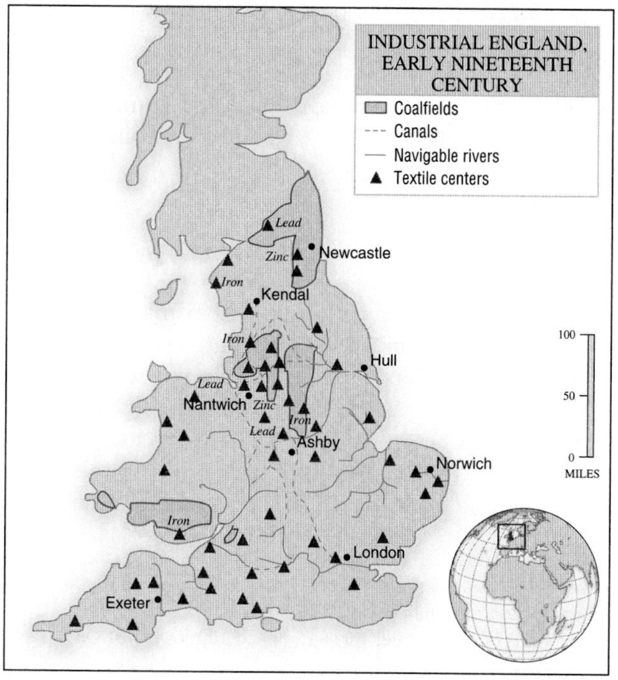

English entrepreneurs established their factories at the beginning of the nineteenth century, not in the traditional population centers such as London, but out of town, close to water power and coal fields and with easy access to markets.

Napoleon's attempt to exclude the British from European markets had hurt economic growth, but it had also spurred the British to look for new manufacturing methods and markets. Once the wars were over, Britain flooded the Continent and the Americas with high-quality, inexpensive goods. No nation could compete against British efficiency.

Industrialized cotton textile production continued to increase in Britain and was supplemented by the arrival of the modern Iron Age. In 1800, Russia and Sweden had exported iron to Britain. By 1815, Britain exported more than five times as much iron as it imported. By 1848, the British produced more iron than the rest of the world combined. As in textile production, a number of inventions in iron-making appeared in response to problems. Improved refining of brittle cast iron made it more malleable and tough so that it could be used in more products. At the same time, more efficient mining processes for both coal and iron ore were used to ensure a dependable supply of raw materials.

To further help Britain dominate the metals market, in the 1850s, Henry Bessemer (1813–1898) developed a process to make steel, a harder and more malleable metal than iron, quickly and cheaply. So effective was the process that, between 1856 and 1870, the price of British steel fell to half the amount formerly charged for the best grade of iron. The drastic reduction in price due to innovations in production, a mark of industrialization, had a positive impact on all areas of the economy.

After mid-century, Britain produced more than two-thirds of the world's coal and more than half its iron and cloth. Industrial development encouraged urbanization, and by 1850, more than half of the population lived in cities and worked in industries. The British continued to enjoy the highest per capita income in the world, and the island nation stood head and shoulders above all others in terms of economic and material strength. With such a position of dominance, the United Kingdom could comfortably advocate Adam Smith's proposals for free-trade.

THE INDUSTRIAL REVOLUTION: CONTINENTAL PHASE

- *How did the Industrial Revolution spread from Britain to the rest of Europe?*

MAP Industrialization in Europe

After mid-century industrialization spread first to the continent and then around the globe as British methods and techniques were imitated and then improved on.

J. M. W. Turner (1775–1851) not only anticipated the innovations of Impressionism in European art, in works such as Rain, Steam, and Speed, *he presented some of the beauty of the industrial age.*

Industrialization and Banking Changes on the Continent

The Continent faced many hurdles to economic growth after the Napoleonic wars. Obstacles to mobility, communication, and cooperation among the classes prevented the social structures there from adapting as easily to change as the British had. The farther one traveled to the south and east, the more repressive the social structure became. In many parts of the Continent, the restored nobilities reclaimed their power, but they were not intellectually, financially, or politically prepared to support industrial development. Fragmented political boundaries, geographical obstacles, and toll-takers along primary river and road systems hampered growth, especially in central Europe. In eastern Europe the middle classes were weaker and more isolated than in the west.

In 1815 the initial stages of industrialization were evident in Belgium, France, and Germany. In Sweden, Russia, and Switzerland there were pockets of potential mechanized production, but these initiatives were tiny compared to Britain's. In 1850 only Belgium could compete with British products in its own markets. There, a combination of favorable governmental policies, good transportation, and stability brought some success.

Governments and businesses sent officials and representatives to Britain to try to discover the secrets of industrialization. The British tried to protect their advantage by banning the export of machines and processes and limiting foreign access to their factories. Industrial espionage existed then as now, and competitors from the Continent did uncover some secrets. Britain's success could be studied, components of it stolen, and its experts hired, but no other European country could combine all the factors that permitted Britain to dominate.

After mid-century, a long period of peace and improved transportation, as well as strategic government assistance, encouraged rapid economic growth in France and the German states. Population increased 25 percent in France and nearly 40 percent in the Germanies, which provided a larger market and labor supply. Two generations of borrowed British technology began to be applied and improved on; but the two most important developments came in banking and in customs and toll reforms.

After 1815, aggressive new banking houses appeared across Europe, strengthened by the profits they had made by extending loans to governments during the Napoleonic wars. They understood the money to be made investing in new industries, such as railroads, and worked with both governments and major capitalists. Firms such as Hope and Baring in London; the Rothschilds in Frankfurt, Paris, Vienna, and London; and numerous Swiss bankers were representative of the private financiers who had well-placed sources and contacts throughout the state and business communities.

Banking changed radically during this period to satisfy the growing demands for money. Long-range **capital** needs were met by the formation of investment banks, while new institutions were created to fill the need for short-term credit. The ultimate source of financial liquidity was the middle classes—the thousands of small investors who put their money in banks to make their own profits through interest earned. More money could be gained from the many small investors than from the few rich families who used to dominate banking.

The *Zollverein*

The Germans led the way in the other major development, the ***Zollverein*** (ZOHL-ver-ein), a customs union which began under Prussian leadership in 1819. This arrangement helped break down the physical and financial barriers imposed at the various state boundaries and, in the next 23 years, came to include most of central and northern Germany. Instead of the more

---

capital—The goods, possessions, or other items of value that constitute wealth and may be used to gain more goods, possessions, or other items of value either through production or investment.

Zollverein—A German customs union, begun under Prussian leadership in 1819, that helped break down the physical and financial barriers imposed at the various boundaries between German states. It allowed goods to circulate free of tolls and tariffs, which reduced prices and stimulated trade.

The interior of the Krupp Steelworks at Essen, Germany, as painted by Otto Bollhagen. Krupp was one of the largest firms in Germany's growing industrial sector.

than 300 divisions fragmenting the German states in 1800, there was a virtual free trade market, something that Britain had enjoyed since the union of Scotland and England in 1707 (and the European Union would create across the Continent at the end of the twentieth century). The significance of the *Zollverein* was that it allowed goods to circulate free of tolls and tariffs, thus reducing prices and stimulating trade.

In the second half of the 1800s, industrialization on the Continent grew rapidly, aided by the increased flow of credit and the elimination of many internal barriers. Tariffs throughout the area fell to a degree not matched until after World War II and the creation of the European Common Market. Major firms, such as the German Krupp steelworks and the French silk industries, controlled portions of the European market and competed effectively with Britain throughout the world.

Agricultural and Transportation Responses to a Growing Population

The industrial revolution coincided with a demographic revolution. A gradual decline in mortality rates, better medical care, more food, earlier marriages, and better sanitary conditions contributed to the European population increase from 175 million to 435 million in the nineteenth century. The number of people grew so rapidly in Europe that although 40 million Europeans emigrated throughout the world, the Continent still showed a population increase in a single century that was greater than that of the previous 20 centuries.

This 130 percent increase between 1800 and 1910 led some observers, such as Thomas Robert Malthus (1766–1834), to forecast a tragic future of massive famine on a global scale. In his "Essay on Population" (1798), Malthus observed the limited food supply and rapidly increasing population of his day and stated that human reproduction would outrun the earth's ability to produce food. He concluded that the inevitable fate of humanity was misery and ruin, since the number of people would rise geometrically while food supply would grow only arithmetically. What Malthus failed to anticipate was the effects of technological innovation in agriculture and transportation.

The vast increase in food production kept up with the population explosion of the nineteenth century. It is estimated that in 1815 around 60 percent of the money and 85 percent of the people in Europe were tied to farming. These large quantities of capital and labor were not used effectively because the advances made in the Netherlands and Britain in the seventeenth and eighteenth centuries had not spread on the Continent. However, progressive landowners gradually introduced these improved methods when they saw the money to be made by feeding the growing populations of the cities.

By the end of the nineteenth century, farmers around the world were plowing new lands and using higher-yielding crop varieties to survive in the worldwide agricultural competition. Industrial nations such as Britain, in which only 10 percent of the population was engaged in farming by 1900, imported more than a fourth of its food. Efficient farmers in the Americas, Australia, and New Zealand competed in the cutthroat global export market, underselling the already impoverished peasants of Ireland and southern and eastern Europe.

To bring the increased food supply to the growing population and to make possible the distribution of raw materials and finished goods to the global market, beginning in 1759, the industrialized countries built the most complete and far-reaching transportation and communication networks ever known.

The Duke of Bridgewater made a major step forward in water transportation when he built a 7 1/2-mile-long canal from his mines to the city of Manchester. Water transport cut the price of his coal in half and gave Britain a vivid lesson in the benefits of canals. By the 1830s, nearly 4000 miles of improved rivers and canals were built, with strong governmental support, making it possible to ship most of the country's products by water. Following the British example, canal building spread through Europe and North America and then to Egypt with the Suez Canal in 1869 and to Latin America with the Panama Canal in 1914. The first project cut the sailing time between London and Bombay, India, by nearly half; the second did away with the need to sail around South America to reach the Pacific Ocean.

Until 1815 most roads were muddy, rutted paths that were impassable during spring thaws and autumn rains. In that year a Scotsman, John McAdam (1756–1836), created the all-weather road by placing small stones in compact layers directly on the roadbed. The pressure of the traffic moving over the highway packed the stones together to give a fairly smooth surface. This practical solution cut the stage-coach time for the 160 miles from London to Sheffield from four days in the 1750s to 28 hours in 1820.

Steam-powered vessels replaced the graceful though less dependable sailing ships in ocean commerce. Clipper ships are among the most beautiful objects ever built, but they cannot move without wind. Sturdy, awkward-looking steamships carried larger cargo with greater regularity and thereby revolutionized world trade. The price of American wheat on the European market dropped by three-fourths in the last part of the century, to a considerable degree the result of the savings made possible by the large, reliable steamships. Transatlantic passenger and mail services were also improved by the use of steam to power seagoing vessels.

The most important element in the European arterial network was the railroad. The Englishman George Stephenson built the first steam locomotive, *Rocket,* in 1829 and by 1860 rails linked every major market in Europe and in the United States. By 1903 the Russians had pushed the Trans-Siberian Railroad to the Pacific Ocean. Railroads cheaply and efficiently carried people and large amounts of material long distances and knit countries and continents closer together. Within cities, urban rail lines and trolleys were widespread by the end of the century; by permitting a wider diffusion of workers, these had an impressive effect on housing and business patterns. In the 1860s London was the first city to establish subways, followed by Budapest in 1896, and Paris in 1900.

Connected with the growth of transportation networks and technological innovation were major improvements in the area of communications. Postal agreements among the various countries made cheap and dependable mail service possible. The introduction of the postage stamp and improved transportation systems brought astronomical increases in the number of letters and packages mailed after 1850. Starting in the 1840s, the electric telegraph, undersea cable, telephone, wireless telegraph, and typewriter expanded the ability to exchange ideas and information. After the transportation and communications revolutions, no longer would distance be an obstacle. The world became a smaller, if not a more unified, place.

MAP
Economic Transformation in Europe: 1750-1850

This ad for Singer Sewing Machines being sold in Zululand shows the impact of Western industry on people in other parts of the world.

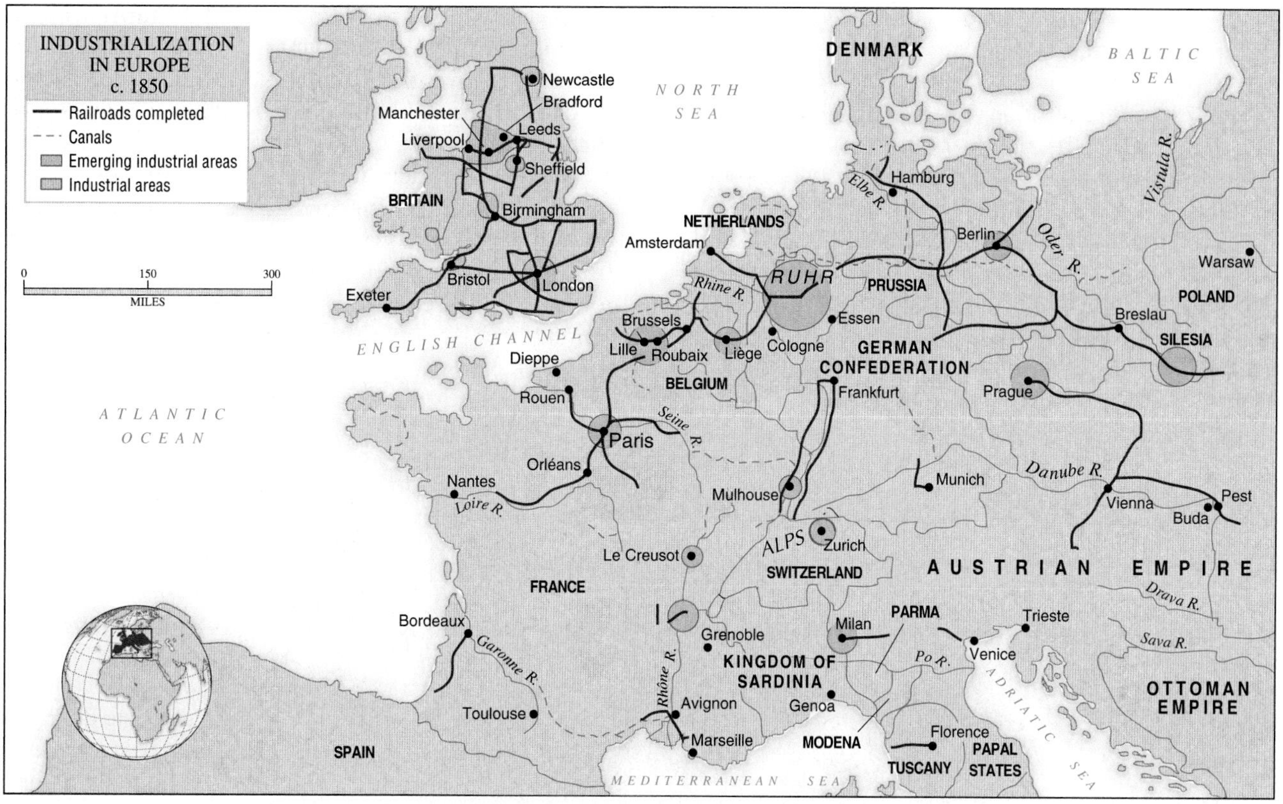

By the middle of the nineteenth century industrialization had spread across Europe, aided by the development of railroad links that brought resources to the new factories and transported their finished goods to world markets.

INDUSTRIALIZATION AND THE WORKERS

- *Why did industrialization fail to bring a decent standard of living to the first generation of industrial workers?*

The first generation of people who worked in the factories did not initially profit from industrialization: instead they paid a heavy price. Everywhere it occurred, industrialization produced wrenching social changes. It drove society away from an agricultural to an urban way of life. The old system, in which peasant families worked the fields during the summer and did their cottage industry work in the winter to their own standards and at their own pace, slowly disappeared. In its place came urban life tied to the factory system. The factory was a place where, for long hours, people did repetitive tasks, using machines to process large amounts of raw materials. This was an efficient way to make a lot of high-quality goods cheaply. But the factories were often dangerous places, and the lifestyle connected to them at first had a terrible effect on the human condition.

The Factory System

In the factory system, the workers worked, and the owners made profits. The owners wanted to make the most they could from their investment and to get the most work they could from their employees. The workers, in turn, felt that they deserved more of the profits because their labor made production possible. This was a situation guaranteed to produce conflict, especially given the wretched conditions the workers faced in the first stages of industrialization.

DOCUMENT Industrial Society and Factory Conditions

The early factories were miserable places, featuring bad lighting, lack of ventilation, dangerous machines, and frequent breakdowns. Safety standards were practically nonexistent, and workers in various industries could expect to contract serious diseases; for example, laborers working with lead paint developed lung problems, pewter workers fell ill to palsy, miners suffered black lung disease, and operators of primitive machines lost fingers, hands, and even lives. Not until late in the nineteenth century did health and disability insurance come into effect. In some factories, workers who suffered accidents were deemed to be at fault; since

DOCUMENT Report on Sanitary Conditions

there was little job security, a worker could be fired for almost any reason.

Women and Child Labor

The demand for plentiful and cheap labor led to the widespread employment of women and children. As we can see in the testimony of eight-year-old Sarah Gooder before a Parliamentary Commission (see Document, "Industrialization and Children"), girls as young as 6 years old were used to haul carts of coal in Lancashire mines, and boys and girls of 4 and 5 years of age worked in textile mills, where their nimble little fingers could easily untangle jams in the machines.

Children who worked in the English mines were called "hurriers." This illustration of children working in the mines appeared in a book titled The White Slaves of England, *published in 1853.*

When they were not laboring, the working families lived in horrid conditions in wretched industrial cities such as Lille, France, and Manchester, England. There were no sanitary, water, or medical services for the workers, and working families were crammed 12 and 15 individuals to a room in damp, dark cellars. Bad diet, alcoholism, cholera, and typhus reduced life spans in the industrial cities. Simultaneous with, and perhaps part of, the industrialization process was a dramatic increase in illegitimate births and prostitution. Up to mid-century, corresponding to the time of maximum upheaval, at least one-third of all births in Europe were out of wedlock.

Later generations profited from the sacrifices made by the first workers in industrialization. Factory owners began to realize that they could make more profit from an efficient factory staffed by contented and healthy workers. But the costs borne by the first generations making the transition between a family-based rural life and the anonymous cruelty of early industrial cities were immense.

Urban Crises

Industrialization prompted massive growth of European cities in the nineteenth century, as can be seen in the following table. In addition, new towns sprang up throughout the Continent and they soon reached the level of more than 100,000 inhabitants. Even in agrarian Russia, where 70 percent of the population worked on the land, there were 17 cities of more than 100,000 by the end of the century.

CASE STUDY
Industrial Side Effects

Political leaders faced serious problems in dealing with mushrooming city growth. The factory system initially forced families to live and work in squalor, danger, and disease, conditions to be found today in countries undergoing the first stages of industrialization. City leaders had the responsibility to maintain a clean environment, provide social and sanitation services, enforce the law, furnish transportation, and—most serious of all—build housing. They uniformly failed to meet the challenges of growth.

Until mid-century, human waste disposal in some parts of Paris was handled by dumping excrement into the street gutters or the Seine River. Not until Baron Georges Haussman (1809–1891) implemented urban renewal in the 1850s and 1860s did the city get an adequate garbage, water, and sewage system. Police protection remained inadequate or corrupt. Other cities shared the same problems to a greater or lesser degree. The new industrial towns that had sprung up were in even worse condition than the older centers.

By the end of the century, however, governments began to deal effectively with urban problems. By 1914 most major European cities began to make clean running water, central heat, adequate street lighting, urban and suburban transport, mass public education,

Nineteenth-Century Urban Growth

City	Population in 1800	Population in 1910
London	831,000	4,521,000
Paris	547,000	2,888,000
Berlin	173,000	2,071,000
Vienna	247,000	2,030,000
St. Petersburg	220,000	1,907,000

Document Industrialization and Children

Early industrialization demanded huge sacrifices, especially from children. Despite the popularity of laissez-faire economic in Great Britain, Parliament began to make inquiries into the working conditions in mines and factories. They discovered that owners preferred to employ little children because their size and dexterity were especially useful in clearing up blockages in looms and in penetrating small spaces in mines. Such owners considered children as legal entities, capable of being equal partners in a legal contract.

Sarah Gooder, Aged 8 Years

I'm a trapper in the Gawber pit. It does not tire me, but I have to trap without a light and I'm scared. I go at four and sometimes half past three in the morning, and come out at five and half past. I never go to sleep. Sometimes I sing when I've light, but not in the dark; I dare not sing then. I don't like being in the pit. I am very sleepy when I go sometimes in the morning. I go to Sunday-schools and read *Reading made Easy.* [She knows her letters and can read little words.] They teach me to pray. [She repeated the Lord's Prayer, not very perfectly, and ran on with the following addition.] "God bless my father and mother, and sister and brother, uncles and aunts and cousins, and everybody else, and God bless me and make me a good servant. Amen. I have heard tell of Jesus many a time. I don't know why he came on earth, I'm sure, and I don't know why he died, but he had stones for his head to rest on. I would like to be at school far better than in the pit."

Questions to Consider

1. Play "devil's advocate" and construct a defense for using children in mines and factories. Take the opposite point of view and construct a critique against the use of children in industrial and mining enterprises.
2. Do you know of any instances in today's economy where children are used in the manufacturing of items used by you or your friends and family?
3. Did liberalism, as seen by John Stewart Mill and Jeremy Bentham, justify the employment of children?

From *Parliamentary Papers* (1842).

dependable sewage systems, and minimal medical care available for their people.

The Labor Movement

The British economy suffered through a difficult time after the end of the Napoleonic wars. High unemployment struck skilled workers, especially non-mechanized loom weavers. In frustration, some of them fought back and destroyed textile machines, the symbol of the forces oppressing them. Strikes, demonstrations, and incidents such as the Peterloo Massacre, August 16, 1819, at St. Peter's Fields, in which soldiers closed down a political meeting, killing 11 and injuring hundreds, vividly expressed the workers' rage. Not until British reformers came forward in the 1820s did the laborers begin to gain some relief.

Their efforts to form labor unions received an important boost in 1825 when the Combination Acts, passed in 1799 against the formation of workers' associations, were repealed. The first unions, such as the half-million-strong Grand National Consolidated Trades Union, were weak and disorganized, split by the gulf between skilled workers and common laborers. Nonetheless, by the end of the century, the workers laid the foundations for the powerful unions that defended them.

Socialism

Political thinkers in France and England responded to the injustices of industrial capitalism by developing the theory of **socialism.** Socialists attacked the system of laissez-faire capitalism as unplanned and unjust. They condemned the increasing concentration of wealth and called for public or worker ownership of business. The nature of the industrial system, dividing worker and owner, also raised serious problems, and socialists insisted that harmony and cooperation, not competition, should prevail.

Socialists believed that human beings are essentially good, and with the proper organization of society there would be a happy future with no wars, crimes,

socialism—An ideology proposing that the community or government have ownership of the means to create wealth.

administration of justice, or government. In this perfectly balanced world, there would also be perfect health and happiness. Karl Marx later derisively labeled socialists who sought such a world as "Utopians."

The first prominent **Utopian socialist** was the French noble Claude Henri de Rouvroy, Comte de Saint-Simon (klod on-REE da hrouv-WHA, komt da san SI-mohn; 1760–1825). He defined a nation as "nothing but a great industrial society" and politics as "the science of production." He advocated that humanity should voluntarily place itself under the rule of the paternalistic despotism of scientists, technicians, and industrialists who would use their collective wisdom to improve the lives of the multitude of poor people.

Charles Fourier (fou-ree-AY; 1772–1837), another French Utopian, believed that the future society must be cooperative and free. He worked out a communal living unit of 1620 people called a *phalanstery*. The members of the group voluntarily chose tasks that appealed to them to do the work needed to ensure the phalanstery's survival. Although his plan was endorsed by many prominent people, attempts made to found cooperative Fourierist communities were unsuccessful. The famous Brook Farm colony in Massachusetts was one such short-lived experiment.

Robert Owen (1771–1858), a successful mill owner in Scotland, was a more practical Utopian socialist. His New Lanark, the site of his textile mills, was a model community. There, between 1815 and 1825, thousands of visitors saw rows of neat, well-kept workers' homes, a garbage collection system, schools for workers' children, and clean factories where workers were treated kindly and no children under age 11 were employed. In 1825 Owen moved to the vicinity of Evansville, Indiana, where he established a short-lived community at New Harmony.

Karl Marx and Communism

Karl Marx (1818–1883) took socialism from its "Utopian" to its "scientific" phase. As was the case with other creators of ideologies to aid the working classes, he came from a comparatively privileged social position, growing up in a pleasant setting in Trier, in the western part of Germany. Marx's Jewish parents converted to Protestantism so that they could participate fully in Prussian society, and then they pushed their son to become a lawyer. Instead of following his parents' wishes, he attended the University of Berlin as a doctoral candidate in philosophy and joined a circle that followed some aspects of Hegel's thought. After finishing his degree, he could not find a university position and so returned to the Rhineland, where he began writing for a local liberal newspaper. The injustices he saw around him and his reading of the French socialists Henri de Saint-Simon and Pierre-Joseph Proudhon (proo-DHON) led him to concentrate on the economic factors in history and pass from philosophical abstractions to the realities of politics and economics.

In 1845 Marx went to Paris to continue his work; there he met Friedrich Engels (1820–1895), the son of a wealthy German businessman who owned factories in England and Germany. Engels had seen firsthand how workers suffered during the first phase of industrialization when he worked at his father's plant in Manchester. In Paris he and Marx spent ten days together sharing their ideas. The two became united in their hatred of what they saw as the inhumane nature of capitalism and spent the rest of their lives attacking it.

Marx was, from the start, the intellectually dominant partner, but Engels gave him lifelong intellectual, material, and personal support. Marx's radical ideas led to his expulsion by the French in 1845. From there, he went first to Belgium and finally to England, where he spent most of his life after 1848.

Almost every day he made his way to the British Museum, where he waged intellectual war on capitalism by doing research for his major works, especially *Das Kapital* ("Capital"; 1867–1894). At night he returned home to write, enduring difficult living conditions and the deaths of three of his children in the 1850s. He wrote prolifically, although he suffered from boils, asthma, spleen and liver problems, and eyestrain. His constant inability to handle money drove him into fits of rage against his creditors. He was increasingly intolerant of anyone who disagreed with him and became an embittered recluse; yet his vision and theories inspired reformers for the next century and a half. Marx constructed a system that gave the oppressed an explanation for their difficult position and hope for their future.

Karl Marx and His Daughter

A materialistic view of history shaped his approach. He wrote that economic forces drove history. He did not deny the existence or importance of spiritual or philosophical values, nor did he doubt that the occasional genius could alter the flow of events. However, the material aspects of life were much more important. Marx believed that "it is not the consciousness of men which determines their existence, but on the contrary, it is the existence which determines their consciousness." As an economic determinist, he believed that when the means of production of a given era changed, the whole social and ideological structure was transformed by the groups who controlled those means of production.

Utopian socialism—A variant of the socialist ideology that proposes that the turning over of the means to create wealth to the community or government can be achieved peacefully.

DOCUMENT
The Communist Manifesto

German philosopher Georg Wilhelm Friedrich Hegel (1770–1831) had written that history is made up of a number of cultural periods, each one the expression of a dominant spirit or idea. After fulfilling its purpose, a given period is replaced by a period of contradictory ideas or values. The original thesis is negated, and that negation is in turn negated once it has run its course. Marx identified the productive forces of society, not culture periods, as the key factor in history. The world is driven by class conflict between those who control the means of production and those who do not, whether master against slave in ancient Greece, patrician against plebeian in Rome, lord against serf in the Middle Ages, noble against bourgeois in early modern times, or capitalist against proletarian in the modern world. History moves in this zigzag pattern through class struggle, a reflection of the Hegelian **dialectic.** Not until the triumph of the proletariat would this pattern stop: The workers controlling the means of production could not logically engage in class conflict, and hence **communism** would be achieved.

The bourgeoisie, or the middle classes, who had erected the new capitalist society by gaining control of the means of production through organizing trade and industry, created its opposition in the proletariat, the class-conscious workers. This latter group would be, according to Marx, "the seeds of the bourgeoisie's own destruction." According to the dialectic, when the workers recognized their true power, they would overthrow the bourgeoisie. Out of this conflict would come the final act of the dialectical process, the classless society in which "each person would work according to his ability and receive according to his need." An interim dictatorship might have to occur because a number of features of the old order would remain and the proletariat would have to be protected. However, as the classless society evolved, the state would wither away.

Through his research, Marx identified a number of defects that foretold the inevitable overthrow of the bourgeoisie, among them alienation and surplus value. The factory system turned workers into cogs in the larger machine and deprived them of satisfaction in their work. In addition, Marx charged that owners did not pay workers for the value they created. A worker could, for example, produce the necessary economic value to supply one individual's needs in seven hours, but the owner would keep the worker laboring for 12 hours. The owner thereby stole the "surplus value" of five working hours from the worker, in effect robbing the worker of the fruits of his or her work.

Finally, Marx noted that in the capitalist system, the rich got richer and fewer and the poor got poorer and more numerous. This gap produced widespread discontent and increased the impetus toward revolution. Further, the masses would be unable to buy all of the goods they produced, and economic crises of overproduction and unemployment would become the rule. In time, once the bourgeois phase of dominance had run its course, the contradictions between the classes would become so great that the proletariat would rise up and take over the means of production.

Socialism and the Labor Movement

Socialist parties of all varieties helped advance the workers' movements in the second half of the nineteenth century by providing a theoretical basis and an aggressive public statement of their case. Marx, who spent his life researching and writing in the defense of the workers—even though he had precious little contact with them—organized the International Workingmen's Association, later known as the First International, in London in 1864. The First International included labor activists ranging from English trade unions to eastern European refugees to anarchists to German theorists. Not much came of the First International's efforts because of constant arguing among the factions and Marx's vindictiveness toward other major figures, such as the Russian anarchist Bakunin (ba-KOO-nin).

In the three decades after Marx's death in 1883, his theories dominated the European workers' movements, though the movements themselves were not united. The French split into three distinct socialist groups. Some British socialists were greatly influenced by the maxims of Christianity, while the socialist Fabian Society—among whose members were the middle-class writers George Bernard Shaw, H. G. Wells, and Sidney and Beatrice Webb—pursued a more prosaic political path. With the spread of industrialization, workers and their leaders found important support in Marx's work even in places such as Russia, where Marx had never foreseen his thoughts as having any influence.

The Social Democrats—Marxist socialists—made important gains in Germany, forcing Bismarck to make concessions (see Chapter 27). The Social Democratic Party became the largest party in the country and the strongest socialist party in Europe under the leadership of its founder, Ferdinand Lassalle. In 1871 there were two socialists in the Reichstag (the lower

dialectic—A process in which a thesis and an antithesis are reconciled in a synthesis.

communism—An ideology which advocates the elimination of private property, the ownership of all goods and means of production by the community, and an elimination of conflict by the creation of a society in which each person works according to his abilities and receives according to his needs.

Socialist Internationals (Labor Unions)

1864–1876	International Workingmen's Association (First International)
1889–1914	Second International, Social Democratic (non-Russian remnants remained until 1972)
1919–1943	Third International, Communist (Leninist, also known as the Comintern)
1923–1970s	Fourth International, Trotskyite (formally organized in 1938)

house of the German legislature); by 1912 the number had risen to 110.

Because of the widespread impact of Marx's ideas in the social sciences and the labor movement, the period of the Second International (1889–1914) was the most important time of his influence. A broad spectrum of thinkers among the 12 million members of the Second International claimed Marx as their inspiration, even though they might differ in opinions about the role of the state, the functions of unions, the crisis of capitalism, the role of the proletariat, and even things he said. There was not a single, monolithic Marxist movement in Europe. Yet, despite their doctrinal differences, the Social Democrats in all countries could agree on essentials for the workers: an eight-hour day, the need to replace standing armies with militias, and a welfare state buttressed by universal suffrage.

The socialist movement strengthened Europe's labor unions, and the workers achieved substantial progress by 1914. Whether by working within the various states' legislatures or by raising the specter of revolution, the socialists helped bring about substantial reforms in the economy, labor practices, civil rights, the courts, and education. They pushed the capitalists to reform, thus, ironically, avoiding the very apocalyptic revolution forecast by Marx.

As industry became more sophisticated and centralized, so did the labor movement. Across Europe the workers could choose anarchist, socialist, or conservative paths to follow. Some unions—the trade or craft unions—centered on a particular occupation. Some found their focus in the various productive stages of an industry, and still others, such as the English Trade Unions Congress, were nationwide and all-encompassing, wielding great power. Whatever the choice, by 1900, unions had made important advances through their solidarity in launching paralyzing strikes.

Although workers could still not negotiate on an equal basis with the owners, they had, by 1914, vastly improved their position over that endured by their grandparents. The British movement had 4 million members and was a powerful force; German unions obtained benefits for their members in a broad number of areas, from life insurance to travel. The income gap between rich and poor began to narrow. Working hours were shortened, and living conditions improved. The real wages of workers—that is, the amount of goods that their income could actually buy—increased by 50 percent in the industrial nations in the last 30 years of the nineteenth century.

THE MIDDLE CLASSES

- *Why were the middle classes interested in reform efforts and other "good works"?*

Although it is difficult to give a strict definition of the middle classes, or **bourgeoisie,** it is easier to say who did not belong. Neither factory workers nor peasants nor the aristocracy were included. In general, the farther south and east one went in Europe, the less numerous and weaker the middle classes were.

But from the mid-eighteenth century through to the opening of World War I, they dominated Europe through their social examples, religious activities, humanitarian work, scientific accomplishment, cultural creations, and ideological work.

"Upstairs, Downstairs"

People socially closer to the laboring classes were considered the lower middle classes, while those near the elite formed the upper middle classes. Included in the lower middle classes were skilled artisans, bureaucrats, clerks, teachers, shopkeepers, and clergy. They realized that very little separated them from the laboring masses and were constantly trying to climb socially. Later in the century, they benefited most from compulsory education laws and were avid consumers of the books written by a new wave of authors, the penny-press newspapers, and state propaganda.

The upper middle classes profited the most from industrialization. It was not easy to break into this level of society, but money, taste, and aggressiveness

bourgeoise—The middle classes, in all of their variations.

could open the doors for the bankers, factory owners, lawyers, architects, doctors, high government officials, and occasionally professors, who tried. Once admitted, they gained many of the benefits of the aristocracy, such as access to the best schools. Because of their greater wealth and leisure time, they controlled politics, the press, and the universities.

The English Example

The model for all middle-class people everywhere was the British upper middle class of the Victorian era, named for Victoria (1837–1901), the long-reigning English queen. The Victorian upper middle class was riddled with contradictions. As Mrs. Beeton in her book on household management indicates, on the surface (see Document), the Victorians had little doubt about what was right and wrong, moral and immoral, proper and improper. Beneath this surface propriety, however, some members of the leading families pursued debauched lives marked by sexual excesses and drug addiction. One of the prime ministers of the era, William Gladstone, devoted considerable attention to "reforming" prostitutes. At the same time, the Victorian literary establishment concentrated on "cleaning up" Shakespeare's plays and toning down some parts of Gibbon's *Decline and Fall of the Roman Empire* so as not to corrupt the class of people in their employ:

The English, the pioneers of the Industrial Revolution, also established the model of how "proper" middle-class people should live. This family at home embodies an ideal of social and domestic life that was copied wherever in the world a middle class came to exist.

Britain had more than 2.5 million servants at the century's end—nearly a million people more than farmed the land.

The British middle classes spearheaded crusades against slavery, alcohol, pornography, and child labor, and for women's rights. Their efforts led to the passage of a series of reforms limiting the employment of young children, setting maximum working hours for teenagers, and regulating working conditions for women—even when the factory owners argued that such changes were bad for the country because they violated the freedom of contract between worker and employer. The churchgoing British upper middle class set the complex model of private excess and public virtue to be imitated by their peers around the world.

Changes in the Christian Churches

Changing times after 1760 posed serious challenges to the Christian churches. The Scientific Revolution and the Enlightenment ate away at the authority of traditional Catholicism and Protestantism. The churches were also reeling under the challenges posed by industrialization and urbanization. The demographic changes that resulted from rapid growth of cities forced the churches to respond to different audiences facing more difficult problems than those of an earlier, simpler age. As the middle-class dominated world of the nineteenth century, the churches not only coped but grew in influence by setting the limits of propriety and expressing concern for the less fortunate.

Among Christian elites, the extreme rationalism of the eighteenth century provoked strong opposition from those who found little warmth or comfort in the thoughts of a world dominated by natural laws and clockwork gods. The responses ranged from Scottish philosopher David Hume's (1711–1776) theory of skepticism to the works of the German philosopher Immanuel Kant (1724–1804), a professor at the University of Königsberg (KEN-igs-berg).

Kant was thoroughly antagonized by the materialistic extremes of the Enlightenment. While appreciating science and dedicated to reason, he worked to shift philosophy back to a more sensible position without giving up much of its newly discovered rational basis. His theories, recorded primarily in the *Critique of Pure Reason* (1781), ushered in a new age of philosophical idealism. Kant agreed with John Locke on the role of the senses in acquiring knowledge of the material world but insisted that sensory experience had to be interpreted by the mind's internal nature. Thus certain ideas—the mind's categories for sorting and recording experiences—were a priori; that is, they existed before the sensory experience

Document *Mrs. Beeton's Book of Household Management* (1861)

Mrs. Beeton's Book of Household Management was first published in 1861. It proved enormously popular; new editions were produced for over half a century. Over 2000 pages long, it covered almost every aspect of middle class life. It was, in effect, a "guide" to successful housewifery.

The Housewife, Home Virtues, Hospitality, Good Temper, Dress and Fashion, Engaging Domestics, Wages of Servants, Visiting, Visiting Cards, Parties, Etc. Etc.

The functions of the mistress of a house resemble those of the general of an army or the manager of a great business concern. Her spirit will be seen in the whole establishment, and if she performs her duties well and intelligently, her domestics will usually follow in her path. Among the gifts that nature has bestowed on woman, few rank higher than the capacity for domestic management, for the exercise of this faculty constantly affects the happiness, comfort, and prosperity of the whole family. In this opinion we are borne out by the author of *The Vicar of Wakefield* [Oliver Goldsmith], who says: "the modest virgin, the prudent wife, and the careful matron are much more serviceable in life than petticoated philosophers, blustering heroines, or virago queans. She who makes her husband and children happy is a much greater character than ladies described in Romances whose whole occupation is to murder mankind with shafts from the quiver of their eyes."

. . . . A woman's home should be first and foremost in her life, but if she allow household cares entirely to occupy her thoughts, she is apt to become narrow in her interests and sympathies, a condition not conducive to domestic happiness. To some overworked women but little rest or recreation may seem possible, but, generally speaking, the leisure to be enjoyed depends upon proper methods of work, punctuality, and early rising. The object of the present work is to give assistance to those who desire practical advice in the government of their home.

Hospitality should be practised; but care must be taken that the love of company, for its own sake, does not become a prevailing passion; such a habit is no longer hospitality, but dissipation. A lady, when she first undertakes the responsibility of a household, should not attempt to retain all the mere acquaintances of her youth. Her true and tried friends are treasures never to be lightly lost, but they, and the friends she will make on entering her husband's circle, and very likely by moving to a new locality, should provide her with ample society.

In conversation one should never dwell unduly on the petty annoyances and trivial disappointments of the day. Many people get into the habit of talking incessantly of the worries of their servants and children, not realizing that to many of their hearers these are uninteresting if not wearisome subjects. From one's own point of view, also, it is well not to start upon a topic without having sufficient knowledge to discuss it with intelligence. Important events, whether of joy or sorrow, should be told to friends whose sympathy or congratulation may be welcome. A wife should never allow a word about any faults of her husband to pass her lips.

Cheerfulness—We cannot too strongly insist on the vital importance of always preserving an equable good temper amidst all the little cares and worries of domestic life. Many women may be heard to declare that men cannot realize the petty anxieties of a household. But a woman must cultivate that tact and forbearance without which no man can hope to succeed in his career. The true woman combines with mere tact that subtle sympathy which makes her the loved companion and friend alike of husband, children, and all around her.

On the important subject of dress and fashion we cannot do better than quote: "Let people write, talk, lecture, satirize, as they may, it cannot be denied that, whatever is the prevailing mode in attire, let it intrinsically be ever so absurd, it will never *look* as ridiculous as another, which however convenient, comfortable, or even becoming is totally opposite in style to that generally worn." A lady's dress should be always suited to her circumstances, and varied for different occasions. The morning dress should be neat and simple, and suitable for the domestic duties that occupy the early part of the day. This dress should be changed before calling hours; but it is not in good taste to wear much jewelry except with an evening dress. . . .

Questions to Consider

1. As you look at your grandmother's generation, how closely do you think her values and practices adhere to those presented by Mrs. Beeton's?
2. What are the most important differences to be found between a woman such as that discussed by Mrs. Beeton in 1861 and women of your generation?

From Mark A. Kishlansky, ed, *Sources of the West*, Vol. 2, (New York: Longman, 2001), pp. 158–160.

occurred. Typical innate ideas of this sort were width, depth, beauty, cause, and God; all were understood yet none was learned directly through the senses. Kant concluded, as René Descartes had, that some truths were derived from material objects, not through the senses but through pure reason. Moral and religious truths, such as God's existence, could not be proved by science yet were known to human beings as rational creatures. Reason, according to Kant, could go beyond the mere interpretation of physical realities.

Even more significant, during this time of political, social, and economic change, was a widespread emotional revival, stressing religion of the heart rather than the mind A new, mass movement, known as *Pietism*, reached full development in England after 1738 when the brothers John Wesley (1703–1791) and Charles Wesley (1708–1788), along with George Whitefield (1714–1770), began a crusade of popular preaching in the Church of England.

The Anglican Pietists discarded traditional formalism and stilted sermons in favor of a glowing religious fervor and hymn singing, producing a vast upsurge of emotional faith among the English lower classes. In February 1739 Whitfield preached to 200 miners from on top of a coal tip; in the following days, thousands of people arrived to hear his words. Breaking out of the ordinary venues for religion, the Wesleys and Whitefield were called "Methodists," at first a term of derision. Later the term came to be the respected and official name for the new movement. After John Wesley's death in 1791, the Methodists officially left the Anglican Church, which proved unable to respond to the needs of large numbers of its adherents, to become the most important independent religious force in England.

On the Continent, Lutheran Pietism, led by Philipp Spener (1635–1705) and Emanuel Swedenborg (1688–1772), responded to the needs of the people dissatisfied with the cold and formulaic state Lutheran church. Swedenborg's movement in Sweden began as an effort to reconcile science and revelation; after his death it became increasingly emotional and mystical. Spener, in Germany, stressed Bible study, hymn singing, and powerful preaching. The Moravian movement sprang from this background. Under the sponsorship of Count Nicholaus von Zinzendorf (1700–1760), it spread to the frontiers of Europe and to the English colonies in America.

The **"Great Awakening,"** a tremendous emotional revival carried across the Atlantic from the European movements, was sustained by Moravians, Methodists, Baptists, and Quakers. It swept the colonial frontier areas of North America from Georgia to New England in the late eighteenth century. Women played prominent roles in this activity, organizing meetings and providing auxiliary services, running charities and providing religious instruction. Among the Quakers, women were often ministers and itinerant preachers. One was Jemima Wilkinson (1752–1819), leader of the Universal Friends; another was Ann Lee (1736–1784), who founded Shaker colonies in New York and New England.

The protestants endured and adapted, deeply affected by the ambitions and values of the ascending middle classes, especially in the rapidly growing Methodist Church in the United Kingdom and the United States. During the nineteenth century, middle-class protestant missionaries went forth as self-proclaimed messengers of the word of God. Once the western states began competing for land around the globe, these missionaries often complemented national policy in their religious work. Buttressed by their complacent sense of speaking God's word, they felt justified in undermining the cultures of the peoples with whom they came in contact—especially if that was the price to be paid for "civilization" and the eternal salvation that came with it.

In England, the Christian Church received another powerful stimulus from the Oxford movement. At the beginning of the nineteenth century, a core of spiritual activists at Oxford University, including the future cardinal John Henry Newman (1801–1890), met to defend the church from the various secular and political forces that were besieging it. During the 1830s, the group split, some members remaining within the Anglican Church and others, including Newman, joining the Catholic Church. During the rest of the century the Oxford movement brought new life to the church in England through its missionary work, participation in social concerns, and improvement of the intellectual level of the faith. Similar developments occurred across the Continent.

The Catholic Church faced a more difficult road, especially after the expulsion of Pope Pius IX (1846–1878) from Rome during the 1848 revolutions. This moderate pope became extraordinarily reactionary, especially after the unification of Italy. He issued the *Syllabus of Errors* in 1864. This document attacked critics who independently examined matters of faith and doctrine. In 1870 he called a general council of the church to proclaim the doctrine of papal infallibility, which states that when speaking *ex cathedra* (kuh-TAY-druh; "from the chair") on issues concerning religion and moral behavior, the pope cannot err.

Pius's successor, Leo XIII (1879–1903), a more flexible and less combative pope, helped bring the church into the modern age. In his encyclical *Rerum Novarum* (RE-rum no-VAR-um; "Concerning New

Great Awakening—The emotional revival of Christianity carried across the Atlantic from the European Pietist movements to the United States.

Things"), issued in 1891, Leo condemned Marxism and upheld capitalism but severely criticized the evils affecting the working classes. By pointing out some of the Christian elements of socialism, Leo placed the church on the side of the workers who were suffering the greatest ills resulting from industrialization. Leo worked to improve relations with Germany, encouraged the passage of social welfare legislation, and supported the formation of Catholic labor unions and political parties.

Humanitarian Movements

The middle classes of Europe generally embraced one of the main tenets of the Enlightenment: the concern for individual human worth. The demand for reform and the belief in human progress came to be tied to traditional Christian principles, such as human communality and God's concern for all people. Religious humanitarianism at the end of the eighteenth and throughout the nineteenth century shunned radical politics and ignored the issue of women's rights, despite the movement's strong support among women. It did, however, seek actively to relieve human suffering and ignorance among children, the urban poor, prisoners, and slaves. This combination of humanitarian objectives and Christian faith achieved remarkable results.

Notable among manifestations of the new desire to help others was the antislavery movement in England. A court case in 1774 ended slavery in that country. From then until 1807, a determined movement sought abolition of the slave trade. Its leader was William Wilberforce (1759–1833), aided by Hannah More (1745–1833) and other Anglican Evangelicals, along with many Methodists and Quakers. Wilberforce repeatedly introduced bills into the House of Commons that would have eliminated the traffic in human bodies. His efforts were rewarded in 1807 when the British trade in slaves was ended, although he and his allies had to continue the struggle for 26 more years before they could achieve abolition in the British colonies.

Religious humanitarians enforced other movements that had been pushed by the rationalist Enlightenment. For example, the movements for both legal reform and prison reform were supported by religious groups. Universal education, extolled by rationalist thinkers, also aroused interest among the denominations. The Sunday School movement, particularly in England, was a forerunner of many private and quasi-public church schools. Finally, concern for the plight of slaves, coupled with rising missionary zeal, increased popular efforts to improve conditions for indigenous peoples in European possessions overseas.

The new middle-class humanitarianism played a significant part in promoting reforms during the worst stages of industrialization. It contributed to a spirit of restlessness and discontent while encouraging independent thought, particularly as it improved education. Its successful campaign against the slave trade also struck a direct blow at the old mercantilist economies, which depended so heavily on plantation agriculture overseas. In time, the messages of the missionaries would also prove to be the most consistent force against colonialism.

Liberalism: The Middle Class Ideology

The rising middle and commercial classes found their interests and ideals best expressed in the doctrine of **liberalism.** Liberalism affirmed the dignity of the individual and the "pursuit of happiness" as an inherent right. The ideology's roots were set firmly in the eighteenth-century soil of constitutionalism, laissez-faire economics, and representative government. Liberals thought in terms of individuals who shared basic rights, were equal before the law, and used government to gain power and carry out gradual reform. In addition, liberals believed that individuals should use their power to ensure that each person would be given the maximum amount of freedom from the state or any other external authority.

In economics, liberals followed the views of Adam Smith (1723–1790) in his *Wealth of Nations.* They believed in fair competition among individuals responding to the laws of supply and demand with a minimum of governmental regulation or interference. They agreed with Smith that society benefited more from competition among individuals motivated by their self-interest than from governmental regulation. The most intelligent and efficient individuals would gain the greatest rewards, society would prosper, and the state would be kept in its proper place, protecting life and property.

Liberals found foes from above and below as they translated their ideas into public policy because nobles and the landed gentry still controlled most countries in Europe. Throughout the century, the middle classes fought to gain political power commensurate with their economic strength. While they were trying to increase their own influence, they sought to limit the political base of the emerging working classes. By the end of the century, the middle classes had consolidated their control over the industrialized world. This was perhaps the major political achievement of the century.

---

liberalism—An ideology founded on the freedom of the individual.

Liberals were freed from the demands of manual labor and possessed enough wealth to spend their spare time in public pursuits. They had the time and leisure to work in government to control state policy to protect their own interests. They gained sufficient security that they undertook the enactment of social reforms to head off revolution. They became the dominant voices in the press and universities and gained commanding authority over public opinion. The liberals' most important contributions came in the areas of civil rights, promotion of the rule of law, government reform, and humanitarian enterprises.

The main interpreters of liberalism came from Britain, and during the first half of the century, Jeremy Bentham (1748–1832) and John Stuart Mill (1806–1873) adapted some liberal theories to modern reality. Bentham devised the concept of **utilitarianism,** or philosophical radicalism, based on the notions of utility and happiness. He connected these ideas by noting that each individual knows what is best for himself or herself and that all human institutions should be measured according to the amount of happiness they give. Bentham built on these two eighteenth-century concepts to form the "pain-and-pleasure" principle. He believed that government's function was to ensure as great a degree of individual freedom as possible, for freedom was the essential precondition of happiness. Utilitarianism in government was thus the securing of the "greatest happiness for the greatest number." If society could provide as much happiness and as little pain as possible, it would be working at maximum efficiency. Bentham recognized what later liberals would eventually espouse—that government would have to work at all levels—but he left no precise prescription as to how to proceed.

Mill spoke more to this issue. He began by noting that, in industry, the interests of the owners and workers did not necessarily coincide. He proposed the theory that government should, if necessary, pass legislation to remedy injustice, pointing out that when the actions of business owners harm the people, the state must step in to protect the citizenry. He challenged the liberal theory of minimal government interference in the economic life of the nation and pointed out that humanitarianism is more important than profit margin. He accepted the principle that maximum freedom should be permitted in business and that natural law should dictate insofar as possible the relationship of citizens.

DOCUMENT
John Stuart Mill on Enfranchisement of Women

He also pointed out that the distribution of wealth depends on the laws and customs of society and that these can be changed by human will. The rights of property and free competition, therefore, should be upheld—but within reasonable limits. Mill pointed out that the liberty of the individual is not absolute—a person has the freedom to do as he or she will as long as it does not harm another But freedom, ultimately, has to be placed under the wider interests of society.

utilitarianism—A doctrine that desires the greatest good for the greatest number, and a balance of life in which pleasure dominates over pain.

SCIENCE, TECHNOLOGY, AND THE SECOND INDUSTRIAL REVOLUTION

- *What was the relationship between science and economics in the leading industrial states of the nineteenth century?*

Until the middle of the eighteenth century, research findings generally served to satisfy the scientifically literate in the royal societies and to provoke further investigation. After 1760, however, industrialists increasingly applied the discoveries of scientists to their production. As the nineteenth century progressed, theoretical research came to have an almost immediate expression in new technologies, which led to the creation of new and profitable chemical, transportation, and electrical industries.

Medicine, Chemistry, and Physics

At the beginning of the nineteenth century, medical practices were making a slow transition away from the indiscriminate use of leeches and bleeding. In the 1840s, physicians began to use ether and chloroform to reduce pain during operations. The Scottish surgeon Joseph Lister (1827–1912) developed new antiseptic practices that made major advances against the spread of infection. By 1900 fairly sophisticated and much safer surgical procedures were available.

Probably the most important single advance came with the substantiation of the germ theory of disease by Louis Pasteur (PAS-tur; 1822–1895) and Robert Koch (1843–1910). During his search for a cure to anthrax—a disease that in the late 1870s destroyed more than 20 percent of the sheep in France—Pasteur established the principle that the injection of a mild form of disease bacterium causes the body to form antibodies that prevent the vaccinated individual from getting the severe form of the particular disease. Koch discovered the specific organisms that caused 11 diseases, including tuberculosis. The work of Pasteur and Koch placed the sciences of bacteriology and immunology on a firm footing and gave promise that the end of

Scientific Advances

1830–1833	Sir Charles Lyell's *Principles of Geology* popularizes James Hutton's concept of geological time
1847	First law of thermodynamics
1859	Darwin publishes *On the Origin of Species*
1869	Dmitri Mendeleev classifies all known elements into the periodic table
1870–1895	Louis Pasteur makes advances in bacteriology
1880–1910	Robert Koch places immunology on firm footing
1876	Dynamo perfected, based on work of Michael Faraday
1896	Pierre and Marie Curie discover radium
1900–1910	Sir Ernest Rutherford advances electron theory

such deadly diseases as typhoid and smallpox might be in sight.

Modern chemistry gained its foundations during the nineteenth century, founded on the atomic theory advanced by an English Quaker schoolmaster, John Dalton (1766–1844). In 1869 Russian chemist Dmitri Mendeleev (dmeet-REE MEN-de-LE-ef; 1834–1907) drew up a "periodic table," in which he classified all known elements according to their weights and properties. From gaps in this table, chemists were able to deduce the existence of undiscovered elements. Other researchers made advances in the field of nutrition and discovered the significance of vitamins. Biochemical research threw light on the presence and function of the ductless (endocrine) glands. Chemotherapy advanced with the discovery of a chemical that could destroy the syphilis bacterium and with procedures that would lead to the discovery of sulfa drugs, penicillin, and other antibiotics.

Revolutionary strides in physics were taken in the areas of electricity and thermodynamics, the first law of which was formulated in 1847. Michael Faraday (1791–1867) prepared the way for the dynamo, a device that made possible changes in communications, the transmission of current over long distances, and the development of the electric motor. The Scottish scientist James Clerk Maxwell (1831–1879) and the German Heinrich Hertz (1857–1894) conducted basic research into the nature of electromagnetic phenomena such as light, radiant heat, and ultraviolet radiation.

Pierre Curie (1859–1906) and his wife, Marie Curie (1867–1934), made major strides toward the discovery of the X-ray and radioactivity. When they extracted radium from uranium ore in 1896, the scientific world became aware of the strength of radioactivity. Marie Curie was the first person to be awarded two Nobel Prizes, one in physics and one in chemistry.

At the beginning of the twentieth century, the British physicist Ernest Rutherford (1871–1937) helped develop electron theory. It had been postulated that the atom contains particles known as electrons. Rutherford contributed the idea that each atom has a central particle, or nucleus, that is positively charged and separate from the negatively charged electrons. These discoveries destroyed one of the foundations of traditional physics, that matter is indivisible and continuous.

Marie Curie, born Manya Sklodowska in Warsaw, Poland, shared with her husband, Pierre, the 1903 Nobel Prize in physics for their work on radioactivity, a term Marie coined in 1898. She won the 1911 Nobel Prize in chemistry for her discovery of radium and polonium and isolation of pure radium. Irène Curie, Marie and Pierre's daughter, shared with her husband, Frédéric Joliot, the 1935 Nobel Prize in chemistry for their work in synthesizing new radioactive isotopes of various elements.

Darwin

In the mid-nineteenth century Charles Darwin (1809–1892) formulated a major scientific theory in *On the Origin of Species by Means of Natural Selection* (1859). This theory of evolution, stating that all complex organisms developed from simple forms through the operation of natural causes, challenged traditionalist Christian beliefs on creation and altered views of life on earth. The theory contended that no species is fixed and changeless. Classical thinkers first stated this view, and contemporary philosophers, such as Hegel, had used the concept of evolutionary change. In the century before Darwin, other research supported the concept of change, both biological and social.

DOCUMENT
On Darwin

Darwin built on the work of Sir Charles Lyell (1797–1875) and Jean-Baptiste Lamarck (1744–1829). Lyell's three-volume *Principles of Geology* (1830–1833) confirmed the views of the Scottish geologist James Hutton (1726–1797), who stated that the earth developed through natural rather than supernatural causes. Lyell helped popularize the notion of geological time operating over a vast span of years. This understanding is essential to the acceptance of any theory of biological evolution, based as it is on changes in species over many thousands of generations. Lamarck, a naturalist, argued that every organism tends to develop new organs to adapt to the changing conditions of its environment. He theorized that these changes are transmitted by heredity to the descendants, which are thereafter changed in structural form.

Though he had originally studied medicine at Edinburgh and prepared for the ministry at Cambridge University, Darwin lost interest in both professions and became a naturalist while in his twenties. From 1831 to 1836 he studied the specimens he had collected while on a five-year surveying expedition aboard the ship *Beagle,* which had sailed along the coast of South America and among the Galápagos Islands. The works of his predecessors, in addition to questions that he had about the theories presented in Malthus's "Essay on Population," helped him define his own theory. When Darwin's book finally appeared, it changed many basic scientific and social assumptions.

In his revolutionary work, Darwin constructed an explanation of how life evolves that negated the literal interpretation of the Bible taught in most Christian churches:

> *Species have been modified, during a long course of descent, chiefly through the natural selection of numerous successive, slight, favorable variations; aided in an important manner by the direct action of external conditions, and by variations which seem to us in our ignorance to arise spontaneously.*[1]

His explanation radically affected the views of the scientific community about the origin and evolution of life on the planet. The hypothesis, in its simplified form, states that all existing plant and animal species are descended from earlier and, generally speaking, more primitive forms. The direct effects of the environment cause species to develop through the inheritance of minute differences in individual structures. As the centuries pass, the more adaptable, stronger species live on, while the weaker, less flexible species die out: the **"survival of the fittest."** Furthermore, a species may also be changed by the cumulative working of sexual selection, which Darwin regarded as the "most powerful means of changing the races of man."

After the announcement of Darwin's theories, other scientists, such as the German biologist August Weismann (VAIS-mahn; 1834–1914) and the Austrian priest Gregor Mendel (1822–1884), worked along similar lines to explore the genetic relationships among living organisms. Weismann proved that acquired characteristics cannot be inherited. Mendel's investigations into the laws of heredity, based on his experiments with the combining of different varieties of garden peas, proved especially valuable in the scientific breeding of plants and animals and demonstrated that the evolution of different species was more complex than Darwin had imagined. Based on their work, biologists hypothesized that there are what would be later called *chromosomes* that carry the characteristics of an organism. Darwin had hinted at and now further research supported the mutation theory, which states that sudden and unpredictable changes within a chromosome can be transmitted by heredity to produce new species. Scientists began to work with the very fundamental building blocks of life and established the groundwork of contemporary bio-technical research.

Technological Growth and Advances

Another reason for the Continent's economic emergence was a wide range of new technologies that took advantage of the scientific discoveries made during the century. Continental competitors, especially the Germans, began with state-of-the-art factories that allowed them to out-produce Britain, whose older factories were less productive.

Electricity

The basic change in the second phase of industrialization was the use of electricity in all aspects of life. Scientists had discovered electricity's basic principles a century earlier, but it was difficult to generate and trans-

survival of the fittest—The notion that in the evolution of species the more adaptable species live on, while the weaker, less fit die out. Later Social Darwinists came to apply this idea to human society.

mit power across long distances. When the first dependable dynamo, which changed energy from mechanical into electrical form, was perfected in 1876, it became possible to generate electricity almost anywhere. Inventors such as the American Thomas A. Edison (1847–1931) began to use the new resource in industry, transportation, entertainment, and the home. Humanity had finally found a source of power that could be transmitted and used easily. The British took the lead in applying electricity to home use. The Germans made the most advanced application of electric technology to industry.

Engines

Another fundamental change came in the use of gas and oil in the newly devised internal combustion engine. Steam power's use was limited by its appetite for huge amounts of fuel and its sheer bulk. Gottlieb Daimler (GOT-leeb DAIM-ler; 1834–1900) perfected the internal combustion engine used in most automobiles today. In 1892 Rudolf Diesel invented the engine that bears his name. It burned fuel instead of harnessing the explosions that drove the Daimler engine.

These new developments led directly to the search for and use of petroleum and the beginning of the passenger car industry. By 1914 the making of cars was a key part of the Italian, German, French, and American economies. Automobile manufacturing called for a number of spin-off industries such as tire, ball-bearing, and windshield manufacturing—the list extends to hundreds of items. Leaving aside the passenger car's economic contribution, the world's cities and people felt the complex impact of this new form of transportation, with consequences, such as expanding the range of an individual's world and increased noise levels and pollution, that changed the character of urban areas.

Laborsaving Devices

Other new machines also changed the quality of life. Bicycles became commonplace in the 1890s, as did sewing machines, cameras, and typewriters, to name a few items. Never before had people had the ability to transform ideas almost instantly into products accessible to the average person. This was another dividend of industrialization and a symbol of a rapidly changing Europe.

CULTURAL RESPONSES TO THE AGE

- *What role does the culture-consuming middle class play in artistic and musical creativity?*

The increasing wealth and leisure time generated by industrialization vastly enlarged the number of consumers of culture. Artists made the transition from responding to the tastes of the noble courts to the new demands of middle-class audiences attending concerts in vast new halls and viewing art in public galleries. However, these transitions were not always universally accepted. In the first part of the century there were three major currents that dominated the cultural scene: conservatism, romanticism, and nationalism. By the end of middle of the century another current, realism, came to fore.

Conservatism

In the nineteenth century **conservatism** was an important cultural and political force. The reaction to the French Revolution, especially as expressed by Edmund Burke (1729–1797), provided the basis of nineteenth-century European conservatism. There were many thinkers who did not believe in the revolutionary slogan of liberty, equality, and brotherhood. They did not believe that liberation could be gained by destroying the historically evolved traditions of the Old Regime. Freedom could be found only in order and be maintained solely by continual reference to precedents. A legitimate political, social, and cultural life needed the framework of tradition to survive.

The conservatives did not have faith in the individual, nor did they share the Romantics' love of pure emotion and spontaneity. Beginning with Burke and continuing through the first part of the nineteenth century to the Frenchman Joseph de Maistre (1753–1821), the Russian Nicholas Karamzin (1766–1826), and the Spaniard Juan Donoso-Cortés (do-NO-so kor-TEZ; 1809–1853), there was a body of intellectuals who found strength, not weakness, in the church and monarchy of the Old Regime; danger, not liberation, in the nationalistic movements; and degradation, not exaltation, in the new Romantic art forms. The conservatives were backward-looking, finding their standards and values in the proven events of the past, not in the untried reforms and emotions of the present.

Romanticism

The Romantic movement unleashed sensitivities that played a major role in forming the literary, artistic, and musical changes of the nineteenth century. The emphasis **Romanticism** places on the individual is apparent in the novels of Johann Wolfgang von Goethe (GEHR-te; 1749–1832) and Friedrich Schiller

---

conservatism—An intellectual movement based on a reaction to the excesses of the French Revolution.

Romanticism—An artistic movement emphasizing the importance of the individual emotional response as contrasted to the measured standards of classicism.

(1759–1805). Goethe's novel *Sorrows of Young Werther* (1774) tells the story of a sensitive, feeling, outcast young man who kills himself with the pistol of his rival after failing to gain his true love. Schiller's play *Wilhelm Tell* (1804) describes the heroic struggle of the Swiss patriots in their drive for independence against tyranny.

Unlike the brittle wit and irony of the authors of the Enlightenment, such as Voltaire, these stories were sentimental and emotional descriptions of people, acting in response to overwhelming and impossible social or political dilemmas, who did what their hearts told them was right. It was better to experience a moving young death or to rise up against impossible odds than to look dispassionately and rationally at life.

The Romantic movement's emphasis on the individual created among some of its participants a truly picturesque lifestyle. For every Victor Hugo (1802–1885) who lived a long, full, excessive life, there were artists, writers, and musicians from London to Moscow who "burned the candle at both ends" in short, passionate, creative lives. To most Romantics, such as Keats, it was better to live briefly and intensely, according to the commandments of the heart, than to die old, fat, rich, bored, lecherous, and bourgeois.

The novel came into prominence in the eighteenth century, but it became the dominant literary form of the nineteenth. Writers such as Victor Hugo and Sir Walter Scott (1771–1832) mined the myths and legends of France and Britain, respectively, to write vastly successful works for the ever-expanding middle-class audiences. Hugo's *Notre Dame de Paris* (1831) and Scott's *Ivanhoe* (1819) detailed their nations' past so effectively that both books were imitated, and sequels and imitations continued to appear into the twentieth century. By 1850 a variety of social and psychological themes challenged the historical novel, along with the gently critical works of William Makepeace Thackeray (1811–1863), who, through deft characterizations in works such as *Vanity Fair* (1848), poked fun at the *nouveau riche* (new-VOH reesh), or "newly rich," social climbers who dominated society.

Poets responded far more pointedly to the challenges thrown down by the Napoleonic and Industrial Revolutions. In 1798 two young British poets, William Wordsworth (1770–1850) and Samuel Taylor Coleridge (1772–1834), published a volume of verse called *Lyrical Ballads.* Wordsworth wrote in the preface that poetry was "the spontaneous overflow of powerful feelings recollected in tranquility." Wordsworth sought to express "universal passions" and the "entire world of nature" through simple, unladen vocabulary. He stressed the intuitive and emotional contemplation of nature as a path to creativity. In an 1802 sonnet he expressed his love of nature and country:

. . . Oft have I looked round
With joy in Kent's green vales; but never found
Myself so satisfied in heart before.
Europe is yet in bonds; but let that pass
Thought for another moment. Thou are free,
My Country! and 'tis joy enough and pride
For one hour's perfect bliss, to tread the grass
Of England once again. . . .[2]

In *Kubla Khan* (1797) and *Rime of the Ancient Mariner* (1798) Coleridge pursued the supernatural and exotic facets of life. His vivid descriptions of distant subjects and nonrational elements of human life served as the precedent for later artists as they examined the areas of fantasy, symbolism, dream states, and the supernatural. The French poet Alphonse de Lamartine (al-FONS de la-mar-TEEN; 1790–1869) led the way

Greats of the Romantic Era

LITERATURE

George Gordon, Lord Byron (1788–1824)
Samuel Taylor Coleridge (1772–1834)
Heinrich Heine (1797–1856)
Victor Hugo (1802–1885)
John Keats (1795–1821)
Alexander Pushkin (1799–1837)
Sir Walter Scott (1771–1832)
Percy Bysshe Shelley (1792–1822)
William Wordsworth (1770–1850)

ART AND ARCHITECTURE

John Constable (1776–1837)
Eugène Delacroix (1798–1863)
Joseph M. W. Turner (1775–1851)
Eugène Viollet-le-Duc (1814–1879)

MUSIC

Ludwig van Beethoven (1770–1827)
Hector Berlioz (1803–1869)
Felix Mendelssohn (1809–1847)
Franz Schubert (1797–1828)
Robert Schumann (1810–1856)
Carl Maria von Weber (1786–1826)

in making the transition from classicism to Romanticism and had an impact across the Continent.

The British poets George Gordon, Lord Byron, (1788–1824) and Percy Bysshe Shelley (1792–1822) rebelled against the constraints of their society and expressed their contempt for the standards of their time through their lives and works. Byron gloried in the cult of freedom. When the Greeks rose up against the Turks in 1821, he joined their cause. He died of fever soon after his arrival. Shelley believed passionately that human perfectibility was possible only through complete freedom of thought and action. On the Continent, Heinrich Heine (HAI-nuh; 1797–1856), who was, like Byron, a cutting satirist and, like Shelley, a splendid lyricist, shared their romantic ideals. Heine is best remembered for his *Buch der Lieder* (book der LEE-der), songs that were put to music by Franz Schubert (1797–1828) and Felix Mendelssohn (MEN-del-son; 1809–1847).

John Keats (1795–1821) was neither social critic nor rebel; for him the worship and pursuit of beauty were of prime importance. In *Ode on a Grecian Urn* (1820) he states:

> *"Beauty is truth, truth beauty"—that is all*
> *Ye know on earth, and all ye need to know.*[3]

Keats believed that the inherent beauty of an object—not some classical formula or social function—justified its existence.

Alexander Pushkin (1799–1837), Russia's greatest poet, liberated his nation's language from the foreign molds and traditions forced on it in the eighteenth century. While serving as the transition between the classical and Romantic ages, Pushkin helped create a truly Russian literature, one that expressed profound depth of his love for his country.

The age of change brought new tendencies to painting as well as to other art forms. There is a great contrast between the precise draftsmanship and formal poses of the classical painters and the unrestrained use of color and new effects of the Romantic artists. Some artists, such as the French master Eugène Delacroix (de-la-CKWAH; 1798–1863), were met with critical resistance. His *Massacre of Chios,* a flamboyant work painted in 1824 upon receiving news of the Turks' slaying of Christians on Chios, was panned by conservative critics as the "massacre of painting."

Less flamboyant but equally part of the Romantic transition are the works of the British painter John Constable (1776–1837). Deeply influenced by Romanticism's emphasis on nature, Constable was in some respects the originator of the modern school of landscape painting. His choice of colors was revolutionary—he used greens freely in his landscape, an innovation considered radical by critics, who favored brown tones. Constable's countryman, Joseph M. W. Turner (1775–1851), sparked controversy with his use of vivid colors and dramatic perspectives that gave him the ability to portray powerful atmospheric effects.

Around 1830, Romanticism's fascination with the medieval period led to a shift from Greek and Roman architectural models to a Gothic revival, in which towers and arches became the chief characteristics. Sir Walter Scott's romances played a major role in this development, and even his house at Abbotsford was designed along Scottish baronial lines. In France, Eugène Viollet-le-Duc (vee-o-LAY-le-DOOK; 1814–1879) spearheaded the movement by writing, teaching, and restoring properties under the aegis of the Commission on Historical Monuments. For the next few decades, architecture was dominated by styles that looked back especially to the Gothic and rococo styles, which were sometimes combined in what some consider aesthetically disastrous presentations.

Nationalism

The writers, musicians, artists, and philosophers caught up in the Romantic movement at the end of the eighteenth century and the beginning of the nineteenth rebelled against the Classicism and the cold logic of the Enlightenment. Instead, they stressed an individual's past, uniqueness, emotions, and creativity as the basis for life. The Romantics investigated history, folklore, linguistics, and myths to define their own identity. They revived the Scandinavian sagas, the French *Chanson de Roland* (shan-SOHN de ro-LAN), and the German *Nibelungen* (KNEE-be-lun-gen) stories. During a time of uncertainty, change, and stress it was both comforting and uplifting to look to the past, even an imagined one. The roots of **nationalism,** the most powerful and longest-lasting of the new ideologies, thus was to be found in Romanticism.

Unique conditions in different parts of Europe produced different variants of nationalism. However, common to them all was a populace consciously embracing a common land, language, folklore, history, enemies, and religion. These elements are the ingredients of the nation's and the individual's identity and pull the members into an indivisible unity. Nationalism can exist where there is no state structure and can thrive in a state where a minority nation is repressed. Nationalism, unlike patriotism, does not need flags and uniforms. All that is needed is a historical and emotional unity around which the members of the nation can gather, a unity that defines a shared identity and entails the total cultural and political loyalty of the individual to the nation.

---

nationalism—A political movement based on shared land, language, folklore, history, and religion.

After 1789 this new force dominated the cultural and political activities of France. The spirit of brotherhood projected by the French Revolution united the French people. On the Continent, Romantics reacted against the French and Napoleonic dominance and helped bring people together in nationalistic opposition, especially in Germany. Georg Wilhelm Friedrich Hegel built on the movement in his lectures and writings at the University of Berlin. For Hegel, history was a process of evolution in which the supremacy of primitive instincts would give way to the reign of clear reason and freedom—the "world spirit"—that would be manifested in the state. The research and writings of the Germans Johann Gottfried von Herder (1744–1803) and brothers Jacob (1785–1863) and Wilhelm Grimm (1786–1859) provided historical support and linguistic bases for the Slavic nationalist movements. Herder conceived of a world spirit, *Weltgeist* (VELT-gaist), made up of component parts of the various national spirits, *Volkgeist* (FOLK-gaist). Each of these national spirits was seen as playing an essential role in the world process, and Herder believed that the Slavs were soon to make an important contribution. The Grimm brothers' philological work aided the literary and linguistic revivals of many Slavic groups.

Romantic nationalism in Britain reacted strongly against the human costs of industrialization and the pretensions of the new merchant classes. It focused on the medieval roots of Britain, as well as on movements such as phil-hellenism (the love of ancient Greece). In France, Spain, Italy, Russia, and other parts of the Continent, the Romantic movement made important contributions to the growth of national identity. In Italy, for example, Giuseppe Mazzini (matz-zee-nee; 1805–1872) and Alessandro Manzoni (1785–1873) played important roles in the unification struggle of the country. Romantic nationalism was also found in the writings of history by Leopold von Ranke (1775–1886) in Germany, Jules Michelet (mish-e-LAY; 1798–1874) in France, Frantisek Palacky (1798–1876) in Bohemia-Moravia, and George Bancroft (1800–1891) in the United States.

Realism

Around 1850, artists and writers began responding to the new age in the realist movement. Artists, especially the French, who were among the most notable early proponents of **realism,** focused on the concrete aspects of life. This led, at the end of the century, to experiments with a range of new forms and structures in the modernist movement (see Chapter 27). At the same time that these movements were developing, a huge new group of consumers, the lower and middle classes, were becoming participants in the new mass culture. They might find little to admire in the fine arts, but through their buying power and their numbers, they would come to have a great effect on large parts of the creative community.

In literature and art, as in politics, realism replaced Romanticism after mid-century. To the realists it was no longer enough to be true to one's instincts and emotions. Their job was to faithfully observe and graphically report all aspects of life in a dispassionate, precise manner so as to depict individuals in their proper setting. In this age of change there was much for writers and artists to portray, and a much larger public now had the leisure time and political interests to respond to their work.

The trend toward the realistic novel had been foreshadowed in the work of Honoré de Balzac (1799–1850), the author of a 90-volume tour de force, *La Comédie Humaine* (la ko-MAY-dee OO-men) (*The Human Comedy*), which depicts French life in the first half of the nineteenth century. A master of characterization, Balzac described life in such detail that his work is a valuable reference on social history for present-day scholars. Gustave Flaubert (floh-BEHR; 1821–1880) was the first French realist writer. His masterpiece, *Madame Bovary* (1856), exhaustively described how the boredom of a young romantic provincial wife led her into adultery, excess, and ultimately suicide. Émile Zola (1840–1902) was the leader of the French naturalist school and a prolific author best known for his novel *Germinal* (1885). He also played a major role as the most influential author of his time by mobilizing French public opinion in 1898 to move against the injustices done to Captain Alfred Dreyfus (see Chapter 27) in his open letter to the French president, which opens *"J'accuse . . ."* (zha-KEUZ) ("I accuse").

British novelist Charles Dickens (1812–1870) protested social conditions in his novels characterizing the everyday life of the middle classes and the poor. In such works as *Oliver Twist* (1838), *Dombey and Son* (1847–1848), and *Hard Times* (1854), he describes some of the worst excesses of industrial expansion and social injustice. Later, Thomas Hardy (1840–1928), in novels such as *Far from the Madding Crowd* (1874), dealt with the struggle—almost always a losing one—of the individual against the impersonal, pitiless forces of the natural and social environment.

American writers such as Henry James (1843–1916), Samuel Clemens, writing under the name of Mark Twain (1835–1910), and Harriet Beecher Stowe (1811–1896) made important contributions to the realist tradition. James tried to catch the "atmosphere of the mind" through an almost clinical examination of the most subtle details. Clemens, better known by

---

realism—An art form focused on the concrete details of real life.

Major Writers and Composers at Mid-Nineteenth-Century

Literature

Honoré de Balzac (1799–1850)

Anton Chekhov (1860–1904)

Charles Dickens (1812–1870)

Feodor Dostoevski (1821–1881)

Gustave Flaubert (1821–1880)

Thomas Hardy (1840–1928)

Henrik Ibsen (1828–1906)

Henry James (1843–1916)

Harriet Beecher Stowe (1811–1896)

Leo Tolstoy (1828–1910)

Mark Twain (Samuel Clemens) (1835–1910)

Music

Johannes Brahms (1833–1897)

Anton Bruckner (1824–1896)

Frédéric Chopin (1810–1849)

Anton Dvořak (1841–1904)

Gustav Mahler (1860–1911)

Modest Mussorgsky (1835–1881)

Sergei Rachmaninov (1873–1943)

Jean Sibelius (1865–1957)

Bedrich Smetana (1824–1884)

Peter Ilich Tchaikovsky (1840–1893)

Richard Wagner (1813–1883)

Giuseppi Verdi (1813–1901)

his pseudonym, Mark Twain, used humor and accurate descriptions of the American Midwest and Far West to underscore social injustice. Stowe's detailed novel *Uncle Tom's Cabin* (1852) captured American hearts and minds and strongly bolstered the antislavery movement.

The Russian novelists Leo Tolstoy (1828–1910) and Feodor Dostoevski (dahs-tah-YEV-skee; 1821–1881) produced the most developed presentation of the realistic novel. Tolstoy stripped every shred of glory and glamor from war in *War and Peace* (1869) and gave an analytical description of the different levels of society. Dostoevski devised a chilling, detailed view of life in St. Petersburg in *Crime and Punishment* (1866), and his *Brothers Karamazov* (1880) offered a painstaking analysis of Russian life during a period of change brought about by the Great Reforms of 1861 (see Chapter 26).

Drama was deeply influenced by realism, as could be seen in the works of the Norwegian Henrik Ibsen (1828–1906), the Irishman George Bernard Shaw (1856–1950), and the Russian Anton Chekhov (1860–1904). *A Doll's House* (1879), Ibsen's understated yet tension-filled work, assailed marriage without love as immoral. Though his characters are not heroic in their dimensions, Ibsen captures the quiet desperation of normal life, and the despair that forces the heroine to leave her husband at the end of the play, in "the door slam heard 'round the world." Shaw used satire and nuance to shock the British public into reassessing conventional attitudes. Chekhov's *Cherry Orchard* (1904) dramatized the changes wrought by emancipation of the serfs on the lives of a gentry family. Lacking obvious plot and action, the play depends on day-to-day detail to build a subtle and exhaustive social portrait.

Beethoven and His Successors

Music did not experience the shift in style from Romantic to realistic that art and literature did. Ludwig van Beethoven (1770–1827) served as a bridge between the classical and Romantic periods. However, the regularity of the minuet, the precision of the sonata, and the elegant but limited small chamber orchestra—all forms Beethoven mastered—were not sufficient to express the powerful forces of the age. A comparison of his relatively measured and restrained First Symphony with the compelling and driven Fifth or the lyrical, nature-dominated Sixth dramatically reveals the changes that he underwent. Beethoven was the ultimate Romantic—a lover of nature, passionate champion of human rights, fighter for freedom. Beethoven spoke to the heart of humanity through his music, especially his magnificent Ninth Symphony, the Ode to Joy.

The momentum of the forces that Beethoven set in motion carried through the entire century. Carl Maria von Weber (1786–1826), Hector Berlioz (BER-lee-oz; 1803–1869), Robert Schumann (1810–1856), along with Felix Mendelssohn and Franz Schubert (1797–1828), made major contributions to the musical repertoire of Europe by mid-century. Thereafter, Johannes Brahms (1833–1897), Anton Bruckner (1824–1896), and Gustav Mahler (1860–1911) made

This idealized portrait of Beethoven reveals the sensitive composer who could write not only the magnificent global message of the last movement of the Ninth Symphony, but also the subtle melodies of his chamber pieces.

lyrical advances in composition and presentation. Each made unique use of the large symphony orchestra, and Brahms also composed three exquisite string quartets along with his four massive symphonies.

In addition, many composers turned to their native folk music and dances for inspiration. Beethoven had used native themes, as Schubert and Schumann did in Austria and Germany. Frédéric Chopin (SHO-pan; 1810–1849), even though he did most of his work in France, drew heavily on Polish folk themes for his mazurkas and polonaises. Jean Sibelius (si-BAI-le-us; 1865–1957) in Finland, Anton Dvořak (DVOR-ak; 1841–1904) and Bedrich Smetana (BAY-drich SME-ta-na; 1824–1884) in Bohemia-Moravia (the modern Czech Republic), and Russians Peter Ilich Tchaikovsky (chai-KOF-skee; 1840–1893), Modest Moussorgsky (1835–1881), and Sergei Rachmaninov (1873–1943) all incorporated folk music in their work. This use of folk themes was both pleasingly familiar and aesthetically satisfying to audiences.

Romanticism and nationalism, with their increasing number of enthusiasts, sparked developments in opera during the century. In his fervid Germanic works, Richard Wagner (1813–1883) infused old Teutonic myths and German folklore with typically Romantic characteristics such as emphasis on the supernatural and the mystical. Wagner's cycle of musical dramas known as *Der Ring des Nibelungen* was the culmination of a long and productive career. His descendants still are involved in the management of the *Festspielhaus* (FEST-shpeel-hous), a theater in Bayreuth (bai-ROOT), Germany, that he designed and his admirers financed.

The greatest operatic composer of the century was Giuseppi Verdi (VEHR-dee; 1813–1901), who composed such masterpieces as *Aïda* (AI-ee-dah), *Rigoletto, Il Trovatore* (tro-va-TOR-ay), and *La Forza del Destino* (la FORT-sa del des-TI-no). His operas, along with those of Wagner, form the core of most of today's major opera house repertoires.

The music world rarely dealt with social problems or harsh realism. Its supporters were by and large the newly ascendant middle classes who had benefited from the economic growth triggered by industrialization. They used the wealth derived from their commercial prosperity to finance the building of new opera houses and symphony halls and maintain the composers and orchestras. Major soloists were the idols of their day, as they showed their virtuosity in compositions that made use of Romantic subject matter infused with sentiment and, not infrequently, showmanship such as that shown by Franz Liszt (1811–1886) in his piano concerts or Jenny Lind, the "Swedish Nightingale" (1820–1887), in her recitals. They drew capacity audiences of contented listeners.

Impressionism in the Arts

Modernism freed painters from the need to communicate surface reality. Gustave Courbet (koor-BAY; 1819–1877) consciously dropped all useless adornments and instead boldly painted the life of the world in which he lived. He was soon surpassed by his countrymen, who became preoccupied with capturing color, light, and atmosphere. Artists such as Édouard Manet (man-AY; 1832–1882), Edgar Degas (day-GAH; 1834–1917), Claude Monet (moh-NAY; 1840–1926), Pierre-Auguste Renoir (ray-NWAH; 1841–1919), and Mary Cassatt (1845–1926) tried to catch the first impression made by a scene or an object on the eye, undistorted by intellect or any subjective attitude. They were called impressionists and worked in terms of light and color rather than solidity of form.

The impressionists found that they could achieve a more striking effect of light by placing one bright area of color next to another without any transitional tones. The also found that shadows could be shown

A barrage of hostility greeted Édouard Manet's Luncheon on the Grass *(1863), which juxtaposed the frank nudity of the female model with two clothed male figures. Although the models and the setting seem realistic, Manet was in fact little concerned with subject matter; he believed that the artist's reality lies in the brush strokes and color rather than in the objects represented in the painting. This attitude later coalesced in the "art for art's sake" school of thought.*

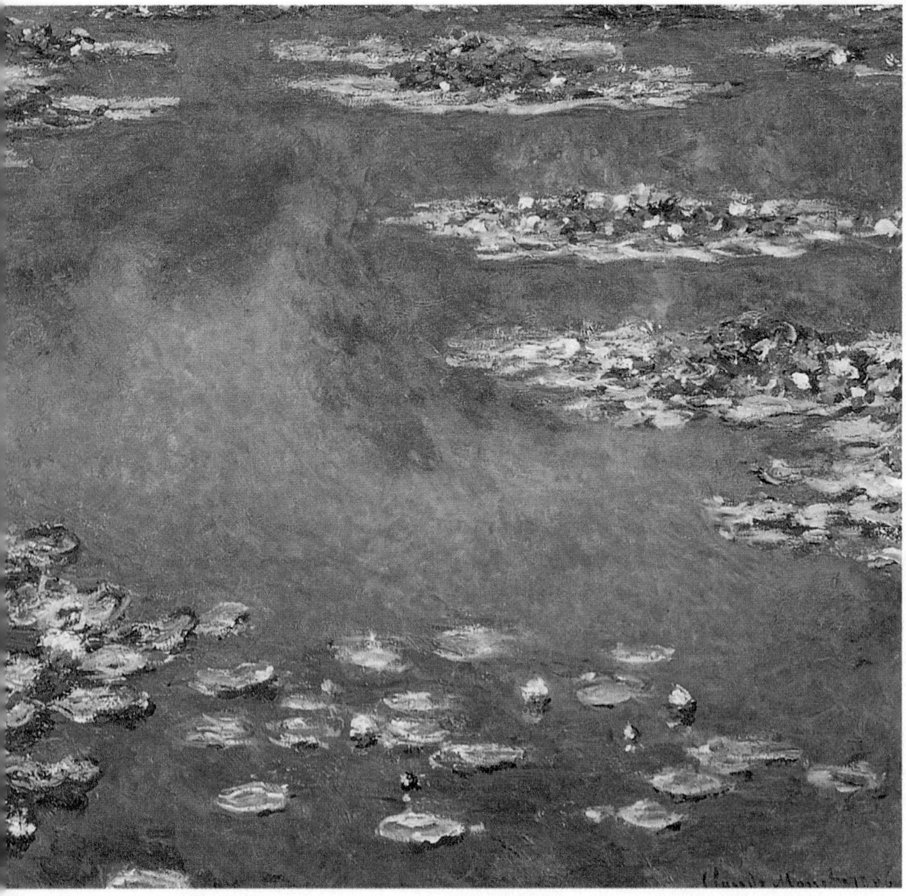

A concern for the effects of light and color united the French impressionists, yet each also developed a personal style. Often regarded as the boldest innovator was Claude Monet, who did a series of paintings of the same subject, such as Water Lilies *(1906).*

not as gray but as colors complementary to those of the objects casting the shadow. At close range, an impressionist painting may seem little more than splotches of unmixed colors, but at a proper distance the eye mixes the colors and allows a vibrating effect of light and emotion to emerge. The impressionists' techniques revolutionized art.

One of the weaknesses of impressionism was that it sacrificed much of the clarity of the classical tradition to gain its effects. Paul Cézanne (SAY-zahn; 1839–1903) addressed that problem. He tried to simplify all natural objects by stressing their essential geometric structure. He believed that everything in nature corresponded to the shape of a cone, cylinder, or sphere. Proceeding from this theory, he was able to get below the surface and give his objects the solidity that had eluded the impressionists, yet he kept the impressionists' striking use of color.

The expressionist Dutch artist Vincent van Gogh (1853–1890), while adapting the impressionist approach to light and color, painted using short strokes of heavy pigment to accentuate underlying forms and rhythms of his subjects. He achieved intensely emotional results, as he was willing to distort what he saw to communicate the sensations he felt. His short life of poverty and loneliness ended in insanity and suicide. Other modernist-inspired forms emerged. French artist Henri Matisse (1869–1954) painted what he felt about an object, rather than just the object itself. He had learned to simplify form partly from his study of African primitive art and the color schemes of oriental carpets.

Sculpture and Architecture

These two most substantial forms of art, sculpture and architecture, went through radical changes during the generation before and after the war. Auguste Rodin (1840–1917) has been called the father of modern sculpture. The realistic honesty and vitality of his work made him the object of stormy controversy during his career. He shared the impressionist painters' dislike of finality in art and preferred to let the viewers' imagination play on his work. Rodin's "rough finish" technique can best be seen in his bronze works, which feature a glittering surface of light and shadow and convey a feeling of immediacy and incompleteness that emphasizes their spontaneous character.

While Rodin was making major contributions in sculpture, architects in Europe were taking advantage of new materials and technologies developed through industrialization to make major improvements in construction. With new resources and methods, architects were able to span greater distances and enclose greater areas than had hitherto been possible.

The Great Chicago Fire of 1871 may have leveled much of the city, but it had the beneficial effect of permitting new building on a large scale. A new form of structure emerged—the steel-skeleton "skyscraper," which enabled builders to erect much taller structures, thanks to the perfecting of the elevator. Before, high buildings had required immensely thick masonry walls or buttresses. Now a metal frame allowed the weight of the structure to be distributed on an entirely different principle. Also, the metal frame permitted a far more extensive use of glass than ever before.

Outstanding among the pioneers in this new approach was American architect Louis Sullivan (1856–1924), who did most of his important work in Chicago. Like others, Sullivan saw the value of the skyscraper in providing a large amount of useful space on a small plot of expensive land. He rejected all attempts to disguise the skeleton of the skyscraper behind a false front and boldly proclaimed it by a clean sweep of line. Sullivan had a far-reaching influence on the approach of choosing function over form.

In Europe the French engineer Alexandre-Gustave Eiffel (1832–1923) planned and erected a 984-foot tower for the Paris International Exposition of 1889. Delicately formed from an iron framework, the tower rests on four masonry piers on a base 330 feet square.

CONCLUSION

The Western middle classes dominated and controlled the industrialization, economic transformations, and scientific advances of the nineteenth century. Their newfound wealth, harnessed to the social and legal changes resulting from the French and Napoleonic Revolutions and the reform movements in Britain and the United States, allowed them to control almost all aspects of Western political life by 1900. Both literate and numerous, they dominated religious, scientific, and cultural affairs, bringing major changes to each area. In the 99 years from the end of the Napoleonic Wars in 1815 to the outbreak of the First World War in 1914, they imposed themselves on the rest of the world through their industrial productivity, scientific and technological discoveries, and economic power.

By the mid-nineteenth century, Britain dominated the world economically, and its middle classes were serving as models for the elites in other societies undergoing industrialization. The British middle classes during the Victorian age were resolutely Christian and correct, conscious as they were of their dominant roles in society. They worked seriously to improve their societies through crusades against alcohol and pornography and for children and women's rights. The middle classes took the lead in changing their societies because the rapid growth of industrialized cities strained the capabilities of local and national authorities to provide utilities, education, law enforcement, and social services. However, charity often began—and remained—at home.

Using the efficiencies of liberal capitalism, the middle classes projected their influences throughout the world. However, they were unable to sustain their triumph. At the beginning of the twentieth century, the peoples in Asia and Africa would see that the Europeans—who had shown such abilities to scale intellectual mountains and spread their power around the globe—had not found the answer to the basic cultural problem of how to get along with one another.

Suggestions for Web Browsing

You can obtain more information about topics included in this chapter at the websites listed below. See also the companion website that accompanies this text, http://www.ablongman.com/brummett, which contains an online study guide and additional resources.

Industrialization
http://www.fordham.edu/halsall/mod/1794woolens.html

A fine selection of primary source documents and contemporary sketches of the first stages of industrialization.

Victorian Web
http://www.victorianweb.org/

Brown University's wonderful overview of the Victorian era in England, offering information about all aspects of Victorian life: social context, political context, economics, religion and philosophy, literature, visual arts, and science and technology.

History of Costumes: Nineteenth Century
http://www.siue.edu/COSTUMES/COSTUME15_INDEX.HTML

Site offers a lively set of images depicting how the various social classes in Europe dressed during the nineteenth century.

Plight of Women's Work in the Industrial Revolution in England and Wales
http://www.womeninworldhistory.com/lesson7.html

Site sponsored by Women in World History Curriculum details the working conditions, home life, and other aspects of British women working in the early 1800s.

Child Labor: British History, 1700–1900
http://www.spartacus.schoolnet.co.uk/IRchild.main.htm

Site presents discussions and images related to child labor in Britain, including information about factory reformers, supporters of child labor, life in the factory, and descriptions of personal experiences.

Enter Evolution: Theory and History
http://www.ucmp.berkeley.edu/history/evolution.html

An extensive site on evolutionary theory, with brief accounts of many eighteenth-century precursors to Charles Darwin, Darwin himself, and Lamarck, Cuvier, and Malthus.

Realism in the Arts
http://martyw.best.vwh.net/Realism.html

A comprehensive collection of images by and intepretations of the realist artists.

Romantic Music
http://www.essentialsofmusic.com/eras/romantic.html

An exhaustive survey of the great romantic composers, with selections of their music.

Images of Leo Tolstoy
http://flag.blackened.net/tolstoy/

A series of sketches and photos of the great Russian writer.

Literature and Film

Romanatic novelists included Sir Walter Scott (*Ivanhoe,*1819) and Victor Hugo (*Notre Dame de Paris,* 1831), whose works were so powerful that they shaped the vision of the past for their countrymen. Their work was paralleled by the poetry of William Wordsworth and Samuel Coleridge. Alphonse de Lamartine in France, Heinrich Heine in Germany, and Alexander Pushkin in Russia enjoyed similar popularity. At mid-century Honoré de Balzac, in his collection *The Human Comedy,* and Gustave Flaubert made realistic portrayals of the contradictions of their age. In English, Charles Dickens and Samuel Clemens made similarly accurate accounts of their nation's strengths and foibles. For each of these writers and artists, there are numerous editions of their collected works.

Numerous video programs on industrialization have been produced by PBS. A compelling series discussing the middle classes at the end of the century in the United Kingdom was *Upstairs, Downstairs* (London Weekend Television, 1971–1975). The theme of marital sadness was touched on by Tolstoy in *Anna Karenina,* Gustave Flaubert in *Madame Bovary,* and Henrik Ibsen, *A Doll's House*. Fine films have been produced of each of these three, especially the Tolstoy and Bovary works.

Suggestions for Reading

For industrialization and its implications, see David S. Landes's classic, *The Unbound Prometheus: Technological Change and Industrial Development in Western Europe from 1750 to the Present* (Cambridge University Press, 2003). For the larger context of the first phase of industrialization, see Eric J. Hobsbawn's classic, *The Age of Revolution* (Vintage, 1996). For the revolutionary impact of industrialization on the American value structure, see James L. Huston, *Securing the Fruits of Labor: The American Concept of Wealth Distribution* (Louisiana State University Press, 1998). On the middle classes in the nineteenth century, see the five volumes of Peter Gay, *The Bourgois Experience: Victoria to Freud,* (Norton, 1984–1998). On J. S. Mill, see Wendy Donner, *The Liberal Self: John Stuart*

Mill's Moral and Political Philosophy (Cornell University Press, 1992). See also Jonathan Beecher, *Charles Fourier: The Visionary and His World* (University of California Press, 1986). Among the large number of works dealing with Karl Marx, the penetrating biography by Isaiah Berlin, *Karl Marx: His Life and Environment*, 4th ed. (Oxford University Press, 1996) is the best introduction. A recent study of change in the church in England is Frances Knight, *The Nineteenth-Century Church and English Society* (Cambridge University Press, 1996). On the complex tie between pretense and culture, see Dianne S. MacLeod, *Art and the Victorian Middle Class: Money and the Making of Cultural Identity* (Cambridge University Press, 1996). David S. Lovejoy, *Religious Enthusiasm and the Great Awakening* (Prentice Hall, 1969), captures the spirit of Pietism and religious humanitarianism. For the arts and music see H. L. C. Jaffee, *The Nineteenth and Twentieth Centuries*, Vol. 5 in *The Dolphin History of Painting*, trans. R. E. Wolf (Thames & Hudson, 1969), and H. C. Colles, *Ideals of the Nineteenth and Twentieth Century*, Vol. 3 in *The Growth of Music* (Oxford University Press, 1956).

CHAPTER

23

Africa and the Middle East During the Age of European Imperialism

CHAPTER CONTENTS

In the eighteenth and nineteenth centuries, the states and empires of Africa and the Middle East underwent a radical restructuring; they faced internal political struggles, the transformation of the world economy, and the military, commercial, and cultural incursions of the Europeans. The economic, technological, and military superiority of certain European states challenged the diverse, complex civilizations of Africa and the Middle East and made them targets in the competition for empire.

In sub-Saharan Africa, Africans did not have a common identity. The diversity of kingdoms and societies made a unified political response to the Europeans impossible. Their responses to European conquest ranged from accommodation to armed resistance. By World War I, most Africans found themselves living within colonies with new political boundaries arbitrarily drawn by the Europeans, without regard for the existing ethnic identities of peoples. They saw their economies restructured to meet the demands of Europeans for their crops and mineral resources. They began the painful process of adapting their cultures and religions to survive in a rapidly industrializing world.

In the Middle East, where empires already existed, politicians and intellectuals discussed ways to keep their empires strong and proposed reforms to enable them to meet the challenges of modernity. The Ottoman Empire at the beginning of the nineteenth century was still large and powerful, but by the end of the century, it had faced bankruptcy, territorial losses, and national separatist movements. The Qajar Empire in Persia was similarly weakened by foreign loans and by the military ambitions of Britain and Russia. From North Africa to central Asia, the citizens of these traditional, polyglot, multiethnic empires found themselves caught up in the great power rivalries of the new imperialists in Europe.

1800

1801 Muhammad Ali arrives in Egypt and seizes power

1808–1839 Mahmud II, reformer, janissary corps destroyed

1820

1821 Greek revolt against Ottoman rule

1839–1876 Ottoman *Tanzimat* reform period

1840

1847 French finalize takeover of Algeria

1848–1896 Reign of Nasir al-Din Shah in Persia

1860

1867 Diamonds discovered in South Africa

1869 Opening of Suez Canal

1876 First Ottoman constitutional revolution

1879 Britain seizes Khyber Pass, dominates Afghanistan

1880

1884 European colonizers meet in Berlin to set ground rules for claiming colonies

1896 Ethiopian army defeats Italians at Aduwa

1899–1902 Anglo-Boer War

1900

1905–1906 Beginning of Persian constitutional revolution

1907 Britain and Russia divide Persia into spheres of influence

1908 Second Ottoman constitutional revolution

EUROPEAN CONQUEST OF AFRICA

■ *What were the motives of European colonizers for conquering most of Africa in the late nineteenth century?*

In 1870 the European nations controlled only 10 percent of the continent. The two most important holdings were at Africa's geographical extremes: French-administered Algeria in the north and the Boer republics and British colonies in the south. Most of the other European holdings were small commercial ones along the West African coast. However, as their rivalries intensified, European nations embarked on a mad scramble to carve up as much of the continent as possible. By World War I, Ethiopia and Liberia were the only African states not under direct European rule.

One of the first European leaders to acquire new African territory was King Leopold II of Belgium, who had long dreamed of creating an empire modeled on Dutch holdings in Asia and the Pacific. When the Belgian government was reluctant to acquire colonies, Leopold took the initiative. In 1876 he organized the International African Association (IAA) and brought the explorer Henry Stanley (1841–1904) into his service. The association, composed of scientists and explorers from many nations, was ostensibly intended to serve humanitarian purposes. But the king had less noble motives. As he put it, he did not want to lose a golden opportunity "to secure . . . a slice of this magnificent African cake."[1] He sent Stanley to central Africa on behalf of the association. Stanley brought along hundreds of blank treaty forms and concluded agreements with various African chiefs, few of whom understood the implications of granting sovereignty to the IAA. By 1882 the organization had laid claim to over 900,000 square miles of territory along the Congo River, an area 75 times the size of Belgium.

DOCUMENT Stanley in Uganda

DOCUMENT Mary Kingsley in Africa

Britain's occupation of Egypt (see p. 695) and Leopold's acquisition of the Congo moved Chancellor Otto von Bismarck to overcome his indifference to colonies and acquire an African empire for Germany. Beginning in February 1884, Bismarck took just a year to annex four colonies: South-West Africa, Togoland, Cameroon, and German East Africa. However, Bismarck's imperial grab was still firmly rooted in his reading of European power politics. He wanted to deflect French hostility to Germany by sparking French interest in acquiring colonies and to put Germany in a position to mediate potential disputes between France and Britain.

MAP Africa Before the Scramble, 1876

While Bismarck was busy acquiring territory, he was also concerned about preventing clashes between colonizers. In 1884 he called the major European powers together in Berlin to discuss potential problems of unregulated African colonization. The conference paid lip service to humanitarian concerns by condemning the slave trade, prohibiting the sale of liquor and firearms in certain areas, and ensuring that European missionaries were not hin-

Representatives of 14 nations, including the United States, met in Berlin in 1884 to set new rules to govern their "scramble for Africa." No representative from Africa was invited to participate.

dered from spreading the Christian faith. Then the European participants moved on to much more important matters.

Seeking to avoid competition for territory that could lead to conflict, they set down the ground rules by which the colonizers were to be guided in their search for colonies. They agreed that the area along the mouth of the Congo River was to be administered by Leopold of Belgium but that it was to be open to free trade and navigation. Drawing on precedents beginning in the sixteenth century, when European nations were creating seaborne empires, they decided that no nation was to stake out claims without first notifying other powers of its intention. No territory could be staked out unless it was effectively occupied, and all disputes were to be settled by arbitration. In spite of these declarations, the competitors often ignored the rules. On several occasions, war was barely avoided.

The humanitarian guidelines were generally disregarded. The methods used to acquire lands continued in many instances to involve deceiving the Africans. European colonists got huge land grants by giving chiefs treaties they could not read and whose contents they did not understand because they were unfamiliar with European concepts of legal rights and property. In return, African chiefs were plied with bottles of gin, red handkerchiefs, and fancy red costumes. The comparison between the European treaty methods and those of the Americans in negotiations with Native American tribes is all too apparent.

The cultural differences between Africans and Europeans were especially vast regarding their conceptions of land ownership. To most African societies, land was not owned privately by individuals but was vested in their chiefs, who allocated it to their people. When chiefs allocated land or mineral rights to Europeans, they had no idea they were disposing of more than its temporary use. When the Europeans later claimed ownership of the land, Africans were indignant, claiming that they had been cheated. In 1888 Charles Rudd, a representative of Cecil Rhodes, signed a treaty with the Ndebele king, Lobengula (c. 1836–1894), in which he was given a monthly stipend and 1000 Martini-Henry rifles in exchange for a concession over minerals and metals. Lobengula was told that the treaty gave Rhodes's company the right to dig a hole in one place, but the treaty actually gave Rhodes unlimited powers.

African leaders who questioned treaty provisions were treated cavalierly. King Jaja (c. 1821–1891) of Opobo, a prosperous trading state in southeastern Nigeria, refused to sign a British treaty unless the wording of clauses on protection and free trade was altered or scrapped. The British agreed to changes, but when the British Consul invited the chiefs to sign the treaty on a ship, they were detained and sent into exile.

The Scrambling of Africa

From the Berlin conference to World War I, European imperialists partitioned the African continent among themselves, with two exceptions—Liberia, which had been established for freed American slaves, and Ethiopia, which fended off Italian invaders. The colonizers were woefully ignorant about the geography of the areas they colonized. Europeans had knowledge of coastal areas, but nineteenth-century explorers had largely concentrated on river explorations and knew little beyond that. Thus, when European statesmen drew boundaries, they were more concerned with strategic interests and potential economic development than with existing kingdoms, ethnic identities, topography, or demography. About half the boundaries were straight lines drawn for simple convenience. As Lord Salisbury, the British prime minister, admitted: "[We] have been engaged in drawing lines upon maps where no white man's foot ever trod, we have been giving away mountains and rivers and lakes to each other, only hindered by the small impediment that we never knew exactly where the mountains and rivers and lakes were."[2]

Colonization in Africa

France and Britain were by far the two leading competitors for African territory. The French vision was to create an empire linking Algeria, West Africa, and the region north of the lower Congo River. To achieve their goal, the French relied on their military to drive eastward from Senegal and northward from the lower Congo. In West Africa the British concentrated on their coastal trading interests and carved out colonies in Gambia, Sierra Leone, the Gold Coast (Ghana), and Nigeria. But they also scooped up possessions elsewhere. In East Africa they laid claim to Kenya and Uganda, and by 1884, they gained control over a stretch of African coast fronting on the Gulf of Aden. Because it guarded the lower approach to the Suez Canal, this protectorate (British Somaliland) was of great strategic value.

Equally important to British control of Egypt were the headwaters of the Nile, situated in the area known as the Anglo-Egyptian Sudan. The French also had their designs on the area as a bargaining chip to force the British to reconsider their exclusive control over Egypt. The French commissioned Captain Jean-Baptiste Marchand to march a force 3000 miles from central Africa to Fashoda on the White Nile south of Khartoum. In July 1898, several months

Document That Was No Brother

Europeans and Africans usually had very different perceptions of the same event. These documents recount two versions of a battle on the Congo River in the 1870s. The first comes from an African chief, Mojimba—recorded by a Catholic priest, Father Joseph Fraessle, several decades after the battle—and the second is by the famed explorer Henry Morton Stanley written for European and American audiences.

When we heard that the man with the white flesh was journeying down the Lualaba (Lualaba-Congo) we were open-mouthed with astonishment. We stood still. All night long the drums announced the strange news—a man with white flesh! . . . He must have got that from the river-kingdom. He will be one of our brothers who were drowned in that river. All life comes from the water, and in the water he has found life. Now he is coming back to us, he is coming home. . . .

We will prepare a feast, I ordered, we will go to meet our brother and escort him into the village with rejoicing! . . . We assembled the great canoes. We listened for the gong which would announce our brother's presence on the Lualaba. Presently the cry was heard: He is approaching the Lualaba. Now he enters the river! . . . We swept forward, my canoe leading, the others following, with songs of joy and with dancing, to meet the first white man our eyes had beheld, and to do him honor.

But as we drew near his canoes there were loud reports, bang! bang! and fire-staves spat bits of iron at us. We were paralyzed with fright; our mouths hung wide open and we could not shut them. Things such as we had never seen, never heard of, never dreamed of—they were the work of evil spirits! Several of my men plunged into the water. . . . What for? Did they fly to safety? No—for others fell down also, in the canoes. Some screamed dreadfully, others were silent—they were dead, and blood flowed from little holes in their bodies. "War! that is war!" I yelled. "Go back!" The canoes sped back to our village with all the strength our spirits could impart to our arms. That was no brother! That was the worst enemy our country had ever seen.

And still those bangs went on; the long staves spat fire, pieces of iron whistled around us, fell into the water with a hissing sound, and our brothers continued to fall. We fell into our village—they came after us. We fled into the forest and flung ourselves on the ground. When we returned that evening our eyes beheld fearful things: our brothers, dead, bleeding, our village plundered and burned, and the water full of dead bodies. . . .

Now tell me: has the white man dealt fairly by us? Oh, do not speak to me of him! You call us wicked men, but you white men are much more wicked! You think because you have guns you can take away our land and our possessions. You have sickness in your heads, for that is not justice.

From Heinrich Schifflers, *The Quest for Africa* (New York: Putnam, 1957), pp. 196–197.

after Marchand planted a French flag at Fashoda, General H. H. Kitchener successfully led an Anglo-Egyptian force against Muslim forces in control of the Sudan. Then Kitchener turned his attention to Marchand, and their forces faced off nervously at Fashoda. The showdown nearly ended in war. To the British, control of the Nile was a strategic necessity. To the French, it was a matter of national prestige, but they were not prepared to go to war over it, and they withdrew Marchand.

Britain was the principal colonizer in southern Africa. British influence expanded northward from the Cape Colony largely through the personal efforts of the diamond magnate Cecil Rhodes, who dreamed of an uninterrupted corridor of British territory from the Cape of Good Hope to Cairo. When the British government hesitated to claim territory north of the Limpopo River, Rhodes took the initiative. Rhodes had heard the stories that King Solomon's mines were

Cecil Rhodes Astride Africa—Cartoon

recruited Africans to fight on their behalf. And Africans, who typically made up the vast majority of European-led units, did the bulk of the fighting.

African states were also at a disadvantage because they did not rethink outmoded battle tactics and because they did not put up a united front. In the face of European expansion, African states sought to preserve as much of their own autonomy and sovereignty as possible. This response usually prevented them from entering into alliances with other African states to confront a common enemy.

Most African societies resisted European conquest at some point, but they first weighed the costs and benefits of European rule and considered whether they should resist, make accommodations, or negotiate with Europeans. They queried European missionaries in their midst for information on the colonizers. They watched developments in neighboring states to see the results of resistance, and they sought advice on the implications of European protection. They assessed their rivalries with neighboring states and the possibility of profit from an alliance with Europeans. They also calculated whether they had the support of their own people. In the East African kingdom of Buganda, a Protestant ruling faction sought British allies to maintain an advantage over Muslim, Catholic, and traditionalist rivals.

African states often changed tactics over the course of time. Moshoeshoe's Basotho kingdom fought the Boers in the Orange Free State on two occasions, appealed for British protection in 1868 to shield it from Afrikaner rule, fought a war against the Cape government in 1880 after the Cape tried to disarm Sotho warriors, and then invited the British to reestablish colonial rule in 1884.

Despite the disparity in firearms, African states sustained resistance to European colonizers until World War I. One of the most durable and innovative resistance leaders was Samori Touré (SA-mor-ee too-RAY; c. 1830–1900), who came from a Dyula trading family in the region of the upper Niger River in West Africa. He built up an army to protect his family's trading interests and then, between 1865 and 1875, created a powerful Islamic kingdom among the Mandinke people that stretched from Sierra Leone to the Ivory Coast. Samori's army could field over 30,000 soldiers and cavalry armed with muskets and rifles, some homemade and some imported from Freetown on the Sierra Leonean coast.

Samori's forces were a formidable opponent when they first clashed with French soldiers probing west from Senegal in 1881. However, the French superiority in weaponry eventually forced Samori to wage a scorched-earth campaign as he moved his kingdom eastward. He then had to deal with internal revolts from his new subjects and also with the British, who refused to declare a protectorate over his kingdom. Squeezed between the French and the British, he fought as long as he could before he was captured and exiled by the French in 1898.

Because of their ability to inspire and unite followers, religious leaders often led the resistance to European invaders. In Sudan, Muhammad Ahmad (1844–1885), a Muslim ***shaykh*** from a village north of Khartoum, proclaimed himself a **Mahdi** ("guided one") in 1881. Muslims believe that in times of crisis a redeemer appears whose mission it is to overthrow tyrannical and oppressive rulers and install just governments in their place. Declaring himself a successor to the prophet Muhammad, Muhammad Ahmad called on people to join him in a *jihad* against the unbelievers, the Egyptian-appointed administrators who were levying taxes and suppressing a profitable slave trade.

From a base 300 miles southwest of Khartoum, Mahdist forces scored numerous successes against Egyptian forces and laid siege to Khartoum in 1884. Despite last-ditch efforts by British officer Charles Gordon to negotiate with the Mahdi, the Mahdists swept into Khartoum in early 1885, killing Gordon and setting up an administration at Omdurman, across the Nile from Khartoum. The Mahdi died a short time later, but his successors founded a Muslim state that lasted until an Anglo-Egyptian force invaded the Sudan in 1898.

A Shona **spirit medium** by the name of Charwe also inspired resistance against the British South Africa Company's (BSAC) colonization of Rhodesia in the 1890s. Shona peoples believed that a person could communicate with God through a dead person's spirit. This spirit can possess a living person who becomes a spirit medium. People especially consulted mediums who were possessed by important figures of the past. These mediums were thought to be guardians of the people and able to ensure good luck in hunting, producing rainfall, and controlling diseases. In the case of Charwe, she claimed to have been possessed by the spirit of Nehanda, a woman who had lived four centuries before.

In 1896, many Shona and Ndebele rose up against the BSAC's exploitative policies. Company officials were expropriating African land, seizing their cattle, levying taxes, and forcing Africans to work on the mines. Some Shona chiefdoms were inspired to revolt by prominent spirit mediums such as Ambuya Nehanda and Kagubi,

---

shaykh—A title given to a high Muslim dignitary or the master of a religious order.

Mahdi—A Muslim spiritual figure and the last *imam* who is expected to appear in the last days of the world.

spirit medium—A religious specialist who serves as an intermediary between the living and prominent spirits.

who secretly spread the message of revolt and urged people to take up arms. Their inspirational leadership sustained the Shona *Chimurenga* ("uprising") for a year. Although the Europeans were nearly expelled, they eventually defeated the rebels. Nehanda and Kagubi were captured and sentenced to hang in March 1898. But Nehanda was defiant to the end. She refused to be converted to Christianity at the last minute and she denounced the Europeans until the moment she was executed. Her prophecy that "my bones will rise" to recapture freedom was remembered by guerillas fighting in the struggle against European domination in the 1970s.[3] They, too, consulted spirit mediums, including an elderly woman who claimed she had been possessed by Nehanda's spirit.

Religious leaders played a leading role in inspiring Shona resistance against white settlers in Zimbabwe in 1896–1897. This photograph is of the spirit mediums Nehanda and Kagubi awaiting trial after they were captured.

Although African armies scored some victories against European forces, only one African state, Ethiopia, successfully repulsed European conquest. In the second half of the nineteenth century, several kings had attempted to revive a unified kingdom of Ethiopia.

Following Tewodros II's suicide in 1868 (p. 581), his successor, Yohannes IV, tried to curb the ambitions of his principal rival, Menelik (1844–1913), the king of Shawa, who had been imprisoned by Tewodros and who had long desired to be emperor. After Yohannes sent a force to confront him, Menelik backed down and pledged his allegiance. However, Menelik took advantage of Yohannes's policy of giving provincial rulers greater autonomy and began conquering territory to Shawa's south.

After Yohannes died in a battle against the Mahdist forces in the Sudan in 1889, Menelik was crowned emperor of Ethiopia. He moved the capital to Addis Ababa ("New Flower") and began modernizing his kingdom by constructing the first railway line between Addis Ababa and the French colony of Djibouti (ji-BOO-tee), laying telephone and telegraph lines for communication with provinces and building bridges. He continued his policy of aggressively expanding Ethiopia's boundaries, more than doubling the kingdom's size. In the end, Menelik could boast that Ethiopia was larger than it had been under any previous emperor.

At the same time, Menelik kept a wary eye on British, French, and Italian intrigues in the region. "I have no intention," he wrote Queen Victoria, "of being an indifferent spectator if the distant Powers hold the idea of dividing up Africa."[4] British and French attentions were focused elsewhere, but the Italians, who had long coveted land on the Red Sea coast, were another matter. In 1889 Italy and Ethiopia signed the Treaty of Wuchale, in which Italy recognized Menelik as emperor of Ethiopia in return for giving the Italians a free hand in an area on the Red Sea coast controlled by one of his rivals. However, the treaty's Italian version stated that Ethiopia had to conduct foreign relations through the Italians, while the **Amharic** version merely stated that Ethiopia could consult with Italy on foreign matters. When Menelik learned through diplomatic exchanges with Britain and France that Italy was claiming a protectorate over Ethiopia, he denounced the treaty and prepared for an eventual showdown with Italy by importing massive quantities of weapons, many of them from Italy.

Amharic—Semitic language spoken by the Amhara people of central and western Ethiopia.

When the Italians mounted an offensive in Tigré province in 1896, Menelik called on his nation to resist them: "Enemies have come who would ruin our country. . . . With God's help I will get rid of them."[5] Menelik's nobles rallied behind him to supply troops, and Ethiopia's army of 100,000 soldiers was more than a match for the 20,000-strong Italian army. At the battle of Aduwa, the Italian generals made a series of tactical blunders, and their force was routed. The Italians were forced to recognize Ethiopia's independence and content themselves with Eritrea, their enclave on the Red Sea coast. However, the memory of this humiliating defeat lingered in Italian minds until Mussolini sought revenge decades later.

THE MINERAL REVOLUTION IN SOUTH AFRICA AND THE ANGLO-BOER WAR

▪ *What difference did the discovery of gold and diamonds have on the relations between the British and Afrikaner and African states?*

The discovery of diamonds in 1867 on the borders of the Cape Colony and the Orange Free State and of gold in 1886 in the Transvaal were to transform the whole of southern Africa economically and politically.

When the diamond fields were opened up, thousands of black and white fortune seekers flocked to the area. The mining town of Kimberley sprang up almost overnight. In the first years of the digs, there were no restrictions on who could stake claims. But in 1873, European diggers, resentful of competition from blacks, successfully lobbied British officials for a law prohibiting Africans from owning claims. This law set the tone for future laws governing who controlled mineral rights and ownership of the land.

Although Africans were excluded from owning claims, there were few restrictions on their movements and where they lived around the mines. Africans typically came to mine for three to six months and left at a time of their own choosing. This freedom changed as European mine owners sought to prevent diamond thefts and to control black workers by preventing desertion and holding down their wages. In 1885 the mine owners began erecting compounds to house black workers. Throughout their stay at a mine, black workers stayed in the compounds and were allowed out only to work in the mine. The compound system was so effective at controlling black labor that it became a fixture in other mining operations throughout southern Africa.

In the early years of the diamond diggings, several thousand people held claims, but by the 1880s, ownership of the mines was falling into the hands of fewer and fewer people. In 1888 the two leading magnates, Cecil Rhodes (1853–1902) and Barney Barnato (1852–1897), pooled their resources to found De Beers, a company that controlled 90 percent of diamond production. Over a century later De Beers continues to dominate the diamond industry not only in South Africa but also around the world.

In 1886, gold discoveries on the Witwatersrand sparked off another rush. The Witwatersrand gold veins were distinctive because they sloped at sharp angles beneath the earth and required shafts to be sunk at depths of up to two miles. The exorbitant costs of deep-level mining as well as of importing skilled labor, mining engineers, and the latest technology required enormous infusions of foreign capital. Profits were hard to sustain, and the main mining houses targeted black wages for cutting costs. They restricted competition for black workers by imposing ceilings on their wages and creating recruiting organizations that eventually developed networks as far north as Zambia and Malawi. The result was a migrant labor system in which tens of thousands of black men came to the mines for six to nine months, while black women stayed home to raise families and look after crops. Another consequence of the mineral discoveries was the extension of railways into the interior of southern Africa.

From 1886 to the end of the century, South Africa's share of world gold production jumped from less than 1 percent to over 25 percent. The center of power in the region shifted from Cape Town to Johannesburg, renewing British interest in controlling the Transvaal. Afrikaner leaders were resolute about protecting their independence, but they feared they would be outnumbered when tens of thousands of *uitlanders* (ATE-lahn-der; "foreigners"), mainly English immigrants, flocked to the gold mines. The Transvaal's president, Paul Kruger (1825–1904), was determined that the *uitlanders* would not gain control. As a boy he had joined in the Great Trek. As a young man, he led Boer commandos conquering African lands. As head of the Transvaal, he was passionately devoted to preserving its independence and the Afrikaners' agrarian way of life.

Kruger's main adversary was Cecil Rhodes, who in 1890 had become prime minister of the Cape Colony. An avowed imperialist, Rhodes now set his sights on bringing down Kruger's republic. He plotted with *uitlanders* in Johannesburg to stage an insurrection. In late 1895 Rhodes's private army, led by Leander Starr Jameson, invaded the Transvaal from neighboring Bechuanaland, but they were quickly captured by Afrikaner commandos. The Jameson raid

While most black migrant workers in the gold mines were men, black women found employment in the urban areas as domestic servants and washerwomen. A Johannesburg regulation of 1899 stated that "every householder or owner of an erf [a plot of land] may keep in his backyard whatever servants he requires for domestic service."

had dire consequences. Rhodes was forced to resign as prime minister, Afrikaners in the Cape were alienated from the British, the Orange Free State formed an alliance with the Transvaal, and the Transvaal began modernizing its army by importing weapons from Europe.

Transvaal leaders were deeply suspicious that the British had been behind Rhodes's reckless actions. Their fears were heightened when in 1897 the British selected Alfred Milner (1854–1925) as the high commissioner for South Africa. He shared Rhodes's imperialist convictions with a passion. He pressured Kruger to reduce the length of time for *uitlanders* to qualify for citizenship in the Transvaal. Although Milner thought Kruger would make significant concessions under pressure, Kruger was unwilling to meet all of Milner's demands.

War broke out in late 1899. Most observers expected the British army to roll over the heavily outnumbered Afrikaner forces. But Afrikaner soldiers were crack shots and expert horsemen. Knowing every inch of ground on which they fought, they frequently outmaneuvered the British troops by resorting to guerrilla tactics. The British countered by conducting a scorched-earth campaign, burning Afrikaner farms and placing Afrikaner women and children and Africans who worked on their farms in unsanitary concentration camps. About 30,000 Afrikaners (half of them children) and 15,000 blacks perished in the camps from disease and starvation. Among Afrikaners the memory of the deaths fueled animosity against the British for generations.

The Boer War and Queen Victoria–Dutch Caricature

COLONIAL RULE IN AFRICA

■ *Why did Islam and Christianity spread so rapidly under European rule?*

The European nations had completed their conquest of African societies by World War I. They then had to figure out how to govern huge colonies with a handful of officials. In 1926 in the Ivory Coast, the French stationed one European official for every 18,000 people, while in southern Nigeria, the British had one for every 70,000. The French, Belgians, Portuguese, and British pragmatically experimented with various policies of administration; whatever their approach, all of them had similar objectives: preserving law and order, quelling disturbances, and spending as little on administration as possible. Thus the common approach was "divide and rule."

"The White Man's Burden" Across Two Centuries

The British, through their experience with administering the Muslim Sokoto **Caliphate** in northern Nigeria, devised a policy of indirect rule, or ruling through African traditional authorities. Frederick Lugard, who had commanded the British troops that conquered the caliphate, stayed on as an administrator. An authoritarian figure who instinctively distrusted educated Africans, Lugard found that he had more in common with the conservative Muslim Fulani aristocrats who ruled the caliphate. Thus

---

caliphate—The territory ruled by a caliph, a leader of the Muslim community.

Lugard favored a policy of colonial officials ruling through indigenous political leaders—chiefs and their councils—who were allowed to continue their day-to-day rule with little interference from the British. However, chiefs were expected to observe colonial laws, carry out the directives of colonial officials, and collect taxes. Because they had difficulty balancing their ties to their subjects with their responsibility to their colonial masters, they found themselves making more and more compromises to conform to colonial rules.

Indirect rule was applied in other British African colonies, even where African societies had structures totally unlike the Sokoto Caliphate. The administrative unit for British rule was the "tribe." For the sake of efficient rule, tribes were arbitrarily created where none had previously existed. The result was an authoritarian structure that barely resembled prior systems of governance. For instance, among the Igbo peoples in southeastern Nigeria, where elders ruled small-scale societies, the British imposed chiefs and issued them warrants to legitimize their authority. The **"warrant chiefs"** provoked resentment among their subjects.

In the late 1920s, as prices for palm oil and palm kernels dropped, the household incomes of women also declined. In 1929, Igbo women, fearing they were going to be taxed, received written assurances they would not be taxed and had a warrant chief arrested for assaulting a woman. One woman in the Oloko district challenged British officials: "What have we women done to warrant our being taxed? We women are like trees which bear fruit. You should tell us the reason why women who bear seeds should be counted."[6] The women's grievances mushroomed into a widespread popular revolt against warrant chiefs and "native" administration in which women attacked jails and released prisoners. Although British troops quelled the revolt and killed 50 women, the women's efforts to reform ruling structures by appointing a council of judges to replace warrant chiefs failed because women could not serve on the courts.

The French had a somewhat different approach to administering their African colonies. Before the scramble for Africa, France had applied the ideals of the French Revolution to a philosophy of assimilation in which selected Africans were immersed in the French language and culture and were treated as French citizens with full political rights. This approach was possible as long as France was governing a small colony like Senegal in West Africa. But once France expanded its holdings in Africa, it was confronted with a large subject population whose cultures were still intact. The French took the attitude that most Africans could not be absorbed into French culture; thus, they relied on direct rule that featured a centralized administration. At the top were French officials; below them were layers of African "chiefs" who ruled over villages, districts, and provinces and were primarily responsible for collecting taxes, maintaining law and order, and recruiting forced labor. If a society did not have a chief, the French would select one based on education, administrative ability, and loyalty.

The Portuguese practiced another form of direct rule. Unlike other colonies in Africa, the territories of Angola and Mozambique were constitutionally part of Portugal and were treated as overseas provinces. As the Industrial Revolution in Europe had largely bypassed Portugal under the longtime rule of Antonio Salazar (1932–1968), Portugal based her economic policies on her African possessions' providing the mother country with cheap raw materials and foodstuffs as well as guaranteeing Portuguese manufacturers a profitable market. Colonial governors reported directly to the Salazar government, and provincial and district administrators gradually took over the collection of taxes and the recruitment of forced labor, tasks that had been previously carried out by African police and chiefs.

In theory, Portuguese officials believed that they, of all the European colonizers, had the unique ability to create a multiracial society. The reality was far different. The Portuguese created a class of *assimilados* ("assimilated people") who were supposed to be treated as equals to Portuguese citizens. To become an *assimilado,* a person had to become Christian (Roman Catholic); read, write, and speak Portuguese; and "practice a Portuguese lifestyle." The numbers of *assimilados,* however, never amounted to more than 3 percent of the African population. The rest were classed as *indigenas* ("indigenous people") and were expected to learn the "dignity of labor" by working on plantations, at public works, and in urban areas. The only way to be exempted from this forced labor system was to be classified as *assimilado* or to seek work as a migrant laborer in neighboring territories. Mozambicans annually supplied over 100,000 members of the labor force for the South African gold mines.

The Colonial Economy

Colonialism imposed a dependent economic relationship between Africa and Europe that continues to shape the economies of independent African nations. Whatever their nationality, European officials shared a common objective: to compel their colonies to produce raw materials for the world market in exchange for finished products from the mother country.

warrant chief—British-appointed chief who derived his authority from a warrant issued by the British.

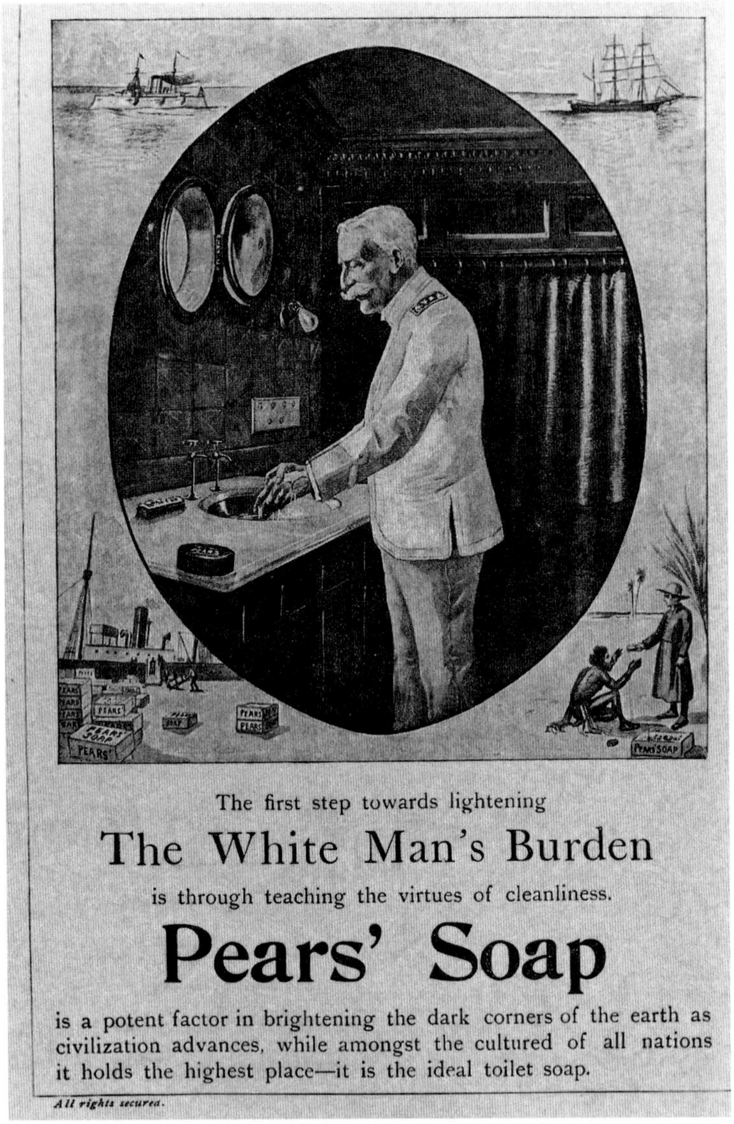

The first step towards lightening
The White Man's Burden
is through teaching the virtues of cleanliness.
Pears' Soap
is a potent factor in brightening the dark corners of the earth as civilization advances, while amongst the cultured of all nations it holds the highest place—it is the ideal toilet soap.
All rights secured.

European businesses linked the expansion of their markets with the spread of European civilization "in the dark corners of the earth." This advertisement for Pear's Soap in McClure's Magazine *draws a direct connection between cleanliness and the acquisition of Western civilization. The bottom right-hand corner of this advertisement depicts a missionary bringing Christianity to an African—with a box of Pear's Soap on the ground next to them.*

Colonial economies took two forms: colonies where European involvement was direct in the form of plantations, mines, and European settlement; and colonies where Africans with small landholdings grew cash crops such as peanuts, oil palms, cotton, rubber, sisal, coffee, and cocoa for export. Because each colony usually produced one cash crop, the colony's well-being was dependent on the price the crop fetched on the world market. The Gold Coast, for example, soon became the world's leading supplier of cocoa, which inspired a song popular in the 1950s:

If you want to send your children to school, it is cocoa,
If you want to want to build your house, it is cocoa,
If you want to marry, it is cocoa,
If you want to buy cloth, it is cocoa,
Whatever you want to do in this world,
It is with cocoa money that you do it.[7]

The introduction of cash crops was extremely disruptive to African agriculture. Cash crops were often grown on the best land at the expense of other crops; thus, overproduction exhausted soils and led to erosion. Colonial officials also favored the interests of African men by granting them the ownership of land on which cash crops were grown. They reaped the lion's share of any proceeds from sales, while women, who had traditionally been responsible for agriculture, were expected to shoulder the burden of tending the new crops as well as performing their normal duties.

European-run plantations and mining operations also played major roles in the colonial economy. Huge estates and mining concessions were ceded to European and American companies. The Firestone Rubber Company took advantage of minimal rents and no income taxes to establish the largest rubber plantation in the world in Liberia. The Belgian giant, Union Minière, had a virtual monopoly over the copper-rich southern Congo, while Anglo-American, a South African company, dominated diamond and gold production in southern Africa.

The worst excesses of economic exploitation were in the Congo, the Belgian monarch Leopold II's private preserve. To recoup the fortune he expended to bankroll his empire, Leopold granted extensive concessions to private companies to build railways and exploit natural and mineral resources. In 1891, he decreed that African land ownership was restricted to areas actually under cultivation. Since most Africans practiced shifting cultivation, vast tracts of land were placed under state control *(domaine privé).*

Belgian King Crushes the Congo Free State—Cartoon

Concession companies were given free rein to exploit regions, first for ivory and then, after the invention of the inflatable bicycle tire, for rubber. The drive to maximize profits encouraged the brutal treatment of Africans pressed into labor service. Leopold's private army held wives hostage to coerce husbands into meeting rubber collection quotas. First-hand reports by courageous individuals such as William Sheppard, an African-American Presbyterian missionary, and Roger Casement, a British Consul, began leaking out of the "Free State" to humanitarian groups and governments about the abuses, atrocities, beatings, and killings sanctioned by Leopold's system. An American missionary reported the details from a Belgian official about the brutal work of an African policeman: "Each time the corporal goes out to get rubber, cartridges are given to him. He must bring back all not used; and for every one used, he must bring back a right hand!"[8]

Leopold's brutalities were responsible for the deaths of millions and were, as contemporary African-American historian George Washington Williams put it, a "crime against humanity."[9] The international outcry over the "Red Rubber" scandal eventually forced the Belgian government to intervene in 1908 and take over administration from Leopold. Conditions in the colony, renamed the Belgian Congo, did not improve for long under the direct administration of the government.

A vast army of migrant laborers was required to run these operations. Because African men were reluctant to leave their families and homes for extended periods, they were compelled to seek work in the towns, mines, and plantations through a head tax on all adult men that had to be paid in cash rather than in kind. Besides paying taxes, workers saved their wages to start up their own businesses back home, to acquire imported goods, and to buy cattle to pay bridewealth for marriages.

Colonialism also introduced new forms of transportation. Built on the backs of unpaid forced labor, railways were constructed from the coastal ports into the interior to extend trading networks and to facilitate the export of commodities, especially minerals. In areas where white settlers had farms, railways not only exported their products but also deliberately skirted the black reserves that supplied laborers to white farms and mines. While ports and railway towns boomed, railways often undermined established trading networks such as the Hausa trade of northern Nigeria with Tripoli in North Africa and the caravan routes in eastern Africa. Cars and trucks also replaced human porters and animals such as donkeys and horses.

The impact of the colonial economy on different regions was uneven. Coastal areas typically benefited more from roads, railways, and economic development than the interior zones, which stagnated and became the primary sources of migrant laborers for the coast. In southern Africa, where mining was the dominant industry, South Africa became an economic powerhouse because most of the roads and railways were built in a north-south direction that steered regional trade through South Africa.

Africans expressed their images of Europeans through art. In the car above, an early twentieth-century work from the Congo, a Belgian mining magnate reclines in the back seat while the African chauffeur drives.

Social and Religious Change

Colonial rule opened up new avenues of social change for Africans. New roads and railways lines created new employment opportunities and the migration of workers to plantations and fast-growing urban centers. Migrant workers, soldiers, students, teachers, and civil servants were exposed to new organizations and associations, dress, music and dance styles, sports, languages, cultures, ideas, values, and faiths.

Imperial cultures had an impact on the new sports that Africans played and how they spent their leisure time. European missionaries initially introduced football (or soccer), which has become the most popular sport in Africa, to students at mission schools because they believed that the sport built morals and character and exposed students to Western civilization. In addition, the sport helped to attract new students. With their policy of assimilation, the French desired to assimilate a black educated elite and develop model French citizens.

Colonial administrators, concerned about the large-scale movement of Africans, especially young men, into the urban areas and the possibilities of social disorder, introduced football to keep men content and provide an outlet for their leisure time activities. The Belgians also introduced football to its African soldiers in the Congo. Because the sport was inexpensive and simple to organize games, the sport achieved a rapid popularity among both players and spectators. Colonial officials sought to control the sport by sponsoring sports bodies and leagues, but because it did not require much capital to form a team, Africans began forming their own football clubs and associations. They were among the few institutions that Africans could own and control. After World War II football clubs became an outlet for expressing opposition to European rule. In Tanganyika African nationalist groups utilized sporting clubs for their meetings. In Nigeria Nnamdi Azikiwe (ah-ZEEK-way), a businessman and nationalist leader who learned football as a boy on the streets of Lagos, founded a network of "Zik" Athletic Clubs across Nigeria. He took advantage of the British allowing his Lagos football club to tour the country by delivering speeches after matches attacking colonial rule.

Christianity and Islam

The colonial era was a period of tremendous growth for both Islam and Christianity, although for contrasting reasons and in different parts of the continent. Christianity experienced its greatest expansion in the southern two-thirds of Africa, while Islam scored successes in the northern third of the continent and along the eastern coast.

Before the advent of colonial rule, Christian missionaries won few converts. Catholic missionaries who accompanied the Portuguese into Africa converted some rulers and their courts but had little influence with commoners. In the late eighteenth and early nineteenth centuries a fresh wave of evangelical Christianity stirred many European Protestant denominations to send missionaries to Africa and elsewhere. They believed they had an obligation to spread the Christian faith to civilize and uplift African "heathens" and to block Islam. They often saw their missions as working hand in hand with the expansion of European commerce globally.

Although some African rulers perceived the missionaries as positive assets who brought technical skills and schools, many questioned whether the missionaries were undermining their authority and restricted their activities. Thus, those who initially converted to Christianity were on the margins of African society—freed slaves, women fleeing bad marriages, famine victims, war refugees, orphans, and people accused of witchcraft.

The next wave of converts consisted of those who wanted access to technical skills and literacy offered at mission schools. Missionaries usually required their students to join their church in order to be admitted to their schools. Because most schooling was at the primary level, few students proceeded on to a handful of secondary schools. Thus high schools such as the École William Ponty in Dakar, Senegal, Achimota in the Gold Coast, and Lovedale and Adams College in South Africa attracted students from whole regions. Friendships at these schools developed into social networks that laid the foundation for anticolonial politics. Those who aspired to university education usually had to go to Europe or America before colleges were established like Fort Hare in South Africa in 1916.

Schooling affected avenues of social advancement. Age, family position, ability, and sex had traditionally determined status in African societies, but in the colonial world, whose missions, schools, civil service, and businesses required a literate elite that was fluent in European languages, education and technical skills became a main avenue to personal advancement.

African Christians continually raised probing questions about Christian missions and Christianity. They especially challenged the attacks of European missionaries on such African cultural practices as **polygyny** and circumcision ceremonies as unchristian and the missionaries' control of leadership and finances in the missions. Some African Christians initiated an African

---

polygyny—A marital practice in which a man has more than one wife.

reformation by breaking away from mission churches to form their own independent churches. These new churches were carbon copies of the mission churches but featured black leadership. Some of the churches adopted the name "Ethiopia" in their titles because Christianity had been established in Ethiopia long before European missionaries arrived in Africa. In 1892, Mangena Mokone (mahn-GAY-nah moh-KOH-nee), a minister near Pretoria, South Africa, left the Wesleyan Methodist Church to "to serve God in his own way" and founded the Ethiopian Church. He criticized European clergy for paying black clergy paltry wages, for continuing to segregate meetings of blacks and whites, and for refusing to allow black clergy to rise to leadership posts.

Some African church leaders drew on the Bible, with its emphasis on justice and equality, for a radical critique of colonial rule. And a few were prepared to take up arms to overthrow the Europeans. One of the most famous anticolonial rebellions was led by John Chilembwe (chee-LIM-bway), a Baptist minister from Nyasaland (currently Malawi) who had been trained at an African-American theological seminary in Virginia. In 1915 he hastily organized an uprising against British colonial rule and the recruitment of Africans to fight in East Africa during World War I. Chilembwe's intention was to "strike a blow and die" in the manner of his hero, American abolitionist John Brown. Although British troops shot and killed Chilembwe as he fled into Mozambique, his example inspired anticolonial protest in later generations.

Dressed in the formal Victorian style favored by the Africans educated in European mission schools, Rev. John Chilembre led an unsuccessful rebellion against British rule and white plantation owners in 1915.

Some black Christians Africanized Christianity by adapting Christian beliefs and rituals to African culture and religious systems. Spirit churches, for instance, were led by healer/prophets who followed African ways of treating disease and illness but invoked the Christian Holy Spirit to cure people. These healer/prophets were especially concerned with coping with diseases such as smallpox, measles, the plague, and influenza that accompanied European conquest and had a devastating impact on African peoples. When the Spanish influenza swept through Africa in late 1918 killing several million people, spirit churches emerged in its wake in many parts of Africa. A variety of Aladura ("one who prays") churches were established among the Yoruba people in Nigeria. A few of these spirit churches established close ties with American and British Pentecostal churches.

Women were especially attracted to spirit churches because they offered unique ways for women to voice their spirituality and express their prophetic talents. A prominent example is the South African charismatic healer Ma' Nku, who left the Dutch Reformed Church to found her own St. John's Apostolic Church. At her central church near Johannesburg, her prayers imbued water with healing properties. So many people flocked to her that she had to install a water-pump for mass healings and baptisms.

Even in churches where women were prophet leaders, men typically filled leadership roles and made decisions. However, women still found ways to carve out personalized spaces. In the Roho churches founded in the 1930s in western Kenya, women composed hymns inspired by the Holy Spirit. Their singing expressed their spirituality in a way that men could not control. In the 1930s the Roho women sang hymns such as "We are women of war, we are women of fire" that boldly proclaimed their faith and their importance to their movement. As they marched around the countryside, they announced their approach to villages by singing their inspirational hymns.

Despite Africa being under European rule, Islam had even greater successes in winning new converts.

"Woman in Street" by an unknown photographer from St. Louis, Senegal. St. Louis was the center of Senegal's artistic and intellectual community for many years.

By World War II an estimated half of all Africans were Muslims, most of which were Sunni Muslims.

The initial response of Muslims to the British and the French in West Africa was either to mount overt resistance or withdraw from contact with Europeans. In Mali *Shaykh* Hamallah (1883–1943) lived an isolated existence and taught only in his own mosque. Because he never expressed himself on African issues or accepted French rule, the French believed that he was organizing resistance. After the French deported him in 1925, his followers prayed towards where he was living in exile rather than to Mecca.

Initially the colonizers took a hostile stance toward Islam. However, the British had experience in dealing with Muslim leaders in India and other colonial possessions. Once resistance died down, the British—and later the French—began courting conservative Muslim leaders who were prepared to establish peaceful relations and maintain the status quo in exchange for certain privileges. Muslim clerics were not restricted to working within colonial boundaries, whereas Christian missionaries were assigned to specific areas and were often not allowed to evangelize in Muslim areas. Ironically the peace that Europeans introduced to certain areas allowed Muslims to travel freely in areas in which they had not operated before. Muslim migrant laborers who worked on plantations spread Islam, and new converts took their new faith back to their home areas. Hausa and Dyula traders moved into "stranger quarters" in towns and won many new adherents to the faith. By the end of the colonial period, costal cities such as Dakar, Freetown and Lagos had Muslim majority populations.

Muslims also took advantage of the fact that they were primarily Africans, not European, and thus were not identified with colonial rulers. They did not expect their converts to abandon their customs and cultures in the way that European Christian missionaries did.

Sufi ***turuq*** or brotherhoods were key agencies of conversion. The Qadiriyya, founded in the twelfth century C.E., was the oldest of the African brotherhoods. It expanded its base in North Africa to northern Nigeria, where it won over the Hausa ruling elite. In Senegal in the early twentieth century, *Shaykh* Ahmad Bamba (1850–1927) founded the Mourides brotherhood. The French exiled him on several occasions because they thought he was leading anti-European resistance. When they allowed him to return in 1912 he had built up a devoted following. Bamba called on his followers to work with the colonial system. He instilled in the Mourides the belief that a disciplined work ethic was necessary for salvation. Mourides *shaykhs* encouraged their disciples to contribute their labor on Mourides farms on the edge of the desert that produced peanuts as a cash crop. The proceeds were dedicated to the spread of Mourides influence. The landless and unemployed were especially drawn to these farms. Between 1912 and 1960 the membership of the order swelled from 60,000 to 400,000.

In eastern Africa, Islam had long been restricted to the Swahili-speaking coast. However, colonial rule

---

turuq—Brotherhoods that are part of Sufism. Each brotherhood has its own separate identity based on initiation ceremonies, practices, and symbolism.

expanded trading networks into the interior. Africans migrating to the coastal areas came into contact with Islam for the first time. Those who converted spread Islam back to their home areas. Muslim traders also expanded their faith by taking advantage of their commercial contacts to develop a communication network that transcended boundaries. Also influential were brotherhoods such as the Shadhiliya and the Qadiriyya. They utilized the Swahili language that was spoken over the region to their advantage.

In eastern Africa, Zanzibar remained a center of Islamic learning. In Tanganyika German officials relied on Muslim police and soldiers to maintain law and order and opened schools for Muslims to train them for the civil service and teaching. Because the German allied with the Ottomans in World War I, they favored Muslims. In Mozambique, however, Portuguese colonizers, who saw themselves on a crusade to spread Roman Catholicism, were hostile to the Islamic presence on the coast. Despite this persecution, Islam maintained a strong following. After the Chilembwe uprising in Nyasaland, British officials worked cooperatively with Muslim chiefs who were perceived as stable leaders. In Uganda, however, where Protestants and Catholics had strong mission operations, British officials did not encourage Islam.

"New Britains": Kenya and Rhodesia

The few Europeans who lived in French and British colonies in Africa were primarily traders, missionaries, and colonial officials who did not think of themselves as permanent settlers. Such was not the case in the British colonies of Kenya and Southern Rhodesia, where European settlers found hospitable climates and staked out extensive land claims at the expense of African societies.

Though located on the equator, a section of central Kenya is a highland area which, at 6000 to 9000 feet above sea level, has a temperate climate that Europeans could tolerate. After conquering African peoples in the region, the British government designated the highlands for white ownership only and encouraged Englishmen and white South Africans to set up farms. The first arrived in 1903; although their numbers were small, they had tremendous influence over British administrators in Nairobi, the capital city. Africans, mostly Kikuyu, who had once tilled the highlands, were classed as squatters and were allowed to farm the land as long as they were needed for labor. In the 1930s thousands of Kikuyu squatters were expelled from white farms and forced to eke out a living in barren reserves or on the streets of Nairobi. This treatment set the stage for a major uprising after World War II.

White settlers in Rhodesia followed a similar path. After conquering Shona and Ndebele kingdoms in several wars in the 1890s, the British South Africa Company turned its attention from a quixotic search for gold to promoting agriculture. White settlers seized additional land from Africans and eventually claimed about half of the country's best land as their own. They were already a potent political force when in 1923 the BSAC gave up administrative control of the colony to the British government. That same year the British gave the largely English settlers a choice of whether they wanted to be incorporated in the Union of South Africa or become a self-governing colony. They chose the latter.

In theory, the British retained certain powers protecting the rights of the African majority. However, as the Rhodesian parliament passed one discriminatory measure after another based on South African laws, the British did not intervene. The Land Apportionment Act of 1930 divided land into black and white areas. Roads, railways, and towns were placed in the white areas; the blacks, in rural reserves, were expected to pay taxes by selling their labor to white employers. Maize and tobacco farming in white areas became profitable through generous price supports, while black farmers were forced to sell their crops at lower prices.

White Exploitation in the Union of South Africa

At the conclusion of the Anglo-Boer war in May 1902, the British could have dictated a settlement to the Afrikaners and extended full political rights to blacks, but they deferred the issue until self-government was extended to the former Afrikaner republics. Milner, the British high commissioner, set about reconstructing the devastated former Afrikaner republics, but he scored few successes. His plan for English speakers to outnumber Afrikaners failed because he could not entice many British immigrants to take up farming in South Africa, and his attempt to Anglicize Afrikaners by setting up English-language schools failed when Afrikaners formed their own independent schools.

Once Milner left South Africa in 1905 following a Liberal party electoral victory in Britain, British officials came to a political understanding with Afrikaner leaders and extended self-government to the former Afrikaner republics, the Orange Free State and the Transvaal, in 1907. The British then moved to unite their four colonies and empowered 30 Afrikaner and English delegates to draft a constitution. Only eight years after a ruinous war, the Union of South Africa became a self-governing dominion in the British Commonwealth.

The first three prime ministers of South Africa were Afrikaners who had led the war against the British. Louis Botha (1863–1919) and Jan Smuts (1870–1950) preached reconciliation with the British, while J. B. M. Hertzog (1866–1942) promoted a separate Afrikaner nationalism. Even though the Afrikaners controlled the government and gained official recognition of their language, Afrikaans, in 1925, English speakers controlled the civil service and dominated the business sector. Despite the deep rift between Britons and Afrikaners, however, they were prepared to work together to preserve and entrench white domination over South Africa's black majority.

The all-white Parliament passed laws protecting whites and hindering the ability of Africans to advance. With the exception of a small number of African and mixed-race males in the Cape Province who could vote in elections, most blacks were excluded from any role in government. In 1936 Prime Minister Hertzog's government struck Cape Africans from the voters' roll. A 1913 law froze the land division between whites and blacks, making it extremely difficult for blacks to buy white land and vice versa. Africans, who comprised over 70 percent of the population, were restricted to reserves that made up about 7 percent of the country. Another 6 percent was later added to the reserves.

Black South African mine workers were required to live in compounds or barracks that they shared with dozens of other miners. They slept on concrete slabs stacked around the room.

In contrast, the government addressed the plight of the numerous unskilled and uneducated whites that lived at or below subsistence level. Ninety percent of these "poor whites" were Afrikaners who, unable to compete on equal terms with blacks, had little choice but to work for pathetically low wages. The government introduced a "civilized labor" policy in the 1920s providing many poor whites with jobs on the railroads, with the post office, and in low-level civil service positions. For every white that won a job, a black had to lose one. The government also reserved supervisory and skilled jobs in the mining industry for whites only. The color bar was extended to most industries and resulted in huge wage disparities. The average wage for Europeans was just under $4 a day, while that for Africans was a little over $3 a week.

THE OTTOMAN EMPIRE REFASHIONED

- *In the nineteenth century what were the pressures for change inside and outside the Ottoman Empire?*

At the beginning of the nineteenth century, the Middle East consisted primarily of two large and loosely structured empires, the Qajar Empire in Persia and the Ottoman Empire, which included Anatolia, the Arab provinces, and most of North Africa. The Ottoman Empire stretched from the Balkans to Sudan and from the **Maghrib** to Arabia, and the Ottoman sultan could still claim a certain preeminence in the Islamic world based on his position as Protector of the Holy Cities. For centuries the Islamic world had extended well beyond the Middle Eastern heartlands. United by their worship of one god, devotion to the Prophet Muhammad, and adherence to the Sharia Islamic law, Muslims looked to Mecca as the sacred site of pilgrimage. Every year the number of believers traveling to Mecca grew, and by 1900 it is estimated that more than 50,000 Indians and 20,000 Malays were making the **hajj** each year. But the Islamic world had been politically divided since the early centuries of Islam, and Muslim states from Southeast Asia to Morocco pursued their own political agendas with little or no reference to the sovereign who controlled the Islamic heartlands.

Maghrib—From an Arabic word meaning "time or place of the sunset." It refers to the western part of North Africa or the present-day countries of Algeria and Morocco.

hajj—A pilgrimage to the holy city of Mecca that every Muslim is expected to make at least once in their lifetime. The hajj is the fifth pillar of Islam.

Challenges to Ottoman Power

In the sixteenth century, the Ottoman administration had been a model of effectiveness. The Ottoman navy dominated the eastern Mediterranean, and Ottoman armies continued to expand the territories of the sultan. The balance of trade was markedly in favor of Asia, with European merchants sending precious coin to procure the goods they wanted from the Ottoman Empire, Persia, and South and Southeast Asia. By the eighteenth century, however, that balance of military and economic power had begun to shift in favor of Europe, where some states were benefiting from industrialization and new military technologies. In this era the Ottoman Empire faced the challenges of decentralizing forces within and vigorous pressure from rivals beyond its boundaries.

Internally, central government power had been weakened by the increasing autonomy of regional governors *(ayan)* in the provinces. These notables mobilized their own provincial forces and resisted or evaded the authority of the central government in Istanbul. They gathered bands of men armed as irregular soldiers in Ottoman military campaigns to serve as their own personal armies. In North Africa the local lords had long enjoyed relative autonomy, and by the end of the eighteenth century, the Ottomans had little real power in the Maghrib.

The ranks of the janissary corps, the premier Ottoman fighting force, had also become grossly inflated. Thousands possessed papers which entitled them to collect military pay and rations but performed no military service; others were forced to take second jobs because inflation had drastically reduced the value of their pay. So the janissaries, once the front line of Ottoman defense, became a source of rebellion and a drain on the government treasury.

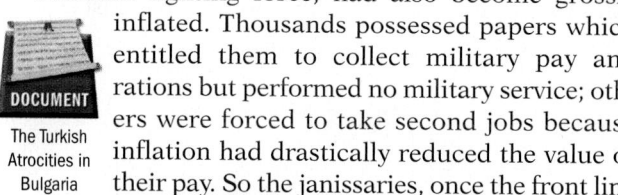

DOCUMENT
The Turkish Atrocities in Bulgaria

Indeed, the most evident signs of Ottoman weakness were military. The Russians defeated the Ottoman armies, and the empire had to sign the humiliating treaty of Küchük Kaynarca in 1774. Not only did the empire lose territory, but the Russians demanded the right to intervene in the affairs of the Orthodox Christian community in the empire. This concession for the first time granted a foreign state the power to meddle directly in Ottoman affairs. In 1798 Napoleon invaded Ottoman Egypt, and although his stay there was short, his easy victory illustrated the tenuousness of Ottoman control over the North African provinces.

The capitulations, treaties that granted special trade privileges to European states, also weakened both Ottoman and Qajar empires. In the sixteenth century the Ottoman and Persian sovereigns had dictated the terms of foreign trade. But as their economies weakened, they granted more and more extensive privileges to European traders, which gave states like Britain and France increasing leverage in commercial affairs. These concessions harmed the businesses of local Ottoman traders who could not compete. As the nineteenth century progressed, European states would extend their influence by granting large loans to Middle Eastern rulers.

Ottoman Reform

To counter these challenges, Sultan Selim III (1789–1806) launched a series of reforms, focusing on the military. He created a new infantry corps composed of Turkish peasants. Selim also opened channels of communication with the European capitals by setting up embassies in London, Paris, Berlin, and Vienna. The janissaries, however, were hostile to Selim's reforms and unwilling to relinquish their centuries-long position of prominence. They deposed the sultan. Still, Selim's reign marks the start of an era of Ottoman reform that would last into the early twentieth century (see Chapter 20).

A much more successful reformer was Sultan Mahmud II (1808–1839). Mahmud restored central authority in the provinces to some degree and cleared the way for military reform by destroying the janissary corps after it revolted in 1826. He then established a new army, modeled on successful European armies and trained by Prussian and French officers. Mahmud also reformed professional education by opening medical and military schools. The language of instruction was French; this, of course, gave an advantage to a new class of young men who were educated in French. Beyond the military sphere, Mahmud's reforms included a restructuring of the bureaucracy, the launching of an official newspaper, and the opening of a translation bureau.

Men trained in the new professional schools and translation bureau would form a new nineteenth-

The Era of Ottoman Reform

1808–1839	Reign of Ottoman reformer Mahmud II
1839–1876	*Tanzimat,* Ottoman reform period
1876	First constitutional revolution
1876–1909	Reign of Sultan Abdülhamid II
1908	Young Turk Revolution reinstates Ottoman constitution

century elite, sometimes called the "French knowers." Able to deal with the European powers on their own terms, these men would both challenge and reform the old Ottoman institutional order. Whereas French-style uniforms were the symbol of the new military, the frock coat was a symbol of the Europeanization of the civil bureaucracy. Mahmud II's reforms were not designed to cast off Ottoman culture and ideology but rather to create systems that would enable the empire to compete with Europe and recoup its status as a world power. Some people resented these changes, preferring the status quo; others saw the new schools and new positions as an opportunity for upward mobility that had been denied them under the old system of elites.

Challenging Ottoman Sovereignty in Europe

Ottoman territorial integrity was challenged in the nineteenth century by a series of separatist movements in the Balkans. The rise of nationalism in Europe and Great Power meddling in Ottoman affairs were both factors in the emergence and evolution of these movements. The Serbs rose in revolt in 1804, followed by the Greeks in 1821, the Romanians in the 1850s, and the Bulgarians in the 1870s.

The Serbs achieved autonomy in 1830 after a long struggle. The Greek Revolt, however, more directly engaged the energies of the Great Powers, who intervened to ensure its success. The Ottomans had crushed the Greek insurrection in its early stages. But Britain, Russia, and France all viewed the rebellion as a focal point in what came to be called the "Eastern Question"—whether the Ottoman Empire would be dismembered, and if so, who would get what (see Chapter 26).

The Greek Revolt captured the imaginations of European intellectuals who were enamored of the Greek classical tradition and saw the revolt as a romantic instance of the forces of freedom triumphing over the forces of despotism. Although that romanticism had little to do with the ground-level realities of the revolt, it did fuel support for the Greeks in the cities of western Europe. Educated Europeans saw themselves as inheritors of the classical Greek traditions and ideals of liberty; conversely, they portrayed the Ottomans as barbarians. In the end a predominantly British fleet sank the Ottoman navy at Navarino in 1827, and Britain, Russia, and France engineered a treaty to establish an independent Greece.

Russia and Britain would encounter each other again over Ottoman territory, but on opposite sides, in the Crimean War (1854–1856). Britain saved Istanbul from Russian conquest, thereby preserving the balance of power. But by the end of the nineteenth century, Europeans were referring to the empire as the "sick man of Europe," and the Ottomans had lost con-

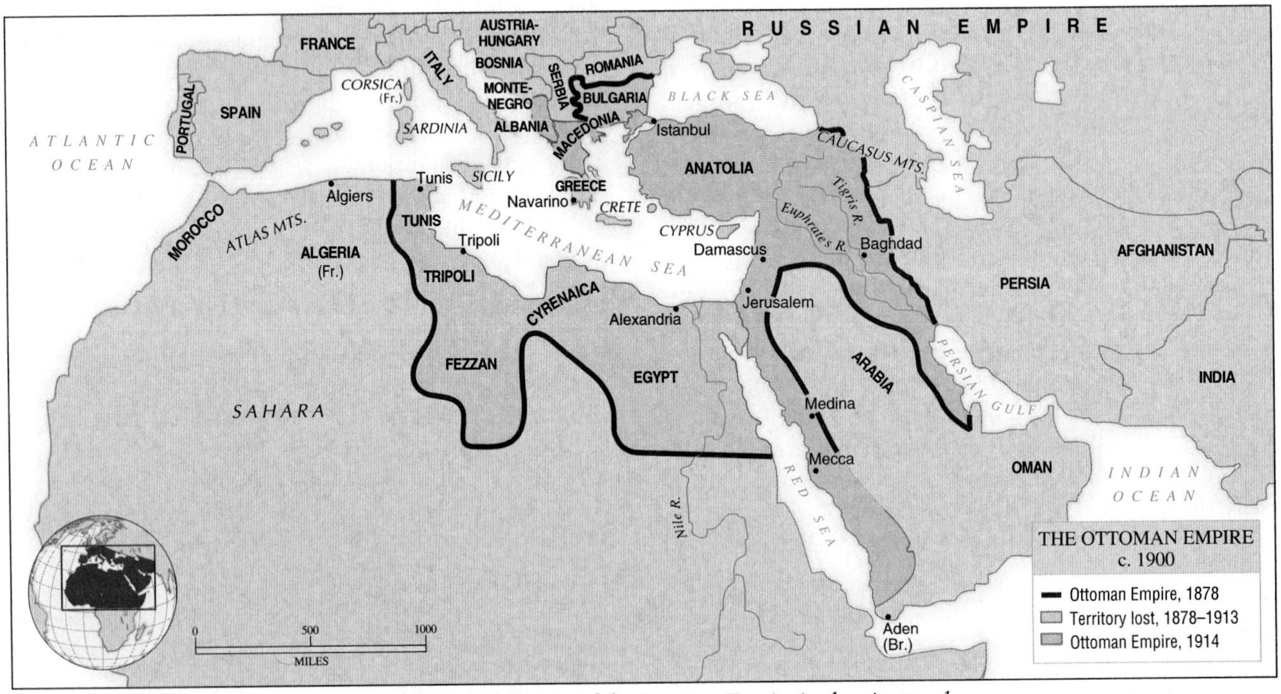

Military defeats and nationalist rebellions diminished the size of the Ottoman Empire in the nineteenth century. However, it still controlled a significant amount of territory in 1914 when the region was engulfed in the conflicts of World War I.

Eugène Delacroix, Massacre at Chios *(1824). European liberals and Romantics such as Delacroix supported the Greeks in their struggle for independence from the Turks, whom they depicted as cruel oppressors.*

trol over most of their Balkan provinces. The nation states carved out of the Balkans have had a complicated history since that time. Borders have been drawn and redrawn (such as those of Yugoslavia in the twentieth century) and ethnic and religious tensions have been exacerbated, as they were in Africa and India for example, by the demands of nations contending for independence.

Egypt and the Rule of Muhammad Ali

Egypt had been a province of the Ottoman Empire since its conquest by Sultan Selim the Grim in 1517. By the late eighteenth century, however, Ottoman rule was little more than nominal as Egypt was controlled in fact by local leaders, the heads of Mamluk households. In the nineteenth century Egypt was conclusively detached from Ottoman rule, first by a highly successful Ottoman military commander named Muhammad Ali and then by the British, who seized Egypt as a strategic link to their colonial empire in India.

Muhammad Ali came to power in Egypt in the aftermath of Napoleon's invasion. The French occupation of Egypt was short-lived, although it served to stimulate European interest in Egyptian civilization. When a joint British-Ottoman expedition arrived in Egypt in 1801 to end the French occupation, Muhammad Ali was one of the Ottoman commanders. He established himself as the dominant military leader, filling the power vacuum left by the French departure.

DOCUMENT
A British View of Egyptian Agriculture, 1840

Muhammad Ali destroyed the Mamluks (as Mahmud II had destroyed the janissaries), organized his military along European lines, and built up a new, conscripted peasant army. This was a radical change for the rural peoples since, traditionally, peasants had not been employed in the military. Muhammad Ali founded new professional schools and a government printing press, reorganized the agricultural and taxation systems of Egypt, sent men to study in France, and launched an ambitious program of industrialization. He also undermined the power of the religious establishment, the *ulama*. Unlike religious leaders (such as the Mahdi) elsewhere in Africa, the *ulama* in Egypt (and in the Ottoman Empire in general) were generally subordinated to the state and did not lead *jihads* or religious revolts.

Muhammad Ali's reforms were more extensive than those of Sultan Mahmud II, but these two contemporaries were both major symbols of Middle Eastern reform. Once Muhammad Ali consolidated his power, he moved to challenge the Ottoman state directly. Initially, he had defended Ottoman interests by defeating the **Wahhabis** (wah-HAH-beez), a puritanical movement, and helping put down the Greek Revolt. But in 1831 he sent his son Ibrahim to invade Syria and Anatolia; Ibrahim marched his armies to within 150 miles of Istanbul.

Here again, Russia, Britain, and France intervened to preserve the Ottoman Empire. Muhammad

Wahhabis—A puritanical movement founded in Arabia by Muhammad ibn Abd al-Wahhab during the 1750s that aimed to cleanse Sunni Islam of innovations like Sufism.

Ali ultimately established an autonomous dynastic state in Egypt where his descendants occupied the throne until the 1950s. His career illustrates the weakness of the Ottoman Empire and its tenuous control over its more distant provinces. European states capitalized on the disruptions caused by Muhammad Ali to negotiate more advantageous commercial agreements with the beleaguered Ottoman sultan, thus undermining the economic foundations of the empire even further.

The Suez Canal

Muhammad Ali's successors pursued parts of his reform programs, with little military or economic success. Egypt benefited from the American Civil War when Egyptian cotton was used to replace the South's cotton exports, which were cut off when the Union blockaded southern ports. But foreign loans and the uncontrolled spending of its rulers left Egypt bankrupt by the 1870s.

The idea of a canal linking the Mediterranean to the Red Sea was not new. The Mamluks, rulers of medieval Egypt, had planned such a canal but lacked the technology to accomplish it. In 1854 the Egyptian ruler, Said, granted a Frenchman, Ferdinand de Lesseps, a concession to build a canal. De Lesseps was only one among many European entrepreneurs and concessionaires pouring into Egypt at this time to take advantage of building opportunities and commercial privileges. Some Middle Eastern people gained employment from these concessionaires but others lost out as more advanced European transport and communication technologies (e.g., the telegraph, steamship, and railroads) began to replace more traditional modes and those who provided them. The building and completion of the canal itself radically disrupted patterns of labor as peasants were forcibly seized from their villages and forced to provide unpaid labor digging the canal. Families were torn apart, women left their farm plots to follow and care for their drafted husbands, and thousands died in the course of the digging.

The Suez Canal was completed in 1869 during the reign of Khedive Ismail (1863–1879). Ismail was committed to the European-style transformation of his realm. But his lavish spending, particularly on his opening ceremonies for the canal, threw Egypt into a financial crisis. The opening ceremonies were a world event. Ismail commissioned the opera *Aïda* (which was not completed in time) and built special pavilions to house visiting dignitaries. His extravagance dazzled even the jaded aristocrats of Europe. The empress

The opening of the Suez Canal in 1869 was an international event attended by numerous heads of state. Lavish spending for this event helped bankrupt Egypt.

Eugénie of France, a notorious clothes horse, was said to have taken 250 dresses with her to the affair.

Plagued by financial troubles, Ismail sold Egypt's shares in the canal to Britain for 4 million pounds sterling in 1875. The stock shares were snapped up by Disraeli, the astute prime minister of Great Britain, while the French dithered over whether to buy them. This sale gave Britain virtual control of this essential water link to its South Asian empire. The following year (the same year the Ottoman Empire defaulted on its loans), Egypt was unable to pay the interest on its foreign loans. Britain and France then forced Egypt to accept European control over its debts and hence its economy.

This assertion of foreign control paved the way for a British invasion of Egypt. The British and French forced Ismail to abdicate in 1879; in 1881 an army officer named Colonel Urabi, of peasant origins, led a military and populist revolt against foreign control in Egypt. He aimed to limit the power of the khedive and to form a national assembly. There was antiforeign rioting in Alexandria, where many Europeans lost their lives. The British, claiming they were acting in the best interests of the Egyptian people, then shelled Alexandria and took Cairo in 1882. Although their occupation was supposedly temporary, they remained until the Egyptian Revolt of 1952 and kept control of the Suez Canal until 1956. Thus, as elsewhere in Africa, the European imperial states used a combination of economic incentive, military force, and treachery to seize control of African empires.

Egypt was part of the Ottoman Empire for more than 350 years. Although the British conquered Egypt in 1882, the Ottomans still thought of it as their own territory. This Ottoman cartoon, published in Istanbul in 1908, expresses bonds of brotherhood between the Ottoman constitutionalist and the Young Egyptian nationalists who were trying to throw off British imperial rule. As the giant symbol of England leans lazily against the pyramids, the tiny Egyptians do not seem to have much of a chance.

Lord Cromer and the Dinshaway Incident

When the British conquered Egypt, they appointed Sir Evelyn Baring, later named Lord Cromer, to reorganize Egyptian finances, eliminate corruption, improve the cotton industry, and oversee the country's affairs from 1883 to 1907. Cromer was an able administrator who stabilized the Egyptian economy, but his harsh policies and contempt for the Egyptian people earned him the hatred of many and helped galvanize the Egyptian nationalist movement.

Those sentiments are symbolized by an episode in 1906 that came to be called the Dinshaway Incident. The affair began simply with British officers on a pigeon shoot in the countryside. The officers, heedless of the fact that Egyptian villagers kept pigeons for food, pursued their hunt and wounded a villager in Dinshaway, in the Nile delta. In the ensuing scuffle, two officers were wounded, and one subsequently died.

What made this episode famous was the British response. Determined to make an example of Dinshaway, the British punished the whole village. They tried dozens of villagers and publicly hanged four. This incident provoked anger throughout Egypt, prompted the penning of patriotic songs, and gave force to the nationalist movement. The Dinshaway Incident showed that the people in the Middle East, and not just the elites, could be mobilized to protect their own economic security and to resist the inroads of European states.

North Africa West of Egypt

The appellation "North Africa" suggests a radical separation between Mediterranean and sub-Saharan Africa. But these two areas have long been linked by networks of trade. North Africa is grouped here with the Middle East because it was Islamized during the early Arab conquests and because it was loosely controlled by the Ottoman Empire during the premodern era. West of Egypt, North Africa contained the state of Morocco, ruled by the Filali dynasty since 1631, and three coastal states based on Tunis, Algiers, and Tripoli that were established under Ottoman rule. These latter three dominated the western Mediterranean for three centuries, remaining nominally under Ottoman control. Semi-autonomous governors, however, exercised the real power in the coastal states, attempting, with limited success, to subordinate tribal leaders in their hinterlands.

Algiers, Tripoli, and, to a lesser extent, Tunis were corsairing states that collected revenues from pirate activity off their coasts. In the eighteenth century they benefited from treaties with various European states that were willing to pay tribute and gifts in exchange for security for their merchant shipping. That shipping was part of a vast web of seaborne trade that reached from Southeast Asia and China to the American colonies.

When the American colonies gained their independence from Britain, they, too, negotiated treaties with these "Barbary States" in order to protect the lucrative American trade with North Africa. Sidi Muhammad (1757–1790) of Morocco granted the fledgling United States its first official trading privileges in 1786. The U.S. Congress authorized $40,000 for a treaty and $25,000 annual tribute for Algiers in 1790 and, shortly thereafter, provided for the building of a navy to gain leverage against the corsair state.

In the nineteenth century, however, European powers began to look to North Africa as an area ripe for conquest. Like Egypt, the rest of North Africa experienced European economic penetration before it suffered actual invasion. That penetration took the form of capitulations, reflecting commercial concessions granted to European states by the Ottomans and the exploitation of North Africa as a market for European goods.

The first target was Algiers. In the 1820s the ruler of Algiers (called the *Dey*) sent ships to aid the Ottomans in putting down the Greek Revolt; he also dealt with internal revolt as Algiers's Berber tribesmen fought against his janissary troops. Meanwhile, the French were enmeshed in conflicts with the Dey over fishing rights, piracy, and a debt the French owed Algiers.

In 1827, using the pretext that the Dey had insulted the French consul by publicly hitting him with a fly whisk, France blockaded Algiers. Pursuing France's imperialist agenda, King Charles X then invaded Algiers in 1830. He sent a large army of occupation, but only after 17 years of fierce resistance could Algeria be directly incorporated as an integral part of the French state. (Over 100 years later, the Algerians would fight just as long and fiercely to free themselves from French rule.)

Algiers then became a base for France to extend its influence in North Africa. Tunis remained singularly autonomous of Ottoman rule and in 1861 established its own constitution. An insurrection, which united tribal and urban elements in 1864, led to the bankrupting of Tunis in 1869. Its French, Italian, and British creditors then gained control of the Tunisian economy. Italy coveted the coastal state with its rich agricultural hinterland, but the French stayed those ambitions by invading in 1881 and making it a protectorate. After that time, much of the country's wealth was siphoned off into French coffers, and most of the population lived in desperate poverty.

From the 1840s to the end of the century, French interests also dominated in Morocco. But Germany was emerging as a significant power in the late nineteenth century and cast its eye on African territory as well, including Morocco. France, however, used its established bases in North Africa and its alliance with the British to win this particular standoff. They promised the Germans territory elsewhere in Africa and took over Morocco in 1912. The French left the Moroccan dynasty in place but did not relinquish their hold on the country until 1956.

The Italians were latecomers in the scramble for Africa. Frustrated by the Ethiopians in their ambitions for northeastern Africa, they decided to seize a piece of the North African pie. Capitalizing on the disruptions caused by the Ottoman constitutional revolution, they declared war on the Ottoman Empire in 1911 and invaded the area around Tripoli, annexing it in the face of a failed Ottoman defense. The Sanusi order of sufis, which had great influence in the region, vigorously resisted Italian (and French) expansionism. This order, established in the area in 1843, worked as both an Islamic reform movement and a political force. It had enormous support among the people both in the cities and in the rural areas. The order would later gain power in the new state of Libya when the colonial powers withdrew. For the time, however, the early twentieth century saw North Africa, like sub-Saharan Africa, divided among the European imperial powers and incorporated into European empires.

Young Ottomans and Constitutional Reform

The challenges to Ottoman sovereignty, combined with the prospect of a newly emerging "modern" world order, prompted a period of reform known as the ***Tanzimat*** ("reorganization") from 1839 to 1876. New professional schools were opened in the empire, the class of "French knowers" expanded, and a more modern and secular civil bureaucracy was established. The power of the *ulama* was diminished by the legal and

The Decline of the Ottoman Empire

Tanzimat—A period of reform (1839–1876) in the Ottoman Empire in which modern schools were opened and the influence of Muslim clerics was curtailed.

Document A Middle Eastern Vision of the West

Middle Easterners traveled to Europe for a variety of reasons in the nineteenth century. Some went for pleasure or educational purposes; others went for medical treatments or business. As European states gained military advantages over Middle Eastern states, more Middle Eastern rulers sent diplomats to gather information on the newly prominent powers. In 1844 France bombarded Moroccan ports and forced a treaty on the Moroccan sultan, Mulay Abd ar-Rahman. The following year, interested in studying the sources of French power, Morocco sent an embassy to France. One of its members was the scholar Muhammad as-Saffar, who later recorded his impressions of French society. As a distinguished visitor, as-Saffar tended to travel in elite circles, and he certainly did not get to see all aspects of French life. But he was intensely interested in French society—from its business practices to its roads, its printing presses, and even its eating habits. Muhammad as-Saffar expressed admiration for French efficiency and military organization, recommending that his ruler imitate these traits in order to ensure Morocco's survival. He also enjoyed the spectacle of men and women dancing together at balls, although he found the French arrogant and uncharitable and their long, drawn-out dinners annoying. All in all, he was an astute observer of French culture, as these excerpts show.

The people of Paris, men and women alike, are tireless in their pursuit of wealth. They are never idle or lazy. The women are like the men in that regard, or perhaps even more so. . . . Even though they have all kinds of amusements and spectacles of the most marvelous kinds, they are not distracted from their work. . . . Nor do they excuse someone for being poor, for indeed death is easier for them than poverty, and the poor man there is seen as vile and contemptible.

Another of their characteristics is a hot-tempered and stubborn arrogance, and they challenge each other to a duel at the slightest provocation. If one of them slanders or insults another, the challenged one has no choice but to respond, lest he be branded a despicable coward for the rest of his life. Then they decide the conditions of the combat—what weapons they will fight with, how it will be done, and the place—and no one in authority interferes with them.

You should know that among the customs of these people is that they sit only in chairs and they know nothing of sitting directly on the floor. . . . Another of their customs is that they do not touch food with their hands, nor do they gather around a single platter. . . . Two people may share one pitcher but each has his own glass from which no one else may drink, for they regard that as the height of uncleanliness. . . . At the end of every course, the servant removes the dishes and other things, and brings fresh ones. The number of dishes piles up, because they change them at every course and no dish is ever eaten from twice. This is due to their excessive concern for cleanliness. . . . [T]hey linger at table for more than two hours, because it is their custom to stretch out the talk during the meal so they can overindulge in food. The Arabs say that perfect hospitality is friendliness at first sight and leisurely talk with one's table companions. But we detested the arrival of mealtimes because of the endless waiting, nor did we understand their conversation. Moreover, much of the food did not agree with us, and we got tired and irritated with the long sitting and waiting.

[At dinner as-Saffar noted the free mingling of the sexes and commented on the women's dress.] Their clothing covered their breasts, which were hidden from view, but the rest of their bosom, face and neck were bare and exposed. They cover their shoulders and upper arms in part with filmy, closefitting sleeves that do not reach the elbow. They bind their waists beneath their dresses with tight girdles which give them a very narrow middle. It is said they are trained into this [shape] from earliest childhood by means of a special mold. . . . In the lower part they drape their clothing in such a way that the backside is greatly exaggerated, but perhaps this is due to something they put underneath [bustles]. . . .

Questions to Consider

1. Why do you think as-Saffar commented on French eating habits? What do you think eating habits and dress styles reveal about a people and their culture?
2. What aspects of a diplomat's life might be enjoyable? What aspects might be unpleasant?

From *Disorienting Encounters: Travels of a Moroccan Scholar in France in 1845–1856*, ed. and trans. Susan G. Miller (Berkeley: University of California Press, 1992).

educational reforms. As new, more secular schools opened, the *ulama* lost their monopoly on education. The government also tried to ward off separatist sentiments by emphasizing the ideology of Ottomanism, the notion that all Ottoman subjects were equal and should be committed to the preservation of the empire, regardless of ethnicity or religion. Of course, not everyone accepted this ideology, but it did hold sway in the government until the end of the empire.

DOCUMENT Reform of the State as an Imperial Project

Out of the reforms of the *Tanzimat* emerged a new civil and military elite, some of whom favored elements of European culture and more democratic forms of government. Among them, a group of intellectuals and bureaucrats, sometimes called the *Young Ottomans,* revitalized Ottoman literature and called for a new synthesis that would combine the best elements of traditional Islamic culture with European ideas and technology. These reformers debated issues such as constitutional freedoms, changing the Ottoman calendar and clocks to European time schemes, "modern" schools, and the "woman question," the rights and education of the "modern" woman.

The reformers also considered the question of slavery. Britain had been trying to force the Ottoman Empire to end the slave trade for some time, but the Young Ottomans tended to conclude that slavery in Muslim countries was fundamentally different from that found in European colonies and in the Americas with the Atlantic slave trade. Ottoman slavery included the elite *kul* system and was primarily domestic rather than agricultural. It was characterized by a predominance of female slaves (rather than the Atlantic slave trade's 2:1 male to female ratio), the use of both white and black slaves, and the provisions of Islamic law which stated that the children of a slave female and her master were free and entitled to inherit.

In 1876 a group of Ottoman reform-minded elites spearheaded a drive to depose Sultan Abdülaziz and install Western-style constitutional government in the Ottoman Empire. They did not wish to eliminate the monarchy, and the new constitution they proposed left considerable power in the hands of the sultan. But they did want an elected assembly, freedom of the press, and equality for all Ottomans. The

One type of European penetration into the Ottoman Empire was the opening of textile factories in western Anatolia. The young girls and women who worked in these factories often made relatively good wages, but their work in factories raised moral issues about "unsupervised" women, much as it did in the factories of Europe. These young women workers in a silk-thread factory pose for the camera in 1878.

Document Halide Edib: Education, Generation, and Class in the Late Ottoman Empire

Halide Edib, born into an elite family in Istanbul in 1883, was a famous Turkish author and nationalist leader. Her father was a progressive who believed women should be educated. Thus Halide was schooled in Turkish, English, and French by tutors. She later became one of the first graduates of the new American College for Girls and wrote a famous novel on the problems of the educated woman. Married at a young age to a prominent scholar many years her senior, she divorced him in 1910 when he decided to take a second wife. Afterward, Edib became a pioneer educator, fought along with her second husband in the War of Turkish Liberation after World War I, and became a prominent international lecturer. She was a member of the Turkish parliament from 1950–1954. Halide Edib's memoirs reflect the era of transformation during which she came of age. Ottoman society during the rule of the Young Turks was refashioning itself and the "Woman Question" was a topic of considerable debate. Here she reflects (for 1913–1914) on the differences between the generations and on a conflict of class and dress that arose while she was pursuing her work in education.

[After her divorce Halide took a house in Istanbul where she lived with her two sons and her beloved grandmother, an elderly woman of the elite class.] Granny was living with me as usual, but I had lost the old sense of nearness to her for the moment. I was constantly out for lessons and lectures; the [Turkish nationalist] club demanded much of my time and my circle of friends had a great deal happen to it. My writing I had to do after ten o'clock at night when the noisy little house slept and left me quiet in my room. Granny also enjoyed those quiet hours; she came to me for talks then. She was much shocked by the new women. Their talk, their walk, their dress, and their general aspect hurt her. She felt lonely, like a stranger in a world where she felt she had stayed too long, like a visitor who has outstayed his welcome; it was as if the newly arrived guests had taken all the room and they looked ever so different from her. She suffered because they shook their arms when they walked, looked into men's eyes, had loud voices, and smoked in public; above all they did not iron their clothes as she did every morning.

[One afternoon Halide took a short cut through a poor section of town, Arasta Street, on the way home from the school where she taught.]

I had on the fashionable [tight] black charshaf [long overgarment] and veil of my class. . . . [U]p and down the street walked a series of little girls. . . . [T]hey had print dresses of the poorest sort, and bare feet shod with wooden clogs which they dragged painfully, but they had a saucy and aggressive way of walking in spite of this impediment. One had a dirty baby in her arms, half her own size, and the baby's nose was running all the time. Another had a broken silk umbrella, which must have had a prosperous past and was evidently stolen property. All lifted their dresses in mock imitation of the chic women of the city; all strutted in a make-believe promenade of great ladies. I must admit they made me ashamedly conscious of how ridiculous our class could be. . . . "Oh, oh, look at her!" shouted the girl with the umbrella—there was neither rain nor sunshine. "On her head she has a cauldron, a silk shawl around her belly has she. She has a well-ring around her throat and wrists [white collar and cuffs] and her shoes are bath clogs [high heels]." A unanimous shout of laughter, accompanied by savage and significant movements, inimitable imitations but openly hostile to me, greeted her speech. . . . I would have given anything to throw off the offending garments, which displayed my class, at whose expense they were laughing, and join in their play. As it was, I was in real danger of being badly stoned, or of having my dress torn in a way that would have been worse than inconvenient. I immediately lifted my veil and joined in the conversation. The human face, especially the human eyes, have their force among their kind. A human being whose eyes and face are invisible is easier to attack. . . . I disarmed the little crowd for a moment. But the moment I made the slightest show of movement, they all bent down, picked up stones from the old pavement and got ready in case I should escape. [Edib was rescued by a shopkeeper who drove the children off. In the future she took care to let her dress "resemble that of the other women of the neighborhood" and not to cover her face when she traveled about Istanbul's poorer districts.]

Questions to Consider

1. Why did Halide's grandmother feel like a stranger in her own home?
2. What does the children's attack on Halide suggest about class and fashion?

From Halide Edib (Adivar), *Memoirs of Halide Edib* (New York: Century Co., n.d. (approximately 1926)), pp. 352, 362–365.

constitutionalists installed a new sultan, Abdülhamid II (1876–1909). But once Abdülhamid consolidated his power, in 1878, he abrogated the constitution and suspended the parliament.

Abdülhamid II and the Young Turk Revolution

Abdülhamid, paradoxically, was both a reformer and an autocrat. He continued many of the trends set in the *Tanzimat* era but controlled opposition through spies, censorship of the press, exile, and imprisonment.

The sultan faced severe challenges on all fronts. Russia declared war on the empire in 1877, resulting in the loss of more Ottoman territory and the creation of a large refugee population fleeing newly acquired Russian lands. Britain occupied Egypt and the island of Cyprus. Meanwhile, the empire, hampered by huge debts that it could not pay, was engaged in trying to redeem its Balkan territories.

Abdülhamid tried to control the centrifugal forces at work on the empire by enhancing central government control, bolstering the military, and establishing closer relations with an increasingly powerful Germany. Kaiser Wilhelm made two state visits, in 1889 and 1898, including a triumphant trip to Jerusalem during which the kaiser, a good politician, declared his friendship with the world's Muslims. Wilhelm's visit had an impact on the architecture of Jerusalem as well as on Ottoman-German relations. The gates of the old walled city of Jerusalem were too narrow to admit the kaiser's carriage. Rather than subject the German empress to the indignity of getting out of her carriage and walking through the gate, Abdülhamid had one of the gates knocked out and enlarged.

The sultan fostered the ideology of Pan-Islam to legitimize his reign and mobilize the support of the world's Muslims. His rhetoric of Islamic unity and his claim to be caliph decidedly did not strike a chord among all Muslims. But his project for a Hijaz railway to bring pilgrims from Damascus to the Holy City of Mecca did generate popular support for the sultan, and schoolchildren across the empire contributed their coins to help ensure its success.

Young Turks march in triumph after their successful coup and overthrow of Abdülhamid II and his government. Like the sultan, the Young Turks used photography to document the events and successes of their government.

The constitutional ideal in the Ottoman Empire, however, had not been lost, and opposition to the sultan mounted as Abdülhamid entered the third decade of his reign. Outside the empire, a group of exiles labored to promote the reinstatement of the constitution. Inside the empire revolutionary sentiments grew among students, bureaucrats, and some members of the military. In 1889 a group of students in the military-medical school founded a secret organization called the Committee for Union and Progress (CUP). This group was instrumental in mobilizing opposition to the regime.

In 1908 a military revolt became the catalyst for the second Ottoman constitutional revolution, known as the Young Turk Revolution. Support for the revolt spread rapidly, and the revolutionaries demanded that Abdülhamid reinstate the constitution. He acceded reluctantly to their demands; elections were held, censorship was suspended, and the **Young Turks** relegated the sultan to a position of secondary importance. Among the issues debated by the new assembly were rehabilitating the navy, reforming the police, and warding off attacks by the empire's neighbors.

DOCUMENT
The Young Turk Revolution, 1908

Young Turks—The name given to a group of army officers who advocated reforming the administration and governance of the Ottoman Empire.

Reactionaries launched a counterrevolution, in which Abdülhamid was implicated, in April 1909; but it was put down by the army. Abdülhamid was promptly deposed, and the CUP came to dominate the Ottoman constitutional regime. Although a new sultan was installed, the revolution marked the end of a centuries-long era of Ottoman monarchical power. The new government remained firmly in the hands of a civilian elite. Discontent simmered in the Arab provinces as the CUP continued the centralizing policies of Abdülhamid. But in general, the government and the remaining provinces stayed committed to the empire until World War I.

DOCUMENT
Political Opposition in the Ottoman Empire

As in other areas of the globe, the population of the empire was affected to varying degrees by this change of regime. The lives of peasants in the countryside were not radically altered, and many of those who held power under the old regime took positions in the new one. There was, however, a greater opportunity for political participation, more freedom of the press, a mass freeing of prisoners, and expanded opportunities for the lower classes to be educated and for women in the middle classes to have a greater role in public society.

PERSIA AND THE GREAT POWER STRUGGLE

- *How did religious and political groups respond to the intrusions of Britain and Russia into Persian Affairs?*

The Ottoman Revolution of 1908 was not the only upheaval to transform government and society in the Middle East. In fact, the same tensions among monarchy, foreign intervention, and Western-style constitutional reform that prompted the Young Turk Revolution also provoked a constitutional revolution in Persia two years earlier. Farther east, a series of Afghan rulers struggled to retain their autonomy while caught between the expansionist powers of British India and tsarist Russia.

Qajar Rule and the Tobacco Rebellion

Persia had been controlled by the Qajar dynasty since 1794. After a military defeat by the Russians in 1828, the Qajar shah was forced to concede extraterritorial rights to Russian merchants and give them special commercial privileges. Soon the British were demanding similar rights. As the nineteenth century progressed, the Qajars found themselves caught in a military and commercial squeeze play between Russia and Britain.

The Political Transformation of Persia

1848–1896	Reign of Nasir al-Din Shah
1891	Tobacco Rebellion and boycott
1896–1906	Reign of Muzaffar al-Din Shah
1905	Constitutional revolution begins
1907–1909	Reign of Muhammad Ali Shah
1909	Constitutionalists depose Muhammad Ali Shah

Foreign incursions reached a climax in the second half of the nineteenth century with the long reign of Nasir al-Din Shah (1848–1896). Unlike the Ottomans or Muhammad Ali, the Qajars remained dependent on the decentralized military power of tribal chiefs to defend Persia. Nasir al-Din implemented some military and educational reforms, but his government remained weak. To bolster his position, the shah negotiated loans, sold concessions to foreign investors, and brought in Russian military advisers to establish a Cossack brigade.

DOCUMENT
Religious Minorities in the Middle East

While Russian influence prevailed in the Qajar military, Britain moved to penetrate various spheres of the Persian economy. The British completed a telegraph line from London to Persia in 1870, symbolizing their increased interest in the area. In 1890 Nasir al-Din granted a British group exclusive rights over the entire Persian tobacco industry. This act alienated the merchant classes, who aligned themselves with the Shi'ite *ulama* to launch a rebellion against the shah and the tobacco concession.

The *ulama* in Persia had never been subordinated by the government to the same degree as in the Ottoman Empire. More like their counterparts in Africa, these religious leaders constituted a powerful force for opposition against the government and would be instrumental in the national revolutions of the twentieth century. During the tobacco rebellion of 1891, the *ulama* engineered a countrywide boycott of tobacco, and the shah was forced to cancel the tobacco concession. This boycott not only illustrated the mobilizing power of the Shi'ite clerics, but (like the Dinshaway Incident in Egypt) also pointed up popular discontent over the increasingly intrusive European presence.

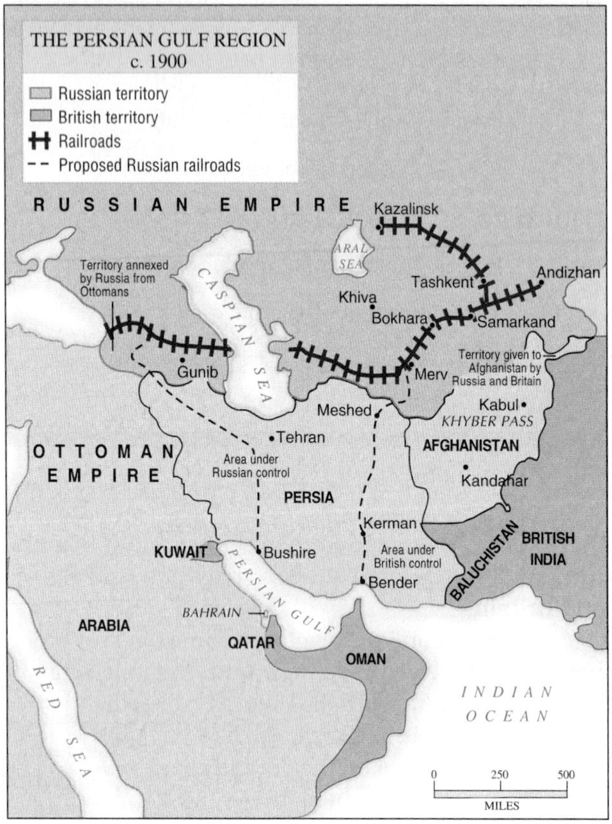

By the late nineteenth century Britain and Russia were both pressing hard to advance their interests in Persia and Afghanistan. Negotiating agreements with local rulers, Britain used the Persian Gulf region as a strategic base for its powerful fleets and as a link to its empire in India. Afghanistan became a contested buffer zone between British India and tsarist Russia.

The Persian Constitutional Revolution

By the beginning of the twentieth century, parts of northern Persia were under the control of the Russians. Tsarist forces trained the Persian army, put up telegraph lines, established a postal system, and developed trade. Some Persian workers crossed into Russia to work in the Caucasus oilfields. The Russian ministry of finance even set up a bank, the Discount and Loan Bank of Persia, with branches in many parts of the nation. This bank lent the Persian government 60 million rubles and provided 120 million rubles to Persian merchants to enable them to buy Russian goods.

The British in turn set up the Imperial Bank of Persia in the southeastern part of the country. In 1901 Muzaffar al-Din Shah (1896–1906) granted a British subject a concession for the oil rights to all of Persia except a few northern provinces. This grant would lead to British control over Persian oil that would continue into the second half of the century. Already crippled by his economic dependence on foreign powers, the shah made three costly trips to Europe during his short reign. These visits were criticized by the Persian public as extravagant. But the shah used these visits to solicit still more foreign loans from the British, the French, and the Russians.

DOCUMENT
The D'Arcy Oil Concession in Persia

Aiming to dominate the sea routes between Suez and their Indian empire, the British also gained footholds in the Persian Gulf region through treaties with a number of *shaykhs,* including the rulers of Muscat, Oman, Bahrain, and Kuwait (1899). In 1903 the British foreign secretary issued what has been called a British Monroe Doctrine over the area: "I say it without hesitation, we should regard the establishment of a naval base or a fortified port in the Persian Gulf by any other power as a very grave menace to British

The shah of Iran from 1896 to 1906, Muzaffer al-Din Shah's reign was noted for encouraging foreign investment and accepting foreign loans. His rule was challenged by popular movements promoting representative government and, after a revolt in 1905, he authorized a Constituent National Assembly.

interests, and we should certainly resist it by all means at our disposal."[10] Thus, the British won the imperialist struggle for control of the Persian Gulf just as France won the struggle for control of the coast of North Africa. Persia had no navy and could not, in any case, match British firepower.

Responding to foreign intervention in Persia, the shah's ineffectual rule, and the growing impetus for representative government, various factions within the nation mobilized a revolt beginning in 1905. This revolution began with a series of protests culminating in a general strike. Mass demonstrations, a strike by the *ulama,* and a massacre of protesters in Tehran by the Cossack brigade followed in 1906.

The shah succumbed to this pressure and authorized a Constituent National Assembly. Elections were held, and new newspapers flourished in the capital. But Muzaffar al-Din died in 1906, and his successor, Muhammad Ali Shah (1907–1909), soon attempted to overturn the constitutional regime, plunging Persia into civil war. The new shah's tyranny and his use of Russian troops against Persians prompted some members of the *ulama* to send a telegram to the Ottoman sultan, asking for his aid to protect fellow Muslims.

After a bitter struggle, the constitutional forces won and deposed Muhammad Ali Shah in July 1909, installing his 12-year-old son in his place. The nation has had a constitutional government ever since, although its power has often been compromised by the preservation of the monarchy.

The Persian constitutional revolution was watched closely in Istanbul and served as a prelude to the Ottoman Revolution, which followed quickly on its heels. The constitutionalists in both empires were inspired by the example of Japan, a modernizing power with a strong military. They were impressed that Japan was an Asian power (with a long history of traditional monarchy) that had successfully modernized and decisively beaten a European power, Russia, in 1905. The new Persian and Ottoman constitutional regimes faced similar problems and were preoccupied with many of the same issues of modernization, freedom, and reform.

The Great Power Struggle for the East

As so often happens, revolution provided the opponents of the Ottoman and Qajar Empires with opportunities to grab territory. European powers extended their hold on onetime Ottoman lands. Between 1908 and 1913 Austria-Hungary annexed Bosnia and Herzegovina, Greece annexed Crete, and Italy—in the course of a short but difficult war—seized Tripoli and Cyrenaica (northeastern Libya). In 1912 and 1913 the Balkan nations fought two wars, which resulted in the partitioning of Macedonia. Although the Ottomans launched popular boycotts against both Austria and Italy (boycotting, for example, Italian spaghetti) they could do nothing to reverse their territorial losses.

In Persia, Russia capitalized on the revolution to seize territory in the northwest. The British and Russians signed a treaty in 1907 dividing Persia into spheres of influence, with the British claiming powers of intervention in the south and Russia claiming the same powers in the north. These two states held Persia in a great pincers, with the British navy protecting its interests in the Persian Gulf and Russia's powerful armies posing a constant threat to Persian sovereignty in the north.

Persia was not, however, the only object of this competition. Afghanistan, to its east, controlled the Khyber Pass, the most direct land route through the mountains from Russia to British-controlled India. The country had been divided previously between the Mughul and Persian empires, but with its mountainous terrain and contending warlords, Afghanistan did not lend itself to unified rule. By the nineteenth century the shah in Kabul, Afghanistan's capital, held tenuous sway over the tribal confederations that controlled the area.

During the first half of the nineteenth century, Persia and Afghanistan were caught up in armed conflicts with the Russians and the British. In an effort to increase their influence in the area and protect India's northern frontiers, the British attempted to install their own handpicked ruler in Afghanistan. The attempt backfired, and the British were forced to retreat. But in 1879 Britain, using its powerful colonial army, seized the Khyber Pass and Kabul and subordinated the Afghan ruler, Yaqub Khan. Between 1881 and 1901 Amir Abdur Rahman consolidated his power over Afghanistan, but Britain retained its hold on Afghanistan's foreign affairs.

Russia, meanwhile, was expanding toward the southeast. Many indigenous peoples, such as the Mongols, Afghans, Turkomans, and Tatars, came within Russia's sphere of influence. Their cities—Samarkand, Tashkent, and Bokhara—became tsarist administrative centers. Russia's advance was accomplished not only by its army but also by the construction of the Trans-Caspian railway, which, at its completion in 1888, reached 1064 miles into the heart of Asia. The Orenburg-Tashkent railway, completed in 1905, stretched 1185 miles farther. Inspired by the feats of both the army and the engineers, some Russian imperialists dreamed of conquering Afghanistan and penetrating India itself. But British pressure blocked Russia's design on Afghanistan, and a British military expedition to Lhasa in 1904 countered Russian influence in Tibet.

By the terms of the Anglo-Russian entente in 1907, Russia and Britain agreed to leave Afghanistan intact. Russia agreed to deal with the sovereign of Afghanistan only through the British government. Great Britain agreed to refrain from occupying or annexing Afghanistan so long as the nation fulfilled its treaty obligations. This partnership was, however, only a marriage of convenience brought on by larger pressures in Europe. Neither side wished to alienate the other in the face of the emerging threat of Germany's war machine.

CONCLUSION

By 1914, European states had established their primacy over Africa and the Middle East. While hundreds of thousands of Africans worked in European-owned mines and plantations, many thousands of Persians crossed into Russia to work in tsarist oilfields. While financiers in London, Berlin, and Paris skimmed the profits from the resources of Africa and Asia, European officials and diplomats dictated policy for much of the region. Although the Young Turk and Persian revolutions brought constitutional governments to the Ottoman and Qajar empires in the Middle East, only Persia would survive the consuming conflicts of World War I. The Young Turks, engaged in rebuilding the Ottoman Empire, chose to enter the war on the German side and suffered disastrous consequences.

Even before 1914, however, the forces that would eventually remove European dominance in the next half century were at work. In Africa and Egypt various indigenous groups mobilized to throw off the European yoke. In Europe citizens and parliamentary representatives debated the relative costs and benefits of empire and colonies. Many remained committed to social Darwinism, the idea of a hierarchy of civilizations expressed in the notions of carrying the "white man's burden" of spreading "civilization" to the "lesser peoples." But despite European military, economic, and technological superiority over the Middle East and Africa, the "white man's burden" would become increasingly onerous as the twentieth century progressed and as the conquered peoples mobilized to gain independence and to assert their own cultural identities.

Culture and identity, of course, are not fixed; they are constantly evolving. The period from 1800 to 1914 in the Middle East and Africa was one of particularly intense and rapid cultural change prompted by marked transformations in economic organization and in the technologies of transportation and communications. The effects of such transformations on African and Middle Eastern societies were compounded as those societies were subjugated by, or subordinated to, European states and economies.

People reacted in different ways to that subordination, depending on their position, class, education, religion, and ethnicity. Some advocated emulation of Europe in order to regain lost powers; others advocated vigorous resistance and adherence to traditional mores; many saw some advantage in compromise, taking technologies and organizational structures from the West while retaining many elements of the old order.

The assertion of European primacy over Africa and the Middle East had dramatic effects. Europeanization altered economic, political, and legal structures. In many cases it radically altered the education systems and even the languages of the conquered territories. French and English cultures were adopted to some degree by many subject peoples, especially among the upper and middle classes. Educated elites used their new skills and literacy to develop critiques of the colonial order. Other African and Middle Eastern peoples rejected the imported European traditions or modified them to suit their own needs.

European influence thus created new cultural syntheses. While upper-class ladies in Istanbul sought out French fashions, upper-class European women dressed in "Turkish" style and consumed Orientalist art. In many ways, however, European culture was a veneer applied to powerful local cultural traditions.

Islam retained its strength in the Middle East and North Africa, and European Christian missionaries met with little success in their efforts to convert Muslims. However, in sub-Saharan Africa, colonial rule expanded the possibilities for communication and the spread of new ideas and religions. Both Christianity and Islam underwent tremendous expansion, usually in different parts of the continent. Many African Christians, dissatisfied with the European missionaries' interpretation of Christianity, adapted the new faith to their own cultural practices.

Suggestions for Web Browsing

You can obtain more information about topics included in this chapter at the websites listed below. See also the companion website that accompanies this text, http://www.ablongman.com/brummett, which contains an online study guide and additional resources.

Sultan Abdul-Hamid II Collection Photography Archives
http://memory.loc.gov/pp/ahiihtml/ahiiabt.html

This site contains nearly 2000 photographs from albums of one of the last sultans of the Ottoman Empire from 1880 to 1893.

Age of European Imperialism: The Partitioning of Africa in the Late Nineteenth Century
http://pw2.netcom.com/~giardina/colony.html

Site discusses the partitioning of Africa and includes an interesting selection of maps tracing the imperial drive in Africa.

Internet Islamic History Sourcebook: Western Intrusion, 1815–1914
http://www.fordham.edu/halsall/islam/islamsbook.html

Extensive online source for links about the history of the Middle East, including short primary documents describing nineteenth-century European imperialism and the end of the Ottoman Empire.

Literature and Film

In *The Days,* trans. Hilary Wayment, 2nd ed. (American University at Cairo Press, 2001), Taha Hussein presents the wonderful three-volume biography of Taha Hussein, the blind village boy who studied at al-Azhar in Cairo and became a famous scholar and author. *The Press and Poetry of Modern Persia* (Kalimat Press, 1984, reprint of 1914 edition) by Edward G. Browne is a collection of prose, poetry, cartoons, and excerpts from the press. Hasan Javadi, in *Satire in Persian Literature* (Fairleigh Dickinson University Press, 1988), offers a survey of satire divided topically, including, for example, satire on women and on religion. W. Morgan Shuster's *The Strangling of Persia* (Image Publishers, 1987, reprint of 1912 edition) is a memoir of the American financial expert brought to Iran in 1911 to manage the empire's finances. Edwin Pears, in *Forty Years in Constantinople, the Recollections of Sir Edwin Pears 1873–1915* (Books for Libraries Press, 1871, reprint of 1916 edition), gives an interesting commentary by an outsider on Ottoman affairs. *The Diary of H.M. The Shah of Persia During His Tour Through Europe in A.D. 1873,* trans. J. W. Redhouse (Mazda, 1995) is a memoir of the Iranian Shah Nasir al-Din's journey to Europe.

Ethiopian filmmaker Haile Gerima's *Adwa* (Mypheduh Films, 1999) chronicles the famous victory of the Ethiopians over the Italians in 1896. Senegalese filmmaker Ousmane Sembene's *Ceddo* (New Yorker Films, 1977) deals with how nineteenth-century West Africans responded to external forces, such as European traders, Christian missionaries, and Muslim jihads. Part of an eight-part series on Africa narrated by Basil Davidson, *The Magnificent African Cake* (Public Media Video, 1984) covers the European scramble for Africa.

Suggestions for Reading

Studies on the European scramble for Africa include David Levering Lewis, *The Race to Fashoda: Colonialism and African Resistance* (Henry Holt, 1995). The use of technology to facilitate conquest is treated in Daniel Headrick, *The Tentacles of Progress: Technology Transfer in the Age of Imperialism, 1850–1940* (Oxford University Press, 1988).

The general subject of African resistance to European conquest is comprehensively treated in Robert Rotberg and Ali Mazrui, *Protest and Power in Black Africa* (Oxford University Press, 1970), and Bruce Vandervort, *Wars of Imperial Conquest in Africa, 1830–1914* (Indiana University Press, 1998). Ethiopia's return to a centralized kingdom and its resistance to European conquest is covered in Harold Marcus, *The Life and Times of Menelik II: Ethiopia, 1844–1913* (Red Sea Press, 1995).

An excellent treatment of the Anglo-Boer War is Bill Nasson, *The South African War, 1899–1902* (Oxford University Press, 1999).

The impact of colonial rule in Africa is examined in Adu Boahen, *African Perspectives on Colonialism* (Johns Hopkins University Press, 1987). Colonialism's impact on social change is covered in Andrew Roberts, ed., *The Colonial Moment in Africa* (Cambridge University Press, 1986). Europe's image of Africa is presented in Jan Nederveen Pieterse, *White on Black: Images of Africa and Blacks in Western Popular Culture* (Yale University Press, 1992).

On the Ottoman Empire in the nineteenth century, see Roderic H. Davison, *Turkey: A Short History,* 3rd ed. (Eothen Press, 1998), for a brief, well-written survey, and see Donald Quataert, *The Ottoman Empire, 1700–1922* (Cambridge University Press, 2000), for a student-friendly survey. On the Young Turk Revolution and its political and cultural impacts, see Palmira Brummett, *Image and Imperialism in the Ottoman Revolutionary Press, 1908–1911* (State University of New York Press, 2000).

Economic issues are covered in Roger Owen, *The Middle East in the World Economy, 1800–1914* (Methuen, 1981).

L. S. Stavrianos, *The Balkans Since 1453* (Holt, Rinehart, and Winston, 1961), provides a treatment of the evolution of the Balkan states in the context of Ottoman rule. On North African politics and culture see Ali Ahmida, *The Making of Modern Libya: State Formation, Colonization, and Resistance, 1830–1932* (State University of New York Press, 1994).

For treatments of the Qajars and the Persian constitutional revolution, see Edmond Bosworth and Carole Hellenbrand, eds., *Qajar Iran: Political, Social and Cultural Change, 1800–1925* (Mazda, 1992).

CHAPTER 24

Asia, 1815–1914

India, Southeast Asia, China, and Japan

CHAPTER CONTENTS

1830

1839–1842 Opium War

1840

1842 Treaty of Nanjing cedes Hong Kong to Britain

1850–1864 Taiping Rebellion

1853 Commodore Perry enters Japan

1857 The Great Revolt in India

1860

1868–1912 Meiji Period in Japan

1880

1885 Indian National Congress founded

1894–1895 Sino-Japanese War

1898 Spanish-American War; United States acquires Philippines, Guam, Puerto Rico

1899–1900 Righteous Harmony Fists (Boxer) Rebellion; Open Door policy in China begins

1900

1904–1905 Russo-Japanese War

1910 Japan annexes Korea

As the nineteenth century opened, Asian countries confronted external pressures and, in many cases, internal turmoil. Indians remained under the centuries-old weak rule of the Mughals (MOO-guls), but British imperialism increasingly modified their lives. The countries of the Indochinese peninsula as well as the islands of the Pacific and Indian Oceans had been subjected to European commercial influences since the sixteenth century, but more coercive forms of imperialism were soon to appear. China under the Manchus remained the world's greatest single power and economy, but it ignored the inevitable pressures of changes among its growing population and among the rapidly rising European countries that would soon threaten its sense of superiority. Japan was entering the third century of its control under the Tokugawa shōguns.

Although most of the world's large cities were in Asia, most Asians, like people elsewhere, lived in villages. In nineteenth-century India, for example, roughly 80 percent of the people lived in communities of fewer than 2000 inhabitants. The area was, and still is, vulnerable to natural disasters such as typhoons, tidal waves, earthquakes, and occasional droughts. Conditions varied greatly throughout the region, but many suffered from poor living conditions, high infant mortality rates, endemic diseases, and inadequate nutrition.

Yet many in Asia were materially better off than their counterparts in the West as the century opened. But by the beginning of the twentieth century, a combination of factors—Western imperialism, population pressures, cultural and ethnic turmoil, and disastrous climatic conditions—conspired to relegate much of Asia to colonial or semicolonial status, although both Japan and Thailand escaped that fate, as conditions there differed. Lack of political independence was by no means the only story in each of these countries. People developed arts, culture, new institutions, economic enterprises, and new ways of relating to one another, which some characterized as "modernization." By 1914, most of Asia rested under the direct or indirect control of Europe, the United States, or Japan, a situation that would endure until World War II.

INDIA

■ *How did British colonialism inspire a subcontinent of fractured principalities to develop a sense of nationalism?*

Internal struggles between the ruling Mughals and the Marathas, the Sikhs, the provincial governors, and other Indian princes offered an opportunity for the British and French to expand militarily and economically in India during the eighteenth century. The British in particular, through the British East India Company, established power in three key towns, Madras, Bombay, and Calcutta, from which they expanded their authority into the interior. By 1757, the Company was the effective ruler of Bengal, following Britain's victory at Plassey. The French and British also fought one another, and India, like North America, was part of the two European powers' world strug-

India: Establishment of the British Raj

1757	The Battle of Plassey; the British East India Company wins control of Bengal
1820s	Indian reformers call for improvement in women's status and education and return to Golden Age of Hindu culture in reaction to British missionary activities
1857–1858	Great Revolt; its suppression ended Mughal rule and brought much of India under the British crown.
1885	Indian National Congress founded
1905	Bengal partitioned, leading to boycott

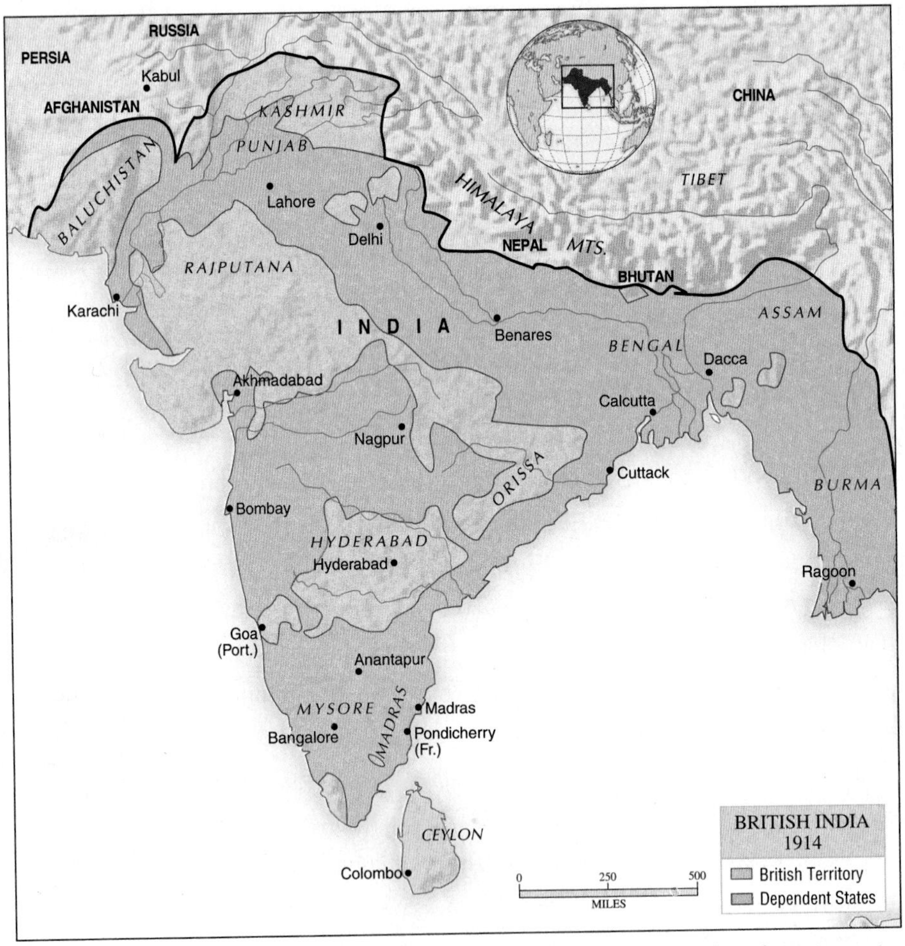

By 1914 the British, on the surface at least, exercised political control over the subcontinent. At the same time, the movement for independence was gaining strength.

This drawing of a British officer of the Bengal regiment shows a British magistrate settling a court case in 1853, during the period of dual control when the British East India Company and the British government shared authority over India.

gle for empire. Following their victory over French forces in India in 1760, the British chipped away at India. During the next century, through absorption of the territory of local princes by conquest or trickery, integration of India's economy with that of the British Empire, and development of an Indian elite expected to be loyal to Britain, India fell increasingly under British dominance.

British traders, particularly the British East India Company, joined with British officials as rulers, assuming the dual roles of businessmen and representatives of a sovereign state. Some Indian princes accepted British domination, but others who resisted lost their land. Until 1858, administration of the subcontinent was divided into two sections: British India was ruled directly by officials sent from London, while in Indian India, the local dynasties ruled under British supervision. The British Parliament, concerned that a profit-seeking company controlled the lives of millions of people while its agents lined their pockets with graft, enacted legislation in 1773 and 1784 that gave it power to control company policies and appoint the governor-general. The governor-general was to adhere to India's "ancient uses and Institutions," but which should those be? The British rulers had Mughal precedents as well as multiple religions and cultures to consider. Britain's stress on differences between Hindus and Muslims as well as on **caste** and hierarchy during the colonial era may have contributed to religious and social tensions in the twentieth century.

DOCUMENT
Arrival of the British in the Punjab

Reform and Rebellion

British missionaries arrived in India before the end of the eighteenth century, opening schools for Indian students and propagating Christian culture. In time, a synthesis of English and Indian culture emerged, which would later fuel the fires of nationalism already sparked by indigenous Indian reformers. By 1820, Indian reformers like Ram Mohan Roy (1772–1833) called for a return to a Golden Age of Hindu culture, when women supposedly enjoyed a higher status. This justified reformers' adding their voices to those of Christian

DOCUMENT
Macaulay's "Minute on Education"

caste—Primarily among Hindus, a religious class designation inherited from one's ancestors and passed on to one's descendents.

missionaries and colonial officials who demanded the prohibition of ***sati*** (sah-TEE)—the burning of widows on the funeral pyres of their deceased husbands—women's seclusion in the home, and female infanticide, as well as the encouragement of girls' education and widows' remarriage. Other reforms included the suppression of banditry and murder called *thugi* (TOO-ghee, from which the English word *thug* is derived), and a multilevel, though not universally widespread, educational system.

DOCUMENT
On Hindu Women and Education

Believing they were "civilizing" the Indians, many of whom were already reformers, the British pushed a variety of social, technological, and economic changes into Indian society. These included English culture (for the elite), railroads to move British products and soldiers into the hinterlands, a public works system, and a telegraph system. In the spring of 1857, a serious rebellion interrupted the flow of modern reforms. Indian troops, called ***sepoys*** (SEE-pois), who formed the bulk of the East India Company's armed forces, started the uprising when they complained that a new cartridge issued to them was smeared with the fat of cows and pigs. This outraged both the Hindus, for whom the cow was a sacred animal, and the Muslims, who considered the pig unclean. The uprising quickly spread, embracing princes and peasants in many provinces. Many other areas remained loyal to the British or at least calm. But elsewhere there was fierce fighting on both sides; the British exterminated whole villages.

DOCUMENT
The Indian Revolt

The Great Revolt of 1857–1858 marked the final collapse of the Mughals. The rebels had proclaimed as their leader the reluctant Mughal emperor. After the British put down the Great Revolt, they exiled him to Burma. The rebellion also put an end to the system of dual control under which the British government and the East India Company shared authority. Parliament eliminated the company's political role, and, after 258 years, the East India Company ended its rule.

Under the new system, the governor-general gained additional duties and a new title—viceroy. The viceroy was responsible to the Secretary of State for India in the British cabinet. In the subcontinent the British maintained direct control of most of the high positions in government, while Indians were trained to carry out administrative responsibilities in the provincial and subordinate systems. Only on rare occasions, however, could native civil officials rise to higher positions in the

sati—The Hindu practice of widow immolation on her husband's funeral pyre.

sepoys—Indian soldiers and policemen working under contract for the British East India Company.

The storming of the Kashmir Gate at Delhi during the Great Revolt of 1857–58.

Document The Great Revolt of 1857–1858

Raging over north and central India in 1857 and 1858, the Great Revolt, known to the British at the time as the "Sepoy Mutiny," engaged far more than the sepoys (Indian troops under British command) alone. Indians serving the British, independent princes, reformers, and peasants joined the soldiers whom the British had counted on to be their loyal supporters. The author of this essay, Sayyid Ahmad Khan (SAI-yid AH-mahd KAHN), an Indian in service to the British who remained loyal to his employers throughout the Revolt, rejected the British assessment that the Great Revolt was the work of some disgruntled sepoys. Rather, as he wrote, the roots went far deeper.

I believe that there was but one primary cause of the rebellion, the others being merely incidental and arising out of it. Nor is this opinion either imaginary or conjectural. It is borne out by the views entertained by wise men of past ages. . . . It has been universally allowed that the admittance of the people to a share in the Government under which they live, is necessary to its efficiency, prosperity, and permanence. . . . The Natives of India, without perhaps a single exception, blame the Government for having deprived them of their position and dignity and for keeping them down. . . . What! Have not [the British officers'] pride and arrogance led them to consider the Natives of India as undeserving the name of human beings?

Questions to Consider

1. According to the author, what was the primary cause of the conflict in 1857–58?
2. Did the author believe that the Indians' love for self-government was a recent development?
3. Did the British realize the importance of respect for Indian customs, or was there an even greater ethnic divide after the Revolt?

From Barbara D. Metcalf and Thomas R. Metcalf, *A Concise History of India* (Cambridge: Cambridge University Press, 2002), p. 99.

bureaucracy. London reorganized the courts and law codes, along with the army and public services. The British applied odd "racial" theories to the military, claiming that some Indians were "racially" suited to military service while others were not. English became the administrative language of the country.

India was governed by and for the British, who viewed themselves as the only people able to rule. In 1900, fully 90 percent of native men and 99 percent of native women were illiterate. Few schools existed at the village level to remedy that situation. While the British supplied improved health standards, better water systems, and political stability, the cost was high. The masses of the rural poor paid for the government and army through taxes on beverages and salt. Moreover, India provided rich resources and vast markets for the British. By 1913, India absorbed more British exports, particularly textiles and steel, than any other country. In return, India sent to England crucial raw materials such as cotton, rice, tea, and indigo.

The English language and British railroads introduced more unity to the country than it had ever known. But the imperial rulers took advantage of the subcontinent's diversity of religions, castes, and principalities (over 700 separate political units) to rule by a policy of "divide and conquer." The British, who encouraged each group to think of itself as distinct, justified their political policies and economic dominance over India by pointing out that they were improving the lives of almost 300 million people. This rationale, however, could not remove the glaring contrasts between the European and Asian ways of life in cities like Bombay, Delhi, and Calcutta.

Resentment against British rule led to the rapid growth of an Indian nationalist movement. In 1885, with the help of several Englishmen who had Indian political ambitions, the Indian National Congress was formed. The Anglo-Indian educational system, although it touched only a minority of the people, served as one of the most potent forces behind the new movement, as the Indians embraced many of the liberal causes popular in England. Especially strong was the drive for women's equality and freedom, away from their traditional position of dependence in which women's legal standing and power derived from their ties to men. Hindu and Muslim women set up schools for girls and widows. Other reformist groups, Hindu, Muslim, and secular, inspired nationalist thinking as well.

DOCUMENT
An Indian Muslim Visits London

As educated Indians learned the history of the rise of self-government in England, their desire for political freedom in their own land grew. The system of British control prevented Indians from rising above a certain level. A pool of thousands of frustrated and unemployed educated Indian youths turned angrily against the government. At the same time, rapacious taxation, disastrous weather conditions, and bubonic plague began a decade of despair in 1896. When the British partitioned Bengal for their own administrative convenience in 1905, nationalist Indians erupted, initiating a very effective boycott of British goods. The partition was later rescinded, but it worsened Hindu-Muslim relations as each reacted differently to the partition policy.

The British responded to the ensuing nationalist violence with some changes in policy between 1907 and 1909. Although the central government's legislature remained under British control, the British allowed the various provincial legislatures to elect Indian majorities, and an Indian was seated in the executive council of the governor-general. These concessions temporarily satisfied some moderates but did not appease the more radical protesters, who saw them as halfway measures. As the twentieth century evolved, the spirit of nationalism and desire for independence became stronger. World War I and its aftermath stoked the nationalist fires.

SOUTHEAST ASIA

- *What combination of local and international factors determined the fate of Southeast Asian countries in the face of European imperialism?*

Throughout continental Southeast Asia and the islands of the Indian and Pacific Oceans, European investors established a plantation economy to grow coffee, tea, pepper, and other products demanded by the world market in the seventeenth and eighteenth centuries. They also discovered and exploited important mineral deposits. To take advantage of these resources, they attempted to limit the chronic civil war and banditry that plagued the region. In some countries, the imperialists saw their role as humanitarian and instituted limited reforms. The impact of these reforms, especially Western-style education, created a new generation of nationalists. In the Dutch East Indies, French Indochina, and the Philippines, young intellectuals aspired to complete independence for themselves and their countries.

The Era of European Dominance

In the eighteenth and nineteenth centuries Great Britain gained control of Sri Lanka (Ceylon), Malaya, and Burma. The first colony, taken from the Dutch in

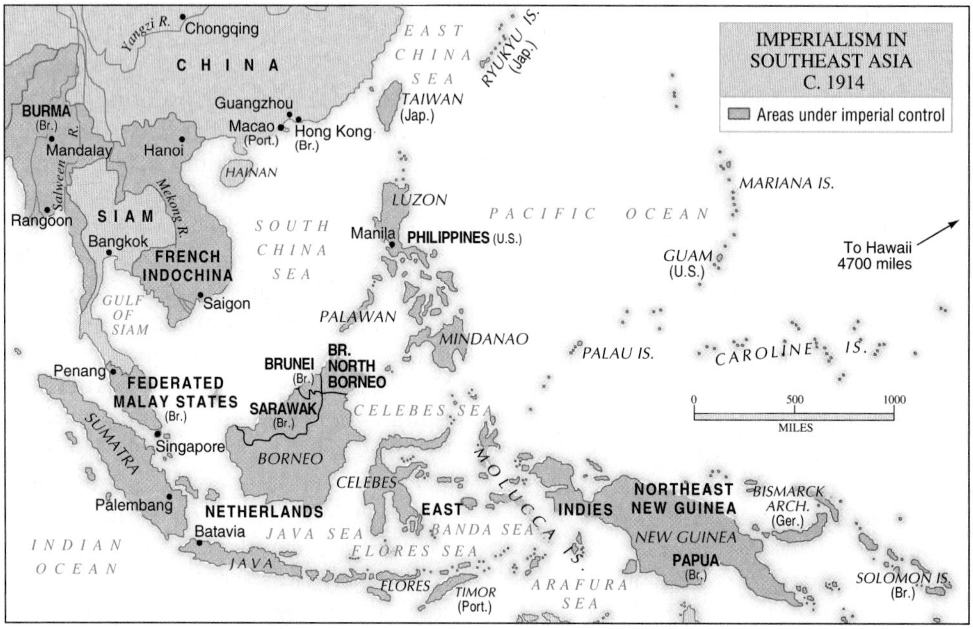

At the beginning of the twentieth century, the map of Southeast Asia showed a mixture of old and new imperialisms, with the Dutch still in Indonesia and the British in Brunei. But the new patterns can be seen too with the French in Vietnam, the British in Hong Kong, and the Americans in the Philippines.

In 1859, on the pretext of preserving Catholicism in Indochina, a French and Spanish expeditionary force stormed and captured the fortress of Saigon.

1796, became one of the most valuable British holdings, producing such prized commodities as tea, rubber, lead, and sapphires. The Malay Peninsula, with the island of Singapore at its tip, provided a vantage point from which Britain could dominate the seas surrounding southern Asia and export valuable supplies of tin and rubber. Although the Burmese struggled valiantly to hold onto national sovereignty through diplomacy and self-defense, the British conquered Burma in three wars between 1824 and 1885 and annexed it to India.

Typical of British attitudes toward Asia, one British governor of Singapore in the 1880s wrote: "I doubt if Asiatics will ever learn to govern themselves; it is contrary to the genius of their race, of their history, of their religious system, that they should. Their desire is a mild, just, and firm despotism."[1]

After a century-long absence, France returned to Southeast Asia in the nineteenth century. French commercial and religious interests had been established as early as the seventeenth century, but it was not until the mid-nineteenth century that France played an imperialist role in Vietnam and Cambodia. Anti-Christian persecutions by Vietnamese monarchs in the 1850s as well as French commercial interests in Southeast Asia sparked a French war with Emperor Tu Duc (TOO DOOK), whose defeat in 1862 forced him to cede several provinces to France and to allow missionaries free reign throughout Vietnam. From that base, France expanded its influence and power through treaties, exploration, and outright annexation. France took Hanoi in 1882, governed Cochin China as a direct colony, and held Annam (central Vietnam), Tonkin, and Cambodia as protectorates that retained some degree of local control. Laos, too, was soon brought under French "protection." By the beginning of the twentieth century France had created an empire in Indochina nearly 50 percent larger than the parent country. But due to French suppression of opposition, an independence movement quickly emerged. By the early twentieth century, Vietnamese nationalists, like their Chinese counterparts, found a model of Asian independence in Japan. During and after World War I, several types of independence movements would challenge French rule.

Thailand alone among Southeast Asian countries retained its independence. Pressed by France in Indochina on its eastern flank and Britain in Burma on its western, Thailand had two remarkable kings, Mongut (MON-goot; r. 1851–1868) and his son Chulalongkorn (CHOO-la-LONG-korn; r. 1868–1910), who successfully modernized the Thai economy and political system to ward off foreign encroachment.

Late in the sixteenth century, the Dutch had taken most of the East Indies from the Portuguese, and in 1602 the Dutch East India Company was organized to exploit the resources of the Moluccas (mo-LOO-kas) in present-day Indonesia. In 1798 the company's holdings were transferred to the Dutch crown, which forced the peasants to grow cash crops for its own benefit. In 1811, Java briefly came under British domination, and the reformist Thomas Raffles liberalized political and economic control. When the Dutch returned in 1816, the Javanese were again subjected to brutal control. The suppression of a ***jihad*** rebellion in the 1820s led the Netherlands to the point of national bankruptcy and took the lives of some 200,000 Javanese. The Dutch response was to run the islands even more brutally as a cash cow for Holland.

In the 1830s the so-called culture system was introduced, under which one-fifth of all local land was set aside to raise crops for the government. One-fifth of all the islanders' time was also required to work the lands. The production of sugar, tobacco, coffee, tea, and other products increased tremendously, ending Dutch fears of bankruptcy and financing Holland's industrial revolution. In the long run, the culture system gave the islands a prosperous means of raising crops, but its implementation deprived the people of sufficient land for their own use and often required torture to force production. Conditions began to improve in 1900 when the Dutch took the first steps to abandon the culture system, which was finally put to rest in 1917. As in other European colonies, discrimination within the education system and elsewhere gave rise to a vigorous independence movement. A Javanese revivalist movement, inspired by the nationalist ideas of Raden Adjeng Kartini (RAH-den AD-yeng kar-TEE-nee), a young woman and member of the elite, sprang up in the first decades of the twentieth century. This was followed in 1912 by the mass-based group Sarekat Islam (SAH-reh-kaht ee-SLAHM; Islamic Association), which forced the Dutch to extend limited rights to Indonesians.

The Philippines

Spanish rule of the Philippines (1571–1898) was increasingly resisted during the nineteenth century. Lay Spaniards lived mainly in the urban areas, while Catholic friars controlled the countryside, converting the masses, other than those in the Muslim areas in Mindanao, to Christianity. Resistance to racial inequality and agrarian exploitation by the friars, common since the mid-1700s, accelerated in the late nineteenth century following the rise of an educated Filipino elite. In the 1880s when the Spanish-educated José Rizal (ho-SAY ri-ZAHL) wrote popular novels calling for reform of colonial injustices, though not for independence, the colonial authorities burned his work, repressed his family, and ultimately executed Rizal in 1896. This incited a militant independence movement. In 1897, the revolutionaries, under Emilio Aguinaldo (eh-MEE-lee-oh AH-ghee-NAHL-doh), declared the independence of the Philippines. Soon thereafter, Aguinaldo was forced into exile in Hong Kong.

At the same time, the United States had been expanding into the Pacific since the end of the Civil War, purchasing Alaska in 1867 and overthrowing the Hawaiian queen in 1893. The United States had just begun to fight Spain in the Caribbean in 1898, and to forestall a Spanish attempt to send help to Cuba from the Philippines, American Commodore George Dewey arranged to bring Aguinaldo back to the Philippines to end Spanish rule there. But Dewey abandoned Aguinaldo, staging a mock naval battle to allow the Spaniards to save face. Then, the United States turned on the Filipinos in a brutal war, killing at least 100,000 men, women, and children and imprisoning 300,000 in barren detention camps where thousands perished. To American soldiers who asked what to do if Filipinos were found outside the camps, one general replied, "Kill and

DOCUMENT
The American Anti-Imperialist League

U.S. atrocities in the Philippines, depicted in an American cartoon, eventually turned U.S. public opinion against the war.

jihad—Religious struggle in Islam.

burn. . . . This is no time to take prisoners. . . . Kill everything over ten."[2]

This radical shift in U.S. foreign policy was inspired by U.S. strategic interests in the western Pacific, social Darwinism, the desire for Asian markets, and Christian evangelism. The three-year war against the Philippines ended in 1902 and ushered in American colonial administration that was surprisingly liberal in light of the bloodshed and racism that had preceded it. In 1913 the legislature became predominantly local, although final authority in the most important matters was still reserved for the U.S. Congress. The Jones Act (1916) created the Commonwealth, increased local self-rule, and called for eventual independence. The Philippine tariff was shaped to favor American trade, and large amounts of capital from the United States were invested in the islands. Increased educational opportunities strengthened the desire for independence among many Filipinos. In their eyes, American government in the Philippines, no matter how efficient or humanitarian, was no substitute for self-government.

DOCUMENT
Imperialism and the White Man's Burden

CHINA: THE LONG NINETEENTH CENTURY

▪ *What domestic and foreign pressures brought about China's decline from being the world's economic engine in the eighteenth century to being a failing monarchy, hobbled by unequal treaties, in the early twentieth century?*

At the end of the 1800s, China's 4 million square miles held 450 million people, more than twice the number a century earlier. The ruling dynasty was the **Qing** (CHING), established by Manchus from Manchuria, who in 1644 had superseded the Ming. Understanding that effective rule as foreigners required an appreciation of Chinese civilization, the Manchus had their subjects cooperating with them within a generation. Although the Qing Dynasty required Chinese men to wear Manchu hairstyles and forbade (unsuccessfully) the binding of Chinese women's feet, the Manchus themselves gradually adopted Chinese attitudes and habits.

MAP
Nineteenth-Century China

One important policy carried over from the Ming Dynasty and earlier was the **tribute system** of foreign relations, which held the Chinese emperor to be morally superior and China itself the Central Kingdom. Subordinate states owed tribute to China in exchange for its paternalistic protection. In reality, the mutual exchange of gifts through official channels constituted a major source of regulated trade. But it also officially placed such exchanges in the context of state-to-state relations, in which China was always the dominant partner.

The reign of the Manchu emperor, Qianlong (chen-LONG; r. 1736–1795), was a time of great expansion. The Qing gained Central Asia, Mongolia, and Tibet. By the end of the eighteenth century, Manchu power extended even into Nepal, and the territory under the Qing control was as extensive as under any previous dynasty. Further, the Qing governed their far-flung and diverse empire with subtle and effective policies on national defense and commercial and political relations with neighboring countries within the framework of the

China in the Imperialist Era

1644	Manchus establish Qing Dynasty
1759	Foreign trade restricted to Guangzhou
1793	Imperial denial of British request for permanent trade representative
1800–1840	British smuggle opium into China
1839	First Opium War, ended by Treaty of Nanjing (1842), which gives Hong Kong to the British
1850–1864	Taiping Rebellion paralyzes China, kills 20 to 30 million people
1856–1858	Second Opium War, ended by Treaty of Tianjin, which opens new ports and permits foreign missionaries to proselytize throughout China
1860	*Tongzhi* restoration movement
1861–1908	Rule by Cixi, the Empress Dowager
1894–1895	China's defeat in Sino-Japanese War
1895–1900	China carved into spheres of influence—areas occupied by United Kingdom, Germany, France, Japan, and Russia
1898	Hundred Days of Reform
1899–1900	Righteous Harmony Fists (Boxer) Uprising
1900	Open Door policy implemented
1911	Revolutionary overthrow of Qing Dynasty; end of monarchy in China

Qing—Manchu Dynasty (1644–1911) in China.

tribute system—China-centered foreign policy whereby subordinate countries give tribute to China and receive gifts (trade) and protection in return.

tribute system. Their overall trade policies maintained a growing economy for their expanding population base.

Global Networks and the Challenges to Manchu Control

Evidence of some of China's problems can be found in the eighteenth-century revolts in Taiwan, Gansu, Hunan, Guizhou (gweh-JOH), and Shandong provinces. China suppressed all of them, but clearly the Central Kingdom faced serious difficulties with its religiously and culturally diverse kingdom. Increasing challenges from the West compounded the threats to the Qing. China, with its vast resources in tea, porcelain, and silk, supplied both its own enormous market and those of Europe and Europe's colonies. From the sixteenth through the eighteenth centuries, Spanish and Portuguese, then Dutch and Japanese, and finally English and American traders called at South China's ports. After 1759, the Qing confined European trade to **"factories"** in the restricted foreigners' quarter in Guangzhou (gwahng-JOH).

By the early nineteenth century, the British East India Company controlled about 90 percent of the foreign trade at the southern port of Guangzhou. The British love for tea was behind the spectacular growth in trade. Britain's tea imports rose from 400,000 pounds in 1720 to 23 million pounds in 1800. One-tenth of Britain's government revenues derived from import taxes on tea alone. By the 1780s, 16 million ounces of silver flowed out to pay for the tea. British merchants and government officials sought ways to bring greater balance to this trade and to conduct it on terms that differed from the tribute system.

For 300 years, the Chinese had been able to regulate trade as they saw fit. Britain's rise as a world power and the expanding liberal trading regime in the Atlantic made the tribute system, under which the Manchus would neither recognize nor receive diplomatic representatives of foreign powers, seem out of date. The British sent Lord George Macartney to the Qing court in 1793 to request a permanent trade representative in Beijing. Macartney refused to perform the ceremonial kowtow (nine full-length prostrations), an important element in the tribute system. Qianlong's response to King George III summarized his view of foreign relations:

> *To send one of your nationals to stay at the Celestial Court to take care of your country's trade with China . . . is not in harmony with the state system of our dynasty and will definitely not be permitted.*

factories—European office and warehouse buildings in India and China.

The waterfront at Guangzhou (Canton) in a nineteenth-century painting. Guangzhou was the first Chinese port regularly visited by European traders. The Portuguese arrived in 1511, followed by the Dutch in the seventeenth century and the French and British in the eighteenth.

. . . There is nothing we lack, as your principal envoy and others have themselves observed. We have never set such store on strange or ingenious objects, nor do we have need of any more of your country's manufactures.[3]

Opium and Trade

Opium smoking had been introduced to China through trade with Southeast Asia in the seventeenth century. At first, it was used for medicinal purposes, but soon it was used to alleviate the emotional and physical strains of work. Its use alarmed Qianlong, who banned its growth in China. This only made imported opium more profitable. Recognizing a great source of income to offset the drain of silver to pay for tea, the British East India Company licensed private trading ships to sell Indian opium on its behalf (the Company feared being implicated in sales of a product the Chinese government had technically prohibited in 1800). Between 1729 and 1838, imports rose from 200 to 40,000 chests per year (one chest contained 150 pounds of opium extract). Though the British were not alone in selling opium to China—Americans made handsome profits as well—the British were able to benefit from selling opium grown in their Indian colony. Soon, the balance of payments shifted, and a net outflow of silver compounded China's problems with widespread addiction and rampant criminality that accompanied the trade.

In the meantime, the empire faced other problems. Corruption spread through the army, and tax farmers defrauded the people. The central bureaucracy declined in efficiency, and the generally weak emperors were unable to meet the challenges of the time. When the East India Company lost its monopoly in 1833 following the rise of Free Trade sentiment in England, new merchant houses pressured the British government to demand more open markets. Viewing the tragedy inflicted on China, Beijing dispatched a tough, brilliant official, Lin Zexu (LIN zeh-SHOO), to Guangzhou. In the spring of 1839 Commissioner Lin confiscated and destroyed the opium. In response, the British confronted Lin's forces with 47 ships.

DOCUMENT
Lin Zexu: Letter to Queen Victoria

In the war that followed, the Chinese could not match the British forces. In 1842 China agreed to the provisions of the Treaty of Nanjing. Hong Kong was ceded to Great Britain, and other ports, including Guangzhou, were opened to British residence and trade. After the Nanjing Treaty's provisions became known, the French and Americans gained the same trading rights as the British in 1844. The advantages granted the three nations by the Chinese set a precedent that would dominate China's relations with the world for the next century.

The British and French defeated China in a second opium war in 1856. By the terms of the Treaty of Tianjin (tee-en-JIN; 1858), the Chinese opened new ports to trading and allowed foreigners to travel in the interior. Christians gained the right to spread their faith and hold property, thus opening up another means of Western penetration. The United States and Russia gained the same privileges in separate treaties.

IMAGE
American Cartoon on Western Powers Carving Up China

Three provisions of these treaties caused long-lasting bitterness among the Chinese: extraterritoriality, customs regulations, and "most favored nation" privileges. Extraterritoriality meant that Westerners, who argued that Chinese concepts of justice were more rigid and harsh than those in the West, had the right to be tried in their own country's consular court. China had to accept a low fixed tariff collected by Europeans, not Chinese customs officials. And the "most favored nation" privileges extended rights automatically to all Europeans (plus the United States) if any one exacted new concessions from China. For the next century, China suffered under these **unequal treaties.** This was a time of unprecedented degradation and humiliation for China.

DOCUMENT
The Treaty of Nanjing

More dangerous for the Qing than the Europeans and Americans was the explosion of revolts in the north, west, and south of the country. The most serious was the Taiping (tai-PING) Rebellion, which lasted from 1850 to 1864. The uprising, fought to attain the Heavenly Kingdom of Great Peace, stemmed from widespread discontent with the social and economic conditions of Manchu rule and the perception of a lack of authority in Beijing. The revolt began near Guangzhou, where opium addiction, unemployment, and the results of foreign penetration were felt most acutely. It centered on the plans of Hong Xiuquan (HONG shoo-CHU-AHN), a man driven to desperation by consistently failing the lowest examination to gain entry into the civil service. After reading Christian tracts, he came to identify himself as a son of God, Jesus's younger brother.

He attracted numerous followers, especially from the poor. For ten years after 1853 he and his forces controlled the southern part of China from Nanjing, and he set out to create a new society detached from the traditional Chinese fabric. Hong struck out at vice, Confucianism, private property, and the landlords. He almost overthrew the central government. However, his vast movement suffered from a lack of effective coordination, giving time for provincial governors to raise new and powerful armies that eventually put

unequal treaties—Treaties forced first on China, then other nominally independent Asian countries, in which the United States or European countries received extraterritoriality, most favored nation privileges, and control of tariffs.

Document Lin Zexu on the Opium Trade

At a time when the West struggles with the influx of illegal drugs from Asia and elsewhere, it is useful to note in the first part of the nineteenth century, the traffic flowed the other way. The British and their Western trading partners flooded China with illegal opium. A Chinese official Lin Zexu saw that the opium trade, which gave Europe such huge profits, undermined his country. He asked Queen Victoria to put a stop to it.

After a long period of commercial intercourse, there appear among the crowd of barbarians both good persons and bad, unevenly. Consequently there are those who smuggle opium to seduce the Chinese people and so cause the spread of the poison to all provinces. Such persons who only care to profit themselves, and disregard their harm to others, are not tolerated by the laws of heaven and are unanimously hated by human beings. His Majesty the Emperor, upon hearing of this, is in a towering rage. He has especially sent me, his commissioner, to come to Guangdong, and together with the governor-general and governor jointly to investigate and settle this matter.

All those people in China who sell opium or smoke opium should receive the death penalty. If we trace the crime of those barbarians who through the years have been selling opium, then the deep harm they have wrought and the great profit they have usurped should fundamentally justify their execution according to law. We take into consideration, however, the fact that the various barbarians have still known how to repent their crimes and return to their allegiance to us by taking the 20,183 chests of opium from their storeships and petitioning us, through their consular officer [superintendent of trade], Elliot, to receive it. It has been entirely destroyed and this has been faithfully reported to the Throne in several memorials by this commissioner and his colleagues.

Fortunately we have received a specially extended favor from His Majesty the Emperor, who considers that for those who voluntarily surrender there are still some circumstances to palliate their crime, and so for the time being he has magnanimously excused them from punishment. But as for those who again violate the opium prohibition, it is difficult for the law to pardon them repeatedly. Having established new regulations, we presume that the ruler of your honorable country, who takes delight in our culture and whose disposition is inclined towards us, must be able to instruct the various barbarians to observe the law with care. It is only necessary to explain to them the advantages and disadvantages and then they will know that the legal code of the Celestial Court must be absolutely obeyed with awe.

We find that your country is sixty or seventy thousand *li* [about 22,000 miles] from China. Yet there are barbarian ships that strive to come here for trade for the purpose of making a great profit. The wealth of China is used to profit the barbarians. That is to say, the great profit made by barbarians is all taken from the rightful share of China. By what right do they then in return use the poisonous drug to injure the Chinese people? Even though the barbarians may not necessarily intend to do us harm, yet in coveting profit to an extreme, they have no regard for injuring others. Let us ask, where is your conscience? I have heard that the smoking of opium is very strictly forbidden by your country; that is because the harm caused by opium is clearly understood. Since it is not permitted to do harm to your own country, then even less should you let it be passed on to the harm of other countries—how much less to China!

Questions to Consider

1. Why did the Western powers, led by the British, sell addictive drugs in China?
2. What do you think were the economic, political, and health effects of the opium trade on China?
3. What comparisons can you make between Commissioner Lin's response to the influx of foreign drugs and that of the United States today?

From Lin Zexu, *Letter to Queen Victoria* (1839).

down the uprising. The Taiping Rebellion was one of the most costly movements in history. It reached into 17 of China's 18 provinces. Estimates of the number of deaths range between 20 and 30 million as the central government brutally repressed the rebels.

Qing Foreign Policy

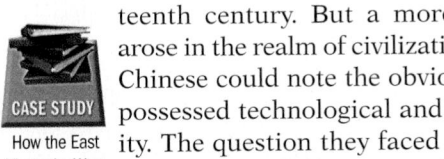

CASE STUDY
How the East Views the West

The Chinese, whose economy was the world's largest in 1800, had been forced to compete with Westerners in military and economic terms through the nineteenth century. But a more serious conflict arose in the realm of civilization and values. The Chinese could note the obvious—that the West possessed technological and military superiority. The question they faced was how to adapt the strength of the West to the core of Chinese civilization in order to become able to compete effectively. In Chinese terms, this was the *ti yong* concept (*ti*="substance"; *yong*="use").

Combining the two elements presented the severe problem of gaining a proper balance. Those who wanted to keep the old culture opposed those who wanted to modernize the country. In 1860 the *Tongzhi* (TONG-juh) restoration movement attempted to strengthen the Manchus. Serious attempts were made to preserve Chinese culture while trying to make use of Western technology. Had these attempts at adaptation been carried out in a time of peace, perhaps the Chinese could have adjusted, but China did not enjoy the luxury of tranquility. Nevertheless, notable investments were made in cotton spinning, coal mining, and shipping as part of a "self-strengthening" movement, although low fixed tariffs prevented the Chinese from protecting infant industries.

After the external buffeting from the West and the internal uprising, the Qing dynasty limped along for another half century, led by a conservative coalition of Manchu and Chinese officials who advised the empress dowager, Cixi (tsih-SHEE), who served from 1861 until her death in 1908. Entering the court as a concubine, Cixi mastered the intricate ceremonial life and intrigue of palace politics. When the senior concubine failed to give birth to a healthy heir to the throne, Cixi bore the emperor a strong and healthy child.

Her position as mother of the heir apparent opened the door to power, and during the reigns of the next three emperors, she was a dominant power, either as sole or joint regent. She built a network of powerful allies and informers that helped her crush internal revolts and restore a measure of prestige to China during a brief period of relative tranquility from 1870 to 1895. Yet at a time when the Japanese were rapidly modernizing and foreign powers were introducing many forms of new technology in their factories, railroads, and communications, Cixi and many of her supporters, holding on to tradition and custom, failed to modernize China.

Carving Up China

During the first wars against the Europeans, the Chinese began the process of ceding territory and spheres of influence to foreigners. By 1860, as a result of the Treaty of Beijing, Russia gained the entire area north of the Amur River and founded the strategic city of Vladivostok. In 1885 France took Indochina, and Britain seized Burma. In 1887 Macao was ceded to Portugal. China was too weak to resist these encroachments on its borders. But the crowning blow came not from the Western nations but from Japan, a land the Chinese had long regarded as inferior.

Trouble had been brewing between China and Japan over the control of Korea for a decade before war broke out in 1894. The brief Sino-Japanese War resulted in a humiliating defeat for China. By the Treaty of Shimonoseki (shi-moh-noh-SEH-kee; 1895), China was forced to recognize the independence of Korea and hand over to Japan the rich Liaodong (lee-ow-DONG) peninsula (soon returned to China under Western pressure) and Taiwan.

The Chinese defeat was the signal for the renewal of aggressive actions by Western powers. Germany demanded a 99-year lease to Jiaozhou (jee-ow-JOH) Bay and was also given exclusive mining and railroad rights throughout Shandong province. Russia obtained a 25-year lease to Liaodong and gained the right to build a railroad across Manchuria, thereby dominating that vast territory. In 1898 Britain obtained the lease of Weihaiwei (WAY-hai-way), a naval base in Shandong, and France leased Guangzhou Bay in southern China.

The United States, acting not from any high-minded desires but rather from the fear that American business was being excluded from China, brought a halt, or at least a hesitation, to the process of dismemberment. In 1899, Secretary of State John Hay asked the major powers to agree to a policy of equal trading privileges. In 1900, several powers did so, and the Open Door policy was born.

The humiliation of the defeat by Japan and the dismemberment of China by the imperialist powers had incensed young Chinese intellectuals, who agitated for liberation from foreign dominance. Enlightened and concerned patriots such as Kang Youwei (KAHNG yoo-WAY), with the support of the young emperor, Cixi's nephew, proposed a wide-ranging series of economic, social, political, and educational reforms, known as the "hundred days of reform" in the summer of 1898. Cixi

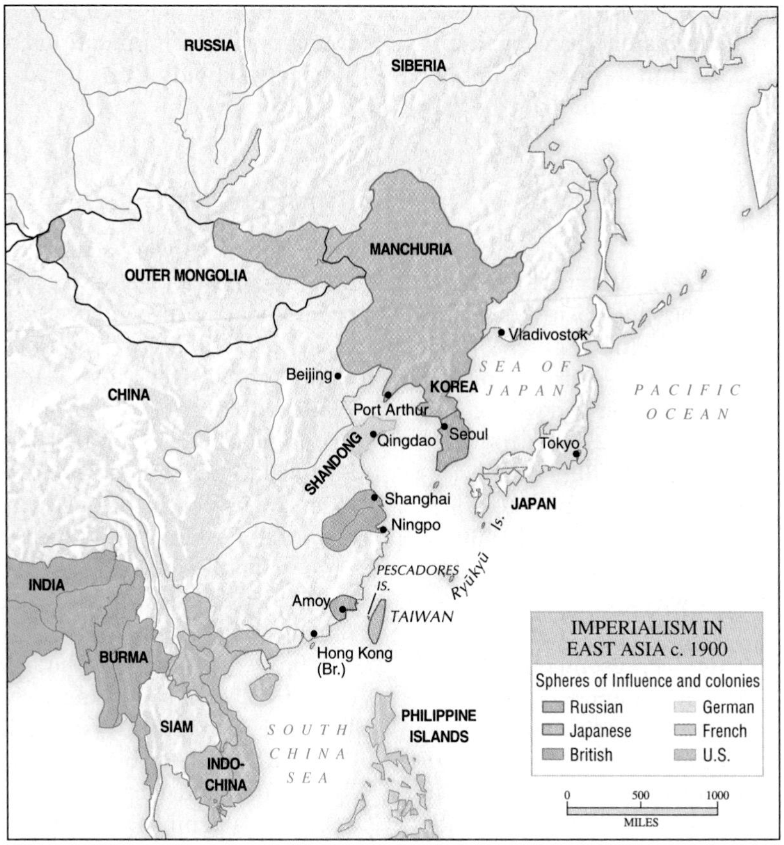

Territorial impositions on East Asia were made by European and American imperialists, as well as China's modernizing neighbor, Japan.

and her advisers opposed the young scholars' attempts to bring about basic reforms because they threatened the interests of Cixi's supporters. She came out of retirement in 1898, imprisoned her nephew, executed several reformers, and revoked the proposed reforms. Kang and a few others fled into exile in Japan.

After the suppression of the reform movement, a group of secret societies united in an organization known as the Righteous Harmony Fists, whose members were called Boxers in the West. At first they were strongly anti-Manchu, but by 1899, the chief object of their hatred had become the foreign nations who were stripping China of land and power. The Boxers started a campaign to rid China of all "foreign devils." Many Europeans were killed, and their legations at Beijing were besieged. In August 1900 a multinational army forced its way to Beijing and released the foreign prisoners. China was forced to apologize for the murder of foreign officials and pay a large indemnity.

MAP Treaty Ports and the Boxer Rebellion in China

By this time, even Cixi acknowledged the need for change. After 1901 she sanctioned reforms in the state examination system, education and governmental structure, and economic life. But these reforms only accelerated the demand for change. Revolutionary movements, many hatched by anti-Manchu exiles in Japan, broke out all over China, and in 1912, the Republic of China was proclaimed with Sun Yat-sen as provisional president. The revolutionary Chinese leaders knew that there had to be radically different approaches taken in China to allow it to survive and compete. As one official wrote in the 1890s:

> *Western nations rely on intelligence and energy to compete with one another. To come abreast of them China should plan to promote commerce and open minds; unless we change, the Westerners will be rich and we poor. We should excel in technology and the manufacture of machinery; unless we change, they will be skillful and we clumsy. . . . Unless we change, the Westerners will cooperate with each other and we shall stand isolated; they will be strong and we shall be weak.*[4]

Unfortunately, the Republic, which had been announced to great fanfare in 1912, was subverted by the assassination in 1913 of many democratically elected leaders and the rise of brutal warlordism.

JAPAN: MODERNITY AND IMPERIALISM

▪ *What was the meaning of "modernity" and what did the Japanese do to attain it in late nineteenth-century Japan?*

At the beginning of the eighteenth century, Japan was administered from Edo (now Tokyo), the largest city in the world at that time, by the head of the Tokugawa clan, whose leader had adopted the title of **shōgun** in 1603. The Japanese emperor, in residence at Kyoto, served as a figurehead with no real function during the Tokugawa (TOH-koo-GAH-wah) period (1600–1868). The Tokugawa controlled the country through their feudal lords, the ***daimyō***. These officials in turn governed their regions with the aid of the samurai, warriors turned bureaucrats during Japan's long centuries of peace. The samurai, about six percent of the population, resided in castle-towns along with merchants and artisans, who together constituted another 10 percent. Most Japanese were farmers, and it was their taxes that supported the government and its functions. The cities were lively, producing a vibrant mass urban culture of arts, theater, poetry, and novels that, in time, also influenced the increasingly literate rural population.

Domestic trade was very vigorous. Samurai and *daimyō* moved across the countryside in massive annual processions to show their loyalty to the shōgun, spreading money and culture throughout the land as they traveled. Merchants moved large quantities of goods by packhorse and by ship. Men and women went on sightseeing trips and pilgrimages to temples and shrines. Japan was a realm of lively interaction in the early modern period. Its population grew from around 12 million in 1600 to 30 million in 1720, but then growth slowed. Urban expansion also slowed down in the eighteenth century, and in 1800 many innovations were taking place in rural villages and towns.

The shōgun's displeasure at the destabilizing effects of Christian missionary activities caused him around 1640 to limit Japan's foreign trade to China, Korea, and the Netherlands. Knowledge of Western science entered Japan through what was called *Rangaku* (RAHN-gah-koo; "Dutch studies"). Scholars of Dutch studies, as well as Confucian scholars, began to question the competence of the shōgun as they observed the disastrous course of events in China under imperialist threat. At the same time, peasant distress intensified with poor administration and abominable weather conditions, leading to riots in the first half of the nineteenth century. The Tokugawa regime was severely challenged in the mid-nineteenth century when it was forced to confront the Western threat.

shōgun—Military overlord in Early Modern Japan.

daimyō—Japanese feudal lord before 1871.

Japan: A Modernizing State

1853–1854	Arrival of Perry; signs Treaty of Kanagawa
1868	Tokugawa overthrown; Meiji Restoration
1868–1873	Capital moved to Tokyo; universal education, universal conscription, land tax reform, factories started
1870s	"Civilization and Enlightenment"
1889	Promulgation of Meiji Constitution
1890	First parliamentary elections
1895	Treaty of Shimonoseki
1902	Anglo-Japanese Treaty
1904–1905	Russo-Japanese War
1912	Death of Emperor Meiji

Western Trade

Both European and American merchants and diplomats tried unsuccessfully to open relations with Japan during the first part of the nineteenth century. Americans, who had just brought California into the Union, were most eager. On July 7, 1853, four U.S. ships under the command of Matthew Perry sailed into Edo Bay and brought the issue of Japanese relations with the West into sharp focus.

A Comic Dialogue, 1855

The four "black ships," as they were called by the Japanese, had been sent by the American government to convince the Japanese that a treaty opening trade relations between the two countries would be of mutual interest. After delivering a letter from the U.S. president, Perry departed, telling the authorities in Edo that he would return in a year for an answer. The Americans returned in February 1854, before the one-year deadline, because they feared that the French or the Russians might gain concessions sooner from the Japanese.

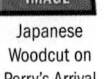

Japanese Woodcut on Perry's Arrival

The shōgun, after a period of intense debate within his country, agreed to Perry's requests. The Treaty of Kanagawa (KAH-nah-GAH-wah), the first formal agreement between Japan and a Western nation, was signed in 1854. By its terms, shipwrecked sailors were to be well treated and two ports were to be opened for provisioning ships and allowing for a limited amount of trade. European traders soon obtained similar privileges, in addition to the right of extraterritoriality. Later treaties, negotiated in 1858, established permanent trade relations and trading ports in Japan for the Americans.

The entry of the West placed a severe strain on the already weakened Japanese political structure. Antiforeign sentiment grew, even as many Japanese recognized that accommodation with the West was bound to come. European and American fleets had bombarded Kagoshima (kah-GOH-shee-mah) and Shimonoseki, two cities with many opponents of opening Japan, in 1863 and 1864, thereby convincing some of the antiforeign elements that their position was hopeless. By 1868, after a time of strife and confusion, the shōgun relinquished his power, and young Japanese reformers initiated radical changes. Edo, renamed Tokyo ("eastern capital"), became the capital of the new Japan.

The Meiji Period (1868–1912)

The new generation of Japanese leaders, most of whom were under 30 years of age and of samurai origin, did not start out with a well-developed plan. They knew they had to unite the country, so they "restored" the emperor, named Meiji (MAY-jee), as a focus for national loyalty and forced the *daimyō* to give up the regional autonomy they had under the Tokugawa. The young leaders of the **Meiji Restoration** next disbanded the old system of statuses in which the samu-

Meiji Restoration—The overthrow of the Tokugawa shōgunate and restoration of imperial rule in 1868.

Document "The Beefeater"

The quest for "Civilization and Enlightenment" inspired legal, social, and cultural changes in the first decades of the Meiji period. Things Japanese were considered old-fashioned, and enlightened men showed their modernity by carrying pocket watches and umbrellas, wearing some items of Western clothing, and above all, according to Kanagaki Robun (KAH-nah-GAH-kee ROH-boon), the author of this satirical monologue by an "enlightened" man, eating beef.

Excuse me, but beef is certainly a most delicious thing, isn't it? . . . I wonder why we in Japan haven't eaten such a clean thing before? . . . We should really be grateful that even people like ourselves can now eat beef, thanks to the fact that Japan is steadily becoming a truly civilized country. . . . In the West, they're free of superstitions. There it's the custom to do everything scientifically, and that's why they've invented amazing things like the steamship and the steam engine. Do you know that they engrave the plates for printing newspapers with telegraphic needles? And that they bring down wind from the sky with balloons? Aren't they wonderful inventions? Of course, there are good reasons behind these inventions. If you look at a map of the world, you'll see some countries marked "tropical," which means that's where the sun shines closest. . . . The king of that part of the world tried all kinds of schemes before he hit on what is called a balloon. That's a big round bag they fill with air high up in the sky. They bring the bag down and open it, causing the cooling air inside the bag to spread out all over the country. That's a great invention. On the other hand, in Russia, which is a cold country where the snow falls even in summer and the ice is so thick the people can't move, they invented the steam engine. You've got to admire them for it. I understand that they modeled the steam engine after the flaming chariot of hell, but anyway, what they do is to load a crowd of people on a wagon and light a fire in a pipe underneath. They keep feeding the fire inside the pipe with coal, so that the people riding on top can travel a great distance completely oblivious to the cold. Those people in the West can think up inventions like that, one after the other.

Questions to Consider

1. Why was being "civilized" identified with Western customs?
2. What kinds of technology seemed to be most impressive to the narrator?
3. Do you think the narrator's understanding of technology would seem strange to his contemporaries in Japan?

From Donald Keene, ed., *Modern Japanese Literature* (New York: Grove Press, 1956), pp. 31–34.

rai alone had ruled. Former samurai—the leaders' own class—could now enter business and former farmers and merchants could enter government. Universal education (1872) and military conscription (1873) were used to level the playing field.

The new leaders felt sufficiently confident in the government's stability that half of them traveled to Europe and the United States in 1871. For 18 months, they sought to renegotiate the unequal treaties forced on them since the 1850s and to study culture, politics, national defense, factories, and schools. When they returned to Japan, they squelched the plans to invade Korea of those who had stayed behind. Many of the latter left the government in anger. Some founded liberal political movements and eventually rejoined the government. But others did not.

Not all samurai had shared the leaders' zeal to eliminate samurai privileges. Starting in 1874 some of those samurai, now even more discontented because the government vetoed the Korean invasion, took part in rebellions. The most important of these was led by an erstwhile friend and fellow leader in the new government, Saigo Takamori (SAI-goh TAH-kah-MOH-ree). In 1877, Saigo led samurai into battle in Satsuma against the "dirt farmer" conscripts he disdained. The samurai were defeated in this brief civil war in which one-third of the 100,000 combatants died.

By the end of the 1870s, a people's rights movement emerged. Former samurai, farmers, merchants and other advocates of Western-style civil rights for men and women joined these nascent efforts to create a constitutional system based on the ***bunmei kaika*** (BOON-may KAI-kah; "Civilization and Enlightenment") ideals—including the political theories of Jean-Jacques Rousseau and John Stuart Mill—eagerly consumed by progressive Japanese. Government leaders had abandoned some of their earlier revolutionary attitudes, so they viewed the people's rights movement as an opposition force. Nevertheless, they helped the movement in 1881 by promising a Constitution and an elected ***Diet*** within a decade. The Constitution was promulgated in 1889, and the first parliamentary elections were held in 1890.

The Constitution was not a particularly liberal document. Drafted mainly by Itō Hirobumi (ee-TOH HEE-roh-BOO-mee), who later became Prime Minister, it made the emperor sovereign and in command of the military. The parliament was bicameral, with a House of Peers (nobility) and a House of Representatives (also called the Lower House). The Peers could veto any proposal passed by the Lower House. Until 1925, the Peers repeatedly rejected legislation passed by the Lower House to expand the electorate to include men of all social classes, including the poor, and continued to veto similar civil rights legislation for women before World War II.

DOCUMENT
The Meiji Constitution, 1889

Equally important, the new government encouraged economic development to create a ***fukoku kyōhei*** (FOO-koh-koo KEE-OH-hay; "rich country,

bunmei kaika—"Civilization and Enlightenment" ideology in Meiji Japan.

Diet—Japanese parliament.

fukoku kyōhei—"Rich country, strong army" policy of Meiji government.

The Meiji Constitution was granted to the Japanese people as a gift of the Emperor, seen here standing under the canopy. Like her husband, the Empress, seated on the throne at the left, wears Western-style clothing for this modern event.

strong military"). This was quite different from the official position taken by the Qing at that time. Model factories in textiles, cement, tools, and other products were set up by the Ministry of Industry in the 1870s. A reformed land tax (1873) siphoned off rural income to fund these initiatives; while this helped the industrial economy, the impact on farmers, many of whom fell into tenancy when they could not pay their taxes, was not as benign. At the same time, agricultural output did grow rapidly to feed the burgeoning population (from 30 million in 1868 to 40 million in 1900 to 73 million in 1940). The government also rapidly built an economic infrastructure to support private industry. This included railroads, telegraph lines, ports, post offices, and schools and universities.

Because the unequal treaties prevented the Japanese from raising tariffs to support new businesses, costs were cut in other ways. Labor bore the brunt. Girls and women worked under often oppressive conditions at very low wages to produce the silk that earned Japan the foreign currency needed to import new technology. Men and women worked together in coal mines. Slum-dwellers picked garbage and did odd jobs. Tuberculosis and other diseases took their toll. Fortunately, by World War I, the worst types of labor exploitation ended as Japan's economy took off and as reforms were implemented.

The other side of the slogan "rich country, strong military" was national defense. The humiliating unequal treaties were finally revised when Japan flexed its muscle in the Sino-Japanese War (1894–1895), the Righteous Harmony Fists (Boxer) Uprising (1900), and the Russo-Japanese War (1904–1905). The colonial world was impressed with Japan's victory over Russia, indicating that it was not a failure of Asia's culture but rather of economic development that kept them from independence. And that, some Asian nations anticipated, could be changed. After each of these wars, Japan not only gained respect in Western eyes—the Anglo-Japanese Alliance of 1902 is one example—it also gained an empire. Imperialism was the evil twin of national defense, as Taiwan and Korea came under Japanese domination and Japan strengthened its claim on northeast Asia. And even respect was spotty; the United States continued to discriminate against Japanese immigrants by passing laws to deprive them of the right to become citizens or own land.

Young women, like this child in a silk reeling mill, plunged their hands into pans of boiling water to remove the silk thread from cocoons. Profits from textile firms, most of whose workers were women and girls, helped fuel Japan's industrialization in the late nineteenth and early twentieth centuries.

When the Emperor Meiji died in 1912, Japanese looked back at 45 years of breathtakingly rapid change. The clang of the railway train, a symbol of modernity, rent the pastoral calm of the countryside. Men of all classes could, in theory, enter any profession, but women still struggled for basic equality, even in marriage. The political parties came to dominate parliamentary government, but an oligarchical **gerontocracy** and a military responsible only to the emperor could circumvent the parliament. Factories produced consumer goods that improved the lives of people rich and poor, but labor was shackled to oppressive conditions and air and water pollution threatened those improvements in the quality of life.

Architects and city planners, writers, and artists produced a tremendous outpouring of culture. Artists used both indigenous methods (after almost two decades of rejection of pre-Meiji art at the beginning of the period) and European methods and themes. Architects built up Japan's modern cities, with their multistoried Western-style buildings. City planners built transportation systems and parks. Writers may have affected the largest number of consumers of new culture, writing stories for publication as books and as installments in the burgeoning newpapers and magazines. Natsume Soseki (NAH-tsoo-may SOH-se-kee; 1868–1912), perhaps modern Japan's most revered writer, wrote of the loneliness of modernity.

In short, Japan was an increasingly modern country. Its poets and writers, its journalists and artists, its reformers and civil and women's rights advocates, served as the conscience of the nation. By the early twentieth century Japan was developing as a democracy, though one in which the people continued to struggle for political rights and economic justice.

CONCLUSION

With the exception of Japan and Thailand (Siam), Asia was dominated by the West at the end of the nine-

---

gerontocracy—Rule by senior citizens; in this case, by elderly former cabinet members or aristocrats.

women had few legal rights and were subordinate to their husbands.

Economic Developments

After independence, Latin American elites were confident that once they escaped the grip of Spanish and Portuguese colonialism, they would develop not only stable political systems but healthy economies. That optimism soon faded as leadership rivalries, regional splits and civil unrest, and ideological and racial divisions frustrated economic development. The elites continued to concentrate wealth in a few hands, and turned to the caudillos to protect their interests.

Most Latin American states suffered economic decline in the initial decades of independence. Independence wars had an adverse impact on production in silver mining in Mexico, Peru, and Bolivia; ranching in Argentina and Uruguay; plantation agriculture in Venezuela; and manufacturing in Ecuador and Mexico. There was little new investment from within Latin America as many *peninsulares* returned to Spain or moved to Cuba and the church withheld its money. Landowners turned inward, preferring to remain self-sufficient rather than producing crops and goods for domestic or international markets. With little revenue coming in, governments had to borrow heavily from Europe. As a result, they had to devote much of their customs revenue and export duties to paying off external debt rather than building up infrastructure such as roads, bridges, railways, and harbors.

With little industrial development taking place, Latin American nations were integrated into Europe's industrial economy but in a subordinate position. They became providers of raw materials such as copper, tin, hides, and agricultural products such as sugar, coffee, and tobacco. Most nations relied heavily on the export of one or two products and thus were at the mercy of international prices. When the price of a product was high, their economies did well, but when the price declined, they suffered. Latin America imported manufactured goods from Europe such as textiles and machinery, but it was slow to introduce new technologies such as the steam engine, which was only introduced in Latin America in the mid-nineteenth century. The mining and textile sectors still heavily depended on outdated technologies.

Britain was by far the leading foreign investor in Latin America until World War I. After colonial rule, Britain quickly recognized the newly independent states, negotiated commercial and navigation treaties, and took the place of Spanish and Portuguese businessmen in controlling the export trade. The British economic empire in Latin America was not based on formal control or direct intervention in the internal affairs of countries. Instead, British businessmen concentrated their investments in key sectors of the economy such as railways and mines and exerted their dominance over commerce to influence the decision-making of local politicians.

At the turn of the twentieth century, Latin America remained largely free of direct political control by Europe and the United States. Instead, Europe and the United States maintained an economic dominance over the region.

Mexico

Mexico suffered a half-century of turmoil after attaining independence in 1821. Agustín Iturbide's empire lasted less than a year, to be replaced by a federal republic. In 1833 state legislatures elected as president General Antonio López de Santa Anna (1795–1876), who eventually served in the office on 11 different occasions. He was a controversial figure. To his supporters he was the "Defender of the Homeland"; to his detractors he was the "Traitor of the Nation." Under his rule he attempted to establish a professional army drafted from Mexico's citizens to put down rebellions by regional caudillos. He also led Mexico into two disastrous wars to the north. In 1836 a group of proslavery Anglo-American settlers had proclaimed independence for Texas. Santa Anna's army defeated them at the Alamo, killing all the defenders, but lost disastrously at San Jacinto shortly thereafter. Texas was eventually annexed to the United States in 1845. Although he was disgraced by the loss of Texas, Santa Anna made several more comebacks. Yet, some ten years after losing Texas, he was drawn into a war with the United States (1846–1848) which resulted in another defeat, the loss of much more land, and even greater humiliation for Mexico. Santa Anna followed these losses up by selling southern New Mexico and Arizona to the United States for $15 million. By the time Santa Anna was toppled for the last time in 1855, Mexico had lost almost half its territory to its neighbor to the north.

An attempt to establish a more representative government came under the leadership of Benito Juárez (1806–1872), a Zapotec Indian who set out to implement a reform program known as the ***Reforma.*** Juarez and the liberals planned to establish a more democratic republic, destroy the political and economic force of the Catholic Church, and include the mestizos and Indians in political life. A terrible civil war followed their anticlerical measures; it ended in 1861 with Juárez's apparent victory.

DOCUMENT
Plan de Ayala

Later, European powers invaded when Mexico was unable to meet the payments on its debts, and a French puppet regime was installed with an Austrian Archduke Ferdinand Maximilian as emperor. Juárez mobilized resistance against the French and, aided in 1867 by pressure from the United States, his forces drove French troops from Mexican soil. Juárez again set out to institute the Reforma, and served in office until his death in 1872.

A coup in 1876 brought a mestizo, Porfirio Díaz (DEE-ahs; 1830–1915), to power. Díaz, who served as president from 1877 to 1880 and again from 1884 to 1911, stabilized Mexico under his firm rule. An adept political manager, he was a master of patron-client relations and balancing the interests of regional caudillos with the Mexico City elite that filled his administration. His primary strategy was to maintain order while building a strong economy. He reorganized the army and slashed the numbers of soldiers; he relied more on an upgraded police force to keep order and rid the countryside of bandits.

Díaz's efforts succeeded in attracting large amounts of foreign investment, especially from the United States. American firms took control of the production of minerals such as gold, silver, lead, copper, and zinc. About one-third of foreign investment flowed to railway construction, which boomed during this period and had profound consequences for Mexico's political and economic life. The new railways stimulated harbor expansions and the creation of new towns and regional identities. It also spurred the commercialization of land near railway lines as large hacienda owners expanded their land holdings at the expense of small landowners.

Díaz relied on the *cientificos* or technocrats for advice on managing the political and economic sys-

Reforma—The name for Benito Juárez's reform program that advocated restricting the powers of the Catholic Church, establishing democratic institutions and giving more political power to mestizos.

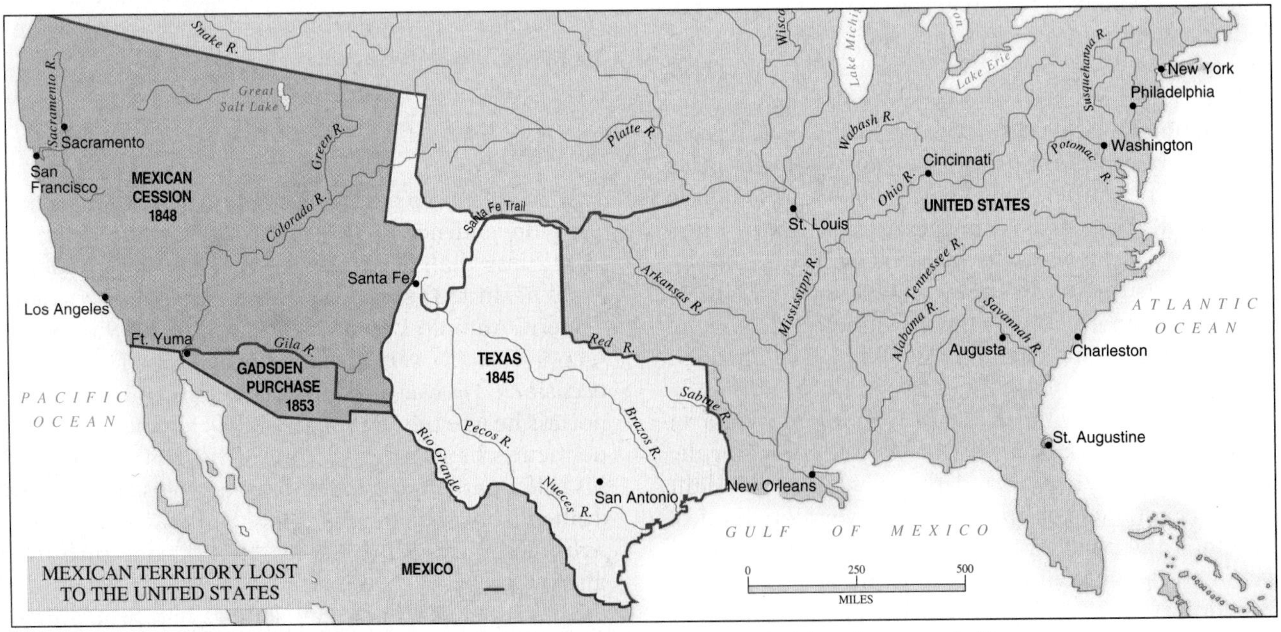

Mexico and the United States, 1846–1853. By the mid-nineteenth century, Mexico had lost almost one-half of its territory to the expanding United States either by war or sale.

President Porfirio Díaz sought to stabilize and modernize Mexico, but his tenure as president from 1877–1880 and 1884–1911 was essentially a dictatorship and established the conditions for the Mexican Revolution.

tem. The *cientificos* wanted to modernize Mexico based on the American model. They poured money into education, expanding free education to all Mexicans and encouraging literacy programs.

Díaz's rule, though outwardly conforming to the constitution, was a dictatorship. If there was much encouragement of arts and letters, there was no liberty. The Indians sank lower and lower into peonage these years. In spite of the anticlerical laws of the Juárez period, the church was quietly permitted to acquire great wealth, and foreign investors exploited Mexico, creating a long-lasting animosity towards foreigners.

Argentina

Until the 1970s, Argentina was probably the wealthiest Spanish-speaking country in the world. Its beginnings as an independent nation were less promising. Spanish colonizers had largely neglected the area because of its lack of minerals. However, Argentina was blessed with the bustling port city of Buenos Aires, whose energetic population sought to encourage European capital and commerce, and the pampas (PAM-puhs), plains that stretched for several hundred miles from Buenos Aires into the interior. The pampas, which contained rich agricultural land that was ideal for cattle ranching, were divided into large **estancias.** The large ranch owners relied on the support of their clients, the gauchos (GOW-chohs)—the independent-minded cowboys and bandits whose way of life has been romanticized in literature and folklore. The gauchos were largely mestizos who were tied to their horse culture.

Argentina's politics were centered around the conflict between landowners who favored a federal system that preserved their powers and the supporters of centralized government (known as *unitarios*) who mostly lived in Buenos Aires. However, from 1829 to 1852, Argentine politics were not controlled by either faction but by a caudillo, Juan Manuel de Rosas, a wealthy landowner and rancher who relied on gaucho support. Although a federalist, as governor of Buenos Aires province, he had no hesitation about stamping his personal authority on every aspect of political life. He favored the interests of the ranching elite, and he paid lip service to the legislature. He did not even bother to issue decrees or laws. He went so far as to require Catholic priests to wear the symbol of his followers, a red ribbon, while they conducted Mass.

estancia—A large estate or cattle ranch in Spanish America.

The gauchos were romanticized in Argentina in much the same way that the cowboys were in the United States.

In 1852 de Rosas was overthrown by an uneasy alliance of Justo José de Urquiza, a former ally of de Rosas, and the *unitarios* of Buenos Aires. A constitution that was remarkably durable was adopted in 1853. It provided for a central administration but with many powers delegated to the provinces. However, it gave power to a president to intervene in the affairs of provinces or depose provincial governors if they did not uphold the central government. Urquiza headed a confederation of interior provinces, while Buenos Aires went its own way until a war between the two resulted in a victory for Buenos Aires and the unification of the country in the 1860s.

Although subsequent presidents were limited to one term each, they generally did not rule in a democratic manner. Domingo Sarmiento (sar-MY-EN-toh), who had been impressed with free public American education while serving as Argentina's minister to Washington, D.C., during the American Civil War, promoted a dramatic expansion of state-sponsored education during his presidency from 1868 to 1874. In 1879–1880, General Julio Roca launched the **"Conquest of the Desert,"** which was actually a campaign to expel nomadic Indian tribes in the southern pampas and neighboring Patagonia. Roca was elected president the same year the war concluded, while the vanquished Indians saw their lands parceled out as a reward to soldiers who had participated in the campaign or bought up by large landowners at cheap prices. European immigrants who did not have the resources to purchase the land were restricted to working as labor tenants on the estancias. The Indians were placed in reservations similar to those in the United States. As a consequence Argentina never saw the development of a peasantry or experienced any pressures for land reform from below.

In the late nineteenth century Argentina benefited from a booming economy that grew at least 5 percent a year between 1880 and World War I. Railway construction into the interior opened up production in the *pampas*, which contain perhaps the most fertile land in the world for growing wheat and lush grazing land for cattle and sheep. In the first half of the nineteenth century, cattle ranches primarily exported hides and beef jerky, which was mainly sold to feed slave populations in Brazil and the Caribbean. Argentina's beef industry dramatically took off with the development of steamships and the introduction of refrigerated ships around 1880 that made it feasible to transport enormous quantities of fresh beef to Europe. Wool and wheat were two additional exports. Sheep farming did not require large numbers of additional laborers, but wheat farms did. They depended on new immigrants for labor because the gauchos, wedded to their horses, refused to take up the plow.

Conquest of the Desert—A military campaign in 1879–1880 led by General Julio Roca against Indian tribes that opened up large areas of Patagonia and the southern pampas for settlement by large estate owners.

The intimate commercial relationship with Britain and other European countries, which lasted until after World War II, affected nearly every aspect of Argentine life. Foreign money, especially British capital, helped develop a sophisticated infrastructure; port facilities, railroads, light industry, and urban conveniences were among the most advanced in the world.

The expansion of the economy required a major increase in workers, and that was provided by a huge influx of European immigrants both to the rural areas as labor tenants and wage laborers and to Buenos Aires as workers in meatpacking plants, in the service sector as dockworkers, and in the government civil service. Between 1870 and World War I, 3 million immigrants—almost one-half were Italians and 32 percent were Spanish-speaking—arrived in Argentina. They made up almost one-third of Argentina's population.

The immigration policies were consciously designed to "Europeanize" the country. In Argentina and other countries such as Brazil, elites shared a common belief that Europeans were superior to indigenous people and African slaves and that the immigrants came with the work ethic and entrepreneurial skills so lacking in local communities.

Many of the immigrants settled in Buenos Aires, which steadily grew in size. By 1936, its population was 2.5 million, which made it the third largest city in the Western Hemisphere after New York and Chicago. Despite its location on a monotonous plain beside a muddy estuary, it developed into a beautiful and vibrant city. Although all sorts of architectural styles were found in buildings, members of its upper class identified with Paris and promoted the construction of wide boulevards. They emulated the European gentry, living grandly in French-styled palaces and closely following Paris fashion trends.

The character of Buenos Aires was also shaped by the massive settlement of new immigrants. They comprised two-thirds of the population of Buenos Aires in 1914. Most of the immigrants were workers and lived either in slums on the city's outskirts or in dilapidated tenements around the city. By and large, these workers were single males with few prospects for finding marriageable partners. They frequented the brothels that were found in every part of the city. Prostitution was legal at this time and operated under the protection of the police and prominent politicians. From the brothels came a sensuous dance, the tango. The lyrics of tango songs reflected the immigrant men's rootlessness and loneliness as well as their misogynistic views of "loose" women. The tango gained widespread acceptance in Argentina after professional dancers

Document Civilization and Barbarism

A liberal Argentine politician Domingo Sarmiento (1881–1888) fled the regime of Juan Manuel de Rosas in the 1840s. While in exile he wrote *Facundo* (1845), a biographical account of the life of General Don Facundo Quiroga, a provincial caudillo and rival to de Rosas. Sarmiento contrasted the barbarism of the caudillos, which he attributed to the lack of sound government and their anarchism, with the civilized behavior found in liberal political systems. Characterizing the pampas as the source of Argentine barbarism and the gauchos as the epitome of cultural backwardness, he maintained that European immigration was necessary to modernize and civilize Argentina.

In the Argentine Republic, it makes one feel pity and shame to compare the German or Scottish colonies to the south of Buenos Aires with the towns existing in the interior. In the first, the little houses are painted, always clean in front, adorned with flowers and nice little shrubs; the furnishings, simple but complete; the dishes made of copper or tin, always shining; the bed with nice curtains; and the inhabitants in constant motion and action. Milking cows, making butter and cheese, some families have been able to amass colossal fortunes, retiring to the city to enjoy its conveniences.

The native town is the disgraceful reverse side of the coin; dirty children covered in rags, living amid packs of dogs; men stretched out on the ground, in utter inactivity; filth and poverty everywhere; a little table and leather chests, the only furnishings; miserable huts for habitation; notably for their generally barbaric and neglected appearance.

This misery, which is now disappearing as a feature of the rural, pastoral areas doubtless motivated the words wrested out of Sir Walter Scott by spite and the humiliation of the English forces: "The vast plains of Buenos Aires," says he, "are populated solely by Christian savages, known by the name of gauchos"—that is, gauchos—"whose principal furnishings are horses' skulls, whose food is raw meat and water, and whose favorite pastime is racing horses until they burst." Unfortunately, adds the good gringo, "they preferred national independence over our cottons and muslins." It would be good to make a proposal to England, just to see how many yards of linen and how many pieces of muslin it would give to own the plains of Buenos Aires. . . .

The man of the city wears European dress, lives a civilized life as we know it everywhere: in the city, there are laws, ideas of progress, means of instruction, some municipal organization, a regular government, etc. Leaving the city district, everything changes in aspect. The man of the country wears other dress, which I will call American, since it is common to all peoples; his way of life is different, his needs, specific and limited. They are like two distinct societies, two people strange to one another. And more still: the man of the country, far from aspiring to resemble the man of the city, rejects with scorn his luxuries and his polite manners; and the clothing of the city dweller, his tailcoat, his cape, his saddle—no such sign of Europe can appear in the countryside with impunity. All that is civilized in the city is blockaded, banished outside of it, and anyone who would dare show up in a frock coat, for example, and mounted in an English saddle, would draw upon himself the peasants' jeers and their brutal aggression. . . .

With young manhood [of the gaucho] comes complete independence—and idleness. Here is what I will call the public life of the gaucho begins, for his education is now finished. We must see these men as Spanish only in language, and in the confused religious notions they maintain, to be able to appreciate their indomitable, haughty character, born of the struggle of man with savage nature, of rational man with the brute. We must see these heavily bearded faces, these grave, serious countenances like those of Asian Arabs, to judge the pitying disdain inspired in them by the sight of a sedentary city dweller, who may have read many books but does not know how to pull down a fierce bull and kill it; who would not know how to provide himself with a horse in the open country, on foot and without help from anyone; who has never stopped a tiger, facing it with a dagger in one hand and a poncho wrapped around the other to stick in its mouth, while he runs it through the heart and leaves it lying at his feet. This habit of triumphing over all resistance, of always proving himself superior to nature, challenging and conquering it, develops a prodigious feeling of individual importance and superiority.

Questions to Consider

1. What are the qualities that Sarmiento associates with gauchos?
2. Is there a connection between Sarmiento's point of view on European culture and the massive immigration from Europe that took place in the late nineteenth century?
3. Are there any similarities or differences between Sarmiento's depiction of the gauchos and those of cowboys in other cultures?

From Domingo Sarmiento, *Facundo: Civilization and Barbarism,* trans. Kathleen Ross (Berkeley: University of California Press, 2003), pp. 52–58.

and amateur bands adopted it; it won even more respectability as it was popularized in Europe just before World War I. After the war prostitution was banned in Argentina, and the tango moved from brothels to cabarets. The content of the lyrics shifted to express the confusion men felt at the growing assertiveness and independence of women. One tango song expressed this sentiment:

Before women were feminine,
now fashion has thrown all that out.
Before only the face and foot showed,
but now they show all there is to be seen.
Today all the women seem to be men,
they smoke, drink whisky, and wear pants.[1]

With the spread of radios in the 1930s, tango songs also developed a mass following among women.

Brazil

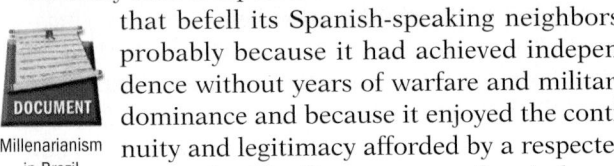

The former Portuguese colony of Brazil maintained its unity and escaped the turbulence and disorders that befell its Spanish-speaking neighbors, probably because it had achieved independence without years of warfare and military dominance and because it enjoyed the continuity and legitimacy afforded by a respected monarchy. The first emperor of an independent Brazil, Pedro I (r. 1822–1831), promulgated a constitution in 1824 that emphasized his own powers and also provided for a General Assembly. The elite were split into two factions. The Portuguese party represented Portuguese-born conservatives who favored the monarchy, while the Brazil party consisted of liberal, southern landowners who supported reducing the power of the monarchy and enhancing provincial autonomy.

DOCUMENT
Millenarianism in Brazil

An economic crisis forced Pedro I to abdicate in 1831. His Brazilian-born 5-year-old son was placed under a regency until he was old enough to take the throne as Pedro II in 1840. For almost the next half-century, two issues—the future of slavery and the monarchy—dominated his reign.

In the early years of his reign Pedro II enjoyed considerable support from political factions and the imperial army, but support for him and the monarchy shifted dramatically during Brazil's five-year war with Paraguay in the late 1860s. The war saw a significant shift in the size of the army with officers demanding more say in the government. Toward the end of the war the emperor tried to limit the influence of the liberals by dissolving the cabinet and relying on conservative advisers. In response, the liberals began agitating for reform and even questioning the legitimacy of the monarchy. Even the Catholic Church retreated from its support for the monarchy. Although there was disaffection from a variety of quarters, the move to overthrow Pedro ultimately came from military officers and republicans who forced the emperor to abdicate without much resistance in 1889 and leave for exile in Portugal.

The End of Brazilian Slavery

Nearly all Latin American countries abolished the slave trade shortly after independence, but slave labor remained the central institution of the economies of Brazil, Cuba, and Puerto Rico. Britain applied pressure on Spain to end the slave trade to Cuba and Puerto Rico in 1820, but as Cuba became the world's largest exporter of sugar in the 1830s, thousands of new slaves continued to be imported. Between 1820 and 1865, about half a million slaves were added to Cuba's slave population.

In Brazil slaves provided cheap labor for the *fazendas* or sugar plantations on its northeast coast, the coffee plantations of the southeastern provinces, and the cattle ranches of the southern provinces. Working conditions on the plantations were very brutal and the slave mortality rate was high. Many more slaves died

Brazilian slaves working in a fazenda *or sugar plantation. The slave trade continued unabated in Brazil until British diplomatic and military pressure forced the emperor to end the trade in 1851. It would take another 37 years, however, before slavery was finally abolished within the country in 1888.*

Document Newspaper Advertisements for Runaway Slaves in Brazil

In nineteenth century Brazil, slaves fleeing their masters was a common occurrence. Because of the costs of replacing slaves who often had skills, slaveholders went to great lengths to recapture them. They ran newspaper advertisements describing in great detail the slaves who had fled and offering substantial rewards for their return or recapture. These descriptions offer insight into the nature of slavery and the reasons why slaves sought to escape from their masters.

$100,000 Reward

Fled on December 3 of this year from the plantation of Major Antonio de Campos Freire one of his slaves named José of the Benguella nation (though he says he is a Creole) from 25 to 30 years of age with the following characteristics: short in stature, thin, well-made body, dark color, face rather long, pale jaw, almost no beard, lips rather full, round head, and is in the habit of going abut with long hair, small eyes, long eyelashes, good teeth, nose medium large, speaks in a refined, humble, and insincere way, may have some old and small marks of punishment on his buttocks. He is a master blacksmith, also knows how to work with copper; also a master at killing ants with his bellows. He is accustomed to getting drunk and in that condition becomes violent. He took some work clothes, a poncho with a yellow lining, a firearm, a hat of rough straw; and whenever he runs away he usually claims to be free and changes his name. Whoever captures him and takes him to his master will receive 100$000 reward, in addition to expenses, which will be paid separately.

O Mercantil (Rio de Janeiro), January 13, 1845

Fled or was led astray a black girl *[moleca]* named Maria of the Cacange nation, who appears to be about 14 years of age and still does not have breasts, black color and thin, wore a dress of white calico with ribbons and pink flowers. The said girl was missing yesterday afternoon when she went to the Campo de Santa Anna to get water, and it appears that she was crying there because someone had stolen her water bucket. Whoever brings her to the Rua de Santa Anna No. 47B, upper floor, will be satisfactorily rewarded, or even someone who gives information about her so that her owner can get her back.

Diario de Rio de Janeiro, December 31, 1847

Fled from Jaraguá from the custody of Mr. Mariz on the 21st of the current month the slave Izidoro, mulatto, 18 years old, tall, long hair; at the sugar mills of Garcatorta and Villa do Norte this slave has a father and relatives; it is very possible that he went to those places; he fled with manacles on his hands and should have some marks on his feet as a result of wearing irons for some days. We appeal to anyone who captures him to deliver him in Maceió to Mr. Antonio Texeira Pinto in the Cambona, and he will be well rewarded. Maceió, December 22, 1855.

O Noticiador Alagoano (Maceió), December 30, 1855

200$000 reward to anyone who captures and brings to the Boa-Vista plantation in the district of Lorena, province of Sao Paulo, the mulatto Camillo, who ran away on the 14th of the present month and belongs to Major Manoel de Freitas Novaes.

Also will pay all expenses of the journey, etc., up to the time of delivery, the aforementioned mulatto having the following features: about 45 years of age, tall in stature, speaks with a high voice and always looks frightened, has some teeth missing in front and lettering on his forehead and on the palms of his hand which says: "Slave of Dona Fortunata," always wearing on his head a cap or handkerchief to hide the letters on his forehead. He wore trousers of woven cloth, a waistcoat of black cloth, a shirt of calico or shirt cloth, and a cloth jacket and poncho. He likes to boast that he is free. He is a master carpenter, sailor, and a coffee, cane sand hydraulic-work machinist. . . .

All authorities and planters are asked to help capture the said slave, and not to trust the submissiveness with which he tries to deceive people of good faith in order to get away.

Diario de Rio de Janeiro, March 24, 1872

Questions to Consider

1. Do these advertisements give you any insights into why slaves fled their masters?
2. What do the advertisements tell you about how slaves acted around white people?
3. Many slaves in the southern United States escaped through the "underground railroad." Was there a similar network in Brazil? How do you think slaves survived in Brazil once they escaped?

From Robert Edgar Conrad, *Children of God's Fire: A Documentary History of Black Slavery in Brazil* (University Park, Pennsylvania: Pennsylvania State University Press, 1984), pp. 362–365.

than were born in the slave population in Brazil, and new shipments of African slaves were constantly required to replenish the labor force. As coffee production increased for the North American and European markets in the 1840s, the main port for slave imports shifted from Bahia (bah-EE-ah) in the northeast to Rio de Janeiro in the south.

Although British investments in Brazil's economy were extensive, the British government was opposed to slavery and tried to prevent ships from bringing additional slaves into Brazil. Britain signed a treaty with Portugal in 1815 banning the slave trade above the equator. In 1826 the British negotiated an agreement with Brazil to end the slave trade by 1830, but this had little effect. Slavers—with the open support of the Brazilian government—found ways to evade British antislavery squadrons and brought over 500,000 slaves from Africa in the 1830s and 1840s alone.

Unlike the United States, there was little division within Brazil's ruling elite about the necessity for slavery. It was popularly accepted at this time that there was no alternative to slave labor. The elite argued that African slaves were much better off in Brazil than they had been in Africa and that their living standard was better than European peasants. Emperor Pedro I, however, was personally opposed to slavery. Pedro II freed his own slaves in 1840, but concern for his own position made him cautious about taking on the plantation aristocracy over the issue of slavery. Abolitionist sentiment was slight, and even the handful of abolitionists did not argue for an immediate end to slavery. In 1850 the British government brought the issue to a head by instructing its navy to aggressively blockade the Brazilian coast and enter Brazilian waters if necessary. The emperor was faced with a choice of defying the British and risking a war or abolishing the trade. The following year he decreed an end to the slave trade.

The institution of slavery, however, lingered on within the country for almost more four decades. Influenced by the American Civil War, Pedro II began considering ways of reducing the number of slaves rather than freeing them outright. Drawing on the experience of abolition in Cuba and former Spanish colonies, he proposed a measure providing that the children of slave mothers would no longer be defined as slaves, but it was not until 1871 that the measure was implemented. Even then, these children were kept in servitude to their mothers' owners until they reached 21. The Brazilian government was also reluctant to set all of the slaves free because of the expense of compensating slave owners for their losses.

Because of the 1871 measure, the slave population shrank from 2.5 million in 1850 to 1 million in 1874. To make up for the lost labor, plantation owners actively recruited European immigrants in the belief that they would be more productive workers and better consumers than freed slaves. Most of the several hundred thousand immigrants who arrived in the 1870s were from southern Europe and worked on coffee plantations.

Another law in 1885 gave freedom to all slaves over the age of 60. Finally, on May 13, 1888, two years after Cuba freed its slaves, Pedro ended Brazilian slavery without any compensation going to the slave owners. Emancipation, however, did not dramatically undermine the power of the plantation owners or improve the status and work condition of freed slaves. A poem of the era aptly captured the plight of freed slaves.

Everything in this world changes,
Only the life of the Negro remains the same;
He works to die of hunger,
The 13th of May fooled him.[2]

The End of Slavery in Brazil

1826	British treaty with Brazil to end slave trade
1840	Emperor Pedro II frees personal slaves
1850	End of slave trade to Brazil
1863	Emancipation Proclamation in United States
1871	Children of slave mothers no longer defined as slaves
1885	Slaves over age of 60 freed
1886	End of slavery in Cuba
1888	Emancipation of slaves in Brazil

Other Latin American Nations

Political turmoil, geographical handicaps, and racial disunity all played a part in the development of the other new nations in Latin America. Bolivia, named so hopefully for the Liberator, Simón Bolívar, underwent countless revolutions. Peru's course was almost as futile. The state of Gran Colombia dissolved by 1830, and its successors—Colombia, Venezuela, and Ecuador—were plagued by instability and civil wars. Paraguay endured a series of dictatorships, and Uruguay, created in 1828 as a buffer between Argentina and Brazil, long suffered from interventions by those two countries.

Nitrates being loaded at Pisagua, the northernmost nitrate port of Chile. Control of the valuable export trade could occasionally lead to war, as it did in the War of the Pacific (1879–1883) in which Chile defeated Peru and Bolivia.

An exception to the prevailing pattern of political chaos was the steady growth of the republic of Chile. In 1830 Chile came under the control of a conservative oligarchy. Although this regime proved to be generally enlightened, the country was kept under tight control for a century and was ruled for the benefit of the large landlords and big business.

Central America narrowly escaped becoming part of Mexico in 1822. After a 15-year effort to create a Central American confederation, Guatemala, El Salvador, Honduras, Nicaragua, and Costa Rica asserted their independence. Except for Costa Rica, where whites comprised the bulk of the population, racial disunity delayed the development of national feeling. On the Caribbean island of Hispaniola, the Dominican Republic, after decades of submission to the more populous but equally underdeveloped Haiti, maintained a precarious independence. The other Caribbean islands remained under foreign dominance—British, Dutch, Spanish, or French—and served their European masters as a source of raw materials—especially coffee, sugar, and tobacco—and later as coaling stations for their steam-powered navies.

TWENTIETH-CENTURY LATIN AMERICA

- *Why did liberal politicians throughout Latin America have such difficulty successfully implementing their programs?*

Limited Political and Economic Reform

At the end of the nineteenth century, politicians who professed to be liberals were ascendant in many Latin American nations such as Mexico, where Porfiro Díaz ruled for over three decades, and Argentina, where General Julio Roca and a series of politicians who represented the small landowning elite took command of government. The political power of the liberals seemed to place them in a position to bring about genuine reform, but this was not to be. Ultimately, the liberals were more concerned with stability and order than they were to their own political ideals. Most notably, the liberals failed to live up to the principles of political accountability and free market economics. Instead, acting against these principles, they expanded the powers of the executive office of government—making this office less accountable to voters and the other branches of government. The liberals, who desired to break Latin America's dependence on the export of raw resources to Europe and the United States, also established government enterprises to oversee key industries such as oil and steel or raised tariffs on imported goods to protect local manufacturers.

CASE STUDY
Brothers in Arms: Comparative Politics and Revolution

While liberal politicians failed to bring about sweeping change in Latin America, new groups became more assertive in political life at this time. Indian peasants and immigrant workers, mostly from Europe, formed organizations to advance their causes. In Argentina immigrant workers brought with them

Argentine suffragists casting symbolic ballots in the 1920s—women would not earn equal voting rights with men until 1947.

the ideas of European anarchists, socialists, and communists and founded new organizations and trade unions. The growing middle class of professionals, small businessmen, and shopkeepers sought a voice in government circles. The vote was gradually extended to more men in many countries, although voting rights meant very little when elections were fraudulent or rigged.

Although women's groups had raised the issue of women's suffrage for many years, the movement gained momentum after World War I when American women won the right to vote in 1920 and women's organizations such as the National Council of Mexican Women and the Brazilian Federation for the Advancement of Women were founded in a number of countries. These organizations not only raised the issue of voting rights, but also other women's issues such as legal reforms, access to education, and divorce. Because their efforts were often ignored at the national level, they turned to organizations associated with the Pan American movement to raise their case with governments. Suffrage rights were placed before such bodies as the American Association for the Advancement of Women and the International Conference of American States.

Finally, in the late 1920s and early 1930s, a handful of states introduced the vote for women but often for reasons having little to do with advancing women's interests. In Ecuador (1929) a conservative ruling elite adopted the vote as a way to broaden its support in the face of continued threats from radical military officers who had staged a coup in 1925. In Brazil (1932) women took advantage of a new reform-minded administration, although both men and women lost the vote after a military coup in 1937. In Uruguay (1932) another ruling elite, threatened by the prospect of new male immigrants winning the vote, extended the vote to women because they thought they would be much more conservative and more likely to preserve the status quo.

In the late nineteenth and early twentieth centuries Latin American economies exported more crops and mineral resources to Europe and the United States in exchange for manufactured goods. Large-scale road and railway construction, often financed by external investors, helped fuel this expansion. Increased crop production, however, was often at the expense of Indians whose land was either bought or confiscated by large landowners. This was a major cause of peasant uprisings in many countries and a contributor to the Mexican Revolution of 1910.

Little was done in Latin American economies to diversify their exports and create industries. The volume of exports expanded, but most national economies were monocultures tied to a few exports. Cuba, Puerto Rico, and the Dominican Republic relied on sugar; Uruguay and Argentina on wool, beef, and wheat; Chile on nitrates and copper; Bolivia on tin, Brazil on rubber, coffee and sugar; and Central American states on coffee and bananas (hence, the origin of the term *banana republic*). It was not until the 1930s that some countries such as Brazil began to promote industrialization through protecting local industries by raising tariffs on imported goods.

The Mexican Revolution

The Mexican Revolution was the first major revolution of the twentieth century and, along with the Russian revolution of 1917, it set a precedent for later revolutionary movements throughout Latin America, Africa, and Asia.

The seeds for the Mexican Revolution were sown during the long rule of Porfirio Díaz. In 1910 he had been president of Mexico for most of the previous 33 years. While his rule may have ushered in a period of unprecedented political stability and economic growth, his policies also laid the foundation for a revolution.

Economic growth had come at a cost. Foreign investors had flocked to the country and had taken control of key sectors of the economy such as mining and agriculture. In the last years of Díaz's rule, a downturn in the American economy and drought and famine in Mexico had an adverse impact on the provinces of northern Mexico. Many workers lost their jobs in mines, farms, ranches, and textile factories. Significant strikes took place among railway and textile factory workers. Peasants deeply resented the loss of their land to commercial landowners. Food riots broke out in some cities.

Although the 80-year-old Díaz had been a master of patronage and buying off competing interest groups, he refused to leave office of his own accord and he made no provision for a peaceful succession. The beneficiaries of his rule were growing concerned about the future. The *cientificos* wanted to create a national political party, while regional caudillos wanted to hold on to their narrow power bases.

Although Díaz easily won reelection in 1910, this time he had to fend off a strong challenge from the son of a wealthy property owner and industrialist named Francisco Madero (1873–1913). After the election he jailed Madero and numerous opposition members for refusing to recognize his regime's legitimacy. Madero moved to San Antonio, Texas, from where he mobilized opposition to Díaz. In late 1910 he issued the **Plan of San Luis Potosi,** which called for democracy, workers' rights, and land reform. His manifesto inspired many groups in Mexico which launched a rebellion against the Díaz regime. Madero—along with Emiliano Zapata (zah-PAH-tah; c. 1877–1923), leader of mestizos and Indians in the south, and Francisco "Pancho" Villa (VEE-yah) and Pasqual Orozco (oh-ROHS-koh), leaders with peasant, cowboy, and farm labor support in the north—carried out the first phase of the revolution. In 1911 Madero crossed the border into Mexico and, with the tacit support of the U.S. government that turned a blind eye to his army buying weapons from American arms dealers, established a provisional government. As the rebel force gained strength, Díaz realized his time was up and negotiated a peaceful exit. As he went to his exile in Paris, he warned: "Francisco Madera has unleashed a tiger; now let's set if he can tame it."[3]

Díaz's words were prophetic. Madero easily won a democratic election and tried to establish his own rule. But he did not reward key supporters such as Villa and Zapata and his proposed reform of state-owned land was a failure. A Mexican bank and an American businessman ended up buying most of the land Madero had opened up because the peasants did not have the resources to purchase it. His military chief of staff and a former supporter of Díaz, General Victoriano Huerta, turned on him and had him assassinated after jailing him in 1913. But Huerta's rule lasted less than a year before he was forced to resign.

The Mexican Revolution

1910	Madero issues Plan of San Luis Potosi
1911	Ousting of Porfiro Díaz
1911	Overthrow of Victoriano Huerta
1912	Overthrow of Francisco Madero
1912	End of Civil War
1913	New constitution adopted
1919	Emiliano Zapata assassinated
1923	Pancho Villa assassinated
1934	Land Reform by Lazaro Cárdenas

Plan of San Luis Potosi—A manifesto issued by Francisco Madero in 1910 that called on Mexicans to overthrow the Díaz regime and supported democratic rights and land reform.

Emiliano Zapata served as the leader of revolutionaries who desired land reform and political change in the south of Mexico.

The power vacuum in Mexico City touched off a civil war that pitted the revolutionary forces of Villa and Zapata against Venustiano Carranza (kahr-RAHN-sah) (1859–1920) and his leading general, Álvero Obregón (OH-bray-GOHN). The latter were staunch nationalists, but since they were less radical than Villa and Zapata, they won the grudging support of the U.S. government, which supplied them with modern weapons and ammunition. The Americans had intervened before against Villa in 1915 after he staged a raid into New Mexico and later sent in an expeditionary force under General John Pershing that ultimately galvanized widespread opposition from Mexicans. Pershing's units returned to American soil a dismal failure. Carranza's forces eventually wore down the resistance of Villa and Zapata, who operated from their respective strongholds in the north and south. The cost in human life was immense. An estimated one million people died in this phase of the revolution. Indeed, few leaders of the revolution died peacefully. Zapata was assassinated in 1919 and Villa four years later.

Cathedral on the Zocalo, Mexico City

In 1917 Carranza wrote a progressive new constitution that provided for a strong president that could not be reelected after a six-year term, an independent judiciary, the right of the government to expropriate land, state control of all resources below the ground such as water and oil, the separation of church and state and the ending of religious education, the legalization of trade unions, an 8-hour work day, and the right of women to divorce. The latter was a major change for a country where marriage was the norm and women were expected to live contentedly in male-dominated households. Many of these provisions, however, were not implemented in the short term.

Carranza was the first of three successive presidents who came from Sonora Province in northern Mexico. All were substantial landowners and were reluctant to carry out the revolution's goals. In the early 1920s President Obregón initiated a modest redistribution of 3 million acres of land to peasants, but subsequent presidents did little to advance the goals of the revolution until Lazaro Cárdenas held the presidency from 1934 to 1940. He opened up 44 million acres of land to peasants by using the ***ejido,*** a traditional Indian institution that held land communally for all the people in a community; 800,000 peasants benefited from the land reform.

Cárdenas nationalized railroads in 1937 and took on the American companies that controlled oil production the following year. He expropriated their holdings and established a state monopoly over oil. Although the American companies appealed to the Roosevelt administration to intervene against Cárdenas, Roosevelt, who was promoting a "Good Neighbor" policy, worked out a compromise in which the

---

ejido—The system of communal ownership of land that was practiced by Indian societies before the arrival of the Spanish.

Party of Revolutionary Institutions (PRI)—The political party founded in 1929 that dominated Mexican political life until the end of the twentieth century.

Mexican government compensated the oil companies for their losses.

Finally, Cárdenas strengthened his party's political machinery. He established a principle that a president had to step down after his 6-year term was over, and that he could choose a successor in consultation with party bosses. Cárdenas renamed the party the *Partido de la Revolución Mexicana* or Mexican Revolutionary Party (PRM). Renamed the **Party of Revolutionary Institutions (PRI)** in 1946, this party dominated Mexican political life for the rest of the century.

Brazil

After the fall of the monarchy in 1889, the new United States of Brazil patterned its federal structure on the U.S. Constitution. But stability was elusive and the nation underwent civil unrest and military upheavals, much like those experienced by other Latin American countries. The centers of power were São Paolo and its coffee plantations that contributed about 30 percent of Brazil's GNP and Minas Gerais (MEE-nahs zhee-RAIS), which was dominated by large ranches. Between them these provinces produced almost all the presidents from 1894 to 1930. The republic was also stable because the army removed itself from politics. Foreign capital continued to enter the country, and, with the end of slavery, immigration from Europe increased. Between 1872 and 1930, 2 million immigrants arrived in Brazil.

Brazil's most important export was coffee, but when the industry slumped in the 1920s because of overproduction and a steep dip in the price of coffee, Brazil had to take on a large amount of foreign debt. After the Wall Street crash of 1929, the demand for coffee dropped even further and the price tumbled from 22.5 to 8 cents a pound. With the economy in tatters, the Brazilian military intervened, maintaining that it had the responsibility to save the country from the misrule of civilians. The army installed Getúlio Vargas (VAHR-gahs) as president; in 1937, he proclaimed the *Estudo Novo* ("New State"), which was little more than a military dictatorship. Democratic rights were suspended and trade unions were brought under state control. The Vargas regime's main economic strategy was industrialization through import substitution. The state protected certain sectors such as manufacturing, mining, oil, steel, electricity, automobile production, and light aircraft by imposing high duties on imports.

Argentina

Argentina's political system was authoritarian with some trappings of democracy. Liberal politicians, primarily drawn from the landowning aristocracy known as the "Oligarchy," dominated Argentina's political affairs. The 1800 individuals who owned most of the land believed in their right to run government. In the executive offices they made decisions among themselves and regularly ignored the legislature. Elections were rife with fraud and vote buying. It was claimed that even the dead came to life to cast their ballots on election days.

The affluent Argentines of the early 1900s sought to make Buenos Aires "the Paris of Latin America."

Twentieth-century Argentine politics were a struggle between the economic power of the land-owning elite and the electoral clout of the urban working and middle classes. A decisive shift in electoral politics came after a reform law was passed in 1912 that provided for universal adult suffrage for males over the age of 18, a secret ballot, and compulsory voting. The reform was designed to co-opt the growing middle class into the political system, but the Radical party that represented the middle class won the next election. Although the Radical party initially reached out for the support of the working class, they became antilabor after harshly repressing a general strike in 1919.

Many working class immigrants were drawn to socialist ideas. Anarchists and syndicalists were initially responsible for organizing among the working class, but after World War I, they lost ground to the Socialist party, which advocated bringing about change through the electoral process, and the Communist party, which directed its energies on building workers' organizations.

Argentina's economy faltered during the Great Depression, prompting the military, which had stayed aloof from politics, to stage a coup in September 1930. Two small army units took over the presidential palace with little opposition. The military, which had become an independent institution with no loyalty to any political party, tried to establish a broad-based political party to run the country. However, they proved to be no more effective than civilian politicians. Civilian politicians regained control of the government before the military intervened again in 1943.

THE COLOSSUS TO THE NORTH: THE UNITED STATES AND LATIN AMERICA

- *Why did the United States repeatedly intervene in Latin America from the late nineteenth century through the 1930s?*

Although the Monroe Doctrine of 1823 declared Latin America off-limits to European colonization, the United States did not have the political or economic power to enforce its policy for many years. Instead, throughout most of the nineteenth century, Britain, through its economic activities, continued to have the most influence in the region. American interests in Mexico and Cuba, however, increased in the mid-nineteenth century after the Mexican-American War and as American sugar interests intensified their desire to annex Cuba to the United States. American investors also began to look to Central America in their efforts to locate a faster route from the eastern United States to the newly opened gold fields of California.

As American economic power grew in the last few decades of the nineteenth century so too did American influence in Latin America. Both American and Latin American business elites generally profited from these arrangements. President Theodore Roosevelt oversaw the introduction of what has been called **"dollar diplomacy"** that coordinated the activities of American foreign investors and the U.S. Department of State to obtain and protect concessions for investors. From 1890 this policy won for American businesses concessions for products such as sugar, bananas, and oil from more than a dozen Latin American republics. Between 1897 and 1914 American investment in Latin America shot up from $1.641 million to $304.3 million. Much of this investment was in minerals and oil, and Latin American products such as cereals, cotton, sugar continued to be exported to Europe since the United States already produced these goods.

The growing importance of the United States was demonstrated in a border dispute between Britain and Venezuela in 1895. When Britain delayed submitting the issue to arbitration, the U.S. State Department took the initiative and delivered a blunt note to London warning the British that refusal to accept arbitration would have grave consequences. The State Department noted U.S. dominance in the Western Hemisphere and boasted that America's geographical position protected it from European pressures. Britain was preoccupied with the Boers in South Africa, the Germans in Europe, and the French in the Sudan and thus could not argue too strenuously against the message. They agreed to resolve the dispute through arbitration.

In 1902–1903 Venezuela again became the subject of American concern. A dispute between Venezuela and a coalition formed by Germany, Great Britain, and Italy provoked the three European powers into blockading the Latin American country and even firing on some of the coastal fortifications to remind the Venezuelan dictator of his obligations to some of their nationals. President Roosevelt at first stood by, watching Venezuela take its punishment. He then became suspicious of German motives and began to match threat with threat, forcing the Europeans to back down and place the issue into international arbitration.

In 1898 the United States went to war with Spain over the way the Spaniards were ruling Cuba; the mis-

dollar diplomacy—A term associated with American foreign policy of the early twentieth century that used economic power to advance foreign policy goals and American business interests.

863,956 The World. 863,956

WORLDS CIRCULATED YESTERDAY

MAINE EXPLOSION CAUSED BY BOMB OR TORPEDO

Capt. Sigsbee and Consul-General Lee Are in Doubt---The World Has Sent a Special Tug, With Submarine Divers, to Havana to Find Out---Lee Asks for an Immediate Court of Inquiry---260 Men Dead.

A SUPPRESSED DESPATCH TO THE STATE DEPARTMENT, THE CAPTAIN SAYS THE ACCIDENT WAS MADE POSSIBLE BY AN ENEMY.

E. C. Pendleton, Just Arrived from Havana, Says He Overheard Talk There of a Plot to Blow Up the Ship---Capt. Zalinski, the Dynamite Expert, and Other Experts Report to The World that the Wreck Was Not Accidental---Washington Officials Ready for Vigorous Action if Spanish Responsibility Can Be Shown---Divers to Be Sent Down to Make Careful Examinations.

American newspapers' coverage of the war with Spain favored the government's imperial ambitions.

treatment of the Cubans also affected American business interests, especially in the sugar industry. The pretext for the war came when the American battleship *Maine* was blown up in Havana's harbor with the loss of 260 crewmen. American President McKinley justified the war "in the name of humanity, in the name of civilization, and on behalf of endangered American interests." Although the U.S. military worked cooperatively with Cuban rebels to defeat Spain, the rebels did not participate in the peace negotiations that established an American protectorate ruled by the U.S. military. Reconstruction favored American business interests, but it also addressed the threat posed by yellow fever, established a system of state education, and introduced local and national government structures with adult male suffrage.

Victory in the brief, dramatic, and well-publicized Spanish-American War won the United States recognition as a world power and possession of a conglomeration of islands in the Pacific Ocean and the Caribbean. The United States annexed Puerto Rico and placed the Philippines, which were halfway around the world, under American rule. Sensitive to accusations of imperialism in Cuba, in 1903 the U.S. government offered Cuba an imperfect, closely tutored independence in which the Cubans were obliged by law to acknowledge the right of the United States to intervene for the "preservation of Cuban independence" and the "maintenance of a government adequate for the protection of life, property, and individual liberty." The United States also retained land at Guantanamo (gwahn-TAH-nah-moh) Bay where a military base was established. These and other restrictions on Cuban independence were embodied in the **Platt Amendment (1901)** to the new Cuban constitution.

Platt Amendment—An amendment to a congressional bill named after Senator Oliver Platt that gave the United States the authority to intervene in Cuba to maintain order and its independence, to keep land at Guantanamo Bay, and to prevent Cuba from making treaties that gave another nation power over Cuba's internal affairs.

A hero of the Cuban independence movement, José Marti gave his life to the cause, dying in 1895, three years before the United States intervened in the struggle and went to war with Spain.

Document José Marti's Observations on the United States and Cuba

Born in Havana, Cuba, José Marti (1853–1895) was a major figure in the Cuban independence struggle against Spain from his youth to his death in 1895 leading a force in the second Cuban war for independence. As a young person he was deported from Cuba for his antigovernment views on several occasions and lived in Spain, Mexico, and Central America before moving to the United States in 1880. He wrote columns for Latin American newspapers on his observations of every aspect of American life, including its political culture, corruption, literature, democratic values, and the contrasts between the rich and the poor. In this letter Marti published in the *New York Evening Post* (March 25, 1889), he responded to attacks in a Philadelphia newspaper, the *Manufacturer,* on Cubans, especially those living in the United States.

This is not the occasion to discuss the question of the annexation of Cuba. It is probable that no self-respecting Cuban would like to see his country annexed to a nation where the leaders of opinion share towards him the prejudices excusable only to vulgar jingoism or rampant ignorance. No honest Cuban will stoop to be received as a moral pest for the sake of the usefulness of his land in a community, where his ability is denied, his morality insulted, and his character despised. There are some Cubans who, from honorable motives, from an ardent admiration for progress and liberty, from a prescience of their own powers under better political conditions, from an unhappy ignorance of the history and tendency of annexation, would like to see the island annexed to the United States. But those who have fought in war and learned in exile, who have built by the work of hands and mind, a virtuous home in the heart of an unfriendly community, who by their successful efforts as scientists and merchants, as railroad builders and engineers, as teachers, artists, lawyers, journalists, orators and poets, as men of alert intelligence and uncommon activity, are honored wherever their powers have been called into action and the people are just enough to understand them, those who have raised, with their less prepared elements, a town of workingmen where the United States had previously a few huts in a barren cliff, those, more numerous than the others, do not desire the annexation of Cuba to the United States. They do not need it. They admired this nation, the greatest ever built by liberty, but they dislike the evil conditions that, like women in the heart, have begun in this mighty republic, their work of destruction. They have made of the heroes of this country their own heroes, and look to the success of the American commonwealth as the crowning glory of mankind, but they cannot honestly believe that excessive individualism, reverence for wealth, and the protracted exultation of a terrible victory are preparing the United States to be the typical nation of liberty, where no opinion is to be based in greed, and no triumph or acquisition reached against charity and justice. We have the country of Lincoln as much as we have the country of Cutting.

We are not the people of destitute vagrants or immoral pigmies that the *Manufacturer* is pleased to picture nor the country of petty talkers, incapable of action, hostile to hard work, that, in a mass with the other countries of Spanish America, we are by arrogant travelers and written represented to be. . . .

The Cubans have, according to the *Manufacturer*, "a distaste for exertion"; they are "helpless," "idle." These "helpless," "idle" men came here twenty years ago empty-handed, with very few exceptions; fought against the climate; mastered the language; lived by their honest labor some in affluence, a few in wealth, rarely in misery; they bought or built homes; they raised families and fortunes; they loved luxury, and worked for it; they were not frequently seen in the dark roads of life; proud self-sustaining, they never feared competition as to intelligence or diligence. . . . In Philadelphia the *Manufacturer* has a daily opportunity to see a hundred Cubans, some of them of heroic history and powerful build, who live by their work in easy comfort. In New York the Cubans are directors in prominent banks, substantial merchants, popular brokers, clerks of recognized ability, physicians with a large practice . . . the "senora" went to work; from a slaveowner she became a slave, took a seat behind the counter, sang in the churches, worked button-holes by the hundred, sewed for a living, curled feathers, gave her soul to duty, withered in work her body. This is the people of "defective morals."

Questions to Consider

1. According to Marti, what are some of the strengths and weaknesses of the United States?
2. What insights do you gain from Marti's letter about the experiences of Cuban immigrants in the United States?

From Philip Foner, ed., *Our American Writings on Latin America and the Struggle for Cuban Independence by José Marti* (New York: Monthly Review Press, 1977), pp. 226–241.

Over the next several decades the United States sent in the marines on numerous occasions to put down revolts or deal with corrupt governments.

Panama also came under American influence through the U.S. desire to build a canal through the isthmus. The idea to build a canal to connect the Pacific and Atlantic oceans had been discussed for several centuries, but it was not until the 1870s that Ferdinand de Lesseps, the builder of the Suez Canal, formed a company to build such a canal. The effort collapsed in 1893 because of a lack of capital. The United States revived the idea of a canal after the Spanish-American War when the U.S. Navy took stock of the new American empire and developed the concept of a two-ocean navy.

In 1901 the British ceded to the United States the exclusive right to control any canal that might be dug through the isthmus. For $40 million the United States bought the rights of de Lesseps' company. A lease was negotiated with Colombia, through whose territory the canal would be built, but that country's senate refused to ratify the treaty, claiming the compensation was too small. Roosevelt is reputed to have responded, "I did not intend that any set of bandits should hold up Uncle Sam." The isthmus erupted in rebellion, encouraged and funded by American officials of the New Panama Canal Company. The new republic of Panama seceded from Colombia in 1903 and promptly concluded a treaty that ceded a 10-mile-wide canal zone "in perpetuity" to the United States. The canal opened in 1914, and the Canal Zone remained in effect an American colony until another treaty eventually brought American control to an end 85 years later.

The Panama Canal

As Latin American states broke away from Spain in the early nineteenth century, its liberal elites had looked up to the United States as a model for progress and political evolution. By the end of the century, when the nation began wielding a "big stick" to keep these states in line, the United States came to be known as the "Colossus of the North." **The Roosevelt Corollary of 1904** stated that the U.S. government reserved the right to collect the debts owed by Latin American nations to outside nations. On numerous occasions the U.S. government subsequently intervened to quell civil unrest, to overthrow governments not operating in American interests, and to install strongmen who served American business investors.

In Nicaragua, where the American-owned **United Fruit Company** was a major investor, the U.S. government regularly dispatched troops to put down civil unrest. In the late 1920s and early 1930s Augusto Sandino (san-DEE-noh) led a spirited resistance to U.S. soldiers. Nicaragua's National Guard killed him in 1934 and the Guard's commander, Anastosio Somoza (soh-MOH-zah), seized control of the government three years later. The government remained a family enterprise until 1979 when the Sandinistas, a rebel group that took its name in Sandino's memory, ousted the Somozas.

American policy took a turn after a pan-American conference in Havana in 1928 in which Latin American countries criticized American interventions in Haiti and Nicaragua in the 1920s. President Herbert Hoover proposed an end to interventionist policies and the creation of a "Good Neighbor" policy that stressed cooperation and trade ties. Hoover's policy was refined by his successor, Franklin Roosevelt. His administration rejected the Platt Amendment and the Roosevelt Corollary and emphasized building mutually beneficial relations through improving trade and investment. Although Roosevelt's administration still attempted to influence the outcome of events in trouble spots, it also showed restraint when the Mexican government nationalized the oil industry in the 1930s.

CONCLUSION

One of the major questions confronting Latin American countries from the early years of independence to World War II was whether they would remain under dictatorial rulers or introduce democratic institutions. After independence autocratic rulers and caudillos dominated the political scene, but in the late nineteenth century politicians who supported liberalism appeared to be in the ascendancy. Liberal politicians gave the impression that they supported the establishment of elected, representative systems. Although many politicians professed their support for liberal ideals, they usually preferred order and stability rather than reform and change. They concentrated power in the hands of strong executives and were reluctant to open up political systems to peasants, workers, and women. Their control, however, broke down in the 1930s

---

The Roosevelt Corollary of 1904—A corollary of President Theodore Roosevelt to the Monroe Doctrine that stated that the United States had the right to intervene in the affairs of Latin American nations in cases of political instability or where they built up large debts to foreign nations.

United Fruit Company—An American-based company established in 1898 that became a major producer of tropical fruits such as bananas and pineapples and had significant economic interests in Central American countries.

because few politicians were capable of coping with the economic crisis of the Great Depression. Militaries, which had previously refrained from direct involvement in government affairs, then began to intervene in such countries as Argentina, Brazil, Chile, Guatemala, Peru, El Salvador, Honduras and Cuba. The military's role in government was to be a recurrent issue after World War II.

Latin American nations were also challenged by economic problems. After independence Latin American economies were dependent on exporting crops and mineral resources to first Europe and then the United States. However, in the last decades of the nineteenth century, many Latin American economies experienced steady growth because of the strong demand for their minerals and crops in Europe and North America. There was little reason to change this relationship because it was cheaper for Latin American nations to import manufactured goods than it was to produce their own. However, after World War I, the demand for Latin American goods dropped sharply as Britain's position as an international power declined and the United States did not import goods such as cotton, sugar and beef that duplicated what American farmers and ranchers were producing. The Great Depression of the 1930s further reduced the demand for Latin American products and sent shock waves through its economies. Latin American nations were divided over what the best path to development was, and the issue continues to be hotly debated until the present.

One of the basic lessons learned by Latin American nations was that the political independence of the early nineteenth century did not necessarily lead to economic development in the twentieth century. This was a hard lesson that was also learned and relearned throughout the twentieth century in newly independent nations in Asia, the Middle East, and Africa as European colonial powers granted freedom to their former colonies.

Suggestions for Web Browsing

You can obtain more information about topics included in this chapter at the websites listed below. See also the companion website that accompanies this text, http://www.ablongman.com/brummett, which contains an online study guide and additional resources.

Mexico: From Empire to Revolution
http://www.getty.edu/art/exhibitions/past/art_mexico2.html

Based on the Getty Research Collection, this website includes visual images on Mexico's history from 1857 to 1923. Included are albums, postcards, photographs, and cabinet cards. The images include leaders as well as ordinary people and railways, bridges, roads, buildings and monuments.

Spanish-American War in Motion Pictures
http://memory.loc.gov/ammem/sawhtml/sawhome.html

This site contains 68 short films produced by the Edison Company and the Mutotope and Biograph Company during the Spanish-American War of 1898 and its aftermath. Some were based on footage shot in Cuba and the Philippines, but others were staged in New Jersey. The website highlights the importance of film for shaping American perceptions and policies towards global issues.

Literature and Film

Some of the best novels on this period examine the lives of generations of families in different settings. Isabel Allende's *House of the Spirits,* trans. Magda Bogm (G. K. Hall, 1986), traces four generations of women in twentieth century Chile. Carlos Fuentes's *The Death of Artemio Cruz,* trans. Alfred MacAdam (Farrar, Straus and Giroux, 1991), chronicles the life of a man who was a leader of the Mexican revolution but who becomes corrupt as he becomes a leading businessman. Gabriel Garcia Márquez's *One Hundred Years of Solitude* (Perennnial, 2004) examines the lives of the Buendiás family in Macondo, Colombia. Elena Poniatowska's *Until We Meet Again* (Pantheon Books, 1993) focuses on the life of a peasant woman from the Mexican Revolution to the post–World War II era.

Suggestions for Reading

General works on Latin American history include Thomas Skidmore and Peter Smith, *Modern Latin America,* 5th ed. (Oxford University Press, 2001); David Bushnell and Neill Macauley, *The Emergence of Latin America in the 19th Century,* 2nd ed. (Oxford University Press, 1994); Edwin Williamson, *Penguin History of Latin America* (Penguin Press, 1992); and Tulio Halperin-Donghi, *The Aftermath of Revolution in Latin America* (Harper and Row, 1973), and *The Contemporary History of Latin America,* trans. John C. Chasteen (Duke University Press, 1993).

Specific studies on Latin American nations include Hugh Thomas, *Cuba, or the Pursuit of Freedom* (Da Capo Press, 1998); David Rock, *Argentina, 1516–1982* (I. B. Taurus, 1986); E. Bradford Burns, *A History of Brazil,* 3rd ed. (Columbia University Press, 1993); Michael Meyer and William Sherman, *The Course of Mexican History,* 3rd ed. (Oxford University Press, 1987);

Ralph Lee Woodward Jr., *Central America: A History Divided,* 3rd ed. (New York: Oxford University Press, 1999); and James Dunkerley, *Power in the Isthmus: A Political History of Central Latin America* (Verso, 1988). Latin America's economic history is treated in Stephen Haber, ed., *How Latin America Fell Behind: Essays on the Economic Histories of Brazil and Mexico, 1800–1914* (Stanford University Press, 1997). A study of Catholic Church-state relations is J. Lloyd Mecham, *Church and State in Latin America: A History of Politico-ecclesiastical Relations* (University of North Carolina Press, 1966).

GENDER

What role has gender played in history?

The Nineteenth Amendment goes to the states.
Harriet Taylor Upton, Maud Wood Park, Mary Garrett Hay and Helen Gardener with House and Senate leaders as Speaker Gillette signs the resolution

The signing of the Nineteenth Amendment, 1920.

Gender—the social roles, relations, and practices constructed around male and female reproductive differences—has shaped human cultures since its very origins. Though gender has been with us from the start, our notions of masculinity and femininity have been anything but immutable. Indeed, over the centuries, the social roles, relations, and practices assigned to men and women have proved to be historically and culturally variable, subject to the influence of religion, ideology, economics, and other factors. This variability has been particularly evident in three areas: sexuality, labor, and women's rights.

The influence of gender on sexuality concerns a range of topics, most notably marriage and reproduction, but also methods of achieving sexual pleasure, sexually transmitted diseases, and forbidden and encouraged sexual practices. Because of the singular importance of reproduction for humanity, most societies have attempted to control sexuality, usually through the state, religious institutions, or social custom. Marriage, as the most fundamental and durable of human social relationships, has stood at the forefront of attempts to regulate sexuality. Historically, most marriages have involved one husband and one wife, but this hasn't always been the case. Marriage could also be a relationship between one husband and more than one wife, as in religions like early Judaism, Islam, or nineteenth-century Mormonism, or in countries like China until the early twentieth century. Marriage could also involve one wife with several husbands, as in some areas of Tibet, or in sequential marriages to brothers in Judaism. In Africa, some societies permitted the marriage of women as "husbands" to other women as "wives." Throughout the world until modern times, marriages and the children they produced have been used to cement political or economic alliances, with little concern for the marital partners' emotions or sexual feelings. Indeed, the political and economic significance of marriage usually meant that parents arranged most marriages rather than the prospective husbands or wives.

Most of the great world religions have attempted to establish acceptable sexual practices. In so doing, most defined subordinate gender roles for women, made female adultery a special concern, created rituals for purification surrounding women's menstrual cycles, and defined and prohibited sexual deviance. As nations and states were strengthened in the early modern period, the secular authority of the state usually stepped in for the religious authorities and attempted to regulate sexuality. In addition to marriage and other areas, states were concerned with the regulation of the socially disruptive practice of prostitution and the devastating effects of sexually transmitted diseases. Eugenics laws in the nineteenth and twentieth centuries in Europe, the United States, and Japan sought to control diseases such as syphilis, especially where it intersected with prostitution. In the late twentieth century, new sexually transmitted diseases such as HIV raised issues around the regulation of sexuality, particularly same-sex practices. Expanding globalization in recent decades has permitted people and pathogens to move with great speed, and the nature of sexuality has allowed the global reach of something as local and intimate as sexually transmitted diseases. Concerns about these diseases, whether at an individual, government, or religious level, all involve issues of gender.

Considerations in the area of labor include the gendered workplace; the impact on gender of the transition from nomadic societies to agricultural ones; the gendered division of labor as the Industrial Revolution encouraged the transition from farm to factory; gender dimensions of the international movement of people and labor under slavery, colonialism, and voluntary migration; and men's and women's different roles in labor movements and resistance.

The early stages of industrialization in New England, for example, moved young women and girls into textile mills, shoe factories, and other mechanized workshops from what had been a cooperative economic and production unit on the farm or in an urban artisan workshop. Wives, husbands, and children in the preindustrial family had earlier worked side by side, often performing gender-differentiated but equally important jobs. The Industrial Revolution increasingly separated home and workplace. Soon, women came to be identified with the home, and men's and women's primary places—the home for married middle-class women, the workplace for all adult men—became gendered. Economic patterns in the West and Japan led to the transition of the family from a cooperative economic and production unit to a place of consumption rather than production, occupied by a mother whose gender role did not include paid labor while the father/husband occupied the public economic sphere.

In more recent times, gender continues to be central to the international labor market. Contemporary factories in the developing world preferentially employ women and girls, whose pay is routinely less than men's. Employment alters the relationship of women to their families and to society at large. In many cases, the migration of women and girls within their own countries to export-processing zones leads to demographic shifts. In Indonesia, girls' power within their families has increased with their exposure to new ideas within their factories, not to mention their economic contribution to their families. Female labor has also been a large component of international migration.

Women's rights are another important focus of gender. Gender was deeply implicated in the creation of the modern nation-state, with masculinity defining the meanings of citizenship and public participation. Modern constitutions devised in the eighteenth and nineteenth centuries articulated a gendered notion of the state. Yet, most also spoke eloquently about the rights of citizens. The contrast between the rhetoric of democracy and its gendered practice gave rise to feminist demands for inclusion in the state. At the same time, gendered social and economic inequalities, such as the legislated subordination of wives to their husbands, harsh conditions in the workplace, and opportunities for education limited by women's gender, gave rise to feminist resistance to the state. In areas under colonial rule, women's rights were closely related to nationalist and anti-imperialist movements, though postcolonial, independent states have, ironically, all too often rejected women's rights as too closely tied to the ideology of their former colonial masters. During the last two or three centuries, the movements we call "feminism" have, thus, been defined by an interesting interaction of simultaneous struggle for inclusion in the state and resistance to the state and society.

As early as 1700, Englishwoman Mary Astell, referring to women's legal subordination to the male family head, responded to the newly emerging political theory that called for (male) citizens' rights against absolute monarchs by declaring, "If all men are born free, how is it that all women are born slaves?" Almost 100 years later, Frenchwoman Olympe de Gouges reacted to the profoundly gendered revolutionary concepts of liberty, equality, and fraternity embodied in *The Declaration of the Rights of Man and Citizen* by writing a feminist challenge, *The Declaration of the Rights of Woman and the Female Citizen*. She was executed not long afterward. Englishwoman Mary Wollstonecraft echoed many of de Gouges's themes in her *Vindication of the Rights of Woman* (1792), which called for equality in education, the family, and political rights. This call for equal treatment in law set the stage for the suffrage and women's rights movements first in England and the United States and in Asia and Latin America later. In England, John Stuart Mill wrote eloquently on women's rights and ran for public office on a rights platform. His words were particularly noted by feminist reformers in Japan and elsewhere.

The most concerted feminist rights efforts were undertaken in the United States in the nineteenth century. The Seneca Falls Convention of 1848 brought together Susan B. Anthony, Elizabeth Cady Stanton, Frederick Douglass, and many others who adopted the "Declaration of Rights and Sentiments" that demanded equality of rights of citizenship and social participation. The U.S. movement was not a unified movement, however. It was characterized by differences over issues of racial justice, class differences, and the role of government in either protecting women or granting them equal rights (the "equality" vs. "difference" debate). The final push for the vote through the Nineteenth Amendment to the U.S. Constitution (1920) represented a concerted effort to overcome differences to accomplish that goal. Likewise, feminist activism around the world has struggled with divisions regarding the adoption of Western feminist ideas, the tensions over Marxist and liberal approaches, and feminism's relationship to cultural, ethnic, and religious differences.

Though historians have only recently discovered gender as a "useful category of analysis,"[1] gender has long been central to our lives, from political debates over marriage and civil rights to feminist calls for protection from labor or sexual exploitation.

Questions

1. Why has marriage, differently defined in various cultures and times, been a central institution in most societies?
2. How has the demand for women's political rights been tied to the rise of the modern nation?
3. How has recent globalization affected gender and disease? Gender and labor? Gender and human rights?

CHAPTER

26

Politics and Diplomacy in the West, 1815–1914

CHAPTER CONTENTS

Western politicians struggled to keep up with and take advantage of the economic and social transformations triggered by industrialization in the nineteenth century. Their political responses ranged from democratic reform to autocratic reaction and were influenced by the new ideas of liberalism, nationalism, and socialism. After the popular revolutions of 1848, each nation in Europe experienced an increase in centralized state power and, concurrently, a growth in the political voice of common people. In response to national ambitions and popular pressures, Realpolitik—realism in politics—became a prevalent theme in Western politics, figuring largely in the unification movements of both Germany and Italy.

By the end of the nineteenth century there was a clear division between the nations that were the most efficient at mastering political change—Germany, France, the United Kingdom, and the United States—and other nations that struggled to stabilize their political and social infrastructures—most notably, Russia, Italy, and Austria-Hungary.

Elsewhere in the world, the peoples of Asia and Africa confronted the threat of European colonization and imperialism. Europeans extended their global domination through emigration—during the nineteenth century millions took part in the greatest mass movement of human beings up to that point in history. Europeans also established colonies for economic gain through the exploitation of natural and human resources.

The opportunistic, short-range focus of Realpolitik blinded Europeans to their larger, long-term interests, however, and the century of European dominance came to an end in 1914 with diplomatic failure and the outbreak of World War I. The destructive forces then unleashed in Europe rippled out across the world and in time would bring an end to European hegemony.

1810

1814–1815 Congress of Vienna

1819 Carlsbad Decrees in Germany; Peterloo Massacre in Great Britain

1830

1830s British reforms in Parliament; beginning of Chartist movement

1830 Paris riots against Charles X; uprisings in Belgium and Poland; Mazzini begins Young Italy Movement

1839 Belgium recognized as an independent "perpetually neutral" state

1840

1845 Potato crop failure in Ireland results in widespread famine

1847 Marx and Engels finish their Communist Manifesto

1848 Revolutions sweep Europe; French Second Republic proclaimed; election of Louis Napoleon

1850

1852 Louis Napoleon proclaims France's Second Empire; Georges Haussmann initiates urban renewal of Paris

1853–1856 Crimean War

1860

1861 Kingdom of Italy proclaimed; Tsar Alexander II issues Emancipation Proclamation; start of American Civil War

1867 The Ausgleich, creation of the Austro-Hungarian monarchy

1870

1870–1871 French defeat in Franco-Prussian war, Paris Commune, proclamation of the Unification of Germany

1880

1881 Tsar Alexander II of Russia assassinated

1888 Kaiser Wilhelm II becomes emperor of Germany

1900

1905 Russian Revolution; October Manifesto issued

1910

1914 Irish Home Rule bill passed; general strike in Italy; start of World War I

THE VIENNA SETTLEMENT AND THE REASSEMBLING OF EUROPE

- *How successful were the diplomats at Vienna in negotiating a peace settlement that prevented another continental war?*

Once Napoleon was "safely" exiled to Elba in 1814, representatives of all the European powers except the Ottoman Empire gathered in September at Vienna. They had the imposing task of building a new political and diplomatic structure for Europe after a quarter century of wars and revolutions. The factor that had brought the British, Prussians, Austrians, and Russians together—Napoleon—was gone, and wartime unity dissolved into peacetime pursuit of self-interest.

The Congress of Vienna

Work went slowly during the 10-month span of the Congress of Vienna. The leaders who gathered at Vienna—Lord Castlereagh of Great Britain, Count von Hardenberg of Prussia, Prince Klemens von Metternich of Austria, Tsar Alexander I of Russia, and Prince Charles-Maurice de Talleyrand of France—met in small secret conferences to decide the future of Europe. Metternich (MET-ter-nick) came to dominate the conference, as much by his diplomatic skills as by his ability to impress on the participants the need for stability.

The Congress dealt with numerous issues: the status of France, the new political boundaries, the response to liberal and national attitudes sweeping the continent, the fate of the powers who had lost territory during the previous 25 years, and the future of dispossessed dynasties. The solutions proposed were moderate. France was allowed to return to its 1792 boundaries; however, after Napoleon's return and the One Hundred Days, the allies cut back the boundaries and imposed penalties. They virtually ignored the democratic, liberal, and nationalistic forces in favor of a more traditional solution to the upheavals of the previous 25 years.

The events since 1789 had drastically altered the map of Europe. For example, the 1000-year-old Holy Roman Empire had disappeared. In an attempt to restore some balance, the Congress followed four principles: legitimacy, encirclement of France, compensation, and balance of power. The Congress ruled that royal houses that had been expelled—such as the Bourbons in France, Spain, and Naples; the House of Savoy in Sardinia-Piedmont; and the House of Orange in the Netherlands—would be placed back

Prince Klemens von Metternich, *portrait by Sir Thomas Lawrence. At the height of his power during the Congress of Vienna, Metternich was largely responsible for the balance of European power agreement worked out by the Congress.*

on their thrones. The redrawn map of Europe resembled the 1789 configuration, except that the Holy Roman Empire remained dissolved. In its place were the 39 states of the German Confederation, dominated by Austria. The redrawing of boundaries created a protective belt of states around France to make future aggression more difficult. The principle of compensation ensured that no important power suffered a loss as the result of the Congress's work. Austria was compensated for the loss of land in the Low Countries by gaining territory in Italy and along the Adriatic. Sweden received Norway in return for permitting Russia to keep Finland.

The desire to construct an effective balance of power remained at the center of the Congress's attention. Each nation had its own idea of what constituted a proper balance, and soon the British and the Austrians found themselves arrayed against the Russians and the Prussians. Russia's ambitions in Poland almost broke up the conference because Britain feared that an enlarged Russia would threaten the balance of power. Prussia wanted all of Saxony, which justified Austria's fears of the growing Berlin-based state. While the four wartime allies split, the clever French representative Talleyrand negotiated a secret treaty binding the French, Austrians, and British to pledge mutual assistance to restrain the Russians and Prussians.

Although the Congress has been criticized for ignoring the democratic impulse in Europe, it has been praised for crafting a general settlement of a complex series of problems, especially compared to the work of the vengeful Allies at Versailles after World War I. The representatives were not totally, blindly reactionary, however; many of the changes of the previous 25 years were retained. The 40 years of general peace that followed, flawed though they may have been, are testimony to the success of Metternich and his colleagues in gaining stability. But, by ignoring the forces of change expressed in the new ideologies, the representatives at Vienna ensured the ultimate failure of the system they created.

The Congress System

The Vienna negotiators set out to coordinate their policies to maintain stability. The first proposal for postwar consultation was symbolic and quixotic. In the fall of 1815, Tsar Alexander I proposed the formation of a "Holy Alliance" to be based on "the precepts of justice, Christian charity, and peace." No one was quite sure what the tsar meant by this pact, but every ruler in Europe signed it except the British king, the Turkish sultan, and the pope. Castlereagh dismissed the Holy Alliance as "a piece of sublime mysticism and nonsense." In November 1815, Austria, Prussia, Russia, and Britain signed the Quadruple Alliance, which became the Quintuple Alliance when France joined in 1818. Under this agreement, the powers pursued their goals through what came to be known as the **Congress System** a concert of the European powers to maintain order, peace, and stability by keeping an eye on France and maintaining the balance of power. This was the first truly functional experiment in collective security in European history.

The Congress System's dedication to the 1815 status quo was challenged in 1820 and 1821 by nationalistic and liberal revolts in Germany, Greece, Spain, Italy, and Latin America. The most violent revolutions occurred in Spain and Italy. Spanish liberals rebelled against the misgovernment of the restored Bourbon king, Ferdinand VII, and their insurrection spread to the army, which mutinied. The general uprising that followed forced the king to give in to the liberals' demands for a constitution and representative government. The Spaniards' success sparked rebellions in Naples and Sicily, governed by the Neapolitan Bourbon king, Ferdinand I. The Italian revolt ran much the same path as that in Spain, and with much the same result: a constitution based on the Spanish model.

Metternich arranged for the Congress allies to meet at Troppau (tro-POW) in 1820, Laibach in 1821, and Verona in 1822 to deal with the uprisings. Ferdinand I came to Laibach, supported Congress System intervention, and reneged on granting a constitution; Austrian troops invaded Italy and placed him back on his throne. In 1822 the Congress allies met to consider the Spanish problem, and the French volunteered to restore the status quo. They sent their armies in to crush the liberals. The repression of the revolts in Spain and Italy marked the high point of the Congress System's success.

Britain began its withdrawal from the Continent into "splendid isolation" in 1820, and the ardent support of British liberals for the 1821 Greek revolt against the Turks further weakened London's interest in cooperating with its former allies. When the Congress System discussed restoring the Spanish king's authority in Latin America, the British objected. Further, U.S. President James Monroe warned the Europeans in 1823 that their intervention into the Western Hemisphere would be regarded as an unfriendly act. By the middle of the decade, the Congress System had withered to an Austrian-Russian alliance in which Metternich set the agenda and the Russians acted as the policemen of European power.

Return of the Bourbons

The restored Bourbon monarch Louis XVIII (r. 1814, 1815–1824) was an unhappy choice for the French

Congress System—An alliance of the signatories of the Vienna settlement dedicated to maintaining the status quo in Europe after 1815.

throne. The new king, a brother of the guillotined Louis XVI, was ill-equipped to lead France out of a quarter century of revolution and Napoleonic charisma. Dull and unpopular, he had been the target of a Talleyrand epigram that "the Bourbons have learned nothing and forgotten nothing." Nonetheless, he tried to hold the country together by blending elements of the revolutionary period with remnants of the Old Regime. Unfortunately, the mixture helped create the instability that plagued the country throughout the century. For 9 years, he suffered the fate of moderates trying to navigate between two extremes: the right wing assailed him for giving too much to the middle classes, while the liberals and radicals said that he had not gone far enough in his policies. Louis was succeeded by his brother, Charles X (r. 1824–1830), who cared nothing about maintaining political balance.

Charles did not accept any of the changes since 1789. In 1829 he announced that he "would rather saw wood than be a king of the English type." So out of tune was he with the times that in July 1830 he drove the usually submissive legislature to the point that it refused to support his proposed ultraroyalist ministry. When elections went badly for him, he issued a set of laws censoring the press and further limiting the already heavily restricted right to vote. These repressive acts drove liberals, radicals, and their journalist allies to revolt. They barricaded the narrow streets of Paris with overturned carts, boxes, tables, and paving stones. Fighting behind these obstacles and from rooftops, they held off the army. Three days later, a less reactionary faction took power after Charles fled across the Channel to Great Britain—the refuge for most political exiles, left or right, during the nineteenth century.

The new government represented the upper middle classes and the landed gentry and stood as a compromise between the republicans—led by the aging Marquis de Lafayette, hero of the American Revolution—and the relatively liberal monarchist supporters of the Orléans branch of the Bourbons. The new king, Louis Philippe (r. 1830–1848), who claimed the title of "citizen king," predictably supported the interests of the wealthy. Louis Philippe took great pains to present a bourgeois image of himself. He received the crown from "the people" and replaced the white Bourbon flag with the revolutionary tricolor. However, Louis Philippe's policies consistently favored the upper bourgeoisie and gentry and shut the workers and middle classes out of the political arena. Of the 32 million French citizens, only 200,000 wealthy male property owners were allowed to vote.

Workers protested that the government was ignoring their interests. Louis Philippe and his advisers were more interested in pursuing a policy of divide and conquer and ignored most suggestions for reform. Restrictive legislation was passed in 1835 to control the growing radical movement. The government kept control, but under the calm surface serious pressures were building. By 1848 France faced a serious crisis.

Eugene Delacroix's Liberty Leading the People, *painted in 1830, presented a romantic vision of the popular demand for social reform and the violence in the streets it wrought.*

The French Influence in Belgium and Poland

The Paris uprising of 1830 encouraged liberals across the Continent, but only in Belgium were there any lasting results. The Vienna Congress had placed the Belgians under the Dutch crown, but this settlement ignored the cultural, economic, religious, and linguistic differences between the two people. The Belgians were primarily Catholic farmers and workers, some of whom spoke Flemish, which was related to Dutch, but most of whom spoke French. The people of the Netherlands were Dutch-speaking protestants and, for the most part, seafarers and traders.

Belgian liberals asked the Dutch king, William I of Orange, to grant them their own administration in August 1830. When he refused, rioting sprouted in Brussels, which the Dutch troops were unable to put down. After expelling the troops, the Belgians declared their independence and drew up a liberal constitution. William asked in vain for help from Tsar Nicholas I. The principle of legitimacy as a pretext for intervention was dead. Stalemate ensued until the summer of 1831 when the Belgian national assembly met in Brussels and chose Prince Leopold of Saxe-Coburg-Gotha (saks-KO-burg-GO-ta) as king. Eight years later the international status of the new state was settled. Belgium was recognized as a "perpetually neutral" state.

The French rebellion had an impact in Poland, where Poles in and around Warsaw rose up in the name of liberal and national principles. After the Congress of Vienna, Poles in this region gained a special status. The area known as Congress Poland had its own constitution and substantial local autonomy. The winds of change and the repressive tendencies of Tsar Nicholas I combined to push the Poles into rebellion in the winter of 1830–1831. The rebels suffered from internal division, and the numerically and militarily superior Russians crushed them. Their major accomplishment was to tie down the Russian troops, whom Nicholas wanted to send to help the Dutch king, for six months and perhaps save the Belgian revolution.

German and Italian Nationalism

The forces of nationalism influenced central Europe from the tip of Italy through the Habsburg lands of central and eastern Europe to the Baltic Sea. Napoleon had performed a great, though unwitting, service for German and Italian nationalists by his direct governing in the area and also by revising the European map. After 1815, the region knew the positive effects of a different style of governing and was divided into a much more rational set of political units.

Metternich had ensured that the Vienna Congress made Austria the dominant partner in the German Confederation. To preserve his country's dominance both in the Confederation and throughout the Habsburg monarchy, he knew that he had to fight continually against nationalism. The currents of Romanticism found forceful expression in the works of German poets and philosophers and in lectures in German classrooms. Nationalism and liberalism found many followers among the young. For example, a great patriotic student festival took place in October 1817 (the three-hundredth anniversary of the Reformation) at Wartburg, where Luther had taken refuge. Liberal students burned reactionary books on a great bonfire to protest their discontent with the status quo. Protests spread both openly and secretly in the *Burschenschaften* (BOUR-shen-shaft-en; "liberal societies"). Metternich moved harshly against the students. He pushed the Carlsbad Decrees (1819) through the Diet of the German Confederation. These acts dissolved student associations, censored the press, and restricted academic freedom. However, the decrees failed to stop the forces of liberalism and nationalism, which grew during the next 20 years.

Italy, which Metternich saw as a "geographical expression" and not a nation, also posed special problems. The Congress of Vienna, in accordance with the principles of legitimacy and compensation, had returned Italy to its geographical status of 1789, divided into areas dominated by the Bourbons, the Papal States, and the Austrians. This settlement ignored the fact that, in the interim, the Italians had experienced more liberty and better government than ever before. The return to the old systems was also a return to high taxes, corruption, favoritism, and banditry.

It was perhaps ironic that this fragmented, individualistic land should produce the most notable Romantic nationalist in Europe, Giuseppe Mazzini. After the Austrians put down the Italian revolutionary movements in 1820 and 1821, Mazzini began to work actively for independence. In 1830 he was implicated in an unsuccessful revolution against the Sardinian royal government and thrown into jail for six months. Once released, he went to London and started a patriotic society that he called **Young Italy.** This organization sent appeals to students and intellectuals to form an Italian nationalist movement. The reactionaries, however, continued to resist the nationalists.

Metternich also feared nationalism in the Habsburg realm, a mosaic composed of many different nationalities, languages, and religions. If nationalism and the desire for self-rule became strong among the Magyars, Czechs, southern Slavs, and Italians, the Habsburg Empire would fall apart. Nationalism

Young Italy—A society created by Giuseppe Mazzini dedicated to the unification of Italy.

threatened the Germans who controlled the empire yet constituted only 20 percent of its population.

By understanding the complex and combustible nature of the region in which Metternich exercised his power, his dread of democratic government and nationalism and his obsession with maintaining the status quo can be understood. Liberalism and nationalism would destroy his power. In a world that was rapidly industrializing, Metternich's power rested on a backward system. Only in Bohemia and the areas immediately around Vienna was there a middle class. The great majority of the inhabitants were peasants, either powerless serfs, as in Hungary, or impoverished tenant farmers who owed half of their time and two-thirds of their crops to the landlord. Government was autocratic, and the regional assemblies had little power and represented mainly the nobility. The social, political, and economic structures were extremely vulnerable to the winds of change that came in 1848.

Revolutionary Outbreaks, 1815–1848

1820–1821	The Germanies, Spain, Italy, Latin America, Greece
1825	Russia
1830	France, Belgium, Poland
1848	France, Prussia, Italy; the Habsburg monarchy: Austria, Bohemia, Hungary, Croatia, Romania

1848: THE REVOLUTIONARY YEAR

- *What forces led to the destruction in 1848 of the international order created at the Congress of Vienna in 1815?*

As it had before, France once again opened a revolutionary era, and the events there set a precedent for what was to occur throughout Europe in 1848. The overthrow of the old order came first in Paris in February and then spread to Berlin, Vienna, Prague, Buda, and Pest in March. Never before had France—or Europe—seen such a fragmented variety of political and social pressures at work at the same time. Romantics, socialists, nationalists, members of the middle class, peasants, and students could all agree that the old structure had to be abandoned, but the ideology espoused by each group envisioned a different path to that goal and a separate view of what the new world should be. Louis Philippe fled Paris, Metternich abandoned Vienna, and the Prussian king, Frederick William IV, gave in. But the movements in France and elsewhere fell apart as soon as they had won because of their diversity, lack of experience, and conflicting ideological goals.

France and the Second Republic

The pressures building since 1830, strengthened by economic depression in 1846 and 1847, erupted in Paris during February 1848. Within the seemingly harmless social arena of the grand dinner party or banquet, liberals and socialists argued for electoral reforms and an end to corruption while they ate and drank at the table. When the government tried to prohibit a banquet scheduled for February 22, the opposition threw up more than 1500 barricades to block the narrow streets of Paris. Violence broke out, and republican leaders took the opportunity to set up a provisional revolutionary government and proclaimed the introduction of universal manhood suffrage. Louis Philippe fled to exile in England.

The new government, the Second Republic, had a brief (1848–1851) and dreary existence. Neither the new leaders nor the voters had any experience with representative government. The forces that united to overthrow the king soon split into moderate and radical wings. The first group wanted middle-class control within the existing social order, while the latter faction desired a social and economic revolution. By the summer the new government faced a major crisis over the issue of national workshops sponsored by the socialist Louis Blanc (BLON; 1811–1882). The workshops were to be the state's means to guarantee every laborer's "right to work." The moderate-dominated government voiced its belief in Blanc's principle of full employment, but the leaders gave the plan's administration to men who wanted to ridicule it. As a result, the workshops became a national joke. Laborers were assigned make-work jobs such as carrying dirt from one end of a park to the other on one day and then carrying it back the next.

The disbanding of the workshops incited a violent insurrection known as the June Days. The unemployed workers raised a red flag as a sign of revolution—the first time that the red flag had been used as a symbol of the proletariat. With the cry of "bread or lead," the demonstrators rebuilt the barricades and tried to overthrow the government. The bloodiest fighting Paris had seen since the Reign of Terror gave the insurgents far more lead than bread, and the movement was crushed. After that, the bourgeoisie and the workers would be on the opposite ends of the political spectrum.

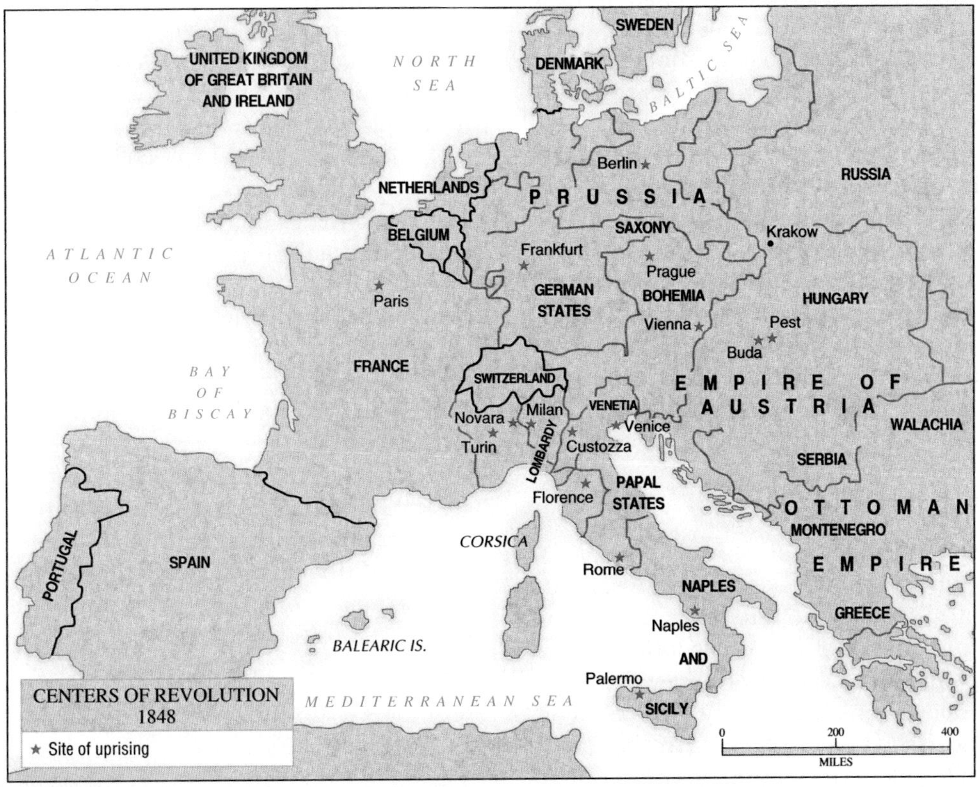

The ideological seeds planted by the French Revolution swept all of the major European continental powers except Russia in 1848. Despite initial successes, the revolutionary wave soon waned.

Germany and the Frankfurt Assembly

The example of the French February revolution quickly crossed the Rhine River and spread to Central Europe. At public assemblies throughout Germany, patriotic liberals demanded unification. Rapid changes came with minimal casualties, largely because of the humane response of the Prussian king, Frederick William IV. When his subjects erected barricades in Berlin on March 15, he decided to make concessions rather than unleash further violence and bloodshed. He ordered the regular army troops out of Berlin and tried to make peace with his "dear Berliners" by promising a parliament, a constitution, and a united Germany. Upon learning of this development, the rulers of the other German states agreed to establish constitutional governments and guarantee basic civil rights.

The **Frankfurt Assembly** opened its first session on May 18. More than 500 delegates attended, coming from the various German states, Austria, and Bohemia. The primarily middle-class membership of the assembly included about 200 lawyers, 100 professors, and many doctors and judges. Popular enthusiasm reached a peak when the assembly's president announced, "We are to create a constitution for Germany, for the whole empire." The assembly deliberated at length over the issues of just what was meant by Germany and what form of government would be best for the new empire. Some debaters wanted a united Germany to include all Germans in Central Europe, even Austria and Bohemia. Others did not want the Austrians included, for a variety of religious and political reasons. Another issue of contention was whether the new imperial crown should be given to the Habsburgs in Vienna or the Hohenzollerns in Berlin.

Germany's history changed tragically when the Assembly failed to unite and bring a liberal solution to political problems. From May to December, the Assembly wasted time in splendid debates over nonessential topics. As the participants talked endlessly, they threw away their chance to take decisive action and contributed to the failed dreams of 1848. Gradually, the conservatives recovered from the shock of the spring revolts and began to rally around their rulers, exhorting them to undo the reformers' work. In Prussia the king regained his confidence, the army remained loyal, and the peasants showed little interest in political affairs. The Berlin liberals soon found themselves isolated, and the king was able to regain control.

Even though the antiliberal forces were at full tide, the Frankfurt Assembly continued its work. It approved the Declaration of the Rights of the German People, an inspiring document that articulated the

Frankfurt Assembly—The meeting held in 1848 to write a constitution for Germany.

progressive political and social ideals of 1848. In April 1849 the Assembly approved a constitution for a united Germany that included an emperor advised by a ministry and a legislature elected by secret ballot. Austria refused to join the new union.

When the leadership of the new German Reich ("nation") was offered to Frederick William, he refused to accept it, later declaring that he could not "pick up a crown from the gutter." After this contemptuous refusal, most of the Assembly's members returned home. Outbreaks against the conservative domination continued, but the Prussian army effectively put them down. Thousands of prominent middle-class liberals fled, many to the United States.

Italy

The news of the revolutions in Paris and Vienna triggered a rash of uprisings on the Italian peninsula. In Sicily, Venice, and Milan, revolutionaries demanded an end to foreign domination and despotic rule. In response, King Charles Albert of Sardinia voluntarily granted a new liberal constitution. Other states, such as Tuscany, also issued constitutions. In the Papal States, meanwhile, reform had begun as early as 1846. Absolute government in Italy almost disappeared.

As in the rest of Europe, the liberal and nationalist triumphs and reforms were quickly swept away by the reactionary tide. The Austrians regained their mastery in the north of Italy in July when they defeated Charles Albert at the decisive battle of Custozza. Another defeat a year later forced him to abdicate in favor of his oldest son, Victor Emmanuel II. Austria helped restore the old rulers and systems of government in Italy to their pre-1848 conditions.

The final blow to the Italian movements came in November 1848 when Pope Pius IX, who had begun a program of reform, refused to join in the struggle against Catholic Austria for a united Italy. His subjects forced him to flee from Rome, and the papal lands were declared a republic, with Mazzini as the head. The pope's flight prompted a hostile reaction from conservative Europe, and the French sent in an army to crush the republic in July 1849. When the pope returned to Rome, he remained bitterly hostile to all liberal causes and ideas until his death in 1878.

The Habsburg Monarchy

The events of 1848 took a tragic toll in the Habsburg lands. When the news of the February uprising reached Vienna, Prague, and Budapest, reformers immediately called for change. In Budapest, the nationalist liberal Lajos Kossuth (la-YOS KOS-sut; 1802–1894) attacked the Habsburg ruler's "stagnant bureaucratic system" and spoke of the "pestilential air blowing from the Vienna charnel house and its deadening effect upon all phases of Hungarian life." He demanded parliamentary government for the whole of the empire.

In Vienna Kossuth's speech inspired some Austrian students and workers to demonstrate in the streets. The movement soon gained the force of a rebellion, and the frightened Austrian emperor forced Metternich, the symbol of European reaction, to resign. Meanwhile, the Hungarian Diet advocated a liberal, parliamentary government under a limited Habsburg monarchy. The Vienna-controlled Danubian region, that mosaic of nationalities, appeared to be on the verge of being transformed into a federation.

MAP Nationalities Within the Habsburg Empire

The empire's diversity soon became mirrored in a characteristic of the revolutionary movements, as the various nationalities divided among themselves. The Hungarians wrote a new constitution that was quite liberal, calling for a guarantee of civil rights, an end to serfdom, and the destruction of special privileges. In

The leader of the Hungarian revolutionary movement of 1848, Lajos Kossuth, gave a liberal constitution to his people but blocked the hopes of neighboring nations such as the Serbs, Croats, and Romanians.

theory, all political benefits guaranteed in the constitution were to extend to all citizens of Hungary, including non-Magyar minorities. The emperor accepted these reforms and promised, in addition, a constitution for Austria. He also promised the Czechs in Bohemia the same reforms granted the Hungarians.

By summer the mood suddenly shifted. German and Czech nationalists began to quarrel, and the Magyars began to oppress the Slavic nationalities and Romanians after they in turn demanded their own political independence. Divisions among the liberal and nationalistic forces gave the conservatives in Vienna time to regroup and suggested to them the obvious tactic to regain their former dominance: divide and conquer the subject nationalities. In June, demonstrations broke out in the streets of Prague, barricades were thrown up, and fighting began. The Austrians lobbed a few shells, Prague surrendered, and any hope for an autonomous kingdom of Bohemia ended.

In Hungary, Kossuth announced that he would offer civil rights, but not national independence, to the minority nationalities under his control. In protest, the South Slavs under the Croat leader Joseph Jellachich (IO-sef ye-LA-chich; 1801–1859) attacked the Magyars, and civil war broke out. The Austrians took advantage of the situation and made Jellachich an imperial general. Following his attack against the Magyars, he was ordered to Vienna, where, in October, he forced the surrender of the liberals who controlled the capital.

By the end of the year, the weak and incapable Emperor Ferdinand I abdicated in favor of his nephew, Franz Joseph—who would rule until 1916. The Austrians began to repeal their concessions to the Hungarians, arguing that their new emperor was not bound by the acts of his predecessor. The Magyars, outraged by this maneuver, declared complete independence for their country. The Austrians, aided by 100,000 Russian troops sent by Tsar Nicholas I and the leadership of the Croatian general Jellachich, defeated the Hungarians in a bloody and one-sided struggle. In the summer of 1849 Kossuth fled the country, and the Hungarian revolution reached its tragic conclusion.

PRUSSIA, GERMAN UNIFICATION, AND THE SECOND REICH

▪ *How did Bismarck manage to unify Germany when the surrounding states of western and eastern Europe were all opposed to unification?*

After 1848, with one exception, Prussia went from strength to strength. Facing a different range of problems in a much more unified state, King Frederick William issued a constitution in 1850 that paid lip service to parliamentary democracy but kept real power in the hands of the king and the upper classes. The Berlin court wanted to form a confederation of northern German states, without Austria. This plan frightened the Austrians and made the Russians uneasy as well. A meeting of the three powers at Olmütz in 1850 forced the Prussians to withdraw their plan. Instead, the 1815 German Confederation was affirmed, with Vienna recognized as the major German power. The embittered Prussians returned to Berlin, pledging revenge for the "humiliation of Olmütz."

Despite this diplomatic setback, Prussia gained success in other areas. Berlin kept the Austrians out of the Zollverein (ZOLL-ver-ine), the customs union of German states, and fought off Austria's efforts to weaken it. The Prussian government, dominated by the nobles, was modern and efficient, especially when compared with that in Vienna. The Prussians extended public education to more of their citizenry than in any other European state. At the start of the 1860s a new ruler, William I (r. 1861–1888), came to power. He had a more permissive interpretation of the 1850 constitution and allowed liberals and moderates the chance to make their voices heard.

Steps to German Unification

1862	Bismarck appointed prime minister
1863	Russian-Prussian accord on Poland
1864	War with Denmark
1866	War with Austria; establishment of North German Confederation
1870	War with France
1871	Proclamation of the Second German Empire (Reich) at Versailles

Bismarck as Prime Minister

A stalemate occurred in 1862 when King William I wanted to strengthen his army but the Chamber of Deputies would not vote to provide the necessary funds. The liberals asserted the constitutional right to approve taxes, while the king equally strongly expressed his right to build up his forces. As the king struggled with this constitutional crisis, he called Otto von Bismarck (1815–1898) home from his post as Prussian ambassador to France and made him prime minister.

Bismarck advised the king to ignore the legislature and collect the needed taxes without the Chamber's approval. Bismarck knew the necessity of armed strength in order to gain Prussia's diplomatic goals. Ironically, his later military victories would gain him the support of many of the liberals whom he had encouraged the king to defy.

Bismarck's entry on the scene in Berlin strengthened not only the king but also the hopes of all who wanted a united German state. Unification appealed to virtually all segments of German society, from the liberals to the conservatives, such as the historian Heinrich von Treitschke (HINE-reesh fon TRITE-shki), who stated, "There is only one salvation! One state, one monarchic Germany under the Hohenzollern dynasty." Berlin, through its leadership of the Zollverein, sponsorship of the confederation of northern German states, and efficient bureaucracy, was the obvious choice for the capital of a unified German state. With the arrival of Bismarck, the Prussians gained the necessary leadership for unification.

The prime minister was a master of the art of **Realpolitik.** He had the intelligence to assess the actual state of conditions, the insight to gauge the character and goals of his opponents, and the talent to move skillfully and quickly. Unlike most of his colleagues, he was an expert image maker, so effective that historians have used his epithet "blood and iron" to describe his career. Few statesmen have ever accomplished so much change with such a comparatively small loss of life in a controlled use of war. Bismarck was a savvy politician who knew that force was the final card to be played, one to be used as the servant of diplomacy and not as its master.

Realpolitik—The nineteenth-century use of Machiavelli's notion that the ends justify the means.

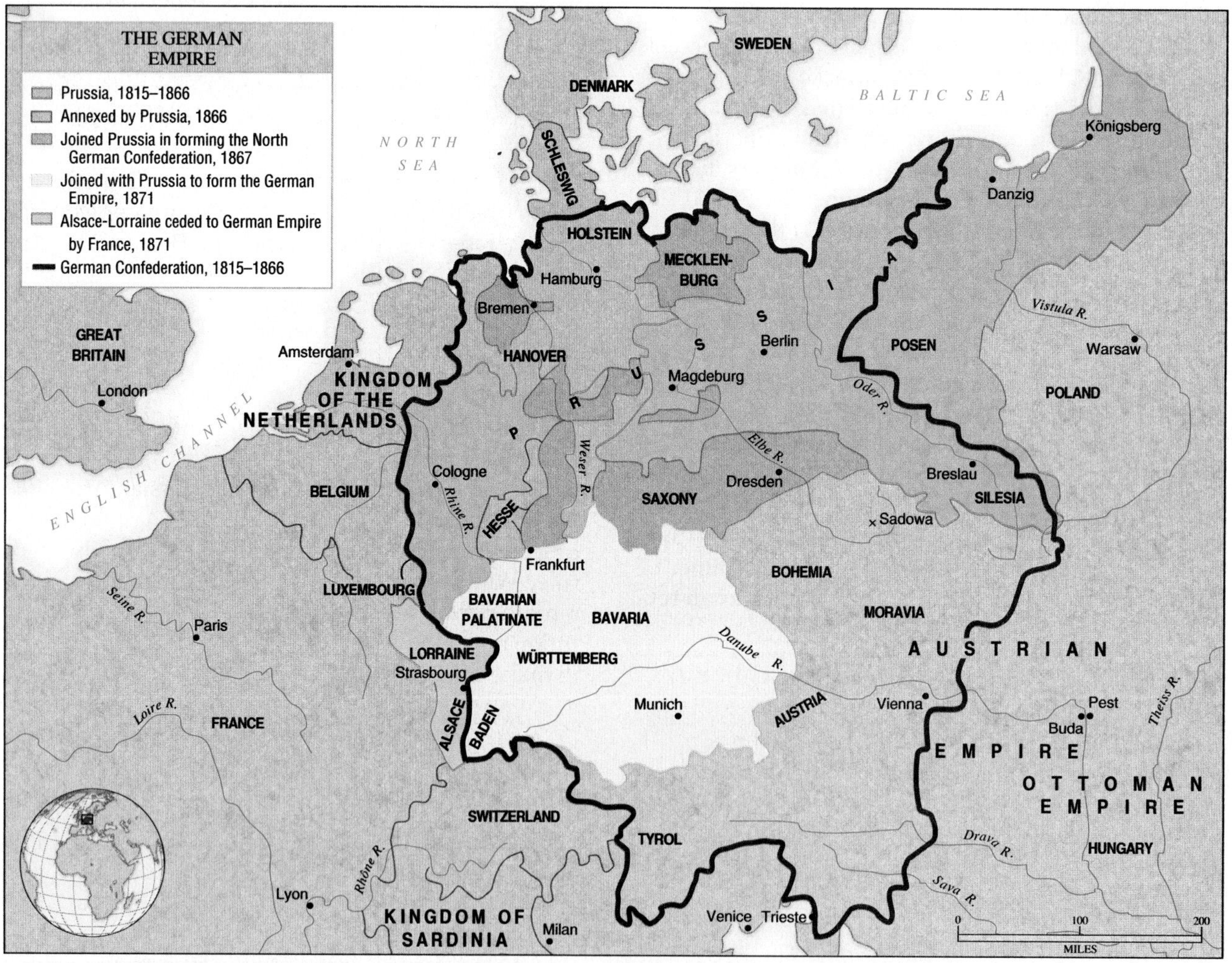

The Hohenzollerns, based in Berlin, began the process of linking their widely spread territories in the seventeenth century. Napoleon contributed to a consolidated German state through his rearrangement of the map after his military conquests, and Bismarck completed the unification of Germany by 1871.

Some historians have attributed his successes to luck, whereas others have deemed them products of genius. An example is his approach to Russia. Bismarck knew that he would have to solidify relations with Russia, and he achieved this in 1863 by promising the Russians that he would aid them in all Polish-related problems. Giving up virtually nothing, he gained a secure eastern flank and proceeded to set up three wars that brought about German unification.

The Danish and Austrian Wars

In 1864 Bismarck invited Austria to join Prussia and wage war on Denmark. The cause of the conflict was the disputed status of two duchies, Schleswig and Holstein, bordering on Prussia and Denmark and claimed by both. The two Germanic powers overwhelmed the modest Danish forces and split the duchies: Austria took Holstein, and Schleswig went to Prussia. With his eastern and northern flanks stabilized, Bismarck set out to isolate Austria.

Italy was already hostile to the Austrians and remained so when Bismarck promised it Venetia in return for its assistance in the future war. He encouraged the French to be neutral by intimating that Prussia might support France should it seek to widen its borders. Severe domestic crises with the Hungarians absorbed Austria, which soon found itself isolated. The Prussian leader provoked war with Vienna by piously expressing alarm at the manner in which the Austrians were ruling Holstein and sending troops into the province. Austria took the bait, entered the war, and was devastated by the Prussians at the battle of Sadowa. In this Seven Weeks' War, the Prussians avenged the "humiliation of Olmütz" of 1850.

Prussia offered a moderate peace settlement that ended the old German Confederation. In its place Bismarck formed the North German Confederation, with Austria and the southern German states excluded. Prussia annexed several territories, including Hanover, Mecklenburg, and other states north of the Main River, in this penultimate stage in the unification of Germany.

The War with France

After 1867 Bismarck turned his attention westward to France and Emperor Napoleon III (1808–1873). The French leader had allowed himself to be talked into neutrality in 1866 because he anticipated a long war between his German neighbors that would weaken them both and because he hoped to expand into the neutral state of Belgium. In August 1866, Napoleon approached Bismarck for his share of the fruits of victory, but the German leader refused to agree to French demands. Frustrated and offended, Napoleon III insisted that Prussia approve France's annexation of Luxembourg and Belgium. In a crafty move, Bismarck invited the French envoy to Berlin to put these demands into writing but still avoided giving a definite response.

Four years later, Bismarck sent the document to the British in order to gain their sympathy for the upcoming war with the French. After France's active participation in the Crimean War, there was no chance that Russia would come to Napoleon's aid. Bismarck let the Austrians know about France's cooperation with the Prussians during the 1866 war, and Italy was not about to help Napoleon III after his activities in 1859. By 1870 France was isolated. It was simply a question now of Bismarck maneuvering the French into war.

The immediate controversy centered on the succession to the Spanish throne left vacant after a revolution had overthrown the reactionary Queen Isabella. The Spaniards asked Leopold, a Hohenzollern prince, to become the constitutional king of their country. France saw this as an unacceptable extension of Prussian influence, and Leopold withdrew his candidacy. But this was not enough for Paris. The French sent their ambassador to Ems, where the Prussian king was vacationing, to gain from him a pledge that he would not again permit Leopold to seek the Spanish throne. The king refused to agree to this unreasonable request. After the interview, he directed that a message be sent to Bismarck, describing the incident. Bismarck altered the message of this Ems dispatch to give the impression that the French ambassador had insulted the Prussian king and that the king had returned the insult. The rumor was leaked to the press and infuriated both the Germans and the French.

France declared war in July. The two countries' forces appeared to be evenly matched in equipment, but the Germans had a better-trained and more experienced army. In 2 months the Prussians overwhelmed the French, delivering the crowning blow at the battle of Sedan, where the emperor and his army were surrounded and forced to surrender. Troops of the combined armies of the German states besieged the north of France for 4 months before the final French capitulation. By the Treaty of Frankfurt in 1871, France lost Alsace and a part of Lorraine to Germany and was required to pay a large indemnity. The call for revenge of France's defeat and humiliation became a major issue in French politics.

Document Bismarck and the Ems Dispatch

Bismarck knew how to manipulate public opinion through press leaks and doctored documents. See how he altered the Ems dispatch to achieve his goals vis-à-vis France.

I made use of the royal authorization communicated to me through Abeken, to publish the contents of the telegram; and in the presence of my two guests I reduced the telegram by striking out words, but without adding or altering, to the following form:

After the news of the renunciation of the hereditary Prince of Hohenzollern had been officially communicated to the imperial government of France by the royal government of Spain, the French ambassador at Ems further demanded of his Majesty the King that he would authorize him to telegraph to Paris that his Majesty the King bound himself for all future time never again to give his consent if the Hohenzollerns should renew their candidature. His Majesty the King thereupon decided not to receive the French ambassador again, and sent to tell him through the aide-de-camp on duty that his Majesty had nothing further to communicate to the ambassador.

The difference in the effect of the abbreviated text of the Ems telegram as compared with that produced by the original was not the result of stronger words but of the form, which made this announcement appear decisive, while Abeken's version only would have been regarded as a fragment of a negotiation still pending, and to be continued at Berlin.

After I had read out the concentrated edition to my two guests, Moltke remarked: "Now it has a different ring; it sounded before like a parley; now it is like a flourish in answer to a challenge."

Questions to Consider

1. How does Bismarck's altering of the Ems dispatch reflect his role as a master of Realpolitik?
2. Do you think government leaders are justified in manipulating truth to gain their political actions? In your lifetime have you seen an example of this?
3. What role do governmental "leaks" such as that of the Ems dispatch play today?

From *Bismarck: The Man and the Statesman,* trans. A. J. Butler (1899).

Judged from the point of view of comparative manpower, the French and German armies appeared in 1870 to be equally strong. However, the Germans took advantage of their superiority in leadership and experience to overwhelm the French in the Franco-Pussian War.

The Second German Reich

The Second Reich came into existence at a ceremony in January 1871 in the Hall of Mirrors at the Palace of Versailles. There King William I became kaiser ("emperor") of a federal union of 26 states with a population of 41 million. The bicameral (two-house) legislature of the new empire consisted of the ***Bundesrat*** (BUN-des-raht), representing the ruling houses of the various states, and the ***Reichstag*** (RIKE-stag), representing the people through its 397 members elected by male suffrage.

Dominant power rested with the kaiser, who controlled military and foreign affairs and the 17 votes in the *Bundesrat* needed to veto any constitutional change. The actual head of government was the chancellor who was appointed by the kaiser and responsible to him only. This arrangement allowed the chancellor to defy or ignore the legislature if it served his purpose. However, he had to operate within the

Bundesrat—The upper class of the German legislature after 1871.

Reichstag—The lower house of the bicameral German legislature after 1871.

constraints of the federal state structure in which large powers of local government were given to the member states.

Bismarck as Chancellor

As chancellor, Otto von Bismarck built modern Germany on his belief in the inherent efficiency of a state based on one faith, one law, and one ruler. He distrusted institutions that did not fit that tripartite formula—specifically, the Catholic Church and the Socialist party. Bismarck was more constrained in domestic than in foreign affairs. It is not surprising, therefore, that he fared better in foreign matters.

The Catholic political party had sent a large bloc of representatives to the Reichstag in 1871, and these members supported the complete independence of the church from state control, denounced divorce, objected to secular education, and questioned freedom of conscience. Many Catholics strongly supported the new dogma of papal infallibility. Within the protestant Prussian part of Germany, Bismarck introduced anti-Catholic policies that triggered a conflict known as the *Kulturkampf* (KUL-ture-kompf; "struggle for civilization"). These so-called May Laws made it an offense for the clergy to criticize the government, regulated the educational activities of the religious orders, and expelled the Jesuits from the country. The state also required civil marriages and dictated that all priests study theology at state universities. Pope Pius IX declared these acts null and void and told loyal Catholics to refuse to obey them. Many of the chancellor's laws applied equally to protestants, who actively protested them.

As opposition spread, Bismarck struck hard at the Catholics, imprisoning priests, confiscating church property, and closing down pulpits. When the tide did not turn in his favor, he realized that he could not afford to create millions of martyrs. Showing his shrewd sense of power, he cut his losses, retreated, and repealed most of the anti-Catholic laws.

The Social Democratic (Marxist) movement posed a greater challenge to Bismarck's rule. The party's founder, Ferdinand Lassalle (1825–1864), rejected violence as a means to gain power and instead advocated working within the existing political structure. After his death the movement retained its nonviolent nature. The party's popularity soared when it was officially established in 1875, and its leaders pushed for true parliamentary democracy and wider-ranging social programs. In 1878 Bismarck used two attempts on the emperor's life as an excuse to launch an all-out campaign to weaken the Social Democrats, even though they had no connection with the assassination attempts. He dissolved extralegal socialist organizations, suppressed their publications, and threw their leaders in jail. Despite these measures, the socialists continued to gain support.

When he failed to weaken the socialists by direct confrontation, the chancellor changed tactics. He decided to undercut them by taking over their program. Through the 1880s, he implemented important social legislation that provided wage earners with sickness, accident, and old-age insurance. He sponsored other laws that responded to many of the abuses workers encountered. Still, the Social Democrats continued to grow in size and influence. However, by creating the first welfare state, the pragmatic Prussian chancellor defused a potential revolution.

Kaiser William II

In 1888 William II, the grandson of the emperor, became head of the Reich. Just as Bismarck had dominated European affairs since 1862, the new emperor would play a key role until 1918. Here was a person who advocated a policy of "blood and iron," but without Bismarck's finesse. Where Bismarck knew the limits and uses of force and appreciated the nuances of public statements, William was a militarist and a bully. Serving in a modern age, the new emperor still believed in the divine right of kings and constantly reminded his entourage that "he and God" worked together for the good of the state. With such a contrast in styles, it is not surprising that William saw Bismarck not as a guide but as a threat. Once William established himself in power, he forced Bismarck to resign in March 1890.

At the beginning of the twentieth century, Germany presented a puzzling picture to the world. On the one hand, the blustering kaiser made fiery and warlike statements. He encouraged militarism and the belief that *"Alles kommt von oben"* (ALL-es kommt fon O-ben; "Everything comes down from above"). On the other hand, his thoroughly advanced country made great scientific and cultural strides. Observers of German affairs noted that one-third of the voters supported the Social Democrats, an indication of a healthy parliamentary system. A commonly held pride in Germany's accomplishments knit the country together.

More important than William's behavior was the fact that, by the beginning of the new century, the Germans competed actively in all areas with the British. Although Germany did not outproduce Britain, long-term projections showed that the island nation's growth had leveled out and that in the next generation the Reich would surpass it. The Germans dominated the world market in the chemical and electrical industries and were making strides in other areas. They boasted a more efficient organization of their industries, a higher literacy rate for their workers, better

Bismarck and the young Kaiser William II meet in 1888. The two disagreed over many issues, and in 1890 William dismissed the aged chancellor.

vocational training, and a more aggressive corps of businessmen. German labor unions were less combative than the British, and the government gave more support to industry than Parliament did. When the kaiser demanded a navy the equal of that of England, alarm bells went off in London.

THE DECLINE OF AUSTRIA

- *Why did the Austrian Empire decline in power and influence after 1867?*

Conservative forces consolidated control in Vienna after 1848, but the Austrian Habsburgs operated from a weakened position. Their victory over the Hungarians brought only temporary comfort. The collapse of the liberal and nationalistic movements in the Habsburg Empire was followed by a harsh repression that did little to address the basic political problems facing Vienna. Centralizing and Germanizing tendencies stimulated nationalist sentiments in the empire. After their losses to the French and Sardinians in 1859, the Austrians considered moving toward a federal system for their lands. The Hungarians, however, demanded equality with Vienna. The government in Vienna became increasingly inept.

The Dual Monarchy

After the Austrians' disastrous defeat by Prussia, Franz Joseph was forced to offer the Hungarians an equal partnership with Vienna in ruling the empire. The offer was accepted, and in 1867 the constitution known as the *Ausgleich* (OUS-glike; "compromise") was enacted. This document created the **Dual Monarchy,** in which the Habsburg ruler was both the king of Hungary and the emperor of Austria—defined as the area that was not part of Hungary. Each country had its own constitution, language, flag, and parliament. Ministers common to both countries handled finance, defense, and foreign affairs, but they were supervised by "delegations," which consisted of 60 members from each parliament who did not meet together, except in emergency circumstances. The *Ausgleich* was to be renegotiated every 10 years.

By the end of the century, the Dual Monarchy contained 12 million Germans, 10 million Hungarians, more than 24 million Slavs, and 4 million Romanians, among other nationalities. Although the Germans of Austria had recognized the equality of the Hungarians, the rest of the nationalities continued to live under alien rule. Now, instead of having to deal with one dominant national group, they had to cope with two. In some cases, as in the prospering, cosmopolitan, and sophisticated area of Bohemia-Moravia, the people wanted an independent state or, at the very least, more rights within the Habsburg realm. Other groups, such as the Serbs, sought the goal of joining their countrymen living in adjacent national states. The nationalities question remained an explosive problem for the authorities in Vienna and Budapest.

The functioning of the Dual Monarchy was best symbolized by the official banknotes, which were printed in eight languages on one side and in Hungarian on the other. In the Hungarian part of the Dual Monarchy, the aristocracy governed under the Kossuth constitution of 1848. The Hungarians refused to share rule with the minorities in their kingdom. A small, powerful landed oligarchy dominated the mass of backward, landless peasants. The conservative leadership carried out a virtual process of Magyarization with their minorities (imposing Hungarian culture as the desired standard) while they continually squabbled with the Austrians.

In the Austrian portion, wealthy German businessmen and the landed aristocracy dominated polit-

Dual Monarchy—The Austro-Hungarian Empire, created in 1867 by the writing of a constitution that defined the relationship between Vienna and Budapest.

It fell to the Habsburgs to exercise power over the ethnic, religious, and linguistic fracture zone of southeastern Europe. Then major nationalities—especially the Hungarians—presented the Vienna-based government with severe challenges.

ical life. But even with this concentration of power, the government was much more democratic, especially after 1907, when the two-house legislature was elected by universal manhood suffrage. Here, too, nationalism was a serious problem, and political parties came to be based not on principle but on nationality. Each nationality had to work with the Germans, even though it might detest them. The nationalities frequently disliked one another, and this prevented the formation of any coalitions among them. By 1914 the Austrians had extended substantial local self-government to their subject nationalities, but this concession did little to quiet discontent.

The *Ausgleich* functioned poorly, yet its defenders could still tell themselves that they were, after all, citizens of a "great empire." The Dual Monarchy occupied a strategic geographical location and had enough military strength to be very influential in the Balkans. In addition, the area had great economic potential, with Hungarian wheat, Croatian and Slovenian livestock, Czech banks and industry, and Austrian commerce. But Franz Joseph ruled over a disjointed conglomeration of peoples who shared only the pretension of being citizens of a great power.

FRANCE: THE SECOND EMPIRE AND THE THIRD REPUBLIC

- *Why was France unable to compete effectively with Germany during the second half of the nineteenth century?*

The Second Empire

In France the violence of the June Days moved the conservatives in the countryside and the moderates in the cities to elect Louis Napoleon, nephew of Napoleon I, to the presidency of the Second Republic in 1848. Although he had failed miserably in his attempts to overthrow the king in 1836 and 1840, he was sure that destiny intended great things for him. When he came back to Paris after the revolution, he was untainted by any involvement in the June Days and appeared to be a unifying force.

Louis Napoleon v. General Cavaignac–British Cartoon

The republic's constitution gave strong powers to the president but limited the office to a single term. Louis Napoleon took advantage of the authority given him and his strong majority to fortify his position. He and his conservative allies dominated France for the next two years, becoming strong enough to overthrow the constitution in a coup d'état in December 1851. Louis Napoleon and his allies brutally put down the workers and peasants who opposed the coup and engineered a plebiscite that gave him virtually unanimous support. In 1852 he proclaimed himself Emperor Napoleon III, and the Second Empire replaced the Second Republic.

During its 18-year span, the Second Empire accomplished a great deal. Industrialization brought prosperity to France. Production doubled. France supported the building of the Suez Canal, and railway mileage in France increased by 500 percent. The partial legalization of labor unions and guarantee of the right to strike improved workers' conditions. Baron Georges Haussmann transformed Paris in an ambitious urban renewal that featured broad boulevards, unified architecture, modern utilities, and improved traffic flow.

The price for the order and stability needed to build this prosperity came in the form of political control. The government remained, in theory, a parliamentary regime. The emperor's agents rigged the elections to ensure a majority in the powerless legislature for the emperor. The secret police hounded opponents, both real and potential, and the state censored the press, which accordingly rarely reported bad news.

At first, the emperor brought glory to France through an interventionist and imperialist foreign policy. He continually claimed to be a man of peace, but he allied with Britain in the Crimean War, supported Count Camillo Benso di Cavour, briefly, in Italy, expanded French influence to ensure a foothold in Indochina, raised the French flag over Tahiti, and penetrated West Africa along the Senegal River. Foreign affairs soured for him in the 1860s when he made an ill-advised attempt to take advantage of the confusion caused by the U.S. Civil War to establish a foothold in the Americas. He placed Maximilian, a Habsburg prince, on the Mexican throne and sent 40,000 troops to support him. Mexican patriots expelled the forces and in 1867 a firing squad executed Maximilian.

After 1866, Louis Napoleon met his match in the Prussian chancellor Otto von Bismarck (1815–1898), when his blundering ambition contributed to a quick Prussian victory over Austria. Finally, in 1870 he gambled on war against Prussia and lost. With this defeat, the Second Empire ended.

The Third Republic

The defeat of France's Second Empire at Sedan in 1870 gave birth to the Third Republic. The humiliating peace terms stripped France of part of Lorraine and all of Alsace and imposed a huge indemnity on the country. The spectacle of the Germans crowning their emperor and proclaiming the Second Reich at Versailles, the symbol of French greatness, left a bitter taste. The stark contrast between the promised grandeur of the Second Empire and the humiliation of 1871 left a legacy of domestic uncertainty and an obsession for revenge against the Germans.

Persistent class conflicts, covered over during Louis Napoleon's reign, also contributed to many years of shaky existence before the republic gained a firm footing. A new and overwhelmingly royalist national assembly was elected to construct a new, conservative government after the signing of the peace with the Germans. This, added to the shock of the defeat, touched off a revolutionary outburst that led to the Paris Commune of 1871.

Parisians had suffered such severe food shortages during the siege of the city that some had been forced to eat rats and zoo animals. When it turned out that their sacrifices had been in vain, republican and radical Parisians joined forces in part of the city to form a commune, in the tradition of the 1792 Paris Commune, to save the republic. The **Communards** advocated government control of prices, wages, and working conditions (including stopping night work in the bakeries). After several weeks of civil strife, the Commune was savagely put down. Class hatred split France further yet.

Because the two monarchist factions that constituted a majority could not agree on an acceptable candidate for the monarchy, they finally settled on a republic as the least disagreeable form of government. The National Assembly approved the new republican constitution in 1875. Under the new system, members of the influential lower house, the Chamber of Deputies, were elected by direct suffrage. There was also a Senate, whose members were elected

---

Communards—Parisians who lived and worked in the Paris Commune in 1871.

indirectly by electoral colleges in the departments. The constitution established a weak executive, elected by the legislature. The ministry exercised real power, but its authority depended on whatever coalition of parties could be assembled to form a tenuous majority in the legislature.

Boulanger and Dreyfus

The stormy tenure of the Third Republic was marked by a series of crises, including anarchist violence culminating in a series of bombings in 1893, financial scandals such as the notorious Panama Canal venture that implicated a wide range of leading figures, and lesser scandals. The two most serious threats were the Boulanger and Dreyfus affairs.

The weak and traumatized republic was both threatened and embarrassed by the public cries for vengeance uttered in 1886 by General Georges Boulanger (ZHORZH boo-lon-ZHAY; 1837–1891), the minister of war. This charismatic, warmongering figure made a series of speeches, which he ended by emotionally proclaiming, "Remember, they are waiting for us in Alsace." The considerable number of antirepublicans saw him as a man on horseback who would sweep away the republic in a coup d'état, much as Louis Napoleon had done in 1851, and bring back French grandeur. The government finally ordered Boulanger's arrest on a charge of conspiracy, and he fled the country. Later he committed suicide.

The Dreyfus case was far more serious because it polarized the entire country, divided and embittered French opinion by the anti-Semitic fervor it unleashed, and challenged the fundamental ideals of French democracy. Captain Alfred Dreyfus (1859–1935), the first Jewish officer on the French general staff, was accused in 1894 of selling military secrets to Germany. His fellow officers tried him, found him guilty, stripped him of his commission, and condemned him to solitary confinement on Devil's Island, a dreadful convict settlement off the northeast coast of South America. Even with the case supposedly settled, military secrets continued to leak to the Germans, and subsequently a royalist, spendthrift officer named Major Esterhazy was accused, tried, and acquitted.

The case became a cause célèbre in 1898 when the French writer Émile Zola (1840–1902) wrote his famous letter *J'accuse* (zha-CUES; "I accuse"), in which he attacked the judge for knowingly allowing the guilty party to go free while Dreyfus remained in jail. The next year Esterhazy admitted his guilt, but by that time the entire country had split into two camps. On the one side were the anti-Dreyfusards—the army, church, and royalists—on the other side were the pro-Dreyfusards—the intellectuals, socialists, and republicans. The case was once again placed under review in the military courts, and even though Esterhazy had confessed, the court continued to find Dreyfus guilty. Finally, the French president pardoned him, and in 1906 the highest civil court in France found him innocent.

The case had greater significance than just the fate of one man. Those who had worked against Dreyfus, especially the church, would pay dearly for their stand. Many republicans believed that the church, a consistent ally of the monarchists, was the natural enemy of democratic government. They demanded an end to the church's official ties to the state. In 1904 and 1905 the government closed all church schools and rescinded the **Napoleonic Concordat.** All ties between church and state were formally ended.

After weathering 40 difficult years, by 1914, the Third Republic had gained prosperity and stability. Workers had found their voice in the country as the

Napoleonic Concordant—Agreement signed between Napoleon and Pope Pius VII in 1801 reestablishing the Catholic Church as the religion of the majority of the French people. The church regained its prominence and role in education, but without its pre-1789 power and wealth.

Captain Alfred Dreyfus had to pass through this "Guard of Dishonor" each day on his way to the courtroom during his second trial in 1899.

various trade and local union groups came together in the General Confederation of Labor. Monarchists and other right-wing parties still had considerable influence, although the Dreyfus affair had weakened them.

French republicanism had wide support across the political spectrum. Most French citizens enjoyed basic democratic rights, which they exercised through the extremely complex multiparty political system of the republic. The various ministries that were constructed from the fragile coalitions came and went with bewildering rapidity. Yet France was strong and prosperous, one of only two republics among the world's great powers.

Count Camillo Benso di Cavour mastered the arts of diplomatic maneuvering to create a unified Italy.

ITALY TO 1914

■ *What challenges did Cavour face in his efforts to unify Italy?*

Italian Unification

After 1848 fighters for Italian unification established their base in the kingdom of Sardinia, where the young monarch, Victor Emmanuel II, refused to withdraw the liberal constitution granted by his father. The prime minister, Count Camillo Benso di Cavour (1810–1861), a liberal influenced by what he had seen in Switzerland, France, and Britain, assumed leadership of the drive to unify the peninsula. After 1852, when he became prime minister, Cavour concentrated on freeing his country from Austrian domination. He knew, however, that Sardinia needed allies to take on the Habsburgs. To that end, in 1855 Sardinia joined Britain and France in their fight against Russia in the Crimean War. This step enabled Cavour to speak at the peace conference after the war, where he stated Italy's desire for unification.

Cavour's presentation won Napoleon III's support, and the two opportunists found that they could both make gains if they could draw the Austrians into war. They agreed that if Cavour could entice the Vienna government into war, France would come to Sardinia's aid and help eject the Austrians from Lombardy and Venetia. In return, France would receive Nice and Savoy from Sardinia. The plan worked to perfection. In April 1859 Cavour lured the Austrians into declaring war. The French and Sardinians defeated them at Magenta and Solferino and drove them out of Lombardy. At the same time, revolts broke out in Tuscany, Modena, Parma, and Romagna. Napoleon was praised and proclaimed as the savior and liberator of Italy.

The Unification of Italy, 1859–1870

Upon receiving his share of the agreement, Napoleon III reversed himself and made peace with Austria before the allies could invade Venetia. The massing of Prussian troops on French borders as well as his second thoughts about the implications of a united Italy drove Napoleon to this move. The Sardinians were outraged, but they could do little but agree to a peace settlement. The agreement awarded Lombardy to Sardinia, restored the exiled rulers of Parma, Modena, Tuscany, and Romagna, and set up an Italian confederation in which Austria was included.

France's duplicity did not stop Cavour. A year later, appealing to the British, he made major changes in the peace settlement. Plebiscites were held in Tuscany, Modena, and Parma, all of which voted to join Sardinia. Even with the loss of Nice and Savoy to France, the addition of the three areas made Sardinia the dominant power in the peninsula.

With the consolidation of power in the north, Giuseppe Garibaldi (1807–1882) became the major figure in the unification struggle. This follower of Mazzini, secretly financed by Cavour, led his 1000 tough adventurers, known as the Red Shirts, to conquer Sicily and Naples. He then prepared to take the Papal States.

Garibaldi Surrendering Power–British Cartoon

This move prompted Cavour, who feared that a march on the pope's holdings might provoke French intervention, to rush troops to Naples. He convinced Garibaldi to surrender his power to Victor Emmanuel II, thus ensuring Sardinian domination of the unification movement. By November 1860, Sardinia had annexed the former kingdom of Naples and Sicily and all the papal lands, except Rome and its environs.

A meeting at Turin in March 1861 formally proclaimed the existence of the kingdom of Italy, a new nation of 22 million people. But Austrian control of Venetia and the pope's jurisdiction over Rome were problems that remained unsolved until after Cavour's death in 1861. Italy gained Venetia in 1866 by allying with Prussia in the Austro-Prussian war. When the Franco-Prussian war broke out in 1870, the French could do little to help the pope. Italian forces took control of Rome, and in 1871, this city became the capital of a unified Italy.

The opportunistic methods used by the Sardinians have been criticized. Cavour made no attempt to hide the true nature of his policies. He once said, "If we did for ourselves what we do for our country, what rascals we should be." He fully understood the rules of the Realpolitik game in the post-1848 state system and played it extraordinarily well.

The New Italian State

Italy faced overwhelming problems. The Italians had to deal with economic, political, and cultural differences between the northern and southern parts of the country, a lack of natural resources, and a politically inexperienced population. It also had too many people for its limited economic base.

Italy's most troubling problem, however, was the question of the papacy, which seriously weakened the state. The pope, the spiritual father of most Italians, refused to accept the incorporation of Rome into the new nation. He called himself the "prisoner of the Vatican," and encouraged—with little effect—his Italian flock not to vote. In an attempt to satisfy the pope, the government in 1871 passed the Law of Papal Guarantees, which set up the Vatican as a sovereign state and allocated the pope an annual sum of $600,000 (roughly the amount of money he had received from his previously held lands). Pius IX rejected the offer, but the state refused to repeal the law.

Despite conflicting and unstable political parties, the new Italian state carried on an impressive program of railroad building, naval construction, and attempts at social and welfare legislation. But major problems remained, especially with the peasantry in the south. Radical political parties made their presence felt after the turn of the century in the form of widespread strikes. In 1900 an anarchist assassinated King Umberto, who had taken the throne in 1878. Change proceeded slowly after that, and not until 1912, a time when there was still widespread illiteracy, did the country gain universal manhood suffrage.

The Italian leaders' ambition to make Italy a world power placed a great burden on the nation. Money spent on the army came at the expense of needed investments in education and social services. National resources were squandered in an unsuccessful attempt in 1896 and 1912 to build an empire in Africa.

Up to the beginning of World War I, Italy faced severe economic crises and labor unrest. In June 1914 a general strike spread through the central part of the peninsula. Benito Mussolini, editor of a socialist journal, played a key role in this movement. Attempts to achieve compulsory education, freedom of the press, and better working conditions did little to ease the economic hardships and high taxes that had driven thousands to emigrate to the United States. The south especially suffered, because it had not shared in the industrial gains of the northern part of the country.

THE UNITED KINGDOM

- *What political and economic factors accounted for the stability of Britain during the nineteenth century?*

Tory Dominance

The post–Napoleonic War period was the most difficult time for Britain, as the transition back to a peacetime economy and the wrenching changes caused by industrialization made their effects felt. Some traditional workers lost their jobs due to the increasing use of machines, and in response, workers smashed the machines and destroyed some factories. Violence broke out when some working-class groups and radicals pushed for rapid reforms. The worst incident took place in August 1819 in what became known as the Peterloo Massacre. In Manchester, a crowd of 60,000 gathered at St. Peter's Fields to push for parliamentary reforms. When the army was sent to disband the meeting, several people were killed and hundreds were injured.

The Tories (Conservatives), Britain's ruling party since the 1770s, were blind to the hardships of the workers. They continued to react to the long-departed excesses of the French Revolution. Instead of dealing with the misfortunes of the poor and the unemployed, they declared that the doctrine of "peace, law, order, and discipline" should be their guide. To that end, they pushed through a series of repressive acts after

1815 that suspended the Habeas Corpus Act, restricted public meetings, repressed liberal newspapers, and placed heavy fines on literature considered to be dangerous. Massive conflict between the rich and poor appeared inevitable.

Britain's political abuses were plain for all to see. Representation in the House of Commons was not at all proportional to the population. Three percent of the people dictated the election of members. The rapidly growing industrial towns such as Manchester and Birmingham—each with more than 100,000 citizens—had no representatives, while other areas, virtually without population, had them. The duke of Wellington's failure to acknowledge the need for reforms aroused the public. In the end, the "Iron Duke" and the Tories were forced to resign when members of his own party voted against Wellington in protest of the Catholic Emancipation Act of 1829, which gave Roman Catholics voting rights and the rights to serve in Parliament and most public offices. The Tories were replaced by a more liberal group, the Whigs. The drive toward self-interested changes by the upper classes had begun in the 1820s, led by Robert Peel (1788–1850) and George Canning (1770–1827). These two set in motion the British reform tradition that continued to 1914. When Wellington was voted out of office, Lord Charles Grey (1764–1845), leader of the Whig party, became head of government. In 1832 Grey pushed immediately to reform Parliament.

Self-Interested Reform

After being blocked by aristocratic interests, first in the House of Commons, and then in the House of Lords, reform bills responding to these electoral abuses were finally passed. But they became law only because King William IV threatened to create enough new members of the House of Lords who would vote for the bills in order to pass them. Grey's reform bills did not bring absolute democracy, but they pointed the way toward a more equitable political system. Reformers pushed through laws that ended capital punishment for more than 100 offenses, created a modern police force for London, recognized labor unions, and repealed old laws that kept non-Anglican protestants from sitting in Parliament. The reform tide increased in the 1830s and 1840s. Abolitionist pressures brought about the ending of slavery in the British Empire in 1833. Parliament passed laws initiating the regulation of working conditions and hours. In 1835 the Municipal Corporations Act introduced a uniform system of town government by popular elections.

Britain's government was far from being a democracy, and in the 1830s and 1840s, a strong popular movement known as **Chartism** developed. Its leaders summarized the country's needs in six demands: universal manhood suffrage, secret voting, no property qualifications for members of Parliament, payment of Parliament members so that the poor could seek election, annual elections, and equal districts. In 1839, 1842, and 1848, the Chartists presented their demands, backed by more than a million signatures on their petitions. But each time, they failed to gain their goals, and the movement declined after 1848. By the end of the century, however, all of their demands, except that for annual parliamentary elections, had been put into law.

Mirroring the ascendancy of the middle classes, economic liberalism became dominant. A policy of free trade came to be favored because, given Britain's overwhelming economic superiority, the country could best profit from that approach. The Corn Laws' protective duties on imported grain, which had favored the gentry since 1815, no longer suited the industrializing British economy. These laws had been designed to encourage exports and to protect British landowners from foreign competition. By the middle of the century, the population had grown to such an extent that British farmers could no longer feed the country, and the price of bread rose alarmingly.

The potato crop famine in Ireland in 1845 spotlighted the situation and the need for low-priced food from abroad. Repeal of the Corn Laws made possible the import of cheaper food. Soon Britain abandoned customs duties of every kind. The economy boomed under the stimulus of cheap imports of raw materials and food.

The Irish Dilemma

One dilemma escaped the solutions of well-meaning reformers, that of the British role in Ireland, which originated in the seventeenth century. The British placed large numbers of Scottish emigrants in the province of Ulster in northern Ireland, which built a strong colony of protestants. In the eighteenth century, the British passed a number of oppressive laws against Irish Catholics, taking what was left of their lands and restricting their political, economic, and religious freedom. Passage of the Act of Union in 1801 forced the Irish to send their representatives to the Parliament in London, not Dublin. Most of the Irish farmland at this time was controlled by parasitic landlords, who leased their newly gained lands in increasingly smaller plots to more and more people. Many peasants could not pay their rent and were

Chartism—A movement active in the middle part of the nineteenth century pushing British politicians to make reforms.

evicted from the land. The Irish lost both their self-government and their livelihood.

The 1845 potato famine and its aftereffects led to a tremendous decline in population. Perhaps as many as 1 million died and 1.5 million emigrated, many to the United States. Between 1841 and 1891, the population fell by more than 40 percent, from 8.8 million to less than 5 million.

For all of their suffering, the Irish gained very few concessions from London during the nineteenth century. The Catholic Emancipation Act (1829) removed legal limitations from the Irish Church while tenants received protection from being arbitrarily evicted by British landlords. The Irish Anglican Church lost its favored position when Roman Catholics were freed of the obligation to pay tax support to a church they did not attend. In the 1880s Irish peasants were given the chance gradually to regain land that had once been theirs.

Victorian Reforms

In the mid-1800s an alliance of the landed gentry and the middle classes worked together to dominate the British government and to keep the lower classes "in their stations." The newly ascendant middle classes believed that political reforms had gone far enough, and the Whig government of Lord Palmerston, who served as prime minister from 1855 to 1865, reflected this view. But the final third of the century would belong to the reforming politicians among the Liberals and Conservatives who had to face the fact that the complacency of government during the "Victorian Compromise" from 1850 to 1865 could not continue. Serious problems plagued the country. Only one adult male in six was entitled to vote. Both parties felt the pressure to make the political system more representative. Both parties also knew that reform must come, and each hoped to take the credit and gain the resultant strength for extending the vote. Thanks to its wealth and adaptability, Britain built a truly democratic political structure by 1914. The state continued to support business even as it became more intimately involved in matters affecting the welfare of its citizens.

Gladstone and Disraeli

Two great statesmen, William Ewart Gladstone (1809–1898), a Liberal, and Benjamin Disraeli (1804–1881), a Conservative, dominated the first part of this period with their policies of gradual reform. They alternated as prime minister from 1867 to 1880. After Disraeli's death, Gladstone prevailed until he retired in 1894. The two leaders came from sharply contrasting backgrounds. The son of a rich Liverpool merchant, Gladstone had every advantage that wealth and good social position could give him. He entered Parliament in 1833 and quickly became one of the great orators of his day. He began as a Conservative, working in the tradition of the Tory reformer Robert Peel. Gradually he shifted his alliance to the newly formed Liberal party in the 1850s, became a strong supporter of laissez-faire economics, and worked to keep government from interfering in business. He was far more effective as a political reformer than as a social or economic one.

Disraeli had few of Gladstone's advantages. The son of a Jew who became a naturalized British subject in 1801, Disraeli was baptized an Anglican. He first made a name for himself as the author of the novel Vivian Grey (1826). In contrast to Gladstone, Disraeli went from liberalism to conservatism in his philosophy. He stood for office as a Conservative throughout his career and became the leader of the party.

The Liberals' turn came first. In 1866 they introduced a moderate reform bill giving city workers the vote. Some Conservatives opposed it, fearful that increasing the franchise would bring the day of revolution closer. When the proposal failed to pass, political agitation and riots rocked the country. The outbreaks evidently impressed the members of Parliament; when the Conservatives came to power in 1867, Disraeli successfully sponsored the Second Reform Bill, which added more than a million city workers to the voting rolls. The measure increased the electorate by 88 percent, although women and farm laborers were still denied the vote.

Even though the Conservatives passed the voter reform bill, the new elections in 1868 brought the Liberals back to power, and Gladstone began his so-called Glorious Ministry, which lasted until 1874. With the granting of the vote to the urban masses, it became imperative to educate their children. The Education Act of 1870 promoted the establishment of local school boards to build and maintain state schools. Private schools received governmental subsidies if they met certain minimal standards. Elementary school attendance, which was compulsory between the ages of 5 and 14, jumped from 1 to 4 million in 10 years.

Other reforms included a complete overhaul of the civil service system. Previously, in both the government and the military, appointments and promotions depended on patronage and favoritism. But in 1870, this method was replaced by open examinations. The government also improved the military by shortening enlistment terms, abolishing flogging, and stopping the sale of officers' ranks. Gladstone's government successfully revamped the justice system and introduced the secret ballot. Finally, some restrictions on labor unions' activities were removed. By 1872 the Glorious Ministry had exhausted itself, and Disraeli referred to Gladstone

Prime Minister William Gladstone introduces the First Home Rule Bill for Ireland before the House of Commons; the bill would go down to defeat.

and his colleagues in the House of Commons as a "range of exhausted volcanoes."

Disraeli's government succeeded the Glorious Ministry in 1874, and he stated that he was going to "give the country a rest." He was no stand-pat Conservative, however. He supported an approach known as Tory democracy, which attempted to weld an alliance between the landed gentry and the workers against the middle class. Even during this "time of rest," Disraeli's government pushed through important reforms in public housing, food and drug legislation, and union rights to strike and picket peacefully.

Gladstone returned to power in 1880 and continued the stream of reforms with the Third Reform Bill, which extended the vote to agricultural workers. This act brought Britain to the verge of universal male suffrage. Gladstone also secured passage of the Employers' Liability Act, which gave workers rights of compensation in case of accidents on the job.

He tried to solve the Irish question, but none of the concessions made up for the lack of home rule, and the Irish patriot Charles Stewart Parnell (1846–1891) began to work actively to force the issue through Parliament. Gladstone introduced home rule bills in 1886 and 1893, but both were defeated. A home rule bill was finally passed in 1914, but by this time the Ulster Protestants strongly opposed the measure and prepared to resist their forced incorporation into Catholic Ireland. The outbreak of war with Germany postponed civil strife, but it was only a 2-year delay until the Easter Uprising of 1916. Not until 1921 did southern Ireland finally gain the status of a British dominion. The home rule bill never went into effect.

The New Liberals

Gladstone's fight for Irish home rule split his party and paved the way for a decade of Conservative rule in Britain (1895–1905). Partly because of foreign and imperial affairs, the Conservatives departed from the reformist traditions of Tory democracy. By 1905 the need for social and political reform again claimed the attention of the parties.

More than 30 percent of the adult male laborers earned a what amounted to sustenance wages, just enough to survive on while employed but not enough to save any money for periods of unemployment, sickness, or family emergency. Workers demonstrated their discontent in a number of strikes. Partly in response to the workers' needs and at the prompting of British socialists, the Labour party was founded in 1900, under the leadership of J. Ramsay MacDonald (1866–1937), a self-made intellectual who had risen from humble status, and the Scottish miner Keir Hardie (1856–1915). The Liberals found themselves threatened on both their left and right flanks. They decided to abandon their laissez-faire economic concepts and embrace a bold program of social legislation. The radical Welsh lawyer David Lloyd George portrayed their program in this way: "Four spectres haunt the poor: Old Age, Accident, Sickness, and Unemployment. We are going to exorcise them."[1]

Led by Prime Minister Herbert Asquith, Lloyd George, and the young Winston Churchill, who had defected from the Conservatives, the Liberal party—with the aid of the Labour bloc—put through a broad program. It provided for old-age pensions, national employment bureaus, workers' compensation protection, and sickness, accident, and unemployment insurance. In addition, labor unions were relieved of financial responsibility for losses caused by strikes. Members of the House of Commons, until that time unpaid, were granted a modest salary. This last act allowed an individual without independent wealth to pursue a political career.

The House of Lords tried to block the Liberal reform plan by refusing to pass the 1909–1910 budget, which laid new tax burdens, including an income tax, on the richer classes in order to pay for the new programs. The Liberals and Labour fought back by directly attacking the rationale for the Lords' existence. They argued that a hereditary, irresponsible upper house was an anachronism in a democracy. The result was the Parliament Bill of 1911, which took away the Lords' power of absolute veto. Asquith announced that the king had promised to create enough new peers to pass the bill if needed (a tactic used with the 1832 Reform Bill). The Lords were forced to approve, and thereafter, they could only delay and force reconsideration of legislation.

By 1914 the evolutionary path to democracy and a modern democratic state structure had, except for women's suffrage, been largely completed. In the previous generation some effort had been made to gain the vote for women, but to little effect. Women's suffrage was not a concern for the major parties, whose leaders for the most part felt that women's proper place was in the home. At the turn of the century, the most effective group working for women's rights was the Women's Social and Political Union (WSPU), whose members were the first to be known as "suffragettes." The founder of the group, Emmeline Pankhurst (1858–1928), first agitated, then disturbed, and then challenged the order and stability of England in the decade before World War I. Pankhurst and her colleagues traveled and worked constantly to make their case, and in 1910 the WSPU abandoned traditional rhetoric in favor of mass marches, hunger strikes, and property damage. In 1913 a young suffragette martyred herself by running in front of the king's horse at the Derby. With the outbreak of the war, the WSPU backed the national effort against the Germans, and finally in 1918, women age 30 and over were granted the vote. Ten years later, they gained equal voting rights with men.

Emmeline Pankhurst, in white scarf, at a rally protesting a government unresponsive to women's issues. After 1910 the women's suffrage movement turned increasingly militant.

The Dominions

Supporting the United Kingdom as allies, customers, and suppliers of raw materials were its Dominions. The British Dominions became self-governing without breaking their political ties to Great Britain. With the exception of South Africa, these new nations were predominantly British in stock, language, culture, and governmental traditions. In the case of Canada, however, a strong French-speaking minority in Quebec, inherited from the original French regime, persisted and preserved its French heritage. In South Africa, following a confused history of rivalry and war between the British and Dutch settlers, a shaky union was achieved. There were no complications of rival Europeans in Australia and New Zealand, which were settled by the British in the beginning and did not have to adjust to an influx of other Europeans. Both Australia and Canada attained political unity by merging a number of colonies into a single government.

In South Africa, after a bloody war with the Boers ended in 1902, the British extended the right of self-government to the Transvaal in 1906 and to the Orange Free State two years later. The Liberal government in Great Britain permitted the Boer and English states to unite and form the Union of South Africa in 1909. Only 7 years after the war, Boer and Briton joined hands to create a new self-governing dominion. The first prime minister of the Union was Louis Botha (1863–1919), who had been a Boer general in the war. Botha's primary purpose was to create neither an English nor a Boer nationality but a blend of the two in a new South African patriotism held together by their shared desire to keep the black majority firmly repressed.

The discovery of Australia dates back to the seventeenth century, when Dutch explorers sighted its shores. Captain Cook's South Seas voyage in 1769, however, paved the way for British settlement. In 1788 Britain transported a group of convicts to Australia and settled them at Sydney. From the parent colony of Sydney, later called New South Wales, five other settlements were founded. Although a majority of the first Europeans in Australia were prisoners, most of them were political prisoners and debtors, rather than hardened criminals. After seven years of servitude, many were liberated and, as "emancipists," became citizens. Quite early in the nineteenth century, many free settlers also came to Australia. They began to protest the dumping of convicts in their new home, and Britain took the first steps to end the practice in 1840. By 1850 the Australian colonies were enjoying a liberal form of self-government. In 1901 the six Australian colonies formed a federal union known as the Commonwealth of Australia, which bears many resemblances to the American system of government.

About 1000 miles from the Australian mainland is a group of islands, two of which are of particular importance. These lonely projections of British influence in the South Pacific constitute the self-governing Dominion of New Zealand. The population of this country, which is slightly smaller than Great Britain in area, is just over 3.3 million. The earliest white settlers were convicts who had escaped from penal settlements in Australia. The activity of other colonizers forced the British government to assume protection of the islands in 1840, and British agents signed a treaty guaranteeing certain rights, especially land rights, to the original inhabitants, the Maoris. However, the New Zealand government was slow to grant full inclusion to the larger society to the Maoris.

Canada came into English control in 1763. London tried to ensure the loyalty of the French Canadians by issuing a royal proclamation guaranteeing the inhabitants' political rights and their freedom to worship as Roman Catholics. These guarantees were strengthened in 1774 when the British government passed the Quebec Act, called the "Magna Carta of the French Canadian race." This act reconfirmed the position of the Catholic Church and perpetuated French laws and customs. However, there was no provision for a representative assembly, such as existed in English-speaking colonies.

The period from 1763 to 1867 is known as the formative stage of Canada. A number of developments took place during this period: the growth of the English-speaking population, the defeat of an attempted conquest by the United States, the grant of local self-government, and finally the confederation of Canada into a dominion. Fear of the United States, the need for a common tariff policy, and a concerted effort to develop natural resources led Canadians into confederation. A plan of union, the British North American Act, was approved by the British government and passed by Parliament in London in 1867. This act united Canada into a federal union of four provinces. The new government had some similarities to the political organization of the United States, but it adopted the British cabinet system, with its principle of ministerial responsibility. As a symbol of its connection with Great Britain, provision was made for a governor-general who was to act as the British monarch's representative to Canada.

THE UNITED STATES

- *Why were the North and South unable to resolve the question of slavery in the first half of the nineteenth century and the issue of the rights of African Americans thereafter?*

Free Land and Unfree People

A new player entered the Western political game in the nineteenth century, the former British colony of United States. The revolutionary movements in Europe during the nineteenth century fought aristocratic domination or foreign rule—or both. The nineteenth-century struggles in the United States were not quite the same. Instead, there were two major related problems. One was the annexation, settlement, and development of land occupied by Native Americans; the other was slavery. Free land and unfree people were the sources of the many political confrontations that culminated in the Civil War, the greatest struggle of nineteenth-century America.

At the conclusion of its successful revolution in 1783, the United States was not a democracy. When the Constitution of the new nation was ratified, only one male in seven had the vote. Religious requirements and property qualifications ensured that only a small elite participated in government. These restrictions allowed patricians from established families in the South and men of wealth and substance in the North to control the country for nearly half a century.

Democratic Advances

The influence of the western frontier helped make America more democratic. Even before the Constitution was ratified, thousands of pioneers crossed the Appalachian Mountains into the new "western country." In the West, land was to be had for the asking, and social caste did not exist—one white person was as good as another—and the indigenous Native Americans came to be seen as an irritant at the least or as a danger to be fought at the most. Vigor, courage, self-reliance, and competence counted, not birth or wealth. Ironically, throughout the nineteenth century, the West was the source of new and liberal movements that challenged the conservative ideas prevalent in the East and South, while at the same time serving as the arena for the uprooting of the Native Americans and the destruction of their way of life.

Until the War of 1812, democracy grew slowly. In 1791 Vermont had been admitted as a manhood suffrage state, in which all men could vote, and the following year, Kentucky followed suit; but Tennessee, Ohio, and Louisiana entered the Union with property and tax qualifications for the vote. After 1817 no new state entered the Union with restrictions on male suffrage except for those regarding slaves. Most appointive offices became elective, and requirements for holding office were liberalized.

Andrew Jackson changed the tone and emphasis of American politics. In 1828 he was elected to the presidency following a campaign that featured the slogan "Down with the aristocrats!" He was the first president produced by the West, the first since George Washington not to have a college education, and the first to have been born in poverty. He owed his election to no congressional clique but rather to the will of the people, who idolized "Old Hickory" as their spokesman and leader.

The triumph of the democratic principle in the 1830s set the direction for political development. With Jackson's election came the idea that any man, by virtue of being an American citizen, could hold any office in the land. Governments widened educational opportunities by enlarging the public school system. With increased access to learning, class barriers became less important. The gaining and keeping of political power came more and more to be tied to satisfying the needs of the people who voted.

DOCUMENT
The Seneca Falls Convention

Andrew Jackson's victories, however, symbolized the change of life for the worse for the Native Americans. After the United States gained independence,

In many regards, Andrew Jackson was the first "people's president," a national leader who looked beyond the demands of the eastern elites to the entire country. Jackson's craggy countenance projects his inner strength and independent spirit.

Discovery Through Maps

An American View of the World in the 1820s

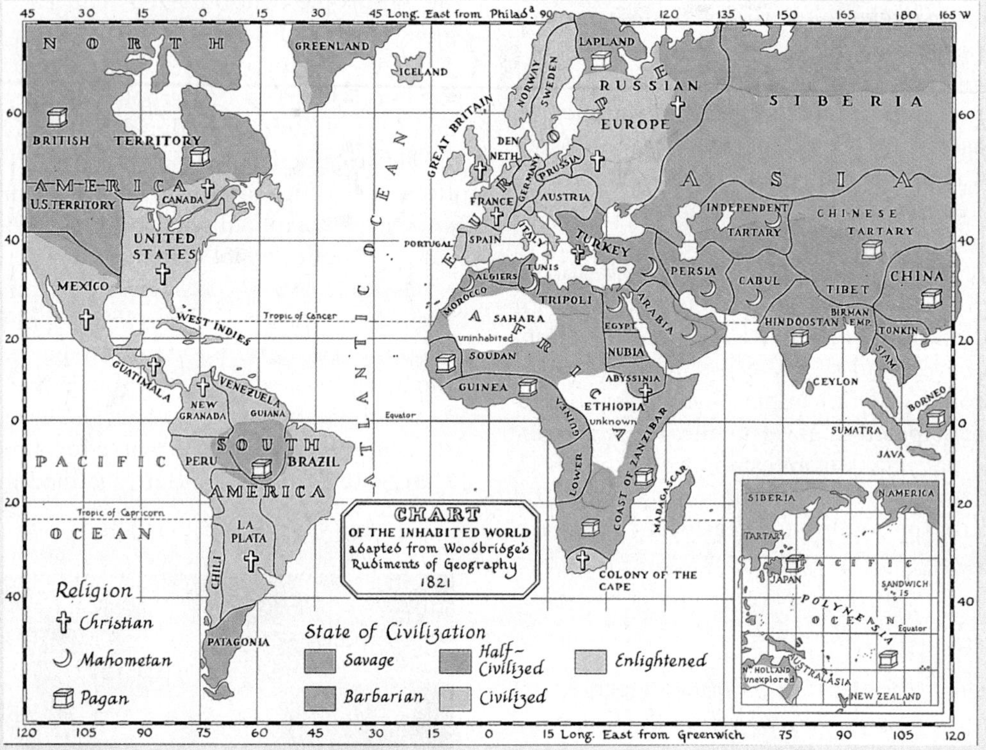

This map, adapted from *The School Atlas to Accompany Woodbridge's Rudiments of Geography* (1821), served to inform students of the status of "civilization" in the world. The color code establishes where the authors believed the various gradations of humanity were: from the "civilized" and "enlightened" to the "savage," with the "barbarians" and "half-civilized" in between. The mapmakers were apparently quite certain that regions where white-skinned Christians were to be found were civilized or at least half-civilized (though they seem to have had their doubts about adherents of Orthodox Christianity in eastern Europe). The people where Islam predominated ranged from half-civilized to barbarian. And much of China, with its four millennia of culture, was classified as barbarian, owing to its "pagan" belief systems.

A complacent arrogance permeates this map, with the area west of the 95th meridian, populated largely by Native Americans, declared to be a savage state, waiting patiently for manifest destiny to bring civilization. Much of Central and South America is admitted to being civilized—but not enlightened. Note also that the cartographer uses Philadelphia as the prime meridian—preferable, he surely thought, to the more traditional but distant Greenwich, a town in England which, after all, had invaded the United States only a decade earlier.

The map shows the dominant role played by religion in viewing the rest of the world in the first part of the nineteenth century. Later, concepts of race would dominate the American worldview, and after 1945 the world would be seen in terms of the Cold War, those areas determined to be democratic and communistic. By the end of the twentieth century, American maps emphasized industrial capacities and potential markets. After September 11, 2001, yet another shift came as the cartographers identified zones where terrorists threatened American interests. Through their emphases, cartographers tell us as much about the spirit of an age as writers and artists.

Questions to Consider

1. After studying this map, what elements do you believe moved the cartographer to identify an area as civilized?
2. When you look at the globe and consider its complexity, what elements do you use to differentiate one area from another?
3. What is the difference between being "civilized" and "enlightened?"

the government had tried to deal with them by placing the various tribes on reservations to control their movements and to aid them in becoming "civilized." As the white population of the United States grew, and the reservation land east of the Mississippi became more valuable, a policy of removal was implemented by leaders such as Jackson. The rationale behind the policy was that the Native Americans, being fundamentally incapable of civilization, should be pushed West into the empty lands. This policy broke the treaties signed at the end of the eighteenth century, which respected the tribes as politically sovereign peoples. Up and down the western frontier, tribes which had entertained friendly relations with the United States under treaty rights, found themselves pushed out of their lands. There were tragedies such as that of the "Trail of Tears" in 1838–1839 when 16,000 Cherokees were forced to leave their homes in the southeast United States. They were rounded up in military stockades where they lived under wretched conditions, and then they were forced to walk to the present-day state of Oklahoma. More than 5000 of them died during those 2 tragic years.

But for the white population, simultaneous with the growth of democracy came the territorial expansion of the country. The Louisiana Territory, purchased from France for about $15 million in 1803 (see Chapter 21), doubled the size of the United States. In 1844, Americans, influenced by **"manifest destiny"**—the belief that their domination of the continent was God's will—demanded "All of Oregon or none." The claim led to a boundary dispute with Great Britain over land between the Columbia River and 54°40′ north latitude. In 1846 the two countries accepted a boundary at the forty-ninth parallel, and the Oregon Territory was settled. The annexation of Texas in 1845 was followed by war with Mexico in 1846. In the peace agreement signed 2 years later, Mexico ceded California, Texas, and the land between the two to the United States. As a result of these acquisitions, by 1860, the area of the United States was two-thirds larger than it had been in 1840.

The addition of the new territories forced the issue of whether slavery should be allowed in those areas. Paralleling developments in Great Britain, abolitionists in the United States, particularly in New England, vigorously condemned slavery. Henry Clay's Missouri Compromise of 1820 permitted slavery in Missouri but forbade it in the rest of the Louisiana Purchase. This settlement satisfied both sides for only a short time. The antislavery forces grew more insistent. In the senatorial campaigns of 1858, candidate Abraham Lincoln declared:

> *A house divided against itself cannot stand. I believe this government cannot endure permanently half slave and half free. I do not expect the Union to be dissolved—I do not expect the house to fall—but I do expect it will cease to be divided. It will become all one thing, or all the other.*

Slavery was an important issue; it served as a focus for the differences and tensions separating the North from the South. However, a more fundamental cause of conflict was that, in a sense, the two sections had become separate societies. The former was industrial, urban, liberal, and democratic; the latter was mainly agricultural, rural, conservative, and dominated by a planter aristocracy. The South strongly opposed the North's desire for higher tariffs, government aid for new railroads, and generous terms for land settlement in the West. These fundamental differences brought North and South to war. Slavery served as a potent symbol and as a moral irritant.

Territorial Growth of the United States

1803	Louisiana Purchase (part or all of present-day Louisiana, Arkansas, Missouri, Iowa, Minnesota, North Dakota, South Dakota, Nebraska, Kansas, Oklahoma, Colorado, Wyoming, Montana)
1810–1819	Florida Cession (parts of present-day Alabama and Mississippi; all of present-day Florida)
1818	British Cession (parts of Minnesota and North Dakota)
1845	Annexation of Texas (part or all of present-day Texas, Oklahoma, Kansas, New Mexico, Colorado)
1846	Oregon Country (parts of present-day Montana, Idaho, Wyoming; all of present-day Oregon and Washington)
1847	Mexican Cession (part or all of present-day Colorado, New Mexico, Utah, Nevada, Arizona, California)
1853	Gadsden Purchase (parts of present-day New Mexico and Arizona)

manifest destiny—An early nineteenth century belief voiced by clergymen in the northeast United States that God meant for white Americans to dominate the continent.

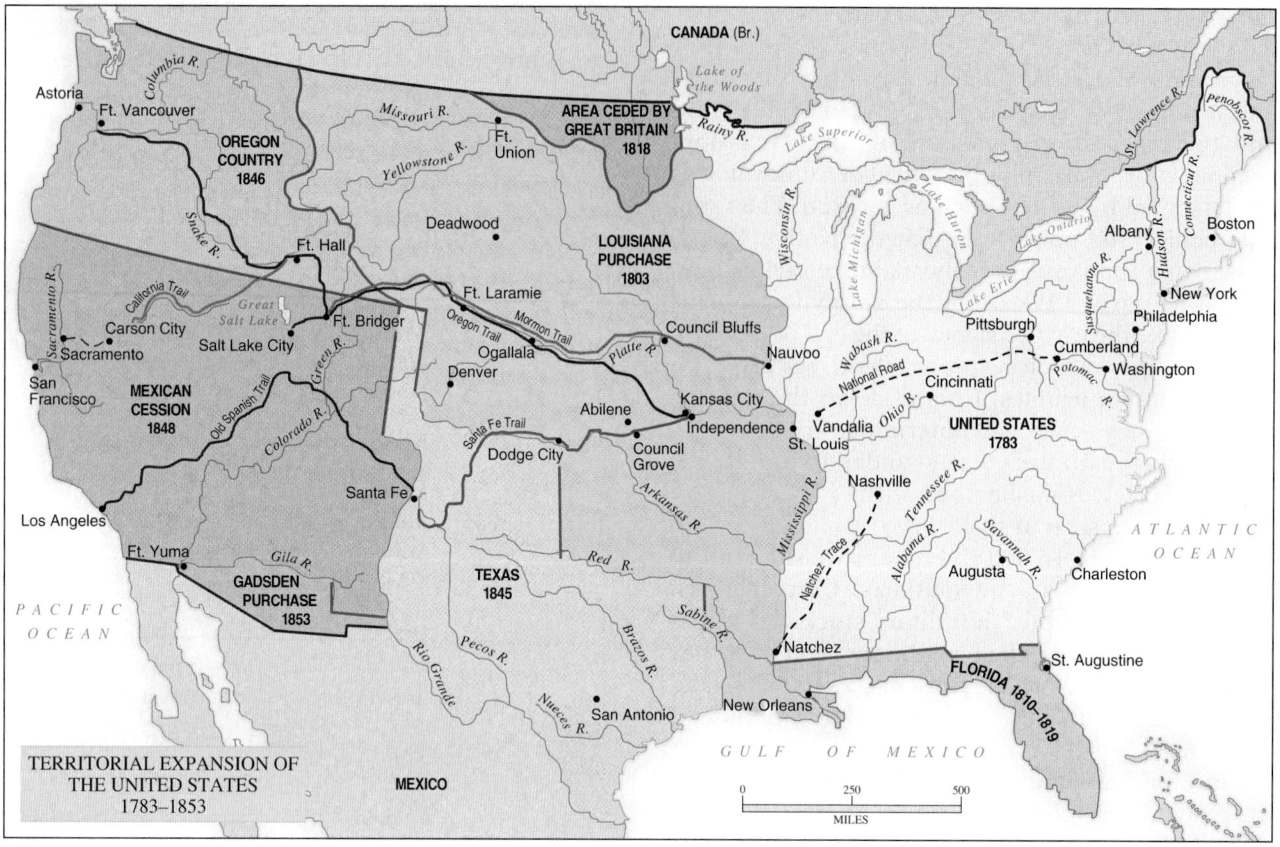

Taking advantage of Napoleon's sale of the Louisiana territory, a militarily weak Mexico, and an otherwise occupied Britain, the United States was able to attain its continental limits by 1853.

The Civil War and Its Results

Soon after Abraham Lincoln was inaugurated as president, the slaveholding southern states seceded from the Union and formed the Confederate States of America. The first shot of the Civil War was fired at Fort Sumter, South Carolina, in 1861, initiating the bloodiest war of American history. Four agonizing years of conflict—in which more than half a million men died and basic elements of the Constitution and law were suspended—ended when General Robert E. Lee surrendered to General Ulysses S. Grant at Appomattox Courthouse in Virginia in April 1865. A few days later, the nation was stunned by the assassination of President Lincoln, who had just begun his second term.

With the final collapse of the Confederacy before the overwhelming superiority of the Union in manpower, industrial resources, and wealth, the Civil War became the grand epic of American history in its heroism, romance, and tragedy. The victorious North used military occupation to try to force the South to extend voting and property rights to the former slaves. Eventually, this so-called Reconstruction period (1865–1877) was ended by a tacit agreement between the northern industrialists and the southern white leaders that enabled the latter to regain political control and to deprive African Americans of their newly won rights. Later, southerners invoked social Darwinist arguments to justify their actions in denying full "blessings of freedom" to the former slaves.

In the century after Reconstruction, Southern politicians deprived African Americans of their voting rights by enacting state laws or employing devices such as poll taxes, literacy tests, property qualifications, and physical threats. Racial segregation in schools, restaurants, parks, and hotels was effectively applied. Laws prohibiting interracial marriage were enacted, and African Americans were generally excluded from unions. Between 1885 and 1918 more than 2500 African Americans were lynched in the United States. As second-class citizens, free but landless, the former slaves essentially formed a sharecropping class, mired in poverty, and deprived of educational opportunities. Not until the 1960s did the political steps occur that began to put into effect that which had been purchased in the sacrifices of the Civil War: full citizenship for African Americans.

If the causes and consequences of the American Civil War are complex, the all-important result was simple. It settled the issue of whether the United States was an indivisible sovereign nation or a collection of sovereign states. The sacrifice of hundreds of

Document "With Malice Toward None": Lincoln's Second Inaugural Address

March 4, 1865, started out dark and rainy. Lincoln spoke only briefly, delivering the shortest inaugural address of any president, before or since. Afterward, as he took the oath of office, the sun came out. Chief Justice Salmon P. Chase, administering the oath, said he hoped that the sunshine would be an "omen of the dispersion of the clouds of war." Indeed it was: The hostilities lasted only a few weeks longer—but they cost Lincoln his life.

At this second appearing to take the oath of the presidential office, there is less occasion for an extended address than there was at the first. Then a statement, somewhat in detail, of a course to be pursued, seemed fitting and proper. Now, at the expiration of four years, during which public declarations have been constantly called forth on every point and phase of the great contest which still absorbs the attention, and engrosses the energies of the nation, little that is new could be presented. The progress of our arms, upon which all else chiefly depends, is as well known to the public as to myself; and it is, I trust, reasonably satisfactory and encouraging to all. With high hope for the future, no prediction in regard to it is ventured.

On the occasion corresponding to this four years ago, all thoughts were anxiously directed to an impending civil-war. All dreaded it—all sought to avert it. While the inaugural address was being delivered from this place, devoted altogether to *saving* the Union without war, insurgent agents were in the city seeking to *destroy* it without war—seeking to dissol[v]e the Union, and divide effects, by negotiation. Both parties deprecated war; but one of them would *make* war rather than let the nation survive; and the other would *accept* war rather than let it perish. And the war came.

One eighth of the whole population were colored slaves, not distributed generally over the Union, but localized in the Southern part of it. These slaves constituted a peculiar and powerful interest. All knew that this interest was, somehow, the cause of the war. To strengthen, perpetuate, and extend this interest was the object for which the insurgents would rend the Union, even by war; while the government claimed no right to do more than to restrict the territorial enlargement of it. Neither party expected for the war, the magnitude, or the duration, which it has already attained. Neither anticipated that the *cause* of the conflict might cease with, or even before, the conflict itself should cease. Each looked for an easier triumph, and a result less fundamental and astounding. Both read the same Bible, and pray to the same God; and each invokes His aid against the other. It may seem strange that any men should dare to ask a just God's assistance in wringing their bread from the sweat of other men's faces; but let us judge not that we be not judged. The prayers of both could not be answered; that of neither has been answered fully. The Almighty has His own purposes. "Woe unto the world because of offences! for it must needs be that offences come; but woe to that man by whom the offence cometh!" If we shall suppose that American Slavery is one of those offences which, in the providence of God, must needs come, but which, having continued through His appointed time, He now wills to remove, and that He gives to both North and South, this terrible war, as the woe due to those by whom the offence came, shall we discern therein any departure from those divine attributes which the believers in a Living God always ascribe to Him? Fondly do we hope—fervently do we pray—that this mighty scourge of war may speedily pass away. Yet, if God wills that it continue, until all the wealth piled by the bond-man's two hundred and fifty years of unrequited toil shall be sunk, and until every drop of blood drawn with the lash, shall be paid by another drawn with the sword, as was said three thousand years ago, so still it must be said "the judgments of the Lord, are true and righteous altogether."

With malice toward none; with charity for all; with firmness in the right, as God gives us to see the right, let us strive on to finish the work we are in; to bind up the nation's wounds; to care for him who shall have borne the battle, and for his widow, and his orphan—to do all which may achieve and cherish a just, and a lasting peace, among ourselves, and with all nations.

Questions to Consider

1. What role does religion play in Lincoln's speech? Do you see his view of God as a mild, New Testament, forgiving God or an vengeful, Old Testament God?
2. How would you characterize his speech: as a celebration of victory or as an accounting of a tragedy?
3. Put yourself in the place of a southern soldier, defeated in the war. How would you view Lincoln's speech? Put yourself in the role of a northern soldier, victorious in the war. Do you think that Lincoln was sufficiently strong in the condemning those who upheld slavery?

From Richard N. Current, ed., *The Political Thought of Abraham Lincoln* (Indianapolis, Ind.: Bobbs-Merrill, 1967), pp. 314–316.

thousands of lives preserved the Union, but the mistreatment of African Americans remained.

Industrialization, Abuse, and Reform

Between 1850 and 1880 the number of cities with a population of 50,000 or more doubled. The number of men employed in industry increased 50 percent. In 1865 there were 35,000 miles of railroads in the country. By 1900 this was estimated to be about 200,000—more than in all of Europe. In 1860 a little more than $1 billion was invested in manufacturing; by 1900 this figure had risen to $12 billion. The value of manufactured products increased proportionately. In 1870 the total production of iron and steel in the United States was far below that of France and Britain. Twenty years later, the United States had outstripped both and was producing about one-third of the world's iron and steel.

The North's victory was a boost for industrialization as well as a result of it, and the economic revolution in the United States that followed was more significant than the conflict itself. Railroads were built across broad prairies, and the first transcontinental line, the Union Pacific, was completed in 1869. Settlers swarmed west, breaking treaties with Native American tribes, altering the environmental balance that supported the lives of the Plains Indians, and destroying the way of life of the original inhabitants of the land.

In the age of rapid industrialism and materialistic expansion, many who pursued profits lost sight of ethical principles in business and in government. William "Boss" Tweed, the chief of the Department of Public Works for the city of New York, rewarded himself and his friends so lavishly through fraudulent contracts, payments under the table, and other corrupt activities that by 1871 he had driven the city to the brink of bankruptcy. Brought to trial, Tweed was convicted of stealing more than $200 million. Ruthless financiers such as Jay Gould and Jim Fisk tampered with the basic financial stability of the nation. The administration of President Ulysses Grant was tainted by scandals and frauds. A new rich class failed to appreciate its responsibilities to society. Corruption was a blatant feature of the new order.

For roughly a century, the gospel for the new nation of America had been rugged individualism. As in Europe, governmental interference in business was unwelcome because of the strong belief that individuals should be free to follow their own inclinations, run their own businesses, and enjoy the profits of their labors. In an expanding nation where land, jobs, and opportunity beckoned, there was little to indicate that the system would not work indefinitely. By 1880, however, the end of the frontier was in sight. Free land of good quality was scarce, and the frontier could no longer serve as a safety valve to release the economic and social pressures of an expanding population.

Between 1850 and 1900 the United States became the most powerful nation in the Western Hemisphere, increased its national wealth from $7 billion to $88 billion, established an excellent system of public education, and fostered the spread of civil liberties for its white citizens and other nations. But there were many disturbing factors in the picture. Unemployment, child labor, and industrial accidents were common in the rapidly growing cities. Slums grew and served as breeding places for disease and crime. Strikes, often accompanied by violence, exacerbated the tension between labor and capital.

In response, the wide-ranging Progressive reform movement flourished between 1890 and 1914. This movement was rooted partly in the agrarian protests against big business sparked by the Populists of the Midwest and the South. The Progressives effectively mobilized the middle classes to work to eliminate sweatshops, the exploitation of labor, and the abuse of natural resources.

The success of the Progressive movement was reflected in the constitutions of the new states admitted to the Union and in their introduction of the direct primary, the initiative and referendum, and the direct election of senators. All these measures tended to give the common people more effective control of the government. After the enactment of the Interstate Commerce Act in 1887, which introduced federal regulation over railroads, a steady expansion of governmental regulation of industry began.

As president of the United States from 1901 to 1909, Theodore Roosevelt launched an aggressive campaign to break up the trusts, conserve natural resources, and regulate railroads, food, and drugs. In 1913 President Woodrow Wilson started a militant campaign of reform called the "New Freedom." His administration reduced the tariff because it was too much the instrument of special economic privilege, enacted banking reform with the Federal Reserve Act of 1913, and regulated businesses in the public interest through the Clayton Antitrust Act and the establishment of the Federal Trade Commission, both in 1914.

In 1914 the United States had risen to the forefront of Western nations. The country's first census, taken in 1790, counted a population of just under 4 million; by 1910 the number was 99 million. During the nineteenth century, more than 25 million immigrants had made their way to America. Since the days of George Washington, the national wealth had increased at least a hundredfold. Once the producer of raw materials only, the United States by 1914 was producing more steel than Britain and Germany combined. A single company, United States Steel, was

Theodore Roosevelt, one of the most flamboyant and effective presidents in the history of the United States, provided cartoonists at the beginning of the twentieth century with almost unlimited possibilities for caricature. Here "T.R." is afflicting the monopolists who dominated the American economy.

capitalized for $1.46 billion, a sum greater than the total estimated wealth of the country in 1790.

The United States and the World

From the first, U.S. foreign policy pursued three goals: national security, trade, and the spread of democracy—and these goals remain largely intact today. During its first quarter century, the United States fought a brief naval war with France, became embroiled with Britain in the War of 1812, and sent two expeditions to the Mediterranean to deal with the Barbary pirates. These complications notwithstanding, Americans spent the next century developing their country. Thomas Jefferson summarized the country's foreign policy with these words: "Peace, commerce, and honest friendship with all nations—entangling alliances with none."[2]

When the country established new foreign contacts, it went across the Pacific. In 1844 the United States made its first treaty with China, opening certain ports to American trade and securing the rights of American merchants and sailors to be tried in American tribunals in China. In 1853 Commodore Matthew Perry visited Japan and, by a show of force, persuaded the Japanese to open some of their harbors to Americans. By 1854 the United States was considering the annexation of the Hawaiian Islands, and in 1867 it purchased Alaska from Russia for the amazingly low price of $7.2 million.

As productivity increased after the Civil War, the United States was forced to seek new outlets for its goods, especially now that the domestic frontier had disappeared. Foreign trade increased from $393 million in 1870 to more than $1.33 billion in 1900. During the same period, investments abroad went from almost nothing to $500 million. This economical group was instrumental in the nation's acquisition of a global empire.

The United States began building a modern navy in 1883, and by 1890 the buildup had accelerated greatly. Care was taken not to alarm the country, however, and the new ships were officially known as "seagoing coastline battleships," a handy nautical contradiction. When this naval program was initiated, the U.S. Navy ranked twelfth among the powers; by 1900 it had advanced to third place. This naval strength served American foreign policy well—particularly in Asia. In 1899 U.S. Secretary of State John Hay initiated the so-called Open Door policy regarding China, an attempt to ensure equal commercial rights for traders of all nations—including, of course, the United States, a latecomer to the China trade. When Chinese patriots fought against the intrusion of foreigners in the Righteous Harmony Fists (Boxer) Rebellion, the United States again took the lead in defending its new outward-looking stance.

America's Latin American neighbors felt the full weight of the Western economic colossus. This drive for markets, raw materials, and outlets for surplus capital led to classic examples of economic imperialism, but both American business and the elites of the local population generally profited from these arrangements (see Chapter 25).

RUSSIA IN REFORM AND REVOLUTION

- *Why did Russia fail to successfully adapt to the political and economic transformations occurring in Western Europe during the nineteenth century?*

The Failed Heritage of Catherine II

In 1815, after its victories in the Napoleonic War, Russia stood as the most powerful country in Europe.

Four decades later, it was defeated in the Crimean War, fought on its own territory. It was evident to most observers, including the tsars, that Russia had neither the economic strength nor the social and political flexibility of the United Kingdom. It could not adapt successfully to the new forces of the nineteenth century. Tsar Alexander I (r. 1801–1825) saw the need for change and understood that the major obstacles to the reform of his empire were its twin foundations: serfdom and autocracy. His grandmother, Catherine II, had educated him in the liberal traditions and assumptions of the Enlightenment, and for the first four years of his reign, he aggressively pursued these notions. During his reign, he attempted major reforms in the areas of education, government, and social welfare. His brother Nicholas II (r. 1825–1855) understood the forces of industrialization, but the Decembrist Revolution led him to impose repressive and reactionary policies during most of his reign.

Enlightenment Dreams

Alexander's experiments with limited serf emancipation, constitutionalism, and federalism demonstrated his desire for change. The tsar was all-powerful in theory, but in reality, he depended on the nobles, who in turn gained their wealth from serfdom. Carrying out the necessary reforms would destroy the foundations of Alexander's power. The fact that his father and grandfather had been killed by nobles made him cautious. Further, it was his misfortune to rule during the Napoleonic wars, and for the first 15 years of his reign, he had to devote immense amounts of money and time to foreign affairs. His liberal reform plans were never carried through to completion, and not until the 1850s, when it was almost too late, would there be another tsar willing and able to make the fundamental social and political reforms needed to make Russia competitive in the industrializing world.

In the reactionary decade after 1815, reformers fell from favor. However, the open discussion of the need for change in the first part of Alexander's reign, the experiences of the soldiers returning from western Europe, and the activities of the expanding number of secret societies kept the dream of change alive. When Alexander failed to reform, the intensity of the reformers' discussions increased. Alexander died in December 1825, and there was confusion over which of his two brothers would succeed to the throne. The days between his death and the confirmation of his younger brother Nicholas I gave a small circle of liberal nobles and army officers the chance to advance their ill-defined demands for a constitution. The officers who led this revolt had been infected with liberal French thought. They sought to end serfdom and establish representative government and civil liberties in Russia. On December 26, these liberals led a small uprising in St. Petersburg. This **Decembrist Revolt,** as it was called, lasted less than a day and could have been put down even earlier had Nicholas been more decisive. This abortive, ill-planned attempt doomed any chance of liberal or democratic reform in Russia for 30 years.

Nicholas I and Russian Reaction

The Decembrist incident shook Nicholas badly, and throughout his reign, he remained opposed to liberal and revolutionary movements. To consolidate his power, he sponsored "official nationalism," whose conservative foundations were "autocracy, orthodoxy, and nationalism"—the Romanov dynasty, the Orthodox Church, and a glorification of the Russian soul. He carried out a thorough policy of censorship that included the screening of foreign visitors, publications, and even musical compositions. The government closely monitored students' activities and curricula in schools and universities. Some 150,000 "dangerous" people were exiled to Siberia. Millions of non-Russians in the empire began to experience limitations on their identities through a forced adherence to Russian customs called "Russification." These activities strengthened Nicholas's immediate control and stopped potential upheaval, but he failed to address adequately the important social and political reforms Russia so badly needed.

Despite his efforts to control intellectual and political currents, Nicholas did not succeed. Reformist activity may have been repressed, but the Russian intellectual circles were creative, tuned as they were to the works of the German philosophers and poets. In the 1840s and 1850s a new breed of intellectuals appeared—thinkers devoted to achieving liberal and socialist political goals. Although they would not make their strength felt until after the 1860s, these thinkers, known as the **intelligentsia,** put down strong roots during Nicholas's reign. Alexander Herzen (1812–1870) and Michael Bakunin (1814–1876) were the pioneers of this peculiarly Russian movement. Herzen was a moderate socialist who advocated emancipating the serfs, liberalizing the government, and freeing the press. In 1847 he went into exile in London, where he founded his famous paper, the *Kolokol* ("Bell"), 10 years later. It was widely read in Russia, supposedly appearing mysteriously on the tsar's table. Bakunin, the father of Russian anarchism,

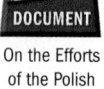

DOCUMENT
On the Efforts of the Polish People

Decembrist Revolt—This, the so-called First Russian Revolution was a failed attempt by liberal nobles to oust Tsar Nicholas I and to introduce a constitution to their country.

intelligentsia—Intellectuals who want to use their ideas to change society.

was more radical. He believed that reform of Russia was useless and advocated terrorism. He preached that anarchy—complete freedom—was the only cure for society's ills. He too went into exile in the West.

The Russian intellectuals debated many questions, most important of which was whether Russia should imitate all aspects of European life or pursue its own tradition of Orthodoxy and a single-centered society. The question had been posed since the reign of Peter the Great. The liberal Westerners argued that if Russia wished to survive, it had to adopt basic aspects of the West and renounce much of its own past. The Slavophiles on the other side of the dialogue, renounced industrial Europe and the modern West, seeing them as materialistic, pagan, and anarchic. They looked to their distant past for guidance for the future.

Nicholas was able to maintain control to the extent that the 1830 and 1848 revolutions had little influence or impact on Russia. Some aspects of industrialization were introduced—for example, the first Moscow–St. Petersburg rail line was put into operation. The government appointed commissions to examine the questions of serfdom and reform, but these extremely serious considerations were kept secret out of fear of provoking a violent reaction from the nobles or a popular uprising among the peasantry. Still, basic doubts about Russia's future remained. Dissident intellectuals, economic and social weakness, and autocratic stagnation were indicators that difficult times were in store for the country.

The Great Reforms

Russia's inept performance in the Crimean War spotlighted the country's weaknesses and the need for reform. When Alexander II (r. 1855–1881) came to the throne, even the conservatives among his subjects acknowledged the need for major change. The new tsar moved quickly to transform the basis of the autocratic structure—the institution of serfdom—but ran into delay from the nobility. Alexander appointed a committee, which, after 5 years of deliberation, drew up the **Emancipation Proclamation,** issued in March 1861. By this reform, 32 million state peasants and 20 million serfs, who had no civil rights, could not own property, and owed heavy dues and services to the nobility, began the transition to land ownership and citizenship.

The government paid the landlords a handsome price for the land that was to be turned over to the peasants. In return, the peasants had to pay the government for the land over a period of 49 years by making payments through their village commune, the *mir*. The drawn-out nature of the land transfer disappointed the former serfs, who had expected a portion of the lords' lands to be turned over to them without charge. Instead, the peasants were trapped in their village communes, which received and allocated all of the land—much of it poor—and divided it among the various families and paid taxes. Even though they were granted ownership of their cottages, farm buildings, garden plots, domestic animals, and implements, the restrictions placed on the peasants by confining them to their villages constituted a serious problem. New generations of peasants increased the population, but there was no corresponding increase in their share of the land.

The emancipation of the serfs was the single most important event in the domestic history of nineteenth-century Russia. It brought about thoroughgoing reforms of the army, judiciary, municipal government, and system of local self-government. One of the most important reforms came in 1864 when local government was transformed by the *Zemstvo* (ZEMST-vo) law. In the countryside, the gentry, middle classes, and peasants elected representatives to local boards *(zemstvos)*. These boards collected taxes and maintained roads, asylums, hospitals, and schools. The zemstvos became perhaps the most successful governmental organizations in Russia.

While Alexander II pushed through the "Great Reforms," the revolutionary movement grew stronger. In the 1850s the nihilist movement developed, questioning all old values, championing the freedom of the individual, and shocking the older generation. At first the nihilists tried to convert the aristocracy to the cause of reform. Failing there, they turned to the peasants in an almost missionary frenzy. Some idealistic young men and women joined the movement to work in the fields with the peasants, while others went to the villages as doctors and teachers to preach the message of reform. This "go to the people" campaign was known as the populist, or *narodnik* (na-ROD-nik), movement. Not surprisingly, the peasants largely ignored the outsiders' message.

Revolutionary Response

Frustrated by this rejection, the idealistic young people turned more and more to terrorism. The radical branch of the nihilists, under the influence of Bakunin's protégé Sergei Nechaev (ne-CHAI-ev; 1847–1882), pursued a program of the total destruction of the status quo, to be accomplished by the revolutionary elite. In Revolutionary Catechism, Nechaev stated that "everything that promotes the success of

Emancipation Proclamation—Called by some the greatest political act of the nineteenth century, the Emancipation Proclamation issued by Tsar Alexander II in March 1861 gave civil and property rights to 52 million state peasants and serfs. It also triggered a series of reforms that changed the military, law, education, and the economy.

Tsar Alexander II instituted sweeping reforms, including the abolition of Russian serfdom in 1861. For many of his subjects, however, they were too little and too late, as this satiric depicting of "The Liberator" suggests.

the revolution is moral and everything that hinders it is immoral." The soldiers in the battle, the revolutionaries, were "doomed men," having "no interests, no affairs, no feelings, no habits, no property, not even a name."[3] The revolution dominated all thoughts and actions of these individuals.

For the 20 years after his emancipation of the serfs, Alexander suffered under increasing revolutionary attack. It was as though the opposition saw each reform not as an improvement but as a weakness to be exploited. In Poland, the tsar had tried to reverse the Russification program of his father and in return saw the Poles revolt in 1863. Would-be assassins made a number of attempts on him, and the violence expanded throughout the 1870s as a number of his officials were attacked by young terrorists such as Vera Zasulich (za-SU-lich; 1851–1919). Finally, Alexander was assassinated in 1881, on the very day he had approved a proposal to call a representative assembly to consider new reforms.

Reaction and Response, 1881–1905

The slain tsar's son, Alexander III (r. 1881–1894), could see only that his father's reforms had resulted in increased opposition and, eventually, death. Consequently, he tried to turn the clock back and reinstate the policy of "autocracy, Orthodoxy, and nationalism." Under the guidance of his chief adviser, Constantine Pobedonostsev (po-bied-do-NOST-sev; 1827–1907), Alexander pursued a policy of censorship, regulation of schools and universities, and increased secret police activities. Along with renewing Russification among the minorities, he permitted the persecution of Jews, who were bullied and sometimes massacred in attacks called pogroms. The tsar may have been successful in driving the revolutionaries underground or executing them, and the nationalities may have been kept in their place, but under Alexander III, Russia lost 13 valuable years in its attempt to become economically and politically competitive with western Europe.

Succeeding Alexander was his son, Nicholas II (r. 1894–1917), a decent but weak man. He inherited and retained both his father's advisers and his father's policies. Larger forces overwhelmed him. Industrialization and rural overpopulation exerted a wide range of political pressures, and the autocratic structure could not cope.

Russia lacked a tradition of gradual reform and habits of compromise such as existed in England. After the assassination of Alexander II, the government increasingly used brutal force to keep order. At the same time, it did little to help the people suffering in the transition from an agrarian to an industrial society. The regime worked energetically to eliminate the opposition by placing secret agents among them, launching violent assaults, and carrying on diversionary anti-Semitic activities with bands of thugs called the Black Hundreds. By attacking the opposition, the tsarist government concentrated on symptoms of Russia's problems—political dissent and critical, social, and economic dilemmas—rather than their causes. The tsars tried to crush all opposition movements, rather than carry out effective reform.

The Liberal party (Constitutional Democrats, or Kadets) wanted a constitutional monarchy and peaceful reform on the British model. Although limited in numbers, because of the elevated social standing of most of their members, the Kadets were a powerful voice for change in Russia.

The much more numerous Social Revolutionaries combined non-Marxist socialism with the *narodnik* tradition and simplistically called for "the whole land for the whole people." These agrarian socialists wanted to give the land to the peasants. However, they lacked a unified leadership and a well-thought-out program.

In this troubled environment, the solutions proposed by Karl Marx attracted a number of supporters. Marx himself did not believe that Russia would be a favorable laboratory for his theories. He expressed surprise when *Das Kapital* was translated into Russian in 1872 but was pleased when he learned of the broad impact of his theories. Many intellectuals looked to Marx to show them the way to a complete social, economic, and political revolution. Not until 1898, however, was there an attempt to establish a Russian Social Democratic party made up of radical intellectuals and politically active workers.

The Russians did not experience the most demanding parts of industrialization until the end of the century and then on a different basis from that of the western European countries. Russia remained an overwhelmingly agrarian society in which the state paid for building factories by using grain produced by the peasants for export on the depressed world market. However, the urban, industrial emphasis of Marx's theories sparked debate over the way in which they applied to Russia.

Lenin and the Bolsheviks

The person who would eventually apply and implement Marxist theory was Vladimir Ilich Ulyanov (VLAD-i-mir EEL-ich oo-LYAN-nov; 1870–1924), who later took the name Lenin. Born in Ulyanovsk (oo-LYAN-ovsk), formerly Simbirsk, a small city along the Volga River, Lenin grew up in the moderate and respectable circumstances provided by his father, a school administrator and teacher.

In 1887 the government arrested and executed Lenin's brother, Alexander, in St. Petersburg on charges of plotting against the life of the tsar. Shortly thereafter, Lenin began to study the writings of Marx and their potential applications to contemporary Russia. He overcame major obstacles from tsarist officials and passed his law exams at St. Petersburg University without formally attending classes. After 1893 he began to compile theories of tactics and strategy that would form the basis of the Soviet Union throughout its 73-year existence.

In 1895 a court sentenced him to exile in Siberia for his political activities. While in exile, he enjoyed complete liberty of movement in the district and could hunt, fish, swim, study, read, and keep up a large correspondence. A political ally, Nadezhda Krupskaia (na-DESH-da KRUP-ska-ia), joined him, and they were married. Later they translated Sidney and Beatrice Webb's *History of Trade Unionism*. When Lenin's exile ended in 1900, he and Krupskaia went to Switzerland, where they joined other Russian Social Democrats in exile in founding the newspaper *Iskra* ("Spark"), whose motto was "From the Spark—the conflagration."

Lenin, the driving force behind the Russian Revolution from which emerged the Soviet Union, spent years studying Marx's theories and adapting them to conditions in Russia.

In applying Marx to Russian conditions, Lenin found it necessary to sketch in several blank spots. Lenin's methods differed greatly from those of western European Marxists, as did his theories. Lenin advocated the formation of a small elite of professional revolutionaries, the **"vanguard of the proletariat."** These professionals, subject to strict party discipline, would anticipate the proletariat's needs and best interests and lead them through the oxymoronic theory of "democratic centralism."

The Social Democrats met in 1903 in London and split into two wings—the Bolsheviks (BOL-shuh-vik) and the Mensheviks (MEN-shuh-vik)—over the questions of the timing of the revolution and the nature of the party. (In Russian, *bolshevik* means "majority" and *menshevik* means "minority," the names stemming

vanguard of the proletariat—The elite revolutionary group that would anticipate the proletariat's needs and lead them through the principle of democratic centralism.

from a vote on party policies in 1903 when the Bolsheviks did prevail. On most occasions until the summer of 1917, however, the Bolsheviks were, in fact, in a distinct minority among the Social Democrats.) The two factions differed sharply on strategy and tactics. The Bolsheviks, following Lenin's revisionist views, were prepared to move the pace of history along through democratic centralism. The Mensheviks believed that Russian socialism should grow gradually and peacefully in accordance with Marxist principles of development and historical evolution, and they were prepared to work within a framework dominated by bourgeois political parties. They knew that their victory was inevitable, given the historical dialectic, and that the proletariat would play the lead role, assisted by the party. After their split in 1903, the two factions never reconciled.

After 1903 Lenin had little success in changing the political conditions of Russia, beyond affecting the most sophisticated part of the workers' movement. However, he continued to make significant doctrinal contributions. Lenin recommended a socialism whose weapon was violence and whose tactics allowed little long-range compromise with the bourgeoisie. However, he also saw the advantages of flexibility and encouraged temporary deviations that might serve the goals of the working class. He took little for granted and reasoned that the development of class unity to destroy the capitalists among the Russian workers might require some assistance. To that end he refined his notion of the way in which the elite party would function. In revolution, the elite party would infiltrate the government, police, and army while participating in legal workers' movements; in government, the party would enforce its dictates on the populace with iron discipline.

Lenin looked out at the undoubted strength of the advanced technological nations and marveled at their extension of power. In *Imperialism, the Highest Stage of Capitalism* (1916) he forecast that the modern capitalist states would destroy themselves. He argued that the wages of the workers did not represent enough purchasing power to absorb the output of the capitalists' factories and that the vast amounts of capital that were accumulated could not be invested profitably in the home country. Therefore, the states would engage in an inevitable competition for markets, resources, and capital that would drive them from cutthroat competition to outright war and their ultimate destruction. At that point, he reasoned, his elite party would be ready to pick up the pieces from the blindly selfish powers.

The Revolution of 1905 and Its Aftermath

As in 1854 at Crimea, a failure in war—this time a "splendid little war" against Japan—exposed the weaknesses of the autocratic tsarist regime. Strikes and protests spread throughout the land in response to the military failure of the Russo-Japanese War during the last days of 1904. On January 22, 1905, the Cossacks opened fire on a peaceful crowd of workers who had advanced on the Winter Palace in St. Petersburg carrying a petition asking for the tsar's help. In response, a general strike broke out, with the strikers demanding a democratic republic, freedom for political prisoners, and the disarming of the police. **Soviets**—councils of workers led by the Social Democrats—appeared in the cities to direct revolutionary activities. Most business and government offices closed, and the whole machinery of Russian economic life creaked to a halt. The country was virtually paralyzed.

After a series of half-measures and stalling in response to strikes and revolutionary activities, the tsar found himself pushed to the wall. Unable to find a dictator to impose order, he was forced to issue the October Manifesto of 1905, which promised "freedom of person, conscience, assembly, and union." A national legislature, the Duma, was to be called without delay. The right to vote would be extended, and no law could be enacted without the Duma's approval. The October Manifesto split the moderate from the socialist opposition and kept Nicholas on the throne, although he was heartbroken for having made the compromise. The socialists tried to start new strikes, but the opposition was now totally split apart.

Most radical forces boycotted the first Duma meeting in the spring of 1906. As a result, the Kadets became the dominant force. Even with this watered-down representation, the tsar was upset by the criticism of the government's handling of the Russo-Japanese War, treatment of minorities, handling of political prisoners, and economic policies. Claiming that the representatives "would not cooperate" with the government, Nicholas dissolved the first Duma. The Russian people turned a cold shoulder to the Kadets' appeals for support. Sensing the decline of political fervor, Nicholas appointed a law-and-order conservative, Peter Stolypin (sto-LEAP-in; 1862–1911), as prime minister. He assumed emergency powers and cracked down on the radicals.

Unlike previous tsarist appointees, Stolypin knew that changes had to be made, especially in the area of agriculture. Despite Nicholas's lack of support, Stolypin set up a process to develop a class of small farmers. He pushed through reforms that abolished all payments still owed by the peasants under the emancipation law and permitted peasants to withdraw from the commune and claim their shares of the land and other wealth as private property. He also opened lands east of the Urals to the peasants and extended financial aid

soviets—Councils of workers led by the Social Democrats in the 1905 Revolution.

Russian Political Movements in 1905

Kadets	Liberals
Octobrists	Moderate liberals
Trudoviks	Populist Labor Party
Socialist Revolutionaries	Agrarian-based socialists—non-Marxist
Bolsheviks	Revisionist democratic centralist Social Democrats (Marxists)
Mensheviks	Social Democrats, Marxist fundamentalists
Monarchist right	Supporters of the tsar
Union of Russian People	Extreme right wing, anti-Semitic and antiliberal
Jewish Bund	Marxist Jewish Workers' party

from the state. He was well on the way to finding a solution to that most enduring of Russian problems, the peasant problem, before he was assassinated in 1911 by a Socialist Revolutionary, who was also an agent of the secret police.

Despite its reactionary tsar and nobility, Russia took major steps toward becoming a constitutional monarchy in the years after 1905. The nation made great economic and social progress. Industrialization increased and generated new wealth. Increased political and civil rights spawned an active public life. Stolypin's death in 1911, however, deprived the country of needed leadership, and World War I gave Russia a test it could not pass.

THE "EASTERN QUESTION" AND THE FAILURE OF EUROPEAN DIPLOMACY TO 1914

- *Why were the European powers unable to come to an agreement about what to do with the Ottoman Empire?*

An Empire in Decline

The Ottoman Empire had played a key role in European history since its creation in the fourteenth century. Until the 1750s, fear of the empire preoccupied the Austrians and the Russians. After that time, the empire went into a state of decline, and its Balkan territories became targets of opportunity for Vienna and St. Petersburg. Because of the empire's vast holdings throughout the Middle East and North Africa, the English, French, and Germans became equally involved with the fate of the Ottoman Empire. There was no easy solution to the question of what to do with the Turks—the so-called **Eastern Question**— and there was no way to partition its holdings without giving one state or another an advantageous position. During the nineteenth century, the European powers settled on a policy of propping up the sultan and maintaining the fiction of the Ottoman Empire being a great power. Unfortunately, the European states failed to devise an answer to the dilemma of what to do with the power vacuum created by the decaying Ottoman Empire and how to manage the various nations of the Balkans who began their struggles for self-determination and independence.

The Balkans Awaken

By the end of the eighteenth century, Ottoman power had substantially declined in the Balkans, just at a time when the various peoples began to experience waves of nationalism. In 1799 Sultan Selim III acknowledged the independence of the mountainous nation of Montenegro, after its long and heroic defense of its liberty. Further proof of Ottoman weakness came in 1804 when some renegade Turkish troops in Belgrade went on a rampage, disobeyed the sultan's orders, and forced the Serbian people to defend themselves. This initial act of self-protection blossomed into a rebellion that culminated in the Serbs gaining an autonomous position within the Ottoman Empire after an 11-year struggle.

Turkish weakness attracted both Russian and British interests. Russia had made a substantial advance toward the Mediterranean during the reign of Catherine II. In 1774 the Treaty of Küchük Kaynarca (kiu-CHUK kay-NAR-tsa), the Russians gained the rights of navigation in the Ottoman waters and the right to intervene in favor of Eastern Orthodox Christians in the Ottoman Empire. The British protested these gains, and in 1791, Prime Minister William Pitt the Younger denounced Russia for its supposed ambitions to dismember the empire. Only the common threat of Napoleon from 1798 to 1815 diverted Great Britain and Russia from their competition in the eastern Mediterranean.

The forces of nationalism in Greece took advantage of the chaotic administration of the Turks in

Eastern Question—The question of how to dispose of the declining Ottoman Empire.

1821. Unlike the Serbian rebellion, the Greek revolution gained substantial outside support from philhellenic ("admiring Greeks") societies of Great Britain. Even though Metternich hoped the revolt would burn itself out, the Greeks were able to take advantage of intervention by the Great Powers to gain their independence.

During the Greek Revolt, the British feared that Russia would use the Greek independence movement as an excuse for further expansion at Turkish expense. The British intervened skillfully, and the Greeks were able to gain their independence without a major Russian advance toward the Straits—the control of which by the Turks blocked their access to the Mediterranean Sea and beyond. Tsar Nicholas I wanted to weaken the Ottoman Empire in order to pave the way for Russia to gain control over the Dardanelles and the Bosporus. So much did he want this expansion of his realm that he set aside his obligations to support the European balance of power. Britain became alarmed at this policy, and the upshot was an agreement in 1827 in which Britain, France, and Russia pledged themselves to secure Greek independence. Russia eventually defeated the Turks, and in 1829 the Treaty of Adrianople gave the Greeks the basis for their independence, while Serbia received autonomy. The Danubian principalities of Moldavia and Wallachia, the basis of the future state of Romania, became Russian protectorates.

By the 1830s it became apparent that the Turks were to be an object of, rather than a participant in, European diplomacy. The sultan's government had few admirers in Europe, but the European powers agreed—at least for the present—to prop up the decaying Ottoman Empire rather than allow one nation to gain dominance in the strategic area.

In 1832 Mehemet Ali, for all intents and purposes the independent governor of Egypt, attacked the sultan, easily putting down the forces of the empire. To prevent the establishment of a new and probably stronger government at the Straits, Nicholas I sent an army to protect Constantinople. In 1833 the Treaty of Unkiar Skelessi (un-key-AR ske-less-ee) gave Russia a dominant position over the Turks.

Britain could not tolerate Russia's advantage and for the next 10 years worked diplomatically to force the tsar to renounce the treaty and sign a general agreement of Turkish independence. This diplomatic game did little to improve the Ottoman Empire's condition. In 1844, while visiting Britain, Nicholas referred to the empire as a "dying man" and proposed that the British join in a dissection of the body.

The Crimean War

The Crimean War, which lasted from 1853 to 1856, was a major turning point in the course of the Eastern Question. The immediate origins of the war were to be found in a quarrel over the management and protection of the holy places in Palestine. Napoleon III, in a move to gain support from Catholics and the military in France, upheld the Roman Catholics' right to perform the housekeeping duties. On the other side, acting under the terms of the treaty signed in Küchük Kaynarca, Nicholas stated that the Orthodox faithful should look after the holy places. From this obscure argument, the Crimean War eventually emerged, as the Great Powers all intervened in the discussions to protect their interests.

The tsar's ambassador to the Turks tried to use the dispute to improve Russia's position in the region, while the British told the sultan to stand firm against the Russians. After the Russians occupied the Danubian principalities in an attempt to show the Turks the seriousness of their demands, the Turks declared war on the Russians in October 1853. By the next summer the French, Sardinians, and British had joined the Turks. Napoleon III saw the war as a chance to enhance his dynasty's reputation, and the Sardinians found an opportunity to gain allies in their drive for Italian unification. Under the impact of antitsarist public opinion, the British took steps to stop the Russians. The stated aim of all the allies was, of course, the defense of the sultan.

A combination of the allies' military strength and the tsarist forces' inefficiency stalemated the Russians. Austria, a former close ally of Russia, took advantage of Russia's difficulties to extend Austrian influence into the Balkans. The Russians sued for peace, and the Treaty of Paris (1856) once again attempted to resolve the Eastern Question. Rather than deal with the weakness of the Ottoman Empire, the treaty affirmed its integrity and Great Power status. The Black Sea was to be a neutral body of water, and the Straits were closed to foreign warships. The treaty declared that no power had the right to intervene on behalf of the sultan's Christian subjects. Russian control of the principalities was ended. The Crimean War momentarily stopped the Russian advance into the Balkans and toward the eastern Mediterranean, but the problems posed by the "sick man of Europe" remained. Further, the various Balkan nations became even more inflamed with the desire for self-rule.

The Unanswered Question

In the generation after the Crimean War the problems posed by the disintegrating Ottoman Empire became more severe. To the north, the Russians, who could do little militarily in the Balkans during this period of intense internal reforms, broadcast the message of pan-Slavic solidarity to their "Orthodox" brothers in the Balkans. The Austrians, their appetites whetted by their part in the Crimean War, kept a wary and opportunistic eye on developments in the Balkans. British loans to the Turks cut into the Turkish tax base and led to the destruction of the indigenous Ottoman textile industry. In addition, with the completion of the Suez Canal in 1869, the eastern Mediterranean came to be even more essential to British interests. Finally, the Germans began to increase their influence in the area after 1871.

Nationalism further complicated the unresolved Eastern Question. The Bulgarians, who had been under the Turkish yoke since the fourteenth century, started their national revival in the late eighteenth century. By the 1860s they had formed a liberation movement, which was strengthened in 1870 when the Turks gave permission to them to found the Bulgarian Exarchate, a Bulgarian wing of the Greek Orthodox faith. This permitted the Bulgarians to establish their churches wherever there were Bulgarian people, a clear invitation for the expansion of the Bulgarian nation. The Bulgarians took strength from the example of the Romanians, who, after centuries of Turkish dominance and a quarter century as a Russian protectorate, had gained their independence in 1861, largely as a result of great power influence. Also, during the 1860s, the Serbian leader Michael Obrenovich (o-BREN-o-vich) had worked toward a Balkan union against the Turks. Amid this maneuvering and ferment, the Turks were unable to strengthen their rule over areas theoretically under their control.

CASE STUDY
Oppression in Bulgaria and Poland

The crisis came to a head in 1875 when peasants revolted in the district of Bosnia, a Turkish-governed province populated by a religiously diverse group of Slavs. Following this insurrection, Serbia and Montenegro declared war on the Turks. In the summer of 1876, the Bulgarians revolted, but the Ottoman forces put down the rebellion. When highly emotional accounts of the Turkish massacres were published in western Europe, the incident became known as the "Bulgarian horrors" and drew British attention to the Balkans. The pan-Slav faithful in St. Petersburg and Moscow were naturally thrilled at the exploits of their "little brothers," and money and volunteers flowed southward.

The series of nationalistic uprisings in the improperly governed Ottoman provinces had captured the attention of the Great Powers, and by the end of 1875 the Eastern Question was once again the main focus of international diplomacy. The "sick man of Europe" was still strong enough to devastate the Serbs and Montenegrins in battle. The insurgents were forced to sue for peace, a move that drew Tsar Alexander II and the Russians into war with the Ottomans in 1877. After a hard-fought campaign, the Russians broke through early in 1878 and were close to achieving their final goal of taking Constantinople when the sultan sued for peace.

The resulting Treaty of San Stefano in March 1878 recognized the complete independence of Serbia and Romania from theoretical Ottoman sovereignty and reaffirmed Montenegro's independence. A large Bulgarian state was set up, nominally tributary to the Ottoman Empire but actually dominated by Russia. The Straits were effectively under Russian control, as the Bulgarian state would have a coast on the Aegean. The Eastern Question was almost solved by the Russians.

Britain and Austria, however, correctly perceived a major shift of the balance of power in Russia's favor, and the two of them forced a reconsideration of the San Stefano treaty at the Congress of Berlin in June and July 1878. Held under the supervision of Bismarck, the self-styled "honest broker," the congress compelled Russia to agree to a revision of Bulgaria's status. The large state created in March was broken into three parts: the northernmost section would be independent, paying tribute to the Turks, while the other two parts would be under Ottoman control. Austria got the right to "occupy and administer" the provinces of Herzegovina and Bosnia.

The congress turned back the Russian advance, stymied the national independence movement, and did little to urge Turkey to put its house in order. The Austrian gains caused great bitterness among the Serbs and Russians, a mood that added to the tension in the Balkans. The Eastern Question remained unanswered, and the Balkans remained an arena of local nationalistic conflicts that would appeal to the imperialistic designs of the Great Powers, especially the Russians and the Austro-Hungarian monarchy.

Appearances and Realities

By 1900 Europeans had many reasons to be optimistic about the future. The growth produced by the previous three generations seemed to support the sturdy belief in progress. There was a substantial amount of unity: Europe was Christian, Caucasian, capitalist, industrialized, and in command of the world. Europeans shared the same vibrant Western traditions, and even the rulers of the various states were all related to one another. As if to symbolize world changes, there were new ways to organize international communication, defuse conflicts, and maintain peace. As early as 1865, a meeting was held in Paris to coordinate the use of telegraph lines and to establish a unified rate structure. Ten years later, the Universal Postal Union was set up to handle the world's mail. To protect the rights of authors, an agreement was drawn up in 1886 for an international copyright union.

Scholars and statesmen worked to strengthen international law, the rules of warfare, and the use of arbitration. A significant example of this was the opening of the Hague Conference in 1899. The Russ-

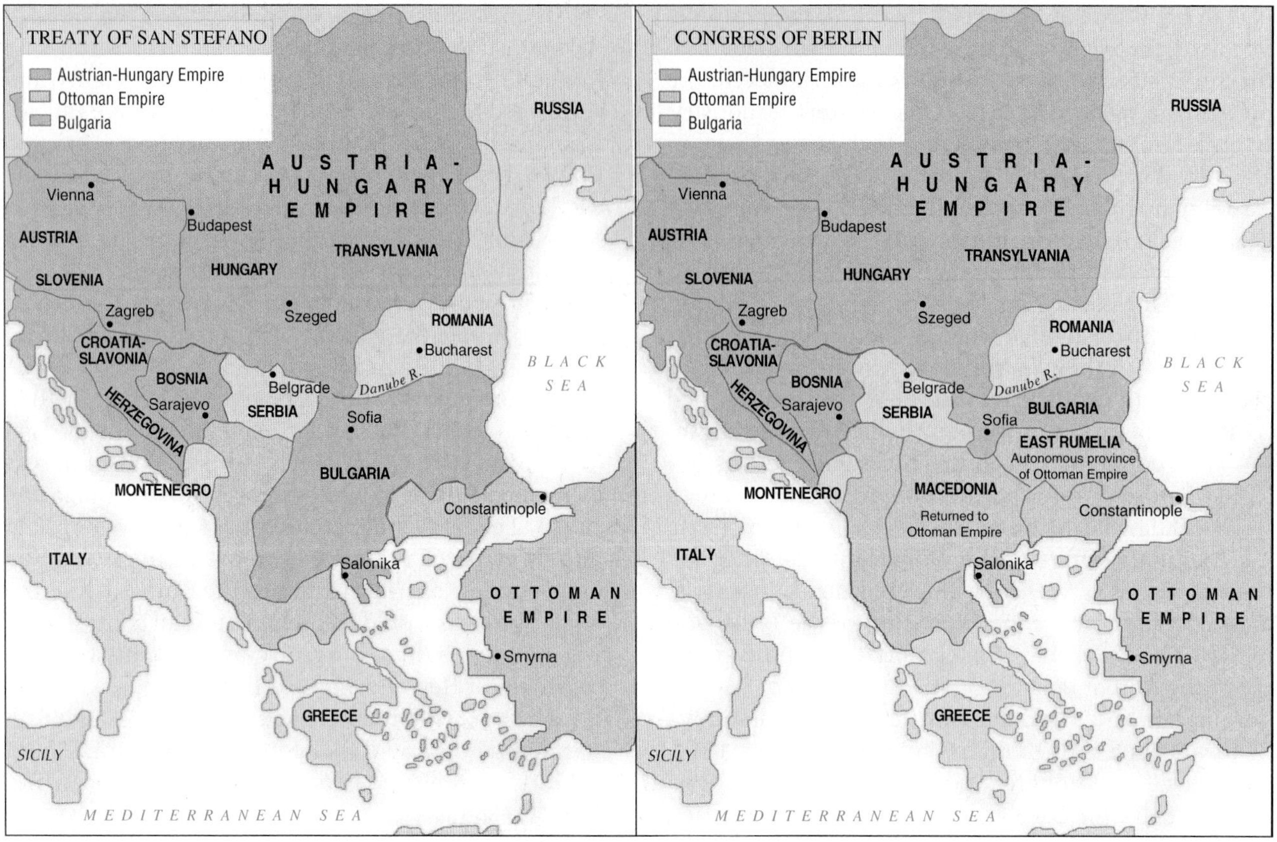

In the spring of 1878, the Russians believed that they had imposed their solution to the Eastern Question in the Treaty of San Stefano. The other European powers disagreed and forced a revision of San Stefano in the Congress of Berlin a few months later. Ultimately, the Eastern Question would remain unanswered until World War I redrew the map of Europe and the Middle East.

ian foreign minister invited the Great Powers to the Dutch city to discuss arms reduction. Although no progress was made on disarmament, the conference did reform the rules of war by improving the treatment of prisoners, outlawing the use of poisonous gas, and defining the conditions of a state of war. In addition, an international court of arbitration, the Hague Tribunal, was established, staffed by an international group of jurists. Appearance before the court was voluntary, as was acceptance of its decisions. The effectiveness of arbitration as a means to solve problems could be seen in the ten years before the war. Various powers signed 162 treaties that pledged the signatories to arbitrate disagreements such as boundary decisions and conflicts over fishing rights.

Alfred Nobel, the Swedish manufacturer of dynamite, personified the contradictions of the age. This international producer of explosives established a peace prize two weeks before his death in November 1896. Andrew Carnegie set up the Carnegie Endowment for International Peace and built a peace palace at The Hague to be used for international conferences. It was finished just weeks before the outbreak of World War I.

All of these developments encouraged believers in progress to envision a peaceful future. They pointed out that all of the wars in the nineteenth century had been generally local and short. They reasoned that if war should break out in the future, the murderous new technologies would ensure that they would not be lengthy or costly. Some social Darwinists asserted that humanity might well evolve beyond the stage of fighting wars altogether. These optimists conveniently ignored the brutal, lengthy, and costly reality of the American Civil War, in many ways the first modern, industrial war. They also ignored the reality that the European state system and military industrial complexes took on a life and momentum of their own.

The End of Bismarck's System

From 1870 to 1890 the German chancellor, Otto von Bismarck, dominated European diplomacy. He built a rational balance-of-power-based foreign policy devoted to the diplomatic isolation of France by depriving it of potential allies. He reasoned that the French would try to take revenge on Germany and regain Alsace and Lorraine, but he knew they could do little without aid from the Austrians or Russians. In 1873 Bismarck made an alliance, known as the Three Emperors' League or *Dreikaiserbund* (dri-KAI-ser-bund), with Russia and Austria-Hungary.

Conflicts between the Austrians and Russians in the Balkans soon put a strain on the league, and at the Congress of Berlin (1878) Bismarck was forced to choose between the conflicting claims of Vienna and St. Petersburg. He chose to support Austria-Hungary for a number of reasons, including fear of alienating Great Britain if he backed the Russians. In addition, he felt that he could probably dominate Austria more easily than Russia. This momentous shift paved the way for a new arrangement. In 1879 Bismarck negotiated the Dual Alliance with the Austro-Hungarian monarchy; in 1882 a new partner, Italy, joined the group, which was now called the Triple Alliance.

The choice of Austria over Russia did not mean that Bismarck abandoned his ties with the tsars. In 1881 the Three Emperors' League was renewed. Rivalries between the Dual Monarchy and Russia in the Balkans put an effective end to the arrangement, and the Dreikaiserbund collapsed for good in 1887. Bismarck negotiated a separate agreement with Russia called the Reinsurance Treaty, in which both sides pledged neutrality—except if Germany attacked France or Russia attacked Austria—and support of the status quo.

Under Bismarck's shrewd hand, Germany kept diplomatic control for 20 years. Bismarck chose his goals carefully and understood the states with which he worked. He made every effort to avoid challenging Britain's interests and to continue isolating France. As a result, Germany was not surrounded by enemies. The chancellor kept from alienating Russia while maintaining his ties with Austria.

In the 1890s, however, the rash actions of the new kaiser, William II, destroyed Germany's favorable position. He dismissed Bismarck in 1890, took foreign policy into his own hands, and arrogantly frittered away the diplomatic advantages the chancellor had built up. France had been attempting to escape from its isolation for some time and had begun, through its bank loans, to make important inroads into Russia even before Bismarck retired. When the kaiser allowed the Reinsurance Treaty to lapse, the Russians decided to look elsewhere. France leapt at the chance, after 20 years, to secure a strong ally. In 1894 the Triple Alliance of Germany, Italy, and Austria-Hungary found itself confronted by the Dual Alliance of Russia and France. Germany's worst fears had come to pass: It was now encircled by enemies.

Major Dates in European Alliances

1872	The Three Emperor's League (Germany, Austria-Hungary, Russia) formed
1879	Dual Alliance (Germany, Austria-Hungary) formed
1882	Triple Alliance (Germany, Austria-Hungary, Italy) formed
1890	Bismarck resigns; Reinsurance Treaty with Russia lapses
1890s	Germany decides to build fleet to compete with British navy
1894	French-Russian Alliance
1904	Britain and France conclude Entente Cordiale
1907	Russia joins Britain and France to form Triple Entente

Britain Ends Its Isolation

At the end of the nineteenth century, Britain found itself involved in bitter rivalries with Russia in the Balkans and in the Middle East and with France in Africa. During the Boer War, all of the Great Powers in Europe were anti-British. However, the supremacy of the British fleet helped discourage intervention. As the new century began, London became concerned that its policy of splendid isolation might need to be abandoned. In these circumstances, the most normal place for Britain to turn would be to Germany.

On the surface nothing seemed more natural than that these two dominant European powers should adjust their national interests to avoid conflict. From the 1880s to 1901 both sides made several approaches to investigate an "understanding" between the major sea power, Britain, and the strongest land power, Germany. Tradition and dynastic relations spoke in favor of a closer tie between the two. By 1900 Berlin and London may have competed in economic and imperialistic terms, but they were far from any major strife in any either area.

The two countries could not, however, come together formally. Even though important figures on both sides could see the advantages of an alliance, strong forces worked against this development. German and British interests did not match sufficiently to permit equal gain from an alliance. The kaiser's numerous bellicose statements and clumsy actions (such as his meddling in British colonial affairs by sending a telegram to South Africa's president, Paul Kruger, in 1896) offended many British leaders. Germany's expanding influence in the Middle East and the Balkans worried the British, as did Germany's tremendous economic progress.

Most threatening for London was Germany's plan to build a fleet that would compete with Britain's. In 1900 Germany initiated a huge naval program providing for, within a 20-year timetable, a fleet strong enough to keep Britain from interfering with German international goals. The British believed that the German program was aimed directly at them. For the island nation, the supremacy of the Royal Navy was a life-or-death matter. Since food and raw materials had to come by sea, it was crucial that the navy be able to protect British shipping.

Challenged by Germany, Britain looked elsewhere for allies. In 1904 officials from London and Paris began to settle their differences and proclaimed the Entente Cordiale ("friendly understanding"), setting aside a tradition of hostility dating back to the Hundred Years' War. The entente and an alliance with Japan in 1902 ended Britain's policy of diplomatic isolation and brought it into the combination that would be pitted against Germany's Triple Alliance. In 1907 London settled its problems with Russia, thereby establishing the Triple Entente. The British made no definite military commitments in the agreements with France and Russia. Theoretically they retained freedom of action, but they were now part of the alliance system.

The North African Crises

In the decade before World War I, Europe experienced a series of crises on its peripheries, none of which vitally threatened the Great Powers' survival individually. However, because of the alliance system, the incidents increased tensions and brought Europe ever closer to war.

The first serious test came in 1905 over Morocco. France sought control of this territory in order to establish a continuous line of dependencies from the Atlantic across the North African coast to Tunisia. Carefully timing their moves, the Germans arranged for the kaiser to visit the Moroccan port of Tangier, where he declared that all powers must respect the independence of the country. The French were forced to give up their immediate plans for taking over Morocco and to agree to Germany's suggestion that an international conference be called at Algeciras (1906) to discuss the matter.

At this meeting the Germans hoped for a split between the British and French. This did not occur. On the contrary, all but one of the nations in attendance—even Italy—supported France rather than Germany. Only Austria-Hungary remained on the kaiser's side. The conference agreed that Morocco should still enjoy its sovereignty but that France and Spain should be given certain rights to police the area.

In 1911 a second Moroccan crisis escalated tensions. When France sent an army into the disputed territory, ostensibly to maintain order, Germany responded by sending the gunboat *Panther* to the Moroccan port of Agadir. Great Britain came out with a blunt warning that all of its power was at the disposal of France in this affair. A diplomatic bargain was finally struck in which France got a free hand in Morocco and Germany gained a small area in equatorial Africa. The two rival alliances managed to avoid war over Morocco. The illusion of progress was maintained—until the alliance system reached the breaking point in the Balkans.

It was in the conduct of diplomacy that the perils of progress took their greatest toll. The vastly stronger states operated more and more under their own views of social Darwinism, building huge defense establishments while ignoring important crises such as those around the declining Ottoman Empire. The Europeans' appetites, egos, and military forces had begun to exceed the terrain left to be taken in the world. The new mass politics, with its popular press, superpatriotic appeals, and blatant aggressiveness, could not adapt easily to the new situation. A century of grabbing territory and reprinting maps showing broader swatches of the globe in the national colors had spoiled the Western states and distorted their foreign policies. The results would bring an end to European dominance.

CONCLUSION

The French and Industrial Revolutions changed the Western world far beyond the comprehension of the leaders gathered at Vienna in 1814. The Congress of Vienna placed a framework of stability on Europe, while accepting many of the changes since 1789. However, it did not deal with the new political forces of liberalism, nationalism, and socialism. This soon became evident with the epidemic of revolutions in the 1820s, 1830s, and 1840s. In 1848 the legacy of the French Revolution and the process of industrialization combined to overpower the political structures of France,

Germany, Italy, and the Habsburg Empire. The 1848 revolutions enjoyed brief, spectacular successes and tragic, lasting failures. The leaders of the revolutions had little or no experience, and they acted under a total infatuation with their ideals. The force of nationalism, so powerful an enemy of autocracy, soon proved to be a fragmenting force among the various liberated nationalities. These factors doomed the idealistic revolutionaries and introduced a new range of political alternatives, such as unification in Italy, the Second Empire in France, and the construction of a unified German state.

Russia and Britain avoided the revolutionary upheavals of 1848, the first through a policy of repression that failed to respond effectively to its overwhelming problems and the second because of an improving standard of living and a flexible, self-interested middle class. For the rest of the century their paths would diverge, as England would grow to establish a world empire while the Russians would struggle with reform and repression until the 1905 Revolution, which would finally bring an end to autocracy. Across the Atlantic, the United States profited by a massive influx of immigrants and became a leading Western power, after enduring a savage and tragic civil war. For the British and the Americans, the triumph of liberalism consolidated the control of industrialization in the hands of the middle classes, who in turn dominated the political arena.

The United Kingdom, through its political stability and continued economic growth, provided an improving standard of living and a flexible, self-interested middle class and established a world empire. In Europe, the German Second Reich came to be the most powerful country on the Continent and challenged the United Kingdom for commercial supremacy. The French consolidated their power after their military and diplomatic defeat in 1870. Thereafter, until 1914, despite the ramshackle nature of the Third Republic and its scandals, France had power and influence. The Italians had achieved unification under the leadership of Cavour and Sardinia, but unification did not bring miraculous improvements in the lives of the Italian people. The Habsburg Empire, after nearly 20 years of trying to deal with its fractious nationalities, redefined itself as the Dual Monarchy in 1867. It managed to hold together until the outbreak of World War I.

The European states were unable to answer the most important challenge facing them throughout the nineteenth century, and that was what to do with the Ottoman Empire—once a world power that held title to far more territory than it could effectively govern. In the political vacuum that developed in the Ottoman-dominated part of Europe—the Balkans—the subjugated nationalities began to claim their independence under their respective banners of nationalism. Crises erupted on the European peripheries of the Ottoman Empire in the 1830s, 1850s, 1870s, and at the beginning of the twentieth century, the countries that had made so much progress domestically were failing to maintain stability internationally.

Suggestions for Web Browsing

You can obtain more information about topics included in this chapter at the websites listed below. See also the companion website that accompanies this text, **http://www.ablongman.com/brummett,** which contains an online study guide and additional resources.

Nationalism and Music
http://acc6.its.brooklyn.cuny.edu/~phalsall/sounds/fnlandia.mid

Through articles and sound files, this site discusses how early-nineteenth-century music reflected growing nationalist feelings in Europe.

Marx-Engels Internet Archive
http://www.marxists.org/archive/marx/index.htm

Extensive site on both Karl Marx and Friedrich Engels offers biographies, a photo gallery, letters, and additional web links.

The Revolution of 1848 in France
http://history.hanover.edu/texts/fr1848.htm

Site includes original source documents from the Revolution of 1848 in France.

Revolutions of 1848
http://www.pvhs.chico.k12.ca.us/~bsilva/projects/revs/1848time.html

Extensive site offers an overview, timeline, biographies, and essays about the revolutions of 1848.

Life of the Tsars
http://www.Alexanderpalace.org/catherinepalace/Alexander.html

Images portraying the luxury of life for the tsars in the nineteenth century.

The Lewis and Clark Expedition
http://www.peabody.harvard.edu/Lewis_and_Clark/default.html

Lewis and Clark brought back an enormous collection of material, which is housed at the Peabody Museum at Harvard.

U.S. Intervention in Latin America
http://www.smplanet.com/imperialism/teddy.html

Site offering a wide range of images, movies, and sound bites regarding intervention in Latin America, particularly the issues surrounding the Panama Canal project.

Theodore Roosevelt
http://www.theodoreroosevelt.org/

A website that touches all aspects of Roosevelt's life and work, including a fine collection of political cartoons.

Benjamin Disraeli
http://projects.vassar.edu/punch/Lockwood.html

Benjamin Disraeli was a controversial figure in British history, as can be seen in the cartoon on this website. Links to William Gladstone and the political setting of the time are also found here.

Nineteenth-Century Austria and Germany
http://www.fordham.edu/halsall/mod/modsbook22.html

A rich crossroads of information about nineteenth-century Austria and Germany is offered by the Internet Modern History Source Book, which contains documents, maps, and images.

Nineteenth-Century Europe in Photos
http://academic.brooklyn.cuny.edu/history/core/pics

Website providing access to a vast array of historical images of the era.

Literature and Film

The nineteenth century was the golden age of the European novel, and across the West, there were powerful talents portraying the complexity and drama of their times. Victor Hugo's *Les Misérables* (1862) is a masterpiece of a book, the subject of both films and musicals. Charles Dickens captured the courage and challenge of the first part of the nineteenth century in England in books such as *Great Expectations* (1860–1861), *A Christmas Carol* (1843), *Hard Times* (1845), *Bleak House* (1852), and *David Copperfield* (1849–1850). Jane Austen's *Pride and Prejudice* (1813), *Sense and Sensibility* (1811), and other novels give an insight into upper-middle-class life and are also the bases of a number of films. The prolific Honoré de Balzac provided detailed portraits of the often cruel social practices of France after the Revolution and Napoleon. *Old Goriot* (1835), *Cousin Bette* (1846), and *Colonel Chabert* (1832) are among his more impressive works. In Russia, Nikolai Gogol skillfully captured the absurdity of the serf system in his *Dead Souls* (1842) and *The Inspector General* (1836). Ivan Turgenev accomplished the finest presentation of generational conflict in his *Fathers and Sons* (1862). Leo Tolstoy published his epochal *War and Peace* in the 1860s, followed by a number of other important works, including *Anna Karenina* (1873–1876). Perhaps the greatest Russian novelist, Fedor Dostoevski, in his finest novel, *The Brothers Karamazov* (1879–1880), described Russia under wrenching transition in the wake of the Great Reforms. His study of human behavior in *Crime and Punishment* (1866) remains one of the finest psychological novels in any language. As were other great titles above, the Russian novels have been presented in several films. Herman Melville's classic, *Moby Dick* (1851), gained instant acceptance as a major contribution to world literature.

The Public Broadcasting System has produced superb studies of the United States in the nineteenth century, available in VHS presentation. See the series on Lincoln (1995), Ken Burns's treatment of the Civil War (1990), and the study of the West and Lewis and Clark (2004). A searching and dramatic portrayal of the struggle for freedom among African Americans is the *Roots of Resistance—A Story of the Underground Railroad* (1995). Edward Zwick directed a stunning portrayal of African Americans fighting for their freedom in the Civil War in *Glory* (Columbia/Tristar, 1989).

As mass education spread and literacy became more widespread, writers went in two separate directions. Poets began to imitate the symbolist work of Paul Verlaine, *Selected Poems* (Oxford University Press, 2000), and Stéphane Mallarmé, *Collected Poems* (University of California Press, 1996), or the popular and widely read works of Rudyard Kipling. See the edition of Kipling's *Kim*, ed. Edward Said (Viking, 1992) for a fine discussion of his work. Other titles by Kipling include *Just So Stories* (1902), *Rikki-Tikki-Tavi* (part of *The Jungle Book*), *The Jungle Book* (1894), and *The Man Who Would Be King* (1889), which became the subject of a fine film of the same name. A person who staked out his own route was the visionary H. G. Wells, who wrote *The Time Machine* (1895), *The Invisible Man* (1897), and *The War of the Worlds* (1898). Other writers became powerful spokesmen for justice, such as Emile Zola, who led the drive to defend Alfred Dreyfus. His *Germinal* (Viking, 1997), one in a series of 19 related novels, stands as one the most important novels at the turn of the century. In the United States, Mark Twain continued his prolific work, but he was joined by authors such as Theodore Dreiser making strong social commentary in his book *Sister Carrie* (1900). Ida Tarbell set the foundations for investigative journalism with her *The History of Standard Oil Company* (1904), a work that was widely read.

Werner Herzog's *Fitzcarraldo* (New World Pictures, 1982) portrays a man with an obsession to establish a trading network along the Amazon and to build a world class opera house there. Claude Berri's *Germinal* (Sony Pictures Classics, 1994) brings Zola's novel to the screen. The diplomatic style of Teddy Roosevelt is captured in John Milius's *The Wind and the Lion* (Columbia, 1975). The Public Broadcasting System has produced a number of documentaries dealing with the period in the United States: *TR, The Story of Theodore Roosevelt* (AMEI–999-FXA, 1998), *Not for Ourselves Alone: The Story of Elizabeth Cady Stanton and Susan B. Anthony* (NFOA-DXO-FXA, 1999), *The Richest Man in the World: Andrew Carnegie* (AMEI–093-FXA, 1997), and America 1900 (AMER-X101-FXA, 1998).

Suggestions for Reading

For a general background to the period see Eric J. Hobsbawm, *Nations and Nationalism since 1780: Programme, Myth, and Reality* (Cambridge University Press, 1993), and Jonathan Sperber, *The European Revolution 1841–1851, New Approaches in European History* (Cambridge University Press, 1994). David Blackbourn's *The Long Nineteenth Century: A History of Germany 1780–1918* (Oxford University Press, 1998) traces the emergence of Prussia as the unifying force. Italian unification is the subject of Derek Bayles' *The Risorgimento and the Unification of Italy* (Allen & Unwin, 1982). Theodore Zeldin's superb study, *France 1848–1945*, 4 Vols. (Oxford University Press, 1973–1975), provides the necessary context to understand that tempestuous century in France. A notion of the complexity of the nationalities question in eastern Europe can be found in Peter F. Sugar and Ivo John Lederer, eds., *Nationalism in Eastern Europe* (University of Washington Press, 1969). J. N. Westwood's *Endurance and Endeavor: Russian History 1812–1992* (Oxford University Press, 1993) is the best one-volume survey. A good overview of the history of the UK during this time is David Thomson's *England in the Nineteenth Century* (Penguin, 1991). For the economic and social changes taking place in nineteenth-century America see James L. Huston, *Securing the Fruits of Labor: The American Concept of Wealth Distribution, 1765–1900* (Louisiana State University Press, 1998). Matthew S. Anderson's *The Eastern Question, 1774–1923* (St. Martin's Press, 1966) remains the best single-volume study of the issue that led to the outbreak of World War I. Joachim Remak's *The Origins of World War I, 1871–1914* (Harcourt Brace Jovanovich, 1997) is a solid analysis of Europe's diplomatic failure.

CHAPTER 27

World War I and Its Economic and Political Consequences

CHAPTER CONTENTS

1905

1908 Austria-Hungary annexes Bosnia-Herzegovina

1910

1912 and 1913 Balkan Wars

1914 Austrian Archduke Francis Ferdinand and his wife assassinated; World War I begins

1916 Battles of Verdun and the Somme

1917 United States enters World War I; Britain pledges support for Jewish homeland in Palestine in Balfour Declaration

1918 Wilson issues Fourteen Points; Russia signs Treaty of Brest-Litovsk with Germany; armistice signed ending World War I

1919 Treaty of Versailles

1920

1924 Dawes Plan; first Labour government in Britain

1929 U.S. stock market crashes

1930

1930–1940 Global depression

Europe's global dominance was brought to an end in August 1914 by a combination of forces—militarism, rival alliances, imperialism, secret diplomacy, and bellicose nationalism. When World War I came to an end four years later, over 10 million soldiers from around the world lay dead on Europe's battlefields, a generation of the best and bravest. Four empires—the German, Austro-Hungarian, Russian, and Ottoman—either faded away or disappeared entirely.

No part of the world remained untouched by these upheavals. The European powers recruited soldiers from their colonies. From Senegal to India to Australia to New Zealand hundreds of thousands of soldiers went to fight and die in the European war. The warring forces waged battles in both East and West Asia, while Asians and Africans went to work in the European countries to replace workers who had been called to the front. The world economy lost what little equilibrium it had and went into a manic cycle of inflation and depression that devastated nations around the globe between 1929 and 1932.

World War I, the "Great War"—the war that was to "make the world safe for democracy"—left a legacy of physical damage, economic disruption, and doubt that threatened the liberal advances of the nineteenth century. The horrible costs of the war made the triumph a hollow one for the democratic victors. After the initial taste for revenge had been satisfied, revulsion for war became widespread. The economic dislocation caused by inflation and depression sapped the strength of the middle classes, the traditional defenders of democracy, and paved the way for extremist dictators.

WORLD WAR I

- *How did European alliances make war all but inevitable?*

As we saw in Chapter 26, the diplomatic structure created by Bismarck, based on a Central Power alliance with Vienna and Rome, began to come apart in the 1890s. The blustering foreign policy of the Kaiser drove England, France, and Russia—three countries that had never worked together—to form the Triple Entente (on-tahnt) in 1907. The two alliances found themselves at odds over the crises in North Africa but managed to avoid going to war. The Central Powers and the Triple Entente entered into World War I in August 1914, however, because of their inability to deal with a series of conflicts in the Balkans.

The Balkan Crises

During the nineteenth century, Russia and Austria competed as they expanded their influences into the Balkan holdings of the Ottoman Empire. Throughout the last part of the nineteenth century, the two openly disagreed on the question of Macedonia, the building of railroads through the peninsula, and boundary revisions. Vienna and St. Petersburg were particularly at odds over the question of the status of Bosnia and Herzegovina (HERTS-ah-GOH-vee-nah).

The Austro-Hungarian monarchy had administered the two areas since the 1878 Congress of Berlin, much to the Russians' and Serbs' displeasure. The Russian Foreign Minister, Count Izvolskii (EEZ-vol-skee), initiated talks with Vienna in 1908 to resolve the situation. In an inexplicable move, he proposed that Russia would approve the Austro-Hungarians to annex the two areas in return for increased Black Sea rights for the Russian navy. The Austrians were pleased to annex Bosnia and Herzegovina, but the Russians never got their part of the bargain.

Serbia was outraged by the incorporation of more Slavs into the Habsburg domain and expected its Slavic, Orthodox protector, Russia, to do something about it. The Russians had been badly bruised in their

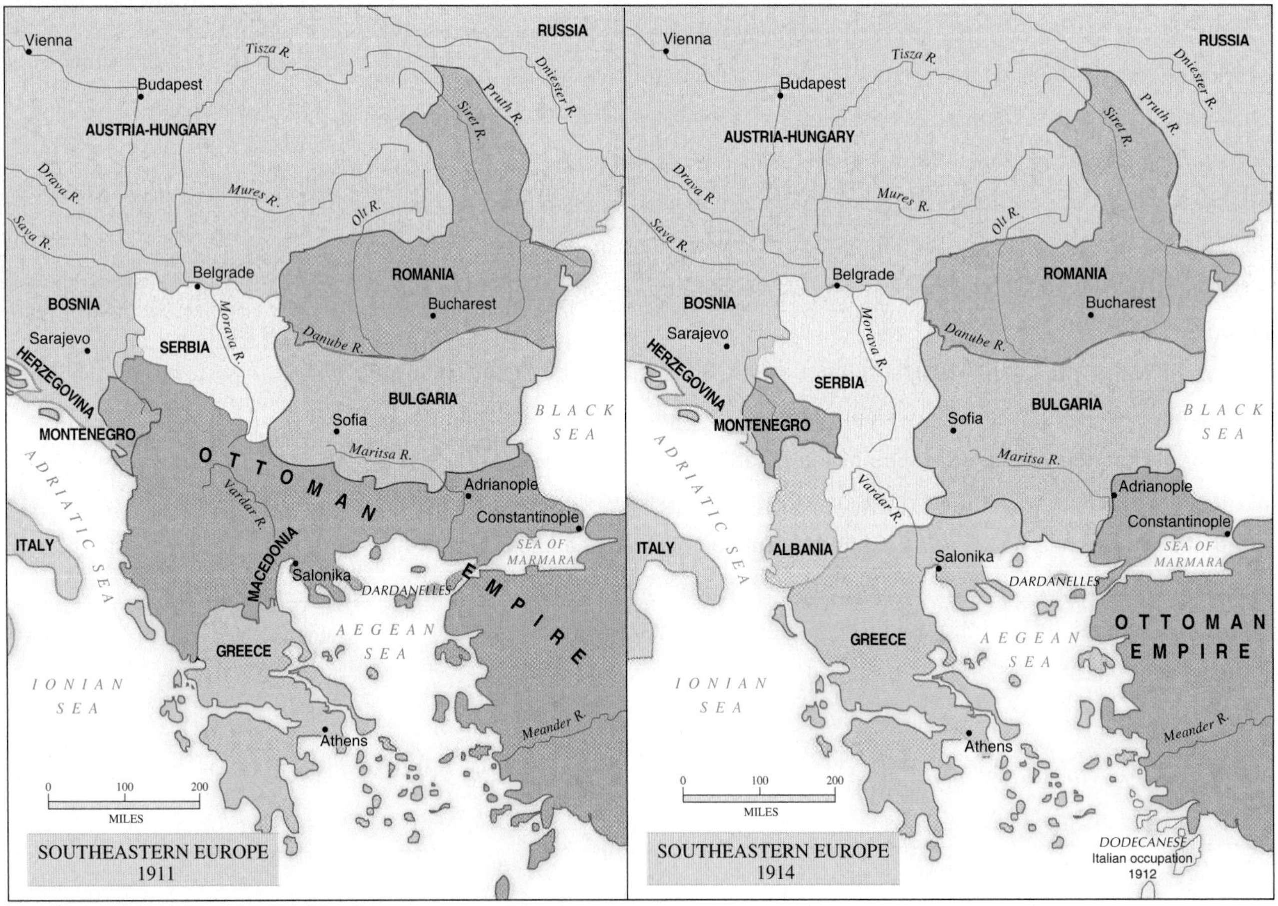

At the end of the nineteenth century (as well as the twentieth), the Balkans were a cauldron of conflicting national memories and ambitions. In the second decade of the twentieth century the Balkans mirrored the weakening of the Austro-Hungarian and Russian Empires.

war with Japan and the Revolution of 1905. Aside from making threatening noises, they could do little to block the annexation, especially in the face of Germany's support for Austria-Hungary.

After 1908, tensions remained high in the Balkans. The Austrians looked to increase their advantage, knowing they had the full backing of Germany. Serbia searched for revenge, while Russia found itself backed into a corner. After the failure of Izvolskii's efforts, the Russians had to support their Balkan allies or lose their influence.

In 1912 Serbia and its neighbors, including Greece and Bulgaria, formed an alliance with the objective of expelling the Turks from Europe. The First Balkan War began later in the year and came to a quick end with the defeat of the Turks. Each of the Balkan allies had its own particular goals in mind in fighting the Ottomans. When the Great Powers stepped in to maintain the balance, problems arose.

Serbia had fought for a seaport on the Adriatic and thought it had gained one with the defeat of the Turks. However, the Italians and Austrians blocked Serbia's access to the sea by overseeing the creation of Albania in the Treaty of London of 1913. Denied their goals, the Serbs turned on their former allies, the Bulgarians, and demanded a part of their spoils from the first war. Bulgaria refused and, emboldened by its successes in the first war, attacked its former allies, starting the Second Balkan War. The Serbs were in turn joined by the Romanians and the Turks. The Bulgarians were no match for the rest of the Balkans and signed a peace that turned over most of the territory that they had earlier gained. The Turks retained only a precarious toehold in Europe, the small pocket from Adrianople to Constantinople.

Had the Great Powers found a way to place a fence around the Balkans and allow the squabbling nations to work out their differences in isolation, the two Balkan wars of 1912 and 1913 would have had little significance. As it was, however, the combative Balkan nations added to the prevailing state of tension between the two competing alliances, whose policies clashed because of their conflicting choices of allies in the Balkans. In effect, the tail wagged the dog, as the alliances reacted to every flare-up in the turbulent peninsula.

Assassination at Sarajevo

By the end of 1913, no permanent solution had been found to the Balkans' problems. Austria was more fearful than ever of Serbia's expansionist desires. Serbian ambitions had grown along with its territory, which had doubled as a result of the recent wars. The Serbian prime minister declared himself satisfied with his gains, and looked forward to a direct challenge of Austria.

The spark that set off World War I was struck on June 28, 1914 with the assassination of the heir to the Austrian throne, Archduke Francis Ferdinand. The archduke and his wife were visiting the town of Sarajevo (SAHR-ah-YAY-voh) in Bosnia, which his realm had recently annexed. While they were driving through the narrow streets in their huge touring car, a 19-year-old Bosnian student named Gavrilo Princip (PRIN-chip), one of seven young terrorists along the route, shot them. Princip had been inspired by propaganda advocating the creation of a greater Serbia and was assisted by Serbian officers serving in a secret organization, the Black Hand. The direct participation of the Serbian government was never proved; even so, the Belgrade authorities were likely to have been involved, at least indirectly.

DOCUMENT
The Murder of Archduke Franz Ferdinand

An illustration from Le Journal de Paris *depicting the Serbian terrorist Gavrilo Princip assassinating Archduke Francis Ferdinand and his wife, Sophie, in Sarajevo on June 28, 1914.*

Threatening the generally held views of inevitable progress at the beginning of the twentieth century were the unanswered Eastern Question in the Balkans and the lingering conflicts over dividing up the prize of North Africa.

The legal details of the case were lost in Vienna's rush to put an end to the problem of Serbia. Count Leopold von Berchtold (BERK-told), the foreign minister, believed that the assassination in Bosnia justified crushing the anti-Austrian propaganda and terrorism coming from the Serbs. The kaiser felt that everything possible must be done to prevent Germany's only reliable ally from being weakened, and he assured the Austrians of his full support. Berchtold received a "blank check" from Germany. Vienna wanted a quick, local Austro-Serbian war, and Germany favored quick action to forestall Russian intervention.

On July 23 the Austro-Hungarian foreign ministry presented an ultimatum to the Serbs. Expecting the list of demands to be turned down, Berchtold insisted on unconditional acceptance within 48 hours. Two days later, the Austro-Hungarian government announced that Serbia's reply, though conciliatory, was not satisfactory. The Austrians immediately mobilized their armed forces.

The Alliances' Inevitable War

The Germans began having second thoughts and urged their ally in late July to negotiate with Russia—which was anxiously following developments. Russia realized that if the Austrians succeeded in humbling the Serbs, Russia's position in the Balkans would suffer irreparably. The French, in the meantime, assured the Russians of their full cooperation and urged full support for Serbia. The British unsuccessfully advised negotiation.

Europe had reached a point of no return: The Austrians had committed themselves to the task of removing an opponent, and the Russians could not permit this removal to happen. Neither side would back down, and each had allies ready to come to its aid. Fearful that Serbia would escape from his clutches, Berchtold succeeded on July 27—in part through deception—in convincing the Habsburg emperor Franz Josef (frahnz YOH-sef) that war was the only way out. The next day, the Austro-Hungarian Empire declared war against Serbia.

As the possibility of a general European war loomed, Berlin sent several frantic telegrams to Vienna. The German ambassador was instructed to tell Berchtold that "as an ally we must refuse to be drawn into a world conflagration because Austria does not respect our advice."[1] Had the Germans spoken to their ally in such tones a month earlier, war might have been avoided. But Austria's belligerence moved the Russians to act. The tsar ordered mobilization on July 30, 1914.

Germany was caught in a dilemma that Bismarck would never have allowed. Surrounded by potential enemies, the Germans had to move decisively or face defeat. The Russian mobilization threatened them, because in the event of war on the eastern front, by treaty, there would also be war on the western front. The best plan for Berlin, one that had been worked out since the beginning of the century by the Chief of the General Staff Alfred von Schlieffen (vun SCHLEEF-en), was to launch a lightning attack against France, which could mobilize faster than Russia, crush France, and then return to meet Russia, which would be slower to mobilize. To allow Russian mobilization to proceed without action would jeopardize this plan.

The Germans set into effect their long-planned strategy to gain European dominance on July 31. They sent ultimatums to St. Petersburg and Paris insisting that the Russians stop their mobilization and demanding a pledge of neutrality from the French. Failing to receive satisfactory replies, Germany declared war on Russia on August 1 and on France two days later. On August 2 the German ambassador in Brussels delivered an ultimatum to the Belgian government announcing his country's intention to send troops through Belgium, in violation of the 1839 treaty guaranteeing Belgian neutrality. The Belgian cabinet refused to grant permission and appealed to the Triple Entente for help.

A majority of the British cabinet did not want war, but with the news of the German ultimatum to Belgium, the tide turned. Sir Edward Grey, the British foreign secretary, sent an ultimatum to Germany demanding that Belgian neutrality be respected. Germany refused, and on August 4 Great Britain declared war.

Because Germany and Austria-Hungary were not waging a defensive war, Italy declined to carry out its obligations under the Triple Alliance and for a time remained neutral. In late August Japan joined the allies. Turkey, fearing Russia, threw in its lot with the Central Powers—which, by the end of 1914, consisted of Germany, Austria-Hungary, Bulgaria, and Turkey.

Diplomats tried desperately to avert a general war. Through confusion, fear, and loss of sleep, the nervous strain among them was almost unbearable. Many broke down and wept when it became apparent they had failed. Grey himself noted in his autobiography that one evening, just before the outbreak of the war, he watched the streetlights being lit from his office window and remarked: "The lamps are going out all over Europe; we shall not see them lit again in our lifetime."[2]

Total War

Although the terrible struggle that racked the world from 1914 to 1918 was fought mainly in Europe, it is rightly called World War I. In the seventeenth and eighteenth centuries, European powers had competed across the globe; however, never had so many fighters and such enormous resources been brought together in a single conflict. Altogether, 27 nations became belligerents, ranging the globe from Japan to Canada and from Argentina to South Africa to Australia.

The Central Powers mobilized 21 million men. The Allies eventually called 40 million men to arms, including 12 million Russians. The two sides were more equally matched than the numbers would indicate, however. Since the Russian divisions were often poorly equipped and ineffectively used, the Allies' apparent advantage was not great. In addition, in the German army, the Central Powers boasted superb generalship and discipline. Another advantage was that the Central Powers fought from a central position and were able to transfer troops quickly and efficiently to various fronts.

The Allies had the advantages of greater resources of finance and raw materials. Britain maintained its naval dominance and could draw on its empire for support. In addition, because Germany was effectively blockaded, the United States, even though officially neutral for most of the war, served as a major source of supplies for the Allies.

The warring nations went into battle in a confident mood. Each side was sure of its strength and felt it had prepared carefully. Each nation's propaganda machine delivered reassuring messages of guaranteed victory. All expected that the war would soon be over—probably by Christmas—and concluded in a few decisive battles. They based their thinking on precedent—but they chose the wrong precedent. They assumed that the next war would be in the model of the efficient Bismarckian wars of the 1860s. Instead, the war came to resemble that of the bloody, four-year-long American Civil War, the first industrialized war.

The First Two Years of War

All of the general staffs had been refining their war plans for years. The Germans knew that Allied naval supremacy would cut them off from needed sources abroad. They realized that they were potentially surrounded and that, according to the Schlieffen Plan, they should strike a quick knockout blow to end the war. They aimed to push the Belgians aside and drive rapidly south into France. The plan then called for the German forces to wheel west of Paris, outflank the French forces, and drive them toward Alsace-Lorraine, where they would be met by another German army. Within six weeks the French would be destroyed, caught between the western hammer and the eastern anvil. Meanwhile, a small German force would be holding the presumably

These German soldiers, shown here huddled in their trench along the western front, try to find a moment of rest during a lull in the war of attrition.

slow-moving Russians on the eastern front, awaiting the arrival, via the excellent German rail system, of the victorious western forces. The plan nearly worked.

The Germans marched according to the plan until they got so close to Paris that they could see the top of the Eiffel Tower. They were hurled back by a bold French offensive through a gap that opened between their armies in the first Battle of the Marne, fought between September 5 and 12. With the assistance of a small British expeditionary force and Parisian taxi drivers who provided transportation, the French then marched north in a race with the Germans to reach and control the vital ports along the English Channel. After much desperate fighting, the enemies established battle positions that stabilized, thus creating the western front, a solid line of opposing trenches that stretched from the Channel to near the Swiss border.

Pilots of the first generation of fighter aircraft in World War I made good use of their maneuverability and fire power, as seen in this dog fight over the Western Front.

For the next four years this line of trenches would be the scene of a grisly **war of attrition,** as the Allies and the Central Powers launched desperate attacks, hoping to gain the decisive "breakthrough" victory that would end the war. The struggle was made all the more bloody by powerful artillery such as the German's gigantic "Big Bertha," more deadly machine guns, silent and devastating clouds of poison gas, and two new weapons: the tank and the airplane. Single battles along that line of death killed more soldiers than those lost by the North and the South combined during the four years of the American Civil War.

The other part of the German scheme that did not go according to plan was the unexpected speed with which the Russians mobilized. They penetrated deeply into East Prussia and overran the Austrian province of Galicia. However, confused leadership resulted in two catastrophic Russian defeats in East Prussia, and Germany never again during the war faced a serious threat on its eastern frontier.

By the end of 1914 all sides knew that they were trapped in a new type of war, one of horrible consequences. Single battles claimed hundreds of thousands of lives, and the toll during the first few months of the conflict ran as high as 1.5 million dead and wounded.

---

war of attrition—A war in which there are no decisive, conclusive battles. Rather, the two sides grind away at each other until one side is exhausted and gives up.

In 1915 the British attempted a major campaign to force open the Dardanelles, closed by Turkey when it joined the Central Powers. This plan, attributed to Winston Churchill, then first lord of the admiralty, was designed to open up the sea route to Russia, which was badly in need of war supplies, and to take the pressure off the western front. After heroic and costly attacks, Allied Australian and New Zealand troops, known as Anzacs, were forced to withdraw from their landing positions on the Gallipoli (ga-LIP-po-lee) peninsula in European Turkey.

Another major Allied setback in 1915 was the defeat of the Russian forces in Poland. More than 1.2 million Russians were killed and wounded, and the Germans took nearly 900,000 prisoners. Although Russia somehow remained in the war and fought well against the Dual Monarchy, it was no longer a concern for the Germans. These defeats generated rising criticism against the tsar's government, and Russian morale deteriorated.

Serbia was the next Central Powers' victim. In September 1915 Bulgaria, still aching from its defeat in the Second Balkan War, entered the war on the side of the Central Powers. Surrounded by enemies, Serbia was helpless, and resistance was quickly crushed. The Austrians had finally gained their goal of the previous summer, but in the context of the continental tragedy, this achievement no longer seemed significant.

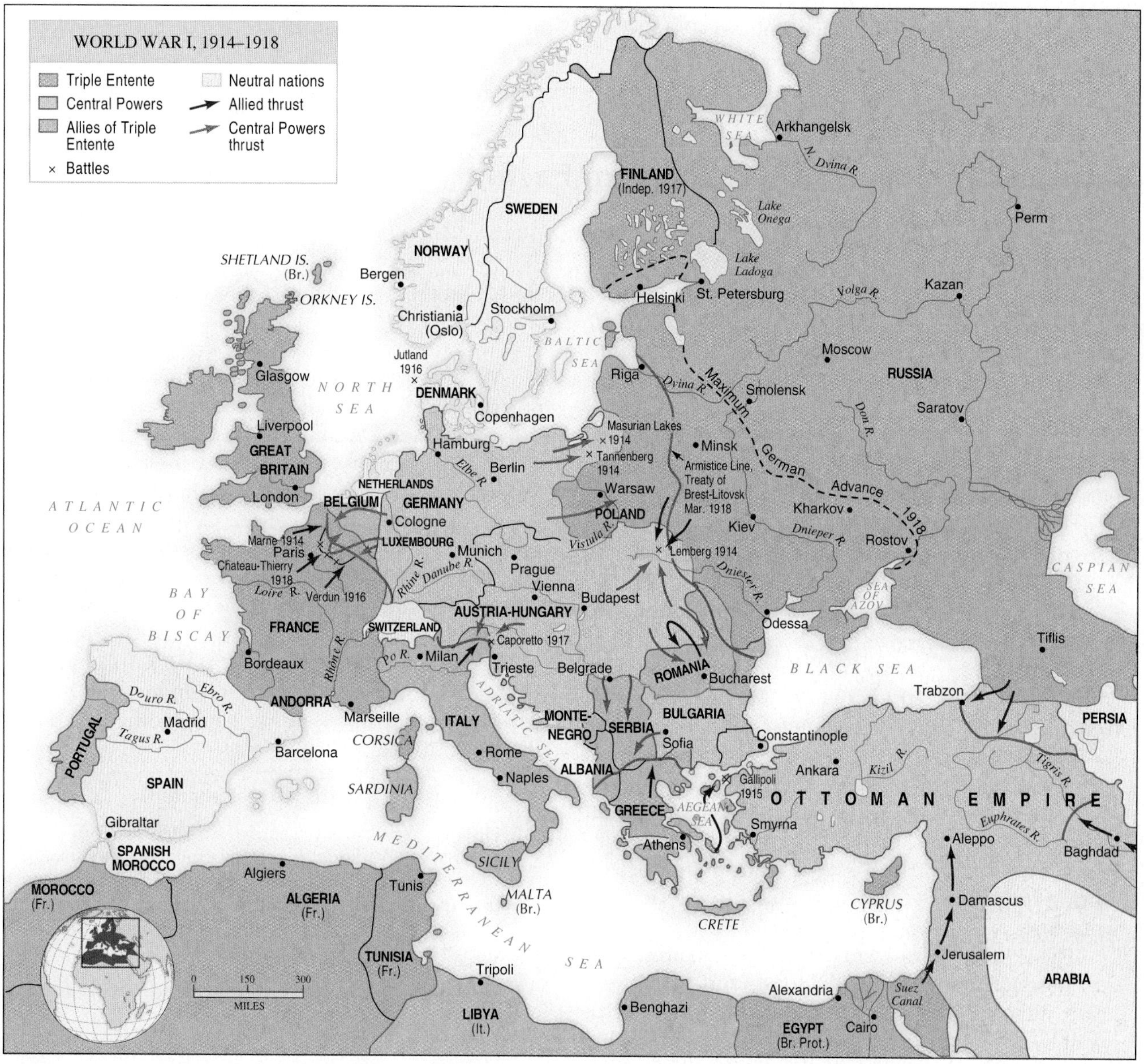

The contrast between the fixed boundary between the Allies and the Central Powers, marked by trenches on the west, and the fluid lines of the eastern front are evident from this map. As much as the Central Powers were blockaded by British control of the North Sea, so too were the Russians blocked by Turkish control of the Dardanelles and the Bosporus and the Germans' control of the Baltic.

The Allies' only bright spot in 1915 was Italy's entry into their ranks. Italy had remained neutral in August 1914 when it had defected from the Triple Alliance, of which it had been at best a token member. Italy joined the Allies following promises made in a secret treaty in London that promised the Italians huge concessions of territory once victory had been attained.

Stalemate

The Allies' strategy on the western front was to restrict attacks to a few concentrated assaults in France, thus saving manpower and at the same time concentrating on their naval blockade. Denied badly needed imports, strategists assumed, the German war effort would be seriously weakened. Countering this tactic, the German high command under General Falkenhayn (FALK-en-hine) launched a massive offensive against the strategic fortress of Verdun (vair-DUN) in February 1916.

After their defeat in 1871 (see Chapter 26), the French had transformed Verdun into a network of 20 forts with powerful artillery, of which the fort of Douaumont (doo-OH-mon) was the most important. Verdun had repulsed the Central Powers' attack in 1914, but the Germans pulled back about 10 miles and set up lines of observation posts and logistical support. So sure were the French of the invincibility of this position that they moved some of their artillery and soldiers to other sites deemed more important. Falkenhayn began in the late autumn of 1915 to build up his strength opposite Verdun, and, night after night, trains arrived loaded with men and matériel. Bad weather forced the Germans to delay their attack, but finally at 7:15 on the morning of February 21, more than 1000 German cannons along a

Document — Diary of Private Tom Easton

British enlisted man Tom Easton recorded the horrors of the battle of the Somme in gripping detail.

A beautiful summer morning, though we'd had a bit of rain earlier. The skylarks were just singing away. Then the grand mine went up, it shook the earth for nearly a minute, and we had to wait for the fallout. The whistles blew and we stepped off one yard apart going straight forward. We were under orders not to stop or look or help the wounded. Carry on if you're fit, it was.

Men began to fall one by one. One officer said we were OK, all the machine-guns were firing over our heads. This was so until we passed our own front line and started to cross No Man's Land. Then trench machine-guns began the slaughter from the La Boiselle salient [German positions]. Men fell on every side screaming. Those who were unwounded dare not attend to them, we must press on regardless. Hundreds lay on the German barbed wire which was not all destroyed and their bodies formed a bridge for others to pass over and into the German front line.

There were few Germans, mainly in machine-gun posts. These were bombed out, and there were fewer still of us, but we consolidated the lines we had taken by preparing firing positions on the rear of the trenches gained, and fighting went on all morning and gradually died down as men and munitions on both sides became exhausted.

When we got to the German trenches we'd lost all our officers. They were all dead, there was no question of wounded. About 25 of us made it there.

Yes, as we made our way over the latter stages of the charge, men dropped all around like ninepins. Apart from machine-guns, the German artillery was also very active, great sheets of earth rose up before one. Every man had to fend for himself as we still had to face the Germans in their trenches when we got there.

I kept shouting for my MOTHER to guide me, strange as it may seem. Mother help me. Not the Virgin Mother but my own maternal Mother, for I was then only 20 years of age.

Questions to Consider

1. How do the combat memories of Private Tom Easton compare with images of war that you have seen in films? Name a movie you have seen that gives an impression of battle similar to that described above and a movie that shows the "glory" of combat.
2. What was "No Man's Land?"
3. How does this passage illustrate the tragedies of trench warfare?

6-mile front fired the first of thousands of shells that descended on Verdun in a bombardment that lasted ten hours. Then the German infantry advanced, equipped with flamethrowers.

The battered and outnumbered French forces fought back bravely and, despite losing some fortified positions, denied the Germans the rapid victory they had desired. This stout resistance gave the Allies time to throw hundreds of thousands of men into the battle, which would rage into the summer and fall. Falkenhayn, who had gambled all on a quick victory, was replaced by Generals Hindenburg and Ludendorff, who decided to abandon the attack on Verdun. The French reclaimed the forts they had lost by the end of the year. The slaughter brought on by massed artillery and infantry charges between the trenches was horrible. The total loss in the battle of Verdun came to 700,000 men.

To ease the pressure against Verdun, the British army on July 1 began an offensive along the Somme River along the western front. Despite their having fired 2 million shells, the attackers' losses on the first day of the battle were catastrophic: 60 percent of the officers and 40 percent of the soldiers—60,000 men in all. Despite these awesome figures, the attacks—with the British making the first use of tanks in August—continued for three months without any substantial gains. General Haig, stymied by the tenacious German resistance, decided to stop the offensive in November. Total German casualties at the Somme were about 550,000, while the British and French lost about 650,000—a staggering 1.2 million men dead or wounded.

1916 Debut of the British Tank

The only major naval engagement of the war, the battle of Jutland (May 31–June 1, 1916), reaffirmed British control of the seas. Taking enormous risks, the Germans maneuvered brilliantly. They could afford to gamble because defeat would in no way worsen their position. The British fleet, however, had to act cautiously and absorbed greater losses. Nevertheless, the Germans finally retreated to their base and remained there for the rest of the war. Only in their submarine warfare did the Germans enjoy success on the high seas during the war.

On the eastern front in 1916 the Russians continued their generally successful campaigns against the Austro-Hungarian forces. But the Germans were always there to save their allies from destruction. Romania, impressed by the Russian victories, finally joined the Allies and launched an attack on the Austrians. After an initial success, the Romanians were soon knocked out of the war by a joint German-Bulgarian invasion.

The Home Front

At the end of 1916, after more than two years of fighting, neither side was close to victory. Instead, the war had turned into a dreary contest of each side trying to bleed the other into submission—a far cry from the glories promised by the propaganda of 1914. War was no longer fought between armies; it was fought between states, and every citizen and office of the state participated.

On the home front, **rationing** was instituted to ensure sufficient supplies for soldiers at the front. As men went off to fight, women took over their jobs in the workplace. Intensive **propaganda** campaigns encouraged civilians to buy more bonds and make more weapons. Nations unleashed a barrage of propaganda inciting total hatred of the enemy, belief in the righteousness of the cause, and unquestioned support for the war effort.

Civil liberties suffered, and in some cases, distinguished citizens were thrown into prison for opposing the war effort. In Britain, for example, the philosopher and mathematician Bertrand Russell was imprisoned for a short time for his pacifistic views. Governments took over control of their national economies and gambled everything on a victory in which the loser would pay all the expenses incurred in the war. The various states outlawed strikes and rigidly controlled currencies and foreign trade.

At the beginning of the war, all was flag waving and enthusiasm. Even the international socialist movement, whose policy it was to promote international proletarian unity, fell victim to the rabid patriotism that infected the Continent. Workers of one country were encouraged to go out and kill workers of the enemy country in the name of the state. There was great idealism, sense of sacrifice, and love of country. At first there was no understanding of the horror, death, and disaster that comes with modern, industrialized war. The British poet Rupert Brooke caught the spirit in his poem "The Soldier":

If I should die, think only this of me:
That there's some corner of a foreign field
That is forever England. There shall be
In that rich earth a richer dust concealed;
A dust whom England bore, shaped, made aware,
Gave, once, her flowers to love, her ways to roam,
A body of England's breathing English air,
Washed by the rivers, blest by suns of home.[3]

But this early idealism, this Romantic conception of death in battle, gradually changed to one of war

---

rationing—A process instituted to control the distribution of resources such as food, clothing, gasoline, sugar, etc. to ensure a sufficient supply during a time of shortage or great need.

propaganda—Publicly disseminated information that has been manipulated to further one's own cause and to damage that of one's opponent.

As the men marched off to war, women left their homes to work in war-related industries. These women are working in a British munitions factory.

weariness and total futility. This growing mood is best seen in the poetry of the young British officer and poet Wilfred Owen, himself a victim on the western front:

What passing-bells for those who die as cattle?
Only the monstrous anger of the guns. . . .
No mockeries for them; no prayers nor bells,
Nor any voice of mourning save the choirs, —
The shrill, demented choirs of wailing shells;
And bugles calling for them from sad shires.[4]

By the end of 1916 a deep yearning for peace dominated Europe. Sensing this mood, leaders on both sides put forth peace feelers. But these halfhearted overtures achieved nothing. Propaganda was used effectively to continue the war and support for it. The populations of the warring states were made to believe that their crusade was somehow divinely inspired. In reality, the Dual Monarchy and France fought for survival; Russia, Germany, and Italy all fought to improve their respective positions in Europe; while Britain fought to save Belgium and a renewed balance of power on the Continent.

Allied Fatigue and American Entry

In 1917 British and French military strength reached its highest point, only to fall precipitously. Allied commanders were hopeful that the long-planned breakthrough might be accomplished, but a large-scale French attack was beaten back, with huge losses. Some French regiments mutinied rather than return to the inferno of "no-man's land" between the trenches. The British sacrificed hundreds of thousands of men without any decisive results in several massive offensives. The Allies also launched unsuccessful campaigns in Italy. Aided by the Germans, the Austrians smashed the Italian front at the Battle of Caporetto (1917), an event vividly described by Ernest Hemingway in *A Farewell to Arms.* Italian resistance finally hardened, and collapse was barely averted.

DOCUMENT

Owen, "Dulce et Decorum Est"

The growing effectiveness of the German submarine menace deepened Allied frustration. By 1917 Allied shipping losses had reached dangerous proportions. In three months 470 British ships fell victim to torpedoes. Britain had no more than six weeks' stores of food on hand, and the supply situation became critical for the Allies. As it turned out, the very weapon that seemed to doom their cause, the submarine, was the source of the Allies' salvation: Germany's decision to use unrestricted submarine warfare brought the United States openly into the war.

The Americans had declared their neutrality in 1914 when President Woodrow Wilson announced that the American people "must be impartial in thought as well as in action." The events of the next

Steps Toward American Entry into World War I

1914	President Wilson proclaims neutrality "in thought and action"; British blockade Germany—including cable
1914–1917	Allied war bond drive
1915	German submarine sinks *Lusitania*
1916	Wilson reelected under slogan "He kept us out of war"
1916–1917	Increased German submarine activity, plots with Mexico
1917	Wilson asks Congress to declare war on Germany (April 6)

two years showed that this would not be the case. American sentiment was overwhelmingly with the Allies from the first. France's help to the colonies in the American Revolution was warmly recalled. Britain and America were closely tied by language, literature, and democratic institutions. Because Britain cut off communications between Germany and the United States, British propaganda and management of the war news dominated U.S. public opinion. Another factor predisposing the United States to the Allied cause was Germany's violation of international law in the invasion of Belgium. This buttressed the widely held view created by the kaiser's saber-rattling speeches that the Germans were undemocratic, unpredictable, and unstable.

These attitudes were reinforced by the fact that the United States had made a substantial investment in the Allied war effort. As the war progressed, it became apparent that the British blockade would permit American trade to be carried on only with the Allies. Before long American factories and farmers were producing weapons and food solely for Great Britain and France. Industry expanded and began to enjoy a prosperity dependent on continued Allied purchases. Between 1914 and 1916 American exports to the Allies quadrupled. Allied bonds totaling about $1.5 billion were sold in the United States in 1915 and 1916. It was quite apparent to the Germans that there was little neutrality on the economic front in the United States.

What triggered the U.S. entry into the war on the Allied side was the German submarine tactics. Blockaded by the British, Germany decided to retaliate by halting all shipping to the Allies. Its submarine campaign began in February 1915, and one of the first victims was the luxury liner *Lusitania,* torpedoed with the loss of more than 1000 lives, including 100 Americans. This tragedy aroused public opinion in the United States. In the fall of 1916, Wilson, campaigning with the slogan "He kept us out of war," was reelected to the presidency. Discovery of German plots to involve Mexico in the war against the United States and more submarine sinkings finally drove Wilson to ask Congress to declare war against Germany on April 6, 1917.

Submarine warfare and a wide range of other causes brought the president to the point of entering the war. Once in the conflict, however, he was intent on making the American sacrifice one "to make the world safe for democracy." Wilson's lofty principles caused a great surge of idealism among Americans.

Germany's Last Drive

The United States mobilized its tremendous resources of men and matériel more rapidly than the Germans had believed possible when they made their calculated risk to increase submarine warfare. Nonetheless, the Central Powers moved to try to gain a decisive victory before U.S. aid could help the Allies.

MAP
Europe at War: World War I, 1914–1919

The fruitless offensives of 1917 had exhausted the British army, and the French had barely recovered from their mutinies. The eastern front collapsed with the February–March revolution in Russia. Eight months later, Lenin and the Bolsheviks took power in Russia and began to negotiate for peace. By the Treaty of Brest-Litovsk early in 1918, Russia made peace with Germany, giving up 1.3 million square miles of territory and 62 million people.

Freed from the necessity of fighting on the east, the Germans unleashed a series of major offensives against the west in the spring of 1918. During one of these attacks, a brigade of American marines symbolized the importance of U.S. support when they stopped a German charge at Château-Thierry (shah-TOH teeah-REE). The Germans made a final effort to knock out the French in July 1918. It was called the *Friedensturm* (FREED-en-sturm), the peace offensive. The Germans made substantial gains but did not score a decisive breakthrough. By this time the German momentum was slowing down, and more than a million American "doughboys" had landed in France. The final German offensive was thrown back after a slight advance.

With the aid of U.S. troops, Marshal Ferdinand Foch (FOSH), the supreme Allied commander, began a counterattack. The badly beaten and continually harassed German troops fell back in rapid retreat. By the end of October, German forces had been driven out of France and Allied armies were advancing into Belgium. The war of fixed positions separated by no-man's land was over. The Allies had smashed the trench defenses and were now in open country.

By October 1 the German high command had already urged the kaiser to sue for peace, and three days later, the German chancellor sent a note to President Wilson seeking an end to hostilities. Wilson responded that peace was not possible as long as Germany was ruled by an autocratic regime. The German chancellor tried to keep the monarchy by instituting certain liberal reforms, but it was too late. Revolution broke out in many parts of Germany. The kaiser abdicated and fled to the Netherlands, and a republic was proclaimed.

While Germany was staggering under the continual pounding of Foch's armies, the German allies were suffering even greater misfortunes. Bulgaria surrendered on September 30, and Turkey a month later. Austria stopped its fighting with Italy on November 3. Nine days later, the Habsburg Empire collapsed when Emperor Charles I fled Vienna to seek sanctuary in Switzerland.

At five o'clock on the morning of November 11, 1918, in a railroad dining car in the Compiègne (kom-PIEN) Forest, the German delegates signed the peace terms presented by Marshal Foch. At eleven o'clock the same day, hostilities were halted. Everywhere except in Germany, the news was received with an outburst of joy. The world was once more at peace, confronted now with the task of binding up its wounds and removing the scars of combat. Delegates from the Allied nations were soon to meet in Paris, where the peace conference would be held.

THE ALLIED PEACE SETTLEMENT

■ *Why was it so much more difficult for the victorious Allies to guarantee a long period of peace than the leaders meeting a century earlier at the Congress of Vienna?*

In November 1918 the Allies stood triumphant, after the costliest war in history. But the Germans could also feel pleased at that moment. They had fought well, avoided being overrun, and escaped being occupied by the Allies. They could acknowledge they had lost the war but hoped that President Wilson would help them.

In February 1918 Wilson had stated that his governing principles would be that there would be no victimization of the defeated and that settlements would have to be approved by the people affected. As events transpired, however, the losers were refused seats at the peace conference. The leaders of the new German Weimar (VI-mar) Republic had no choice but to sign a dictated settlement—an act that simultaneously discredited the republic among the German people and served as the first step toward World War II.

Idealism and Realities

The destructiveness of World War I made a fair peace settlement impossible. The war had been fought on a winner-take-all basis, and now it was time for the Central Powers to pay. At the peace conference the winning side was dominated by a French realist, a British politician, and an American idealist. The French representative was the aged Premier Georges Clemenceau (KLEM-on-soh); representing Britain was the Prime Minister David Lloyd George; and the U.S. representative was President Woodrow Wilson. The three were joined by the Italian prime minister, Vittorio Orlando, who attended to make sure his country gained adequate compensation for its large sacrifices. These four men made most of the key decisions, even though most

The "Big Four" at the Versailles Peace Conference were, left to right, Prime Minister David Lloyd George of Britain, Prime Minister Vittorio Orlando of Italy, Premier Georges Clemenceau of France, and President Woodrow Wilson of the United States. Representatives from Germany were excluded from the negotiating tables. The Big Four became the Big Three when Orlando withdrew abruptly because the conference refused to give Italy all it demanded.

of the interested nations and factions in the world were represented in Paris, except for the Russians.

Clemenceau had played a colorful and important role in French politics for half a century. He had fought continuously for his political beliefs, opposing corruption, racism, and antidemocratic forces. He wanted to ensure French security in the future by pursuing restitution, reparations, and guarantees. Precise programs, not idealistic statements, would protect France.

The two English-speaking members of the Big Three represented the extremes in dealing with the Germans. Lloyd George had been reelected in December on a program of "squeezing the German lemon until the pips are squeaked." He wanted to destroy Berlin's naval, commercial, and colonial position and to ensure his own political future at home. In January 1918 President Wilson had given Congress a list known as the **Fourteen Points,** describing his plan for peace. Wilson wanted to break the world out of its tradition of armed anarchy and establish a framework for peace that would favor America's traditions of democracy and trade. At the peace conference this shy and sensitive man communicated his beliefs with a coldness and an imperiousness that offended his colleagues.

The Great War had not been a "war to end all wars" or a war "to make the world safe for democracy." The United States had hardly been neutral in its loans and shipments of supplies to the Allies before 1917. In

Fourteen Points—President Woodrow Wilson's program to establish and maintain peace after World War I.

Document John Maynard Keynes on Clemenceau

The British economist John Maynard Keynes served as a staff member of the British delegation negotiating in Paris at the end of the First World War. He caught the spirit of the peacemakers at Versailles in *The Economic Consequences of the Peace.* His portrait of Clemenceau is especially revealing.

He felt about France what Pericles felt of Athens—unique value in her, nothing else mattering; but his theory of politics was Bismarck's. He had one illusion—France; and one disillusion—mankind, including Frenchmen, and his colleagues not least. His principles for the peace can be expressed simply. In the first place, he was a foremost believer in the view of German psychology that the German understands and can understand nothing but intimidation, that he is without generosity or remorse in negotiation, that there is no advantage he will not take of you, and no extent to which he will not demean himself for profit, that he is without honor, pride, or mercy. Therefore you must never negotiate with a German or conciliate him; you must dictate to him. On no other terms will he respect you, or will you prevent him from cheating you. But it is doubtful how far he thought these characteristics peculiar to Germany, or whether his candid view of some other nations was fundamentally different. His philosophy had, therefore, no place for "sentimentality" in international relations. Nations are real things, of whom you love one and feel for the rest indifference—or hatred. The glory of the nation you love is a desirable end—but generally to be obtained at your neighbor's expense. The politics of power are inevitable, and there is nothing very new to learn about this war or the end it was fought for; England had destroyed, as in each preceding century, a trade rival; a mighty chapter had been closed in the secular struggle between the glories of Germany and of France.

Prudence required some measure of lip service to the "ideals" of foolish Americans and hypocritical Englishmen; but it would be stupid to believe that there is much room in the world, as it really is, for such affairs as the League of Nations, or any sense in the principle of self-determination except as an ingenious formula for rearranging the balance of power in one's own interest.

Questions to Consider

1. Do you find the description of Clemenceau to be favorable or critical? How do you feel about Clemenceau's views of the Germans, as reported by Keynes?
2. Do you find Clemenceau, and his views of the nation as reported by Keynes, to be an example of Realpolitik as practiced by Bismarck? Explain your answer.
3. What do you believe Clemenceau's views of President Woodrow Wilson and the League of Nations were?

From John Maynard Keynes, *The Economic Consequences of the Peace* (New York: Harcourt, Brace, 1920).

fact, during the war the financial and political center of balance for the world had crossed the ocean. The Americans made a rather abrupt shift from debtor to creditor status. The United States had entered the war late and had profited from it, and Wilson could afford to wear a rather more idealistic mantle.

The Europeans had paid for the war with the blood of their young and the coin of their realms. The Allies now looked forward to a healthy return on their investment. The extent of that harvest had long been mapped out in secret treaties, copies of which the Bolsheviks released for the world to see.

Open Covenants, Secret Treaties

Wilson wanted to use his Fourteen Points as the basis for a lasting peace. He wanted to place morality and justice ahead of power and revenge as considerations in international affairs. The first five points were general and guaranteed "open covenants openly arrived at," freedom of the seas in war and peace alike, removal of all economic barriers and establishment of an equality of trade among all nations, reductions in national armaments, and readjustment of all colonial claims, giving the interests of the population concerned equal weight with the claim of the government whose title was to be determined. The next eight points dealt with specific issues involving the evacuation and restoration of Allied territory, self-determination for minority nationalities, and the redrawing of European boundaries along national lines.

The fourteenth point contained the germ of the **League of Nations,** a general association of all nations whose purpose was to guarantee political independence and territorial integrity to great and small states alike. When Wilson arrived in Europe, the crowds on the streets and the victorious and the defeated nations alike greeted him as a messiah. His program had received great publicity, and its general, optimistic nature had earned him great praise.

The victorious Allies came to Paris to gain the concrete rewards promised them in the various secret treaties. Under these pacts, which would not come to public knowledge until the beginning of 1919, the Allies had promised the Italians concessions that would turn the Adriatic into an Italian sea, the Russians the right to take over the Bosporus and Dardanelles Straits and Constantinople, the Romanians the right to take over large amounts of Austro-Hungarian territory, and the Japanese the right to keep the German territory of Kiaochow in China. In addition, the British and French divided what was formerly Ottoman-controlled Iraq and Syria into their respective spheres of influence. As for Palestine, on November 2, 1917, the British—with the agreement of President Wilson—in the declaration by Lord Arthur James Balfour, stated that "His Majesty's government looks favorably on the establishment of a national home for the Jewish people." Lord Balfour went on to affirm that nothing would be done that would "prejudice the civil and religious rights" of the non-Jewish communities in Palestine.

League of Nations—International peacekeeping and humanitarian organization created in 1919 at the Paris peace conferences.

Wilson refused to consider these agreements, which many of the victors regarded as IOUs now due to be paid in return for their role in the war, but the contracting parties in the treaties would not easily set aside their deals to satisfy Wilson's ideals. Even before the beginning of formal talks—negotiations that would be unprecedented in their complexity—the Allies were split. Lloyd George and Clemenceau discovered early that Wilson had his price, and that was the League of Nations. They played on his desire for this organization to water down most of the 13 other points. They were also aware that Wilson's party had suffered a crushing defeat in the 1918 elections and that strong factions in the United States were drumming up opposition to his program.

The League of Nations

When the diplomats began full meetings, the first issue was the formation of the League of Nations. Wilson insisted that the first work of the conference must be to provide for such a league as part of the peace treaty. After much negotiation, the covenant was approved by the full conference in April 1919. To gain support for the League, however, Wilson compromised on other matters. Many of his Fourteen Points were repudiated, but he believed that an imperfect treaty incorporating the League was better than a perfect one without it.

The covenant of the League of Nations specified its aims: "to guarantee international cooperation and to achieve international peace and security." To achieve this goal, Article 10, the key section of the document, provided that

> *. . . the Members of the League undertake to respect and preserve against external aggression the territorial integrity and existing political independence of all Members of the League. In case of any such aggression or in case of any threat or danger of such aggression, the Council shall advise upon the means by which this obligation shall be fulfilled.*

The League of Nations was the first systematic and thorough attempt to create an organization designed to prevent war and promote peace. Though ultimately unsuccessful, it was a valiant effort to curb the abuses of the state system while maintaining the individual sovereignty of each member of the community of nations.

The League's main organs were the Council, the Assembly, and the Secretariat. Dominated by the Great Powers, the Council was the most important body. It dealt with most of the emergencies arising in international affairs. The Assembly served as a platform from which all League members could express their views. It could make recommendations to the Council on specific issues, but all-important decisions required the unanimous consent of its members, and every nation in the Assembly had one vote. Two important bodies created by the covenant of the League were the Permanent Court of International Justice (the World Court) and the International Labor Organization (ILO).

Redrawing German Boundaries

After establishing the League, the diplomats got down to the business of dealing with Germany. France reclaimed Alsace-Lorraine, and plebiscites gave parts of the former German Empire to Denmark and Belgium. The French wanted to build a buffer state, made up of former German territory west of the Rhine, to be dominated by France. The Americans and the British proposed a compromise to Clemenceau, which he accepted. The territory in question would be occupied by Allied troops for a period of 5 to 15 years, and a zone extending 30 miles east of the Rhine was to be demilitarized.

In addition, the French claimed the Saar basin, a rich coal-mining area. Although they did not take outright control of the area, which reverted to League administration, they did gain ownership of the mines in compensation for the destruction of their own installations in northern France. It was agreed that after 15 years a plebiscite would be held in the area. Finally, Wilson and Lloyd George agreed that the United States and Great Britain would, by treaty, guarantee France against aggression.

In the aftermath of World War I, Europe lost four empires—the Russian, Ottoman, Austro-Hungarian, and German—and gained a number of successor states, each unhappy with its new boundaries.

In Eastern Europe the conference created the "Polish corridor," which separated East Prussia from the rest of Germany, in order to give the newly created state of Poland access to the sea. This raised grave problems, as it included territory in which there were large numbers of Germans. (The land in question had been taken from Poland by Prussia in the eighteenth century.) A portion of Silesia, north of the new state of Czechoslovakia, was also ceded to Poland, but Danzig, a German city, was placed under League jurisdiction. All in all, Germany lost 25,000 square miles inhabited by 6 million people—a fact seized on by German nationalist leaders in the 1920s.

The Mandate System and Reparations

A curious mixture of idealism and revenge determined the allocation of the German colonies and certain territories belonging to Turkey. Because outright annexation would look too much like unvarnished imperialism, it was suggested that the colonies be turned over to the League, which in turn would give them to certain of its members to administer. The colonies were to be known as ***mandates,*** and precautions were taken to ensure that they would be administered for the wellbeing and development of the inhabitants. Once a year, the mandatory powers were to present a detailed account of their administration of the territories of the League. The mandate system was a step forward in colonial administration, but Germany nevertheless was deprived of all colonies, with the excuse that it could not rule them justly or efficiently.

As the **Treaty of Versailles** (ver-SIGH) took shape, the central concept was that Germany had been responsible for the war. Article 231 of the treaty stated explicitly:

> *The Allied and Associated Governments affirm and Germany accepts the responsibility of Germany and her allies for causing all the loss and damage to which the Allied and Associated Governments and their nationals have been subjected as a consequence of the war imposed upon them by the aggression of Germany and her Allies.*

Britain and France demanded that Germany pay the total cost of the war, including pensions. The United States protested this demand, and, eventually, a compromise emerged in which, with the exception of Belgium, Germany had to pay only war damages, including those suffered by civilians, and the cost of pensions. These payments, called ***reparations*** (implying repair), were exacted on the ground that Germany should bear responsibility for the war.

Although the Allies agreed that Germany should pay reparations, they could not agree on how much should be paid. Some demands ran as high as $200 billion. Finally, it was decided that a committee should fix the amount; in the meantime, Germany was to begin making payments. By the time the committee report appeared in May 1921, the payments totaled nearly $2 billion. The final bill came to $32.5 billion, to be paid off by Germany by 1963.

The Allies required Germany, as part of in-kind reparations payments, to hand over most of its merchant fleet, construct 1 million tons of new shipping for the Allies, and deliver vast amounts of coal, equipment, and machinery to them. The conference permitted Germany a standing army of only 100,000 men, a greatly reduced fleet, and no military aircraft. Munitions plants were to be closely supervised.

The treaty also called for the kaiser to be tried for a "supreme offense against international morality and the sanctity of treaties," thus setting a precedent for the Nuremberg tribunals after World War II. Nothing came of this demand, however. The kaiser remained in Holland, protected in his exile by the Dutch government.

Dictated Treaties

Before coming to Paris in April 1919 to receive the Treaty of Versailles, the German delegation was given no official information about its terms and thus no opportunity to debate points it found to be unjust. Allied governments stated that "Germany and its people were alone guilty." The Weimar delegation had no alternative but to sign. The continued blockade created great hardships in Germany, and the Allies threatened an invasion if the Germans did not accept the peace. The treaty was signed on June 28, the fifth anniversary of the assassination of Archduke Francis Ferdinand, in the Hall of Mirrors at Versailles, the same room where the German Empire had been proclaimed. As one American wrote, "The affair was elaborately staged and made as humiliating to the enemy as it well could be."[5]

The Mask Falls—German Cartoon Reacting to the Treaty of Versailles

The Allies imposed equally harsh treaties on Germany's supporters. The Treaty of St. Germain (1919) with Austria recognized the nationalist movements of the Czechs, Poles, and southern Slavs. These groups had already formed states and reduced the remnants of the former Dual Monarchy into the separate states

---

mandates—A grant of authority from the League of Nation to a state to set up a government and other institutions in former German colonies.

Treaty of Versailles—During the peace conferences to end World War I, the actual negotiations with the various Central Powers took place at selected suburbs around Paris.The conference dealing with Germany took place at the former residence of French kings, Versailles.

reparations—Payments demanded from Germany to pay for the costs of the war.

MAP The Division of Germany and Austria

of Austria and Hungary. Austria became a landlocked country of 32,000 square miles and 6 million people. It was forbidden to seek ***Anschluss*** (ON-schlus)—union with Germany. Italy acquired sections of Austria, South Tyrol, Trentino (with its 250,000 Austrian Germans), and the northeastern coast of the Adriatic, with its large numbers of Slavs.

To complete their control of the Adriatic, the Italians wanted a slice of the Dalmatian coast and the port of Fiume (fee-YOU-may). That city, however, was the natural port for the newly created state of Yugoslavia, and it had not been promised to the Italians in 1915. Wilson declared the Italian claim to be a contradiction of the principle of self-determination, and the ensuing controversy almost wrecked the peace conference. The issue was not settled until 1920, when Italy renounced its claim to Dalmatia and Fiume became an independent state. Four years later it was ceded to Italy.

By the Treaty of Sèvres (SEV-ruh) (1920), the Ottoman Empire was placed on the operating table of power politics and divided among Greece, Britain, and France. An upheaval in August 1920 in Constantinople led to the emergence of the Nationalists under Mustafa Kemal, who refused to accept the treaty. Not until July 1923 did Turkey's postwar status become clear in the milder Treaty of Lausanne (loo-ZAHN), which guaranteed Turkish control of Anatolia (see Chapter 30).

Hungary (Treaty of Trianon, 1920) and Bulgaria (Treaty of Neuilly, 1919) did not fare as well as Turkey in dealing with the Allies. The Hungarians lost territory to Czechoslovakia, Yugoslavia, and Romania. Bulgaria lost access to the Aegean Sea and territory populated by nearly 1 million people, had to pay a huge indemnity, and underwent demilitarization.

The eastern European states that profited from the settlements proved to be useful allies for France in the first 15 years of the interwar period. Those that suffered were easy prey for the Nazis in the 1930s.

Anschluss—Union between Austria and Germany.

Peace Treaties Ending World War I

Versailles	Germany (1919)
St. Germaine	Austria (1919)
Neuilly	Bulgaria (1919)
Sèvres	Turkey (1920 refused; Lausanne 1923)
Trianon	Hungary (1920)

Evaluating the Peacemakers

The treaties ending World War I have received heavy criticism from diplomatic historians, especially when compared with the work of the Congress of Vienna. The peace that emerged brought only weariness, new disagreements, and inflation.

Russia was completely disregarded. The new Bolshevik government (see Chapter 28), in its weak position, indicated a willingness to deal with the West on the issue of prewar debts and border conflicts, if the West would extend financial aid and withdraw its expeditionary forces. The anti-Bolshevik forces in Paris did not take the offer seriously. By missing this opportunity, the Allies took a course that had tremendous consequences for "the long-term future of both the Russian and the American people and indeed of mankind generally."[6]

Many commentators have laid the genesis of World War II just one generation later at the feet of the Paris peacemakers. Other critics point out that the United States' reversion to isolationism doomed the work of the conference. Furthermore, there were never any broad plans made for European economic recovery.

The Costs of the War

It is impossible to give a true accounting of the costs of any war because there is no way to calculate the contributions that might have been made by the individuals killed in battle. About 2 to 3 million Russians died, and more perished in the 1918–1921 civil war. Among the other major participants, almost 2 million Germans, over 1.5 million French, close to 1 million English, 500,000 Italians, 1.2 million Austro-Hungarians, and 325,000 Turks died in battle. These figures do not count the wounded, whose lives may have been shortened or altered as a result of their injuries. Furthermore, the young paid the highest price: Scholars estimate that Germany and France each lost over 15 percent of their young men.

Estimates of the financial drain of the war range between $250 billion and $300 billion in early 1920s dollars. These figures do not bring home the depth of the war's impact on trade, shipping, and monetary stability. Belgium, for example, lost over 300,000 houses and thousands of factories, and 15,000 square miles of northeastern France were in ruins. How does one calculate the cost of taking the 75 million men who were mobilized away from their jobs and their homes? How can the mental carnage inflicted on the combatants and their families be measured? No balance sheet can measure the psychological toll of the conflict on the women and children who had to bear the tension of fear and loneliness for their loved ones at the front.

Political institutions felt the effects of the war in different ways. The German, Habsburg, Russian, and Ottoman Empires crumbled and disappeared from the historical stage. Replacing them were uncertain republics or dictatorships. The colonial empires that remained were weakened, and indigenous nationalist movements made substantial progress.

The roots of the economic problems that plagued Europe after the war—agricultural overproduction, bureaucratic regulations, and protectionism—could be seen before 1914. Compounding these factors were the traditional challenges encountered in shifting from a wartime to a peacetime economy, especially that of demobilizing millions of soldiers and bringing them back into the labor market. Finally, the globe reeled under the blows of an influenza outbreak that ultimately killed twice as many people as the war did. The epidemic was both a tragic conclusion to the war years and a tragic first step toward the future.

Postwar Economic Events

1919–1923	Inflation (except in Britain and Czechoslovakia)
1922	Great Britain pledges to moderate debt collections
1923–1924	German hyperinflation
1924	Dawes Plan for liberalized reparations and loans for German recovery
1929	U.S. stock market crash (October 29)
1930–1940	Great Depression

ECONOMIC DISASTERS

■ *In what ways did the First World War destroy global economic equilibrium?*

One of the most serious problems facing the survivors of World War I was the confused and desperate situation of the world economy. Much of the direct and indirect cost of the war had been covered by borrowing, and now the bills were coming due in a world unable to pay them. The lasting results of the war touched many areas. The conflict altered global trading patterns, reduced shipping, and weakened Europe's former economic dominance. The various peace treaties multiplied the number of European boundaries, which soon became obstacles to the flow of goods, especially in the successor states of the Habsburg monarchy and in Poland. Rail and communications lines had to be reconfigured to reflect the interest of newly created states.

The Debt Problem

During the war, a radical change had taken place in Europe's economic relationship with the United States. In 1914 the United States had been a debtor nation for the amount of $3.75 billion, owed mostly to Europe. The war totally reversed this situation. The United States lent billions of dollars and sold tons of supplies to the Allies. British blockades kept the United States from being able to deal with the Germans, precluding further profits, but by 1919 Europeans owed the United States more than $10 billion. This tremendous debt posed what economists call a transfer problem. The international obligations could be paid only by the actual transfer of gold or by the sale of goods.

Complicating the picture, Allied powers in Europe had also lent each other funds, with the British acting as the chief banker, lending more than 1.7 billion pounds sterling. When the Allies' credit dried up, they turned to the United States for financial help. Even though Britain owed huge sums to U.S. financiers, it remained a net creditor of $4 billion because of money owed it by European debtors. France, by contrast, stood as a net debtor of $3.5 billion. In addition to its own war debts, the French government suffered greatly when the Bolsheviks renounced repayment of the tsarist debt, amounting to some 12 billion francs—one-quarter of France's foreign holdings.

Some of the Allies argued that the inter-Allied debts were political, that all of them had, in effect, been poured into a common pool for victory. These people wondered how France's contribution in the lives of its young men could be figured into the equation in terms of francs, dollars, or pounds. They proposed that, with victory, all debts should be canceled. The United States, which had gone to Paris with a conciliatory spirit toward Germany in the treaty negotiations, changed its tune when dollars and cents were involved. This attitude was best expressed in a remark attributed to American president Calvin Coolidge, who expected full repayment, when he is alleged to have said: "They hired [borrowed] the money, didn't they?" Beneath the extremes of these positions were the understandable motives of getting out of paying a huge debt or gaining from the payment of debts owed.

Weimar Germany: Debt, Reparations, and Inflation

Reparations complicated Germany's debt problem and the challenge of converting the country back to a peacetime economy. In the first three years after the war the German government, like other European states, spent much more than its income. This policy was masked by "floating debts . . . in other words, by the printing press."[7] The mark, which had been valued at 4.2 to the dollar in 1914, went to 75 in July 1921, to 186 in January 1922, to 402 in July, and to 4000 by December of that year. The situation became so serious in the summer of 1922 that Great Britain proposed collecting no more from its debtors—Allied and German alike—than the United States collected from Britain itself. Such "statesmanship" was prompted by the fact that London had gained what it wanted from the peace settlement: Germany's navy was destroyed, Germany's merchant ships were transferred as reparations, and Germany's empire was gone. No more could be squeezed out.

Britain saw that Germany would not be able to meet its reparations payments. Without those payments, the victors would not be able to make their own payments on the inter-Allied debts, especially debts owed to the United States. Although the United States insisted that there was no connection between the inter-Allied debts and German reparations, negotiations were carried on, and debt payment plans were set up with 13 nations. No reductions were made in principal, but in every case the interest rate was radically decreased. Still, the total amount owed came to more than $22 billion.

At the end of 1922 the Germans asked for a delay in their reparations obligations and then defaulted on some payments. In response, in January 1923, French troops, supported by Belgian and Italian contingents, marched into the rich industrial district of the Ruhr, undeterred by American and British objections. This shortsighted French move contributed nothing to the solution of Europe's problems and played into the hands of radical German politicians.

Encouraged by the Berlin government, German workers defied the French army and went on strike; many ended up in jail. The French toyed for a while with the idea of establishing a separate state in the Rhineland to act as a buffer between Germany and France. Chaotic conditions in the Ruhr encouraged the catastrophic inflation of the German currency to make up for the loss of exports and to support the striking workers. The value of the mark to the dollar went from 7200 in January 1923 to 160,000 in July to 1 million in August to 4.2 trillion in December. During the worst part of the inflation, the Reichsbank had 150 firms using 2000 presses running day and night to print banknotes. To get out of their dilemma, the Germans made an effective transition to a more stable currency by simply abandoning the old one. The French, in return, gained very little benefit from the occupation.

Inflation in Germany during the 1920s grew so drastic that the German mark became nearly worthless. It was cheaper, for example, for this German woman to start fires with marks than to use them to purchase kindling.

Inflation and Its Consequences

All European nations encountered a rocky path as they attempted to gain equilibrium after the war. Britain had minimal price increases and returned to prewar levels within two years after the signing of the Versailles treaty. On the Continent price and monetary stability came less easily. Only Czechoslovakia seemed to have its economic affairs well in hand.

France did not stabilize its currency until 1926, when the franc was worth 50 to the dollar (one-tenth its value in 1914). In Austria prices rose to 14,000 times their prewar level until stability of sorts came in 1922. Hungary's prices went to 23,000 times prewar level, but this increase is dwarfed by Poland's (2.5

million times prewar level) and Russia's (4 billion times prewar level).

Inflation had massive social and political consequences, most notably in Germany. Millions of middle-class Germans, small property owners who were the hoped-for base of the new Weimar Republic, found themselves caught in the wage-price squeeze. Prices for the necessities of life rose far faster than income or savings. As mothers wheeled baby carriages full of money to bakeries to buy bread, fathers watched a lifetime of savings dwindle to insignificance. Pensioners on fixed incomes suffered doubly under this crisis. The bourgeoisie, the historical champions of liberal politics throughout Europe, suffered blows more devastating than those of war, since inflation stole not only the value of their labor but also the worth of their savings and insurance.

Where the middle classes and liberal traditions were strong, democracy could weather the inflationary storm. But in central Europe, where they were not—especially in Germany, where the inflation was worst—the cause of future totalitarianism received an immense boost. Alan Bullock, a biographer of Adolf Hitler, wrote that "the result of inflation was to undermine the foundations of German society in a way which neither the war nor the revolution of 1918 nor the Treaty of Versailles had ever done."[8]

Temporary Improvements

After 1923, the liberal application of U.S. funds brought some calm to the economic storm. Business was more difficult to conduct because protectionism became more and more the dominant trait of international trade. **Autarky,** the goal of gaining total economic self-sufficiency and freedom from reliance on any other nation, increasingly became the unstated policy of many governments.

Nonetheless, production soon reached 1913 levels, currencies began to stabilize, and the French finally recalled their troops from the Ruhr. Most significant, in September 1924 a commission under the leadership of U.S. banker Charles Dawes formulated a more liberal reparations policy in order to get the entire repayment cycle back into motion. Dawes's plan, replaced in 1929 by the Young plan (named for its principal formulator, U.S. businessman Owen Young), reduced installments and extended them over a longer period. A loan of $200 million, mostly from the United States, was floated to aid German recovery. The Berlin government resumed payments to the Allies, and the Allies paid their debt installments to the United States—which in effect received its own money back again.

Prosperity of a sort returned to Europe. As long as the circular flow of cash from the United States to Germany to the Allies to the United States continued, the international monetary system functioned. The moment the cycle broke down, the world economy headed for the rocks of **depression.** One economic historian has written:

> *In 1924–31 Germany drew some one [billion] pounds [sterling] from abroad and the irony was that Germany, in fact, received far more in loans, including loans to enable her to pay interest on earlier loans than she paid out in reparations, thus gaining in the circular flow and re-equipping her industries and her public utilities with American funds in the processes in the 1920s before repudiating her debts in the 1930s.*[9]

Danger Signs

The system broke down in 1928 and 1929 when U.S. and British creditors needed their capital for investments in their own countries. Extensions on loans, readily granted a year earlier, were refused. Even before the U.S. stock market crash on October 29, 1929, disaster was on the horizon.

Few people in America could admit such a possibility during the decade, however. The United States had become the commercial center of the world, and its policies were central to the world's financial health. The United States still had an internal market in the 1920s with a seemingly inexhaustible appetite for new products such as radios, refrigerators, electrical appliances, and automobiles. This expansion, based on consumer goods and supported by a seemingly limitless supply of natural resources, gave the impression of solid and endless growth.

Tragically, the contradictions of the postwar economic structure were making themselves felt. The cornerstones of pre-1914 prosperity—multilateral trade, the gold standard, and interchangeable currencies—were crumbling. The policies of autarky, with high tariff barriers to protect home products against foreign competition, worked against international economic health. Ironically, the United States led the way toward higher tariffs, and other nations quickly retaliated. American foreign trade declined seriously, and the volume of world trade decreased.

There were other danger signals. Europe suffered a population decline. There were 22 million fewer people in the 1920s in the western part of the Continent than had been expected. The decrease in internal markets affected trade, as did the higher external barriers. Around the globe, the agricultural sector suffered

---

autarky—The program of total economic self-sufficiency.

depression—A time of stagnant economic activity in which high unemployment occurs.

from declining prices during the 1920s. At the same time that farmers received less for their products, they had to pay more to live—a condition that negatively affected peasants in Europe and Asia and farmers and ranchers in the United States.

In the hopes of reaching a wider market, farmers around the world borrowed money to expand production early in the 1920s. Temporarily, the food surplus benefited consumers, but across the world, agricultural interests suffered from overproduction. Tariff barriers prevented foodstuffs from circulating to the countries where hunger existed. By the end of the decade, people in Asia were starving while wheat farmers in Whitman County, Washington, dumped their grain into the Snake River and coffee growers in Brazil saw their product burned to fuel steam locomotives. Many farmers went bankrupt, unable to keep up with payments on these debts. The countryside preceded the cities into the economic tragedy.

The Great Crash

Because of America's central position in the world economy, any development on Wall Street, positive or negative, reverberated around the globe. The United States, with roughly 3 percent of the world's population, produced 46 percent of the globe's industrial output. The country was too shortsighted to use its newfound power wisely. Its financial life in the 1920s was dominated by the activities of daring and sometimes unscrupulous speculators who made the arena of high finance a precarious and exciting world of its own. The businessmen creating this world were not pursuing long-term stability. Their blind rush for profit led to America's crash, which in turn sparked a world disaster. Even before the stock market crash, Wall Street had been showing signs of distress, such as capital shortfalls, excessively large inventories, and agricultural bankruptcies. But nothing prepared financiers for the disaster that struck on October 29, 1929—Black Thursday. By noon Wall Street was caught in a momentum of chaotic fear, and stock prices began plummeting. The end of the trading session halted the initial hemorrhage of stock values, but the damage was done.

The economist John Kenneth Galbraith has written: "On the whole, the great stock market crash can be much more readily explained than the depression that followed it."[10] Overspeculation, loose controls, dishonest investors, and a loss of confidence in the ever-upward market trend can be identified as causes for the crash. Further causes can be traced to the inequitable distribution of wealth, with the farmers and workers left out while the top 3 percent of Americans grew incredibly rich and irresponsible. Industrial overexpansion was fueled by speculators buying stock "on margin," with insufficient cash backing for the investments. In addition, the government's hands-off policies permitted massive abuses to take place unchecked.

The international impact of the crash can be explained by the involvement in the U.S. market of investors and bankers from a number of countries, the interdependent world economic structure, the peculiar Allied debt and reparations structure, the growing agricultural crisis, and the inadequate banking systems of the world.

Some economic historians believe that the cycle of highs and lows hit a particularly vicious low point in 1929. Crashes had occurred before, but never with such widespread repercussions over such a long period of time. In the United States, stock prices declined one-third overall within a few weeks, wiping out fortunes, shattering confidence in business, and destroying consumer demand. The disaster spread worldwide as American interests demanded payment on foreign loans and imports decreased. The Kredit-Anstalt (kre-DIT an-SHTALT) bank of Vienna did not have enough money to fill demands for funds from French banks and failed in 1931. This collapse set in motion a dominolike banking crisis throughout Europe. Forecasts by Washington politicians and New York financiers that the worst was over and that the

Bankrupt investor Walter Thornton attempts to sell his car for $100 following the stock market crash of October 29, 1929, "Black Thursday."

world economy was fundamentally sound after a "technical readjustment" convinced nobody. There would be no easy recovery.

The World Depression

DOCUMENT The Great Depression

By 1932 the value of industrial shares had fallen close to 60 percent on the New York and Berlin markets. Unemployment doubled in Germany, and 25 percent of the labor force was out of work in the United States. The middle classes, which had invested in the stock market, saw their investments and savings wiped out. In nation after nation, industry declined, prices fell, banks collapsed, and economies stagnated. In the western democracies the depression heightened the feelings of uneasiness that had existed since 1918. In other countries the tendency to seek authoritarian solutions became even more pronounced. Throughout the world, people feared a future marked by lowered standards of living, unemployment, and hunger.

The middle classes on the Continent, which had suffered from inflation during the 1920s, became caught in a whiplash effect during the depression. Adherence to old liberal principles collapsed in the face of economic insecurity, and state control of the economies increased. Governments raised tariffs to restrict imports and reverted to command economies, an expedient usually reserved for wartime. As conditions deteriorated, fear caused most governments to look no farther than their own boundaries. Under the competing systems of autarky, each nation tried to increase exports and decrease imports.

After almost a century of free trade, modified by a comparatively few protective duties levied during and after World War I, Great Britain finally enacted a high tariff in 1932 with provisions to protect members of its empire. In the United States, the Hawley-Smoot Tariff of 1930 increased the value-added duty to 50 percent on a wide variety of agricultural and manufactured imports.

Another technique to increase exports at the expense of others was to depreciate a nation's currency—that is, to reduce the value of its money. When Japan depreciated the yen, for example, a U.S. dollar or British pound could buy more Japanese goods. In effect, lowering the yen reduced the price of Japanese exports. In most cases, however, devaluation brought only a temporary trade advantage. Other nations could play the same game, as the United States did in 1934 when it abandoned the gold standard and reduced the amount of gold backing for the dollar by 40 percent.

The debt problem that grew out of the war worsened during the depression. In 1931 President Herbert Hoover gained a one-year moratorium on all intergovernmental debts. The next year, European leaders meeting at Lausanne practically canceled German reparations payments in the hope that the United States would make corresponding concessions in reducing war debts. The Americans, for a variety of domestic financial and political reasons, refused to concede that there was a logical connection between reparations and war debts. As the depression deepened, the debtors could not continue their payments. France refused outright in 1932; Germany after 1933 completely stopped paying reparations; Britain and four other nations made token payments for a time and then stopped entirely in 1934. Only Finland continued to meet its schedule of payments.

Families had at least as many problems in paying their bills as the governments of the world. Factories closed down and laid off their workers. Harvests rotted in the fields as the price of wheat fell to its lowest price in 300 years and other agricultural commodities suffered similar price declines. The lives of the cacao grower along Africa's Gold Coast, the coffee grower in Brazil, and the plantation worker in the Netherlands East Indies were as affected as those of the factory worker in Pittsburgh, Lille, or Frankfurt.

The 1929 crash occurred in an economic framework still suffering from the dislocations of World War I. It began a downturn in the world economy that would not end until the world armed for another global conflict. Whether the depression ended because of World War II or whether the world would have eventually recovered on its own is a question that will always be debated. The weaknesses in American stock market operations were by and large addressed in a series of reforms.

From the major banks to the soup lines in villages, the depression had profound implications for politics. The combination of inflation and depression threatened representative government. Unemployed and starving masses were tempted to turn to dictators who promised jobs and bread. The hardships of economic stability, even in countries where the liberal tradition was strongest, led to a massive increase in state participation in the daily life of the individual.

POLITICS IN THE DEMOCRACIES

- *What were the effects of the economic crises on democratic governments between the war?*

During the interwar period, there was a loss of belief in the genius of big business and free market capitalism in most parts of the world, as business itself had to turn more and more to the powers of the state to survive. After 1918, parliamentary government—the foundation of all that the liberals of the nineteenth century had worked for—came under attack everywhere.

For the most part, only in Scandinavia—in Norway, Sweden, and Denmark—did representative government operate smoothly throughout the interwar period. Economic prosperity prevailed there throughout the 1920s, and the depression was less severe than in Britain, France, or the United States. Switzerland, the Netherlands, and Belgium also maintained relatively high standards of living and kept their governments on the democratic road. But in the 20 years after peace came to the West, Britain, France, the United States, and most of the other democracies exhibited lethargy and shortsightedness in the face of fascist aggression.

Interwar Western Society: Mass Escapism and Despair

After the devastating losses of the War and during the political and economic crises of the 1920s, the urban working and lower middle classes found escape in the popular cultural products of their countries. More leisure time and money enabled them to fill the music halls and public sporting arenas. They would rarely be found in the concert halls, art galleries, or serious bookstores. Rather, they read the penny press and the dime novel, both of which featured simple vocabulary and easy-to-follow information and plots. The penny press served many functions: to inform, entertain, and sell goods. Sensationalism, whether the confessions of a "fallen woman" or the account of some adventurer, was the main attraction of the dime novel. Comic strips first appeared in central Europe in the 1890s and then spread rapidly throughout the Western world. By the interwar period, mass culture offered relief from the bad news of the time.

A number of technological advances—coated celluloid film, improved shutter mechanisms, reliable projectors, and a safe source of illumination—were combined to introduce the cinema—motion pictures, or movies—to the world. These developments seem to have come together almost simultaneously in France, Britain, and the United States. The first public motion picture performances took place in Paris in 1895 and soon after in London and New York. Even though another 20 years passed before feature-length films were produced, movies were an immediate success, attracting an infinitely larger audience than live performances could ever reach. By the 1920s, movies had become the most popular, most universal art form of the twentieth century. From the theaters of Main Street, USA, to the private projection rooms of the Kremlin, artists such as Charlie Chaplin and Marlene Dietrich became universal favorites.

Technology touched the common people in many ways and vastly expanded leisure possibilities. Henry Ford's affordable Model T made automobiles widely accessible and opened up the world to those who cared to drive. In cities, virtually every home had electricity, which powered bright lights, refrigeration, and other conveniences. Radio brought drama, sports, and news into millions of living rooms. And the new technology vastly increased access to music.

Through radio and phonograph records millions of people discovered jazz, formerly the special preserve of black musicians and their audiences. Louis Armstrong and his trumpet and Paul Whiteman and his band became known worldwide. At the same time, Rosa Ponselle, Arturo Toscanini, and other figures from the opera and concert world became celebrities known to millions more than could ever have seen them perform in person.

The German actress, Marlene Dietrich, became an internationally known celebrity through her performances in films such as The Blue Angel.

The combination of increased leisure time, greater mobility, and improved communications led to the development of the modern "star" system in sports and entertainment. Sports, including football in its North American and European forms, bicycle racing, cricket, baseball, and boxing, captured the popular imagination. As times became more difficult and front-page news turned grim after World War I the world's citizens could find some diversion in reading about their boxers—Jack Dempsey, Max Schmeling, and Georges Carpentier. In the United States golfers and baseball stars became better known and better paid than presidents.

While the masses escaped, the elites found little hope. Among writers, Franz Kafka (1883–1924) perhaps best captured the nightmarish nature of the post–World War I world. In works such as *The Metamorphosis* and *The Trial,* he portrayed a ritualistic society in which a well-organized insanity prevails. Rational, well-meaning individuals run a constant maze from which there is no exit, only more structures.

Many sensitive artists and writers cast serious doubt on the Renaissance notion that "man is the measure of all things." Writers such as Thomas Mann (1875–1955) in his *Magic Mountain* gave testimony that the Western world had gone very far off course, and the best that could be hoped for was survival. Historians worked under the profound influence of Oswald Spengler's *Decline of the West.* The book, finished one year before the defeat of the Central Powers, was more widely quoted than read. In it the German historian traced the life span of cultures, from birth through maturity to death, and identified the symptoms of the West's demise. Other writers expressed a similar fascination with the death of their civilization, but perhaps more significant was that people in the West knew Spengler's name and general message. And they found the pessimistic tone justified by events.

Britain, 1919–1939

The 1920s was not a tranquil decade for Great Britain. The country endured a number of social and political crises tied to the bitter labor disputes and unemployment that disrupted the nation. Neither Liberals nor Conservatives could do much to alter the flow of events immediately after the war. From 1919 to 1922, David Lloyd George led a coalition, but it broke apart, leading to the division and decline of the Liberals. From May 1923 to January 1924, Stanley Baldwin led an unsuccessful Conservative government.

Ramsay MacDonald formed the first Labour government and became the first socialist prime minister. For ten months he and his party pursued a program to introduce socialism slowly and within the democratic framework. His move to recognize the newly established Soviet Union (USSR) was controversial. When the London *Times* published the so-called Zinoviev (zi-NOH-vee-EF) letter, a document in which the Communist Third International supposedly laid out a program for revolution in Britain, the public backlash defeated the Labour government in the October 1924 elections.

For the next five years, the Conservatives under Baldwin held power. After renouncing the treaties the Labour cabinet had made with the USSR, the Conservatives set out on a generally unsuccessful and stormy tenure. Britain returned its currency to the gold standard in 1925, a policy that led indirectly to an increase in labor unrest. The government struggled through a coal strike and a general strike in which more than 2.5 million of the nation's 6 million workers walked out. Baldwin reduced taxes on business, but this move did little to remedy the deflationary effect of a return to the gold standard.

In May 1929 Labour under MacDonald won another victory. Once again, the Labourites resumed relations with the Soviet Union and attempted their measured socialist program. The effects of the depression, however, condemned MacDonald and his government to failure. In two years, exports and imports declined 35 percent and close to 3 million unemployed people roamed the streets. Labour could do little to address the basic causes of the disaster; in fact, no single party could. When MacDonald's government fell in 1931, it was replaced by a national coalition government dominated by the Conservatives. The coalition government initiated a recovery program featuring a balanced budget, limited social spending, and encouragement of private enterprise. By 1933 a substantial measure of prosperity had been regained, and productivity had increased by 23 percent over the 1929 level.

To achieve this comeback, some of what remained of laissez-faire policy was discarded. The government regulated the currency, levied high tariffs, gave farmers subsidies, and imposed a heavy burden of taxation. The taxes went to expanded educational and health facilities, better accident and unemployment insurance, and more adequate pensions. As for the rich, they had a large portion of their income taxed away, and what might be left at death was decimated by inheritance taxes. It was ruefully declared that the rich could hardly afford to live, much less to die.

During the 20 years between the wars, Britain's political parties lacked forward-looking programs. The parties seemed unable to measure up to the demands of a difficult new age. In the empire, demands for home rule grew during the interwar period, especially in India, Sri Lanka, Burma, and Egypt. An ominous trend was the growing antagonism between the Arab inhabitants of mandated Palestine and the Jewish Zionist immigrants. Yet these issues would not come to a crisis until after World War II.

Happier developments could be seen in the attainment of home rule by the Irish Free State (the southern part of Ireland) in 1921 and Britain's recognition in the Statute of Westminister (1931) of a new national status for the dominions (Canada, Australia, New Zealand, and South Africa). Collectively, the four states were then known as the British Commonwealth of Nations and would be held together henceforth only by loyalty to the crown and by common language, legal principles, traditions, and economic interests. For most of the dominions, democratic traditions for the white populations survived the pressures of the depression, even though they were painfully susceptible to the effects of the world slump.

Interwar France

France suffered from World War I the most of any of the democracies; loss of lives as a proportion of the population and direct property damage were enormous. More than two out of every ten French men died. Years later, the nation, which had historically experienced less rapid population growth than other European states, still felt the war's heavy losses.

Victory did not address any of France's basic political problems. The French labored under much the same political and social stagnation after 1918 as it had before 1914. The economic impact of the war and the social disruptions that occurred during and after the conflict exacerbated these conditions. A dangerous inflation plagued France and undermined its rather shallow prosperity. The multiparty system hampered the parliamentary structure of the Third Republic, and the governments formed from shaky coalitions. The exhausted country lacked vitality and a sense of national purpose after gaining revenge against the Germans.

After 1919 the British wished to withdraw from continental Europe to look after their imperial interests, and the United States shrank back into isolationism. Working from a dispirited domestic base, France had to bear the burden of overseeing international affairs on the Continent. Overall, with the exception of the counterproductive occupation of the Ruhr, the French carried their duties well in the 1920s. In the next decade, however, France retreated into the so-called Maginot (MAH-zhi-noh) mentality, named after the construction of the Maginot Line, a supposedly impenetrable line of fortresses to the east.

The depression struck France later than it did other countries, but in some ways the damage was greater. French leadership was no more astute than that of the other democracies before and during the depression. For a while, France managed to maintain a false prosperity from the 1920s, partly because of its large gold holdings; but by the early 1930s, it suffered much the same fate as the other countries. Tourism dried up, contributing to the already rising unemployment rate and budget deficits. In the face of these problems, the French carried the additional financial burden of rearming to face a renewed German threat.

Ministry after ministry took power, only to collapse a few months later. Citizens became impatient with the government, especially when the press exposed corruption in high places. One of the more shocking scandals was that surrounding the schemes of Alexander Stavisky, a rogue who had bribed officials and cheated French investors out of some 600 million francs. When the ministry in power in December 1933 refused to authorize an investigation after Stavisky's assumed suicide, thousands of angry citizens took to the streets of Paris in protest. In February 1934 right-wing mobs tried to storm the Chamber of Deputies.

The outcome of this affair was a new government, the National Union, a rightist coalition that endured strikes and avoided civil war for the next two years. France was becalmed. The leftists were unable to reorganize their forces quickly to gain control, and the rightists failed to deal with either domestic or foreign problems. In the spring of 1936 the leftist Popular Front took power.

This coalition, under the leadership of Léon Blum (1872–1950), won a national election and set in motion a program to bring socialist reforms to France's struggling economy. Blum's government tried to reduce the domination of the traditional

Léon Blum served as Prime Minister of the French Popular Front in 1936–1937, a time of diplomatic and economic upheaval.

ruling elite over the finances of the country on the one hand, and on the other, to work with the Communists to help block the growing fascist influences. The cooperation with the Communists caused serious problems, including the usual one of how to work with the Soviet-dominated party without being captured by it. Many French voters refused to support the Popular Front for fear that it might commit France to fight against Germany for the benefit of the Soviet Union.

In foreign affairs the Popular Front worked closely with Great Britain and supported the work of the League of Nations. It also attempted to appease Germany, though it remained hostile to Italy. During the Spanish civil war (1936–1939), fearing civil war at home, Blum's government, along with the British, declared neutrality in the face of fascist aggression.

In this atmosphere of social, economic, and international turmoil, Blum was unable to govern successfully. Further, an epidemic of sit-down strikes involving some 300,000 workers embarrassed the government. Gradually, laws introducing a 40-hour workweek, higher wages, collective bargaining, and paid vacations were enacted to satisfy many of labor's demands. In addition, the government extended its control over the Bank of France and instituted a public works program. Blum navigated as best he could, favoring the worker against monopoly and big business while avoiding the totalitarian extremes of fascism and communism. After only a year in office, however, he was forced to resign. The unfavorable trade balance, huge public debt, and unbalanced budget brought down the Popular Front government. France swung back to the right with a government that ended the 40-hour week and put down strikes.

The National Union and the Popular Front mirrored the widening split between the upper and lower classes. The workers believed that the Popular Front's reforms had been sabotaged and that a France ruled by a wealthy clique deserved little or no allegiance. Conversely, some business owners and financiers were horrified at the prospect of communism and openly admired Hitler's fascism. Soviet and German propagandists subtly encouraged the widening of the gulf.

While the French quarreled and France's economic strength declined, Germany—regimented and working feverishly—outstripped France in the manufacture of armaments. There were no leaders to bring France together, and the pieces were in place for the easy and tragic fall of the country to German troops at the start of World War II in the spring of 1940.

Eastern Europe

With the exception of Finland and Czechoslovakia, democratic governments fared poorly in eastern Europe in the interwar period. By 1938 most of the states retained only the false front of parliamentary forms. Real power was exercised by varying combinations of secret police, official censors, armed forces, and corrupt politicians. Except in the western parts of Czechoslovakia and among the Jewish communities, there was a welcoming attitude toward the German National Socialists (Nazis) and their programs.

Most of these countries had an unhappy legacy of oppression by powerful neighbors, minority problems, economic weakness, and peasant societies. Poland, the Baltic states, Finland, Czechoslovakia, Yugoslavia, and Albania had not existed as states before 1913. Hungary, Bulgaria, and Austria had been on the losing side in World War I and paid dearly for that alliance in the treaties ending the war. Romania, which had been among the victors, gained large amounts of land and also a number of non-Romanian minorities.

For the first decade after World War I, the small countries of eastern Europe had the opportunity to develop without undue external influence or interference. However, the exclusivist, aggressive, and perhaps paranoid nationalism that dominated each nation thwarted any possibility of regional cooperation. The peace treaties had settled few of the problems plaguing the area and instead constructed a series of arbitrary political boundaries that brought far more conflict than accord. The countries in the region all sought autarkist solutions to their economic problems by erecting huge tariff barriers, which only served to emphasize the states' weaknesses.

Among the eastern European states, Czechoslovakia, with its combination of a strong middle class, accumulation of capital, technology base, and high literacy rate, had the greatest potential for successful democratic government. Four hundred years of Austrian domination had not crushed the Czech national spirit. After the collapse of the Dual Monarchy in November 1918, the Czechs joined with the Slovaks, who had been under Hungarian domination for 1000 years, to establish a republic.

The new state possessed a literate and well-trained citizenry and a solid economic base, and it managed to avoid the roller-coaster ride of inflation in the immediate postwar period. Its solid financial institutions, advanced industry, and a small-farm-based agricultural sector made it an island of prosperity. Like the other eastern European successor states, it had serious minority problems. But of all the new states, Czechoslovakia extended the most liberal policies toward minorities. By the time of the depression, Czechoslovakia showed every indication of growing into a mature democratic country. The depression, however, heavily affected the country's export trade and hit especially hard in the textile industry, which was centered in the German-populated Sudetenland (soo-DAY-ten-land). By 1935 the economic blows had made the area ripe for Nazi agitation and infiltration.

After Czechoslovakia, Poland had the best chance of the successor states to form a democratic government. The Poles, however, had to overcome several problems: a border conflict with the Soviet Union, the dilemma of the Polish Corridor to Danzig, minority issues, and the fact that Poland had been partitioned for over a century. When the country was reunited after the war, the Poles chose to imitate the constitutional system of the French Third Republic. The multiplicity of parties, a weak executive, and the resultant succession of governments led to political paralysis until 1926, when Marshal Josef Pilsudski (1867–1935) led a military revolt against the Warsaw government.

For the next nine years Pilsudski imposed his generally benevolent rule on the country. After his death in 1935, a group of colonels ruled Poland, and they permitted the formation of several protofascist organizations. By the time the Poles turned back toward a more liberal government in 1938, it was too late. For three years they had played up to the Nazis, and now they stood isolated before Hitler's advance.

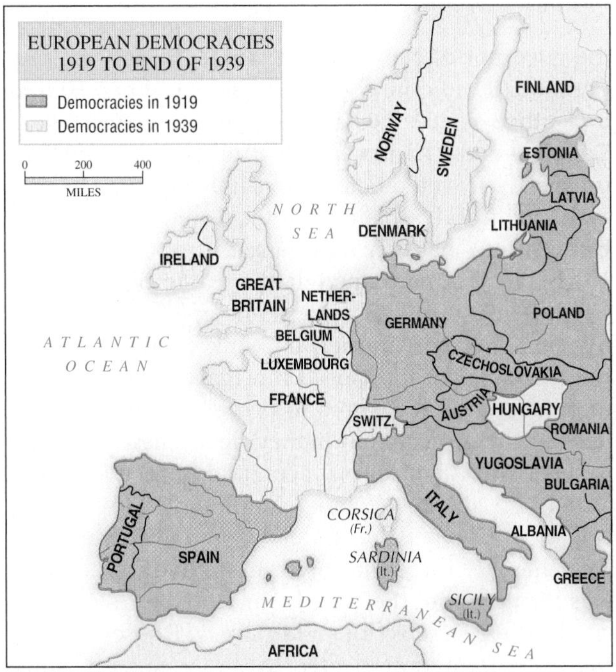

Democracy waned in the uncertain years after World War I as people turned increasingly toward more authoritarian leaders whom they hoped would bring them stability and prosperity.

Problems with being trapped between powerful neighbors plagued the Baltic states of Latvia, Lithuania, and Estonia, which came into existence in 1918. The democratic governments of these countries endured much political and economic strife before they eventually gave way to dictatorial forms of government to survive with the Nazis.

The Balkan states of Yugoslavia, Albania, and Greece were buffeted by the ambitions of Italian imperialism, economic upheaval, and political corruption. Disintegration seemed a real possibility for Yugoslavia in the 1920s, but the conglomerate state stubbornly attempted to hold together the six major ethnic groups within its boundaries. King Alexander established himself as dictator in 1929 and ruled until 1934, when he was assassinated by Croatian separatists. Thereafter, the rising Nazi state drew parts of economically depressed Yugoslavia into its orbit, deeply splitting the country. By the end of the 1930s, both Greece and Albania were ruled by dictators.

Romania, another of the Balkan states, gained greatly from World War I, doubling its area and its population. Although the state had great economic potential, the government was unable to impose a stable rule during the interwar period. Severe problems with minorities and peasants and foreign control of the economy foiled the attempts of moderate politicians to rule, until, by the 1930s, fascist groups wielded a large amount of influence. In 1938 King Carol tried unsuccessfully to counter the pro-Nazi forces in Romania. Two years later the country lost one-third of its territory and population to the Bulgarians, Russians, and Hungarians, and Carol fled to Spain.

Portugal and Spain

During the interwar period, economic problems, aristocratic privilege, and peasant misery worked against successful democratic or parliamentary government in the Iberian peninsula. After the end of World War I, Portugal endured ten years of political indecision until Antonio de Oliveira Salazar (1889–1970), a professor of economics, became minister of finance in 1928. After helping straighten out some of the country's financial problems, Salazar became Portugal's premier and virtual dictator. He maintained Portugal's close ties with Britain while lending assistance to right-wing elements in Spain.

None of the political parties could deal adequately with Spain's problems in the 1920s. Revolts and strikes plagued the country until 1931, when the king abdicated and left the country. At the end of the year a new liberal constitution was adopted, and a republic was proclaimed. The new constitution was extremely liberal, but it had the support of neither the left nor the right. Mob violence and the threat of military coups continually harassed the republic.

By 1936 the peasants and workers were beginning to take matters into their own hands. At the same time, the military, under Generalissimo Francisco Franco, sought to pursue its own political ends. In July the army made its move and attacked the republican government. This marked the start of a civil war in Spain, a war that in retrospect seems inevitable because of the country's indigenous social antagonisms.

The United States

The United States emerged from World War I as the strongest country in the world. But while other states looked to Washington to continue to play a political and diplomatic role in the world, the U.S. government turned inward, away from the international scene. Americans shelved Wilson's wartime idealism, ignored the League of Nations, and returned to domestic politics. At the same time, however, American businessmen played an active role in international business until 1929: Not until the 1980s would a larger percentage of American financial activities take place abroad.

During the 1920s, three Republican presidents—Warren G. Harding, Calvin Coolidge, and Herbert Hoover—benefited from the well-being of the country and the generally carefree spirit of the times. Although refusing to join the League of Nations, the United States did participate in the Washington Naval Conference in 1921–1922 to limit the race in warship construction, the Dawes and Young plans for economic stabilization, and the Kellogg-Briand pact (1928) to outlaw war.

Harding's domestic policies were marked by protectionist economics, probusiness legislation, and scandal. After Harding died suddenly in 1923, the widespread corruption of his administration was exposed. His vice president, Coolidge, easily weathered the storm and, after his 1924 election, advocated high tariffs, tax reduction, and a hands-off policy on federal regulation of business. Only nagging problems in the agricultural sphere detracted from the dazzling prosperity and honest government that marked his administration.

In the 1928 presidential elections, Herbert Hoover—a successful mining engineer who had directed Belgian relief during the war, had been present at the Versailles negotiations, and had overseen the Russian relief plan in the early 1920s—overwhelmed

The Great Depression and the environmental disaster that accompanied it, the Dust Bowl, devastated the American economy and brought ruin to hundreds of families. Dorothea Lange's photograph of a migrant mother captured the love, strength, patience, and pain of the mothers that held those families together.

the governor of New York, Alfred E. Smith, the first Catholic to be nominated for president. When Hoover took office in 1929, he had the support of a Republican Congress and a nation enjoying unbounded industrial prosperity. It would be his incredibly bad luck to have to deal with and be blamed for the worst depression the United States has ever experienced.

By 1932 Americans felt the tragic blows of the Great Depression—25 percent unemployment, 30,000 business failures, numerous bank collapses, and a huge number of foreclosed mortgages. Hoover tried unprecedented measures to prop up faltering businesses with government money, devise new strategies to deal with the farm problem, and build confidence among the shaken citizenry. Yet he failed to shift the tide of the depression. Indeed, some observers note that the only force that brought an end to the crisis was the arrival of the World War II.

In the 1932 elections Franklin D. Roosevelt, only the third Democrat elected to the presidency since 1860, defeated Hoover by assembling a coalition of labor, intellectuals, minorities, and farmers—a coalition the Democratic party could count on for nearly a half century. The country had reached a crisis point by the time Roosevelt was inaugurated in 1933, and quick action had to be taken in the face of a wave of bank closings.

Under Roosevelt's leadership, the **New Deal**—a sweeping, pragmatic, often hit-or-miss program—was developed to cope with the emergency. The New Deal's three objectives were relief, recovery, and reform. Millions of dollars flowed from the federal treasury to feed the hungry, create jobs for the unemployed through public works, and provide for the sick and elderly through such reforms as the Social Security Act. In addition, Roosevelt's administration substantially reformed the banking and investment industries, greatly increased the rights of labor unions, invested in massive public power and conservation projects, and supported families who were in danger of losing their homes or who simply needed homes.

The Democrats' programs created much controversy among those who believed that they went too far toward creating a socialistic government and those who believed that they did not go far enough toward attacking the depression. Hated or loved, Roosevelt was in control, and the strength and leadership he provided were unparalleled in the interwar democracies.

Interwar Latin America

The huge wartime demand for Latin American mineral and agricultural products resulted in an economic boom that, with a minor contraction, continued on into the 1920s. However, the area's crucial weakness remained—its economic dependence on only a few products. Among Latin America's 20 republics, Brazil based its prosperity on coffee, Cuba depended on sugar, Venezuela on oil, Bolivia on tin, Mexico on oil and silver, Argentina on wheat and meat, and the various Central American countries on bananas.

Another problem was land distribution. On many large estates conditions resembled medieval serfdom. Because the Catholic Church was a great landowner, certain members of the clergy combined with the landed interests to oppose land reforms.

During the 1920s, Mexico spearheaded the movement for social reform in Latin America. A series of governments, each claiming to be faithful to the spirit of the 1910 revolt, sought to gain more control over the vast oil properties run by foreign investors. The government solved the agrarian problem at the expense of the large landowners. These changes were accompanied by a wave of anticlericalism. Under these attacks, the Catholic Church lost much property, saw many churches destroyed, and had to work through an underground priesthood for a time.

Mexico exerted a strong influence over other Latin American countries. Between 1919 and 1929, seven nations adopted new, liberal constitutions. In addition, there were growing demands for better economic and social opportunities, a breakdown of the barriers that divided the few extremely rich from the many abysmally poor, and improvements in health, education, and the status of women. Above all there was an increasing desire for more stable conditions.

Because of their dependence on raw-material exports, the Latin American countries suffered a serious economic crisis during the Great Depression. Largely as a result of the disaster, revolutions broke out in six South American countries in 1930.

During the 1930s, the "colossus of the north," the United States, attempted to improve its relations with Latin America and to stimulate trade. The Good Neighbor policy, originated in Hoover's administration and begun in 1933, asserted that "no state has the right to intervene in the internal or external affairs of another." Less pious, but more effective, was the $560 million worth of inter-American trade that the new policy encouraged.

Rivalries among industrialized nations for the Latin American market became intense during the 1930s. Nazi Germany concluded many barter agreements with Latin American customers and at the same time penetrated the countries politically by organizing German immigrants into pro-Nazi groups, supporting fascist politicians, and developing powerful propaganda networks. When war came, however, most of Latin America lined up with the democracies.

THE WESTERN TRADITION IN TRANSITION: CHANGING CERTAINTIES

- *Some historians believe that the First World War delivered a death blow to classic Western Civilization. Looking at the changes in science, literature, and the arts, do you agree?*

The world was in the process of change even before World War I. All of the basic definitions were changing. At the dawn of twentieth century, science made

---

New Deal—President Franklin D. Roosevelt's series of programs to deal with the effects of the depression.

great strides, and such figures as Max Planck, Albert Einstein, Ivan Pavlov, and Sigmund Freud enlarged understanding of the universe and the individual. Even before the war, which had dealt a deathblow to the nineteenth-century legacy of optimism, these physicists and psychologists pointed out that the old foundations and beliefs on which the European world rested had to be rethought.

Science and Society

At the beginning of the twentieth century, the basic view of human nature changed. The Russian scientist Ivan Pavlov (1849–1936) gave the study of psychology a new impetus. In 1900 he carried out a series of experiments in which food was given to a dog at the same time that a bell was rung. After a time the dog identified the sound of the bell with food. Henceforth, the sound of the bell alone conditioned the dog to salivate, just as if food had been presented. Pavlov demonstrated the influence of physical stimuli on an involuntary process in all animals.

The psychology of "conditioned reflexes," based on Pavlov's work, achieved wide popularity, especially in the United States, as the basis for behaviorism, which considered the human as analogous to a machine responding mechanically to stimuli. Behaviorism stressed experimentation and observational techniques and did much to create relatively valid intelligence and aptitude tests. It also served to strengthen the materialist philosophies of the period.

Probably the most famous and controversial name associated with psychology is that of Sigmund Freud (1856–1939). Placing far greater stress than any predecessor on the role of the unconscious, Freud pioneered the theory and methods of **psychoanalysis.** This theory is based on the idea that human beings are born with unconscious drives that from the very beginning seek some sort of outlet or expression. Young children often express their drives in ways that violate social conventions for proper behavior. Parents typically forbid these behaviors and punish children for performing them. As a result, many innate drives are *repressed*—pushed out of conscious awareness. Repressed drives, however, continue to demand some kind of expression. Freud believed that many repressed drives were *sublimated,* or channeled into some kind of tolerated or even highly praised behavior.

psychoanalysis—A method of dealing with emotional problems in which the psychoanalyst encourages his patients to speak and reveal their innermost thoughts and dreams—especially dealing with events during their infancy.

Albert Einstein overturned the Newtonian universe of order and replaced it with his special theory of relativity, which provided new ways to view time and space. He is shown here with his wife.

Freud was particularly interested in psychological disorders, and he treated emotional disturbances by encouraging patients to bring back to the surface deeply repressed drives and memories. By making patients aware of their unconscious feelings, Freud hoped that they would understand themselves better and be able to respond more effectively to the problems they faced. Freud used the techniques of free association and dream interpretation to explore how unconscious feelings might be related to patients' symptoms. He believed that many of his patients' symptoms resulted from repressed sexual and aggressive drives. Freud's theories have had a tremendous influence not only on the science of psychology but also on our culture as a whole, although his theories were falling out of favor as the twentieth century ended.

The old Newtonian understanding of the world changed. The scientific giant of the first half of the twentieth century, Albert Einstein (1879–1955) contended in 1905 that light is propagated through space in the form of particles, which he called *photons*. Moreover, the energy contained in any particle of matter, such as the photon, is equal to the mass of that body multiplied by the square of the velocity of light (approximately 186,300 miles per second). This theory, expressed in the equation $E=mc^2$, provided the answer to many mysteries of physics. For example, questions such as how radioactive substances like radium and uranium are able to eject particles at enormous velocities and to go on doing so for millions of years could be examined in a new light. The magnitude of energy contained in the nuclei of atoms could be revealed. Above all, $E=mc^2$ showed that mass and energy are equatable. In 1906 Einstein formulated his special theory of **relativity,** which set out a radically new approach to explain the concepts of time, space, and velocity.

Ten years later Einstein proposed his general theory, in which he incorporated gravitation into relativity. He showed that gravitation is identical to acceleration and that light rays would be deflected in passing through a gravitational field—a prediction confirmed by observation of an eclipse in 1919 and by various experiments carried out in the American space programs in the 1960s and 1970s and the Hubble telescope in 1994. The theory of relativity has been subsequently confirmed in other ways as well. The conversion of mass into energy was dramatically demonstrated in the atomic bomb, which obtains its energy by the annihilation of part of the matter of which it is composed.

Einstein's theories upset the Newtonian views of the universe. Einstein's universe is not Newton's three-dimensional figure of length, breadth, and thickness. It is, instead, a four-dimensional space-time continuum in which time itself varies with velocity. Such a cosmic model calls for the use of non-Euclidean geometry. Einstein's theory changed scientists' attitude toward the structure and mechanics of the universe. On a broader scale, his relativistic implications penetrated many of the philosophical, moral, and aesthetic concepts of the twentieth century.

The fundamental discoveries in physics came before World War I. The British physicist Ernest Rutherford (1871–1937) advanced the theory in 1911 that each atom has a central particle, or nucleus, which is positively charged. Rutherford's argument repudiated the belief that the atom was indivisible. On the Continent, discoveries with even greater consequences were being made. German physicist Max Planck (1858–1947) studied radiant heat, which comes from the sun and is identical in nature with light. He found that the energy emitted from a vibrating electron proceeds not in a steady wave, as was traditionally believed, but discontinuously in the form of calculable "energy packages." Planck called each such package a *quantum;* thus the quantum theory was born. This jolt to traditional physics was to prove extremely valuable in the rapidly growing study of atomic physics.

Planck and Einstein investigated the infinite extent of the external universe, with a massive impact on the state of knowledge. At the same time, the equally infinite extent of the universe known as the mind also began to be studied in greater depth than ever before.

The Transformation of Literature and Music

Romanticism had broken the classical molds and opened the way for diversity in forms, styles, and themes. Romantics followed their emotions, while realists advocated a more objective way of portraying the world by stressing accuracy and precision. By the end of the nineteenth century a new movement, modernism—fragmented, disorganized, and united only in its reaction to the past—came to hold sway among Europe's writers, artists, and musicians.

By the beginning of the twentieth century, modernism freed the writer from all rules of composition and form and all obligations to communicate to a large audience. Poetry was especially affected by this new tendency. Toward the end of the century, in reaction to the demands of realism, French poets Stéphane Mallarmé (1842–1898) and Paul Verlaine (ver-LEN; 1844–1896) inaugurated the symbolist movement. Poetry rather than prose best fit the symbolists' goal of conveying ideas by suggestion rather than by precise, photographic word-pictures. In a sense, all modern literature stems from the symbolist movement. By increasing the power of the poet to reach the readers' imagination through expanded combinations of allusion, symbol, and double meaning, symbolism gave new obscurity to the written word.

Modernism affected music as it had affected poetry and art. The French composer Claude Debussy (de-BYEU-see; 1862–1918) tried in his music to imitate what he read in poetry and saw in impressionist paintings. He engaged in "tone painting" to achieve a special mood or atmosphere. This device can be heard in his "symphonic poem" *Prelude to the Afternoon of a Faun,* which shocked the musical world when it was first performed in 1894. The impressionist painters had gained their effects by juxtapos-

---

relativity—A radically new approach to view time and motion.

ing widely different colors. The composers juxtaposed widely separate chords to create similarly brilliant, shimmering effects.

Before 1914, a number of other composers had also been rebelling strongly against lyrical Romanticism and engaged in striking experimentation. Breaking with the "major-minor" system of tonality, which had been the musical tradition since the Renaissance, some of them used several different keys simultaneously, a device known as *polytonality*. Outstanding among such composers was Igor Stravinsky (1882–1971), who was less concerned with melody than with achieving effects by means of polytonality, dissonant harmonies, and percussive rhythms. Other composers, such as the Austrian-born Arnold Schoenberg (1874–1951), experimented with atonality, the absence of any fixed key. Schoenberg developed the 12-tone system, an approach in which compositions depart from all tonality and harmonic progressions while at the same time stressing extreme dissonances. Stravinsky's and Schoenberg's music may strike the first-time listener as harsh and unpleasant, but these experiments with polytonality and atonality were symbolic of their time, when the old absolute values were crumbling—a time of clashing dissonance.

Not only was Pablo Picasso the most prolific artist of the twentieth century, but he also taught the public over the course of his long life that there was a number of different ways that one could see and portray traditional subjects, as in Les Demoiselles d'Avignon *(1907). Pablo Picasso, "Les Demoiselles d'Avignon, Paris" (June–July 1907). Acquired through the Lillie P. Bliss Bequest (333.1939). © The Museum of Modern Art/Licensed by Scala/Art Resource, NY. ©2003 Estate of Pablo Picasso/Artists Rights Society (ARS), New York.*

Changes in the Visual Arts

The Spanish artist Pablo Picasso (1881–1974) and others helped develop the school called **cubism.** Cubists would choose an object, then construct an abstract pattern from it, giving the opportunity to view it simultaneously from several points. Such a pattern is evident in much of Picasso's work, including the pivotal *Les Demoiselles D'Avignon* (lay day-MWAH-sels dah-veen-YON; 1907). During the interwar period Picasso modified his cubist style and became a public figure through paintings such as *Guernica* (GWEHR-nee-kah), a mural that captures vividly the human horrors of the destruction of a small town in Spain by fascist air forces during that country's civil war. Henri Matisse (1869–1954) continued to exercise a major influence on young painters through his abstract works.

Another movement that came out of the 1920s was surrealism, led by artists such as Georgio de Chirico (KIR-e-KOH; 1888–1978) and René Magritte (mah-GREET; 1898–1967). The proponents of this approach saw the subconscious mind as the vehicle that could free people from the shackles of modern society and lead them to total creative freedom. They felt an affinity with "primitive art" and its close associations with magical and mythological themes. They exalted the irrational, the violent, and the absurd in human experience and saw World War I as proof that rationality did not exist and that, therefore, neither did artistic standards. Salvador Dalí (1904–1989) perhaps indicated his convictions about the artistic establishment and the society it represented when he gave a lecture on art while wearing a diver's helmet. Man Ray (1890–1976) and Marcel Duchamp (1887–1968) took the themes of irrationality and anti-traditionalism to their extremes in the artistic movement known as Dada.

Architecture

In the decade prior to World War I, an "international" style of architecture, which broke sharply with tradition, developed in Germany. This style, which stressed the use of various techniques from the machine age, was particularly well suited to early-twentieth-century industrialization. In 1914 one of the outstanding leaders of this movement, Walter Gropius (GRO-pei-us; 1883–1969), designed an exhibition hall in Cologne that emphasized horizontal lines, used glass, exposed staircases, and did not hide its functionalism. Nearly a century later, this hall is still regarded as contemporary. Proponents of this new movement in architecture established a highly influential school of functional art and architecture, the Bauhaus, in 1918.

One of Louis Sullivan's pupils, Frank Lloyd Wright (1867–1959), originated revolutionary designs for houses. One feature of Wright's structures was the interweaving of interiors and exteriors through the use of terraces and cantilevered roofs. He felt that a building should look appropriate on its site; it should "grow out of the land." His "prairie houses," with their long, low lines, were designed to blend in with the flat land of the Midwest. Much of what is today taken for granted in domestic architecture stems directly from Wright's experiments at the beginning of the twentieth century.

Architectural Pioneers

Alexandre Gustave Eiffel (1832–1923)	Planned and built the tower that bears his name for the 1889 Paris International Exposition
Walter Gropius (1883–1969)	One of founders of the Bauhaus movement; built avant-garde exposition hall in Cologne
Louis Sullivan (1856–1924)	Chicago architect who chose function over form in his skyscrapers
Frank Lloyd Wright (1867–1959)	Greatest twentieth-century American architect

CONCLUSION

Germany's rapid economic growth, military buildup, ambitious foreign policy, and inability to control its Austro-Hungarian ally helped bring the normally competitive European economic arena to a crisis in the summer of 1914. By violating Belgian neutrality and declaring war on Russia and France, Germany stood as the state most responsible for the outbreak of the First World War, a fact for which it was severely punished in the Treaty of Versailles. Its actions had provided the spark to the volatile environment of the aggressive state system and set in motion four years in which the science, wealth, and power of Europe were concentrated on the business of destroying much of what the Continent had accomplished in the previous century.

cubism—An art form that permits the portrayal of a subject from several different points of view simultaneously.

After the war, the non-European world took advantage of the exhaustion of the colonial powers to increase their drives toward national independence. In the Middle East, Arab national ambitions had flared in 1916 into a revolt against Ottoman rule. The immigration of European Jews to Palestine led to conflict between Arabs and Jews, which was to increase as time passed. The peoples of North Africa, the Middle East, India, southeastern Asia, and Oceania were gathering strength in their battle to oust the Europeans and govern themselves. In the huge colonial area south of the Sahara, Africans were beginning to stir restlessly against European rule. Even China, tradition-bound for centuries, turned to revolution to regain the power and prestige it had lost during the era of imperialism. Although Jiang Jieshi (Chiang Kai-shek) won an internal power struggle and organized the government, the country remained poor and weak. Meanwhile, Japan embarked on its amazing technological, industrial, and military growth and became a world power.

Suggestions for Web Browsing

You can obtain more information about topics included in this chapter at the websites listed below. See also the companion website that accompanies this text, **http://www.ablongman.com/brummett**, which contains an online study guide and additional resources.

The Great War
http://www.pitt.edu/~pugachev/greatwar/ww1.html

Vast site devoted to all aspects of World War I.

World War I
http://www.worldwar1.com/

Another extensive site on all aspects of World War I.

The Great Depression
http://history.searchbeat.com/greatdepression.htm

The SearchBeat Guide to the Great Depression offers resources on the Great Depression.

Spanish Civil War
http://www.spartacus.schoolnet.co.uk/Spanish-Civil-War.htm

Extensive site includes links to maps, history, and biographies regarding the Spanish civil war.

Museo Picasso Virtual: Online Picasso Project
http://www.tamu.edu/mocl/picasso/

Extensive online project, in multiple languages, offering a tour of the life, family, travels, and works of this twentieth-century master.

Literature and Film

As noted in the chapter, this period was an incredibly rich period for novels, films, and poetry. The person who best captured the era's complexity and perversity was Franz Kafka; see a collection of his work in *The Complete Stories of Kafka* (Schocken Books, 1995). One of the finest novels about war ever written was Erich Maria Remarque's *All Quiet on the Western Front* (many editions). Alexander Solzhenitsyn's *August 1914* (Bantam, 1974) is an important piece of literature describing Russia's entry into the war. The poet T. S. Eliot captured the deceptions of the age in poems such as "The Wasteland" and "The Love Songs of J. Alfred Prufrock" (see *Collected Poems: 1909–1962*, Harcourt, 1963). Andre Gide's *Journals* 1928–*1939* (University of Illinois Press, 2000) give a window into the tumultuous age of the 1930s in Paris. American writers—such as F. Scott Fitzgerald—*The Great Gatsby* (1925), *This Side of Paradise* (1920), *The Beautiful and the Damned* (1922); Ernest Hemingway—*A Farewell to Arms* (1929), *For Whom the Bells Toll* (1940), *The Sun Also Rises* (1926); and Sinclair Lewis—*Main Street* (1920), *Elmer Gantry* (1927)—dealt with lost idealism and hypocrisy in their works. Films have been made of each of the American novels that are listed above, in addition to *All Quiet on the Western Front* (Universal, 1930).

Suggestions for Reading

The most accessible general study of the war is Martin Gilbert, *The First World War: A Complete History* (Henry Holt, 1996). Alistair Horne, *The Price of Glory: Verdun, 1916* (Penguin, 1994) deals with a key event in the war. Paul Fussell captures the brutal nature and impact of the war in *The Great War and Modern Memory*, 25th anniv. ed. (Oxford University Press, 2000). On the crisis in the French army, see Leonard V. Smith, *Between Mutiny and Obedience: The Case of the French Fifth Infantry* (Princeton University Press, 1994). See Arthur S. Link, *Wilson the Diplomatist* (Hopkins, 1957), regarding the U.S. president's participation at Paris. The responsibilities of winning the war are discussed in William Laird Kleine-Ahlbrandt, *The* Burden of Victory: France, Britain, and the Enforcement of the Versailles Peace, 1919–*1925* (University Press of America, 1995).

For a recent analysis of Weimar's social and economic crises, see Richard Bessel, *Germany After the First World War* (Clarendon Press, 1993). Charles P. Kindelberger, *The World in Depression, 1929–1939*, rev. ed. (University of California Press, 1986), covers the global perspective of the 1930s. Charles S. Maier surveys the social and political consequences of the difficult interwar period in *Recasting Bourgeois Europe: Stabilization in France, Germany, and Italy in the Decade After World War I* (Princeton University Press, 1988). For events in the successor states, see Joseph Rothschild, *East Central Europe Between the Two World Wars* (University of Washington Press, 1974). John Stevenson provides a good survey of British life between the wars in *Social Conditions in Britain Between the Wars* (Penguin, 1977). For developments in France in the 1930s, see John T. Marcus, *French Socialism in the Crisis Years, 1933–1936* (Praeger, 1963). For the United States, see William E. Leuchtenberg, *The FDR Years: On Roosevelt and His Legacy* (Columbia University Press, 1995).

An understanding of the interwar scene can be gained from reading some of the biographies of the participants. See, for example, Albrecht Fölsing, *Albert Einstein: A Biography,* trans. Ewald Osers (Viking, 1997); Meryle Secrest, *Frank Lloyd Wright*: A Biography (University of Chicago Press, 1998); Ian Gibson, *The Shameful Life of Salvador Dalí* (Norton, 1998); and Michael Oliver, *Stravinsky* (Phaidon, 1995). Michael Fitzgerald, *Making Modernism: Picasso and the Creation of the Market for Twentieth-Century Art* (Farrar, Straus & Giroux, 1995), details the pioneering work of Picasso in exploiting the huge market for art among the ever-increasing upper middle classes.

CHAPTER

28

The USSR, Italy, Germany, and Japan

Democratic Failure and Authoritarian Government in the Interwar Period

CHAPTER CONTENTS

After the final shots of World War I were fired and the last peace treaties were signed, an uneasy 20-year period of peace began. The victorious Allies made their transitions from wartime to peacetime economies, and the United Kingdom, France, and the United States tried to resume their usual political pursuits. But it was impossible to return to a normal, pre-1914 life. The world had changed. Woodrow Wilson had foreseen the global suffering caused by World War I to be a prelude for a world "made safe for democracy." Instead, the war's aftershocks and the destruction of global economic stability shook democratic governments to their core, as we saw in Chapter 27, and aided the development of nondemocratic rule in Russia, Italy, and Germany. Japan, like the European governments of the prewar period, entered a period of increasing democratization in the immediate post-1919 era, but disillusionment with international cooperation following the breakdown of the world economy in 1929 and the rising tensions on the Asian continent turned Japan toward militaristic, nondemocratic rule in the late 1930s as well.

To the democratic nations watching the developments in these four countries in the 1930s, the USSR, Italy, Germany, and Japan seemed to have had greater success in mobilizing their economies. Their respective political programs seemed, to some in the West, to inspire their populations to work harder and accomplish more. Important public figures in the United States, the United Kingdom, and France—in despair at the seeming weakness of their own systems—praised the methods and the results of the dictators. As Italy, Germany, and Japan invaded other countries and ignored the League of Nations, the democratic world stood still, as if stunned by what was happening (see Chapter 31). When the Germans signed treaties with Japan in 1936 and 1940, Italy in 1937 and 1940, and the USSR in 1939, it seemed as if the nondemocratic forces had built up an unstoppable momentum.

Each of the nondemocratic powers pursued its own, unique path in the 20-year period between the world wars. The Bolshevik victory in 1917 in Russia led to the imposition of a Marxist-Leninist-Stalinist strategy on the governing of the USSR. Italy and Germany developed a new ideology, *fascism,* during the interwar period. In Japan, military-dominated cabinets easily destroyed democratic institutions that had only

1910

1912 Mussolini becomes editor of socialist newspaper *Avanti*

1912–1931 Taishō Democracy in Japan

1915

1915 Twenty-One Demands

1917 February-March Revolution overthrows Romanov dynasty; October-November Revolution overthrows provisional government; Communist rule established

1918 Treaty of Brest-Litovsk; World War I ends; revolutions in Germany

1919 Weimar Constitution adopted; Weimar Republic begins

1920

1921 Mussolini elected to Chamber of Deputies, established National Fascist party

1922 Fascists march on Rome; USSR formed

1923 Hitler's *Putsch* fails

1924 Lenin dies

1925

1925 Universal Manhood Suffrage in Japan

1928 Stalin institutes first five-year plan

1930

1931 Manchurian Incident

1933 Hitler elected chancellor of Germany, proclaims Third Reich

1937 War with China (Japan)

1940

1940 Tripartite Pact

1940 Trotsky assassinated in Mexico

recently emerged. Each of these countries went through the failure of democratic institutions (however brief in Russia), severe economic problems, governmental change leading to one-party control, and finally state mobilization of the masses. Even though they arrived at their political systems in different ways, the governments of the USSR, Italy, Germany, and Japan developed antidemocratic, antiliberal, anti-free-trade policies, and each limited individual freedom for its citizens. Though they signed treaties with one another, in the end, most saw their national strength dependent on their own military expansion and rejected the multilateral world order championed by the democracies after World War I.

REVOLUTIONS IN RUSSIA: 1917 AND 1928–1939

- *How did each of the two revolutions—the November 1917 Revolution of Lenin and the 1928–1939 changes imposed by Stalin—transform Russia?*

Russia entered the war in August 1914 in a buoyant and patriotic mood. It took only two months to dampen initial optimism and to expose the army's weakness and the tsarist government's corruption and inefficiency. By the middle of 1915, drastic losses (more than 2 million casualties) and food and fuel shortages lowered morale. Strikes increased among the factory workers during 1916, and the peasants, whose sons were dying in large numbers and whose desire for land reform was being ignored, became discontented. The enormous costs of Russia's participation in World War I and the incompetence of the government led in March to the first Russian Revolution of 1917, and the end of the Romanov dynasty.

The First, "Spontaneous" 1917 Revolution

A spontaneous event from below sparked the 1917 Russian Revolution. In the first part of March,[1] a strike broke out in a Petrograd factory. By March 8, sympathy strikes had virtually paralyzed the city. At the same time, a bread shortage occurred, which brought more people into the streets. Scattered fighting broke out between the strikers and protesters on one side and the police on the other. Tsar Nicholas II ordered the strikers back to work and dismissed the Duma (parliament) on March 11. His orders touched off the revolutionary crisis. The Duma refused to go home, and the strikers defied the government and held mass meetings. The next day the army and police openly sided with the workers.

Three events occurring between March 12 and March 15 marked the end of the old regime. On March 12 the Duma declared the formation of a provisional committee (renamed the *Provisional Government* on March 15) to serve as a caretaker administration until a Constituent Assembly could be elected to write a constitution for the future Russian republic. On the same day, Marxist socialists and Socialist Revolutionaries in Petrograd formed the **Soviet** ("council") of Workers' Deputies (renamed three days later the *Soviet of Workers' and Soldiers' Deputies*). Nicholas abdicated on March 15 in favor of his brother Michael, who turned down the throne the next day in favor of the Provisional Government. After more than three centuries in power, the Romanov dynasty ceased to rule.

For the next six months Russia proceeded under a system Leon Trotsky, the great Marxist theoretician and revolutionary, described as "dual power"—the Provisional Government and the Soviet. The moderates and liberals in the Provisional Government quickly produced a program of civil rights and liberties that gave Russia a springtime of freedom in 1917, the likes of which the country had never known before and would not experience again for 70 years. From the first, however, the Provisional Government was hampered by its temporary nature: It refused to take permanent action on major issues until the Constituent Assembly, elected by all Russians, could convene to write a constitution.

Soviet—A council. First used in Russia during the 1905 Revolution when the Social Democrats organized Soviets (councils) of workers.

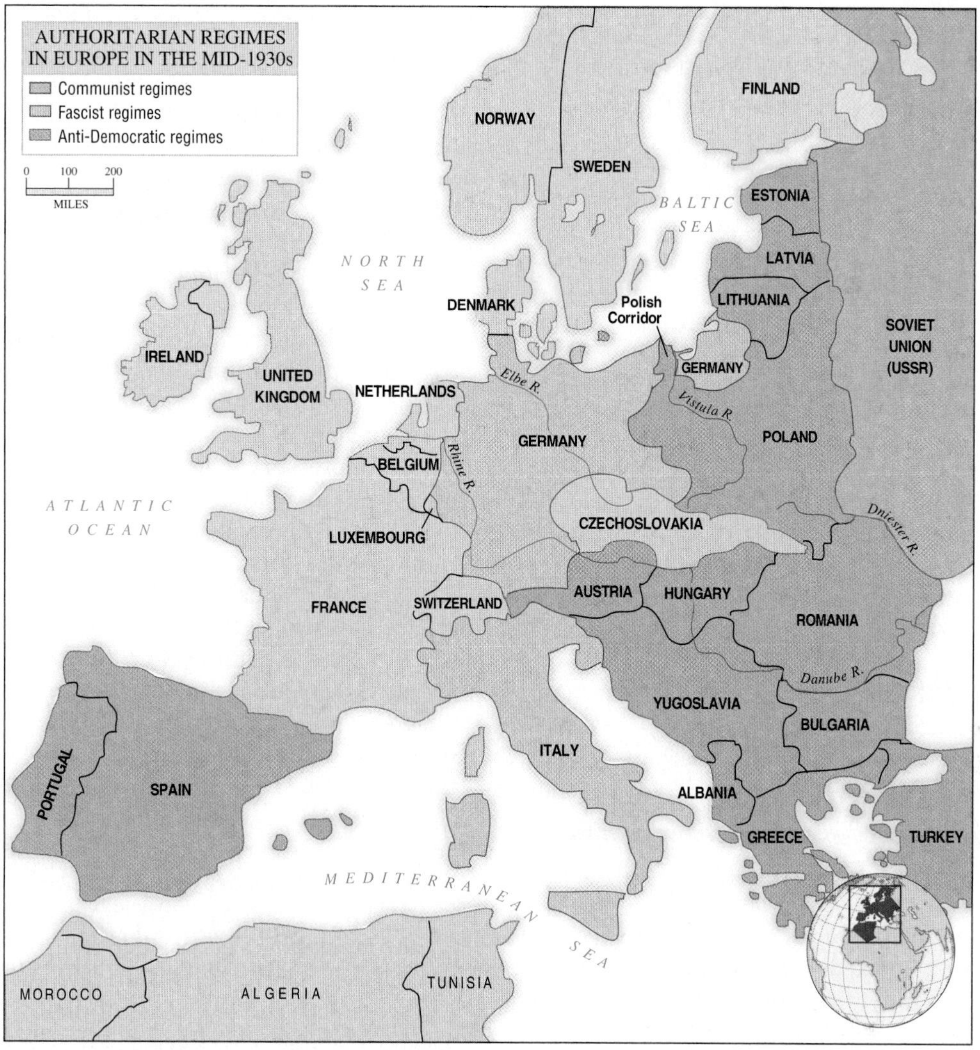

The self-proclaimed democracies may have won World War I, but they lost the peace. By the end of the 1930s, they were greatly outnumbered by fascist, authoritarian, and communist regimes.

The Soviet was dominated by the **Menshevik** wing of the Russian Social Democratic party along with the Socialist Revolutionaries. The Mensheviks closely followed Marx's teachings and believed that a liberal, bourgeois phase of history had to run its course. Even though they had greater popular support than the Provisional Government, they refused to take power. They did not believe 1917 to be the historically proper moment, as defined by Marx's theories, and they doubted their own capacity to maintain order. After the fall of the tsar, power passed to those who could not or would not rule.

From the first, the dual power system functioned in a contradictory and ineffective way. On March 14 the Soviet issued its first law, Order No. 1, which placed the running of the army on a democratic basis, through a committee structure. Soldiers were to obey only those orders that agreed with the official position of the Soviet, which wanted peace. At the same time, the Provisional Government insisted on living up to Russia's commitments to the Allies, carrying out the war, in hopes of gaining the Bosporus, Constantinople, and the Dardanelles from the crumbling Ottoman Empire.

As the months wore on, the position of moderates in both parts of the system weakened, and all the involved parties became discredited. The Provisional Government put off calling the Constituent Assembly and thereby deferred any possibility of finding solutions to the problems Russia faced. It continued to

---

Menshevik—The Russian Social Democrats meeting in London split into two wings in 1903—the Bolsheviks (the majority) and the Mensheviks (the minority)—reflecting from the results of a vote on party policies. The Mensheviks went on to become the most powerful branch of the Social Democrats in Russia until 1907. The Bolsheviks, led by Lenin, finally gained power in November 1917.

End of the Romanov Dynasty: The February-March Revolution of 1917

All dates are according to the Gregorian calendar, which replaced the Julian calendar in use in Russia at the time.

March 8	Sympathy strikes paralyze city
March 11	Tsar orders strikers back to work, dismisses Duma
March 12	Army and police disobey orders; Duma declares formation of provisional committee—Provisional Government on March 15; Socialists proclaim formation of Soviet of Workers' Deputies—Soviet of Workers' and Soldiers' Deputies on March 15
March 15	Tsar Nicholas I abdicates, passes power to his brother, Michael
March 16	Michael renounces power, empowerment of Provisional Government

pursue the war to "honor its commitments" and to gain the prizes promised in the secret treaties. The Provisional Government's actions, combined with the refusal of the Mensheviks to take control for ideological reasons, meant that the masses, who suffered from economic hardships or fought and died on the front lines, could find little consolation in either branch of dual power.

By July the liberals and moderates had given up the reins of power. Alexander Kerensky (1881–1970), who had been the only real revolutionary in the original cabinet, became the head of the Provisional Government. He was in an impossible situation. Leftists accused the Provisional Government of heartlessly pursuing the war, while rightists condemned it for tolerating too many leftists. In the meantime, the Soviet extended its organization throughout Russia by setting up local affiliates. Through the summer, however, the Soviets lacked the forceful leadership they needed to take control of the country.

The Second, "Bolshevik" Revolution of 1917

In 1917 Lenin returned to Russia from exile in Switzerland, intent on giving the revolution the leadership it lacked. He had spelled out his tactics and ideas in the previous decade, and his disciples in Russia, the **Bolsheviks,** had built up a core of supporters in the factories and the army. As late as December 1916, he had stated that the revolution would not occur within his lifetime. Four months later, working through Swiss contacts and with German assistance, he returned to Russia. The Germans gave him transportation and financial support in the hope that he would cause widespread chaos, forcing Russia to withdraw from the war.

From the moment he stepped off the train in Petrograd on the evening of April 16, Lenin tried to control the revolution. He proposed immediately stopping the war against Germany and starting one against "social oppressors." He called for giving all power to the Soviets and nationalizing all land. He also pushed for calling all Social Democrats, of whatever persuasion, communists. Lenin badly misjudged his audience, and the Mensheviks and Social Revolutionaries rejected his program.

During the summer and fall of 1917 the Provisional Government and the Soviet continued their misgovernment. Kerensky tried to rule through a series of coalitions in which the political balance continually shifted to the left. By the middle of July, after a moderately successful offensive against the Austrians, soldiers began to desert in large numbers rather than face a useless death in World War I. The Russian front, along with the army, disintegrated. In the capital, the Mensheviks persisted in refusing to take power through the Soviet: The historical time was not right. As if to match the ineptness of dual power, the Bolsheviks made an ill-conceived attempt to take power. The move backfired, and Lenin was forced to flee in disguise to Finland.

After surviving the Bolshevik crisis, Kerensky faced a new threat from the right when General Lavr Kornilov tried to "help" the government by sending his troops to the capital. Kerensky and the Soviet interpreted this action as a right-wing counterrevolutionary move and mobilized to head it off. Kornilov's ill-advised maneuver failed, and ironically, he weakened the people he wanted to help.

Between March and October 1917 the force of the revolution ground to bits all of Russia's structures and parties, from monarchist to Menshevik. The economic system fell apart as the rhythms of planting and commerce were disrupted by the uproar. To the people caught in this chaos, the moderates' political dreams, the Mensheviks' revolutionary timing, and the Bolsheviks' schemes for the seizure of power were all totally irrelevant.

Bolshevik—The branch of the Social Democratic party, led by Lenin, that governed Russia after 1917. The official name came to be the Communist party.

K. N. Aksyonov's portrayal of V. I. Lenin's arrival at the Finland Station in Petrograd, received by an adoring throng, idealizes what in fact was a difficult time for the Bolshevik leader, in April 1917.

The actual revolution took place far away from the politicians and "great men." The army withered away as mass desertions and the execution of officers became commonplace. In the countryside the peasants began carrying out land reform on their own, expelling landowners and killing those who would not leave. In the cities workers began to take over factories. The Russian Empire broke apart from internal conflicts, the continued pressure of war, and the rising spirits of the nationalities who had been oppressed for centuries.

Only the Bolsheviks seemed to have an answer to Russia's crisis; even their slogans, such as "Peace, Land, and Bread," reflected what was already happening. Furthermore, they had the discipline and adaptability to take advantage of events. By October 1917 the Bolsheviks had discarded their slogan, "All Power to the Soviets." Frankly, Lenin, the unchallenged Bolshevik leader, now controlled the Petrograd Soviet. After much hesitation, he decided to move on November 6. The Military Revolutionary Committee, led by Leon Trotsky and supported by the Communist-dominated crew of the battleship *Aurora,* took control of the communications and police centers in Petrograd. With the exception of sporadic fighting around the Winter Palace, Trotsky's military forces had little trouble. They arrested all members of the Provisional Government who could be found. Kerensky escaped from the capital in a car flying the U.S. flag. Lenin then found himself leading a party of more than 200,000 people (an increase from 23,600 in February), which claimed control of a state with more than 170 million inhabitants.

Power, Allied Intervention, and Civil War

The Bolsheviks assumed power over a war-weakened, revolution-ravaged state that was in terrible condition. Lenin's takeover split the Soviet itself when the Mensheviks and the Social Revolutionaries refused to participate. Lenin had a bare majority at the Soviet's first postrevolutionary meeting. In the free elections held in December to form a Constituent Assembly, the Bolsheviks received just one-fourth of the votes. Yet such details as democratic representation did not stop Lenin. He proceeded to rule Russia. The Bolsheviks immediately put through decrees to declare peace and settle the land question. In the meantime, his cadres imposed their control over Moscow and the other cities in the country.

Lenin then began to lay the foundations for a single-party dictatorship that endured until 1991. When the Constituent Assembly convened in Petrograd on January 18, 1918, and proved that it would not be a tool for Lenin, the Bolsheviks closed it down at bayonet point the next day. By dissolving the Constituent Assembly, Lenin crushed all remnants of the briefly flowering democracy. This decisive step sealed the fate of the Mensheviks and most other opposition leftist parties. Not for 71 years would there be contested elections, open criticism of the central power, and the possibility of a potential democratic opposition.

Almost immediately the revolutionary government came under attack from the White forces, the Allied Expeditionary Forces, and the new Polish state. The Whites, a powerful but fragmented group of anti-Bolsheviks, responded to the overthrow of the Provisional Government and the dissolution of the Constituent Assembly by attacking the revolutionary government. The resulting Civil War would claim as many casualties in three years as the country had lost in World War I. The Allied Powers sent several small expeditionary armies to Russia for the stated purpose of controlling matériel they had sent the former tsarist army. In reality, they helped the Whites.

Lenin also had to make peace with Germany and after two months of negotiations concluded the Treaty of Brest-Litovsk (1918). This agreement drastically reduced the territory under Russian control and made the centers of government much more exposed to attack. In reality, Lenin sacrificed territory over which he had no control and took his country out of a war it could not fight.

The Allies, still at war with Germany, feared that the Bolsheviks were in a conspiracy with the Germans, especially after the terms of the Brest-Litovsk treaty became known. They also hoped that if Lenin could be overthrown, the Whites might reopen fighting against the Central Powers. The last of the expeditionary forces, the Japanese, did not leave until 1922. War broke out between Russia and Poland over a disputed boundary.

From its new capital at Moscow, the Red (Bolshevik) government took all means to defend the revolution. Lenin's forces reimposed the death penalty (it had been abolished in all areas—except in the Russian army at the front—by the Provisional Government) and unleashed a reign of terror. The Red Army and the Cheka (secret police) systematically destroyed the enemies of the revolution as well as individuals who were only lukewarm in their support of the new regime. Prison camps and repressive terror harsher than any since Ivan IV dominated life in the Russian state. In July 1918 the former tsar and his family, under house arrest since the outbreak of the revolution, were herded into the cellar of the house in which they were being held and were executed. They would not receive their final burial until 1998.

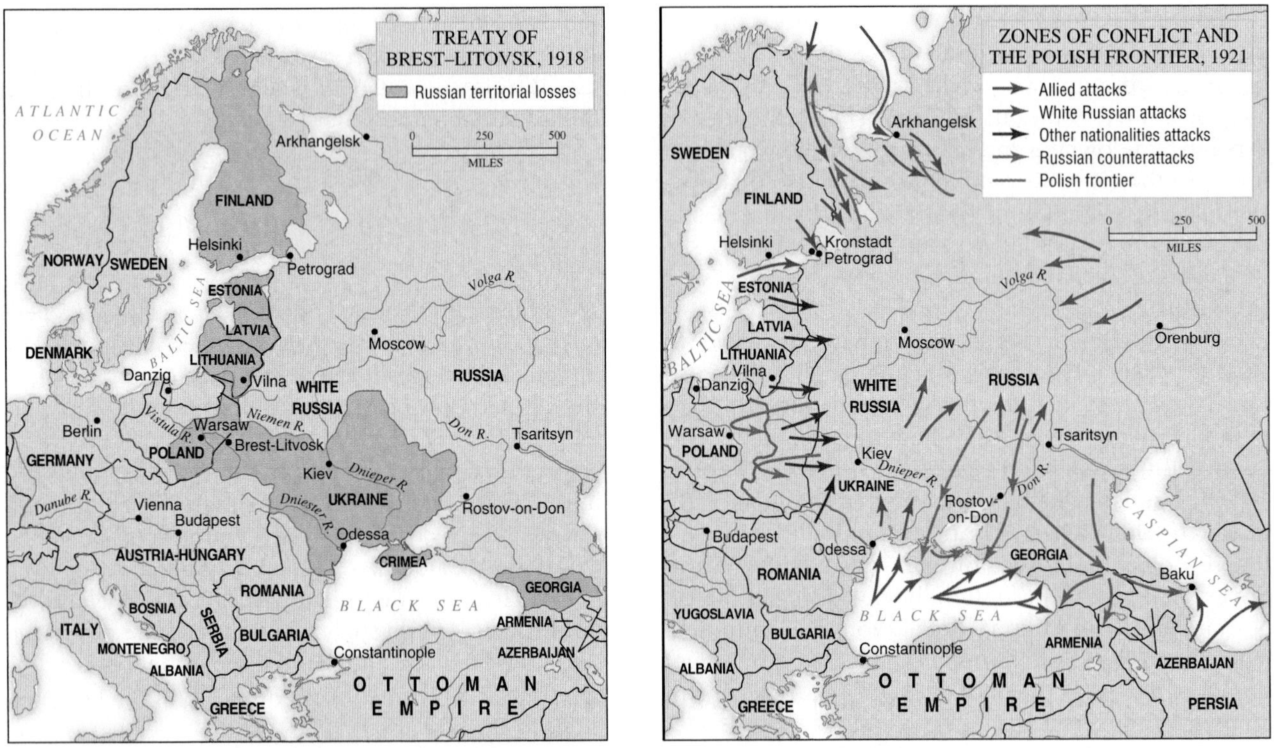

Germany took advantage of Russian weaknesses after the 1917 revolution to deprive the revolutionary state of much of its economic base and territory. Not only did the fledgling Moscow-based communist state face intervention by the Western Allies in 1918, but it also had a war with the newly reunited Polish state over the western borderlands formerly controlled by the tsars.

After the Central Powers surrendered in November 1918, Allied intervention in Russia ceased, and the Bolsheviks concentrated their energies against the Whites. Trotsky turned the Red Army into a disciplined, centralized force. The disorganized and dispersed White opposition, whose units ranged from Siberia to the Caucasus to Europe, could not match the Red forces. Taking advantage of their shorter supply lines, ideological unity, and dislike of Allied intervention, the Bolsheviks put an end to White resistance by 1920. The Whites were united on few issues besides their hatred of the Bolsheviks. After their defeat, nearly a million of them scattered across the globe.

Theory, Reality, and the State

Lenin had no hesitation about revising Marx's doctrines to fit Russian conditions. He had long opposed all democratic parliamentary procedures, especially the concept of an officially recognized opposition party. He advocated instead a revolutionary "dictatorship of the **proletariat"** under Bolshevik leadership. The new order would rule in accordance with "democratic centralism," in which the vanguard party would anticipate the best interests of the masses and rule for them.

Lenin altered certain aspects of the Marxist concept of the historical process. He accepted the view that the proletarian-socialist revolution must be preceded by a bourgeois-democratic revolution. He interpreted the March 1917 events as the first democratic revolution and his own coup d'état in November as the second, or proletarian-socialist, revolution. This approach drastically shortened the historical process by which the bourgeois stage was to run its course. Lenin justified dissolving the Constituent Assembly on the grounds that a higher form of democratic principle had now been achieved, making the assembly superfluous. The November Revolution had vested all power in the Russian Republic in the people themselves, as expressed in their revolutionary committees, the soviets.

The new state acted in many spheres. In policies reminiscent of Robespierre's tenure during the French Revolution, the new government attacked the church, changed the calendar (adopting the Gregorian and rejecting the Julian system), and simplified the alphabet. The Cheka enforced ideological unity with a level of terror that set the standard for later Soviet secret police organizations.

In the first six years after Lenin seized power, there were three major developments relating to the Communist party, the name adopted by the Bolsheviks in 1918. First, all other parties were suppressed. Second,

Russian children help carry the propaganda for Stalin's campaign for collectivization of agriculture. The banner reads, in part, "Everybody to the collective farm!" These happy faces belie the tragedy resulting from the collectivization program in which millions fell victim to slaughter or starvation.

the function of the party was changed from that of carrying out the revolution to that of governing the country. Third, within the party itself, a small elite group called the **Politburo,** which set policy, consolidated power in its hands. Among the members of the first Politburo were Lenin, Trotsky, and Stalin. The second major organ of the party was the Secretariat for the Central Committee, which oversaw the implementation of policy into practice.

The state itself became known as the Russian Socialist Federated Soviet Republic (RSFSR). As the Moscow-based Communist government extended its authority after the civil war, the jurisdiction of the RSFSR grew. In 1922 the Union of Soviet Socialist Republics (USSR) was formed, consisting of the four constituent socialist republics: the RSFSR, the Ukraine, White Russia (Belorussia), and Transcaucasia; and the USSR would soon expand to reflect the multinational nature of the Eurasian state. Although it appeared that the state exercised sovereign power, the USSR actually was governed by the Communist party. So great did the authority of the Communist party become over the formation and administration

proletariat—In Marxist theory, the proletariat is the politically class-conscious portion of the working classes who would move to achieve the socialist revolution.

Politburo—The small, elite group of the Communist party that established policy.

of policy that, before Lenin's death in early 1924, it could be said that party and state were one. Consequently, whoever controlled the party controlled the state, and in the new Soviet state the key person would be Joseph Stalin.

War Communism and the NEP

From 1918 to 1921 Lenin tried to apply undiluted Marxist principles to eliminate private ownership of land; nationalize banks, railways, and shipping; and restrict the money economy. This policy, known as *war communism,* was widely unpopular. The peasants, who had just attained their centuries-long goal of controlling their own land, did not like the prospects of collectivization and the surrender of their surplus grain to the state. Many workers did not want to be forced to work in factories. Former managers showed little enthusiasm for running enterprises for the state's benefit.

In the early months of 1920, the new government faced its most dangerous crisis to date. Six years of war and civil strife had left Russia exhausted. Industrial production was 13 percent of what it had been in 1914. Crop failures, poor management, and transportation breakdowns contributed to the disaster. Famine brought more than 20 million people to the brink of starvation. The government was forced to ask for help, and organizations such as Herbert Hoover's American project to bring relief to Russia helped the country through the crisis, but not before some 5 million people died.

Lenin Calls for Electrification of All Russia

Internal chaos, in addition to controversy with Poland over disputed borders, further plagued Lenin's government. From 1918 to 1921 other areas of the former Russian Empire—Finland, Estonia, Latvia, Lithuania, and Bessarabia—chose to go their own way. In February 1921 sailors at Kronstadt, formerly supporters of the regime, rebelled against the Bolsheviks and were massacred by the Red Army. Lenin said that the revolt "illuminated reality like a flash of lightning,"[2] and chose to make an ideological retreat.

War communism was a total failure. Lenin decided that it was necessary "to take one step backward in order to go two steps forward." He explained that Russia had tried to do too much too soon in attempting to change everything at once. He also noted that there had not been a firestorm of complementary communist revolutions sweeping the globe. The outbreaks in Germany and Hungary had been brutally quashed. Russia stood alone. Compromise was necessary to survive, and besides altering his diplomatic front abroad, he recommended a return to certain practices of capitalism, the so-called New Economic Policy, or NEP.

This retreat from war communism lasted until 1928 and allowed the Soviet state to get on its feet. Peasants were relieved from the wholesale appropriation of grain. After paying a fixed tax, they were permitted to sell their surplus produce in the open market. Private management could once again run firms and factories employing fewer than 20 employees. Workers in state industries received a graduated wage scale. Foreign commerce and technology were actively sought. These compromises proved to be highly beneficial, and the Soviet economy revived.

Ideological purists criticized the policy and pointed out that private businesses and the **kulaks,** as the ambitious peasants who accumulated property were called, profited greatly. Lenin's concessions and compromises gave the Communists time to regroup and recover, and the Russian people gained much-needed breathing space. Lenin emphasized the absolute necessity for the party to "control the commanding heights of the economy." The state continued to manage banking, transportation, heavy industry, and public utilities.

The NEP was Lenin's last major contribution. In broken health since surviving a would-be assassin's bullet in 1918, he worked as much as he could until his death in January 1924.

Trotsky Versus Stalin

A weakness of all dictatorships is that there is no well-defined mechanism to pass power from one leader to the next. Lenin was the one person in the party who possessed unchallenged authority and whose decrees were binding. After his death, Leon Trotsky and Joseph Stalin, rivals with conflicting policies and personalities, fought for power.

Leon Trotsky (1879–1940), born Lev Davidovich Bronstein, was a star in the political arena. He was a magnificent, charismatic orator; an energetic and magnetic leader in all areas; and a first-rate intellectual and theoretician. He turned to Marxism as a teenager and, like Lenin, had been exiled to Siberia for his revolutionary activities. He participated in the major events of Russian social democracy. Trotsky was a member of the *Iskra* (EES-craw) group of Russian exiles in Zurich, had been present in London in 1903 and opposed Lenin in the Bolshevik-Menshevik split, played a key role in the 1905 Russian Revolution, and was an essential figure in the 1917 revolutions and the Civil War. His egocentricity and arrogance contrasted sharply with the shrewd and cunning nature of his less colorful but more calculating rival.

Joseph Stalin (1879–1953), born in Georgia as Joseph Vissarionovich Dzhugashvili (zhu-GOSH-vee-

---

kulaks—Farmers in the USSR who owned major farm implements or employed others.

lee), labored for the revolution in obscurity. While Trotsky played the star, Stalin worked behind the scenes. Trotsky was a crowd-pleasing orator; Stalin, when he spoke in Russian (his second language—Georgian was his first), was not an inspiring speaker. Admitted to a seminary to be trained for the priesthood, the young Stalin was later expelled for radical opinions. In the years before the revolutions Stalin served the Bolsheviks by robbery to gain funds for the party's organization and propaganda activities. In all ways he faithfully supported Lenin—unlike Trotsky, who had not been a uniformly obedient disciple between 1903 and 1917. Stalin was exiled east of the Urals a number of times before he returned to Petrograd in 1917 to play an active role in the events of that year. He knew his own strengths and weaknesses. He also formed his opinion of Trotsky rather early on, characterizing him in 1907 as "beautifully useless."

After the 1917 revolutions, Stalin did much of the less glamorous organizational work of the party; he was also responsible for dealing with the various nationalities. While others in the Politburo dealt with ideological questions or fought the civil war, Stalin created a network of people—loyal to him alone—who worked in the bureaucratic apparatus and came to be known as *apparatchiks* (ap-pa-RAT-cheeks). With and through them he controlled the bureaucracy. In 1922 *Pravda* ("Truth"), the official party newspaper, carried a brief announcement that the Central Committee had confirmed Stalin as general secretary of the secretariat, a position that became the most powerful in the Soviet Union.

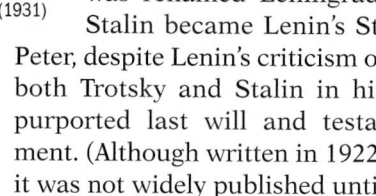

After Lenin's death, Stalin moved to construct a new secular religion for the Soviet Union, Leninism, formed in 1924 and powerful for more than 60 years. The mark of faith came to be unquestioning loyalty to Lenin. The city of Petrograd, for example, was renamed Leningrad. Stalin became Lenin's St. Peter, despite Lenin's criticism of both Trotsky and Stalin in his purported last will and testament. (Although written in 1922, it was not widely published until the 1950s.)

CASE STUDY
Lenin (1920) vs. Stalin (1931)

In the competition with Trotsky, Stalin won because he was the better organizer and the more skillful manipulator of people. Staying in the background, Stalin, the modest "helper," played the game of "divide and conquer" as members of the Politburo fought among themselves. By 1926 party members realized that Stalin had consolidated his position and had the full support of the party apparatus. By the end of that year, Trotsky and other opponents were removed from the Politburo. By 1929 Stalin was referred to as the "Lenin of today." Stalin's supporters occupied the key posts in both government and party, and he became the chairman of the Politburo. By 1940 he had eliminated all of the old Bolsheviks, including Trotsky, who was exiled and finally struck down by an assassin in Mexico, on Stalin's orders.

More than just an opportunist or a super-bureaucrat, Stalin had his own ideological views on the future of the country. Trotsky and others had believed, along with Lenin, that the USSR could not survive indefinitely as a socialist island in a capitalist ocean. It was the duty, they held, of Russian Communists to push for revolution elsewhere. Stalin, less a theorist than a political realist, viewed the idea of a world revolution as premature. He correctly noted that Marxism had made little headway outside the USSR, despite the existence of what, from the Marxist standpoint, were advanta-

Joseph Vissarionovich Dzhugashvili, fourth from the right in the first row, chose to call himself Stalin ("steel") and came close to gaining totalitarian control of the USSR during the 1930s working through his chosen men of the apparatus, the apparatchiks, pictured with him here, many of whom would remain in power for a half-century.

geous conditions for revolution in Germany and Italy. Stalin called for a new policy of building up socialism in a single state. (Lenin had once hinted at that alternative in 1921.) He put an end to the NEP and began taking "two steps forward"—with brutal and far-reaching results.

Stalin's Economics: Revolution from Above, 1928–1939

Russia had begun industrialization at a late date and from the 1890s on was continuously aware of its backwardness. The drastic destruction of World War I and the Civil War reversed much of the progress that had been made, and by the late 1920s Stalin was deeply concerned with the country's economic weakness in the face of foreign invasion. He ordered a radical overhaul of the entire country and society designed to make 50 years' progress in ten.

The NEP was scrapped in 1928, and Stalin imposed collectivization of agriculture and a series of five-year plans calling for heavy industrialization. Long working hours and a six-day workweek were instituted in an attempt to revolutionize the Soviet Union's economic structure. For the first time in history, a government controlled all significant economic activity through a central planning apparatus. This was an attempt to remove the old market-based system and replace it with new framework. To drive the entire population along, Stalin strengthened his secret police so that they could force the nation through what would be a decade of convulsive internal struggle. By 1939 Stalin had consolidated his personal dictatorship, at the cost of 10 to 20 million lives.

War on the Peasants

Stalin wanted to transform the peasants into a rural proletariat, raising food on state and collective farms, not on their own plots. He had little doctrinal help from Marx, who had not considered that the revolution he forecast could take place in a peasant-dominated society. Marx left little guidance about what to do with the peasants beyond mention of collectivized agriculture. He had assumed that capitalism would convert peasants into day laborers before the socialist revolution took place; hence farming would continue, except that now the state would own the farms.

Lenin's war communism programs had failed, yet Stalin went back to them as he drew up his guidelines to transform agriculture. The major problem he faced was to convince the peasants to surrender their private lands, which they had finally got in 1917, to the state and collective farms.

Under Stalin's program, the state farms, *sovkhoz* (sof-HOHS), would be owned outright by the government, which would pay the workers' wages. The collective farms, *kolkhoz* (KOLK-hohs), would be created from land taken from the kulaks and from the peasants who would voluntarily accept the government's decree to merge their own holdings. *Kolkhoz* members would work the land under the management of a board of directors. At the end of the year each farm's net earnings would be totaled in cash and in kind, and the members would be paid on the basis of the amount and skill of their labor.

The theoretical advantages of large-scale mechanized farming over small-scale peasant agriculture were obvious. In addition, the government intended the reforms to permit the more efficient political education of the peasants. Further, the new programs would liquidate the kulaks, successful farmers who owned more property than their neighbors and who represented a disturbing element on the socialist landscape.

The vast majority of peasants disagreed violently with Stalin's agricultural program. They did not want to give up their land. One of the party leaders, Lazar Kaganovich, noted that "women in the countryside in many cases played the most 'advanced' role in the reaction against collective farms."[3] When the peasants did not flock to the government's banners, Stalin ordered harsher methods. When the class war between the poor peasants and the kulaks did not take place, he sent the secret police and the army to the villages. The transition to collectivization was carried out under some of the most barbarous and brutal measures ever enacted by a government against its own people.

In the tragedy that followed, millions of people, especially in the Ukraine, died from direct attack, from famine, or in work camps. By a decree in February 1930 the state forced about 1 million kulaks off their land and took their possessions. Many peasants opposed these measures, slaughtering their herds and destroying their crops rather than hand them over to the state. In 1933 the number of horses was less than half the number there had been in 1928, and there were 40 percent fewer cattle and half as many sheep and goats. After nine years of war on the peasants, however, 90 percent of the land and 100 million peasants were in the collective and state farms.

The Five-Year Plans

Stalin introduced the system of central planning in 1928. He and his advisers assumed that by centralizing all aspects of the allocation of resources and removing market forces from the economy, they could ensure a swift buildup of capital goods and heavy industries. The five-year plans, which began in 1929, restricted the manufacture of consumer goods and abolished capitalism in the forms permitted under the NEP. Citizens were allowed to own certain types of private property, houses, furniture, clothes, and personal effects. They could not own property that could be used to make profits by hiring workers. The state was to be the only employer.

The first five-year plan called for a 250 percent increase in overall industrial productivity. The state and police turned their entire effort to this goal. Even in the chaos that occurred—buildings were erected to house nonexistent machines, and machines were shipped to places where there were no buildings—growth did take place.

The party cited statistics to prove that the plan had been achieved in four and one-half years. Whether these were accurate or not—and they have been vigorously challenged—Soviet industry and society were totally transformed. The costs were disastrous, but Stalin portrayed the Soviet Union as being in a form of war with the world, and without strength, he pointed out, the USSR would be crushed.

The second five-year plan began in 1933 and sought to resolve some of the mistakes of the first. The government placed greater emphasis on improving the quality of industrial products and on making more consumer goods. The third plan, begun in 1938, emphasized national defense. State strategies called for industrial plants to be shifted east of the Urals, and efforts were made to develop new sources of oil and other important commodities. Gigantism was the key, as the world's largest tractor factory was built in Chelyabinsk (chel-EE-AH-binsk), greatest power station in Dnepropetrovsk (dnie-pro-PET-rovsk), and largest automobile plant in Gorki.

The plans achieved remarkable results. In 1932 Soviet authorities claimed an increase in industrial output of 334 percent over 1914 levels; 1937 output was 180 percent over that of 1932. But the high volume of production was often tied to mediocre quality, and the achievements were gained only with an enormous cost in human life and suffering and massive damage to the environment. At first the burdensome cost of importing heavy machinery, tools, equipment, and finished steel from abroad forced a subsistence scale of living on the people. These purchases were paid for by the sale of food and raw material in the world's markets at a time when the prices for such goods had fallen drastically.

DOCUMENT
Stalin Demands Rapid Industrialization

In the rush to industrialize, basic aspects of Marxism were set aside. The dictatorship *of* the proletariat increasingly became the dictatorship *over* the proletariat. Another ideological casualty was the basic concept of economic egalitarianism. In 1931 Stalin declared that equality of wages was "alien and detrimental to Soviet production" and a "petit bourgeois deviation." So much propaganda was used to implant this twist that the masses came to accept the doctrine of inequality of wages as a fundamental communist principle.

The Great Purges

During the 1930s, Stalin consolidated his hold over the Communist party and created the political system that would last until the ascent to power of Mikhail Gorbachev in 1985. Stalin established an all-powerful, personal, dictatorial rule by doing away with all of his rivals, real and potential, in purges. He also took the opportunity to remove all scientific, cultural, and educational figures who did not fit in with his plans for the future. By 1939 Stalin had destroyed what was left of the Russian revolutionary tradition and replaced it with the rule of his people—the apparatchiks—who lived well in comparison with the rest of the Soviet population.

The long arm of the secret police gathered in thousands of Soviet citizens to face the kangaroo court and the firing squad. All six original members of the 1920 Politburo who survived Lenin were purged by Stalin. Old Bolsheviks who had been loyal comrades of Lenin, high officers of the Red Army, directors of industry, and rank-and-file party members were liquidated. Millions more were sent to forced labor camps. It has been estimated that between 5 and 6 percent of the population spent time in the pretrial prisons of the secret police.

Party discipline and fear prevented party members from turning against Stalin, who controlled the party. The world watched a series of show trials in which loyal Communists confessed to an amazing array of charges, generally tied, after 1934, to the assassination of Sergei Kirov, Leningrad party chief and one of Stalin's chief aides. Western journalists reported news of the trials to the world while the drugged, tortured, and intimidated defendants confessed to crimes they had not committed. By 1939 fully 70 percent of the members of the Central Committee elected in 1934 had been purged. Among officers in the armed forces, the purges claimed 3 of 5 army marshals, 14 of 16 army commanders, all 8 admirals, 60 of 67 corps commanders, 136 of 199 divisional commanders, 221 of 397 brigade commanders, and roughly one-half of the remaining officers, or some 35,000 men. A large portion of the leadership of the USSR was destroyed.

In a sense, the purges culminated in Mexico with Trotsky's assassination in 1940. The lessons of the purges were chilling and effective. The way to succeed,

Document Stalin and State Terror

Stalin's totalitarianism brought the development of state terror to unparalleled heights as the regime victimized not only innocent people but also their families during the purges. Nadezhda Mandelstam's husband, Osip, had been rounded up in 1934 for having created a clever epigram criticizing Stalin and placed in exile in provincial Voronezh. Once the purges went into their next phase, he was re-arrested in 1938 and died en route to a labor camp near Vladivostok on the Pacific coast. Nadezhda Mandelstam described the nature of the terror, and its effect on the human soul.

When I used to read about the French Revolution as a child, I often wondered whether it was possible to survive during a reign of terror. I now know beyond doubt that it is impossible. Anybody who breathes the air of terror is doomed, even if nominally he manages to save his life. Everybody is a victim—not only those who die, but also all the killers, ideologists, accomplices and sycophants who close their eyes and wash their hands—even if they are secretly consumed with remorse at night. Every section of the population has been through the terrible sickness caused by terror, and none has so far recovered, or become fit again for normal civic life. It is an illness that is passed on to the next generation, so that the sons pay for the sins of the fathers and perhaps only the grandchildren begin to get over it—or at least it takes on a different form with them.

The principles and aims of mass terror have nothing in common with ordinary police work or with security. The only purpose of terror is intimidation. To plunge the whole country into a state of chronic fear, the number of victims must be raised to astronomical levels, and on every floor of every building there must always be several apartments from which the tenants have suddenly been taken away. The remaining inhabitants will be model citizens for the rest of their lives—this will be true for every street and every city through which the broom has swept. The only essential thing for those who rule by terror is not to overlook the new generations growing up without faith in their elders, and to keep on repeating the process in systematic fashion. Stalin ruled for a long time and saw to it that the waves of terror recurred from time to time, always on an even greater scale than before. But the champions of terror invariably leave one thing out of account—namely, that they can't kill everyone, and among their cowed, half-demented subjects there are always witnesses who survive to tell the tale.

Questions to Consider

1. Why did Stalin take writers so seriously that he persecuted and executed so many of them? How could words hurt him, he who had all of the power?
2. What does Nadezhda Mandelstam say is the goal of terror?
3. Have you ever been affected by terrorists or a terrorist act? Do you agree with Mandelstam as to the effect of terrorism on you, directly or indirectly?

to survive, was to be devotedly, unquestioningly, a follower of Joseph Stalin.

Changes in Soviet Society

In the 20 years after 1917, all aspects of Soviet society came under the control of the party. The atomization of society, a prime characteristic of dictatorial government, did not permit such secret, self-contained, and mutually trusting groups as the family to exist at ease. After the Revolution, the party dealt in contradictory terms with various aspects of social life, but, by and large, the government worked to weaken the importance of the family. Until 1936, divorces required no court proceedings, abortions were legal, women were encouraged to take jobs outside the home, and communist nurseries were set up to care for children while their mothers worked. Pressure on the family continued under Stalin, but in different ways. Children were encouraged to report to the authorities "antirevolutionary" statements made by their parents.

Women paid a heavy price for the Stalin revolutions in industry and agriculture. In the cities they often did heavy labor, using the same tools and working the same hours men worked and suffering equally from the industrial accidents of the time. In the countryside they carried the burden of laboring on the collective farm, doing all of the work in the home, and doing 80 percent of the work on the private plots, which provided food for the family and money from sales in the markets. Alarm spread in Moscow at the lack of population growth during the 1930s. By a law of June 27, 1936, intended to strengthen the family unit, it became harder to gain a divorce; abortions were prohibited; and to increase the birthrate, the government held out the promise of subsidies to women: the more children, the larger the subsidy. As one scholar noted in a study of these conditions, "having been mobilized for production, women would henceforth be mobilized for reproduction."[4]

The party did work to upgrade medical care, improve—for a time—the treatment of the more than 100 national groups that made up the USSR, and extend educational opportunities. But even here political goals outweighed humanitarian objectives. Education—almost exclusively in the Russian language—existed primarily to indoctrinate non-Russian pupils with communist precepts and Russian cultural values. Religious persecution was widespread, and the strong wave of anti-Semitism seen at the end of the nineteenth century returned under Stalin. Jews were referred to as people to be suspected: "rootless cosmopolitans." Also, in their internal passports, Jews were identified by their ethnicity and not as Russians or Ukrainians. The Orthodox Church lost most of its power in education, and religious training was prohibited, except in the home.

In the first decade after the 1917 revolutions, intellectuals and artists experienced much more freedom than they would in the 1930s. The party emphasized the tenets of social realism but permitted some innovation. The Bolsheviks initially tolerated and even encouraged writers with independent leanings. Even though a large number of artists and writers fled the country after the Revolution, others, including the poets Alexander Blok (1880–1921) and Vladimir Mayakovsky (mai-ah-KOF-skee; 1893–1930), remained and continued to write. During the NEP and after, cultural life bloomed in many areas, especially the cinema, as can be seen in the works of the great director Sergei Eisenstein (1898–1948). In music, composers Sergei Prokofiev (proh-KOF-ee-yev; 1891–1953) and Dmitri Shostakovich (1906–1975) contributed works that added to the world's musical treasury, although the latter had to apologize to Stalin for the "bourgeois nature" of one of his symphonies. Once Stalin gained control, he dictated that all art, science, and thought should serve the party's program and philosophy. Artists and thinkers were to become, in Stalin's words, "engineers of the mind." Art for art's sake was counterrevolutionary. Socialist realism in its narrowest sense was to be pursued. History became a means to prove the correctness of Stalin's policies.

FASCISM

▪ *What are the basic principles of fascism?*

World War I put an end to the Western world's belief in continual improvement, a democratic society, and liberal economics. In the pessimism of the 1920s a new social and political model was embraced in many parts of Europe. A half-century before Mussolini led his "March on Rome" and Hitler gained power in 1933, European thinkers had established the roots of a new political ideology: fascism, an ideology that rejected the liberal, progressive values of the nineteenth century and advocated the superiority of one group over all others.

Europe in the 1920s and 1930s

Justifications for Superiority

One of the bases of fascism can be found in the willful misreading of nineteenth-century scientific research. Charles Darwin's hypotheses (see Chapter 22), for example, were very attractive to the middle classes, especially when misapplied to areas Darwin never dreamed of discussing—human social, economic, and political activities. Popularizers of the theory of evolution—social Darwinists—evoked the inevitability of progress, the perfectibility of humanity, and Anglo-Saxon racial dominance. The most popular adherent of **social Darwinism** in Europe and the United States was the English philosopher Herbert Spencer (1820–1903), who applied Darwin's theories to all aspects of human social and political life and to justify the superiority of one group over another.

European thinkers such as Joseph-Arthur de Gobineau (goh-bee-NOH; 1816–1882) devised racial hierarchies with, of course, themselves at the top. Gobineau applied biological theory to politics, regarding nations as organisms. He argued that different races are innately unequal in ability and worth and that the genius of a race depended on heredity, not external factors. Gobineau stated a widely held belief among Europeans that white people alone were capable of cultural creativity and that intermixture with other races would destroy that creativity. Social Darwinist arguments and Gobineau's pseudoscientific

social Darwinism—A misapplication of Darwin's theories of evolution, applied to human society to justify the temporary dominance of predominantly Caucasian nations at the end of the nineteenth century.

theories in support of white superiority gave "rational" justifications to blatant bigotry and provided a reassuring sanction for European domination over Asians and Africans. Spencer and Gobineau laid the foundations for modern racism.

One of the manifestations of this notion of superiority was the Anglo-Saxon movement. In Britain and Germany, writers and speakers presented the case for the superiority of northern Europeans. They stated that world leadership should naturally reside in London and Berlin because the people living there possessed the proper combination of religion, racial qualities, and culture to enable them to dictate the world's future. People as diverse as Kaiser William II and U.S. President Woodrow Wilson shared this outlook. In addition, a Pan-Germanic League was organized in Berlin in the 1890s to spread the belief in the superiority of the German race and culture. In the United States, the destruction of the way of life of the Native Americans was justified by the demands of the unstoppable tide of progress.

Modern Anti-Semitism

Another support for superiority of one group over another was anti-Semitism. This systematic hostility toward the Jews had persisted in Europe since Constantine the Great made Christianity the religion of the Eastern Roman Empire in the fourth century. But the movement attained new strength and vigor in the last part of the nineteenth century. In Germany the historian Heinrich von Treitschke (TRITE-shkee; 1834–1896) stated that "the Jews are our calamity." In France anti-Semitism played a significant role in the Dreyfus affair (see Chapter 26). In eastern Europe the Jews suffered many injustices; in Russia they were murdered in **pogroms.** Anti-Semitism became stronger because of the economic dislocation that modernization introduced and of the work of cranks who turned out pseudoscientific tracts and forgeries such as the *Protocols of the Elders of Zion* that encouraging bigoted attitudes. Politicians in central and eastern Europe were not slow to take advantage of the prevailing anti-Semitism.

Jews, in response, expressed a growing desire for a homeland where they would be safe and free. In 1896, Theodor Herzl (HEHRT-zel) founded the movement known as *Zionism,* promoting the creation of an independent Jewish state in Palestine, the ancestral home of the Jews. The first general congress of Zionists was held in Switzerland in 1897, and so began a small-scale emigration to Palestine, despite the fact that the region was principally populated by Arabs.

pogrom—A planned massacre of defenseless people, usually Jews, at the end of the nineteenth century.

Theodor Herzl founded the Zionist movement to bring to fruition the longing of the Jews of the Diaspora for a homeland in the land of their ancestors, Palestine. He was driven not only by his faith but also by the rabid anti-Semitism that was resurgent in central Europe toward the end of the nineteenth century.

The End of Rationality

The social Darwinists and racialist writers advocated the superiority of white Christian people over others. Other middle-class thinkers in the generation before World War I provided new insights that ate away at the foundations of classic Western civilization. In France Henri Bergson wrote that "vital instinct," not reason, was the most important part of creativity. In Italy Benedetto Croce (be-ne-DET-toh KROH-chee) rebelled against the positivism and rationalism of the age. At the same time that Albert Einstein began to undermine the classic Newtonian universe, Sigmund Freud questioned the whole notion of rationality. As the social Darwinists misinterpreted the carefully reasoned hypotheses of Charles Darwin, so did opportunistic political activists begin to fill the definitional void by advocating a new kind of state based on emotion, charisma, antiliberalism, anticonservatism, antirationalism, and radical nationalism.[5]

Classic liberalism advocated freedom and equality and led to the introduction of mass democratic politics in the second half of the nineteenth century. Some European elites did not like the idea of universal manhood suffrage and the rules and restrictions of free and fair elections. Especially among younger Europeans, this resentment sparked an emotional, often irrational reaction against the values of the older generation and the desire for action—any kind of action. The writings of Friedrich Nietzsche (FREED-reesh NEET-shee; 1844–1900) calling for the dominance of an *Übermensch* (OO-ber-mensh), a "superior man" who despised the mediocrity of the bourgeoisie, became popular. In France, Georges Sorel (1847–1922), a retired engineer, stated the need for action and violence to replace parliamentary democracy from a leftist point of view. Sorel advocated the use of violence as a justifiable means to deal with the corruption of bourgeois society and to bring together like-minded people in a common crusade. To Sorel the victims of violence paid the necessary price for progress, and their suffering was more than justified by the advances that brutality could bring.

As the end of the century approached, the notion of the bourgeois corruption and the decadence of Western civilization, especially the purported weakening of the white race, was discussed everywhere in the West. This mode of thinking was especially prevalent in Germany and Austria, and its most influential spokesman was Houston Stewart Chamberlain (1855–1927), who wrote that the blond-haired, blue-eyed "Aryan" (northern Indo-European) had a very special "race soul" whose existence was threatened by Jews.

These thoughts and tendencies found fertile ground in the boredom of the middle classes. Stanley Payne writes that "quite aside from any specific political proclivity, a concern for new approaches and new values—and possibly a new style of life" was fed by this bourgeois boredom. This, plus the growth of a "youth culture," with its roots in the well-to-do middle classes, provided an audience for these ideas. "A mood of rejection of some of the dominant values of preceding generations had set in. Faith in rationalism, the positivist approach, and the worship of materialism came increasingly under fire. Hostility toward bureaucracy, the parliamentary system, and the drive for 'mere' equality often accompanied this spirit of rejection."[6] This "spirit of rejection" grew stronger after the disappointments and deceptions of the World War I, and in 1919 Benito Mussolini first used the word *fascism* to encapsulate all of these tendencies.

The Italian leader may be seen as the father of fascism, but he had no precise definition of what the movement was. Unlike communism, fascism has no basic text and takes on different forms in different countries. Robert O. Paxton, however, has established that there are certain characteristics at the core of fascism. There is:

- *a sense of overwhelming crisis beyond the reach of any traditional solutions;*
- *the primacy of the group, toward which one has duties superior to every right, whether individual or universal, and the subordination of the individual to it;*
- *the belief that one's group is a victim, a sentiment that justifies any action, without legal or moral limits, against its enemies, both internal and external;*
- *dread of the group's decline under the corrosive effects of individualistic liberalism, class conflict, and alien influences;*
- *the need for a closer integration of a purer community, by consent if possible, or by exclusionary violence if necessary;*
- *the need for authority by natural chiefs (always male), culminating in a national chieftain who alone is capable of incarnating the group's historical destiny;*
- *the superiority of the leader's instincts over abstract and universal reason;*
- *the beauty of violence and the efficacy of will, when they are devoted to the group's success;*
- *the right of the chosen people to dominate others without restraint from any kind of human or divine law, right being decided by the sole criterion of the group's prowess within a Darwinian struggle."*[7]

ITALY AND MUSSOLINI

- *How was Mussolini able to take and hold power in Italy?*

After entering the war on the Allied side in 1915, the kingdom of Italy joined the peace negotiations with great expectations. The Italians had joined the Allies with the understanding that with victory they would gain Trieste, Dalmatia, Trentino, and some territory in Asia Minor. They came away from Versailles with minor gains, however, not nearly enough, in their minds, to justify the deaths of 700,000 of their soldiers.

Postwar Italy suffered social and economic damage similar to that of the other combatants. Inflation—the lira fell to one-third of its prewar value—and disrupted trade patterns hampered recovery. These ailments worsened the domestic crises the country had been struggling with before the war. There were not enough jobs for the returning soldiers, and unemployed veterans were ripe targets for the growing extremist parties. In some cities residents refused to pay their rent in protest over poor living conditions. In the countryside peasants took land from landlords. Everywhere, food was in short supply.

In the four years after the armistice, five premiers came and went, either because of their own incompetence or because of the insolubility of the problems they faced. Liberal democracy was not equal to the challenge of post–World War I government in Italy.

The situation favored the appearance of a strong man, a dictator. Such a man was a blacksmith's son named Mussolini, who bore the Christian name Benito, in honor of the liberal Mexican President Benito Juárez (HWA-rez). During his youth, Benito Mussolini (1883–1945) received an education dominated by left-wing political thinkers. Even though he became editor of the influential socialist newspaper *Avanti* ("Forward") in 1912, he was far from consistent in his political views. Early on, he demonstrated his opportunistic and pragmatic nature. For example, when a majority of the Italian Socialist party called for neutrality in World War I, Mussolini came out for intervention. Party officials removed *Avanti* from his control and expelled him from the party. He then proceeded to put out his own paper, *Il Pòpolo d'Italia* (PO-po-lo dee-TAL-ee-uh; "The People of Italy"), in which he continued to call for Italian entry in the war on the Allied side.

To carry out his interventionist campaign, Mussolini organized formerly leftist groups into bands called *fasci,* a named derived from the Latin *fasces,* a bundle of rods bound around an ax, which was the symbol of authority in ancient Rome. When Italy entered the war, Mussolini volunteered for the army, saw active service at the front, and was wounded. When he returned to civilian life, he reorganized the *fasci* into the *fasci di combattimento* (FASH-ee dee kom-bat-tee-MEN-toh; "fighting groups") to attract war veterans and try to gain control of Italy.

Mussolini's Rise to Power

1919	Italian discontent with peace treaties
1919–1920	Gabriele D'Annunzio and his followers occupy Fiume
1919–1922	Series of ineffective governments and postwar economic crises
1922	Unsuccessful union antifascist protest; March on Rome; King Victor Emmanuel III asks Mussolini to form a government

The Path to Power

In the 1919 elections, the freest in Italy until after World War II, the Socialists capitalized on mass unemployment and hardship to become the strongest party. But the party lacked effective leadership and failed to take advantage of its position. Although the extreme right-wing groups did not elect a single candidate to the Chamber of Deputies, they pursued power in other ways.

The fiery writer and nationalist leader Gabriele D'Annunzio (ga-bree-EL-eh dan NOON-zee-oh; 1863–1938) had occupied the disputed city of Fiume with his corps of followers, in direct violation of the mandates of the Paris peace conference. This defiance of international authority appealed to the fascist movement. D'Annunzio provided lessons for the observant Mussolini, who copied many of the writer's methods and programs, especially D'Annunzio's flare for the dramatic. During his 15-month control of Fiume, D'Annunzio and his followers wore black shirts, carried daggers, and used the so-called Roman salute—raising the right arm in a rigid, ramrodlike gesture. Ironically, D'Annunzio and his band were wrong: In antiquity, slaves saluted their masters by raising their right hands; free men shook hands.

The fascists gained the backing of landowning and industrial groups, who feared the victory of Marxist socialism in Italy. Mussolini's toughs beat up opponents, broke strikes, and disrupted opposition meetings in 1919 and 1920, while the government did nothing. Despite these activities, the extreme right-wing politicians still failed to dominate the 1921 elections. Only 35 fascists, Mussolini among them, gained seats in the Chamber of Deputies, while the Liberal and Democratic parties gained a plurality. Failing to succeed through the existing system, Mussolini established the National Fascist party in November.

The Liberal-Democratic government of 1922 proved as ineffective as its predecessors, and the Socialists continued to bicker among themselves. Mussolini's party, however, attracted thousands of disaffected middle-class people, cynical and opportunistic intellectuals, and workers. Frustration with the central government's incompetence, not fear of the left, fueled the fascist rise.

In August 1922 the trade unions called a general strike to protest the rise of fascism. Mussolini's forces smashed their efforts. In October, after a huge rally in Naples, 50,000 fascists swarmed into Rome, and soon thereafter, King Victor Emmanuel III invited Mussolini to form a new government. During the next month, Mussolini assembled a cabinet composed of his party members and nationalists and gained dictatorial powers to bring stability to the country. The fascists remained a distinct minority in Italy, but by gaining control of the central government, they could place their members and allies in positions of power. The October March on Rome ushered in Mussolini's 20-year reign.

Building the Fascist State

The new Italian leader followed no strict ideology as he consolidated his dictatorial rule. He threw out all the democratic procedures of the postwar years and dissolved rival political parties. He and his colleagues ruthlessly crushed free expression and banished critics of their government to prison settlements off Italy's southern coast. They censored the press and set up tribunals for the defense of the state (not the citizens). Although he retained the shell of the old system, the fascist leader established a totally new state.

Mussolini controlled all real power through the Fascist Grand Council, whose members occupied the government's ministerial posts. At one time, he personally held no fewer than eight offices. All this activity and centralization of power provided a striking contrast to the lethargy of the four years immediately after the war. Encouraged by the popular support for his regime, Mussolini passed a series of laws in 1925 and 1926, under which the Italian cities lost their freely elected self-governments and all units of local and provincial government were welded into a unified structure controlled from Rome.

Once he had centralized Italian political life, Mussolini pursued the development of his ideology in a pragmatic manner. In his rise to power, Mussolini lashed out against the capitalists, the church, the monarchy, and the middle classes. But he would learn to work with all of those elements in his flexible pursuit of power. He once stated in an interview, "I am all for motion."[8] Movement, not consistency and science, marked his ideology.

This portrait of Mussolini by futurist Geraldo Dottoli portrays him as a man of the power.

Early in the 1920s Mussolini, a former atheist, began to tie the church into the structure of his new society. In 1928 he negotiated the Lateran Treaty with church representatives in order to settle the long-standing controversy between Rome and the Vatican. The new pact required compulsory religious instruction and recognized Catholicism as the state religion. Vatican City, a new state of 108 acres located within Rome itself, was declared to be fully sovereign and independent. In addition, the state promised the Vatican $91 million. Mussolini gained a measure of approval from devout Italians and the Vatican's support for his fascist government.

Mussolini's economic system, which has come to be known as *state capitalism,* aimed to abolish class conflict through cooperation between labor and capital, by state force if necessary. In communist theory, labor is the basis of society. In fascism, labor and capital are both instruments of the state. The fascists constructed a corporate state, in which the country was divided into *syndicates,* or corporations—13 at first, later 22. Initially, six of these came from labor and an equal number represented capital or management. The thirteenth group was established for the professions. Under state supervision, these bodies were to deal with labor disputes, guarantee adequate wage scales, control prices, and supervise working conditions. After 1926, strikes by workers and lockouts by employers were prohibited.

The pragmatic leader believed that private enterprise was the most efficient method of production: "The state intervenes in economic production only when private enterprise fails or is insufficient or when the political interests of the state are involved."[9] Mussolini liked to claim that his structure embodied a classless economic system that stood as one of fascism's greatest contributions to political theory.

Reflecting the practice of the time, the Italians sought economic self-sufficiency, especially in the areas of food supply, power resources, and foreign trade. Wheat production and hydroelectric-generating capacity both increased, but the drive for self-sufficiency was carried to an unprofitable extreme. The state, in its quest for economic independence, launched many projects to provide for a home supply of products that could be obtained much more cheaply from other nations.

Military training began early in Mussolini's fascist state. There were youth organizations for every age group over the age of 4.

State and Struggle: Mussolini's Legacy

As in the case of the other dictatorships, Mussolini's programs had some worthwhile features, including slum clearance, rural modernization, and campaigns against illiteracy and malaria. The trains *did* run on time, as Mussolini boasted, and the omnipresent Mafia was temporarily dispersed, with many of its more notable figures fleeing to the United States. But these positive achievements were more than outweighed by the ruinous war with Ethiopia (see Chapter 31), excessive military spending, and special benefits to large landowners and industrialists. In 1930 real wages remained low in comparison to the rest of industrialized Europe.

The Great Depression hit Italy later than other countries, but it lasted longer, and its effects were devastating to Mussolini's economy. The 33 percent increase in 1929 gross national product over that of 1914 was soon wiped out, and the old problems of inadequate natural resources, unfavorable balance of trade, and expanding population made the country vulnerable to economic disaster. In 1933 the number of unemployed reached 1 million and the public debt soared to an alarming level. Despite a reorganization of the nation in 1934 into 22 government-controlled corporations, a massive public works program, and agricultural reforms, Italy continued to suffer. In the 1930s, Italy's fate and future came to be closely tied to that of Germany, whose leaders embraced the ideology haphazardly begun by Mussolini.

Mussolini's fascist ideology built on the cult of the leader, *Il Duce* (eel deu-CHAY; "the Great Man") and the all-powerful corporate state. But it was Mussolini's charisma that held the movement together. The Italian dictator asserted that "life for the fascist is a continuous, ceaseless fight" and that "struggle is at the origin of all things." Mirroring the nonintellectual nature of its creator, fascism never had a text, as Marxism did. But its basis was an extreme nationalism that asserted that Italy in its present form was corrupt. Mussolini believed that it was possible to regain the nation's pure form by rejecting substantial portions of the present age: In his speeches, Mussolini referred constantly to the legacy of the Roman Empire. *Il Duce* and his followers sensed that they lived at a watershed between the tarnished old and the possible gleaming new and that it was their duty to save their nation by bringing in a new breed of man.

Mussolini's movement was antiliberal, characterized by real hatred of the bourgeoisie and all that it created in the nineteenth century. *Il Duce* encouraged a high birthrate but noted that individuals were significant only insofar as they were part of the state. Children were indoctrinated with the party line. The movement was also anticonservative, rejecting the traditional role of the monarchy and cynically using the church. Mussolini's party rejected traditional laissez-faire capitalism and the hierarchies that came with it, and, in that sense, it was socialist. Rather than waiting for the "invisible hand" to furnish the motive force of their country, Italian fascists, as good totalitarians, looked to the state to engineer life at all levels. The Italian fascists were also racists and sought to link up with like-minded people around the world. The strength of Mussolini's fascism was that it could be adapted to any ideological or cultural setting, because to be a fascist, one needed only to hate, believe, obey, and fight.

Beneath the talk of struggle and the trappings of grandeur was the reality of Italy. Mussolini was no Stalin or Hitler, and his fascism was a far milder form of totalitarianism than that seen in the USSR or Germany. The Italian people simply defused many of the potentially atrocious elements of his fascist rule. There was no class destruction or genocide in Italy. The Italians, who had endured control by the Goths, the Normans, the French, and the Austrians before unification, were survivors.

THE GERMAN TRAGEDY

■ *What economic and social factors contributed to the rise of Adolf Hitler?*

In the first week of November 1918, as World War I came to a close, revolutions broke out all over Germany. Sailors stationed at Kiel rebelled; leftists in Munich revolted. The kaiser fled to the Netherlands after the authority of his government crumbled. On November 9 the chancellor transferred his power to Friedrich Ebert, leader of the majority party, the Social Democrats, and the new leader announced the establishment of a republic.

Europe Between the Wars: 1919–1939

Violence spread quickly. The Spartacists, led by Karl Liebknecht (LEEB-knect) and Rosa Luxemburg, who formed the German Communist party at the end of 1918, wanted a complete social and political revolution. Ebert's Social Democrats favored a democratic system in which property rights would be maintained. At the beginning of 1919 the radical and moderate socialists clashed violently. Experiments in revolutionary government in Bavaria and Berlin horrified traditionalists and even the Social Democrats. In the spring a coalition of forces, ranging from moderate socialists to right-wing bands of unemployed veterans, crushed the leftists and murdered Liebknecht and Luxemburg.

By the end of the year, Germany had weathered the threat of a leftist revolution. Meanwhile, the moderate parties triumphed in elections to select a constitutional convention, with the Social Democrats winning the most votes. The constitution they wrote at Weimar (VI-mar) and adopted in mid-1919 created some of the problems that would plague the new government.

The liberal document provided for a president, a chancellor who was responsible to the Reichstag (RIKE-shtag), and national referenda. In addition, the constitution guaranteed the rights of labor, personal liberty, and compulsory education for everyone up to the age of 18. Once the new system was put into operation, its weaknesses were readily apparent. The multitude of parties permitted by the constitution condemned the government to function solely by shaky coalitions that often broke apart and forced the president to rule by emergency decree, thus bypassing legal constitutional procedures.

Failure of the Weimar Republic

The new Weimar Republic faced overwhelming obstacles. First, it had to live with the stigma of having accepted the Versailles treaty, with its infamous war guilt clause. The defeatist image, combined with opposition from both right- and left-wing extremists, plagued the Weimar moderates. The myth of betrayal in accepting the Versailles treaty helped Field Marshal Paul von Hindenburg, a stalwart Prussian and war hero, win election to the presidency in 1925. In 1927 he formally renounced the theory of war guilt, a politically popular move but one with little effect on the obligation to pay reparations. Although these payments did not noticeably affect the standard of living after 1925, they continued to be a visible sign of defeat, especially since the money used to pay the victorious Allies had to come from foreign loans.

France Demands War Reparations from Germany—Cartoon

The Weimar government ruled during an economically chaotic period. The government caused inflation, wiped out savings, and destroyed much of the confidence of the middle class, shaking the resolve of the group on whom the fate of the republic rested. Even after 1923, when the economy took a turn for the better, perceptive observers noted that the new prosperity rested on shaky foundations.

During the five years before the onset of the Great Depression, Germany rebuilt its industrial plants with the most up-to-date equipment and techniques available, becoming the second-ranking industrial nation in the world, behind the United States. Rebuilding, however, was financed largely with foreign loans, including some $800 million from the Americans. In fact, the Germans borrowed almost twice as much money as they paid out. When the short-term loans came due, the economic bubble burst.

The Economic Cycle and the Nazis

1919	Transition to peacetime economy, massive unemployment
1920	Formation of National Socialist German Workers' (Nazi) party, drawing from out-of-work soldiers
1923	The Munich *Putsch,* massive inflation
1928	High point of economic normalization; Nazis have only 12 seats in the Reichstag
1930	Beginning of Great Depression; Nazis increase seats in Reichstag to 107
1932	Depth of Great Depression; Nazis make strong showing in July elections
1933	Social discontent caused by depression brings increased business support of Nazis; Hitler gains power with 44 percent of deputies, buttressed by Nationalist party's 8 percent

In addition to these economic difficulties, other problems plagued the Weimar government. Many people in Germany still idealized the authoritarian Prussian state. The German general staff and its numerous and powerful supporters were not placed under effective civilian control. Disregarding the Versailles restrictions on military growth, Germany increased its armed forces in the 1920s, in cooperation with the Soviet Union, the other European outcast. Probably more dangerous to the Weimar Republic's existence was that group of individuals described by Peter Gay as the *Vernunftrepublikaner* (ver-NUNFT-re-pub-li-kah-ner) or "rational republicans from intellectual choice rather than passionate conviction." These intellectuals, politicians, and businessmen, who should have been the strength of Weimar, "learned to live with the Republic but they never learned to love it and never believed in its future."[10]

The insecurity of the middle classes was the factor most responsible for the failure of the Weimar Republic. After the war and inflation, what professionals, white-collar workers, and skilled trades people feared most was being dragged down to the level of the masses. Right-wing orators played on such fears and warned that the Weimar Republic could not stop the growth of communism. After 1929, the fear and discontent of the middle classes crystallized around their children, who blamed their parents for the catastrophe of 1918 and the humiliations that followed. German youth, many of them unemployed after 1929, repudiated the Weimar Republic and sought a new savior for their country and themselves. In their rise to power, the Nazis skillfully exploited the fears and hopes of German middle-class youth.

During the Weimar period in Germany, (1918–1933), George Grosz in satirical paintings such as The Pillars of Society *(1926) powerfully expressed his scorn for militarism, capitalism, the complacent middle classes, and the corrupt society of his time. bpk, Berlin/Art Resource, NY/© Estate of George Grosz/Licensed by VAGA, New York, NY.*

Adolf Hitler

The man who was to "save the fatherland" came from outside its borders. Adolf Hitler (1889–1945) was born in Austria, the son of a minor customs official in the Austro-Hungarian monarchy. A mediocre student and something of a loner during his school days, he went to Vienna in 1908 hoping to become an architect or an artist. When he failed to gain admission to the art institute, he abandoned pursuing a career in art.

In the cosmopolitan capital of Vienna, surrounded by a rich diversity of nationalities and religions, Hitler formed a personal political philosophy. He avidly read pamphlets written by racists who advocated the leader concept and variations of social Darwinism. In addition, anti-Semitism was a popular political platform, and the city's mayor openly espoused it. Hitler also dabbled in pan-Germanism and Marxist socialism. The swirl of ideas and theories percolated in the brain of the impoverished and aimless young man and furnished him with the motivations and ambitions that drove him forward.

A year before World War I, Hitler moved to Munich, where he earned a meager living by selling his drawings. When the conflict erupted in 1914, he joined a German regiment and was sent to France, where he fought bravely. At the time of the armistice in 1918, he was in a hospital recovering from being blinded in a gas attack. He later said that news of Germany's defeat caused him to turn his face to the wall and weep bitterly.

Following his recovery, Hitler returned to Munich, where he was hired by city authorities to act as a special agent to investigate extremists. In the line of duty he checked on a small organization called the German Workers' party. Hitler became attracted to the group's fervently nationalistic doctrine and agreed with their antidemocratic, anticommunist, and anti-Semitic beliefs. He joined the party and soon dominated it.

In 1920 the party renamed itself the National Socialist German Workers' party, the first two syllables of which are pronounced *"Nazi"* in German. That same year, the party founded a newspaper to spread its views; formed a paramilitary organization from out-of-work veterans, the *Sturmabteilung* (shtirm-AB-tai-lung) or SA; and adopted a symbol, the swastika set on a red background. The swastika has been used by many cultures to express the unending cycle of life. The red background symbolized the community of German blood.

More important than the party or its symbol was Hitler, who became widely known for his remarkable powers as a speaker. His ability to arouse and move mass audiences drew large crowds in Munich. Even those who hated all that he stood for were fascinated by his performances. In the early days he would hire a number of beer halls for his adherents and speed from one to the next delivering his emotion-filled message. He called for land reform, the nationalization of trusts, the abolition of all unearned incomes, expansion to include all German-speaking peoples in Europe, and the cancellation of the Versailles treaty. The points of his arguments were less important than the way he delivered them. As the ultimate demagogue, he could package his concepts to fit whatever audience he addressed, and his popularity soared.

In November 1923, at the depth of Germany's inflationary crisis, Hitler staged a *Putsch,* or revolt, in Munich. Poorly planned and premature, the attempt failed. Hitler was sent to prison after his arrest, and there, in comparatively luxurious conditions, he dictated his statement of principles in *Mein Kampf* ("My Struggle"). Far from a literary masterpiece, the work was both an autobiography and a long-winded exposition of Nazi philosophy and objectives.

In *Mein Kampf* Hitler writes that history is fashioned by great races, of which the Aryan is the finest. The noblest Aryans, according to Hitler, are the Germans, who should rule the world. He charges that the Jews are the archcriminals of all time, that democracy is decadent, and that communism is criminal. He states that expansion into the Soviet Ukraine and the destruction of France are rightful courses for the Germans, who will use war and force, the proper instruments of the strong, to achieve their goals. The book, initially dismissed as the ravings of a wild man, was widely read in the 1930s. Its sales made Hitler a wealthy man.

Hitler's Chance

Hitler's first attempt to take advantage of economic disaster failed, but he would not fail the second time. After 1930 the Führer (FIU-rher; "leader") took advantage of the desperate conditions resulting from closed banks, 6 million unemployed, and people roaming the streets for food. Night after night, civil and military police battled mobs of rioting communists and Nazis. The depression was "the last ingredient in a complicated witches' brew" that led to Hitler's takeover.[11]

The depression brought on the collapse of the moderates' position in the Weimar government. In the 1930 elections the Nazis increased their number of seats in the Reichstag (the German legislative assembly) from 12 to 107. As conditions grew worse, the hungry and frightened, as well as the rich and powerful, turned to Hitler. The latter groups feared the communists and saw the Führer as a useful shield against a proletarian revolution.

As the Nazi movement grew in popularity, Hitler's brilliant propaganda chief, Joseph Goebbels (GEHR-bels), used every communications device available to convert the masses to Nazism. He staged huge spectacles all over Germany in which thousands of storm troopers and the audiences themselves all became supporting players to the star of the drama, Adolf Hitler. Such controlled hysteria was more important than the message Hitler continued to repeat.

Despite Goebbels's work, Hitler lost the March 1932 presidential elections to the aged World War I hero Hindenburg. But after a strong showing by the Nazis in the July Reichstag elections, Hindenburg, following the advice of his supporters and the business community, asked Hitler to join a coalition government. The Führer refused, demanding instead the equivalent of dictatorial power.

The stalemate led to the dissolution of the Reichstag in September, and for the next two months, the government limped along until a second general election was held. This costly campaign nearly emptied the Nazis' treasury. It was also politically costly in that they lost some of their seats in the Reichstag.

Some observers believed that the Nazis had passed the crest of their power. At this critical point, however, a clique of aristocratic nationalists and powerful industrialists, fearing a leftist revolution, offered Hitler the chancellorship. In January 1933, a mixed cabinet was created with Hitler at the head. Because he did not have a clear majority in the Reichstag, Hitler called another general election for March 5.

The Nazis used all the muscle at their disposal during this campaign. They monopolized the radio broadcasts and the press, and the SA bullied and beat the voters. Many Germans became disgusted with the strong-arm methods, and the tide definitely swung against the Nazis. Hitler needed a dramatic incident to gain a clear majority in the election.

On the evening of February 27, a fire gutted the Reichstag building. The blaze had been set by a 24-year-old Dutchman, Marinus van der Lubbe, as a statement against capitalism. Apparently acting alone, van der Lubbe gave the Nazis the issue they needed to mobilize their support. Goebbels's propaganda machine went into action to blame the fire on the international communist movement. Uncharacteristically, the propaganda minister overplayed the story, and most of the outside world came to believe that the Nazis themselves had set the fire.

Adolf Hitler's ability to communicate effectively and persuasively with a majority of the German population was a major asset in his rise to power and popularity. Here he is shown (front right) speaking with young members of his Nazi party.

Hitler may not have made much profit from the incident internationally, but he did use it to win the election. The Nazis captured 44 percent of the deputies, a result which—with the 8 percent controlled by the Nationalist party—gave them a bare majority. Quickly, Hitler's forces put through the Enabling Act, which gave the Führer the right to rule by decree for the next four years.

Every aspect of the Weimar government was overturned, legally. The Nazis crushed all opposition parties and put aside the Weimar constitution, which was never formally abolished. Germany for the first time became a unitary national, rather than federal, state. After Hindenburg died in 1934, Hitler became both chancellor and president. As if to put the world on notice that a renewed German force was rising in central Europe, he withdrew Germany from the League of Nations in 1933. Two years later, he introduced conscription, in defiance of the Versailles treaty.

Hitler proclaimed his regime the Third Reich, succeeding the First Reich of Otto the Great, which had lasted from 962 to 1806, and Bismarck's Second Reich, from 1871 to 1918. Hitler quickly introduced aspects of his Nazi variant of fascism, which was much more pernicious than Mussolini's. Hitler's ideology united the diverse Germans and expressed resentment against the rapid industrialization that had cut many of the people away from their traditional values. But it was primarily the racist elements of Aryan supremacy and hatred of the Jews that set Nazism apart.

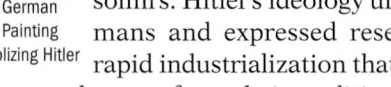

IMAGE
German Painting Idolizing Hitler

War on the Jews

An essential part of the Nazi ideology was an absolute hatred of the Jews, an element of society the Nazis considered unfit to continue in the new world they envisioned. After crushing all opposition, real and potential, Hitler began to destroy the Jews. When he took power, there were only 500,000 Jews out of a population of 66 million Germans. Since 1880 the number of Jews in the population had been declining and would have continued to do so through assimilation. Hitler, however, proclaimed that Jews were everywhere, plotting to gain control of the world, and he pledged to destroy them. His beliefs reflected his own contempt for the Jews, not any demographic reality.

All Jewish officials in the government lost their jobs, Jews were forbidden to pursue their business and industrial activities, and Jewish businesses were boycotted. Non-Jews snatched up at bargain prices valuable properties formerly owned by Jews. Non-Jewish doctors and lawyers profited when Jewish professionals were forced from their practices. Hitler gained solid supporters among the business and professional classes as he pursued his racist policies. Germans willingly believed that the Jews deserved their fate as the price they had to pay for the Versailles treaty, for the harmful aspects of capitalism, and for internationalism. Half-hearted international protests failed to limit the anti-Semitic policies. Hitler had many fervent supporters both inside and outside Germany.

The Nazis set to building concentration camps; in time these would turn into death camps. In the meantime, the immediate pressures of government policies pushed many Jews into committing suicide. It has been estimated that in 1933 alone, 19,000 German citizens killed themselves and 16,000 more died from unexplained causes.

In 1935 the so-called **Nuremberg laws** came into force. Marriages between Aryans and non-Aryans were forbidden. Jews (defined as all persons with one-fourth or more Jewish blood) lost their citizenship, and anti-

Nuremberg laws—The collection of laws issued in 1935 depriving Jews in the Third Reich of most of their civil rights and dispossessing them of their legal rights and occupational possibilities.

Semitic signs were posted in all public places. (During the 1936 Berlin Olympic Games, these notices were taken down so as not to upset visitors.) Increasingly, there was public mention of the "inferior blood" of the Jews. As the state came to need more and more money for armaments, the Jews would be made to pay. This enterprise reached a climax with vicious attacks on Jews and their businesses and synagogues on November 9, 1938, known as ***Kristallnacht*** (KRIS-tel-nakht; "Night of Broken Glass"). Nazi sympathizers smashed the windows of 7500 shops and burned 267 synagogues, killing 91 people in the process. The police rounded up 30,000 Jews and sent them to concentration camps. Adding insult to injury, a fine of 1 billion marks was imposed on the Jewish community in retaliation for the murder of a German diplomat in Paris.

Attacked, deprived of their citizenship and economic opportunities, and barred from public service, the Jews of Germany, who considered themselves good German citizens, bore the barbaric blows with remarkable resilience. Some, including a number of Germany's best scientific minds, were able to flee the country—a loss that may well have doomed Hitler's efforts in World War II. Most stayed. They, like the outside world, which showed little concern, did not realize that Hitler's true goal was the "Final Solution," the extermination of the Jews. His mad quest, known as the *Holocaust,* would lead to the deaths of more than 6 million Jews throughout all of Europe and the USSR and at least 4 million others not lucky enough to be "Aryan."

DOCUMENT
The Holocaust: Memoirs from the Commandant of Auschwitz

The Nazi Impact on Culture, Church, Education, and Society

Hitler and Goebbels controlled all of the media in the totalitarian Third Reich. A Reich culture cabinet was set up to instill a single pattern of thought in literature, the press, broadcasting, drama, music, art, and the cinema. Forbidden books, including works of some of Germany's most distinguished writers, were seized and destroyed in huge bonfires. The cultural vitality of the Weimar Republic, represented by the likes of Thomas Mann, Erich Maria Remarque (re-MARK), Kurt Weill (VILE), and Bertolt Brecht (BREKHT), was replaced by the sterile social realism of the Third Reich.

Religion became entrapped in the dictatorial mechanism. Since Nazism elevated the state above all else, a movement was started to subordinate religion to the Hitler regime. The organized churches originally backed the Nazis warmly, until it became apparent that they were to serve the larger aim of the Aryan cause. Protestant churches suffered under the Nazi attempt to make them an arm of the state, and several dissident ministers were imprisoned. By the end of the decade, the Catholic Church, too, came under subtle but constant attack.

German universities, once renowned for their academic freedom, became agencies for propagating the racial myths of Nazism and for carrying out far-fetched experiments in human genetic engineering on selected concentration camp inmates. Only good Nazis could go to universities, and professors who did not cooperate with the regime were fired. The rich traditions of German scholarship became perverted by governmental pressure and many professors who were more than glad to collaborate with the Nazis.

The state used mass popular education, integrated with the German Youth movement, to drill and regiment boys and girls to be good Nazis. Boys learned, above all else, to be ready to fight and die for their Führer. The girls were prepared for their ultimate task, bearing and rearing the many babies to be needed by the Third Reich.

When they took power, the Nazis made it clear that they viewed the political and professional activity of

This painting shows a blissful Nazi family, close to nature, with the blond mother carrying out her duties of bearing and bringing up children for the Third Reich while the sturdy and caring father watches over his nursing baby.

Kristallnacht—The "night of the broken glass" when, on November 9, 1938, Nazi sympathizers smashed the windows of Jewish shops, burned synagogues, and killed 91 people. In addition, more than 30,000 Jews were sent to concentration camps and a fine of 1 billion DM was imposed on the Jewish community, all in response to the murder of a minor German diplomat in Paris.

women during the Weimar period as a sign of general decadence. Like the other authoritarian states in the 1930s, they declared that the prime role of women was to stay home and bear children—in this case, racially pure German children. As in Stalin's USSR, the state gave subsidies and other financial incentives to large families, and abortion was illegal. However, after 1937, women were first encouraged—and six years later, compelled—to contribute to the economy by performing whatever work the state demanded—usually in armaments factories and always at lower wages than received by men. As in Stalin's Soviet Union, the women also had to bear the burden of their housework, carrying a disproportionate share of the workload.

Document The New German Woman

Paula Siber served as the acting head of the National Socialist Party (Nazi) Association of German Women in 1933. She established the basic guidelines for the Party's expectations of what the new German woman should be. Women were not to be in the forefront, making political, economic, or military decisions. Rather, they were to be the most important actors in the creation of the new, purified national community both in giving birth to a large number of children and to passing on the essence of the German tradition to their children.

To be a woman means to be a mother, means affirming with the whole conscious force of one's soul the value of being a mother and making it a law of life. The role of motherhood assigned to woman by nature and fully endorsed by National Socialism in no way means, however, that the task of National Socialist woman within the framework of the National Community should be simply that of knowing herself to be the carrier of race and blood, and hence of the biological conservation of the people.

Over and above the duty intrinsic to her gender of conserving her race and people there is also the holy task entrusted to man and woman of enhancing and developing the inner, spiritual, and human qualities. This in the case of woman culminates in the motherhood of the soul as the highest ennoblement of any woman, whether she is married or not.

Therefore, a woman belongs at the side of a man not just as a person who brings children into the world, not just as an adornment to delight the eye, not just as a cook and cleaner. Instead woman has the holy duty to be a life companion, which means being a comrade who pursues her vocation as woman with clarity of vision and spiritual warmth. . . .

To be a woman in the deepest and most beautiful sense of the word is the best preparation for being a mother. For the highest calling of the National Socialist woman is not just to bear children, but consciously and out of total devotion to her role and duty as mother to raise children for her people. . . .

The mother is also the intermediary for the people and national culture . . . to which she and her child belong. For she is the custodian of its culture, which she provides her child with thorough fairy-tales, legends, games, and customs in a way which is decisive for the whole relationship which he will later have to his people. . . . In a National Socialist Germany, the sphere of social services . . . is predominantly the sphere of the woman. For woman belongs wherever social services or human care is required.

Apart from these tasks of conserving the people, educating the people, and helping the people, the final area of responsibility for the woman, one not to be undervalued, is her contribution to the national economy. Women manage 75 per cent of the total income of the people, which passes through her hands simply in running the home. . . .

The national economy includes agriculture. It is today less possible than ever to imagine the struggle for existence and the toil involved in the economics of improving crops, refining breeds, and farming new land, activities which demand constant attention and maintenance, without the contribution of woman to agriculture in overseeing and running the farm.

Questions to Consider

1. Do you believe that the Nazi party believed women to be equal in their possibilities to men?
2. What does Ms. Siber mean when she says that women are "the custodians of the [national] culture?
3. What would be your response if a national political leader issued such a statement today? Would you agree with it? Why? Would you disagree with it? Why?

From G. Kallmeyer, "The Women's Issue and Its National Socialist Solution," Wolfenbuttel, Berlin, 1933, in *Fascism: Oxford Readers*, Roger Griffin, ed. (Oxford University Press, 1995).

Discovery Through Maps

Wishful Thinking: A Nazi Tourism Map

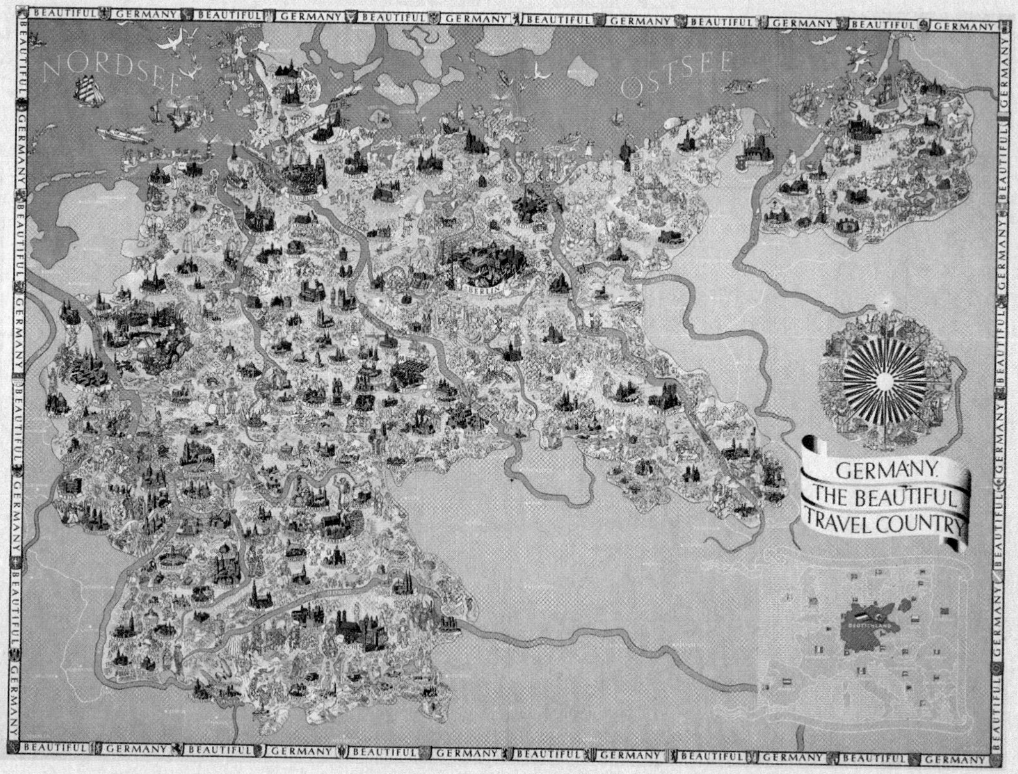

States promote tourism for a number of reasons. Tourists come, spend money, and go home: It is much like harvesting a crop, without having to do all of the difficult work. Tourists tend to be the most curious and best informed people of given society: They can have their views of a given country positively affected by their travels. Tourists go home, and if they have had a good time, encourage others to come in sort of a multiplier effect—to visit and bring their money and their impressions.

With the exception of a few hermit regimes, most countries in the twentieth century worked hard to encourage tourists to come, for the reasons pointed out above. The Third Reich was no exception. The Reich's Tourist Information Office issued a map to entice foreigners to come around the time of the 1936 Olympics called *Germany, the Beautiful Travel Country.* It is chock full of portrayals of Germany's diverse population and historic and natural sites: except for Jews. Tourist campaigns emphasize what they take to be the positive aspects of their country, the Third Reich did just that.

Germany, in this detail from the map, is a prosperous place under the control of the National Socialist Worker's Party and the beautiful Aryan people are truly happy. There are workers shown—in gleaming new factories, picture perfect peasant lands, sturdy fishing boats, and artisans workshops. There are also lots of recreational activities from swimming to skiing to gamboling and gambling to hunting and bird watching. The culture of the Reich can be seen in the exhortations to visit the fine art museums, music festivals, and observe artists at work. Germany was a beautiful country to travel in, if one stayed on the proper path and didn't look too closely at what was going on.

Many people did come to Germany, and admired the work of the Nazis and their allies. English royalty, American heroes such as Charles Lindbergh, and admiring travelers from eastern Europe all came and accepted at face value what they saw. Most tourists are like that. Not until the end of the 1930s did it become apparent that beneath the busy and happy facade a malignant force gained strength.

Questions to Consider

1. As you look at the map, do you see it as overtly propagandistic, or as simply a solid piece of advertising? Is there a difference between the two?
2. What image does the map attempt to give the observer of Germany under the Nazis?
3. Do you notice any obvious signs of the Nazi presence, such as soldiers, or images of German leaders?

Economic Policies

As in Italy, fascism in Germany revolved around a form of state capitalism. In theory and practice, Nazism retained capitalism and private property. The state, however, rigidly controlled both business and labor. The Nazis dissolved labor unions and enrolled workers and employers in a new organization, the Labor Front. As in Mussolini's corporate state, the right of the workers to strike or of management to call a lockout was denied. The Nazis took compulsory dues from the workers' wages to support Nazi organizations. As a standard operating procedure, the state set up the "Strength Through Joy" movement, which provided sports events, musical festivals, plays, movies, and vacations at low cost.

The Nazis' ultimate goal was self-sufficiency—autarky—which they would try to reach through complete state control of the economy. They assumed, as the fascists did in Italy, that only the state could ensure the social harmony needed to attain the maximum productive potential for the state's benefit.

The government tried to solve the nation's very serious economic problems by confiscating valuable Jewish property, laying a huge tax load on the middle class, and increasing the national debt by one-third to provide work for the unemployed. To create jobs, the first four-year plan, established in 1933, undertook an extensive program of public works and rearmament. The unemployed were put to work on public projects (especially in the system of superhighways, the *Autobahnen*), in munitions factories, and in the army.

Overlapping the first program, the second four-year plan was initiated in 1936. The objective of this plan was to set up an autarkist state. In pursuit of self-sufficiency, substitute commodities—frequently inferior in quality and more costly than similar goods available on the world market—were produced by German laboratories, factories, and mills. The gross national product increased by 68 percent by 1938, but the standard of living did not rise in proportion to the higher economic growth rate. When World War II began in 1939, German industry still produced insufficient munitions, even after Hitler took over the Czech Skoda works. Germany's war economy did not hit its stride until 1942.

By then, the economic picture didn't matter. Hitler controlled Germany. How an advanced, "civilized" nation like Germany could have thrown itself willingly under this madman's control is one of history's great questions. Other nations had stronger authoritarian traditions, greater economic problems, and more extreme psychological strain. Some observers maintain that there could have been no Third Reich without this unprecedented demagoguery that found a willing audience in the troubled conditions after 1918.

JAPAN

- *What role did economic crises and challenges play in the rise to power of the militarists in Japan?*

Japan was the rising international star in the first years of the twentieth century. A constitutional monarchy with a growing modern, industrial sector, it was one of the few Asian or African countries to escape Western imperialism. Western observers hailed Japan's entry onto the world stage. At the same time, Japan's victory in the Russo–Japanese War in 1904–1905 ushered in an era of hope to colonized people around the world. For the first time in centuries, a non-European power seemed to offer a model of liberation through modernization. Attitudes in Asia began to change by 1914, however, when Japan, under the Anglo-Japanese Naval Treaty of 1902, joined the Western powers in the war against Germany. Sensing an opportunity to stabilize China, which was wracked by instability and warlordism at the time, Japan's foreign minister issued Twenty-One Demands to the warlord of Beijing in 1915. While most of these demands went no further than asking for economic concessions, several threatened China's sovereignty. Patriotic young Chinese were enraged, setting the stage for the deterioration of Sino-Japanese relations. As one of the victorious Allies at Versailles, Japan gained German-held territories in China and in the Pacific, exacerbating Chinese animosity. Japan had become one of the world's major democracies, part of the multilateral alliance that included the United States, Britain, France, and Italy. But its growing clash with rising Asian nationalism sowed the seeds for its unilateral approach to foreign relations that challenged and eventually destroyed Japan's democracy in the 1930s.

Post–World War I Japan

Unlike the experience for European countries, World War I was a good war for Japan. The horrors of war were never visited on Japan. On the contrary, the temporary withdrawal of European and American interests in East Asia during World War I offered Japan tremendous economic opportunities. Japan's sales to Asia and to its domestic market exploded during the war. A new middle class emerged almost overnight in the years after the war, with women joining men in new professions in Tokyo and other vibrant, modern cities. Lively cosmopolitan life, with its jazz bars, glittering department stores, mass circulation magazines, and growing access to education that introduced young people to a wealth of ideas from abroad, tied Japanese youth to international cultural currents. College men—and some women—demanded human rights, universal suffrage, and support for the still-oppressed working class. "New Women" and "Modern Girls," many of them holding new middle-class jobs as schoolteachers, shop clerks, nurses, journalists, and telephone operators, strolled down Tokyo's fashionable Ginza. On Sundays, they were joined by their working-class counterparts from the textile mills who also enjoyed the freedom of urban culture, if only for one day a week, far from their parents' watchful eyes.

Many Japanese women struggled for women's rights, worked in offices and factories, and joined progressive movements in the interwar period. Later, during World War II, many would be swept up in groups working on behalf of the militarist state. Here, a group of patriotic women bows toward the imperial palace to honor the crown prince during the war.

Emblematic of modernity, young men and women created a culture the press dubbed *ero/guro/nansensu* (EH-roh GOO-roh nahn-SEN-soo; "erotic, grotesque and nonsensical"). They read poetry by feminist poet Yosano Akiko (YOH-sah-noh AH-kee-koh); essays on democracy by highly regarded university professor Yoshino Sakuzō (YOH-shee-noh SAH-koo-zoh) and on women's liberation by feminists Ichikawa Fusae (IH-chee-KAH-wah foo-SAI) and Hiratsuka Raichō (hee-RAHTS-kah RAI-choh); novels by Tanizaki Jun'ichirō (TAH-nee-ZAH-kee JOON-ih-chee-ROH) and by Akutagawa Ryūnosuke (AHK-tah-GAH-wah ryoo-NOH-skeh), author of *Rashomon;* and movies and plays from Hollywood and Europe. Philosopher Bertrand Russell and birth-control advocate Margaret Sanger attracted crowds when they visited Japan.

But deep economic divisions also developed in Japan. Immediately after World War I, rampant inflation of commodity prices led to a nation-wide outburst of what came to be called Rice Riots. The countryside stagnated while the cities grew, and rich enterprises called ***zaibatsu*** (vast conglomerates like Mitsubishi and Mitsui, with up to 600 subsidiaries) offered their workers and managers stability and good wages while other laborers toiled in fly-by-night workshops. The visible inequalities in Japan's modern society led to a host of popular movements: university students came together in groups demanding social reform for the poor; proletarian men and their liberal supporters in the Diet (parliament) struggled for, and won in 1925, votes for all men, thus removing the tax qualifications in place since 1890; feminists demanded complete social equality in the private sphere of the family and rights of equal citizenship in the public realm; tenant farmers formed unions to fend off high rents and rural social inequal-

---

zaibatsu—Powerful, complex, multifaceted enterprises that produced many different products while building up a family-like loyalty among their middle- and upper-level managers.

ity; union organizers struggled for both better working conditions and human dignity and respect for workers; and reformers implemented internationally encouraged labor reforms such as an end to night shifts for women and children in textile mills and coal mines.

In many cases, these struggles for democratic change were successful. And even when the changes were not accomplished, the advocates of change saw the interwar period as a period of hope and democracy. Though the reign of the emperor Taishō lasted only from 1912 to 1926, many contemporaries considered the long period from 1905 till the rise of Japanese militarism at home and abroad in the 1930s as the era of "Taishō *Demokurashii*" (Democracy). Japan enjoyed rather good relations with the Western powers, even though relations with China began to sour and oppressive treatment of Koreans under Japanese colonialism was replicated in the discriminatory treatment of Koreans resident in Japan. In Western eyes, Japan was one of the imperialist democracies. What was understood neither in Japan nor in Europe nor America at the time was that it was impossible to be an imperialist and a democracy at the same time. By the 1930s, this contradiction would become clear for Japan's case.

Japan's democratic government in the interwar period took a form different from many others at the time. Like many European governments, Japan had a constitutional monarchy. But unlike the European case, the head of the majority party in the Diet did not automatically become prime minister. Instead, an unelected group of elder statesmen, most of them aristocrats and former prime ministers, nominated the prime minister and cabinet. This changed in 1918 when the head of the majority party was asked to form a cabinet for the first time. Until right-wing terrorists frightened the elder statesmen away from nominating party leaders after 1932, elected party leaders held the dominant position in a power structure made up of elites from the Diet, the bureaucracy, the military, and big business. These party governments were not entirely democratic, however. Despite their expansion of rights and promotion of social reforms, they also passed laws that limited free expression of leftist ideas in order to undercut the attraction of socialist voices.

Japan in the Interwar Era

1912–1931	Taishō Democracy
1915	Twenty-One Demands
1923	Tokyo Earthquake
1925	Universal Manhood Suffrage in Japan
1931	Manchurian Incident
1937–1945	War with China
1940	Tripartite Pact (Japan, Germany, Italy)

Interwar Foreign Policy and Economic Crises

During the 1920s, Japanese foreign policy tended to support Western-led multilateral systems, such as the Washington Conference system and the League of Nations (see Chapter 29). With the very significant exception of America's humiliation of Japan through prohibition of Japanese immigration to the United States and through America's refusal to insert a racial equality clause—Japan's key demand—in the 1919 Versailles treaty, Japan was treated as a "Western" power.

On the continent, meanwhile, Japanese soldiers in territories through which the Japanese-held South Manchurian Railway passed became ideologues for a point of view opposed to both the liberal individualism and capitalism that characterized Japan in the 1920s. They hoped to carry out their ideas far from Tokyo's eyes. In 1927, these soldiers assassinated the warlord of Manchuria, and in September 1931, they carried out an explosion along the Railway. Fighting broke out between Japanese and Chinese forces, and by 1932, the Japanese controlled Manchuria. Though some statesmen hoped to continue a cooperative policy in international affairs, others were swayed by the unilateral approach of the military stationed in Manchuria. The events of 1931 triggered continuing skirmishes between Chinese nationalist forces and the Japanese military, and in 1933, when the League of Nations condemned Japan's actions, Japan walked out, thus ending the hope that an international body like the League could guarantee peace.

Economic distress was one reason for Japan's policy shifts from liberal internationalism to increasing militarism and a unilateral approach to foreign relations. In 1923, Tokyo had been hit by one of the largest earthquakes on record. At least 100,000 were killed, and millions were made homeless. The government lent generously to rebuild—too generously

Konoe Fumimaro, Prime Minister at the beginning of the 1937 war against China, was selected because his princely heritage suggested he could manage the nation during war. He resigned in October 1941, less than two months before the attack on Pearl Harbor.

perhaps, as the loans often went unpaid, leading to bank failures in 1927. Japan had not yet recovered from that crisis when the New York Stock Exchange crashed, starting a worldwide depression in 1929. Japanese factories closed, and workers returned to their villages, leading to more violent tenant disputes when landlords took back land to allow their returning children to farm. As U.S. consumers stopped buying silk stockings, Japanese farm families who relied on silk sales found themselves selling their daughters into prostitution. Japan started to pull out of the depression sooner than other industrial nations when its finance minister pioneered deficit financing that would, four years later, come to be called **Keynesianism.** Urban areas rebounded, but the countryside remained poor.

Keynesianism—An economic theory devised by the British economist John Maynard Keynes and his followers that advocated government fiscal and monetary intervention to enhance economic activity and employment.

The Rise of Militarism

Right-wing fanatics, no longer confined to Manchuria, took up the cause of destitute farmers and developed an antiurban, antimodern ideology. They made several attempts to overthrow the government by assassination. The prime minister was killed in 1932, and a major coup attempt, lasting three days, killed several high-ranking government officials, bureaucrats, business leaders, and generals in February 1936. Party-led governments were replaced by increasingly military-dominated cabinets. Urban Japanese continued to enjoy vibrant material culture until the end of the 1930s, but changes were beginning to alter their lives.

Japan's cooperation with Western democracies, especially in multilateral treaty systems and in mutual support for one another's colonial possessions—treaties with the United States, France, and England supported their common imperialism—gave way in 1936 to Japan's Anti-Comintern Pact with Nazi Germany (signed by Fascist Italy in 1937) which was directed against the Soviet Union, and in 1940 to the Tripartite Pact, with the same three signatories and directed against the United States. In addition, the Japanese signed a neutrality pact with the Soviet Union in April 1941. Japan's full-scale involvement in World War II had begun in July 1937 with the war with China (see Chapters 29 and 31 for the war in China and elsewhere in Asia from 1937 to 1945). The war with the United States, begun on December 7, 1941, when Japan launched a major attack on Pearl Harbor in Hawaii, followed several years of rapidly deteriorating relations. In the next several years, Japanese leaders destroyed human rights in Japan and the war zone.

CONCLUSION

Russia, Italy, Germany, and Japan had separate and distinct cultural, social, and political roots that gave unique qualities to their nondemocratic governments. Each of the states however, shared similar circumstances. Each faced economic upheavals, had weak traditions of liberal rule, and were easy targets for ambitious individuals or groups ready to take command. In the absence of dynamic democratic forces at home, these circumstances produced the interwar government structures of the nondemocratic states.

For the European powers, to be sure, the fascists and the communists differed in theory: The fascists used capitalism while the communists opposed it; fascism emphasized nationalism while communism preached internationalism; fascism had a weak dogmatic basis while communism was based on Marx's scientific socialism; fascism made use of religion while communism attacked it. But by 1939, the common interests of Berlin and Moscow were much more important than the theoretical differences. Although they may have been philosophically separate, in their policies, the states were remarkably similar—and could share foreign policy goals, as would be seen in the Nazi-Soviet pact of September 1939. In Japan, the interwar period began with a push toward greater democratization and internationalism of cultural, diplomatic, and economic ties. It ended, however, with war and expansionism in Asia, isolation from and eventually war with its earlier allies, an alliance with Germany and Italy, and after a bloody war against Russia at Nomonhan in 1939, a neutrality pact with the Soviets.

Suggestions for Web Browsing

You can obtain more information about topics included in this chapter at the websites listed below. See also the companion website that accompanies this text, http://www.ablongman.com/brummett, which contains an online study guide and additional resources.

The Italian Fascist Youth Movement
http://www.library.wisc.edu/libraries/dpf/fascism/youth.html

A spectacular collection of images in the Italian Fascist Youth Movement from University of Wisconsin's superb Fascism series, Italian Life Under Fascism.

Library of Congress: Soviet Archive Exhibit
http://www.ncsa.uiuc.edu/SDG/Experimental/soviet.exhibit/soviet.archive.html

A magnificent exhibition at the Library of Congress on the Soviet years. Documents on both the foreign and domestic aspects of the USSR, with stunning evidence concerning collectivization.

A USSR Purge Trial
http://art-bin.com/art/omosc20e.html

A transcript from a purge trial. One can see the methods of Andrei Vyshinsky as he grills I. N. Smirnov.

The War Between Japan and China
http://www.fas.harvard.edu/~asiactr/sino-japanese/

Resources on the war between Japan and China, 1931–1945.

Literature and Film

In Italy the works of Curzio Malaparte capture the spirit of the interwar period and the opening of World War II. His best known work is *Kaputt* (1944), a brilliant witness to the period. In Germany, Erich Maria Remarque's book *All Quiet on the Western Front* (1929) captured the cruelty of the first war while the works of Thomas Mann (*Buddenbrooks* (1901) and *Death in Venice* (1912)) drew the wrath of the Nazis in the interwar period. He along with the playwright Bertolt Brecht (*Three Penny Opera* (1922), *Mother Courage* (1939)) and Remarque found themselves on the list of the unacceptables. The film director Leni Riefenstahl produced two cinematic triumphs for the Nazis in her *Triumph of the Will* (1934) and a documentary on the 1936 Berlin Olympics (1938).

The period 1919–1939 was a difficult time for writers and film makers in Russia, Italy, and Germany. In these authoritarian states, an arid form of Socialist Realism prevailed. In poetry, Russia suffered from the early deaths of A. A. Blok (1921) and V. V. Mayakovsky, the first a reformed noble and the second a revolutionary figure. Blok's greatest poems, *The Twelve* and *The Scythians,* capture the dread and the essence of the revolution. Mayakovsky personified the avant-garde, but in his satirical plays *The Bathhouse* (1930) and *The Bedbug* (1928), he wrote two cutting critiques of the bureaucratic revolution (1930) just before he committed suicide. Anna Akmatova began her brilliant, controversial career in 1935 with her epic *The Requiem,* not to be published until 1988. At this time Mikhail Sholokhov wrote more to the regime's liking in his novel *And Quiet Flows the Don* (1928–1940)—which has a Tolstoyan sweep. Evgeny Zamyatin in *We* (1920) anticipated by 30 years George Orwell's themes in *1984* and Mikhail Bulgakov in *The Master and Margarita* (1928–1940) gave an impression of the world of Stalinian totalitarianism. In film, the great Soviet director Sergei Eisenstein created magnificent epics with *Ivan the Terrible* (Home Vision Entertainment, 1947) and *Alexander Nevsky* (White Star, 1939) complete with a spectacular musical score by Prokofiev. Andrei Konchalovsky's 1991 film, *The Inner Circle/The Projectionist* (Columbia/Tristar) is a chilling, subtle look into what life among Stalin's immediate circle might have been like.

Many films produced after the war capture the suffering at the war era. Akira Kurosawa's *No Regrets for Our Youth* (Home Vision Entertainment, 1946) is a moving condemnation of militarism as seen through the eyes of a brave widow of a dissident journalist; Kinoshita Keisuke's *Twenty-four Eyes* (Shochiku Films, 1954) chronicles the lives and wartime deaths of the kindergarten children of one teacher. Tanizaki Jun'ichirō's novel, *The Makioka Sisters* (Vintage, 1995), written during World War II, focuses on a family with four adult sisters, each one symbolic of a different type of modern Japanese.

Suggestions for Reading

Orlando Figes provides an excellent perspective of Russia's inability to avoid revolution in *A People's Tragedy: The Russian Revolution, 1891–1924* (Penguin, 1998). Sheila Fitzpatrick, *The Russian Revolution, 1917–1932* (Oxford University Press, 1982), is a first-rate analysis that establishes the themes undergirding the Stalinist society that emerged in the 1930s. See also her perceptive *Everyday Stalinism: Ordinary Life in Extraordinary Times in the 1930s* (Oxford University Press, 2000). Robert Conquest details the campaign against the peasantry in *Harvest of Sorrow* (Oxford University Press, 1986). J. Arch Getty and Oleg. V. Naumov, *The Road to Terror: Stalin and the*

Self-Destruction of the Bolsheviks (1932–1939) (Yale University Press, 1999) provides documents essential to understanding the purges.

Essential introductions and guides to the complex world of fascism are Robert O. Paxton, *The Anatomy of Fascism* (Knopf, 2004), and Stanley G. Payne, *A History of Fascism, 1914–1945* (University of Wisconsin Press, 1995). Adrian Lyttelton's *The Seizure of Power: Fascism in Italy, 1919–1939,* 2nd ed. (Princeton University Press, 1988) remains a useful introduction. Ian Kershaw's *Hitler: 1889–1936 Hubris* (Norton, 2000) and *Hitler: 1936–1945 Nemesis* (Norton, 2001) give the best biography of the German dictator.

On Japan's politics, foreign policy, and expansion, see Louise Young, *Japan's Total Empire: Manchuria and the Culture of Wartime Imperialism* (University of California Press, 1998), and Joshua Fogel, *The Nanjing Massacre in History and Historiography* (University of California Press, 2000). See also Sheldon Garon, *Molding Japanese Minds* (Princeton University Press, 1997) and Vera Mackie, *Creating Socialist Women in Japan* (Cambridge University Press, 2002).

CHAPTER

29

Forging New Nations in Asia, 1910–1950

CHAPTER CONTENTS

Fifty years of aggressive expansion by Europe, the United States and, later, Japan had spread those countries' ideas, investments, colonists, and control to much of the world. Even Asian societies that were not directly colonized were influenced by the politics, cultures, and economies of the imperialist states. It was in the period between the world wars and immediately afterward that many of these societies adopted—or had imposed on them—the nation-state model of political organization. Japan adopted the nation-state model and, like the European and American nation-states, gained an empire. As it turned toward militarism in the 1930s, Japan is discussed in Chapter 28.

The idea of the nation took hold among anti-imperialists throughout colonial Asia. The 1919 peace conference at Versailles, which ended World War I, promised "self-determination of nations," and independence fighters from throughout Asia took the victorious powers at their word. When it became clear that only European states were to be accorded the rights of self-determination, independence movements took on the task of nationalist liberation with renewed energy. Some nationalists, inspired by the revolutionary anti-imperialist rhetoric of Marxism and the victory of the Soviets in Russia, embraced socialism as the path of liberation. Others, inspired by the democratic and modernist ideologies espoused, ironically, by the imperialists themselves, used the language of Western liberalism. The message of liberalism was enhanced by the artistic and intellectual ferment that grew from the repudiation of the old social orders that had dominated culture until World War I.

Thus, nationalist anti-imperialism of the interwar period was characterized not only by the quest to build new nations but also by a struggle between various forms of progressivism—especially socialism versus capitalism. Civil wars were, therefore, embedded within the struggles for independence.

Both indigenous changes and global forces of modernity, as well as the economic and strategic actions of the world powers, led to the evolution of Asian states at this time. This era witnessed a dramatic movement of people from the countryside to the city, with accompanying social and economic turmoil. The processes that gained momentum in the nineteenth century in the realms of industrialization, education,

1910

1910 Korea becomes Japanese colony

1912 Republic of China declared

1915

1919 Rowlett Act and Amritsar Massacre; May Fourth Incident in China; March First movement in Korea

1920

1920 Indian National Congress launches policy of noncooperation

1921 Founding of Chinese Communist Party

1930

1930 Muslim League founded

1934–35 The Long March: Chinese Communists escape to Shaanxi

1935

1937–1945 China at war with Japan

1940

1941 Ho Chi Minh establishes the Viet Minh

1942 Quit India Movement

1945

1946 Philippines gain independence from the United States

1947 Independence and Partition of India

1949 People's Republic of China founded

transportation, and communication remained vigorous. New leaders emerged, and even in the absence of full political rights of independence, systems of government, law, economics, and social values began to change. While many economies in Asia remained primarily agrarian, others abandoned traditional modes of economic organization. Often the transformation caused dramatic changes in the lives of individuals and families within a single generation—as when rural girls and women migrated to mills and towns in search of factory or domestic labor or when men and women migrated across the ocean to seek work.

World War I and its aftershocks strengthened independence movements in Asia. Nationalist campaigns, active in most of the colonies before the war, grew rapidly in virtually all of the European and Japanese possessions and mandates. China endured revolution and civil strife, and the areas of Southeast Asia pursued independence. India's independence movement grew in several different directions, most notably that of Mohandas Gandhi, with his tactic of nonviolence. These movements, together with the blow to European imperialism dealt by the war with Japan and the Europeans' exhaustion with fighting after World War II, finally persuaded the imperialists to pull up their stakes in the decades after that war. Across Asia, nations struggled to redefine themselves, adapt to global economic reorganization, and throw off the yoke of colonial domination.

CHINA: REVOLUTION AND REPUBLIC

- *How did cultural, political, and nationalistic forces come together to build a new nation from the ruins of a 2000-year-old imperial state?*

At the dawn of the twentieth century, the Qing Dynasty maintained a tenuous grip on power. The failed Righteous Harmony Fists (Boxer) Uprising had persuaded the Empress Dowager Cixi to reform the monarchy or else lose the right to rule. Reforms in education, governance, the military, and other areas were quickly promulgated. New schools were educating 10 million boys and girls by 1910 (the government had approved girls' education in 1907, and by 1910 1.6 million girls were already attending school). The Qing began working on a constitution in 1908. Provincial assemblies, though selected by an electorate severely limited by gender and wealth, sat for the first time in 1909. And a modern-style military, under General Yuan Shikai (yoo-AHN shuh-KAI), was commissioned.

Rather than shoring up the monarchy, however, these measures undermined it in the eyes of those who sought broader and deeper change. Similarly, the visible growth of a modern sector—with railroads, shipping companies, and banks—rather than promoting support for a modernizing state, only served to highlight its failings, as these industries were dominated by foreign investors. Protests against Russia for its occupation of Manchuria after the Righteous Harmony Fists (Boxer) Uprising (1903) and the United States for discriminatory immigration laws (1905) were additional indications of popular dissatisfaction.

The Revolution of 1911

Many young nationalists, even while despising the dismemberment of their country, sought the tools for challenging both the foreign threat and Manchu rule in modern, and often foreign, ideas. They often were introduced to these ideas—and forged alliances with like-minded Chinese—while overseas. Japan, only a few hundred miles away from China and using a writing system many Chinese could understand, was the schoolroom for China's revolutionaries. Most of the 8000 Chinese students in Japan at the end of the Qing were men, but some were women. The most famous martyr of the Revolution of 1911, a woman who never lived to see the overthrow of the Manchus, was Qiu Jin (CHOO JIN). Qiu joined the Revolutionary Alliance *(Tongmenghui)* while a student in Japan, returned to China to promote revolution and feminism, and was executed for her role in an abortive coup in 1907.

More influential in the long run was Sun Yat-sen (1866–1925). Sun had studied in Hawaii and Hong Kong, founded the Revolutionary Alliance in Tokyo in 1905, and developed what he called the "Three Principles of the People"—nationalism, democracy, and the people's livelihood. Like the thousands of their compatriots who studied revolutionary thought overseas, Qiu and Sun eagerly sought out Western ideas, espe-

peasant uprisings planned by the CCP for that year. Mao's "Autumn Harvest Uprising" failed and the peasants were severely repressed. Despite that failure, the report Mao produced following the uprising set the stage for the kind of peasant revolution he would eventually lead to victory in China two decades later. Praising violence as necessary for revolution, Mao believed that "Several hundred million peasants will rise like a mighty storm, like a hurricane, a force so swift and violent that no power, however great, will be able to hold it back."[2]

For the time being, though, the Communists hardly seemed capable of leading a mighty storm. Under attack from the Nationalist government, they set up their own government in Jiangxi province, where they established land reform and other policies while constantly fending off the Nanjing government's "annihilation campaigns." In the fall of 1934, Jiang Jieshi successfully blockaded the Communists, who were forced out of their province and began the **Long March.** Many people, especially women and children, were left behind and suffered reprisals, but the 100,000 Communists on the Long March endured extraordinary hardships as they climbed mountains, crossed gorges, trudged through swamps, and succumbed to illness. Less than ten percent survived the 6000-mile ordeal to arrive in October 1935 in Shaanxi (shahn-SHI) province where the Communists remained until after World War II. Until after the death of Deng Xiaoping (DUHNG show-PING) in 1997, leaders of post-1949 China all were survivors of the Long March. The other important result of the Long March was the emergence of Mao Zedong as the premier leader of the Communists.

World War II

The most significant events in China's history in the decades after the fall of the Qing were part of the struggle for national unity. Foreign relations were always important but took a back seat to domestic issues. By the 1930s, this would change, as Japan emerged as the main international player in East Asia. European imperialists continued to play a role in China's coastal areas, but the growing tensions and China's eventual war with Japan, together with internal civil war, ultimately led to the Communists' victory in 1949.

Challenged, as China was, by Western imperialism, Japan had adopted an expansive position in East Asia by the end of the nineteenth century. Taiwan was made a Japanese colony in 1895, followed by Korea in 1910. Japan's victory over Russia in the Russo-Japanese War gave it railroad rights in Manchuria in 1905. These created a Japanese presence in areas of interest to the Chinese, but Japan continued to be praised by reformist Chinese as Asia's leader until 1915. The humiliating Twenty-one Demands of that year, while mostly rejected, made Japan appear as aggressive as the worst imperialists—and more dangerous because of its proximity. At the end of World War I, Japan (along with the United States, Britain, France and Canada) invaded Siberia to try to stop the Bolshevik revolution in Russia, and Japanese troops remained in Northeast Asia until 1922. Japan's hold on Shandong (as a result of the Versailles Conference) from 1919 till 1922 was a bitter pill for Chinese to swallow. In 1922, however, relations appeared to improve, at least temporarily. The Washington Conference of 1921–1922 produced several treaties, one of which, the Nine-Power, was signed by China and Japan and guaranteed China's territorial integrity.

Mao Zedong, Chairman of the Chinese Communist Party until his death in 1976.

Long March—Chinese Communist escape to Shaanxi, 1934–35; established leadership in CCP.

At the same time, Japanese soldiers stationed in Northeast Asia were conducting a foreign policy of their own which eventually undermined the Washington Conference treaties. Believing the warlord of Manchuria, Zhang Zuolin (JAHNG zoo-aw-LIN), whom they had supported because of his assistance with Japanese interests in Manchuria, was not sufficiently helpful, rogue members of the Japanese army assassinated him. Although the Japanese government eventually distanced itself from this terrorist incident, the Japanese army in Manchuria could not be controlled and carried out a much more significant incident on September 18, 1931. This Manchurian Incident led to major combat and the creation in 1932 of the state of "Manchukuo" (MAHN-joo-goo-aw), headed by the last Qing emperor, but really ruled by the Japanese army. This action was condemned by the League of Nations, but Japan simply abandoned the League in 1933.

Tensions, which often took a military form, continued between Japan and China in the next several years. In 1936, the son of the assassinated Zhang Zuolin kidnapped Jiang Jieshi, head of the Nationalist government of the Republic of China, for not moving against Japanese encroachment. Forced under the threat of death to agree to a united front with the Communists, whom he had just driven into the Shaanxi caves during the previous year's Long March, Jiang was viewed by the Japanese military as a threat to its continental ambitions. Full-scale warfare between China and Japan broke out on July 7, 1937, following an incident at a bridge outside Beijing. Thus began World War II in Asia.

By December 1937, Japanese forces had conquered Beijing, Tianjin (tee-un-JIN), and Shanghai. Chinese soldiers took a stand at Nanjing and were brutally defeated. In the weeks after the defeat, as the Nationalist government decamped to the backwater town of Chongqing, Japanese soldiers went on a rampage in Nanjing so brutal that it came to be known throughout the world as the **"Rape of Nanking."** ("Nanjing" is an alternate spelling of "Nanking.") Many tens of thousands of civilians were killed, around 20,000 women were raped, and the city was ransacked. Despite brave fighting by the Nationalists in their areas and the Communists in their areas, the war dragged on. At the same time, despite the united front, Jiang continued to fight against the Communists, blockading them in 1941. U.S. President Franklin Roosevelt and British Prime Minister Winston Churchill envisioned a postwar order in which Jiang's government would play a major international role, but the continuing tensions with the Communists made that seem unlikely. After the Allied victory over Japan in 1945, civil war broke out in China. The Communists won, driving the Nationalists to Taiwan, and declared the founding of the People's Republic of China on October 1, 1949.

KOREA: FROM MONARCHY TO COLONY

- *How did Koreans attempt to build a nation while under the Japanese colonial rule?*

The Chosŏn dynasty (1392–1910) faced the same pressures from Western imperialists encountered by other East Asian countries in the late nineteenth century. American and French naval invasions were repulsed in 1866 and 1871. In 1876 Japan, embarking on its own program of modernization, forced a trade treaty on Korea, the Treaty of Kangwha (KAHNG-wah). In short order, unequal treaties with the United States, England, France, Germany, Russia, Italy, and Belgium opened the door to influence by Christian missionaries and trade. The Chosŏn king, Kojŏng, sent study missions to Japan and the West to decide whether to modernize Korea to save it from imperialism. While many conservative Confucianists opposed any changes, others welcomed them, particularly young reformers who called themselves the Enlightenment Party. Calling for major changes in the style of Meiji Japan, these upper-class or **yangban** reformers, led by Kim Ok-kyun (KIM ohk-kee-OON), attempted a coup in 1884. Japanese advisers had backed them up, but they were defeated by Chinese forces in Korea.

Tensions appeared temporarily resolved by a diplomatic agreement between the Qing and Japan that removed the bulk of those nations' forces from Korea in 1885. But China continued to meddle closely in the Korean court's foreign relations, and Korea's open ports permitted Japanese merchants to dominate trade and drive up rice prices. In 1893 and 1894, famine sparked regional uprisings, and the **Tonghak** (tong-hahk; "Eastern Learning") religious movement, suppressed in the 1860s, reemerged. Tonghak was a blend of Buddhism and folk religions, and with its respect for the downtrodden, including women, it appealed to many. King Kojŏng called in Chinese troops to put down the rebels, and under the provisions of the 1885 Sino-Japanese agreement, Japan felt compelled to send in its own

Rape of Nanking—Military violence by Japanese soldiers in Nanjing, December 1937; 100,000 to 200,000 Chinese killed.

yangban—Korean aristocracy in Chosŏn dynasty.

Tonghak—"Eastern Learning" movement in Korea; uprising set stage for Sino-Japanese War.

troops. The Sino-Japanese War (1894–95) was a major victory for Japan.

China withdrew from Korea, and modernizers came to the fore. The increasingly powerful Japanese pushed the Korean government to institute the Kabo Reforms (1894–1896) which called for a constitutional monarchy, modernizing schools, banking, and the military, and eliminating class distinctions. When conservatives opposed these changes, however, the Japanese instigated the murder of the conservative Queen Min, wife of King Kojŏng. Despite this extreme example of Japan's meddling in Korea's affairs, the cause of progressive change, championed by those who saw modernizing Japan as Korea's model, was not extinguished. Men and women—some educated in the Protestant schools dating from the 1880s, others educated in Japan or the West—established the Independence Club in 1896. The Club's newspaper, the *Independent*, was published in han'gul, a Korean script, rather than using Chinese characters and celebrated Korean heroes, independence, and need to modernize. Inspired by the nationalism of the Independence Club, Koreans flocked to meetings about progressive change, including people's rights, women's rights, and representative government. King Kojŏng banned the Club and its newspaper in 1898, but both were a school for independence movements of the future, and one member would become the first president of the Republic of Korea half a century later.

Downtown Seoul with modern buildings built during the colonial period.

Japan's victory in the Russo-Japanese War (1904–1905) expanded its role in Northeast Asia. Despite Korean protest, Japan made Korea a protectorate in 1905 and a full-scale colony in 1910. One of the first instances of Korean women organizing for national independence occurred in 1907 with the National Debt Compensation Campaign, when women activists attempted, unsuccessfully, to diminish Japan's presence through repaying Korean debts to Japan. Colonial rule was harsh. Koreans lost rights to join movements or speak freely, and many were deprived of rights to lands they had farmed for centuries. As in China, Korean nationalists took seriously the Wilsonian promise of self-determination of nations, and demonstrated against Japanese colonialism on March 1, 1919. Brutally repressed—thousands of Koreans were killed—what was meant to be a peaceful demonstration set in motion an independence movement.

Japan's Territorial Ambitions

Japanese colonial policy in the next decade was a reaction to the brutality of 1919. Substituting "cultural rule" for the previous "military rule," the colonial government permitted an expansion of political movements, including newspapers; organizations that studied Korean history, language, and culture; and limited political discussions about the nation. The political organization **Sin'ganhoe** (SHIN-gahn-HOH-eh) brought together Korean cultural nationalists, many of them people of wealth, and members of the Korean Communist Party, many of them advocating social revolution accompanying national liberation from Japan. As in China, the two groups split. The Communists went underground or into exile but came back after the end of the colonial period in 1945, eventually becoming the government of North Korea.

The 1930s ended the period of cultural rule. As rising militarism repressed Japanese life at home, Japanese rule became increasingly harsh in Korea. Much of Korea's rice production was shipped to Japan, starving the Korean people; the language of instruction in Korea's schools was restricted to Japanese after 1934; Koreans were required to adopt Japanese surnames in 1940; several million Korean men were forced to serve in the Japanese military or work in Japanese factories and mines after 1938; and several hundred thousand Korean women and girls were forced into sexual slavery as **"comfort women"** for the Japanese military during World War II. This painful legacy of colonialism made the prospect of nation-building in the postwar era difficult—and the onset of the Cold War worsened those prospects.

Sin'ganhoe—New Korea Society, pro-independence movement, 1927–1931.

comfort women—Euphemism for the sexual slaves, mostly Korean women, used by the Japanese military in World War II.

NATIONALISM IN SOUTHEAST ASIA

- *How did Southeast Asians use Western ideas of self-governance and modernity in their struggles for independence?*

The drive for independence became stronger in Southeast Asia between the two world wars. Taking advantage of the war-weakened colonialists, local leaders adapted the ideologies of the day—Wilson's "self-determination of nations," socialism, or a combination of the two—to their campaigns for freedom. The example of Japan's rise to the status of a Great Power showed that the West had no monopoly on harnessing technology and organization to national goals.

Populations grew dramatically in Southeast Asia during the interwar period. From 1930 to 1960 the number of people in Thailand, Malaya, and the Philippines increased more than 100 percent; in Indonesia, Burma, and Indochina the number increased more than 50 percent.

Economic trends also had great influence on most of the region. The imperialist powers continued to exploit their colonies, ignoring the democratic rhetoric they had used during World War I. Their draining of the area's resources, coupled with an unpredictable world market that crashed in 1929, led to increased hardship in much of the region. The Chinese played an increasingly important role as merchants in the local economies. In Burma, Indians played the same role. European and Chinese capital investment encouraged rapid growth in exports of minerals and forest products. In Siam (Thailand), Vietnam, and a few other countries, rice production grew more rapidly than population, and as a result those countries became rice exporters during this period.

Water Buffalo in Southeast Asia

Throughout the area, some among the elite became accustomed to Western culture as more and more young people went to the "parent countries" to be educated. The masses, however, were barely touched by this process. The result was a growing cultural and social divide between the local leadership and the people at large. Few among the imperialist powers undertook to prepare their colonies for eventual self-government, since they had no intention of letting them go.

Indochina

France's Indochinese Union—made up of three Vietnamese territories (the colony of Cochin China and protectorates of Annam and Tonkin), as well as the protectorates of Cambodia and Laos, annexed one-by-one between 1862 and 1893—was ruled by a French governor-general residing in Hanoi. Though the Vietnamese emperor was retained, he had little power. Indochina was run for the benefit of France. Huge landholdings came under French control, producing rice, rubber, coffee, tea, and sugar for the French market. Coal mines, also controlled by the French, shipped coal to run industries at home. Impoverished peasants from the northern part of the Indochinese Union were sent as coolie laborers to Cochin China in the south or to French Pacific colonies like Tahiti.

People and products were not only shipped out of Vietnam, but other goods were brought in, from which the French also derived revenues. Opium, salt, and wine were sold to Vietnamese consumers and taxed at very high rates.

Though most of the profits of the Indochinese colonies went to France, some Vietnamese as well as Chinese immigrants to Vietnam took part in shipping and marketing the colonies' products. In addition, a new cosmopolitan professional class, including doctors, lawyers, and teachers, emerged in Saigon (Ho Chi Minh City). As in other East Asian colonies, it was among these urban professionals that anticolonial nationalism first stirred. Although the French espoused a goal of "civilizing" the Indochinese—that is, making them more like the French—they extended the benefits of education only to a few. But those few began to read texts by Chinese and Japanese reformers, often translations of Rousseau, Locke, and Mill. Phan Boi Chau (FAHN BOI CHOW; 1867–1940) and Phan Chu Trinh (FAN CHOO TRIN; 1872–1926) both studied in Japan, encountering Chinese and Korean revolutionaries. Others went to France and were inspired by the ideals of the French Revolution, which were utterly unfulfilled in Vietnam. One nationalist was even convicted in 1926 for the treasonous act of translating Rousseau's *Social Contract* into Vietnamese.

The urban intelligentsia in the 1920s took up the issues that had inspired the May Fourth generation in China. To build a new Vietnam, many were saying, new social relations, including those between men and women, must be encouraged. Other radical ideas were developing in the 1920s. One hundred thousand Vietnamese had been sent to France during World War I to take the places of French workers drafted into the army. Exposed to French working-class radicalism, many later worked for the independence they believed Vietnam deserved. Ho Chi Minh (1890–1969) went to the Versailles peace conference with a petition for independence, which, like all the other non-European petitions, was denied. Vietnamese increasingly turned to political organizing for independence, establishing, in 1927, the Nationalist Party of Vietnam and in 1930, the Indochinese Communist Party.

A Vietnamese nationalist poster dating from the end of the French colonial period. A Viet Minh supporter crushes the French soldier and his flag.

DOCUMENT
Vietnamese Declaration of Independence

The French (Vichy) government continued to administer Vietnam while the Japanese military moved in between 1941 and 1945. Hoping to defeat both the Japanese and the French, Ho Chi Minh established a united front movement, the Viet Minh (League of the Independence of Vietnam) in 1941, that anticipated the end of colonialism. Ho and other Vietnamese nationalists would be surprised and disappointed when the French moved back in between 1945 and 1954.

The Philippines

DOCUMENT
The American Anti-Imperialist League

The American war against Filipino independence fighters spawned an anti-imperialist movement in the United States. U.S. President McKinley had to devise a face-saving way to end the embarrassment of that colonial war and sent U.S. officials to strike a deal with the Filipino elite. The governor-general in the war-torn Philippines, Judge (later President) William Howard Taft, allowed the elite to participate in administration at the local level while U.S. officials governed at the national level. Though an elected legislative assembly was established in 1907, it could be vetoed by the top American administrators.

By 1908, Taft feared that the expedient tactic of pacifying the Philippines' desire for self-rule by co-opting the elite was stifling the development of democracy and potentially creating an aristocratic government. Believing that a longer period of tutelage was necessary before the Filipinos could govern themselves, Taft did not support a rapid transition to independence. The U.S. position changed in 1912. Under Francis B. Harrison, appointed governor-general by President Wilson that year, the Filipinos increasingly took over administration. **The Jones Act** of 1916 became the basis for the development of constitutional government. Sergio Osmeña (SEHR-hee-oh os-MEN-yah) and Manuel Quezon (mahn-oo-EL kay-ZON), leaders of the nationalist movement, publicly advocated independence at the earliest possible time and went to the United States in 1919 to request it. The two worried privately, however, about problems with defense, currency, and free trade should the Philippines gain independence soon. The election of President Warren Harding made the question of immediate independence a moot point, as the Republican position was to take a slower approach.

The U.S. position changed radically again with the onset of the Depression in 1929. U.S. industry groups that earlier fought against independence switched to the other side as a way to keep Filipino products out of the United States. Workers wanted to deny Filipinos access to the U.S. labor market (colonial subjects were exempt from the immigration laws which kept out other Asians). These groups joined President Franklin Roosevelt in supporting liberation. The Tydings-McDuffie Act of 1934 promised complete independence within a decade, although, postponed by World War II, it was not granted until July 4, 1946.

Throughout the period of American colonialism, a sense of nationalism developed in the Philippines. While deep divisions among rich and poor worsened, almost all Filipinos came to identify with the nation, overcoming some, though certainly not all, linguistic and ethnic divisions. Education was probably the greatest legacy of U.S. rule, with 50 percent of the population literate on the eve of World War II. Public health was also radically improved, and life expectancy jumped from 14 years in 1900 to 40 years in 1940.

Indonesia/Dutch East Indies

New schools for Indonesians, called Dutch Native Schools, trained thousands of civil servants, lawyers,

---

The Jones Act—U.S. law, 1916, promising eventual independence to Philippines.

doctors, and other professionals. Many of this group of educated young men, dissatisfied with traditional status hierarchies as well as with Dutch racial superiority, joined the anti-imperialist organization **Sarekat Islam** (SAH-reh-kaht ee-SLAHM) in 1912. Both anti-Dutch and anti-Chinese, Sarekat Islam claimed 2 million members by 1919. (Chinese merchants played a large role in the Indonesian economy, which was resented by nationalist Indonesians.)

Sarekat Islam's leader, Umar Sayed Tjokrominoto (oo-MAHR sah-YED tee-OH-kroh-mee-NOH-toh) used a modernist form of Islam as a means of promoting Indonesian nationalism, modernization, and socialism. In 1920, the leftists in Sarekat broke away as the Partai Kommunis Indonesia (PKI, Communist Party of Indonesia). The PKI grew quickly, especially among highly educated, though underemployed young men, frustrated with Dutch authoritarianism. In November 1926, the PKI proclaimed a republic and started an uprising. The Dutch cracked down, throwing 13,000 PKI members into concentration camps or forcing them into exile. That ended the PKI until the Dutch were driven out of Indonesia.

Sarekat was not much more fortunate. Though the Dutch had introduced modest political reforms in response to Sarekat's demands, the pace of change was glacially slow, only adding to the nationalists' frustration. In 1927, Achmed Sukarno (soo-KAHR-noh; 1901–1970), Tjokrominoto's son-in-law, established the Indonesian Nationalist Party. The next year, the Party adopted key elements of nationalist identity—a flag, a single national language, and a national anthem. In 1930, Sukarno was arrested by the Dutch authorities; he was released in 1931, then arrested again along with other nationalist leaders, and was not freed till the Japanese defeated the Dutch in 1942.

The Japanese appeared to expand rights, but in reality granted little to Indonesians. Japan's defeat in August 1945 brought the Dutch, and the struggle for independence, back to Indonesia until 1947.

Siam (Thailand)

In the interwar period, Siam, which changed its name to Thailand ("Land of the Free") in 1939, continued to modernize. Educational improvements, economic growth, and increased political sophistication contrasted sharply, however, with the political and administrative domination of the country by the extensive royal family. Educated, elite nonaristocrats chafed at continuing favoritism for aristocrats. In 1932 a French-trained law professor, Pridi Phanomyung (PREE-dee FAH-noh-mee-yung), led a bloodless coup d'état, and a new constitution was promulgated with the agreement of the king, turning him into a reigning, not ruling, monarch. Since then, the country has been ruled by an alliance of army and oligarchy. During the 1930s, Thailand became increasingly nationalistic, repressing Chinese merchants and limiting Chinese immigration, treating Christians as aliens, and admiring the military successes of Japan in China. In mid-1944, when it appeared Japan would lose the Pacific War, Thailand switched allegiance to the United States to preserve its independence.

Burma and Malaya

In Burma, the British colonials wiped out the old social and political system. Buddhism, which had been the glue that held Burmese society together, was sidelined, especially in the Christian-oriented schools the British had established. British insults, together with anger over the presence of Indian moneylenders in Burma, fueled an independence movement. Despite their feelings about Indians in Burma, the Burmese independence movement modeled itself on the tactics practiced by the highly respected **Indian National Congress.** Buddhism, however, provided the focus for organizational activity. The Young Men's Buddhist Association, formed in 1906, organized the General Council of Burmese Associations in 1921. The General Council brought nationalism to the village level.

British promises after World War I to promote Indian self-government created a similar demand in Burma. A Buddhist-inspired uprising spread through many Burmese villages before it was crushed in 1937. Some reforms did occur. In 1937, Burma was administratively split off from India. A parliamentary system was begun with a Burmese prime minister under a British governor, who held responsibility for foreign relations, defense, and finance. The Japanese promise of independence during World War II led Burma to side with Japan against the British, but cruel behavior by the Japanese led many Burmese to join an underground resistance.

No strong nationalist movement developed in Malaya, perhaps because the large ethnic groups living there were given ample space to succeed in a pluralist society. The agricultural rights of the Malay people were not taken away, despite the formation of large, foreign-owned tin and rubber operations. The Chinese in Malaya, as elsewhere throughout Southeast Asia, were involved in commerce and allowed to expand their import-export businesses. The Indians, for the most part workers on plantations and in mines, were loyal to India as their homeland. The only seri-

Sarekat Islam—Indonesian independence movement, founded 1912, also known as the Islamic Association.

Indian National Congress—Secular independence movement in India, founded 1885.

Discovery Through Maps

What's in a Name? Siam or Thailand?

Maps nominally show the world "as it really is." But peoples, nations, and boundaries are always evolving, often very quickly. Thus, maps tend to depict the world as it used to be or as it was imagined to be. While mapmakers may have a difficult time keeping up with the ways in which states and national identities change, there are other reasons why maps may reflect different visions of reality. Maps institutionalize points of view, ways of seeing or naming parts of the world. Should a map call a country by the name used by its own people or by the name used by those who buy the map? Older Western maps, for example, might designate the capital of China as Peking rather than Beijing. Suppose there is a political conflict in some part of the world and the contending parties call their country by two different names. Which name should the mapmaker employ? When a new government comes to power and changes the name of a state, it may take months or even years to change the name on maps, stamps, currency, and textbooks.

The frontispiece of a book published in the United States demonstrates the problems of naming and of demarcating borders in Southeast Asia. This 1941 work by Virginia Thompson is called *Thailand: The New Siam,* reflecting both the old and new names of a country in Southeast Asia. The accompanying map shows Southeast Asia in transition. The name *Siam* was officially changed to *Thailand* in 1939, but two years later this mapmaker thought it wise to include both names on the map. Nor does the map reflect the political realities of the day. In 1941 the borders of Thailand were being contested. In the context of World War II, the Japanese had entered Thailand, and the Thai government was challenging the French in Cambodia. Maps also reflect the progress and losses of imperialism. Thus this map's designation "French Indo-China" shows the empire that France carved out in Southeast Asia in the nineteenth century. The sweeping title "Netherlands India" across the islands of Sumatra and Borneo suggests the long-term interests and conquests of the Dutch in this region. Compare this map to a current map of Southeast Asia (see p. 1059), and to nineteenth century maps (see p. 712), and see how the names and borders have changed.

Questions to Consider

1. What types of identity are suggested in the names of countries?
2. Why might a people or a political group want to change the name of their country? What difficulties might they face in doing so?

ous source of tension arose among the Chinese, many of whom supported opposing sides—the Nationalists versus the Communists—in the civil war at home. And when Japan occupied the Malay Peninsula during World War II, the Chinese mounted a resistance, which led to harsh treatment of that population by the occupiers. After World War II, the British tried to disarm the anti-Japanese guerrillas. Ethnic Malays demanded independence, which Britain was reluctant to grant as long as a Communist Chinese insurgency continued. Eventually, the British handed over rule to the non-Communist Malayan Chinese Association and the United Malay National Association in 1957.

INDIA: THE DRIVE FOR INDEPENDENCE

- *What important innovations in the struggle for independence were developed in India and permitted a disunited country to gain its freedom from one of the world's great imperial powers?*

As in East Asia, World War I accelerated Indians' demands for independence—or at first, self-rule. It awakened new pride in India but at the same time set the stage for the sectarian differences that would be India's tragedy at the time of independence. When World War I began, nearly all anti-British activity in India ceased and thousands of Indian troops were mobilized to fight in World War I on the side of their colonial masters, the British. Soon, however, the irony of Indians fighting in a struggle between civilization and slavery or barbarism—as the battle between England and its allies, on the one hand, and Germany and its allies, on the other was characterized—was too great to swallow. In addition, India's 60 million Muslims were torn by Britain's war against the Ottoman Empire, one of the Central Powers. The large numbers of Indians who fought in Europe on the side of the British Empire were struck by the greater freedom accorded all classes of people in Europe.

South Asia

Gradual Steps Toward Self-Rule

By 1917 Indian nationalists expected immediate compensation for their loyalty in terms of more self-government. The British, however, pursued a policy stressing gradual development of self-government within the British Empire. To this end, in 1918, a British commission under the more liberal Secretary of State for India, Edwin S. Montagu, recommended a new constitution.

Taj Majal, India

India on the Road to Independence

1914–1918	Indians fight for Britain in WWI
1918	Rowlatt Acts imposed
1919	Amritsar Massacre
1920	Indian National Congress launches policy of noncooperation
1930	Salt Marches
1930	Muslim League
1933	Muslim students propose new state, to be called Pakistan
1942	Quit India Movement
1947	Independence and partition

Reforms emerged in 1919 from that commission and were codified in the Government of India Act of 1921. These provided for a system of dual government in the provinces by which certain powers were reserved to the British while the provincial legislatures were granted other, generally lesser, powers. Montagu called for an increase in Indian representation on the Imperial Legislative Council.

To Indian nationalists these reforms represented only a small step toward self-rule. Indian suspicion was hardly surprising in the context of other repressive legislation passed earlier, the Rowlatt Acts, called the "Black Acts" by Indians. These laws, passed in 1919 through the Imperial Legislative Council without a single vote by an elected Indian member, denied press freedom and allowed the police and other officials extraordinary powers in searching out anti-imperialist activities. Disheartened by the limited reforms as well as the violence that followed under the Rowlatt Acts, many nationalists demanded sweeping changes. Britain, however, lacked a comprehensive plan to grant independence, and a diehard segment of British public opinion, led by the Conservative leader Winston Churchill, strongly opposed any such suggestion of the breakup of the empire.

Gandhi and Civil Disobedience

The foremost nationalist leader in India was Mohandas Gandhi (moh-HAHN-das GAHN-dee; 1869–1948). Born of middle-class parents, Gandhi went to London to study law; later he went to South Africa to defend Indians there against the abuses of the planters. Gandhi's encounter with South African discrimination against "nonwhites" transformed him. In South Africa, Indians were subject to numerous legal restrictions that hampered their freedom of movement, prevented them from buying property, and imposed added taxes on them. Gandhi worked aggressively for the legal and political rights of the oppressed. He repudiated wealth, practiced ascetic self-denial, condemned violence, and advocated service to others. He launched a community *(ashram)* that served as a model for living out those principles. With Gandhi as their leader, the Indians in South Africa adopted the tactic of "civil disobedience"—they carried out various protests, refused to work, held mass demonstrations, and marched into areas where their presence was forbidden by law. Through "passive resistance" and noncooperation, Gandhi forced the government to remove some restrictions, thereby attracting worldwide attention.

When he returned to his native land shortly after the outbreak of World War I, Gandhi was welcomed as a hero. Initially, he supported the British in the war effort, but soon he went on the offensive. A crucial factor in his decision was a journey he took in 1917 to Champaran, in Bihar in northeastern India, at the invitation of an impoverished peasant. The peasant had dogged Gandhi's steps until he persuaded him to come and see the terrible conditions of the indigo sharecroppers in his district. Gandhi already had a reputation; his visit alarmed the authorities, who threatened to jail him. But the intrepid lawyer mobilized support and launched a nonviolent campaign for reform and justice for the peasants. Gandhi viewed this episode as seminal. "What I did," he explained, "was a very ordinary thing. I declared that the British could not order me around in my own country."[3]

In India Gandhi founded another ashram based on service, living simply, and self-reliance. He lived there off and on for the rest of his life, but his attention was increasingly turned to agitating for British withdrawal. In response to the Rowlatt Acts, Gandhi and other nationalists launched a campaign of civil disobedience. A mass strike was declared in which all work was to cease and the population was to pray and fast. Gandhi argued that moral force would triumph over physical force. How could the Rowlatt Acts, designed to punish revolutionary actions against the British, be applied, Gandhi reasoned, to those who did not engage with the government at all?

Contrary to Gandhi's plan, however, riots and violence occurred in some areas. Although the British had forbidden public gatherings, 10,000 to 20,000 men, women, and children assembled in a large walled courtyard in the sacred Sikh city of Amritsar (ahm-REET-sahr) in the Punjab. In an infamous action, known as the Amritsar Massacre, the local British general, Reginald Dyer, marched armed soldiers into the courtyard and opened fire without warning on the unarmed crowd who had gathered not for political reasons but to celebrate a religious festival in April 1919. The soldiers mowed down the stampeding men, women, and children, slaughtering 379 and wounding over 1000. Dyer noted afterward that he expected to teach the Indians a lesson and do "a jolly lot of good." Days after the massacre, the general exacerbated matters by ordering that all Indians must crawl on all fours as they passed the house of a British schoolteacher who had been assaulted by some rioters. Dyer was forced to resign, but many British colonials supported the bloody suppression of the Amritsar "demonstrators." To many Indians, Dyer's actions suggested the true bottom line of Britain's rule over India.

Mohandas Gandhi used the weapons of nonviolent protest and noncooperation in his struggle to win independence for India. An immensely popular and beloved leader, Gandhi was called Mahatma, or "Great Soul," by the people of India.

The Amritsar Massacre and other acts of cruelty thus inflamed public opinion and prompted Gandhi and other nationalists to intensify their efforts for independence. The Indian National Congress launched a policy of noncooperation with the government in 1920, and Gandhi was arrested in 1922 and sentenced to six years in prison. Gandhi's imprisonment served as a symbol of Indian resistance and earned him the devotion of the Indian people. The intrepid attorney also worked for other goals besides freeing India. He sought to end the drinking of alcohol, raise the status of women, remove the stigma attached to the Depressed Classes (untouchables), and bring about cooperation between Hindus and Muslims. These objectives chal-

Document Gandhi and "Truth-Force"

Gandhi developed tactics of noncooperation and passive resistance while a young lawyer in South Africa and applied those methods to India's struggle upon his return home shortly after the beginning of World War I. The prospect of violence within the anti-imperialist movement concerned him deeply, and by 1920, he began to urge Indians to adopt his methods of *Satyagraha*, literally "truth-force," as superior to passive resistance. Only through complete *ahimsa* (nonviolence), coupled with a strict adherence to truth, even if truth and nonviolence did not appear to work in the short term, would the oppressed succeed. Gandhi adopted this tactic not only because it fit his spiritual orientation but also because he was pragmatic enough to know that the Indians were no match, militarily, for the British.

I have drawn the distinction between passive resistance as understood and practiced in the West and *Satyagraha* before I had evolved the doctrine of the latter to its full logical and spiritual extent. I often used "passive resistance" and "Satyagraha" as synonymous terms: but as the doctrine of Satyagraha developed, the expression "passive resistance" ceases even to be synonymous. . . . Moreover passive resistance does not necessarily involve complete adherence to truth under every circumstance. . . . Satyagraha is a weapon of the strong; it admits of no violence under any circumstance whatever; and it ever insists upon truth. . . . (From a letter written by Gandhi, 25 January 1920.)

In the application of Satyagraha, I discovered, in the earliest stages, that pursuit of Truth did not admit of violence being inflicted on one's opponent, but that he must be weaned from error by patience and sympathy. . . . And patience means self-suffering. . . .

As an individual:

1. A satyagrahi, i.e., a civil resister, will harbour no anger.
2. He will suffer the anger of the opponent.
3. In so doing he will put up with assaults from the opponent, never retaliate; but he will not submit, out of fear of punishment or the like, to any order given in anger.
4. When any person in authority seeks to arrest a civil resister, he will voluntarily submit to the arrest, and he will not resist the attachment or removal of his own property, if any, when it is sought to be confiscated by the authorities.
5. If a civil resister has any property in his possession as a trustee, he will refuse to surrender it, even though in defending it he will lose his own life. He will, however, never retaliate.
6. Non-retaliation excludes swearing and cursing.
7. Therefore a civil resister will never insult his opponent, and therefore not take part in many of the newly coined cries which are contrary to the spirit of *ahimsa*.
8. A civil resister will not salute the Union Jack, nor will he insult it or officials, English or Indian.
9. In the course of the struggle if anyone insults an official of commits an assault upon him, a civil resister will protect such official or officials from the insult or attack even at the risk of his life. (From *Young India*, 27 February 1930.)

Questions to Consider

1. Gandhi claimed that satyagraha had nothing in common with the methods used in the struggles for freedom in the West before his time. Was he correct?
2. To what extent was this tactic secular and to what extent religious?
3. What important American leader later adapted Gandhian methods for the U.S. civil rights movement? Could they be effectively applied outside a colonial context?

Both quotations are from The Indian Ministry of External Affairs Website, at http://meadev.nic.in/Gandhi/satyagrahya.htm.

lenged the fundamental social order of India and earned him many enemies.

In 1927 the Congress demanded full dominion status, the same constitutional equality enjoyed by white settler dominions like Canada and Australia. But many Muslims refused to support Congress's "Commonwealth of India" plan, as it rejected set-aside seats on the central legislative body for Muslims who, as a minority, were afraid of being excluded.

At the same time, Gandhi launched a new campaign of civil disobedience in 1930. In a well-publicized "salt march," Gandhi led thousands of men and women to the sea, where he broke British law by panning salt. Salt was a necessity of life. Taxes on salt were a vital source of revenue for the British government in India, especially after nationalist boycotts of British cloth and alcohol cut revenues from those sources. At first, Gandhi prohibited women from participating in the **salt marches,** but feminist nationalism had been growing for decades, and women such as Sarojini Naidu (sah-roh-JEE-nee NAI-doo; 1879–1949), the first Indian woman elected president of the Indian National Congress, demanded a role for women. Gandhi relented, women joined the marches, and Naidu shouted, "Hail, law breaker!" as Gandhi walked into the sea to pick up a lump of salt.[4] The British authorities attacked and beat the nonviolent marchers, whose passive resistance—captured on film—presented a picture at once noble and heartrending of Indian resolve. Eighty thousand marchers, of whom 17,000 were women, were arrested. Women, on whom Gandhi also called to manufacture homespun cloth to wean India from British imports, now became a significant part of Gandhian nationalism.

The Continuing Struggle

In 1930 the British arranged a series of roundtable conferences in London. A total of 112 Indian delegates were invited, but with the exception of Gandhi and a few others, all were carefully selected by the British viceroy in India. In 1932, the British proposed the Communal Award, which sought to give special treatment to religious and social "minorities," including Muslims and "untouchables." Though a lifelong supporter of the rights of the downtrodden untouchables, Gandhi, while in jail in 1932, started a fast in opposition to this proposal which, he felt, would undermine the equal treatment of all. In 1935, the British passed a new Government of India Act, which advocated a federal union to bring the British provinces and the princely states of India into a central government.

Gandhi's visit to England in the early 1930s caused a sensation, and he was in great demand for speeches and visits. As an advocate of nonviolence and self-determination, he attracted like-minded groups and leaders from all over the world. For others he was a curiosity, braving the English winter in his typical garb of loincloth, shawl, and sandals. When Gandhi was invited to visit King George V and Queen Mary for tea, the press had a field day, speculating on what he might wear to the royal occasion. Gandhi dressed in his customary fashion. Later, when someone inquired whether he had worn too little clothing, Gandhi answered with characteristic wit, "The King had enough on for both of us."[5]

The primary moving force in the independence movement was the powerful Indian National Congress, which had become the dominant party for Indian nationalists after 1935. Its membership of several million was predominantly Hindu but also included many Muslims, not all of whom had joined the **Muslim League,** and members of other religious groups. The Congress ignored the demands of Muslims to stress communal differences, however, and focused on nationalism and getting the British out of India. Opinion varied on how to get the British out. Gandhi's opposite was Bal Gangadhar Tilak (BAHL gahn-GAH-dar TEE-lahk), a firebrand brahman, who, until his death in 1920, advocated Hindu supremacy and the use of violence to evict the British. But soon after World War I, the Congress came under Gandhi's leadership; his personal following among the people was the chief source of the party's tremendous influence. Gandhi transformed the Congress, which had been primarily a highly educated, male, middle-class organization, into a mass movement that included the peasants. It became the spearhead of nationalist efforts to negotiate with the British for self-rule. It would dominate the Indian elections of 1937 and lead India upon achieving independence in 1947.

Another prominent leader of the Congress was Jawaharlal Nehru (ja-WAH-ar-lahl NEH-roo; 1889–1964), who came from a brahman family of ancient lineage. In his youth Nehru had all of the advantages of wealth: English tutors and enrollment in the English public school of Harrow and later Trinity College, Cambridge, where he obtained his B.A. in 1910. Two years afterward, he was admitted to the bar. On his return to India, however, he showed little interest in practicing law and gradually became completely absorbed in his country's fight for freedom.

A devoted friend and disciple of Gandhi, Nehru could not agree with the older leader's spiritual rejection of much of the modern world. At heart Nehru

---

salt marches—1930 marches led by Gandhi to protest British salt monopoly in India.

Muslim League—Political organization of anti-imperialist Muslims in India, founded 1930.

Jawaharlal Nehru, along with Gandhi one of the paramount leaders of Indian nationalism, later served as prime minister of independent India.

was a rationalist, an agnostic, an ardent believer in science, and a foe of all supernaturalism. As he himself said, "I have become a queer mixture of the East and the West, out of place everywhere, at home nowhere. Perhaps my thoughts and approach to life are more akin to what is called Western than Eastern, but India calls me."[6] Nehru expressed the sentiments of many Asians and Africans under colonial rule. They had been given a European education that alienated them from their own cultures and failed to secure for them equality with the Europeans. Nehru would later become the first prime minister of independent India. Gandhi and Nehru represented two strands of Indian nationalism. Though their visions of the ideal Indian society differed, they were in agreement that Britain must leave and allow the Indians to govern themselves.

The Hindu-Muslim Divide

As Britain's imperial control over India began to loosen, tensions between the Muslim and Hindu communities increased. Many Muslims believed that after independence they would become a powerless minority, the target of Hindu retaliation for centuries of Muslim (Mughal) rule. Some feared that the Hindu-dominated Congress party would have no place for Muslims once the British left India. Thus the conflict that emerged was a struggle for political and cultural survival.

In the early 1930s the Muslim League, a political party, began to challenge the claim of the Indian National Congress to represent all of India. The leader of the Muslim League, Muhammad Ali Jinnah (moo-HAH-mad AH-lee JIN-nah; 1876–1948), had originally been a prominent member of the Congress party. Jinnah, once dubbed by Indian nationalists the "ambassador of Hindu-Muslim unity," became alienated by what he considered Hindu domination of the Congress and its claim to be the sole agent of Indian nationalism.

The Muslim League began to advance the "two-nation theory," and, in 1933, a group of Muslim students at Cambridge University circulated a pamphlet advocating the establishment of a new state in South Asia to be known as Pakistan. This leaflet was the opening act of what later became a bloody drama. In 1939 the Muslim League emphatically denounced any scheme of self-government of India that would mean majority Hindu rule.

Britain's declaration that India was at war with Germany in September 1939 rekindled angry memories of World War I when India's aid was thanked only by increased British repression. While Nehru and other Indian nationalists sympathized with Britain in its struggle against Nazi Germany, they demanded equality with Britain as a necessary condition of coming to its aid. Denied independence, Indian leaders ordered the provincial ministries of Congress to resign in protest. Muslim leaders such as Jinnah saw this as an opportunity for independent action by Muslim areas, which they had demanded of Congress for the past decade. Gandhi's entreaties to Jinnah to remain united against imperialism went unheeded. When a British delegation tried to get Gandhi to agree to allow Muslim areas to opt out of an Indian dominion to be formed after World War II, Gandhi would not budge, instead launching the **"Quit India"** movement in 1942. Other Indian nationalists created an army of the thousands of Indian soldiers the British had lost in Singapore when the Japanese captured the city. While many Indians supported England during the War, others, later viewed as heroes of Indian nationalism, did not.

DOCUMENT
Gandhi Speaks

In the years after World War II, Britain looked for a way out of India, but the rise of sectarian violence

Quit India—Militant movement started in 1942 to eliminate British rule.

CASE STUDY The Partition of India

made them hesitant to leave. Negotiations repeatedly broke down, and in the end, India was partitioned into predominantly Hindu India and predominantly Muslim Pakistan. Bloodletting was not over, as many millions died in the 1947 transition to independence.

CONCLUSION

Between the two world wars, imperialism went on the defensive before the rise of nationalism in Asia. In the opening decades of the twentieth century, Japan, as noted in Chapter 28, served as the model of the successful Asian nation-state; it made amazing progress in industrialization and implemented a constitutional government. By 1919 the island nation had become one of the world's leading powers.

Although China was not, strictly speaking, part of the colonial world, in many ways this vast land was under the indirect influence of the Great Powers. Chinese Nationalists, led by Sun Yat-sen, overthrew the Manchu dynasty and established a republic. After years of conflict among rival factions, Jiang Jieshi consolidated power in the Guomindang regime. The nascent Chinese Communist movement, under Mao Zedong, survived World War II to go on to build a nation in the post-1949 era.

Other East Asian countries also undertook nation-building, often using the rhetoric of national strength and people's rights learned from the imperialists, to get rid of foreign domination. Koreans, Indonesians, Vietnamese, Filipinos, Burmese, and Malays all built nationalist movements on a combination of indigenous and Western thinking about independence. Many were bitterly disappointed in Western hypocrisy over the issue of self-determination of nations. In the end, World War II destroyed both Western and Japanese imperialism in East and Southeast Asia.

India also exposed colonial hypocrisy. It became a model of democratic nationalism under the leadership of Mohandas Gandhi. He preached a message of nonviolence and civil disobedience to force Britain to grant a substantial measure of self-government to the Indians. Ultimately, World War II also dissolved British imperialism in India. Though Indians had worked the longest and hardest of all nationalists to build a nation since the 1880s, however, sectarian differences tore independent South Asia apart in 1947, creating two nations, India and Pakistan.

Suggestions for Web Browsing

You can obtain more information about topics included in this chapter at the websites listed below. See also the companion website that accompanies this text, **http://www.ablongman.com/brummett**, which contains an online study guide and additional resources.

History of China
http://www-chaos.umd.edu/history/toc.html

This is the table of contents for the University of Maryland's exceptionally broad coverage of sites for Chinese history, including documents, images, and explanatory texts.

Modern India
http://www.clas.ufl.edu/users/gthursby/ind/history.htm

Extensive list of history sites dedicated to India.

Gandhi
http://www.gandhimuseum.org/papers.html

An extensive collection of Gandhi's writings compiled by India's National Gandhi Museum.

Literature and Film

China's greatest fiction writers of the early twentieth century, Lu Xun and Ding Ling, portray the tensions in the struggle for justice in the modernizing state. Lu Xun's short stories are arguably the best and most accessible examples of May Fourth literature. See Lu Xun, *Diary of a Madman and Other Stories* (University of Hawaii Press, 1980). Ding Ling's short stories depict the quest for women's liberation. See Ding Ling, *I Myself Am a Woman*, ed. Tani Barlow (Beacon Press, 1989). For a satire of modernization in 1930s Vietnam, see Vu Trong Phung, *Dumb Luck* (trans. Nguyen Nguyet Cam and Peter Zinoman, University of Michigan, 2002). Gong Li's 1991 film, *Raise the Red Lantern*, depicts the struggle for autonomy of an educated young Chinese woman in a polygamous household of the 1920s.

Suggestions for Reading

For an overview of Chinese history, see Patricia Buckley Ebrey, *The Cambridge Illustrated History of China* (Cambridge, University Press, 1996) and Jonathan D. Spence, *The Search for Modern China* (W.W. Norton, 1999). Wang Zheng's *Women in the Chinese Enlightenment* (University of California Press, 1999) is an excellent study of progressive women in the interwar period.

Harry J. Benda and John A. Larkin, *The World of Southeast Asia* (Harper & Row, 1967), and D.S. Sar Desai, *Southeast Asia: Past and Present* (Westview, 1989), provide good general coverage of Southeast Asia. For Vietnam, see Hue-tam Ho Tai, *Radicalism and the Origins of the Vietnamese Revolution* (Harvard University Press, 1992). On Korea, see Carter J. Eckert, *Korea Old and New* (Harvard University Press, 1990).

Gandhi's autobiography makes fascinating reading: *Mohandas Gandhi, An Autobiography: The Story of My Experiments with Truth*, trans. M. Desai (Boston: Beacon Press, 1957). New and accessible histories of India include John Keay, *India: A History* (Grove Press, 2000) and Barbara D. Metcalf and Thomas R. Metcalf, *A Concise History of India* (Cambridge University Press, 2002).

CHAPTER

30

Emerging National Movements in the Middle East and Africa from the 1920s to 1950s

CHAPTER CONTENTS

1910

1912 African National Congress established in South Africa

1917 Balfour Declaration

1920

1920 Mandates established, Treaty of Sèvres

1923 Turkish Republic recognized

1925 Pahlavi dynasty established in Iran

1930

1933 Ibn Sa'ud grants oil concession to Standard Oil

1935 Italian invasion of Ethiopia

1940

1945 Fifth Pan-African Congress, Manchester, England

1950

1951 Outbreak of Mau Mau Rebellion, Kenya

Fifty years of aggressive expansion by the West had spread European ideas, factories, and colonists to much of the world. Those African and Middle Eastern societies that were not directly colonized by European powers were nonetheless dramatically influenced by the politics, cultures, and economies of imperialist Western states. It was in the period between the world wars and immediately afterward that many of these societies adopted—or had imposed on them—the nation-state model of political organization. During this period certain African and Middle Eastern peoples who had been subordinated to Europe began to gain their political independence.

But European imperialism is only one element, albeit an important one, of the evolution of African and Middle Eastern states in this time frame. This era also witnessed a dramatic movement of people from the countryside to the city, with the accompanying social and economic turmoil. The modernization processes that gained momentum in the nineteenth century in the realms of industrialization, education, transportation, and communication remained vigorous. The automobile and the airplane, though still exciting innovations, became facts of life. New leaders emerged, and there was a radical transformation in systems of government, law, economics, and traditional social values. While many areas of Africa and the Middle East retained their traditional agrarian economies, others lost or abandoned traditional modes of economic organization. Often the transformation caused dramatic changes in the lives of individuals and families within a single generation—when rural girls were forced into factory or domestic labor in the cities or when men migrated across the ocean to seek work, for example.

World War I and its aftershocks strengthened independence movements in Africa and Middle East, in part because the power of the dominant imperial states—Britain, France, and Germany—had been diminished by the war. Nationalist campaigns, present in embryonic form in most of the colonies before the war, grew rapidly in virtually all of the European possessions and mandates. India's independence movement and Mohandas Gandhi's tactics of nonviolence were an inspiration to African political leaders. Across the Middle East and Africa, nations struggled to redefine themselves, adapt to global economic reorganization, and throw off the yoke of European domination.

THE MIDDLE EAST DIVIDED

■ *What impact did the outcome of World War I have on Middle Eastern politics?*

World War I dramatically altered the political, cultural, and geographical configuration of the Middle East. Before the war, the Middle East was divided primarily into two large agrarian empires, the Ottoman and the Persian (or Iranian). Most of the North African Muslim states had, by this time, fallen under the control of European overlords. North Africa's premier cultural center, Egypt, was seized by the British in 1882; France had gained control of Tunis and Algiers; and Italy took parts of Libya from the Ottomans in 1911. After World War I, Persia (hereafter called Iran), which had remained neutral, maintained its territorial integrity. But the centuries-long rule of the Ottoman Empire in the Middle East was swept away, and its territories were parceled out among the victors. The peoples of the Middle East in the ensuing period can be divided between those who remained independent and those who were governed by Britain and France. That division would prove critical in the evolution of the modern nation-states of the region.

MAP Europe and the Middle East After World War I

The War Years

The events of World War I cannot be understood without a grasp of the competing interests involved. There had long been speculation over who might get what, when (and if) the Ottoman Empire fell. The Russians coveted a Mediterranean port. The British wished to dominate the area around the Suez Canal, the sea route to their Indian empire. The French had long-standing connections along the eastern Mediterranean coast, which they aspired to control. The Germans wanted a

MAP The Middle East in the 1920s

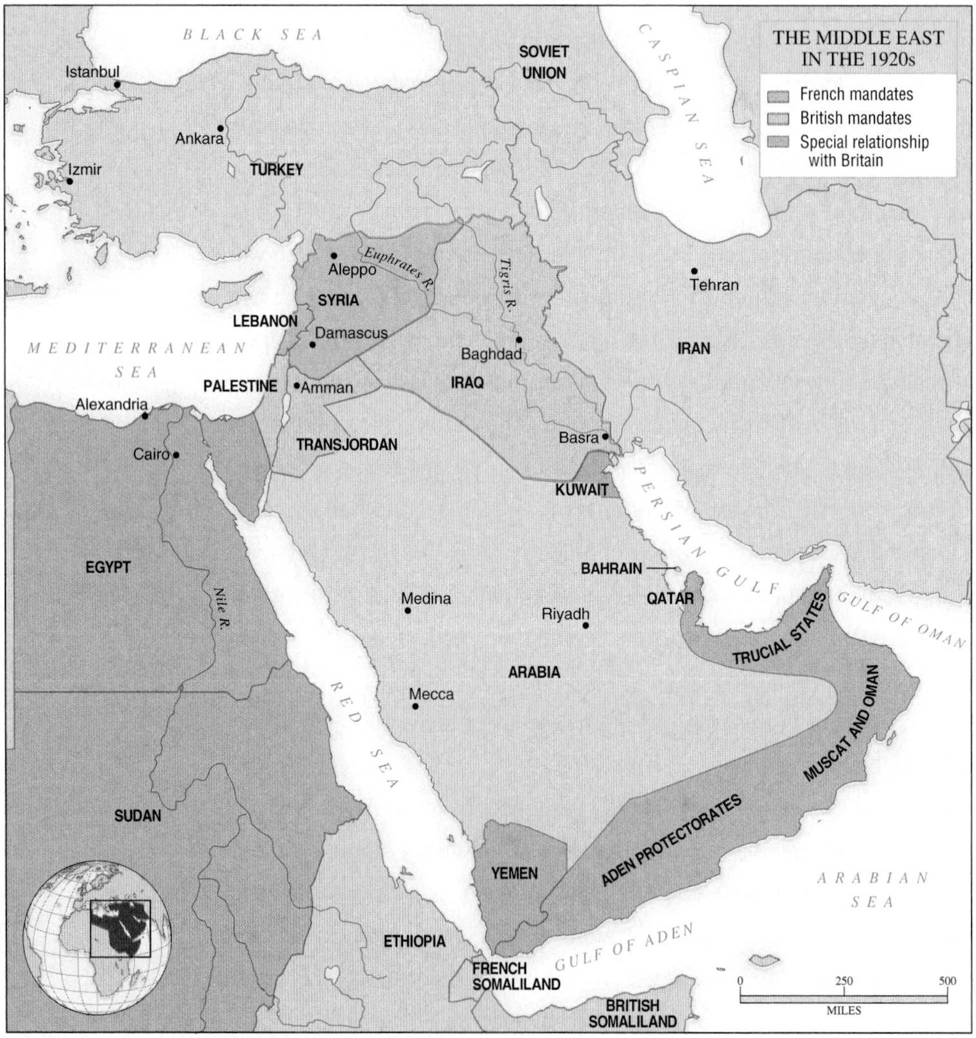

After World War I the British and French controlled Egypt, Palestine, Syria, and Iraq. Transjordan had a special status under Emir Abdullah.

The Middle East Between the Wars

1917	Balfour Declaration
1919	Wafd-led rebellion in Egypt
1920	Mandates set up in conquered Ottoman territory
1923	Sa'd Zaghlul becomes first prime minister of Egypt
1923–1938	Mustafa Kemal Atatürk rules the Turkish Republic
1925	Pahlavi dynasty established in Iran (Persia)
1932	Ibn Sa'ud's new state named kingdom of Saudi Arabia

base in the eastern Mediterranean and some North African territory as well. Perhaps the most hotly contested territory of all was the city of Jerusalem, not a rich or strategic city but sacred to Jews, Christians, and Muslims. Jerusalem had been under Ottoman rule for centuries, but in the early twentieth century a new set of claimants to Jerusalem, the **Zionists,** had emerged on the world stage.

Prompted by a long-standing military liaison with the Germans, and at the urging of Enver Pasha, the Minister of War, the Ottoman Empire joined the Central Powers in the war. The British then used their conquered territory in Egypt as a staging base for military operations against the Germans and the Ottomans. To mobilize support, they also made a series of conflicting agreements concerning the disposition of Ottoman territories. British High Commissioner Sir Henry McMahon in Cairo began correspondence with Sharif Husain of Mecca (1856–1931), guardian of Islam's holy places. The British told Husain that in the event of an Arab revolt against the Ottoman regime, Britain would recognize Arab independence. About the same time, in 1916, Britain, France, and Russia signed the secret **Sykes-Picot Agreement.** It provided for the division of Syria and Iraq between Britain and France, with Russia receiving parts of Asiatic Turkey. Palestine was to be placed under an international administration. These great powers were dividing up the spoils of war before they had won them.

Believing that the British were promising him an Arab state, Husain launched a revolt in 1916. The Arab forces were commanded by his third son, Faisal (1885–1933). The Arab Revolt was not particularly large (most Arabs remained loyal to the Ottoman regime), but it was tactically significant and a blow to Ottoman prestige. It also garnered a lot of attention in the Western press, which crafted a romantic adventure story around the exploits of a British officer, T. E. Lawrence (1888–1935), "Lawrence of Arabia," who fought alongside the Arabs.

The Ottoman forces fought well during the war, but the empire was short of money, supplies, and ammunition; it could not match British firepower. When the Ottoman forces were defeated in Syria in October 1918, the Ottoman sultan was forced to sign an armistice. The British allowed Faisal to march into Damascus, the capital of Greater Syria, where he began to set up his own administration. In March 1920 the General Syrian Congress, with high hopes for the birth of a new Arab state, proclaimed Faisal king of Syria.

When Faisal attended the postwar Paris Peace Conference to plead the cause of Arab independence, however, he found he had no real standing. In April 1920, at the San Remo Conference, it was decided to turn over all Arab territories formerly in the Ottoman Empire to the Allied powers to be administered as **mandates.** Syria and Lebanon were mandated to France, Iraq and Palestine to Britain. Husain's dream of a large and independent Arab state was thus short-lived. The French, in line with the Sykes-Picot Agreement, marched troops into Damascus in July 1920 and forced Faisal to relinquish his newly established kingdom.

To mollify their former allies, the British later established Faisal as king of their mandate in Iraq and set up his brother Abdullah as ruler of a desert province based in Amman and carved out of the mandate for Palestine. This new territory was called Transjordan. These two episodes demonstrate the gamelike quality of the partition of the Ottoman Empire. The people of Iraq had no desire for a Hashemite king from Arabia, and there was no logic to the lines drawn around Transjordan except that it was a sparsely populated territory that neither the British nor the Zionists particularly wanted. But these things were imposed on the region and its people to serve British interests.

The Husain-McMahon correspondence and the Sykes-Picot Agreement were not the only significant promises made during the war. The promise with the

Zionists—Supporters of a movement to establish a Jewish homeland in Palestine.

Sykes-Picot Agreement—A secret agreement concluded in 1916 between Britain and France that divided the Middle East into British and French spheres of influence.

mandates—Former territories and colonies of Germany and the Ottoman Empire that were placed under the administration of major powers such as Britain and France. The mandate system was overseen by the League of Nations.

The sons of Sharif Husain of Mecca were rewarded by the victors for their assistance in World War I. Faisal (seated left), a leader of the Arab Revolt, was first named king of Syria and then king of Iraq after the French forced him out of Damascus. He is shown here with his brothers, Abdullah (center), king of Transjordan, and Ali (right), who briefly ruled the Hijaz.

broadest ramifications was the **Balfour Declaration,** which in 1917 promised British support to Zionists in their aspirations for a Jewish "National Home" in Palestine. The Zionist movement—that is, the political movement aimed at establishing a Jewish state preferably in the "Holy Land" of Palestine—geared up in the late nineteenth century as the persecution of Jews continued in Russia and anti-Semitism spread in Europe. In 1897 the World Zionist Organization was founded under the leadership of Theodor Herzl (see Chapter 28). Following Herzl's death in 1904, leadership of the Zionist movement was assumed by Chaim Weizmann (1874–1952), a Russian Jew who had become a British subject. An intimate intellectual friendship developed between Weizmann and the English statesman Arthur James Balfour (1848–1930), who came to support the Zionist program. That association culminated in the Balfour Declaration, which was designed to mobilize Jewish support for Britain during World War I:

> *His Majesty's Government views with favour the establishment in Palestine of a national home for the Jewish people, and will use their best endeavors to facilitate the achievement of that object, it being clearly understood that nothing shall be done which may prejudice the civil and religious rights of existing non-Jewish communities in Palestine or the rights and political status enjoyed by Jews in any other country.*

The carefully worded statement did not specify what the nature of such a Jewish "national home" would be. The population of Palestine, according to British estimates, was only about 9 percent Jewish at the time, but the Balfour Declaration referred to the majority Arab population of Palestine only as "the existing non-Jewish community." Many European and American Jews were fearful that the establishment of a Jewish state would subject them to further discrimination in or even expulsion from their own countries. Nor was the indigenous Jewish population in Palestine necessarily in sympathy with the Zionists, who were considered by many as European outsiders. Nevertheless, the Balfour Declaration provided a great boost to Zionist aspirations in Palestine.

Balfour Declaration—A statement that the British foreign minister, Arthur Balfour, issued in 1917 promising British support to Zionists for a Jewish "national home" in Palestine.

Document Memorandum of the General Syrian Congress

World War I and its destruction of the old empires paved the way for the rise of Arab nationalism. This memorandum of the General Syrian Congress sounded themes that would be heard throughout the twentieth century. It reflects fear of Zionist encroachments, admiration of the United States as a defender of self-determination, and dismay at the social Darwinistic assumption that the Syrians were among those peoples not yet ready to rule themselves. Despite the desires of the congress, the French soon deposed Emir Faisal as ruler of Syria and took control of the area. Note that Palestine was considered part of Greater Syria as it had been under Ottoman rule.

We the undersigned members of the General Syrian Congress, meeting in Damascus on Wednesday, July 2nd, 1919, made up of representatives from the three Zones, viz., the Southern, Eastern, and Western, provided with credentials and authorizations by the inhabitants of our various districts, Moslems, Christians, and Jews, have agreed upon the following statement of the desires of the people of the country who have elected us.

1. We ask absolutely complete political independence for Syria.
2. We ask that the Government of this Syrian country should be a democratic civil constitutional Monarchy on broad decentralization principles, safeguarding the rights of minorities, and that the King be the Emir Faisal, who carried on a glorious struggle in the cause of our liberation and merited our full confidence and entire reliance.
3. Considering the fact that the Arabs inhabiting the Syrian area are not naturally less gifted than other more advanced races and that they are by no means less developed than the Bulgarians, Serbians, Greeks, and Roumanians at the beginning of their independence, we protest against Article 22 of the Covenant of the League of Nations, placing us among the nations in their middle stage of development which stand in need of a mandatory power.
4. In the event of the rejection of the Peace Conference of this just protest for certain considerations that we may not understand, we, relying on the declarations of President Wilson that his object in waging war was to put an end to the ambition of conquest and colonization, can only regard the mandate mentioned in the Covenant of the League of Nations as equivalent to the rendering of economical and technical assistance that does not prejudice our complete independence. And desiring that our country should not fall a prey to colonization and believing that the American Nation is farthest from any thought of colonization and has no political ambition in our country, we will seek the technical and economic assistance from the United States of America, provided that such assistance does not exceed 20 years.
5. In the event of America not finding herself in a position to accept our desire for assistance, we will seek this assistance from Great Britain, also provided that such does not prejudice our complete independence and unity of our country and that the duration of such assistance does not exceed that mentioned in the previous article.
6. We do not acknowledge any right claimed by the French Government in any part whatever of our Syrian country and refuse that she should assist us or have a hand in our country under any circumstances and in any place.
7. We oppose the pretensions of the Zionists to create a Jewish commonwealth in the southern part of Syria, known as Palestine, and oppose Zionist migration to any part of our country; for we do not acknowledge their title but consider them a grave peril to our people from the national, economical, and political points of view. Our Jewish compatriots [that is, Jews living in Syria] shall enjoy our common rights and assume the common responsibilities.

Questions to Consider

1. Why do the members of the Congress prefer to be under a mandate of the United States if they cannot be free? Why are they opposed to France having any power over Syria?
2. Why do the delegates here make a point (in no. 3) of comparing themselves to the Bulgarians, Roumanians, and Greeks?
3. Was U.S. President Wilson's ambition of putting an end to conquest and colonization realistic? Why or why not?

From *Foreign Relations of the United States: Paris Peace Conference,* Vol. 12 (Washington, D.C.: U.S. Government Printing Office, 1919), pp. 780–781.

The war and the treaties that followed exacted a high human cost. Besides those killed in the war, thousands of Ottoman citizens starved. The Armenian population was greatly reduced by Ottoman massacres. When the victors divided Ottoman territory, they did so with little consideration for natural ethnic or linguistic affinities. Families were separated and now had to develop new "national" identities; one branch of a family might reside in the new British mandate of Palestine and another in the new country of Transjordan. Over a million Turks and Greeks were uprooted from their homes in forced population transfers after the war. The Young Turk Revolution had imagined a nation based on a multilingual, multiethnic, multireligious citizenship. The new nations and mandates, instead, divided citizens along those same lines.

Mustafa Kemal and the New Secular Model of Turkey

The intention of the victors was to partition the Ottoman lands among the French, the Italians, the British, and the Greeks. The hated capitulations, canceled by the Young Turks, were restored. When World War I ended, the sultan dismissed the Ottoman parliament, British warships patrolled the Bosporus and the Dardanelles, and the Greeks occupied Izmir in western Anatolia. The once great Ottoman Empire was dismembered and humiliated.

MAP
The Decline of the Ottoman Empire

A group of Ottoman patriots, however, rallied around Mustafa Kemal (1880–1938), hero of the Gallipoli campaign in World War I. After the Ottoman defeat, he had been sent by the sultan to demobilize the Turkish troops in Anatolia. Disregarding instructions, Kemal, along with a group of other officers, reorganized the troops and defied the Allies. From their base in eastern Anatolia and later Ankara, these men formed their own government, electing Kemal as president. They upheld self-determination for all peoples, including the Turks, and proclaimed the abolition of all special rights enjoyed by foreigners in Turkey.

As president of the Turkish Republic from its beginning until his death in 1938, Mustafa Kemal instituted many civil and cultural reforms. He was called Atatürk, "Father Turk."

Kemal and his forces "liberated" Izmir from the Greeks, thus reestablishing Turkish control over western Anatolia, and gained the support of the new Soviet Union and France. Britain, exhausted by the war, was unwilling to mobilize a major initiative to stop them. Meanwhile, Mustafa Kemal established himself in power, abolishing the sultanate and declaring Turkey a republic in 1922. The Allies agreed to a revision of the Treaty of Sèvres, and the Treaty of Lausanne, signed in 1923, recognized Turkish sovereignty. The Turkish heartland, Anatolia, remained intact, and no reparations were demanded. Thus Turkey was resurrected as an independent nation-state and escaped the fate of the Arab provinces of the empire, which became mandates under Britain and France.

DOCUMENT
The Six Arrows of Kemalism

The circumstances of Turkey's founding gave Mustafa Kemal tremendous power and prestige; he was viewed as the "savior" of the new country. That power and prestige enabled him to dominate Turkish politics and implement a series of radical secularizing reforms. This forceful leader, later called Atatürk, or "Father Turk," established a new democratic constitution, but he regarded autocratic rule under a single political party as a necessary stage in raising his people to the level of education and social well-being that democratic government and parliamentary rule required. Committed to Westernization and secularization, he based his model of progress on the European nation-state.

Atatürk's reforms radically transformed Turkish society. He closed down the popular sufi orders and the traditional religious schools. Determined to enforce the separation of church and state, he abolished the Islamic Sharia law and replaced it with a civil code based on a Swiss model. Kemal also banned the traditional male headgear, the fez. The fez was a symbol of Ottoman identity, and many Turks resented the antifez law as an instance of unjust government intervention in people's personal lives and an affront to Islam as well. Atatürk did not try to legislate women's dress, but he did campaign actively for Western-style education and attire for women. In 1935 women were given the vote in Turkey and permitted to run for seats in the national assembly.

CASE STUDY
Soviet and Turkish Plans for Industrialization

Perhaps Atatürk's most drastic reform was changing the Turkish script from the Arabic to the Latin alphabet (the same alphabet used in Britain, France, and the United States). Turkey's leader believed that this radical change would turn his country toward the West, make it truly modern, and divorce it from its traditions linked to the Ottoman monarchy. Thousands of teachers had to be trained in the use of the new script; government documents, printing presses, textbooks, newspapers, and street signs had to be changed. The alphabet reform permeated almost all aspects of everyday life; more than any other, this reform decisively divorced Turkey from its past. By the time Atatürk died in 1938, Turkey was a new and different nation.

Blue Mosque in Instanbul, Turkey

Iran

Iran remained neutral in World War I, but Qajar rule did not long survive the war. The Russian occupation was ended by the 1917 revolutions, but the British had discovered oil in western Iran shortly before the war and were determined to protect their oil concession. As a result, there was widespread antiforeign sentiment in the region, provoked in part by British attempts to dominate Iranian economic and foreign policy. Iran, meanwhile, was economically devastated, and the Qajars could not control the tribal chiefs in their provinces.

Under these chaotic circumstances, Reza Khan, a commander of the nation's Cossack brigade, began a campaign in 1921 to take over the government. By 1925 he had succeeded, persuading the assembly to depose the Qajar shah. The shah was already in Europe, having found it expedient to follow Reza Khan's "suggestion" that he take a "vacation." Reza Khan thus founded a new dynasty, the Pahlavi dynasty. Like Mustafa Kemal in Turkey, the new shah combined a constitutional system with an authoritarian regime. He launched a program of modernizing and secularizing reforms modeled on Kemal's. He adopted a new legal system, thus weakening the power of the *ulama,* and opened the secular Tehran University in 1935.

Reza Shah imposed Western dress for males, but he went even further in 1936, banning the veil for women. This law, and the shah's insistence that his officials bring their wives to mixed-sex entertainments like dinners and balls, caused an uproar. It violated long-standing customs of modesty. Many older women, accustomed to the veil, were terribly embarrassed and refused to leave the house. Some officials said they would rather divorce or lose their jobs than expose their wives and daughters to the eyes of strange men. Radical reform based on Western models was thus not necessarily welcome; it often violated social custom. Reza Shah was successful in many of his modernizing and economic reforms, but secularization did not succeed in Iran to the same degree that it did in Turkey.

Iran was no longer at the mercy of foreign loans, but neither was it free of foreign intervention. The British-owned Anglo-Iranian Oil Company held a concession dating from 1901 to exploit Iranian oil. In 1933 the shah renegotiated his country's agreement with the company, but Iran still received only 20 percent of the oil revenues. To counteract British influence, the shah cultivated ties with Germany, but when World War II began, Iran remained neutral. Fearful of German intervention, however, Britain and Russia again used military force to intervene in Iranian affairs.

Arabia

Like Turkey and Iran, Arabia remained independent in the aftermath of World War I. The British controlled the Persian Gulf and preserved a series of treaty arrangements with local *shaykhs* along the southern and eastern coasts of Arabia. But the victors saw no particular profit in trying to control the bulk of the Arabian peninsula; its mostly forbidding terrain was sparsely populated, and it had no apparent strategic or natural resource value. Sharif Husain was discredited in the eyes of many Muslims because he had collaborated with the British and proclaimed himself "caliph" after the war. He retained control of the Hijaz for a time, but while his sons ruled in Transjordan and Iraq, he was soon to lose power in Arabia.

The man who would rule Arabia and unite the tribes was Abd el-Aziz ibn Sa'ud (sah-OOD; 1881–1953). Ibn Sa'ud was a tribal chief who had seized the city of Riyadh in 1902 and from that base launched a campaign to unify the peninsula under his rule. Like his predecessor a century before, Ibn Sa'ud established himself as both a successful warrior and defender of the puritanical Wahhabi doctrine that aimed to purge Islam of all innovations. In 1924 he captured the holy cities of Mecca and Medina, which have remained under Sa'udi rule ever since. Britain recognized the new king in exchange for his recognition of their special position in the Gulf. The new state was officially named the Kingdom of Saudi Arabia in 1932. Ibn Sa'ud preserved some of the Arabian customs of consultative rule and based his authority on royal decree legitimized by the consent of the *ulama.* Unlike the other Middle Eastern states, his kingdom had no constitution; the law of the land was the Sharia, Islamic law.

Saudi Arabia was impoverished but it was free, unlike most of the Arab provinces. It was a sparsely populated nation composed mostly of commercial cities and seminomadic tribes. The lives of its people and the country's economic situation began to change in 1933 when the king granted a concession to the Standard Oil

Company (later known as Arabian American Oil). Oil was discovered in 1938 but did not become a significant factor in Arabia until after World War II.

Egypt

Egypt and most of North Africa had been subordinated to European rule before World War I. Nationalist movements were agitating for independence across North Africa but, as in India, Britain and France had no intentions of granting real independence to these conquered territories. That would not be achieved until after World War II.

During World War I, Egypt was ruled by the British high commissioner and was forced to participate militarily and economically in the war, which caused great hardship. In 1918 some prominent Egyptians, led by Sa'd Zaghlul (c. 1860–1927), formed the **Wafd** ("Delegation") and asked the high commissioner to let them represent Egypt at the Paris Peace Conference. The request was denied. The Wafd then mobilized popular support throughout the country, culminating in widespread rebellion in 1919. Students joined workers demonstrating in the streets for independence. The British put down the demonstrations by force but conceded to popular pressure by allowing Zaghlul and others to attend the peace conference. This series of events began a long period, lasting into World War II during which the Wafd was the dominant party in Egyptian politics.

In 1922 the British declared Egypt independent, but (as had been the case in 1920s India) it was a hollow victory for Egyptian nationalists because Britain retained control over defense, foreign affairs, the economy, the Sudan, and the Suez Canal. The capitulations remained in place, and British troops remained in Egypt. In the 1923 elections the Wafd won an overwhelming victory and Zaghlul became the first Egyptian prime minister. The khedive, a descendent of Muhammad Ali, became "king," but England continued to dominate the political life of Egypt. The nature of this relationship is illustrated by the mutual defense pact England forced on Egypt in 1936 and by its reoccupation of the country after World War II.

One interesting ramification of European influence and educational institutions in Egypt was the emergence of a women's movement. Led by upper-class Egyptian women, often with Western-style educations, the Egyptian Feminist Union was founded in 1923. It took an active role in the nationalist struggle and advocated rights for women: suffrage, education for girls, and marriage reform. The founder of the union, Huda Sha'rawi, is famous for publicly removing her veil in the Cairo train station after returning from a feminist congress in Europe. At this time, the women's movement in Egypt remained mostly an urban phenomenon. Most of Egypt's population was a rural one of villagers and peasants—they were little affected by many of the social and political movements in Cairo and Alexandria.

Another highly significant movement that began in Egypt in this era and continues to have influence to the present day is the **Muslim Brotherhood.** The Brotherhood was founded in 1928 by Hasan al-Banna, a teacher and member of the *ulama*. Hasan al-Banna called for the restoration of the Sharia, but the Muslim Brotherhood was not a movement of purification in the same way that the Wahhabi movement in Arabia was. Rather, the Brotherhood was a movement of religious, social, and political reform. It developed social programs such as adult education, job training, and free clinics; it had a special attraction among the poor and became popular in both the cities and the countryside. With its message of traditional Islamic law and values, combined with social services and respect for modern technology, the Brotherhood had a powerful appeal; chapters rapidly spread beyond the borders of Egypt. The Brotherhood stands as an early and visible example of a modern Islamist movement, one that took into consideration the people and their culture as well as the demands of "modernity."

Minarets and Mosque, Egypt

The Mandates

Unlike Egypt and the states of North Africa, the rest of the Arab world had been, at least nominally, under Ottoman control until World War I. The treaties after the war gave Britain the mandates for Iraq and Palestine (out of which Transjordan was carved) and France the mandate for Syria, which it divided into Syria and Lebanon. One historian has called the mandate system "little more than nineteenth-century imperialism repackaged to give the appearance of self-determination."[1] Mandates were territories, and their people, who were considered incapable of self-rule, were to be governed by "more advanced" nations until such time as they were able to govern themselves. The mandate system was a reflection of social Darwinism, which ranked various societies on the basis of a hierarchical civilizational ladder. The European victors, of course, considered themselves to be at the top of that ladder.

Wafd—An Egyptian political party founded in 1918 that challenged British rule.

Muslim Brotherhood—An organization founded in 1928 in Egypt by Hasan al-Banna. The Muslim Brotherhood promoted religious, political, and social reforms and sponsored social programs.

Document We Have Not Come as Conquerors, But as Liberators

As the Ottoman Empire was partitioned, the British were given responsibility for three provinces that were arbitrarily united as Iraq. As British troops entered Baghdad on March 19, 1917, Lieutenant General Stanley Maude issued a proclamation to the city's inhabitants assuring them of the benevolent intentions of the British.

In the name of my King, and in the name of the peoples over whom he rules, I address you as follows:—

Our military operations have as their object the defeat of the enemy, and the driving of him from these territories. In order to complete this task, I am charged with absolute and supreme control of all regions in which British troops operate; but our armies do not come into your cities and lands as conquerors or enemies, but as liberators. Since the days of Halaka your city and your lands have been subject to the tyranny of strangers, your palaces have been subject to the tyranny of strangers, your palaces have fallen into ruins, your gardens have sunk in desolation, and your forefathers and yourselves have groaned in bondage. Your sons have been carried off to wars not of your seeking, your wealth has been stripped from you by unjust men and squandered in distant places. . . .

It is the wish not only of my King and his peoples, but it is also the wish of the great nations with whom he is in alliance, that you should prosper even as in the past, when your lands were fertile, when your ancestors gave to the world literature, science, and arts, and when Baghdad city was one of the wonders of the world.

Between your people and the dominions of my King there has been a close bond of interest. For 200 years have the merchants of Baghdad and Great Britain traded together in mutual profit and friendship. On the other hand, the Germans and the Turks, who have despoiled you and yours, have for 20 years made Baghdad a center of power from which to assail the power of the British and the Allies of the British in Persia and Arabia. Therefore the British Government cannot remain indifferent as to what takes place in your country now or in the future. . . .

But you people of Baghdad, whose commercial prosperity and whose safety from oppression and invasion must ever be a matter of the close concern to the British government, are not to understand that it is the wish of the British Government to impose upon you alien institutions. It is the hope of the British Government that the aspirations of your philosophers and writers shall be realized and that once again the people of Baghdad shall flourish, enjoying their wealth and substance under institutions which are inconsonance with their sacred laws and their racial ideas. . . .

Many noble Arabs have perished in the cause of Arab freedom, at the hands of those alien rulers, the Turks, who oppressed them. It is the determination of the Government of Great Britain and the great Powers allied to Great Britain that these noble Arabs shall not have suffered in vain. It is the hope and desire of the British people and the nations in alliance with them that the Arab race may rise once more to greatness and renown among the peoples of the earth, and that it shall bind itself together to this end in unity and concord.

O people of Baghdad remember that for 26 generations you have suffered under strange tyrants who have ever endeavoured to set one Arab house against another in order that they might profit by your dissensions. This policy is abhorrent to Great Britain and her Allies, for there can be neither peace nor prosperity where there is enmity and misgovernment. Therefore I am commanded to invite you, through your nobles and elders and representatives, to participate in the management of your civil affairs in collaboration with the political representatives of Great Britain who accompany the British Army, so that you may be united with your kinsmen in North, East, South, and West in realizing the aspirations of your race.

Questions to Consider

1. What was the experience of Iraq with British rule? Did the British act as conquerors or liberators?
2. How did British rule compare with Ottoman rule over Iraq?

From "The Proclamation of Baghdad," Readings, War, *Harper's Magazine* (online edition), December 4, 2003, http://www.harpers.org/ProclamationBaghdad.html.

Iraq was not a country at all but a mandate with a highly diverse population carved out of three Ottoman provinces. For the British, Iraq was a link between their strategic bases in the Persian Gulf and their oil interests in Iran. When British troops reached the capital, Baghdad, in 1917, they announced that they had come as liberators and not conquerors. However, a few months after the San Remo conference, the jailing of a *shaykh* sparked an insurrection that spread to a third of Iraq and took the British three months to put down. The British then brought in the outsider Faisal to rule. He was crowned king as the band played "God Save the King," an ironic statement on imported British culture. Britain retained control of finances and the military, and Iraq was declared a constitutional monarchy. Faisal's government had considerably greater autonomy than the French allowed Syria, and in 1932 Iraq became independent. It was, however, independence with strings attached. Britain retained air bases in the country and had negotiated a 75-year lease to exploit Iraqi oil. During World War II, British forces reoccupied the country, a clear reminder that Iraqi freedom was in part a function of British strategic interests.

The French brought in a large military force to enforce their rule in Syria. There they divided the territory in such a way as to emphasize and exacerbate religious and ethnic differences and to favor the Christian community. Lebanon's population was predominantly Arab but religiously divided among Christians (Maronites were the largest group), Muslims (Sunni and Shi'ite), and Druze (originally a heterodox offshoot of Shi'ite Islam). The French carved Lebanon out of the Syrian mandate in order to set up a majority Christian state that would retain close ties with France even after independence.

France kept tight control over its mandates, prompting widespread rebellion in Syria from 1925 to 1927. Syria remained without real political representation and without independence until after World War II. Conversely, in Lebanon, the French set up a constitutional regime in 1926, but election to office was based on religious affiliation, and France kept control of foreign and military affairs. When World War II began, France suspended the constitution. In the end, the French withdrew only grudgingly from Syria and Lebanon in 1943. They left Lebanon with a system of religiously based politics that has plagued the nation ever since.

The Question of Palestine

The mandate for Palestine was unique from its beginning because Palestine was not just another territory. It was the Holy Land—an object of Jewish, Christian, and Muslim fervor—and consequently, a focus of world attention. The British had to contend with the demands of the Zionists, who felt they had been promised Palestine by the Balfour Declaration, and with the majority Palestinian Arab population, who wanted independence.

The Ottoman government had tried to prevent the Zionists' acquisition of land in Palestine, with little success. Once Palestine became a British mandate, the Jewish population was granted certain privileges—not necessarily because of British sympathy for the Zionists but because the Zionists were Europeans, not "Orientals." Thus they were allowed their own flag; Hebrew was made one of the official languages of the mandate; Jews in service to the British were paid more than Arabs; and the Zionist community, the ***Yishuv,*** was allowed to arm itself while the Arab community was not. Many of the early Zionists were proponents of socialism, an ideology that manifested itself in the founding of communal farms called ***kibbutzim*** (ki-BOOTS-im). In this context it is important to remember that the struggle between the Zionists and the Palestinian Arabs was not primarily a struggle over religion (many of the Zionists were secular Jews, and the Arabs were Muslim, Christian, or secular); it was a struggle over land.

The British failed in trying to balance their own interests with those of the Arabs and Zionists. Unlike other mandates, Palestine never had an assembly or a constitution. Instead, the British advanced a series of abortive proposals, trying to satisfy both sides but tending to favor the Zionists. The Arab population was not unified; its leaders lacked connections in Britain and failed to mobilize the same organizational power as the Zionists. The most visible Arab leader was Hajj Amin al-Husayni, the chief Islamic jurist of Jerusalem, but he did not speak for the whole Palestinian community.

Waves of Jewish immigration between 1919 and 1926 seemed to confirm the fears of the Arab population that the British meant to deliver Palestine into the hands of the Zionists. In 1929 Jews and Arabs clashed over activities at the Wailing Wall (a remnant of Solomon's Temple in Jerusalem and part of the sanctuary of the Dome of the Rock, a sacred Muslim shrine). Then, the rise of Hitler prompted a dramatic exodus of Jews fleeing Nazi Germany. Many were not Zionists, but restrictive immigration quotas in countries like the United States made Palestine a reasonable option for emigrating Jews. The enormous influx

Yishuv—A Hebrew word meaning "settlement" that the Zionist movement used to refer to Jewish settlers in Palestine before it became Israel.

kibbutzim—A type of agriculture established by Jewish settlers in Palestine in which agricultural land and resources are owned by the community and in which all decisions are made collectively by the community.

Jewish immigrants arriving by sea to the British controlled mandate of Palestine in the 1930s. For Jews, immigration to Palestine represented one of the few options they had to escape rising anti-Semitism in central and eastern Europe. For the Palestinians, Jewish immigration coupled with British colonial rule represented a European effort to divest them of their land.

of immigrants between 1933 and 1936 further alarmed the Arab population, prompting a revolt that included demonstrations, rioting, and mass strikes. The revolt was aimed both at the Zionists and at the British administration; the British crushed it after six months but could not crush the frustration and hostility that prompted it. As in other countries where large-scale immigration occurs, the Palestinians, most of whom were small farmers, were afraid of being dislocated from their lands and jobs.

In 1937 the British Peel Commission found that the mandate could not satisfy its contradictory objectives; it recommended that Palestine be partitioned into an Arab state and a Jewish state. Britain would control a corridor stretching from the Mediterranean to Jerusalem. This recommendation was rejected by both sides; it also prompted another Arab rebellion that lasted until 1939. The rebellion symbolized the intractability of the Palestine question; it was a portent of more violence to come.

Throughout the 1930s, the "Palestine question" provoked heated discussion in many parts of the world. Zionists argued that Jews had a historical right to the Holy Land, that they had been promised a state by the Balfour Declaration, and that Jewish colonization constituted a "democratic and progressive" influence in the Middle East. The Palestinians responded that Palestine had been their country for more than a 1000 years and declared that the Balfour Declaration did not bind them because they had not been consulted in its formulation. They asked how any people could be expected to stand idly by and watch an alien immigrant group be transformed from a minority into a majority. For the Palestinians, the Zionists were yet another variety of European imperialism in a particularly virulent form.

With the threat of war looming in 1939, Britain eagerly sought to regain Arab goodwill and thereby strengthen its position in the Middle East. It issued a "white paper" declaring that it was Britain's aim to have as an ally an independent Palestine, to be established at the end of 10 years, with guarantees for both Palestinian and Jewish populations. During this 10-year period land sales were to be restricted. Jewish immigration would be limited to 75,000 people over 5 years; and then, no more immigration would take place without the consent of the Palestinians. That, of course, was an unfulfillable promise; no one could yet imagine the full extent of Hitler's atrocities. After the war, the Zionists would achieve their Jewish state in Palestine, but the Palestine question would not be resolved.

THE CHALLENGE TO COLONIAL RULE IN AFRICA

- *Were there significant differences between African protest movements challenging colonial rule before and after World War II?*

By World War I European nations had taken control of Africa and the armed resistance of Africans had ended. However, colonial rule was harsh and Africans explored other ways of voicing their many grievances—forced conscription during World War I and forced labor to build roads and railways, the demand for cash crops such as cocoa and groundnuts in rural areas, competition from European businesses that undercut African entrepreneurs, excessive taxes, higher prices on goods after World War I, attacks on African cultural institutions, and discrimination against African civil servants in appointments and promotions.

Although colonial rule was built on European domination and control, the economic and social changes that colonialism stimulated—urbanization, transportation, and Western education—ironically laid the foundations for African challenges to colonial rule. Urbanization brought many Africans from different areas to cities, where they interacted and communicated with each other and developed new identities. Transportation such as buses and trains carried rural migrants back to their villages with news, fresh ideas and different political views. Western education in government and mission schools created a literate elite that could read and write and follow discussions on nationalism and independence elsewhere in Africa and the world. This elite established dozens of newspapers (mainly in the British colonies) such as the *Lagos Weekly Record*, the *West African Pilot*, and *Imvo Zabantsundu* ("African Opinion") that vigorously criticized white rule. Literate Africans read the black press and then disseminated news and opinions to a much wider network of people.

The initial challenges to colonial rule were often based on local grievances. Protest organizations were usually based on kinship, ethnicity, or regional identities and took up issues that advanced their particular interests and improved economic conditions. However, once Africans began to recognize that their grievances were shared more widely, they explored creating organizations that embraced larger numbers of people and ethnic groups. They began to think in terms of nationalist movements that covered a whole colony.

An urbanized educated and professional elite (lawyers, doctors, clerks in the civil service, teachers, traders, commercial farmers, and clergy) dominated the early African nationalist movements. They were well-read and aware of what was happening in other parts of the world, and they borrowed their concepts of nationalism from European examples that emphasized the concept of a nation state. European nations had gone through a long process of developing national identities, but African colonies were arbitrarily created by European colonizers and did not have common identities.

Political movements in British colonies before World War II were moderate. They did not call for independence from European colonizers but for the

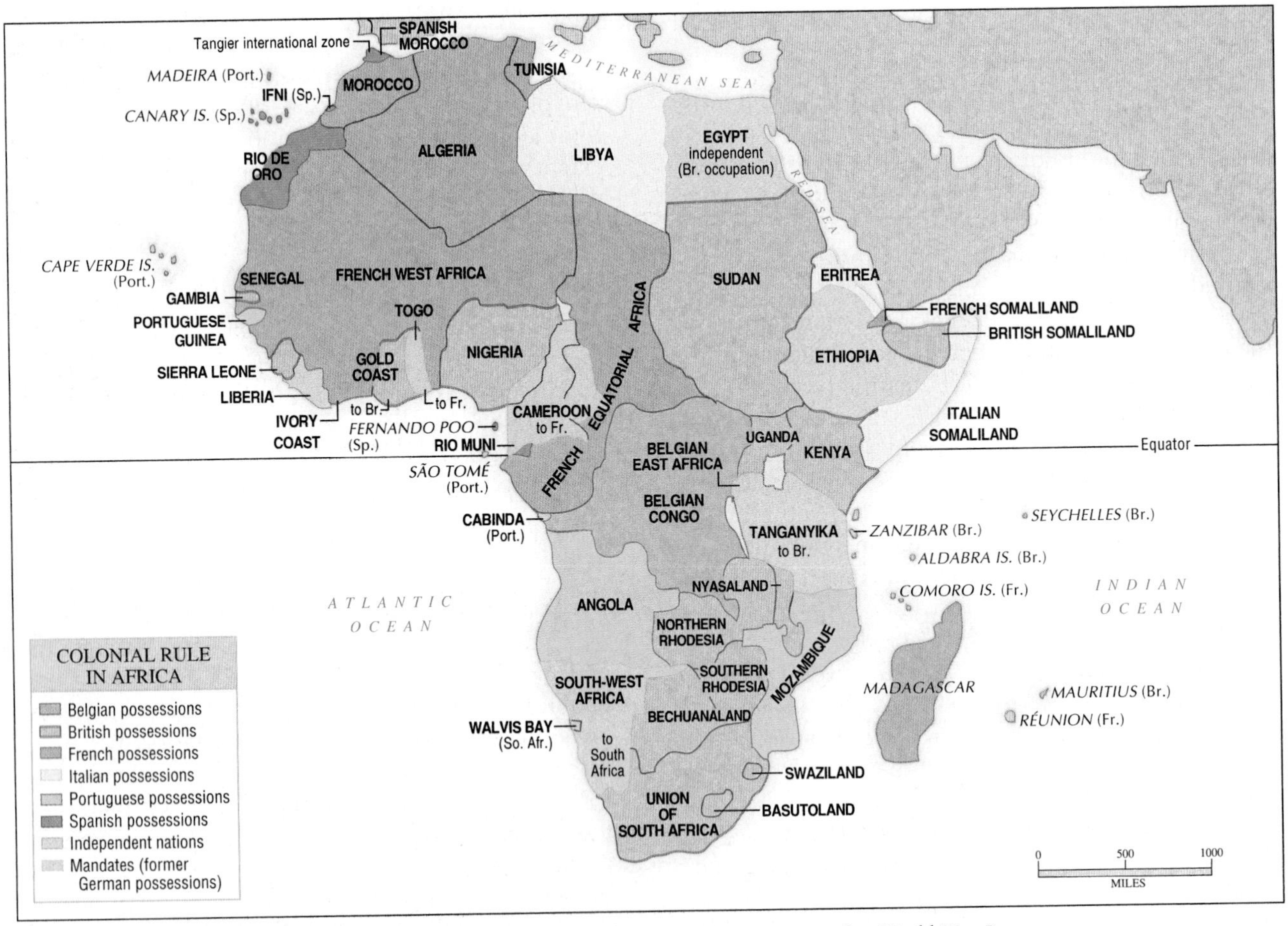

After colonial rule was firmly established in Africa, the only change in possessions came after World War I. Germany's four colonies were placed under the League of Nations, which established a mandate system for other colonizers to administer the territories.

Africa	
1912	Founding of African National Congress in South Africa
1935	Italy invades Ethiopia
1944	Formation of ANC Youth League in South Africa
1945	Fifth Pan-African Congress
1951	Beginning of Mau Mau rebellion in Kenya

redress of specific grievances. Even when they criticized aspects of colonial rule, they made sure to express their loyalty to the British crown. In 1920 African professionals in the British colonies of Gold Coast (later Ghana), Gambia, Nigeria and Sierra Leone established the **National Congress of British West Africa (NCBWA).** Its most prominent spokesperson was J. E. Casely-Hayford, a Gold Coast lawyer. The NCBWA favored using constitutional methods to achieve gradual change and protected its members' interests by calling for improved education and for new constitutions in which they would be allowed to join Legislative Councils that advised British officials. They wrongly thought the British would allow the Councils to evolve into Parliaments.

National Congress of British West Africa—An organization founded in 1920 by African professionals in West Africa to give greater influence to educated Africans in colonial decision-making.

Although the challenges of elite organizations were usually restrained, some of their protests ended in violent confrontations. In Kenya the East African Association (EAA), a largely Kikuyu organization, was formed to protest against forced labor, pass laws, high taxes, and reductions in black wages. In March 1922, its leader, Harry Thuku, was arrested in Nairobi for agitation. Demonstrators that gathered outside his jail charged the police, who then shot and killed 56 people. The EAA was banned the following year.

The Portuguese and Belgians effectively clamped down on dissent in their colonies, while the French encouraged Africans in their colonies to follow a path the French designed. One element of French policy was to assimilate a small number of Africans and give them full rights as French citizens. By 1926, about 50,000 of 13 million Africans in France's African colonies were French citizens. Most of them lived in Senegal, where four communes had elected a single deputy to the Chamber of Deputies in Paris since the nineteenth century. Europeans and Creoles had represented the communes until the 1914 election, the first time a secret ballot was used and the first time an African, Blaise Diagne, was elected to the Chamber of

The first African elected to the French Chamber of Deputies in 1914, Blaise Diagne (in bowler hat on the right) was the highest elected African official in the French colonies until after World War II.

Deputies. A former customs official, Diagne had served in French colonial outposts in the Caribbean and Southeast Asian. He remained in the Chamber of Deputies for the next two decades and was the highest elected African official in the French colonies until after World War II. He advocated racial equality and dignity for Africans, but not an end to French rule. He successfully challenged a colonial decree that severely limited the number of French citizens in the colonies but only by agreeing to recruit Africans into the French army after the outbreak of World War I.

PAN-AFRICANISM

- *What was the impact of the Italian invasion of Ethiopia on black opinion around the world?*

The African challenge to colonial rule was strengthened by international support from Pan-Africanism. This was a movement that grew out of the shared experiences of blacks in many parts of the world with European domination through the slave trade, racism, and colonialism. Although Pan-Africanism's primary aim was to unify and strengthen blacks, its leaders disagreed about who their main audience was. Some Pan-Africanists limited their message exclusively to Africans in sub-Saharan Africa, while others appealed more broadly to Africans throughout the continent or to blacks throughout Africa and the **African diaspora,** including the Caribbean and the Americas.

In the late nineteenth and early twentieth centuries, the leading lights of the Pan-Africanist movement were blacks of the diaspora such as W. E. B. Du Bois and Marcus Garvey. Born and raised in Massachusetts, Du Bois (1868–1963), an organizer of the **National Association for the Advancement of Colored People (NAACP)** and editor of its magazine, *The Crisis,* was most comfortable in intellectual circles. He asserted the right of blacks to participate in national governments and advocated the eventual self-rule of African countries. He was a prominent force behind a series of pan-African conferences held in Europe and the United States. One of the congresses, with representatives from 15 countries attending, was convened in Paris in 1919. The congress coincided with the Versailles Peace Conference, and Du Bois urged the gathering to place the former German colonies under an international agency, rather than under the rule of one of the victorious powers, such as Britain.

Du Bois's primary rival in the Pan-Africanist movement was Marcus Garvey (1887–1940), who immigrated from Jamaica to the United States in 1916 and founded the Universal Negro Improvement Association. A charismatic showman, Garvey won a mass following not only in the United States but also in the Caribbean, Great Britain, and many parts of Africa. Rallying his followers around the popular slogan "Africa for the Africans," he called for black self-awareness, economic self-sufficiency, and Africa's immediate independence. He founded the Black Star shipping line to repatriate blacks to Africa. His activities drew the ire of the American government, which jailed him on tax evasion charges and deported him in 1929. He spent the rest of his life in Jamaica and Britain.

An event that galvanized black opinion throughout the world was the Italian invasion of Ethiopia. As the

The Jamaican-born Marcus Garvey was a fiery Pan-Africanist. After settling in the Harlem neighborhood of New York City in 1916, he won a large black following not only in the United States but throughout the world.

African diaspora—Consists of all the individuals and communities scattered around the world who claim African descent.

National Association for the Advancement of Colored People (NAACP)—An organization founded in 1909 to improve the legal, educational, economic, and political lives of African Americans.

Crowned emperor of Ethiopia in 1930, Haile Selassie (1892–1975) gained international attention when his country was invaded by Italy in 1935. Haile Selassie's reign extended until 1974, when he was overthrown by a military coup.

only African state beside Liberia that survived the scramble for Africa, Ethiopia—and its emperor, Haile Selassie (HI-le se-la-SEE)—symbolized Africa's independence and freedom. Ethiopia fell victim, however, to the expansionist designs of the Italian dictator Benito Mussolini, who sought an Italian East African empire and revenge for the Italian defeat at Aduwa in 1896. Late in 1934, fighting broke out between the Ethiopians and the Italians, and in the following year, Mussolini's forces used the pretext of a skirmish on the Italian Somaliland border to invade the country. Emperor Haile Selassie made a dramatic appearance before the League of Nations to appeal for help. Before he could speak, however, he had to endure the catcalls and whistles of the Italian journalists in the hall.

The League tried to arrange for arbitration. Unconvinced by the shameless Italian argument that Ethiopia, not Italy, was the aggressor, the League voted to prohibit shipment of certain goods to Italy and to deny it credit. But the effect of the sanctions was minor because oil—without which no modern army could fight—was not included in the list of prohibited articles. France and Britain gave only lukewarm support to the sanctions because they did not want to alienate Italy. The United States, which had not joined the League, and Germany, which had left it by that time, largely ignored the prohibitions. Only outraged public opinion, moved by newspaper photographs showing barefooted Ethiopians fighting the modern Italian army, drove the governments to even the pretense of action.

A quarter of a million poorly trained and inadequately armed Ethiopian soldiers were no match for the mechanized Italian army. The Ethiopians could field only 13 unarmed planes against the Italian air force, which had no compunction about using poison gas. In July 1936 when sanctions were removed, Haile Selassie, an emperor without a country, went to live in exile in Britain until the Italians were driven out in 1941.

Ethiopia's downfall had a stirring impact on black nationalists all over the world. When Kwame Nkrumah (in-KROO-mah), a nationalist from the Gold Coast arrived in London and heard of the invasion, he said, "At that moment it was almost as if the whole of London had declared war on me personally. . . . My nationalism surged to the fore."[2] Groups of blacks in the United States and Britain founded organizations to support the Ethiopian war effort and later began to take on the larger issue of European colonialism.

As World War II was drawing to a close, several hundred black delegates met in Manchester, England, for the **Fifth Pan-African Congress.** Pan-African veteran Du Bois attended, as well as the Afro-Caribbean organizers of the Manchester congress, C. L. R. James, George Padmore, and Ras Makonnen. However, the most influential participants were Africans such as Nkrumah and Kenya's Jomo Kenyatta, who pressed the congress to adopt resolutions demanding immediate freedom in Africa by any means necessary. They resolved that "if the Western world is still determined to rule mankind by force, then Africans, as a last resort, may have to appeal to force in the effort to achieve Freedom, even if force destroys them and the world."[3] Henceforth, the struggle for African independence was to be waged not in European centers of power but in Africa itself as leaders such as Nkrumah and Kenyatta returned home to lead the independence struggles in their countries.

Fifth Pan-African Congress—A meeting of pan Africanists held in Manchester, England in 1945 that called for the immediate independence of African colonies.

Document

The Awakening of a Pan-African Spirit

In the period before World War II, pan-African ideas spread rapidly throughout the black world. In this passage from his autobiography, black South African writer Peter Abrahams (b. 1918) recounts the profound impact of African-American political ideas and music and culture on his personal development. After leaving South Africa in 1940, he lived in England and attended the Fifth Pan African Congress in 1945. In the 1950s he moved to Jamaica, where he still resides.

I found the Bantu Men's Social Centre on the outer rim of Johannesburg, on the way to Langlaagte and the white mountains of sand that towered beyond it. It was a huge building that stood in its own grounds.

I hesitated uncertainly on the pavement till two well-dressed black men speaking English passed me and went in. I followed them. There was a passage that widened into a rectangular hall. Doors led off to right and left. On the first door on the left was the word: "Secretary." The two men passed that and entered the second door on the left. I knocked on the door marked "Secretary." . . .

From the other side of the huge door that faced the passage came a deep voice, touched with the velvet quality of organ notes, singing a familiar song.

The organ notes stopped. Another, lighter voice, without the magic quality of the first, sang the same words, tried to make them sound the same, but failed. Then the magnificent voice sang a little more of the song. And again the lighter voice repeated it. If only the lighter voice would leave the other alone! Others must have shared my feeling, for a man came out of the door where the two had gone in earlier. He pushed the great door open. I saw part of a huge hall.

"Hlubi, man!" the man called. "The fellows want to hear Robeson. Turn it up!"

"All right."

Black men appeared from everywhere and stood in silence.

That was a black man, one of us! I knew it. I needed no proof. The men about me, their faces, their bearing, carried all the proof. That was a black man! The voice of a black man!

"Some voice, heh, son?" a man said to me.

"Yessir!"

"He's an American Negro," the man said, and moved away.

I followed him through the door where the greatest number went. It was a long room, spacious, and with big windows that let in light.

I moved over to the bookshelves. I wanted to touch the books, but held back. Perhaps it was not permitted. Typed slips showed what each shelf held: novels, history, sociology, travel, Africans, political science, American Negro literature . . . I stopped there, American Negro literature. The man had said Robeson was an American Negro.

A man got up and came over. He ran his finger along the American Negro literature shelf and took out a book.

"Excuse me. Can I look at these?"

"Of course," he smiled.

I reached up and took out a fat black book. *The Souls of Black Folk*, by W. E. B. Du Bois. I turned the pages. It spoke about a people in a valley. And they were black, and dispossessed, and denied. I skimmed through the pages, anxious to take it all in. I read:

"For this much all men know: despite compromise, war, struggle, the Negro is not free."

"The Negro is not free." . . . I remembered those "Reserved for Europeans Only" signs; I remembered no white boys ever carried bags at the market or ran from the police; I remembered my long walks in the white sections of the city, and the lavatories, and the park benches, and the tearooms . . . "The Negro is not free."

But why had I not thought of it myself? Now, having read the words, I knew that I had known this all along. But until now I had had no words to voice that knowledge. Du Bois's words had the impact of a revelation.

Elsewhere I read:

> *I have seen a land right merry with the sun, where children sing, and rolling hills lie like passioned women wanton with harvest. And there in the King's Highway sat and sits a figure veiled and bowed, by which the traveler's footsteps hasten as they go. On the tainted air broods fear. Three centuries' thought has been the raising and unveiling of that bowed human heart, and now behold a century new for the duty and the deed. The problem of the Twentieth Century is the problem of the colour-line.*

Questions to Consider

1. Why were African Americans such as Paul Robeson and W. E. B. Du Bois an inspirational example for black South Africans?
2. As you examine the events of the last century, how do you respond to Du Bois's assertion that the primary problem of the twentieth century is the color line?

Jomo Kenyatta (1894–1978), president of Kenya African Union. The British arrested him in 1952 and charged him with conspiring to organize the Mau Mau rebellion. He was finally released in 1961. He served as independent Kenya's first prime minister from 1963 until his death.

WORLD WAR II AND ITS AFTERMATH

- *What influences did World War II have on African political thought?*

World War II made a dramatic impact on the lives of many Africans whose political consciousness was raised and who began posing questions about the continuation of colonial rule. These changes stimulated new and more aggressive African nationalist movements to challenge colonizers after the war and to begin the process of ending colonial rule.

The people whose lives were most directly affected by the war were African soldiers. When Germany invaded France in May 1940, about 80,000 Africans from French colonies were serving in France. About a quarter lost their lives in the fighting, while many others were captured and sent to German prisoner-of-war camps in which they were treated poorly. The Vichy government then declared that France's colonies were neutral and that no more African soldiers would be recruited. The only African governor, Felix Ebouè, was also the lone governor to oppose this decision and support the Free French.

In the British colonies, African soldiers joined the British army in huge numbers and served as combat troops and supply carriers in many theatres of war. British West Africa contributed 167,000 soldiers, while British East Africa provided 280,000 men. On the other hand, South Africa's white rulers were wary of exposing blacks to modern weapons and restricted their black units' service to laborers.

African units assisted the Allies in driving the Italians out from Somalia, Eritrea, and Ethiopia; the Germans from North Africa and southern Europe; and the Japanese from Burma, where African troops adapted well to the tropical environment. Helping to defeat the Japanese army was significant because the Japanese had driven out the British and French from their colonies in Southeast Asia.

The experiences of African servicemen exploded the myth of European invincibility and superiority. They served as equals and interacted with white soldiers, many of whom were uneducated. They saw Europeans living in abject poverty and fighting one another. Many African servicemen, who returned home with expectations of employment and better conditions and treatment, were disillusioned by the lack of change. They took a more critical view of colonial rule and were prepared to confront it by joining nationalist parties. One returned serviceman expressed his feelings in a biting parody of Psalm 23 he submitted to a Gold Coast (Ghana) newspaper:

The European merchant is my shepherd,
And I am in want;
He maketh me to lie down in cocoa farms;
He leadeth me beside the waters of great need;
The general managers and producers frighten me.
Thou preparedst a reduction in my salary
In the presence of my creditors.
Thou anointest my income with taxes;
My expense runs over my income
And I will dwell in a rented house for ever![4]

African politicians also began questioning the motives of Britain and France for involving them in the war. The Allies claimed that they stood for democracy and racial equality in the struggle against fascism and racism. A clause of the Atlantic Charter of 1941 stipulated that the Allies supported "the right of all peoples to choose the form of government under which they all live."[5] Many Africans interpreted this to mean that steps would be taken to assure their independence after the war, but Churchill let it be known that he was not prepared to preside over the dissolution of the British Empire. On the other hand, President Roosevelt openly opposed imperialism and expressed his concerns for African rights. His position was critical in a postwar world in which the influence of Britain and France was greatly reduced and two nations with no African colonies, the United States and the Soviet Union, became the major global powers.

The political parties that African politicians organized after the war were of a different character than prewar organizations. They were mass parties that had full-time organizers and reached out to urban and rural people. Party leaders closely watched the independence struggle in India and Burma. Some such as Nkrumah in the Gold Coast and Kenneth Kaunda in Northern Rhodesia (Zambia) became disciples of Mahatma Gandhi and his philosophy of nonviolent civil disobedience. African politicians were very direct about their goals. They wanted self-rule without delay.

A passionate advocate of African unity, Kwame Nkrumah was the leader of Ghana's drive for independence from Great Britain and served as its first president from 1957 until his overthrow by the military in 1966.

In Tanzania anticolonial protest after World War II was fuelled by unpopular British agricultural policies that were deeply resented by African peasants. Initially protests were organized along ethnic and regional lines, but as local groups realized that a national front was necessary, they supported the founding of the Tanganyika African National Union (TANU) in 1954. TANU's leader was Julius Nyerere, a teacher trained in Scotland and England. TANU effectively used the UN Trusteeship Council established to monitor colonial administration in the former mandated territories of the League of Nations. One case TANU brought to the Trusteeship Council involved 3000 African farmers in the Meru district who were losing their land to white settlers.

While political organizations developed in each British colony, the pace of political activities in the French colonies was tied to political developments in France. The French Constituent Assembly elected in 1945 contained five African delegates (in the total of 64 from French colonies) out of 586 delegates. The African deputies allied with the left-wing Socialists and Communists, which had a majority in the Assembly, but in 1946, conservative parties won a majority in fresh elections and adopted a new constitution that closed the door on African independence and weakened the provisions for French citizenship in the colonies. African deputies organized a meeting in Bamako, Mali, to discuss how to respond, but they split because of divisions in the French left. One group supported the Communists, which backed independence for the colonies, while the others allied with the Socialists, which opposed the Bamako meeting. Participants in Bamako established the *Rassemblement démocratique africain* ("African Democratic Assembly" or RDA), an alliance of individual parties from each of the colonies. A leading member was Felix Houphouët-Boigny, a wealthy planter and a communist, but after colonial officials began a wave of repression against the RDA, Houphouët retreated from his opposition to the French government.

Most African nationalist movements, even when they engaged in confrontational protests against colonial officials, did not turn to armed resistance to bring about change. In colonies such as Algeria, Southern Rhodesia, South Africa, South West Africa, and Kenya in which armed resistance developed, it was usually associated with the presence of European settlers and the expropriation of African land.

In Kenya, a small community of about 60,000 white settlers was concentrated in the fertile highlands north of Nairobi, where they took huge chunks of land, especially from the Kikuyu people (see p. 689). White farmers were vocal about protecting their interests and lobbied British officials to put off any political concessions to Africans.

The Kikuyu were split into moderates, who preferred continued negotiations, and radicals, who wanted immediate action, even if it meant taking up arms. The moderates were represented by Jomo Kenyatta who had returned home after World War II to take up the leadership of the Kenyan African Union. The radicals formed the **Land and Freedom Army** (more popularly known as Mau Mau). Its supporters went through mass oathing ceremonies in which they totally committed themselves to the movement. When their rebellion broke out in 1951, they not only attacked Europeans but also Africans who remained loyal to the British. Mau Mau fighters killed a handful of whites as well as over 1000 loyalists who supported the British by joining Homeguard units. Women played prominent roles in Mau Mau not only as fighters, but also as spies, intelligence gatherers, and carriers of supplies and food to guerrillas in the forests.

To quell the rebellion, the British launched a ruthless counterinsurgency campaign and detained 80,000 people, including Kenyatta, in jails and camps. The British suspected him of masterminding Mau Mau, although he actually had no links to it. After hostilities ended in 1955, the British kept a state of emergency in

Land and Freedom Army—More popularly known as Mau Mau, this army was established by Kikuyu radicals in Kenya to attack white settlers and British colonial officials.

Langata Detention Camp, Kenya, 1954. As part of its counterinsurgency tactics, the British established detention camps such as Langata to imprison Mau Mau rebels as well as other opponents such as Jomo Kenyatta.

Document — Pass Laws and African Women in South Africa

A key way in which the white minority maintained its dominance in South Africa was through pass laws that controlled where adult Africans could live, seek work, and move in white areas. In 1912, after African women in the Orange Free State province protested against these laws by organizing demonstrations and writing petitions, the government backed down and rarely enforced these laws against women. However, in January 1956, the government announced that African women had to join men and carry passes. This decision provoked tremendous resistance from black women. However, the government continued to enforce the law for another three decades.

Petition of the Native and Coloured Women of the Province of the Orange Free State

11 March, 1912

To the Right Honourable General Louis Botha, PC., M.L.A., Prime Minister of the Union of South Africa, CAPE TOWN,

Sir,

The petition of the undersigned humbly showeth:—

2. That your petitioners, as inhabitants of the said Province, are under a burden of having to carry Residential Passes in terms of Section 2 of Law 8 of 1893 (Orange Free State Statutes).

3. That this law is a source of grievance to your petitioners in that:—

(a) It renders them liable to interference by any policeman at any time, and in that way deprives them of that liberty enjoyed by their women-folk in other Provinces.

(b) It has a barbarous tendency of ignoring the consequences of marriage in respect of natives, especially the right of parents to control their children, a right which parents ought to exercise without interference from outside, and the effect of its operation upon the minds of our children is that it inculcates upon them the idea that as soon as they become liable to comply with the requirements of the law, their age of majority also commences, and, can, therefore, act independently of their parents.

(c) It is an effective means of enforcing labour and throws to pieces every element of respect to which they are entitled; and for this reason it has no claim to recognition as a just, progressive and protective law, necessary for their elevation in the scale of civilization; moreover it does not improve their social status. . . .

Wherefore your petitioners humbly pray that the Right Honourable the Prime Minister may be pleased:—

1. To grant them immediate relief from this burdensome law by introducing a Bill in Parliament repealing it. . . .

Lilian Ngoyi, Presidential Address to the African National Congress Women's League, Transvaal, November 1956.

. . . Hardly any other South Africa Law has caused so much suffering and hardship to Africans as the pass laws. Hardly any other measure has created so much suffering and racial friction and hostility between black and white. Any policeman may at any time demand to see your pass and failure to produce it for any reason means imprisonment or a fine. It makes it permissible to violate the sanctity and privacy of our homes. An African, sleeping peacefully in his house, may be woken up at night asked to produce one and failure to do so may lead to his arrest and imprisonment even though he has committed no crime whatsoever. . . .

The pass law is the basis and cornerstone of the system of oppression and exploitation in this country. It is a device to ensure cheap labour for the mines and the farms. It is a badge of slavery in terms whereof all sorts of insults and humiliation may be committed on Africans by members of the ruling class. It is because of these reasons that the Congress has always regarded the pass laws as the principal target of the struggle for freedom. . . . *Only direct mass action will deter the Government and stop it from proceeding with its cruel laws*. . . . STRIJDOM, STOP AND THINK FOR YOU HAVE AROUSED THE WRATH OF THE WOMEN OF SOUTH AFRICA and that wrath might put you and your evil deeds out of action sooner than you expect.

Questions to Consider

1. What do we learn from these documents about the impact of passes on African women and African family life?
2. Compare the language and tone of the petition of 1913 and Lilian Ngoyi's speech 40 years later. In both cases what do they tell you about the state and style of black protest at that time and African attitudes towards the white government?

From M. J. Daymond et al., eds., *Women Writing Africa: The Southern Region* (Witwatersrand University Press, 2003), pp. 159–161 and 242–243.

effect until 1959 and did not release Kenyatta until 1961. Two years later he became the first president of an independent Kenya.

South Africa had a much larger white population than Kenya, but Black South African protest was distinct from other African nationalist movements because it did not challenge a colonial ruler. Britain had pulled out from formal control when the Union of South Africa was established in 1910 and handed over power to Afrikaner and English settlers, who began passing discriminatory laws.

The primary opposition to white rule was the South African Native National Congress, founded in 1912 (and renamed the **African National Congress (ANC)** in 1923) to bring Africans from all black ethnic groups together into one organization. Led by Africans educated in Christian mission schools, the ANC initially had modest goals. African leaders did not immediately call for black majority rule. They wanted blacks to be treated as equals with whites and to remove discriminatory laws. They concluded that waging armed struggle was futile, and they sought change through nonviolent constitutional means such as signing petitions, making representations to the government, and even sending delegations to the British government to pressure the South African government to change legislation. The British government, however, was deaf to all their appeals.

The ANC's first president was a Congregational minister named John Dube (1871–1946), who, while receiving his education at Oberlin College in the United States, became a disciple of the American educator Booker T. Washington and his philosophy of industrial education for advancing blacks. After returning to Natal, Dube founded his own school, Ohlange Institute, modeled on Washington's Tuskegee Institute. He also started up a Zulu/English language newspaper.

Women were not represented in the ANC's leadership, but there were prominent women activists. One was Charlotte Maxeke (1874–1939), who also had studied at Ohio's Wilberforce College in the 1890s, where she was a student of W. E. B. DuBois. On her return to South Africa, she and her husband founded a high school, Wilberforce Institute, sponsored by the African Methodist Episcopal Church. She had an avid interest in social welfare issues and, as President of the Bantu Women's League, she led a campaign against pass laws.

With only a few thousand members, the ANC's challenge to white rule was very restrained until World War II, when tens of thousands of Africans, who streamed into the urban centers like Johannesburg to take up jobs, became involved in protests over housing shortages, the high costs of transportation, and pass laws. Sensing this mood of militancy, a younger generation of politicians formed a Youth League within the ANC in 1944 to push their elders to challenge white rule more aggressively. The Youth League's first president was Anton Lembede, a lawyer. He died in 1947, but other Youth Leaguers such as Nelson Mandela, Walter Sisulu, and Oliver Tambo continued to play important roles as resistance leaders for over a half century.

Opposing the ANC was a narrow form of nationalism advocated by many Afrikaners. The ANC aimed at bringing together Africans from many different ethnic groups in a common body, while Afrikaner nationalists focused exclusively on unifying and mobilizing Afrikaners. In 1948, the Afrikaner-dominated National Party won the white election and began implementing the rigid system of racial separation known as **apartheid.** ANC Youth Leaguers responded by forcing a change of ANC leadership in 1949 and pressing the movement to adopt a Program of Action that advocated direct action such as strikes, boycotts, and civil disobedience. During the 1950s, as the ANC engaged in mass protests against apartheid laws, its membership rose to over 100,000.

CONCLUSION

From World War I to the years after World War II, imperialism went on the defensive before the rise of nationalism in the Middle East and Africa. Independence movements against European dominance took root and flourished.

In the Islamic heartlands, one traditional empire, Qajar Persia, maintained its territorial integrity but witnessed the establishment of a new dynasty, a new name, and a program of modernizing reforms. The other, the Ottoman Empire, was broken up in the aftermath of the war and divided among independent states and mandates controlled by Britain and France. Arab nationalists bitterly contested European control in the mandated areas, while Zionists, aspiring to a Jewish homeland, challenged both the British and the indigenous Arab populace for control of Palestine. The

African National Congress (ANC)—A political organization founded in 1912 in South Africa to promote equal rights for black people and to abolish discriminatory laws and segregation.

apartheid—An Afrikaans word meaning "separateness," it was the policy of rigid racial segregation introduced by the National party in South Africa after 1948.

mandates in the Arab territories stood in stark contrast to the independent states of Arabia and Turkey, the latter redeemed by Mustafa Kemal Atatürk from the ruins of the Ottoman Empire. In the background of these political struggles, a new economic factor, oil, emerged as a resource that would later bring untold riches to some parts of the Middle East. But oil would not become a primary factor in global politics until after World War II.

African nationalists were not dealing with the breakup of existing empires but with challenging the European imperial presence. They sought to replace colonial rule with self-government and to bring about the political and cultural resurgence of a people whose way of life was challenged by Western imperialism. Their political activity took place at the village, regional, national and international levels, where the pan-African movement drew supporters from the black diaspora in North America, the Caribbean and Europe. World War II, like World War I, had a dramatic impact on Africa as well as France and Britain, which came out of the war with less influence in the world. The efforts of nationalist movements gained momentum after the war and forced the French and British to consider granting independence to their colonies much sooner than they planned. During the 1950s and 1960s most British and French colonies won their independence, thus setting the stage for the independence of the rest of Africa in the last decades of the twentieth century.

Suggestions for Web Browsing

You can obtain more information about topics included in this chapter at the websites listed below. See also the companion website that accompanies this text, **http://www.ablongman.com/brummett,** which contains an online study guide and additional resources.

Internet Islamic History Sourcebook: The Islamic World, 1918–1945
http://www.fordham.edu/halsall/islam/islamsbook.html#Islamic%20Nationalism

Online source for links about the history of the Middle East, 1918–1945.

Internet African History Sourcebook: The Fight for Independence
http://www.fordham.edu/halsall/africa/africasbook.html#

Online source of links about the African struggle for independence. Includes sources such as the Manifesto of the Second Pan African Congress, 1922.

Historical Documents Archive African National Congress
http://www.anc.org.za/ancdocs/history/

This archive contains hundreds of documents and biographical profiles relating to the history of the African National Congress, founded in 1912 to protest segregation and white rule in South Africa.

Literature and Film

For an interesting combination of fiction and memoirs on Arab society see Siham Tergeman, *Daughter of Damascus* (University of Texas Press, 1994), and Hanna Mina, *Fragments of Memory: A Story of a Syrian Family* (University of Texas Press, 1993) an autobiographical novel, both on Syria; see also Fadia Faqir, *Pillars of Salt* (Interlink, 1997), set in Jordan. Driss Chraibi's *Mother Comes of Age* (Three Continents Press, 1994) is a wonderful autobiographical novel about a middle-aged Moroccan woman coming to terms with technological and ideological change in the WWII era. Nobel laureate Naguib Mahfouz writes of Egypt under British occupation and its struggle for independence in *Palace Walk* (Doubleday, 1990) and *Midaq Alley* (Doubleday, 1975). Abdel Rahman al-Sharqawi's *Egyptian Earth* (Saqi, 1990) is a tale of peasant life and the dilemmas of war during the 1973 Arab-Israeli war.

Chinua Achebe's trilogy—*Things Fall Apart, No Longer at Ease,* and *Arrow of God*—traces a Nigerian family through the span of the colonial period (Anchor, 1989–1994). Modikwe Dikobe's *The Marabi Dance* (Heinemann, 1984) is a novel set in a black township in South Africa in the 1930s that highlights popular culture and the urbanization of black migrant workers. Buchi Emecheta's *The Joys of Motherhood* (George Braziller, 1980) treats the difficulty of being a woman in African society and under British colonial rule.

Films include *Black and White in Color* (Warner Home Video, 1976), a satirical treatment of a skirmish between French and German colonials in West Africa at the outset of World War I. Based on a novel by Joyce Cary, *Mister Johnson* (Artemis, 1991) is a portrait of an African clerk who faces numerous problems adjusting to his role as a civil servant under colonial administration in Nigeria.

Suggestions for Reading

A lucid and balanced survey of the modern Middle East is William Cleveland, *A History of the Modern Middle East* (Westview, 2000). A study of the nature of change in the Islamic world is John Voll, *Islam: Continuity and Change in the Modern World*, 2nd ed. (Syracuse, 1994). For a good introduction on the mandate for Palestine, see Charles D. Smith, *Palestine and the Arab Israeli Conflict,* 4th ed. (St. Martin's Press, 2000). On the years of World War I and the British role, see the account by David Fromkin, *A Peace to End All Peace* (Avon Books, 1988). On the history of the Jewish people see Raymond Scheindlin, *A Short History of the Jewish People* (Oxford University Press, 1998). Ann M. Lesch, *Arab Politics in Palestine* (Cornell University Press, 1979), traces the rise of Arab nationalism in Palestine.

On the emergence of Turkey and of Mustafa Kemal Atatürk, see Feroz Ahmad, *The Making of Modern Turkey* (Routledge, 1993). On Iran in this era, see Ervand Abrahamian, *Iran Between*

Two Revolutions (Princeton University Press, 1982). For a nice summary on Egypt, see Afaf Lutfi al-Sayyid Marsot, *A Short History of Modern Egypt* (Cambridge University Press, 1986). For the Iraq mandate, see Peter Sluglett, *Britain in Iraq, 1914–1932* (Ithaca Press, 1976).

African protest and nationalist movement during the colonial era are examined in the series *UNESCO General History of Africa,* Vols. 7 and 8 (University of California Press, 1985). Black protest against white rule in South Africa is examined in Vols. 1 and 2 of Thomas Karis and Gwendolen M. Carter, *From Protest to Challenge: A Documentary History of African Politics in South Africa, 1882–1964* (Hoover Institution Press, 1971). The Mau Mau rebellion is treated in David Throup, *Economic and Social Origins of Mau Mau, 1945–1953* (Ohio University Press, 1988). The Pan-Africanist movement is assessed in Imanuel Geiss, *The Pan-African Movement* (Methuen, 1974).

CHAPTER

31

World War II

Origins and Consequences, 1919–1946

CHAPTER CONTENTS

1920

1922 Germany and the USSR conclude Rapallo Pact

1930

1931 Japan invades Manchuria

1935

1936 Germany occupies the Rhineland; Hitler and Mussolini form the Rome-Berlin Axis; Germany and Japan sign Anti-Comintern Pact

1936–1939 Spanish Civil War; Spanish Republic falls; Franco becomes dictator

1937 Japan invades China; World War II begins in Asia

1938 Anschluss with Austria; Munich Pact

1939 Germany and Russia sign nonaggression pact; Germany invades Poland; World War II begins in Europe

1940

1940 France falls to the Axis

1941 Lend-Lease Act; Atlantic Charter; Japan attacks Pearl Harbor; United States enters war

1943 Russians defeat Germans at Stalingrad

1945

1945 Germany surrenders; U.S. drops atomic bombs on Hiroshima and Nagasaki; Japan surrenders

The victorious Allied states went their separate ways after World War I. The United States refused participation in most postwar diplomatic activities but remained active in international business. Great Britain withdrew from the Continent of Europe and looked after the Commonwealth and empire. Italy plunged into five years of governmental failure, leading to Mussolini's takeover. France was left holding the responsibility for overseeing democratic interests in Europe.

In the first decade after the war, statesmen with global vision made serious attempts to control conflict through international organizations and treaties limiting arms and outlawing war. The economic disasters of the Wall Street Crash and the Great Depression at the end of the 1920s, however, forced the democracies to look inward.

At the same time, aggressive nations took advantage of the democracies' retreat to advance their interests: Japan invaded Manchuria and, later, China and Southeast Asia; Italy attacked Ethiopia, and Germany expanded its influence in Central Europe. Burdened by domestic concerns and the memories of the losses in World War I, the representatives of the democracies tried unsuccessfully to reason with the militarists. World War II, which started in July 1937 in Asia, reached Europe in 1939.

From 1937 to 1945 the world experienced slaughter and destruction on an unprecedented scale. New and horrible technologies ravaged the globe as large bombers carried the war to civilians hundreds of miles behind what used to be known as the front line in Europe and Asia. While fighting his enemies, Hitler made use of industrial technology to try to exterminate the Jews in a genocide that has come to be known as the Holocaust. In the Pacific theater, primitive means of warfare—hand-to-hand combat—joined technologically sophisticated methods—advanced aerial warfare launched from aircraft carriers—in the military actions between the Americans and the Japanese. For perhaps 20 million other Asians in Japan, China, and Southeast Asia, death came from starvation and from the skies in the form of bombing, including the only uses of nuclear weapons in the world's history. After nuclear weapons made direct conflicts between great powers unthinkable, war took on a new form. A bipolar Cold War between the USSR and the United States ensued, in which Moscow and Washington avoided fighting each other directly but competed worldwide through every other method.

THE TROUBLED CALM: THE WEST IN THE 1920S

■ *Why were the European democracies unable to maintain the advantage they had gained in winning World War I?*

The aftershocks of World War I overwhelmed the interwar period. The horror, expense, and exhaustion of the tragedy haunted losers and winners alike. Many of the younger generation had died and political leadership fell to either the old or the untried. It was in this uncertain environment that the League of Nations began its work.

The League of Nations

The League's record from 1919 to 1929 was modest, neither one of failure nor one of triumph. Such threats to peace as disputes between Sweden and Finland and between Britain and Turkey were resolved. When a major power defied the League, however, as in the case of Italy's quarrel with Greece over Corfu, the organization could do nothing. The refusal of the United States, the world's strongest democracy, to join weakened the League's peacekeeping possibilities.

Through no fault of the League's, little progress was made in the field of disarmament; however, the League had a distinguished list of accomplishments in other areas. It supervised the exchange and repatriation of prisoners of war and saved thousands of refugees from starvation. It helped Austria, Bulgaria, and Hungary secure badly needed loans. The League also provided valuable services in administering the region of the Saar Basin and the Free City of Danzig. It investigated the existence of slavery in certain parts of the world, sought to stanch traffic in dangerous drugs, and stood ready to offer assistance when disasters brought suffering and destruction.

In the intellectual and cultural realm the League published books and periodicals dealing with national and international problems of all kinds and from its own radio station broadcast important information, particularly in the field of health. Unfortunately, the League's excellent record in these areas has been obscured by its failure to maintain a lasting peace.

The French Quest for Security

Because the United States chose to play a limited role in international affairs and Great Britain returned to its traditional focus on the empire and the Commonwealth, France assumed the leadership of postwar Europe. In 1919 the French pursued a very simple but difficult foreign policy goal: absolute security. Since the Napoleonic grandeur a century earlier, the French had seen their power and authority diminish while German economic and military strength had increased. Twice in 50 years, Germany had invaded France, with horrendous results.

France spent much of the postwar decade trying to guarantee its own safety by keeping Germany weak. In the first five years after the armistice, the French wanted to impose maximum financial penalties on the Germans. In 1923, assisted by the Belgians, they occupied the Ruhr region in a move that had immense short- and long-range implications (see Chapter 27). Some historians have seen in this act the first step toward World War II because it hardened the German desire for revenge. Even though the Dawes Plan eased the situation, the French attitude divided the former Allies and provided ammunition to German ultranationalists.

The rift between the French and the Germans was papered over in Locarno, Switzerland, in 1925. In the Locarno Pact, Germany, Great Britain, France, and Italy agreed to guarantee the existing frontiers along the Rhine, to establish a demilitarized zone 30 miles deep along the east bank of the Rhine, and to refrain from attacking one another. The problems along France's eastern frontier would be dealt with by international guarantee (although the British dominions stated their disagreement) and U.S. money. Germany received, and accepted, an invitation to join the League of Nations, a symbolic act that seemed to indicate its return to the international community. Still, the Locarno Pact addressed only Germany's western frontier and left unresolved the controversial issues of the territories of the newly formed and contentious nations of eastern Europe.

Another well-meaning but ultimately ineffectual agreement was the **Kellogg-Briand Pact** (1928), developed by U.S. Secretary of State Frank Kellogg and French Foreign Minister Aristide Briand. This pact, eventually signed by 62 nations, outlawed war as an instrument of national policy but omitted provisions to enforce the agreement.

The Paris government had little faith in the Covenant of the League of Nations as a guarantee of France's survival. The French, instead, depended more and more on their own diplomats. They tried to construct a wall of allies along Germany's eastern

---

Kellogg-Briand Pact—An international treaty named after the American Secretary of State Frank Kellogg and French Foreign Minister Aristide Briand that outlawed war. Sixty-two nations signed the treaty, which had little effect because there were no enforcement provisions.

Document Erich Maria Remarque, *The Road Back*

Erich Maria Remarque, who wrote so eloquently of the horrors of war in *All Quiet on the Western Front,* compellingly expressed the despair and frustration of German veterans in *The Road Back.* In the discussion of the inflation and the bitterness of his "brother," he captures the mood that helped Hitler gain power.

Demonstrations in the streets have been called for this afternoon. Prices have been soaring everywhere for months past, and the poverty is greater even than it was during the war. Wages are insufficient to buy the bare necessities of life, and even though one may have the money it is often impossible to buy anything with it. But ever more and more gin palaces and dance halls go up, and ever more and more blatant is the profiteering and swindling.

Scattered groups of workers on strike march through the streets. Now and again there is a disturbance. A rumour is going about that troops have been concentrated at the barracks. But there is no sign of it as yet.

Here and there one hears cries and counter-cries. Somebody is haranguing at a street corner. Then suddenly everywhere is silence.

A procession of men in the faded uniforms of the front-line trenches is moving slowly toward us.

It was formed up by sections, marching in fours. Big white placards are carried before: *Where is the Fatherland's gratitude?—The War Cripples are starving.*

It was no good to go on assuming that a common basis for all the different groups and classes in Germany could be found. The break between them became daily wider and more irreparable. The plebiscite of the Right "against the Young Plan and the war-guilt lie" proved just as unsuccessful as those arranged in former years by the Left, but the poison of the defamatory agitation remained in the body of the community, and we watched its effects with anxiety.

In my own family the political antagonism was growing past endurance. In October Fritz had finished his apprenticeship in an old-established export house, at the precise moment when the firm went bankrupt—a minor incident compared with such events as the breakdown of the Frankfurt General Insurance Company and the Civil Servants' Bank or the enforced reorganization and amalgamation of the Deutsche Bank and the Disconto-Gesellschaft, which all happened in the course of the year and dangerously damaged the whole economic life of Germany. Yet for my brother the bankruptcy of his firm overshadowed all other happenings, since it meant that he lost his job. His three years' training was in vain—there was not a single export firm which was not forced to dismiss as many of its employees as possible.

"Yes, that's just it—millions! If it isn't my fault, whose fault is it? I tell you—your friends, the French, the English, the Americans, all those damnable nations who inflict on us one dishonorable penalty after the other—they are to blame for all this. Before the war the whole world bought German goods. My firm exported to Africa, to the German colonies. Hundreds of thousands we turned over every year. But they have robbed us of our colonies, of all our foreign markets. They have stolen the coal mines in the Saar and in Upper Silesia, they squeeze millions of marks out of our bleeding country. We'll never rise again unless we free ourselves by another war."

"Don't be foolish, Fritz. Things are bad in the whole world."

"I don't care about the world, I care only about Germany, which you and your pacifists have delivered into the hands of our enemies. I despise you, you are not worthy to call yourself a German."

Questions to Consider

1. What were some of the most important elements in the creation of German anger after World War I?
2. Whom does Fritz blame for his situation? Do you agree?
3. In Fritz's point of view, after his argument with the author, who is worthy to call himself German?

frontier that would simultaneously surround the Germans and isolate the Soviet Union. As long as Germany was weak and dependent on Western loans, France could operate as the major diplomatic power on the Continent. But even in the 1920s, France lacked the strength or the vision to lead Europe. When Germany and Italy began to flex their muscles in the 1930s, France—even with British help—responded to fascist aggression from a position of weakness.

Soviet and German Cooperation

The Soviet Union and Germany, the two diplomatic outcasts of the 1920s, quickly forged a working relationship that was useful to both of them. The USSR had isolated itself by signing the **Treaty of Brest-Litovsk,** nationalizing foreign property, and repudiating foreign debts as well as by espousing its communist ideology internationally. Probably the greatest barrier was the ideological one, as expressed through the activities of the **Third Communist International,** or Comintern. That body, organized in 1919, was dedicated to the overthrow of capitalism throughout the world.

In the 1920s the Comintern spread communist propaganda, established Communist parties, and infiltrated labor unions and other working-class groups throughout the world. Even after Lenin had given up hope for an immediate world revolution and started to normalize relations with the West, the Comintern encouraged radicals who had broken off from moderate socialist groups to organize Communist parties. Communists of all countries became members of the Comintern, meeting in congresses held in Moscow and setting up committees to coordinate their activities. Communist parties were different from other national political groups because they owed their allegiance to an international organization rather than to the nations in which they resided.

By 1922 the Soviet Union was pursuing a two-pronged foreign policy. One approach used the Communist parties abroad to achieve ideological goals, as in China, where the Communists worked together with Jiang Jieshi's Nationalists until 1927, when they were forced to develop an independent movement (see Chapter 29). The other approach worked through normal international channels for traditional economic and diplomatic goals, generally in Europe.

From the time Lenin left Switzerland to return to Petrograd with Berlin's assistance, the Soviet Union enjoyed a mutually advantageous relationship with Germany. At the beginning of the 1920s, the two nations ratified secret agreements allowing for joint military training enterprises. Their first major open diplomatic contact came at Rapallo, Italy, in 1922, where they renounced the concept of reparations. In the Rapallo Pact, the Germans and Russians agreed to cooperate in a number of areas. Germany was extremely bitter about the treatment it had received at Versailles; the Soviets had faced Allied intervention during their civil war. It naturally followed that a main feature of the foreign policies of both countries would be either to ignore the Versailles settlement or to escape from its consequences. Both countries shared the ambition to dominate Poland, against whom the USSR had fought at the beginning of the decade.

Although, as Lenin perceptively noted, Russia wanted revolution while Germany sought revenge, the two nations cooperated closely until 1933. Then, after a six-year gap, they cooperated again in the Nazi-Soviet nonaggression pact.

The Weimar government under Gustav Stresemann wanted to rearm but was forbidden to do so by the Versailles treaty. Stresemann backed the cooperation between his government and the Soviet Union to build up German military might. Berlin supplied technical aid to the USSR while German pilots and specialists went on maneuvers in Russia. Even after the proclamation of the so-called spirit of Locarno, the two nations worked with each other. In 1926 the Rapallo Pact was renewed for another five years.

Soviet-German Relations, 1917–1939

1917	Germans financially support Bolsheviks
1918	Treaty of Brest-Litovsk
1919–1922	Weimar-Soviet secret joint military agreements
1922	Rapallo Pact formalizes German-Russian cooperation
1926	Rapallo Pact extended five years
1933–1937	Stalin unsuccessfully advocates common front against Germany
1933–1937	Hitler speaks out against USSR, signs Anti-Comintern Pact
1938–1939	Renewed secret negotiations between Moscow and Berlin
1939	USSR-German nonaggression pact

Treaty of Brest-Litovsk—The treaty between the USSR and Germany signed in March 1918 in which peace was declared between the two countries and the USSR gave up more than a million square miles of land and more than 60 million people.

Third Communist International—The Comintern, organized in 1919, was an organization dedicated to the overthrow of capitalism.

EPOCH OF THE AGGRESSORS

- *Why did Great Britain, France, and the United States not take a more vigorous stand against Japanese, Italian, and German aggression before 1939?*

The awful toll taken by World War I convinced the democracies that never again should humanity have to endure such a tragedy. Multilateral efforts, especially the League of Nations, were made to prevent the kinds of alliances that were blamed for the inevitability of that war. By the mid-1930s, however, governments in Tokyo, Rome, and Berlin viewed multilateralism as weak and ineffective and saw the era as opportune for taking unilateral approaches to expansionism.

Japan Invades Manchuria, 1931

Throughout the 1920s, Japan's foreign policy was characterized by multilateral agreements and treaties. The Washington Conference system (see Chapter 29) tied Japan diplomatically to Western democracies. At the same time, close economic ties with those countries aided trade and economic growth. When, at the end of the 1920s, rogue members of the Japanese military stationed along the Japanese-owned railroad in Manchuria tried to implement their own foreign policy in opposition to what they called Tokyo's "weak-kneed" cooperation with the West, they failed to gain much support in Japan.

But the Great Depression discredited global multilateralism in the eyes of many in Japan, making the call for a Japanese-dominated economic sphere in northeast Asia and a unilateral approach to national security increasingly attractive in the 1930s. When another group of Japanese soldiers set off a bomb on the South Manchurian Railroad on September 18, 1931, Tokyo was thrust into conflict in Manchuria, triggering military action against Nationalist Chinese forces there. A Japanese puppet state was established in Manchuria in 1932. China appealed to the League of Nations, which condemned the aggression, but Japan's withdrawal from the League in 1933 indicated the limits of its ability to guarantee world peace. Some historians consider this the beginning of what they call "Japan's 15-year war."

In 1930 the Washington Conference system had taken a hit when the Japanese Prime Minister was assassinated for trying to continue the cooperative policy of reductions in naval buildup. Although Japan did not have the funds to begin building up its navy in the early 1930s, by the middle of the decade, the government felt released from the arms limitations negotiated in 1922 at Washington and 1930 at London.

There was, however, no unified point of view among Japan's leaders. Many government leaders were not interested in escalating continental expansion by military means, though they were firmly committed to increasing Japanese economic penetration of China in the 1920s and 1930s. The Japanese army focused on the Soviet Union as a potential threat, while navy leaders worried about the United States and England. Even on the eve of World War II, the army and navy took opposing points of view. Japan's business leaders desperately wanted to preserve trade ties with the West as well as with Asia, and American business interests were committed to supporting good relations with Japan even in the late 1930s when American church groups and others raised the alarm about brutal actions by the Japanese military in China. The Japanese Foreign Ministry in the 1930s claimed to be perplexed that the Western countries told Japan to roll back its imperialist attacks on Asia while failing to grant independence to their own colonies. The situation in East Asia did not seem to present itself in black and white terms at first.

One important link among Japanese, even those who wished to maintain multilateral ties, was an increasing belief that Japan would have to rely on its own resources for national security. And that, in turn, led to an acceptance, at first grudging and later more enthusiastic, of Japanese military expansionism.

The Chinese Nationalists responded to Japan's creation of the Manchurian puppet state by boycotts of Japanese goods. Shanghai, which had large settlements controlled by foreign forces, most notably England but also Japan and other treaty powers, staged a particularly effective boycott in 1932. The local Japanese commandant demanded an end to the boycott, and a small skirmish broke out between Chinese and Japanese troops. The commandant took this as an insult and retaliated by bombing Chinese troops in a congested urban area. Though the Tokyo government objected to these actions and did not escalate military

Aggression and Democratic Nonresponse, 1931–1938

1931	Japanese invade Manchuria
1932	Japanese attack Shanghai
1934–1935	Italians invade Ethiopia
1935	Remilitarization of the Rhineland by Germany
1936	Spanish General Francisco Franco rebels against the government of republican Spain
1937	Japanese begin full-scale war in China
1938	German *Anschluss* with Austria; dismemberment of Czechoslovakia in the wake of the Munich Accords

actions around Shanghai at that time, the United States and England expressed shock and Chinese nationalists became determined to drive the Japanese out of Shanghai.

At the same time, in North China, Japanese forces undertook much more aggressive action. The same forces based in Manchuria who had engineered the Manchurian Incident in 1931 decided they needed more security on the border with North China. They began a gradual but steady encroachment on Chinese territory in 1933. The Chinese Nationalist government at Nanjing, more concerned about consolidating its political control in China than about Japanese actions in the north, signed an agreement called the Tanggu (TONG-geu) truce establishing a demilitarized zone around Beijing and extending Japanese control to the Great Wall in May 1933. By 1935, Japanese forces in North China, hoping to create a buffer zone between the Nationalists and the Japanese state in Manchuria, pushed further into North China. Jiang Jieshi (ZHANG SHIE-shi), leader of the Nationalists, was preoccupied with the Communists, and did little to oppose the Japanese forces at first (see Chapter 29). Following the December 1936 truce between the Communists and Nationalists, China presented a united front. Jiang now joined the struggle against Japan.

In Japan, right-wing young officers had attempted to overthrow the Japanese government, which they viewed as too capitalistic, too liberal, too individualistic, and too modern. They staged a massive coup on February 26, 1936. Though these rebels were cut down by the Emperor's command that they return to their barracks as well as the training of the big guns of naval warships in Tokyo Bay on their positions, the real loser was the civilian government. After 1936, either military officers or defense-oriented civilians took over the reins of government in Tokyo. In June 1937, one of those civilians, Prince Konoe Fumimaro (fu-mee-mah-roh), became Prime Minister. When a small skirmish between Japanese and Chinese soldiers at Marco Polo Bridge in North China broke out on July 7, 1937, Konoe authorized full-scale war in August. Chinese bombers hit the Japanese settlement in Shanghai, and Japanese commanders swiftly retaliated, moving down the Yangzi River and reaching Nanjing by December 1937. The Japanese soldiers committed brutal carnage in Nanjing in the winter of 1937–1938 (see Chapter 29 on the Rape of Nanjing). Interestingly, the generals who had been the architects of the war in Manchuria were dismayed over the war in China, believing that Japan's national interests were best served by defending Korea, Manchuria, and North China against the Soviets. But Konoe did not agree. He declared that Japan would never negotiate with Jiang and the Nationalist Chinese government, and in November 1938, declared a "New Order in East Asia."

The New Order's objectives were to expel Western interests, defined as "Anglo-American imperialism," from East Asia and establish a self-sufficient economic bloc including Japan, Manchuria, and China, "have-not" nations that had been excluded from their place in the world by the West. Three years later, Konoe attempted to give concrete form to the "New Order" policy by proclaiming a **"Greater East Asia Co-Prosperity Sphere,"** a Japanese-dominated economic zone from which Japan could procure raw materials and markets for its industry and expanding population as well as for production of munitions. The "New Order in East Asia" had its domestic counterpart in

Greater East Asia Co-Prosperity Sphere—The projected Japanese-dominated colonial zone, most importantly including Manchuria and China, that would enable Japan to be self-sufficient economically.

An abandoned Chinese baby cries out during the Japanese attack on Nanjing.

policies to promote "national spiritual mobilization," an effort to get people to conserve energy and food and to reject decadent and wasteful habits like permanent waves and fancy kimono; the obliteration of independent unions, women's groups, and political parties and their replacement with government-run groups; and rationing and controls on scarce commodities.

As for foreign policy, Japan had few friends. The United States ended its long-time commercial treaty with Japan in 1939 to protest Japan's actions in China, setting the stage for U.S. embargoes first of iron and steel in the summer of 1940 and then of oil in the summer of 1941, following Japan's entry into southern Vietnam (with the assent of the Vichy French government). In 1936, Japan had signed its first treaty with Nazi Germany, the Anti-Comintern Pact. This was followed by a brief war against the Soviets in 1939; the **Tripartite Pact** (with Germany and Italy) against the United States in September 1940; and a neutrality pact with the Soviets in April 1941. The German invasion of the Soviet Union did more to relieve Japan of its fear of the Russians than the neutrality pact, and Japan then moved troops into southern Vietnam in preparation for operations against the Dutch East Indies (Indonesia). Dependent on U.S. oil, Japan had two options in the summer of 1941—give in to America's conditions for negotiating a return of oil shipments, which meant abandoning all the gains on the continent, or invade the oil-rich Dutch East Indies.

Italian forces occupying Ethiopia at the beginning of World War II. Rome's investment in African conquest produced negligible returns.

Italy Attacks Ethiopia

While Japan pursued continental expansionism, Italy set out to claim a prize it had failed to take in 1896—Ethiopia, one of only two independent states left in Africa. Late in 1934, fighting broke out between the Ethiopians and the Italians, and in the following year, Mussolini's forces invaded the country. Emperor Haile Selassie made a dramatic appearance before the League to appeal for help. Before he could speak, however, he had to endure the catcalls and whistles of the Italian journalists in the hall.

The League tried to arrange for arbitration. Unconvinced by the shameless Italian argument that Ethiopia, not Italy, was the aggressor, the League voted to prohibit shipment of certain goods to Italy and to deny it credit. But the effect of the sanctions was minor because oil—without which no modern army could fight—was not included in the list of prohibited articles. France and Britain gave only lukewarm support to the sanctions because they did not want to alienate Italy. The United States, which had not joined the League, and Germany, which had left it by that time, largely ignored the prohibitions. Only outraged public opinion, moved by newspaper photographs showing barefooted Ethiopians fighting the modern Italian army, drove the governments to even the pretense of action.

Using bombs, mustard gas, and tanks, the Italians advanced swiftly into Ethiopia and crushed Haile Selassie's army. Meanwhile, the German reoccupation of the Rhineland in March helped shift international attention away from the conflict in Africa. The whole sorry story ended in July 1936 when sanctions were removed. Haile Selassie, an emperor without a country, went to live in Britain, the first of several royal exiles who would be forced from their thrones in the next decade.

The Rhineland and the Axis

Soon after taking power, Hitler carried out the revisions the Germans wanted in the Versailles Treaty. He also won his country's support by seeking revenge against the Allies. As George F. Kennan noted at the time, "The man is acting in the best traditions of German nationalism, and his conception of his own mission is perhaps clearer than that of his predecessors because it is uncomplicated by any sense of responsibility to European culture as a whole."[1] During his first two years in

Tripartite Pact—The agreement Japan signed with Germany and Italy in 1940 against the United States.

power, Hitler paid lip service to peace while increasing the tempo of rearmament. In March 1935 he negated the disarmament clauses of the Versailles treaty and a year later reoccupied the Rhineland.

The move, which Hitler described as producing the most nerve-racking moments of his life, sent German troops marching boldly into the Rhineland in defiance of the Versailles treaty and the Locarno agreements. The Germans could not have resisted had the British and French moved in response. But London did nothing, and Paris mobilized 150,000 troops behind the **Maginot** (MAZH-ee-noh) **line** but did no more. Hitler later confessed that had the French advanced against him, "We would have had to withdraw with our tails between our legs, for the military resources at our disposal would have been totally inadequate for even a moderate resistance."[2]

The League's weak response to the Japanese invasion of China and the Italian attack on Ethiopia, combined with the feeble British and French reaction to German reoccupation of the Rhineland, encouraged the aggressors and served as a prelude to the formation of the Axis alliance. Until Hitler gained power, Germany had been without close allies. After the Ethiopian crisis and the League sanctions, Italy and Germany began to work more closely together. In 1936 they formalized the friendship in the Rome-Berlin Axis, and one year later, Mussolini followed Hitler's lead by withdrawing from the League of Nations.

Japan, the third major member of the Axis, joined forces with Germany in 1936 in the Anti-Comintern Pact. A year later, Italy also joined in that agreement, which effectively encircled the Soviet Union. Relations between Moscow and Berlin had cooled after 1934, and the Soviet Union now became the object of anticommunist rhetoric. Many right-wing leaders in the West hoped that the "Red menace" would be taken care of by Hitler and his allies.

All in all, 1936 was a banner year for Hitler. He had gained allies, pleased his own people by remilitarizing the Rhineland, learned the weakness of the democratic powers and the League, and gained international prestige from his successful staging of the Olympic Games. He also found a successful device to distract potential opponents' attention: the Spanish Civil War.

The Spanish Tragedy

By 1936 the five-year-old Spanish republic was disintegrating. It had brought neither prosperity nor stability to Spain. Reactionary forces had tried to gain control of the government while left-wing groups had resorted to terrorism. The liberal approach had failed, and in the summer of 1936, the army revolted against the legal government in Madrid.

General Francisco Franco (1892–1975) commanded the insurgents, who included in their ranks most of the regular army troops. Mussolini strongly backed Franco, and the rightist forces expected a quick victory. many groups, however, stood by the republic, and they put up a strong resistance against the insurgents, stopping them at the outskirts of Madrid.

By the end of 1936, each side had gained the backing of a complicated alliance of forces. Franco had the support of the Italians, who sent large numbers of planes, troops, and weapons, and the Germans, who tested their latest military technology against the republicans. The republic gained the support of the Soviet Union, which sent arms, "advisers," and other supplies, as well as a large contingent of disorganized but idealistic antifascist fighters, including a number from Britain and the United States.

The insurgents capitalized on Soviet support for the republic, and Franco pronounced his cause to be strictly an anticommunist crusade—a cunning oversimplification of dubious validity, considering that the communists were never in control of more than a snippet of republican Spain, and that for only a few months in 1938 until Stalin decided to pull his support. While Spain bled, suffering more than 700,000 deaths, outside forces took advantage of the tragic situation for their own selfish purposes.

The democratic powers—Great Britain, France, and the United States—attempted to stay out of the conflict. Britain did not want to risk a Continental war. France suffered from internal divisions that made its leaders fear that their country, too, might dissolve in civil war. The United States declared its official neutrality. Instead of permitting arms to be sent to the recognized, legally constituted republican government, which had the right under international law to purchase weapons for self-defense, Britain and France set up a nonintervention system by which the nations of Europe agreed not to send arms to either side. Only the democracies adhered to this arrangement, which was meant to limit the scope of the conflict. The various dictators continued to send support to their respective sides.

After the last holdout, Barcelona, fell in March 1939, the Spanish republic was no more. Franco, at the head of the new state, gained absolute power, which he held until his death in 1975. The Spanish Civil War was a national catastrophe that left permanent scars on the country's people.

Appeasement

In 1937 Neville Chamberlain (1869–1940) became Britain's prime minister. Years before he took office,

Maginot line—A supposedly impenetrable line of fortresses constructed by France along its eastern frontier between Switzerland and Belgium in the 1920s.

the British had tried to achieve **détente** with the Germans, backed by an air force which concentrated its resources on bombers. Chamberlain tried a new strategy: a defense policy based on a fighter air force and centered solely on protecting Britain. He wanted to reassure Germany, acknowledge her legitimate complaints, and reach the settlement of outstanding issues peacefully by recognizing mutual interests and establishing well-defined spheres of influence. Chamberlain's name came to symbolize the policy of **appeasement,** the policy of meeting German demands and grievances without demanding firm reciprocal advantages and asking instead only for future "mutual understandings."

Chamberlain took the direction of foreign policy on his own shoulders in his attempt to explore every possibility for reaching an understanding with the dictators. He dedicated himself to an effort to ease international tensions despite snubs from those he wished to placate and warnings from his military and foreign policy advisers. He based his policy on the most humane of motives—peace—and on the most civilized of assumptions—that Hitler could be reasonable and fair-minded. By showing good faith and by withdrawing from any possibility of being able to wage war on the Continent, Chamberlain froze himself into a position of having to avoid war at any cost. His policies were strongly supported in Britain and throughout most of the British Commonwealth.

France had shown that it would not move militarily without British backing, and under Chamberlain, the entente with France was put on the back burner, a development that hurt French resolve. The democratic world became uneasily aware of its growing weakness in comparison with the dictators. As the European balance of power shifted, the small states began to draw away from the impotent League of Nations.

The prestige of the Axis blossomed. Some nations tried to make deals with Germany and Italy, while others, including the Scandinavian countries and the Netherlands, withdrew into the shelter of neutrality and "innocent isolation." In eastern Europe, semifascist regimes became the order of the day, as the states in that unhappy region lined up to get in Germany's good graces. In 1934 Poland had signed a nonaggression pact with Germany. Belgium gave up its alliance with France. In eastern Europe, only Czechoslovakia remained loyal to Paris.

Hitler became increasingly aware of the opportunity presented by Britain's "peace at any price" policy and the decline of the French alliance system. On November 5, 1937, in a meeting at the Reich Chancellery in Berlin that lasted for more than four hours, Hitler laid out his plans and ideas for the future. According to the notes of the meeting taken by Colonel Friedrich Hossbach, the Führer gave a statement that was to be regarded "in the event of his death, as his last will and testament."

"The aim of German policy," Hitler stated, "was to make secure and to preserve the racial community and to enlarge it. It was therefore a question of space. Germany's future was wholly conditional upon the need for space." The answer to that question was force, which was to be applied in the next six years, because, after 1943, German technological and military superiority would be lost. Hossbach noted that "the Führer believed that almost certainly Britain, and probably France as well, had already tacitly written off the Czechs."[3]

Historians still debate the importance of the Chancellery meeting. Hitler's message was not favorably received by the military staff present, since they knew full well that Germany was in no shape to fight. Yet the significance of the message can be found in the wholesale changes in personnel Hitler introduced at the end of 1937 and in the contrast it affords to the views of Chamberlain. The prime minister wanted peace at any price. The Führer wanted space at any price.

Toward Austria and the Sudetenland

When Hitler announced the military reoccupation of the Rhineland in the spring of 1936, he stated, "We have no territorial demands to make in Europe." He lied. By 1938, with the German army growing in strength and the air force becoming a powerful unit, the Führer began to implement one of his foreign policy goals—placing the German-speaking peoples under one Reich. The first step on that path was to unite Austria and Germany in the ***Anschluss*** (ON-schleus; "joining").

In 1934 the Nazis had badly bungled an attempt to annex Austria. Two years later, softening-up operations began again, and by 1938, intense pressure had been levied against Austrian chancellor Kurt von Schuschnigg to cooperate with Berlin. After a stormy meeting with Hitler in February, Schuschnigg restated his country's desire to be independent, although concessions would be made to Germany. He called for a plebiscite in March to prove his point. Outraged at this independent action, Hitler ordered Schuschnigg to resign and to cancel the vote. Both actions were taken, but Hitler sent his forces into Austria anyway.

---

détente—A state of reduced tensions between two countries.

appeasement—The policy of meeting German demands and grievances without demanding firm reciprocal advantages and asking instead only for future "mutual understandings."

Anschluss—The German word for "joining."

Document The Hossbach Memorandum

Two years before the outbreak of World War II, Adolf Hitler recapitulated his goals in a secret meeting. Colonel Friedrich Hossbach took down Hitler's comments.

The aim of German policy was to make secure and to preserve the racial community and to enlarge it. It was therefore a question of space.

The German racial community comprised over 85 million people and, because of their number and the narrow limits of habitable space in Europe, constituted a tightly packed racial core such as was not to be met in any other country and such as implied the right to a greater living space than in the case of other peoples. . . .

Germany's future was therefore wholly conditional upon the solving of the need for space, and such a solution could be sought, of course, only for a foreseeable period of about one to three generations. . . .

The question for Germany ran: where could she achieve the greatest gain at the lowest cost? . . .

Case 1: Period 1943–1945

After this date only a change for the worse, from our point of view, could be expected.

The equipment of the army, navy, and *Luftwaffe*, as well as the formation of the officer corps, was nearly completed. Equipment and armament were modern; in further delay there lay the danger of their obsolescence. In particular, the secrecy of "special weapons" could not be preserved forever. The recruiting of reserves was limited to current age groups; further drafts from older untrained age groups were no longer available.

Our relative strength would decrease in relation to the rearmament which would by then have been carried out by the rest of the world. If we did not act by 1943–45, any year could, in consequence of a lack of reserves, produce the food crisis, to cope with which the necessary foreign exchange was not available, and this must be regarded as a "waning point of the regime." Besides, the world was expecting our attack and was increasing its counter-measures from year to year. It was while the rest of the world was still preparing its defenses that we were obliged to take the offensive. . . .

Case 2

If internal strife in France should develop into such a domestic crisis as to absorb the French Army completely and render it incapable of use for war against Germany, then the time for action against the Czechs had come.

Case 3

If France is so embroiled by a war with another state that she cannot "proceed" against Germany.

For the improvement of our politico-military position our first objective, in the event of our being embroiled in war, must be to overthrow Czechoslovakia and Austria simultaneously in order to remove the threat to our flank in any possible operation against the West. In a conflict with France it was hardly to be regarded as likely that the Czechs would declare war on us on the very same day as France. The desire to join in the war would, however, increase among the Czechs in proportion to any weakening on our part and then her participation could clearly take the form of an attack toward Silesia, toward the north or toward the west. . . .

The Führer saw case 3 coming definitely nearer; it might emerge from the present tensions in the Mediterranean, and he was resolved to take advantage of it whenever it happened, even as early as 1938.

Questions to Consider

1. When Hitler spoke of the "racial community," to what is he referring?
2. Why did Hitler want to move against the Czechs?
3. What was the single most important goal for Hitler, in his defense of the "racial community"?

From *Auswärtiges Amt: Documents on German Foreign Policy,* Series D, Vol. 1 (Washington, D.C.: U.S. Government Printing Office, 1949), pp. 29–49.

By March 13, 1938, a new chancellor, approved by Hitler, announced the union of Austria and Germany. After a month in which all opposition was silenced, Hitler held his own plebiscite and gained a majority of 99.75 percent in favor of union. The democratic powers did not intervene to help Austria. In fact, the British ambassador to Germany voiced no opposition to the annexation of Austria, as long as it was done in a peaceful manner.[4]

Following his success in Austria, Hitler moved on to his next objective, the annexation of the Sudetenland. This area along the western border of Czechoslovakia was populated mainly by German textile workers who had suffered economically during the depression. The Sudetenland was also the site of the extremely well-fortified Czech defenses. In September 1938 the Führer bluntly informed Chamberlain that he was determined to gain self-determination for the Sudeten Germans. He charged, falsely, that the Czechs had mistreated the German minorities. In fact, among the eastern European states, Czechoslovakia had the best record in dealing with minority nationalities. But in this affair, Britain and France consistently overlooked both the record of the Prague government and the Czech statesmen themselves.

Chamberlain persuaded French premier Édouard Daladier (da-LAD-dee-ay) that the sacrifice of Czechoslovakia would save the peace. When the French joined the British to press the Czechs to accept the Nazi demands, the Prague government had little choice but to agree. Chamberlain informed Hitler of Czechs' willingness to compromise, only to find that the German demands had increased considerably. Angered by the Führer's duplicity, Chamberlain refused to accept the new terms, which included Czech evacuation of some areas and the cession of large amounts of matériel and agricultural goods.

Munich and Democratic Betrayal

The crisis over Czechoslovakia would be the last major international issue decided only by European powers. Symbolically, it would be viewed as a failure that would affect diplomatic decisions for generations to come. On September 28, 1938, Chamberlain received a note from Hitler inviting him to attend a conference at Munich. The following day, Chamberlain flew to Germany to meet with Hitler, Mussolini, and Daladier at Nazi headquarters. They worked for 13 hours on the details of the surrender of the Sudetenland. No Czech representative was present, nor were the Soviets—outspoken allies of the Czechs—consulted.

The **Munich Conference** accepted all of Hitler's demands and, in addition, rewarded Poland and Hungary with slices of unfortunate Czechoslovakia. The tragedy for the Czechs brought relief for millions of Europeans, half-crazed with fear of war. But thoughtful individuals pondered whether this settlement would be followed by another crisis. Winston Churchill, who

Munich Conference—Conference in Munich on September 28 including Germany, Italy, France, and the United Kingdom in which the Western Allies agreed to Hitler's demands on the surrender of the Sudetenland.

At the Munich Conference in September 1938, British prime minister Neville Chamberlain (left) and French premier Édouard Daladier (next to him) capitulated to Hitler's demands regarding Czechoslovakia. Italian dictator Benito Mussolini stands to the right of Hitler.

was then in political eclipse in Britain, solemnly warned: "Do not suppose that this is the end. This is only the beginning of the reckoning."[5]

The mounting fears of French and British statesmen were confirmed in 1939. Deprived of its military perimeter, the Czech government stood unprotected against the Nazi pressure that came in March. Hitler summoned Czech president Emil Hacha to Berlin. Subjected to all kinds of threats during an all-night session, Hacha finally capitulated and signed a document placing his country under the "protection" of Germany. His signature was a mere formality, however, for German troops were already crossing the Czech frontier. Not to be outdone, Mussolini seized Albania the following month. The two dictators then celebrated by signing a military alliance, the so-called Pact of Steel.

In response to the taking of Czechoslovakia and violation of the Munich pledges, Great Britain ended its appeasement policy and, for the first time in its history, authorized a peacetime draft. In Paris, Daladier gained special emergency powers to push forward national defense.

In the United States, isolationism reigned supreme. Between 1935 and 1937, in response to feelings of revulsion stemming from World War I, the U.S. Congress passed neutrality acts that made it unlawful for any nation at war to obtain munitions from the United States. At the same time, in response to events in Ethiopia, in Spain, and along the Rhine, President Franklin D. Roosevelt and the State Department worked quietly to alert the American people to the dangers of the world situation. In October 1937, Roosevelt pointed out that "the peace, the freedom, and the security of 90 percent of the population of the world is being jeopardized by the remaining 10 percent who are threatening a breakdown of all international order and law."[6] The president's call, in this so-called quarantine speech, for positive endeavors to preserve peace brought forth a hostile reaction from the press and public. Two years later Roosevelt told political leaders that the Germans and Italians could win the next war. His warnings went unheeded, as a significant portion of the American public hoped that the Nazis could do away with the Communists in the Soviet Union.

The Nazi-Soviet Pact

The final step on the road to World War II was Germany's attack on Poland. The Treaty of Versailles had turned over West Prussia to Poland as a corridor to the sea. Though 90 percent of the corridor's population was Polish, the Baltic city of Danzig—a free city under a League of Nations high commissioner—was nearly all German. Late in March 1939, Hitler proposed to Poland that Danzig be ceded to Germany and that the Nazis be allowed to occupy the narrow strip of land connecting Germany with East Prussia. Chamberlain, with French concurrence, warned the Nazis that "in the event of any action that clearly threatens Polish independence," the British would "at once lend the Polish government all support in their power." This was an essentially symbolic gesture, since Poland's location made any useful Western aid impossible.

In the months that followed the Allied warnings, France and Britain competed with Germany for an alliance with Russia. Stalin had closely observed the actions of the democratic powers since Hitler's rise to power. He was aware of the hope expressed in some Western conservative circles that Hitler might effectively put an end to the Soviet regime. Further, he pledged to stay out of a war between "imperialists." He had to make a closely reasoned choice between the two sets of suitors competing for Soviet partnership.

Chamberlain and Daladier had ignored Moscow at Munich, and, generally, British relations with the Communists were quite cool. Now, with the Polish question of paramount importance, the French and British approaches appeared optimistic to Stalin. In May, Vyacheslav Molotov became the Soviet foreign minister. While Molotov negotiated publicly with the British and French, who sent negotiators not empowered to make agreements, he was also in secret contact with the highest levels in Berlin.

For centuries, Germany and Russia had shared a concern over the fate of Poland. They had been able to reach agreement at Poland's expense in the eighteenth and nineteenth centuries. From late 1938 on, Moscow and Berlin pondered yet another division of the country. Negotiations between the two proceeded intensely from June through August 1939. While top-ranking German and Soviet diplomats flew between the two capitals, the lower-ranking mission sent to Moscow by Britain traveled leisurely by boat.

By 1939 Stalin had to choose wisely between the Western democracies, with their spotty record of defending their friends, and Nazi Germany, which could offer him concrete advantages in eastern Europe. On August 21, to the world's great amazement, the Soviet Union and Germany signed a **nonaggression pact.**

In retrospect, it is not at all surprising that Stalin chose to work with the Nazis. Through this agreement, Stalin gave Hitler a free hand in Poland and the assurance of not having to fight a two-front war. After the British and French guarantees to the Poles in March, Hitler knew that his attack on Poland would precipitate a general European war. The Führer had

Nazi-Soviet Nonaggression Pact—Diplomatic agreement in which the USSR and Germany agreed not to take up arms against each other.

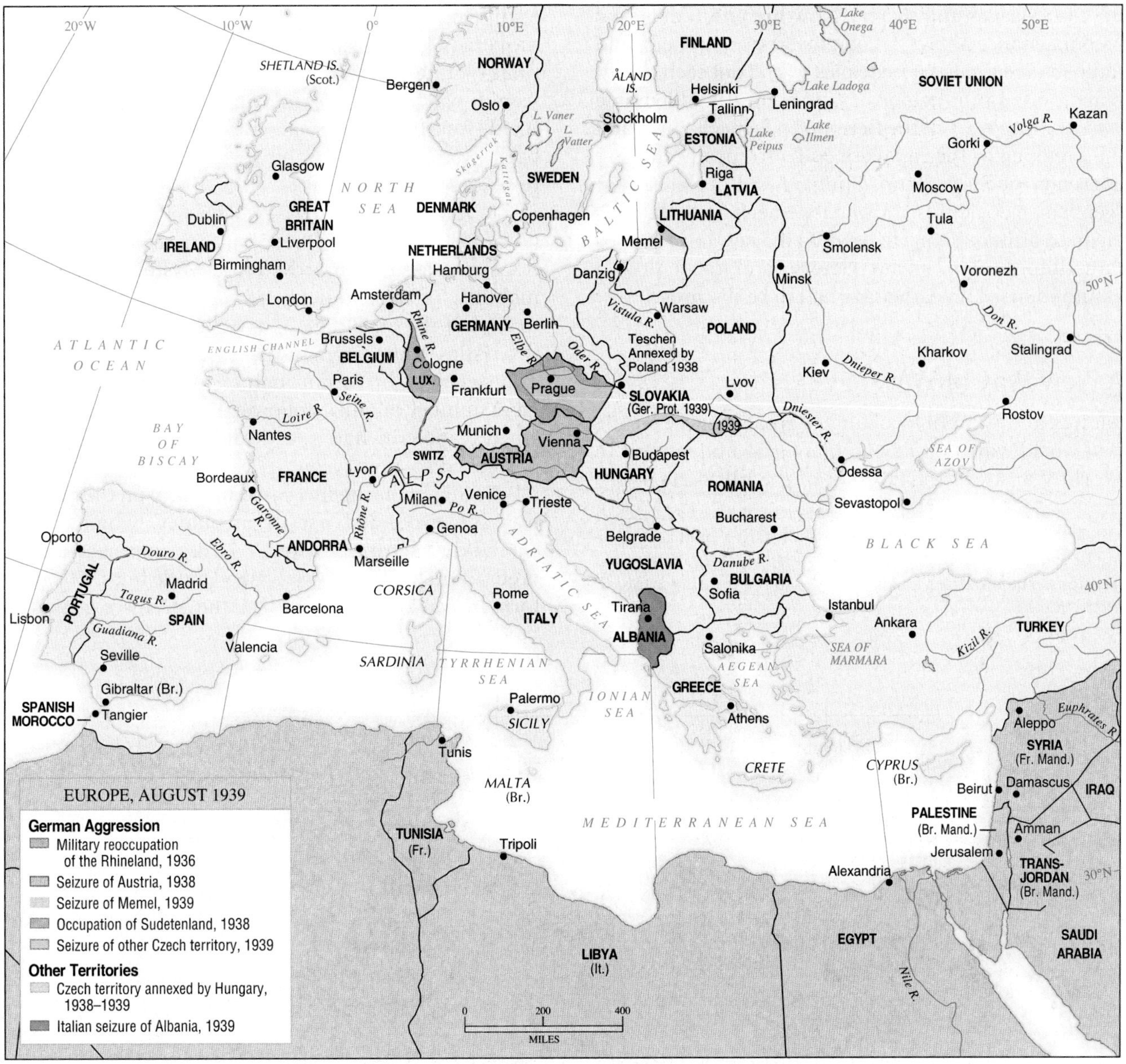

The extent of Hitler's gains in expanding German hegemony by 1939 can be seen here. By using less violence than Bismarck, he took advantage of Allied weakness to become more successful than the old chancellor.

prepared plans that called for the invasion to begin in August 1939, and thanks to the nonaggression pact, Hitler could attack without fear of Moscow's intervention. Furthermore, he did not believe that Britain and France would dare oppose him.

The nonaggression pact gave the Soviets time to build up strength while the imperialists weakened themselves in war. In addition, the USSR was secretly promised Finland, Estonia, Latvia, eastern Poland, and Bessarabia (the region principally to be found in present-day Moldova). Germany would get everything to the west, including Lithuania. The Nazis also got guarantees of valuable raw materials and grain from the Soviets. Ideological differences could be set aside for such a mutually profitable pact.

WORLD WAR II

▪ *Why did the Axis powers lose World War II?*

When Nazi forces crossed the Polish border early on the morning of September 1, 1939, they set off the European portion of World War II, the conflict that killed more people more efficiently than any previous war. In all areas the latest scientific and technological advances were placed in the service of a new kind of war that killed civilians as well as soldiers and sailors. New techniques and attitudes revolutionized the field of intelligence. Scientists made major advances in both codemaking and codebreaking. Intelligence-gathering no longer depended on the old cloak-and-dagger stealing of messages and secrets. Now high-altitude aerial reconnaissance aircraft, radar, the first computers, and radio intercepts allowed enemies to find out each other's plans. Among the major advances on the Allied side were the discovery of the German code mechanism and the breaking of the Japanese code. Ironically, in 1929 Secretary of State Henry Stimson had declared that "gentlemen do not read other gentlemen's mail," but this civilized attitude soon changed. In the new style of warfare, information meant victory, and the cultured assumptions of an earlier age had to be discarded.

A New Way of War

Tactics and weaponry changed greatly between the two world wars. Tanks and planes had been used in World War I, but the concept of the **blitzkrieg**—literally "lightning war," massive mobile mechanized movements and saturation bombings behind the lines—made the weapons far more lethal. The trench warfare of World War I and the concept of fixed, fortified positions, such as the Maginot line built by the French in the 1920s and 1930s, proved to be useless.

Mobility was the key—even more so than superior numbers of men and weapons. Better communications, provided by improved radio systems, increased mobility. To strike quickly, with great force, and then to exploit the advantage proved to be the main characteristics of the German successes in 1939 and 1940. The Germans broke through enemy lines by using a large number of tanks, followed by the infantry. Rarely since Napoleon had speed and concentrated force been used so effectively.

Complementing increased mobility on the ground was the expanded use of airplanes, which could spread devastating firepower across continents, hundreds of miles behind established battle lines. The new forms of war, however, sparked the inventive genius of

blitzkrieg—Literally "lightning war," the blitzkrieg emphasized the use of rapid mechanized mobility to overwhelm dug-in, fortified positions. The blitzkrieg was a response to the trench warfare of World War I.

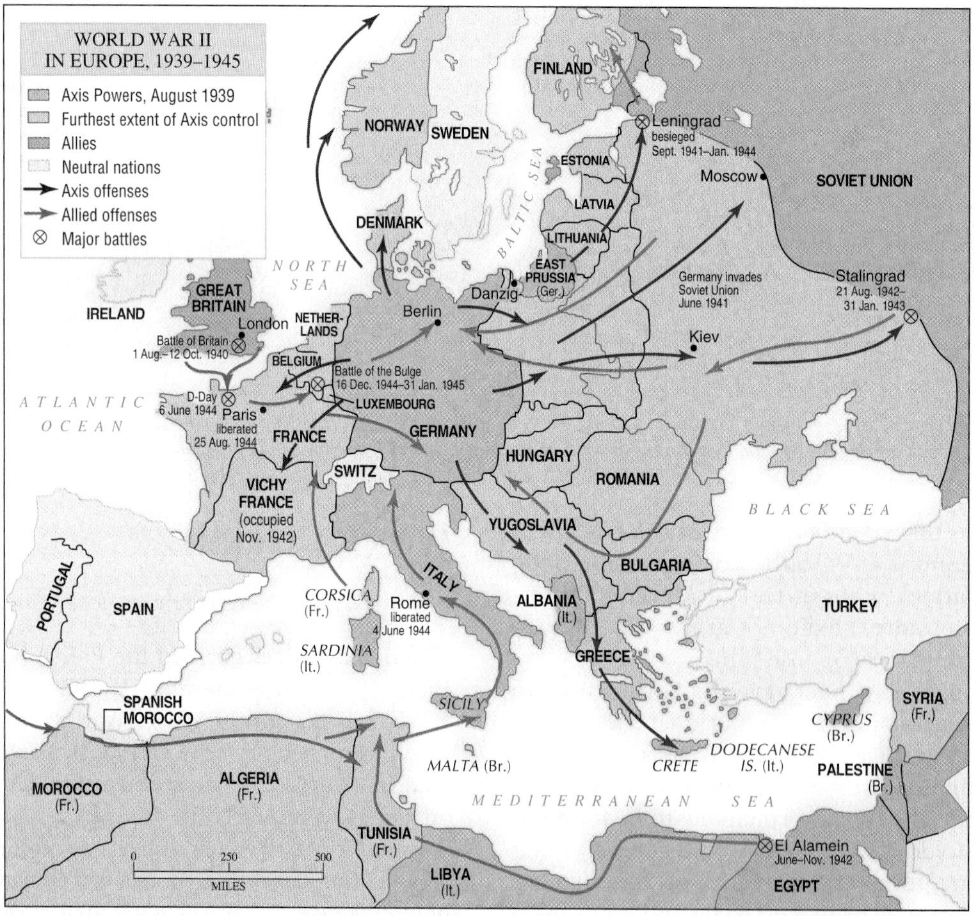

Aided by the Nazi-Soviet pact of August 1939, which allowed them to concentrate their fighting on a single front, the Germans, in one of the most successful military campaigns in history, ripped through the Low Countries and France. The Maginot line of defense constructed by the French proved totally useless.

the scientists as each technological advance elicited a response—long-range German bombers brought the need for improved radar; improved propeller-driven aircraft set off the development of jet-powered airplanes. No matter how sophisticated the aerial technology became, however, the war proved that, with the exception of nuclear weapons, air power alone could not bring an enemy to its knees.

Other innovations appeared during the war—paratroopers, advanced landing crafts, and the German flying bombs such as the V–1 and rockets such as the V–2. Aircraft carriers and amphibious forces played an important part in the war in the Pacific. The Japanese used carriers in their attack on Pearl Harbor, and the Americans used amphibious forces in "island hopping" across the Pacific.

As in World War I, however, military success lay in the ability of the states to mobilize their populations and resources. During World War II, governments came to control all aspects of life. But the final, deciding factor was the ability of the individual soldier, following the directions of such brilliant commanders as Rommel or Eisenhower, to apply all of these resources. In the end, all of these factors were overwhelmed by the ultimate scientific and technological accomplishment, the atomic bomb. Ironically, although created to protect state interests, this ultimate weapon could destroy civilization.

Blitzkrieg and *Sitzkrieg*

After staging an "incident" on the morning of September 1, 1939, Nazi troops crossed the Polish frontier without a declaration of war, using the new tactics of the blitzkrieg. At the same time, the German *Luftwaffe* (air force) began to bomb Polish cities. On the morning of September 3, Chamberlain sent an ultimatum to Germany demanding that the invasion be halted. The time limit was given as 11:00 A.M. the same day. At 11:15 Chamberlain announced in a radio broadcast that Britain was now at war. France also soon declared war. After 21 years, Europe was once again immersed in war.

The world now had the chance to see the awesome speed and power of Nazi arms. The Polish forces collapsed, crushed between the German advance from the west and, two weeks later, a Soviet invasion from the east. By the end of the month, after a brave but hopeless resistance, the Poles once again saw their country partitioned between the Germans and the Russians.

Britain and France did not try to breach Germany's western defensive line, the Siegfried line along the Rhine. With their blockade and mastery of the seas, they hoped to defeat Hitler by attrition. During the winter of 1939–1940, there was little fighting along the Franco-German frontier. The lull in action came to be referred to as the phony war, or *Sitzkrieg*.

The Soviets took advantage of the lull to attack Finland in November. This campaign revealed, to Moscow's embarrassment, the Finns' toughness and the Soviet Union's military unpreparedness in the wake of recent purges. After an unexpectedly difficult four-month-long campaign, the immense Soviet Union forced tiny Finland to cede substantial amounts of territory.

"Blood, Toil, Tears, and Sweat"

In the spring of 1940, the Nazi high command launched its attack on western Europe. In its scope, complexity, and accomplishments it was one of the most successful military campaigns ever carried out. In April, Nazi forces invaded Norway and Denmark. The Norwegians fought back fiercely for three weeks before being vanquished, and Denmark was taken in even less time. In the second week of May, the German armies overran the neutral Netherlands, Belgium, and Luxembourg. The next week they went into northern France all the way to the English Channel. In the process, they trapped an Anglo-French army of nearly 400,000 on the beach at Dunkirk.

The reversals in Norway and the Low Countries and the military crisis in France led to Chamberlain's resignation. Winston Churchill (1874–1965) became prime minister of Great Britain. Churchill had had uneven success in both his political and military careers. In the 1930s, his warnings against Hitler and Mussolini had been largely ignored. He was viewed as a "might-have-been; a potentially great man flawed by flashiness, irresponsibility, unreliability, and inconsistency."[7] Yet in 1940, at the age of 66, Churchill offered qualities of leadership equal to the nation's peril. For the next five years, he was the voice and symbol of a defiant and indomitable Britain.

Facing the prospect of the destruction of the British army at Dunkirk, Churchill refused to be publicly dismayed. Appearing before Parliament as the new prime minister, he announced, "I have nothing to offer but blood, toil, tears, and sweat." He prepared his people for a long and desperate conflict, knowing full well that only the Channel, a thin screen of fighter aircraft, and an untried device called radar protected Britain. Churchill's example inspired his people. Hitler had found his match in the area of charismatic leadership.

Hitler hesitated to quash the forces trapped at Dunkirk, thereby allowing time for hundreds of small craft protected by the Royal Air Force to evacuate across the Channel 335,000 soldiers, including more than 100,000 French troops. Military leaders had hoped that they might be able to save 30,000 of the trapped men; now they had 11 times that number. An army had been saved, though it had lost all of its heavy equipment.

After Dunkirk, the fall of France was inevitable. Eager to be in on the kill, Mussolini declared war on France on June 10. Designated as an open city by the French in order to spare its destruction, Paris fell on June 14. As the German advance continued, the members of the French government who wanted to continue resistance were voted down. Marshal Philippe Pétain (PAY-tan; 1856–1951), the 84-year-old hero of Verdun in World War I, became premier. He immediately asked Hitler for an armistice, and in the same dining car in which the French had imposed armistice terms on the Germans in 1918, the Nazis and French on June 22, 1940, signed another peace agreement. The Germans had gained revenge for their shame in 1918.

France was split into two zones, occupied and unoccupied. In unoccupied France, Pétain's government at Vichy was supposedly free from interference, but in reality, it became a puppet of the Nazis. The Third Republic, created in 1871 from the debris of defeat suffered at Germany's hands, now came to an end with a blow from the same country.

A remarkable patriot, Brigadier-General Charles de Gaulle (1890–1970), fled to London and organized the Free French Government, which adopted as its symbol the red cross of Lorraine, flown by Joan of Arc in her fight to liberate France five centuries earlier. De Gaulle worked to keep alive the idea of France as a great power and continued to aid the Allied cause in his sometimes quixotic way throughout the war.

Only Britain remained in opposition to Hitler, and the odds against the British seemed overwhelming. The Nazis planned a cross-Channel assault, while in Buckingham Palace, the queen took pistol lessons, saying, "I shall not go down like the others."[8] All Britain had to pin its hopes on was its navy, an army whose best equipment was still at Dunkirk, radar, and fast fighter aircraft flown by brave pilots. Churchill's eloquence inspired his people:

> *We shall go on to the end. . . . We shall defend our island, whatever the cost may be, we shall fight on the beaches, we shall fight on the landing grounds, we shall fight in the fields and in the streets, we shall fight in the hills; we shall never surrender.*[9]

The Germans sent an average of 200 bombers over London every night for nearly two months in the summer and fall of 1940. They suffered heavy losses to the Royal Air Force, which profited from a combination of superior aircraft, pilots, radar sightings, and visual detection. Yet all through the fall and winter of 1940–1941, Britain continued to be racked by terrible raids. Night bombing destroyed block after block of British cities. Evacuating their children and old people to the north, going to work by day and sleeping in air raid shelters and underground stations at night, Britain's people stood firm—proof that bombing civilians would not break their will.

Beginning in the summer of 1940, German bombers struck indiscriminately at England. This Nazi aerial photo shows a bomber over the Thames River in London.

Mastery of Europe

During the fall and winter of 1940–1941, Hitler strengthened his position in the Balkans, but not without some difficulty. By March 1941, Hungary, Bulgaria, and

St. Paul's Cathedral, glimpsed through the smoke and fire in the aftermath of a German bombing raid over London, December 31, 1940.

Romania had joined the Axis. Hitler had to control the Hungarians and Bulgarians, who were pursuing ancient ambitions for Romanian land. In the process, Romania lost a third of its population and territory to its two neighbors. The Romanians emerged, however, as helpful allies for the Germans, and Marshal Ion Antonescu became Hitler's favorite foreign general.

Mussolini, eager to gain some glory for his forces, invaded neutral Greece in October 1940. This thrust proved a costly failure when, in December, the Greeks successfully counterattacked. The Italians met other defeats in North Africa and Ethiopia, which the British recaptured.

Partly in an attempt to pull Mussolini out of a humiliating position, the Germans, in the first four months of 1941, overran Yugoslavia and Greece. Two months of intense aerial and infantry attacks were needed to defeat the Yugoslavs and Greeks, forcing Hitler to spend considerable amounts of men and resources. But when the job was done, the Führer had secured his right flank prior to his invasion of the Soviet Union, an event for which he had prepared during the previous year.

The results of these forays into the Balkans may have been positive for the Axis in the short run. But by going into the Balkans, Hitler delayed his attack on the Soviets by six to eight weeks. This delay, in addition to inadequate intelligence and bad planning, may have cost him victory on the eastern front. The Germans and the Italians also controlled only the major cities of Yugoslavia. Large bands of resistance fighters and partisans roamed the area, among them Communist forces led by Josip Tito. Hitler had to leave behind German troops formerly committed to the Soviet invasion and replace them with less effective Bulgarian and Hungarian forces.

By the spring of 1941, nearly all of Europe had come under German control. Only Portugal, Switzerland, Sweden, Ireland, Spain, and Turkey remained neutral. For the Swiss, Swedes, and Spaniards, this was a strange kind of neutrality. The Swiss played an important role as "Germany's central banker." Swiss banks absorbed the accounts of Jews who were in the concentration camps, handled transfers of German looted gold—some of which was gold later melted down from the fillings of the death camp inmates—

and financed German purchases of goods from neutral countries. The Swedes permitted German troops to cross their territory for the attack on the USSR, allowed the Germans to use their railroad system, and used their navy to provide escort services for German supply ships. After the German ball-bearing factories were knocked out by Allied aircraft, replacements for that all-important commodity were found in Sweden. Spain under Franco was pro-Nazi, sending 40,000 "volunteers" to fight on the eastern front. Not all the neutrals were as blatant as the Swedes or the Swiss or as pro-German as Franco. The true neutrals were trapped in a difficult position and made the best of their situation. The others profiteered and probably prolonged the war by their activities.[10]

War with the Soviet Union

Hitler and Stalin had signed the nonaggression pact for their own specific, short-term advantages. From the first, there was tension and mistrust between the two, and neither side had any illusions about a long-lasting friendship. Stalin had hoped for a much more difficult war in the west among the "imperialists" and had not expected that Hitler would so quickly become the master of Europe.

As early as July 1940, Hitler resolved to attack the Soviets in an operation code-named *Barbarossa*. In the fall of the year, he decided not to invade Britain but instead to pursue his original goal of obtaining *Lebensraum* ("living space") and resources. During 1941, British and American intelligence experts told Stalin of Hitler's intentions to attack, but the Soviet dictator clung to his obligations under the nonaggression pact. Even while the Nazis were invading in June 1941, shipments of Soviet grain were headed to Germany.

Operation Barbarossa required an enormous amount of effort and resources. Along a battlefront 1800 miles long, 9 million men became locked in struggle. At the outset, the Nazi tank units were unstoppable as they killed or captured enormous numbers of Soviet troops. In October, Hitler's army neared the center of Moscow (a monument today between the city's Sheremetevo Airport and the Kremlin marks the farthest advance of the German army). A month earlier, the Nazis had besieged Leningrad, beginning a two-year struggle in which over 1 million civilians died. The USSR appeared to be on the verge of collapse.

When winter came earlier, and more severely, than usual, the Nazi offensive broke down. Weapons froze, troops were inadequately clothed, and heavy snows blocked the roads. The German attack halted, and in the spring of 1942, the Red Army recovered some territory. One reason the Soviets could bounce back was the success of the five-year plans in relocating industry behind the Urals. Another reason was the sheer bravery and tenacity of the Soviet people. In addition, the United States and Britain had begun sending supplies to the USSR.

The United States Enters the War

Following the collapse of France and during the battle of Britain, the American people had begun to understand the dangerous implications of an Axis victory. After Dunkirk, the United States sent arms to Britain, embarked on a rearmament program, and introduced a peacetime draft. The Lend-Lease Act of 1941 empowered the president to make arms available to any country whose defense was thought to be vital to the U.S. national interest. Despite ideological differences, America sent more than $11 billion worth of munitions to the Soviet Union.

An integral part of German success in World War II was the firepower and mobility of their armored divisions. Here are tanks and soldiers breaking through the Stalin Line during the German invasion of the Soviet Union in 1941.

The magazine of the destroyer U.S.S. Shaw *explodes during the Japanese attack on Pearl Harbor, Hawaii, December 7, 1941.*

To define the moral purpose and principles of the struggle, Roosevelt and Churchill drafted the Atlantic Charter in August 1941. Meeting somewhere in the Atlantic, the two pledged that "after the final destruction of Nazi tyranny," they hoped to see a peace in which "men in all the lands may live out their lives in freedom from fear and want." Though the United States had not yet declared itself at war in the fall of 1941, it was far from neutral.

One event brought the full energies of the American people into the war against the European dictators and the Japanese militarists: the Japanese attack on Pearl Harbor on December 7, 1941, capping several years of deteriorating relations. Even though Hitler was considered the more dangerous enemy, it was Japan's expansionist policy that brought the United States into the war.

Alarmed by Tokyo's ambitions for the New Order in Asia and widely published accounts of Japanese atrocities, the United States had failed to renew the commercial treaty, frozen Japanese funds, and refused to sell Japan war matériel. Despite these measures, Japan pursued its expansion, even while attempting to negotiate an agreement with the U.S. to restart the flow of oil if Japan left Vietnam. In October 1941, Konoe resigned after failing to secure a direct meeting with U.S. President Roosevelt, and General Tōjō Hideki (1884–1948) was appointed Prime Minister in anticipation of a preemptive strike against the United States. On Sunday, December 7, while secretaries at the Japanese embassy in Washington were typing a translation of the final letter breaking off diplomatic relations with the United States, Japanese planes, launched from aircraft carriers, attacked the American bases at Pearl Harbor, Hawaii. The stunningly successful attack wiped out many American aircraft on the ground and crippled half of the United States' Pacific fleet.

The following day, the United States declared war on Japan; Britain followed suit. The British dominions, the refugee governments of Europe, and many Latin American nations soon joined the American and British cause. Four days later, Germany declared war on the United States. On January 2, 1942, the 26 nations that stood against Germany, Italy, and Japan solemnly pledged themselves to uphold the principles of the Atlantic Charter and declared themselves united for the duration of the war.

The Apogee of the Axis

For the 9 months after Pearl Harbor, Japanese power expanded over the Pacific and into Southeast Asia. Tokyo conquered Hong Kong, Singapore, the Netherlands East Indies, Malaya, Burma, and Indochina (Vietnam). The Philippines fell when an American force surrendered at Bataan. Much of China fell under Japanese control, with the exception of interior regions around Chongqing under the Nationalists and in northwest China around Shaanxi (shon-shee) under the Communists.

The summer of 1942 was an agonizing period for the nations allied against the Axis. A new German offensive pushed deeper into Russia, threatening the important city of Stalingrad. The forces of the gifted German general Rommel menaced Egypt and inflicted a stinging defeat on the British army in Libya. All over the globe, the Axis powers were in the ascendancy. But their advantage was to be short-lived.

Japanese expansion in the Pacific was halted by two major American naval victories, the Coral Sea in May and Midway in June. In the first, the Americans sank more than 100,000 tons of Japanese shipping and stopped the Japanese advance toward Australia. In the second, the Americans turned back the advance toward Hawaii by devastating the Japanese carrier force. In both cases, the American forces benefited by having broken the Japanese code and intercepting key messages. After these spectacular victories, U.S. marines began the tortuous conquest of the Japanese at Guadalcanal and driving them back, island by island, while the Navy destroyed most of the Japanese merchant fleet. The destruction of shipping spelled the end of the Japanese Empire, as it was dependent on raw materials from Asia.

By 1943 the main islands of Japan were cut off from their sources of raw materials and their markets. The government was forced to draft young men into the military, and older men, teenaged boys and girls, and unmarried women were drafted into the labor force. Controls over daily life—rationing of food and clothing and regimenting of films, newspapers, religion, and other aspects of civil society—destroyed civic life. In a time before instant news, the government lied to the people to retain their support while depriving them of food and necessities, telling them Japan was winning spectacular victories when, in fact, their ships lay at the bottom of the sea and thousands of soldiers were killed. Married women were told to "be fruitful and multiply for the prosperity of the nation." Millions of children were evacuated to the countryside, where those over 12 were taken from school and put to work. Colonial subjects fared even worse, as Korean and Chinese men were drafted to work in Japanese mines and factories and between 100,000 and 200,000 Korean and other Asian women were forced into sexual slavery as "comfort women" for the Japanese military.

Thousands of young women, 80 to 90 percent of them Korean, were rounded up and forced to work as sex slaves for the Japanese Army after 1937. Pictured here is a group of so-called "comfort women" in Manila following their liberation by the Allies.

In November 1942, British and American troops landed in North Africa, and the British defeated Axis troops at El Alamein in Egypt. By May 1943, all Axis troops in North Africa had been destroyed or captured. In July 1943, the Allied forces invaded and captured Sicily. On the twenty-fifth of that month, the whole edifice of Italian fascism collapsed when Mussolini was stripped of his office and held captive. (He was rescued by Nazi agents in September.) In the meantime, the Allies began their slow and bitter advance up the Italian boot. The new Italian government signed an armistice in September 1943, months before Rome was taken in June 1944. German resistance in northern Italy continued until the end of the war.

The Russian Turning Point

As important as the victories in the Pacific, North Africa, and Italy were, the decisive campaign took place in Russia. Hitler threw the bulk of his men and resources against the Soviet troops in the hope of knocking them out of the war and of gaining badly needed resources and food supplies. Hitler's strategy and operations along the eastern front constituted one mistake after another.

The Nazis lost a great opportunity to encourage the disintegration of the Soviet Union in 1941 because they treated the peoples they encountered as ***Untermenschen,*** or subhumans. Often the Nazis, far from encountering resistance, would be treated as liberators by the villages they entered and were given the traditional gifts of bread and salt. Often, peasants dissolved the unpopular collective farms in the hope that private ownership would be restored. The separatist Ukrainians looked forward to German support for reinstituting their state. The Nazi occupation negated all of these potential advantages. The Nazis carried their mobile killing operations of genocide with them, conscripted Slavs for slave labor in Germany, and generally mistreated the population in areas that they occupied.

Hitler's campaign gave Stalin the opportunity to wrap himself in the flag of patriotism. He replaced the ideological standards with those of nationalism and orthodoxy. He even went so far as to announce the end of the Comintern in 1943, an act more symbolic than

Untermenschen—Literally "subhumans." The term used by Nazi race theorists to describe non-Aryans.

Grieving families in the USSR try to identify the dead. The Nazi marches through Russia produced innumerable massacres.

real. For the first and perhaps the only time, the Communist party and the Soviet people were truly united in a joint enterprise.

The long (September 14, 1942, to February 2, 1943) and bloody battle between the Germans and the Soviets was focused on the strategic industrial city of Stalingrad on the Volga River. Hitler had fanatically sought to take the city, which, under the constant pounding of artillery, had little of importance left in it. His generals advised him to stop the attempt and retreat to a more defensible line. Hitler refused, and the German Sixth Army of 270,000 men was surrounded and finally captured in February 1943. A German soldier trapped at Stalingrad wrote in a letter:

> *Around me everything is collapsing, a whole army is dying, day and night are on fire, and four men busy themselves with daily reports on temperatures and cloud ceilings. I don't know much about war. No human being has died by my hand. I haven't even fired live ammunition from my pistol. But I know this much: the other side would never show such a lack of understanding for its men.*[11]

Along the long front, 500,000 German and affiliated troops were killed or taken prisoner. By the autumn of 1943, an army of 2.5 million Germans faced a Soviet force of 5.5 million.

The initiative had definitely passed to the Allies in the European theater. The Germans lost their air dominance, and the American industrial machine was cranking up to full production. By the beginning of 1944 the Germans were being pushed out of the Soviet Union, and in August Soviet troops accepted the surrender of Romania. Bulgaria was next to be liberated by the Soviet Union, while the Allies continued doggedly fighting their way north in Italy. But whereas the western Allies were, in their fashion, fighting the war to its military end, Stalin placed the postwar political objectives in the forefront of his advance into Europe.

An example of the Soviet use of military tactics to gain political goals could be seen in the action around Warsaw in August and September 1944 when the Red Army deferred the capture of the Polish capital to allow the Nazis to destroy potential opponents. The Polish resistance, which was centered in Warsaw and in contact with the exile government in London, had noted the arrival of Soviet forces in Warsaw's eastern suburbs. When the Nazis prepared to evacuate the city, the resistance rose up to claim control of the capital. Since these were non-Communist Poles, Stalin's forces refused to advance to the city, choosing instead to withdraw back across the Vistula River.

During the next five months, the Soviets refused to permit the British and the Americans, who wanted to air-drop supplies to the resistance, to land and refuel in the Ukraine. Because the flight to Warsaw from London was too far to make in a round trip, the Allies could not supply the resistance. The Nazis stopped their retreat, returned to Warsaw, and totally destroyed the resistance. Soviet forces then advanced and took the capital in January. Poland was now deprived of many of its potential postwar non-Communist leaders. When the Soviets advanced, they brought with them their own properly prepared Polish forces, both military and political, to control the country (see Chapter 32).

Axis Collapse

Operation Overlord, Normandy, 1944

Following months of intense planning and days of difficult decision making, the Allies on June 6, 1944—D-Day—launched a vast armada

The color guard of the 30th infantry division marching down the Champs Elysée during the liberation of Paris.

of ships that landed half a million men on the beaches of Normandy. The Allied armies broke through the German defenses and liberated Paris at the end of August and Brussels at the beginning of September. The combined forces wheeled toward Germany. After fending off a major German offensive in the battle of the Bulge in December, the Allies were ready to march on Germany.

It took four more months for the Allies from the west and the Soviets from the east to crush the German Third Reich. By May 1, the battle of Berlin had reached a decisive point, and the Russians were about to take the city. In contrast with World War I, German civilians suffered greatly in World War II. The Allies gained total command of the skies, and for every ton of bombs that fell on English cities, more than 300 tons fell on German towns and cities; Dresden and Cologne, in particular, were essentially leveled by extensive fire-bombing.

With victory in sight, Stalin, Roosevelt, and Churchill met at Yalta in the Crimea in February 1945 to discuss the peace arrangements. They agreed that the Soviet Union should have a preponderant influence in eastern Europe, decided that Germany should be divided into four occupation zones, discussed the makeup and functioning of the United Nations (a proposed successor to the defunct League of Nations), and confirmed that the Soviets would enter the war against Japan after the defeat of Germany, which they did—two days after the atomic bomb was dropped on Hiroshima. Yalta was the high point of the alliance. After this conference, relations between the Western powers and the Soviets rapidly deteriorated.

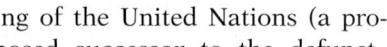

The "Big Three" at Yalta

The European Axis leaders did not live to see defeat. Mussolini was seized by antifascist partisan fighters and shot to death, and his mutilated body and that of his mistress were hung by the heels in a public square in Milan on April 28, 1945. Hitler committed suicide two days later. His body and that of his mistress, Eva Braun, whom he had just married, were soaked in gasoline and set afire.

President Roosevelt also did not live to see the end of the war. He died suddenly on April 12, 1945, less than a month before the German armies capitulated. The final surrender in Europe took place in Berlin on May 8, 1945, proclaimed by the newly installed president, Harry Truman, as V-E Day, Victory in Europe Day.

The Holocaust

As the Allied armies liberated Europe and marched through Germany and Poland, they came on sites that testified to the depths to which human beings can sink—the Nazi death camps. Nazi Propaganda Minister Joseph Goebbels wrote in his diary on March 14, 1945, that "it's necessary to exterminate these Jews like rats, once and for all. In Germany, thank God, we've taken care of that. I hope the world will follow this example."[12]

Poland and the Death Camps

He was only too accurate in saying that Germany had "already taken care of that." In Belsen, Buchenwald (BOO-ken-vold), Dachau (DAH-kow), Auschwitz (OWSH-vits), and other permanent camps and in

In his Self-Portrait with a Jewish Identity Card *(1943), Felix Nussbaum visually defines the sheer terror, anxiety, and helplessness felt by Jews under the Third Reich. Nussbaum and his wife were arrested in 1944; both died at the Auschwitz extermination camp.*

mobile killing operations that moved with the armies, Hitler's forces sought to "purify the German race" and to "remove the lesser breeds as a source of biological infection." Working under the efficient efforts of the Gestapo (secret police), led by Chief Heinrich Himmler, and with the aid of hardworking Deputy Chief Reinhard Heydrich, the Nazis set out to gain the **"Final Solution"** to the Jewish question.

Genocide

Although preparations had been under way for ten years, the completed plan for the Final Solution came in 1942. More than 3 million men, women, and children were put to death at Auschwitz alone. At Auschwitz more than 2000 people at a time could be gassed in half an hour; the operation could be repeated four times a day. The able-bodied were forced to work until they could work no more, and then they too were gassed. Millions more died from starvation, on diets that averaged 600 to 700 calories a day.[13] Torture, medical experimentation, and executions all claimed a large toll. The victims' eyeglasses were collected, their hair was shaved off for use in the wig trade, their gold fillings were removed as plunder, and their bodies were either burned or buried.

Memoirs from the Commandant of Auschwitz

Final Solution—Term used to define the goal of the Holocaust, to eliminate all Jews from the earth.

Thus the captured Jews, along with assorted *Untermenschen* (Gypsies, homosexuals, petty criminals, and conquered non-Aryans), made an economic contribution on their way to extermination. The Nazis did not act alone: they were aided by anti-Semitic citizens in Poland, Romania, France, Hungary, the Baltic States, and the Soviet Union. Few of the more than 4 million Polish Jews survived the war, sharing the fate of those 1200 Jews killed and burned in July 1941 by their fellow Polish villagers in Jedwabne.[14] Similar devastation occurred among the Romanian Jewry.

All of this was done with bureaucratic efficiency, coldness, discipline, and professionalism. Himmler believed that his new variety of knights must "make this people disappear from the face of the earth." Had this been done in a fit of insanity and madness by barbarians, it could perhaps be comprehended. But that it was done by educated bureaucrats and responsible officials from a "civilized" nation made the enterprise all the more chilling and incredible. The question of the complicity of the German people in the Holocaust continues to be debated.[15] Between 1939 and 1945 the Jewish population in Nazi-occupied Europe decreased from 9,739,200 to 3,505,800. Six million were killed in Nazi gas chambers or in executions, and another 6 million non-Jews fell victim to the Nazi slaughter.[16]

The Atomic Bomb

While the Allied armies finished off the Germans, the Americans continued the advance toward Japan begun in the summer of 1943, capturing on the way the islands of Tarawa, Kwajalein, and Saipan after bloody, hand-to-hand struggles on sandy beaches and in the jungles of the interior. In October 1944, with their victory in the battle of Leyte Gulf, the greatest naval engagement in history, the Allies ended the threat of the Japanese fleet.

Furthest Limits of Japanese Conquests

The Allies then took Iwo Jima and Okinawa, only a few hundred miles from Japan. From these bases, waves of American bombers rained destruction on Japanese cities. This virtually nonstop bombing claimed a huge toll of civilian casualties. One hundred Japanese cities were fire-bombed; the fire-bombing of Tokyo left 100,000 dead and 1.5 million homeless in one night of incendiary attacks. The attacks on Japan's civilian population made it clear that the Japanese government had lied to its people about wartime success.

The war was devastating to non-Japanese as well, including Korean and Chinese forced laborers, comfort women, and prisoners of war who received brutal treatment such as that accorded the Americans in the

Document The Nazi Death Camps

Henry Friedlander gave a dispassionate description of the functioning of the Nazi death camps.

The largest killing operation took place in Auschwitz, a regular concentration camp. There Auschwitz Commandant Rudolf Hess improved the method used by Christian Wirth, substituting crystallized prussic acid—known by the trade name Zyklon B—for carbon monoxide. In September, 1941, an experimental gassing, killing about 250 ill prisoners and about 600 Russian POWs, proved the value of Zyklon B. In January, 1942, systematic killing operations, using Zyklon B, commenced with the arrival of Jewish transports from Upper Silesia. These were soon followed without interruption by transports of Jews from all occupied countries of Europe.

The Auschwitz killing center was the most modern of its kind. The SS built the camp at Birkenau, also known as Auschwitz II. There, they murdered their victims in newly constructed gas chambers and burned their bodies in crematoria constructed for this purpose. A postwar court described the killing process:

Prussic acid fumes developed as soon as Zyklon B pellets seeped through the opening into the gas chamber and came into contact with the air. Within a few minutes, these fumes agonizingly asphyxiated the human beings in the gas chamber. During these minutes horrible scenes took place. The people who now realized that they were to die an agonizing death screamed and raged and beat their fists against the locked doors and against the walls. Since the gas spread from the floor of the gas chamber upward, small and weak people were the first to die. The others, in their death agony, climbed on top of the dead bodies on the floor, in order to get a little more air before they too painfully choked to death.

Questions to Consider

1. Why did the Nazis choose to use Zyklon B for the destruction of the Jews and others?
2. When did the systematic killing operations using Zyklon B begin?
3. Do you believe that it is possible that there will be other genocides in your lifetime? Why? Where?

From Henry Friedlander, "The Nazi Camps," in *Genocide: Critical Issues of the Holocaust,* eds. Alex Grobman and David S. Landes (Los Angeles: Simon Wiesenthal Center, 1983), pp. 222–223.

American GIs entering the Nazi concentration camps were aghast at what they found. In some camps they forced local Germans to view the piles of Jews who had been murdered before the Allies could liberate them and before the Nazis could burn or bury their bodies—both to make ordinary Germans aware of the unspeakable horror their government had committed and to preclude official denials that the genocide had taken place.

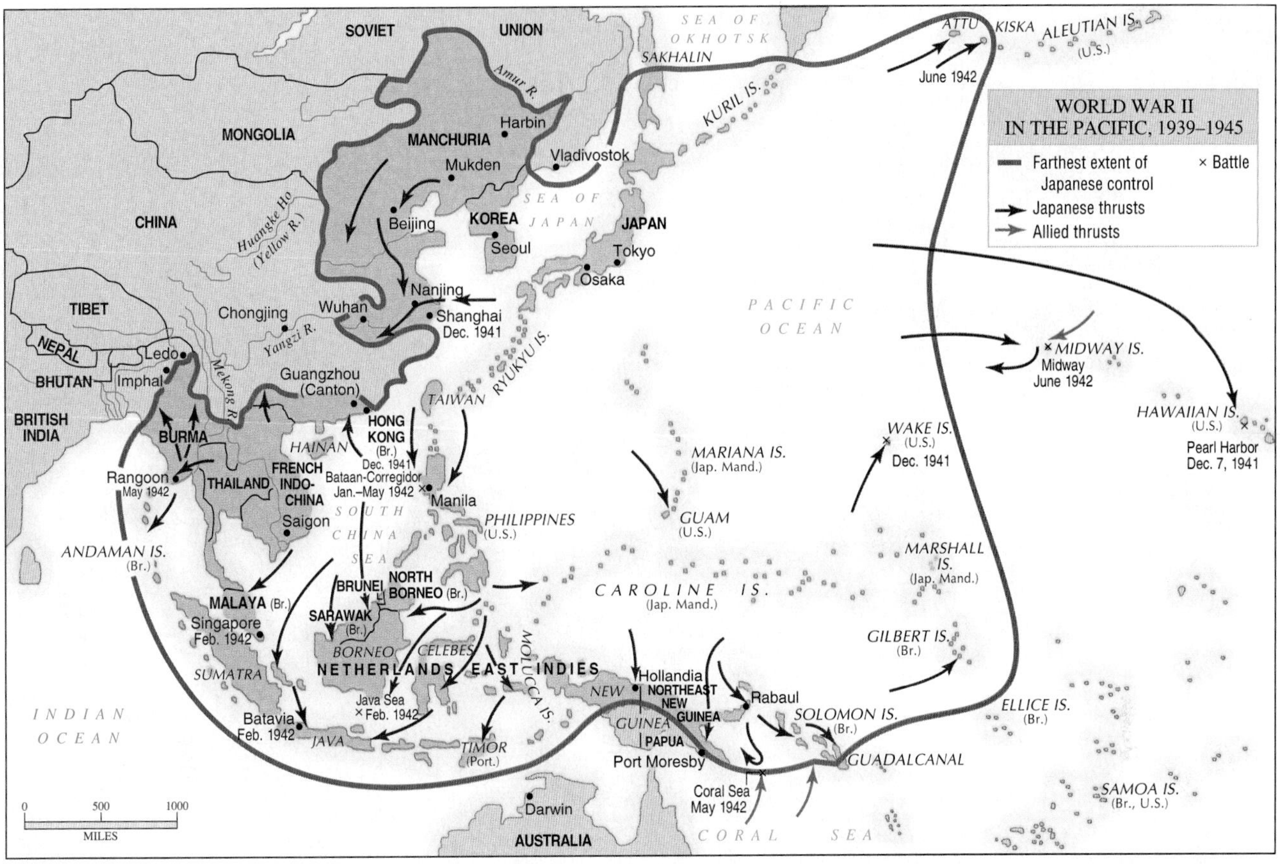

For a decade after the invasion of Manchuria in 1931, the Japanese expanded their control over the region known as the "Greater East Asian Co-Prosperity Sphere." Not until the battle of Midway in June 1942 was their momentum broken.

Bataan Death March in the Philippines and the Allies in the slave labor camps throughout Southeast Asia. Japan's notorious Unit 731 performed heinous medical experiments on prisoners.

In the China-Burma-India theater, the Chinese, with U.S. aid, made inroads into areas previously captured by Japan. As the Allies come closer to defeating Japan, they became aware of the desperation tactics inspired by loyalty to the Emperor, symbolized most effectively by the *kamakaze* pilots, who, in a final suicidal gesture, flew their bomb-loaded airplanes directly into American ships. Based on figures from the island-hopping campaigns, the projected casualty rate for the taking of the main island of Japan ran into the hundreds of thousands.

The decisive developments in the Pacific war took place in the American state of New Mexico, where by 1945, U.S. scientists, with the help of physicists who had fled central Europe to escape Hitler, invented a new and terrible weapon, the atomic bomb. After the defeat of Germany, the Japanese began to seek ways to end the war short of the "unconditional surrender" demanded by the Allies by approaching the Soviets to serve as mediators. But the Russians had already agreed to enter the war. The Potsdam Declaration, issued by U.S. President Truman and British Prime Minister Clement Atlee in July, reiterated the demand that Japan unconditionally surrender or face "utter destruction." Japanese Prime Minister Suzuki Kantarō, unwilling to abandon the emperor, which he believed would be required under unconditional surrender, decided to "silently ignore" the declaration. On August 6, an American bomber dropped an atomic bomb on the city of Hiroshima. As the mushroom-shaped cloud rose over the city, only charred ruins were left behind. An expanse of approximately 3 square miles, 60 percent of the city, was pulverized. Estimates of those killed instantly range from 78,000 to 140,000; an additional 100,000 were seriously, often mortally, wounded and 200,000 left homeless. Two days later, the Soviets declared war on Japan. The next day, August 9, a second bomb was dropped on the city of Nagasaki, killing about 70,000. Deaths from radiation sickness caused by the two bombs continued into the 1950s.

DOCUMENT
An Eyewitness to Hiroshima

President Harry Truman's controversial decision to drop the atomic bombs on Hiroshima and Nagasaki in 1945 helped end the war in the Pacific. However, as nuclear competition between the United States and the USSR led to devices of enormously greater destructiveness than the bombs dropped in 1945, the mushroom cloud came to symbolize the reality that scientists had created weapons that could extinguish humanity. Détente between Moscow and Washington brought a period of relaxation in the 1980s and 1990s, but fears of nuclear proliferation remain.

On August 15, the Japanese population stood silent and dazed as they heard the emperor's high-pitched voice for the first time on the radio, telling them to "endure the unendurable." The war was over, the losses now meaningless. The surrender ceremony took place aboard the battleship *Missouri* on September 2, 1945, almost six years to the day after Hitler plunged the world into World War II.

POSTWAR SETTLEMENTS

- *Why were victorious allies unable to establish a lasting peace after the end of World War II?*

In Asia, the census for 1950 showed a loss of some 55 million people, even after a five-year period of recuperation. Many had died as wartime casualties of

Japan's military actions, forced labor camps, and disease and hunger. Among the Japanese, a total of 1.7 million of their soldiers were killed in battle and almost one million Japanese civilians died during the war from the firebombs and nuclear weapons that had depopulated and irradiated parts of the country. War and revolution continued for the next generation from Indonesia to Korea, claiming more lives.

The Japanese were left reeling from the devastation and profoundly disgusted with the war and the government that had led them into that conflict. They were ready, after defeat, to resume the democratic trends they had experienced in the 1920s, under the rule of the Allied Occupation headed by American General Douglas MacArthur.

Europeans faced the challenges of economically and politically reconstructing their countries. One-fourth of Germany's cities were in rubble, as were numerous places in Italy and Central Europe. Many of the people who had escaped battle and bombing combed through the ruins to try to find food in their struggle to survive. In places like Yugoslavia, the war against the Germans and Italians and the civil wars that followed claimed 10 percent of the population and left a legacy of bitterness that would erupt in bitter conflicts 40 years later. Twenty-five million people died in the Soviet Union, and the country lost a third of its national wealth as well as the next generation of leaders—condemning the country to be ruled a generation later by leaders who were old, ill, and weak.

Europe faced two other problems at the end of the war: dealing with Nazi collaborators and resettling millions of labor slaves. In countries that had been occupied by the Germans, victorious resistance groups began to take vigilante justice against those who had worked with the invaders. Across Europe they executed thousands of collaborators. In France alone, 800 were sent to their deaths. After the war and into the mid-1990s, courts sentenced thousands more to prison terms. Eight million foreign laborers who had been exploited as slaves by the Nazis remained to be resettled. Five million of them had been sent home by the end of 1945, including many Soviet citizens who were repatriated against their will. Some of them chose suicide rather than return to Stalin's rule.

In Germany the Allies began to carry out a selective process of denazification. Some former Nazis were sent to prison, but thousands of others remained free because of large-scale declarations of amnesty. Many ex-Nazis were employed by the scientific and intelligence services of each of the Allies. Symbolically, the most important denazification act came at the 1945–1946 trials of war criminals held at **Nuremberg.** Critics condemned the trials as an act of vengeance, "a political act by the victors against the vanquished." The prosecution declared, however, that the Nazis' crimes were so terrible that "civilization cannot tolerate their being ignored because it cannot survive their being repeated." As Telford Taylor, the American prosecutor of the German general staff, stated, "The gas chambers, mountains of corpses, human-skin lampshades, shrunken skulls, freezing experiments, and bank vaults filled with gold teeth" were the "poisoned fruit" of the tree of German militarism. Taylor brushed aside the generals' arguments that they were "just following orders." He made the point that they still had to exercise moral judgment.[17] An international panel of jurists conducted the proceedings; it condemned 12 leading Nazis to be hanged and sent seven to prison for crimes against humanity. The panel also acquitted three high officials. Nuremberg established the precedent for War Crimes tribunals that have subsequently taken place in the Hague under the aegis of the United Nations.

Following the Yalta agreement, the Allies established four occupation zones in Germany: French, British, American, and Soviet. They divided the capital, Berlin, located in the Soviet sector, into four similar parts. The Soviets promised free access from the western zones to Berlin. Growing hostility between the Soviet Union and the United States by the end of the war blocked a comprehensive peace settlement for Germany.

CONCLUSION

By 1945, the victorious allies had put an end to German, Italian, and Japanese aggression. In contrast with World War I, which has spawned many historiographical controversies concerning its causes, there is no doubt that the key figure in the starting of World War II was Adolf Hitler. He was the essential link, the man whose policies and ideas welded the dictators together.

Unlike the Japanese and the Italians, whose global influence was limited by either geographical or internal problems, Hitler could build on Germany's industrial might and central location to forge a force for world conquest. Historians vary sharply on his goals and motivations. Some see him as a politician playing the traditional game of European power politics in a

---

Nuremberg Trials—After World War II, trials of Nazi war criminals for crimes against humanity that took place in Nuremberg, formerly the site of Hitler's mass rallies.

most skillful way, while others view him as a single-minded fanatic pursuing the plans for conquest laid out in *Mein Kampf.* Between these two extremes are the scholars who believe that the Führer had thought out long-term goals but pursued them haphazardly as opportunities presented themselves.

Hitler struck the spark that set off the worldwide conflagration. Aiding and abetting his ambitions was the obsessive desire of the democracies for peace. By 1939 the lesson had been learned that appeasement does not guarantee peace, nor does it take two equally belligerent sides to make a war.

Suggestions for Web Browsing

You can obtain more information about topics included in this chapter at the websites listed below. See also the companion website that accompanies this text, http://www.ablongman.com/brummett, which contains an online study guide and additional resources.

The Nanjing Massacres
http://www.gotrain.com/dan/nanking1.htm

The page attempts a full portrayal of the horrors of the Japanese taking of Nanjing.

Lycos Guide to World War II
http://www.lycos.com/wguide/network/net 969250.html

This portal provides a rich compilation of websites regarding all aspects of World War II.

Battle of Stalingrad
http://www.stalingrad.net/

This website offers rare photos of this pivotal battle of World War II.

Role of American Women in World War II
http://www.pomperaug.com/socstud/stumuseum/web/arhhome.htm

This site provides a rich repository of photos, primary interviews, and other materials detailing the role of women on the American side of the war.

D-Day
http://www.isidore-of-seville.com/d-day/

Extensive site provides information on D-Day.

The Holocaust
http://www.wiesenthal.com/

The Simon Wiesenthal Center provides a wide range of information about the Holocaust.

National Holocaust Museum
http://www.remember.org

Site provides the most exhaustive support for students searching for information on genocide and the Holocaust.

Hiroshima Archive
http://www.kyohaku.go.jp

A poignant research and educational guide for all who wish to expand their knowledge of the atomic bombing of Japan.

Literature and Film

Some major novels dealing with World War II are (all in many different editions) James Michener, *Tales of the South Pacific,* Thomas Heggen, *Mr. Roberts,* Leon Uris, *Battle Cry,* and Norman Mailer, *The Naked and the Dead*. Herman Wouk's epic *Winds of War* and *War and Remembrance* trace the war from 1939 through to the discovery of the death camps. Jerzy Kosinski's *Painted Bird* traces the path of an orphan through Poland during the war. Günter Grass's *Tin Drum* follows the Nazi progress through Danzig while Joseph Heller captures the insanity of war in *Catch 22.* Curzio Malaparte in *Kaputt* traces the course of the war from the Axis side. Kenzaburo Oe's *Fire from the Ashes: Short Stories about Hiroshima and Nagasaki* gives the reader the perspective of the victims of the first nuclear attack.

Filmmakers have presented various aspects of the war. All of the novels above have served as the basis for films. Bernhard Wicki's *The Longest Day* (Fox, 1962) and Franklin J. Schaffner's *Patton* (Fox, 1970) are masterpieces. Recently, Jean-Jacques Annaud captured the drama of the battle of Stalingrad in *Enemy at the Gates* (Paramount, 2001). Terrence Malick's *The Thin Red Line* (Fox, 1999) caught the horror of the Pacific War. Four of Steven Spielberg's most important films have dealt with various aspects of the conflict: The home front was portrayed in *1941* (Universal Studios, 1979). The Japanese invasion and occupation of China were shown through the eyes of a child in *Empire of the Sun* (Warner, 1987). *Schindler's List* (Universal Studios, 1993) captured the tragedy of the holocaust, and the bravery and suffering of the American GIs were presented in *Saving Private Ryan* (Universal/MCA, 1998). Robert Benigni *La Vita È Bella* ("Life Is Beautiful"; Miramax, 1998) gives a bittersweet view of Italian Fascism and life in a concentration camp.

Suggestions for Reading

Hans Gatzke, ed., *European Diplomacy Between the Two Wars, 1919–1939* (Quadrangle, 1972), remains a useful survey. Gerhard Weinberg gives a penetrating analysis in his two books: *The Foreign Policy of Hitler's Germany: Diplomatic Revolution in Europe, 1933–1936* (University of Chicago Press, 1970) and *The Foreign Policy of Hitler's Germany, 1937–1939* (University of Chicago Press, 1980). For a study of the pressures affecting Franklin Roosevelt as he responded to the European crisis, see Barbara Rearden Farnham, *Roosevelt and the Munich Crisis: A Study of Political Decision Making* (Princeton University Press, 1997).

A study that reveals the multifaceted background of Chamberlain's policy is Gaines Post, *Dilemmas of Appeasement: British Deterrence and Defense, 1934–1937* (Cornell University Press, 1993). Michael Alpert provides an overview of the tragic events in Spain in *A New International History of the Spanish Civil War* (St. Martin's Press, 1998). For Hitler, see also Ian Kershaw's two-volume biography cited in Chapter 29. Albert Seaton, *The Russo-German War, 1941–1945* (Praeger, 1970), is especially strong in its analysis of Soviet strategy.

See also the study edited by Akira Iriye, *Pearl Harbor and the Coming of the Pacific War* (Bedford/St. Martins, 1999), for a series of essays and documents on the origins of the Pacific War.

Yoshiaki Yashimi carried out interviews with survivors and archival research to produce *Comfort Women: Sexual Slavery in the Japanese Military During World War II* (Columbia University Press, 2001). Two indispensable studies are John Dower, *War Without Mercy: Race and Power in the Pacific War* (Pantheon Books, 1986), and Haruko Taya Cook and Theodore Cook, *Japan at War: An Oral History* (New Press, 1992).

The role of advanced technology in the Allied victory is discussed by Richard Overy, *Why the Allies Won* (W. W. Norton, 1997). The Nazis' genocide policies are analyzed in Raul Hilberg, *The Destruction of the European Jews* (Quadrangle, 1961). Telford Taylor's memoir, *The Anatomy of the Nuremberg Trials* (Knopf, 1994), is a thorough and compelling discussion of these unprecedented hearings.

GLOBAL ISSUES

WAR AND INTERNATIONAL LAW

How have nations sought to prevent the worst atrocities of war such as genocide?

Skulls at Ntmara Church, Kigali, Rwanda.

Humans have fought wars and committed atrocities against their enemies throughout recorded history. In an effort to minimize the most destructive aspects of armed conflict, most civilizations established codes of conduct for warfare. Ancient examples of such codes include prohibitions against attacking neutral parties, religious sites, and enemies approaching under a flag of truce. Codes such as these constituted the very first rules of war. Despite their intent, the effect these rules had on warfare was limited. In some conflicts, the participants might observe codes of conduct; in many others, though, they breached them freely. The codes, moreover, were not universally respected among nations. Codes that might apply in one culture might carry little or no weight in another.

Over the centuries, war after war was fought around the world, some more brutally than others, but little changed concerning the rules of war. This state of affairs only came to an end in the nineteenth century, when the first international laws codifying the rules of war were written. These laws came about as a necessity. The introduction of industrialized technology to combat made warfare more destructive than ever before.

The first Geneva Conference of 1864, held partially in response to the carnage of the American Civil War, laid the foundation for the rules of war that were later written into international law in the Hague conferences of 1899 and 1907 and the Geneva Conventions of 1906, 1929, and 1949. The rules of war established a legal framework for warfare in five major areas: (1) the status of combatants; (2) the conduct of hostilities; (3) the occupation of enemy territory and the treatment of enemy noncombatants; (4) the treatment of neutral parties; and (5) the management of armistices and truces. Under international law, the breach of the rules of war in any one of these areas legally constitutes a war crime.

As the history of the twentieth century has shown, however, international law carries little weight if the nations of world choose not to enforce it. One of the first large-scale breaches of the rules of war occurred during World War I. At the time, the Ottoman Empire viewed its substantial Armenian minority suspiciously, seeing the Orthodox Christian community as a potential fifth-column that could aid the Russians on its eastern flank. In the spring of 1915 Turkish authorities began to round up the Armenian populations near its border with Russia. The situation quickly deteriorated further when the government massacred thousands of Armenian civilian and business leaders. Thereafter, in towns and villages across the country, the government imprisoned and killed Armenian men and forcibly relocated Armenian women and children. In cities around Lake Van, where the majority of Armenians had lived, the entire Armenian population was destroyed.[1] In the end, between 1 and 1.5 million Armenians died.[2]

While the scope of the Ottoman atrocities slowly gained international recognition after World War I, the victorious Allies took no actions to prosecute those responsible for the massacre. The interwar period that followed, however, did see some international attempts to control arms at the Washington Conference, further amendments to the Geneva Conventions, and even an effort to outlaw war in Kellogg-Briand Pact of 1928. Nevertheless, with the collapse of the League of Nations there was no international authority to enforce the rules of war. It would take the horrors of World War II to shock the international community into changing the status quo.

World War II was unquestionably the bloodiest war in world history—as many as 50 million people died in the conflict. While there were thousands of individual war crimes committed in both the war's European and Pacific theaters, one particular atrocity stands above them all in the scale of its carnage: the Holocaust.

The Holocaust, "whose intent was to exterminate the Jewish people from the face of the earth and to obliterate their identity and all its dimensions,"[3] was the most thoroughgoing attempt to destroy an entire people in history. Embracing discredited scientific theories, the Nazis identified themselves as the master race and Jews as a lower form of humanity and a threat to the purity of their own race. Their "final solution" to this problem was to kill over 6 million Jews, along with another 5 million "undesirables," including gypsies, homosexuals, handicapped people, communists, ethnic Slavs, criminals, and others.

Even before World War II was concluded, the Allies created the United Nations Commission for the Investigation of War Crimes. In 1945 and 1946, building on the Commission's work, the Allies established tribunals in Nuremberg and Tokyo to try German and Japanese leaders for violating the rules of war set forth in the Hague and Geneva conventions. The tribunal at Nuremberg represented the first international war crimes trial in history. Of the 22 men tried by the tribunal, 19 were found guilty and 11 were subsequently executed. Later, during the Tokyo tribunal, 28 Japanese leaders were tried for war crimes and seven received the death sentence.

In 1948 and 1949, the United Nations legally defined the destruction of one people by another as *genocide,* a crime against humanity:

". . . a public policy whose intent is either (a) the extermination of a collectivity or category, usually a communal group or class, or (b) the killing of a large fraction of a collectivity or category including the families of its members, and the destruction of its social and cultural identity in most or all of its aspects."[4]

Neither the lessons of World War II nor the precedents of Nuremberg and Tokyo, however, prevented serious violations of the rules of war, including genocide, from occurring again. During the 1970s, the communist Khmer Rouge regime set out to eliminate Cambodia's professional and middle classes, leading to the death of 1.6 million people, or 20 percent of the population. While the world condemned this outrage, the international community did nothing to punish those who had committed war crimes and crimes against humanity.

The international community was again confronted by serious war crimes and genocide in the 1990s. In 1992, after the republic of Bosnia and Herzegovina voted to secede from the crumbling Yugoslavian nation, Serbian forces began a process of population transfer and murder known as "ethnic cleansing." In places like Vukovar and Srebenica, Serbian militias rounded up and executed Bosnian men. Serbian forces also used gang rape as a weapon to terrorize Bosnian women. Croats and, to a lesser extent, Bosnian forces responded with similar outrages until the Dayton Peace Accords in 1995 brought the war to an end. Some 200,000 people were killed and 2 million people displaced in the fighting. Four years later, the Serbs repeated their policies of ethnic cleansing in Kosovo, driving nearly 800,000 Albanian residents out of the country.

While the fighting raged in the former Yugoslavia, an even greater atrocity occurred in the Central African nation of Rwanda. There, between April and August of 1994, radicalized Hutus slaughtered some 800,000 Tutsis and moderate Hutus. A Hutu elite organized the genocide, training and arming radical Hutu militias in advance, and nobody—not the old nor the young, neither women nor children—was to be spared. Instructions on how to kill the Tutsis were broadcast over the national radio stations. The killing was a preindustrial, personalized massacre, done for the large part with machetes, clubs with nails, farm tools, or even kitchen implements.[5]

While the international community was unable to prevent the atrocities committed in either the former Yugoslavia or Rwanda, in both instances it attempted to punish the perpetrators. In 1993, the United Nations Security Council established the International Criminal Tribunal for the former Yugoslavia (ICTY), based in The Hague, to try war-crimes cases. The tribunal began its work in July 1994, and a decade later it is still trying war criminals. Its most important trial to date is of ex-Yugoslav president Slobodan Milosevic, who is charged with more than 60 war crimes. In 1994, the United Nations Security Council also established an International Criminal Tribunal for Rwanda (ICTR) in Arusha, Tanzania. So far it has tried nine people for genocide and another 40 are waiting to be tried.

In 1998 the United Nations celebrated the fiftieth anniversary of the Universal Declaration of Human Rights—which proclaimed the basic civil, political, social, and economic rights of all of the world's citizens. Even against the tide of atrocities cited above there is no doubt that international law in the area of war crimes is making progress. Nongovernmental organizations (NGOs) such as Amnesty International and Human Rights Watch monitor conflicts throughout the world and issue reports identifying war crimes and crimes against humanity. Law schools around the world have changed their curricula to include courses on both human rights and international law and the number of lawyers working in these areas has increased.

Questions

1. Why is it so difficult to reconcile national sovereignty and international law? In your answer consider the United States' refusal to participate in the International Criminal Court.
2. What are the strengths and weaknesses that the United Nations brings to the task of enforcing international laws concerning the rules of war?
3. At what point does ethnic cleansing end and genocide begin?

CHAPTER

32

The Bipolar World

Cold War and Decolonization, 1945–1991

CHAPTER CONTENTS

1940

1945 Yalta Conference; Potsdam Conference; WWII ends; UN chartered; Ho Chi Minh establishes Republic of Vietnam

1947 Truman Doctrine; Marshall Plan begins

1949 NATO formed; COMECON established; Berlin blockade; People's Republic of China proclaimed

1950

1950–1953 Korean War

1954–1962 Algerian War of Independence

1956 Khrushchev begins de-Stalinization; Hungarian Revolt; Suez Crisis

1957 Ghana becomes independent

1960

1962 Cuban Missile Crisis

1968 Prague Spring; Soviet Bloc invasion of Czechoslovakia

1970

1975 Reunification of Vietnam

1980

1985 Gorbachev declares policies of *glasnost* and *perestroika*

1989–1990 Collapse of Communism in eastern Europe

Two countries, the Union of Soviet Socialist Republics and the United States, dominated the globe in the half-century after the end of World War II. Their ideologies presented starkly different views about the nature of politics, society, and religion and the role of the individual. The two powers also proposed two different economic systems to the world. The United States and its allies wished to avoid the errors of protectionism during the 1930s and constructed a range of institutions at Bretton Woods to encourage capitalism. Those areas linked with the Soviet Union adopted the central planning model of the Soviet Union and worked in the COMECON system by 1948 (see p. 943).

Moscow and Washington's competition—which came to be known as the "Cold War" because it was a time of neither all-out war nor true peace—divided Europe into two spheres along the "Iron Curtain" until 1989. Though the two sides concentrated millions of troops and targeted hundreds of nuclear weapons against each other, a stalemate resulted that gave that continent the longest period of peace in its recorded history. In other parts of the world, the Soviet-American conflict led to almost continual warfare because this bipolar struggle occurred at the same time that many of the world's peoples were breaking the bonds of their colonial past. The United States tended to support those governments representing the status quo while the Soviet Union invested heavily in those forces seeking national liberation. Those countries undergoing decolonization tried to benefit as best they could from the conflicting attentions of the USSR and the United States.

During the 50 years of the Cold War, the nature of the bipolar competition changed. The conflict had its beginnings in a world in which dominance came from the capacity to use force and ended in a world in which dominance went to those who had the capacity to construct a sound economy. The Cold War came to a conclusion not as the result of a surprise nuclear attack, but because the USSR's social and economic infrastructure crumbled while the United States survived considerable social and economic stress.

COMPETING ECONOMIC MODELS

- *What are the comparative advantages and disadvantages of the Soviet centrally planned economy and the Western market-based economy?*

Even before the defeat of the Axis in World War II, the Western allies made plans to avoid the horrendous economic crisis that had followed World War I. Forty-four nations, the core of the original membership of the United Nations, met in July 1944 at the New Hampshire resort town of Bretton Woods to put the peacetime world economy on a solid footing. Recalling the lessons of **protectionism** and **autarky** in the 1930s, the financial leaders devised plans to ensure a free flow of international trade. The Soviet Union later refused to participate in the Western plans for protecting and extending capitalism. Instead, they expanded their central planning model to the states in their new sphere of influence.

A New Capitalist Framework

The **Bretton Woods Conference** created the **International Monetary Fund (IMF),** chartered in 1945, to restore the money system that had collapsed in previous decades when countries abandoned the gold standard and resorted to export-enhancing devices such as currency devaluation and protectionist measures such as tariffs and quotas. The conference intended that the IMF would oversee a system of fixed exchange rates, founded on the dollar, which could be easily exchanged for gold at the rate of $35 an ounce. The IMF was based on a foundation of currencies paid in by the member states. These deposits served as a world savings account from which a member state could take short-term loans to handle debt payments without having to resort to the disruptive tactics of manipulating exchange rates or devaluation. The standard for the exchange rates among the various currencies was that in existence as of the first day of the Bretton Woods conference. Member countries could not change their currency's values without approval of the IMF. Although the system faced some problems based on the weaknesses of many of the member states' postwar economies, the IMF supported a generation of monetary stability that allowed businesses to pursue their international plans with confidence in a stable market.

The conference also established the International Bank for Reconstruction and Development, more commonly known as the World Bank, chartered in December 1945. In its first 10 years the World Bank focused mostly on the rebuilding of Europe. Over the next three decades the bank devoted the bulk of its resources to aiding states undergoing development or rebuilding.

A key development in reforming the world economy was the establishment in 1947 of the **General Agreement on Tariffs and Trade (GATT)** under U.S. leadership. Having absorbed the lessons of the protectionist and autarkic 1930s, the Allies put together an international institution to set up worldwide rules for business that would give nations the confidence to break down old barriers that blocked free trade. GATT operated through a series of meetings between nations to remove protectionist restrictions. The assurance a nation received for entering the GATT framework was the "most favored nation" clause, which guaranteed that any trade advantage worked out in a nation-to-nation agreement would be automatically shared by all members of GATT.

The Soviet Alternative

Stalin and his successors, until Gorbachev, chose not to participate in the Western economic structure. They maintained the central planning model installed in the late 1920s and implanted it in the Eastern European countries that came under their influence after the end of World War II. Under this economic system, known as **COMECON,** Moscow followed the "Socialism in One Country" theory in which international communists had to sacrifice for the benefit of Russia. At first, the Eastern European allies—which had been, with few exceptions, dominated by the Nazis—indirectly helped pay for the reconstruction of the war-damaged Soviet Union. Then, in the 1950s, Moscow attempted to organize the various socialist economies for the greater good of the socialist whole. The Soviet Union wanted each of its allied nations to specialize in producing certain items for the entire

---

protectionism—An economic policy of favoring domestic interests by imposing limits and tariffs on foreign trade and economic competition.

autarky—The policy of economic independence and self-sufficiency.

Bretton Woods Conference—In July 1944, 44 nations met at the New Hampshire resort town of Bretton Woods to put the peacetime economy on a solid footing. The participants wanted to avoid the economic mistakes of the interwar period.

International Monetary Fund (IMF)—Chartered in 1945, the International Monetary Fund was created to restore the money system that had collapsed in previous decades.

General Agreement on Tariffs and Trade (GATT)—Established in 1947, the General Agreements on Tariffs and Trade sought to avoid the protectionist and autarkist errors of the interwar period and establish a framework that would permit free trade among nations.

COMECON—The economic bloc coordinated by the Soviet Union.

Soviet Bloc. This was an unpopular idea in the allied nations such as Romania, which saw itself condemned to raising corn and wheat while other countries could industrialize.

The central planning system in its USSR and Soviet Bloc versions provided for economic growth until the 1970s. New technological challenges and domestic priorities overtaxed COMECON thereafter, and the system was unable to reform itself.

THE COLD WAR: 1945–1962

▪ *What were some of the factors that permitted the United States and the Soviet Union to avoid direct conflict during the Cold War?*

August 1945 signaled a new age in world history. Within 5 years the United States and the Union of Soviet Socialist Republics, the sole possessors of nuclear weapons, stood alone in their bipolar confrontation. A five-century-long epoch in world history in which the most powerful countries maintained their domination through the use of superior military technology had arrived at its final act.

The Roots of the Cold War

American and British slowness in opening the Second Front in Europe while his country bore the brunt of Nazi attacks irritated Stalin by the beginning of 1943. He was also upset by the lack of information from the Western Allies on their activities in North Africa and Italy. Finally, he saw the lack of increased financial support from the United States as a sign of insufficient appreciation for the suffering and contributions of the USSR.

During the war, the Western Allies expressed their discontent at the lack of Soviet public recognition of their assistance and the USSR's unwillingness to share information. As the Russians advanced into Eastern Europe, Washington and London noted with disapproval Stalin's imposition of procommunist leaders in positions of power in Eastern Europe. The activities of Soviet spies in the United States and the United Kingdom also spread suspicions of Stalin and the Soviet Union.

The breakdown of wartime cooperation that developed into the half-century of Cold War is the subject of a wide-ranging and passionate disagreement among historians. One school of interpretation accuses the United States of putting Stalin in an untenable position and of being responsible for the Cold War. Others accuse Stalin of a consistent and long-term search for the extension of communism, especially after the battle of Stalingrad, and find the Soviet Union responsible for the Cold War.

Historians who take a more centralist approach note that the United States and USSR had differed in their views on economics, politics, social organization,

Germany: The European Epicenter of the Cold War

1945	Russians take Berlin; Four Power Agreement on the governing of Germany; quadripartite division of Berlin
1946	Russians begin reneging on economic agreements; British and U.S. zones merged
1947	Truman Doctrine announced; start of containment strategy; Marshall Plan
1948	USSR consolidates control over Eastern Europe, blockades Berlin; French zone merges with British and U.S. zones
1949	NATO established; COMECON established; German Federal Republic (West Germany) established, Konrad Adenauer becomes chancellor; German "economic miracle" begins
1953	Workers revolt in East Germany (German Democratic Republic) over food shortage and increased working hours
1955–1961	USSR demands withdrawal of Western forces; Berlin a "free city"
1961	Khrushchev demands Western withdrawal from Berlin; construction of Berlin Wall; German Democratic Republic sealed off from West
1982–1983	Missile debate
1988	East German leaders begin censoring Russian papers
1989	East Germans flee to West through Czechoslovakia and Hungary; Berlin Wall opened up
1990	Germany reunited

Soviet Bloc—The allies of the Soviet Union in Europe and Asia.

religion, and the role of the individual in society since the November Revolution of 1917. The Nazi invasion of Russia temporarily brought the two sides together, but fractures in the anti-Axis alliance began to appear toward the end of 1943. The decline of the traditional European powers created a power vacuum around the globe into which the forces of Moscow and Washington entered, and came into competition.

No matter which view is accepted, it is clear that the devastating power of nuclear weapons ensured that the United States and the Soviet Union never directly fought each other. However, "proxy wars" fought by their client nations and their own occasional political and economic intervention cost millions of lives in the areas of Asia, Africa, and Latin America undergoing decolonization.

The Cold War in Europe to 1953

Soon after the February 1945 Yalta Conference, it became clear that Stalin's view of the composition of postwar Eastern Europe was very different from that of Roosevelt and Churchill. As early as April 1, 1945, Roosevelt sent a telegram to Stalin protesting the latter's violation of Yalta pledges. A month later Churchill sent a similar message of protest.

MAP
Europe in the Cold War

From 1945 to 1948, Stalin carefully expanded his control over the region, working through his allies' domination of the various coalition governments. The Communists occupied the most powerful positions in the coalition governments; opposition parties gained largely symbolic posts. By the end of 1948, when the Americans had largely withdrawn from Europe, the governments in Warsaw, East Berlin, Prague, Budapest, Bucharest, Sofia, and Tirana operated as satellites orbiting the political center of Moscow. Stalin used the Soviet Bloc as a 400-mile-deep buffer against capitalist invasion and as a source to help the USSR rebuild. He blocked any political, economic, or cultural contact with the West. Only Yugoslavia, led by Marshal Josip Tito, remained outside of Moscow's hegemonic control.

Meanwhile, in the 3 years after 1945, the four-power agreement on the governing of Germany soon broke apart. In the fall of 1946, Britain and America merged their zones into one economic unit, which came to be known as Bizonia. The French joined that union in 1948. Germany was now split into two parts, one administered by the Western Allies and the other by the Soviets. It would remain divided until the line between the two powers—dubbed the "Iron Curtain" by Churchill—fell in 1989.

The Soviets did not return their armies to peacetime status after 1945. They challenged the West in Turkey and Iran while the Yugoslav and Albanian communist governments supported the Greek partisans against the British-sponsored government in Athens. Britain, however, was too weak to play its former dominant role in the region. The Americans, as they would subsequently do throughout the globe, filled the gap left by their British allies.

President Harry Truman responded to Soviet pressure by announcing that the United States would support any country threatened by communist aggression. Soon after this proclamation of the **Truman Doctrine** in 1947 (see Document, "The Truman Doctrine"), the United States sent economic and military aid to Greece and Turkey, a move traditionally held to mark the American entry into the Cold War: And in the early 1950s the United States sponsored the overthrow of the elected government of Iran. Whereas the Soviet threat to American interests might have been real in Turkey and Iran, in Greece the Soviet Union had no interest in seeing a leftist victory because that would have fortified their ideological enemy, the Yugoslav leader Josip Tito.

DOCUMENT
The Truman Doctrine

The Americans, comfortable with their nuclear monopoly, had looked forward to a peaceful postwar world. By the end of 1946, they were angered by Soviet actions in the United Nations, Eastern Europe, and China and by the growth of Communist parties in Western Europe. Truman, who felt he could do business with Stalin as one politician to another, indicated he had changed his mind when he wrote in his journal in November 1946 that there was no difference among the government in Moscow, that of the tsars, or that of the Hitler regime.

American diplomat George F. Kennan explained that the correct stance to take toward Stalin's policies was one of **containment.** In an article titled "The Sources of Soviet Conduct," written anonymously in the July 1947 issue of *Foreign Affairs,* Kennan proposed a "realistic understanding of the profound and deep-rooted difference between the United States and the Soviet Union" and the exercise of "a long-term, patient but firm and vigilant containment of Russian expansive tendencies."[1] This advice successfully shaped U.S. policy throughout Europe but later was tragically misapplied in Southeast Asia.

The broad economic and political arms of containment came into play. Secretary of State George C. Marshall proposed a plan of economic aid to help Europe solve its postwar financial problems. Western

---

Truman Doctrine—The policy proclaimed in 1947 that the United States would support any country threatened by communist aggression.

containment—The doctrine proposed by George F. Kennan that stated that the best way to deal with the Soviet Union was through the exercise of a containment of Russian expansive tendencies. Kennan believed that once the forward momentum of the Soviet advance was blocked, internal contradictions would weaken the Soviet Union.

Document The Truman Doctrine

Conflicting Western and Soviet interests in the Balkans, Turkey, and Iran caught the United States unprepared to respond. Once the Americans recovered from their post-1945 euphoria, President Truman spelled out his response to perceived Soviet aggression. The Truman Doctrine was one of the primary foreign policy statements of the United States since the end of the World War II.

The peoples of a number of countries of the world have recently had totalitarian regimes forced upon them against their will. The Government of the United States has made frequent protests against coercion and intimidation, in violation of the Yalta agreement, in Poland, Rumania, and Bulgaria. I must also state that in a number of other countries there have been similar developments.

At the present moment in world history nearly every nation must choose between alternative ways of life. The choice is too often not a free one.

One way of life is based upon the will of the majority, and is distinguished by free institutions, representative government, free elections, guaranties of individual liberty, freedom of speech and religion, and freedom from political oppression.

The second way of life is based upon the will of a minority forcibly imposed upon the majority. It relies upon terror and oppression, a controlled press and radio, fixed elections, and the suppression of personal freedoms.

I believe that it must be the policy of the United States to support free peoples who are resisting attempted subjugation by armed minorities or by outside pressures.

I believe that we must assist free peoples to work out their own destinies in their own way.

I believe that our help should be primarily through economic and financial aid, which is essential to economic stability and orderly political processes.

Questions to Consider

1. What caused President Truman to issue this doctrine?
2. Do you see this document to be more a statement of idealism or self-interest?
3. A number of critics of post–World War II U.S. foreign policy see the Truman Doctrine as a tool to impose the American way of life and American interests on the rest of the world. Do you agree?

From U.S. Congress, *Congressional Record,* 80th Congress, 1st Session, Vol. 93, (Washington, D.C.: U.S. Government Printing Office, 1947), p. 1981; U.S. Congress, Senate Committee on Foreign Relations, *A Decade of American Foreign Policy: Basic Documents, 1941–1949* (Washington, D.C.: U.S. Government Printing Office, 1950), pp. 1270–1271.

European nations eagerly accepted the **Marshall Plan,** but the Soviet Union rejected American aid for itself and its bloc. Congress authorized the plan, known as the European Recovery Program, and within 4 years, the industrial output of the recipients climbed to 64 percent over 1947 levels and 41 percent over prewar levels. The program supplied most of the capital and technical assistance the Western European states needed for reconstruction. The Marshall Plan funds came with strict conditions: The recipients had to promise to balance their budgets, free prices, fight inflation, establish a stable currency, and eliminate protectionist trade measures. No similar aid plan was extended to Japan, although American military requisitions for the Korean War greatly helped Japan's economy to recovery after 1950.

In July 1948, after opposing a Western series of currency and economic reforms in Germany, the Soviets blocked all land and water transport to Berlin from the West. For the next 10 months, the allies supplied West Berlin by air. They made over 277,000 flights to bring 2.3 million tons of food and other vital materials to the besieged city. Rather than risk war over the city, with the threat of American nuclear weapons, the Soviets removed their blockade in May 1949. In the same month, the Federal Republic of Germany came into existence, made up of the three Western allied zones. Almost immediately, the Soviet Union established the German Democratic Republic in the Soviet zone. Germany would remain divided for the next 41 years.

Marshall Plan—The U.S. plan to aid Europe in solving its postwar economic problems. The goals were not only the economic reconstruction of Europe, but also the blocking of the domestic communist movements in each country.

To try to force the Western powers out of Berlin in July 1948, the Russians imposed a blockade on the city. In response, the Allies organized an airlift to fly in supplies to the city and its beleaguered citizens. In May 1949 the Soviets lifted the blockade.

In the spring of 1949, the United States and its allies established the **North Atlantic Treaty Organization (NATO),** an alliance for mutual assistance. The initial members were Great Britain, France, Belgium, Luxembourg, the Netherlands, Norway, Denmark, Portugal, Italy, Iceland, the United States, and Canada. Greece and Turkey joined in 1952, followed by West Germany in 1955. At the beginning, NATO was essentially a paper organization. The Americans had disarmed so quickly after World War II that military planners in 1949 drew up plans for a retreat behind the Pyrenees in Spain and across the Channel to England in case of a Soviet attack. Soon, the Americans crafted their strategic response to the communists in a document known as NSC–68, which led to the creation of an immense military system and a vast expansion of the newly created Central Intelligence Agency (CIA) to counter the communist advance anywhere in the world by any means necessary.

In 1955 the Soviets created the **Warsaw Pact,** which formalized the already existing unified military command in Soviet-dominated Eastern Europe. Warsaw Pact members included, in addition to the Soviet Union, Albania, Bulgaria, Romania, Czechoslovakia, Hungary, Poland, and East Germany. The alliance lasted until 1989.

China and Korea: 1949–1953

The communist leader Mao Zedong's victory in China in 1949 (see Chapters 29 and 35) shocked the United States even more than did the communist advances in Eastern Europe in 1948. Suddenly, the global maps featured a large part of Eurasia colored in red. But few people in the West were prepared for what was about to happen in Korea.

North Atlantic Treaty Organization (NATO)—The United States and its allies constructed this alliance for mutual assistance, establishing NATO in 1949.

Warsaw Pact—The military alliance of the Soviet Bloc, established in 1955.

After Japan's surrender in World War II, Korea had been divided at the 38th parallel into American and Soviet zones of occupation (see Chapter 35). When the occupying troops left, they were replaced by two hostile forces, each claiming jurisdiction over the entire country. On June 25, 1950, North Korean troops crossed the 38th parallel into South Korea. The United States immediately called for a special meeting of the **UN Security Council,** whose members demanded a cease-fire and withdrawal of the invaders. The Soviet delegate was boycotting the council at the time and was not present to veto the action.

When North Korea ignored the UN's demand, the Security Council sent troops to help the South Korean government. In what the United States termed a "police action," 3 years of costly fighting followed. United Nations forces led by the United States repelled the invaders, who were supported by the USSR and the People's Republic of China. An armistice was signed in July 1953, after Stalin's death in March and a U.S. threat to use nuclear weapons against China. Two million Koreans, north and south, perished. About half a million Chinese and over 50,000 Americans lost their lives before the armistice was signed by representatives of North Korea, China, and the United States (on behalf of the United Nations). There were no South Korean representatives present. A new border between the two parts of the country was established near the 38th parallel, and South Korea's independence was maintained. After a period of improving relations between the two Koreas, serious tensions reemerged in the early twenty-first century.

UN Security Council—The arm of the UN made up of representatives of the permanent members of the UN plus other states that serve limited terms. Its function is to maintain peace and order.

The Korean conflict was the first in which the United States military forces were racially integrated.

The Khrushchev Years: 1953–1962

After World War II, Josef Stalin returned to the policies he had imposed in the 1930s—a command economy based on 5-year plans enforced by the security police. Until his death in 1953, Stalin oversaw the extension of communist governments throughout eastern Europe and in China. Stalin came to occupy the same all-commanding position in the communist controlled countries abroad as he did in the Soviet Union.

Stalin's death in March 1953 introduced a period of collective leadership in the Soviet Union. The transition from an all-powerful despot to a clique of competing apparatchiks brought a change to the nature and scope of Soviet foreign policy for the 2 years after 1953. A committee made up of Lavrenti Beria (secret police), Georgi Malenkov (chief Stalin aide), and Vyacheslav Molotov (foreign affairs) succeeded Stalin. Within 3 years, the initial triumvirate had disappeared, elbowed aside by Nikita Sergeyevich Khrushchev (1894–1971).

IMAGE
Red Square Military Parade, Moscow

Khrushchev's greatest contribution to the history of world communism was to launch the de-Stalinization campaign. In February 1956 at the Twentieth Party Congress, he gave a speech titled "The Crimes of the Stalin Era." He attacked his former patron as a bloodthirsty tyrant and revealed many of the cruelties of the purges and the mistakes of World War II. He carefully heaped full responsibility on the dead dictator for the excesses of the past 25 years, removing the blame from the apparatchiks such as himself whom Stalin had placed in power. Khrushchev blamed Stalin's crimes on the dictator's "cult of the personality."

Khrushchev's speech echoed throughout the communist world, sparking uprisings in Poland and Hungary and widening the gulf between China and the Soviet Union. Chinese-Soviet relations soured drastically after 1956, and by 1960, Khrushchev had pulled all Soviet technicians and assistance out of China. During the next decade, the split grew still wider as Mao proclaimed himself to be Khrushchev's equal in ideological affairs, and the Chinese tried to extend their own power in the developing world against both the Soviet Union and the United States by sending out the same sorts of technicians and money as the others.

CASE STUDY
Lenin (1920) vs. Khrushchev (1960)

Khrushchev also imposed his point of view that nuclear war would be suicidal for all concerned. He returned to the Leninist doctrine of **peaceful coexistence** and renounced the idea that open war between the socialist and capitalist worlds was inevitable. Peaceful coexistence ushered in momentarily better relations between Moscow and Washington and led to a summit meeting in Geneva in 1955. Later, the Americans refrained from interfering in the Polish and Hungarian crises that erupted in 1956, and Moscow and Washington worked together during the Suez Crisis that same year.

Two Soviet technological triumphs, however, in 1957 escalated the tensions between the United States and the USSR. Soviet scientists put the first artificial satellite, *Sputnik,* into orbit around the earth and began building a powerful fleet of intercontinental ballistic missiles (ICBMs). These advances gave the Soviet Union the ability to land a nuclear weapon on U.S. territory in 25 minutes. The Cold War was becoming much more dangerous.

DOCUMENT
Khrushchev Challenges the West to Disarm

A series of conflicts between Moscow and Washington in the early 1960s brought the superpowers closer to nuclear war. A summit convened in Paris in 1960 broke up angrily when the Soviets shot down an American U–2 reconnaissance plane over Siberia. Khrushchev, sensing the presence of an ailing, lame-duck president in Eisenhower, seized the opportunity to denounce the West in a series of provocative moves. He demanded the resignation of UN Secretary-General Dag Hammarskjold (HAM-mer-shold), who he believed

---

peaceful coexistence—The Leninist doctrine that refutes the notion that open war between the socialist and capitalist worlds is inevitable—competition between the two systems would continue in all other areas, however.

Stalin's chief supporters surround the bier at his funeral, March 6, 1953. Left to right, they are Vyacheslav Molotov, Kliment Voroshilov, Lavrenti Beria, Georgi Malenkov, Nikolai Bulganin, Nikita Khrushchev, Lazar Kaganovich, and Anastas Mikoyan. Khrushchev was the victor in the power struggle to succeed Stalin.

opposed the Soviet-backed side in the civil war currently raging in the Congo.

Khrushchev and Kennedy

In the spring of 1961, with John F. Kennedy, a young and inexperienced president, in office, Moscow stepped up all of its pressures around the world. The failure of a U.S. attempt to land forces of Cuban exiles at the Bay of Pigs to overcome Premier Fidel Castro gave Khrushchev a victory in the competition for influence in the decolonizing world. Russian and American interests increasingly collided in all perceived power vacuums. These zones, such as in Laos and Vietnam, in which imperial powers had withdrawn but in which there were no stable governments to replace them, threatened to become theaters of war.

DOCUMENT
Kennedy and Cuba

In Europe, the Soviets once again demanded the withdrawal of the allies from West Berlin. Once again, citing postwar agreements, the West refused to back down. This time, the East Germans, acting under Soviet supervision, erected a wall between the two halves of the city, thereby blocking escape routes formerly used by thousands. To a generation of leaders in the United States, students of the lessons of appeasement in Munich a quarter century earlier and of the success of containment, it seemed evident that force had to be met with force.

IMAGE
Brandenberg Gate, Berlin, Germany

In October 1962 the world came as close as it ever has to full-scale nuclear war. Three years earlier, Fidel Castro had led a successful revolution against the right-wing Cuban dictator Fulgencio Batista (bah-TEES-tah). Castro immediately began to transform the island into a communist state. After the failure of the American effort to overthrow him at the Bay of Pigs, the Soviets began to install missiles in Cuba.

To the United States these missiles were a dangerous threat to the Cold War balance of power. Kennedy ordered what was, in effect, a naval blockade around Cuba and demanded that Moscow withdraw the offensive weapons. After a few days of "eyeball-to-eyeball" crisis in which one incident might have triggered direct military—even nuclear—action between Moscow and Washington, Khrushchev "blinked"—he ordered the missiles removed in exchange for assurances that the United States would respect Cuba's territory and other concessions such as the removal of American missiles in Turkey.

During this time, people on both sides of the "Iron Curtain" became painfully aware of the fragility of the peace between Moscow and Washington and of the capacity of the two powers to put an end to human life on the planet. Children in Russian and American schools practiced the routine of "duck and cover" and learned where bomb shelters were.

Khrushchev was forced from office in 1964, after his blunders in Cuba. Before he left, however, he worked with the Americans to avoid future nuclear confrontations.

After the frightening confrontation in October 1962, the United States and the Soviet Union never again came so close to a nuclear war. They established a series of agreements that assured full communication—such as the "Hotline" between Moscow and Washington—and began to limit the growth of their nuclear arsenals. The Cuban missile crisis convinced leaders in Washington and Moscow of the need to reduce the peril of nuclear war and ushered in a 30-year process of complex negotiations dealing with all

Document Khrushchev's Address to the Twentieth Party Congress

After a quarter century of Stalinist rule, the USSR badly needed a policy change and a break from the iron-handed treatment of the "Vozhd." Three year's after Stalin's death, Nikita S. Khrushchev emerged as the most important Soviet political figure. In March 1956, Khrushchev justified change on the grounds that Stalin had departed from Leninist norms and pursued the "cult of the personality."

When we analyze the practice of Stalin in regard to the direction of the party and of the country, when we pause to consider everything which Stalin perpetrated, we must be convinced that Lenin's fears were justified. The negative characteristics of Stalin, which, in Lenin's time, were only incipient, transformed themselves during the last years into a grave abuse of power by Stalin, which caused untold harm to our party.

We have to consider seriously and analyze correctly this matter in order that we may preclude any possibility of a repetition in any form whatever of what took place during the life of Stalin, who absolutely did not tolerate collegiality in leadership and in work, and who practiced brutal violence, not only toward everything which opposed him, but also toward that which seemed to his capricious and despotic character, contrary to his concepts.

Stalin acted not through persuasion, explanation, and patient cooperation with people, but by imposing his concepts and demanding absolute submission to his opinion. Whoever opposed this concept or tried to prove his viewpoint, and the correctness of his position, was doomed to removal from the leading collective and to subsequent moral and physical annihilation. This was especially true during the period following the 17th party congress, when many prominent party leaders and rank-and-file party workers, honest and dedicated to the cause of communism, fell victim to Stalin's despotism. . . .

Lenin's traits—patient work with people; stubborn and painstaking education of them; the ability to induce people to follow him without using compulsion, but rather through the ideological influence on them of the whole collective—were entirely foreign to Stalin. [Stalin] discarded the Leninist method of convincing and educating; he abandoned the method of ideological struggle for that of administrative violence, mass repressions, and terror. He acted on an increasingly larger scale and more stubbornly through punitive organs, at the same time often violating all existing norms of morality and of Soviet laws. . . .

During Lenin's life party congresses were convened regularly; always when a radical turn in the development of the party and the country took place Lenin considered it absolutely necessary that the party discuss at length all the basic matters pertaining to internal and foreign policy and to questions bearing on the development of party and government. . . .

Were our party's holy Leninist principles observed after the death of Vladimir Ilyich?

Whereas during the first few years after Lenin's death party congresses and central committee plenums took place more or less regularly; later, when Stalin began increasingly to abuse his power, these principles were brutally violated. This was especially evident during the last 15 years of his life. Was it a normal situation when 13 years elapsed between the 18th and 19th party congresses, years during which our party and our country had experienced so many important events? These events demanded categorically that the party should have passed resolutions pertaining to the country's defense during the patriotic war and to peacetime construction after the war. Even after the end of the war a congress was not convened for over 7 years. . . .

In practice Stalin ignored the norms of party life and trampled on the Leninist principle of collective party leadership.

Questions to Consider

1. What is the cult of the personality, and why is it a bad thing?
2. How did Khrushchev note that Stalin departed from Leninist norms?
3. Why do you think Khrushchev made these charges against the very man who was responsible for his present position as General Secretary of the Communist Party?

From U.S. Congress, *Congressional Record,* 84th Congress, 2nd Session, Vol. 102, (Washington, D.C.: U.S. Government Printing Office, 1956), pp. 9389–9403.

Discovery Through Maps

Massive Retaliatory Power, 1954

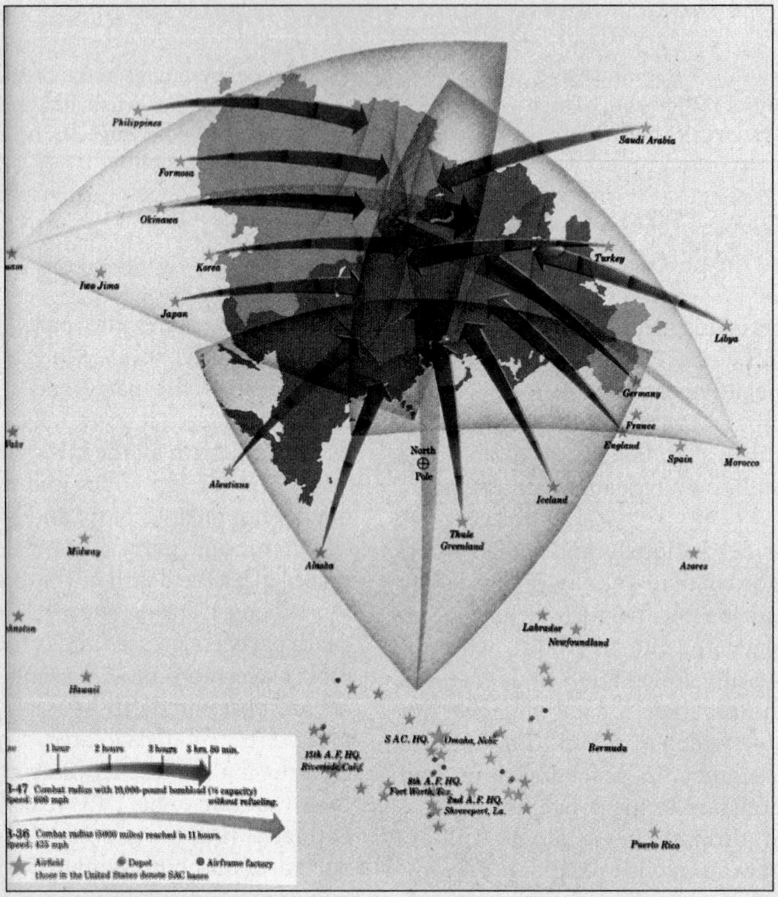

The decisive fact of life for citizens of the United States and the Soviet Union in the 1950s and 1960s was the possibility, perhaps the probability, that a cataclysmic nuclear conflict would bring an end to the human race. While open air nuclear testing spread and polluted the earth's atmosphere, Moscow and Washington pursued a race to develop delivery systems to gain an added advantage in case of war.

Students in schools practiced the maneuver of "duck and cover" to protect themselves from incoming warheads. Homeowners were encouraged to build backyard bomb shelters. Radio stations broadcast "test emergency warnings." In the northern part of the United States, volunteers scanned the skies for incoming aircraft.

This is an example of a Cold War map published in *Fortune* magazine in May 1954 after John Foster Dulles, the U.S. Secretary of State, announced a new policy based on "massive retaliation." This map was meant to reassure Americans that the major Soviet targets were well covered and that Moscow dared not attack first.

This propaganda effort was accompanied by a program to present the Russians as evil, in order to justify the buildup of Americans arms. Only a few people dared consider that similar maps were circulating in Moscow, showing American targets, and that the likeliest outcome of the retaliation strategy would be mutual destruction.

After the Cuban Missile Crisis of October 1962, the Soviet Union and the United States started a long process to lessen the possibility of a nuclear nightmare. Forty years later, George W. Bush, the President of the United States, and Vladimir Putin, the President of Russia, signed a treaty to reduce the number of their nuclear weapons by two-thirds.

Questions to Consider

1. Attack or defend the following statement: "Nuclear weapons are the only factors that have prevented a World War III."
2. In your opinion, what role did manipulation of public opinion play in justifying the U.S. arms buildup?
3. What were the advantages for the United States in their policy of "Massive Retaliation?"

Berlin was Europe's flashpoint for the greater part of the Cold War. The Soviet Bloc had failed to win the confrontation during the Berlin Blockade (1948–1949). In 1961, testing the resolve of the new U.S. president, John F. Kennedy, the East Germans erected a wall—shown in its early stages here—separating their zone from the sectors controlled by the Western powers. The Berlin Wall was the site of numerous brave and tragic escape attempts until it was torn down in 1989.

aspects of the risk of nuclear war. A limited test ban treaty was signed in August 1963 and later treaties were agreed to outlawing the testing of nuclear devices in outer space, in the earth's atmosphere, or underwater. Latin America was declared to be a nuclear free zone in 1968, and nonproliferation treaties followed in 1970 and 1978.

The greatest proof of the superpowers interdependence could be found in the Strategic Arms Limitation Talks (SALT I and SALT II). In these two negotiations, the United States and the USSR acknowledged, in effect, an equivalence of killing power that led to the capacity for "mutual assured destruction" (MAD). After 2 years of complicated talks, President Richard Nixon and General Secretary Leonid Brezhnev signed the SALT I treaty in Moscow in the spring of 1972. The treaty limited the number of intercontinental ballistic missiles (ICBMs) that could be deployed by each side for 5 years and restricted the construction of antiballistic missile systems to two sites in each country in order to maintain MAD. SALT II dealing with ICBMs that could be equipped with multiple independently targeted reentry vehicles (MIRVs) was eventually signed in 1979. In 1982, the Strategic Arms Reduction Talks (START) began but were interrupted in 1983 and were not renewed until Mikhail Gorbachev became the Soviet leader.

VIETNAM AND AFGHANISTAN

- *What were the implications of the U.S. failure in Vietnam and the Soviet failure in Afghanistan?*

While the superpowers carefully avoided fighting each other, they invested heavily in groups representing them in areas undergoing decolonization: Generally each side had a proxy it financed which fought for it (see Chapters 34 and 35).

There were two exceptions to this rule: The United States became caught up in Vietnam, and, at the end of the period, the Soviet Union became mired in a swamp of its own in Afghanistan. The Russians gave enormous support to the forces opposing the United States in Vietnam, while the Americans financed and trained the

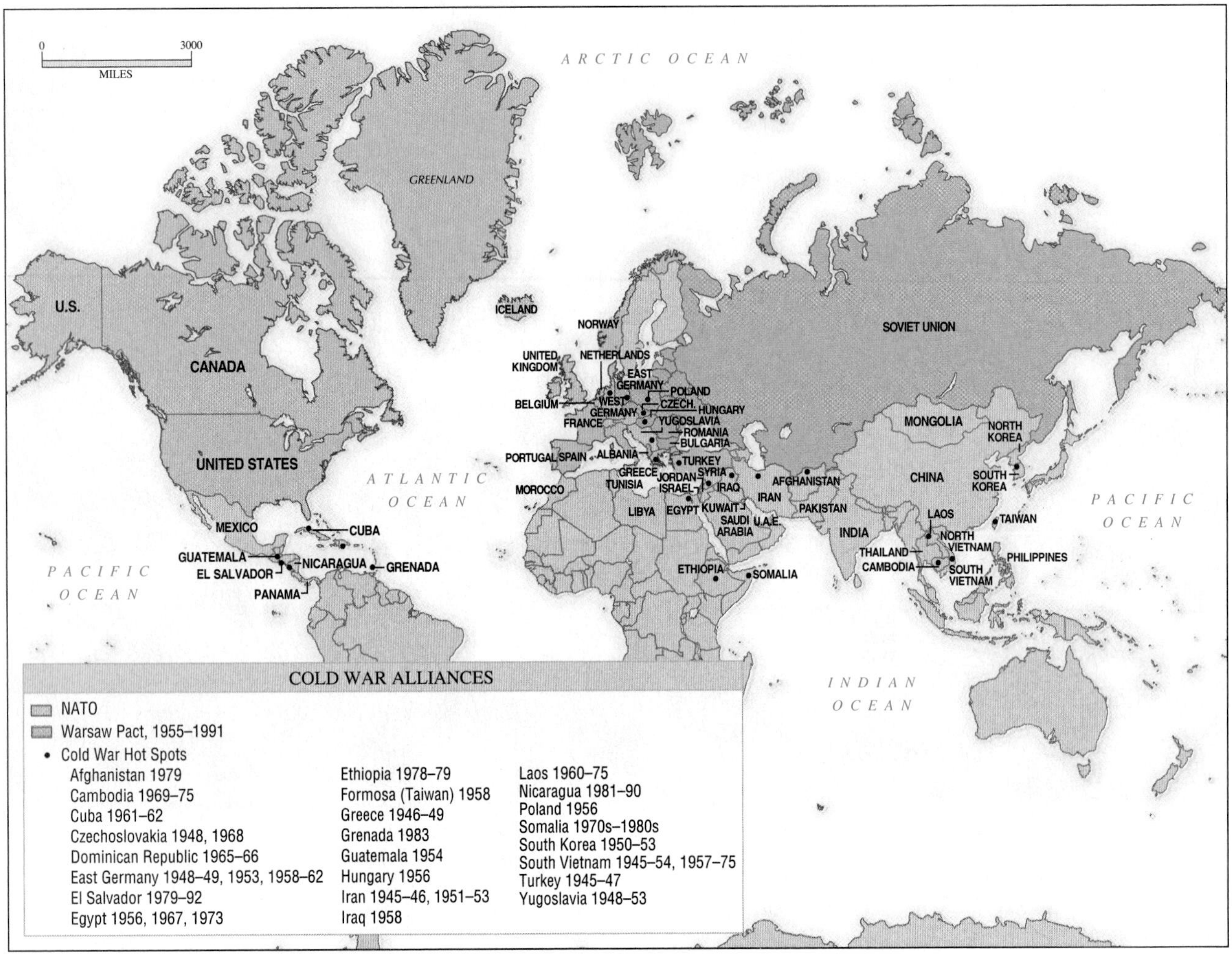

Most of South America, Asia, and Africa served as arenas for Moscow and Washington's bipolar competition during the Cold War.

forces opposing the Russians in Afghanistan. The wars had devastating effects on both countries.

The Americanization of the Vietnamese Civil War

The United States initially opposed the reinstatement of French rule in Vietnam after World War II. When the Russians and Chinese recognized the government of the Democratic Republic of Vietnam (DRV) under Ho Chi Minh, however, the U.S. policy shifted to support the French against the DRV, now deemed an agent of international communism. France's defeat at Dienbienphu (dee-EN-bee-EN-FOO) in 1954 led the United States to assume the role of protector of the noncommunist forces in the southern part of Vietnam, while the DRV in the north was supported by the USSR and China. Civil war continued in the south, as communists and others rebelled against the U.S.-supported government.

In 1960 there were only 800 U.S. military advisers in South Vietnam. Four years later, this figure had risen to 23,000. Thereafter, the war in all of its aspects became increasingly Americanized. By 1968 there were more than 500,000 U.S. troops in the country. In 1965 the United States turned the southern civil war into a war against the DRV, which had been aiding the communist forces in the south, by starting an intensive air campaign against the north. The aerial campaign failed to intimidate the North Vietnamese and became a subject of bitter controversy in the United States. Support of the DRV and southern communist forces by the Russians and the Chinese made the Vietnam conflict part of the larger Cold War.

Many Americans began to question the U.S. role in Vietnam. Their doubts were sharpened in the early spring of 1968 when the Viet Cong (pro-Communist South Vietnamese guerrillas) launched the Tet Offensive against the Saigon forces and the Americans. Widely covered by television and print journalists, the offensive turned into a military disaster for the Viet

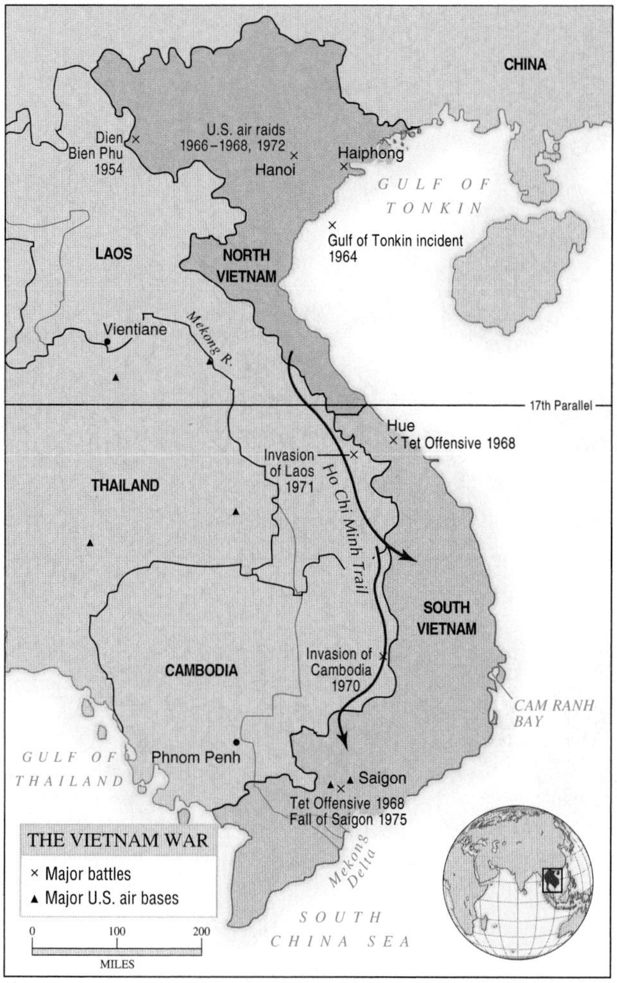

After 1945, Indochina returned temporarily to French dominance. A successful national liberation movement drove the French out in 1954, and thereafter, the United States became increasingly involved in the struggle between Saigon in South Vietnam and Hanoi in North Vietnam.

Cong and DRV, but the images of death and destruction communicated a notion of helplessness to the American people. The U.S. military victory became a political defeat for President Johnson.

During the final months of President Lyndon Johnson's administration, peace talks began in Paris with all interested parties represented. The Nixon administration continued the talks through 3 years of frustrating negotiations until, in January 1973, an accord was signed. It provided for a cease-fire, the withdrawal of U.S. troops, and the release of all prisoners of war.

Once the Americans withdrew, the North Vietnamese continued their advance into the south to unite the whole country. In early 1975, the Hanoi forces, soon to be the fifth largest military in the world, began a massive offensive. Deprived of U.S. support, the southern forces fell apart once the northern frontiers were overrun. Saigon was captured in late April and renamed Ho Chi Minh City. Many South Vietnamese fled their homeland, and some 140,000 gained sanctuary in the United States.

Repercussions of the U.S. Failure

The United States expanded the fighting into neutral Cambodia in the spring of 1970, invading it with the goal of cutting North Vietnamese supply lines and driving the DRV army from its sanctuaries there. Following the North Vietnamese victory in 1975, Communists took control of Cambodia and Laos. The brutal Khmer Rouge (KMEHR REUZH) regime embarked on a reign of terror in Cambodia, which was renamed *Kampuchea.* In Phnom Penh, the capital, nearly all the inhabitants—more than 2 million people—were driven into the countryside, regardless of age or infirmity.

People in other cities suffered the same fate; many died from sickness or starvation. A new social system of farm units with labor brigades and communal kitchens was set up. The slightest sign of disobedience resulted in death. The leader of the Chinese-supported Khmer Rouge regime was Pol Pot. His regime's goal seems to have been a self-sufficient agricultural society in which most people would have food and shelter but no pay. It is estimated that between 1975 and 1980 more than 2 million Cambodians died, most of them savagely murdered.

After the United States withdrew its troops from Vietnam in 1973, many South Vietnamese fled the country. Here a mother and her children struggle across a river to escape the aerial bombardment of their village.

Pictured here are some of the results of Pol Pot's policy to purify Cambodian society. The slaughter of approximately two million people turned the beautiful country of Cambodia into a "Killing Field."

By the end of the 1990s, comparative stability had returned to the region. Normal diplomatic and trade relations were restored between the United States and Vietnam. In Cambodia a massive UN operation stabilized the country and permitted an election in 1993 that included all parties. By 1994 the Khmer Rouge, because of their continued military activities, were expelled from participation in the Phnom Penh government. Finally, after the death of Pol Pot, the Cambodian government reached an accord with the Khmer Rouge to bring peace to Cambodia.

The USSR's "Vietnam": Afghanistan

The USSR had signed a "friendship treaty" with Afghanistan in 1978, a symbolic document testifying to the close ties between Moscow and Kabul. By 1979, however, it appeared that the Soviet-supported government of President Hafizullah Amin (hah-fee-ZOO-lah ah-MEEN) would be toppled by a rebellion. Earlier, the Soviets had sent in 5000 military and civilian advisers to assist him. Moscow had made such a large investment that it could not tolerate the loss of its client state. Further, the occupation of the American embassy in Teheran, Iran, in November 1979 and the loss of U.S. "listening posts" in that country testified to a major shift in the regional balance of power.

In late December, thousands of Soviet troops crossed the border, captured the airport, and stormed the presidential palace in Kabul. They killed their erstwhile ally Amin and installed Babrak Kamal. The Soviet advance, however, sputtered to a stop during the next few years. Moscow was caught in a destructive quagmire. The Afghan resistance, led by the **mujahideen** (moo-JAH-he-DEEN), aided by soldiers from Saudi Arabia and other Islamic countries and lavishly supported by the United States, stalemated the Soviets and their puppets. The one advantage the USSR had in the battlefield—air power—was negated by the Afghans' effective use of American-supplied Stinger antiaircraft missiles.

As the decade wore on, Afghanistan became for the USSR what Vietnam had been for the United States: a costly, demoralizing, divisive conflict. Similarly, the cost to the Afghan people was immense. Millions were uprooted, villages were destroyed, and many areas were littered with mines and booby traps. The Soviet Union

---

mujahideen—Muslim guerrilla warriors involved in a holy war *(jihad)*.

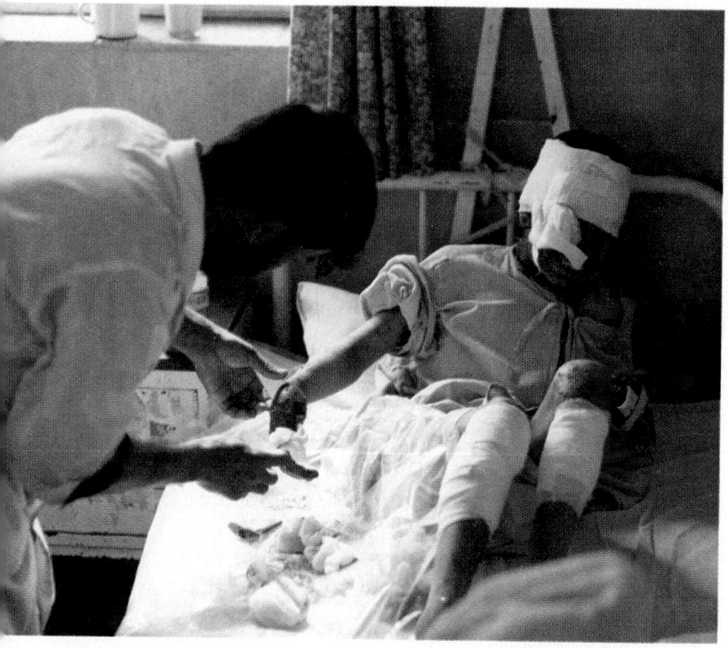

Landmines planted during the Afghan war had and continue to have devastating effects on the civilian population.

finally withdrew its forces in 1989. The civil war continued into the 1990s, and Afghanistan returned to its tradition of tribal competition until a puritanical religious party, the Taliban, aided by Osama bin Laden and his al-Qaeda terrorist group, imposed its control on 80 percent of the country at the end of the 1990s (see Chapter 34).

GORBACHEV AND THE END OF THE COLD WAR

■ *How successful was Gorbachev in reforming the Soviet political and economic system?*

Mikhail Gorbachev, the leader of the Soviet Union from 1985 to 1991, made major contributions in the foreign policy arena. In acknowledgment of his accomplishments, he received the Nobel Peace Prize in 1990.

DOCUMENT
Gorbachev on the Need for Economic Reform

He renounced the Brezhnev doctrine that permitted Soviet armed intervention into socialist states. By doing so, he allowed the Soviet Bloc and its Warsaw Pact military commitments to disintegrate; in fact, they no longer existed by the end of 1989. He pulled Soviet troops out of Afghanistan in 1989 and worked to bring peace to several hot spots in Africa, including Angola. Most remarkably, he chose not to obstruct the reunification of Germany. He joined in UN resolutions condemning

MAP
Breakup of the Soviet Union

Early in his first administration, President Ronald Reagan referred to the Soviet Union as the "Evil Empire" and showed little interest in cooperating in any way with Moscow. After the accession of Mikhail Gorbachev, Reagan changed his attitude, and the two men worked closely to ease tensions between the two great powers.

Iraq's takeover of Kuwait in 1990 and cooperated in the alliance's military defeat of the invading forces in 1991.

In arms control, Gorbachev brought the process to a logical conclusion. In November 1985 he met with President Ronald Reagan in Geneva to continue the discussion of arms control issues. The two powers were able to sign the Intermediate Nuclear Forces (INF) agreement in Washington in 1987. The INF accord set up the destruction of all intermediate- and shorter-range missiles within 3 years. Further, the treaty would be monitored by on-site verification, with Soviet and U.S. experts confirming the fulfillment of the treaty's provisions in each other's country.

The end of the Cold War removed from the world the nightmare of bipolar nuclear annihilation. The signing of the Strategic Arms Reduction Treaty (START) in July 1991 marked the first step in cutting down the large stockpiles of nuclear warheads on each side. In 1994 Moscow and Washington formally altered the targeting software in their missiles, removing each other's strategic areas from the target list. The two countries also pledged to work together to fight nuclear proliferation.

DECOLONIZATION

- *What were two of the most important factors in bringing about decolonization?*

The end of the twentieth century marked a major watershed in world history. The two World Wars had destroyed the dominant position of the traditional European powers such as England, France, and Germany. The Munich pact signed in 1938 would be the last major diplomatic note signed solely by these traditional powers. After 1945, political dominance moved to the periphery of the Western zone—to Moscow and to Washington, where it remained for the relatively brief period of the Cold War. It is evident that the United States stands in 2005 as the last of the major, Western powers.

After 1945 the non-Western world led by Japan, India, and China asserted itself, and as the third millennium begins, countries that were colonies a century earlier are making important steps to become regional and world powers. Decolonization is the essential step by which the non-Western world passed from being an object of to being a major subject of world affairs.

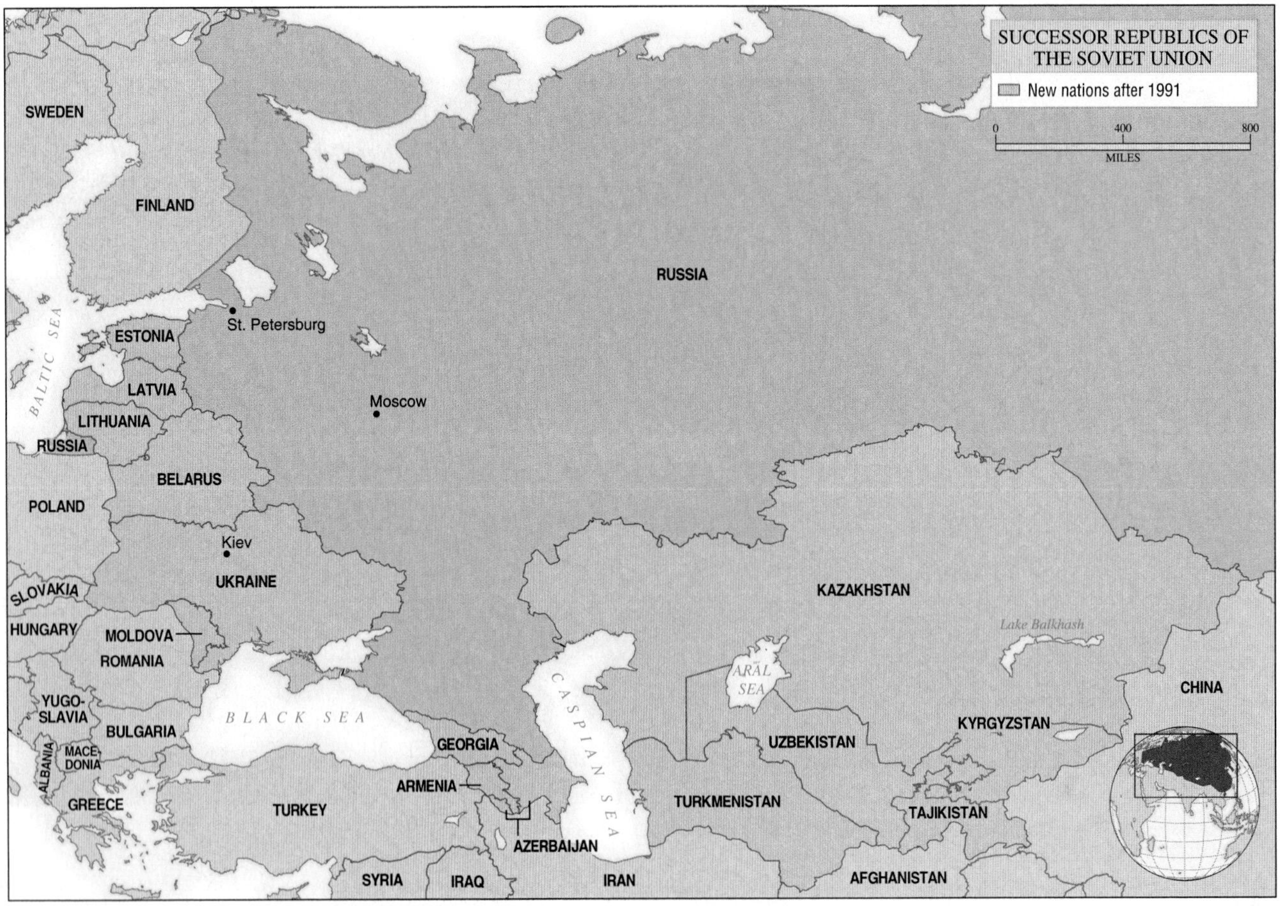

The end of the Union of Soviet Socialist Republics in 1991 led to the birth of 14 new states.

Asia

The most powerful Asian nations—China, Japan, and India—each followed a different path after World War II (see Chapter 35). The Civil War in China between the communists and Nationalists, begun in 1927, had been interrupted by the Japanese invasion and the subsequent events of World War II. It reignited in 1945 and would end with a communist victory in 1949. Japan emerged from its defeat and devastation slowly after 1945, but under the indirect control of the Americans, it would again become a major industrial power by the end of the 1950s. The subcontinent gained its independence from Great Britain in 1947, in the successor states of India and Pakistan (see Chapters 29 and 35). Those countries in Asia still remaining under colonial rule began their journeys to independence.

French rule in Indochina (comprising the territories of Laos, Cambodia, and Vietnam) was in some ways the least enlightened of all the colonial regimes in Southeast Asia. In 1941, for example, the colonial government had the highest proportion of Europeans in its service of any in the region. Eighty percent of the Vietnamese population was illiterate, and less than three percent of the population received any higher education. After World War II, France, which had been a power in Indochina for 80 years, was forced to grant a measure of autonomy to Cambodia and Laos, its former colonial possessions in Southeast Asia. The status of Vietnam posed a greater problem. In 1945 a nationalist and procommunist movement led by Ho Chi Minh had established the independent Democratic Republic of Vietnam, also referred to as the Vietminh regime.

Negotiations between the Vietminh and the French led nowhere, and war broke out in December 1946. The cruel and violent struggle, anticolonial as well as ideological, lasted for nearly 8 years. In May 1950 the United States began sending substantial financial and military support to the French. The end came dramatically in 1954 when the French surrendered their isolated outpost at Dienbienphu, along with 10,000 troops.

In a conference at Geneva later that year, a truce line was established at the 17th parallel, to be regarded as a temporary boundary pending nationwide elections. These elections were never held; instead in 1955, Bao Dai, a puppet of the French, installed his prime minister Ngo Dinh Diem as head of a new Republic of Vietnam, based in Saigon. The United States gave its full support to this Vietnamese Catholic leader. Meanwhile, the tension between the DRV regime in Hanoi and the Saigon government increased.

As discussed previously, the United States shipped advisors and weapons to Saigon in an attempt to create a South Vietnamese state capable of holding its own against the DRV and their allies in South Vietnam. Washington also sponsored the establishment of the Southeast Asia Treaty Organization (SEATO) to stop the spread of communism into Cambodia, Laos, and South Vietnam. At the same time, the communists, thwarted in their aim to unite North and South by an election, began guerrilla operations against the South Vietnamese leader Ngo Dinh Diem. Diem, in the face of a rising crisis, became even more autocratic and less inclined to make reforms, perhaps reflecting Washington's shift in policy from President Eisenhower's emphasis on "nation building" to Kennedy's strategy of "counterinsurgency."

In the Philippines, Japanese occupation during World War II brought most of the Filipinos closer to the United States. However, the drive for independence continued. Independence was granted in July 1946. In the former Dutch East Indies, local liberation movements began almost immediately after the war for the expulsion of the European imperialists. Indonesia succeeded in gaining independence in December 1949.

The Middle East and North Africa

European colonizers fully expected their rule in the Middle East and North Africa to extend for the rest of the twentieth century, but events of World War II set off forces that accelerated the Arab and African nationalist challenges to colonial rule. One change the war brought was that tens of thousands of colonial subjects served as soldiers and laborers in theaters of war in North Africa, Europe, the Middle East, and Asia. As they witnessed the collapse of colonial power elsewhere, the myth of European invincibility was punctured. When they returned home to find massive unemployment and rampant inflation, they joined nationalist movements to express their dissatisfaction with colonial rule.

In the twentieth century the disintegration of the vast Ottoman Empire made the Middle East and North Africa a difficult area in which to establish successor states. Not only were there Arab-Turk conflicts, there were also the competing claims of the various royal houses. After World War II the area became a powder keg of conflicting interests when the Western powers carved the state of Israel out of lands predominantly occupied by the Palestinians. The arrival of European survivors of the holocaust, augmented by the influx of "oriental" Jews from North Africa and southwest Asia, created a legacy of conflicting claims to holy places that has threatened world peace for the past 60 years (see Chapter 34). Control of the region's oil supply has become one of the key diplomatic interests of the industrialized world since 1945.

World War II was a dividing line for the types of organizations Africans formed to voice their grievances and concerns. Before the war, groups were established to represent the particular interests of teachers, clerks, clergy, traders, chiefs, and commercial farmers and usually concentrated on local, cultural, or ethnic issues. However, after the war, political movements developed with more ambitious goals that mobilized people on a national level. Their leaders were typically educated in mission and government schools or overseas in Europe and America.

The Algerian revolutionaries were inspired by the actions of nationalist leaders in other countries. In Iran, Mohammad Mosaddeq (MOS-a-dek) nationalized oil, introduced liberal reforms to government, and challenged the shah so successfully that the ruler was forced to flee. Mosaddeq later was overthrown by a CIA-sponsored military coup in 1954. In addition, Habib Bourguiba (ha-BEEB bor-GHEE-ba) in Tunisia and Abdel Gamel Nasser in Egypt led successful national movements. Emboldened by the French failure at Dienbienphu in 1954, the National Liberation Front (*Front de libération nationale*; FLN) declared a war against the French in November, a war that eventually led to the death of 250,000 Algerians and 25,000 French soldiers. Indirectly, the Algerian revolt led to the fall of the French Fourth Republic and the return of nearly 2 million embittered French residents of Algeria to their homeland.

The pressure of the two Great Powers hastened the end of colonization. A rare instance of the United States and the USSR working together came in the context of the Suez Crisis of 1956. The French and the English, as well as the Israelis, were eager to remove the charismatic Egyptian leader Abdel Gamal Nasser. The French were furious with him for his work in undermining their authority in North Africa. The British wanted to regain their holdings in the Suez Canal—which Nasser had nationalized—and enhance their presence in the region. The Israelis welcomed the weakening of a major Arab leader and hoped to gain the Sinai Peninsula. In November 1956, without first consulting the United States, the countries attacked and defeated Egypt. The United States and the Soviet Union, working through the United Nations, blocked the advance by the three countries and forced them to withdraw from their territorial gains. The bipolar powers would not tolerate interlopers in their global domination.

Sub-Saharan Africa

The British colony of Gold Coast set the pace for independence in sub-Saharan Africa. The British believed that the best approach for their colonies was to groom Africans for a gradual takeover of government. They introduced a constitution in 1945 that allowed for a Legislative Council with an African majority that was not directly elected. Several years later a coalition of lawyers, teachers, and businessmen, many with ties to chiefs, formed the United Gold Coast Convention (UGCC) to counter the new constitution. UGCC leaders selected the recently returned Kwame Nkrumah as its organizing secretary, but he proved too radical for both the UGCC and British officials.

After Nkrumah formed a rival party, the Convention People's Party (CPP), in 1949, he set out to mobilize a mass following. When his "Positive Action" campaign sparked off widespread protests, he was jailed. After his party overwhelmingly won elections in 1951 for the Legislative Council, the British recog-

The charismatic Egyptian leader, Gamal Abdel Nasser, served as a model to national liberation leaders around the globe. He overthrew King Faruq, declared Egypt to be a republic in 1953, and ended British control of the Suez Canal.

nized the inevitable and released Nkrumah and appointed him leader of government business. After winning several more elections, Nkrumah's party called for independence, and the British granted it in 1957. The former Gold Coast colony became the new nation of Ghana.

Ghana's route to independence set a pattern for the freedom struggle in many other colonies throughout the continent. African nationalist parties won over mass followings and challenged colonial rulers, who initially resisted concessions but finally agreed to transfer power through negotiations.

However, France, Belgium, and especially Portugal, were reluctant to follow Britain's lead. They still clung to the belief that their colonies were better off under colonial rule. In 1958 President Charles de Gaulle established the French Community, in which France maintained control over economic development and the external and military affairs of its colonies. De Gaulle was so confident that France's African territories preferred to stay under French rule that he offered them a choice in a referendum of joining a French-controlled federation or independence.

The only French colony to defy de Gaulle was Guinea, where a trade union leader, Sekou Touré (SAY-koo TOO-ray), mobilized his followers to vote against continued French rule. Guinea was granted immediate independence in 1958, although the French punitively pulled out their civil servants and equipment (even ripping out telephones) and refused to offer any economic assistance. However, Guinea's independence was a turning point, and 13 other French colonies in Africa followed suit in 1960. Over the next decade most of the other colonies gained their freedom. The exceptions were the Portuguese colonies and the white-ruled states of Rhodesia and South Africa, who resisted any transfer of power to the African majority. Independence in those territories would take much longer and require African nationalist movements to take up arms to force change.

Farther to the south, and again caught up in the cold war conflict, was Angola, where the Portuguese were eventually pushed out. West Africa came closer to independence, especially the British sector. However, in the Belgian Congo, a collapse of imperial rule set in motion a series of disasters that continue up to the present day. In Latin America the Cubans carried out their revolution in 1958, with the nationalist communist Fidel Castro coming to control. (See Chapter 34 for the details of all of these independence movements.) In each of these liberation movements, and in many others, the pressures of the U.S.-USSR conflict were felt.

The Cold War competition between Moscow and Washington was felt in the former Portuguese colony of Angola where Cuban advisers supported the pro-Soviet side and South Africans worked for the pro-American side.

The United Nations: Midwife for National Independence Movements

Anxious to prevent the return of another global conflict, the wartime allies created the United Nations and new economic institutions. The United Nations and its Trusteeship Council, which had a responsibility for colonial territories under the old League of Nations, would serve as the arena in which those struggling for independence would voice their desires for freedom.

Great Britain and the United States laid the foundations for the United Nations in 1941 when they proposed "the establishment of a wider and permanent system of general security" so that "men in all lands may live out their lives in freedom from fear and want." Subsequent meetings in Moscow and Yalta led representatives of 50 governments, meeting in San Francisco from April to June 1945, to draft the Charter of the United Nations. The membership of the UN grew from 51 members in 1945 to 191 in 2002.

To pursue its goals of peace and an improved standard of living for the world, the UN would work through six organizations: the Security Council, to maintain peace and order; the General Assembly, to function as a sort of "town meeting of the world"; the Economic and Social Council, to improve living standards and extend human rights; the Trusteeship Council, to advance the interests of the colonial peoples; the International Court of Justice, to resolve disputes between nations; and the Secretariat, headed by the secretary-general, to serve the needs of the other organizations.

The greatest controversy at San Francisco arose over the right of veto in the Security Council. The smaller countries held that it was unjust for the big powers to be able to block the wishes of the majority. But the Big Five—the United States, the Soviet Union, China, France, and Great Britain—affirmed that, singly and collectively, they had special interests and responsibilities in maintaining world peace and security. The UN charter therefore provided that the Security Council should consist of 11 members: five permanent members representing the Great Powers and six elected by the General Assembly for a term of 2 years. On purely procedural matters a majority of seven votes was sufficient; on matters of substance, all permanent members had to agree.

UN Universal Declaration of Human Rights

The United Nations proved to be more effective than the League of Nations. Like its predecessor, the UN lacks the sovereign power of its member states, and there are serious questions in the United States as to its effectiveness. However, as was shown in the Korean conflict in the 1950s, the Persian Gulf War in 1991, and in Afghanistan in the early 2000s, it has become more wide-ranging and effective in its influence.

CONCLUSION

The Union of Soviet Socialist Republics and the United States of America had been divided conceptually and philosophically since November 1917. The time of cooperation to defeat Adolf Hitler in a classic balance of power war was the exception rather than the rule. After World War II, the two nations, led by Harry S Truman and Josef Stalin, stood as the only surviving superpowers, and they set forth on an epic global competition in all arenas, except for war with each other.

With the exception of the Cuban missile crisis in 1962, their struggle came down, finally, to the question of economic efficiency. The West's economy had always been more productive than that of the Soviet Bloc. The USSR and its allies suffered drastic damage during World War II, and it took the better part of the next decade to recover to even the prewar levels. The Communist nations' centrally planned economic system worked reasonably well when focused on a single, well-defined goal: military buildup. However, after the mid-1970s, the West presented challenges beyond those of a military nature. Citizens of the Warsaw Pact, who had constantly lagged behind the citizens in the NATO alliance in terms of standards of living and quality of life, began to demand improvements. In response, the Soviet Bloc leaders were forced to reform, and the rigid centrally planned system was ill-equipped to produce the needed changes. This economic failure contributed to the breakup of the Warsaw Pact, the end of the Cold War, and the end of the USSR itself.

While the Euratlantic nations attempted to reestablish some manner of stability in Europe after World War II, there was a flourishing of the prewar national independence movements throughout the rest of the world. From Burma's departure from the British Empire in 1948, to Mao Zedong's victory in China in 1949, to Abdel Gamel Nasser's uprising in Egypt in 1952, the tide of decolonization was sweeping across the globe. National leaders were trying to master the complex calculus of decaying imperial power, aggressive new ideological forces, and their own historical circumstances as they drove to independence.

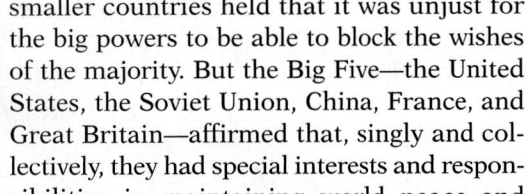

Suggestions for Web Browsing

You can obtain more information about topics included in this chapter at the websites listed below. See also the companion website that accompanies this text, **http://www.ablongman.com/brummett,** which contains an online study guide and additional resources.

Cold War International History Project
http://wwics.si.edu/index.cfm?topic_id=1409&fuseaction=topics.home

This website offers a wide range of scholarly discussions of the conflict.

National Security Archive
http://www.gwu.edu/~nsarchiv/

This online project provides up-to-date revelations of Cold War events based on newly opened archives.

National Security Agency Venona Project
http://www.nsa.gov/venona/index.cfm

The National Security Agency's Central Security Service provides an in-depth account of the U.S. infiltration of Soviet cryptology, revealing the extent of the USSR's attempt to penetrate the highest levels of the American national security apparatus.

National Security Agency Cuba Missile Crisis
http://www.nsa.gov/publications/publi00033.cfm

Site reveals the importance of spies and spy planes in the incident that almost led to a nuclear confrontation.

Cable News Network's Series on the Cold War
http://www.cnn.com/SPECIALS/cold.war/

CNN series offers a wide range of interviews with participants and never-seen-before photographs.

Brookings Institution's U.S. Nuclear Weapons Study Project
http://www.brook.edu/fp/projects/nucwcost/weapons.htm

This site contains documents covering the assumptions that nuclear weapons brought "more bang for the buck."

Russia: How Has Change Affected the Former USSR?
http://www.learner.org/exhibits/russia/

Site sponsored by the Annenberg/CPB Project Exhibits Collection details the enormous changes that have taken place in the former Soviet Union since 1991.

Literature and Film

Jean Larteguy detailed the frustration of the French in their withdrawal from their colonial world in *The Centurions.* The best chronicler of the deceptions and deceit of post-1945 world is John Le Carré in a series ranging from the 1960s into the new century with titles such as *The Spy Who Came in From the Cold; Smiley's People; The Little Drummer Girl; Tinker, Tailor, Soldier, Spy; A Perfect Spy; A Small Town in Germany; The Honourable Schoolboy; The Russia House;* and *The Looking Glass War.*

In *The Scent of Green Papaya* (Columbia/Tristar, 1993) a servant weds a pianist in 1950s Saigon. This tranquilly beautiful film depicts a lost, peaceful Vietnam. Régis Wargnier's *Indochine* (Columbia/Tristar, 1992) portrays the tragic transition of a French family in Vietnam at a revolutionary time. Gillo Pontecorvo's *Battle of Algiers* (Rhino Video, 1966) is the ultimate film about a war of national liberation. The Australian Peter Weir's *The Year of Living Dangerously* (Warner, 1983) presents the complexities of transitions in Indonesia. Stanley Kubrick captured the insanity of the nuclear age in *Dr. Strangelove or How I Learned to Stop Worrying and Love the Bomb* (Columbia/Tristar, 1964).

America's involvement in Vietnam attracted the best efforts of Oliver Stone in *Platoon* (MGM/UA, 1986), Francis Ford Coppola in *Apocalypse Now* (Paramount, 1979), and Michael Cimino in *The Deer Hunter* (Universal Studios, 1978). The CNN series on the Cold War is marked by frank interviews with most of the surviving players. PBS has produced a number of programs dealing with the epoch, such as *The Marshall Plan: Against the Odds* (MPAO-DXO-FXA); *Spy in the Sky* (AMEI–809-FXA), a study of the use of surveillance aircraft in the early years of the Cold War; and several documentaries in the *NOVA* series. The BBC's presentation of John LeCarré's *Tinker, Tailor, Soldier, Spy* (1979), starring Alec Guiness, was a triumph.

Suggestions for Reading

The origins of the Cold War remain a major issue of debate among historians. Perhaps the best overview on the historiographical conflict is Louis J. Halle, *The Cold War as History* (HarperCollins, 1994). John Lewis Gaddis's magisterial study *We Know Now: Rethinking the Cold War* (Oxford University Press, 1998) is based on both declassified U.S. and former USSR archives. On the Vietnam War, see Stanley Karnow, *Vietnam: A History* (Penguin, 1984). The best summary of the tragedy in the Indochina peninsula is Marilyn Young, *The Vietnam Wars, 1945–1990* (HarperCollins, 1994). Stephen White, *Gorbachev and After* (Cambridge University Press, 1991), gives a solid account of the dénouement of the Gorbachev revolution. Easily the best coverage of the collapse of communism in Eastern Europe is Gale Stokes, *The Walls Came Tumbling Down* (Oxford University Press, 1993). William E. Odom's authoritative *The Collapse of the Soviet Military* (Yale University Press, 1999) is essential to understanding the dilemmas facing Gorbachev. J. L. H. Keep's *Last of the Empires: A History of the Soviet Union 1945–1991* (Oxford University Press, 1995) is the best general study of the factors bringing an end to the USSR.

For detailed suggestions for readings on the countries experiencing decolonization, see Chapters 34 and 35.

CHAPTER 33

The United States and Europe Since 1945

Politics in an Age of Conflict and Change

CHAPTER CONTENTS

1940

1944 Bretton Woods Conference

1945 International Monetary Fund (IMF) chartered; World Bank chartered

1947 General Agreement on Trade and Tariffs (GATT) approved

1950

1950 European Coal and Steel Community established

1957 European Economic Community founded

1960

1963 President Kennedy assassinated

1968 Martin Luther King Jr. assassinated

1970

1974 President Nixon resigns

1990

1989–1990 Collapse of Communism in eastern Europe; Unification of Germany

1995 World Trade Organization (WTO) established

2000

2001 al-Qaeda terrorist attacks in New York and Washington

2002 European Union introduces the Euro

2004 Madrid train bombing; the European Union adds nine new states

At the same time that the Cold War dominated international affairs, a revolution in the way people live began in the so-called developed world and spread to other parts of the world. In the past half-century, with the development of more effective means of population control, women have entered the workplace in large numbers, which has altered the nature of family life. Major advances in technology have changed the way people live, work, and use their time. Many have viewed these changes as positive developments, but with them have also come issues of global economic interdependence and environmental concerns. As in the nineteenth century, social and technological developments have run ahead of the vision of politicians. The political parties that succeed now are those that can adapt their programs to reflect these changes.

As all the developed countries emerged from the Cold War and began to work within the framework of market economics, some observers believed that the world had arrived at the "end of history," the triumph of the liberal political and economic model. A certain complacency set in that was exploded on September 11, 2001, when the al-Qaeda organization hijacked four airliners and attacked the symbols of American power: the World Trade Center in New York and the Pentagon and the White House in Washington, D.C. They succeeded in striking three of their four targets. Later terrorists struck in Spain, Morocco, Turkey, and Indonesia. The terrorists have come, by-and-large, from well-educated and prosperous families. The support they receive in developing areas of the Islamic world, however, indicates that by striking at the wealthy, the terrorists tap the frustrations of the poor, seemingly condemned to lag behind the comfortable life of the developed world.

As a new, liberal global market has emerged, world economies have become divided. The economies of the least developed countries are devoted primarily to jobs dealing with raw materials, such as farming, mining, and fishing. The more advanced developing countries are more and more involved in the manufacturing, assembly, and production of clothing, shoes, and a wide range of other consumer goods. In the developed countries, the service sector employs most of the people. More than 90 percent of the babies being born in the world today, however, are in the less developed and developing regions—by definition the poorest. The rest are born in the developed countries, the industrial and postindustrial world—the richest. Two manifestations of this disequilibrium can be increasingly seen: massive population movements and terrorism.

TECHNOLOGICAL AND SOCIAL CHANGES

- *How have recent technological innovations influenced modern society?*

Two great changes in the past, the Neolithic Revolution and the Industrial Revolution, brought about fundamental changes in the way people lived. Since 1945, humanity has been undergoing another such revolution brought about by computers and robotics. These machines have changed the way that work is done and, consequently, the way that people live, relate to one another, and spend their leisure time. These machines, and a demand for a richer life, have led to the vast increase in the number of women entering the work force. The impact of this change on the traditional family structure has led to strains and stresses on roles within the family.

Technological Revolutions

Propelling the developed world's economic growth was the exceedingly fruitful work of its scientists and engineers. Atomic energy continued to present the double-sided prospect of unlimited energy and great danger, with the latter revealed dramatically in the disastrous meltdown at Chernobyl (cher-NOH-bul), Ukraine, in 1986. Advances in biology and biochemistry produced a similar mixed picture.

In 1953 James D. Watson and Francis H. C. Crick revealed a model of the structure of the DNA (deoxyribonucleic acid) molecule, the basic genetic building block of all living things. Research stemming from their work brought new insights into processes of heredity and led to the possibility of shaping the future of numerous species. Like the problems raised by nuclear power, this capability to mold genetics poses profound social and ethical issues. The new research promises to help cure maladies ranging from Alzheimer's disease to Parkinson's disease to various birth defects, but the procedures to make this progress involve using fetal tissue and stem cells, violating the moral codes of certain religions. The cloning of animals, including the sheep Dolly who suffered from premature arthritis, and the possibility of cloning human beings pose serious challenges to governments and spiritual leaders alike. Other spin-offs of the advances in the use of DNA came in the criminal justice system, where the use of DNA evidence in judicial appeals led to the reversal of death penalties levied on innocent people.

The potential for automation in industry was vastly enhanced by the development of the silicon chip, a complex miniature electric circuit etched onto a tiny wafer of silicon crystal. One type of chip, the microprocessor, could serve as the "brain" of a computer. Besides being able to carry out computing functions in a very small space, no larger than a thumbnail, it was much cheaper than earlier technology and much more reliable. Microtechnology markedly affected corporate structures and organization, as well as the nature and extent of work. Communications systems became more sophisticated and widely available. In the space of 20 years the personal computer became as common as television sets in the homes and businesses of the developed world. For individuals, everything from financial planning to training to basic communications can now be done on computers. For businesses, inventories can be more effectively monitored, and financial operations have been simplified. These new systems have led to the increased use of robotics in assembly lines, cheaper and more effective than humans for carrying out repetitive work.

By the beginning of the twenty-first century all parts of the world were industrializing. There were major petrochemical complexes in the Middle East, automated steel mills in India, computer factories in Brazil, and sophisticated hydroelectric installations in Africa. All around the Pacific Rim, nations big and small experienced technological transformation. India benefited from all aspects of the international use of computers: A large part of the new developments in software took place there and much of the customer service business for American software and hardware companies has been routed to English-speaking Indian technicians. In Senegal, French industries outsourced some of their work to the skilled techni-

In more and more applications such as this automotive assembly line, robots are being used to replace human laborers in work.

cians and consultants of Dakar. A vast network of highways, pipelines, railways, shipping and air lanes, fiber-optic cables, and communications satellites united the world. All of these served the needs of multinational firms and publicly owned enterprises.

Technology, in turn, transformed agriculture and diet. Food canning and refrigeration, together with the bulk transport of grains, permitted the shipping of perishable goods to all parts of the world. Food production was increased by plant genetics, new managerial methods, and large-scale agribusinesses, with machines steadily reducing the number of workers doing menial labor. New business methods and technology made the world a smaller and more profitable place. However, this also made the nations of the world more interdependent than ever before.

The Postwar Social Revolution: Women and Family

While the Cold War in its various manifestations captured the attention of politicians and the public alike in the half century after World War II and Western leaders devised a new international economic system, a social revolution was taking place in the developed world, where the vast majority of the population no longer makes its living raising food or processing natural materials. In the 40 or 50 developed countries, less than 6 percent of the population engages in such activities.

Today most people of the developed world do what would be considered "white-collar" work in the services industry. In addition, the government is now a much greater factor in every stage of the life of the average person: at the beginning of the twentieth century in the United States, government spending took up 1.8 percent of the GDP; at the end of the century, it was 34 percent—and much more in European countries.

A whole new range of technological products in the homes of the developed world—microwave ovens, television and stereo systems, computers, and other vastly improved appliances make housekeeping much less work and connect the family unit to a larger universe—the positive or negative effects of which have yet to be determined for traditional culture. Thanks to revolutions in science and technology, people in the capitalist world live longer, grow larger, and are healthier during their lives—a trend that promises to continue. One of the scientific discoveries, the birth control pill, and enhanced birth control procedures made it possible for women to pursue their own destinies.

The biggest postwar revolution has come in the change in the status of women. In Europe and America—as well as in Japan and the Philippines—women are beginning to be elected in significant numbers in regional and local government and in national legislative assemblies, but still not in numbers reflecting their proportion of the population. After 30 years of organized work by groups such as the National Organization for Women (NOW), women are becoming the dominant political force in the United States, even though an Equal Rights Amendment has failed to be enacted.

Immediately after World War II, most women who had gone to work in the war effort returned home. A half-century later, most women work outside the home (60–80 percent of women age 25–54 in the developed world). Even though the labor force is more than one-half female, the average woman continues to earn only about 70 percent of what the average man earns doing the same job. The so-called **glass ceiling** is still in place for most women in the developed

glass ceiling—The limitation placed on a woman's rise within a bureaucracy. It is not seen, but it is real.

Although women slightly outnumber men in the United States, there are only 14 women in the Senate. Still, this is a great increase in the past 20 years.

world; only a very small—but increasing—percentage of women make it to the levels of senior management positions in government and in business. A recent survey, however, has found that in western Europe and North America, most women would want to work "whether or not they needed the money." The same survey found that close to 60 percent of working women in Europe contributed half or more of family income—with French women leading the way, providing 72 percent. The change in women's status is clear from a Gallup poll taken 60 years ago. At that time, 82 percent of people in the United States, men and women, believed that "a married woman should not earn money if her husband was capable of supporting her."[1]

The post-Soviet era in eastern Europe and Russia has been far more difficult for women. The social safety net that was there under the Communist regimes disappeared. It is difficult to find dependable medical and dental care, and loss of a job now usually means loss of a home. Important changes in governments and economics have had few beneficial effects for women, who are not only full-time workers outside the house but also responsible for keeping the home running and acting as caregivers. Traditional male attitudes remain despite the political revolutions since 1991. Women earn as much as one-third less than men for the same job, but worse, women are cut off from important positions in business and government. In Lithuania, for example, women occupy only 15 of the 141 seats in parliament and hold the same low level of participation in important government jobs.

The family in the United States and western Europe experienced a fundamental redefinition in the past half century from that presented in 1950s American television series *Father Knows Best*, which consisted of the genial and patriarchal working father, the attentive and loving housewife, the adorable but mischievous two or three children, the dog, the house in the suburbs, the car, and so on. It is doubtful that this iconic presentation reflected reality, but it was part of the mythology of the United States. At the end of the century, with divorce rates in Europe and parts of the United States leading to the breakup of one out of two marriages each year, the single-parent family was more reflective of reality. Economic demands and the liberation of women from traditional roles led to a majority of working mothers and the appearance in increasing numbers of the "house husband."

As the global economy produces more and more changes in the world, the institution of the family is undergoing further redefinition. In France in 1998 and 1999, for example, a law was instituted that allows nontraditional couples—homosexuals or unmarried men and women living together—to have the same legal rights as traditionally married couples. In some

Document Simone de Beauvoir, *The Second Sex*

A profound, far-reaching postwar movement was the struggle undertaken to improve the status of women. In *The Second Sex*, an analysis of women's secondary status in society, Simone de Beauvoir likened women's status to that of other oppressed groups. The work has become a classic of feminist literature.

The parallel drawn . . . between women and the proletariat is valid in that neither ever formed a minority or a separate collective unit of mankind. And instead of a single historical event it is in both cases a historical development that explains their status as a class and accounts for the membership of particular individuals in that class. But proletarians have not always existed, whereas there have always been women. They are women in virtue of their anatomy and physiology. Throughout history they have always been subordinated to men, and hence their dependency is not the result of a historical even or social change—it was not something that occurred.

Questions to Consider

1. In de Beauvoir's view, what is the link between two oppressed groups, the proletariat and women?
2. Do you believe that de Beauvoir sees a liberation of women from their second class status?
3. Do you believe that de Beauvoir sees anatomy as destiny?

From Simone de Beauvoir, *The Second Sex*, trans. H. M. Parshley (New York: Alfred A. Knopf, 1952).

states in the United States, marriage between people of the same sex has become legal. The controversial and emotional debate about the nature of the family and the roles of men and women in the new global society shows no signs of being resolved.

THE UNITED STATES

▪ *What factors contributed to make the United States the world's most dominant power?*

As we saw in Chapter 32, for most of the half-century after the end of World War II, the United States devoted a large part of its energies to the pursuit of the Cold War. It had emerged from World War II with its landscape unscathed and its economy the most powerful in the world. And this wealth enabled the United States over the next 40 years to assume vast responsibilities such as the Marshall Plan and the maintenance of a global military presence.

MAP The United States in World History: A Chronological Perspective

Domestically, until 1981, both Democratic and Republic administrations based their policies firmly on the legacy of Franklin D. Roosevelt's New Deal. Politicians who opposed the Roosevelt programs suffered decisive defeats. In addition, the major parties after 1965 generally lent their support to the emerging civil rights movement that finally removed the legal restrictions to equal citizenship to the African-American population and extended the possibility of equal treatment for women. However, starting in the 1980s, conservative leaders began questioning various aspects of the New Deal legacy because there were no longer sufficient resources to satisfy the demands of an expanding population.

Postwar Leadership

In addition to his foreign policy accomplishments after 1945, Harry S Truman, who served as president from 1945 to 1953, continued to crusade for the rights of the "common man" and against the "fat cats" as he extended the New Deal. Truman reached out to the African-American population as he integrated the armed forces and extended federal programs to a formerly ignored group.

Republican Dwight David Eisenhower, the former supreme commander of Allied forces in Europe, was twice elected to the presidency with overwhelming victories. He continued, with somewhat less enthusiasm, to oversee the growth of federal programs and the beginnings of racial integration in public schools. Eisenhower's appointment of judges such as Earl Warren to the Supreme Court established a liberal core of judges that would make its mark felt in the civil rights decisions during the 1960s.

Eisenhower's successor, the Democrat John F. Kennedy, was elected president in 1961 and promised a "New Frontier" spirit for America. While speaking out for programs to aid the poor and minorities, he was unable to push his programs through Congress. He captured the nation's idealism, especially with the Peace Corps, but his assassination in November 1963 cut his presidency short.

The Crisis of the Presidency

Kennedy's vice president, Lyndon B. Johnson, picked up the burden of the slain chief executive and completed a series of major domestic reforms. Johnson could claim credit for the **Civil Rights Act of 1964,** the War on Poverty, Medicare, important environmental legislation, and the creation of the Department of Housing and Urban Development. However, major problems such as environmental pollution, decay of the inner cities, and minority discontent—the crisis of rising expectations—remained unsolved.

In foreign affairs the increasingly unpopular Vietnam conflict (see Chapter 32) plagued Johnson's presidency. The war alone cost more than $30 billion annually, and this outlay, along with expensive domestic programs, fueled the inflation that would come in the 1970s. Congress was hesitant to provide the funds needed to improve conditions for minorities and the inner cities while at the same time conducting a costly war. These priorities angered many Americans, spurring the development of a powerful protest movement, and many average citizens found themselves in deep and serious opposition to their government's policies. The ensuing political turmoil turned especially ugly in 1968 with the assassinations of civil rights leader Martin Luther King Jr. (see Document, "Martin Luther King Jr., 'Beyond Vietnam: A Time to Break Silence' ") and of Senator Robert F. Kennedy, brother of the former president, who was close to gaining the Democratic presidential nomination.

The fragmentation of the Democratic opposition led to the 1968 election by a razor-thin margin of Republican Richard M. Nixon. Nixon had served as Eisenhower's vice president for two terms, before being narrowly defeated by John Kennedy in 1960. Nixon, reelected by a landslide in 1972, shifted toward a more pragmatic philosophy of government. To fight inflation, caused in part by the costs of the Vietnam War and social programs, the administration, for the first and only time after World War II, imposed a wage and price freeze from August to November 1971 and wage and price controls from November 1971 to January 1973. These measures helped reduce the rate of inflation to about 3 percent. But when the administration returned to a free market policy at the end of April 1974, prices began to rise. The oil embargo imposed by the **OPEC** nations to protest American support of Israel contributed to the rise in inflation rates to 12 percent and a 6 percent unemployment rate.

During this time, the Nixon administration also concentrated on foreign affairs—especially matters related to ending the war in Vietnam, keeping peace in the Middle East, opening relations with China, and maintaining détente with the Soviet Union. In each area Nixon and his chief adviser, Henry Kissinger, compiled a substantial record of success. This record, however, was overshadowed by scandal.

Nixon's vice president, Spiro T. Agnew, resigned under the weight of charges of bribery, extortion, and kickbacks dating from his time as governor of Maryland. (Under the Twenty-Fifth Amendment to the U.S. Constitution, passed just six years earlier, Nixon appointed a new vice president, Gerald R. Ford.) Far more serious, several men connected with Nixon's 1972 reelection campaign were arrested and charged with burglarizing the Democratic party's campaign headquarters at the Watergate, an apartment and hotel complex in Washington, D.C. Citing "presidential confidentiality," Nixon withheld information concerning these activities from a special prosecutor, a grand jury, and the public. When lengthy televised hearings led to the conviction of his closest associates, Nixon lost the confidence of most of the nation. The Judiciary Committee of the House of Representatives in July 1974 voted to recommend impeachment. Repudiated and disgraced, Nixon resigned in August. His handpicked successor, Gerald Ford, granted Nixon a full pardon.

The Limited Presidency

Economic problems—including high inflation that reduced the value of the dollar and high unemployment—continued to plague the nation. In 1976 Ford ran against the relatively unknown Jimmy Carter, former governor of Georgia. Carter campaigned on promises to restore trust in government, extend social programs, and improve economic conditions. Carter won the close election, becoming the first president from the Deep South since before the Civil War.

Carter inherited the same problems as his predecessors and incurred some new ones. To deal with the crisis in the Middle East, he brought the leaders of Egypt and Israel together at the presidential retreat in Camp David, Maryland. He continued to pursue limitations on nuclear arms. But for many observers, his

Civil Rights Act of 1964—Legislation that imposed equal voting rights, outlawed racial discrimination, and continued to demand desegregation at all levels of society, among other reforms.

OPEC—Organization of Petroleum Exporting Countries created in 1960. An organization created by several petroleum producing states to gain control over their oil output and pricing.

Document Martin Luther King Jr., "Beyond Vietnam: A Time to Break Silence"

One of the most powerful moral voices of the postwar United States was the Reverend Dr. Martin Luther King Jr. He knew his own flaws, and also those of the country in which he lived. As he overcame his own limits, he worked to make his country a place truly more moral, just, kind, and caring. He gave voice to the demands and needs of African Americans that helped achieve the Civil Rights acts of the 1960s that gave, for the first time, equal citizenship rights to all Americans. In this speech at Riverside Church in New York City in 1967, he addressed the moral dilemma posed by the war in Vietnam.

I have come to this magnificent house of worship tonight because my conscience leaves me no other choice. I join with you in this meeting because I am in deepest agreement with the aims and work of the organization which has brought us together: Clergy and Laymen Concerned about Vietnam. The recent statement of your executive committee are the sentiments of my own heart and I found myself in full accord when I read its opening lines: "A time comes when silence is betrayal." That time has come for us in relation to Vietnam. . . .

Since I am a preacher by trade, I suppose it is not surprising that I have seven major reasons for bringing Vietnam into the field of my moral vision. There is at the outset a very obvious and almost facile connection between the war in Vietnam and the struggle I, and others, have been waging in America. A few years ago there was a shining moment in that struggle. It seemed as if there was a real promise of hope for the poor—both black and white—through the poverty program. There were experiments, hopes, new beginnings. Then came the buildup in Vietnam and I watched the program broken and eviscerated as if it were some idle political plaything of a society gone mad on war, and I knew that America would never invest the necessary funds or energies in rehabilitation of its poor so long as adventures like Vietnam continued to draw men and skills and money like some demonic destructive suction tube. So I was increasingly compelled to see the war as an enemy of the poor and to attack it as such.

Perhaps the more tragic recognition of reality took place when it became clear to me that the war was doing far more than devastating the hopes of the poor at home. It was sending their sons and their brothers and their husbands to fight and to die in extraordinarily high proportions relative to the rest of the population. We were taking the black young men who had been crippled by our society and sending them eight thousand miles away to guarantee liberties in Southeast Asia which they had not found in southwest Georgia and East Harlem. So we have been repeatedly faced with the cruel irony of watching Negro and white boys on TV screens as they kill and die together for a nation that has been unable to seat them together in the same schools. So we watch them in brutal solidarity burning the huts of a poor village, but we realize that they would never live on the same block in Detroit. I could not be silent in the face of such cruel manipulation of the poor.

My third reason moves to an even deeper level of awareness, for it grows out of my experience in the ghettoes of the North over the last three years—especially the last three summers. As I have walked among the desperate, rejected and angry young men I have told them that Molotov cocktails and rifles would not solve their problems. I have tried to offer them my deepest compassion while maintaining my conviction that social change comes most meaningfully through nonviolent action. But they asked—and rightly so—what about Vietnam? They asked if our own nation wasn't using massive doses of violence to solve its problems, to bring about the changes it wanted. Their questions hit home, and I knew that I could never again raise my voice against the violence of the oppressed in the ghettos without having first spoken clearly to the greatest purveyor of violence in the world today—my own government. For the sake of those boys, for the sake of this government, for the sake of hundreds of thousands trembling under our violence, I cannot be silent. . . .

Questions to Consider

1. What are Dr. King's arguments against the American involvement in Vietnam?
2. Is Dr. King's argument a political or a moral one?

From Rev. Martin Luther King Jr., "Beyond Vietnam: A Time to Break Silence," April 4, 1967, http://www.hartford-hwp.com/archives/45a/058.html.

greatest accomplishment was that he made human rights considerations an operative part of American foreign policy. Domestically, Carter attempted to enact an extremely ambitious program of social and economic benefits while maintaining sufficient military strength. Not surprisingly, spending increased despite the goal of a balanced budget.

Rising fuel prices and declining per capita output exacerbated the economic difficulties. American helplessness and frustration grew when Iranian militants captured 53 hostages during a takeover of the U.S. embassy in Tehran. The combination of economic problems, the foreign policy crisis surrounding the Soviet invasion of Afghanistan, and the hostage dilemma led to Carter's defeat in November 1980 by Ronald Reagan, former actor and governor of California. As a final snub to Carter, the Iranians released the American hostages just as Reagan took the oath of office in January 1981.

Reagan won the presidency by an overwhelming margin, and he promised to set about reversing a half-century of increasing federal involvement in American life by making drastic cuts in federal programs. These cuts were part of his "New Federalism" program, also known as "Reaganomics." The president believed that, at the same time, he could cut personal and business taxes and increase military spending. The assumption underlying the policy was that the budget cuts and tax cuts would simultaneously cure inflation and bring about economic growth.

The tax cuts were not matched by reduced federal spending, however. The percentage of gross domestic product spent by government increased during Reagan's first term. By the time he left office in 1988, the federal deficit had soared to unprecedented heights spurred primarily by increased defense costs. Inflation rates fell significantly, but interest rates remained high.

The economic problems posed little obstacle to Reagan in the 1984 election, in which he carried 49 of the 50 states. Not even his bitterest critic could deny the effect of his will and personality on the office of president. Observers looked back to Franklin D. Roosevelt to find Reagan's equal as a communicator and master of the legislative process. Reagan won major tax and budget victories in the Democrat-controlled House of Representatives and gained backing in the Senate for such controversial diplomatic initiatives as the sale of sophisticated equipment to Saudi Arabia and the Intermediate-Range and Shorter-Range Nuclear Forces (INF) treaty. He survived an assassination attempt in March 1981, and this display of stamina and his considerable charm gave him an aura of authority and respect—despite a sometimes shocking lack of mastery of the details of his own programs—that no president since Eisenhower had enjoyed.

The United States moved increasingly into the role of participating in international peacekeeping efforts. In October 1983, a suicide bomber in a truck killed 241 Marines in Beirut, Lebanon.

Reagan faced a number of foreign policy challenges in the Middle East and North Africa. A bombing in October 1983 killed 241 marines Reagan had sent to Lebanon in 1982 to act as part of an international peacekeeping force. This attack forced Reagan to withdraw U.S. troops from the area. Relations with Israel cooled when Israeli forces bombed an Iraqi nuclear facility, annexed the Golan Heights (wrested from Syria in 1967), and invaded Lebanon. The aggressive policies of Libyan leader Muammar al-Qadhafi (mu-am-MAR al-ga-DHA-fi) led to conflicts with the United States, which triggered U.S. air attacks on Libya in the spring of 1986. In another controversial move, Reagan sent U.S. naval forces to the Persian Gulf when war between Iran and Iraq threatened to disrupt international oil shipments.

Festering social and economic problems in Latin America erupted into revolutionary movements in El Salvador and Nicaragua. The Reagan administration sent in military advisers and millions of dollars to support the factions it considered "democratic." When Congress withdrew support for the rebels known as the Contras, who were fighting the leftist Sandinista government of Nicaragua, officials in the Reagan administration conspired to carry out illegal maneuvers, including the selling of weapons to supposed moderates in Iran and diverting the proceeds to the Nicaraguan rebels. The "Iran-Contra affair" cast a pall over the last two years of the administration and led to felony convictions for high-ranking Reagan aides.

The Republicans maintained their hold on the White House with the election of George H. W. Bush in 1988. The new president failed to maintain the Reagan momentum in extending American influence favorably to affect the development of democracy and free markets in the Soviet Union. Bush instead drew back, choosing to be "prudent" and to consult closely with allies and opponents alike to maintain stability during the enormous changes occurring in eastern Europe and the Soviet Union during 1989.

Bush's major success in foreign policy was his leadership of the anti-Iraq coalition during the Persian Gulf War in 1990 and 1991, mounted after Iraq invaded and annexed neighboring Kuwait. Deftly working through the United Nations and mobilizing a powerful coalition, Bush effectively stymied the Iraq government diplomatically and then sent U.S. troops to lead the UN coalition forces in a massive bombing campaign against Iraq. A 100-hour ground offensive ultimately drove Saddam Hussein's Iraqi forces out of Kuwait. The coalition constructed by Bush did not go on to Baghdad, however, because of the terms under which the coalition was assembled. Also Bush and his advisers understood that the taking of Baghdad would spark an insurgency in Iraq. This in turn would be followed by a probable Kurdish drive for an independent state, which would threaten the interests of Iran, Turkey, and Syria. Finally, there was the fear that a power vacuum in Iraq would allow the Shi'ite Iranian regime to expand its power into southern Iraq.

Bush's administration faced worsening economic problems: a growing budget deficit, productivity declines, balance-of-trade problems, the failure of many savings and loan institutions, and the fear of recession. Makeshift solutions to foreign opportunities, the deficit crisis, and other pressing domestic problems contributed to the president's decline in public opinion polls.

Nagging economic problems helped ensure the 1992 victory of Bill Clinton, who used a succinct catchphrase to keep his campaign staff focused: "It's the economy, stupid!" In his first two years the former Arkansas governor attempted to take the Democratic party to a more centrist position, responding to the conditions in the bond market more than to his presumed constituency of labor, the poor, and the disaffected. Despite successes such as gaining U.S. acceptance of the **North American Free Trade Agreement (NAFTA),** the cloud of earlier personal improprieties and inadequate staff work gave the Clinton administration an image of muddling inefficiency in both domestic and foreign affairs that contributed to a sweeping Republican victory in the 1994 midterm elections, giving the GOP control of both houses of Congress.

Clinton and his advisers learned their lessons from that defeat and moved increasingly to the political center. In the 1996 elections he ran on a program that was ideologically to the right of George H. W. Bush's positions in 1992 and easily defeated the Republican candidate, former Senate leader Robert Dole. Clinton benefited from the booming economy, which resulted from a basic overhaul of American management and manufacturing techniques, and the generally peaceful world situation. In his second term, Clinton worked continuously to find a solution to the Israeli-Palestinian crisis. He used the prestige of his presidency to try to bring the two peoples together, personally intervening in conferences in the United States and overseas to try to produce a joint agreement on such thorny issues as the status of Jerusalem and an independent Palestinian state. He also placed the United States fully into the complex questions revolving around the ethnic cleansing activities of the Yugoslav state in Bosnia, Croatia, and Kosovo. That he did not find a solution to these difficult problems is a

Rabin and Arafat Shake Hands at the White House, 1993

North American Free Trade Agreement (NAFTA)—North American Free Trade Agreement, agreed to by Canada, the United States, and Mexico and put into effect in 1994. NAFTA created a free-trade zone in North America and removed obstacles to cross-border investment.

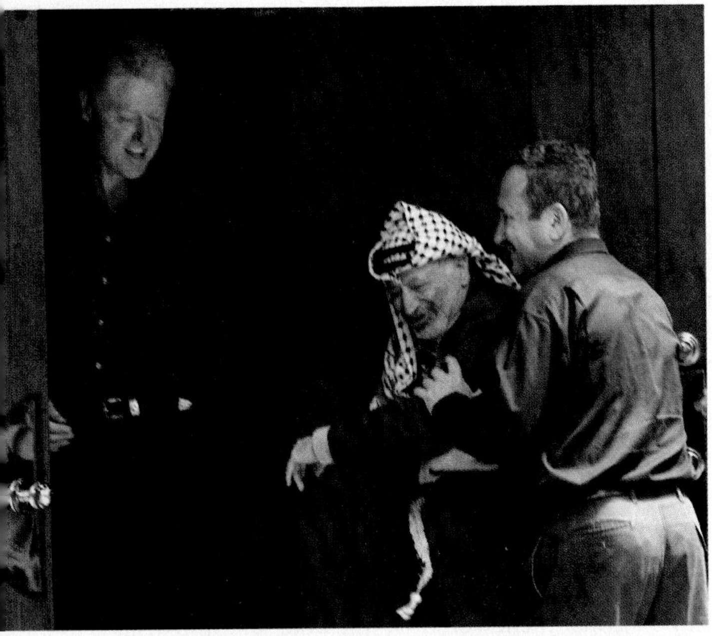

In the last months of his presidency, President Clinton convinced the Israeli leader Ehud Barak to make substantial concessions to resolve the question of Jerusalem. At the last moment, however, Arafat announced he could not make any concessions. The next four years have led to bloody conflict between the Palestinians and the Israelis.

reflection more on the nature of ethnic conflicts than on the efforts of his administration.

A tawdry scandal plagued the president throughout 1998; after finally admitting to improper behavior and lying to the American people, Clinton was impeached by the House of Representatives and his case was sent to the Senate for trial. But the economy continued to be strong and no Americans were dying in foreign wars; perhaps that is why the public seemed more embarrassed than embittered by the entire spectacle and greeted his acquittal by the Senate in 1999 with a collective yawn.

The New Century: Electoral Crisis and Terrorism

The United States greeted the new millennium with a sense of optimism. There was an unprecedented, if uneven, growth in wealth, and the stock markets leapt from one record high to another, riding on the back of companies dealing in the new computer based technologies, the so-called dot-coms. Public opinion focused blithely on the imagined triumphs and tragedies of athletes, actors and actresses, and politicians. As the country became richer, it became less and less concerned with the rest of the world, and the major television networks and newspapers, with few exceptions, reduced their coverage of international affairs.

The 2000 presidential campaign between Vice President Albert Gore and the Governor of Texas George W. Bush, a son of the forty-first president, served to excite more jokes than serious attention. The near dead heat in the November elections was followed by more than a month of recounts in the state of Florida and the juridical jousting of attorneys for the Republican and Democratic parties. In December, the Supreme Court severed the Gordian knot of challenges with a decision that effectively handed the presidency to George Bush. Subsequent surveys showed that Bush would have won the state of Florida had the recounts been permitted, and by taking Florida he would have won the Electoral College. In any event, he finished more than a half-million votes behind Albert Gore in the popular vote.

President Bush's team effectively oversaw three months of successes for the Republican program, before the balance of power swung to the Democratic side in the Senate in the wake of a change-of-party decision by a Republican senator. At the same time, the stock market began a rather severe decline, as the dot-coms experienced the evaporation of their value. This event was heralded by Wall Street observers as a long-overdue market correction. In fact, it was the beginning of a recession. In foreign policy, the Bush team dealt with challenges such as the emergency landing of an American surveillance aircraft in China, began a substantial change in relations with Russia, and irritated its allies by a series of unilateral withdrawals from major international accords.

In the morning of September 11, 2001, the benign contentment and even boredom that characterized public discourse came to an abrupt end when four passenger jets belonging to U.S. companies were hijacked by al-Qaeda terrorists acting on orders from Osama bin Laden. (See Chapter 34 for a discussion of Osama bin Laden and al-Qaeda.) In a skillfully orchestrated set of maneuvers, hijacked jumbo jets, fully loaded with enough fuel to make a transcontinental flight, crashed into the two World Trade Center towers in New York. The combination of the impact of the Boeing jumbos and the heat generated by the burning jet fuel brought down the twin towers, killing nearly 3000 people. Two other airliners attempted *kamikaze*-like attacks on Washington, D.C. One crashed into the Pentagon in Washington, D.C., cutting a huge gash in the five-sided building. Another plane also targeted the White House or the Capitol. It crashed in Pennsylvania after passengers fought back and thwarted the hijackers' plans.

These events, seen live on TV across the globe, had a traumatic effect on the United States matched only, perhaps, by the effects of the Japanese attacks on Pearl Harbor in 1941. The images of the collapsing buildings, their inhabitants jumping to their deaths from

At 8:46 a.m. (Eastern Daylight Time) on September 11, 2001, hijacked American Airlines flight 11 from Boston crashed into the north tower of the World Trade Center. Seventeen minutes later, hijacked United Airlines flight 175, also from Boston, shown here, crashed into the south tower. These two events launched the United States of America into a new millennium, and a new world.

the top floors, and the bravery of fire, police, and emergency personnel, along with ordinary citizens, galvanized the United States into a unity and purpose not seen in generations.

George W. Bush proclaimed a global assault against terrorism in all of its forms and struck at and destroyed the Taliban regime in Afghanistan, a state that had served as the host for, and protector of, Osama bin Laden and al-Qaeda. Public opinion polls gave the president overwhelming support for whatever he wanted to do and the House and Senate voted through authority to pursue the terrorists wherever necessary. At the same time, new legislation, the **Patriot Act,** was passed by the House and Senate and signed into law by the president. This Act gave the government unprecedented authority to delve into the personal lives of Americans and to limit certain civil rights. In addition, a new agency was created, the Homeland Security Office, that was supposed to coordinate police and information gathering activities at all levels to block terrorist attacks.

President Bush and his advisers, after removing Taliban control in Afghanistan, turned their attention to Iraq, where they deemed that Saddam Hussein had close relations with al-Qaeda and possessed concealed stores of chemical and biological weapons, or **weapons of mass destruction.** After a year of trying to gain international cooperation through the United Nations, the Americans with their British allies constructed a coalition of small powers and struck at Iraq in a preemptive attack in the spring of 2003. They quickly

Patriot Act—The Patriot Act was signed into law in October 2001. Its goals can be seen by its official title: "The uniting and strengthening [of] America by providing appropriate tools required to intercept and obstruct terrorism (USA Patriot Act) of 2001."

weapons of mass destruction—Chemical, biological, and nuclear weapons whose capacity to inflict massive casualties far outstrips conventional weapons.

Former president George H. W. Bush takes the hand of his son, President George W. Bush, after the latter's participation in the memorial service at the Washington National Cathedral for those killed in the September 11 terrorist attacks.

defeated Saddam Hussein and his forces militarily, but there appeared to be no well-conceived plan for the postwar period. The vacuum created by the removal of Saddam's Ba'th party by the allies led to all manner of looting and violence. In January of 2005, even though a new Iraqi government had been installed, nearly 150,000 American soldiers remained in Iraq, unable to stop an Iraqi insurgency—aided by anti-American forces coming in from outside. Bush's "go-it-alone" policies toward Iraq had negated all of the pro-American sentiment that had developed in Europe and around the world after September 11, 2001. Polling data indicated that sentiments toward the United States had fallen to an all-time low.

Domestically, President Bush lost the wave of high public support he had had after September 11. By the summer of 2004, public approval of his handling of the war on terrorism had declined, and a majority of Americans questioned the war and occupation of Iraq. The absence of proof of a close Iraqi tie with al-Qaeda combined with the failure to discover weapons of mass destruction in Iraq led many Americans to become cynical about the Bush administration's involvement in the Middle East. In addition, federal investigations indicated a state of passivity and unpreparedness on the eve of September 11 attacks and grave failures in the intelligence community. This provided an opportunity for the Democratic presidential candidate Senator John Kerry from Massachusetts to regain the White House for the Democrats. The United States electorate was split down the middle in their attitudes toward the president—one side overwhelmingly favorable and the other overwhelming unfavorable, and there was precious little middle ground to be won.

The campaign for the presidency in the autumn of 2004 was marked by sharp differences between President Bush and Senator Kerry over issues of foreign policy—especially American activities in Iraq, homeland security, social security reform, and other domestic issues. As political analysts and polling experts studied the responses of the American people to the two candidates, it became apparent that the division of America between the heartland and the West and East coasts and the north industrial states that was seen in the 2000 campaign still existed.

In the November elections the intensity of the passions of the supporters for each candidate and the unprecedented efforts to mobilize voters produced the highest turnout in recent elections. George W. Bush in 2004 again won a close victory in the Electoral College: But, unlike in 2000, he gained a sizeable majority in the popular vote. Thus armed with what he termed "political capital," the President set out to implement an ambitious, if controversial, program in domestic and international affairs.

WESTERN EUROPE

- *What factors contributed to the creation of the European Union?*

The most significant development in postwar western Europe was the progress toward integration. The desire for cooperation came from the lessons learned during World War II, taught by visionaries such as the French statesmen Jean Monnet and Robert Schumann. In 1950 Monnet and Schumann put forth a program to create the European Coal and Steel Community to coordinate the supply of those two essential industrial commodities in West Germany, France, Italy, Belgium, the Netherlands, and Luxembourg. Five years later the European Atomic Energy Community was created.

The same six nations that participated in these supranational organizations in 1957 established the **European Economic Community (EEC),** the Common Market. The organization's goal was to build enduring foundations for the closer union between European peoples. To that end it reduced tariffs among its members and created a great free trade union that became the fastest-growing market in the Western world. In 1992, after the Treaty of Maastricht was approved by the member states, the Common Market became the European Union. In May 2004, the number of states participating in the European Union grew to 25, with other nations waiting to be admitted.

DOCUMENT
A Common Market and European Integration

Economic Growth and the Dilemma of Legal and Illegal Immigration

From EEC headquarters in Brussels, a staff of thousands of experts administered the organization's affairs. In the 1950s the income of its members doubled. While the U.S. economy grew at a rate of 3.8 percent, that of France expanded by 7.1 percent, Italy by 8.4 percent, and West Germany by 9.6 percent. During the rest of the decade, trade nearly doubled among EEC members. Their factories and power plants hummed with activity, their workforce augmented by more than 10.5 million workers who migrated, many with their families, from southern Europe.

Lagging far behind these advances, Britain became a member of the Common Market in 1973; Ireland and Denmark also joined in that year. The admission of Spain and Portugal in 1986 brought the number to 12. While the member nations jealously guarded their sovereignty, they made substantial strides toward total economic integration. Various advances have been made toward adopting a common passport, setting a basic workweek and holiday policy for all workers, and equalizing welfare benefits.

Europe became a single market, the European Union (EU), at the end of 1992 with the approval of the Treaty of Maastricht, an act similar to the 1707 Act of Union between England and Scotland, the Constitution of the United States, and the North German *Zollverein* (TSOHL-fer-ain) in the first part of the nineteenth century. Reaching the goal of "Europe 1992" was not easy. Serious controversies over agricultural policy, banking policies, and tax differences had to be overcome. The European leaders worked hard to reassure the rest of the world that their 12-nation market would not be protectionist while they put together the more than 300 directives that would form the laws for the commercial union.

The program entailed opening up the 12 nations' boundaries so that there would be no restriction to the movement of goods and people and establishing a "social dimension" to define the "rights of ordinary people in the great market and to help the poorer among them." There was also a more difficult drive toward economic and monetary unity, including a single European currency and central bank. One indication of the EU's success was the introduction of the currency, the Euro, across most of Europe in January 2002. Economic union also included single standards on electricity, pipeline pressures, safety, and health.

IMAGE
European Money Before the Euro

The momentum toward political unity slowed somewhat during the 1990s. Obstacles born of 1000 years of nationalism remained. Unresolved issues included a state's favoring its own industries in the purchase of supplies and equipment, protection of particular industries by sovereign states, and the value-added tax.

Political changes brought challenges of expansion. In the 1990s, the remaining members of the rival European Free Trade Association—Finland, Austria, Iceland, and Sweden—had gained membership in the EU. Norway voted not to join. Despite the problems experienced in integrating the poorer nations of Europe, especially Greece, the EU's leadership was still eager to extend full membership to some of the former Soviet Bloc states and Mediterranean islands. In May 2004, Poland, the Czech Republic, Slovakia, Hungary, Lithuania, Latvia, Estonia, the Greek part of Cyprus, and Malta entered the European Union. The next step for the European Union is to agree on a constitution by the end of 2005.

Another response to the Common Market's success has been a massive influx of foreigners into the region. These included emigrants from Turkey who came to Germany as *Gastarbeiter* (gahst-ahr-bait-er; "guest workers") and Scandinavia, North Africans who came to France and Spain, people from the Balkans who entered Italy, and a wide variety of workers from the former imperial holdings who came to Europe to pursue their futures. Given the comparatively low birthrate of Europeans, countries such as Germany are encouraging the continuation of legal immigration. Engineers and computer technicians from Turkey and the Balkan states are being encouraged to move to Germany to fill the gaps in the nation's workforce as more and more German workers take early retirement.

A more difficult problem is that of illegal immigrants. The wealth of the European Union has attracted a large number of people entering illegally

---

European Economic Community (EEC)—A free trade union among West Germany, France, Italy, Belgium, the Netherlands, and Luxemburg created in 1957. This initial group served as the basis for the enlarged European Union.

Document Jean Monnet on European Unity

Jean Monnet was a pioneer in building the foundations for a unified Europe. In a 1953 speech he expressed his hopes for the future, to be attained in 1992.

Mr. President, Ladies and Gentlemen, on behalf of my colleagues . . . and myself, I wish to say how very pleased we are to have this meeting to-day with the members of the Common Assembly and the members of the Consultative Assembly. The co-operation between the Council of Europe and the European Coal and Steel Community has now definitely entered a concrete phase. . . .

In respect of coal and steel, the community has set up a huge European market of more than 150 million consumers, i.e., equal in number to the population of the United States of America. Under the terms of the Treaty, customs duties and quota restrictions have been abolished between Germany, Belgium, France, Italy, Luxembourg and the Netherlands; the principal discriminations in respect of transport have been done away with.... The road along which the six countries of the Community have set out is the right road, but we must continue to seek even more zealously ways and means of achieving a more complete understanding with the other countries of Europe. When they have seen and understood, as we have done, what this new and living Europe means for them, they will, one of these days, I hope, themselves join in.

Questions to Consider

1. What advantages are there to European unity?
2. Why do you think that commodities like coal and steel were the first to be chosen for the free trade zone?
3. Do you think Monnet saw trade as a way to achieve political change?

From the Joint Meeting of the Members of the Consultative Assembly of the Council of Europe and of the Members of the Common Assembly of the European Community of Coal and Steel, *Official Report of the Debate,* Strasbourg, June 22, 1953.

from Ukraine, Moldova, Romania, and other countries of the former Soviet Bloc. Smuggling people from China and Africa is a high-profit enterprise for unscrupulous individuals who place their customers in difficult conditions to get them into the European area. Those who succeed in making it to a European city generally find themselves crowded into substandard public housing in industrial suburbs surrounding the city center. Because of their illegal status, the jobs they can find are badly paid with no benefits. Unemployment runs as high as 30 percent among illegal immigrants in countries like France and Germany—where unemployment among citizens is already higher than 9 percent. They also suffer from the disdain of the local population, attacks from right-wing parties such as the National Front in France and the Neo-Nazis in Germany and Austria, and a lack of hope. It is from the ranks of such migrants that terrorist networks such al-Qaeda draw recruits and organized crime networks find a receptive audience.

Despite these problems, and in response to the Common Market's successes, other trade zones have been established: NAFTA, which linked Canada, Mexico, and the United States; and the Asia Pacific Economic Cooperation (APEC), which included the Pacific Rim states of Australia, Brunei, Canada, China, Hong Kong, Indonesia, Japan, South Korea, Malaysia, New Zealand, the Philippines, Singapore, Taiwan, and the United States.

Great Britain

Great Britain emerged from World War II at the height of its prestige in the twentieth century, but the glow of victory and the glory earned by its sacrifices served only to conceal Britain's dismal condition. The country was in a state of near-bankruptcy. As a result of the war, its investments had drastically declined and huge bills had been run up for the support of British armies overseas. In addition, increases in welfare benefits drained the economy.

After 1945 the London government could not reinstate the delicately balanced formula under which Britain had paid for massive imports of food and raw materials through exports and income from foreign investments, banking, and insurance. The British people, who had paid dearly to defeat the Axis Powers, did not produce the necessary export surplus to restore

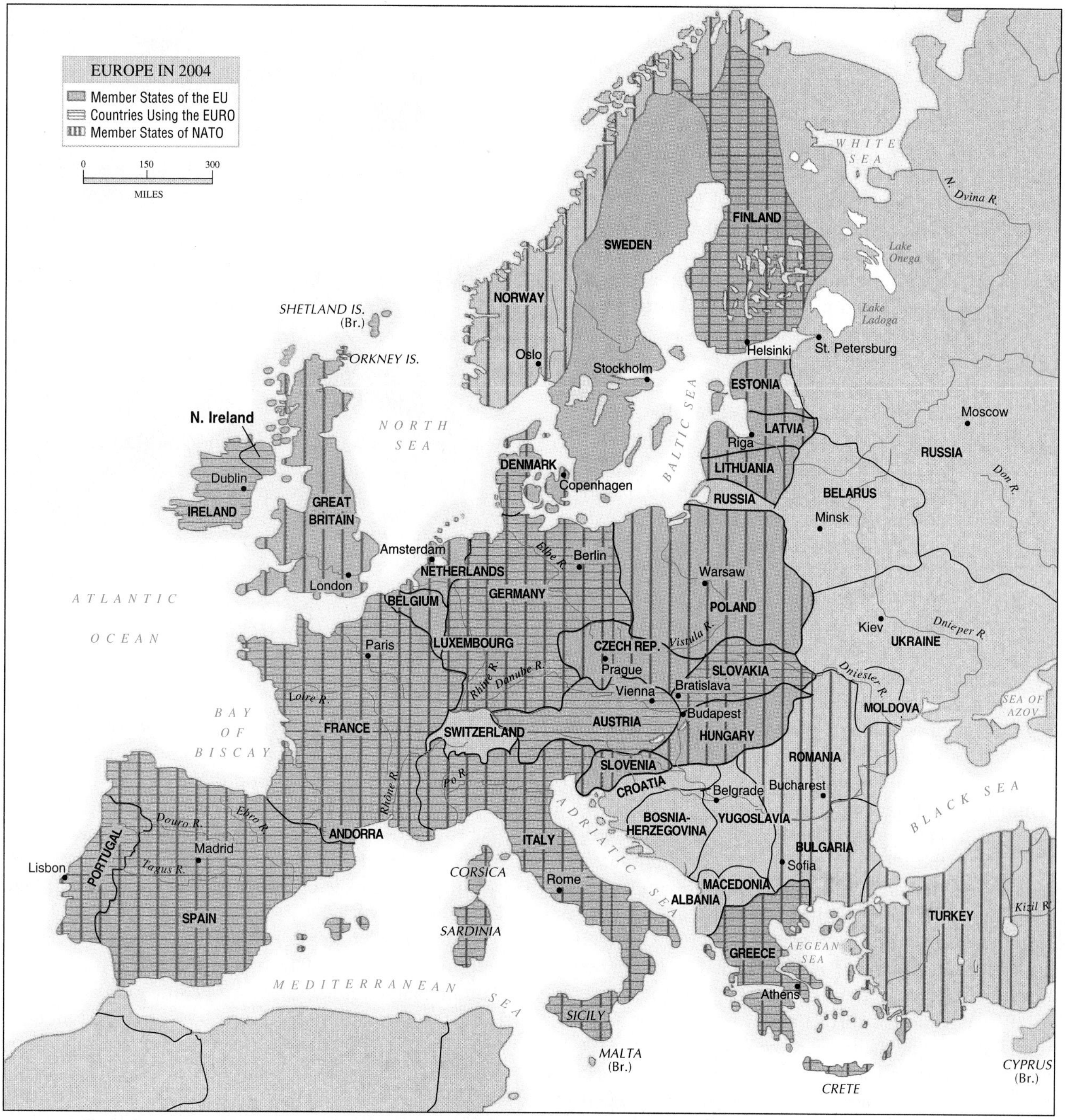

The European Union and NATO are in the process of expanding toward the east. As of 2004, the states of Europe were arrayed in the European Union, NATO, and Euro common currency zone, and those states awaiting admission to one or all three groups.

Britain's wealth. Over the next 40 years, they would watch their vanquished enemies become wealthy while they struggled with aging industrial facilities and extremely costly welfare programs.

The Conservatives have dominated British politics since the end of the war, with interludes of Labour rule. The Conservatives oppose nationalization of industry, encourage private enterprise, and favor a reduced social welfare program. Labour supports nationalization of industry and a thorough welfare state. Neither party has been able to find a wholesale cure for the serious ailments afflicting the country.

After the wartime coalition government of Conservatives and Labour, the country held its first peacetime regular election in July 1945, and to the amazement of many, Labourite Clement Attlee defeated wartime leader Winston Churchill. Attlee was a low-key, hardworking, honest politician who came from a comfortable middle-class background. In foreign affairs, the Labour government continued to work closely with the United States, and in domestic policy, it set out to improve basic living standards while converting to a peacetime economic base. Within two years, most major industrial and financial functions had been nationalized. In Britain's mixed economy, 80 percent of the workforce was employed by private enterprise. The Labour party suffered, as it would for the next 40 years, from factionalism between its left wing, which was inclined to be anti-American and pro-Russian, and the mainstream. Weakened by this split, Labour lost the general election in 1951, and the Conservatives began a 13-year span of dominance.

Churchill returned as prime minister until 1955, when he resigned and was succeeded by Anthony Eden. Eden resigned in January 1957 following the Suez Crisis, and Harold Macmillan took the party's leadership until July 1963. During the 1950s, economic conditions slowly improved until 1959, when they rapidly deteriorated. Britain went deeply in the red in its balance of payments. By the end of 1960, the economic outlook was grim. The next year the government applied for membership in the Common Market, in the belief that a closer trading association with the Continent would reverse the terrible domestic economic situation. The issue of membership in the EEC split both the Conservative and Labour parties. But debate became moot when French president Charles de Gaulle moved successfully to block Britain's admittance.

The long period of Conservative rule ended in 1964 with the election of a small Labour majority headed by Harold Wilson, who had previously been the youngest cabinet minister in 150 years. Under his leadership, Labour made important advances in education, slum clearance, and housing. But the old economic problems remained to plague the government. In 1967 Wilson was forced to devalue the pound sterling. Labour's lackluster performance in the late 1960s led to a victory in the 1970 election for the Conservatives under the leadership of Edward Heath. Heath's only significant achievement was bringing the country into the Common Market. Labor unrest in 1973 and the Arab oil embargo dealt crippling blows to the British economy, and Heath's bland leadership could not save his party from defeat in the 1974 elections. Labour returned once again, led by Wilson, who commanded a narrow majority. Continued industrial unrest, declining production, and alarming inflation led to major changes.

In 1975 Wilson resigned, to be succeeded by James Callaghan, a pragmatic moderate. He warned that "we are still not earning the standard of living we are enjoying. We are only keeping up our standards by borrowing, and this cannot go on indefinitely." During 1976, Britain had to borrow $5.3 billion from ten other countries. Massive cuts were proposed for social services and the armed forces. Many unions denounced this action, but it seemed imperative to all responsible leaders. Callaghan's inability to deal with the fiscal and economic problems in his country led to new elections and yet another change in the spring of 1979.

Margaret Thatcher was the first woman to head a major British party (the Conservative Party) and the first woman to serve as prime minister of Great Britain, a post she held for 11 years.

Margaret Thatcher led her Conservative forces to victory—and herself into the role of Britain's first woman prime minister—by proposing radical changes in Britain's economic and social programs. Thatcher's success in carrying out her programs gave her overwhelming victories in 1983 and again in 1987. She demanded—and received—sacrifices from her own people, more favorable treatment from the Common Market, and firm backing from the United States. She built a solid political base against a disorganized Labour opposition. From there she proceeded to change the nature of the Conservative party and to attempt to reform British society, until she was removed by her party in 1990 and replaced by John Major, who barely kept power in the 1992 elections.

Major never enjoyed the standing or the success of Thatcher and was ousted by the pragmatic leader of the Labour party, Tony Blair, in 1997. The Conservatives suffered a massive defeat, and Blair found himself in the position to change the basic thrust of the Thatcherite programs. After he had taken control of the Labour party, Blair had effectively neutralized its radical element and later took a centrist path, which pleased British business. In presenting socialism with a capitalist face Blair set a trend in European politics that was followed by Lionel Jospin in France and Gerhard Schroeder in Germany. The success of Blair's approach could be seen in his overwhelming victory for a second term in the spring of 2001, and his survival in the face of powerful opposition to his policies on Iraq and higher education.

Slow economic growth and unemployment were constant problems in the half-century after the war. Britain continued to try to find the difficult balance between making an industrial comeback without seriously sacrificing its extensive welfare services. Another serious dilemma was the stark contrast between the rich southeastern part of the country and the permanently depressed areas of the Midlands, Scotland, and Wales. Friction between protestants and Catholics remained a flashpoint in Northern Ireland. Racial problems generated by English resentment over the influx of nonwhite British subjects from the **Commonwealth** defied easy solution. But in 2003 the United Kingdom and Ireland were both riding an economic wave that drove real GDP beyond $28,000 per capita for the British and $29,000 for the Irish. This gave support to the hope that the perennial infrastructure problems were finally solved.

France: Grandeur and Reality

While most of France agreed to do the "rational" thing and capitulate to the Nazis in June 1940, Charles de Gaulle urged the government to move to North Africa and continue the struggle. During the war he personified France as a Great Power rather than a humiliated Nazi victim. In a famous broadcast to the French people from his exile in London, de Gaulle declared:

> *Whatever happens, the flame of French resistance must not and shall not die. . . . Must we abandon all hope? Is our defeat final and irremediable? To those questions I answer—No!*[2]

After the liberation of Paris in August 1944, de Gaulle was proclaimed provisional president and for 14 months was a virtual dictator by consent. Elections held in October 1945 confirmed that the people wanted a new constitution. Sharp differences, however, developed between de Gaulle and members of the government. The general resigned in January 1946, occupying himself with the writing of his memoirs. In the fall of that year the Fourth Republic was established. Unfortunately, the old confusing patterns of the Third Republic were repeated. Too many parties and too much bickering precluded any significant action; nevertheless, the regime lasted a dozen years.

The Fourth Republic collapsed over the issue of Algeria. Revolt against the French colonial government there began in 1954 and for the next eight years drained French resources. The French population in Algeria, more than a million people, insisted that Algeria be kept French. Army leaders supported them. Plots to overthrow the government in Paris were started. Facing the prospect of a civil war, the ineffectual French government, which had been referred to as a "regime of mediocrity and chloroform," resigned in 1958, naming de Gaulle as president. His new government was granted full power for six months.

De Gaulle had been awaiting his nation's call in his country home. Eager to reenter the political arena, he returned to Paris and oversaw the drafting of a new constitution, this for the Fifth French Republic. The new code was overwhelmingly approved by referendum in September 1958. De Gaulle was named president for seven years and proceeded to make this office the most important in the government. In both the Third and Fourth Republics the legislature had been dominant, but now the president and cabinet held supreme power. During a crisis, the executive could assume nearly total power. De Gaulle once commented, "The assemblies debate, the ministers govern, the constituent council thinks, the president of the Republic decides."

De Gaulle ended the Algerian war and shrugged off assassination plots and armed revolts. Then, he set forth on his foremost objective to make France a Great Power, to give it grandeur. He noted in his memoirs that "France cannot be France without greatness." For the next seven years he worked to make France the dominant power in Europe, a third force free of either U.S. or Soviet domination. To this end, he persisted in making France an independent nuclear power. In 1966 he withdrew French military forces from active participation in NATO, although France remained a consultative member of the alliance. Above all, de Gaulle was opposed to membership in any supranational agency. For this reason, while he tolerated the Common Market, he blocked any attempts to transform it into a political union. Even though he wielded great influence internationally, at home his position weakened.

A serious upheaval of university students and workers' strikes in 1968 further diminished de Gaulle's authority. A national referendum had been called to reorganize the government on a regional basis. De Gaulle unnecessarily made it a vote of confidence. When the referendum failed, he resigned his office

---

Commonwealth—A loose alliance of nations with the United Kingdom based on loyalty to the crown and a common language. When created by the Statute of Westminster in 1931, the Commonwealth included only Canada, Australia, New Zealand, and South Africa, but it now contains 54 member countries.

and retired to his country estate, where he died 18 months later. His successor was Georges Pompidou, an able administrator who gave evidence of vision in his leadership. When Pompidou died unexpectedly in 1974, the country elected Valéry Giscard d'Estaing (ZHEES-car des-TANG) as president. A resistance hero and a brilliant student, he had entered government service and become a high-ranking civil servant by the age of 26. The new president initiated a series of important reforms relating to urban growth, real estate, and divorce. He also favored lowering the voting age to 18.

Despite the generally high quality of leadership in France, the country was afflicted by the international economic difficulties relating to the energy crisis and American financial woes after 1973. Problems of inflation and housing shortages helped the rise to power of the Communist and Socialist parties, whose active participation in the wartime resistance had increased their popularity. There was a real possibility that a combined political program by the two parties might lead to a Marxist domination of the government. This did not happen in the elections of March 1978. Nevertheless, the strength of the left was evident and continued to grow in the face of economic problems and discontent with Giscard's personal rule. In May 1981 Socialist leader François Mitterrand was elected president, and 20 years of right-of-center government came to an end.

In June the Socialist party gained a majority in the National Assembly, and Mitterrand set out to reverse two centuries of French tradition by decentralizing the governmental apparatus installed by Napoleon. In addition, he pursued a program to nationalize some of France's largest business and banking enterprises. Mitterrand's honeymoon did not last long, as the parties to his right began to practice stalling tactics in the Assembly to block his programs. The Communists, who had lost badly in the 1981 elections, received four relatively insignificant seats in the cabinet, in return for which they promised cooperation with the new government. Mitterrand had to deal with the economic problems of slow industrial growth, inflation, and unemployment, and he found these as resistant to solution as Giscard did. By the end of 1985 the economy began to improve. The president lost his majority in elections in March 1986 but regained it in 1988 before losing it again in 1993.

Mitterrand died in 1996 and was succeeded by the centrist leader Jacques Chirac. Despite serious charges of corruption he has remained as president. During his presidency, he has worked with a prime minister of his own party, Alain Juppé, then with Lionel Jospin—a prime minister of the Socialist party—in an awkward system known as cohabitation, and finally in the spring of 2002 Chirac overcame a serious challenge from the extreme right wing to be reelected for a five-year term and to carry a powerful majority in the National Assembly. Chirac gained temporary popular support in 2003 and 2004 with his opposition to the American campaign in Iraq. However, the deeper, underlying social and economic problems remained.

France's challenge remains that of balancing pride in its culture and way of doing things with the demands of an increasingly economically internationalized, American-dominated world. After the events of September 11, 2001, the French were reminded of their own problems with terrorism throughout the 1990s, as there were celebrations of al-Qaeda's striking the World Trade Center and the Pentagon in the Arab-dominated suburbs of Marseilles and an increase in tensions between French and Arab citizens of the Republic. Increasing incidents of anti-Jewish and anti-Muslim activities further added to the feeling of unease.

Germany: Recovery to Reunification

West Germany to 1989

The most dramatic postwar European transformation has been that of West Germany. Recovering from the death, disaster, and destruction of World War II, the Bonn government accomplished political and economic miracles. When the Soviet Bloc disintegrated in 1989, the Bonn government moved rapidly to extend economic aid and work for reunification. By October 1990 unification had been accomplished, justifying the dreams of postwar Germany's most important leader, Konrad Adenauer, who led his country from the status of despised outcast to that of valued Western ally.

Born in 1876, Adenauer entered politics in 1906 as a member of the city council of Cologne. In 1917 he became mayor of the city, holding office until 1933, when the Nazis dismissed him. During Hitler's regime, he was imprisoned twice but lived mostly in retirement at home, cultivating his rose garden. After 1945 he entered German national politics, becoming leader of the new Christian Democratic party. With the approval of the Allied occupation authorities, German representatives drafted a constitution for the German Federal Republic, which was ratified in 1949. Adenauer, at the age of 73, became chancellor of West Germany.

In the new democratic government the presidency was made weak, while the real executive, the chancellor, was given specific authority to determine "the fundamental policies of the government." The chancellor was responsible to the *Bundestag*, a popularly elected legislative body. One of the weaknesses of the Weimar Republic had been the existence of many small parties, leading to unstable multiparty coalitions. In the new government, a party, to be recognized, had to win at least 5 percent of the votes in a given election.

Adenauer assumed power when Germany was still an outcast and its economy was in ruins. His one driving obsession was to get his people to work. Taking advantage of the tensions of the Cold War, he succeeded admirably. Under the force of his autocratic and sometimes domineering leadership, the Germans rebuilt their destroyed cities and factories using some $3 billion in Marshall Plan assistance. As early as 1955, West German national production exceeded prewar figures, with only 53 percent of former German territory. Providing the initial economic guidance for this recovery was Adenauer's minister of economics, Ludwig Erhard, a professional economist and a firm believer in laissez-faire economics. Germany's economic growth was accompanied by little inflation, practically no unemployment, and few labor problems.

Adenauer's achievements in foreign affairs were as remarkable as his leadership in domestic affairs. The Federal Republic of Germany gained full sovereignty in 1955. At that same time, West Germany was admitted into the NATO alliance. Adenauer decided to align closely with the West and cultivated close ties with the United States. In 1963 he signed a treaty of friendship with France, ending a century-long period of hostility. Adenauer expressed his attitude toward foreign affairs when he said, "Today I regard myself primarily as a European and only in second place as a German." It was natural that he brought his nation into Europe's new institutions, the European Coal and Steel Community and the Common Market. Adenauer's great frustration in foreign affairs was his failure to achieve the reunification of Germany.

In 1963, after 14 years in office, Adenauer retired and was succeeded as chancellor by Ludwig Erhard, who was, in turn, succeeded by Kurt Kiesinger. The big change in German politics occurred in 1969 with the victory of the Social Democratic party. This moderate, nondoctrinaire socialist party was led by Willy Brandt, who became chancellor. A foe of the Nazis, Brandt had fled to Norway, where he became a member of the resistance after Hitler's conquest. After the war he returned to Germany and became prominent in the Social Democratic party. In 1957 he became mayor of West Berlin, and then, in 1966, foreign minister in Bonn. Brandt was very active in setting West Germany's foreign policy. He was instrumental in getting Great Britain into the Common Market, and he tried to improve relations with eastern Europe and the Soviet Union through *Ostpolitik*, a policy of cooperation with Warsaw Pact nations. In journeys to both Moscow and Warsaw in 1970 he negotiated a treaty with the USSR renouncing the use of force and an agreement with Poland recognizing its western border along the Oder and Neisse Rivers. A treaty was also signed with East Germany for improving contacts and reducing tensions. These negotiations and others paved the way for the entry of the two Germanies into the United Nations.

Brandt's concentration on foreign affairs led to the appearance of neglect of domestic issues such as inflation and rising unemployment. Important segments of German public opinion attacked him on the policy of *Ostpolitik*. After a spy scandal rocked the government, Brandt resigned in the spring of 1974. Helmut Schmidt, who succeeded him, paid closer attention to domestic affairs.

Under Schmidt's leadership Germany continued its strong economic growth in the wake of the oil embargo. German workers did not suffer the unemployment problems of other countries because of the practice of firing and sending home foreign workers when job cutbacks were needed. Germany's economy in the 1980s was not immune to issues such as foreign trade fluctuations and oil imports. Still, Schmidt, as head of the most powerful Western European nation, had the prestige and record to ensure his victory in the 1980 elections.

In the late 1970s Schmidt had asked the United States to counter the Soviet placement of SS–20 intermediate-range missiles by placing intermediate-range ballistic missiles in Europe, thereby setting off a debate that did not end until 1983. Schmidt faced both the disapproval of antinuclear demonstrators, who did not want the missiles, and the displeasure of conservatives in his country and the United States over German economic ties with the Soviet Union. In the autumn of 1982 political power passed again to the Christian Democratic party, now led by Helmut Kohl.

Helmut Kohl's party proved to be a staunch supporter of the United States, in particular of its program to place U.S. intermediate-range missiles in Europe. In the face of strident Soviet protests, Kohl guided a bill through the West German parliament in November 1983 to deploy the missiles. After that success and a strong victory in 1987, Kohl, despite his reputation as a plodding politician, came to play a strong role in European affairs and in relations with the Soviet Union. In the course of his tenure, Kohl changed with the times to deal with environmental issues brought forcefully to the public forum by the environmentally focused Green party.

East Germany to 1989

After 1945, eastern Europe reflected the changes that took place in the USSR. Nowhere was this more evident than in East Germany from 1945 to 1990. Following the organization of the eastern zone of Germany into the German Democratic Republic, Communist authorities broke up large private farms and expanded heavy industry. Thousands of discontented East Germans fled each week to West Germany through Berlin. In June

1953, severe food shortages coupled with new decrees establishing longer working hours touched off a workers' revolt, which was quickly put down. The westward flow of refugees continued, however, until 1961, when the Berlin Wall was constructed.

The wall stopped the exodus of people, and East Germany stabilized. For the next 28 years, the country had the highest density of armed men per square mile in the Soviet Bloc and the Communist world's highest economic growth rate. The country's athletes and businesses did well in world competition, and slowly and subtly, under Erich Honecker and a new generation of bureaucrats, the German Democratic Republic improved relations with West Germany.

Gorbachev's program of liberalization threatened Honecker and his colleagues. After 1988, East German authorities stopped the circulation of Soviet periodicals that carried stories considered to be too liberal. At the same time, analysts noted the slowing economic growth rate of East Germany and the fact that the standard of living in West Germany was far higher. Old facilities, old managers, and old ideas eroded the economy of East Germany.

Unification

In September 1989, East Germans, looking for a better life, again fled by the thousands to the West, this time through Hungary and Czechoslovakia. This exodus, followed by Gorbachev's visit to Berlin in October, helped precipitate a crisis, bringing hundreds of thousands of protesters to the streets of Berlin. Honecker was removed in October, and on November 9, the Berlin Wall was breached. Once that symbolic act took place, both East and West Germans began to call for a unified Germany. Press exposés revealed corruption and scandals among the Communist elite. In the East German elections of March 1990, pro-Western parties won overwhelmingly. By October, Germany was reunited, with the first free all-German elections since Hitler took power. By 2000, Berlin was once again to be the capital of united Germany.

Helmut Kohl masterfully took advantage of the breakdown of the German Democratic Republic to claim the issue of reunification for himself and his party. In the next five years Kohl devoted most of his time and his country's money into integrating the former German Democratic Republic into the new German state. He had to privatize inefficient East German firms, draw investment from the West, and convince the former communist state to participate fully in the German democracy. A distrust and disdain sprang up between the two parts of the country, the East and the West: The West found the Easterners *(Ossis)* to be lazy and not sufficiently grateful, while the East saw the Westerners *(Wessis)* to be arrogant and cold.

By the end of 1994, Kohl had confounded critics who had contempt for his intellect and thought him politically naive. He overcame all the opposition for election, and his three-party coalition once again

The new generation of European leaders is shown here with Vladimir Putin, the president of Russia, and his wife Ludmila at the left and the German Prime Minister Gerhard Schroeder and his wife Doris Schroeder-Koepf to the right.

enabled him to remain chancellor. The cost of incorporating East Germany into the republic continued to be immense and has led to a high unemployment rate, centered in the east, which will need at least another decade to catch up with its neighbors to the west. Yet after a brief downswing, German industries have reformed themselves and are reclaiming parts of the world market, especially in automobiles, that they lost in the 1980s. None of this resurgence helped Kohl in the September 1998 elections, as his center-right coalition was replaced by a center-left coalition headed by the moderate Socialist Gerhard Schroeder.

The charismatic and colorful Schroeder was initially aided by a scandal stemming from an illegal use of funds by Kohl and his Christian Democratic party. His coalition with the Greens and other liberal parties withstood the challenges posed by the NATO bombing of Yugoslavia during the Kosovo conflict at the end of the decade, and Schroeder moved to have his country take its proper military and diplomatic place in the world, including vigorously opposing the U.S.-led attack against Iraq. Economic problems remained, however, as Germany continued a recession that started in 2004 and carried an unemployment rate that approached 10 percent. These problems threatened the Social Democrat's hold on power, and the chancellor's attempts to reform the Social Security system provoked revolts within his own ranks.

Italy: Political Instability, Economic Growth

Following the end of Mussolini's regime, Italy voted by a narrow margin to end the monarchy. A new constitution, adopted in 1947, provided for a premier and a ministry responsible to the legislature. The Christian Democratic party—strongly Catholic, pro-Western, and anticommunist—was the leading middle-of-the-road group. Its spokesman and leader was Alcide de Gasperi (al-CHEE-da da gas-SPAR-ee), whose ministry governed the country from 1947 to 1953. Like Adenauer, de Gasperi was a strong adherent of democracy and supported European unity. Italy joined NATO in 1949 and the Common Market in 1957.

In little more than a decade, the Italian economy changed from predominantly agricultural to industrial. For a time, in the late 1950s and early 1960s, industry advanced faster in Italy than in any other part of Europe. In 1960 the output of manufacturing tripled pre-1939 levels, and in 1961, steel production exceeded 1 million tons. By the end of the 1980s, Italy ranked among the world's leaders in high-tech industry, fashion, furniture design, and banking. Most economic development occurred in northern Italy around the thriving cities of Turin, Milan, and Bologna.

Southern Italy did not progress as rapidly. Too many people, too few schools, inadequate roads, and inefficient, fragmented farms worked by poor peasants were among the problems besetting the area. The government offered help in the form of subsidies, tax concessions, and programs for flood control and better highways, but southern Italy remained a challenging problem.

If the Italian economy was a source of optimism, politics was another story. After de Gasperi's retirement in 1953, politics became increasingly characterized by a series of cabinet crises, shaky coalitions, and government turnovers. Between the end of World War II and the end of the century, Italy had had more than 50 governments.

In the 1970s, labor unrest, unemployment, and inflation posed problems that politicians could not deal with, even in coalitions in which the Communist party joined with other factions. For a while terrorism dominated political life. In 1978, the anarchist Red Brigade kidnapped one of Italy's most prominent public figures, former premier Aldo Moro, and assassinated him nearly two months later, leaving his body in a car parked equidistant between the Christian Democratic and Communist party headquarters in Rome. Terrorists spread chaos among business and political leaders. Finally, during the 1980s, the government, dominated by Bettino Craxi and Ciriaco de Mita, improved conditions. The terrorist networks were broken, and law enforcement agencies began to combat organized crime in southern Italy and Sicily.

Widespread corruption and inefficiency in the Christian Democratic–dominated system were exposed in a series of trials that reached to the highest levels of Italian society and government in the 1990s. Exposure of the nationwide network of corruption in 1992 sent some of the most powerful Italian leaders to jail, where some committed suicide. Revulsion provoked by the widespread corruption led in 1993 to a reform of the political system from that of a senate based on a proportional system of representation to a scheme in which power went to the group claiming the majority of votes. In 1994, a national election to form the new parliament resulted in victory for the charismatic television businessman, soccer team owner, and right-winger Silvio Berlusconi. Berlusconi's *Forza Italia* ("Let's Go, Italy") coalition included openly fascist politicians. Predictably, within six months, Berlusconi's government itself was embroiled in crisis, and in 1998 the man himself was sentenced to two years in prison for corruption. But because of the appeals process and his political power he avoided going to jail.

The businesslike late-1990s government of Romano Prodi stabilized the Italian economy and politics, and Italy was one of the first European countries to meet the standards for entry into the Euro system. He was replaced at the end of the century by the scandal-ridden Berlusconi who managed to escape his legal problems to become an ardent upholder of Prodi's status quo. The swashbuckling Berlusconi kept power by the sheer force of his personality and his control of most of the televised media in Italy, even maintaining his position while supporting the unpopular American involvement in Iraq.

Italy continues to face the split between the industrialized and wealthy north and the more rural and poorer south of the country. It continues to have a new government more or less once a year, as the fragile coalitions are dispersed over controversial issues. Italy also suffers from the problem of illegal immigrants, especially from Albania, who overtax the country's social welfare structure and funnel illegal drugs into western Europe.

Portugal

Portugal was an incredibly corrupt monarchy until 1910. The country then became a republic, but its record of internal turmoil continued. Between 1910 and 1930 there were 21 popular uprisings and 43 cabinets. Toward the end of that period, the army ousted the politicians and took control of the government. In 1932 the generals called on Antonio de Oliveira Salazar to run the country. This former economics professor, a fervent and austere Catholic, shunned social life and was content to live on a very small salary. He devoted all of his time to running an authoritarian government. The press was censored, and education—in a country in which two-thirds of the population was illiterate—was neglected. Some economic improvement did take place, but the people, who were frozen out of politics, remained poor. In 1955 a five-year program to stimulate the economy was launched, but its gains were canceled out by population increases and the huge costs resulting from wars in Portugal's African colonies.

Salazar retired in 1968 because of ill health, and six years later, a group of junior army officers overthrew the government. Serious divisions appeared between the moderate liberal factions and the Communists. In the summer of 1976, however, elections confirmed the victory of the moderate Socialists. A new constitution was enacted, establishing a democratic system. The government faced difficult economic problems—600,000 refugees from Portuguese Africa had to be absorbed, fueling high unemployment and runaway inflation. After the 1974 revolution, workers had seized many businesses, large farms, and hotels. In most instances, private ownership had to be restored under efficient management. During the 1980s, political and economic stability returned to the country, led in the latter part of the decade by Mario Soares (SWA-rush), ruling through a Socialist coalition. Compared with the northern Europe, Portugal remained poor, but it has stabilized its economy with a 3 percent inflation rate and increased literacy rates. It also, in the new millennium, maintained its substantial cultural and financial influence in Brazil.

Spain

In the four decades after World War II, Spain passed from the Franco dictatorship to a rapidly industrializing, modern European state. Franco ruled over an almost ruined country after taking control in 1939. Many of Spain's most talented and productive people had fled, and 700,000 people had died in the civil war. So horrible was the conflict and so great the losses that Franco gained a grudging toleration from the majority of the exhausted population. Those who did not cooperate faced his secret police.

Cold War tensions eased Spain's reentry into the community of nations in the 1950s. The United States resumed diplomatic relations, and Spain became a member of the UN in 1955. The following year, the Pact of Madrid provided naval and air bases for the Americans, in return for which Spain received more than $2 billion a year in aid. In the 1960s and 1970s, the widespread poverty and backwardness that had long characterized Spain began to diminish. Inspired by the Portuguese Revolution of 1974, workers and students began to demonstrate and show their unrest. In the summer of 1975, Franco died. He had named Prince Juan Carlos as his successor, thereby indicating his wish that the monarchy be restored.

The young king was crowned in November 1975, and in his speech of acceptance he promised to represent all Spaniards, recognizing that the people were asking for "profound improvements." In 1976 the reformed government announced amnesty for political prisoners, freedom of assembly, and more rights for labor unions. An orderly general election took place in the spring of 1977. Post-Franco Spain began its parliamentary-monarchy phase with impressive stability. Underneath, deep ideological divisions remained, which decreased over time. The major crisis came in February 1981 when radical elements of the army invaded the parliament building to attempt a coup. Juan Carlos put his life on the line by going to parliament and intervening to block the overthrow attempt. It immediately became apparent that there was no support for the coup among the public at large, and the attempt was brushed aside.

In May 1982 Spain joined NATO—still a controversial decision—and later that year, elected Felipe Gonzales of the Socialist party to run the country. Gonzales brought Spain into the Common Market and worked hard to diversify the country's economy. He strengthened his position in the 1986 elections and by 1990 was governing a country attractive to investors in high-tech industries. Gonzales's party became complacent in their years in power and lost the 1996 elections to the Conservatives led by José Maria Aznar, who imposed a strict program of fiscal responsibility on the country.

A major challenge to Spain remains the Basque separatist movement, ETA, in the northwestern part of the country. Bombings and assassinations were a weekly event throughout the country at the beginning of the century, as the separatists successfully resisted international efforts to penetrate their ranks and destroy them. The al-Qaeda bombing of a Madrid train station in March 2004—purportedly as punishment for Spain's participation in the occupation of Iraq—and the Aznar government's attempt to blame the atrocity on ETA led to the return of the Socialists to power under the leadership of Jose Luis Rodriguez-Zapatero.

Greece

Greece, since its modern creation in 1821, has rarely enjoyed political stability. From that year until 1945, there were 15 different types of government with 176 premiers, who, obviously, averaged less than one year in office. Inefficiency in government, economic backwardness, and political crises have continued to plague Greece since 1945. In the Greek Civil War (1946–1949) pro-Western forces, who controlled only the major cities, turned back a powerful Communist surge for power and reestablished the monarchy. Greek politicians ignored the complex economic issues affecting the peasants, preferring instead to attempt to regain various islands and territories controlled by Greeks in the long-distant past known as *irredentas* (ir-re-DENT-as). In the spring of 1967 a group of army colonels seized power. A dictatorship was established that jailed many political figures and harshly punished any criticism of its rule. Many Greeks fled into exile. The military junta made a serious miscalculation in 1974 when it connived to increase Greek authority on Cyprus, a move that led to a Turkish invasion of the island. This blunder led to the junta's downfall.

Thereafter, the Greeks created a republic, complete with a new constitution. They applied for membership in the Common Market in 1975 and were admitted in 1981. In its application the government stated that its desire to join the European Economic Community was "based on our earnest desire to consolidate democracy in Greece within the broader democratic institutions of the European Community to which Greece belongs." Since that time, Greek leaders have maintained their democratic traditions. In November 1981 the Socialist party, led by Andreas Papandreou (AN-dre-as pa-pan-DRAY-oo), gained power and held it through 1989. He led his party back to power four years later. Papandreou ran on pledges to evict U.S. forces from Greek bases and to move Greek foreign policy away from its Western orientation. In the middle of the decade, Papandreou followed traditional Greek tendencies to reclaim land lost to Turkey in the past 500 years and to mobilize the nation by actively opposing the independence of the former Yugoslav republic of Macedonia on political, economic, and historical grounds.

Yet the Greeks remained active participants in NATO and the Common Market. Like Portugal, Greece is, by European standards, a poor country with a stagnant economy and an inflation rate of 18 percent. In the 1989 elections these factors, plus scandals surrounding Papandreou's personal life, led to the defeat of the Socialists and the forming of an unlikely coalition made up of the Communist and Conservative parties, which enjoyed a short tenure in power. As the decade came to an end, the Greek prime minister, Costas Simitis, walked a political tightrope between nationalist expectations, fired up by the conflicts in Yugoslavia to his north, and the need for sound fiscal policies. The difficult relationship with Turkey, which has plagued the country for most of its existence, remains at the forefront of Greek consciousness, along with problems of domestic terrorism. The Greeks temporarily put all of that behind them as they successfully hosted the 2004 Olympic games.

EASTERN EUROPE

- *How successful have the eastern European states been in moving from the Soviet Bloc to European Union?*

After consolidating political control over eastern Europe by 1948, Moscow attempted to organize its allies through the trade organization COMECON. The USSR set up COMECON in 1949 as a response to the Marshall Plan and other Western projects to promote economic growth. In its first decade the organization served Soviet postwar recovery needs. Moscow worked a reverse system of mercantilism on the region, exporting raw materials at high prices and buying back finished goods at low cost. Eastern Europe suffered greatly under this system, and nowhere could the contrast between the capitalist and communist systems be seen more dramatically than in the divided city of Berlin.

In the 1960s and 1970s the Soviet Bloc states began to profit from buying cheap energy supplies

Discovery Through Maps

The Euro Comes to Greece

Greece, the southeasternmost member of the European Union, joined most of the other countries in the EU in the introduction of a common currency, the Euro, on January 1, 2002. After a brief period of transition in which the former, national currencies could be used along with the Euro, most of Europe easily converted to the new money. As the dollar can be used throughout the United States, so too can the Euro be used throughout most of the European continent.

The Euro bills (five Euros up to 500) feature generic designs with European motifs along with a map of Europe. Note that no individuals are featured. The coins (one cent, two cent, five cent, ten cent, 20 cent, 50 cent, one Euro, two Euro) have the value of the piece on one side and a national symbol on the other, much like the new quarters in the United States featuring individual states. After a month or two of awkwardness in which people became accustomed to the new pieces, the Euros became easily and widely accepted. This is surprising because some of the national monies had existed for more than five centuries.

The Euro eliminates the need for currency conversion, with the accompanying service charges, when people travel or do business within the Euro zone. More importantly, the acceptance of the Euro indicates that a united Europe is becoming more of a fact, and less of a dream. The new currency is no guarantee that the Europeans will end their millennia history of violence against each other. But it makes it more difficult for states to isolate themselves from their neighbors.

Greece is an active part of the European Union, and hosted the 2004 Olympic games. But soon it will be joined by other countries in eastern Europe and the Balkans as the European community becomes bigger and bigger. In 1914, Europe stood preeminent in the world. Two world wars and the Cold War reduced its global importance. Perhaps the Euro heralds the end of a century of discord and disagreement and will help produce a continent more concerned with joint peace and prosperity and not individual national ambition.

In the first half-year, at least, aside from complaints of a general rise of prices across the Continent with the introduction of the Euro, there is every evidence that the new currency will bring the various parts of the European Union closer together.

Questions to Consider

1. What advantages will the European community gain by using a common currency? What disadvantages?
2. Do you believe that a strong and a united Europe is in the interest of the United States? Why or why not?
3. If the United States were to join with Canada and Mexico in a common North American currency, which portions of the population would have the greatest difficulties in making the adjustment?

from the USSR in return for which they could send goods they could not market to the West. Their standard of living began to improve along with their economic growth rates. By the end of the 1970s, however, COMECON faced a serious crisis. The region fell behind the rest of the world economically because of the rigidity of the centrally planned system used in the Bloc economies and the restrictive bilateral nature of COMECON—everything had to go through Moscow. Prague and Budapest, for instance, could not work directly to achieve production or trade efficiency. COMECON countries faced far more barriers than the Common Market countries did. Further, each country's currency was nonconvertible; it could be spent only within that country.

Aggravating the situation was the fact that, as world energy prices fell in the latter part of the 1980s, the eastern Europeans were trapped into paying premium prices for Soviet oil and gas. Several eastern European states borrowed heavily from the West and invested the proceeds unwisely. Far more damaging than these purely fiscal concerns were the environmental disasters spawned by the Soviet-model centrally planned economies. Eastern Europe, as well as the former USSR, was one of the most devastatingly polluted areas in the world. Fifty years of Soviet domination were a terrible burden for the peoples of eastern Europe.

After 2004, the northern half of the former Soviet Bloc entered the European Union. The southern half, Romania and the Balkan states, remains plagued by corruption, ethnic strife, and lawlessness. It remains to be seen if the north will go on to economic and political progress while the south remains largely poor and unstable.

Poland

In Poland, as in Yugoslavia, communism acquired a national character after a slow, subtle struggle that broke open in the fall of 1956 following Khrushchev's "Crimes of the Stalin Era" speech. Polish leader Wladyslaw Gomulka (vlad-EE-slov goh-mul-KAH) set out on a difficult path to satisfy both Moscow and Warsaw, Soviet power and Polish nationalism. Gomulka governed skillfully through the 1960s until 1970, when he fell victim to the pressures of economic discontent and an increasingly corrupt Communist party.

Demonstrations and strikes broke out around the country, and some, such as those at the Baltic port city of Gdansk (formerly Danzig), were bloodily repressed. Gomulka was replaced by Edward Gierek, who, throughout the 1970s, walked the same narrow line as Gomulka between satisfying Moscow and Poland. Gierek borrowed extensively from the West and made several ill-advised economic decisions. By 1980 Poland was laboring to pay the interest on a foreign debt of $28 billion, and in the summer of 1980, the delicate compromise created by Gomulka and Gierek fell apart in a series of strikes caused by increases in food prices.

A nationwide labor movement, *Solidarnosc*, or Solidarity, came into being. By October, around 10 million Poles from all segments of society had joined this movement, which stood for reform, equality, and workers' rights. In many ways, Solidarity's programs were protests against the Leninist concept of the party. It was Solidarity's proletarian base that made it so appealing to the world and so threatening to the other Marxist-Leninist leaders of the Soviet Bloc. Unfortunately, the problems that had brought down Gierek remained. A year of Solidarity-dominated government brought no solutions, only continued frustration.

Conflict with the government, now headed by General Wojciech Jaruzelski (vui-CHEK ya-ruh-ZEL-skee), appeared inevitable. Solidarity's leader, Lech Walesa—an out-of-work electrician who had been fired for earlier attempts to organize a trade union in Gdansk—showed an instinctive genius for dealing effectively with every element of the Polish spectrum and the Soviet Union. He attempted to maintain a moderate position.

When Walesa's backers pushed him to call for a national vote to establish a noncommunist government, the Jaruzelski government responded with force, in part to maintain itself and in part to avoid Soviet intervention. Jaruzelski declared martial law, and security forces rounded up Solidarity's leaders. Outward shows of protest were squelched within two weeks.

Through the 1980s, Communist party morale dipped as membership fell 20 percent. Although banned, Solidarity retained the genuine affection of the Poles and the support of the Roman Catholic Church, headed by Pope John Paul II, a former Polish cardinal. To the embarrassment of the Polish state, Lech Walesa was awarded the Nobel Peace Prize in 1983. The economic situation deteriorated as inflation increased, the standard of living plummeted, and foreign debt soared to $40 billion. The party could not solve the problems it faced, and in desperation it turned to Solidarity, which it had outlawed eight years earlier. The June 1989 elections resulted in an overwhelming victory for the union, and in July it took its place in the Polish parliament, the *Sejm* (SAYM), as the first opposition party to win free elections in Eastern Europe since 1948. Solidarity won 99 out of 100 seats in the upper house and 161 seats (35 percent) in the lower house—all that was allotted to it in a preparatory roundtable.

In January 1990 Poland decided to adopt a market economy. Even with substantial financial support from the West, the country faced rising unemployment and recession. The strains produced by the shift to a market economy tested even the Solidarity movement, which split into two wings, one led by Mazowiecki Tadeuszi (ma-zo-VIET-skee ta-dei-USH-ee), who briefly became prime minister in 1990, and one led by Lech Walesa, who eventually became the president of Poland.

Despite political roadblocks, Poland made amazing success toward privatization and market reforms. Even when Poland's former Communists, now called Social Democrats, took power in 1993, they did not reverse course. Poland stands as one of the success stories in the former Soviet Bloc, with economic growth of 5 percent in 1996, a thriving stock market, and a successful market economy. From 1993 to 2004, foreign investment in Poland has more than doubled and the per capita gross domestic product reached nearly $11,000, still 35 percent that of Western industrialized countries. Symbolic of Poland's progress from Soviet Bloc state to a member of the European community was the fact that it was admitted as a full member of the North Atlantic Treaty Organization in 1998.

Czechoslovakia and the Czech and Slovak Republics

After the fall of the democratic government in 1948, the Czechoslovak Communist party, the most Stalinist of the European parties, imposed harsh control for 20 years. In the spring of 1968, however, the country's liberal traditions came into the open. Under the influence of Marxist moderates, a new form of communism—"socialism with a human face"—was put into effect by the Slovak leader Alexander Dubcek (DOOB-chek). As in Yugoslavia under Tito, the Czechoslovaks chose not to rebel against Moscow but rather to adapt communism to their own conditions. But in August 1968, the Soviet Union and four Soviet Bloc allies invaded Prague with more than 500,000 troops. Within 20 hours, the liberal regime, which advocated policies strikingly similar to those to be supported by Gorbachev 20 years later, was overthrown. The Soviets captured Dubcek and took him to Moscow to confront Brezhnev.

The Soviets took their action against Czechoslovakia pursuant to the so-called Brezhnev Doctrine,

Under the leadership of Alexander Dubcek in 1968, the Czechoslovak Communist party sought to reverse 20 years of Stalinist policies by instituting "socialism with a human face." This prompted the nation's invasion, for a variety of geopolitical and ideological reasons, by the joint forces of five socialist nations in August of that year.

under which Communist states were obliged to aid their fraternal colleagues against "aggression," even when the fraternal colleague does not ask for aid, in order to safeguard the communal gains of the socialist movement. The Soviet-led forces crushed the Czechoslovak reforms to "protect the progress of socialism." Like that of East Germany, the Czech economy by the late 1980s was hampered by outmoded technology, timid leadership, and discredited ideology. The country suffered greatly from polluted air and acid rain, and the population suffered under a declining standard of living.

Events in East Germany precipitated the October 1989 events in Prague, when a prodemocracy meeting by over 10,000 demonstrators was savagely broken up by the police. Protests in November met similar results. Still the Czechoslovaks were not deterred. In the "Velvet Revolution" of November 1989 some 200,000 demonstrators in Prague demanded free elections and the resignation of the Communist leaders. The wave of change from Moscow initiated by Mikhail Gorbachev after 1985 was unable to adapt to the new conditions, and dissidents, including president-to-be Vaclav Havel (VAT-swof HAV-el), who in January 1989 had been thrown in jail for human rights protests, found themselves running the country by December of that year. Symbolic of the new freedom, Dubcek came out of internal exile, and in the June 1990 elections, Havel was confirmed as president. As in the other eastern European states, however, the high spirits of the 1989 revolution were soon replaced by the sober realities of repairing the effects of two generations of Communist rule.

Serious political problems and Slovak separatist demands drove Czechoslovakia to split into its constituent parts, the Czech Republic and the Slovak Republic, on January 1, 1993. The Czech Republic suffered little from the dissolution of the 65-year-old federation, but the Slovaks suffered from economic decline and political instability under the rule of the former Communist hard-liner Vladimir Meciar. A year after the split, unemployment in Slovakia exceeded 15 percent, compared to 3.5 percent among the Czechs, and since then, the gap between the two countries has remained the same. Ten years later, Slovakia achieved a remarkable economic growth with a GDP per capita of more than $13,000, but with a high unemployment rate too.

The Czech Republic's economic growth faltered briefly in the 1990s but rebounded in the first part of the new century. A combination of corruption and a high trade deficit led to a new government under the Socialists being formed in the spring of 1998. Vaclav Havel remained a stabilizing force, and with a nearly $16,000 GDP per capita, the Czech citizens are comfortably absorbing the good times and bad times of the transition.

Hungary

After the Stalin purges, the Hungarian Communist party became increasingly inept until October 1956, when discontent with Soviet dominance erupted into revolution. For a week, a popular government existed, and Russian troops withdrew from Budapest. When the new government announced its intentions to leave the Warsaw Pact and be neutral, Soviet forces returned and crushed the rebellion. More than 200,000 refugees fled to the West.

Over the next 30 years, Janos Kadar (1912–1989) oversaw an initially bloody repression of the revolution and the execution of Hungarian premier Imre Nagy (EEM-re NAHZH). Later, Kadar led a subtle pursuit of a Hungarian variant of communism. In the process, the Hungarians gained a higher standard of living than the Soviets, an active intellectual life, and a range of economic reforms. In the mid-1980s, however, the Hungarian economic system, which encouraged more private initiative and decentralization, ran into difficulties. Hungary's foreign debt and inflation both increased. Gorbachev encouraged the Hungarians to pursue their reforms, sometimes at the discomfort of Kadar, who was gently moved from power in 1987.

In 1989 the Hungarians dismantled the barriers, fences, and minefields between themselves and the Austrians. Hungary imposed the first income tax and value-added tax in eastern Europe, allowed 100 percent foreign ownership of Hungarian firms, opened a stock market, and set up institutions to teach Western management methods to Hungarian businessmen. The economy remains competitive, with a $13,900 GDP per capita, but government officials say that it will take ten years before Hungary can reach western European standards of living.

By March 1990, Hungary had installed a multiparty system and was holding free elections, which led to the installation of a right-of-center government led by Joszef Antall and the overwhelming repudiation of the Communists. The next four years proved to be frustrating to the Hungarians, however. Substantial Western investment came in, but the suffering among the poorer population in the country increased.

Tragically, in this area stripped of Jews by the Holocaust, anti-Semitism reemerged as a political force. Anti-Gypsy feelings also intensified. Elections in 1994 resulted in a victory for the Communist Social Democrats, who promised to maintain the free market reforms while extending social justice. Although they fulfilled these promises, a rise in organized crime and growing doubts about the Social Democrats' competence led back to a right-of-center government in the summer of 1998 under the young Viktor Orban. Despite substantial foreign debt, Hungary has exhibited impressive governmental and social stability and entered NATO as the third nation from the former Soviet Bloc. Tensions remain with its neighbors, however, as Orban's government in 2001 attempted to gain special status for Hungarians living in Romania, Slovakia, and Serbia. The Social Democrats regained control of the government in 2002 when Peter Medgyessy (MED-zhes-see) became prime minister.

Bulgaria

Bulgaria proved to be a loyal ally of Moscow after 1945, and its standard of living greatly improved. The Bulgarian economy averaged a growth rate of close to 3 percent a year and became increasingly diversified. Todor Zhivkov (TOE-dor ZHIV-kov) skillfully followed the Soviet lead and showed flexibility in responding to the early Gorbachev programs, especially the agricultural reforms. Until the autumn of 1989, the party appeared to be conservative and nationalist, as shown in its campaign against the country's Turkish minority (nearly 8 percent of the population) to deprive them of their heritage.

The wave of freedom hit Bulgaria at the end of 1989. Zhivkov was ousted in a party-led coup and replaced by Peter Mladenov. It seemed in the free elections in May 1990 that Mladenov and his allies would be the only party group to make the transition and maintain power in eastern Europe. But even he was thrown out in July, when his role as orchestrator of the Zhivkov coup was noted, and the noncommunist philosopher Zhelyu Zhelev became president.

The Bulgarians avoided making the hard economic choices needed to reform their country, and at the end of 1996, they experienced a virtual economic collapse. Inflation soared, wiping out savings and driving prices up. At the same time, the government proved unable to pay the interest on the foreign debt. The International Monetary Fund has imposed an austerity program on Bulgaria that has caused widespread distress. Local mafias have prospered, conducting black market trade with the various factions in the Yugoslav conflict and serving as a conduit for the international drug trade. As if in despair, the country voted in 2001 to elect its former king, Simeon II, as president of the country.

Romania

After the 1960s, Romania under Nicolae Ceausescu (chow-SESH-koo) was the most independent of the Warsaw Pact countries in foreign policy. Domestically, the country labored under one of the most hard-line and corrupt regimes in the Bloc, a regime whose economic policies of self-sufficiency plunged the standard of living to unprecedented depths. Ceausescu achieved his goal to become free of foreign debts by the summer of 1989, but at a cruel cost in human suffering.

Ceausescu, accused by critics of desiring to achieve "socialism in one family," developed the cult of the personality to new heights. While imposing severe economic hardship on the nation, he built grandiose monuments to himself. Protected by his omnipresent secret police, the *Securitate,* he seemed untouchable. But the 1989 wave of democracy spread even to Romania, which was the only country to experience widespread violence during that revolutionary year. Ceausescu and his wife were taken into custody and executed, thus bringing their dreadful regime to an end.

The Romanian pattern of political corruption continued, and Ion Iliescu manipulated the elections of May 1990 to keep power. Later in the summer, the National Salvation Front made shameless use of miners and former *Securitate* officials to terrorize its critics. An uneasy equilibrium was attained, but little progress was made to heal the devastating wounds inflicted by the Ceausescu regime. Under Iliescu the Leninist heritage remained strong in Romania, whose authoritarianism had a chilling effect on the pluralistic tendencies in the region.

Finally in 1996, the neo-Communists lost power when Emil Constantinescu became president. The country faces many of the same problems as neighboring Bulgaria—the need to privatize inefficient state industries, to introduce efficient management methods, and to gain some sort of control over the rampant corruption that plagues its economy. Many Romanians placed high and unrealistic hopes on being invited to join NATO. When that did not happen, there was a backlash against the West among a segment of the population who support the neo-fascist politics of Vadim Tudor. In the 2000 elections, however, Iliescu again returned to power as the Romanians chose to go with a familiar face. Despite the corruption that characterizes business relations in the country, foreigners are investing in the automotive sector (France), oil and gas (Russia), and telecommunications (Greece). The GDP per capita has reached nearly $7000, but with the flight of technicians and young people abroad, it will be difficult to maintain a long-term trend of economic progress.

Albania

Albania under Enver Hoxha (HOD-zha; 1908–1985) worked closely with the Soviet Union until 1956. After Khrushchev's denunciation of Stalin, the country switched its allegiance to the Chinese until 1978. For the next decade Albania—the poorest and most backward country in Europe—went its own way in seeming isolation, only reluctantly entering into trade, diplomatic, and sports relations with other nations. Yet even Albania was not immune to the unrest sweeping Eastern Europe in 1989. In the summer of 1990, people desperate to escape the country flocked into foreign embassies, and soon thereafter, some 40,000 Albanians fled to Italy and Greece. Democratic elections were held in March 1991, but even there, the Albanians marched to their own tune as the Communists carried two-thirds of the vote. Two years later, the Democratic party won an overwhelming victory. Albania remained the poorest and most backward country in Europe.

Tragically, the economically inexperienced Albanians flocked to "get rich quick" pyramid schemes that collapsed in December 1996 when those who were in first started to pull their money out. Civil order collapsed in the country as factions gained control of the army's weapons and the country dissolved into regions controlled by local warlords. European intervention led by the Italians brought order, but then Albanians living in Yugoslavian provinces began to rebel against their Belgrade overlords. At the beginning of the new century, Albania remains a fragmented nation and a potential tinderbox, overwhelmed by the hundreds of thousands of Kosovar Albanians seeking refuge there. Its weak economy forces thousands of its young to seek work elsewhere in Italy and Austria, legally or illegally.

Yugoslavia and After

One of Stalin's major failures after 1945 was in his dealings with Marshal Josip Broz Tito of Yugoslavia. Tito had been a loyal Communist and a good Stalinist in the 1930s. During the war, he was an effective resistance leader, surviving attacks from Germans, Italians, and various right-wing factions in Yugoslavia. He had been in close contact with the Western allies and, after the war, began to receive substantial assistance from them. Tito led the liberation of Yugoslavia from the Nazis and kept the country out of Moscow's orbit.

Stalin noted Tito's independence and from 1946 on, sought measures to oppose him. Ethnically divided, Yugoslavia overcame its internal divisions and a 10 percent casualty rate during the war to unite behind Tito. The Yugoslav leader's national backing, geographical distance from the Soviet Union, and support from the West enabled him to stand firm against increasing Soviet meddling in his country.

Tito became the first national communist, a firm believer in Marxism who sought to apply the ideology within the context of his nation's objective conditions. This position placed him directly against Stalin, who believed that communists the world over must work for the greater glory and support of the Soviet Union. Tito believed that the setting in which ideology was found had to be taken into consideration, pointing out that Lenin had to adapt Marxist doctrine to conditions in Russia. Stalin insisted that Moscow's orders and examples must be slavishly followed. In 1948 Yugoslavia was expelled from the Soviet Bloc. Successfully withstanding Stalin's pressures, including assassination attempts, Tito emerged as a key figure in the development of world communism.

After 1948, the six republics, containing ten ethnic groups, that formed Yugoslavia survived the pressures of national diversity, the political stresses of the bipolar world, and serious economic difficulties. Many observers doubted that the country could survive Tito's death in 1980. However, Yugoslavia remained tenuously united under its unique system of annually rotating the head of state—despite an 80 percent inflation rate and a 30 percent decline in the standard of living.

Ethnic strife among Serbs and Croats and the Albanians of Kosovo finally destroyed the unity of the multinational state in 1991. Armed conflict broke out as the various constituent republics sought to break away from the Serbian-dominated coalition led by Slobodan Milosevic (SLO-bo-dahn mee-LOSH-eh-vich). Slovenia and Croatia won their freedom in June, and Macedonia declared its independence in November 1991, followed by Bosnia-Herzegovina in December. Serbia and tiny Montenegro were all that remained in the Yugoslav "federation."

Serbs, Croats, and Bosnian Muslims fought in a continually shifting multiple-front war to claim what each side saw as its legitimate patrimony. The Bosnian Serbs, inheriting the bulk of the old Yugoslav

The former Yugoslavia after 1991.

The Serbian "ethnic cleansing" produced atrocities such as the mass murders at Srebrenica. International War Crimes Tribunal investigators uncover a mass grave as they collect evidence for use at the court in The Hague.

armed forces' supplies and weapons and backed by Belgrade, gained 70 percent of Bosnia-Herzegovina and in the process became international pariahs. They carried out genocidal attacks—**"ethnic cleansing"**—on the Bosnian Muslims, who labored under an arms embargo nominally imposed by the West. In reality, the Americans tacitly permitted Islamic states to arm the Bosnians.

The Western allies made noises of protest and even got the Russians to share in the token condemnations of the Serbs, but the only tangible Western aid for the Bosnians came from a U.S. airlift, which in its first year made more sorties over the region and dumped more supplies in the general region than did the U.S. Air Force supplying Berlin in 1948. NATO forces also launched air strikes and periodically bluffed the Serbs into pulling back from Muslim enclaves such as Sarajevo and Gorazde. Truces and peace plans came and went, resolving nothing, while the West hoped that the economic sanctions against Serbia would finally yield some results. Finally the Western powers, joined by Russia, placed forces in the region, and a negotiated truce was arrived at in 1995 at the unlikely site of Dayton, Ohio. The war had led to the deaths of more than 200,000 people and forced more than 3 million to leave their homes.

A peacekeeping force led by the Americans remained in Bosnia, imposing order on the contesting forces and monitoring the activities of the Belgrade government led by Slobodan Milosevic, elected president of rump Yugoslavia in July 1997. The next year, he began to use the ethnic cleansing tactics he had used in Bosnia in the southern province of Kosovo, a province that contains the spiritual center of the Serbs, the battlefield where the Ottoman forces defeated them in 1389. Kosovo's population was 90 percent Kosovar Albanians; after a decade of frustration, some Albanians had formed the Kosovo Liberation Army, which threatened Serb control in parts of the province. All through 1998, the Belgrade government built up its military and paramilitary presence there. Fearing a repeat of the events in Bosnia at the beginning of the decade, the Western allies in October 1998 and February–March 1999 tried to convince Milosevic to change his tactics through diplomatic means. When he did

ethnic cleansing—The process by which a state removes—either by murder or forcing out of their homes—groups not desired. As carried out by the Belgrade government in the 1990s, some of these acts reached the level of genocide.

not, NATO forces began a bombing campaign at the end of March to "degrade" the Yugoslav military forces. What had been a comparative trickle of refugees and sporadic atrocities became a flood of 1 million people forced from their homes and mass murders. At the same time, the NATO bombing, which was stated to be against Milosevic and his forces and not the Yugoslav people, produced numerous civilian casualties. Thanks to the NATO coalition holding together, the energizing of Russia to support an end to the conflict, and the impact of the bombardments, peace of sorts returned to Kosovo in the middle of June. As the Yugoslavs pulled out of the province, to be replaced by the UN-sponsored peacekeeping forces, the reintegration of the almost 1 million Kosovars who fled the region proved to be a difficult task.

As stability came in Kosovo, revolution occurred in Belgrade. In October 2000, an uprising ousted Slobodan Milosevic from power. Elections held in December confirmed the loss of his party's dominance. In the spring of 2001, Milosevic was taken to The Hague in the Netherlands to be tried by an international tribunal for crimes against humanity and genocide. In Kosovo, elections were held for the first multiethnic parliament—a contest won by the moderate Albanian factions. However, by this time, the destabilization of the previous decade had spilled over into Macedonia (officially known as the Former Yugoslav Republic of Macedonia). A combination of European Union and NATO pressures managed to keep the lid on the threat of a full-fledged war between the Slavic and Albanian populations of Macedonia.

THE SOVIET UNION AND THE RUSSIAN REPUBLIC

▪ *Why was the USSR unable to carry out adequate economic reforms in the post-1945 period?*

Soviet Postwar Policies

To achieve equality with the United States after World War II, Stalin launched the fourth 5-year plan in 1946, pushing growth in heavy industry and military goods. To increase Soviet output, he imposed double shifts on many workers. Those whose loyalty to Stalin was in the least suspect were sent to a network of camps spread from Siberia to central Asia to the Arctic region. As they served their punishment, they contributed economically. Tragically, thousands died in the camps from overwork, inadequate food, and the bitter cold. To rebuild the devastated farming regions, Stalin returned to his collectivization policies.

MAP Post-Cold War Russia

The dictator continued to place his supporters in all important offices, combining "the supreme command of the party with the supreme administration of the state." He made entry into the Communist party more difficult and purged many people who had slipped in through the relaxed membership standards during wartime. In the early 1950s, Stalin lashed out more ruthlessly and unpredictably than ever before, as he came to suspect everyone. His half-million-strong security police quashed any sign of dissent, criticism, or free expression. He ordered genocidal attacks on entire peoples, such as the Crimean Tatars. There were indications that the dictator was preparing a major purge that would go beyond "elite self-renewal." In January 1953 the police announced that a "doctors' plot" had been uncovered and that a group of physicians serving high military and governmental officials had been planning to undermine their patients' health. Because seven of the nine accused were Jewish, an anti-Zionist campaign was feared. The purge did not occur, however, because, on March 5, 1953, Stalin died after a painful illness.

From Khrushchev to Chernenko

Stalin's death introduced a period of collective leadership in the Soviet Union. Within three years, the initial triumvirate had disappeared, elbowed aside by Nikita Sergeyevich Khrushchev (khroo-SHCHOV; 1894–1971). Unlike many of the **apparatchiks,** Khrushchev came from peasant stock, and he worked his way up from being a shepherd to being a factory worker and then joining the party in 1918. He rose rapidly in the 1930s, especially after pushing through, at great human cost, the Moscow subway system, to become a Politburo member. He made no claim to being an urban intellectual, instead he delighted in using crude and brutal language around those he considered to be pretentious people. This behavior masked the fact that he was both bright and cunning, able to spot the flaws and weaknesses in his opponents and to take advantage of both at the proper time.

One of Khrushchev's main goals was to reform agriculture. He proposed increasing incentives for the peasants and enlarging the area under production in Soviet Siberia and Central Asia—the virgin lands. Between 1953 and 1958, production rose by 50 percent. Thereafter, farming in the virgin lands proved to be economically wasteful and environmentally disastrous.

Khrushchev's de-Stalinization campaign in February 1956 at the Twentieth Party Congress had an earthquakelike effect on the international communist movement but led to a breathing space inside of

---

apparatchiks—Officials working within the Stalinist bureaucracy, the party apparatus, who gained their livelihood and status from their position within the ruling structure.

the Soviet Union. By blaming all of past ills on the dead dictator, he justified the activities of the present leadership (which had all gained their places because of their slavish adherence to Stalin). Khrushchev also worked to improve the quality and quantity of consumer goods available in Soviet stores. In cultural affairs also, there was a brief relaxation in the "Socialist Realism Only" government policy toward the arts and the printing and publication of important novels, such as *One Day in the Life of Ivan Denisovich* (1962) by Alexandr Solzhenitsyn.

Not all of his colleagues were happy with him, and in 1957 there was a failed attempt by members of the original triumvirate and their allies to remove him, and thereafter, they remained vigilant, ready to remove him after the failure of his agricultural reforms and the aftermath of the Cuban Missile Crisis. Following Khrushchev's "retirement" in 1964, a classic apparatchik, Leonid Brezhnev (1906–1982), dominated the next stage of Cold War and Soviet history. Working with Aleksei Kosygin (1904–1980), he constructed an alliance with the military to deliver support that would enable the USSR to gain military parity with the United States.

From 1964 to 1974, Brezhnev and Kosygin split power, Brezhnev acting as general secretary and Kosygin as premier, overseeing sporadic reform attempts. Brezhnev later became president of the country under terms of the 1977 constitution. Serious health problems limited his effectiveness in the last years of his tenure. Politics remained based on Stalin's foundations, as modified by Khrushchev. The central planners continued to emphasize industrial growth and slowly increase the supply of consumer goods. In foreign policy the new team pursued peaceful coexistence at the same time that they greatly strengthened the Soviet armed forces.

While the USSR gained military parity with the West, its civilian economy ground to a halt. The long-standing agricultural crisis grew worse. The Soviets spent huge amounts to import grain from abroad to cope with food shortages at home. Especially maddening to the Soviet leaders was the extraordinary amount of crops that rotted in the fields or en route to market. Private plots worked by peasants after hours for their own profit, which accounted for only 3 percent of sown land, provided 30 percent of all the table food in the Soviet Union.

Brezhnev was succeeded in 1982 by Yuri Andropov (1914–1984), a railway worker's son who rose to the peak of Soviet power as head of the KGB. Andropov's jobs put him at the crossroads of all information. Recognizing the disastrous condition of the USSR's infrastructure, he brought a large number of people from the provinces to work in high party positions in Moscow and set out immediately to increase output, fight corruption, and strengthen the military. He started campaigns to combat alcoholism and cheating and fired people who did not perform up to his standards. His health, however, deteriorated, and from the summer of 1983 until his announced death in February 1984, Andropov was out of public view.

The last of the Stalin protégés was Konstantin Chernenko (1912–1985), who succeeded Andropov to the posts of first secretary and president. Chernenko had ridden Brezhnev's coattails since the 1950s but had been soundly defeated by Andropov for the top job in 1982. His age and poor health signified that he would be a transition figure between the old guard and a new generation. The strain of leadership almost immediately broke Chernenko's fragile health, and even before his death in March 1985, wholesale changes were taking place in the highest levels of the Soviet government.

The economies of the Soviet Bloc states stagnated after the middle of the 1970s. By the end of the 1980s, the economic gap between the two sides forced Moscow and its allies in COMECON to seek admission to the International Monetary Fund (IMF) and to the General Agreement on Trade and Tariffs (GATT). It was apparent that the global political economy had become one of the most important factors in world relations.

Mikhail Gorbachev: Glasnost and Perestroika

After Chernenko's death in 1985, a new generation of Soviet leaders came to the fore, led by Mikhail Gorbachev (b. 1931). No less devoted to Marxism-Leninism than the former generation, the new leaders—many of whom had been placed in positions of influence by Andropov—more openly attacked the economic and social problems the USSR faced.

CASE STUDY
Gorbachev (1987), vs. Lenin (1920), and Stalin (1931)

Gorbachev moved rapidly to take power by implementing a platform based on **glasnost** ("openness") and **perestroika** ("restructuring") to try to bring new life to the Soviet system. Glasnost was Gorbachev's way of motivating the Soviet people to be more creative and work harder. Perestroika attempted to remove the structural blocks to modernization. These two themes launched the final act in the de-Stalinization campaign begun by Khrushchev in 1956.

For the first time the party acknowledged mistakes, such as the Chernobyl nuclear disaster in April 1986. Past tragedies—especially those of the 1930s that had long been common knowledge—were now openly discussed. Gorbachev permitted unprecedented criticism of party and political leaders by the

---

glasnost—"Openness" or "transparency." Opening the party and government structures of the Soviet Union to bring in the most progressive elements of society to reform the system.

perestroika—Literally "restructuring," a basic reform of the Soviet political and economic system.

press and television. One of the unexpected results of glasnost was a revival of separatist movements in the various Soviet republics.

Gorbachev originally sought to use perestroika to fine-tune the traditional central planning apparatus and party and state procedures, but the total failure of the Stalinist system demanded a more wide-ranging program. By 1990 the depth and severity of the Soviet Union's problems drove Gorbachev to attempt to impose a market economy, reduce the role of the Leninist "vanguard party," and alter the governmental structure.

Gorbachev became the undisputed master of the party and the state, putting down rivals with great skill and using public opinion and free elections to neutralize opponents while building a new power base. After being named president in October 1988, he set out to reform that most secret and powerful of all Soviet institutions, the KGB, urging its new leaders to imitate the structure of the American CIA.

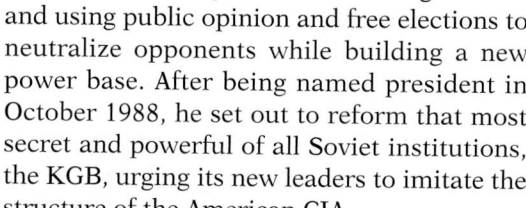

DOCUMENT
Mikhail Gorbachev on the Need for Economic Reform

Until 1989 the Supreme Soviet was a carefully preselected rubber-stamp body. Real power was concentrated in the Council of Ministers, headed by a prime minister. In elections in March and April 1989, many powerful officials were voted down, even though they had run unopposed. The Congress of People's Deputies, which was to meet annually and be reelected every five years, replaced the old Supreme Soviet.

The Communist party posed a special problem for Gorbachev, a dedicated Leninist. It was so inflexible that Gorbachev had to diminish its role after the July 1990 party congress. Thereafter, no major party member sat on the Politburo, with the exception of the Soviet president. The party became subordinate to the state, losing its leading role. Millions gave up their party memberships after 1989, many of them going to work in city and republic governments, where there was greater opportunity.

Gorbachev invoked glasnost and perestroika to jump-start the moribund economy. Although gross domestic product figures continued to indicate that the Soviet economy was the second largest in the world, the reality was that the infrastructure was undermined by outmoded technologies, inefficient factories, a dispirited and underemployed workforce, and environmental disasters. Unlike the Chinese, who had in 1978 started their economic reforms in the countryside so as to ensure an adequate supply of food, Gorbachev relied on a more Leninist, democratic centralist approach and failed miserably. The Communist party, which Lenin had seen as the elite cadre that would anticipate the needs of the proletariat for the proletariat, had been turned by Stalin and his successors into an institution of privilege of, by, and for the party.

Everything went bad at once for Gorbachev. As economic conditions deteriorated, he increased concessions to party hard-liners and bureaucratic opportunists, buying time to hold power. In the spring of 1991, hundreds of thousands of people marched in the streets of Moscow to protest the premier's retreat from liberalism. Separatist protests increased in the Baltic republics of Estonia, Latvia, and Lithuania as well as in Georgia, the Ukraine, and Moldavia. Standards of living throughout the nation plummeted.

On August 19, while Gorbachev was on vacation in the Crimea, an eight-man "state emergency committee" made up of leaders of the KGB, the military, the interior department, and other offices of the central government—all appointed by Gorbachev—mounted an attempt to take power. Gorbachev's vice president announced that his leader was ill and that a state of emergency was to be imposed for six months.

The attempted coup was immediately denounced by Boris Yeltsin (b. 1931), who had been popularly elected President of the Russian Republic and who barricaded himself inside the offices of the Russian parliament building in Moscow. He instructed all army and KGB units not to obey the coup leaders' orders. The next day 50,000 people turned out in Moscow to face down tanks sent by the central government. Larger groups mobilized in Leningrad and Kishinev. Several units of KGB and army forces refused to obey the central command's orders, and the coup began to unravel. By August 21 the crisis was over, and Yeltsin had emerged as the man of the hour.

Six days after the attempted coup, the reality of the situation became clear. Gorbachev resigned as leader of the Soviet Communist party and recommended dissolution of the Central Committee. Yeltsin claimed control of party archives and KGB records, and across the Soviet Union, in a vast revolution, the Communist party—after 74 years of almost total power—was cut off from all its vanguard roles in running the country. In

On August 19, 1991, president of the Russian Republic Boris Yeltsin stands atop an armed carrier in Moscow to read a statement urging people to resist the attempted hard-line coup.

MAP Break-up of the Soviet Union

addition, the party had to surrender its wealth and property to the parliaments of the various republics. Gorbachev remained as president of the Soviet Union, at least until popular elections could be held. But the USSR itself would last only four more months, ending its 69-year existence on December 21, 1991. It was replaced by a smaller and looser confederation, the Commonwealth of Independent States.

Boris Yeltsin and the Russian Republic

After August 1991, Boris Yeltsin was the most important Russian politician. Like other leaders at the end of a revolution, he found that a change in government did not remove the terrible problems facing Russia such as inflation, budget deficits, and declining living standards. To deal with these problems, Yeltsin set in motion programs of privatization and the construction of a new infrastructure for international trade and commerce. There were also serious problems with ethnic minorities—especially in Chechnya.

Almost immediately, Yeltsin had to deal with opposition from the apparatchik-laden Congress of People's Deputies, elected under the old Soviet model. The Congress consistently blocked Yeltsin's attempts to implement a series of market-oriented economic reforms, such as liberalizing prices on most nonfood goods. In addition, Yeltsin faced problems from deputies who accused him of caving in to Western pressures in both domestic and foreign policy. The Russian president remained personally popular; however, this had little effect on the Congress, which continued to block his initiatives.

Yeltsin's contest with the parliament reached a stalemate in September 1993. When the Congress threatened to take much of his authority away, he responded by dissolving the Congress and calling for new elections in December. He then sent troops to surround the parliament building—the Russian White House—and told deputies that they would have to leave the building by October 4. These actions provoked widespread criticism throughout Russia, and leaders of 62 out of 89 regional councils called for Yeltsin to remove the troops.

On October 3, forces opposing the president took over the office of the mayor of Moscow and attacked the state television center. To an audience watching these events live on international television, it was remarkable that only 62 people died in the fighting. The next day, Yeltsin sent tanks and artillery against the Russian White House and battered the resisters into submission.

Yeltsin's forces and a new constitution barely carried the vote in the December elections, winning enough seats in parliament to prevent the opposition from being able to impeach the president. To maintain power in the face of an extremist coalition that was seemingly held together only by its opposition to Yeltsin, the president took a centrist course, advocating a rebirth of the Great Russian state, damping down essential programs to produce a privatized economy, and distancing himself from the West in foreign affairs—especially the extension of early NATO membership to the former eastern European states and Western intervention in disintegrating Yugoslavia. Aided by substantial American support in financing and carrying out his campaign, Yeltsin was reelected in 1996, defeating the leader of the Communist party.

Russia's economy during the Yeltsin years proved unable to make the comparatively rapid change to a market system, as had the economies of Poland, the Czech Republic, and Hungary. The ethnic and social diversity of the continent-sized state made a "cold turkey" transition to the market system difficult. For the large majority of the Russian people, the change from a communist to a modified free market system brought no improvement to their lives. Cities such as St. Petersburg began to lose population as residents moved out to villages where they winterized huts and became full-time gardeners. For two-thirds of Russia's citizens, the quality of life declined more than 50 percent in the ten years after 1991.

DOCUMENT Scientists Examine Russia's Economy and Environment 1991–1993

But for a few young, well-connected individuals, Yeltsin's haphazard privatization allowed them to gain control of Russia's basic resources of nickel, aluminum, natural gas, and oil. Russia has proven oil reserves of nearly 55 billion barrels, barely one-fifth that of Saudi Arabia, but substantial nonetheless—enough to allow Russia to be the second largest oil exporter in most years. The young capitalists, who became known as *oligarchs*, gained control of the basic resources of the country for around ten percent of their real value between 1993 and 1996. Thereafter, they took advantage of the disarray and corruption of Yeltsin's government to avoid most of the taxes they should have paid. By 2003, 17 of the world's richest men were Russian oligarchs between the ages of 36 and 54. One of them, Mikhail Khodorkovsky, who controlled Yukos Oil, was the twenty-sixth richest person in the world at that time.

Yeltsin's ill health and the popular perception that he was the tool of the Russian "mafia" combined to force him to step down at the end of 1999. In preparation for that event, he named Vladimir V. Putin—one of his aides, a former KGB officer, and head of that group's successor, the Federal Security Bureau (FSB)—to be the prime minister of Russia in the summer of 1999. On the last day of the year, Yeltsin formally resigned and named Putin the acting president.

Vladimir Putin

Presidential elections in March 2000 confirmed Putin as president. He inherited the host of problems Yeltsin had not solved: massive corruption in all spheres of political life, control of major economic sectors by the "mafia" and the oligarchs, slow economic growth, the war in Chechnya, and other problems dealing with national groups within the Russian Federation. It became immediately apparent that he would be a different kind of president than Yeltsin. His major immediate goal was reassert the power of the political center in Moscow over the provinces. He used to good effect the concern over terrorist incidents in Moscow—tied to the renewed warfare in Chechnya—and his control over the most important newspapers and television stations to muster support for his position. Within the government, he began to dismiss members of the former Yeltsin team and to replace them with colleagues from the former KGB and other security agencies.

By 2004 he had broken the "mafia" and the oligarchs, imprisoning Mikhail Khodorkovsky and forcing other oligarchs to leave the country. For this, and other reasons, Putin has a popularity rating above 80 percent in Russia. He has successfully recentralized power. More efficient courts seem to be succeeding in reducing the widespread corruption that had flourished in the 1990s. There has been a large increase in tax collections. Russia's economy has stabilized, and in 2001–2003 the country experienced a considerable economic growth. The Duma acts more and more like a western representative assembly.

Critics in the West still point out that Putin achieved these results by clearly undemocratic means. His party, United Russia, had a virtual monopoly on television screens in the run up to the presidential elections in March 2004. Writers and reporters who knew too much or criticized too openly were murdered by unknown assailants. Popular television stations have been silenced and commentators deemed too independent have lost their jobs. Still, within Russia, the president enjoys broad support.

Russia has a long way to go. It continues to fight a demographic crisis that has men dying at an average age of 61, 12 years sooner than men in Western countries and a lowering birthrate. Economically, President Putin has stated that Russia's goal was to equal the GDP rate of Portugal by 2015, a difficult task given that Russia's GDP at the end of 2004 was $8900, $10,000 behind the Portuguese level. Still, after the terrorist attacks on the United States, the Russian president used his friendly relationship with the American president, George W. Bush, to make economic and foreign policy gains, especially in regard to the use of force to put down opponents along his southern frontiers.

In the successor states along Russia's western border, economic and political developments ranged from the tragic in the Caucasian republics to the corrupt and inefficient in Ukraine and Belarus. Kiev had nuclear weapons, untapped economic potential, and a disastrously corrupt and inept government. In July 1994 the Western powers offered to loan Ukraine $4 billion and to aid in the rebuilding or replacing of the damaged Chernobyl nuclear power plant. But Ukraine's economy continued to limp along despite a new constitution in 1996 that gave President Leonid Kuchma the power to impose major structural reforms. Belarus, under its Stalinist leader Alexander Lukashenka, is marching resolutely backward, crushing domestic political opponents and lashing out at international critics. Like Moldova and the Ukraine, Belarus's economy is in a tragic state, and only energy imports from Russia keep its infrastructure intact. Moldova took heroic measures to introduce the discipline and quality needed to compete in the international market at the beginning of the 1990s but now ranks as the poorest country in Europe.

It was only the imposition of Russian arms that brought a tenuous peace to the Caucasus. Armenians and Azeris battled over control of Nagorno-Karabakh; Georgians and Abkhazians and roving bands of independent mercenaries fought over long-disputed lands. And in the Chechnya region of Russia, a full-scale war between Moscow and Chechen separatists in 1995 and 1996 ended with an armed truce that left the Chechens in control of vital oil and gas pipelines. The war reignited two years later, and the Russians resumed their brutal response against a combined force of mujahideen, Arab fighters, and the local population. The Chechens have spread their struggle from the Caucasus into bomb attacks in Moscow and provincial capitols.

In Central Asia, the countries of Tajikstan, Turkmenistan, Uzbekistan, and Kazakhstan made little progress toward pluralistic democratic structures. The presidents of these countries, such as Nursultan A. Nazarbayev (na-zar-BAI-ev) in Kazkahstan, gained power early in the 1990s and spend little time encouraging the development of a democratic opposition, preferring instead to enrich their own friends and family—as they had during the former USSR. The rich petroleum and mineral deposits, however, made them important players in the post-1991 global economic scene. Their importance became even greater during the military action in Afghanistan in the fall of 2001 in which they extended landing rights to the American forces, in return for less international scrutiny.

INTERDEPENDENCE IN A CHANGING WORLD

- *Has globalization made the Unites States richer and more secure, or more wealthy, yet more exposed to danger?*

As the twenty-first century began, it was evident that global interdependence placed pressures on private citizens and political leaders. On the one hand there was the struggle by non-Western individuals to maintain their cultures and values in the face of the on-rushing Western-dominated globalization. On the other hand, political leaders everywhere found themselves more and more at the mercy of international currents over which they had little control: globalization, terrorism, global warming, and pollution. The Internet, satellite television, and cell phones joined traditional media such as radio and newspapers to inundate people on all continents with a flood of information. There were a few individuals isolated from the on-rushing tide of interdependence. But there were no political leaders—neither George W. Bush or Vladimir Putin—who claim to be control of events.

The Global Economy

After 1945 the world experienced unprecedented economic growth and development and increasing interdependence. But trade flows changed. The international monetary system of exchange rates pegged to the dollar and the fixed price of gold lasted until 1971, when trade imbalances led to gold outflows from major importing nations such as the United States. President Richard Nixon dealt a fatal blow to the Bretton Woods system by severing the link between gold and the dollar. His move opened the way for "floating rates," the determination of exchange rates by market mechanisms.

This policy change aided multinational firms, headquartered in one country but with operations throughout the world, because, by shifting operations, they could take advantage of exchange rate differences to reduce cost. In response, countries whose economies depended on the export of raw materials began to band together in an attempt to affect the price of their goods, because the price of their goods determined the value of their currency.

The oil embargo of the 1970s imposed by the OPEC countries, originally intended to punish the nations that supported Israel in the 1973 Arab-Israeli war, dealt a serious blow to international stability. Quadrupling their prices, the OPEC nations gained in wealth at the expense of oil-importing nations. Poor oil-importing nations borrowed on international markets to finance their oil purchases. Banks in the United States, Europe, and Japan made substantial loans to countries in eastern Europe, Latin America, and Africa—whose total debt by the end of the 1970s topped $1.3 trillion. Brazil's debt was nearly $100 billion; Mexico's was close to $90 billion. To ensure their survival, nations such as Brazil, Hungary, and Poland allowed World Bank personnel to impose regulations on domestic economic policy in return for loans, an unprecedented sacrifice of national sovereignty to an international body. Nonetheless, nonpayment by the debtor nations threatened to topple the world's banking structure as it became apparent that these poor nations could not repay their loans. The debt crisis of the 1980s pressed the IMF to the limit. Debts continued to be rescheduled, but the largest debtors showed an ever-declining ability to pay. In January 2002, Argentina faced a severe economic and political crisis as it was unable to pay even the interest on its foreign debts and faced draconian solutions to stabilize its economy.

This situation, and the world recession of 1978–1985, had different effects on different parts of the globe. Unemployment soared around the world, especially in the less developed countries, which were also plagued with rising population rates. In the United States the recession contributed to huge trade deficits and federal budget deficits. The United States was the first nation to recover from the recession, largely by generating a huge national debt and borrowing heavily from foreigners. A creditor since 1917, the United States now became a debtor nation.

In the late 1980s the United States momentarily lost its financial dominance to the Japanese, who themselves would later be challenged by Asia's "Four Tigers"—South Korea, Taiwan, Hong Kong, and Sin-

Global Economic Milestones

1944	Bretton Woods Conference plans peacetime economy
1945	International Monetary Fund, World Bank chartered
1947	General Agreement on Tariffs and Trade established
1948	Marshall Plan in Europe
1949	COMECON instituted
1950	Dodge Plan instituted in Japan
1971	President Nixon takes dollar off gold standard
1973–1974	OPEC oil crisis
1980s	Banking crises in Latin America and eastern Europe
1987	U.S. stock market crash
1989	USSR and Soviet Bloc abandon central planning model
1995	World Trade Organization established
1997–1998	Asian economic crisis
2002	Euro introduced

gapore. New technologies and cheaper labor overseas produced high-quality items that cost less than U.S.-manufactured goods. Competition was especially severe for Americans in the advanced technology and automobile markets until the early 1990s.

The resulting foreign trade deficits increased the desire for protectionist legislation in the 1980s, especially in the United States. Many congressional members argued that Japanese trade restrictions and subsidies harmed U.S. agricultural and technological exports while American markets remained relatively open to foreign imports. The GATT mechanism was pushed to the breaking point. In 1989 the United States invoked Section 301 of the Trade Act of 1974 to levy sanctions against India, Brazil, and Japan for unfair trade practices.

By the end of the 1990s Japan, South Korea, Indonesia, and Malaysia faced serious economic problems as a combination of vastly overvalued real estate investments, currency speculation, and corruption led to a collapse of those countries' currencies and fears of a meltdown of the Asian economic system that would threaten the global economy. Once again the IMF stepped into the crisis with its prescriptions of closing down weak banks and businesses, austerity budgets, and fiscal conservatism. Also, the United States plunged billions of dollars into the region to stabilize the situation. The Asian crisis had a damaging effect on the new capitalist economies of the former Soviet Bloc. Russia's inability to take the serious steps to reform its economy and the crooked nature of its economy made the Russian market rickety even before the Asian crisis. Westerners found themselves on the horns of a dilemma: whether to let Russia suffer through its crisis with the possibility that the democratic experiment might fail or to pour more billions of dollars in with the knowledge that most of it would never help most ordinary Russians anyway.

Given the turbulence of the previous half century, however, the foundation established at Bretton Woods allowed the world to avoid the inflation and depression that marked the 1920s and 1930s. The long-running Uruguay Round of the GATT talks, in which the United States worked with 115 other states to update the GATT rules, ended successfully in December 1993. This led to the establishment of the **World Trade Organization (WTO),** a streamlined approach to continuing the fight against trade barriers that had been successfully waged by GATT since World War II, which in 2001 admitted China into its ranks. At the same time, the interdependence of the world economy made it impossible to isolate the economic shocks produced by the September 11, 2001, attacks on the World Trade Center and its effects. Also, the recession in the United States that began after two quarters of negative economic growth in 2001 affected the entire world, leading to increased unemployment, declining profits, and decreased investment in research for new products.

The economic interdependence produced a number of shared transformations. Global economic growth produced an affiliated global challenge to the environment. A population explosion led to the demand for more resources and raw materials. In response, the rain forests of Southeast Asia and South America—essential for the recycling of air and water—were being destroyed at a rapid rate. Technological advancement made fishermen more efficient, and they began to reduce the essential stocks of the worlds' fisheries. Larger industries, especially in Mexico, China, and Brazil, created more pollution of the air and water. The North Americans—who consumed 20 times as much water as South Americans—through their automobile-based lifestyles

With the end of the Cold War and the decade of wars in the former Yugoslavia, illegal immigration from eastern Europe and the Balkans became a serious issue, especially for the Italians. Shown here is a boatload of Albanian refugees being turned away at Brindisi Italy in March 1997.

World Trade Organization (WTO)—The successor organization to GATT (the General Agreement on Trades and Tariffs), established in 1995. As with its predecessor, the organization carried on the fight against trade barriers.

added to the forces producing global warming and the holes in the ozone layer.

Economic interdependence and the demand for more workers brought women massively into the workforce. Even though labor-saving devices permitted housework to be done in one-tenth the time, the traditional family underwent a fundamental change. The advances in the equality of women with men were not everywhere the same, but it is not to be doubted that a social revolution is taking place.

As the world becomes more interdependent, it also becomes more vulnerable. The magnetic lure of one-fourth of the world being rich while three-fourths of the world remains poor has produced a demographic movement not seen since the nineteenth century. National boundaries have become porous, a development which favors the work of terrorists. Al-Qaeda may have been acting more to destabilize governments in the Middle East—especially oil-rich Saudi Arabia—when it struck at the United States on September 11, 2001. The statements of Osama bin Laden say precious little about poverty. But it cannot be doubted that as long as the disparity between the rich and the poor remains, and grows, the capitalist world will be the target of more attacks. All of the advanced military technology of the United States and its allies in the war against terrorism cannot remove the fact that in striking at violence, the rich countries are attacking the symptom of a crisis, not the cause.

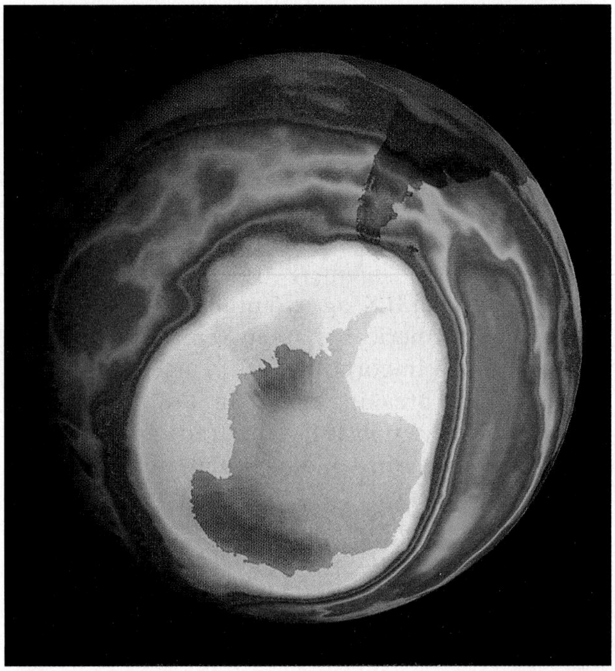

Although there are debates over the causes of the global warming that is taking place, satellite images such as this prove that there is no doubt that the holes in the protective ozone layers are becoming larger, as are the threats to the planet's people.

Environmental Challenges

Increased consumption of resources through generation of electricity, transportation, and manufacturing processes has threatened the world's environment. In this new, interdependent world, the postwar international economic growth and the technological revolutions generated an unwelcome by-product: pollution. The UN Conference on the Human Environment held in Stockholm in 1972 produced no serious negotiations but did sound the call that environmental problems know no national boundaries. Since then, a number of international congresses and conventions have discussed the damage of global pollution: the destruction of air quality, the damage to the oceans, and the threat to the world's supply of drinking water.

For every victory in the war against pollution—such as meaningful programs to preserve the oceans' capacity to replenish their fish, local campaigns to reclaim polluted lakes and rivers, and new technology to cut the damage to the environment of automobiles—there were setbacks in other areas. Global warming and the destruction of the ozone layer posed serious dangers to the world's increasing population ranging from increased rates of skin cancer to the threat of rising levels of the world's oceans that threatened cities such as Venice. It is difficult to deal with the damage created when modern industry and technology generate by-products that destroy the environment and, at an equivalent pace, the planet's forests. The slashing and burning of forests in Southeast Asia and the Amazon basin threatened the earth's natural capacity to replenish the water supply and the cleanse the air.

Massive environmental problems plagued the former Soviet Bloc, especially in Central Asia where the fourth largest body of fresh water in the world—the Aral Sea—is in process of disappearing. The abysmal conditions in which the centrally planned economies left eastern Europe and Russia overwhelmed planners and reformers. The capitalist world has yet to work out the conflict between economic development and environmental safety for itself, let alone the peoples of the former Soviet Bloc and the developing world. Admittedly tentative steps to control the process of global warming such as the Kyoto protocol could not gain, for example, the participation of the United States, which valued its economic development over global approaches to shared problems.

CONCLUSION

The United States, experiencing its longest-running economic growth cycle, still faces the challenges of making its pluralistic system work and preserving its basic civil liberties in the face of the terrorist attacks of September 11, 2001. Its investments in antiterrorist campaigns and the Iraq and Afghan wars have led to a federal budget deficit of close to $500 billion and a dependence on imported capital, to the tune of $1 billion a day.

If Europe can continue to work out the old problems of political and cultural particularism, its economic union holds the promise that in the twenty-first century, as in the nineteenth, economic power will return to the Europeans. Its success will depend on its being able to integrate the states of eastern Europe.

In 1989 the Soviet Union disintegrated in a revolutionary change not seen since 1848. After 15 years the results were varied. The former Soviet republics in the north entered the European Union, after gaining their independence. Those to the south faced corruption and ethnic conflict. In general, except for the top 10 percent, the Russians endured a general decline in the quality of life but seemed to be adapting to their new system of democracy under Putin.

All of these political entities must adapt to meet the changing challenges of technological development and the changes in the role of women and the family. The pressures of globalization demand increasing efficiencies from the countries of the "North," as many jobs move to the developing world. Maintaining the rich diversity of national identities in the face of a globalized culture perpetuated almost exclusively by American media also poses a challenge. And with all that, international concerns for the degrading of the environment remain acute.

Suggestions for Web Browsing

You can obtain more information about topics included in this chapter at the websites listed below. See also the companion website that accompanies this text, **http://www.ablongman.com/brummett**, which contains an online study guide and additional resources.

NATO Official Home Page
http://www.nato.int

Official documents for the rapidly changing European scene in the 1900s.

The European Union
http://www.eurunion.org

Information on events within the European Union.

The New European Politics of the 1990s
http://nwl.newsweek.com/nw-srv/inetguide/guide 2023877.html

A new kind of politics emerged in Europe during the 1990s—the so-called third way between traditional socialism and conservatism. Prime Minister Tony Blair exemplifies that path and his career can be traced on the site.

Literature and Film

Thomas Wolfe's novels and essays—for example, *The Bonfire of the Vanities* (1987) and *Radical Chic & Mau-Mauing the Flack Catchers* (1970)—cast a cynical eye on the realities of the 1960s and 1970s. Neal Stephenson's *Snow Crash* (1992) opened up new horizons in the writing of science fiction. John Updike's and Norman Mailer's novels and short stories show as much about their evolution as the countries. Marguerite Duras dealt with love in a difficult time in *The Lover* (1984) and *Hiroshima Mon Amour* (1959). John le Carré brought the spy novel to new heights in *Tinker, Tailor, Soldier, Spy* (1974) and *The Spy Who Came in from the Cold* (1963). The Oxford Don J. R. R. Tolkien brought the epic into the late twentieth century in his work on the Hobbits in his trilogy. Heinrich Böll was awarded the 1972 Nobel Prize for his contribution to German literature, particularly his novel of German life from World War I (1914–1918) through the 1970s, *Gruppenbild mit Dame* (*Group Portrait with Lady;* 1971).

In film, the Italian Frederico Fellini dealt with the insanities of the nuclear age in *La Dolce Vita* (Republic, 1960) and *Amarcord* (Home Vision Entertainment, 1974), a portrayal of growing up in Fascist Italy, which had a contemporary relevance. In France François Truffaut led a new wave of French film makers with films such as *Jules et Jim* (Fox Lorber, 1962) and the film version of Ray Bradbury's *Fahrenheit 451* (Universal, 1966). Ingmar Bergman's *Seventh Seal* (Home Vision Entertainment, 1957) captured the apocalyptic nature of the time. Oliver Stone provided a compelling, particularist viewpoint of America in *JFK* (Warner, 1991), *Nixon* (PBS, 1995), *Wall Street* (Twentieth Century Fox, 1987), and *Born on the Fourth of July* (Universal, 1989). Sam Mendes held a magnifying glass up against the tensions and fractures of American families in the Academy Award–winning *American Beauty* (Universal/MCA, 1999). Spike Lee's *Malcolm X* (Warner, 1992) traced a leader's saga. Michael Wadleigh's *Woodstock* (Warner, 1970) caught a movement's life at its apogee. Joel Schumacher's *St. Elmo's Fire* (Columbia/Tristar, 1985) provides a window into the lives of an idealistic generation's process of coming to terms. Gary Ross's *Pleasantville* (New Line, 1998) is a time warp into the conformity of the 1950s. Alan J. Pakula's *All the President's Men* (Warner, 1976) examines the reporters who brought down a president. Barry Levinson's *Wag the Dog* (New Line, 1997) lays bare the role of spin doctors in American political life. Woody Allen's *Annie Hall* (MGM/UA, 1977) sparred with the concept of romantic love.

Suggestions for Reading

For a fine new synthesis see John R. McNeill, *Something New Under the Sun: An Environmental History of the Twentieth-Century World* (W. W. Norton, 2001). On the profound transformation in women's roles in the twentieth century, see the classics by Simone de Beauvoir, *The Second Sex* (Vintage, 1989), and Betty Friedan, *The Feminine Mystique* (W. W. Norton, 2001).

At the end of the 1980s, Joseph S. Nye Jr. wrote a magisterial analysis of the United States' role in *Bound to Lead: The Changing Nature of American Power* (Basic Books, 1989). Most of the postwar presidents have produced memoirs.

The resurgence of western Europe is dealt with in J. Robert Wegs, *Europe Since 1945* (St. Martin's Press, 1991). Michael Emerson et al., *The Economics of 1992: The E.C. Commission's Assessment of the Economic Effects of Completing the Internal Market* (Oxford University Press, 1988), is a wise assessment of the challenges and promises of the united Europe. Easily the best coverage of the collapse of communism in Eastern Europe is Gale Stokes, *The Walls Came Tumbling Down* (Oxford University Press, 1993).

Roger Cohen, *Hearts Grown Brutal: Sagas of Sarajevo* (Random House, 1998), captures the human tragedy of the Yugoslav crises. J. L. H. Keep's *Last of the Empires: A History of the Soviet Union 1945–1991* (Oxford University Press, 1995) is the best general study of the factors bringing an end to the USSR. A new compilation of articles on the political situation in Russia after 1991 see Michael McFaul, Nikolai Petrov, and Andrei Ryabov, eds., *Between Dictatorship and Democracy: Russian Post-Communist Political Reform* (Carnegie Endowment for International Peace, 2004).

CHAPTER 34

The Middle East, Africa, and Latin America Since 1945

The Struggle for Survival

CHAPTER CONTENTS

The Middle East and Africa comprise new countries created after 1945 when the old European empires disappeared, while the nations of Latin America won their independence in previous centuries. Whatever their origins, during the Cold War, these nations served as an arena for competition between Washington and Moscow; some of its leaders were successful in manipulating that contest to their own advantage, and others were not. In addition to the Cold War, political leadership, population pressure, health crises, external debt, and economic dependence were major factors in the evolution of Latin American, Middle Eastern, and African nations in the second half of the twentieth century.

At the turn of the century the vast majority of the nations of the developing world remained trapped by poverty, overpopulation, and the indifference of the developed world. More than 92 percent of the world's population (much of it in the Middle East, Africa, and Latin America) lived in areas where per capita GDP (gross domestic product) did not exceed $3000. Different factors (varying by place) accounted for this widespread backwardness, among them: corrupt leadership, the dominance of a peasant subsistence economy, the residual effects of colonialism, the lack of capital, the lack of education, rising fuel prices, inflation, inadequate health care, and overpopulation. Large areas of each of these three regions are sparsely populated, isolated, and lacking in adequate transport systems. Conversely, Latin America, Africa, and the Middle East all contain exceptionally large cities that have become magnets for rural in-migration in the last 50 years. Millions of people have left stagnant rural areas for densely populated urban megacenters that are plagued by crumbling infrastructure, air and water pollution, and joblessness. The end of the Cold War and the increased threat of terrorism, however, have signaled a worldwide reconfiguring of economies, governments, allegiances, and identity politics. Whether the nations of the Middle East, Africa, and Latin America will benefit or suffer from that evolving set of circumstances remains to be seen.

1940

1948 State of Israel proclaimed; National party wins white election in South Africa and institutes apartheid

1950

1957 Ghana becomes first sub-Saharan nation to gain independence; Suez Canal Crisis

1959 Cuban revolution brings Castro and the communists to power

1960

1960 Eighteen African nations gain independence

1967 Arab-Israeli War

1970

1973 Military coup overthrows Salvador Allende in Chile

1976 Soweto uprising in South Africa

1979 Iranian Revolution; start of Iran-Iraq War

1980

1980 Zimbabwe institutes black majority rule

1990

1994 Nelson Mandela elected president of South Africa; Rwandan genocide; creation of NAFTA

1995 Islamic party wins election in Turkey

1995 Vicente Fox elected as president of Mexico

2000

2000 Vicente Fox elected as president of Mexico

THE MIDDLE EAST: RELIGION AND POLITICS

■ *Why have Islamist movements become popular in so many Muslim countries?*

Four major factors conditioned the evolution of the Middle East in the second half of the twentieth century: the creation of the state of Israel, decolonization, the exploitation of oil resources, and the Cold War. (The latter three factors, it is important to note, also characterized regions of Africa and South America.) Toward the end of the century, a fifth element, the growing popularity of **Islamist** movements, has challenged the established secular governments of Middle Eastern nations and drawn world attention to the region in the aftermath of the attack on the World Trade Center, which was carried out by the radical Islamist group al-Qaeda.

Decolonization was a gradual process. Although some of the Arab states were granted independence in the interwar period, the mandate powers, Britain and France, retained a significant military and economic presence. During World War II, England reoccupied Iraq and used Egypt as a staging ground for its war effort. Only in the generation after the war did all the nation-states of the Middle East truly gain their independence. In the meantime, the arrival of European Jews seeking refuge in the area after the war, Zionist mobilization (which aimed at the establishment of a Jewish state in Palestine), and Great Power political pressure led to the creation of the state of Israel in 1948. This touched off a bitter conflict between the

Islamist—Political groups that advocate government based on a strict interpretation of Islamic religious and legal tenets.

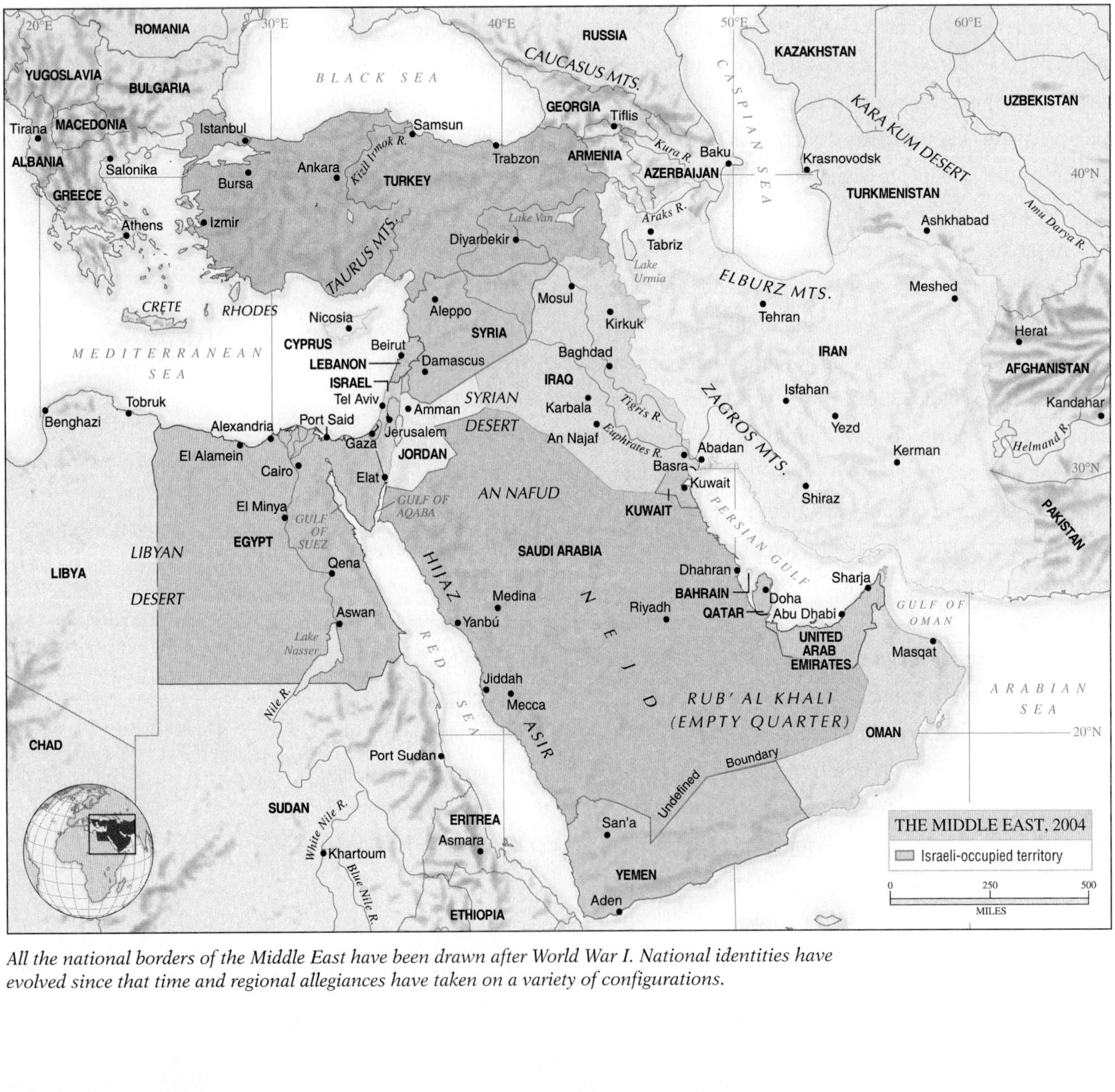

All the national borders of the Middle East have been drawn after World War I. National identities have evolved since that time and regional allegiances have taken on a variety of configurations.

new state and its Arab neighbors, who viewed Israel as a symbol of continued European imperialism in the region. Israel's creation provided a homeland for Jews brutalized by the Holocaust, but it produced an immediate refugee problem as thousands of Palestinian residents fled or were driven from their homes. It also created the dilemma of how a Westernized state with a significant Muslim and Christian population could also be a Jewish state. Israel was then, and remains, one of the most significant factors in Middle East politics, although its relationships with the Palestinians and with each of its regional neighbors have evolved along significantly different lines.

In the aftermath of the creation of Israel, a determined group of Egyptian army officers decided to free Egypt from the British yoke once and for all. Colonel Gamal Abdel Nasser of Egypt helped lead the revolution that overthrew King Faruq in 1952, made Egypt a republic in 1953, and ended British control over the Suez Canal. Nasser became a hero of Arab nationalism and of the Nonaligned Nations movement in the context of the Cold War, playing the United States and the Soviet Union against each other. He envisioned Egypt becoming a dominant power in the Arab world, the Muslim world, and Africa, but many of his ambitious modernizing schemes failed, as did his attempt to merge Egypt and Syria into one Arab state. Egypt and Israel formed the two poles around which the Arab-Israeli conflict was to revolve in the decades to come.

The Modern Middle East

The Arab-Israeli Conflict

1948	State of Israel proclaimed; Arab states attack
1956	Israel joins Britain and France in war on Egypt for control of Suez Canal
1964	Palestine Liberation Organization (PLO) founded
1967	Israel wins Arab-Israeli war (Six-Day War), occupies conquered territories; UN Resolution 242
1973	Egypt and Syria attack Israel (Yom Kippur War)
1977	Egyptian president Anwar Sadat talks peace in Jerusalem
1978	Camp David Accords
1982	Israel invades Lebanon
1993	Israel and Palestinians negotiate limited autonomy for the Palestinians
2001	Ariel Sharon becomes prime minister of Israel; new Palestinian *intifada*

The Arab-Israeli Conflict

In 1947, plagued by Zionist terror tactics, Britain referred the question of the mandate for Palestine to the United Nations. The resulting partition plan, which gave most of the territory of Palestine to the Jews, was rejected by the **Arab League.** As with its precipitous withdrawal from (and partition of) India about the same time, Britain responded to the deteriorating situation in Palestine by announcing the end of the mandate. In the ensuing chaos and civil war, the armed and well-organized Zionist community seized Palestine and proclaimed the independent state of Israel in May 1948.

Conscious of its hostile surroundings, the fledgling Israeli state took steps to become militarily, economically, and politically strong. The success of those efforts became quite evident in 1956 when Nasser nationalized the Suez Canal. As allies of the British and French, the Israelis retaliated and overwhelmed the Egyptians in a war for control of the canal. International pressure applied by the United States, the USSR, and the United Nations forced the Israelis to withdraw from their territorial gains. But Israel's successful partnership with the old colonial powers was a slap in the face to the Arab states, still smarting from their failure to prevent Israeli statehood in 1948.

External pressure, however, brought only a temporary reprieve from hostilities. The issues of Palestinian rights and statehood, the security of the state of Israel, and free access to the Suez Canal continued to be contested, monopolizing the attention of foreign policy makers in the region, as well as in Moscow and Washington. In 1967 Nasser sought a military solution to the Arab-Israeli conflict by mobilizing his forces and those of the Arab states surrounding Israel, requesting the withdrawal of UN peacekeeping forces, and blockading the Gulf of Aqaba, Israel's access to the Red Sea. Israel retaliated, and within 72 hours, had completely overwhelmed and humiliated Nasser and his Arab allies. When a cease-fire was arranged after only six days of fighting, Israel occupied the Sinai peninsula, including the east bank of the Suez Canal, East Jerusalem, the west bank of the Jordan River, and the tactically important Golan Heights inside Syria.

Meanwhile, the Palestinians, disillusioned by the failure of the Arab states to liberate Palestine, had begun to mobilize to fight Israel on their own. The

Arab League—An organization of 21 Arab states formed in 1945 to coordinate policies on economic affairs, communication, social and health issues, and international affairs.

Discovery Through Maps

Borders and Identities: The UN Partition Plan

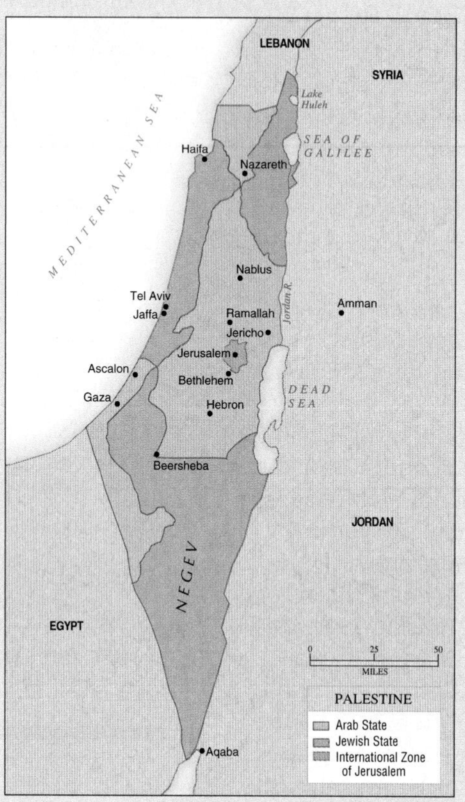

The borders of new nations can be planned and mapped, but those plans and maps are often radically different from ground-level realities. The United Nations' partition plan for the British mandate of Palestine is a case in point. After World War II, the Zionists in Palestine began aggressively to push for the establishment of a Jewish state. Violence in the mandate, created out of the Ottoman Empire by the treaties of World War I, escalated between 1944 and 1947. Then Britain's foreign secretary, Ernest Bevin, reflecting Britain's loss of control in the area, referred the "Palestine Question" to the United Nations. The UN created a special committee in 1947 that proposed the end of the mandate and its partition into one Arab and one Jewish state, with Jerusalem as a special internationalized city. The proposal was accepted by Zionist leaders and rejected by Arab leaders. After hard lobbying by U.S. President Harry Truman, the partition plan passed in the UN General Assembly. But the plan, shown on this map, never became a reality. Britain's planned withdrawal from Palestine caused a panic in the mandate. Zionist forces seized the initiative, gained control of Palestine, and proclaimed an Israeli state on May 14, 1948.

The drawing of borders in the Middle East for mandates after World War I, and later for nation-states often did not take into account the identities or wishes of the people living there. But the drawing of these borders ultimately did create new national identities, like those of Israelis and Jordanians, residents of newly created states. Others, like the Palestinians, were dispossessed by the new boundary lines and began a struggle for their own nations and "national" identities. The UN partition plan for Palestine was designed by a committee that spent only five weeks in the mandate. It had to take into account the political, religious, and strategic interests and demands of many competing parties outside of Palestine. The resulting map was an awkward patchwork of divided territories. Over 50 years later the ultimate shape of the map of Israel is still contested.

Questions to Consider

1. Look at a series of maps of this region beginning in 1900; how frequently have the boundaries changed?
2. The mandate for Palestine was a small territory and not rich. Why did so many groups and states have an interest in what happened there?
3. What factors prevented the creation of a Palestinian state out of the mandate for Palestine?

Palestine Liberation Organization (PLO) was founded in 1964. A secular umbrella organization aiming to establish an independent Palestine, it rejected the idea of an Israeli state. The PLO was given added impetus by the Six-Day War, a triumph for Israel but a disaster for the Palestinians. The conquest of the occupied territories created new waves of refugees and made the Israelis masters over a large and unwilling population. Now Israel had three types of residents: Jewish citizens, Palestinian citizens (Muslim and Christian) with second-class citizenship status, and individuals under military occupation who had no citizen's rights.

The UN responded to the 1967 war with Resolution 242, which recognized Israel's right to exist but ordered the return of the occupied territories. Arguing both that they were essential for the defense of Israel and that they constituted part of the Promised Land, the Israelis refused to give up the territories and launched a program of Jewish settlements designed to make the newly conquered lands indelibly Jewish. These territories thus became the focal point of an ongoing struggle between Israel, the Palestinians, and the surrounding Arab states. The Arab states each pursued their own national agendas and Cold War alliances, but they were united in their opposition to Israel.

After 1967 the PLO worked to organize resistance to Israel. It supported political activities, schools for Palestinians, work programs, and military and guerrilla training. Tensions mounted as attacks by Palestinian guerrillas were met with Israeli counterattacks. The Soviet Union was a major supplier of arms, aid, and technicians to the Arab states. The United States provided arms and aid to some Arab states but committed itself to the existence of Israel, investing billions of dollars a year in aid. That support was a reflection of American perceptions that Israel, as a "Western" state founded by European immigrants, was a natural ally, but it also reflected the support of many Americans for the Judeo-Christian tradition and biblical promises of a return to Zion.

Realizing the danger of a Soviet-American confrontation in the Middle East should a new round of war explode, Britain, France, the United States, and the USSR explored ways to bring the contending parties to agreement. Acceptance of a cease-fire in the summer of 1970 gave some hope for a settlement, but the situation deteriorated a few months later when Israel charged Egypt with cease-fire violations. Then Nasser died suddenly, which was a great blow to the Egyptian people, and Egypt needed time to reestablish itself under a new leader, Anwar Sadat. But soon overt conflict between Egypt and Israel resumed. On October 6, 1973, the Jewish holy day of Yom Kippur, the Egyptians and Syrians launched a coordinated attack on Israel. For the first few days, the Arabs held the initiative, but Israeli forces counterattacked, crossing the Suez Canal into Egypt and driving to within 25 miles of Damascus, the capital of Syria. In some of the most concentrated armored combat since World War II, thousands of lives were lost and 1800 tanks and 200 aircraft were destroyed.

During the fighting, the United States organized a large airlift of arms to Israel, and the Soviets responded with troop movements. Soviet and American leaders, however, averted a possible showdown through consultations, and the UN arranged a cease-fire. In January 1974, Egypt and Israel signed a pact, providing for mutual troop withdrawals, the return of the east bank of the canal to Egypt, a UN buffer zone, and an exchange of prisoners. Fighting continued between Israel and Syria in the strategic Golan Heights area.

The Yom Kippur War and its spin-offs were costly for the Middle East. Israel spent $5 billion and suffered 5000 casualties in addition to an ever-increasing rate of inflation generated by war expenses. Arab casualties were more than five times the Israeli losses. But whereas the Israelis came to a sober realization of their demographic and financial limitations, the Egyptians came out of the war with improved morale.

Oil Politics

As the Cold War was gaining momentum and the state of Israel was establishing itself, a new economic weapon was emerging in the Middle East. Oil had first been exploited by the British in Iran early in the twentieth century. In 1933 Ibn Sa'ud, sovereign of the newly constituted kingdom of Saudi Arabia, granted an oil concession to the American Oil Company (ARAMCO). Bahrain began exporting oil in 1934 and became the first Gulf state to develop an oil-based economy. Oil was soon discovered in Arabia and in the kingdom of Kuwait (a British protectorate from the end of World War I until 1961).

Saudi Arabia, Kuwait, and the other Gulf states now control at least 50 percent of the world's proven oil reserves. But major production did not gear up until after World War II, and foreign companies tended to control the revenues and organization of Middle Eastern oil resources in the 1950s. Their dominance began to change in 1960 when the Organization of Petroleum Exporting Countries (OPEC) was founded by Iran, Iraq, Kuwait, Saudi Arabia, and Venezuela to gain control over their oil output and pricing. For these states, oil began to mean global power. Oil also meant an influx of foreign workers for

---

Palestine Liberation Organization (PLO)—A group founded in 1964 whose goal was to establish an independent state of Palestine.

the petroleum-producing states: Western technical workers, South Asian laborers, and workers from neighboring Middle Eastern states seeking higher wages. These workers were part of a world phenomenon of migration for labor that intensified in the twentieth century, affecting Africa and Latin America as well as the Middle East. While foreign technical workers enjoyed excellent wages and a high standard of living, foreign domestics often worked under conditions reminiscent of slave labor. Neither group was well integrated into their host Middle Eastern societies.

DOCUMENT
The Saudi-Aramco "50/50" Agreement

In 1973, OPEC's Arab member states deployed the oil weapon in the aftermath of the October Arab-Israeli war. Saudi Arabia placed an embargo on oil shipments to the United States, and the Arab oil-producing states cut production, creating panic in the industrialized world and long lines at gas pumps. The embargo symbolized a new balance in systems of world power. It harshly affected the Japanese and the Western Europeans, who respectively received 82 and 72 percent of their oil from the Middle East.

The United States, which imported only 11 percent of its oil supplies from the Middle East, suffered substantial disruption in its economic activity, and a shocked American public began to rail against Saudi "oil *shaykhs*." The embargo was lifted in 1974, but the industrialized nations had been forced into a greater appreciation of oil as a world-class weapon wielded by states that otherwise had little leverage in world politics. Oil prices have fluctuated since then and have risen in recent years. OPEC has used its control over price and production levels to gain for its member states a greater voice in world affairs. Indeed, OPEC serves as a model for newly independent oil-producing nations among the one-time Soviet republics that hope to use current and projected oil resources as leverage to gain a share of world economic and political power.

Egyptian-Israeli Détente

In September 1975, Egypt and Israel reached an agreement by which additional territory in the Sinai peninsula was returned to Egypt and both sides resolved not to resort to force. The United States agreed to provide up to 200 civilian technicians to maintain a precautionary warning system between the two sides. Washington also committed additional arms and financial support to Israel and Egypt (who are still the two largest recipients of U.S. aid).

In late November 1977, President Anwar Sadat initiated a dramatic shift in regional affairs when he flew to Jerusalem to conduct peace talks with Israeli leaders. Sadat, born of a peasant family, had excelled in school and entered the Royal Military Academy. He had worked with other officers to rid Egypt of British domination and in the coup to expel King Faruq. A loyal follower of Nasser, Sadat succeeded him as president in 1970, Thereafter, he gravitated increasingly into the U.S. sphere, eventually ordering the 18,000-member corps of Soviet military and technical advisers out of his country. Sadat faced serious problems at home, brought on by a faltering economy and a rapidly increasing population. These problems led to severe riots, sparked by runaway inflation. In part as a result of these internal conflicts, Sadat came to believe that Egypt's most compelling need was for peace and recovery.

The United States strongly supported Sadat's peace overtures, and President Jimmy Carter invited

Israeli prime minister Menachem Begin, standing beside U.S. president Jimmy Carter, shakes hands with Egyptian president Anwar Sadat. Carter had invited Begin and Sadat to a summit meeting at Camp David in September 1978 to work out a peace agreement between Israel and Egypt. This agreement was celebrated in the West, but it failed to produce the hoped-for resolution to the Arab-Israeli conflict.

Sadat and Israel's prime minister, Menachem Begin, to meet at Camp David, outside Washington, in September 1978. After intense negotiations, the three leaders produced a framework for peace. Israel agreed to return all the Sinai to Egypt, but no definite agreement was reached on the status of the West Bank, where 1 million displaced Palestinians lived. It was proposed that negotiations should begin to set up an elected self-governing authority for the Palestinians and to end the Israeli military government. The Camp David Accords recognized that the Palestinian question was inextricably linked to the question of Middle East peace. Nonetheless, while Egypt and Israel have maintained a sometimes precarious peace, the Palestinian question over two decades later has not been resolved, and the final status of the West Bank remains a critical issue.

Sadat and Begin received the Nobel Peace Prize in 1978. The Sinai was returned to Egypt and the Suez Canal opened to Israeli ships. In 1980 the two nations opened their borders to each other, exchanged ambassadors, and began air service between the countries. But Sadat was viewed as a traitor in the Arab world, and Egypt was expelled from the Arab League, losing the dominant position in the region that Nasser had secured for it.

Separate Destinies: The Evolution of Turkey and Lebanon

Once nation-states were created in the Middle East, they evolved in very different ways. Some became rich as a result of the exploitation of oil; others remained poor. Most developed secular governmental systems; others, like Saudi Arabia, retained the Sharia (Islamic law) as the basis of their political and legal systems. In the Cold War competition between the United States and the Soviet Union, Middle Eastern states chose sides, cultivated alliances, or tried to remain aloof. A good example of the divergent ways in which Middle Eastern states evolved is found in the cases of Turkey and Lebanon. The former became a model of Western-style secularism in the Middle East; the latter was devastated by civil war, rooted in religion-based politics and the dislocations caused by the Israeli-Palestinian conflict.

Unlike much of the Middle East, Turkey escaped the fate of becoming a tributary of Britain or France after World War I. Its attainment of independence early in the century and the success of Atatürk's radical secularizing reforms made Turkey a model of sorts for those who envisioned Western-style, secular government as the proper course for Middle Eastern nations. Yet Atatürk's transformation of the institutions of government, education, religion, and law did not eliminate Islam as a powerful force in Turkish society. After Atatürk's death Turkey entered an inevitable period of readjustment, during which it struggled to reach an equilibrium between its religious and cultural traditions on the one hand and the Westernized secularism of Atatürk on the other.

Turkey's first multiparty elections were held in 1946, and in 1950 the opposition Democratic party won a substantial majority of the votes. One of its first acts was to legalize the call to prayer in Arabic, reverting to a traditional practice that Atatürk had outlawed. Over time other aspects of the secularizing policies of Atatürk were moderated, reflecting the religious sentiments of much of the Turkish populace, which is 99 percent Muslim. Despite these changes, however, Atatürk remains a dominant figure in the Turkish public imagination, and the Turkish government, particularly the military, remains committed to secularism. The tensions between secular nationalism and the cultural and religious practices of the population are not, of course, unique to Turkey. Indeed, such tensions have marked the evolution of the world's nations in the twentieth and twenty-first centuries. What makes the case of Turkey particularly remarkable is the short time frame in which Atatürk enacted his radical secularizing reforms.

After World War II both Turkish and Iranian sovereignty were threatened by Soviet expansionism, which drove each state into the U.S. camp. From the late 1940s on, the United States perceived Turkey and Iran as strategic bulwarks against the Soviet Union and poured military and economic aid into both. Turkey permitted the Americans to establish military bases on its territory and built up its own military with U.S. aid. Although it remained an important ally of the Americans throughout the Cold War period, that relationship was seriously strained in the 1960s and 1970s when the United States supported Greece in the struggle for the Mediterranean island of Cyprus. Since that time, Turkey has explored closer relations with other Middle Eastern states (including Israel) and is seeking to establish itself as a regional power and as a broker in relations between Europe and the newly constituted Central Asian republics spun off from the Soviet Union.

DOCUMENT
Voices of Protest

Since the 1950s, Turkey has retained its secular, democratic, multiparty government, although coups in 1960, 1971, and 1980 each brought interludes of military rule. Turkish society now faces a series of challenges ranging from devastating inflation and devaluation of its currency to an undeclared civil war with elements of its Kurdish population in the eastern provinces to new political challenges mounted by Islamist parties.

In the 1990s the Turks elected their first female prime minister, Tansu Ciller, leader of the True Path party, and Turkey's first Islamist prime minister, Necmettin Erbakan, a member of the Refah party. These elections suggest the divergent strains in Turkish politics. The Refah party, which promised a series of Islamic reforms, won substantial victories in 1994 in the major centers of Istanbul and Ankara. This populist party, with its appeal to Islamic values and its vigorous social programs, struck a sympathetic chord, especially among the poor and the millions of rural Turks who had recently migrated to the large urban centers. Refah won the 1995 national elections by a slim margin and ultimately constructed a precarious coalition government with Erbakan as prime minister from 1996 to 1997. But the military, interpreting Refah's successes as a threat to Turkey's secular system of government, maneuvered to oust Erbakan, and in 1998 the Turkish High Court outlawed the Refah party.

In 2002, the moderate Islamist Justice and Development party won a two-thirds majority in Parliament and Recep Erdogan, who had been jailed in 1999 for encouraging religious hatred, was selected as Prime Minister. This time the military refrained from directly involvement in the political process. One of the first acts of the new government was to refuse the U.S. military access to Turkey's military bases to launch the invasion of Iraq in 2003.

Unlike Turkey, Lebanon became a mandate of the French after World War I, and that era of colonial rule indelibly marked its evolution as an independent state. Lebanon's capital, Beirut, was once one of the most beautiful and affluent cities in the Middle East, a center for commerce and a crossroads of cultures and religions. But in the 1970s, it became an arena in which competing factions played out their ambitions.

First, Lebanon became a battleground in the Israeli-Palestinian conflict. The Palestine Liberation Organization (PLO) led by Yassir Arafat had been driven out of Jordan in the early 1970s. It set up its headquarters in Lebanon and stepped up demands for Israeli withdrawal from the west bank of the Jordan River and the Gaza Strip, both captured by Israel during the 1967 war. The PLO wanted an independent Palestinian state and, in pursuit of that goal, launched guerrilla raids from its bases in southern Lebanon and encouraged demonstrations to harass Israeli authorities. In response, beginning in 1978, Israel made repeated incursions into Lebanese territory to strike back at the PLO bases.

Civil war added to Lebanon's troubles. This small, ethnically mixed nation, its area slightly less than that of Connecticut, is divided among Muslim, Christian, and Druze factions. The Druze originated as a Shi'ite splinter group in the medieval era; they now constitute a separate religious faction. Syria and Lebanon had been declared independent in 1941, but the French relinquished control only grudgingly and waited five years to withdraw their troops. When they left, they set the stage for political and religious violence. The Christians held a slight majority in Lebanon, and France wanted to ensure the continuity of that Christian dominance. So they set up a political system for Lebanon based on confessional politics—political office allocated by religious affiliation. Under this system, the various factions maintained for a time a somewhat precarious balance. But high Muslim birthrates—in addition to the influx of Palestinians after the creation of Israel, the 1967 Arab-Israeli War, and civil strife in Jordan in the early 1970s—tipped that balance. The Christians, initially supported by Syria, fought the Muslim and Druze factions in the streets of Beirut until an October 1976 cease-fire. The cost was 25,000 dead, thou-

Tansu Ciller greets supporters in Istanbul in 1998. Although this photo shows the prime minister dressed conservatively in a headscarf, Ciller was educated in the United States and, like many Turkish women, routinely wears "Western" style professional clothing. The headscarf in Turkey has, however, become a symbol of women's right to choose their dress and their identity.

sands more wounded, and sections of the city gutted. The country's once flourishing economy was at a standstill.

In the summer of 1981, PLO forces in southern Lebanon fired rockets into Israel, which responded with massive air attacks on Palestinian strongholds in Beirut. Hundreds of civilians were killed. In the summer of 1982, the Israelis invaded the city, surrounding Muslim-held West Beirut. Under siege, the PLO agreed to evacuate Beirut in September, under the direction of a French, Italian, and U.S. multinational contingent. But after this multinational force departed, the violence resumed; the newly elected president, Bashir Gemayel, a Christian, and 26 of his colleagues were killed by a bomb. In apparent response, Christian militiamen, unchecked by the Israelis, massacred over 1000 Palestinian men, women, and children in two refugee camps. Although the Israeli invasion forced the PLO out of Lebanon, the state remained a battleground, and Israel supported an occupied buffer zone in southern Lebanon until the end of the twentieth century.

In the succeeding decade, the skeletal outlines of bombed buildings, shadowy videotapes of hostages, and pictures of young and old darting through streets to avoid gunfire made Lebanon a symbol to the world of the costs of civil strife. Many of Beirut's citizens fled during the course of the civil war; others remained hopeful that an equilibrium could once again be reached. Although the civil war eventually ended, Syria capitalized on the chaos to extend its power over parts of Lebanon, and Israel in the 1990s continued periodic air strikes. Today Beirut has in many ways recovered from the civil war. Lebanon remains, however, tainted by intercommunal violence, its uneasy position vis-à-vis Syria, and the deep-seated hostilities that the Arab-Israeli conflict has produced.

The Iranian Revolution

Iran, which had served as an area of competition between the British and the Russians since the nineteenth century, became a bone of contention between the United States and the Soviet Union after World War II. Shah Mohammad Reza Pahlavi ascended the Iranian throne in 1941 after the Allies forced his father to abdicate for supporting Germany in World War II. After the war, he asked foreign troops to withdraw from his country. But the continued presence of Soviet troops on his borders, the aggressive activities of the Iranian Communist party (Tudeh), and a shared interest in exploiting Iranian oil moved the shah increasingly into the U.S. camp as the Cold War geared up. By the early 1950s, Pahlavi had gained a reputation as an American ally who wished to continue the traditions of authoritarian monarchy but who was, politically, rather weak.

Meanwhile, some segments of the Iranian population were chafing under the monarchy and the continued control of Iranian oil by Britain. They found a hero in a member of the traditional landed class named Mohammad Mosaddeq (MOS-a-dek). Elected Prime Minister, Mosaddeq in 1953 advocated a set of liberalizing reforms and nationalization of Iranian oil. His program directly challenged the shah, who fled the country. But the United States had committed to Pahlavi as a Cold War ally and saw Mosaddeq as a threat. It boycotted Iranian oil, used the CIA to support a military coup that overthrew Mosaddeq in 1954, and helped restore the shah to power. For the next 25 years, Iran rested firmly within the orbit of the United States, a valuable source of oil and a bulwark against Soviet expansion. In return, the Americans supplied the shah's arsenal. Mosaddeq remained under house arrest and became a symbol of Iranian resistance to both Western imperialism and kingly authority.

The shah attempted a rapid modernization of his country, but his so-called White Revolution threatened the integrity of Iranian culture. Pahlavi imagined himself a benevolent father, dragging an unwilling and ignorant Iran into the twentieth century. But many Iranians saw him as brutal dictator and a Western pawn. The presence of over 100,000 foreigners (especially oil industry technicians and military advisers) in the country, including 47,000 Americans, alienated many Iranians, who perceived the shah as undermining both Islam and Iran's political and economic base. Opposition to the shah's rule spread widely in the 1970s, from militant communists to Shi'ite clergy to discontented nationalists. Inflation angered the business classes and the laborers. Peasants who were disenchanted with the shah's land reforms and who had swelled the ranks of impoverished migrants in the capital city, Tehran, also resented the shah's rule.

The plight of these peasants and their resentment toward the shah, with his fancy palaces, lavish celebrations, and affluent, Westernized retainers, is graphically depicted in children's stories by the Iranian author Samad Behrangi. In one of those stories, a ragged and hungry village boy, who has come to Tehran with his father to find work, describes the fancy neighborhood where the rich, Westernized Iranians live.

> *I came to the streets where there wasn't any smoke or dirty smell. The children and adults all had clean, fresh clothing. Their faces shone.... Whenever I came to such areas, I thought I was sitting in a theatre and watching a movie. I was never able to imagine what kind of food they ate, how they slept or spoke, or what kind of clothing they wore in such tall, clean houses.*[1]

The boy and his father ultimately decide to go home, thinking it better to starve in the village surrounded by family and friends than to starve homeless and alone in the city. The characters in Behrangi's stories symbolized the suffering of many of the Iranian people despite Iran's oil wealth and the shah's Westernizing reforms.

To stem the growing opposition to his regime, the shah launched a reign of terror. The storm broke in January 1978 when large numbers of students demonstrated in the streets. Many were killed and wounded by the shah's troops. Strikes and demonstrations spread throughout the country until they became a revolution. The army and secret police (SAVAK) proved helpless in the face of the revolt. In January 1979 the shah fled the country, seeking asylum in the United States, then in Panama, and finally in Egypt, where he died in 1980.

The main objective of the disparate factions participating in this revolution was to get rid of the shah. Once that task was accomplished, the coalition broke down and the Shi'ite clergy used its organizational apparatus to gain ascendancy. The diffuse and widespread revolution found its focus in the aged Ayatollah Ruhollah Khomeini (ko-MAY-nee), a Shi'ite holy man who had been exiled in 1963 for speaking out against the shah. From Iraq and then from Paris, he had carried on an incessant propaganda effort directed at the shah's "godless and materialistic" rule. Khomeini's rhetoric struck a sympathetic chord among Iranians offended by the shah's anti-Islamic reforms, ostentatious lifestyle, and "selling out" of Iran's resources to the West.

When the shah was finally forced out, Khomeini returned in triumph to Iran where, by popular mandate, he took up the reins of power. The monarchy was abolished, and Iran became a republic with a single-house parliament (the Islamic Consultative Assembly). Khomeini promptly banned Western music on radio and television, "provocative" bathing suits, liquor, and a broad range of other items deemed "un-Islamic." Consolidating his power after the revolution, the Ayatollah retained Iran's constitutional government but based it firmly on the Sharia (Islamic law). He then changed the curriculum and textbooks of Iran's schools to reflect the ideology of the new regime. The implementation of sexual segregation in the schools and the mandatory re-veiling of women in public provoked a reexamination, and considerable debate on the status (and proper place) of women in society.

Ayatollah Khomeini

Khomeini viewed the United States as the "Great Satan," a power intimately associated with the abusive rule of the shah and a symbol of imperialism, materialism, and godlessness. He encouraged the expression of anti-American sentiments. In November 1979 a mob of young Iranians stormed and seized the U.S. embassy and took 53 hostages, whom they held for over a year. This act and other consequences of the revolution alienated Iran from its previously warm relations with Western powers, who were fearful of the implications of Islamic rule and of the potential for destabilization of the Middle East.

Iran's regional neighbors were also alarmed at Khomeini's rise to power, fearing that he might export his Islamic revolution. In the aftermath of the revolution, Iraqi leader Saddam Hussein, hoping for a speedy victory over a weakened Iran, attacked Iranian airfields and oil refineries in September 1980. This attack provoked a war that devastated the Iranian economy, already severely disrupted by the revolution. The financial drain of the war helped force the Iranians to release the U.S. hostages in return for the United States' release of Iranian assets frozen in response to the hostage taking.

The Iran-Iraq war dragged on for nearly a decade until an armistice in 1989—brought on by exhaustion. It had been a war of attrition in which both sides suffered enormous losses. The Iranians employed all of their resources, including 12- and 13-year-old boys, in attacks against the well-ensconced but smaller Iraqi army. The Iraqis violated the accepted international rules of combat by using chemical weapons.

Khomeini died in June 1989, but the idea of Islamic revolution lived on. Iran became a worldwide model for people disenchanted with secularism and interested in new state formations that might combine representative government with traditional religious culture and law. Within Iran, as in Turkey after the death of Atatürk, a period of adjustment was inevitable. While the new Islamic government better reflected the religious and cultural beliefs of many Iranians, a government controlled by the mullahs (Islamic religious authorities) was too conservative, too restrictive, or too religious for many segments of the society. Iran also has a very youthful population; in 1991, 44.3 percent were under age 15 and 71 percent under age 30. In 1997, with strong support from young people, women, and intellectuals, Mohammad Khatami (a moderate member of the *ulama*) was elected president by a nearly 70 percent vote. Khatami advocated a less restrictive interpretation of Islamic law, fewer restrictions on the media, and the opening up of relations with the West. His election (and reelection in 2001), in which women voters played a prominent role, reflects the struggle going on in Iran over the social and political interpretation of the 1979 revolution. As Khatami pushes for further liberalization and reform in government, Iranian journalists and filmmakers are testing the limits of censorship with a vibrant and satirical press and film industry. Meanwhile, the enormous Iranian student population—

Ayatollah Khomeini's Vision of Islamic Government

Document Ayatollah Khomeini, *Message to the Pilgrims*

The following message was written in September 1978 while Khomeini, in exile in Iraq, was preparing to leave for Paris. An appeal for solidarity of all Muslims with the Iranian people in their struggle against the shah, it circulated among those making the sacred pilgrimage to Mecca. It was translated into Arabic, Turkish, Urdu, Malay-Indonesian, French, and English. The Saudi Arabian government was fearful of Khomeini's brand of Islam, and many Muslims felt little affinity for the Ayatollah's Shi'ite beliefs. But Khomeini's call to support oppressed peoples against the forces of imperialism and despotism was calculated to strike a sympathetic chord worldwide among all Muslims suffering under repressive regimes or Western dominance.

Now that it is the season of Pilgrimage to the sacred House of God and Muslims have come from all over the world to visit God's House, it is necessary that they pay attention to one of the most important aspects of this great gathering while they are performing the noble rites of the hajj, and examine the social and political circumstances of the Islamic countries. They must inform themselves of the hardships that their brothers in faith are suffering and strive to relieve those hardships, in accordance with their Islamic and moral duty.... For fifty years Iran, which has about thirty million Muslims, has been in the grip of the Pahlavi dynasty, a self-proclaimed servant of foreign powers. During those fifty dark years, the great people of Iran have been writhing under police repression, suffocation, and spiritual torture.

The Shah has given foreigners all the subterranean wealth and vital interests belonging to the people. He has given oil to America; gas to the Soviet Union; pastureland, forests and part of the oil to England and other countries. The people have been deprived of all the necessities of life and kept in a state of backwardness. The imperialist system has taken control of the army, the education, and the economy of our country....

Now that our people in recent years have awakened, risen up to gain their rights, and cried out against oppression, they have been answered with machine guns, tanks, and cannons. The massacres that have occurred in the cities of Iran in recent months are a cause of shame to history. With the support of America and with all the infernal means at his disposal, the Shah has fallen on our oppressed people, turning Iran into one vast graveyard. General strikes engulf the country.... Martial law has cast its sinister shadow over the people, and his mercenaries and commandoes are busy killing young and old, men and women.

I have not been permitted to continue my activity in any Islamic country, my activity that consists of conveying to the world the cry of my oppressed people. Because I must at all events fulfill my religious and ethical duty, I have been obliged to leave the Islamic world in the hope of alerting human society to the suffering of the oppressed people of Iran.

Now, O Muslims of the world, show concern for the problem of Iran, and convey to the world the cry of thirty million oppressed Muslims. The Most Noble Messenger [the Prophet, Muhammad] (peace and blessings be upon him) is reported to have said: "He who arises in the morning and gives no thought to the affairs of the Muslims is not a Muslim."

O God, I have conveyed the message, and peace be upon those who follow true guidance.

Questions to Consider

1. How does Khomeini characterize the regime of the shah?
2. What language does he use to draw a picture of the plight of the Iranian people? Is it effective?
3. In Khomeini's view, what is the role of foreign countries in contributing to the suffering of the Iranians?

From Ruhollah Khomeini, *Islam and Revolution: Writings and Declarations of Imam Khomenini,* trans. Hamid Algar (New York: Kegan Paul, 2002).

male and female alike—is engaging in its own persistent revolution, demonstrating for more freedoms and pushing back the veil required by law for women in public places. However, reformist advances in recent years were dealt a severe blow in the parliamentary election of 2004 when the Council of Guardians, which screens candidates, disqualified over 2000 reformists from participating in the election. As a result, those opposed to reform won an overwhelming victory.

Pro-Iranian Muslims in Lebanon raise their hands in salute to the Ayatollah Khomeini during a symbolic funeral held in Beirut to honor the deceased Iranian spiritual leader. Khomeini had become an important world symbol of self-determination and opposition to Western dominance. For some Muslims he was a hero; many others, however, rejected Khomeini's brand of Islam and found his conservatism, subordination of women, and intrusive moral control unpalatable.

Toward a New Balance

During the first part of the 1980s, Egypt remained an outcast among Arab countries because of its détente with Israel. In October 1981 a small group of Islamic militants assassinated Sadat while he was reviewing a military parade. Shortly before his death, he had ordered a crackdown on the **Muslim Brotherhood,** which opposed his reconciliation with Israel and Egypt's increasingly secular nature.

Sadat's successor, Hosni Mubarak, pledged to continue Sadat's commitments and welcomed U.S. support in dollars and weapons. During the 1980s, Mubarak improved Egypt's relations with other moderate Arab states as he struggled with his country's overwhelming economic problems, brought on by a mushrooming population along the Nile and chronic problems of corruption within the authoritarian regime. Mubarak solidified his position, maintained Sadat's foreign policies, and has proved remarkably durable after 20 years in office and significant challenges from Islamist factions.

In Israel, huge outlays for defense drove the inflation rate to average over 50 percent in the last part of the 1980s. The Israelis came to depend more and more on aid from the United States, whose annual announced subsidies exceeded $3 billion a year. Meanwhile, world and American public opinion became increasingly sympathetic to the Palestinians as their ***intifada*** ("uprising") within Israel drew harsh Israeli responses extensively covered on world television. Indeed, from the Iranian Revolution to the Palestinian *intifada* to the Persian Gulf War, television coverage began to play an increasingly influential role in the crafting of Middle Eastern politics.

While committed to Israel's security, the United States, especially during the administration of President George H. W. Bush (1989–1993), continued to aid friendly Arab states who opposed Israel. This was particularly the case with Saudi Arabia, the main supplier of American oil imports. The United States sold the Saudis large quantities of sophisticated weapons and sent the U.S. Navy to keep the Persian Gulf oil shipment lanes open during the latter stages of the Iran-Iraq war.

Iraq, a country with immense oil reserves and agricultural potential, had expended huge sums on the war with Iran. Under Saddam Hussein, the Iraqis had developed extensive military capabilities. Saddam, whose secular nationalist Ba'th party regime had vigorously suppressed all political opposition in Iraq, imagined himself filling the power vacuum left in the Middle East by Nasser's death. But his aspirations to nuclear power were set back when the Israelis bombed his nuclear reactor in 1981. During the Iran-Iraq war, more than a million people died in the fighting, and the Iraqi leader used chemical weapons on Iraqi Kurdish villagers to intimidate the large Kurdish minority in northern Iraq.

Soon after the Iran-Iraq war ended, Saddam Hussein launched another offensive in the region. In August 1990, Iraqi troops invaded and overran the oil-rich nation of Kuwait. This aggressive act, and its implied threat to Saudi Arabia, produced an immedi-

Muslim Brotherhood—An organization founded in 1928 in Egypt by Hasan al-Banna. The Muslim Brotherhood promoted religious, political, and social reforms and sponsored social programs.

intifada—In Arabic, "shaking off." The name given to two separate Palestinian uprisings against Israel in the occupied West Bank and Gaza Strip, the first between 1987–1993 and the second from 2000 through the publication date of this text.

ate response. The fear that if Iraq took the Saudi oilfields, it would control one-third of the global oil reserves moved the UN Security Council to impose a series of strict sanctions on Baghdad. The Soviet Union and the United States, both former patrons of Hussein, lined up in opposition to the Iraqi dictator.

For the next six months the UN, led by a coalition assembled by the United States, increased pressure on Saddam Hussein by imposing sanctions and embargoes on his country. The Iraqi leader received the support of the PLO and Jordan, but much of the Arab world viewed his aggression with fear and anger. When sanctions and embargoes failed to move Iraq to withdraw from Kuwait, an American-led 26-nation coalition (including Egypt, Saudi Arabia, Syria, Turkey, France, Italy, and the United Kingdom) began heavy bombardment of Iraq in January 1991. A month later the allies launched a land offensive that, in 100 hours, evicted Iraq's soldiers from Kuwait and left the coalition in possession of one-fifth of Iraq. This smashing of Iraq's forces represented a post–Cold War reconfiguration of Middle Eastern alliances. It was clear that each nation-state in the Middle East was pursuing its own agenda and that pro-U.S. or pro-Soviet designations were no longer adequate to explain Middle Eastern policy.

Kuwait had been redeemed, but Saddam Hussein remained firmly in power. He brutally put down uprisings by Shi'ite groups in the south of Iraq and by Kurds in the north. Hundreds of thousands of Kurds fled and became refugees. Wartime oil spills and oil wells torched by the retreating Iraqis left an ecological disaster in the Gulf region. Although soundly beaten, Saddam Hussein was a survivor. For over a decade after the Gulf War, he successfully resisted postwar, U.N.-mandated weapons inspections and maintained a tight grasp on Iraqi politics. The suffering of ordinary Iraqis under a prolonged international boycott was terrible. After the U.S. government overthrew the Taliban regime in Afghanistan in 2002 for its support of Osama bin Laden's al-Qaeda network, it focused its attention on Iraq. Claiming that the Hussein regime was a threat to regional and global stability because of its weapons of mass destruction and its support for international terrorism, the administration of President George W. Bush pushed ahead without a UN mandate and organized a coalition that toppled Hussein in a short war in 2003. The campaign split America's traditional allies, with Britain, Spain, Italy, and Japan supporting the United States, and France, Germany, and Canada refusing to participate. The aftermath of this second Gulf War has been messy. Insurgents have organized a resistance against coalition forces and and it remains uncertain whether a stable government in Iraq will emerge.

Once the battles of the first Gulf War were concluded, diplomatic activity in the major capitals of the world prepared the way for conferences that were expected to bring peace to the region. A step in that direction took place in September 1993 when PLO leader Yassir Arafat and Israeli leader Yitzhak Rabin met in Washington to sign an agreement to turn certain parts of the occupied territories over to the Palestinians in return for guarantees of peace for Israel. Secret negotiations had brought the bitter enemies together.

DOCUMENT
Israel-PLO Declaration

The PLO, isolated from much of its financial support because of its backing of Iraq and challenged by the increasing popularity of Islamist factions, saw the negotiations as perhaps a last chance to maintain a position in the Middle East and gain a foothold for a future Palestinian state. Israel saw an opportunity to construct a peace that would fragment its opponents and bring some relief to an Israeli populace weary of war.

The agreement set up a 5-year-long framework of limited autonomy for the Palestinians in Jericho and the Gaza Strip and continuing negotiations for a permanent solution. The Palestinian Authority assumed control over certain designated areas. For the first time Palestinian schools were permitted texts that openly taught their pupils about "Palestine." But the settlement proved largely unworkable. Prime Minister Rabin was assassinated by an Israeli right-wing extremist in 1995; and many Palestinians have become disillusioned with their limited gains under the new administration. The Israeli government has refused to alter its policies promoting Jewish settlements (which have increased by 60 percent since 1993) in the occupied territories and has stepped up its annexation of Palestinian lands around Jerusalem. Suicide bombings by Palestinian factions in Tel Aviv and Jerusalem have terrified Israelis and helped derail peace negotiations.

In 1998 Israelis celebrated 50 years of Israeli statehood, while Palestinians remained frustrated in their hopes for independence. Both peoples remain deeply divided over the limits of Palestinian autonomy and over the future character of the Israeli state. Those divisions manifested themselves at the beginning of the new millennium through increased violence in the occupied territories and a reassertion of the Palestinian *intifada*. Frustrated by the failure to achieve peace and security, Israelis in 2001 elected the aging warhorse Ariel Sharon as prime minister. A war hero, Likud party stalwart, ardent proponent of Israeli settlement in the occupied territories, and principal engineer of the invasion of Lebanon, Sharon promised Israel security and strong leadership. To the Palestinians, however, Sharon, whom they hold responsible for the refugee camp massacres in 1982, is a symbol of Israeli intransigence and their dashed hopes for a Palestinian state. Arafat's control

Israel has been erecting a controversial security fence between Israel and Palestine's West Bank. Israel claims the fence is necessary to prevent Palestinian terrorists from entering Israel and killing civilians, while Palestinian officials maintain that Israel is expanding its borders by building parts of the fence on Palestinian land.

over the Palestinian Authority was weakened by infighting and corruption, and the situation in Israel and Palestine devolved into civil war. Following Arafat's death in late 2004, Mahmoud Abbas was elected president of the Palestinian Authority in early 2005.

The attack on the World Trade Center in September 2001 compounded the anxiety of Israel and the Palestinians alike. Israel is concerned that U.S. efforts at forming a world alliance against terrorism will enhance the bargaining power of Arab states at Israel's expense. The Palestinians fear that they will be tarred with the broad accusation of "supporters of terrorism" and hence lose what little bargaining power they have. Meanwhile, Islamist groups in the region point to U.S. support for Israel and the continuing plight of the Palestinians as a primary justification for the World Trade Center attack.

Islamist Factions

After three generations of independence, some segments of Middle Eastern society have become disillusioned with the promises of Western-style secular nationalism. Their hopes for prosperity and freedom under the new national regimes have often failed to materialize, and their frustration has found expression in support for Islamist movements. These movements, which assert the central role of Islam in culture, politics, and law, are not a new phenomenon (and they are not limited to the Middle East). They have their roots in the Islamic reform movements—the Muslim Brotherhood, for example—of the nineteenth and early twentieth centuries. But Islamist factions have been given impetus in recent decades by the success of the Iranian Revolution, the economic failures of secular regimes, and the corruption of moral and family values associated by some Muslims with the importation of Western culture.

In the context of widespread poverty and political strife, some Islamist factions have gained support in the Middle East, particularly among the poor. These factions span a broad range of ideological and political positions. They may advocate a return to "traditional" piety and communal values, a rejection of Western consumerism and cultural imperialism, a more significant role for Islam in schools and government, or a discarding of secular rule altogether. Often they augment their political base of support by providing social services such as adult education, job training, and relief services. The assassination of Sadat in Egypt and the victories of the Refah party in

Turkey are indicators of the success of Islamist rhetorics among certain segments of the Middle Eastern populace. So too is the popularity of Hamas among Palestinians. Hamas is an Islamist party that rejects Israel and advocates the implementation of Sharia law. It became increasingly popular during the *intifada* as many Palestinians became disenchanted with PLO leadership.

Radical variants of Islamism came dramatically to the fore in world consciousness in 2001 when members of the al-Qaeda network—a clandestine, international, terrorist organization financed by the wealthy Saudi national Osama bin Laden—launched an attack on the World Trade Center in New York and the Pentagon in Washington, D.C. Bin Laden, a multimillionaire adopted a form of militant Islam (that most Muslims reject) as a young man and joined other Muslim volunteers fighting a holy war against Soviet troops from Afghanistan in the 1980s. From his bases in Afghanistan (see Chapter 32) and elsewhere he trained young men to die as "martyrs" in attacks against nations he considered "enemies of Islam." Originally, bin Laden's primary target was Saudi Arabia, whose ruling regime he criticized for impiety, corruption, and allowing U.S. troops on Saudi soil during the Gulf War. But, increasingly, the United States, as world hegemon, has become his primary target. Most Muslims have denounced al-Qaeda's activities as un-Islamic, but some have responded with sympathy to bin Laden's charges that the United States is an intrusive and greedy imperial power that has backed the persecution of Palestinians and Iraqis.

Governments in the Middle East fear bin Laden's repressive and extremist interpretation of Islam, a puritanical and violent interpretation that rejects their legitimacy and preaches their overthrow. Most administrations in the Middle East remain committed to secular rule, as do many citizens of Middle Eastern states. But the successes of Islamist factions in the area are a reflection of a worldwide process of self-examination among peoples suffering from economic deprivation, critical of the systems imposed during the period of Western imperial dominance, and interested in incorporating their own cultural traditions and values more directly into the institutions of government, education, and law.

AFRICA: THE SEARCH FOR NATIONAL IDENTITIES

▪ *What was the legacy of European colonialism in Africa?*

In 1945 there were four independent African nations; at the end of the century, there were 53 sovereign states. The critical years were from the mid-1950s to the end of the 1960s, when dozens of African states won their independence. Africa's postindependence leaders generally embraced Kwame Nkrumah's dictum to "seek ye first the political kingdom." They were optimistic that once they had thrown off the shackles of colonial rule, they could build viable nation-states and tackle the poverty and underdevelopment that gripped the continent. But their optimism was short-lived as they underestimated the long-term impact of the colonial legacy and the fragility of the new states. The disillusionment of many Africans with their newly independent states is captured in the lament of Joshua Nkomo, a veteran leader of the freedom struggle in Zimbabwe: "The hardest lesson of my life has come to me late. It is that a nation can win freedom without the people becoming free."[2]

One of the most pressing problems the new states faced was how to build and maintain national unity among different and sometimes antagonistic religious, cultural, regional, and ethnic groups. In most cases, the new African states were not the product of a long historical process such as took place in Europe. Most African boundaries were arbitrary creations of the imperialists and had little relation to the people who lived there. Nigeria, for example, was known as the "linguistic crossroads of Africa" because it encompassed hundreds of diverse ethnic groups, all competing for a share of national resources. When African countries founded the **Organization of African Unity (OAU)** in 1963, however, they decided to maintain existing boundaries rather than to open up conflicts by redrawing them.

In most newly independent countries, the men who led the freedom struggle took over the reins of power. However, politicians had little experience with running governments, political parties were immature, and civil cultures were weak. The authoritarian governing styles of colonial rulers shaped the outlooks of many politicians, who did not tolerate opposition parties. A democratic culture did not take root, and power became increasingly concentrated in the hands of executive presidents who often proclaimed themselves "president for life." There was little difference between a president's pronouncements and official policy.

Civilian leaders in many African countries did not last long, however, because soldiers were prepared to stage coups against governments. African armies are generally small, but they have the means to topple civilian governments with ease. Soldiers usually justi-

Organization of African Unity (OAU)—An organization founded in 1963 to promote African unity and economic cooperation between member states and to advance Africa in science and technology, defense and security, and education and culture. It had 53 members and was replaced in 2002 by the African Union.

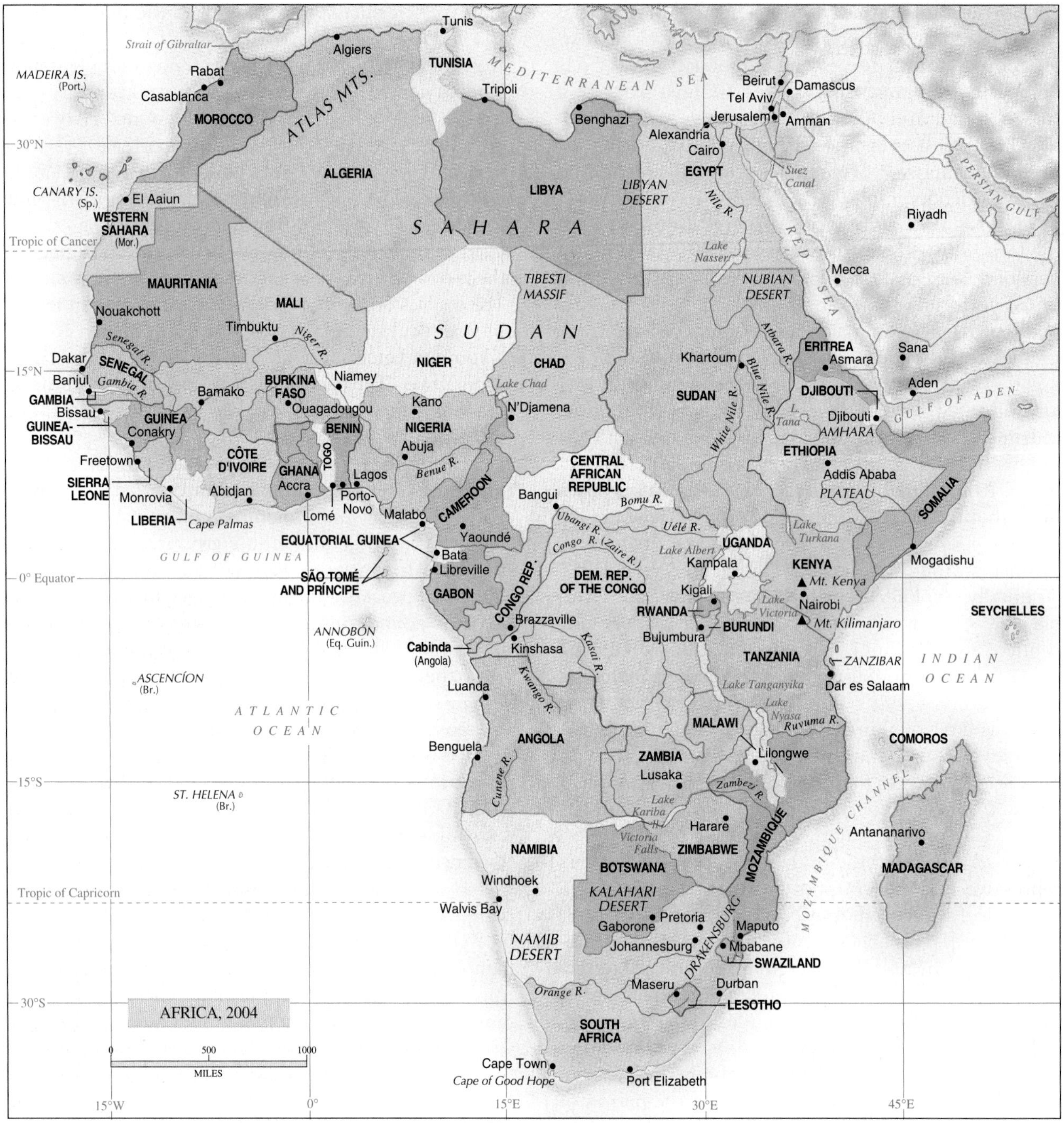

When African nations gained their independence, they maintained the boundaries drawn by European colonizers in the late nineteenth century. Eritrea, which won its independence from Ethiopia in 1993 after a long war, is the only African nation to secede successfully from an existing country.

fied a coup by portraying themselves as guardians of the public interest who were saving their country from corrupt and inefficient politicians. As in Nigeria, they also intervened to protect regional interests. More than half of all African states have experienced military takeovers in the past four decades. Between 1952 and 1985, independent African states experienced 54 military coups. A common cycle was for the military to stage a coup, return to the barracks in favor of civilians, and then intervene again. One of the few African states to sustain a multiparty system is Botswana, which succeeded in fostering political diversity, despite living for many decades in the shadow of neighboring white regimes.

Since the end of the Cold War, however, a second wave of independence has swept through Africa. Grassroots people and civic organizations around the continent have stepped up their calls for democratic

Africa

1957	Independence of Ghana
1963	Creation of Organization of African Unity
1975	Intervention of United States and USSR in Angolan Civil War
1976	Soweto uprising in South Africa
1990	Release of Nelson Mandela from prison
1994	Genocide in Rwanda
2000	Election of Olesegun Obasanjo as President of Nigeria

government, and some promising steps have been made toward implanting democratic rule. Since the late 1980s, Africa has witnessed dozens of elections. Some of them have installed genuine democratic governments, while others have been manipulated by autocratic rulers and military officers trying to stay in power.

Both Islam and Christianity rapidly expanded over the last century. In most African countries Christians and Muslims coexist peacefully, but in countries such as Nigeria and Sudan, religious rivalries have been divisive. The Sudan has been in the throes of a long civil war because its central government, dominated by Muslims who live in the north of the country, has discriminated against southerners who are either Christians or adhere to indigenous African religious beliefs.

Another critical part of the colonial inheritance was that independent African nations were saddled with underdeveloped economies that were closely tied to their former colonial rulers. In the 1960s African countries depended on primary products such as minerals and crops for about 80 percent of their exports. That dependence has not changed appreciably since then. Thus the health of African economies is still largely dependent on the prices their raw materials receive in world commodity markets.

Some African nations, such as Kenya and the Ivory Coast, adopted the view that the capitalist path was the correct path to development and prosperity. They modeled their policies after western Europe and the United States, encouraged foreign investment and private businesses, and promoted rapid industrialization.

Other African leaders took the attitude that African economies, because of their marginal position in the global economy, were doomed to perpetual underdevelopment and poverty. They tried to break their states' dependency on the West by adopting socialism and developing close relations with the Soviet Union or China. African socialism typically meant state ownership of public enterprises, mines and industries, and banks and insurance companies, but socialist policies came in many varieties. Some states, such as Ethiopia, Angola, and Mozambique, practiced an orthodox brand of Marxism, while others, such as Tanzania, experimented with a socialism based on African communal values.

Regardless of the path taken, most African economies have not prospered. The nations of Africa import more goods than they export, they have to import food to feed their own citizens, they have not attracted significant amounts of foreign assistance and foreign investment, and they have been plagued by enormous debts to lending institutions. African states devote about four times as much on repaying debts as they do on providing health services. The net result is that most African states had GDPs smaller than the endowments of top Ivy League universities. Thirty-two of the 47 countries classified by the World Bank as "least developed" are in Africa. And the poorer countries are even poorer than they were in the 1960s.

In the first decades after independence, most African states retained close ties with their former colonial rulers economically and politically, leading some observers to charge that independence was really another form of colonialism, or **neocolonialism.** Of the former colonizers, France retained a unique status in its former colonies. French culture and language persisted among African elites, and France maintained its financial, technical, and military links. The French military intervened on several dozen occasions to rescue African leaders under fire from their own people. Francophone (French-speaking) African leaders usually paid more attention to their ties with France than to those with the OAU.

By the 1980s, African states were shackled with enormous debts, declining standards of living, and sluggish economies. GDP growth rates in the 1980s averaged only 2.1 percent per year, while the population growth rate increased to 3.1 percent per year. As a result, since the mid-1980s, African governments have shifted their ties with their former colonial rulers to international lending agencies such as the World Bank and the International Monetary Fund (IMF).

The World Bank and IMF cure for ailing African economies has been **Structural Adjustment Programs (SAPs)** that compel African governments to

---

neocolonialism—The control exerted by developed nations over developing nations, usually former colonies that are still dependent on their former colonizers in economic and/or cultural areas even though they are politically independent.

Structural Adjustment Programs (SAPs)—Economic policies such as selling off state-owned enterprises and devaluing currencies that countries must follow to qualify for new World Bank and International Monetary Fund loans and to make loan repayments on existing debt owed to commercial banks and the World Bank.

promote market economies, liberalize foreign investment codes, and sell off state-owned enterprises to the private sector. More than two-thirds of African countries have adopted SAPs, but the cure has often been worse than the illness. The conditions for loans—currency devaluations, an end to the subsidies of staple foods, and wage freezes—have imposed enormous pressures on governments to carry out highly unpopular policies that have provoked protests. Some countries and individuals have benefited from SAPs, but many others have suffered. Women and children have suffered the most from these policies as various government support programs for food staples, education, and health care have been ended.

DOCUMENT World Bank-Supported Day Care

The gravest challenge confronting many nations in Africa and the world is the AIDS (acquired immunodeficiency syndrome) pandemic, which infected an estimated 34 million Africans and killed 12 million in the last 20 years of the twentieth century. One death in five in Africa is attributed to AIDS, and an estimated 6000 Africans are dying of AIDS every day. In some countries, funeral parlors are staying open 24 hours a day.

AIDS has particularly been devastating in southern Africa, where life expectancy is expected to decline to age 47 by 2005. AIDS spread rapidly in the region because thousands of migrant laborers move from urban to rural areas, condoms have not been extensively used, people are already infected with other sexually transmitted diseases or have weak immune systems because of malnourishment, and AIDS sufferers are ostracized if their condition is publicly known. AIDS has adversely affected every aspect of African life, ranging from agriculture, where farmers stricken with AIDS can no longer till their fields, to the commercial sector, where businesses have to train many more workers because a certain percentage of the staff are out with AIDS-related illnesses, and to African governments, which find it very difficult for their health care systems and providers to cope with the staggering cost of treating so many AIDS patients. In recent years, cheaper generic drugs have made it possible for more countries to provide antiretrovirals to their citizens.

Some African countries such as Senegal and Uganda have had more success in keeping AIDS rates lower because their political and religious leaders have

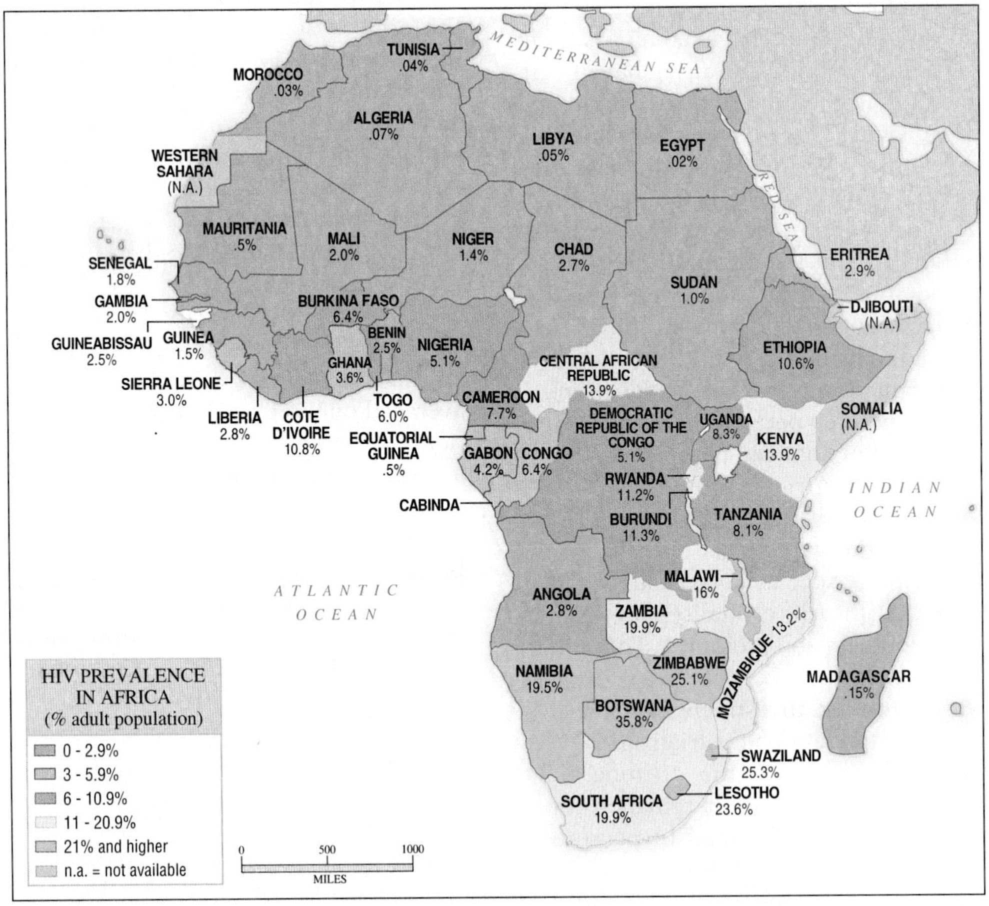

The spread of AIDS over the last two decades has hit the hardest in the continent of Africa. This map shows the estimated percentages of those infected with the HIV virus in African countries in 2000.

Document The Village That Has "Eaten Itself Limb by Limb"

In 2000 the global estimate for HIV/AIDS deaths was 3 million. HIV/AIDS deaths number about 20,000 annually in North America, while the figure for sub-Saharan Africa is 2.4 million. This is the equivalent of two World Trade Center/Pentagon tragedies each and every day. Besides its toll on human life, HIV/AIDS has left a profound mark on social and economic life and has become a major threat to human security. The following newspaper article comments on the impact of HIV/AIDS on a village in Zimbabwe.

In Charumbira village in Masvingo province, Zimbabwe, Wednesday is a sacred day. According to custom, it is the chief's chosen day and no one is allowed to work in the fields or dig—unless it is a grave that's being dug up. All women are to remain at home while the men gather under a barren fig tree to discuss matters arising in the village.

However, this custom has changed over the past two years. Now every Wednesday, 200 to 300 widows meet under the fig tree, to learn how to live with the HIV/AIDS virus.

The widows, whose husbands began dying of HIV/AIDS in the late 1980s, have now come together to form a support group that will help them to cope with the impact of HIV/AIDS. The group has been further divided into smaller groups of 30 to 40 women who meet regularly and visit each other to share their experiences or pay visits to the sick. The groups also help children with food and money for school, in families where both parents have died.

Each group chooses three or four people to go for training, and on their return to impart their newly acquired knowledge about HIV/AIDS and how to live with it.

Although many women in the village have not been tested for HIV/AIDS, most believe they are HIV-positive. Miriro Mukeda (30), whose husband died a few weeks ago, believes she is also infected. "I was still sleeping with Jacob when he fell sick, and unless there is some miracle, there is no doubt that I am infected with AIDS as well."

Another widow, Susan Charumbira (44), who lost her husband 12 years ago, says villagers have been avoiding talking about AIDS. The cause of death is left to speculation. "People never wanted to talk about it, but my husband was HIV-positive, and I don't know how I have lived to this day. I thought I was going to die, and so was my child, who was then only one and half years. It is difficult to believe he is now finishing high school. However, I am getting sickly these days," she says, touching blisters on her face.

According to Maget Madenga, also a widow, and one of the leaders and founders of the support group, the idea of a support group started in 1994, but could not take off because many widows feared to be associated with AIDS and they refused to join. "It was only two years ago, that women started facing financial problems in sending children to school and feeding them, that started turning to support groups."

AIDS has destroyed the economic base of the village and provoked changes in its social fabric. Mupazi Tsveta (76), one of the village elders, has lost four sons to the pandemic and now has to care for their four widows and children.

"The village has eaten itself limb by limb and it is now hanging on the balance," he says. "Once the women start to die there will be no village to talk about anymore."

"It is difficult to establish how many people have succumbed to the pandemic in Charumbira." Tsveta stretches out his fingers, only to lose count after a few names, and all he can say is, "*Pasi radya* [the land has swallowed up countless villagers]."

Chief Fortune Charumbira says all men who were between the ages of 20 and 45 in 1990 have now died and most of them have left children and wives.

A survey done by a local secondary school, Mudavanhu, shows that at least 18 students in a class of more than 40 pupils have no fathers. "It was after we saw an increasing number of very bright pupils dropping out of school, missing lessons and losing concentration that we decided to look into the matter," says deputy principal Reason Tsvakiwa.

Tsvakiwa says HIV/AIDS is causing major disruptions in school. Children can no longer afford to pay school fees and as a result the school has resorted to fundraising to keep operations running.

"Being a teacher has become more than classroom work. We have to ensure the school has minimum resources to continue operating. Sometimes teachers contribute from their own salaries to help children who come to school on an empty stomach."

Questions to Consider

1. What impact is HIV/AIDS having on family and social structure in this village?
2. What does this article tell you about the challenge of combating HIV/AIDS in rural areas?

From Scotch Tagwiyeri, "The village that has 'eaten itself limb by limb,'" *Weekly Mail and Guardian* (Johannesburg, South Africa), March 12, 2001.

vigorously supported frank public education programs on how to deal with the disease.

North Africa

France's two protectorates in North Africa, Tunisia and Morocco, gained independence in a relatively peaceful way in 1956. In sharp contrast stands the transfer of autonomy to Algeria. France had invested millions of dollars in the development of this territory, largely for the benefit of French immigrants who, by 1960, constituted about one-tenth of the population.

Although Algeria was an integral part of France and sent representatives to the French National Assembly, resentment against foreign control grew among the Muslim majority. Following a mounting campaign of violence, revolution broke out in 1958. After four years of savage warfare whose repercussions brought down the French Fourth Republic, Charles de Gaulle paved the way for Algeria's independence in 1962. Most of the 1 million Europeans living there left the scarred and battered country for France.

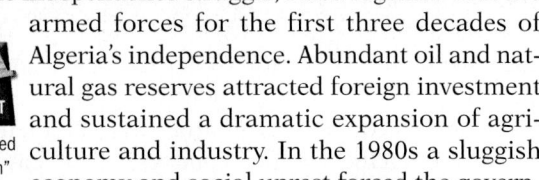

DOCUMENT
"The Wretched of the Earth"

The **Front for National Liberation (FLN),** which led the independence struggle, ruled together with the armed forces for the first three decades of Algeria's independence. Abundant oil and natural gas reserves attracted foreign investment and sustained a dramatic expansion of agriculture and industry. In the 1980s a sluggish economy and social unrest forced the government to introduce political reforms and allow the first multiparty elections for local government in 1990. When parliamentary elections were held in 1992, the Islamic Salvation Front (FIS) won an unexpected victory over the FLN. However, the military intervened, voided the elections results, and banned the FIS. General Liamine Zéroual won elections without the FIS participating in 1995, but his government has not been able to reach a settlement with opposition parties or to slow bloody war between the military and radical Islamists in which tens of thousands of people have been brutally murdered. In 1999 an election was boycotted by the main opposition parties.

Libya made the transition from Italian colony to independent nation in 1951 following a period of French-British supervision. Inspired by Nasser's revolution in Egypt, a group of young army officers led by Colonel Muammar al-Qadhafi (gha-DAH-fee) overthrew the monarchy in 1969. As "leader of the revolution," Qadhafi has remained Libya's head of state, promoting a *jamahiriya* ("state of the masses") philosophy, a blend of socialist and Islamic ideas. Because he opposed the formation of political parties and parliamentary democracy, Qadhafi established a government based on people's committees and popular congresses. In 1977 Libya proclaimed itself the Socialist People's Libyan Arab Jamahiriya.

Oil revenues have been the main source of Libya's economic growth, financing industrial development and paying for social programs, housing, health care, and education for many of its citizens. Qadhafi's regime nationalized all foreign-owned property, but declining oil prices led to the opening up of the private sector in the 1990s.

Libya's oil wealth allowed Qadhafi to promote an idiosyncratic foreign policy based on pan-Arab nationalism and support for revolutionary movements such as the PLO. Libya's intervention in Middle Eastern and African Affairs led to confrontations with western European nations and the United States, which accused Libya of sponsoring international terrorism. When Libyan agents were implicated after bombs exploded on a Pan American Airlines flight over Lockerbie, Scotland, and a French UTA flight over Niger, the UN imposed a trade and international flight embargo on Libya. The embargo was lifted in 1999 after Libya handed over the accused bombers of the Pan American flight for a trial in the Netherlands in which one of the bombers was convicted. After the United States ousted Saddam Hussein's regime in Iraq in 2003, Qadhafi committed Libya to give up advanced weapons systems and has been rewarded with increased cooperation from the United States and European states.

Middle Africa

DOCUMENT
Kwame Nkrumah on African Unity

Ghana was the first nation south of the Sahara to gain independence. In 1957 Kwame Nkrumah (c. 1909–1972), its prime minister, was the idol of African nationalists for championing African unity, and his newly freed nation was the symbol of freedom and democracy in Africa. But in the year after taking power, Nkrumah began to muzzle the press and imprison the opposition. In 1964 he made Ghana a one-party state. As he developed into an outright dictator, he embarked on ruinous economic policies such as a showy hydroelectric dam and support of a large military establishment. Nkrumah's controlled press called him the "Great Redeemer" and "His Messianic Majesty," while his economy slid downhill under the weight of extravagant spending and corruption.

IMAGE
Kwame Nkrumah

In 1966 a group of army officers seized control of the country. Eager to speed economic recovery and restore some semblance of political freedom, the army leaders permitted the return to parliamentary institutions in 1969. Ghana thus became

---

Front for National Liberation (FLN)—A political organization established in 1954 that led the Algerian struggle for independence from France.

the first African country to return to multiparty government after being under military rule. During the 1970s, another military junta staged a coup, but by the end of the decade, civilian rule had been restored. In 1981 the military under Flight Lieutenant Jerry Rawlings (b. 1947) resumed control until 1996, when Rawlings was elected president in multiparty elections. Ghana made a major step towards entrenching democratic rule when Rawlings stepped down following elections in 2000 that brought John Kufuor into office.

When it gained independence in 1960, Nigeria, Africa's most populous nation, offered the greatest promise of a prosperous and stable future among all new African states. It had several thousand well-trained civil servants, more than 500 doctors, an equal number of lawyers, a substantial body of engineers and urban professionals, and vibrant universities. It was endowed with a variety of important natural resources, especially oil.

Between 1962 and 1966, a series of crises—disputed elections, corruption, and crime waves—undermined the government's stability. In 1966 military officers took control of the country in a bloody coup. The following year, Ibo groups in southeastern Nigeria seceded and proclaimed the independent Republic of Biafra (bee-A-frah). The Nigerian government launched military offensives as well as an economic blockade against the rebel state. Hundreds of thousands, especially children, died of starvation. In 1970 Biafra surrendered and was reincorporated into Nigeria.

After 13 years of military rule, civilian government was restored in 1979, along with a new constitution patterned after that of the United States. Designed to prevent a return of the ethnic and regional feuds that had wrecked the first republic, the new constitution created a federal system providing for the allocation of powers between a central and 19 state governments. However, following a sharp drop in petroleum prices, the military intervened again in 1983 and banned all political parties.

In the early 1990s, it appeared that the military was preparing to hand over power to civilians. But after newspaper publisher Moshood Abiola (ah-bee-OH-lah) was elected president in 1993, the governing military council declared the election results null and void, and jailed Abiola. Following the deaths in 1998 of Abiola in prison and of military strongman Sani Abacha, military leaders allowed elections and a return to civilian rule. In the 1993 and 2003 elections, Olesegun Obasanjo (oh-bah-SAHN-joh) was elected

A child soldier of the Liberia Peace Council, one of the factions that fought for power in Liberia's civil war between 1997 and 2003. In many civil wars around the world, children have been forced into combatant roles as they have been separated from their families and kinfolk.

and reelected president. As an army general, Obasanjo had served as head of state under a military government from 1976 to 1979, but he had distinguished himself then by advocating the return of government to civilians. Abacha also jailed him in 1995 for three years. Obasanjo's major task is creating national unity in the face of regional, ethnic, and religious rivalries and ensuring that oil revenues are distributed more evenly around the country.

By contrast, the Democratic Republic of the Congo, a country as large as western Europe but lacking any ethnic or political unity, has made little progress toward creating a stable political environment. In 1959 the Belgian colonizers, in the face of general protest and serious rioting, promised independence. When self-government came the next year, 120 political parties representing regional and ethnic interests contested elections. The new government lacked unity and stability. A civil war broke out almost immediately, and Katanga province, which produced 70 percent of the country's mineral wealth, seceded. At the request of the Congolese government, UN peacekeeping forces intervened to restore order and quell the Katanga secession, which they did by 1964.

The government still lacked coherence, and the army commander, General Joseph Mobutu Sese Seko (1930–1997), staged a coup in 1965. He renamed the Congo Zaïre, but his style of rule mirrored that of King Leopold of Belgium a century earlier. Mobutu was a "kleptocrat": He and his elite bilked the mineral-rich country of billions of dollars while leaving their people with one of the lowest per capita incomes in the world. Mobutu cleverly played Cold War politics and won support from the West by portraying himself as a bulwark against communism. When the Cold War ended, Mobutu made halfhearted attempts at negotiating with opposition groups for a democratic constitution. His regime was finally toppled in 1997 by an insurgency led by Laurent Kabila, who was supported by several neighboring states. In turn, Kabila spent most of his energy dealing with a rebel force sponsored by several neighbors, Uganda and Rwanda, until he was assassinated in 2000. Although his son succeeded him and the war shows signs of ending, Congo's future is not very promising.

Northeastern Africa, known as the Horn of Africa, consisted of Ethiopia, Somalia, and several small states. It became geopolitically significant after 1945 because of its proximity to the sea-lanes of the Red Sea and the Persian Gulf. After Emperor Haile Selassie (1892–1975) returned to Ethiopia following the expulsion of the Italians in 1941, he kept the anachronistic feudal system largely in place. In the 1960s, in the face of student and ethnic protests, the emperor failed to move decisively on land reform or reduce the dominance of his Amhara ethnic group in government. The crisis that led to his downfall began with a famine in 1973 that killed an estimated 200,000 people. Blame was pinned on his government for mismanaging drought relief, and strikes, student unrest, and scandal among the royal family all combined to bring success to a military coup that dethroned the emperor in 1974.

The new military rulers were bitterly divided among moderates and radicals. Following three years of disputes, the radicals, led by Mengistu Haile Meriam (b. 1937), seized control. Their governing council, the Dergue, immediately set to abolishing the country's feudal system, transforming Ethiopia into a socialist state with a Stalinist one-party system. The council nationalized businesses and land, introduced collective farms, censored the media, imprisoned opponents, and executed at least 10,000 opponents.

The Dergue then turned to addressing a host of secessionist movements in Ogaden, a province adjacent to Somalia, and Eritrea, which had been governed first by the Italians and then by the British until being absorbed into Ethiopia in 1961. Somalia had taken possession of Ogaden in 1977, but the next year the Ethiopians broke with their longtime American allies and signed a treaty with the Soviet Union that gave them $1 billion in aid, 17,000 Cuban troops, and up-to-date weapons. The Ethiopians launched a counteroffensive and pushed the Somalis back.

In the late 1970s the Dergue also became bogged down in protracted wars with Eritrean and Tigrean guerrillas, who were fighting for independence in provinces bordering each other. When Eritrea won its independence in 1993, it was the first case in which an African state successfully seceded.

Mengistu finally began to loosen his tight grip on the country. He reversed disastrous economic policies and moderated his political line. However, his efforts were too little and too late to make any difference. Tigrean rebels toppled his regime in 1991 and have governed the country since then. Ethiopia and Eritrea engaged in two brief but bloody wars after 1998 over an unresolved border dispute. Although a cease-fire is in effect, relations between the two countries remain tense.

In Somalia, where clan rivalries dominated national politics, Siad Barré (b. 1919) maintained himself and his Maréhan clan in power for several decades by manipulating clan rivalries. However, insurgencies, droughts, and refugees contributed to the collapse of the Barré regime in 1991, and a civil war between clans broke out. Food shortages in the rural areas of southern Somalia led to some 300,000 dying of starvation. Televised pictures of dead and dying infants moved the international community to action, and in 1992 a UN peacekeeping force intervened to facilitate food relief.

What started out as a humanitarian crusade, however, ended in disaster when the UN force attempted to disarm warring Somali factions and stabilize the situation. A number of UN and American troops lost their lives attempting to disarm the soldiers of one of the clan leaders, Mohammed Aydeed. The American contingent of the UN force was withdrawn in 1994 and the remaining UN forces a year later. Since then, unity talks between clan leaders have faltered and no faction or coalition has been able to form a cohesive central government.

One of the most tragic events in recent African history was the genocide that took place in Rwanda in 1994 as Hutu extremists massacred an estimated 1 million Tutsis. This tragedy had been in the making during the colonial era. German and Belgian colonial officials had reinforced Tutsi dominance over the Hutus by favoring Tutsi chiefs, replacing Hutu chiefs with Tutsi chiefs, and compelling the Hutu to provide forced labor for the colonial economy. Catholic missionaries compounded the problem by catering to the Tutsis and excluding Hutus in their schools.

Antagonisms between the Hutus and the Tutsis intensified. Before Rwanda's independence in 1962, the Tutsi monarchy was deposed and some Hutus took vengeance and massacred thousands of Tutsis. After independence, the Hutu majority took power and excluded Tutsis from political life and discriminated against them. Many Tutsis fled into exile in neighboring states. After 1972, the dominant figure in Hutu politics was a military officer, Juvenal Habyarimana (hah-byah-ree-MAH-nah; 1936–1994), who seized power in a military coup in 1972 but who won elections from 1983 on.

In 1990 a Tutsi-led rebel force invaded Rwanda from Uganda, sparking off a civil war that forced thousands of refugees to flee the country. Habyarimana and the rebels negotiated a transitional government, but in April 1994, as Habyarimana and the president of Burundi were returning from peace talks, a rocket from an unknown source shot down their plane, killing them both. Hutu extremists who opposed Habyarimana's negotiations with the Tutsi rebels blamed his death on a Tutsi conspiracy. They methodically incited violence against the Tutsis. Mobilizing Hutu militia groups, known as ***interahamwe*** (in-ter-ah-HAHM-way), and the presidential guard, they launched a reign of terror against Tutsis and any Hutu moderates who opposed them. Within a few months, their genocidal campaign had killed hundreds of thousands and forced more than 2 million refugees into exile. In the chaos the Tutsi-led rebels seized power and ousted the Hutu-dominated regime. Many Tutsi and Hutu refugees have returned to Rwanda, and the government led by Paul Kagame has attempted to reconcile the ethnic factions.

Southern Africa

In southern Africa in the 1950s and 1960s, white-ruled regimes resisted the calls for black majority rule, and African nationalist movements turned to armed struggle to bring about change. Self-governing white regimes in Rhodesia and South Africa dug in their heels and defied the "winds of change" to the north. Portugal clung to its African colonies because they were profitable and enhanced Portugal's prestige in the world and because large numbers of Portuguese, especially the rural poor, had emigrated to the African colonies after World War II. Frustrated by the lack of political change, African nationalist movements launched wars of liberation in the Portuguese colonies in the early 1960s. By 1970, Portugal was committing over 40 percent of its budget and more than 150,000 soldiers to the African insurgencies. A decisive moment came in April 1974 when the Portuguese military, weary of the protracted African wars, revolted against the dictatorship that had ruled Portugal for nearly 50 years. The new military junta quickly concluded settlements with African political movements in Angola, Mozambique, and Guinea-Bissau. The last two gained independence with little difficulty as power was transferred to the leading party.

Freedom for Angola was complicated by superpower rivalries and three Angolan political parties contesting for power. Following the granting of independence in 1975, the parties were supposed to share power in a government of unity, but bloody strife broke out between them. The United States covertly assisted the National Union for the Total Independence of Angola (UNITA), while the Soviet Union and Cuba backed the Movement for the Popular Liberation of Angola (MPLA). When the South African military invaded in support of UNITA, the Cubans sent troops to aid the MPLA. The South Africans pulled back their forces, but a civil war continued between UNITA and the MPLA and their external backers for the next two decades until UNITA's leader, Jonas Savimbi, was killed in 2002. Savimbi's death created the possibility of stability, although the future of this oil-rich country is unclear.

Zimbabwe, the successor to Rhodesia, also suffered a painful war. In the 1960s, some 250,000 whites ruled more than 5 million Africans in Rhodesia. In 1965 the white minority declared its independence from Great Britain, which declared that it would not recognize Rhodesia's independence until full political

---

interahamwe—Literally, "those who work together"; Hutu militia groups that helped carry about the Rwandan genocide against the minority Tutsi and moderate Hutus.

Robert Mugabe has been Zimbabwe's only president since its independence in 1980. Although he has stated that he will step down as president in 2008, his policies since the mid-1990s have contributed to a sharp decline in Zimbabwe's economy.

rights had been granted to the African majority. Britain did not send troops to end the rebellion, but neither a trade embargo imposed by Britain nor economic sanctions levied by the UN could force the whites to give up power. In the early 1970s, Britain and Rhodesia negotiated an agreement that would have allowed whites to maintain power indefinitely. But the agreement foundered because African nationalists were virtually unanimous in their opposition to it.

In the mid-1960s, African nationalists launched a guerrilla war to overthrow white rule. A decade later the war intensified. Zambia and newly independent Mozambique allowed guerrillas to infiltrate into Rhodesia, while South African troops joined Rhodesian forces in search-and-destroy missions, often crossing the borders into neighboring countries. White leaders struck a bargain with several black leaders that placed blacks in political leadership but protected white privilege and landholdings and allowed whites to maintain control of the civil service, army, and police. Black factions led by Joshua Nkomo (1917–1999) and Robert Mugabe (b. 1924) boycotted the elections held in April 1978 and continued the war. After Britain brought all the parties together for fresh negotiations and brokered a settlement, new elections were held in April 1980, and Mugabe won a decisive victory.

Mugabe was elected president of the nation, renamed Zimbabwe, and in four subsequent elections, entrenched himself and his political party in firm command of the government. Mugabe changed his ideology from Marxist socialism to market socialism, and he promoted pragmatic reforms rather than a radical transformation of the economy and society. The most sensitive issue has been the continued control of a small number of white farmers over the best land. In the first decade of his rule, Mugabe's government bought some white farms but usually for the benefit of the government's ruling elite. However, in recent years, as Mugabe lost support among urban Africans and war veterans of the freedom struggle, he tried to appeal to rural Africans by unleashing bands of thugs to seize white farms and turn them over to the landless poor. As a result, Zimbabwe's economy has plummeted and millions of Zimbabweans have sought refuge in neighboring states.

South Africa was the dominant actor in the region, and its white minority defied the winds of change the longest. In 1948 the Afrikaner-dominated National party won a surprise victory in white elections and began implementing its policies of rigid racial separation known as apartheid. Parliament passed hundreds of new laws entrenching inequality. The Population Registration Act separated South Africans according to arbitrary racial classifications. The Group Areas Act segregated residential and business areas in cities along racial lines.

The cornerstone of apartheid was its program of territorial segregation, based on the historical fiction that all racial groups belonged to distinct nations and that Africans belonged to ten "autonomous" states known as **Bantustans,** or homelands. These bogus states, carved out of land of little value to white South Africans, were, not surprisingly, poor and underdeveloped, forcing a constant exodus of blacks to find employment on white farms and in urban areas as migrant workers. Those who could not find work and housing and meet other requirements were classed as illegal immigrants and shipped back to the homelands. Millions of people, almost all of them black, were forcibly moved from their homes to achieve the apartheid vision.

In the 1960s the Bantustans were offered self-governing status and, in the mid-1970s, full indepen-

---

Bantustans—An official name that the South African government gave in the 1950s to land reserves occupied by the Africans. These reserves comprised about 13% of the country's total land. The government later changed the name to "homelands."

dence. Four homelands accepted it, but—because recognition meant conceding that Africans were no longer citizens of South Africa—no country outside South Africa recognized their independence. In the 1970s, the government began experimenting with piecemeal reforms to prolong white domination into the next century. Laws were repealed prohibiting sexual relations and marriages across the color line and segregating racial groups in public places. In 1984 a new constitution established a tricameral parliament that featured legislative bodies for whites, Indians, and Coloureds (people of mixed-race ancestry) but pointedly left out Africans. The reforms, however, came too late to satisfy most blacks.

Black political groups had waged nonviolent protest campaigns for many decades. Thus, when new laws required African women to start carrying passes, 20,000 antiapartheid women of all races marched on the prime minister's offices in Pretoria in 1956 to present petitions. They sang a song composed for the occasion that became an anthem for women's groups: "Now you have touched the women.... You have struck a rock. You have dislodged a boulder. You will be crushed."[3] As these and other protests persisted, the government banned the African National Congress (ANC) and the Pan Africanist Congress in 1960. Their members responded by forming underground groups and turning to armed struggle. The government ruthlessly clamped down on the opposition, wielding new laws that allowed detention without trial. Many opposition leaders such as Nelson Mandela (b. 1918) were imprisoned for lengthy jail terms, while others were forced into exile to organize resistance from African states to the north.

Resistance was dampened for a few years until black workers and students renewed the protest. In 1976 black students rebelled against the government's education policies, which prevented most blacks from acquiring skills. When police and soldiers clamped down on their protests, thousands of youths left the country to take up the armed struggle. When the ANC and PAC renewed their guerrilla activities, South Africa launched a campaign of destabilization against southern African countries that supported them. To bring regional states into line, the South African government applied a variety of economic pressures, unleashed cross-border raids against ANC bases in neighboring states, and supported antigovernment guerrillas in Angola, Mozambique, and Lesotho. The cost of the wars and economic destabilization to southern African countries has been estimated at close to $1 billion.

DOCUMENT
A White Journalist on Apartheid

By the late 1980s, South Africa was under pressure on a number of fronts to end apartheid. International economic, arms, and sporting sanctions were hurting and isolating the country. The economy was stagnating, new government programs were at a standstill, and repression of antiapartheid activists was not silencing opposition. Moreover, time and demographics were on the side of the black majority, whose members were gaining clout in trade unions and the economy. Without a decisive break from its apartheid past, long-term prospects for change without considerable bloodshed looked remote.

F. W. de Klerk (b. 1936), who replaced Botha as president in September 1989, made a bold move in early 1990 by legalizing all banned political parties and freeing Mandela, the symbolic leader of many South African blacks, from almost three decades of imprisonment. De Klerk, who had not been known as a reformer, and Mandela, the inveterate foe of apartheid, were unlikely partners. However, they and their negotiating teams began the arduous process of dismantling apartheid and preparing the way for the writing of a new constitution. They had to contend with ultra-right-wing whites that disrupted meetings and hoped to polarize the country as well as conservative blacks that wanted to prevent an ANC government.

Although thousands died in political conflicts leading up to the elections of April, 1994, amazingly, the elections proceeded with few problems. The ANC

Nelson Mandela and Frederik W. de Klerk led the negotiations that brought about an end to white majority rule and elections in South Africa in 1994. Mandela was elected president, and de Klerk served for three years as a deputy vice president.

decisively won the election, and Mandela was inaugurated as president, with de Klerk serving as a vice president (he stepped down in 1997). A crisis that a decade earlier seemed destined for a tragic end had been resolved through compromise and democratic elections. Mandela's government concentrated on healing the divisions between whites and blacks and tackling apartheid's legacy of inequality in housing, health care, land redistribution, education, and water resources. Mandela stepped down, and in the 1999 and 2004 elections the ANC and President Thabo Mbeki stayed in power. South Africa has one of the highest percentages of HIV-positive people in the world, but Mbeki's government was slow to address the disease until 2003 when it introduced a treatment program.

While the South African government was undergoing its own transformation, it was moving to grant independence to Namibia in 1990. A German colony until 1919, the area was known as South-West Africa and administered as a mandate by South Africa under the supervision of the League of Nations. Following World War II South Africa treated South-West Africa as one of its provinces and refused to transfer its jurisdiction to the UN, which had formally ended South Africa's mandate in 1966. Inhabited by 1 million blacks and 100,000 whites, Namibia contained valuable mineral deposits, but even more important, it served as a buffer against the tide of liberation in black countries to the north.

In 1985 South Africa concluded an agreement with a coalition of blacks and whites for a form of self-rule, but it refused to negotiate with the South-West African Peoples' Organization (SWAPO), which had been waging a guerrilla war from neighboring Angola and Zambia since the late 1960s. The stalemate was broken in the late 1980s when Cuba agreed to withdraw its troops over several years from neighboring Angola. South Africa likewise offered to withdraw and then worked with the United Nations to oversee a transition to independence. Elections were held in 1989 with SWAPO winning nearly 60 percent of the vote. SWAPO's leader, Sam Nujoma held the presidency for three terms until he agreed to step down in 2004. Namibia has maintained its commitment to democracy and has held national and local elections on a regular basis.

LATIN AMERICA: REFORM, REPRESSION, OR REVOLT

- *What has been the impact of external debt on the economies of Latin American countries over the past 25 years?*

Modern Latin America

After World War II Latin America shared many of the problems experienced by the developing countries of the world outside Europe. Formerly competitive economies—such as those of Argentina, Mexico, and Brazil—fell far behind rapidly advancing areas, such as South Korea, Taiwan, and Singapore. Whether in countries of primarily European stock (Argentina, Uruguay, and Chile), dualistic Indian-Spanish societies (Peru, Bolivia, Ecuador, and Mexico), racially diverse societies such as Brazil and Venezuela, or single-crop economies such as those of Central America, Latin America faces serious challenges.

The Perils of the Postwar Era

The years since 1945 witnessed many economic challenges and much political instability and social unrest in the region. For example, until an opposition party candidate was elected president in Mexico in 2000, the only countries with continuously elected governments after 1950 were those dominated by a single major party. Between 1950 and 1966 a total of 14 governments were forcefully overthrown, and dictatorial rule was imposed on more than half the Latin American population. However, in the last two decades, many military regimes have handed over the reins of government to civilian politicians.

The political instability and the seeds of social upheaval spring from appalling socioeconomic disparities. Latin America has the most uneven distribution of income in the world. Educational and health services are inadequate, and literacy rates remain low. Life expectancy for Latin American males is around 55 years—17 years less than in the United States and Canada. The population increases by about 2 percent yearly. By 1990 the region's population topped 500 million.

Because agricultural productivity is inefficient and low, millions of people have moved from the rural areas to urban centers. Shantytowns on the edges of large cities house thousands amid filth, disease, hunger, and crime. Mexico City and São Paulo, Brazil, two of the world's largest cities, boast populations of about 20 million people.

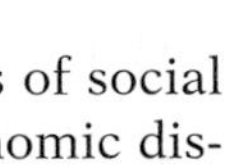

Pope John Paul II Address

Latin American countries have faced serious economic challenges. After World War II their principal economic strategy was to reduce reliance on European and American goods by producing their own manufactured goods. This strategy faltered, however, because it did not create many jobs and because there was not a large enough consumer market for locally produced goods. In addition, the economic health of many Latin American states depended on the world market prices for one or two leading exports such as copper, wheat, and coffee. In the 1960s, as the international prices for these products declined, economies stagnated.

A recent problem of Latin American states is a crippling external debt. With the fivefold rise in the price of oil following the 1973 Arab-Israel war and another jump in 1979, governments turned to international banks for loans as a way of stimulating their economies. The debt Latin American states owed to banks rose from $27.6 billion in 1970 to $231 billion in 1980 and to $417.6 billion dollars in 1990. Many Latin American states found it very difficult to pay off the interest on the debt, let alone the debt itself. Many of those that agreed to structural adjustment programs of the International Monetary Fund (IMF) made some progress in paying or restructuring debt repayments. For some Latin American countries, the debt forced them to improve transportation and communications and make their economies more attractive to foreign investment, but for others such as Argentina, the debt has led to enormous economic hardships and political instability.

Over the last two decades the international drug trade has plagued many Latin American states, which have served as producers of cocaine and heroin or as centers for distribution to North America, Europe, and Asia. Colombia, Peru, Bolivia, and Mexico are major producers of drugs, while Central America and the Caribbean are important intermediaries for shipping drugs to North America. The coca bush and opium poppy grow wild, especially in the foothills of the Andes Mountains. Small farmers in less-developed areas are reluctant to give up their production because they provide important sources of income.

The drug trade has presented a major challenge to governments because it creates a parallel economy that is not under their control and because it leads to lawlessness as guerrilla groups and drug cartels finance themselves on its profits. Bribery and corruption have undermined the police, soldiers, judges, and politicians. Officials who combat drug traffickers have been targeted for assassination. In Colombia the government declared war on the drug cartels centered in the cities of Medellin and Cali, but even after their leaders were jailed or killed, smaller cartels sprouted up in their place. The United States, in cooperation with Latin American governments, scored some successes in the war on drugs through seizing illegal drug shipments and convincing growers to shift from coca or opium to alternative crops. In Colombia, small growers have been encouraged to produce coffee. But with the price of coffee slumping in 2001, some growers returned to coca production.

Latin America

1946	Election of Juan Perón as president of Argentina
1947	Establishment of Organization of American States
1959	Fidel Castro assumes power in Cuba
1960	Brasília becomes capital of Brazil
1968	Mexico City hosts Olympic games
1973	Overthrow of Salvador Allende in Chile
1999	American transfer of Panama Canal to Panama
2000	Election of Vicente Fox as president of Mexico

The Yankee Factor

A key element in Latin America is the relationship between the United States and its neighbors. American economic involvement in Latin America remains massive. American companies continue to employ about 2 million people, pay 25 percent of the region's taxes, and produce one-third of its exports.

In the aftermath of World War II, Latin America was not significant to American policymakers, who focused their attention on rebuilding the economies of Europe and Japan. However, as American fears of the spread of Soviet influence escalated, the United States paid increasing interest to keeping Latin American nations in its orbit. The **Organization of American States (OAS)** was created in 1948 to bring 35 North and South American countries together for foreign policy consultations. The United States pressured Latin American states to abolish their Communist parties and break off diplomatic relations with the Soviet Union. All except Mexico, Argentina, and Uruguay did so. The United States signed bilateral defense pacts with governments that forged closer ties between the American military and Latin American military elites. Finally, the United States assisted in overthrowing regimes whose policies were perceived to be threatening American interests. In 1954 the CIA aided in ousting Guatemala's president, Jacobo Arbenz, because his land reform policies were opposed by the United Fruit Company, an American corporation and Guatemala's largest landowner.

Organization of the American States (OAS)—An organization composed of North and South American states originally founded as the International Union of American Republics. It changed its name to the OAS in 1948 and now has 35 members. Its primary objectives are to promote peace and security, representative democracy, conflict resolution, and economic development among member states.

Although most Latin American nations won their independence in the nineteenth century, they have struggled to free themselves of authoritarian regimes and to pursue economic stability and growth in the shadow of the United States, which has long dominated the region.

As part of its war on illegal drugs, the U.S. government has cooperated with Latin American nations to stop drug production at its source. This photo shows a plane spraying defoliant on a Colombian plantation growing poppies, the source of opium.

After the failure of the American-sponsored invasion attempt at the Bay of Pigs in Cuba in 1961 (see Chapter 32), President John F. Kennedy initiated the **Alliance for Progress** to improve the quality of life and strengthen democratic institutions in Latin American nations. The United States pledged $20 billion, to be matched by the other members of the alliance, but the Alliance failed by 1970 as little economic growth took place and the United States backed military regimes that took over in many Latin American countries.

One long-standing source of discord between the United States and Latin America was removed in 1978 when the U.S. Senate approved the treaty that returned the Panama Canal Zone to the Republic of Panama in 1999 while safeguarding American interests in the area. This agreement, negotiated over a period of 14 years under four American presidents, was a sign to some that the United States was eager to improve relations with its neighbors. However, there were some excesses the United States would not tolerate: Allegations that Panamanian President Manuel Noriega cooperated in drug running and overturned democratic elections moved U.S. President George W. Bush to order an American military invasion of Panama to oust Noriega in December 1989. Noriega was tried in an American court on charges of drug trafficking and is currently serving a lengthy jail term in Florida.

Alliance for Progress—A U.S. government assistance program initiated in 1961 by President John F. Kennedy aimed at improving relations between the United States and Latin American nations by promoting democratic government and economic development and addressing economic inequalities.

South America

In the period after World War II, many countries of South America followed a similar pattern. Civilian governments were overthrown by military elites, who blamed civilian politicians for economic failures and corruption. However, in the last two decades, most states have made the transition from military to civilian rule, although the new democracies remain fragile.

Brazil is the world's fifth largest country and South America's largest country, comprising almost half of the continent's land surface. Although Brazil's plantations historically had been the mainstay of its economy, its contributions to Brazil's GDP have declined to about one-third. Brazil is the world's largest producer of coffee and exports a range of tropical products such as bananas, cacao, black pepper, and palm oils. Brazil has lessened its imports of gasoline by processing sugar cane and cassava and converting them into ethanol.

Although Brazil maintained democratic rule in the decades after World War II, its military loomed in the background and often served as a power broker. President Juscelino Kubitshek (1953–1961) built on a strong sense of Brazilian nationalism by promoting the idea that Brazil was destined to play a major role as a global power. Developing the Brazilian interior was a major priority, and one of Kubitshek's boldest decisions was to move the capital 600 miles from Rio de Janeiro to an underdeveloped region in the center of the country. Brasília became Brazil's capital in 1960.

The delicate balance between civilian politicians and the military broke down during the presidency of João Goulart (1961–1964). A populist, Goulart's policies appealed to the left but alienated some of Brazil's most powerful groups: large landowners, who resisted Goulart's land reform for peasants, and senior military officers, who opposed his proposal to create a trade union for soldiers. In 1964 the military ousted Goulart and, clamping down on dissent, recognized only two parties—one representing the government and the

DOCUMENT
Chico Mendes on the Rainforest

other the opposition. They suppressed a guerrilla movement active between 1969 and 1973. Although the regime's economic policies encouraged rapid economic growth from 1968 to 1974, the "Brazilian miracle" faded by 1980 as inflation reached more than 100 percent and foreign debt escalated. In 1982 the foreign debt reached $87 billion, the highest in the world at the time.

A return to civilian rule in 1985 did not stabilize the economy. Inflation ran out of control, reaching 1585 percent in 1991 and almost 2500 percent in 1993. Although President Fernando Cardoso, elected in 1994 and reelected in 1998, curbed inflation by linking a new currency, the *real,* to the U.S. dollar, the Brazilian government has not controlled huge budget deficits and currency devaluations, which slowed economic growth.

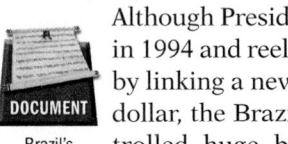

DOCUMENT Brazil's Constitution of 1988

Argentina's political system following World War II was dominated by military-civilian rivalries and by the personality and policies of Juan Perón (pay-ROHN), a middle-aged army colonel who won the 1946 election. Perón's most loyal following came from urban workers whose wages he increased. His charismatic second wife, Eva (popularly known as Evita), a former radio actress who died at 33 in 1952, headed the Peronist Women's Party, which appealed to working class and poor women. Her party established centers that provided many services for women—day care, free legal and medical advice, and meeting halls. In the 1952 election women voters gave Juan Perón a resounding 64 percent of their votes.

DOCUMENT Perón and Postwar Populism

Perón also favored state control of the economy and developed the industrial sector at the expense of rural areas, where beef and wheat had been traditional mainstays of the economy. Perón's clashes with the Catholic Church brought about his downfall. Perón alienated Catholic leaders by legalizing divorce and placing church schools under state control. In 1955, the military removed him from power.

Although Perón was in exile and military officers ran government, his Perónist followers continued to influence Argentina's political life. Perón returned

Chile's military regime in the 1970s rounded up thousands of its opponents and summarily executed many of them. Demonstrations by the Mothers of the Plaza de Mayo became a constant reminder to the Chileans and the international community of the human rights abuses of Chile's military rulers. Here, Argentine supporters carry on the vigil in Buenos Aires.

from Spain to recapture the presidency in 1973 elections. After his death a year later, his third wife Isabel succeeded him, but she did not have the same flair for politics. After the military expelled her in 1976, they took brutal steps to stifle dissent. About 10,000 to 20,000 people "disappeared" after being picked up by security squads. **The Mothers of the Plaza del Mayo** sought information on the fate of their missing relatives and children by carrying on a lengthy vigil at the plaza in front of the presidential palace.

In 1982, the military junta made a major blunder by asserting a long-standing claim to the Falkland Islands (called the *Malvinas* by Argentina), a British possession. After invading the islands, the Argentine army was easily defeated by the British in a 70-day war. As a consequence, the discredited Argentine military restored the government to civilian hands.

Carlos Menem's election in 1989 marked the first time since 1928 that a transfer was made from one sitting president to another without military interference. Menem, however, had to placate the military by issuing pardons to former members of the military junta implicated in human rights abuses.

Menem also addressed economic problems by adopting neoliberal policies of privatizing state-owned corporations and linking a new Argentine currency, the peso, to the American dollar. His policies brought economic stability in the short run. Inflation, which had reached 150 percent per year at the beginning of his term of office, dramatically dropped to 4 percent by 1994 and the GDP grew at a healthy rate. In 1997, however, a recession hit and unemployment grew to 14 percent. Financial turmoil plagued Menem's successor, Fernando de la Rúa, elected in 1999. In late 2001, his administration's inability to pay off a debt of $132 billion to foreign and domestic creditors caused a major crisis. He resigned and was quickly followed by four other presidents. The government declared bankruptcy and dramatically devalued the peso.

In the post–World War II period, Chile sustained a healthy democratic system with a number of political parties vying in elections. The Christian Democrats, who controlled government in the 1960s, promoted moderate reforms to give more land to peasants and attempted to gain more ownership of the copper industry, which was dominated by American corporations and accounted for about 80 percent of Chile's exports in the early 1970s.

The 1970 presidential election was a closely contested race with three parties splitting most of the vote. Although the Communist-Socialist candidate, Salvador Allende (al-YIN-day), took office with only 36 percent of the vote, he immediately implemented a socialist agenda, redistributing landholdings and nationalizing important sectors of the economy: the copper, steel, and coal industries and 60 percent of private banks. His policies prompted strong opposition from the business sector and especially from U.S. interests. Allende's rule came to a bloody end in a 1973 coup. Military leaders, with covert financial assistance from the CIA, ousted the president, who died—by his own hand—when the army laid siege to the presidential palace.

The new regime, led by General Auguste Pinochet (PEE-noh-SHAY), dissolved Congress, suspended the constitution, banned all political parties, and clamped down on opposition groups. Pinochet's free-market policies—reducing tariffs, government subsidies, and the size of the civil service—appealed to property and business owners. On several occasions he called plebiscites to endorse his continued rule, but in 1988, the political opposition united to mobilize voters to vote no to continued military rule.

When moderate politician Patricio Aylwin took office in 1989, he had to carry out a difficult balancing act—investigating human rights abuses under the military regime, while keeping the military content. A Commission for Truth and Reconciliation was established to record the experiences of the several thousand people killed by the military and compensate families of victims. The Commission did not have the authority to prosecute the guilty. Hence, Pinochet, who was implicated in the killings, was not put on trial, and he continued to wield influence as head of the armed forces until his retirement in 1998. That same year, he was arrested in Great Britain at the request of Spanish authorities who held him accountable for crimes against Spanish citizens in Chile in 1973. Pinochet was eventually allowed to return to Chile and was given immunity to prosecution since he retained a seat for life in the Chilean Senate.

The economic policies of Aylwin and his successor, Edwardo Frei Ruiz-Tagle, worked to promote Chile's economy at 6.7 percent per annum from 1990 to 1998. Chile's economy slowed to less than 1 percent in 1999, however, and the economy has remained sluggish.

The Caribbean

In the Caribbean the British successfully ushered in independence in the West Indies—Jamaica, Trinidad and Tobago, Barbados, and numerous other colonies became sovereign nations. Although most of these states have maintained multiparty systems, they remain economically weak because of their lack of capital and their reliance on exporting a few crops or min-

The Mothers of the Plaza del Mayo—A group of Argentine mothers who began demonstrating in 1977 every Thursday at the Plaza del Mayo in front of the presidential palace. They were challenging the military government to explain what happened to their children who disappeared at the hands of the government.

Argentina's economy collapsed in 2001, and its government took the drastic step of declaring bankruptcy. Many of its citizens took to the streets to protest the government's mismanagement of the economy.

erals. Although 12 nations of the Caribbean encourage regional integration through the **Caribbean Community and Common Market (Caricom),** established in 1973, most Caribbean states send the bulk of their exports to the United States and Canada. A key source of revenue is tourists from Latin America and North America, but because so few jobs have been created, there has been a massive emigration of people to the United States and other countries.

Jamaica, which gained its independence in 1962, has a more varied economy than most Caribbean nations. While the sugar industry has declined, tourism, citrus fruits, and bauxite exports have become the mainstays of the Jamaican economy. However, the unemployment rate has consistently remained at between 20 to 30 percent.

Since independence in 1962, Jamaica's main political rivalry has been between the Jamaican Labour party (JLP) and the People's National party (PNP). The PNP's most prominent leader, Michael Manley, served as president over two periods. In his first term (1972–1980) he preached "democratic socialism" and advocated a strong role for the state in the economy. He was also a prominent spokesman for Third World causes. Manley was succeeded by the JLP's Edward Seaga whose policies were more sympathetic to private enterprise and who favored U.S. interests. As Jamaica's economy faltered, however, Manley was reelected in 1989 as a moderate and an advocate of free-market policies. Although he retired because of poor health in 1992, his successor, Percival Patterson, maintained the PNP in power.

Cuba's modern history has been dominated by its revolution of 1958. Before the revolution, Cuba had been controlled by a former army sergeant, Fulgencio Batista, who had ruled on his own or through civilian presidents since 1934. Cuba's economy largely depended on sugar exports and American investment, and Cuba's capital, Havana, was a haven for American tourists (and gangsters), lured by gambling casinos.

Cuba's revolutionary movement was led by Fidel Castro (b. 1926). The son of a well-to-do sugar cane farmer, Castro was introduced to revolutionary politics while a law student at the University of Havana. In July 1953 he organized a disastrous attack on a garrison at Santiago. After serving a short prison term, he fled to Mexico and plotted a return. He and his rebel band of 80 sailed on the *Granma* in late 1956, but they were nearly all killed when they landed in Oriente Province. Castro and a small band of rebels escaped to the Sierra Maestra Mountains in southeast Cuba from which they waged a guerrilla war. With popular support for Castro's movement growing and Batista's National Guard collapsing, Batista abruptly fled after his annual party on New Year's Eve. Castro's rebels marched unopposed into Havana.

DOCUMENT
Castro Defends the Revolution

Although he billed himself as a nationalist reformer when he took power, Castro moved sharply to the left and eventually proclaimed himself a Communist. His rhetoric became stridently anti-American. Shortly after John Kennedy became the U.S. president in 1961, the United States supported an ill-fated invasion by Cuban exiles at the Bay of Pigs off the southern coast of Cuba. By then, the Cuban government was forging close ties with the socialist bloc, especially the Soviet Union.

CASE STUDY
The Cold War and Cuba

Castro's policies were dogmatically socialist. He built up the Communist party and jailed thousands of opponents, including former comrades. His govern-

Caribbean Community and Common Market (Caricom)—An organization founded in 1973 to serve as a forum for promoting democracy and human rights and to encourage multilateral discussions on issues of common concern such as trade, regional security, and transport. It has 15 members.

ment seized American property and nationalized businesses. It also addressed social problems and launched successful campaigns to eradicate illiteracy and to provide basic health to the lower classes. Educational and health standards rose appreciably, as did living conditions among the peasants, who constituted the great majority of the population. The professional and middle classes, however, suffered losses in both living standards and personal liberties, and many hundreds of thousands fled to the United States.

After the U.S. government imposed a rigid trade embargo on Cuba, Cuba was drawn even closer to the Soviet Bloc and exported much of its sugar crop in exchange for oil, food, and other subsidies. In 1975 some 16 members of the OAS voted to end the embargo, and the United States intimated a desire for détente. This last possibility was made remote with the intervention of thousands of Cuban troops and advisers supporting pro-Soviet regimes in Angola, Mozambique, and Ethiopia.

By the mid-1990s, global political changes had created new challenges for Castro. Cuba's role overseas ended with peace talks in Angola. The Soviet Union could no longer afford the luxury of propping up Castro's faltering economy and virtually abandoned him. His version of Marxism-Leninism was shared only by North Korea. Castro, however, defying predictions that his regime would quickly collapse, extended his rule by modifying certain of his policies. He invited Pope John Paul II to pay a state visit in 1998 and allowed Christmas to be celebrated as a public holiday for the first time in three decades. He tolerated some private enterprise, especially in the area of attracting foreign tourism, although that did not benefit many Cubans. He eased the impact of the American economic boycott against Cuba by improving trade ties with Latin American, Caribbean, and European nations.

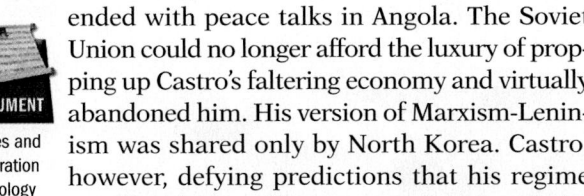

DOCUMENT
Torres and Liberation Theology

Although the American government has generally taken a hard-line stance toward Cuba, there are slight differences from one branch of government to another. The U.S. Congress passed the Helms-Burton Act in 1996 to punish non-American businesses operating in Cuba; several years later, the Clinton administration eased restrictions on humanitarian assistance and medicines being sent to Cuba. George W. Bush's administration has resumed tightening the embargo.

One of the world's poorest countries, Haiti passed through a series of military rulers and dictators after World War II. In 1957, François Duvalier, popularly known as "Papa Doc," seized power. He used the police, military and secret police, known as the *Tontons Macoutes,* to terrorize opponents. Declaring himself president for life, he looted the state treasury for his personal enrichment. After his death in 1971, his son, Jean-Claude or "Baby Doc," served as president until he was forced out of office and fled the country in 1986.

There have been many obstacles to creating democratic institutions in Haiti. In February 1991 Jean-Bertrand Aristide, a Catholic priest, was elected president. Seven months later, the army expelled him. In response, the UN imposed an oil and arms embargo on the country, which led to a compromise, under which Aristide would be allowed back in the country. When the compromise collapsed, a wave of reprisals and random murders swept the country and led to the frantic exodus of thousands of Haitians on fragile craft to avoid punishment. By autumn 1994 after the coup leaders refused to give in to international demands for Aristide's return, the United States and its Caribbean allies negotiated the departure of the coup leaders and restored Aristide to power—but only after he agreed not to run for reelection.

After Aristide's party's candidate, René Préval, succeeded him as president in 1996, Aristide grew dissatisfied with Préval's performance and formed his own political party, *La Fanmi Lavalas*. In 2000 Aristide captured the presidency in elections boycotted by the opposition parties. In 2004, after a rebellion against Aristide erupted, he was forced to leave the country. However, with an unemployment rate of 70 percent and a per capita annual income of $250 in Haiti, any successor has to cope with a difficult situation.

Mexico and Central America

With a population of around 100 million people, Mexico is the largest Spanish-speaking country in the world, is the fourteenth largest country in the world, and has the eleventh largest world economy. From 1950 to 1995, the number of people living in urban centers rose from 10 million to 69 million.

Mexico's political life for most of the twentieth century was dominated by the *Partido Revolucionaro Institucional* (PRI; Institutional Revolutionary party). Although the PRI's roots were in the Mexican revolution of the early twentieth century, the post–World War II PRI's policies largely favored middle-class and urbanized citizens. Until the 1980s, the primary political competition was between factions of the PRI. The sitting president, chosen every six years, had enormous powers because he selected his successor and nominated party officials.

The PRI's near monopoly over the political system began to weaken in the 1980s. One factor was a major earthquake that struck Mexico City in 1985, killing an estimated 7000 people. The PRI was blamed for not conducting an aggressive rescue mission and for allowing violations of construction regulations.

PRI rule was also shaken by economic problems. Despite oil discoveries in the Gulf of Mexico in the 1970s that generated $13 billion in earnings in 1981 and made Mexico the fifth largest petroleum exporter in the world, Mexico's economy could not overcome a slump in oil prices in 1981. By 1982 Mexico's debt amounted to $90 billion, and it was unable to repay its creditors. It had to be bailed out by the U.S. government and international financial institutions. Although Mexico's economy eventually recovered, another debt crisis was narrowly averted in 1994.

In recent years, Mexico's economy has benefited from the creation of the North American Free Trade Association (NAFTA). Responding to the development of the European Union and the possibility of a unified Asian market, the United States pushed for the creation of NAFTA, which was put into effect on January 1, 1994, after Canada, Mexico, and the United States ratified the agreement. This agreement marked one of the great successes of Mexican president Carlos Salinas as NAFTA expanded Mexican exports going to the United States and attracted American investment. In 1999 almost 90 percent of Mexican exports went to the United States.

Despite this success, the PRI's control steadily declined after 1994. During the presidential campaign of 1994, the PRI's candidate was assassinated. The brother of former president Carlos Salinas was arrested for his complicity in the murder and, eventually, was convicted. Afterward, Carlos Salinas decided it was prudent for him to move to Ireland. The PRI government faced a determined guerrilla movement in Chiapas, a southern province with widespread poverty.

In 1997 the PRI lost its absolute majority of Mexico's congress to opposition parties for the first time in over 50 years. Then, in the 2000 presidential election, Vicente Fox Quesada, the candidate for an opposition coalition Alliance for Change, defeated the PRI's Francisco Labastida 44% to 37%. Fox's election was historic because it marked the first time that a candidate of the PRI had lost a national election.

The election of Vicente Fox as Mexico's president in 2000 brought an end to the dominance of the Partido Revolucionaro Institucional in Mexican politics for the most of the twentieth century.

In contrast to Mexico's political stability, most Central American states underwent long periods of turmoil as guerrilla movements challenged oligarchies that controlled most of the land and political systems. In Nicaragua three generations of dictators from the Somosa family ruled the country from 1937 to 1979 before Anastasio Somosa had to resign in the face of a popular uprising and the collapse of his national guard. The successor government was an uneasy coalition between representatives of business and the guerrilla movement, the Sandinista National Liberation Front (named after a guerrilla leader of the 1930s, César Sandino).

In 1984 the Sandinista leader, Daniel Ortega, won an election and began implementing socialist policies. However he was staunchly opposed by the Reagan administration, which imposed an embargo on Nicaragua in 1985 and began funneling support to a counterrevolutionary group called the Contras. A peace accord was signed in 1987, and national elections were held in 1990. The National Opposition Union, a coalition of anti-Sandinista parties, won that election and all subsequent ones as the Liberal Constitution party. Despite charges of government corruption and a slumping economy, the ruling party candidate Enrique Bolaños won the presidency in 2001, beating back a vigorous challenge from Ortega.

El Salvador also struggled through a bloody civil war in the 1970s and 1980s. The war erupted when Napoleon Duarte, who won the election in 1972, was denied the presidency. The military took on leftist guerrillas of the Farabunde Marti National Liberation Front (FMLN). Death squads from both right and left brought terror to the countryside. The warfare ended in 1991 when the government signed a peace agreement with the FMLN. A right-of-center party, the National Republican party, has ruled the country since then. Because of the war, hundreds of thousands of Salvadorean immigrants left for the United States. It is estimated that they send back over a billion dollars a year to their families in El Salvador.

CONCLUSION

All the countries of the Middle East, Africa, and Latin America, from richest to poorest, have been affected by decolonization, the Cold War and its conclusion, the technological revolution, and shifts in the global economic system. All of them entered the modern era in a period of European dominance that often provoked violent encounters. Many face major economic and demographic issues that find expression in political instability. The creation of new nation-states after World War II as imperial powers withdrew from territories such as Palestine and Nigeria created massive refugee problems or inflamed ethnoreligious tensions in ways that have significantly shaped—and continue to shape—the destinies of nations of the Middle East and Africa.

In the Middle East the politics of oil have reconfigured global economic relations and split the region very dramatically into haves and have-nots. Cold War divisions of the political space no longer split the region into pro–United States, pro-Soviet, and "neutral" states; rather, new configurations of allegiance based on economics, ideology, and strategic interest (including varied relationships to Israel) are still emerging. Meanwhile, conflicts over the right to self-determination and the degree to which Islam will have an integral role in national identity, law, and government have taken center stage as the Israeli-Palestinian struggle devolves into civil war and as Islamist movements (through peaceful and violent means) move to more directly challenge the legitimacy of secular governments.

African nations succeeded in gaining their independence from European colonizers and white-settler regimes in southern Africa. However, they have been plagued by a host of problems in creating viable nation-states—regional, religious, and ethnic factionalism, dictators and military coups, Cold War rivalries, lack of trained administrators, and weak physical infrastructures. From the 1990s to the present, high HIV/AIDS rates ravaged many African countries, killing millions of people. In addition, despite Africa's abundant natural resources, most African countries are economically underdeveloped and have high rates of poverty. Despite the challenges of independence, a growing number of African nations have introduced democratic political systems and policies that have improved their economic performance.

Unlike African nations, Latin American states have not had to create new national identities. They still face daunting challenges in building nations, however. From the 1950s to the 1980s, many Latin American governments were burdened with the repressive rule of dictators and military regimes, but most have turned to democratic systems in the last few decades. Their societies remain divided between a wealthy few and the poor masses. These disparities provided a rich opportunity for revolutionaries in nations such as Cuba, El Salvador, and Nicaragua. Although some Latin American states have attempted to develop their own self-sustaining economies, the region's accumulation of massive debts and its continuing reliance on the export of oil or agricultural products have not dramatically shifted its vulnerability and dependence on the United States and other industrialized powers.

Suggestions for Web Browsing

You can obtain more information about topics included in this chapter at the websites listed below. See also the companion website that accompanies this text, http://www.ablongman.com/brummett, which contains an online study guide and additional resources.

Internet Islamic History Sourcebook: The Islamic World Since 1945
http://www.fordham.edu/halsall/islam/islamsbook.html#

The Islamic World Since 1945

Extensive online source for links about the history of the Middle East since 1945, including country studies, international affairs, and the Israel-Palestine conflict.

Internet African History Sourcebook: Modern Africa
http://www.fordham.edu/halsall/africa/africasbook.html#

Detailed online source for links about the history of Africa since 1945, including primary documents regarding country studies, continuing imperialism, international affairs, and gender and sexuality.

Internet Modern History Sourcebook: Latin America
http://www.fordham.edu/halsall/mod/modsbook55.html#

Detailed online source for documents regarding specific countries, common themes and issues, and indigenous peoples.

Literature and Film

Elias Khoury, *The Kingdom of Strangers* (University of Arkansas Press, 1996), is a rich interweaving of stories set in war-ravaged Lebanon and Palestine. Samar Attar, *Lina: Portrait of a Damascene Girl* (Three Continents, 1994), is a memoir of life and family in the Syrian capital seen through the eyes of a young girl. Gholam-Hossein Sa'edi, *Fear and Trembling* (Three Continents, 1984), is a critique of politics, society, and Westernization by one of Iran's premier literati.

Yusuf Al-Qa'id, *War in the Land of Egypt* (Interlink, 1998), is an interesting and antiwar presentation of the effects of the 1973 war on an Egyptian village. Samad Behrangi, *The Little Black Fish and Other Stories,* 2nd ed. (Three Continents, 1987), tells tales of the poor, set in Tehran and in Iranian villages under the shah's rule. Shusha Guppy, *The Blindfold Horse: Memories of a Persian Childhood* (Beacon, 1988), is the memoir of an elite young woman growing up in an increasingly Westernized Iran.

Gabriel Garcia Marquez's *One Hundred Years of Solitude* (Perennial, 2004) deals with a century of life in a small town. Octavio Paz's *Labyrinth of Solitude* (Viking Penguin, 1985) addresses the creation of Mexican identity in the twentieth century and relations between Mexicans of Native American and European ancestry. Isabel Allende's *House of the Spirits* (Alfred A. Knopf, 1986) portrays the life history of a poor woman who rises to wealth and influence.

Chinua Achebe's *A Man of the People* (Anchor, 1989) is a biting social commentary on the personal and political corruption of African leaders. Mariama Ba's *So Long a Letter* (Heinemann, 1989) treats the struggles of a middle-aged woman in a Muslim society after her former husband dies. Set in the apartheid era of South Africa, Andre Brink's *A Dry White Season* (HarperCollins, 1979) deals with a conservative Afrikaner teacher coming to terms with the brutalities of white oppression and the challenges of black resistance. Tsitsi Dangaremba's *Nervous Conditions,* 3rd ed. (Seal Press, 2002) is the story of a young African woman seeking education in white-dominated Zimbabwe in the 1960s.

A Veiled Revolution (Icarus Films, 1982), directed by Marilyn Gaunt, presents the voices of Egyptian women in the 1970s on the issue of veiling. *The Battle of Algiers* (Stella Productions, 1965), directed by Gillo Pontecorvo, is a feature film on Algeria's struggle for independence. *The Palestinian People Do Have Rights* (Icarus Films, 1979), is a UN documentary on the plight of the Palestinian people after the creation of the state of Israel. *But You Speak Such Good English* (30 Bird Productions, 1999), directed by Marjan Safinia, is a short and humorous documentary on Iranian expatriates and their children growing up in London.

Mapantsula's (California Newsreel, 1988) lead character is an African gangster faced with the painful choice of becoming a police informant or supporting the freedom struggle in South Africa. *Xala* (California Newsreel, 1975) is Ousmane Sembene's satirical portrayal of the African elite in Senegal. *Lumumba* (Zeitgeist Video, 2001) recounts the rise of nationalist leader Patrice Lumumba to become Congo's first president in 1960 and his assassination a year later. Two documentaries treat recent African events. *Hopes on the Horizon* (Blackside, 2001) examines African struggles for democracy in the 1990s, while *Mandela's Fight for Freedom* (Discovery Networks, 1995) covers South Africa's transition from apartheid in the 1980s to the first democratic election in 1994.

A Cuban-produced film, *Memories of Underdevelopment* (New Yorker Films, 1973), is an honest portrait of a well-off young man who grapples with the implications of the Cuban revolution. *La Historia Oficial* (The Official Story; Fox Lorber, 1985) is an Argentine film about a family who learns that their adopted child was taken from "disappeared" family. *The Buena Vista Social Club* (Artisan Entertainment, 1999) is a documentary on Cuban popular music of the 1940s and 1950s featuring legendary performers.

Suggestions for Reading

A good survey of the Middle East in the late twentieth century is William Cleveland, *A History of the Modern Middle East* (Westview, 2001). The best survey of the Arab-Israeli conflict is Charles D. Smith, *Palestine and the Arab-Israeli Conflict,* 4th ed. (St. Martin's Press, 2000). On the United Nations' original partition plan, see Walter Laqueur and Barry Rubin, eds., *The Israeli-Arab Reader: A Documentary History of the Middle East Conflict,* 5th ed. (Penguin, 1995).

An insightful book on Iran is Said Arjomand, *The Turban for the Crown: The Islamic Revolution in Iran* (Oxford University Press, 1988). On Turkey, see Feroz Ahmad, *The Making of Modern Turkey* (Routledge, 1993). Daniel Yergin, *The Prize* (Touchstone Press, 1991), is a beautifully written and acutely analytical study of the impact of oil on politics and diplomacy in the world.

A general study on contemporary African political and economic development is William Tordoff, *Government and Politics in Africa,* 3rd ed. (Indiana University Press, 1997).

Recent developments in specific African countries are covered in Kinfe Abraham, *Ethiopia* (Red Sea Press, 1994), and Paul Beckett and Crawford Young, *Dilemmas of Democracy in Nigeria* (University of Rochester Press, 1997). Rwanda's genocide is examined in Fergal Keane, *Season of Blood: A Rwandan Journey* (Viking, 1995).

Afrikaner politics and the construction of the apartheid system are covered in Dan O'Meara, *Forty Lost Years: The Apartheid State and the Politics of the National Party, 1948–1994*

(Ohio University Press, 1996). The African challenge to apartheid is treated in Thomas Karis and Gail Gerhart, *From Protest to Challenge: A Documentary History of African Politics in South Africa,* Vols. 3 and 5 (Indiana University Press, 1997). The ending of apartheid and the transition to democratic rule in South Africa is covered in Allister Sparks, *Tomorrow Is Another Country: The Inside Story of South Africa's Road to Change* (University of Chicago Press, 1996)

General studies on Latin America include Leslie Bethell, ed., *Latin America: Economy and Society Since 1930* (Cambridge University Press, 1998). In the 1990s, scholars have focused on the transition from military to civilian governments. Among the key studies is John Peeler, *Building Democracy in Latin America* (Lynne Rienner, 1999).

A general study on Mexican politics is Roderic Al Camp, *Mexico: Politics in Mexico,* 2nd ed. (Oxford University Press, 1996). A specific study on Brazil is Javier Martinez-Lara, *Building Democracy in Brazil: The Politics of Constitutional Change, 1985–1995* (St. Martin's Press, 1996). A recent work on Cuba is Miguel Angel Centeno and Mauricio Font, eds., *Toward a New Cuba: Legacies of a Revolution* (Lynne Rienner, 1997).

American foreign policy toward Latin America is examined in Lars Schoultz, *Beneath the United States: A History of U.S. Policy Toward Latin America* (Harvard University Press, 1998).

CHAPTER

35

Asia Since 1945

Political, Economic, and Social Revolutions

CHAPTER CONTENTS

In post-World War II Asia, a complex range of concerns faced those who had survived the war—decolonization, the Cold War, the rise of new technologies, and the need to come to terms with the legacy of the wartime years, as well as the development of nations based on the nationalist thought incubated in the previous decades. Japan examined the negative aspects of the type of state building that it had embarked on in the early decades of the twentieth century when it had joined the modern imperialists.

Nation-building has not occurred painlessly. Wars of decolonization took place against the backdrop of the Cold War, turning them into proxy wars for the United States and Soviet Union while inflicting the greatest carnage on the former colonial states. Armistices failed to bring lasting peace, as retribution along ideological or ethnic lines continued for some decades. In 1945, few could possibly imagine that the devastated lands of East Asia and the religiously divided lands of South Asia would reassert themselves as pivotal players in the global economy by the end of the twentieth century—as they had 300 years earlier.

Asia's nations are linked to the rest of the world through military, environmental, and economic globalization. An economic crisis in East Asia in 1997 spread viruslike across the Eurasian landmass. President George W. Bush's decision to protect U.S. steel in 2002 (later rescinded) had an immediate effect on Asian steel makers. Hollywood has had a profound effect on Asian filmmakers while India's "Bollywood" is starting to find a bigger share of the market in the West. Chinese and Japanese films routinely find large Western audiences. The World Cup of Football (soccer) hosted by South Korea and Japan drew the gaze of the world in the spring of 2002, just as the talents of the latest Japanese and Korean baseball phenoms intrigue American sports fans.

In the geopolitical realm, international terror organizations as well as international movements for human rights cross boundaries from Asia to Europe to North America. Politics and economics in Asia matter deeply to countries at great distances from Asia. India-Pakistan relations affect the whole world; North Korea's nuclear programs alter the East Asian balance of power; and the state of Japan's economy affects the global economy.

1940

1947 India and Pakistan become independent

1949 People's Republic of China established; Republic of Indonesia formed

1950

1950–1953 Korean War

1952 U.S. occupation of Japan ends; Japanese obtain political independence

1958 Mao initiates Great Leap Forward

1960

mid-1960s to mid-1970s China's Cultural Revolution

1968 Suharto becomes Indonesian head of state

1970

1971 Civil war in East Pakistan leads to war between Pakistan and India; Bangladesh formed out of East Pakistan

1978–1985 Deng Xiaoping introduces market reforms to China

1979 Soviet invasion of Afghanistan

1980

1984 Indira Gandhi assassinated

1988 Benazir Bhutto becomes first woman elected to lead Pakistan

1989 Tiananmen Square Massacre in China

1990

1998 Hindu nationalist BJP wins Indian elections

2000

2001 China enters WTO

2001 United States invades Afghanistan, ousting the Taliban regime

2002 East Timor gains independence from Indonesia

2004 Congress Party wins elections in India

THE PEOPLE'S REPUBLIC OF CHINA AND OTHER CHINESE COUNTRIES

- *Why has China shifted course so frequently in its post-1949 quest for political integration and economic growth?*

Announcing that the "Chinese people have now stood up," Mao Zedong proclaimed the founding of the People's Republic of China on October 1, 1949. Decades of war and revolution were then to give way to nation-building. But the trajectory of China's nation-building in the next half-century was anything but smooth. Moving from land reform and industrial reconstruction, to collectivization and communization, and later to increasing market incentives, economic development made frequent changes in course. In the realm of foreign policy, China shifted from a close relationship with the Soviet Union and a bitter enmity with the United States to a rupture of relations with the former and a rebuilding of ties with the latter. And China's approach to human rights in free expression, artistic license, women's rights, and other social and cultural areas often changed direction.

The Communist Victory

Between 1927 and 1937 the Nationalist or Guomindang (GWAW-min-dang) government of Jiang Jieshi (jee-AHNG jeh-SHEE; also known as Chiang Kai-shek) had initiated useful reforms in the areas under its control. The Japanese war in China prevented the expansion of those policies to the rest of the country. At the end of World War II, Jiang insisted that Japanese forces surrender only to the Nationalists. But the Soviets, who had declared war on Japan in the last week of the Pacific War, held Jiang's forces out of Manchuria while the Russians plundered Japanese investments there. In the meantime, Mao Zedong's Communist forces moved into Manchuria. The Nationalists appeared to be much stronger than the Communists, having larger numbers of troops and a government recognized by the rest of the world. Jiang sent 500,000 Nationalist troops to Manchuria.

The tensions between the Communists and Nationalists threatened to reopen the civil war in China, and United States President Harry S. Truman sent the U.S. Army chief of staff, General George C. Marshall, to China to mediate between the two sides. Newly appointed as American secretary of state, Marshall returned home in January 1947, his mission a failure. In his final report he blasted extremists on both sides for failing to make peace.

Jiang felt confident in his rejection of the American's advice. His armies swiftly moved to capture Communist strongholds. In July 1947, however, the tide of war had changed. Jiang's assassination of Nationalist critics, the Guomindang's brutal suppression of the Taiwanese, and the failure of the economy eroded support for the Nationalist government. In addition, Jiang's army—poorly equipped, miserably paid, and suffering low morale—began to disintegrate. The Communists began to capture city after city in mid-1947, frequently facing only token resistance. Economic problems added to Jiang's military dilemma. The Nationalists had been unable to rebuild the economy after 1945, and inflation soared. The U.S. dollar was worth 93,000 Chinese dollars on the black market. Serious riots broke out, and in Shanghai thousands of workers went on strike. By the end of 1947, the Nationalist forces went into retreat, and in 1948 the Nationalist presence in Manchuria collapsed. The complete defeat of Jiang's armies occurred in 1949 when Mao's "People's Liberation Army" captured the major cities in China. Mao proclaimed the establishment of the People's Republic of China (PRC) on October 1, 1949, and by the middle of 1950, Mao ruled all of mainland China's 550,000,000 people. Jiang's Nationalists fled to the island of Taiwan.

Right-wing Americans, influenced by the anti-Communist demagoguery of Wisconsin Senator Joseph McCarthy, charged that liberals and "fellow travelers" (anyone who espoused social aims similar to the Communists') had lost China.[1] In fact, U.S. American military aid to China during World War II totaled $845 million; from 1945 to 1949 it came to

China

1949	Founding of People's Republic of China
1950–1952	Land Reform program
1950	Marriage reform
1956–1957	Hundred Flowers campaign
1958–1961	Great Leap Forward
1960–1989	Sino-Soviet rupture in relations
1966–1976	Cultural Revolution
1972	Nixon goes to China
1976	Death of Mao, arrest of Gang of Four
1978	Deng Xiaoping introduces Four Modernizations
1989	Tiananmen demonstrations
1997	Hong Kong reverts to China

slightly more than $2 billion. It is extremely doubtful whether additional American military aid to China would have changed the final outcome of the civil war. The bulk of the Nationalist forces had lost the will to fight; in any case, China was not America's to "lose."

The period from 1949 to 1952 was one of consolidation of power and structuring of the new state. China had been at war for decades—first the struggles among the warlords, followed by the war against Japan, and finally the civil war of the late 1940s. A new state that could start rebuilding was a top priority. At first, China was divided into provinces, some to be under direct central government control and some to be ruled as "autonomous regions." Mao Zedong's administration extended to Manchuria, Inner Mongolia, and Chinese Turkestan. In 1950 his armies moved into Tibet. The Beijing government continued to seek to regain the traditional holdings of the Qing Dynasty, including the lands gained by Russia during the nineteenth century. Such a policy caused serious problems not only for the Soviet Union but also for Vietnam, Burma, and India.

Relations with the United States deteriorated during this period and were put on a Cold War footing until the 1970s. The United States supported Jiang in his struggle against the Communists, but relations declined even farther with the outbreak of the Korean War in June 1950. The United States began to give massive economic and military aid to the Nationalists on Taiwan, and when U.S. forces in Korea moved toward the Chinese border, China entered the Korean War. U.S.-China relations hardened into complete opposition for the next two decades.

Mao's domestic policies were intended to build support among the masses of the Chinese population. He called for a program of reform that was moderate compared to later initiatives. It included, on the one hand, state control of large businesses and redistribution of farm land from landlords to the tenant farmers who tilled the land, and on the other, protection of small private concerns, rapid industrialization under state control, and increased benefits to labor, such as social insurance. Though the elimination of private ownership was an ultimate Communist goal, Mao needed the support of technical and manufacturing specialists to rebuild China's economy. He considered members of the "national bourgeoisie," as he called capitalists without ties to the Guomindang or to the Western and Japanese imperialists, to be initially helpful.

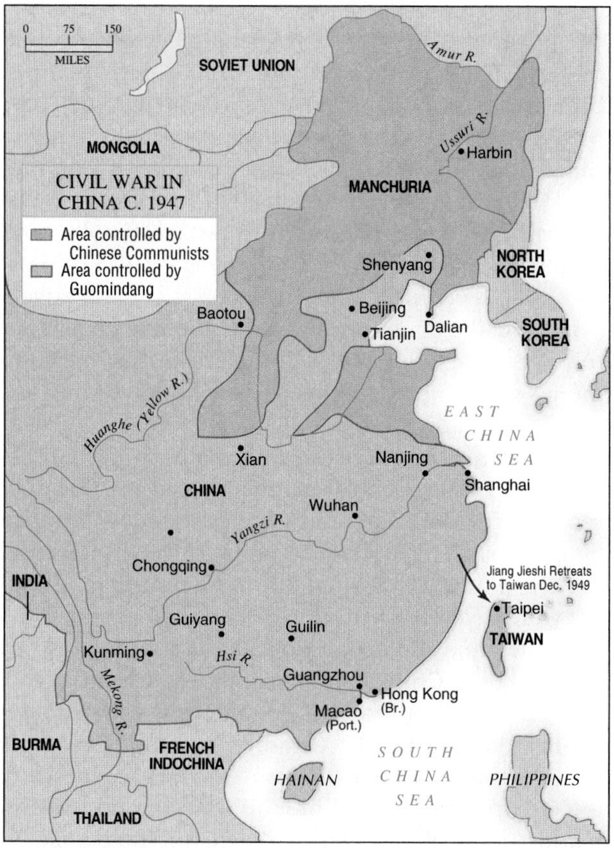

In 1947, Mao's Communist forces were engaged in a civil war with the Nationalist government's army.

Mao's Government

After 1949, Mao used his version of Marxism to change the whole order of Chinese society from its traditional patterns. He concentrated power in the Chinese Communist party (CCP), which was led by the party's **Central Committee.** Though democratic forces were at first tolerated, they were soon subsumed under the power of the CCP, which held all major civil and military positions. The day-to-day work of the Central Committee fell to a smaller Politburo, headed by Mao, who was also Chairman of the CCP and head of the government of the PRC.

The new government brought both inflation and corruption under control. Mao's interest in rural reform dated back to the 1920s, so early on, he turned his attention to the plight of the countryside. Since more than 70 percent of farmland was owned by 10 percent of the landlords, the government encouraged angry landless peasants to confiscate large holdings and redistribute them. This process included violent actions against large landlords, but it was very popular with the bulk of the formerly land-poor peasants. Owning their own land, peasants increased productivity and allowed for a surplus that would be shifted to industrial development. The land-to-the-tiller policy was a successful policy. But it was not to last.

Central Committee—Body of approximately 300 members elected by CCP National Congress held every 5 years. The Central Committee selects the ruling Politburo.

Women heading off to work on a collective farm, around 1965, made up about half the agrarian work force at that time. As China's economy modernized in later decades, women played an even greater role in farming when men headed off to factory and other jobs.

Mao Zedong's interpretation of Marxism was different from most other Marxists' views. While Marx had stated that people's ideology was strongly influenced by their class identity, Mao believed that individuals could change their ideology much more quickly. Wanting to move to a more Communist state, Mao believed he could change people's outlook overnight by changing their material circumstances. As peasants became small holders with the land reform of 1950–1952, they could be encouraged to embrace communism, he figured, by moving first, in 1953, to "mutual aid teams" which allowed farmers to pool their machinery and resources, then, from 1955 to 1957, to full **collectivization** of farms. Nearly all peasants were made members of rural collectives in which all labor, farm equipment, and land were controlled by the state.

Mao made plans for the industrial sector as well. A Soviet-style 5-year plan for economic development in industry was initiated in 1953. The Russians sent machinery and thousands of advisers. The Chinese made impressive advances in heavy industry, and the success of the first plan led to a second 5-year plan. But Mao was distressed that the industrial sector had outpaced the agrarian sector. After all, China's revolution was led by peasants, and it would not do to have farmers' livelihoods fall behind those of urban workers. Mao also expressed concern about inequalities between average workers and the privileged party bureaucrats. Thus, in 1956 and 1957, he urged intellectuals and others to speak out against bureaucratic corruption. Dubbed the **"Hundred Flowers"** campaign, Mao's efforts were at first ignored by frightened intellectuals. Later, promised freedom of speech, many spoke out. Mao cracked down severely, purging hundreds of thousands from their jobs, jailing countless others, and destroying the fledgling literary and artistic worlds. When Mao announced his **Great Leap Forward** in 1958, no intellectuals dared to criticize its obvious shortcomings.

Mao launched the Great Leap Forward with a huge propaganda campaign and galvanized millions of urban and rural workers into a frenzied effort to tremendously increase the production of steel, electricity, and coal. Thousands of small backyard furnaces sprang up to produce steel. The Chinese boldly predicted that they would surpass British industrial capacity in 15 years.

In the countryside Mao installed "people's communes." The state created some 26,000 of these units, each averaging 5000 households, or about 25,000 people. The heads of the communes collected taxes and ran schools, childcare centers, dormitories, communal kitchens, and even cemeteries in a massive social experiment. Mao tried to convert peasants into a rural proletariat paid in wages. Until the late 1970s, almost all land, dwellings, and livestock were effectively owned by the communes. Among the few benefits of the otherwise failed policy of the creation of the communes were improvements in distribution of medical care and literacy.

The Great Leap Forward ultimately proved disastrous for China. Central planners erred in allocating resources and capital, and farm production dropped dangerously. The steel and iron produced in the rural backyard furnaces turned out to be unusable. Farmers were often left without the tools to produce the food they and the urban population required. From 1959 to 1961 Chinese industry lacked essential raw materials, and millions of people went without adequate food. Between 1960 and 1962, a combination of bad weather and chaos bequeathed by the failure of the Great Leap resulted in malnutrition and the premature death of between 16 and 30 million people. At the same time that the Great Leap was failing, the Soviet Union withdrew its technological and financial

---

collectivization—Merging of previously privately held farms into one large unit owned jointly and farmed collectively.

Hundred Flowers—Movement urging intellectuals to speak out against corruption, first encouraged and later repressed by Mao.

Great Leap Forward—1958–1961 attempt to equalize output of industrial and agricultural sectors by forming rural communes, requiring all to work, and providing extensive social services. Its failure led to starvation.

Document Mao on Communism in China

Mao Zedong adapted Marxism to China. After paying tribute to the Soviet Union in a speech delivered in 1949, he stated his goals for the future.

Communists the world over are wiser than the bourgeoisie, they understand the laws governing the existence and development of things, they understand dialectics and they can see farther. The bourgeoisie does not welcome this truth because it does not want to be overthrown.

As everyone knows, our Party passed through these twenty-eight years not in peace but amid hardships, for we had to fight enemies, both foreign and domestic, both inside and outside the Party. We thank Marx, Engels, Lenin and Stalin for giving us a weapon. This weapon is not a machine-gun, but Marxism-Leninism. . . .

The Russians made the October Revolution and created the world's first socialist state. Under the leadership of Lenin and Stalin, the revolutionary energy of the great proletariat and labouring people of Russia, hitherto latent and unseen by foreigners, suddenly erupted like a volcano, and the Chinese and all mankind began to see the Russians in a new light. Then, and only then, did the Chinese enter an entirely new era in their thinking and their life. They found Marxism-Leninism, the universally applicable truth, and the face of China began to change....

There are bourgeois republics in foreign lands, but China cannot have a bourgeois republic because she is a country suffering under imperialist oppression. The only way is through a people's republic led by the working class. . . .

Twenty-four years have passed since Sun Yat-sen's death, and the Chinese revolution, led by the Communist Party of China, has made tremendous advances in both theory and practice and has radically changed the face of China. Up to now the principal and fundamental experience the Chinese people have gained is twofold:

1. Internally, arouse the masses of the people. That is, unite the working class, the peasantry, the urban petty bourgeoisie and the national bourgeoisie, form a domestic united front under the leadership of the working class, and advance from this to the establishment of a state which is a people's democratic dictatorship under the leadership of the working class and based on the alliance of workers and peasants.
2. Externally, unite in a common struggle with those nations of the world which treat us as equals and unite with the peoples of all countries. That is, ally ourselves with the Soviet Union, with the People's Democracies and with the proletariat and the broad masses of the people in all other countries, and form an international united front.

To sum up our experience and concentrate it into one point, it is: the people's democratic dictatorship under the leadership of the working class (through the Communist Party) and based upon the alliance of workers and peasants. This dictatorship must unite as one with the international revolutionary forces. This is our formula, our principal experience, our main programme. . . .

The Communist Party of the Soviet Union is our best teacher and we must learn from it. The situation both at home and abroad is in our favor, we can rely fully on the weapon of the people's democratic dictatorship, unite the people throughout the country, the reactionaries excepted, and advance steadily to our goal.

Questions to Consider

1. How was Mao's application of Communism different from that of the leaders of the Soviet Union?
2. Why are the Communists wiser than the bourgeoisie, according to Mao?
3. What is a "democratic dictatorship?" Is this an oxymoron, or a viable concept?

From Mao Zedong, "In Commemoration of the 28th Anniversary of the Communist Party of China, June 30, 1949," in *Selected Works,* Vol. 5 (New York: International Publishers, n.d.), pp. 411–423.

support. Indeed, this marked the beginning of a Sino-Soviet split that rivaled the Cold War tensions as a threat to world peace. Soviet premier Khrushchev's attack on Stalin in 1956 was taken by Mao as an implicit criticism of himself; the Soviets' refusal to help China take back Taiwan and the Soviets' support of India, which had given refuge to Tibet's Dalai Lama and others fleeing Chinese suppression in Tibet, sealed the break. A three-power Cold War scenario—Russia, China, and the United States—emerged, complicating international affairs and promoting proxy wars around the world for the next three decades.

Faced with these crises, Mao, who had championed the Great Leap Forward, was bypassed by more pragmatic leaders in the Communist Part, especially Liu Shaoqi (lee-OO show-CHEE) and Zhou Enlai (JOH en-LAI). The government radically changed its economic policy in 1961. In the communes, which were not yet dismantled, social experimentation and centralized control were somewhat relaxed. Working conditions were improved, and private plots in which peasants were allowed to keep or sell the crops and animals they raised were used as incentives to increase agricultural production. Between 1961 and 1964, industry also recovered, and the discovery of petroleum provided new energy sources. China made advances in light industry, especially in consumer goods and cotton production. Signs of technological progress included the detonation of a nuclear device in 1964 and of a hydrogen bomb in 1967.

The Cultural Revolution and International Recognition

By the early 1960s, an ideological schism had widened between Mao and the longtime comrades who signaled the rejection of his more rigid ideology by referring to Mao as an "ancestor"—revered and even worshipped but ignored in everyday life. Moderates advocated gradual social change and economic development, while radicals like Mao sought to pursue the drastic restructuring of Chinese society. Mao believed that many in the Communist party had lost their revolutionary zeal.

When a historical play written by a government official was taken as a thinly veiled criticism of Mao, the revered ancestor struck back, calling on supporters in the army and especially among young people to attack the party leadership for their conservatism. High school and college students fell under the spell of utopian Maoism, forming themselves into bands called **Red Guards,** determined to wipe out what they considered old fashioned art, ideas, and even the old guard of the CCP. Top leaders like Liu Shaoqi were arrested—he later died in prison—universities were closed, and scholarship ceased. Young people replicated the fabled "Long March" and went down to the countryside to live among the peasants, most of whom where not flattered by the Red Guards' adulation but rather resented having to take care of city slickers. Placing political purity above economic growth and applying Maoist ideas from *Quotations from Chairman Mao (*nick-

Red Guards—During the Cultural Revolution, school-age youth inspired by Mao to attack vestiges of pre-1949 Chinese life and culture.

From 1966 to 1969, schools in the PRC closed down as students, waving books of Mao's quotations or carrying his image, demonstrated throughout the country as Red Guards of the Cultural Revolution.

named the "Little Red Book"), the Red Guards hampered production and research. Their rallies and demonstrations disrupted the entire educational system. "Redness" (ideological purity) was favored over technical expertise. Only nuclear research was spared the attacks of the anti-intellectual Red Guards; guarded by the People's Liberation Army (PLA), the nuclear labs were a protected space.

The effects of these events, called the **Cultural Revolution,** were dire. By 1967, industrial production had plummeted and basic education and most research had ceased; some areas of the country were approaching anarchy. Eventually, Mao called on the PLA to bring the Red Guards under control, restore order, and put an end to the excesses of the Cultural Revolution.

Premier Zhou Enlai (1898–1976), Mao's longtime associate, gradually helped to restore the country's industrial productivity. The return to political stability was more difficult, but Zhou managed to hold the country together while rival factions intrigued for power. Zhou removed China from the diplomatic isolation in which it had resided since 1958. He responded to a diplomatic initiative made by the Nixon administration in 1971 and moved closer to the United States, motivated perhaps by the armed border clashes with the Soviet Union that had begun to occur along the Amur River. In 1971, the United Nations voted to seat the PRC rather than the Nationalist government of Taiwan. The American policy shift signaled to other nations, such as Japan and some NATO countries, that the United States would not object to the restoration of diplomatic relations with the PRC. The United States recognized the PRC and withdrew diplomatic recognition of Taiwan in 1979. In addition, China sought to develop its industrial capacity through the use of foreign technology and to bring in foreign currency through both an expanded banking system based in the British crown colony of Hong Kong and the development of a tourist industry.

The Shanghai Communiquè, 1972

Deng Xiaoping's Pragmatic Reforms

After Zhou and Mao died in 1976, politicians jockeyed for control with varying intensity. Leading the most militant faction, known as the **Gang of Four,** was Mao's widow, Jiang Qing (jee-AHNG CHING; 1914–1991), who was overthrown, disgraced, and brought to a televised show trial in 1980. Jiang, as one of the leading ideologues of the Cultural Revolution, was blamed for its excesses. The trial of the Gang of Four deflected blame for the Cultural Revolution to a few people, thereby paving the way for the advent of a more moderate, pragmatic group of officials led by Deng Xiaoping (DUHNG show-PING).

Deng was a political survivor whose roots in the party went back to the 1920s. He endured political exile and the Cultural Revolution to introduce his variant of reform Marxism, in which the party kept control of the "commanding heights" of the economy. Aided by his moderate chief lieutenants, Hu Yaobang (HOO yow-BAHNG) and Zhao Ziyang (JOW zee-YAHNG), Deng introduced a pragmatic series of economic reforms called the **Four Modernizations** (agriculture, industry, science, and defense). The first major move to introduce a more market-oriented economy came in the countryside in 1978. The party allowed greater personal profit for the peasants, and this resulted in a vast increase in productivity. Individual peasants gained access to the land through a long-term rental scheme to till farms as their own. In 1982, communes were stripped of their political authority and replaced by cities, towns, and villages. The incentive-based plan gave China a grain surplus in 6 of the next 7 years. With an increased food supply and a contented peasantry, Deng in 1985 encouraged the introduction of market incentives in the cities, with the goal of gaining similar economic gains there. To foster more rapid development, Deng permitted the entry of Western experts and technology, a process called the "Open Door Policy." Western, especially American, influence grew in the cities in China during the 1980s, along with foreign trade and an influx of other foreigners.

The government continued to keep the cost of medicine low and supplemented wages with accident insurance, medical coverage, day care centers, and maternity benefits. The standard of living in China improved, but the removal of price controls on food and other staple items led to inflation. Even with economic progress, the standard of living in China remained far below the standards in industrialized countries.

The educational system changed drastically under the Communists. In the 1930s, only 20 percent of the people had been literate. By 2001, the figure had risen to 81 percent. Across China a crash program of schooling was initiated, and "spare-time" schools with work-study programs for those unable to attend school full time were established. Thousands of Chinese students emigrated abroad to study, including some 200,000 to the United States.

Cultural Revolution—Maoist movement, 1966–1976, to destroy traditional culture and modern "bourgeois" culture; founded on utopian, revolutionary dreams.

Gang of Four—Four of the many leaders of the Cultural Revolution who were blamed for the failures and brutality of that movement. The group included Mao's widow.

Four Modernizations—Vigorous program designed by Deng Xiaoping to reject vestiges of the Cultural Revolution by embracing Western methods in military, science, industry, and agriculture.

Deng had worked for the economic liberalization of his country but failed to sponsor similar reform on the political front. Students and workers began to express discontent with inflation, corruption, and a lack of democracy in China. In December 1978, a young worker was arrested for calling for a fifth "Modernization"—democracy. The newly liberalizing state did not know how to deal with ideological diversity. Greater opportunities for expression alternated with periods of crackdowns in the next decade. New ideas flowed into China in the 1980s—music from Japan, movies from Hong Kong, and literature from around the world. By the end of the 1980s, even relations with Russia were improving. As the world's media were gathering in Beijing to witness the historic restoration of ties between the Soviet Union and China in the spring of 1989, students were carrying out massive demonstrations for democratization. In the spring of 1989 students across China demonstrated in honor of the liberal politician Hu Yaobang, who had died in March. The demonstrators went on to criticize Deng's government. The protest reached a climax in May and June when thousands of demonstrators calling for democracy occupied the ceremonial center of modern China, Tiananmen Square in Beijing. Both the students and the government were aware of the historic timing of their demonstrations—May 4, 1989, was the seventieth anniversary of the May Fourth Movement that also started with demonstrations in Tiananmen. The whole world was watching.

The party split over how to deal with the protesters and their supporters, sometimes numbering 1 million strong. Zhao advocated accommodation, but the hard-line prime minister, Li Peng (LEE PUHNG), called for a crackdown. By the end of May, the students had won the enthusiastic support of the workers and citizens of Beijing, Shanghai, and Chengdu. In June the People's Liberation Army, using tanks and machine guns, cleared the square and the surrounding area of the student demonstrators. More than 3000 people were killed in the massacre.

Premier Zhao Ziyang, who had counseled a moderate approach to the demonstrators, was forced from office. Jiang Zemin (jee-AHNG zuh-MIN; 1926–), who replaced him, continued economic liberalization and international ties, but also continued his policy of strict political controls.

A Beijing citizen faces down a convoy of tanks rolling down the Avenue of Eternal Peace during the prodemocracy demonstrations in Tiananmen Square in June 1989.

China in the 1990s and Beyond

During the 1990s, China's export trade expanded dramatically, and foreign economic interests increased their activities in China. Economic ties between the Chinese and the United States grew rapidly, and China enjoyed most favored nation trading status with the United States. It maintains a high level of trade with Europe and Japan but of even greater importance are its ties with Taiwan and Singapore. Inflationary pressures resulting from rapid economic growth threatened to create major social problems for the Chinese Communist leadership. At the same time, the Chinese continued to construct enterprise zones along the coast in which the most modern technology was used by Chinese businesses working closely with world banking and commercial interests for joint profits. Beijing joined the World Trade Organization (WTO) in 2000.

Culture blossomed in the 1990s and 2000s. Rock stars delighted Chinese audiences; public intellectuals founded journals on a variety of subjects from fashion to environmentalism; painters used techniques from a variety of traditions and showed their works around the world; architects created new urban cityscapes. Chinese filmmakers gained an international audience of millions, even as many filmmakers had to fight censorship. Chinese artists worked throughout Asia, Europe, North America, and Australia, enriching cultural styles wherever they went.

The Communist party remained fairly strong, counting around 52 million members in 1992, even though fewer than 10 percent of those applying for

Despite astounding economic modernization over the past 20 years, China remains a country of startling contrasts. Here the very latest in electronic goods are transported by a traditional three-wheel bicycle.

party membership were admitted. When Deng Xiaoping died in 1997, China had weathered the transition in leadership and had become a world power in the twenty-first century, a full member of the World Trade Organization, and an active participant in the world coalition against terrorism.

There is a great disparity, however, in the benefits of the new, market economy between those living along the special economic zones on the Pacific coasts and those living in the interior. Among the 1.25 billion Chinese are those who, living in cities such as Guangzhou, have profited from participating in the globalized economy.

Opportunities for women remain a major issue in China. The 1950 Marriage Law was a significant advance for Chinese women, offering them legal freedom within marriage. Men as well as women earned rights to land under the land reform policies of 1950–1952. The Great Leap Forward, for all its economic disasters, enhanced women's equality by expanding their opportunities to earn money, even though women did not earn equal pay for equal work. Slogans such as "Women Hold Up Half the Sky" suggested the goal of gender equality during the Cultural Revolution.

And yet women were not treated equally, despite laws and policies. Ding Ling (see Chapter 29) was persecuted for demanding that the PRC recognize gender as a category as important as class. When Deng Xiaoping instituted the Four Modernizations in 1978, he called for limiting family size to one child per family in order to enhance economic growth. Important though population control was, the burden of implementing it fell on wives. Pressured by their families to produce sons—sons were greatly favored over daughters—wives were often punished for giving birth to daughters. Baby girls were at times abandoned or killed, and their families thought they could try again to have a boy. Infanticide was illegal, but some families tried to circumvent the law. Modern ultrasound technology has made infanticide less common because it permits sex-selective abortion—also illegal but still practiced. As a result, China today faces the twin crises of female infanticide and of too many boys. Many men will never marry and the government fears the consequences of an explosion in the population of adolescent boys. The one-child policy has been relaxed, and two children are permitted in rural areas and unlimited children in ethnic minority areas, but overall, the sex ratio remains greatly unbalanced.

DOCUMENT
China's One-Child Family Policy

Jiang Zemin stepped down as General Secretary of the CCP in 2002, and his replacement, Hu Jintao (HOO jin-TOW; 1942–), seems to take a similar approach to the development of a market economy while maintaining political controls. Economic liberalization did, however, help society become somewhat more liberal. Individuals' homes, cars, and other possessions became increasingly important. Some tensions common to industrial societies have begun to be felt, however. The water has also become dangerously polluted, the air so dirty that a permanent haze envelopes the cities, and deforestation so pervasive that desertification has spread in the northwest. China will have to rigorously address these problems as its economy grows.

China in the coming years faces several major challenges, including reducing the disparities in income between coastal and interior areas; deciding how to deal with the ethnic minorities, especially in Tibet and in the northwest provinces where the Uigurs want an autonomous status; responding to environmental degradation; widening democratic opportunities in a globalizing society; and expanding and equalizing the rights of women, from infancy through education, employment, marriage, motherhood, and old age.

Hong Kong

The leaders in Beijing planned in 1984 to restore Chinese authority over Hong Kong when its lease to Great Britain ran out in 1997. The PRC promised that Hong Kong would retain its own laws for 50 years after the transfer, but democracy advocates are already feeling an erosion of their rights. The PRC would like to continue to use Hong Kong as an economic engine in the Southeast, and so must juggle its desire for control with the need for economic liberalization. The former British colony, roughly six times the size of the District of Columbia, has remained an economic powerhouse. The 7.2 million citizens enjoy a per capita GDP of $25,400 as they pursue economic activities ranging from high tech industries to banking to clothing manufacture. Hong Kong continues to profit from its position as an economic bridge between the capitalist world and the rest of China, despite the competition from Guangzhou and Singapore. Beijing exercises an increasingly tight control over the city, and in return, the local officials try to anticipate the demands of the capital, especially in questions of immigration.

Modern Hong Kong

Taiwan

Taiwan had experienced modern economic development under Japanese colonialism. Though many of Taiwan's leading intellectuals were wiped out by the Chinese Nationalists in 1947, Taiwan was later rebuilt with Nationalist funds, U.S. aid, and Japanese investment. The Guomindang government has been on Taiwan since 1949. In 1975, Jiang Jieshi died. His son, Jiang Jingguo (jee-AHNG jing-GWAW; 1910–1988), then took over and encouraged high tech development. After China regained sovereignty over Hong Kong in 1997 and Macao in 1999, the Beijing government renewed its efforts to extend control over Taiwan. China tried to influence the 2000 presidential elections, but to no avail, as the Independent party led by President Chen Shui-Bian (CHEN shwee-bee-AHN; 1951–) and feminist Vice President Lu Xiulian (LOO-shoo-lee-AHN; 1944–) gained power. While Taiwan labors in diplomatic obscurity—recognized by few nation-states—it continues to be economically and militarily strong. With its considerable wealth, Taiwan is able to arm itself with the most up-to-date weapons. At the same time, it exists under the protective umbrella of the United States. Although economic relations between Taiwan and China have been warming as the natural logic of business opportunities and a shared cultural background encourage financial and tourist ties, strategic tensions remain, and, in fact, have increased as Taiwanese politicians call for abandoning the old notion of "one China" in favor of recognizing two Chinas.

By 2000 Taiwan's gross national product had reached $386 billion, an average annual per capita income of close to $17,400. By comparison, the growing economy of the PRC produced a gross national product of $4.5 trillion, with a per capita income of $3,600. One-fifth of the PRC's imports and exports are with Taiwan, and investors from Taiwan outpace those from other countries.

Singapore

Singapore, part of the British Empire in Malaya, was a magnet for Chinese immigration in its colonial era. Geographically distant from China and not under any form of political control by China, its majority Chinese population nevertheless makes it a culturally Chinese state. Decolonization in the 1950s produced ethnic violence before Singapore gained its independence from Malaysia in 1965. The tiny city-state has been dominated by the People's Action party since independence and by the PAP's leader, Lee Kwan Yew, until 1991. Lee's rule was characterized by stability brought on by a conservative Confucian-based government and high economic growth. What the city-state lacked in political freedoms, it made up for with a high standard of living for its 4.3 million inhabitants—a per capita GDP of $26,500 in 2001. The economy consistently registers a growth rate of more than 4 percent.

JAPAN: FROM DEFEAT TO DOMINANCE TO DOUBT

- *Did postwar Japanese prefer growth at any cost over protection of the environment, women's rights, consumer benefits, and improvements in the workplace?*

On August 28, 1945, just three weeks after atomic bombs were dropped on Hiroshima and Nagasaki, an advance party of 150 Americans, the lead group of a substantial army of occupation, landed in Japan.

Japan

1945–1952	American Occupation of Japan
1947	Reverse course in Occupation
1955	Formation of Liberal Democratic party
1960	Demonstrations against U.S.-Japan Security Treaty
1970s–1980s	Trade tensions with United States
1989–1990	Beginning of recession

Supreme Commander General Douglas MacArthur soon arrived to preside over Japan's transition from one military authority to another. The Japanese had successfully recast their infrastructure during the Meiji Restoration. They would make another massive—and successful—adjustment after 1945.

Postwar Japan

The Americans were convinced that a program of demilitarization and democratization would create a new Japan. Many believed that Japan would become a peaceful agrarian country. Little did the Americans, very few of whom had any knowledge of Japan, imagine that the program of change was just what Japan needed to emerge in two decades as one of the great economic powers. Japan's democratic movements and quest for modernity in the years before the war had already accustomed many to the kinds of values and institutions necessary for rapid reconstruction. Despite the beliefs of the members of the U.S. Occupation, democracy and individualism, though suppressed during the war, were not unfamiliar concepts to many Japanese. Significantly, defeat itself opened up an opportunity to start afresh. Social inequalities were leveled when rich and poor alike were homeless and without food. When Japan rebuilt, it built from the bottom up. Until the last two decades, class differences in postwar Japan were far smaller than those in other industrialized countries. The devastation of the war had another effect: Disillusioned with their own wartime leaders, the Japanese offered no resistance to the Occupation.

The Occupation—nominally international but in reality dominated by the Americans—cut Japan's territorial possessions back to the four main islands. Korea was decolonized, and Manchuria and other semicolonial areas were removed from Japanese control. Millions of soldiers, sailors, and colonists, some of them with no home in Japan, were forced to return to the home islands. Others were taken prisoner by the Russians and died in Siberian gulags. The military was demobilized, reservist organizations disbanded, and key wartime military and civilian leaders were placed on trial. Japanese Prime Minister Tōjō Hideki (TOH-joh hee-DEH-kee) and six of his colleagues were executed. Two hundred thousand governmental and business leaders were blocked from resuming their jobs, though many were able to go back to work when the Americans left in 1952. For a while, industries were dismantled for reparations, particularly by the Russians in Northeast Asia, but this practice was soon stopped.

The final authority during the Occupation was the American military, but day-to-day administration was carried out by Japanese bureaucrats. While most of the institutions of government were purged, the bureaucracy was little affected, and daily life could get back to normal more quickly. Every document had to be translated into English for the Occupation's approval, and as a result, the records of this time

Homeless and without food, Japanese widows and children struggled to survive in the bleak months after Japan's surrender. It would take a decade for Japan's economy to recover to its prewar level.

period, stored in the U.S. National Archives, are unusually rich and detailed.

Unlike the case of Europe, the Americans did not pay for the rebuilding of Japan's industrial infrastructure. In the first winter after the end of the war, Japan faced massive starvation and disease. The Americans did supply food and medicines, but most people still had to resort to the black market to survive.

One of the first public policies changed was civil rights for women. The feminist activists of the prewar era lost no time appealing for women's rights to the Prime Minister. Knowing that the Occupation would soon demand those rights, he granted them to the feminist petitioners. Women voted for the first time in the elections of April 1946. For his New Year's message to the people of Japan, the emperor stated that he was not divine, a concept some though not all Japanese had believed. In the next few months, a new Constitution was written, ostensibly by the Japanese, but in reality by a committee of Americans, one of whom was a 21-year-old young woman, Beate Sirota (Gordon). The Constitution was promulgated in 1947 and modified the Meiji-era document in several important ways: The people rather than the emperor were sovereign; two fully elected houses of Parliament were the governing body at the national level; the Supreme Court had the right of judicial review; all rights were made absolute, not reversible as in the Meiji document; and **Article IX** renounced war as a way to settle international disputes.

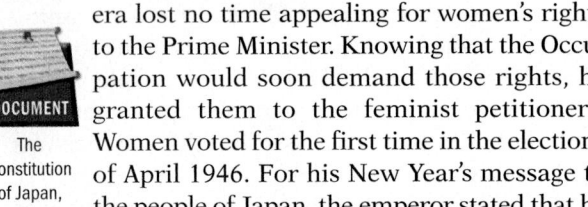

DOCUMENT The Constitution of Japan, 1947

Social changes included a new educational system based on the American pattern of decentralized public schools, with textbooks rewritten to delete militant nationalism. Almost all schools were open to boys and girls, and both sexes could attend universities. Admission was to be based on merit, but in later years, merit came to be measured by passing exams based on extensive memory work. Another important social change was the constitutional guarantee of equal rights of men and women; while often ignored in practice, the Constitution may be used to demand rights in a court of law. Labor unions were once more permitted to exist. The Americans at first encouraged them as a way of liberating labor from wartime restrictions. By February 1947, however, the Americans cracked down on some labor activists and outlawed a planned general strike, claiming to be concerned that a strike would slow Japan's economic recovery. Cold War fears, however, especially of the impending victory of the CCP in nearby China, were the major reason why the Occupation prevented the strike; the unions were seen as moving too far to the left. The era of unbridled democratization, lasting from the fall of 1945 to the spring of 1947 came to an end in what contemporaries called the "reverse course."

To be sure, democratic changes did continue even after February 1947. Two key areas of economic change also had social implications. Perhaps most important, especially in the creation of a conservative rural electorate, was land reform. As in China, land was taken from rich landlords and given to poor tenant farmers. But the process was much more benign, and wartime agricultural policies had already begun the shift in ownership of land. The other major change was the forced dismantling of the large industrial combines known as *zaibatsu*. The Americans believed that small enterprises would foster competition, improve economic growth, and ensure fairness. By 1947, the "trust-busting" policy was seen as slowing economic recovery and was stopped. In time, many of the large firms regrouped, but in new ways that avoided breaking the laws against economic concentration.

Recovery was also slowed by devastating inflation. The Occupation instituted a policy of deflation, which threw many workers out of their already tenuous jobs. The real recovery came when the Americans began to place orders for equipment to be used in the Korean War.

As a result of the Cold War in Europe and the Communist invasion of South Korea in 1950, Japan became the United States' principal ally in the Pacific. Despite Soviet opposition and without the participation of the USSR, a peace treaty was signed in 1951 and went into effect the next year, giving Japan full political independence. A security pact between Japan and the United States allowed Americans to station troops in Japan. The Socialist party and the Japanese peace movement continued to protest against that pact as damaging to Japan's national sovereignty in subsequent years.

Political and Social Change

Conservatives have consistently, with brief interruptions, controlled the Japanese government. In 1955, responding to a merger of two Socialist parties, two conservative parties merged to form the Liberal Democratic party, which was friendly to big business, favored modest rearmament, and backed the alliance with the United States. Allied with professional civil servants and business interests, it was sufficiently strong to endure periodic charges of corruption for the next 38 years. The Socialist party, the major opposi-

Article IX—Article in Japan's 1947 constitution outlawing war and the use of force as a way to resolve international tensions.

tion, demanded retention of Article IX, opposed the 1952 security pact with the United States, and favored neutrality in foreign affairs. The small Communist party was vocal but weak. In the first half of the postwar era, rural voters tended to vote for conservative candidates, while most urban areas had Socialist mayors. Many people voted for their local candidate less for reasons of ideology and more because the candidate had a record of getting things done for his (or, rarely, her) constituency.

The new system was flexible enough to absorb the radical transformation Japan has experienced in the past half-century, although charges of corruption brought the political system to near-paralysis in the late 1980s and early 1990s. In 1994 alone, there were three prime ministers, including a Socialist. After a half-century, reformers seemed ready to shake off the legacy of the Liberal Democratic party and attack problems in the economy, politics, and society. But the Liberal Democratic party showed considerable tenacity and kept power, leading a coalition government under Prime Minister Koizumi Junichirō (KOH-ee-ZOO-mee JUN-ee-chee-ROH).

Rapid urbanization and industrialization posed enormous social challenges. Rural areas lost population while city populations—and consequent environmental problems—skyrocketed. With more than 23 million people, the Tokyo metropolitan region became one of the largest urban areas in the world. The cities of Tokyo, Osaka, and Nagoya occupied only 1 percent of the country's land area but contained over one-fourth of the country's population.

In a headlong rush to rebuild, pollution affected Japan more seriously than any other industrial country in the 1960s. Prime Minister Ikeda Hayato (EE-kay-dah HAH-yah-toh) promised the Japanese people that he would double per capita income within a decade. The Japanese were dispirited by the government's parliamentary maneuvering and strong-arm reaction to demonstrations against the renewal of the U.S.-Japan Security Treaty in 1960, and to regain popular support, the Prime Minister focused on satisfying consumer needs. Within 7 years, the GDP had doubled and Japanese enjoyed televisions, cars, and more comfortable, though still cramped, homes. Factories churned out these products, refineries produced

Outside of the massive megalopolis that stretches from Tokyo to Osaka, smaller cities such as the one pictured here integrate urban and farming districts in an environmentally conscious mix.

oil, and mining dug up hillsides. By 1970, industrial waste produced deadly mercury poisoning, and the air was so foul that authorities told Tokyo children to stay indoors and not breathe the air. In 1970, the Japanese people had had enough. At what price should middle-class lifestyles be bought? In the early 1970s, Japan therefore took the international lead in overcoming pollution, producing less polluting cars, requiring antipollution devices on smokestacks, and requiring recycling at home.

Urban living also caused traditional values and attitudes to change. Parental authority and family ties weakened as young married couples, forsaking the traditional three-generation household, set up their own homes. The stresses and strains of urbanization were reflected in student riots and in the appearance, for the first time in Japanese history, of juvenile delinquency. International influences—seen in fashions, television, sports, and beauty contests and heard in rock music—became embedded in Japanese culture. Today, high fashion and popular culture alike are as likely, if not more so, to originate in Japan as in Europe or the United States.

The early 1950s were a time of intense labor strife and union clashes with industrial management. But by the 1960s, as the economy was booming, labor became more complacent. A cooperative spirit developed between labor and management as long as jobs were plentiful. Male workers worked long hours, and in exchange, were promised lifetime career security. Industrial concerns seemed to be characterized by a kind of harmony. Young people, however, more interested in meeting the individual needs of their families, began to question unstinting dedication to their companies. Men claimed they wished to spend more time with their families, and women workers were under intense social pressure to care for their families if they had children. This trend toward individualism began in the 1970s, parallel to the questioning of growth at the expense of the environment or personal health. And it certainly accelerated in the 1990s when corporations themselves went back on the promise of job security as Japan faced economic recession. Guaranteed lifetime employment came increasingly under challenge. Corporate paternalism had to be discarded to satisfy the demands of efficiency. Slowly but surely, the communalism that had dominated Japanese life weakened under the impact of economic and cultural individualism.

Perhaps the greatest changes were those affecting women. Before World War II, many Japanese women were part of the workforce, especially young women. The poor worked in textiles, domestic service, farming, or the sex trades, and middle-class women worked in offices, department stores, nursing, and teaching. But no women had full civil rights. There was an active movement for women's civil rights, but like other movements it was suppressed in the 1930s. After 1945 women gained the right to own property, sue for divorce, pursue educational opportunities, and vote. Despite the existence of these rights, women still faced an uphill battle toward equality. Women were socially expected to shoulder the entire burden of taking care of the home, leaving little opportunity to obtain more than a part-time, underpaid job with no benefits. A series of legal challenges, the passage of equal employment legislation and family care leave laws, convenience foods, and other home aids have made it somewhat easier for women to enter the workforce. By 2002, women constituted 50 percent of the nation's workforce—although an even thicker glass ceiling prevailed in Japan than in other industrialized countries, preventing women from reaching top management positions. More than 30 percent of women high school graduates attended postsecondary institutions.

Politics has been even harder for women to break into. Japan has fewer women members of parliament than most advanced industrial countries. Feminists speak out about continuing inequalities. But what may be most telling is the extraordinarily low birthrate. Japanese society still places barriers on mothers' full participation in the workforce. Schools assume mothers will be home during the day, and companies hesitate to hire mothers for fear of absenteeism. So, many women never marry, and those who do marry have one or no children. Japan's birthrate, the world's lowest, is below replacement level. The government is concerned about the graying of the population as Japanese live longer—Japan also has the world's greatest longevity—and few young people are coming along to replenish the social security funds to support retirees.

Economic Dominance and Doubt

Japan's developmental trajectory from the early postwar years shows a shift from anxiety about survival, to growth at all costs, to responsible balancing of health and other human needs with wealth, and finally to worrying about the outsourcing of jobs and the rise of serious global competition. Japan encountered serious obstacles in its path to economic development. Farmland is scarce, and Japan is self-sufficient only in rice. It has to import much of its other food for its population (126 million by 2001) and most of the raw materials for its industries. The Korean War in 1950 gave Japan an initial boost, as American forces spent lavishly. In 1950 the GDP was $10 billion. The 1973 oil embargo and subsequent price increases hit Japan hard. Inflation skyrocketed, economic growth plunged, and for a while, the balance of trade was negative.

Japan's business managers made the necessary adjustments for recovery.

By the end of the 1970s, the Japanese built half the world's tonnage in shipping and had become the world's biggest producer of motorcycles, bicycles, transistor radios, and sewing machines. The Japanese soon outpaced the United States in automobile production and drove the American domestic television industry virtually out of business. After the October 1987 U.S. stock market slide, Tokyo temporarily became the world financial center, as it dominated banking.

In the late 1980s, the Japanese began to watch uneasily as South Korea, Taiwan, Hong Kong, and Singapore, using the Japanese formula of a strong and disciplined workforce and efficient use of new technology, became effective competitors in the world market. South Korea especially launched a direct challenge to Japan in the high-technology and automotive markets.

Recession in Japan was not as serious as in some Asian countries, but it hit hard after 1991 because of the overinflated prices for stocks and real estate in the 1980s. A vastly overpriced real estate market—at one time, the listed real estate value for Tokyo alone exceeded the value of the entire United States; a weakening management structure, with a parade of industrial chiefs solemnly apologizing for running their firms into ruin and atoning by resigning from their companies; and a disastrous series of bad loans that ruined several large banks brought the nation to the brink of a financial crash. Japan's annualized GDP fell 5.3 percent in the first three months of 1998—and that in a part of the globe that saw the annualized GDP of South Korea, Malaysia, Thailand, and Indonesia, who imitated the Japanese policy of export at any cost, fall by 20 percent in 1997. The yen continued to decline against the dollar into 2002. As Japan entered another recession, observers held their breath to see if the Japanese government would take the necessary steps to put its financial structure in shape.[2] But the Japanese economy remained one of the world's strongest. Japan's per capita GDP in 2001 was $36,280, compared with $27,280 in the United States. In recent years, the recession has ended, and the yen has recovered against the dollar.

While the Japanese economy may not be the model it once seemed, Japanese culture and the arts are now at the forefront. In the area of popular culture, Japanese anime sets the standard for postmodern youth culture. Japanese architects' buildings are found throughout the world. Writers such as Yoshimoto Banana (YOH-shee-MOH-toh bah-NAH-nah; 1964–) and other young women and men are the pop writers of the youth generation. Unlike the writers, filmmakers, and painters of earlier generations, the work of these artists is part of a global culture that need not be interpreted as Japanese.

KOREA: A NATION DIVIDED

▪ *Will economic and political differences continue to outweigh the Korean desire for reunification?*

After Japan's surrender on August 15, 1945, Koreans, who had been anticipating liberation from foreign rule, were deeply disappointed. Japanese colonial rule was replaced by American occupation in the south and by Soviet in the north. The Soviet Union, which had maintained neutrality with Japan throughout World War II, entered the war after the United States had dropped the atomic bomb on Hiroshima. In the next days, Russian forces moved into Northeast Asia—Manchuria and Korea had been under Japanese control—and when the Japanese surrendered, the Russians joined the Americans in accepting that surrender. Koreans, eagerly awaiting independence, felt betrayed. The departing Japanese occupying force actually handpicked its successor. They chose the populist (but noncommunist) Yŏ Un-hyŏng (YOH oon-hee-ONG), who negotiated a treaty ensuring that the Japanese would not be part of any Korean peacekeeping. The new leader set up the Committee for the Preparation of Korean Independence (CPKI) in Seoul, which attempted to make itself into a national government. Local self-governance committees sprang up throughout Korea, ready to take up local administration as the Japanese departed. The CPKI convened a meeting of representatives of these committees in September 1945.

The Politics of Decolonization, Occupation, and Division

The CPKI proclaimed the formation of the Korean People's Republic on September 6, 1945. Its agenda was decolonization. In addition to land reform that

Korea

1948	North Korea and South Korea created
1950–1953	Korean War
1961–1979	Pak Chŏnghŏi rules as president
1980–1988	Chŏn Tuwhan as president
1988	Seoul Olympics, beginning of democratization
1994	Death of Kim Ilsŏng; rule by his son Kim Jongil

would take land away from the Japanese and those who had collaborated with them, to nationalizing such major industries as mining and railways, and to establishing labor laws to protect adult and child labor, the CPKI worked to remove from civilian administration those Koreans who had benefited from Japanese colonial power or who had held positions in the colonial government. This government was rejected by both the American and Soviet occupying forces, who divided Korea at the 38th parallel and proclaimed that Korea would be under American and Soviet "trusteeships" until it could govern itself.

The U.S. government of occupation outlawed the Korean People's Republic and set up another foreign government of occupation, the United States Army Military Government in Korea (USAMGIK). Koreans were bitterly disappointed not only by the loss of self-government so soon after they had gained it, but also by the fact that the U.S. forces relied on those the Koreans considered collaborators with the Japanese colonialists. The U.S. forces gave positions of authority to collaborationist Koreans who had already been purged by the people's committees. Over 80 percent of police officers in the Korean National Police in October 1945 had worked for the Japanese Government General as police officers, the most detested arm of the state.

The following February, in P'yŏngyang (pee-ong-YAHNG) in the Soviet sector, the guerrilla fighter General Kim Ilsŏng (KIM il-SONG; also spelled "Il-Sung") was proclaimed head of the Interim People's Committee. In the South, U.S. authorities established a Republic of Korea (ROK) in August 1948. The Americans chose the anticommunist Syngman Rhee, an octogenarian who had been involved in anticolonial actions at the dawn of the Japanese occupation in the early twentieth century, as the first president of the ROK. In response, the Soviets proclaimed Kim Ilsŏng to be Premier of the Democratic People's Republic of Korea (DPRK) which the Soviets created. Then, in late 1948, the Soviet Union ended its occupation of Korea, and during the following spring, American troops withdrew from south of the 38th parallel. Both governments—the ROK and the DPRK—claimed jurisdiction over the entire country.

Within 2 years, the two new governments were embroiled in a Korean civil war that lasted from 1950 to 1953 (the war is technically not over, as only an armistice has been signed). This war led to the devastation of a people barely beginning to recover from colonial rule. During those 3 years, families were divided, and over 1 million Koreans were killed, wounded, kidnapped, or declared missing. The destruction of industrial infrastructure and housing by incendiary bombing along with the numbers of refugees in camps can be measured, but the psychological damage caused by this warfare is just beginning to be understood.

Cold War tensions produced conflicting views of the start of the war, though recent archival findings increasingly corroborate the view that northern forces, encouraged by the Soviet Union, crossed the 38th parallel into South Korea on June 25, 1950. Washington immediately called for a special meeting of the UN Security Council, whose members demanded a ceasefire and withdrawal of the invaders. The Soviet delegate was boycotting the council at the time and was not present to veto the action. When North Korea ignored the UN's demand, the Security Council sent troops, led by General Douglas MacArthur who had recently been directing the U.S. occupation of Japan, to help the South Korean government. Three years of costly fighting followed, in what the UN termed a "police action." Led by the United States, United Nations forces, which suffered over 140,000 casualties, repelled the northern forces, who were supported by the USSR and later the People's Republic of China. After Stalin's death in March 1953 and a U.S. threat to use nuclear weapons against China, an armistice was signed in July 1953. A new border between the two parts of the country was established near the 38th parallel. Until that time, more than 2 million Koreans, mostly civilians, were killed.

North Korea and South Korea

Since its inception, North Korea has been a familial dictatorship of General Kim Ilsŏng until his death in 1994, followed by his son Kim Jongil. The general and his son perfected the art of the cult of the personality in their dictatorships. North Korea is the last of the totalitarian states built on a Stalinist model of constant mobilization against external enemies and of continuous economic mismanagement. Despite its investments in long-range nuclear missiles and nuclear research, North Korea cannot feed itself. Only international food aid has stopped a massive famine. Although the state has achieved full literacy among its population, it prohibits contact with outside ideas and influences. There are elections, but there is only one party, the Korean Workers party—no opposition parties are tolerated.

The record of this regime, aside from impressive mass demonstrations of love for the regime for the benefit of visiting foreigners and constant mobilization, has been to create the most centrally planned, autarchic economy in the world, which is in a state of near collapse from lack of investment in needed infrastructure. The dictators have made the decision to invest upward of one-third of their economy in the military, while their country faces malnutrition and declining standards of living. The GDP in North Korea in 2000 was $1000; the GDP for South Korea, $8600.

The economic condition of North Korea is very weak. The collapse of Communist governments in Eastern Europe and Russia meant that North Korean goods no longer had a market; thus North Korea's "self-reliance" policy collapsed, leading to famine. Moreover, North Korea's diplomatic actions have recently been highly suspect, exacerbating its self-imposed isolation.

Movements for reform that are increasingly common in the South, such as human rights initiatives, women's rights and student movements, and environmental concerns, are unheard of in the DPRK.

South Korea has had an entirely difference experience since the 1953 armistice. The first years of the postwar ROK were marked by poverty, homelessness, and a failed economy. Foreign aid kept South Koreans from starving. The South Korean government of the 1950s was characterized by favoritism and corruption. President Syngman Rhee maintained control with the aid of the National Security Law of 1948, which allowed for the imprisonment of tens of thousands of suspected communists. His 1959 extension of the National Security Law outlawed all criticism of his regime. The following year, however, Rhee met his downfall. Popular dissatisfaction with the president was expressed in massive demonstrations by university and high school students. After over 100 students were killed by police firing point-blank into their crowd, Rhee had no choice but to resign. He was followed by the democratically elected Chang Myŏng (CHAHNG mee-ONG), who was overthrown by a military coup in 1961.

The Pak Chŏnghŏi (PAHK chuhng-hoo-EE; also spelled "Park Chung Hee") era of military rule followed. The "Korean-style democracy," of Pak's junta, lasting from 1961 until 1979, contained no democratic elements. In 1961, South Korea was placed under martial law, and the Korean Central Intelligence Agency (KCIA) was established. By the time martial law was ended in 1963, the KCIA system of domestic and international surveillance was well established. Once order had been established, Pak's priority was economic growth. To that end he rounded up "illicit profiteers" and adopted a practice from the Chinese Cultural Revolution—convicted businessmen were paraded through the streets, with signs that said, "I am a corrupt swine," "I ate the people," and other denunciations. He also instituted "Export Day," which celebrated family, filial piety, and loyalty. Although one key phrase was "treat employees like family," Pak's success had more to do with industrial planning under the direction of the central Economic Planning Board, a concept borrowed from the colonial Japanese in Manchuria and from postwar Japan.

In the 1970s and 1980s, South Korea underwent a rapid economic growth, labeled an "economic miracle" by several observers. The nation earned an important portion of international trade in the areas of ship-building, automobiles, computers, and insurance. Pak supported the economic dominance of **chaebŏl** (CHAI-bol)—industrial/banking/marketing combines. These chaebŏl had close ties to the government. Pak's export-oriented approach was not invulnerable to the ups and downs of the global trading cycle, however. In 1972, the combination of recession and depression, in part due to America's protectionism regarding textiles, preceded the declaration of a state of emergency. Pak suspended the constitution and banned all political parties and exercise of civil liberties. In place of the freedoms he had suspended, Pak called for a "revitalizing" *(yushin)* including the new ***"yushin* constitution."** The new order, an obvious dictatorship, was followed by arbitrary arrests, forced confessions under torture, and detentions in prison. Neither politicians, religious leaders, professors, nor students escaped punishment. In response to Pak's repressions, a student movement, supported by intellectuals, workers, and ordinary housewives, gained in momentum. By 1979, demonstrations by students and workers were out of control, and the Pak dictatorship was brought to a violent end. After arguing about political means of bringing dissent under control, Pak's KCIA director Kim Jaekyu shot and killed Pak and the head of his presidential security force.

South Korea Enters the U.S. Auto Market

Jockeying for power following Pak's assassination led to victory of yet another junta under General Chŏn Tuwhan (CHON doo-WAHN; also spelled "Chun Doo-whan," 1931–), more state repression, and another round of demonstrations. The 1980 Kwangju (KWAHNG-joo) uprising began with student demonstrations against martial law and led to an insurrection during which Kwangju citizens seized weapons in order to drive out paratroopers responsible for atrocities. Within little more than a week, up to 2000 people had been killed. The leading opposition leader, Kim Taejung (KIM DAI-joong; also spelled "Kim Dae Jung," 1925–), was sentenced to death. Under Chŏn there were some reforms such as the abolition of a curfew existing since the Korean War and of school uniforms that had been introduced by the Japanese colonial government. However, the pattern of state repression, including torture and violent popular unrest, continued.

---

chaebŏl—Korean economic conglomerates similar to Japanese *zaibatsu* before World War II.

***yushin* constitution**—constitution written by Pak's government in 1972 that guaranteed Pak a permanent position as the president. Pak was assassinated in 1979, and the *yushin* constitution was replaced in 1980.

The people's movement or *minjung* movement, which began to take shape in the early 1970s, was a leading force in political activism. The movement provided an organizational force not only for intellectuals, students, and workers, who had already been active, but also for members of the new white-collar class. Chŏn, who was to become the most hated leader in postwar South Korean history, responded by throwing journalists, civil servants, labor organizers, teachers, and all others suspected of sedition into "purification camps" where they were starved and beaten. The "Korean Model" of economic success was based on such state control, but by the mid-1980s, the Chŏn regime was to be challenged by labor unrest, and many Korean youths were committing suicide as a form of protest.

In 1987, a year before the Olympics were set to open in Seoul, Chŏn provoked another crisis by selecting a successor—and a general at that. Rioting ensued, but it was pacified by the desire to show the world that Korea could handle a massive undertaking like the Olympics. Repression abated as No Tae'u (NOH tai-OO; also spelled "Roh Tae-woo," 1932–) the new president, calmed dissent. Greater economic and social liberalization accompanied the growth of personal income and Koreans' increasing identification as part of the middle class. In 1993, Kim Yŏngsam (KIM yong-SAHM; also spelled "Kim Young-sam," 1927–) became South Korea's first civilian president in 30 years. Kim Taejung, once sentenced to death, was elected president in 1997. Kim Taejung was hampered by a strongly entrenched opposition and by the collapse of Korea's and other Asian economies in 1997. International bailouts were necessary to keep South Korea afloat. In addition, relations with Japan—with whom Korea hosted the World Cup of Football (soccer) in the summer of 2002—remained rocky. Korean women who had been abused as "comfort women" by Japanese troops during World War II gained neither an apology nor compensation for their suffering. Japanese textbooks minimizing atrocities during the war have also caused outrage in Korea. Kim Taejung nevertheless continued to try to improve relations.

One long-term problem, relations between the South and North, began to be addressed. Kim Taejung and Kim Jongil began talks to open contacts between Seoul and Pyŏngyang in 2000 as part of South Korea's **"Sunshine Policy."** After that, there have been family visits and improved relations. In 2003, the North declared it had nuclear weapons capability, precipitating a change in diplomatic relations. While the ROK government under current president Roh Moo Hyun (ROH MOO hee-OON) would like to continue improving relations, the United States and China are particularly concerned about the foreign policy implications of a nuclear North Korea.

DOCUMENT North-South Korean Accord

Japan and Korea cosponsored the 2002 World Cup competition, hoping to improve relations still affected by the period of Japan's colonial control of Korea. Here Korean fans urge on their national soccer team.

South Korea faces a number of crucial issues in the future, including its relations with the North, the need to improve the status of women, and the recovery, after 60 years, from the humiliation of colonialism.

Sunshine Policy—South Korean investment in North Korea, encouragement of visits by South Koreans to northern family members; President Kim Taejung received the Nobel Peace Prize for the Sunshine Policy.

SOUTHEAST ASIA

- *What were the roles of nationalism, ethnicity, ideology, and religion in the building of Southeast Asian nations in the post–World War II era?*

One of the first indications that the whole structure of European imperialism would quickly collapse came in the late 1940s when Indonesian nationalists demanded a complete break with the Netherlands and forces for independence began their drive for freedom in Indochina.

MAP Modern Southeast Asia

Indonesia

Immediately after Japan's surrender, independence fighters Achmed Sukarno and Mohammed Hatta proclaimed Indonesia's independence on August 17, 1945. But the Dutch would not leave, and the United States and Great Britain initially supported the return of the Dutch. An ugly war against the Dutch colonial masters then broke out. Finally in 1949, through UN mediation, the Netherlands East Indies formally became the Republic of Indonesia, achieving nationhood at roughly the same time as the states of India and Israel. Although it is the biggest and potentially richest nation in Southeast Asia, Indonesia has enjoyed little tranquility since it gained independence.

Today, the state—which has the fourth largest population in the world—is 87 percent Muslim but encompasses a mixture of many cultures on more than 3000 islands, ranging from hunter-gatherers to urban professionals and intellectuals. Complicating the situation is the prominence of the Chinese minority. Chinese Indonesians, making up less than 3 percent of Indonesia's more than 200 million people, control two-thirds of the nation's economy. Anti-Chinese riots and plots against the central government in Java have arisen in various places.

For the first 15 years after independence, Indonesia experienced inflation, food shortages, and declining exports. Its population increased while its economy declined. A large portion of the blame for this situation rested with Indonesia's flamboyant president, Achmed Sukarno. He contracted huge Russian loans for arms, fought a costly guerrilla campaign against Malaysia, confiscated foreign businesses, and wasted money on expensive, flashy enterprises. Sukarno had come to power as a prominent leader in the preindependence nationalist movement. After experimenting with what he called "guided democracy" in the 1950s, Sukarno assumed dictatorial power in 1959 and declared himself president for life in 1963.

Muslim students in Indonesia triggered the events that led to Sukarno's downfall. After an attempted Communist coup in 1965, they launched attacks on Indonesians they believed to have Communist con-

The states of East and Southeast Asia wield considerable influence in world politics and economies.

nections. The Chinese minority was targeted, and 500,000 to 750,000 people were executed or killed during several months of lawlessness. The army's chief of staff, General T. N. J. Suharto, who put down the coup, became effective head of state and in March 1968 officially became president.

Suharto initially installed a more Western-oriented government and, in return, received substantial American aid for the country. He rehabilitated the Indonesian economy by continuing Sukarno's "guided democracy" and developed highly successful literacy programs. But over the next 25 years, Suharto's military regime engaged in several violent incidents. In 1971 and again in 1974, there were serious racial outbursts during which thousands of students went on rampages, looting and damaging Chinese shops and homes. The Indonesians invaded East Timor, the Portuguese half of one of its islands, in 1975 and initiated a savage occupation that led to the death of over 200,000 people. During the 1970s, some 30,000 political dissidents were imprisoned, while rampant corruption dominated government, the civil service, and business. Enormous wealth remained concentrated in the hands of a very few individuals.

The end of Suharto's regime was strangely reminiscent of its beginning. Indonesia shared in a radical slowdown of East Asian economies that began in 1997. As economic discontent simmered, mass demonstrations of Indonesian students turned violent. The students demanded democratization, an end to government corruption, new elections, and the ouster of Suharto. As in the earlier crises, violence was both random and directed at the economically privileged Chinese minority. Terrified shopkeepers painted notices on the fronts of their buildings saying they were "good Muslims" or Hindus, in other words, not Chinese. In 1998, in the midst of mass protests and widespread looting and burning, Suharto was forced to step down. The Indonesian students celebrated his resignation as a victory over autocracy. Since 1998, Indonesia has had four presidents, including Megawati Sukarnoputri, daughter of Sukarno. In 2004, Susilo Bambang Yudhoyono was elected president.

A series of national liberation movements, combined with the downturn in the economy, placed huge challenges to the leadership of this important country. The territory of East Timor conducted an August 1999 plebiscite in which 98 percent of the people voted; 80 percent opted for independence. A group of quasi-independent militias took issues into their own hands and began a campaign of terror against the people of East Timor. The resulting murders and rapes moved the international community, acting through the United Nations, to send a force to restore calm. The tragic success of the East Timorese prompted other groups in the 17,000 island archipelago to seek independence.

Indonesia and Malaysia

1949	Independence of Indonesia
1950s	Sukarno's "guided democracy" policy in Indonesia
1957	Malaysia admitted into British Commonwealth
1965	Anti-Sukarno coup; rise of Suharto in Indonesia
1981	Mahathir assumes power in Malaysia
1998	Suharto forced out; democratic elections instituted in Indonesia

Malaysia

Created out of former British holdings, the Federation of Malaysia was admitted into the British Commonwealth in 1957. In 1963 it became independent and immediately faced Sukarno-sponsored guerrilla attacks. As in Indonesia, a major problem in Malaysia was the country's racial mix and the resulting hostilities. The largest group (45 percent of the population) is Malay and Muslim, but the mainly Buddhist Chinese (35 percent) hold the majority of the wealth, and what they do not control is owned largely by the small Hindu Indian minority (10 percent). In the late 1960s and early 1970s, Malays attacked the other two groups, and ethnoreligious conflicts continue to plague the region.

Political organizations are structured around ethnicity: the dominant United Malays National Organization (UMNO); the Malayan Chinese Association (MCA); and the Malayan Indian Congress (MIC). The three formed the Alliance party, which held power until 1969. Thereafter, sectarian riots tore them apart, and UMNO demanded precedence. After 1989, the Alliance was reconstituted.

The prime minister, Mohamad Mahathir (moh-HAH-mahd MAH-hah-teer), who has been in power since 1981, has struggled to impose calm on the ethnic conflicts and maintain a fiscal balance. He called on Malaysians to "Look East"—that is, to Japan and not to the United States or Europe. However, at the end of the 1990s, the Asian economic crash deeply affected Malaysia as it did other Asian countries. Since then, the Islamic majority of the country—most of the world's Muslims live in Southeast Asia, not the Middle East—has attempted to increase its influence in the country in ways ranging from the use of Islamic law in the regions it controls to the requirement that women wear the veil. Malaysia and Indonesia, like other countries in the region, are working out the dynamics of democratic versus theocratic rule in the contexts of rapidly changing economics and ethnoreligious tensions of long standing. Religious nationalism is likely to remain a significant and enduring factor in the evolution of those societies.

Indochina: Vietnam, Laos, Cambodia, and Myanmar (Burma)

Japanese forces moved into Vietnam, Laos, and Cambodia in July 1941. Though they maintained a military presence until the last months of the war, they did not assume any role in civil administration, which remained in French hands. The emperor remained in place in Annam and Tonkin. Meanwhile, Ho Chi Minh contacted Americans to collaborate against the Japanese. Unknown to Vietnamese independence fighters, the United States was not prepared to back up Ho when he declared Vietnam's independence in September 1945. Rather, the United States and its World War II allies agreed to let China accept Japan's surrender in the northern part of Vietnam and Britain to accept it in the southern part. Soon the French reasserted control over the hapless Vietnamese.

Fighting a losing war with Vietnamese who wanted their country's independence, the French set up Bao Dai as the monarch of Vietnam. Ho Chi Minh's Democratic Republic of Vietnam (DRV) was recognized by the Soviet Union and the PRC in 1948, and the United States decided that Vietnam was now part of the Cold War. The United States threw its support to France, offering massive funding and other forms of aid. In March 1954, Vietnamese forces, now increasingly Communist, decisively defeated France. France called for an international meeting to end its colonial occupation of Vietnam. The conference at Geneva, Switzerland, was attended by Britain, the USSR, France, China, the DRV, and Laos and Cambodia. The United States attended as an observer so that it need not feel bound to accept the terms of the conference. The conference called for a cease-fire at the 17th parallel and elections within 2 years. France left Vietnam, but elections never took place. The temporary armistice line hardened into a long-lasting boundary between two countries, the DRV (North Vietnam) and the Republic of Vietnam (South Vietnam).

The United States then supported a succession of leaders in the South as Vietnam became a pawn in the Cold War. On a more-or-less belligerent footing, liberties were suppressed, though a democratic artistic culture did begin to emerge for a while in the South. In the North, Ho Chi Minh suppressed those he deemed "class enemies."

Vietnam

1945–1954	Anticolonial war against France
1954	Geneva Conference; Founding of Republic of Vietnam (South Vietnam)
1960	Creation of National Liberation Front
1964	Gulf of Tonkin Incident, escalation of U.S. war in Vietnam
1973	Withdrawal of U.S. forces
1975	Reunification of Vietnam
1994	United States and Vietnam restore diplomatic relations

The ruler of South Vietnam, Ngo Dinh Diem (NOH DIN zee-EM) favored his family members, Catholics, and sycophants and ignored the pressing problems of the countryside. Buddhist reformers, as well as secular, leftist opponents of the regime who came together in the National Liberation Front (NLF), stepped up pressure against Diem. Viewing the struggle in Vietnam as part of the global communist threat, President Kennedy sent 11,000 troops to Vietnam. In the next decade, the number of U.S. troops reached 543,000, and large amounts of modern munitions—including aircraft, defoliants, and bombs—were used against the NLF, now joined by North Vietnamese forces. The Soviets and the PRC helped to supply the Communist forces. Life in both the North and the South was brutal. Recognizing the United States could not win, President Nixon negotiated an end to the U.S. involvement in 1973. In 1975, Northern forces moved into the South and defeated the South Vietnamese state. The first years of a reunited Vietnam were focused on rebuilding the chemically polluted, mercilessly bombed-out country. At the same time, bitter reprisals against southerners began. Many fled, especially those who were ethnically Chinese. By 1986, exhausted, the Vietnamese Communist party adopted a program of economic liberalization similar to China's Four Modernizations.

The communist government in Hanoi embarked on a policy of maintaining its ideological base and political stability while opening to the world economic community. But ideology began to erode, and the communist government periodically shifted from greater openness to greater repression. Vietnam also lost technological and economic assistance with the end of the USSR in 1991. The Asian financial crisis at the end of the 1990s temporarily stalled economic growth, but since 2000, Vietnam has returned to a pattern of improvement. In March of that year, William Cohen, the U.S. Secretary of Defense at that time, led a high-level delegation to Vietnam to discuss the question of American prisoners of war and those declared missing in action during the war. Discussions also extended to commercial contacts and possible limited military cooperation. Ties with the U.S. have improved greatly. In addition to formal diplomatic relations achieved under President Clinton, President George W. Bush normalized trade relations in 2002. However, Vietnam's per capita GDP hovers around $2500 as of 2003. In addition, freedom of expression is not universally guaranteed, although artists have increasing latitude to express themselves.

Other countries of the former Indochina have not fared as well. Laos is one of the few remaining communist states in the world. This single-party dictatorship, founded in 1975, has made very little improvement in the infrastructure of the country: there are no railroads, few roads, and only a few urban areas have electricity. The leadership has attempted some tentative improvements in decentralizing its economy since 1986, but to little effect—its per capita GDP in 2001 was $1700.

After the Khmer Rouge genocidal attacks on the urban classes that led to the deaths of over 2 million people from 1975 to 1979, Cambodia has made slow but steady progress. The UN-sponsored elections in 1993 brought back something close to a normal political life under the Cambodian monarch King Norodom Sihanouk (NOR-oh-dom SEE-hah-nook)—who reigned from 1953 to 2004. His son Sihamoni follows in his father's footsteps. The country has regained some of its former tourist trade, and it is this that led to annual economic improvements until 1997, when the Asian financial crisis made its effects felt. In 1998, the remnants of the Khmer Rouge surrendered and another successful election was held. For the first time in 30 years, the country enjoyed living in state of peace, but its GDP remains low, at $1700 per capita.

Myanmar (Burma) has been run by a military junta since 1991. It is principally known for its extremely profitable trade in illegal drugs and a high rate of AIDS—some 500,000 out of the 41 million population. Economic indices become less than dependable in the face of the extremely active black market activities, but latest figures indicate a per capita GDP of $1900. The Nobel Peace Prize Laureate Aung San Suu Kyi (OWNG SAN SOO KEE), who has struggled for democracy in her country, was placed under house arrest for most of the time between 1991 and 2002, when restrictions were tentatively lifted by the junta.

The Philippines

The Philippines since World War II have had a complex relationship with the United States. For almost half a century, the United States ruled the Philippines as a colony. In 1946, the country became politically independent—though militarily and economically dominated by the United States for the next 20 years. Wealthy families dominated the democratically elected government, postponing the necessary changes to overcome poverty, rural landlessness, and underdevelopment. While Manila and other cities became showcases of modernity, other sectors lagged. When Ferdinand Marcos and his wife Imelda took power in 1965, he

Philippine President Gloria Macapagal Arroyo addresses her people as she arrives at the presidential palace for the first time in January 2001.

instituted a policy he called "constitutional authoritarianism." His authoritarian rule was hardened in 1972 when he declared martial law. Unfortunately, U.S. presidents, fearful of the spread of communism, supported the Marcos dictatorship. His wife was put in charge of building Manila, and in the process the two Marcoses plundered the Philippines economy, while ruling with an iron fist. Communist and Islamic insurgencies developed under this repression. Finally, in the 1980s, even business interests in the Philippines were alienated from the Marcoses, and together with religious interests, the poor, the intellectuals, and brave people throughout the islands, they ousted Marcos.

Marcos was forced from office in 1986 by the "People Power" election of Corazon Aquino, widow of the heroic opposition leader murdered by Marcos's forces in 1983. The built-up resentment against Marcos and his U.S. backers as well as volcanic eruptions led to the Americans' closing their last base in the Philippines in 1992. Since then, the country has made considerable economic progress, and it is one of the few bright lights in the region. Throughout the 1990s, the Philippines maintained a favorable balance of trade and saw its GDP climb to $3800 per capita. Politically, factionalism within the government led to the unseating of Joseph Estrada, who was elected in 1998, in 2001. More than 100,000 of his opponents demonstrated in the streets for his removal from office on the grounds of massive corruption. When the leaders of the armed forces joined them, Estrada left office, to be succeeded by his vice president, Gloria Macapagal Arroyo, who was reelected in 2004.

Since 2000, the Philippines government has had to deal with the continual threat of communist guerrillas and Muslim separatists. The former have been contained, while the latter group—a minority within the 5 percent of the country that is Muslim—has carried out kidnappings that have embarrassed the government. Linkages with international terrorist movements have increased concern in the Philippines. For the first time in 10 years, American military forces are back on Philippine soil to assist the army in combating the Muslim separatist forces.

THE SUBCONTINENT

▪ *What role did ethnicity and religion play in the formation of new nations in South Asia after 1947?*

In the Indian subcontinent, the western thrust of the Japanese armies in World War II and the appeal of Subhas Chandra Bose's alliance with Japan against Britain induced the British government to negotiate with Indian nationalist leaders. In 1942 Britain offered India independence and the option of joining the British Commonwealth when the war ended. But Gandhi called this a "postdated cheque on a failing bank" and called for a forceful "Quit India" movement. During and immediately after the war, tensions between the Muslim and Hindu populations in India, which had been compounded by the British administration, were inflamed. The minority Muslim population was fearful that when the British withdrew, it would be targeted and dominated by the Hindu majority.

Partition

When World War II ended and it became apparent that the British would indeed leave India, the shape the new state would take was vigorously contested. The Indian National Congress, founded in 1885 and the primary Indian nationalist organization, had had great success in the 1936–1937 elections and took the lead in negotiations for independence with the British government. Congress included many Muslim members, but in the late 1930s the Muslim League, guided by onetime Congress member Muhammad Ali Jinnah, began to agitate vigorously for separate Muslim seats, though not at first for a separate Muslim state. Muslims constituted one-fifth of the population of the subcontinent, and many Muslims feared majority Hindu rule. Gandhi had envisioned an independent India where all communal groups shared in governance and lived in harmony. But India had a long history of ethnic hostilities dating to the medieval era.

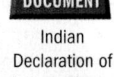

DOCUMENT
Indian Declaration of Independence

DOCUMENT
Gandhi: Against the Partition of India

This religious animosity and mistrust, the presence of armed, demobilized World War II soldiers in the countryside, and the insecurity produced by negotiations over the future nature of the Indian state resulted in communal violence and chaos in some provinces as the British prepared to leave India. Jinnah sought strength for his vision of "Pakistan"—a collection of Muslim-majority provinces within a unified India and equal voice for Muslims and Hindus. This would weaken the central government while strengthening the provinces. Jawaharlal Nehru, the leader of the Congress party, rejected this proposal in favor of a strong central state that would encourage economic development. Talks broke down, and violent riots broke out. Thousands were killed as Hindus, Muslims, and now Sikhs took to the streets. The Muslim League decided to support a separate state.

DOCUMENT
Jinnah, the "Father" of Pakistan

Lord Mountbatten arrived in India as British viceroy in March 1947 to help settle the turmoil but promptly determined that the date for British withdrawal should be moved up. Although the Muslim League's demand for a separate state called Pakistan did not represent the wishes of all Muslims, Mountbatten was persuaded that India must be partitioned along religious lines. Accordingly, when the British withdrew, they divided the subcontinent into Hindu and Muslim sectors. On August 12, 1947, they handed over the reins of government to two new sovereign states, India and Pakistan. India was a huge nation comprising most of the subcontinent. The new Muslim state of Pakistan consisted, awkwardly, of two chunks of land separated by 1000 miles of Indian territory. Although Jinnah was not satisfied with the land allocated to the new state, he had little choice but to accept the British division. As it turned out, however, the borders drawn in 1947 would not be final.

Defining the boundaries of the new states was not easily accomplished. For one thing, the British had not directly ruled all of India. Nearly 600 Indian princes were governing about 40 percent of the subcontinent in autonomous or semiautonomous states. These principalities, based primarily on timeworn landlord-client relations and peasant labor, had to be incorporated into the new political entities. The boundary lines of the two new nations, which took months to formalize, also sacrificed existing economic, ethnic, and linguistic affinities in order to ensure religious divisions. Partition radically disrupted longstanding patterns of commerce, social relations, and people's day-to-day lives. As occurred with the drawing of new national boundaries in the Middle East, families were separated—some members residing in one state, while others nearby resided in another.

DOCUMENT
The Tandon Family at Partition

As the boundaries were drawn, many Indians, fearful of discrimination and communal violence, left their homes: Muslims to migrate or flee to Pakistan and Hindus to the new state of India. Millions became refugees. Hundreds of thousands died in the relocation process or in the riots, killings, and panic produced by the hastily imposed partition. This terrible slaughter is engraved in the memories of the citizens of the two nations and has contributed to the continuation of communal violence. One example of the chaos and instability created out of this ill-conceived slashing of new national boundaries is the princely state of Jammu and Kashmir. Jammu and Kashmir had an overwhelmingly Muslim population but a Hindu ruler who had submitted to the British crown; furthermore, it was located in the wide swath of contested borderlands between the two proposed states. Although Kashmir was ultimately allocated to the new state of India, that allocation has been contested on and off ever since partition. Kashmir remains a critical source of conflict in the tense relationship between India and Pakistan. Following the shedding of much blood over Kashmir, serious negotiations between India and Pakistan began in 2004.

Partition had additional painful consequences. Thousands of women were raped and kidnapped, to be distributed as spoils of war. The two governments attempted to right this wrong by repatriating these women to their "rightful" country. But their former families often did not want them back and many of the women themselves had made new families, so the problem could not be easily resolved. Another painful outcome was the murder of Mahatma Gandhi on January 30, 1948, by a Hindu nationalist. In subsequent years, violent Hindu nationalism would challenge India's democracy.

DOCUMENT
Women in Karimpur, India

India: The World's Largest Democracy

Of the long list of states that became independent after 1945, few have retained genuine liberal regimes. Until 1975 the sole outstanding example was India, the world's largest democratically governed state. In its first half-century of independence, India's government was dominated by the Congress party, which had in turn emerged out of the nationalist struggle in the context of British rule. But as the fledgling nation established itself, new indigenous forces began to percolate to the top, expressing a certain unease with secular government and those who endorsed it. Especially from the late 1970s onward, separatist movements also challenged the notion of Indian unity, posing the threat of a new partition.

After independence, India's parliament functioned with little friction. This success was due to the efforts of a cadre of very skilled and capable men in the Congress party (see Chapter 29). One of them was Jawaharlal Nehru, the country's first prime minister, who held that office from 1947 to 1964 and was an Anglophile of sorts and an ardent devotee of democratic government. Nehru asserted the power of strong central government while trying to manage the decentralizing tendencies of his large, polyglot, multiethnic state. He sought to maintain close relations with both the Soviet Union and China, often to the discomfort of the United States. Relations with China, however, were compromised by a border conflict that led to a major military action in the first part of the 1960s and acted as a drain on India's economy. Nehru, along with Egypt's President Nasser and Yugoslavian President Tito, was a founder of the **Nonaligned Nations Movement,** which aimed to avoid commitment to either the

Nonaligned Nations Movement—Organization of approximately 100 countries not formally allied with a major power bloc. Founded in 1961, the movement struggles to find relevance in a post–Cold War era.

Document Nehru and the Two Sides of Kashmir

On August 15, 1947, the Indian Independence Act came into effect. The princely states like Jammu and Kashmir (here called "Kashmir") were allowed to decide which new state, India or Pakistan, they would join. Hari Singh, the Hindu prince (maharaja) of Kashmir, which had a predominantly Muslim population, delayed his decision. Meanwhile, by October 1947, communal violence has exploded in the Punjab, and India accused Pakistan of sponsoring raids and incursions into Kashmir. The maharaja of Kashmir requested military assistance from India and ultimately acceded to union with that state. Jawaharlal Nehru, India's new prime minister, then sent troops into Kashmir. What follows is Nehru's defense of the Indian invasion. Although the union of Kashmir to India was completed, parts of the original territory remained under Pakistani control, and the two states have fought an on-again, off-again war over the province. Within Kashmir, certain segments of the population (divided along communal and linguistic lines) have supported India; others have supported Pakistan; still others have struggled for Kashmiri independence. (Sheikh Abdullah was a prominent Muslim leader who supported a secular state and worked for Kashmiri autonomy; he became prime minister of Kashmir in 1948 but was later imprisoned for 11 years for refusing to pledge loyalty to India.)

[Speech of Nehru before Constituent Assembly of India, November 25, 1947, on the defense of Kashmir]. . . . In accepting the accession, however, we made it perfectly clear to the Maharaja that his government must be carried on in future according to the popular will and that Sheikh Abdullah should be charged with the formation of an interim government. . . . Sheikh Abdullah, in our opinion, had undoubtedly the support of the large majority of the people of Kashmir, Muslims, Hindus, and Sikhs. Further, we made it clear that as soon as law and order had been restored in Kashmir and her soil cleared of the invaders, the question of the State's accession should be settled by reference to the people. . . .

The civilian population, completely unarmed, with the enemy within a few miles of the city, behaved in a manner which showed extraordinary courage and coolness. They did so, because they had a great leader and because Hindus, Muslims, and Sikhs all joined together under him to throw back the enemy and to save Kashmir, their common heritage. . . .

I should like to say here that certain events happened near Jammu early in November which I regret very deeply. The Muslim convoys of evacuees [to Pakistan] were being taken away from Jammu when they were attacked by non-Muslim refugees and others and a large number of casualties were inflicted. The troops escorting them did not play a creditable role. I might add that none of our troops were present or had anything to do with this. . . .

The House is aware that the Pakistan Government have protested emphatically against our action in Kashmir. In doing so they have used language which is not becoming in any government and have alleged fraud and conspiracy on our part. I need only say that I am completely convinced that every action that the Government of India has taken in regard to Kashmir has been straight and above board and it can defend it at any time before the world. . . .

I cannot say this of the Pakistan Government. Their case is that the genesis of the trouble was the extensive killing of Muslims in Eastern Punjab and Kashmir and that the raid on Kashmir was a spontaneous reaction to this on the part of the tribesmen. I think this is completely untrue. I regret deeply that in parts of the Jammu province Muslims were killed and driven out. This of course has had nothing to do with our Government or our forces. But this mutual killing has been a very tragic feature during these past months in the Punjab, and Jammu was powerfully affected by this. We have sufficient evidence in our possession to demonstrate that the whole business of the Kashmir raids both in the Jammu province and in Kashmir proper was deliberately organized by the high officials of the Pakistan Government. . . . It is impossible to escape the conclusion that the raids on Kashmir were carefully planned and well organized by the Pakistan authorities with the deliberate object of seizing the State [Kashmir] by force and then declaring accession to Pakistan. . . . If we had allowed this scheme to succeed, we would have been guilty of the betrayal of the people of Kashmir and of a grave dereliction of duty to India. . . . The issue in Kashmir is whether violence and naked force should decide the future or the will of the people. . . .

Questions to Consider

1. Without trying to decide which state was "entitled" to Kashmir, look at the language of Nehru's speech. How does he legitimize India's action?
2. Under conditions such as occurred with the Partition of India, how might the "will of the people," in any given place, be determined?
3. Nehru suggests that India's troops had no part in or responsibility for the communal violence. Compare this situation to other situations of conflict and violence that you have encountered in world history.

From Dorothy Norman, ed., *Nehru, The First Sixty Years*, Vol. 2 (New York: John Day, 1965), pp. 349–352.

United States or the Soviet Union in the context of the Cold War. Through this movement, states like India hoped to assert their autonomy and to have a real voice in world affairs.

Nehru's daughter, Indira Gandhi (no relation to Mohandas Gandhi), was elected prime minister in 1966. The Congress party hoped to use her, as Nehru's daughter and a well-loved and highly visible public figure, to guarantee its position of power. But she proved to be less malleable than Congress leaders had expected and moved to consolidate her own power and achieve a new political stability for India. Her popularity reached a peak with the defeat of Pakistan in a 1971 war that led to the creation of the country of Bangladesh out of East Pakistan. From 1972 to 1974, however, India's mildly socialist economy was battered by serious crop failures, food riots, strikes, and student unrest. In the face of mounting opposition, and claiming to act in defense of national unity, Gandhi declared a state of emergency in June 1975 and took over direct control of the government. She jailed 10,000 of her critics, imposed press censorship, and suspended fundamental civil rights.

With the opposition muzzled, the people were exhorted to "work more and talk less." After a year, the new order claimed numerous gains, advances in productivity, a drop in inflation, curbs in the black market, and more widespread birth control measures to alleviate India's population pressures. Although Gandhi declared that her drastic measures were only temporary, some critics observed that she was trying to move "from dictatorship to dynasty."

In 1977 Gandhi released political prisoners and announced that national elections would be held. But many Indians had been alienated by her draconian policies, which included forced sterilizations, in an attempt to control India's skyrocketing population, and the bulldozing of some of the Delhi slums. These "reforms" targeted the poor. A coalition of opposition parties defeated Gandhi in the elections and brought Moraji Desai (moh-RAH-jee de-SAI) to the prime ministry. Democratic freedoms were restored, but the coalition failed to hold together, and Indian voters returned Gandhi to power in 1979. She promised the country strong leadership, with no more "excesses." For the next 4 years she pursued a neutral course, reflecting the geopolitical position in which India found itself. India's close ties with the USSR served as a defensive shield against China. The 1979 Soviet invasion of Afghanistan constituted an indirect threat to India, but Gandhi refrained from criticizing the action.

Although India achieved a certain economic success and political prominence under Indira Gandhi, it also faced serious ethnic and communal conflicts. In the south and in Sri Lanka, the culturally and linguistically distinct Tamils agitated for independence. In the north, the religiously and linguistically distinct Sikhs, who constitute a majority in the state of Punjab, also entertained separatist aspirations.

The Sikh religion dates to the early sixteenth century when the mystic Nanak founded a monotheistic creed that was influenced by both Hinduism and Islam. The Sikhs, whose territories were divided in the 1947 partition, had a golden temple in their sacred city of Amritsar. When Sikh extremists took over and occupied the temple in 1984, Gandhi sent in the army to blast them out. This reckless act was considered a desecration of the Sikh temple and led to an explosion of rioting and violence. In October of that year Gandhi was assassinated by members of her Sikh bodyguard.

Indira Gandhi was succeeded by her son Rajiv, a former pilot and political novice who soon showed a surprising degree of confidence and competence in governing the world's largest democracy, with more than 800 million citizens. Rajiv consolidated his political position and moved India toward a more Westernized, capitalist orientation. Still, the country's widespread poverty, exploding population, and internal divisions, especially the long-standing Kashmir border dispute with Pakistan and the continued challenges of Sikh and Tamil separatism, posed significant problems for Gandhi's administration. He was defeated in elections at the end of 1989 and replaced by V. P. Singh of the

India After Independence

1947	Independence from Britain
1947–1964	Jawaharlal Nehru, prime minister
1966	Indira Gandhi, Nehru's daughter, becomes prime minister
1971	India defeats Pakistan; Bangladesh formed
1975	Indira Gandhi declares emergency, assumes dictatorial powers
1977	Moraji Desai, prime minister
1979	Indira Gandhi reelected
1984	Gandhi assassinated; son Rajiv succeeds her
1991	Rajiv Gandhi assassinated
1998	Bharatiya Janata (BJP), Hindu nationalist party, wins elections
2004	Congress under Sonia Gandhi's leadership wins elections; Manmohan Singh becomes Prime Minister

National Front party, which proved unable to consolidate its power. In 1991 new elections returned the Congress party to power, but not before Rajiv Gandhi was assassinated by a Tamil separatist.

After independence, the Indian government had pursued Mohandas Gandhi's ideal of self-sufficiency. It insisted on indigenous control of the economy and emphasized developing the production of consumer goods at home rather than relying on imports. It demanded 51 percent Indian control of foreign companies on its soil, even refusing to let the Coca-Cola Company operate in India unless it shared its secret formula. In these efforts, India was relatively successful, developing many locally produced goods. During the first half of the 1990s, however, Indian leaders abandoned many of the socialist foundations of their economic structure and introduced various aspects of the capitalist market economy. Analysts had pointed out during the 1980s that India possessed the largest essentially untapped middle-class market in the world. With the entry of market forces into the country, the Indian economy expanded. The countryside had gained self-sufficiency in the 1970s and 1980s. Now it was the turn of the cities and the business community to become major players in the international economy.

In 1995 P. V. Narasimha Rao was the only prime minister not in the bloodline of the Nehru-Gandhi dynasty to have lasted through the first half of a parliamentary term. Working with his finance minister, Manmohan Singh, and enjoying the total support of the business community, he continued to pursue market reforms. India's economy continued to grow under the changes in the central government in the 1990s.

While the large cities of India developed an upwardly mobile and cosmopolitan middle class, those same cities have seen their infrastructures overwhelmed by population growth, in-migration from the countryside, and the air pollution produced by industrialization and the increasing numbers of the middle classes who own motorized vehicles. Delhi and Bombay, for example, are crammed with squatters' huts that have become permanent settlements. Large swathes of huts, in places like public parks and along railroad tracks, are periodically bulldozed. Thousands of residents then either promptly rebuild them or are forced into the streets to search for living space elsewhere. Although municipal governments try to regulate the movement of trucks, the large numbers of diesel-powered vehicles create air pollution that has increased the incidence of respiratory and heart disease, even among the young.

The communal hostilities inflamed by partition have not ended half a century after independence. The constitution of India aimed to make all citizens equal before the law. All Indians were entitled to receive an education in their own language and in the language of the state, Hindi. But caste, class, and communal differences (as elsewhere in the world) were not so readily eradicated. Upper-caste Hindus resisted privileges, such as guaranteed slots in university and civil service positions, given by the government to the members of the Untouchable caste. In response, the **Untouchables,** taking the name *Dalits* ("the oppressed"), organized politically.

In the 1980s, Hindu parties mobilized to make India an indelibly Hindu state, rejecting the secular and egalitarian ideals of Gandhi and Nehru and of the Indian constitution. Hindu-Muslim tensions crystallized around a sixteenth-century mosque at Ayodhya, which was said to be the birthplace of the Hindu Lord Ram. Stirred by Hindu nationalist politicians, Hindu militants tore the mosque down by hand in 1992, prompting further intercommunal violence. In the 1996 elections, the Hindu nationalist Bharatiya Janata

Untouchables—Persons outside the four *varnas,* historically employed in leatherwork, burials, and similar occupations.

Hindu militants attack the mosque at Ayodhya, which became a symbol of Hindu-Muslim conflict in India.

party (bah-RAH-tee-ya jah-NAH-tah; BJP), representing business and entrepreneurial interests, won 186 seats in parliament, up from only two seats in 1984. In 1998 the BJP won the Indian elections, prompting new fears that Muslims, Sikhs, and other minorities would suffer under Hindu rule. Shortly after coming to power, the BJP enhanced its popularity among Indians and sent a message of warning to China and Pakistan when it set off a series of nuclear bomb tests. In so doing, India initially alienated its Western allies but staked its claim as a major power for the next century. Prime Minister Vajpayee of the BJP, however, began to move toward better relations with Pakistan, especially over the issue of Kashmir, and supported modern high-tech development in the years before the BJP's defeat at the polls in 2004. The Congress party was returned to power with Manmohan Singh (mahn-MOH-hahn SING) as prime minister, and though it promised greater assistance to the poor, who were left behind as the Indian economy boomed in recent years, the trend of increasing internationalization and economic growth is likely to continue.

Modern South Asia

Pakistan

Pakistan's two distant parts had religion in common but not language or culture. When Jinnah, the primary voice for the creation of Pakistan and its constitutional government, died in 1948, the artificially constructed state splintered as each region pursued its own local agenda. Meanwhile, Pakistan had to contend with challenges on its borders with India and Afghanistan. In a broader frame, Pakistan joined U.S.-backed alliances to contain the Soviet Union and, in return, benefited from U.S. aid.

In 1958 General Mohammad Ayub Khan came to power. His regime gave Pakistan reasonable stability and some relief from corrupt politicians, and under his tutelage, the country made economic progress. Ten years later, however, pent-up dissatisfaction against corruption in the government led to a new military dictatorship under General Yahya Khan. Regionalism continued to be a major problem. The more prosperous West Pakistan dominated and exploited East Pakistan, and the East's grievances escalated into riots and threats of secession.

The Pakistani government sent troops into East Pakistan in 1971 in response to an uprising. This attack and the depredations committed by the troops caused an influx of East Pakistani refugees into India. India intervened on behalf of East Pakistan, defeating the central government's forces and encouraging the region to break away. In 1972 East Pakistan became the new state of Bangladesh. Bangladesh, covering an area not much larger than the state of Arkansas, was an instantaneous economic disaster with twice the population density of Japan. The Bangladeshi population in 2000 was approximately 130 million (about half the population of the United States), while the per capita GNP was a mere $260. Like Indonesia, Bangladesh is home to a significant percentage of the world's Muslims; the number of Bangladeshi pilgrims journeying to Mecca every year is second only to the number of Indonesians.

A civilian government was established in Pakistan in 1970, led by Zulkifar Ali Bhutto (1928–1979), a populist leader who had been educated at universities in Oxford and Berkeley. Throughout the 1970s, Pakistan's economic problems persisted, along with its domestic instability. Bhutto was overthrown in 1977 by General Mohammad Zia ul-Haq (ZEE-ah ool-HAHK), who had him executed in 1979. The new military dictator, who faced widespread opposition, invoked martial law and postponed elections. Like his predecessors, he had to contend with both Indian hostility and potential Soviet intervention. Pakistan retained its traditional alignment with China, while India kept close ties with Moscow.

In 1979 the Iranian Revolution and the Soviet invasion of Afghanistan enhanced the importance of Pakistan's Cold War alliance with the West. Meanwhile, a contingent of 36 Islamic foreign ministers meeting in Pakistan condemned the Soviet aggression against the Afghan people. In 1981 Pakistan negotiated for a substantial American aid agreement, providing for $3.2 billion in arms over a period of 6 years. Pakistan thereafter served as the American support base for the Afghan resistance against the Soviets. Meanwhile, thousands of Afghan refugees flooded into Pakistan where many of them led lives of misery, crowded into refugee camps and challenging an already overburdened Pakistani economy.

In 1985 Zia ul-Haq lifted martial law; he was killed in 1988 in a plane crash. Bhutto's daughter Benazir, the first woman elected to govern a Muslim nation, succeeded him at the age of 35. She remained in office for 20 months, but her power was circumscribed. Under pressure from the army, she was dismissed after accusations of incompetence and corruption. She returned to prominence in the early 1990s and serves as an example of both the strength of political dynasties in South Asia and the ability of well-placed Muslim women to hold positions of great power. In the fall of 1999, the military under General Parvez Musharraf again seized power in Pakistan, demonstrating the continued power of the military in politics and popular discontent with its civilian governments.

Like India, Pakistan continues to grapple with the problems of high population growth and uneven economic development. Relations between India and Pakistan remain tense, especially over the issue of

Document Benazir Bhutto at Harvard

Benazir Bhutto became Pakistan's first female prime minister in 1988. She came from an elite Muslim family and had led a life of wealth and privilege. Her father, elected president by popular mandate in 1970, was executed in 1979 by the military dictator Zia ul-Haq (1977–1988). In Pakistan, Benazir Bhutto's election held the promise of a new era of democracy and progress. In the West, she was viewed as a leader likely to modernize, Westernize, and ally her nation with the United States. She had, after all, attended Radcliffe College, Harvard University. Bhutto's memoirs provide interesting insight into the Western-style education many prominent South Asians received; they also suggest the dilemma of being a "foreign" student abroad during an era of political turmoil for both Pakistan and the United States.

I was born in Karachi on June 21, 1953. . . . In our house education was a top priority. Like his father before him, my father wanted to make examples of us, the next generation of educated and progressive Pakistanis. At three I was sent to Lady Jennings Nursery School, then at five to one of the top schools in Karachi, the Convent of Jesus and Mary. Instruction at CJM was in English, the language we spoke at home more often than my parents' native languages of Sindhi and Persian or the national language, Urdu. And though the Irish nuns who taught there divided the older students into houses with inspirational names like "Discipline," "Courtesy," "Endeavor," and "Service," they made no effort to convert us to Christianity. . . .

There was no question in my family that my sister and I would be given the same opportunities in life as our brothers. Nor was there in Islam. We learned at an early age that it was men's interpretation of our religion that restricted women's opportunities, not our religion itself. . . .

[Bhutto's father was determined that she study abroad (he himself had studied at Berkeley) and at the age of sixteen she was admitted to Radcliffe.]

. . . "Pak-i-stan? Where's Pak-i-stan?" My new classmates had asked me when I first arrived at Radcliffe. "Pakistan is the largest Muslim country in the world," I replied, sounding like a handout from our embassy. "There are two wings of Pakistan separated by India." "Oh, India," came the relieved response, "You're next to India." I smarted every time I heard the reference to India, with whom we had had two bitter wars. Pakistan was supposed to be one of America's strongest allies. . . . Yet Americans seemed completely unaware of the existence of my country.

[In 1970 Bhutto's father was elected, and the union between East and West Pakistan began to break down. In March 1971 the Pakistani army attacked the East Pakistani rebels.] Looting. Rape. Kidnappings. Murder. Whereas no one had cared about Pakistan when I arrived at Harvard, now everyone did. And the condemnation of my country was universal. At first I refused to believe the accounts of the Western press of atrocities being committed by our army in what the East Bengal rebels were now calling Bangladesh. According to the government-controlled Pakistani papers my parents sent me every week, the brief rebellion had been quelled. What were these charges then, that Dacca had been burned to the ground and firing squads sent into the university to execute students, teachers, poets, novelists, doctors and lawyers? I shook my head in disbelief. . . . I found security in the official jingoistic line in our part of the world that the reports in the Western press were "exaggerated" and a "Zionist Plot" against an Islamic state. My classmates at Harvard were harder to convince. "Your army is barbaric," the accusations would come. . . . "You people are fascist dictators." . . . "We are fighting an Indian-backed insurgency," I'd lash back. "We are fighting to hold our country together, just as you did during your own Civil War." How many times since have I asked God to forgive me for my ignorance. I didn't see then that the democratic mandate for Pakistan had been grossly violated. The majority province of East Pakistan was basically treated as a colony by the minority West. . . . Eighty percent of government jobs were filled by people from the West. The central government had even declared Urdu our national language, a language few in East Pakistan understood, further handicapping the Bengalis in competing for jobs in government or education. . . . I was too young and naïve at Harvard to understand that the Pakistani army was capable of committing the same atrocities as any army let loose in a civilian population. The psychology can be deadly, as it was when U.S. forces massacred innocent civilians in My Lai [Vietnam] in 1968.

Questions to Consider

1. Bhutto's memoir was published in 1989. How might that affect her portrayal of herself, her father, and her country and its conflicts?
2. Why would an elite Muslim family send its children to an English language missionary school in Pakistan and to college in the United States?
3. What does this excerpt suggest about the ways a foreigner like Bhutto could and could not adjust to college in the United States?

From *Benazir Bhutto, Daughter of Destiny* (New York: Simon and Schuster, 1989), pp. 45–46, 54–55, 58–64.

Nuclear tests by India and Pakistan in 1998 prompted the launching of this hot-air protest balloon, which sails past the Taj Mahal in Agra, northern India.

Kashmir. In 1998 India asserted its sovereignty and defied Western nations by conducting nuclear tests. Pakistan replied shortly thereafter by exploding its own nuclear bombs, claiming that it had no choice in the face of the Indian nuclear threat. While the United Nations and established nuclear powers like the United States condemned these tests as the beginning of another nuclear arms race, citizens of Pakistan and India celebrated their respective states' tests as symbols of national power and autonomy.

The Pakistan-Afghanistan Connection

Along with the development of nuclear weapons and the long-standing conflict with India over Kashmir, the flood of Afghan refugees in the aftermath of the 1979 Soviet invasion created serious turmoil for Pakistan in both its domestic and its foreign affairs. Afghanistan, like India, had been forced to assert its independence in the context of British dominance in the region. After it gained independence in 1919, Afghanistan established a special relationship with the Soviet Union that would endure throughout much of the twentieth century. As the Cold War evolved in the 1950s and 1960s, Afghanistan became a significant client of the Soviets, while the United States cultivated Pakistan as a bulwark against Soviet expansion. The two Asian nations, however, shared many similarities. Like the boundaries between India and Pakistan, what became the boundary between Afghanistan and Pakistan had been rather arbitrarily drawn by the British. There was nothing "natural" about this national boundary; it split ethnolinguistically similar communities and caused chronic friction between the two nations. Nonetheless, Pakistan and Afghanistan shared Islam as their majority religion along with many ethnic and cultural connections. When the Soviets invaded Afghanistan in 1979, millions of Afghan refugees flooded into Pakistan, disrupting its politics and economy. As the Soviet occupation dragged on, despite significant Afghan resistance, those refugees became semipermanent residents of Pakistan.

Both Pakistan and the United States supported Afghan resistance against the Soviet occupation. Arabs from the Middle East also traveled to Afghanistan to assist in what they deemed a "holy war" against the Soviets. Among them was a young Saudi millionaire named Osama bin Laden, who would later launch the clandestine, international terrorist network known as al-Qaeda. Ultimately the Afghan resistance was successful and the Soviets began to withdraw from Afghanistan in 1988. But that withdrawal sparked a vicious civil war in Afghanistan as various factions struggled for dominance. The violence of the occupation was succeeded by the violence of civil war for the Afghan people, and a new force called the Taliban emerged to dominate Afghan politics. The Taliban ("students") were a core group of very conservative Muslim clerics and theology students who had been trained in the madrasahs (Islamic schools) of Afghanistan and Pakistan. These men, preaching "law and order" and an ultraconservative vision of Islam, mobilized followers and secured support from Pakistan. They managed to seize military control of the bulk of Afghan territory. There they established an order of sorts, and then implemented a repressive Islamic government that included the banning of music and alcohol and the sequestering of women in their homes (forbidden to attend school or work).

The Taliban regime was considered a threat by its neighbors, Iran and the newly independent Central Asian Republics; Pakistan was one of its few supporters. Ultimately, the Taliban leadership entered into an alliance with Osama bin Laden, from whom they received funding and to whom they provided sanctuary. When, in September 2001, bin Laden masterminded the attacks on the World Trade Center and Pentagon, the United States demanded that the Taliban hand him over. They refused. The United States secured the support of Pakistan (which abandoned its former clients, the Taliban) and launched a concerted air attack on Afghanistan. The Taliban were toppled from power, and Pakistan took a leading role in helping to negotiate the establishment of a new Afghan regime. But General Musharraf's support for the U.S. war effort was not popular among many of Pakistan's people, and the Afghan war provoked new hostilities between Pakistan and India, especially after an Islamic militant group based in Pakistan sent gunmen to attack the Indian parliament in December 2001. As 2002 began, troops were massed on both sides of the India-Pakistan border; those tensions have abated and India and Pakistan began negotiating improved relations in 2004. The new regime in Afghanistan remains in a precarious position, however, trying to establish some stability in a country devastated by war and by factional politics. Although there were successful elections in 2004, Taliban and other forces continue to play a role outside the capital at Kabul.

CONCLUSION

In the second half of the twentieth century, Asia remained a theater of conflicts, including those in Afghanistan, Kashmir, the Korean peninsula, Vietnam, and Indonesia. There is a complex set of reasons for these regions becoming centers of violence. These countries hold the world's fastest-growing populations, its most essential resources, and the most politically explosive situations stemming from either politics or ideology. All these countries, from richest to poorest, have been deeply affected by decolonization, the Cold War and its conclusion, and the technological revolution. All of them entered the modern era in a period of European, American, and Japanese dominance that often provoked violent encounters. Many face major economic and demographic issues that find expression in political instability. The drawing of new nation-state boundaries after World War II as imperial powers withdrew from territories like India, Korea, maritime Southeast Asia, and Indochina created massive refugee problems and inflamed ethnoreligious tensions in ways that have significantly shaped—and continue to shape—the destinies of nations in Asia.

China fought its own ideological battles before entering a period of rapid modernization after 1978. Japan emerged from the radioactive ruins of World War II to become the second largest economy in the world. South Korea, Singapore, Hong Kong, and Taiwan constructed their own economic miracles to become major players in the global economy. Indonesia and Malaysia freed themselves from the yoke of European dominance and enjoyed substantial economic progress. However, independence unleashed powerful ethnic and religious antagonisms, many of which remain unresolved. The countries of Indochina—Vietnam, Laos, Cambodia, and Burma—slowly emerged out of the generation of wars after 1945, but faced a long an difficult road to equal the progress made by other Asian nations.

After the British withdrew from the subcontinent, India and Pakistan entered a half-century of sometimes peaceful competition. The increasing power of Hindu nationalism now signals an era of continued communal violence in India, the second most populous nation in the world.

Suggestions for Web Browsing

You can obtain more information about topics included in this chapter at the websites listed below. See also the companion website that accompanies this text, **http://www.ablongman.com/brummett**, which contains an online study guide and additional resources.

Internet East Asia History Sourcebook: China Since World War II
http://www.fordham.edu/halsall/eastasia/eastasiasbook.html#
Extensive online source for links about the history of China after 1949.

History: People's Republic of China
http://www.hartford-hwp.com/archives/55/index-b.html
Numerous recent articles about economic, political, and social events in China.

Changing Relationships Between the United States and Japan
http://www.mofa.go.jp/region/n-america/us/
The relationship between the United States and Japan is a rapidly changing one. This Japanese Ministry of Foreign Affairs site provides both information and the opportunity for interchange.

Postwar Japan
http://www.lib.duke.edu/ias/eac/histwww.htm#postwar
Excellent collection assembled by the Duke University library.

Itihaas: Chronology—Independent India
http://sify.com/itihaas/independent_india/index.php
In-depth chronology of independence; most entries include subsites with text and images.

Korea
http://www.koreasociety.org

Resources for all levels of historical study. The guide for teachers is especially informative.

Southeast Asia
http://www.ocf.berkeley.edu/~sdenney

Extensive collection of documents on Vietnam, Laos, and Cambodia.

Literature and Film

In *Wild Swans: Three Daughters of China* (Doubleday, 1991) Jung Chang gives an autobiographical account of the Cultural Revolution. *White Badge, A Novel of Korea*, by Ahn Junghyo (Soho Press, 1989) relates the story of Korean soldiers who fought in the Vietnam War on the U.S. side. The book was made into a fine movie in 1992, directed by Ji-yeong Jeong. *The Rainy Spell and Other Korean Stories*, rev. ed. (M. E. Sharpe, 1997), trans. Suh Ji-moon, includes a wonderful translation of Yun Hung-gil's title story. *The Sacred Willow* (Oxford University Press, 2000), by Duong Van Mai Elliott, describes four generations in the life of a Vietnamese family. *When Heaven & Earth Changed Places* (Plume, 1993), by Le Ly Hayslip with Jay Wurts, describes a peasant girl growing up in Vietnam, Vietnamese-G.I. relationships, and her journey to America.

Difficult Daughters (Penguin, 1998), by Manju Kapur, is an intriguing exploration of gender relations and women's place. Bapsi Sidwa, in *Cracking India* (Milkweed, 1991), presents the story, at once terrifying and funny, of family relations (especially in the Parsi minority community) and the communal violence that ensued in the aftermath of Partition. Arundhati Roy's *The God of Small Things* (HarperCollins, 1998) is a literary tour de force set amid the Syriac Christian community of Kerala in the last decades of the twentieth century. The author captures many facets of contemporary Indian cultural and social life.

The Oxford Book of Japanese Short Stories, ed. Theodore W. Goosen (Oxford University Press, 2002), is an excellent collection of contemporary Japanese prose writing. The film *Ikiru* (Toho, 1952), directed by Japanese master Akira Kurosawa, is the moving portrayal of a gentle civil servant after World War II. *The Blue Kite* (Beijing Film Studio, 1993) allows a wonderful look at how political changes can even touch the smallest of lives, it is also harshly critical, in a subdued sort of way, of what happened in China during the 1950s and 1960s.

In *Two Daughters* (Columbia, 1961), the celebrated director Satyajit Ray relates a tale of poverty, kindness, and abuse in the village, and marriage customs in the city. In Ray's trilogy *Pather Panchali, Aparajito*, and *The World of Apu* (Columbia, 1955–1959), he details the life of a young man in the village, his struggles in college, marriage, and decision to become a writer.

Suggestions for Reading

An excellent survey of the first decades of the People's Republic of China is Maurice Meisner, *Mao's China and After: A History of the People's Republic* (Free Press, 1986). A useful local study of one village through war and revolution is *Chinese Village, Socialist State*, by Edward Friedman, Paul Pickowicz, Mark Selden, and Kay Ann Johnson (Yale University Press, 1991). William A. Joseph, Christine Wong, and David Zweig, *New Perspectives on the Cultural Revolution* (Harvard University Press, 1991), offers an incisive treatment of that cataclysmic era. Merle Goldman and Roderick MacFarquhar, eds., *The Paradox of China's Post-Mao Reforms* (Harvard University Press, 1999), is an excellent treatment of the last three decades. The lives of women in the post-Mao decade are cogently treated by Gail Hershatter and Emily Honig in *Personal Voices: Chinese Women in the 1980s* (Stanford University Press, 1988).

The best book on the immediate postwar era in Japan is John Dower, *Embracing Defeat: Japan in the Wake of World War II* (W. W. Norton, 1999). *Postwar Japan as History*, ed. Andrew Gordon (University of California Press, 1993), is a fine collection of essays on a wide range of topics. For an insightful examination of the meaning of late-twentieth-century history, see Norma Field, *In the Realm of a Dying Emperor: A Portrait of Japan at Century's End* (Pantheon Books, 1991).

For a comprehensive collection of excellent articles on Southeast Asia, see Nicholas Tarling, *The Cambridge History of Southeast Asia: Nineteenth and Twentieth Centuries* (Cambridge University Press, 1992). On the Philippines, see Jose Arcilla, *An Introduction to Philippine History*, 4th ed. (Ateneo de Manila Press, 1999), and Stanley Karnow, *In Our Image: America's Empire in the Philippines* (Ballantine Books, 1990). Women in Southeast Asia and other Asian countries are treated in Louise Edwards and Mina Roces, eds., *Women in Asia: Tradition, Modernity and Globilisation* (University of Michigan Press, 2000).

Robert Dujarric has edited a solid study dealing with the complexities of bringing North and South Korea together in *Korean Unification and After: U.S. Policy Toward a Unified Korea* (Hudson Institute, 2000). The role of Korean women in national definition is studied in Elaine H. Kim and Chungmoo Choi, eds., *Dangerous Women: Gender and Korean Nationalism* (Routledge, 1997).

Some valuable surveys of modern India include Stanley Wolpert, *A New History of India*, 7th ed. (Oxford University Press, 2004); Sugata Bose and Ayesha Jalal, *Modern South Asia: History, Culture, and Political Economy* (Routledge, 1998); and Barbara D. Metcalf and Thomas R. Metcalf, *A Concise History of India* (Cambridge University Press, 2001). On Afghanistan, see Ahmed Rashid, *Taliban* (Yale University Press, 2000).

Credits

Chapter 1

2 University of Pennsylvania Museum (neg #30-12-702); **3** John Reader/Science Photo Library/Photo Researchers, Inc.; **4** John Reader/Science Photo Library/Photo Researchers, Inc.; **6** Drawing of Paleolithic tools; **7** Des & Jen Bartlett/Bruce Coleman; **8** James Mellaart; **11** Erich Lessing/Art Resource, NY; **16** Courtesy, The Oriental Institute of the University of Chicago. Photo by Victor J. Boswell, Jr. (sm8601); **18** Kurt Scholz/Egyptian National Museum, Cairo/SuperStock; **20** ©The Trustees of the British Museum (EA 921); **21** ©The Trustees of the British Museum; **23** ©The Trustees of the British Museum; **24** ©Sandro Vannini/CORBIS; **26** The Metropolitan Museum of Art, Gift of Norbert Schimmel Trust, 1989. (1989.281.10) Photograph ©1992 The Metropolitan Museum of Art; **32** ©The Trustees of The British Museum

Chapter 2

38 Gansu Provincial Museum,Wang Lu/China Stock; **41** The Avery Brundage Collection, B60P377 ©Asian Art Museum of San Francisco, Chong-Moon Lee Center For Asian Art and Culture. Used by permission.; **43** Imagine China; **44** Musée Cernuschi, Musées des Arts de l'Asie de la Ville de Paris; **48** ©Bettmann/CORBIS; **53** Don Hamilton Photo & Film; **55** Werner Forman/Art Resource, NY; **58** Christie's Images; **58** Robert Harding Picture Library Ltd.

Chapter 3

65 Jean-Louis Nou/akg – images; **67** MacQuitty International Collection, London; **68** Jean-Louis Nou/akg – images; **68** National Museum of India, New Delhi/Bridgeman Art Library; **76** Jean-Louis Nou/akg – images; **82** Burstein Collection/CORBIS; **84** British Library/The Art Archive; **85** Ministero per I Beni e le Attivitá Culturali Soprintendenza Archeologica; **86** Jean-Louis Nou /akg – images; **90** ©Adam Woolfitt/CORBIS; **91** "Vessel in the Form of an Ax," 2nd cent. B.C. to 5th cent. A.D. The Metropolitan Museum of Art, Purchase, George McFadden Gift and Edith Perry Chapman Fund, 1993. (1993.525) Photograph by Bruce White. ©1993 The Metropolitan Museum of Art

Global Issue Essay

94 ©Reuters/CORBIS

Chapter 4

97 Scala/Art Resource, NY; **99** Michael Holford Photographs; **100** Nimatallah/Art Resource, NY; **101** Scala/Art Resource, NY; **105** Réunion des Musées Nationaux/Art Resource, NY; **113** Courtesy, The Manchester Museum, The University of Manchester (Fx 568); **118** akg – images; **119** © Charles O'Rear/CORBIS; **121** "Dionysos, Ariadne & Pan." Hellenic Ministry of Culture/Archaeological Receipts Fund/TAP Service; **126** Erich Lessing /Art Resource, NY; **127** ©Araldo de Luca/Corbis

Chapter 5

130 Vanni/Art Resource, NY; **133** Scala/Art Resource, NY; **136** Scala/Art Resource, NY; **143** Archivo Fotografico Musei Capitolini/INDEX, Firenze; **146** Werner Forman Archive/Art Resource, NY; **148** The Art Archive/Museo della Civilta Romana Rome/Dagli Orti; **149** Scala/Art Resource, NY; **149** The J. Paul Getty Museum, Villa Collection, Malibu, California. ©J. Paul Getty Museum; **150** Scala/Art Resource, NY; **151** Israel Museum, Jerusalem, Israel/Ancient Art and Architecture Collection Ltd/Bridgeman Art Library; **156** ©Araldo de Luca/Corbis;**159** Scala/Art Resource, NY

Chapter 6

164 ©Diego Lezama Orezzoli/CORBIS; **167** Duane Preble; **171** ©Christel Gerstenberg/CORBIS; **171** Woodfin Camp & Associates; **172** Ronald Sheridan/Art Resource, NY; **174** akg – images; **176** The Granger Collection, New York; **179** Scala/Art Resource, NY; **183** Bibliothèque Nationale, Paris, France/Bridgeman Art Library; **187** Roger-Violett/Getty Images; **190** ©The State Russian Museum/CORBIS

Chapter 7

194 Bibliotek Nationale/akg – Images; **198** By permission of the British Library; **201** "The Night Journey of Muhammad on His Steed, Buraq," 1514. Leaf from the "Bustan" (underline) of Sa'di, copied by calligrapher Sultan-Muhammad Nur. The Metropolitan Museum of Art, Purchase, Louis V. Bell Fund and Astor Foundation Gift, 1974. (1974.294.2) Photograph by Schecter Lee. Photograph ©1986, The Metropolitan Museum of Art; **204** Qisas al-Anibiya, folio 152v, illustration: "Jesus Performs Miracle of Loaves." (Spencer Persian MS 46) Spencer Collection, The New York Public Library, Astor, Lenox and Tilden Foundations; **204** Qisas al-Anibiya, "Moses Turns Staff into a Dragon." Spencer Persian Manuscript, 46, folio 82. Courtesy, the Spencer Collection, The New York Public Library, Astor, Lenox and Tilden Foundations; **205** Reproduced by kind permission of the Trustees of the Chester Beatty Library, Dublin; **210** The Imagebank Films/Getty Images; **210** The Bodleian Library, University of Oxford (MS Ouseley Add 24 folio 55v); **212** Bibliothèque Nationale de France (Ms. Ar. 5847 fol. 138v.); **212** akg – images; **215** The Art Archive/Egyptian Museum Cairo/Dagli Orti; **216** The Bodleian Library, University of Oxford (MS Pococke 375 folio 3v-4r); **219** ©SuperStock, Inc.

Global Issue Essay

223 ©Gianni Dagli Orti/CORBIS

Chapter 8

224 bpk, Berlin/Art Resource, NY; **228** Sarha Errington/Hutchinson Library of Holland Park, Ltd.; **229** Erich Lessing/Art Resource, NY; **230** Werner Forman/Art Resource, NY; **234** Georger Gerster/Photo Researchers, Inc.; **236** Marc & Evelyn Bernheim/Woodfin Camp & Associates; **238** Bibliothèque Nationale de France, Paris; **241** Bibliothèque Nationale de France, Paris; **244** Bibliothèque Nationale de France, Paris; **244** ©Ferdinando Scianna/Magnum Photos, Inc.; **246** ©Paul Almasy/CORBIS; **249** akg – images; **250** National Palace Museum, Taipei, Taiwan, Republic of China; **251** Marc & Evelyn Bernheim/Woodfin Camp & Associates; **252** Robert Aberman/Art Resource, NY

Chapter 9

256 ©Archivo Iconografico, S.A./CORBIS; **259** The Pierpont Morgan Library/Art Resource, NY; **259** Belt Buckle, Visigothic (Spain), Migration Period, c. 525–560. Bronze with garnets, mother-of-pearl, green glass, traces of gilding, gold foil, W 6.7 x LL 13.3 cm. ©The Cleveland Museum of Art, 2004. Purchase from the J.H. Wade Fund, 2001.119; **262** Foto Marburg /Art Resource, NY; **270** ©Archivo Iconografico, S.A./CORBIS; **271** "Des Proprietez des Choses," 1482. British Library, London, UK/Bridgeman Art Library; **273** St. Francis Receives Approval of his 'Regula Prima' from Pope Innocent III (1160–1216) in 1210, 1297–1299 (fresco), Giotto di Bondone (c.1266–1337)/San Francesco, Upper Church, Assisi, Italy, Giraudon/Bridgeman Art Library; **279** Giraudon/Art Resource, NY; **281** Carrow Psalter detail: "The Martyrdom of Thomas a Becket," English, 1250. MS W. 34 f. 15v. The Walters Art Museum, Baltimore; **282** The Metropolitan Museum of Art, Gift of George Blumenthal, 1941. (41.100.157) Photograph ©1986 The Metropolitan Museum of Art

Chapter 10

286 Werner Forman/Art Resource, NY; **291** "Krishna Battling the Horse Demon, Keshi," 5th cent. The Metropolitan Museum of Art, Purchase, Florence and Herbert Irving Gift, 1991. (1991.300) Photograph by Bruce White. Photograph ©1994 The Metropolitan Museum of Art; **292** Ric Ergenbright Photography; **296** ©Wolfgang Kaehler/CORBIS; **298** Anonymous, Chinese, Equestrienne, Tang dynasty (618–907 CE), 2nd quarter of 8th century, Earthenware with traces of polychromy, 56.2 x 48.2 cm. Mr. and Mrs. Potter Palmer Collection, 1970.1073 Photography ©The Art Institute of Chicago; **304** Fan Kuan, "Snow Mountain and Forest." China-Stock (WL-16); **305** Bibliothèque Nationale de France, Paris; **305** Victoria & Albert Museum, London/Art Resource, NY; **307** The National Palace Museum, Taipei, Taiwan, Republic of China (detail); **309** Special Collections, New York Public Library, Astor, Lenox and Tilden Foundations; **311** Art Resource, NY; **312** TNM Image Archives Source:http://TnmArchives.jp/; **314** Kyoto News Service; **316** Tokugawa Reimeikai Foundation, Tokyo, Japan/Bridgeman Art Library; **317** ©Sakamoto Photo Research Library/CORBIS; **319** ©Royalty-Free/CORBIS

Chapter 11

322 ©Werner Forman/CORBIS; **327** Bruce Coleman; **329** Justin Kerr; **330** Museo Nacional de Antropologia, Mexico City/Werner Forman/Art Resource, NY; **334** Ewing Krainin; **338** Mark C. Burnett, Ohio Historical Society, Columbus/Photo Researchers, Inc.; **339** Cahokia Mounds State Historic Site; **340** International Color Stock, Ltd./eStock Photo; **341** ©L. Clarke/CORBIS

Global Issue Essay

344 ©Asian Art & Archaeology, Inc./CORBIS

Chapter 12

346 British Library/Art Archive; **349** By permission of the British Library (Or. 5736.f.172v); **351** Weltkarte des piri Reis, 1513. Istanbul, Topkapi. Serail-Museum/akg – images; **352** "Suleyman the Magnificent," mid-16th cent. The Metropolitan Museum of Art, Rogers Fund, 1938. (38.149.1) Photograph ©1986 The Metropolitan Museum of Art; **354** From: Title page of Baudier's "Histoire . . . empereur des Turcs," 1631. Rare Books Division, Department of Rare Books and Special Collections, Princeton University Library; **356** "Portrait of a Sufi," 16th century. The Metropolitan Museum of Art, The Cora Timken Burnett Collection of Persian Miniatures and Other Persian Art Objects, Bequest of Cora Timken Burnett, 1956 (57.51.27). Photograph ©1989 The Metropolitan Museum of Art; **359** "Adam & Eve," detail, from a Falnama (Book of Omens), Iran, c.1550. Arthur M. Sackler Gallery, Smithsonian Institution, Washington, D.C.: Smithsonian Unrestricted Trust Funds, Smithsonian Collections Acquisition Program, and Dr. Arthur M. Sackler, S1986.251; **360** Folio from the "Haft Awrang" of Jami Iran, 1556–1565. Freer Gallery of Art, Smithsonian Institution, Washington, D.C.: Purchase, F1946.12.59a; **362** By Permission of the British Library (Or.3714. f.478); **364** J. Vidler/©SuperStock, Inc.; **365** Abu'l Hasan, "Allegorical Representation of Emperor Jahangir and Shah 'Abbas of Persia," South Asian, Mughal, c.1618. From the St. Petersburg Album. Full color and gold on paper; 23.8 x 15.4 cm. Freer Gallery of Art, Smithsonian Institution, Washington, D.C.: Purchase, (F1945.9a); **367** "Birth of a Prince" from an illustrated manuscript of the Jahangir-nama, Bishndas (Attributed to), Northern India, Mughal, c. 1620. Museum of Fine Arts, Boston, Francis Bartlett Donation of 1912 and Picture Fund (14.657)

Chapter 13

370 ©Craig Lovell/CORBIS; **374** "Portrait of Hung-Wu." National Palace Museum, Taipei. Photograph by Wan-go H. C. Weng; **375** By permission of the British Library, (Maps 33.c.13); **379** National Palace Museum, Taipei, Taiwan, Republic of China; **380** Victoria & Albert Museum, London/Art Resource, NY; **380** National Palace Museum, Taipei, Taiwan, Republic of China; **383**; **383** Courtesy, The Trustees of the Victoria and Albert Museum, Photograph by Ian Thomas; **388** ©Mike Yamashita/CORBIS; **390** ©Michael Maslan Historic Photographs/CORBIS; **393** ©Richard Bickel/CORBIS

Chapter 14

397 Vatican Museums and Galleries, Vatican City, Italy/Bridgeman Art Library; **401** Scala/Art Resource, NY; **402** Scala/Art Resource, NY; **402** Erich Lessing/Art Resource, NY; **404** SCALA/Art Resource, NY; **405** Erich Lessing/Art Resource, NY; **405** Scala/Art Resource, NY; **406** Bibliothèque de l'Institute de France, Paris; **407** Erich Lessing/Art Resource, NY; **408** Scala/Art Resource, NY; **408** Kunsthistorisches Museum, Vienna, Austria/Bridgeman Art Library; **409** akg – images; **410** Giraudon/Art Resource, NY; **411** ©National Gallery, London (NG 186); **411** ©Archivo Iconografico, S.A./CORBIS; **412** SCALA/Art Resource, NY; **413** Réunion des Musées Nationaux/Art Resource, NY; **417** Lucas Cranach the Younger, "Martin Luther and the Wittenberg Reformers," c.1543. Toledo Museum of Art (1926.55). Purchased with funds from the Libbey Endowment, Gift of Edward Drummond Libbey; **420** Erich Lessing/Art Resource, NY; **423** Giraudon/Art Resource, NY; **428** Scala/Art Resource, NY

Chapter 15

432 Elizabeth I, Armada portrait, c.1588 (oil on panel), English School, (16th century)/Private Collection/Bridgeman Art Library; **434** Giraudon/Art Resource, NY; **436** Ken Walsh Private Collection/Bridgeman Art Library; **437** ©CORBIS; **439** ©Austrian Archives; Haus-, Hof- und Staatsarchiv, Vienna/CORBIS; **444** Scala/Art Resource, NY; **446** Erich Lessing/Art Resource, NY; **449** ©Archivo Iconografico, S.A./CORBIS; **451** ©Archivo Iconografico, S.A./CORBIS; **455** Wallach Collection, New York Public Library, Astor, Lenox and Tilden Foundations; **456** Les Musées de la Ville de Strasbourg

Global Issue Essay

461 ©Bettmann/Corbis

Chapter 16

462 British Museum, London, UK/Bridgeman Art Library; **465** National Maritime Museum, Greenwich (HC0705); **466** ©Bettmann/CORBIS; **468** The Art Archive/Museo de Arte Antiga Lisbon/Dagli Orti; **470** Werner Forman /Art Resource, NY; **475** Bibliothèque Nationale de France, Paris; **477** ©The Trustees of the British Museum (1950AM22 1); **481** akg – images; **483** Musées Royaux des Beaux-Arts de Belgique; **487** Library of Congress (LC-USZ62-14987)

Chapter 17

490 ©Rijksmuseum, Amsterdam; **493** ©CORBIS; **495** ©CORBIS; **497** ©CORBIS; **503** Erich Lessing/Art Resource, NY; **505** Réunion des Musées Nationaux/Art Resource, NY; **506** Réunion des Musées Nationaux/Art Resource, NY; **510** Danish Royal Collections at Rosenborg Castle (#1612); **510** ©Archivo Iconografico, S.A./CORBIS; **513** Ursula Edelmann; **515** ©Bettmann/CORBIS

Chapter 18

527 Giraudon/Art Resource, NY; **529** By permission of the British Library (Maps C.6.c.3 bet 22 & 23); **531** Erich Lessing/Art Resource, NY; **533** National Portrait Gallery, London (NPG 3846); **540** Sovfoto; **542** Giraudon/Art Resource, NY; **548** Giraudon/Art Resource, NY; **549** Giraudon/Art Resource, NY; **552** Erich Lessing/Art Resource, NY

Chapter 19

560 ©Gianni Dagli Orti/CORBIS; **563** Library of Congress/Fairstreet Pictures; **564** Library of Congress/Fairstreet Pictures; **568** Jean-Loup Charmet/Bridgeman Art Library; **573** By Permission of the British Library (1047.h.16 opp.p.58 in book); **573** South African Library of Capetown/Panos Pictures; **576** Mary Evans Picture Library; **576** George McAll Theal map of South Africa; **579** Peter Newark's Pictures; **580** Roger-Viollet/Getty Images

Global Issue Essay

584 ©Bettman/CORBIS

Chapter 20

586 Museum of Fine Arts, Boston. William Sturgis Bigelow Collection, 11.19687. Photograph ©2004 Museum of Fine Arts, Boston; **590** "Birth in a Harem," late 18th century. Los Angeles County Museum of Art, The Edward Binney, 3rd Collection of Turkish Art at the Los Angeles County Museum of Art. Photograph ©2005 Museum Associates/LACMA; **593**

Mary Evans Picture Library; **597** Victoria & Albert Museum, London/Art Resource, NY; **598** ©Otto Money (photography by AIC Photographic Services); **600** Photograph Courtesy Peabody Essex Museum (Neg# 19184); **601** ©Pierre Colombel/CORBIS; **602** Giuseppe Castiglione, Italian (worked in China), 1688–1766. "Inauguration Portraits of Emperor Quianlong, the Empress, and the Eleven Imperial Consorts," 1736. Handscroll, ink and color on silk, 52.9 x 688.3 cm. ©The Cleveland Museum of Art. John L. Severance Fund, 1969.31; **605** Réunion des Musées Nationaux/Art Resource, NY; **608** Erich Lessing/Art Resource, NY; **611** Isoda Koryusai, "Hinagata Wakana Hatsumoyo" series, c.1775. Collection of The Newark Museum, Louis V. Ledoux Collection. The Newark Museum/Art Resource, NY

Chapter 21

619 ©Gianni Dagli Orti/CORBIS; **622** Museo de America; **623** ©CORBIS; **624** akg – images; **625** University of Minnesota, James Ford Bell Library; **626** ©Stapleton Collection/CORBIS; **632** The Granger Collection, New York; **632** Ohio Historical Society; **637** Georgetown University Library, Special Collections; **637** Organization of American States

Chapter 22

642 The Granger Collection, New York; **646** Erich Lessing/Art Resource, NY; **647** Historisches Archiv Fried. Krupp AG; **648** Library of Congress (LC-USZC4-2763); **655** Culver Pictures, Inc.; **660** ©Hulton-Deutsch/CORBIS; **667** akg – images; **668** Giraudon/Art Resource, NY; **668** Claude Monet, French, 1840–1926, Water Lilies, 1906, oil on canvas, 34 1/2 x 36 1/2 in. (87.6 x 92.7 cm), Mr. and Mrs. Martin A. Ryerson Collection, 1933.1157 Reproduction, The Art Institute of Chicago.

Chapter 23

672 ©Bettmann/CORBIS; **674** Culver Pictures, Inc.; **680** National Archives, Zimbabwe; **682** Africana Museum, JPL; **684** Wisconsin Historical Society; **685** Werner Forman/Art Resource, NY; **687** Centre of African Studies, University of Edinburgh, Scotland; **688** Revue Noire; **690** ©CORBIS; **693** Erich Lessing/Art Resource, NY; **694** Mary Evans Picture Library; **695** Ottoman Gazette Kalem; **698** Roger-Viollet/Getty Images; **700** Brown Brothers; **702** Réunion des Musées Nationaux/Art Resource, NY

Chapter 24

707 "Admiral Perry's Arrival in Japan in 1853," (detail). Carl H. Boehringer Collection, The Mariners' Museum, Newport News, VA; **709** The Granger Collection, New York; **713** The Granger Collection, New York; **714** General Research Division, The New York Public Library, Astor, Lenox and Tilden Foundation; **716** Photograph Courtesy Peabody Essex Museum (E79708); **723** The Metropolitan Museum of Art, Gift of Lincoln Kirstein, 1959. (JP3233-3235) Photograph ©1993 The Metropolitan Museum of Art; **724** ©Horace Bristol/CORBIS

Chapter 25

726 Photos12.com – Oasis; **731** ©Bettmann/CORBIS; **731** ©Bettmann/CORBIS; **734** ©Bettmann/CORBIS; **738** Archivo General de la Nacion, Buenos Aires, Argentina; **740** ©CORBIS; **741** Archivo General de la Nacion, Buenos Aires, Argentina; **743** New York Historical Society; **743** ©Bettmann/CORBIS

Global Issue Essay

748 ©CORBIS

Chapter 26

750 bpk, Berlin/Art Resource, NY; **752** Giraudon/Art Resource, NY; **754** Erich Lessing/Art Resource, NY; **758** ©CORBIS; **762** ©Gianni Dagli Orti/CORBIS; **764** Hulton Archive/Getty Images; **767** Hulton Archive/Getty Images; **768** Mansell Collection/Time Life Pictures/Getty Images; **772** ©Bettmann/CORBIS; **773** Courtesy, the Museum of London (#11274); **775** Ralph E.W. Earl, "Portrait of General Andrew Jackson President of the United States." Memphis Brooks Museum of Art, Memphis, TN; Memphis Park Commission Purchase 46.2; **781** The Granger Collection, New York; **784** ©Hulton-Deutsch Collection/CORBIS; **785** Stock Montage

Chapter 27

796 ©Hulton-Deutsch Collection/CORBIS; **799** ©Leonard de Selva/CORBIS; **802** ©CORBIS; **796** ©CORBIS; **806** Imperial War Museum, London; **808** Brown Brothers; **815** ©CORBIS; **817** ©Bettmann/CORBIS; **819** ©Bettmann/CORBIS; **821** Hulton Archive/Getty Images; **824** Dorothea Lange/Library of Congress; **826** Underwood & Underwood/Corbis

Chapter 28

832 ©Bettmann/CORBIS; **837** Museum of the Revolution/Sovfoto; **839** Sovfoto; **841** Sovfoto; **846** The Granger Collection, New York; **849** Erich Lessing/Art Resource, NY; **850** ©CORBIS; **854** Popperfoto/Robertstock.com; **857** David Tatlock/Petersham Book Loft; **859** ©Bettmann/CORBIS; **861** ©Bettmann/CORBIS

Chapter 29

865 ©Henri-Cartier Bresson/Magnum Photos, Inc.; **867** ©Bettmann/CORBIS; **869** ©ENA/Popperfoto/Robertstock/Retrofile; **871** akg – images; **873** Library of Congress; **875** Photos12.com – Oasis; **879** Margaret Bourke-White/Time Life Picture Collection/Getty Images; **882** AP/Wide World Photos

Chapter 30

884 ©CORBIS; **888** ©CORBIS; **890** Hulton Archive/Getty Images; **895** ©Hulton-Deutsch/CORBIS; **897** Keystone Press Agency; **898** ©CORBIS; **899** ©CORBIS; **901** Newslink Africa, London; **903** Tomham, London/The Image Works

Chapter 31

908 ©Hulton-Deutsch Collection/CORBIS; **914** The National Archives (NWDNS-208-AA-132N(2)); **915** Index s.a.s.; **919** ©CORBIS; **924** AP/Wide World Photos; **925** Hulton Archive/Getty Images; **926** ©CORBIS; **928** ©Bettmann/CORBIS; **929** Dmitry Baltermants/Sovfoto; **930** akg – images; **932** ©CORBIS; **934** ©Roger Ressmeyer/CORBIS

Global Issue Essay

938 ©Gideon Mendel/CORBIS

Chapter 32

940 ©CORBIS; **947** Sovfoto; **947** Consulate General of Germany; **947** ©CORBIS; **951** Flip Schulke/Stock Photo; **953** ©CORBIS; **954** AP/Wide World Photos; **955** ©Peter Turnley/CORBIS; **955** ©CORBIS; **958** AP/Wide World Photos; **959** Patrick Aventurier/Gamma Press, Inc.

Chapter 33

962 ©Guillermo Navarro/COVER/CORBIS; **965** ©Charles O'Rear/CORBIS; **966** ©Ron Sachs/CORBIS; **970** ©CORBIS; **972** ©Reuters/CORBIS; **973** Robert Clark/Aurora & Quanta Productions; **974** AP/Wide World Photos; **978** Peter Jordan; **982** ©CORBIS; **986** Yannis Kontos/Gamma Press, Inc.; **988** Popperfoto/Robertstock.com; **992** AP/Wide World Photos; **995** Sovfoto/Eastfoto; **999** AP/Wide World Photos; **1000** Photo Researchers, Inc.

Chapter 34

1003 AP/Wide World Photos; **1008** Dirck Halstead/Getty Images; **1010** AP/Wide World Photos; **1014** ©Bettmann/CORBIS; **1016** ©REINHARD KRAUSE/Reuters/CORBIS; **1023** ©Patrick Robert/Sygma/CORBIS; **1026** ©Reuters/CORBIS; **1027** ©CORBIS; **1031** ©Reuters/CORBIS; **1032** AP/Wide World Photos; **1033** Robert Nickelsberg/Time Life Pictures/Getty Images; **1036** Clasos Press/Gamma Press, Inc.

Chapter 35

1040 Courtesy of Mainichi Shimbun Information Center, Tokyo; **1044** ©Rene Burri/Magnum Photos, Inc.; **1046** ©Bettmann/CORBIS; **1048** ©Reuters New Media Inc./CORBIS; **1049** Time Life Pictures/Getty Images; **1051** ©CORBIS; **1053** ©Cary Wolinsky/IPN/AURORA; **1058** ©Reuters/CORBIS; **1062** ©AFP/CORBIS; **1067** Pablo Bartholomew/Getty Images; **1070** "Greenpeace Action Against Indian Nuclear Test," Taj Mahal, Agra, India. GREENPEACE/Morgan

Notes

Chapter 1

1. Harold C. Conklin, *The Relation of Hanunóo Culture to the Plant World*, doctoral dissertation, Yale University, 1954 (microfilm), p. 9. See also Claude Levi-Strauss, *The Savage Mind* (Chicago: University of Chicago Press, 1970), Chapter 1, "The Science of the Concrete."
2. Rob Stein, *Archaeology: Astronomical Structures in Ancient Egypt* (Washington, D.C.: Washington Post Company, 1998).
3. *The Code of Hammurabi*, Reverse Side, xxiv: 43–48, as quoted in Jean Bottero, *Mesopotamia: Writing, Reasoning, and the Gods* (Chicago: University of Chicago Press, 1992).
4. *The Code of Hammurabi*, Reverse Side, xxiv: 43–48.
5. From the *Epic of Gilgamesh*, trans. E. A. Speiser, in *Ancient Near Eastern Texts Relating to the Old Testament*, 2nd ed., ed. James B. Pritchard. Copyright © 1950, 1955, 1969, renewed 1978 by Princeton University Press. Reprinted by permission of Princeton University Press.
6. From the *Epic of Gilgamesh*, in Pritchard.
7. From Miriam Lichtheim, *Ancient Egyptian Literature: A Book of Readings, Three Volumes*, Vol. 2. Copyright © 1973–1980 Regents of the University of California. Reprinted by permission of the University of California Press.
8. John A. Wilson, *The Burden of Egypt* (Chicago: University of Chicago Press, 1951), p. 117.
9. Lichtheim, *Ancient Egyptian Literature*, Vol. 2, pp. 96, 98.
10. John Foster, *Love Songs of the New Kingdom* (New York: Charles Scribner's Sons, 1974), p. 72.
11. Amy Dockser Marcus, *The View from Nebo* (Little, Brown, and Company: 2000), pp. 22–28.
12. I. Finkelstein and Neil A. Silberman, *The Bible Unearthed* (New York: The Free Press, 2002), pp. 123–145 passim.

Chapter 2

1. From *The Book of Songs*, quoted in Patricia Buckley Ebrey, *The Cambridge Illustrated History of China* (Cambridge: Cambridge University Press, 1996), p. 34.
2. Michael Loewe, *The Pride That Was China* (New York: St. Martin's Press, 1990), p. 99.
3. Loewe, p. 99.
4. Loewe, p. 99.
5. Mencius, VA:5, in W. Theodore de Bary et al., trans., *Sources of Chinese Tradition* (New York: Columbia University Press, 1960), p. 96.
6. From the *Laozi*, quoted in Ebrey, p. 48.
7. Arthur Waldron, *The Great Wall of China: From History to Myth* (Cambridge: Cambridge University Press, 1990).
8. Loewe, p. 106.
9. W. Theodore de Bary, *East Asian Civilizations: A Dialogue in Five Stages* (Cambridge, Mass.: Harvard University Press, 1988), p. 19.
10. R. G. Collingwood, *The Idea of History* (New York: Galaxy Books, 1956), p. 22.
11. Kwang-Chih Chang, *The Archaeology of Ancient China*, 4th ed. (New Haven, Conn.: Yale University Press, 1987), p. 5.
12. Christopher Cullen, *Astronomy and Mathematics in Ancient China: The Zhou bi suan jing* (Cambridge: Cambridge University Press, 1996).
13. Nancy Lee Swann, *Pan Chao: Foremost Woman Scholar of China* (Ann Arbor, Mich.: University of Michigan, 2001) pp. 84–85.
14. See Loewe, ch. 18.

Chapter 3

1. Kautilya, *The Kautiliyan Arthasastra*, Part II, 2nd ed., trans. R. P. Kangle (Bombay: University of Bombay, 1972), pp. 327, 339–341.
2. Kautilya, pp. 327, 339–341.
3. Quoted in Vincent Smith, *The Oxford History of India* (Oxford: Oxford University Press, 1958), p. 131.
4. Quoted in Charles Drekmeier, *Kingship and Community in Early India* (Stanford, Calif.: Stanford University Press, 1962), p. 175.
5. From *The Interior Landscape: Love Poems from a Classical Tamil Anthology*, trans. A. K. Ramanujan (Bloomington: Indiana University Press, 1975), p. 54.
6. *The Bhagavad-Gita*, trans. Barbara Stoler Miller (New York: Bantam, 1986), pp. 46–47.
7. *The Ramayana of Valmiki*, Vol. 1, trans. Robert P. Goldman (Princeton, N.J.: Princeton University Press, 1984), p. 121.

Global Issues: Migration

1. B. Weiss, "The Decline of Late Bronze Age Civilizations as a Possible Response to Climatic Change," *Climatic Change*, Vol. 4 (1982), pp. 172–198.

Chapter 6

1. Procopius of Caesarea, *History of the Wars*, Vol. 1, 24:36–38, trans. S. R. Rosenbaum, in Charles Diehl, *Theodora: Empress of Byzantium* (New York: Ungar, 1972), pp. 87–88.
2. Geoffrey de Villehardouin, "The Conquest of Constantinople," in M. R. B. Shaw, *Chronicles of the Crusades* (Baltimore: Penguin, 1963), pp. 79, 92.
3. *The Russian Primary Chronicle*, trans. Samuel H. Cross and O. P. Sherbowitz-Wetzor (Cambridge: Mediaeval Academy of America, 1953), pp. 110–118.

Chapter 7

1. *Rubáiyát of Omar Khayyám*, trans. Edward Fitzgerald, stanzas 12, 13, 71, and 72.
2. Ibn Khaldun, *The Muqaddimah: An Introduction to History*, Vol.1, trans. Franz Rosenthal (London: Routledge & Kegan Paul, 1958), p. 71.
3. John Williams, ed., *Islam* (New York: Braziller, 1962), p. 142.

Chapter 8

1. Kevin Shillington, *History of Africa* (New York: St. Martin's Press, 1989), p. 10.
2. Terry Childs and David Killick, "Indigenous African Metallurgy: Nature and Culture," *Annual Review of Anthropology* (1993), pp. 326–327.
3. The latest synthesis of research on Bantu migrations is Jan Vansina, "A Slow Revolution: Farming in Subequatorial Africa," *Azania* 29–30 (1994–1995), pp. 15–26.
4. Richard Pankhurst, *The Ethiopians: A History* (Oxford: Blackwells, 1998), p. 40.

5. Al Omari, quoted in Tadesse Tamrat, "The Horn of Africa: The Solomonids in Ethiopia and the States of the Horn of Africa," in D. T. Niane, ed., *UNESCO General History of Africa: Africa from the Twelfth to the Sixteenth Century* (Berkeley: University of California Press, 1984), p. 435.
6. Donald Crummey, *Land and Society in the Christian Kingdom of Ethiopia from the Thirteenth to the Twentieth Century* (Oxford: James Currey, 2000), p. 29.
7. Joseph Vogel, *Encyclopedia of Precolonial Africa: Archaeology, History, Languages, Cultures, and Environment* (Walnut Creek, Calif.: AltaMira Press, 1997), p. 490.
8. Ralph Austen, "Slave Trade: Trans-Saharan Trade," in Seymour Drescher and Stanley Engerman, eds., *A Historical Guide to World Slavery* (Oxford: Oxford University Press, 1998), p. 368.
9. Al Omari, quoted in Vogel, *Encyclopedia of Precolonial Africa,* p. 492.
10. Barbara Callaway, *Muslim Hausa Women in Nigeria: Tradition and Change* (Syracuse University Press, 1989), p. 9.
11. Adu Boahen, *Topics in West African History* (Longman, 1966), p. 9.
12. Michael Pearson, *Port Cities and Intruders: The Swahili Coast, India, and Portugal in the Early Modern Era* (Johns Hopkins University Press, 1998), pp. 36–37. Pearson defines the Afrasian Sea as extending from Sofala in Mozambique to the southern tip of India.
13. Al Masudi, quoted in G. S. P. Freeman-Grenville, *The East African Coast* (Oxford: Oxford University Press, 1962), pp. 15–17.
14. A. H. J. Prins, *The Swahili-Speaking Peoples of Zanzibar and the East African Coast* (International African Institute, 1961), p. 93, quoted in Chapurukha Kusimba, *The Rise and Fall of Swahili States* (AltaMira Press, 1999), pp. 134– 5.
15. Eric Gilbert and Jonathan Reynolds, *Africa in World History from Prehistory to the Present* (Upper Saddle River, N.J.: Pearson, 2004), p. 113.

Chapter 10

1. Stanley Wolpert, *A New History of India,* 7th ed. (New York: Oxford University Press, 2004), p. 79.
2. Hermann Kulke and Dietmar Rothermund, *History of India,* 3rd ed. (London: Routledge, 1998), p. 147.
3. *Alberuni's India,* trans. Edward Sachau (New York: Norton, 1971), p. 100.
4. Minhaju-s Siraj, quoted in John Keay, *India: A History* (New York: Grove Press, 2000), p. 245.
5. Excerpt from poem by Xu Yeueying, in Kan-I Sun Chang and Haun Saussy, eds., *Women Writers of Traditional China* (Stanford, Calif.: Stanford University Press, 1999), p. 78.
6. Quoted in H. H. Gowen and H. W. Hall, *An Outline History of China* (New York: Appleton, 1926), p. 117.
7. *The Works of Li Po,* trans. Shigeyoshi Obata (New York: Dutton, 1950), no. 71.
8. Du Fu, "A Song of War Chariots," in Cyril Birch, ed., *Anthology of Chinese Literature* (New York: Grove Press, 1965), pp. 240–241.
9. Marco Polo, *The Travels of Marco Polo* (New York: Grosset & Dunlap, 1931), pp. 30, 133–149.
10. Donald Keene, ed., *Anthology of Japanese Literature: From the Earliest Era to the Mid-Nineteenth Century* (New York: Grove Press, 1955), pp. 39–41.
11. Murasaki Shikibu, "The Diary of Murasaki Shikibu," in Donald Keene, ed., *Anthology of Japanese Literature* (New York: Grove Press, 1960), p. 152.

Chapter 11

1. Quoted by Clements Markham, in Edward Hyams and George Ordish, *The Last of the Incas* (New York: Simon & Schuster, 1963), p. 88.

Global Issues: Location and Identity

1. Emanuel Bowen, *Complete Atlas of the Known World* (London, 1752), cited in Martin W. Lewis and Kären Wigen, *The Myth of Continents: A Critique of Metageography* (Berkeley: University of California Press, 1997), p. 29.
2. Just as the European-initiated paradigm of East and West influenced people outside of Europe in the past century, China's view of itself as the "Middle Kingdom" has influenced non-Chinese views of the rest of Asia. On maps of Asia, Japan sometimes gets chopped off, and in teaching about East Asia, Korea and Vietnam have only recently joined China and Japan as deserving of treatment.
3. Cited by Lewis and Wigen, p. 69.
4. Robert B. Marks, *The Origins of the Modern World: A Global and Ecological Narrative* (Lanham, Md.: Rowman and Littlefield, 2002), pp. 52–53.
5. Lewis and Wigen, p. 23.
6. An early critic of the arbitrary binary divide between East and West is Edward W. Said, *Orientalism* (New York: Pantheon, 1978).
7. Karl Wittfogel, *Oriental Despotism: A Comparative Study of Total Power* (New Haven, Conn.: Yale University Press, 1957). Because Asian agriculture—uniquely—required irrigation, Wittfogel alleged, autocratic government came into being there. The argument may be logical, but the ecological premise is wrong.

Chapter 12

1. Vincent A. Smith, *Akbar, the Great Mogul,* 2nd ed. (Mystic, Conn.: Verry, 1966), p. 522.
2. Zahiruddin Muhammad Babur, *Baburnama,* trans. and ed. Wheeler Thackston (New York: Oxford University Press, 1996), pp. 350–351.
3. Babur, p. 351.
4. Quoted in Bamber Gascoigne, *The Great Moghuls* (New York: Harper & Row, 1971), p. 128.

Chapter 14

1. Quoted in Roland Bainton, *Here I Stand: A Life of Martin Luther* (New York: Abingdon Cokesbury, 1950), p. 54.
2. Quoted in Heiko A. Oberman, *Luther, Between God and the Devil* (New Haven, Conn.: Yale University Press, 1982) p. 190, see also pp. 187–188.
3. From Henry Bettenson, ed., *Documents of the Christian Church* (New York: Oxford University Press, 1963), pp. 280–283.
4. Quoted in Harold Grim, *The Reformation Era* (New York: Macmillan, 1968), p. 17.
5. From "Institutes of the Christian Religion," in Harry J. Carroll et al., eds., *The Development of Civilization* (Glenview, Ill.: Scott, Foresman, 1970), pp. 91–93.
6. From Lowell H. Zuck, ed., *Christianity and Revolution* (Philadelphia: Temple University Press, 1975), pp. 95–97.

Chapter 15

1. Charles Tilly, ed., *The Formation of the National States in Western Europe* (Princeton, N.J.: Princeton University Press, 1975), p. 42.
2. See Charles Tilly, *Coercion, Capital, and European States, AD 990–1992* (Oxford: Blackwell, 1992).
3. Lonnie R. Johnson, *Central Europe: Enemies, Neighbors, Friends* (New York/Oxford: Oxford University Press, 1996), p. 63.
4. See K. Bosl, A. Gieysztor, F. Graus, M. M. Postan, F. Seibt, *Eastern and Western Europe in the Middle Ages,* ed. Geoffrey Barraclough (London: Thames and Hudson, 1970).
5. Wallace T. MacCaffrey, *Elizabeth I, War and Politics 1558–1603* (Princeton, N.J.: Princeton University Press, 1992), p. 6.

6. Peter F. Sugar, *Southeastern Europe under Ottoman Rule: 1354–1804,* Vol. 5 of Peter F. Sugar and Donald W. Treadgold, eds., *A History of East Central Europe* (Seattle and London: University of Washington Press, 1977), pp. 55–59, 273–274.

Chapter 16

1. Quoted in David Killingray, *A Plague of Europeans* (New York: Penguin, 1973), p. 20.
2. Quoted in Robert Rotberg, *A Political History of Tropical Africa* (New York: Harcourt Brace, 1965), pp. 85–86.
3. Quoted in John Middleton, *The World of the Swahili: An African Mercantile Civilization* (New Haven, Conn.: Yale University Press, 1992), pp. 46–47.

Chapter 17

1. Quoted in F. Tyler, *The Modern World* (New York: Farrar & Rinehart, 1939), p. 186.
2. Quoted in Robert B. Asprey, *Frederick the Great: The Magnificent Enigma* (New York: Ticknor & Fields, 1986).
3. See the superb book by Simon Schama, *The Embarrassment of Riches: An Interpretation of Dutch Culture in the Golden Age* (New York: Vintage, 1997).
4. Quoted in Pierre Gaxotte, *Frederick the Great* (London: Bell, 1941), p. 357.

Chapter 18

1. Quoted in Stillman Drake, *Galileo at Work* (Chicago: University of Chicago Press, 1978), p. 41.
2. Quoted in Stephen F. Mason, *A History of Sciences* (New York: Collier Books, 1962), p. 206.
3. Quoted in James Harvey Robinson and Charles A. Beard, *Readings in European History,* Vol. 1 (Boston: Ginn and Co., 1908), pp. 202–205.
4. Quoted in E. Neville Williams, *The Ancient Régime in Europe* (New York: Harper & Row, 1970), p. 424.

Chapter 19

1. Hilary Beckles, *Natural Rebels: A Social History* (New Brunswick, N.J.: Rutgers University Press, 1989), p. 155.
2. Richard Pankhurst, *The Ethiopians* (London: Blackwell Publishers, 1998), p. 109.
3. Donald Crummey, *Land and Society in the Christian Kingdom of Ethiopia from the Thirteenth to the Twentieth Century* (James Currey, 2000), p. 95.
4. Crummey, p. 131.

Chapter 20

1. From Walter Andrews et al., trans., *Ottoman Lyric Poetry* (Austin: University of Texas Press, 1997), p. 137.
2. Matsuo Bashō, cited in Harold G. Henderson, *An Introduction to Haiku* (New York: Doubleday, 1958), p. 18.

Chapter 21

1. Quoted in Clinton L. Rossiter, *The First American Revolution* (New York: Harcourt Brace, 1956), prefatory note.
2. Quoted in Madison Smartt Bell, *Master of the Crossroads* (New York: Pantheon, 2000).

Chapter 22

1. Charles Darwin "The Origin of Species," in *Introduction to Contemporary Civilization in the West,* Vol. 2 (New York: Columbia University Press, 1955), pp. 453–454.
2. William Wordsworth, "Composed in the Valley near Dover on the Day of Landing," in *Selected Poetry of William Wordsworth* (New York: Modern Library, 1950).
3. From John Keats, "Ode on a Grecian Urn" from *Poems* (1820).

Chapter 23

1. Adam Hochschild, *King Leopold's Ghost* (New York: Houghton Mifflin Co., 1998), p. 58.
2. *London Times,* Aug. 7, 1890.
3. David Lan, *Guns and Rain: Guerrillas and Spirit Mediums in Zimbabwe* (Berkeley: University of California Press, 1985), p. 6.
4. Adu Boahen, *Africa under Colonial Domination, 1880–1935,* UNESCO General History of Africa, Vol. VII (Berkeley: University of California Press, 1985), p. 4.
5. Harold Marcus, *The Life and Times of Menelik II Ethiopia 1844–1913* (Oxford: Clarendon, 1975), p. 160.
6. Nina Mba, *Nigerian Women Mobilized: Women's Political Activity in Southern Nigeria, 1900–1945* (Berkeley, Calif.: Institute of International Studies, 1982), p. 76.
7. Quoted in William Tordoff, *Government and Politics in Africa,* 3rd ed. (Indiana University Press, 1997), p. 39.
8. Patrick Manning, *Francophone Sub-Saharan Africa, 1880–1985* (Cambridge: Cambridge University Press, 1988), p. 45.
9. Adam Hochschild, *King Leopold's Ghost* (New York: Houghton Mifflin Co., 1998), p. 112.
10. Quoted in N. D. Harris, *Europe and the East* (Boston: Houghton Mifflin, 1926), p. 285.

Chapter 24

1. Frederick Weed, quoted in D. R. Sar Desai, *Southeast Asia: Past and Present* (Boulder, Colo.: Westview Press, 1989), p. 101.
2. General Jacob F. Smith, quoted in Sar Desai, p. 149.
3. Quoted in Franz H. Michael and George E. Taylor, *The Far East in the Modern World* (New York: Holt, Rinehart and Winston, 1956), p. 122.
4. Quoted in Ch'u Chai and Winberg Chai, *The Changing Society of China* (New York: Mentor Books, 1962), p. 189.

Chapter 25

1. Donald Castro, "Women in the World of the Tango," in Gertrude Yeager, ed., *Confronting Change, Challenging Tradition: Women in Latin American History* (Wilmington, Del.: Scholarly Resources, 1994), p. 68.
2. E. Bradford Burns, *A History of Brazil,* 2nd ed. (New York: Columbia University Press, 1980), p. 274.
3. Michael C. Meyer and William H. Beezley, eds., *Oxford History of Mexico* (Oxford: Oxford University Press, 2000), p. 403.

Global Issues: Gender

1. Joan W. Scott, "Gender, A Useful Category of Historical Analysis," *American Historical Review* 91:5 (December 1986): 1053–1075.

Chapter 26

1. Quoted in F. Owen, *Tempestuous Journey: Lloyd George, His Life and Times* (London: Hutchinson), p. 186.
2. Quoted in Foster Rhea Dulles, *America's Rise to World Power, 1898–1954* (New York: Harper & Row, 1955), p. 4.
3. Quoted in Basil Dmystryshyn, ed., *Imperial Russia: A Source Book, 1700–1917* (New York: Holt, Rinehart, and Winston, 1967), p. 241.

Chapter 27

1. Quoted by C. J. H. Hayes, *A Political and Cultural History of Modern Europe,* Vol. 2 (New York: Macmillan, 1939), p. 572.
2. Edward Grey, Viscount of Fallodon, *25 Years,* Vol. 2 (New York: Stokes, 1925), p. 20.
3. "The Soldier," in *The Collected Poems of Rupert Brooke* (New York: Dodd, Mead, 1915).
4. Anthem for a Doomed Youth," in *The Collected Poems of Wilfred Owen*. Copyright © 1963 by Chatto & Windus, Ltd., 1946. Reprinted by permission of New Directions Publishing Corporation and Chatto & Windus on behalf of the estate of Wilfred Owen.
5. Quoted in R. J. Sontag, *European Diplomatic History, 1871–1932* (New York: Century, 1933), p. 392.
6. George F. Kennan, *The Decision to Intervene* (Princeton, N.J.: Princeton University Press, 1958), p. 471.
7. A. J. Ryder, *Twentieth-Century Germany: From Bismarck to Brandt* (New York: Columbia University Press, 1973), p. 216.
8. Alan Bullock, *Hitler: A Study in Tyranny* (New York: Harper Torchbooks, 1964), p. 91.
9. Sidney Pollard, *European Economic Integration, 1815–1970* (New York: Harcourt Brace Jovanovich, 1974), p. 138.
10. John Kenneth Galbraith, *The Great Crash, 1929* (Boston: Houghton Mifflin, 1961), p. 173.

Chapter 28

1. After 1917, the Communist authorities adopted the Western-style, Gregorian calendar. In the calendar in use at that time, however, the Julian calendar, the first Russian revolution took place in February.
2. J. N. Westwood, *Endurance and Endeavour: Russian History, 1812–1986* (Oxford: Oxford University Press, 1987), p. 276.
3. Lynne Viola, "Bab'i i Bunty and the Peasant Worker's Protest During Collectivization," in Beatrice Farnsworth and Lynne Viola, eds., *Russian Peasant Women* (Oxford: Oxford University Press, 1992), pp. 191, 198.
4. Roberta Manning, "Women in the Soviet Countryside on the Eve of World War II, 1935–1940," in Farnsworth and Viola, *Russian Peasant Women,* pp. 206–207.
5. Roger Griffin, *Fascism: An Oxford Reader* (Oxford: Oxford University Press, 1995), pp. 4–9.
6. Stanley G. Payne, *A History of Fascism, 1914–1945* (Madison: University of Wisconsin Press, 1995), ch. 1.
7. Robert O. Paxton, *The Anatomy of Fascism* (London: Penguin Books, 2004), pp. 219–220.
8. Benito Mussolini, *Fascism: Doctrine and Institutions* (New York: Fertig, 1968), p. 38.
9. Elizabeth Wiskemann, *Fascism in Italy: Its Development and Influence* (New York: St. Martin's Press, 1969), p. 23.
10. Peter Gay, *Weimar Culture* (New York: Harper Torchbooks, 1968), p. 23.
11. David S. Landes, *The Unbound Prometheus: Technological Change and Industrial Development in Western Europe from 1750 to the Present* (Cambridge: Cambridge University Press, 1969), p. 398.

Chapter 29

1. Chen Duxiu, inaugural issue of *New Youth,* 1915, cited in Ebrey, 270.
2. Mao Tse-tung, "Report on an Investigation of a Peasant Movement in Hunan," in *Selected Works of Mao Tse-tung* (Beijing: Foreign Languages Press, 1967), Vol. 1.
3. Louis Fischer, *The Life of Mahatma Gandhi* (New York: Collier Books, 1966), p. 159.
4. Sarojini Naidu, cited in Stanley Wolpert, *A New History of India,* 5th ed. (New York: Oxford University Press, 1997), p. 315.
5. Fischer, p. 285.
6. Jawaharlal Nehru, *Toward Freedom* (New York: Day, 1942), p. 353.

Chapter 30

1. William Cleveland, *A History of the Modern Middle East* (Boulder, Colo.: Westview Press, 1994), p. 155.
2. Kwame Nkrumah, *Ghana: The Autobiography of Kwame Nkrumah* (London: Nelson, 1957), p. 27.
3. Ali Mazrui and Michael Tidy, *Nationalism and New States in Africa* (London: Heinemann, 1984), p. 22.
4. Basil Davidson, *Modern Africa: A Social and Political History,* 2nd ed. (Longman, 1989), p. 66.
5. Michael Crowder, *West Africa Under Colonial Rule* (London: Hutchinson and Co., 1968), p. 482.

Chapter 31

1. George F. Kennan, *Memoirs* (New York: Bantam Books, 1969), p. 122.
2. John Toland, *Adolf Hitler* (New York: Ballantine Books, 1977), pp. 522, 529.
3. Francis L. Loewenheim, *Peace or Appeasement* (Boston: Houghton Mifflin, 1965), pp. 2, 4.
4. Middlemas, *Strategy of Appeasement,* p. 177.
5. Winston L. S. Churchill, *Blood, Sweat, and Tears* (New York: Putnam, 1941), p. 66.
6. Franklin D. Roosevelt, "Address at Chicago, October 5, 1937," in *The Literature of the United States,* eds. W. Blair, T. Hornberger, and R. Stewart, Vol. 2 (Chicago: Scott, Foresman, 1955), p. 831.
7. S. E. Ayling, *Portraits of Power* (New York: Barnes & Noble, 1963), p. 159.
8. Nigel Nicolson, ed., *Harold Nicolson: The War Years, 1939–1945* (New York: Atheneum, 1967), p. 100.
9. Churchill, *Blood, Sweat, and Tears,* p. 297.
10. James Risen, "U.S. Details 6 Neutral Countries' Role in Aiding Nazis," *New York Times,* June 21, 1998.
11. *Last Letters from Stalingrad,* trans. Franz Schneider and Charles Gullas (New York: Signet Books, 1965), p. 20.
12. Quoted in John Vinocur, "Goebbels in Published 1945 Diary Blames Goring for Nazi's Collapse," *New York Times,* Jan. 3, 1978.
13. For important testimony about life in Auschwitz, see Primo Levi, *Survival in Auschwitz* (Touchstone Books, Simon and Schuster, New York, 1996).
14. For a summation of this story, see Jan T. Gross, "Neighbors," *The New Yorker,* March 12, 1991, pp. 64–77. For fuller coverage, see *Gross's Neighbors: The Destruction of the Jewish Community in Jedwabne, Poland* (Princeton, N.J.: Princeton University Press, 1991.
15. See Daniel Jonah Goldhagen, *Hitler's Willing Executioners: Ordinary Germans and the Holocaust* (New York: Knopf, 1996). The most outspoken criticism of Goldhagen's thesis is to be found in Norman G. Finkelstein and Ruth Bettina Birn, *A Nation on Trial: The Goldhagen Thesis and Historical Truth* (New York: Henry Holt, 1998).
16. Raul Hilberg, *The Destruction of the European Jews* (Chicago: Quadrangle Books, 1961); Maurice Crouzet, *Histoire Générale des Civilisations,* Vol. 7 (Paris: Presses Universitaires de France, 1957), pp. 358–359.
17. "Obituary, Telford Taylor," *The Economist,* May 30, 1998, p. 95.

Global Issues: War and International Law

1. Arnold Toynbee as quoted in Robert Melson, *Revolution and Genocide: On the Origins of the Armenian Genocide and the*

Holocaust (Chicago and London: The University of Chicago Press, 1992), p. 145.

2. Bernard Lewis, *The Emergence of Modern Turkey* (Oxford: Oxford University Press, 1961), p. 356.
3. Melson, p. 26.
4. Melson, p. 26.
5. Philip Gourevitch captured this tragedy in his book, *We Wish to Inform You that Tomorrow We Will Be Killed With Our Families: Stories from Rwanda* (New York: Farrar, Straus & Giroux, 1998).

Chapter 32

1. Quoted in David Rees, *The Age of Containment* (New York: St. Martin's Press, 1967), p. 23.

Chapter 33

1. Bill Emmott, "Freedom's Journey," *The Economist,* September 18, 1999 (special supplement), pp. 10, 11, 37, 38.
2. Charles de Gaulle, *The Call to Honor* (New York: Viking, 1955), p. 33.

Chapter 34

1. Samad Behrangi, *The Little Black Fish and Other Stories,* trans. Eric and Mary Hooglund (Washington, D.C.: Three Continents Press, 1982), p. 37.
2. Joshua Nkomo, *The Story of My Life* (New York: Methuen, 1984), p. 245.
3. Elizabeth Schmidt, *"Now You Have Touched the Women": African Women's Resistance to the Pass Laws in South Africa, 1950–1960,* Notes and Documents 6/83. (New York: United Nations Centre Against Apartheid, March, 1983), p. 19.

Chapter 35

1. Richard Rovere, *Senator Joe McCarthy* (London: Methuen, 1959), p. 24.
2. "As Japan Goes . . . ," *The Economist,* June 20, 1998.

Index

Note: Page numbers followed by letters *i* and *m* indicate illustrations and maps, respectively. Boldface page numbers indicate key terms.

D

J

K

M

X

Primary Source Documents

How to Analyze Primary Source Documents

Historians study sources to reconstruct the lifestyles and events of previous generations. By examining the ideas and thoughts conveyed in primary sources, we can attempt to understand the past as the people who lived it did. By using sources, historians craft an understanding of the people, events, ideas, trends, and themes of the past based upon interpretation of those sources.

Primary sources are generally first-hand accounts or records. They may have been written or created during the time period under investigation, or they may have been written at a later date by someone who lived through earlier events. Most crucially, primary sources have not been interpreted by anyone else, though they may offer interpretations of the events they describe.

The primary source documents presented here give you the opportunity to put your investigative skills to the test by analyzing the sources yourself, rather than by reading others' interpretations.

WHEN ANALYZING A PRIMARY SOURCE, YOU SHOULD ASK SEVEN KEY QUESTIONS.

1. **Who is the author?**
   Who wrote or created this? Is there a single or multiple authors? An author's identity sometimes helps you answer the later questions.
2. **What type of source is this?**
   All the sources here are documents, but what type? Is it a biography or a government document? This is a simple but crucial step because you must consider what you can expect to learn from the document.
3. **What is the message of this source?**
   What is the author describing? What is happening in the text? What is the story?
4. **Who is the intended audience?**
   Who is the author addressing? Was the source intended for private or public consumption? Identifying the audience will help you answer the next question.
5. **Why was this source created?**
   Does the author have an agenda, a larger purpose? Is the author trying to persuade the audience? Is the document or source simply a compilation or facts, or does it include opinion, inference, or interpretation?
6. **Is this source credible and accurate?**
   Historians must examine every source with a critical eye. What do you know about the author? Does the document make sense? Do the facts presented by the author or what you know about the time period support the thesis, statement, assertion, or story the author is conveying? Why should you trust, or distrust, this source?
7. **How is this source valuable to me?**
   How does the source relate to other sources from the time period or along the same issue or theme? Does it support or contradict them? Does it repeat information from other sources or add new information? How relevant is the source to your topic of inquiry? Does it extensively cover your topic, or only marginally or not at all? Remember, you should explore enough sources to obtain a variety of viewpoints.

Let's take a look at a portion of a document to see how this process works. Reading the full document selection, of course, provides even more clues to understanding this source.

Galileo Galilei, Letter to the Duchess Christina

Galileo Galilei (1564–1642) was one of the primary figures in the Scientific Revolution. In 1608 Galileo, then a professor of mathematics at the University of Pisa, heard of a new technology, the telescope. Galileo quickly built his own telescope and used it to observe the planets and the stars. His observations provided evidence in favor of the Copernican theory of heliocentrism. For a variety of reasons, many religious leaders considered heliocentrism dangerous, and Galileo was initially commanded by the Roman Catholic Church to avoid teaching it. After the publication in 1632 of his most important work, Dialogue on the Two World Systems, *which was supposed to be impartial but favored heliocentrism, he was forced to recant his claim that the earth moves in relation to the sun. He spent the remainder of his life under house arrest. Galileo is also famous for his work in theoretical mechanics, particularly for his formulation of the law of inertia. In the following selection, Galileo describes how the results of the new science can be reconciled with the Bible.*

My goal is this alone; that if, among errors that may abound in these considerations of a subject remote from my profession, there is anything that may be serviceable to the holy Church in making a decision concerning the Copernican system, it may be taken and utilized as seems best to the superiors. And if not, let my book be torn and burnt, as I neither intend nor pretend to gain from it any fruit that is not pious and Catholic. And though many of the things I shall reprove have been heard by my own ears, I shall freely grant to those who have spoken them that they never said them, if that is what they wish, and I shall confess myself to have been mistaken. Hence let whatever I reply be addressed not to them, but to whoever may have held such opinions.

The reason produced for condemning the opinion that the earth moves and the sun stands still is that in many places in the Bible one may read that the sun moves and the earth stands still. Since the Bible cannot err, it follows as a necessary consequence that anyone takes an erroneous and heretical position who maintains that the sun is inherently motionless and the earth movable . . .

. . . Hence I think that I may reasonably conclude that whenever the Bible has occasion to speak of any physical conclusion (especially those which are very abstruse and hard to understand), the rule has been observed of avoiding confusion in the minds of the common people which would render them contumacious toward the higher mysteries. Now the Bible, merely to condescend to popular capacity, has not hesitated to obscure some very important pronouncements, attributing to God himself some qualities extremely remote from (and even contrary to) His essence. Who then, would positively declare that this principle has been set aside, and the Bible has confined itself rigorously to the bare and restricted sense of its words, when speaking but casually of the earth, of water, of the sun, or of any other created thing? Especially in view of the fact that these things in no way concern the primary purpose of the sacred writings, which is the service of God and the salvation of souls—matters infinitely beyond the comprehension of the common people.

This being granted, I think that in discussions of physical problems we ought to begin not from the authority of scriptural passages, but from sense-experiences and necessary demonstrations; for the holy Bible and the phenomena of nature proceed alike from the divine Word, the former as the dictate of the Holy Ghost and the latter as the observant executrix of God's commands. It is necessary for the Bible, in order to be accommodated to the understanding of every man, to speak many things which appear to differ from the absolute truth so far as the bare meaning of the words is concerned. But Nature, on the other hand, is inexorable and immutable: she never transgresses the laws imposed upon her, or cares a whit whether her abstruse reasons and methods of operation are understandable to men. For that reason it appears that nothing physical which sense-experience sets before our eyes, or which necessary demonstrations prove to us, ought to be called in question (much less condemned) upon the testimony of biblical passages which may have some different meaning beneath their words. For the Bible is not chained in every expression to conditions as strict as those which govern all physical effects; nor is God any less excellently revealed in Nature's actions than in the sacred statements of the Bible.

NOW LET'S LOOK AT WHAT WE CAN LEARN FROM THIS TEXT.

1. **Who is the author?**
   From the header we know that the author is Galileo Galilei (1564–1642), a key figure during the Scientific Revolution.
2. **What type of source is this?**
   This is an open letter Galileo wrote to the Grand Duchess Christina to defend his position in the conflict between the scientific community and the Catholic Church.
3. **What is the message of this source?**
   Galileo's message is that the Copernican system, even though it appears to be in conflict with certain Biblical passages, must be viewed as the truth. He wants readers to understand that in spiritual matters the Bible is the unquestioned authority, but in matters of Nature, human observation must be considered the final authority.
4. **Who is the intended audience?**
   The source is titled Letter to the Grand Duchess Christina, as it was written to the Grand Duchess at her request to answer her questions regarding the contradictions between the Bible and science. Letters of this sort were circulated among the elites, so Galileo wrote it with the anticipation that it would be widely distributed.
5. **Why was this source created?**
   As the header suggests, Galileo was in the middle of a controversy surrounding the relationship between science and religion. Galileo intended this document to defend the role of science and to argue man's observational powers should stand alongside Christian doctrine.
6. **Is this source credible and accurate?**
   Galileo was constantly under duress from the Catholic Church, as he was forced to recant some of his scientific claims and was placed under house arrest by the Church. He was writing a letter to someone in a position of power who, although she was Protestant, was certain to circulate his writings among members of the Catholic Church hierarchy. Despite this, Galileo appears to have written a letter outlining his argument that the findings of science must not be constrained by the Church's desire to avoid confusing "the common people." You must weigh the various outside factors and decide if this letter may be taken as an accurate representation of Galileo's position in the matter and what that position means in the overall debate.
7. **How is this source valuable to you?**
   This source would be an invaluable central component if you were researching:
   - The debate between science and religion
   - Galileo's writings and his position in the debate

   It would be an important part of a paper on:
   - The resistance to scientific knowledge by the Catholic Church
   - The origins of modern science

   It would be crucial background information if you were researching:
   - The writings and opinions of Galileo
   - The evolution of Catholic Church policy regarding scientific discovery

You now have the basic tools to begin analyzing historical documents yourself. As you apply these skills to the documents contained here, you will likely find that your skill level will increase rapidly. You may even find yourself reading others' interpretations of primary source documents with a more critical eye.

DOCUMENT 1.1
Papyrus of Ani, "The Egyptian Book of the Dead" (1200 B.C.E.)
From the translation by E. A. Wallis Budge

In the Egyptian belief system, Ra was the sun god and Osiris was the god of the dead. The excerpt below is from the Papyrus of Ani, a wonderfully preserved papyrus scroll (though Egyptologists describe it as a "book") entombed with the scribe Ani. The purpose of such scrolls was to assist the deceased in the afterlife, where every person possessed three spirits called the Ka, the Ba, and the Akh. These spirits could survive only if the deceased's body did not decay.

A Hymn of Praise to Ra When He Riseth in the Eastern Part of Heaven:

Behold, the Osiris Ani, the scribe of the holy offerings of all the gods, saith: Homage to thee, O thou who hast come as Khepera, Khepera the creator of the gods, Thou art seated on thy throne, thou risest up in the sky, illumining thy mother [Nut], thou art seated on thy throne as the king of the gods. [Thy] mother Nut stretcheth out her hands, and performeth an act of homage to thee. The domain of Manu receiveth thee with satisfaction. The goddess Maat embraceth thee at the two seasons of the day. May Ra give glory, and power, and thruth-speaking, and the appearance as a living soul so that he may gaze upon Heru-khuti, to the KA of the Osiris the Scribe Ani, who speaketh truth before Osiris, and who saith: Hail, O all ye gods of the House of the Soul, who weigh heaven and earth in a balance, and who give celestial food [to the dead]. Hail, Tatun, [who art] One, thou creator of mortals [and] of the Companies of the Gods of the South and of the North, of the West and of the East, ascribe ye praise to Ra, the lord of heaven, the KING, Life, Strength, and Health, the maker of the gods. Give ye thanks unto him in his beneficent form which is enthroned in the Atett Boat; beings celestial praise thee, beings terrestial praise thee. Thoth and the goddess Maat mark out thy course for thee day by day and every day. Thine enemy the Serpent hath been given over to the fire. The Serpent-fiend Sebau hath fallen headlong, his forelegs are bound in chains, and his hind legs hath Ra carried away from him. The Sons of Revolt shall never more rise up. The House of the Aged One keepeth festival, and the voices of those who make merry are in the Great Place. The gods rejoice when they see Ra crowned upon his throne, and when his beams flood the world with light. The majesty of this holy god setteth out on his journey, and he goeth onwards until he reacheth the land of Manu; the earth becometh light at his birth each day; he proceedeth until he reacheth the place where he was yesterday. O be thou at peace with me. Let me gaze upon thy beauties. Let me journey above the earth. Let me smite the Ass. Let me slit asunder the Serpent-fiend Sebau. Let me destroy Aepep at the moment of his greatest power. Let me behold the Abtu Fish at his season, and the Ant Fish with the Ant Boat as it piloteth it in its lake. Let me behold Horus when he is in charge of the rudder [of the Boat of Ra], with Thoth and the goddess Maat on each side of him. Let me lay hold of the tow-rope of the Sektet Boat, and the rope at the stern of the Matett Boat. Let Ra grant to me a view of the Disk (the Sun), and a sight of Ah (the Moon) unfailingly each day. Let my Ba-soul come forth to walk about hither and thither and whithersoever it pleaseth. Let my name be called out, let it be found inscribed on the tablet which recordeth the names of those who are to receive offerings. Let meals from the sepulchral offerings be given to me in the presence [of Osiris], as to those who are in the following of Horus. Let there be prepared for me a seat in the Boat of the Sun on the day wheron the god saileth. Let me be received in the presence of Osiris in the Land of Truth-speaking—the Ka of Osiris Ani.

DOCUMENT ANALYSIS

1. What can we learn about a culture from its funereal rites?

______

______

______

2. What does this document seek to do for Ani?

______

______

______

DOCUMENT 1.2
Hammurabi's Law Code (1792 B.C.E.)
Source: James B. Pritchard, ed. *Ancient Near Eastern Texts Relating to the Old Testament,* trans. Theophile J. Meek (Princeton, NJ: Princeton University Press, 1955), pp. 166–7, 170–7. Language modernized by Wayne Ackerson.

Originally one of many small city-state empires in Mesopotamia, Babylon became the center of a large empire under its king, Hammurabi. Hammurabi ruled from approximately 1792 to 1750 B.C.E., and was a tremendously successful ruler. Not only did he build an empire for his city, he also helped that city become the new Near Eastern cultural center. Hammurabi's scribes carefully maintained old Sumerian records, encouraged literacy among the upper classes, and made religious changes (elevating Babylon's patron god, Marduk, to the top divine position).

Notwithstanding Hammurabi's military skill, his most noted contribution was the creation of the world's first written, comprehensive law code. Law codes had always existed (usually passed down orally), and some had been written, but even the previous written ones were not complete and comprehensive. Though usually called Hammurabi's law code, the collection of laws is more a list of decisions made by judges in the past than laws passed by the king himself. Hammurabi claimed that these laws were sanctioned by the gods, and had copies carved on markers to be placed in prominent locations such as temple courtyards. Despite Hammurabi's efforts at empire-building, within a few years of his death his kingdom began to crumble.

1. If an upper class man accused another upper class man and brought a charge of murder against him, but has not proven it, his accuser shall be executed.

3. If an upper class man came forward with false testimony in a case, and has not proven the word he spoke, if that case was a death-penalty case, that man shall be put to death.

4. If he came forward with false testimony concerning grain or money, he shall bear the punishment in that case.

14. If an upper class man has kidnapped the young son of another upper class man, he shall be executed.

15. If an upper class man has helped either a male slave owned by the government or a male slave of a private citizen or a female slave of a private citizen to escape the city, he shall be executed.

17. If an upper class man caught a runaway slave in the open and has taken him to his owner, the slave's owner shall pay him two shekels of silver.

19. If he has kept the slave in his house and later the slave has been found in his possession, that upper class man shall be executed.

21. If an upper class man broke into a home through the wall, he shall be executed in front of the hole and then walled in.

22. If an upper class man is caught committing robbery, he shall be executed.

128. If an upper class man marries a woman but did not draw up the marriage contracts for her, she is not his wife.

129. If the wife of an upper class man has been caught while sleeping with another man, they shall tie them both up and throw them into the water. If the husband of the woman wishes to spare his wife, then the king may in turn order his subject spared.

131. If an upper class man's wife was accused by her husband of adultery, but was not caught while sleeping with another man, she shall swear she is innocent before god and return home.

134. If an upper class man was kidnapped and there was not enough money and food in his home for his wife to survive, she may enter the home of another, with no blame incurred by the wife.

149. If that woman has refused to live in her husband's home, he shall return her dowry to her and she may leave.

153. If an upper class man's wife has caused her husband's death because of another man, the woman shall be impaled on stakes.

154. If an upper class man sleeps with his daughter, he shall be forced to leave the city.

155. If an upper class man chose a bride for his son and his son has slept with her, but later the man is caught sleeping with her, that upper class man shall be tied up and thrown into the water.

157. If an upper class man sleeps with his mother after his father dies, both mother and son shall be burned to death.

162. If, when an upper class man gets married, and his wife bears him children and later dies, the dowry belongs to her children and her father cannot claim it.

185. If an upper class man adopted a boy and has raised him, that foster child shall never be reclaimed.

186. If an upper class man, upon adopting a boy, seeks out the boy's parents, that child may return to his father's home.

188. If an artisan took a son as a foster child and taught him his trade or craft, he may never be reclaimed.

189. If he has not taught him his trade or craft, that child may return to his father's home.

195. If a son hits his father, the son's hand shall be cut off.

196. If an upper class man destroyed the eye of another noble, his eye shall also be destroyed.

197. If he has broken another noble's bone, his bone shall also be broken.

198. If he destroyed the eye or broken the bone of a commoner, he shall pay one mina of silver.

199. If he has destroyed the eye or broken a bone of an upper class man's slave, he shall pay half the slave's value.

202. If an upper class man slaps the face of an upper class man who is superior to him, he shall be whipped sixty times with an oxtail whip in public.

203. If a noble slaps another noble's face who is of the same rank, he shall pay one mina of silver.

204. If a commoner slaps the face of another commoner, he shall pay ten shekels of silver.

205. If an upper class man's slave has slapped the face of a noble, his ear shall be cut off.

228. If a builder built a house for an upper class man and finished it, the man shall pay the builder two shekels of silver per sar (a measurement of about 42 square yards).

229. If a builder built a house for an upper class man but the house falls down due to poor craftsmanship and kills the upper class man, the builder shall be executed.

230. If it has caused the death of a son of the home's owner, the son of the builder shall be executed.

282. If a male slave has said to his master, "you do not own me," his master shall prove him to be his slave and cut off the slave's ear.

DOCUMENT ANALYSIS

1. Are there any business-related laws here?

____

____

____

2. What happens if someone lies in court?

____

____

____

3. What happens to someone who harbors a runaway slave in his home?

____

____

____

4. Would you say that these laws are "fair"? Why or why not?

____

____

____

5. Would you say that women have any rights, according to Hammurabi's code?

____

____

____

DOCUMENT 2.1
Confucius, from *Analects* (441–479 B.C.E.)

Source: *Confucian Analects, the Great Learning, and the Doctrine of the Mean,* in *Chinese Classics Series of the Clarendon Press,* Vol. 1, trans. James Legge (Oxford: Clarendon Press, 1893).

Confucius was a scholar who lived between ca. 551 and 479 B.C.E. During this time, China experienced political decentralization and social instability as a result of rivalry among difference princes. In his search for restoration of social order, Confucius argued that this chaotic situation was due to the breakdown of China's social foundation, which was based on the principle of proper relationships. According to Confucius, the key relationships included those between ruler and subject, father and son, husband and wife, elder brother and younger brother, and friend and friend. Only by fixing these relationships could China regain peace and order. Confucius' ideas, however, were not well accepted by the ruling class of his time, and he spent the rest of his lifetime teaching. After Confucius, China sank into an even worse period known as the Warring States (475–221 B.C.E.). Confucius did not leave any written works, but his disciples recorded and further enriched his ideas by putting together—in a rather unsystematic way—a collection of his teachings and arguments. These Analects, which describe what we commonly know as Confucianism, would reshape the Chinese way of thinking in the millennia to come. Confucius's ideas on good government and proper relationships in the society are clearly reflected in the following arguments.

FILIAL PIETY

Zi, you asked what filial piety was. The Master said, "The filial piety of now-a-days means the support of one's parents. But dogs and horses likewise are able to do something in the way of support;—without reverence, what is there to distinguish the one support giver from the other?"

The Master said, "In serving his parents, a son may remonstrate with them, but gently; when he sees that they do not incline to follow his advice, he shows an increased degree of reverence, but does not abandon his purpose; and should they punish him, he does not allow himself to murmur."

Mang I asked what filial piety was. The Master said, "It is not being disobedient." Soon after, as Fan Chih was driving him, the Master told him, saying, "Mang Sun asked me what filial piety was, and I answered him, 'not being disobedient.'" Fan Chih said, "What did you mean?" The Master replied, "That parents, when alive, should be served according to propriety; that, when dead, they should be buried according to propriety; and that they should be sacrificed to according to propriety."

PROPRIETY

The Master said, "Respectfulness, without the rules of propriety, becomes laborious bustle; carefulness, without the rules of propriety, becomes timidity; boldness, without the rules of propriety, becomes insubordination; straightforwardness, without the rules of propriety, becomes rudeness."

IDEAL GOVERNMENT

The Master said, "When rulers love to observe the rules of propriety, the people respond readily to the calls on them for service."

The Master said, "If the people be led by laws, and uniformity sought to be given them by punishments, they will try to avoid the punishment, but have no sense of shame.

"If they be led by virtue, and uniformity sought to be given them by the rules of propriety, they will have the sense of shame, and moreover will become good."

The Master said, "He who exercises government by means of his virtue may be compared to the north polar star, which keeps its place and all the stars turn towards it."

The duke Ai asked, saying, "What should be done in order to secure the submission of the people?" Confucius replied, "Advance the upright and set aside the crooked, then the people will submit. Advance the crooked and set aside the upright, then the people will not submit."

Ji Kang asked how to cause the people to reverence their ruler, to be faithful to him, and to go on to nerve themselves to virtue. The Master said, "Let him preside over them with gravity;—then they will reverence him. Let him be filial and kind to all;—then they will be faithful to him. Let him advance the good and teach the incompetent;—then they will eagerly seek to be virtuous."

Ji Kang asked Confucius about government. Confucius replied, "To govern means to rectify. If you lead on the people with correctness, who will dare not to be correct?"

. . . . . .

The Master said, "If a minister makes his own conduct correct, what difficulty will he have in assisting in government? If he cannot rectify himself, what has he to do with rectifying others?"

The Master said, "If good men were to govern a country in succession for a hundred years, they would be able to transform the violently bad, and dispense with capital punishments." True indeed is this saying!

THE SUPERIOR MAN

Confucius said, "There are three things of which the superior man stands in awe. He stands in awe of the ordinances of Heaven. He stands in awe of great men. He stands in awe of the words of sages.

"The mean man does not know the ordinances of Heaven, and consequently does not stand in awe of them. He is disrespectful to great men. He makes sport of the words of sages."

Zi Gong asked what constituted the superior man. The Master said, "He acts before he speaks, and afterward speaks according to his actions."

The Master said, "The mind of the superior man is conversant with righteousness; the mind of the mean man is conversant with gain."

The Master said, "If the will be set on virtue, there will be no practice of wickedness."

The Master said, "Riches and honors are what men desire. If it cannot be obtained in the proper way, they should not be held. Poverty and meanness are what men dislike. If it cannot be obtained in the proper way, they should not be avoided.

"If a superior man abandon virtue, how can he fulfill the requirements of that name?

"The superior man does not, even for the space of a single meal, act contrary to virtue. In moments of haste, he cleaves to it. In seasons of danger, he cleaves to it."

The Master said, "By nature, men are nearly alike; by practice, they get to be wide apart."

. . . . . .

The Master said, "By extensively studying all learning, and keeping himself under the restraint of the rules of propriety, one may thus likewise not err from what is right."

The Master said, "The accomplished scholar is not a utensil."

SPIRITS

The subjects on which the Master did not talk, were extraordinary things, feats of strength, disorder, and spiritual beings.

. . . . . .

Ji Lu asked about serving the spirits of the dead. The Master said, "While you are not able to serve men, how can you serve their spirits?"

Ji Lu added, "I venture to ask about death?" He was answered, "While you do not know life, how can you know about death?"

DOCUMENT ANALYSIS

1. From this document, what can be seen as the major themes in Confucianism?

2. Summarize Confucius's idea of an ideal government.

3. What should be the major qualities of a superior man, according to Confucius?

4. Why does Confucius consider propriety important for individuals and family, as well as the state?

5. Why was the Warring States period so important for the development of Confucianism?

DOCUMENT 2.2

Laozi, from *Daodejing* (500s–400s B.C.E.)

Source: *The Sacred Books of the East,* Vol. 39, ed. F. Max Müller, (Oxford: Clarendon Press, 1886). 1.

Daoism was associated with a legendary scholar, Laozi, who was believed to be a contemporary of Confucius. Laozi 's view of restoring peace in the face of China's collapsing social order was quite different from that of Confucius. According to Laozi, the proper way to escape from war and political entanglement is to retreat into seclusion and embrace the harmony of nature. Through this contemplation of nature, one could become attuned to the Dao ("the way" in Chinese). Daoist views on government and human relationships were also different from those of Confucius. Daoism suggests a less active role for the government and more freedom for the people. Because of this retreatist attitude toward politics and society, Daoism gradually evolved into a popular religion absorbing its rites and organizational forms from Buddhism and local superstitions.

THE WAY

The Dao that can be trodden is not the enduring and unchanging Dao. The name that can be named is not the enduring and unchanging name.

Conceived of as having no name, it is the Originator of heaven and earth; conceived of as having a name, it is the Mother of all things.

. . . . . .

The Dao produces all things and nourishes them; it produces them and does not claim them as its own; it does all, and yet does not boast of it; it presides over all, and yet does not control them. This is what is called "The mysterious quality" of the Dao.

When the Great Dao ceased to be observed, benevolence and righteousness came into vogue.

Then appeared wisdom and shrewdness, and there ensued great hypocrisy.

Man takes his law from the Earth; the Earth takes its law from Heaven; Heaven takes its law from the Dao. The law of the Dao is its being what it is.

All-pervading is the Great Dao! It may be found on the left hand and on the right.

All things depend on it for their production, which it gives to them, not one refusing obedience to it. When its work is accomplished, it does not claim the name of having done it. It clothes all things as with a garment, and makes no assumption of being their lord;—it may be named in the smallest things; . . . it may be named in the greatest things.

. . . . . .

He who has in himself abundantly the attributes of the Dao is like an infant.

. . . . . .

The Dao in its regular course does nothing, for the sake of doing it, and so there is nothing which it does not do.

THE WISE PERSON

When we renounce learning we have no troubles.

If we could renounce our sageness and discard our wisdom, it would be better for the people a hundredfold. If we could renounce our benevolence and discard our righteousness, the people would again become filial and kindly. If we could renounce our artful contrivances and discard our scheming for gain, there would be no thieves nor robbers.

. . . . . .

The sage manages affairs without doing anything, and conveys his instructions without the use of speech.

. . . . . .

Therefore the sage holds in his embrace the one thing of humility, and manifests it to all the world. He is free from self-display, and therefore he shines; from self-assertion, and therefore he is distinguished; from self-boasting, and therefore his merit is acknowledged; from self-complacency, and therefore he acquires superiority. It is because he is thus free from striving that therefore no one in the world is able to strive with him.

THE IDEAL GOVERNMENT

A state may be ruled by measures of correction; weapons of war may be used with crafty dexterity; but the kingdom is made one's own only by freedom from action and purpose.

How do I know that it is so? By these facts:—In the kingdom the multiplication of prohibitive enactments increases the poverty of the people; the more implements to add to their profit that the people have, the greater disorder is there in the state and clan; the more acts of crafty dexterity that men possess, the more do strange contrivances appear; the more display there is of legislation, the more thieves and robbers there are.

Therefore a sage has said, "I will do nothing, and the people will be transformed of themselves; I will be fond of keeping still, and the people will of themselves become correct. I will take no trouble about it, and the people will of themselves become rich; I will manifest no ambition, and the people will of themselves attain to the primitive simplicity."

Not to value and employ men of superior ability is the way to keep the people from rivalry among themselves; not to prize articles which are difficult to procure is the way to keep them from becoming thieves; not to show them what is likely to excite their desires is the way to keep their minds from disorder.

Therefore the sage, in the exercise of his government, empties their minds, fills their bellies, weakens their wills, and strengthens their bones.

He constantly tries to keep them without knowledge and without desire, and where there are those who have knowledge, to keep them from presuming to act on it. When there is this abstinence from action, good order is universal.

DOCUMENT ANALYSIS

1. How different is the Daoist idea an ideal government from that of Confucianism?

____

____

____

2. How does Daoism portray the relationship between people and nature? Why is harmony between man and nature important?

____

____

____

3. What is the Daoist view of "good order"?

4. What is the Way in Daoist interpretation?

5. What kind of people in China's classical society were likely to be attracted by Daoist teaching?

DOCUMENT 3.1
Buddhist Stories (300 B.C.E.)

These Buddhist stories or "Jataka tales" are very old and have a long tradition of being passed on from generation to generation serving as source for moral behavior for humans in general. These stories are stories of wisdom and morals written around 300 B.C. in a language called Pali, which were later translated and distributed to people across the world. They are mainly about past incarnations of Buddha, and are meant to teach the values of self-sacrifice, honesty, morality, and others to a common person.

A Poor Man Wins Spiritual Treasure

Should one see, as it were, a revealer of hidden treasures. This religious instruction was given by the Teacher while he was in residence at Jetavana with reference to Venerable Rādha. [104]

We are told that before Rādha became a monk he was a poor Brahman living at Sāvatthi. Deciding to live with the monks, he went to the monastery and took up his residence there, performing various duties such as cutting the grass, sweeping the cells, and preparing water for bathing the face. The monks treated him kindly, but were not willing to admit him to the Order. The result of this was that he began to lose flesh.

Now one day, early in the morning, the Teacher surveyed the world and seeing the Brahman, considered within himself what would become of him. Perceiving that he would become an Arahat, he went in the evening, feigning that he was making a tour of the monastery, to the Brahman's quarters and said to him, "Brahman, what are you doing here?" "Performing the major and minor duties for the monks, Reverend Sir." [105] "Do they treat you kindly?" "Yes, Reverend Sir, I receive sufficient food, but they are not willing to admit me to the Order." Accordingly the Teacher convoked an assembly of the monks and questioned them about the matter, saying, "Monks, is there anyone who remembers any act of this Brahman?"

Said the Elder Sāriputta, "Reverend Sir, I remember something. When I was making my round in Rājagaha, he brought me a ladleful of his own food and gave it to me. I remember this good office of his." Said the Teacher, "Sāriputta, is it not proper to release from suffering one who has performed such a service?" "Very well, Reverend Sir, I will receive him into the Order." Sāriputta accordingly received him into the Order. He received a seat in the refectory in the outer circle of seats. Even with rice-porridge and other kinds of food, he grew weary.

The Elder took him with him on his rounds and constantly admonished and instructed him, saying, "You must do this; you must not do that." The monk was amenable to discipline and respectful, and followed his preceptor's instructions so faithfully that in but a few days he attained the Arahatship. The Elder went with him to the Teacher, paid obeisance to the Teacher, and sat down. The Teacher gave him a friendly welcome and said to him, "Sāriputta, is your pupil amenable to discipline?" "Yes, Reverend Sir, he is thoroughly amenable to discipline; no matter what fault I mention, he never shows resentment." [106] "Sāriputta, if you could have pupils like this monk, how many would you take?" "I would take all I could get, Reverend Sir."

Now one day the monks began a discussion in the Hall of Truth: "They say the Elder Sāriputta is grateful and thankful. When a poor Brahman gave him but a ladleful of food, he remembered his kindness and made a monk of him. Moreover the Elder Rādha, patient of admonition, received a patient teacher." The Teacher, hearing their talk, said, "Monks, this is not the first time Sāriputta has shown himself grateful and thankful. He showed the same disposition in a previous state of existence also." And to illustrate his meaning, he related the Alīnacitta Jātaka, found in the Second Book, as follows:

Because of Alīnacitta, a mighty host was defeated; Alīnacitta captured alive the king of Kosala, dissatisfied with his army.

Even so a monk alert of will, directed aright,
By cultivating good qualities, by the attainment of Nibbāna,
Will in due time bring about the destruction of all Attachments.

Said the Teacher, "The Elder Sāriputta was at that time the solitary elephant which presented the pure white elephant his son to the carpenters, in recognition of the service they did him in healing his foot." Having thus related the Jātaka about the Elder Sāriputta, he said with reference to the Elder Rādha, "Monks, when a fault is pointed out to a monk, he ought to be amenable to discipline like Rādha; and when he is admonished, he should not take offense. Indeed he who gives admonition should be looked upon as one who points out where treasures are to be found." So saying, [107] he joined the connection and, instructing them in the Law, pronounced the following Stanza,

76. Should one see, as it were, a revealer of hidden treasures, one who points out what should be avoided, Who administers reproof where there is occasion for reproof, a man of intelligence, One should follow so wise a man; It will be better, not worse, for one to follow so wise a man.

The Insolent Monks

Let a man admonish and instruct. This religious instruction was given by the Teacher while he was in residence at Jetavana with reference to the Assajipunabbasuka monks. [109] But the story begins at Kītāgiri.

These monks, we are told, were two pupils of the Chief Disciples, but in spite of that fact were shameless and wicked. While they were in residence at Kītāgiri with their retinues of five hundred monks, they planted and caused to be planted flowering trees sand were guilty of all manner of misconduct besides. They violated homes and procured thence the monastic requisites on which they lived. They rendered the monastery uninhabitable for the amiable monks.

Hearing of their doings, the Teacher determined to expel them from the Order. For this purpose he summoned the two Chief Disciples, together with their retinues, and said to them, "Expel those who will not obey your commands, but admonish and instruct those who will obey. He who admonishes and instructs is hated by those that lack wisdom, but is loved and cherished by the wise." And joining the connection and instructing them in the Law, he pronounced the following Stanza,

77. Let a man admonish and instruct, and forbid what is improper;
For if he do so, he will be loved by the good, but hated by the wicked. [110]

Sāriputta and Moggallāna went there and admonished and instructed the Elders and corrected their behavior, others returned to the house-life, while still others were expelled from the Order.

DOCUMENT ANALYSIS

1. The selection, "A Poor Man Wins Spiritual Treasure," deals with Rādha's efforts to become a monk. What information does it provide about Buddhist views concerning the gaining of wisdom and stature?

______

______

______

2. What information do the two selections give about the importance of the proper order of things in Buddhism?

DOCUMENT 4.1

Plutarch on Alexander the Great, from Plutarch, *Lives* (1st c. B.C.E.)

Source: Plutarch, *Lives.* Vol. 7. trans. Bernadotte Perrin (Cambridge, MA: Harvard University Press, 1919), pp. 225, 231, 233, 235, 241, 43, 245, 289, 291, 339, 341, 355, 359, 361, 399, 401.

The Hellenistic Age was an era of great change for the eastern Mediterranean. Ushered in by Philip of Macedon's conquest of Greece in 338 B.C.E. and lasting until Rome's takeover of Egypt in 31 B.C.E., this age saw the spread of a Greek-like culture throughout the Middle East and Egypt. This change was made possible by the empire-building of Alexander III of Macedon, or "Alexander the Great."

Alexander the Great is often cited by military historians as the greatest military figure in human history. It is certainly true that, as a general, he never lost a battle, and he overcame serious obstacles to conquer a huge empire stretching from Greece to western India in just over ten years. As with most major historical figures, however, Alexander is still a subject of controversy. Some historians call him one of the world's great visionaries—a leader who wanted to create a unified, peaceful Greek world. Others call Alexander little more than a drunken brawler, prone to violence and excess. These scholars say that it was after a night of extreme revelry that Alexander died in 323 B.C.E.

One of the surviving sketches written by the Greek historian Plutarch is on Alexander the Great.

It is the life of Alexander the king . . . that I am writing in this book, and the multitude of the deeds to be treated is so great that I shall make no other preface than to entreat my readers, in case I do not tell of all the famous actions of these men, nor even speak exhaustively at all in each particular case, but in epitome for the most part, not to complain.

. . . The outward appearance of Alexander is best represented by the statues of him which Lysippus made, and it was by this artist alone that Alexander himself thought it fit that he should be modelled. For those peculiarities which many of his successors and friends afterwards tried to imitate, namely, the poise of the neck, which was bent slightly to the left, and the melting glance of his eyes, this artist has accurately observed. Appelles, however, in painting him as wielder of the thunder-bolt, did not reproduce his complexion, but made it too dark and swarthy. Whereas he was of a fair colour, as they say, and his fairness passed into ruddiness on his breast particularly, and in his face. Moreover, that a very pleasant odour exhaled from his skin and that there was a fragrance about his mouth and all his flesh, so that his garments were filled with it.

But while he was still a boy his self-restraint showed itself in the fact that, although he was impetuous and violent in other matters, the pleasures of the body had little hold upon him, and he indulged in them with great moderation, while his ambition kept his spirit serious and lofty in advance of his years. For it was neither every kind of fame nor fame from every source that he courted, as Philip did, who plumed himself like a sophist on the power of his oratory, and took care to have the victories of his chariots at Olympia engraved upon his coins; nay, when those about him inquired whether he would be willing to contend in the foot-race at the Olympic games, since he was swift of foot, "Yes," said he, "if I could have kings as my contestants." And in general, too, Alexander appears to have been averse to the whole race of athletes; at any rate, though he instituted very many contests, not only for tragic poets and players on the flute and players on the lyre, but also for rhapsodists, as well as for hunting of every sort and for fighting with staves, he took no interest in offering prizes either for boxing or for the pancratium.

[Alexander's father, Philip, employed Aristotle as his son's tutor.]

. . . Aristotle he admired at the first, and loved him, as he himself used to say, more than he did his father, for that the one had given him life, but the other had taught him a noble life; later, however, he held him in more or less of suspicion, not to the extent of doing him any harm, but his kindly attentions lacked their former ardour and affection towards him, and this was proof of estrangement. However, that eager yearning for philosophy which was imbedded in his nature and which ever grew with his growth, did not subside from his soul.

. . . Alexander was naturally munificent, and became still more so as his wealth increased. His gifts, too, were accompanied by a kindly spirit, with which alone, to tell the truth, a giver confers a favour. . . . [A] common Macedonian was driving a mule laden with some of the royal gold, and when the beast gave out, took the load on his own shoulders and tried to carry it. The king, then, seeing the man in great distress and learning the facts of the case, said, as the man was about to lay his burden down, "Don't give out, but finish your journey by taking this load to your own tent." Furthermore, he was generally more displeased with those who would not take his gifts than with those who asked for them.

[The Greeks considered anyone who did not speak Greek to be a "barbarian." Alexander and his armies obviously encountered many non-Greek speakers, but here Plutarch is probably referring to the Parthians. Parthia, a Middle Eastern kingdom, was attacked in late 330 B.C.E.]

. . . [H]e marched into Parthia, where, during a respite from fighting, he first put on the barbaric dress, [perhaps] from a desire to adapt himself to the native customs, believing that community of race and custom goes far towards softening the hearts of men. . . . At first he wore this only in intercourse with the Barbarians and with his companions at home, then people generally saw him riding forth or giving audience in this attire. The sight was offensive to the Macedonians, but they admired his other high qualities and thought they ought to yield to him in some things which made for his pleasure or his fame.

Under these circumstances, too, he adapted his own mode of life still more to the customs of the country, and tried to bring these into closer agreement with Macedonian customs, thinking that by a mixture and community of practice which produced good will, rather than by force, his authority would be kept secure while he was far away. For this reason, too, he chose out thirty thousand boys and gave orders that they should learn the Greek language and be trained to use Macedonian weapons, appointing many instructors for this work. His marriage to Roxana [from Bactria, a kingdom to the east of the Persian Empire], whom he saw in her youthful beauty taking part in a dance at a banquet, was a love affair, and yet it was thought to harmonize well with the matters which he had in hand. For the Barbarians were encouraged by the partnership into which the marriage brought them, and they were beyond measure fond of Alexander, because, most temperate of all men that he was in these matters, he would not consent to approach even the only woman who ever mastered his affections, without the sanction of law.

[By late 326 B.C.E., Alexander and his armies had conquered Persia and had crossed the Indus River Valley. After a major battle, Alexander wished to continue eastward.]

. . . [H]aving had all they could do to repulse an enemy who mustered only twenty thousand infantry and two thousand horse, they violently opposed Alexander when he insisted on crossing the river Ganges. . . . For they were told that [local] kings were awaiting them with eighty thousand horsemen, two hundred thousand footmen, eight thousand chariots, and six thousand fighting elephants.

At first, then, Alexander shut himself up in his tent from displeasure and wrath and lay there, feeling no gratitude for what he had already achieved unless he should cross the Ganges, nay, counting a retreat a confession of defeat. But his friends gave him fitting consolation, and his soldiers crowded about his door and besought him with loud cries and wailing, until at last he relented and began to break camp.

DOCUMENT ANALYSIS

1. Do you notice any negative observations in this account?

2. Does Plutarch say anything positive about Alexander, and would you characterize this account as generally positive?

3. Is there any evidence in this selection to support those historians who argue that Alexander wished for peace and unity? If so, what is it?

4. What kinds of leisure activities does Alexander seem to have enjoyed?

5. What reaction did the other Macedonians have when Alexander wore his "barbarian" clothes in public?

Course Name and Number ______________________ Instructor ______________________

DOCUMENT 5.1

Aelius Aristides, from "The Roman Oration" (2nd c. C.E.)

Source: Moses Hadas, *A History of Rome* (1956)

The period of Roman history between the rise of Nerva to the imperial throne in 96 C.E. and the death of the emperor Marcus Aurelius in 180 C.E. is known as the Pax Romana (Roman Peace), and its rulers during that time have been called the "Five Good Emperors." During this time, Rome reached the height of its military expansion and wealth. The pride and confidence of the Roman elite is clearly on display in the following document. The Roman Oration is one of the most important works of one of the most celebrated orators of the period. Aelius Aristides (120–189 C.E.) was a leader of the literary movement to revive the style of the Greek sophists. In The Roman Oration, *Aelius praises the accomplishments of Rome. His purpose was not to give an accurate account of Roman conquest and governance, but to dazzle his audience with hyperbolic eloquence. Even so, it gives us a glimpse of how Romans wished to think of themselves.*

"If one considers the vast extent of your empire he must be amazed that so small a fraction of it rules the world, but when he beholds the city and its spaciousness it is not astonishing that all the habitable world is ruled by such a capital. . . . Your possessions equal the sun's course. . . . You do not rule within fixed boundaries, nor can anyone dictate the limits of your sway. . . . Whatever any people produces can be found here, at all times and in abundance. . . . Egypt, Sicily, and the civilized part of Africa are your farms; ships are continually coming and going. . . .

"Vast as it is, your empire is more remarkable for its thoroughness than its scope: there are no dissident or rebellious enclaves. . . . The whole world prays in unison that your empire may endure forever.

"Governors sent out to cities and peoples each rule their charges, but in their relations to each other they are equally subjects. The principal difference between governors and their charges is this—they demonstrate the proper way to be a subject. So great is their reverence for the great Ruler [the emperor], who administers all things. Him they believe to know their business better than they themselves do, and hence they respect and heed him more than one would a master overseeing a task and giving orders. No one is so self-assured that he can remain unmoved upon hearing the emperor's name: he rises in prayer and adoration and utters a twofold prayer—to the gods for the Ruler, and to the Ruler for himself. And if the governors are in the least doubt concerning the justice of claims or suits of the governed, public or private, they send to the Ruler for instructions at once and await his reply, as a chorus awaits its trainer's directions. Hence the Ruler need not exhaust himself by traveling to various parts to settle matters in person. It is easy for him to abide in his place and manage the world through letters; these arrive almost as soon as written, as if borne on wings.

"But the most marvelous and admirable achievement of all, and the one deserving our fullest gratitude, is this. . . . You alone of the imperial powers of history rule over men who are free. You have not assigned this or that region to this nabob or that mogul; no people has been turned over as a domestic and bound holding—to a man not himself free. But just as citizens in an individual city might designate magistrates, so you, whose city is the whole world, appoint governors to protect and provide for the governed, as if they were elective, not to lord it over their charges. As a result, so far from disputing the office as if it were their own, governors make way for their successors readily when their term is up, and may not even await their coming. Appeals to a higher jurisdiction are as easy as appeals from parish to county. . . .

"But the most notable and praiseworthy feature of all, a thing unparalleled, is your magnanimous conception of citizenship. All of your subjects (and this implies the whole world) you have divided into two parts: the better endowed and more virile, wherever they may be, you have granted citizenship and even kinship; the rest you govern as obedient subjects. Neither the seas nor expanse of land bars citizenship; Asia and Europe are not differentiated. Careers are open to talent. . . . Rich and poor find contentment and profit in your system; there is no other way of life. Your polity is a single and all-embracing harmony. . . .

"You have not put walls around your city, as if you were hiding it or avoiding your subjects; to do so you considered ignoble and inconsistent with your principles, as if a master should show fear of his slaves. You did not overlook walls, however, but placed them round the empire, not the city. The splendid and distant walls you erected are worthy of you; to men within their circuit they are visible, but it requires a journey of months and years from the city to see them. Beyond the outermost ring of the civilized world you drew a second circle, larger in radius and easier to defend, like the outer fortifications of a city. Here you built walls and established cities in diverse parts. The cities you filled with colonists; you introduced arts and crafts and established an orderly culture. . . . Your military organization makes all others childish. Your soldiers and officers you train to prevail not only over the enemy but over themselves. The soldier lives under discipline daily, and none ever deserts the post assigned him.

"You alone are, so to speak, natural rulers. Your predecessors were masters and slaves in turn; as rulers they were counterfeits, and reversed their positions like players in a ball game. . . . You have measured out the world, bridged rivers, cut roads through mountains, filled the wastes with posting stations, introduced orderly and refined modes of life. . . .

"Be all gods and their offspring invoked to grant that this empire and this city flourish forever and never cease until stones float upon the sea and trees forbear to sprout in the springtide. May the great Ruler and his sons be preserved to administer all things well."

DOCUMENT ANALYSIS

1. In the modern world, most people regard imperialism as unequivocally oppressive. Based on this document, how might the Romans justify their conquests?

____

____

____

2. Pushing past the obvious exaggeration, what does this document tell us about how the Romans ruled?

____

____

____

3. The phrase "rule over men who are free" seems like an oxymoron to a modern person. What does the author mean by this?

4. This speech reflected the opinion of the Roman elite. If you asked a member of the Roman aristocracy what the special abilities of Romans were, how would he respond?

5. What are this author's criteria for the greatness of the Roman Empire?

Name ______________________ Date ______________________

Course Name and Number ______________________ Instructor ______________________

DOCUMENT 6.1

Nestor-Iskander on the fall of Constantinople (1450s)

Source: *Anthology of Old Russian Literature,* ed. Ad. Stender-Petersen in collaboration with Stefan Congrat-Butlar. (New York: Columbia University Press, 1954).

Nestor-Iskander was, insofar as we know, a Slav of Orthodox background who converted to Islam. His account of the fall of Constantinople has been preserved in Russian language sources, and tells the story of the battle from the Byzantine perspective—that is, from inside the city. Nestor-Iskander apparently was actually present for the siege and fall of the city.

This document paints a noble picture of the Byzantine Emperor, Constantine XI. More importantly, it highlights the intimate relationship between the Byzantine ruler, the Orthodox Church, and the elite of Byzantine society.

Nestor-Iskander concludes his tale by mentioning an old Byzantine "prophecy" that held that one day a people called the rhusios would gain control of Constantinople. Russian sources interpreted rhusios, which in Greek means "red-haired," as russkii, which means Russian. This "prophecy" would inspire some Russians to understand that Russia would take Constantinople's place as the heir of Rome, and the seat of true Christianity.

The godless [Sultan] Mohammed [II, 1451–1481], son of Murad [II, 1421–1451], who at that time ruled the Turks, took note of all the problems [that plagued Constantinople]. And, although he professed peace, he wanted to put an end to Emperor Constantine [XI, 1449–1453]. Towards that end he assembled a large army and, by land and by sea, suddenly appeared with that large force before the city [of Constantinople] and laid siege to it. . . . [The Emperor], therefore, sent his envoys to Sultan Mohammed in order to discuss peace and past [relations]. But Mohammed did not trust them, and as soon as the envoys departed, he ordered cannons and guns to fire at the city. Others were commanded to make ready wall-scaling equipment and build assault structures. Such city inhabitants as Greek, Venetian, and Genoese [mercenaries] left because they did not want to fight the Turks. . . .

On the fourteenth day, after they had said their heathen prayers, the Turks sounded trumpets, beat their drums, and played on all other of their musical instruments. . . . Because of continued heavy shooting, city defenders could not stand safely on the wall. Some crouched down awaiting the attack; others fired their cannons and guns as much as they could, killing many Turks. The Patriarch, bishops, and all clergy prayed constantly, pleading for God's mercy and for [His help in] saving the city.

When the Turks surmised that they had killed all the defenders on the wall, they ordered their forces to give a loud shout [before the assault]. Some soldiers carried incendiary devices, others ladders, still others wall-destroying equipment, and the rest many other instruments of destruction. They were ordered to attack and capture the city. City defenders, too, cried out and shouted back and engaged them in a fierce battle. The Emperor toured the city, encouraging his people, promising them God's help and ordering the ringing of church bells so as to summon all the inhabitants [to defend their city]. When the Turks heard the ringing of church bells, they ordered their trumpets, flutes, and thousands of other musical instruments to sound out. And there was a great and terrible slaughter! . . .

When Mohammed saw such a multitude of his men killed, and when he was told of Emperor's bravery, he could not sleep. [On May 27, 1453] he called in his Council and informed them that he wanted to lift the siege that night, before a large [Papal] fleet arrived in the city to reinforce [its defenses]. But then there appeared an unexpected miracle of God! The anticipated [Papal] help failed to materialize. Instead, at 7:00 p.m. that evening the entire city was suddenly engulfed by a great darkness. The air suddenly thickened and, in a moaning way, it hovered above the city. Then, big black drops of rain, as large as the eye of a buffalo, began to fall. People were shocked and horrified by this unusual occurrence. Patriarch Athanasius gathered all of his clergy and members of the Imperial Council, went to the Emperor, and told him the following: "Your Illustrious Majesty! All citizens of the city believe in its vitality. But they also think that the Holy Spirit has abandoned it. Now every living creature is foretelling the demise of this city. We beseech you to leave the city. All of us will perish here. For God's sake, please leave!". . . The Emperor did not listen to them. He replied instead: "Let God's will be done!"

. . . When they noticed the determination of the godless [Mohammed], [the Byzantine] military commanders, officials, and nobles joined the battle and implored the Emperor to leave in order to escape death. He wept bitterly and told them: "Remember the words I said earlier! Do not try to protect me! I want to die with you!" and they replied: "All of us will die for God's church and for you!"

Then they escorted him to [relative] safety and many people told him to leave the city. After they pledged their allegiance to him, they lamented and cried and returned to their posts. . . . There was fierce fighting, more vicious than all previous encounters. Many [Byzantine] military commanders, officials, and nobles perished and the few who survived went to the Emperor to report to him about the disaster. There is no way to give an accurate number of Byzantine and Turkish casualties. The select Turkish force of 3000, like wild animals, dispersed and searched all corners of the city in an effort to capture the Emperor.

The impious Mohammed then ordered all of his forces to occupy all city streets and gates in order to capture the Emperor. In his camp he retained only the Janissaries, who readied their cannons and guns in fear of a sudden attack by the Emperor. Sensing God's command, the Emperor went to the Great Church [St. Sophia?], where he fell to the ground pleading for God's mercy and forgiveness for his sins. Then he bade farewell to the Patriarch, the clergy, and the Empress, bowed to those who were present and left the church. . . . As he left the church the Emperor said: "If you want to suffer for God's church and for the Orthodox faith, then follow me!"

Then he mounted his horse and went to the Golden Gate, hoping to encounter there the godless. He was able to attract some 3000 [Byzantine] soldiers. Near the Gate they met a multitude of Turks whom they defeated. The Emperor wanted to reach the Gate but could not on account of many corpses. Then he encountered another large Turkish force and they fought till darkness. In this manner the Orthodox Emperor Constantine suffered for God's churches and for the Orthodox faith. On May 29 [1453], according to eyewitnesses, he killed more than 600 Turks with his own hand. And the saying was fulfilled. *It started with Constantine and it ended with Constantine.* . . .

. . . City inhabitants in streets and courtyards refused to surrender to the Turks. They fought them and on that day [May 29] many died, including women and children. Others were taken into captivity. Brave soldiers stationed themselves in windows and refused to surrender and give up their posts. . . . During daylight they ran and hid themselves in various abysses and at night they came out and fought the Turks. Others, especially women and children, threw bricks, tiles, and burning pieces of wood at them and thereby caused them great trouble.

[This form of resistance] stunned the pashas and sanjak-beys. Because they did not know what to do, they sent a messenger to the Sultan with the following information: "The city will not be pacified until you enter it!" He ordered that a search be made for the Emperor and the Empress. He [the Sultan] himself was afraid to enter the city and that fact troubled him greatly. He then called in [Byzantine] nobles and military commanders who had been captured in the battle and were held as war prisoners by the pashas. He gave them his resolute word and some gifts, and sent them, together with the pashas and sanjak-beys, to deliver the following message to [the defiant] city inhabitants in streets and courtyards: "All fighting must stop! There should be neither fear, nor killings nor taking people into captivity! If you disobey this order, all of you, including your wives and children, will be put to the sword!" And so it was. The fighting stopped. . . .

When he heard this the Sultan was pleased. . . .

. . . [H]eresy caused the downfall of old Rome. The Turks used their axes to shatter the doors of all churches of the Second Rome, the city of

Constantinople. Now [in Moscow], the new Third Rome, the Holy Ecumenical Apostolic Church of your sovereign state shines brighter than the sun in the universal Orthodox Christian faith throughout the world. Pious Tsar! Let [people of] your state know that all states of the Orthodox faith have now merged into one, your state. You are the only true Christian ruler under the sky!

DOCUMENT ANALYSIS

1. How do the two sides view the "great darkness" that enveloped the city on 27 May 1543?

2. How does Muhammed II view the Byzantine Emperor, the Orthodox Patriarch, and the other elites of Byzantine society?

3. What role does religion play in the outcome of the conflict, according to this source?

4. What weapons were the most critical to the fall of the city?

5. Which leader is portrayed as the better military commander, Constantine XI or Muhammed II?

DOCUMENT 7.1

From "The Holy *Qur'an*"

Source: *The Koran Interpreted,* trans. Arthur J. Arberry, 2 vols. (London: George Allen and Unwin, 1955), Vol. 1, pp. 41–46, 50–55, 65, 71–72.

The religion of Islam was revealed to an Arabian merchant named Muhammad in 610 C.E. Within about twenty years, by the time of Muhammad's death in 632, the religion was on firm footing within the Arabian Peninsula. The next few decades would see Islam spread quickly into Egypt and North Africa, as well as into the Middle East.

Shortly after Muhammad's death, in the 650s, an "official" version of God's words to Muhammad, as well as Muhammad's sayings, was written down. The Qu'ran is a document much like the Judeo-Christian Old Testament, containing the mythos of the religion, as well as its basic tenets and practices. Not surprisingly, given the influence of both Judaism and Christianity (or perhaps because, as some scholars suggest, the supreme God in each is actually the same being), there are many things that the three religions share in common. The following excerpt not only discusses some of the basic beliefs of Islam, but also illustrates some of the similarities between these three monotheistic religions.

Those unbelievers of the **People of the Book**
and the idolaters wish not that any good
should be sent down upon you from your Lord;
but God singles out for His mercy whom he will;
God is of bounty abounding. . . .

Many of the People of the Book wish they might
restore you as unbelievers, after you have believed,
in the jealousy of their souls, after the truth
has become clear to them; yet do you pardon
and be forgiving, till God brings His command;
truly God is powerful over everything.
And perform the prayer, and pay the alms;
whatever good you shall forward to your souls' account,
you shall find it with God; assuredly God
sees the things you do.
And they say, "None shall enter Paradise
except that they be Jews or Christians."
Such are their fancies. Say: "Produce your
proof, if you speak truly."
Nay, but whosoever submits his will to God,
being a good-doer, his wage is with his Lord,
and no fear shall be on them, neither shall
they sorrow.

The Jews say, "The Christians stand not on anything";
the Christians say, "The Jews stand not on anything";
yet they recite the Book. So too the ignorant
say the like of them. God shall decide
between them on the Day of Resurrection
touching their differences.
And who does greater evil than he who bars
God's places of worship, so that His Name
be not rehearsed in them, and strives to
destroy them?
Such men might never enter them, save in
fear; for them is degradation in the present world,
and in the world to come a mighty
chastisement.

To God belong the East and the West;
whithersoever you turn, there is the
Face of God;
God is All-embracing, All-knowing. . . .
Children of Israel, remember My blessing
wherewith I blessed you, and that I have
preferred you above all beings. . . .

And when his Lord tested Abraham
with certain words, and he fulfilled them.
He said, "Behold, I make you a leader
for the people." Said he, "And of my seed?"
He said "My covenant shall not reach
the evildoers."
And when We appointed the House to be
a place of visitation for the people,
and a sanctuary,
and: "Take to yourselves Abraham's station
for a place of prayer." And We made covenant
with Abraham and Ishmael, "Purify
My House for those that shall go about it
and those that cleave to it, to those who bow
and prostrate themselves." . . .

When his Lord said to him, "Surrender,"
he said, "I have surrendered me to
the Lord of all Being."
And Abraham charged his sons with this
and Jacob likewise: My sons, God has
chosen for you the religion;
see that you die not
save in surrender."

Why, were you witnesses, when death came
to Jacob? When he said to his sons,
"What will you serve after me?" They said,
"We will serve thy God and the God of thy fathers
Abraham, Ishmael, and Isaac, One God;
to Him we surrender."
That is a nation that has passed away;
there awaits them that they have earned,
and there awaits you that you have earned;
you shall not be questioned concerning
the things they did.

And they say, "Be Jews or Christians and
you shall be guided." Say thou: "Nay, rather
the creed of Abraham, a man of pure faith;
he was no idolater."
Say you: "We believe in God, and
in that which has been sent down on us
and sent down on Abraham, Ishmael,
Isaac and Jacob, and the Tribes,
and that which was given to Moses and Jesus
and the Prophets, of their Lord; we
make no division between any of them, and
to Him we surrender."
And if they believe in the like of that you
believe in, then they are truly guided; but if
they turn away, then they are clearly in
schism,
God will suffice you for them; He is
the All-hearing, the All-knowing;
the baptism of God; and who is there
that baptizes fairer than God?
Him we are serving.
Say: "Would you then dispute with us
concerning God, who is our Lord
and your Lord? Our deeds belong to us,
and to you belong your deeds; Him
we serve sincerely. . . . "

It is not piety, that you turn your faces
to the East and to the West.
True piety is this:
to believe in God, and the Last Day,
the angels, the Book, and the Prophets,
to give of one's substance, however cherished,
to kinsmen, and orphans,
the needy, the traveler, beggars,
and to ransom the slave,
to perform the prayer, to pay the alms.
And they who fulfill their covenant
when they have engaged in a covenant,
and endure with fortitude
misfortune, hardship, and peril,
these are they who are true in their faith,
these are the truly godfearing. . . .
O believers, prescribed for you is
the Fast, even as it was prescribed for
those that were before you—haply you
will be godfearing—
for days numbered; and if any of you
be sick, or if he be on a journey,
then a number of other days. . . .
And fight in the way of God with those
who fight with you, but aggress not: God
loves not the aggressors.
And slay them wherever you come upon them,
and expel them from where they expelled you;
persecution is more grievous than slaying.
But fight them not by the Holy Mosque
until they should fight you there;
then, if they fight you, slay them—
such is the recompense of unbelievers—
but if they give over, surely God is

All-forgiving, All-compassionate.
Fight them, till there is no persecution
and the religion is God's; then if they
give over, there shall be no enmity
save for evildoers.
The holy month for the holy month;
holy things demand retaliation.
Whoso commits aggression against you,
do you commit aggression against him
like as he has committed against you;
and fear you God, and know that God is
with the godfearing.
And expend in the way of God;
and cast not yourselves by your own hands
into destruction, but be good-doers; God
loves the good-doers.
Fulfill the Pilgrimage and the Visitation
unto God; but if you are prevented,
then such offering as may be feasible. . . .
And when you have performed your holy rites
remember God, as you remember your fathers
or yet more devoutly. . . .
God
there is no god but He, the
Living, the Everlasting.
Slumber seizes Him not, neither sleep;
to Him belongs
all that is in the heavens and the earth.
Who is there that shall intercede with Him
save by his leave?
He knows what lies before them and
what is after them,
and they comprehend not anything of
His knowledge save such as He
wills.
His Throne comprises the heavens and
earth;
the preserving of them oppresses Him not;
He is the All-high, the All-glorious.
No compulsion is there in religion.
Rectitude has become clear from error.
So whosoever disbelieves in idols
and believes in God, has laid hold of
the most firm handle, unbreaking; God is
All-hearing, All-knowing.
God is the Protector of the believers;
He brings them forth from the shadows
into the light. . . .
Those who believe and do deeds of
righteousness,
and perform the prayer, and pay the alms—
their wage awaits them with their Lord,
and no fear shall be on them, neither shall
they sorrow. . . .
God charges no soul save to its capacity;
standing to its account is what it has earned,
and against its account what it has merited.
Our Lord,
take us not to task
if we forget, or make mistake.
Our Lord,
charge us not with a load such
as Thou didst lay upon those before us.
Our Lord,
do Thou not burden us
beyond what we have the strength to bear.
And pardon us,
and forgive us,
and have mercy on us;
Thou art our Protector.
And help us against the people
of the unbelievers.

DOCUMENT ANALYSIS

1. From this excerpt, would you say that Islam is similar at all to Judaism and Christianity? If so, how?

2. How are Muslims supposed to fight?

3. What is the "Pilgrimage" referred to in this excerpt?

4. What sorts of good deeds should Muslims do?

5. Will Jews or Christians enter "Paradise" after death?

DOCUMENT 8.1

From *Sundiata: An Epic of Old Mali* (1235)

Source: D. T. Niane, *Sundiata: An Epic of Old Mali,* trans. G. D. Pickett (Essex, England: Longman House, 1988).

A powerful rival to Mandingo power in the Sudan was the pagan people called Soso. In order to check the influence of the Mali Empire, the Soso king, Soumaoro, killed the eleven brothers who were heirs to the throne of Mali. There was a twelfth, Sundiata, whom they spared because he was crippled.

The story of Sundiata's rise to power reveals much of the early history of the Mandingo king and his thrilling defeat of Soumaoro in 1235. The epic of old Mali contains a fascinating description of palace intrigue in the capital city of Niani. Sundiata emerges as the central hero of the tale through magic, cunning, strength and providence. Sundiata becomes a great king noted for his Muslim piety, wisdom, justice and military strength. Under his reign, the Mali Empire recovers from war and returns to prosperity. Caravans of many riches traveled to Niani, and people from distant lands spoke of this great king. Sundiata is still regarded by the Mandingo as their national hero.

The oral history excerpted below is primarily the work of an obscure griot from the village of Djeliba Koro. A "griot" is a member of a hereditary caste in West Africa whose job it is to keep the oral history of the tribe or village. As explained by author D.T. Niane, at one time "griots were the counsellors of kings, they conserved the constitutions of kingdoms by memory work alone; each princely family had its griot appointed to preserve tradition; it was from among the griots that kings used to choose the tutors for young princes. In the very hierarchical society of Africa before colonization, . . . the griot appears as one of the most important of this society, because it is he who, for want of archives, records the customs, traditions and governmental principles of kings."

Soumaoro sent a detachment under his son Sosso Balla to block Sundiata's route to Tabon. Sosso Balla was about the same age as Sundiata. He promptly deployed his troops at the entrance to the mountains to oppose Sundiata's advance to Tabon. . . .

Sundiata was immovable, so the orders were given and the war drums began to beat. On his proud horse Sundiata turned to right and left in front of his troops. He entrusted the rearguard, composed of a part of the Wagadou cavalry, to his younger brother Manding Bory. Having drawn his sword, Sundiata led the charge, shouting his war cry.

The Sossos were surprised by this sudden attack for they all thought that the battle would be joined the next day. The lightning that flashes across the sky is slower, the thunderbolts less frightening and floodwaters less surprising than Sundiata swooping down on Sosso Balla and his smiths. In a trice, Sundiata was in the middle of the Sossos like a lion in the sheepfold. The Sossos, trampled under the hooves of his fiery charger, cried out. When he turned to the right the smiths of Soumaoro fell in their tens, and when he turned to the left his sword made heads fall as when someone shakes a tree of ripe fruit. The horsemen of Mema wrought a frightful slaughter and their long lances pierced flesh like a knife sunk into a paw-paw. Charging ever forwards, Sundiata looked for Sosso Balla; he caught sight of him and like a lion bounded towards the son of Soumaoro, his sword held aloft. His arm came sweeping down but at that moment a Sosso warrior came between Djata and Sosso Balla and was sliced like a calabash. Sosso Balla did not wait and disappeared from amidst his smiths. Seeing their chief in flight, the Sossos gave way and fell into a terrible rout. . . .

The news of the battle of Tabon spread like wildfire in the plains of Mali. It was known that Soumaoro was not present at the battle, but the mere fact that his troops had retreated before Sundiata sufficed to give hope to all the peoples of Mali. Soumaoro realized that from now on he would have to reckon with this young man. He got to know of the prophecies of Mali, yet he was still too confident. When Sosso Balla returned with the remnant he had managed to save at Tabon, he said to his father, 'Father, he is worse than a lion; nothing can withstand him.'. . .

The son of Sogolon had already decided on his plan of campaign—to beat Soumaoro, destroy Sosso and return triumphantly to Niani. He now had five army corps at his disposal. . . .

Sundiata caught sight of him and tried to cut a passage through to him. He struck to the right and struck to the left and trampled underfoot. The murderous hooves of his 'Daffeké' dug into the chests of the Sossos. Soumaoro was now within spear range and Sundiata reared up his horse and hurled his weapon. It whistled away and bounced off Soumaoro's chest as off a rock and fell to the ground. Sogolon's son bent his bow but with a motion of the hand Soumaoro caught the arrow in flight and showed it to Sundiata as if to say 'Look, I am invulnerable.'

Furious, Sundiata snatched up his spear and with his head bent charged at Soumaoro, but as he raised his arm to strike his enemy he noticed that Soumaoro had disappeared. Manding Bory riding at his side pointed to the hill and said, 'Look, brother.'

Sundiata saw Soumaoro on the hill, sitting on his black-coated horse. How could he have done it, he who was only two paces from Sundiata? By what power had he spirited himself away on to the hill? The son of Sogolon stopped fighting to watch the king of Sosso. The sun was already very low and Soumaoro's smiths gave way but Sundiata did not give the order to pursue the enemy. Suddenly, Soumaoro disappeared! . . .

The battle of Neguéboria showed Djata, if he needed to be shown, that to beat the king of Sosso other weapons were necessary.

The evening of Neguéboria, Sundiata was master of the field, but he was in a gloomy mood. He went away from the field of battle with its agonized cries of the wounded, and Manding Bory and Tabon Wana watched him go. He headed for the hill where he had seen Soumaoro after his miraculous disappearance. . . .

But it was time to return to his native Mali. Sundiata assembled his army in the plain and each people provided a contingent to accompany the Mansa to Niani. . . .

Sundiata and his men had to cross the Niger in order to enter old Mali. One might have thought that all the dug-out canoes in the world had arranged to meet at the port of Ka-ba. It was the dry season and there was not much water in the river. The fishing tribe of Somono, to whom Djata had given the monopoly of the water, were bent on expressing their thanks to the son of Sogolon. They put all their dug-outs side by side across the Niger so that Sundiata's sofas could cross without wetting their feet.

When the whole army was on the other side of the river, Sundiata ordered great sacrifices. A hundred oxen and a hundred rams were sacrificed. It was thus that Sundiata thanked God on returning to Mali.

The villages of Mali gave Maghan Sundiata an unprecedented welcome. At normal times a traveller on foot can cover the distance from Ka-ba to Niani with only two halts, but Sogolon's son with his army took three days. The road to Mali from the river was flanked by a double human hedge. Flocking from every corner of Mali, all the inhabitants were resolved to see their saviour from close up. The women of Mali tried to create a sensation and they did not fail. At the entrance to each village they had carpeted the road with their multi-coloured pagnes, so that Sundiata's horse would not so much as dirty its feet on entering their village. . . .

Sundiata was leading the van. He had donned his costume of a hunter king—a plain smock, skin-tight trousers and his bow slung across his back. At his side Balla Fasséké was still wearing his festive garments gleaming with gold. Between Djata's general staff and the army Sosso Balla had been placed, amid his father's fetishes. But his hands were no longer tied. As at Ka-ba, abuse was everywhere heaped upon him and the prisoner did not dare look up at the hostile crowd. . . .

The troops were marching along singing the 'Hymn to the Bow', which the crowd took up. New songs flew from mouth to mouth. Young women offered the soldiers cool water and cola nuts. And so the triumphal march across Mali ended outside Niani, Sundiata's city.

It was a ruined town which was beginning to be rebuilt by its inhabitants. A part of the ramparts had been destroyed and the charred walls still bore the marks of the fire. From the top of the hill Djata looked on Niani, which looked like a dead city. He saw the plain of Sounkarani, and he also saw the site of the young baobab tree. The survivors of the catastrophe were standing in rows on the Mali road. The children were waving branches, a few young women were singing, but the adults were mute. . . .

With Sundiata peace and happiness entered Niani. Lovingly Sogolon's son had his native city rebuilt. He restored in the ancient style his father's old enclosure where he had grown up. People came from all the villages of Mali to settle in Niani. The walls had to be destroyed to enlarge the town, and new quarters were built for each kin group in the enormous army. . . .

After a year Sundiata held a new assembly at Niani, but this one was the assembly of dignitaries and kings of the empire. The kings and notables of all the tribes came to Niani. The kings spoke of their administration and the dignitaries talked of their kings. Fakoli, the nephew of Soumaoro, having proved himself too independent, had to flee to evade the Mansa's anger. His lands were confiscated and the taxes of Sosso were payed directly into the granaries of Niani. In this way, every year, Sundiata gathered about him all the kings and notables; so justice prevailed everywhere, for the kings were afraid of being denounced at Niani.

Djata's justice spared nobody. He followed the very word of God. He protected the weak against the strong and people would make journeys lasting several days to come and demand justice of him. Under his sun the upright man was rewarded and the wicked one punished.

In their new-found peace the villages knew prosperity again, for with Sundiata happiness had come into everyone's home. Vast fields of millet, rice, cotton, indigo and fonio surrounded the villages. Whoever worked always had something to live on. Each year long caravans carried the taxes in kind to Niani.

You could go from village to village without fearing brigands. A thief would have his right hand chopped off and if he stole again he would be put to the sword.

New villages and new towns sprang up in Mali and elsewhere. 'Dyulas', or traders, became numerous and during the reign of Sundiata the world knew happiness.

There are some kings who are powerful through their military strength. Everybody trembles before them, but when they die nothing but ill is spoken of them. Others do neither good nor ill and when they die they are forgotten. Others are feared because they have power, but they know how to use it and they are loved because they love justice. Sundiata belonged to this group. He was feared, but loved as well. He was the father of Mali and gave the world peace. After him the world has not seen a greater conqueror, for he was the seventh and last conqueror. He had made the capital of an empire out of his father's village, and Niani became the navel of the earth. . . .

The griots, fine talkers that they were, used to boast of Niani and Mali saying: 'If you want salt, go to Niani, for Niani is the camping place of the Sahel caravans. If you want gold, go to Niani, for Bouré, Bambougou and Wagadou work for Niani. If you want fine cloth, go to Niani, for the Mecca road passes by Niani. If you want fish, go to Niani, for it is there that the fishermen of Maouti and Djenné come to sell their catches. If you want meat, go to Niani, the country of the great hunters, and the land of the ox and the sheep. If you want to see an army, go to Niani, for it [is] there that the united forces of Mali are to be found. If you want to see a great king, go to Niani, for it is there that the son of Sogolon lives, the man with two names.'. . .

After him many kings and many Mansas reigned over Mali and other towns sprang up and disappeared. Hajji Mansa Moussa, of illustrious memory, beloved of God, built houses at Mecca for pilgrims coming from Mali, but the towns which he founded have all disappeared, Karanina, Bouroun-Kouna—nothing more remains of these towns. Other kings carried Mali far beyond Djata's frontiers, for example Mansa Samanka and Fadima Moussa, but none of them came near Djata.

Maghan Sundiata was unique. In his own time no one equalled him and after him no one had the ambition to surpass him. He left his mark on Mali for all time and his taboos still guide men in their conduct.

Mali is eternal. To convince yourself of what I have said go to Mali.

DOCUMENT ANALYSIS

1. In what manner does the king of Timbuktu (Tombuto) consolidate and maintain political and economic power?

2. Reading the geographic descriptions provided by Leo proved very useful to geographers of the period. What is the importance of the Niger River to kingdom-building in the Sudanic region?

3. The role of merchants is well described by this Arab traveler. What are the most important trade goods of the region? How is the trade conducted, and by whom?

4. What is Leo Africanus' opinion of the people of Mali (Melli)?

5. What is the role of Islam to kingdom-building in West Africa?

DOCUMENT 9.1

Usamah Ibn-Munqidh, "An Arab-Syrian Gentleman and Warrior in the Period of the Crusades" (1100s C.E.)

Source: Usamah Ibn-Munqidh, *An Arab-Syrian Gentleman and Warrior in the Period of the Crusades,* trans. Philip K. Hitti (New York: Columbia University Press, 2000), pp. 70, 158–61, 163–65.

The Crusades were a crucial series of events for both Europe and the Middle East. Scholars continue to debate exactly how much of Europe's Crusading efforts were truly religious, and how much motivated by other interests. Irrespective of this, the Crusades contributed to an expanding worldview for both Europeans and the peoples they encountered. Just as Westerners were learning about the Middle East, Middle Easterners were learning about Westerners.

In the mid-twelfth century C.E., a Syrian named Usamah Ibn-Muniqidh wrote a memoir about his life and times that included discussions of his experiences with Frankish (French) Crusaders. While other parts of his memoirs address his travels throughout Egypt and Lebanon and include a section eulogizing his father, it is his portrayal of the European Crusaders for which his work is most remembered.

A Moslem cavalier survives a Frankish thrust which cuts his heart vein.—I once witnessed in an encounter between us and the **Franks** one of our cavaliers, named Badi ibn-TalIl al-Qushayri, who was one of our brave men, receive in his chest, while clothes with only two pieces of garment, a lance thrust from a Frankish knight. The lance cut the vein in his chest and issued from his side. He turned back right away, but we never thought he would make his home alive. But as **Allah** (worthy of admiration is he!) had predestined, he survived and his wound was healed. But for one year after that, he could not sit up in case he was lying on his back unless somebody held him by the shoulders and helped him. At last what he suffered from entirely disappeared and he reverted to his old ways of living and riding. My only comment is: How mysterious are the works of him whose will is always executed among his creatures! He giveth life and he causeth death, but he is living and dieth not. In his hand is all good, and he is over all things potent.

An artisan dies from a needle prick.—We had once with us an artisan, 'Attab by name, who was one of the most corpulent and tall of men. He entered his home one day, and as he was sitting down he leaned on his hand against a robe which happened to be near him and in which there was a needle. The needle went through the palm of his hand and he died because of it. And, by Allah, as he moaned in the lower town, his moan could be heard from the citadel on account of the bulk of his body and the volume of his voice. This man dies of a needle, whereas al-Qushayri is pierced with a lance which penetrates through his chest and issues out of his side and yet suffers no harm!

A Shayzar woman captures three Franks.—The following will serve as an illustration of women's love of adventure:

A group of Frankish pilgrims, after making the pilgrimage, returned to Rafaniyyah, which at that time belonged to them. They then left it for Afamiyah. During the night they lost their way and landed in Shayzar, which at that time had no wall. They entered the city, numbering about seven or eight hundred men, women and children. The army of Shayzar had already gone out of the town in the company of my two uncles, 'Izz-al-DIn abu-al-'Asakir Sultan and Fakhr-al-DIn abu-Kamil Shafi' (may Allah's mercy rest upon their souls!), to meet two brides, whom my uncles had married, who were sisters and belonged to the banu-al-Sufi, the Aleppines. My father (may Allah's mercy rest upon his soul!) remained in the castle. One of our men, going out of the city at night on business, suddenly saw a Frank. He went back and got his sword, then went out and killed him. The battle cry sounded all over the town. The inhabitants went out, killed the Franks and took as booty all the women, children, silver and beasts of burden they had.

At that time there was in Shayzar a woman named Nadrah, daughter of Buzarmat, who was the wife of one of our men. This woman went out with our men, captured a Frank and introduced him into her house. She went out again, captured another Frank and brought him in. Again she went out and captured still another. Thus she had three Franks in her house. After taking as booty what they had and what suited her of their possessions, she went out and called some of her neighbors, who killed them.

During the same night my two uncles, with the army, arrived. Some of the Franks had taken to flight and were pursued by certain men from Shayzar, who killed them in the environs of the town. The horses of my uncles' army, on entering the town in the nighttime, began to stumble over corpses without knowing what they were stumbling over, until one of the cavaliers dismounted and saw the corpses in the darkness. This terrified our men, for they thought the town had been raided by surprise. In fact, it was booty which Allah (exalted and majestic is he!) had delivered into the hands of our people.

Prefers to be a Frankish shoemaker's wife to life in a Moslem castle.—A number of maids taken captive from the Franks were brought into the home of my father (may Allah's mercy rest upon his soul!). The Franks (may Allah's curse be upon them!) are an accursed race, the members of which do not assimilate except with their own kin. My father saw among them a pretty maid who was in the prime of youth, and said to his housekeeper, "Introduce this woman into the bath, repair her clothing and prepare her for a journey." This she did. He then delivered the maid to a servant of his and sent her to al-AmIr Shihab-al-DIn Malik ibn-Salim, the lord of the Castle of Ja'bar, who was a friend of his. He also wrote him a letter, saying, "We have won some booty from the Franks, from which I am sending thee a share." The maid suited Shihab-al-DIn, and he was pleased with her. He took her to himself and she bore him a boy, whom he called Badran. Badran's father named him his heir apparent, and he became of age. On his father's death, Badran became the governor of the town and its people, his mother being the real power. She entered into conspiracy with a band of men and let herself down from the castle by a rope. The band took her to Saruj, which belonged at that time to the Franks. There she married a Frankish shoemaker, while her son was the lord of the Castle of Ja'bar.

Their lack of sense.—Mysterious are the works of the Creator, the author of all things! When one comes to recount cases regarding the Franks, he cannot but glorify Allah (exalted is he!) and sanctify him, for he sees them as animals possessing the virtues of courage and fighting, but nothing else; just as animals have only the virtues of strength and carrying loads. I shall now give some instances of their doings and their curious mentality.

Newly arrived Franks are especially rough.—Everyone who is a fresh emigrant from the Frankish lands is ruder in character than those who have become acclimatized and have held long association with the Moslems.

Franks lack jealousy in sex affairs.—The Franks are void of all zeal and jealousy. One of them may be walking along with his wife. He meets another man who takes the wife by the hand and steps aside to converse with her while the husband is standing on one side waiting for his wife to conclude the conversation. If she lingers too long for him, he leaves her alone with the conversant and goes away.

Here is an illustration which I myself witnessed:

When I used to visit Nablus, I always took lodging with a man named Mu'izz, whose home was a lodging house for the Moslems. The house had windows which opened to the road, and there stood opposite to it on the other side of the road a house belonging to a Frank who sold wine for the merchants. He would take some wine in a bottle and go around announcing it by shouting, "So and so, the merchant, has just opened a cask full of this wine. He who wants to buy some of it will find it in such and such a place." The Frank's pay for the announcement made would be the wine in that bottle. One day this Frank went home and found a man with his wife in the same bed. He asked him, "What could have made thee enter into my wife's room?" The man replied, "I was tired, so I went in to rest." "But how," asked he, "didst thou get into my bed?" The other replied, "I found a bed that was spread, so I slept in it." "But," said he, "my wife was sleeping together with thee!" The other replied, "Well, the bed is hers. How could I therefore have prevented her from using her own bed?" "By the truth of my religion," said the husband, "if thou shouldst do it again, thou and I would have a quarrel." Such was for the Frank the entire expression of his disapproval and the limit of his jealousy.

DOCUMENT ANALYSIS

1. Does the author seem to favor women using their abilities or not? Why?

2. How diligently do the Frankish men work to keep their wives faithful, according to the author?

3. How does the author view the Franks?

4. Is there anything positive that the author recounts about the Franks?

5. What is the character of the new arrivals from Frankish territory?

DOCUMENT 10.1
Dandin, from *Tales of the Ten Princes* (500s)

Source: Dandin, *Tales of the Ten Princes,* in A. L. Basham, *The Wonder That Was India* (New York: Grove Press, 1954), pp. 444–6.

Much as Latin was long considered the "high" language of Christianity, the learned language of Hinduism is Sanskrit. Though few people could actually read it, scholars, intellectuals, and writers used it frequently in early India. One of the most well-known writers of Sanskrit literature in the early period was Dandin, who lived sometime in the late 500s to early 600s C.E.

Dandin's most noted work is Tales of the Ten Princes, *a collection of tales connected by an ongoing narrative. Focusing on the experiences of Prince Rajavahana, a Hindu prince, the tales are more secular than religious. Many of Dandin's tales tend to be sensual in nature, or deal with leading a virtuous life. Despite being written in a language that most Hindus could not understand, Dandin's stories provide quite a bit of detail about the lives and attitudes of common people. In this excerpt, Dandin uses his story to discuss the characteristics of the perfect wife.*

"In the land of the **Dravidians** is a city called Kañci. Therein dwelt the very wealthy son of a merchant, by name Saktikumara. When he was nearly eighteen he thought: 'There's no pleasure in living without a wife or with one of bad character. Now how can I find a really good one?' So, dubious of his chance of finding wedded bliss with a woman taken at the word of others, he became a fortune-teller, and roamed the land with a measure of unhusked rice tied in the skirts of his robe; and parents, taking him for an interpreter of birthmarks, showed their daughters to him. Whenever he saw a girl of his own class, whatever her birthmarks, he would say to her: 'My dear girl, can you cook me a good meal from this measure of rice?' And so, ridiculed and rejected, he wandered from house to house.

One day in the land of the Sibis, in a city on the banks of the Kaveri, he examined a girl who was shown to him by her nurse. She wore little jewellery, for her parents had spent their fortune, and had nothing left but their dilapidated mansion. As soon as he set eyes on her he thought: 'This girl is shapely and smooth in all her members. Not one limb is too fat or too thin, too short or too long. Her fingers are pink; her hands are marked with auspicious lines—the barleycorn, the fish, the lotus and the vase; her ankles are shapely; her feet are plump and the veins are not prominent; her thighs curve smoothly; her knees can barely be seen, for they merge into her rounded thighs; her buttocks are dimpled and round as chariot wheels; her navel is small, flat and deep; her stomach is adorned with three lines; the nipples stand out from her large breasts, which cover her whole chest; her palms are marked with signs which promise corn, wealth and sons; her nails are smooth and polished like jewels; her fingers are straight and tapering and pink; her arms curve sweetly from the shoulder, and are smoothly jointed; her slender neck is curved like a conch-shell; her lips are rounded and of even red; her pretty chin does not recede; her cheeks are round, full and firm; her eyebrows do not join above her nose, and are curved, dark and even; her nose is like a half-blown sesamum flower; her wide eyes are large and gentle and flash with three colours, black, white and brown; her brow is fair as the new moon; her curls are lovely as a mine of sapphires; her long ears are adorned doubly, with earrings and charming lotuses, hanging limply; her abundant hair is not brown, even at the tips, but long, smooth, glossy and fragrant. The character of such a girl cannot but correspond to her appearance, and my heart is fixed upon her, so I'll test her and marry her. For one regret after another is sure to fall on the heads of people who don't take precautions!' So, looking at her affectionately, he said, 'Dear girl, can you cook a good meal for me with this measure of rice?'

"Then the girl glanced at her old servant, who took the measure of rice from his hand and seated him on the veranda, which had been well sprinkled and swept, giving him water to cool his feet. Meanwhile the girl bruised the fragrant rice, dried it a little at a time in the sun, turned it repeatedly, and beat it with a hollow cane on a firm flat spot, very gently, so as to separate the grain without crushing the husk. Then she said to the nurse, 'Mother, goldsmiths can make good use of these husks for polishing jewellery. Take them, and, with the coppers you get for them, buy some firewood, not too green and not too dry, a small cooking pot, and two earthen dishes.'

"When this was done she put the grains of rice in a shallow wide-mouthed, round-bellied mortar, and took a long and heavy pestle of acacia-wood, its head shod with a plate of iron. . . . With skill and grace she exerted her arms, as the grains jumped up and down in the mortar. Repeatedly she stirred them and pressed them down with her fingers; then she shook the grains in a winnowing basket to remove the beard, rinsed them several times, worshipped the hearth, and placed them in water which had been five times brought to the boil. When the rice softened, bubbled and swelled, she drew the embers of the fire together, put a lid on the cooking pot, and strained off the gruel. Then she patted the rice with a ladle and scooped it out a little at a time; and when she found that it was thoroughly cooked she put the cooking pot on one side, mouth downward. Next she damped down those sticks which were not burnt through, and when the fire was quite out she sent them to the dealers to be sold as charcoal, saying, 'With the coppers that you get for them, buy as much as you can of green vegetables, ghee, curds, sesamum oil, myrobalans and tamarind.'

"When this was done she offered him a few savouries. Next she put the rice-gruel in a new dish immersed in damp sand, and cooled it with the soft breeze of a palm-leaf fan. She added a little salt, and flavoured it with the scent of the embers; she ground the myrobalans to a smooth powder, until they smelt like a lotus; and then, by the lips of the nurse, she invited him to take a bath. This he did, and when she too had bathed she gave him oil and myrobalans [as an unguent].

"After he had bathed he sat on a bench in the paved courtyard, which had been thoroughly sprinkled and swept. She stirred the gruel in the two dishes, which she set before him on a piece of pale green plantain leaf, cut from a tree in the courtyard. He drank it and felt rested and happy, relaxed in every limb. Next she gave him two ladlefuls of the boiled rice, served with a little ghee and condiments. She served the rest of the rice with curds, three spices, and fragrant and refreshing buttermilk and gruel. He enjoyed the meal to the last mouthful.

"When he asked for a drink she poured him water in a steady stream from the spout of a new pitcher—it was fragrant with incense, and smelt of fresh trumpet-flowers and the perfume of full-blown lotuses. He put the bowl to his lips, and his eyelashes sparkled with rosy drops as cool as snow; his ears delighted in the sound of the trickling water; his rough cheeks thrilled and tingled at its pleasant contact; his nostrils opened wide at its sweet fragrance; and his tongue delighted in its lovely flavour, as he drank the pure water in great gulps. Then, at his nod, the girl gave him a mouthwash in another bowl. The old woman took away the remains of his meal, and he slept awhile in his ragged cloak, on the pavement plastered with fresh cowdung.

"Wholly pleased with the girl, he married her with due rites, and took her home. Later he neglected her awhile and took a mistress, but the wife treated her as a dear friend. She served her husband indefatigably, as she would a god, and never neglected her household duties; and she won the loyalty of her servants by her great kindness. In the end her husband was so enslaved by her goodness that he put the whole household in her charge, made her sole mistress of his life and person, and enjoyed the three aims of life—virtue, wealth and love. So I maintain that virtuous wives make their lords happy and virtuous."

DOCUMENT ANALYSIS

1. According to Dandin, what sorts of attributes does an ideal wife possess?

2. Do domestic activities appear to be a primary concern for Indian men? Why or why not?

3. Does the author seem more concerned about the wife's moral nature or her physical appearance?

4. Does this excerpt seem to paint a picture of a "typical" husband and wife relationship throughout much of history? Why or why not?

5. What things does the husband in this excerpt do for his wife?

DOCUMENT 10.2

Marco Polo on Chinese society under the Mongol rule (1270s)

Source: W. Marsden, trans., *The Travels of Marco Polo (1818)*; rendered into modern English by A. J. Andrea.

Marco Polo was the son of an Italian merchant who traveled the Silk Road to Mongol China in the year 1275. A gifted linguist and master of four languages, Marco Polo was appointed by emperor Kublai Khan as an official in the Privy Council in 1277 and for three years he was a tax inspector in Yanzhou, a city on the Grand Canal near the northeastern coast. He also visited Karakorum, the old capital of the original Mongol empire. Marco Polo stayed in Khan's court for seventeen years, acquiring great wealth in gold and jewelry.

Reportedly, Marco Polo kept a detailed dairy about his travels and his experiences in China. He recalled in great detail the moment when he and other members of his family first met the Emperor Kublai Khan: "They knelt before him and made obeisance with the utmost humility. The Great Khan bade them rise and received them honorably and entertained them with good cheer. He asked many questions about their condition and how they fared after their departure . . . Then they presented the privileges and letters which the Pope had sent, with which he was greatly pleased, and handed over the holy oil, which he received with joy and prized very highly."

Marco Polo's account of his life under the Mongols and his personal experience in China's Yuan Dynasty caused both curiosity and doubts among Westerners. Many questioned the validity of his records, wondering if he had ever reached China. The controversy led to a book in 1995 entitled Did Marco Polo Go to China? *by Frances Wood, head of Chinese Studies at the British Library. Wood argued that Marco Polo probably only went as far as Constantinople, where he gathered information on China from Arabs and Persians who returned from their China trip.*

It is their custom that the bodies of all deceased grand khans and other great lords from the family of Chinggis Khan are carried for internment to a great mountain called **Altai.** No matter where they might die, even if it is a hundred days' journey away, they nevertheless are brought here for burial. It is also their custom that, in the process of conveying the bodies of these princes, the escort party sacrifices whatever persons they happen to meet along the route, saying to them: "Depart for the next world and there serve your deceased master." They believe that all whom they kill in this manner will become his servants in the next life. They do the same with horses, killing all the best, so that the dead lord might use them in the next world. When the corpse of **Mongke** Khan was transported to this mountain, the horsemen who accompanied it slew upward of 20,000 people along the way.

Now that I have begun speaking about the **Tartars,** I will tell you more about them. They never remain fixed in one location. As winter approaches they move to the plains of a warmer region in order to find sufficient pasturage for their animals. In summer they inhabit cool regions in the mountains where there is water and grass and their animals are free of the annoyance of gad-flies and other biting insects. They spend two or three months progressively climbing higher and grazing as they ascend, because the grass is not sufficient in any one spot to feed their extensive herds.

Their huts, or tents, are circular and formed by covering a wooden frame with felt. These they transport on four-wheeled carts wherever they travel, since the framework is so well put together that it is light to carry. Whenever they set their huts up, the entrance always faces south. They also have excellent two-wheeled vehicles so well covered with black felt that, no matter how long it rains, rain never penetrates. These are drawn by oxen and camels and serve to carry their wives, children, and all necessary utensils and provisions.

It is the women who tend to their commercial concerns, buying and selling, and who tend to all the needs of their husbands and households. The men devote their time totally to hunting, hawking, and warfare. They have the best falcons in the world, as well as the best dogs. They subsist totally on meat and milk, eating the produce of their hunting, especially a certain small animal, somewhat like a hare, which our people call Pharaoh's rats, which are abundant on the steppes in summer. They likewise eat every manner of animal: horses, camels, even dogs, provided they are fat. They drink mare's milk, which they prepare in such a way that it has the qualities and taste of white wine. In their language they call it *kemurs.*

Their women are unexcelled in the world so far as their chastity and decency of conduct are concerned, and also in regard to their love and devotion toward their husbands. They regard marital infidelity as a vice which is not simply dishonorable but odious by its very nature. Even if there are ten or twenty women in a household, they live in harmony and highly praiseworthy concord, so that no offensive word is ever spoken. They devote full attention to their tasks and domestic duties, such as preparing the family's food, managing the servants, and caring for the children, whom they raise in common. The wives' virtues of modesty and chastity are all the more praiseworthy because the men are allowed to wed as many women as they please. The expense to the husband for his wives is not that great, but the benefit he derives from their trading and from the work in which they are constantly employed is considerable. For this reason, when he marries he pays a dowry to his wife's parents. The first wife holds the primary place in the household and is reckoned to be the husband's most legitimate wife, and this status extends to her children. Because of their unlimited number of wives, their offspring is more numerous than that of any other people. When a father dies, his son may take all of his deceased father's wives, with the exception of his own mother. They also cannot marry their sisters, but upon a brother's death they may marry their sisters-in-law. Every marriage is solemnized with great ceremony.

. . .

Their weapons are bows, iron maces, and in some instances, spears. The bow, however, is the weapon at which they are the most expert, being accustomed to use it in their sports from childhood. They wear armor made from the hides of buffalo and other beasts, fire-dried and thus hard and strong.

They are brave warriors, almost to the point of desperation, placing little value on their lives, and exposing themselves without hesitation to every sort of danger. They are cruel by nature. They are capable of undergoing every manner of privation, and when it is necessary, they can live for a month on the milk of their mares and the wild animals they catch. Their horses feed on grass alone and do not require barley or other grain. The men are trained to remain on horseback for two days and two nights without dismounting, sleeping in the saddle while the horse grazes. No people on the earth can surpass them in their ability to endure hardships, and no other people shows greater patience in the face of every sort of deprivation. They are most obedient to their chiefs, and are maintained at small expense. These qualities, which are so essential to a soldier's formation, make them fit to subdue the world, which in fact they have largely done.

When one of the great Tartar chiefs goes to war, he puts himself at the head of an army of 100,000 horsemen and organizes them in the following manner. He appoints an officer to command every ten men and others to command groups of 100, 1,000, and 10,000 men respectively. Thus ten of the officers who command ten men take their orders from an officer who commands 100; ten of these captains of a 100 take their orders from an officer in charge of a 1,000; and ten of these officers take orders from one who commands 10,000. By this arrangement, each officer has to manage only ten men or ten bodies of men. . . . When the army goes into the field, a body of 200 men is sent two days' march in advance, and parties are stationed on each flank and in the rear, to prevent surprise attack.

When they are setting out on a long expedition, they carry little with them. . . . They subsist for the most part on mare's milk, as has been said. . . . Should circumstances require speed, they can ride for ten days without lighting a fire or taking a hot meal. During this time they subsist on the blood drawn from their horses, each man opening a vein and drinking the blood. They also have dried milk. . . . When setting off on an expedition, each man takes about ten pounds. Every morning they put about half a pound of this into a leather flask, with as much water as necessary. As they ride, the motion violently shakes the contents, producing a thin porridge which they take as dinner. . . .

All that I have told you here concerns the original customs of the Tartar lords. Today, however, they are corrupted. Those who live in China have adopted the customs of the idol worshippers, and those who inhabit the eastern provinces have adopted the ways of the Muslims.

DOCUMENT ANALYSIS

1. Could Marco Polo tell the difference between Chinese culture and Mongol traditions?

___

___

___

2. How Chinese was the Mongol governor in his perspective and his rule?

___

___

___

3. How different or similar are the views of the Mongol governor and Marco Polo concerning the Mongol Empire?

___

___

___

4. To what can you attribute the success of the Mongol rule in China?

Name ______________________ Date ______________________

Course Name and Number ______________________ Instructor ______________________

DOCUMENT 11.1

Xicohtencatl the Elder, "I Say This" (15th–16th c. C.E.)

Source: Xicohtencatl, the Elder, "I Say This," in *Fifteen Poets of the Aztec World,* ed. Miguel Leon-Portilla (Norman, OK: University of Oklahoma Press, 1992), pp. 239–40.

*Xicohtencatl, the Elder, was Lord of Tizatlan. He was also a composer of songs. What is known is that he was born in about 1425 and lived until 1522 C.E., after the arrival of the Spanish. Xicohtencatl was also a warrior. It is said he took part in important battles and conquests involving the Mexicas (Aztecs), but in the end Xicohtencatl was forced to come to an agreement making Tizatlan an ally of other chiefdoms in the lake region near Mexico-**Tenochtitlán.***

Warfare for these people, in this era, had very specific rules. A field needed to be marked, and the battle could not go beyond its boundaries. The battles provided an opportunity for sons of lords to practice warfare, but they could not attempt to gain land for chiefdoms out of the war. The warriors captured would be sacrificed to the gods.

Warfare was about the political ambitions of the combatants and brought out the Mexican "worldview" that they were the chosen people of Huitzelopochi, the god of war. Xicohtencatl made a decision to take advantage of the arrival of the Spanish to aid in his fight against surrounding chiefdoms. However, the Spanish were ultimately not interested in helping native groups, but in conquering them.

*The **Flowery Wars** tells of the past struggles of the people of Tlazcala (the wider confederacy of cities of which Tizatlan was a part). The poem speaks to the value of war in the life of Tlazcala, because "flowery war" is sacred war. However, there is irony in telling the glory of wars that eventually, with the coming of the Spanish, brought doom to the people of Tlazcala.*

I say this, I the lord Xicohtencatl:
Do not go forth in vain!
Take up your shield, the vessel of flowery water!
Your little bowl with a handle.
Your precious vessel, color of obsidian, stands upright,
with it, we will bring the water on our shoulders,
we will carry it there in Mexico,
from Chapolco, on the shore of the lake.

Do not go forth in vain,
my nephew, my little children, my nephews,
you, children of the water!
I make the water flow,
O Lord Cuauhtencoztli,
let us all go!

We will bring the water on our shoulders,
truly we are going to carry it!

Captain Motelchiuhtzin wants to announce it,
my friends!
He says it is not yet dawn.
We take up our burden of water:
crystal clear, precious, color of turquoise,
which moves in waves.
Thus you will come there, to the place of the vessels,
do not go forth in vain!

Nanahuatl [the god] will perhaps make noise there.
My little son!
You, leader of men, you, precious creature,
a painting with gold in the Toltec manner,
paint the precious bowl, Lord Axayacatl.
We go together to partake,
we approach the precious waters.
They are falling, drops rain down,
there, close to the small canals.

He who carries my flowery water, Huanitzin,
now comes to give it to me,
O my uncles, Tlaxcalans, Chichimecs!
Do not go forth in vain!

The flowery war, the shield's flower,
have opened their corollas.
They resound,
the sweet-smelling flowers rain down,
Thus perhaps for this,
he came to conceal gold and silver;
for this I take the painted books.
O my little canal, with my vessel the water flows!
O my old ones!

DOCUMENT ANALYSIS

1. Both documents refer to the "field." What is the significance? Why would there be a specific place for warfare?

____

____

____

2. How do the documents speak of the warriors?

____

____

____

3. How do you see the place of warfare in the life of a people? Would it have been the most important thing in a communityís life? What does it tell us about the overall culture?

____

____

____

4. What is the relationship of the gods to the warriors? What part do the gods play in war?

5. What is the significance of flowers? What is the connection between flowers and warfare?

DOCUMENT 11.2

Anonymous Aztec (mid-1500s), "The Midwife Addresses the Woman Who Has Died in Childbirth"

Source: "The Midwife Addresses the Woman Who Has Died in Childbirth," trans. John Bierhorst in Nahuatl (1994).

The Florentine Codex was one of several permanent records of Aztec culture. Like other codices, the Florentine Codex was written down by the Spanish, who had Aztec elders tell them the stories of the Aztec people. It is known as the General History of the Things of New Spain.

In Aztec culture, the parents of a married couple who are expecting a child choose a midwife for the pregnant mother. After some ritualistic protests, the midwife accepts the task of delivering the child and assumes care of the expectant mother. The midwife and the woman prepare for the birth. The midwife prepares the "flower house," or birthing room. The expectant woman is urged to be like Cihuacoatl Quilaztli, source of the human race, and bring forth another human in, to the world. The woman is also likened to a warrior in battle.

If the woman successfully gives birth, she is addressed as a great warrior, but reminded to be humble. She should respect the Creator who gives life and takes it away. If she dies in childbirth, she is spoken of as one of the great warriors in the sky. She will become one of the women who accept the sun at midday and lead it down to the west.

In the document that follows, the midwife addresses a woman who has died in childbirth. We see that the midwife treats the woman as a god. She prays to the woman, who lies silent in death in front of her.

Precious feather, child,
Eagle woman, dear one,
Dove, daring daughter,
You have labored, you have toiled,
Your task is finished.
You came to the aid of your Mother, the noble lady, Cihuacoatl Quilaztli.
You received, raised up, and held the shield, the little buckler that she laid in your hands: she your Mother, the noble lady, Cihuacoatl Quilaztli.
Now wake! Rise! Stand up!
Comes the daylight, the daybreak:
Dawn's house has risen crimson, it comes up standing.
The crimson swifts, the crimson swallows, sing,
And all the crimson swans are calling.
Get up, stand up! Dress yourself!
Go! Go seek the good place, the perfect place, the home of your Mother,
your Father, the Sun,
The place of happiness, joy,
Delight, rejoicing.
Go! Go follow your Mother, your Father, the Sun.
May his elder sisters bring you to him: they the exalted, the celestial women,
who always and forever know happiness, joy, delight, and rejoicing, in the company and in the presence of our Mother, our Father, the Sun; who make him happy with their shouting.
My child, darling daughter, lady,
You spent yourself, you labored manfully:
You made yourself a victor, a warrior for Our Lord, though not without consuming all your strength; you sacrificed yourself.
Yet you earned a compensation, a reward: a good, perfect, precious death.
By no means did you die in vain.
And are you truly dead? You have made a sacrifice. Yet how else could you have become worthy of what you now deserve?
You will live forever, you will be happy, you will rejoice in the company and in the presence of our holy ones, the exalted women. Farewell, my daughter, my child. Go be with them, join them. Let them hold you and take you in.
May you join them as they cheer him and shout to him: our Mother, our Father, the Sun;
And may you be with them always, whenever they go in their rejoicing.

But my little child, my daughter, my lady,
You went away and left us, you deserted us, and we are but old men and old women.
You have cast aside your mother and your father.
Was this your wish? No, you were summoned, you were called.
Yet without you, how can we survive?
How painful will it be, this hard old age?
Down what alleys or in what doorways will we perish?
Dear lady, do not forget us! Remember the hardships that we see, that we suffer, here on earth:
The heat of the sun presses against us; also the wind, icy and cold:
This flesh, this clay of ours, is starved and trembling. And we, poor prisoners of our stomachs! There is nothing we can do.
Remember us, my precious daughter, O eagle woman, O lady!
You lie beyond in happiness. In the good place, the perfect place,
You live.
In the company and in the presence of our lord,
You live.
You as living flesh can see him, you as living flesh can call to him.
Pray to him for us!
Call to him for us!
This is the end,
We leave the rest to you.

DOCUMENT ANALYSIS

1. How does the midwife address the woman who has just died?

____

____

____

2. How does the midwife describe life for those left behind?

____

____

____

3. How does the midwife describe what it will be like in "the good place"?

4. How is the woman like a warrior?

5. What evidence of Aztec theology is evident in this song?

Name ______________________ Date ______________________

Course Name and Number ______________________ Instructor ______________________

DOCUMENT 12.1

Gianfrancesco Morosini, "Turkey Is a Republic of Slaves" (late 16th c.)

Source: Gianfrancensco Morosini, "Turkey Is a Republic of Slaves," in *Pursuit of Power: Venetian Ambassadors' Reports on Spain, Turkey, and France in the Age of Phillip II,* 1560–1600 (New York: Torchbook/Harper and Row, 1970), pp. 127–9, 131–4.

Constantinople was conquered in 1453 by the Ottoman Empire. The city was renamed Istanbul and was soon on its way back to the greatness it had enjoyed during the height of the Byzantine Empire. Indeed, just as the city had been the cultural, intellectual, and political heart for the Byzantines, so, too, would it be for the Ottoman Empire.

But, in many ways, the history of the Ottoman Empire was of a quick, decisive rise to power followed by a long, steady decline. Even by the seventeenth century, European observers (who admittedly tended to be biased against Muslim institutions anyway) were noticing signs of decay and weakness. One such individual was a Venetian ambassador to Istanbul, who was in Turkey during the 1580s. His reports Gianfrancesco Morosini not only discuss the organization of the military and the government, but also provide a European view of the perceived strengths and weaknesses of the Turkish people. These and other dispatches also describe the Turkish capital.

They succeed to the throne without any kind of ceremony of election or coronation. According to Turkish law of succession, which resembles most countries' laws in this respect, the oldest son should succeed to the throne as soon as the father dies. But in fact, whichever of the sons can first enter the royal compound in Constantinople is called the sultan and is obeyed by the people and by the army. Since he has control of his father's treasure he can easily gain the favor of the janissaries and with their help control the rest of the army and the civilians.

Because this government is based on force, the brother who overcomes the others is considered the lord of all. The same obedience goes to a son who can succeed in overthrowing his father, a thing which bothers the Turks not at all. As a result, when his sons are old enough to bear arms, the sultan generally does not allow them near him, but sends them off to some administrative district where they must live under continual suspicion until their father's death. And just as the fathers do not trust their own sons, the sons do not trust their fathers and are always afraid of being put to death. This is the sad consequence of unbridled ambition and hunger for power—a miserable state of affairs where there is no love between father and sons, and much less between sons and father.

This lord has thirty-seven kingdoms covering enormous territory. His dominion extends to the three principal parts of the world, Africa, Asia, and Europe; and since these lands are joined and contiguous with each other, he can travel for a distance of eight thousand miles on a circuit through his empire and hardly need to set foot in another prince's territories.

The principal cities of the Turks are Constantinople, **Adrianople,** and Bursa, the three royal residence places of the sultans. Buda is also impressive, as are the Asian cities—Cairo, Damascus, Aleppo, Bagdad and others—but none of these have the things which usually lend beauty to cities. Even Constantinople, the most important of them all, which is posted in the most beautiful and enchanting situation that can be imagined, still lacks those amenities that a great city should have, such as beautiful streets, great squares, and handsome palaces. Although Constantinople has many mosques, royal palaces, inns, and public baths, the rest of the city is mazy and filthy; even these [public buildings], with their leaded domes studded with gilded bronze ornaments, only beautify the long-distance panorama of the city.

The security of the empire depends more than anything else on the large numbers of land and sea forces which the Turks keep continually under arms. These are what make them feared throughout the world.

The sultan always has about 280,000 well-paid men in his service. Of them about 80,000 are paid every three months out of his personal treasury. These include roughly 16,000 janissaries, who form the Grand Signor's advance guard; six legions, or about 12,000 cavalry called "spahi," who serve as his rear guard; and about 1,500 other defenders. . . . The other 200,000 cavalry . . . are not paid with money like the others, but are assigned landholdings [called timars].

The timariots are in no way inferior as fighting men to the soldiers paid every three months with cash, because the timars are inherited like the fiefs distributed by Christian rulers.

What about the fighting qualities of these widely feared Turkish soldiers? I can tell you the opinion I formed at Scutari, where I observed the armies of Ferrad Pasha and Osman Pasha (Ferrad's army was there for more than a month, and Osman's for a matter of weeks). I went over to Scutari several times to confer with the two pashas and also, unofficially, to look at the encampment, and I walked through the whole army and carefully observed every detail about the caliber of their men, their weapons, and the way they organize a bivouac site and fortify it. I think I can confidently offer this conclusion: they rely more on large numbers and obedience than they do on organization and courage.

Although witnesses who saw them in earlier times claim they are not as good as they used to be, it appears that the janissaries are still the best of the Turkish soldiers. They are well-made men, and they can handle their weapons—the arquebus, club, and scimitar—quite well. These men are accustomed to hardships, but they are only used in battle in times of dire necessity.

As for the cavalry, some are lightly armed with fairly weak lances, huge shields, and scimitars.

If I compare these men with Christian soldiers, such as those I saw in the wars in France or in the Christian King's conquest of Portugal, I would say they are much better than Christian soldiers in respect to obedience and discipline. However, in courage and enthusiasm, and in physical appearance and weapons, they are distinctly inferior.

The naval forces which the Great Turk uses to defend his empire are vast and second to none in the world. . . . True, at present they do not have at hand all the armaments they would need to outfit the as yet uncompleted galleys, . . . But his resources are so great that if he wanted to he could quickly assemble what he needs; he has already begun to attend to this.

DOCUMENT ANALYSIS

1. From the document, how does it appear that a new king is selected in the Ottoman Empire?

____

____

____

2. How does the author evaluate the Ottoman army?

3. Is Constantinople considered an attractive city by the author?

4. What are the three principal Turkish cities?

5. Would you consider this a positive or a negative account? Why?

Name ______________________ Date ______________________

Course Name and Number ______________________ Instructor ______________________

DOCUMENT 13.1

Ieyasu Tokugawa, "Closed Country Edict of 1635" and "Exclusion of the Portuguese, 1639" (1630s)

Source: *Japan: A Documentary History,* trans. and ed. David John Lu (Armonk, NY: M. E. Sharpe, 1997).

Ieyasu Tokugawa was granted the title of shogun in 1603 after defeating his rivals by using guns brought into Japan by the Europeans. His successors, however, began to fear that the growing trade with the West and influence of Christianity would directly challenge the Japanese value system. Below are two major shogun edicts intended to force foreign trade and missionaries out of Japan. Japan remained an isolated country for the next two hundred years, until the Americans tried to open relations with Japan in 1853.

CLOSED COUNTRY EDICT OF 1635

1. Japanese ships are strictly forbidden to leave for foreign countries.

2. No Japanese is permitted to go abroad. If there is anyone who attempts to do so secretly, he must be executed. The ship so involved must be impounded and its owner arrested, and the matter must be reported to the higher authority.

3. If any Japanese returns from overseas after residing there, he must be put to death.

4. If there is any place where the teachings of padres is practiced, the two of you must order a thorough investigation.

5. Any informer revealing the whereabouts of the followers of padres must be rewarded accordingly. If anyone reveals the whereabouts of a high ranking padre, he must be given one hundred pieces of silver. For those of lower ranks, depending on the deed, the reward must be set accordingly.

6. If a foreign ship has an objection [to the measures adopted] and it becomes necessary to report the matter to **Edo,** you may ask the **Omura** domain to provide ships to guard the foreign ship. . . .

7. If there are any **Southern Barbarians** who propagate the teachings of padres, or otherwise commit crimes, they may be incarcerated in the prison. . . .

8. All incoming ships must be carefully searched for the followers of padres.

9. No single trading city shall be permitted to purchase all the merchandise brought by foreign ships.

10. Samurai are not permitted to purchase any goods originating from foreign ships directly from Chinese merchants in Nagasaki.

11. After a list of merchandise brought by foreign ships is sent to Edo, as before you may order that commercial dealings may take place without waiting for a reply from Edo.

12. After settling the price, all white yarns brought by foreign ships shall be allocated to the five trading cities and other quarters as stipulated.

13. After settling the price of white yarns, other merchandise [brought by foreign ships] may be traded freely between the [licensed] dealers. However, in view of the fact that Chinese ships are small and cannot bring large consignments, you may issue orders of sale at your discretion. Additionally, payment for goods purchased must be made within twenty days after the price is set.

14. The date of departure homeward of foreign ships shall not be later than the twentieth day of the ninth month. Any ships arriving in Japan later than usual shall depart within fifty days of their arrival. As to the departure of Chinese ships, you may use your discretion to order their departure after the departure of the Portuguese ***galeota.***

15. The goods brought by foreign ships which remained unsold may not be deposited or accepted for deposit.

16. The arrival in Nagasaki of representatives of the five trading cities shall not be later than the fifth day of the seventh month. Anyone arriving later than that date shall lose the quota assigned to his city.

17. Ships arriving in Hirado must sell their raw silk at the price set in Nagasaki, and are not permitted to engage in business transactions until after the price is established in Nagasaki.

You are hereby required to act in accordance with the provisions set above. It is so ordered.

EXCLUSION OF THE PORTUGUESE, 1639

1. The matter relating to the proscription of Christianity is known [to the Portuguese]. However, heretofore they have secretly transported those who are going to propagate that religion.

2. If those who believe in that religion band together in an attempt to do evil things, they must be subjected to punishment.

3. While those who believe in the preaching of padres are in hiding, there are incidents in which that country [Portugal] has sent gifts to them for their sustenance.

In view of the above, hereafter entry by the Portuguese galeota is forbidden. If they insist on coming [to Japan], the ships must be destroyed and anyone aboard those ships must be beheaded. We have received the above order and are thus transmitting it to you accordingly.

The above concerns our disposition with regard to the galeota.

Memorandum

With regard to those who believe in Christianity, you are aware that there is a proscription, and thus knowing, you are not permitted to let padres and those who believe in their preaching to come aboard your ships. If there is any violation, all of you who are aboard will be considered culpable. If there is anyone who hides the fact that he is a Christian and boards your ship, you may report it to us. A substantial reward will be given to you for this information.

This memorandum is to be given to those who come on Chinese ships. [A similar note to the Dutch ships.]

DOCUMENT ANALYSIS

1. How would these two edicts affect Japan's relations with the outside world?

____

____

____

2. What was the argument behind the shogun's decision of 1639 to expel the Christians?

____

____

____

3. What was the primary purpose of the 1635 Edict?

4. What were the major restrictions imposed upon the Japanese?

5. What were the major restrictions on foreign traders?

DOCUMENT 14.1
Giorgio Vasari, from "Life of Leonardo Da Vinci" (1550)

This description of Leonardo barely does justice to its brilliant subject. Da Vinci gave meaning to the phrase "Renaissance Man." He was an artist, a scientist, an inventor par excellence. This short piece was written by Vasari, a contemporary of Leonardo, and a keen observer of Renaissance Rome. It is believed that Vasari actually coined the term "renaissance."

The richest gifts are occasionally seen to be showered, as by celestial influence, upon certain human beings; nay, they sometimes supernaturally and marvelously congregate in a single person,—beauty, grace, and talent being united in such a manner that to whatever the man thus favored may turn himself, his every action is so divine as to leave all other men far behind him. This would seem manifestly to prove that he has been specially endowed by the hand of God himself, and has not obtained his preeminence through human teaching or the powers of man.

This was perceived and acknowledged by all men in the case of Leonardo da Vinci, in whom (to say nothing of his beauty of person, which yet was such that it has never been sufficiently extolled) there was a grace beyond expression, which was manifest without thought or effort in every act and deed, and who had besides so rare a gift of talent and ability that to whatever subject he turned his attention, no matter how difficult, he presently made himself absolute master of it.

In him extraordinary power was combined with remarkable facility, a mind of regal boldness and magnanimous daring. His gifts were such that the celebrity of his name was spread abroad, and he was held in the highest estimation not only in his own time but also, and even to a greater degree, after his death,—nay, he has continued, and will continue, to be held in the highest esteem by all succeeding generations.

Truly remarkable, indeed, and divinely endowed was Leonardo da Vinci. He was the son of Ser Piero da Vinci. He would without doubt have made great progress in learning and knowledge of the sciences had he not been so versatile and changeful. The instability of his character led him to undertake many things which having commenced he afterwards abandoned. In arithmetic, for example, he made such rapid progress in the short time that he gave his attention to it, that he often confounded the master who was teaching him by the perpetual doubts that he started and by the difficult questions that he proposed.

He also commenced the study of music, and resolved to acquire the art of playing the lute, when, being by nature of an exalted imagination and full of the most graceful vivacity, he sang to the instrument most divinely, improvising at once both the verse and the music.

[Verocchio, an esteemed artist of the period, upon seeing some of the drawings which Leonardo had made, gladly agreed to take him into his shop.] Thither the boy resorted with the utmost readiness, and not only gave his attention to one branch of art but to all those of which design makes a portion. Endowed with such admirable intelligence and being also an excellent geometrician, Leonardo not only worked in sculpture but in architecture; likewise he prepared various designs for ground plans and the construction of entire buildings. He too it was who, while only a youth, first suggested the formation of a canal from Pisa to Florence by means of certain changes to be effected in the river Arno. Leonardo likewise made designs for mills, fulling machines, and other engines which were run by water. But as he had resolved to make painting his profession, he gave the greater part of his time to drawing from nature.

DOCUMENT ANALYSIS

1. To what does Vasari attribute da Vinci's talents?

______

______

______

2. For many, Leonardo da Vinci embodies the idea of the multi-talented Renaissance man. According to Vasari, in what areas did da Vinci excel?

______

______

______

DOCUMENT 14.2
Dante, from *The Divine Comedy* (1321)

Dante Alighieri's long narrative poem, The Divine Comedy, *describes the author's imaginary journeys through hell (Inferno), purgatory (Purgatorio), and heaven (Paradiso). It is considered to be one of the great works of Western literature and it assured its author of celebrity status in Renaissance Italy. Here is a brief excerpt from the Paradiso.*

II. Humanism

We were still a little distant from it, yet not so far that I could not partially discern that honorable folk possessed that place. "O thou that honorest both science and art, these, who are they, that have such honor that from the condition of the others it sets them apart?" and he to me, "The honorable fame of them which resounds above in thy life wins grace in heaven that so advances them." At this a voice was heard by me, "Honor the loftiest Poet! His shade returns that was departed." When the voice had ceased and was quiet, I saw four great shades coming to us: they had a semblance neither sad nor glad. The good Master [Virgil] began to say, "Look at him with that sword in hand who cometh before the three, even as lord. He is Homer, the sovereign poet; the next who comes is Horace, the satirist; Ovid is the third, and the last is Lucan. Since each shares with me the name that the solitary voice sounded, they dome honor, and in that do well."

Thus I saw assembled the fair school of that Lord of the loftiest song which above the others as an eagle flies. After they had discoursed somewhat together, they turned to me with sign of salutation; and my Master smiled thereat. And fat more of honor yet they did me, for they made me of their band, so that I was the sixth amid so much wit. Thus we went on as far as the light, speaking things concerning which silence is becoming, even as was speech there where I was.

We came to the foot of a noble castle, seven times circled by high walls, defended roundabout by a fair streamlet. This we passed as if hard ground; through seven gates I entered with these sages; we came to a meadow of fresh verdure. People were there with eyes slow and grave, of great authority in their looks; they spake seldom and with soft voices. Thus we drew apart, on one side, into a place open, luminous, and high, so that they all could be seen. There opposite upon the green enamel were shown to me the great spirits, whom to have seen I inwardly exalt myself.

I saw Electra with many companions, among whom I knew Hector and Æneas, Cæsar in armor, with his gerfalcon eyes; I saw Camilla and Pentheliea on the other side, and I saw the King Latinus, who was seated with Lavinia, his daughter. I saw that Brutus who drove out Tarquin; Lucretia, Julia, Marcia, and Cornelia; and alone, apart, I saw the Saladin. When I raised my brow a little more, I saw the Master of those who know, seated amid the philosophic family; all regard him, all do him honor. Here I saw both Socrates and Plato, who before the others stand nearest to him; Democritus, who ascribes the world to chance; Diogenes, Anaxagoras, and Thales, Empedocles, Heraclitus, and Zeno; and I saw the good collector of the qualities, Dioscorides, I mean; and I saw Orpheus, Tully, and Linus, and moral Seneca, Euclid the geometer, and Ptolemy, Hippocrates, Avicenna, Galen, and Averroës, who made the great comment. I cannot report of all in full, because the long theme so drives me that many times speech comes short of fact.

DOCUMENT ANALYSIS

1. What does this selection tell us about Dante's views regarding humanism?

____

____

____

2. Who is Dante talking about when he refers to "the Master of those who know"? Who does Dante place around the Master?

____

____

____

DOCUMENT 15.1
James I, "The Divine Right of Kings" (1616)

From *The Political Works of James I,* reprinted from the edition of 1616 with an introduction by Charles Howard McIlwain (Cambridge, Mass.: Harvard University Press, 1918), pp. 53–70.

James Stuart (James VI of Scotland, 1567–1625; James I of England, 1603–1625) was an intellectual who was rarely able to implement his ideas. He had hoped to unify England, Scotland, and Ireland, but was thwarted by both political realities and his own personal failings. He sought to ease international tensions, but his efforts to prevent the conflict that would become the Thirty Years' War were unsuccessful. The outbreak of the Thirty Years' War also destroyed his hope of brokering a European religious compromise. In addition to his duties as monarch, James I wrote on a variety of topics. His most famous work, the True Law of a Free Monarchy, is a classic argument for divine-right monarchy. Interestingly, although James penned this work in 1598, before he assumed the throne of England, he never tried to implement divine-right rule in England. He firmly believed that his power and authority derived solely from God, but acknowledged that as king of England, he had sworn oaths to govern according to the "laws and customs of England."

As there is not a thing so necessarie to be knowne by the people of any land, next the knowledge of their God, as the right knowledge of their alleageance, according to the forme of governement established among them, especially in a Monarchie (which forme of government, as resembling the Divinitie, approacheth nearest to perfection, as all the learned and wise men from the beginning have agreed upon; Unitie being the perfection of all things,) So hath the ignorance, and (which is worse) the seduced opinion of the multitude blinded by them, who thinke themselves able to teach and instruct the ignorants, procured the wracke and overthrow of sundry flourishing Common-wealths; and heaped heavy calamities, threatening utter destruction upon others. And the smiling successe, that unlaw rebellions have oftentimes had against Princes in ages past (such hath bene the misery, and the iniquitie of the time) hath by way of practise strengthened many of their errour: albeit there cannot be a more deceivable argument; then to judge by the justnesse of the cause by the event thereof; as hereafter shall be proved more at length. And among others, no Common-wealth, that ever hath bene since the beginning, hath had greater need of the trew knowledge of this ground, then this our so long disordered, and distracted Common-wealth hath: the misknowledge hereof being the onely spring, from whence have flowed so many endlesse calamities, miseries, and confusions, as is better felt by many, then the cause thereof well knowne, and deepely considered. The naturall zeale therefore, that I beare to this my native countrie, with the great pittie I have to see the so-long disturbance thereof for lack of the trew knowledge of this ground (as I have said before) hath compelled me at last to breake silence, to discharge my conscience to you my deare country men herein, that knowing the ground from whence these your many endlesse troubles have proceeded, as well as ye have already too-long tasted the bitter fruites thereof, ye may by knowledge, and eschewing of the cause escape, and divert the lamentable effects that ever necessarily follow thereupon. I have chosen the onely to set downe in this short Treatise, the trew grounds of the mutuall deutie, and alleageance betwixt a free and absolute Monarche, and his people.

First then, I will set downe the trew grounds, whereupon I am to build, out of the Scriptures, since Monarchie is the trew paterne of Divinitie, as I have already said: next, from the fundamental Lawes of our own Kingdome, which nearest must concerne us: thirdly, from the law of Nature, by divers similitudes drawne out of the same.

By the Law of Nature the King becomes a naturall Father to all his Lieges at his Coronation: And as the Father of his fatherly duty is bound to care for the nourishing, education, and vertuous government of his children; even so is the king bound to care for all his subjects. As all the toile and paine that the father can take for his children, will be thought light and well bestowed by him, so that the effect thereof redound to their profite and weale; so ought the Prince to doe towards his people. As the kindly father ought to foresee all inconvenients and dangers that may arise towards his children, and though with the hazard of his owne person presse to prevent the same; so ought the King towards his people. As the fathers wrath and correction upon any of his children that offendeth, ought to be by a fatherly chastisement seasoned with pitie, as long as there is any hope of amendment in them; so ought the King towards any of his Lieges that offend in that measure. And shortly, as the Fathers chiefe joy ought to be in procuring his childrens welfare, rejoycing at their weale, sorrowing and pitying at their evil, to hazard for their safetie, travell for their rest, wake for their sleepe; and in a word, to thinke that his earthly felicitie and life standeth and liveth more in them, nor in himself; so ought a good Prince thinke of his people.

As to the other branch of this mutuall and reciprock band, is the duety and alleageance that the Lieges owe to their King: the ground whereof, I take out of the words of Samuel, dited by Gods Spirit, when God had given him commandement to heare the peoples voice in choosing and annointing them a King. And because that place of Scripture being well understood, is so pertinent for our purpose, I have insert herein the very words of the Text.

10. So Samuel tolde all the wordes of the Lord unto the people that asked a King of him.

11. And he said, this shall be the maner of the King that shall raigne over you: hee will take your sonnes, and appoint them to his Charets, and to be his horsemen, and some shall runne before his Charet.

12. Also, hee will make them his captaines over thousands, and captaines over fifties, and to eare his ground, and to reape his harvest, and to make instruments of warre and the things that serve for his charets:

13. Hee will also take your daughters, and make them Apothicaries, and Cookes, and Bakers.

14. And hee will take your fields, and your vineyards, and your best Olive trees, and give them to his servants.

15. And hee will take the tenth of your seed, and of your Vineyards, and give it to his Eunuches, and to his servants.

16. And hee will take your men servants, and your maid-servants, and the chief of your young men, and your asses, and put them to his worke.

17. Hee will take the tenth of your sheepe: and ye shall be his servants.

18. And ye shall cry out at that day, because of your King, whom ye have chosen you: and the Lord God will not heare you at that day.

19. But the people would not heare the voice of Samuel, but did say: Nay, but there shalbe a King over us.

20. And we also will be all like other Nations, and our King shall judge us, and goe out before us, and fight out battles.

As likewise, although I have said, a good king will frame all his actions to be according to the Law; yet is hee not bound thereto but of his good will, and for good example—giving to his subjects: For as in the law of abstaining from eating of flesh in Lenton, the king will, for examples sake, make his owne house to observe the Law; yet no man will thinke he needs to take a licence to eate flesh. And although by our Lawes, the bearing and wearing of hag-buts, and pistolets be forbidden, yet no man can find any fault in the King, for causing his traine use them in any raide upon the Borderers, or other malefactours or rebellious subjects. So as I have alreadie said, a good King, although hee be above the Law, will subject and frame his actions thereto, for examples sake to his subjects, and of his owne free-will, but not as subject or bound thereto.

And the agreement of the Law of nature in this our ground with the Lawes and constitutions of God, and man, already alleged, will by two similitudes easily appeare. The King towards his people is rightly compared to a father of children, and to a head of a body composed of divers members: For as fathers, the good Princes, and Magistrates of the people of God acknowledged themselves to their subjects. And for all other well ruled Common-wealths, the stile of Pater patriae was ever, and is commonly used to Kings. And the proper office of a King towards his Subjects, agrees very wel with the office of the head towards the body, and all members thereof: For from the head, being the seate of Judgement, proceedeth the care and foresight of guiding, and preventing all evill that may come to the body, so doeth the King for his people. As the discourse and direction flowes from the head, and the execution according thereunto belongs to the rest of the members, every one according to their office: so it is betwixt a wise Prince, and his people. As the judgement coming from the head may not onely imploy the members, every one in their owne office, as long as they are able for it; but likewise in case any of them be affected with any infirmitie must care and provide for their remedy, in-case it be curable, and if otherwise, gar cut them off for feare of infecting of the rest: even so is it betwixt the Prince, and his people. And as there is ever hope of curing any diseased member of the direction of the head, as long as it is whole; but by contrary, if it be troubled, all the members are partakers of that paine, so is it betwixt the Prince and his people.

And now first for the fathers part (whose naturally love to his children I described in the first part of this my discourse, speaking of the dutie that Kings owe to their Subjects) consider, I pray you what duetie his children owe to him, & whether upon any pretext whatsoever, it wil not be thought monstrous and unnaturall to his sons, to rise up against him, to control him at their appetite, and when they thinke good to sley him, or to cut him off, and adopt to themselves any other they please in his roome: Or can any pretence of wickedness or rigor on his part be a just excuse for his children to put hand into him? And although wee see by the course of nature, that love useth to descend more than to ascend, in case it were trew, that the father hated and wronged the children never so much, will any man, endued with the least sponke of reason, thinke it lawful for them to meet him with the line? Yea, suppose the father were furiously following his sonnes with a drawen sword, is it lawful for them to turne and strike againe, or make any resistance but by flight? I thinke surely, if there were no more but the example of bruit beasts & unreasonable creatures, it may serve well enough to qualifie and prove this my argument. We reade often the pietie that the Storkes have to their olde and decayed parents: And generally wee know, that there are many sorts of beasts and fowles, that with violence and many bloody strokes will beat and banish their yong ones from them, how soone they perceive them to be able to fend themselves; but wee never read or heard of any resistance on their part, except among the vipers; which prooves such persons, as ought to be reasonable creatures, and yet unnaturally follow this example, to be endued with their viperous nature.

And it is here likewise to be noted, that the duty and alleageance, which the people sweareth to their prince, is not bound to themselves, but likewise to their lawfull heires and posterity, the lineall to their lawfull heires and posterity, the lineall succession of crowns being begun among the people of God, and happily continued in divers Christian commonwealths: So as no objection either of heresie, or whatsoever private statute or law may free the people from their oathgiving to their king, and his succession, established by the old fundamentall lawes of the kingdom: For, as hee is their heritable over-lord, and so by birth, not by any right in the coronation, commeth to his crowne; it is a like unlawful (the crowne ever standing full) to displace him that succeedeth thereto, as to eject the former: For at the very moment of the expiring of the king reigning, the nearest and lawful heire entreth in his place: And so to refuse him, or intrude another, is not to holde out uncomming in, but to expell and put out their righteous King. And I trust at this time whole France acknowledgeth the superstitious rebellion of the liguers, who upon pretence of heresie, by force of armes held so long out, to the great desolation of their whole country, their native and righteous king from possessing of his owne crowne and naturall kingdome.

Not that by all this former discourse of mine, and Apologie for kings, I meane that whatsoever errors and intollerable abominations a sovereigne prince commit, hee ought to escape all punishment, as if thereby the world were only ordained for kings, & they without controlment to turne it upside down at their pleasure: but by the contrary, by remitting them to God (who is their onely ordinary Judge) I remit them to the sorest and sharpest school-master that can be devised for them: for the further a king is preferred by God above all other ranks & degrees of men, and the higher that his seat is above theirs, the greater is his obligation to his maker. And therfore in case he forget himselfe (his unthankfulness being in the same measure of height) the sadder and sharper will be correction be; and according to the greatnes of the height he is in, the weight of his fall wil recompense the same: for the further that any person is obliged to God, his offence becomes and growes so much the greater, then it would be in any other. Joves thunderclaps light oftner and sorer upon the high & stately oaks, then on the low and supple willow trees: and the highest bench is sliddriest to sit upon. Neither is it ever heard that any king forgets himself towards God, or in his vocation; but God with the greatnesse of the plague revengeth the greatnes of his ingratitude: Neither thinke I by the force of argument of this my discourse so to perswade the people, that none will hereafter be raised up, and rebell against wicked Princes. But remitting to the justice and providence of God to stirre up such scourges as pleaseth him, for punishment of wicked kings (who made the very vermine and filthy dust of the earth to bridle the insolencie of proud Pharaoh) my onely purpose and intention in this treatise is to perswade, as farre as lieth in me, by these sure and infallible grounds, all such good Christian readers, as beare not onely the naked name of a Christian, but kith the fruites thereof in their daily forme of life, to keep their hearts and hands free from such monstrous and unnaturall rebellions, whensoever the wickednesse of a Prince shall procure the same at Gods hands: that, when it shall please God to cast such scourges of princes, and instruments of his fury in the fire, ye may stand up with cleane handes, and unspotted consciences, having prooved your selves in all your actions trew Christians toward God, and dutifull subjects towards your King, having remitted the judgement and punishment of all his wrongs to him, whom to onely of right it appertaineth.

But craving at God, and hoping that God shall continue his blessing with us, in not sending such fearefull desolation, I heartily wish our kings behaviour so to be, and continue among us, as our God in earth, and loving Father, endued with such properties as I described a King in the first part of this Treatise. And that ye (my deare countreymen, and charitable readers) may presse by all means to procure the prosperitie and welfare of your King; that as hee must on the one part thinke all his earthly felicitie and happiness grounded upon your weale, caring more for himselfe for your sake then for his owne, thinking himselfe onely ordained for your weale; such holy and happy emulation may arise betwixt him and you, as his care for your quietnes, and your care for his honor and preservation, may in all your actions daily strive together, that the Land may thinke themselves blessed with such a King, and the king may thinke himself most happy in ruling over so loving and obedient subjects.

DOCUMENT ANALYSIS

1. Are there any limits on the power of a king? What are they?

2. What are James's motives in this essay?

DOCUMENT 16.1
Christopher Columbus, Letter from the 'New World' (1493)

There was no more fateful encounter in human history than Columbus's "discovery" of the so-called New World. In this letter, he describes his initial encounters with the native peoples of the Caribbean.

The Discovered Islands.

Because my undertakings have attained success, I know that it will be pleasing to you: these I have determined to relate, so that you may be made acquainted with everything done and discovered in this our voyage. On the thirty-third day after I departed from Cadiz, I came to the Indian Sea, where I found many islands inhabited by men without number, of all which I took possession for our most fortunate king, with proclaiming heralds and flying standards, no one objecting. To the first of these I gave the name of the blessed Saviour, on whose aid relying I had reached this as well as the other island. But the Indians call it Guanahany. I also called each one of the others by a new name. For I ordered one island to be called Santa Maria of the Conception, another Fernandina, another Isabella, another Juana, and so on with the rest. As soon as we had arrived at that island which I have just now said was called Juana, I proceeded along its coast towards the west for some distance; I found it so large and without perceptible end, that I believed it to be not an island, but the continental country of Cathay; seeing, however, no towns or cities situated on the sea-coast, but only some villages and rude farms, with whose inhabitants I was unable to converse, because as soon as they saw us they took flight. I proceeded farther, thinking that I would discover some city or large residences. At length, perceiving that we had gone far enough, that nothing new appeared, and that this way was leading us to the north, which I wished to avoid, because it was winter on the land, and it was my intention to go to the south, moreover the winds were becoming violent, I therefore determined that no other plans were practicable, and so, going back, I returned to a certain bay that I had noticed, from which I sent two of our men to the land, that they might find out whether there was a king in this country, or any cities. These men traveled for three days, and they found people and houses without number, but they were small and without any government, therefore they returned. Now in the meantime I had learned from certain Indians, whom I had seized there, that this country was indeed an island, and therefore I proceeded towards the east, keeping all the time near the coast, for 322 miles, to the extreme ends of this island. From this place I saw another island to the east, distant from this Juana 54 miles, which I called forthwith Hispana; and I sailed to it; and I steered along the northern coast, as at Juana, towards the east, 564 miles. And the said Juana and the other island there appear very fertile. This island is surrounded by many very safe and wide harbors, not excelled by any others that I have ever seen. Many great and salubrious rivers flow through it. There are also many very high mountains there. All these island are very beautiful, and distinguished by various qualities; they are accessible, and full of a great variety of trees stretching up to the stars; the leaves of which I believe are never shed, for I saw them as green and flourishing as they are usually in Spain in the month of May; some of them were blossoming, some were bearing fruit, some were in other conditions; each one was thriving in its own way. The nightingale and various other birds without number were singing, in the month of November, when I was exploring them. There are besides in the said island Juana seven or eight kinds of palm trees, which far excel ours in height and beauty, just as all the other trees, herbs, and fruits do. There are also excellent pine trees, vast plains and meadows, a variety of birds, a variety of honey, and a variety of metals, excepting iron. In the one which was called Hispana, as we said above, there are great and beautiful mountains, vast fields, groves, fertile plains, very suitable for planting and cultivating, and for the building of houses. The convenience of the harbors in this island, and the remarkable number of rivers contributing to the healthfulness of man, exceed belief, unless one has seen them. The trees, pasturage, and fruits of this island differ greatly from those of Juana. This Hispana, moreover, abounds in different kinds of spices, in gold, and in metals. On this island, indeed, and on all the others which I have seen, and of which I have knowledge, the inhabitants of both sexes go always naked, just as they came into the world, except some of the women, who use a covering of a leaf or some foliage, or a cotton cloth, which they make themselves for that purpose. All these people lack, as I said above, every kind of iron; they are also without weapons, which indeed are unknown; nor are they competent to use them, not on account of deformity of body, for they are well formed, but because they are timid and full of fear. The carry for weapons, however, reeds baked in the sun, on the lower ends of which they fasten some shafts of dried wood rubbed down to a point; and indeed they do not venture to use these always; for it frequently happened when I sent two or three of my men to some of the villages, that they might speak with the natives, a compact troop of the Indians would march out, and as soon as they saw our men approaching, they would quickly take flight, children being pushed aside by their fathers, and fathers by their children.

DOCUMENT ANALYSIS

1. Upon what sources did Columbus draw in naming the islands he encountered?

____

____

____

2. What were the key physical attributes of the islands that Columbus noted?

____

____

____

3. How did Columbus view the native peoples he encountered?

____

____

____

DOCUMENT 16.2
Bartolomé de las Casas, from *In Defense of the Indians* (1500)

Source: Bartolomé de las Casas, "In Defense of the Indians," in *In Defense of the Indians,* ed. and trans. Stafford Poole (Dekalb, IL: Northern Illinois University Press, 1974), pp. 42-46.

As Spain struggled in the mid 1500s to consolidate control over its New World possessions, a great debate erupted over the status and treatment of the Indians. At the heart of the debate lay the issue of whether Indians were civilized. An Aristotle treatise enshrined in Spanish law gave civilized peoples the right to wage war upon uncivilized peoples and take them as slaves. Consequently, assessments of Indians as barbarian benefited many Spanish settlers who sought both to impose their jurisdiction on the Indians and to take advantage of their labor. The Iberian scholar and theologian Juan Ines de Sepúlveda became a spokesperson for such interests.

Sepúlveda faced stiff opposition. Bartolomé de las Casas, who had served several years as a bishop in Mexico, represented the other side of the debate. Arguing that Indians were civilized, the theologian sought on behalf of both Indians and priests outraged at the settlers' excesses to persuade the Spanish Crown to impose stricter controls on its colonists. The debate's outcome would determine and shape Spain's policy toward all of its New World inhabitants.

Now if we shall have shown that among our Indians of the western and southern shores (granting that we call them barbarians and that they are barbarians) there are important kingdoms, large numbers of people who live settled lives in a society, great cities, kings, judges and laws, persons who engage in commerce, buying, selling, lending, and the other contracts of the law of nations, will it now stand proved that the Reverend Doctor Sepúlveda has spoken wrongly and viciously against peoples like these, either out of malice or ignorance of Aristotle's teaching, and, therefore, has falsely and perhaps irreparably slandered them before the entire world? From the fact that the Indians are barbarians it does not necessarily follow that they are incapable of government and have to be ruled by others, except to be taught about the Catholic faith and to be admitted to the holy sacraments. They are not ignorant, inhuman, or bestial. Rather, long before they had heard the word Spaniard they had properly organized states, wisely ordered by excellent laws, religion, and custom. They cultivated friendship and, bound together in common fellowship, lived in populous cities in which they wisely administered the affairs of both peace and war justly and equitably, truly governed by laws that at very many points surpass ours, and could have won the admiration of the sages of Athens, as I will show in the second part of this Defense.

Now if they are to be subjugated by war because they are ignorant of polished literature, let Sepúlveda hear Trogus Pompey:

Nor could the Spaniards submit to the yoke of a conquered province until Caesar Augustus, after he had conquered the world, turned his victorious armies against them and organized that barbaric and wild people as a province, once he had led them by law to a more civilized way of life.

Now see how he called the Spanish people barbaric and wild. I would like to hear Sepúlveda, in his cleverness, answer this question: Does he think that the war of the Romans against the Spanish was justified in order to free them from barbarism? And this question also: Did the Spanish wage an unjust war when they vigorously defended themselves against them?

Next, I call the Spaniards who plunder that unhappy people torturers. Do you think that the Romans, once they had subjugated the wild and barbaric peoples of Spain, could with secure right divide all of you among themselves, handing over so many head of both males and females as allotments to individuals? And do you then conclude that the Romans could have stripped your rulers of their authority and consigned all of you, after you had been deprived of your liberty, to wretched labors, especially in searching for gold and silver lodes and mining and refining the metals? And if the Romans finally did that, as is evident from Diodorus, [would you not judge] that you also have the right to defend your freedom, indeed your very life, by war? Sepúlveda, would you have permitted Saint James to evangelize your own people of Córdoba in that way? For God's sake and man's faith in him, is this the way to impose the yoke of Christ on Christian men? Is this the way to remove wild barbarism from the minds of barbarians? Is it not, rather, to act like thieves, cut-throats, and cruel plunderers and to drive the gentlest of people headlong into despair? The Indian race is not that barbaric, nor are they dull witted or stupid, but they are easy to teach and very talented in learning all the liberal arts, and very ready to accept, honor, and observe the Christian religion and correct their sins (as experience has taught) once priests have introduced them to the sacred mysteries and taught them the word of God. They have been endowed with excellent conduct, and before the coming of the Spaniards, as we have said, they had political states that were well founded on beneficial laws.

. . . From this it is clear that the basis for Sepúlveda's teaching that these people are uncivilized and ignorant is worse than false. Yet even if we were to grant that this race has no keenness of mind or artistic ability, certainly they are not, in consequence, obliged to submit themselves to those who are more intelligent and to adopt their ways, so that, if they refuse, they may be subdued by having war waged against them and be enslaved, as happens today. For men are obliged by the natural law to do many things they cannot be forced to do against their will. We are bound by the natural law to embrace virtue and imitate the uprightness of good men. No one, however, is punished for being bad unless he is guilty of rebellion. Where the Catholic faith has been preached in a Christian manner and as it ought to be, all men are bound by the natural law to accept it, yet no one is forced to accept the faith of Christ. No one is punished because he is sunk in vice, unless he is rebellious or harms the property and persons of others. No one is forced to embrace virtue and show himself as a good man. One who receives a favor is bound by the natural law to return the favor by what we call antidotal obligation. Yet no one is forced to this, nor is he punished if he omits it, according to the common interpretation of the jurists.

DOCUMENT ANALYSIS

1. How does las Casas's position on the role of Christianity in the New World differ from that which he ascribes to Sepúlveda? What are some of the implications of this division within the Church?

2. In comparing the Spaniards to the Romans, what do you think las Casas was trying to achieve?

3. Las Casas was a master of rhetoric. How does his language in describing the Spanish settlers and their actions incline his audience to accept his bias or position? Do you think he was successful?

4. On what grounds does las Casas argue that the Indians are civilized?

5. Referring to the reading, say how important you think legal and philosophical precedents were in making a successful case before the Spanish Crown? Do you think this form of logic and argument was itself based upon Roman precedent? Why or why not?

DOCUMENT 17.1

Lomonosov, "Panegyric to the Sovereign Emperor Peter the Great" (1741)

Source: From *On the Corruption of Morals in Russia* by Prince M. M. Shcherbatov. Edited and translated by A. Lentin.

Peter the Great was both canonized and vilified by people of his time (and has been similarly treated by historians of today). Many condemned his methods of bringing a backward nation into the modern era. Probably the biggest critic of Peter's "Westernization" of Russia was the Russian Orthodox Church, a powerful force that controlled many theologically-based aspects of Russian culture—for example, the wearing of beards. As Peter encouraged travel between western Europe and Russia, new ideas—both secular and religious—were introduced to Russia, and the Russian Orthodox Church began to feel threatened.

There were those in Russia, however, that welcomed the things Peter did. After Peter died, these admirers began to mythologize his accomplishments. The ***panegyric*** *included here was written after Peter's death on the occasion of the coronation of his daughter, Elizabeth, in 1741. Some people feel its purpose was to remind Elizabeth of the policies and deeds of her father. It was also an early contribution to the myth that has surrounded Peter the Great ever since.*

. . . As a part of His grand designs the all-wise Monarch provided as a matter of absolute necessity for the dissemination of all kinds of knowledge in the homeland, and also for an increase in the numbers of persons skilled in the higher branches of learning, together with artists and craftsmen; though I have given His paternal solicitude in this matter the most prominent place, my whole speech would not be long enough to describe it in detail. For, having repeatedly made the rounds of European states like some swift-soaring eagle, He did induce (partly by command and partly by His own weighty example) a great multitude of His subjects to leave their country for a time and to convince themselves by experience how great an advantage a person and an entire state can derive from a journey of inquiry in foreign regions. Then were the wide gates of great Russia opened up; then . . . the sons of Russia, journey(ed) forth to acquire knowledge in the various sciences and arts, and, in the other direction, foreigners arriving with various skills, books, and instruments. Then to the study of Mathematics and Physics, previously thought of as forms of sorcery and witchcraft, but now arrayed in purple, crowned with laurels, and placed on the Monarch's throne, reverential respect was accorded in the sanctified Person of Peter. What benefit was brought to us by all the different sciences and arts, bathed in such a glow of grandeur, is proved by the superabundant richness of our most varied pleasures, of which our forefathers, before the days of Russia's Great Enlightener, were not only deprived but in many cases had not even any conception. How many essential things which previously came to Russia from distant lands with difficulty and at great cost are now produced inside the state, and not only provide for our needs but also with their surplus supply other lands. There was a time when the neighbors on our borders boasted that Russia, a great and powerful state, was unable properly to carry out military operations or trade without their assistance, since its mineral resources included neither precious metals for the stamping of coins nor even iron, so needful for the making of weapons with which to stand against an enemy. This reproach disappeared through the enlightenment brought by Peter; the bowels of the mountains have been opened up by his mighty and industrious hand. Metals pour out of them, and are not only freely distributed within the homeland but are also given back to foreign peoples as if in repayment of loans. The brave Russian army turns against the enemy weapons produced from Russian mines and Russian hands.

In the establishment of the sizable army needed for the defense of the homeland, the security of His subjects, and the unhindered carrying out of important enterprises within the country, how great was the solicitude of the Great Monarch, how impetuous His zeal, how assiduous His search of ways and means! . . . The impossible was made possible by extraordinary zeal, and above all by an unheard-of-example. In former times the Roman Senate, beholding the Emperor Trajan standing before the Consul to receive from him the dignity of Consul, exclaimed: "Through this thou art the greater, the more majestic!" What exclamations, what applause were due to Peter the Great for His unparalleled self-abasement? Our fathers beheld their crowned Sovereign not among the candidates for a Roman consulship but in the ranks of common soldiers, not demanding power over Rome, but obedient to the bidding of His subjects. O you beautiful regions, fortunate regions which beheld a spectacle so wondrous! Oh, how you marveled at the friendly contest of the regiments of a single Sovereign, both commander and subordinate, giving orders and obeying them! Oh, how you admired the siege, defense, and capture of new Russian fortresses, not for immediate mercenary gain but for the sake of future glory, not for putting down enemies but to encourage fellow country-men. Looking back at those past years, we can now imagine the great love for the Sovereign and the ardent devotion with which the newly instituted army was fired, seeing Him in their company at the same table, eating the same food, seeing His face covered with dust and sweat, seeing that He was no different from them, except that in training and in diligence He was superior to all. By such an extraordinary example the most wise Sovereign, rising in rank alongside His subjects, proved that Monarchs can in no other way increase their majesty, glory, and eminence so well as by such gracious condescension. The Russian army was toughened by such encouragement, and during the twenty years' war with the Swedish Crown, and later in other campaigns, filled the ends of the universe with the thunder of its weapons and with the noise of its triumphs. It is true that the first battle of Narva was not successful; but the superiority of our foes and the retreat of the Russian army have, through envy and pride, been exaggerated to their glorification and our humiliation, out of all proportion to the actual event. For although most of the Russian army had seen only two years' service and faced a veteran army accustomed to battle, although disagreement arose between our commanders, and a malicious turncoat revealed to the enemy the entire position in our camp, and Charles XII [of Sweden] by a sudden attack did not give the Russians time to form ranks—yet even in their retreat they destroyed the enemy's willingness to fight on to final victory. Thus the only reason the Russian Life Guard, which had remained intact, together with another sizable part of the army, did not dare to attack the enemy thereafter was the absence of its main leaders, who had been summoned by Charles for peace talks and detained as prisoners. For this reason the Guards and the rest of the army returned to Russia with their arms and war chest, drums beating and banners flying. That this failure occurred more through the unhappy circumstances described than through any lack of skill in the Russian troops and that Peter's new army could, even in its infancy, defeat the seasoned regiments of the enemies, was proved in the next year and subsequently by many glorious victories won over them. . . .

. . . But was it merely out of sheer curiosity or, at the most, for purposes of instruction and command, that He did in Holland and Britain attain perfection in the theory and practice of equipping a fleet and in navigational science? Everywhere the Great Sovereign aroused His subjects to labor, not only by command and reward, but also by His own example! I call you to witness, O great Russian rivers; I address myself to you, O happy shores, sanctified by Peter's footsteps and watered by His sweat. How many times you resounded with high-spirited and eager cries as the heavy timbers, ready for launching of the ship, were being slowly moved by the workmen and then, at the touch of His hand, made a sudden spurt toward the swift current, inspiring the multitude, encouraged by His example, to finish off the huge hulks with incredible speed. To what a marvelous and rousing spectacle were the assembled people treated as these great structures moved nearer to launching! When their indefatigable Founder and Builder, now moving topside, now below, now circling round, tested the soundness of each part, the power of the machinery, and the precision of all the preparations and by command, encouragement, ingenuity, and the quick skill of His tireless hands, rectified the defects which He had detected. In this unflagging zeal, this invincible persistence in labor, the legendary prowess of the ancients was shown in Peter's day to have been not fiction but the very truth! . . .

DOCUMENT ANALYSIS

1. How does he describe the effects of Peter's tour of western Europe and the new knowledge that returns with Peter to Russia?

2. How would this document contribute to the myth of Peter the Great? Do you think that was the intention of the author? Why?

3. One of Peter's greatest achievements was his navy. How does the author portray the extremes to which Peter went to have his navy?

4. What does Lomonosov see as Peter's virtues or qualities?

5. What is the relationship between Peter and his subjects?

DOCUMENT 17.2

Letter from Louis XIV to his son (1661)

Source: Louis XIV, *A King's Lessons in Statecraft: Louis XIV: Letters to His Heirs with Introduction and Notes by Jean Longnon.* Trans. Herbert Wilson. (Port Washington, NY: Kennikat Press, 1970), pp. 39–40, 48–51.

During the sixteenth and seventeenth centuries, England, for various reasons, was moving toward what we might call a "Constitutional Monarchy." In such a system, the power of a king or a queen is limited by a written constitution (or, in England's case, where there is no written constitution, a series of documents that serve the same general purpose as a constitution). In general, such a system tends to be more decentralized than centralized, as power is delegated to bodies such as a parliament. In contrast, France during the same period was developing, to the envy of the rest of Western Europe, a strong, centralized absolute monarchy, where the king's position was not limited in any way. Louis XIV, who ruled from 1643 to 1715, became the prototypical absolute monarch, even developing a sort of "cult of personality" around him.

Because ruling over and maintaining such a centralized system required care and attention, Louis XIV in 1661 wrote a series of memoirs to his son, the dauphin. These memoirs not only provided practical advice for the king's heir, they also provide us with insight into royal attitudes and priorities. Sadly for Louis XIV, the dauphin died before his father, and it was Louis's great-grandson who became Louis XV in 1714.

MANY REASONS, all very important, my son, have decided me, at some labour to myself, but one which I regard as forming one of my greatest concerns, to leave you these Memoirs of my reign and of my principal actions. I have never considered that kings, feeling in themselves, as they do, all paternal affection, are dispensed from the obligation common to fathers of instructing their children by example and by precept.

I have even hoped that in this purpose I might be able to be more helpful to you, and consequently to my subjects, than any one else in the world; for there cannot be men who have reigned of more talents and greater experience than I, nor who have reigned in France; and I do not fear to tell you that the higher the position the greater are the number of things which cannot be viewed or understood save by one who is occupying that position.

I have considered, too, what I have so often experienced myself—the throng who will press round you, each for his own ends, the trouble you will have in finding disinterested advice, and the entire confidence you will be able to feel in that of a father who has no other interest but your own, no ardent wish but for your greatness.

I have given, therefore, some consideration to the condition of Kings—hard and rigorous in this respect—who owe, as it were, a public account of their actions to the whole world and to all succeeding centuries, and who, nevertheless, are unable to do so to all and sundry at the time without injury to their greatest interests, and without divulging the secret reasons of their conduct.

[Louis talks briefly about his own reign]

Two things without doubt were absolutely necessary: very hard work on my part, and a wise choice of persons capable of seconding it.

As for work, it may be, my son, that you will begin to read these Memoirs at an age when one is far more in the habit of dreading than loving it, only too happy to have escaped subjection to tutors and to have your hours regulated no longer, nor lengthy and prescribed study laid down for you.

There is something more, my son, and I hope that your own experience will never teach it to you: nothing could be more laborious to you than a great amount of idleness if you were to have the misfortune to fall into it through beginning by being disgusted with public affairs, then with pleasure, then with idleness itself, seeking everywhere fruitlessly for what can never be found, that is to say, the sweetness of repose and leisure without having the preceding fatigue and occupation.

I laid a rule on myself to work regularly twice every day, and for two or three hours each time with different persons, without counting the hours which I passed privately and alone, nor the time which I was able to give on particular occasions to any special affairs that might arise. There was no moment when I did not permit people to talk to me about them, provided that they were urgent; with the exception of foreign ministers who sometimes find too favourable moments in the familiarity allowed to them, either to obtain or to discover something, and whom one should not hear without being previously prepared.

I cannot tell you what fruit I gathered immediately I had taken this resolution. I felt myself, as it were, uplifted in thought and courage; I found myself quite another man, and with joy reproached myself for having been too long unaware of it. This first timidity, which a little self-judgment always produces and which at the beginning gave me pain, especially on occasions when I had to speak in public, disappeared in less than no time. The only thing I felt then was that I was King, and born to be one. I experienced next a delicious feeling, hard to express, and which you will not know yourself except by tasting it as I have done. For you must not imagine, my son, that the affairs of State are like some obscure and thorny path of learning which may possibly have already wearied you, wherein the mind strives to raise itself with effort above its purview, more often to arrive at no conclusion, and whose utility or apparent utility is repugnant to us as much as its difficulty. The function of Kings consists principally in allowing good sense to act, which always acts naturally and without effort. What we apply ourselves to is sometimes less difficult than what we do only for our amusement. Its usefulness always follows. A King, however skilful and enlightened be his ministers, cannot put his own hand to the work without its effect being seen. Success, which is agreeable in everything, even in the smallest matters, gratifies us in these as well as in the greatest, and there is no satisfaction to equal that of noting every day some progress in glorious and lofty enterprises, and in the happiness of the people which has been planned and thought out by oneself. All that is most necessary to this work is at the same time agreeable; for, in a word, my son, it is to have one's eyes open to the whole earth; to learn each hour the news concerning every province and every nation, the secrets of every court, the mood and the weaknesses of each Prince and of every foreign minister; to be well-informed on an infinite number of matters about which we are supposed to know nothing; to elicit from our subjects what they hide from us with the greatest care; to discover the most remote opinions of our own courtiers and the most hidden interests of those who come to us with quite contrary professions. I do not know of any other pleasure we would not renounce for that, even if curiosity alone gave us the opportunity.

I have dwelt on this important subject longer than I had intended, and far more for your sake than for my own; for while I am disclosing to you these methods and these alleviations attending the greatest cares of royalty I am not unaware that I am likewise depreciating almost the sole merit which I can hope for in the eyes of the world. But in this matter, my son, your honour is dearer to me than my own; and if it should happen that God call you to govern before you have yet taken to this spirit of application and to public affairs of which I am speaking, the least deference you can pay to the advice of a father, to whom I make bold to say you owe much in every kind of way, is to begin to do and to continue to do for some time, even under constraint and dislike, for love of me who beg it of you, what you will do all your life from love of yourself, if once you have made a beginning.

DOCUMENT ANALYSIS

1. Does Louis XIV seem arrogant, or is he simply offering experienced advice?

2. Is there anything Louis suggests not to do?

3. List three things Louis believes a successful ruler must do.

4. Overall, do you feel Louis gives his son good or bad advice? Why?

5. What do you think Louis XIV means when we writes "the function of kings consists principally in allowing good sense to act"?

DOCUMENT 18.1
Letter from Galileo Galilei to the Duchess Christina (1632)

Galileo Galilei (1564–1642) was one of the primary figures in the Scientific Revolution. In 1608 Galileo, then a professor of mathematics at the University of Pisa, heard of a new technology, the telescope. Galileo quickly built his own telescope and used it to observe the planets and the stars. His observations provided evidence in favor of the Copernican theory of heliocentrism. For a variety of reasons, many religious leaders considered heliocentrism dangerous, and Galileo was initially commanded by the Roman Catholic Church to avoid teaching it. After the publication in 1632 of his most important work, Dialogue on the Two World Systems, which was supposed to be impartial but favored heliocentrism, he was forced to recant his claim that the earth moves in relation to the sun. He spent the remainder of his life under house arrest. Galileo is also famous for his work in theoretical mechanics, particularly for his formulation of the law of inertia. In the following selection, Galileo describes how the results of the new science can be reconciled with the Bible.

My goal is this alone; that if, among errors that may abound in these considerations of a subject remote from my profession, there is anything that may be serviceable to the holy Church in making a decision concerning the Copernican system, it may be taken and utilized as seems best to the superiors. And if not, let my book be torn and burnt, as I neither intend nor pretend to gain from it any fruit that is not pious and Catholic. And though many of the things I shall reprove have been heard by my own ears, I shall freely grant to those who have spoken them that they never said them, if that is what they wish, and I shall confess myself to have been mistaken. Hence let whatever I reply be addressed not to them, but to whoever may have held such opinions.

The reason produced for condemning the opinion that the earth moves and the sun stands still is that in many places in the Bible one may read that the sun moves and the earth stands still. Since the Bible cannot err, it follows as a necessary consequence that anyone takes an erroneous and heretical position who maintains that the sun is inherently motionless and the earth movable . . .

. . . Hence I think that I may reasonably conclude that whenever the Bible has occasion to speak of any physical conclusion (especially those which are very abstruse and hard to understand), the rule has been observed of avoiding confusion in the minds of the common people which would render them contumacious toward the higher mysteries. Now the Bible, merely to condescend to popular capacity, has not hesitated to obscure some very important pronouncements, attributing to God himself some qualities extremely remote from (and even contrary to) His essence. Who then, would positively declare that this principle has been set aside, and the Bible has confined itself rigorously to the bare and restricted sense of its words, when speaking but casually of the earth, of water, of the sun, or of any other created thing? Especially in view of the fact that these things in no way concern the primary purpose of the sacred writings, which is the service of God and the salvation of souls—matters infinitely beyond the comprehension of the common people.

This being granted, I think that in discussions of physical problems we ought to begin not from the authority of scriptural passages, but from sense-experiences and necessary demonstrations; for the holy Bible and the phenomena of nature proceed alike from the divine Word, the former as the dictate of the Holy Ghost and the latter as the observant executrix of God's commands. It is necessary for the Bible, in order to be accommodated to the understanding of every man, to speak many things which appear to differ from the absolute truth so far as the bare meaning of the words is concerned. But Nature, on the other hand, is inexorable and immutable: she never transgresses the laws imposed upon her, or cares a whit whether her abstruse reasons and methods of operation are understandable to men. For that reason it appears that nothing physical which sense-experience sets before our eyes, or which necessary demonstrations prove to us, ought to be called in question (much less condemned) upon the testimony of biblical passages which may have some different meaning beneath their words. For the Bible is not chained in every expression to conditions as strict as those which govern all physical effects; nor is God any less excellently revealed in Nature's actions than in the sacred statements of the Bible. Perhaps this is what Tertullian meant by these words.

"We conclude that God is known first through Nature, and then again, more particularly, by doctrine; by Nature in His works, and by doctrine in His revealed word."

From this I do not mean to infer that we need not have an extraordinary esteem for the passages of holy Scripture. On the contrary, having arrived at any certainties in physics, we ought to utilize these as the most appropriate aids in the true exposition of the Bible and in the investigation of those meanings which are necessarily contained therein, for these must be concordant with demonstrated truths. I should judge that the authority of the Bible was designed to persuade men of those articles and propositions which, surpassing all human reasoning, could not be made credible by science, or by any other means than through the very mouth of the Holy Spirit.

Yet even in those propositions which are not matters of faith, this authority ought to be preferred over that of all human writings which are supported only by bare assertions or probable arguments, and not set forth in a demonstrative way. This I hold to be necessary and proper to the same extent that divine wisdom surpasses all human judgment and conjecture . . .

. . . From these things it follows as a necessary consequence that, since the Holy Ghost did not intend to teach us whether heaven moves or stands still, whether its shape is spherical or like a discus or extended in a plane, nor whether the earth is located at its center or off to one side, then so much the less was it intended to settle for us any other conclusion of the same kind. And the motion or rest of the earth and the sun is so closely linked with the things just named, that without a determination of the one, neither side can be taken in the other matters. Now if the Holy Spirit has purposely neglected to teach us propositions of this sort as irrelevant to the highest goal (that is, to our salvation), how can anyone affirm that it is obligatory to take sides on them, and that one belief is required by faith, while the other side is erroneous? Can an opinion be heretical and yet have no concern with the salvation of souls? Can the Holy Ghost be asserted not to have intended teaching us something that does concern our salvation? I would say here something that was heard from an ecclesiastic of the most eminent degree: "That the intention of the Holy Ghost is to teach us how one goes to heaven, not how heaven goes." . . .

. . . . This granted, and it being true that two truths cannot contradict one another, it is the function of wise expositors to seek out the true senses of scriptural texts. These will unquestionably accord with the physical conclusions which manifest sense and necessary demonstrations have previously made certain to us. Now the Bible, as has been remarked, admits in many places expositions that are remote from the signification of the words for reasons we have already given. Moreover, we are unable to affirm that all interpreters of the Bible speak by divine inspiration, for if that were so there would exist no differences between them about the sense of a given passage. Hence I should think it would be the part of prudence not to permit anyone to usurp scriptural texts and force them in some way to maintain any physical conclusion to be true, when at some future time the sense and demonstrative or necessary reasons may show the contrary. Who indeed will set bounds to human ingenuity? Who will assert that everything in the universe capable of being perceived is already discovered and known? Let us rather confess quite truly that "Those truths which we know are very few in comparison with those which we do not know."

We have it from the very mouth of the Holy Ghost that God delivered up the world to disputations, so that man cannot find out the work that God hath done from the beginning event to the end. In my opinion no one, in contradiction to that dictum, should close the road to free philosophizing about mundane and physical things, as if everything had already been discovered and revealed with certainty. Nor should it be considered rash not to be satisfied with those opinions which have become common. No one should be scorned in physical disputes for not holding to the opinions which happen to please other people best, especially concerning problems which have been debated among the greatest philosophers for thousands of years.

DOCUMENT ANALYSIS

1. Both Galileo and Luther have been seen as champions of freedom of expression. From these documents, do you think that is an accurate assessment of what these men were trying to do?

2. Given the religious situation of the time, why do you think Galileo's defense was unsuccessful?

3. What is the purpose of the Bible for Galileo? For Luther? How are they similar? Why do you think Luther rejected heliocentrism?

4. With regard to understanding the natural world, what is the relationship between Biblical authority and science for Galileo?

DOCUMENT 18.2

Sor Juana Inéz de la Cruz, from *La Respuesta* (1695)

Source: The Spanish text for this seventeenth-century declaration of women's intellectual freedom was discovered by Gabriel North Seymour during her Fulbright Scholarship in Mexico in 1980, following graduation from Princeton University. The English language translation by Margaret Sayers Peden was commissioned by Lime Rock Press, Inc., a small independent press in Connecticut, and was originally published in 1982 in a limited edition that included Ms. Seymour's black-and-white photographs of Sor Juana sites, under the title, "A Woman of Genius: The Intellectual Autobiography of Sor Juana Inés de la Cruz." The publication was honored at a special convocation of Mexican and American scholars at the Library of Congress. Copyright 1982 by Lime Rock Press, Inc. Reprinted by permission.

Arguably one of the greatest divides in the contact zone was that between the sexes. The patriarchal nature of Spanish rule and of the Catholic Church ensured that legally, at least, women were restricted to inferior positions and to lives with few rights. This was as true of Spanish women as it was of indigenous women. Perhaps the most impressive example of gender conflict involved Sor Juana Inéz de la Cruz, a Mexican nun in the late 1600s.

A brilliant and talented scholar, Sor Juana in 1690 wrote a daring critique of an earlier Jesuit sermon. Her critique prompted the Bishop of Puebla to admonish her for having overstepped herself as a woman. Sor Juana subsequently defended herself in a lengthy reply (respuesta) that challenged the foundations of the society in which she lived. Her 1695 response to the Bishop set off a struggle that highlighted not only divisions between the sexes, but also those within the Church, and between the Church and the Spanish government, in which Sor Juana found many powerful and influential supporters.

. . . I see many and illustrious women; some blessed with the gift of prophecy, like Abigail, others of persuasion, like Esther; others with pity, like Rehab; others with perseverance, like Anna, the mother of Samuel; and an infinite number of others, with diverse gifts and virtues . . .

. . . for all were nothing more than learned women, held, and celebrated—and venerated as well—as such by antiquity. Without mentioning an infinity of other women whose names fill books. For example, I find the Egyptian Catherine, studying and influencing the wisdom of all the wise men of Egypt. I see a Gertrudis studying, writing, and teaching. And not to overlook examples close to home, I see my most holy mother Paula, learned in Hebrew, Greek, and Latin, and most able in interpreting the Scriptures. And what greater praise than, having as her chronicler a Jeronimus Maximus, that Saint scarcely found himself competent for his task, and says, with that weighty deliberation and energetic precision with which he so well expressed himself: "If all the members of my body were tongues, they still would not be sufficient to proclaim the wisdom and virtue of Paula."

. . . The venerable Doctor Arce (by his virtue and learning a worthy teacher of the Scriptures) in his scholarly *Bibliorum* raises this question: *Is it permissible for women to dedicate themselves to the study of the Holy Scriptures, and to their interpretation?* and he offers as negative arguments the opinions of many saints, especially that of the Apostle: *Let women keep silence in the churches; for it is not permitted them to speak,* etc. He later cites other opinions and, from the same Apostle, verses from his letter to Titus: *The aged women in like manner, in holy attire . . . teaching well,* with interpretations by the Holy Fathers. Finally he resolves, with all prudence, that teaching publicly from a University chair, or preaching from the pulpit, is not permissible for women; but that to study, write, and teach privately not only is permissible, but most advantageous and useful. It is evident that this is not to be the case with all women, but with those to whom God may have granted special virtue and prudence, and who may be well advanced in learning, and having the essential talent and requisites for such a sacred calling. This view is indeed just, so much so that not only women, who are held to be so inept, but also men, who merely for being men believe they are wise, should be prohibited from interpreting the Sacred Word if they are not learned and virtuous and of gentle and well-inclined natures; that this is not so has been, I believe, at the root of so much sectarianism and so many heresies. For there are many who study but are ignorant, especially those who are in spirit arrogant, troubled, and proud, so eager for new interpretations of the Word (which itself rejects new interpretations) that merely for the sake of saying what no one else has said they speak a heresy, and even then are not content. Of these the Holy Spirit says: *For wisdom will not enter into a malicious soul.* To such as these more harm results from knowing than from ignorance. A wise man has said: he who does not know Latin is not a complete fool; but he who knows it is well qualified to be. And I would add that a fool may reach perfection (if ignorance may tolerate perfection) by having studied his title of philosophy and theology and by having some learning of tongues, by which he may be a fool in many sciences and languages: a great fool cannot be contained solely in his mother tongue.

For such as these, I reiterate, study is harmful, because it is as if to place a sword in the hands of a madman; which, though a most noble instrument for defense, is in his hands his own death and that of many others. So were the Divine Scriptures in the possession of the evil Pelagius and the intractable Arius, of the evil Luther, and the other heresiarchs like our own Doctor (who was neither ours nor a doctor) Cazalla. To these men, wisdom was harmful; although it is the greatest nourishment and the life of the soul; in the same way that in a stomach of sickly constitution and adulterated complexion, the finer the nourishment it receives, the more arid, fermented, and perverse are the humors it produces; thus these evil men: the more they study, the worse opinions they engender, their reason being obstructed with the very substance meant to nourish it, and they study much and digest little, exceeding the limits of the vessel of their reason. Of which the Apostle says: *For I say, by the grace that is given me, to all that are among you, not to be more wise than it behoveth to be wise, but to be wise unto sobriety, and according as God hath divided to every one the measure of faith.* And in truth, the Apostle did not direct these words to women, but to men; and that keep silence is intended not only for women, but for all incompetents. If I desire to know as much, or more, than Aristotle or Saint Augustine, and if I have not the aptitude of Saint Augustine or Aristotle, though I study more than either, not only will I not achieve learning, but I will weaken and dull the workings of my feeble reason with the disproportionateness of the goal.

DOCUMENT ANALYSIS

1. How does Sor Juana turn her agreement with Arce into an attack on the male-dominated society in which she lived? Do you think the Church in particular would have found Sor Juana's argument more threatening than, say, the average male Spaniard? Why or why not?

2. In her *Respuesta,* Sor Juana treats intellect as a veritable weapon. To what extent do you agree with her? What examples might you provide that would support or contradict her?

3. On what grounds does Sor Juana defend her right to exercise her intellect?

4. What examples does Sor Juana offer of noted and influential women? What does the variety of sources from which she draws her examples tell us of Sor Juana's education?

5. What reasons does Sor Juana give for agreeing with Doctor Arce's argument for barring women from the pulpit?

DOCUMENT 19.1

Mungo Park on slavery in Africa (late 1700s)

Source: Mungo Park, *Travels* (London: J. M. Dent & Sons, 1932).

During the late eighteenth and early nineteenth centuries in Europe, the scientific revolution and the Enlightenment were inspiring new attitudes and outlooks on the world. Educated Europeans were interested in what lay beyond their immediate horizon. It is no surprise, then, that this period marked the beginning of a new era of exploration and discovery, as European explorers delved deeper into areas of the world largely unknown to them. Underlying most, if not all, of these journeys, however, was the potential for economic gain for those who sponsored the travels.

One such explorer was Mungo Park, a Scotsman who traveled along the Gambia and Niger Rivers in west Africa from 1795 to 1797 and 1805 to 1806. Park, who died on his second trip, was keenly aware that his purpose was to "scout out" economic potential. Nonetheless, Park's journals provide an insightful glimpse into life in west Africa. Abolitionists especially liked his commentary on slavery within Africa, and quoted his writing to support their cause.

The slaves in Africa, I suppose, are nearly in the proportion of three to one to the free men. They claim no reward for their services except food and clothing, and are treated with kindness or severity, according to the good or bad disposition of their masters. Custom, however, has established certain rules with regard to the treatment of slaves, which it is thought dishonourable to violate. Thus, the domestic slaves, or such as are born in a man's own house, are treated with more lenity than those which are purchased with money. The authority of the master over the domestic slave, extends only to reasonable correction; for the master cannot sell his domestic without having first brought him to a public trial before the chief men of the place. But these restrictions on the power of the master extend not to the case of prisoners taken in war, nor to that of slaves purchased with money. All these unfortunate beings are considered as strangers and foreigners, who have no right to the protection of the law, and may be treated with severity, or sold to a stranger, according to the pleasure of their owners. There are, indeed, regular markets, where slaves of this description are bought and sold; and the value of a slave in the eye of an African purchaser, increases in proportion to his distance from his native kingdom; for when slaves are only a few days' journey from the place of their nativity, they frequently effect their escape; but when one or more kingdoms intervene, escape being more difficult, they are more readily reconciled to their situation. On this account, the unhappy slave is frequently transferred from one dealer to another, until he has lost all hopes of returning to his native kingdom. The slaves which are purchased by the Europeans on the coast are chiefly of this description; a few of them are collected in the petty wars, hereafter to be described, which take place near the coast; but by far the greater number are brought down in large caravans from the inland countries, of which many are unknown even by name to the Europeans. The slaves which are thus brought from the interior may be divided into two distinct classes; first, such as were slaves from their birth, having been born of enslaved mothers; secondly, such as were born free, but who afterwards, by whatever means, became slaves. Those of the first description are by far the most numerous; for prisoners taken in war (at least such as are taken in open and declared war, when one kingdom avows hostilities against another), are generally of this description.

Slaves of the second description generally become such by one or other of the following causes:—1. *Captivity*; 2. *Famine*; 3. *Insolvency*; 4. *Crimes*. A free man may, by the established customs of Africa, become a slave by being taken in war. War is, of all others, the most productive source, and was probably the origin of slavery.

Be this as it may, it is a known fact, that prisoners of war in Africa are the slaves of the conquerors; and when the weak or unsuccessful warrior begs for mercy beneath the uplifted spear of his opponent, he gives up at the same time his claim to liberty, and purchases his life at the expense of his freedom.

War, therefore, is certainly the most general and most productive source of slavery, and the desolations of war often (but not always) produce the second cause of slavery, famine, in which case a free man becomes a slave to avoid a greater calamity. During a great scarcity, which lasted for three years, in the countries of the Gambia, great numbers of people became slaves in this manner.

The third cause of slavery is insolvency. Of all the offences (if insolvency may be so called) to which the laws of Africa have affixed the punishment of slavery, this is the most common.

The fourth cause above enumerated is *the commission of crimes, on which the laws of the country affix slavery as a punishment.* In Africa, the only offences of this class are murder, adultery, and witchcraft; and I am happy to say that they did not appear to me to be common. In cases of murder, I was informed that the nearest relation of the deceased had it in his power, after conviction, either to kill the offender with his own hand, or sell him into slavery. When adultery occurs, it is generally left to the option of the person injured, either to sell the culprit, or accept such a ransom for him as he may think equivalent to the injury he has sustained. By witchcraft is meant pretended magic, by which the lives or healths of persons are affected; in other words, it is the administering of poison. No trial for this offence, however, came under my observation while I was in Africa, and I therefore suppose that the crime and its punishment occur but very seldom.

When a free man has become a slave by any one of the causes before mentioned, he generally continues so for life, and his children (if they are born of an enslaved mother) are brought up in the same state of servitude. There are, however, a few instances of slaves obtaining their freedom, and sometimes even with the consent of their masters; as by performing some singular piece of service, or by going to battle, and bringing home two slaves as a ransom; but the common way of regaining freedom is by escape; and when slaves have once set their minds on running away, they often succeed. Some of them will wait for years before an opportunity presents itself, and during that period show no signs of discontent. In general, it may be remarked, that slaves who come from a hilly country, and have been much accustomed to hunting and travel, are more apt to attempt their escape than such as are born in a flat country, and have been employed in cultivating the land.

[Regarding the Atlantic slave trade, Park says the following:]

How far it is maintained and supported by the slave traffic, which for two hundred years the nations of Europe have carried on with the natives of the coast, it is neither within my province nor in my power to explain. If my sentiments should be required concerning the effect which a discontinuance of that commerce would produce on the manners of the natives, I should have no hesitation in observing, that, in the present unenlightened state of their minds, my opinion is, the effect would neither be so extensive or beneficial as many wise and worthy persons fondly expect.

DOCUMENT ANALYSIS

1. Does Mungo Park appear to favor an end to the slave trade? Explain.

2. If a person becomes a slave in one of these four ways, how long does he/she generally stay a slave?

3. Is Park's account objective? Does it indicate any bias, or is it "fair"?

4. What are the four most common ways for a person to become a slave?

5. What two classes of slaves are brought to the coast from the interior?

DOCUMENT 19.2
Anonymous, "A Defense of the Slave Trade" (1740)

Source: From "A Defense of the African Slave Trade, 1740," London Magazine, 9 (1740), 493–494, in Elizabeth Donnan, *Documents Illustrative of the History of the Slave Trade to America* (Washington, D.C.: Carnegie Institution, 1930), II, 469–470.

Justifying European involvement in the trans-Atlantic slave trade often involved the use of ideas that made the endeavor seem moral; it was considered part of the "white man's burden" to release Africans from a worst bondage at home. Merchants, in particular, felt the need for some justification for transporting and selling human cargo. In this document, an anonymous person writes about conditions along the Guinea Coast of West Africa and the cruel power of the local kings to control African slaves. The anonymous writer is responding to a letter published in the Gentleman's Magazine *under the pseudonym Mercator Honestus, which argued against slavery and the slave trader.*

It is well known that many of the great kingdoms of West Africa had dealt in a local slave trade for centuries. Slaves were used in agricultural production, in households, and as part of court life. These slaves were under varying degrees of bondage outside the realm of what we call ***"chattel slavery,"*** *that is, under African customs, the condition of slavery was not hereditary and even slaves had some rights. What is interesting about this account is the heavy emphasis on* ***Enlightenment*** *ideas such as the right of every human being to liberty and happiness. European merchants believed they were freeing Africans from an even worst fate, slavery without Western laws and Christianity.*

Sir, The Guinea Trade, by the Mistake of some, or Misrepresentation of others, hath been charged with Inhumanity, and a Contradiction to good Morals. Such a Charge at a Time when private and publick Morals are laugh'd at, as the highest Folly, by a powerful Faction; and Self-interest set up as the only Criterion of true Wisdom, is certainly very uncourtly: But yet as I have a profound Regard for those superannuated Virtures; you will give me Leave to justify the African Trade, upon those Stale Principles, from the Imputations of "Mercator Honestus"; and shew him that there are People in some boasted Regions of Liberty, under a more wretched Slavery, than the Africans transplanted to our American Colonies.

The Inhabitants of Guinea are indeed in a most deplorable State of Slavery, under the arbitrary Powers of their Princes both as to Life and Property. In the several Subordinations to them, every great Man is absolute lord of his immediate Dependents. And lower still; every Master of a Family is Proprietor of his Wives, Children, and Servants; and may at his Pleasure consign them to Death, or a better Market. No doubt such a State is contrary to Nature and Reason, since every human Creature hath an absolute Right to Liberty. But are not all arbitrary Governments, as well in Europe, as Africa, equally repugnant to that great Law of Nature? And yet it is not in our Power to cure the universal Evil, and set all the Kingdoms of the Earth free from the Domination of Tyrants, whose long Possession, supported by standing Armies, and flagitious Ministers, renders the Thraldom without Remedy, while the People under it are by Custom satisfied with, or at least quiet under Bondage.

All that can be done in such a Case is, to communicate as much Liberty, and Happiness, as such circumstances will admit, and the People will consent to: And this is certainly by the Guinea Trade. For, by purchasing, or rather ransoming the Negroes from their national Tyrants, and transplanting them under the benign Influences of the Law, and Gospel, they are advanced to much greater Degrees of Felicity, tho' not to absolute Liberty.

That this is truly the Case cannot be doubted by any one acquainted with the Constitution of our Colonies, where the Negroes are governed by Laws, and suffer much less Punishment in Proportion to their Crimes, than the People in other Countries more refined in the Arts of Wickedness; and where Capital Punishment is inflicted only by the Civil Magistrates. . . .

Perhaps my Antagonist calls the Negroes Allowance of a Pint of Corn and an Herring, penurious, in Comparison of the full Meals of Gluttony: But if not let him compare that Allowance, to what the poor Labourer can purchase for Tenpence per Day to subsist himself and Family, and he will easily determine the American's Advantage. . . .

Nevertheless, Mercator will say, the Negroes are Slaves to their Proprietors: How Slaves? Nominally: Not really so much Slaves, as the Peasantry of all Nations is to Necessity; not so much as those of Corruption, or Party Zeal; not in any Sense, such abject Slaves, as every vicious Man is to his own Appetites. Indeed there is this Difference between Britons, and the Slaves of all other Nations; that the latter are so by Birth, or tyrannical Necessity; the former can never be so, but by a wicked Choice, or execrable Venality. . . .

Glossary

Chattel Slavery
Slavery based upon the principle that men and women who are slaves enjoy no rights and can hold no property. In most cases, this type of slavery is hereditary, and humans are bought and sold as property by the owners. It was the prevalent form of slavery used by Europeans during the age of the Atlantic slave trade, from the sixteenth to the eighteenth century.

Enlightenment
The period in Europe when thinkers supported scientific advances and social scientific knowledge based upon rational laws. Most important, the Enlightenment produced a set of basic principles about human affairs: human beings were good, could be educated, and were entitled to basic rights of life, liberty, and the pursuit of wealth. In sixteenth-century Europe, the enslavement of "barbarians" or nonbelievers was seen as positive—as a way to civilize others; however, during the Enlightenment, slavery came to be seen as backward and immoral. The slave trade in particular was criticized. It was the symbol of slavery's inhumanity and cruelty.

DOCUMENT ANALYSIS

1. In addition to arguments based on moral principles, what other justifications against the slave trade might Mercator Honestus have used to criticize merchants involved in the traffic of human lives? Do you think these are valid claims? Why or why not?

____

____

____

2. What can we deduce from this document about the relationship between merchants and other elements of European society regarding the slave trade? Who might be particularly interested in the content and flavor of this publication?

____

____

____

3. What do the descriptions of African life along the west coast of Africa tell us about European perceptions of African slavery?

4. What role do Enlightenment ideas play in justifying the trans-Atlantic slave trade? To what degree do you think English ideas on law, government, and justice contributed to merchant activity in the slave trade?

5. What was the author's attitude toward African indigenous slavery? Are there religious overtones to the passage? If so, describe and explain them.

DOCUMENT 20.1

Abu Taleb on the West and Western influence (late 1700s)

Source: Abu Taleb, "The Travels of Mirza Abu Taleb Khan," in *Sources of Indian Tradition,* ed. Theodore de Bary (New York: Columbia University Press, 1958), pp. 561–5.

Muslims filled the top positions in much of India during the Mughal Dynasty. As European influence and trade increased, however, the Muslim empires and kingdoms weakened substantially. Upper-caste Hindus began to have their children educated in Western schools, and, while relatively few Hindus had the chance to travel to Europe, many started to affect English ways and attitudes. The same cannot be said for Indian Muslims, who generally resisted Western influence on their lives and customs, but who were often more able to travel (unlike Hindus, they had no religious prohibitions against foreign travel).

One of the first educated Indians to travel to Europe was Abu Taleb. Born in 1752, Abu Taleb served the Mughal government for much of his early life, and, after retiring, spent three years in Europe. When he returned to Calcutta, he wrote The Travels of Mirza Abu Taleb Khan. *Written in Persian for his Muslim audience, the book illustrates Abu Taleb's interest in English ways and life, but also displays the attitudes between the English and Indian Muslims.*

Glory be to God, the Lord of all worlds, who has conferred innumerable blessings on mankind, and accomplished all the laudable desires of his creatures. Praise be also to the Chosen of Mankind [Muhammad], the traveler over the whole expanse of the heavens, and benedictions without end on his descendants and companions.

The wanderer over the face of the earth, Abk Tleb, the son of Mohammed of Ispahan, begs leave to inform the curious in biography, that, owing to several adverse circumstances, finding it inconvenient to remain at home, he was compelled to undertake many tedious journeys, during which he associated with men of all nations and beheld various wonders, both by sea and by land.

It therefore occurred to him, that if he were to write all the circumstances of his journey through Europe, to describe the curiosities and wonders which he saw, and to give some account for the manner and customs of the various nations he visited, all of which are little known to Asiatics, it would afford a gratifying banquet to his countrymen.

He was also of opinion, that many of the customs, inventions, sciences, and ordinances of Europe, the good effects of which are apparent in those countries, might with great advantage be imitated by Mohammedans.

Impressed with these ideas, he, on his first setting out on his travels, commenced a journal, in which he daily inserted every event, and committed to writing such reflections as occurred to him at the moment: and on his return to Calcutta, in the year of the Hejira 1218 (A.D. 1803), having revised and abridged his notes, he arranged them in the present form.

[Here Abk Tleb changes from the third to the first person, and laments:] I have named this work . . . "The Travels of Tleb in the Regions of Europe"; but when I reflect on the want of energy and the indolent dispositions of my countrymen, and the many erroneous customs which exist in all Mohammedan countries and among all ranks of Mussulmans, I am fearful that my exertions will be thrown away. The great and the rich, intoxicated with pride and luxury, and puffed up with the vanity of their possessions, consider universal science as comprehended in the circle of their own scanty acquirements and limited knowledge; while the poor and common people, from the want of leisure, and overpowered by the difficulty of procuring a livelihood, have not time to attend to their personal concerns, much less to form desires for the acquirement of information on new discoveries and inventions; although such a passion has been implanted by nature in every human breast, as an honor and an ornament to the species. I therefore despair of their reaping any fruit from my labors, being convinced that they will consider this book of no greater value than the volumes of tales and romances which they peruse merely to pass away their time, or are attracted thereto by the easiness of the style. It may consequently be concluded, that as they will find no pleasure in reading a work which contains a number of foreign names, treats on uncommon subjects, and alludes to other matters which cannot be understood at the first glance, but require a little time for consideration, they will, under pretense of zeal for their religion, entirely abstain and refrain from perusing it.

Ode to London

Henceforward we will devote our lives to London, and its heart-alluring Damsels:
Our hearts are satiated with viewing fields, gardens, rivers, and palaces.

We have no longing for the Toba, Sudreh, or other trees of Paradise:
We are content to rest under the shade of these terrestrial Cypresses.

If the Shaikh of Mecca is displeased at our conversion, who cares?
May the Temple which has conferred such blessings on us, and its Priests, flourish!

Fill the goblet with wine! If by this I am prevented from returning
To my old religion, I care not; nay, I am the better pleased.

If the prime of my life has been spent in the service of an Indian Cupid,
It matters not: I am now rewarded by the smiles of the British Fair.

Adorable creatures! Whose flowing tresses, whether of flaxen or of jetty hue,
Or auburn gay, delight my soul, and ravish all my senses!

Whose ruby lips would animate the torpid clay, or marble statue!
Had I a renewal of life, I would, with rapture, devote it to your service!

These wounds of Cupid, on your heart, Tleba, are not accidental:
They were engendered by Nature, like the streaks on the leaf of a tulip.

The first and greatest defect I observed in the English is their want of faith in religion, and their great inclination to philosophy [atheism]. The effects of these principles, or rather want of principle, is very conspicuous in the lower orders of people, who are totally devoid of honesty. They are, indeed, cautious how they transgress against the laws, from fear of punishment; but whenever an opportunity offers of purloining any thing without the risk of detection, they never pass it by. They are also ever on the watch to appropriate to themselves the property of the rich, who, on this account, are obliged constantly to keep their doors shut, and never to permit an unknown person to enter them. At present, owing to the vigilance of the magistrates, the severity of the laws, and the honor of the superior classes of people, no very bad consequences are to be apprehended; but if ever such nefarious practices should become prevalent and should creep in among the higher classes, inevitable ruin must ensue.

The second defect most conspicuous in the English character is pride, or insolence. Puffed up with their power and good fortune for the last fifty years, they are not apprehensive of adversity, and take no pains to avert it. Thus, when the people of London, some time ago, assembled in mobs on account of the great increase of taxes and high price of provisions, and were nearly in a state of insurrection—although the magistrates, by their vigilance in watching them, and by causing parties of soldiers to patrole the streets day and night, to disperse all persons whom they saw assembling together, succeeded in quieting the disturbance—yet no pains were afterwards taken to eradicate the evil. Some of the men in power said it had been merely a plan of the artificers to obtain higher wages (an attempt frequently made by the English tradesmen); others were of opinion that no remedy could be applied; therefore no further notice was taken of the affair. All this, I say, betrays a blind confidence, which, instead of meeting the danger and endeavoring to prevent it, waits till the misfortune arrives, and then attempts to remedy it. Such was the case with the late king of France, who took no step to oppose the Revolution till it was too late. This self-confidence is to be found, more or less, in every Englishman; it however differs much from the pride of the Indians and Persians.

Their third defect is a passion for acquiring money and their attachment to worldly affairs. Although these bad qualities are not so reprehensible in them as in countries more subject to the vicissitudes of fortune, (because, in England, property is so well protected by the laws that every person reaps the fruits of his industry, and, in his old age, enjoys the earnings or economy of his youth,) yet sordid and illiberal habits are generally found to accompany avarice and parsimony, and, consequently, render the possessor of them contemptible; on the contrary, generosity, if it does not launch into prodigality, but is guided by the hand of prudence, will render a man respected and esteemed.

DOCUMENT ANALYSIS

1. In the first section of the excerpt, does Abu Taleb think Muslims are going to take to Western learning? Explain.

___

___

___

2. Is the poem about London positive or negative? What makes you think so?

___

___

___

3. What appears to you to be the biggest problem pointed out? Why?

___

___

___

4. List two of the defects of the English pointed out by Abu Taleb.

___

___

___

5. What appears to you to be the biggest problem pointed out? Why?

___

___

___

6. What is the overall consequence of the English arrogance toward social problems, according to the author?

___

___

___

DOCUMENT 20.2

Baktha'war Kahn on Aurangzeb, Mughal Ruler (late 1600s)

Source: Henry M. Elliot and John Dowson, eds., *The History of India as Told by Its Own Historians*, 8 vols. (London: Truebner, 1867–1877), vol. 7, pp. 157–162.

India's Mughal Empire was constantly trying to address the practical problems facing a minority Muslim population ruling over a much larger Hindu population. Some rulers, such as Akbar the Great (1556–1605), proved tolerant and accommodating to Hindus and other local religious groups. Akbar even attempted, unsuccessfully, to create a new religion that brought together elements from Islam, Hinduism, and Zoroastrianism, among others. Akbar's successors generally continued his tolerant policies.

There was, of course, another approach to the Mughal problem. Rather than accommodating Hindus, a ruler might oppress them to solve some of the problems of governance. A ruler who is remembered for doing so is Aurangzeb, who ruled from 1658–1707 and even executed his brother for being too tolerant of other faiths. In the early 1680s, an advisor of Aurangzeb, Baktha'war Khan, wrote a history of the world up through the time of Aurangzeb's reign. The following excerpt not only discusses the ruler's religious attitudes, it also addresses his personality and overall attitudes.

Be it known to the readers of this work that this humble slave of the Almighty is going to describe in a correct manner the excellent character, the worthy habits and the refined morals of this most virtuous monarch, Aurangzeb, according as he has witnessed them with his own eyes. The Emperor, a great worshiper of God by natural propensity, is remarkable for his rigid attachment to religion. . . . Having made his ablutions [ritual washings], he always occupies a great part of his time in adoration of the Deity, and says the usual prayers, first in the mosque and then at home, both in congregation and in private, with the most heartfelt devotion. He keeps the appointed fasts on Fridays and other sacred days, and he reads the Friday prayers in the mosque with the common people of the Muslim faith. He keeps vigils during the whole of the sacred nights, and with the light of the favor of God illumines the lamps of religion and prosperity. From his great piety, he passes whole nights in the mosque which is in his palace, and keeps company with men of devotion. In privacy he never sits on a throne. He gave away in alms before his accession a portion of his allowance of lawful food and clothing, and now devotes to the same purpose the income of a few villages in the district of Delhi, and the proceeds of two or three salt-producing tracts, which are appropriated to his private purse. . . . During the whole month of Ramadan he keeps fast, says the prayers appointed for that month, and reads the holy Qur'an in the assembly of religious and learned men, with whom he sits for that purpose during six, and sometimes nine hours of the night. During the last ten days of the month, he performs worship in the mosque, and although, on account of several obstacles, he is unable to proceed on a pilgrimage to Mecca, yet the care which he takes to promote facilities for pilgrims to that holy place may be considered equivalent to the pilgrimage.

Though he has collected at the foot of his throne those who inspire ravishment in joyous assemblies of pleasure, in the shape of singers who possess lovely voices and clever instrumental performers, and in the commencement of his reign sometimes used to hear them sing and play, and though he himself understands music well, yet now for several years past, on account of his great restraint and self-denial . . . he entirely abstains from this amusement. If any of the singers and musicians becomes ashamed of his calling, he makes an allowance for him or grants him land for his maintenance. . . .

In consideration of their rank and merit, he shows much honor and respect to the saints and learned men, and through his cordial and liberal exertions, the sublime doctrines of our pure religion have obtained such prevalence throughout the wide territories of **Hindustan** as they never had in the reign of any former king.

Hindu writers have been entirely excluded from holding public offices, and all the worshiping places of the infidels [Hindus] and the great temples of these infamous people have been thrown down and destroyed in a manner which excites astonishment at the successful completion of so difficult a task. . . .

As it is a great object with this Emperor that all Muslims should follow the principles of the religion. . . and as there was no book which embodied them all, and as until many books had been collected and a man had obtained sufficient leisure, means and knowledge of theological subjects, he could not satisfy his inquiries on any disputed point, therefore His Majesty, the protector of the faith, determined that a body of eminently learned and able men of Hindustan should take up the voluminous and most trustworthy works which were collected in the royal library, and having made a digest of them, compose a book which might form a standard canon of the law, and afford to all an easy and available means of ascertaining the proper and authoritative interpretation. The chief conductor of this difficult undertaking was the most learned man of the time, Shaikh Nizam, and all the members of the society were very handsomely and liberally paid, so that up to the present time a sum of about two hundred thousand rupees has been expended in this valuable compilation, which contains more than one hundred thousand lines. When the work, with God's pleasure, is completed, it will be for all the world the standard exposition of the law. . . .

The Emperor is perfectly acquainted with the commentaries, traditions, and law. . . . One of the greatest excellences of this virtuous monarch is, that he has learned the Qur'an by heart. Though in his early youth he had committed to memory some chapters of that sacred book, yet he learned the whole by heart after ascending the throne. He took great pains and showed much perseverance in impressing it upon his mind. He writes in a very elegant hand, and has acquired perfection in this art. He has written two copies of the holy book with his own hand, and having finished and adorned them with ornaments and marginal lines, at the expense of seven thousand rupees, he sent them to the holy cities of Mecca and Medina . . . . He is a very elegant writer in prose, and has acquired proficiency in versification, but agreeably to the words of God, "Poets deal in falsehoods," he abstains from practicing it. He does not like to hear verses except those which contain a moral. "To please Almighty God he never turned his eye towards a flatterer, nor gave his ear to a poet."

The Emperor has given a very liberal education to his fortunate and noble children, who, by virtue of his attention and care, have reached to the summit of perfection, and made great advances in rectitude, devotion, and piety, and in learning the manners and customs of princes and great men. Through his instruction they have learned the Book of God by heart, obtained proficiency in the sciences and polite literature, writing the various hands, and in learning the Turkish and the Persian languages.

In like manner, the ladies of the household also, according to his orders, have learned the fundamental and necessary tenets of religion, and all devote their time to the adoration and worship of the Deity, to reading the sacred Qur'an, and performing virtuous and pious acts. The excellence of character and the purity of morals of this holy monarch are beyond all expression. As long as nature nourishes the tree of existence, and keeps the garden of the world fresh, may the plant of the prosperity of this preserver of the garden of dignity and honor continue fruitful!

DOCUMENT ANALYSIS

1. Does the author claim the king was dedicated to his religion? Explain.

____

____

____

2. What do you think Aurangzeb's attitudes were toward what we might call "social welfare"?

____

____

____

3. What qualities does the author seem to respect in his ruler?

4. What was Aurangzeb's attitude toward Hinduism?

5. Why didn't Aurangzeb generally listen to poetry?

DOCUMENT 21.1

D. F. Sarmiento, "Symbolism and Contested Identities in Argentina" (1810s)

Source: D. F. Sarmiento, *Life in the Argentine Republic in the Days of the Tyrants; or, Civilization and Barbarism*, trans. Mrs. Horace Mann (New York: Hafner Press, 1868), pp. 62–4, 137–40.

While Argentina had no large indigenous population to factor into its quest for national identity, racial considerations, nevertheless, played a critical part in how Argentines viewed themselves, especially in an era shaped by ideas of scientific racism. Indeed, Domingo Sarmiento's famous essay on civilization and barbarism in Latin American—a sustained critique of how Argentine caudillo Facundo Quiroga had prevented Argentina from taking its place on the world stage of civilized countries—used a racial duality as a means of understanding Argentina's post-independence successes and failures. The white upper-class population of Buenos Aires—of whom Sarmiento was an example—sought to mimic European culture, fashion, and political traditions. The caudillos who represented their rural counterparts, by contrast, were less impressed by all things European. In the following section, Sarmiento discusses how political symbolism embodied and reflected the essential dualities—civilization versus barbarism, and pure versus mixed blood—of Argentine society.

. . . Like all civil wars in which deep differences of education, belief, and motives divide the parties engaged in them, the internal warfare of the Argentine Republic was long and obstinate, until one of the elements of the strife was victorious. The Argentine Revolutionary War was twofold: 1st, a civilized warfare of the cities against Spain; 2d, a war against the cities on the part of the country chieftains with the view of shaking off all political subjection and satisfying their hatred of civilization. The cities overcame the Spaniards, and were in their turn overcome by the country districts. This is the explanation of the Argentine Revolution, the first shot of which was fired in 1810, and the last is still to be heard.

. . . To make the ruin and decadence of civilization and the rapid progress of barbarism perceptible to the reader, I must select two cities—one already annihilated, the other insensibly proceeding towards barbarism—La Rioja and San Juan. La Rioja was formerly a city of some account, but its own sons would fail to recognize it in its present condition.

. . . Let us now look at the condition of La Rioja, as exhibited by the answers given to one of the many inquiries I have instituted for the purpose of gaining a thorough knowledge of the facts on which I base my theories. These are the statements of a reliable person, who was unacquainted with my object in investigating his memory of matters that must have been fresh in his mind, for it was only four months before that he left Rioja.

1. What is about the actual amount of the population of Rioja city?

   Ans. About fifteen hundred souls. It is said that only fifteen adult males reside in the city.

2. How many persons of note live in it?

   Ans. Six or eight in the city.

3. How many lawyers' offices are open there?

   Ans. None.

4. How many men wear dress-coats?

   Ans. None.

5. How many young men from La Rioja are studying at Cordova or Buenos Ayres?

   Ans. I know of only one.

. . . This was the famous fight at Tala, the first exploit of Quiroga beyond the limits of his province. He had conquered "the bravest of the brave," and kept his sword as a trophy of the victory. Will he stop there? But let us see the force which sustained itself against the colonel of the 13th regiment, who overthrew a government to equip his company. Facundo raised at Tala a flag which was not Argentine, but of his own invention; namely, a black ground with a skull and cross-bones in the center. This was the flag which he had lost early in the engagement, and which he intended to recover, as he said to his routed soldiers, even at the mouth of hell. Terror, death, hell, were represented on the banner and in the proclamations of this general of the Llanos.

And there was still another revelation of the Arab-Tartar spirit of that power which was to destroy the cities. The Argentine colors are blue and white; the clear sky of a fair day, and the bright light of the disk of the sun: "peace and justice for all." In our hatred of tyranny and violence, we reject on our national flag warlike devices. Two hands, as a sign of union, support the Phrygian cap of Liberty. "The United Cities" says this symbol, "will sustain their acquired liberty." The sun begins to illumine the background of this device, while the darkness of night is disappearing. The armies of the Republic, which were to spread over the whole country to enforce the coming of that promised light, wear a uniform of dark blue. But now, in the very heart of the Republic, the color red appears on the national banners, in the dress of the soldiers, and in the cockade which every native Argentine must wear under pain of death. Let us look up the significance of the color red. I have before me a picture of all the national flags of the world. In civilized Europe there is but one in which this color prevails, notwithstanding the barbaric origin of its banners. The red ones are: Algiers, a red flag with skull and cross-bones; Tunis, a red flag; Mongolia, the same; Turkey, a red flag with a crescent; Morocco; Japan, red with the exterminating knife; Siam has the same.

I remember that travelers in the interior of Africa provide themselves with *red* cloth for the Negro princes. "The king of Elve," say the brothers Lander, "wore a Spanish coat of *red* cloth and pantaloons of the same color."

I remember that the presents sent by the government of Chili to the **caciques** of Aranco, were *red* cloaks and coats, because savages liked this color especially.

Siam, the Africans, the savages, the Roman Neros, the barbarian kings, the hangmen, the Rosas, should be clothed in a color now proscribed by Christian and civilized communities? No, it is because red is the symbol of violence, blood, and barbarism. If not, why this antagonism?

The Argentine revolution of independence was symbolized by two blue stripes and one white one; signifying, *justice, peace, justice.*

The amendment made by Facundo and approved by Rosas, was a red band, signifying *terror, blood, barbarism.*

In all ages this significance has been given to the color purple or red; study the history of those nations who have hoisted this color, and you will always find a Rosas and a Facundo—terror, barbarism, and blood always prevailing. In Morocco, the emperor has the singular prerogative of killing criminals with his own hand. Each phase of civilization is expressed in its garments, and every style of apparel is indicative of an entire system of ideas. Why do we wear beards at the present day? Because of the researches recently made in mediæval history; the direction given to romantic literature is reflected in the fashions of the day. And why are these constantly changing? Because of the freedom of thought in Europe; let thought be stationary, enslaved, and the costume will remain unchanged. Thus in Asia, where men live under such governments as that of Rosas, the same style of dress has been worn since the time of Abraham. . . .

DOCUMENT ANALYSIS

1. How does Sarmiento characterize the Argentine wars for independence?

2. To what extent does Sarmiento draw parallels between political symbolism and the civilization-barbarism issue? How does he use language to persuade his readers?

3. To what key internal division does Sarmiento link his "civilization versus barbarism" duality?

4. What evidence does Sarmiento use in assessing Argentine barbarism? What does Sarmiento's evidence tell you of his own prejudices?

5. What symbols do Argentines use in their politics?

DOCUMENT 22.1

Evidence of a Female Millhand to the Parliamentary Commissioners (early 1800s)

Source: John Carey, ed., *Eyewitness to History* (New York: Avon Books, 1987), pp. 295–8.

The Industrial Revolution had a profound impact on the European economy. The transition form rural craft-based economies to urban industrialization revolutionized the manufacturing of goods. The organization of labor also took a dramatic shift as human or animal power was replaced by mechanical power with the development of the efficient steam engine by James Watt in the 1780s. The application of steam to machinery revolutionized the textile industry and the transportation industries. The factory system appeared, and capitalism reigned triumphant.

Socially, the Industrial Revolution also wrought tremendous change. The new industrial working class that emerged found itself mired in monotonous, low paying, and often dangerous jobs. Employment was never secure, sick workers received no pay, and any protests caused immediate dismissal. Unfortunately for many families, one worker in the family could not earn enough to supply the family's needs, so working class families became families where every member, including children, contributed by taking employment. Children in Britain had always worked, but their employment in the textile mills deprived them of an education and often subjected them to harsh discipline. Working conditions for children finally attracted Parliamentary attention in Britain, and in 1815 a Parliamentary commission heard testimony from mill employees from across Great Britain.

Factory Conditions, c. 1815
Evidence of a Female Millhand to the Parliamentary Commissioners

Elizabeth Bentley

What age are you?
Twenty-three.

Where do you live?
At Leeds.

What time did you begin work at the factory?
When I was six years old.

At whose factory did you work?
Mr Burk's.

What kind of mill is it?
Flax mill.

What was your business in that mill?
I was a little doffer.

What were your hours of labour in that mill?
From 5 in the morning till 9 at night, when they were thronged.

For how long a time together have you worked that excessive length of time?
For about a year.

What were the usual hours of labour when you were not so thronged?
For six in the morning till 7 at night.

What time was allowed for meals?
Forty minutes at noon.

Had you any time to get your breakfast or drinking?
No, we had to get it as we could.

Do you consider doffing a laborious employment?
Yes.

Explain what you had to do?
When the frames are full, they have to stop the frames, and take the flyers off, and take the full bobbins off, and carry them to the roller, and then put empty ones on, and set the frame going again.

Does that keep you constantly on your feet?
Yes, there are so many frames and they run so quick.

Your labour is very excessive?
Yes, you have not time for anything.

Suppose you flagged a little, or were late, what would they do?
Strap us.

And they are in the habit of strapping those who are last in doffing?
Yes.

Constantly?
Yes.

Girls as well as boys?
Yes.

Have you ever been strapped?
Yes.

Severely?
Yes.

Is the strap used so as to hurt you excessively?
Yes it is . . . I have seen the overlooker go to the top end of the room, where the little girls hug the can to the backminders; he has taken a strap, and a whistle in his mouth, and sometimes he has got a chain and chained them, and strapped them all down the room.

What was his reason for that?
He was very angry.

Did you live far from the mill?
Yes, two miles.

Had you a clock?
No, we had not.

Were you generally there in time?
Yes, my mother has been up at 4 o'clock in the morning, and at 2 o'clock in the morning; the colliers used to go to their work at 3 or 4 o'clock, and when she heard them stirring she has got up out of her warm bed, and gone out and asked them the time; and I have sometimes been at Hunslet Car at 2 o'clock in the morning, when it was streaming down with rain, and we have had to stay till the mill was opened.

You are considerably deformed in person as a consequence of this labour?
Yes I am.

And what time did it come on?
I was about 13 years old when it began coming, and it has got worse since; it is five years since my mother died, and my mother was never able to get me a good pair of stays to hold me up, and when my mother died I had to do for myself, and got me a pair.

Were you perfectly straight and healthy before you worked at a mill?
Yes, I was as straight a little girl as ever went up and down town.

Were you straight till you were 13?
Yes, I was.

Did your deformity come upon you with much pain and weariness?
Yes, I cannot express the pain all the time it was coming.

Do you know of anybody that has been similarly injured in their health?
Yes, in their health, but not many deformed as I am.

It is very common to have weak ankles and crooked knees?
Yes, very common indeed.

This is brought on by stopping the spindle?
Yes.

Where are you now?
In the poorhouse.

State what you think as to the circumstances in which you have been placed during all this time of labour, and what you have considered about it as to the hardship and cruelty of it.
The witness was too much affected to answer the question.

DOCUMENT ANALYSIS

1. Describe a typical workday for this worker.

2. How well did employees eat? What did they eat? Was this very healthy?

3. What was discipline like in the factory? How were children disciplined if they dozed off or failed in their duty?

4. Why do you think parents allowed their children to be subjected to this type of work?

5. Would you expect this woman's experience to be typical or atypical of factory work in this period? Why or why not?

DOCUMENT 22.2
Elizabeth Cady Stanton on the Seneca Falls Convention (1848)

Source: Elizabeth Cady Stanton, *A History of Woman Suffrage*, vol. 1 (Rochester, N.Y.: Fowler and Wells, 1889), pp. 70–71.

The 1848 Seneca Falls Convention is often regarded as the beginning of the feminist movement in America. However, the idea for the convention may have originated in the 1840 World Anti-Slavery Convention in London where women, despite their efforts to rid the world of slavery, were not allowed to speak and were forced to sit behind a partition.

Elizabeth Cady Stanton, who attended the meeting in London, was repulsed by the treatment women received and began to refine her anger into a statement based on Thomas Jefferson's Declaration of Independence. The draft was first proposed before the 300 participants at the Seneca Falls Convention in July 1848. This first meeting, and the proposals found in the Declaration of Sentiments, would provide a framework for the struggle of women to achieve equal rights and the right to vote.

When, in the course of human events, it becomes necessary for one portion of the family of man to assume among the people of the earth a position different from that which they have hitherto occupied, but one to which the laws of nature and of nature's God entitle them, a decent respect to the opinions of mankind requires that they should declare the causes that impel them to such a course.

We hold these truths to be self-evident: that all men and women are created equal; that they are endowed by their Creator with certain inalienable rights; that among these are life, liberty, and the pursuit of happiness; that to secure these rights governments are instituted, deriving their just powers from the consent of the governed. Whenever any form of government becomes destructive of these ends, it is the right of those who suffer from it to refuse allegiance to it, and to insist upon the institution of a new government, laying its foundation on such principles, and organizing its powers in such form, as to them shall seem most likely to effect their safety and happiness. Prudence, indeed, will dictate that governments long established should not be changed for light and transient causes; and accordingly all experience hath shown that mankind are more disposed to suffer, while evils are sufferable, than to right themselves by abolishing the forms to which they are accustomed. But when a long train of abuses and usurpations, pursuing invariably the same object, evinces a design to reduce them under absolute despotism, it is their duty to throw off such government, and to provide new guards for their future security. Such has been the patient sufferance of the women under this government, and such is now the necessity which constrains them to demand the equal station to which they are entitled. The history of mankind is a history of repeated injuries and usurpations on the part of man toward woman, having in direct object the establishment of an absolute tyranny over her. To prove this, let facts be submitted to a candid world.

He has never permitted her to exercise her inalienable right to the elective franchise.

He has compelled her to submit to laws, in the formation of which she had no voice.

He has withheld from her rights which are given to the most ignorant and degraded men—both natives and foreigners.

Having deprived her of this first right of a citizen, the elective franchise, thereby leaving her without representation in the halls of legislation, he has oppressed her on all sides.

He has made her, if married, in the eye of the law, civilly dead.

He has taken from her all right in property, even to the wages she earns.

He has made her, morally, an irresponsible being, as she can commit many crimes with impunity, provided they be done in the presence of her husband. In the covenant of marriage, she is compelled to promise obedience to her husband, he becoming, to all intents and purposes, her master—the law giving him power to deprive her of her liberty, and to administer chastisement.

He has so framed the laws of divorce, as to what shall be the proper causes, and in case of separation, to whom the guardianship of the children shall be given, as to be wholly regardless of the happiness of women—the law, in all cases, going upon a false supposition of the supremacy of man, and giving all power into his hands.

After depriving her of all rights as a married woman, if single, and the owner of property, he has taxed her to support a government which recognizes her only when her property can be made profitable to it.

He has monopolized nearly all the profitable employments, and from those she is permitted to follow, she receives but a scanty remuneration. He closes against her all the avenues to wealth and distinction which he considers most honorable to himself. As a teacher of theology, medicine, or law, she is not known.

He has denied her the facilities for obtaining a thorough education, all colleges being closed against her.

He allows her in church, as well as state, but a subordinate position, claiming apostolic authority for her exclusion from the ministry, and, with some exceptions, from any public participation in the affairs of the church.

He has created a false public sentiment by giving to the world a different code of morals for men and women, by which moral delinquencies which exclude women from society, are not only tolerated, but deemed of little account in man.

He has usurped the prerogative of Jehovah himself, claiming it as his right to assign for her a sphere of action, when that belongs to her conscience and to her God.

He has endeavored, in every way that he could, to destroy her confidence in her own powers, to lessen her self-respect, and to make her willing to lead a dependent and abject life.

Now, in view of this entire disfranchisement of one-half the people of this country, their social and religious degradation—in view of the unjust laws above mentioned, and because women do feel themselves aggrieved, oppressed, and fraudulently deprived of their most sacred rights, we insist that they have immediate admission to all the rights and privileges which belong to them as citizens of the United States.

DOCUMENT ANALYSIS

1. How convincing is the argument? Do you agree with what the Declaration is proposing?

____

____

____

2. What are some of the main limitations on the rights of women listed in the Declaration? What is said about marriage, for example?

____

____

____

3. What are some of the resolutions proposed in the document?

DOCUMENT 23.1
Halide Edib, from *Memoirs of Halide Edib*

Source: Halide Edib [Ady'var], *Memoirs of Halide Edib* (New York: The Century Co., 1926), pp. 252–3, 256–9.

Halide Edib Ady'var (1884–1964) is best known as a prominent spokesperson for women's rights, and an ardent supporter of the Turkish nationalist movement following World War I. Educated at the American-run Istanbul Women's College, Halide Edib authored several novels, and two volumes of memoirs, covering the period from her childhood through the foundation of the Turkish Republic in 1923. After her husband, Adnan Ady'var, ran afoul of the regime of Mustafa Kemal Atatürk, Halide Edib spent the late 1920s and 1930s living, teaching and writing in Europe, the United States, and India, before returning to Turkey following Atatürk's death.

On the morning of July 11,1908, I was sitting in the spacious hall of Antigone, with my old friends from Beshiktash, Auntie Peyker and her husband Hamdi Effendi. Their son was the young officer who had escaped to Europe and joined the Young Turks, and they often came to me to talk of him and to get his letters, for they corresponded with him through an American friend of mine. They had no hope of ever seeing their son alive. Hamidian rule had a finality and inevitability which made one almost laugh at the idea that it could be changed by a few pamphlets published occasionally in Paris and sent to Constantinople in secret.

I well remember the silence before Salih Zeki Bey came into the hall with the morning paper open in his hands. Granny, who lived with me at the time, was peacefully settled on the corner sofa.

Salih Zeki Bey walked slowly, his eyes on the first page of the paper, and with a strange look of surprise on his face. Then he read aloud the imperial communiquê of four lines. The cringing praise of the sultan was even more exaggerated than usual, but the communiquê was written in concise terms and said that his Majesty the sultan was to restore the constitution of 1876.

As we listened in the old-fashioned hall, with the wide stretch of wonderful blue sea expanding behind a line of dark green pines, consternation overcame us.

The old pair sat in silence, the tears rolling down their wrinkled cheeks. Laconic as were those lines, they transfigured the minds of these old people with the radiant hope that they might see their son again. Granny, who hardly understood the meaning, looked over her spectacles as she asked:

"What does it mean, Halidé?"

What did it mean? I hardly realized that a long scene of heaven and hell was to be enacted in the smothered land of Turkey and that I was to be called to act, to suffer, to knock my foolish young head against the realities of life, struggling endlessly, watching the interminable tragedy to its bitter end. This was to be my education in life after my education in school.

But now to return to our little group. The subject seemed alien and hard to discuss. The word "constitution," after its exile from the dictionary, was now suddenly used again in an imperial communiquê. The indestructibility of thought is marvelous; it is always there, blind to individual suffering and cost, boring its way from mind to mind, leaping large gaps and periods; but triumphant always, it marches on regardless of time, ceaselessly developing and maturing in the mind of man. . . .

What was the effect of this thunderbolt in the city of Istamboul? How would the city act, or how had it already acted? These were the enigmas we tried to solve that morning.

It was Hussein Jahid who brought us the news in the evening. The city had looked hesitatingly at the constitution so suddenly and simply announced. The people gathered at street corners and tried to talk in undertones, but there was a feeling of uncertainty, even of distrust, a vague questioning as to the meaning of this sudden change; some went so far as to take it for a trap in which to catch the people of Istamboul. Hussein Jahid had written enthusiastic editorials for "Sabah" and "Ikdam," the two prominent papers of the capital, for the next morning.

We had a sleepless night, sometimes talking but mostly thinking. I wandered restlessly in the large hall, walking out into the warm July night that was so sweet and balmy. Something invisible and new in the air haunted us. We had queer dreams and visions about the terror and blood which accompany revolutions, but we did not allow them utterance.

The words "equality, liberty, justice, and fraternity" sounded most strange. Fraternity was added on account of the Christians. The great ideals of Tanzimat, expressed as the Union of the Elements, had taken this familiar form. There had never been a more passionate desire in the peoples of Turkey to love each other, to work for the realization of this new Turkey, where a free government and a free life was to start.

Poor granny was restless. "No good comes out of new things. What you call constitution was given at the time of **Midhat Pasha,** and he lost his head for it," she said.

In the evening of July 12, Hussein Jahid brought us news from the city once more. Usually so impassive and calm, he also seemed affected by the enthusiasm of the city. The papers might have been printed on goldleaf, so high were the prices paid for them. People were embracing each other in the streets in mad rejoicing. Hussein Juhid smilingly added, "I had to wash my face well in the evening, for hundreds who did not know me from Adam, hundreds whom I have never seen, kissed me as I walked down the road of the **Sublime Porte;** the ugly sides of revolution, vengeance and murder, will not stain ours."

The next day I went down to see Istamboul. The scene on the bridge caught me at once. There was a sea of men and women all cockaded in red and white, flowing like a vast human tide from one side to the other. The tradition of centuries seemed to have lost its effect. There was no such thing as sex or personal feeling. Men and women in a common wave of enthusiasm moved on, radiating something extraordinary, laughing, weeping in such intense emotion that human deficiency and ugliness were for the time completely obliterated. Thousands swayed and moved on. Before each official building there was an enormous crowd calling to the minister to come out and take the oath of allegiance to the new régime.

As I drove along the Sublime Porte the butchers of Istamboul were leaving its austere portals in their white chemises. They also had come to get assurance from the highest that this new joy was to be safeguarded and that they, the butchers, also were going to share in this great task.

In three days the whole empire had caught the fever of ecstasy. No one seemed clear about its meaning. The news of the change had come from Saloniki through several young officers whose names were shouted as its symbol. To the crowd the change in its clearest sense spelled the pulling down of a régime which meant oppression, corruption, and tyranny, while the new, whatever it was, spelled happiness and freedom.

I went down to the city twice that week and came back stirred to the very depths of my being. The motley rabble, the lowest pariahs, were going about in a sublime emotion, with tears running down their unwashed faces, the shopkeepers joining the procession without any concern for their goods. There seemed to be no thieves and no criminals. Dr. Riza Tewfik and Selim Sirry paraded their handsome figures on horseback, solving the judicial difficulties of the people with long speeches. It looked like the millennium.

DOCUMENT ANALYSIS

1. How does Halide Edib portray the regime of Abd̦lhamid?

2. How does the author characterize the public reaction to the news of the restoration of the constitution? Why was the reaction so strong?

3. How would you compare Halide Edib's account of the reaction to the Young Turk Revolution of 1908 and Tevfik Fikret's account of the Young Turk's coup of 1912?

4. What impact did the event have on the interaction between men and women, and between Muslims and non-Muslims? What accounts for this impact?

5. What were the public's expectations from the Young Turk revolution and restoration of the constitution?

DOCUMENT 24.1

Syed Ahmed Khan, "An Indian Muslim Visits London" (mid 1800s)

Source: Syed Ahmed Khan, *Life and Work of Sir Syed Ahmed Khan, in Sources of Indian Tradition: Volume Two: Modern India and Pakistan,* Stephen Hay, ed. (New York: Columbia University Press, 1988), pp. 186–90

Muslims have always been a minority population in India, even during the Mughal Empire. Only around twenty percent of the population then had been Muslim. Nonetheless, in terms of culture, the Muslim population was never absorbed into the larger Hindu population. During the eighteenth and into the nineteenth century, there existed vibrant and active cultures and scholarship from both sides of the religious divide. While many Hindus tried to acclimate themselves to the arriving British, generally Muslims did not.

A notable exception to that general trend was Syed Ahmed Khan, born in 1817. Khan, like Rammohun Roy, welcomed British influence. He wished to show Muslims, usually hesitant to get too close to the British, that not only was this contact acceptable, it was a positive thing with only good results. Khan also wanted to prove to the British that protecting and aiding the Muslims in India was in their best interest. Khan had some success in each of these goals, though Muslims lagged behind Hindus in Western education and government service. Khan also visited London in 1869—a visit he writes about in one of the following documents. He also discusses the impact of Western education on Indian Muslims.

It is nearly six months since I arrived in London, and [I] have been unable to see many things I should have liked, been able to see a good deal, and have been in the society of lords and dukes at dinners and evening parties. Artisans and the common working-man I have seen in numbers, I have visited famous and spacious mansions, museums, engineering works, shipbuilding establishments. gun-foundries, ocean-telegraph companies which connect continents, vessels of war (in one of which I walked for miles, the Great Eastern steamship), have been present at the meetings of several societies, and have dined at clubs and private houses. The result of all this is, that although I do not absolve the English in India of discourtesy, and of looking upon the natives of that country as animals and beneath contempt, I think they do so from not understanding us; and I am afraid I must confess that they are not far wrong in their opinion of us. Without flattering the English, I can truly say that the natives of India, high and low, merchants and petty shopkeepers, educated and illiterate, when contrasted with the English in education, manners, and uprightness, are as like them as a dirty animal is to an able and handsome man. The English have reason for believing us in India to be imbecile brutes. Although my countrymen will consider this opinion of mine an extremely harsh one, and will wonder what they are deficient in, and in what the English excel, to cause me to write as I do, I maintain that they have no cause for wonder, as they are ignorant of everything here, which is really beyond imagination and conception. . . . I only remark on politeness, knowledge, good faith, cleanliness, skilled workmanship, accomplishments, and thoroughness, which are the results of education and civilisation. All good things, spiritual and worldly, which should be found in man, have been bestowed by the Almighty on Europe, and especially on England. By spiritual good things I mean that the English carry out all the details of the religion which they believe to be the true one, with a beauty and excellence which no other nation can compare with. This is entirely due to the education of the men and women . . . If Hindustanis can only attain to civilisation, it will probably, owing to its many excellent natural powers, become, if not the superior, at least the equal of England.

Look at this young girl Elizabeth Matthews [a servant in the house in which he was living], who, in spite of her poverty, invariably buys a half-penny paper called the "Echo" and reads it when at leisure. If she comes across a "Punch," in which there are pictures of women's manners and customs, she looks at them, and enjoys the editor's remarks thereon. All the shops have the names of their occupants written in front in splendid golden letters, and servants requiring anything have only to read and enter. Cabmen and coachmen keep a paper or a book under their seats and after taking the passenger to his destination, or in case the coach has to wait, they take out their newspaper and start reading.

Until the education of the masses is pushed on as it is here, it is impossible for a native to become civilised and honoured.

The cause of England's civilisation is that all the arts and sciences are in the language of the country. . . . Those who are really bent on improving and bettering India must remember that the only way of compassing this is by having the whole of the arts and sciences translated into their own language.

[From a letter to Mawlawi Tasadduq]

I have been accused by people, who do not understand, of being disloyal to the culture of Islam, even to Islam itself. There are men who say that I have become a Christian. All this I have drawn upon myself because I advocate the introduction of a new system of education which will not neglect the Islamic basis of our culture, nor, for that matter, the teaching of Islamic theology itself, but which will surely take account of the changed conditions in this land. Today there are no Muslim rulers to patronize those who are well versed in the old Arabic and Persian learning. The new rulers insist upon a knowledge of their language for all advancement in their services and in some of the independent professions like practising law as well. If the Muslims do not take to the system of education introduced by the British, they will not only remain a backward community but will sink lower and lower until there will be no hope of recovery left to them. Is this at all a pleasing prospect? . . .

The adoption of the new system of education does not mean the renunciation of Islam. It means its protection. We are justly proud of the achievements of our forefathers in the fields of learning and culture. We should, however, remember that these achievements were possible only because they were willing to act upon the teachings of the Prophet upon whom be peace and blessings of God. He said that knowledge is the heritage of the believer, and that he should acquire it wherever he can find it. He also said that the Muslims should seek knowledge even if they have to go to China to find it. . . . Islam, Islamic culture, and the Muslims themselves prospered as long as the Prophet was followed in respect of these teachings; when we ceased to take interest in the knowledge of others, we began to decline in every respect. Did the early Muslims not take to Greek learning avidly? Did this in any respect undermine their loyalty to Islam? . . .

How can we remain true Muslims or serve Islam, if we sink into ignorance?

. . .

The Muslims have nothing to fear from the adoption of the new education if they simultaneously hold steadfast to their faith, because Islam is not irrational superstition; it is a rational religion which can march hand in hand with the growth of human knowledge. Any fear to the contrary betrays lack of faith in the truth of Islam.

DOCUMENT ANALYSIS

1. Does Khan seem to like London?

____

____

____

2. How do the "natives of India" stack up against the English?

3. Is Islam in any danger from Western education, according to Khan?

4. What was so special about the servant girl, Elizabeth Matthews?

5. Why should Muslims undertake Western education, according to Khan?

DOCUMENT 25.1

Euclides de Cunha, "Canudos: Millenarianism in Late-Nineteenth-Century Brazil" (1952)

Source: Euclides da Cunha, *Rebellion in the Backlands* (Chicago: University of Chicago Press, 1952), pp. 127–9, 152–4, 160–2.

Despite claims of "color-blindness," Brazilians, like the rest of their Latin American counterparts, tended to view and interpret their society in racial terms. Brazilians' flirtation with European positivism and scientific racism exacerbated their biases. Several years after the fall of the Brazilian monarchy in 1889, a millenarian backlands rebellion involving mixed-blood inhabitants of the Northeastern interior provided the new republic with a new "voice from below" as well as its first serious challenge. As the inhabitants of Canudos delivered unexpected setbacks to the Brazilian military, which recently had defeated several plots to restore the monarchy, public interest in the conflict grew accordingly. A journalist by training, Euclides da Cunha did more than report the news; he interpreted it through a lens shaped by the social and political biases of his time. As a fervent supporter of the republican regime, da Cunha's diatribes against Canudos grew increasingly savage as the conflict wore on. This excerpt is from his classic Os Sertões.

HOW A MONSTER IS FORMED

And so there appeared in Baía the somber anchorite with hair down to his shoulders, a long tangled beard, an emaciated face, and a piercing eye a—monstrous being clad in a blue canvas garment and leaning on the classic staff which is used to stay the pilgrim's tottering steps.

What his life had been over so long a period of time, no one knows. An aged caboclo, captured in Canudos in the last days of the campaign, had something to tell me about this, but he was very vague and could give no exact dates or specific details. He had known Antonio Maciel in the backlands of Pernambuco, a year or two after the latter had left Crato. From what this witness told me, I gathered that, while still a youth, Antonio Maciel had made a vivid impression upon the imagination of the sertanejos. He had come there a vagabond, without any fixed destination, and he never referred to his past. His conversation was made up of short phrases and an occasional monosyllable. From one stop to the next he went, seemingly careless as to what direction he took, indifferent to danger, taking no thought of his life, eating little or nothing, and now and again sleeping out in the open, along the roadside, as if in fulfillment of a rude and prolonged penance.

It is not surprising, then, if to these simple folk he became a fantastic apparition, with something unprepossessing about him; nor is it strange if, when this singular old man of a little more than thirty years drew near the farmhouses of the tropeiros, the festive guitars at once stopped strumming and the improvisations ceased. This was only natural. Filthy and battered in appearance, clad in his threadbare garment and silent as a ghost, he would spring up suddenly out of the plains, peopled by hobgoblins. Then he would pass on, bound for other places, leaving the superstitious backwoodsmen in a daze. And so it was, in the end, he came to dominate them without seeking to do so.

In the midst of a primitive society which, by its own ethnic qualities and through the malevolent influence of the holy missions, found it easier to comprehend life in the form of incomprehensible miracles, this man's mysterious way of living was bound to surround him with a more than ordinary amount of prestige, which merely served to aggravate his delirious temperament. All the legends and conjectures which sprang up about him were a propitious soil for the growth of his own hallucinations. His insanity therewith became externalized. The intense admiration and the absolute respect which were accorded him gradually led to his becoming the unconditional arbiter in all misunderstandings and disputes, the favored Counselor in all decisions. The multitude thus spared him an agonizing quest in search of his own emotional state, all the effort, the anguish-laden questionings, the entire process of delirious introspection such as ordinarily accompanies the evolution of madness in sickly brains. The multitude created him, refashioning him in its own image. It broadened his life immeasurably by impelling him into those errors that were common two thousand years ago. The people needed someone to translate for them their own vague idealizations, someone to guide them in the mysterious paths of heaven.

And so the evangelist arose, a monstrous being, but an automaton. This man who swayed the masses was but a puppet. Passive as a shade, he moved them. When all is said, he was doing no more than to condense the obscurantism of three separate races. And he grew in stature until he was projected into History. . . .

He looked upon the Republic with an evil eye and consistently preached rebellion against the new laws. From 1893 on he assumed an entirely new and combative attitude. This was due to an incident of no great moment in itself. The autonomy of the municipalities having been decreed, the chambers of the various localities in the interior of Baía had posted up on the traditional bulletin boards, taking the place of newspapers, the regulations governing the collection of taxes and the like. Antonio Conselheiro was in Bom Conselho at the time this novel procedure was instituted. He did not like the new taxes and planned an immediate retaliation. On a day of the fair he gathered the people and, amid seditious cries and noisy demonstrations, had them make a bonfire of the bulletin boards in the public square. And, raising his voice above this "audo-da-fé," which the authorities out of weakness had failed to prevent, he began openly preaching insurrection against the laws of the country. Then, realizing the gravity of his offense, he left town, taking the Monte Santo Road, to the north.

WHY NOT PREACH AGAINST THE REPUBLIC?

He preached against the Republic, there is no denying that. This antagonism was an inevitable derivative of his mystic exacerbation, a variant of his religious delirium that was forced upon him. Yet he did not display the faintest trace of a political intuition; for your jagunço is quite as inapt at understanding the republican form of government as he is the constitutional monarchy. Both to him are abstractions, beyond the reach of his intelligence. He is instinctively opposed to both of them, since he is in that phase of evolution in which the only rule he can conceive is that of a priestly or a warrior chieftain.

We must insist upon this point: the war of Canudos marked an ebb, a backward flow, in our history. What we had to face here was the unlooked-for resurrection, under arms, of an old society, a dead society, galvanized into life by a madman. We were not acquainted with this society; it was not possible for us to have been acquainted with it. The adventurers of the seventeenth century, it is true, would encounter in it conditions with which they were familiar, just as the visionaries of the Middle Ages would be at home among the *demonopaths* of Varzenis or the Stundists of Russia; for these epidemic psychoses make their appearance in all ages and in all places, as obvious anachronisms, inevitable contrasts in the uneven evolution of the peoples—contrasts which become especially evident at a time when a broad movement is vigorously impelling the backward peoples toward a higher and civilized way of life. We then behold the exaggerated Perfectionists breaking through the triumphant industrialism of North America, or the somber *Stürmisch* sect, inexplicably inspired by the genius of Klopstock, sharing the cradle of the German renascence.

. . . . Instead, we looked at it from the narrow-minded point of view of partisan politics. In the presence of these monstrous aberrations, we had a revealing fit of consternation; and, with an intrepidity that was worthy of a better cause, we proceeded to put them down with bayonets, thereby causing history to repeat itself, as we made yet another inglorious incursion into these unfortunate regions, opening up once more the grass-grown trails of the bandeiras.

In the backlands agitator, whose revolt was a phase of rebellion against the natural order of things, we beheld a serious adversary, a mighty foeman representing a regime that we had done away with, one who was capable of overthrowing our nascent institutions.

DOCUMENT ANALYSIS

1. According to da Cunha, what were the motivations guiding the residents of Canudos as they came into conflict with other Brazilians?

2. How does da Cunha characterize backlands' society and its peoples?

3. In assessing the Canudos movement, what important questions remain unasked? How might they reveal a different perspective than that of da Cunha?

4. What are da Cunha's impressions of the Counselor? Are they positive or negative?

5. What kinds of biases (political, social, racial, etc.) do you detect in da Cunha's account of what took place?

Name ______________________ Date ______________________

Course Name and Number ______________________ Instructor ______________________

DOCUMENT 26.1

José Rufino Echenique, "I Met Vidal on His Way to the Palace" (1840s)

Source: José Rufino Echenique, "I Met Vidal on His Way to the Palace," in *Problems in Modern Latin American History: A Reader,* eds. John Charles Chasteen and Joseph S. Tulchin, trans. John Charles Chasteen (Wilmington, D.E.: Scholarly Resources, 1994), pp. 45–8.

The proliferation of caudillos (military leaders) in the post-independence era added to the fledgling republics' fragility. Extensive militarization in the course of the revolutionary wars left the Latin American landscape littered with out-of-work generals at a time when national governments were unable to field and sustain large armies. Capable of overwhelming the national government, caudillos' motivations tended to be more pragmatic than ideological. Indeed, caudillos succeeded where politicians failed in terms of gauging or representing the identity of the people they led. Coming from diverse socioeconomic backgrounds, caudillos provided a voice for those at the bottom. The most successful caudillos, like Peru's José Rufino Echenique, moved skillfully through multiple layers of society and built their alliances on personal, as opposed to strictly political, loyalties. The excerpt from Echenique's memoirs provides a window into Peru in the 1840s, when efforts to create a national identity out of political alliances and divisions in Lima were outmatched by the more personal movements of caudillos in the countryside.

Echenique's Reflections on Revolutions

I had left my hacienda and come to Lima to buy some mules that I had heard were on sale near the port. Passing the street which runs in front of the Palace of Government, I met my friend Colonel Ros, who told me of Hercelles's defeat. He also said that Hercelles himself had been captured and was presently being brought as a prisoner to Lima, but that an order had been issued to execute him before arriving. Ros added that I could probably save Hercelles if I tried, because of the great influence that I had with [Acting President] Vidal. It was true that I did have influence with Vidal, and since I was Hercelles's friend I went straight to the Palace. Vidal was not there, but they told me that I might speak with La Fuente, a government minister with particular sway over Vidal, so I went to speak with him about the matter. I found him surrounded by many important figures, among them the minister Lazo, all talking about Hercelles. With his characteristic emphasis, La Fuente spoke of the order which had been given, saying that Hercelles should be shot the moment it was received, and declared that the government would do the same five hundred times to stop revolutions. Several of his interlocutors voiced their agreement. You may be sure that this resolution wounded my patriotism because I considered it tyranny. Overcome by my feelings, I said nothing, but withdrew, determined to reach Vidal. They had told me he was at his house, and I headed that way.

As it happened, I met Vidal on his way to the Palace, and we returned there together. As soon as we were alone, I told him why I was looking for him, and I was astonished to hear him simply repeat the same words I had heard from La Fuente. Sensitive by nature, I also have an unfortunately violent temper, and I took offense that he should speak to me in that way. His arbitrary threats constituted a horrible tyranny for the nation, and furthermore, the man he intended to destroy was my good friend. I made up my mind first to save my friend, and then to help overthrow a government of methods so antithetical to laws and rights. This decision, unhappily, became the cause of all that befell me later: the loss of my privileged situation and of the bright future that corresponded to it . . .

. . . Shortly thereafter we learned of a revolution in favor of General Vivanco, which had taken place in Arequipa. The well-known patriotism, ability, honesty, and honorable sentiments of General Vivanco gave everyone high hopes for the future progress and stability of the country. By this time the government had fallen into complete disrepute. Besides not doing anything to benefit the nation, the government had lost even institutional legitimacy because, at the death of Gamarra, the presidency should have gone to Menéndez, who was chairman of the Executive Council, or to Vice President Figuerola, and not to Vidal, who had been merely assistant to the Vice President. Consequently, the revolution spread quickly to Cuzco, and then to Ayacucho, where General Pezet joined with his division. In Lima, there were four corps which I decided to bring into the revolution without having communicated with Vivanco. I began by establishing contact with some of the officers, and I found them favorably disposed. When Figuerola assumed the presidency and made Castilla Minister of War, these corps were now under his command. But I could not turn back because I had already made commitments to some supporters of Vivanco. In addition, I had the highest opinion of Vivanco and felt it my patriotic duty to help put him in power. Foolishly, I thought that my responsibilities would end with the triumph of the revolution and that I would then be able to return to the peace and quiet of my hacienda. Most important, two high officers had solemnly committed themselves to move the moment that I gave the command.

I do not know whether or not Castilla found out about the revolutionary plans, but for some reason he sent the four corps under his command to spend the night in the main plaza of Lima. I received word of this maneuver, which was taken for a sign that the revolution had been discovered, and without hesitation I went to talk with the officers loyal to me, judging that the time was ripe. We encountered little resistance from the officers in command of the other two corps. They, too, put themselves at my orders when I proclaimed Vivanco to be Supreme Chief of the Republic. The next day, most of the leading citizens of the city met to proclaim the same thing. They also named me mayor and military commander of Lima. I could find no way to decline these honors and so accepted them, trusting that it would be only until the arrival of Vivanco, at which time I could get rid of these responsibilities and go back to my private occupations. In the meantime, I persecuted no one and allowed Castilla himself to remain free in his own house.

A few days later I heard that Castilla was conspiring with another officer to bring down the revolution on a certain night. That night I went to the barracks where the reaction was supposed to begin, and I stayed there until dawn. Nothing happened, and people's apprehension began to dissipate. Then I learned that Colonel Alvarado Ortiz was on his way to Lima from Jauja with two battalions. Some said that he supported Vivanco; and others, that he meant to restore the constitutional government. When he arrived, I had him bivouac his troops in Lurín as a precaution, but without letting him know that I did not trust him. Next, General Pezet arrived with the force which had announced for Vivanco in Ayacucho. Because of his rank I put my soldiers at his disposition, but I continued in the office of mayor.

Everyone knows how well I executed my duties as mayor. It is enough to say that I neglected nothing and enjoyed wide popularity. Pezet and I got along excellently. He continued the policy of not bothering anyone for political reasons. Still, we could not rest easy because we had no news of Vivanco, not a word, and all the time we heard rumors of thriving conspiracies to bring back the constitutional government.

Finally, we learned that Vivanco had arrived in Jauja and was continuing to Lima, so we prepared him a splendid reception with the enthusiastic participation of the people, who seemed well pleased with the new order of things. Immediately after reporting on everything concerning the current situation of Lima, I asked Vivanco to appoint a new mayor, explaining my determination to return to my personal affairs, which were suffering from my neglect. But he asked me—one could even say he begged me—not to desert him at a time when my services were urgently needed for the regeneration of our country. I have always been too soft to deny a favor to a friend, and, believing that it would be unpatriotic to abandon Vivanco at this moment, I agreed to continue.

DOCUMENT ANALYSIS

1. Do Echenique's stated reasons for remaining involved in politics, despite pressing "personal affairs," ring true with you? Why or why not?

2. Given the document's insights into the inner workings of mid-nineteenth-century Peruvian politics, what do you believe were the country's prospects for political and/or social stability?

3. What evidence do you find to suggest that personal ties or loyalties in mid-nineteenth-century Peru may have superceded more formal obligations and legalities when it came to accounting for people's actions?

4. What sense, if any, do you gain of the various actors' identities or agendas?

5. Why does Echenique decide to lead a revolution?

DOCUMENT 27.1

A Turkish Officer Describes the Armenian Massacres (1915–6)

Source: From the Armenian National Institute; www.armenian-genocide.org

The term "genocide" has become synonymous with the suffering of European Jews during World War II. Largely forgotten is the suffering of Turkish Armenians during World War I. Indeed, since so little was said by the international community at the time, the Armenian genocide may have provided the blueprint for the Nazi treatment of the Jews.

The Armenians, a racial and religious minority in Turkey, had lived peacefully in Turkish society for hundreds of years. Armenian Christianity existed alongside Islam until a governmental change led by the Young Turk movement set into motion events that would result in the first genocide of the twentieth century. The Young Turks began their rise to power in Turkey in 1908, and became determined to purify their country by removing the Armenians. Using World War I as a cover, the Turks from 1915 to 1916 systematically removed thousands of Armenians from their homes and forcibly relocated them to labor camps where they were denied food and water. The United Nations estimates that over one million Armenians were killed as a result of these policies.

CIRCULATED TO THE KING AND WAR CABINET
[December 26, 1916]
ARMENIAN MASSACRES.
Report by an Eye-Witness, Lieutenant Sayied Ahmed Moukhtar Baas.

In April 1915 I was quartered at Erzeroum. An order came from Constantinople that Armenians inhabiting the frontier towns and village be deported to the interior. It was said then that this was only a precautional measure. I saw at that time large convoys of Armenians go through Erzeroum. They were mostly old men, women and children. Some of the able-bodied men had been recruited in the Turkish Army and many had fled to Russia. The massacres had not begun yet. In May 1915 I was transferred to Trebizond. In July an order came to deport to the interior all the Armenians in the Vilayet of Trebizond. Being a member of the Court Martial I knew that deportations meant massacres.

The Armenian Bishop of Trebizond was ordered to proceed under escort to Erzeroum to answer for charges trumped up against him. But instead of Erzeroum he was taken to Baipurt and from there to Gumush-Khana. The Governor of the latter place was then Colonel Abdul-Kadar Aintabli of the General Staff. He is famous for his atrocities against the Armenians. He had the Bishop murdered at night. The Bishop of Erzeroum was also murdered at Gumish-Khana.

Besides the deportation order referred to above an Imperial "Iradeh" was issued ordering that all deserters when caught, should be shot without trial. The secret order read "Armenians" in lieu of "deserters." The Sultan's "Iradeh" was accompanied by a "fatwa" from Sheikh-ul-Islam stating that the Armenians had shed Moslem blood and their killing was lawful. Then the deportations started. The children were kept back at first. The Government opened up a school for the grown-up children and the American Consul of Trebizond instituted an asylum for the infants. When the first batches of Armenians arrived at Gumish-Khana all able-bodied men were sorted out with the excuse that they were going to be given work. The women and children were sent ahead under escort with the assurance by the Turkish authorities that their final destination was Mosul and that no harm will befall them. The men kept behind, were taken out of town in batches of 15 and 20, lined up on the edge of ditches prepared beforehand, shot and thrown into the ditches. Hundreds of men were shot every day in a similar manner. The women and children were attacked on their way by the ("Shotas"), the armed bands organised by the Turkish Government who attacked them and seized a certain number. After plundering and committing the most dastardly outrages on the women and children they massacred them in cold blood. These attacks were a daily occurrence until every woman and child had been got rid of. The military escorts had strict orders not to interfere with the "Shotas."

The children that the Government had taken in charge were also deported and massacred.

The infants in the care of the American Consul of Trebizond were taken away with the pretext that they were going to be sent to Sivas where an asylum had been prepared for them. They were taken out to sea in little boats. At some distance out they were stabbed to death, put in sacks and thrown into the sea. A few days later some of their little bodies were washed up on the shore at Trebizond.

In July 1915 I was ordered to accompany a convoy of deported Armenians. It was the last batch from Trebizond. There were in the convoy 120 men, 700 children and about 400 women. From Trebizond I took them to Gumish-Khana. Here the 120 men were taken away, and, as I was informed later, they were all killed. At Gumish-Khana I was ordered to take the women and children to Erzinjian. On the way I saw thousands of bodies of Armenians unburied. Several bands of "Shotas" met us on the way and wanted me to hand over to them women and children. But I persistently refused. I did leave on the way about 300 children with Moslem families who were willing to take care of them and educate them. The "Mutessarrif" of Erzinjian ordered me to proceed with the convoy to Kamack. At the latter place the authorities refused to take charge of the women and children. I fell ill and wanted to go back, but I was told that as long as the Armenians in my charge were alive I would be sent from one place to the other. However I managed to include my batch with the deported Armenians that had come from Erzeroum. In charge of the latter was a colleague of mine, Mohamed Effendi from the Gendarmerie. He told me afterwards that after leaving Kamach they came to a valley where the Euphrates ran. A band of Shotas sprang out and stopped the convoy. They ordered the escort to keep away and then shot every one of the Armenians and threw them in the river.

At Trebizond the Moslems were warned that if they sheltered Armenians they would be liable to the death penalty.

Government officials at Trebizond picked up some of the prettiest Armenian women of the best families. After committing the worst outrages on them they had them killed.

Cases of rape of women and girls even publicly are very numerous. They were systematically murdered after the outrage.

The Armenians deported from Erzeroum started with their cattle and whatever possessions they could carry. When they reached Erzinjian they became suspicious seeing that all the Armenians had already been deported. The Vali of Erzeroum allayed their fears and assured them most solemnly that no harm would befall them. He told them that the first convoy should leave for Kamach, the others remaining at Erzeroum until they received word from their friends informing of their safe arrival to destination. And so it happened. Word came that the first batch had arrived safely at Kamach, which was true enough. But the men were kept at Kamach and shot, and the women were massacred by the Shotas after leaving that town.

The Turkish officials in charge of the deportation and extermination of the Armenians were: At Erzeroum, Bihas Eddin Shaker Bey; At Trebizond, Naiil Bey, Tewfik Bey Monastirly, Colonel of Gendarmerie, The Commissioner of Police; At Kamach, the member of Parliament for Erzinjian. The Shotas headquarters were also at Kamach. Their chief was the Kurd Murzabey who boasted that he alone had killed 70,000 Armenians. Afterwards he was thought to be dangerous by the Turks and thrown into prison charged with having hit a gendarme. He was eventually executed in secret.

DOCUMENT ANALYSIS

1. Could this happen today?

2. Describe some of the horrors that were perpetrated on the Armenians.

3. How do you think this could happen? What are the motivations?

4. What happened to Armenian woman?

DOCUMENT 27.2

The Great Depression: An Oral Account (1932)

Source: Jim Sheridan, "The March," in *Hard Times: An Oral History of the Great Depression,* by Studs Terkel (New York: Pantheon, 1986), pp. 13–16.

No one incident from the catastrophic Great Depression can sum up the misery, hopelessness, and fear felt by those who lived through it. From 1928 until the outbreak of World War II, most Western nations suffered from a sagging economy due to America's financial collapse. President Herbert Hoover was reluctant to offer any direct governmental assistance to those suffering, including veterans of the first world war.

In response, as many as 20,000 veterans staged the Bonus March on Washington, D.C., to protest their situation and petition Congress and the President for an early payment of their service bonus of $1000, which was scheduled to be paid in 1945. They received little sympathy from the government, including President Hoover, who ordered the veterans be dispersed from the city. In the oral history that follows, one witness describes how those orders were carried out.

The soldiers were walking the streets, the fellas who had fought for democracy in Germany. They thought they should get the bonus right then and there because they needed the money. A fella by the name of Waters, I think, got up the idea of these ex-soldiers would go to Washington, make the kind of trip the hoboes made with Coxey in 1898, they would be able to get the government to come through.

D. C. Webb organized a group from Bughouse Square to go on this bonus march. Not having been in the army—I was too young for World War I and too old for World War II (laughs)—I was wondering if I would be a legitimate marcher. But the ten or fifteen other fellas were all soldiers, and they thought it would be O.K. for me to go. Webb said, "Come along, you're a pretty good bum." (Laughs.)

We went down to the railyards and grabbed a freight train. . . .

Sometimes there'd be fifty, sixty people in a boxcar. We'd just be sprawled out on the floor. The toilet . . . you had to hold it till you got a division point. (Laughs.) That's generally a hundred miles. You didn't carry food with you. You had to bum the town. It was beggary on a grand scale.

In one town, D. C. Webb got up on the bandstand and made a speech. We passed the hat, even, among the local citizenry. The money was used to buy cigarettes for the boys. Townspeople, they were very sympathetic.

There was none of this hatred you see now when strange people come to town, or strangers come to a neighborhood. They resent it, I don't know why. That's one of the things about the Depression. There was more camaraderie than there is now. . . .

When we got to Washington, there was quite a few ex-servicemen there before us. There was no arrangements for housing. Most of the men that had wives and children were living in. This was across the Potomac River—what was known as Anacostia Flats. They had set up housing there, made of cardboard and of all kinds. I don't know how they managed to get their food. Most other contingents was along Pennsylvania Avenue.

They were tearing down a lot of buildings along that street, where they were going to do some renewal, build some federal buildings. A lot of ex-servicemen just sort of turned them into barracks. They just sorta bunked there. Garages that were vacant, they took over. Had no respect for private property. They didn't even ask permission of the owners. They didn't even know who the hell the owners was.

They had come to petition Hoover, to give them the bonus before it was due. And Hoover refused this. He told them they couldn't get it because it would make the country go broke. They would hold midnight vigils around the White House and march around the White House in shifts.

The question was now: How were they going to get them out of Washington? They were ordered out four or five times, and they refused. The police chief was called to send them out, but he [General Pelham D. Glassford] refused. I also heard that the marine commander, who was called to bring out the marines, also refused. Finally, the one they did get to shove these bedraggled ex-servicemen out of Washington was none other than the great **MacArthur.**

The picture I'll always remember . . . here is MacArthur coming down Pennsylvania Avenue. And, believe me, ladies and gentlemen, he came on a white horse. He was riding a white horse. Behind him were tanks, troops of the regular army.

This was really a riot that wasn't a riot, in a way. When these ex-soldiers wouldn't move, they'd poke them with their bayonets, and hit them on the head with the butt of a rifle. First, they had a hell of a time getting them out of the buildings they were in. Like a sit-in.

They managed to get them out. A big colored soldier, about six feet tall, had a big American flag he was carrying. He was one of the bonus marchers. He turned to one of the soldiers who was pushing him along, saying: "Get along there, you big black bastard." That was it. He turned and said, "Don't try to push me. I fought for this flag. I fought for this flag in France and I'm gonna fight for it here on Pennsylvania Avenue." The soldier hit him on the side of the legs with the bayonet. I think he was injured. But I don't know if he was sent to the hospital.

This was the beginning of a riot, in a way. These soldiers were pushing these people. They didn't want to move, but they were pushing them anyway.

As night fell, they crossed the Potomac. They were given orders to get out of Anacostia Flats, and they refused. The soldiers set those shanties on fire. They were practically smoked out. I saw it from a distance. I could see the pandemonium. The fires were something like the fires you see nowadays that are started in these ghettoes. But they weren't started by the people that live there.

The soldiers threw tear gas at them and vomiting gas. It was one assignment they reluctantly took on. They were younger than the marchers. It was like sons attacking their fathers. The next day the newspapers deplored the fact and so forth, but they realized the necessity of getting these men off. Because they were causing a health hazard to the city, MacArthur was looked upon as a hero.

And so the bonus marchers straggled back to the various places they came from without their bonuses.

DOCUMENT ANALYSIS

1. Since the author tells us that he was not a veteran, do you think he was an effective witness?

____

____

____

2. What happened to the black veteran who was protesting? What was his response to being forced out?

____

____

____

3. What was the purpose of the Bonus March and who participated?

4. Who was responsible for the removal of the veterans?

5. Why do you think President Hoover ordered the veterans to be removed?

DOCUMENT 28.1

Speech Delivered at the First All-Union Conference of Leading Personnel of Socialist Industry (1931)

Source: From J. Stalin: *Works* July 1930–January 1934 Volume 13 by J. Stalin. Lawrence and Wishart, London, 1955. Reprinted by Permission.

Stalin consolidated his leadership of the Soviet Union by the end of 1927. He immediately turned to the industrialization of the nation with the first Five-Year Plan, which began in November 1928. The plan called for the gradual, voluntary collectivization of Soviet agriculture, yet Stalin began forcing farmers into collectives within a year of the plan's start. Despite a temporary retreat from coercion in the spring of 1930 (peasant resistance to coercion had endangered the spring planting), Stalin continued forcing peasants into collective farms throughout the 1930s. Against this backdrop of violence in the countryside, the industrialization drive continued.

This document presents Stalin's views on the contemporary problems of the ongoing industrialization process early in 1931. Speaking to a group of what we would now call "business executives," Stalin sets forth the challenge to complete the industrialization of the country within a decade. His reasons include foreign and domestic concerns, and draw upon both Russian nationalism and proletarian internationalism as critical factors.

About ten years ago a slogan was issued: "Since Communists do not yet properly understand the technique of production, since they have yet to learn the art of management, let the old technicians and engineers—the experts—carry on production, and you, Communists, do not interfere with the technique of the business; but, while not interfering, study technique, study the art of management tirelessly, in order later on, together with the experts who are loyal to us, to become true managers of production, true masters of the business." Such was the slogan. But what actually happened? The second part of this formula was cast aside, for it is harder to study than to sign papers; and the first part of the formula was vulgarised: non-interference was interpreted to mean refraining from studying the technique of production. The result has been nonsense, harmful and dangerous nonsense, which the sooner we discard the better.

Life itself has more than once warned us that all was not well in this field. The Shakhty affair was the first grave warning. The Shakhty affair showed that the Party organisations and the trade unions lacked revolutionary vigilance. It showed that our business executives were disgracefully backward in technical knowledge; that some of the old engineers and technicians, working without supervision, rather easily go over to wrecking activities, especially as they are constantly being besieged by "offers" from our enemies abroad.

The second warning was the "Industrial Party" trial.

Of course, the underlying cause of wrecking activities is the class struggle. Of course, the class enemy furiously resists the socialist offensive. This alone, however, is not an adequate explanation for the luxuriant growth of wrecking activities.

How is it that wrecking activities assumed such wide dimensions? Who is to blame for this? We are to blame. Had we handled the business of managing production differently, had we started much earlier to learn the technique of the business, to master technique, had we more frequently and efficiently intervened in the management of production, the wreckers would not have succeeded in doing so much damage.

We must ourselves become experts, masters of the business; we must turn to technical science—such was the lesson life itself was teaching us. But neither the first warning nor even the second brought about the necessary change. It is time, high time that we turned towards technique. It is time to discard the old slogan, the obsolete slogan of non-interference in technique, and ourselves become specialists, experts, complete masters of our economic affairs.

It is frequently asked: Why have we not one-man management? We do not have it and we shall not get it until we have mastered technique. Until there are among us Bolsheviks a sufficient number of people thoroughly familiar with technique, economy and finance, we shall not have real one-man management. You can write as many resolutions as you please, take as many vows as you please, but, unless you master the technique, economy and finance of the mill, factory or mine, nothing will come of it, there will be no one-man management.

Hence, the task is for us to master technique ourselves, to become masters of the business ourselves. This is the sole guarantee that our plans will be carried out in full, and that one-man management will be established.

This, of course, is no easy matter; but it can certainly be accomplished. Science, technical experience, knowledge, are all things that can be acquired. We may not have them today, but tomorrow we shall. The main thing is to have the passionate Bolshevik desire to master technique, to master the science of production. Everything can be achieved, everything can be overcome, if there is a passionate desire for it.

It is sometimes asked whether it is not possible to slow down the tempo somewhat, to put a check on the movement. No, comrades, it is not possible! The tempo must not be reduced! On the contrary, we must increase it as much as is within our powers and possibilities. This is dictated to us by our obligations to the workers and peasants of the U.S.S.R. This is dictated to us by our obligations to the working class of the whole world.

To slacken the tempo would mean falling behind. And those who fall behind get beaten. But we do not want to be beaten. No, we refuse to be beaten! One feature of the history of old Russia was the continual beatings she suffered because of her backwardness. She was beaten by the Mongol khans. She was beaten by the Turkish beys. She was beaten by the Swedish feudal lords. She was beaten by the Polish and Lithuanian gentry. She was beaten by the British and French capitalists. She was beaten by the Japanese barons. All beat her—because of her backwardness, because of her military backwardness, cultural backwardness, political backwardness, industrial backwardness, agricultural backwardness. They beat her because to do so was profitable and could be done with impunity. You remember the words of the pre-revolutionary poet: "You are poor and abundant, mighty and impotent, Mother Russia." Those gentlemen were quite familiar with the verses of the old poet. They beat her, saying: "You are abundant," so one can enrich oneself at your expense. They beat her, saying: "You are poor and impotent," so you can be beaten and plundered with impunity. Such is the law of the exploiters—to beat the backward and the weak. It is the jungle law of capitalism. You are backward, you are weak—therefore you are wrong; hence you can be beaten and enslaved. You are mighty—therefore you are right; hence we must be wary of you.

That is why we must no longer lag behind.

In the past we had no fatherland, nor could we have had one. But now that we have overthrown capitalism and power is in our hands, in the hands of the people, we have a fatherland, and we will uphold its independence. Do you want our socialist fatherland to be beaten and to lose its independence? If you do not want this, you must put an end to its backwardness in the shortest possible time and develop a genuine Bolshevik tempo in building up its socialist economy. There is no other way. That is why Lenin said on the eve of the October Revolution: "Either perish, or overtake and outstrip the advanced capitalist countries."

We are fifty or a hundred years behind the advanced countries. We must make good this distance in ten years. Either we do it, or we shall go under.

That is what our obligations to the workers and peasants of the U.S.S.R. dictate to us.

But we have yet other, more serious and more important, obligations. They are our obligations to the world proletariat. They coincide with our obligations to the workers and peasants of the U.S.S.R. But we place them higher. The working class of the U.S.S.R. is part of the world working class. We achieved victory not solely through the efforts of the working class of the U.S.S.R., but also thanks to the support of the working class of the world. Without this support we would have been torn to pieces long ago. It is said that our country is the shock brigade of the proletariat of all countries. That is well said. But it imposes very serious obligations upon us. Why does the international proletariat support us? How did we merit this support? By the fact that we were the first to hurl ourselves into the battle against capitalism, we were the first to establish working-class state power, we were the first to begin building socialism. By the fact that we are engaged on a cause which, if successful, will transform the whole world and free the entire working class. But what is needed for success? The elimination of our backwardness, the development of a high Bolshevik tempo of construction. We must march forward in such a way that the working class of the whole world, looking at us, may say: There you have my advanced detachment, my shock brigade, my working-class state power, my fatherland; they are engaged on their cause, our cause, and they are working well; let us support them against the capitalists and promote the cause of the world revolution. Must we not justify the hopes of the world's working class, must we not fulfil our obligations to them? Yes, we must if we do not want to utterly disgrace ourselves.

Such are our obligations, internal and international.

As you see, they dictate to us a Bolshevik tempo of development.

I will not say that we have accomplished nothing in regard to management of production during these years. In fact, we have accomplished a good deal. We have doubled our industrial output compared with the pre-war level. We have created the largest-scale agricultural production in the world. But we could have accomplished still more if we had tried during this period really to master production, the technique of production, the financial and economic side of it.

In ten years at most we must make good the distance that separates us from the advanced capitalist countries. We have all the "objective" possibilities for this. The only thing lacking is the ability to make proper use of these possibilities. And that depends on us. Only on us! It is time we learned to make use of these possibilities. It is time to put an end to the rotten line of non-interference in production. It is time to adopt a new line, one corresponding to the present period—the line of interfering in everything. If you are a factory manager—interfere in all the affairs of the factory, look into everything, let nothing escape you, learn and learn again. Bolsheviks must master technique. It is time Bolsheviks themselves became experts. In the period of reconstruction, technique decides everything. And a business executive who does not want to study technique, who does not want to master technique, is a joke and not an executive.

It is said that it is hard to master technique. That is not true! There are no fortresses that Bolsheviks cannot capture. We have solved a number of most difficult problems. We have overthrown capitalism. We have assumed power. We have built up a huge socialist industry. We have transferred the middle peasants on to the path of socialism. We have already accomplished what is most important from the point of view of construction. What remains to be done is not so much: to study technique, to master science. And when we have done that we shall develop a tempo of which we dare not even dream at present.

And we shall do it if we really want to.

DOCUMENT ANALYSIS

1. How did Lenin view the relationship between the bulk of the Russian people and the Bolshevik regime?

____

____

____

2. What role should education play in the modernization process, according to Lenin?

____

____

____

3. What time frame did Lenin consider appropriate for completion of the modernization process?

____

____

____

4. Why did Lenin believe that the Bolsheviks had to modernize Russia rapidly?

____

____

____

5. Why did Lenin see electrification of the entire country as such an urgent necessity?

____

____

____

Name ______________________ Date ______________________

Course Name and Number ______________________ Instructor ______________________

DOCUMENT 29.1
A Letter on British Imperialism (1915)

Rabindranath Tragore won the 1912 Nobel Prize for Literature and was known for his lyrical writing style. However, he was also a keen observer and critic of British colonial policy in his native India. He was knighted in 1915, only to renounce his knighthood in protest of the British massacre of Indian civilians at Amritsar in that year. He was an early supporter of Gandhi but a severe critic of nationalist extremism.

From ***Letters to a Friend.***
Calcutta, *July* 11th, 1915

Conscientious men are comfortable men; they live within the bounds of their duties, and consequently enjoy their fixed proportion of leisure. But I shirk my duties in order to create works that eat up all my time; and then I suddenly leave my work and try to elope with unmitigated indolence.

I shall be floating on the Padma before the next week is out, and shall forget to imagine that my presence in the Council of Creation is imperatively necessary for the betterment of Humanity. I am a born nomad—as I am sure you are—and my work has to be fluid, if it is to be my work. But absolute fluidity in work can only be had at its commencement. Therefore my duty is to start things and then leave them. Unless I leave them and keep at a distance, I cannot help them in maintaining their ideal character. But, this time, it is the fatigue of my body and mind that is driving me into solitude. The kind of work that I can do in a particular scheme requires freshness of mind more than perseverance. Therefore there must be a break before I resume my duties.

It is easy for me to understand the stress of pain that you are feeling now about the wrongs of the world, and especially among the weaker races of mankind, who are oppresses by the strong. Human wrongs are not pitiable, they are terrible. Those who are in power forget every day that it is for their very power's sake that they have to be just. When God's appeal comes from the weak and the poor, then it is full of danger for those who are in power; for then they are apt to think that they can disregard it with impunity, especially if it upsets their office arrangements in the very least degree. They have more faith in their pitiful system and their prestige than in moral providence.

In India, when the upper classes ruled over the lower, they forged their own chains. Europe is closely following Brahmin India, when she looks upon Asia and Africa as her legitimate fields for exploitation. The problem would be simpler if she could altogether denude other continents of their population; but so long as there are alien races, it will be difficult for Europe to realize her moral responsibility with regard to them. The gravest danger is when Europe deceives herself into thinking that she is helping the cause of humanity by helping herself; that men are essentially different, and what is good for her people is not good for others who are inferior. Thus Europe, gradually and imperceptibly, is losing faith in her own ideals and weakening her own moral supports.

But I must not go on weaving truisms; and on our own side I must equally acknowledge this truth, that weakness is heinous because it is a menace to the strong and the surest cause of downfall for others than those who own it. It is a moral duty for every race to cultivate strength, so as to be able to help the world's balance of power to remain even. We are doing England the greatest disservice possible by making it easy for her to despise us and yet to rule; to feel very little sympathy for us and yet to judge us.

Will Europe never understand the genesis of the present war, and realize that the true cause lies in her own growing skepticism towards her own ideals—those ideas that have helped her to be great? She seems to have exhausted the oil that once lighted her lamp. Now she is feeling a distrust against the oil itself, as if it were not at all necessary for her light.

DOCUMENT ANALYSIS

1. What did Tragore see as the greatest weakness of Britain's colonial policy?

____

____

____

2. Tragore stated that the Indians were "making it easy for her [England] to despise us." To what is he referring?

____

____

____

DOCUMENT 29.2
Mahatma Gandhi on civil disobedience (1910s)

Mahatma Gandhi was one of the most important historical personages of the 20th century. He led the fight against imperialism world-wide and led India to independence in 1948. In this early speech, Gandhi defends the tactic of non-violent civil disobedience in the confrontation with power.

Civil disobedience was on the lips of every one of the members of the All-India Congress Committee. Not having really ever tried it, every one appeared to be enamoured of it from a mistaken belief in it as a soverign [sic] remedy for present day ills. I feel sure that it can be made such if we can produce the necessary atmosphere for it. For individuals there always is that atmosphere except when their civil disobedience is certain to lead to bloodshed. I discovered this exception during the Satyagraha days. But even so a call may come which one dare not neglect, cost it what it may. I can clearly see that time is coming to me when I must refuse obedience to every single State-made law even though there might be a certainty of bloodshed. When neglect of the call means a denial of God, civil disobedience becomes a peremptory duty.

Mass civil disobedience stands on a different footing. It can only be tried in a calm atmosphere. It must be the calmness of strength not weakness, knowledge not ignorance. Individual civil disobedience may be and often is vicarious. Mass civil disobedience may be and often is selfish in the sense that individuals expect personal gain from their disobedience. Thus in South Africa, Kallenbach and Polak offered vicarious civil disobedience. They had nothing to gain. Thousands offered it because they expected personal gain also in the shape say of the removal of the annual poll-tax levied upon ex-indentured men and their wives and grown up children. It is sufficient in mass civil disobedience if the resisters understand the working of the doctrine.

It was in a practically uninhabited tract of country that I was arrested in South Africa when I was marching into prohibited with over two to three thousand men and some women. The company included several Pathans and others who were able-bodied men. It was the greatest testimony of merit the Government of South Africa gave to the movement. They know that we were as harmless as we were determined. It was easy enough for that body of men to cut to pieces those who arrested me. It would have not only been a most cowardly thing to do, but it would have been a treacherous breach of their own pledge, and it would have meant ruin to the struggle of freedom and the forcible deportation of every Indian from South Africa. But the men were no rabble. They were disciplined soldiers and all the better for being unarmed. Though I was to inform them, they did not disperse, nor did they turn back. They marched on to their destination till they were every one of them arrested and imprisoned. So far as I am aware, this was one instance of discipline and nonviolence for which there is no parallel in history. Without such restraint I see no hope of successful mass civil disobedience here.

We must dismiss the idea of overawing the Government by huge demonstrations every time some one is arrested. On the contrary we must treat arrest as the normal condition of the life of a non-cooperator. For we must seek arrest and imprisonment as a soldier who goes to a battle to seek death. We expect to bear down the opposition of the Government by courting and not by avoiding imprisonment even though it be by showing our supposed readiness to be arrested and imprisoned. Civil disobedience then emphatically means our desire to surrender to a single unarmed policeman. Our triumph consists in thousands being led to the prisons like lambs to a slaughterhouse. If the lambs of the world had been willingly led they had long ago saved themselves from the butcher's knife. Our triumph consists again in being imprisoned for no wrong whatever. The greater our innocence, the greater our strength and the swifter our victory.

As it is, the Government is cowardly. We are afraid of imprisonment. The Government takes advantage of our fear of gaols. If only our men and women welcome gaols as health-resorts, we will cease to worry about the dear ones put in gaols which our countrymen in South Africa need to nickname, His Majesty's Hotels.

We have too long been mentally disobedient to the laws of the State and have too often surreptitiously evaded them, to be fired all of a sudden for civil disobedience. Disobedience to be civil has to be open and nonviolent.

Complete civil disobedience is a state of peaceful rebellion—a refusal to obey every single State-made law. It is certainly more dangerous than an armed rebellion. For it can never be down if the civil resisters are prepared to face extreme hardship. It is based upon an implicit belief in the absolute efficacy of innocent suffering. By noiselessly going to prison a civil resister ensures a calm atmosphere. The wrong-doer wearies of wrong doing in the absence of resistance. All pleasure is lost when the victim betrays no resistance. A full grasp of the conditions of successful civil resistance is necessary at least on the part of the representatives of the people before we can launch out on an enterprise of such magnitude. The quickest remedies are always fraught with the greatest danger and require the utmost skill in handling them. It is my firm conviction that if we bring about a successful boycott of foreign cloth we shall have produced an atmosphere that would enable us to inaugurate civil disobedience on a scale that no Government can resist. I would therefore urge patience and concentration on Swadeshu upon those who are impatient to embark on mass civil disobedience.

DOCUMENT ANALYSIS

1. What lessons in conducting civil disobedience did Gandhi learn from his experiences in South Africa?

____

____

____

2. Why did Gandhi believe that civil disobedience could be successful in India?

____

____

____

DOCUMENT 30.1
Program of the People's Party of the Republic (1935)

C. H. P. Programi (Ankara: Cumhuriyet Halk Partisi, 1935); translated into English as *Program of the People's Party of the Republic* (Ankara: People's Republican Party, 1935), adopted by fourth party congress.

Following the Ottoman defeat in World War I, a group of Turkish nationalists regrouped in eastern Anatolia to begin a struggle against Allied and Greek occupation of Anatolia. The nationalists, led by Mustafa Kemal (Atatürk), Ismet (Inonü), Kazym (Karabekir), and other former Ottoman officers, created a parliament in their headquarters, Ankara, and vested sovereignty in the Grand National Assembly. In 1923, along with declaring the Turkish Republic, Mustafa Kemal led the creation of a political party, the People's Party (later Republican People's Party, or RPP), which dominated Turkish politics until its defeat by the Democrat Party in 1950. Throughout the 1920s, the People's Party was the center of politics, and two experiments, in 1924 and 1929, with the formation of an opposition party ended unsuccessfully. In response to the impact of the Great Depression and expressions of popular discontent with single-party rule, party leaders decided in 1931 to articulate a set of guiding principles, or arrows, of the RPP. The following selection was published following the fourth party congress in 1935.

ADOPTED BY THE FOURTH GRAND CONGRESS OF THE PARTY, MAY 1935

INTRODUCTION

The fundamental ideas that constitute the basis of the Program of the Republican Party of the People are evident in the acts and realizations which have taken place from the beginning of our Revolution until today.

On the other hand, the main ideas have been formulated in the general principles of the Statutes of the Party, adopted also by the Grand Congress of the Party in 1927, as well as in the Declaration published on the occasion of the elections to the Grand National Assembly in 1931.

The main lines of our intentions, not only for a few years, but for the future as well, are here put together in a compact form. All of these principles which are the fundamentals of the Party constitute Kamâlism.

PART I

PRINCIPLES

1—The Fatherland

2—The Nation

3—The Constitution of the State

4—The Public Rights

1—THE FATHERLAND. The Fatherland is the sacred country within our present political boundaries, where the Turkish Nation lives with its ancient and illustrious history, and with its past glories still living in the depths of its soil.

The Fatherland is a Unity which does not accept separation under any circumstance.

2—THE NATION. The Nation is the political Unit composed of citizens bound together with the bonds of language, culture and ideal.

3—CONSTITUTIONAL ORGANIZATION OF THE STATE. Turkey is a nationalist, populist, étatist, secular [laïque], and revolutionary Republic.

The form of administration of the Turkish nation is based on the principle of the unity of power. There is only one Sovereignty, and it belongs to the nation without restriction or condition.

The Grand National Assembly exercises the right of sovereignty in the name of the nation. The legislative authority and the executive power are embodied in the Grand National Assembly. The Assembly exercises its legislative power itself. It leaves its executive authority to the President of the Republic, elected from among its members, and to the Council of Ministers appointed by him. The courts in Turkey are independent.

The Party is convinced that this is the most suitable of all State organizations.

4—PUBLIC RIGHTS.

(a) It is one of the important principles of our Party to safeguard the individual and social rights of liberty, of equality, of inviolabilty, and of property. These rights are within the bounds of the State's authority. The activity of the individuals and of legal persons shall not be in contradiction with the interests of the public. Laws are made in accordance with this principle.

(b) The Party does not make any distinction between men and women in giving rights and duties to citizens.

(c) The Law on the election of deputies shall be renewed. We find it more suitable to the real requirements of democracy to leave the citizen free to elect electors whom he knows well and trusts, in accordance with the general conditions of our country. The election of the deputies shall take place in this manner.

PART II

THE ESSENTIAL CHARACTERISTICS OF THE REPUBLICAN PARTY OF THE PEOPLE

5—The Republican Party of the People is: (a) Republican (b) Nationalist (c) Populist (d) Étatist (e) Secular (f) Revolutionary.

(a) The Party is convinced that the Republic is the form of government which represents and realizes most safely the ideal of national sovereignty. With this un-shakable conviction, the Party defends, with all its means, the Republic against all danger.

(b) The Party considers it essential to preserve the special character and the entirely independent identity of the Turkish social community in the sense explained in Art. 2. The Party follows, in the meantime, a way parallel to and in harmony with all the modern nations in the way of progress and development, and in international contacts and relations.

(c) The source of Will and Sovereignty is the Nation. The Party considers it an important principle that this Will and Sovereignty be used to regulate the proper fulfillment of the mutual duties of the citizen to the State and of the State to the citizen.

We consider the individuals who accept an absolute equality before the Law, and who recognize no privileges for any individual, family, class, or community, to be of the people and for the people (populist).

It is one of our main principles to consider the people of the Turkish Republic, not as composed of different classes, but as a community divided into various professions according to the requirements of the division of labor for the individual and social life of the Turkish people.

The farmers, handicraftsmen, laborers and workmen, people exercising free professions, industrialists, merchants, and public servants are the main groups of work constituting the Turkish community. The functioning of each of these groups is essential to the life and happiness of the others and of the community.

The aims of our Party, with this principle, are to secure social order and solidarity instead of class conflict, and to establish harmony of interests. The benefits are to be proportionate to the aptitude to the amount of work.

(d) Although considering private work and activity a basic idea, it is one of our main principles to interest the State actively in matters where the general and vital interests of the nation are in question, especially in the economic field, in order to lead the nation and the country to prosperity in as short a time as possible.

The interest of the State in economic matters is to be an actual builder, as well as to encourage private enterprises, and also to regulate and control the work that is being done.

The determination of the economic matters to be undertaken by the State depends upon the requirements of the greatest public interest of the nation. If the enterprise, which the State itself decides to undertake actively as a result of this necessity, is in the hands of private entrepreneurs, its appropriation shall, each time, depend upon the enactment of a law, which will indicate the way in which the State shall indemnify the loss sustained by the private enterprise as a result of this appropriation. In the estimation of the loss the possibility of future earnings shall not be taken into consideration.

(e) The Party considers it a principle to have the laws, regulations, and methods in the administration of the State prepared and applied in conformity with the needs of the world and on the basis of the fundamentals and methods provided for modern civilization by Science and Technique.

As the conception of religion is a matter of conscience, the Party considers it to be one of the chief factors of the success of our nation in contemporary progress, to separate ideas of religion from politics, and from the affairs of the world and of the State.

(f) The Party does not consider itself bound by progressive and evolutionary principles in finding measures in the State administration. The Party holds it essential to remain faithful to the principles born of revolutions which our nation has made with great sacrifices, and to defend these principles which have since been elaborated.

Glossary

Grand National Assembly (Türkiye Büyük Millet Meclisi)

The parliament of the Turkish Republic was first convened in Ankara on April 23, 1920, during the Turkish War of Independence. Among its first acts were to name Mustafa Kemal (Atatürk), president of the Assembly, and to proclaim itself the sole legitimate representative of the entire Turkish nation in the struggle against Allied and Greek occupation forces and the government of the Ottoman Sultan.

Ismet Inonü (1884–1972)

Mustafa Ismet (Inonü), popularly known as Ismet Pasha, trained at the Ottoman War College before serving as an officer in World War I. Following the war, he joined the nationalist cause, was named commander of the nationalist forces in 1920, and led Turkish troops to major victories over the Greeks at Inonü, in western Anatolia. In 1922–1923 he led the Turkish negotiations at Lausanne, which recognized the independence and sovereignty of the Ankara government. From 1923 to 1937, he served almost continuously as Prime Minister of the Turkish Republic. Following the death of Atatürk in 1938, Inonü became the second President of Turkey, a position he held until the RPP's electoral defeat in 1950. He remained in the Grand National Assembly, serving as Prime Minister in the early 1960s, until his retirement in 1971.

Kamâlism (Kemalism)

Named after Mustafa Kemal Atatürk, Kemalism is the ideological underpinning of a series of legal, political, economic and cultural reforms carried out during Atatürk's presidency, 1923–1938, and after. The reforms include the six arrows, or guiding principles of republicanism, nationalism, secularism, populism, reformism, and statism.

Kâzym Karabekir (1882–1948)

Trained at the Ottoman War College, Kâzym Pasha served as commander of the Caucasian front in World War I. Following the war, he was one of the first Ottoman commanders to begin gathering support for nationalist defense of Anatolia. After accepting the overall leadership of Mustafa Kemal, Karabekir continued to serve as commander of the nationalist forces on the eastern front, and defeated Armenian efforts to form an independent state in 1920. Karabekir eventually clashed with Atatürk over the latter's control in the RPP and the National Assembly, and was arrested and tried for conspiracy to assassinate Atatürk in 1926. Acquitted, Karabekir retired from public life until Atatürk's death in 1938, when Ismet Inonü asked him to take a seat in the Assembly.

DOCUMENT ANALYSIS

1. According to the fourth principle, Ètatism, what role should the Turkish state play in the economy, and why? How does this principle affect views of the role of private enterprise?

___

___

___

2. Compare this document to the Hatt-i Şerif of Gühane (1839) of Sultan Abdülmecid I (doc. 27.1). In what ways are the two documents similar and different, in terms of defining the rights and obligations of citizens, and in terms of the role of the state in economic and cultural matters?

___

___

___

3. How does the document define secularism? Why does the party advocate secularism?

___

___

___

4. How does the document define the Turkish nation? What is the connection between the nation and the fatherland?

___

___

___

5. What are the six characteristics, or arrows, of the RPP? Why does the party reject the notion of class division or conflict in Turkish society? In whose interest does the party claim to serve?

___

___

___

DOCUMENT 31.1

Rudolf Hoess, from *Commandant to Auschwitz* (1940s)

Source: Rudolf Hoess, *Commandant to Auschwitz* (Wiedenfeld & Nicolson, Ltd.)

The Holocaust, the systematic slaughter of over six million European Jews during World War II, was the most horrific aspect of the Nazi reign in Germany. The origins of the Holocaust were as early as 1935, with the passage of the Nuremberg Laws, which strictly regulated Jewish involvement in German society. The laws forbid Jews from government service, intermarriage with other (non-Jewish) Germans, or holding public office. By January 1942, Nazi leaders were openly discussing the "Final Solution": a removal of European Jews through any means necessary, including extermination.

The Nazi government removed many Jews from their towns and villages and placed them in concentration camps located in various parts of Europe. The most infamous of these was Auschwitz, located in German-occupied Poland. Upon arrival, Jews unfit for work were immediately exterminated; others were spared only to be worked to death in forced labor camps. The selection that follows is from the Commandant of Auschwitz, Rudolf Hoess, who wrote his memoirs while in prison after the war. He was executed for his crimes in 1947.

In the spring of 1942 the first transports of Jews, all earmarked for extermination, arrived from Upper Silesia.

They were taken from the detraining platform to the "cottage"—to bunker I—across the meadows where later building site II was located. The transport was conducted by Aumeier and Palitzisch and some of the block leaders. They talked with the Jews about general topics, inquiring concerning their qualifications and trades, with a view to misleading them. On arrival at the "cottage," they were told to undress. At first they went calmly into the rooms where they were supposed to be disinfected. But some of them showed signs of alarm, and spoke of death by suffocation and of annihilation. A sort of panic set in at once. Immediately all the Jews still outside were pushed into the chambers, and the doors were screwed shut. With subsequent transports the difficult individuals were picked out early and most carefully supervised. At the first signs of unrest, those responsible were unobtrusively led behind the building and killed with a small-caliber gun, that was inaudible to the others. The presence and calm behavior of the Special Detachment [of Sonderkommandos] served to reassure those who were worried or who suspected what was about to happen. A further calming effect was obtained by members of the Special Detachment accompanying them into the rooms and remaining with them until the last moment, while an SS man also stood in the doorway until the end.

It was most important that the whole business of arriving and undressing should take place in an atmosphere of the greatest possible calm. People reluctant to take off their clothes had to be helped by those of their companions who had already undressed, or by men of the Special Detachment.

The refractory ones were calmed down and encouraged to undress. The prisoners of the Special Detachment also saw to it that the process of undressing was carried out quickly, so that the victims would have little time to wonder what was happening. . .

Many of the women hid their babies among the piles of clothing. The men of the Special Detachment were particularly on the lookout for this, and would speak words of encouragement to the woman until they had persuaded her to take the child with her. The women believed that the disinfectant might be bad for their smaller children, hence their efforts to conceal them.

The smaller children usually cried because of the strangeness of being undressed in this fashion, but when their mothers or members of the Special Detachment comforted them, they became calm and entered the gas chambers, playing or joking with one another and carrying their toys.

I noticed that women who either guessed or knew what awaited them nevertheless found the courage to joke with the children to encourage them, despite the mortal terror visible in their own eyes.

One woman approached me as she walked past and, pointing to her four children who were manfully helping the smallest ones over the rough ground, whispered:

"How can you bring yourself to kill such beautiful, darling children? Have you no heart at all?"

One old man, as he passed by me, hissed:

"Germany will pay a heavy penance for this mass murder of the Jews."

His eyes glowed with hatred as he said this. Nevertheless he walked calmly into the gas chamber, without worrying about the others.

One young woman caught my attention particularly as she ran busily hither and thither, helping the smallest children and the old women to undress. During the selection she had had two small children with her, and her agitated behavior and appearance had brought her to my notice at once. She did not look in the least like a Jewess. Now her children were no longer with her. She waited until the end, helping the women who were not undressed and who had several children with them, encouraging them and calming the children. She went with the very last ones into the gas chamber. Standing in the doorway, she said:

"I knew all the time that we were being brought to Auschwitz to be gassed. When the selection took place I avoided being put with the able-bodied ones, as I wished to look after the children. I wanted to go through it all, fully conscious of what was happening. I hope that it will be quick. Goodbye!"

From time to time women would suddenly give the most terrible shrieks while undressing, or tear their hair, or scream like maniacs. These were immediately led away behind the building and shot in the back of the neck with a small-caliber weapon.

It sometimes happened that, as the men of the Special Detachment left the gas chamber, the women would suddenly realize what was happening, and would call down every imaginable curse upon our heads.

I remember, too, a woman who tried to throw her children out of the gas chamber, just as the door was closing. Weeping, she called out:

"At least let my precious children live."

There were many such shattering scenes, which affected all who witnessed them.

During the spring of 1942 hundreds of vigorous men and women walked all unsuspecting to their death in the gas chambers, under the blossom-laden fruit trees of the "cottage" orchard. This picture of death in the midst of life remains with me to this day.

The process of selection, which took place on the unloading platforms, was in itself rich in incident.

The breaking up of families, and the separation of the men from the women and children, caused much agitation and spread anxiety throughout the whole transport. This was increased by the further separation from the others of those capable of work. Families wished at all costs to remain together. Those who had been selected ran back to rejoin their relations. Mothers with children cried to join their husbands, or old people attempted to find those of their children who had been selected for work, and who had been led away.

Often the confusion was so great that the selections had to be begun all over again. The limited area of standing room did not permit better sorting arrangements. All attempts to pacify these agitated mobs were useless. It was often necessary to use force to restore order.

As I have already frequently said, the Jews have strongly developed family feelings. They stick together like limpets. . .

Then the bodies had to be taken from the gas chambers, and after the gold teeth had been extracted, and the hair cut off, they had to be dragged to the pits or to the crematoria. Then the fires in the pits had to be stoked, the surplus fat drained off, and the mountain of burning corpses constantly turned over so that the draught might fan the flames . . .

It happened repeatedly that Jews of the Special Detachment would come upon the bodies of close relatives among the corpses, and even among the living as they entered the gas chambers. They were obviously affected by this, but it never led to any incident.

DOCUMENT ANALYSIS

1. How did Hess and the Nazis view the Jews? Does he ever refer to them with any emotion?

___

___

___

2. How does Hess seem to view the process? Does he see it as horrible, or does he view it with pride, especially in terms of the efficiency of the process?

___

___

___

3. What do you feel was the most horrifying experience faced by the Jews in the camp?

___

___

___

4. What happened to the bodies after the gassing process?

___

___

___

5. What role did the Sonderkommandos, or Special Detachment troops, play in the process?

___

___

___

DOCUMENT 31.2

Father John A. Siemes, "Hiroshima—August 6th, 1945"

Source: "Hiroshima—August 6th, 1945" by Father John A. Siemes, professor of modern philosophy at Tokyo's Catholic University.

The war effort surrounding World War II brought about surprising scientific advancement. Jet propulsion, radar, and sonar all trace their origins back to the conflict, as does nuclear fission. The American effort to develop an atomic bomb, code-named the Manhattan Project, began in earnest in 1942 under the military direction of General Leslie R. Groves. Groves gathered together a group of scientists, physicists, and engineers to construct a bomb that derived its explosive power from the splitting of atoms rather than a chemical reaction. They successfully created three nuclear weapons (code-named Trinity) and exploded the first bomb in May 1945, in New Mexico.

The remaining two bombs were sent to Tinian Island to be used against Japan, which still remained at war with the United States. President Truman, faced with the choice of either invading the Japanese home islands in an all-out assault or using the new weapon, decided that the atomic bombs should be used despite the enormous loss of civilian life. On August 6, 1945, the first bomb exploded over the city of Hiroshima. Three days later, on August 9, the second bomb exploded over Nagasaki. Total casualties may never be known due to the effects of radiation, but most figures indicate that more than 200,000 Japanese were either killed or injured. These devastating losses contributed to the Japanese surrender on August 15, 1945. The selection that follows is from Father John A. Siemes, professor of modern philosophy at Tokyo's Catholic University, and an eyewitness to the first explosion in Hiroshima.

Up to August 6th, occasional bombs, which did no great damage, had fallen on Hiroshima. Many cities roundabout, one after the other, were destroyed, but Hiroshima itself remained protected. There were almost daily observation planes over the city but none of them dropped a bomb. The citizens wondered why they alone had remained undisturbed for so long a time. There were fantastic rumors that the enemy had something special in mind for this city, but no one dreamed that the end would come in such a fashion as on the morning of August 6th.

August 6th began in a bright, clear, summer morning. About seven o'clock, there was an air raid alarm which we had heard almost every day and a few planes appeared over the city. No one paid any attention and at about eight o'clock, the all-clear was sounded. I am sitting in my room at the Novitiate of the Society of Jesus in Nagatsuke; during the past half year, the philosophical and theological section of our Mission had been evacuated to this place from Tokyo. The Novitiate is situated approximately two kilometers from Hiroshima, half-way up the sides of a broad valley which stretches from the town at sea level into this mountainous hinterland, and through which courses a river. From my window, I have a wonderful view down the valley to the edge of the city.

Suddenly—the time is approximately 8:14—the whole valley is filled by a garish light which resembles the magnesium light used in photography, and I am conscious of a wave of heat. I jump to the window to find out the cause of this remarkable phenomenon, but I see nothing more than that brilliant yellow light. As I make for the door, it doesn't occur to me that the light might have something to do with enemy planes. On the way from the window, I hear a moderately loud explosion which seems to come from a distance and, at the same time, the windows are broken in with a loud crash. There has been an interval of perhaps ten seconds since the flash of light. I am sprayed by fragments of glass. The entire window frame has been forced into the room. I realize now that a bomb has burst and I am under the impression that it exploded directly over our house or in the immediate vicinity.

I am bleeding from cuts about the hands and head. I attempt to get out of the door. It has been forced outwards by the air pressure and has become jammed. I force an opening in the door by means of repeated blows with my hands and feet and come to a broad hallway from which open the various rooms. Everything is in a state of confusion. All windows are broken and all the doors are forced inwards. The bookshelves in the hallway have tumbled down. I do not note a second explosion and the fliers seem to have gone on. Most of my colleagues have been injured by fragments of glass. A few are bleeding but none has been seriously injured. All of us have been fortunate since it is now apparent that the wall of my room opposite the window has been lacerated by long fragments of glass.

We proceed to the front of the house to see where the bomb has landed. There is no evidence, however, of a bomb crater; but the southeast section of the house is very severely damaged. Not a door nor a window remains. The blast of air had penetrated the entire house from the southeast, but the house still stands. It is constructed in a Japanese style with a wooden framework, but has been greatly strengthened by the labor of our Brother Gropper as is frequently done in Japanese homes. Only along the front of the chapel which adjoins the house, three supports have given way (it has been made in the manner of Japanese temple, entirely out of wood).

Down in the valley, perhaps one kilometer toward the city from us, several peasant homes are on fire and the woods on the opposite side of the valley are aflame. A few of us go over to help control the flames. While we are attempting to put things in order, a storm comes up and it begins to rain. Over the city, clouds of smoke are rising and I hear a few slight explosions. I come to the conclusion that an incendiary bomb with an especially strong explosive action has gone off down in the valley. A few of us saw three planes at great altitude over the city at the time of the explosion. I, myself, saw no aircraft whatsoever.

Perhaps a half-hour after the explosion, a procession of people begins to stream up the valley from the city. The crowd thickens continuously. A few come up the road to our house. We give them first aid and bring them into the chapel, which we have in the meantime cleaned and cleared of wreckage, and put them to rest on the straw mats which constitute the floor of Japanese houses. A few display horrible wounds of the extremities and back. The small quantity of fat which we possessed during this time of war was soon used up in the care of the burns. Father Rektor who, before taking holy orders, had studied medicine, ministers to the injured, but our bandages and drugs are soon gone. We must be content with cleansing the wounds.

More and more of the injured come to us. The least injured drag the more seriously wounded. There are wounded soldiers, and mothers carrying burned children in their arms. From the houses of the farmers in the valley comes word: "Our houses are full of wounded and dying. Can you help, at least by taking the worst cases?" The wounded come from the sections at the edge of the city. They saw the bright light, their houses collapsed and buried the inmates in their rooms. Those that were in the open suffered instantaneous burns, particularly on the lightly clothed or unclothed parts of the body. Numerous fires sprang up which soon consumed the entire district. We now conclude that the epicenter of the explosion was at the edge of the city near the Jokogawa Station, three kilometers away from us. We are concerned about Father Kopp who that same morning, went to hold Mass at the Sisters of the Poor, who have a home for children at the edge of the city. He had not returned as yet.

Toward noon, our large chapel and library are filled with the seriously injured. The procession of refugees from the city continues. Finally, about one o'clock, Father Kopp returns, together with the Sisters. Their house and the entire district where they live has burned to the ground. Father Kopp is bleeding about the head and neck, and he has a large burn on the right palm. He was standing in front of the nunnery ready to go home. All of a sudden, he became aware of the light, felt the wave of heat and a large blister formed on his hand. The windows were torn out by the blast. He thought that the bomb had fallen in his immediate vicinity. The nunnery, also a wooden structure made by our Brother Gropper, still remained but soon it is noted that the house is as good as lost because the fire, which had begun at many points in the neighborhood, sweeps closer and closer, and water is not available. There is still time to rescue certain things from the house and to bury them in an open spot. Then the house is swept by flame, and they fight their way back to us along the shore of the river and through the burning streets.

Soon comes news that the entire city has been destroyed by the explosion and that it is on fire.

DOCUMENT ANALYSIS

1. Do you think Father Siemes is a reliable witness? Why or why not?

2. How effective do you think the detonation of the atomic bomb was in driving Japan to surrender?

3. How prepared are the priests or the population for this explosion?

4. What are some of the problems faced by the priests after the blast?

5. What were some of the immediate effects of the nuclear explosion?

Name ______________________ Date ______________________

Course Name and Number ______________________ Instructor ______________________

DOCUMENT 32.1
Ho Chi Minh on self-determination (1954)

Ho Chi Minh led the Vietnamese people in their struggles against European colonialism and then American military power. Often the process of de-colonization ran up against the exigencies of Cold War geopolitics. In this document, Ho discusses the impact of the 1954 Geneva Conference.

Appeal Made After the Successful Conclusion of the Geneva Agreements

Compatriots all over the country,

Armymen and Cadres,

The Geneva Conference has come to an end. It is a great victory for our diplomacy.

On behalf of the Government, I cordially make the following appeal:

1 – For the sake of peace, unity, independence and democracy of the Fatherland, our people, armymen, cadres and government have, during these eight years or so, joined in a monolithic bloc, endured hardship and overcome all difficulties to resolutely carry out the Resistance and have won many brilliant victories. On this occasion, on behalf of the Government, I cordially congratulate you, from North to South. I respectfully bow to the memory of the armymen and people who have sacrificed their lives for the Fatherland, and send my homages of comfort to the wounded and sick armymen.

This great victory is also due to the support given us in our just struggle by the peoples of our brother countries, by the French people and the peace-loving people of the world.

Thanks to these victories and the efforts made by the delegation of the Soviet Union at the Berlin Conference, negotiations were opened between our country and France at the Geneva Conference. At this conference the struggle of our delegation and the assistance given by the delegations of the Soviet Union and China have ended in a great victory for us: the French government has recognized the independence, sovereignty, unity and territorial integrity of our country; it has agreed to withdraw French troops from our country, etc.

From now on, we must make every effort to consolidate peace and achieve reunification, independence and democracy throughout our country.

2 – In order to re-establish peace, the first step to take is that the armed forces of both parties should cease fire.

The regroupment in two regions is a temporary measure; it is a transitional step for the implementation of the armistice and restoration of peace, and paves the way for a national reunification through general elections. Regroupment in regions is in no way a partition of our country, neither is it an administrative division.

During the armistice, our army is regrouped in the North; the French troops are regrouped in the South, that is to say, there is a change of regions. A number of regions which were formerly occupied by the French, now become our free zones. Vice versa, a number of regions formerly liberated by us, will now be temporarily occupied by the French troops before they leave for France.

This is a necessity; North, Central and South Viet Nam are territories of ours. Our country will certainly be unified, our entire people will surely be liberated.

Our compatriots in the South were the first to wage the war of Resistance. They possess a high political consciousness. I am confident that they will place national interests above local interests, permanent interests above temporary interests and join their efforts with the entire people in strengthening peace, achieving unity, independence and democracy all over the country. The Party, Government and I, always follow the efforts of our people and we are sure that our compatriots will be victorious.

3 – The struggle to consolidate peace and achieve reunification, independence and democracy, is also a long and hard struggle. In order to carry the day, our people, armymen and cadres from North to South, must unite closely. They must be at one in thought and deed.

We are resolved to abide by the agreements entered into with the French Government. At the same time we demand that the French Government should correctly implement the agreements they have signed with us.

We must do our utmost to strengthen peace, and be vigilant to check the manœuvres of peace wreckers.

We must endeavor to struggle for the holding of free general elections throughout the country to reunify our territory.

We must exert all our efforts to restore, build, strengthen and develop our forces in every field so as to attain complete independence.

We must do our utmost to carry out social reforms in order to improve our people's livelihood and realize genuine democracy.

We further tighten our fraternal relations with Cambodia and Laos.

We strengthen the great friendship between us and the Soviet Union, China and other brother countries. To maintain peace, we enhance our solidarity with the French people, the Asian people and people all over the world.

4 – I call on all our compatriots, armymen and cadres to strictly follow the lines and policies laid down by the Party and Government, to struggle for the consolidation of peace, and the achievement of national reunification, independence and democracy throughout the country.

I eagerly appeal to all genuine patriots, irrespective of their social class, creed, political stand and former affiliation, sincerely to co-operate with us and fight for the sake of our country and our people so as to bring about peace and achieve reunification, independence and democracy for our beloved Viet Nam.

If our people are as one, if thousands of men are like one, victory will certainly be ours.

Long live a peaceful, unified, independent and democratic Viet Nam.

DOCUMENT ANALYSIS

1. What is Ho Chi Minh referring to in section two when he discusses the "regroupment" of Vietnam into two regions? Was he correct in his assessment of the situation?

____

____

____

2. What political efforts did Ho see as being necessary to create a viable, independent Vietnam?

____

____

____

3. Why did the Soviet Union and China support the Vietnamese independence movement?

Name ______________________ Date ______________________

Course Name and Number ______________________ Instructor ______________________

DOCUMENT 33.1
European Interaction and the Common Market (1960)

Ravaged by two world wars, Europe looked to end the long suffering. Western European leaders believed that economic conflicts had played major roles in those earlier conflicts and launched the continent on the road to economic and political integration. Here is a justification for an economic common market published by the European Community Information Service.

Tomorrow Has Already Begun

Already, for well over three years, the Common market has been facing the political and economic challenge presented to the Europeans by the rapidly changing postwar world.

The drive for European unification, which began ten years ago with the Schuman Plan, and whose ultimate aim is a unified Europe, has reached a decisive stage. Within the Community, which at present comprises Belgium, France, Germany (Federal Republic), Italy, Luxembourg and the Netherlands, the customs union is rapidly taking shape and common policies are being hammered out—sometimes painfully, but nonetheless surely. Among the Community's neighbors, Britain, in a spectacular change of policy which may have historic consequences, has formally applied for membership and other countries have followed her.

The revolution now taking place in Europe stems from the radically changed continent which in 1945 emerged from six years of devastating war. The divided nations of Western Europe were no longer great world powers; their weakness, political and economic, before the new military giant in the East made nonsense of old nationalistic policies. Colonialism was dying. New ideas and new methods were needed.

The European Community is building a Europe which will be capable of standing on its own feet and playing a full part in this new world. It is not an alliance or an inter-governmental organization; the technical and economic nature of its work should not mask the fundamental political significance of what is being done.

An economic union of 170 million people is being created; the first steps are being taken towards political unity; and the decision of the British Government offers the bright hope that the Community, nucleus of European unity, will expand into an even stronger union, determined, as part of the wider Atlantic community, to defend the values of freedom and democracy in which it believes.

DOCUMENT ANALYSIS

1. According to this document, what were the reasons behind the founding of the European Community?

____

____

____

2. What goals does the European Community hope to accomplish?

____

____

____

DOCUMENT 33.2
From *Environmental and Health Atlas of Russia* (1995)

Source: Murray Feshbach, ed., *Environmental and Health Atlas of Russia* (Moscow: PAIMS Publishing House, 1995), pp. 2–11 through 2–20.

When the Soviet Union disintegrated in 1991, Russian and outside observers could, for the first time, openly analyze and discuss the consequences of the country's industrialization. Only then did the other side of Russia's frenetic transformation in the twentieth century begin to become clear.

In 1995, the first surveys of Russian scientific analysis of the state of the Russian environment were published in Moscow. This document includes excerpts from the introduction to an atlas of over 300 maps designed to graphically portray environmental and demographic problems directly related to the industrialization drive. It discusses the country's economic situation in 1993, and summarizes problems with radioactivity and air and water pollution throughout the Russian Federation.

2.2.2. THE CURRENT ECONOMIC SITUATION

A. S. Martynov, V. G. Vinogradov, A. V. Denisov, A. N. Yelokhin and A. A. Sorogin

The economic situation in Russia in 1991–1993 can be simply characterized as a crisis. In this part of the Atlas, indicators are shown which illustrate mostly the process of the disintegration of the economic system while touching upon the standard of living and social mood of the population.

The fall of output from the beginning of reforms enables us to identify the regions in which the highest intensity of socially significant changes occurred. It is completely unimportant whether these changes are linked only to the disintegration of the old structures, or if they occurred simultaneously with the growth of new economic relations. Both translated at social and household levels into an uncomfortable feeling among the people (loss of jobs, changes of jobs, learning new specialties at a mature age, erratic work schedules, etc.). On a mass scale, all these processes led to an accumulation of social stress, losses in the material guarantees of the standard of living, and reductions in expenditures for health care. At the regional level, the situation was aggravated by reductions in expenditures for municipal health care systems (when output drops, tax receipts decrease); for the individual, medicines become inaccessible, the system of preventive measures disintegrated, and chronic diseases were neglected. On the other hand, the decline in production in most cases almost meant an overall reduction of emissions into the air and of discharges of contaminated water.

Purely economic factors such as the level of debts of enterprises to banks, suppliers and consumers relative to the financial assets of enterprises have serious ecological and social consequences. The regions having the greatest financial difficulties are those in which industries do not occupy a monopolistic position in the markets of Russia (mostly agricultural). The same reason explains the relatively [sic] well-being of some Siberian regions which produce raw materials, while Kamchatka oblast, which does not have any significant raw materials, is experiencing full financial collapse.

Financial difficulties cause problems of supplying industry with necessary spare parts, resources and maintenance. Enterprise indebtedness leads to unstable salary payments to their workforce, which consequently leads to social instability and stress. In particular, there is a correlation between those areas where enterprises are experiencing financial problems and areas where results from the referendum of April 25, 1993 and the elections of December 12, 1993 were unfavorable to the authorities.

But the greatest danger for the people working at enterprises in economic disarray, as well as for the environment, arises when enterprises continue to work using worn-out equipment, do not perform preventive maintenance, violating work regimes and regulations, and use of inappropriate raw materials due to breakdowns in supply.

Less obvious, but no less important for the health of the population is the overall breakdown of social services, including medicines, which is a consequence of the financial difficulties of enterprises. This process will have the most serious consequences in Siberia and the Far East, where due to the uncompleted developmental processes in these regions, the infrastructure of the cities and especially of the workers' settlements, depends on the industrial enterprises.

The maps showing the rate of industrial accidents in the regions of Russia shows the relationship of its growth to the simultaneous reduction in the volume of output. The level of danger of accidents and losses connected with them are growing. The very "age" of these industrial centers represents a set of factors which lead to a high accident rate. Those "centers" which were created and intensively developed in the years before and during the war, such as the Urals, the Kuzbass, and Tula have reached the period of extreme aging of their capital stock. Similarly, work on very worn-out equipment, explains the high accident rates in such poorly developed regions as Kalmykiya and Tuva. The grave financial situation of enterprises, among a number of factors, determines the level of accidents in the North Caucasus.

The greatest accident rate increase in 1992–1993 occurred in those regions which have highly developed metallurgical and chemical industries, while in the northern and Siberian mining regions it was decreasing or at best increasing at a lower rate. Due to economic disarray, the number of skilled personnel in large industry has declined as competent cadres departed. . . .

The significance of a poorly developed infrastructure is much clearer in the materials on Emergency Situations (ES). . . Given equal industrial activity, ecological and ecologically-significant emergency situations occur less often in industrially developed centers, than in less developed regions. Given the weakness of the systems for prevention and clean-up of accidents, even a small accident may develop ecological consequences, and threaten to become an Emergency Situation.

This situation reflects a mutual compensation in the increased frequency of Emergency Situations and in reduced production activity. Murmansk and Astrakhan oblasts can be pointed to as dangerous places. Nonetheless, one also should note the steadily increasing, but not yet maximal level frequency of Emergency Situations in the entire Lower Volga region. This region has ecologically dangerous industries but a considerable potential for further development during the post-crisis period. This potential is based on a combination of freed-up reserves from military sites and plants, a good transportation infrastructure, the lack of acute ethnic conflicts, successful implementation of agricultural reforms ("setting up new farmers"), an intensive concentration of migrants from Central Asia, and a returning German population which has a strong work ethic along with a very probable investment support from Germany. In the aggregate, these factors can provide a steady increase in industrial activity in this region which, taking into account the frequency of Emergency Situations, may create serious ecological safety problems . . .

DOCUMENT ANALYSIS

1. How do the scientists view the relationship between central and regional authorities in Russia?

____

____

____

DOCUMENT 34.1

UN Secretariat, "Israel-PLO Declaration of Principles on Interim Self-Government Arrangements, September 13, 1993" (1993)

Source: United Nations Secretariat Israel-PLO Declaration of Principles on Interim Self-Government Arrangements, September 13, 1993, (April 16, 2001).

On September 13, 1993, Yasir Arafat, Chairman of the Palestine Liberation Organization (PLO) and Yitzhak Rabin, Prime Minister of Israel, met on the lawn of the White House to witness the signing of a historic accord between the Israelis and Palestinians. After the signing, Arafat extended his hand to Rabin, who hesitated for some time before President Bill Clinton nudged him on the back then he shook Arafat's hand. The event, watched around the world, signaled the culmination of more than a year of secret and open negotiations between representatives of the PLO and the government of Israel. As the world was just learning, beginning in April of 1992, Norwegian academics and diplomats with ties to both the PLO and the Israeli Labour Party had offered to act as intermediaries to bring together the two sides. Over several months, more than a dozen secret meetings were held, in London and Norway. In August of 1992, representatives of the PLO and Israel signed a declaration of principles, known as the Oslo Accord. The declaration, which formed the basis for subsequent negotiations, committed the PLO to removing the clause in its Charter calling for the destruction of Israel and renouncing the use of violence against Israelis, while Israel accepted the PLO as the legitimate representative of the Palestinian people—those living in the occupied West Bank and Gaza Strip, as well as those living in exile.

Although the compromises in the Oslo Accord were hotly contested by both Israeli and Palestinian opponents, Rabin and Arafat convinced their supporters that the risks of not having an accord were now greater than the risks of reaching a compromise. On September 13th, the two leaders, longtime adversaries, met to show their commitment to replacing a decades-long struggle marked by violence with a new relationship based on mutual trust. On November 4, 1995, Yitzhak Rabin was assassinated by an opponent of the peace process. Confronting huge political, economic, and cultural barriers, the Israelis and Palestinians continue to struggle with the meaning and implications of the Declaration of Principles, which remains more a blueprint for future possibilities than a record of accomplishments.

Israel-PLO Declaration of Principles on Interim Self-Government Arrangements
September 13, 1993

The Government of the State of Israel and the P.L.O. team (in the Jordanian-Palestinian delegation to the Middle East Peace Conference) (the "Palestinian Delegation"), representing the Palestinian people, agree that it is time to put an end to decades of confrontation and conflict, recognize their mutual legitimate and political rights, and strive to live in peaceful coexistence and mutual dignity and security and achieve a just, lasting and comprehensive peace settlement and historic reconciliation through the agreed political process. Accordingly, the two sides agree to the following principles:

ARTICLE I: AIM OF THE NEGOTIATIONS

The aim of the Israeli-Palestinian negotiations within the current Middle East peace process is, among other things, to establish a Palestinian Interim Self-Government Authority, the elected Council (the "Council"), for the Palestinian people in the West Bank and the Gaza Strip, for a transitional period not exceeding five years, leading to a permanent settlement based on Security Council Resolutions 242 and 338.

It is understood that the interim arrangements are an integral part of the whole peace process and that the negotiations on the permanent status will lead to the implementation of Security Council Resolutions 242 and 338. . . .

ARTICLE III: ELECTIONS

1. In order that the Palestinian people in the West Bank and Gaza Strip may govern themselves according to democratic principles, direct, free and general political elections will be held for the Council under agreed supervision and international observation, while the Palestinian police will ensure public order. . . .

3. These elections will constitute a significant interim preparatory step toward the realization of the legitimate rights of the Palestinian people and their just requirements. . . .

ARTICLE VI: PREPARATORY TRANSFER OF POWERS AND RESPONSIBILITIES

1. Upon the entry into force of this Declaration of Principles and the withdrawal from the Gaza Strip and the Jericho area, a transfer of authority from the Israeli military government and its Civil Administration to the authorised Palestinians for this task, as detailed herein, will commence. This transfer of authority will be of a preparatory nature until the inauguration of the Council.

2. Immediately after the entry into force of this Declaration of Principles and the withdrawal from the Gaza Strip and Jericho area, with the view to promoting economic development in the West Bank and Gaza Strip, authority will be transferred to the Palestinians on the following spheres: education and culture, health, social welfare, direct taxation, and tourism. The Palestinian side will commence in building the Palestinian police force, as agreed upon. Pending the inauguration of the Council, the two parties may negotiate the transfer of additional powers and responsibilities, as agreed upon. . . .

ARTICLE VIII: PUBLIC ORDER AND SECURITY

In order to guarantee public order and internal security for the Palestinians of the West Bank and the Gaza Strip, the Council will establish a strong police force, while Israel will continue to carry the responsibility for defending against external threats, as well as the responsibility for overall security of Israelis for the purpose of safeguarding their internal security and public order. . . .

ARTICLE XIII: REDEPLOYMENT OF ISRAELI FORCES

1. After the entry into force of this Declaration of Principles, and not later than the eve of elections for the Council, a redeployment of Israeli military forces in the West Bank and the Gaza Strip will take place, in addition to withdrawal of Israeli forces carried out in accordance with Article XIV.

2. In redeploying its military forces, Israel will be guided by the principle that its military forces should be redeployed outside populated areas.

3. Further redeployments to specified locations will be gradually implemented commensurate with the assumption of responsibility for public order and internal security by the Palestinian police force pursuant to Article VIII above. . . .

ANNEX II: PROTOCOL ON WITHDRAWAL OF ISRAELI FORCES FROM THE GAZA STRIP AND JERICHO AREA

1. The two sides will conclude and sign within two months from the date of entry into force of this Declaration of Principles, an agreement on the withdrawal of Israeli military forces from the Gaza Strip and Jericho area. This agreement will include comprehensive arrangements to apply in the Gaza Strip and the Jericho area subsequent to the Israeli withdrawal.

2. Israel will implement an accelerated and scheduled withdrawal of Israeli military forces from the Gaza Strip and Jericho area, beginning immediately with the signing of the agreement on the Gaza Strip and Jericho area and to be completed within a period not exceeding four months after the signing of this agreement.

3. The above agreement will include, among other things:

a. Arrangements for a smooth and peaceful transfer of authority from the Israeli military government and its Civil Administration to the Palestinian representatives.

b. Structure, powers and responsibilities of the Palestinian authority in these areas, except: external security, settlements, Israelis, foreign relations, and other mutually agreed matters.

c. Arrangements for the assumption of internal security and public order by the Palestinian police force consisting of police officers recruited locally and from abroad holding Jordanian passports and Palestinian documents issued by Egypt. Those who will participate in the Palestinian police force coming from abroad should be trained as police and police officers.

d. A temporary international or foreign presence, as agreed upon.

e. Establishment of a joint Palestinian-Israeli Coordination and Cooperation Committee for mutual security purposes.

f. An economic development and stabilization program, including the establishment of an Emergency Fund, to encourage foreign investment, and financial and economic support. Both sides will coordinate and cooperate jointly and unilaterally with regional and international parties to support these aims.

g. Arrangements for a safe passage for persons and transportation between the Gaza Strip and Jericho area. . . .

Done at Washington, D.C., this thirteenth day of September, 1993.

For the Government of Israel Shimon Peres
For the P.L.O. Mahmud Abbas
Witnessed By: The United States of America Warren Christopher
The Russian Federation Andrei Kozyrev

DOCUMENT 35.1
From Sichuan Province's "One-Child Family Policy" (1970s)

Source: Patricia Buckley Ebrey, ed., *Chinese Civilization: A Sourcebook* (New York: The Free Press, 1993), pp. 478–81.

In the early 1970s, the Chinese government announced that China's population reached one billion. In order to control population growth, the Chinese government worked out a strategy, known as the one-child family policy, which was applicable to all couples getting married and preparing to have a child. The policy regulates that the newly wedded couple is allowed to have only one child, and any ensuing pregnancy will have to be terminated by abortion. In order to encourage citizens to comply with the birth-planning policy, the government also provided benefits such as free medical care for both the parents and the one child, free education for the one child, and other incentives at the workplace for the parents. Penalties for not abiding by the rule lead to fines, demotions, being fired, laid off, or removed from Communist Party membership. The policy has become compulsory, with various measures to reinforce it.

The major barrier for a smooth implementation of the one-child family policy has been the traditional Chinese concept of having the male heir to continue the family name. The policy has been working more effectively in urban areas than in rural areas, largely because employment for the urban population imposes pressures on them to observe the policy. The rural population, on the other hand, relies exclusively on a family-centered work force in the field, especially the male labors. Therefore, a female child is not desirable, and having one will compel the family to have the second, or the third, until they have a male.

The following document is the version from Sichuan Province—the most populated province in China. The document is closely identified with the version from the Central Committee of the Chinese government in terms of regulations and rules.

SICHUAN PROVINCIAL BIRTH-PLANNING RULES

Article 1. To practice birth planning, exercise control over the population, and improve the quality of the population so that population growth would be suited to economic and social development plans, these regulations are enacted in accordance with the People's Republic of China (PRC) Constitution, PRC Marriage Law, and relevant regulations of the state, and in connection with Sichuan's actual realities.

Article 2. Both husband and wife have the duty to practice birth planning.

Article 6. Late marriage and late births are encouraged. Late marriage means that both men and women are married three years later than the lawful age [of 20 for women and 22 for men]. Late births mean births by women aged 24 and above.

Article 7. Births should occur in a planned manner. Each couple is encouraged to give birth to one child. No births must occur without marriage.

Article 8. Couples who can meet the following requirements may have a second child:

1. The first child has a nonhereditary disease and cannot become a normal laborer;
2. Marriage between an only son and an only daughter;
3. In the rural areas, the groom moves to the house of the bride, who is an only daughter, after marriage;
4. Only sons and daughters of martyrs in rural areas;
5. Disabled demobilized soldiers in rural areas with Merit Citation Class II, A;
6. Those in rural areas who were disabled while on duty and are equivalent to the disabled demobilized soldiers with Merit Citation Class II, A;
7. The person is the only one of several brothers in rural areas who is capable of having children;
8. In the rural areas, the husband or wife is the only son or daughter for two generations;
9. In the rural areas of the Pengzhou mountain counties and the mountain townships (not including the flatland, hilly land, and valleys) within the basin approved by the cities (prefectures) of the economic construction zone, families with only daughters that have labor shortages;
10. In the rural areas of the remote mountain areas in Pengzhou mountain counties, families with only sons and daughters; and
11. Both husband and wife are returned overseas Chinese who have settled down in Sichuan.

Article 9. Couples who have no children many years after marriage, but the wife has become pregnant after adopting a child, may give birth to a child.

Article 10. Those who can meet one of the following requirements may have a second child:

1. A widower or widow remarries and before the remarriage, the widower or widow has fewer than two children, while the spouse has no children; and
2. Husband or wife who remarries after a divorce and before the remarriage, one side has only one child, while the other has no children.

Article 11. For those who can meet the requirements of Articles 8, 9, and 10 and who want to bear children, both husband and wife should submit an application, which will be examined and brought into line with birth planning by the departments at the county level responsible for birth planning work. Second births should occur after an interval of four years.

Article 23. Those who refuse education and give birth to children not covered by the plan will be fined from the month the child is born. The wages or annual income of both husband and wife will be decreased by ten to twenty percent for seven years; the total sum deducted should not be less than five hundred yuan. Those who give birth to another child after the birth permitted according to Articles 8, 9, and 10 of these regulations will be fined at a minimum of eight hundred yuan. A heavy fine will be imposed on those giving births not covered by the plan.

Regarding pregnancy not covered by the plan, both husband and wife will be imposed a fine of twenty to thirty yuan a month during the period of pregnancy. If the pregnancy is terminated, the fine imposed will be returned.

The fine imposed will be used for birth planning work only. The provincial birth planning committee and finance department will work out use and management methods.

Article 24. If those giving births not covered by the plan are cadres and staff members, apart from imposing a fine, the units where they work should also apply disciplinary sanctions according to the seriousness of the case.

Article 25. Those who have received certificates for only children and are allowed to give birth to a second child should return their certificates and will no longer get rewards and preferential treatment from the month they are allowed to give birth to a second child. Those who give birth to another child without approval, apart from the measures stipulated in Articles 23 and 24, will no longer get rewards and preferential treatment for only children and must return the certificates and health care benefits for only children.

Article 26. Regarding doctors, nurses, and working personnel in charge of birth planning work and marriage registration and state functionaries who violate these regulations, practice fraud, and accept bribes, the units where they work or the higher level competent departments should educate them through criticisms and disciplinary sanctions. If their practices constitute an offense, the judicial organs will investigate and affix the responsibility for the offense according to law.

Persons holding direct responsibility for accidents in ligation operations due to negligence will be handled according to relevant regulations.

Article 27. Regarding those who insult, threaten, and beat doctors, nurses, and working personnel in charge of birth planning work or use other methods to obstruct birth planning, the public security organs will handle the cases in light of the "PRC Regulations Concerning Public

Security Management and Punishment." If the practices constitute an offense, the judicial organs will investigate and affix the responsibility for the offense according to law.

Article 28. Drowning, abandoning, selling, and maltreatment of girl babies and their mothers are prohibited. Regarding those involved in any of these practices, the units where they work or the leading organs concerned should educate them through criticisms and disciplinary sanction in light of the seriousness of the case. If their practices constitute an offense, the judicial organs will investigate and affix the responsibility for the offense according to law.

Illegal removal of intrauterine devices is prohibited. In addition to confiscating the income obtained from illegally taking out the intrauterine device, a fine of over five hundred yuan will be imposed. A heavy fine will be imposed on those who commit the offense repeatedly. The judicial organs will, according to law, investigate and affix the responsibility for injuries and deaths caused therefrom.

DOCUMENT ANALYSIS

1. How does the government encourage the Chinese citizens to adhere to the policy?

2. Under what conditions can a couple have a second child without paying the fine?

3. What are the major punishments for violating the policy?

4. What are the major reasons given by the Chinese government to promote the one-child family policy?

5. What practices are prohibited?

DOCUMENT 35.2

Extract from speeches by Mahatma Gandhi against the partition of India (1947)

Source: Extracts from writings and words of Mahatma Gandhi as compiled in *The Essential Gandhi: An Anthology,* edited by Louis Fischer, 1962. Reprinted by permission of the Navajivan Trust.

Despite its leaders' high hopes for a peaceful transition from British colony to independent nation, India had no such luck. There had been no real consensus among nationalist leaders about the new nation's relationship with Britain, and tensions between Hindus and Muslims had long existed. These tensions had been partially covered over by the desire to expel the British, but almost immediately upon independence in 1947, they returned to the surface. Some more extreme leaders on both sides of the issue had called for separate countries for the two groups, but many Indian leaders pleaded against division and in favor of unity.

The most well-known Indian nationalist was Mohandas Gandhi (1869–1948). Gandhi was the dominant force in the Indian National Congress (the main nationalist organization) through much of the early 20th century, and remained in many ways India's guiding light until his assassination in 1948.

Gandhi had always worked diligently to pull together Hindus and Muslims, and believed that a successful nation included both. While many Hindus supported Gandhi's efforts towards Muslims, it was in fact a Hindu, upset with conciliatory approach, who eventually murdered him. In this series of quotes, Gandhi pleads for a unified India.

[The demand for Pakistan] as put forth by the Moslem League is un-Islamic and I have not hesitated to call it sinful. Islam stands for unity and the brotherhood of mankind, not for disrupting the oneness of the human family. Therefore, those who want to divide India into possibly warring groups are enemies alike of India and Islam. They may cut me to pieces but they cannot make me subscribe to something which I consider to be wrong.

A friend from Eastern Pakistan asks how can I declare myself an inhabitant of undivided India when it is cut into two, and when to be of one part excludes you from the other? Whatever the legal pundits may say, they cannot dominate the mind of man. Who can prevent the friend from declaring himself as a citizen of the world even though legally he is not, and though he may be, as he will be, prevented from entering many States under their laws? Legal status should not worry a man who has not reduced himself to the state of a machine as many of us have. So long as the moral condition is sound, there is no warrant for anxiety. What every one of us has to guard against is the harboring of ill-will against a State or its people. . . .

In actual life, it is impossible to separate us into two nations. We are not two nations. Every Moslem will have a Hindu name if he goes back far enough in his family history. Every Moslem is merely a Hindu who has accepted Islam. That does not create nationality. . . . We in India have a common culture. In the North, Hindi and Urdu are understood by both Hindus and Moslems. In Madras, Hindus and Moslems speak Tamil, and in Bengal, they both speak Bengali and neither Hindi nor Urdu. When communal riots take place, they are always provoked by incidents over cows and by religious processions. That means that it is our superstitions that create the trouble and not our separate nationalities.

. . . We must not cease to aspire, in spite of [the] wild talk, to befriend all Moslems and hold them fast as prisoners of our love.

[If] India is divided she will be lost forever. Therefore . . . if India is to remain undivided, Hindus and Moslems must live together in brotherly love, not in hostile camps organized either for defensive action or retaliation. . . .

DOCUMENT ANALYSIS

1. Does it appear that there are any circumstances under which Gandhi would accept the separation of the two groups?

____

____

____

2. What common language is shared in Bengal?

____

____

____

3. What common languages do Hindus and Muslims share in northern India?

____

____

____

4. Why does Gandhi call the idea of a separate Pakistan "sinful"?

____

____

____

DOCUMENT 35.3

"North and South Korean Declaration Text, June 2000" (2000)

Source: "North and South Korean Declaration Text: June 2000." Reprinted by permission of the Embassy of Korea in Washington D.C.

The legacy of the Korean War was a divided peninsula and a long-term hostility between people who used to share a unified country. The war also created two different states that have gone in opposite directions in their political and economic development.

With the end of the Cold War and economic reforms in the Pacific, South Korea has emerged as one of the Four Little Dragons in the region, while North Korea remains isolated from the rest of the international community. The Korean families, separated by the war and the 1953 cease-fire, have been longing for union and dialogue. Starting in the 1980s, exchange programs of family visits and communication between the South and North have been gradually taking place.

The summit between leaders of South Korea and North Korea in June, 2000, was a historic event that marked a step toward unification of the peninsula and further cooperation. Most importantly, the Koreans are going to resolve the issue of unification among themselves, through cooperation and understanding.

Upholding the lofty wishes of the Korean people yearning for peaceful reunification of the fatherland, President Kim Dae-jung of the Republic of (South) Korea and Kim Jong II, chairman of the National Defense Commission of the Democratic Peoples' Republic of (North) Korea, held a historic meeting and summit talks on June 13–15, 2000. Noting that the meeting and talks held for the first time in the divided Korean history carry grave significance in promoting mutual understanding and developing South-North relations and achieving peaceful, national reunification, the top leaders of South and North Korea declared as follows:

(1) The South and North, as masters of national unification, will join hands in efforts to resolve the issue of national unification independently.

(2) Acknowledging common elements in the South's proposal for a consideration and the North's proposal for a federation of lower stage, the South and the North agreed to promote reunification.

(3) The South and North will exchange groups of dispersed family members and their relatives around Aug. 15 and resolve as soon as possible humanitarian issues, including the repatriation of communist prisoners.

(4) The South and North will pursue a balanced development of their national economies and build mutual trust by accelerating exchange in the social, cultural, sports, health and environmental sectors.

(5) In order to put these agreements into practice, the South and North will hold a dialogue between government authorities at an early date. President Kim Dae-jung cordially invited National Defense Commission chairman Kim Jong II to visit Seoul and he agreed to do that at an appropriate time.

DOCUMENT ANALYSIS

1. Given the fact that both the United States (under the United Nations banner) and China were involved in the Korean War, why are these two powers not included in this accord?

2. How important is this accord to the future cooperation of both South and North Korea?

3. What are the major differences between North Korea and South Korea?

4. What is the main goal for both the South and North Korean people in the summit?

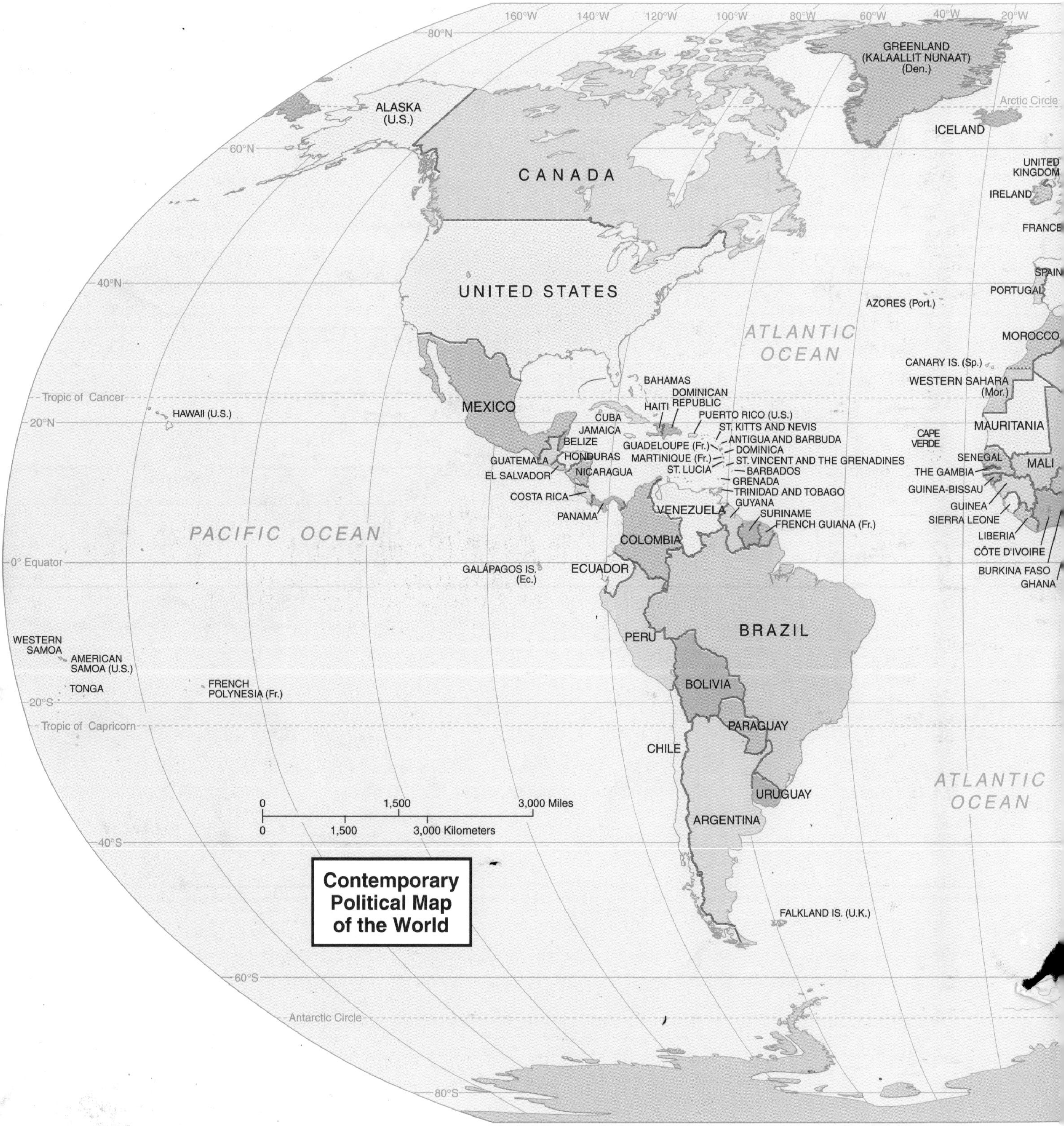
Contemporary Political Map of the World
160°W
140°W
120°W
100°W
80°W
60°W
40°W
20°W
80°N
60°N
40°N
20°N
0° Equator
20°S
40°S
60°S
80°S
Arctic Circle
Tropic of Cancer
Tropic of Capricorn
Antarctic Circle
GREENLAND
(KALAALLIT NUNAAT)
(Den.)
ALASKA
(U.S.)
ICELAND
CANADA
UNITED KINGDOM
IRELAND
FRANCE
SPAIN
PORTUGAL
UNITED STATES
AZORES (Port.)
ATLANTIC OCEAN
MOROCCO
CANARY IS. (Sp.)
WESTERN SAHARA
(Mor.)
BAHAMAS
DOMINICAN REPUBLIC
HAITI
MEXICO
HAWAII (U.S.)
CUBA
PUERTO RICO (U.S.)
ST. KITTS AND NEVIS
JAMAICA
ANTIGUA AND BARBUDA
BELIZE
GUADELOUPE (Fr.)
DOMINICA
CAPE VERDE
MAURITANIA
GUATEMALA
HONDURAS
MARTINIQUE (Fr.)
ST. VINCENT AND THE GRENADINES
SENEGAL
MALI
EL SALVADOR
NICARAGUA
ST. LUCIA
BARBADOS
THE GAMBIA
GRENADA
GUINEA-BISSAU
COSTA RICA
TRINIDAD AND TOBAGO
GUINEA
GUYANA
PANAMA
VENEZUELA
SURINAME
SIERRA LEONE
FRENCH GUIANA (Fr.)
PACIFIC OCEAN
COLOMBIA
LIBERIA
CÔTE D'IVOIRE
GALÁPAGOS IS.
(Ec.)
ECUADOR
BURKINA FASO
GHANA
BRAZIL
PERU
WESTERN SAMOA
AMERICAN SAMOA (U.S.)
TONGA
FRENCH POLYNESIA (Fr.)
BOLIVIA
PARAGUAY
CHILE
ATLANTIC OCEAN
URUGUAY
0
1,500
3,000 Miles
0
1,500
3,000 Kilometers
ARGENTINA
FALKLAND IS. (U.K.)